Hazardous Materials

49 CFR Parts 100-185

Including:
Hazardous Materials Registration Program and Forms
Guide for Preparing Hazardous Materials Incidents Reports
Enhancing Security of Hazardous Materials Shipments Against Acts of Terrorism or Sabotage
Infectious Substances Pamphlet — What You Need to Know
What Hazardous Materials Regulations Apply to Agricultural Transportation?
Complying with the October 1, 1998 Intrastate Commerce Requirements (HM-200)
What Hazardous Materials Regulations Apply to Materials of Trade?
Regional Office Locations
Department of Transportation Organizational Chart

Updated through June 6, 2003

This publication is also available on CD-Rom 

Changing the Complex Into Compliance®

Mangan Communications, Inc.
http://www.mancomm.com

® 629-M

Patent Pending

315 West Fourth Street
Davenport, Iowa 52801
(563) 323-6245
(800) 767-3759
Fax: (888) 398-6245

Website: http://www.mancomm.com
E-Mail: safetyinfo@mancomm.com

While every effort has been made to ensure that the information contained herein is accurate and complete at the time of printing, the frequency of changes in the regulations makes it impossible to guarantee the complete accuracy of the information that follows. Therefore, neither Mangan Communications, Inc., nor its subsidiaries shall be liable for any damages resulting from the use of or reliance upon this publication. Furthermore, the appearance of products, services, companies, organizations or causes in the 49 CFR does not in any way imply endorsement by Mangan Communications, Inc., or its subsidiaries.

This publication is constructed to provide accurate information in regard to the material included. It is sold with the understanding that the publisher is not involved in providing accounting, legal, or other professional service. If legal consultation or other expert advice is required, the services of a professional person should be engaged.

Library of Congress Control Number: 2002112165
ISBN: 0-9718080-6-6

Introducing a better way to look at 49 CFR . . .

RegLogic™

This CFR is superior to other publications presenting OSHA regulations because it has been modernized with **RegLogic™**. This unique formatting will aid you in finding information faster and understanding it easier.

RegLogic™ includes:

Color-Coding.
This CFR is reproduced in two colors, so all subdividers and important headers jump out at you in color. No more highlighting!

Headings.
Most paragraphs begin with a bold, colored, or italic heading for faster reference.

Outline form.
Extensive use of indenting, as in outline form, makes it much easier for you to locate and understand each regulation.

Enhanced Graphics.
All the graphics have been completely redrawn in high-resolution for super-sharp reproduction, and special shading and coloring have been added for increased clarity and understanding.

Subpart B - Loading, Unloading, and Handling

§175.75 Quantity limitations aboard aircraft.

(a) Except as provided in §175.85(c)(3), no person may carry on an aircraft:

- (1) *A hazardous material except as permitted by this subchapter;*
- (2) *More than 25 kg* (55 pounds) net weight of hazardous material (and in addition thereto, 75 kg (165 pounds) net weight of Division 2.2 (non-flammable compressed gas) materials permitted to be carried aboard passenger-carrying aircraft:
  - (i) *In an inaccessible cargo compartment,*
  - (ii) *In any freight container* within an accessible cargo compartment, or
  - (iii) *In any accessible* cargo compartment in a cargo aircraft only in a manner that makes it inaccessible unless in a freight container;
- (3) *Packages containing* Class 7 (radioactive) materials when their combined transport index number (determined by adding together the transport index numbers shown on the labels of the individual packages and/or overpacks):
  - (i) *In passenger carrying aircraft,* exceeds 50.0 or, for any single package, exceeds 3.0, or
  - (ii) *In cargo aircraft only,* exceeds 200.00 (for fissile Class 7 (radioactive) materials, see §175.702(b)(2)(iv)) or, for any single package, exceeds 10.0.

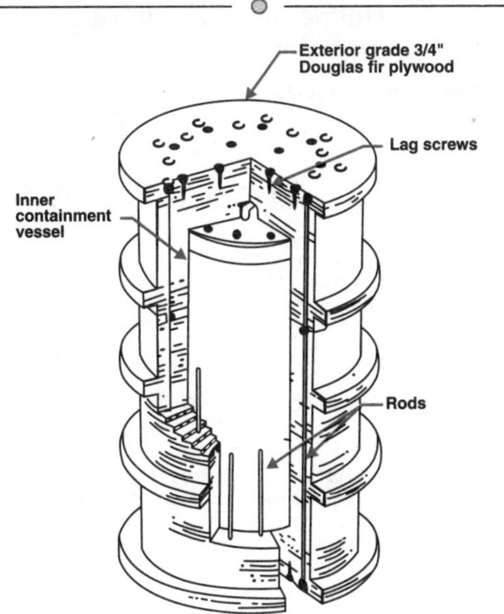

(5) *A project narrative statement* of the goals and objectives of each proposed project, including the following:
(i) *A background statement* describing the applicant's long-term goals and objectives with respect to:
[A] The current abilities and authorities of the applicant's program for preparedness planning;
[B] The need to sustain or increase program capability;
[C] Current degree of participation in or intention to assess the need for a regional hazardous materials emergency response team; and
[D] The impact that the grant will have on the program.

Bracket Revisions.
Square brackets [ ] in the lower subdivisions give you a better sense of organization within the regulation.

Appendix C to Part 178
Nominal and minimum thicknesses of steel drums and jerricans.
For each listed packaging capacity, the following table compares the ISO Standard 3574 nominal thickness with the corresponding ISO Standard 3574 minimum thickness.

Maximum capacity (L)	ISO nominal (mm)	Corresponding ISO minimum (mm)
20	0.7	0.63
30	0.8	0.73
40	0.8	0.73
60	1.0	0.92
120	1.0	0.92
220	1.0	0.92
450	1.9	1.77

Tables.
All dotted lines have been replaced with lines and colors for easier use and faster reference.

Index.
This book contains an easy-to-use index, including section numbers *and* page numbers in color for easy access.

Online forms available.
Full-size versions of every form in this book are available free of charge at www.dotcfr.com

RegLogic™ is a one-of-a-kind approach that you will find only from Mangan Communications, Inc.

Recent changes in regulations:

November 2002:
- Several sections have been revised to contain the new requirements for shippers and carriers. These changes were originally published on July 12, 2002, and revised again on Nov. 1, 2002.

January 2003:
- Sections 107.612 and 107.616 have been revised to reflect changes in registration fees.
- Section 171.7 has been updated to include the most recent amendments to incorporation by reference materials.

March 2003:
- The definition of "Administrator" was revised in 107.1
- Requirements for an aircraft operator transporting a hazardous material were revised in Parts 171 and 175.
- Part 172 was revised, including the addition of a new Subpart I, to establish new requirements to enhance the security of hazardous materials transported in commerce.

April 2003:
- Changes have been made throughout the Hazardous Materials regulations to update and clarify rules on the construction and maintenance of cargo tank motor vehicles.

May 2003:
- An interim final rule was incorporated into Parts 107, 171, 176, and 177 to reflect a requirement that shippers and transporters of certain hazardous materials comply with Federal security regulations that apply to motor carrier and vessel transportation.
- In response to appeals submitted to an Aug. 8, 2002 final rule, a May 8 final rule amended certain requirements, extended certain compliance dates, and made minor editorial corrections.
- The table in §171.6 was updated to coincide with a final rule passed in March.
- Parts 171, 173, 177, and 178 were revised to permit, for an interim period and subject to certain unloading conditions, the unloading of IM and UN portable tanks transporting certain liquid hazardous materials when those tanks are not equipped with a thermal means of remote activation of the internal self-closing stop-valves fitted on the bottom discharge outlets. Permitting such unloading for an interim period affords operators time to bring the portable tanks into conformance with the regulations.

June 2003:
- A correction to the final rule published May 8, 2003 was in the Federal Register on June 2, 2003. These corrections had an effective date of June 2, 2003.

Table of Contents

Subchapter C - Hazardous Materials Regulations

Part 180 - Continuing Qualification and Maintenance of Packagings

Addendum

Subchapter A - Hazardous Materials and Oil Transportation

Part 105 - Hazardous Materials Program Definitions and General Procedures

Subpart A - Definitions

§105.5 Definitions.

(a) **This part contains the definitions** for certain words and phrases used throughout this subchapter (49 CFR parts 105 through 110). At the beginning of each subpart, the Research and Special Programs Administration ("RSPA" or "we") will identify the defined terms that are used within the subpart — by listing them — and refer the reader to the definitions in this part. This way, readers will know that RSPA has given a term a precise meaning and will know where to look for it.

(b) **Terms used in this part are defined as follows:**

Associate Administrator means Associate Administrator for Hazardous Materials Safety, Research and Special Programs Administration.

Approval means written consent, including a competent authority approval, from the Associate Administrator or other designated Department official, to perform a function that requires prior consent under subchapter C of this chapter (49 CFR parts 171 through 180).

Competent Authority means a national agency that is responsible, under its national law, for the control or regulation of some aspect of hazardous materials (dangerous goods) transportation. Another term for Competent Authority is "Appropriate authority" which is used in the International Civil Aviation Organization's (ICAO) Technical Instructions for the Safe Transport of Dangerous Goods by Air. The Associate Administrator is the United States Competent Authority for purposes of 49 CFR part 107.

Competent Authority Approval means an approval by the competent authority that is required under an international standard (for example, the ICAO Technical Instructions for the Safe Transport of Dangerous Goods by Air and the International Maritime Dangerous Goods Code). Any of the following may be considered a competent authority approval if it satisfies the requirement of an international standard:

(1) *A specific regulation in subchapter A or C of this chapter.*

(2) *An exemption or approval* issued under subchapter A or C of this chapter.

(3) *A separate document* issued to one or more persons by the Associate Administrator.

Exemption means a document issued by the Associate Administrator under the authority of 49 U.S.C. 5117. The document permits a person to perform a function that is not otherwise permitted under subchapter A or C of this chapter, or other regulations issued under 49 U.S.C. 5101 et seq. (e.g., Federal Motor Carrier Safety routing requirements.)

Federal hazardous material transportation law means 49 U.S.C. 5101 et seq.

File or **Filed** means received by the appropriate RSPA or other designated office within the time specified in a regulation or rulemaking document.

Hazardous material means a substance or material that the Secretary of Transportation has determined is capable of posing an unreasonable risk to health, safety, and property when transported in commerce, and has designated as hazardous under section 5103 of Federal hazardous materials transportation law (49 U.S.C. 5103). The term includes hazardous substances, hazardous wastes, marine pollutants, elevated temperature materials, materials designated as hazardous in the Hazardous Materials Table (see 49 CFR 172.101), and materials that meet the defining criteria for hazard classes and divisions in part 173 of subchapter C of this chapter.

Hazardous Materials Regulations or **HMR** means the regulations at 49 CFR parts 171 through 180.

Indian tribe has the same meaning given that term in section 4 of the Indian Self-Determination and Education Assistance Act (25 U.S.C. 450b).

Person means an individual, firm, copartnership, corporation, company, association, or joint-stock association (including any trustee, receiver, assignee, or similar representative); or a government or Indian tribe (or an agency or instrumentality of any government or Indian tribe) that transports a hazardous material to further a commercial enterprise or offers a hazardous material for transportation in commerce. Person does not include the following:

(1) *The United States Postal Service.*

(2) *Any agency or instrumentality* of the Federal government, for the purposes of 49 U.S.C. 5123 (civil penalties) and 5124 (criminal penalties).

(3) *Any government or Indian tribe* (or an agency or instrumentality of any government or Indian tribe) that transports hazardous material for a governmental purpose.

Political subdivision means a municipality; a public agency or other instrumentality of one or more States, municipalities, or other political body of a State; or a public corporation, board, or commission established under the laws of one or more States.

Preemption determination means an administrative decision by the Associate Administrator that Federal hazardous materials law does or does not void a specific State, political subdivision, or Indian tribe requirement.

Regulations issued under Federal hazardous materials transportation law means regulations contained in subchapter A of this chapter (49 CFR parts 105 through 110) and in subchapter C of this chapter (49 CFR parts 171 through 180).

State means a State of the United States, the District of Columbia, the Commonwealth of Puerto Rico, the Commonwealth of the Northern Mariana Islands, the Virgin Islands, American Samoa, Guam, or any other territory or possession of the United States designated by the Secretary.

Transports or **Transportation** means the movement of property and loading, unloading, or storage incidental to the movement.

Waiver of Preemption means a decision by the Associate Administrator to forego preemption of a non-Federal requirement — that is, to allow a State, political subdivision or Indian tribe requirement to remain in effect. The non-Federal requirement must provide at least as much public protection as the Federal hazardous materials transportation law and the regulations issued under Federal hazardous materials transportation law, and may not unreasonably burden commerce.

Subpart B - General Procedures

§105.15 Defined terms used in this subpart.

The following defined terms (see subpart A of this part) appear in this subpart: Approval; Exemption; Federal hazardous material transportation law; Hazardous material; Hazardous materials regulations; Indian tribe; Preemption determination; State; Transportation; Waiver of preemption.

Obtaining Guidance and Public Information

§105.20 Guidance and interpretations.

(a) **Hazardous materials regulations.** You can obtain information and answers to your questions on compliance with the hazardous materials regulations (49 CFR parts 171 through 180) and interpretations of those regulations by contacting RSPA's Office of Hazardous Materials Safety as follows:

(1) *Call* the Hazardous Materials Information Center at 1-800-467-4922 (in Washington, DC, call 202-366-4488). The Center is staffed from 9 a.m. through 5 p.m. Eastern time, Monday through Friday except Federal holidays. After hours, you can leave a recorded message and your call will be returned by the next business day.

(2) *E-mail* the Hazardous Materials Information Center at infocntr @rspa.dot.gov.

(3) *Access* the Office of Hazardous Materials Safety home page via the Internet at http://hazmat.dot.gov.

(4) *Send a letter,* with your return address and a daytime telephone number, to: Office of Hazardous Materials Standards, Research and Special Programs Administration, Attn: DHM-10, U.S. Department of Transportation, 400 7th Street SW., Washington, DC 20590-0001.

(b) **Federal hazardous materials transportation law** and preemption. You can obtain information and answers to your questions on Federal hazardous materials transportation law, 49 U.S.C. 5101 et seq., and Federal preemption of State, local, and Indian tribe hazardous material transportation requirements, by contacting RSPA's Office of the Chief Counsel as follows:

(1) *Call* the Office of the Chief Counsel at (202) 366-4400 from 9 a.m. to 5 p.m. Eastern time, Monday through Friday except Federal holidays.

(2) *Access* the Office of the Chief Counsel's home page via the Internet at http://rspa-atty.dot.gov.

(3) *Send a letter,* with your return address and a daytime telephone number, to: Office of the Chief Counsel, Research and Special Programs Administration, Attn: DCC-10, U.S. Department of Transportation, Washington, DC 20590-0001.

(4) *Contact* the Office of the Chief Counsel for a copy of applications for preemption determinations, waiver of preemption determinations, and inconsistency rulings received by RSPA before February 1, 1997.

§105.25 Reviewing public documents.

RSPA is required by statute to make certain documents and information available to the public. You can review and copy publicly available documents and information at the locations described in this section.

(a) **DOT Docket Management System.** Unless a particular document says otherwise, the following documents are available for public review and copying at the Department of Transportation's Docket Management System, Room PL 401, 400 7th Street, SW., Washington, DC 20590-0001, or for review and downloading through the Internet at http://dms.dot.gov:

(1) *Rulemaking documents* in proceedings started after February 1, 1997, including notices of proposed rulemaking, advance notices of proposed rulemaking, public comments, related Federal Register notices, final rules, appeals, and RSPA's decisions in response to appeals.

(2) *Applications for exemption* numbered DOT-E 11832 and above. Also available are supporting data, memoranda of any informal meetings with applicants, related Federal Register notices, public comments, and decisions granting or denying exemptions applications.

(3) *Applications for preemption* determinations and waiver of preemption determinations received by RSPA after February 1, 1997. Also available are public comments, Federal Register notices, and RSPA's rulings, determinations, decisions on reconsideration, and orders issued in response to those applications.

(b) **Office of Hazardous Materials Safety.**

(1) *You may obtain documents* (e.g., proposed and final rules, notices, letters of clarification, safety notices, DOT forms and other documents) by using the "Fax On Demand" system. To reach the "Fax On Demand" system, dial 1-800-467-4922 and select Option 2. You may choose documents to be faxed to your machine.

(2) *Upon your written request,* we will make the following documents and information available to you:

(i) *Appeals under 49 CFR part 107* and RSPA's decisions issued in response to those appeals.

(ii) *Records of compliance* order proceedings and RSPA compliance orders.

(iii) *Applications for approvals,* including supporting data, memoranda of any informal meetings with applicants, and decisions granting or denying approvals applications.

(iv) *Applications for exemptions* numbered below DOT-E 11832 and related background information are available for public review and copying at the Office of Hazardous Materials Safety, Office of Hazardous Materials Exemptions and Approvals, U.S. Department of Transportation, Room 8100, 400 7th Street, SW., Washington, DC 20590-0001.

(v) *Other information* about RSPA's hazardous materials program required by statute to be made available to the public for review and copying and any other information RSPA decides should be available to the public.

(3) *Your written request* to review documents should include the following:

(i) *A detailed description of the documents you wish to review.*

(ii) *Your name, address, and telephone number.*

(4) *Send your written request to:* Associate Administrator for Hazardous Materials Safety, Research and Special Programs Administration, Attn: DHM-1, U.S. Department of Transportation, 400 7th Street, SW., Washington, DC 20590-0001.

§105.26 Obtaining records on file with RSPA.

To obtain records on file with RSPA, other than those described in §105.25, you must file a request with RSPA under the Freedom of Information Act (FOIA) (5 U.S.C. 552). The procedures for filing a FOIA request are contained in 49 CFR part 7.

§105.30 Information made available to the public and request for confidential treatment.

When you submit information to RSPA during a rulemaking proceeding, as part of your application for exemption or approval, or for any other reason, we may make that information publicly available unless you ask that we keep the information confidential.

(a) **Asking for confidential treatment.** You may ask us to give confidential treatment to information you give to the agency by taking the following steps:

(1) *Mark "confidential"* on each page of the original document you would like to keep confidential.

(2) *Send us,* along with the original document, a second copy of the original document with the confidential information deleted.

(3) *Explain why* the information you are submitting is confidential (for example, it is exempt from mandatory public disclosure under the Freedom of Information Act, 5 U.S.C. 552 or it is information referred to in 18 U.S.C. 1905).

(b) **RSPA Decision.** RSPA will decide whether or not to treat your information as confidential. We will notify you, in writing, of a decision to grant or deny confidentiality at least five days before the information is publicly disclosed, and give you an opportunity to respond.

Serving Documents

§105.35 Serving documents in RSPA proceedings.

(a) **Service by RSPA.** We may serve the document by one of the following methods, except where a different method of service is specifically required:

(1) *Registered or certified mail.*

(i) *If we serve a document* by registered or certified mail, it is considered served when mailed.

(ii) *An official* United States Postal Service receipt from the registered or certified mailing is proof of service.

(iii) *We may serve* a person's authorized representative or agent by registered or certified mail, or in any other manner authorized by law. Service on a person's authorized agent is the same as service on the person.

(2) *Personal service.*

(3) *Publication in the Federal Register.*

(b) **Service by others.** If you are required under this subchapter to serve a person with a document, serve the document by one of the following methods, except where a different method of service is specifically required:

(1) *Registered or certified mail.*

(i) *If you serve a document* by registered or certified mail, it is considered served when mailed.

(ii) *An official* United States Postal Service receipt from the registered or certified mailing is proof of service.

(iii) *You may serve* a person's authorized representative or agent by registered or certified mail or in any other manner authorized by law. Service on a person's authorized agent is the same as service on the person.

(2) *Personal service.*

(3) *Electronic service.*

(i) *In a proceeding* under §107.317 of this subchapter (an administrative law judge proceeding), you may electronically serve documents on us.

(ii) *Serve documents* electronically through the Internet at http://dms.dot.gov.

§105.40 Designated agents for non-residents.

(a) **General requirement.** If you are not a resident of the United States but are required by this subchapter or subchapter C of this chapter to designate a permanent resident of the United States to act as your agent and receive documents on your behalf, you must prepare a designation and file it with us.

(b) **Agents.** An agent:

(1) *May be an individual, a firm, or a domestic corporation.*

(2) *May represent any number of principals.*

(3) *May not reassign* responsibilities under a designation to another person.

(c) **Preparing a designation.** Your designation must be written and dated, and it must contain the following information:

(1) *The section in the HMR that requires you to file a designation.*

(2) *A certification* that the designation is in the correct legal form required to make it valid and binding on you under the laws, corporate

bylaws, and other requirements that apply to designations at the time and place you are making the designation.

(3) *Your full legal name,* the principal name of your business, and your mailing address.

(4) *A statement* that your designation will remain in effect until you withdraw or replace it.

(5) *The legal name and mailing address of your agent.*

(6) *A declaration of acceptance signed by your agent.*

(d) **Address.** Send your designation to:
Office of Hazardous Materials Exemptions and Approvals Research and Special Programs Administration, Attn: DHM-30, U.S. Department of Transportation 400 7th Street, SW., Washington, DC 20590-0001.

(e) **Designations are binding.** You are bound by your designation of an agent, even if you did not follow all the requirements in this section, until we reject your designation.

Subpoenas

§105.45 Issuing a subpoena.

(a) **Subpoenas explained.** A subpoena is a document that may require you to attend a proceeding, produce documents or other physical evidence in your possession or control, or both. RSPA may issue a subpoena either on its initiative or at the request of someone participating in a proceeding. Anyone who requests that RSPA issue a subpoena must show that the subpoena seeks information that will materially advance the proceeding.

(b) **Attendance and mileage expenses.**

(1) *If you receive* a subpoena to attend a proceeding under this part, you may receive money to cover attendance and mileage expenses. The attendance and mileage fees will be the same as those paid to a witness in a proceeding in the district courts of the United States.

(2) *If RSPA issues* a subpoena to you based upon a request, the requester must serve a copy of the original subpoena on you, as required in §105.50. The requester must also include attendance and mileage fees with the subpoena unless the requester asks RSPA to pay the attendance and mileage fees because of demonstrated financial hardship and RSPA agrees to do so.

(3) *If RSPA issues* a subpoena at the request of an officer or agency of the Federal government, the officer or agency is not required to include attendance and mileage fees when serving the subpoena. The officer or agency must pay the fees before you leave the hearing at which you testify.

§105.50 Serving a subpoena.

(a) **Personal service.** Anyone who is not an interested party and who is at least 18 years of age may serve you with a subpoena and fees by handing the subpoena and fees to you, by leaving them at your office with the individual in charge, or by leaving them at your house with someone who lives there and is capable of making sure that you receive them. If RSPA issues a subpoena to an entity, rather than an individual, personal service is made by delivering the subpoena and fees to the entity's registered agent for service of process or to any officer, director or agent in charge of any of the entity's offices.

(b) **Service by mail.** You may be served with a copy of a subpoena and fees by certified or registered mail at your last known address. Service of a subpoena and fees may also be made by registered or certified mail to your agent for service of process or any of your representatives at that person's last known address.

(c) **Other methods.** You may be served with a copy of a subpoena by any method where you receive actual notice of the subpoena and receive the fees before leaving the hearing at which you testify.

(d) **Filing after service.** After service is complete, the individual who served a copy of a subpoena and fees must file the original subpoena and a certificate of service with the RSPA official who is responsible for conducting the hearing.

§105.55 Refusal to obey a subpoena.

(a) **Quashing or modifying a subpoena.** If you receive a subpoena, you can ask RSPA to overturn ("quash") or modify the subpoena within 10 days after the subpoena is served on you. Your request must briefly explain the reasons you are asking for the subpoena to be quashed or modified. RSPA may then do the following:

(1) *Deny your request.*

(2) *Quash or modify the subpoena.*

(3) *Grant your request* on the condition that you satisfy certain specified requirements.

(b) **Failure to obey.** If you disobey a subpoena, RSPA may ask the Attorney General to seek help from the United States District Court for the appropriate District to compel you, after notice, to appear before RSPA and give testimony, produce subpoenaed documents or physical evidence, or both.

Notes

Part 106 - Rulemaking Procedures

Subpart A - RSPA Rulemaking Documents

§106.5 Defined terms used in this subpart.

The following defined terms (see part 105, subpart A, of this subchapter) appear in this subpart: File; Person; State.

§106.10 Process for issuing rules.

(a) **RSPA ("we") uses informal rulemaking procedures** under the Administrative Procedure Act (5 U.S.C. 553) to add, amend, or delete regulations. To propose or adopt changes to a regulation, RSPA may issue one or more of the following documents. We publish the following rulemaking documents in the Federal Register unless we name and personally serve a copy of a rule on every person subject to it:
  (1) *An advance notice of proposed rulemaking.*
  (2) *A notice of proposed rulemaking.*
  (3) *A final rule.*
  (4) *An interim final rule.*
  (5) *A direct final rule.*

(b) **Each of the rulemaking documents in paragraph** (a) of this section generally contains the following information:
  (1) *The topic involved in the rulemaking document.*
  (2) *RSPA's legal authority for issuing the rulemaking document.*
  (3) *How interested persons* may participate in the rulemaking proceeding (for example, by filing written comments or making oral presentations).
  (4) *Whom to call if you have questions about the rulemaking document.*
  (5) *The date,* time, and place of any public meetings being held to discuss the rulemaking document.
  (6) *The docket number* and regulation identifier number (RIN) for the rulemaking proceeding.

§106.15 Advance notice of proposed rulemaking.

An advance notice of proposed rulemaking (ANPRM) tells the public that RSPA is considering an area for rulemaking and requests written comments on the appropriate scope of the rulemaking or on specific topics. An advance notice of proposed rulemaking may or may not include the text of potential changes to a regulation.

§106.20 Notice of proposed rulemaking.

A notice of proposed rulemaking (NPRM) contains RSPA's specific proposed regulatory changes for public comment and contains supporting information. It generally includes proposed regulatory text.

§106.25 Revising regulations without first issuing an ANPRM or NPRM.

RSPA may add, amend, or delete regulations without first issuing an ANPRM or NPRM in the following situations:

(a) **We may go directly to a final rule or interim final rule** if, for good cause, we find that a notice of proposed rulemaking is impracticable, unnecessary, or contrary to the public interest. We must place that finding and a brief statement of the reasons for it in the final rule or interim final rule.

(b) **We may issue a direct final rule (see §106.40).**

§106.30 Final rule.

A final rule sets out new regulatory requirements and their effective date. A final rule will also identify issues raised by commenters in response to the notice of proposed rulemaking and give the agency's response.

§106.35 Interim final rule.

An interim final rule is issued without first issuing a notice of proposed rulemaking and accepting public comments and sets out new regulatory requirements and their effective date. RSPA may issue an interim final rule if it finds, for good cause, that notice and public procedure are impracticable, unnecessary, or contrary to the public interest. RSPA will clearly set out this finding in the interim final rule. After receiving and reviewing public comments, as well as any other relevant documents, RSPA may revise the interim final rule and then issue a final rule.

§106.40 Direct final rule.

A direct final rule makes regulatory changes and states that the regulatory changes will take effect on a specified date unless RSPA receives an adverse comment or notice of intent to file an adverse comment within the comment period — generally 60 days after the direct final rule is published in the Federal Register.

(a) **Actions taken by direct final rule.** We may use direct final rulemaking procedures to issue rules that do any of the following:
  (1) *Make minor substantive changes to regulations.*
  (2) *Incorporate by reference* the latest edition of technical or industry standards.
  (3) *Extend compliance dates.*
  (4) *Make noncontroversial changes to regulations.* We must determine and publish a finding that use of direct final rulemaking, in this situation, is in the public interest and unlikely to result in adverse comment.

(b) **Adverse comment.** An adverse comment explains why a rule would be inappropriate, or would be ineffective or unacceptable without a change. It may challenge the rule's underlying premise or approach. Under the direct final rule process, we do not consider the following types of comments to be adverse:
  (1) *A comment recommending* another rule change, in addition to the change in the direct final rule at issue, unless the commenter states why the direct final rule would be ineffective without the change.
  (2) *A frivolous or irrelevant comment.*

(c) **Confirmation of effective date.** We will publish a confirmation document in the Federal Register, generally within 15 days after the comment period closes, if we have not received an adverse comment or notice of intent to file an adverse comment. The confirmation document tells the public the effective date of the rule — either the date stated in the direct final rule or at least 30 days after the publication date of the confirmation document, whichever is later.

(d) **Withdrawing a direct final rule.**
  (1) *If we receive* an adverse comment or notice of intent to file an adverse comment, we will publish a document in the Federal Register before the effective date of the direct final rule advising the public and withdrawing the direct final rule in whole or in part.
  (2) *If we withdraw* a direct final rule because of an adverse comment, we may incorporate the adverse comment into a later direct final rule or may publish a notice of proposed rulemaking.

(e) **Appeal.** You may appeal RSPA's issuance of a direct final rule (see §106.115) only if you have previously filed written comments (see §106.60) to the direct final rule.

§106.45 Tracking rulemaking actions.

The following identifying numbers allow you to track RSPA's rulemaking activities:

(a) **Docket number.** We assign an identifying number, called a docket number, to each rulemaking proceeding. Each rulemaking document that RSPA issues in a particular rulemaking proceeding will display the same docket number. This number allows you to do the following:
  (1) *Associate related documents that appear in the Federal Register.*
  (2) *Search* the DOT Docket Management System ("DMS") for information on particular rulemaking proceedings — including notices of proposed rulemaking, public comments, petitions for rulemaking, appeals, records of additional rulemaking proceedings and final rules. There are two ways you can search the DMS:
    (i) *Visit the public docket room* and review and copy any docketed materials during regular business hours. The DOT Docket Management System is located at the U.S. Department of Transportation, Plaza Level 401, 400 7th Street, SW., Washington, DC 20590-0001.
    (ii) *View and download* docketed materials through the Internet at http://dms.dot.gov.

(b) **Regulation identifier number.** The Department of Transportation publishes a semiannual agenda of all current and projected Department of Transportation rulemakings, reviews of existing regulations, and completed actions. This semiannual agenda appears in the Unified Agenda of Federal Regulations that is published in the Federal Register in April and October of each year. The semiannual agenda tells the public about the Department's — including RSPA's — regulatory activities. The Department assigns a regulation identifier number (RIN) to each individual rulemaking proceeding in the semiannual agenda. This number appears on all rulemaking documents published in the Federal Register and makes it easy for you to track those rulemaking proceedings in both the Federal Register and the semiannual regulatory agenda itself, as well as to locate all documents in the Docket Management System pertaining to a particular rulemaking.

Subpart B - Participating in the Rulemaking Process

§106.50 Defined terms used in this subpart.

The following defined terms (see part 105, subpart A, of this subchapter) appear in this subpart: File; Person; Political subdivision; State.

§106.55 Public participation in the rulemaking process.

You may participate in RSPA's rulemaking process by doing any of the following:

(a) **File written comments on any rulemaking document** that asks for comments, including an advance notice of proposed rulemaking, notice of proposed rulemaking, interim final rule, or direct final rule.

(b) **Ask that we hold a public meeting** in any rulemaking proceeding and participate in any public meeting that we hold.

(c) **File a petition for rulemaking that asks us** to add, amend, or delete a regulation.

(d) **File an appeal that asks us to reexamine our decision** to issue all or part of a final rule, interim final rule, or direct final rule.

Written Comments

§106.60 Filing comments.

Anyone may file written comments about proposals made in any rulemaking document that requests public comments, including any State government agency, any political subdivision of a State, and any interested person invited by RSPA to participate in the rulemaking process.

§106.65 Required information for written comments.

Your comments must be in English and must contain the following:

(a) **The docket number of the rulemaking document** you are commenting on, clearly set out at the beginning of your comments.

(b) **Information, views, or arguments** that follow the instructions for participation that appear in the rulemaking document on which you are commenting.

(c) **All material that is relevant to any statement of fact** in your comments.

(d) **The document title and page number of any material** that you reference in your comments.

§106.70 Where and when to file comments.

(a) **Unless you are told to do otherwise** in the rulemaking document on which you are commenting, send your comments to us in either of the following ways:

(1) *By mail to:* Docket Management System, U.S. Department of Transportation, Room PL 401, Washington, DC 20590-0001.

(2) *Through the Internet to http://dms.dot.gov.*

(b) **Make sure that your comments reach us** by the deadline set out in the rulemaking document on which you are commenting. We will consider late-filed comments to the extent possible.

(c) **We may reject comments that are not relevant** to the rulemaking. We may reject comments you file electronically if you do not follow the electronic filing instructions at the DOT Web site.

§106.75 Extension of time to file comments.

You may ask for more time to file comments on a rulemaking proceeding. If RSPA grants your request, it is granted to all persons. We will notify the public of the extension by publishing a document in the Federal Register. If RSPA denies your request, RSPA will notify you of the denial. To ask for more time, you must do the following:

(a) **File a request for extension at least ten days** before the end of the comment period established in the rulemaking document.

(b) **Show that you have good cause for the extension** and that an extension is in the public interest.

(c) **Include the docket number of the rulemaking document** you are seeking additional time to comment on, clearly set out at the beginning of your request.

(d) **Send your request to:** Docket Management System, U.S. Department of Transportation, Room PL 401, 400 7th Street, SW., Washington, DC 20590-0001.

Public Meetings and Other Proceedings

§106.80 Public meeting procedures.

A public meeting is a non-adversarial, fact-finding proceeding conducted by a RSPA representative. Generally, public meetings are announced in the Federal Register. Interested persons are invited to attend and to present their views to the agency on specific issues. There are no formal pleadings and no adverse parties, and any regulation issued afterward is not necessarily based exclusively on the record of the meeting. Sections 556 and 557 of the Administrative Procedure Act (5 U.S.C. 556 and 557) do not apply to public meetings under this part.

§106.85 Requesting a public meeting.

(a) **You may ask for a public meeting** by filing a written request with RSPA no later than 20 days before the expiration of the comment period specified in the rulemaking document. Send your request for a public meeting to: Docket Management System, U.S. Department of Transportation, Room PL 401, 400 7th Street, SW., Washington, DC 20590-0001.

(b) **RSPA will review your request** and, if you have shown good cause for a public meeting, we will grant it and publish a notice of the meeting in the Federal Register.

§106.90 Other rulemaking proceedings.

During a rulemaking proceeding, RSPA may invite you to do the following:

(a) **Participate in a conference at which minutes are taken.**

(b) **Make an oral presentation.**

(c) **Participate in any other public proceeding** to ensure that RSPA makes informed decisions during the rulemaking process and to protect the public interest, including a negotiated rulemaking or work group led by a facilitator.

Petitions for Rulemaking

§106.95 Requesting a change to the regulations.

You may ask RSPA to add, amend, or delete a regulation by filing a petition for rulemaking as follows:

(a) **For regulations in 49 CFR parts 110, 130, 171 through 180,** submit the petition to: Office of Hazardous Materials Standards, Research and Special Programs Administration, Attn: DHM-10, U.S. Department of Transportation, 400 7th Street, SW., Washington, DC 20590-0001.

(b) **For regulations in 49 CFR parts 105, 106, or 107,** submit the petition to: Office of the Chief Counsel, Research and Special Programs Administration, Attn: DCC-10, U.S. Department of Transportation, 400 7th Street, SW., Washington, DC 20590-0001.

§106.100 Required information for a petition for rulemaking.

(a) **You must include the following information** in your petition for rulemaking:

(1) *A summary* of your proposed action and an explanation of its purpose.

(2) *The language* you propose for a new or amended rule, or the language you would delete from a current rule.

(3) *An explanation* of your interest in your proposed action and the interest of anyone you may represent.

(4) *Information and arguments* that support your proposed action, including relevant technical and scientific data available to you.

(5) *Any specific cases* that support or demonstrate the need for your proposed action.

(b) **If the impact of your proposed action is substantial,** and data or other information about that impact are available to you, we may ask that you provide information about the following:

(1) *The costs and benefits* of your proposed action to society in general, and identifiable groups within society in particular.

(2) *The direct effects,* including preemption effects under section 5125 of Federal hazardous materials transportation law, of your proposed action on States, on the relationship between the Federal government and the States, and on the distribution of power and responsibilities among the various levels of government. (See 49 CFR part 107, subpart C, regarding preemption.)

(3) *The regulatory burden* of your proposed action on small businesses, small organizations, small governmental jurisdictions, and Indian tribes.

(4) *The recordkeeping* and reporting burdens of your proposed action and whom they would affect.

(5) *The effect* of your proposed action on the quality of the natural and social environments.

§106.105 RSPA response to a petition for rulemaking.

We will review and respond to your petition for rulemaking as follows:

If your petition is . . .	And if we determine that . . .	Then . . .
(a) Incomplete		We may return your petition with a written explanation.
(b) Complete	Your petition does not justify a rulemaking action.	We will notify you in writing that we will not start a rulemaking proceeding.
(c) Complete	Your petition does justify a rulemaking action.	We will notify you in writing that we will start a rulemaking proceeding.

Appeals

§106.110 Appealing a RSPA action.

You may appeal the following RSPA actions:

(a) **RSPA's issuance of a final rule** or RSPA's withdrawal of a notice of proposed rulemaking under the rulemaking procedures in this part. However, you may appeal RSPA's issuance of a direct final rule only if you previously filed comments to the direct final rule (see §106.40(e)).

(b) **Any RSPA decision on a petition for rulemaking.**

§106.115 Required information for an appeal.

(a) **Appeal of a final rule or withdrawal of a notice** of proposed rulemaking. If you appeal RSPA's issuance of a final rule or RSPA's withdrawal of a notice of proposed rulemaking, your appeal must include the following:

(1) *The docket number* of the rulemaking you are concerned about, clearly set out at the beginning of your appeal.

(2) *A brief statement* of your concern about the final rule or the withdrawal of notice of proposed rulemaking at issue.

(3) *An explanation* of why compliance with the final rule is not practical, reasonable, or in the public interest.

(4) *If you want RSPA* to consider more facts, the reason why you did not present those facts within the time given during the rulemaking process for public comment.

(b) **Appeal of a decision.** If you appeal RSPA's decision on a petition for rulemaking, you must include the following:

(1) *The contested aspects of the decision.*

(2) *Any new arguments or information.*

§106.120 Appeal deadline.

(a) **Appeal of a final rule or withdrawal of a notice** of proposed rulemaking. If you appeal RSPA's issuance of a final rule or RSPA's withdrawal of a proposed rulemaking, your appeal document must reach us no later than 30 days after the date RSPA published the regulation or the withdrawal notice in the Federal Register. After that time, RSPA will consider your petition to be one for rulemaking under §106.100.

(b) **Appeal of a decision.** If you appeal RSPA's decision on a petition for rulemaking, your appeal document must reach us no later than 30 days from the date RSPA served you with written notice of RSPA's decision.

§106.125 Filing an appeal.

Send your appeal to: Docket Management System, U.S. Department of Transportation, Room PL 401, 400 7th Street, SW., Washington, DC 20590-0001.

§106.130 RSPA response to an appeal.

Unless RSPA provides otherwise, filing an appeal will not keep a final rule from becoming effective. We will handle an appeal according to the following procedures:

(a) **Appeal of a final rule or withdrawal of a notice** of proposed rulemaking.

(1) *We may consolidate* your appeal with other appeals of the same rule.

(2) *We may grant or deny your appeal,* in whole or in part, without further rulemaking proceedings, unless granting your appeal would result in the issuance of a new final rule.

(3) *If we decide to grant your appeal,* we may schedule further proceedings and an opportunity to comment.

(4) *RSPA will notify you,* in writing, of the action on your appeal within 90 days after the date that RSPA published the final rule or withdrawal of notice of proposed rulemaking at issue in the Federal Register. If we do not issue a decision on your appeal within the 90-day period and we anticipate a substantial delay, we will notify you directly about the delay and will give you an expected decision date. We will also publish a notice of the delay in the Federal Register.

(b) **Appeal of a decision.**

(1) *We will not consider your appeal* if it merely repeats arguments that RSPA has previously rejected.

(2) *RSPA will notify you,* in writing, of the action on your appeal within 90 days after the date that RSPA served you with written notice of its decision on your petition for rulemaking. If we do not issue a decision on your appeal within the 90-day period, and we anticipate a substantial delay, we will notify you directly about the delay and will give you an expected decision date.

Notes

Part 107 - Hazardous Materials Program Procedures

Subpart A - Definitions

§107.1 Definitions.

All terms defined in 49 U.S.C. 5102 are used in their statutory meaning. Other terms used in this part are defined as follows:

Acting knowingly means acting or failing to act while

(1) *Having actual knowledge of the facts giving rise to the violation, or*

(2) *Having the knowledge* that a reasonable person acting in the same circumstances and exercising due care would have had.

Administrator means the Administrator, Research and Special Programs Administration or his or her delegate.

Applicant means the person in whose name an exemption, approval, registration, a renewed or modified exemption or approval, or party status to an exemption is requested to be issued.

Application means a request under subpart B of this part for an exemption, a renewal or modification of an exemption, party status to an exemption, or a request under subpart H of this part for an approval, or renewal or modification of an approval.

Approval means written consent, including a competent authority approval, from the Associate Administrator, or other designated Department official, to perform a function that requires prior consent under subchapter C of this chapter (49 CFR parts 171 through 180).

Approval Agency means an organization or a person designated by the RSPA to certify packagings as having been designed, manufactured, tested, modified, marked or maintained in compliance with applicable DOT regulations.

Associate Administrator means the Associate Administrator for Hazardous Materials Safety, Research and Special Programs Administration.

Competent Authority means a national agency that is responsible, under its national law, for the control or regulation of some aspect of hazardous materials (dangerous goods) transportation. Another term for "Competent Authority" is "Appropriate Authority," which is used in the International Civil Aviation Organization's (ICAO) Technical Instructions for the Safe Transport of Dangerous Goods by Air. The Associate Administrator is the United States Competent Authority for purposes of this part 107.

Competent Authority Approval means an approval by the competent authority that is required under an international standard (for example, the ICAO Technical Instructions for the Safe Transport of Dangerous Goods by Air or the International Maritime Dangerous Goods Code). Any of the following may be considered a competent authority approval if it satisfies the requirement of an international standard:

(1) *A specific regulation in subchapter A or C of this chapter.*

(2) *An exemption or approval* issued under subchapter A or C of this chapter.

(3) *A separate document* issued to one or more persons by the Associate Administrator.

DOT or **Department** means U.S. Department of Transportation.

Exemption means a document issued by the Associate Administrator under the authority of 49 U.S.C. 5117. The document permits a person to perform a function that is not otherwise permitted under subchapter A or C of this chapter, or other regulations issued under 49 U.S.C. 5101-5127 (e.g., Federal Motor Carrier Safety routing requirements).

Federal hazardous material transportation law means 49 U.S.C. 5101 et seq.

Filed means received by the appropriate RSPA or other designated office within the time specified in a regulation or rulemaking document.

Holder means the person in whose name an exemption or approval has been issued.

Imminent Hazard means the existence of a condition which presents a substantial likelihood that death, serious illness, severe personal injury, or substantial endangerment to health, property, or the environment may occur before the reasonably foreseeable completion of an administrative hearing or other formal proceeding initiated to abate the risks of those effects.

Incident means an event resulting in the unintended and unanticipated release of a hazardous material or an event meeting incident reporting requirements in §171.15 or §171.16 of this chapter.

Indian Tribe has the same meaning given that term in section 4 of the Indian Self-Determination and Education Assistance Act (25 U.S.C. 450b).

Investigation includes investigations authorized under 49 U.S.C. 5121 and inspections authorized under 49 U.S.C. 5118 and 5121.

Manufacturing exemption means an exemption from compliance with specified requirements that otherwise must be met before representing, marking, certifying (including requalifying, inspecting, and testing), selling or offering a packaging or container as meeting the requirements of subchapter C of this chapter governing its use in the transportation in commerce of a hazardous material. A manufacturing exemption is an exemption issued to a manufacturer of packagings who does not offer for transportation or transport hazardous materials in packagings subject to the exemption.

Party means a person, other than a holder, authorized to act under the terms of an exemption.

Person means an individual, firm, copartnership, corporation, company, association, or joint-stock association (including any trustee, receiver, assignee, or similar representative); or a government or Indian tribe (or an agency or instrumentality of any government or Indian tribe) that transports a hazardous material to further a commercial enterprise or offers a hazardous material for transportation in commerce. "Person" does not include the following:

(1) *The United States Postal Service,*

(2) *Any agency or instrumentality* of the Federal government, for the purposes of 49 U.S.C. 5123 (civil penalties) and 5124 (criminal penalties).

(3) *Any government or Indian tribe* (or an agency or instumentality of any government or Indian tribe) that transports hazardous material for a governmental purpose.

Registration means a written acknowledgment from the Associate Administrator that a registrant is authorized to perform a function for which registration is required under subchapter C of this chapter (e.g., registration in accordance with 49 CFR 178.503 regarding marking of packagings). For purposes of subparts A through E, "registration" does not include registration under subpart F or G of this part.

Report means information, other than an application, registration or part thereof, required to be submitted to the Associate Administrator pursuant to this subchapter, subchapter B or subchapter C of this chapter.

Respondent means a person upon whom the RSPA has served a notice of probable violation.

State means a State of the United States, the District of Columbia, the Commonwealth of Puerto Rico, the Commonwealth of the Northern Mariana Islands, the Virgin Islands, American Samoa, Guam, or any other territory or possession of the United States designated by the Secretary.

Transports or **transportation** means the movement of property and loading, unloading, or storage incidental to the movement.

Subpart B - Exemptions

§107.101 Purpose and scope.

This subpart prescribes procedures for the issuance, modification and termination of exemptions from requirements of this subchapter, subchapter C of this chapter, or regulations issued under chapter 51 of 49 U.S.C.

§107.105 Application for exemption.

(a) **General.** Each application for an exemption or modification of an exemption must be written in English and must —

(1) *Be submitted* for timely consideration, at least 120 days before the requested effective date, in duplicate to: Associate Administrator for Hazardous Materials Safety (Attention: Exemptions, DHM-31), Research and Special Programs Administration, U.S. Department of Transportation, 400 7th Street, SW., Washington, DC 20590-0001. Alternatively, the application with any attached supporting documentation submitted in an appropriate format may be sent by facsimile (fax) to: (202) 366-3753 or (202) 366-3308 or by electronic mail (e-mail) to: Exemptions@rspa.dot.gov;

(2) *State the name,* street and mailing addresses, e-mail address optional, and telephone number of the applicant; if the applicant is not an individual, state the name, street and mailing addresses, e-mail address optional, and telephone number of an individual designated as an agent of the applicant for all purposes related to the application;

(3) *If the applicant* is not a resident of the United States, a designation of agent for service in accordance with §105.40 of this part; and

(4) *For a manufacturing exemption,* a statement of the name and street address of each facility where manufacturing under the exemption will occur.

(b) **Confidential treatment.** To request confidential treatment for information contained in the application, the applicant shall comply with §105.30.

(c) **Description of exemption proposal.** The application must include the following information that is relevant to the exemption proposal:

(1) *A citation* of the specific regulation from which the applicant seeks relief;

(2) *Specification of the proposed mode or modes of transportation;*
(3) *A detailed description* of the proposed exemption (e.g., alternative packaging, test, procedure or activity) including, as appropriate, written descriptions, drawings, flow charts, plans and other supporting documents;
(4) *A specification* of the proposed duration or schedule of events for which the exemption is sought;
(5) *A statement* outlining the applicant's basis for seeking relief from compliance with the specified regulations and, if the exemption is requested for a fixed period, a description of how compliance will be achieved at the end of that period;
(6) *If the applicant* seeks emergency processing specified in §107.117, a statement of supporting facts and reasons;
(7) *Identification and description* of the hazardous materials planned for transportation under the exemption;
(8) *Description* of each packaging, including specification or exemption number, as applicable, to be used in conjunction with the requested exemption;
(9) *For alternative packagings,* documentation of quality assurance controls, package design, manufacture, performance test criteria, in-service performance and service-life limitations.

(d) **Justification of exemption proposal.** The application must demonstrate that an exemption achieves a level of safety at least equal to that required by regulation, or if a required safety level does not exist, is consistent with the public interest. At a minimum, the application must provide the following:
(1) *Information describing* all relevant shipping and incident experience of which the applicant is aware that relates to the application;
(2) *A statement* identifying any increased risk to safety or property that may result if the exemption is granted, and a description of the measures to be taken to address that risk; and
(3) *Either* —
(i) *Substantiation,* with applicable analyses, data or test results, that the proposed alternative will achieve a level of safety that is at least equal to that required by the regulation from which the exemption is sought; or
(ii) *If the regulations* do not establish a level of safety, an analysis that identifies each hazard, potential failure mode and the probability of its occurrence, and how the risks associated with each hazard and failure mode are controlled for the duration of an activity or life-cycle of a packaging.

FEDERAL REGISTER UPDATES

An Interim Final Rule affecting §107.105 was published in the May 5, 2003 Federal Register.

(c) [1]

(10) *A certification that the applicant* is in compliance with transportation security laws and regulations. When a Class 1 material is forbidden for transportation by air except under an exemption (see Columns 9A and 9B in the table in 49 CFR 172.101), an applicant for an exemption to transport such Class 1 material on passenger-carrying or cargo-only aircraft must also certify that no person within the categories listed in 18 U.S.C. 842(i) will participate in the transportation of the Class 1 material. [2]

1. Paragraph (c) is the same as before.
2. Paragraph (c)(10) was added.

§107.107 Application for party status.

(a) **Any person eligible to apply for an exemption** may apply to be made party to an application or an existing exemption, other than a manufacturing exemption.

(b) **Each application filed under this section must** —
(1) *Be submitted in duplicate to:* Associate Administrator for Hazardous Materials Safety (Attention: Exemptions, DHM-31), Research and Special Programs Administration, U.S. Department of Transportation, 400 7th Street, SW, Washington, DC 20590-0001. Alternatively, the application with any attached supporting documentation submitted in an appropriate format may be sent by facsimile (fax) to: (202) 366-3753 or (202) 366-3308 or by electronic mail (e-mail) to: Exemptions@rspa.dot.gov;
(2) *Identify by number* the exemption application or exemption to which the applicant seeks to become a party;
(3) *State the name,* street and mailing addresses, e-mail address optional, and telephone number of the applicant; if the applicant is not an individual, state the name, street and mailing addresses, e-mail address optional, and telephone number of an individual designated as the applicant's agent for all purposes related to the application; and
(4) *If the applicant* is not a resident of the United States, provide a designation of agent for service in accordance with §105.40.

(c) **The Associate Administrator grants or denies** an application for party status in the manner specified in §107.113(e) and (f) of this subpart.

(d) **A party to an exemption is subject to all terms** of that exemption, including the expiration date. If a party to an exemption wishes to renew party status, the exemption renewal procedures set forth in §107.109 apply.

§107.109 Application for renewal.

(a) **Each application for renewal of an exemption** or party status to an exemption must —
(1) *Be submitted in duplicate to:* Associate Administrator for Hazardous Materials Safety (Attention: Exemptions, DHM-31), Research and Special Programs Administration, U.S. Department of Transportation, 400 7th Street, SW, Washington, DC 20590-0001. Alternatively, the application with any attached supporting documentation submitted in an appropriate format may be sent by facsimile (fax) to: (202) 366-3753 or (202) 366-3308 or by electronic mail (e-mail) to: Exemptions@rspa.dot.gov;
(2) *Identify by number the exemption for which renewal is requested;*
(3) *State the name,* street and mailing addresses, e-mail address optional, and telephone number of the applicant; if the applicant is not an individual, state the name, street and mailing addresses, e-mail address optional, and telephone number of an individual designated as an agent of the applicant for all purposes related to the application;
(4) *Include either* a certification by the applicant that the original application, as it may have been updated by any application for renewal, remains accurate and complete; or include an amendment to the previously submitted application as is necessary to update and assure the accuracy and completeness of the application, with certification by the applicant that the application as amended is accurate and complete; and
(5) *Include a statement* describing all relevant shipping and incident experience of which the applicant is aware in connection with the exemption since its issuance or most recent renewal. If the applicant is aware of no incidents, the applicant shall so certify. When known to the applicant, the statement should indicate the approximate number of shipments made or packages shipped, as the case may be, and number of shipments or packages involved in any loss of contents, including loss by venting other than as authorized in subchapter C.

(b) **If at least 60 days before an existing exemption expires** the holder files an application for renewal that is complete and conforms to the requirements of this section, the exemption will not expire until final administrative action on the application for renewal has been taken.

FEDERAL REGISTER UPDATES

An Interim Final Rule affecting §107.109 was published in the May 5, 2003 Federal Register.

(a) [1]

(6) *Include a certification that the applicant* is in compliance with transportation security laws and regulations. When a Class 1 material is forbidden for transportation by air except under an exemption (see Columns 9A and 9B in the table in 49 CFR 172.101), an applicant for an exemption to transport such Class 1 material on passenger-carrying or cargo-only aircraft must also certify that no person within the categories listed in 18 U.S.C. 842(i) will participate in the transportation of the Class 1 material. [2]

1. Paragraph (a) is the same as before.
2. Paragraph (a)(6) was added.

§107.111 Withdrawal.

An application may be withdrawn at any time before a decision to grant or deny it is made. Withdrawal of an application does not authorize the removal of any related records from the RSPA dockets or files. Applications that are eligible for confidential treatment under §105.30 will remain confidential after the application is withdrawn. The duration of this confidential treatment for trade secrets and commercial or financial information is indefinite, unless the party requesting the confidential treatment of the materials notifies the Associate Administrator that the confidential treatment is no longer required.

§107.113 Application processing and evaluation.

(a) **The Associate Administrator reviews an application** for exemption, modification of exemption, party to exemption, or renewal of an exemption to determine if it is complete and conforms with the requirements of this subpart. This determination will be made within 30 days of receipt of the application for exemption, modification of exemption, or party to exemption, and within 15 days of receipt of an application for renewal of an exemption. If an application is determined to be incomplete, the applicant is informed of the reasons.

(b) **An application, other than a renewal,** party to, or emergency exemption application, that is determined to be complete is docketed. Notice of the application is published in the Federal Register, and an opportunity for public comment is provided. All comments received during the comment period are considered before final action is taken on the application.

(c) **No public hearing or other formal proceeding** is required under this subpart before the disposition of an application. Unless emergency processing under §107.117 is requested and granted, applications are usually processed in the order in which they are filed.

(d) **During the processing and evaluation of an application,** the Associate Administrator may request additional information from the applicant. If the applicant does not respond to a written request for additional information within 30 days of the date the request was received, the application may be deemed incomplete and denied. However, if the applicant responds in writing within the 30-day period requesting an additional 30 days within which it will gather the requested information, the Associate Administrator may grant the 30-day extension.

(e) **The Associate Administrator may grant or deny** an application, in whole or in part. In the Associate Administrator's discretion, an application may be granted subject to provisions that are appropriate to protect health, safety or property. The Associate Administrator may impose additional provisions not specified in the application or remove conditions in the application that are unnecessary.

(f) **The Associate Administrator may grant an application** on finding that —

(1) *The application complies with this subpart;*

(2) *The application demonstrates* that the proposed alternative will achieve a level of safety that:

(i) *Is at least equal to* that required by the regulation from which the exemption is sought, or

(ii) *If the regulations* do not establish a level of safety, is consistent with the public interest and adequately will protect against the risks to life and property inherent in the transportation of hazardous materials in commerce;

(3) *The application states* all material facts, and contains no materially false or materially misleading statement;

(4) *The applicant meets* the qualifications required by applicable regulations; and

(5) *The applicant* is fit to conduct the activity authorized by the exemption. This assessment may be based on information in the application, prior compliance history of the applicant, and other information available to the Associate Administrator.

(g) **An applicant is notified in writing** whether the application is granted or denied. A denial contains a brief statement of reasons.

(h) **An exemption and any renewal thereof** terminates according to its terms or, if not otherwise specified, two years after the date of issuance. A grant of party status to an exemption, unless otherwise stated, terminates on the date that the exemption expires.

(i) **The Associate Administrator, on determining** that an application concerns a matter of general applicability and future effect and should be the subject of rulemaking, may initiate rulemaking under part 106 of this chapter in addition to or instead of acting on the application.

(j) **The Associate Administrator publishes** in the Federal Register a list of all exemption grants, denials, and modifications and all exemption applications withdrawn under this section.

§107.117 Emergency processing.

(a) **An application is granted emergency processing** if the Associate Administrator, on the basis of the application and any inquiry undertaken, finds that —

(1) *Emergency processing* is necessary to prevent significant injury to persons or property (other than the hazardous material to be transported) that could not be prevented if the application were processed on a routine basis; or

(2) *Emergency processing* is necessary for immediate national security purposes or to prevent significant economic loss that could not be prevented if the application were processed on a routine basis.

(b) **Where the significant economic loss is to the applicant,** or to a party in a contractual relationship to the applicant with respect to the activity to be undertaken, the Associate Administrator may deny emergency processing if timely application could have been made.

(c) **A request for emergency processing** on the basis of potential economic loss must reasonably describe and estimate the potential loss.

(d) **An application submitted under this section** must conform to §107.105 to the extent that the receiving Department official deems necessary to process the application. An application on an emergency basis must be submitted to the Department modal contact official for the initial mode of transportation to be utilized, as follows:

(1) *Certificate-Holding Aircraft:* The Federal Aviation Administration Civil Aviation Security Office that serves the place where the flight will originate or that is responsible for the aircraft operator's overall aviation security program. The nearest Civil Aviation Security Office may be located by calling the FAA Duty Officer, 202-267-3333 (any hour).

(2) *Noncertificate-Holding Aircraft* (Those Which Operate Under 14 CFR Part 91): The Federal Aviation Administration Civil Aviation Security Office that serves the place where the flight will originate. The nearest Civil Aviation Security Office may be located by calling the FAA Duty Officer, 202-267-3333 (any hour).

(3) *Motor Vehicle Transportation:* Chief, Hazardous Materials Division, Federal Motor Carrier Safety Administration, U.S. Department of Transportation, Washington, DC 20590-0001, 202-366-6121 (day); 1-800-424-8802 (night).

(4) *Rail Transportation:* Staff Director, Hazardous Materials Division, Office of Safety Assurance and Compliance, Federal Railroad Administration, U.S. Department of Transportation, Washington, DC 20590-0001, 202-493-6248 or 202-493-6244 (day); 1-800-424-8802 (night).

(5) *Water Transportation:* Chief, Hazardous Materials Standards Division, Office of Operating and Environmental Standards, United States Coast Guard, U.S. Department of Transportation, Washington, DC 20593-0001, 202-267-1577 (day); 1-800-424-8802 (night).

(e) **On receipt of all information necessary** to process the application, the receiving Department official transmits to the Associate Administrator, by the most rapid available means of communication, an evaluation as to whether an emergency exists under §107.117(a) and, if appropriate, recommendations as to the conditions to be included in the exemption. If the Associate Administrator determines that an emergency exists under §107.117(a) and that, with reference to the criteria of §107.113(f), granting of the application is in the public interest, the Associate Administrator grants the application subject to such terms as necessary and immediately notifies the applicant. If the Associate Administrator determines that an emergency does not exist or that granting of the application is not in the public interest, the applicant immediately is so notified.

(f) **A determination that an emergency does not exist** is not subject to reconsideration under §107.123 of this part.

(g) **Within 90 days following issuance** of an emergency exemption, the Associate Administrator will publish, in the Federal Register, a notice of issuance with a statement of the basis for the finding of emergency and the scope and duration of the exemption.

§107.121 Modification, suspension or termination of exemption or grant of party status.

(a) **The Associate Administrator may modify** an exemption or grant of party status on finding that —

(1) *Modification is necessary* so that an exemption reflects current statutes and regulations; or

(2) *Modification is required* by changed circumstances to meet the standards of §107.113(f).

(b) **The Associate Administrator may modify,** suspend or terminate an exemption or grant of party status, as appropriate, on finding that —

(1) *Because of a change* in circumstances, the exemption or party status no longer is needed or no longer would be granted if applied for;

(2) *The application* contained inaccurate or incomplete information, and the exemption or party status would not have been granted had the application been accurate and complete;

(3) *The application* contained deliberately inaccurate or incomplete information; or

(4) *The holder or party* knowingly has violated the terms of the exemption or an applicable requirement of this chapter, in a manner demonstrating the holder or party is not fit to conduct the activity authorized by the exemption.

(c) **Except as provided in paragraph (d) of this section,** before an exemption or grant of party status is modified, suspended or terminated, the Associate Administrator notifies the holder or party in writing of the proposed action and the reasons for it, and provides an opportunity to show cause why the proposed action should not be taken.

(1) *The holder or party* may file a written response that shows cause why the proposed action should not be taken within 30 days of receipt of notice of the proposed action.

(2) *After considering* the holder's or party's written response, or after 30 days have passed without response since receipt of the

notice, the Associate Administrator notifies the holder or party in writing of the final decision with a brief statement of reasons.

(d) The Associate Administrator, if necessary to avoid a risk of significant harm to persons or property, may in the notification declare the proposed action immediately effective.

§107.123 Reconsideration.

(a) An applicant for exemption, an exemption holder, or an applicant for party status to an exemption may request that the Associate Administrator reconsider a decision under §107.113(g), §107.117(e) or §107.121(c) of this part. The request must —
  (1) *Be in writing and filed within 20 days of receipt of the decision;*
  (2) *State in detail any alleged errors of fact and law;*
  (3) *Enclose any additional information* needed to support the request to reconsider; and
  (4) *State in detail the modification of the final decision sought.*

(b) The Associate Administrator grants or denies, in whole or in part, the relief requested and informs the requesting person in writing of the decision. If necessary to avoid a risk of significant harm to persons or property, the Associate Administrator may, in the notification, declare the action immediately effective.

§107.125 Appeal.

(a) A person who requested reconsideration under §107.123 and is denied the relief requested may appeal to the Administrator. The appeal must —
  (1) *Be in writing and filed* within 30 days of receipt of the Associate Administrator's decision on reconsideration;
  (2) *State in detail any alleged errors of fact and law;*
  (3) *Enclose any additional information* needed to support the appeal; and
  (4) *State in detail the modification of the final decision sought.*

(b) The Administrator, if necessary to avoid a risk of significant harm to persons or property, may declare the Associate Administrator's action effective pending a decision on appeal.

(c) The Administrator grants or denies, in whole or in part, the relief requested and informs the appellant in writing of the decision. The Administrator's decision is the final administrative action.

§107.127 Availability of documents for public inspection.

(a) Documents related to an application under this subpart, including the application itself, are available for public inspection, except as specified in paragraph (b) of this section, at the Office of the Associate Administrator for Hazardous Materials Safety, Research and Special Programs Administration, Office of Hazardous Materials Exemptions and Approvals, U.S. Department of Transportation, 400 7th Street, SW, Washington, DC 20590-0001, Room 8100. Office hours are 8:30 a.m. to 5:00 p.m., Monday through Friday, except holidays when the office is closed. Copies of available documents may be obtained as provided in part 7 of this title. Documents numbered 11832 and above may also be viewed at the internet website address http://dms.dot.gov.

(b) Documents available for inspection do not include materials determined to be withheld from public disclosure under §105.30 and in accordance with the applicable provisions of section 552(b) of title 5, United States Code, and part 7 of this title.

Subpart C - Preemption

§107.201 Purpose and scope.

(a) This subpart prescribes procedures by which:
  (1) *Any person,* including a State, political subdivision, or Indian tribe, directly affected by any requirement of a State, political subdivision, or Indian tribe, may apply for a determination as to whether that requirement is preempted under 49 U.S.C. 5125, or regulations issued thereunder; and
  (2) *A State,* political subdivision, or Indian tribe may apply for a waiver of preemption with respect to any requirement that the State, political subdivision, or Indian tribe acknowledges to be preempted by 49 U.S.C. 5125, or regulations issued thereunder, or that has been determined by a court of competent jurisdiction to be so preempted.

(b) For purposes of this subpart, **political subdivision** includes a municipality; a public agency or other instrumentality of one or more States, municipalities, or other political subdivisions of a State; or a public corporation, board, or commission established under the laws of one or more States.

(c) For purposes of this subpart, **regulations issued under the Federal hazardous material transportation law** means the regulations contained in this subchapter and subchapter C of this chapter.

(d) Unless otherwise ordered by the Associate Administrator, an application for a preemption determination which includes an application for a waiver of preemption will be treated and processed solely as an application for a preemption determination.

§107.202 Standards for determining preemption.

(a) Except as provided in §107.221 and unless otherwise authorized by Federal law, any requirement of a State or political subdivision thereof or an Indian tribe, that concerns one of the following subjects and that is not substantively the same as any provision of the Federal hazardous material transportation law, this subchapter or subchapter C that concerns that subject, is preempted:
  (1) *The designation,* description, and classification of hazardous material.
  (2) *The packing,* repacking, handling, labeling, marking, and placarding of hazardous material.
  (3) *The preparation,* execution, and use of shipping documents pertaining to hazardous material and requirements related to the number, content, and placement of those documents.
  (4) *The written notification,* recording, and reporting of the unintentional release in transportation of hazardous material.
  (5) *The design,* manufacturing, fabrication, marking, maintenance, reconditioning, repairing, or testing of a packaging or a container which is represented, marked, certified, or sold as qualified for use in the transportation of hazardous material.

(b) Except as provided in §107.221 and unless otherwise authorized by Federal law, any requirement of a State or political subdivision or Indian tribe is preempted if —
  (1) *Complying with* a requirement of the State, political subdivision, or Indian tribe and a requirement under the Federal hazardous material transportation law or regulations issued thereunder is not possible;
  (2) *The requirement* of the State, political subdivision, or Indian tribe, as applied or enforced, is an obstacle to accomplishing and carrying out the Federal hazardous material transportation law or regulations issued thereunder; or
  (3) *It is preempted under 49 U.S.C. 5125 (c).*

(c) A State, political subdivision, or Indian tribe may impose a fee related to transporting hazardous material only if the fee is fair and used for a purpose related to transporting hazardous material, including enforcement and planning, developing and maintaining a capability for emergency response.

(d) For purposes of this section, "substantively the same" means that the non-Federal requirement conforms in every significant respect to the Federal requirement. Editorial and other similar de minimis changes are permitted.

Preemption Determinations

§107.203 Application.

(a) With the exception of highway routing matters covered under 49 U.S.C. 5125(c), any person, including a State or political subdivision thereof or an Indian tribe, directly affected by any requirement of a State or political subdivision thereof or an Indian tribe, may apply to the Associate Administrator for a determination of whether that requirement is preempted by §107.202 (a) or (b).

(b) Each application filed under this section for a determination must:
  (1) *Be submitted* to Associate Administrator for Hazardous Materials Safety, Research and Special Programs Administration, U.S. Department of Transportation, Washington, DC 20590-0001. Attention: Hazardous Materials Preemption Docket;
  (2) *Set forth* the text of the State or political subdivision or Indian tribe requirement for which the determination is sought;
  (3) *Specify each requirement* of the Federal hazardous material transportation law or the regulations issued thereunder with which the applicant seeks the State or political subdivision or Indian tribe requirement to be compared;
  (4) *Explain why* the applicant believes the State or political subdivision or Indian tribe requirement should or should not be preempted under the standards of §107.202; and
  (5) *State how* the applicant is affected by the State or political subdivision or Indian tribe requirement.

(c) The filing of an application for a determination under this section does not constitute grounds for noncompliance with any requirement of the Federal hazardous material transportation law or the regulations issued thereunder.

(d) Once the Associate Administrator has published notice in the Federal Register of an application received under paragraph (a) of this section, no applicant for such determination may seek relief with respect to the same or substantially the same issue in any court until final action has been taken on the application or until 180 days after filing of the application, whichever occurs first.

Nothing in §107.203(a) prohibits a State or political subdivision or Indian tribe, or any other person directly affected by any requirement of a State or political subdivision thereof or Indian tribe, from seeking a determination of preemption in any court of competent jurisdiction in lieu of applying to the Associate Administrator under paragraph (a) of this section.

§107.205 Notice.

(a) **If the applicant is other than a State,** political subdivision, or Indian tribe, the applicant shall mail a copy of the application to the State, political subdivision, or Indian tribe concerned accompanied by a statement that the State, political subdivision, or Indian tribe may submit comments regarding the application to the Associate Administrator. The application filed with the Associate Administrator must include a certification that the applicant has complied with this paragraph and must include the names and addresses of each State, political subdivision, or Indian tribe official to whom a copy of the application was sent.

(b) **The Associate Administrator will publish notice of,** including an opportunity to comment on, an application in the Federal Register and may notify in writing any person readily identifiable as affected by the outcome of the determination.

(c) **Each person submitting written comments** to the Associate Administrator with respect to an application filed under this section shall send a copy of the comments to the applicant and certify to the Associate Administrator that he or she has complied with this requirement. The Associate Administrator may notify other persons participating in the proceeding of the comments and provide an opportunity for those other persons to respond. Late-filed comments are considered so far as practicable.

§107.207 Processing.

(a) **The Associate Administrator may initiate an investigation** of any statement in an application and utilize in his or her evaluation any relevant facts obtained by that investigation. The Associate Administrator may solicit and accept submissions from third persons relevant to an application and will provide the applicant an opportunity to respond to all third person submissions. In evaluating an application, the Associate Administrator may consider any other source of information. The Associate Administrator on his or her own initiative may convene a hearing or conference, if he or she considers that a hearing or conference will advance his or her evaluation of the application.

(b) **The Associate Administrator may dismiss the application** without prejudice if:

(1) *He or she determines* that there is insufficient information upon which to base a determination; or

(2) *He or she requests* additional information from the applicant and it is not submitted.

§107.209 Determination.

(a) **Upon consideration of the application** and other relevant information received, the Associate Administrator issues a determination.

(b) **The determination includes a written statement** setting forth the relevant facts and the legal basis for the determination, and provides that any person aggrieved thereby may file a petition for reconsideration with the Associate Administrator.

(c) **The Associate Administrator provides a copy** of the determination to the applicant and to any other person who substantially participated in the proceeding or requested in comments to the docket to be notified of the determination. A copy of each determination is placed on file in the public docket. The Associate Administrator will publish the determination or notice of the determination in the Federal Register.

(d) **A determination issued under this section** constitutes an administrative determination as to whether a particular requirement of a State or political subdivision or Indian tribe is preempted under the Federal hazardous material transportation law or regulations issued thereunder. The fact that a determination has not been issued under this section with respect to a particular requirement of a State or political subdivision or Indian tribe carries no implication as to whether the requirement is preempted under the Federal hazardous material transportation law or regulations issued hereunder.

§107.211 Petition for reconsideration.

(a) **Any person aggrieved by a determination** issued under §107.209 may file a petition for reconsideration with the Associate Administrator. The petition must be filed within 20 days of publication of the determination in the Federal Register.

(b) **The petition must contain a concise statement** of the basis for seeking review, including any specific factual or legal error alleged. If the petition requests consideration of information that was not previously made available to the Associate Administrator, the petition must include the reasons why such information was not previously made available.

(c) **The petitioner shall mail a copy of the petition** to each person who participated, either as an applicant or commenter, in the preemption determination proceeding, accompanied by a statement that the person may submit comments concerning the petition to the Associate Administrator within 20 days. The petition filed with the Associate Administrator must contain a certification that the petitioner has complied with this paragraph and include the names and addresses of all persons to whom a copy of the petition was sent. Late-filed comments are considered so far as practicable.

(d) **The Associate Administrator's decision** constitutes final agency action.

§107.213 Judicial review.

A party to a proceeding under §107.203(a) may seek review by the appropriate district court of the United States of a decision of the Associate Administrator by filing a petition with the court within 60 days after the Associate Administrator's determination becomes final. The determination becomes final when it is published in the Federal Register.

Waiver of Preemption Determinations

§107.215 Application.

(a) **With the exception of requirements preempted** under 49 U.S.C. 5125(c), any State or political subdivision thereof, or Indian tribe may apply to the Associate Administrator for a waiver of preemption with respect to any requirement that the State or political subdivision thereof or an Indian tribe acknowledges to be preempted under the Federal hazardous material transportation law or the regulations issued thereunder, or that has been determined by a court of competent jurisdiction to be so preempted. The Associate Administrator may waive preemption with respect to such requirement upon a determination that such requirement —

(1) *Affords an equal or greater level* of protection to the public than is afforded by the requirements of the Federal hazardous material transportation law or the regulations issued thereunder, and

(2) *Does not unreasonably burden commerce.*

(b) **Each application filed under this section** for a waiver of preemption determination must:

(1) *Be submitted* to the Associate Administrator for Hazardous Materials Safety, Research and Special Programs Administration, U.S. Department of Transportation, Washington, DC 20590-0001. Attention: Hazardous Materials Preemption Docket;

(2) *Set forth the text* of the State or political subdivision requirement for which the determination is being sought;

(3) *Include a copy* of any court order and any ruling issued under §107.209 having a bearing on the application;

(4) *Contain an express acknowledgment* by the applicant that the State, political subdivision, or Indian tribe requirement is preempted under the Federal hazardous material transportation law or the regulations issued thereunder, unless it has been so determined by a court of competent jurisdiction or in a determination issued under §107.209;

(5) *Specify each requirement* of the Federal hazardous material transportation law or the regulations issued thereunder that preempts the State, political subdivision, or Indian tribe requirement;

(6) *State why* the applicant believes the State, political subdivision or Indian tribe requirements affords an equal or greater level of protection to the public than is afforded by the requirements of the Federal hazardous material transportation law or the regulations issued thereunder;

(7) *State why* the applicant believes the State, political subdivision or Indian tribe requirement does not unreasonably burden commerce; and

(8) *Specify what steps* the State, political subdivision or Indian tribe is taking to administer and enforce effectively its inconsistent requirement.

§107.217 Notice.

(a) **The applicant shall mail a copy of the application** and any subsequent amendments or other documents relating to the application to each person who is reasonably ascertainable by the applicant as a person who will be affected by the determination sought. The copy of the application must be accompanied by a statement that the person may submit comments regarding the application to the Associate Administrator within 45 days. The application filed with the Associate Administrator must include a certification that the application has complied with this paragraph and must include the names and addresses of each person to whom the application was sent.

(b) **Notwithstanding the provisions of paragraph (a)** of this section, if the State or political subdivision determines that compliance with paragraph (a) of this section would be impracticable, the applicant shall:

(1) *Comply with the requirements* of paragraph (a) of this section with regard to those persons whom it is reasonable and practicable to notify; and

(2) *Include with the application* filed with the Associate Administrator a description of the persons or class or classes of persons to whom notice was not sent.

(c) **The Associate Administrator may require the applicant** to provide notice in addition to that required by paragraphs (a) and (b) of this section, or may determine that the notice required by paragraph (a) of the section is not impracticable, or that notice should be published in the Federal Register. Late-filed comments are considered so far as practicable.

(d) **The Associate Administrator may notify** any other persons who may be affected by the outcome of a determination on the application.

(e) **Any person submitting written comments** to the Associate Administrator with respect to an application filed under this section shall send a copy of the comments to the applicant. The person shall certify to the Associate Administrator that he has complied with the requirements of this paragraph. The Associate Administrator may notify other persons participating in the proceeding of the comments and provide an opportunity for those other persons to respond.

§107.219 Processing.

(a) **The Associate Administrator may initiate** an investigation of any statement in an application and utilize in his or her evaluation any relevant facts obtained by that investigation. The Associate Administrator may solicit and accept submissions from third persons relevant to an application and will provide the applicant an opportunity to respond to all third person submissions. In evaluating an application, the Associate Administrator on his or her own initiative may convene a hearing or conference, if he or she considers that a hearing or conference will advance his or her evaluation of the application.

(b) **The Associate Administrator may dismiss the application** without prejudice if:

(1) *He or she determines* that there is insufficient information upon which to base a determination;

(2) *Upon his or her request,* additional information is not submitted by the applicant; or

(3) *The applicant fails to provide the notice required by §107.217.*

(c) **Except as provided in §107.201(c),** the Associate Administrator will only consider an application for a waiver of preemption determination if:

(1) *The applicant* State or political subdivision thereof or Indian tribe expressly acknowledges in its application that the State or political subdivision thereof or Indian tribe requirement for which the determination is sought is inconsistent with the requirements of the Federal hazardous material transportation law or the regulations issued thereunder; or

(2) *The State* or political subdivision thereof or Indian tribe requirement has been determined by a court of competent jurisdiction or in a ruling issued under §107.209 to be inconsistent with the requirements of the Federal hazardous material transportation law or the regulations issued thereunder.

(d) **When the Associate Administrator has received** all substantive information it considers necessary to process an application for a waiver of preemption determination, it serves notice of that fact upon the applicant and all other persons who received notice of the proceeding pursuant to §107.217.

(e) **To the extent possible, each application** for a waiver of preemption determination will be acted upon in a manner consistent with the disposition of previous applications for waiver of preemption determinations.

§107.221 Determination.

(a) **After considering the application** and other relevant information received or obtained during the proceeding, the Associate Administrator issues a determination.

(b) **The Associate Administrator may issue** a waiver of preemption only on finding that the requirement of the State or political subdivision thereof or Indian tribe affords the public a level of safety at least equal to that afforded by the requirements of the Federal hazardous material transportation law or the regulations issued thereunder and does not unreasonably burden commerce. In determining if the requirement of the State or political subdivision thereof or Indian tribe unreasonably burdens commerce, the Associate Administrator considers:

(1) *The extent* to which increased costs and impairment of efficiency result from the requirement of the State or political subdivision thereof or Indian tribe.

(2) *Whether the requirement* of the State or political subdivision thereof or Indian tribe has a rational basis.

(3) *Whether the requirement* of the State or political subdivision thereof or Indian tribe achieves its stated purpose.

(4) *Whether there is need* for uniformity with regard to the subject concerned and if so, whether the requirement of the State or political subdivision thereof or Indian tribe competes or conflicts with those of other States or political subdivisions thereof or Indian tribes.

(c) **The determination includes a written statement** setting forth relevant facts and legal bases and providing that any person aggrieved by the determination may file a petition for reconsideration with the Associate Administrator.

(d) **The Associate Administrator provides a copy** of the determination to the applicant and to any other person who substantially participated in the proceeding or requested in comments to the docket to be notified of the determination. A copy of the determination is placed on file in the public docket. The Associate Administrator will publish the determination or notice of the determination in the Federal Register.

(e) **A determination under this section constitutes** an administrative finding of whether a particular requirement of a State or political subdivision thereof or Indian tribe is preempted under the Federal hazardous material transportation law or any regulation issued thereunder, or whether preemption is waived.

§107.223 Petition for reconsideration.

(a) **Any person aggrieved by a determination** under §107.221 may file a petition for reconsideration with the Associate Administrator. The petition must be filed within 20 days of publication of the determination in the Federal Register.

(b) **The petition must contain a concise statement** of the basis for seeking review, including any specific factual or legal error alleged. If the petition requests consideration of information that was not previously made available to the Associate Administrator, the petition must include the reasons why such information was not previously made available.

(c) **The petitioner shall mail a copy of the petition** to each person who participated, either as an applicant or commenter, in the waiver of preemption proceeding, accompanied by a statement that the person may submit comments concerning the petition to the Associate Administrator within 20 days. The petition filed with the Associate Administrator must contain a certification that the petitioner has complied with this paragraph and include the names and addresses of all persons to whom a copy of the petition was sent. Late-filed comments are considered so far as practicable.

(d) **The Associate Administrator's decision** constitutes final agency action.

§107.227 Judicial review.

A party to a proceeding under §107.215(a) may seek review by the appropriate district court of the United States of a decision of the Associate Administrator by filing a petition with the court within 60 days after the Associate Administrator's determination becomes final. The determination becomes final when it is published in the Federal Register.

Subpart D - Enforcement

§107.301 Delegated authority for enforcement.

Under redelegation from the Administrator, Research and Special Programs Administration, the Associate Administrator for Hazardous Materials Safety and the Office of the Chief Counsel exercise their authority for enforcement of the Federal hazardous material transportation law, this subchapter, and subchapter C of this subchapter, in accordance with §1.53 of this title.

§107.303 Purpose and scope.

This subchapter describes the various enforcement authorities exercised by the Associate Administrator for Hazardous Materials Safety and the Office of Chief Counsel and the associated sanctions and prescribes the procedures governing the exercise of those authorities and the imposition of those sanctions.

§107.305 Investigations.

(a) **General.** In accordance with its delegated authority under part 1 of this title, the Associate Administrator may initiate investigations relating to compliance by any person with any provisions of this subchapter or subchapter C of this chapter, or any exemption, approval, or order issued thereunder, or any court decree relating thereto. The Associate Administrator encourages voluntary production of documents in accordance with and subject to §105.45, and hearings may be conducted, and depositions taken pursuant to 49 U.S.C. 5121(a). The Associate Administrator may conduct investigative conferences and hearings in the course of any investigation.

(b) **Investigations and Inspections.** Investigations under 49 U.S.C. 5121(a) are conducted by personnel duly authorized for that purpose by the Associate Administrator. Inspections under 49 U.S.C. 5121(c) are conducted by Hazardous Materials Enforcement Specialists, also known as "hazmat inspectors" or "inspectors," whom the Associate Administrator has designated for that purpose.

(1) *An inspector* will, on request, present his or her credentials for examination, but the credentials may not be reproduced.

(2) *An inspector* may administer oaths and receive affirmations in any matter under investigation by the Associate Administrator.

(3) *An inspector* may gather information by reasonable means including, but not limited to, interviews, statements, photocopying, photography, and video- and audio-recording.

(4) *With concurrence* of the Director, Office of Hazardous Materials Enforcement, Research and Special Programs Administration, an inspector may issue a subpoena for the production of documentary or other tangible evidence if, on the basis of information available to the inspector, the documents and evidence materially will advance a determination of compliance with this subchapter or subchapter C. Service of a subpoena shall be in accordance with §105.50. A person to whom a subpoena is directed may seek review of the subpoena by applying to the Office of Chief Counsel in accordance with §105.55(a). A subpoena issued under this paragraph may be enforced in accordance with §105.55(b).

(c) **Notification.** Any person who is the subject of an Associate Administrator investigation and who is requested to furnish information or documentary evidence is notified as to the general purpose for which the information or evidence is sought.

(d) **Termination.** When the facts disclosed by an investigation indicate that further action is unnecessary or unwarranted at that time, the person being investigated is notified and the investigative file is closed without prejudice to further investigation by the Associate Administrator.

(e) **Confidentiality.** Information received in an investigation under this section, including the identity of the person investigated and any other person who provides information during the investigation, shall remain confidential under the investigatory file exception, or other appropriate exception, to the public disclosure requirements of 5 U.S.C. 552.

Compliance Orders and Civil Penalties

§107.307 General.

(a) **When the Associate Administrator and the Office** of the Chief Counsel have reason to believe that a person is knowingly engaging or has knowingly engaged in conduct which is a violation of the Federal hazardous material transportation law or any provision of this subchapter or subchapter C of this chapter, or any exemption, or order issued thereunder, for which the Associate Administrator or the Office of the Chief Counsel exercise enforcement authority, they may —

(1) *Issue a warning letter, as provided in §107.309;*

(2) *Initiate proceedings* to assess a civil penalty, as provided in either §§107.310 or 107.311;

(3) *Issue an order* directing compliance, regardless of whether a warning letter has been issued or a civil penalty assessed; and

(4) *Seek any other remedy* available under the Federal hazardous material transportation law.

(b) **In the case of a proceeding initiated** for failure to comply with an exemption, the allegation of a violation of a term or condition thereof is considered by the Associate Administrator and the Office of the Chief Counsel to constitute an allegation that the exemption holder or party to the exemption is failing, or has failed to comply with the underlying regulations from which relief was granted by the exemption.

§107.309 Warning letters.

(a) **The Associate Administrator may issue a warning letter** to any person whom the Associate Administrator believes to have committed a probable violation of the Federal hazardous material transportation law or any provision of this subchapter, subchapter C of this chapter, or any exemption issued thereunder.

(b) **A warning letter issued under this section includes:**

(1) *A statement* of the facts upon which the Associate Administrator bases its determination that the person has committed a probable violation;

(2) *A statement* that the recurrence of the probable violations cited may subject the person to enforcement action; and

(3) *An opportunity* to respond to the warning letter by submitting pertinent information or explanations concerning the probable violations cited therein.

§107.310 Ticketing.

(a) **For an alleged violation that does not have** a direct or substantial impact on safety, the Associate Administrator may issue a ticket.

(b) **The Associate Administrator issues a ticket** by mailing it by certified or registered mail to the person alleged to have committed the violation. The ticket includes:

(1) *A statement* of the facts on which the Associate Administrator bases the conclusion that the person has committed the alleged violation;

(2) *The maximum penalty* provided for by statute, the proposed full penalty determined according to RSPA's civil penalty guidelines and the statutory criteria for penalty assessment, and the ticket penalty amount; and

(3) *A statement* that within 45 days of receipt of the ticket, the person must pay the penalty in accordance with paragraph (d) of this section, make an informal response under §107.317, or request a formal administrative hearing under §107.319.

(c) **If the person makes an informal response** or requests a formal administrative hearing, the Associate Administrator forwards the inspection report, ticket and response to the Office of the Chief Counsel for processing under §§107.307-107.339, except that the Office of the Chief Counsel will not issue a Notice of Probable Violation under §107.311. The Office of the Chief Counsel may impose a civil penalty that does not exceed the proposed full penalty set forth in the ticket.

(d) **Payment of the ticket penalty amount** must be made in accordance with the instructions on the ticket.

(e) **If within 45 days of receiving the ticket** the person does not pay the ticket amount, make an informal response, or request a formal administrative hearing, the person has waived the right to make an informal response or request a hearing, has admitted the violation and owes the ticket penalty amount to RSPA.

§107.311 Notice of probable violation.

(a) **The Office of Chief Counsel may serve a notice** of probable violation on a person alleging the violation of one or more provisions of the Federal hazardous material transportation law or any provision of this subchapter or subchapter C of this chapter, or any exemption, or order issued thereunder.

(b) **A notice of probable violation issued** under this section includes the following information:

(1) *A citation* of the provisions of the Federal hazardous material transportation law, an order issued thereunder, this subchapter, subchapter C of this chapter, or the terms of any exemption issued thereunder which the Office of Chief Counsel believes the respondent is violating or has violated.

(2) *A statement* of the factual allegations upon which the demand for remedial action, a civil penalty, or both, is based.

(3) *A statement* of the respondent's right to present written or oral explanations, information, and arguments in answer to the allegations and in mitigation of the sanction sought in the notice of probable violation.

(4) *A statement* of the respondent's right to request a hearing and the procedures for requesting a hearing.

(5) *In addition,* in the case of a notice of probable violation proposing a compliance order, a statement of the proposed actions to be taken by the respondent to achieve compliance.

(6) *In addition,* in the case of a notice of probable violation proposing a civil penalty:

(i) *A statement* of the maximum civil penalty for which the respondent may be liable;

(ii) *The amount of the preliminary civil* penalty being sought by the Office of Chief Counsel, constitutes the maximum amount the Chief Counsel may seek throughout the proceeding; and

(iii) *A description of the manner in* which the respondent makes payment of any money due the United States as a result of the proceeding.

(c) **The Office of Chief Counsel may amend a notice** of probable violation at any time before issuance of a compliance order or an order assessing a civil penalty. If the Office of Chief Counsel alleges any new material facts or seeks new or additional remedial action or an increase in the amount of the proposed civil penalty, it issues a new notice of probable violation under this section.

§107.313 Reply.

(a) **Within 30 days of receipt of a notice** of probable violation, the respondent must either:
(1) *Admit the violation under §107.315;*
(2) *Make an informal response under §107.317; or*
(3) *Request a hearing under §107.319.*

(b) **Failure of the respondent to file a reply** as provided in this section constitutes a waiver of the respondent's right to appear and contest the allegations and authorizes the Chief Counsel, without further notice to the respondent, to find the facts to be as alleged in the notice of probable violation and issue an order directing compliance or assess a civil penalty, or, if proposed in the notice, both. Failure to request a hearing under paragraph (a)(3) of this section constitutes a waiver of the respondent's right to a hearing.

(c) **Upon the request of the respondent,** the Office of Chief Counsel may, for good cause shown and filed within the 30 days prescribed in the notice of probable violation, extend the 30-day response period.

§107.315 Admission of violations.

(a) **In responding to a notice of probable violation** issued under §107.311, the respondent may admit the alleged violations and agree to accept the terms of a proposed compliance order or to pay the amount of the preliminarily assessed civil penalty, or, if proposed in the notice, both.

(b) **If the respondent agrees to the terms** of a proposed compliance order, the Chief Counsel issues a final order prescribing the remedial action to be taken by the respondent.

(c) **Payment of a civil penalty, when the amount** of the penalty exceeds $10,000, must be made by wire transfer, through the Federal Reserve Communications System (Fedwire), to the account of the U.S. Treasury. Detailed instructions on making payments by wire transfer may be obtained from the Financial Operations Division (AMZ-320), Federal Aviation Administration, Mike Monroney Aeronautical Center, P.O. Box 25880, Oklahoma City, OK 73125.

(d) **Payment of a civil penalty, when the amount** of the penalty is $10,000 or less, must be made either by wire transfer, as set forth in paragraph (c) of this section, or certified check or money order payable to "U.S. Department of Transportation" and submitted to the Financial Operations Division (AMZ-320), Federal Aviation Administration, Mike Monroney Aeronautical Center, P.O. Box 25880, Oklahoma City, OK 73125.

§107.317 Informal response.

(a) **In responding to a notice of probable violation** under §107.311, the respondent may submit to the official who issued the notice, written explanations, information, or arguments in response to the allegations, the terms of a proposed compliance order, or the amount of the preliminarily assessed civil penalty.

(b) **The respondent may include in his informal response** a request for a conference. Upon the request of the respondent, the conference may be either in person or by telephone. A request for a conference must set forth the issues the respondent will raise at the conference.

(c) **Upon receipt of a request for a conference** under paragraph (b) of this section, the Chief Counsel's Office, in consultation with the Associate Administrator, arranges for a conference as soon as practicable at a time and place of mutual convenience.

(d) **The respondent's written explanations, information,** and arguments as well as the respondent's presentation at a conference are considered by the Chief Counsel in reviewing the notice of probable violation. Based upon a review of the proceeding, the Chief Counsel may dismiss the notice of probable violation in whole or in part. If he does not dismiss it in whole, he issues an order directing compliance or assessing a civil penalty, or, if proposed in the notice, both.

§107.319 Request for a hearing.

(a) **In responding to a notice of probable violation** under §107.311, the respondent may request a formal administrative hearing on the record before an Administrative Law Judge (ALJ) obtained by the Office of the Chief Counsel.

(b) **A request for a hearing under paragraph (a) of this section must:**
(1) *State the name and address* of the respondent and of the person submitting the request if different from the respondent;
(2) *State which allegations of violations, if any, are admitted; and*
(3) *State generally* the issues to be raised by the respondent at the hearing. Issues not raised in the request are not barred from presentation at the hearing; and
(4) *Be addressed to the official who issued the notice.*

(c) **After a request for a hearing that complies with** the requirements of paragraph (b) of this section, the Chief Counsel obtains an ALJ to preside over the hearing and notifies the respondent of this fact. Upon assignment of an ALJ, further matters in the proceeding generally are conducted by and through the ALJ, except that the Chief Counsel and respondent may compromise or settle the case under §107.327 of this subpart without order of the ALJ or voluntarily dismiss the case under Rule 41(a)(1) of the Federal Rules of Civil Procedure without order of the ALJ; in the event of such a compromise, settlement or dismissal, the Chief Counsel expeditiously will notify the ALJ thereof.

(d) **At any time after requesting a formal administrative hearing** but prior to the issuance of a decision and final order by the ALJ, the respondent may withdraw such request in writing, thereby terminating the jurisdiction of the ALJ in the case. Such a withdrawal constitutes an irrevocable waiver of respondent's right to such a hearing on the facts, allegations, and proposed sanction presented in the notice of probable violation to which the request for hearing relates.

§107.321 Hearing.

(a) **To the extent practicable, the hearing is held** in the general vicinity of the place where the alleged violation occurred or at a place convenient to the respondent. Testimony by witnesses shall be given under oath and the hearing shall be recorded verbatim.

(b) **Hearings are conducted in accordance with** the Federal Rules of Evidence and Federal Rules of Civil Procedure; however, the ALJ may modify them as he determines necessary in the interest of a full development of the facts. In addition, the ALJ may:
(1) *Administer oaths and affirmations;*
(2) *Issue subpoenas as provided by §105.45;*
(3) *Adopt procedures* for the submission of motions, evidence, and other documents pertinent to the proceeding;
(4) *Take or cause depositions to be taken;*
(5) *Rule on offers of proof and receive relevant evidence;*
(6) *Examine witnesses at the hearing;*
(7) *Convene, recess,* reconvene, adjourn and otherwise regulate the course of the hearing;
(8) *Hold conferences* for settlement, simplification of the issues, or any other proper purpose; and
(9) *Take any other action* authorized by, or consistent with, the provisions of this subpart and permitted by law which may expedite the hearing or aid in the disposition of an issue raised therein.

(c) **The official who issued the notice of probable violation,** or his representative, has the burden of proving the facts alleged therein.

(d) **The respondent may appear and be heard** on his own behalf or through counsel of his choice. The respondent or his counsel may offer relevant information including testimony which he believes should be considered in opposition to the allegations or which may bear on the sanction being sought and conduct such cross-examination as may be required for a full disclosure of the facts.

§107.323 ALJ's decision.

(a) **After consideration of all matters of record** in the proceeding, the ALJ shall issue an order dismissing the notice of probable violation in whole or in part or granting the sanction sought by the Office of Chief Counsel in the notice. If the ALJ does not dismiss the notice of probable violation in whole, he issues an order directing compliance or assessing a civil penalty, or, if proposed in the notice, both. The order includes a statement of the findings and conclusions, and the reasons therefore, on all material issues of fact, law, and discretion.

(b) **If, within 20 days of receipt of an order issued** under paragraph (a) of this section, the respondent does not submit in writing his acceptance of the terms of an order directing compliance, or, where appropriate, pay a civil penalty, or file an appeal under §107.325, the case may be referred to the Attorney General with a request that an action be brought in the appropriate United States District Court to enforce the terms of a compliance order or collect the civil penalty.

§107.325 Appeals.

(a) **Hearing proceedings.** A party aggrieved by an ALJ's decision and order issued under §107.323, may file a written appeal in accordance with paragraph (c) of this section with the Administrator, Research and Special Programs Administration (RSPA), 400 Seventh Street, SW., Washington, DC 20590-0001.

(b) **Non-Hearing proceedings.** A respondent aggrieved by an order issued under §107.317, may file a written appeal in accordance with paragraph (c) of this section with the Administrator, RSPA, 400 Seventh Street, SW., Washington, DC 20590-0001.

(c) **An appeal of an order issued under this subpart must:**
  (1) *Be filed* within 20 days of receipt of the order by the appealing party; and
  (2) *State with particularity* the findings in the order that the appealing party challenges, and include all information and arguments pertinent thereto.

(d) **If the Administrator, RSPA, affirms the order** in whole or in part, the respondent must comply with the terms of the decision within 20 days of the respondent's receipt thereof, or within the time prescribed in the order. If the respondent does not comply with the terms of the decision within 20 days of receipt, or within the time prescribed in the order, the case may be referred to the Attorney General for action to enforce the terms of the decision.

(e) **The filing of an appeal stays the effectiveness** of an order issued under §107.317 or §107.323. However, if the Administrator, RSPA, determines that it is in the public interest, he may keep an order directing compliance in force pending appeal.

§107.327 Compromise and settlement.

(a) **At any time before an order issued** under §107.317 or §107.323 is referred to the Attorney General for enforcement, the respondent or the Office of Chief Counsel may propose a compromise as follows:
  (1) *In civil penalty cases,* the respondent or Chief Counsel may offer to compromise the amount of the penalty by submitting an offer for a specific amount to the other party. An offer of compromise by the respondent shall be submitted to the Chief Counsel who may, after consultation with the Associate Administrator, accept or reject it.
    (i) *A compromise offer* stays the running of any response period then outstanding.
    (ii) *If a compromise* is agreed to by the parties, the respondent is notified in writing. Upon receipt of payment by Office of Chief Counsel, the respondent is notified in writing that acceptance of payment is in full satisfaction of the civil penalty proposed or assessed, and Office of Chief Counsel closes the case with prejudice to the respondent.
    (iii) *If a compromise* cannot be agreed to, the respondent is notified in writing and is given 10 days or the amount of time remaining in the then outstanding response period, whichever is longer, to respond to whatever action was taken by the Office of Chief Counsel or the Administrator, RSPA.
  (2) *In compliance order cases,* the respondent may propose a consent agreement to the Chief Counsel. If the Chief Counsel accepts the agreement, he issues an order in accordance with its terms. If the Chief Counsel rejects the agreement, he directs that the proceeding continue. An agreement submitted to the Chief Counsel must include:
    (i) *A statement* of any allegations of fact which the respondent challenges;
    (ii) *The reasons* why the terms of a compliance order or proposed compliance order are or would be too burdensome for the respondent, or why such terms are not supported by the record in the case;
    (iii) *A proposed* compliance order suitable for issuance by the Chief Counsel;
    (iv) *An admission of all jurisdictional facts; and*
    (v) *An express waiver* of further procedural steps and all right to seek judicial review or otherwise challenge or contest the validity of the order.

(b) **Notwithstanding paragraph (a)(1) of this section,** the respondent or Office of Chief Counsel may propose to settle the case. If the Chief Counsel agrees to a settlement, the respondent is notified and the case is closed without prejudice to the respondent.

§107.329 Maximum penalties.

(a) **A person who knowingly violates a requirement** of the Federal hazardous material transportation law, an order issued thereunder, this subchapter, subchapter C of this chapter, or an exemption issued under this subchapter applicable to the transporting of hazardous materials or the causing of them to be transported or shipped is liable for a civil penalty of not more than $25,000 ($27,500 for a violation occurring after January 21, 1997) and not less than $250 for each violation. When the violation is a continuing one, each day of the violation constitutes a separate offense.

(b) **A person who knowingly violates a requirement** of the Federal hazardous material transportation law, an order issued thereunder, this subchapter, subchapter C of this chapter, or an exemption issued under this subchapter applicable to the manufacture, fabrication, marking, maintenance, reconditioning, repair, or testing of a packaging or container which is represented, marked, certified or sold by that person as being qualified for use in the transportation of hazardous materials in commerce is liable for a civil penalty of not more than $25,000 ($27,500 for a violation occurring after January 21, 1997) and not less than $250 for each violation.

§107.331 Assessment considerations.

After finding a knowing violation under this subpart, the Office of Chief Counsel assesses a civil penalty taking the following into account:
(a) **The nature and circumstances of the violation;**
(b) **The extent and gravity of the violation;**
(c) **The degree of the respondent's culpability;**
(d) **The respondent's prior violations;**
(e) **The respondent's ability to pay;**
(f) **The effect on the respondent's ability to continue in business; and**
(g) **Such other matters as justice may require.**

Criminal Penalties

§107.333 Criminal penalties generally.

A person who knowingly violates §171.2(g) or willfully violates a provision of the Federal hazardous material transportation law or an order or regulation issued thereunder shall be fined under title 18, United States Code, or imprisoned for not more than 5 years, or both.

§107.335 Referral for prosecution.

If the Associate Administrator becomes aware of a possible willful violation of the Federal hazardous material transportation law, this subchapter, subchapter C of this chapter, or any exemption, or order issued thereunder, for which the Associate Administrator exercises enforcement responsibility, it shall report it to the Office of the Chief Counsel, Research and Special Programs Administration, U.S. Department of Transportation, Washington, DC 20590-0001. If appropriate, the Chief Counsel refers the report to the Department of Justice for criminal prosecution of the offender.

§107.336 Limitation on fines and penalties.

If a State or political subdivision or Indian tribe assesses any fine or penalty determined by the Secretary to be appropriate for a violation concerning a subject listed in §107.202(a), no additional fine or penalty may be assessed for such violation by any other authority.

Injunctive Action

§107.337 Injunctions generally.

Whenever it appears to the Office of Chief Counsel that a person has engaged, or is engaged, or is about to engage in any act or practice constituting a violation of any provision of the Federal hazardous material transportation law, this subchapter, subchapter C of this chapter, or any exemption, or order issued thereunder, for which the Office of Chief Counsel exercises enforcement responsibility, the Administrator, RSPA, or his delegate, may request the Attorney General to bring an action in the appropriate United States District Court for such relief as is necessary or appropriate, including mandatory or prohibitive injunctive relief, interim equitable relief, and punitive damages as provided by 49 U.S.C. 5122(a).

§107.339 Imminent hazards.

Whenever it appears to the Office of the Chief Counsel that there is a substantial likelihood that death, serious illness, or severe personal injury will result from the transportation of a particular hazardous material or hazardous materials container, before a compliance order proceeding or other administrative hearing or formal proceeding to abate the risk of that harm can be completed, the Administrator, RSPA, or his delegate, may bring an action under 49 U.S.C. 5122(b) in the appropriate United States District Court for an order suspending or restricting the transportation of that hazardous material or those containers or for such other equitable relief as is necessary or appropriate to ameliorate the hazard.

Appendix A to Subpart D of Part 107
Guidelines for civil penalties.

I. **This appendix sets forth the guidelines** used by the Office of Hazardous Materials Safety (as of January 18, 1995) in making initial baseline determinations for recommending civil penalties. The first part of these guidelines is a list of baseline amounts or ranges for probable violations frequently cited in enforcement reports referred for action. Following the list of violations are general guidelines used by OHMS in making initial penalty determinations in enforcement cases.

II. List of Frequently Cited Violations

Violation description	Section or cite	Baseline assessment
PART 107 — REQUIREMENTS		
Failure to register as a carrier or shipper of hazardous material.	107.608	$1,000 +, $500 each add'l year
PART 171 — REQUIREMENTS		
Failure to give immediate telephone notice of a reportable hazardous materials incident.	171.15	$3,000
Failure to file a DOT 5800.1 Hazardous Materials Incident Report within 30 days following an unintentional release of hazardous materials in transportation.	171.16	$500 to $2,500
PART 172 — REQUIREMENTS		
Shipping Papers (§172.200-172.205):		
Failure to execute a shipping paper for a shipment of hazardous materials.	172.201	$3,000 to $6,000
Failure to follow one or more of the three approved formats for listing hazardous materials on a shipping paper.	172.201(a)(1)	$1,200
Failure to include a proper shipping name in the shipping description or using an incorrect proper shipping name.	172.202	$800 to $1,600
Failure to include a hazard class/division number in the shipping description.	172.202	$1,000 to $2,000
Using an incorrect hazard class/identification number: — that does not affect compatibility requirements — that affects compatibility requirements	172.202	 $800 $3,000 to $6,000
Failure to include an identification number in the shipping description.	172.202	$1,000 to $2,000
Using an incorrect identification number: — that does not change the response information — that changes the response information	172.202	 $800 $3,000 to $6,000
Using a shipping description that includes additional unauthorized information (extra or incorrect words).	172.202	$800
Using a shipping description not in required sequence.	172.202	$500
Using a shipping description with two or more required elements missing or incorrect: — such that the material is misdescribed — such that the material is misclassified	172.202	 $3,000 $6,000
Failure to include the total quantity of hazardous material covered by a shipping description.	172.202(c)	$400
The letters "RQ" are not used in the shipping description to identify materials that are hazardous substances.	172.203(c)(2)	$500
Using a shipping description for Class 7 (radioactive) material that fails to contain the required additional entries, or contains incorrect information for these additional entries.	172.203(d)	$2,000 to $4,000
Failure to include a required technical name in parentheses for a listed generic or "n.o.s." material.	172.203(k)	$1,000
Failure to list an exemption number in association with the shipping description.	172.203(a)	$800
Failure to include the required shipper's certification on a shipping paper.	172.204(a)	$1,000
Failure to execute the required shipper's certification on a shipping paper.	172.204	$800
Emergency Response Information Requirements (§172.600-172.604):		
1. Providing or listing incorrect emergency response information with or on a shipping paper: a. no significant difference in response b. significant difference in response	172.602	 $800 $3,000 to $6,000
2. Failure to include an emergency response telephone number on a shipping paper.	172.604	$2,600
3. Failure to have the emergency response telephone number monitored while a hazardous material is in transportation or listing multiple telephone numbers (without specifying the times for each) that are not monitored 24 hours a day.	172.604	$1,300
4. Listing an unauthorized emergency response telephone number on a shipping paper.	172.604	$2,600 to $4,200
5. Listing an incorrect or non-working emergency response telephone number on a shipping paper.	172.604	$1,300
6. Failure to provide required technical information when the listed emergency response telephone number is contacted.	172.604	$1,300
Package Marking Requirements (§172.300-172.338):		
Failure to mark the proper shipping name on a package or marking an incorrect shipping name on a package.	172.301(a)	$800 to $1,600
Failure to mark the identification number on a package.	172.301(a)	$1,000 to $2,000
Marking a package with an incorrect identification number: — that does not change the response information — that changes the response information	172.301(a)	 $800 $3,000 to $6,000
Failure to mark the proper shipping name and identification number on a package.	172.301(a)	$3,000 to $6,000
Marking a package with an incorrect shipping name and identification number: — that does not change the response information — that changes the response information	172.301(a)	 $1,500 to $3,000 $3,000 to $6,000
Failure to include the required technical name(s) in parentheses for a listed generic or "no" entry.	172.301(c)	$1,000
Failure to mark a package containing liquid hazardous materials with required orientation marks.	172.312	$2,500 to $3,500.
Package Labeling Requirements (§172.400-172.450):		
Failure to label a package.	172.400	$5,000
Placing a label that represents a hazard other than the hazard presented by the hazardous material in the package.	172.400	$5,000
Placing a label on a package that does not contain a hazardous material.	172.401(a)	$800
Placing a label on Class 7 (radioactive) material that understates the proper label category.	172.403	$5,000
Placing a label on Class 7 (radioactive) material that fails to contain, or has erroneous, entries for the name of the radionuclide(s), activity, and transport index.	172.403(g)	$2,000 to $4,000
Placing a label not conforming to size requirements on a package.	172.407(c)	$800
Placing a label on a different surface of the package than, or far away from, the proper shipping name.	172.406(a)	$800
Placing a label that does not meet color specification requirements on a package (depending on the variance).	172.407(d)	$600 to $2,500
Failure to place a required subsidiary label on a package.	172.402	$500 to $2,500
Failure to provide an appropriate class or division number on a label.	172.411	$2,500

Violation description	Section or cite	Baseline assessment
Placarding Requirements (§172.500-172.560):		
Failure to properly placard a freight container or vehicle containing hazardous materials when table 1 is applicable.	172.504	$1,000 to $9,000
Failure to properly placard a freight container or vehicle containing hazardous materials when table 2 is applicable.	172.504	$800 to $7,500
Training Requirements (§172.700-172.704):		
Failure to train hazmat employees in the three required areas of training: — more than 10 hazmat employees — 10 hazmat employees or less	172.702	 $2,400 and up $1,500 and up
Failure to train hazmat employees in any one of the three required areas of training: — more than 10 hazmat employees — 10 hazmat employees or less	172.702	 $800 and up $500 and up
Failure to maintain training records: — more than 10 hazmat employees — 10 hazmat employees or less	172.704	 $800 and up $500 and up
PART 173 — REQUIREMENTS		
Overpack Requirements (§173.25):		
Failure to mark an overpack with a statement indicating that the inside packages comply with prescribed specifications when specification packaging is required.	173.25(a)(4)	$3,000
Reconditioner Requirements (§173.28):		
1. Representing, marking, or certifying a drum as a reconditioned UN standard packaging, when the drum did not meet a UN standard.	173.28(c), (d)	$6,000 to $10,800
2. Marking an incorrect registration number on a reconditioned packaging: a. Incorrect number b. Use of another reconditioner's number	173.28(b)(2)(ii)	 $800 $7,200
3. Failure to properly conduct alternate leakage test: a. improper test b. no test at all	173.28(b)(2)(i)	 $2,000 $4,000
4. Representing, marking, or certifying a drum as altered from one standard to another, when the drum had not actually been altered.	173.28(d)	$500
Portable and IM Tank Requirements (§§173.32(e), 173.32c, 173.315):		
Offering hazardous materials for transportation in a DOT specification or exemption portable tank which is out of test.	173.32(a)(1), 173.315(a), Applicable Exemption	$3,500 to $7,000
Offering an IM portable tank for transportation that has not been hydrostatically tested within the last 2 1/2 years per 173.32b(a).	173.32c(c)	$3,500
Offering an IM portable tank for transportation that has not been visually inspected in last five years per 173.32b(b).	173.32c(c)	$3,500
Offering an IM portable tank for transportation that has not been visually or hydrostatically tested as required, or failing to remove the safety relief valves during testing.	173.32c(c)	$7,000
Offering a hazardous material for transportation in an IM portable tank equipped with bottom outlets, when the material contained is prohibited from being offered in this type of packaging: — Packing Group II — Packing Group III	173.32c(g)	 $7,000 $5,000
Failure to provide the required outage for a shipment of hazardous materials, that results in the release of hazardous materials.	173.32c(k)	$6,000 to $12,000
Offering a hazardous material for transportation in an DOT, exemption, or IM portable tank which fails to bear markings that it has been properly retested.	173.32(e)(3), 173.32b(d)	$3,000
Cylinder Retesters (§§173.23, 173.34, and 173.302):		
Failure to remark as DOT 3AL an aluminum cylinder manufactured under a former exemption.	173.23(c)	$600
Certifying or marking as retested a nonspecification cylinder.	173.34	$800
Marking a cylinder in or on the sidewall area when not permitted by the applicable specification.	173.34(c)(1)	$6,000 to $10,800
Failure to maintain legible markings on a cylinder.	173.34(c)	$800
Failure to perform hydrostatic retesting at the minimum of 5/3 times the service pressure, or at the minimum specified test pressure.	173.34(e)	$2,100 to $5,200
Failure to conduct a complete visual external and internal examination.	173.34(e)(3)	$2,100 to $5,200
Failure to have a retester's identification number (RIN).	173.34(e)(2)(i)	$4,000
Failure to have current authority due to failure to renew a retester's identification number.	173.34(e)(2)(i)	$2,000
Failure to have a retester's identification number and marking another RIN on a cylinder.	173.34(e)(2)(i)	$7,200
Marking a RIN before successfully completing a hydrostatic retest.	173.34(e)(1)(ii)	$800
Requalifying a DOT cylinder without performing the visual inspection or hydrostatic retest.	173.34(e)(1)(ii)	$4,200 to $10,400
Performing hydrostatic retesting without demonstrating the accuracy of the testing equipment.	173.34(e)(4)	$2,100 to $5,200
Failure to hold hydrostatic test pressure for 30 seconds or sufficiently longer to allow for complete expansion.	173.34(e)(4)	$3,100
Failure to perform a second retest, after equipment failure, at a pressure of 10% more or 100 psi more, whichever is less (includes exceeding 90% of test pressure prior to conducting a retest).	173.34(e)(4)	$3,100
Failure to condemn a cylinder with permanent expansion of 10% or greater (5% for certain exemption cylinders); failure to condemn cylinders with evidence of internal or external corrosion, denting, bulging, or rough usage.	173.34(e)(6)	$10,000
Marking an FRP cylinder with steel stamps in the FRP area of the cylinder such that the integrity of the cylinder is compromised.	Applicable Exemption	$6,000 to $10,800
Failure to keep complete and accurate records of cylinder reinspection and retest: — no records kept — incomplete or inaccurate records	 173.34(e)(8)	 $4,000 $1,000 to $3,000
Improper marking of the RIN or retest date on a cylinder.	173.34(e)(7)	$800
Marking a DOT 3HT cylinder with a steel stamp other than a low-stress steel stamp.	173.34(e)(15)	$6,000 to $10,800
Marking a "+" sign on a cylinder without determining the average or maximum wall stress, by calculation or reference to CGA Pamphlet C-5.	173.302(c)(3)	$3,000 to $4,000
Representing, marking, or certifying a cylinder as meeting the requirements of an exemption, when the cylinder was not maintained or retested in accordance with the exemption.	171.2(c), Applicable Exemption	$2,000 to $6,000

Violation description	Section or cite	Baseline assessment
Rebuilder Requirements (§173.34):		
Representing a DOT-4 series cylinder as meeting the requirements of the Hazardous Materials Regulations without being authorized to do so by the Associate Administrator for Hazardous Materials Safety.	173.34(l)	$6,000 to $10,800
Offeror Requirements (General):		
Offering a hazardous material for transportation in an unauthorized non-UN standard or nonspecification packaging (includes the failure to comply with the terms of an exemption authorizing the use of a nonstandard or nonspecification packaging): — Packing Group I (includes §172.504 table 1 materials) — Packing Group II — Packing Group III	Various	 $9,000 $7,000 $5,000
Offering a hazardous material for transportation in a packaging that has successfully been tested to an applicable UN standard, but is not marked with the required UN marking.	178.3(a), 178.503(a)	$3,600
Offering a hazardous material for transportation in a packaging that leaks during conditions normally incident to transportation. — Packing Group I (includes §172.504 table 2 materials) — Packing Group II — Packing Group III	173.24(b)	 $12,000 $9,000 $6,000
Overfilling a package so that the effectiveness is substantially reduced. — Packing Group I (includes §172.504 table 1 materials) — Packing Group II — Packing Group III	173.24(b)	 $9,000 $6,000 $3,000
Offering a hazardous material for transportation after October 1, 1996, in an unauthorized non-UN standard packaging marked as manufactured to a DOT specification: — packaging meets DOT specification — packaging does not meet DOT specification	171.14	 $3,000 $5,000 to $9,000
Offeror Requirements (Class 1 — Explosives):		
Failing to mark the "EX" approval number on a package containing an explosive.	172.320	$1,200
Offering an unapproved explosive for transportation: — Div 1.3 & 1.4 fireworks meeting the chemistry requirements (both quantity and type) of APA Standard 87-1 — all other explosives (including forbidden explosives)	173.54 and 173.56(b)	 $5,000 to $10,000 $10,000 to $27,500
Offering a leaking or damaged package of explosives for transportation.	173.54(c)	$10,000 to $27,500
Offeror Requirements (Class 7 — Radioactive Materials):		
1. Offering a DOT specification 7A packaging without maintaining complete documentation of tests and an engineering evaluation or comparative data: a. tests and evaluation not performed b. complete records not maintained	173.415(a), 173.461	 $8,400 $2,000 to $5,000
2. Offering a Type B packaging without holding a valid NRC approval certificate: a. never having obtained one b. holding an expired certificate	173.471(a).	 $2,500 $1,000
3. Offering a limited quantity of radioactive materials without marking the inner (or single) packaging "Radioactive".	173.421(a)(4)	$5,000 and up
4. Offering low specific activity (LSA) radioactive materials consigned as exclusive use without providing instructions for maintenance of exclusive use shipment controls.	173.427(a)(6)	$800
5. Offering a package that exceeds the permitted limits for surface radiation or transport index.	173.441	$10,000 and up
6. Offering a package without determining the level of removable external contamination, or that exceeds the limit for removable external contamination.	173.443	$5,000 and up
7. Storing packages of radioactive material in a group with a total transport index more than 50.	173.447(a)	$5,000 and up
8. Offering special form radioactive materials without maintaining a complete safety analysis or Certificate of Competent Authority.	173.476(a), (b)	$2,500
Offeror Requirements (Cylinders):		
Offering a compressed gas for transportation in a cylinder that is out of test.	173.301(c)	$4,200 to $10,400
Failure to check each day the pressure of a cylinder charged with acetylene that is representative of that day's compression, after the cylinder has cooled to a settled temperature, or failure to keep a record of this test for at least 30 days.	173.303(d)	$5,000
Offering a limited quantity of a compressed gas in a metal container for the purpose of propelling a nonpoisonous material and failing to heat the cylinder until the pressure is equivalent to the equilibrium pressure at 130 °F, without evidence of leakage, distortion, or other defect.	173.306(a)(3), (h)	$1,500 to $6,000
PART 178 — REQUIREMENTS		
Third-Party Packaging Certifiers (General):		
1. Issuing a certification that directs the packaging manufacturer to improperly mark a packaging (e.g., steel drum to be marked UN 4G).	171.2(e), 178.2(b), 178.3(a), 178.503(a)	$500 per item
Manufacturers (General):		
1. Failure to insure a packaging certified as meeting the UN standard is capable of passing the required performance testing: a. Packing Group I (includes Section 172.504 table 1 materials) b. Packing Group II c. Packing Group III	178.601(b)	 $10,800 $8,400 $6,000
2. Certifying a packaging as meeting a UN standard when design qualification testing was not performed: a. Packing Group I (includes Section 172.504 table 1 materials) b. Packing Group II c. Packing Group III	178.601(d)	 $10,800 $8,400 $6,000
3. Failure to conduct periodic retesting on UN standard packaging (depending on length of time and Packing Group).	178.601(e)	$2,000 to $10,800
4. Failure to properly conduct testing for UN standard packaging (e.g., testing with less weight than marked on packaging; drop testing from lesser height than required; failing to condition fiberboard boxes before design test): a. design qualification testing b. periodic retesting	 178.601(d) 178.601(e)	 $2,000 to $10,800 $500 to $10,800
5. Marking, or causing the marking of, a packaging with the symbol of a manufacturer or packaging certifier other than the company that actually manufactured or certified the packaging.	178.2(b), 178.3(a), 178.503(a)(8)	$7,200
6. Failure to maintain testing records: a. design qualification testing b. periodic retesting	178.601(1)	 $1,000 to $5,000 $500 to $2,000
7. Improper marking of UN certification.	178.503	$500 per item

Violation description	Section or cite	Baseline assessment
8. Manufacturing DOT specification packaging after October 1, 1994 that is not marked as meeting a UN performance standard: a. if packaging does meet DOT specification b. if packaging does not meet DOT specification	171.14	 $3,000 $6,000 to $10,800
Manufacturing Requirements — Drums:		
1. Failure to properly conduct production leakproofness test: a. improper testing b. no testing performed	 178.604(b)(1) 173.28	 $2,000 $2,000 to $10,800
Manufacturing Requirements — Cylinders:		
1. Manufacturing, representing, marking, certifying, or selling a DOT high-pressure cylinder that was not inspected and verified by an approved independent inspection agency.	Various	$7,500 to $15,000
2. Failure to have a registration number or failure to mark the registration number on the cylinder.	Various	$800
3. Marking another company's number on a cylinder.	Various	$7,200
4. Failure to mark the date of manufacture or lot number on a DOT-39 cylinder.	178.65	$3,000
5. Failure to have a chemical analysis performed in the US for a material manufactured outside the US/failure to obtain a chemical analysis from the foreign manufacturer.	Various	$5,000
6. Failure to meet wall thickness requirements.	Various	$7,500 to $15,000
7. Failure to heat treat cylinders prior to testing.	Various	$5,000 to $15,000
8. Failure to conduct a complete visual internal examination.	Various	$2,500 to $6,200
9. Failure to conduct a hydrostatic test, or conducting a hydrostatic test with inaccurate test equipment.	Various	$2,500 to $6,200
10. Failure to conduct a flattening test.	Various	$7,500 to $15,000
11. Failure to conduct a burst test on a DOT-39 cylinder.	178.65(f)(2)	$5,000 to $15,000
12. Failure to have inspections and verifications performed by an inspector.	Various	$7,500 to $15,000
13. Failure to maintain a required inspector's reports: a. no reports at all b. incomplete or inaccurate reports	Various	 $5,000 $1,000 to $4,000
Other Requirements		
Carrier Requirements:		
Transporting packages of hazardous materials that have not been secured against movement within the vehicle.	177.834(a) & (g)	$3,000
Transporting explosives in a motor vehicle containing metal or other articles or materials likely to damage such explosives or any package in which they are contained, without segregating in different parts of the load or securing them in place in or on the motor vehicle and separated by bulkheads or other suitable means to prevent such damage.	177.835(i)	$5,200
Transporting railway track torpedoes outside of flagging kits, in violation of E-7991.	171.2(b)	$7,000
Transporting Class 7 (radioactive) material having a total transport index more than 50.	177.842(a)	$5,000 and up
Transporting Class 7 (radioactive) material without maintaining the required separation distance.	177.842(b)	$5,000 and up
Failing to comply with requirements of an exemption authorizing the transportation of Class 7 (radioactive) material having a total transport index more than 50: — failure to have the radiation survey record required by Paragraphs 7(f), 8(b)(3). — failure to have other accompanying documents required by Paragraph 8(b). — other violations of Paragraphs 7 and 8.	171.2(b)	 $5,000 $500 each $5,000 and up
Exemptions:		
Offering or transporting hazardous materials, or otherwise performing a function, covered by an exemption after expiration of the exemption.	171.2(a), (b), (c), Various	$1,000 + $500 each add'l year

III. Consideration of Statutory Criteria

A. *These guidelines* are used by the Office of Hazardous Materials Safety (OHMS) in setting initial proposed penalties for hazmat violations. They indicate baseline amounts or ranges for probable violations frequently cited in enforcement reports and set forth general OHMS policy for considering statutory criteria.

B. *The initial baseline determination* partially considers the nature, extent, circumstances, and gravity of the alleged violation. That determination then is adjusted to consider all other evidence concerning the nature, extent, circumstances, and gravity of the alleged violation; degree of culpability; history of prior violations; ability to pay; effect of the penalty on ability to continue to do business; and such other matters as justice may require (a major component of which is corrective action taken by a respondent to prevent a recurrence of similar violations). In making a penalty recommendation, the baseline or range may be increased or decreased on the basis of evidence pertaining to these factors.

C. *The following miscellaneous factors* are used to implement one or more of the statutory assessment criteria.

IV. Miscellaneous Factors Affecting Penalty Amounts

A. *Corrective Action*

1. *A proposed penalty* is mitigated for documented corrective action of alleged violations taken by a respondent. Corrective action may occur: (1) After an inspection and before a Notice of Probable Violation (NOPV) is issued; (2) on receipt of an NOPV; or (3) after receipt of an NOPV (possibly after it is solicited by an RSPA attorney). In general, corrective action may reduce a penalty up to 25%. Mitigation may be taken into account in the referral memo or may be recommended prior to issuance of an Order by RSPA's Chief Counsel.
2. *The two primary factors* in determining the penalty reduction are extent and timing of the corrective action. In other words, mitigation will be determined on the basis of how much corrective action was taken and when it was taken. Systemic action to prevent future violations is given greater consideration than action simply to remedy violations identified during the inspection.
3. *Mitigation is applied* to individual violations. Thus, in a case with two violations, if corrective action for the first violation is more extensive than for the second, the penalty for the first will be mitigated more than that for the second.

B. *Respondents That Re-Ship*

A shipper that reships materials received from another company, in the same packaging and without opening or altering the package, independently is responsible for ensuring that the shipment complies with Federal hazmat law, and independently may be subject to enforcement action if the package does not comply. Nevertheless, the reshipper is considered to have a lesser level of responsibility for compliance in those respects in which it reasonably relies on the compliance of the package as received. In most cases of this type, OHMS will discount the applicable baseline standard by about 25%. The specific knowledge and expertise of all parties must be considered in discounting for reliance on a prior shipper. This discount is applied before any consideration of mitigation based on corrective action.

C. *Penalty Increases for Multiple Counts*
Under the Federal hazmat law, 49 U.S.C. 5213(a), each violation of the HMR and each day of a continuing violation (except for violations pertaining to packaging manufacture or qualification) is subject to a civil penalty of up to $25,000 ($27,500 for a violation occurring after January 21, 1997). Absent aggravating factors, OHMS, in its exercise of discretion, ordinarily will apply a single penalty for multiple counts or days of violation. In a number of cases, particularly those involving shippers, an inspector may cite two or more similar packaging violations for different hazardous materials. For example, the inspector may cite the same marking violation for two or more packages. OHMS usually will consider those additional violations as counts of the same violation and will not recommend multiples of the same baseline penalty. Rather, OHMS usually will recommend the baseline penalty for a single violation, increased by 25% for each additional violation.

D. *Financial Considerations*

1. *Mitigation is appropriate* when the baseline penalty would (1) exceed an amount that the respondent is able to pay, or (2) have an adverse effect on the respondent's ability to continue in business. These criteria relate to a respondent's entire business, and not just the product line or part of its operations involved in the violation(s). Beyond the overall financial size of the respondent's business, the relevant items of information on a respondent's balance sheet include the current ratio (current assets to current liabilities), the nature of current assets, and net worth (total assets minus total liabilities).
2. *These figures* are considered on a case-by-case basis. In general, however, a current ratio close to or below 1.0 means that the company may have difficulty in paying a large penalty, and may justify reduction of the penalty or an installment payment plan. A small amount of cash on hand representing limited liquidity, even with substantial other current assets (such as accounts receivable or inventory), may warrant a short-term payment plan. Respondent's income statement also will be reviewed to determine whether a payment plan is appropriate.
3. *Many companies* are able to continue in business for extended periods of time with a small or negative net worth, and many respondents have paid substantial civil penalties in installments even though net worth was negative. For this reason, negative net worth alone does not always warrant reduction of a proposed penalty or even, in the absence of factors discussed above, a payment plan.
4. *In general,* an installment payment plan may be justified where reduction of a proposed penalty is not, but the appropriateness of either (or both) will depend on the circumstances of the case. The length of a payment plan should be as short as possible, but the plan may consider seasonal fluctuations in a company's income if the company's business is seasonal (e.g., swimming pool chemical sales, fireworks sales) or if the company has documented specific reasons for current non-liquidity.
5. *Evidence of financial condition* is used only to decrease a penalty, and not to increase it.

E. *Penalty Increases for Prior Violations*

1. *The baseline penalty* presumes an absence of prior violations. If prior violations exist, generally they will serve to increase a proposed penalty. The general standard for increasing a baseline proposed penalty on the basis of prior violations is as follows:
   a. *One prior case* — 25% increase over the pre-mitigation recommended penalty
   b. *Two prior cases* — 50% increase over the pre-mitigation recommended penalty
   c. *Three prior cases* — 75% increase over the pre-mitigation recommended penalty
   d. *Four or more prior cases* — 100% increase over the pre-mitigation recommended penalty
2. *A case of prior violations* closed more than five years previously normally will not be considered in determining a proposed penalty.

F. *Penalty Increases for Use of Expired Exemptions*
Adjustments to the base line figures for use of expired exemptions can be made depending on how much material has been shipped during the period between the expiration date and the renewal date. If the company previously has been found to have operated under an expired exemption, the penalty is normally doubled. If the company has been previously cited for other violations, the penalty generally will be increased by about 25%.

Subpart E - Designation of Approval and Certification Agencies

§107.401 Purpose and scope.

(a) **This subpart establishes procedures** for the designation of agencies to issue approval certificates and certifications for types of packagings designed, manufactured, tested, or maintained in conformance with the requirements of this subchapter, subchapter C of this chapter, and standards set forth in the United Nations (U.N.) Recommendations (Transport of Dangerous Goods). Except for certifications of compliance with U.N. packaging standards, this subpart does not apply unless made applicable by a rule in subchapter C of this chapter.

(b) **The Associate Administrator may issue** approval certificates and certifications addressed in paragraph (a) of this section.

§107.402 Application for designation as an approval or certification agency.

(a) **Any organization or person seeking designation** as an approval or certification agency shall apply in writing to the Associate Administrator for Hazardous Materials Safety (DHM-32), Department of Transportation, 400 Seventh Street, SW., Washington DC 20590-0001. Alternatively, the application with any attached supporting documentation in an appropriate format may be submitted by facsimile (fax) to: (202) 366-3753 or (202) 366-3308 or by electronic mail (e-mail) to: Approvals@rspa.dot.gov.Each application must be signed and certified to be correct by the applicant or, if the applicant is an organization, by an authorized officer or official representative of the organization. Any false statement or representation, or the knowing and willful concealment of a material fact, may subject the applicant to prosecution under the provisions of 18 U.S.C. 1001, result in the denial or termination of a designation.

(b) **Each application for designation must be** in English and include the following information:

(1) *Name and address* of the applicant, including place of incorporation if a corporation. In addition, if the applicant is not a resident of the United States, the name and address of a permanent resident of the United States designated in accordance with §105.40 to serve as agent for service of process.

(2) *If the applicant's* principal place of business is in a country other than the United States, a copy of the designation from the Competent Authority of that country delegating to the applicant an approval or designated agency authority for the type of packaging for which a DOT designation is sought, and a statement that the Competent Authority also delegates similar authority to U.S. Citizens or organizations having designations under this subpart from the RSPA.

(3) *A listing,* by DOT specification (or exemption) number, or U.N. designation, of the types of packagings for which approval authority is sought.

(4) *A personnel qualifications plan* listing the qualifications that the applicant will require of each person to be used in the performance of each packaging approval or certification function. As a minimum, these qualifications must include:

(i) *The ability* to review and evaluate design drawings, design and stress calculations;

(ii) *A knowledge* of the applicable regulations of subchapter C of this chapter and, when applicable, U.N. standards; and

(iii) *The ability* to conduct or monitor and evaluate test procedures and results; and

(iv) *The ability* to review and evaluate the qualifications of materials and fabrication procedures.

(5) *A statement* that the applicant will perform its functions independent of the manufacturers and owners of the packagings concerned.

(6) *A statement* that the applicant will allow the Associate Administrator or his representative to inspect its records and facilities in so far as they relate to the approval or certification of specification packagings and shall cooperate in the conduct of such inspections.

(c) **The applicant shall furnish any additional information** relevant to the applicant's qualifications, if requested by the Associate Administrator.

§107.403 Designation of approval agencies.

(a) **If the Associate Administrator determines** that an application contains all the required information, the applicant is sent a letter of designation and assigned an identification code.

(b) **If the Associate Administrator determines** that an application does not contain all the required information, the application is denied and the applicant is sent a written notice containing all the reasons for the denial.

(c) **Within 30 days of an initial denial of an application** under paragraph (b) of this section, the applicant may file an amended application. If after considering the amended application, the Associate Administrator determines that it should be denied, he notifies the applicant, and the denial constitutes the final action of the Associate Administrator on the application. Within 60 days of receipt of the final denial the applicant may appeal the denial to the Administrator, RSPA, setting forth in writing where the Associate Administrator for Hazardous Materials Safety erred in this determination.

§107.404 Conditions of designation.

(a) **Each designation made under this subpart** contains the following conditions:
  (1) *The designated approval* or certification agency may use only testing equipment that it has determined, through personal inspection, to be suitable for the purpose.
  (2) *Each approval certificate* and certification issued by the designated approval agency must contain the name and identification code of the approval agency.
  (3) *Each approval certificate* and certification must be in a format acceptable to the Associate Administrator.
(b) **The designated approval agency shall notify** the Associate Administrator within 20 days after the date there is any change in the information submitted under §107.402.
(c) **The designated approval agency shall comply** with all of the terms and conditions stated in its letter of designation under the subpart.
(d) **Nothing in this part relieves a manufacturer or owner** of a packaging of responsibility for compliance with any of the applicable requirements of this title.

§107.405 Termination of designation.

(a) **Any designation issued under §107.403** of this subchapter may be suspended or terminated if the Associate Administrator determines that:
  (1) *The application* for designation contained a misrepresentation, or the applicant willfully concealed a material fact.
  (2) *The approval agency* failed to comply with a term or condition stated in the agency's letter of designation.
  (3) *The Competent Authority* of an approval agency of a country outside the United States has failed to initiate, maintain or recognize a qualified U.S. approval agency.
(b) **Before a designation is suspended or terminated,** the Associate Administrator shall give to the approval agency:
  (1) *Written notice* of the facts or conduct believed to warrant suspension or termination of the designation.
  (2) *Sixty days* in which to show in writing why the designation should not be suspended or terminated.

Subpart F - Registration of Cargo Tank and Cargo Tank Motor Vehicle Manufacturers and Repairers and Cargo Tank Motor Vehicle Assemblers

FEDERAL REGISTER UPDATES

In the April 18, 2003 Federal Register, the title of Subpart F of Part 107 was revised, effective October 1, 2003. The revisions were as follows:

Subpart F - Registration of Cargo Tank and Cargo Tank Motor Vehicle Manufacturers, Assemblers, Repairers, Inspectors, Testers, and Design Certifying Engineers

§107.501 Scope.

(a) **This subpart establishes a registration procedure** for persons who are engaged in the manufacture, assembly, inspection and testing, certification, or repair of a cargo tank or a cargo tank motor vehicle manufactured in accordance with a DOT specification under subchapter C of this chapter or under terms of an exemption issued under this part.
(b) **Persons engaged in continuing qualification** and maintenance of cargo tanks and cargo tank motor vehicles must be familiar with the requirements set forth in part 180, subpart E, of this chapter.

§107.502 General registration requirements.

(a) **Definitions:** For purposes of this subpart —
  (1) **Assembly** means the assembly of one or more tanks or cargo tanks to a motor vehicle or to a motor vehicle suspension component and involves no welding on the cargo tank wall.
  (2) *The terms* **Authorized Inspector, Cargo tank, Cargo tank motor vehicle, Design Certifying Engineer, Registered Inspector,** and **Person** are defined in §171.8 of this chapter.
  (3) *The terms* **cargo tank wall** and **manufacturer** are defined in §178.320(a), and repair is defined in §180.403 of this chapter.
(b) **No person may engage in the manufacture, assembly,** certification, inspection or repair of a cargo tank or cargo tank motor vehicle manufactured under the terms of a DOT specification under subchapter C of this chapter or an exemption issued under this part unless the person is registered with the Department in accordance with the provisions of this subpart. A person employed as an inspector or design certifying engineer is considered to be registered if the person's employer is registered.
(c) **A person who performs functions which are subject** to the provisions of this subpart may perform only those functions which have been identified to the Department in accordance with the procedures of this subpart.
(d) **Registration statements must be in English,** contain all of the information required by this subpart, and be submitted to: Approvals Branch (Attn.: DHM-32), Associate Administrator for Hazardous Materials Safety, Research and Special Programs Administration, Department of Transportation, Washington, DC 20590-0001. Alternatively, a statement with any attached supporting documentation in an appropriate format may be submitted by facsimile (fax) to: (202) 366-3753 or (202) 366-3308 or by electronic mail (e-mail) to: Approvals@rspa.dot.gov.
(e) **Upon determination that a registration statement** contains all the information required by this subpart, the Department will send the registrant a letter confirming receipt of the registration application and assigning a registration number to that person. A separate registration number will be assigned for each cargo tank manufacturing, assembly, repair facility or other place of business identified by the registrant.

FEDERAL REGISTER UPDATES

In the April 18, 2003 Federal Register, §107.502 was revised, effective October 1, 2003.

(a) [1]
  (1) **Assembly** means the performance of any of the following functions when the function does not involve welding on the cargo tank wall: [2]
    (i) *The mounting* of one or more tanks or cargo tanks on a motor vehicle or to a motor vehicle suspension component;
    (ii) *The installation* of equipment or components necessary to meet the specification requirements prior to the certification of the cargo tank motor vehicle; or
    (iii) *The installation* of linings, coatings, or other materials to the inside of a cargo tank wall.

(d) **Registration statements must be in English,** contain all of the information required by this subpart, and be submitted to: FMCSA Hazardous Materials Division — MC-ECH, Room 8310, 400 7th Street SW., Washington, DC 20590. [3]

1. Paragraph (a) is the same as before.
2. Paragraph (a)(1) was revised.
3. Paragraph (d) text was revised.

§107.503 Registration statement.

(a) **Each registration statement must be in English** and contain the following information:
  (1) *Name;*
  (2) *Street address,* mailing address and telephone number for each facility or place of business;
  (3) *A statement* signed by the person responsible for compliance with the applicable requirements of this chapter, certifying knowledge of those requirements and that each employee who is a Registered Inspector or Design Certifying Engineer meets the minimum qualification requirements set forth in §171.8 of this chapter for "Registered Inspector" or "Design Certifying Engineer". The following language may be used.

  I certify that all Registered Inspectors and Design Certifying Engineers used in performance of the prescribed functions meet the minimum qualification requirements set forth in 49 CFR 171.8, that I am the person responsible for ensuring compliance with the applicable requirements of this chapter, and that I have knowledge of the requirements applicable to the functions to be performed.

  (4) *A description* of the specific functions to be performed on cargo tanks or cargo tank motor vehicles, e.g.:
    (i) *Manufacture,*
    (ii) *Assembly,*
    (iii) *Inspection and testing* (specify type, e.g., external or internal visual inspection, lining inspection, hydrostatic pressure test, leakage test, thickness test),
    (iv) *Certification,*
    (v) *Repair, or*
    (vi) *Equipment manufacture;*
  (5) *An identification* of the types of DOT specification and exemption cargo tanks or cargo tank motor vehicles which the registrant intends to manufacture, assemble, repair, inspect, test or certify;

(6) *A statement* indicating whether the registrant employs Registered Inspectors or Design Certifying Engineers to conduct certification, inspection or testing functions addressed by this subpart. If the registrant engages a person who is not an employee of the registrant to perform these functions, provide the name, address and registration number of that person; and

(7) *If the registrant* is not a resident of the United States, the name and address of a permanent resident of the United States designated in accordance with §105.40 to serve as agent for service of process.

(b) **In addition to the information required** under paragraph (a) of this section, each person who manufactures a cargo tank or cargo tank motor vehicle must submit a copy of the manufacturer's current ASME Certificate of Authorization for the use of the ASME "U" stamp.

(c) **In addition to the information required** under paragraph (a) of this section, each person who repairs a cargo tank or cargo tank motor vehicle must submit a copy of the repair facility's current National Board Certificate of Authorization for the use of the "R" stamp or ASME Certificate of Authorization for the use of the ASME "U" stamp. Any person who repairs MC-series cargo tanks which are not certified to the ASME Code must submit a copy of the National Board or ASME Certificate of Authorization to RSPA before June 30, 1992.

FEDERAL REGISTER UPDATES

In the April 18, 2003 Federal Register, §107.503 was revised, effective October 1, 2003.

(a) [1]

(3) *A statement indicating* whether the facility uses mobile testing/inspection equipment to perform inspections, tests, or repairs at a location other than the address listed in paragraph (a)(2) of this section. [2]

1. Paragraph (a) is the same as before.
2. Paragraphs (a)(3), (a)(4), (a)(5), (a)(6), and (a)(7) of §107.503 were redesignated as paragraphs (a)(4), (a)(5), (a)(6), (a)(7), and (a)(8) respectively, and new paragraph (a)(3) was added.

§107.504 Period of registration, updates, and record retention.

(a) **Registration will be for a maximum of six years** from the date of the original registration.

(b) **Any correspondence with the Department** must contain the registrant's name and registration number.

(c) **A registration must be renewed every six years** or within thirty days of reissuance of an ASME or National Board Certification, whichever occurs first, by submitting an up-to-date registration statement containing the information prescribed by §107.503. Any person initially registered under the provisions of §107.502 and who is in good standing is eligible for renewal.

(d) **A registrant shall provide written notification** to the Department within thirty days of any of the following occurrences:

(1) *Any change* in the registration information submitted under §107.503;

(2) *Replacement* of the person responsible for compliance with the requirements in §107.503(a)(3). If this occurs, the registrant shall resubmit the required certification;

(3) *Loss of ASME or National Board Certificate of Authorization; or*

(4) *A change in function;* such as, from assembly to manufacture, an addition of a function, or a change to the types of inspections, tests or certifications of cargo tanks or cargo tank motor vehicles.

(e) **Each registrant shall maintain a current copy** of the registration information submitted to the Department and a current copy of the registration number identification received from the Department at the location identified in §107.503(a)(2) during such time the person is registered with the Department and for two years thereafter.

(f) **The issuance of a registration number** under this subpart is not an approval or endorsement by the Department of the qualifications of any person to perform the specified functions.

Subpart G - Registration of Persons Who Offer or Transport Hazardous Materials

§107.601 Applicability.

(a) **The registration and fee requirements of this subpart** apply to any person who offers for transportation, or transports, in foreign, interstate or intrastate commerce —

(1) *A highway route-controlled quantity* of a Class 7 (radioactive) material, as defined in §173.403 of this chapter;

(2) *More than 25 kg* (55 pounds) of a Division 1.1,1.2, or 1.3 (explosive) material (see §173.50 of this chapter) in a motor vehicle, rail car or freight container;

(3) *More than one L* (1.06 quarts) per package of a material extremely toxic by inhalation (i.e., "material poisonous by inhalation," as defined in §171.8 of this chapter, that meets the criteria for "hazard zone A," as specified in §§173.116(a) or 173.133(a) of this chapter);

(4) *A shipment* of a quantity of hazardous materials in a bulk packaging (see §171.8 of this chapter) having a capacity equal to or greater than 13,248 L (3,500 gallons) for liquids or gases or more than 13.24 cubic meters (468 cubic feet) for solids;

(5) *A shipment* in other than a bulk packaging of 2,268 kg (5,000 pounds) gross weight or more of one class of hazardous materials for which placarding of a vehicle, rail car, or freight container is required for that class, under the provisions of subpart F of part 172 of this chapter; or

(6) *Except as provided* in paragraph (b) of this section, a quantity of hazardous material that requires placarding, under provisions of subpart F of part 172 of this chapter.

(b) **Paragraph (a)(6) of this section does not apply** to those activities of a farmer, as defined in §171.8 of this chapter, that are in direct support of the farmer's farming operations.

(c) **In this subpart,** the term "shipment" means the offering or loading of hazardous material at one loading facility using one transport vehicle, or the transport of that transport vehicle.

§107.606 Exceptions.

(a) **The following are excepted from the requirements** of this subpart:

(1) *An agency of the Federal government.*

(2) *A State agency.*

(3) *An agency of a political subdivision of a State.*

(4) *An employee* of any of those agencies in paragraphs (a)(1) through (a)(3) of this section with respect to the employee's official duties.

(5) *A hazmat employee* (including, for purposes of this subpart, the owner-operator of a motor vehicle that transports in commerce hazardous materials, if that vehicle at the time of those activities, is leased to a registered motor carrier under a 30-day or longer lease as prescribed in 49 CFR part 376 or an equivalent contractual agreement).

(6) *A person* domiciled outside the United States, who offers solely from a location outside the United States, hazardous materials for transportation in commerce, provided that the country of which such a person is a domiciliary does not require persons domiciled in the United States, who solely offer hazardous materials for transportation to the foreign country from places in the United States, to file a registration statement or to pay a registration fee.

(b) **Upon making a determination that persons domiciled** in the United States, who offer hazardous materials for transportation to a foreign country solely from places in the United States, must file registration statements or pay fees to that foreign country, the U.S. Competent Authority will provide notice of such determination directly to the Competent Authority of that foreign country and by publication in the Federal Register. Persons who offer hazardous materials for transportation to the United States from that foreign country must file a registration statement and pay the required fee no later than 60 days following publication of the determination in the Federal Register.

§107.608 General registration requirements.

(a) **Except as provided in §107.616(d),** each person subject to this subpart must submit a complete and accurate registration statement on DOT Form F 5800.2 not later than June 30 for each registration year, or in time to comply with paragraph (b) of this section, whichever is later. Each registration year begins on July 1 and ends on June 30 of the following year.

(b) **No person required to file a registration statement** may transport a hazardous material or cause a hazardous material to be transported or shipped, unless such person has on file, in accordance with §107.620, a current Certificate of Registration in accordance with the requirements of this subpart.

(c) **A registrant whose name or principal place of business** has changed during the year of registration must notify RSPA of that change by submitting an amended registration statement not later than 30 days after the change.

(d) **Copies of DOT Form F 5800.2 and instructions** for its completion may be obtained from the Hazardous Materials Registration Program, DHM-60, U.S. Department of Transportation, Washington, DC 20590-0001, by calling 617-494-2545 or 202-366-4109, or via the Internet at "http://hazmat.dot.gov".

(e) **If the registrant is not a resident of the United States,** the registrant must attach to the registration statement the name and address of a permanent resident of the United States, designated in accordance with §105.40, to serve as agent for service of process.

§107.612 Amount of fee.

(a) **Registration year 1999-2000 and earlier.** For all registration years through 1999-2000, each person subject to the requirements of §107.601(a)(1)-(5) of this subpart must pay an annual fee of $300 (which includes a $50 processing fee).

(b) **Registration years 2000-2001, 2001-2002 and 2002-2003.** For the registration years 2000-2001, 2001-2002, and 2002-2003, each person subject to the requirements of this subpart must pay an annual fee as follows:

(1) *Small business.* Each person that qualifies as a small business under criteria specified in 13 CFR part 121 applicable to the North American Industry Classification System (NAICS) code that describes that person's primary commercial activity must pay an annual fee of $275 and the processing fee required by paragraph (b)(3) of this section.

(2) *Other than a small business.* Each person that does not meet criteria specified in paragraph (b)(1) of this section must pay an annual fee of $1,975 and the processing fee required by paragraph (b)(3) of this section.

(3) *Processing fee.* The processing fee is $25 for each registration statement filed. A single statement may be filed for one, two, or three registration years as provided in §107.616(c).

(c) **Registration years 2003-2004, 2004-2005 and 2005-2006.** For registration years 2003-2004, 2004-2005, and 2005-2006, each person subject to the requirements of this subpart must pay an annual registration fee as follows:

(1) *Small business.* Each person that qualifies as a small business, under criteria specified in 13 CFR part 121 applicable to the North American Industry Classification System (NAICS) code that describes that person's primary commercial activity, must pay an annual registration fee of $125 and the processing fee required by paragraph (c)(4) of this section.

(2) *Not-for-profit organization.* Each not-for-profit organization must pay an annual registration fee of $125 and the processing fee required by paragraph (c)(4) of this section. A not-for-profit organization is an organization exempt from taxation under 26 U.S.C. 501(a).

(3) *Other than* a small business or not-for-profit organization. Each person that does not meet the criteria specified in paragraph (c)(1) or (c)(2) of this section must pay an annual registration fee of $275 and the processing fee required by paragraph (c)(4) of this section.

(4) *Processing fee.* The processing fee is $25 for each registration statement filed. A single statement may be filed for one, two, or three registration years as provided in §107.616(c).

(d) **Registration years 2006-2007 and following.** For each registration year beginning with 2006-2007, each person subject to the requirements of this subpart must pay an annual fee as follows:

(1) *Small business.* Each person that qualifies as a small business, under criteria specified in 13 CFR part 121 applicable to the North American Industry Classification System (NAICS) code that describes that person's primary commercial activity, must pay an annual registration fee of $250 and the processing fee required by paragraph (d)(4) of this section.

(2) *Not-for-profit organization.* Each not-for-profit organization must pay an annual registration fee of $250 and the processing fee required by paragraph (d)(4) of this section. A not-for-profit organization is an organization exempt from taxation under 26 U.S.C. 501(a).

(3) *Other than a small business* or not-for-profit organization. Each person that does not meet the criteria specified in paragraph (d)(1) or (d)(2) of this section must pay an annual registration fee of $975 and the processing fee required by paragraph (d)(4) of this section.

(4) *Processing fee.* The processing fee is $25 for each registration statement filed. A single statement may be filed for one, two, or three registration years as provided in §107.616(c).

§107.616 Payment procedures.

(a) **Except as provided in paragraph (d) of this section,** each person subject to the requirements of this subpart must mail the registration statement and payment in full to the U.S. Department of Transportation, Hazardous Materials Registration, P.O. Box 740188, Atlanta, Georgia 30374-0188, or submit the statement and payment electronically through the Department's e-Commerce Internet site. Access to this service is provided at http://hazmat.dot.gov/register.htm. A registrant required to file an amended registration statement under §107.608(c) must mail it to the same address or submit it through the same Internet site.

(b) **Payment must be made by certified check,** cashier's check, personal check, or money order in U.S. funds and drawn on a U.S. bank, payable to the U.S. Department of Transportation and identified as payment for the "Hazmat Registration Fee," or by completing an authorization for payment by credit card or other electronic means of payment acceptable to the Department on the registration statement or as part of an Internet registration as provided in paragraph (a) of this section.

(c) **Payment must correspond to the total fees** properly calculated in the "Amount Due" block of the DOT form F 5800.2. A person may elect to register and pay the required fees for up to three registration years by filing one complete and accurate registration statement.

(d) **A person may obtain a temporary registration number,** valid for 45 days from the date of issuance, through an expedited registration process as follows:

(1) *Contact RSPA* by telephone (800-942-6990 or 617-494-2545) and provide name, principal place of business, and credit card payment information;

(2) *Pay a registration and processing fee as follows:*

(i) *For registration year 2002-2003,* pay a registration fee of $275, a processing fee of $25, and an expedited handling fee of $50. The total fee is $350. Persons who do not meet the criteria for a small business, as specified in §107.612(b)(1), must enclose an additional registration fee payment of $1,700 with the expedited follow-up material, for a total of $2,050 (registration fee — $1,975; processing fee — $25; expedited handling fee — $50);

(ii) *For registration years* 2003-2004, 2004-2005, and 2005-2006, pay a registration fee of $125, a processing fee of $25, and an expedited handling fee of $50. The total fee is $200. Persons who do not meet the criteria for a small business or are not a not-for-profit organization, as specified in §107.612(c), must enclose an additional registration fee payment of $150 with the expedited follow-up material, for a total of $350 (registration fee — $275; processing fee — $25; expedited handling fee — $50); and

(iii) *For registration years beginning with 2006-2007,* pay a registration fee of $250, a processing fee of $25, and an expedited handling fee of $50. The total fee is $325. Persons who do not meet the criteria for a small business or are not a not-for-profit organization, as specified in §107.612(d), must enclose an additional registration fee payment of $725 with the expedited follow-up material, for a total of $1,050 (registration fee — $975; processing fee — $25; expedited handling fee — $50); and

(3) *Submit a completed* registration statement and proof of payment to RSPA before the expiration date of the temporary registration number.

§107.620 Recordkeeping requirements.

(a) **Each person subject to the requirements of this subpart,** or its agent designated under §107.608(e), must maintain at its principal place of business for a period of three years from the date of issuance of each Certificate of Registration:

(1) *A copy of the registration statement filed with RSPA; and*

(2) *The Certificate of Registration issued to the registrant by RSPA.*

(b) **After January 1, 1993, each motor carrier** subject to the requirements of this subpart must carry a copy of its current Certificate of Registration issued by RSPA or another document bearing the registration number identified as the "U.S. DOT Hazmat Reg. No." on board each truck and truck tractor (not including trailers and semi-trailers) used to transport hazardous materials subject to the requirements of this subpart. The Certificate of Registration or document bearing the registration number must be made available, upon request, to enforcement personnel.

(c) **In addition to the requirements of paragraph (a)** of this section, after January 1, 1995, each person who transports by vessel a hazardous material subject to the requirements of this subpart must carry on board the vessel a copy of its current Certificate of Registration or another document bearing the current registration number identified as the "U.S. DOT Hazmat Reg. No."

(d) **Each person subject to this subpart must furnish** its Certificate of Registration (or a copy thereof) and all other records and information pertaining to the information contained in the registration statement to an authorized representative or special agent of DOT upon request.

Subpart H - Approvals, Registrations, and Submissions

§107.701 Purpose and scope.

(a) **This subpart prescribes procedures** for the issuance, modification and termination of approvals, and the submission of registrations and reports, as required by this chapter.

(b) **The procedures of this subpart are in addition** to any requirements in subchapter C of this chapter applicable to a specific approval, registration or report. If compliance with both a specific requirement of subchapter C of this chapter and a procedure of this subpart is not possible, the specific requirement applies.

(c) **Registration under subpart F or G of this part** is not subject to the procedures of this subpart.

§107.705 Registrations, reports, and applications for approval.

(a) **A person filing a registration, report, or application** for an approval, or a renewal or modification of an approval subject to the provisions of this subpart must —

(1) *File the registration,* report, or application with the Associate Administrator for Hazardous Materials Safety (Attention: Approvals, DHM-32), Research and Special Programs Administration, U.S. Department of Transportation, 400 7th Street, SW., Washington, DC 20590-0001. Alternatively, the document with any attached supporting documentation in an appropriate format may be filed by facsimile (fax) to: (202) 366-3753 or (202) 366-3308 or by electronic mail (e-mail) to: Approvals@rspa.dot.gov.

(2) *Identify the section* of the chapter under which the registration, report, or application is made;

(3) *If a report is required* by an approval, a registration or an exemption, identify the approval, registration or exemption number;

(4) *Provide the name,* street and mailing addresses, e-mail address optional, and telephone number of the person on whose behalf the registration, report, or application is made and, if different, the person making the filing;

(5) *If the person* on whose behalf the filing is made is not a resident of the United States, provide a designation of agent for service in accordance with §105.40;

(6) *Provide a description* of the activity for which the registration or report is required; and

(7) *Provide additional information* as requested by the Associate Administrator, if the Associate Administrator determines that a filing lacks pertinent information or otherwise does not comply with applicable requirements.

(b) **In addition to the provisions in paragraph (a)** for an approval, an application for an approval, or an application for modification or renewal of an approval, the applicant must provide —

(1) *A description of the activity for which the approval is required;*

(2) *The proposed duration of the approval;*

(3) *The transport mode or modes affected, as applicable;*

(4) *Any additional information* specified in the section containing the approval; and

(5) *For an approval* which provides exceptions from regulatory requirements or prohibitions —

(i) *Identification of any* increased risk to safety or property that may result if the approval is granted, and specification of the measures that the applicant considers necessary or appropriate to address that risk; and

(ii) *Substantiation,* with applicable analyses or evaluations, if appropriate, demonstrating that the proposed activity will achieve a level of safety that is at least equal to that required by the regulation.

(c) **For an approval with an expiration date,** each application for renewal or modification must be filed in the same manner as an original application. If a complete and conforming renewal application is filed at least 60 days before the expiration date of an approval, the Associate Administrator, on written request from the applicant, will issue a written extension to permit operation under the terms of the expired approval until a final decision on the application for renewal has been made. Operation under an expired approval is prohibited absent a written extension. This paragraph does not limit the authority of the Associate Administrator to modify, suspend or terminate an approval under §107.713.

(d) **To request confidential treatment for information** contained in the application, the applicant shall comply with §105.30(a).

§107.709 Processing of an application for approval, including an application for renewal or modification.

(a) **No public hearing or other formal proceeding** is required under this subpart before the disposition of an application.

(b) **At any time during the processing of an application,** the Associate Administrator may request additional information from the applicant. If the applicant does not respond to a written request for additional information within 30 days of the date the request was received, the application may be deemed incomplete and denied. However, if the applicant responds in writing within the 30-day period requesting an additional 30 days within which it will gather the requested information, the Associate Administrator may grant the 30-day extension.

(c) **The Associate Administrator may grant or deny** an application, in whole or in part. At the Associate Administrator's discretion, an application may be granted subject to provisions that are appropriate to protect health, safety and property. The Associate Administrator may impose additional provisions not specified in the application, or delete conditions in the application which are unnecessary.

(d) **The Associate Administrator may grant an application** on finding that —

(1) *The application complies with this subpart;*

(2) *The application demonstrates* that the proposed activity will achieve a level of safety that —

(i) *Is at least equal to that required by the regulation, or*

(ii) *If the regulations* do not establish a level of safety, is consistent with the public interest and adequately will protect against the risks to life and property inherent in the transportation of hazardous materials in commerce;

(3) *The application* states all material facts, and contains no materially false or materially misleading statement;

(4) *The applicant* meets the qualifications required by applicable regulations; and

(5) *The applicant* is fit to conduct the activity authorized by the approval, or renewal or modification of approval. This assessment may be based on information in the application, prior compliance history of the applicant, and other information available to the Associate Administrator.

(e) **Unless otherwise specified in this chapter** or by the Associate Administrator, an approval in which a term is not specified does not expire.

(f) **The Associate Administrator notifies the applicant** in writing of the decision on the application. A denial contains a brief statement of reasons.

§107.711 Withdrawal.

An application may be withdrawn at any time before a decision to grant or deny it is made. Withdrawal of an application does not authorize the removal of any related records from the RSPA dockets or files. Applications that are eligible for confidential treatment under §105.30 will remain confidential after the application is withdrawn. The duration of this confidential treatment for trade secrets and commercial or financial information is indefinite, unless the party requesting the confidential treatment of the materials notifies the Associate Administrator that the confidential treatment is no longer required.

§107.713 Approval modification, suspension or termination.

(a) **The Associate Administrator may modify an approval** on finding that —

(1) *Modification is necessary* to conform an existing approval to relevant statutes and regulations as they may be amended from time to time; or

(2) *Modification is required* by changed circumstances to enable the approval to continue to meet the standards of §107.709(d).

(b) **The Associate Administrator may modify, suspend** or terminate an approval, as appropriate, on finding that —

(1) *Because of a change* in circumstances, the approval no longer is needed or no longer would be granted if applied for;

(2) *The application* contained inaccurate or incomplete information, and the approval would not have been granted had the application been accurate and complete;

(3) *The application* contained deliberately inaccurate or incomplete information; or

(4) *The holder* knowingly has violated the terms of the approval or an applicable requirement of this chapter in a manner demonstrating lack of fitness to conduct the activity for which the approval is required.

(c) **Except as provided in paragraph (d) of this section,** before an approval is modified, suspended or terminated, the Associate Administrator notifies the holder in writing of the proposed action and the reasons for it, and provides an opportunity to show cause why the proposed action should not be taken.
  (1) *The holder* may file a written response with the Associate Administrator within 30 days of receipt of notice of the proposed action.
  (2) *After considering* the holder's or party's written response, or after 30 days have passed without response since receipt of the notice, the Associate Administrator notifies the holder in writing of the final decision with a brief statement of reasons.
(d) **The Associate Administrator, if necessary to avoid** a risk of significant harm to persons or property, may in the notification declare the proposed action immediately effective.

§107.715 Reconsideration.

(a) **An applicant or a holder may request** that the Associate Administrator reconsider a decision under §107.709(f) or §107.713(c). The request must:
  (1) *Be in writing and filed within 20 days of receipt of the decision;*
  (2) *State in detail any alleged errors of fact and law;*
  (3) *Enclose any additional information* needed to support the request to reconsider; and
  (4) *State in detail the modification of the final decision sought.*
(b) **The Associate Administrator considers** newly submitted information on a showing that the information could not reasonably have been submitted during application processing.
(c) **The Associate Administrator grants or denies,** in whole or in part, the relief requested and informs the requesting person in writing of the decision.

§107.717 Appeal.

(a) **A person who requested reconsideration** under §107.715 may appeal to the Administrator the Associate Administrator's decision on the request. The appeal must:
  (1) *Be in writing and filed* within 30 days of receipt of the Associate Administrator's decision on reconsideration;
  (2) *State in detail any alleged errors of fact and law;*
  (3) *Enclose any additional information* needed to support the appeal; and
  (4) *State in detail the modification of the final decision sought.*
(b) **The Administrator, if necessary to avoid a risk** of significant harm to persons or property, may declare the Associate Administrator's action effective pending a decision on appeal.
(c) **The Administrator grants or denies,** in whole or in part, the relief requested and informs the appellant in writing of the decision on appeal. The Administrator's decision on appeal is the final administrative action.

Subpart I - Approval of Independent Inspection Agencies, Cylinder Requalifiers, and Non-domestic Chemical Analyses and Tests of DOT Specification Cylinders

§107.801 Purpose and scope.

(a) **This subpart prescribes procedures for —**
  (1) *A person* who seeks approval to be an independent inspection agency to perform cylinder inspections and verifications required by parts 178 and 180 of this chapter;
  (2) *A person* who seeks approval to engage in the requalification (e.g., inspection, testing, or certification), rebuilding, or repair of a cylinder manufactured in accordance with a DOT specification under subchapter C of this chapter or under the terms of an exemption issued under this part;
  (3) *A person* who seeks approval to perform the manufacturing chemical analyses and tests of DOT specification or exemption cylinders outside the United States.
(b) **No person may engage in a function** identified in paragraph (a) of this section unless approved by the Associate Administrator in accordance with the provisions of this subpart. Each person must comply with the applicable requirements in this subpart. In addition, the procedural requirements in subpart H of this part apply to the filing, processing, and termination of an approval issued under this subpart.

§107.803 Approval of independent inspection agency.

(a) **General.** Prior to performing cylinder inspections and verifications required by parts 178 and 180 of this chapter, a person must apply to the Associate Administrator for an approval as an independent inspection agency. A person approved as an independent inspection agency is not an RSPA agent or representative.
(b) **Criteria.** No applicant for approval as an independent inspection agency may be engaged in the manufacture of cylinders for use in the transportation of hazardous materials, or be directly or indirectly controlled by, or have a financial involvement with, any entity that manufactures cylinders for use in the transportation of hazardous materials, except for providing services as an independent inspector.
(c) **Application information.** Each applicant must submit an application in conformance with §107.705 containing the information prescribed in §107.705(a). In addition, the application must contain the following information:
  (1) *Name and address* of each facility where tests and inspections are to be performed.
  (2) *Detailed description* of the inspection and testing facilities to be used by the applicant.
  (3) *Detailed description* of the applicant's qualifications and ability to perform the inspections and to verify the inspections required by part 178 of this chapter or under the terms of an exemption issued under this part.
  (4) *Name, address,* and principal business activity of each person having any direct or indirect ownership interest in the applicant greater than three percent and any direct or indirect ownership interest in each subsidiary or division of the applicant.
  (5) *Name of* each individual whom the applicant proposes to employ as an inspector and who will be responsible for certifying inspection and test results, and a statement of that person's qualifications.
  (6) *An identification* or qualification number assigned to each inspector who is supervised by a certifying inspector identified in paragraph (c)(3) of this section.
  (7) *A statement* that the applicant will perform its functions independent of the manufacturers and owners of the cylinders.
  (8) *The signature* of the person certifying the approval application and the date on which it was signed.
(d) **Facility inspection.** Upon the request of the Associate Administrator, the applicant must allow the Associate Administrator or the Associate Administrator's designee to inspect the applicant's facilities and records. The person seeking approval must bear the cost of the inspection.
(e) **After approval, the Associate Administrator** may authorize, upon request, the independent inspection agency to perform other inspections and functions for which the Associate Administrator finds the applicant to be qualified. Such additional authorizations will be noted on each inspection agency's approval documents.

§107.805 Approval of cylinder requalifiers.

(a) **General.** A person must meet the requirements of this section to be approved to inspect, test, certify, repair, or rebuild a cylinder in accordance with a DOT specification under subpart C of part 178 or subpart C of part 180 of this chapter or under the terms of an exemption issued under this part.
(b) **Independent Inspection Agency Review.** Each applicant must arrange for an independent inspection agency, approved by the Associate Administrator pursuant to this subpart, to perform a review of its inspection or requalification operation. The person seeking approval must bear the cost of the inspection. A list of approved independent inspection agencies is available from the Associate Administrator at the address listed in §107.705. Assistance in obtaining an approval is available from the same address.
(c) **Application for approval.** If the inspection performed by an independent inspection agency is completed with satisfactory results, the applicant must submit a letter of recommendation from the independent inspection agency, an inspection report, and an application containing the information prescribed in §107.705(a). In addition, the application must contain —
  (1) *The name of the facility manager;*
  (2) *The DOT* specification/exemption cylinders that will be inspected, tested, repaired, or rebuilt at the facility;
  (3) *A certification* that the facility will operate in compliance with the applicable requirements of subchapter C of this chapter; and
  (4) *The signature* of the person making the certification and the date on which it was signed.

(d) **Issuance of requalifier identification number (RIN).** The Associate Administrator issues a RIN as evidence of approval to requalify DOT specification/exemption cylinders if it is determined, based on the applicant's submission and other available information, that the applicant's qualifications and, when applicable, facility are adequate to perform the requested functions in accordance with the criteria prescribed in subpart C of Part 180 of this chapter.

(e) **Expiration of RIN.** Unless otherwise provided in the issuance letter, an approval expires five years from the date of issuance, provided the applicant's facility and qualifications are maintained at or above the level observed at the time of inspection by the independent inspection agency, or at the date of the certification in the application for approval for requalifiers only performing inspections made under §180.209(g) of this chapter.

(f) **Exceptions.** Notwithstanding the requirements in paragraphs (b) and (c) of this section, a person who only performs inspections in accordance with §180.209(g) of this chapter may submit an application that, in addition to the information prescribed in §107.705(a), identifies the DOT specification/exemption cylinders to be inspected; certifies the requalifier will operate in compliance with the applicable requirements of subchapter C of this chapter; certifies the persons performing inspections have been trained and have the information contained in each applicable CGA pamphlet incorporated by reference in §171.7 of this chapter applicable to the requalifiers' activities; and includes the signature of the person making the certification and the date on which it was signed. Each person must comply with the applicable requirements in this subpart. In addition, the procedural requirements in subpart H of this part apply to the filing, processing and termination of an approval issued under this subpart. After September 30, 2003, no person may requalify a DOT specification/ exemption cylinder in accordance with §180.209(g) of this chapter unless that person has been issued a RIN as provided in paragraph (d) of this section.

(g) **Each holder of a current RIN** shall report in writing any change in its name, address, ownership, testing equipment, or management or personnel performing any function under this section, to the Associate Administrator (DHM-32) within 20 days of the change.

§107.807 Approval of non-domestic chemical analyses and tests.

(a) **General.** A person who seeks to manufacture DOT specification or exemption cylinders outside the United States must seek an approval from the Associate Administrator to perform the chemical analyses and tests of those cylinders outside the United States.

(b) **Application for approval.** Each applicant must submit an application containing the information prescribed in §107.705(a). In addition, the application must contain —

(1) *The name, address,* and a description of each facility at which cylinders are to be manufactured and chemical analyses and tests are to be performed;

(2) *Complete details* concerning the dimensions, materials of construction, wall thickness, water capacity, shape, type of joints, location and size of openings and other pertinent physical characteristics of each specification or exemption cylinder for which approval is being requested, including calculations for cylinder wall stress and wall thickness, which may be shown on a drawing or on separate sheets attached to a descriptive drawing;

(3) *The name of the independent inspection agency to be used; and*

(4) *The signature* of the person making the certification and the date on which it was signed.

(c) **Facility inspections.** Upon the request of the Associate Administrator, the applicant must allow the Associate Administrator or the Associate Administrator's designee to inspect the applicant's cylinder manufacturing and testing facilities and records, and must provide such materials and cylinders for analyses and tests as the Associate Administrator may specify. The applicant or holder must bear the cost of the initial and subsequent inspections, analyses, and tests.

Part 110 - Hazardous Materials Public Sector Training and Planning Grants

§110.1 Purpose.

This part sets forth procedures for reimbursable grants for public sector planning and training in support of the emergency planning and training efforts of States, Indian tribes, and local communities to deal with hazardous materials emergencies, particularly those involving transportation. These grants will enhance the implementation of the Emergency Planning and Community Right-to-Know Act of 1986 (42 U.S.C. 11001).

§110.5 Scope.

(a) **This part applies to States and Indian tribes** and contains the program requirements for public sector training and planning grants to support hazardous materials emergency planning and training efforts.

(b) **The requirements contained in 49 CFR part 18,** "Uniform Administrative Requirements for Grants and Cooperative Agreements to State and Local Governments", apply to grants issued under this part.

(c) **Copies of standard forms and OMB circulars** referenced in this part are available from the HMTUSA Grants Manager, Research and Special Programs Administration, U.S. Department of Transportation, 400 Seventh Street, SW., Washington DC 20590-0001.

§110.7 Control number under the Paperwork Reduction Act.

The Office of Management and Budget control number assigned to collection of information in §§110.30, 110.70, 110.80, and 110.90 is 2137-0586.

§110.10 Eligibility.

This part applies to States and Indian tribes. States may apply for planning and training grants. Federally-recognized Indian tribes may apply for training grants.

§110.20 Definitions.

Unless defined in this part, all terms defined in 49 U.S.C. 5102 are used in their statutory meaning and all terms defined in 49 CFR part 18 and OMB Circular A-102, with respect to administrative requirements for grants, are used as defined therein. Other terms used in this part are defined as follows:

Allowable costs means those costs that are: eligible, reasonable, necessary, and allocable to the project permitted by the appropriate Federal cost principles, and approved in the grant.

Associate Administrator means the Associate Administrator for Hazardous Materials Safety, Research and Special Programs Administration.

Budget period means the period of time specified in the grant agreement during which the project manager may expend or obligate project funds.

Cost review means the review and evaluation of costs to determine reasonableness, allocability, and allowability.

Indian country means Indian country as defined in 18 U.S.C. 1151. That section defines Indian country as all land within the limits of any reservation under the jurisdiction of the U.S. Government, notwithstanding the issuance of any patent, and, including rights-of-way running through the reservation; all dependent Indian communities within the borders of the United States whether within the original or subsequently acquired territory thereof, and whether within or without the limits of a State; and all Indian allotments, the Indian titles to which have not been extinguished, including rights-of-way running through the same.

Indian tribe means a tribe "Federally-recognized" by the Secretary of the Interior under 25 CFR 272.2.

Local Emergency Planning Committee (LEPC) means a committee appointed by the State Emergency Response Commission under section 301(c) of the Emergency Planning and Community Right-to-Know Act of 1986 (42 U.S.C. 11001(c)) that includes at a minimum, representatives from each of the following groups or organizations: elected State and local officials; law enforcement, firefighting, civil defense, first aid, health, local environmental, hospital, and transportation personnel; broadcast and print media; community groups; and owners and operators of facilities subject to the emergency planning requirements.

National curriculum means the curriculum required to be developed under 49 U.S.C. 5115 and necessary to train public sector emergency response and preparedness teams, enabling them to comply with performance standards as stated in 49 U.S.C. 5115(c).

Political subdivision means a county, municipality, city, town, township, local public authority (including any public and Indian housing agency under the United States Housing Act of 1937 (42 U.S.C. 1401 et seq.), school district, special district, intrastate district, council of governments (whether or not incorporated as a nonprofit corporation under State law), any other regional or interstate government entity, or any agency or instrumentality of a local government.

Project means the activities and tasks identified in the grant agreement.

Project manager means the State or Indian tribal official designated in a grant as the recipient agency's principal program contact with the Federal Government.

Project officer means the Federal official designated in a grant as the program contact with the project manager. The project officer is responsible for monitoring the project.

Project period means the length of time specified in a grant for completion of all work associated with that project.

State Emergency Response Commission (SERC) means the State Emergency Response Commission appointed by the Governor of each State and Territory under the Emergency Planning and Community Right-to-Know Act of 1986.

Statement of Work means that portion of a grant that describes the purpose and scope of activities and tasks to be carried out as part of the proposed project.

§110.30 Grant application.

(a) **General.** An applicant for a planning or training grant shall use only the standard application forms approved by the Office of Management and Budget (OMB) (SF-424 and SF-424A) under the Paperwork Reduction Act of 1980 (44 U.S.C. 3502). Applicants are required to submit an original and two copies of the application package to: Grants Manager, Research and Special Programs Administration, U.S. Department of Transportation, 400 7th Street, SW., Washington, DC 20590-0001. Applications received on or before January 1st and July 1st of each year will be considered in that cycle of the semi-annual review and award process. An initial round of the review and award process will consider applications received on or before November 15, 1992. Requests and continuation applications must include an original and two copies of the affected pages; previously submitted pages with information that is still current do not have to be resubmitted. The application must include the following:

(1) *Application for Federal Assistance* for non-construction programs (SF-424) and Budget sheets (SF-424A). A single application may be used for both planning and training if the budgets for each are entered separately on all budget sheets.

(2) *For States,* a letter from the Governor designating the State agency that is authorized to apply for a grant and to provide the written certifications required to receive a grant.

(3) *For Indian tribes,* a letter from the tribal government, governing body, or tribal council to the effect that the applicant is authorized to apply for a grant and to provide the written certifications required to receive a grant.

(4) *A written statement* explaining whether the State or tribe assesses and collects fees on the transportation of hazardous materials and whether such assessments or fees are used solely to carry out purposes related to the transportation of hazardous materials.

(5) *A statement* designating a project manager and providing the name, position, address and phone number of that individual who will be responsible for coordinating the funded activities with other agencies/organizations.

(6) *A project narrative statement* of the goals and objectives of the proposed project, project design, and long range plans. The proposed grant project and budget periods may be one or more years.

(7) *A statement of work* in support of the proposed project that describes and sets priorities for the activities and tasks to be conducted, the costs associated with each activity, the number and types of deliverables and products to be completed, and a schedule for implementation.

(8) *A description* of the major items of costs needed to implement the statement of work and a copy of any cost or price analysis if conducted.

(9) *Drug-Free Workplace Certification.* The applicant must certify as specified in appendix C of 49 CFR part 29 that it will comply with the Drug-Free Workplace Act of 1988 (Pub. L. 100-690, title V, subtitle D; 51 U.S.C. 701 et seq.).

(10) *Anti-Lobbying Certification.* The applicant must certify as specified in appendix A of 49 CFR part 20 that no Federal funds will be expended to pay any person for influencing or attempting to influence an officer or employee of any agency, a Member of

Congress, an officer or employee of Congress, or an employee of a Member of Congress (section 319 of Pub. L. 101-121, 31 U.S.C. 1352).

(11) *Debarment and Suspension Certification.* The applicant must certify as specified in subpart G of 49 CFR part 29 that it will not make an award or permit any award to any party which is debarred or suspended or is otherwise excluded from or ineligible for participation in Federal assistance programs.

(b) **Planning.** In addition to the requirements specified in paragraph (a) of this section, eligible State applicants must include the following in their application package:

(1) *A written certification* that the State is complying with sections 301 and 303 of the Emergency Planning and Community Right-to-Know Act of 1986, including a brief explanation of how compliance has been achieved.

(2) *A written statement* specifying the aggregate expenditure of funds of the State, exclusive of Federal funds, for each of its last two fiscal years for developing, improving, and implementing emergency plans under the Emergency Planning and Community Right-to-Know Act of 1986, including an explanation specifying the sources of these funds. A written certification that the State's aggregate expenditures, as defined by the State, of funds for this purpose, exclusive of Federal funds, will not fall below the average level of its expenditures for its last two fiscal years. The applicant may not claim any of these expenditures for cost-sharing.

(3) *A written statement* agreeing to make at least 75 percent of the Federal funds awarded available to LEPCs and an explanation of how the applicant intends to make such funds available to them for developing, improving, or implementing emergency plans.

(4) *Designation* of a project manager to serve as contact for coordinating planning funds under this program.

(5) *A project narrative statement* of the goals and objectives of each proposed project, including the following:

(i) *A background statement* describing the applicant's long-term goals and objectives with respect to:

[A] The current abilities and authorities of the applicant's program for preparedness planning;

[B] The need to sustain or increase program capability;

[C] Current degree of participation in or intention to assess the need for a regional hazardous materials emergency response team; and

[D] The impact that the grant will have on the program.

(ii) *A discussion* of whether the applicant's program currently knows, or intends to assess, transportation flow patterns of hazardous materials within the State and between that State and another State.

(iii) *A schedule for implementing the proposed grant activities.*

(iv) *A statement* describing the ways in which planning will be monitored by the project manager.

(v) *A statement* indicating that all members of the State Emergency Response Commission were provided the opportunity to review the grant application.

(c) **Training.** In addition to the requirements specified in paragraph (a) of this section, eligible State and Indian tribe applicants must include the following in their application package:

(1) *For a State applicant,* a written certification explaining how the State is complying with sections 301 and 303 of the Emergency Planning and Community Right-to-Know Act.

(2) *A written statement* specifying the aggregate expenditure of funds of the State or Indian tribe, exclusive of Federal funds, for each of its last two fiscal years for training public sector employees to respond to accidents and incidents involving hazardous materials, including an explanation specifying the sources of these funds. A written certification that the applicant's aggregate expenditure, as defined by the State or tribe, of funds for this purpose, exclusive of Federal funds, will not fall below the average level of its expenditures for its last two fiscal years. The applicant may not claim any of these expenditures for cost-sharing purposes.

(3) *For a State applicant,* a written statement agreeing to make at least 75 percent of the Federal funds awarded available for the purpose of training public sector employees employed or used by political subdivisions. A State applicant may elect to pass all or some portion of the grant on to political subdivisions for this purpose. The applicant must include a specific explanation of how it intends to meet this requirement.

(4) *Designation of a primary point of contact* for coordinating training funded under this program. Identification of a single repository for copies of course materials delivered under the grant as specified in §110.90 of this part.

(5) *A project narrative statement* of the long-range goals and objectives of each proposed project, including the following:

(i) *A background statement describing:*

[A] The current hazardous materials training program(s);

[B] Training audience, including numbers and levels of training and accreditation program for each level or criterion required to advance to the next level;

[C] Estimated total number of persons to be trained under the proposed project;

[D] The ways in which training grants will support the integrated delivery of training to meet the needs of individualized geographic and resource needs and time considerations of local responders. When appropriate, a statement describing how the proposed project will accommodate the different training needs for rural versus urban environments; and

[E] The impact that the grant and the National Curriculum will have on the program.

(ii) *A statement* describing how the National Curriculum will be used or modified to train public sector employees at the local level to respond to accidents and incidents involving hazardous materials.

(iii) *A statement* describing the ways in which effectiveness of training will be monitored by the project manager, including, but not limited to, examinations, critiques, and instructor evaluations.

(iv) *A schedule* for implementing the proposed training grant activities.

(v) *A statement* indicating that all members of the State or Tribal Emergency Response Commission were provided the opportunity to review the grant application.

§110.40 Activities eligible for funding.

(a) **Planning.** Eligible State applicants may receive funding for the following activities:

(1) *Development, improvement, and implementation* of emergency plans required under the Emergency Planning and Community Right-to-Know Act of 1986, as well as exercises which test the emergency plan. Enhancement of emergency plans to include hazard analysis as well as response procedures for emergencies involving transportation of hazardous materials, including radioactive materials.

(2) *An assessment* to determine flow patterns of hazardous materials within a State, between a State and another State or Indian country, and development and maintenance of a system to keep such information current.

(3) *An assessment* of the need for regional hazardous materials emergency response teams.

(4) *An assessment of local response capabilities.*

(5) *Conduct of emergency response* drills and exercises associated with emergency preparedness plans.

(6) *Provision of technical staff to support the planning effort.*

(7) *Additional activities* the Associate Administrator deems appropriate to implement the scope of work for the proposed project plan and approved in the grant.

(b) **Training.** Eligible State and Indian tribe applicants may receive funding for the following activities:

(1) *An assessment* to determine the number of public sector employees employed or used by a political subdivision who need the proposed training and to select courses consistent with the National Curriculum.

(2) *Delivery of comprehensive* preparedness and response training to public sector employees. Design and delivery of preparedness and response training to meet specialized needs. Financial assistance for trainees and for the trainers, if appropriate, such as tuition, travel expenses to and from a training facility, and room and board while at the training facility.

(3) *Emergency response* drills and exercises associated with training, a course of study, and tests and evaluation of emergency preparedness plans.

(4) *Expenses associated* with training by a person (including a department, agency, or instrumentality of a State or political subdivision thereof or an Indian tribe) and activities necessary to monitor such training including, but not limited to, examinations, critiques and instructor evaluations.

(5) *Provision of staff* to manage the training effort designed to result in increased benefits, proficiency, and rapid deployment of local and regional responders.

(6) *Additional activities* the Associate Administrator deems appropriate to implement the scope of work for the proposed project and approved in the grant.

§110.50 Disbursement of Federal funds.

(a) **Preaward expenditures may not be reimbursed.**

(b) **Reimbursement may not be made** for a project plan unless approved in the grant award.

(c) **If a recipient agency seeks additional funds,** the amendment request will be evaluated on the basis of needs, performance and availability of funds. An existing grant is not a commitment of future Federal funding.

§110.60 Cost sharing for planning and training.

(a) **The recipient agency must provide 20 percent** of the direct and indirect costs of all activities covered under the grant award program with non-Federal funds. Recipients may either use cash (hard-match), in-kind (soft-match) contributions, or a combination of in-kind plus hard-match to meet this requirement. In-kind (soft-match) contributions are in addition to the maintenance of effort required of recipients of grant awards. The types of contributions allowed are as follows:

(1) *Any funds* from a State, local, or other non-Federal source used for an eligible activity as defined in §110.40 in this part.

(2) *The dollar equivalent value* of an eligible activity as defined in §110.40 of this part provided by a State, local, or other non-Federal source.

(3) *The value* of participants' salary while attending a planning or training activity contained in the approved grant application provided by a State, local, or other non-Federal source.

(4) *Additional types* of in-kind contributions the Associate Administrator deems appropriate.

(b) **Funds used for matching purposes** under any other Federal grant or cooperative agreement may not be used for matching purposes. The funds expended by a recipient agency to qualify for the grant may not be used for cost-sharing purposes.

(c) **Acceptable contributions for matching** and cost sharing purposes must conform to 49 CFR part 18.

§110.70 Financial administration.

(a) **A State must expend and account for grant funds** in accordance with State laws and procedures for expending and accounting for its own funds. Fiscal control and accounting procedures of the State, as well as its subgrantees and cost-type contractors, must be sufficient to:

(1) *Permit the preparation* of reports required by 49 CFR part 18 and this part, including the tracing of funds provided for planning to a level of expenditure adequate to establish that at least 75 percent of the funds provided were made available to LEPCs for developing, improving, and implementing emergency plans; and the tracing of funds provided for training to a level of expenditure adequate to establish that at least 75 percent of the funds provided were made available for the purposes of training public sector employees employed or used by political subdivisions.

(2) *Permit the tracing of funds* to a level of expenditure adequate to establish that such funds have not been used in violation of the restrictions and prohibitions of applicable statutes.

(b) **The financial management systems of Indian tribes** and any subgrantees must meet the standards of 49 CFR 18.20, including the ability to trace funds provided for training to a level of expenditure adequate to establish that at least 75 percent of the funds provided were made available for the purposes of training public sector employees employed or used by political subdivisions.

(c) **Advances shall be made to States and Indian tribes** consistent with 49 CFR part 18 and 31 CFR part 205. The Associate Administrator shall base these advances on demonstrated need, which will be determined on a case-by-case basis, considering such factors as State/Tribal budget constraints and reductions in amounts budgeted for hazardous materials activities. To obtain an advance, a State or Indian tribe must comply with the following requirements:

(1) *A letter* from the Governor or Tribal leader or their designee is required specifying the extenuating circumstances requiring the funding advance for the grant;

(2) *The maximum advance request* may not be more than $25,000 for each State or Indian tribe;

(3) *Recipients of advance funding* must obligate those funds within 3 months of receipt;

(4) *Advances including interest* will be deducted from the initial reimbursement to the State or Indian tribe; and

(5) *The State or Indian tribe* will have its allocation of current grant funds reduced and will not be permitted to apply for future grant funds until the advance is covered by a request for reimbursement. For example, if $25,000 is advanced for personnel costs, this advance would be deducted from the initial reimbursement in the year the advance was made.

(d) **To be allowable, costs must be eligible,** reasonable, necessary, and allocable to the approved project in accordance with OMB Circular A-87 and included in the grant award. Costs incurred prior to the award of any grant are not allowable. Recipient agencies are responsible for obtaining audits in accordance with the Single Audit Act of 1984 (31 U.S.C. 7501), 49 CFR part 90, and OMB Circular A-128. Audits shall be made by an independent auditor in accordance with generally accepted government auditing standards covering financial and compliance audits. The Associate Administrator may audit a recipient agency at any time.

§110.80 Procurement.

Project managers shall use procurement procedures and practices which reflect applicable State laws and regulations and Federal requirements as specified in 49 CFR 18.36.

§110.90 Grant monitoring, reports, and records retention.

(a) **Grant monitoring.** Project managers are responsible for managing the day-to-day operations of grant, subgrant and contract-supported activities. Project managers must monitor performance of supported activities to assure compliance with applicable Federal requirements and achievement of performance goals. Monitoring must cover each program, function, activity, or task covered by the grant. Monitoring and reporting requirements for planning and training are contained in this part; general grant reporting requirements are specified in 49 CFR 18.40.

(b) **Reports.**

(1) *The project manager* shall submit a performance report at the completion of an activity for which reimbursement is being requested or with a request to amend the grant. The final performance report is due 90 days after the expiration or termination of the grant.

(2) *Project managers* shall submit an original and two copies of all performance reports. Performance reports for planning and training must include comparison of actual accomplishments to the stated goals and objectives established for the performance period, and the reasons for not achieving those goals and objectives, if applicable.

(3) *Project managers* shall report developments or events that occur between the required performance reporting dates which have significant impact upon the planning and training activity such as:

(i) *Problems, delays, or adverse conditions* which will impair the ability to meet the objective of the grant; and

(ii) *Favorable developments* which enable meeting time schedules and objectives sooner or at less cost than anticipated or producing more beneficial results than originally planned.

(4) *Financial reporting,* except as provided in §110.70 and 49 CFR 18.41, shall be supplied quarterly using Standard Form 270, Request for Advance or Reimbursement, to report the status of funds. The project manager shall report separately on planning and training.

(c) **Records retention.** In accordance with 49 CFR 18.42, all financial and programmatic records, supporting documents, statistical records, training materials, and other documents generated under a grant shall be maintained by the project manager for three years from the date the project manager submits the final financial status report (SF 269) or Request for Advance or Reimbursement (SF 270). The project manager shall designate a repository and single-point of contact for planning and for training, or both, for these purposes. If any litigation, claim, negotiation, audit or other action involving the records has been started before the expiration of the 3-year period, the records must be retained until completion of the action and resolution of all issues which arise from it, or until the end of the regular 3-year period, whichever is later.

§110.100 Enforcement.

If a recipient agency fails to comply with any term of an award (whether stated in a Federal statute or regulation, an assurance, a State plan or application, a notice of award, or elsewhere) a noncompliance action may be taken as specified in 40 CFR 18.43. The recipient agency may appeal any such actions as specified in 49 CFR part 18. Costs incurred by the recipient agency during a suspension or after termination of an award are not allowable unless the Associate Administrator authorizes it in writing. Grant awards may be terminated in whole or in part with the consent of the recipient at any agreed upon effective date, or by the recipient upon written notification.

§110.110 After-grant requirements.

The Associate Administrator will close out the award upon determination that all applicable administrative actions and all required work of the grant are complete in accordance with subpart D of 49 CFR part 18. The project manager must submit all financial, performance, and other reports required as a condition of the grant, within 90 days after the expiration or termination of the grant. This time frame may be extended by the Associate Administrator for Hazardous Materials Safety for cause.

§110.120 Deviation from this part.

Recipient agencies may request a deviation from the non-statutory provisions of this part. The Associate Administrator will respond to such requests in writing. If appropriate, the decision will be included in the grant agreement. Request for deviations from part 110 must be submitted to: Grants Manager, Research and Special Programs Administration, U.S. Department of Transportation, 400 7th Street, SW., Washington, DC 20590-0001.

§110.130 Disputes.

Disputes should be resolved at the lowest level possible, beginning with the project manager and the project officer. If an agreement cannot be reached, the Administrator, RSPA, will serve as the dispute resolution official, whose decision will be final.

Subchapter B - Oil Transportation

Part 130 - Oil Spill Prevention and Response Plans

§130.1 Purpose.

This part prescribes prevention, containment and response planning requirements of the Department of Transportation applicable to transportation of oil by motor vehicles and rolling stock.

§130.2 Scope.

(a) The requirements of this part apply to —
- (1) *Any liquid petroleum oil* in a packaging having a capacity of 3,500 gallons or more; and
- (2) *Any liquid petroleum* or non-petroleum oil in a quantity greater than 42,000 gallons per packaging.

(b) The requirements of this part have no effect on —
- (1) *The applicability* of the Hazardous Materials Regulations set forth in subchapter C of this chapter; and
- (2) *The discharge* notification requirements of the United States Coast Guard (33 CFR part 153) and EPA (40 CFR part 110).

(c) The requirements of this part do not apply to —
- (1) *Any mixture or solution* in which oil is in a concentration by weight of less than 10 percent.
- (2) *Transportation of oil by aircraft or vessel.*
- (3) *Any petroleum oil* carried in a fuel tank for the purpose of supplying fuel for propulsion of the transport vehicle to which it is attached.
- (4) *Oil transport* exclusively within the confines of a non-transportation-related or terminal facility in a vehicle not intended for use in interstate or intrastate commerce (see 40 CFR part 112, appendix A).

(d) The requirements in §130.31(b) of this part do not apply to mobile marine transportation-related facilities (see 33 CFR part 154).

§130.3 General requirements.

No person may offer or accept for transportation or transport oil subject to this part unless that person —

(a) Complies with this part; and

(b) Has been instructed on the applicable requirements of this part.

§130.5 Definitions.

In this subchapter:

Animal fat means a non-petroleum oil, fat, or grease derived from animals, not specifically identified elsewhere in this part.

Contract or other means is:
- (1) *A written contract* with a response contractor identifying and ensuring the availability of the necessary personnel or equipment within the shortest practicable time;
- (2) *A written certification* by the owner or operator that the necessary personnel or equipment can and will be made available by the owner or operator within the shortest practicable time; or
- (3) *Documentation of membership* in an oil spill response organization that ensures the owner's or operator's access to the necessary personnel or equipment within the shortest practicable time.

EPA means the U.S. Environmental Protection Agency.

Liquid means a material that has a vertical flow of over two inches (50 mm) within a three-minute period, or a material having one gram or more liquid separation, when determined in accordance with the procedures specified in ASTM D 4359-84, "Standard Test Method for Determining Whether a Material is a Liquid or a Solid," 1990 edition, which is incorporated by reference.

NOTE: This incorporation by reference has been approved by the Director of the Federal Register in accordance with 5 U.S.C. 552(a) and 1 CFR part 51. A copy may be obtained from the American Society for Testing and Materials, 1916 Race Street, Philadelphia, PA 19103. Copies may be inspected at the Office of Hazardous Materials Safety, Office of Hazardous Materials Standards, Room 8422, DOT headquarters building, 400 7th St., SW, Washington, DC 20590, or at the Office of the Federal Register, 800 North Capitol St., NW, Room 700, Washington, DC 20002.

Maximum extent practicable means the limits of available technology and the practical and technical limits on an owner or operator of an onshore facility in planning the response resources required to provide the on-water recovery capability and the shoreline protection and cleanup capability to conduct response activities for a worst-case discharge of oil in adverse weather.

Non-petroleum oil means any animal fat, vegetable oil or other non-petroleum oil.

Oil means oil of any kind or in any form, including, but not limited to, petroleum, fuel oil, sludge, oil refuse, and oil mixed with wastes other than dredged spoil.

NOTE: This definition does not include hazardous substances (see 40 CFR part 116).

Other non-petroleum oil means a non-petroleum oil of any kind that is not an animal fat or vegetable oil.

Packaging means a receptacle and any other components or materials necessary for the receptacle to perform its containment function in conformance with the packaging requirements of this part. A compartmented tank is a single packaging.

Person means an individual, firm, corporation, partnership, association, State, municipality, commission, or political subdivision of a State, or any interstate body, as well as a department, agency, or instrumentality of the executive, legislative or judicial branch of the Federal Government.

Petroleum oil means any oil extracted or derived from geological hydrocarbon deposits, including fractions thereof.

Qualified individual means an individual familiar with the response plan, trained in his or her responsibilities in implementing the plan, and authorized, on behalf of the owner or operator, to initiate all response activities identified in the plan, to enter into response-related contracts and obligate funds for such contracts, and to act as a liaison with the on-scene coordinator and other responsible officials. The qualified individual must be available at all times the owner or operator is engaged in transportation subject to part 130 (alone or in conjunction with an equally qualified alternate), must be fluent in English, and must have in his or her possession documentation of the required authority.

Transports or **Transportation** means any movement of oil by highway or rail, and any loading, unloading, or storage incidental thereto.

Vegetable oil means a non-petroleum oil or fat derived from plant seeds, nuts, kernels or fruits, not specifically identified elsewhere in this part.

Worst-case discharge means "the largest foreseeable discharge in adverse weather conditions," as defined at 33 U.S.C. 1321(a)(24). The largest foreseeable discharge from a motor vehicle or rail car is the capacity of the cargo container. The term "maximum potential discharge," used in §130.31(a), is synonymous with "worst-case discharge."

§130.11 Communication requirements.

(a) No person may offer oil subject to this part for transportation unless that person provides the person accepting the oil for transportation a document indicating the shipment contains oil.

(b) No person may transport oil subject to this part unless a readily available document indicating that the shipment contains oil is in the possession of the transport vehicle operator during transportation.

(c) A material subject to the requirements of this part need not be specifically identified as oil when the shipment document accurately describes the material as: aviation fuel, diesel fuel, fuel oil, gasoline, jet fuel, kerosene, motor fuel, or petroleum.

§130.21 Packaging requirements.

Each packaging used for the transportation of oil subject to this part must be designed, constructed, maintained, closed, and loaded so that, under conditions normally incident to transportation, there will be no release of oil to the environment.

§130.31 Response plans.

(a) After September 30, 1993, no person may transport oil subject to this part unless that person has a current basic written plan that:
- (1) *Sets forth* the manner of response to discharges that may occur during transportation;
- (2) *Takes into account* the maximum potential discharge of the contents from the packaging;
- (3) *Identifies private personnel* and equipment available to respond to a discharge;
- (4) *Identifies the appropriate* persons and agencies (including their telephone numbers) to be contacted in regard to such a discharge and its handling, including the National Response Center; and
- (5) *For each motor carrier,* is retained on file at that person's principal place of business and at each location where dispatching of motor vehicles occurs; and for each railroad, is retained on file at that person's principal place of business and at the dispatcher's office.

(b) **After February 18, 1993, no person may transport** an oil subject to this part in a quantity greater than 1,000 barrels (42,000 gallons) unless that person has a current comprehensive written plan that:

(1) *Conforms* with all requirements specified in paragraph (a) of this section;

(2) *Is consistent* with the requirements of the National Contingency Plan (40 CFR part 300) and Area Contingency Plans;

(3) *Identifies* the qualified individual having full authority to implement removal actions, and requires immediate communications between that individual and the appropriate Federal official and the persons providing spill response personnel and equipment;

(4) *Identifies,* and ensures by contract or other means the availability of, private personnel (including address and phone number), and the equipment necessary to remove, to the maximum extent practicable, a worst case discharge (including a discharge resulting from fire or explosion) and to mitigate or prevent a substantial threat of such a discharge;

(5) *Describes* the training, equipment testing, periodic unannounced drills, and response actions of facility personnel, to be carried out under the plan to ensure the safety of the facility and to mitigate or prevent the discharge, or the substantial threat of such a discharge; and

(6) *Is submitted,* and resubmitted in the event of any significant change, to the Federal Railroad Administrator (for tank cars), or to the Federal Highway Administrator (for cargo tanks) at 400 Seventh Street SW, Washington, DC 20590-0001. (Approved by the Office of Management and Budget under control number 2137-0591)

§130.33 Response plan implementation.

If, during transportation of oil subject to this part, a discharge occurs — into or on the navigable waters of the United States; on the adjoining shorelines to the navigable waters; or that may affect natural resources belonging to, appertaining to, or under the exclusive management authority of, the United States — the person transporting the oil shall implement the plan required by §130.31, in a manner consistent with the National Contingency Plan, 40 CFR part 300, or as otherwise directed by the Federal on-scene coordinator.

Subchapter C - Hazardous Materials Regulations

Part 171 - General Information, Regulations, and Definitions

§171.1 Purpose and scope.

(a) **This subchapter prescribes requirements** of the Department governing —

(1) *The offering* of hazardous materials for transportation and transportation of hazardous materials in interstate, intrastate, and foreign commerce by rail car, aircraft, motor vehicle, and vessel (except as delegated at §1.46(t) of this title).

(2) *The representation* that a hazardous material is present in a package, container, rail car, aircraft, motor vehicle, or vessel.

(3) *The manufacture,* fabrication, marking, maintenance, reconditioning, repairing, or testing of a packaging or container which is represented, marked, certified, or sold for use in transportation of hazardous materials.

(4) *The use* of terms and symbols prescribed in this subchapter for the marking, labeling, placarding and description of hazardous materials and packagings used in their transport.

(b) **Any person who, under contract with any department,** agency, or instrumentality of the executive, legislative, or judicial branch of the Federal Government, transports, or causes to be transported or shipped, a hazardous material or manufactures, fabricates, marks, maintains, reconditions, repairs, or tests a package or container which is represented, marked, certified, or sold by such person as qualified for use in the transportation of a hazardous material shall be subject to and comply with all provisions of the Federal hazardous materials transportation law, all orders and regulations issued thereunder, and all other substantive and procedural requirements of Federal, State, and local governments and Indian tribes (except any such requirements that have been preempted by the Federal hazardous materials transportation law or any other Federal law), in the same manner and to the same extent as any person engaged in such activities that are in or affect commerce is subject to such provisions, orders, regulations, and requirements.

(c) **Any person who knowingly violates a requirement** of the Federal hazardous material transportation law, an order issued thereunder, subchapter A, an exemption issued under subchapter A, of this subchapter, is liable for a civil penalty of not more than $25,000 ($27,500 for a violation that occurs after January 21, 1997) and not less than $250 for each violation. When the violation is a continuing one and involves the transporting of hazardous materials or the causing of them to be transported or shipped, each day of the violation constitutes a separate offense. Any person who knowingly violates §171.2(g) of this subchapter or willfully violates a provision of the Federal hazardous material transportation law or an order or regulation issued thereunder shall be fined under Title 18, United States Code, or imprisoned for not more than 5 years, or both.

§171.2 General requirements.

(a) **No person may offer or accept a hazardous material** for transportation in commerce unless that person is registered in conformance with subpart G of part 107 of this chapter, if applicable, and the hazardous material is properly classed, described, packaged, marked, labeled, and in condition for shipment as required or authorized by applicable requirements of this subchapter, or an exemption, approval or registration issued under this subchapter or subchapter A of this chapter.

(b) **No person may transport a hazardous material** in commerce unless that person is registered in conformance with subpart G of part 107 of this chapter, if applicable, and the hazardous material is handled and transported in accordance with applicable requirements of this subchapter, or an exemption, approval or registration issued under this subchapter or subchapter A of this chapter.

(c) **No person may represent, mark, certify, sell, or offer** a packaging or container as meeting the requirements of this subchapter or an exemption, approval or registration issued under this subchapter or subchapter A of this chapter, governing its use in the transportation in commerce of a hazardous material, whether or not it is used or intended to be used for the transportation of a hazardous material, unless the packaging or container is manufactured, fabricated, marked, maintained, reconditioned, repaired and retested, as appropriate, in accordance with applicable requirements of this subchapter, or an exemption, approval or registration issued under this subchapter or subchapter A of this chapter.

(d) **The representations, markings, and certifications** subject to the prohibitions of paragraph (c) of this section include, but are not limited to —

(1) *Specification identifications* that include the letters "ICC," "DOT," "CTC," "MC," or "UN";

(2) *Exemption, approval,* and registration numbers that include the letters "DOT," "EX," "M," or "R"; and

(3) *Test dates* associated with specification, registration, approval, retest, exemption, or requalification identification number (RIN) markings indicating compliance with a test or retest requirement of this subchapter, or an exemption, an approval, or a registration issued under this subchapter or subchapter A of this chapter.

(e) **When a person performs a function covered by** or having an effect on a specification prescribed in part 178, 179 or 180 of this subchapter, an approval issued under this subchapter, or an exemption issued under subpart B of this chapter, that person must perform the function in accordance with that specification, approval, or exemption, as appropriate.

(f) **No person shall, by marking or otherwise, represent that —**

(1) *A container or package* for the transportation of hazardous materials is safe, certified, or in compliance with the requirements of this title unless it meets the requirements of all applicable regulations issued under the Federal hazardous material transportation law; or

(2) *A hazardous material* is present in a package, container, motor vehicle, rail car, aircraft, or vessel, if the hazardous material is not present.

(g) **No person shall unlawfully alter, remove, deface,** destroy, or otherwise tamper with —

(1) *Any marking,* label, placard, or description on a document required by the Federal hazardous material transportation law, or the regulations issued thereunder; or

(2) *Any package,* container, motor vehicle, rail car, aircraft, or vessel used for the transportation of hazardous materials.

(h) **No person shall —**

(1) *Falsify or alter* an exemption, approval, registration or other grant of authority issued under this subchapter or subchapter A of this chapter; or

(2) *Offer a hazardous material* for transportation or transport a hazardous material in commerce, or represent, mark, certify, or sell a packaging or container, under a false or altered exemption, approval, registration or other grant of authority issued under this subchapter or subchapter A of this chapter.

§171.3 Hazardous waste.

(a) **No person may offer for transportation** or transport a hazardous waste (as defined in §171.8 of this subchapter) in interstate or intrastate commerce except in accordance with the requirements of this subchapter.

(b) **No person may accept for transportation,** transport, or deliver a hazardous waste for which a manifest is required unless that person:

(1) *Has marked* each motor vehicle used to transport hazardous waste in accordance with §390.21 or §1058.2 of this title even though placards may not be required;

(2) *Complies with* the requirements for manifests set forth in §172.205 of this subchapter; and

(3) *Delivers,* as designated on the manifest by the generator, the entire quantity of the waste received from the generator or a transporter to:

(i) *The designated facility* or, if not possible, to the designated alternate facility;

(ii) *The designated subsequent carrier; or*

(iii) *A designated place outside the United States.*

NOTE: Federal law specifies penalties up to $250,000 fine for an individual and $500,000 for a company and 5 years imprisonment for the willful discharge of hazardous waste at other than designated facilities. 49 U.S.C. 5124.

(c) **If a discharge of hazardous waste** or other hazardous material occurs during transportation, and an official of a State or local government or a Federal agency, acting within the scope of his official responsibilities, determines that immediate removal of the waste is necessary to prevent further consequence, that official may authorize the removal of the waste without the preparation of a manifest. [NOTE: In such cases, EPA does not require carriers to have EPA identification numbers.]

NOTE 1: EPA requires shippers (generators) and carriers (transporters) of hazardous wastes to have identification numbers which must be displayed on hazardous waste manifests. See 40 CFR parts 262 and 263. (Identification number application forms may be obtained from EPA regional offices.)

NOTE 2: In 40 CFR part 263, the EPA sets forth requirements for the cleanup of releases of hazardous wastes.

§171.4 Marine pollutants.

(a) Except as provided in paragraph (c) of this section, no person may offer for transportation or transport a marine pollutant, as defined in §171.8, in intrastate or interstate commerce except in accordance with the requirements of this subchapter.

(b) The requirements of this subchapter for the transportation of marine pollutants are based on the provisions of Annex III of the 1973 International Convention for Prevention of Pollution from Ships, as modified by the Protocol of 1978 (MARPOL 73/78).

(c) Exceptions. Except when transported aboard vessel, the requirements of this subchapter specific to marine pollutants do not apply to non-bulk packagings transported by motor vehicles, rail cars or aircraft.

§171.6 Control numbers under the Paperwork Reduction Act.

(a) Purpose and scope. This section collects and displays the control numbers assigned to the HMR collections of information by the Office of Management and Budget (OMB) under the Paperwork Reduction Act of 1995. This section complies with the requirements of 5 CFR 1320.7(f), 1320.12, 1320.13 and 1320.14 (OMB regulations implementing the Paperwork Reduction Act of 1995) for the display of control numbers assigned by OMB to collections of information of the HMR.

(b) OMB control numbers. The table in paragraph (b)(2) of this section sets forth the control numbers assigned to collection of information in the HMR by the Office of Management and Budget (OMB) under the Paperwork Reduction Act of 1995.

(1) *Column 1* lists the OMB control number assigned to the HMR collections of information. Column 2 contains the Report Title of the approved collection of information. Column 3 lists the part(s) or section(s) in 49 CFR identified or described in the collection of information.

(2) *Table.*

Current OMB control No.	Title	Title 49 CFR part or section where identified and described
2137-0014	Cargo Tank Specification Requirements	§§107.503, 107.504, 178.320, 178.337, 178.338, 178.345, 180.407, 180.409, 180.413, 180.417
2137-0018	Inspection and Testing of Portable Tank and IBC's	§§173.24, 173.32, 178.3, 178.245, 178.255, 178.270, 178.273, 178.274, 178.703, 178.801, 180.352, 180.605
2137-0022	Testing, Inspection, and Marking Requirements for Cylinders	§§173.302a, 173.303, 173.304, 173.309, 178.2, 178.3, 178.35, 178.44, 178.45, 178.46, 178.57, 178.59, 178.60, 178.61, 178.68, 180.205, 180.209, 180.211, 180.213, 180.215
2137-0034	Hazardous Materials Shipping Papers and Emergency Response Information	§§172.200, 172.201, 172.203, 172.204, 172.205, 172.600, 172.602, 172.604, 172.606, 173.6, 173.7, 173.22, 173.56, 174.24, 174.26, 174.114, 175.30, 175.31, 175.33, 175.35, 176.24, 176.27, 176.30, 176.36, 176.89, 177.817
2137-0039	Hazardous Materials Incident Report	§§171.15, 171.16
2137-0051	Rulemaking and Exemptions Petitions	§§105.30, 105.40, 106.95, 106.110, 107.105, 107.107, 107.109, 107.113, 107.117, 107.121, 107.123, 107.125, 107.205, 107.211, 107.215, 107.217, 107.219, 107.221, 107.223
2137-0510	RAM Transportation Requirements	Part 173, Subpart I, §§173.22, 173.411, 173.415, 173.416, 173.417, 173.457, 173.471, 173.472, 173.473, 173.476
2137-0542	Cryogenic Liquids Requirements	§§173.318, 177.816, 177.840, 180.405
2137-0557	Approvals for Hazardous Materials	§§107.402; 107.403; 107.405; 107.503; 107.705; 107.713; 107.715; 107.717; 107.803; 107.805; 107.807; 110.30; 172.101; 172.102, Special Provisions 26, 19, 53, 55, 60, 105, 118, 121, 125, 129, 131, 133, 136; 172.102, Special Provisions B45, B55, B61, B69, B77, B81, N10, N72, Code: T42; 173.2a; 173.4; 173.7; 173.21; 173.22; 173.24; 173.38; 173.31; 173.51; 173.56; 173.58; 173.59; 173.124; 173.128; 173.159; 173.166; 173.171; 173.214; 173.222; 173.224; 173.225; 173.245; 173.301; 173.305; 173.306; 173.314; 173.315; 173.316; 173.318; 173.334; 173.340; 173.411; 173.433; 173.457; 173.471; 173.472; 173.473; 173.476; 174.50; 174.63; 175.10; 175.701; 176.168; 176.340; 176.704; 178.3; 178.35; 178.47; 178.53; 178.58; 178.270-3; 178.270-13; 178.273; 178.274; 178.503; 178.509; 178.605; 178.606; 178.608; 178.801; 178.813; 180.213
2137-0559	Rail Carriers and Tank Car Tank Requirements	§§172.102, Special provisions: B45, B46, B55, B61, B69, B77, B78, B81; 173.10, 173.31, 174.20, 174.50, 174.63, 174.104, 174.114, 174.204, 179.3, 179.4, 179.5, 179.6, 179.7, 179.11, 179.18, 179.22, 179.100-9, 179.100-12, 179.100-13, 179.100-16, 179.100-17, 179.102-4, 179.102-17, 179.103-1, 179.103-2, 179.103-3, 179.103-5, 179.200-10, 179.200-14, 179.200-15, 179.200-16, 179.200-17, 179.200-19, 179.201-3, 179.201-8, 179.201-9, 179.220-4, 179.220-7, 179.220-8, 179.220-13, 179.220-15, 179.220-17, 179.220-18, 179.220-20, 179.220-22, 179.300-3, 179.300-7, 179.300-9, 179.300-12, 179.300-13, 179.300-15, 179.300-20, 179.400-3, 179.400-4, 179.400-11, 179.400-13, 179.400-16, 179.400-17, 179.400-19, 179.400-20, 179.500-5, 179.500-8, 179.500-12, 179.500-18, 180.505, 180.509, 180.515, 180.517
2137-0572	Testing Requirements for Non-Bulk Packaging	§§178.2, 178.601
2137-0582	Container Certification Statement	§§176.27, 176.172
2137-0586	Hazardous Materials Public Sector Training and Planning Grants	Part 110
2137-0595	Cargo Tank Motor Vehicles in Liquefied Compressed Gas Service	§§173.315, 178.337-8, 178.337-9, 180.405, 180.416
2137-0612	Hazardous Materials Security Plans	Part 172, Subpart I, §§172.800, 172.802, 172.804

§171.7 Reference material.

(a) Matter incorporated by reference —

(1) *General.* There is incorporated, by reference in parts 170-189 of this subchapter, matter referred to that is not specifically set forth. This matter is hereby made a part of the regulations in parts 170-189 of this subchapter. The matter subject to change is incorporated only as it is in effect on the date of issuance of the regulation referring to that matter. The material listed in paragraph (a)(3) has been approved for incorporation by reference by the Director of the Federal Register in accordance with 5 U.S.C 552(a) and 1 CFR part 51. Material is incorporated as it exists on the date of the approval and a notice of any change in the material will be published in the Federal Register. Matters referenced by footnote are included as part of the regulations of this subchapter.

(2) *Accessibility of materials.* All incorporated matter is available for inspection at:

(i) *The Office of Hazardous Materials Safety,* Office of Hazardous Materials Standards, Room 8422, NASSIF Building, 400 7th Street, SW., Washington, DC 20590; and

(ii) *The Office of the Federal Register,* 800 North Capitol Street, NW., suite 700, Washington, DC.

(3) *Table of material incorporated by reference.* The following table sets forth material incorporated by reference. The first column lists the name and address of the organization from which the material is available and the name of the material. The second column lists the section(s) of this subchapter, other than §171.7, in which the matter is referenced. The second column is presented for information only and may not be all inclusive.[1]

Source and name of material	49 CFR reference
Air Transport Association of America, 1301 Pennsylvania Avenue, N.W., Washington, DC 20004-1707	
ATA Specification No. 300 Packaging of Airline Supplies, Revision 19, July 31, 1996	172.102
The Aluminum Association, 420 Lexington Avenue, New York, NY 10017	
Aluminum Standards and Data, Seventh Edition, June 1982	172.102; 178.46; 178.65
American National Standards Institute, Inc., 25 West 43rd Street, New York, NY 10036	
ANSI/ASHRAE 15-94, Safety Code for Mechanical Refrigeration	173.306
ANSI B16.5-77, Steel Pipe Flanges, Flanged Fittings	178.345; 178.360
ANSI N14.1 Uranium Hexafluoride — Packaging for Transport, 1971, 1982, 1987, 1990, 1995 and 2001 Editions	173.417; 173.420
American Pyrotechnics Association (APA), P.O. Box 213, Chestertown, MD 21620	
APA Standard 87-1, Standard for Construction and Approval for Transportation of Fireworks, Novelties, and Theatrical Pyrotechnics, January 23, 1998 version	173.56

Source and name of material	49 CFR reference
American Society of Mechanical Engineers, ASME International, 22 Law Drive, P.O. Box 2900, Fairfield, NJ 07007-2900	
ASME Code, Sections II (Parts A and B), V, VIII (Division 1), and IX of 1998 Edition of American Society of Mechanical Engineers Boiler and Pressure Vessel Code	173.32; 173.306; 173.315; 173.318; 173.420; 178.245; 178.255; 178.270; 178.271; 178.272; 178.337; 178.338; 178.345; 178.346; 178.347; 178.348; 179.400; 180.407; 180.417
ASME Code, Section V (FR Nondestructive Examination), 1977	180.407
ASME Code, Section IX (FR Welding and Brazing Qualification), 1977 and Addendum (1979)	178.245; 178.270; 178.337; 178.338
American Society for Testing and Materials, 100 Barr Harbor Drive, West Conshohocken, PA 19428 Noncurrent ASTM Standards are available from: Engineering Societies Library, 354 E. 47th Street, New York, NY 10017	
ASTM A 20/A 20M-93a Standard Specification for General Requirements for Steel Plates for Pressure Vessels	178.337-2; 179.102-4; 179.102-17
ASTM A 47-68 Malleable Iron Castings	179.200
ASTM A 240/A 240M-99b Standard Specification for Heat-Resisting Chromium and Chromium-Nickel Stainless Steel Plate, Sheet and Strip for Pressure Vessels	178.57; 178.358-5; 179.100-7; 179.100-10; 179.102-1; 179.102-4; 179.102-17; 179.200-7; 179.201-5; 179.220-7; 179.400-5
ASTM A 242-81 Standard Specification for High-Strength Low-Alloy Structural Steel	179.100
ASTM A 262-93a Standard Practices for Detecting Susceptibility to Intergranular Attack in Austenitic Stainless Steels	179.100-7; 179.200-7; 179.201-4
ASTM A 300-58 Steel Plates for Pressure Vessels for Service at Low Temperatures	178.337
ASTM A 302/A 302M-93 Standard Specification for Pressure Vessel Plates, Alloy Steel, Manganese-Molybdenum and Manganese-Molybdenum Nickel	179.100-7; 179.200-7; 179.220-7
ASTM A 333-67 Seamless and Welded Steel Pipe for Low-Temperature Service	178.45
ASTM A 366/A 366M-91 (1993)e1 Standard Specification for Steel, Sheet, Carbon, Cold-Rolled, Commercial Quality	178.601
ASTM A 370-94 Standard Test Methods and Definitions for Mechanical Testing of Steel Products	179.102-1; 179.102-4; 179.102-17
ASTM A 441-81 Standard Specification for High-Strength Low-Alloy Structural Manganese Vanadium Steel	178.338
ASTM A 514-81 Standard Specification for High-Yield Strength Quenched and Tempered Alloy Steel Plate, Suitable for Welding	178.338
ASTM A 516/A 516M-90 Standard Specification for Pressure Vessel Plates, Carbon Steel, for Moderate and Lower-Temperature Service	178.337-2; 179.100-7; 179.100-20; 179.102-1; 179.102-2; 179.102-4; 179.102-17; 179.200-7; 179.220-7
ASTM A 537/A 537M-91 Standard Specification for Pressure Vessel Plates, Heat-Treated, Carbon-Manganese-Silicon Steel	179.100-7; 179.102-4; 179.102-17
ASTM A 568/A 568M-95 Standard Specification for Steel, Sheet, Carbon, and High-Strength, Low-Alloy, Hot-Rolled and Cold-Rolled, General Requirements for	178.601
ASTM A 572-82 Standard Specification for High-Strength Low-Alloy Columbian-Vanadium Steels of Structural Quality	178.338; 179.100
ASTM A 588-81 Standard Specification for High-Strength Low-Alloy Structural Steel with 50 Ksi Minimum Yield Point to 4 in. Thick	179.100; 178.338
ASTM A 606-75 Standard Specification for Steel Sheet and Strip Hot-Rolled and Cold-Rolled, High-Strength, Low-Alloy, with Improved Atmospheric Corrosion Resistance, 1975 (Reapproved 1981)	178.338
ASTM A 612-72a High Strength Steel Plates for Pressure Vessels for Moderate and Lower Temperature Service	178.337
ASTM A 633-79a Standard Specification for Normalized High-Strength Low-Alloy Structural Steel, 1979 Edition	178.338
ASTM A 715-81 Standard Specification for Steel Sheet and Strip, Hot-Rolled, High-Strength, Low-Alloy with Improved Formability, 1981	178.338
ASTM B 162-93a Standard Specification for Nickel Plate, Sheet, and Strip	179.200-7
ASTM B 209-93 Standard Specification for Aluminum and Aluminum-Alloy Sheet and Plate	179.100-7; 179.200-7; 179.220-7
ASTM B 557-84 Tension Testing Wrought and Cast Aluminum and Magnesium-Alloy Products	178.46
ASTM B 580-79 Standard Specification for Anodic Oxide Coatings on Aluminum, (Re-approved 2000)	173.316; 173.318; 178.338-17

Source and name of material	49 CFR reference
ASTM D 56-97a Standard Test Method for Flash Point by Tag Closed Tester.	173.120
ASTM D 93-97 Standard Test Methods for Flash Point by Pensky-Martens Closed Cup Tester	173.120
ASTM D 445-88 Kinematic Viscosity of Transparent and Opaque Liquids (and the Calculation of Dynamic Viscosity)	171.8
ASTM D 1200-88 Viscosity by Ford Viscosity Cup	171.8
ASTM D 1709-01 Standard Test Methods for Impact Resistance of Plastic Film by the Free-Falling Dart Method	173.197
ASTM D 1835-97 Standard Specification for Liquefied Petroleum (LP) Gases	180.209
ASTM D 1838-64 Copper Strip Corrosion by Liquefied Petroleum (LP) Gases	173.315
ASTM D 1922-00a Standard Test Method for Propagation Tear Resistance of Plastic Film and Thin Sheeting by Pendulum Method	173.197
ASTM D 3278-96 Standard Test Methods for Flash Point of Liquids by Small Scale Closed-Cup Apparatus	173.120
ASTM D 3828-97, Standard Test Methods for Flash Point by Small Scale Closed Tester	173.120
ASTM D 4206-96 Standard Test Method for Sustained Burning of Liquid Mixtures Using the Small Scale Open-Cup Apparatus	173.120
ASTM D 4359-90 Standard Test Method for Determining Whether a Material is a Liquid or a Solid	171.8
ASTM E 8-99 Standard Test Methods for Tension Testing of Metallic Materials	178.36; 178.37; 178.38; 178.39; 178.44; 178.45; 178.50; 178.51; 178.53; 178.55; 178.56; 178.57; 178.58; 178.59; 178.60; 178.61; 178.68
ASTM E 23-98 Standard Test Methods for Notched Bar Impact Testing of Metallic Materials	178.57
ASTM E 112-88 Standard Test Methods for Determining Average Grain Size	178.44
ASTM E 112-96 Standard Test Methods for Determining Average Grain Size, 1996 Edition	178.274
ASTM E 213-98, Standard Practice for Ultrasonic Examination of Metal Pipe and Tubing	178.45
ASTM E 290-92 Standard Test Method for Semi-Guided Bend Test for Ductility of Metallic Materials	178.46
ASTM E 681-85 Standard Test Method for Concentration Limits of Flammability of Chemicals	173.115
ASTM G 23-69 Standard Recommended Practice for Operating Light-and-Water Exposure Apparatus (Carbon-Arc Type) for Exposure of Nonmetallic Materials	172.407; 172.519
ASTM G 26-70 Standard Recommended Practice for Operating Light-and-Water Exposure Apparatus (Xenon-Arc-Type) for Exposure of Nonmetallic Materials	172.407; 172.519
ASTM G 31-72 (Reapproved 1995) Standard Practice for Laboratory Immersion Corrosion Testing of Metals	173.137
American Water Works Association, 1010 Vermont Avenue, NW., Suite 810, Washington, DC 20005	
AWWA Standard C207-55, Steel Pipe Flanges, 1955	178.360
American Welding Society, 550 N. W. Le Jeune Road, Miami, Florida 33126	
AWS Code B 3.0; Standard Qualification Procedure; 1972 (FRB 3.0-41, rev. May 1973)	178.356
AWS Code D 1.0; Code for Welding in Building Construction (FR D 1.0-66)	178.356
Association of American Railroads, American Railroads Building, 50 F Street, NW., Washington, DC 20001	
AAR Manual of Standards and Recommended Practices, Section C — Part III, Specifications for Tank Cars, Specification M-1002, September 1992	173.31
AAR Manual of Standards and Recommended Practices, Section C — Part III, Specifications for Tank Cars, Specification M-1002, January 1996	174.63; 179.6; 179.7; 179.12; 179.15; 179.16; 179.20; 179.22; 179.100; 179.101; 179.102; 179.103; 179.200; 179.201; 179.220; 179.300; 179.400; 180.509; 180.513; 180.515; 180.517
AAR Manual of Standards and Recommended Practices, Section I, Specially Equipped Freight Car and Intermodal Equipment, 1988	174.55; 174.63
AAR Specifications for Design, Fabrication and Construction of Freight Cars, Volume 1, 1988	179.16

Source and name of material	49 CFR reference
Chlorine Institute, Inc., 2001 L Street, NW., Suite 506, Washington, DC 20036	
Type 1 1/2 JQ 225, Dwg, H51970, Revision D, April 5, 1989; or Type 1 1/2 JQ 225, Dwg. H50155, Revision F, April 4, 1989	173.315
Section 3, Pamphlet 57, Emergency Shut-Off Systems for Bulk Transfer of Chlorine, 3rd Edition, October 1997	177.840
Standard Chlorine Angle Valve Assembly, Dwg. 104-8, July 1993	178.337-9
Excess Flow Valve with Removable Seat, Dwg. 101-7, July 1993	178.337-8
Excess Flow Valve with Removable Basket, Dwg. 106-6, July 1993	178.337-8
Standards for Housing and Manway Covers for Steel Cargo Tanks, Dwg. 137-3, September 1, 1982	178.337-10
Compressed Gas Association, Inc., 4221 Walney Road, 5th Floor, Chantilly, Virginia 20151	
CGA Pamphlet C-3, Standards for Welding on Thin-Walled Steel Cylinders, 1994	178.47; 178.50; 178.51; 178.53; 178.56; 178.57; 178.58; 178.59; 178.60; 178.61; 178.65; 178.68; 180.211
CGA Pamphlet C-5, Cylinder Service Life — Seamless Steel High Pressure Cylinders, 1991	173.302a
CGA Pamphlet C-6, Standards for Visual Inspection of Steel Compressed Gas Cylinders, 1993	173.198; 180.205; 180.209; 180.211; 180.519
CGA Pamphlet C-6.1, Standards for Visual Inspection of High Pressure Aluminum Compressed Gas Cylinders, 1995	180.205; 180.209
CGA Pamphlet C-6.2, Guidelines for Visual Inspection and Requalification of Fiber Reinforced High Pressure Cylinders, 1988	180.205
CGA Pamphlet C-6.3, Guidelines for Visual Inspection and Requalification of Low Pressure Aluminum Compressed Gas Cylinders, 1991	180.205; 180.209
CGA Pamphlet C-7, A Guide for the Preparation of Precautionary Markings for Compressed Gas Containers, appendix A, issued 1992 (6th Edition)	172.400a
CGA Pamphlet C-8, Standard for Requalification of DOT-3HT Cylinder Design, 1985	180.205
CGA Pamphlet C-11, Recommended Practices for Inspection of Compressed Gas Cylinders at Time of Manufacture, 1993	178.35
CGA Pamphlet C-12, Qualification Procedure for Acetylene Cylinder Design, 1994	173.301; 173.303; 178.59; 178.60
CGA Pamphlet C-13, Guidelines for Periodic Visual Inspection and Requalification of Acetylene Cylinders, 1992	173.303; 180.205; 180.209
CGA Pamphlet C-14, Procedures for Fire Testing of DOT Cylinder Pressure Relief Device Systems, 1979	173.301
CGA Pamphlet G-2.2 Tentative Standard Method for Determining Minimum of 0.2% Water in Anhydrous Ammonia, 1985	173.315
CGA Pamphlet G-4.1, Cleaning Equipment for Oxygen Service, 1985	178.338
CGA Pamphlet P-20, Standard for the Classification of Toxic Gas Mixtures, 1995	173.115
CGA Pamphlet S-1.1., Pressure Relief Device Standards — Part 1 — Cylinders for Compressed Gases, 1994 (with the exception of paragraph 9.1.1.1)	173.301; 173.304a
CGA Pamphlet S-1.2, Safety Relief Device Standards Part 2 — Cargo and Portable Tanks for Compressed Gases, 1980	173.315; 173.318
CGA Pamphlet S-7, Method for Selecting Pressure Relief Devices for Compressed Gas Mixtures in Cylinders, 1996	173.301
CGA Technical Bulletin TB-2, Guidelines for Inspection and Repair of MC-330 and MC-331 Cargo Tanks, 1980	180.413
Department of Defense (DOD), 2461 Eisenhower Avenue, Alexandria, VA 22331	
DOD TB 700-2; NAVSEAINST 8020.8B; AFTO 11A-1-47; DLAR 8220.1: Explosives Hazard Classification Procedures, January 1998	173.56
Department of Energy (USDOE), 100 Independence Avenue SW., Washington, DC 20545 USDOE publications available from: Superintendent of Documents, Government Printing Office (GPO) or The National Technical Information Service (NTIS)	
USDOE, CAPE-1662, Revision 1, and Supplement 1, Civilian Application Program Engineering Drawings	178.356; 178.358
USDOE, Material and Equipment Specification No. SP-9, Rev. 1, and Supplement — Fire Resistant Phenolic Foam	178.356; 178.358
USDOE, ORO 651 — Uranium Hexafloride; A Manual of Good Practices, Revision 6, 1991 edition	173.417
USDOE, KSS-471, November 30, 1986 — Proposal for Modifications to U.S. Department of Transportation Specification 21PF-1, Fire and Shock Resistant Phenolic Foam — Insulated Metal Overpack	178.358

Source and name of material	49 CFR reference
General Services Administration, Specification Office, Rm. 6662, 7th and D Street, SW., Washington, DC 20407	
Federal Specification RR-C-901C, Cylinders, Compressed Gas: High Pressure Steel DOT 3AA, and Aluminum Applications, January 15, 1981 (Superseding RR-C-901B, August 1, 1967).	173.302; 173.336; 173.337
Health and Human Services, Centers for Disease Control and Prevention, 1600 Clifton Road N.E., Atlanta GA 30333 Also available from: Superintendent of Documents, Government Printing Office (GPO), HHS Publication No. (CDC) 93-8395, Biosafety in Microbiological and Biomedical Laboratories, 3rd Edition, May 1993, Section II	173.134
Institute of Makers of Explosives, 1120 19th Street, Suite 310, Washington, DC 20036-3605	
IME Safety Library Publication No. 22 (IME Standard 22), Recommendation for the Safe Transportation of Detonators in a Vehicle with Certain Other Explosive Materials, May 1993	173.63; 177.835
International Atomic Energy Agency (IAEA), P.O. Box 100, Wagramer Strasse 5, A-1400 Vienna, Austria Also available from: Bernan Associates, 4611-F Assembly Drive, Lanham, MD 20706-4391, USA; or Renouf Publishing Company, Ltd., 812 Proctor Avenue, Ogdensburg, New York 13669, USA	
IAEA, Regulations for the Safe Transport of Radioactive Material, No. TS-R-1, 1996 Edition (Revised), (ST-1, Revised).	171.12
IAEA, Regulations for the Safe Transport of Radioactive Material, Safety Series No. 6, 1985 Edition (as Amended 1990)	171.12; 173.415; 173.416; 173.417; 173.473
International Civil Aviation Organization (ICAO), P.O. Box 400, Place de l'Aviation Internationale, 1000 Sherbrooke Street West, Montreal, Quebec, Canada H3A 2R2 ICAO Technical Instructions available from: INTEREG, International Regulations, Publishing and Distribution Organization, P.O. Box 60105, Chicago, IL 60660	
Technical Instructions for the Safe Transport of Dangerous Goods by Air (ICAO Technical Instructions), DOC 9284-AN/905, 2003-2004 Edition, including Erratum.	171.11; 172.202; 172.401; 172.512; 172.602
International Maritime Organization (IMO), 4 Albert Embankment, London, SE17SR, United Kingdom or New York Nautical Instrument & Service Corporation, 140 W. Broadway, New York, NY 10013	
International Maritime Dangerous Goods (IMDG) Code, 2000 edition, including Amendment 30-00 (English edition)	171.12; 172.401; 172.502; 173.21; 176.2; 176.5; 176.11; 176.27; 176.30
International Maritime Dangerous Goods (IMDG Code), 2002 Edition, including Amendment 31-02 (English Edition).	171.12; 172.202; 172.401; 172.502; 172.602; 173.21; 176.2; 176.5; 176.11; 176.27; 176.30
International Organization for Standardization, Case Postale 56, CH-1211, Geneve 20, Switzerland Also available from: ANSI 25 West 43rd Street, New York, NY 10036	
ISO-82-1974(E) Steels Tensile Testing	178.270-3
ISO 535-1991(E) Paper and board — Determination of water absorptiveness — Cobb method	178.516
ISO 1496-3 Series 1 freight containers — Specification and testing, Part 3: Tank containers for liquids, gases and pressurized dry bulk, March 1, 1995, Fourth Edition	178.274
ISO 1496-3-1995(E) - Series 1 Freight Containers — Specification and Testing — Part 3: Tank Containers for Liquids, Gases and Pressurized Dry Bulk	173.411
ISO-2431-1984(E) Standard Cup Method	173.121
ISO 2592-1973(E) Petroleum products — Determination of flash and fire points — Cleveland open cup method	173.120
ISO 2919-1980(E) - Sealed radioactive sources — Classification	173.469
ISO 3036-1975(E) Board — Determination of puncture resistance	178.708
ISO 3574-1986(E) Cold-reduced carbon steel sheet of commercial and drawing qualities	178.503
ISO 4126-1 Safety valves — Part 1: General Requirements, December 15, 1991, First Edition	178.274
ISO/TR 4826-1979(E) - Sealed radioactive sources — Leak test methods	173.469
ISO 6892 Metallic materials — Tensile testing, July 15, 1984, First Edition	178.274
ISO 8115 Cotton bales — Dimensions and density, 1986 Edition.	172.102
ISO 9328-1 — 1991(E) Steel plates and strips for pressure purposes — Technical delivery conditions — Part 1: General requirements	173.137
National Board of Boiler and Pressure Vessel Inspectors, 1055 Crupper Avenue, Columbus, Ohio 43229	
National Board Inspection Code, A Manual for Boiler and Pressure Vessel Inspectors, NB-23, 1992 Edition	180.413

Source and name of material	49 CFR reference
National Fire Protection Association, Batterymarch Park, Quincy, MA 02269	
NFPA Pamphlet No. 58 — Standard for the Storage and Handling of Liquefied Petroleum Gases, 1979	173.315
National Institute of Standards and Technology, Department of Commerce, 5285 Port Royal Road, Springfield, VA 22151	
USDC, NBS Handbook H-28 (1957), 1957 Handbook of Screw-Thread Standards for Federal Services, Part II, December 1966 Edition	178.45, 178.46
National Motor Freight Traffic Association, Inc., Agent 1616 P Street, NW., Washington, DC 20036	
National Motor Freight Classification NMF 100-I, 1982	177.841
Organization for Economic Cooperation and Development (OECD), OECD Publications and Information Center, 2001 L Street, Suite 700, Washington, DC 20036	
OECD Guideline for Testing of Chemicals, No.404 "Acute Dermal Irritation/Corrosion," 1992	173.137
Transport Canada, TDG Canadian Government Publishing Center, Supply and Services, Canada, Ottawa, Ontario, Canada K1A 059	
Transportation of Dangerous Goods Regulations, 1 July 1985, SOR/85/77, incorporating the following Registration Numbers: SOR/85-314, SOR/85-585, SOR/85-609, SOR/86-526, SOR/88-635, SOR/87-335, SOR/87-186, SOR/89-39, SOR/89-294, SOR/90-847, SOR/91-711, SOR/91-712, SOR/92-447, SOR/92-600, SOR/93-203, SOR/93-274, SOR/93-525, SOR/94-146 and SOR/94-264 (English edition), SOR/95-241, and SOR/95-547	171.12a; 172.401; 172.502
Truck Trailer Manufacturers Association, 1020 Princess Street, Alexandria, Virginia 22314	
TTMA RP No. 81, Performance of Spring Loaded Pressure Relief Valves on MC 306, MC 307, and MC 312 Tanks, May 24, 1989 Edition	178.345-10
TTMA RP No. 61-94, Performance of Manhole and/or Fill Opening Assemblies on MC 306 and DOT 406 Cargo Tanks, December 28, 1994 Edition	180.405
TTMA TB No. 107, Procedure for Testing Inservice, Unmarked, and/or Uncertified MC 306 Type Cargo Tank Manhole Covers, May 24, 1989 Edition	180.405
United Nations, United Nations Sales Section, New York, NY 10017	
UN Recommendations on the Transport of Dangerous Goods, Twelfth Revised Edition (2001)	172.202; 172.401; 172.502; 173.24
UN Recommendations on the Transport of Dangerous Goods, Manual of Tests and Criteria, Third Revised Edition (1999)	172.102; 173.21; 173.56; 173.57; 173.124; 173.128; 173.166; 173.185

(b) **List of informational materials** not requiring incorporation by reference. The materials listed in this paragraph do not require approval for incorporation by reference and are included for informational purposes. These materials may be used as noted in those sections in which the material is referenced.

Source and name of material	49 CFR reference
American Biological Safety Association, 1202 Allanson Road, Mundelein, IL 60060	
Risk Group Classification for Infectious Agents, 1998	173.134
Association of American Railroads, American Railroads Building, 50 F Street, NW., Washington, DC 20001	
AAR Catalog Nos. SE60CHT; SE60CC; SE60CHTE; SE60CE; SE60DC; SE60DE	179.14
AAR Catalog Nos. SE67CC; SE67CE; SE67BHT; SE67BC; SE67BHTE; SE67BE	179.14
AAR Catalog Nos. SE68BHT; SE68BC; SE68BHTE; SE68BE	179.14
AAR Catalog Nos. SE69AHTE; SE69AE	179.14
AAR Catalog Nos. SF70CHT; SF70CC; SF70CHTE; SF70CE	179.14
AAR Catalog Nos. SF73AC; SF73AE; SF73AHT; SF73AHTE	179.14
AAR Catalog Nos. SF79CHT; SF79CC; SF79CHTE; SF79CE	179.14
Bureau of Explosives, Hazardous Materials Systems (BOE), Association of American Railroads, American Railroads Building, 50 F Street, NW., Washington, DC 20001	
Fetterley's Formula (The Determination of the Relief Dimensions for Safety Valves on Containers in which Liquefied gas is charged and when the exterior surface of the container is exposed to a temperature of 1,200 °F.)	173.315
Pamphlet 6, Illustrating Methods for Loading and Bracing Carload and Less-Than-Carload Shipments of Explosives and Other Dangerous Articles, 1962.	174.55; 174.101; 174.112; 174.115; 174.290
Pamphlet 6A (includes appendix No. 1, October 1944 and appendix 2, December 1945), Illustrating Methods for Loading and Bracing Carload and Less-Than-Carload Shipments of Loaded Projectiles, Loaded Bombs, etc., 1943	174.101; 174.290
Pamphlet 6C, Illustrating Methods for Loading and Bracing Trailers and Less-Than-Trailer Shipments of Explosives and Other Dangerous Articles Via Trailer-on-Flatcar (TOFC) or Container-on-Flatcar (COFC), 1985	174.55; 174.63; 174.101; 174.112; 174.115
Emergency Handling of Hazardous Materials in Surface Transportation, 1989	171.7
Centers for Disease Control and Prevention, 1600 Clifton Road, Atlanta, GA 30333	
Biosafety in Microbiological and Biomedical Laboratories, Fourth Edition, April 1999	173.134
National Association of Corrosion Engineers, 1440 South Creek, Houston, Texas 77084	
NACE Standard TM-01-69, Test Method Laboratory Corrosion Testing of Metals for the Process Industries, 1969	173.136
National Institutes of Health, Bethesda, MD 20892	
NIH Guidelines for Research Involving Recombinant DNA Molecules (NIH Guidelines), January 2001, Appendix B	173.134
Society of Plastics Industries, Inc., Organic Peroxide Producers Safety Division, 1275 K Street, NW., Suite 400, Washington, DC 20005	
Self Accelerating Decomposition Temperature Test, 1972	173.21

FEDERAL REGISTER UPDATES

In the April 18, 2003 Federal Register, §171.7(a)(3) was revised, effective October 1, 2003.

1

Source and name of material	49 CFR reference
American Petroleum Institute, 1220 L Street, NW, Washington, D.C. 20005-4070	
API Recommended Practice 1604 Closures of Underground Petroleum Storage Tanks, 3rd Edition, March 1996	172.102

2

Source and name of material	49 CFR reference
TTMA RP No. 61-98, Performance of Manhole and/or Fill Opening Assemblies on MC 306, DOT 406, Non-ASME MC 312 and Non-ASME DOT 412 Cargo Tanks, June 1, 1998	180.405(g)
TTMA RP No. 81-97, Performance of Spring Loaded Pressure Relief Valves on MC 306, MC 307, MC 312, DOT 406, DOT 407, and DOT 412 Tanks, July 1, 1997 Edition	178.345-10
TTMA TB No. 107, Procedure for Testing In-Service Unmarked and/or Uncertified MC 306 and Non-ASME MC 312 Type Cargo Tank Manhole Covers, June 1, 1998 Edition	180.405(g)

1. A new entry for "American Petroleum Institute" was added in appropriate alphabetical order.
2. Under "Truck Trailer Manufacturers Association," the entries "TTMA TB No. 81" and "TTMA RP No. 61-94" were removed, the entry "TTMA TB No. 107" was revised and two new entries were added in appropriate alpha-numeric order.

§171.8 Definitions and abbreviations.

In this subchapter,

Aerosol means any non-refillable receptacle containing a gas compressed, liquefied or dissolved under pressure, the sole purpose of which is to expel a nonpoisonous (other than a Division 6.1 Packing Group III material) liquid, paste, or powder and fitted with a self-closing release device allowing the contents to be ejected by the gas.

Agricultural product means a hazardous material, other than a hazardous waste, whose end use directly supports the production of an agricultural commodity including, but not limited to a fertilizer, pesticide, soil amendment or fuel. An agricultural product is limited to a material in Class 3, 8 or 9, Division 2.1, 2.2, 5.1, or 6.1, or an ORM-D material.

Approval means a written authorization, including a competent authority approval, from the Associate Administrator or other designated Department official, to perform a function for which prior authorization by the Associate Administrator is required under subchapter C of this chapter (49 CFR parts 171 through 180).

Approved means approval issued or recognized by the Department unless otherwise specifically indicated in this subchapter.

Asphyxiant gas means a gas which dilutes or replaces oxygen normally in the atmosphere.

Associate Administrator means the Associate Administrator for Hazardous Materials Safety, Research and Special Programs Administration.

Atmospheric gases means air, nitrogen, oxygen, argon, krypton, neon and xenon.

Authorized Inspection Agency means:
(1) *A jurisdiction* which has adopted and administers one or more sections of the ASME Boiler and Pressure Vessel Code as a legal requirement and has a representative serving as a member of the ASME Conference Committee; or
(2) *An insurance company* which has been licensed or registered by the appropriate authority of a State of the United States or a Province of Canada to underwrite boiler and pressure vessel insurance in such State or Province.

Authorized Inspector means an Inspector who is currently commissioned by the National Board of Boiler and Pressure Vessel Inspectors and employed as an Inspector by an Authorized Inspection Agency.

Bag means a flexible packaging made of paper, plastic film, textiles, woven material or other similar materials.

Bar means 1 BAR = 100 kPa (14.5 psi).

Barge means a non-selfpropelled vessel.

Biological product. See §173.134 of this subchapter.

Bottle means an inner packaging having a neck of relatively smaller cross section than the body and an opening capable of holding a closure for retention of the contents.

Bottom shell means that portion of a tank car tank surface, excluding the head ends of the tank car tank, that lies within two feet, measured circumferentially, of the bottom longitudinal center line of the tank car tank.

Box means a packaging with complete rectangular or polygonal faces, made of metal, wood, plywood, reconstituted wood, fiberboard, plastic, or other suitable material. Holes appropriate to the size and use of the packaging, for purposes such as ease of handling or opening, or to meet classification requirements, are permitted as long as they do not compromise the integrity of the packaging during transportation, and are not otherwise prohibited in this subchapter.

Break-bulk means packages of hazardous materials that are handled individually, palletized, or unitized for purposes of transportation as opposed to bulk and containerized freight.

Btu means British thermal unit.

Bulk packaging means a packaging, other than a vessel or a barge, including a transport vehicle or freight container, in which hazardous materials are loaded with no intermediate form of containment and which has:
(1) *A maximum capacity* greater than 450 L (119 gallons) as a receptacle for a liquid;
(2) *A maximum net mass* greater than 400 kg (882 pounds) and a maximum capacity greater than 450 L (119 gallons) as a receptacle for a solid; or
(3) *A water capacity* greater than 454 kg (1000 pounds) as a receptacle for a gas as defined in §173.115 of this subchapter.

Bureau of Explosives means the Bureau of Explosives (B of E) of the Association of American Railroads.

C means Celsius or Centigrade.

Captain of the Port (COTP) means the officer of the Coast Guard, under the command of a District Commander, so designated by the Commandant for the purpose of giving immediate direction to Coast Guard law enforcement activities within an assigned area. As used in this subchapter, the term Captain of the Port includes an authorized representative of the Captain of the Port.

Carfloat means a vessel that operates on a short run on an irregular basis and serves one or more points in a port area as an extension of a rail line or highway over water, and does not operate in ocean, coastwise, or ferry service.

Cargo aircraft only means an aircraft that is used to transport cargo and is not engaged in carrying passengers. For purposes of this subchapter, the terms cargo aircraft only, cargo-only aircraft and cargo aircraft have the same meaning.

Cargo tank means a bulk packaging which:
(1) *Is a tank intended primarily* for the carriage of liquids or gases and includes appurtenances, reinforcements, fittings, and closures (for tank, see 49 CFR 178.345-1(c), 178.337-1, or 178.338-1, as applicable);
(2) *Is permanently attached to* or forms a part of a motor vehicle, or is not permanently attached to a motor vehicle but which, by reason of its size, construction or attachment to a motor vehicle is loaded or unloaded without being removed from the motor vehicle; and
(3) *Is not fabricated* under a specification for cylinders, portable tanks, tank cars, or multi-unit tank car tanks.

Cargo tank motor vehicle means a motor vehicle with one or more cargo tanks permanently attached to or forming an integral part of the motor vehicle.

Cargo vessel means:
(1) *Any vessel other than a passenger vessel; and*
(2) *Any ferry* being operated under authority of a change of character certificate issued by a Coast Guard Officer-in-Charge, Marine Inspection.

Carrier means a person engaged in the transportation of passengers or property by:
(1) *Land or water, as a common, contract, or private carrier, or*
(2) *Civil aircraft.*

CC means closed-cup.

Character of vessel means the type of service in which the vessel is engaged at the time of carriage of a hazardous material.

Class means hazard class. See hazard class.

Class 1. See §173.50 of this subchapter.

Class 2. See §173.115 of this subchapter.

Class 3. See §173.120 of this subchapter.

Class 4. See §173.124 of this subchapter.

Class 5. See §173.128 of this subchapter.

Class 6. See §173.132 of this subchapter.

Class 7. See §173.403 of this subchapter.

Class 8. See §173.136 of this subchapter.

Class 9. See §173.140 of this subchapter.

Closure means a device which closes an opening in a receptacle.

COFC means container-on-flat-car.

Combination packaging means a combination of packaging, for transport purposes, consisting of one or more inner packagings secured in a non-bulk outer packaging. It does not include a composite packaging.

Combustible liquid. See §173.120 of this subchapter.

Compatibility group letter means a designated alphabetical letter used to categorize different types of explosive substances and articles for purposes of stowage and segregation. See §173.52 of this subchapter.

Competent Authority means a national agency responsible under its national law for the control or regulation of a particular aspect of the transportation of hazardous materials (dangerous goods). The term Appropriate Authority, as used in the ICAO Technical Instructions (see §171.7), has the same meaning as Competent Authority. For purposes of this subchapter, the Associate Administrator is the Competent Authority for the United States.

Composite packaging means a packaging consisting of an outer packaging and an inner receptacle, so constructed that the inner receptacle and the outer packaging form an integral packaging. Once assembled it remains thereafter an integrated single unit; it is filled, stored, shipped and emptied as such.

Compressed gas. See §173.115 of this subchapter.

Consumer commodity means a material that is packaged and distributed in a form intended or suitable for sale through retail sales agencies or instrumentalities for consumption by individuals for purposes of personal care or household use. This term also includes drugs and medicines.

Containership means a cargo vessel designed and constructed to transport, within specifically designed cells, portable tanks and freight containers which are lifted on and off with their contents intact.

Corrosive material. See §173.136 of this subchapter.

Crate means an outer packaging with incomplete surfaces.

Crewmember means a person assigned to perform duty in an aircraft during flight time.

Cryogenic liquid. See §173.115(g) of this subchapter.

Cultures and stocks. See §173.134 of this subchapter.

Cylinder means a pressure vessel designed for pressures higher than 40 psia and having a circular cross section. It does not include a portable tank, multi-unit tank car tank, cargo tank, or tank car.

Dangerous when wet material. See §173.124 of this subchapter.

Design Certifying Engineer means a person registered with the Department in accordance with subpart F of part 107 of this chapter who has the knowledge and ability to perform stress analysis of pressure vessels and to otherwise determine whether a cargo tank design and construction meets the applicable DOT specification. In addition, Design Certifying Engineer means a person who meets, at a minimum, any one of the following:
(1) *Has an engineering degree* and one year of work experience in cargo tank structural or mechanical design.
(2) *Is currently registered* as a professional engineer by the appropriate authority of a State of the United States or a Province of Canada.
(3) *Has at least three years' experience* in performing the duties of a Design Certifying Engineer by September 1, 1991, and was registered with the Department by December 31, 1995.

Designated facility means a hazardous waste treatment, storage, or disposal facility that has been designated on the manifest by the generator.

Diagnostic specimen. See §173.134 of this subchapter.

District Commander means the District Commander of the Coast Guard, or his authorized representative, who has jurisdiction in the particular geographical area.

Division means a subdivision of a hazard class.

DOD means the U.S. Department of Defense.

Domestic transportation means transportation between places within the United States other than through a foreign country.

DOT or **Department** means U.S. Department of Transportation.

Drum means a flat-ended or convex-ended cylindrical packaging made of metal, fiberboard, plastic, plywood, or other suitable materials. This definition also includes packagings of other shapes made of metal or plastic (e.g., round taper-necked packagings or pail-shaped packagings) but does not include cylinders, jerricans, wooden barrels or bulk packagings.

Elevated temperature material means a material which, when offered for transportation or transported in a bulk packaging:

(1) *Is in a liquid phase* and at a temperature at or above 100 °C (212 °F);

(2) *Is in a liquid phase* with a flash point at or above 37.8 °C (100 °F) that is intentionally heated and offered for transportation or transported at or above its flash point; or

(3) *Is in a solid phase* and at a temperature at or above 240 °C (464 °F).

Engine means a locomotive propelled by any form of energy and used by a railroad.

EPA means U.S. Environmental Protection Agency.

Etiologic agent. See §173.134 of this subchapter.

EX number means a number preceded by the prefix "EX", assigned by the Associate Administrator, to an item that has been evaluated under the provisions of §173.56 of this subchapter.

Exemption means a document issued by the Associate Administrator under the authority of 49 U.S.C. 5117. The document permits a person to perform a function that is not otherwise permitted under subchapter A or C of this chapter, or other regulations issued under 49 U.S.C. 5101 through 5127 (e.g., Federal Motor Carrier Safety routing).

Explosive. See §173.50 of this subchapter.

F means degree Fahrenheit.

Farmer means a person engaged in the production or raising of crops, poultry, or livestock.

Federal hazardous material transportation law means 49 U.S.C. 5101 et seq.

Ferry vessel means a vessel which is limited in its use to the carriage of deck passengers or vehicles or both, operates on a short run on a frequent schedule between two points over the most direct water route, other than in ocean or coastwise service, and is offered as a public service of a type normally attributed to a bridge or tunnel.

Filling density has the following meanings:

(1) *For compressed gases in cylinders,* see §173.304a(a)(2) table note 1.

(2) *For compressed gases in tank cars,* see §173.314(c) table note 1.

(3) *For compressed gases* in cargo tanks and portable tanks, see §173.315(a) table note 1.

(4) *For cryogenic liquids in cylinders, except hydrogen,* see §173.316 (c)(1).

(5) *For hydrogen, cryogenic liquid in cylinders,* see §173.316(c)(3) table note 1.

(6) *For cryogenic liquids in cargo tanks,* see §173.318(f)(1).

(7) *For cryogenic liquids in tank cars,* see §173.319(d)(1).

Flammable gas. See §173.115 of this subchapter.

Flammable liquid. See §173.120 of this subchapter.

Flammable solid. See §173.124 of this subchapter.

Flash point. See §173.120 of this subchapter.

Freight container means a reusable container having a volume of 64 cubic feet or more, designed and constructed to permit being lifted with its contents intact and intended primarily for containment of packages (in unit form) during transportation.

Fuel tank means a tank other than a cargo tank, used to transport flammable or combustible liquid, or compressed gas for the purpose of supplying fuel for propulsion of the transport vehicle to which it is attached, or for the operation of other equipment on the transport vehicle.

Fumigated lading. See §§172.302(g) and 173.9.

Gas means a material which has a vapor pressure greater than 300 kPa (43.5 psia) at 50 °C (122 °F) or is completely gaseous at 20 °C (68 °F) at a standard pressure of 101.3 kPa (14.7 psia).

Gross weight or **Gross mass** means the weight of a packaging plus the weight of its contents.

Hazard class means the category of hazard assigned to a hazardous material under the definitional criteria of part 173 of this subchapter and the provisions of the §172.101 table. A material may meet the defining criteria for more than one hazard class but is assigned to only one hazard class.

Hazard zone means one of four levels of hazard (Hazard Zones A through D) assigned to gases, as specified in §173.116(a) of this subchapter, and one of two levels of hazards (Hazard Zones A and B) assigned to liquids that are poisonous by inhalation, as specified in §173.133(a) of this subchapter. A hazard zone is based on the LC50 value for acute inhalation toxicity of gases and vapors, as specified in §173.133(a).

Hazardous material means a substance or material that the Secretary of Transportation has determined is capable of posing an unreasonable risk to health, safety, and property when transported in commerce, and has designated as hazardous under section 5103 of Federal hazardous materials transportation law (49 U.S.C. 5103). The term includes hazardous substances, hazardous wastes, marine pollutants, elevated temperature materials, materials designated as hazardous in the Hazardous Materials Table (see 49 CFR 172.101), and materials that meet the defining criteria for hazard classes and divisions in part 173 of subchapter C of this chapter.

Hazardous substance for the purposes of this subchapter, means a material, including its mixtures and solutions, that —

(1) *Is listed in the appendix A to §172.101 of this subchapter;*

(2) *Is in a quantity,* in one package, which equals or exceeds the reportable quantity (RQ) listed in the appendix A to §172.101 of this subchapter; and

(3) *When in a mixture or solution —*

(i) *For radionuclides,* conforms to paragraph 7 of the appendix A to §172.101.

(ii) *For other than radionuclides,* is in a concentration by weight which equals or exceeds the concentration corresponding to the RQ of the material, as shown in the following table:

RQ pounds (kilograms)	Concentration by weight	
	Percent	PPM
5000 (2270)	10	100,000
1000 (454)	2	20,000
100 (45.4)	0.2	2,000
10 (4.54)	0.02	200
1 (0.454)	0.002	20

The term does not include petroleum, including crude oil or any fraction thereof which is not otherwise specifically listed or designated as a hazardous substance in appendix A to §172.101 of this subchapter, and the term does not include natural gas, natural gas liquids, liquefied natural gas, or synthetic gas usable for fuel (or mixtures of natural gas and such synthetic gas).

Hazardous waste, for the purposes of this chapter, means any material that is subject to the Hazardous Waste Manifest Requirements of the U.S. Environmental Protection Agency specified in 40 CFR part 262.

Hazmat employee means a person who is employed by a hazmat employer and who in the course of employment directly affects hazardous materials transportation safety. This term includes an owner-operator of a motor vehicle which transports hazardous materials in commerce. This term includes an individual, including a self-employed individual, employed by a hazmat employer who, during the course of employment:

(1) *Loads, unloads, or handles hazardous materials;*

(2) *Manufactures, tests,* reconditions, repairs, modifies, marks, or otherwise represents containers, drums, or packagings as qualified for use in the transportation of hazardous materials;

(3) *Prepares hazardous materials for transportation;*

(4) *Is responsible for safety of transporting hazardous materials; or*

(5) *Operates a vehicle used to transport hazardous materials.*

Hazmat employer means a person who uses one or more of its employees in connection with: transporting hazardous materials in commerce; causing hazardous materials to be transported or shipped in commerce; or representing, marking, certifying, selling, offering, manufacturing, reconditioning, testing, repairing, or modifying containers, drums, or packagings as qualified for use in the transportation of hazardous materials. This term includes an owner-operator of a motor vehicle which transports hazardous materials in commerce. This term also includes any department, agency, or instrumentality of the United States, a State, a political subdivision of a State, or an Indian tribe engaged in an activity described in the first sentence of this definition.

Hermetically sealed means closed by fusion, gasketing, crimping, or equivalent means so that no gas or vapor can enter or escape.

IAEA means International Atomic Energy Agency.

IATA means International Air Transport Association.

ICAO means International Civil Aviation Organization.

IMO means International Maritime Organization.

Infectious substance (etiologic agent). See §173.134 of this subchapter.

Inner packaging means a packaging for which an outer packaging is required for transport. It does not include the inner receptacle of a composite packaging.

Inner receptacle means a receptacle which requires an outer packaging in order to perform its containment function. The inner receptacle may be an inner packaging of a combination packaging or the inner receptacle of a composite packaging.

Intermediate bulk container or **IBC** means a rigid or flexible portable packaging, other than a cylinder or portable tank, which is designed for mechanical handling. Standards for IBCs manufactured in the United States are set forth in subparts N and O of part 178 of this subchapter.

Intermediate packaging means a packaging which encloses an inner packaging or article and is itself enclosed in an outer packaging.

Intermodal container means a freight container designed and constructed to permit it to be used interchangeably in two or more modes of transport.

Intermodal portable tank or **IM portable tank** means a specific class of portable tanks designed primarily for international intermodal use.

International transportation means transportation —

(1) *Between any place* in the United States and any place in a foreign country;

(2) *Between places in the United States through a foreign country; or*

(3) *Between places* in one or more foreign countries through the United States.

Irritating material. See §173.132(a)(2) of this subchapter.

Jerrican means a metal or plastic packaging of rectangular or polygonal cross-section.

Large packaging means a packaging that —

(1) *Consists of an outer packaging* which contains articles or inner packagings;

(2) *Is designated for mechanical handling;*

(3) *Exceeds 400 kg net mass or 450 liters (118.9 gallons) capacity;*

(4) *Has a volume* of not more than 3 m^3 (see §178.801(i) of this subchapter); and

(5) *Conforms to the requirements* for the construction, testing and marking of large packagings as specified in the UN Recommendations.

Limited quantity, when specified as such in a section applicable to a particular material, means the maximum amount of a hazardous material for which there is a specific labeling or packaging exception.

Liquid means a material, other than an elevated temperature material, with a melting point or initial melting point of 20 °C (68 °F) or lower at a standard pressure of 101.3 kPa (14.7 psia). A viscous material for which a specific melting point cannot be determined must be subjected to the procedures specified in ASTM D 4359 "Standard Test Method for Determining Whether a Material is Liquid or Solid" (see §171.7).

Liquid phase means a material that meets the definition of liquid when evaluated at the higher of the temperature at which it is offered for transportation or at which it is transported, not at the 37.8 °C (100 °F) temperature specified in ASTM D 4359-84.

Magazine vessel means a vessel used for the receiving, storing, or dispensing of explosives.

Magnetic material. See §173.21(d) of this subchapter.

Marine pollutant, means a material which is listed in appendix B to §172.101 of this subchapter (also see §171.4) and, when in a solution or mixture of one or more marine pollutants, is packaged in a concentration which equals or exceeds:

(1) *Ten percent by weight* of the solution or mixture for materials listed in the appendix; or

(2) *One percent by weight* of the solution or mixture for materials that are identified as severe marine pollutants in the appendix.

Marking means a descriptive name, identification number, instructions, cautions, weight, specification, or UN marks, or combinations thereof, required by this subchapter on outer packagings of hazardous materials.

Material of trade means a hazardous material, other than a hazardous waste, that is carried on a motor vehicle —

(1) *For the purpose* of protecting the health and safety of the motor vehicle operator or passengers;

(2) *For the purpose* of supporting the operation or maintenance of a motor vehicle (including its auxiliary equipment); or

(3) *By a private motor carrier* (including vehicles operated by a rail carrier) in direct support of a principal business that is other than transportation by motor vehicle.

Material poisonous by inhalation means:

(1) *A gas* meeting the defining criteria in §173.115(c) of this subchapter and assigned to Hazard Zone A, B, C, or D in accordance with §173.116(a) of this subchapter;

(2) *A liquid* (other than as a mist) meeting the defining criteria in §173.132(a)(1)(iii) of this subchapter and assigned to Hazard Zone A or B in accordance with §173.133(a) of this subchapter; or

(3) *Any material* identified as an inhalation hazard by a special provision in column 7 of the §172.101 table.

MAWP means maximum allowable working pressure.

Maximum capacity means the maximum inner volume of receptacles or packagings.

Maximum net mass means the allowable maximum net mass of contents in a single packaging, or as used in subpart M of part 178 of this subchapter, the maximum combined mass of inner packaging, and the contents thereof.

Metered delivery service means a cargo tank unloading operation conducted at a metered flow rate of 378.5 L (100 gallons) per minute or less through an attached delivery hose with a nominal inside diameter of 3.175 cm (1 1/4 inches) or less.

Miscellaneous hazardous material. See §173.140 of this subchapter.

Mixture means a material composed of more than one chemical compound or element.

Mode means any of the following transportation methods; rail, highway, air, or water.

Motor vehicle includes a vehicle, machine, tractor, trailer, or semitrailer, or any combination thereof, propelled or drawn by mechanical power and used upon the highways in the transportation of passengers or property. It does not include a vehicle, locomotive, or car operated exclusively on a rail or rails, or a trolley bus operated by electric power derived from a fixed overhead wire, furnishing local passenger transportation similar to street-railway service.

Name of contents means the proper shipping name as specified in §172.101 of this subchapter.

Navigable waters means, for the purposes of this subchapter, waters of the United States, including the territorial seas.

Non-bulk packaging means a packaging which has:

(1) *A maximum capacity* of 450 L (119 gallons) or less as a receptacle for a liquid;

(2) *A maximum net mass* of 400 kg (882 pounds) or less and a maximum capacity of 450 L (119 gallons) or less as a receptacle for a solid; or

(3) *A water capacity* of 454 kg (1000 pounds) or less as a receptacle for a gas as defined in §173.115 of this subchapter.

Nonflammable gas. See §173.115 of this subchapter.

N.O.S. means not otherwise specified.

N.O.S. description means a shipping description from the §172.101 table which includes the abbreviation n.o.s.

NPT means an American Standard taper pipe thread conforming to requirements of Federal Standard H28, part II, section VII. See §171.7.

NRC (non-reusable container) means a packaging (container) whose reuse is restricted in accordance with the provisions of §173.28 of this subchapter.

Occupied caboose means a rail car being used to transport non-passenger personnel.

Officer in Charge, Marine Inspection means a person from the civilian or military branch of the Coast Guard designated as such by the Commandant and who under the supervision and direction of the Coast Guard District Commander is in charge of a designated inspection zone for the performance of duties with respect to the enforcement and administration of title 52, Revised Statutes, acts amendatory thereof or supplemental thereto, rules and regulations thereunder, and the inspection required thereby.

Offshore supply vessel means a cargo vessel of less than 500 gross tons that regularly transports goods, supplies or equipment in support of exploration or production of offshore mineral or energy resources.

Operator means a person who controls the use of an aircraft, vessel, or vehicle.

Organic peroxide. See §173.128 of this subchapter.

ORM means other regulated material. See §173.144 of this subchapter.

Outage or **ullage** means the amount by which a packaging falls short of being liquid full, usually expressed in percent by volume.

Outer packaging means the outermost enclosure of a composite or combination packaging together with any absorbent materials, cushioning and any other components necessary to contain and protect inner receptacles or inner packagings.

Overpack, except as provided in subpart K of part 178 of this subchapter, means an enclosure that is used by a single consignor to provide protection or convenience in handling of a package or to consolidate two or more packages. Overpack does not include a transport vehicle, freight container, or aircraft unit load device. Examples of overpacks are one or more packages:
(1) *Placed or stacked* onto a load board such as a pallet and secured by strapping, shrink wrapping, stretch wrapping, or other suitable means; or
(2) *Placed in a protective outer packaging such as a box or crate.*

Oxidizer. See §173.127 of this subchapter.

Oxidizing gas means a gas which may, generally by providing oxygen, cause or contribute to the combustion of other material more than air does.

Oxygen generator (chemical) means a device containing chemicals that upon activation release oxygen as a product of chemical reaction.

Package or **Outside Package** means a packaging plus its contents. For radioactive materials, see §173.403 of this subchapter.

Packaging means a receptacle and any other components or materials necessary for the receptacle to perform its containment function in conformance with the minimum packing requirements of this subchapter. For radioactive materials packaging, see §173.403 of this subchapter.

Packing group means a grouping according to the degree of danger presented by hazardous materials. Packing Group I indicates great danger; Packing Group II, medium danger; Packing Group III, minor danger. See §172.101(f) of this subchapter.

Passenger (With respect to vessels and for the purposes of part 176 only) means a person being carried on a vessel other than:
(1) *The owner or his representative;*
(2) *The operator;*
(3) *A bona fide member* of the crew engaged in the business of the vessel who has contributed no consideration for his carriage and who is paid for his services; or
(4) *A guest* who has not contributed any consideration directly or indirectly for his carriage.

Passenger-carrying aircraft means an aircraft that carries any person other than a crewmember, company employee, an authorized representative of the United States, or a person accompanying the shipment.

Passenger vessel means —
(1) *A vessel subject* to any of the requirements of the International Convention for the Safety of Life at Sea, 1974, which carries more than 12 passengers;
(2) *A cargo vessel* documented under the laws of the United States and not subject to that Convention, which carries more than 16 passengers;
(3) *A cargo vessel* of any foreign nation that extends reciprocal privileges and is not subject to that Convention and which carries more than 16 passengers; and
(4) *A vessel* engaged in a ferry operation and which carries passengers.

Person means an individual, firm, copartnership, corporation, company, association, or joint-stock association (including any trustee, receiver, assignee, or similar representative); or a government or Indian tribe (or an agency or instrumentality of any government or Indian tribe) that transports a hazardous material to further a commercial enterprise or offers a hazardous material for transportation in commerce. Person does not include the following:
(1) *The United States Postal Service.*
(2) *Any agency* or instrumentality of the Federal government, for the purposes of 49 U.S.C. 5123 (civil penalties) and 5124 (criminal penalties.).
(3) *Any government* or Indian tribe (or an agency or instrumentality of any government or Indian tribe) that transports hazardous material for a governmental purpose.

Placarded car means a rail car which is placarded in accordance with the requirements of part 172 of this subchapter.

Poisonous gas. See §173.115 of this subchapter.

Poisonous materials. See §173.132 of this subchapter.

Portable tank means a bulk packaging (except a cylinder having a water capacity of 1000 pounds or less) designed primarily to be loaded onto, or on, or temporarily attached to a transport vehicle or ship and equipped with skids, mountings, or accessories to facilitate handling of the tank by mechanical means. It does not include a cargo tank, tank car, multi-unit tank car tank, or trailer carrying 3AX, 3AAX, or 3T cylinders.

Preferred route or **Preferred highway** is a highway for shipment of highway route controlled quantities of radioactive materials so designated by a State routing agency, and any Interstate System highway for which an alternative highway has not been designated by such State agency as provided by §397.103 of this title.

Primary hazard means the hazard class of a material as assigned in the §172.101 table.

Private track or **Private siding** means track located outside of a carrier's right-of-way, yard, or terminals where the carrier does not own the rails, ties, roadbed, or right-of-way and includes track or portion of track which is devoted to the purpose of its user either by lease or written agreement, in which case the lease or written agreement is considered equivalent to ownership.

Proper shipping name means the name of the hazardous material shown in Roman print (not italics) in §172.101 of this subchapter.

Psi means pounds per square inch.

Psia means pounds per square inch absolute.

Psig means pounds per square inch gauge.

Public vessel means a vessel owned by and being used in the public service of the United States. It does not include a vessel owned by the United States and engaged in a trade or commercial service or a vessel under contract or charter to the United States.

Pyrophoric liquid. See §173.124(b) of this subchapter.

Radioactive materials. See §173.403 of this subchapter for definitions relating to radioactive materials.

Rail car means a car designed to carry freight or non-passenger personnel by rail, and includes a box car, flat car, gondola car, hopper car, tank car, and occupied caboose.

Railroad means a person engaged in transportation by rail.

Receptacle means a containment vessel for receiving and holding materials, including any means of closing.

Registered Inspector means a person registered with the Department in accordance with subpart F of part 107 of this chapter who has the knowledge and ability to determine whether a cargo tank conforms with the applicable DOT specification. In addition, Registered Inspector means a person who meets, at a minimum, any one of the following:
(1) *Has an engineering degree and one year of work experience.*
(2) *Has an associate degree in engineering* and two years of work experience.
(3) *Has a high school diploma* (or General Equivalency Diploma) and three years of work experience.
(4) *Has at least three years' experience* in performing the duties of a Registered Inspector by September 1, 1991, and was registered with the Department by December 31, 1995.

Regulated medical waste. See §173.134 of this subchapter.

Reportable quantity (RQ) for the purposes of this subchapter means the quantity specified in column 2 of the appendix to §172.101 for any material identified in column 1 of the appendix.

Research means investigation or experimentation aimed at the discovery of new theories or laws and the discovery and interpretation of facts or revision of accepted theories or laws in the light of new facts.

Residue means the hazardous material remaining in a packaging, including a tank car, after its contents have been unloaded to the maximum extent practicable and before the packaging is either refilled or cleaned of hazardous material and purged to remove any hazardous vapors.

Risk group. See §173.134 of this subchapter.

RSPA means the Research and Special Programs Administration, U.S. Department of Transportation, Washington, DC 20590.

SADT means self-accelerated decomposition temperature. See §173.21(f) of this subchapter.

Salvage packaging means a special packaging conforming to §173.3 of this subchapter into which damaged, defective or leaking hazardous materials packages, or hazardous materials that have spilled or leaked, are placed for purposes of transport for recovery or disposal.

SCF (standard cubic foot) means one cubic foot of gas measured at 60 °F and 14.7 psia.

Self-defense spray means an aerosol or non-pressurized device that:
(1) *Is intended to have* an irritating or incapacitating effect on a person or animal; and
(2) *Meets no hazard criteria* other than for Class 9 (for example, a pepper spray; see §173.140(a) of this subchapter) and, for an aerosol, Division 2.1 or 2.2 (see §173.115 of this subchapter), except that it may contain not more than two percent by mass of a tear gas substance (e.g., chloroacetophenone (CN) or 0-chlorobenzylmalonitrile (CS); see §173.132(a)(2) of this subchapter.)

Sharps. See §173.134 of this subchapter.

Sheathing means a covering consisting of a smooth layer of wood placed over metal and secured to prevent any movement.

Shipping paper means a shipping order, bill of lading, manifest or other shipping document serving a similar purpose and containing the information required by §§172.202, 172.203 and 172.204.

Siftproof packaging means a packaging impermeable to dry contents, including fine solid material produced during transportation.

Single packaging means a non-bulk packaging other than a combination packaging.

Solid means a material which is not a gas or a liquid.

Solution means any homogeneous liquid mixture of two or more chemical compounds or elements that will not undergo any segregation under conditions normal to transportation.

Specification packaging means a packaging conforming to one of the specifications or standards for packagings in part 178 or part 179 of this subchapter.

Spontaneously combustible material. See §173.124(b) of this subchapter.

Stabilized means that the hazardous material is in a condition that precludes uncontrolled reaction. This may be achieved by methods such as adding an inhibiting chemical, degassing the hazardous material to remove dissolved oxygen and inerting the air space in the package, or maintaining the hazardous material under temperature control.

State means a State of the United States, the District of Columbia, the Commonwealth of Puerto Rico, the Commonwealth of the Northern Mariana Islands, the Virgin Islands, American Samoa, Guam, or any other territory or possession of the United States designated by the Secretary.

State-designated route means a preferred route selected in accordance with U.S. DOT "Guidelines for Selecting Preferred Highway Routes for Highway Route Controlled Quantities of Radioactive Materials" or an equivalent routing analysis which adequately considers overall risk to the public.

Stowage means the act of placing hazardous materials on board a vessel.

Strong outside container means the outermost enclosure which provides protection against the unintentional release of its contents under conditions normally incident to transportation.

Subsidiary hazard means a hazard of a material other than the primary hazard. (See primary hazard).

Table in §172.101 or **§172.101 table** means the Hazardous Materials Table in §172.101 of this subchapter.

Technical name means a recognized chemical name or microbiological name currently used in scientific and technical handbooks, journals, and texts. Generic descriptions are authorized for use as technical names provided they readily identify the general chemical group, or microbiological group. Examples of acceptable generic chemical descriptions are organic phosphate compounds, petroleum aliphatic hydrocarbons and tertiary amines. For proficiency testing only, generic microbiological descriptions such as bacteria, mycobacteria, fungus, and viral samples may be used. Except for names which appear in subpart B of part 172 of this subchapter, trade names may not be used as technical names.

TOFC means trailer-on-flat-car.

Top shell means the tank car tank surface, excluding the head ends and bottom shell of the tank car tank.

Toxin. See §173.134 of this subchapter.

Trailership means a vessel, other than a carfloat, specifically equipped to carry motor transport vehicles and fitted with installed securing devices to tie down each vehicle. The term trailership includes Roll-on/Roll-off (RO/RO) vessels.

Train means one or more engines coupled with one or more rail cars, except during switching operations or where the operation is that of classifying and assembling rail cars within a railroad yard for the purpose of making or breaking up trains.

Trainship means a vessel other than a rail car ferry or carfloat, specifically equipped to transport railroad vehicles, and fitted with installed securing devices to tie down each vehicle.

Transport vehicle means a cargo-carrying vehicle such as an automobile, van, tractor, truck, semitrailer, tank car or rail car used for the transportation of cargo by any mode. Each cargo-carrying body (trailer, rail car, etc.) is a separate transport vehicle.

UFC means Uniform Freight Classification.

UN means United Nations.

UN portable tank means a intermodal tank having a capacity of more than 450 liters (118.9 gallons). It includes a shell fitted with service equipment and structural equipment, including stabilizing members external to the shell and skids, mountings or accessories to facilitate mechanical handling. A UN portable tank must be capable of being filled and discharged without the removal of its structural equipment and must be capable of being lifted when full. Cargo tanks, rail tank car tanks, non-metallic tanks, non-specification tanks, bulk bins, and IBCs and packagings made to cylinder specifications are not UN portable tanks.

UN Recommendations means the UN Recommendations on the Transport of Dangerous Goods.

UN standard packaging means a packaging conforming to standards in the UN Recommendations.

Unit load device means any type of freight container, aircraft container, aircraft pallet with a net, or aircraft pallet with a net over an igloo.

United States means a State of the United States, the District of Columbia, the Commonwealth of Puerto Rico, the Commonwealth of the Northern Mariana Islands, the Virgin Islands, American Samoa, Guam, or any other territory or possession of the United States designated by the Secretary.

Vessel includes every description of watercraft, used or capable of being used as a means of transportation on the water.

Viscous liquid means a liquid material which has a measured viscosity in excess of 2500 centistokes at 25 °C (77 °F) when determined in accordance with the procedures specified in ASTM Method D 445-72 "Kinematic Viscosity of Transparent and Opaque Liquids (and the Calculation of Dynamic Viscosity)" or ASTM Method D 1200-70 "Viscosity of Paints, Varnishes, and Lacquers by Ford Viscosity Cup."

Volatility refers to the relative rate of evaporation of materials to assume the vapor state.

Water reactive material. See §173.124(c) of this subchapter.

Water resistant means having a degree of resistance to permeability by and damage caused by water in liquid form.

Wooden barrel means a packaging made of natural wood, of round cross-section, having convex walls, consisting of staves and heads and fitted with hoops.

W.T. means watertight.

FEDERAL REGISTER UPDATES

In the April 18, 2003 Federal Register, §171.8 was revised, effective October 1, 2003.

Cargo tank[1] means a bulk packaging that:

(1) *Is a tank intended primarily* for the carriage of liquids or gases and includes appurtenances, reinforcements, fittings, and closures (for the definition of a tank, see 49 CFR 178.320, 178.337-1, or 178.338-1, as applicable);

(2) *Is permanently attached to* or forms a part of a motor vehicle, or is not permanently attached to a motor vehicle but which, by reason of its size, construction or attachment to a motor vehicle is loaded or unloaded without being removed from the motor vehicle; and

(3) *Is not fabricated* under a specification for cylinders, intermediate bulk containers, multi-unit tank car tanks, portable tanks, or tank cars.

Design Certifying Engineer[2] means a person registered with the Department in accordance with subpart F of part 107 of this chapter who has the knowledge and ability to perform stress analysis of pressure vessels and otherwise determine whether a cargo tank design and construction meets the applicable DOT specification. A Design Certifying Engineer meets the knowledge and ability requirements of this section by meeting any one of the following requirements:

(1) *Has an engineering degree* and one year of work experience in cargo tank structural or mechanical design;

(2) *Is currently registered* as a professional engineer by appropriate authority of a state of the United States or a province of Canada; or

(3) *Has at least three years' experience* in performing the duties of a Design Certifying Engineer prior to September 1, 1991.

Maximum allowable working pressure or **MAWP**[3]**:** For DOT specification cargo tanks used to transport liquid hazardous materials, see §178.320(c) of this subchapter.

Registered Inspector[4] means a person registered with the Department in accordance with subpart F of part 107 of this chapter who has the knowledge and ability to determine whether a cargo tank conforms to the applicable DOT specification. A Registered Inspector meets the knowledge and ability requirements of this section by meeting any one of the following requirements:

(1) *Has an engineering degree* and one year of work experience relating to the testing and inspection of cargo tanks;

(2) *Has an associate degree in engineering* and two years of work experience relating to the testing and inspection of cargo tanks;

(3) *Has a high school diploma* (or General Equivalency Diploma) and three years of work experience relating to the testing and inspection of cargo tanks; or

(4) *Has at least three years' experience* performing the duties of a Registered Inspector prior to September 1, 1991.

1. The definition for "Cargo tank" was revised.
2. The definition for "Design Certifying Engineer" was revised.
3. The definition for "MAWP" was removed and a definition for "Maximum allowable working pressure or MAWP" was added in its place.
4. The definition for "Registered Inspector" was revised.

§171.9 Rules of construction.

(a) In this subchapter, unless the context requires otherwise:

(1) *Words imparting the singular include the plural;*

(2) *Words imparting the plural include the singular; and*

(3) *Words imparting the masculine gender include the feminine;*

(b) In this subchapter, the word:

(1) *"Shall" is used in an imperative sense;*

(2) *"Must" is used in an imperative sense;*

(3) *"Should" is used in a recommendatory sense;*

(4) *"May"* is used in a permissive sense to state authority or permission to do the act described, and the words "no person may * * *" or "a person may not * * *" means that no person is required, authorized, or permitted to do the act described; and

(5) *"Includes" is used as a word of inclusion not limitation.*

§171.10 Units of measure.

(a) General. To ensure compatibility with international transportation standards, most units of measure in this subchapter are expressed using the International System of Units ("SI" or metric). Where SI units appear, they are the regulatory standard. U.S. standard or customary units, which appear in parentheses following the SI units, are for information only and are not intended to be the regulatory standard.

(b) Abbreviations for SI units of measure generally used throughout this subchapter are as shown in paragraph (c) of this section. Customary units shown throughout this subchapter are generally not abbreviated.

(c) Conversion values.

(1) *Conversion values* are provided in the following table and are based on values provided in ASTM E 380-89, "Standard for Metric Practice."

(2) *If an exact conversion is needed,* the following conversion table should be used.

Table of Conversion Factors for SI Units

Measurement	SI to U.S. standard	U.S. standard to SI
Activity	1 TBq = 27 Ci	1 Ci = 0.037 TBq
Length	1 cm = 0.3937008 in 1 m = 3.280840 ft	1 in = 2.540000 cm 1 ft = 0.3048000 m
Thickness	1 mm = 0.03937008 in	1 in = 25.40000 mm
Mass (weight)	1 kg = 2.204622 lb 1 g = 0.03527397 oz	1 lb = 0.4535924 kg 1 oz = 28.34952 g
Pressure	1 kPa = 0.1450377 psi 1 Bar = 100 kPa = 14.504 psi 1 kPa = 7.5 mm Hg	1 psi = 6.894757 kPa 1 psi = 0.06895 Bar
Radiation level	1 Sv/hr = 100 rem/hr	1 rem/hr = 0.01 Sv/hr
Volume (liquid)	1 L = 0.2641720 gal 1 mL = 0.03381402 oz 1 m^3 = 35.31466 ft^3	1 gal = 3.785412 L 1 oz = 29.57353 mL 1 ft^3 = 0.02831685 m^3
Density	1 kg/m^3 = 0.06242797 lb/ft^3	1 lb/ft^3 = 16.01846 kg/m^3
Force	1 Newton = 0.2248 Pound-force	1 Pound-force = 4.483 N

Abbreviation for units of measure are as follows:

Unit of measure and abbreviation:

(SI): millimeter, mm; centimeter, cm; meter, m; gram, g; kilogram, kg; kiloPascal, kPa; liter, L; milliliter, mL; cubic meter, m^3; Terabecquerel, TBq; Gigabecquerel, GBq; millisievert, mSv; Newton, N;

(U.S.): Inch, in; foot, ft; ounce, oz; pound, lb; psig, psi; gallon, gal; cubic feet, ft^3; Curie, Ci; millicurie, mCi; millirem, mrem.

§171.11 Use of ICAO Technical Instructions.

Notwithstanding the requirements of parts 172 and 173 of this subchapter, a hazardous material may be transported by aircraft, and by motor vehicle either before or after being transported by aircraft, in accordance with the ICAO Technical Instructions (incorporated by reference, see §171.7) if the hazardous material:

(a) Is packaged, marked, labeled, classified, described and certified on a shipping paper and otherwise in a condition for shipment as required by the ICAO Technical Instructions;

(b) Is within the quantity limits prescribed for transportation by either passenger-carrying or cargo aircraft, as appropriate, as specified in the ICAO Technical Instructions;

(c) Is not a forbidden material or package according to §173.21 of this subchapter or column 3 of the §172.101 table; and

(d) Fulfills the following additional requirements as applicable:

(1) *For a material* that meets the definition of a hazardous substance as defined in this subchapter, the shipping paper and package markings must conform to the provisions in §§172.203(c) and 172.324, respectively, of this subchapter.

(2) *When a hazardous material,* which is subject to the requirements of the ICAO Technical Instructions, is also a hazardous waste as defined in this subchapter:

(i) *The word "Waste"* must precede the proper shipping name on shipping papers and package markings; and

(ii) *It must comply* with §172.205 with respect to the hazardous waste manifests.

(3) *When a hazardous material* is not subject to the requirements of the ICAO Technical Instructions, it must be transported as required by this subchapter.

(4) *When a hazardous material* that is regulated by this subchapter for transportation by highway is transported by motor vehicle on a public highway under the provisions of this section, the following requirements apply:

(i) *The motor vehicle* must be placarded in accordance with subpart F of part 172 of this subchapter; and

(ii) *The shipping paper* may include an indication that the shipment is being made under the provisions of this section or the letters "ICAO."

(5) *Except for* a Division 2.2 air bag, air bag module, or seat-belt pretensioner, the shipping paper description must conform to the requirements of §173.166(c) of this subchapter.

(6) *For radioactive materials:*

(i) *Shipping papers* for highway route controlled quantity radioactive materials shipments must meet the requirements of §172.203(d)(4) of this subchapter.

(ii) *Competent authority certification* and any necessary revalidation for Type B, Type B(U), Type B(M), and fissile materials packages must be obtained from the appropriate authorities as specified in §§173.471, 173.472 and 173.473 of this subchapter, and all requirements of the certificates and revalidations must be met.

(iii) *Except for limited quantities* of Class 7 (radioactive) material, the provisions of §§172.204(c)(4), 173.448(e), (f) and (g)(3) of this subchapter apply.

(iv) *Limited quantities* of radioactive materials must meet the provisions of §173.421, §173.424 or §173.426 as appropriate of this subchapter.

(v) *Type A package contents* shall be limited in accordance with §173.431 of this subchapter.

(vi) *The definition* for "radioactive material" in §173.403 of this subchapter applies to radioactive materials transported under the provisions of this section.

(7) *If a United States variation* is indicated in the ICAO Technical Instructions for any provision governing the transport of the hazardous material, the hazardous material is transported in conformance with that variation.

(8) *Abbreviations* may not be used in shipping paper entries or package markings unless they are specifically authorized by this subchapter. ICAO class or division numbers are not considered to be abbreviations.

(9) *When a hazardous material,* which is subject to the requirements of the ICAO Technical Instructions, is a material poisonous by inhalation (see §171.8 of this subchapter) —

(i) *The shipping description* must include the words "Toxic Inhalation Hazard" or "Poison-Inhalation Hazard" or "Inhalation Hazard", as required in §172.203(m) of this subchapter;

(ii) *The material* must be packaged in accordance with the requirements of this subchapter; and

(iii) *The package* must be marked in accordance with §172.313 of this subchapter and labeled with "POISON INHALATION HAZARD" or "POISON GAS", as appropriate, in accordance with subpart E of part 172 of this subchapter.

(10) *Shipments of hazardous materials* under this section must conform to the requirements for emergency response information as prescribed in subpart G of part 172 of this subchapter.

(11) *Packages of Class 1* (explosive) materials must be marked in accordance with §172.320 of this subchapter.

(12) *If an ammonium nitrate fertilizer* or ammonium nitrate mixed fertilizer, must not meet the definition and criteria of a Class 1 (explosive) material.

(13) *Transportation of marine pollutants,* as defined in §171.8 of this subchapter, in bulk packagings must conform to the requirements of §§172.203(l) and 172.322 of this subchapter.

(14) *Except as provided* for limited quantities of compressed gases in containers of not more than 4 fluid ounces capacity under §173.306(a)(1) of this subchapter, aerosols must meet the definition for "Aerosol" in §171.8. In addition, an aerosol must be in a metal packaging if the packaging exceeds 7.22 cubic inches.

(15) *A chemical oxygen generator* is forbidden for transportation aboard a passenger-carrying aircraft and must be approved, classed, described and packaged in accordance with the requirements of this subchapter for transportation on cargo-only aircraft. A chemical oxygen generator (spent) is forbidden for transportation on aircraft.

(16) *A cylinder containing* Oxygen, compressed, may not be transported on a passenger-carrying aircraft or in an inaccessible cargo location aboard a cargo-only aircraft unless it is packaged as required by Part 173 and Part 178 of this subchapter and is placed in an overpack or outer packaging that satisfies the requirements of Special Provision A52 in §172.102.

(17) *An organic peroxide* that is not identified by technical name in the Organic Peroxide Table in §173.225(b) of this subchapter must be approved by the Associate Administrator in accordance with the requirements of §173.128(d) of this subchapter.

§171.12 Import and export shipments.

(a) **Importer's responsibility.** Except in the case of a shipment from Canada conforming to §171.12a of this subchapter, each person importing a hazardous material into the United States shall provide the shipper and the forwarding agent at the place of entry into the United States timely and complete information as to the requirements of this subchapter that will apply to the shipment of the material within the United States. The shipper, directly or through the forwarding agent at the place of entry, shall provide the initial carrier in the United States the certificate of compliance required by §172.204 of this subchapter. The carrier may not accept the material for transportation unless the required certification is provided. All shipping paper information required under paragraph (b) or (d) of this section must be in English.

(b) **IMDG Code (see §171.7 of this subchapter).** The IMDG Code sets forth descriptions, classifications, packagings, labeling and vessel stowage requirements. Notwithstanding the provisions of this subchapter, a material which is packaged, marked, classed, labeled, placarded, described, stowed and segregated, and certified (including a container packing certification, if applicable) in accordance with the IMDG Code, and otherwise conforms to the requirements of this section, may be offered and accepted for transportation and transported within the United States. The following conditions and limitations apply:

(1) *The provisions* of this paragraph (b) apply only if all or part of the transportation is by vessel.

(2) *A number of materials* listed in the IMDG Code are not subject to the requirements of this subchapter. The provisions of this subchapter do not apply to materials listed in the IMDG Code which are not designated as hazardous materials under this subchapter. These materials may, however, be transported in the U.S. when described, marked and labeled in accordance with the IMDG Code.

(3) *A material designated* as a hazardous material under this subchapter which is not subject to the requirements of the IMDG Code may not be transported under the provisions of this section. For example, internal combustion engines, and viscous flammable liquids having a flash point of 23 °C (73.4 °F) or greater and less than or equal to 60.5 °C (140.9 °F) as provided in 2.3.2.5 of the IMDG Code may not be transported under the provisions of this section and are subject to the requirements of this subchapter.

(4) *A forbidden material or package* according to §173.21 of this subchapter or column 3 of the §172.101 table may not be transported under the provisions of this section.

(5) *Except for IBCs and UN portable tanks* intended for liquids or solids, bulk packagings must conform to the requirements of this subchapter. For UN portable tanks, Special Provisions TP37, TP38, TP44 and TP45 must be met when applicable. Except as specified in paragraph (b)(8) of this section for a material poisonous (toxic) by inhalation (see §171.8 of this subchapter), the T Codes specified for specific hazardous materials in Column 13 of the Dangerous Goods List of the IMDG Code may be applied to the transportation of those materials in IM, IMO and DOT Specification 51 portable tanks when these portable tanks are authorized in accordance with the requirements of this subchapter.

(6) *For export,* packagings must conform to the applicable requirements in §§173.24, 173.24a and 173.28 of this subchapter.

(7) *A Class 1 material* must be classed and approved under the procedures in subpart C of part 173 of this subchapter and conform to the requirements of §172.320 and part 176 of this subchapter.

(8) *When a hazardous material,* which is subject to the requirements of the IMDG Code, is a material poisonous by inhalation (see §171.8 of this subchapter) —

(i) *The shipping description* must include the words "Toxic Inhalation Hazard" or "Poison-Inhalation Hazard" or "Inhalation Hazard", as required in §172.203(m) of this subchapter;

(ii) *The material* must be packaged in accordance with the requirements of this subchapter;

(iii) *The package* must be marked in accordance with §172.313 of this subchapter;

(iv) *Except as provided* in paragraph (b)(8)(v) of this section, the package must be labeled or placarded POISON GAS or POISON INHALATION HAZARD, as appropriate, in accordance with subparts E and F of this subchapter;

(v) *A label or placard* that conforms to IMDG Code specifications for a "Class 2.3" or "Class 6.1" label or placard may be substituted for the POISON GAS or POISON INHALATION HAZARD label or placard required by paragraph (b)(8)(iv) of this section on a package transported in a closed transport vehicle or freight container. The transport vehicle or freight container must be marked with identification numbers for the hazardous material, regardless of the total quantity contained in the transport vehicle or freight container, in the manner specified in §172.313(c) of this subchapter and placarded as required by subpart F of this subchapter;

(vi) *A package,* freight container, or transport vehicle may be placarded in conformance with IMDG Code placard specifications for "Class 2.3" or "Class 6.1", as appropriate, in place of the POISON GAS or POISON INHALATION HAZARD placard required by paragraph (b)(8)(iv) of this section when moving within a single port area, including contiguous harbor.

(9) *Class 7 materials* must conform to the provisions of paragraph (d) of this section.

(10) *For a hazardous waste, as defined in this subchapter —*

(i) *The word "Waste"* must precede the proper shipping name on shipping papers and packages; and

(ii) *The requirements* of §172.205 of this subchapter with respect to hazardous waste manifests are applicable.

(11) *A hazardous substance* as defined in this subchapter must conform to the requirements of §§172.203(c) and 172.324 of this subchapter.

(12) *A poisonous material* must conform to the requirements of §172.203(m) of this subchapter.

(13) *[Reserved]*

(14) *Any ammonium nitrate fertilizer* or ammonium nitrate mixed fertilizer must not meet the definition and criteria of a Class 1 (explosive) material.

(15) *Cylinders not manufactured* to a DOT specification must conform to the requirements of §173.301(j) through (m) of this subchapter or, for Canadian manufactured cylinders, to the requirements of §171.12a(b)(13).

(16) *Shipments of hazardous materials* under this section must conform to the requirements for emergency response information as prescribed in subpart G of part 172 of this subchapter.

(17) *Except as provided* for limited quantities of compressed gases in containers of not more than 4 fluid ounces capacity under §173.306(a)(1) of this subchapter, aerosols must meet the definition for "Aerosol" in §171.8.

(18) *A chemical oxygen generator* must be approved in accordance with the requirements of this subchapter. A chemical oxygen generator and a chemical oxygen generator (spent) must be classed, described and packaged in accordance with the requirements of this subchapter.

(19) *Except for Division 2.2,* the shipping paper description for an air bag, air bag module, or seat-belt pretensioner must conform to the requirements of §173.166(c) of this subchapter.

(20) *An organic peroxide* that is not identified by technical name in the Organic Peroxide Table in §173.225(b) of this subchapter must be approved by the Associate Administrator in accordance with the requirements of §173.128(d) of this subchapter.

(c) **Use of IMDG Code in port areas.** Section 171.2 notwithstanding, a hazardous material (other than Division 1.1 or 1.2 or Class 7) being imported into or exported from the United States or passing through the United States in the course of being shipped between places outside the United States may be offered and accepted for transportation and transported by motor vehicle within a single port area (including contiguous harbors) when packaged, marked, classed, labeled, stowed and segregated in accordance with the IMDG Code, if the hazardous material is offered and accepted in accordance with the requirements of subparts C and F of part 172 of this subchapter pertaining to shipping papers and placarding and otherwise conforms to the applicable requirements of part 176 of this subchapter. The requirement in §172.201(d) of this subchapter for an emergency telephone number does not apply to shipments made in accordance with the IMDG Code if the hazardous material:

(1) *Is not offloaded from the vessel;*

(2) *Is offloaded* between ocean vessels at a U.S. port facility without being transported by public highway.

(d) **Use of International Atomic Energy Agency (IAEA)** regulations for Class 7 (radioactive) materials. Class 7 (radioactive) materials being imported into or exported from the United States, or passing through the United States in the course of being shipped between places outside the United States, may be offered and accepted for transportation when packaged, marked, labeled, and otherwise prepared for shipment in accordance with IAEA "Regulations for the Safe Transport of Radioactive Material," Safety Series No. 6 or TS-R-1 (incorporated by reference, see §171.7), if —

(1) *Highway route* controlled quantities (see §173.403 of this subchapter) are shipped in accordance with §§172.203(d)(4), 172.507 and 173.22(c) of this subchapter;

(2) *For fissile materials* and Type B packages, the competent authority certification and any necessary revalidation is obtained from the appropriate competent authorities as specified in §§173.471, 173.472 and 173.473 of this subchapter and all requirements of the certificates and revalidations are met;

(3) *Type A package contents* are limited in accordance with §173.431 of this subchapter;

(4) *The country of origin* for the shipment has adopted the corresponding edition (Safety Series No. 6, 1985 Edition, or TS-R-1, 1996 Edition) of the IAEA "Regulations for the Safe Transport of Radioactive Material';

(5) *The requirements* of §§173.448(e), 173.448(f), and 173.448(g)(3) of this subchapter are fulfilled, when applicable;

(6) *Shipments comply* with the requirements for emergency response information prescribed in subpart G of part 172 of this subchapter; and

(7) *The definition* for "radioactive material" in §173.403 of this subchapter is applied to radioactive materials transported under the provisions of this section.

(e) **Shipments to or from Mexico.** Unless otherwise excepted, hazardous materials shipments from Mexico to the United States or from the United States to Mexico must conform to all applicable requirements of this subchapter. When a hazardous material that is a material poisonous by inhalation (see §171.8) is transported by highway or rail from Mexico to the United States, or from the United States to Mexico, the following requirements apply:

(1) *The shipping description* must include the words "Toxic Inhalation Hazard" or "Poison-Inhalation Hazard" or "Inhalation Hazard", as required in §172.203(m) of this subchapter.

(2) *The material* must be packaged in accordance with requirements of this subchapter.

(3) *The package* must be marked in accordance with §172.313 of this subchapter.

(4) *Except as provided* in paragraph (e)(5) of this section, the package must be labeled or placarded POISON GAS or POISON INHALATION HAZARD, as appropriate, in accordance with subparts E and F of this subchapter.

(5) *A label or placard* that conforms to the UN Recommendations on the Transport of Dangerous Goods specifications for a "Division 2.3" or "Division 6.1" label or placard may be substituted for the POISON GAS or POISON INHALATION HAZARD label or placard required by §§172.400(a) and 172.504(e) of this subchapter on a package transported in a closed transport vehicle or freight container. The transport vehicle or freight container must be marked with identification numbers for the material, regardless of the total quantity contained in the transport vehicle or freight container, in the manner specified in §172.313(c) of this subchapter and placarded as required by subpart F of this subchapter.

FEDERAL REGISTER UPDATES

In the May 30, 2003 Federal Register, §171.12 was revised, effective June 30, 2003.

(b) [1]

(21) *No person may offer* an IM or UN portable tank containing liquid hazardous materials of Class 3, PG I or II, or PG III with a flash point less than 100 °F (38 °C); Division 5.1, PG I or II; or Division 6.1, PG I or II, for unloading while it remains on a transport vehicle with the motive power unit attached, unless it conforms to the requirements in §177.834(o) of this subchapter. [2]

1. Paragraph (b) is the same as before.
2. Paragraph (b)(21) was added.

§171.12a Canadian shipments and packagings.

(a) **Scope and applicability.** This section sets forth provisions for the transportation by rail or highway of shipments of hazardous materials which conform to the regulations of the Government of Canada but which may differ from the requirements of this subchapter with regard to hazard communication, classification or packaging. Except as provided in paragraph (b)(5)(iv) of this section, the provisions apply only to shipments which originate in Canada and either terminate in the U.S. or transit the U.S. to a Canadian or foreign destination, and to the return to Canada of empty bulk packages containing residues of hazardous materials which originally were imported into the U.S. Reciprocal provisions, applicable to exports from the U.S., appear in the regulations of the Government of Canada.

(b) **Conditions and limitations.** Notwithstanding the requirements of parts 172, 173, and 178 of this subchapter, and subject to the limitations of paragraph (a) of this section, a hazardous material that is classed, marked, labeled, placarded, described on a shipping paper, and packaged in accordance with the Transportation of Dangerous Goods (TDG) Regulations issued by the Government of Canada may be offered for transportation and transported to or through the United States by motor vehicle or rail car. Copies of the TDG Regulations may be obtained from the Canadian Government Publishing Centre, Ottawa, Ontario K1A 059; Telephone (819) 956-4800. The following conditions and limitations apply:

(1) *A number of materials listed* in the TDG Regulations may not be subject to the requirements of this subchapter. The provisions of this subchapter do not apply to materials listed in the TDG Regulations which are not designated as hazardous materials under this subchapter. These materials may, however, be transported in the U.S. when described, marked and labeled in accordance with the TDG Regulations.

(2) *A material designated* as a hazardous material under this subchapter which is not subject to the requirements of the TDG Regulations may not be transported under the provisions of this section.

(3) *A forbidden material or package* according to §173.21 of this subchapter or column 3 of the §172.101 table may not be transported under the provisions of this section.

(4) *A Class 1 material* must be classed and approved under the procedures in subpart C of part 173 of this subchapter, and packages of Class 1 materials must be marked in accordance with §172.320 of this subchapter.

(5) *When a hazardous material,* which is a material poisonous by inhalation under the provisions of this subchapter (see §171.8 of this subchapter), is subject to the requirements of the TDG Regulations —

(i) *The shipping description* must include the words "Toxic Inhalation Hazard" or "Poison Inhalation Hazard" or "Inhalation Hazard", as required in §172.203(m) of this subchapter;

(ii) *The material* must be packaged in accordance with the requirements of this subchapter;

(iii) *The package* must be marked in accordance with §172.313 of this subchapter;

(iv) *Except as provided* in paragraph (b)(5)(v) of this section and for a package containing anhydrous ammonia, the package must be labeled or placarded POISON GAS or POISON INHALATION HAZARD, as appropriate, in accordance with subparts E and F of this subchapter;

(v) *A label or placard* that conforms to the specifications in the TDG Regulations for a "Class 2.3" or "Class 6.1" label or placard may be substituted for the POISON GAS or POISON INHALATION HAZARD label or placard required by paragraph (b)(5)(iv) of this section on a package transported in a closed transport vehicle or freight container. The transport vehicle or freight container must be marked with identification numbers for the material, regardless of quantity, in the manner specified in §172.313(c) of this subchapter and placarded as required by subpart F of this subchapter. When moving in the United States, the transport vehicle or freight container may also be placarded in accordance with the appropriate TDG regulations in addition to the POISON GAS or POISON INHALATION HAZARD placards required by paragraph (b)(5)(iv) of this section;

(vi) *For shipments of anhydrous ammonia,* the shipping paper must contain an indication that the markings, labels and placards have been applied in conformance with the TDG Regulations and this paragraph (b)(5).

(6) *Required shipping descriptions* and package markings must be in English. Abbreviations may not be used unless specifically

authorized by this subchapter. Identification numbers must be preceded by "UN" or "NA". The use of an identification number preceded by "PIN" is not authorized.

(7) *Shipments must conform* to the requirements for emergency response information in subpart G of part 172 of this subchapter.

(8) *A Class 7 material* must conform to the provisions of §171.12(d) of this subchapter;

(9) *For a hazardous waste as defined in this subchapter* —

(i) *The word "Waste"* must precede the proper shipping name on shipping papers and packages; and

(ii) *The requirements* of §172.205 of this subchapter with respect to hazardous waste manifests are applicable;

(10) *A hazardous substance* as defined in this subchapter must conform to the requirements of §§172.203(c) and 172.324 of this subchapter; and

(11) *A poisonous material* must conform to the requirements of §172.203(m) of this subchapter.

(12) *[Reserved]*

(13) *When the provisions* of this subchapter require that a DOT specification or UN standard packaging must be used for a hazardous material, a packaging authorized by the TDG Regulations may be used only if it corresponds to the DOT specification or UN packaging authorized by this subchapter. Cylinders not manufactured to DOT specifications must conform to the requirements of §173.301(j) through (m) of this subchapter.

(14) *Any ammonium nitrate fertilizer* or ammonium nitrate mixed fertilizer must not meet the definition and criteria of a Class 1 (explosive) material.

(15) *Transportation of marine pollutants,* as defined in §171.8 of this subchapter, must conform to the requirements of §§172.203(l) and 172.322 of this subchapter.

(16) *Except as provided* for limited quantities of compressed gases in containers of not more than 4 fluid ounces capacity under §173.306(a)(1) of this subchapter, aerosols must meet the definition for "Aerosol" in §171.8.

(17) *A chemical oxygen generator* must be approved in accordance with the requirements of this subchapter. A chemical oxygen generator and a chemical oxygen generator (spent) must be classed, described and packaged in accordance with the requirements of this subchapter.

(18) *An organic peroxide* that is not identified by technical name in the Organic Peroxide Table in §173.225(b) of this subchapter must be approved by the Associate Administrator in accordance with the requirements of §173.128(d) of this subchapter.

FEDERAL REGISTER UPDATES

An Interim Final Rule affecting §171.12a was published in the May 5, 2003 Federal Register.

(b) [1]

(19) *Rail and motor carriers* must comply with 49 CFR 1572.9 and 49 CFR 1572.11 to the extent those regulations apply, when transporting Class 1 materials. [2]

1. Paragraph (b) is the same as before.
2. Paragraph (b)(19) was added.

FEDERAL REGISTER UPDATES

In the May 30, 2003 Federal Register, §171.12a was revised, effective June 30, 2003.

(b) [1]

(20) *No person may offer* an IM or UN portable tank containing liquid hazardous materials of Class 3, PG I or II, or PG III with a flash point less than 100 °F (38 °C); Division 5.1, PG I or II; or Division 6.1, PG I or II, for unloading while it remains on a transport vehicle with the motive power unit attached, unless it conforms to the requirements in §177.834(o) of this subchapter. [2]

1. Paragraph (b) is the same as before.
2. Paragraph (b)(20) was added.

§171.14 Transitional provisions for implementing certain requirements.

General. The purpose of the provisions of this section is to provide an orderly transition to certain new requirements so as to minimize any burdens associated with them.

(a) Previously filled packages —

(1) *Packages filled prior to October 1, 1991.* Notwithstanding the marking and labeling provisions of subparts D and E, respectively, of part 172, and the packaging provisions of part 173 and subpart B of part 172 of this subchapter, a package may be offered for transportation and transported prior to October 1, 2001, if it —

(i) *Conforms to* the old requirements of this subchapter in effect on September 30, 1991;

(ii) *Was filled with a hazardous material prior to October 1, 1991;*

(iii) *Is marked* "Inhalation Hazard" if appropriate, in accordance with §172.313 of this subchapter or Special Provision 13, as assigned in the §172.101 table; and

(iv) *Is not emptied and refilled on or after October 1, 1991.*

(2) *Non-bulk packages* filled prior to October 1, 1996. Notwithstanding the packaging provisions of subpart B of part 172 and the packaging provisions of part 173 of this subchapter with respect to UN standard packagings, a non-bulk package other than a cylinder may be offered for transportation and transported domestically prior to October 1, 1999, if it —

(i) *Conforms* to the requirements of this subchapter in effect on September 30, 1996;

(ii) *Was filled* with a hazardous material prior to October 1, 1996; and

(iii) *Is not emptied and refilled on or after October 1, 1996.*

(b) Transitional placarding provisions. Until October 1, 2001, placards which conform to specifications for placards in effect on September 30, 1991, or placards specified in the December 21, 1990 final rule may be used, for highway transportation only, in place of the placards specified in subpart F of part 172 of this subchapter, in accordance with the following table:

Placard Substitution Table

Hazard class or division No.	Current placard name	Old (Sept. 30, 1991) placard name
Division 1.1	Explosives 1.1	Explosives A
Division 1.2	Explosives 1.2	Explosives A
Division 1.3	Explosives 1.3	Explosives B
Division 1.4	Explosives 1.4	Dangerous
Division 1.5	Explosives 1.5	Blasting agents
Division 1.6	Explosives 1.6	Dangerous
Division 2.1	Flammable gas	Flammable gas
Division 2.2	Nonflammable gas	Nonflammable gas
Division 2.3[1]	Poison gas	Poison gas
Class 3	Flammable	Flammable
Combustible liquid	Combustible	Combustible
Division 4.1	Flammable solid	Flammable solid
Division 4.2	Spontaneously combustible	Flammable solid
Division 4.3	Dangerous when wet	Flammable solid W
Division 5.1	Oxidizer	Oxidizer
Division 5.2	Organic peroxide	Organic peroxide
Division 6.1, (inhalation hazard, Zone A or B)[1]	Poison inhalation hazard	Poison
Division 6.1, PG I (other than Zone A or B inhalation hazard), PG II, or PG III	Poison	Poison
Class 7	Radioactive	Radioactive
Class 8	Corrosive	Corrosive
Class 9	Class 9	(none required)

1. For materials poisonous by inhalation, by all modes of transportation, until October 1, 2001, placards may be used that conform to specifications for placards (1) in effect on September 30, 1991, (2) specified in the December 21, 1990 final rule, or (3) specified in the July 22, 1997 final rule.

(c) Non-specification fiber drums. A non-specification fiber drum with a removable head is authorized for a liquid hazardous material in Packing Group III that is not poisonous by inhalation for which the packaging was authorized under the requirements of part 172 or part 173 of this subchapter in effect on September 30, 1991. This authorization expires on the date on which funds are authorized to be appropriated to carry out chapter 51 of title 49, United States Code (related to transportation of hazardous materials), for fiscal years beginning after September 30, 1997. Information concerning this funding authorization date may be obtained by contacting the Office of the Associate Administrator.

(d) A final rule published in the Federal Register on June 21, 2001, effective October 1, 2001, resulted in revisions to this subchapter. During the transition period, until October 1, 2002, as provided in paragraph (d)(1) of this section, a person may elect to comply with either the applicable requirements of this subchapter in effect on September 30, 2001, or the requirements published in the June 21, 2001 final rule.

(1) *Transition dates.* The effective date of the June 21, 2001 final rule is October 1, 2001. A delayed compliance date of October 1, 2002 is authorized. On October 1, 2002, all applicable regulatory requirements adopted in the June 21, 2001 final rule in effect on October 1, 2001 must be met.

(2) *Intermixing old and new requirements.* Prior to October 1, 2002, it is recommended that the hazard communication requirements be consistent where practicable. Marking, labeling, placarding, and shipping paper descriptions should conform to either the old requirements of this subchapter in effect on September 30, 2001, or the new requirements of this subchapter in the June 21, 2001 final rule without intermixing communication elements. However, intermixing is permitted, during the applicable transition period, for packaging, hazard communication, and handling provisions, as follows:

(i) *If either* shipping names or identification numbers are identical, a shipping paper may display the old shipping description even if the package is marked and labeled under the new shipping description;

(ii) *If either* shipping names or identification numbers are identical, a shipping paper may display the new shipping description even if the package is marked and labeled under the old shipping description; and

(iii) *Either old or new placards* may be used regardless of whether old or new shipping descriptions and package markings are used.

(3) *Until October 1, 2003,* the KEEP AWAY FROM FOOD labeling and placarding requirements in effect on September 30, 1999, may continue to be used in place of the new requirements for Division 6.1, Packing Group III materials.

(4) *Until January 1, 2010,* a hazardous material may be transported in an IM or IMO portable tank in accordance with the T Codes (Special Provisions) assigned to a hazardous material in Column (7) of the HMT in effect on September 30, 2001. (See §173.32(c) of this subchapter for the continued use and manufacture of portable tanks.)

(5) *Until October 1, 2005,* proper shipping names that included the word "inhibited" prior to the June 21, 2001 final rule in effect on October 1, 2001, may continue to be shown on packagings in place of "stabilized."

(e) **A Division 6.2 label conforming to specifications** in §172.432 of this subchapter in effect on September 30, 2002, may be used until October 1, 2005.

FEDERAL REGISTER UPDATES

In the March 25, 2003 Federal Register, paragraph (f) was added to §171.14, effective October 1, 2003.

(f) **49 CFR 175.33 sets out requirements** regarding the availability of information for hazardous materials transported by aircraft. Until October 1, 2004, a person may elect to comply with either the applicable requirements of 49 CFR 175.33 in effect on September 30, 2003, and contained in 49 CFR Part 175 revised as of October 1, 2002, or the requirements of that section contained in 49 CFR Part 175 revised as of October 1, 2003. On October 1, 2004, all applicable regulatory requirements in 49 CFR 175.33 in effect on October 1, 2003 must be met.

§171.15 Immediate notice of certain hazardous materials incidents.

(a) **At the earliest practicable moment,** each carrier who transports hazardous materials (including hazardous wastes) shall give notice in accordance with paragraph (b) of this section after each incident that occurs during the course of transportation (including loading, unloading and temporary storage) in which —

(1) *As a direct result of hazardous materials —*

(i) *A person is killed; or*

(ii) *A person receives injuries requiring his or her hospitalization; or*

(iii) *Estimated carrier or other property damage exceeds $50,000; or*

(iv) *An evacuation* of the general public occurs lasting one or more hours; or

(v) *One or more* major transportation arteries or facilities are closed or shut down for one hour or more; or

(vi) *The operational flight pattern or routine of an aircraft is altered; or*

(2) *Fire, breakage,* spillage, or suspected radioactive contamination occurs involving shipment of radioactive material; or

(3) *Fire, breakage,* spillage, or suspected contamination occurs involving shipment of infectious substances; or

(4) *There has been* a release of a marine pollutant in a quantity exceeding 450 L (119 gallons) for liquids or 400 kg (882 pounds) for solids; or

(5) *A situation exists* of such a nature (e.g., a continuing danger to life exists at the scene of the incident) that, in the judgment of the carrier, it should be reported to the National Response Center even though it does not meet the criteria of paragraph (a) (1), (2) or (3) of this section.

(b) **Except for transportation by aircraft,** each notice required by paragraph (a) of this section shall be given to the National Response Center by telephone (toll-free) on 800-424-8802. Notice involving shipments transported by aircraft must be given to the nearest FAA Civil Aviation Security Office by telephone at the earliest practical moment after each incident in place of the notice to the National Response Center. Notice involving infectious substances may be given to the Director, Centers for Disease Control, U.S. Public Health Service, Atlanta, Ga. (800) 232-0124, in place of the notice to the National Response Center or (toll call) on 202-267-2675; however, a written report is still required as stated in paragraph (c) of this section. Each notice must include the following information:

(1) *Name of reporter.*

(2) *Name and address of carrier represented by reporter.*

(3) *Phone number where reporter can be contacted.*

(4) *Date, time, and location of incident.*

(5) *The extent of injuries, if any.*

(6) *Classification, name, and quantity* of hazardous materials involved, if such information is available.

(7) *Type of incident* and nature of hazardous material involvement and whether a continuing danger to life exists at the scene.

(c) **Each carrier making a report under this section** shall also make the report required by §171.16.

NOTE: Under 40 CFR 302.6 EPA requires persons in charge of facilities (including transport vehicles, vessels and aircraft) to report any release of a hazardous substance in a quantity equal to or greater than its reportable quantity, as soon as that person has knowledge of the release, to the U.S. Coast Guard National Response Center at (toll free) 800-424-8802 or (toll) 202-267-2675.

§171.16 Detailed hazardous materials incident reports.

(a) **Each carrier who transports hazardous materials** shall report in writing, in duplicate, on DOT Form F 5800.1 (Rev. 6/89) to the Department within 30 days of the date of discovery, each incident that occurs during the course of transportation (including loading, unloading, and temporary storage) in which any of the circumstances set forth in 171.15(a) occurs or there has been an unintentional release of hazardous materials from a package (including a tank) or any quantity of hazardous waste has been discharged during transportation. If a report pertains to a hazardous waste discharge:

(1) *A copy* of the hazardous waste manifest for the waste must be attached to the report; and

(2) *An estimate* of the quantity of the waste removed from the scene, the name and address of the facility to which it was taken, and the manner of disposition of any removed waste must be entered in Section IX of the report form (Form F 5800.1) (Rev. 6/89).

(b) **Each carrier making a report under this section** shall send the report to the Information Systems Manager, DHM-63, Research and Special Programs Administration, Department of Transportation, Washington, DC 20590-0001; a copy of the report shall be retained, for a period of two years, at the carrier's principal place of business, or at other places as authorized and approved in writing by an agency of the Department of Transportation.

(c) **Except as provided in paragraph (d) of this section,** the requirements of paragraph (a) of this section do not apply to incidents involving the unintentional release of a hazardous material —

(1) *Transported under one of the following proper shipping names:*

(i) *Consumer commodity.*

(ii) *Battery, electric storage, wet, filled with acid or alkali.*

(iii) *Paint and paint-related material* when shipped in a packaging of five gallons or less.

(2) *Prepared and transported* as a limited quantity shipment in accordance with this subchapter.

(d) **The exceptions to incident reporting** provided in paragraph (c) of this section do not apply to:

(1) *Incidents required to be reported under 171.15(a);*

(2) *Incidents involving transportation aboard aircraft;*

(3) *Except for consumer commodities, materials in Packing Group I; or*

(4) *Incidents involving the transportation of hazardous waste.*

NOTE: A guideline document for assisting in the completion of DOT Form F 5800.1 (Rev. 6/89) may be obtained from the Office of Hazardous Materials Transportation, DHM-51, U.S. Department of Transportation, Washington, DC 20590-0001.

§§171.17-171.18 [Reserved]

§171.19 Approvals or authorizations issued by the Bureau of Explosives.

Effective December 31, 1998, approvals or authorizations issued by the Bureau of Explosives (BOE), other than those issued under part 179 of this subchapter, are no longer valid.

§171.20 Submission of Examination Reports.

(a) **When it is required in this subchapter** that the issuance of an approval by the Associate Administrator be based on an examination by the Bureau of Explosives (or any other test facility recognized by RSPA), it is the responsibility of the applicant to submit the results of the examination to the Associate Administrator.

(b) **Applications for approval submitted** under paragraph (a) of this section, must be submitted to the Associate Administrator for Hazardous Materials Safety, Research and Special Programs Administration, Washington, DC 20590-0001.

(c) **Any applicant for an approval aggrieved** by an action taken by the Associate Administrator, under this subpart may file an appeal with the Administrator, RSPA within 30 days of service of notification of a denial.

§171.21 Assistance in investigations and special studies.

(a) **A carrier who is responsible for reporting** an incident under the provisions of §171.16 shall make all records and information pertaining to the incident available to an authorized representative or special agent of the Department upon request. The carrier shall give an authorized representative or special agent of the Department reasonable assistance in the investigation of the incident.

(b) **If the Department makes an inquiry** to a carrier of hazardous materials in connection with a study of incidents, the carrier shall —

(1) *Respond to the inquiry* within 30 days after its receipt or within such other time as the inquiry may specify; and

(2) *Provide full,* true, and correct answers to any questions included in the inquiry.

Part 172 - Hazardous Materials Table, Special Provisions, Hazardous Materials Communications, Emergency Response Information, and Training Requirements

Subpart A - General

§172.1 Purpose and scope.

This part lists and classifies those materials which the Department has designated as hazardous materials for purposes of transportation and prescribes the requirements for shipping papers, package marking, labeling, and transport vehicle placarding applicable to the shipment and transportation of those hazardous materials.

§172.3 Applicability.

(a) This part applies to —

(1) *Each person* who offers a hazardous material for transportation, and

(2) *Each carrier* by air, highway, rail, or water who transports a hazardous material.

(b) When a person, other than one of those provided for in paragraph (a) of this section, performs a packaging labeling or marking function required by this part, that person shall perform the function in accordance with this part.

Subpart B - Table of Hazardous Materials and Special Provisions

§172.101 Purpose and use of hazardous materials table.

(a) The Hazardous Materials Table (Table) in this section designates the materials listed therein as hazardous materials for the purpose of transportation of those materials. For each listed material, the Table identifies the hazard class or specifies that the material is forbidden in transportation, and gives the proper shipping name or directs the user to the preferred proper shipping name. In addition, the Table specifies or references requirements in this subchapter pertaining to labeling, packaging, quantity limits aboard aircraft and stowage of hazardous materials aboard vessels.

(b) Column 1: Symbols. Column 1 of the Table contains six symbols ("+", "A", "D", "G", "I" and "W") as follows:

(1) *The plus (+) sign* fixes the proper shipping name, hazard class and packing group for that entry without regard to whether the material meets the definition of that class, packing group or any other hazard class definition. When the plus sign is assigned to a proper shipping name in Column (1) of the §172.101 Table, it means that the material is known to pose a risk to humans. When a plus sign is assigned to mixtures or solutions containing a material where the hazard to humans is significantly different from that of the pure material or where no hazard to humans is posed, the material may be described using an alternative shipping name that represents the hazards posed by the material. An appropriate alternate proper shipping name and hazard class may be authorized by the Associate Administrator.

(2) *The letter "A"* denotes a material that is subject to the requirements of this subchapter only when offered or intended for transportation by aircraft, unless the material is a hazardous substance or a hazardous waste. A shipping description entry preceded by an "A" may be used to describe a material for other modes of transportation provided all applicable requirements for the entry are met.

(3) *The letter "D"* identifies proper shipping names which are appropriate for describing materials for domestic transportation but may be inappropriate for international transportation under the provisions of international regulations (e.g., IMO, ICAO). An alternate proper shipping name may be selected when either domestic or international transportation is involved.

(4) *The letter "G"* identifies proper shipping names for which one or more technical names of the hazardous material must be entered in parentheses, in association with the basic description. (See §172.203(k).)

(5) *The letter "I"* identifies proper shipping names which are appropriate for describing materials in international transportation. An alternate proper shipping name may be selected when only domestic transportation is involved.

(6) *The letter "W"* denotes a material that is subject to the requirements of this subchapter only when offered or intended for transportation by vessel, unless the material is a hazardous substance or a hazardous waste. A shipping description entry preceded by a "W" may be used to describe a material for other modes of transportation provided all applicable requirements for the entry are met.

(c) Column 2: Hazardous materials descriptions and proper shipping names. Column 2 lists the hazardous materials descriptions and proper shipping names of materials designated as hazardous materials. Modification of a proper shipping name may otherwise be required or authorized by this section. Proper shipping names are limited to those shown in Roman type (not italics).

(1) *Proper shipping names* may be used in the singular or plural and in either capital or lower case letters. Words may be alternatively spelled in the same manner as they appear in the ICAO Technical Instructions or the IMDG Code. For example "aluminum" may be spelled "aluminium" and "sulfur" may be spelled "sulphur". However, the word "inflammable" may not be used in place of the word "flammable".

(2) *Punctuation marks* and words in italics are not part of the proper shipping name, but may be used in addition to the proper shipping name. The word "or" in italics indicates that terms in the sequence may be used as the proper shipping name, as appropriate.

(3) *The word "poison" or "poisonous"* may be used interchangeably with the word "toxic" when only domestic transportation is involved. The abbreviation "n.o.i." or "n.o.i.b.n." may be used interchangeably with "n.o.s.".

(4) *Except for hazardous wastes,* when qualifying words are used as part of the proper shipping name, their sequence in the package markings and shipping paper description is optional. However, the entry in the Table reflects the preferred sequence.

(5) *When one entry* references another entry by use of the word "see", if both names are in Roman type, either name may be used as the proper shipping name (e.g., Ethyl alcohol, see Ethanol).

(6) *When a proper shipping name* includes a concentration range as part of the shipping description, the actual concentration, if it is within the range stated, may be used in place of the concentration range. For example, an aqueous solution of hydrogen peroxide containing 30 percent peroxide may be described as "Hydrogen peroxide, aqueous solution with not less than 20 percent but not more than 40 percent hydrogen peroxide" or "Hydrogen peroxide, aqueous solution with 30 percent hydrogen peroxide".

(7) *Use of the prefix "mono"* is optional in any shipping name, when appropriate. Thus, Iodine monochloride may be used interchangeably with Iodine chloride. In "Glycerol alpha-monochlorohydrin" the term "mono" is considered a prefix to the term "chlorohydrin" and may be deleted.

(8) *Use of the word "liquid" or "solid".* The word "liquid" or "solid" may be added to a proper shipping name when a hazardous material specifically listed by name may, due to differing physical states, be a liquid or solid. When the packaging specified in Column 8 is inappropriate for the physical state of the material, the table provided in paragraph (i)(4) of this section should be used to determine the appropriate packaging section.

(9) *Hazardous wastes.* If the word "waste" is not included in the hazardous material description in Column 2 of the Table, the proper shipping name for a hazardous waste (as defined in §171.8 of this subchapter), shall include the word "Waste" preceding the proper shipping name of the material. For example: Waste acetone.

(10) *Mixtures and solutions.*

(i) *A mixture or solution* not identified specifically by name, comprised of a hazardous material identified in the Table by technical name and non-hazardous material, shall be described using the proper shipping name of the hazardous material and the qualifying word "mixture" or "solution", as appropriate, unless —

[A] Except as provided in §172.101(i)(4) the packaging specified in Column 8 is inappropriate to the physical state of the material;

[B] The shipping description indicates that the proper shipping name applies only to the pure or technically pure hazardous material;

[C] The hazard class, packing group, or subsidiary hazard of the mixture or solution is different from that specified for the entry;

[D] There is a significant change in the measures to be taken in emergencies;

[E] The material is identified by special provision in Column 7 of the §172.101 Table as a material poisonous by inhalation; however, it no longer meets the definition of poisonous by inhalation or it falls within a different hazard zone than that specified in the special provision; or

[F] The material can be appropriately described by a shipping name that describes its intended application, such as "Coating solution", "Extracts, flavoring" or "Compound, cleaning liquid".

(ii) *If one or more* of the conditions specified in paragraph (c)(10)(i) of this section is satisfied, then a proper shipping name shall be selected as prescribed in paragraph (c)(12)(ii) of this section.

(iii) *A mixture or solution* not identified in the Table specifically by name, comprised of two or more hazardous materials in the same hazard class, shall be described using an appropriate shipping description (e.g., "Flammable liquid, n.o.s."). The name that most appropriately describes the material shall be used; e.g., an alcohol not listed by its technical name in the Table shall be described as "Alcohol, n.o.s." rather than "Flammable liquid, n.o.s.". Some mixtures may be more appropriately described according to their application, such as "Coating solution" or "Extracts, flavoring liquid" rather than by an n.o.s. entry. Under the provisions of subparts C and D of this part, the technical names of at least two components most predominately contributing to the hazards of the mixture or solution may be required in association with the proper shipping name.

(11) *Except for a material* subject to or prohibited by §§173.21, 173.54, 173.56(d), 173.56(e), 173.224(c) or 173.225(c) of this subchapter, a material that is considered to be a hazardous waste or a sample of a material for which the hazard class is uncertain and must be determined by testing may be assigned a tentative proper shipping name, hazard class, identification number and packing group, if applicable, based on the shipper's tentative determination according to:

(i) *Defining criteria in this subchapter;*

(ii) *The hazard precedence prescribed in §173.2a of this subchapter;*

(iii) *The shippers knowledge of the material;*

(iv) *In addition* to paragraphs (c)(11)(i) through (iii) of this section, for a sample of a material, other than a waste, the following must be met:

[A] Except when the word "Sample" already appears in the proper shipping name, the word "Sample" must appear as part of the proper shipping name or in association with the basic description on the shipping paper;

[B] When the proper shipping description for a sample is assigned a "G" in Column (1) of the §172.101 Table, and the primary constituent(s) for which the tentative classification is based are not known, the provisions requiring a technical name for the constituent(s) do not apply; and

[C] A sample must be transported in a combination packaging which conforms to the requirements of this subchapter that are applicable to the tentative packing group assigned, and may not exceed a net mass of 2.5 kg. (5.5 pounds) per package.

Note to Paragraph (c)(11): For the transportation of self-reactive, organic peroxide and explosive samples, see §§173.224(c)(3), 173.225(c)(2) and 173.56(d) of this subchapter, respectively.

(12) *Except when* the proper shipping name in the Table is preceded by a plus (+) —

(i) *If it is specifically determined* that a material meets the definition of a hazard class, packing group or hazard zone, other than the class, packing group or hazard zone shown in association with the proper shipping name, or does not meet the defining criteria for a subsidiary hazard shown in Column 6 of the Table, the material shall be described by an appropriate proper shipping name listed in association with the correct hazard class, packing group, hazard zone, or subsidiary hazard for the material.

(ii) *Generic or n.o.s. descriptions.* If an appropriate technical name is not shown in the Table, selection of a proper shipping name shall be made from the generic or n.o.s. descriptions corresponding to the specific hazard class, packing group, hazard zone, or subsidiary hazard, if any, for the material. The name that most appropriately describes the material shall be used; e.g., an alcohol not listed by its technical name in the Table shall be described as "Alcohol, n.o.s." rather than "Flammable liquid, n.o.s.". Some mixtures may be more appropriately described according to their application, such as "Coating solution" or "Extracts, flavoring, liquid", rather than by an n.o.s. entry, such as "Flammable liquid, n.o.s." It should be noted, however, that an n.o.s. description as a proper shipping name may not provide sufficient information for shipping papers and package markings. Under the provisions of subparts C and D of this part, the technical name of one or more constituents which makes the product a hazardous material may be required in association with the proper shipping name.

(iii) *Multiple hazard materials.* If a material meets the definition of more than one hazard class, and is not identified in the Table specifically by name (e.g., acetyl chloride), the hazard class of the material shall be determined by using the precedence specified in §173.2a of this subchapter, and an appropriate shipping description (e.g., "Flammable liquid, corrosive n.o.s.") shall be selected as described in paragraph (c)(12)(ii) of this section.

(iv) *If it is specifically determined* that a material is not a forbidden material and does not meet the definition of any hazard class, the material is not a hazardous material.

(13) *Self-reactive materials and organic peroxides.* A generic proper shipping name for a self-reactive material or an organic peroxide, as listed in Column 2 of the Table, must be selected based on the material's technical name and concentration, in accordance with the provisions of §§173.224 or 173.225 of this subchapter, respectively.

(14) *A proper shipping name* that describes all isomers of a material may be used to identify any isomer of that material if the isomer meets criteria for the same hazard class or division, subsidiary risk(s) and packing group, unless the isomer is specifically identified in the Table.

(15) *Hydrates of inorganic substances* may be identified using the proper shipping name for the equivalent anhydrous substance if the hydrate meets the same hazard class or division, subsidiary risk(s) and packing group, unless the hydrate is specifically identified in the Table.

(16) *Unless it is already included* in the proper shipping name in the §172.101 Table, the qualifying words "liquid" or "solid" may be added in association with the proper shipping name when a hazardous material specifically listed by name in the §172.101 Table may, due to the differing physical states of the various isomers of the material, be either a liquid or a solid (for example "Dinitrotoluenes, liquid" and "Dinitrotoluenes, solid"). Use of the words "liquid" or "solid" is subject to the limitations specified for the use of the words "mixture" or "solution" in paragraph (c)(10) of this section. The qualifying word "molten" may be added in association with the proper shipping name when a hazardous material, which is a solid in accordance with the definition in §171.8 of this subchapter, is offered for transportation in the molten state (for example, "Alkylphenols, solid, n.o.s., molten").

(d) Column 3: Hazard class or Division. Column 3 contains a designation of the hazard class or division corresponding to each proper shipping name, or the word "Forbidden".

(1) *A material* for which the entry in this column is "Forbidden" may not be offered for transportation or transported. This prohibition does not apply if the material is diluted, stabilized or incorporated in a device and it is classed in accordance with the definitions of hazardous materials contained in part 173 of this subchapter.

(2) *When a reevaluation* of test data or new data indicates a need to modify the "Forbidden" designation or the hazard class or packing group specified for a material specifically identified in the Table, this data should be submitted to the Associate Administrator.

(3) *A basic description* of each hazard class and the section reference for class definitions appear in §173.2 of this subchapter.

(4) *Each reference* to a Class 3 material is modified to read "Combustible liquid" when that material is reclassified in accordance with §173.150 (e) or (f) of this subchapter or has a flash point above 60.5 °C (141 °F) but below 93 °C (200 °F).

(e) Column 4: Identification number. Column 4 lists the identification number assigned to each proper shipping name. Those preceded by the letters "UN" are associated with proper shipping names considered appropriate for international transportation as well as domestic transportation. Those preceded by the letters "NA" are associated with proper shipping names not recognized for international transportation, except to and from Canada. Identification numbers in the "NA9000" series are associated with proper shipping names not appropriately covered by international hazardous materials (dangerous goods) transportation standards, or not appropriately addressed by international transportation standards for emergency response information purposes, except for transportation between the United States and Canada.

(f) Column 5: Packing group. Column 5 specifies one or more packing groups assigned to a material corresponding to the proper shipping name and hazard class for that material. Class 2, Class 7, Division 6.2 (other than regulated medical wastes), and ORM-D materials, do not have packing groups. Packing Groups I, II and III indicate the degree of danger presented by the material is either great, medium or minor, respectively. If more than one packing group is indicated for an entry, the packing group for the hazardous material is determined using the criteria for assignment of packing groups specified in subpart D of part 173. When a reevaluation of test data or new data indicates a need to modify the specified packing group(s), the data should be submitted to the Associate Administrator. Each reference in this column to a material which is a hazardous waste or a hazardous substance, and whose proper shipping name is preceded in Column 1 of the Table by the letter "A" or "W", is modified to read "III" on those occasions when the material is offered for transportation or transported by a mode in which its transportation is not otherwise subject to requirements of this subchapter.

(g) **Column 6: Labels.** Column 6 specifies codes which represent the hazard warning labels required for a package filled with a material conforming to the associated hazard class and proper shipping name, unless the package is otherwise excepted from labeling by a provision in subpart E of this part, or part 173 of this subchapter. The first code is indicative of the primary hazard of the material. Additional label codes are indicative of subsidiary hazards. Provisions in §172.402 may require that a label other than that specified in Column 6 be affixed to the package in addition to that specified in Column 6. No label is required for a material classed as a combustible liquid or for a Class 3 material that is reclassed as a combustible liquid. For "Empty" label requirements, see §173.428 of this subchapter. The codes contained in Column 6 are defined according to the following table:

Label Substitution Table

Label code	Label name
1	Explosive
1.1[1]	Explosive 1.1[1]
1.2[1]	Explosive 1.2[1]
1.3[1]	Explosive 1.3[1]
1.4[1]	Explosive 1.4[1]
1.5[1]	Explosive 1.5[1]
1.6[1]	Explosive 1.6[1]
2.1	Flammable Gas
2.2	Non-Flammable Gas
2.3	Poison Gas
3	Flammable Liquid
4.1	Flammable Solid
4.2	Spontaneously Combustible
4.3	Dangerous When Wet
5.1	Oxidizer
5.2	Organic Peroxide
6.1 (inhalation hazard, Zone A or B)	Poison Inhalation Hazard
6.1 (other than inhalation hazard, Zone A or B)[2]	Poison
6.2	Infectious substance
7	Radioactive
8	Corrosive
9	Class 9

1. Refers to the appropriate compatibility group letter.
2. The packing group for a material is indicated in column 5 of the table.

(h) **Column 7: Special provisions.** Column 7 specifies codes for special provisions applicable to hazardous materials. When Column 7 refers to a special provision for a hazardous material, the meaning and requirements of that special provision are as set forth in §172.102 of this subpart.

(i) **Column 8: Packaging authorizations.** Columns 8A, 8B and 8C specify the applicable sections for exceptions, non-bulk packaging requirements and bulk packaging requirements, respectively, in part 173 of this subchapter. Columns 8A, 8B and 8C are completed in a manner which indicates that "§173." precedes the designated numerical entry. For example, the entry "202" in Column 8B associated with the proper shipping name "Gasoline" indicates that for this material conformance to non-bulk packaging requirements prescribed in §173.202 of this subchapter is required. When packaging requirements are specified, they are in addition to the standard requirements for all packagings prescribed in §173.24 of this subchapter and any other applicable requirements in subparts A and B of part 173 of this subchapter.

(1) *Exceptions.* Column 8A contains exceptions from some of the requirements of this subchapter. The referenced exceptions are in addition to those specified in subpart A of part 173 and elsewhere in this subchapter. A "None" in this column means no packaging exceptions are authorized, except as may be provided by special provisions in Column 7.

(2) *Non-bulk packaging.* Column 8B references the section in part 173 of this subchapter which prescribes packaging requirements for non-bulk packagings. A "None" in this column means non-bulk packagings are not authorized, except as may be provided by special provisions in Column 7. Each reference in this column to a material which is a hazardous waste or a hazardous substance, and whose proper shipping name is preceded in Column 1 of the Table by the letter "A" or "W", is modified to include "§173.203" or "§173.213", as appropriate for liquids and solids, respectively, on those occasions when the material is offered for transportation or transported by a mode in which its transportation is not otherwise subject to the requirements of this subchapter.

(3) *Bulk packaging.* Column 8C specifies the section in part 173 of this subchapter which prescribes packaging requirements for bulk packagings, subject to the limitations, requirements and additional authorizations of Column 7. A "None" in this column means bulk packagings are not authorized, except as may be provided by special provisions in Column 7. Additional authorizations and limitations for use of IM portable tanks are set forth in Column 7. For each reference in this column to a material which is a hazardous waste or a hazardous substance, and whose proper shipping name is preceded in Column 1 of the Table by the letter "A" or "W" and which is offered for transportation or transported by a mode in which its transportation is not otherwise subject to the requirements of this subchapter:

(i) *The column reference is §173.240 or §173.241, as appropriate.*

(ii) *For a solid material,* the exception provided in Special provision B54 is applicable.

(iii) *For a Class 9 material* which meets the definition of an elevated temperature material, the column reference is §173.247.

(4) *For a hazardous material* which is specifically named in the Table and whose packaging sections specify packagings not applicable to the form of the material (e.g., packaging specified is for solid material and the material is being offered for transportation in a liquid form) the following table should be used to determine the appropriate packaging section:

Packaging section reference for solid materials	Corresponding packaging section for liquid materials
§173.187	§173.181
§173.211	§173.201
§173.212	§173.202
§173.213	§173.203
§173.240	§173.241
§173.242	§173.243

(j) **Column 9: Quantity limitations.** Columns 9A and 9B specify the maximum quantities that may be offered for transportation in one package by passenger-carrying aircraft or passenger-carrying rail car (Column 9A) or by cargo aircraft only (Column 9B), subject to the following:

(1) *"Forbidden"* means the material may not be offered for transportation or transported in the applicable mode of transport.

(2) *The quantity limitation* is "net" except where otherwise specified, such as for "Consumer commodity" which specifies "30 kg gross."

(3) *When articles or devices* are specifically listed by name, the net quantity limitation applies to the entire article or device (less packaging and packaging materials) rather than only to its hazardous components.

(4) *A package* offered or intended for transportation by aircraft and which is filled with a material forbidden on passenger-carrying aircraft but permitted on cargo aircraft only, or which exceeds the maximum net quantity authorized on passenger-carrying aircraft, shall be labelled with the CARGO AIRCRAFT ONLY label specified in §172.448 of this part.

(5) *The total net quantity* of hazardous material for an outer non-bulk packaging that contains more than one hazardous material may not exceed the lowest permitted maximum net quantity per package as shown in Column 9A or 9B, as appropriate. If one material is a liquid and one is a solid, the maximum net quantity must be calculated in kilograms. See §173.24a(c)(1)(iv).

(k) **Column 10: Vessel stowage requirements.** Column 10A [Vessel stowage] specifies the authorized stowage locations on board cargo and passenger vessels. Column 10B [Other provisions] specifies codes for stowage requirements for specific hazardous materials. The meaning of each code in Column 10B is set forth in §176.84 of this subchapter. Section 176.63 of this subchapter sets forth the physical requirements for each of the authorized locations listed in Column 10A. (For bulk transportation by vessel, see 46 CFR parts 30 to 40, 70, 98, 148, 151, 153 and 154.) The authorized stowage locations specified in Column 10A are defined as follows:

(1) **Stowage category "A"** means the material may be stowed "on deck" or "under deck" on a cargo vessel and on a passenger vessel.

(2) **Stowage category "B"** means —

(i) *The material* may be stowed "on deck" or "under deck" on a cargo vessel and on a passenger vessel carrying a number of passengers limited to not more than the larger of 25 passengers, or one passenger per each 3 m of overall vessel length; and

(ii) *"On deck only"* on passenger vessels in which the number of passengers specified in paragraph (k)(2)(i) of this section is exceeded.

(3) **Stowage category "C"** means the material must be stowed "on deck only" on a cargo vessel and on a passenger vessel.

(4) **Stowage category "D"** means the material must be stowed "on deck only" on a cargo vessel and on a passenger vessel carrying a number of passengers limited to not more than the larger of 25 passengers or one passenger per each 3 m of overall vessel length, but the material is prohibited on passenger vessels in which the limiting number of passengers is exceeded.

(5) **Stowage category "E"** means the material may be stowed "on deck" or "under deck" on a cargo vessel and on a passenger vessel carrying a number of passengers limited to not more than the larger of 25 passengers, or one passenger per each 3 m of overall vessel length, but is prohibited from carriage on passenger vessels in which the limiting number of passengers is exceeded.

(6) **Stowage category "01"** means the material may be stowed "on deck" or "under deck" on a cargo vessel (up to 12 passengers) and on a passenger vessel.

(7) **Stowage category "02"** means the material may be stowed "on deck" or "under deck" on a cargo vessel (up to 12 passengers) and "on deck" in closed cargo transport units or "under deck" in closed cargo transport units on a passenger vessel.

(8) **Stowage category "03"** means the material may be stowed "on deck" or "under deck" on a cargo vessel (up to 12 passengers) and "on deck" in closed cargo transport units on a passenger vessel.

(9) **Stowage category "04"** means the material may be stowed "on deck" or "under deck" on a cargo vessel (up to 12 passengers) but the material is prohibited on a passenger vessel.

(10) **Stowage category "05"** means the material may be stowed "on deck" in closed cargo transport units or "under deck" on a cargo vessel (up to 12 passengers) and on a passenger vessel.

(11) **Stowage category "06"** means the material may be stowed "on deck" in closed cargo transport units or "under deck" on a cargo vessel (up to 12 passengers) and "on deck" in closed cargo transport units or "under deck" in closed cargo transport units on a passenger vessel.

(12) **Stowage category "07"** means the material may be stowed "on deck" in closed cargo transport units or "under deck" on a cargo vessel (up to 12 passengers) and "on deck" only in closed cargo transport units on a passenger vessel.

(13) **Stowage category "08"** means the material may be stowed "on deck" in closed cargo transport units or "under deck" on a cargo vessel (up to 12 passengers) but the material is prohibited on a passenger vessel.

(14) **Stowage category "09"** means the material may be stowed "on deck only" in closed cargo transport units or "under deck" in closed cargo transport units on a cargo vessel (up to 12 passengers) and on a passenger vessel.

(15) **Stowage category "10"** means the material may be stowed "on deck" in closed cargo transport units or "under deck" in closed cargo transport units on a cargo vessel (up to 12 passengers) and "on deck" only in closed cargo transport units on a passenger vessel.

(16) **Stowage category "11"** means the material may be stowed "on deck" in closed cargo transport units or "under deck" in magazine stowage type "c" on a cargo vessel (up to 12 passengers) and "on deck" only in closed cargo transport units on a passenger vessel.

(17) **Stowage category "12"** means the material may be stowed "on deck" in closed cargo transport units or "under deck" in magazine stowage type "c" on a cargo vessel (up to 12 passengers) but the material is prohibited on a passenger vessel.

(18) **Stowage category "13"** means the material may be stowed "on deck" in closed cargo transport units or "under deck" in magazine stowage type "A" on a cargo vessel (up to 12 passengers) and "on deck" only in closed cargo transport units on a passenger vessel.

(19) **Stowage category "14"** means the material may be stowed "on deck" in closed cargo transport units on a cargo vessel (up to 12 passengers) but the material is prohibited on a passenger vessel.

(20) **Stowage category "15"** means the material may be stowed "on deck" in closed cargo transport units or "under deck" in closed cargo transport units on a cargo vessel (up to 12 passengers) but the material is prohibited on a passenger vessel.

(l) **Changes to the Table.**

(1) *Unless specifically stated otherwise* in a rule document published in the Federal Register amending the Table —

(i) *Such a change* does not apply to the shipment of any package filled prior to the effective date of the amendment; and

(ii) *Stocks of preprinted* shipping papers and package markings may be continued in use, in the manner previously authorized, until depleted or for a one-year period, subsequent to the effective date of the amendment, whichever is less.

(2) *Except as otherwise provided* in this section, any alteration of a shipping description or associated entry which is listed in the §172.101 Table must receive prior written approval from the Associate Administrator.

(3) *The proper shipping name* of a hazardous material changed in the May 6, 1997 final rule, in effect on October 1, 1997, only by the addition or omission of the word "compressed," "inhibited," "liquefied" or "solution" may continue to be used to comply with package marking requirements, until January 1, 2003.

§172.101 - Hazardous Materials Table

Symbols	Hazardous materials descriptions and proper shipping names	Hazard class or Division	Identification Numbers	PG	Label Codes	Special provisions (§172.102)	(8) Packaging (§173.***)			(9) Quantity limitations		(10) Vessel stowage	
							Exceptions	Non-bulk	Bulk	Passenger aircraft/rail	Cargo aircraft only	Location	Other
(1)	(2)	(3)	(4)	(5)	(6)	(7)	(8A)	(8B)	(8C)	(9A)	(9B)	(10A)	(10B)
	Accellerene, see **p-Nitrosodimethylaniline**												
	Accumulators, electric, see **Batteries, wet** *etc.*												
	Acetal	3	UN1088	II	3	IB2, T4, TP1	150	202	242	5 L	60 L	E	
	Acetaldehyde	3	UN1089	I	3	A3, B16, T11, TP2, TP7	None	201	243	Forbidden	30 L	E	
A	**Acetaldehyde ammonia**	9	UN1841	III	9	IB8, IP6	155	204	240	200 kg	200 kg	A	34
	Acetaldehyde oxime	3	UN2332	III	3	B1, IB3, T4, TP1	150	203	242	60 L	220 L	A	
	Acetic acid, glacial *or* **Acetic acid solution,** *with more than 80 percent acid, by mass*	8	UN2789	II	8, 3	A3, A6, A7, A10, B2, IB2, T7, TP2	154	202	243	1 L	30 L	A	
	Acetic acid solution, *not less than 50 percent but not more than 80 percent acid, by mass*	8	UN2790	II	8	A3, A6, A7, A10, B2, IB2, T7, TP2	154	202	242	1 L	30 L	A	
	Acetic acid solution, *with more than 10 percent and less than 50 percent acid, by mass*	8	UN2790	III	8	IB3, T4, TP1	154	203	242	5 L	60 L	A	
	Acetic anhydride	8	UN1715	II	8, 3	A3, A6, A7, A10, B2, IB2, T7, TP2	154	202	243	1 L	30 L	A	40
	Acetone	3	UN1090	II	3	IB2, T4, TP1	150	202	242	5 L	60 L	B	
	Acetone cyanohydrin, stabilized	6.1	UN1541	I	6.1	2, A3, B9, B14, B32, B76, B77, N34, T20, TP2, TP13, TP38, TP45	None	227	244	Forbidden	Forbidden	D	25, 40, 49
	Acetone oils	3	UN1091	II	3	IB2, T4, TP1, TP8	150	202	242	5 L	60 L	B	
	Acetonitrile	3	UN1648	II	3	IB2, T7, TP2	150	202	242	5L	60 L	B	40
	Acetyl acetone peroxide with more than 9 percent by mass active oxygen	Forbidden											
	Acetyl benzoyl peroxide, solid, or with more than 40 percent in solution	Forbidden											
	Acetyl bromide	8	UN1716	II	8	B2, IB2, T8, TP2, TP12	154	202	242	1 L	30 L	C	40
	Acetyl chloride	3	UN1717	II	3, 8	A3, A6, A7, IB1, N34, T8, TP2, TP12	None	202	243	1 L	5 L	B	40
	Acetyl cyclohexanesulfonyl peroxide, with more than 82 percent wetted with less than 12 percent water	Forbidden											
	Acetyl iodide	8	UN1898	II	8	B2, IB2, T7, TP2, TP13	154	202	242	1 L	30 L	C	40
	Acetyl methyl carbinol	3	UN2621	III	3	B1, IB3, T2, TP1	150	203	242	60 L	220 L	A	
	Acetyl peroxide, solid, or with more than 25 percent in solution	Forbidden											
	Acetylene, dissolved	2.1	UN1001		2.1		None	303	None	Forbidden	15 kg	D	25, 40, 57
	Acetylene (liquefied)	Forbidden											
	Acetylene silver nitrate	Forbidden											
	Acetylene tetrabromide, see **Tetrabromoethane**												
	Acid butyl phosphate, see **Butyl acid phosphate**												
	Acid, sludge, *see* **Sludge acid**												
	Acridine	6.1	UN2713	III	6.1	IB8, IP3	153	213	240	100 kg	200 kg	A	
	Acrolein dimer, stabilized	3	UN2607	III	3	B1, IB3, T2, TP1	150	203	242	60 L	220 L	A	40
	Acrolein, stabilized	6.1	UN1092	I	6.1, 3	1, B9, B14, B30, B42, B72, B77, T22, TP2, TP7, TP13, TP38, TP44	None	226	244	Forbidden	Forbidden	D	40
	Acrylamide	6.1	UN2074	III	6.1	IB8, IP3, T4, TP1	153	213	240	100 kg	200 kg	A	12
	Acrylic acid, stabilized	8	UN2218	II	8, 3	B2, IB2, T7, TP2	154	202	243	1 L	30 L	C	25, 40
	Acrylonitrile, stabilized	3	UN1093	I	3, 6.1	B9, T14, TP2, TP13	None	201	243	Forbidden	30 L	E	40
	Actuating cartridge, explosive, see **Cartridges, power device**												

§172.101 - Hazardous Materials Table

Symbols	Hazardous materials descriptions and proper shipping names	Hazard class or Division	Identification Numbers	PG	Label Codes	Special provisions (§172.102)	(8) Packaging (§173.***) Exceptions	Non-bulk	Bulk	(9) Quantity limitations Passenger aircraft/rail	Cargo aircraft only	(10) Vessel stowage Location	Other
(1)	(2)	(3)	(4)	(5)	(6)	(7)	(8A)	(8B)	(8C)	(9A)	(9B)	(10A)	(10B)
	Adhesives, *containing a flammable liquid*	3	UN1133	I	3	B42, T11, TP1, TP8, TP27	150	201	243	1 L	30 L	B	
				II	3	B52, IB2, T4, TP1, TP8	150	173	242	5 L	60 L	B	
				III	3	B1, B52, IB3, T2, TP1	150	173	242	60 L	220 L	A	
	Adiponitrile	6.1	UN2205	III	6.1	IB3, T3, TP1	153	203	241	60 L	220 L	A	
	Aerosols, *corrosive, Packing Group II or III, (each not exceeding 1 L capacity)*	2.2	UN1950		2.2, 8	A34	306	None	None	75 kg	150 kg	A	40, 48, 85
	Aerosols, *flammable, (each not exceeding 1 L capacity)*	2.1	UN1950		2.1	N82	306	None	None	75 kg	150 kg	A	40, 48, 85
	Aerosols, flammable, n.o.s. *(engine starting fluid) (each not exceeding 1 L capacity)*	2.1	UN1950		2.1	N82	306	None	None	Forbidden	150 kg	A	40, 48, 85
	Aerosols, *non-flammable, (each not exceeding 1 L capacity)*	2.2	UN1950		2.2		306, 307	None	None	75 kg	150 kg	A	48, 85
	Aerosols, *poison, each not exceeding 1 L capacity*	2.2	UN1950		2.2		306	None	None	Forbidden	Forbidden	A	40, 48, 85
	Air bag inflators, compressed gas *or* **Air bag modules, compressed gas** *or* **Seat-belt pretensioners, compressed gas**	2.2	UN3353		2.2	133	166	166	166	75 kg	150 kg	A	
	Air bag inflators, *pyrotechnic or* **Air bag modules,** *pyrotechnic or* **Seat-belt pretensioner,** *pyrotechnic*	1.4G	UN0503	II	1.4G		166	166	166	Forbidden	75 kg	02	24E
	Air bag inflators, *pyrotechnic or* **Air bag modules,** *pyrotechnic or* **Seat-belt pretensioner,** *pyrotechnic*	9	UN3268	III	9		166	166	166	25 kg	100 kg	A	
	Air, compressed	2.2	UN1002		2.2	78	306	302	302	75 kg	150 kg	A	
	Air, refrigerated liquid, *(cryogenic liquid)*	2.2	UN1003		2.2, 5.1	T75, TP5, TP22	320	316	318, 319	Forbidden	150 kg	D	51
	Air, refrigerated liquid, *(cryogenic liquid) non-pressurized*	2.2	UN1003		2.2, 5.1	T75, TP5, TP22	320	316	318, 319	Forbidden	Forbidden	D	51
	Aircraft engines (including turbines), see **Engines, internal combustion**												
	Aircraft evacuation slides, see **Life saving appliances** *etc.*												
	Aircraft hydraulic power unit fuel tank *(containing a mixture of anhydrous hydrazine and monomethyl hydrazine) (M86 fuel)*	3	UN3165	I	3, 6.1, 8		None	172	None	Forbidden	42 L	E	
	Aircraft survival kits, see **Life saving appliances** *etc.*												
G	**Alcoholates solution, n.o.s.,** *in alcohol*	3	UN3274	II	3, 8	IB2	None	202	243	1 L	5 L	B	
	Alcoholic beverages	3	UN3065	II	3	24, B1, IB2, T4, TP1	150	202	242	5 L	60 L	A	
				III	3	24, B1, IB3, N11, T2, TP1	150	203	242	60 L	220 L	A	
	Alcohols, n.o.s.	3	UN1987	I	3	T11, TP1, TP8, TP27	None	201	243	1 L	30 L	E	
				II	3	IB2, T7, TP1, TP8, TP28	150	202	242	5 L	60 L	B	
				III	3	B1, IB3, T4, TP1, TP29	150	203	242	60 L	220 L	A	
G	**Alcohols, flammable, toxic, n.o.s.**	3	UN1986	I	3, 6.1	T14, TP2, TP13, TP27	None	201	243	Forbidden	30 L	E	40
				II	3, 6.1	IB2, T11, TP2, TP27	None	202	243	1 L	60 L	B	40
				III	3, 6.1	B1, IB3, T7, TP1, TP28	None	203	242	60 L	220 L	A	
	Aldehydes, n.o.s.	3	UN1989	I	3	T11, TP1, TP27	None	201	243	1 L	30 L	E	
				II	3	IB2, T7, TP1, TP8, TP28	150	202	242	5 L	60 L	B	
				III	3	B1, IB3, T4, TP1, TP29	150	203	242	60 L	220 L	A	

§172.101 - Hazardous Materials Table

Symbols	Hazardous materials descriptions and proper shipping names	Hazard class or Division	Identification Numbers	PG	Label Codes	Special provisions (§172.102)	(8) Packaging (§173.***)			(9) Quantity limitations		(10) Vessel stowage	
							Exceptions	Non-bulk	Bulk	Passenger aircraft/ rail	Cargo aircraft only	Location	Other
(1)	(2)	(3)	(4)	(5)	(6)	(7)	(8A)	(8B)	(8C)	(9A)	(9B)	(10A)	(10B)
G	**Aldehydes, flammable, toxic, n.o.s.**	3	UN1988	I II III	3, 6.1 3, 6.1 3, 6.1	T14, TP2, TP13, TP27 IB2, T11, TP2, TP27 B1, IB3, T7, TP1, TP28	None None 150	201 202 203	243 243 242	Forbidden 1 L 60 L	30 L 60 L 220 L	E B A	40 40
	Aldol	6.1	UN2839	II	6.1	IB2, T7, TP2	None	202	243	5 L	60 L	A	12
G	**Alkali metal alcoholates, self-heating, corrosive, n.o.s.**	4.2	UN3206	II III	4.2, 8 4.2, 8	64, IB5, IP2 64, IB8, IP3	None None	212 213	242 242	15 kg 25 kg	50 kg 100 kg	B B	
	Alkali metal alloys, liquid, n.o.s.	4.3	UN1421	I	4.3	A2, A3, B48, N34	None	201	244	Forbidden	1 L	D	
	Alkali metal amalgam, liquid	4.3	UN1389	I	4.3	A2, A3, N34	None	201	244	Forbidden	1 L	D	40
	Alkali metal amalgam, solid	4.3	UN1389	I	4.3	IB4, IP1, N40	None	211	242	Forbidden	15 kg	D	
	Alkali metal amides	4.3	UN1390	II	4.3	A6, A7, A8, A19, A20, IB7, IP2	151	212	241	15 kg	50 kg	E	40
	Alkali metal dispersions, *or* **Alkaline earth metal dispersions**	4.3	UN1391	I	4.3	A2, A3	None	201	244	Forbidden	1 L	D	
	Alkaline corrosive liquids, n.o.s., see **Caustic alkali liquids, n.o.s.**												
G	**Alkaline earth metal alcoholates, n.o.s.**	4.2	UN3205	II III	4.2 4.2	65, IB6, IP2 65, IB8, IP3	None None	212 213	241 241	15 kg 25 kg	50 kg 100 kg	B B	
	Alkaline earth metal alloys, n.o.s.	4.3	UN1393	II	4.3	A19, IB7, IP2	151	212	241	15 kg	50 kg	E	
	Alkaline earth metal amalgams	4.3	UN1392	I	4.3	A19, IB4, IP1, N34, N40	None	211	242	Forbidden	15 kg	D	
G	**Alkaloids, liquid, n.o.s.,** *or* **Alkaloid salts, liquid, n.o.s.**	6.1	UN3140	I II III	6.1 6.1 6.1	A4, T14, TP2, TP27 IB2, T11, TP2, TP27 IB3, T7, TP1, TP28	None None 153	201 202 203	243 243 241	1 L 5 L 60 L	30 L 60 L 220 L	A A A	
G	**Alkaloids, solid, n.o.s.** *or* **Alkaloid salts, solid, n.o.s.** *poisonous*	6.1	UN1544	I II III	6.1 6.1 6.1	IB7, IP1 IB8, IP2, IP4 IB8, IP3	None None 153	211 212 213	242 242 240	5 kg 25 kg 100 kg	50 kg 100 kg 200 kg	A A A	
	Alkyl sulfonic acids, liquid *or* **Aryl sulfonic acids, liquid** *with more than 5 percent free sulfuric acid*	8	UN2584	II	8	B2, IB2, T8, TP2, TP12, TP13	154	202	242	1 L	30 L	B	
	Alkyl sulfonic acids, liquid *or* **Aryl sulfonic acids, liquid** *with not more than 5 percent free sulfuric acid*	8	UN2586	III	8	IB3, T4, TP1	154	203	241	5 L	60 L	B	
	Alkyl sulfonic acids, solid *or* **Aryl sulfonic acids, solid,** *with more than 5 percent free sulfuric acid*	8	UN2583	II	8	IB8, IP2, IP4	154	212	240	15 kg	50 kg	A	
	Alkyl sulfonic acids, solid *or* **Aryl sulfonic acids, solid** *with not more than 5 percent free sulfuric acid*	8	UN2585	III	8	IB8, IP3	154	213	240	25 kg	100 kg	A	
	Alkylphenols, liquid, n.o.s. *(including C2-C12 homologues)*	8	UN3145	I II III	8 8 8	T14, TP2 IB2, T11, TP2, TP27 IB3, T7, TP1, TP28	None 154 154	201 202 203	243 242 241	0.5 L 1 L 5 L	2.5 L 30 L 60 L	B B A	
	Alkylphenols, solid, n.o.s. *(including C2-C12 homologues)*	8	UN2430	I II III	8 8 8	IB7, IP1, T10, TP2, TP28 IB8, IP2, IP4, T3, TP2 IB8, IP3, T3, TP1	None 154 154	211 212 213	242 240 240	1 kg 15 kg 25 kg	25 kg 50 kg 100 kg	B B A	
	Alkylsulfuric acids	8	UN2571	II	8	B2, IB2, T8, TP2, TP12, TP13	154	202	242	1 L	30 L	C	14
	Allethrin, see **Pesticides, liquid, toxic, n.o.s.**												
	Allyl acetate	3	UN2333	II	3, 6.1	IB2, T7, TP1, TP13	None	202	243	1 L	60 L	E	40
	Allyl alcohol	6.1	UN1098	I	6.1, 3	2, B9, B14, B32, B74, B77, T20, TP2, TP13, TP38, TP45	None	227	244	Forbidden	Forbidden	D	40
	Allyl bromide	3	UN1099	I	3, 6.1	T14, TP2, TP13	None	201	243	Forbidden	30 L	B	40
	Allyl chloride	3	UN1100	I	3, 6.1	T14, TP2, TP13	None	201	243	Forbidden	30 L	E	40
	Allyl chlorocarbonate, see **Allyl chloroformate**												

§172.101 - Hazardous Materials Table

Symbols	Hazardous materials descriptions and proper shipping names	Hazard class or Division	Identification Numbers	PG	Label Codes	Special provisions (§172.102)	(8) Packaging (§173.***)			(9) Quantity limitations		(10) Vessel stowage	
							Exceptions	Non-bulk	Bulk	Passenger aircraft/rail	Cargo aircraft only	Location	Other
(1)	(2)	(3)	(4)	(5)	(6)	(7)	(8A)	(8B)	(8C)	(9A)	(9B)	(10A)	(10B)
	Allyl chloroformate	6.1	UN1722	I	6.1, 3, 8	2, A3, B9, B14, B32, B74, N41, T20, TP2, TP13, TP38, TP45	None	227	244	Forbidden	Forbidden	D	40
	Allyl ethyl ether	3	UN2335	II	3, 6.1	IB2, T7, TP1, TP13	None	202	243	1 L	60 L	E	40
	Allyl formate	3	UN2336	I	3, 6.1	T14, TP2, TP13	None	201	243	Forbidden	30 L	E	40
	Allyl glycidyl ether	3	UN2219	III	3	B1, IB3, T2, TP1	150	203	242	60 L	220 L	A	
	Allyl iodide	3	UN1723	II	3, 8	A3, A6, IB1, N34, T7, TP2, TP13	None	202	243	1 L	5 L	B	40
	Allyl isothiocyanate, stabilized	6.1	UN1545	II	6.1, 3	A3, A7, IB2, T7, TP2	None	202	243	Forbidden	60 L	D	40
	Allylamine	6.1	UN2334	I	6.1, 3	2, B9, B14, B32, B74, T20, TP2, TP13, TP38, TP45	None	227	244	Forbidden	Forbidden	D	40
	Allyltrichlorosilane, stabilized	8	UN1724	II	8, 3	A7, B2, B6, IB2, N34, T7, TP2, TP13	None	202	243	Forbidden	30 L	C	40
	Aluminum alkyl halides	4.2	UN3052	I	4.2, 4.3	B9, B11, T21, TP2, TP7	None	181	244	Forbidden	Forbidden	D	
	Aluminum alkyl hydrides	4.2	UN3076	I	4.2, 4.3	B9, B11, T21, TP2, TP7	None	181	244	Forbidden	Forbidden	D	
	Aluminum alkyls	4.2	UN3051	I	4.2, 4.3	B9, B11, T21, TP2, TP7	None	181	244	Forbidden	Forbidden	D	
	Aluminum borohydride *or* **Aluminum borohydride in devices**	4.2	UN2870	I	4.2, 4.3	B11	None	181	244	Forbidden	Forbidden	D	
	Aluminum bromide, anhydrous	8	UN1725	II	8	IB8, IP2, IP4	154	212	240	15 kg	50 kg	A	40
	Aluminum bromide, solution	8	UN2580	III	8	IB3, T4, TP1	154	203	241	5 L	60 L	A	
	Aluminum carbide	4.3	UN1394	II	4.3	A20, IB7, IP2, N41	151	212	242	15 kg	50 kg	A	
	Aluminum chloride, anhydrous	8	UN1726	II	8	IB8, IP2, IP4	154	212	240	15 kg	50 kg	A	40
	Aluminum chloride, solution	8	UN2581	III	8	IB3, T4, TP1	154	203	241	5 L	60 L	A	
	Aluminum dross, wet or hot	Forbidden											
	Aluminum ferrosilicon powder	4.3	UN1395	II III	4.3, 6.1 4.3, 6.1	A19, IB5, IP2 A19, A20, IB4	151 151	212 213	242 241	15 kg 25 kg	50 kg 100 kg	A A	40, 85, 103 40, 85, 103
	Aluminum hydride	4.3	UN2463	I	4.3	A19, N40	None	211	242	Forbidden	15 kg	E	
D	**Aluminum, molten**	9	NA9260	III	9	IB3, T1, TP3	None	None	247	Forbidden	Forbidden	D	
	Aluminum nitrate	5.1	UN1438	III	5.1	A1, A29, IB8, IP3	152	213	240	25 kg	100 kg	A	
	Aluminum phosphate solution, see **Corrosive liquids,** *etc.*												
	Aluminum phosphide	4.3	UN1397	I	4.3, 6.1	A8, A19, N40	None	211	242	Forbidden	15 kg	E	40, 85
	Aluminum phosphide pesticides	6.1	UN3048	I	6.1	A8, IB7, IP1	None	211	242	Forbidden	15 kg	E	40, 85
	Aluminum powder, coated	4.1	UN1309	II III	4.1 4.1	IB8, IP2, IP4 IB8, IP3	151 151	212 213	240 240	15 kg 25 kg	50 kg 100 kg	A A	13, 39, 101 13, 39, 101
	Aluminum powder, uncoated	4.3	UN1396	II III	4.3 4.3	A19, A20, IB7, IP2 A19, A20, IB8, IP4	151 151	212 213	242 241	15 kg 25 kg	50 kg 100 kg	A A	39 39
	Aluminum resinate	4.1	UN2715	III	4.1	IB6	151	213	240	25 kg	100 kg	A	
	Aluminum silicon powder, uncoated	4.3	UN1398	III	4.3	A1, A19, IB8, IP4	151	213	241	25 kg	100 kg	A	40, 85, 103
	Aluminum smelting by-products *or* **Aluminum remelting by-products**	4.3	UN3170	II III	4.3 4.3	128, B115, IB7, IP2 128, B115, IB8, IP4	None None	212 213	242 241	15 kg 25 kg	50 kg 100 kg	B B	85, 103 85, 103
	Amatols, see **Explosives, blasting, type B**												
G	**Amines, flammable, corrosive, n.o.s.** *or* **Polyamines, flammable, corrosive, n.o.s.**	3	UN2733	I II III	3, 8 3, 8 3, 8	T14, TP1, TP27 IB2, T11, TP1, TP27 B1, IB3, T7, TP1, TP28	None None 150	201 202 203	243 243 242	0.5 L 1 L 5 L	2.5 L 5 L 60 L	D B A	40 40 40
G	**Amines, liquid, corrosive, flammable, n.o.s.** *or* **Polyamines, liquid, corrosive, flammable, n.o.s.**	8	UN2734	I II	8, 3 8, 3	A3, A6, N34, T14, TP2, TP27 IB2, T11, TP2, TP27	None None	201 202	243 243	0.5 L 1 L	2.5 L 30 L	A A	

§172.101 - Hazardous Materials Table

Symbols	Hazardous materials descriptions and proper shipping names	Hazard class or Division	Identification Numbers	PG	Label Codes	Special provisions (§172.102)	(8) Packaging (§173.***)			(9) Quantity limitations		(10) Vessel stowage	
							Exceptions	Non-bulk	Bulk	Passenger aircraft/ rail	Cargo aircraft only	Location	Other
(1)	(2)	(3)	(4)	(5)	(6)	(7)	(8A)	(8B)	(8C)	(9A)	(9B)	(10A)	(10B)
G	**Amines, liquid, corrosive, n.o.s.,** *or* **Polyamines, liquid, corrosive, n.o.s.**	8	UN2735	I	8	A3, A6, B10, N34, T14, TP2, TP27	None	201	243	0.5 L	2.5 L	A	
				II	8	B2, IB2, T11, TP1, TP27	154	202	242	1 L	30 L	A	
				III	8	IB3, T7, TP1, TP28	154	203	241	5 L	60 L	A	
G	**Amines, solid, corrosive, n.o.s.,** *or* **Polyamines, solid, corrosive n.o.s.**	8	UN3259	I	8	IB7, IP1	None	211	242	1 kg	25 kg	A	
				II	8	IB8, IP2, IP4	154	212	240	15 kg	50 kg	A	
				III	8	IB8, IP3	154	213	240	25 kg	100 kg	A	
	2-Amino-4-chlorophenol	6.1	UN2673	II	6.1	IB8, IP2, IP4	None	212	242	25 kg	100 kg	A	
	2-Amino-5-diethylaminopentane	6.1	UN2946	III	6.1	IB3, T4, TP1	153	203	241	60 L	220 L	A	
	2-Amino-4,6-Dinitrophenol, wetted *with not less than 20 percent water by mass*	4.1	UN3317	I	4.1	23, A8, A19, A20, N41	None	211	None	1 kg	15 kg	E	28, 36
	2-(2-Aminoethoxy) ethanol	8	UN3055	III	8	IB3, T4, TP1	154	203	241	5 L	60 L	A	
	N-Aminoethylpiperazine	8	UN2815	III	8	IB3, T4, TP1	154	203	241	5 L	60 L	A	12
+	**Aminophenols (o-; m-; p-)**	6.1	UN2512	III	6.1	IB8, IP3, T4, TP1	153	213	240	100 kg	200 kg	A	
	Aminopropyldiethanolamine, see **Amines, *etc.***												
	n-Aminopropylmorpholine, see **Amines, *etc.***												
	Aminopyridines *(o-; m-; p-)*	6.1	UN2671	II	6.1	IB8, IP2, IP4, T7, TP2	None	212	242	25 kg	100 kg	B	12, 40
I	**Ammonia, anhydrous**	2.3	UN1005		2.3, 8	4, T50	None	304	314, 315	Forbidden	25 kg	D	40, 57
D	**Ammonia, anhydrous**	2.2	UN1005		2.2	13, T50	None	304	314, 315	Forbidden	25 kg	D	40, 57
D	**Ammonia solution,** *relative density less than 0.880 at 15 degrees C in water, with more than 50 percent ammonia*	2.2	UN3318		2.2	13, T50	None	304	314, 315	Forbidden	25 kg	D	40, 57
I	**Ammonia solution,** *relative density less than 0.880 at 15 degrees C in water, with more than 50 percent ammonia*	2.3	UN3318		2.3, 8	4, T50	None	304	314, 315	Forbidden	25 kg	D	40, 57
	Ammonia solutions, *relative density between 0.880 and 0.957 at 15 degrees C in water, with more than 10 percent but not more than 35 percent ammonia*	8	UN2672	III	8	IB3, T7, TP1	154	203	241	5 L	60 L	A	40, 85
	Ammonia solutions, *relative density less than 0.880 at 15 degrees C in water, with more than 35 percent but not more than 50 percent ammonia*	2.2	UN2073		2.2		306	304	314, 315	Forbidden	150 kg	E	40, 57
	Ammonium arsenate	6.1	UN1546	II	6.1	IB8, IP2, IP4	None	212	242	25 kg	100 kg	A	
	Ammonium azide	Forbidden											
	Ammonium bifluoride, solid, see **Ammonium hydrogen difluoride, solid**												
	Ammonium bifluoride solution, see **Ammonium hydrogen difluoride, solution**												
	Ammonium bromate	Forbidden											
	Ammonium chlorate	Forbidden											
	Ammonium dichromate	5.1	UN1439	II	5.1	IB8, IP2, IP4	152	212	242	5 kg	25 kg	A	
	Ammonium dinitro-o-cresolate	6.1	UN1843	II	6.1	IB8, IP2, IP4, T7, TP2	None	212	242	25 kg	100 kg	B	36, 65, 66, 77
	Ammonium fluoride	6.1	UN2505	III	6.1	IB8, IP3	153	213	240	100 kg	200 kg	A	26
	Ammonium fluorosilicate	6.1	UN2854	III	6.1	IB8, IP3	153	213	240	100 kg	200 kg	A	26
	Ammonium fulminate	Forbidden											
	Ammonium hydrogen sulfate	8	UN2506	II	8	IB8, IP2, IP4	154	212	240	15 kg	50 kg	A	40
	Ammonium hydrogendifluoride, solid	8	UN1727	II	8	IB8, IP2, IP4, N34	154	212	240	15 kg	50 kg	A	25, 26, 40
	Ammonium hydrogendifluoride, solution	8	UN2817	II	8, 6.1	IB2, N34, T8, TP2, TP12, TP13	None	202	243	1 L	30 L	B	40
				III	8, 6.1	IB3, T4, TP1, TP12, TP13	154	203	241	5 L	60 L	B	40, 95
	Ammonium hydrosulfide, solution, see **Ammonium sulfide solution**												

§172.101 - Hazardous Materials Table

Symbols	Hazardous materials descriptions and proper shipping names	Hazard class or Division	Identification Numbers	PG	Label Codes	Special provisions (§172.102)	(8) Packaging (§173.***)			(9) Quantity limitations		(10) Vessel stowage	
							Exceptions	Non-bulk	Bulk	Passenger aircraft/ rail	Cargo aircraft only	Location	Other
(1)	(2)	(3)	(4)	(5)	(6)	(7)	(8A)	(8B)	(8C)	(9A)	(9B)	(10A)	(10B)
D	**Ammonium hydroxide,** *see* **Ammonia solutions,** *etc.*												
	Ammonium metavanadate	6.1	UN2859	II	6.1	IB8, IP2, IP4	None	212	242	25 kg	100 kg	A	
D	**Ammonium nitrate fertilizers**	5.1	NA2072	III	5.1	7, IB8	152	213	240	25 kg	100 kg	B	48, 59, 60, 117
	Ammonium nitrate fertilizers; *uniform non-segregating mixtures of ammonium nitrate with added matter which is inorganic and chemically inert towards ammonium nitrate, with not less than 90 percent ammonium nitrate and not more than 0.2 percent combustible material (including organic material calculated as carbon), or with more than 70 percent but less than 90 percent ammonium nitrate and not more than 0.4 percent total combustible material*	5.1	UN2067	III	5.1	52, IB8, IP3	152	213	240	25 kg	100 kg	B	48, 59, 60, 117
A W	**Ammonium nitrate fertilizers:** *uniform non-segregating mixtures of nitrogen/phosphate or nitrogen/postash types or complete fertilizers of nitrogen/ phosphate/postash type, with not more than 70 percent ammonium nitrate and not more than 0.4 percent total added combustible material or with not more than 45 percent ammonium nitrate with unrestricted combustible material*	9	UN2071	III	9	132, IB8	155	213	240	200 kg	200 kg	A	
D	**Ammonium nitrate-fuel oil mixture** *containing only prilled ammonium nitrate and fuel oil*	1.5D	NA0331	II	1.5D		None	62	None	Forbidden	Forbidden	10	19E
	Ammonium nitrate, liquid *(hot concentrated solution)*	5.1	UN2426		5.1	B5, T7	None	None	243	Forbidden	Forbidden	D	59, 60
D	**Ammonium nitrate mixed fertlizers**	5.1	NA2069	III	5.1	10, IB8	152	213	240	25 kg	100 kg	B	48, 59, 60, 117
	Ammonium nitrate, *with more than 0.2 percent combustible substances, including any organic substance calculated as carbon, to the exclusion of any other added substance*	1.1D	UN0222	II	1.1D		None	62	None	Forbidden	Forbidden	10	19E
	Ammonium nitrate, *with not more than 0.2 percent of combustible substances, including any organic substance calculated as carbon, to the exclusion of any other added substance*	5.1	UN1942	III	5.1	A1, A29, IB8, IP3	152	213	240	25 kg	100 kg	A	48, 59, 60, 116
	Ammonium nitrite	Forbidden											
	Ammonium perchlorate	1.1D	UN0402	II	1.1D	107	None	62	None	Forbidden	Forbidden	10	19E
	Ammonium perchlorate	5.1	UN1442	II	5.1	107, A9, IB6, IP2	152	212	242	5 kg	25 kg	E	58, 69, 106
	Ammonium permanganate	Forbidden											
	Ammonium persulfate	5.1	UN1444	III	5.1	A1, A29, IB8, IP3	152	213	240	25 kg	100 kg	A	
	Ammonium picrate, *dry or wetted with less than 10 percent water, by mass*	1.1D	UN0004	II	1.1D		None	62	None	Forbidden	Forbidden	10	5E, 19E
	Ammonium picrate, wetted *with not less than 10 percent water, by mass*	4.1	UN1310	I	4.1	23, A2, N41	None	211	None	0.5 kg	0.5 kg	D	28, 36
	Ammonium polysulfide, solution	8	UN2818	II	8, 6.1	IB2, T7, TP2, TP13	None	202	243	1 L	30 L	B	12, 26, 40
				III	8, 6.1	IB3, T4, TP1, TP13	154	203	241	5 L	60 L	B	12, 26, 40
	Ammonium polyvanadate	6.1	UN2861	II	6.1	IB8, IP2, IP4	None	212	242	25 kg	100 kg	A	
	Ammonium silicofluoride, see **Ammonium fluorosilicate**												
	Ammonium sulfide solution	8	UN2683	II	8, 6.1, 3	IB1, T7, TP2, TP13	None	202	243	1 L	30 L	B	12, 22, 26, 100
	Ammunition, blank, see **Cartridges for weapons, blank**												
	Ammunition, illuminating *with or without burster, expelling charge or propelling charge*	1.2G	UN0171	II	1.2G			62	None	Forbidden	Forbidden	03	
	Ammunition, illuminating *with or without burster, expelling charge or propelling charge*	1.3G	UN0254	II	1.3G			62	None	Forbidden	Forbidden	03	

§172.101 - Hazardous Materials Table

Symbols	Hazardous materials descriptions and proper shipping names	Hazard class or Division	Identification Numbers	PG	Label Codes	Special provisions (§172.102)	(8) Packaging (§173.***)			(9) Quantity limitations		(10) Vessel stowage	
							Exceptions	Non-bulk	Bulk	Passenger aircraft/ rail	Cargo aircraft only	Location	Other
(1)	(2)	(3)	(4)	(5)	(6)	(7)	(8A)	(8B)	(8C)	(9A)	(9B)	(10A)	(10B)
	Ammunition, illuminating *with or without burster, expelling charge or propelling charge*	1.4G	UN0297	II	1.4G			62	None	Forbidden	75 kg	02	
	Ammunition, incendiary *liquid or gel, with burster, expelling charge or propelling charge*	1.3J	UN0247	II	1.3J			62	None	Forbidden	Forbidden	04	23E
	Ammunition, incendiary (water-activated contrivances) with burster, expelling charge or propelling charge, see **Contrivances, water-activated, etc.**												
	Ammunition, incendiary, white phosphorus, *with burster, expelling charge or propelling charge*	1.2H	UN0243	II	1.2H			62	None	Forbidden	Forbidden	08	8E, 14E, 15E, 17E
	Ammunition, incendiary, white phosphorus, *with burster, expelling charge or propelling charge*	1.3H	UN0244	II	1.3H			62	None	Forbidden	Forbidden	08	8E, 14E, 15E, 17E
	Ammunition, incendiary *with or without burster, expelling charge, or propelling charge*	1.2G	UN0009	II	1.2G			62	None	Forbidden	Forbidden	03	
	Ammunition, incendiary *with or without burster, expelling charge, or propelling charge*	1.3G	UN0010	II	1.3G			62	None	Forbidden	Forbidden	03	
	Ammunition, incendiary *with or without burster, expelling charge or propelling charge*	1.4G	UN0300	II	1.4G			62	None	Forbidden	75 kg	02	
	Ammunition, practice	1.4G	UN0362	II	1.4G			62	None	Forbidden	75 kg	02	
	Ammunition, practice	1.3G	UN0488	II	1.3G			62	None	Forbidden	Forbidden	03	
	Ammunition, proof	1.4G	UN0363	II	1.4G			62	None	Forbidden	75 kg	02	
	Ammunition, rocket, see **Warheads, rocket** *etc.*												
	Ammunition, SA (small arms), see **Cartridges for weapons,** *etc.*												
	Ammunition, smoke (water-activated contrivances), white phosphorus, with burster, expelling charge or propelling charge, see **Contrivances, water-activated,** *etc. (UN 0248)*												
	Ammunition, smoke (water-activated contrivances), without white phosphorus or phosphides, with burster, expelling charge or propelling charge, see **Contrivances, water-activated,** *etc. (UN 0249)*												
	Ammunition smoke, white phosphorus *with burster, expelling charge, or propelling charge*	1.2H	UN0245	II	1.2H			62	None	Forbidden	Forbidden	08	8E, 14E, 15E, 17E
	Ammunition, smoke, white phosphorus *with burster, expelling charge, or propelling charge*	1.3H	UN0246	II	1.3H			62	None	Forbidden	Forbidden	08	8E, 14E, 15E, 17E
	Ammunition, smoke *with or without burster, expelling charge or propelling charge*	1.2G	UN0015	II	1.2G, 8			62	None	Forbidden	Forbidden		8E, 17E, 20E
	Ammunition, smoke *with or without burster, expelling charge or propelling charge*	1.3G	UN0016	II	1.3G, 8			62	None	Forbidden	Forbidden		8E, 17E, 20E
	Ammunition, smoke *with or without burster, expelling charge or propelling charge*	1.4G	UN0303	II	1.4G, 8			62	None	Forbidden	75 kg		7E, 8E, 14E, 15E, 17E
	Ammunition, sporting, see **Cartridges for weapons,** *etc. (UN 0012; UN 0328; UN 0339)*												
	Ammunition, tear-producing, non-explosive, *without burster or expelling charge, non-fuzed*	6.1	UN2017	II	6.1, 8		None	212	None	Forbidden	50 kg	E	13, 40
	Ammunition, tear-producing *with burster, expelling charge or propelling charge*	1.2G	UN0018	II	1.2G, 8, 6.1			62	None	Forbidden	Forbidden		8E, 17E, 20E
	Ammunition, tear-producing *with burster, expelling charge or propelling charge*	1.3G	UN0019	II	1.3G, 8, 6.1			62	None	Forbidden	Forbidden		8E, 17E, 20E

§172.101 - Hazardous Materials Table

Sym-bols	Hazardous materials descriptions and proper shipping names	Hazard class or Division	Identifi-cation Numbers	PG	Label Codes	Special provisions (§172.102)	(8) Packaging (§173.***)			(9) Quantity limitations		(10) Vessel stowage	
							Excep-tions	Non-bulk	Bulk	Passen-ger aircraft/ rail	Cargo aircraft only	Loca-tion	Other
(1)	(2)	(3)	(4)	(5)	(6)	(7)	(8A)	(8B)	(8C)	(9A)	(9B)	(10A)	(10B)
	Ammunition, tear-producing *with burster, expelling charge or propelling charge*	1.4G	UN0301	II	1.4G, 8, 6.1			62	None	Forbidden	75 kg		7E, 8E, 14E, 15E, 17E
	Ammunition, toxic, non-explosive, *without burster or expelling charge, non-fuzed*	6.1	UN2016	II	6.1		None	212	None	Forbidden	100 kg	E	13, 40
	Ammunition, toxic (water-activated contrivances), with burster, expelling charge or propelling charge, see **Contrivances, water-activated,** *etc.*												
G	**Ammunition, toxic** *with burster, expelling charge, or propelling charge*	1.2K	UN0020	II	1.2K, 6.1			62	None	Forbidden	Forbidden	08	8E, 14E, 15E, 17E
G	**Ammunition, toxic** *with burster, expelling charge, or propelling charge*	1.3K	UN0021	II	1.3K, 6.1			62	None	Forbidden	Forbidden	08	8E, 14E, 15E, 17E
	Amyl acetates	3	UN1104	III	3	B1, IB3, T2, TP1	150	203	242	60 L	220 L	A	
	Amyl acid phosphate	8	UN2819	III	8	IB3, T4, TP1	154	203	241	5 L	60 L	A	
	Amyl butyrates	3	UN2620	III	3	B1, IB3, T2, TP1	150	203	242	60 L	220 L	A	
	Amyl chlorides	3	UN1107	II	3	IB2, T4, TP1	150	202	242	5 L	60 L	B	
	Amyl formates	3	UN1109	III	3	B1, IB3, T2, TP1	150	203	242	60 L	220 L	A	
	Amyl mercaptans	3	UN1111	II	3	A3, IB2, T4, TP1	None	202	242	5 L	60 L	B	95, 102
	n-Amyl methyl ketone	3	UN1110	III	3	B1, IB3, T2, TP1	150	203	242	60 L	220 L	A	
	Amyl nitrate	3	UN1112	III	3	B1, IB3, T2, TP1	150	203	242	60 L	220 L	A	40
	Amyl nitrites	3	UN1113	II	3	IB2, T4, TP1	150	202	242	5 L	60 L	E	40
	Amylamines	3	UN1106	II III	3, 8 3, 8	IB2, T7, TP1 B1, IB3, T4, TP1	None 150	202 203	243 242	1 L 5 L	5 L 60 L	B A	
	Amyltrichlorosilane	8	UN1728	II	8	A7, B2, B6, IB2, N34, T7, TP2, TP13	None	202	242	Forbidden	30 L	C	40
	Anhydrous ammonia, *see* **Ammonia, anhydrous**												
	Anhydrous hydrofluoric acid, see **Hydrogen fluoride, anhydrous**												
+	**Aniline**	6.1	UN1547	II	6.1	IB2, T7, TP2	None	202	243	5 L	60 L	A	40
	Aniline hydrochloride	6.1	UN1548	III	6.1	IB8, IP3	153	213	240	100 kg	200 kg	A	
	Aniline oil, see **Aniline**												
	Anisidines	6.1	UN2431	III	6.1	IB3, T4, TP1	153	203	241	60 L	220 L	A	
	Anisole	3	UN2222	III	3	B1, IB3, T2, TP1	150	203	242	60 L	220 L	A	
	Anisoyl chloride	8	UN1729	II	8	B2, IB2, T7, TP2	154	202	242	1 L	30 L	C	40
	Anti-freeze, liquid, see **Flammable liquids, n.o.s.**												
	Antimonous chloride, see **Antimony trichloride**												
	Antimony compounds, inorganic, liquid, n.o.s.	6.1	UN3141	III	6.1	35, IB3, T7, TP1, TP28	153	203	241	60 L	220 L	A	
	Antimony compounds, inorganic, solid, n.o.s.	6.1	UN1549	III	6.1	35, IB8, IP3	153	213	240	100 kg	200 kg	A	
	Antimony lactate	6.1	UN1550	III	6.1	IB8, IP3	153	213	240	100 kg	200 kg	A	
	Antimony pentachloride, liquid	8	UN1730	II	8	B2, IB2, T7, TP2	None	202	242	1 L	30 L	C	40
	Antimony pentachloride, solutions	8	UN1731	II III	8 8	B2, IB2, T7, TP2 IB3, T4, TP1	154 154	202 203	242 241	1 L 5 L	30 L 60 L	C C	40 40
	Antimony pentafluoride	8	UN1732	II	8, 6.1	A3, A6, A7, A10, IB2, N3, T7, TP2	None	202	243	Forbidden	30 L	D	40
	Antimony potassium tartrate	6.1	UN1551	III	6.1	IB8, IP3	153	213	240	100 kg	200 kg	A	
	Antimony powder	6.1	UN2871	III	6.1	IB8, IP3	153	213	240	100 kg	200 kg	A	
	Antimony sulfide and a chlorate, mixtures of	Forbidden											
	Antimony sulfide, solid, see **Antimony compounds, inorganic, n.o.s.**												
	Antimony trichloride, liquid	8	UN1733	II	8	B2, IB2	154	202	242	1 L	30 L	C	40
	Antimony trichloride, solid	8	UN1733	II	8	IB8, IP2, IP4	154	212	240	15 kg	50 kg	A	40
	Aqua ammonia, see **Ammonia solution,** *etc.*												

§172.101 - Hazardous Materials Table

Symbols	Hazardous materials descriptions and proper shipping names	Hazard class or Division	Identification Numbers	PG	Label Codes	Special provisions (§172.102)	(8) Packaging (§173.***) Exceptions	Non-bulk	Bulk	(9) Quantity limitations Passenger aircraft/rail	Cargo aircraft only	(10) Vessel stowage Location	Other
(1)	(2)	(3)	(4)	(5)	(6)	(7)	(8A)	(8B)	(8C)	(9A)	(9B)	(10A)	(10B)
	Argon, compressed	2.2	UN1006		2.2		306	302	314, 315	75 kg	150 kg	A	
	Argon, refrigerated liquid *(cryogenic liquid)*	2.2	UN1951		2.2	T75, TP5	320	316	318	50 kg	500 kg	B	
	Arsenic	6.1	UN1558	II	6.1	IB8, IP2, IP4	None	212	242	25 kg	100 kg	A	
	Arsenic acid, liquid	6.1	UN1553	I	6.1	T20, TP2, TP7, TP13	None	201	243	1 L	30 L	B	46
	Arsenic acid, solid	6.1	UN1554	II	6.1	IB8, IP2, IP4	None	212	242	25 kg	100 kg	A	
	Arsenic bromide	6.1	UN1555	II	6.1	IB8, IP2, IP4	None	212	242	25 kg	100 kg	A	12, 40
	Arsenic chloride, see **Arsenic trichloride**												
	Arsenic compounds, liquid, n.o.s. *inorganic, including arsenates, n.o.s.; arsenites, n.o.s.; arsenic sulfides, n.o.s.; and organic compounds of arsenic, n.o.s.*	6.1	UN1556	I II III	6.1 6.1 6.1	 IB2 IB3	None None 153	201 202 203	243 243 241	1 L 5 L 60 L	30 L 60 L 220 L	B B B	40 40 40
	Arsenic compounds, solid, n.o.s. *inorganic, including arsenates, n.o.s.; arsenites, n.o.s.; arsenic sulfides, n.o.s.; and organic compounds of arsenic, n.o.s.*	6.1	UN1557	I II III	6.1 6.1 6.1	IB7, IP1 IB8, IP2, IP4 IB8, IP3	None None 153	211 212 213	242 242 240	5 kg 25 kg 100 kg	50 kg 100 kg 200 kg	A A A	
	Arsenic pentoxide	6.1	UN1559	II	6.1	IB8, IP2, IP4	None	212	242	25 kg	100 kg	A	
	Arsenic sulfide and a chlorate, mixtures of	Forbidden											
	Arsenic trichloride	6.1	UN1560	I	6.1	2, B9, B14, B32, B74, T20, TP2, TP13, TP38, TP45	None	227	244	Forbidden	Forbidden	B	40
	Arsenic trioxide	6.1	UN1561	II	6.1	IB8, IP2, IP4	None	212	242	25 kg	100 kg	A	
	Arsenic, white, solid, see **Arsenic trioxide**												
	Arsenical dust	6.1	UN1562	II	6.1	IB8, IP2, IP4	None	212	242	25 kg	100 kg	A	
	Arsenical pesticides, liquid, flammable, toxic, *flash point less than 23 degrees C*	3	UN2760	I II	3, 6.1 3, 6.1	T14, TP2, TP13, TP27 IB2, T11, TP2, TP13, TP27	None None	201 202	243 243	Forbidden 1 L	30 L 60 L	B B	40 40
	Arsenical pesticides, liquid, toxic	6.1	UN2994	I II III	6.1 6.1 6.1	T14, TP2, TP13, TP27 IB2, T11, TP2, TP13, TP27 IB3, T7, TP2, TP28	None None 153	201 202 203	243 243 241	1 L 5 L 60 L	30 L 60 L 220 L	B B A	40 40 40
	Arsenical pesticides, liquid, toxic, flammable *flash point not less than 23 degrees C*	6.1	UN2993	I II III	6.1, 3 6.1, 3 6.1, 3	T14, TP2, TP13, TP27 IB2, T11, TP2, TP13, TP27 B1, IB3, T7, TP2, TP28	None None 153	201 202 203	243 243 242	1 L 5 L 60 L	30 L 60 L 220 L	B B A	40 40 40
	Arsenical pesticides, solid, toxic	6.1	UN2759	I II III	6.1 6.1 6.1	IB7, IP1 IB8, IP2, IP4 IB8, IP3	None None 153	211 212 213	242 242 240	5 kg 25 kg 100 kg	50 kg 100 kg 200 kg	A A A	40 40 40
	Arsenious acid, solid, see **Arsenic trioxide**												
	Arsenious and mercuric iodide solution, see **Arsenic compounds, liquid, n.o.s.**												
	Arsine	2.3	UN2188		2.3, 2.1	1	None	192	245	Forbidden	Forbidden	D	40
	Articles, explosive, extremely insensitive *or* **Articles, EEI**	1.6N	UN0486	II	1.6N	101	None	62	None	Forbidden	Forbidden	07	
G	**Articles, explosive, n.o.s.**	1.4S	UN0349	II	1.4S	101	None	62	None	25 kg	100 kg	05	
G	**Articles, explosive, n.o.s.**	1.4B	UN0350	II	1.4B	101	None	62	None	Forbidden	Forbidden	06	
G	**Articles, explosive, n.o.s.**	1.4C	UN0351	II	1.4C	101	None	62	None	Forbidden	75 kg	06	
G	**Articles, explosive, n.o.s.**	1.4D	UN0352	II	1.4D	101	None	62	None	Forbidden	75 kg	06	
G	**Articles, explosive, n.o.s.**	1.4G	UN0353	II	1.4G	101	None	62	None	Forbidden	75 kg	06	
G	**Articles, explosive, n.o.s.**	1.1L	UN0354	II	1.1L	101	None	62	None	Forbidden	Forbidden	08	8E, 14E, 15E, 17E
G	**Articles, explosive, n.o.s.**	1.2L	UN0355	II	1.2L	101	None	62	None	Forbidden	Forbidden	08	8E, 14E, 15E, 17E
G	**Articles, explosive, n.o.s.**	1.3L	UN0356	II	1.3L	101	None	62	None	Forbidden	Forbidden	08	8E, 14E, 15E, 17E
G	**Articles, explosive, n.o.s.**	1.1C	UN0462	II	1.1C	101	None	62	None	Forbidden	Forbidden	07	

§172.101 - Hazardous Materials Table

Symbols	Hazardous materials descriptions and proper shipping names	Hazard class or Division	Identification Numbers	PG	Label Codes	Special provisions (§172.102)	(8) Packaging (§173.***)			(9) Quantity limitations		(10) Vessel stowage	
							Exceptions	Non-bulk	Bulk	Passenger aircraft/ rail	Cargo aircraft only	Location	Other
(1)	(2)	(3)	(4)	(5)	(6)	(7)	(8A)	(8B)	(8C)	(9A)	(9B)	(10A)	(10B)
G	**Articles, explosive, n.o.s.**	1.1D	UN0463	II	1.1D	101	None	62	None	Forbidden	Forbidden	07	
G	**Articles, explosive, n.o.s.**	1.1E	UN0464	II	1.1E	101	None	62	None	Forbidden	Forbidden	07	
G	**Articles, explosive, n.o.s.**	1.1F	UN0465	II	1.1F	101	None	62	None	Forbidden	Forbidden	08	
G	**Articles, explosive, n.o.s.**	1.2C	UN0466	II	1.2C	101	None	62	None	Forbidden	Forbidden	07	
G	**Articles, explosive, n.o.s.**	1.2D	UN0467	II	1.2D	101	None	62	None	Forbidden	Forbidden	07	
G	**Articles, explosive, n.o.s.**	1.2E	UN0468	II	1.2E	101	None	62	None	Forbidden	Forbidden	07	
G	**Articles, explosive, n.o.s.**	1.2F	UN0469	II	1.2F	101	None	62	None	Forbidden	Forbidden	08	
G	**Articles, explosive, n.o.s.**	1.3C	UN0470	II	1.3C	101	None	62	None	Forbidden	Forbidden	07	
G	**Articles, explosive, n.o.s.**	1.4E	UN0471	II	1.4E	101	None	62	None	Forbidden	75 kg	06	
G	**Articles, explosive, n.o.s.**	1.4F	UN0472	II	1.4F	101	None	62	None	Forbidden	Forbidden	08	
	Articles, pressurized pneumatic *or* **hydraulic** *containing non-flammable gas*	2.2	UN3164		2.2		306	302, 304	None	No limit	No limit	A	
	Articles, pyrophoric	1.2L	UN0380	II	1.2L		None	62	None	Forbidden	Forbidden	08	8E, 14E, 15E, 17E
	Articles, pyrotechnic *for technical purposes*	1.1G	UN0428	II	1.1G		None	62	None	Forbidden	Forbidden	07	
	Articles, pyrotechnic *for technical purposes*	1.2G	UN0429	II	1.2G		None	62	None	Forbidden	Forbidden	07	
	Articles, pyrotechnic *for technical purposes*	1.3G	UN0430	II	1.3G		None	62	None	Forbidden	Forbidden	07	
	Articles, pyrotechnic *for technical purposes*	1.4G	UN0431	II	1.4G		None	62	None	Forbidden	75 kg	06	
	Articles, pyrotechnic *for technical purposes*	1.4S	UN0432	II	1.4S		None	62	None	25 kg	100 kg	05	
D	**Asbestos**	9	NA2212	III	9	IB8, IP2, IP4	155	216	240	200 kg	200 kg	A	34, 40
	Ascaridole (organic peroxide)	Forbidden											
D	**Asphalt,** *at or above its flash point*	3	NA1999	III	3	IB3, T1, TP3	150	203	247	Forbidden	Forbidden	D	
D	**Asphalt, cut back,** *see* **Tars, liquid,** *etc.*												
	Automobile, motorcycle, tractor, other self-propelled vehicle, engine, or other mechanical apparatus, see **Vehicles** *or* **Battery** *etc.*												
A G	**Aviation regulated liquid, n.o.s.**	9	UN3334		9	A35	155	204		No limit	No limit	A	
A G	**Aviation regulated solid, n.o.s.**	9	UN3335		9	A35	155	204		No limit	No limit	A	
	Azaurolic acid (salt of) (dry)	Forbidden											
	Azido guanidine picrate (dry)	Forbidden											
	5-Azido-1-hydroxy tetrazole	Forbidden											
	Azido hydroxy tetrazole (mercury and silver salts)	Forbidden											
	3-Azido-1,2-Propylene glycol dinitrate	Forbidden											
	Azidodithiocarbonic acid	Forbidden											
	Azidoethyl nitrate	Forbidden											
	1-Aziridinylphosphine oxide-(tris), see **Tris-(1-aziridinyl) phosphine oxide, solution**												
	Azodicarbonamide	4.1	UN3242	II	4.1	38, IB8	151	212	240	Forbidden	Forbidden	D	12, 61, 74
	Azotetrazole (dry)	Forbidden											
	Barium	4.3	UN1400	II	4.3	A19, IB7, IP2	151	212	241	15 kg	50 kg	E	
	Barium alloys, pyrophoric	4.2	UN1854	I	4.2		None	181	None	Forbidden	Forbidden	D	
	Barium azide, *dry or wetted with less than 50 percent water, by mass*	1.1A	UN0224	II	1.1A, 6.1	111, 117	None	62	None	Forbidden	Forbidden	12	
	Barium azide, wetted *with not less than 50 percent water, by mass*	4.1	UN1571	I	4.1, 6.1	A2	None	182	None	Forbidden	0.5 kg	D	28
	Barium bromate	5.1	UN2719	II	5.1, 6.1	IB8, IP2, IP4	None	212	242	5 kg	25 kg	A	56, 58, 106
	Barium chlorate	5.1	UN1445	II	5.1, 6.1	A9, IB6, IP2, N34, T4, TP1	None	212	242	5 kg	25 kg	A	56, 58, 106
	Barium compounds, n.o.s.	6.1	UN1564	II III	6.1 6.1	IB8, IP2, IP4 IB8, IP3	None 153	212 213	242 240	25 kg 100 kg	100 kg 200 kg	A A	
	Barium cyanide	6.1	UN1565	I	6.1	IB7, IP1, N74, N75	None	211	242	5 kg	50 kg	A	26, 40
	Barium hypochlorite *with more than 22 percent available chlorine*	5.1	UN2741	II	5.1, 6.1	A7, A9, IB8, IP2, IP4, N34	152	212	None	5 kg	25 kg	B	56, 58, 106

§172.101 - Hazardous Materials Table

Symbols	Hazardous materials descriptions and proper shipping names	Hazard class or Division	Identification Numbers	PG	Label Codes	Special provisions (§172.102)	(8) Packaging (§173.***)			(9) Quantity limitations		(10) Vessel stowage	
							Exceptions	Non-bulk	Bulk	Passenger aircraft/ rail	Cargo aircraft only	Location	Other
(1)	(2)	(3)	(4)	(5)	(6)	(7)	(8A)	(8B)	(8C)	(9A)	(9B)	(10A)	(10B)
	Barium nitrate	5.1	UN1446	II	5.1, 6.1	IB8, IP2, IP4	None	212	242	5 kg	25 kg	A	
	Barium oxide	6.1	UN1884	III	6.1	IB8, IP3	153	213	240	100 kg	200 kg	A	
	Barium perchlorate	5.1	UN1447	II	5.1, 6.1	IB6, IP2, T4, TP1	None	212	242	5 kg	25 kg	A	56, 58, 106
	Barium permanganate	5.1	UN1448	II	5.1, 6.1	IB6, IP2	None	212	242	5 kg	25 kg	D	56, 58, 69, 106, 107
	Barium peroxide	5.1	UN1449	II	5.1, 6.1	IB6, IP2	None	212	242	5 kg	25 kg	A	13, 75, 106
	Barium selenate, see **Selenates** *or* **Selenites**												
	Barium selenite, see **Selenates** *or* **Selenites**												
	Batteries, containing sodium	4.3	UN3292	II	4.3		189	189	189	Forbidden	No limit	A	
	Batteries, dry, containing potassium hydroxide solid, *electric, storage*	8	UN3028	III	8		None	213	None	25 kg gross	230 kg gross	A	
	Batteries, wet, filled with acid, *electric storage*	8	UN2794	III	8		159	159	159	30 kg gross	No limit	A	
	Batteries, wet, filled with alkali, *electric storage*	8	UN2795	III	8		159	159	159	30 kg gross	No limit	A	
	Batteries, wet, non-spillable, *electric storage*	8	UN2800	III	8		159	159	159	No Limit	No Limit	A	
	Batteries, dry, *not subject to the requirements of this subchapter*					130							
	Battery fluid, acid	8	UN2796	II	8	A3, A7, B2, B15, IB2, N6, N34, T8, TP2, TP12	154	202	242	1 L	30 L	B	
	Battery fluid, alkali	8	UN2797	II	8	B2, IB2, N6, T7, TP2	154	202	242	1 L	30 L	A	
	Battery lithium type, see **Lithium batteries** *etc.*												
	Battery-powered vehicle *or* **Battery-powered equipment**	9	UN3171		9	134	220	220	None	No limit	No limit		
	Battery, wet, filled with acid or alkali with vehicle or mechanical equipment containing an internal combustion engine, see **Vehicle,** *etc. or* **Engines, internal combustion,** *etc.*												
+	**Benzaldehyde**	9	UN1990	III	9	IB3, T2, TP1	155	203	241	100 L	220 L	A	
	Benzene	3	UN1114	II	3	IB2, T4, TP1	150	202	242	5 L	60 L	B	40
	Benzene diazonium chloride (dry)	Forbidden											
	Benzene diazonium nitrate (dry)	Forbidden											
	Benzene phosphorus dichloride, see **Phenyl phosphorus dichloride**												
	Benzene phosphorus thiodichloride, see **Phenyl phosphorus thiodichloride**												
	Benzene sulfonyl chloride	8	UN2225	III	8	IB3, T4, TP1	154	203	241	5 L	60 L	A	40
	Benzene triozonide	Forbidden											
	Benzenethiol, see **Phenyl mercaptan**												
	Benzidine	6.1	UN1885	II	6.1	IB8, IP2, IP4	None	212	242	25 kg	100 kg	A	
	Benzol, **see Benzene**												
	Benzonitrile	6.1	UN2224	II	6.1	IB2, T7, TP2	None	202	243	5 L	60 L	A	26, 40
	Benzoquinone	6.1	UN2587	II	6.1	IB8, IP2, IP4	None	212	242	25 kg	100 kg	A	
	Benzotrichloride	8	UN2226	II	8	B2, IB2, T7, TP2	154	202	242	1 L	30 L	A	40
	Benzotrifluoride	3	UN2338	II	3	IB2, T4, TP1	150	202	242	5 L	60 L	B	40
	Benzoxidiazoles (dry)	Forbidden											
	Benzoyl azide	Forbidden											
	Benzoyl chloride	8	UN1736	II	8	B2, IB2, T8, TP2, TP12, TP13	154	202	242	1 L	30 L	C	40
	Benzyl bromide	6.1	UN1737	II	6.1, 8	A3, A7, IB2, N33, N34, T8, TP2, TP12, TP13	None	202	243	1 L	30 L	D	13, 40
	Benzyl chloride	6.1	UN1738	II	6.1, 8	A3, A7, B70, IB2, N33, N42, T8, TP2, TP12, TP13	None	202	243	1 L	30 L	D	13, 40

§172.101 - Hazardous Materials Table

Symbols	Hazardous materials descriptions and proper shipping names	Hazard class or Division	Identification Numbers	PG	Label Codes	Special provisions (§172.102)	(8) Packaging (§173.***)			(9) Quantity limitations		(10) Vessel stowage	
							Exceptions	Non-bulk	Bulk	Passenger aircraft/ rail	Cargo aircraft only	Location	Other
(1)	(2)	(3)	(4)	(5)	(6)	(7)	(8A)	(8B)	(8C)	(9A)	(9B)	(10A)	(10B)
	Benzyl chloride *unstabilized*	6.1	UN1738	II	6.1, 8	A3, A7, B8, B11, IB2, N33, N34, N43, T8, TP2, TP12, TP13	None	202	243	1 L	30 L	D	13, 40
	Benzyl chloroformate	8	UN1739	I	8	A3, A6, B4, N41, T10, TP2, TP12, TP13	None	201	243	Forbidden	2.5 L	D	40
	Benzyl iodide	6.1	UN2653	II	6.1	IB2, T7, TP2	None	202	243	5 L	60 L	B	12, 40
	Benzyldimethylamine	8	UN2619	II	8, 3	B2, IB2, T7, TP2	154	202	243	1 L	30 L	A	40, 48
	Benzylidene chloride	6.1	UN1886	II	6.1	IB2, T7, TP2	None	202	243	5 L	60 L	D	40
	Beryllium compounds, n.o.s.	6.1	UN1566	II	6.1	IB8, IP2, IP4	None	212	242	25 kg	100 kg	A	
				III	6.1	IB8, IP3	153	213	240	100 kg	200 kg	A	
	Beryllium nitrate	5.1	UN2464	II	5.1, 6.1	IB8, IP2, IP4	None	212	242	5 kg	25 kg	A	
	Beryllium, powder	6.1	UN1567	II	6.1, 4.1	IB8, IP2, IP4	None	212	242	15 kg	50 kg	A	
	Bicyclo [2,2,1] hepta-2,5-diene, stabilized *or* **2,5-Norbornadiene, stabilized**	3	UN2251	II	3	IB2, T7, TP2	150	202	242	5 L	60 L	D	
	Biphenyl triozonide	Forbidden											
	Bipyridilium pesticides, liquid, flammable, toxic, *flash point less than 23 degrees C*	3	UN2782	I	3, 6.1	T14, TP2, TP13, TP27	None	201	243	Forbidden	30 L	E	
				II	3, 6.1	IB2, T11, TP2, TP13, TP27	None	202	243	1 L	60 L	B	40
	Bipyridilium pesticides, liquid, toxic	6.1	UN3016	I	6.1	T14, TP2, TP13, TP27	None	201	243	1 L	30 L	B	40
				II	6.1	IB2, T11, TP2, TP13, TP27	None	202	243	5 L	60 L	B	40
				III	6.1	IB3, T7, TP2, TP28	153	203	241	60 L	220 L	A	40
	Bipyridilium pesticides, liquid, toxic, flammable, *flash point not less than 23 degrees C*	6.1	UN3015	I	6.1, 3	T14, TP2, TP13, TP27	None	201	243	1 L	30 L	B	21, 40
				II	6.1, 3	IB2, T11, TP2, TP13, TP27	None	202	243	5 L	60 L	B	21, 40
				III	6.1, 3	B1, IB3, T7, TP2, TP28	153	203	242	60 L	220 L	A	21, 40
	Bipyridilium pesticides, solid, toxic	6.1	UN2781	I	6.1	IB7, IP1	None	211	242	5 kg	50 kg	A	40
				II	6.1	IB8, IP2, IP4	None	212	242	25 kg	100 kg	A	40
				III	6.1	IB8, IP3	153	213	240	100 kg	200 kg	A	40
	Bis (Aminopropyl) piperazine, see **Corrosive liquid, n.o.s.**												
	Bisulfate, aqueous solution	8	UN2837	II	8	A7, B2, IB2, N34, T7, TP2	154	202	242	1 L	30 L	A	
				III	8	A7, IB3, N34, T4, TP1	154	203	241	5 L	60 L	A	
	Bisulfites, aqueous solutions, n.o.s.	8	UN2693	III	8	IB3, T7, TP1, TP28	154	203	241	5 L	60 L	A	26, 40
	Black powder, compressed *or* **Gunpowder, compressed** *or* **Black powder, in pellets** *or* **Gunpowder, in pellets**	1.1D	UN0028	II	1.1D		None	62	None	Forbidden	Forbidden	10	
	Black powder *or* **Gunpowder,** *granular or as a meal*	1.1D	UN0027	II	1.1D		None	62	None	Forbidden	Forbidden	10	
D	**Black powder for small arms**	4.1	NA0027	I	4.1	70	None	170	None	Forbidden	Forbidden	E	
	Blasting agent, n.o.s., see **Explosives, blasting** *etc.*												
	Blasting cap assemblies, see **Detonator assemblies, non-electric,** *for blasting*												
	Blasting caps, electric, see **Detonators, electric** *for blasting*												
	Blasting caps, non-electric, see **Detonators, non-electric,** *for blasting*												
	Bleaching powder, see **Calcium hypochlorite mixtures,** *etc.*												
I	**Blue asbestos** *(Crocidolite) or* **Brown asbestos** *(amosite, mysorite)*	9	UN2212	II	9	IB8, IP2, IP4	155	216	240	Forbidden	Forbidden	A	34, 40
	Bombs, photo-flash	1.1F	UN0037	II	1.1F			62	None	Forbidden	Forbidden	08	
	Bombs, photo-flash	1.1D	UN0038	II	1.1D			62	None	Forbidden	Forbidden	03	
	Bombs, photo-flash	1.2G	UN0039	II	1.2G			62	None	Forbidden	Forbidden	03	
	Bombs, photo-flash	1.3G	UN0299	II	1.3G			62	None	Forbidden	Forbidden	03	

§172.101 - Hazardous Materials Table

Symbols	Hazardous materials descriptions and proper shipping names	Hazard class or Division	Identification Numbers	PG	Label Codes	Special provisions (§172.102)	(8) Packaging (§173.***)			(9) Quantity limitations		(10) Vessel stowage	
							Exceptions	Non-bulk	Bulk	Passenger aircraft/ rail	Cargo aircraft only	Location	Other
(1)	(2)	(3)	(4)	(5)	(6)	(7)	(8A)	(8B)	(8C)	(9A)	(9B)	(10A)	(10B)
	Bombs, smoke, non-explosive, *with corrosive liquid, without initiating device*	8	UN2028	II	8		None	160	None	Forbidden	50 kg	E	40
	Bombs, *with bursting charge*	1.1F	UN0033	II	1.1F			62	None	Forbidden	Forbidden	08	
	Bombs, *with bursting charge*	1.1D	UN0034	II	1.1D			62	None	Forbidden	Forbidden	03	
	Bombs, *with bursting charge*	1.2D	UN0035	II	1.2D			62	None	Forbidden	Forbidden	03	
	Bombs, *with bursting charge*	1.2F	UN0291	II	1.2F			62	None	Forbidden	Forbidden	08	
	Bombs with flammable liquid, *with bursting charge*	1.1J	UN0399	II	1.1J			62	None	Forbidden	Forbidden	04	23E
	Bombs with flammable liquid, *with bursting charge*	1.2J	UN0400	II	1.2J			62	None	Forbidden	Forbidden	04	23E
	Boosters with detonator	1.1B	UN0225	II	1.1B		None	62	None	Forbidden	Forbidden	11	
	Boosters with detonator	1.2B	UN0268	II	1.2B		None	62	None	Forbidden	Forbidden	07	
	Boosters, *without detonator*	1.1D	UN0042	II	1.1D		None	62	None	Forbidden	Forbidden	07	
	Boosters, *without detonator*	1.2D	UN0283	II	1.2D		None	62	None	Forbidden	Forbidden	07	
	Borate and chlorate mixtures, see **Chlorate and borate mixtures**												
	Borneol	4.1	UN1312	III	4.1	A1, IB8, IP3	None	213	240	25 kg	100 kg	A	
+	**Boron tribromide**	8	UN2692	I	8, 6.1	2, A3, A7, B9, B14, B32, B74, N34, T20, TP2, TP12, TP13, TP38, TP45	None	227	244	Forbidden	Forbidden	C	12
	Boron trichloride	2.3	UN1741		2.3, 8	3, B9, B14	None	304	314	Forbidden	Forbidden	D	25, 40
	Boron trifluoride, compressed	2.3	UN1008		2.3	2, B9, B14	None	302	314, 315	Forbidden	Forbidden	D	40
	Boron trifluoride acetic acid complex	8	UN1742	II	8	B2, B6, IB2, T8, TP2, TP12	154	202	242	1 L	30 L	A	
	Boron trifluoride diethyl etherate	8	UN2604	I	8, 3	A19, T10, TP2	None	201	243	0.5 L	2.5 L	D	40
	Boron trifluoride dihydrate	8	UN2851	II	8	IB8, IP2, IP4, T7, TP2	154	212	240	15 kg	50 kg	B	12, 40
	Boron trifluoride dimethyl etherate	4.3	UN2965	I	4.3, 8, 3	A19, T10, TP2, TP7	None	201	243	Forbidden	1 L	D	21, 28, 40, 49, 100
	Boron trifluoride propionic acid complex	8	UN1743	II	8	B2, IB2, T8, TP2, TP12	154	202	242	1 L	30 L	A	
	Box toe gum, see **Nitrocellulose** *etc.*												
	Bromates, inorganic, aqueous solution, n.o.s.	5.1	UN3213	II	5.1	IB2, T4, TP1	152	202	242	1 L	5 L	B	56, 58, 106
	Bromates, inorganic, n.o.s.	5.1	UN1450	II	5.1	IB8, IP2, IP4	152	212	242	5 kg	25 kg	A	56, 58, 106
	Bromine azide	Forbidden											
+	**Bromine** *or* **Bromine solutions**	8	UN1744	I	8, 6.1	1, A3, A6, B9, B64, B85, N34, N43, T22, TP2, TP10, TP12, TP13	None	226	249	Forbidden	Forbidden		12, 40, 66, 74, 89, 90
	Bromine chloride	2.3	UN2901		2.3, 8, 5.1	2, B9, B14	None	304	314, 315	Forbidden	Forbidden	D	40, 89, 90
+	**Bromine pentafluoride**	5.1	UN1745	I	5.1, 6.1, 8	1, B9, B14, B30, B72, T22, TP2, TP12, TP13, TP38, TP44	None	228	244	Forbidden	Forbidden	D	25, 40, 66, 90
+	**Bromine trifluoride**	5.1	UN1746	I	5.1, 6.1, 8	2, B9, B14, B32, B74, T22, TP2, TP12, TP13, TP38, TP45	None	228	244	Forbidden	Forbidden	D	25, 40, 66, 90
	4-Bromo-1,2-dinitrobenzene	Forbidden											
	4-Bromo-1,2-dinitrobenzene (unstable at 59 degrees C.)	Forbidden											
	1-Bromo-3-chloropropane	6.1	UN2688	III	6.1	IB3, T4, TP1	153	203	241	60 L	220 L	A	
	1-Bromo-3-methylbutane	3	UN2341	III	3	B1, IB3, T2, TP1	150	203	242	60 L	220 L	A	
	1-Bromo-3-nitrobenzene (unstable at 56 degrees C)	Forbidden											
	2-Bromo-2-nitropropane-1,3-diol	4.1	UN3241	III	4.1	46, IB8, IP3	151	213	None	25 kg	50 kg	C	12, 25, 40
	Bromoacetic acid, *solid*	8	UN1938	II	8	A7, IB8, IP2, IP4, N34, T7	154	212	240	15 kg	50 kg	A	
	Bromoacetic acid, *solution*	8	UN1938	II	8	B2, IB2, T7, TP2	154	202	242	1 L	30 L	A	40
+	**Bromoacetone**	6.1	UN1569	II	6.1, 3	2, T20, TP2, TP13	None	193	245	Forbidden	Forbidden	D	40

§172.101 - Hazardous Materials Table

Symbols	Hazardous materials descriptions and proper shipping names	Hazard class or Division	Identification Numbers	PG	Label Codes	Special provisions (§172.102)	(8) Packaging (§173.***)			(9) Quantity limitations		(10) Vessel stowage	
							Exceptions	Non-bulk	Bulk	Passenger aircraft/ rail	Cargo aircraft only	Location	Other
(1)	(2)	(3)	(4)	(5)	(6)	(7)	(8A)	(8B)	(8C)	(9A)	(9B)	(10A)	(10B)
	Bromoacetyl bromide	8	UN2513	II	8	B2, IB2, T8, TP2, TP12	154	202	242	1 L	30 L	C	40
	Bromobenzene	3	UN2514	III	3	B1, IB3, T2, TP1	150	203	242	60 L	220 L	A	
	Bromobenzyl cyanides, *liquid*	6.1	UN1694	I	6.1	T14, TP2, TP13	None	201	243	Forbidden	30 L	D	12, 40
	Bromobenzyl cyanides, *solid*	6.1	UN1694	I	6.1	T14, TP2, TP13	None	211	242	Forbidden	50 kg	D	12, 40
	1-Bromobutane	3	UN1126	II	3	IB2, T4, TP1	150	202	242	5L	60 L	B	40
	2-Bromobutane	3	UN2339	II	3	B1, IB2, T4, TP1	150	202	242	5 L	60 L	B	40
	Bromochloromethane	6.1	UN1887	III	6.1	IB3, T4, TP1	153	203	241	60 L	220 L	A	
	2-Bromoethyl ethyl ether	3	UN2340	II	3	IB2, T4, TP1	150	202	242	5 L	60 L	B	40
	Bromoform	6.1	UN2515	III	6.1	IB3, T4, TP1	153	203	241	60 L	220 L	A	12, 40
	Bromomethylpropanes	3	UN2342	II	3	IB2, T4, TP1	150	202	242	5 L	60 L	B	
	2-Bromopentane	3	UN2343	II	3	IB2, T4, TP1	150	202	242	5 L	60 L	B	
	Bromopropanes	3	UN2344	II III	3 3	IB2, T4, TP1 IB3, T2, TP1	150 150	202 203	242 242	5 L 60 L	60 L 220 L	B A	40
	3-Bromopropyne	3	UN2345	II	3	IB2, T4, TP1	150	202	242	5 L	60 L	D	40
	Bromosilane	Forbidden											
	Bromotoluene-alpha, see **Benzyl bromide**												
	Bromotrifluoroethylene	2.1	UN2419		2.1		None	304	314, 315	Forbidden	150 kg	B	40
	Bromotrifluoromethane *or* **Refrigerant gas, R 13B1**	2.2	UN1009		2.2	T50	306	304	314, 315	75 kg	150 kg	A	
	Brucine	6.1	UN1570	I	6.1	IB7, IP1	None	211	242	5 kg	50 kg	A	
	Bursters, *explosive*	1.1D	UN0043	II	1.1D		None	62	None	Forbidden	Forbidden	07	
	Butadienes, stabilized	2.1	UN1010		2.1	T50	306	304	314, 315	Forbidden	150 kg	B	40
	Butane *see also* **Petroleum gases, liquefied**	2.1	UN1011		2.1	19, T50	306	304	314, 315	Forbidden	150 kg	E	40
	Butane, butane mixtures and mixtures having similar properties in cartridges each not exceeding 500 grams, see **Receptacles,** *etc.*												
	Butanedione	3	UN2346	II	3	IB2, T4, TP1	150	202	242	5 L	60 L	B	
	1,2,4-Butanetriol trinitrate	Forbidden											
	Butanols	3	UN1120	II III	3 3	IB2, T4, TP1, TP29 B1, IB3, T2, TP1	150 150	202 203	242 242	5 L 60 L	60 L 220 L	B A	
	tert-Butoxycarbonyl azide	Forbidden											
	Butyl acetates	3	UN1123	II III	3 3	IB2, T4, TP1 B1, IB3, T2, TP1	150 150	202 203	242 242	5 L 60 L	60 L 220 L	B A	
	Butyl acid phosphate	8	UN1718	III	8	IB3, T4, TP1	154	203	241	5 L	60 L	A	
	Butyl acrylates, stabilized	3	UN2348	III	3	B1, IB3, T2, TP1	150	203	242	60 L	220 L	A	
	Butyl alcohols, see **Butanols**												
	Butyl benzenes	3	UN2709	III	3	B1, IB3, T2, TP1	150	203	242	60 L	220 L	A	
	n-Butyl bromide, see **1-Bromobutane**												
	n-Butyl chloride, see **Chlorobutanes**												
D	**sec-Butyl chloroformate**	6.1	NA2742	I	6.1, 3, 8	2, B9, B14, B32, B74, T20, TP4, TP12, TP13, TP38, TP45	None	227	244	1 L	30 L	A	12, 13, 22, 25, 40, 48, 100
	n-Butyl chloroformate	6.1	UN2743	I	6.1, 8, 3	2, B9, B14, B32, B74, T20, TP2, TP13, TP38, TP45	None	227	244	Forbidden	Forbidden	A	12, 13, 21, 25, 40, 100
	Butyl ethers, see **Dibutyl ethers**												
	Butyl ethyl ether, see **Ethyl butyl ether**												
	n-Butyl formate	3	UN1128	II	3	IB2, T4, TP1	150	202	242	5 L	60 L	B	
	tert-Butyl hydroperoxide, with more than 90 percent with water	Forbidden											
	tert-Butyl hypochlorite	4.2	UN3255	I	4.2, 8		None	211	243	Forbidden	Forbidden	D	
	N-n-Butyl imidazole	6.1	UN2690	II	6.1	IB2, T7, TP2	None	202	243	5 L	60 L	A	

§172.101 - Hazardous Materials Table

Symbols	Hazardous materials descriptions and proper shipping names	Hazard class or Division	Identification Numbers	PG	Label Codes	Special provisions (§172.102)	(8) Packaging (§173.***)			(9) Quantity limitations		(10) Vessel stowage	
							Exceptions	Non-bulk	Bulk	Passenger aircraft/rail	Cargo aircraft only	Location	Other
(1)	(2)	(3)	(4)	(5)	(6)	(7)	(8A)	(8B)	(8C)	(9A)	(9B)	(10A)	(10B)
	tert-Butyl isocyanate	6.1	UN2484	I	6.1, 3	1, A7, B9, B14, B30, B72, T22, TP2, TP13, TP38, TP44	None	226	244	Forbidden	Forbidden	D	40
	n-Butyl isocyanate	6.1	UN2485	I	6.1, 3	2, A7, B9, B14, B32, B74, B77, T20, TP2, TP13, TP38, TP45	None	227	244	Forbidden	Forbidden	D	40
	Butyl mercaptans	3	UN2347	II	3	A3, IB2, T4, TP1	150	202	242	5 L	60 L	D	26, 95
	n-Butyl methacrylate, stabilized	3	UN2227	III	3	B1, IB3, T2, TP1	150	203	242	60 L	220 L	A	
	Butyl methyl ether	3	UN2350	II	3	IB2, T4, TP1	150	202	242	5 L	60 L	B	
	Butyl nitrites	3	UN2351	I II III	3 3 3	T11, TP1, TP8, TP27 IB2, T4, TP1 B1, IB3, T2, TP1	150 150 150	201 202 203	243 242 242	1 L 5 L 60 L	30 L 60 L 220 L	E B A	40 40 40
	tert-Butyl peroxyacetate, with more than 76 percent in solution	Forbidden											
	n-Butyl peroxydicarbonate, with more than 52 percent in solution	Forbidden											
	tert-Butyl peroxyisobutyrate, with more than 77 percent in solution	Forbidden											
	Butyl phosphoric acid, see **Butyl acid phosphate**												
	Butyl propionates	3	UN1914	III	3	B1, IB3, T2, TP1	150	203	242	60 L	220 L	A	
	5-tert-Butyl-2,4,6-trinitro-m-xylene *or* **Musk xylene**	4.1	UN2956	III	4.1		None	214	None	Forbidden	Forbidden	D	12
	Butyl vinyl ether, stabilized	3	UN2352	II	3	IB2, T4, TP1	150	202	242	5 L	60 L	B	40
	n-Butylamine	3	UN1125	II	3, 8	IB2, T7, TP1	None	202	242	1 L	5 L	B	40
	N-Butylaniline	6.1	UN2738	II	6.1	IB2, T7, TP2	None	202	243	5 L	60 L	A	
	tert-Butylcyclohexylchloroformate	6.1	UN2747	III	6.1	IB3, T4, TP1	153	203	241	60 L	220 L	A	12, 13, 25
	Butylene *see also* **Petroleum gases, liquefied**	2.1	UN1012		2.1	19, T50	None	304	314, 315	Forbidden	150 kg	E	40
	1,2-Butylene oxide, stabilized	3	UN3022	II	3	IB2, T4, TP1	150	202	242	5 L	60 L	B	49
	Butyltoluenes	6.1	UN2667	III	6.1	IB3, T4, TP1	153	203	241	60 L	220 L	A	
	Butyltrichlorosilane	8	UN1747	II	8, 3	A7, B2, B6, IB2, N34, T7, TP2, TP13	None	202	243	Forbidden	30 L	C	40
	1,4-Butynediol	6.1	UN2716	III	6.1	A1, IB8, IP3	None	213	240	100 kg	200 kg	A	61, 70
	Butyraldehyde	3	UN1129	II	3	IB2, T4, TP1	150	202	242	5 L	60 L	B	
	Butyraldoxime	3	UN2840	III	3	B1, IB3, T2, TP1	150	203	242	60 L	220 L	A	
	Butyric acid	8	UN2820	III	8	IB3, T4, TP1	154	203	241	5 L	60 L	A	12
	Butyric anhydride	8	UN2739	III	8	IB3, T4, TP1	154	203	241	5 L	60 L	A	
	Butyronitrile	3	UN2411	II	3, 6.1	IB2, T7, TP1, TP13	None	202	243	1 L	60 L	E	40
	Butyryl chloride	3	UN2353	II	3, 8	IB2, T8, TP2, TP12, TP13	None	202	243	1 L	5 L	C	40
	Cacodylic acid	6.1	UN1572	II	6.1	IB8, IP2, IP4	None	212	242	25 kg	100 kg	E	26
	Cadmium compounds	6.1	UN2570	I II III	6.1 6.1 6.1	IB7, IP1 IB8, IP2, IP4 IB8, IP3	None None 153	211 212 213	242 242 240	5 kg 25 kg 100 kg	50 kg 100 kg 200 kg	A A A	
	Caesium hydroxide	8	UN2682	II	8	IB8, IP2, IP4	154	212	240	15 kg	50 kg	A	
	Caesium hydroxide solution	8	UN2681	II III	8 8	B2, IB2, T7, TP2 IB3, T4, TP1	154 154	202 203	242 241	1 L 5 L	30 L 60 L	A A	
	Calcium	4.3	UN1401	II	4.3	IB7, IP2	151	212	241	15 kg	50 kg	E	
	Calcium arsenate	6.1	UN1573	II	6.1	IB8, IP2, IP4	None	212	242	25 kg	100 kg	A	
	Calcium arsenate and calcium arsenite, mixtures, solid	6.1	UN1574	II	6.1	IB8, IP2, IP4	None	212	242	25 kg	100 kg	A	
	Calcium bisulfite solution, see **Bisulfites, aqueous solutions, n.o.s.**												
	Calcium carbide	4.3	UN1402	I II	4.3 4.3	A1, A8, B55, B59, IB4, IP1, N34 A1, A8, B55, B59, IB7, IP2, N34	None 151	211 212	242 241	Forbidden 15 kg	15 kg 50 kg	B B	
	Calcium chlorate	5.1	UN1452	II	5.1	IB8, IP2, IP4, N34	152	212	242	5 kg	25 kg	A	56, 58, 106

§172.101 - Hazardous Materials Table

Symbols	Hazardous materials descriptions and proper shipping names	Hazard class or Division	Identification Numbers	PG	Label Codes	Special provisions (§172.102)	(8) Packaging (§173.***) Exceptions	Non-bulk	Bulk	(9) Quantity limitations Passenger aircraft/ rail	Cargo aircraft only	(10) Vessel stowage Location	Other
(1)	(2)	(3)	(4)	(5)	(6)	(7)	(8A)	(8B)	(8C)	(9A)	(9B)	(10A)	(10B)
	Calcium chlorate aqueous solution	5.1	UN2429	II	5.1	A2, IB2, N41, T4, TP1	152	202	242	1 L	5 L	B	56, 58, 106
				III	5.1	A2, IB2, N41, T4, TP1	152	203	241	2.5 L	30 L	B	56, 68, 106
	Calcium chlorite	5.1	UN1453	II	5.1	A9, IB8, IP2, IP4, N34	152	212	242	5 kg	25 kg	A	56, 58, 106
	Calcium cyanamide *with more than 0.1 percent of calcium carbide*	4.3	UN1403	III	4.3	A1, A19, IB8, IP4	151	213	241	25 kg	100 kg	A	
	Calcium cyanide	6.1	UN1575	I	6.1	IB7, IP1, N79, N80	None	211	242	5 kg	50 kg	A	26, 40
	Calcium dithionite *or* **Calcium hydrosulfite**	4.2	UN1923	II	4.2	A19, A20, IB6, IP2	None	212	241	15 kg	50 kg	E	13
	Calcium hydride	4.3	UN1404	I	4.3	A19, N40	None	211	242	Forbidden	15 kg	E	
	Calcium hydrosulfite, *see* **Calcium dithionite**												
	Calcium hypochlorite, dry *or* **Calcium hypochlorite mixtures dry** *with more than 39 percent available chlorine (8.8 percent available oxygen)*	5.1	UN1748	II	5.1	A7, A9, IB8, IP2, IP4, N34, W9	152	212	None	5 kg	25 kg	D	4, 5, 25, 48, 56, 58, 69
	Calcium hypochlorite, hydrated *or* **Calcium hypochlorite, hydrated mixtures,** *with not less than 5.5 percent but not more than 10 percent water*	5.1	UN2880	II	5.1	IB8, IP2, IP4, W9	152	212	240	5 kg	25 kg	D	4, 5, 25, 48, 56, 58, 69
	Calcium hypochlorite mixtures, dry, *with more than 10 percent but not more than 39 percent available chlorine*	5.1	UN2208	III	5.1	A1, A29, IB8, IP3, N34, W9	152	213	240	25 kg	100 kg	D	4, 5, 25, 48, 56, 58, 69
	Calcium manganese silicon	4.3	UN2844	III	4.3	A1, A19, IB8, IP2, IP4	151	213	241	25 kg	100 kg	A	85, 103
	Calcium nitrate	5.1	UN1454	III	5.1	34, IB8, IP3	152	213	240	25 kg	100 kg	A	
A	**Calcium oxide**	8	UN1910	III	8	IB8, IP3	154	213	240	25 kg	100 kg	A	
	Calcium perchlorate	5.1	UN1455	II	5.1	IB6, IP2	152	212	242	5 kg	25 kg	A	56, 58, 106
	Calcium permanganate	5.1	UN1456	II	5.1	IB6, IP2	152	212	242	5 kg	25 kg	D	56, 58, 69, 106, 107
	Calcium peroxide	5.1	UN1457	II	5.1	IB6, IP2	152	212	242	5 kg	25 kg	A	13, 75, 106
	Calcium phosphide	4.3	UN1360	I	4.3, 6.1	A8, A19, N40	None	211	242	Forbidden	15 kg	E	40, 85
	Calcium, pyrophoric *or* **Calcium alloys, pyrophoric**	4.2	UN1855	I	4.2		None	187	None	Forbidden	Forbidden	D	
	Calcium resinate	4.1	UN1313	III	4.1	A1, A19, IB6	None	213	240	25 kg	100 kg	A	
	Calcium resinate, fused	4.1	UN1314	III	4.1	A1, A19, IB4	None	213	240	25 kg	100 kg	A	
	Calcium selenate, see **Selenates** *or* **Selenites**												
	Calcium silicide	4.3	UN1405	II	4.3	A19, IB7, IP2	151	212	241	15 kg	50 kg	B	85, 103
				III	4.3	A1, A19, IB8, IP4	151	213	241	25 kg	100 kg	B	85, 103
	Camphor oil	3	UN1130	III	3	B1, IB3, T2, TP1	150	203	242	60 L	220 L	A	
	Camphor, *synthetic*	4.1	UN2717	III	4.1	A1, IB8, IP3	None	213	240	25 kg	100 kg	A	
	Cannon primers, see **Primers, tubular**												
	Caproic acid	8	UN2829	III	8	IB3, T4, TP1	154	203	241	5 L	60 L	A	
	Caps, blasting, see **Detonators,** *etc.*												
	Carbamate pesticides, liquid, flammable, toxic, *flash point less than 23 degrees C*	3	UN2758	I	3, 6.1	T14, TP2, TP13, TP27	None	201	243	Forbidden	30 L	B	40
				II	3, 6.1	IB2, T11, TP2, TP13, TP27	None	202	243	1 L	60 L	B	40
	Carbamate pesticides, liquid, toxic	6.1	UN2992	I	6.1	T14, TP2, TP13, TP27	None	201	243	1 L	30 L	B	40
				II	6.1	IB2, T11, TP2, TP13, TP27	None	202	243	5 L	60 L	B	40
				III	6.1	IB3, T7, TP2, TP28	153	203	241	60 L	220 L	A	40
	Carbamate pesticides, liquid, toxic, flammable, *flash point not less than 23 degrees C*	6.1	UN2991	I	6.1, 3	T14, TP2, TP13, TP27	None	201	243	1 L	30 L	B	40
				II	6.1, 3	IB2, T11, TP2, TP13, TP27	None	202	243	5 L	60 L	B	40
				III	6.1, 3	B1, IB3, T7, TP2, TP28	153	203	242	60 L	220 L	A	40
	Carbamate pesticides, solid, toxic	6.1	UN2757	I	6.1	IB7, IP1	None	211	242	5 kg	50 kg	A	40
				II	6.1	IB8, IP2, IP4	None	212	242	25 kg	100 kg	A	40
				III	6.1	IB8, IP3	153	213	240	100 kg	200 kg	A	40

§172.101 - Hazardous Materials Table

Sym-bols	Hazardous materials descriptions and proper shipping names	Hazard class or Division	Identifi-cation Numbers	PG	Label Codes	Special provisions (§172.102)	(8) Packaging (§173.***)			(9) Quantity limitations		(10) Vessel stowage	
							Excep-tions	Non-bulk	Bulk	Passen-ger aircraft/ rail	Cargo aircraft only	Loca-tion	Other
(1)	(2)	(3)	(4)	(5)	(6)	(7)	(8A)	(8B)	(8C)	(9A)	(9B)	(10A)	(10B)
	Carbolic acid, see **Phenol, solid** *or* **Phenol, molten**												
	Carbolic acid solutions, see **Phenol solutions**												
I	**Carbon, activated**	4.2	UN1362	III	4.2	IB8, IP3	None	213	241	0.5 kg	0.5 kg	A	12
I	**Carbon,** *animal or vegetable origin*	4.2	UN1361	II III	4.2 4.2	IB6 IB8, IP3	None None	212 213	242 241	Forbidden Forbidden	Forbidden Forbidden	A A	12 12
	Carbon bisulfide, see **Carbon disulfide**												
	Carbon dioxide	2.2	UN1013		2.2		306	302, 304	302, 314, 315	75 kg	150 kg	A	
	Carbon dioxide and nitrous oxide mixtures	2.2	UN1015		2.2		306	None	314, 315	75 kg	150 kg	A	
	Carbon dioxide and oxygen mixtures, compressed	2.2	UN1014		2.2, 5.1	77	306	304	314, 315	75 kg	150 kg	A	
	Carbon dioxide, refrigerated liquid	2.2	UN2187		2.2	T75, TP5	306	304	314, 315	50 kg	500 kg	B	
A W	**Carbon dioxide, solid** *or* **Dry ice**	9	UN1845	III	None		217	217	240	200 kg	200 kg	C	40
	Carbon disulfide	3	UN1131	I	3, 6.1	B16, T14, TP2, TP7, TP13	None	201	243	Forbidden	Forbidden	D	18, 40, 115
	Carbon monoxide, compressed	2.3	UN1016		2.3, 2.1	4	None	302	314, 315	Forbidden	25 kg	D	40
	Carbon monoxide and hydrogen mixture, compressed	2.3	UN2600		2.3, 2.1	6	None	302	302	Forbidden	Forbidden	D	40
D	**Carbon monoxide, refrigerated liquid** *(cryogenic liquid)*	2.3	NA9202		2.3, 2.1	4, T75, TP5	None	316	318	Forbidden	Forbidden	D	
	Carbon tetrabromide	6.1	UN2516	III	6.1	IB8, IP3	153	213	240	100 kg	200 kg	A	25
	Carbon tetrachloride	6.1	UN1846	II	6.1	IB2, N36, T7, TP2	None	202	243	5 L	60 L	A	40
	Carbonyl chloride, see **Phosgene**												
	Carbonyl fluoride, compressed	2.3	UN2417		2.3, 8	2	None	302	None	Forbidden	Forbidden	D	40
	Carbonyl sulfide	2.3	UN2204		2.3, 2.1	3, B14	None	304	314, 315	Forbidden	25 kg	D	40
	Cartridge cases, empty primed, see **Cases, cartridge, empty, with primer**												
	Cartridges, actuating, for aircraft ejector seat catapult, fire extinguisher, canopy removal or apparatus, see **Cartridges, power device**												
	Cartridges, explosive, see **Charges, demolition**												
	Cartridges, flash	1.1G	UN0049	II	1.1G		None	62	None	Forbidden	Forbidden	07	
	Cartridges, flash	1.3G	UN0050	II	1.3G		None	62	None	Forbidden	75 kg	07	
	Cartridges for weapons, blank	1.1C	UN0326	II	1.1C		None	62	None	Forbidden	Forbidden	07	
	Cartridges for weapons, blank	1.2C	UN0413	II	1.2C		None	62	None	Forbidden	Forbidden	07	
	Cartridges for weapons, blank *or* **Cartridges, small arms, blank**	1.4S	UN0014	II	None		63	62	None	25 kg	100 kg	05	
	Cartridges for weapons, blank *or* **Cartridges, small arms, blank**	1.3C	UN0327	II	1.3C		None	62	None	Forbidden	Forbidden	07	
	Cartridges for weapons, blank *or* **Cartridges, small arms, blank**	1.4C	UN0338	II	1.4C		None	62	None	Forbidden	75 kg	06	
	Cartridges for weapons, inert projectile	1.2C	UN0328	II	1.2C		None	62	None	Forbidden	Forbidden	03	
	Cartridges for weapons, inert projectile *or* **Cartridges, small arms**	1.4S	UN0012	II	None		63	62	None	25 kg	100 kg	05	
	Cartridges for weapons, inert projectile *or* **Cartridges, small arms**	1.4C	UN0339	II	1.4C		None	62	None	Forbidden	75 kg	06	
	Cartridges for weapons, inert projectile *or* **Cartridges, small arms**	1.3C	UN0417	II	1.3C		None	62	None	Forbidden	Forbidden	06	
	Cartridges for weapons, *with bursting charge*	1.1F	UN0005	II	1.1F		None	62	None	Forbidden	Forbidden	08	
	Cartridges for weapons, *with bursting charge*	1.1E	UN0006	II	1.1E		None	62	None	Forbidden	Forbidden	03	
	Cartridges for weapons, *with bursting charge*	1.2F	UN0007	II	1.2F		None	62	None	Forbidden	Forbidden	08	
	Cartridges for weapons, *with bursting charge*	1.2E	UN0321	II	1.2E		None	62	None	Forbidden	Forbidden	03	
	Cartridges for weapons, *with bursting charge*	1.4F	UN0348	II	1.4F		None	62	None	Forbidden	Forbidden	08	

§172.101 - Hazardous Materials Table

Sym-bols	Hazardous materials descriptions and proper shipping names	Hazard class or Division	Identifi-cation Numbers	PG	Label Codes	Special provisions (§172.102)	(8) Packaging (§173.***)			(9) Quantity limitations		(10) Vessel stowage	
							Excep-tions	Non-bulk	Bulk	Passen-ger aircraft/ rail	Cargo aircraft only	Loca-tion	Other
(1)	(2)	(3)	(4)	(5)	(6)	(7)	(8A)	(8B)	(8C)	(9A)	(9B)	(10A)	(10B)
	Cartridges for weapons, *with bursting charge*	1.4E	UN0412	II	1.4E		None	62	None	Forbidden	75 kg	02	
	Cartridges, oil well	1.3C	UN0277	II	1.3C		None	62	None	Forbidden	Forbidden	07	
	Cartridges, oil well	1.4C	UN0278	II	1.4C		None	62	None	Forbidden	75 kg	06	
	Cartridges, power device	1.3C	UN0275	II	1.3C		None	62	None	Forbidden	75 kg	07	
	Cartridges, power device	1.4C	UN0276	II	1.4C	110	None	62	None	Forbidden	75 kg	06	
	Cartridges, power device	1.4S	UN0323	II	1.4S	110	63	62	None	25 kg	100 kg	05	
	Cartridges, power device	1.2C	UN0381	II	1.2C		None	62	None	Forbidden	Forbidden	07	
	Cartridges, safety, blank, see **Cartridges for weapons, blank** *(UN 0014)*												
	Cartridges, safety, see **Cartridges for weapons,** *other than blank or* **Cartridges, power device** *(UN 0323)*												
	Cartridges, signal	1.3G	UN0054	II	1.3G		None	62	None	Forbidden	75 kg	07	
	Cartridges, signal	1.4G	UN0312	II	1.4G		None	62	None	Forbidden	75 kg	06	
	Cartridges, signal	1.4S	UN0405	II	1.4S		None	62	None	25 kg	100 kg	05	
D	**Cartridges, small arms**	ORM-D			None		63	None	None	30 kg gross	30 kg gross	A	
	Cartridges, sporting, see **Cartridges for weapons,** *other than blank*												
	Cartridges, starter, jet engine, see **Cartridges, power device**												
	Cases, cartridge, empty with primer	1.4S	UN0055	II	1.4S	50	None	62	None	25 kg	100 kg	05	
	Cases, cartridges, empty with primer	1.4C	UN0379	II	1.4C	50	None	62	None	Forbidden	75 kg	06	
	Cases, combustible, empty, without primer	1.4C	UN0446	II	1.4C		None	62	None	Forbidden	75 kg	06	
	Cases, combustible, empty, without primer	1.3C	UN0447	II	1.3C		None	62	None	Forbidden	Forbidden	07	
	Casinghead gasoline see **Gasoline**												
A W	**Castor beans** *or* **Castor meal** *or* **Castor pomace** *or* **Castor flake**	9	UN2969	II	None	IB8, IP2, IP4	155	204	240	No limit	No limit	E	34, 40
G	**Caustic alkali liquids, n.o.s.**	8	UN1719	II	8	B2, IB2, T11, TP2, TP27	154	202	242	1 L	30 L	A	
				III	8	IB3, T7, TP1, TP28	154	203	241	5 L	60 L	A	
	Caustic potash, see **Potassium hydroxide** *etc.*												
	Caustic soda, (etc.) see **Sodium hydroxide** *etc.*												
	Cells, containing sodium	4.3	UN3292	II	4.3		189	189	189	25 kg gross	No limit	A	
	Celluloid, *in block, rods, rolls, sheets, tubes, etc., except scrap*	4.1	UN2000	III	4.1		None	213	240	25 kg	100 kg	A	
	Celluloid, scrap	4.2	UN2002	III	4.2	IB8, IP3	None	213	241	Forbidden	Forbidden	D	
	Cement, see **Adhesives** *containing flammable liquid*												
	Cerium, *slabs, ingots, or rods*	4.1	UN1333	II	4.1	IB8, IP2, IP4, N34	None	212	240	15 kg	50 kg	A	74, 91
	Cerium, *turnings or gritty powder*	4.3	UN3078	II	4.3	A1, IB7, IP2	151	212	242	15 kg	50 kg	E	
	Cesium *or* **Caesium**	4.3	UN1407	I	4.3	A19, IB1, IP1, N34, N40	None	211	242	Forbidden	15 kg	D	
	Cesium nitrate *or* **Caesium nitrate**	5.1	UN1451	III	5.1	A1, A29, IB8, IP3	152	213	240	25 kg	100 kg	A	
D	**Charcoal** *briquettes, shell, screenings, wood, etc.*	4.2	NA1361	III	4.2	IB8	151	213	240	25 kg	100 kg	A	12
	Charges, bursting, plastics bonded	1.1D	UN0457	II	1.1D		None	62	None	Forbidden	Forbidden	07	
	Charges, bursting, plastics bonded	1.2D	UN0458	II	1.2D		None	62	None	Forbidden	Forbidden	07	
	Charges, bursting, plastics bonded	1.4D	UN0459	II	1.4D		None	62	None	Forbidden	75 kg	06	
	Charges, bursting, plastics bonded	1.4S	UN0460	II	1.4S		None	62	None	25 kg	100 kg	05	
	Charges, demolition	1.1D	UN0048	II	1.1D		None	62	None	Forbidden	Forbidden	03	
	Charges, depth	1.1D	UN0056	II	1.1D		None	62	None	Forbidden	Forbidden	03	
	Charges, expelling, explosive, for fire extinguishers, see **Cartridges, power device**												

§172.101 - Hazardous Materials Table

Symbols	Hazardous materials descriptions and proper shipping names	Hazard class or Division	Identification Numbers	PG	Label Codes	Special provisions (§172.102)	(8) Packaging (§173.***) Exceptions	Non-bulk	Bulk	(9) Quantity limitations Passenger aircraft/rail	Cargo aircraft only	(10) Vessel stowage Location	Other
(1)	(2)	(3)	(4)	(5)	(6)	(7)	(8A)	(8B)	(8C)	(9A)	(9B)	(10A)	(10B)
	Charges, explosive, commercial *without detonator*	1.1D	UN0442	II	1.1D		None	62	None	Forbidden	Forbidden	07	
	Charges, explosive, commercial *without detonator*	1.2D	UN0443	II	1.2D		None	62	None	Forbidden	Forbidden	07	
	Charges, explosive, commercial *without detonator*	1.4D	UN0444	II	1.4D		None	62	None	Forbidden	75 kg	06	
	Charges, explosive, commercial *without detonator*	1.4S	UN0445	II	1.4S		None	62	None	25 kg	100 kg	05	
	Charges, propelling	1.1C	UN0271	II	1.1C		None	62	None	Forbidden	Forbidden	07	
	Charges, propelling	1.3C	UN0272	II	1.3C		None	62	None	Forbidden	Forbidden	07	
	Charges, propelling	1.2C	UN0415	II	1.2C		None	62	None	Forbidden	Forbidden	07	
	Charges, propelling	1.4C	UN0491	II	1.4C		None	62	None	Forbidden	75 kg	06	
	Charges, propelling, for cannon	1.3C	UN0242	II	1.3C		None	62	None	Forbidden	Forbidden	10	
	Charges, propelling, for cannon	1.1C	UN0279	II	1.1C		None	62	None	Forbidden	Forbidden	10	
	Charges, propelling, for cannon	1.2C	UN0414	II	1.2C		None	62	None	Forbidden	Forbidden	10	
	Charges, shaped, flexible, linear	1.4D	UN0237	II	1.4D		None	62	None	Forbidden	75 kg	06	
	Charges, shaped, flexible, linear	1.1D	UN0288	II	1.1D	101	None	62	None	Forbidden	Forbidden	07	
	Charges, shaped, *without detonator*	1.1D	UN0059	II	1.1D		None	62	None	Forbidden	Forbidden	07	
	Charges, shaped, *without detonator*	1.2D	UN0439	II	1.2D		None	62	None	Forbidden	Forbidden	07	
	Charges, shaped, *without detonator*	1.4D	UN0440	II	1.4D		None	62	None	Forbidden	75 kg	06	
	Charges, shaped, *without detonator*	1.4S	UN0441	II	1.4S		None	62	None	25 kg	100 kg	05	
	Charges, supplementary explosive	1.1D	UN0060	II	1.1D		None	62	None	Forbidden	Forbidden	10	
D	**Chemical kit**	8	NA1760	II	8		154	161	None	1 L	30 L	B	40
	Chemical kits	9	UN3316		9	15	None	None	None	10 kg	10 kg	A	
	Chloral, anhydrous, stabilized	6.1	UN2075	II	6.1	IB2, T7, TP2	None	202	243	5 L	60 L	D	40
	Chlorate and borate mixtures	5.1	UN1458	II	5.1	A9, IB8, IP2, IP4, N34	152	212	240	5 kg	25 kg	A	56, 58, 106
				III	5.1	A9, IB8, IP3, N34	152	213	240	25 kg	100 kg	A	56, 58, 106
	Chlorate and magnesium chloride mixtures	5.1	UN1459	II	5.1	A9, IB8, IP2, IP4, N34, T4, TP1	152	212	240	5 kg	25 kg	A	56, 58, 106
				III	5.1	A9, IB8, IP3, N34, T4, TP1	152	213	240	25 kg	100 kg	A	56, 58, 106
	Chlorate of potash, see **Potassium chlorate**												
	Chlorate of soda, see **Sodium chlorate**												
	Chlorates, inorganic, aqueous solution, n.o.s.	5.1	UN3210	II	5.1	IB2, T4, TP1	152	202	242	1 L	5 L	B	56, 58, 106
	Chlorates, inorganic, n.o.s.	5.1	UN1461	II	5.1	A9, IB6, IP2, N34	152	212	242	5 kg	25 kg	A	56, 58, 106
	Chloric acid aqueous solution, *with not more than 10 percent chloric acid*	5.1	UN2626	II	5.1	IB2	None	229	None	Forbidden	Forbidden	D	56, 58, 106
	Chloride of phosphorus, see **Phosphorus trichloride**												
	Chloride of sulfur, see **Sulfur chloride**												
	Chlorinated lime, see **Calcium hypochlorite mixtures,** *etc.*												
	Chlorine	2.3	UN1017		2.3, 8	2, B9, B14, T50, TP19	None	304	314, 315	Forbidden	Forbidden	D	40, 51, 55, 62, 68, 89, 90
	Chlorine azide	Forbidden											
D	**Chlorine dioxide, hydrate, frozen**	5.1	NA9191	II	5.1, 6.1		None	229	None	Forbidden	Forbidden	E	
	Chlorine dioxide (not hydrate)	Forbidden											
	Chlorine pentafluoride	2.3	UN2548		2.3, 5.1, 8	1, B7, B9, B14	None	304	314	Forbidden	Forbidden	D	40, 89, 90
	Chlorine trifluoride	2.3	UN1749		2.3, 5.1, 8	2, B7, B9, B14	None	304	314	Forbidden	Forbidden	D	40, 89, 90
	Chlorite solution	8	UN1908	II	8	A3, A6, A7, B2, IB2, N34, T7, TP2, TP24	154	202	242	1 L	30 L	B	26
				III	8	A3, A6, A7, B2, IB3, N34, T4, TP2, TP24	154	203	241	5 L	60 L	B	26
	Chlorites, inorganic, n.o.s.	5.1	UN1462	II	5.1	A7, IB6, IP2, N34	152	212	242	5 kg	25 kg	A	56, 58, 106
	1-Chloro-1,1-difluoroethane *or* **Refrigerant gas R 142b**	2.1	UN2517		2.1	T50	306	304	314, 315	Forbidden	150 kg	B	40

§172.101 - Hazardous Materials Table

Symbols (1)	Hazardous materials descriptions and proper shipping names (2)	Hazard class or Division (3)	Identification Numbers (4)	PG (5)	Label Codes (6)	Special provisions (§172.102) (7)	(8) Packaging (§173.***) Exceptions (8A)	Non-bulk (8B)	Bulk (8C)	(9) Quantity limitations Passenger aircraft/rail (9A)	Cargo aircraft only (9B)	(10) Vessel stowage Location (10A)	Other (10B)
	3-Chloro-4-methylphenyl isocyanate	6.1	UN2236	II	6.1	IB2	None	202	243	5 L	60 L	B	40
	1-Chloro-1,2,2,2-tetrafluoroethane *or* **Refrigerant gas R 124**	2.2	UN1021		2.2	T50	306	304	314, 315	75 kg	150 kg	A	
	4-Chloro-o-toluidine hydrochloride	6.1	UN1579	III	6.1	IB8, IP3	153	213	240	100 kg	200 kg	A	
	1-Chloro-2,2,2-trifluoroethane *or* **Refrigerant gas R 133a**	2.2	UN1983		2.2	T50	306	304	314, 315	75 kg	150 kg	A	
	Chloroacetic acid, molten	6.1	UN3250	II	6.1, 8	IB1, T7, TP3	None	202	243	Forbidden	Forbidden	C	40
	Chloroacetic acid, solid	6.1	UN1751	II	6.1, 8	A3, A7, IB8, IP4, N34	None	212	242	15 kg	50 kg	A	40
	Chloroacetic acid, solution	6.1	UN1750	II	6.1, 8	A7, IB2, N34, T7, TP2	None	202	243	1 L	30 L	C	40
	Chloroacetone, stabilized	6.1	UN1695	I	6.1, 3, 8	2, B9, B14, B32, B74, N12, N32, N34, T20, TP2, TP13, TP38, TP45	None	227	244	Forbidden	Forbidden	D	21, 40, 100
	Chloroacetone (unstabilized)	Forbidden											
+	**Chloroacetonitrile**	6.1	UN2668	II	6.1, 3	2, B9, B14, B32, B74, IB99, T20, TP2, TP38, TP45	None	227	244	Forbidden	Forbidden	A	12, 26, 40
	Chloroacetophenone *(CN), liquid*	6.1	UN1697	II	6.1	A3, IB2, N12, N32, N33, T11, TP2, TP13, TP27	None	202	243	Forbidden	60 L	D	12, 40
	Chloroacetophenone *(CN), solid*	6.1	UN1697	II	6.1	A3, IB8, IP2, IP4, N12, N32, N33, N34, T7, TP2, TP13	None	212	None	Forbidden	100 kg	D	12, 40
	Chloroacetyl chloride	6.1	UN1752	I	6.1, 8	2, A3, A6, A7, B3, B8, B9, B14, B32, B74, B77, N34, N43, T20, TP2, TP13, TP38, TP45	None	227	244	Forbidden	Forbidden	D	40
	Chloroanilines, liquid	6.1	UN2019	II	6.1	IB2, T7, TP2	None	202	243	5 L	60 L	A	
	Chloroanilines, solid	6.1	UN2018	II	6.1	IB8, IP2, IP4, T7, TP2	None	212	242	25 kg	100 kg	A	
	Chloroanisidines	6.1	UN2233	III	6.1	IB8, IP3	153	213	240	100 kg	200 kg	A	
	Chlorobenzene	3	UN1134	III	3	B1, IB3, T2, TP1	150	203	242	60 L	220 L	A	
	Chlorobenzol, see **Chlorobenzene**												
	Chlorobenzotrifluorides	3	UN2234	III	3	B1, IB3, T2, TP1	150	203	242	60 L	220 L	A	40
	Chlorobenzyl chlorides	6.1	UN2235	III	6.1	IB3, T4, TP1	153	203	241	60 L	220 L	A	
	Chlorobutanes	3	UN1127	II	3	IB2, T4, TP1	150	202	242	5 L	60 L	B	
	Chlorocresols, *liquid*	6.1	UN2669	II	6.1	IB2, T7, TP2	None	202	243	5 L	60 L	A	12
	Chlorocresols, *solid*	6.1	UN2669	II	6.1	IB8, IP2, IP3, T7	None	212	242	25 kg	100 kg	A	12
	Chlorodifluorobromomethane *or* **Refrigerant gas R 12B1**	2.2	UN1974		2.2	T50	306	304	314, 315	75 kg	150 kg	A	
	Chlorodifluoromethane and chloropentafluoroethane mixture *or* **Refrigerant gas R 502** *with fixed boiling point, with approximately 49 percent chlorodifluoromethane*	2.2	UN1973		2.2	T50	306	304	314, 315	75 kg	150 kg	A	
	Chlorodifluoromethane *or* **Refrigerant gas R 22**	2.2	UN1018		2.2	T50	306	304	314, 315	75 kg	150 kg	A	
+	**Chlorodinitrobenzenes**	6.1	UN1577	II	6.1	IB8, IP2, IP4, T7, TP2	None	212	242	25 kg	100 kg	A	91
	2-Chloroethanal	6.1	UN2232	I	6.1	2, B9, B14, B32, B74, T20, TP2, TP13, TP38, TP45	None	227	244	Forbidden	Forbidden	D	40
	Chloroform	6.1	UN1888	III	6.1	IB3, N36, T7, TP2	153	203	241	60 L	220 L	A	40
G	**Chloroformates, toxic, corrosive, flammable, n.o.s.**	6.1	UN2742	II	6.1, 8, 3	5, IB1, T7, TP2	None	202	243	1 L	30 L	A	12, 13, 21, 25, 40, 100
G	**Chloroformates, toxic, corrosive, n.o.s.**	6.1	UN3277	II	6.1, 8	IB2, T8, TP2, TP13, TP28	None	202	243	1 L	30 L	A	12, 13, 25, 40
	Chloromethyl chloroformate	6.1	UN2745	II	6.1, 8	IB2, T7, TP2, TP13	None	202	243	1 L	30 L	A	12, 13, 21, 25, 40, 100
	Chloromethyl ethyl ether	3	UN2354	II	3, 6.1	IB2, T7, TP1, TP13	None	202	243	1 L	60 L	E	40

§172.101 - Hazardous Materials Table

Symbols	Hazardous materials descriptions and proper shipping names	Hazard class or Division	Identification Numbers	PG	Label Codes	Special provisions (§172.102)	(8) Packaging (§173.***)			(9) Quantity limitations		(10) Vessel stowage	
							Exceptions	Non-bulk	Bulk	Passenger aircraft/ rail	Cargo aircraft only	Location	Other
(1)	(2)	(3)	(4)	(5)	(6)	(7)	(8A)	(8B)	(8C)	(9A)	(9B)	(10A)	(10B)
	Chloronitroanilines	6.1	UN2237	III	6.1	IB8, IP3	153	213	240	100 kg	200 kg	A	
+	**Chloronitrobenzene,** *ortho, liquid*	6.1	UN1578	II	6.1	IB2, T11, TP2, TP13, TP27	None	202	243	5 L	60 L	A	
+	**Chloronitrobenzenes** *meta or para, solid*	6.1	UN1578	II	6.1	IB8, IP2, IP4, T7, TP2	None	212	242	25 kg	100 kg	A	
	Chloronitrotoluenes, *liquid*	6.1	UN2433	III	6.1	IB3, T4, TP1	153	203	241	60 L	220 L	A	
	Chloronitrotoluenes, *solid*	6.1	UN2433	III	6.1	IB8, IP3	153	213	240	100 kg	200 kg	A	
	Chloropentafluoroethane *or* **Refrigerant gas R 115**	2.2	UN1020		2.2	T50	306	304	314, 315	75 kg	150 kg	A	
	Chlorophenolates, liquid *or* **Phenolates, liquid**	8	UN2904	III	8	IB3	154	203	241	5 L	60 L	A	
	Chlorophenolates, solid *or* **Phenolates, solid**	8	UN2905	III	8	IB8, IP3	154	213	240	25 kg	100 kg	A	
	Chlorophenols, liquid	6.1	UN2021	III	6.1	IB3, T4, TP1	153	203	241	60 L	220 L	A	
	Chlorophenols, solid	6.1	UN2020	III	6.1	IB8, IP3, T4, TP1	153	213	240	100 kg	200 kg	A	
	Chlorophenyltrichlorosilane	8	UN1753	II	8	A7, B2, B6, IB2, N34, T7, TP2	None	202	242	Forbidden	30 L	C	40
+	**Chloropicrin**	6.1	UN1580	I	6.1	2, B7, B9, B14, B32, B46, B74, T20, TP2, TP13, TP38, TP45	None	227	244	Forbidden	Forbidden	D	40
	Chloropicrin and methyl bromide mixtures	2.3	UN1581		2.3	2, B9, B14, T50	None	193	314, 315	Forbidden	Forbidden	D	25, 40
	Chloropicrin and methyl chloride mixtures	2.3	UN1582		2.3	2, T50	None	193	245	Forbidden	Forbidden	D	25, 40
	Chloropicrin mixture, flammable (pressure not exceeding 14.7 psia at 115 degrees F flash point below 100 degrees F) see **Toxic liquids, flammable,** *etc.*												
	Chloropicrin mixtures, n.o.s.	6.1	UN1583	I II III	6.1 6.1 6.1	5 IB2 IB3	None None 153	201 202 203	243 243 241	Forbidden Forbidden Forbidden	Forbidden Forbidden Forbidden	C C C	40 40 40
D	**Chloropivaloyl chloride**	6.1	NA9263	I	6.1, 8	2, B9, B14, B32, B74, T20, TP4, TP12, TP13, TP38, TP45	None	227	244	Forbidden	Forbidden	B	40
	Chloroplatinic acid, solid	8	UN2507	III	8	IB8, IP3	154	213	240	25 kg	100 kg	A	
	Chloroprene, stabilized	3	UN1991	I	3, 6.1	B57, T14, TP2, TP13	None	201	243	Forbidden	30 L	D	40
	Chloroprene, uninhibited	Forbidden											
	2-Chloropropane	3	UN2356	I	3	N36, T11, TP2, TP13	150	201	243	1 L	30 L	E	
	3-Chloropropanol-1	6.1	UN2849	III	6.1	IB3, T4, TP1	153	203	241	60 L	220 L	A	
	2-Chloropropene	3	UN2456	I	3	A3, N36, T11, TP2	150	201	243	1 L	30 L	E	
	2-Chloropropionic acid	8	UN2511	III	8	IB3, T4, TP2	154	203	241	5 L	60 L	A	8
	2-Chloropyridine	6.1	UN2822	II	6.1	IB2, T7, TP2	None	202	243	5 L	60 L	A	40
	Chlorosilanes, corrosive, flammable, n.o.s.	8	UN2986	II	8, 3	IB2, T11, TP2, TP27	None	202	243	1 L	30 L	C	40
	Chlorosilanes, corrosive, n.o.s.	8	UN2987	II	8	B2, IB2, T14, TP2, TP27	154	202	242	1 L	30 L	C	40
	Chlorosilanes, flammable, corrosive, n.o.s.	3	UN2985	II	3, 8	IB1, T11, TP2, TP13, TP27	None	201	243	1 L	5 L	B	40
	Chlorosilanes, water-reactive, flammable, corrosive, n.o.s.	4.3	UN2988	I	4.3, 3, 8	A2, T10, TP2, TP7, TP13	None	201	244	Forbidden	1 L	D	21, 28, 40, 49, 100
+	**Chlorosulfonic acid** *(with or without sulfur trioxide)*	8	UN1754	I	8, 6.1	2, A3, A6, A10, B9, B10, B14, B32, B74, T20, TP2, TP12, TP38, TP45	None	227	244	Forbidden	Forbidden	C	40
	Chlorotoluenes	3	UN2238	III	3	B1, IB3, T2, TP1	150	203	242	60 L	220 L	A	
	Chlorotoluidines *liquid*	6.1	UN2239	III	6.1	IB3, T7, TP1, TP28	153	203	241	60 L	220 L	A	
	Chlorotoluidines *solid*	6.1	UN2239	III	6.1	IB8, IP3, T4, TP1	153	213	240	100 kg	200 kg	A	

§172.101 - Hazardous Materials Table

Symbols (1)	Hazardous materials descriptions and proper shipping names (2)	Hazard class or Division (3)	Identification Numbers (4)	PG (5)	Label Codes (6)	Special provisions (§172.102) (7)	(8) Packaging (§173.***) Exceptions (8A)	Non-bulk (8B)	Bulk (8C)	(9) Quantity limitations Passenger aircraft/rail (9A)	Cargo aircraft only (9B)	(10) Vessel stowage Location (10A)	Other (10B)
	Chlorotrifluoromethane and trifluoromethane azeotropic mixture *or* **Refrigerant gas R 503** *with approximately 60 percent chlorotrifluoromethane*	2.2	UN2599		2.2		306	304	314, 315	75 kg	150 kg	A	
	Chlorotrifluoromethane *or* **Refrigerant gas R 13**	2.2	UN1022		2.2		306	304	314, 315	75 kg	150 kg	A	
	Chromic acid solution	8	UN1755	II III	8 8	B2, IB2, T8, TP2, TP12 IB3, T4, TP1, TP12	154 154	202 203	242 241	1 L 5 L	30 L 60 L	C C	40 40
	Chromic anhydride, see **Chromium trioxide, anhydrous**												
	Chromic fluoride, solid	8	UN1756	II	8	IB8, IP2, IP4	154	212	240	15 kg	50 kg	A	26
	Chromic fluoride, solution	8	UN1757	II III	8 8	B2, IB2, T7, TP2 IB3, T4, TP1	154 154	202 203	242 241	1 L 5 L	30 L 60 L	A A	
	Chromium nitrate	5.1	UN2720	III	5.1	A1, A29, IB8, IP3	152	213	240	25 kg	100 kg	A	
	Chromium oxychloride	8	UN1758	I	8	A3, A6, A7, B10, N34, T10, TP2, TP12	None	201	243	0.5 L	2.5 L	C	40, 66, 74, 89, 90
	Chromium trioxide, anhydrous	5.1	UN1463	II	5.1, 8	IB8, IP4	None	212	242	5 kg	25 kg	A	
	Chromosulfuric acid	8	UN2240	I	8	A3, A6, A7, B4, B6, N34, T10, TP2, TP12, TP13	None	201	243	0.5 L	2.5 L	B	40, 66, 74, 89, 90
	Chromyl chloride, see **Chromium oxychloride**												
	Cigar and cigarette lighters, charged with fuel, see **Lighters for cigars, cigarettes,** *etc.*												
	Coal briquettes, hot	Forbidden											
	Coal gas, compressed	2.3	UN1023		2.3, 2.1	3	None	302	314, 315	Forbidden	25 kg	D	40
	Coal tar distillates, flammable	3	UN1136	II III	3 3	IB2, T4, TP1 B1, IB3, T4, TP1, TP29	150 150	202 203	242 242	5 L 60 L	60 L 220 L	B A	
	Coal tar dye, corrosive, liquid, n.o.s, see **Dyes, liquid** *or* **solid, n.o.s.** *or* **Dye intermediates, liquid** *or* **solid, corrosive, n.o.s.**												
	Coating solution *(includes surface treatments or coatings used for industrial or other purposes such as vehicle undercoating, drum or barrel lining)*	3	UN1139	I II III	3 3 3	T11, TP1, TP8, TP27 IB2, T4, TP1, TP8 B1, IB3, T2, TP1	150 150 150	201 202 203	243 242 242	1 L 5 L 60 L	30 L 60 L 220 L	E B A	
	Cobalt naphthenates, powder	4.1	UN2001	III	4.1	A19, IB8, IP3	151	213	240	25 kg	100 kg	A	
	Cobalt resinate, precipitated	4.1	UN1318	III	4.1	A1, A19, IB6	151	213	240	25 kg	100 kg	A	
	Coke, hot	Forbidden											
	Collodion, see **Nitrocellulose** *etc.*												
D G	**Combustible liquid, n.o.s.**	Combustible	NA1993	III	None	IB3,T1, T4, TP1	150	203	241	60 L	220 L	A	
G	**Components, explosive train, n.o.s.**	1.2B	UN0382	II	1.2B	101	None	62	None	Forbidden	Forbidden	11	
G	**Components, explosive train, n.o.s.**	1.4B	UN0383	II	1.4B	101	None	62	None	Forbidden	75 kg	06	
G	**Components, explosive train, n.o.s.**	1.4S	UN0384	II	1.4S	101	None	62	None	25 kg	100 kg	05	
G	**Components, explosive train, n.o.s.**	1.1B	UN0461	II	1.1B	101	None	62	None	Forbidden	Forbidden	11	
	Composition B, see **Hexolite,** *etc.*												
D G	**Compounds, cleaning liquid**	8	NA1760	I II III	8 8 8	A7, B10, T14, TP2, TP9, TP27 B2, IB2, N37, T11, TP2, TP27 IB3, N37, T7, TP1, TP28	None 154 154	201 202 203	243 242 241	0.5 L 1 L 5 L	2.5 L 30 L 60 L	B B A	40 40 40
D G	**Compounds, cleaning liquid**	3	NA1993	I II III	3 3 3	T11, TP1, TP9 IB2, T7, TP1, TP8, TP28 B1, B52, IB3, T4, TP1, TP29	150 150 150	201 202 203	243 242 242	1 L 5 L 60 L	30 L 60 L 220 L	E B A	

§172.101 - Hazardous Materials Table

Symbols	Hazardous materials descriptions and proper shipping names	Hazard class or Division	Identification Numbers	PG	Label Codes	Special provisions (§172.102)	(8) Packaging (§173.***) Exceptions	Non-bulk	Bulk	(9) Quantity limitations Passenger aircraft/ rail	Cargo aircraft only	(10) Vessel stowage Location	Other
(1)	(2)	(3)	(4)	(5)	(6)	(7)	(8A)	(8B)	(8C)	(9A)	(9B)	(10A)	(10B)
D G	**Compounds, tree killing, liquid** *or* **Compounds, weed killing, liquid**	8	NA1760	I	8	A7, B10, T14, TP2, TP9, TP27	None	201	243	0.5 L	2.5 L	B	40
				II	8	B2, IB2, N37, T11, TP2, TP27	154	202	242	1 L	30 L	B	40
				III	8	IB3, N37, T7, TP1, TP28	154	203	241	5 L	60 L	A	40
D G	**Compounds, tree killing, liquid** *or* **Compounds, weed killing, liquid**	3	NA1993	I	3	T11, TP1, TP9	150	201	243	1 L	30 L	E	
				II	3	IB2, T7, TP1, TP8, TP28	150	202	242	5 L	60 L	B	
				III	3	B1, B52, IB3, T4, TP1, TP29	150	203	242	60 L	220 L	A	
D G	**Compounds, tree killing, liquid** *or* **Compounds, weed killing, liquid**	6.1	NA2810	I	6.1	T14, TP2, TP13, TP27	None	201	243	1 L	30 L	B	40
				II	6.1	IB2, T11, TP2, TP27	None	202	243	5 L	60 L	B	40
				III	6.1	IB3, T7, TP1, TP28	153	203	241	60 L	220 L	A	40
G	**Compressed gas, flammable, n.o.s.**	2.1	UN1954		2.1		306	302, 305	314, 315	Forbidden	150 kg	D	40
G	**Compressed gas, n.o.s.**	2.2	UN1956		2.2		306, 307	302, 305	314, 315	75 kg	150 kg	A	
G	**Compressed gas, oxidizing, n.o.s.**	2.2	UN3156		2.2, 5.1		306	302	314, 315	75 kg	150 kg	D	
G I	**Compressed gas, toxic, corrosive, n.o.s.** *Inhalation Hazard Zone A*	2.3	UN3304		2.3, 8	1	None	192	245	Forbidden	Forbidden	D	40
G I	**Compressed gas, toxic, corrosive, n.o.s.** *Inhalation Hazard Zone B*	2.3	UN3304		2.3, 8	2	None	302, 305	314, 315	Forbidden	Forbidden	D	40
G I	**Compressed gas, toxic, corrosive, n.o.s.** *Inhalation Hazard Zone C*	2.3	UN3304		2.3, 8	3	None	302, 305	314, 315	Forbidden	Forbidden	D	40
G I	**Compressed gas, toxic, corrosive, n.o.s.** *Inhalation Hazard Zone D*	2.3	UN3304		2.3, 8	4	None	302, 305	314, 315	Forbidden	Forbidden	D	40
G I	**Compressed gas, toxic, flammable, corrosive, n.o.s.** *Inhalation Hazard Zone A*	2.3	UN3305		2.3, 2.1, 8	1	None	192	245	Forbidden	Forbidden	D	17, 40
G I	**Compressed gas, toxic, flammable, corrosive, n.o.s.** *Inhalation Hazard Zone B*	2.3	UN3305		2.3, 2.1, 8	2	None	302, 305	314, 315	Forbidden	Forbidden	D	17, 40
G I	**Compressed gas, toxic, flammable, corrosive, n.o.s.** *Inhalation Hazard Zone C*	2.3	UN3305		2.3, 2.1, 8	3	None	302, 305	314, 315	Forbidden	Forbidden	D	17, 40
G I	**Compressed gas, toxic, flammable, corrosive, n.o.s.** *Inhalation Hazard Zone D*	2.3	UN3305		2.3, 2.1, 8	4	None	302, 305	314, 315	Forbidden	Forbidden	D	17, 40
G	**Compressed gas, toxic, flammable, n.o.s.** *Inhalation hazard Zone A*	2.3	UN1953		2.3, 2.1	1	None	192	245	Forbidden	Forbidden	D	40
G	**Compressed gas, toxic, flammable, n.o.s.** *Inhalation hazard Zone B*	2.3	UN1953		2.3, 2.1	2, B9, B14	None	302, 305	314, 315	Forbidden	Forbidden	D	40
G	**Compressed gas, toxic, flammable, n.o.s.** *Inhalation Hazard Zone C*	2.3	UN1953		2.3, 2.1	3, B14	None	302, 305	314, 315	Forbidden	Forbidden	D	40
G	**Compressed gas, toxic, flammable, n.o.s.** *Inhalation Hazard Zone D*	2.3	UN1953		2.3, 2.1	4	None	302, 305	314, 315	Forbidden	Forbidden	D	40
G	**Compressed gas, toxic, n.o.s.** *Inhalation Hazard Zone A*	2.3	UN1955		2.3	1	None	192	245	Forbidden	Forbidden	D	40
G	**Compressed gas, toxic, n.o.s.** *Inhalation Hazard Zone B*	2.3	UN1955		2.3	2, B9, B14	None	302, 305	314, 315	Forbidden	Forbidden	D	40
G	**Compressed gas, toxic, n.o.s.** *Inhalation Hazard Zone C*	2.3	UN1955		2.3	3, B14	None	302, 305	314, 315	Forbidden	Forbidden	D	40
G	**Compressed gas, toxic, n.o.s.** *Inhalation Hazard Zone D*	2.3	UN1955		2.3	4	None	302, 305	314, 315	Forbidden	Forbidden	D	40
G I	**Compressed gas, toxic, oxdizing, corrosive, n.o.s.** *Inhalation Hazard Zone A*	2.3	UN3306		2.3, 5.1, 8	1	None	192	244	Forbidden	Forbidden	D	40, 89, 90
G I	**Compressed gas, toxic, oxidizing, corrosive, n.o.s.** *Inhalation Hazard Zone B*	2.3	UN3306		2.3, 5.1, 8	2	None	302, 305	314, 315	Forbidden	Forbidden	D	40, 89, 90
G I	**Compressed gas, toxic, oxidizing, corrosive, n.o.s.** *Inhalation Hazard Zone C*	2.3	UN3306		2.3, 5.1, 8	3	None	302, 305	314, 315	Forbidden	Forbidden	D	40, 89, 90
G I	**Compressed gas, toxic, oxidizing, corrosive, n.o.s.** *Inhalation Hazard Zone D*	2.3	UN3306		2.3, 5.1, 8	4	None	302, 305	314, 315	Forbidden	Forbidden	D	40, 89, 90
G	**Compressed gas, toxic, oxidizing, n.o.s.** *Inhalation Hazard Zone A*	2.3	UN3303		2.3, 5.1	1	None	192	245	Forbidden	Forbidden	D	40

§172.101 - Hazardous Materials Table

Symbols	Hazardous materials descriptions and proper shipping names	Hazard class or Division	Identification Numbers	PG	Label Codes	Special provisions (§172.102)	(8) Packaging (§173.***)			(9) Quantity limitations		(10) Vessel stowage	
							Exceptions	Non-bulk	Bulk	Passenger aircraft/rail	Cargo aircraft only	Location	Other
(1)	(2)	(3)	(4)	(5)	(6)	(7)	(8A)	(8B)	(8C)	(9A)	(9B)	(10A)	(10B)
G	**Compressed gas, toxic, oxidizing, n.o.s.** *Inhalation Hazard Zone B*	2.3	UN3303		2.3, 5.1	2	None	302, 305	314, 315	Forbidden	Forbidden	D	40
G	**Compressed gas, toxic, oxidizing, n.o.s.** *Inhalation Hazard Zone C*	2.3	UN3303		2.3, 5.1	3	None	302, 305	314, 315	Forbidden	Forbidden	D	40
G	**Compressed gas, toxic, oxidizing, n.o.s.** *Inhalation Hazard Zone D*	2.3	UN3303		2.3, 5.1	4	None	302, 305	314, 315	Forbidden	Forbidden	D	40
D	**Consumer commodity**	ORM-D			None		156, 306	156, 306	None	30 kg gross	30 kg gross	A	
	Contrivances, water-activated, *with burster, expelling charge or propelling charge*	1.2L	UN0248	II	1.2L	101	None	62	None	Forbidden	Forbidden	08	8E, 14E, 15E, 17E
	Contrivances, water-activated, *with burster, expelling charge or propelling charge*	1.3L	UN0249	II	1.3L	101	None	62	None	Forbidden	Forbidden	08	8E, 14E, 15E, 17E
	Copper acetoarsenite	6.1	UN1585	II	6.1	IB8, IP2, IP4	None	212	242	25 kg	100 kg	A	
	Copper acetylide	Forbidden											
	Copper amine azide	Forbidden											
	Copper arsenite	6.1	UN1586	II	6.1	IB8, IP2, IP4	None	212	242	25 kg	100 kg	A	
	Copper based pesticides, liquid, flammable, toxic, *flash point less than 23 degrees C*	3	UN2776	I	3, 6.1	T14, TP2, TP13, TP27	None	201	243	Forbidden	30 L	B	40
				II	3, 6.1	IB2, T11, TP2, TP13, TP27	None	202	243	1 L	60 L	B	40
	Copper based pesticides, liquid, toxic	6.1	UN3010	I	6.1	T14, TP2, TP13, TP27	None	201	243	1 L	30 L	B	40
				II	6.1	IB2, T11, TP2, TP13, TP27	None	202	243	5 L	60 L	B	40
				III	6.1	IB3, T7, TP2, TP28	153	203	241	60 L	220 L	A	40
	Copper based pesticides, liquid, toxic, flammable *flash point not less than 23 degrees C*	6.1	UN3009	I	6.1, 3	T14, TP2, TP13, TP27	None	201	243	1 L	30 L	B	40
				II	6.1, 3	IB2, T11, TP2, TP13, TP27	None	202	243	5 L	60 L	B	40
				III	6.1, 3	B1, IB3, T7, TP2, TP28	153	203	242	60 L	220 L	A	40
	Copper based pesticides, solid, toxic	6.1	UN2775	I	6.1	IB7, IP1	None	211	242	5 kg	50 kg	A	40
				II	6.1	IB8, IP2, IP4	None	212	242	25 kg	100 kg	A	40
				III	6.1	IB8, IP3	153	213	240	100 kg	200 kg	A	40
	Copper chlorate	5.1	UN2721	II	5.1	A1, IB8, IP2, IP4	152	212	242	5 kg	25 kg	A	56, 58, 106
	Copper chloride	8	UN2802	III	8	IB8, IP3	154	213	240	25 kg	100 kg	A	
	Copper cyanide	6.1	UN1587	II	6.1	IB8, IP2, IP4	None	204	242	25 kg	100 kg	A	26
	Copper selenate, see **Selenates** *or* **Selenites**												
	Copper selenite, see **Selenates** *or* **Selenites**												
	Copper tetramine nitrate	Forbidden											
A W	**Copra**	4.2	UN1363	III	4.2	IB8, IP3, IP6	None	213	241	Forbidden	Forbidden	A	13, 19, 48, 119
	Cord, detonating, *flexible*	1.1D	UN0065	II	1.1D	102	63(a)	62	None	Forbidden	Forbidden	07	
	Cord, detonating, *flexible*	1.4D	UN0289	II	1.4D		None	62	None	Forbidden	75 kg	06	
	Cord detonating *or* **Fuse detonating** *metal clad*	1.2D	UN0102	II	1.2D		None	62	None	Forbidden	Forbidden	07	
	Cord, detonating *or* **Fuse, detonating** *metal clad*	1.1D	UN0290	II	1.1D		None	62	None	Forbidden	Forbidden	07	
	Cord, detonating, mild effect *or* **Fuse, detonating, mild effect** *metal clad*	1.4D	UN0104	II	1.4D		None	62	None	Forbidden	75 kg	06	
	Cord, igniter	1.4G	UN0066	II	1.4G		None	62	None	Forbidden	75 kg	06	
	Cordeau detonant fuse, see **Cord, detonating,** *etc;* **Cord, detonating,** *flexible*												
	Cordite, see **Powder, smokeless**												
G	**Corrosive liquid, acidic, inorganic, n.o.s.**	8	UN3264	I	8	B10, T14, TP2, TP27	None	201	243	0.5 L	2.5 L	B	40
				II	8	B2, IB2, T11, TP2, TP27	154	202	242	1 L	30 L	B	40
				III	8	IB3, T7, TP1, TP28	154	203	241	5 L	60 L	A	40

§172.101 - Hazardous Materials Table

Symbols	Hazardous materials descriptions and proper shipping names	Hazard class or Division	Identification Numbers	PG	Label Codes	Special provisions (§172.102)	(8) Packaging (§173.***)			(9) Quantity limitations		(10) Vessel stowage	
							Exceptions	Non-bulk	Bulk	Passenger aircraft/rail	Cargo aircraft only	Location	Other
(1)	(2)	(3)	(4)	(5)	(6)	(7)	(8A)	(8B)	(8C)	(9A)	(9B)	(10A)	(10B)
G	**Corrosive liquid, acidic, organic, n.o.s.**	8	UN3265	I	8	B10, T14, TP2, TP27	None	201	243	0.5 L	2.5 L	B	40
				II	8	B2, IB2, T11, TP2, TP27	154	202	242	1 L	30 L	B	40
				III	8	IB3, T7, TP1, TP28	154	203	241	5 L	60 L	A	40
G	**Corrosive liquid, basic, inorganic, n.o.s.**	8	UN3266	I	8	B10, T14, TP2, TP27	None	201	243	0.5 L	2.5 L	B	40
				II	8	B2, IB2, T11, TP2, TP27	154	202	242	1 L	30 L	B	40
				III	8	IB3, T7, TP1, TP28	154	203	241	5 L	60 L	A	40
G	**Corrosive liquid, basic, organic, n.o.s.**	8	UN3267	I	8	B10, T14, TP2, TP27	None	201	243	0.5 L	2.5 L	B	40
				II	8	B2, IB2, T11, TP2, TP27	154	202	242	1 L	30 L	B	40
				III	8	IB3, T7, TP1, TP28	154	203	241	5 L	60 L	A	40
G	**Corrosive liquid, self-heating, n.o.s.**	8	UN3301	I	8, 4.2	B10	None	201	243	0.5 L	2.5 L	D	
				II	8, 4.2	B2, IB1	154	202	242	1 L	30 L	D	
G	**Corrosive liquids, flammable, n.o.s.**	8	UN2920	I	8, 3	B10, T14, TP2, TP27	None	201	243	0.5 L	2.5 L	C	25, 40
				II	8, 3	B2, IB2, T11, TP2, TP27	None	202	243	1 L	30 L	C	25, 40
G	**Corrosive liquids, n.o.s.**	8	UN1760	I	8	A7, B10, T14, TP2, TP27	None	201	243	0.5 L	2.5 L	B	40
				II	8	B2, IB2, T11, TP2, TP27	154	202	242	1 L	30 L	B	40
				III	8	IB3, T7, TP1, TP28	154	203	241	5 L	60 L	A	40
G	**Corrosive liquids, oxidizing, n.o.s.**	8	UN3093	I	8, 5.1		None	201	243	Forbidden	2.5 L	C	89
				II	8, 5.1	IB2	None	202	243	1 L	30 L	C	89
G	**Corrosive liquids, toxic, n.o.s.**	8	UN2922	I	8, 6.1	A7, B10, T14, TP2, TP13, TP27	None	201	243	0.5 L	2.5 L	B	40
				II	8, 6.1	B3, IB2, T7, TP2	None	202	243	1 L	30 L	B	40
				III	8, 6.1	IB3, T7, TP1, TP28	154	203	241	5 L	60 L	B	40
G	**Corrosive liquids, water-reactive, n.o.s.**	8	UN3094	I	8, 4.3		None	201	243	Forbidden	1 L	E	
				II	8, 4.3		None	202	243	1 L	5 L	E	
G	**Corrosive solid, acidic, inorganic, n.o.s.**	8	UN3260	I	8	IB7, IP1	None	211	242	1 kg	25 kg	B	
				II	8	IB8, IP2, IP4	154	212	240	15 kg	50 kg	B	
				III	8	IB8, IP3	154	213	240	25 kg	100 kg	A	
G	**Corrosive solid, acidic, organic, n.o.s.**	8	UN3261	I	8	IB7, IP1	None	211	242	1 kg	25 kg	B	
				II	8	IB8, IP2, IP4	154	212	240	15 kg	50 kg	B	
				III	8	IB8, IP3	154	213	240	25 kg	100 kg	A	
G	**Corrosive solid, basic, inorganic, n.o.s.**	8	UN3262	I	8	IB7, IP1	None	211	242	1 kg	25 kg	B	
				II	8	IB8, IP2, IP4	154	212	240	15 kg	50 kg	B	
				III	8	IB8, IP3	154	213	240	25 kg	100 kg	A	
G	**Corrosive solid, basic, organic, n.o.s.**	8	UN3263	I	8	IB7, IP1	None	211	242	1 kg	25 kg	B	
				II	8	IB8, IP2, IP4	154	212	240	15 kg	50 kg	B	
				III	8	IB8, IP3	154	213	240	25 kg	100 kg	A	
G	**Corrosive solids, flammable, n.o.s.**	8	UN2921	I	8, 4.1	IB6	None	211	242	1 kg	25 kg	B	12, 25
				II	8, 4.1	IB8, IP2, IP4	None	212	242	15 kg	50 kg	B	12, 25
G	**Corrosive solids, n.o.s.**	8	UN1759	I	8	IB7, IP1	None	211	242	1 kg	25 kg	B	
				II	8	128, IB8, IP2, IP4	154	212	240	15 kg	50 kg	A	
				III	8	128, IB8, IP3	154	213	240	25 kg	100 kg	A	
G	**Corrosive solids, oxidizing, n.o.s.**	8	UN3084	I	8, 5.1		None	211	242	1 kg	25 kg	C	
				II	8, 5.1	IB6, IP2	None	212	242	15 kg	50 kg	C	
G	**Corrosive solids, self-heating, n.o.s.**	8	UN3095	I	8, 4.2		None	211	243	1 kg	25 kg	C	
				II	8, 4.2	IB6, IP2	None	212	242	15 kg	50 kg	C	
G	**Corrosive solids, toxic, n.o.s.**	8	UN2923	I	8, 6.1	IB7	None	211	242	1 kg	25 kg	B	40
				II	8, 6.1	IB8, IP2, IP4	None	212	240	15 kg	50 kg	B	40
				III	8, 6.1	IB8, IP3	154	213	240	25 kg	100 kg	B	40, 95
G	**Corrosive solids, water-reactive, n.o.s.**	8	UN3096	I	8, 4.3	IB4, IP1	None	211	243	1 kg	25 kg	D	
				II	8, 4.3	IB6, IP2	None	212	242	15 kg	50 kg	D	
D W	**Cotton**	9	NA1365		9	137, IB8, IP2, IP4, W41	None	None	None	No limit	No limit	A	
A W	**Cotton waste, oily**	4.2	UN1364	III	4.2	IB8, IP6	None	213	None	Forbidden	Forbidden	A	54
A I W	**Cotton, wet**	4.2	UN1365	III	4.2	IB8, IP6	None	204	241	Forbidden	Forbidden	A	

§172.101 - Hazardous Materials Table

Symbols	Hazardous materials descriptions and proper shipping names	Hazard class or Division	Identification Numbers	PG	Label Codes	Special provisions (§172.102)	(8) Packaging (§173.***)			(9) Quantity limitations		(10) Vessel stowage	
							Exceptions	Non-bulk	Bulk	Passenger aircraft/rail	Cargo aircraft only	Location	Other
(1)	(2)	(3)	(4)	(5)	(6)	(7)	(8A)	(8B)	(8C)	(9A)	(9B)	(10A)	(10B)
	Coumarin derivative pesticides, liquid, flammable, toxic, *flash point less than 23 degrees C*	3	UN3024	I	3, 6.1	T14, TP2, TP13, TP27	None	201	243	Forbidden	30 L	B	40
				II	3, 6.1	IB2, T11, TP2, TP13, TP27	None	202	243	1 L	60 L	B	40
	Coumarin derivative pesticides, liquid, toxic	6.1	UN3026	I	6.1	T14, TP2, TP13, TP27	None	201	243	1 L	30 L	B	40
				II	6.1	IB2, T11, TP2, TP27	None	202	243	5 L	60 L	B	40
				III	6.1	IB3, T7, TP1, TP28	153	203	241	60 L	220 L	A	40
	Coumarin derivative pesticides, liquid, toxic, flammable *flash point not less than 23 degrees C*	6.1	UN3025	I	6.1, 3	T14, TP2, TP13, TP27	None	201	243	1 L	30 L	B	40
				II	6.1, 3	IB2, T11, TP2, TP13, TP27	None	202	243	5 L	60 L	B	40
				III	6.1, 3	B1, IB3, T7, TP1, TP28	153	203	242	60 L	220 L	A	40
	Coumarin derivative pesticides, solid, toxic	6.1	UN3027	I	6.1	IB7, IP1, T14, TP2, TP27	None	211	242	5 kg	50 kg	A	40
				II	6.1	IB8, IP2, IP4, T11, TP2, TP27	None	212	242	25 kg	100 kg	A	40
				III	6.1	IB8, IP3, T7, TP1, TP28	153	213	240	100 kg	200 kg	A	40
	Cresols	6.1	UN2076	II	6.1, 8	IB8, IP2, IP4, T7, TP2	None	202	243	1 L	30 L	B	
	Cresylic acid	6.1	UN2022	II	6.1, 8	IB2, T7, TP2, TP13	None	202	243	1 L	30 L	B	
	Crotonaldehyde, stabilized	6.1	UN1143	I	6.1, 3	2, B9, B14, B32, B74, B77, T20, TP2, TP13, TP38, TP45	None	227	244	Forbidden	Forbidden	B	40
	Crotonic acid *liquid*	8	UN2823	III	8	IB3, T4, TP1	154	203	241	5 L	60 L	A	12
	Crotonic acid, *solid*	8	UN2823	III	8	IB8, IP3	154	213	240	25 kg	100 kg	A	12
	Crotonylene	3	UN1144	I	3	T11, TP2	150	201	243	1 L	30 L	E	
	Cupriethylenediamine solution	8	UN1761	II	8, 6.1	IB2, T7, TP2	None	202	243	1 L	30 L	A	
				III	8, 6.1	IB3, T7, TP1, TP28	154	203	242	5 L	60 L	A	95
	Cutters, cable, explosive	1.4S	UN0070	II	1.4S		None	62	None	25 kg	100 kg	05	
	Cyanide or cyanide mixtures, dry, see **Cyanides, inorganic, solid, n.o.s.**												
	Cyanide solutions, n.o.s.	6.1	UN1935	I	6.1	B37, T14, TP2, TP13, TP27	None	201	243	1 L	30 L	B	40, 52
				II	6.1	IB2, T11, TP2, TP13, TP27	None	202	243	5 L	60 L	A	40, 52
				III	6.1	IB3, T7, TP2, TP13, TP28	153	203	241	60 L	220 L	A	40, 52
	Cyanides, inorganic, solid, n.o.s.	6.1	UN1588	I	6.1	IB7, IP1, N74, N75	None	211	242	5 kg	50 kg	A	52
				II	6.1	IB8, IP2, IP4, N74, N75	None	212	242	25 kg	100 kg	A	52
				III	6.1	IB8, IP3, N74, N75	153	213	240	100 kg	200 kg	A	52
	Cyanogen	2.3	UN1026		2.3, 2.1	2	None	304	245	Forbidden	Forbidden	D	40
	Cyanogen bromide	6.1	UN1889	I	6.1, 8	A6, A8	None	211	242	1 kg	15 kg	D	40
	Cyanogen chloride, stabilized	2.3	UN1589		2.3, 8	1	None	192	245	Forbidden	Forbidden	D	40
	Cyanuric chloride	8	UN2670	II	8	IB8, IP2, IP4	None	212	240	15 kg	50 kg	A	12, 40
	Cyanuric triazide	Forbidden											
	Cyclobutane	2.1	UN2601		2.1		306	304	314, 315	Forbidden	150 kg	B	40
	Cyclobutyl chloroformate	6.1	UN2744	II	6.1, 8, 3	IB1, T7, TP2, TP13	None	202	243	1 L	30 L	A	12, 13, 21, 25, 40, 100
	1,5,9-Cyclododecatriene	6.1	UN2518	III	6.1	IB3, T4, TP1	153	203	241	60 L	220 L	A	40
	Cycloheptane	3	UN2241	II	3	IB2, T4, TP1	150	202	242	5 L	60 L	B	40
	Cycloheptatriene	3	UN2603	II	3, 6.1	IB2, T7, TP1, TP13	None	202	243	1 L	60 L	E	40
	Cycloheptene	3	UN2242	II	3	B1, IB2, T4, TP1	150	202	242	5 L	60 L	B	
	Cyclohexane	3	UN1145	II	3	IB2, T4, TP1	150	202	242	5 L	60 L	E	
	Cyclohexanone	3	UN1915	III	3	B1, IB3, T2, TP1	150	203	242	60 L	220 L	A	
	Cyclohexene	3	UN2256	II	3	IB2, T4, TP1	150	202	242	5 L	60 L	E	
	Cyclohexenyltrichlorosilane	8	UN1762	II	8	A7, B2, IB2, N34, T7, TP2, TP13	None	202	242	Forbidden	30 L	C	40
	Cyclohexyl acetate	3	UN2243	III	3	B1, IB3, T2, TP1	150	203	242	60 L	220 L	A	

§172.101 - Hazardous Materials Table

Symbols	Hazardous materials descriptions and proper shipping names	Hazard class or Division	Identification Numbers	PG	Label Codes	Special provisions (§172.102)	(8) Packaging (§173.***)			(9) Quantity limitations		(10) Vessel stowage	
							Exceptions	Non-bulk	Bulk	Passenger aircraft/rail	Cargo aircraft only	Location	Other
(1)	(2)	(3)	(4)	(5)	(6)	(7)	(8A)	(8B)	(8C)	(9A)	(9B)	(10A)	(10B)
	Cyclohexyl isocyanate	6.1	UN2488	I	6.1, 3	2, B9, B14, B32, B74, B77, T20, TP2, TP13, TP38, TP45	None	227	244	Forbidden	Forbidden	D	40
	Cyclohexyl mercaptan	3	UN3054	III	3	B1, IB3, T2, TP1	150	203	242	60 L	220 L	A	40, 95
	Cyclohexylamine	8	UN2357	II	8, 3	IB2, T7, TP2	None	202	243	1 L	30 L	A	40
	Cyclohexyltrichlorosilane	8	UN1763	II	8	A7, B2, IB2, N34, T7, TP2, TP13	None	202	242	Forbidden	30 L	C	40
	Cyclonite and cyclotetramethylenetetranitramine mixtures, wetted *or* **desensitized** *see* **RDX and HMX mixtures, wetted** *or* **desensitized** *etc.*												
	Cyclonite and HMX mixtures, wetted *or* **desensitized** *see* **RDX and HMX mixtures, wetted** *or* **desensitized** *etc.*												
	Cyclonite and octogen mixtures, wetted *or* **desensitized** *see* **RDX and HMX mixtures, wetted** *or* **desensitized** *etc.*												
	Cyclonite, *see* **Cyclotrimethylenetrinitramine,** *etc.*												
	Cyclooctadiene phosphines, *see* **9-Phosphabicyclononanes**												
	Cyclooctadienes	3	UN2520	III	3	B1, IB3, T2, TP1	150	203	242	60 L	220 L	A	
	Cyclooctatetraene	3	UN2358	II	3	IB2, T4, TP1	150	202	242	5 L	60 L	B	
	Cyclopentane	3	UN1146	II	3	IB2, T7, TP1	150	202	242	5 L	60 L	E	
	Cyclopentane, methyl, see **Methylcyclopentane**												
	Cyclopentanol	3	UN2244	III	3	B1, IB3, T2, TP1	150	203	242	60 L	220 L	A	
	Cyclopentanone	3	UN2245	III	3	B1, IB3, T2, TP1	150	203	242	60 L	220 L	A	
	Cyclopentene	3	UN2246	II	3	IB2, T7, TP2	150	202	242	5 L	60 L	E	40
	Cyclopropane	2.1	UN1027		2.1	T50	306	304	314, 315	Forbidden	150 kg	E	40
	Cyclotetramethylene tetranitramine (dry or unphlegmatized) (HMX)	Forbidden											
	Cyclotetramethylenetetranitramine, desensitized *or* **Octogen, desensitized** *or* **HMX, desensitized**	1.1D	UN0484	II	1.1D		None	62	None	Forbidden	Forbidden	10	
	Cyclotetramethylenetetranitramine, wetted *or* **HMX, wetted** *or* **Octogen, wetted** *with not less than 15 percent water, by mass*	1.1D	UN0226	II	1.1D		None	62	None	Forbidden	Forbidden	10	
	Cyclotrimethylenetrinitramine and cyclotetramethylenetetranitramine mixtures, wetted *or* **desensitized** *see* **RDX and HMX mixtures, wetted** *or* **desensitized** *etc.*												
	Cyclotrimethylenenitramine and octogen, mixtures, wetted *or* **desensitized** *see* **RDX and HMX mixtures, wetted** *or* **desensitized** *etc.*												
	Cyclotrimethylenetrinitramine and HMX mixtures, wetted *or* **desensitized** *see* **RDX and HMX mixtures, wetted** *or* **desensitized** *etc.*												
	Cyclotrimethylenetrinitramine, desensitized *or* **Cyclonite, desensitized** *or* **Hexogen, desensitized** *or* **RDX, desensitized**	1.1D	UN0483	II	1.1D		None	62	None	Forbidden	Forbidden	10	
	Cyclotrimethylenetrinitramine, wetted *or* **Cyclonite, wetted** *or* **Hexogen, wetted** *or* **RDX, wetted** *with not less than 15 percent water by mass*	1.1D	UN0072	II	1.1D		None	62	None	Forbidden	Forbidden	10	
	Cymenes	3	UN2046	III	3	B1, IB3, T2, TP1	150	203	242	60 L	220 L	A	
	Dangerous Goods in Machinery *or* **Dangerous Goods in Apparatus**	9	UN3363			136	None	222	None	No limit	No limit	A	
	Decaborane	4.1	UN1868	II	4.1, 6.1	A19, A20, IB6, IP2	None	212	None	Forbidden	50 kg	A	
	Decahydronaphthalene	3	UN1147	III	3	B1, IB3, T2, TP1	150	203	242	60 L	220 L	A	

§172.101 - Hazardous Materials Table

Symbols	Hazardous materials descriptions and proper shipping names	Hazard class or Division	Identification Numbers	PG	Label Codes	Special provisions (§172.102)	(8) Packaging (§173.***)			(9) Quantity limitations		(10) Vessel stowage	
							Exceptions	Non-bulk	Bulk	Passenger aircraft/ rail	Cargo aircraft only	Location	Other
(1)	(2)	(3)	(4)	(5)	(6)	(7)	(8A)	(8B)	(8C)	(9A)	(9B)	(10A)	(10B)
	n-Decane	3	UN2247	III	3	B1, IB3, T2, TP1	150	203	242	60 L	220 L	A	
	Deflagrating metal salts of aromatic nitroderivatives, n.o.s.	1.3C	UN0132	II	1.3C		None	62	None	Forbidden	Forbidden	10	5E
	Delay electric igniter, see **Igniters**												
	Depth charges, see **Charges, depth**												
	Detonating relays, see **Detonators**, *etc.*												
	Detonator assemblies, non-electric *for blasting*	1.1B	UN0360	II	1.1B		None	62	None	Forbidden	Forbidden	11	
	Detonator assemblies, non-electric, *for blasting*	1.4B	UN0361	II	1.4B	103	63(f), 63(g)	62	None	Forbidden	75 kg	06	
	Detonator, assemblies, non-electric *for blasting*	1.4S	UN0500	II	1.4S		63(f), 63(g)	62	None	25 kg	100 kg	05	
	Detonators, electric, *for blasting*	1.1B	UN0030	II	1.1B		63(f), 63(g)	62	None	Forbidden	Forbidden	11	
	Detonators, electric, *for blasting*	1.4B	UN0255	II	1.4B	103	63(f), 63(g)	62	None	Forbidden	75 kg	06	
	Detonators, electric *for blasting*	1.4S	UN0456	II	1.4S		63(f), 63(g)	62	None	25 kg	100 kg	05	
	Detonators for ammunition	1.1B	UN0073	II	1.1B		None	62	None	Forbidden	Forbidden	11	
	Detonators for ammunition	1.2B	UN0364	II	1.2B		None	62	None	Forbidden	Forbidden	11	
	Detonators for ammunition	1.4B	UN0365	II	1.4B	103	None	62	None	Forbidden	75 kg	06	
	Detonators for ammunition	1.4S	UN0366	II	1.4S		None	62	None	25 kg	100 kg	05	
	Detonators, non-electric, *for blasting*	1.1B	UN0029	II	1.1B		None	62	None	Forbidden	Forbidden	11	
	Detonators, non-electric, *for blasting*	1.4B	UN0267	II	1.4B	103	63(f), 63(g)	62	None	Forbidden	75 kg	06	
	Detonators, non-electric, *for blasting*	1.4S	UN0455	II	1.4S		63(f), 63(g)	62	None	25 kg	100 kg	5	
	Deuterium, compressed	2.1	UN1957		2.1		306	302	None	Forbidden	150 kg	E	40
	Devices, small, hydrocarbon gas powered *or* **Hydrocarbon gas refills for small devices** *with release device*	2.1	UN3150		2.1		306	304	None	Forbidden	150 kg	B	40
	Di-n-amylamine	3	UN2841	III	3, 6.1	B1, IB3, T4, TP1	150	203	242	60 L	220 L	A	
	Di-n-butyl peroxydicarbonate, with more than 52 percent in solution	Forbidden											
	Di-n-butylamine	8	UN2248	II	8, 3	IB2, T7, TP2	None	202	243	1 L	30 L	A	
	2,2-Di-(tert-butylperoxy) butane, with more than 55 percent in solution	Forbidden											
	Di-(tert-butylperoxy) phthalate, with more than 55 percent in solution	Forbidden											
	2,2-Di-(4,4-di-tert-butylperoxycyclohexyl) propane, with more than 42 percent with inert solid	Forbidden											
	Di-2,4-dichlorobenzoyl peroxide, with more than 75 percent with water	Forbidden											
	1,2-Di-(dimethylamino)ethane	3	UN2372	II	3	IB2, T4, TP1	150	202	242	5 L	60 L	B	
	Di-2-ethylhexyl phosphoric acid, see **Diisooctyl acid phosphate**												
	Di-(1-hydroxytetrazole) (dry)	Forbidden											
	Di-(1-naphthoyl) peroxide	Forbidden											
	a,a'-Di-(nitroxy) methylether	Forbidden											
	Di-(beta-nitroxyethyl) ammonium nitrate	Forbidden											
	Diacetone alcohol	3	UN1148	II III	3 3	IB2, T4, TP1 B1, IB3, T2, TP1	150 150	202 203	242 242	5 L 60 L	60 L 220 L	B A	
	Diacetone alcohol peroxides, with more than 57 percent in solution with more than 9 percent hydrogen peroxide, less than 26 percent diacetone alcohol and less than 9 percent water; total active oxygen content more than 9 percent by mass	Forbidden											
	Diacetyl, see **Butanedione**												
	Diacetyl peroxide, solid, or with more than 25 percent in solution	Forbidden											
	Diagnostic specimen	6.2				A82	134	199	None	4 L or 4 kg	4L or 4 kg	A	40

§172.101 - Hazardous Materials Table

Symbols	Hazardous materials descriptions and proper shipping names	Hazard class or Division	Identification Numbers	PG	Label Codes	Special provisions (§172.102)	(8) Packaging (§173.***)			(9) Quantity limitations		(10) Vessel stowage	
							Exceptions	Non-bulk	Bulk	Passenger aircraft/rail	Cargo aircraft only	Location	Other
(1)	(2)	(3)	(4)	(5)	(6)	(7)	(8A)	(8B)	(8C)	(9A)	(9B)	(10A)	(10B)
	Diallylamine	3	UN2359	II	3, 6.1, 8	IB2, T7, TP1	None	202	243	1 L	5 L	B	21, 40, 100
	Diallylether	3	UN2360	II	3, 6.1	IB2, N12, T7, TP1, TP13	None	202	243	1 L	60 L	E	40
	4,4'-Diaminodiphenyl methane	6.1	UN2651	III	6.1	IB8, IP3, T4, TP1	153	213	240	100 kg	200 kg	A	
	p-Diazidobenzene	Forbidden											
	1,2-Diazidoethane	Forbidden											
	1,1'-Diazoaminonaphthalene	Forbidden											
	Diazoaminotetrazole (dry)	Forbidden											
	Diazodinitrophenol (dry)	Forbidden											
	Diazodinitrophenol, wetted *with not less than 40 percent water or mixture of alcohol and water, by mass*	1.1A	UN0074	II	1.1A	111, 117	None	62	None	Forbidden	Forbidden	12	
	Diazodiphenylmethane	Forbidden											
	Diazonium nitrates (dry)	Forbidden											
	Diazonium perchlorates (dry)	Forbidden											
	1,3-Diazopropane	Forbidden											
	Dibenzyl peroxydicarbonate, with more than 87 percent with water	Forbidden											
	Dibenzyldichlorosilane	8	UN2434	II	8	B2, IB2, T7, TP2, TP13	154	202	242	1 L	30 L	C	40
	Diborane, compressed	2.3	UN1911		2.3, 2.1	1	None	302	None	Forbidden	Forbidden	D	40, 57
D	**Diborane mixtures**	2.1	NA1911		2.1	5	None	302	245	Forbidden	Forbidden	D	40, 57
	Dibromoacetylene	Forbidden											
	1,2-Dibromobutan-3-one	6.1	UN2648	II	6.1	IB2	None	202	243	5 L	60 L	B	40
	Dibromochloropropane	6.1	UN2872	III	6.1	IB3, T4, TP1	153	203	241	60 L	220 L	A	
A	**Dibromodifluoromethane,** *R12B2*	9	UN1941	III	None	T11, TP2	155	203	241	100 L	220 L	A	25
	1,2-Dibromoethane, see **Ethylene dibromide**												
	Dibromomethane	6.1	UN2664	III	6.1	IB3, T4, TP1	153	203	241	60 L	220 L	A	
	Dibutyl ethers	3	UN1149	III	3	B1, IB3, T2, TP1	150	203	242	60 L	220 L	A	
	Dibutylaminoethanol	6.1	UN2873	III	6.1	IB3, T4, TP1	153	203	241	60 L	220 L	A	
	N,N'-Dichlorazodicarbonamidine (salts of) (dry)	Forbidden											
	1,1-Dichloro-1-nitroethane	6.1	UN2650	II	6.1	IB2, T7, TP2	None	202	243	5 L	60 L	A	12, 40
D	**3,5-Dichloro-2,4,6-trifluoropyridine**	6.1	NA9264	I	6.1	2, B9, B14, B32, B74, T20, TP4, TP12, TP13, TP38, TP45	None	227	244	Forbidden	Forbidden	A	40
	Dichloroacetic acid	8	UN1764	II	8	A3, A6, A7, B2, IB2, N34, T8, TP2, TP12	154	202	242	1 L	30 L	A	
	1,3-Dichloroacetone	6.1	UN2649	II	6.1	IB8, IP2, IP4	None	212	242	25 kg	100 kg	B	12, 40
	Dichloroacetyl chloride	8	UN1765	II	8	A3, A6, A7, B2, B6, IB2, N34, T7, TP2	154	202	242	1 L	30 L	D	40
	Dichloroacetylene	Forbidden											
+	**Dichloroanilines, liquid**	6.1	UN1590	II	6.1	IB2, T7, TP2	None	202	243	5 L	60 L	A	40
+	**Dichloroanilines, solid**	6.1	UN1590	II	6.1	IB8, IP2, IP4, T7, TP2	None	212	242	25 kg	100 kg	A	40
+	**o-Dichlorobenzene**	6.1	UN1591	III	6.1	IB3, T4, TP1	153	203	241	60 L	220 L	A	
	2,2'-Dichlorodiethyl ether	6.1	UN1916	II	6.1, 3	IB2, N33, N34, T7, TP2	None	202	243	5 L	60 L	A	
	Dichlorodifluoromethane and difluoroethane azeotropic mixture *or* **Refrigerant gas R 500** *with approximately 74 percent dichlorodifluoromethane*	2.2	UN2602		2.2	T50	306	304	314, 315	75 kg	150 kg	A	
	Dichlorodifluoromethane *or* **Refrigerant gas R 12**	2.2	UN1028		2.2	T50	306	304	314, 315	75 kg	150 kg	A	
	Dichlorodimethyl ether, symmetrical	6.1	UN2249	I	6.1		None	201	243	Forbidden	Forbidden	D	40
	1,1-Dichloroethane	3	UN2362	II	3	IB2, T4, TP1	150	202	242	5 L	60 L	B	40

§172.101 - Hazardous Materials Table

Symbols	Hazardous materials descriptions and proper shipping names	Hazard class or Division	Identification Numbers	PG	Label Codes	Special provisions (§172.102)	(8) Packaging (§173.***)			(9) Quantity limitations		(10) Vessel stowage	
							Exceptions	Non-bulk	Bulk	Passenger aircraft/ rail	Cargo aircraft only	Location	Other
(1)	(2)	(3)	(4)	(5)	(6)	(7)	(8A)	(8B)	(8C)	(9A)	(9B)	(10A)	(10B)
	1,2-Dichloroethane, see **Ethylene dichloride**												
	Dichloroethyl sulfide	Forbidden											
	1,2-Dichloroethylene	3	UN1150	II	3	IB2, T7, TP2	150	202	242	5 L	60 L	B	
	Dichlorofluoromethane *or* **Refrigerant gas R21**	2.2	UN1029		2.2	T50	306	304	314, 315	75 kg	150 kg	A	
	Dichloroisocyanuric acid, dry *or* **Dichloroisocyanuric acid salts**	5.1	UN2465	II	5.1	28, IB8, IP4	152	212	240	5 kg	25 kg	A	13
	Dichloroisopropyl ether	6.1	UN2490	II	6.1	IB2, T7, TP2	None	202	243	5 L	60 L	B	
	Dichloromethane	6.1	UN1593	III	6.1	IB3, N36, T7, TP2	153	203	241	60 L	220 L	A	
	Dichloropentanes	3	UN1152	III	3	B1, IB3, T2, TP1	150	203	242	60 L	220 L	A	
	Dichlorophenyl isocyanates	6.1	UN2250	II	6.1	IB8, IP2, IP4, T7, TP2	None	212	242	25 kg	100 kg	B	25, 40, 48
	Dichlorophenyltrichlorosilane	8	UN1766	II	8	A7, B2, B6, IB2, N34, T7, TP2, TP13	None	202	242	Forbidden	30 L	C	40
	1,2-Dichloropropane	3	UN1279	II	3	IB2, N36, T4, TP1	150	202	242	5 L	60 L	B	
	1,3-Dichloropropanol-2	6.1	UN2750	II	6.1	IB2, T7, TP2	None	202	243	5 L	60 L	A	12, 40
	Dichloropropene and propylene dichloride mixture, see **1,2-Dichloropropane**												
	Dichloropropenes	3	UN2047	II III	3 3	IB2, T4, TP1 B1, IB3, T2, TP1	150 150	202 203	242 242	5 L 60 L	60 L 220 L	B A	
	Dichlorosilane	2.3	UN2189		2.3, 2.1, 8	2, B9, B14	None	304	314, 315	Forbidden	Forbidden	D	17, 40
	1,2-Dichloro-1,1,2,2-tetrafluoroethane *or* **Refrigerant gas R 114**	2.2	UN1958		2.2	T50	306	304	314, 315	75 kg	150 kg	A	
	Dichlorovinylchloroarsine	Forbidden											
	Dicycloheptadiene, see **Bicyclo [2,2,1] hepta-2,5-diene, stabilized**												
	Dicyclohexylamine	8	UN2565	III	8	IB3, T4, TP1	154	203	241	5 L	60 L	A	
	Dicyclohexylammonium nitrite	4.1	UN2687	III	4.1	IB8, IP3	151	213	240	25 kg	100 kg	A	48
	Dicyclopentadiene	3	UN2048	III	3	B1, IB3, T2, TP1	150	203	242	60 L	220 L	A	
	Didymium nitrate	5.1	UN1465	III	5.1	A1, IB8, IP3	152	213	240	25 kg	100 kg	A	
D	**Diesel fuel**	3	NA1993	III	None	B1, IB3, T4, TP1, TP29	150	203	242	60 L	220 L	A	
I	**Diesel fuel**	3	UN1202	III	3	B1, IB3, T2, TP1	150	203	242	60 L	220 L	A	
	Diethanol nitrosamine dinitrate (dry)	Forbidden											
	Diethoxymethane	3	UN2373	II	3	IB2, T4, TP1	150	202	242	5 L	60 L	E	
	3,3-Diethoxypropene	3	UN2374	II	3	IB2, T4, TP1	150	202	242	5 L	60 L	B	
	Diethyl carbonate	3	UN2366	III	3	B1, IB3, T2, TP1	150	203	242	60 L	220 L	A	
	Diethyl cellosolve, see **Ethylene glycol diethyl ether**												
	Diethyl ether *or* **Ethyl ether**	3	UN1155	I	3	T11, TP2	150	201	243	1 L	30 L	E	40
	Diethyl ketone	3	UN1156	II	3	IB2, T4, TP1	150	202	242	5 L	60 L	B	
	Diethyl peroxydicarbonate, with more than 27 percent in solution	Forbidden											
	Diethyl sulfate	6.1	UN1594	II	6.1	IB2, T7, TP2	None	202	243	5 L	60 L	C	
	Diethyl sulfide	3	UN2375	II	3	IB2, T7, TP1, TP13	None	202	243	5 L	60 L	E	
	Diethylamine	3	UN1154	II	3, 8	IB2, N34, T7, TP1	None	202	243	1 L	5 L	E	40
	2-Diethylaminoethanol	8	UN2686	II	8, 3	B2, IB2, T7, TP2	None	202	243	1 L	30 L	A	
	Diethylaminopropylamine	3	UN2684	III	3, 8	B1, IB3, T4, TP1	150	203	242	5 L	60 L	A	
+	**N, N-Diethylaniline**	6.1	UN2432	III	6.1	IB3, T4, TP1	153	203	241	60 L	220 L	A	
	Diethylbenzene	3	UN2049	III	3	B1, IB3, T2, TP1	150	203	242	60 L	220 L	A	
	Diethyldichlorosilane	8	UN1767	II	8, 3	A7, B6, IB2, N34, T7, TP2, TP13	None	202	243	Forbidden	30 L	C	40
	Diethylene glycol dinitrate	Forbidden											
	Diethyleneglycol dinitrate, desensitized *with not less than 25 percent non-volatile water-insoluble phlegmatizer, by mass*	1.1D	UN0075	II	1.1D		None	62	None	Forbidden	Forbidden	13	21E
	Diethylenetriamine	8	UN2079	II	8	B2, IB2, T7, TP2	154	202	242	1 L	30 L	A	40

§172.101 - Hazardous Materials Table

Symbols	Hazardous materials descriptions and proper shipping names	Hazard class or Division	Identification Numbers	PG	Label Codes	Special provisions (§172.102)	(8) Packaging (§173.***) Exceptions	Non-bulk	Bulk	(9) Quantity limitations Passenger aircraft/rail	Cargo aircraft only	(10) Vessel stowage Location	Other
(1)	(2)	(3)	(4)	(5)	(6)	(7)	(8A)	(8B)	(8C)	(9A)	(9B)	(10A)	(10B)
	N,N-Diethylethylenediamine	8	UN2685	II	8, 3	IB2, T7, TP2	None	202	243	1 L	30 L	A	
	Diethylgold bromide	Forbidden											
	Diethylthiophosphoryl chloride	8	UN2751	II	8	B2, IB2, T7, TP2	None	212	240	15 kg	50 kg	D	12, 40
	Diethylzinc	4.2	UN1366	I	4.2, 4.3	B11, T21, TP2, TP7	None	181	244	Forbidden	Forbidden	D	18
	Difluorochloroethanes, see **1-Chloro-1,1-difluoroethanes**												
	1,1-Difluoroethane *or* **Refrigerant gas R 152a**	2.1	UN1030		2.1	T50	306	304	314, 315	Forbidden	150 kg	B	40
	1,1-Difluoroethylene *or* **Refrigerant gas R 1132a**	2.1	UN1959		2.1		306	304	None	Forbidden	150 kg	E	40
	Difluoromethane *or* **Refrigerant gas R 32**	2.1	UN3252		2.1	T50	306	302	314, 315	Forbidden	150 kg	D	40
	Difluorophosphoric acid, anhydrous	8	UN1768	II	8	A6, A7, B2, IB2, N5, N34, T8, TP2, TP12	None	202	242	1 L	30 L	A	40
	2,3-Dihydropyran	3	UN2376	II	3	IB2, T4, TP1	150	202	242	5 L	60 L	B	
	1,8-Dihydroxy-2,4,5,7-tetranitroanthraquinone (chrysamminic acid)	Forbidden											
	Diiodoacetylene	Forbidden											
	Diisobutyl ketone	3	UN1157	III	3	B1, IB3, T2, TP1	150	203	242	60 L	220 L	A	
	Diisobutylamine	3	UN2361	III	3, 8	B1, IB3, T4, TP1	150	203	242	5 L	60 L	A	
	Diisobutylene, isomeric compounds	3	UN2050	II	3	IB2, T4, TP1	150	202	242	5 L	60 L	B	
	Diisooctyl acid phosphate	8	UN1902	III	8	IB3, T4, TP1	154	203	241	5 L	60 L	A	
	Diisopropyl ether	3	UN1159	II	3	IB2, T4, TP1	150	202	242	5 L	60 L	E	40
	Diisopropylamine	3	UN1158	II	3, 8	IB2, T7, TP1	None	202	243	1 L	5 L	B	
	Diisopropylbenzene hydroperoxide, with more than 72 percent in solution	Forbidden											
	Diketene, stabilized	6.1	UN2521	I	6.1, 3	2, B9, B14, B32, B74, T20, TP2, TP13, TP38, TP45	None	227	244	Forbidden	Forbidden	D	40, 49
	1,2-Dimethoxyethane	3	UN2252	II	3	IB2, T4, TP1	150	202	242	5 L	60 L	B	
	1,1-Dimethoxyethane	3	UN2377	II	3	IB2, T7, TP1	150	202	242	5 L	60 L	B	
	Dimethyl carbonate	3	UN1161	II	3	IB2, T4, TP1	150	202	242	5 L	60 L	B	
	Dimethyl chlorothiophosphate, see **Dimethyl thiophosphoryl chloride**												
	2,5-Dimethyl-2,5-dihydroperoxy hexane, with more than 82 percent with water	Forbidden											
	Dimethyl disulfide	3	UN2381	II	3	IB2, T4, TP1	150	202	242	5 L	60 L	B	40
	Dimethyl ether	2.1	UN1033		2.1	T50	306	304	314, 315	Forbidden	150 kg	B	40
	Dimethyl-N-propylamine	3	UN2266	II	3, 8	IB2, T7, TP2, TP13	None	202	243	1 L	5 L	B	40
	Dimethyl sulfate	6.1	UN1595	I	6.1, 8	2, B9, B14, B32, B74, B77, T20, TP2, TP13, TP38, TP45	None	227	244	Forbidden	Forbidden	D	40
	Dimethyl sulfide	3	UN1164	II	3	IB1, T7, TP2	None	202	242	5 L	60 L	E	40
	Dimethyl thiophosphoryl chloride	6.1	UN2267	II	6.1, 8	IB2, T7, TP2	None	202	243	1 L	30 L	B	25
	Dimethylamine, anhydrous	2.1	UN1032		2.1	T50	None	304	314, 315	Forbidden	150 kg	D	40
	Dimethylamine solution	3	UN1160	II	3, 8	IB2, T7, TP1	None	202	243	1 L	5 L	B	
	2-Dimethylaminoacetonitrile	3	UN2378	II	3, 6.1	IB2, T7, TP1	None	202	243	1 L	60 L	A	26, 40
	2-Dimethylaminoethanol	8	UN2051	II	8, 3	B2, IB2, T7, TP2	154	202	243	1 L	30 L	A	
	2-Dimethylaminoethyl acrylate	6.1	UN3302	II	6.1	IB2, T7, TP2	None	202	243	5 L	60 L	D	25
	2-Dimethylaminoethyl methacrylate	6.1	UN2522	II	6.1	IB2, T7, TP2	None	202	243	5 L	60 L	B	40
	N,N-Dimethylaniline	6.1	UN2253	II	6.1	IB1, T7, TP2	None	202	243	5 L	60 L	A	
	2,3-Dimethylbutane	3	UN2457	II	3	IB2, T7, TP1	150	202	242	5 L	60 L	E	
	1,3-Dimethylbutylamine	3	UN2379	II	3, 8	IB2, T7, TP1	None	202	243	1 L	5 L	B	
	Dimethylcarbamoyl chloride	8	UN2262	II	8	B2, IB2, T7, TP2	154	202	242	1 L	30 L	A	40
	Dimethylcyclohexanes	3	UN2263	II	3	IB2, T4, TP1	150	202	242	5 L	60 L	B	
	Dimethylcyclohexylamine	8	UN2264	II	8, 3	B2, IB2, T7, TP2	154	202	243	1 L	30 L	A	40

§172.101 - Hazardous Materials Table

Symbols	Hazardous materials descriptions and proper shipping names	Hazard class or Division	Identification Numbers	PG	Label Codes	Special provisions (§172.102)	(8) Packaging (§173.***)			(9) Quantity limitations		(10) Vessel stowage	
							Exceptions	Non-bulk	Bulk	Passenger aircraft/rail	Cargo aircraft only	Location	Other
(1)	(2)	(3)	(4)	(5)	(6)	(7)	(8A)	(8B)	(8C)	(9A)	(9B)	(10A)	(10B)
	Dimethyldichlorosilane	3	UN1162	II	3, 8	B77, IB2, T7, TP2, TP13	None	202	243	Forbidden	Forbidden	B	40
	Dimethyldiethoxysilane	3	UN2380	II	3	IB2, T4, TP1	150	202	242	5 L	60 L	B	
	Dimethyldioxanes	3	UN2707	II III	3 3	IB2, T4, TP1 B1, IB3, T2, TP1	150 150	202 203	242 242	5 L 60 L	60 L 220 L	B A	
	N,N-Dimethylformamide	3	UN2265	III	3	B1, IB3, T2, TP2	150	203	242	60 L	220 L	A	
	Dimethylhexane dihydroperoxide (dry)	Forbidden											
	Dimethylhydrazine, symmetrical	6.1	UN2382	I	6.1, 3	2, A7, B9, B14, B32, B74, B77, T20, TP2, TP13, TP38, TP45	None	227	244	Forbidden	Forbidden	D	40
	Dimethylhydrazine, unsymmetrical	6.1	UN1163	I	6.1, 3, 8	2, B7, B9, B14, B32, B74, T20, TP2, TP13, TP38, TP45	None	227	244	Forbidden	Forbidden	D	21, 38, 40, 100
	2,2-Dimethylpropane	2.1	UN2044		2.1		306	304	314, 315	Forbidden	150 kg	E	40
	Dimethylzinc	4.2	UN1370	I	4.2, 4.3	B11, B16, T21, TP2, TP7	None	181	244	Forbidden	Forbidden	D	18
	Dinitro-o-cresol, *solid*	6.1	UN1598	II	6.1	IB8, IP2, IP4, T7, TP2	None	212	242	25 kg	100 kg	A	
	Dinitro-o-cresol, *solution*	6.1	UN1598	II	6.1	IB2, IP2, IP4, T7, TP2	None	202	243	5 L	60 L	A	
	1,3-Dinitro-5,5-dimethyl hydantoin	Forbidden											
	Dinitro-7,8-dimethylglycoluril (dry)	Forbidden											
	1,3-Dinitro-4,5-dinitrosobenzene	Forbidden											
	1,4-Dinitro-1,1,4,4-tetramethylolbutanetetranitrate (dry)	Forbidden											
	2,4-Dinitro-1,3,5-trimethylbenzene	Forbidden											
	Dinitroanilines	6.1	UN1596	II	6.1	IB8, IP2, IP4, T7, TP2	None	212	242	25 kg	100 kg	A	91
	Dinitrobenzenes, *liquid*	6.1	UN1597	II	6.1	11, IB2, T7, TP2	None	202	243	5 L	60 L	A	91
	Dinitrobenzenes, *solid*	6.1	UN1597	II	6.1	11, IB8, IP2, IP4	None	212	242	25 kg	100 kg	A	91
	Dinitrochlorobenzene, see **Chlorodinitrobenzene**												
	1,2-Dinitroethane	Forbidden											
	1,1-Dinitroethane (dry)	Forbidden											
	Dinitrogen tetroxide	2.3	UN1067		2.3, 5.1, 8	1, B7, B14, B45, B46, B61, B66, B67, B77, T50, TP21	None	336	314	Forbidden	Forbidden	D	40, 89, 90
	Dinitroglycoluril *or* **Dingu**	1.1D	UN0489	II	1.1D		None	62	None	Forbidden	Forbidden	10	
	Dinitromethane	Forbidden											
	Dinitrophenol, *dry or wetted with less than 15 percent water, by mass*	1.1D	UN0076	II	1.1D, 6.1		None	62	None	Forbidden	Forbidden	10	5E
	Dinitrophenol solutions	6.1	UN1599	II III	6.1 6.1	IB2, T7, TP2 IB3, T4, TP1	None 153	202 203	243 241	5 L 60 L	60 L 220 L	A A	36 36
	Dinitrophenol, wetted *with not less than 15 percent water, by mass*	4.1	UN1320	I	4.1, 6.1	23, A8, A19, A20, N41	None	211	None	1 kg	15 kg	E	28, 36
	Dinitrophenolates *alkali metals, dry or wetted with less than 15 percent water, by mass*	1.3C	UN0077	II	1.3C, 6.1		None	62	None	Forbidden	Forbidden	10	5E
	Dinitrophenolates, wetted *with not less than 15 percent water, by mass*	4.1	UN1321	I	4.1, 6.1	23, A8, A19, A20, N41	None	211	None	1 kg	15 kg	E	28, 36
	Dinitropropylene glycol	Forbidden											
	Dinitroresorcinol, *dry or wetted with less than 15 percent water, by mass*	1.1D	UN0078	II	1.1D		None	62	None	Forbidden	Forbidden	10	5E
	2,4-Dinitroresorcinol (heavy metal salts of) (dry)	Forbidden											
	4,6-Dinitroresorcinol (heavy metal salts of) (dry)	Forbidden											
	Dinitroresorcinol, wetted *with not less than 15 percent water, by mass*	4.1	UN1322	I	4.1	23, A8, A19, A20, N41	None	211	None	1 kg	15 kg	E	28, 36
	3,5-Dinitrosalicylic acid (lead salt) (dry)	Forbidden											
	Dinitrosobenzene	1.3C	UN0406	II	1.3C		None	62	None	Forbidden	Forbidden	10	

§172.101 - Hazardous Materials Table

Symbols	Hazardous materials descriptions and proper shipping names	Hazard class or Division	Identification Numbers	PG	Label Codes	Special provisions (§172.102)	(8) Packaging (§173.***) Exceptions	Non-bulk	Bulk	(9) Quantity limitations Passenger aircraft/ rail	Cargo aircraft only	(10) Vessel stowage Location	Other
(1)	(2)	(3)	(4)	(5)	(6)	(7)	(8A)	(8B)	(8C)	(9A)	(9B)	(10A)	(10B)
	Dinitrosobenzylamidine and salts of (dry)	Forbidden											
	2,2-Dinitrostilbene	Forbidden											
	Dinitrotoluenes, *liquid*	6.1	UN2038	II	6.1	IB2, T7, TP2	None	202	243	5 L	60 L	A	
	Dinitrotoluenes, molten	6.1	UN1600	II	6.1	T7, TP3	None	202	243	Forbidden	Forbidden	C	
	Dinitrotoluenes, *solid*	6.1	UN2038	II	6.1	IB8, IP2, IP4, T7, TP2	None	212	242	25 kg	100 kg	A	
	1,9-Dinitroxy pentamethylene-2,4, 6,8-tetramine (dry)	Forbidden											
	Dioxane	3	UN1165	II	3	IB2, T4, TP1	150	202	242	5 L	60 L	B	
	Dioxolane	3	UN1166	II	3	IB2, T4, TP1	150	202	242	5 L	60 L	B	40
	Dipentene	3	UN2052	III	3	B1, IB3, T2, TP1	150	203	242	60 L	220 L	A	
	Diphenylamine chloroarsine	6.1	UN1698	I	6.1		None	201	None	Forbidden	Forbidden	D	40
	Diphenylchloroarsine, liquid	6.1	UN1699	I	6.1	A8, B14, B32, N33, N34, T14, TP2, TP13, TP27	None	201	243	Forbidden	30 L	D	40
	Diphenylchloroarsine, solid	6.1	UN1699	I	6.1	A8, B14, B32, IB7, IP1, N33, N34	None	211	242	Forbidden	15 kg	D	40
	Diphenyldichlorosilane	8	UN1769	II	8	A7, B2, IB2, N34, T7, TP2, TP13	None	202	242	Forbidden	30 L	C	40
	Diphenylmethyl bromide	8	UN1770	II	8	IB8, IP2, IP4	154	212	240	15 kg	50 kg	D	40
	Dipicryl sulfide, *dry or wetted with less than 10 percent water, by mass*	1.1D	UN0401	II	1.1D		None	62	None	Forbidden	Forbidden	10	
	Dipicryl sulfide, wetted *with not less than 10 percent water, by mass*	4.1	UN2852	I	4.1	A2, N41	None	211	None	Forbidden	0.5 kg	D	28
	Dipicrylamine, *see* **Hexanitrodiphenylamine**												
	Dipropionyl peroxide, with more than 28 percent in solution	Forbidden											
	Di-n-propyl ether	3	UN2384	II	3	IB2, T4, TP1	150	202	242	5 L	60 L	B	
	Dipropyl ketone	3	UN2710	III	3	B1, IB3, T2, TP1	150	203	242	60 L	220 L	A	
	Dipropylamine	3	UN2383	II	3, 8	IB2, T7, TP1	None	202	243	1 L	5 L	B	
G	**Disinfectant, liquid, corrosive, n.o.s.**	8	UN1903	I	8	A7, B10, T14, TP2, TP27	None	201	243	0.5 L	2.5 L	B	
G	**Disinfectants, liquid, corrosive n.o.s.**	8	UN1903	II III	8 8	B2, IB2, T7, TP2 IB3, T4, TP1	154 154	202 203	242 241	1 L 5 L	30 L 60 L	B A	
G	**Disinfectants, liquid, toxic, n.o.s.**	6.1	UN3142	I II III	6.1 6.1 6.1	A4, T14, TP2, TP27 IB2, T11, TP2, TP27 IB3, T7, TP1, TP28	None None 153	201 202 203	243 243 241	1 L 5 L 60 L	30 L 60 L 220 L	A A A	40 40 40
G	**Disinfectants, solid, toxic, n.o.s.**	6.1	UN1601	II III	6.1 6.1	IB8, IP2, IP4 IB8, IP3	None 153	212 213	242 240	25 kg 100 kg	100 kg 200 kg	A A	40 40
	Disodium trioxosilicate	8	UN3253	III	8	IB8, IP3	154	213	240	25 kg	100 kg	A	
G	**Dispersant gases, n.o.s.** *see* **Refrigerant gases, n.o.s.**												
	Divinyl ether, stabilized	3	UN1167	I	3	T11, TP2	None	201	243	1 L	30 L	E	40
	Dodecyltrichlorosilane	8	UN1771	II	8	A7, B2, B6, IB2, N34, T7, TP2, TP13	None	202	242	Forbidden	30 L	C	40
	Dry ice, *see* **Carbon dioxide, solid**												
G	**Dyes, liquid, corrosive, n.o.s. or Dye intermediates, liquid, corrosive, n.o.s.**	8	UN2801	I II III	8 8 8	11, B10, T14, TP2, TP27 11, B2, IB2, T11, TP2, TP27 11, IB3, T7, TP1, TP28	None 154 154	201 202 203	243 242 241	0.5 L 1 L 5 L	2.5 L 30 L 60 L	A A A	
G	**Dyes, liquid, toxic, n.o.s.** *or* **Dye intermediates, liquid, toxic, n.o.s.**	6.1	UN1602	II III	6.1 6.1	IB2 IB3	None 153	202 203	243 241	5 L 60 L	60 L 220 L	A A	
G	**Dyes, solid, corrosive, n.o.s.** *or* **Dye intermediates, solid, corrosive, n.o.s.**	8	UN3147	I II III	8 8 8	IB7, IP1 IB8, IP2, IP4 IB8, IP3	None 154 154	211 212 213	242 240 240	1 kg 15 kg 25 kg	25 kg 50 kg 100 kg	A A A	
G	**Dyes, solid, toxic, n.o.s.** *or* **Dye intermediates, solid, toxic, n.o.s.**	6.1	UN3143	I II III	6.1 6.1 6.1	A5, IB7, IP1, T14, TP2, TP27 IB8, IP2, IP4 IB8, IP3	None None 153	211 212 213	242 242 240	5 kg 25 kg 100 kg	50 kg 100 kg 200 kg	A A A	

§172.101 - Hazardous Materials Table

Symbols	Hazardous materials descriptions and proper shipping names	Hazard class or Division	Identification Numbers	PG	Label Codes	Special provisions (§172.102)	(8) Packaging (§173.***) Exceptions	Non-bulk	Bulk	(9) Quantity limitations Passenger aircraft/ rail	Cargo aircraft only	(10) Vessel stowage Location	Other
(1)	(2)	(3)	(4)	(5)	(6)	(7)	(8A)	(8B)	(8C)	(9A)	(9B)	(10A)	(10B)
	Dynamite, see **Explosive, blasting, type A**												
	Electrolyte (acid or alkali) for batteries, see **Battery fluid, acid** *or* **Battery fluid, alkali**												
	Elevated temperature liquid, flammable, n.o.s., *with flash point above 37.8 C, at or above its flash point*	3	UN3256	III	3	IB1, T3, TP3, TP29	None	None	247	Forbidden	Forbidden	A	
	Elevated temperature liquid, n.o.s., *at or above 100 C and below its flash point (including molten metals, molten salts, etc.)*	9	UN3257	III	9	IB1, T3, TP3, TP29	None	None	247	Forbidden	Forbidden	A	85
	Elevated temperature solid, n.o.s., *at or above 240 C, see §173.247(h)(4)*	9	UN3258	III	9		247(h)(4)	None	247	Forbidden	Forbidden	A	85
	Engines, internal combustion, *flammable gas powered*	9	UN3166		9	135	220	220	220	Forbidden	No limit	A	
	Engines, internal combustion, *flammable liquid powered*	9	UN3166		9	135	220	220	220	No limit	No limit	A	
G	**Environmentally hazardous substances, liquid, n.o.s.**	9	UN3082	III	9	8, IB3, T4, TP1, TP29	155	203	241	No limit	No limit	A	
G	**Environmentally hazardous substances, solid, n.o.s.**	9	UN3077	III	9	8, B54, IB8, N20	155	213	240	No limit	No limit	A	
	Epibromohydrin	6.1	UN2558	I	6.1, 3	T14, TP2, TP13	None	201	243	Forbidden	Forbidden	D	40
+	**Epichlorohydrin**	6.1	UN2023	II	6.1, 3	IB2, T7, TP2, TP13	None	202	243	5 L	60 L	A	40
	1,2-Epoxy-3-ethoxypropane	3	UN2752	III	3	B1, IB3, T2, TP1	150	203	242	60 L	220 L	A	
	Esters, n.o.s.	3	UN3272	II III	3 3	IB2, T7, TP1, TP8, TP28 B1, IB3, T4, TP1, TP29	150 150	202 203	242 242	5 L 60 L	60 L 220 L	B A	
	Etching acid, liquid, n.o.s., see **Hydrofluoric acid, solution** *etc.*												
	Ethane	2.1	UN1035		2.1		306	304	302	Forbidden	150 kg	E	40
D	**Ethane-Propane mixture, refrigerated liquid**	2.1	NA1961		2.1	T75, TP5	None	316	314, 315	Forbidden	Forbidden	D	40
	Ethane, refrigerated liquid	2.1	UN1961		2.1	T75, TP5	None	None	315	Forbidden	Forbidden	D	40
	Ethanol amine dinitrate	Forbidden											
	Ethanol *or* **Ethyl alcohol** *or* **Ethanol solutions** *or* **Ethyl alcohol solutions**	3	UN1170	II III	3 3	24, IB2, T4, TP1 24, B1, IB3, T2, TP1	150 150	202 203	242 242	5 L 60 L	60 L 220 L	A A	
	Ethanolamine *or* **Ethanolamine solutions**	8	UN2491	III	8	IB3, T4, TP1	154	203	241	5 L	60 L	A	
	Ether, see **Diethyl ether**												
	Ethers, n.o.s.	3	UN3271	II III	3 3	IB2, T7, TP1, TP8, TP28 B1, IB3, T4, TP1, TP29	150 150	202 203	242 242	5 L 60 L	60 L 220 L	B A	
	Ethyl acetate	3	UN1173	II	3	IB2, T4, TP1	150	202	242	5 L	60 L	B	
	Ethyl acrylate, stabilized	3	UN1917	II	3	IB2, T4, TP1, TP13	150	202	242	5 L	60 L	B	40
	Ethyl alcohol, *see* **Ethanol**												
	Ethyl aldehyde, see **Acetaldehyde**												
	Ethyl amyl ketone	3	UN2271	III	3	B1, IB3, T2, TP1	150	203	242	60 L	220 L	A	
	N-Ethyl-N-benzylaniline	6.1	UN2274	III	6.1	IB3, T4, TP1	153	203	241	60 L	220 L	A	
	Ethyl borate	3	UN1176	II	3	IB2, T4, TP1	150	202	242	5 L	60 L	B	
	Ethyl bromide	6.1	UN1891	II	6.1	IB2, T7, TP2, TP13	None	202	243	5 L	60 L	B	40, 85
	Ethyl bromoacetate	6.1	UN1603	II	6.1, 3	IB2, T7, TP2	None	202	243	Forbidden	Forbidden	D	40
	Ethyl butyl ether	3	UN1179	II	3	B1, IB2, T4, TP1	150	202	242	5 L	60 L	B	
	Ethyl butyrate	3	UN1180	III	3	B1, IB3, T2, TP1	150	203	242	60 L	220 L	A	
	Ethyl chloride	2.1	UN1037		2.1	B77, T50	None	322	314, 315	Forbidden	150 kg	B	40
	Ethyl chloroacetate	6.1	UN1181	II	6.1, 3	IB2, T7, TP2	None	202	243	5 L	60 L	A	

§172.101 - Hazardous Materials Table

Symbols	Hazardous materials descriptions and proper shipping names	Hazard class or Division	Identification Numbers	PG	Label Codes	Special provisions (§172.102)	(8) Packaging (§173.***)			(9) Quantity limitations		(10) Vessel stowage	
							Exceptions	Non-bulk	Bulk	Passenger aircraft/rail	Cargo aircraft only	Location	Other
(1)	(2)	(3)	(4)	(5)	(6)	(7)	(8A)	(8B)	(8C)	(9A)	(9B)	(10A)	(10B)
	Ethyl chloroformate	6.1	UN1182	I	6.1, 3, 8	2, A3, A6, A7, B9, B14, B32, B74, N34, T20, TP2, TP13, TP38, TP45	None	227	244	Forbidden	Forbidden	D	21, 40, 100
	Ethyl 2-chloropropionate	3	UN2935	III	3	B1, IB3, T2, TP1	150	203	242	60 L	220 L	A	
+	**Ethyl chlorothioformate**	8	UN2826	II	8, 6.1, 3	2, B9, B14, B32, B74, T20, TP2, TP38, TP45	None	227	244	Forbidden	Forbidden	A	40
	Ethyl crotonate	3	UN1862	II	3	IB2, T4, TP2	150	202	242	5 L	60 L	B	
	Ethyl ether, *see* **Diethyl ether**												
	Ethyl fluoride *or* **Refrigerant gas R161**	2.1	UN2453		2.1		306	304	314, 315	Forbidden	150 kg	E	40
	Ethyl formate	3	UN1190	II	3	IB2, T4, TP1	150	202	242	5 L	60 L	E	
	Ethyl hydroperoxide	Forbidden											
	Ethyl isobutyrate	3	UN2385	II	3	IB2, T4, TP1	150	202	242	5 L	60 L	B	
+	**Ethyl isocyanate**	3	UN2481	I	3, 6.1	1, A7, B9, B14, B30, B72, T22, TP2, TP13, TP38, TP44	None	226	244	Forbidden	Forbidden	D	40
	Ethyl lactate	3	UN1192	III	3	B1, IB3, T2, TP1	150	203	242	60 L	220 L	A	
	Ethyl mercaptan	3	UN2363	I	3	T11, TP2, TP13	None	201	243	Forbidden	30 L	E	95, 102
	Ethyl methacrylate	3	UN2277	II	3	IB2, T4, TP1	150	202	242	5 L	60 L	B	
	Ethyl methyl ether	2.1	UN1039		2.1		None	201	314, 315	Forbidden	150 kg	B	40
	Ethyl methyl ketone *or* **Methyl ethyl ketone**	3	UN1193	II	3	IB2, T4, TP1	150	202	242	5 L	60 L	B	
	Ethyl nitrite solutions	3	UN1194	I	3, 6.1		None	201	None	Forbidden	Forbidden	E	40, 105
	Ethyl orthoformate	3	UN2524	III	3	B1, IB3, T2, TP1	150	203	242	60 L	220 L	A	
	Ethyl oxalate	6.1	UN2525	III	6.1	IB3, T4, TP1	153	203	241	60 L	220 L	A	
	Ethyl perchlorate	Forbidden											
D	**Ethyl phosphonothioic dichloride, anhydrous**	6.1	NA2927	I	6.1, 8	2, B9, B14, B32, B74, T20, TP4, TP12, TP13, TP38, TP45	None	227	244	Forbidden	Forbidden	D	40
D	**Ethyl phosphonous dichloride, anhydrous** *pyrophoric liquid*	6.1	NA2845	I	6.1, 4.2	2, B9, B14, B32, B74, T20, TP4, TP12, TP13, TP38, TP45	None	227	244	Forbidden	Forbidden	D	18
D	**Ethyl phosphorodichloridate**	6.1	NA2927	I	6.1, 8	2, B9, B14, B32, B74, T20, TP4, TP12, TP13, TP38, TP45	None	227	244	Forbidden	Forbidden	D	40
	Ethyl propionate	3	UN1195	II	3	IB2, T4, TP1	150	202	242	5 L	60 L	B	
	Ethyl propyl ether	3	UN2615	II	3	IB2, T4, TP1	150	202	242	5 L	60 L	E	
	Ethyl silicate, see **Tetraethyl silicate**												
	Ethylacetylene, stabilized	2.1	UN2452		2.1		None	304	314, 315	Forbidden	150 kg	B	40
	Ethylamine	2.1	UN1036		2.1	B77, T50	None	321	314, 315	Forbidden	150 kg	D	40
	Ethylamine, aqueous solution *with not less than 50 percent but not more than 70 percent ethylamine*	3	UN2270	II	3, 8	IB2, T7, TP1	None	202	243	1 L	5 L	B	40
	N-Ethylaniline	6.1	UN2272	III	6.1	IB3, T4, TP1	153	203	241	60 L	220 L	A	
	2-Ethylaniline	6.1	UN2273	III	6.1	IB3, T4, TP1	153	203	241	60 L	220 L	A	
	Ethylbenzene	3	UN1175	II	3	IB2, T4, TP1	150	202	242	5 L	60 L	B	
	N-Ethylbenzyltoluidines liquid	6.1	UN2753	III	6.1	IB3, T7, TP1	153	203	241	60 L	220 L	A	
	N-Ethylbenzyltoluidines solid	6.1	UN2753	III	6.1	IB8, IP3, T7, TP1	153	213	240	100 kg	200 kg	A	
	2-Ethylbutanol	3	UN2275	III	3	B1, IB3, T2, TP1	150	203	242	60 L	220 L	A	
	Ethylbutyl acetate	3	UN1177	III	3	B1, IB3, T2, TP1	150	203	242	60 L	220 L	A	
	2-Ethylbutyraldehyde	3	UN1178	II	3	B1, IB2, T4, TP1	150	202	242	5 L	60 L	B	
	Ethyldichloroarsine	6.1	UN1892	I	6.1	2, B9, B14, B32, B74, T20, TP2, TP13, TP38, TP45	None	227	244	Forbidden	Forbidden	D	40
	Ethyldichlorosilane	4.3	UN1183	I	4.3, 8, 3	A2, A3, A7, N34, T10, TP2, TP7, TP13	None	201	244	Forbidden	1 L	D	21, 28, 40, 49, 100

§172.101 - Hazardous Materials Table

Symbols	Hazardous materials descriptions and proper shipping names	Hazard class or Division	Identification Numbers	PG	Label Codes	Special provisions (§172.102)	(8) Packaging (§173.***)			(9) Quantity limitations		(10) Vessel stowage	
							Exceptions	Non-bulk	Bulk	Passenger aircraft/rail	Cargo aircraft only	Location	Other
(1)	(2)	(3)	(4)	(5)	(6)	(7)	(8A)	(8B)	(8C)	(9A)	(9B)	(10A)	(10B)
	Ethylene, acetylene and propylene in mixture, refrigerated liquid *with at least 71.5 percent ethylene with not more than 22.5 percent acetylene and not more than 6 percent propylene*	2.1	UN3138		2.1	T75, TP5	None	304	314, 315	Forbidden	Forbidden	D	40
	Ethylene chlorohydrin	6.1	UN1135	I	6.1, 3	2, B9, B14, B32, B74, T20, TP2, TP13, TP38, TP45	None	227	244	Forbidden	Forbidden	D	40
	Ethylene, compressed	2.1	UN1962		2.1		306	304	302	Forbidden	150 kg	E	40
	Ethylene diamine diperchlorate	Forbidden											
	Ethylene dibromide	6.1	UN1605	I	6.1	2, B9, B14, B32, B74, B77, T20, TP2, TP13, TP38, TP45	None	227	244	Forbidden	Forbidden	D	40
	Ethylene dibromide and methyl bromide liquid mixtures, see **Methyl bromide and ethylene dibromide, liquid mixtures**												
	Ethylene dichloride	3	UN1184	II	3, 6.1	IB2, T7, TP1	None	202	243	1 L	60 L	B	40
	Ethylene glycol diethyl ether	3	UN1153	III	3	B1, IB3, T2, TP1	150	203	242	60 L	220 L	A	
	Ethylene glycol dinitrate	Forbidden											
	Ethylene glycol monoethyl ether	3	UN1171	III	3	B1, IB3, T2, TP1	150	203	242	60 L	220 L	A	
	Ethylene glycol monoethyl ether acetate	3	UN1172	III	3	B1, IB3, T2, TP1	150	203	242	60 L	220 L	A	
	Ethylene glycol monomethyl ether	3	UN1188	III	3	B1, IB3, T2, TP1	150	203	242	60 L	220 L	A	
	Ethylene glycol monomethyl ether acetate	3	UN1189	III	3	B1, IB3, T2, TP1	150	203	242	60 L	220 L	A	
	Ethylene oxide and carbon dioxide mixture *with more than 87 percent ethylene oxide*	2.3	UN3300		2.3, 2.1	4	None	304	314, 315	Forbidden	Forbidden	D	40
	Ethylene oxide and carbon dioxide mixtures *with more than 9 percent but not more than 87 percent ethylene oxide*	2.1	UN1041		2.1	T50	306	304	314, 315	Forbidden	25 kg	B	40
	Ethylene oxide and carbon dioxide mixtures *with not more than 9 percent ethylene oxide*	2.2	UN1952		2.2		306	304	314, 315	75 kg	150 kg	A	
	Ethylene oxide and chlorotetrafluoroethane mixture *with not more than 8.8 percent ethylene oxide*	2.2	UN3297		2.2	T50	306	304	314, 315	75 kg	150 kg	A	
	Ethylene oxide and dichlorodifluoromethane mixture, *with not more than 12.5 percent ethylene oxide*	2.2	UN3070		2.2	T50	306	304	314, 315	75 kg	150 kg	A	
	Ethylene oxide and pentafluoroethane mixture *with not more than 7.9 percent ethylene oxide*	2.2	UN3298		2.2	T50	306	304	314, 315	75 kg	150 kg	A	
	Ethylene oxide and propylene oxide mixtures, *with not more than 30 percent ethylene oxide*	3	UN2983	I	3, 6.1	5, A11, N4, N34, T14, TP2, TP7, TP13	None	201	243	Forbidden	30 L	E	40
	Ethylene oxide and tetrafluoroethane mixture *with not more than 5.6 percent ethylene oxide*	2.2	UN3299		2.2	T50	306	304	314, 315	75 kg	150 kg	A	
	Ethylene oxide *or* **Ethylene oxide with nitrogen** *up to a total pressure of 1MPa (10 bar) at 50 degrees C*	2.3	UN1040		2.3, 2.1	4, T50, TP20	None	323	323	Forbidden	25 kg	D	40
	Ethylene, refrigerated liquid *(cryogenic liquid)*	2.1	UN1038		2.1	T75, TP5	None	316	318, 319	Forbidden	Forbidden	D	40
	Ethylenediamine	8	UN1604	II	8, 3	IB2, T7, TP2	154	202	243	1 L	30 L	A	40
	Ethyleneimine, stabilized	6.1	UN1185	I	6.1, 3	1, B9, B14, B30, B72, B77, N25, N32, T22, TP2, TP13, TP38, TP44	None	226	244	Forbidden	Forbidden	D	40
	Ethylhexaldehyde, see **Octyl aldehydes** *etc.*												
	2-Ethylhexyl chloroformate	6.1	UN2748	II	6.1, 8	IB2, T7, TP2, TP13	None	202	243	1 L	30 L	A	12, 13, 21, 25, 40, 100
	2-Ethylhexylamine	3	UN2276	III	3, 8	B1, IB3, T4, TP1	150	203	242	5 L	60 L	A	40
	Ethylphenyldichlorosilane	8	UN2435	II	8	A7, B2, IB2, N34, T7, TP2, TP13	None	202	242	Forbidden	30 L	C	

§172.101 - Hazardous Materials Table

Symbols	Hazardous materials descriptions and proper shipping names	Hazard class or Division	Identification Numbers	PG	Label Codes	Special provisions (§172.102)	(8) Packaging (§173.***) Exceptions	Non-bulk	Bulk	(9) Quantity limitations Passenger aircraft/ rail	Cargo aircraft only	(10) Vessel stowage Location	Other
(1)	(2)	(3)	(4)	(5)	(6)	(7)	(8A)	(8B)	(8C)	(9A)	(9B)	(10A)	(10B)
	1-Ethylpiperidine	3	UN2386	II	3, 8	IB2, T7, TP1	None	202	243	1 L	5 L	B	
	N-Ethyltoluidines	6.1	UN2754	II	6.1	IB2, T7, TP2	None	202	243	5 L	60 L	A	
	Ethyltrichlorosilane	3	UN1196	II	3, 8	A7, IB1, N34, T7, TP2, TP13	None	202	243	1 L	5 L	B	40
	Etiologic agent, see **Infectious substances,** *etc.*												
	Explosive articles, see **Articles, explosive , n.o.s.** *etc.*												
	Explosive, blasting, type A	1.1D	UN0081	II	1.1D		None	62	None	Forbidden	Forbidden	10	21E
	Explosive, blasting, type B	1.1D	UN0082	II	1.1D		None	62	None	Forbidden	Forbidden	10	
	Explosive, blasting, type B *or* **Agent blasting, Type B**	1.5D	UN0331	II	1.5D	105, 106	None	62	None	Forbidden	Forbidden	10	
	Explosive, blasting, type C	1.1D	UN0083	II	1.1D	123	None	62	None	Forbidden	Forbidden	10	22E
	Explosive, blasting, type D	1.1D	UN0084	II	1.1D		None	62	None	Forbidden	Forbidden	10	
	Explosive, blasting, type E	1.1D	UN0241	II	1.1D		None	62	None	Forbidden	Forbidden	10	19E
	Explosive, blasting, type E *or* **Agent blasting, Type E**	1.5D	UN0332	II	1.5D	105, 106	None	62	None	Forbidden	Forbidden	10	
	Explosive, forbidden. See §173.54	Forbidden											
	Explosive substances, see **Substances, explosive, n.o.s.** *etc.*												
	Explosives, slurry, see **Explosive, blasting, type E**												
	Explosives, water gels, see **Explosive, blasting, type E**												
	Extracts, aromatic, liquid	3	UN1169	II III	3 3	IB2, T4, TP1, TP8 B1, IB3, T2, TP1	150 150	202 203	242 242	5 L 60 L	60 L 220 L	B A	
	Extracts, flavoring, liquid	3	UN1197	II III	3 3	IB2, T4, TP1, TP8 B1, IB3, T2, TP1	150 150	202 203	242 242	5 L 60 L	60 L 220 L	B A	
	Fabric with animal or vegetable oil, see **Fibers** *or* **fabrics,** *etc.*												
	Ferric arsenate	6.1	UN1606	II	6.1	IB8, IP2, IP4	None	212	242	25 kg	100 kg	A	
	Ferric arsenite	6.1	UN1607	II	6.1	IB8, IP2, IP4	None	212	242	25 kg	100 kg	A	
	Ferric chloride, anhydrous	8	UN1773	III	8	IB8, IP3	154	213	240	25 kg	100 kg	A	
	Ferric chloride, solution	8	UN2582	III	8	B15, IB3, T4, TP1	154	203	241	5 L	60 L	A	
	Ferric nitrate	5.1	UN1466	III	5.1	A1, A29, IB8, IP3	152	213	240	25 kg	100 kg	A	
	Ferrocerium	4.1	UN1323	II	4.1	59, A19, IB8, IP2, IP4	151	212	240	15 kg	50 kg	A	
	Ferrosilicon, *with 30 percent or more but less than 90 percent silicon*	4.3	UN1408	III	4.3, 6.1	A1, A19, IB8, IP4	151	213	240	25 kg	100 kg	A	13, 40, 85, 103
	Ferrous arsenate	6.1	UN1608	II	6.1	IB8, IP2, IP4	None	212	242	25 kg	100 kg	A	
D	**Ferrous chloride, solid**	8	NA1759	II	8	IB8, IP2, IP4	154	212	240	15 kg	50 kg	A	
D	**Ferrous chloride, solution**	8	NA1760	II	8	B3, IB2, T11, TP2, TP27	154	202	242	1 L	30 L	B	40
	Ferrous metal borings *or* **Ferrous metal shavings** *or* **Ferrous metal turnings** *or* **Ferrous metal cuttings** *in a form liable to self-heating*	4.2	UN2793	III	4.2	A1, A19, IB8, IP3, IP6	None	213	241	25 kg	100 kg	A	
	Fertilizer ammoniating solution *with free ammonia*	2.2	UN1043		2.2		306	304	314, 315	Forbidden	150 kg	E	40
A W	**Fibers** *or* **Fabrics, animal** *or* **vegetable** *or* **Synthetic, n.o.s.** *with animal or vegetable oil*	4.2	UN1373	III	4.2	137, IB8, IP3	None	213	241	Forbidden	Forbidden	A	
	Fibers *or* **Fabrics impregnated with weakly nitrated nitrocellulose, n.o.s.**	4.1	UN1353	III	4.1	A1, IB8, IP3	None	213	240	25 kg	100 kg	D	
	Films, nitrocellulose base, from which gelatine has been removed; film scrap, see **Celluloid scrap**												
	Films, nitrocellulose base, *gelatine coated (except scrap)*	4.1	UN1324	III	4.1		None	183	None	25 kg	100 kg	D	91
	Fire extinguisher charges, *corrosive liquid*	8	UN1774	II	8	N41	154	202	None	1 L	30 L	A	
	Fire extinguisher charges, expelling, explosive, see **Cartridges, power device**												

§172.101 - Hazardous Materials Table

Sym-bols	Hazardous materials descriptions and proper shipping names	Hazard class or Division	Identifi-cation Numbers	PG	Label Codes	Special provisions (§172.102)	(8) Packaging (§173.***)			(9) Quantity limitations		(10) Vessel stowage	
							Excep-tions	Non-bulk	Bulk	Passen-ger aircraft/ rail	Cargo aircraft only	Loca-tion	Other
(1)	(2)	(3)	(4)	(5)	(6)	(7)	(8A)	(8B)	(8C)	(9A)	(9B)	(10A)	(10B)
	Fire extinguishers *containing compressed or liquefied gas*	2.2	UN1044		2.2	18, 110	309	309	None	75 kg	150 kg	A	
	Firelighters, solid *with flammable liquid*	4.1	UN2623	III	4.1	A1, A19	None	213	None	25 kg	100 kg	A	
	Fireworks	1.1G	UN0333	II	1.1G	108	None	62	None	Forbidden	Forbidden	07	
	Fireworks	1.2G	UN0334	II	1.2G	108	None	62	None	Forbidden	Forbidden	07	
	Fireworks	1.3G	UN0335	II	1.3G	108	None	62	None	Forbidden	Forbidden	07	
	Fireworks	1.4G	UN0336	II	1.4G	108	None	62	None	Forbidden	75 kg	06	
	Fireworks	1.4S	UN0337	II	1.4S	108	None	62	None	25 kg	100 kg	05	
	First aid kits	9	UN3316		9	15	None	None	None	10 kg	10 kg	A	
W	**Fish meal, stabilized** *or* **Fish scrap, stabilized**	9	UN2216	III	None	IB8	155	218	218	No limit	No limit	A	88
	Fish meal, unstablized *or* **Fish scrap, unstabilized**	4.2	UN1374	II	4.2	A1, A19, IB8, IP2	None	212	241	15 kg	50 kg	A	119, 120
	Fissile radioactive materials, see **Radioactive material, fissile, n.o.s.**												
	Flammable compressed gas, see **Compressed** *or* **Liquefied gas, flammable,** *etc.*												
	Flammable compressed gas (small receptacles not fitted with a dispersion device, not refillable), see **Receptacles,** *etc.*												
	Flammable gas in lighters, see **Lighters** *or* **lighter refills,** *cigarettes, containing flammable gas*												
G	**Flammable liquid, toxic, corrosive, n.o.s.**	3	UN3286	I II	3, 6.1, 8 3, 6.1, 8	T14, TP2, TP13, TP27 IB2, T11, TP2, TP13, TP27	None None	201 202	243 243	Forbidden 1 L	2.5 L 5 L	E B	21, 40, 100 21, 40, 100
G	**Flammable liquids, corrosive, n.o.s.**	3	UN2924	I II III	3, 8 3, 8 3, 8	T14, TP2 IB2, T11, TP2, TP27 B1, IB3, T7, TP1, TP28	None None 150	201 202 203	243 243 242	0.5 L 1 L 5 L	2.5 L 5 L 60 L	E B A	40 40 40
G	**Flammable liquids, n.o.s.**	3	UN1993	I II III	3 3 3	T11, TP1 IB2, T7, TP1, TP8, TP28 B1, B52, IB3, T4, TP1, TP29	150 150 150	201 202 203	243 242 242	1 L 5 L 60 L	30 L 60 L 220 L	E B A	
G	**Flammable liquids, toxic, n.o.s.**	3	UN1992	I II III	3, 6.1 3, 6.1 3, 6.1	T14, TP2, TP13, TP27 IB2, T7, TP2, TP13 B1, IB3, T7, TP1, TP28	None None 150	201 202 203	243 243 242	Forbidden 1 L 60 L	30 L 60 L 220 L	E B A	40 40
G	**Flammable solid, corrosive, inorganic, n.o.s.**	4.1	UN3180	II III	4.1, 8 4.1, 8	A1, IB6, IP2 A1, IB6	151 151	212 213	242 242	15 kg 25 kg	50 kg 100 kg	D D	40 40
G	**Flammable solid, inorganic, n.o.s.**	4.1	UN3178	II III	4.1 4.1	A1, IB8, IP2, IP4 A1, IB8, IP3	151 151	212 213	240 240	15 kg 25 kg	50 kg 100 kg	B B	
G	**Flammable solid, organic, molten, n.o.s.**	4.1	UN3176	II III	4.1 4.1	IB1, T3, TP3, TP26 IB1, T1, TP3, TP26	151 151	212 213	240 240	Forbidden Forbidden	Forbidden Forbidden	C C	
G	**Flammable solid, oxidizing, n.o.s.**	4.1	UN3097	II III	4.1, 5.1 4.1, 5.1	131 131	None None	214 214	214 214	Forbidden Forbidden	Forbidden Forbidden	E D	40 40
G	**Flammable solid, toxic, inorganic, n.o.s.**	4.1	UN3179	II III	4.1, 6.1 4.1, 6.1	A1, IB6, IP2 A1, IB6	151 151	212 213	242 242	15 kg 25 kg	50 kg 100 kg	B B	40 40
G	**Flammable solids, corrosive, organic, n.o.s.**	4.1	UN2925	II III	4.1, 8 4.1, 8	A1, IB6, IP2 A1, IB6	None 151	212 213	242 242	15 kg 25 kg	50 kg 100 kg	D D	40 40
G	**Flammable solids, organic, n.o.s.**	4.1	UN1325	II III	4.1 4.1	A1, IB8, IP2, IP4, T3, TP1 A1, IB8, IP3, T1, TP1	151 151	212 213	240 240	15 kg 25 kg	50 kg 100 kg	B B	
G	**Flammable solids, toxic, organic, n.o.s.**	4.1	UN2926	II III	4.1, 6.1 4.1, 6.1	A1, IB6, IP2 A1, IB6	None 151	212 213	242 242	15 kg 25 kg	50 kg 100 kg	B B	40 40
	Flares, aerial	1.3G	UN0093	II	1.3G		None	62	None	Forbidden	75 kg	07	
	Flares, aerial	1.4G	UN0403	II	1.4G		None	62	None	Forbidden	75 kg	06	
	Flares, aerial	1.4S	UN0404	II	1.4S		None	62	None	25 kg	100 kg	05	

§172.101 - Hazardous Materials Table

Symbols	Hazardous materials descriptions and proper shipping names	Hazard class or Division	Identification Numbers	PG	Label Codes	Special provisions (§172.102)	(8) Packaging (§173.***) Exceptions	(8) Packaging Non-bulk	(8) Packaging Bulk	(9) Quantity limitations Passenger aircraft/ rail	(9) Quantity limitations Cargo aircraft only	(10) Vessel stowage Location	(10) Vessel stowage Other
(1)	(2)	(3)	(4)	(5)	(6)	(7)	(8A)	(8B)	(8C)	(9A)	(9B)	(10A)	(10B)
	Flares, aerial	1.1G	UN0420	II	1.1G		None	62	None	Forbidden	Forbidden	07	
	Flares, aerial	1.2G	UN0421	II	1.2G		None	62	None	Forbidden	Forbidden	07	
	Flares, airplane, see **Flares, aerial**												
	Flares, signal, see **Cartridges, signal**												
	Flares, surface	1.3G	UN0092	II	1.3G		None	62	None	Forbidden	75 kg	07	
	Flares, surface	1.1G	UN0418	II	1.1G		None	62	None	Forbidden	Forbidden	07	
	Flares, surface	1.2G	UN0419	II	1.2G		None	62	None	Forbidden	Forbidden	07	
	Flares, water-activated, see **Contrivances, water-activated,** *etc.*												
	Flash powder	1.1G	UN0094	II	1.1G		None	62	None	Forbidden	Forbidden	15	
	Flash powder	1.3G	UN0305	II	1.3G		None	62	None	Forbidden	Forbidden	15	
	Flue dusts, poisonous, see **Arsenical dust**												
	Fluoric acid, see **Hydrofluoric acid,** *etc.*												
	Fluorine, compressed	2.3	UN1045		2.3, 5.1, 8	1	None	302	None	Forbidden	Forbidden	D	40, 89, 90
	Fluoroacetic acid	6.1	UN2642	I	6.1	IB7, IP1	None	211	242	1 kg	15 kg	E	
	Fluoroanilines	6.1	UN2941	III	6.1	IB3, T4, TP1	153	203	241	60 L	220 L	A	
	Fluorobenzene	3	UN2387	II	3	IB2, T4, TP1	150	202	242	5 L	60 L	B	
	Fluoroboric acid	8	UN1775	II	8	A6, A7, B2, B15, IB2, N3, N34, T7, TP2	154	202	242	1 L	30 L	A	
	Fluorophosphoric acid anhydrous	8	UN1776	II	8	A6, A7, B2, IB2, N3, N34, T8, TP2, TP12	None	202	242	1 L	30 L	A	
	Fluorosilicates, n.o.s.	6.1	UN2856	III	6.1	IB8, IP3	153	213	240	100 kg	200 kg	A	26
	Fluorosilicic acid	8	UN1778	II	8	A6, A7, B2, B15, IB2, N3, N34, T8, TP2, TP12	None	202	242	1 L	30 L	A	
	Fluorosulfonic acid	8	UN1777	I	8	A3, A6, A7, A10, B6, B10, N3, T10, TP2, TP12	None	201	243	0.5 L	2.5 L	D	40
	Fluorotoluenes	3	UN2388	II	3	IB2, T4, TP1	150	202	242	5 L	60 L	B	40
	Forbidden materials. See §173.21	Forbidden											
	Formaldehyde, solutions, flammable	3	UN1198	III	3, 8	B1, IB3, T4, TP1	150	203	242	5 L	60 L	A	40
	Formaldehyde, solutions, *with not less than 25 percent formaldehyde*	8	UN2209	III	8	IB3, T4, TP1	154	203	241	5 L	60 L	A	
	Formalin, see **Formaldehyde, solutions**												
	Formic acid	8	UN1779	II	8	B2, B28, IB2, T7, TP2	154	202	242	1 L	30 L	A	40
	Fracturing devices, explosive, *without detonators for oil wells*	1.1D	UN0099	II	1.1D		None	62	None	Forbidden	Forbidden	07	
	Fuel, aviation, turbine engine	3	UN1863	I II III	3 3 3	T11, TP1, TP8 IB2, T4, TP1, TP8 B1, IB3, T2, TP1	150 150 150	201 202 203	243 242 242	1 L 5 L 60 L	30 L 60 L 220 L	E B A	
D	**Fuel oil** *(No. 1, 2, 4, 5, or 6)*	3	NA1993	III	3	B1, IB3, T4, TP1, TP29	150	203	242	60 L	220 L	A	
	Fuel system components (including fuel control units (FCU), carburetors, fuel lines, fuel pumps) see **Dangerous Goods in Apparatus** *or* **Dangerous Goods in Machinery**												
	Fulminate of mercury (dry)	Forbidden											
	Fulminate of mercury, wet, see **Mercury fulminate,** *etc.*												
	Fulminating gold	Forbidden											
	Fulminating mercury	Forbidden											
	Fulminating platinum	Forbidden											
	Fulminating silver	Forbidden											
	Fulminic acid	Forbidden											
	Fumaryl chloride	8	UN1780	II	8	B2, IB2, T7, TP2	154	202	242	1 L	30 L	C	8, 40
	Fumigated lading, see **§§172.302(g), 173.9 and 176.76(h)**												

§172.101 - Hazardous Materials Table

Symbols (1)	Hazardous materials descriptions and proper shipping names (2)	Hazard class or Division (3)	Identification Numbers (4)	PG (5)	Label Codes (6)	Special provisions (§172.102) (7)	(8) Packaging (§173.***) Exceptions (8A)	Non-bulk (8B)	Bulk (8C)	(9) Quantity limitations Passenger aircraft/rail (9A)	Cargo aircraft only (9B)	(10) Vessel stowage Location (10A)	Other (10B)
	Fumigated transport vehicle or freight container see 173.9												
	Furaldehydes	6.1	UN1199	II	6.1, 3	IB2, T7, TP2	None	202	243	5 L	60 L	A	
	Furan	3	UN2389	I	3	T12, TP2, TP13	None	201	243	1 L	30 L	E	40
	Furfuryl alcohol	6.1	UN2874	III	6.1	IB3, T4, TP1	153	203	241	60 L	220 L	A	26, 74
	Furfurylamine	3	UN2526	III	3, 8	B1, IB3, T4, TP1	150	203	242	5 L	60 L	A	40
	Fuse, detonating, *metal clad, see* **Cord, detonating,** *metal clad*												
	Fuse, detonating, mild effect, *metal clad, see* **Cord, detonating, mild effect,** *metal clad*												
	Fuse, igniter *tubular metal clad*	1.4G	UN0103	II	1.4G		None	62	None	Forbidden	75 kg	06	
	Fuse, non-detonating *instantaneous or quickmatch*	1.3G	UN0101	II	1.3G		None	62	None	Forbidden	Forbidden	07	
	Fuse, safety	1.4S	UN0105	II	1.4S		None	62	None	25 kg	100 kg	05	
D	**Fusee** *(railway or highway)*	4.1	NA1325	II	4.1		None	184	None	15 kg	50 kg	B	
	Fusel oil	3	UN1201	II III	3 3	IB2, T4, TP1 B1, IB3, T2, TP1	150 150	202 203	242 242	5 L 60 L	60 L 220 L	B A	
	Fuses, tracer, see **Tracers for ammunition**												
	Fuzes, combination, percussion and time, see **Fuzes, detonating** *(UN0257, UN0367);* **Fuzes, igniting** *(UN0317, UN0368)*												
	Fuzes, detonating	1.1B	UN0106	II	1.1B		None	62	None	Forbidden	Forbidden	11	
	Fuzes, detonating	1.2B	UN0107	II	1.2B		None	62	None	Forbidden	Forbidden	11	
	Fuzes, detonating	1.4B	UN0257	II	1.4B	116	None	62	None	Forbidden	75 kg	06	
	Fuzes, detonating	1.4S	UN0367	II	1.4S	116	None	62	None	25 kg	100 kg	05	
	Fuzes, detonating, *with protective features*	1.1D	UN0408	II	1.1D		None	62	None	Forbidden	Forbidden	07	
	Fuzes, detonating, *with protective features*	1.2D	UN0409	II	1.2D		None	62	None	Forbidden	Forbidden	07	
	Fuzes, detonating, *with protective features*	1.4D	UN0410	II	1.4D	116	None	62	None	Forbidden	75 kg	06	
	Fuzes, igniting	1.3G	UN0316	II	1.3G		None	62	None	Forbidden	Forbidden	07	
	Fuzes, igniting	1.4G	UN0317	II	1.4G		None	62	None	Forbidden	75 kg	06	
	Fuzes, igniting	1.4S	UN0368	II	1.4S		None	62	None	25 kg	100 kg	05	
	Galactsan trinitrate	Forbidden											
	Gallium	8	UN2803	III	8		None	162	240	20 kg	20 kg	B	48
	Gas cartridges, *(flammable) without a release device, non-refillable*	2.1	UN2037		2.1		306	304	None	1 kg	15 kg	B	40
	Gas generator assemblies (aircraft), *containing a non-flammable non-toxic gas and a propellant cartridge*	2.2			2.2		None	335	None	75 kg	150 kg	A	
D	**Gas identification set**	2.3	NA9035		2.3	6	None	194	None	Forbidden	Forbidden	D	
	Gas oil	3	UN1202	III	3	B1, IB3, T2, TP1	150	203	242	60 L	220 L	A	
G	**Gas, refrigerated liquid, flammable, n.o.s.** *(cryogenic liquid)*	2.1	UN3312		2.1	T75, TP5	None	316	318	Forbidden	Forbidden	D	40
G	**Gas, refrigerated liquid, n.o.s.** *(cryogenic liquid)*	2.2	UN3158		2.2	T75, TP5	320	316	318	50 kg	500 kg	D	
G	**Gas, refrigerated liquid, oxidizing, n.o.s.** *(cryogenic liquid)*	2.2	UN3311		2.2, 5.1	T75, TP5	320	316	318	Forbidden	Forbidden	D	
	Gas sample, non-pressurized, flammable, n.o.s., *not refrigerated liquid*	2.1	UN3167		2.1		306	302, 304	None	1 L	5 L	D	
	Gas sample, non-pressurized, toxic, flammable, n.o.s., *not refrigerated liquid*	2.3	UN3168		2.3, 2.1		306	302	None	Forbidden	1 L	D	
	Gas sample, non-pressurized, toxic, n.o.s., *not refrigerated liquid*	2.3	UN3169		2.3		306	302, 304	None	Forbidden	1 L	D	
D	**Gasohol** *gasoline mixed with ethyl alcohol, with not more than 20 percent alcohol*	3	NA1203	II	3		150	202	242	5 L	60 L	E	
	Gasoline	3	UN1203	II	3	B33, IB2, T4, TP1	150	202	242	5 L	60 L	E	

§172.101 - Hazardous Materials Table

Symbols	Hazardous materials descriptions and proper shipping names	Hazard class or Division	Identification Numbers	PG	Label Codes	Special provisions (§172.102)	(8) Packaging (§173.***)			(9) Quantity limitations		(10) Vessel stowage	
							Exceptions	Non-bulk	Bulk	Passenger aircraft/ rail	Cargo aircraft only	Location	Other
(1)	(2)	(3)	(4)	(5)	(6)	(7)	(8A)	(8B)	(8C)	(9A)	(9B)	(10A)	(10B)
	Gasoline, casinghead, see **Gasoline**												
	Gelatine, blasting, see **Explosive, blasting, type A**												
	Gelatine dynamites, see **Explosive, blasting, type A**												
	Germane	2.3	UN2192		2.3, 2.1	2	None	302	245	Forbidden	Forbidden	D	40
	Glycerol-1,3-dinitrate	Forbidden											
	Glycerol gluconate trinitrate	Forbidden											
	Glycerol lactate trinitrate	Forbidden											
	Glycerol alpha-monochlorohydrin	6.1	UN2689	III	6.1	IB3, T4, TP1	153	203	241	60 L	220 L	A	
	Glyceryl trinitrate, see **Nitroglycerin,** *etc.*												
	Glycidaldehyde	3	UN2622	II	3, 6.1	IB2, T7, TP1	150	202	243	1 L	60 L	A	40
	Grenades, *hand or rifle, with bursting charge*	1.1D	UN0284	II	1.1D			62	None	Forbidden	Forbidden	07	
	Grenades, *hand or rifle, with bursting charge*	1.2D	UN0285	II	1.2D			62	None	Forbidden	Forbidden	07	
	Grenades, *hand or rifle, with bursting charge*	1.1F	UN0292	II	1.1F			62	None	Forbidden	Forbidden	08	
	Grenades, *hand or rifle, with bursting charge*	1.2F	UN0293	II	1.2F			62	None	Forbidden	Forbidden	08	
	Grenades, illuminating, see **Ammunition, illuminating,** *etc.*												
	Grenades, practice, *hand or rifle*	1.4S	UN0110	II	1.4S			62	None	25 kg	100 kg	05	
	Grenades, practice, *hand or rifle*	1.3G	UN0318	II	1.3G			62	None	Forbidden	Forbidden	07	
	Grenades, practice, *hand or rifle*	1.2G	UN0372	II	1.2G			62	None	Forbidden	Forbidden	07	
	Grenades practice *Hand or rifle*	1.4G	UN0452	II	1.4G			62	None	Forbidden	75 kg	06	
	Grenades, smoke, see **Ammunition, smoke,** *etc.*												
	Guanidine nitrate	5.1	UN1467	III	5.1	A1, IB8, IP3	152	213	240	25 kg	100 kg	A	73
	Guanyl nitrosaminoguanylidene hydrazine (dry)	Forbidden											
	Guanyl nitrosaminoguanylidene hydrazine, wetted *with not less than 30 percent water, by mass*	1.1A	UN0113	II	1.1A	111, 117	None	62	None	Forbidden	Forbidden	12	
	Guanyl nitrosaminoguanyltetrazene (dry)	Forbidden											
	Guanyl nitrosaminoguanyltetrazene, wetted *or* **Tetrazene, wetted** *with not less than 30 percent water or mixture of alcohol and water, by mass*	1.1A	UN0114	II	1.1A	111, 117	None	62	None	Forbidden	Forbidden	12	
	Gunpowder, compressed *or* **Gunpowder in pellets,** *see* **Black powder** *(UN 0028)*												
	Gunpowder, *granular or as a meal, see* **Black powder** *(UN 0027)*												
	Hafnium powder, dry	4.2	UN2545	I II III	4.2 4.2 4.2	 A19, A20, IB6, IP2, N34 IB8, IP3	None None None	211 212 213	242 241 241	Forbidden 15 kg 25 kg	Forbidden 50 kg 100 kg	D D D	
	Hafnium powder, wetted *with not less than 25 percent water (a visible excess of water must be present) (a) mechanically produced, particle size less than 53 microns; (b) chemically produced, particle size less than 840 microns*	4.1	UN1326	II	4.1	A6, A19, A20, IB6, IP2, N34	None	212	241	15 kg	50 kg	E	
	Hand signal device, see **Signal devices, hand**												
	Hazardous substances, liquid or solid, n.o.s., see **Environmentally hazardous substances,** *etc.*												
D G	**Hazardous waste, liquid, n.o.s.**	9	NA3082	III	9	IB3, T2, TP1	155	203	241	No limit	No limit	A	
D G	**Hazardous waste, solid, n.o.s.**	9	NA3077	III	9	B54, IB8, IP2	155	213	240	No limit	No limit	A	
	Heating oil, light	3	UN1202	III	3	B1, IB3, T2, TP1	150	203	242	60 L	220 L	A	
	Helium, compressed	2.2	UN1046		2.2		306	302	302, 314	75 kg	150 kg	A	85
	Helium-oxygen mixture, see **Rare gases and oxygen mixtures**												

§172.101 - Hazardous Materials Table

Symbols (1)	Hazardous materials descriptions and proper shipping names (2)	Hazard class or Division (3)	Identification Numbers (4)	PG (5)	Label Codes (6)	Special provisions (§172.102) (7)	(8) Packaging (§173.***) Exceptions (8A)	Non-bulk (8B)	Bulk (8C)	(9) Quantity limitations Passenger aircraft/ rail (9A)	Cargo aircraft only (9B)	(10) Vessel stowage Location (10A)	Other (10B)
	Helium, refrigerated liquid *(cryogenic liquid)*	2.2	UN1963		2.2	T75, TP5	320	316	318	50 kg	500 kg	B	
	Heptafluoropropane *or* **Refrigerant gas R 227**	2.2	UN3296		2.2	T50	306	304	314, 315	75 kg	150 kg	A	
	n-Heptaldehyde	3	UN3056	III	3	B1, IB3, T2, TP1	150	203	242	60 L	220 L	A	
	Heptanes	3	UN1206	II	3	IB2, T4, TP1	150	202	242	5 L	60 L	B	
	n-Heptene	3	UN2278	II	3	IB2, T4, TP1	150	202	242	5 L	60 L	B	
	Hexachloroacetone	6.1	UN2661	III	6.1	IB3, T4, TP1	153	203	241	60 L	220 L	B	12, 40
	Hexachlorobenzene	6.1	UN2729	III	6.1	IB3	153	203	241	60 L	220 L	A	
	Hexachlorobutadiene	6.1	UN2279	III	6.1	IB3, T4, TP1	153	203	241	60 L	220 L	A	
	Hexachlorocyclopentadiene	6.1	UN2646	I	6.1	2, B9, B14, B32, B74, B77, T20, TP2, TP13, TP38, TP45	None	227	244	Forbidden	Forbidden	D	40
	Hexachlorophene	6.1	UN2875	III	6.1	IB8, IP3	153	213	240	100 kg	200 kg	A	
	Hexadecyltrichlorosilane	8	UN1781	II	8	A7, B2, B6, IB2, N34, T7, TP2	None	202	242	Forbidden	30 L	C	40
	Hexadienes	3	UN2458	II	3	IB2, T4, TP1	None	202	242	5 L	60 L	B	
	Hexaethyl tetraphosphate and compressed gas mixtures	2.3	UN1612		2.3	3	None	334	None	Forbidden	Forbidden	D	40
	Hexaethyl tetraphosphate, *liquid*	6.1	UN1611	II	6.1	IB2, IP2, IP4, N76	None	202	243	5 L	60 L	E	40
	Hexaethyl tetraphosphate, *solid*	6.1	UN1611	II	6.1	IB8, IP2, IP4, N76	None	212	242	25 kg	100 kg	E	40
	Hexafluoroacetone	2.3	UN2420		2.3, 8	2, B9, B14	None	304	314, 315	Forbidden	Forbidden	D	40
	Hexafluoroacetone hydrate	6.1	UN2552	II	6.1	IB2, T7, TP2	None	202	243	5 L	60 L	B	40
	Hexafluoroethane, compressed *or* **Refrigerant gas R 116**	2.2	UN2193		2.2		306	304	314, 315	75 kg	150 kg	A	
	Hexafluorophosphoric acid	8	UN1782	II	8	A6, A7, B2, IB2, N3, N34, T8, TP2, TP12	None	202	242	1 L	30 L	A	
	Hexafluoropropylene compressed *or* **Refrigerant gas R 1216**	2.2	UN1858		2.2	T50	306	304	314, 315	75 kg	150 kg	A	
	Hexaldehyde	3	UN1207	III	3	B1, IB3, T2, TP1	150	203	242	60 L	220 L	A	
	Hexamethylene diisocyanate	6.1	UN2281	II	6.1	IB2, T7, TP2, TP13	None	202	243	5 L	60 L	C	13, 40
	Hexamethylene triperoxide diamine (dry)	Forbidden											
	Hexamethylenediamine, solid	8	UN2280	III	8	IB8, IP3, T4, TP1	154	213	240	25 kg	100 kg	A	12
	Hexamethylenediamine solution	8	UN1783	II III	8 8	IB2, T7, TP2 IB3, T4, TP1	None 154	202 203	242 241	1 L 5 L	30 L 60 L	A A	
	Hexamethyleneimine	3	UN2493	II	3, 8	IB2, T7, TP1	None	202	243	1 L	5 L	B	40
	Hexamethylenetetramine	4.1	UN1328	III	4.1	A1, IB8, IP3	151	213	240	25 kg	100 kg	A	
	Hexamethylol benzene hexanitrate	Forbidden											
	Hexanes	3	UN1208	II	3	IB2, T4, TP1	150	202	242	5 L	60 L	E	
	2,2',4,4',6,6'-Hexanitro-3,3'-dihydroxyazobenzene (dry)	Forbidden											
	Hexanitroazoxy benzene	Forbidden											
	N,N'-(hexanitrodiphenyl) ethylene dinitramine (dry)	Forbidden											
	Hexanitrodiphenyl urea	Forbidden											
	2,2',3',4,4',6-Hexanitrodiphenylamine	Forbidden											
	Hexanitrodiphenylamine *or* **Dipicrylamine** *or* **Hexyl**	1.1D	UN0079	II	1.1D		None	62	None	Forbidden	Forbidden	10	
	2,3',4,4',6,6'-Hexanitrodiphenylether	Forbidden											
	Hexanitroethane	Forbidden											
	Hexanitrooxanilide	Forbidden											
	Hexanitrostilbene	1.1D	UN0392	II	1.1D		None	62	None	Forbidden	Forbidden	10	
	Hexanoic acid, see **Corrosive liquids, n.o.s.**												
	Hexanols	3	UN2282	III	3	B1, IB3, T2, TP1	150	203	242	60 L	220 L	A	
	1-Hexene	3	UN2370	II	3	IB2, T4, TP1	150	202	242	5 L	60 L	E	

§172.101 - Hazardous Materials Table

Symbols	Hazardous materials descriptions and proper shipping names	Hazard class or Division	Identification Numbers	PG	Label Codes	Special provisions (§172.102)	(8) Packaging (§173.***) Exceptions	Non-bulk	Bulk	(9) Quantity limitations Passenger aircraft/ rail	Cargo aircraft only	(10) Vessel stowage Location	Other
(1)	(2)	(3)	(4)	(5)	(6)	(7)	(8A)	(8B)	(8C)	(9A)	(9B)	(10A)	(10B)
	Hexogen and cyclotetramethylenetetranitramine mixtures, wetted *or* **desensitized** *see* **RDX and HMX mixtures, wetted** *or* **desensitized** *etc.*												
	Hexogen and HMX mixtures, wetted *or* **desensitized** *see* **RDX and HMX mixtures, wetted** *or* **desensitized** *etc.*												
	Hexogen and octogen mixtures, wetted *or* **desensitized** *see* **RDX and HMX mixtures, wetted** *or* **desensitized** *etc.*												
	Hexogen, *see* **Cyclotrimethylenetrinitramine,** *etc.*												
	Hexolite, *or* **Hexotol** *dry or wetted with less than 15 percent water, by mass*	1.1D	UN0118	II	1.1D		None	62	None	Forbidden	Forbidden	10	
	Hexotonal	1.1D	UN0393	II	1.1D		None	62	None	Forbidden	Forbidden	10	
	Hexyl, *see* **Hexanitrodiphenylamine**												
	Hexyltrichlorosilane	8	UN1784	II	8	A7, B2, B6, IB2, N34, T7, TP2, TP13	None	202	242	Forbidden	30 L	C	40
	High explosives, see individual explosives' entries												
	HMX, *see* **Cyclotetramethylenete tranitramine,** *etc.*												
	Hydrazine, anhydrous *or* **Hydrazine aqueous solutions** *with more than 64 percent hydrazine, by mass*	8	UN2029	I	8, 3, 6.1	A3, A6, A7, A10, B7, B16, B53	None	201	243	Forbidden	2.5 L	D	21, 40, 42, 100
	Hydrazine, aqueous solution *with not more than 37 percent hydrazine, by mass*	6.1	UN3293	III	6.1	IB3, T4, TP1	153	203	241	60 L	220 L	A	
	Hydrazine azide	Forbidden											
	Hydrazine chlorate	Forbidden											
	Hydrazine dicarbonic acid diazide	Forbidden											
	Hydrazine hydrate *or* **Hydrazine aqueous solutions,** *with not less than 37 percent but not more than 64 percent hydrazine, by mass*	8	UN2030	II	8, 6.1	B16, B53, IB2, T7, TP2, TP13	None	202	243	Forbidden	30 L	D	40, 42, 82
	Hydrazine perchlorate	Forbidden											
	Hydrazine selenate	Forbidden											
	Hydriodic acid, anhydrous, see **Hydrogen iodide, anhydrous**												
	Hydriodic acid	8	UN1787	II III	8 8	A3, A6, B2, IB2, N41, T7, TP2 IB3, T4, TP1	154 154	202 203	242 241	1 L 5 L	30 L 60 L	C C	 8
	Hydrobromic acid, anhydrous, see **Hydrogen bromide, anhydrous**												
	Hydrobromic acid, *with more than 49 percent hydrobromic acid*	8	UN1788	II III	8 8	B2, B15, IB2, N41, T7, TP2 IB3, T4, TP1	154 154	202 203	242 241	Forbidden Forbidden	Forbidden Forbidden	C C	 8
	Hydrobromic acid, *with not more than 49 percent hydrobromic acid*	8	UN1788	II III	8 8	A3, A6, B2, B15, IB2, N41, T7, TP2 IB3, T4, TP1	154 154	202 203	242 241	1 L 5 L	30 L 30 L	C C	 8
	Hydrocarbon gas mixture, compressed, n.o.s.	2.1	UN1964		2.1		306	302	314, 315	Forbidden	150 kg	E	40
	Hydrocarbon gas mixture, liquefied, n.o.s.	2.1	UN1965		2.1	T50	306	304	314, 315	Forbidden	150 kg	E	40
	Hydrocarbons, liquid, n.o.s.	3	UN3295	I II III	3 3 3	T11, TP1, TP8 IB2, T7, TP1, TP8, TP28 B1, IB3, T4, TP1, TP29	150 150 150	201 202 203	243 242 242	1 L 5 L 60 L	30 L 60 L 220 L	E B A	
	Hydrochloric acid, anhydrous, see **Hydrogen chloride, anhydrous**												
	Hydrochloric acid	8	UN1789	II III	8 8	A3, A6, B3, B15, IB2, N41, T8, TP2, TP12 IB3, T4, TP1, TP12	154 154	202 203	242 241	1 L 5 L	30 L 60 L	C C	 8

§172.101 - Hazardous Materials Table

Symbols	Hazardous materials descriptions and proper shipping names	Hazard class or Division	Identification Numbers	PG	Label Codes	Special provisions (§172.102)	(8) Packaging (§173.***)			(9) Quantity limitations		(10) Vessel stowage	
							Exceptions	Non-bulk	Bulk	Passenger aircraft/ rail	Cargo aircraft only	Location	Other
(1)	(2)	(3)	(4)	(5)	(6)	(7)	(8A)	(8B)	(8C)	(9A)	(9B)	(10A)	(10B)
	Hydrocyanic acid, anhydrous, see **Hydrogen cyanide** *etc.*												
	Hydrocyanic acid, aqueous solutions *or* **Hydrogen cyanide, aqueous solutions** *with not more than 20 percent hydrogen cyanide*	6.1	UN1613	I	6.1	2, B61, B65, B77, B82, T20, TP2, TP13	None	195	244	Forbidden	Forbidden	D	40
D	**Hydrocyanic acid, aqueous solutions** *with less than 5 percent hydrogen cyanide*	6.1	NA1613	II	6.1	IB1, T14, TP2, TP13, TP27	None	195	243	Forbidden	5 L	D	40
	Hydrocyanic acid, liquefied, see **Hydrogen cyanide,** *etc.*												
	Hydrocyanic acid (prussic), unstabilized	Forbidden											
	Hydrofluoric acid and Sulfuric acid mixtures	8	UN1786	I	8, 6.1	A6, A7, B15, B23, N5, N34, T10, TP2, TP12, TP13	None	201	243	Forbidden	2.5 L	D	40
	Hydrofluoric acid, anhydrous, see **Hydrogen fluoride, anhydrous**												
	Hydrofluoric acid, *with more than 60 percent strength*	8	UN1790	I	8, 6.1	A6, A7, B4, B15, B23, N5, N34, T10, TP2, TP12, TP13	None	201	243	0.5 L	2.5 L	D	12, 40
	Hydrofluoric acid, *with not more than 60 percent strength*	8	UN1790	II	8, 6.1	A6, A7, B15, IB2, N5, N34, T8, TP2, TP12	None	202	243	1 L	30 L	D	12, 40
	Hydrofluoroboric acid, see **Fluoroboric acid**												
	Hydrofluorosilicic acid, see **Fluorosilicic acid**												
	Hydrogen and Methane mixtures, compressed	2.1	UN2034		2.1		306	302	302, 314, 315	Forbidden	150 kg	E	40
	Hydrogen bromide, anhydrous	2.3	UN1048		2.3, 8	3, B14	None	304	314, 315	Forbidden	25 kg	D	40
	Hydrogen chloride, anhydrous	2.3	UN1050		2.3, 8	3	None	304	None	Forbidden	Forbidden	D	40
	Hydrogen chloride, refrigerated liquid	2.3	UN2186		2.3, 8	3, B6	None	None	314, 315	Forbidden	Forbidden	B	40
	Hydrogen, compressed	2.1	UN1049		2.1		306	302	302, 314	Forbidden	150 kg	E	40, 57
	Hydrogen cyanide, solution in alcohol *with not more than 45 percent hydrogen cyanide*	6.1	UN3294	I	6.1, 3	2, B9, B14, B32, B74, T20, TP2, TP13, TP38, TP45	None	227	244	Forbidden	Forbidden	D	40
	Hydrogen cyanide, stabilized *with less than 3 percent water*	6.1	UN1051	I	6.1, 3	1, B35, B61, B65, B77, B82	None	195	244	Forbidden	Forbidden	D	40
	Hydrogen cyanide, stabilized, *with less than 3 percent water and absorbed in a porous inert material*	6.1	UN1614	I	6.1	5	None	195	None	Forbidden	Forbidden	D	25, 40
	Hydrogen fluoride, anhydrous	8	UN1052	I	8, 6.1	3, B7, B46, B71, B77, T10, TP2	None	163	243	Forbidden	Forbidden	D	40
	Hydrogen iodide, anhydrous	2.3	UN2197		2.3	3, B14	None	304	314, 315	Forbidden	Forbidden	D	40
	Hydrogen iodide solution, see **Hydriodic acid, solution**												
	Hydrogen peroxide and peroxyacetic acid mixtures, stabilized *with acids, water and not more than 5 percent peroxyacetic acid*	5.1	UN3149	II	5.1, 8	A2, A3, A6, B53, IB2, IP5, T7, TP2, TP6, TP24	None	202	243	1 L	5 L	D	25, 66, 75, 106
	Hydrogen peroxide, aqueous solutions *with more than 40 percent but not more than 60 percent hydrogen peroxide (stabilized as necessary)*	5.1	UN2014	II	5.1, 8	12, A3, A6, B53, B80, B81, B85, IB2, IP5, T7, TP2, TP6, TP24, TP37	None	202	243	Forbidden	Forbidden	D	25, 66, 75, 106
	Hydrogen peroxide, aqueous solutions *with not less than 20 percent but not more than 40 percent hydrogen peroxide (stabilized as necessary)*	5.1	UN2014	II	5.1, 8	A2, A3, A6, B53, IB2, IP5, T7, TP2, TP6, TP24, TP37	None	202	243	1 L	5 L	D	25, 66, 75, 106
	Hydrogen peroxide, aqueous solutions *with not less than 8 percent but less than 20 percent hydrogen peroxide (stabilized as necessary)*	5.1	UN2984	III	5.1	A1, IB2, IP5, T4, TP1, TP6, TP24, TP37	152	203	241	2.5 L	30 L	B	25, 75, 106
	Hydrogen peroxide, stabilized *or* **Hydrogen peroxide aqueous solutions, stabilized** *with more than 60 percent hydrogen peroxide*	5.1	UN2015	I	5.1, 8	12, A3, A6, B53, B80, B81, B85, T10, TP2, TP6, TP24, TP37	None	201	243	Forbidden	Forbidden	D	25, 66, 75, 106

§172.101 - Hazardous Materials Table

Symbols	Hazardous materials descriptions and proper shipping names	Hazard class or Division	Identification Numbers	PG	Label Codes	Special provisions (§172.102)	(8) Packaging (§173.***)			(9) Quantity limitations		(10) Vessel stowage	
							Exceptions	Non-bulk	Bulk	Passenger aircraft/ rail	Cargo aircraft only	Location	Other
(1)	(2)	(3)	(4)	(5)	(6)	(7)	(8A)	(8B)	(8C)	(9A)	(9B)	(10A)	(10B)
	Hydrogen, refrigerated liquid *(cryogenic liquid)*	2.1	UN1966		2.1	T75, TP5	None	316	318, 319	Forbidden	Forbidden	D	40
	Hydrogen selenide, anhydrous	2.3	UN2202		2.3, 2.1	1	None	192	245	Forbidden	Forbidden	D	40
	Hydrogen sulfate, see **Sulfuric acid**												
	Hydrogen sulfide	2.3	UN1053		2.3, 2.1	2, B9, B14	None	304	314, 315	Forbidden	Forbidden	D	40
	Hydrogendifluorides, n.o.s. *solid*	8	UN1740	II III	8 8	IB5, IP2, IP4, N3, N34 IB8, IP3, N3, N34	None 154	212 213	240 240	15 kg 25 kg	50 kg 100 kg	A A	25, 26, 40 25, 26, 40
	Hydrogendifluorides, n.o.s. *solutions*	8	UN1740	II III	8 8	IB2, N3, N34 IB3, IP3, N3, N34	None 154	202 203	242 241	1 L 5 L	30 L 60 L	A A	25, 26, 40 25, 26, 40
	Hydroquinone	6.1	UN2662	III	6.1	IB8, IP3, T4, TP1	153	213	240	100 kg	200 kg	A	
	Hydrosilicofluoric acid, see **Fluorosilicic acid**												
	Hydroxyl amine iodide	Forbidden											
	Hydroxylamine sulfate	8	UN2865	III	8	IB8, IP3	154	213	240	25 kg	100 kg	A	
	Hypochlorite solutions	8	UN1791	II III	8 8	A7, B2, B15, IB2, IP5, N34, T7, TP2, TP24 IB3, N34, T4, TP2, TP24	154 154	202 203	242 241	1 L 5 L	30 L 60 L	B B	26 26
	Hypochlorites, inorganic, n.o.s.	5.1	UN3212	II	5.1	IB8, IP2, IP4	152	212	240	5 kg	25 kg	D	48, 56, 58, 69, 106, 116, 118
	Hyponitrous acid	Forbidden											
	Igniter fuse, metal clad, see **Fuse,** *igniter, tubular, metal clad*												
	Igniters	1.1G	UN0121	II	1.1G		None	62	None	Forbidden	Forbidden	07	
	Igniters	1.2G	UN0314	II	1.2G		None	62	None	Forbidden	Forbidden	07	
	Igniters	1.3G	UN0315	II	1.3G		None	62	None	Forbidden	Forbidden	07	
	Igniters	1.4G	UN0325	II	1.4G		None	62	None	Forbidden	75 kg	06	
	Igniters	1.4S	UN0454	II	1.4S		None	62	None	25 kg	100 kg	05	
	3,3'-Iminodipropylamine	8	UN2269	III	8	IB3, T4, TP2	154	203	241	5 L	60 L	A	
G	**Infectious substances, affecting animals** *only*	6.2	UN2900		6.2	A81, A82	134	196	None	50 mL or 50g	4 L or 4 kg	B	40
G	**Infectious substances, affecting humans**	6.2	UN2814		6.2	A81, A82	134	196	None	50 mL or 50g	4 L or 4 kg	B	40
	Inflammable, see Flammable												
	Initiating explosives (dry)	Forbidden											
	Inositol hexanitrate (dry)	Forbidden											
G	**Insecticide gases, n.o.s.**	2.2	UN1968		2.2		306	304	314, 315	75 kg	150 kg	A	
G	**Insecticide gases, flammable, n.o.s.**	2.1	UN3354		2.1	T50	306	304	314, 315	Forbidden	150 kg	D	40
G	**Insecticide gases, toxic, flammable, n.o.s.** *Inhalation hazard Zone A*	2.3	UN3355		2.3, 2.1	1	None	192	245	Forbidden	Forbidden	D	40
G	**Insecticide gases, toxic, flammable, n.o.s.** *Inhalation hazard Zone B*	2.3	UN3355		2.3, 2.1	2, B9, B14	None	302, 305	314, 315	Forbidden	Forbidden	D	40
G	**Insecticide gases, toxic, flammable, n.o.s.** *Inhalation hazard Zone C*	2.3	UN3355		2.3, 2.1	3, B14	None	302, 305	314, 315	Forbidden	Forbidden	D	
G	**Insecticide gases, toxic, flammable, n.o.s.** *Inhalation hazard Zone D*	2.3	UN3355		2.3, 2.1	4	None	302, 305	314, 315	Forbidden	Forbidden	D	
G	**Insecticide gases, toxic, n.o.s.**	2.3	UN1967		2.3	3	None	193, 334	245	Forbidden	Forbidden	D	40
	Inulin trinitrate (dry)	Forbidden											
	Iodine azide (dry)	Forbidden											
	Iodine monochloride	8	UN1792	II	8	B6, IB8, IP2, IP4, N41, T7, TP2	None	212	240	Forbidden	50 kg	D	40, 66, 74, 89, 90
	Iodine pentafluoride	5.1	UN2495	I	5.1, 6.1, 8		None	205	243	Forbidden	2.5 L	D	25, 40, 66, 90
	2-Iodobutane	3	UN2390	II	3	IB2, T4, TP1	150	202	242	5 L	60 L	B	
	Iodomethylpropanes	3	UN2391	II	3	IB2, T4, TP1	150	202	242	5 L	60 L	B	
	Iodopropanes	3	UN2392	III	3	B1, IB3, T2, TP1	150	203	242	60 L	220 L	A	
	Iodoxy compounds (dry)	Forbidden											
	Iridium nitratopentamine iridium nitrate	Forbidden											

§172.101 - Hazardous Materials Table

Symbols	Hazardous materials descriptions and proper shipping names	Hazard class or Division	Identification Numbers	PG	Label Codes	Special provisions (§172.102)	(8) Packaging (§173.***) Exceptions	(8) Packaging Non-bulk	(8) Packaging Bulk	(9) Quantity limitations Passenger aircraft/rail	(9) Quantity limitations Cargo aircraft only	(10) Vessel stowage Location	(10) Vessel stowage Other
(1)	(2)	(3)	(4)	(5)	(6)	(7)	(8A)	(8B)	(8C)	(9A)	(9B)	(10A)	(10B)
	Iron chloride, see **Ferric chloride**												
	Iron oxide, spent, *or* **Iron sponge, spent** *obtained from coal gas purification*	4.2	UN1376	III	4.2	B18, IB8, IP3	None	213	240	Forbidden	Forbidden	E	
	Iron pentacarbonyl	6.1	UN1994	I	6.1, 3	1, B9, B14, B30, B72, B77, T22, TP2, TP13, TP38, TP44	None	226	244	Forbidden	Forbidden	D	40
	Iron sesquichloride, see **Ferric chloride**												
	Irritating material, see **Tear gas substances,** *etc.*												
	Isobutane *see also* **Petroleum gases, liquefied**	2.1	UN1969		2.1	19, T50	306	304	314, 315	Forbidden	150 kg	E	40
	Isobutanol *or* **Isobutyl alcohol**	3	UN1212	III	3	B1, IB3, T2, TP1	150	203	242	60 L	220 L	A	
	Isobutyl acetate	3	UN1213	II	3	IB2, T4, TP1	150	202	242	5 L	60 L	B	
	Isobutyl acrylate, stabilized	3	UN2527	III	3	B1, IB3, T2, TP1	150	203	242	60 L	220 L	A	
	Isobutyl alcohol, *see* **Isobutanol**												
	Isobutyl aldehyde, *see* **Isobutyraldehyde**												
D	**Isobutyl chloroformate**	6.1	NA2742	I	6.1, 3, 8	2, B9, B14, B32, B74, T20, TP4, TP12, TP13, TP38, TP45	None	227	244	1 L	30 L	A	12, 13, 22, 25, 40, 48, 100
	Isobutyl formate	3	UN2393	II	3	IB2, T4, TP1	150	202	242	5 L	60 L	B	
	Isobutyl isobutyrate	3	UN2528	III	3	B1, IB3, T2, TP1	150	203	242	60 L	220 L	A	
+	**Isobutyl isocyanate**	3	UN2486	I	3, 6.1	1, B9, B14, B30, B72, T22, TP2, TP13, TP27	None	226	244	Forbidden	Forbidden	D	40
	Isobutyl methacrylate, stabilized	3	UN2283	III	3	B1, IB3, T2, TP1	150	203	242	60 L	220 L	A	
	Isobutyl propionate	3	UN2394	III	3	B1, IB3, T2, TP1	150	203	242	60 L	220 L	B	
	Isobutylamine	3	UN1214	II	3, 8	IB2, T7, TP1	None	202	243	1 L	5 L	B	40
	Isobutylene *see also* **Petroleum gases, liquefied**	2.1	UN1055		2.1	19, T50	306	304	314, 315	Forbidden	150 kg	E	40
	Isobutyraldehyde *or* **Isobutyl aldehyde**	3	UN2045	II	3	IB2, T4, TP1	150	202	242	5 L	60 L	E	40
	Isobutyric acid	3	UN2529	III	3, 8	B1, IB3, T4, TP1	150	203	242	5 L	60 L	A	
	Isobutyronitrile	3	UN2284	II	3, 6.1	IB2, T7, TP2, TP13	None	202	243	1 L	60 L	E	40
	Isobutyryl chloride	3	UN2395	II	3, 8	IB1, T7, TP2	None	202	243	1 L	5 L	C	40
G	**Isocyanates, flammable, toxic, n.o.s.** *or* **Isocyanate solutions, flammable, toxic, n.o.s.** *flash point less than 23 degrees C*	3	UN2478	II	3, 6.1	5, A3, A7, IB2, T11, TP2, TP13, TP27	None	202	243	1 L	60 L	D	40
G	**Isocyanates, toxic, flammable, n.o.s.** *or* **Isocyanate solutions, toxic, flammable, n.o.s.,** *flash point not less than 23 degrees C but not more than 61 degrees C and boiling point less than 300 degrees C*	6.1	UN3080	II	6.1, 3	IB2, T11, TP2, TP13, TP27	None	202	243	5 L	60 L	B	25, 40, 48
G	**Isocyanates, toxic, n.o.s.** *or* **Isocyanate solutions, toxic, n.o.s.,** *flash point more than 61 degrees C and boiling point less than 300 degrees C*	6.1	UN2206	II	6.1	IB2, T11, TP2, TP13, TP27	None	202	243	5 L	60 L	E	25, 40, 48
				III	6.1	IB3, T7, TP1, TP13, TP28	153	203	241	60 L	220 L	E	25, 40, 48
	Isocyanatobenzotrifluorides	6.1	UN2285	II	6.1, 3	5, IB2, T7, TP2	None	202	243	5 L	60 L	D	25, 40, 48
	Isoheptenes	3	UN2287	II	3	IB2, T4, TP1	150	202	242	5 L	60 L	B	
	Isohexenes	3	UN2288	II	3	IB2, T11, TP1	150	202	242	5 L	60 L	E	
	Isooctane, see **Octanes**												
	Isooctenes	3	UN1216	II	3	IB2, T4, TP1	150	202	242	5 L	60 L	B	
	Isopentane, see **Pentane**												
	Isopentanoic acid, see **Corrosive liquids, n.o.s.**												
	Isopentenes	3	UN2371	I	3	T11, TP2	150	201	243	1 L	30 L	E	
	Isophorone diisocyanate	6.1	UN2290	III	6.1	IB3, T4, TP2	153	203	241	60 L	220 L	B	40
	Isophoronediamine	8	UN2289	III	8	IB3, T4, TP1	154	203	241	5 L	60 L	A	

§172.101 - Hazardous Materials Table

Symbols	Hazardous materials descriptions and proper shipping names	Hazard class or Division	Identification Numbers	PG	Label Codes	Special provisions (§172.102)	(8) Packaging (§173.***)			(9) Quantity limitations		(10) Vessel stowage	
							Exceptions	Non-bulk	Bulk	Passenger aircraft/rail	Cargo aircraft only	Location	Other
(1)	(2)	(3)	(4)	(5)	(6)	(7)	(8A)	(8B)	(8C)	(9A)	(9B)	(10A)	(10B)
	Isoprene, stabilized	3	UN1218	I	3	T11, TP2	150	201	243	1 L	30 L	E	
	Isopropanol *or* **Isopropyl alcohol**	3	UN1219	II	3	IB2, T4, TP1	150	202	242	5 L	60 L	B	
	Isopropenyl acetate	3	UN2403	II	3	IB2, T4, TP1	150	202	242	5 L	60 L	B	
	Isopropenylbenzene	3	UN2303	III	3	B1, IB3, T2, TP1	150	203	242	60 L	220 L	A	
	Isopropyl acetate	3	UN1220	II	3	IB2, T4, TP1	150	202	242	5 L	60 L	B	
	Isopropyl acid phosphate	8	UN1793	III	8	IB8, IP3, T4, TP1	154	213	240	25 kg	100 kg	A	
	Isopropyl alcohol, *see* **Isopropanol**												
	Isopropyl butyrate	3	UN2405	III	3	B1, IB3, T2, TP1	150	203	242	60 L	220 L	A	
	Isopropyl chloroacetate	3	UN2947	III	3	B1, IB3, T2, TP1	150	203	242	60 L	220 L	A	
	Isopropyl chloroformate	6.1	UN2407	I	6.1, 3, 8	2, B9, B14, B32, B74, B77, T20, TP2, TP13, TP38, TP44	None	227	244	Forbidden	Forbidden	B	40
	Isopropyl 2-chloropropionate	3	UN2934	III	3	B1, IB3, T2, TP1	150	203	242	60 L	220 L	A	
	Isopropyl isobutyrate	3	UN2406	II	3	IB2, T4, TP1	150	202	242	5 L	60 L	B	
+	**Isopropyl isocyanate**	3	UN2483	I	3, 6.1	1, B9, B14, B30, B72, T22, TP2, TP13, TP38, TP44	None	226	244	Forbidden	Forbidden	D	40
	Isopropyl mercaptan, see **Propanethiols**												
	Isopropyl nitrate	3	UN1222	II	3	IB2, IP7	150	202	None	5 L	60 L	D	
	Isopropyl phosphoric acid, see **Isopropyl acid phosphate**												
	Isopropyl propionate	3	UN2409	II	3	IB2, T4, TP1	150	202	242	5 L	60 L	B	
	Isopropylamine	3	UN1221	I	3, 8	T11, TP2	None	201	243	0.5 L	2.5 L	E	
	Isopropylbenzene	3	UN1918	III	3	B1, IB3, T2, TP1	150	203	242	60 L	220 L	A	
	Isopropylcumyl hydroperoxide, with more than 72 percent in solution	Forbidden											
	Isosorbide dinitrate mixture *with not less than 60 percent lactose, mannose, starch or calcium hydrogen phosphate*	4.1	UN2907	II	4.1	IB6, IP2	None	212	None	15 kg	50 kg	E	
	Isosorbide-5-mononitrate	4.1	UN3251	III	4.1	66, IB8	151	213	240	Forbidden	Forbidden	D	12
	Isothiocyanic acid	Forbidden											
	Jet fuel, see **Fuel aviation, turbine engine**												
D	**Jet perforating guns, charged oil well, with detonator**	1.1D	NA0124	II	1.1D	55, 56	None	62	None	Forbidden	Forbidden	07	
D	**Jet perforating guns, charged oil well, with detonator**	1.4D	NA0494	II	1.4D	55, 56	None	62	None	Forbidden	Forbidden	06	
	Jet perforating guns, charged *oil well, without detonator*	1.1D	UN0124	II	1.1D	55	None	62	None	Forbidden	Forbidden	07	
	Jet perforating guns, charged, *oil well, without detonator*	1.4D	UN0494	II	1.4D	55, 114	None	62	None	Forbidden	300 kg	06	
	Jet perforators, see **Charges, shaped,** *etc.*												
	Jet tappers, without detonator, see **Charges, shaped,** *etc.*												
	Jet thrust igniters, for rocket motors or Jato, see **Igniters**												
	Jet thrust unit (Jato), see **Rocket motors**												
	Kerosene	3	UN1223	III	3	B1, IB3, T2, TP2	150	203	242	60 L	220 L	A	
G	**Ketones, liquid, n.o.s.**	3	UN1224	I	3	T11, TP1, TP8, TP27	None	201	243	1 L	30 L	E	
				II	3	IB2, T7, TP1, TP8, TP28	150	202	242	5 L	60 L	B	
				III	3	B1, IB3, T4, TP1, TP29	150	203	242	60 L	220 L	A	
	Krypton, compressed	2.2	UN1056		2.2		306	302	None	75 kg	150 kg	A	
	Krypton, refrigerated liquid *(cryogenic liquid)*	2.2	UN1970		2.2	T75, TP5	320	None	None	50 kg	500 kg	B	
	Lacquer base or lacquer chips, nitrocellulose, dry, see **Nitrocellulose,** *etc. (UN 2557)*												

§172.101 - Hazardous Materials Table

Symbols	Hazardous materials descriptions and proper shipping names	Hazard class or Division	Identification Numbers	PG	Label Codes	Special provisions (§172.102)	(8) Packaging (§173.***) Exceptions	(8) Packaging Non-bulk	(8) Packaging Bulk	(9) Quantity limitations Passenger aircraft/rail	(9) Quantity limitations Cargo aircraft only	(10) Vessel stowage Location	(10) Vessel stowage Other
(1)	(2)	(3)	(4)	(5)	(6)	(7)	(8A)	(8B)	(8C)	(9A)	(9B)	(10A)	(10B)
	Lacquer base or lacquer chips, plastic, wet with alcohol or solvent, see **Nitrocellulose** *(UN2059, UN2555, UN2556, UN2557) or* **Paint** *etc.(UN1263)*												
	Lead acetate	6.1	UN1616	III	6.1	IB8, IP3	153	213	240	100 kg	200 kg	A	
	Lead arsenates	6.1	UN1617	II	6.1	IB8, IP2, IP4	None	212	242	25 kg	100 kg	A	
	Lead arsenites	6.1	UN1618	II	6.1	IB8, IP2, IP4	None	212	242	25 kg	100 kg	A	
	Lead azide (dry)	Forbidden											
	Lead azide, wetted *with not less than 20 percent water or mixture of alcohol and water, by mass*	1.1A	UN0129	II	1.1A	111, 117	None	62	None	Forbidden	Forbidden	12	
	Lead compounds, soluble, n.o.s.	6.1	UN2291	III	6.1	138, IB8, IP3	153	213	240	100 kg	200 kg	A	
	Lead cyanide	6.1	UN1620	II	6.1	IB8, IP2, IP4	None	212	242	25 kg	100 kg	A	26
	Lead dioxide	5.1	UN1872	III	5.1	A1, IB8, IP3	152	213	240	25 kg	100 kg	A	
	Lead dross, see **Lead sulfate,** *with more than 3 percent free acid*												
	Lead nitrate	5.1	UN1469	II	5.1, 6.1	IB8, IP2, IP4	None	212	242	5 kg	25 kg	A	
	Lead nitroresorcinate (dry)	Forbidden											
	Lead perchlorate, solid	5.1	UN1470	II	5.1, 6.1	IB6, IP2, T4, TP1	None	212	242	5 kg	25 kg	A	56, 58, 106
	Lead perchlorate, solution	5.1	UN1470	II	5.1, 6.1	IB1, T4, TP1	None	202	243	1 L	5 L	A	56, 58, 106
	Lead peroxide, see **Lead dioxide**												
	Lead phosphite, dibasic	4.1	UN2989	II III	4.1 4.1	IB8, IP2, IP4 IB8, IP3	None 151	212 213	240 240	5 kg 15 kg	25 kg 50 kg	B B	34 34
	Lead picrate (dry)	Forbidden											
	Lead styphnate (dry)	Forbidden											
	Lead styphnate, wetted *or* **Lead trinitroresorcinate, wetted** *with not less than 20 percent water or mixture of alcohol and water, by mass*	1.1A	UN0130	II	1.1A	111, 117	None	62	None	Forbidden	Forbidden	12	
	Lead sulfate *with more than 3 percent free acid*	8	UN1794	II	8	IB8, IP2, IP4	154	212	240	15 kg	50 kg	A	
	Lead trinitroresorcinate, *see* **Lead styphnate,** *etc.*												
	Life-saving appliances, not self inflating *containing dangerous goods as equipment*	9	UN3072		None	143	None	219	None	No limit	No limit	A	
	Life-saving appliances, self inflating	9	UN2990		None		None	219	None	No limit	No limit	A	
	Lighter replacement cartridges containing liquefied petroleum gases (and similar devices, each not exceeding 65 grams), see **Lighters** *or* **lighter refills** *etc. containing flammable gas*												
	Lighters, fuse	1.4S	UN0131	II	1.4S		None	62	None	25 kg	100 kg	05	
	Lighters *or* **Lighter refills** *cigarettes, containing flammable gas*	2.1	UN1057		2.1	N10	None	21, 308	None	1 kg	15 kg	B	40
	Lime, unslaked, see **Calcium oxide**												
G	**Liquefied gas, flammable, n.o.s.**	2.1	UN3161		2.1	T50	306	304	314, 315	Forbidden	150 kg	D	40
G	**Liquefied gas, n.o.s.**	2.2	UN3163		2.2	T50	306	304	314, 315	75 kg	150 kg	A	
G	**Liquefied gas, oxidizing, n.o.s.**	2.2	UN3157		2.2, 5.1		306	304	314, 315	75 kg	150 kg	D	
G I	**Liquefied gas, toxic, corrosive, n.o.s.** *Inhalation Hazard Zone A*	2.3	UN3308		2.3, 8	1	None	192	245	Forbidden	Forbidden	D	40
G I	**Liquefied gas, toxic, corrosive, n.o.s.** *Inhalation Hazard Zone B*	2.3	UN3308		2.3, 8	2	None	304	314, 315	Forbidden	Forbidden	D	40
G I	**Liquefied gas, toxic, corrosive, n.o.s.** *Inhalation Hazard Zone C*	2.3	UN3308		2.3, 8	3	None	304	314, 315	Forbidden	Forbidden	D	40
G I	**Liquefied gas, toxic, corrosive, n.o.s.** *Inhalation Hazard Zone D*	2.3	UN3308		2.3, 8	4	None	304	314, 315	Forbidden	Forbidden	D	40
G I	**Liquefied gas, toxic, flammable, corrosive, n.o.s.** *Inhalation Hazard Zone A*	2.3	UN3309		2.3, 2.1, 8	1	None	192	245	Forbidden	Forbidden	D	17, 40
G I	**Liquefied gas toxic, flammable, corrosive, n.o.s.** *Inhalation Hazard Zone B*	2.3	UN3309		2.3, 2.1, 8	2	None	304	314, 315	Forbidden	Forbidden	D	17, 40

§172.101 - Hazardous Materials Table

Symbols (1)	Hazardous materials descriptions and proper shipping names (2)	Hazard class or Division (3)	Identification Numbers (4)	PG (5)	Label Codes (6)	Special provisions (§172.102) (7)	(8) Packaging (§173.***) Exceptions (8A)	Non-bulk (8B)	Bulk (8C)	(9) Quantity limitations Passenger aircraft/rail (9A)	Cargo aircraft only (9B)	(10) Vessel stowage Location (10A)	Other (10B)
G I	**Liquefied gas, toxic, flammable, corrosive, n.o.s.** *Inhalation Hazard Zone C*	2.3	UN3309		2.3, 2.1, 8	3	None	304	314, 315	Forbidden	Forbidden	D	17, 40
G I	**Liquefied gas, toxic, flammable, corrosive, n.o.s.** *Inhalation Hazard Zone D*	2.3	UN3309		2.3, 2.1, 8	4	None	304	314, 315	Forbidden	Forbidden	D	17, 40
G	**Liquefied gas, toxic, flammable, n.o.s.** *Inhalation Hazard Zone A*	2.3	UN3160		2.3, 2.1	1	None	192	245	Forbidden	Forbidden	D	40
G	**Liquefied gas, toxic, flammable, n.o.s.** *Inhalation Hazard Zone B*	2.3	UN3160		2.3, 2.1	2, B9, B14	None	304	314, 315	Forbidden	Forbidden	D	40
G	**Liquefied gas, toxic, flammable, n.o.s.** *Inhalation Hazard Zone C*	2.3	UN3160		2.3, 2.1	3, B14	None	304	314, 315	Forbidden	Forbidden	D	40
G	**Liquefied gas, toxic, flammable, n.o.s.** *Inhalation Hazard Zone D*	2.3	UN3160		2.3, 2.1	4	None	304	314, 315	Forbidden	Forbidden	D	40
G	**Liquefied gas, toxic, n.o.s.** *Inhalation Hazard Zone A*	2.3	UN3162		2.3	1	None	192	245	Forbidden	Forbidden	D	40
G	**Liquefied gas, toxic, n.o.s.** *Inhalation Hazard Zone B*	2.3	UN3162		2.3	2, B9, B14	None	304	314, 315	Forbidden	Forbidden	D	40
G	**Liquefied gas, toxic, n.o.s.** *Inhalation Hazard Zone C*	2.3	UN3162		2.3	3, B14	None	304	314, 315	Forbidden	Forbidden	D	40
G	**Liquefied gas, toxic, n.o.s.** *Inhalation Hazard Zone D*	2.3	UN3162		2.3	4	None	304	314, 315	Forbidden	Forbidden	D	40
G I	**Liquefied gas, toxic, oxidizing, corrosive, n.o.s.** *Inhalation Hazard Zone A*	2.3	UN3310		2.3, 5.1, 8	1	None	192	245	Forbidden	Forbidden	D	40, 89,90
G I	**Liquefied gas, toxic, oxidizing, corrosive, n.o.s.** *Inhalation Hazard Zone B*	2.3	UN3310		2.3, 2.1, 8	2	None	304	314, 315	Forbidden	Forbidden	D	40, 89,90
G I	**Liquefied gas, toxic, oxidizing, corrosive, n.o.s.** *Inhalation Hazard Zone C*	2.3	UN3310		2.3, 2.1, 8	3	None	304	314, 315	Forbidden	Forbidden	D	40, 89, 90
G I	**Liquefied gas, toxic, oxidizing, corrosive, n.o.s.** *Inhalation Hazard Zone D*	2.3	UN3310		2.3, 2.1, 8	4	None	304	314, 315	Forbidden	Forbidden	D	40, 89, 90
G	**Liquefied gas, toxic, oxidizing, n.o.s.** *Inhalation Hazard Zone A*	2.3	UN3307		2.3, 5.1	1	None	192	245	Forbidden	Forbidden	D	40
G	**Liquefied gas, toxic, oxidizing, n.o.s.** *Inhalation Hazard Zone B*	2.3	UN3307		2.3, 5.1	2	None	304	314, 315	Forbidden	Forbidden	D	40
G	**Liquefied gas, toxic, oxidizing, n.o.s.** *Inhalation Hazard Zone C*	2.3	UN3307		2.3, 5.1	3	None	304	314, 315	Forbidden	Forbidden	D	40
G	**Liquefied gas, toxic, oxidizing, n.o.s.** *Inhalation Hazard Zone D*	2.3	UN3307		2.3, 5.1	4	None	304	314, 315	Forbidden	Forbidden	D	40
	Liquefied gases, *non-flammable charged with nitrogen, carbon dioxide or air*	2.2	UN1058		2.2		306	304	None	75 kg	150 kg	A	
	Liquefied hydrocarbon gas, see **Hydrocarbon gas mixture, liquefied, n.o.s.**												
	Liquefied natural gas, see **Methane,** *etc. (UN 1972)*												
	Liquefied petroleum gas *see* **Petroleum gases, liquefied**												
	Lithium	4.3	UN1415	I	4.3	A7, A19, IB1, IP1, N45	None	211	244	Forbidden	15 kg	E	
	Lithium acetylide ethylenediamine complex, see **Water reactive solid** *etc.*												
	Lithium alkyls	4.2	UN2445	I	4.2, 4.3	B11, T21, TP2, TP7	None	181	244	Forbidden	Forbidden	D	
	Lithium aluminum hydride	4.3	UN1410	I	4.3	A19	None	211	242	Forbidden	15 kg	E	
	Lithium aluminum hydride, ethereal	4.3	UN1411	I	4.3, 3	A2, A3, A11, N34	None	201	244	Forbidden	1 L	D	40
	Lithium batteries, contained in equipment	9	UN3091	II	9	29	185(i)	185	None	5 kg	5 kg	A	
	Lithium batteries packed with equipment	9	UN3091	II	9	29	185	185	None	5 kg gross	35 kg gross	A	
	Lithium battery	9	UN3090	II	9	29	185	185	None	5 kg gross	35 kg gross	A	
	Lithium borohydride	4.3	UN1413	I	4.3	A19, N40	None	211	242	Forbidden	15 kg	E	

§172.101 - Hazardous Materials Table

Symbols	Hazardous materials descriptions and proper shipping names	Hazard class or Division	Identification Numbers	PG	Label Codes	Special provisions (§172.102)	(8) Packaging (§173.***)			(9) Quantity limitations		(10) Vessel stowage	
							Exceptions	Non-bulk	Bulk	Passenger aircraft/ rail	Cargo aircraft only	Location	Other
(1)	(2)	(3)	(4)	(5)	(6)	(7)	(8A)	(8B)	(8C)	(9A)	(9B)	(10A)	(10B)
	Lithium ferrosilicon	4.3	UN2830	II	4.3	A19, IB7, IP2	151	212	241	15 kg	50 kg	E	40, 85, 103
	Lithium hydride	4.3	UN1414	I	4.3	A19, N40	None	211	242	Forbidden	15 kg	E	
	Lithium hydride, fused solid	4.3	UN2805	II	4.3	A8, A19, A20, IB4	151	212	241	15 kg	50 kg	E	
	Lithium hydroxide, monohydrate *or* **Lithium hydroxide, solid**	8	UN2680	II	8	IB8, IP2, IP4	154	212	240	15 kg	50 kg	A	
	Lithium hydroxide, solution	8	UN2679	II III	8 8	B2, IB2, T7, TP2 IB3, T4, TP2	154 154	202 203	242 241	1 L 5 L	30 L 60 L	A A	 96
	Lithium hypochlorite, dry *with more than 39% available chlorine (8.8% available oxygen) or* **Lithium hypochlorite mixtures, dry** *with more than 39% available chlorine (8.8% available oxygen)*	5.1	UN1471	II	5.1	A9, IB8, IP2, IP4, N34	152	212	240	5 kg	25 kg	A	48, 56,58, 69, 106, 116
	Lithium in cartridges, see **Lithium**												
	Lithium nitrate	5.1	UN2722	III	5.1	A1, IB8, IP3	152	213	240	25 kg	100 kg	A	
	Lithium nitride	4.3	UN2806	I	4.3	A19, IB4, IP1, N40	None	211	242	Forbidden	15 kg	E	
	Lithium peroxide	5.1	UN1472	II	5.1	A9, IB6, IP2, N34	152	212	None	5 kg	25 kg	A	13, 75, 106
	Lithium silicon	4.3	UN1417	II	4.3	A19, A20, IB7, IP2	151	212	241	15 kg	50 kg	A	85, 103
	LNG, see **Methane** *etc. (UN 1972)*												
	London purple	6.1	UN1621	II	6.1	IB8, IP2, IP4	None	212	242	25 kg	100 kg	A	
	LPG, see **Petroleum gases, liquefied**												
	Lye, see **Sodium hydroxide, solutions**												
	Magnesium alkyls	4.2	UN3053	I	4.2, 4.3	B11, T21, TP2, TP7	None	181	244	Forbidden	Forbidden	D	18
	Magnesium aluminum phosphide	4.3	UN1419	I	4.3, 6.1	A19, N34, N40	None	211	242	Forbidden	15 kg	E	40, 85
+	**Magnesium arsenate**	6.1	UN1622	II	6.1	IB8, IP2, IP4	None	212	242	25 kg	100 kg	A	
	Magnesium bisulfite solution, see **Bisulfites, aqueous solutions, n.o.s.**												
	Magnesium bromate	5.1	UN1473	II	5.1	A1, IB8, IP4	152	212	242	5 kg	25 kg	A	56, 58, 106
	Magnesium chlorate	5.1	UN2723	II	5.1	IB8, IP2, IP4	152	212	242	5 kg	25 kg	A	56, 58, 106
	Magnesium diamide	4.2	UN2004	II	4.2	A8, A19, A20, IB6	None	212	241	15 kg	50 kg	C	
	Magnesium diphenyl	4.2	UN2005	I	4.2		None	187	244	Forbidden	Forbidden	C	
	Magnesium dross, wet or hot	Forbidden											
	Magnesium fluorosilicate	6.1	UN2853	III	6.1	IB8, IP3	153	213	240	100 kg	200 kg	A	26
	Magnesium granules, coated, *particle size not less than 149 microns*	4.3	UN2950	III	4.3	A1, A19, IB8, IP4	151	213	240	25 kg	100 kg	A	
	Magnesium hydride	4.3	UN2010	I	4.3	A19, N40	None	211	242	Forbidden	15 kg	E	
	Magnesium *or* **Magnesium alloys** *with more than 50 percent magnesium in pellets, turnings or ribbons*	4.1	UN1869	III	4.1	A1, IB8, IP3	151	213	240	25 kg	100 kg	A	39
	Magnesium nitrate	5.1	UN1474	III	5.1	A1, IB8, IP3	152	213	240	25 kg	100 kg	A	
	Magnesium perchlorate	5.1	UN1475	II	5.1	IB6, IP2	152	212	242	5 kg	25 kg	A	56, 58, 106
	Magnesium peroxide	5.1	UN1476	II	5.1	IB6, IP2	152	212	242	5 kg	25 kg	A	13, 75, 106
	Magnesium phosphide	4.3	UN2011	I	4.3, 6.1	A19, N40	None	211	None	Forbidden	15 kg	E	40, 85
	Magnesium, powder *or* **Magnesium alloys, powder**	4.3	UN1418	I II III	4.3, 4.2 4.3, 4.2 4.3, 4.2	A19, B56 A19, B56, IB5, IP2 A19, B56, IB8, IP4	None None None	211 212 213	244 241 241	Forbidden 15 kg 25 kg	15 kg 50 kg 100 kg	A A A	39 39 39
	Magnesium scrap, see **Magnesium,** *etc. (UN 1869)*												
	Magnesium silicide	4.3	UN2624	II	4.3	A19, A20, IB7, IP2	151	212	241	15 kg	50 kg	B	85, 103
	Magnetized material, see §173.21												
	Maleic anhydride	8	UN2215	III	8	IB8, IP3, T4, TP1	154	213	240	25 kg	100 kg	A	
	Malononitrile	6.1	UN2647	II	6.1	IB8, IP2, IP4	None	212	242	25 kg	100 kg	A	12
	Mancozeb (manganese ethylenebisdithiocarbamate complex with zinc) see **Maneb**												
	Maneb *or* **Maneb preparations** *with not less than 60 percent maneb*	4.2	UN2210	III	4.2, 4.3	57, A1, A19, IB6	None	213	242	25 kg	100 kg	A	34
	Maneb stabilized *or* **Maneb preparations, stabilized** *against self-heating*	4.3	UN2968	III	4.3	54, A1, A19, IB8, IP4	151	213	242	25 kg	100 kg	B	34

§172.101 - Hazardous Materials Table

Symbols	Hazardous materials descriptions and proper shipping names	Hazard class or Division	Identification Numbers	PG	Label Codes	Special provisions (§172.102)	(8) Packaging (§173.***)			(9) Quantity limitations		(10) Vessel stowage	
							Exceptions	Non-bulk	Bulk	Passenger aircraft/ rail	Cargo aircraft only	Location	Other
(1)	(2)	(3)	(4)	(5)	(6)	(7)	(8A)	(8B)	(8C)	(9A)	(9B)	(10A)	(10B)
	Manganese nitrate	5.1	UN2724	III	5.1	A1, IB8, IP3	152	213	240	25 kg	100 kg	A	
	Manganese resinate	4.1	UN1330	III	4.1	A1, IB6	151	213	240	25 kg	100 kg	A	
	Mannitan tetranitrate	Forbidden											
	Mannitol hexanitrate (dry)	Forbidden											
	Mannitol hexanitrate, wetted *or* **Nitromannite, wetted** *with not less than 40 percent water, or mixture of alcohol and water, by mass*	1.1D	UN0133	II	1.1D	121	None	62	None	Forbidden	Forbidden	10	
	Marine pollutants, liquid or solid, n.o.s., see **Environmentally hazardous substances, liquid** *or* **solid, n.o.s.**												
	Matches, block, see **Matches, 'strike anywhere'**												
	Matches, fusee	4.1	UN2254	III	4.1		186	186	None	Forbidden	Forbidden	A	
	Matches, safety *(book, card or strike on box)*	4.1	UN1944	III	4.1		186	186	None	25 kg	100 kg	A	
	Matches, strike anywhere	4.1	UN1331	III	4.1		186	186	None	Forbidden	Forbidden	B	
	Matches, wax, Vesta	4.1	UN1945	III	4.1		186	186	None	25 kg	100 kg	B	
	Matting acid, see **Sulfuric acid**												
	Medicine, liquid, flammable, toxic, n.o.s.	3	UN3248	II III	3, 6.1 3, 6.1	36, IB2 36, IB3	None 150	202 203	None None	1 L 5 L	5 L 5 L	B A	40
	Medicine, liquid, toxic, n.o.s.	6.1	UN1851	II III	6.1 6.1		153 153	202 203	243 241	5 L 5 L	5 L 5 L	C C	40 40
	Medicine, solid, toxic, n.o.s.	6.1	UN3249	II III	6.1 6.1	36 36	153 153	212 213	None None	5 kg 5 kg	5 kg 5 kg	C C	40 40
	Memtetrahydrophthalic anhydride, see **Corrosive liquids, n.o.s.**												
	Mercaptans, liquid, flammable, n.o.s. *or* **Mercaptan mixture, liquid, flammable, n.o.s.**	3	UN3336	I II III	3 3 3	T11, TP2 IB2, T7, TP1, TP8, TP28 B1, B52, IB3, T4, TP1, TP29	150 150 150	201 202 203	243 242 241	1 L 5 L 60 L	30 L 60 L 220 L	E B B	95 95 95
	Mercaptans, liquid, flammable, toxic, n.o.s. *or* **Mercaptan mixtures, liquid, flammable, toxic, n.o.s.**	3	UN1228	II III	3, 6.1 3, 6.1	IB2, T11, TP2, TP27 B1, IB3, T7, TP1, TP28	None 150	202 203	243 242	Forbidden 5 L	60 L 220 L	B A	40, 95 40, 95
	Mercaptans, liquid, toxic, flammable, n.o.s. *or* **Mercaptan mixtures, liquid, toxic, flammable, n.o.s.,** *flash point not less than 23 degrees C*	6.1	UN3071	II	6.1, 3	IB2, T11, TP2, TP13, TP27	None	202	243	5 L	60 L	C	40, 121
	5-Mercaptotetrazol-1-acetic acid	1.4C	UN0448	II	1.4C		None	62	None	Forbidden	75 kg	09	
	Mercuric arsenate	6.1	UN1623	II	6.1	IB8, IP2, IP4	None	212	242	25 kg	100 kg	A	
	Mercuric chloride	6.1	UN1624	II	6.1	IB8, IP2, IP4	None	212	242	25 kg	100 kg	A	
	Mercuric compounds, see **Mercury compounds,** *etc.*												
	Mercuric nitrate	6.1	UN1625	II	6.1	IB8, IP2, IP4, N73	None	212	242	25 kg	100 kg	A	
+	**Mercuric potassium cyanide**	6.1	UN1626	I	6.1	IB7, IP1, N74, N75	None	211	242	5 kg	50 kg	A	26
	Mercuric sulfocyanate, see **Mercury thiocyanate**												
	Mercurol, see **Mercury nucleate**												
	Mercurous azide	Forbidden											
	Mercurous compounds, see **Mercury compounds,** *etc.*												
	Mercurous nitrate	6.1	UN1627	II	6.1	IB8, IP2, IP4	None	212	242	25 kg	100 kg	A	
A W	**Mercury**	8	UN2809	III	8		164	164	240	35 kg	35 kg	B	40, 97
	Mercury acetate	6.1	UN1629	II	6.1	IB8, IP2, IP4	None	212	242	25 kg	100 kg	A	
	Mercury acetylide	Forbidden											
	Mercury ammonium chloride	6.1	UN1630	II	6.1	IB8, IP2, IP4	None	212	242	25 kg	100 kg	A	
	Mercury based pesticides, liquid, flammable, toxic, *flash point less than 23 degrees C*	3	UN2778	I II	3, 6.1 3, 6.1	T14, TP2, TP13, TP27 IB2, T11, TP2, TP13, TP27	None None	201 202	243 243	Forbidden 1 L	30 L 60 L	B B	40 40

§172.101 - Hazardous Materials Table

Symbols	Hazardous materials descriptions and proper shipping names	Hazard class or Division	Identification Numbers	PG	Label Codes	Special provisions (§172.102)	(8) Packaging (§173.***)			(9) Quantity limitations		(10) Vessel stowage	
							Exceptions	Non-bulk	Bulk	Passenger aircraft/rail	Cargo aircraft only	Location	Other
(1)	(2)	(3)	(4)	(5)	(6)	(7)	(8A)	(8B)	(8C)	(9A)	(9B)	(10A)	(10B)
	Mercury based pesticides, liquid, toxic	6.1	UN3012	I	6.1	T14, TP2, TP13, TP27	None	201	243	1 L	30 L	B	40
				II	6.1	IB2, T11, TP2, TP13, TP27	None	202	243	5 L	60 L	B	40
				III	6.1	IB3, T7, TP2, TP28	153	203	241	60 L	220 L	A	40
	Mercury based pesticides, liquid, toxic, flammable, *flash point not less than 23 degrees C*	6.1	UN3011	I	6.1, 3	T14, TP2, TP13, TP27	None	201	243	1 L	30 L	B	40
				II	6.1, 3	IB2, T11, TP2, TP13, TP27	None	202	243	5 L	60 L	B	40
				III	6.1, 3	IB3, T7, TP2, TP28	153	203	242	60 L	220 L	A	40
	Mercury based pesticides, solid, toxic	6.1	UN2777	I	6.1	IB7, IP1	None	211	242	5 kg	50 kg	A	40
				II	6.1	IB8, IP2, IP4	None	212	242	25 kg	100 kg	A	40
				III	6.1	IB8, IP3	153	213	240	100 kg	200 kg	A	40
	Mercury benzoate	6.1	UN1631	II	6.1	IB8, IP2, IP4	None	212	242	25 kg	100 kg	A	
	Mercury bromides	6.1	UN1634	II	6.1	IB8, IP2, IP4	None	212	242	25 kg	100 kg	A	
	Mercury compounds, liquid, n.o.s.	6.1	UN2024	I	6.1		None	201	243	1 L	30 L	B	40
				II	6.1	IB2	None	202	243	5 L	60 L	B	40
				III	6.1	IB3	153	203	241	60 L	220 L	B	40
	Mercury compounds, solid, n.o.s.	6.1	UN2025	I	6.1	IB7, IP1	None	211	242	5 kg	50 kg	A	
				II	6.1	IB8, IP2, IP4	None	212	242	25 kg	100 kg	A	
				III	6.1	IB8, IP3	153	213	240	100 kg	200 kg	A	
A	**Mercury** *contained in manufactured articles*	8	UN2809	III	8		None	164	None	No limit	No limit	B	40, 97
	Mercury cyanide	6.1	UN1636	II	6.1	IB8, IP2, IP4, N74, N75	None	212	242	25 kg	100 kg	A	26
	Mercury fulminate, wetted *with not less than 20 percent water, or mixture of alcohol and water, by mass*	1.1A	UN0135	II	1.1A	111, 117	None	62	None	Forbidden	Forbidden	12	
	Mercury gluconate	6.1	UN1637	II	6.1	IB8, IP2, IP4	None	212	242	25 kg	100 kg	A	
	Mercury iodide, *solid*	6.1	UN1638	II	6.1	IB2, IP2, IP4	None	212	242	25 kg	100 kg	A	
	Mercury iodide aquabasic ammonobasic (Iodide of Millon's base)	Forbidden											
	Mercury iodide, *solution*	6.1	UN1638	II	6.1	IB8, IP2, IP4	None	202	243	5 L	60 L	A	
	Mercury nitride	Forbidden											
	Mercury nucleate	6.1	UN1639	II	6.1	IB8, IP2, IP4	None	212	242	25 kg	100 kg	A	
	Mercury oleate	6.1	UN1640	II	6.1	IB8, IP2, IP4	None	212	242	25 kg	100 kg	A	
	Mercury oxide	6.1	UN1641	II	6.1	IB8, IP2, IP4	None	212	242	25 kg	100 kg	A	
	Mercury oxycyanide	Forbidden											
	Mercury oxycyanide, desensitized	6.1	UN1642	II	6.1	IB8, IP2, IP4	None	212	242	25 kg	100 kg	A	26, 91
	Mercury potassium iodide	6.1	UN1643	II	6.1	IB8, IP2, IP4	None	212	242	25 kg	100 kg	A	
	Mercury salicylate	6.1	UN1644	II	6.1	IB8, IP2, IP4	None	212	242	25 kg	100 kg	A	
+	**Mercury sulfates**	6.1	UN1645	II	6.1	IB8, IP2, IP4	None	212	242	25 kg	100 kg	A	
	Mercury thiocyanate	6.1	UN1646	II	6.1	IB8, IP2, IP4	None	212	242	25 kg	100 kg	A	
	Mesityl oxide	3	UN1229	III	3	B1, IB3, T2, TP1	None	203	242	60 L	220 L	A	
	Metal alkyl halides, water-reactive n.o.s. *or* **Metal aryl halides, water-reactive, n.o.s.**	4.2	UN3049	I	4.2, 4.3	B9, B11, T21, TP2, TP7	None	181	244	Forbidden	Forbidden	D	
	Metal alkyl hydrides, water-reactive, n.o.s. *or* **Metal aryl hydrides, water-reactive, n.o.s.**	4.2	UN3050	I	4.2, 4.3	B9, B11, T21, TP2, TP7	None	181	244	Forbidden	Forbidden	D	
	Metal alkyls, water-reactive, n.o.s. *or* **Metal aryls, water-reactive n.o.s.**	4.2	UN2003	I	4.2, 4.3	B11, T21, TP2, TP7	None	181	244	Forbidden	Forbidden	D	
	Metal carbonyls, n.o.s.	6.1	UN3281	I	6.1	5, T14, TP2, TP13, TP27	None	201	243	1 L	30 L	B	40
				II	6.1	IB2, T11, TP2, TP27	None	202	243	5 L	60 L	B	40
				III	6.1	IB3, T7, TP1, TP28	153	203	241	60 L	220 L	A	40
	Metal catalyst, dry	4.2	UN2881	I	4.2	N34	None	187	None	Forbidden	Forbidden	C	
				II	4.2	IB6, IP2, N34	None	187	242	Forbidden	50 kg	C	
				III	4.2	IB8, IP3, N34	None	187	241	25 kg	100 kg	C	
	Metal catalyst, wetted *with a visible excess of liquid*	4.2	UN1378	II	4.2	A2, A8, IB1, N34	None	212	None	Forbidden	50 kg	C	
	Metal hydrides, flammable, n.o.s.	4.1	UN3182	II	4.1	A1, IB4	151	212	240	15 kg	50 kg	E	
				III	4.1	A1, IB4	151	213	240	25 kg	100 kg	E	

§172.101 - Hazardous Materials Table

Symbols	Hazardous materials descriptions and proper shipping names	Hazard class or Division	Identification Numbers	PG	Label Codes	Special provisions (§172.102)	(8) Packaging (§173.***)			(9) Quantity limitations		(10) Vessel stowage	
							Exceptions	Non-bulk	Bulk	Passenger aircraft/ rail	Cargo aircraft only	Location	Other
(1)	(2)	(3)	(4)	(5)	(6)	(7)	(8A)	(8B)	(8C)	(9A)	(9B)	(10A)	(10B)
	Metal hydrides, water reactive, n.o.s.	4.3	UN1409	I II	4.3 4.3	A19, N34, N40 A19, IB4, N34, N40	None 151	211 212	242 242	Forbidden 15 kg	15 kg 50 kg	D D	
	Metal powder, self-heating, n.o.s.	4.2	UN3189	II III	4.2 4.2	IB6, IP2 IB8, IP3	None None	212 213	241 241	15 kg 25 kg	50 kg 100 kg	C C	
	Metal powders, flammable, n.o.s.	4.1	UN3089	II III	4.1 4.1	IB8, IP2, IP4 IB6	151 151	212 213	240 240	15 kg 25 kg	50 kg 100 kg	B B	
	Metal salts of methyl nitramine (dry)	Forbidden											
G	**Metal salts of organic compounds, flammable, n.o.s.**	4.1	UN3181	II III	4.1 4.1	A1, IB8, IP2, IP4 A1, IB8, IP3	151 151	212 213	240 240	15 kg 25 kg	50 kg 100 kg	B B	40 40
	Metaldehyde	4.1	UN1332	III	4.1	A1, IB8, IP3	151	213	240	25 kg	100 kg	A	
G	**Metallic substance, water-reactive, n.o.s.**	4.3	UN3208	I II III	4.3 4.3 4.3	IB4 IB7, IP2 IB8, IP4	None 151 151	211 212 213	242 242 241	Forbidden 15 kg 25 kg	15 kg 50 kg 100 kg	E E E	40 40 40
G	**Metallic substance, water-reactive, self-heating, n.o.s.**	4.3	UN3209	I II III	4.3, 4.2 4.3, 4.2 4.3, 4.2	 IB5, IP2 IB8, IP4	None None None	211 212 213	242 242 242	Forbidden 15 kg 25 kg	15 kg 50 kg 100 kg	E E E	40 40 40
	Methacrylaldehyde, stabilized	3	UN2396	II	3, 6.1	45, IB2, T7, TP1, TP13	None	202	243	1 L	60 L	E	40
	Methacrylic acid, stabilized	8	UN2531	II	8	IB3, T4, TP1, TP18	154	202	242	1 L	30 L	A	
+	**Methacrylonitrile, stabilized**	3	UN3079	I	3, 6.1	2, B9, B14, B32, B74, T20, TP2, TP13, TP38, TP45	None	227	244	Forbidden	Forbidden	D	12, 40, 48
	Methallyl alcohol	3	UN2614	III	3	B1, IB3, T2, TP1	150	203	242	60 L	220 L	A	
	Methane and hydrogen, mixtures, see **Hydrogen and methane, mixtures,** *etc.*												
	Methane, compressed *or* **Natural gas, compressed** *(with high methane content)*	2.1	UN1971		2.1		306	302	302	Forbidden	150 kg	E	40
	Methane, refrigerated liquid *(cryogenic liquid) or* **Natural gas, refrigerated liquid** *(cryogenic liquid), with high methane content)*	2.1	UN1972		2.1	T75, TP5	None	None	318	Forbidden	Forbidden	D	40
	Methanesulfonyl chloride	6.1	UN3246	I	6.1, 8	2, B9, B14, B32, B74, T20, TP2, TP12, TP13, TP38, TP45	None	227	244	Forbidden	Forbidden	D	40
+ I	**Methanol**	3	UN1230	II	3, 6.1	IB2, T7, TP2	150	202	242	1 L	60 L	B	40
D	**Methanol**	3	UN1230	II	3	IB2, T7, TP2	150	202	242	1 L	60 L	B	40
	Methazoic acid	Forbidden											
	4-Methoxy-4-methylpentan-2-one	3	UN2293	III	3	B1, IB3, T2, TP1	150	203	242	60 L	220 L	A	
	1-Methoxy-2-propanol	3	UN3092	III	3	B1, IB3, T2, TP1	150	203	242	60 L	220 L	A	
+	**Methoxymethyl isocyanate**	3	UN2605	I	3, 6.1	1, B9, B14, B30, B72, T22, TP2, TP13, TP38, TP44	None	226	244	Forbidden	Forbidden	D	40
	Methyl acetate	3	UN1231	II	3	IB2, T4, TP1	150	202	242	5 L	60 L	B	
	Methyl acetylene and propadiene mixtures, stabilized	2.1	UN1060		2.1	T50	306	304	314, 315	Forbidden	150 kg	B	40
	Methyl acrylate, stabilized	3	UN1919	II	3	IB2, T4, TP1, TP13	150	202	242	5 L	60 L	B	
	Methyl alcohol, see **Methanol**												
	Methyl allyl chloride	3	UN2554	II	3	IB2, T4, TP1, TP13	150	202	242	5 L	60 L	E	
	Methyl amyl ketone, see **Amyl methyl ketone**												
	Methyl bromide	2.3	UN1062		2.3	3, B14, T50	None	193	314, 315	Forbidden	25 kg	D	40
	Methyl bromide and chloropicrin mixtures with more than 2 percent chloropicrin, see **Chloropicrin and methyl bromide mixtures**												
	Methyl bromide and chloropicrin mixtures with not more than 2 percent chloropicrin, see **Methyl bromide**												

§172.101 - Hazardous Materials Table

Symbols	Hazardous materials descriptions and proper shipping names	Hazard class or Division	Identification Numbers	PG	Label Codes	Special provisions (§172.102)	(8) Packaging (§173.***) Exceptions	Non-bulk	Bulk	(9) Quantity limitations Passenger aircraft/rail	Cargo aircraft only	(10) Vessel stowage Location	Other
(1)	(2)	(3)	(4)	(5)	(6)	(7)	(8A)	(8B)	(8C)	(9A)	(9B)	(10A)	(10B)
	Methyl bromide and ethylene dibromide mixtures, liquid	6.1	UN1647	I	6.1	2, B9, B14, B32, B74, N65, T20, TP2, TP13, TP38, TP44	None	227	244	Forbidden	Forbidden	C	40
	Methyl bromoacetate	6.1	UN2643	II	6.1	IB2, T7, TP2	None	202	243	5 L	60 L	D	40
	2-Methyl-1-butene	3	UN2459	I	3	T11, TP2	None	201	243	1 L	30 L	E	
	2-Methyl-2-butene	3	UN2460	II	3	IB2, T7, TP1	None	202	242	5 L	60 L	E	
	3-Methyl-1-butene	3	UN2561	I	3	T11, TP2	None	201	243	1 L	30 L	E	
	Methyl tert-butyl ether	3	UN2398	II	3	IB2, T7, TP1	150	202	242	5 L	60 L	E	
	Methyl butyrate	3	UN1237	II	3	IB2, T4, TP1	150	202	242	5 L	60 L	B	
	Methyl chloride, *or* **Refrigerant gas R 40**	2.1	UN1063		2.1	T50	306	304	314, 315	5 kg	100 kg	D	40
	Methyl chloride and chloropicrin mixtures, see **Chloropicrin and methyl chloride mixtures**												
	Methyl chloride and methylene chloride mixtures	2.1	UN1912		2.1	T50	306	304	314, 315	Forbidden	150 kg	D	40
	Methyl chloroacetate	6.1	UN2295	I	6.1, 3	T14, TP2, TP13	None	201	243	1 L	30 L	D	
	Methyl chlorocarbonate, see **Methyl chloroformate**												
	Methyl chloroform, see **1,1,1-Trichloroethane**												
	Methyl chloroformate	6.1	UN1238	I	6.1, 3, 8	1, B9, B14, B30, B72, N34, T22, TP2, TP13, TP38, TP44	None	226	244	Forbidden	Forbidden	D	21, 40, 100
	Methyl chloromethyl ether	6.1	UN1239	I	6.1, 3	1, B9, B14, B30, B72, T22, TP2, TP38, TP44	None	226	244	Forbidden	Forbidden	D	40
	Methyl 2-chloropropionate	3	UN2933	III	3	B1, IB3, T2, TP1	150	203	242	60 L	220 L	A	
	Methyl dichloroacetate	6.1	UN2299	III	6.1	IB3, T4, TP1	153	203	241	60 L	220 L	A	
	Methyl ethyl ether, see **Ethyl methyl ether**												
	Methyl ethyl ketone, *see* **Ethyl methyl ketone**												
	Methyl ethyl ketone peroxide, in solution with more than 9 percent by mass active oxygen	Forbidden											
	2-Methyl-5-ethylpyridine	6.1	UN2300	III	6.1	IB3, T4, TP1	153	203	241	60 L	220 L	A	
	Methyl fluoride, *or* **Refrigerant gas R 41**	2.1	UN2454		2.1		306	304	314, 315	Forbidden	150 kg	E	40
	Methyl formate	3	UN1243	I	3	T11, TP2	150	201	243	1 L	30 L	E	
	2-Methyl-2-heptanethiol	6.1	UN3023	I	6.1, 3	2, B9, B14, B32, B74, T20, TP2, TP13, TP38, TP45	None	227	244	Forbidden	Forbidden	D	40, 102
	Methyl iodide	6.1	UN2644	I	6.1	2, B9, B14, B32, B74, T20, TP2, TP13, TP38, TP45	None	227	244	Forbidden	Forbidden	A	12, 40
	Methyl isobutyl carbinol	3	UN2053	III	3	B1, IB3, T2, TP1	150	203	242	60 L	220 L	A	
	Methyl isobutyl ketone	3	UN1245	II	3	IB2, T4, TP1	150	202	242	5 L	60 L	B	
	Methyl isobutyl ketone peroxide, in solution with more than 9 percent by mass active oxygen	Forbidden											
	Methyl isocyanate	6.1	UN2480	I	6.1, 3	1, B9, B14, B30, B72, T22, TP2, TP13, TP38, TP44	None	226	244	Forbidden	Forbidden	D	26, 40
	Methyl isopropenyl ketone, stabilized	3	UN1246	II	3	IB2, T4, TP1	150	202	242	5 L	60 L	B	
	Methyl isothiocyanate	6.1	UN2477	I	6.1, 3	2, B9, B14, B32, B74, T20, TP2, TP13, TP38, TP45	None	227	244	Forbidden	Forbidden	A	
	Methyl isovalerate	3	UN2400	II	3	IB2, T4, TP1	150	202	242	5 L	60 L	B	
	Methyl magnesium bromide, in ethyl ether	4.3	UN1928	I	4.3, 3		None	201	243	Forbidden	1 L	D	
	Methyl mercaptan	2.3	UN1064		2.3, 2.1	3, B7, B9, B14, T50	None	304	314, 315	Forbidden	25 kg	D	40

§172.101 - Hazardous Materials Table

Symbols	Hazardous materials descriptions and proper shipping names	Hazard class or Division	Identification Numbers	PG	Label Codes	Special provisions (§172.102)	(8) Packaging (§173.***) Exceptions	Non-bulk	Bulk	(9) Quantity limitations Passenger aircraft/rail	Cargo aircraft only	(10) Vessel stowage Location	Other
(1)	(2)	(3)	(4)	(5)	(6)	(7)	(8A)	(8B)	(8C)	(9A)	(9B)	(10A)	(10B)
	Methyl mercaptopropionaldehyde, see **Thia-4-pentanal**												
	Methyl methacrylate monomer, stabilized	3	UN1247	II	3	IB2, T4, TP1	150	202	242	5 L	60 L	B	40
	Methyl nitramine (dry)	Forbidden											
	Methyl nitrate	Forbidden											
	Methyl nitrite	Forbidden											
	Methyl norbornene dicarboxylic anhydride, see **Corrosive liquids, n.o.s.**												
	Methyl orthosilicate	6.1	UN2606	I	6.1, 3	2, B9, B14, B32, B74, T20, TP2, TP13, TP38, TP45	None	227	244	Forbidden	Forbidden	E	40
D	**Methyl phosphonic dichloride**	6.1	NA9206	I	6.1, 8	2, A3, B9, B14, B32, B74, N34, N43, T20, TP4, TP12, TP13, TP38, TP45	None	227	244	Forbidden	Forbidden	C	
	Methyl phosphonothioic dichloride, anhydrous, see **Corrosive liquid, n.o.s.**												
D	**Methyl phosphonous dichloride,** *pyrophoric liquid*	6.1	NA2845	I	6.1, 4.2	2, B9, B14, B16, B32, B74, T20, TP4, TP12, TP13, TP38, TP45	None	227	244	Forbidden	Forbidden	D	18
	Methyl picric acid (heavy metal salts of)	Forbidden											
	Methyl propionate	3	UN1248	II	3	IB2, T4, TP1	150	202	242	5 L	60 L	B	
	Methyl propyl ether	3	UN2612	II	3	IB2, T7, TP2	150	202	242	5 L	60 L	E	40
	Methyl propyl ketone	3	UN1249	II	3	IB2, T4, TP1	150	202	242	5 L	60 L	B	
	Methyl sulfate, see **Dimethyl sulfate**												
	Methyl sulfide, see **Dimethyl sulfide**												
	Methyl trichloroacetate	6.1	UN2533	III	6.1	IB3, T4, TP1	153	203	241	60 L	220 L	A	
	Methyl trimethylol methane trinitrate	Forbidden											
	Methyl vinyl ketone, stabilized	6.1	UN1251	I	6.1, 3, 8	1, B9, B14, B30, B72, T22, TP2, TP13, TP38, TP44	None	226	244	Forbidden	Forbidden	B	40
	Methylal	3	UN1234	II	3	IB2, T7, TP2	None	202	242	5 L	60 L	E	
	Methylamine, anhydrous	2.1	UN1061		2.1	T50	306	304	314, 315	Forbidden	150 kg	B	40
	Methylamine, aqueous solution	3	UN1235	II	3, 8	B1, IB2, T7, TP1	150	202	243	1 L	5 L	E	41
	Methylamine dinitramine and dry salts thereof	Forbidden											
	Methylamine nitroform	Forbidden											
	Methylamine perchlorate (dry)	Forbidden											
	Methylamyl acetate	3	UN1233	III	3	B1, IB3, T2, TP1	150	203	242	60 L	220 L	A	
	N-Methylaniline	6.1	UN2294	III	6.1	IB3, T4, TP1	153	203	241	60 L	220 L	A	
	alpha-Methylbenzyl alcohol	6.1	UN2937	III	6.1	IB3, T4, TP1	153	203	241	60 L	220 L	A	
	3-Methylbutan-2-one	3	UN2397	II	3	IB2, T4, TP1	150	202	242	5 L	60 L	B	
	N-Methylbutylamine	3	UN2945	II	3, 8	IB2, T7, TP1	None	202	243	1 L	5 L	B	40
	Methylchlorosilane	2.3	UN2534		2.3, 2.1, 8	2, A2, A3, A7, B9, B14, N34	None	226	314, 315	Forbidden	Forbidden	D	17, 40
	Methylcyclohexane	3	UN2296	II	3	B1, IB2, T4, TP1	150	202	242	5 L	60 L	B	
	Methylcyclohexanols, *flammable*	3	UN2617	III	3	B1, IB3, T2, TP1	150	203	242	60 L	220 L	A	
	Methylcyclohexanone	3	UN2297	III	3	B1, IB3, T2, TP1	150	203	242	60 L	220 L	A	
	Methylcyclopentane	3	UN2298	II	3	IB2, T4, TP1	150	202	242	5 L	60 L	B	
D	**Methyldichloroarsine**	6.1	NA1556	I	6.1	2, T20, TP4, TP12, TP13, TP38, TP45	None	192	None	Forbidden	Forbidden	D	40
	Methyldichlorosilane	4.3	UN1242	I	4.3, 8, 3	A2, A3, A7, B6, B77, N34, T10, TP2, TP7, TP13	None	201	243	Forbidden	1 L	D	21, 28, 40, 49, 100
	Methylene chloride, see **Dichloromethane**												
	Methylene glycol dinitrate	Forbidden											

§172.101 - Hazardous Materials Table

Symbols	Hazardous materials descriptions and proper shipping names	Hazard class or Division	Identification Numbers	PG	Label Codes	Special provisions (§172.102)	(8) Packaging (§173.***)			(9) Quantity limitations		(10) Vessel stowage	
							Exceptions	Non-bulk	Bulk	Passenger aircraft/rail	Cargo aircraft only	Location	Other
(1)	(2)	(3)	(4)	(5)	(6)	(7)	(8A)	(8B)	(8C)	(9A)	(9B)	(10A)	(10B)
	2-Methylfuran	3	UN2301	II	3	IB2, T4, TP1	150	202	242	5 L	60 L	E	
	a-Methylglucoside tetranitrate	Forbidden											
	a-Methylglycerol trinitrate	Forbidden											
	5-Methylhexan-2-one	3	UN2302	III	3	B1, IB3, T2, TP1	150	203	242	60 L	220 L	A	
	Methylhydrazine	6.1	UN1244	I	6.1, 3, 8	1, B7, B9, B14, B30, B72, B77, N34, T22, TP2, TP13, TP38, TP44	None	226	244	Forbidden	Forbidden	D	21, 40, 49, 100
	4-Methylmorpholine *or* **n-methylmorpholine**	3	UN2535	II	3, 8	B6, IB2, T7, TP1	None	202	243	1 L	5 L	B	40
	Methylpentadienes	3	UN2461	II	3	IB2, T4, TP1	150	202	242	5 L	60 L	E	
	2-Methylpentan-2-ol	3	UN2560	III	3	B1, IB3, T2, TP1	150	203	242	60 L	220 L	A	
	Methylpentanes, see **Hexanes**												
	Methylphenyldichlorosilane	8	UN2437	II	8	IB2, T7, TP2, TP13	154	202	242	1 L	30 L	C	40
	1-Methylpiperidine	3	UN2399	II	3, 8	IB2, T7, TP1	None	202	243	1 L	5 L	B	
	Methyltetrahydrofuran	3	UN2536	II	3	IB2, T4, TP1	150	202	242	5 L	60 L	B	
	Methyltrichlorosilane	3	UN1250	I	3, 8	A7, B6, B77, N34, T11, TP2, TP13	None	201	243	Forbidden	2.5 L	B	40
	alpha-Methylvaleraldehyde	3	UN2367	II	3	B1, IB2, T4, TP1	150	202	242	5 L	60 L	B	
	Mine rescue equipment containing carbon dioxide, see **Carbon dioxide**												
	Mines *with bursting charge*	1.1F	UN0136	II	1.1F			62	None	Forbidden	Forbidden	08	
	Mines *with bursting charge*	1.1D	UN0137	II	1.1D			62	None	Forbidden	Forbidden	03	
	Mines *with bursting charge*	1.2D	UN0138	II	1.2D			62	None	Forbidden	Forbidden	03	
	Mines *with bursting charge*	1.2F	UN0294	II	1.2F			62	None	Forbidden	Forbidden	08	
	Mixed acid, see **Nitrating acid, mixtures** *etc.*												
	Mobility aids, see **Battery powered equipment** *or* **Battery powered vehicle'**												
D	**Model rocket motor**	1.4C	NA0276	II	1.4C	51	None	62	None	Forbidden	75 kg	06	
D	**Model rocket motor**	1.4S	NA0323	II	1.4S	51	None	62	None	25 kg	100 kg	05	
	Molybdenum pentachloride	8	UN2508	III	8	IB8, IP3, T4, TP1	154	213	240	25 kg	100 kg	C	40
	Monochloroacetone (unstabilized)	Forbidden											
	Monochloroethylene, see **Vinyl chloride, stabilized**												
	Monoethanolamine, see **Ethanolamine, solutions**												
	Monoethylamine, see **Ethylamine**												
	Morpholine	8	UN2054	I	8, 3	T10, TP2	None	201	243	.5 L	2.5 L	C	25, 40
	Morpholine, aqueous, mixture, see **Corrosive liquids, n.o.s.**												
	Motor fuel anti-knock compounds *see* **Motor fuel anti-knock mixtures**												
+	**Motor fuel anti-knock mixtures**	6.1	UN1649	I	6.1, 3	14, B9, B90, T14, TP2, TP13	None	201	244	Forbidden	30 L	D	25, 40
	Motor spirit, *see* **Gasoline**												
	Muriatic acid, see **Hydrochloric acid**												
	Musk xylene, *see* **5-tert-Butyl-2,4,6-trinitro-m-xylene**												
	Naphtha see **Petroleum distillates n.o.s.**												
	Naphthalene, crude *or* **Naphthalene, refined**	4.1	UN1334	III	4.1	A1, IB8, IP3	151	213	240	25 kg	100 kg	A	
	Naphthalene diozonide	Forbidden											
	beta-Naphthylamine	6.1	UN1650	II	6.1	IB8, IP2, IP4, T7, TP2	None	212	242	25 kg	100 kg	A	
	alpha-Naphthylamine	6.1	UN2077	III	6.1	IB8, IP3, T3, TP1	153	213	240	100 kg	200 kg	A	
	Naphthalene, molten	4.1	UN2304	III	4.1	A1, IB1, T1, TP3	151	213	241	Forbidden	Forbidden	C	
	Naphthylamineperchlorate	Forbidden											

§172.101 - Hazardous Materials Table

Symbols	Hazardous materials descriptions and proper shipping names	Hazard class or Division	Identification Numbers	PG	Label Codes	Special provisions (§172.102)	(8) Packaging (§173.***)			(9) Quantity limitations		(10) Vessel stowage	
							Exceptions	Non-bulk	Bulk	Passenger aircraft/ rail	Cargo aircraft only	Location	Other
(1)	(2)	(3)	(4)	(5)	(6)	(7)	(8A)	(8B)	(8C)	(9A)	(9B)	(10A)	(10B)
	Naphthylthiourea	6.1	UN1651	II	6.1	IB8, IP2, IP4	None	212	242	25 kg	100 kg	A	
	Naphthylurea	6.1	UN1652	II	6.1	IB8, IP2, IP4	None	212	242	25 kg	100 kg	A	
	Natural gases (with high methane content), see **Methane,** *etc. (UN 1971, UN 1972)*												
	Neohexane, see **Hexanes**												
	Neon, compressed	2.2	UN1065		2.2		306	302	302	75 kg	150 kg	A	
	Neon, refrigerated liquid *(cryogenic liquid)*	2.2	UN1913		2.2	T75, TP5	320	316	None	50 kg	500 kg	B	
	New explosive or explosive device, see §§173.51 and 173.56												
	Nickel carbonyl	6.1	UN1259	I	6.1, 3	1	None	198	None	Forbidden	Forbidden	D	18, 40
	Nickel cyanide	6.1	UN1653	II	6.1	IB8, IP2, IP4, N74, N75	None	212	242	25 kg	100 kg	A	26
	Nickel nitrate	5.1	UN2725	III	5.1	A1, IB8, IP3	152	213	240	25 kg	100 kg	A	
	Nickel nitrite	5.1	UN2726	III	5.1	A1, IB8, IP3	152	213	240	25 kg	100 kg	A	56, 58
	Nickel picrate	Forbidden											
	Nicotine	6.1	UN1654	II	6.1	IB2	None	202	243	5 L	60 L	A	
	Nicotine compounds, liquid, n.o.s. *or* **Nicotine preparations, liquid, n.o.s.**	6.1	UN3144	I II III	6.1 6.1 6.1	A4 IB2, T11, TP2, TP27 IB3, T7, TP1, TP28	None None 153	201 202 203	243 243 241	1 L 5 L 60 L	30 L 60 L 220 L	B B B	40 40 40
	Nicotine compounds, solid, n.o.s. *or* **Nicotine preparations, solid, n.o.s.**	6.1	UN1655	I II III	6.1 6.1 6.1	IB7, IP1 IB8, IP2, IP4 IB8, IP3	None None 153	211 212 213	242 242 240	5 kg 25 kg 100 kg	50 kg 100 kg 200 kg	B A A	
	Nicotine hydrochloride *or* **Nicotine hydrochloride solution**	6.1	UN1656	II	6.1	IB2, IP2, IP4	None	202	243	5 L	60 L	A	
	Nicotine salicylate	6.1	UN1657	II	6.1	IB8, IP2, IP4	None	212	242	25 kg	100 kg	A	
	Nicotine sulfate, *solid*	6.1	UN1658	II	6.1	IB8, IP2, IP4	None	212	242	25 kg	100 kg	A	
	Nicotine sulfate, *solution*	6.1	UN1658	II	6.1	IB2, T7, TP2	None	202	243	5 L	60 L	A	
	Nicotine tartrate	6.1	UN1659	II	6.1	IB8, IP2, IP4	None	212	242	25 kg	100 kg	A	
	Nitrated paper (unstable)	Forbidden											
	Nitrates, inorganic, aqueous solution, n.o.s.	5.1	UN3218	II III	5.1 5.1	58, IB2, T4, TP1 58, IB2, T4, TP1	152 152	202 203	242 241	1 L 2.5 L	5 L 30 L	B B	46 46
	Nitrates, inorganic, n.o.s.	5.1	UN1477	II III	5.1 5.1	IB8, IP2, IP4 IB8, IP3	152 152	212 213	240 240	5 kg 25 kg	25 kg 100 kg	A A	46 46
	Nitrates of diazonium compounds	Forbidden											
	Nitrating acid mixtures, spent *with more than 50 percent nitric acid*	8	UN1826	I	8, 5.1	T10, TP2, TP12, TP13	None	158	243	Forbidden	2.5 L	D	40, 66
	Nitrating acid mixtures spent *with not more than 50 percent nitric acid*	8	UN1826	II	8	B2, IB2, T8, TP2, TP12	None	158	242	Forbidden	30 L	D	40
	Nitrating acid mixtures *with more than 50 percent nitric acid*	8	UN1796	I	8, 5.1	T10, TP2, TP12, TP13	None	158	243	Forbidden	2.5 L	D	40, 66
	Nitrating acid mixtures *with not more than 50 percent nitric acid*	8	UN1796	II	8	B2, IB2, T8, TP2, TP12, TP13	None	158	242	Forbidden	30 L	D	40
	Nitric acid *other than red fuming, with more than 70 percent nitric acid*	8	UN2031	I	8, 5.1	B47, B53, T10, TP2, TP12, TP13	None	158	243	Forbidden	2.5 L	D	44, 66, 89, 90, 110, 111
	Nitric acid *other than red fuming, with not more than 70 percent nitric acid*	8	UN2031	II	8	B2, B47, B53, IB2, T8, TP2, TP12	None	158	242	Forbidden	30 L	D	44, 66, 89, 90, 110, 111
+	**Nitric acid, red fuming**	8	UN2032	I	8, 5.1, 6.1	2, B9, B32, B74, T20, TP2, TP12, TP13, TP38, TP45	None	227	244	Forbidden	Forbidden	D	40, 66, 74, 89, 90
	Nitric oxide, compressed	2.3	UN1660		2.3, 5.1, 8	1, B37, B46, B50, B60, B77	None	337	None	Forbidden	Forbidden	D	40, 89, 90
	Nitric oxide and dinitrogen tetroxide mixtures *or* **Nitric oxide and nitrogen dioxide mixtures**	2.3	UN1975		2.3, 5.1, 8	1, B7, B9, B14, B45, B46, B61, B66, B67, B77	None	337	None	Forbidden	Forbidden	D	40, 89, 90
G	**Nitriles, flammable, toxic, n.o.s.**	3	UN3273	I II	3, 6.1 3, 6.1	T14, TP2, TP13, TP27 IB2, T11, TP2, TP13, TP27	None None	201 202	243 243	Forbidden 1 L	30 L 60 L	E B	40, 52 40, 52

§172.101 - Hazardous Materials Table

Symbols	Hazardous materials descriptions and proper shipping names	Hazard class or Division	Identification Numbers	PG	Label Codes	Special provisions (§172.102)	(8) Packaging (§173.***)			(9) Quantity limitations		(10) Vessel stowage	
							Exceptions	Non-bulk	Bulk	Passenger aircraft/rail	Cargo aircraft only	Location	Other
(1)	(2)	(3)	(4)	(5)	(6)	(7)	(8A)	(8B)	(8C)	(9A)	(9B)	(10A)	(10B)
G	**Nitriles, toxic, flammable, n.o.s.**	6.1	UN3275	I	6.1, 3	5, T14, TP2, TP13, TP27	None	201	243	1 L	30 L	B	40
				II	6.1, 3	IB2, T11, TP2, TP13, TP27	None	202	243	5 L	60 L	B	40
G	**Nitriles, toxic, n.o.s.**	6.1	UN3276	I	6.1	5, T14, TP2, TP13, TP27	None	201	243	1 L	30 L	B	
				II	6.1	IB2, T11, TP2, TP27	None	202	243	5 L	60 L	B	
				III	6.1	IB3, T7, TP1, TP28	153	203	241	60 L	220 L	A	
	Nitrites, inorganic, aqueous solution, n.o.s.	5.1	UN3219	II	5.1	IB1, T4, TP1	152	202	242	1 L	5 L	B	46, 56, 58
				III	5.1	IB2, T4, TP1	152	203	241	2.5 L	30 L	B	46, 56, 58
	Nitrites, inorganic, n.o.s.	5.1	UN2627	II	5.1	33, IB8, IP4	152	212	None	5 kg	25 kg	A	46, 56, 58
	3-Nitro-4-chlorobenzotrifluoride	6.1	UN2307	II	6.1	IB2, T7, TP2	None	202	243	5 L	60 L	A	40
	6-Nitro-4-diazotoluene-3-sulfonic acid (dry)	Forbidden											
	Nitro isobutane triol trinitrate	Forbidden											
	N-Nitro-N-methylglycolamide nitrate	Forbidden											
	2-Nitro-2-methylpropanol nitrate	Forbidden											
	Nitro urea	1.1D	UN0147	II	1.1D		None	62	None	Forbidden	Forbidden	10	
	N-Nitroaniline	Forbidden											
+	**Nitroanilines** *(o-; m-; p-;)*	6.1	UN1661	II	6.1	IB8, IP2, IP4, T7, TP2	None	212	242	25 kg	100 kg	A	
+	**Nitroanisole**	6.1	UN2730	III	6.1	IB8, IP3, T4, TP1	153	213	240	100 kg	200 kg	A	
+	**Nitrobenzene**	6.1	UN1662	II	6.1	IB2, T7, TP2	None	202	243	5 L	60 L	A	40
	m-Nitrobenzene diazonium perchlorate	Forbidden											
	Nitrobenzenesulfonic acid	8	UN2305	II	8	IB2	154	202	242	1 L	30 L	A	
	Nitrobenzol, see **Nitrobenzene**												
	5-Nitrobenzotriazol	1.1D	UN0385	II	1.1D		None	62	None	Forbidden	Forbidden	10	
	Nitrobenzotrifluorides	6.1	UN2306	II	6.1	IB2, T7, TP2	None	202	243	5 L	60 L	A	40
	Nitrobromobenzenes *liquid*	6.1	UN2732	III	6.1	IB3, T4, TP1	153	203	241	60 L	220 L	A	
	Nitrobromobenzenes *solid*	6.1	UN2732	III	6.1	IB8, IP3, T4, TP1	153	213	240	100 kg	200 kg	A	
	Nitrocellulose, *dry or wetted with less than 25 percent water (or alcohol), by mass*	1.1D	UN0340	II	1.1D		None	62	None	Forbidden	Forbidden	13	27E
	Nitrocellulose membrane filters, *with not more than 12.6% nitrogen, by dry mass*	4.1	UN3270	II	4.1	43, A1	151	212	240	1 kg	15 kg	D	
	Nitrocellulose, plasticized *with not less than 18 percent plasticizing substance, by mass*	1.3C	UN0343	II	1.3C		None	62	None	Forbidden	Forbidden	10	
	Nitrocellulose, solution, flammable *with not more than 12.6 percent nitrogen, by mass, and not more than 55 percent nitrocellulose*	3	UN2059	II	3	IB2, T4, TP1, TP8	150	202	242	5 L	60 L	B	
				III	3	B1, IB3, T2, TP1	150	203	242	60 L	220 L	A	
	Nitrocellulose, *unmodified or plasticized with less than 18 percent plasticizing substance, by mass*	1.1D	UN0341	II	1.1D		None	62	None	Forbidden	Forbidden	13	27E
	Nitrocellulose, wetted *with not less than 25 percent alcohol, by mass*	1.3C	UN0342	II	1.3C		None	62	None	Forbidden	Forbidden	10	
	Nitrocellulose with alcohol *with not less than 25 percent alcohol by mass, and with not more than 12.6 percent nitrogen, by dry mass*	4.1	UN2556	II	4.1		151	212	None	1 kg	15 kg	D	28
	Nitrocellulose, *with not more than 12.6 percent nitrogen, by dry mass, or* **Nitrocellulose mixture with pigment** *or* **Nitrocellulose mixture with plasticizer** *or* **Nitrocellulose mixture with pigment and plasticizer**	4.1	UN2557	II	4.1	44	151	212	None	1 kg	15 kg	D	28
	Nitrocellulose with water *with not less than 25 percent water, by mass*	4.1	UN2555	II	4.1		151	212	None	15 kg	50 kg	E	28
	Nitrochlorobenzene, see **Chloronitrobenzenes** *etc.*												
	Nitrocresols	6.1	UN2446	III	6.1	IB8, IP3	153	213	240	100 kg	200 kg	A	

§172.101 - Hazardous Materials Table

Symbols	Hazardous materials descriptions and proper shipping names	Hazard class or Division	Identification Numbers	PG	Label Codes	Special provisions (§172.102)	(8) Packaging (§173.***)			(9) Quantity limitations		(10) Vessel stowage	
							Exceptions	Non-bulk	Bulk	Passenger aircraft/rail	Cargo aircraft only	Location	Other
(1)	(2)	(3)	(4)	(5)	(6)	(7)	(8A)	(8B)	(8C)	(9A)	(9B)	(10A)	(10B)
	Nitroethane	3	UN2842	III	3	B1, IB3, T2, TP1	150	203	242	60 L	220 L	A	
	Nitroethyl nitrate	Forbidden											
	Nitroethylene polymer	Forbidden											
	Nitrogen, compressed	2.2	UN1066		2.2		306	302	314, 315	75 kg	150 kg	A	
	Nitrogen dioxide, *see* **Dinitrogen tetroxide**												
	Nitrogen fertilizer solution, see **Fertilizer ammoniating solution** *etc.*												
	Nitrogen, mixtures with rare gases, see **Rare gases and nitrogen mixtures**												
	Nitrogen peroxide, see Dinitrogen tetroxide												
	Nitrogen, refrigerated liquid *cryogenic liquid*	2.2	UN1977		2.2	T75, TP5	320	316	318	50 kg	500 kg	D	
	Nitrogen tetroxide and nitric oxide mixtures, see **Nitric oxide and nitrogen tetroxide mixtures**												
	Nitrogen tetroxide, see **Dinitrogen tetroxide**												
	Nitrogen trichloride	Forbidden											
	Nitrogen trifluoride, compressed	2.2	UN2451		2.2, 5.1		None	302	None	75 kg	150 kg	D	40
	Nitrogen triiodide	Forbidden											
	Nitrogen triiodide monoamine	Forbidden											
	Nitrogen trioxide	2.3	UN2421		2.3, 5.1, 8	1	None	336	245	Forbidden	Forbidden	D	40, 89, 90
	Nitroglycerin, desensitized *with not less than 40 percent non-volatile water insoluble phlegmatizer, by mass*	1.1D	UN0143	II	1.1D, 6.1	125	None	62	None	Forbidden	Forbidden	13	21E
	Nitroglycerin, liquid, not desensitized	Forbidden											
	Nitroglycerin mixture, desensitized, liquid, flammable, n.o.s. *with not more than 30 percent nitroglycerin, by mass*	3	UN3343		3	129	None	214	None	Forbidden	Forbidden	D	
	Nitroglycerin mixture, desensitized, liquid, n.o.s. *with not more than 30% nitroglycerin, by mass*	3	UN3357	II	3	142	None	202	243	5 L	60 L	E	
	Nitroglycerin mixture, desensitized, solid, n.o.s. *with more than 2 percent but not more than 10 percent nitroglycerin, by mass*	4.1	UN3319	II	4.1	118	None	None	None	Forbidden	0.5 kg	E	
	Nitroglycerin, solution in alcohol, *with more than 1 percent but not more than 5 percent nitroglycerin*	3	UN3064	II	3	N8	None	202	None	Forbidden	5 L	E	
	Nitroglycerin, solution in alcohol, *with more than 1 percent but not more than 10 percent nitrogylcerin*	1.1D	UN0144	II	1.1D		None	62	None	Forbidden	Forbidden	10	21E
	Nitroglycerin solution in alcohol *with not more than 1 percent nitroglycerin*	3	UN1204	II	3	IB2, N34	None	202	None	5 L	60 L	B	
	Nitroguanidine nitrate	Forbidden											
	Nitroguanidine *or* **Picrite,** *dry or wetted with less than 20 percent water, by mass*	1.1D	UN0282	II	1.1D		None	62	None	Forbidden	Forbidden	10	
	Nitroguanidine, wetted *or* **Picrite, wetted** *with not less than 20 percent water, by mass*	4.1	UN1336	I	4.1	23, A8, A19, A20, N41	None	211	None	1 kg	15 kg	E	28
	1-Nitrohydantoin	Forbidden											
	Nitrohydrochloric acid	8	UN1798	I	8	A3, B10, N41, T10, TP2, TP12, TP13	None	201	243	Forbidden	2.5 L	D	40, 66, 74, 89, 90
	Nitromannite (dry)	Forbidden											
	Nitromannite, wetted, *see* **Mannitol hexanitrate,** *etc.*												
	Nitromethane	3	UN1261	II	3		150	202	None	Forbidden	60L	A	
	Nitromuriatic acid, see **Nitrohydrochloric acid**												
	Nitronaphthalene	4.1	UN2538	III	4.1	A1, IB8, IP3	151	213	240	25 kg	100 kg	A	

§172.101 - Hazardous Materials Table

Symbols (1)	Hazardous materials descriptions and proper shipping names (2)	Hazard class or Division (3)	Identification Numbers (4)	PG (5)	Label Codes (6)	Special provisions (§172.102) (7)	(8) Packaging (§173.***) Exceptions (8A)	(8) Packaging Non-bulk (8B)	(8) Packaging Bulk (8C)	(9) Quantity limitations Passenger aircraft/rail (9A)	(9) Quantity limitations Cargo aircraft only (9B)	(10) Vessel stowage Location (10A)	(10) Vessel stowage Other (10B)
+	**Nitrophenols** *(o-; m-; p-;)*	6.1	UN1663	III	6.1	IB8, IP3, T4, TP3	153	213	240	100 kg	200 kg	A	
	m-Nitrophenyldinitro methane	Forbidden											
	Nitropropanes	3	UN2608	III	3	B1, IB3, T2, TP1	150	203	242	60 L	220 L	A	
	p-Nitrosodimethylaniline	4.2	UN1369	II	4.2	A19, A20, IB6, IP2, N34	None	212	241	15 kg	50 kg	D	34
	Nitrostarch, *dry or wetted with less than 20 percent water, by mass*	1.1D	UN0146	II	1.1D		None	62	None	Forbidden	Forbidden	10	
	Nitrostarch, wetted *with not less than 20 percent water, by mass*	4.1	UN1337	I	4.1	23, A8, A19, A20, N41	None	211	None	1 kg	15 kg	D	28
	Nitrosugars (dry)	Forbidden											
	Nitrosyl chloride	2.3	UN1069		2.3, 8	3, B14	None	304	314, 315	Forbidden	Forbidden	D	40
	Nitrosylsulfuric acid	8	UN2308	II	8	A3, A6, A7, B2, IB2, N34, T8, TP2, TP12	154	202	242	1 L	30 L	D	40, 66, 74, 89, 90
	Nitrotoluenes, *liquid o-; m-; p-;*	6.1	UN1664	II	6.1	IB2, IP2, IP4, T7, TP2	None	202	243	5 L	60 L	A	
	Nitrotoluenes, *solid m-, or p-*	6.1	UN1664	II	6.1	IB8, IP2, IP4, T7, TP2	None	212	242	25 kg	100 kg	A	
	Nitrotoluidines (mono)	6.1	UN2660	III	6.1	IB8, IP3	153	213	240	100 kg	200 kg	A	
	Nitrotriazolone *or* **NTO**	1.1D	UN0490	II	1.1D		None	62	None	Forbidden	Forbidden	10	
	Nitrous oxide and carbon dioxide mixtures, see **Carbon dioxide and nitrous oxide mixtures**												
	Nitrous oxide	2.2	UN1070		2.2, 5.1		306	304	314, 315	75 kg	150 kg	A	40
	Nitrous oxide, refrigerated liquid	2.2	UN2201		2.2, 5.1	B6, T75, TP5, TP22	None	304	314, 315	Forbidden	Forbidden	B	40
	Nitroxylenes, (o-; m-; p-)	6.1	UN1665	II	6.1	IB2, IP2, IP4, T7, TP2	None	202	243	5 L	60 L	A	
	Nitroxylol, see **Nitroxylenes**												
	Nonanes	3	UN1920	III	3	B1, IB3, T2, TP1	150	203	242	60 L	220 L	A	
	Non-flammable gas, n.o.s., see **Compressed gas,** *etc. or* **Liquefied gas,** *etc.*												
	Nonliquefied gases, see **Compressed gases,** *etc.*												
	Nonliquefied hydrocarbon gas, see **Hydrocarbon gas mixture, compressed, n.o.s.**												
	Nonyltrichlorosilane	8	UN1799	II	8	A7, B2, B6, IB2, N34, T7, TP2, TP13	None	202	242	Forbidden	30 L	C	40
	Nordhausen acid, see **Sulfuric acid, fuming** *etc.*												
	2,5-Norbornadiene, stabilized, *see* **Bicyclo 2,2,1 hepta-2,5-diene, stabilized**												
	Octadecyltrichlorosilane	8	UN1800	II	8	A7, B2, B6, IB2, N34, T7, TP2, TP13	None	202	242	Forbidden	30 L	C	40
	Octadiene	3	UN2309	II	3	B1, IB2, T4, TP1	150	202	242	5 L	60 L	B	
	1,7-Octadine-3,5-diyne-1,8-dimethoxy-9-octadecynoic acid	Forbidden											
	Octafluorobut-2-ene *or* **Refrigerant gas R 1318**	2.2	UN2422		2.2		None	304	314, 315	75 kg	150 kg	A	
	Octafluorocyclobutane, *or* **Refrigerant gas RC 318**	2.2	UN1976		2.2	T50	None	304	314, 315	75 kg	150 kg	A	
	Octafluoropropane *or* **Refrigerant gas R 218**	2.2	UN2424		2.2	T50	None	304	314, 315	75 kg	150 kg	A	
	Octanes	3	UN1262	II	3	IB2, T4, TP1	150	202	242	5 L	60 L	B	
	Octogen, *etc. see* **Cyclotetramethylene tetranitramine,** *etc.*												
	Octolite *or* **Octol,** *dry or wetted with less than 15 percent water, by mass*	1.1D	UN0266	II	1.1D		None	62	None	Forbidden	Forbidden	10	
	Octonal	1.1D	UN0496		1.1D		None	62	None	Forbidden	Forbidden	10	
	Octyl aldehydes	3	UN1191	III	3	B1, IB3, T2, TP1	150	203	242	60 L	220 L	A	

§172.101 - Hazardous Materials Table

Symbols	Hazardous materials descriptions and proper shipping names	Hazard class or Division	Identification Numbers	PG	Label Codes	Special provisions (§172.102)	(8) Packaging (§173.***) Exceptions	Non-bulk	Bulk	(9) Quantity limitations Passenger aircraft/ rail	Cargo aircraft only	(10) Vessel stowage Location	Other
(1)	(2)	(3)	(4)	(5)	(6)	(7)	(8A)	(8B)	(8C)	(9A)	(9B)	(10A)	(10B)
	Octyltrichlorosilane	8	UN1801	II	8	A7, B2, B6, IB2, N34, T7, TP2, TP13	None	202	242	Forbidden	30 L	C	40
	Oil gas, compressed	2.3	UN1071		2.3, 2.1	6	None	304	314, 315	Forbidden	25 kg	D	40
	Oleum, see **Sulfuric acid, fuming**												
	Organic peroxide type A, liquid or solid	Forbidden											
G	**Organic peroxide type B, liquid**	5.2	UN3101	II	5.2, 1	53	152	225	None	Forbidden	Forbidden	D	12, 40
G	**Organic peroxide type B, liquid, temperature controlled**	5.2	UN3111	II	5.2, 1	53	None	225	None	Forbidden	Forbidden	D	2, 40
G	**Organic peroxide type B, solid**	5.2	UN3102	II	5.2, 1	53	152	225	None	Forbidden	Forbidden	D	12, 40
G	**Organic peroxide type B, solid, temperature controlled**	5.2	UN3112	II	5.2, 1	53	None	225	None	Forbidden	Forbidden	D	2, 40
G	**Organic peroxide type C, liquid**	5.2	UN3103	II	5.2		152	225	None	5 L	10 L	D	12, 40
G	**Organic peroxide type C, liquid, temperature controlled**	5.2	UN3113	II	5.2		None	225	None	Forbidden	Forbidden	D	2, 40
G	**Organic peroxide type C, solid**	5.2	UN3104	II	5.2		152	225	None	5 kg	10 kg	D	12, 40
G	**Organic peroxide type C, solid, temperature controlled**	5.2	UN3114	II	5.2		None	225	None	Forbidden	Forbidden	D	2, 40
G	**Organic peroxide type D, liquid**	5.2	UN3105	II	5.2		152	225	None	5 L	10 L	D	12, 40
G	**Organic peroxide type D, liquid, temperature controlled**	5.2	UN3115	II	5.2		None	225	None	Forbidden	Forbidden	D	2, 40
G	**Organic peroxide type D, solid**	5.2	UN3106	II	5.2		152	225	None	5 kg	10 kg	D	12, 40
G	**Organic peroxide type D, solid, temperature controlled**	5.2	UN3116	II	5.2		None	225	None	Forbidden	Forbidden	D	2, 40
G	**Organic peroxide type E, liquid**	5.2	UN3107	II	5.2		152	225	None	10 L	25 L	D	12, 40
G	**Organic peroxide type E, liquid, temperature controlled**	5.2	UN3117	II	5.2		None	225	None	Forbidden	Forbidden	D	2, 40
G	**Organic peroxide type E, solid**	5.2	UN3108	II	5.2		152	225	None	10 kg	25 kg	D	12, 40
G	**Organic peroxide type E, solid, temperature controlled**	5.2	UN3118	II	5.2		None	225	None	Forbidden	Forbidden	D	2, 40
G	**Organic peroxide type F, liquid**	5.2	UN3109	II	5.2	IB52, IP5, T23	152	225	225	10 L	25 L	D	12, 40
G	**Organic peroxide type F, liquid, temperature controlled**	5.2	UN3119	II	5.2	IB52, IP5, T23	None	225	225	Forbidden	Forbidden	D	2, 40
G	**Organic peroxide type F, solid**	5.2	UN3110	II	5.2	IB52, T23	152	225	225	10 kg	25 kg	D	12, 40
G	**Organic peroxide type F, solid, temperature controlled**	5.2	UN3120	II	5.2	T23	None	225	225	Forbidden	Forbidden	D	2, 40
D	**Organic phosphate, mixed with compressed gas** *or* **Organic phosphate compound, mixed with compressed gas** *or* **Organic phosphorus compound, mixed with compressed gas**	2.3	NA1955		2.3	3	None	334	None	Forbidden	Forbidden	D	40
	Organic pigments, self-heating	4.2	UN3313	II	4.2	IB8, IP4	None	212	241	15 kg	50 kg	C	
				III	4.2	IB8, IP3	None	213	241	25 kg	100 kg	C	
	Organoarsenic compound, n.o.s.	6.1	UN3280	I	6.1	5, IB7, IP1, T14, TP2, TP27	None	211	242	5 kg	50 kg	B	
				II	6.1	IB8, IP2, IP4, T11, TP2, TP27	None	212	242	25 kg	100 kg	B	
				III	6.1	IB8, IP3, T7, TP1, TP28	153	213	240	100 kg	200 kg	A	
	Organochlorine pesticides liquid, flammable, toxic, *flash point less than 23 degrees C*	3	UN2762	I	3, 6.1	T14, TP2, TP13, TP27	None	201	243	Forbidden	30 L	B	40
				II	3, 6.1	IB2, T11, TP2, TP13, TP27	None	202	243	1 L	60 L	B	40
	Organochlorine pesticides, liquid, toxic	6.1	UN2996	I	6.1	T14, TP2, TP13, TP27	None	201	243	1 L	30 L	B	40
				II	6.1	IB2, T11, TP2, TP13, TP27	None	202	243	5 L	60 L	B	40
				III	6.1	IB3, T7, TP2, TP28	153	203	241	60 L	220 L	A	40
	Organochlorine pesticides, liquid, toxic, flammable, *flash point not less than 23 degrees C*	6.1	UN2995	I	6.1, 3	T14, TP2, TP13, TP27	None	201	243	1 L	30 L	B	40
				II	6.1, 3	IB2, T11, TP2, TP13, TP27	None	202	243	5 L	60 L	B	40
				III	6.1	B1, IB3, T7, TP2, TP28	153	203	242	60 L	220 L	A	40

§172.101 - Hazardous Materials Table

Symbols	Hazardous materials descriptions and proper shipping names	Hazard class or Division	Identification Numbers	PG	Label Codes	Special provisions (§172.102)	(8) Packaging (§173.***) Exceptions	(8) Packaging (§173.***) Non-bulk	(8) Packaging (§173.***) Bulk	(9) Quantity limitations Passenger aircraft/ rail	(9) Quantity limitations Cargo aircraft only	(10) Vessel stowage Location	(10) Vessel stowage Other
(1)	(2)	(3)	(4)	(5)	(6)	(7)	(8A)	(8B)	(8C)	(9A)	(9B)	(10A)	(10B)
	Organochlorine pesticides, solid, toxic	6.1	UN2761	I	6.1	IB7, IP1	None	211	242	5 kg	50 kg	A	40
				II	6.1	IB8, IP2, IP4	None	212	242	25 kg	100 kg	A	40
				III	6.1	IB8, IP3	153	213	240	100 kg	200 kg	A	40
G	**Organometallic compound** *or* **Compound solution** *or* **Compound dispersion, water-reactive, flammable, n.o.s.**	4.3	UN3207	I	4.3, 3	T13, TP2, TP7	None	201	244	Forbidden	1 L	E	40
				II	4.3, 3	IB1, IP2, T7, TP2, TP7	None	202	243	1 L	5 L	E	40
				III	4.3, 3	IB2, IP4, T7, TP2, TP7	None	203	242	5 L	60 L	E	40
G	**Organometallic compound, toxic n.o.s.**	6.1	UN3282	I	6.1	IB7, IP1, T14, TP2, TP27	None	211	242	5 kg	50 kg	B	
				II	6.1	IB8, IP2, IP4, T11, TP2, TP27	None	212	242	25 kg	100 kg	B	
				III	6.1	IB8, IP3, T7, TP1, TP28	153	213	240	100 kg	200 kg	A	
	Organophosphorus compound, toxic, flammable, n.o.s.	6.1	UN3279	I	6.1, 3	5, T14, TP2, TP13	None	201	243	1 L	30 L	B	40
				II	6.1, 3	IB2, T11, TP2, TP13, TP27	None	202	243	5 L	60 L	B	40
	Organophosphorus compound, toxic n.o.s.	6.1	UN3278	I	6.1	5, IB7, T14, TP2, TP13, TP27	None	201	243	1 L	30 L	B	
				II	6.1	IB2, T11, TP2, TP27	None	202	243	5 L	60 L	B	
				III	6.1	IB3, T7, TP1, TP28	153	203	241	60 L	220 L	A	
	Organophosphorus pesticides, liquid, flammable, toxic, *flash point less than 23 degrees C*	3	UN2784	I	3, 6.1	T14, TP2, TP13, TP27	None	201	243	Forbidden	30 L	B	40
				II	3, 6.1	IB2, T11, TP2, TP13, TP27	None	202	243	1 L	60 L	B	40
	Organophosphorus pesticides, liquid, toxic	6.1	UN3018	I	6.1	N76, T14, TP2, TP13, TP27	None	201	243	1 L	30 L	B	40
				II	6.1	IB2, N76, T11, TP2, TP13, TP27	None	202	243	5 L	60 L	B	40
				III	6.1	IB3, N76, T7, TP2, TP28	153	203	241	60 L	220 L	A	40
	Organophosphorus pesticides, liquid, toxic, flammable, *flash point not less than 23 degrees C*	6.1	UN3017	I	6.1, 3	N76, T14, TP2, TP13, TP27	None	201	243	1 L	30 L	B	40
				II	6.1, 3	IB2, N76, T11, TP2, TP13, TP27	None	202	243	5 L	60 L	B	40
				III	6.1, 3	B1, IB3, N76, T7, TP2, TP28	153	203	242	60 L	220 L	A	40
	Organophosphorus pesticides, solid, toxic	6.1	UN2783	I	6.1	IB7, IP1, N77	None	211	242	5 kg	50 kg	A	40
				II	6.1	IB8, IP2, IP4, N77	None	212	242	25 kg	100 kg	A	40
				III	6.1	IB8, IP3, N77	153	213	240	100 kg	200 kg	A	40
	Organotin compounds, liquid, n.o.s.	6.1	UN2788	I	6.1	A3, N33, N34, T14, TP2, TP13, TP27	None	201	243	1 L	30 L	B	40
				II	6.1	A3, IB2, N33, N34, T11, TP2, TP13, TP27	None	202	243	5 L	60 L	A	40
				III	6.1	IB3, T7, TP2, TP28	153	203	241	60 L	220 L	A	40
	Organotin compounds, solid, n.o.s.	6.1	UN3146	I	6.1	A5, IB7, IP1	None	211	242	5 kg	50 kg	B	40
				II	6.1	IB8, IP2, IP4	None	212	242	25 kg	100 kg	A	40
				III	6.1	IB8, IP3	153	213	240	100 kg	200 kg	A	40
	Organotin pesticides, liquid, flammable, toxic, *flash point less than 23 degrees C*	3	UN2787	I	3, 6.1	T14, TP2, TP13, TP27	None	201	243	Forbidden	30 L	B	40
				II	3, 6.1	IB2, T11, TP2, TP13, TP27	None	202	243	1 L	60 L	B	40
	Organotin pesticides, liquid, toxic	6.1	UN3020	I	6.1	T14, TP2, TP13, TP27	None	201	243	1 L	30 L	B	40
				II	6.1	IB2, T11, TP2, TP13, TP27	None	202	243	5 L	60 L	B	40
				III	6.1	IB3, T7, TP2, TP28	153	203	241	60 L	220 L	A	40
	Organotin pesticides, liquid, toxic, flammable, *flash point not less than 23 degrees C*	6.1	UN3019	I	6.1, 3	T14, TP2, TP13, TP27	None	201	243	1 L	30 L	B	40
				II	6.1, 3	IB2, T11, TP2, TP13, TP27	None	202	243	5 L	60 L	B	40
				III	6.1, 3	B1, IB3, T7, TP2, TP28	153	203	242	60 L	220 L	A	40
	Organotin pesticides, solid, toxic	6.1	UN2786	I	6.1	IB7, IP1	None	211	242	5 kg	50 kg	A	40
				II	6.1	IB8, IP2, IP4	None	212	242	25 kg	100 kg	A	40
				III	6.1	IB8, IP3	153	213	240	100 kg	200 kg	A	40
	Orthonitroaniline, see **Nitroanilines** *etc.*												

§172.101 - Hazardous Materials Table

Symbols	Hazardous materials descriptions and proper shipping names	Hazard class or Division	Identification Numbers	PG	Label Codes	Special provisions (§172.102)	(8) Packaging (§173.***)			(9) Quantity limitations		(10) Vessel stowage	
							Exceptions	Non-bulk	Bulk	Passenger aircraft/rail	Cargo aircraft only	Location	Other
(1)	(2)	(3)	(4)	(5)	(6)	(7)	(8A)	(8B)	(8C)	(9A)	(9B)	(10A)	(10B)
	Osmium tetroxide	6.1	UN2471	I	6.1	A8, IB7, IP1, N33, N34	None	211	242	5 kg	50 kg	B	40
D G	**Other regulated substances, liquid, n.o.s.**	9	NA3082	III	9	IB3, T2, TP1	155	203	241	No limit	No limit	A	
D G	**Other regulated substances, solid, n.o.s.**	9	NA3077	III	9	B54, IB8, IP2	155	213	240	No limit	No limit	A	
G	**Oxidizing liquid, corrosive, n.o.s.**	5.1	UN3098	I	5.1, 8		None	201	244	Forbidden	2.5 L	D	13, 56, 58, 69, 106
				II	5.1, 8	IB1	None	202	243	1 L	5 L	B	34, 56, 58, 69, 106
				III	5.1, 8	IB2	152	203	242	2.5 L	30 L	B	34, 56, 58, 69, 106
G	**Oxidizing liquid, n.o.s.**	5.1	UN3139	I	5.1	127, A2	None	201	243	Forbidden	2.5 L	D	56, 58, 69, 106
				II	5.1	127, A2, IB2	152	202	242	1 L	5 L	B	56, 58, 69, 106
				III	5.1	127, A2, IB2	152	203	241	2.5 L	30 L	B	56, 58, 69, 106
G	**Oxidizing liquid, toxic, n.o.s.**	5.1	UN3099	I	5.1, 6.1		None	201	244	Forbidden	2.5 L	D	56, 58, 69, 106
				II	5.1, 6.1	IB1	None	202	243	1 L	5 L	B	56, 58, 95, 106
				III	5.1, 6.1	IB2	152	203	242	2.5 L	30 L	B	56, 58, 95, 106
G	**Oxidizing solid, corrosive, n.o.s.**	5.1	UN3085	I	5.1, 8		None	211	242	1 kg	15 kg	D	13, 56, 58, 69, 106
				II	5.1, 8	IB6, IP2	None	212	242	5 kg	25 kg	B	13, 34, 56, 58, 69, 106
				III	5.1, 8	IB8, IP3	152	213	240	25 kg	100 kg	B	13, 34, 56, 58, 69, 106
G	**Oxidizing solid, flammable, n.o.s.**	5.1	UN3137	I	5.1, 4.1		None	214	214	Forbidden	Forbidden		
G	**Oxidizing solid, n.o.s.**	5.1	UN1479	I	5.1	IB6, IP1	None	211	242	1 kg	15 kg	D	56, 58, 69, 106
				II	5.1	IB8, IP2, IP4	152	212	240	5 kg	25 kg	B	56, 58, 69, 106
				III	5.1	IB8, IP3	152	213	240	25 kg	100 kg	B	56, 58, 69, 106
G	**Oxidizing solid, self-heating, n.o.s.**	5.1	UN3100	II	5.1, 4.2		None	214	214	Forbidden	Forbidden		
G	**Oxidizing solid, toxic, n.o.s.**	5.1	UN3087	I	5.1, 6.1		None	211	242	1 kg	15 kg	D	56, 58, 69, 106
				II	5.1, 6.1	IB6, IP2	None	212	242	5 kg	25 kg	B	56, 58, 69, 95, 106
				III	5.1, 6.1	IB8, IP3	152	213	240	25 kg	100 kg	B	56, 58, 69, 95, 106
G	**Oxidizing solid, water-reactive, n.o.s.**	5.1	UN3121		5.1, 4.3		None	214	214	Forbidden	Forbidden		
	Oxygen and carbon dioxide mixtures, see **Carbon dioxide and oxygen mixtures**												
	Oxygen, compressed	2.2	UN1072		2.2, 5.1	A52	306	302	314, 315	75 kg	150 kg	A	
	Oxygen difluoride, compressed	2.3	UN2190		2.3, 5.1, 8	1	None	304	None	Forbidden	Forbidden	D	13, 40, 89, 90
	Oxygen generator, chemical *(including when contained in associated equipment, e.g., passenger service units (PSUs), portable breathing equipment (PBE), etc.)*	5.1	UN3356	II	5.1	60, A51	None	212	None	Forbidden	25 kg gross	D	56, 58, 69, 106
+	**Oxygen generator, chemical, spent**	9	NA3356	III	9	61	None	213	None	Forbidden	Forbidden	A	
	Oxygen, mixtures with rare gases, see **Rare gases and oxygen mixtures**												
	Oxygen, refrigerated liquid *(cryogenic liquid)*	2.2	UN1073		2.2, 5.1	T75, TP5, TP22	320	316	318	Forbidden	Forbidden	D	
	Paint *including paint, lacquer, enamel, stain, shellac solutions, varnish, polish, liquid filler, and liquid lacquer base*	3	UN1263	I	3	T11, TP1, TP8	150	201	243	1 L	30 L	E	
				II	3	B52, IB2, T4, TP1, TP8	150	173	242	5 L	60 L	B	
				III	3	B1, B52, IB3, T2, TP1	150	173	242	60 L	220 L	A	
	Paint *or* **Paint related material**	8	UN3066	II	8	B2, IB2, T7, TP2	154	173	242	1 L	30 L	A	
				III	8	B52, IB3, T4, TP1	154	173	241	5 L	60 L	A	

§172.101 - Hazardous Materials Table

Symbols (1)	Hazardous materials descriptions and proper shipping names (2)	Hazard class or Division (3)	Identification Numbers (4)	PG (5)	Label Codes (6)	Special provisions (§172.102) (7)	(8) Packaging (§173.***)			(9) Quantity limitations		(10) Vessel stowage	
							Exceptions (8A)	Non-bulk (8B)	Bulk (8C)	Passenger aircraft/rail (9A)	Cargo aircraft only (9B)	Location (10A)	Other (10B)
	Paint related material *including paint thinning, drying, removing, or reducing compound*	3	UN1263	I II III	3 3 3	T11, TP1, TP8 B52, IB2, T4, TP1, TP8 B1, B52, IB3, T2, TP1	150 150 150	201 173 173	243 242 242	1 L 5 L 60 L	30 L 60 L 220 L	E B A	
	Paper, unsaturated oil treated *incompletely dried (including carbon paper)*	4.2	UN1379	III	4.2	IB8, IP3	None	213	241	Forbidden	Forbidden	A	
	Paraformaldehyde	4.1	UN2213	III	4.1	A1, IB8, IP3	151	213	240	25 kg	100 kg	A	
	Paraldehyde	3	UN1264	III	3	B1, IB3, T2, TP1	150	203	242	60 L	220 L	A	
	Paranitroaniline, solid, see **Nitroanilines** *etc.*												
D	**Parathion and compressed gas mixture**	2.3	NA1967		2.3	3	None	334	245	Forbidden	Forbidden	E	40
	Paris green, solid, see **Copper acetoarsenite**												
A W	**PCB,** *see* **Polychlorinated biphenyls**												
+	**Pentaborane**	4.2	UN1380	I	4.2, 6.1	1	None	205	245	Forbidden	Forbidden	D	
	Pentachloroethane	6.1	UN1669	II	6.1	IB2, T7, TP2	None	202	243	5 L	60 L	A	40
	Pentachlorophenol	6.1	UN3155	II	6.1	IB8, IP2, IP4	None	212	242	25 kg	100 kg	A	
	Pentaerythrite tetranitrate (dry)	Forbidden											
	Pentaerythrite tetranitrate mixture, desensitized, solid, n.o.s. *with more than 10 percent but not more than 20 percent PETN, by mass*	4.1	UN3344	II	4.1	118	None	214	None	Forbidden	Forbidden	E	40
	Pentaerythrite tetranitrate *or* **Pentaerythritol tetranitrate** *or* **PETN,** *with not less than 7 percent wax by mass*	1.1D	UN0411	II	1.1D		None	62	None	Forbidden	Forbidden	10	
	Pentaerythrite tetranitrate, wetted *or* **Pentaerythritol tetranitrate, wetted,** *or* **PETN, wetted** *with not less than 25 percent water, by mass, or* **Pentaerythrite tetranitrate,** *or* **Pentaerythritol tetranitrate** *or* **PETN, desensitized** *with not less than 15 percent phlegmatizer by mass*	1.1D	UN0150	II	1.1D	121	None	62	None	Forbidden	Forbidden	10	
	Pentaerythritol tetranitrate, *see* **Pentaerythrite tetranitrate,** *etc.*												
	Pentafluoroethane *or* **Refrigerant gas R 125**	2.2	UN3220		2.2	T50	306	304	314, 315	75 kg	150 kg	A	
	Pentamethylheptane	3	UN2286	III	3	B1, IB3, T2, TP1	150	203	242	60 L	220 L	A	
	Pentane-2,4-dione	3	UN2310	III	3, 6.1	B1, IB3, T4, TP1	150	203	242	60 L	220 L	A	
	[PG II only] Pentanes	3	UN1265	II	3	IB2, T4, TP1	150	202	242	5 L	60 L	E	
	Pentanitroaniline (dry)	Forbidden											
	Pentanols	3	UN1105	II III	3 3	IB2, T4, TP1, TP29 B1, B3, IB3, T2, TP1	150 150	202 203	242 242	5 L 60 L	60 L 220 L	B A	
	1-Pentene *(n-amylene)*	3	UN1108	I	3	T11, TP2	150	201	243	1 L	30 L	E	
	1-Pentol	8	UN2705	II	8	B2, IB2, T7, TP2	154	202	242	1 L	30 L	B	38
	Pentolite, *dry or wetted with less than 15 percent water, by mass*	1.1D	UN0151	II	1.1D		None	62	None	Forbidden	Forbidden	10	
	Pepper spray, see **Aerosols,** *etc. or* **Self-defense spray, non-pressurized**												
	Perchlorates, inorganic, aqueous solution, n.o.s.	5.1	UN3211	II III	5.1 5.1	IB2, T4, TP1 IB2, T4, TP1	152 152	202 202	242 241	1 L 2.5 L	5 L 30 L	B B	46, 56,58 56, 58, 69, 106
	Perchlorates, inorganic, n.o.s.	5.1	UN1481	II III	5.1 5.1	IB6, IP2 IB8, IP3	152 152	212 213	242 240	5 kg 25 kg	25 kg 100 kg	A A	46, 56 46, 56
	Perchloric acid, with more than 72 percent acid by mass	Forbidden											
	Perchloric acid *with more than 50 percent but not more than 72 percent acid, by mass*	5.1	UN1873	I	5.1, 8	A2, A3, N41, T10, TP1, TP12	None	201	243	Forbidden	2.5 L	D	66
	Perchloric acid *with not more than 50 percent acid by mass*	8	UN1802	II	8, 5.1	IB2, N41, T7, TP2	None	202	243	Forbidden	30 L	C	66

§172.101 - Hazardous Materials Table

Symbols	Hazardous materials descriptions and proper shipping names	Hazard class or Division	Identification Numbers	PG	Label Codes	Special provisions (§172.102)	(8) Packaging (§173.***) Exceptions			(9) Quantity limitations Passenger aircraft/ rail		(10) Vessel stowage Location	
							Exceptions	Non-bulk	Bulk	Passenger aircraft/ rail	Cargo aircraft only	Location	Other
(1)	(2)	(3)	(4)	(5)	(6)	(7)	(8A)	(8B)	(8C)	(9A)	(9B)	(10A)	(10B)
	Perchloroethylene, see **Tetrachloroethylene**												
	Perchloromethyl mercaptan	6.1	UN1670	I	6.1	2, A3, A7, B9, B14, B32, B74, N34, T20, TP2, TP13, TP38, TP45	None	227	244	Forbidden	Forbidden	D	40
	Perchloryl fluoride	2.3	UN3083		2.3, 5.1	2, B9, B14	None	302	314, 315	Forbidden	Forbidden	D	40
	Percussion caps, see **Primers, cap type**												
	Perfluoro-2-butene, see **Octafluorobut-2-ene**												
	Perfluoro(ethyl vinyl ether)	2.1	UN3154		2.1		306	302, 304, 305	314, 315	Forbidden	150 kg	E	40
	Perfluoro(methyl vinyl ether)	2.1	UN3153		2.1	T50	306	302, 304, 305	314, 315	Forbidden	150 kg	E	40
	Perfumery products *with flammable solvents*	3	UN1266	II	3	IB2, T4, TP1, TP8	150	202	242	15 L	60 L	B	
				III	3	B1, IB3, T2, TP1	150	203	242	60 L	220 L	A	
	Permanganates, inorganic, aqueous solution, n.o.s.	5.1	UN3214	II	5.1	26, IB2, T4, TP1	152	202	242	1 L	5 L	D	56, 58, 69, 106, 107
	Permanganates, inorganic, n.o.s.	5.1	UN1482	II	5.1	26, A30, IB6, IP2	152	212	242	5 kg	25 kg	D	56, 58, 69, 106, 107
				III	5.1	26, A30, IB8, IP3	152	213	240	25 kg	100 kg	D	56, 58, 69, 106, 107
	Peroxides, inorganic, n.o.s.	5.1	UN1483	II	5.1	A7, A20, IB6, IP2, N34	None	212	242	5 kg	25 kg	A	13, 75, 106
				III	5.1	A7, A20, IB8, IP3, N34	152	213	240	25 kg	100 kg	A	13, 75, 106
	Peroxyacetic acid, with more than 43 percent and with more than 6 percent hydrogen peroxide	Forbidden											
	Persulfates, inorganic, aqueous solution, n.o.s.	5.1	UN3216	III	5.1	IB2, T4, TP1, TP29	152	203	241	2.5 L	30 L	A	
	Persulfates, inorganic, n.o.s.	5.1	UN3215	III	5.1	IB8, IP3	152	213	240	25 kg	100 kg	A	
G	**Pesticides, liquid, flammable, toxic,** *flash point less than 23 degrees C*	3	UN3021	I	3, 6.1	B5, T14, TP2, TP13, TP27	None	201	243	Forbidden	30 L	B	
				II	3, 6.1	IB2, T11, TP2, TP13, TP27	None	202	243	1 L	60 L	B	
G	**Pesticides, liquid, toxic, flammable, n.o.s.** *flash point not less than 23 degrees C*	6.1	UN2903	I	6.1, 3	T14, TP2, TP13, TP27	None	201	243	1 L	30 L	B	40
				II	6.1, 3	IB2, T11, TP2, TP13, TP27	None	202	243	5 L	60 L	B	40
				III	6.1, 3	B1, IB3, T7, TP2	153	203	242	60 L	220 L	A	40
G	**Pesticides, liquid, toxic, n.o.s.**	6.1	UN2902	I	6.1	T14, TP2, TP13, TP27	None	201	243	1 L	30 L	B	40
				II	6.1	IB2, T11, TP2, TP13, TP27	None	202	243	5 L	60 L	B	40
				III	6.1	IB3, T7, TP2, TP28	153	203	241	60 L	220 L	A	40
G	**Pesticides, solid, toxic, n.o.s.**	6.1	UN2588	I	6.1	IB7	None	211	242	5 kg	50 kg	A	40
				II	6.1	IB8, IP2, IP4	None	212	242	25 kg	100 kg	A	40
				III	6.1	IB8, IP3	153	213	240	100 kg	200 kg	A	40
	PETN, *see* **Pentaerythrite tetranitrate**												
	PETN/TNT, *see* **Pentolite,** *etc.*												
	Petrol, *see* **Gasoline**												
	Petroleum crude oil	3	UN1267	I	3	T11, TP1, TP8	None	201	243	1 L	30 L	E	
				II	3	IB2, T4, TP1, TP8	150	202	242	5 L	60 L	B	
				III	3	B1, IB3, T2, TP1	150	203	242	60 L	220 L	A	
	Petroleum distillates, n.o.s. *or* **Petroleum products, n.o.s.**	3	UN1268	I	3	T11, TP1, TP8	150	201	243	1 L	30 L	E	
				II	3	IB2, T7, TP1, TP8, TP28	150	202	242	5 L	60 L	B	
				III	3	B1, IB3, T4, TP1, TP29	150	203	242	60 L	220 L	A	
	Petroleum gases, liquefied *or* **Liquefied petroleum gas**	2.1	UN1075		2.1	T50	306	304	314, 315	Forbidden	150 kg	E	40
D	**Petroleum oil**	3	NA1270	I	3	T11, TP1, TP9	None	201	243	1 L	30 L	E	
				II	3	IB2, T7, TP1, TP8, TP28	150	202	242	5 L	60 L	B	
				III	3	B1, IB3, T4, TP1, TP29	150	203	242	60 L	220 L	A	
	Phenacyl bromide	6.1	UN2645	II	6.1	IB8, IP2, IP4	None	212	242	25 kg	100 kg	B	40

§172.101 - Hazardous Materials Table

Symbols	Hazardous materials descriptions and proper shipping names	Hazard class or Division	Identification Numbers	PG	Label Codes	Special provisions (§172.102)	(8) Packaging (§173.***) Exceptions	(8) Packaging Non-bulk	(8) Packaging Bulk	(9) Quantity limitations Passenger aircraft/rail	(9) Quantity limitations Cargo aircraft only	(10) Vessel stowage Location	(10) Vessel stowage Other
(1)	(2)	(3)	(4)	(5)	(6)	(7)	(8A)	(8B)	(8C)	(9A)	(9B)	(10A)	(10B)
+	**Phenetidines**	6.1	UN2311	III	6.1	IB3, T4, TP1	153	203	241	60 L	220 L	A	
	Phenol, molten	6.1	UN2312	II	6.1	B14, T7, TP3	None	202	243	Forbidden	Forbidden	B	40
+	**Phenol, solid**	6.1	UN1671	II	6.1	IB8, IP2, IP4, N78, T6, TP2	None	212	242	25 kg	100 kg	A	
	Phenol solutions	6.1	UN2821	II III	6.1 6.1	IB2, T7, TP2 IB3, T4, TP1	None 153	202 203	243 241	5 L 60 L	60 L 220 L	A A	
	Phenolsulfonic acid, liquid	8	UN1803	II	8	B2, IB2, N41, T7, TP2	154	202	242	1 L	30 L	C	14
	Phenoxyacetic acid derivative pesticide, liquid, flammable, toxic *flash point less than 23 degrees C*	3	UN3346	I II	3, 6.1 3, 6.1	T14, TP2, TP13, TP27 IB2, T11, TP2, TP13, TP27	None None	201 202	243 243	Forbidden 1 L	30 L 60 L	B B	40 40
	Phenoxyacetic acid derivative pesticide, liquid, toxic	6.1	UN3348	I II III	6.1 6.1 6.1	T14, TP2, TP13, TP27 IB2, T11, TP2, TP27 IB3, T7, TP2, TP28	None 153 153	201 202 203	243 243 241	1 L 5 L 60 L	30 L 60 L 220 L	B B A	40 40 40
	Phenoxyacetic acid derivative pesticide, liquid, toxic, flammable, *flash point not less than 23 degrees C*	6.1	UN3347	I II III	6.1, 3 6.1, 3 6.1, 3	T14, TP2, TP13, TP27 IB2, T11, TP2, TP13, TP27 IB3, T7, TP2, TP28	None 153 153	201 202 203	243 243 241	1 L 5 L 60 L	30 L 60 L 220 L	B B A	40 40 40
	Phenoxyacetic acid derivative pesticide, solid, toxic	6.1	UN3345	I II III	6.1 6.1 6.1	IB7, IP1 IB8, IP2, IP4 IB8, IP3	None 153 153	211 212 213	242 242 240	5 kg 25 kg 100 kg	50 kg 100 kg 200 kg	A A A	40 40 40
	Phenyl chloroformate	6.1	UN2746	II	6.1, 8	IB2, T7, TP2, TP13	None	202	243	1 L	30 L	A	12, 13, 21, 25, 40, 100
	Phenyl isocyanate	6.1	UN2487	I	6.1, 3	2, B9, B14, B32, B74, B77, N33, N34, T20, TP2, TP13, TP38, TP45	None	227	244	Forbidden	Forbidden	D	40
	Phenyl mercaptan	6.1	UN2337	I	6.1, 3	2, B9, B14, B32, B74, B77, T20, TP2, TP13, TP38, TP45	None	227	244	Forbidden	Forbidden	B	26, 40
	Phenyl phosphorus dichloride	8	UN2798	II	8	B2, B15, IB2, T7, TP2	154	202	242	Forbidden	30 L	B	40
	Phenyl phosphorus thiodichloride	8	UN2799	II	8	B2, B15, IB2, T7, TP2	154	202	242	Forbidden	30 L	B	40
	Phenyl urea pesticides, liquid, toxic	6.1	UN3002	I II III	6.1 6.1 6.1	T14, TP2, TP27 T7, TP2 T4, TP1	None None 153	201 202 203	243 243 241	1 L 5 L 60 L	30 L 60 L 220 L	B B A	40 40 40
	Phenylacetonitrile, liquid	6.1	UN2470	III	6.1	IB3, T4, TP1	153	203	241	60 L	220 L	A	26
	Phenylacetyl chloride	8	UN2577	II	8	B2, IB2, T7, TP2	154	202	242	1 L	30 L	C	40
	Phenylcarbylamine chloride	6.1	UN1672	I	6.1	2, B9, B14, B32, B74, T20, TP2, TP13, TP38, TP45	None	227	244	Forbidden	Forbidden	D	40
	m-Phenylene diaminediperchlorate (dry)	Forbidden											
+	**Phenylenediamines** *(o-, m-, p-)*	6.1	UN1673	III	6.1	IB8, IP3, T7, TP1	153	213	240	100 kg	200 kg	A	
	Phenylhydrazine	6.1	UN2572	II	6.1	IB2, T7, TP2	None	202	243	5 L	60 L	A	40
	Phenylmercuric acetate	6.1	UN1674	II	6.1	IB8, IP2, IP4	None	212	242	25 kg	100 kg	A	
	Phenylmercuric compounds, n.o.s.	6.1	UN2026	I II III	6.1 6.1 6.1	IB7, IP1 IB8, IP2, IP4 IB8, IP3	None None 153	211 212 213	242 242 240	5 kg 25 kg 100 kg	50 kg 100 kg 200 kg	A A A	
	Phenylmercuric hydroxide	6.1	UN1894	II	6.1	IB8, IP2, IP4	None	212	242	25 kg	100 kg	A	
	Phenylmercuric nitrate	6.1	UN1895	II	6.1	IB8, IP2, IP4	None	212	242	25 kg	100 kg	A	
	Phenyltrichlorosilane	8	UN1804	II	8	A7, B6, IB2, N34, T7, TP2	None	202	242	Forbidden	30 L	C	40
	Phosgene	2.3	UN1076		2.3, 8	1, B7, B46	None	192	314	Forbidden	Forbidden	D	40
	9-Phosphabicyclononanes *or* **Cyclooctadiene phosphines**	4.2	UN2940	II	4.2	A19, IB6, IP2	None	212	241	15 kg	50 kg	A	
	Phosphine	2.3	UN2199		2.3, 2.1	1	None	192	245	Forbidden	Forbidden	D	40

§172.101 - Hazardous Materials Table

Sym-bols	Hazardous materials descriptions and proper shipping names	Hazard class or Division	Identifi-cation Numbers	PG	Label Codes	Special provisions (§172.102)	(8) Packaging (§173.***)			(9) Quantity limitations		(10) Vessel stowage	
							Excep-tions	Non-bulk	Bulk	Passen-ger aircraft/ rail	Cargo aircraft only	Loca-tion	Other
(1)	(2)	(3)	(4)	(5)	(6)	(7)	(8A)	(8B)	(8C)	(9A)	(9B)	(10A)	(10B)
	Phosphoric acid, *liquid or solid*	8	UN1805	III	8	A7, IB3, IP3, N34, T4, TP1	154	203	241	5 L	60 L	A	
	Phosphoric acid triethyleneimine, see **Tris-(1-aziridiyl)phosphine oxide, solution**												
	Phosphoric anhydride, see **Phosphorus pentoxide**												
	Phosphorous acid	8	UN2834	III	8	IB8, IP3, T3, TP1	154	213	240	25 kg	100 kg	A	48
	Phosphorus, amorphous	4.1	UN1338	III	4.1	A1, A19, B1, B9, B26, IB8, IP3	None	213	243	25 kg	100 kg	A	74
	Phosphorus bromide, see **Phosphorus tribromide**												
	Phosphorus chloride, see **Phosphorus trichloride**												
	Phosphorus heptasulfide, *free from yellow or white phosphorus*	4.1	UN1339	II	4.1	A20, IB4, N34	None	212	240	15 kg	50 kg	B	74
	Phosphorus oxybromide	8	UN1939	II	8	B8, IB8, IP2, IP4, N41, N43, T7, TP2	None	212	240	Forbidden	50 kg	C	12, 40
	Phosphorus oxybromide, molten	8	UN2576	II	8	B2, B8, IB1, N41, N43, T7, TP3, TP13	None	202	242	Forbidden	Forbidden	C	40
+	**Phosphorus oxychloride**	8	UN1810	II	8, 6.1	2, A7, B9, B14, B32, B74, B77, N34, T20, TP2, TP38, TP45	None	227	244	Forbidden	Forbidden	C	40
	Phosphorus pentabromide	8	UN2691	II	8	A7, IB8, IP2, IP4, N34	154	212	240	Forbidden	50 kg	B	12, 40
	Phosphorus pentachloride	8	UN1806	II	8	A7, IB8, IP2, IP4, N34	None	212	240	Forbidden	50 kg	C	40
	Phosphorus pentafluoride, compressed	2.3	UN2198		2.3, 8	2, B9, B14	None	302, 304	314, 315	Forbidden	Forbidden	D	40
	Phosphorus pentasulfide, *free from yellow or white phosphorus*	4.3	UN1340	II	4.3, 4.1	A20, B59, IB4	151	212	242	15 kg	50 kg	B	74
	Phosphorus pentoxide	8	UN1807	II	8	A7, IB8, IP2, IP4, N34	154	212	240	15 kg	50 kg	A	
	Phosphorus sesquisulfide, *free from yellow or white phosphorus*	4.1	UN1341	II	4.1	A20, IB4, N34	None	212	240	15 kg	50 kg	B	74
	Phosphorus tribromide	8	UN1808	II	8	A3, A6, A7, B2, B25, IB2, N34, N43, T7, TP2	None	202	242	Forbidden	30 L	C	40
	Phosphorus trichloride	6.1	UN1809	I	6.1, 8	2, B9, B14, B15, B32, B74, B77, N34, T20, TP2, TP13, TP38, TP45	None	227	244	Forbidden	Forbidden	C	40
	Phosphorus trioxide	8	UN2578	III	8	IB8, IP3	154	213	240	25 kg	100 kg	A	12
	Phosphorus trisulfide, *free from yellow or white phosphorus*	4.1	UN1343	II	4.1	A20, IB4, N34	None	212	240	15 kg	50 kg	B	74
	Phosphorus, white dry *or* **Phosphorus, white, under water** *or* **Phosphorus white, in solution** *or* **Phosphorus, yellow dry** *or* **Phosphorus, yellow, under water** *or* **Phosphorus, yellow, in solution**	4.2	UN1381	I	4.2, 6.1	B9, B26, N34, T9, TP3	None	188	243	Forbidden	Forbidden	E	
	Phosphorus white, molten	4.2	UN2447	I	4.2, 6.1	B9, B26, N34, T21, TP3, TP7, TP26	None	188	243	Forbidden	Forbidden	D	
	Phosphorus (white or red) and a chlorate, mixtures of	Forbidden											
	Phosphoryl chloride, see **Phosphorus oxychloride**												
	Phthalic anhydride *with more than .05 percent maleic anhydride*	8	UN2214	III	8	IB8, IP3, T4, TP3	154	213	240	25 kg	100 kg	A	
	Picolines	3	UN2313	III	3	B1, IB3, T4, TP1	150	203	242	60 L	220 L	A	40
	Picric acid, *see* **Trinitrophenol,** *etc.*												
	Picrite, *see* **Nitroguanidine,** *etc.*												
	Picryl chloride, *see* **Trinitrochlorobenzene**												
	Pine oil	3	UN1272	III	3	B1, IB3, T2, TP1	150	203	242	60 L	220 L	A	

§172.101 - Hazardous Materials Table

Symbols	Hazardous materials descriptions and proper shipping names	Hazard class or Division	Identification Numbers	PG	Label Codes	Special provisions (§172.102)	(8) Packaging (§173.***) Exceptions	Non-bulk	Bulk	(9) Quantity limitations Passenger aircraft/rail	Cargo aircraft only	(10) Vessel stowage Location	Other
(1)	(2)	(3)	(4)	(5)	(6)	(7)	(8A)	(8B)	(8C)	(9A)	(9B)	(10A)	(10B)
	alpha-Pinene	3	UN2368	III	3	B1, IB3, T2, TP1	150	203	242	60 L	220 L	A	
	Piperazine	8	UN2579	III	8	IB8, IP3, T4, TP1	154	213	240	25 kg	100 kg	A	12
	Piperidine	8	UN2401	I	8, 3	T10, TP2	None	201	243	0.5 L	2.5 L	B	
	Pivaloyl chloride, see **Trimethylacetyl chloride**												
	Plastic molding compound *in dough, sheet or extruded rope form evolving flammable vapor*	9	UN3314	III	9	32, IB8, IP6	155	221	221	100 kg	200 kg	A	85, 87
	Plastic solvent, n.o.s., see **Flammable liquids, n.o.s.**												
	Plastics, nitrocellulose-based, self-heating, n.o.s.	4.2	UN2006	III	4.2		None	213	None	Forbidden	Forbidden	C	
	Poisonous gases, n.o.s., see **Compressed** *or* **liquefied gases, flammable** *or* **toxic, n.o.s.**												
	Polyalkylamines, n.o.s., see **Amines,** *etc.*												
	Polychlorinated biphenyls, liquid	9	UN2315	II	9	9, 81, 140, IB3, T4, TP1	155	202	241	100 L	220 L	A	95
	Polychlorinated biphenyls, solid	9	UN2315	II	9	9, 81, 140, IB7	155	212	240	100 kg	200 kg	A	95
	Polyester resin kit	3	UN3269		3	40	152	225	None	5 kg	5 kg	B	
	Polyhalogenated biphenyls, liquid *or* **Polyhalogenated terphenyls liquid**	9	UN3151	II	9	IB3	155	204	241	100 L	220 L	A	95
	Polyhalogenated biphenyls, solid *or* **Polyhalogenated terphenyls, solid**	9	UN3152	II	9	IB8, IP2, IP4	155	204	241	100 kg	200 kg	A	95
	Polymeric beads, expandable, *evolving flammable vapor*	9	UN2211	III	9	32, IB8, IP6, IP7	155	221	221	100 kg	200 kg	A	85, 87
	Potassium	4.3	UN2257	I	4.3	A19, A20, B27, IB1, IP1, N6, N34, T9, TP3, TP7	None	211	244	Forbidden	15 kg	D	
	Potassium arsenate	6.1	UN1677	II	6.1	IB8, IP2, IP4	None	212	242	25 kg	100 kg	A	
	Potassium arsenite	6.1	UN1678	II	6.1	IB8, IP2, IP4	None	212	242	25 kg	100 kg	A	
	Potassium bisulfite solution, see **Bisulfites, aqueous solutions, n.o.s.**												
	Potassium borohydride	4.3	UN1870	I	4.3	A19, N40	None	211	242	Forbidden	15 kg	E	
	Potassium bromate	5.1	UN1484	II	5.1	IB8, IP4	152	212	242	5 kg	25 kg	A	56, 58, 106
	Potassium carbonyl	Forbidden											
	Potassium chlorate	5.1	UN1485	II	5.1	A9, IB8, IP4, N34	152	212	242	5 kg	25 kg	A	56, 58, 106
	Potassium chlorate, aqueous solution	5.1	UN2427	II III	5.1 5.1	A2, IB2, T4, TP1 A2, IB2, T4, TP1	152 152	202 203	241 241	1 L 2.5 L	5 L 30 L	B B	56, 58, 106 56, 58, 69, 106
	Potassium chlorate mixed with mineral oil, see **Explosive, blasting, type C**												
	Potassium cuprocyanide	6.1	UN1679	II	6.1	IB8, IP2, IP4	None	212	242	25 kg	100 kg	A	26
	Potassium cyanide	6.1	UN1680	I	6.1	B69, B77, IB7, IP1, N74, N75, T14, TP2, TP13	None	211	242	5 kg	50 kg	B	52
	Potassium dichloro isocyanurate or Potassium dichloro-s-triazinetrione, see **Dichloroisocyanuric acid, dry** *or* **Dichloroisocyanuric acid salts** *etc.*												
	Potassium dithionite *or* **Potassium hydrosulfite**	4.2	UN1929	II	4.2	A8, A19, A20, IB6, IP2	None	212	241	15 kg	50 kg	E	13
	Potassium fluoride	6.1	UN1812	III	6.1	IB8, IP3, T4, TP1	153	213	240	100 kg	200 kg	A	26
	Potassium fluoroacetate	6.1	UN2628	I	6.1	IB7, IP1	None	211	242	5 kg	50 kg	E	
	Potassium fluorosilicate	6.1	UN2655	III	6.1	IB8, IP3	153	213	240	100 kg	200 kg	A	26
	Potassium hydrate, see **Potassium hydroxide, solid**												
	Potassium hydrogen fluoride, see **Potassium hydrogen difluoride**												
	Potassium hydrogen fluoride solution, see **Corrosive liquid, n.o.s.**												

§172.101 - Hazardous Materials Table

Symbols	Hazardous materials descriptions and proper shipping names	Hazard class or Division	Identification Numbers	PG	Label Codes	Special provisions (§172.102)	(8) Packaging (§173.***)			(9) Quantity limitations		(10) Vessel stowage	
							Exceptions	Non-bulk	Bulk	Passenger aircraft/ rail	Cargo aircraft only	Location	Other
(1)	(2)	(3)	(4)	(5)	(6)	(7)	(8A)	(8B)	(8C)	(9A)	(9B)	(10A)	(10B)
	Potassium hydrogen sulfate	8	UN2509	II	8	A7, IB8, IP2, IP4, N34	154	212	240	15 kg	50 kg	A	
	Potassium hydrogendifluoride, *solid*	8	UN1811	II	8, 6.1	IB8, IP2, IP4, N3, N34, T7, TP2	154	212	240	15 kg	50 kg	A	25, 26, 40
	Potassium hydrogendifluoride, *solution*	8	UN1811	II	8, 6.1	IB8, IP2, IP4, N3, N34, T7, TP2	154	202	243	1 L	30 L	A	25, 26, 40
	Potassium hydrosulfite, *see* **Potassium dithionite**												
	Potassium hydroxide, liquid, see **Potassium hydroxide solution**												
	Potassium hydroxide, solid	8	UN1813	II	8	IB8, IP2, IP4	154	212	240	15 kg	50 kg	A	
	Potassium hydroxide, solution	8	UN1814	II III	8 8	B2, IB2, T7, TP2 IB3, T4, TP1	154 154	202 203	242 241	1 L 5 L	30 L 60 L	A A	
	Potassium hypochlorite, solution, see **Hypochlorite solutions,** *etc.*												
	Potassium, metal alloys	4.3	UN1420	I	4.3	A19, A20, B27, IB4, IP1	None	211	244	Forbidden	15 kg	D	
	Potassium metal, liquid alloy, see **Alkali metal alloys, liquid, n.o.s.**												
	Potassium metavanadate	6.1	UN2864	II	6.1	IB8, IP2, IP4	None	212	242	25 kg	100 kg	A	
	Potassium monoxide	8	UN2033	II	8	IB8, IP2, IP4	154	212	240	15 kg	50 kg	A	
	Potassium nitrate	5.1	UN1486	III	5.1	A1, A29, IB8, IP3	152	213	240	25 kg	100 kg	A	
	Potassium nitrate and sodium nitrite mixtures	5.1	UN1487	II	5.1	B78, IB8, IP4	152	212	240	5 kg	25 kg	A	56, 58
	Potassium nitrite	5.1	UN1488	II	5.1	IB8, IP4	152	212	242	5 kg	25 kg	A	56, 58
	Potassium perchlorate, solid	5.1	UN1489	II	5.1	IB6, IP2	152	212	242	5 kg	25 kg	A	56, 58, 106
	Potassium perchlorate, solution	5.1	UN1489	II	5.1	IB2, T4, TP1	152	202	242	1 L	5 L	A	56, 58, 106
	Potassium permanganate	5.1	UN1490	II	5.1	IB8, IP4	152	212	240	5 kg	25 kg	D	56, 58, 69, 106, 107
	Potassium peroxide	5.1	UN1491	I	5.1	A20, IB6, IP1, N34	None	211	None	Forbidden	15 kg	B	13, 75, 106
	Potassium persulfate	5.1	UN1492	III	5.1	A1, A29, IB8, IP3	152	213	240	25 kg	100 kg	A	
	Potassium phosphide	4.3	UN2012	I	4.3, 6.1	A19, N40	None	211	None	Forbidden	15 kg	E	40, 85
	Potassium selenate, see **Selenates** *or* **Selenites**												
	Potassium selenite, see **Selenates** *or* **Selenites**												
	Potassium sodium alloys	4.3	UN1422	I	4.3	A19, B27, IB4, IP1, N34, N40, T9, TP3, TP7	None	211	244	Forbidden	15 kg	D	
	Potassium sulfide, anhydrous *or* **Potassium sulfide** *with less than 30 percent water of crystallization*	4.2	UN1382	II	4.2	A19, A20, B16, IB6, IP2, N34	None	212	241	15 kg	50 kg	A	
	Potassium sulfide, hydrated *with not less than 30 percent water of crystallization*	8	UN1847	II	8	IB8, IP2, IP4	154	212	240	15 kg	50 kg	A	26
	Potassium superoxide	5.1	UN2466	I	5.1	A20, IB6, IP1	None	211	None	Forbidden	15 kg	B	13, 75, 106
	Powder cake, wetted *or* **Powder paste, wetted** *with not less than 17 percent alcohol by mass*	1.1C	UN0433	II	1.1C		None	62	None	Forbidden	Forbidden	10	
	Powder cake, wetted *or* **Powder paste, wetted** *with not less than 25 percent water, by mass*	1.3C	UN0159	II	1.3C		None	62	None	Forbidden	Forbidden	10	
	Powder paste, *see* **Powder cake,** *etc.*												
	Powder, smokeless	1.1C	UN0160	II	1.1C		None	62	None	Forbidden	Forbidden		26E
	Powder, smokeless	1.3C	UN0161	II	1.3C		None	62	None	Forbidden	Forbidden		26E
	Power device, explosive, see **Cartridges, power device**												
	Primers, cap type	1.4S	UN0044	II	None		None	62	None	25 kg	100 kg	05	
	Primers, cap type	1.1B	UN0377	II	1.1B		None	62	None	Forbidden	Forbidden	11	
	Primers, cap type	1.4B	UN0378	II	1.4B		None	62	None	Forbidden	75 kg	06	
	Primers, small arms, see **Primers, cap type**												
	Primers, tubular	1.3G	UN0319	II	1.3G		None	62	None	Forbidden	Forbidden	07	

§172.101 - Hazardous Materials Table

Symbols	Hazardous materials descriptions and proper shipping names	Hazard class or Division	Identification Numbers	PG	Label Codes	Special provisions (§172.102)	(8) Packaging (§173.***)			(9) Quantity limitations		(10) Vessel stowage	
							Exceptions	Non-bulk	Bulk	Passenger aircraft/ rail	Cargo aircraft only	Location	Other
(1)	(2)	(3)	(4)	(5)	(6)	(7)	(8A)	(8B)	(8C)	(9A)	(9B)	(10A)	(10B)
	Primers, tubular	1.4G	UN0320	II	1.4G		None	62	None	Forbidden	75 kg	06	
	Primers, tubular	1.4S	UN0376	II	None		None	62	None	25 kg	100 kg	05	
	Printing ink, *flammable or* **Printing ink related material** *(including printing ink thinning or reducing compound), flammable*	3	UN1210	I II III	3 3 3	T11, TP1, TP8 IB2, T4, TP1, TP8 B1, IB3, T2, TP1	150 150 150	173 173 173	243 242 242	1 L 5 L 60 L	30 L 60 L 220 L	E B A	
	Projectiles, illuminating, see **Ammunition, illuminating,** *etc.*												
	Projectiles, *inert with tracer*	1.4S	UN0345	II	1.4S			62	None	25 kg	100 kg	01	
	Projectiles, *inert, with tracer*	1.3G	UN0424	II	1.3G			62	None	Forbidden	Forbidden	03	
	Projectiles, *inert, with tracer*	1.4G	UN0425	II	1.4G			62	None	Forbidden	75 kg	02	
	Projectiles, *with burster or expelling charge*	1.2D	UN0346	II	1.2D			62	None	Forbidden	Forbidden	03	
	Projectiles, *with burster or expelling charge*	1.4D	UN0347	II	1.4D			62	None	Forbidden	75 kg	02	
	Projectiles, *with burster or expelling charge*	1.2F	UN0426	II	1.2F			62	None	Forbidden	Forbidden	08	
	Projectiles, *with burster or expelling charge*	1.4F	UN0427	II	1.4F			62	None	Forbidden	Forbidden	08	
	Projectiles, *with burster or expelling charge*	1.2G	UN0434	II	1.2G			62	None	Forbidden	Forbidden	03	
	Projectiles, *with burster or expelling charge*	1.4G	UN0435	II	1.4G			62	None	Forbidden	75 kg	02	
	Projectiles, *with bursting charge*	1.1F	UN0167	II	1.1F			62	None	Forbidden	Forbidden	08	
	Projectiles, *with bursting charge*	1.1D	UN0168	II	1.1D			62	None	Forbidden	Forbidden	03	
	Projectiles, *with bursting charge*	1.2D	UN0169	II	1.2D			62	None	Forbidden	Forbidden	03	
	Projectiles, *with bursting charge*	1.2F	UN0324	II	1.2F			62	None	Forbidden	Forbidden	08	
	Projectiles, *with bursting charge*	1.4D	UN0344	II	1.4D			62	None	Forbidden	75 kg	02	
	Propadiene, stabilized	2.1	UN2200		2.1		None	304	314, 315	Forbidden	150 kg	B	40
	Propadiene mixed with methyl acetylene, see **Methyl acetylene and propadiene mixtures, stabilized**												
	Propane *see also* **Petroleum gases, liquefied**	2.1	UN1978		2.1	19, T50	306	304	314, 315	Forbidden	150 kg	E	40
	Propanethiols	3	UN2402	II	3	IB2, T4, TP1, TP13	150	202	242	5 L	60 L	E	95, 102
	n-Propanol *or* **Propyl alcohol, normal**	3	UN1274	II III	3 3	B1, IB2, T4, TP1 B1, IB3, T2, TP1	150 150	202 203	242 242	5 L 60 L	60 L 220 L	B A	
	Propellant, liquid	1.3C	UN0495	II	1.3C	37	None	62	None	Forbidden	Forbidden	10	
	Propellant, liquid	1.1C	UN0497	II	1.1C	37	None	62	None	Forbidden	Forbidden	10	
	Propellant, solid	1.1C	UN0498	II	1.1C		None	62	None	Forbidden	Forbidden		26E
	Propellant, solid	1.3C	UN0499	II	1.3C		None	62	None	Forbidden	Forbidden		26E
	Propellant, solid	1.4C	UN0501		1.4C		None	62	None	Forbidden	Forbidden	A	24E
	Propionaldehyde	3	UN1275	II	3	IB2, T7, TP1	150	202	242	5 L	60 L	E	
	Propionic acid	8	UN1848	III	8	IB3, T4, TP1	154	203	241	5 L	60 L	A	
	Propionic anhydride	8	UN2496	III	8	IB3, T4, TP1	154	203	241	5 L	60 L	A	
	Propionitrile	3	UN2404	II	3, 6.1	IB2, T7, TP1, TP13	None	202	243	Forbidden	60 L	E	40
	Propionyl chloride	3	UN1815	II	3, 8	IB1, T7, TP1	None	202	243	1 L	5 L	B	40
	n-Propyl acetate	3	UN1276	II	3	IB2, T4, TP1	150	202	242	5 L	60 L	B	
	Propyl alcohol, *see* **Propanol**												
	n-Propyl benzene	3	UN2364	III	3	B1, IB3, T2, TP1	150	203	242	60 L	220 L	A	
	Propyl chloride	3	UN1278	II	3	IB2, N34, T7, TP2	None	202	242	Forbidden	60 L	E	
	n-Propyl chloroformate	6.1	UN2740	I	6.1, 3, 8	2, A3, A6, A7, B9, B14, B32, B74, B77, N34, T20, TP2, TP13, TP38, TP44	None	227	244	Forbidden	Forbidden	B	21, 40, 100
	Propyl formates	3	UN1281	II	3	IB2, T4, TP1	150	202	242	5 L	60 L	B	
	n-Propyl isocyanate	6.1	UN2482	I	6.1, 3	1, B9, B14, B30, B72, T22, TP2, TP13, TP38, TP44	None	226	244	Forbidden	Forbidden	D	40

§172.101 - Hazardous Materials Table

Symbols	Hazardous materials descriptions and proper shipping names	Hazard class or Division	Identification Numbers	PG	Label Codes	Special provisions (§172.102)	(8) Packaging (§173.***)			(9) Quantity limitations		(10) Vessel stowage	
							Exceptions	Non-bulk	Bulk	Passenger aircraft/ rail	Cargo aircraft only	Location	Other
(1)	(2)	(3)	(4)	(5)	(6)	(7)	(8A)	(8B)	(8C)	(9A)	(9B)	(10A)	(10B)
	Propyl mercaptan, see **Propanethiols**												
	n-Propyl nitrate	3	UN1865	II	3	IB2, IP7	150	202	None	5 L	60 L	D	
	Propylamine	3	UN1277	II	3, 8	IB2, N34, T7, TP1	None	202	243	1 L	5 L	E	40
	Propylene *see also* **Petroleum gases, liquefied**	2.1	UN1077		2.1	19, T50	306	304	314, 315	Forbidden	150 kg	E	40
	Propylene chlorohydrin	6.1	UN2611	II	6.1, 3	IB2, T7, TP2, TP13	None	202	243	5 L	60 L	A	12, 40, 48
	Propylene oxide	3	UN1280	I	3	A3, N34, T11, TP2, TP7	None	201	243	1 L	30 L	E	40
	Propylene tetramer	3	UN2850	III	3	B1, IB3, T2, TP1	150	203	242	60 L	220 L	A	
	1,2-Propylenediamine	8	UN2258	II	8, 3	A3, A6, IB2, N34, T7, TP2	None	202	243	1 L	30 L	A	40
	Propyleneimine, stabilized	3	UN1921	I	3, 6.1	A3, N34, T14, TP2, TP13	None	201	243	1 L	30 L	B	40
	Propyltrichlorosilane	8	UN1816	II	8, 3	A7, B2, B6, IB2, N34, T7, TP2, TP13	None	202	243	Forbidden	30 L	C	40
	Prussic acid, see **Hydrogen cyanide**												
	Pyrethroid pesticide, liquid, flammable, toxic, *flash point less than 23 degrees C*	3	UN3350	I	3, 6.1	T14, TP2, TP13, TP27	None	201	243	Forbidden	30 L	B	40
				II	3, 6.1	IB2, T11, TP2, TP13, TP27	None	202	243	1 L	60 L	B	40
	Pyrethroid pesticide, liquid toxic	6.1	UN3352	I	6.1	T14, TP2, TP13, TP27	None	211	242	1 L	30 L	A	40
				II	6.1	IB2, T11, TP2, TP27	153	212	242	5 L	60 L	A	40
				III	6.1	IB3, T7, TP2, TP28	153	213	240	60 L	220 L	A	40
	Pyrethroid pesticide, liquid, toxic, flammable, *flash point not less than 23 degrees C*	6.1	UN3351	I	6.1, 3	T14, TP2, TP13, TP27	None	201	243	1 L	30 L	B	40
				II	6.1, 3	IB2, T11, TP2, TP13, TP27	None	202	243	5 L	60 L	B	40
				III	6.1, 3	IB3, T7, TP2, TP28	153	203	241	60 L	220 L	B	40
	Pyrethroid pesticide, solid, toxic	6.1	UN3349	I	6.1	IB7, IP1	None	211	242	5 kg	50 kg	A	40
				II	6.1	IB8, IP2, IP4	153	212	242	25 kg	100 kg	A	40
				III	6.1	IB8, IP3	153	213	240	100 kg	200 kg	A	40
	Pyridine	3	UN1282	II	3	IB2, T4, TP2	None	202	242	5 L	60 L	B	21, 100
	Pyridine perchlorate	Forbidden											
G	**Pyrophoric liquid, inorganic, n.o.s.**	4.2	UN3194	I	4.2		None	181	244	Forbidden	Forbidden	D	18
G	**Pyrophoric liquids, organic, n.o.s.**	4.2	UN2845	I	4.2	B11, T22, TP2, TP7	None	181	244	Forbidden	Forbidden	D	18
G	**Pyrophoric metals, n.o.s.,** *or* **Pyrophoric alloys, n.o.s.**	4.2	UN1383	I	4.2	B11	None	187	242	Forbidden	Forbidden	D	
G	**Pyrophoric organometallic compound, water-reactive, n.o.s.**	4.2	UN3203	I	4.2, 4.3	T21, TP2, TP7	None	187	242	Forbidden	Forbidden	D	18
G	**Pyrophoric solid, inorganic, n.o.s.**	4.2	UN3200	I	4.2		None	187	242	Forbidden	Forbidden	D	
G	**Pyrophoric solids, organic, n.o.s.**	4.2	UN2846	I	4.2		None	187	242	Forbidden	Forbidden	D	
	Pyrosulfuryl chloride	8	UN1817	II	8	B2, IB2, T8, TP2, TP12	154	202	242	1 L	30 L	C	40
	Pyroxylin solution or solvent, see **Nitrocellulose**												
	Pyrrolidine	3	UN1922	II	3, 8	IB2, T7, TP1	None	202	243	1 L	5 L	B	40
	Quebrachitol pentanitrate	Forbidden											
	Quicklime, see **Calcium oxide**												
	Quinoline	6.1	UN2656	III	6.1	IB3, T4, TP1	153	203	241	60 L	220 L	A	12
	R 12, see **Dichlorodifluoromethane**												
	R 12B1, see **Chlorodifluorobromomethane**												
	R 13, see **Chlorotrifluoromethane**												
	R 13B1, see **Bromotrifluoromethane**												
	R 14, see **Tetrafluoromethane**												
	R 21, see **Dichlorofluoromethane**												
	R 22, see **Chlorodifluoromethane**												

§172.101 - Hazardous Materials Table

Symbols	Hazardous materials descriptions and proper shipping names	Hazard class or Division	Identification Numbers	PG	Label Codes	Special provisions (§172.102)	(8) Packaging (§173.***) Exceptions	(8) Packaging (§173.***) Non-bulk	(8) Packaging (§173.***) Bulk	(9) Quantity limitations Passenger aircraft/ rail	(9) Quantity limitations Cargo aircraft only	(10) Vessel stowage Location	(10) Vessel stowage Other
(1)	(2)	(3)	(4)	(5)	(6)	(7)	(8A)	(8B)	(8C)	(9A)	(9B)	(10A)	(10B)
	R 114, see **Dichlorotetrafluoroethane**												
	R 115, see **Chloropentafluoroethane**												
	R 116, see **Hexafluoroethane**												
	R 124, see **Chlorotetrafluoroethane**												
	R 133a, see **Chlorotrifluoroethane**												
	R 152a, see **Difluoroethane**												
	R 500, see **Dichlorodifluoromethane and difluoroethane,** *etc.*												
	R 502, see **Chlorodifluoromethane and chloropentafluoroethane mixture,** *etc.*												
	R 503, see **Chlorotrifluoromethane and trifluoromethane,** *etc.*												
D	**Radioactive material, excepted package-articles manufactured from natural** *or* **depleted uranium** *or* **natural thorium**	7	UN2910		None		422, 426	422, 426	422, 426			A	
I	**Radioactive material, excepted package-articles manufactured from natural uranium** *or* **depleted uranium** *or* **natural thorium**	7	UN2909		None		422, 426	422, 426	422, 426			A	
D	**Radioactive material, excepted package-empty package** *or* **empty packaging**	7	UN2910		Empty		428	428	428			A	
I	**Radioactive material, excepted package-empty packaging**	7	UN2908		Empty		422, 428	422, 428	422, 428			A	
D	**Radioactive material, excepted package-instruments** *or* **articles**	7	UN2910		None		422, 424	422, 424	422, 424			A	
I	**Radioactive material, excepted package-instruments** *or* **articles**	7	UN2911		None		422, 424	422, 424	422, 424			A	
	Radioactive material, excepted package-limited quantity of material	7	UN2910		None		421, 422	421, 422	421, 422			A	
D	**Radioactive material, fissile, n.o.s.**	7	UN2918		7		453	417	417			A	40, 95
I	**Radioactive material, low specific activity (LSA-I)** *non fissile or fissile-excepted*	7	UN2912		7	T5, TP4, W7	421, 422, 428	427	427			A	95
I	**Radioactive material, low specific activity (LSA-II)** *non fissile or fissile-excepted*	7	UN3321		7	T5, TP4, W7	421, 422, 428	427	427			A	95
I	**Radioactive material, low specific activity (LSA-III)** *non fissile or fissile excepted*	7	UN3322		7	T5, TP4, W7	421, 422, 428	427	427			A	95
D	**Radioactive material, low specific activity, n.o.s.** *or* **Radioactive material, LSA, n.o.s.**	7	UN2912		7	T5, TP4	421, 428	427	427			A	95
D	**Radioactive material, n.o.s.**	7	UN2982		7		421, 428	415, 416	415, 416			A	40, 95
D	**Radioactive material, special form, n.o.s.**	7	UN2974		7		421, 424	415, 416	415, 416			A	95
D	**Radioactive material, surface contaminated object** *or* **Radioactive material, SCO**	7	UN2913		7		421, 424, 426	427	427			A	95
I	**Radioactive material, surface contaminated objects (SCO-I** *or* **SCO-II)** *non fissile or fissile-excepted*	7	UN2913		7		421, 422, 428	427	427			A	95
I	**Radioactive material, transported under special arrangement,** *non fissile or fissile excepted*	7	UN2919		7	139							
I	**Radioactive material, transported under special arrangement, fissile**	7	UN3331		7	139							
I	**Radioactive material, Type A package, fissile** *non-special form*	7	UN3327		7	W7, W8	453	417	417			A	95
I	**Radioactive material, Type A package** *non-special form, non fissile or fissile-excepted*	7	UN2915		7	W7, W8		415	415			A	95
I	**Radioactive material, Type A package, special form** *non fissile or fissile-excepted*	7	UN3332		7	W7, W8		415, 476	415, 476			A	95

§172.101 - Hazardous Materials Table

Symbols	Hazardous materials descriptions and proper shipping names	Hazard class or Division	Identification Numbers	PG	Label Codes	Special provisions (§172.102)	(8) Packaging (§173.***)			(9) Quantity limitations		(10) Vessel stowage	
							Exceptions	Non-bulk	Bulk	Passenger aircraft/ rail	Cargo aircraft only	Location	Other
(1)	(2)	(3)	(4)	(5)	(6)	(7)	(8A)	(8B)	(8C)	(9A)	(9B)	(10A)	(10B)
I	**Radioactive material, Type A package, special form, fissile**	7	UN3333		7	W7, W8	453	417, 476	417, 476			A	
I	**Radioactive material, Type B(M) package, fissile**	7	UN3329		7		453	417	417			A	
I	**Radioactive material, Type B(M) package** *non fissile or fissile-excepted*	7	UN2917		7			416	416			A	95
I	**Radioactive material, Type B(U) package, fissile**	7	UN3328		7		453	417	417			A	
I	**Radioactive material, Type B(U) package** *non fissile or fissile-excepted*	7	UN2916		7			416	416			A	95
I	**Radioactive material, uranium hexafluoride** *non fissile or fissile-excepted*	7	UN2978		7, 8		423	420, 427	420, 427			A	95
I	**Radioactive material, uranium hexafluoride, fissile**	7	UN2977		7, 8		453	417, 420	417, 420			A	
	Railway torpedo, see **Signals, railway track, explosive**												
	Rare gases and nitrogen mixtures, compressed	2.2	UN1981		2.2		306	302	None	75 kg	150 kg	A	
	Rare gases and oxygen mixtures, compressed	2.2	UN1980		2.2	79	306	302	None	75 kg	150 kg	A	
	Rare gases mixtures, compressed	2.2	UN1979		2.2		306	302	None	75 kg	150 kg	A	
	RC 318, see **Octafluorocyclobutane**												
	RDX and cyclotetramethylenetetranitramine, wetted *or* **desensitized** *see* **RDX and HMX mixtures, wetted or desensitized**												
	RDX and HMX mixtures, wetted *with not less than 15 percent water by mass or* **RDX and HMX mixtures, desensitized** *with not less than 10 percent phlegmatizer by mass*	1.1D	UN0391	II	1.1D		None	62	None	Forbidden	Forbidden	10	
	RDX and Octogen mixtures, wetted *or* **desensitized** *see* **RDX and HMX mixtures, wetted** *or* **desensitized** *etc.*												
	RDX, see **Cyclotrimethylene trinitramine,** *etc.*												
	Receptacles, small, containing gas (gas cartridges) *flammable, without release device, not refillable and not exceeding 1 L capacity*	2.1	UN2037		2.1		306	304	None	1 kg	15 kg	B	40
	Receptacles, small, containing gas (gas cartridges) *non-flammable, without release device, not refillable and not exceeding 1 L capacity*	2.2	UN2037		2.2		306	304	None	1 kg	15 kg	B	40
	Red phosphorus, see **Phosphorus, amorphous**												
	Refrigerant gas R 404A	2.2	UN3337		2.2	T50	306	304	314, 315	75 kg	150 kg	A	
	Refrigerant gas R 407A	2.2	UN3338		2.2	T50	306	304	314, 315	75 kg	150 kg	A	
	Refrigerant gas R 407B	2.2	UN3339		2.2	T50	306	304	314, 315	75 kg	150 kg	A	
	Refrigerant gas R 407C	2.2	UN3340		2.2	T50	306	304	314, 315	75 kg	150 kg	A	
G	**Refrigerant gases, n.o.s.**	2.2	UN1078		2.2	T50	306	304	314, 315	75 kg	150 kg	A	
D	**Refrigerant gases, n.o.s.** *or* **Dispersant gases, n.o.s.**	2.1	NA1954		2.1	T50	306	304	314, 315	Forbidden	150 kg	D	40
	Refrigerating machines, *containing flammable, non-toxic, liquefied gas*	2.1	UN3358		2.1		306	306	306	Forbidden	Forbidden	C	40
	Refrigerating machines, *containing non-flammable, non-toxic, liquefied gas or ammonia solution (UN2672)*	2.2	UN2857		2.2	A53	306, 307	306	306, 307	450 kg	450 kg	A	
	Regulated medical waste	6.2	UN3291	II	6.2	A13	134, 197	197	197	No limit	No limit	A	40
	Release devices, explosive	1.4S	UN0173	II	1.4S		None	62	None	25 kg	100 kg	05	
	Resin solution, *flammable*	3	UN1866	I	3	B52, T11, TP1, TP8	150	201	243	1 L	30 L	E	
				II	3	B52, IB2, T4, TP1, TP8	150	173	242	5 L	60 L	B	
				III	3	B1, B52, IB3, T2, TP1	150	173	242	60 L	220 L	A	

§172.101 - Hazardous Materials Table

Symbols	Hazardous materials descriptions and proper shipping names	Hazard class or Division	Identification Numbers	PG	Label Codes	Special provisions (§172.102)	(8) Packaging (§173.***)			(9) Quantity limitations		(10) Vessel stowage	
							Exceptions	Non-bulk	Bulk	Passenger aircraft/rail	Cargo aircraft only	Location	Other
(1)	(2)	(3)	(4)	(5)	(6)	(7)	(8A)	(8B)	(8C)	(9A)	(9B)	(10A)	(10B)
	Resorcinol	6.1	UN2876	III	6.1	IB8, IP3	153	213	240	100 kg	200 kg	A	
	Rifle grenade, see **Grenades,** *hand or rifle, etc.*												
	Rifle powder, see **Powder, smokeless** *(UN 0160)*												
	Rivets, explosive	1.4S	UN0174	II	1.4S		None	62	None	25 kg	100 kg	05	
	Road asphalt or tar liquid, see **Tars, liquid,** *etc.*												
	Rocket motors	1.3C	UN0186	II	1.3C	109	None	62	None	Forbidden	220 kg	03	
	Rocket motors	1.1C	UN0280	II	1.1C	109	None	62	None	Forbidden	Forbidden	03	
	Rocket motors	1.2C	UN0281	II	1.2C	109	None	62	None	Forbidden	Forbidden	03	
	Rocket motors, liquid fueled	1.2J	UN0395	II	1.2J	109	None	62	None	Forbidden	Forbidden	04	23E
	Rocket motors, liquid fueled	1.3J	UN0396	II	1.3J	109	None	62	None	Forbidden	Forbidden	04	23E
	Rocket motors with hypergolic liquids *with or without an expelling charge*	1.3L	UN0250	II	1.3L	109	None	62	None	Forbidden	Forbidden	08	8E, 14E, 15E
	Rocket motors with hypergolic liquids *with or without an expelling charge*	1.2L	UN0322	II	1.2L	109	None	62	None	Forbidden	Forbidden	08	8E, 14E, 15E
	Rockets, line-throwing	1.2G	UN0238	II	1.2G		None	62	None	Forbidden	Forbidden	07	
	Rockets, line-throwing	1.3G	UN0240	II	1.3G		None	62	None	Forbidden	75 kg	07	
	Rockets, line-throwing	1.4G	UN0453	II	1.4G		None	62	None	Forbidden	75 kg	06	
	Rockets, liquid fueled *with bursting charge*	1.1J	UN0397	II	1.1J		None	62	None	Forbidden	Forbidden	04	23E
	Rockets, liquid fueled *with bursting charge*	1.2J	UN0398	II	1.2J		None	62	None	Forbidden	Forbidden	04	23E
	Rockets, *with bursting charge*	1.1F	UN0180	II	1.1F		None	62	None	Forbidden	Forbidden	08	
	Rockets, *with bursting charge*	1.1E	UN0181	II	1.1E		None	62	None	Forbidden	Forbidden	03	
	Rockets, *with bursting charge*	1.2E	UN0182	II	1.2E		None	62	None	Forbidden	Forbidden	03	
	Rockets, *with bursting charge*	1.2F	UN0295	II	1.2F		None	62	None	Forbidden	Forbidden	08	
	Rockets, *with expelling charge*	1.2C	UN0436	II	1.2C		None	62	None	Forbidden	Forbidden	03	
	Rockets, *with expelling charge*	1.3C	UN0437	II	1.3C		None	62	None	Forbidden	Forbidden	03	
	Rockets, *with expelling charge*	1.4C	UN0438	II	1.4C		None	62	None	Forbidden	75 kg	02	
	Rockets, *with inert head*	1.3C	UN0183	II	1.3C		None	62	None	Forbidden	Forbidden	03	
	Rockets, *with inert head*	1.2C	UN0502		1.2C		None	62	None	Forbidden	Forbidden	B	1E, 5E
	Rosin oil	3	UN1286	II III	3 3	IB2, T4, TP1 B1, IB3, T2, TP1	150 150	202 203	242 242	5 L 60 L	60 L 220 L	B A	
	Rubber solution	3	UN1287	II III	3 3	IB2, T4, TP1, TP8 B1, IB3, T2, TP1	150 150	202 203	242 242	5 L 60 L	60 L 220 L	B A	
	Rubidium	4.3	UN1423	I	4.3	22, A7, A19, IB1, IP1, N34, N40, N45	None	211	242	Forbidden	15 kg	D	
	Rubidium hydroxide	8	UN2678	II	8	IB8, IP2, IP4, T7, TP2	154	212	240	15 kg	50 kg	A	
	Rubidium hydroxide solution	8	UN2677	II III	8 8	B2, IB2, T7, TP2 IB3, T4, TP1	154 154	202 203	242 241	1 L 5 L	30 L 60 L	A A	
	Safety fuse, see **Fuse, safety**												
G	**Samples, explosive,** *other than initiating explosives*		UN0190	II		113	None	62	None	Forbidden	Forbidden	14	12E
	Sand acid, see **Fluorosilicic acid**												
	Seed cake, *containing vegetable oil solvent extractions and expelled seeds, with not more than 10 percent of oil and when the amount of moisture is higher than 11 percent, with not more than 20 percent of oil and moisture combined*	4.2	UN1386	III	None	IB8, IP3, IP6, N7	None	213	241	Forbidden	Forbidden	A	13
I	**Seed cake** *with more than 1.5 percent oil and not more than 11 percent moisture*	4.2	UN1386	III	None	IB8, IP3, IP6, N7	None	213	241	Forbidden	Forbidden	E	13
I	**Seed cake** *with not more than 1.5 percent oil and not more than 11 percent moisture*	4.2	UN2217	III	None	IB8, IP3, IP6, N7	None	213	241	Forbidden	Forbidden	A	13
	Selenates *or* **Selenites**	6.1	UN2630	I	6.1	IB7, IP1	None	211	242	5 kg	50 kg	E	

§172.101 - Hazardous Materials Table

Symbols	Hazardous materials descriptions and proper shipping names	Hazard class or Division	Identification Numbers	PG	Label Codes	Special provisions (§172.102)	(8) Packaging (§173.***) Exceptions	Non-bulk	Bulk	(9) Quantity limitations Passenger aircraft/ rail	Cargo aircraft only	(10) Vessel stowage Location	Other
(1)	(2)	(3)	(4)	(5)	(6)	(7)	(8A)	(8B)	(8C)	(9A)	(9B)	(10A)	(10B)
	Selenic acid	8	UN1905	I	8	IB7, IP1, N34	None	211	242	Forbidden	25 kg	A	
	Selenium compound, n.o.s.	6.1	UN3283	I	6.1	IB7, IP1, T14, TP2, TP27	None	211	242	5 kg	50 kg	B	
				II	6.1	IB8, IP2, IP4, T11, TP2, TP27	None	212	242	25 kg	100 kg	B	
				III	6.1	IB8, IP3, T7, TP1, TP28	153	213	240	100 kg	200 kg	A	
	Selenium disulfide	6.1	UN2657	II	6.1	IB8, IP2, IP4	None	212	242	25 kg	100 kg	A	
	Selenium hexafluoride	2.3	UN2194		2.3, 8	1	None	302	None	Forbidden	Forbidden	D	40
	Selenium nitride	Forbidden											
	Selenium oxychloride	8	UN2879	I	8, 6.1	A3, A6, A7, N34, T10, TP2, TP12, TP13	None	201	243	0.5 L	2.5 L	E	40
	Self-defense spray, aerosol, see **Aerosols**, *etc.*												
+ A D	**Self-defense spray, non-pressurized**	9	NA3334	III	9	A37	155	203	None	No limit	No limit	A	
G	**Self-heating liquid, corrosive, inorganic, n.o.s.**	4.2	UN3188	II III	4.2, 8 4.2, 8	IB2 IB2	None None	202 203	243 241	1 L 5 L	5 L 60 L	C C	
G	**Self-heating liquid, corrosive, organic, n.o.s.**	4.2	UN3185	II III	4.2, 8 4.2, 8	IB2 IB2	None None	202 203	243 241	1 L 5 L	5 L 60 L	C C	
G	**Self-heating liquid, inorganic, n.o.s.**	4.2	UN3186	II III	4.2 4.2	IB2 IB2	None None	202 203	242 241	1 L 5 L	5 L 60 L	C C	
G	**Self-heating liquid, organic, n.o.s.**	4.2	UN3183	II III	4.2 4.2	IB2 IB2	None None	202 203	242 241	1 L 5 L	5 L 60 L	C C	
G	**Self-heating liquid, toxic, inorganic, n.o.s.**	4.2	UN3187	II III	4.2, 6.1 4.2, 6.1	IB2 IB2	None None	202 203	243 241	1 L 5 L	5 L 60 L	C C	
G	**Self-heating liquid, toxic, organic, n.o.s.**	4.2	UN3184	II III	4.2, 6.1 4.2, 6.1	IB2 IB2	None None	202 203	243 241	1 L 5 L	5 L 60 L	C C	
G	**Self-heating solid, corrosive, inorganic, n.o.s.**	4.2	UN3192	II III	4.2, 8 4.2, 8	IB5, IP2 IB8, IP3	None None	212 213	242 242	15 kg 25 kg	50 kg 100 kg	C C	
G	**Self-heating, solid, corrosive, organic, n.o.s.**	4.2	UN3126	II III	4.2, 8 4.2, 8	IB5, IP2 IB8, IP3	None None	212 213	242 242	15 kg 25 kg	50 kg 100 kg	C C	
G	**Self-heating solid, inorganic, n.o.s.**	4.2	UN3190	II III	4.2 4.2	IB6, IP2 IB8, IP3	None None	212 213	241 241	15 kg 25 kg	50 kg 100 kg	C C	
G	**Self-heating, solid, organic, n.o.s.**	4.2	UN3088	II III	4.2 4.2	IB6, IP2 IB8, IP3	None None	212 213	241 241	15 kg 25 kg	50 kg 100 kg	C C	
G	**Self-heating, solid, oxidizing, n.o.s.**	4.2	UN3127		4.2, 5.1		None	214	214	Forbidden	Forbidden		
G	**Self-heating solid, toxic, inorganic, n.o.s.**	4.2	UN3191	II III	4.2, 6.1 4.2, 6.1	IB5, IP2 IB8, IP3	None None	212 213	242 242	15 kg 25 kg	50 kg 100 kg	C C	
G	**Self-heating, solid, toxic, organic, n.o.s.**	4.2	UN3128	II III	4.2, 6.1 4.2, 6.1	IB5, IP2 IB8, IP3	None None	212 213	242 242	15 kg 25 kg	50 kg 100 kg	C C	
	Self-propelled vehicle, see **Engines** *or* **Batteries** *etc.*												
G	**Self-reactive liquid type B**	4.1	UN3221	II	4.1	53	None	224	None	Forbidden	Forbidden	D	61
G	**Self-reactive liquid type B, temperature controlled**	4.1	UN3231	II	4.1	53	None	224	None	Forbidden	Forbidden	D	2, 61
G	**Self-reactive liquid type C**	4.1	UN3223	II	4.1		None	224	None	5 L	10 L	D	61
G	**Self-reactive liquid type C, temperature controlled**	4.1	UN3233	II	4.1		None	224	None	Forbidden	Forbidden	D	2, 61
G	**Self-reactive liquid type D**	4.1	UN3225	II	4.1		None	224	None	5 L	10 L	D	61
G	**Self-reactive liquid type D, temperature controlled**	4.1	UN3235	II	4.1		None	224	None	Forbidden	Forbidden	D	2, 61
G	**Self-reactive liquid type E**	4.1	UN3227	II	4.1		None	224	None	10 L	25 L	D	61
G	**Self-reactive liquid type E, temperature controlled**	4.1	UN3237	II	4.1		None	224	None	Forbidden	Forbidden	D	2, 61
G	**Self-reactive liquid type F**	4.1	UN3229	II	4.1		None	224	None	10 L	25 L	D	61
G	**Self-reactive liquid type F, temperature controlled**	4.1	UN3239	II	4.1		None	224	None	Forbidden	Forbidden	D	2, 61
G	**Self-reactive solid type B**	4.1	UN3222	II	4.1	53	None	224	None	Forbidden	Forbidden	D	61
G	**Self-reactive solid type B, temperature controlled**	4.1	UN3232	II	4.1	53	None	224	None	Forbidden	Forbidden	D	2, 61
G	**Self-reactive solid type C**	4.1	UN3224	II	4.1		None	224	None	5 kg	10 kg	D	61
G	**Self-reactive solid type C, temperature controlled**	4.1	UN3234	II	4.1		None	224	None	Forbidden	Forbidden	D	2, 61

§172.101 - Hazardous Materials Table

Symbols	Hazardous materials descriptions and proper shipping names	Hazard class or Division	Identification Numbers	PG	Label Codes	Special provisions (§172.102)	(8) Packaging (§173.***) Exceptions	Non-bulk	Bulk	(9) Quantity limitations Passenger aircraft/rail	Cargo aircraft only	(10) Vessel stowage Location	Other
(1)	(2)	(3)	(4)	(5)	(6)	(7)	(8A)	(8B)	(8C)	(9A)	(9B)	(10A)	(10B)
G	**Self-reactive solid type D**	4.1	UN3226	II	4.1		None	224	None	5 kg	10 kg	D	61
G	**Self-reactive solid type D, temperature controlled**	4.1	UN3236	II	4.1		None	224	None	Forbidden	Forbidden	D	2, 61
G	**Self-reactive solid type E**	4.1	UN3228	II	4.1		None	224	None	10 kg	25 kg	D	61
G	**Self-reactive solid type E, temperature controlled**	4.1	UN3238	II	4.1		None	224	None	Forbidden	Forbidden	D	2, 61
G	**Self-reactive solid type F**	4.1	UN3230	II	4.1		None	224	None	10 kg	25 kg	D	61
G	**Self-reactive solid type F, temperature controlled**	4.1	UN3240	II	4.1		None	224	None	Forbidden	Forbidden	D	2, 61
	Shale oil	3	UN1288	I	3	T11, TP1, TP8, TP27	None	201	243	1 L	30 L	B	
				II	3	IB2, T4, TP1, TP8	150	202	242	5 L	60 L	B	
				III	3	B1, IB3, T2, TP1	150	203	242	60 L	220 L	A	
	Shaped charges, see **Charges, shaped,** *etc.*												
	Signal devices, hand	1.4G	UN0191	II	1.4G		None	62	None	Forbidden	75 kg	06	
	Signal devices, hand	1.4S	UN0373	II	1.4S		None	62	None	25 kg	100 kg	05	
	Signals, distress, *ship*	1.1G	UN0194	II	1.1G		None	62	None	Forbidden	Forbidden	07	
	Signals, distress, *ship*	1.3G	UN0195	II	1.3G		None	62	None	Forbidden	75 kg	07	
	Signals, highway, see **Signal devices, hand**												
	Signals, railway track, explosive	1.1G	UN0192	II	1.1G		None	62	None	Forbidden	Forbidden	07	
	Signals, railway track, explosive	1.4S	UN0193	II	1.4S		None	62	None	25 kg	100 kg	05	
	Signals, railway track, explosive	1.3G	UN0492		1.3G		None	62	None	Forbidden	Forbidden	07	
	Signals, railway track, explosive	1.4G	UN0493		1.4G		None	62	None	Forbidden	75 kg	06	
	Signals, ship distress, water-activated, see **Contrivances, water-activated,** *etc.*												
	Signals, smoke	1.1G	UN0196	II	1.1G		None	62	None	Forbidden	Forbidden	07	
	Signals, smoke	1.4G	UN0197	II	1.4G		None	62	None	Forbidden	75 kg	06	
	Signals, smoke	1.2G	UN0313	II	1.2G		None	62	None	Forbidden	Forbidden	07	
	Signals, smoke	1.3G	UN0487	II	1.3G		None	62	None	Forbidden	Forbidden	07	
	Silane, compressed	2.1	UN2203		2.1		None	302	None	Forbidden	Forbidden	E	40, 57, 104
	Silicofluoric acid, see **Fluorosilicic acid**												
	Silicon chloride, see **Silicon tetrachloride**												
	Silicon powder, amorphous	4.1	UN1346	III	4.1	A1, IB8, IP3	None	213	240	25 kg	100 kg	A	
	Silicon tetrachloride	8	UN1818	II	8	A3, A6, B2, B6, IB2, T7, TP2, TP7	154	202	242	1 L	30 L	C	40
	Silicon tetrafluoride, compressed	2.3	UN1859		2.3, 8	2	None	302	None	Forbidden	Forbidden	D	40
	Silver acetylide (dry)	Forbidden											
	Silver arsenite	6.1	UN1683	II	6.1	IB8, IP2, IP4	None	212	242	25 kg	100 kg	A	
	Silver azide (dry)	Forbidden											
	Silver chlorite (dry)	Forbidden											
	Silver cyanide	6.1	UN1684	II	6.1	IB8, IP2, IP4	None	212	242	25 kg	100 kg	A	26, 40
	Silver fulminate (dry)	Forbidden											
	Silver nitrate	5.1	UN1493	II	5.1	IB8, IP4	152	212	242	5 kg	25 kg	A	
	Silver oxalate (dry)	Forbidden											
	Silver picrate (dry)	Forbidden											
	Silver picrate, wetted *with not less than 30 percent water, by mass*	4.1	UN1347	I	4.1		None	211	None	Forbidden	Forbidden	D	28, 36
	Sludge, acid	8	UN1906	II	8	A3, A7, B2, IB2, N34, T8, TP2, TP12	None	202	242	Forbidden	30 L	C	14
D	**Smokeless powder for small arms** *(100 pounds or less)*	4.1	NA3178	I	4.1	16	None	171	None	Forbidden	7.3 kg	A	
	Soda lime *with more than 4 percent sodium hydroxide*	8	UN1907	III	8	IB8, IP3	154	213	240	25 kg	100 kg	A	

§172.101 - Hazardous Materials Table

Symbols	Hazardous materials descriptions and proper shipping names	Hazard class or Division	Identification Numbers	PG	Label Codes	Special provisions (§172.102)	(8) Packaging (§173.***)			(9) Quantity limitations		(10) Vessel stowage	
							Exceptions	Non-bulk	Bulk	Passenger aircraft/ rail	Cargo aircraft only	Location	Other
(1)	(2)	(3)	(4)	(5)	(6)	(7)	(8A)	(8B)	(8C)	(9A)	(9B)	(10A)	(10B)
	Sodium	4.3	UN1428	I	4.3	A7, A8, A19, A20, B9, B48, B68, IB4, IP1, N34, T9, TP3, TP7, TP46	None	211	244	Forbidden	15 kg	D	
	Sodium aluminate, solid	8	UN2812	III	8	IB8, IP3	154	213	240	25 kg	100 kg	A	
	Sodium aluminate, solution	8	UN1819	II III	8 8	B2, IB2, T7, TP2 IB3, T4, TP1	154 154	202 203	242 241	1 L 5 L	30 L 60 L	A A	
	Sodium aluminum hydride	4.3	UN2835	II	4.3	A8, A19, A20, IB1	151	212	242	Forbidden	50 kg	E	
	Sodium ammonium vanadate	6.1	UN2863	II	6.1	IB8, IP2, IP4	None	212	242	25 kg	100 kg	A	
	Sodium arsanilate	6.1	UN2473	III	6.1	IB8, IP3	153	213	240	100 kg	200 kg	A	
	Sodium arsenate	6.1	UN1685	II	6.1	IB8, IP2, IP4	None	212	242	25 kg	100 kg	A	
	Sodium arsenite, aqueous solutions	6.1	UN1686	II III	6.1 6.1	IB2, T7, TP2 IB3, T4, TP2	None 153	202 203	243 241	5 L 60 L	60 L 220 L	A A	
	Sodium arsenite, solid	6.1	UN2027	II	6.1	IB8, IP2, IP4	None	212	242	25 kg	100 kg	A	
	Sodium azide	6.1	UN1687	II	6.1	IB8, IP2, IP4	None	212	242	25 kg	100 kg	A	36, 52, 91
	Sodium bifluoride, see **Sodium hydrogendifluoride**												
	Sodium bisulfite, solution, see **Bisulfites, aqueous solutions, n.o.s.**												
	Sodium borohydride	4.3	UN1426	I	4.3	N40	None	211	242	Forbidden	15 kg	E	
	Sodium borohydride and sodium hydroxide solution, *with not more than 12 percent sodium borohydride and not more than 40 percent sodium hydroxide by mass*	8	UN3320	II III	8 8	B2, IB2, N34, T7, TP2 B2, IB3, N34, T4, TP2	154 154	202 203	242 241	1 L 5 L	30 L 60 L	A A	26
	Sodium bromate	5.1	UN1494	II	5.1	IB8, IP4	152	212	242	5 kg	25 kg	A	56, 58, 106
	Sodium cacodylate	6.1	UN1688	II	6.1	IB8, IP2, IP4	None	212	242	25 kg	100 kg	A	26
	Sodium chlorate	5.1	UN1495	II	5.1	A9, IB8, IP4, N34, T4, TP1	152	212	240	5 kg	25 kg	A	56, 58, 106
	Sodium chlorate, aqueous solution	5.1	UN2428	II III	5.1 5.1	A2, IB2, T4, TP1 A2, IB2, T4, TP1	152 152	202 203	241 241	1 L 2.5 L	5 L 30 L	B B	56, 58, 106 56, 58, 69, 106
	Sodium chlorate mixed with dinitrotoluene, see **Explosive blasting, type C**												
	Sodium chlorite	5.1	UN1496	II	5.1	A9, IB8, IP2, IP4, N34, T4, TP1	None	212	242	5 kg	25 kg	A	56, 58,106
	Sodium chloroacetate	6.1	UN2659	III	6.1	IB8, IP3	153	213	240	100 kg	200 kg	A	
	Sodium cuprocyanide, solid	6.1	UN2316	I	6.1	IB7, IP1	None	211	242	5 kg	50 kg	A	26
	Sodium cuprocyanide, solution	6.1	UN2317	I	6.1	T14, TP2, TP13	None	201	243	1 L	30 L	B	26, 40
	Sodium cyanide	6.1	UN1689	I	6.1	B69, B77, IB7, IP1, N74, N75, T14, TP2, TP13	None	211	242	5 kg	50 kg	B	52
	Sodium dichloroisocyanurate or Sodium dichloro-s-triazinetrione, see **Dichloroisocyanuric acid** *etc.*												
	Sodium dinitro-o-cresolate, *dry or wetted with less than 15 percent water, by mass*	1.3C	UN0234	II	1.3C		None	62	None	Forbidden	Forbidden	10	5E
	Sodium dinitro-o-cresolate, wetted *with not less than 15 percent water, by mass*	4.1	UN1348	I	4.1, 6.1	23, A8, A19, A20, N41	None	211	None	1 kg	15 kg	E	28, 36
	Sodium dithionite *or* **Sodium hydrosulfite**	4.2	UN1384	II	4.2	A19, A20, IB6, IP2	None	212	241	15 kg	50 kg	E	13
	Sodium fluoride	6.1	UN1690	III	6.1	IB8, IP3, T4, TP1	153	213	240	100 kg	200 kg	A	26
	Sodium fluoroacetate	6.1	UN2629	I	6.1	IB7, IP1	None	211	242	5 kg	50 kg	E	
	Sodium fluorosilicate	6.1	UN2674	III	6.1	IB8, IP3	153	213	240	100 kg	200 kg	A	26
	Sodium hydrate, see **Sodium hydroxide, solid**												
	Sodium hydride	4.3	UN1427	I	4.3	A19, N40	None	211	242	Forbidden	15 kg	E	
	Sodium hydrogendifluoride, *solid*	8	UN2439	II	8	IB8, IP2, IP4, N3, N34	154	212	240	15 kg	50 kg	A	12, 25, 26, 40

§172.101 - Hazardous Materials Table

Symbols	Hazardous materials descriptions and proper shipping names	Hazard class or Division	Identification Numbers	PG	Label Codes	Special provisions (§172.102)	(8) Packaging (§173.***)			(9) Quantity limitations		(10) Vessel stowage	
							Exceptions	Non-bulk	Bulk	Passenger aircraft/ rail	Cargo aircraft only	Location	Other
(1)	(2)	(3)	(4)	(5)	(6)	(7)	(8A)	(8B)	(8C)	(9A)	(9B)	(10A)	(10B)
	Sodium hydrogendifluoride *solution*	8	UN2439	II	8	IB8, IP2, IP4, N3, N34	154	202	242	1 L	30 L	A	12, 25, 26, 40
	Sodium hydrosulfide, *with less than 25 percent water of crystallization*	4.2	UN2318	II	4.2	A7, A19, A20, IB6, IP2	None	212	241	15 kg	50 kg	A	
	Sodium hydrosulfide *with not less than 25 percent water of crystallization*	8	UN2949	II	8	A7, IB8, IP2, IP4, T7, TP2	154	212	240	15 kg	50 kg	A	26
	Sodium hydrosulfite, *see* **Sodium dithionite**												
	Sodium hydroxide, solid	8	UN1823	II	8	IB8, IP2, IP4	154	212	240	15 kg	50 kg	A	
	Sodium hydroxide solution	8	UN1824	II III	8 8	B2, IB2, N34, T7, TP2 IB3, N34, T4, TP1	154 154	202 203	242 241	1 L 5 L	30 L 60 L	A A	
	Sodium hypochlorite, solution, see **Hypochlorite solutions** *etc.*												
	Sodium metal, liquid alloy, see **Alkali metal alloys, liquid, n.o.s.**												
	Sodium methylate	4.2	UN1431	II	4.2, 8	A19, IB5, IP2	None	212	242	15 kg	50 kg	B	
	Sodium methylate solutions *in alcohol*	3	UN1289	II III	3, 8 3, 8	IB2, T7, TP1, TP8 B1, IB3, T4, TP1	None 150	202 203	243 242	1 L 5 L	5 L 60 L	B A	
	Sodium monoxide	8	UN1825	II	8	IB8, IP2, IP4	154	212	240	15 kg	50 kg	A	
	Sodium nitrate	5.1	UN1498	III	5.1	A1, A29, IB8, IP3	152	213	240	25 kg	100 kg	A	
	Sodium nitrate and potassium nitrate mixtures	5.1	UN1499	III	5.1	A1, A29, IB8, IP3	152	213	240	25 kg	100 kg	A	
	Sodium nitrite	5.1	UN1500	III	5.1, 6.1	A1, A29, IB8, IP3	152	213	240	25 kg	100 kg	A	56, 58
	Sodium pentachlorophenate	6.1	UN2567	II	6.1	IB8, IP2, IP4	None	212	242	25 kg	100 kg	A	
	Sodium perchlorate	5.1	UN1502	II	5.1	IB6, IP2	152	212	242	5 kg	25 kg	A	56, 58, 106
	Sodium permanganate	5.1	UN1503	II	5.1	IB6, IP2	152	212	242	5 kg	25 kg	D	56, 58, 69, 106, 107
	Sodium peroxide	5.1	UN1504	I	5.1	A20, IB6, IP1, N34	None	211	None	Forbidden	15 kg	B	13, 75, 106
	Sodium peroxoborate, anhydrous	5.1	UN3247	II	5.1	IB8, IP4	152	212	240	5 kg	25 kg	A	13, 25, 106
	Sodium persulfate	5.1	UN1505	III	5.1	A1, IB8, IP3	152	213	240	25 kg	100 kg	A	
	Sodium phosphide	4.3	UN1432	I	4.3, 6.1	A19, N40	None	211	None	Forbidden	15 kg	E	40, 85
	Sodium picramate, *dry or wetted with less than 20 percent water, by mass*	1.3C	UN0235	II	1.3C		None	62	None	Forbidden	Forbidden	10	5E
	Sodium picramate, wetted *with not less than 20 percent water, by mass*	4.1	UN1349	I	4.1	23, A8, A19, N41	None	211	None	Forbidden	15 kg	E	28, 36
	Sodium picryl peroxide	Forbidden											
	Sodium potassium alloys, see **Potassium sodium alloys**												
	Sodium selenate, see **Selenates** *or* **Selenites**												
	Sodium sulfide, anhydrous *or* **Sodium sulfide** *with less than 30 percent water of crystallization*	4.2	UN1385	II	4.2	A19, A20, IB6, IP2, N34	None	212	241	15 kg	50 kg	A	
	Sodium sulfide, hydrated *with not less than 30 percent water*	8	UN1849	II	8	IB8, IP2, IP4, T7, TP2	154	212	240	15 kg	50 kg	A	26
	Sodium superoxide	5.1	UN2547	I	5.1	A20, IB6, IP1, N34	None	211	None	Forbidden	15 kg	E	13, 75, 106
	Sodium tetranitride	Forbidden											
G	**Solids containing corrosive liquid, n.o.s.**	8	UN3244	II	8	49, IB5	154	212	240	15 kg	50 kg	B	40
G	**Solids containing flammable liquid, n.o.s.**	4.1	UN3175	II	4.1	47, IB6, IP2	151	212	240	15 kg	50 kg	B	
G	**Solids containing toxic liquid, n.o.s.**	6.1	UN3243	II	6.1	48, IB2	None	212	240	25 kg	100 kg	B	40
	Sounding devices, explosive	1.2F	UN0204	II	1.2F		None	62	None	Forbidden	Forbidden	08	
	Sounding devices, explosive	1.1F	UN0296	II	1.1F		None	62	None	Forbidden	Forbidden	08	
	Sounding devices, explosive	1.1D	UN0374	II	1.1D		None	62	None	Forbidden	Forbidden	07	
	Sounding devices, explosive	1.2D	UN0375	II	1.2D		None	62	None	Forbidden	Forbidden	07	
	Spirits of salt, see **Hydrochloric acid**												
	Squibs, see **Igniters** *etc.*												
	Stannic chloride, anhydrous	8	UN1827	II	8	B2, IB2, T7, TP2	154	202	242	1 L	30 L	C	

§172.101 - Hazardous Materials Table

Symbols	Hazardous materials descriptions and proper shipping names	Hazard class or Division	Identification Numbers	PG	Label Codes	Special provisions (§172.102)	(8) Packaging (§173.***)			(9) Quantity limitations		(10) Vessel stowage	
							Exceptions	Non-bulk	Bulk	Passenger aircraft/rail	Cargo aircraft only	Location	Other
(1)	(2)	(3)	(4)	(5)	(6)	(7)	(8A)	(8B)	(8C)	(9A)	(9B)	(10A)	(10B)
	Stannic chloride pentahydrate	8	UN2440	III	8	IB8, IP3	154	213	240	25 kg	100 kg	A	
	Stannic phosphide	4.3	UN1433	I	4.3, 6.1	A19, N40	None	211	242	Forbidden	15 kg	E	40, 85
	Steel swarf, see **Ferrous metal borings,** *etc.*												
	Stibine	2.3	UN2676		2.3, 2.1	1	None	304	None	Forbidden	Forbidden	D	40
	Storage batteries, wet, see **Batteries,** *wet etc.*												
	Strontium arsenite	6.1	UN1691	II	6.1	IB8, IP2, IP4	None	212	242	25 kg	100 kg	A	
	Strontium chlorate	5.1	UN1506	II	5.1	A1, A9, IB8, IP2, IP4, N34	152	212	242	5 kg	25 kg	A	56, 58, 106
	Strontium nitrate	5.1	UN1507	III	5.1	A1, A29, IB8, IP3	152	213	240	25 kg	100 kg	A	
	Strontium perchlorate	5.1	UN1508	II	5.1	IB6, IP2	152	212	242	5 kg	25 kg	A	56, 58, 106
	Strontium peroxide	5.1	UN1509	II	5.1	IB6, IP2	152	212	242	5 kg	25 kg	A	13, 75, 106
	Strontium phosphide	4.3	UN2013	I	4.3, 6.1	A19, N40	None	211	None	Forbidden	15 kg	E	40, 85
	Strychnine *or* **Strychnine salts**	6.1	UN1692	I	6.1	IB7, IP1	None	211	242	5 kg	50 kg	A	40
	Styphnic acid, *see* **Trinitroresorcinol,** *etc.*												
	Styrene monomer, stabilized	3	UN2055	III	3	B1, IB3, T2, TP1	150	203	242	60 L	220 L	A	
G	**Substances, explosive, n.o.s.**	1.1L	UN0357	II	1.1L	101	None	62	None	Forbidden	Forbidden		8E, 14E, 15E, 17E
G	**Substances, explosive, n.o.s.**	1.2L	UN0358	II	1.2L	101	None	62	None	Forbidden	Forbidden		8E, 14E, 15E, 17E
G	**Substances, explosive, n.o.s.**	1.3L	UN0359	II	1.3L	101	None	62	None	Forbidden	Forbidden		8E, 14E, 15E, 17E
G	**Substances, explosive, n.o.s.**	1.1A	UN0473	II	1.1A	101, 111	None	62	None	Forbidden	Forbidden	12	
G	**Substances, explosive, n.o.s.**	1.1C	UN0474	II	1.1C	101	None	62	None	Forbidden	Forbidden	10	
G	**Substances, explosive, n.o.s.**	1.1D	UN0475	II	1.1D	101	None	62	None	Forbidden	Forbidden	10	
G	**Substances, explosive, n.o.s.**	1.1G	UN0476	II	1.1G	101	None	62	None	Forbidden	Forbidden	08	
G	**Substances, explosive, n.o.s.**	1.3C	UN0477	II	1.3C	101	None	62	None	Forbidden	Forbidden	10	
G	**Substances, explosive, n.o.s.**	1.3G	UN0478	II	1.3G	101	None	62	None	Forbidden	Forbidden	08	
G	**Substances, explosive, n.o.s.**	1.4C	UN0479	II	1.4C	101	None	62	None	Forbidden	75 kg	09	
G	**Substances, explosive, n.o.s.**	1.4D	UN0480	II	1.4D	101	None	62	None	Forbidden	75 kg	09	
G	**Substances, explosive, n.o.s.**	1.4S	UN0481	II	1.4S	101	None	62	None	25 kg	75 kg	05	
G	**Substances, explosive, n.o.s.**	1.4G	UN0485	II	1.4G	101	None	62	None	Forbidden	75 kg	08	
G	**Substances, explosive, very insensitive, n.o.s.,** *or* **Substances, EVI, n.o.s.**	1.5D	UN0482	II	1.5D	101	None	62	None	Forbidden	Forbidden	10	
	Substituted nitrophenol pesticides, liquid, flammable, toxic, *flash point less than 23 degrees C*	3	UN2780	I II	3, 6.1 3, 6.1	T14, TP2, TP13, TP27 IB2, T11, TP2, TP13, TP27	None None	201 202	243 243	Forbidden 1 L	30 L 60 L	B B	40 40
	Substituted nitrophenol pesticides, liquid, toxic	6.1	UN3014	I II III	6.1 6.1 6.1	T14, TP2, TP13, TP27 IB2, T11, TP2, TP13, TP27 IB3, T7, TP2, TP28	None None 153	201 202 203	243 243 241	1 L 5 L 60 L	30 L 60 L 220 L	B B A	40 40 40
	Substituted nitrophenol pesticides, liquid, toxic, flammable *flash point not less than 23 degrees C*	6.1	UN3013	I II III	6.1, 3 6.1, 3 6.1, 3	T14, TP2, TP13, TP27 IB2, T11, TP2, TP13, TP27 B1, IB3, T7, TP2, TP28	None None 153	201 202 203	243 243 242	1 L 5 L 60 L	30 L 60 L 220 L	B B A	40 40 40
	Substituted nitrophenol pesticides, solid, toxic	6.1	UN2779	I II III	6.1 6.1 6.1	IB7, IP1 IB8, IP2, IP4 IB8, IP3	None None 153	211 212 213	242 242 240	5 kg 25 kg 100 kg	50 kg 100 kg 200 kg	A A A	40 40 40
	Sucrose octanitrate (dry)	Forbidden											
	Sulfamic acid	8	UN2967	III	8	IB8, IP3	154	213	240	25 kg	100 kg	A	
D	**Sulfur**	9	NA1350	III	9	30, IB8, IP2	None	None	240	No limit	No limit	A	19, 74
I	**Sulfur**	4.1	UN1350	III	4.1	30, IB8, IP3, T1, TP1	None	None	240	No limit	No limit	A	19, 74
	Sulfur and chlorate, loose mixtures of	Forbidden											

§172.101 - Hazardous Materials Table

Symbols	Hazardous materials descriptions and proper shipping names	Hazard class or Division	Identification Numbers	PG	Label Codes	Special provisions (§172.102)	(8) Packaging (§173.***)			(9) Quantity limitations		(10) Vessel stowage	
							Exceptions	Non-bulk	Bulk	Passenger aircraft/rail	Cargo aircraft only	Location	Other
(1)	(2)	(3)	(4)	(5)	(6)	(7)	(8A)	(8B)	(8C)	(9A)	(9B)	(10A)	(10B)
	Sulfur chlorides	8	UN1828	I	8	5, A3, B10, B77, N34, T20, TP2, TP12	None	201	243	Forbidden	2.5 L	C	40
	Sulfur dichloride, see **Sulfur chlorides**												
	Sulfur dioxide	2.3	UN1079		2.3, 8	3, B14, T50, TP19	None	304	314, 315	Forbidden	25 kg	D	40
	Sulfur dioxide solution, see **Sulfurous acid**												
	Sulfur hexafluoride	2.2	UN1080		2.2		306	304	314, 315	75 kg	150 kg	A	
D	**Sulfur, molten**	9	NA2448	III	9	IB3, T1, TP3	None	213	247	Forbidden	Forbidden	C	61
I	**Sulfur, molten**	4.1	UN2448	III	4.1	IB1, T1, TP3	None	213	247	Forbidden	Forbidden	C	61
	Sulfur tetrafluoride	2.3	UN2418		2.3, 8	1	None	302	245	Forbidden	Forbidden	D	40
+	**Sulfur trioxide, stabilized**	8	UN1829	I	8, 6.1	2, A7, B9, B14, B32, B49, B74, B77, N34, T20, TP4, TP12, TP13, TP25, TP26, TP38, TP45	None	227	244	Forbidden	Forbidden	A	40
	Sulfuretted hydrogen, see **Hydrogen sulfide**												
	Sulfuric acid, fuming *with less than 30 percent free sulfur trioxide*	8	UN1831	I	8	A3, A7, B84, N34, T20, TP2, TP12, TP13	None	201	243	Forbidden	2.5 L	C	14, 40
+	**Sulfuric acid, fuming** *with 30 percent or more free sulfur trioxide*	8	UN1831	I	8, 6.1	2, A3, A6, A7, B9, B14, B32, B74, B77, B84, N34, T20, TP2, TP12, TP13	None	227	244	Forbidden	Forbidden	C	14, 40
	Sulfuric acid, spent	8	UN1832	II	8	A3, A7, B2, B83, B84, IB2, N34, T8, TP2, TP12	None	202	242	Forbidden	30 L	C	14
	Sulfuric acid *with more than 51 percent acid*	8	UN1830	II	8	A3, A7, B3, B83, B84, IB2, N34, T8, TP2, TP12	154	202	242	1 L	30 L	C	14
	Sulfuric acid *with not more than 51% acid*	8	UN2796	II	8	A3, A7, B2, B15, IB2, N6, N34, T8, TP2, TP12	154	202	242	1 L	30 L	B	
	Sulfuric and hydrofluoric acid mixtures, *see* **Hydrofluoric and sulfuric acid mixtures**												
	Sulfuric anhydride, see **Sulfur trioxide, stabilized**												
	Sulfurous acid	8	UN1833	II	8	B3, IB2, T7, TP2	154	202	242	1 L	30 L	B	40
+	**Sulfuryl chloride**	8	UN1834	I	8, 6.1	1, A3, B6, B9, B10, B14, B30, B74, B77, N34, T22, TP2, TP12, TP38, TP44	None	226	244	Forbidden	Forbidden	C	40
	Sulfuryl fluoride	2.3	UN2191		2.3	4	None	304	314, 315	Forbidden	25 kg	D	40
	Tars, liquid *including road asphalt and oils, bitumen and cut backs*	3	UN1999	II	3	B13, IB2, T3, TP3, TP29	150	202	242	5 L	60 L	B	
				III	3	B1, B13, IB3, T1, TP3	150	203	242	60 L	220 L	A	
	Tear gas candles	6.1	UN1700	II	6.1, 4.1		None	340	None	Forbidden	50 kg	D	40
	Tear gas cartridges, see **Ammunition, tear-producing,** *etc.*												
D	**Tear gas devices** *with more than 2 percent tear gas substances, by mass*	6.1	NA1693	I	6.1		None	340	None	Forbidden	Forbidden	D	40
				II	6.1		None	340	None	Forbidden	Forbidden	D	40
	Tear gas devices, with not more than 2 percent tear gas substances, by mass, see **Aerosols,** *etc.*												
	Tear gas grenades, see **Tear gas candles**												
G	**Tear gas substances, liquid, n.o.s.**	6.1	UN1693	I	6.1		None	201	None	Forbidden	Forbidden	D	40
				II	6.1	IB2	None	202	None	Forbidden	5 L	D	40
G	**Tear gas substances, solid, n.o.s.**	6.1	UN1693	I	6.1		None	211	None	Forbidden	15 kg	D	40
				II	6.1	IB8, IP2, IP4	None	212	None	Forbidden	25 kg	D	40

§172.101 - Hazardous Materials Table

Symbols	Hazardous materials descriptions and proper shipping names	Hazard class or Division	Identification Numbers	PG	Label Codes	Special provisions (§172.102)	(8) Packaging (§173.***)			(9) Quantity limitations		(10) Vessel stowage	
							Exceptions	Non-bulk	Bulk	Passenger aircraft/ rail	Cargo aircraft only	Location	Other
(1)	(2)	(3)	(4)	(5)	(6)	(7)	(8A)	(8B)	(8C)	(9A)	(9B)	(10A)	(10B)
	Tellurium compound, n.o.s.	6.1	UN3284	I	6.1	IB7, IP1, T14, TP2, TP27	None	211	242	5 kg	50 kg	B	
				II	6.1	IB8, IP2, IP4, T11, TP2, TP27	None	212	242	25 kg	100 kg	B	
				III	6.1	IB8, IP3, T7, TP1, TP28	153	213	240	100 kg	200 kg	A	
	Tellurium hexafluoride	2.3	UN2195		2.3, 8	1	None	302	None	Forbidden	Forbidden	D	40
	Terpene hydrocarbons, n.o.s.	3	UN2319	III	3	B1, IB3, T4, TP1, TP29	150	203	242	60 L	220 L	A	
	Terpinolene	3	UN2541	III	3	B1, IB3, T2, TP1	150	203	242	60 L	220 L	A	
	Tetraazido benzene quinone	Forbidden											
	Tetrabromoethane	6.1	UN2504	III	6.1	IB3, T4, TP1	153	203	241	60 L	220 L	A	
	Tetrachloroethane	6.1	UN1702	II	6.1	IB2, N36, T7, TP2	None	202	243	5 L	60 L	A	40
	Tetrachloroethylene	6.1	UN1897	III	6.1	IB3, N36, T4, TP1	153	203	241	60 L	220 L	A	40
	Tetraethyl dithiopyrophosphate	6.1	UN1704	II	6.1	IB8, IP2, IP4	None	212	242	25 kg	100 kg	D	40
	Tetraethyl silicate	3	UN1292	III	3	B1, IB3, T2, TP1	150	203	242	60 L	220 L	A	
	Tetraethylammonium perchlorate (dry)	Forbidden											
	Tetraethylenepentamine	8	UN2320	III	8	IB3, T4, TP1	154	203	241	5 L	60 L	A	
	1,1,1,2-Tetrafluoroethane *or* **Refrigerant gas R 134a**	2.2	UN3159		2.2	T50	306	304	314, 315	75 kg	150 kg	A	
	Tetrafluoroethylene, stabilized	2.1	UN1081		2.1		306	304	None	Forbidden	150 kg	E	40
	Tetrafluoromethane, compressed *or* **Refrigerant gas R 14**	2.2	UN1982		2.2		None	302	None	75 kg	150 kg	A	
	1,2,3,6-Tetrahydrobenzaldehyde	3	UN2498	III	3	B1, IB3, T2, TP1	150	203	242	60 L	220 L	A	
	Tetrahydrofuran	3	UN2056	II	3	IB2, T4, TP1	None	202	242	5 L	60 L	B	
	Tetrahydrofurfurylamine	3	UN2943	III	3	B1, IB3, T2, TP1	150	203	242	60 L	220 L	A	
	Tetrahydrophthalic anhydrides *with more than 0.05 percent of maleic anhydride*	8	UN2698	III	8	IB8, IP3	154	213	240	25 kg	100 kg	A	
	1,2,3,6-Tetrahydropyridine	3	UN2410	II	3	IB2, T4, TP1	150	202	242	5 L	60 L	B	
	Tetrahydrothiophene	3	UN2412	II	3	IB2, T4, TP1	150	202	242	5 L	60 L	B	
	Tetramethylammonium hydroxide	8	UN1835	II	8	B2, IB2, T7, TP2	154	202	242	1 L	30 L	A	
	Tetramethylene diperoxide dicarbamide	Forbidden											
	Tetramethylsilane	3	UN2749	I	3	T14, TP2	None	201	243	Forbidden	30 L	D	
	Tetranitro diglycerin	Forbidden											
	Tetranitroaniline	1.1D	UN0207	II	1.1D		None	62	None	Forbidden	Forbidden	10	
+	**Tetranitromethane**	5.1	UN1510	I	5.1, 6.1	2, B9, B14, B32, B74, T20, TP2, TP13, TP38, TP44	None	227	None	Forbidden	Forbidden	D	40, 66, 106
	2,3,4,6-Tetranitrophenol	Forbidden											
	2,3,4,6-Tetranitrophenyl methyl nitramine	Forbidden											
	2,3,4,6-Tetranitrophenylnitramine	Forbidden											
	Tetranitroresorcinol (dry)	Forbidden											
	2,3,5,6-Tetranitroso-1,4-dinitrobenzene	Forbidden											
	2,3,5,6-Tetranitroso nitrobenzene (dry)	Forbidden											
	Tetrapropylorthotitanate	3	UN2413	III	3	B1, IB3, T4, TP1	150	203	242	60 L	220 L	A	
	Tetrazene, *see* **Guanyl nitrosaminoguanyltetrazene**												
	Tetrazine (dry)	Forbidden											
	Tetrazol-1-acetic acid	1.4C	UN0407	II	1.4C		None	62	None	Forbidden	75 kg	09	
	1H-Tetrazole	1.1D	UN0504		1.1D		None	62	None	Forbidden	Forbidden	B	1E, 5E
	Tetrazolyl azide (dry)	Forbidden											
	Tetryl, *see* **Trinitrophenylmethylnitramine**												
	Thallium chlorate	5.1	UN2573	II	5.1, 6.1	IB6, IP2	None	212	242	5 kg	25 kg	A	56, 58, 106
	Thallium compounds, n.o.s.	6.1	UN1707	II	6.1	IB8, IP2, IP4	None	212	242	25 kg	100 kg	A	
	Thallium nitrate	6.1	UN2727	II	6.1, 5.1	IB6, IP2	None	212	242	5 kg	25 kg	A	

§172.101 - Hazardous Materials Table

Symbols	Hazardous materials descriptions and proper shipping names	Hazard class or Division	Identification Numbers	PG	Label Codes	Special provisions (§172.102)	(8) Packaging (§173.***)			(9) Quantity limitations		(10) Vessel stowage	
							Exceptions	Non-bulk	Bulk	Passenger aircraft/ rail	Cargo aircraft only	Location	Other
(1)	(2)	(3)	(4)	(5)	(6)	(7)	(8A)	(8B)	(8C)	(9A)	(9B)	(10A)	(10B)
	4-Thiapentanal	6.1	UN2785	III	6.1	IB3, T4, TP1	153	203	241	60 L	220 L	D	25, 49
	Thioacetic acid	3	UN2436	II	3	IB2, T4, TP1	150	202	242	5 L	60 L	B	
	Thiocarbamate pesticide, liquid, flammable, toxic, *flash point less than 23 degrees C*	3	UN2772	I II	3, 6.1 3, 6.1	T14, TP2, TP13, TP27 IB2, T11, TP13, TP27	None None	201 202	243 243	Forbidden 1 L	30 L 60 L	B B	40 40
	Thiocarbamate pesticide, liquid, toxic, flammable, *flash point not less than 23 degrees C*	6.1	UN3005	I II III	6.1, 3 6.1, 3 6.1, 3	T14, TP2, TP13 IB2, T11, TP2, TP13, TP27 IB3, T7, TP2, TP28	None None 153	201 202 203	243 243 242	1 L 5 L 60 L	30 L 60 L 220 L	B B A	40 40 40
	Thiocarbamate pesticide, liquid, toxic	6.1	UN3006	I II III	6.1 6.1 6.1	T14, TP2, TP13 IB2, T11, TP2, TP13, TP27 IB3, T7, TP2, TP28	None None 153	201 202 203	243 243 241	1 L 5 L 60 L	30 L 60 L 220 L	B B A	40 40 40
	Thiocarbamate pesticides, solid, toxic	6.1	UN2771	I II III	6.1 6.1 6.1	IB7, IP1 IB8, IP2, IP4 IB8, IP3	None None 153	211 212 213	242 242 240	5 kg 25 kg 100 kg	50 kg 100 kg 200 kg	A A A	40 40 40
	Thiocarbonylchloride, see **Thiophosgene**												
	Thioglycol	6.1	UN2966	II	6.1	IB2, T7, TP2	None	202	243	5 L	60 L	A	
	Thioglycolic acid	8	UN1940	II	8	A7, B2, IB2, N34, T7, TP2	154	202	242	1 L	30 L	A	
	Thiolactic acid	6.1	UN2936	II	6.1	IB2, T7, TP2	None	202	243	5 L	60 L	A	
	Thionyl chloride	8	UN1836	I	8	A7, B6, B10, N34, T10, TP2, TP12, TP13	None	201	243	Forbidden	Forbidden	C	40
	Thiophene	3	UN2414	II	3	IB2, T4, TP1	150	202	242	5 L	60 L	B	40
+	**Thiophosgene**	6.1	UN2474	II	6.1	2, A7, B9, B14, B32, B74, N33, N34, T20, TP2, TP38, TP45	None	227	244	Forbidden	Forbidden	B	26, 40
	Thiophosphoryl chloride	8	UN1837	II	8	A3, A7, B2, B8, B25, IB2, N34, T7, TP2	None	202	242	Forbidden	30 L	C	40
	Thiourea dioxide	4.2	UN3341	II III	4.2 4.2	IB6, IP2 IB8, IP3	None None	212 213	241 241	15 kg 25 kg	50 kg 100 kg	D D	
D	**Thorium metal, pyrophoric**	7	UN2975		7, 4.2		None	418	None	Forbidden	Forbidden	D	95
D	**Thorium nitrate, solid**	7	UN2976		7, 5.1		None	419	None	Forbidden	15 kg	A	95
	Tin chloride, fuming, see **Stannic chloride, anhydrous**												
	Tin perchloride or Tin tetrachloride, see **Stannic chloride, anhydrous**												
	Tinctures, medicinal	3	UN1293	II III	3 3	IB2, T4, TP1, TP8 B1, IB3, T2, TP1	150 150	202 203	242 242	5 L 60 L	60 L 220 L	B A	
	Tinning flux, see **Zinc chloride**												
	Titanium disulphide	4.2	UN3174	III	4.2	IB8, IP3	None	213	241	25 kg	100 kg	A	
	Titanium hydride	4.1	UN1871	II	4.1	A19, A20, IB4, N34	None	212	241	15 kg	50 kg	E	
	Titanium powder, dry	4.2	UN2546	I II III	4.2 4.2 4.2	 A19, A20, IB6, IP2, N5, N34 IB8, IP3	None None None	211 212 213	242 241 241	Forbidden 15 kg 25 kg	Forbidden 50 kg 100 kg	D D D	
	Titanium powder, wetted *with not less than 25 percent water (a visible excess of water must be present) (a) mechanically produced, particle size less than 53 microns; (b) chemically produced, particle size less than 840 microns*	4.1	UN1352	II	4.1	A19, A20, IB6, IP2, N34	None	212	240	15 kg	50 kg	E	
	Titanium sponge granules *or* **Titanium sponge powders**	4.1	UN2878	III	4.1	A1, IB8, IP3	None	213	240	25 kg	100 kg	D	
+	**Titanium tetrachloride**	8	UN1838	II	8, 6.1	2, A3, A6, B7, B9, B14, B32, B74, B77, T20, TP2, TP13, TP38, TP45	None	227	244	Forbidden	Forbidden	C	40

§172.101 - Hazardous Materials Table

Symbols	Hazardous materials descriptions and proper shipping names	Hazard class or Division	Identification Numbers	PG	Label Codes	Special provisions (§172.102)	(8) Packaging (§173.***) Exceptions			(9) Quantity limitations Passenger aircraft/rail		(10) Vessel stowage Location	
							Exceptions	Non-bulk	Bulk	Passenger aircraft/rail	Cargo aircraft only	Location	Other
(1)	(2)	(3)	(4)	(5)	(6)	(7)	(8A)	(8B)	(8C)	(9A)	(9B)	(10A)	(10B)
	Titanium trichloride mixtures	8	UN2869	II	8	A7, IB8, IP2, IP4, N34	154	212	240	15 kg	50 kg	A	40
				III	8	A7, IB8, IP3, N34	154	213	240	25 kg	100 kg	A	40
	Titanium trichloride, pyrophoric *or* **Titanium trichloride mixtures, pyrophoric**	4.2	UN2441	I	4.2, 8	A7, A8, A19, A20, N34	None	181	244	Forbidden	Forbidden	D	40
	TNT mixed with aluminum, see **Tritonal**												
	TNT, *see* **Trinitrotoluene**, *etc.*												
	Toluene	3	UN1294	II	3	IB2, T4, TP1	150	202	242	5 L	60 L	B	
+	**Toluene diisocyanate**	6.1	UN2078	II	6.1	IB2, T7, TP2, TP13	None	202	243	5 L	60 L	D	25, 40
	Toluene sulfonic acid, see **Alkyl**, *or* **Aryl sulfonic acid** *etc.*												
+	**Toluidines** *liquid*	6.1	UN1708	II	6.1	IB2, T7, TP2	None	202	243	5 L	60 L	A	
+	**Toluidines** *solid*	6.1	UN1708	II	6.1	IB8, IP2, IP4, T7, TP2	None	212	242	25 kg	100 kg	A	
	2,4-Toluylenediamine *or* **2,4-Toluenediamine**	6.1	UN1709	III	6.1	IB8, IP3, T4, TP1	153	213	240	100 kg	200 kg	A	
	Torpedoes, liquid fueled, *with inert head*	1.3J	UN0450	II	1.3J			62	None	Forbidden	Forbidden	04	23E
	Torpedoes, liquid fueled, *with or without bursting charge*	1.1J	UN0449	II	1.1J			62	None	Forbidden	Forbidden	04	23E
	Torpedoes *with bursting charge*	1.1E	UN0329	II	1.1E			62	None	Forbidden	Forbidden	03	
	Torpedoes *with bursting charge*	1.1F	UN0330	II	1.1F			62	None	Forbidden	Forbidden	08	
	Torpedoes *with bursting charge*	1.1D	UN0451	II	1.1D			62	None	Forbidden	Forbidden	03	
G	**Toxic liquid, corrosive, inorganic, n.o.s.**	6.1	UN3289	I	6.1, 8	T14, TP2, TP13, TP27	None	201	243	0.5 L	2.5 L	A	
				II	6.1, 8	IB2, T11, TP2, TP27	None	202	243	1 L	30 L	A	
G	**Toxic liquid, corrosive, inorganic, n.o.s.** *Inhalation Hazard, Packing Group I, Zone A*	6.1	UN3289	I	6.1, 8	1, B9, B14, B30, B72, T22, TP2, TP13, TP27, TP38, TP44	None	226	244	Forbidden	Forbidden	B	40
G	**Toxic liquid, corrosive, inorganic, n.o.s.** *Inhalation Hazard, Packing Group I, Zone B*	6.1	UN3289	I	6.1, 8	2, B9, B14, B32, B74, T20, TP2, TP13, TP27, TP38, TP45	None	227	244	Forbidden	Forbidden	B	40
G	**Toxic liquid, inorganic, n.o.s.**	6.1	UN3287	I	6.1	T14, TP2, TP13, TP27	None	201	243	1 L	30 L	A	
				II	6.1	IB2, T11, TP2, TP27	None	202	243	5 L	60 L	A	
				III	6.1	IB3, T7, TP1, TP28	153	203	241	60 L	220 L	A	
G	**Toxic liquid, inorganic, n.o.s.** *Inhalation Hazard, Packing Group I, Zone A*	6.1	UN3287	I	6.1	1, B9, B14, B30, B72, T22, TP2, TP13, TP27, TP38, TP44	None	226	244	Forbidden	Forbidden	B	40
G	**Toxic liquid, inorganic, n.o.s.** *Inhalation Hazard, Packing Group I, Zone B*	6.1	UN3287	I	6.1	2, B9, B14, B32, B74, T20, TP2, TP13, TP27, TP38, TP45	None	227	244	Forbidden	Forbidden	B	40
G	**Toxic liquids, corrosive, organic, n.o.s.**	6.1	UN2927	I	6.1, 8	T14, TP2, TP13, TP27	None	201	243	0.5 L	2.5 L	B	40
				II	6.1, 8	IB2, T11, TP2, TP27	None	202	243	1 L	30 L	B	40
G	**Toxic liquids, corrosive, organic, n.o.s.,** *inhalation hazard, Packing Group I, Zone A*	6.1	UN2927	I	6.1, 8	1, B9, B14, B30, B72, T22, TP2, TP13, TP27, TP38, TP44	None	226	244	Forbidden	Forbidden	D	40
G	**Toxic liquids, corrosive, organic, n.o.s.,** *inhalation hazard, Packing Group I, Zone B*	6.1	UN2927	I	6.1, 8	2, B9, B14, B32, B74, T20, TP2, TP13, TP27, TP38, TP45	None	227	244	Forbidden	Forbidden	D	40
G	**Toxic liquids, flammable, organic, n.o.s.**	6.1	UN2929	I	6.1, 3	T14, TP2, TP13, TP27	None	201	243	1 L	30 L	B	40
				II	6.1, 3	IB2, T11, TP2, TP13, TP27	None	202	243	5 L	60 L	B	40

§172.101 - Hazardous Materials Table

Symbols (1)	Hazardous materials descriptions and proper shipping names (2)	Hazard class or Division (3)	Identification Numbers (4)	PG (5)	Label Codes (6)	Special provisions (§172.102) (7)	(8) Packaging (§173.***) Exceptions (8A)	Non-bulk (8B)	Bulk (8C)	(9) Quantity limitations Passenger aircraft/rail (9A)	Cargo aircraft only (9B)	(10) Vessel stowage Location (10A)	Other (10B)
G	**Toxic liquids, flammable, organic, n.o.s.,** *inhalation hazard, Packing Group I, Zone A*	6.1	UN2929	I	6.1, 3	1, B9, B14, B30, B72, T22, TP2, TP13, TP27, TP38, TP44	None	226	244	Forbidden	Forbidden	D	40
G	**Toxic liquids, flammable, organic, n.o.s.,** *inhalation hazard, Packing Group I, Zone B*	6.1	UN2929	I	6.1, 3	2, B9, B14, B32, B74, T20, TP2, TP13, TP27, TP38, TP45	None	227	244	Forbidden	Forbidden	D	40
G	**Toxic, liquids, organic, n.o.s.**	6.1	UN2810	I II III	6.1 6.1 6.1	T14, TP2, TP13, TP27 IB2, T11, TP2, TP13, TP27 IB3, T7, TP1, TP28	None None 153	201 202 203	243 243 241	1 L 5 L 60 L	30 L 60 L 220 L	B B A	40 40 40
G	**Toxic, liquids, organic, n.o.s.** *Inhalation hazard, Packing Group I, Zone A*	6.1	UN2810	I	6.1	1, B9, B14, B30, B72, T22, TP2, TP13, TP27, TP38, TP44	None	226	244	Forbidden	Forbidden	D	40
G	**Toxic, liquids, organic, n.o.s.** *Inhalation hazard, Packing Group I, Zone B*	6.1	UN2810	I	6.1	2, B9, B14, B32, B74, T20, TP2, TP13, TP27, TP38, TP45	None	227	244	Forbidden	Forbidden	D	40
G	**Toxic liquids, oxidizing, n.o.s.**	6.1	UN3122	I II	6.1, 5.1 6.1, 5.1	A4 IB2	None None	201 202	243 243	Forbidden 1 L	2.5 L 5 L	C C	
G	**Toxic liquids, oxidizing, n.o.s.** *Inhalation hazard, Packing Group I, Zone A*	6.1	UN3122	I	6.1, 5.1	1, B9, B14, B30, B72, T22, TP2, TP13, TP38, TP44	None	226	244	Forbidden	Forbidden	C	
G	**Toxic liquids, oxidizing, n.o.s.** *Inhalation Hazard, Packing Group I, Zone B*	6.1	UN3122	I	6.1, 5.1	2, B9, B14, B32, T20, TP2, TP13, TP38, TP44	None	227	244	Forbidden	Forbidden	C	
G	**Toxic liquids, water-reactive, n.o.s.**	6.1	UN3123	I II	6.1, 4.3 6.1, 4.3	A4 IB2	None None	201 202	243 243	Forbidden 1 L	1 L 5 L	E E	40 40
G	**Toxic liquids, water-reactive, n.o.s.** *Inhalation hazard, packing group I, Zone A*	6.1	UN3123	I	6.1, 4.3	1, B9, B14, B30, B72, T22, TP2, TP13, TP38, TP44	None	226	244	Forbidden	Forbidden	E	40
G	**Toxic liquids, water-reactive, n.o.s.** *Inhalation hazard, packing group I, Zone B*	6.1	UN3123	I	6.1, 4.3	2, B9, B14, B32, B74, T20, TP2, TP13, TP38, TP44	None	227	244	Forbidden	Forbidden	E	40
G	**Toxic solid, corrosive, inorganic, n.o.s.**	6.1	UN3290	I II	6.1, 8 6.1, 8	IB7 IB6, IP2	None None	211 212	242 242	1 kg 15 kg	25 kg 50 kg	A A	
G	**Toxic solid, inorganic, n.o.s.**	6.1	UN3288	I II III	6.1 6.1 6.1	IB7 IB8, IP2, IP4 IB8, IP3	None None 153	211 212 213	242 242 240	5 kg 25 kg 100 kg	50 kg 100 kg 200 kg	A A A	
G	**Toxic solids, corrosive, organic, n.o.s.**	6.1	UN2928	I II	6.1, 8 6.1, 8	IB7 IB6, IP2	None None	211 212	242 242	1 kg 15 kg	25 kg 50 kg	B B	40 40
G	**Toxic solids, flammable, organic, n.o.s.**	6.1	UN2930	I II	6.1, 4.1 6.1, 4.1	IB6 IB8, IP2, IP4	None None	211 212	242 242	1 kg 15 kg	15 kg 50 kg	B B	
G	**Toxic solids, organic, n.o.s.**	6.1	UN2811	I II III	6.1 6.1 6.1	IB7 IB8, IP2, IP4 IB8, IP3	None None 153	211 212 213	242 242 240	5 kg 25 kg 100 kg	50 kg 100 kg 200 kg	B B A	
G	**Toxic solids, oxidizing, n.o.s.**	6.1	UN3086	I II	6.1, 5.1 6.1, 5.1	 IB6, IP2	None None	211 212	242 242	1 kg 15 kg	15 kg 50 kg	C C	
G	**Toxic solids, self-heating, n.o.s.**	6.1	UN3124	I II	6.1, 4.2 6.1, 4.2	A5 IB6, IP2	None None	211 212	242 242	5 kg 15 kg	15 kg 50 kg	D D	40 40
G	**Toxic solids, water-reactive, n.o.s.**	6.1	UN3125	I II	6.1, 4.3 6.1, 4.3	A5 IB6, IP2	None None	211 212	242 242	5 kg 15 kg	15 kg 50 kg	D D	40 40
G	**Toxins, from living sources, liquid, n.o.s.**	6.1	UN3172	I II III	6.1	141 141 141	None None 153	201 202 203	243 243 241	1 L 5 L 60 L	30 L 60 L 220 L	B B A	40 40 40
G	**Toxins, from living sources, solid, n.o.s.**	6.1	UN3172	I II III	6.1	141 141 141	None None 153	211 212 213	243 243 241	5 kg 25 kg 100 kg	50 kg 100 kg 200 kg	B B A	
D	**Toy Caps**	1.4S	NA0337	II	1.4S		None	62	None	25 kg	100 kg	05	
	Tracers for ammunition	1.3G	UN0212	II	1.3G		None	62	None	Forbidden	Forbidden	07	
	Tracers for ammunition	1.4G	UN0306	II	1.4G		None	62	None	Forbidden	75 kg	06	
	Tractors, see **Vehicle**, *etc.*												
	Tri-(b-nitroxyethyl) ammonium nitrate	Forbidden											
	Triallyl borate	6.1	UN2609	III	6.1	IB3	153	203	241	60 L	220 L	A	13

§172.101 - Hazardous Materials Table

Symbols	Hazardous materials descriptions and proper shipping names	Hazard class or Division	Identification Numbers	PG	Label Codes	Special provisions (§172.102)	(8) Packaging (§173.***)			(9) Quantity limitations		(10) Vessel stowage	
							Exceptions	Non-bulk	Bulk	Passenger aircraft/rail	Cargo aircraft only	Location	Other
(1)	(2)	(3)	(4)	(5)	(6)	(7)	(8A)	(8B)	(8C)	(9A)	(9B)	(10A)	(10B)
	Triallylamine	3	UN2610	III	3, 8	B1, IB3, T4, TP1	None	203	242	5 L	60 L	A	40
	Triazine pesticides, liquid, flammable, toxic, *flash point less than 23 degrees C*	3	UN2764	I	3, 6.1	T14, TP2, TP13, TP27	None	201	243	Forbidden	30 L	B	40
				II	3, 6.1	IB2, T11, TP2, TP13, TP27	None	202	243	1 L	60 L	B	40
	Triazine pesticides, liquid, toxic	6.1	UN2998	I	6.1	T14, TP2, TP13, TP27	None	201	243	1 L	30 L	B	40
				II	6.1	IB2, T11, TP2, TP13, TP27	None	202	243	5 L	60 L	B	40
				III	6.1	IB3, T7, TP2, TP28	153	203	241	60 L	220 L	A	40
	Triazine pesticides, liquid, toxic, flammable, *flash point not less than 23 degrees C*	6.1	UN2997	I	6.1, 3	T14, TP2, TP13, TP27	None	201	243	1 L	30 L	B	40
				II	6.1, 3	IB2, T11, TP2, TP13, TP27	None	202	243	5 L	60 L	B	40
				III	6.1, 3	IB3, T7, TP2, TP28	153	203	242	60 L	220 L	A	40
	Triazine pesticides, solid, toxic	6.1	UN2763	I	6.1	IB7, IP1	None	211	242	5 kg	50 kg	A	40
				II	6.1	IB8, IP2, IP4	None	212	242	25 kg	100 kg	A	40
				III	6.1	IB8, IP3	153	213	240	100 kg	200 kg	A	40
	Tributylamine	6.1	UN2542	II	6.1	IB2, T7, TP2	None	202	243	5 L	60 L	A	
	Tributylphosphane	4.2	UN3254	I	4.2		None	211	242	Forbidden	Forbidden	D	
	Trichloro-s-triazinetrione dry, with more than 39 percent available chlorine, see **Trichloroisocyanuric acid, dry**												
	Trichloroacetic acid	8	UN1839	II	8	A7, IB8, IP2, IP4, N34	154	212	240	15 kg	50 kg	A	
	Trichloroacetic acid, solution	8	UN2564	II	8	A3, A6, A7, B2, IB2, N34, T7, TP2	154	202	242	1 L	30 L	B	
				III	8	A3, A6, A7, IB3, N34, T4, TP1	154	203	241	5 L	60 L	B	8
+	**Trichloroacetyl chloride**	8	UN2442	II	8, 6.1	2, A3, A7, B9, B14, B32, B74, N34, T20, TP2, TP38, TP45	None	227	244	Forbidden	Forbidden	D	40
	Trichlorobenzenes, liquid	6.1	UN2321	III	6.1	IB3, T4, TP1	153	203	241	60 L	220 L	A	
	Trichlorobutene	6.1	UN2322	II	6.1	IB2, T7, TP2	None	202	243	5 L	60 L	A	25, 40
	1,1,1-Trichloroethane	6.1	UN2831	III	6.1	IB3, N36, T4, TP1	153	203	241	60 L	220 L	A	40
	Trichloroethylene	6.1	UN1710	III	6.1	IB3, N36, T4, TP1	153	203	241	60 L	220 L	A	40
	Trichloroisocyanuric acid, dry	5.1	UN2468	II	5.1	IB8, IP4	152	212	240	5 kg	25 kg	A	13
	Trichloromethyl perchlorate	Forbidden											
	Trichlorosilane	4.3	UN1295	I	4.3, 3, 8	A7, N34, T14, TP2, TP7, TP13	None	201	244	Forbidden	Forbidden	D	21, 28, 40, 49, 100
	Tricresyl phosphate *with more than 3 percent ortho isomer*	6.1	UN2574	II	6.1	A3, IB2, N33, N34, T7, TP2	None	202	243	5 L	60 L	A	
	Triethyl phosphite	3	UN2323	III	3	B1, IB3, T2, TP1	150	203	242	60 L	220 L	A	
	Triethylamine	3	UN1296	II	3, 8	IB2, T7, TP1	None	202	243	1 L	5 L	B	40
	Triethylenetetramine	8	UN2259	II	8	B2, IB2, T7, TP2	154	202	242	1 L	30 L	B	40
	Trifluoroacetic acid	8	UN2699	I	8	A3, A6, A7, B4, N3, N34, T10, TP2, TP12	None	201	243	0.5 L	2.5 L	B	12, 40
	Trifluoroacetyl chloride	2.3	UN3057		2.3, 8	2, B7, B9, B14, T50, TP21	None	304	314, 315	Forbidden	Forbidden	D	40
	Trifluorochloroethylene, stabilized	2.3	UN1082		2.3, 2.1	3, B14, T50	None	304	314, 315	Forbidden	Forbidden	D	40
	1,1,1-Trifluoroethane, compressed *or* **Refrigerant gas R 143a**	2.1	UN2035		2.1	T50	306	304	314, 315	Forbidden	150 kg	B	40
	Trifluoromethane *or* **Refrigerant gas R 23**	2.2	UN1984		2.2		306	304	314, 315	75 kg	150 kg	A	
	Trifluoromethane, refrigerated liquid	2.2	UN3136		2.2	T75, TP5	306	None	314, 315	50 kg	500 kg	D	
	2-Trifluoromethylaniline	6.1	UN2942	III	6.1	IB3	153	203	241	60 L	220 L	A	
	3-Trifluoromethylaniline	6.1	UN2948	II	6.1	IB2, T7, TP2	None	202	243	5 L	60 L	A	40
	Triformoxime trinitrate	Forbidden											
	Triisobutylene	3	UN2324	III	3	B1, IB3, T4, TP1	150	203	242	60 L	220 L	A	
	Triisopropyl borate	3	UN2616	II	3	IB2, T4, TP1	150	202	242	5 L	60 L	A	
				III	3	B1, IB3, T2, TP1	150	203	242	60 L	220 L	A	

§172.101 - Hazardous Materials Table

Symbols	Hazardous materials descriptions and proper shipping names	Hazard class or Division	Identification Numbers	PG	Label Codes	Special provisions (§172.102)	(8) Packaging (§173.***)			(9) Quantity limitations		(10) Vessel stowage	
							Exceptions	Non-bulk	Bulk	Passenger aircraft/ rail	Cargo aircraft only	Location	Other
(1)	(2)	(3)	(4)	(5)	(6)	(7)	(8A)	(8B)	(8C)	(9A)	(9B)	(10A)	(10B)
D	**Trimethoxysilane**	6.1	NA9269	I	6.1, 3	2, B9, B14, B32, B74, T20, TP4, TP12, TP13, TP38, TP45	None	227	244	Forbidden	Forbidden	E	40
	Trimethyl borate	3	UN2416	II	3	IB2, T7, TP1	150	202	242	5 L	60 L	B	
	Trimethyl phosphite	3	UN2329	III	3	B1, IB3, T2, TP1	150	203	242	60 L	220 L	A	
	1,3,5-Trimethyl-2,4,6-trinitrobenzene	Forbidden											
	Trimethylacetyl chloride	6.1	UN2438	I	6.1, 8, 3	2, A3, A6, A7, B3, B9, B14, B32, B74, N34, T20, TP2, TP13, TP38, TP45	None	227	244	Forbidden	Forbidden	D	25, 40
	Trimethylamine, anhydrous	2.1	UN1083		2.1	T50	306	304	314, 315	Forbidden	150 kg	B	40
	Trimethylamine, aqueous solutions *with not more than 50 percent trimethylamine by mass*	3	UN1297	I II III	3, 8 3, 8 3, 8	T11, TP1 B1, IB2, T7, TP1 B1, IB3, T7, TP1	None None 150	201 202 203	243 243 242	0.5 L 1 L 5 L	2.5 L 5 L 60 L	D B A	40, 41 40, 41 40, 41
	1,3,5-Trimethylbenzene	3	UN2325	III	3	B1, IB3, T2, TP1	None	203	242	60 L	220 L	A	
	Trimethylchlorosilane	3	UN1298	II	3, 8	A3, A7, B77, IB2, N34, T7, TP2, TP13	None	202	243	1 L	5 L	E	40
	Trimethylcyclohexylamine	8	UN2326	III	8	IB3, T4, TP1	154	203	241	5 L	60 L	A	
	Trimethylene glycol diperchlorate	Forbidden											
	Trimethylhexamethylene diisocyanate	6.1	UN2328	III	6.1	IB3, T4, TP2, TP13	153	203	241	60 L	220 L	B	
	Trimethylhexamethylenediamines	8	UN2327	III	8	IB3, T4, TP1	154	203	241	5 L	60 L	A	
	Trimethylol nitromethane trinitrate	Forbidden											
	Trinitro-meta-cresol	1.1D	UN0216	II	1.1D		None	62	None	Forbidden	Forbidden	10	5E
	2,4,6-Trinitro-1,3-diazobenzene	Forbidden											
	2,4,6-Trinitro-1,3,5-triazido benzene (dry)	Forbidden											
	Trinitroacetic acid	Forbidden											
	Trinitroacetonitrile	Forbidden											
	Trinitroamine cobalt	Forbidden											
	Trinitroaniline *or* **Picramide**	1.1D	UN0153	II	1.1D		None	62	None	Forbidden	Forbidden	10	
	Trinitroanisole	1.1D	UN0213	II	1.1D		None	62	None	Forbidden	Forbidden	10	
	Trinitrobenzene, *dry or wetted with less than 30 percent water, by mass*	1.1D	UN0214	II	1.1D		None	62	None	Forbidden	Forbidden	10	
	Trinitrobenzene, wetted *with not less than 30 percent water, by mass*	4.1	UN1354	I	4.1	23, A2, A8, A19, N41	None	211	None	0.5 kg	0.5 kg	E	28
	Trinitrobenzenesulfonic acid	1.1D	UN0386	II	1.1D		None	62	None	Forbidden	Forbidden	10	5E
	Trinitrobenzoic acid, *dry or wetted with less than 30 percent water, by mass*	1.1D	UN0215	II	1.1D		None	62	None	Forbidden	Forbidden	10	
	Trinitrobenzoic acid, wetted *with not less than 30 percent water, by mass*	4.1	UN1355	I	4.1	23, A2, A8, A19, N41	None	211	None	0.5 kg	0.5 kg	E	28
	Trinitrochlorobenzene *or* **Picryl chloride**	1.1D	UN0155	II	1.1D		None	62	None	Forbidden	Forbidden	10	
	Trinitroethanol	Forbidden											
	Trinitroethylnitrate	Forbidden											
	Trinitrofluorenone	1.1D	UN0387	II	1.1D		None	62	None	Forbidden	Forbidden	10	
	Trinitromethane	Forbidden											
	1,3,5-Trinitronaphthalene	Forbidden											
	Trinitronaphthalene	1.1D	UN0217	II	1.1D		None	62	None	Forbidden	Forbidden	10	
	Trinitrophenetole	1.1D	UN0218	II	1.1D		None	62	None	Forbidden	Forbidden	10	
	Trinitrophenol *or* **Picric acid,** *dry or wetted with less than 30 percent water, by mass*	1.1D	UN0154	II	1.1D		None	62	None	Forbidden	Forbidden	10	5E
	Trinitrophenol, wetted *with not less than 30 percent water, by mass*	4.1	UN1344	I	4.1	23, A8, A19, N41	None	211	None	1 kg	15 kg	E	28, 36
	2,4,6-Trinitrophenyl guanidine (dry)	Forbidden											
	2,4,6-Trinitrophenyl nitramine	Forbidden											

§172.101 - Hazardous Materials Table

Symbols	Hazardous materials descriptions and proper shipping names	Hazard class or Division	Identification Numbers	PG	Label Codes	Special provisions (§172.102)	(8) Packaging (§173.***)			(9) Quantity limitations		(10) Vessel stowage	
							Exceptions	Non-bulk	Bulk	Passenger aircraft/rail	Cargo aircraft only	Location	Other
(1)	(2)	(3)	(4)	(5)	(6)	(7)	(8A)	(8B)	(8C)	(9A)	(9B)	(10A)	(10B)
	2,4,6-Trinitrophenyl trimethylol methyl nitramine trinitrate (dry)	Forbidden											
	Trinitrophenylmethylnitramine *or* **Tetryl**	1.1D	UN0208	II	1.1D		None	62	None	Forbidden	Forbidden	10	
	Trinitroresorcinol *or* **Styphnic acid,** *dry or wetted with less than 20 percent water, or mixture of alcohol and water, by mass*	1.1D	UN0219	II	1.1D		None	62	None	Forbidden	Forbidden	10	5E
	Trinitroresorcinol, wetted *or* **Styphnic acid, wetted** *with not less than 20 percent water, or mixture of alcohol and water by mass*	1.1D	UN0394	II	1.1D		None	62	None	Forbidden	Forbidden	10	5E
	2,4,6-Trinitroso-3-methyl nitraminoanisole	Forbidden											
	Trinitrotetramine cobalt nitrate	Forbidden											
	Trinitrotoluene and Trinitrobenzene mixtures *or* **TNT and trinitrobenzene mixtures** *or* **TNT and hexanitrostilbene mixtures** *or* **Trinitrotoluene and hexanitrostilnene mixtures**	1.1D	UN0388	II	1.1D		None	62	None	Forbidden	Forbidden	10	
	Trinitrotoluene mixtures containing Trinitrobenzene and Hexanitrostilbene *or* **TNT mixtures containing trinitrobenzene and hexanitrostilbene**	1.1D	UN0389	II	1.1D		None	62	None	Forbidden	Forbidden	10	
	Trinitrotoluene *or* **TNT,** *dry or wetted with less than 30 percent water, by mass*	1.1D	UN0209	II	1.1D		None	62	None	Forbidden	Forbidden	10	
	Trinitrotoluene, wetted *with not less than 30 percent water, by mass*	4.1	UN1356	I	4.1	23, A2, A8, A19, N41	None	211	None	0.5 kg	0.5 kg	E	28
	Tripropylamine	3	UN2260	III	3, 8	B1, IB3, T4, TP1	150	203	242	5 L	60 L	A	40
	Tripropylene	3	UN2057	II III	3 3	IB2, T4, TP1 B1, IB3, T2, TP1	150 150	202 203	242 242	5 L 60 L	60 L 220 L	B A	
	Tris-(1-aziridinyl)phosphine oxide, solution	6.1	UN2501	II III	6.1 6.1	IB2, T7, TP2 IB3, T4, TP1	None 153	202 203	243 241	5 L 60 L	60 L 220 L	A A	
	Tris, bis-bifluoroamino diethoxy propane (TVOPA)	Forbidden											
	Tritonal	1.1D	UN0390	II	1.1D		None	62	None	Forbidden	Forbidden	10	
	Tungsten hexafluoride	2.3	UN2196		2.3, 8	2	None	338	None	Forbidden	Forbidden	D	40
	Turpentine	3	UN1299	III	3	B1, IB3, T2, TP1	150	203	242	60 L	220 L	A	
	Turpentine substitute	3	UN1300	I II III	3 3 3	T11, TP1, TP8, TP27 IB2, T4, TP1 B1, IB3, T2, TP1	None 150 150	201 202 203	243 242 242	1 L 5 L 60 L	30 L 60 L 220 L	B B A	
	Undecane	3	UN2330	III	3	B1, IB3, T2, TP1	150	203	242	60 L	220 L	A	
D	**Uranium hexafluoride,** *fissile excepted or non-fissile*	7	UN2978		7, 8		423	420, 427	420, 427				
D	**Uranium hexafluoride, fissile** *(with more than 1 percent U-235)*	7	UN2977		7, 8		453	417, 420	417, 420			A	95
D	**Uranium metal, pyrophoric**	7	UN2979		7, 4.2		None	418	None			D	95
D	**Uranium nitrate hexahydrate solution**	7	UN2980		7, 8		421, 427	415, 416, 417	415, 416, 417			D	95
D	**Uranyl nitrate, solid**	7	UN2981		7, 5.1		None	419	None	Forbidden	15 kg	A	95
	Urea hydrogen peroxide	5.1	UN1511	III	5.1, 8	A1, A7, A29, IB8, IP3	152	213	240	25 kg	100 kg	A	13
	Urea nitrate, *dry or wetted with less than 20 percent water, by mass*	1.1D	UN0220	II	1.1D	119	None	62	None	Forbidden	Forbidden	10	
	Urea nitrate, wetted *with not less than 20 percent water, by mass*	4.1	UN1357	I	4.1	39, A8, A19, N41	None	211	None	1 kg	15 kg	A	28
	Urea peroxide, see **Urea hydrogen peroxide**												
	Valeraldehyde	3	UN2058	II	3	IB2, T4, TP1	150	202	242	5 L	60 L	B	
	Valeric acid, see **Corrosive liquids, n.o.s.**												
	Valeryl chloride	8	UN2502	II	8, 3	A3, A6, A7, B2, IB2, N34, T7, TP2	154	202	243	1 L	30 L	C	40

§172.101 - Hazardous Materials Table

Symbols	Hazardous materials descriptions and proper shipping names	Hazard class or Division	Identification Numbers	PG	Label Codes	Special provisions (§172.102)	(8) Packaging (§173.***) Exceptions	Non-bulk	Bulk	(9) Quantity limitations Passenger aircraft/ rail	Cargo aircraft only	(10) Vessel stowage Location	Other
(1)	(2)	(3)	(4)	(5)	(6)	(7)	(8A)	(8B)	(8C)	(9A)	(9B)	(10A)	(10B)
	Vanadium compound, n.o.s.	6.1	UN3285	I II III	6.1 6.1 6.1	IB7, IP1, T14, TP2, TP27 IB8, IP2, IP4, T11, TP2, TP27 IB8, IP3, T7, TP1, TP28	None None 153	211 212 213	242 242 240	5 kg 25 kg 100 kg	50 kg 100 kg 200 kg	B B A	
	Vanadium oxytrichloride	8	UN2443	II	8	A3, A6, A7, B2, B16, IB2, N34, T7, TP2	154	202	242	Forbidden	30 L	C	40
	Vanadium pentoxide, *non-fused form*	6.1	UN2862	III	6.1	IB8, IP3	153	213	240	100 kg	200 kg	A	40
	Vanadium tetrachloride	8	UN2444	I	8	A3, A6, A7, B4, N34, T10, TP2	None	201	243	Forbidden	2.5 L	C	40
	Vanadium trichloride	8	UN2475	III	8	IB8, IP3	154	213	240	25 kg	100 kg	A	40
	Vanadyl sulfate	6.1	UN2931	II	6.1	IB8, IP2, IP4	None	212	242	25 kg	100 kg	A	
	Vehicle, flammable gas powered	9	UN3166		9	135	220	220	220	Forbidden	No limit	A	
	Vehicle, flammable liquid powered	9	UN3166		9	135	220	220	220	No limit	No limit	A	
	Very signal cartridge, see **Cartridges, signal**												
	Vinyl acetate, stabilized	3	UN1301	II	3	IB2, T4, TP1	150	202	242	5 L	60 L	B	
	Vinyl bromide, stabilized	2.1	UN1085		2.1	T50	306	304	314, 315	Forbidden	150 kg	B	40
	Vinyl butyrate, stabilized	3	UN2838	II	3	IB2, T4, TP1	150	202	242	5 L	60 L	B	
	Vinyl chloride, stabilized	2.1	UN1086		2.1	21, B44, T50	306	304	314, 315	Forbidden	150 kg	B	40
	Vinyl chloroacetate	6.1	UN2589	II	6.1, 3	IB2, T7, TP2	None	202	243	5 L	60 L	A	
	Vinyl ethyl ether, stabilized	3	UN1302	I	3	A3, T11, TP2	None	201	243	1 L	30 L	D	
	Vinyl fluoride, stabilized	2.1	UN1860		2.1		306	304	314, 315	Forbidden	150 kg	E	40
	Vinyl isobutyl ether, stabilized	3	UN1304	II	3	IB2, T4, TP1	150	202	242	5 L	60 L	B	
	Vinyl methyl ether, stabilized	2.1	UN1087		2.1	B44, T50	306	304	314, 315	Forbidden	150 kg	B	40
	Vinyl nitrate polymer	Forbidden											
	Vinylidene chloride, stabilized	3	UN1303	I	3	T12, TP2, TP7	150	201	243	1 L	30 L	E	40
	Vinylpyridines, stabilized	6.1	UN3073	II	6.1, 3, 8	IB1, T7, TP2, TP13	None	202	243	1 L	30 L	B	40
	Vinyltoluenes, stabilized	3	UN2618	III	3	B1, IB3, T2, TP1	150	203	242	60 L	220 L	A	
	Vinyltrichlorosilane, stabilized	3	UN1305	I	3, 8	A3, A7, B6, N34, T11, TP2, TP13	None	201	243	Forbidden	2.5 L	B	40
	Warheads, rocket *with burster or expelling charge*	1.4D	UN0370	II	1.4D		None	62	None	Forbidden	75 kg	02	
	Warheads, rocket *with burster or expelling charge*	1.4F	UN0371	II	1.4F		None	62	None	Forbidden	Forbidden	08	
	Warheads, rocket *with bursting charge*	1.1D	UN0286	II	1.1D		None	62	None	Forbidden	Forbidden	03	
	Warheads, rocket *with bursting charge*	1.2D	UN0287	II	1.2D		None	62	None	Forbidden	Forbidden	03	
	Warheads, rocket *with bursting charge*	1.1F	UN0369	II	1.1F		None	62	None	Forbidden	Forbidden	08	
	Warheads, torpedo *with bursting charge*	1.1D	UN0221	II	1.1D		None	62	None	Forbidden	Forbidden	03	
G	**Water-reactive liquid, corrosive, n.o.s.**	4.3	UN3129	I II III	4.3, 8 4.3, 8 4.3, 8	 IB1 IB2	None None None	201 202 203	243 243 242	Forbidden 1 L 5 L	1 L 5 L 60 L	D E E	 85
G	**Water-reactive liquid, n.o.s.**	4.3	UN3148	I II III	4.3 4.3 4.3	 IB1 IB2	None None None	201 202 203	244 243 242	Forbidden 1 L 5 L	1 L 5 L 60 L	E E E	40 40 40
G	**Water-reactive liquid, toxic, n.o.s.**	4.3	UN3130	I II III	4.3, 6.1 4.3, 6.1 4.3, 6.1	A4 IB1 IB2	None None None	201 202 203	243 243 242	Forbidden 1 L 5 L	1 L 5 L 60 L	D E E	 85 85
G	**Water-reactive solid, corrosive, n.o.s.**	4.3	UN3131	I II III	4.3, 8 4.3, 8 4.3, 8	IB4, IP1, N40 IB6, IP2 IB8, IP4	None 151 151	211 212 213	242 242 241	Forbidden 15 kg 25 kg	15 kg 50 kg 100 kg	D E E	 85 85
G	**Water-reactive solid, flammable, n.o.s.**	4.3	UN3132	I II III	4.3, 4.1 4.3, 4.1 4.3, 4.1	IB4, N40 IB4 IB6	None 151 151	211 212 213	242 242 241	Forbidden 15 kg 25 kg	15 kg 50 kg 100 kg	D E E	
G	**Water-reactive solid, n.o.s.**	4.3	UN2813	I II III	4.3 4.3 4.3	IB4, N40 IB7, IP2 IB8, IP4	None 151 151	211 212 213	242 242 241	Forbidden 15 kg 25 kg	15 kg 50 kg 100 kg	E E E	40 40 40
G	**Water-reactive, solid, oxidizing, n.o.s.**	4.3	UN3133	II III	4.3, 5.1 4.3, 5.1		None None	214 214	214 214	Forbidden Forbidden	Forbidden Forbidden	E E	40 40

§172.101 - Hazardous Materials Table

Symbols	Hazardous materials descriptions and proper shipping names	Hazard class or Division	Identification Numbers	PG	Label Codes	Special provisions (§172.102)	(8) Packaging (§173.***)			(9) Quantity limitations		(10) Vessel stowage	
							Exceptions	Non-bulk	Bulk	Passenger aircraft/rail	Cargo aircraft only	Location	Other
(1)	(2)	(3)	(4)	(5)	(6)	(7)	(8A)	(8B)	(8C)	(9A)	(9B)	(10A)	(10B)
G	**Water-reactive solid, self-heating, n.o.s.**	4.3	UN3135	I II III	4.3, 4.2 4.3, 4.2 4.3, 4.2	N40 IB5, IP2 IB8, IP4	None None None	211 212 213	242 242 241	Forbidden 15 kg 25 kg	15 kg 50 kg 100 kg	E E E	
G	**Water-reactive solid, toxic, n.o.s.**	4.3	UN3134	I II III	4.3, 6.1 4.3, 6.1 4.3, 6.1	A8, IB4, IP1, N40 IB5, IP2 IB8, IP4	None 151 151	211 212 213	242 242 241	Forbidden 15 kg 25 kg	15 kg 50 kg 100 kg	D E E	 85 85
	Wheel chair, electric, see **Battery powered vehicle** *or* **Battery powered equipment**												
	White acid, see **Hydrofluoric acid**												
I	**White asbestos** *(chrysotile, actinolite, anthophyllite, tremolite)*	9	UN2590	III	9	IB8, IP2, IP3	155	216	240	200 kg	200 kg	A	34, 40
	Wood preservatives, liquid	3	UN1306	II III	3 3	IB2, T4, TP1, TP8 B1, IB3, T2, TP1	150 150	202 203	242 242	5 L 60 L	60 L 220 L	B A	40 40
	Xanthates	4.2	UN3342	II III	4.2 4.2	IB6, IP2 IB8, IP3	None None	212 213	241 241	15 kg 25 kg	50 kg 100 kg	D D	40 40
	Xenon, compressed	2.2	UN2036		2.2		306	302	None	75 kg	150 kg	A	
	Xenon, refrigerated liquid *(cryogenic liquids)*	2.2	UN2591		2.2	T75, TP5	320	None	None	50 kg	500 kg	B	
	Xylenes	3	UN1307	II III	3 3	IB2, T4, TP1 B1, IB3, T2, TP1	150 150	202 203	242 242	5 L 60 L	60 L 220 L	B A	
	Xylenols	6.1	UN2261	II	6.1	IB8, IP2, IP4, T7, TP2	None	212	242	25 kg	100 kg	A	
	Xylidines, solid	6.1	UN1711	II	6.1	IB8, IP2, IP4, T7, TP2	None	212	242	25 kg	100 kg	A	
	Xylidines, solution	6.1	UN1711	II	6.1	IB2, T7, TP2	None	202	243	5 L	60 L	A	
	Xylyl bromide	6.1	UN1701	II	6.1	A3, A6, A7, IB2, N33, T7, TP2, TP13	None	340	None	Forbidden	60 L	D	40
	p-Xylyl diazide	Forbidden											
	Zinc ammonium nitrite	5.1	UN1512	II	5.1	IB8, IP4	None	212	242	5 kg	25 kg	E	
	Zinc arsenate *or* **Zinc arsenite** *or* **Zinc arsenate and zinc arsenite mixtures**	6.1	UN1712	II	6.1	IB8, IP2, IP4	None	212	242	25 kg	100 kg	A	
	Zinc ashes	4.3	UN1435	III	4.3	A1, A19, IB8, IP4	151	213	241	25 kg	100 kg	A	
	Zinc bisulfite solution, see **Bisulfites, aqueous solutions, n.o.s.**												
	Zinc bromate	5.1	UN2469	III	5.1	A1, A29, IB8, IP3	152	213	240	25 kg	100 kg	A	56, 58, 106
	Zinc chlorate	5.1	UN1513	II	5.1	A9, IB8, IP2, IP4, N34	152	212	242	5 kg	25 kg	A	56, 58, 106
	Zinc chloride, anhydrous	8	UN2331	III	8	IB8, IP3	None	213	240	25 kg	100 kg	A	
	Zinc chloride, solution	8	UN1840	III	8	IB3, T4, TP1	154	203	241	5 L	60 L	A	
	Zinc cyanide	6.1	UN1713	I	6.1	IB7, IP1	None	211	242	5 kg	50 kg	A	26
	Zinc dithionite *or* **Zinc hydrosulfite**	9	UN1931	III	None	IB8	155	204	240	100 kg	200 kg	A	49
	Zinc ethyl, see **Diethylzinc**												
	Zinc fluorosilicate	6.1	UN2855	III	6.1	IB8, IP3	153	213	240	100 kg	200 kg	A	26
	Zinc hydrosulfite, *see* **Zinc dithionite**												
	Zinc muriate solution, see **Zinc chloride, solution**												
	Zinc nitrate	5.1	UN1514	II	5.1	IB8, IP4	152	212	240	5 kg	25 kg	A	
	Zinc permanganate	5.1	UN1515	II	5.1	IB6, IP2	152	212	242	5 kg	25 kg	D	56, 58, 69, 106, 107
	Zinc peroxide	5.1	UN1516	II	5.1	IB6, IP2	152	212	242	5 kg	25 kg	A	13, 75, 106
	Zinc phosphide	4.3	UN1714	I	4.3, 6.1	A19, N40	None	211	None	Forbidden	15 kg	E	40, 85
	Zinc powder *or* **Zinc dust**	4.3	UN1436	I II III	4.3, 4.2 4.3, 4.2 4.3, 4.2	A19, IB4, IP1, N40 A19, IB7, IP2 IB8, IP4	None None None	211 212 213	242 242 242	Forbidden 15 kg 25 kg	15 kg 50 kg 100 kg	A A A	
	Zinc resinate	4.1	UN2714	III	4.1	A1, IB6	151	213	240	25 kg	100 kg	A	
	Zinc selenate, see **Selenates** *or* **Selenites**												
	Zinc selenite, see **Selenates** *or* **Selenites**												
	Zinc silicofluoride, see **Zinc fluorosilicate**												

§172.101 - Hazardous Materials Table

Symbols	Hazardous materials descriptions and proper shipping names	Hazard class or Division	Identification Numbers	PG	Label Codes	Special provisions (§172.102)	(8) Packaging (§173.***)			(9) Quantity limitations		(10) Vessel stowage	
							Exceptions	Non-bulk	Bulk	Passenger aircraft/ rail	Cargo aircraft only	Location	Other
(1)	(2)	(3)	(4)	(5)	(6)	(7)	(8A)	(8B)	(8C)	(9A)	(9B)	(10A)	(10B)
	Zirconium, dry, *coiled wire, finished metal sheets, strip (thinner than 254 microns but not thinner than 18 microns)*	4.1	UN2858	III	4.1	A1, IB8	151	213	240	25 kg	100 kg	A	
	Zirconium, dry, *finished sheets, strip or coiled wire*	4.2	UN2009	III	4.2	A1, A19, IB8	None	213	240	25 kg	100 kg	D	
	Zirconium hydride	4.1	UN1437	II	4.1	A19, A20, IB4, N34	None	212	240	15 kg	50 kg	E	
	Zirconium nitrate	5.1	UN2728	III	5.1	A1, A29, IB8, IP3	152	213	240	25 kg	100 kg	A	
	Zirconium picramate, *dry or wetted with less than 20 percent water, by mass*	1.3C	UN0236	II	1.3C		None	62	None	Forbidden	Forbidden	10	5E
	Zirconium picramate, wetted *with not less than 20 percent water, by mass*	4.1	UN1517	I	4.1	23, N41	None	211	None	1 kg	15 kg	D	28, 36
	Zirconium powder, dry	4.2	UN2008	I II III	4.2 4.2 4.2	 A19, A20, IB6, IP2, N5, N34 IB8, IP3	None None None	211 212 213	242 241 241	Forbidden 15 kg 25 kg	Forbidden 50 kg 100 kg	D D D	
	Zirconium powder, wetted *with not less than 25 percent water (a visible excess of water must be present) (a) mechanically produced, particle size less than 53 microns; (b) chemically produced, particle size less than 840 microns*	4.1	UN1358	II	4.1	A19, A20, IB6, IP2, N34	None	212	241	15 kg	50 kg	E	
	Zirconium scrap	4.2	UN1932	III	4.2	IB8, IP3, N34	None	213	240	Forbidden	Forbidden	D	
	Zirconium suspended in a liquid	3	UN1308	I II III	3 3 3	 IB2 B1, IB2	None None 150	201 202 203	243 242 242	Forbidden 5 L 60 L	Forbidden 60 L 220 L	B B B	
	Zirconium tetrachloride	8	UN2503	III	8	IB8, IP3	154	213	240	25 kg	100 kg	A	

FEDERAL REGISTER UPDATES

In the April 18, 2003 Federal Register, the §172.101 Hazardous Materials Table was revised, effective October 1, 2003. The following entries were revised to read as follows:

§172.101 - Hazardous Materials Table

Symbols	Hazardous materials descriptions and proper shipping names	Hazard class or Division	Identification Numbers	PG	Label Codes	Special provisions (§172.102)	(8) Packaging (§173.***)			(9) Quantity limitations		(10) Vessel stowage	
							Exceptions	Nonbulk	Bulk	Passenger aircraft/ rail	Cargo aircraft only	Location	Other
(1)	(2)	(3)	(4)	(5)	(6)	(7)	(8A)	(8B)	(8C)	(9A)	(9B)	(10A)	(10B)
D	**Diesel fuel**	3	NA1993	III	None	144, B1, IB3, T4, TP1, TP29	150	203	242	60 L	220 L	A	
I	**Diesel fuel**	3	UN1202	III	3	144, B1, IB3, T2, TP1	150	203	242	60 L	220 L	A	
	Fuel, aviation, turbine engine	3	UN1863	I II III	3 3 3	144, T11, TP1, TP8 144, IB2, T4, TP1, TP8 144, B1, IB3, T2, TP1	150 150 150	210 202 203	243 242 242	1 L 5 L 60 L	30 L 60 L 220 L	E B A	
D	**Fuel Oil** *(No. 1, 2, 4, 5, or 6)*	3	NA1993	III	3	144, B1, IB3, T4, TP1, TP29	150	203	242	60 L	220 L	A	
	Gas oil	3	UN1203	III	3	144, B1, IB3, T2, TP1	150	203	242	60 L	220 L	A	
D	**Gasohol** *gasoline mixed with ethyl alcohol, with not more than 20 percent alcohol.*	3	NA1203	I	3	144	150	202	242	5 L	60 L	E	
	Gasoline	3	UN1203	II	3	144, B33, IB2, T4, TP1	150	202	242	5 L	60 L	3	
	Hydrocarbons, liquid, n.o.s.	3 3 3	UN3295	I II III	3 3 3	144, T11, TP1, TP8 144, IB2, T7, TP1, TP8, TP28 144, B1, IB3, T4, TP1, TP29	150 150 150	201 202 203	243 242 242	1 L 5 L 60 L	30 L 60 L 220 L	E B A	
	Kerosene	3	UN1223	III	3	144, B1, IB3, T2, TP2	150	203	242	60 L	220 L	A	
	Petroleum crude oil	3	UN1267	I II III	3 3 3	144, T11, TP1, TP8 144, IB2, T4, TP1, TP8 144, B1, IB3, T2, TP1	None 150 150	201 202 203	243 242 242	1 L 5 L 60 L	39 L 60 L 220 L	E B A	
	Petroleum distillates, n.o.s. *or* **Petroleum products, n.o.s.**	3	UN1268	I II III	3 3 3	144, T11, TP1, TP8 144, IB2, T7, TP1, TP8, TP28 144, B1, IB3, T4, TP1, TP29	150 150 150	201 202 203	243 242 242	1 L 5 L 60 L	30 L 60 L 220 L	E B A	
D	**Petroleum oil**	3	NA1270	I II III	3 3 3	144, T11, TP1, TP9 144, IB2, T7, TP1, TP8, TP28 144, B1, IB3, T4, TP1, TP29	None 150 150	201 202 203	243 242 242	1 L 5 L 60 L	30 L 60 L 220 L	E B A	

§172.101 App. A List of hazardous substances and reportable quantities.

1. **This appendix lists materials** and their corresponding reportable quantities (RQ's) that are listed or designated as "hazardous substances" under section 101(14) of the Comprehensive Environmental Response, Compensation, and Liability Act, 42 U.S.C. 9601(14) (CERCLA; 42 U.S.C. 9601 et seq). This listing fulfills the requirement of CERCLA, 42 U.S.C. 9656(a), that all "hazardous substances," as defined in 42 U.S.C. 9601(14), be listed and regulated as hazardous materials under 49 U.S.C. 5101-5127. That definition includes substances listed under sections 311(b)(2)(A) and 307(a) of the Federal Water Pollution Control Act, 33 U.S.C. 1321(b)(2)(A) and 1317(a), section 3001 of the Solid Waste Disposal Act, 42 U.S.C. 6921, and section 112 of the Clean Air Act, 42 U.S.C. 7412. In addition, this list contains materials that the Administrator of the Environmental Protection Agency has determined to be hazardous substances in accordance with section 102 of CERCLA, 42 U.S.C. 9602. It should be noted that 42 U.S.C. 9656(b) provides that common and contract carriers may be held liable under laws other than CERCLA for the release of a hazardous substance as defined in that Act, during transportation that commenced before the effective date of the listing and regulating of that substance as a hazardous material under 49 U.S.C. 5101-5127.
2. **This appendix is divided into two TABLES** which are entitled "TABLE 1 — HAZARDOUS SUBSTANCES OTHER THAN RADIONUCLIDES" and "TABLE 2 — RADIONUCLIDES." A material listed in this appendix is regulated as a hazardous material and a hazardous substance under this subchapter if it meets the definition of a hazardous substance in §171.8 of this subchapter.
3. **The procedure for selecting a proper shipping name** for a hazardous substance is set forth in §172.101(c).
4. **Column 1 of TABLE 1, entitled "Hazardous substance"**, contains the names of those elements and compounds that are hazardous substances. Following the listing of elements and compounds is a listing of waste streams. These waste streams appear on the list in numerical sequence and are referenced by the appropriate "D", "F", or "K" numbers. Column 2 of TABLE 1, entitled "Reportable quantity (RQ)", contains the reportable quantity (RQ), in pounds and kilograms, for each hazardous substance listed in Column 1 of TABLE 1.
5. **A series of notes is used throughout TABLE 1 and TABLE 2** to provide additional information concerning certain hazardous substances. These notes are explained at the end of each TABLE.
6. **TABLE 2 lists radionuclides** that are hazardous substances and their corresponding RQ's. The RQ's in table 2 for radionuclides are expressed in units of curies and terabecquerels, whereas those in table 1 are expressed in units of pounds and kilograms. If a material is listed in both table 1 and table 2, the lower RQ shall apply. Radionuclides are listed in alphabetical order. The RQ's for radionuclides are given in the radiological unit of measure of curie, abbreviated "Ci", followed, in parentheses, by an equivalent unit measured in terabecquerels, abbreviated "TBq".
7. **For mixtures of radionuclides,** the following requirements shall be used in determining if a package contains an RQ of a hazardous substance:
   (i) *if the identity and quantity* (in curies or terabecquerels) of each radionuclide in a mixture or solution is known, the ratio between the quantity per package (in curies or terabecquerels) and the RQ for the radionuclide must be determined for each radionuclide. A package contains an RQ of a hazardous substance when the sum of the ratios for the radionuclides in the mixture or solution is equal to or greater than one;
   (ii) *if the identity* of each radionuclide in a mixture or solution is known but the quantity per package (in curies or terabecquerels) of one or more of the radionuclides is unknown, an RQ of a hazardous substance is present in a package when the total quantity (in curies or terabecquerels) of the mixture or solution is equal to or greater than the lowest RQ of any individual radionuclide in the mixture or solution; and
   (iii) *if the identity* of one or more radionuclides in a mixture or solution is unknown (or if the identity of a radionuclide by itself is unknown), an RQ of a hazardous substance is present when the total quantity (in curies or terabecquerels) in a package is equal to or greater than either one curie or the lowest RQ of any known individual radionuclide in the mixture or solution, whichever is lower.

Table 1 to Appendix A - Hazardous Substances Other Than Radionuclides

Hazardous substance	Reportable quantity (RQ) pounds (kilograms)
Acenaphthene	100 (45.4)
Acenaphthylene	5000 (2270)
Acetaldehyde	1000 (454)
Acetaldehyde, chloro-	1000 (454)
Acetaldehyde, trichloro-	5000 (2270)
Acetamide	100 (45.4)
Acetamide, N-(aminothioxomethyl)-	1000 (454)
Acetamide, N-(4-ethoxyphenyl)-	100 (45.4)
Acetamide, N-fluoren-2-yl-	1 (0.454)
Acetamide, 2-fluoro-	100 (45.4)
Acetic acid	5000 (2270)
Acetic acid (2,4-dichlorophenoxy)-	100 (45.4)
Acetic acid, ethyl ester	5000 (2270)
Acetic acid, fluoro-, sodium salt	10 (4.54)
Acetic acid, lead (2+) salt	10 (4.54)
Acetic acid, thallium(I+) salt	1000 (454)
Acetic anhydride	5000 (2270)
Acetone	5000 (2270)
Acetone cyanohydrin	10 (4.54)
Acetonitrile	5000 (2270)
Acetophenone	5000 (2270)
2-Acetylaminofluorene	1 (0.454)
Acetyl bromide	5000 (2270)
Acetyl chloride	5000 (2270)
1-Acetyl-2-thiourea	1 (0.454)
Acrolein	1(0.454)
Acrylamide	5000 (2270)
Acrylic acid	5000 (2270)
Acrylonitrile	100 (45.4)
Adipic acid	5000 (2270)
AldicarbD	1 (0.454)
Aldrin	1 (0.454)
Allyl alcohol	100 (45.4)
Allyl chloride	1000 (454)
Aluminum phosphide	100 (45.4)
Aluminum sulfate	5000 (2270)
4-Aminobiphenyl	1 (0.454)
5-(Aminomethyl)-3-isoxazolol	1000 (454)
4-Aminopyridine	1000 (454)
Amitrole	10 (4.54)
Ammonia	100 (45.4)
Ammonium acetate	5000 (2270)
Ammonium benzoate	5000 (2270)
Ammonium bicarbonate	5000 (2270)
Ammonium bichromate	10 (4.54)
Ammonium bifluoride	100 (45.4)
Ammonium bisulfite	5000 (2270)
Ammonium carbamate	5000 (2270)
Ammonium carbonate	5000 (2270)
Ammonium chloride	5000 (2270)
Ammonium chromate	10 (4.54)
Ammonium citrate, dibasic	5000 (2270)
Ammonium dichromate @	10 (4.54)
Ammonium fluoborate	5000 (2270)
Ammonium fluoride	100 (45.4)
Ammonium hydroxide	1000 (454)
Ammonium oxalate	5000 (2270)
Ammonium picrate	10 (4.54)

Table 1 to Appendix A - Hazardous Substances Other Than Radionuclides

Hazardous substance	Reportable quantity (RQ) pounds (kilograms)
Ammonium silicofluoride	1000 (454)
Ammonium sulfamate	5000 (2270)
Ammonium sulfide	100 (45.4)
Ammonium sulfite	5000 (2270)
Ammonium tartrate	5000 (2270)
Ammonium thiocyanate	5000 (2270)
Ammonium vanadate	1000 (454)
Amyl acetate iso-Amyl acetate sec-Amyl acetate tert-Amyl acetate	5000 (2270)
Aniline	5000 (2270)
o-Anisidine	100 (45.4)
Anthracene	5000 (2270)
Antimony ¢	5000 (2270)
Antimony pentachloride	1000 (454)
Antimony potassium tartrate	100 (45.4)
Antimony tribromide	1000 (454)
Antimony trichloride	1000 (454)
Antimony trifluoride	1000 (454)
Antimony trioxide	1000 (454)
Argentate(1-), bis(cyano-C)-, potassium	1 (0.454)
Aroclor 1016	1 (0.454)
Aroclor 1221	1 (0.454)
Aroclor 1232	1 (0.454)
Aroclor 1242	1 (0.454)
Aroclor 1248	1 (0.454)
Aroclor 1254	1 (0.454)
Aroclor 1260	1 (0.454)
Arsenic ¢	1 (0.454)
Arsenic acid	1 (0.454)
Arsenic acid H_3AsO_4	1 (0.454)
Arsenic disulfide	1 (0.454)
Arsenic oxide As_20_3	1 (0.454)
Arsenic oxide As_20_5	1 (0.454)
Arsenic pentoxide	1 (0.454)
Arsenic trichloride	1 (0.454)
Arsenic trioxide	1 (0.454)
Arsenic trisulfide	1 (0.454)
Arsine, diethyl-	1 (0.454)
Arsinic acid, dimethyl-	1 (0.454)
Arsonous dichloride, phenyl-	1 (0.454)
Asbestos ¢¢	1 (0.454)
Auramine	100 (45.4)
Azaserine	1 (0.454)
Aziridine	1 (0.454)
Aziridine, 2-methyl-	1 (0.454)
Azirino[2',3':3,4]pyrrolo(1,2-a)indole-4,7-dione,6-amino-8-[[(aminocarbonyl)oxy] methyl]-1,1a,2,8,8a, 8b-hexahydro-8a-methoxy-5-methyl-, [1aS-[aalpha,8beta,8aalpha,8balpha)]-	10 (4.54)
Barium cyanide	10 (4.54)
Benz[j]aceanthrylene, 1,2-dihydro-3-methyl-	10 (4.54)
Benz[c]acridine	100 (45.4)
3,4-Benzacridine	100 (45.4)
Benzal chloride	5000 (2270)
Benzamide, 3,5-dichloro-N-(1,1-dimethyl-2-propynyl)	5000 (2270)
Benz[a]anthracene	10 (4.54)
1,2-Benzanthracene	10 (4.54)
Benz[a]anthracene, 7,12-dimethyl-	1 (0.454)
Benzenamine	5000 (2270)

Table 1 to Appendix A - Hazardous Substances Other Than Radionuclides

Hazardous substance	Reportable quantity (RQ) pounds (kilograms)
Benzenamine, 4,4'-carbonimidoylbis (N,N-dimethyl-	100 (45.4)
Benzenamine, 4-chloro-	1000 (454)
Benzenamine, 4-chloro-2-methyl-, hydrochloride	100 (45.4)
Benzenamine, N,N-dimethyl-4-(phenylazo)-	10 (4.54)
Benzenamine, 2-methyl-	100 (45.4)
Benzenamine, 4-methyl-	100 (45.4)
Benzenamine, 4,4'-methylenebis(2-chloro-	10 (4.54)
Benzenamine, 2-methyl-, hydrochloride	100 (45.4)
Benzenamine, 2-methyl-5-nitro-	100 (45.4)
Benzenamine, 4-nitro-	5000 (2270)
Benzene	10 (4.54)
Benzene, 1-bromo-4-phenoxy-	100 (45.4)
Benzene, chloro-	100 (45.4)
Benzene, chloromethyl-	100 (45.4)
Benzene, 1,2-dichloro-	100 (45.4)
Benzene, 1,3-dichloro-	100 (45.4)
Benzene, 1,4-dichloro-	100 (45.4)
Benzene, 1,1'-(2,2-dichloroethylidene)bis[4-chloro	1 (0.454)
Benzene, dichloromethyl-	5000 (2270)
Benzene, 1,3-diisocyanatomethyl	100 (45.4)
Benzene, dimethyl-	100 (45.4)
Benzene, m-dimethyl-	1000 (454)
Benzene, o-dimethyl-	1000 (454)
Benzene, p-dimethyl-	100 (45.4)
Benzene, hexachloro-	10 (4.54)
Benzene, hexahydro-	1000 (454)
Benzene, hydroxy-	1000 (454)
Benzene, methyl-	1000 (454)
Benzene, 1-methyl-2,4-dinitro-	10 (4.54)
Benzene, 2-methyl-1,3-dinitro-	100 (45.4)
Benzene, 1-methylethyl-	5000 (2270)
Benzene, nitro-	1000 (454)
Benzene, pentachloro-	10 (4.54)
Benzene, pentachloronitro-	100 (45.4)
Benzene, 1,2,4,5-tetrachloro-	5000 (2270)
Benzene, 1,1'-(2,2,2-trichloroethylidene)bis[4-chloro-	1 (0.454)
Benzene, 1,1'-(2,2,2-trichloroethylidene)bis[4-methoxy)	1 (0.454)
Benzene, (trichloromethyl)	10 (4.54)
Benzene, 1,3,5-trinitro-	10 (4.54)
Benzeneacetic acid, 4-chloro-alpha-(4-chlorophenyl)-alpha-hydroxy-, ethyl ester	10 (4.54)
Benzenebutanoic acid, 4-[bis(2-chloroethyl)amino]-	10 (4.54)
Benzenediamine, ar-methyl-	10 (4.54)
1,2-Benzenedicarboxylic acid, [bis(2-ethylhexyl)] ester	100 (45.4)
1,2-Benzenedicarboxylic acid, dibutyl ester	10 (4.54)
1,2-Benzenedicarboxylic acid, diethyl ester	1000 (454)
1,2-Benzenedicarboxylic acid, dimethyl ester	5000 (2270)
1,2-Benzenedicarboxylic acid, dioctyl ester	5000 (2270)
1,3-Benzenediol	5000 (2270)
1,2-Benzenediol,4-[1-hydroxy-2-(methylamino)ethyl]-	1000 (454)
Benzeneethanamine, alpha,alpha-dimethyl-	5000 (2270)
Benzenesulfonic acid chloride	100 (45.4)
Benzenesulfonyl chloride	100 (45.4)
Benzenethiol	100 (45.4)
Benzidine	1 (0.454)
1,2-Benzisothiazol-3(2H)-one,1,1-dioxide	100 (45.4)
Benzo[a]anthracene	10 (4.54)
1,3-Benzodioxole, 5-(2-propenyl)-	100 (45.4)
1,3-Benzodioxole, 5-(1-propenyl)-	100 (45.4)

Table 1 to Appendix A - Hazardous Substances Other Than Radionuclides

Hazardous substance	Reportable quantity (RQ) pounds (kilograms)
1,3-Benzodioxole, 5-propyl-	10 (4.54)
Benzo[b]fluoranthene	1 (0.454)
Benzo[k]fluoranthene	5000 (2270)
Benzo[j,k]fluorene	100 (45.4)
Benzoic acid	5000 (2270)
Benzonitrile	5000 (2270)
Benzo[g,h,i]perylene	5000 (2270)
2H-1-Benzopyran-2-one, 4-hydroxy-3-(3-oxo-1-phenyl-butyl)-, & salts, when present at concentrations greater than 0.3%	100 (45.4)
Benzo[a]pyrene	1 (0.454)
3,4-Benzopyrene	1 (0.454)
p-Benzoquinone	10 (4.54)
Benzo [rst]pentaphene	10 (4.54)
Benzotrichloride	10 (4.54)
Benzoyl chloride	1000 (454)
1,2-Benzphenanthrene	100 (45.4)
Benzyl chloride	100 (45.4)
Beryllium ¢	10 (4.54)
Beryllium chloride	1 (0.454)
Beryllium dust ¢	10 (4.54)
Beryllium fluoride	1 (0.454)
Beryllium nitrate	1 (0.454)
alpha - BHC	10 (4.54)
beta - BHC	1 (0.454)
delta - BHC	1 (0.454)
gamma - BHC	1 (0.454)
2,2'Bioxirane	10 (4.54)
Biphenyl	100 (45.4)
(1,1'-Biphenyl)-4,4'-diamine	1 (0.454)
(1,1'-Biphenyl)-4,4'-diamine,3,3'-dichloro-	1 (0.454)
(1,1'-Biphenyl)-4,4'-diamine,3,3'-dimethoxy-	10 (4.54)
(1,1'-Biphenyl)-4,4'-diamine,3,3'-dimethyl-	10 (4.54)
Bis(2-chloroethoxy) methane	1000 (454)
Bis(2-chloroethyl) ether	10 (4.54)
Bis(2-ethylhexyl)phthalate	100 (45.4)
Bromoacetone	1000 (454)
Bromoform	100 (45.4)
4-Bromophenyl phenyl ether	100 (45.4)
Brucine	100 (45.4)
1,3-Butadiene	10 (4.54)
1,3-Butadiene, 1,1,2,3,4,4-hexachloro-	1 (0.454)
1-Butanamine, N-butyl-N-nitroso-	10 (4.54)
1-Butanol	5000 (2270)
2-Butanone	5000 (2270)
2-Butanone, 3,3-dimethyl-1-(methylthio)-,O-[(methylamino) carbonyl] oxime	100 (45.4)
2-Butanone peroxide	10 (4.54)
2-Butenal	100 (45.4)
2-Butene, 1,4-dichloro-	1 (0.454)
2-Butenoic acid, 2-methyl-,7[[2,3-dihydroxy-2-(1-methoxyethyl)-3-methyl-1-oxobutoxy]methyl]-2,3,5,7a-tetrahydro-1H-pyrrolizin-1-yl ester, [1S-[1alpha(Z),7(2S*, 3R*), 7alpha]]-	10 (4.54)
Butyl acetate iso-Butyl acetate sec-Butyl acetate tert-Butyl acetate	5000 (2270)
n-Butyl alcohol	5000 (2270)
Butylamine iso-Butylamine sec-Butylamine tert-Butylamine	1000 (454)
Butyl benzyl phthalate	100 (45.4)
n-Butyl phthalate	10 (4.54)
Butyric acid iso-Butyric acid	5000 (2270)
Cacodylic acid	1 (0.454)
Cadmium ¢	10 (4.54)
Cadmium acetate	10 (4.54)
Cadmium bromide	10 (4.54)
Cadmium chloride	10 (4.54)
Calcium arsenate	1 (0.454)
Calcium arsenite	1 (0.454)
Calcium carbide	10 (4.54)
Calcium chromate	10 (4.54)
Calcium cyanamide	1000 (454)
Calcium cyanide	10 (4.54)
Calcium cyanide $Ca(CN)_2$	10 (4.54)
Calcium dodecylbenzene sulfonate	1000 (454)
Calcium hypochlorite	10 (4.54)
Camphene, octachloro-	1 (0.454)
Captan	10 (4.54)
Carbamic acid, ethyl ester	100 (45.4)
Carbamic acid, methylnitroso-, ethyl ester	1 (0.454)
Carbamic chloride, dimethyl-	1 (0.454)
Carbamide, thio-	10 (4.54)
Carbamimidoselenoic acid	1000 (454)
Carbamothioic acid, bis (1-methylethyl)-, S-(2,3-dichloro-2-propenyl) ester	100 (45.4)
Carbaryl	100 (45.4)
Carbofuran	10 (4.54)
Carbon bisulfide	100 (45.4)
Carbon disulfide	100 (45.4)
Carbonic acid, dithallium (I+)	100 (45.4)
Carbonic dichloride	10 (4.54)
Carbonic difluoride	1000 (454)
Carbonochloridic acid, methyl ester	1000 (454)
Carbon oxyfluoride	1000 (454)
Carbon tetrachloride	10 (4.54)
Carbonyl sulfide	100 (45.4)
Catechol	100 (45.4)
Chloral	5000(2270)
Chloramben	100 (45.4)
Chlorambucil	10 (4.54)
Chlordane	1 (0.454)
Chlordane, alpha & gamma isomers	1 (0.454)
Chlordane, technical	1 (0.454)
Chlorine	10 (4.54)
Chlornaphazine	100 (45.4)
Chloroacetaldehyde	1000 (454)
Chloroacetic acid	100 (45.4)
2-Chloroacetophenone	100 (45.4)
p-Chloroaniline	1000 (454)
Chlorobenzene	100 (45.4)
Chlorobenzilate	10 (4.54)
4-Chloro-m-cresol	5000 (2270)
p-Chloro-m-cresol	5000 (2270)
Chlorodibromomethane	100 (45.4)
Chloroethane	100 (45.4)
2-Chloroethyl vinyl ether	1000 (454)
Chloroform	10 (4.54)
Chloromethane	100 (45.4)
Chloromethyl methyl ether	10 (4.54)

Table 1 to Appendix A - Hazardous Substances Other Than Radionuclides

Hazardous substance	Reportable quantity (RQ) pounds (kilograms)
beta-Chloronaphthalene	5000 (2270)
2-Chloronaphthalene	5000 (2270)
2-Chlorophenol	100 (45.4)
o-Chlorophenol	100 (45.4)
4-Chlorophenyl phenyl ether	5000 (2270)
1-(o-Chlorophenyl)thiourea	100 (45.4)
Chloroprene	100 (45.4)
3-Chloropropionitrile	1000 (454)
Chlorosulfonic acid	1000 (454)
4-Chloro-o-toluidine, hydrochloride	100 (45.4)
Chlorpyrifos	1 (0.454)
Chromic acetate	1000 (454)
Chromic acid	10 (4.54)
Chromic acid H_2CrO_4, calcium salt	10 (4.54)
Chromic sulfate	1000 (454)
Chromium ¢	5000 (2270)
Chromous chloride	1000 (454)
Chrysene	100 (45.4)
Cobaltous bromide	1000 (454)
Cobaltous formate	1000 (454)
Cobaltous sulfamate	1000 (454)
Coke Oven Emissions	1 (0.454)
Copper ¢	5000 (2270)
Copper chloride @	10 (4.54)
Copper cyanide	10 (4.54)
Copper cyanide CuCN	10 (4.54)
Coumaphos	10 (4.54)
Creosote	1 (0.454)
Cresols (isomers and mixture)	100 (45.4)
m-Cresol	100 (45.4)
o-Cresolo	100 (45.4)
p-Cresol	100 (45.4)
Cresylic acid (isomers and mixture)	100 (45.4)
m-Cresylic acid	100 (45.4)
o-Cresylic acid	100 (45.4)
p-Cresylic acid	100 (45.4)
Crotonaldehyde	100 (45.4)
Cumene	5000 (2270)
Cupric acetate	100 (45.4)
Cupric acetoarsenite	1 (0.454)
Cupric chloride	10 (4.54)
Cupric nitrate	100 (45.4)
Cupric oxalate	100 (45.4)
Cupric sulfate	10 (4.54)
Cupric sulfate ammoniated	100 (45.4)
Cupric tartrate	100 (45.4)
Cyanides (soluble salts and complexes) not otherwise specified	10 (4.54)
Cyanogen	100 (45.4)
Cyanogen bromide	1000 (454)
Cyanogen bromide (CN)Br	1000 (454)
Cyanogen chloride	10 (4.54)
Cyanogen chloride (CN)Cl	10 (4.54)
2,5-Cyclohexadiene-1,4-dione	10 (4.54)
Cyclohexane	1000 (454)
Cyclohexane, 1,2,3,4,5,6-hexachloro-, (1alpha,2alpha,3beta,4alpha,5alpha,6beta)-	1 (0.454)
Cyclohexanone	5000 (2270)
2-Cyclohexyl-4,6-dinitrophenol	100 (45.4)
1,3-Cyclopentadiene, 1,2,3,4,5,5-hexachloro-	10 (4.54)

Table 1 to Appendix A - Hazardous Substances Other Than Radionuclides

Hazardous substance	Reportable quantity (RQ) pounds (kilograms)
Cyclophosphamide	10 (4.54)
2,4-D Acid	100 (45.4)
2,4-D Ester	100 (45.4)
Daunomycin	10 (4.54)
DDD	1 (0.454)
4,4'-DDD	1 (0.454)
DDE	1 (0.454)
4,4'-DDE	1 (0.454)
DDT	1 (0.454)
4,4'-DDT	1 (0.454)
Diallate	100 (45.4)
Diamine	1 (0.454)
Diazinon	1 (0.454)
Diazomethane	100 (45.4)
Dibenz[a,h]anthracene	1 (0.454)
1,2:5,6-Dibenzanthracene	1 (0.454)
Dibenzo[a,h]anthracene	1 (0.454)
Dibenzofuran	100 (45.4)
Dibenz[a,i]pyrene	10 (4.54)
1,2-Dibromo-3-chloropropane	1 (0.454)
Dibutyl phthalate	10 (4.54)
Di-n-butyl phthalate	10 (4.54)
Dicamba	1000 (454)
Dichlobenil	100 (45.4)
Dichlone	1 (0.454)
Dichlorobenzene	100 (45.4)
1,2-Dichlorobenzene	100 (45.4)
1,3-Dichlorobenzene	100 (45.4)
1,4-Dichlorobenzene	100 (45.4)
m-Dichlorobenzene	100 (45.4)
o-Dichlorobenzene	100 (45.4)
p-Dichlorobenzene	100 (45.4)
3,3'-Dichlorobenzidine	1 (0.454)
Dichlorobromomethane	5000 (2270)
1,4-Dichloro-2-butene	1 (0.454)
Dichlorodifluoromethane	5000 (2270)
1,1-Dichloroethane	1000 (454)
1,2-Dichloroethane	100 (45.4)
1,1-Dichloroethylene	100 (45.4)
1,2-Dichloroethylene	1000 (454)
Dichloroethyl ether	10 (4.54)
Dichloroisopropyl-ether	1000 (454)
Dichloromethane @	1000 (454)
Dichloromethoxy ethane	1000 (454)
Dichloromethyl ether	10 (4.54)
2,4-Dichlorophenol	100 (45.4)
2,6-Dichlorophenol	100 (45.4)
Dichlorophenylarsine	1 (0.454)
Dichloropropane 1,1-Dichloropropane 1,3-Dichloropropane	1000 (454)
1,2-Dichloropropane	1000 (454)
Dichloropropane - Dichloropropene (mixture)	100 (45.4)
Dichloropropene 2,3-Dichloropropene	100 (45.4)
1,3-Dichloropropene	100 (45.4)
2,2-Dichloropropionic acid	5000 (2270)
Dichlorvos	10 (4.54)
Dicofol	10 (4.54)
Dieldrin	1 (0.454)

Table 1 to Appendix A - Hazardous Substances Other Than Radionuclides

Hazardous substance	Reportable quantity (RQ) pounds (kilograms)
1,2:3,4-Diepoxybutane	10 (4.54)
Diethanolamine	100 (45.4)
Diethylamine	1000 (454)
N,N-diethylaniline	1000 (454)
Diethylarsine	1 (0.454)
1,4-Diethylenedioxide	100 (45.4)
Diethylhexyl phthalate	100 (45.4)
N,N'-Diethylhydrazine	10 (4.54)
O,O-Diethyl S-methyl dithiophosphate	5000 (2270)
Diethyl-p-nitrophenyl phosphate	100 (45.4)
Diethyl phthalate	1000 (454)
O,O-Diethyl O-pyrazinyl phosphorothioate	100 (45.4)
Diethylstilbestrol	1 (0.454)
Diethyl sulfate	10 (4.54)
Dihydrosafrole	10 (4.54)
Diisopropyl fluorophosphate	100 (45.4)
1,4,5,8-Dimethanonaphthalene 1,2,3,4,10,10-hexachloro-1,4,4a,5,8,8a-hexahydro, (1alpha,4alpha,4abeta,5abeta,8beta,8abeta)-	1 (0.454)
1,4,5,8-Dimethanonaphthalene, 1,2,3,4,10,10-10-hexachloro-1,4,4a,5,8,8a-hexahydro-, (1alpha,4alpha,4abeta,5alpha,8alpha,8abeta)-	1 (0.454)
2,7:3,6-Dimethanonaphth[2,3-b]oxirene, 3,4,5,6,9,9-hexachloro-1a,2,2a,3,6,6a,7,7a-octahydro-,(1aalpha,2beta,2abeta,3alpha,6alpha,6abeta,7beta,7aalpha)-	1 (0.454)
2,7:3,6-Dimethanonaphth[2,3-b]oxirene, 3,4,5,6,9,9-hexachloro-1a,2,2a,3,6,6a,7,7a-octahydro-,(1aalpha,2beta,2aalpha,3beta,6beta,6aalpha,7beta,7aalpha)-	1 (0.454)
Dimethoate	10 (4.54)
3,3'-Dimethoxybenzidine	10 (4.54)
Dimethylamine	1000 (454)
p-Dimethylaminoazobenzene	10 (4.54)
N,N-dimethylaniline	100 (45.4)
7,12-Dimethylbenz[a]anthracene	1 (0.454)
3,3'-Dimethylbenzidine	10 (4.54)
alpha,alpha-Dimethylbenzylhydroperoxide	10 (4.54)
Dimethylcarbamoyl chloride	1 (0.454)
Dimethylformamide	100 (45.4)
1,1-Dimethylhydrazine	10 (4.54)
1,2-Dimethylhydrazine	1 (0.454)
Dimethylhydrazine, unsymmetrical @	10 (4.54)
alpha,alpha-Dimethylphenethylamine	5000 (2270)
12,4-Dimethylphenol	100 (45.4)
Dimethyl phthalate	5000 (2270)
Dimethyl sulfate	100 (45.4)
Dinitrobenzene (mixed) m-Dinitrobenzene o-Dinitrobenzene p-Dinitrobenzene	100 (45.4)
4,6-Dinitro-o-cresol and salts	10 (4.54)
Dinitrogen tetroxide @	10 (4.54)
Dinitrophenol 2,5-Dinitrophenol	10 (4.54)
2,4-Dinitrophenol	10 (4.54)
Dinitrotoluene 3,4-Dinitrotoluene	10 (4.54)
2,4-Dinitrotoluene	10 (4.54)
2,6-Dinitrotoluene	100 (45.4)
Dinoseb	1000 (454)
Di-n-octyl phthalate	5000 (2270)
1,4-Dioxane	100 (45.4)
1,2-Diphenylhydrazine	10 (4.54)

Table 1 to Appendix A - Hazardous Substances Other Than Radionuclides

Hazardous substance	Reportable quantity (RQ) pounds (kilograms)
Diphosphoramide, octamethyl-	100 (45.4)
Diphosphoric acid, tetraethyl ester	10 (4.54)
Dipropylamine	5000 (2270)
Di-n-propylnitrosamine	10 (4.54)
Diquat	1000 (454)
Disulfoton	1 (0.454)
Dithiobiuret	100 (45.4)
Diuron	100 (45.4)
Dodecylbenzenesulfonic acid	1000 (454)
2,4-D, salts and esters	100 (45.4)
Endosulfan	1 (0.454)
alpha-Endosulfa	1 (0.454)
beta-Endosulfan	1 (0.454)
Endosulfan sulfate	1 (0.454)
Endothall	1000 (454)
Endrin	1 (0.454)
Endrin, & metabolites	1 (0.454)
Endrin aldehyde	1 (0.454)
Epichlorohydrin	100 (45.4)
Epinephrine	1000 (454)
1,2-Epoxybutane	100 (45.4)
Ethanal	1000 (454)
Ethanamine, N-ethyl-N-nitroso-	1 (0.454)
Ethane, 1,2-dibromo-	1 (0.454)
Ethane, 1,1-dichloro-	1000 (454)
Ethane, 1,2-dichloro-	100 (45.4)
Ethane, hexachloro-	100 (45.4)
Ethane, 1,1'-[methylenebis(oxy)]bis(2-chloro-	1000 (454)
Ethane, 1,1'-oxybis-	100 (45.4)
Ethane, 1,1'-oxybis(2-chloro-	10 (4.54)
Ethane, pentachloro-	10 (4.54)
Ethane, 1,1,1,2-tetrachloro-	100 (45.4)
Ethane, 1,1,2,2-tetrachloro-	100 (45.4)
Ethane, 1,1,2-trichloro-	100 (45.4)
Ethane, 1,1,1-trichloro-	1000 (454)
1,2-Ethanediamine, N,N-dimethyl-N'-2-pyridinyl-N'-(2-thienyl-methyl)-	5000 (2270)
Ethanedinitrile	100 (45.4)
Ethanenitrile	5000 (2270)
Ethanethioamide	10 (4.54)
Ethanimidothioic acid, N-[[(methylamino)carbonyl] oxy]-, methyl ester	100 (45.4)
Ethanol, 2-ethoxy-	1000 (454)
Ethanol, 2,2'-(nitrosoimino)bis-	1 (0.454)
Ethanone, 1-phenyl-	5000 (2270)
Ethanoyl chloride	5000 (2270)
Ethene, chloro-	1 (0.454)
Ethene, 2-chloroethoxy-	1000 (454)
Ethene, 1,1-dichloro-	100 (45.4)
Ethene, 1,2-dichloro- (E)	1000 (454)
Ethene, tetrachloro-	100 (45.4)
Ethene, trichloro-	100 (45.4)
Ethion	10 (4.54)
Ethyl acetate	5000 (2270)
Ethyl acrylate	1000 (454)
Ethylbenzene	1000 (454)
Ethyl carbamate (Urethan)	100 (45.4)
Ethyl chloride @	100 (45.4)
Ethyl cyanide	10 (4.54)
Ethylene dibromide	1 (0.454)

Table 1 to Appendix A - Hazardous Substances Other Than Radionuclides

Hazardous substance	Reportable quantity (RQ) pounds (kilograms)
Ethylene dichloride	100 (45.4)
Ethylene glycol	5000 (2270)
Ethylene glycol monoethyl ether	1000 (454)
Ethylene oxide	10 (4.54)
Ethylenebisdithiocarbamic acid	5000 (2270)
Ethylenebisdithiocarbamic acid, salts and esters	5000 (2270)
Ethylenediamine	5000 (2270)
Ethylenediamine tetraacetic acid (EDTA)	5000 (2270)
Ethylenethiourea	10 (4.54)
Ethylenimine	1 (0.454)
Ethyl ether	100 (45.4)
Ethylidene dichloride	1000 (454)
Ethyl methacrylate	1000 (454)
Ethyl methanesulfonate	1 (0.454)
Ethyl methyl ketone @	5000 (2270)
Famphurdimethylester	1000 (454)
Ferric ammonium citrate	1000 (454)
Ferric ammonium oxalate	1000 (454)
Ferric chloride	1000 (454)
Ferric fluoride	100 (45.4)
Ferric nitrate	1000 (454)
Ferric sulfate	1000 (454)
Ferrous ammonium sulfate	1000 (454)
Ferrous chloride	100 (45.4)
Ferrous sulfate	1000 (454)
Fluoranthene	100 (45.4)
Fluorene	5000 (2270)
Fluorine	10 (4.54)
Fluoroacetamide	100 (45.4)
Fluoroacetic acid, sodium salt	10 (4.54)
Formaldehyde	100 (45.4)
Formic acid	5000 (2270)
Fulminic acid, mercury(2+)salt	10 (4.54)
Fumaric acid	5000 (2270)
Furan	100 (45.4)
Furan, tetrahydro-	1000 (454)
2-Furancarboxaldehyde	5000 (2270)
2,5-Furandione	5000 (2270)
Furfural	5000 (2270)
Furfuran	100 (45.4)
Glucopyranose, 2-deoxy-2-(3-methyl-3-nitrosoureido)-	1 (0.454)
D-Glucose, 2-deoxy-2-[[methylnitrosoamino)-carbonyl]amino]-	1 (0.454)
Glycidylaldehyde	10 (4.54)
Guanidine, N-methyl-N'-nitro-N-nitroso-	10 (4.54)
Guthion	1 (0.454)
Heptachlor	1 (0.454)
Heptachlor epoxide	1 (0.454)
Hexachlorobenzene	10 (4.54)
Hexachlorobutadiene	1 (0.454)
Hexachlorocyclohexane (gamma isomer)	1 (0.454)
Hexachlorocyclopentadiene	10 (4.54)
Hexachloroethane	100 (45.4)
1,2,3,4,10-10-Hexachloro-1,4,4a,5,8,8a-hexahydro-1,4:5,8-endo,exo-dimethanonaphthalene	1 (0.454)
Hexachlorophene	100 (45.4)
Hexachloropropene	1000 (454)
Hexaethyl tetraphosphate	100 (45.4)
Hexamethylene-1,6-diisocyanate	100 (45.4)
Hexamethylphosphoramide	1 (0.454)
Hexane	5000 (2270)
Hydrazine	1 (0.454)
Hydrazine, 1,2-diethyl-	10 (4.54)
Hydrazine, 1,1-dimethyl-	10 (4.54)
Hydrazine, 1,2-dimethyl-	1 (0.454)
Hydrazine, 1,2-diphenyl-	10 (4.54)
Hydrazine, methyl-	10 (4.54)
Hydrazinecarbothioamide	100 (45.4)
Hydrochloric acid	5000 (2270)
Hydrocyanic acid	10 (4.54)
Hydrofluoric acid	100 (45.4)
Hydrogen chloride	5000 (2270)
Hydrogen cyanide	10 (4.54)
Hydrogen fluoride	100 (45.4)
Hydrogen phosphide	100 (45.4)
Hydrogen sulfide	100 (45.4)
Hydrogen sulfide H_2S	100 (45.4)
Hydroperoxide, 1-methyl-1-phenylethyl-	10 (4.54)
Hydroquinone	100 (45.4)
2-Imidazolidinethione	10 (4.54)
Indeno(1,2,3-cd)pyrene	100 (45.4)
1,3-Isobenzofurandione	5000 (2270)
Isobutyl alcohol	5000 (2270)
Isodrin	1 (0.454)
Isophorone	5000 (2270)
Isoprene	100 (45.4)
Isopropanolamine dodecylbenzene sulfonate	1000 (454)
Isosafrole	100 (45.4)
3(2H)-Isoxazolone, 5-(aminomethyl)-	1000 (454)
Keponedecachloroc-tahydro-	1 (0.454)
Lasiocarpine	10 (4.54)
Lead ¢	10 (4.54)
Lead acetate	10 (4.54)
Lead arsenate	1 (0.454)
Lead, bis(acetato-O)tetrahydroxytri	10 (4.54)
Lead chloride	10 (4.54)
Lead fluoborate	10 (4.54)
Lead fluoride	10 (4.54)
Lead iodide	10 (4.54)
Lead nitrate	10 (4.54)
Lead phosphate	10 (4.54)
Lead stearate	10 (4.54)
Lead subacetate	10 (4.54)
Lead sulfate	10 (4.54)
Lead sulfide	10 (4.54)
Lead thiocyanate	10 (4.54)
Lindane	1 (0.454)
Lithium chromate	10 (4.54)
Malathion	100 (45.4)
Maleic acid	5000 (2270)
Maleic anhydride	5000 (2270)
Maleic hydrazide	5000 (2270)
Malononitrile	1000 (454)
MDI	5000 (2270)
Melphalan	1 (0.454)
Mercaptodimethur	10 (4.54)
Mercuric cyanide	1 (0.454)
Mercuric nitrate	10 (4.54)

Table 1 to Appendix A - Hazardous Substances Other Than Radionuclides

Hazardous substance	Reportable quantity (RQ) pounds (kilograms)
Mercuric sulfate	10 (4.54)
Mercuric thiocyanate	10 (4.54)
Mercurous nitrate	10 (4.54)
Mercury	1 (0.454)
Mercury, (acetato-O)phenyl-	100 (45.4)
Mercury fulminate	10 (4.54)
Methacrylonitrile	1000 (454)
Methanamine, N-methyl-	1000 (454)
Methanamine, N-methyl-N-nitroso	10 (4.54)
Methane, bromo-	1000 (454)
Methane, chloro-	100 (45.4)
Methane, chloromethoxy-	10 (4.54)
Methane, dibromo-	1000 (454)
Methane, dichloro-	1000 (454)
Methane, dichlorodifluoro-	5000 (2270)
Methane, iodo-	100 (45.4)
Methane, isocyanato-	10 (4.54)
Methane, oxybis(chloro-	10 (4.54)
Methane, tetrachloro-	10 (4.54)
Methane, tetranitro-	10 (4.54)
Methane, tribromo-	100 (45.4)
Methane, trichloro-	10 (4.54)
Methane, trichlorofluoro-	5000 (2270)
Methanesulfenyl chloride, trichloro-	100 (45.4)
Methanesulfonic acid, ethyl ester	1 (0.454)
Methanethiol	100 (45.4)
6,9-Methano-2,4,3-benzodioxathiepin, 6,7,8,9,10,10-hexachloro-1,5,5a,6,9,9a-hexahydro-, 3-oxide	1 (0.454)
Methanoic acid	5000 (2270)
4,7-Methano-1H-indene, 1,4,5,6,7,8,8-heptachloro-a,4,7,7a-tetrahydro-	1 (0.454)
4,7-Methano-1H-indene, 1,4,5,6,7,8,8-octachloro-2,3,3a,4,7,7a-hexahydro-	1 (0.454)
Methanol	5000 (2270)
Methapyrilene	5000 (2270)
1,3,4-Metheno-2H-cyclobutal[cd]-pentalen-2-one, 1,1a,3,3a,4,5,5,5a,5b,6-decachloroctahydro-	1 (0.454)
Methomyl	100 (45.4)
Methoxychlor	1 (0.454)
Methyl alcohol	5000 (2270)
Methylamine @	100 (45.4)
Methyl bromide	1000 (454)
1-Methylbutadiene	100 (45.4)
Methyl chloride	100 (45.4)
Methyl chlorocarbonate	1000 (454)
Methyl chloroform	1000 (454)
Methyl chloroformate	1000 (454)
Methylchloromethyl ether @	1 (0.454)
3-Methylcholanthrene	10 (4.54)
4,4'-Methylenebis(2-chloroaniline)	10 (4.54)
Methylene bromide	1000 (454)
Methylene chloride	1000 (454)
4,4'-Methylenedianiline	10 (4.54)
Methylene diphenyl diisocyanate	5000 (2270)
Methylene oxide	100 (45.4)
Methyl ethyl ketone (MEK)	5000 (2270)
Methyl ethyl ketone peroxide	10 (4.54)
Methyl hydrazine	10 (4.54)
Methyl iodide	100 (45.4)
Methyl isobutyl ketone	5000 (2270)
Methyl isocyanate	10 (4.54)

Table 1 to Appendix A - Hazardous Substances Other Than Radionuclides

Hazardous substance	Reportable quantity (RQ) pounds (kilograms)
2-Methyllactonitrile	10 (4.54)
Methyl mercaptan	100 (45.4)
Methyl methacrylate	1000 (454)
Methyl parathion	100 (45.4)
4-Methyl-2-pentanone	5000 (2270)
Methyl tert-butyl ether	1000 (454)
Methylthiouracil	10 (4.54)
Mevinphos	10 (4.54)
Mexacarbate	1000 (454)
Mitomycin C	10 (4.54)
MNNG	10 (4.54)
Monoethylamine	100 (45.4)
Monomethylamine	100 (45.4)
Muscimol	1000 (454)
Naled	10 (4.54)
5,12-Naphthacenedione, 8-acetyl-10-[3-amino-2,3,6-trideoxy-alpha-L-lyxo-hexopyranosyl) oxy]-7,8,9,10-tetrahydro-6,8,11-trihydroxy-1-methoxy-, (8S-cis)-	10 (4.54)
Naphthalenamine, N,N-bis(2-chloroethyl)-	100 (45.4)
Naphthalene	100 (45.4)
Naphthalene, 2-chloro-	5000 (2270)
1,4-Naphthalenedione	5000 (2270)
2,7-Naphthalenedisulfonic acid, 3,3'-[(3,3'-dimethyl-(l,1'-biphenyl)-4,4'-diyl)-bis(azo)]bis(5-amino-4-hydroxy)-tetrasodium salt	10 (4.54)
Naphthenic acid	100 (45.4)
1,4-Naphthoquinone	5000 (2270)
alpha-Naphthylamine	100 (45.4)
beta-Naphthylamine	1 (0.454)
1-Naphthylamine	100 (45.4)
2-Naphthylamine	1 (0.454)
alpha-Naphthylthiourea	100 (45.4)
Nickel ¢	100 (45.4)
Nickel ammonium sulfate	100 (45.4)
Nickel carbonyl	10 (4.54)
Nickel carbonyl $Ni(CO)_4$,(T-4)-	10 (4.54)
Nickel chloride	100 (45.4)
Nickel cyanide	10 (4.54)
Nickel cyanide $Ni(CN)_2$	10 (4.54)
Nickel hydroxide	10 (4.54)
Nickel nitrate	100 (45.4)
Nickel sulfate	100 (45.4)
Nicotine and salts	100 (45.4)
Nitric acid	1000 (454)
Nitric acid, thallium(1+) salt	100 (45.4)
Nitric oxide	10 (4.54)
p-Nitroaniline	5000 (2270)
Nitrobenzene	1000 (454)
4-nitrobiphenyl	10 (4.54)
Nitrogen dioxide	10 (4.54)
Nitrogen oxide NO	10 (4.54)
Nitrogen oxide NO_2	10 (4.54)
Nitroglycerine	10 (4.54)
Nitrophenol (mixed) m- o- p-	100 (45.4)
o-Nitrophenol	100 (45.4)
p-Nitrophenol	100 (45.4)
2-Nitrophenol	100 (45.4)
4-Nitrophenol	100 (45.4)
2-Nitropropane	10 (4.54)

Table 1 to Appendix A - Hazardous Substances Other Than Radionuclides

Hazardous substance	Reportable quantity (RQ) pounds (kilograms)
N-Nitrosodi-n-butylamine	10 (4.54)
N-Nitrosodiethanolamine	1 (0.454)
N-Nitrosodiethylamine	1 (0.454)
N-Nitrosodimethylamine	10 (4.54)
N-Nitrosodiphenylamine	100 (45.4)
N-Nitroso-N-ethylurea	1 (0.454)
N-Nitroso-N-methylurea	1 (0.454)
N-Nitroso-N-methylurethane	1 (0.454)
N-Nitrosomethylvinylamine	10 (4.54)
n-Nitrosomorpholine	1 (0.454)
N-Nitrosopiperidine	10 (4.54)
N-Nitrosopyrrolidine	1 (0.454)
Nitrotoluene m-Nitrotoluene o-Nitrotoluene p-Nitrotoluene	1000 (454)
5-Nitro-o-toluidine	100 (45.4)
Octamethylpyrophosphoramide	100 (45.4)
Osmium oxide OsO_4 (T-4)-	1000 (454)
Osmium tetroxide	1000 (454)
7-Oxabicyclo[2.2.1]heptane-2,3-dicarboxylic acid	1000 (454)
1,2-Oxathiolane, 2,2-dioxide	10 (4.54)
2H-1,3,2-Oxazaphosphorin-2-amine, N,N-bis(2-chloroethyl)tetrahydro-, 2-oxide	10 (4.54)
Oxirane	10 (4.54)
Oxiranecarboxyaldehyde	10 (4.54)
Oxirane, (chloromethyl)-	100 (45.4)
Paraformaldehyde	1000 (454)
Paraldehyde	1000 (454)
Parathion	10 (4.54)
Pentachlorobenzene	10 (4.54)
Pentachloroethane	10 (4.54)
Pentachloronitrobenzene (PCNB)	100 (45.4)
Pentachlorophenol	10 (4.54)
1,3-Pentadiene	100 (45.4)
Perchloroethylene	100 (45.4)
Perchloromethyl mercaptan @	100 (45.4)
Phenacetin	100 (45.4)
Phenanthrene	5000 (2270)
Phenol	1000 (454)
Phenol, 2-chloro-	100 (45.4)
Phenol, 4-chloro-3-methyl-	5000 (2270)
Phenol, 2-cyclohexyl-4,6-dinitro-	100 (45.4)
Phenol, 2,4-dichloro-	100 (45.4)
Phenol, 2,6-dichloro-	100 (45.4)
Phenol, 4,4'-(1,2-diethyl-1,2-ethenediyl)bis-, (E)	1 (0.454)
Phenol, 2,4-dimethyl-	100 (45.4)
Phenol, 2,4-dinitro-	10 (4.54)
Phenol, methyl-	100 (45.4)
Phenol, 2-methyl-4,6-dinitro-	10 (4.54)
Phenol, 2,2'-methylenebis[3,4,6-trichloro-	100 (45.4)
Phenol, 2-(1-methylpropyl)-4,6-dinitro	1000 (454)
Phenol, 4-nitro-	100 (45.4)
Phenol, pentachloro-	10 (4.54)
Phenol, 2,3,4,6-tetrachloro-	10 (4.54)
Phenol, 2,4,5-trichloro-	10 (4.54)
Phenol, 2,4,6-trichloro-	10 (4.54)
Phenol, 2,4,6-trinitro-, ammonium salt	10 (4.54)
L-Phenylalanine, 4-[bis(2-chloroethyl)aminol]	1 (0.454)
p-Phenylenediamine	5000 (2270)

Table 1 to Appendix A - Hazardous Substances Other Than Radionuclides

Hazardous substance	Reportable quantity (RQ) pounds (kilograms)
1,10-(1,2-Phenylene)pyrene	100 (45.4)
Phenyl mercaptan @	100 (45.4)
Phenylmercuric acetate	100 (45.4)
Phenylthiourea	100 (45.4)
Phorate	10 (4.54)
Phosgene	10 (4.54)
Phosphine	100 (45.4)
Phosphoric acid	5000 (2270)
Phosphoric acid, diethyl 4-nitrophenyl ester	100 (45.4)
Phosphoric acid, lead(2+) salt (2:3)	10 (4.54)
Phosphorodithioic acid, O,O-diethyl S-[2-(ethylthio)ethyl]ester	1 (0.454)
Phosphorodithioic acid, O,O-diethyl S-(ethylthio) methyl ester	10 (4.54)
Phosphorodithioic acid, O,O-diethyl S-methyl ester	5000 (2270)
Phosphorodithioic acid, O,O-dimethyl S-[2 (methylamino)-2-oxoethyl] ester	10 (4.54)
Phosphorofluoridic acid, bis(1-methylethyl) ester	100 (45.4)
Phosphorothioic acid, O,O-diethyl O-(4-nitrophenyl) ester	10 (4.54)
Phosphorothioic acid, O,O-diethyl O-pyrazinyl ester	100 (45.4)
Phosphorothioic acid, O,O-dimethyl O-(4-nitrophenyl) ester	100 (45.4)
Phosphorothioic acid, O,[4-[(dimethylamino)sulfonyl] phenyl] O,O-dimethyl ester	1000 (454)
Phosphorus	1 (0.454)
Phosphorus oxychloride	1000 (454)
Phosphorus pentasulfide	100 (45.4)
Phosphorus sulfide	100 (45.4)
Phosphorus trichloride	1000 (454)
Phthalic anhydride	5000 (2270)
2-Picoline	5000 (2270)
Piperidine, 1-nitroso-	10 (4.54)
Plumbane, tetraethyl-	10 (4.54)
POLYCHLORINATED BIPHENYLS (PCBs)	1 (0.454)
Potassium arsenate	1 (0.454)
Potassium arsenite	1 (0.454)
Potassium bichromate	10 (4.54)
Potassium chromate	10 (4.54)
Potassium cyanide	10 (4.54)
Potassium cyanide K(CN)	10 (4.54)
Potassium hydroxide	1000 (454)
Potassium permanganate	100 (45.4)
Potassium silver cyanide	1 (0.454)
Pronamide	5000 (2270)
Propanal, 2-methyl-2-(methylthio)-,O-[(methylamino)carbonyl]oxime	1 (0.454)
1-Propanamine	5000 (2270)
1-Propanamine, N-nitroso-N-propyl-	10 (4.54)
1-Propanamine, N-propyl-	5000 (2270)
Propane, 1,2-dibromo-3-chloro-	1 (0.454)
Propane, 1,2-dichloro-	1000 (454)
Propane, 2-nitro-	10 (4.54)
Propane, 2,2'-oxybis [2-chloro-	1000 (454)
1,3-Propane sultone	10 (4.54)
Propanedinitrile	1000 (454)
Propanenitrile	10 (4.54)
Propanenitrile, 3-chloro-	1000 (454)
Propanenitrile, 2-hydroxy-2-methyl-	10 (4.54)
1,2,3-Propanetriol, trinitrate-	10 (4.54)
1-Propanol, 2,3-dibromo-, phosphate (3:1)	10 (4.54)
1-Propanol, 2-methyl-	5000 (2270)
2-Propanone	5000 (2270)
2-Propanone, 1-bromo-	1000 (454)
Propargite	10 (4.54)

Table 1 to Appendix A - Hazardous Substances Other Than Radionuclides

Hazardous substance	Reportable quantity (RQ) pounds (kilograms)
Propargyl alcohol	1000 (454)
2-Propenal	1 (0.454)
2-Propenamide	5000 (2270)
1-Propene, 1,3-dichloro-	100 (45.4)
1-Propene, 1,1,2,3,3,3-hexachloro-	1000 (454)
2-Propenenitrile	100 (45.4)
2-Propenenitrile, 2-methyl-	1000 (454)
2-Propenoic acid	5000 (2270)
2-Propenoic acid, ethyl ester	1000 (454)
2-Propenoic acid, 2-methyl-, ethyl ester	1000 (454)
2-Propenoic acid, 2-methyl-, methyl ester	1000 (454)
2-Propen-1-ol	100 (45.4)
beta-Propioaldehyde	1000 (454)
Propionic acid	5000 (2270)
Propionic acid, 2-(2,4,5-trichlorophenoxy)-	100 (45.4)
Propionic anhydride	5000 (2270)
Propoxur (baygon)	100 (45.4)
n-Propylamine	5000 (2270)
Propylene dichloride	1000 (454)
Propylene oxide	100 (45.4)
1,2-Propylenimine	1 (0.454)
2-Propyn-1-ol	1000 (454)
Pyrene	5000 (2270)
Pyrethrins	1 (0.454)
3,6-Pyridazinedione, 1,2-dihydro-	5000 (2270)
4-Pyridinamine	1000 (454)
Pyridine	1000 (454)
Pyridine, 2-methyl-	5000 (2270)
Pyridine, 3-(1-methyl-2-pyrrolidinyl)-, (S)	100 (45.4)
2,4-(1H,3H)-Pyrimidinedione, 5-[bis(2-chloroethyl)amino]-	10 (4.54)
4(1H)-Pyrimidinone, 2,3-dihydro-6-methyl-2-thioxo-	10 (4.54)
Pyrrolidine, 1-nitroso-	1 (0.454)
Quinoline	5000 (2270)
RADIONUCLIDES	See table 2
Reserpine	5000 (2270)
Resorcino	5000 (2270)
Saccharin and salts	100 (45.4)
Safrole	100 (45.4)
Selenious acid	10 (4.54)
Selenious acid, dithallium(1+) salt	1000 (454)
Selenium ¢	100 (45.4)
Selenium dioxide	10 (4.54)
Selenium oxide	10 (4.54)
Selenium sulfide	10 (4.54)
Selenium sulfide SeS_2	10 (4.54)
Selenourea	1000 (454)
L-Serine, diazoacetate (ester)	1 (0.454)
Silver ¢	1000 (454)
Silver cyanide	1 (0.454)
Silver cyanide Ag(CN)	1 (0.454)
Silver nitrate	1 (0.454)
Silvex(2,4,5-TP)	100 (45.4)
Sodium	10 (4.54)
Sodium arsenate	1 (0.454)
Sodium arsenite	1 (0.454)
Sodium azide	1000 (454)
Sodium bichromate	10 (4.54)
Sodium bifluoride	100 (45.4)

Table 1 to Appendix A - Hazardous Substances Other Than Radionuclides

Hazardous substance	Reportable quantity (RQ) pounds (kilograms)
Sodium bisulfite	5000 (2270)
Sodium chromate	10 (4.54)
Sodium cyanide	10 (4.54)
Sodium cyanide Na(CN)	10 (4.54)
Sodium dodecylbenzene sulfonate	1000 (454)
Sodium fluoride	1000 (454)
Sodium hydrosulfide	5000 (2270)
Sodium hydroxide	1000 (454)
Sodium hypochlorite	100 (45.4)
Sodium methylate	1000 (454)
Sodium nitrite	100 (45.4)
Sodium phosphate, dibasic	5000 (2270)
Sodium phosphate, tribasic	5000 (2270)
Sodium selenite	100 (45.4)
Streptozotocin	1 (0.454)
Strontium chromate	10 (4.54)
Strychnidin-10-one	10 (4.54)
Strychnidin-10-one, 2,3-dimethoxy-	100 (45.4)
Strychnine and salts	10 (4.54)
Styrene	1000 (454)
Styrene oxide	100 (45.4)
Sulfur chloride @	1000 (454)
Sulfur monochloride	1000 (454)
Sulfur phosphide	100 (45.4)
Sulfuric acid	1000 (454)
Sulfuric acid, dimethyl ester	100 (45.4)
Sulfuric acid, dithallium(I+) salt	100 (45.4)
2,4,5-T	1000 (454)
2,4,5-T acid	1000 (454)
2,4,5-T amines	5000 (2270)
2,4,5-T esters	1000 (454)
2,4,5-T salts	1000 (454)
TDE	1 (0.454)
1,2,4,5-Tetrachlorobenzene	5000 (2270)
2,3,7,8-Tetrachlorodibenzo-p-dioxin (TCDD)	1 (0.454)
1,1,1,2-Tetrachloroethane	100 (45.4)
1,1,2,2-Tetrachloroethane	100 (45.4)
Tetrachloroethane @	100 (45.4)
Tetrachloroethene	100 (45.4)
Tetrachloroethylene	100 (45.4)
2,3,4,6-Tetrachlorophenol	10 (4.54)
Tetraethyl lead	10 (4.54)
Tetraethyl pyrophosphate	10 (4.54)
Tetraethyldithiopyrophosphate	100 (45.4)
Tetrahydrofuran	1000 (454)
Tetranitromethane	10 (4.54)
Tetraphosphoric acid, hexaethyl ester	100 (45.4)
Thallic oxide	100 (45.4)
Thallium ¢	1000 (454)
Thallium(I) acetate	100 (45.4)
Thallium(I) carbonate	100 (45.4)
Thallium(I) chloride	100 (45.4)
Thallium chloride TlCl	100 (45.4)
Thallium(I) nitrate	100 (45.4)
Thallium oxide Tl_2O_3	100 (45.4)
Thallium selenite	1000 (454)
Thallium(I) sulfate	100 (45.4)
Thioacetamide	10 (4.54)

Table 1 to Appendix A - Hazardous Substances Other Than Radionuclides

Hazardous substance	Reportable quantity (RQ) pounds (kilograms)
Thiodiphosphoric acid, tetraethyl ester	100 (45.4)
Thiofanox	100 (45.4)
Thioimidodicarbonic diamide $[(H_2N)C(S)]_2NH$	100 (45.4)
Thiomethanol	100 (45.4)
Thioperoxydicarbonic diamide $[(H_2N)C(S)]_2S_2$, tetramethyl-	10 (4.54)
Thiophenol	100 (45.4)
Thiosemicarbazide	100 (45.4)
Thiourea	10 (4.54)
Thiourea, (2-chlorophenyl)-	100 (45.4)
Thiourea, 1-naphthalenyl-	100 (45.4)
Thiourea, phenyl-	100 (45.4)
Thiram	10 (4.54)
Titanium tetrachloride	1000 (454)
Toluene	1000 (454)
Toluenediamine	10 (4.54)
Toluene diisocyanate	100 (45.4)
o-Toluidine	100 (45.4)
p-Toluidine	100 (45.4)
o-Toluidine hydrochloride	100 (45.4)
Toxaphene	1 (0.454)
2,4,5-TP acid	100 (45.4)
2,4,5-TP acid esters	100 (45.4)
1H-1,2,4-Triazol-3-amine	10 (4.54)
Trichlorfon	100 (45.4)
1,2,4-Trichlorobenzene	100 (45.4)
1,1,1-Trichloroethane	1000 (454)
1,1,2-Trichloroethane	100 (45.4)
Trichloroethene	100 (45.4)
Trichloroethylene	100 (45.4)
Trichloromethanesulfenyl chloride	100 (45.4)
Trichloromonofluoromethane	5000 (2270)
Trichlorophenol 2,3,4-Trichlorophenol 2,3,5-Trichlorophenol 2,3,6-Trichlorophenol 2,4,5-Trichlorophenol 2,4,6-Trichlorophenol 3,4,5-Trichlorophenol	10 (4.54)
2,4,5-Trichlorophenol	10 (4.54)
2,4,6-Trichlorophenol	10 (4.54)
Triethanolamine dodecylbenzene sulfonate	1000 (454)
Triethylamine	5000 (2270)
Trifluralin	10 (4.54)
Trimethylamine	100 (45.4)
2,2,4-Trimethylpentane	1000 (454)
1,3,5-Trinitrobenzene	10 (4.54)
1,3,5-Trioxane, 2,4,6-trimethyl-	1000 (454)
Tris(2,3-dibromopropyl) phosphate	10 (4.54)
Trypan blue	10 (4.54)
Uracil mustard	10 (4.54)
Uranyl acetate	100 (45.4)
Uranyl nitrate	100 (45.4)
Urea, N-ethyl-N-nitroso-	1 (0.454)
Urea, N-methyl-N-nitroso-	1 (0.454)
Vanadic acid, ammonium salt	1000 (454)
Vanadium oxide V_2O_5	1000 (454)
Vanadium pentoxide	1000 (454)
Vanadyl sulfate	1000 (454)
Vinyl acetate	5000 (2270)
Vinyl acetate monomer	5000 (2270)
Vinylamine, N-methyl-N-nitroso-	10 (4.54)

Table 1 to Appendix A - Hazardous Substances Other Than Radionuclides

Hazardous substance	Reportable quantity (RQ) pounds (kilograms)
Vinyl bromide	100 (45.4)
Vinyl chloride	1 (0.454)
Vinylidene chloride	100 (45.4)
Warfarin, & salts, when present at concentrations greater than 0.3%	100 (45.4)
Xylene	100 (45.4)
m-Xylene	1000 (454)
o-Xylene	1000 (454)
p-Xylene	100 (45.4)
Xylene (mixed)	100 (45.4)
Xylenes (isomers and mixture)	100 (45.4)
Xylenol	1000 (454)
Yohimban-16-carboxylic acid,11,17-dimethoxy-18-[(3,4,5-trimethoxybenzoyl)oxy]-, methyl ester (3beta,16beta,17alpha,18beta,20alpha)-	5000 (2270)
Zinc ¢	1000 (454)
Zinc acetate	1000 (454)
Zinc ammonium chloride	1000 (454)
Zinc borate	1000 (454)
Zinc bromide	1000 (454)
Zinc carbonate	1000 (454)
Zinc chloride	1000 (454)
Zinc cyanide	10 (4.54)
Zinc cyanide $Zn(CN)_2$	10 (4.54)
Zinc fluoride	1000 (454)
Zinc formate	1000 (454)
Zinc hydrosulfite	1000 (454)
Zinc nitrate	1000 (454)
Zinc phenolsulfonate	5000 (2270)
Zinc phosphide	100 (45.4)
Zinc phosphide Zn_3P_2, when present at concentrations greater than 10%	100 (45.4)
Zinc silicofluoride	5000 (2270)
Zinc sulfate	1000 (454)
Zirconium nitrate	5000 (2270)
Zirconium potassium fluoride	1000 (454)
Zirconium sulfate	5000 (2270)
Zirconium tetrachloride	5000 (2270)
D001 Unlisted Hazardous Wastes Characteristic of Ignitability	100 (45.4)
D002 Unlisted Hazardous Wastes Characteristic of Corrosivity	100 (45.4)
D003 Unlisted Hazardous Wastes Characteristic of Reactivity	100 (45.4)
D004-D043 Unlisted Hazardous Wastes Characteristic of Toxicity	
D004 Arsenic	1 (0.454)
D005 Barium	1000 (454)
D006 Cadmium	10 (4.54)
D007 Chromium	10 (4.54)
D008 Lead	10 (4.54)
D009 Mercury	1 (0.454)
D010 Selenium	10 (4.54)
D011 Silver	1 (0.454)
D012 Endrin	1 (0.454)
D013 Lindane	1 (0.454)
D014 Methoxychlor	1 (0.454)
D015 Toxaphene	1 (0.454)
D016 2,4-D	100 (45.4)
D017 2,4,5-TP	100 (45.4)
D018 Benzene	10 (4.54)
D019 Carbon tetrachloride	10 (4.54)
D020 Chlordane	1 (0.454)
D021 Chlorobenzene	100 (45.4)
D022 Chloroform	10 (4.54)

Table 1 to Appendix A - Hazardous Substances Other Than Radionuclides

Hazardous substance	Reportable quantity (RQ) pounds (kilograms)
D023 o-Cresol	100 (45.4)
D024 m-Cresol	100 (45.4)
D025 p-Cresol	100 (45.4)
D026 Cresol	100 (45.4)
D027 1,4-Dichlorobenzene	100 (45.4)
D028 1,2-Dichloroethane	100 (45.4)
D029 1,1-Dichloroethylene	100 (45.4)
D030 2,4-Dinitrotoluene	10 (4.54)
D031 Heptachlor (and hydroxide)	1 (0.454)
D032 Hexachlorobenzene	10 (4.54)
D033 Hexachlorobutadiene	1 (0.454)
D034 Hexachloroethane	100 (45.4)
D035 Methyl ethyl ketone	5000 (2270)
D036 Nitrobenzene	1000 (454)
D037 Pentachlorophenol	10 (4.54)
D038 Pyridine	1000 (454)
D039 Tetrachloroethylene	100 (45.4)
D040 Tricholorethylene	100 (45.4)
D041 2,4,5-Trichlorophenol	10 (4.54)
D042 2,4,6-Trichlorophenol	10 (4.54)
D043 Vinyl chloride	1 (0.454)
F001 The following spent halogenated solvents used in degreasing; all spent solvent mixtures/blends used in degreasing containing, before use, a total of ten percent or more (by volume) of one or more of the below listed halogenated solvents or those solvents listed in F002, F004 and F005; and still bottoms from the recovery of these spent solvents and spent solvent mixtures	10 (4.54)
(a) Tetrachloroethylene	100 (45.4)
(b) Trichloroethylene	100 (45.4)
(c) Methylene chloride	1000 (454)
(d) 1,1,1-Trichloroethane	1000 (454)
(e) Carbon tetrachloride	10 (4.54)
(f) Chlorinated fluorocarbons	5000 (2270)
F002 The following spent halogenated solvents; all spent solvent mixtures/blends containing, before use, a total of ten percent or more (by volume) of one or more of the below listed halogenated solvents or those listed in F001, F004, F005; and still bottoms from the recovery of these spent solvents and spent solvent mixtures	10 (4.54)
(a) Tetrachloroethylene	100 (45.4)
(b) Methylene chloride	1000 (454)
(c) Trichloroethylene	100 (45.4)
(d) 1,1,1-Trichloroethane	1000 (454)
(e) Chlorobenzene	100 (45.4)
(f) 1,1,2-Trichloro-1,2,2-trifluoroethane	5000 (2270)
(g) o-Dichlorobenzene	100 (45.4)
(h) Trichlorofluoromethane	5000 (2270)
(i) 1,1,2 Trichloroethane	100 (45.4)
F003 The following spent non-halogenated solvents and solvents:	100 (45.4)
(a) Xylene	1000 (454)
(b) Acetone	5000 (2270)
(c) Ethyl acetate	5000 (2270)
(d) Ethylbenzene	1000 (454)
(e) Ethyl ether	100 (45.4)
(f) Methyl isobutyl ketone	5000 (2270)
(g) n-Butyl alcohol	5000 (2270)
(h) Cyclohexanone	5000 (2270)
(i) Methanol	5000 (2270)

Table 1 to Appendix A - Hazardous Substances Other Than Radionuclides

Hazardous substance	Reportable quantity (RQ) pounds (kilograms)
F004 The following spent non-halogenated solvents and the still bottoms from the recovery of these solvents:	100 (45.4)
(a) Cresols/Cresylic acid	1000 (454)
(b) Nitrobenzene	100 (45.4)
F005 The following spent non-halogenated solvents and the still bottoms from the recovery of these solvents:	100 (45.4)
(a) Toluene	1000 (454)
(b) Methyl ethyl ketone	5000 (2270)
(c) Carbon disulfide	100 (45.4)
(d) Isobutanol	5000 (2270)
(e) Pyridine	1000 (454)
F006 Wastewater treatment sludges from electroplating operations except from the following processes: (1) sulfuric acid anodizing of aluminum, (2) tin plating on carbon steel, (3) zinc plating (segregated basis) on carbon steel, (4) aluminum or zinc-aluminum plating on carbon steel, (5) cleaning/stripping associated with tin, zinc and aluminum plating on carbon steel, and (6) chemical etching and milling of aluminum	10 (4.54)
F007 Spent cyanide plating bath solutions from electroplating operations	10 (4.54)
F008 Plating bath residues from the bottom of plating baths from electroplating operations where cyanides are used in the process	10 (4.54)
F009 Spent stripping and cleaning bath solutions from electroplating operations where cyanides are used in the process	10 (4.54)
F010 Quenching bath residues from oil baths from metal heat treating operations where cyanides are used in the process	10 (4.54)
F011 Spent cyanide solutions from salt bath pot cleaning from metal heat treating operations (except for precious metals heat treating spent cyanide solutions from salt bath pot cleaning)	10 (4.54)
F012 Quenching wastewater treatment sludges from metal heat treating operations where cyanides are used in the process	10 (4.54)
F019 Wastewater treatment sludges from the chemical conversion coating of aluminum — except from zirconium phosphating in aluminum can washing when such phosphating is an exclusive conversion coating process	10 (4.54)
F020 Wastes (except wastewater and spent carbon from hydrogen chloride purification) from the production or manufacturing use (as a reactant, chemical intermediate, or component in a formulating process) of tri- or tetrachlorophenol, or of intermediates used to produce their pesticide derivatives. (This listing does not include wastes from the production of hexachlorophene from highly purified 2,4,5-trichlorophenol.)	1 (0.454)
F021 Wastes (except wastewater and spent carbon from hydrogen chloride purification) from the production or manufacturing use (as a reactant, chemical intermediate, or component in a formulating process) of pentachlorophenol, or of intermediates used to produce its derivatives	1 (0.454)
F022 Wastes (except wastewater and spent carbon from hydrogen chloride purification) from the manufacturing use (as a reactant, chemical intermediate, or component in a formulating process) of tetra-, penta-, or hexachlorobenzenes under alkaline conditions	1 (0.454)
F023 Wastes (except wastewater and spent carbon from hydrogen chloride purification) from the production of materials on equipment previously used for the production or manufacturing use (as a reactant, chemical intermediate, or component in a formulating process) of tri- and tetrachlorophenols. (This listing does not include wastes from equipment used only for the production or use of hexachlorophene from highly purified 2,4,5-trichlorophenol.)	1 (0.454)
F024 Wastes, including but not limited to distillation residues, heavy ends, tars, and reactor cleanout wastes, from the production of chlorinated aliphatichydrocarbons, having carbon content from one to five, utilizing free radical catalyzed processes. (This listing does not include light ends, spent filters and filter aids, spent dessicants(sic), wastewater, wastewater treatment sludges, spent catalysts, and wastes listed in 40 CFR 261.32.)	1 (0.454)

Table 1 to Appendix A - Hazardous Substances Other Than Radionuclides

Hazardous substance	Reportable quantity (RQ) pounds (kilograms)
F025 Condensed light ends, spent filters and filter aids, and spent desiccant wastes from the production of certain chlorinated aliphatic hydrocarbons, by free radical catalyzed processes. These chlorinated aliphatic hydrocarbons are those having carbon chain lengths ranging from one to and including five, with varying amounts and positions of chlorine substitution	1 (0.454)
F026 Wastes (except wastewater and spent carbon from hydrogen chloride purification) from the production of materials on equipment previously used for the manufacturing use (as a reactant, chemical intermediate, or component in a formulating process) of tetra-, penta-, or hexachlorobenzene under alkaline conditions	1 (0.454)
F027 Discarded unused formulations containing tri-, tetra-, or pentachlorophenol or discarded unused formulations containing compounds derived from these chlorophenols. (This listing does not include formulations containing hexachlorophene synthesized from prepurified 2,4,5-trichlorophenol as the sole component.)	1 (0.454)
F028 Residues resulting from the incineration or thermal treatment of soil contaminated with EPA Hazardous Waste Nos. F020, F021, F022, F023, F026, and F027	1 (0.454)
F032	1 (0.454)
F034	1 (0.454)
F035	1 (0.454)
F037	1 (0.454)
F038	1 (0.454)
F039 Multi source leachate	1 (0.454)
K001 Bottom sediment sludge from the treatment of wastewaters from wood preserving processes that use creosote and/or pentachlorophenol	1 (0.454)
K002 Wastewater treatment sludge from the production of chrome yellow and orange pigments	10 (4.54)
K003 Wastewater treatment sludge from the production of molybdate orange pigments	10 (4.54)
K004 Wastewater treatment sludge from the production of zinc yellow pigments	10 (4.54)
K005 Wastewater treatment sludge from the production of chrome green pigments	10 (4.54)
K006 Wastewater treatment sludge from the production of chrome oxide green pigments (anhydrous and hydrated)	10 (4.54)
K007 Wastewater treatment sludge from the production of iron blue pigments	10 (4.54)
K008 Oven residue from the production of chrome oxide green pigments	10 (4.54)
K009 Distillation bottoms from the production of acetaldehyde from ethylene	10 (4.54)
K010 Distillation side cuts from the production of acetaldehyde from ethylene	10 (4.54)
K011 Bottom stream from the wastewater stripper in the production of acrylonitrile	10 (4.54)
K013 Bottom stream from the acetonitrile column in the production of acrylonitrile	10 (4.54)
K014 Bottoms from the acetonitrile purification column in the production of acrylonitrile	5000 (2270)
K015 Still bottoms from the distillation of benzyl chloride	10 (4.54)
K016 Heavy ends or distillation residues from the production of carbon tetrachloride	1 (0.454)
K017 Heavy ends (still bottoms) from the purification column in the production of epichlorohydrin	10 (4.54)
K018 Heavy ends from the fractionation column in ethyl chloride production	1 (0.454)
K019 Heavy ends from the distillation of ethylene dichloride in ethylene dichloride production	1 (0.454)
K020 Heavy ends from the distillation of vinyl chloride in vinyl chloride monomer production	1 (0.454)

Table 1 to Appendix A - Hazardous Substances Other Than Radionuclides

Hazardous substance	Reportable quantity (RQ) pounds (kilograms)
K021 Aqueous spent antimony catalyst waste from fluoromethanes production	10 (4.54)
K022 Distillation bottom tars from the production of phenol/acetone from cumene	1 (0.454)
K023 Distillation light ends from the production of phthalic anhydride from naphthalene	5000 (2270)
K024 Distillation bottoms from the production of phthalic anhydride from naphthalene	5000 (2270)
K025 Distillation bottoms from the production of nitrobenzene by the nitration of benzene	10 (4.54)
K026 Stripping still tails from the production of methyl ethyl pyridines	1000 (454)
K027 Centrifuge and distillation residues from toluene diisocyanate production	10 (4.54)
K028 Spent catalyst from the hydrochlorinator reactor in the production of 1,1,1-trichloroethane	1 (0.454)
K029 Waste from the product steam stripper in the production of 1,1,1-trichloroethane	1 (0.454)
K030 Column bottoms or heavy ends from the combined production of trichloroethylene and perchloroethylene	1 (0.454)
K031 By-product salts generated in the production of MSMA and cacodylic acid	1 (0.454)
K032 Wastewater treatment sludge from the production of chlordane	10 (4.54)
K033 Wastewater and scrub water from the chlorination of cyclopentadiene in the production of chlordane	10 (4.54)
K034 Filter solids from the filtration of hexachlorocyclopentadiene in the production of chlordane	10 (4.54)
K035 Wastewater treatment sludges generated in the production of creosote	1 (0.454)
K036 Still bottoms from toluene reclamation distillation in the production of disulfoton	1 (0.454)
K037 Wastewater treatment sludges from the production of disulfoton	1 (0.454)
K038 Wastewater from the washing and stripping of phorate production	10 (4.54)
K039 Filter cake from the filtration of diethylphosphorodithioic acid in the production of phorate	10 (4.54)
K040 Wastewater treatment sludge from the production of phorate	10 (4.54)
K041 Wastewater treatment sludge from the production of toxaphene	1 (0.454)
K042 Heavy ends or distillation residues from the distillation of tetrachlorobenzene in the production of 2,4,5-T	10 (4.54)
K043 2,6-dichlorophenol waste from the production of 2,4-D	10 (4.54)
K044 Wastewater treatment sludges from the manufacturing and processing of explosives	10 (4.54)
K045 Spent carbon from the treatment of wastewater containing explosives	10 (4.54)
K046 Wastewater treatment sludges from the manufacturing, formulation and loading of lead-based initiating compounds	10 (4.54)
K047 Pink/red water from TNT operations	10 (4.54)
K048 Dissolved air flotation (DAF) float from the petroleum refining industry	10 (4.54)
K049 Slop oil emulsion solids from the petroleum refining industry	10 (4.54)
K050 Heat exchanger bundle cleaning sludge from the petroleum refining industry	10 (4.54)

Table 1 to Appendix A - Hazardous Substances Other Than Radionuclides

Hazardous substance	Reportable quantity (RQ) pounds (kilograms)
K051 API separator sludge from the petroleum refining industry	10 (4.54)
K052 Tank bottoms (leaded) from the petroleum refining industry	10 (4.54)
K060 Ammonia still lime sludge from coking operations	1 (0.454)
K061 Emission control dust/sludge from the primary production of steel in electric furnaces	10 (4.54)
K062 Spent pickle liquor generated by steel finishing operations of facilities within the iron and steel industry	10 (4.54)
K064 Acid plant blowdown slurry/sludge resulting from thickening of blowdown slurry from primary copper production	10 (4.54)
K065 Surface impoundment solids contained in and dredged from surface impoundments at primary lead smelting facilities	10 (4.54)
K066 Sludge from treatment of process wastewater and/or acid plant blowdown from primary zinc production	10 (4.54)
K069 Emission control dust/sludge from secondary lead smelting	10 (4.54)
K071 Brine purification muds from the mercury cell process in chlorine production, where separately prepurified brine is not used	1 (0.454)
K073 Chlorinated hydrocarbon waste from the purification step of the diaphragm cell process using graphite anodes in chlorine production	10 (4.54)
K083 Distillation bottoms from aniline extraction	100 (45.4)
K084 Wastewater treatment sludges generated during the production of veterinary pharmaceuticals from arsenic or organo-arsenic compounds	1 (0.454)
K085 Distillation or fractionation column bottoms from the production of chlorobenzenes	10 (4.54)
K086 Solvent washes and sludges, caustic washes and sludges, or water washes and sludges from cleaning tubs and equipment used in the formulation of ink from pigments, driers, soaps, and stabilizers containing chromium and lead	10 (4.54)
K087 Decanter tank tar sludge from coking operations	100 (45.4)
K088 Spent potliners from primary aluminum reduction	10 (4.54)
K090 Emission control dust or sludge from ferrochromiumsilicon production	10 (4.54)
K091 Emission control dust or sludge from ferrochromium production	10 (4.54)
K093 Distillation light ends from the production of phthalic anhydride from ortho-xylene	5000 (2270)
K094 Distillation bottoms from the production of phthalic anhydride from ortho-xylene	5000 (2270)
K095 Distillation bottoms from the production of 1,1,1-trichloroethane	100 (45.4)
K096 Heavy ends from the heavy ends column from the production of 1,1,1-trichloroethane	100 (45.4)
K097 Vacuum stripper discharge from the chlordane chlorinator in the production of chlordane	1 (0.454)
K098 Untreated process wastewater from the production of toxaphene	1 (0.454)
K099 Untreated wastewater from the production of 2,4-D	10 (4.54)
K100 Waste leaching solution from acid leaching of emission control dust/ sludge from secondary lead smelting	10 (4.54)
K101 Distillation tar residues from the distillation of aniline-based compounds in the production of veterinary pharmaceuticals from arsenic or organo-arsenic compounds	1 (0.454)

Table 1 to Appendix A - Hazardous Substances Other Than Radionuclides

Hazardous substance	Reportable quantity (RQ) pounds (kilograms)
K102 Residue from the use of activated carbon for decolorization in the production of veterinary pharmaceuticals from arsenic or organo-arsenic compounds	1 (0.454)
K103 Process residues from aniline extraction from the production of aniline	100 (45.4)
K104 Combined wastewater streams generated from nitrobenzene/aniline chlorobenzenes	10 (4.54)
K105 Separated aqueous stream from the reactor product washing step in the production of chlorobenzenes	10 (4.54)
K106 Wastewater treatment sludge from the mercury cell process in chlorine production	1 (0.454)
K107 Column bottoms from product seperation from the production of 1,1-dimethylhydrazine (UDMH) from carboxylic acid hydrazines	10 (4.54)
K108 Condensed column overheads from product seperation and condensed reactor vent gases from the production of 1,1-dimethylhydrazine (UDMH) from carboxylic acid hydrazides	10 (4.54)
K109 Spent filter cartidges from product purification from the production of 1,1-dimethylhydrazine (UDMH) from carboxylic acid hydazides	10 (4.54)
K110 Condensed column overheads from intermediate separation from the production of 1,1-dimethylhydrazines (UDMH) from carboxylic acid hydrazides	10 (4.54)
K111 Product washwaters from the production of dinitrotoluene via nitration of toluene	10 (4.54)
K112 Reaction by-product water from the drying column in the production of toluenediamine via hydrogenation of dinitrotoluene	10 (4.54)
K113 Condensed liquid light ends from the purification of toluenediamine in the production of toluenediamine via hydrogenation of dinitrotoluene	10 (4.54)
K114 Vicinals from the purification of toluenediamine in the production of toluenediamine via hydrogenation of dinitrotoluene	10 (4.54)
K115 Heavy ends from the purification of toluenediamine in the production of toluenediamine via hydrogenation of dinitrotoluene	10 (4.54)
K116 Organic condensate from the solvent recovery column in the production of toluene diisocyanate via phosgenation of toluenediamine	10 (4.54)
K117 Wastewater from the reaction vent gas scrubber in the production of ethylene bromide via bromination of ethene	1 (0.454)
K118 Spent absorbent solids from purification of ethylene dibromide in the production of ethylene dibromide	1 (0.454)
K123 Process wastewater (including supernates, filtrates, and washwaters) from the production of ethylenebisdithiocarbamic acid and its salts	10 (4.54)
K124 Reactor vent scrubber water from the production of ethylenebisdithiocarbamic acid and its salts	10 (4.54)
K125 Filtration, evaporation, and centrifugation solids from the production of ethylenebisdithiocarbamic acid and its salts	10 (4.54)
K126 Baghouse dust and floor sweepings in milling and packaging operations from the production or formulation of ethylenebisdithiocarbamic acid and its salts	10 (4.54)
K131 Wastewater from the reactor and spent sulfuric acid from the acid dryer in the production of methyl bromide	100 (45.4)
K132 Spent absorbent and wastewater solids from the production of methyl bromide	1000 (454)
K136 Still bottoms from the purification of ethylene dibromide in the production of ethylene dibromide via bromination of ethene	1 (0.454)
K141	1 (0.454)
K142	1 (0.454)
K143	1 (0.454)

Table 1 to Appendix A - Hazardous Substances Other Than Radionuclides

Hazardous substance	Reportable quantity (RQ) pounds (kilograms)
K144	1 (0.454)
K145	1 (0.454)
K147	1 (0.454)
K148	1 (0.454)
K149	10 (4.54)
K150	10 (4.54)
K151	10 (4.54)
K156	1 (0.454)
K157	1 (0.454)
K158	1 (0.454)
K169	10 (4.54)
K170	1 (0.454)
K171	1 (0.454)
K172	1 (0.454)
K174	1 (0.454)
K175	1 (0.454)
K176	1 (0.454)
K177	5000 (2270)
K178	1 (0.454)

Footnotes:

¢ The RQ for these hazardous substances is limited to those pieces of the metal having a diameter smaller than 100 micrometers (0.004 inches).

¢¢ The RQ for asbestos is limited to friable forms only.

@ Indicates that the name was added by RSPA because (1) the name is a synonym for a specific hazardous substance and (2) the name appears in the Hazardous Materials Table as a proper shipping name.

List of Hazardous Substances and Reportable Quantities

Table 2 to Appendix A - Radionuclides

(1) Radionuclide	(2) Atomic Number	(3) Reportable Quantity (RQ) Ci (TBq)
Actinium-224	89	100 (3.7)
Actinium-225	89	1 (.037)
Actinium-226	89	10 (.37)
Actinium-227	89	0.001 (.000037)
Actinium-228	89	10 (.37)
Aluminum-26	13	10 (.37)
Americium-237	95	1000 (37)
Americium-238	95	100 (3.7)
Americium-239	95	100 (3.7)
Americium-240	95	10 (.37)
Americium-241	95	0.01 (.00037)
Americium-242	95	100 (3.7)
Americium-242m	95	0.01 (.00037)
Americium-243	95	0.01 (.00037)
Americium-244	95	10 (.37)
Americium-244m	95	1000 (37)
Americium-245	95	1000 (37)
Americium-246	95	1000 (37)
Americium-246m	95	1000 (37)
Antimony-115	51	1000 (37)
Antimony-116	51	1000 (37)
Antimony-116m	51	100 (3.7)
Antimony-117	51	1000 (37)
Antimony-118m	51	10 (.37)
Antimony-119	51	1000 (37)
Antimony-120 (16 min)	51	1000 (37)
Antimony-120 (5.76 day)	51	10 (.37)
Antimony-122	51	10 (.37)

Table 2 to Appendix A - Radionuclides

(1) Radionuclide	(2) Atomic Number	(3) Reportable Quantity (RQ) Ci (TBq)
Antimony-124	51	10 (.37)
Antimony-124m	51	1000 (37)
Antimony-125	51	10 (.37)
Antimony-126	51	10 (.37)
Antimony-126m	51	1000 (37)
Antimony-127	51	10 (.37)
Antimony-128 (10.4 min)	51	1000 (37)
Antimony-128 (9.01 hr)	51	10 (.37)
Antimony-129	51	100 (3.7)
Antimony-130	51	100 (3.7)
Antimony-131	51	1000 (37)
Argon-39	18	1000 (37)
Argon-41	18	10 (.37)
Arsenic-69	33	1000 (37)
Arsenic-70	33	100 (3.7)
Arsenic-71	33	100 (3.7)
Arsenic-72	33	10 (.37)
Arsenic-73	33	100 (3.7)
Arsenic-74	33	10 (.37)
Arsenic-76	33	100 (3.7)
Arsenic-77	33	1000 (37)
Arsenic-78	33	100 (3.7)
Astatine-207	85	100 (3.7)
Astatine-211	85	100 (3.7)
Barium-126	56	1000 (37)
Barium-128	56	10 (.37)
Barium-131	56	10 (.37)
Barium-131m	56	1000 (37)
Barium-133	56	10 (.37)
Barium-133m	56	100 (3.7)
Barium-135m	56	1000 (37)
Barium-139	56	1000 (37)
Barium-140	56	10 (.37)
Barium-141	56	1000 (37)
Barium-142	56	1000 (37)
Berkelium-245	97	100 (3.7)
Berkelium-246	97	10 (.37)
Berkelium-247	97	0.01 (.00037)
Berkelium-249	97	1 (.037)
Berkelium-250	97	100 (3.7)
Beryllium-10	4	1 (.037)
Beryllium-7	4	100 (3.7)
Bismuth-200	83	100 (3.7)
Bismuth-201	83	100 (3.7)
Bismuth-202	83	1000 (37)
Bismuth-203	83	10 (.37)
Bismuth-205	83	10 (.37)
Bismuth-206	83	10 (.37)
Bismuth-207	83	10 (.37)
Bismuth-210	83	10 (.37)
Bismuth-210m	83	0.1 (.0037)
Bismuth-212	83	100 (3.7)
Bismuth-213	83	100 (3.7)
Bismuth-214	83	100 (3.7)
Bromine-74	35	100 (3.7)
Bromine-74m	35	100 (3.7)
Bromine-75	35	100 (3.7)
Bromine-76	35	10 (.37)
Bromine-77	35	100 (3.7)

Table 2 to Appendix A - Radionuclides

(1) Radionuclide	(2) Atomic Number	(3) Reportable Quantity (RQ) Ci (TBq)
Bromine-80	35	1000 (37)
Bromine-80m	35	1000 (37)
Bromine-82	35	10 (.37)
Bromine-83	35	1000 (37)
Bromine-84	35	100 (3.7)
Cadmium-104	48	1000 (37)
Cadmium-107	48	1000 (37)
Cadmium-109	48	1 (.037)
Cadmium-113	48	0.1 (.0037)
Cadmium-113m	48	0.1 (.0037)
Cadmium-115	48	100 (3.7)
Cadmium-115m	48	10 (.37)
Cadmium-117	48	100 (3.7)
Cadmium-117m	48	10 (.37)
Calcium-41	20	10 (.37)
Calcium-45	20	10 (.37)
Calcium-47	20	10 (.37)
Californium-244	98	1000 (37)
Californium-246	98	10 (.37)
Californium-248	98	0.1 (.0037)
Californium-249	98	0.01 (.00037)
Californium-250	98	0.01 (.00037)
Californium-251	98	0.01 (.00037)
Californium-252	98	0.1 (.0037)
Californium-253	98	10 (.37)
Californium-254	98	0.1 (.0037)
Carbon-11	6	1000 (37)
Carbon-14	6	10 (.37)
Cerium-134	58	10 (.37)
Cerium-135	58	10 (.37)
Cerium-137	58	1000 (37)
Cerium-137m	58	100 (3.7)
Cerium-139	58	100 (3.7)
Cerium-141	58	10 (.37)
Cerium-143	58	100 (3.7)
Cerium-144	58	1 (.037)
Cesium-125	55	1000 (37)
Cesium-127	55	100 (3.7)
Cesium-129	55	100 (3.7)
Cesium-130	55	1000 (37)
Cesium-131	55	1000 (37)
Cesium-132	55	10 (.37)
Cesium-134	55	1 (.037)
Cesium-134m	55	1000 (37)
Cesium-135	55	10 (.37)
Cesium-135m	55	100 (3.7)
Cesium-136	55	10 (.37)
Cesium-137	55	1 (.037)
Cesium-138	55	100 (3.7)
Chlorine-36	17	10 (.37)
Chlorine-38	17	100 (3.7)
Chlorine-39	17	100 (3.7)
Chromium-48	24	100 (3.7)
Chromium-49	24	1000 (37)
Chromium-51	24	1000 (37)
Cobalt-55	27	10 (.37)
Cobalt-56	27	10 (.37)
Cobalt-57	27	100 (3.7)
Cobalt-58	27	10 (.37)

Table 2 to Appendix A - Radionuclides

(1) Radionuclide	(2) Atomic Number	(3) Reportable Quantity (RQ) Ci (TBq)
Cobalt-58m	27	1000 (37)
Cobalt-60	27	10 (.37)
Cobalt-60m	27	1000 (37)
Cobalt-61	27	1000 (37)
Cobalt-62m	27	1000 (37)
Copper-60	29	100 (3.7)
Copper-61	29	100 (3.7)
Copper-64	29	1000 (37)
Copper-67	29	100 (3.7)
Curium-238	96	1000 (37)
Curium-240	96	1 (.037)
Curium-241	96	10 (.37)
Curium-242	96	1 (.037)
Curium-243	96	0.01 (.00037)
Curium-244	96	0.01 (.00037)
Curium-245	96	0.01 (.00037)
Curium-246	96	0.01 (.00037)
Curium-247	96	0.01 (.00037)
Curium-248	96	0.001 (.000037)
Curium-249	96	1000 (37)
Dysprosium-155	66	100 (3.7)
Dysprosium-157	66	100 (3.7)
Dysprosium-159	66	100 (3.7)
Dysprosium-165	66	1000 (37)
Dysprosium-166	66	10 (.37)
Einsteinium-250	99	10 (.37)
Einsteinium-251	99	1000 (37)
Einsteinium-253	99	10 (.37)
Einsteinium-254	99	0.1 (.0037)
Einsteinium-254m	99	1 (.037)
Erbium-161	68	100 (3.7)
Erbium-165	68	1000 (37)
Erbium-169	68	100 (3.7)
Erbium-171	68	100 (3.7)
Erbium-172	68	10 (.37)
Europium-145	63	10 (.37)
Europium-146	63	10 (.37)
Europium-147	63	10 (.37)
Europium-148	63	10 (.37)
Europium-149	63	100 (3.7)
Europium-150 (12.6 hr)	63	1000 (37)
Europium-150 (34.2 yr)	63	10 (.37)
Europium-152	63	10 (.37)
Europium-152m	63	100 (3.7)
Europium-154	63	10 (.37)
Europium-155	63	10 (.37)
Europium-156	63	10 (.37)
Europium-157	63	10 (.37)
Europium-158	63	1000 (37)
Fermium-252	100	10 (.37)
Fermium-253	100	10 (.37)
Fermium-254	100	100 (3.7)
Fermium-255	100	100 (3.7)
Fermium-257	100	1 (.037)
Fluorine-18	9	1000 (37)
Francium-222	87	100 (3.7)
Francium-223	87	100 (3.7)
Gadolinium-145	64	100 (3.7)
Gadolinium-146	64	10 (.37)

Table 2 to Appendix A - Radionuclides

(1) Radionuclide	(2) Atomic Number	(3) Reportable Quantity (RQ) Ci (TBq)
Gadolinium-147	64	10 (.37)
Gadolinium-148	64	0.001 (.000037)
Gadolinium-149	64	100 (3.7)
Gadolinium-151	64	100 (3.7)
Gadolinium-152	64	0.001 (.000037)
Gadolinium-153	64	10 (.37)
Gadolinium-159	64	1000 (37)
Gallium-65	31	1000 (37)
Gallium-66	31	10 (.37)
Gallium-67	31	100 (3.7)
Gallium-68	31	1000 (37)
Gallium-70	31	1000 (37)
Gallium-72	31	10 (.37)
Gallium-73	31	100 (3.7)
Germanium-66	32	100 (3.7)
Germanium-67	32	1000 (37)
Germanium-68	32	10 (.37)
Germanium-69	32	10 (.37)
Germanium-71	32	1000 (37)
Germanium-75	32	1000 (37)
Germanium-77	32	10 (.37)
Germanium-78	32	1000 (37)
Gold-193	79	100 (3.7)
Gold-194	79	10 (.37)
Gold-195	79	100 (3.7)
Gold-198	79	100 (3.7)
Gold-198m	79	10 (.37)
Gold-199	79	100 (3.7)
Gold-200	79	1000 (37)
Gold-200m	79	10 (.37)
Gold-201	79	1000 (37)
Hafnium-170	72	100 (3.7)
Hafnium-172	72	1 (.037)
Hafnium-173	72	100 (3.7)
Hafnium-175	72	100 (3.7)
Hafnium-177m	72	1000 (37)
Hafnium-178m	72	0.1 (.0037)
Hafnium-179m	72	100 (3.7)
Hafnium-180m	72	100 (3.7)
Hafnium-181	72	10 (.37)
Hafnium-182	72	0.1 (.0037)
Hafnium-182m	72	100 (3.7)
Hafnium-183	72	100 (3.7)
Hafnium-184	72	100 (3.7)
Holmium-155	67	1000 (37)
Holmium-157	67	1000 (37)
Holmium-159	67	1000 (37)
Holmium-161	67	1000 (37)
Holmium-162	67	1000 (37)
Holmium-162m	67	1000 (37)
Holmium-164	67	1000 (37)
Holmium-164m	67	1000 (37)
Holmium-166	67	100 (3.7)
Holmium-166m	67	1 (.037)
Holmium-167	67	100 (3.7)
Hydrogen-3	1	100 (3.7)
Indium-109	49	100 (3.7)
Indium-110 (4.9 hr)	49	10 (.37)
Indium-110 (69.1 min)	49	100 (3.7)
Indium-111	49	100 (3.7)
Indium-112	49	1000 (37)
Indium-113m	49	1000 (37)
Indium-114m	49	10 (.37)
Indium-115	49	0.1 (.0037)
Indium-115m	49	100 (3.7)
Indium-116m	49	100 (3.7)
Indium-117	49	1000 (37)
Indium-117m	49	100 (3.7)
Indium-119m	49	1000 (37)
Iodine-120	53	10 (.37)
Iodine-120m	53	100 (3.7)
Iodine-121	53	100 (3.7)
Iodine-123	53	10 (.37)
Iodine-124	53	0.1 (.0037)
Iodine-125	53	0.01 (.00037)
Iodine-126	53	0.01 (.00037)
Iodine-128	53	1000 (37)
Iodine-129	53	0.001 (.000037)
Iodine-130	53	1 (.037)
Iodine-131	53	0.01 (.00037)
Iodine-132	53	10 (.37)
Iodine-132m	53	10 (.37)
Iodine-133	53	0.1 (.0037)
Iodine-134	53	100 (3.7)
Iodine-135	53	10 (.37)
Iridium-182	77	1000 (37)
Iridium-184	77	100 (3.7)
Iridium-185	77	100 (3.7)
Iridium-186	77	10 (.37)
Iridium-187	77	100 (3.7)
Iridium-188	77	10 (.37)
Iridium-189	77	100 (3.7)
Iridium-190	77	10 (.37)
Iridium-190m	77	1000 (37)
Iridium-192	77	10 (.37)
Iridium-192m	77	100 (3.7)
Iridium-194	77	100 (3.7)
Iridium-194m	77	10 (.37)
Iridium-195	77	1000 (37)
Iridium-195m	77	100 (3.7)
Iron-52	26	100 (3.7)
Iron-55	26	100 (3.7)
Iron-59	26	10 (.37)
Iron-60	26	0.1 (.0037)
Krypton-74	36	10 (.37)
Krypton-76	36	10 (.37)
Krypton-77	36	10 (.37)
Krypton-79	36	100 (3.7)
Krypton-81	36	1000 (37)
Krypton-83m	36	1000 (37)
Krypton-85	36	1000 (37)
Krypton-85m	36	100 (3.7)
Krypton-87	36	10 (.37)
Krypton-88	36	10 (.37)
Lanthanum-131	57	1000 (37)
Lanthanum-132	57	100 (3.7)
Lanthanum-135	57	1000 (37)
Lanthanum-137	57	10 (.37)

Table 2 to Appendix A - Radionuclides

(1) Radionuclide	(2) Atomic Number	(3) Reportable Quantity (RQ) Ci (TBq)
Lanthanum-138	57	1 (.037)
Lanthanum-140	57	10 (.37)
Lanthanum-141	57	1000 (37)
Lanthanum-142	57	100 (3.7)
Lanthanum-143	57	1000 (37)
Lead-195m	82	1000 (37)
Lead-198	82	100 (3.7)
Lead-199	82	100 (3.7)
Lead-200	82	100 (3.7)
Lead-201	82	100 (3.7)
Lead-202	82	1 (.037)
Lead-202m	82	10 (.37)
Lead-203	82	100 (3.7)
Lead-205	82	100 (3.7)
Lead-209	82	1000 (37)
Lead-210	82	0.01 (.00037)
Lead-211	82	100 (3.7)
Lead-212	82	10 (.37)
Lead-214	82	100 (3.7)
Lutetium-169	71	10 (.37)
Lutetium-170	71	10 (.37)
Lutetium-171	71	10 (.37)
Lutetium-172	71	10 (.37)
Lutetium-173	71	100 (3.7)
Lutetium-174	71	10 (.37)
Lutetium-174m	71	10 (.37)
Lutetium-176	71	1 (.037)
Lutetium-176m	71	1000 (37)
Lutetium-177	71	100 (3.7)
Lutetium-177m	71	10 (.37)
Lutetium-178	71	1000 (37)
Lutetium-178m	71	1000 (37)
Lutetium-179	71	1000 (37)
Magnesium-28	12	10 (.37)
Manganese-51	25	1000 (37)
Manganese-52	25	10 (.37)
Manganese-52m	25	1000 (37)
Manganese-53	25	1000 (37)
Manganese-54	25	10 (.37)
Manganese-56	25	100 (3.7)
Mendelevium-257	101	100 (3.7)
Mendelevium-258	101	1 (.037)
Mercury-193	80	100 (3.7)
Mercury-193m	80	10 (.37)
Mercury-194	80	0.1 (.0037)
Mercury-195	80	100 (3.7)
Mercury-195m	80	100 (3.7)
Mercury-197	80	1000 (37)
Mercury-197m	80	1000 (37)
Mercury-199m	80	1000 (37)
Mercury-203	80	10 (.37)
Molybdenum-101	42	1000 (37)
Molybdenum-90	42	100 (3.7)
Molybdenum-93	42	100 (3.7)
Molybdenum-93m	42	10 (.37)
Molybdenum-99	42	100 (3.7)
Neodymium-136	60	1000 (37)
Neodymium-138	60	1000 (37)
Neodymium-139	60	1000 (37)

Table 2 to Appendix A - Radionuclides

(1) Radionuclide	(2) Atomic Number	(3) Reportable Quantity (RQ) Ci (TBq)
Neodymium-139m	60	100 (3.7)
Neodymium-141	60	1000 (37)
Neodymium-147	60	10 (.37)
Neodymium-149	60	100 (3.7)
Neodymium-151	60	1000 (37)
Neptunium-232	93	1000 (37)
Neptunium-233	93	1000 (37)
Neptunium-234	93	10 (.37)
Neptunium-235	93	1000 (37)
Neptunium-236 (1.2 E 5 yr)	93	0.1 (.0037)
Neptunium-236 (22.5 hr)	93	100 (3.7)
Neptunium-237	93	0.01 (.00037)
Neptunium-238	93	10 (.37)
Neptunium-239	93	100 (3.7)
Neptunium-240	93	100 (3.7)
Nickel-56	28	10 (.37)
Nickel-57	28	10 (.37)
Nickel-59	28	100 (3.7)
Nickel-63	28	100 (3.7)
Nickel-65	28	100 (3.7)
Nickel-66	28	10 (.37)
Niobium-88	41	100 (3.7)
Niobium-89 (122 min)	41	100 (3.7)
Niobium-89 (66 min)	41	100 (3.7)
Niobium-90	41	10 (.37)
Niobium-93m	41	100 (3.7)
Niobium-94	41	10 (.37)
Niobium-95	41	10 (.37)
Niobium-95m	41	100 (3.7)
Niobium-96	41	10 (.37)
Niobium-97	41	100 (3.7)
Niobium-98	41	1000 (37)
Osmium-180	76	1000 (37)
Osmium-181	76	100 (3.7)
Osmium-182	76	100 (3.7)
Osmium-185	76	10 (.37)
Osmium-189m	76	1000 (37)
Osmium-191	76	100 (3.7)
Osmium-191m	76	1000 (37)
Osmium-193	76	100 (3.7)
Osmium-194	76	1 (.037)
Palladium-100	46	100 (3.7)
Palladium-101	46	100 (3.7)
Palladium-103	46	100 (3.7)
Palladium-107	46	100 (3.7)
Palladium-109	46	1000 (37)
Phosphorus-32	15	0.1 (.0037)
Phosphorus-33	15	1 (.037)
Platinum-186	78	100 (3.7)
Platinum-188	78	100 (3.7)
Platinum-189	78	100 (3.7)
Platinum-191	78	100 (3.7)
Platinum-193	78	1000 (37)
Platinum-193m	78	100 (3.7)
Platinum-195m	78	100 (3.7)
Platinum-197	78	1000 (37)
Platinum-197m	78	1000 (37)
Platinum-199	78	1000 (37)
Platinum-200	78	100 (3.7)

Table 2 to Appendix A - Radionuclides

(1) Radionuclide	(2) Atomic Number	(3) Reportable Quantity (RQ) Ci (TBq)
Plutonium-234	94	1000 (37)
Plutonium-235	94	1000 (37)
Plutonium-236	94	0.1 (.0037)
Plutonium-237	94	1000 (37)
Plutonium-238	94	0.01 (.00037)
Plutonium-239	94	0.01 (.00037)
Plutonium-240	94	0.01 (.00037)
Plutonium-241	94	1 (.037)
Plutonium-242	94	0.01 (.00037)
Plutonium-243	94	1000 (37)
Plutonium-244	94	0.01 (.00037)
Plutonium-245	94	100 (3.7)
Polonium-203	84	100 (3.7)
Polonium-205	84	100 (3.7)
Polonium-207	84	10 (.37)
Polonium-210	84	0.01 (.00037)
Potassium-40	19	1 (.037)
Potassium-42	19	100 (3.7)
Potassium-43	19	10 (.37)
Potassium-44	19	100 (3.7)
Potassium-45	19	1000 (37)
Praseodymium-136	59	1000 (37)
Praseodymium-137	59	1000 (37)
Praseodymium-138m	59	100 (3.7)
Praseodymium-139	59	1000 (37)
Praseodymium-142	59	100 (3.7)
Praseodymium-142m	59	1000 (37)
Praseodymium-143	59	10 (.37)
Praseodymium-144	59	1000 (37)
Praseodymium-145	59	1000 (37)
Praseodymium-147	59	1000 (37)
Promethium-141	61	1000 (37)
Promethium-143	61	100 (3.7)
Promethium-144	61	10 (.37)
Promethium-145	61	100 (3.7)
Promethium-146	61	10 (.37)
Promethium-147	61	10 (.37)
Promethium-148	61	10 (.37)
Promethium-148m	61	10 (.37)
Promethium-149	61	100 (3.7)
Promethium-150	61	100 (3.7)
Promethium-151	61	100 (3.7)
Protactinium-227	91	100 (3.7)
Protactinium-228	91	10 (.37)
Protactinium-230	91	10 (.37)
Protactinium-231	91	0.01 (.00037)
Protactinium-232	91	10 (.37)
Protactinium-233	91	100 (3.7)
Protactinium-234	91	10 (.37)
RADIONUCLIDES $ †		1 (.037)
Radium-223	88	1 (.037)
Radium-224	88	10 (.37)
Radium-225	88	1 (.037)
Radium-226 **	88	0.1 (.0037)
Radium-227	88	1000 (37)
Radium-228	88	0.1 (.0037)
Radon-220	86	0.1 (.0037)
Radon-222	86	0.1 (.0037)
Rhenium-177	75	1000 (37)

Table 2 to Appendix A - Radionuclides

(1) Radionuclide	(2) Atomic Number	(3) Reportable Quantity (RQ) Ci (TBq)
Rhenium-178	75	1000 (37)
Rhenium-181	75	100 (3.7)
Rhenium-182 (12.7 hr)	75	10 (.37)
Rhenium-182 (64.0 hr)	75	10 (.37)
Rhenium-184	75	10 (.37)
Rhenium-184m	75	10 (.37)
Rhenium-186	75	100 (3.7)
Rhenium-186m	75	10 (.37)
Rhenium-187	75	1000 (37)
Rhenium-188	75	1000 (37)
Rhenium-188m	75	1000 (37)
Rhenium-189	75	1000 (37)
Rhodium-100	45	10 (.37)
Rhodium-101	45	10 (.37)
Rhodium-101m	45	100 (3.7)
Rhodium-102	45	10 (.37)
Rhodium-102m	45	10 (.37)
Rhodium-103m	45	1000 (37)
Rhodium-105	45	100 (3.7)
Rhodium-106m	45	10 (.37)
Rhodium-107	45	1000 (37)
Rhodium-99	45	10 (.37)
Rhodium-99m	45	100 (3.7)
Rubidium-79	37	1000 (37)
Rubidium-81	37	100 (3.7)
Rubidium-81m	37	1000 (37)
Rubidium-82m	37	10 (.37)
Rubidium-83	37	10 (.37)
Rubidium-84	37	10 (.37)
Rubidium-86	37	10 (.37)
Rubidium-87	37	10 (.37)
Rubidium-88	37	1000 (37)
Rubidium-89	37	1000 (37)
Ruthenium-103	44	10 (.37)
Ruthenium-105	44	100 (3.7)
Ruthenium-106	44	1 (.037)
Ruthenium-94	44	1000 (37)
Ruthenium-97	44	100 (3.7)
Samarium-141	62	1000 (37)
Samarium-141m	62	1000 (37)
Samarium-142	62	1000 (37)
Samarium-145	62	100 (3.7)
Samarium-146	62	0.01 (.00037)
Samarium-147	62	0.01 (.00037)
Samarium-151	62	10 (.37)
Samarium-153	62	100 (3.7)
Samarium-155	62	1000 (37)
Samarium-156	62	100 (3.7)
Scandium-43	21	1000 (37)
Scandium-44	21	100 (3.7)
Scandium-44m	21	10 (.37)
Scandium-46	21	10 (.37)
Scandium-47	21	100 (3.7)
Scandium-48	21	10 (.37)
Scandium-49	21	1000 (37)
Selenium-70	34	1000 (37)
Selenium-73	34	10 (.37)
Selenium-73m	34	100 (3.7)
Selenium-75	34	10 (.37)

Table 2 to Appendix A - Radionuclides

(1) Radionuclide	(2) Atomic Number	(3) Reportable Quantity (RQ) Ci (TBq)
Selenium-79	34	10 (.37)
Selenium-81	34	1000 (37)
Selenium-81m	34	1000 (37)
Selenium-83	34	1000 (37)
Silicon-31	14	1000 (37)
Silicon-32	14	1 (.037)
Silver-102	47	100 (3.7)
Silver-103	47	1000 (37)
Silver-104	47	1000 (37)
Silver-104m	47	1000 (37)
Silver-105	47	10 (.37)
Silver-106	47	1000 (37)
Silver-106m	47	10 (.37)
Silver-108m	47	10 (.37)
Silver-110m	47	10 (.37)
Silver-111	47	10 (.37)
Silver-112	47	100 (3.7)
Silver-115	47	1000 (37)
Sodium-22	11	10 (.37)
Sodium-24	11	10 (.37)
Strontium-80	38	100 (3.7)
Strontium-81	38	1000 (37)
Strontium-83	38	100 (3.7)
Strontium-85	38	10 (.37)
Strontium-85m	38	1000 (37)
Strontium-87m	38	100 (3.7)
Strontium-89	38	10 (.37)
Strontium-90	38	0.1 (.0037)
Strontium-91	38	10 (.37)
Strontium-92	38	100 (3.7)
Sulfur-35	16	1 (.037)
Tantalum-172	73	100 (3.7)
Tantalum-173	73	100 (3.7)
Tantalum-174	73	100 (3.7)
Tantalum-175	73	100 (3.7)
Tantalum-176	73	10 (.37)
Tantalum-177	73	1000 (37)
Tantalum-178	73	1000 (37)
Tantalum-179	73	1000 (37)
Tantalum-180	73	100 (3.7)
Tantalum-180m	73	1000 (37)
Tantalum-182	73	10 (.37)
Tantalum-182m	73	1000 (37)
Tantalum-183	73	100 (3.7)
Tantalum-184	73	10 (.37)
Tantalum-185	73	1000 (37)
Tantalum-186	73	1000 (37)
Technetium-101	43	1000 (37)
Technetium-104	43	1000 (37)
Technetium-93	43	100 (3.7)
Technetium-93m	43	1000 (37)
Technetium-94	43	10 (.37)
Technetium-94m	43	100 (3.7)
Technetium-96	43	10 (.37)
Technetium-96m	43	1000 (37)
Technetium-97	43	100 (3.7)
Technetium-97m	43	100 (3.7)
Technetium-98	43	10 (.37)
Technetium-99	43	10 (.37)

Table 2 to Appendix A - Radionuclides

(1) Radionuclide	(2) Atomic Number	(3) Reportable Quantity (RQ) Ci (TBq)
Technetium-99m	43	100 (3.7)
Tellurium-116	52	1000 (37)
Tellurium-121	52	10 (.37)
Tellurium-121m	52	10 (.37)
Tellurium-123	52	10 (.37)
Tellurium-123m	52	10 (.37)
Tellurium-125m	52	10 (.37)
Tellurium-127	52	1000 (37)
Tellurium-127m	52	10 (.37)
Tellurium-129	52	1000 (37)
Tellurium-129m	52	10 (.37)
Tellurium-131	52	1000 (37)
Tellurium-131m	52	10 (.37)
Tellurium-132	52	10 (.37)
Tellurium-133	52	1000 (37)
Tellurium-133m	52	1000 (37)
Tellurium-134	52	1000 (37)
Terbium-147	65	100 (3.7)
Terbium-149	65	100 (3.7)
Terbium-150	65	100 (3.7)
Terbium-151	65	10 (.37)
Terbium-153	65	100 (3.7)
Terbium-154	65	10 (.37)
Terbium-155	65	100 (3.7)
Terbium-156	65	10 (.37)
Terbium-156m (24.4 hr)	65	1000 (37)
Terbium-156m (5.0 hr)	65	1000 (37)
Terbium-157	65	100 (3.7)
Terbium-158	65	10 (.37)
Terbium-160	65	10 (.37)
Terbium-161	65	100 (3.7)
Thallium-194	81	1000 (37)
Thallium-194m	81	100 (3.7)
Thallium-195	81	100 (3.7)
Thallium-197	81	100 (3.7)
Thallium-198	81	10 (.37)
Thallium-198m	81	100 (3.7)
Thallium-199	81	100 (3.7)
Thallium-200	81	10 (.37)
Thallium-201	81	1000 (37)
Thallium-202	81	10 (.37)
Thallium-204	81	10 (.37)
Thorium (Irradiated)	90	***
Thorium (Natural)	90	**
Thorium-226	90	100 (3.7)
Thorium-227	90	1 (.037)
Thorium-228	90	0.01 (.00037)
Thorium-229	90	0.001 (.000037)
Thorium-230	90	0.01 (.00037)
Thorium-231	90	100 (3.7)
Thorium-232 **	90	0.001 (.000037)
Thorium-234	90	100 (3.7)
Thulium-162	69	1000 (37)
Thulium-166	69	10 (.37)
Thulium-167	69	100 (3.7)
Thulium-170	69	10 (.37)
Thulium-171	69	100 (3.7)
Thulium-172	69	100 (3.7)
Thulium-173	69	100 (3.7)

Table 2 to Appendix A - Radionuclides

(1) Radionuclide	(2) Atomic Number	(3) Reportable Quantity (RQ) Ci (TBq)
Thulium-175	69	1000 (37)
Tin-110	50	100 (3.7)
Tin-111	50	1000 (37)
Tin-113	50	10 (.37)
Tin-117m	50	100 (3.7)
Tin-119m	50	10 (.37)
Tin-121	50	1000 (37)
Tin-121m	50	10 (.37)
Tin-123	50	10 (.37)
Tin-123m	50	1000 (37)
Tin-125	50	10 (.37)
Tin-126	50	1 (.037)
Tin-127	50	100 (3.7)
Tin-128	50	1000 (37)
Titanium-44	22	1 (.037)
Titanium-45	22	1000 (37)
Tungsten-176	74	1000 (37)
Tungsten-177	74	100 (3.7)
Tungsten-178	74	100 (3.7)
Tungsten-179	74	1000 (37)
Tungsten-181	74	100 (3.7)
Tungsten-185	74	10 (.37)
Tungsten-187	74	100 (3.7)
Tungsten-188	74	10 (.37)
Uranium (Depleted)	92	***
Uranium (Irradiated)	92	***
Uranium (Natural)	92	**
Uranium Enriched 20% or greater	92	***
Uranium Enriched less than 20%	92	***
Uranium-230	92	1 (.037)
Uranium-231	92	1000 (37)
Uranium-232	92	0.01 (.00037)
Uranium-233	92	0.1 (.0037)
Uranium-234 **	92	0.1 (.0037)
Uranium-235 **	92	0.1 (.0037)
Uranium-236	92	0.1 (.0037)
Uranium-237	92	100 (3.7)
Uranium-238 **	92	0.1 (.0037)
Uranium-239	92	1000 (37)
Uranium-240	92	1000 (37)
Vanadium-47	23	1000 (37)
Vanadium-48	23	10 (.37)
Vanadium-49	23	1000 (37)
Xenon-120	54	100 (3.7)
Xenon-121	54	10 (.37)
Xenon-122	54	100 (3.7)
Xenon-123	54	10 (.37)
Xenon-125	54	100 (3.7)
Xenon-127	54	100 (3.7)

Table 2 to Appendix A - Radionuclides

(1) Radionuclide	(2) Atomic Number	(3) Reportable Quantity (RQ) Ci (TBq)
Xenon-129m	54	1000 (37)
Xenon-131m	54	1000 (37)
Xenon-133	54	1000 (37)
Xenon-133m	54	1000 (37)
Xenon-135	54	100 (3.7)
Xenon-135m	54	10 (.37)
Xenon-138	54	10 (.37)
Ytterbium-162	70	1000 (37)
Ytterbium-166	70	10 (.37)
Ytterbium-167	70	1000 (37)
Ytterbium-169	70	10 (.37)
Ytterbium-175	70	100 (3.7)
Ytterbium-177	70	1000 (37)
Ytterbium-178	70	1000 (37)
Yttrium-86	39	10 (.37)
Yttrium-86m	39	1000 (37)
Yttrium-87	39	10 (.37)
Yttrium-88	39	10 (.37)
Yttrium-90	39	10 (.37)
Yttrium-90m	39	100 (3.7)
Yttrium-91	39	10 (.37)
Yttrium-91m	39	1000 (37)
Yttrium-92	39	100 (3.7)
Yttrium-93	39	100 (3.7)
Yttrium-94	39	1000 (37)
Yttrium-95	39	1000 (37)
Zinc-62	30	100 (3.7)
Zinc-63	30	1000 (37)
Zinc-65	30	10 (.37)
Zinc-69	30	1000 (37)
Zinc-69m	30	100 (3.7)
Zinc-71m	30	100 (3.7)
Zinc-72	30	100 (3.7)
Zirconium-86	40	100 (3.7)
Zirconium-88	40	10 (.37)
Zirconium-89	40	100 (3.7)
Zirconium-93	40	1 (.037)
Zirconium-95	40	10 (.37)
Zirconium-97	40	10 (.37)

$ The RQs for all radionuclides apply to chemical compounds containing the radionuclides and elemental forms regardless of the diameter of pieces of solid material.

† The RQ of one curie applies to all radionuclides not otherwise listed. Whenever the RQs in TABLE 1 — HAZARDOUS SUBSTANCES OTHER THAN RADIONUCLIDES and this table conflict, the lowest RQ shall apply. For example, uranyl acetate and uranyl nitrate have RQs shown in TABLE 1 of 100 pounds, equivalent to about one-tenth the RQ level for uranium-238 in this table.

** The method to determine the RQs for mixtures or solutions of radionuclides can be found in paragraph 7 of the note preceding TABLE 1 of this appendix. RQs for the following four common radionuclide mixtures are provided: radium-226 in secular equilibrium with its daughters (0.053 curie); natural uranium (0.1 curie); natural uranium in secular equilibrium with its daughters (0.052 curie); and natural thorium in secular equilibrium with its daughters (0.011 curie).

*** Indicates that the name was added by RSPA because it appears in the list of radionuclides in 49 CFR 173.435. The reportable quantity (RQ), if not specifically listed elsewhere in this appendix, shall be determined in accordance with the procedures in paragraph 7 of this appendix.

§172.101 App. B List of marine pollutants.

1. **See §171.4 of this subchapter** for applicability to marine pollutants. This appendix lists potential marine pollutants as defined in §171.8 of this subchapter.
2. **Marine pollutants listed in this appendix** are not necessarily listed by name in the §172.101 Table. If a marine pollutant not listed by name or by synonym in the §172.101 Table meets the definition of any hazard Class 1 through 8, then you must determine the class and division of the material in accordance with §173.2a of this subchapter. You must also select the most appropriate hazardous material description and proper shipping name. If a marine pollutant not listed by name or by synonym in the §172.101 Table does not meet the definition of any Class 1 through 8, then you must offer it for transportation under the most appropriate of the following two Class 9 entries: "Environmentally hazardous substances, liquid, n.o.s.," UN3082, or "Environmentally hazardous substances, solid, n.o.s." UN3077.
3. **This appendix contains two columns.** The first column, entitled "S.M.P." (for severe marine pollutants), identifies whether a material is a severe marine pollutant. If the letters "PP" appear in this column for a material, the material is a severe marine pollutant, otherwise it is not. The second column, entitled "Marine Pollutant," lists the marine pollutants.
4. **If a material not listed in this appendix** meets the criteria for a marine pollutant, as provided in the General Introduction of the IMDG Code, Guidelines for the Identification of Harmful Substances in Packaged Form, the material may be transported as a marine pollutant in accordance with the applicable requirements of this subchapter.
5. **If approved by the Associate Administrator,** a material listed in this appendix which does not meet the criteria for a marine pollutant, as provided in the General Introduction of the IMDG Code, Guidelines for the Identification of Harmful Substances in Packaged Form, is excepted from the requirements of this subchapter as a marine pollutant.

List of Marine Pollutants

S.M.P. (1)	Marine pollutant (2)
	Acetone cyanohydrin, stabilized
	Acetylene tetrabromide
	Acetylene tetrachloride
	Acraldehyde, inhibited
	Acrolein, inhibited
	Acrolein, stabilized
	Acrylic aldehyde, inhibited
	Alcohol C-12 - C-16 poly(1-6) ethoxylate
	Alcohol C-13 - C-15 poly(1-6) ethoxylate
	Alcohol C-6 - C-17 (secondary)poly(3-6) ethoxylate
	Aldicarb
PP	Aldrin
	Alkyl (c12-c14) dimethylamine
	Alkyl (c7-c9) nitrates
	Alkylbenzenesulphonates, branched and straight chain
	Alkylphenols, liquid, n.o.s. *(including C2-C12 homologues)*
	Alkylphenols, solid, n.o.s. *(including C2-C12 homologues)*
	Allyl bromide
	ortho-Aminoanisole
	Aminocarb
	Ammonium dinitro-o-cresolate
	n-Amylbenzene
PP	Azinphos-ethyl
PP	Azinphos-methyl
	Barium cyanide
	Bendiocarb
	Benomyl
	Benquinox
	Benzyl chlorocarbonate
	Benzyl chloroformate
PP	Binapacryl
	N,N-Bis (2-hydroxyethyl) oleamide (LOA)
PP	Brodifacoum

List of Marine Pollutants

S.M.P. (1)	Marine pollutant (2)
	Bromine cyanide
	Bromoacetone
	Bromoallylene
	Bromobenzene
	ortho-Bromobenzyl cyanide
	Bromocyane
	Bromoform
PP	Bromophos-ethyl
	3-Bromopropene
	Bromoxynil
	Butanedione
	2-Butenal, stabilized
	Butyl benzyl phthalate
	N-tert-butyl-*N*-cyclopropyl-6-methylthio-1,3,5-triazine-2,4-diamine
	2,4-Di-tert-butylphenol
	2,6-Di-tert-butylphenol
	para-tertiary-butyltoluene
PP	Cadmium compounds
	Cadmium sulphide
	Calcium arsenate
	Calcium arsenate and calcium arsenite, mixtures, solid
	Calcium cyanide
PP	Camphechlor
	Carbaryl
	Carbendazim
	Carbofuran
	Carbon tetrabromide
	Carbon tetrachloride
PP	Carbophenothion
	Cartap hydrochloride
PP	Chlordane
	Chlorfenvinphos
PP	Chlorinated paraffins (C-10 - C-13)
PP	Chlorinated paraffins (C14-C17), with more than 1% shorter chain length
	Chlorine
	Chlorine cyanide, inhibited
	Chlormephos
	Chloroacetone, stabilized
	1-Chloro-2,3-Epoxypropane
	2-Chloro-6-nitrotoluene
	4-Chloro-2-nitrotoluene
	Chloro-ortho-nitrotoluene
	2-Chloro-5-trifluoromethylnitrobenzene
	para-Chlorobenzyl chloride, liquid or solid
	Chlorodinitrobenzenes, liquid or solid
	1-Chloroheptane
	1-Chlorohexane
	Chloronitroanilines
	Chloronitrotoluenes, *liquid*
	Chloronitrotoluenes, *solid*
	1-Chlorooctane
PP	Chlorophenolates, liquid
PP	Chlorophenolates, solid
	Chlorophenols, liquid
	Chlorophenols, solid
	Chlorophenyltrichlorosilane
	alpha-Chloropropylene
	Chlorotoluenes (meta-;para-)
PP	Chlorpyriphos
PP	Chlorthiophos

List of Marine Pollutants

S.M.P. (1)	Marine pollutant (2)
	Cocculus
	Coconitrile
	Copper acetoarsenite
	Copper arsenite
	Copper chloride
PP	Copper chloride solution
PP	Copper cyanide
PP	Copper metal powder
PP	Copper sulphate, anhydrous, hydrates
	Coumachlor
PP	Coumaphos
PP	Cresyl diphenyl phosphate
	Crotonaldehyde, stabilized
	Crotonic aldehyde, stabilized
	Crotoxyphos
	Cupric arsenite
PP	Cupric chloride
PP	Cupric cyanide
PP	Cupric sulfate
	Cupriethylenediamine solution
PP	Cuprous chloride
	Cyanide mixtures
	Cyanide solutions
	Cyanides, inorganic, n.o.s.
	Cyanogen bromide
	Cyanogen chloride, inhibited
	Cyanogen chloride, stabilized
	Cyanophos
PP	1,5,9-Cyclododecatriene
PP	Cyhexatin
PP	Cymenes (o-;m-;p-)
PP	Cypermethrin
PP	DDT
	Decycloxytetrahydrothiophene dioxide
	DEF
	Desmedipham
	Di-allate
	Di-n-Butyl phthalate
PP	Dialifos
	4,4'-Diaminodiphenylmethane
PP	Diazinon
	1,3-Dibromobenzene
PP	Dichlofenthion
	Dichloroanilines
	1,3-Dichlorobenzene
	1,2-Dichlorobenzene
	1,4-Dichlorobenzene
	Dichlorobenzene (meta-; para-)
	2,2-Dichlorodiethyl ether
	Dichlorodimethyl ether, symmetrical
	Di-(2-chloroethyl) ether
	1,1-Dichloroethylene, inhibited
	1,6-Dichlorohexane
	Dichlorophenyltrichlorosilane
PP	Dichlorvos
PP	Diclofop-methyl
	Dicrotophos
PP	Dieldrin
	Diisopropylbenzenes
	Diisopropylnaphthalenes, mixed isomers

List of Marine Pollutants

S.M.P. (1)	Marine pollutant (2)
PP	Dimethoate
PP	N,N-Dimethyldodecylamine
	Dimethylhydrazine, symmetrical
	Dimethylhydrazine, unsymmetrical
	Dinitro-o-cresol, *solid*
	Dinitro-o-cresol, *solution*
	Dinitrochlorobenzenes, liquid or solid
	Dinitrophenol, *dry or wetted with less than 15 percent water, by mass*
	Dinitrophenol solutions
	Dinitrophenol, *wetted with not less than 15 percent water, by mass*
	Dinitrophenolates alkali metals, *dry or wetted with less than 15 percent water, by mass*
	Dinitrophenolates, wetted *with not less than 15 percent water, by mass*
	Dinobuton
	Dinoseb
	Dinoseb acetate
	Dioxacarb
	Dioxathion
	Dipentene
	Diphacinone
	Diphenyl
	Diphenyl oxide and biphenyl phenyl ether mixtures
PP	Diphenylamine chloroarsine
PP	Diphenylchloroarsine, solid *or* liquid
	Disulfoton
	1,4-Di-tert-butylbenzene
	DNOC
	DNOC (pesticide)
	Dodecyl diphenyl oxide disulphonate
PP	Dodecyl hydroxypropyl sulfide
	1-Dodecylamine
PP	Dodecylphenol
	Drazoxolon
	Edifenphos
PP	Endosulfan
PP	Endrin
	Epibromohydrin
	Epichlorohydrin
PP	EPN
PP	Esfenvalerate
PP	Ethion
	Ethoprophos
	Ethyl fluid
	Ethyl mercaptan
	2-Ethylhexyl nitrate
	5-Ethyl-2-picoline
	Ethyl propenoate, inhibited
	2-Ethyl-3-propylacrolein
	Ethyl tetraphosphate
	Ethyldichloroarsine
	Ethylene dibromide and methyl bromide mixtures, liquid
	2-Ethylhexaldehyde
	Fenamiphos
PP	Fenbutatin oxide
PP	Fenchlorazole-ethyl
PP	Fenitrothion
PP	Fenoxapro-ethyl
PP	Fenoxaprop-P-ethyl
PP	Fenpropathrin
	Fensulfothion

List of Marine Pollutants

S.M.P. (1)	Marine pollutant (2)
PP	Fenthion
PP	Fentin acetate
PP	Fentin hydroxide
	Ferric arsenate
	Ferric arsenite
	Ferrous arsenate
PP	Fonofos
	Formetanate
PP	Furathiocarb (ISO)
PP	gamma-BHC
	Gasoline, leaded
PP	Heptachlor
	Heptenophos
	n-Heptaldehyde
	n-Heptylbenzene
	normal-Heptyl chloride
PP	Hexachlorobutadiene
PP	1,3-Hexachlorobutadiene
	Hexaethyl tetraphosphate *liquid*
	Hexaethyl tetraphosphate, *solid*
	normal-Hexyl chloride
	n-Hexylbenzene
	Hydrocyanic acid, anhydrous, stabilized, containing less than 3% water
	Hydrocyanic acid, anhydrous, stabilized, containing less than 3% water and absorbed in a porous inert material
	Hydrocyanic acid, aqueous solutions *not more than 20% hydrocyanic acid*
	Hydrogen cyanide solution in alcohol, *with not more than 45% hydrogen cyanide*
	Hydrogen cyanide, stabilized *with less than 3% water*
	Hydrogen cyanide, stabilized *with less than 3% water and absorbed in a porous inert material*
	Hydroxydimethylbenzenes, liquid or solid
	Ioxynil
	Isoamyl mercaptan
	Isobenzan
	Isobutyl butyrate
	Isobutylbenzene
	Isodecyl acrylate
	Isodecyl diphenyl phosphate
	Isofenphos
	Isooctyl nitrate
	Isoprocarb
	Isopropenylbenzene
	Isotetramethylbenzene
PP	Isoxathion
	Lead acetate
	Lead arsenates
	Lead arsenites
	Lead compounds, soluble, n.o.s.
	Lead cyanide
	Lead nitrate
	Lead perchlorate, solid or solution
	Lead tetraethyl
	Lead tetramethyl
PP	Lindane
	Linuron
	London Purple
	Magnesium arsenate
	Malathion
	Mancozeb (ISO)
	Maneb

List of Marine Pollutants

S.M.P. (1)	Marine pollutant (2)
	Maneb preparations *with not less than 60% maneb*
	Maneb preparation, stabilized against self-heating
	Maneb stabilized *or* Maneb preparations, stabilized *against self-heating*
	Manganese ethylene-1,2-bis-dithiocarbamate
	Manganese ethylene-1,2-bis-dithiocarbamate, stabilized against self-heating
	Mecarbam
	Mephosfolan
	Mercaptodimethur
PP	Mercuric acetate
PP	Mercuric ammonium chloride
PP	Mercuric arsenate
PP	Mercuric benzoate
PP	Mercuric bisulphate
PP	Mercuric bromide
PP	Mercuric chloride
PP	Mercuric cyanide
PP	Mercuric gluconate
	Mercuric iodide
PP	Mercuric nitrate
PP	Mercuric oleate
PP	Mercuric oxide
PP	Mercuric oxycyanide, desensitized
PP	Mercuric potassium cyanide
PP	Mercuric Sulphate
PP	Mercuric thiocyanate
PP	Mercurol
PP	Mercurous acetate
PP	Mercurous bisulphate
PP	Mercurous bromide
PP	Mercurous chloride
PP	Mercurous nitrate
PP	Mercurous salicylate
PP	Mercurous sulphate
PP	Mercury acetates
PP	Mercury ammonium chloride
PP	Mercury based pesticide, liquid, flammable, toxic
PP	Mercury based pesticides, liquid, toxic, flammable
PP	Mercury based pesticides, liquid, toxic
PP	Mercury based pesticides, solid, toxic
PP	Mercury benzoate
PP	Mercury bichloride
PP	Mercury bisulphates
PP	Mercury bromides
PP	Mercury compounds, liquid, n.o.s.
PP	Mercury compounds, solid, n.o.s.
PP	Mercury cyanide
PP	Mercury gluconate
PP	Mercury (I) (mercurous) compounds (pesticides)
PP	Mercury (II) (mercuric) compounds (pesticides)
	Mercury iodide
PP	Mercury nucleate
PP	Mercury oleate
PP	Mercury oxide
PP	Mercury oxycyanide, desensitized
PP	Mercury potassium cyanide
PP	Mercury potassium iodide
PP	Mercury salicylate
PP	Mercury sulfates
PP	Mercury thiocyanate
	Metam-sodium

List of Marine Pollutants

S.M.P. (1)	Marine pollutant (2)
	Methamidophos
	Methanethiol
	Methidathion
	Methomyl
	ortho-Methoxyaniline
	Methyl bromide and ethylene dibromide mixtures, liquid
	Methyl mercaptan
	3-Methylacroleine, stabilized
	Methylchlorobenzenes
	Methylnitrophenols
	3-Methylpyradine
	Methyltrithion
	Methylvinylbenzenes, inhibited
PP	Mevinphos
	Mexacarbate
	Mirex
	Monocrotophos
	Motor fuel anti-knock mixtures
	Motor fuel anti-knock mixtures or compounds
	Nabam
	Naled
PP	Nickel carbonyl
PP	Nickel cyanide
PP	Nickel tetracarbonyl
	3-Nitro-4-chlorobenzotrifluoride
	Nitrobenzene
	Nitrobenzotrifluorides, liquid or solid
	Nonylphenol
	normal-Octaldehyde
	Oleylamine
PP	Organotin compounds, liquid, n.o.s.
PP	Organotin compounds (pesticides)
PP	Organotin compounds, solid, n.o.s.
PP	Organotin pesticides, liquid, flammable, toxic, n.o.s., *flash point less than 23 °C*
PP	Organotin pesticides, liquid, toxic, flammable, n.o.s.
PP	Organotin pesticides, liquid, toxic, n.o.s.
PP	Organotin pesticides, solid, toxic, n.o.s.
	Orthoarsenic acid
PP	Osmium tetroxide
	Oxamyl
	Oxydisulfoton
	Paraoxon
PP	Parathion
PP	Parathion-methyl
PP	PCBs
	Pentachloroethane
PP	Pentachlorophenol
	Pentalin
	Pentanethiols
	n-Pentylbenzene
	Perchloroethylene
	Perchloromethylmercaptan
	Petrol, leaded
PP	Phenarsazine chloride
	d-Phenothrin
PP	Phenthoate
	1-Phenylbutane
	2-Phenylbutane
	Phenylcyclohexane

List of Marine Pollutants

S.M.P. (1)	Marine pollutant (2)
PP	Phenylmercuric acetate
PP	Phenylmercuric compounds, n.o.s.
PP	Phenylmercuric hydroxide
PP	Phenylmercuric nitrate
	2-Phenylpropene
PP	Phorate
PP	Phosalone
	Phosmet
PP	Phosphamidon
PP	Phosphorus, white, molten
PP	Phosphorus, white *or* yellow dry *or* under water *or* in solution
PP	Phosphorus white, *or* yellow, molten
PP	Phosphorus, yellow, molten
	Pindone (and salts of)
	Pirimicarb
PP	Pirimiphos-ethyl
PP	Polychlorinated biphenyls
PP	Polyhalogenated biphenyls, liquid *or* Terphenyls liquid
PP	Polyhalogenated biphenyls, solid *or* Terphenyls, solid
PP	Potassium cuprocyanide
	Potassium cyanide, solid
	Potassium cyanide, solution
PP	Potassium cyanocuprate (I)
PP	Potassium cyanomercurate
PP	Potassium mercuric iodide
	Promecarb
	Propachlor
	Propaphos
	Propenal, inhibited
	Propoxur
	Prothoate
	Prussic acid, anhydrous, stabilized
	Prussic acid, anhydrous, stabilized, absorbed in a porous inert material
PP	Pyrazophos
	Quinalphos
PP	Quizalofop
PP	Quizalofop-p-ethyl
	Rotenone
	Salithion
PP	Silafluofen
	Silver arsenite
	Silver cyanide
	Silver orthoarsenite
PP	Sodium copper cyanide, solid
PP	Sodium copper cyanide solution
PP	Sodium cuprocyanide, solid
PP	Sodium cuprocyanide, solution
	Sodium cyanide, solid
	Sodium cyanide, solution
	Sodium dinitro-o-cresolate, *dry or wetted with less than 15 percent water, by mass*
	Sodium dinitro-ortho-cresolate, wetted *with not less than 15 percent water, by mass*
PP	Sodium pentachlorophenate
	Strychnine *or* Strychnine salts
	Sulfotep
PP	Sulprophos
	Tallow nitrile
	Temephos
	TEPP
PP	Terbufos

List of Marine Pollutants

S.M.P. (1)	Marine pollutant (2)
	Tetrabromoethane
	Tetrabromomethane
	1,1,2,2-Tetrachloroethane
	Tetrachloroethylene
	Tetrachloromethane
	Tetrachlorophenol
	Tetraethyl dithiopyrophosphate
PP	Tetraethyl lead, liquid
	Tetramethrin
	Tetramethyllead
	Thallium chlorate
	Thallium compounds, n.o.s.
	Thallium compounds (pesticides)
	Thallium nitrate
	Thallium sulfate
	Thallous chlorate
	Thiocarbonyl tetrachloride
	Triaryl phosphates, isopropylated
PP	Triaryl phosphates, n.o.s.
	Triazophos
	Tribromomethane
PP	Tributyltin compounds
	Trichlorfon
PP	1,2,3 — Trichlorobenzene
	Trichlorobenzenes, liquid
	Trichlorobutene
	Trichlorobutylene
	Trichloromethane sulphuryl chloride
	Trichloromethyl sulphochloride
	Trichloronat
	Tricresyl phosphate (less than 1% ortho-isomer)
PP	Tricresyl phosphate, not less than 1% ortho-isomer but not more than 3% orthoisomer
PP	Tricresyl phosphate *with more than 3 percent ortho-isomer*
	Triethylbenzene
	Triisopropylated phenyl phosphates
	Trimethylene dichloride
PP	Triphenylphosphate
	Triphenyl phosphate/tert-butylated triphenyl phosphates mixtures containing 5% to 10% triphenyl phosphates
PP	Triphenyl phosphate/tert-butylated triphenyl phosphates mixtures containing 10% to 48% triphenyl phosphates
PP	Triphenyltin compounds
	Tritolyl phosphate (less than 1% ortho-isomer)
PP	Tritolyl phosphate (not less than 1% ortho-isomer)
	Trixylenyl phosphate
	Vinylidene chloride, stabilized
	Warfarin (and salts of)
PP	White phosphorus, dry
PP	White phosphorus, wet
	White spirit, low (15-20%) aromatic
PP	Yellow phosphorus, dry
PP	Yellow phosphorus, wet
	Zinc bromide
	Zinc cyanide

§172.102 Special provisions.

(a) **General.** When column 7 of the §172.101 table refers to a special provision for a hazardous material, the meaning and requirements of that provision are as set forth in this section. When a special provision specifies packaging or packaging requirements —

(1) *The special provision* is in addition to the standard requirements for all packagings prescribed in §173.24 of this subchapter and any other applicable packaging requirements in subparts A and B of part 173 of this subchapter; and

(2) *To the extent* a special provision imposes limitations or additional requirements on the packaging provisions set forth in column 8 of the §172.101 table, packagings must conform to the requirements of the special provision.

(b) **Description of codes for special provisions.** Special provisions contain packaging provisions, prohibitions, exceptions from requirements for particular quantities or forms of materials and requirements or prohibitions applicable to specific modes of transportation, as follows:

(1) *A code consisting* only of numbers (for example, "11") is multi-modal in application and may apply to bulk and non-bulk packagings.

(2) *A code containing* the letter "A" refers to a special provision which applies only to transportation by aircraft.

(3) *A code containing* the letter "B" refers to a special provision which applies only to bulk packaging requirements. Unless otherwise provided in this subchapter, these special provisions do not apply to IM portable tanks.

(4) *A code containing* the letter "H" refers to a special provision which applies only to transportation by highway.

(5) *A code containing* the letter "N" refers to a special provision which applies only to non-bulk packaging requirements.

(6) *A code containing* the letter "R" refers to a special provision which applies only to transportation by rail.

(7) *A code containing* the letter "T" refers to a special provision which applies only to transportation in IM portable tanks.

(8) *A code containing* the letter "W" refers to a special provision which applies only to transportation by water.

(c) **Tables of special provisions.** The following tables list, and set forth the requirements of, the special provisions referred to in column 7 of the §172.101 table.

(1) *Numeric provisions.* These provisions are multi-modal and apply to bulk and non-bulk packagings:

Code/Special Provisions

1. **This material is poisonous by inhalation** (see §171.8 of this subchapter) in Hazard Zone A (see §173.116(a) or §173.133(a) of this subchapter), and must be described as an inhalation hazard under the provisions of this subchapter.
2. **This material is poisonous by inhalation** (see §171.8 of this subchapter) in Hazard Zone B (see §173.116(a) or §173.133(a) of this subchapter), and must be described as an inhalation hazard under the provisions of this subchapter.
3. **This material is poisonous by inhalation** (see §171.8 of this subchapter) in Hazard Zone C (see §173.116(a) of this subchapter), and must be described as an inhalation hazard under the provisions of this subchapter.
4. **This material is poisonous by inhalation** (see §171.8 of this subchapter) in Hazard Zone D (see §173.116(a) of this subchapter), and must be described as an inhalation hazard under the provisions of this subchapter.
5. **If this material meets the definition for a material** poisonous by inhalation (see §171.8 of this subchapter), a shipping name must be selected which identifies the inhalation hazard, in Division 2.3 or Division 6.1, as appropriate.
6. **This material is poisonous by inhalation** and must be described as an inhalation hazard under the provisions of this subchapter.
7. **An ammonium nitrate fertilizer** is a fertilizer formulation, containing 90% or more ammonium nitrate and no more than 0.2% organic combustible material (calculated as carbon), which does not meet the definition and criteria of a Class 1 (explosive) material (See §173.50 of this subchapter).
8. **A hazardous substance that is not a hazardous waste** may be shipped under the shipping description "Other regulated substances, liquid or solid, n.o.s.", as appropriate. In addition, for solid materials, special provision B54 applies.

9. **Packaging for certain PCBs for disposal and storage** is prescribed by EPA in 40 CFR 761.60 and 761.65.
10. **An ammonium nitrate mixed fertilizer** is a fertilizer formulation, containing less than 90% ammonium nitrate and other ingredients, which does not meet the definition and criteria of a Class 1 (explosive) material (See §173.50 of this subchapter).
11. **The hazardous material must be packaged** as either a liquid or a solid, as appropriate, depending on its physical form at 55 °C (131 °F) at atmospheric pressure.
12. **In concentrations greater than 40 percent,** this material has strong oxidizing properties and is capable of starting fires in contact with combustible materials. If appropriate, a package containing this material must conform to the additional labeling requirements of §172.402 of this subchapter.
13. **The words "Inhalation Hazard" shall be entered** on each shipping paper in association with the shipping description, shall be marked on each non-bulk package in association with the proper shipping name and identification number, and shall be marked on two opposing sides of each bulk package. Size of marking on bulk package must conform to §172.302(b) of this subchapter. The requirements of §§172.203(m) and 172.505 of this subchapter do not apply.
14. **Motor fuel antiknock mixtures are:**
    a. *Mixtures of one or more* organic lead mixtures (such as tetraethyl lead, triethylmethyl lead, diethyldimethyl lead, ethyltrimethyl lead, and tetramethyl lead) with one or more halogen compounds (such as ethylene dibromide and ethylene dichloride), hydrocarbon solvents or other equally efficient stabilizers; or
    b. *tetraethyl lead.*
15. **Chemical kits and first aid kits** are boxes, cases, etc., containing small amounts of various compatible dangerous goods which are used for medical, analytical, or testing purposes and for which exceptions are provided in this subchapter. For transportation by aircraft, any hazardous materials forbidden in passenger aircraft may not be included in these kits. Inner packagings may not exceed 250 mL for liquids or 250 g for solids and must be protected from other materials in the kit. The total quantity of hazardous materials in any one kit may not exceed either 1 L or 1 kg. The packing group assigned to the kit as a whole must be the most stringent packing group assigned to any individual substance contained in the kit. Kits must be packed in wooden boxes (4C1, 4C2), plywood boxes (4D), reconstituted wood boxes (4F), fiberboard boxes (4G) or plastic boxes (4H1, 4H2); these packagings must meet the requirements appropriate to the packing group assigned to the kit as a whole. The total quantity of hazardous materials in any one package may not exceed either 10 L or 10 kg. Kits which are carried on board transport vehicles for first-aid or operating purposes are not subject to the requirements of this subchapter.
16. **This description applies to smokeless powder** and other solid propellants that are used as powder for small arms and have been classed as Division 1.3 and 4.1 in accordance with §173.56 of this subchapter.
18. **This description is authorized only for fire extinguishers** listed in §173.309(b) of this subchapter meeting the following conditions:
    a. *Each fire extinguisher* may only have extinguishing contents that are nonflammable, non-poisonous, non-corrosive and commercially free from corroding components.
    b. *Each fire extinguisher* must be charged with a nonflammable, non-poisonous, dry gas that has a dew-point at or below minus 46.7 °C (minus 52 °F) at 101 kPa (1 atmosphere) and is free of corroding components, to not more than the service pressure of the cylinder.
    c. *A fire extinguisher* may not contain more than 30% carbon dioxide by volume or any other corrosive extinguishing agent.
    d. *Each fire extinguisher* must be protected externally by suitable corrosion-resisting coating.
19. **For domestic transportation only,** the identification number "UN1075" may be used in place of the identification number specified in column (4) of the §172.101 table. The identification number used must be consistent on package markings, shipping papers and emergency response information.
21. **This material must be stabilized by appropriate means** (e.g., addition of chemical inhibitor, purging to remove oxygen) to prevent dangerous polymerization (see §173.21(f) of this subchapter).
22. **If the hazardous material is in dispersion in organic liquid,** the organic liquid must have a flash point above 50 °C (122 °F).
23. **This material may be transported under the provisions** of Division 4.1 only if it is so packed that the percentage of diluent will not fall below that stated in the shipping description at any time during transport. Quantities of not more than 500 g per package with not less than 10 percent water by mass may also be classed in Division 4.1, provided a negative test result is obtained when tested in accordance with test series 6(c) of the UN Manual of Tests and Criteria (see §171.7 of this subchapter).
24. **Alcoholic beverages containing more than 70 percent** alcohol by volume must be transported as materials in Packing Group II. Alcoholic beverages containing more than 24 percent but not more than 70 percent alcohol by volume must be transported as materials in Packing Group III.
26. **This entry does not include ammonium permanganate,** the transport of which is prohibited except when approved by the Associate Administrator.
28. **The dihydrated sodium salt of dichloroisocyanuric acid** is not subject to the requirements of this subchapter.
29. **Lithium cells and batteries and equipment** containing or packed with lithium cells and batteries which do not comply with the provisions of §173.185 of this subchapter may be transported only if they are approved by the Associate Administrator.
30. **Sulfur is not subject to the requirements** of this subchapter if transported in a non-bulk packaging or if formed to a specific shape (e.g., prills, granules, pellets, pastilles, or flakes).
31. **Materials which have undergone sufficient heat treatment** to render them non-hazardous are not subject to the requirements of this subchapter.
32. **Polymeric beads and molding compounds** may be made from polystyrene, poly(methyl methacrylate) or other polymeric material.
33. **Ammonium nitrites and mixtures** of an inorganic nitrite with an ammonium salt are prohibited.
34. **The commercial grade of calcium nitrate fertilizer,** when consisting mainly of a double salt (calcium nitrate and ammonium nitrate) containing not more than 10 percent ammonium nitrate and at least 12 percent water of crystallization, is not subject to the requirements of this subchapter.
35. **Antimony sulphides and oxides** which do not contain more than 0.5 percent of arsenic calculated on the total mass do not meet the definition of Division 6.1.
36. **The maximum net quantity per package** is 5 L (1 gallon) or 5 kg (11 pounds).
37. **Unless it can be demonstrated by testing** that the sensitivity of the substance in its frozen state is no greater than in its liquid state, the substance must remain liquid during normal transport conditions. It must not freeze at temperatures above -15 °C (5 °F).
38. **If this material shows a violent effect** in laboratory tests involving heating under confinement, the labeling requirements of Special Provision 53 apply, and the material must be packaged in accordance with packing method OP6 in §173.225 of this subchapter. If the SADT of the technically pure substance is higher than 75 °C, the technically pure substance and formulations derived from it are not self-reactive materials and, if not meeting any other hazard class, are not subject to the requirements of this subchapter.
39. **This substance may be carried** under provisions other than those of Class 1 only if it is so packed that the percentage of water will not fall below that stated at any time during transport. When phlegmatized with water and inorganic inert material, the content of urea nitrate must not exceed 75 percent by mass and the mixture should not be capable of being detonated by test 1(a)(i) or test 1(a)(ii) in the UN Recommendations Tests and Criteria (see §171.7 of this subchapter).
40. **Polyester resin kits consist of two components:** a base material (Class 3, Packing Group II or III) and an activator (organic peroxide), each separately packed in an inner packaging. The organic peroxide must be type D, E, or F, not requiring temperature control, and be limited to a quantity of 125 mL (4.22 ounces) per inner packaging if liquid, and 500 g (1 pound) if solid. The components may be placed in the same outer packaging provided they will not interact dangerously in the event of leakage. Packing group will be II or III, according to the criteria for Class 3, applied to the base material.
43. **The membrane filters, including paper separators** and coating or backing materials, that are present in transport, must not be able to propagate a detonation as tested by one of the tests described in the UN Manual of Tests and Criteria, Part I, Test series 1(a) (see §171.7 of this subchapter). On the basis of the results of suitable burning rate tests, and taking into account the standard tests in the UN Manual of Tests and Criteria, Part III, subsection 33.2.1 (see §171.7 of this subchapter), nitrocellulose membrane filters in the form in which they are to be transported that do not meet the criteria for a Division 4.1 material are not subject to the requirements of this subchapter. Packagings must be so con-

structured that explosion is not possible by reason of increased internal pressure. Nitrocellulose membrane filters covered by this entry, each with a mass not exceeding 0.5 g, are not subject to the requirements of this subchapter when contained individually in an article or a sealed packet.

44. **The formulation must be prepared** so that it remains homogeneous and does not separate during transport. Formulations with low nitrocellulose contents and neither showing dangerous properties when tested for their ability to detonate, deflagrate or explode when heated under defined confinement by the appropriate test methods and criteria in the UN Recommendations, Tests and Criteria, not classed as a Division 4.1 (flammable solid) when tested in accordance with the procedures specified in §173.124 of this subchapter (chips, if necessary, crushed and sieved to a particle size of less than 1.25 mm) are not subject to the requirements of this subchapter.

45. **Temperature should be maintained** between 18 °C (64.4 °F) and 40 °C (104 °F). Tanks containing solidified methacrylic acid must not be reheated during transport.

46. **This material must be packed in accordance** with packing method OP6 (see §173.225 of this subchapter). During transport, it must be protected from direct sunshine and stored (or kept) in a cool and well-ventilated place, away from all sources of heat.

47. **Mixtures of solids which are not subject** to this subchapter and flammable liquids may be transported under this entry without first applying the classification criteria of Division 4.1, provided there is no free liquid visible at the time the material is loaded or at the time the packaging or transport unit is closed. Each packaging must correspond to a design type that has passed a leakproofness test at the Packing Group II level. Small inner packagings consisting of sealed packets containing less than 10 mL of a Class 3 liquid in Packing Group II or III absorbed onto a solid material are not subject to this subchapter provided there is no free liquid in the packet.

48. **Mixtures of solids which are not subject** to this subchapter and toxic liquids may be transported under this entry without first applying the classification criteria of Division 6.1, provided there is no free liquid visible at the time the material is loaded or at the time the packaging or transport unit is closed. Each packaging must correspond to a design type that has passed a leakproofness test at the Packing Group II level. This entry may not be used for solids containing a Packing Group I liquid.

49. **Mixtures of solids which are not subject** to this subchapter and corrosive liquids may be transported under this entry without first applying the classification criteria of Class 8, provided there is no free liquid visible at the time the material is loaded or at the time the packaging or transport unit is closed. Each packaging must correspond to a design type that has passed a leakproofness test at the Packing Group II level.

50. **Cases, cartridge, empty with primer** which are made of metallic or plastic casings and meeting the classification criteria of Division 1.4 are not regulated for domestic transportation.

51. **This description applies to items** previously described as "Toy propellant devices, Class C" and includes reloadable kits. Model rocket motors containing 30 grams or less propellant are classed as Division 1.4S and items containing more than 30 grams of propellant but not more than 62.5 grams of propellant are classed as Division 1.4C.

52. **Ammonium nitrate fertilizers** may not meet the definition and criteria of Class 1 (explosive) material (see §173.50 of this subchapter).

53. **Packages of these materials** must bear the subsidiary risk label, "EXPLOSIVE", unless otherwise provided in this subchapter or through an approval issued by the Associate Administrator, or the competent authority of the country of origin. A copy of the approval shall accompany the shipping papers.

54. **Maneb or maneb preparations** not meeting the definition of Division 4.3 or any other hazard class are not subject to the requirements of this subchapter when transported by motor vehicle, rail car, or aircraft.

55. **This device must be approved** in accordance with §173.56 of this subchapter by the Associate Administrator.

56. **A means to interrupt and prevent detonation** of the detonator from initiating the detonating cord must be installed between each electric detonator and the detonating cord ends of the jet perforating guns before the charged jet perforating guns are offered for transportation.

57. **Maneb or maneb preparations** stabilized against self-heating need not be classified in Division 4.2 when it can be demonstrated by testing that a volume of 1 m^3 of substance does not self-ignite and that the temperature at the center of the sample does not exceed 200 °C, when the sample is maintained at a temperature of not less than 75 °C $\pm$ 2 °C for a period of 24 hours, in accordance with procedures set forth for testing self-heating materials in the UN Manual of Tests and Criteria (see §171.7 of this subchapter).

58. **Aqueous solutions of Division 5.1** inorganic solid nitrate substances are considered as not meeting the criteria of Division 5.1 if the concentration of the substances in solution at the minimum temperature encountered in transport is not greater than 80% of the saturation limit.

59. **Ferrocerium, stabilized against corrosion,** with a minimum iron content of 10 percent is not subject to the requirements of this subchapter.

60. **After September 30, 1997,** an oxygen generator, chemical, that is shipped with its means of initiation attached must incorporate at least two positive means of preventing unintentional actuation of the generator, and be classed and approved by the Associate Administrator. The procedures for approval of a chemical oxygen generator that contains an explosive means of initiation (e.g., a primer or electric match) are specified in §173.56 of this subchapter. Each person who offers a chemical oxygen generator for transportation after September 30, 1997, shall: (1) ensure that it is offered in conformance with the conditions of the approval; (2) maintain a copy of the approval at each facility where the chemical oxygen generator is packaged; and (3) mark the approval number on the outside of the package.

61. **A chemical oxygen generator is spent** if its means of ignition and all or a part of its chemical contents have been expended.

64. **The group of alkali metals** includes lithium, sodium, potassium, rubidium, and caesium.

65. **The group of alkaline earth metals** includes magnesium, calcium, strontium, and barium.

66. **Formulations of these substances** containing not less than 30 percent non-volatile, non-flammable phlegmatizer are not subject to this subchapter.

70. **Black powder that has been classed** in accordance with the requirements of §173.56 of this subchapter may be reclassed and offered for domestic transportation as a Division 4.1 material if it is offered for transportation and transported in accordance with the limitations and packaging requirements of §173.170 of this subchapter.

74. **During transport, this material must be protected** from direct sunshine and stored or kept in a cool and well-ventilated place, away from all sources of heat.

77. **For domestic transportation,** a Division 5.1 subsidiary risk label is required only if a carbon dioxide and oxygen mixture contains more than 23.5% oxygen.

78. **This entry may not be used to describe** compressed air which contains more than 23.5 percent oxygen. An oxidizer label is not required for any oxygen concentration of 23.5 percent or less.

79. **This entry may not be used for mixtures** that meet the definition for oxidizing gas.

81. **Polychlorinated biphenyl items,** as defined in 40 CFR 761.3, for which specification packagings are impractical, may be packaged in non-specification packagings meeting the general packaging requirements of subparts A and B of part 173 of this subchapter. Alternatively, the item itself may be used as a packaging if it meets the general packaging requirements of subparts A and B of part 173 of this subchapter.

101. **The name of the particular substance or article must be specified.**

102. **The ends of the detonating cord** must be tied fast so that the explosive cannot escape. The articles may be transported as in Division 1.4 Compatibility Group D (1.4D) if all of the conditions specified in §173.63(a) of this subchapter are met.

103. **Detonators which will not mass detonate** and undergo only limited propagation in the shipping package may be assigned to 1.4B classification code. Mass detonate means that more than 90 percent of the devices tested in a package explode practically simultaneously. Limited propagation means that if one detonator near the center of a shipping package is exploded, the aggregate weight of explosives, excluding ignition and delay charges, in this and all additional detonators in the outside packaging that explode may not exceed 25 grams.

105. **The word "Agents" may be used** instead of "Explosives" when approved by the Associate Administrator.

106. **The recognized name of the particular explosive** may be specified in addition to the type.

107. **The classification of the substance** is expected to vary especially with the particle size and packaging but the border lines have not been experimentally determined; appropriate classifi-

cations should be verified following the test procedures in §§173.57 and 173.58 of this subchapter.

108. **Fireworks must be so constructed and packaged** that loose pyrotechnic composition will not be present in packages during transportation.

109. **Rocket motors must be nonpropulsive** in transportation unless approved in accordance with §173.56 of this subchapter. A rocket motor to be considered "nonpropulsive" must be capable of unrestrained burning and must not appreciably move in any direction when ignited by any means.

110. **Fire extinguishers transported under UN1044** may include installed actuating cartridges (cartridges, power device of Division 1.4C or 1.4S), without changing the classification of Division 2.2, provided the aggregate quantity of deflagrating (propellant) explosives does not exceed 3.2 grams per extinguishing unit.

111. **Explosive substances of Division 1.1** Compatibility Group A (1.1A) are forbidden for transportation if dry or not desensitized, unless incorporated in a device.

113. **The sample must be given a tentative approval** by an agency or laboratory in accordance with §173.56 of this subchapter.

114. **Jet perforating guns, charged, oil well,** without detonator may be reclassed to Division 1.4 Compatibility Group D (1.4D) if the following conditions are met:
   a. *The total weight* of the explosive contents of the shaped charges assembled in the guns does not exceed 90.5 kg (200 pounds) per vehicle; and
   b. *The guns are packaged* in accordance with Packing Method US 1 as specified in §173.62 of this subchapter.

115. **Boosters with detonator, detonator assemblies** and boosters with detonators in which the total explosive charge per unit does not exceed 25 g, and which will not mass detonate and undergo only limited propagation in the shipping package may be assigned to 1.4B classification code. Mass detonate means more than 90 percent of the devices tested in a package explode practically simultaneously. Limited propagation means that if one booster near the center of the package is exploded, the aggregate weight of explosives, excluding ignition and delay charges, in this and all additional boosters in the outside packaging that explode may not exceed 25 g.

116. **Fuzes, detonating may be classed in Division 1.4** if the fuzes do not contain more than 25 g of explosive per fuze and are made and packaged so that they will not cause functioning of other fuzes, explosives or other explosive devices if one of the fuzes detonates in a shipping packaging or in adjacent packages.

117. **If shipment of the explosive substance** is to take place at a time that freezing weather is anticipated, the water contained in the explosive substance must be mixed with denatured alcohol so that freezing will not occur.

118. **This substance may not be transported** under the provisions of Division 4.1 unless specifically authorized by the Associate Administrator.

119. **This substance, when in quantities** of not more than 11.5 kg (25.3 pounds), with not less than 10 percent water, by mass, also may be classed in Division 4.1, provided a negative test result is obtained when tested in accordance with test series 6(c) of the UN Manual of Tests and Criteria.

120. **The phlegmatized substance** must be significantly less sensitive than dry PETN.

121. **This substance, when containing less alcohol,** water or phlegmatizer than specified, may not be transported unless approved by the Associate Administrator.

123. **Any explosives, blasting, type C containing chlorates** must be segregated from explosives containing ammonium nitrate or other ammonium salts.

125. **Lactose or glucose or similar materials** may be used as a phlegmatizer provided that the substance contains not less than 90%, by mass, of phlegmatizer. These mixtures may be classified in Division 4.1 when tested in accordance with test series 6(c) of the UN Manual of Tests and Criteria (see §171.7 of this subchapter) and approved by the Associate Administrator. Testing must be conducted on at least three packages as prepared for transport. Mixtures containing at least 98%, by mass, of phlegmatizer are not subject to the requirements of this subchapter. Packages containing mixtures with not less than 90% by mass, of phlegmatizer need not bear a POISON subsidiary risk label.

127. **Mixtures containing oxidizing and organic materials** transported under this entry may not meet the definition and criteria of a Class 1 material. (See §173.50 of this subchapter.)

128. **Regardless of the provisions of §172.101(c)(12),** aluminum smelting by-products and aluminum remelting by-products described under this entry, meeting the definition of Class 8, Packing Group II and III may be classed as a Division 4.3 material and transported under this entry. The presence of a Class 8 hazard must be communicated as required by this Part for subsidiary hazards.

129. **These materials may not be classified and transported** unless authorized by the Associate Administrator on the basis of results from Series 2 Test and a Series 6(c) Test from the UN Manual of Tests and Criteria (see §171.7 of this subchapter) on packages as prepared for transport. The packing group assignment and packaging must be approved by the Associate Administrator for Hazardous Materials Safety on the basis of the criteria in §173.21 of this subchapter and the package type used for the Series 6(c) test.

130. **Batteries, dry are not subject to the requirements** of this subchapter only when they are offered for transportation in a manner that prevents the dangerous evolution of heat (for example, by the effective insulation of exposed terminals).

131. **This material may not be offered for transportation** unless approved by the Associate Administrator.

132. **Ammonium nitrate fertilizers of this composition** are not subject to the requirements of this subchapter if shown by a trough test (see United Nations Recommendations on the Transport of Dangerous Goods, Manual Tests and Criteria, Part III, sub-section 38.2) (see §171.7 of this subchapter) not to be liable to self-sustaining decomposition and provided that they do not contain an excess of nitrate greater than 10% by mass (calculated as potassium nitrate).

133. **This description applies to articles which are used** as life-saving vehicle air bag inflators or air bag modules or seat-belt pretensioners, containing a gas or a mixture of compressed gases classified under Division 2.2, and with or without small quantities of pyrotechnic material. For units with pyrotechnic material, initiated explosive effects must be contained within the pressure vessel (cylinder) such that the unit may be excluded from Class 1 in accordance with paragraphs 1.11(b) and 16.6.1.4.7(a)(ii) of the UN Manual of Tests and Criteria, Part 1 (see §171.7 of this subchapter). In addition, units must be designed or packaged for transport so that when engulfed in a fire there will be no fragmentation of the pressure vessel or projection hazard. This may be determined by analysis or test. The pressure vessel must be in conformance with the requirements of this subchapter for the gas(es) contained in the pressure vessel or as specifically authorized by the Associate Administrator.

134. **This entry only applies to vehicles,** machinery and equipment which are powered by wet batteries or sodium batteries and which are transported with these batteries installed. Examples of such items are electrically-powered cars, lawn mowers, wheelchairs and other mobility aids. Self-propelled vehicles which also contain an internal combustion engine must be consigned under the entry "Vehicle, flammable gas powered" or "Vehicle, flammable liquid powered", as appropriate.

135. **The entries "Vehicle, flammable gas powered"** or "Vehicle, flammable liquid powered", as appropriate, must be used when internal combustion engines are installed in a vehicle.

136. **This entry only applies to machinery and apparatus** containing hazardous materials as in integral element of the machinery or apparatus. It may not be used to describe machinery or apparatus for which a proper shipping name exists in the §172.101 Table. Except when approved by the Associate Administrator, machinery or apparatus may only contain hazardous materials for which exceptions are referenced in Column (8) of the §172.101 Table and are provided in part 173, subpart D, of this subchapter. Hazardous materials shipped under this entry are excepted from the labeling requirements of this subchapter unless offered for transportation or transported by aircraft and are not subject to the placarding requirements of part 172, subpart F, of this subchapter. Orientation markings as described in §172.312 (a)(2) are required when liquid hazardous materials may escape due to incorrect orientation. The machinery or apparatus, if unpackaged, or the packaging in which it is contained shall be marked "Dangerous goods in machinery" or "Dangerous goods in apparatus", as appropriate, with the identification number UN3363. For transportation by aircraft, machinery or apparatus may not contain any material forbidden for transportation by passenger or cargo aircraft. The Associate Administrator may except from the requirements of this subchapter, equipment, machinery and apparatus provided:
   a. *It is shown that it does not pose a significant risk in transportation;*
   b. *The quantities* of hazardous materials do not exceed those specified in §173.4 of this subchapter; and

c. *The equipment,* machinery or apparatus conforms with §173.222 of this subchapter.

137. **Cotton, dry is not subject to the requirements** of this subchapter when it is baled in accordance with ISO 8115, "Cotton Bales — Dimensions and Density" to a density of at least 360 kg/m^3 (22.4lb/ft^3) and it is transported in a freight container or closed transport vehicle.

138. **Lead compounds which,** when mixed in a ratio of 1:1000 with 0.07M (Molar concentration) hydrochloric acid and stirred for one hour at a temperature of 23 °C ± 2 °C, exhibit a solubility of 5% or less are considered insoluble.

139. **Use of the "special arrangement"** proper shipping names for international shipments must be made under an IAEA Certificate of Competent Authority issued by the Associate Administrator in accordance with the requirements in §173.471, §173.472, or §173.473 of this subchapter. Use of these proper shipping names for domestic shipments may be made only under a DOT exemption, as defined in, and in accordance with the requirements of subpart B of part 107 of this subchapter.

140. **This material is regulated only when it meets** the defining criteria for a hazardous substance or a marine pollutant. In addition, the column 5 reference is modified to read "III" on those occasions when this material is offered for transportation or transported by highway or rail.

141. **A toxin obtained from a plant, animal,** or bacterial source containing an infectious substance, or a toxin contained in an infectious substance, must be classed as Division 6.2, described as an infectious substance, and assigned to UN 2814 or UN 2900, as appropriate.

142. **These hazardous materials may not be classified** and transported unless authorized by the Associate Administrator. The Associate Administrator will base the authorization on results from Series 2 tests and a Series 6(c) test from the UN Manual of Tests and Criteria (see §171.7 of this subchapter) on packages as prepared for transport in accordance with the requirements of this subchapter.

143. **These articles may contain:**
   a. *Division 2.2 compressed gases, including oxygen;*
   b. *Signal devices* (Class 1) which may include smoke and illumination signal flares. Signal devices must be packed in plastic or fiberboard inner packagings;
   c. *Electric storage batteries;*
   d. *First aid kits; or*
   e. *Strike anywhere matches.*

FEDERAL REGISTER UPDATES

In the April 18, 2003 Federal Register, §172.102 was revised, effective October 1, 2003.

(c) [1]

(1) [2]

Code/Special Provisions [3]

144. **If transported as a residue** in an underground storage tank (UST), as defined in 40 CFR 180.12, that has been cleaned and purged or rendered inert according to the American Petroleum Institute (API) Standard 1604 (incorporated by reference; see §171.7 of this subchapter), then the tank and this material are not subject to any other requirements of this subchapter. However, sediments remaining in the tank that meet the definition for a hazardous material are subject to the applicable regulations of this subchapter. [4]

1. Paragraph (c) is the same as before.
2. Paragraph (c)(1) is the same as before.
3. This reads the same as before.
4. Special provision 144 was added in numerical order.

(2) *"A" codes.* These provisions apply only to transportation by aircraft:

Code/Special Provisions

A1. **Single packagings are not permitted on passenger aircraft.**

A2. **Single packagings are not permitted on aircraft.**

A3. **For combination packagings,** if glass inner packagings (including ampoules) are used, they must be packed with absorbent material in tightly closed metal receptacles before packing in outer packagings.

A4. **Liquids having an inhalation toxicity** of Packing Group I are not permitted on aircraft.

A5. **Solids having an inhalation toxicity** of Packing Group I are not permitted on passenger aircraft and may not exceed a maximum net quantity per package of 15 kg (33 pounds) on cargo aircraft.

A6. **For combination packagings,** if plastic inner packagings are used, they must be packed in tightly closed metal receptacles before packing in outer packagings.

A7. **Steel packagings must be corrosion-resistant** or have protection against corrosion.

A8. **For combination packagings,** if glass inner packagings (including ampoules) are used, they must be packed with cushioning material in tightly closed metal receptacles before packing in outer packagings.

A9. **For combination packagings,** if plastic bags are used, they must be packed in tightly closed metal receptacles before packing in outer packagings.

A10. **When aluminum or aluminum alloy** construction materials are used, they must be resistant to corrosion.

A11. **For combination packagings,** when metal inner packagings are permitted, only specification cylinders constructed of metals which are compatible with the hazardous material may be used.

A13. **Bulk packagings are not authorized for transportation by aircraft.**

A19. **Combination packagings consisting of** outer fiber drums or plywood drums, with inner plastic packagings, are not authorized for transportation by aircraft.

A20. **Plastic bags as inner receptacles** of combination packagings are not authorized for transportation by aircraft.

A29. **Combination packagings consisting of** outer expanded plastic boxes with inner plastic bags are not authorized for transportation by aircraft.

A30. **Ammonium permanganate is not authorized** for transportation on aircraft.

A34. **Aerosols containing a corrosive liquid** in Packing Group II charged with a gas are not permitted for transportation by aircraft.

A35. **This includes any material which is not covered** by any of the other classes but which has an anesthetic, narcotic, noxious or other similar properties such that, in the event of spillage or leakage on an aircraft, extreme annoyance or discomfort could be caused to crew members so as to prevent the correct performance of assigned duties.

A37. **This entry applies only to a material** meeting the definition in §171.8 of this subchapter for self-defense spray.

A51. **When transported by cargo-only aircraft,** an oxygen generator must conform to the provisions of an approval issued under Special Provision 60 and be contained in a packaging prepared and originally offered for transportation by the approval holder.

A52. **A cylinder containing Oxygen, compressed,** may not be loaded into a passenger-carrying aircraft or in an inaccessible cargo location on a cargo-only aircraft unless it is placed in an overpack or outer packaging that conforms to the performance criteria of Air Transport Association (ATA) Specification 300 for Category I shipping containers.

A53. **Refrigerating machines** and refrigerating machine components are not subject to the requirements of this subchapter when containing less than 12 kg (26.4 pounds) of a non-flammable gas or when containing 12 L (3 gallons) or less of ammonia solution (UN2672) (see §173.307 of this subchapter).

A81. **The quantity limits in columns (9A) and (9B)** do not apply to body fluids known to contain or suspected of containing an infectious substance when transported in primary receptacles not exceeding 1,000 mL (34 ounces) and in outer packagings not exceeding 4 L (1 gallon) and packaged in accordance with §173.196 of this subchapter.

A82. **The quantity limits in columns (9A) and (9B)** do not apply to human or animal body parts, whole organs or whole bodies known to contain or suspected of containing an infectious substance.

(3) *"B" codes.* These provisions apply only to bulk packagings, other than IBCs:

Code/Special Provisions

B1. **If the material has a flash point** at or above 38 °C (100 °F) and below 93 °C (200 °F), then the bulk packaging requirements of §173.241 of this subchapter are applicable. If the material has a flash point of less than 38 °C (100 °F), then the bulk packaging requirements of §173.242 of this subchapter are applicable.

B2. **MC 300, MC 301, MC 302,** MC 303, MC 305, and MC 306 and DOT 406 cargo tanks are not authorized.

B3. **MC 300, MC 301, MC 302,** MC 303, MC 305, and MC 306 and DOT 406 cargo tanks and DOT 57 portable tanks are not authorized.

B4. **MC 300, MC 301, MC 302,** MC 303, MC 305, and MC 306 and DOT 406 cargo tanks are not authorized.

B5. Only ammonium nitrate solutions with 35 percent or less water that will remain completely in solution under all conditions of transport at a maximum lading temperature of 116 °C (240 °F) are authorized for transport in the following bulk packagings: MC 307, MC 312, DOT 407 and DOT 412 cargo tanks with at least 172 kPa (25 psig) design pressure. The packaging shall be designed for a working temperature of at least 121 °C (250 °F). Only Specifications MC 304, MC 307 or DOT 407 cargo tank motor vehicles are authorized for transportation by vessel.

B6. Packagings shall be made of steel.

B7. Safety relief devices are not authorized on multi-unit tank car tanks. Openings for safety relief devices on multi-unit tank car tanks shall be plugged or blank flanged.

B8. Packagings shall be made of nickel, stainless steel, or steel with nickel, stainless steel, lead or other suitable corrosion resistant metallic lining.

B9. Bottom outlets are not authorized.

B10. MC 300, MC 301, MC 302, MC 303, MC 305, and MC 306 and DOT 406 cargo tanks, and DOT 57 portable tanks are not authorized.

B11. Tank car tanks must have a test pressure of at least 2,068.5 kPa (300 psig). Cargo and portable tanks must have a design pressure of at least 1,207 kPa (175 psig).

B13. A nonspecification cargo tank motor vehicle authorized in §173.247 of this subchapter must be at least equivalent in design and in construction to a DOT 406 cargo tank or MC 306 cargo tank (if constructed before August 31, 1995), except as follows:

a. *Packagings equivalent* to MC 306 cargo tanks are excepted from the certification, venting, and emergency flow requirements of the MC 306 specification.

b. *Packagings equivalent* to DOT 406 cargo tanks are excepted from §§178.345-7(d)(5), circumferential reinforcements; 178.345-10, pressure relief; 178.345-11, outlets; 178.345-14, marking, and 178.345-15, certification.

c. *Packagings are excepted* from the design stress limits at elevated temperatures, as described in the ASME Code. However, the design stress limits may not exceed 25 percent of the stress, as specified in the Aluminum Association's "Aluminum Standards and Data" (7th Edition June 1982), for 0 temper at the maximum design temperature of the cargo tank.

B14. Each bulk packaging, except a tank car or a multi-unit-tank car tank, must be insulated with an insulating material so that the overall thermal conductance at 15.5 °C (60 °F) is no more than 1.5333 kilojoules per hour per square meter per degree Celsius (0.075 Btu per hour per square foot per degree Fahrenheit) temperature differential. Insulating materials must not promote corrosion to steel when wet.

B15. Packagings must be protected with non-metallic linings impervious to the lading or have a suitable corrosion allowance.

B16. The lading must be completely covered with nitrogen, inert gas or other inert materials.

B18. Open steel hoppers or bins are authorized.

B23. Tanks must be made of steel that is rubber lined or unlined. Unlined tanks must be passivated before being placed in service. If unlined tanks are washed out with water, they must be repassivated prior to return to service. Lading in unlined tanks must be inhibited so that the corrosive effect on steel is not greater than that of hydrofluoric acid of 65 percent concentration.

B25. Packagings must be made from monel or nickel or monel-lined or nickel-lined steel.

B26. Tanks must be insulated. Insulation must be at least 100 mm (3.9 inches) except that the insulation thickness may be reduced to 51 mm (2 inches) over the exterior heater coils. Interior heating coils are not authorized. The packaging may not be loaded with a material outside of the packaging's design temperature range. In addition, the material also must be covered with an inert gas or the container must be filled with water to the tank's capacity. After unloading, the residual material also must be covered with an inert gas or the container must be filled with water to the tank's capacity.

B27. Tanks must have a service pressure of 1,034 kPa (150 psig). Tank car tanks must have a test pressure rating of 1,379 kPa (200 psig). Lading must be blanketed at all times with a dry inert gas at a pressure not to exceed 103 kPa (15 psig).

B28. Packagings must be made of stainless steel.

B30. MC 312, MC 330, MC 331 and DOT 412 cargo tanks and DOT 51 portable tanks must be made of stainless steel, except that steel other than stainless steel may be used in accordance with the provisions of §173.24b(b) of this subchapter. Thickness of stainless steel for tank shell and heads for cargo tanks and portable tanks must be the greater of 7.62 mm (0.300 inch) or the thickness required for a tank with a design pressure at least equal to 1.5 times the vapor pressure of the lading at 46 °C (115 °F). In addition, MC 312 and DOT 412 cargo tank motor vehicles must:

a. *Be ASME Code (U) stamped* for 100% radiography of all pressure-retaining welds;

b. *Have accident damage protection* which conforms with §178.345-8 of this subchapter;

c. *Have a MAWP or design pressure of at least 87 psig: and*

d. *Have a bolted manway cover.*

B32. MC 312, MC 330, MC 331, DOT 412 cargo tanks and DOT 51 portable tanks must be made of stainless steel, except that steel other than stainless steel may be used in accordance with the provisions of §173.24b(b) of this subchapter. Thickness of stainless steel for tank shell and heads for cargo tanks and portable tanks must be the greater of 6.35 mm (0.250 inch) or the thickness required for a tank with a design pressure at least equal to 1.3 times the vapor pressure of the lading at 46 °C (115 °F). In addition, MC 312 and DOT 412 cargo tank motor vehicles must:

a. *Be ASME Code (U) stamped* for 100% radiography of all pressure-retaining welds;

b. *Have accident damage protection* which conforms with §178.345-8 of this subchapter;

c. *Have a MAWP or design pressure of at least 87 psig; and*

d. *Have a bolted manway cover.*

B33. MC 300, MC 301, MC 302, MC 303, MC 305, MC 306, and DOT 406 cargo tanks equipped with a 1 psig normal vent used to transport gasoline must conform to table 1 of this Special Provision. Based on the volatility class determined by using ASTM D439 and the Reid vapor pressure (RVP) of the particular gasoline, the maximum lading pressure and maximum ambient temperature permitted during the loading of gasoline may not exceed that listed in table I.

Table I - Maximum Ambient Temperature — Gasoline

ASTM D439 volatility class	Maximum lading and ambient temperature[1]
A (RVP<=9.0 psia)	131 °F
B (RVP<=10.0 psia)	124 °F
C (RVP<=11.5 psia)	116 °F
D (RVP<=13.5 psia)	107 °F
E (RVP<=15.0 psia)	100 °F

1. Based on maximum lading pressure of 1 psig at top of cargo tank.

B35. Tank cars containing hydrogen cyanide may be alternatively marked "Hydrocyanic acid, liquefied" if otherwise conforming to marking requirements in subpart D of this part. Tank cars marked "HYDROCYANIC ACID" prior to October 1, 1991 do not need to be remarked.

B37. The amount of nitric oxide charged into any tank car tank may not exceed 1,379 kPa (200 psig) at 21 °C (70 °F).

B42. Tank cars must have a test pressure of 34.47 Bar (500 psig) or greater and conform to Class 105J. Each tank car must have a reclosing pressure relief device having a start-to-discharge pressure of 10.34 Bar (150 psig). The tank car specification may be marked to indicate a test pressure of 13.79 Bar (200 psig).

B44. All parts of valves and safety relief devices in contact with lading must be of a material which will not cause formation of acetylides.

B45. Each tank must have a reclosing combination pressure relief device equipped with stainless steel or platinum rupture discs approved by the AAR Tank Car Committee.

B46. The detachable protective housing for the loading and unloading valves of multi-unit tank car tanks must withstand tank test pressure and must be approved by the Associate Administrator.

B47. Each tank may have a reclosing pressure relief device having a start-to-discharge pressure setting of 310 kPa (45 psig).

B48. Portable tanks in sodium metal service may be visually inspected at least once every 5 years instead of being retested hydrostatically. Date of the visual inspection must be stenciled on the tank near the other required markings.

B49. Tanks equipped with interior heater coils are not authorized. Single unit tank car tanks must have a reclosing pressure relief device having a start-to-discharge pressure set at no more than 1551 kPa (225 psig).

B50. Each valve outlet of a multi-unit tank car tank must be sealed by a threaded solid plug or a threaded cap with inert luting or gasket material. Valves must be of stainless steel and the caps, plugs, and valve seats must be of a material that will not deteriorate as a result of contact with the lading.

B52. Notwithstanding the provisions of §173.24b of this subchapter, non-reclosing pressure relief devices are authorized on DOT 57 portable tanks.

B53. Packagings must be made of either aluminum or steel.

B54. Open-top, sift-proof rail cars are also authorized.

B55. Water-tight, sift-proof, closed-top, metal-covered hopper cars, equipped with a venting arrangement (including flame arrestors) approved by the Associate Administrator are also authorized.

B56. Water-tight, sift-proof, closed-top, metal-covered hopper cars are also authorized if the particle size of the hazardous material is not less than 149 microns.

B57. Class 115A tank car tanks used to transport chloroprene must be equipped with a non-reclosing pressure relief device of a diameter not less than 305 mm (12 inches) with a maximum rupture disc pressure of 310 kPa (45 psig).

B59. Water-tight, sift-proof, closed-top, metal-covered hopper cars are also authorized provided that the lading is covered with a nitrogen blanket.

B60. DOT Specification 106A500X multi-unit tank car tanks that are not equipped with a pressure relief device of any type are authorized. For the transportation of phosgene, the outage must be sufficient to prevent tanks from becoming liquid full at 55 °C (130 °F).

B61. Written procedures covering details of tank car appurtenances, dome fittings, safety devices, and marking, loading, handling, inspection, and testing practices must be approved by the Associate Administrator before any single unit tank car tank is offered for transportation.

B64. Each single unit tank car tank built after December 31, 1990 must be equipped with a tank head puncture resistance system that conforms to §179.16 of this subchapter.

B65. Tank cars must have a test pressure of 34.47 Bar (500 psig) or greater and conform to Class 105A. Each tank car must have a pressure relief device having a start-to-discharge pressure of 15.51 Bar (225 psig). The tank car specification may be marked to indicate a test pressure of 20.68 Bar (300 psig).

B66. Each tank must be equipped with gas tight valve protection caps. Outage must be sufficient to prevent tanks from becoming liquid full at 55 °C (130 °F). Specification 110A500W tanks must be stainless steel.

B67. All valves and fittings must be protected by a securely attached cover made of metal not subject to deterioration by the lading, and all valve openings, except safety valve, must be fitted with screw plugs or caps to prevent leakage in the event of valve failure.

B68. Sodium must be in a molten condition when loaded and allowed to solidify before shipment. Outage must be at least 5 percent at 98 °C (208 °F). Bulk packagings must have exterior heating coils fusion welded to the tank shell which have been properly stress relieved. The only tank car tanks authorized are Class DOT 105 tank cars having a test pressure of 2,069 kPa (300 psig) or greater.

B69. Dry sodium cyanide or potassium cyanide may be shipped in sift-proof weather-resistant metal covered hopper cars, covered motor vehicles, portable tanks or non-specification bins. Siftproof, water-resistant, fiberboard IBCs are permitted when transported in closed freight containers or transport vehicles. Bins must be approved by the Associate Administrator.

B70. If DOT 103ANW tank car tank is used: All cast metal in contact with the lading must have 96.7 percent nickel content; and the lading must be anhydrous and free from any impurities.

B71. Tank cars must have a test pressure of 20.68 Bar (300 psig) or greater and conform to Class 105, 112, 114 or 120.

B72. Tank cars must have a test pressure of 34.47 Bar (500 psig) or greater and conform to Class 105J, 106, or 110.

B74. Tank cars must have a test pressure of 20.68 Bar (300 psig) or greater and conform to Class 105S, 106, 110, 112J, 114J or 120S.

B76. Tank cars must have a test pressure of 20.68 Bar (300 psig) or greater and conform to Class 105S, 112J, 114J or 120S. Each tank car must have a reclosing pressure relief device having a start-to-discharge pressure of 10.34 Bar (150 psig). The tank car specification may be marked to indicate a test pressure of 13.79 Bar (200 psig).

B77. Other packaging are authorized when approved by the Associate Administrator.

B78. Tank cars must have a test pressure of 4.14 Bar (60 psig) or greater and conform to Class 103, 104, 105, 109, 111, 112, 114 or 120. Heater pipes must be of welded construction designed for a test pressure of 500 psig. A 25 mm (1 inch) woven lining of asbestos or other approved material must be placed between the bolster slabbing and the bottom of the tank. If a tank car tank is equipped with a non-reclosing pressure relief device, the rupture disc must be perforated with a 3.2 mm (0.13 inch) diameter hole. If a tank car tank is equipped with a reclosing pressure relief valve, the tank must also be equipped with a vacuum relief valve.

B80. Each cargo tank must have a minimum design pressure of 276 kPa (40 psig).

B81. Venting and pressure relief devices for tank car tanks and cargo tanks must be approved by the Associate Administrator.

B82. Cargo tanks and portable tanks are not authorized.

B83. Bottom outlets are prohibited on tank car tanks transporting sulfuric acid in concentrations over 65.25 percent.

B84. Packagings must be protected with non-metallic linings impervious to the lading or have a suitable corrosion allowance for sulfuric acid or spent sulfuric acid in concentration up to 65.25 percent.

B85. Cargo tanks must be marked with the name of the lading in accordance with the requirements of §172.302(b).

B90. Steel tanks conforming or equivalent to ASME specifications which contain solid or semisolid residual motor fuel antiknock mixture (including rust, scale, or other contaminants) may be shipped by rail freight or highway. The tank must have been designed and constructed to be capable of withstanding full vacuum. All openings must be closed with gasketed blank flanges or vapor tight threaded closures.

B115. Rail cars, highway trailers, roll-on/roll-off bins, or other non-specification bulk packagings are authorized. Packagings must be sift-proof, prevent liquid water from reaching the hazardous material, and be provided with sufficient venting to preclude dangerous accumulation of flammable, corrosive, or toxic gaseous emissions such as methane, hydrogen, and ammonia. The material must be loaded dry.

(4) *Table 1, Table 2, and Table 3* — IB Codes, Organic Peroxide IBC Code, and IP Special IBC Packing Provisions. These provisions apply only to transportation in IBCs. IBCs may be used for the transportation of hazardous materials when no IBC code is assigned in the §172.101 Table for the specific material only when approved by the Associate Administrator. The letter "Z" shown in the marking code for composite IBCs must be replaced with a capital code letter designation found in §178.702(a)(2) of this subchapter to specify the material used for the outer packaging. Tables 1, 2, and 3 follow:

Table 1 - IB Codes (IBC Codes)

IBC Code	Authorized IBCs
IB1	Authorized IBCs: Metal (31A, 31B and 31N). Additional Requirement: Only liquids with a vapor pressure less than or equal to 110 kPa at 50 °C (1.1 bar at 122 °F), or 130 kPa at 55 °C (1.3 bar at 131 °F) are authorized.
IB2	Authorized IBCs: Metal (31A, 31B and 31N); Rigid plastics (31H1 and 31H2); Composite (31HZ1). Additional Requirement: Only liquids with a vapor pressure less than or equal to 110 kPa at 50 °C (1.1 bar at 122 °F), or 130kPa at 55 °C (1.3 bar at 131 °F) are authorized.
IB3	Authorized IBCs: Metal (31A, 31B and 31N); Rigid plastics (31H1 and 31H2); Composite (31HZ1 and 31HA2, 31HB2, 31HN2, 31HD2 and 31HH2). Additional Requirement: Only liquids with a vapor pressure less than or equal to 110 kPa at 50 °C (1.1 bar at 122 °F), or 130 kPa at 55 °C (1.3 bar at 131 °F) are authorized.
IB4	Authorized IBCs: Metal (11A, 11B, 11N, 21A, 21B, 21N, 31A, 31B and 31N).
IB5	Authorized IBCs: Metal (11A, 11B, 11N, 21A, 21B, 21N, 31A, 31B and 31N); Rigid plastics (11H1, 11H2, 21H1, 21H2, 31H1 and 31H2); Composite (11HZ1, 21HZ1 and 31HZ1).
IB6	Authorized IBCs: Metal (11A, 11B, 11N, 21A, 21B, 21N, 31A, 31B and 31N); Rigid plastics (11H1, 11H2, 21H1, 21H2, 31H1 and 31H2); Composite (11HZ1, 11HZ2, 21HZ1, 21HZ2, 31HZ1 and 31HZ2). Additional Requirement: Composite IBCs 11HZ2 and 21HZ2 may not be used when the hazardous materials being transported may become liquid during transport.
IB7	Authorized IBCs: Metal (11A, 11B, 11N, 21A, 21B, 21N, 31A, 31B and 31N); Rigid plastics (11H1, 11H2, 21H1, 21H2, 31H1 and 31H2); Composite (11HZ1, 11HZ2, 21HZ1, 21HZ2, 31HZ1 and 31HZ2); Wooden (11C, 11D and 11F). Additional Requirement: Liners of wooden IBCs must be sift-proof.
IB8	Authorized IBCs: Metal (11A, 11B, 11N, 21A, 21B, 21N, 31A, 31B and 31N); Rigid plastics (11H1, 11H2, 21H1, 21H2, 31H1 and 31H2); Composite (11HZ1, 11HZ2, 21HZ1, 21HZ2, 31HZ1 and 31HZ2); Fiberboard (11G); Wooden (11C, 11D and 11F); Flexible (13H1, 13H2, 13H3, 13H4, 13H5, 13L1, 13L2, 13L3, 13L4, 13M1 or 13M2).
IB99	IBCs are only authorized if approved by the Associate Administrator.

Table 2 - Organic Peroxide IBC Code (IB52)
[This IBC Code applies to organic peroxides of type F. For formulations not listed in this table, only IBCs that are approved by the Associate Administrator may be used.]

UN No.	Organic peroxide	Type of IBC	Maximum quantity (liters)	Control temperature	Emergency temperature
3109	ORGANIC PEROXIDE, TYPE F, LIQUID				
	tert-Butyl hydroperoxide, not more than 72% with water.	31A	1250		
	tert-Butyl peroxyacetate, not more than 32% in diluent type A.	31A 31HA1	1250 1000		
	tert-Butyl peroxy-3,5,5-trimethylhexanoate, not more than 32% in diluent type A.	31A 31HA1	1250 1000		
	Cumyl hydroperoxide, not more than 90% in diluent type A.	31HA1	1250		
	Dibenzoyl peroxide, not more than 42% as a stable dispersion.	31H1	1000		
	Di-tert-butyl peroxide, not more than 52% in diluent type A.	31A 31HA1	1250 1000		
	1,1-Di-(tert-butylperoxy) cyclohexane, not more than 42% in diluent type A.	31H1	1000		
	Dilauroyl peroxide, not more than 42%, stable dispersion, in water.	31HA1	1000		
	Isopropyl cumyl hydroperoxide, not more than 72% in diluent type A.	31HA1	1250		
	p-Menthyl hydroperoxide, not more than 72% in diluent type A.	31HA1	1250		
	Peroxyacetic acid, stabilized, not more than 17%.	31H1 31HA1 31A	1500 1500 1500		
3110	Organic peroxide type F, solid.	31A 31H1 31HA1			
	Dicumyl peroxide.	31A 31H1 31HA1			
3119	ORGANIC PEROXIDE, TYPE F, LIQUID, TEMPERATURE CONTROLLED				
	tert-Butyl peroxy-2-ethylhexanoate, not more than 32% in diluent type B.	31HA1 31A	1000 1250	+30 °C +30 °C	+35 °C +35 °C
	tert-Butyl peroxyneodecanoate, not more than 32% in diluent type A.	31A	1250	0 °C	+10 °C
	tert-Butyl peroxyneodecanoate, not more than 42% stable dispersion, in water.	31A	1250	-5 °C	+5 °C
	tert-Butyl peroxypivalate, not more than 27% in diluent type B.	31HA1 31A	1000 1250	+10 °C +10 °C	+15 °C +15 °C
	Cumyl peroxyneodecanoate, not more than 52%, stable dispersion, in water.	31A	1250	-15 °C	-5 °C
	Di-(4-tert-butylcyclohexyl) peroxydicarbonate, not more than 42%, stable dispersion, in water.	31HA1	1000	+30 °C	+35 °C
	Dicetyl peroxydicarbonate, not more than 42%, stable dispersion, in water.	31HA1	1000	+30 °C	+35 °C
	Di-(2-ethylhexyl) peroxydicarbonate, not more than 52%, stable dispersion, in water.	31A	1250	-20 °C	-10 °C
	Dimyristyl peroxydicarbonate, not more than 42%, stable dispersion, in water.	31HA1	1000	+15 °C	+20 °C
	Di-(3,5,5-trimethylhexanoyl) peroxide, not more than 38% in diluent type A.	31HA1 31A	1000 1250	+10 °C +10 °C	+15 °C +15 °C
	Di-(3,5,5-trimethylhexanoyl) peroxide, not more than 52%, stable dispersion, in water.	31A	1250	+10 °C	+15 °C
	1,1,3,3-Tetramethylbutyl peroxyneodecanoate, not more than 52%, stable dispersion, in water.	31A	1250	-5 °C	+5 °C

Table 3 - IP Codes

Code	Provision
IP1	IBCs must be packed in closed freight containers or a closed transport vehicle.
IP2	When IBCs other than metal or rigid plastics IBCs are used, they must be offered for transportation in a closed freight container or a closed transport vehicle.
IP3	Flexible IBCs must be sift-proof and water-resistant or must be fitted with a sift-proof and water-resistant liner.
IP4	Flexible, fiberboard or wooden IBCs must be sift-proof and water-resistant or be fitted with a sift-proof and water-resistant liner.
IP5	IBCs must have a device to allow venting. The inlet to the venting device must be located in the vapor space of the IBC under maximum filling conditions.
IP6	Non-specification bulk bins are authorized.
IP7	For UN identification numbers 1327, 1363, 1364, 1365, 1386, 1841, 2211, 2217, 2793 and 3314, IBCs are not required to meet the IBC performance tests specified in part 178, subpart N of this subchapter.

(5) *"N" codes.* These provisions apply only to non-bulk packagings:

Code/Special Provisions

N3. Glass inner packagings are permitted in combination or composite packagings only if the hazardous material is free from hydrofluoric acid.

N4. For combination or composite packagings, glass inner packagings, other than ampoules, are not permitted.

N5. Glass materials of construction are not authorized for any part of a packaging which is normally in contact with the hazardous material.

N6. Battery fluid packaged with electric storage batteries, wet or dry, must conform to the packaging provisions of §173.159 (g) or (h) of this subchapter.

N7. The hazard class or division number of the material must be marked on the package in accordance with §172.302 of this subchapter. However, the hazard label corresponding to the hazard class or division may be substituted for the marking.

N8. Nitroglycerin solution in alcohol may be transported under this entry only when the solution is packed in metal cans of not more than 1 L capacity each, overpacked in a wooden box containing not more than 5 L. Metal cans must be completely surrounded with absorbent cushioning material. Wooden boxes must be completely lined with a suitable material impervious to water and nitroglycerin.

N10. Lighters and their inner packagings, which have been approved by the Associate Administrator (see §173.21(i) of this subchapter), must be packaged in one of the following outer packagings at the Packing Group II level: 4C1 or 4C2 wooden boxes; 4D plywood boxes; 4F reconstituted wood boxes; 4G fiberboard boxes; or 4H1 or 4H2 plastic boxes. The approval number (e.g., T-* * *) must be marked on each outer package and on the shipping paper.

N11. This material is excepted for the specification packaging requirements of this subchapter if the material is packaged in strong, tight non-bulk packaging meeting the requirements of subparts A and B of part 173 of this subchapter.

N12. Plastic packagings are not authorized.

N20. A 5M1 multi-wall paper bag is authorized if transported in a closed transport vehicle.

N25. Steel single packagings are not authorized.

N32. Aluminum materials of construction are not authorized for single packagings.

N33. Aluminum drums are not authorized.

N34. Aluminum construction materials are not authorized for any part of a packaging which is normally in contact with the hazardous material.

N36. Aluminum or aluminum alloy construction materials are permitted only for halogenated hydrocarbons that will not react with aluminum.

N37. This material may be shipped in an integrally-lined fiber drum (1G) which meets the general packaging requirements of subpart B of part 173 of this subchapter, the requirements of part 178 of this subchapter at the packing group assigned for the material and to any other special provisions of column 7 of the §172.101 table.

N40. This material is not authorized in the following packagings:

a. *A combination packaging* consisting of a 4G fiberboard box with inner receptacles of glass or earthenware;

b. *A single packaging of a 4C2 sift-proof, natural wood box; or*

c. *A composite packaging 6PG2* (glass, porcelain or stoneware receptacles within a fiberboard box).

N41. Metal construction materials are not authorized for any part of a packaging which is normally in contact with the hazardous material.

N42. 1A1 drums made of carbon steel with thickness of body and heads of not less than 1.3 mm (0.050 inch) and with a corrosion-resistant phenolic lining are authorized for stabilized benzyl chloride if tested and certified to the Packing Group I performance level at a specific gravity of not less than 1.8.

N43. Metal drums are permitted as single packagings only if constructed of nickel or monel.

N45. Copper cartridges are authorized as inner packagings if the hazardous material is not in dispersion.

N65. Outage must be sufficient to prevent cylinders or spheres from becoming liquid full at 55 °C (130 °F). The vacant space (outage) may be charged with a nonflammable nonliquefied compressed gas if the pressure in the cylinder or sphere at 55 °C (130 °F) does not exceed 125 percent of the marked service pressure.

N72. Packagings must be examined by the Bureau of Explosives and approved by the Associate Administrator.

N73. Packagings consisting of outer wooden or fiberboard boxes with inner glass, metal or other strong containers; metal or fiber drums; kegs or barrels; or strong metal cans are authorized and need not conform to the requirements of part 178 of this subchapter.

N74. Packages consisting of tightly closed inner containers of glass, earthenware, metal or polyethylene, capacity not over 0.5 kg (1.1 pounds) securely cushioned and packed in outer wooden barrels or wooden or fiberboard boxes, not over 15 kg (33 pounds) net weight, are authorized and need not conform to the requirements of part 178 of this subchapter.

N75. Packages consisting of tightly closed inner packagings of glass, earthenware or metal, securely cushioned and packed in outer wooden barrels or wooden or fiberboard boxes, capacity not over 2.5 kg (5.5 pounds) net weight, are authorized and need not conform to the requirements of part 178 of this subchapter.

N76. For materials of not more than 25 percent active ingredient by weight, packages consisting of inner metal packagings not greater than 250 mL (8 ounces) capacity each, packed in strong outer packagings together with sufficient absorbent material to completely absorb the liquid contents are authorized and need not conform to the requirements of part 178 of this subchapter.

N77. For materials of not more than two percent active ingredients by weight, packagings need not conform to the requirements of part 178 of this subchapter, if liquid contents are absorbed in an inert material.

N78. Packages consisting of inner glass, earthenware, or polyethylene or other nonfragile plastic bottles or jars not over 0.5 kg (1.1 pounds) capacity each, or metal cans not over five pounds capacity each, packed in outer wooden boxes, barrels or kegs, or fiberboard boxes are authorized and need not conform to the requirements of part 178 of this subchapter. Net weight of contents in fiberboard boxes may not exceed 29 kg (64 pounds). Net weight of contents in wooden boxes, barrels or kegs may not exceed 45 kg (99 pounds).

N79. Packages consisting of tightly closed metal inner packagings not over 0.5 kg (1.1 pounds) capacity each, packed in outer wooden or fiberboard boxes, or wooden barrels, are authorized and need not conform to the requirements of part 178 of this subchapter. Net weight of contents may not exceed 15 kg (33 pounds).

N80. Packages consisting of one inner metal can, not over 2.5 kg (5.5 pounds) capacity, packed in an outer wooden or fiberboard box, or a wooden barrel, are authorized and need not conform to the requirements of part 178 of this subchapter.

N82. See §173.306 of this subchapter for classification criteria for flammable aerosols.

(6) *"R" codes.* These provisions apply only to transportation by rail. [Reserved]

(7) *"T" codes.*

(i) *These provisions* apply to the transportation of hazardous materials in UN and IM Specification portable tanks. Portable tank instructions specify the requirements applicable to a portable tank when used for the transportation of a specific hazardous material. These requirements must be met in addition to the design and construction specifications in part 178 of this subchapter. Portable tank instructions T1 through T22 specify the applicable minimum test pressure, the minimum shell thickness (in reference steel), bottom opening requirements and pressure relief requirements. In T23, the organic peroxides and self-reactive substances which are authorized to be transported in portable tanks are listed along with the applicable control and emergency temperatures. Liquefied compressed gases are assigned to portable tank instruction T50. T50 provides the maximum allowable working pressures, bottom opening requirements, pressure relief requirements and degree of filling requirements for liquefied compressed gases permitted for transport in portable tanks. Refrigerated liquefied gases which are authorized to be transported in portable tanks are specified in tank instruction T75.

(ii) *The following table* specifies the portable tank requirements applicable to T Codes T1 through T22. Column 1 specifies the T Code. Column 2 specifies the minimum test pressure, in bar (1 bar = 14.5 psig), at which the periodic hydrostatic testing required by §180.605 of this subchapter must be conducted. Column 3 specifies the section reference for minimum shell thickness or, alternatively, the minimum shell thickness value. Column 4 specifies the applicability of §178.275(g)(3) of this subchapter for the pressure relief devices. When the word "Normal" is indicated, §178.275(g)(3) of this subchapter does not apply. Column 5 references the applicable requirements for bottom openings in part 178 of this subchapter or references "Prohibited" which means bottom openings are prohibited. The table follows:

Table of Portable Tank T Coder T1-T22
[Portable tank code T1-T22 apply to liquid and solid hazardous materials of Classes 3 through 9 which are transported in portable tanks.]

Portable tank instruction (1)	Minimum test pressure (bar) (2)	Minimum shell thickness (in mm-reference steel) (See §178.274(d)) (3)	Pressure-relief requirements (See §178.275(g)) (4)	Bottom opening requirements (See §178.275(d)) (5)
T1	1.5	§178.274(d)(2)	Normal	§178.275(d)(2)
T2	1.5	§178.274(d)(2)	Normal	§178.275(d)(3)
T3	2.65	§178.274(d)(2)	Normal	§178.275(d)(2)
T4	2.65	§178.274(d)(2)	Normal	§178.275(d)(3)
T5	2.65	§178.274(d)(2)	§178.275(g)(3)	Prohibited
T6	4	§178.274(d)(2)	Normal	§178.275(d)(2)
T7	4	§178.274(d)(2)	Normal	§178.275(d)(3)
T8	4	§178.274(d)(2)	Normal	Prohibited
T9	4	6 mm	Normal	Prohibited
T10	4	6 mm	§178.275(g)(3)	Prohibited
T11	6	§178.274(d)(2)	Normal	§178.275(d)(3)
T12	6	§178.274(d)(2)	§178.275(g)(3)	§178.275(d)(3)
T13	6	6 mm	Normal	Prohibited
T14	6	6 mm	§178.275(g)(3)	Prohibited
T15	10	§178.274(d)(2)	Normal	§178.275(d)(3)
T16	10	§178.274(d)(2)	§178.275(g)(3)	§178.275(d)(3)
T17	10	6 mm	Normal	§178.275(d)(3)
T18	10	6 mm	§178.275(g)(3)	§178.275(d)(3)
T19	10	6 mm	§178.275(g)(3)	Prohibited
T20	10	8 mm	§178.275(g)(3)	Prohibited
T21	10	10 mm	Normal	Prohibited
T22	10	10 mm	§178.275(g)(3)	Prohibited

(iii) *The following table* specifies the portable tank requirements applicable to T23 for self-reactive substances of Division 4.1 and organic peroxides of Division 5.2 which are authorized to be transported in portable tanks:

Portable Tank Code T23
[Portable tank code T23 applies to self-reactive substances of Division 4.1 and organic peroxides of Division 5.2.]

UN No.	Hazardous material	Minimum test pressure (bar)	Minimum shell thinkness (mm-reference steel) See . . .	Bottom opening requirements See . . .	Pressure-relief requirements See . . .	Filling limits	Control temperature	Emergency temperature
3109	Organic peroxide, Type F, liquid	4	§178.274(d)(2)	§178.275(d)(3)	§178.275(g)(1)	Not more than 90% at 59 °F (15 °C)		
	tert-Butyl hydroperoxide, not more than 72% with water. *Provided that steps have been taken to achieve the safety equivalence of 65% tert-Butyl hydroperoxide and 35% water	4	§178.274(d)(2)	§178.275(d)(3)	§178.275(g)(1)	Not more than 90% at 59 °F (15 °C)		
	Cumyl hydro-peroxide, not more than 90% in diluent type A	4	§178.274(d)(2)	§178.275(d)(3)	§178.275(g)(1)	Not more than 90% at 59 °F (15 °C)		
	Di-tert-butyl peroxide, not more than 32% in diluent type A	4	§178.274(d)(2)	§178.275(d)(3)	§178.275(g)(1)	Not more than 90% at 59 °F (15 °C)		
	Isopropyl cumyl hydro-peroxide, not more than 72% in diluent type A	4	§178.274(d)(2)	§178.275(d)(3)	§178.275(g)(1)	Not more than 90% at 59 °F (15 °C)		
	p-Menthyl hydro-peroxide, not more than 72% in diluent type A	4	§178.274(d)(2)	§178.275(d)(3)	§178.275(g)(1)	Not more than 90% at 59 °F (15 °C)		
	Pinanyl hydro-peroxide, not more than 50% in diluent type A	4	§178.274(d)(2)	§178.275(d)(3)	§178.275(g)(1)	Not more than 90% at 59 °F (15 °C)		
3110	Organic peroxide, Type F, solid	4	§178.274(d)(2)	§178.275(d)(3)	§178.275(g)(1)	Not more than 90% at 59 °F (15 °C)		
	Dicumyl peroxide *Maximum quantity per portable tank 2,000 kg							
3119	Organic peroxide, Type F, liquid, temperature controlled	4	§178.274(d)(2)	§178.275(d)(3)	§178.275(g)(1)	Not more than 90% at 59 °F (15 °C)	As approved by Assoc. Admin.	As approved by Assoc. Admin.
	tert-Butyl peroxyacetate, not more than 32% in diluent type B	4	§178.274(d)(2)	§178.275(d)(3)	§178.275(g)(1)	Not more than 90% at 59 °F (15 °C)	+30 °C	+35 °C
	tert-Butyl peroxy-2-ethylhexanoate, not more than 32% in diluent type B	4	§178.274(d)(2)	§178.275(d)(3)	§178.275(g)(1)	Not more than 90% at 59 °F (15 °C)	+15 °C	+20 °C
	tert-Butyl peroxypivalate, not more than 27% in diluent type B	4	§178.274(d)(2)	§178.275(d)(3)	§178.275(g)(1)	Not more than 90% at 59 °F (15 °C)	-5 °C	+10 °C
	tert-Butyl peroxy-3,5,5-trimethyl-hexanoate, not more than 32% in dileunt type B	4	§178.274(d)(2)	§178.275(d)(3)	§178.275(g)(1)	Not more than 90% at 59 °F (15 °C)	+35 °C	+40 °C

Portable Tank Code T23
[Portable tank code T23 applies to self-reactive substances of Division 4.1 and organic peroxides of Division 5.2.]

UN No.	Hazardous material	Minimum test pressure (bar)	Minimum shell thinkness (mm-reference steel) See . . .	Bottom opening requirements See . . .	Pressure-relief requirements See . . .	Filling limits	Control temperature	Emergency temperature
	Di-(3,5,5-trimethyl-hexanoyl) peroxide, not more than 38% in diluent type A	4	§178.274(d)(2)	§178.275(d)(3)	§178.275(g)(1)	Not more than 90% at 59 °F (15 °C)	0 °C	+5 °C
3120	Organix peroxide, Type F, solid, temperature controlled	4	§178.274(d)(2)	§178.275(d)(3)	§178.275(g)(1)	Not more than 90% at 59 °F (15 °C)	As approved by Assoc. Admin.	As approved by Assoc. Admin.
3229	Self-reactive liquid Type F	4	§178.274(d)(2)	§178.275(d)(3)	§178.275(g)(1)	Not more than 90% at 59 °F (15 °C)		
3230	Self-reactive solid Type F	4	§178.274(d)(2)	§178.275(d)(3)	§178.275(g)(1)	Not more than 90% at 59 °F (15 °C)		
3239	Self-reactive liquid Type F, temperature controlled	4	§178.274(d)(2)	§178.275(d)(3)	§178.275(g)(1)	Not more than 90% at 59 °F (15 °C)	As approved by Assoc. Admin.	As approved by Assoc. Admin.
3240	Self-reactive solid Type F, temperature controlled	4	§178.274(d)(2)	§178.275(d)(3)	§178.275(g)(1)	Not more than 90% at 59 °F (15 °C)	As approved by Assoc. Admin.	As approved by Assoc. Admin.

(iv) *The following* portable tank instruction applies to portable tanks used for the transportation of liquefied compressed gases. The T50 table provides the UN identification number and proper shipping name for each liquefied compressed gas authorized to be transported in a T50 portable tank. The table provides maximum allowable working pressures, bottom opening requirements, pressure relief device requirements and degree of filling requirements for each liquefied compressed gases permitted for transportation in a T50 portable tank. In the minimum test pressure column, "small" means a portable tank with a diameter of 1.5 meters or less when measured at the widest part of the shell, "sunshield" means a portable tank with a shield covering at least the upper third of the shell, "bare" means no sunshield or insulation is provided, and "insulated" means a complete cladding of sufficient thickness of insulating material necessary to provide a minimum conductance of not more than 0.67 $w/m^2/k$. In the pressure relief requirements column, the word "Normal" denotes that a frangible disc as specified in §178.276(e)(3) of this subchapter is not required. The T50 table follows:

Portable Tank Code T50
[Portable tank code T50 applies to liquefied compressed gases.]

UN No.	Non-refrigerated liquefied compressed gases	Max. allowable working pressure (bar) small; bare; sunshield; insulated	Openings below liquid level	Pressure relief requirements (see §178.27(e))	Maximum filling density (kg/l)
1005	Ammonia, anhydrous	29.0 25.7 22.0 19.7	Allowed	§178.276(e)(3)	0.53
1009	Bromotrifluoromethane *or* Refrigerant gas R 13B1	38.0 34.0 30.0 27.5	Allowed	Normal	1.13
1010	Butadienes, stabilized	7.5 7.0 7.0 7.0	Allowed	Normal	0.55
1011	Butane	7.0 7.0 7.0 7.0	Allowed	Normal	0.51
1012	Butylene	8.0 7.0 7.0 7.0	Allowed	Normal	0.53
1017	Chlorine	19.0 17.0 15.0 13.5	Not Allowed	§178.276(e)(3)	1.25
1018	Chlorodifluoromethane *or* Refrigerant gas R 22	26.0 24.0 21.0 19.0	Allowed	Normal	1.03
1020	Chloropentafluoroethane *or* Refrigerant gas R 115	23.0 20.0 18.0 16.0	Allowed	Normal	1.06
1021	1-Chloro-1,2,2,2-tetrafluoroethane *or* Refrigerant gas R 124	10.3 9.8 7.9 7.0	Allowed	Normal	1.2
1027	Cyclopropane	18.0 16.0 14.5 13.0	Allowed	Normal	0.53
1028	Dichlorodifluoromethane *or* Refrigerant gas R 12	16.0 15.0 13.0 11.5	Allowed	Normal	1.15

Portable Tank Code T50
[Portable tank code T50 applies to liquefied compressed gases.]

UN No.	Non-refrigerated liquefied compressed gases	Max. allowable working pressure (bar) small; bare; sunshield; insulated	Openings below liquid level	Pressure relief requirements (see §178.27(e))	Maximum filling density (kg/l)
1029	Dichlorofluoromethane *or* Refrigerant gas R 21	7.0 7.0 7.0 7.0	Allowed	Normal	1.23
1030	1,1-Difluoroethane *or* Refrigerant gas R 152a	16.0 14.0 12.4 11.0	Allowed	Normal	0.79
1032	Dimethylamine, anhydrous	7.0 7.0 7.0 7.0	Allowed	Normal	0.59
1033	Dimethyl ether	15.5 13.8 12.0 10.6	Allowed	Normal	0.58
1036	Ethylamine	7.0 7.0 7.0 7.0	Allowed	Normal	0.61
1037	Ethyl chloride	7.0 7.0 7.0 7.0	Allowed	Normal	0.8
1040	Ethylene oxide with *nitrogen up to a total pressure of 1MPa (10 bar) at 50 °C*	Only authorized in 10 bar insulated portable tanks	Not allowed	§178.276(e)(3)	0.78
1041	Ethylene oxide and carbon dioxide mixture *with more than 9% but not more than 87% ethylene oxide*	See MAWP definition in §178.276(a)	Allowed	Normal	See §173.32(f)
1055	Isobutylene	8.1 7.0 7.0 7.0	Allowed	Normal	0.52
1060	Methyl acetylene and propadiene mixture, stabilized	28.0 24.5 22.0 20.0	Allowed	Normal	0.43
1061	Methylamine, anhydrous	10.8 9.6 7.8 7.0	Allowed	Normal	0.58
1062	Methyl bromide	7.0 7.0 7.0 7.0	Not allowed	§178.276(e)(3)	1.51
1063	Methyl chloride *or* Refrigerant gas R 40	14.5 12.7 11.3 10.0	Allowed	Normal	0.81
1064	Methyl mercaptan	7.0 7.0 7.0 7.0	Not allowed	§178.276(e)(3)	0.78
1067	Dinitrogen tetroxide	7.0 7.0 7.0 7.0	Not allowed	§178.276(e)(3)	1.3
1075	Petroleum gas, liquefied	See MAWP definition in §178.276(a)	Allowed	Normal	See §173.32(f)
1077	Propylene	28.0 24.5 22.0 20.0	Allowed	Normal	0.43
1078	Refrigerant gas, n.o.s.	See MAWP definition in §178.276(a)	Allowed	Normal	See §173.32(f)
1079	Sulphur dioxide	11.6 10.3 8.5 7.6	Not allowed	§178.276(e)(3)	1.23
1082	Trifluorochloroethylene, stabilized *or* Refrigerant gas R 1113	17.0 15.0 13.1 11.6	Not allowed	§178.276(e)(3)	1.13
1083	Trimethylamine, anhydrous	7.0 7.0 7.0 7.0	Allowed	Normal	0.56

Portable Tank Code T50
[Portable tank code T50 applies to liquefied compressed gases.]

UN No.	Non-refrigerated liquefied compressed gases	Max. allowable working pressure (bar) small; bare; sunshield; insulated	Openings below liquid level	Pressure relief requirements (see §178.27(e))	Maximum filling density (kg/l)
1085	Vinyl bromide, stabilized	7.0 7.0 7.0 7.0	Allowed	Normal	1.37
1086	Vinyl chloride, stabilized	10.6 9.3 8.0 7.0	Allowed	Normal	0.81
1087	Vinyl methyl ether, stabilized	7.0 7.0 7.0 7.0	Allowed	Normal	0.67
1581	Chloropicrin and methyl bromide mixture	7.0 7.0 7.0 7.0	Not Allowed	§178.276(e)(3)	1.51
1582	Chloropicrin and methyl chloride mixture	19.2 16.9 15.1 13.1	Not allowed	§178.276(e)(3)	0.81
1858	Hexafluoropropylene compressed *or* Refrigerant gas R 1216	19.2 16.9 15.1 13.1	Allowed	Normal	1.11
1912	Methyl chloride and methylene chloride mixture	15.2 13.0 11.6 10.1	Allowed	Normal	0.81
NA 1954	Insecticide gases, *flammable*, n.o.s.	See MAWP definition in §178.276(a)	Allowed	Normal	§173.32(f)
1958	1,2-Dichloro-1,1,2,2-tetrafluoroethane *or* Refrigerant gas R 114	7.0 7.0 7.0 7.0	Allowed	Normal	1.3
1965	Hydrocarbon gas, mixture liquefied, n.o.s.	See MAWP definition in §178.276(a)	Allowed	Normal	See §173.32(f)
1969	Isobutane	8.5 7.5 7.0 7.0	Allowed	Normal	0.49
1973	Chlorodifluoromethane and chloropentafluoroethane mixture *with fixed boiling point, with approximately 49% chlorodifluoromethane or Refrigerant gas R502*	28.3 25.3 22.8 20.3	Allowed	Normal	1.05
1974	Chlorodifluorobromomethane *or* Refrigerant gas R 12B1	7.4 7.0 7.0 7.0	Allowed	Normal	1.61
1976	Octafluorocyclobutane *or* Refrigerant gas RC 318	8.8 7.8 7.0 7.0	Allowed	Normal	1.34
1978	Propane	22.5 20.4 18.0 16.5	Allowed	Normal	0.42
1983	1-Chloro-2,2,2-trifluoroethane *or* Refrigerant gas R 133a	7.0 7.0 7.0 7.0	Allowed	Normal	1.18
2035	1,1,1-Trifluoroethane compressed *or* Refrigerant gas R 143a	31.0 27.5 24.2 21.8	Allowed	Normal	0.76
2424	Octafluoropropane *or* Refrigerant gas R 218	23.1 20.8 18.6 16.6	Allowed	Normal	1.07
2517	1-Chloro-1,1-difluoroethane *or* Refrigerant gas R 142b	8.9 7.8 7.0 7.0	Allowed	Normal	0.99
2602	Dichlorodifluoromethane and difluoroethane azeotropic mixture *with approximately 74% dichlorodifluoromethane or* Refrigerant gas R 500	20.0 18.0 16.0 14.5	Allowed	Normal	1.01

Portable Tank Code T50
[Portable tank code T50 applies to liquefied compressed gases.]

UN No.	Non-refrigerated liquefied compressed gases	Max. allowable working pressure (bar) small; bare; sunshield; insulated	Openings below liquid level	Pressure relief requirements (see §178.27(e))	Maximum filling density (kg/l)
3057	Trifluoroacetyl chloride	14.6 12.9 11.3 9.9	Not allowed	§178.276(e)(3)	1.17
3070	Ethylene oxide and dichlorodifluoromethane mixture *with not more than 12.5% ethylene oxide*	14.0 12.0 11.0 9.0	Allowed	§178.276(e)(3)	1.09
3153	Perfluoro (methyl vinyl ether)	14.3 13.4 11.2 10.2	Allowed	Normal	1.14
3159	1,1,1,2-Tetrafluoroethane *or* Refrigerant gas R 134a	17.7 15.7 13.8 12.1	Allowed	Normal	1.04
3161	Liquefied gas, flammable, n.o.s.	See MAWP definition in §178.276(a)	Allowed	Normal	§173.32(f)
3163	Liquefied gas, n.o.s.	See MAWP definition in §178.276(a)	Allowed	Normal	§173.32(f)
3220	Pentafluoroethane *or* Refrigerant gas R 125	34.4 30.8 27.5 24.5	Allowed	Normal	0.95
3252	Difluoromethane *or* Refrigerant gas R 32	43.0 39.0 34.4 30.5	Allowed	Normal	0.78
3296	Heptafluoropropane *or* Refrigerant gas R 227	16.0 14.0 12.5 11.0	Allowed	Normal	1.2
3297	Ethylene oxide and chlorotetrafluoroethane mixture, *with not more than 8.8% ethylene oxide*	8.1 7.0 7.0 7.0	Allowed	Normal	1.16
3298	Ethylene oxide and pentafluoroethane mixture, *with not more than 7.9% ethylene oxide*	25.9 23.4 20.9 18.6	Allowed	Normal	1.02
3299	Ethylene oxide and tetrafluoroethane mixture, *with not more than 5.6% ethylene oxide*	16.7 14.7 12.9 11.2	Allowed	Normal	1.03
3318	Ammonia solution, *relative density less than 0.880 at 15 °C in water, with more than 50% ammonia*	See MAWP definition in §178.276(a)	Allowed	§178.276(e)(3)	§173.32(f)
3337	Refrigerant gas R 404A	31.6 28.3 25.3 22.5	Allowed	Normal	0.84
3338	Refrigerant gas R 407A	31.3 28.1 25.1 22.4	Allowed	Normal	0.95
3339	Refrigerant gas R 407B	33.0 29.6 26.5 23.6	Allowed	Normal	0.95
3340	Refrigerant gas R 407C	29.9 26.8 23.9 21.3	Allowed	Normal	0.95

(v) *When portable* tank instruction T75 is referenced in Column (7) of the §172.101 Table, the applicable refrigerated liquefied gases are authorized to be transported in portable tanks in accordance with the requirements of §178.277 of this subchapter.

(vi) *UN and IM* portable tank codes/special provisions. When a specific portable tank instruction is specified by a T Code in Column (7) of the §172.101 Table for a specific hazardous material, a Specification portable tank conforming to an alternative tank instruction may be used if:

[A] the alternative portable tank has a higher or equivalent test pressure (for example, 4 bar when 2.65 bar is specified);

[B] the alternative portable tank has greater or equivalent wall thickness (for example, 10 mm when 6 mm is specified);

[C] the alternative portable tank has a pressure relief device as specified in the T Code. If a frangible disc is required in series with the reclosing pressure relief device for the specified portable tank, the alternative portable tank must be fitted with a frangible disc in series with the reclosing pressure relief device; and

[D] With regard to bottom openings —

[1] When two effective means are specified, the alternative portable tank is fitted with bottom openings having two or three effective means of closure or no bottom openings; or

[2] When three effective means are specified, the portable tank has no bottom openings or three effective means of closure; or

[3] When no bottom openings are authorized, the alternative portable tank must have bottom openings.

(vii) *When a hazardous material* is not assigned a portable tank T Code or TP 9 is referenced in Column (7) of the §172.101 Table, the hazardous material may only be transported in a portable tank if approved by the Associate Administrator.

(viii) *Portable tank special provisions* are assigned to certain hazardous materials to specify requirements that are in addition to those provided by the portable tank instructions or the requirements in part 178 of this subchapter. Portable tank special provisions are designated with the abbreviation TP (tank provision) and are assigned to specific hazardous materials in Column (7) of the §172.101 Table. The following is a list of the portable tank special provisions:

Code/Special Provisions

TP1. The maximum degree of filling must not exceed the degree of filling determined by the following:

$$\left(\text{Degree of filling} = \frac{97}{1+\alpha(t_r - t_f)}\right)$$

Where:

t_r is the maximum mean bulk temperature during transport, and t_f is the temperature in degrees celsius of the liquid during filling.

TP2 a. *The maximum degree of filling* must not exceed the degree of filling determined by the following:

$$\left(\text{Degree of filling} = \frac{95}{1+\alpha(t_r - t_f)}\right)$$

Where:

t_r is the maximum mean bulk temperature during transport,

t_f is the temperature in degrees celsius of the liquid during filling, and

α is the mean coefficient of cubical expansion of the liquid between the mean temperature of the liquid during filling (t_f) and the maximum mean bulk temperature during transportation (t_r) both in degrees celsius.

b. *For liquids transported* under ambient conditions α may be calculated using the formula:

$$\alpha = \frac{d_{15} - d_{50}}{35\ d_{50}}$$

Where:

d_{15} and d_{50} are the densities (in units of mass per unit volume) of the liquid at 15 °C (59 °F) and 50 °C (122 °F), respectively.

TP3. For liquids transported under elevated temperature, the maximum degree of filling is determined by the following:

$$\left(\text{Degree of filling} = 95\frac{d_t}{d_f}\right)$$

Where:

d_t is the density of the material at the maximum mean bulk temperature during transport; and

d_f is the density of the material at the temperature in degrees celsius of the liquid during filling; and

d_f is the density of the liquid at the mean temperature of the liquid during filling, and d_t is the maximum mean bulk temperature during transport.

TP4. The maximum degree of filling for portable tanks must not exceed 90%.

TP5. For a portable tank used for the transport of flammable refrigerated liquefied gases or refrigerated liquefied oxygen, the maximum rate at which the portable tank may be filled must not exceed the liquid flow capacity of the primary pressure relief system rated at a pressure not exceeding 120 percent of the portable tank's design pressure. For portable tanks used for the transport of refrigerated liquefied helium and refrigerated liquefied atmospheric gas (except oxygen), the maximum rate at which the tank is filled must not exceed the liquid flow capacity of the pressure relief device rated at 130 percent of the portable tank's design pressure. Except for a portable tank containing refrigerated liquefied helium, a portable tank shall have an outage of at least two percent below the inlet of the pressure relief device or pressure control valve, under conditions of incipient opening, with the portable tank in a level attitude. No outage is required for helium.

TP6. To prevent the tank from bursting in an event, including fire engulfment (the conditions prescribed in CGA pamphlet S-1.2 (see §171.7 of this subchapter) may be used to consider the fire engulfment condition), it must be equipped with pressure relief devices that are adequate in relation to the capacity of the tank and the nature of the hazardous material transported.

TP7. The vapor space must be purged of air by nitrogen or other means.

TP8. A portable tank having a minimum test pressure of 1.5 bar (150 kPa) may be used when the flash point of the hazardous material transported is greater than 0 °C (32 °F).

TP9. A hazardous material assigned to special provision TP9 in Column (7) of the §172.101 Table may only be transported in a portable tank if approved by the Associate Administrator.

TP10. The portable tank must be fitted with a lead lining at least 5 mm (0.2 inches) thick. The lead lining must be tested annually to ensure that it is intact and functional. Another suitable lining material may be used if approved by the Associate Administrator.

TP12. This material is considered highly corrosive to steel.

TP13. Self-contained breathing apparatus must be provided when this hazardous material is transported by sea.

TP16. The portable tank must be protected against over and under pressurization which may be experienced during transportation. The means of protection must be approved by the approval agency designated to approve the portable tank in accordance with the procedures in part 107, subpart E, of this subchapter. The pressure relief device must be preceded by a frangible disk in accordance with the requirements in §178.275(g)(3) of this subchapter to prevent crystallization of the product in the pressure relief device.

TP17. Only inorganic non-combustible materials may be used for thermal insulation of the tank.

TP18. The temperature of this material must be maintained between 18 °C (64.4 °F) and 40 °C (104 °F) while in transportation. Portable tanks containing solidified methacrylic acid must not be reheated during transportation.

TP19. The calculated wall thickness must be increased by 3 mm at the time of construction. Wall thickness must be verified ultrasonically at intervals midway between periodic hydraulic tests (every 2.5 years). The portable tank must not be used if the wall thickness is less than that prescribed by the applicable T code in Column (7) of the Table for this material.

TP20. This hazardous material must only be transported in insulated tanks under a nitrogen blanket.

TP21. The wall thickness must not be less than 8 mm. Portable tanks must be hydraulically tested and internally inspected at intervals not exceeding 2.5 years.

TP22. Lubricants for portable tank fittings (for example, gaskets, shut-off valves, flanges) must be oxygen compatible.

TP24. The portable tank may be fitted with a device to prevent the build up of excess pressure due to the slow decomposition of the hazardous material being transported. The device must be in the vapor space when the tank is filled under maximum filling conditions. This device must also prevent an unacceptable amount of leakage of liquid in the case of overturning.

TP25. Sulphur trioxide 99.95% pure and above may be transported in tanks without an inhibitor provided that it is maintained at a temperature equal to or above 32.5 °C (90.5 °F).

TP26. The heating device must be exterior to the shell. For UN 3176, this requirement only applies when the hazardous material reacts dangerously with water.

TP27. A portable tank having a minimum test pressure of 4 bar (400 kPa) may be used provided the calculated test pressure is 4 bar or less based on the MAWP of the hazardous material, as defined in §178.275 of this subchapter, where the test pressure is 1.5 times the MAWP.

TP28. A portable tank having a minimum test pressure of 2.65 bar (265 kPa) may be used provided the calculated test pressure is 2.65 bar or less based on the MAWP of the hazardous material, as defined in §178.275 of this subchapter, where the test pressure is 1.5 times the MAWP.

TP29. A portable tank having a minimum test pressure of 1.5 bar (150.0 kPa) may be used provided the calculated test pressure is 1.5 bar or less based on the MAWP of the hazardous materials, as defined in §178.275 of this subchapter, where the test pressure is 1.5 times the MAWP.

TP30. This hazardous material may only be transported in insulated tanks.

TP31. This hazardous material may only be transported in tanks in the solid state.

TP37. IM portable tanks are only authorized for the shipment of hydrogen peroxide solutions in water containing 72% or less hydrogen peroxide by weight. Pressure relief devices shall be designed to prevent the entry of foreign matter, the leakage of liquid and the development of any dangerous excess pressure. In addition, the portable tank must be designed so that internal surfaces may be effectively cleaned and passivated. Each tank must be equipped with pressure relief devices conforming to the following requirements:

Concentration of hydrogen per peroxide solution	Total[1]
52% or less	11
Over 52%, but not greater than 60%	22
Over 60%, but not greater than 72%	32

1. Total venting capacity in standard cubic feet hour (S.C.F.H.) per pound of hydrogen peroxide solution.

TP38. Each portable tank must be insulated with an insulating material so that the overall thermal conductance at 15.5 °C (60 °F) is no more than 1.5333 kilojoules per hour per square meter per degree Celsius (0.075 Btu per hour per square foot per degree Fahrenheit) temperature differential. Insulating materials may not promote corrosion to steel when wet.

TP44. Each portable tank must be made of stainless steel, except that steel other than stainless steel may be used in accordance with the provisions of §173.24b(b) of this subchapter. Thickness of stainless steel for tank shell and heads must be the greater of 7.62 mm (0.300 inch) or the thickness required for a portable tank with a design pressure at least equal to 1.5 times the vapor pressure of the hazardous material at 46 °C (115 °F).

TP45. Each portable tank must be made of stainless steel, except that steel other than stainless steel may be used in accordance with the provisions of 173.24b(b) of this subchapter. Thickness of stainless steel for portable tank shells and heads must be the greater of 6.35 mm (0.250 inch) or the thickness required for a portable tank with a design pressure at least equal to 1.3 times the vapor pressure of the hazardous material at 46 °C (115 °F).

TP46. Portable tanks in sodium metal service are not required to be hydrostatically retested.

(8) *"W" codes.* These provisions apply only to transportation by water:

Code/Special Provisions

W7. Vessel stowage category for uranyl nitrate hexahydrate solution is "D" as defined in §172.101(k)(4).

W8. Vessel stowage category for pyrophoric thorium metal or pyrophoric uranium metal is "D" as defined in §172.101(k)(4).

W9. When offered for transportation by water, the following Specification packagings are not authorized unless approved by the Associate Administrator: woven plastic bags, plastic film bags, textile bags, paper bags, IBCs and bulk packagings.

W41. When offered for transportation by water, this material must be packaged in bales and be securely and tightly bound with rope, wire or similar means.

Subpart C - Shipping Papers

§172.200 Applicability.

(a) **Description of hazardous materials required.** Except as otherwise provided in this subpart, each person who offers a hazardous material for transportation shall describe the hazardous material on the shipping paper in the manner required by this subpart.

(b) **This subpart does not apply to any material,** other than a hazardous substance, hazardous waste or marine pollutant, that is —

(1) *Identified by the letter "A"* in column 1 of the §172.101 table, except when the material is offered or intended for transportation by air; or

(2) *Identified by the letter "W"* in column 1 of the §172.101 table, except when the material is offered or intended for transportation by water; or

(3) *An ORM-D,* except when the material is offered or intended for transportation by air.

§172.201 Preparation and retention of shipping papers.

(a) **Contents.** When a description of hazardous material is required to be included on a shipping paper, that description must conform to the following requirements:

(1) *When a hazardous material and a* material not subject to the requirements of this subchapter are described on the same shipping paper, the hazardous material description entries required by §172.202 and those additional entries that may be required by §172.203:

(i) *Must be entered first, or*

(ii) *Must be entered* in a color that clearly contrasts with any description on the shipping paper of a material not subject to the requirements of this subchapter, except that a description on a reproduction of a shipping paper may be highlighted, rather than printed, in a contrasting color (the provisions of this paragraph apply only to the basic description required by §172.202(a)(1), (2), (3), and (4)), or

(iii) *Must be identified* by the entry of an "X" placed before the proper shipping name in a column captioned "HM." (The "X" may be replaced by "RQ," if appropriate.)

(2) *The required* shipping description on a shipping paper and all copies thereof used for transportation purposes, must be legible and printed (manually or mechanically) in English.

(3) *Unless it is specifically authorized* or required in this subchapter, the required shipping description may not contain any code or abbreviation.

(4) *A shipping paper* may contain additional information concerning the material provided the information is not inconsistent with the required description. Unless otherwise permitted or required by this subpart, additional information must be placed after the basic description required by §172.202(a).

(b) **[Reserved]**

(c) **Continuation page.** A shipping paper may consist of more than one page, if each page is consecutively numbered and the first page bears a notation specifying the total number of pages included in the shipping paper. For example, "Page 1 of 4 pages."

(d) **Emergency response telephone number.** Except as provided in §172.604(c), a shipping paper must contain an emergency response telephone number, as prescribed in subpart G of this part.

(e) **Each person who provides a shipping paper** must retain a copy of the shipping paper required by §172.200(a), or an electronic image thereof, that is accessible at or through its principal place of business and must make the shipping paper available, upon request, to an authorized official of a Federal, State, or local government agency at reasonable times and locations. For a hazardous waste, the shipping paper copy must be retained for three years after the material is accepted by the initial carrier. For all other hazardous materials, the shipping paper copy must be retained for 375 days after the material is accepted by the initial carrier. Each shipping paper copy must include the date of acceptance by the initial carrier, except that, for rail, vessel, or air shipments, the date on the shipment waybill, airbill, or bill of lading may be used in place of the date of acceptance by the initial carrier. A motor carrier (as defined in §390.5 of Subchapter B of Chapter III of Subtitle B) that uses a shipping paper without change for multiple shipments of a single hazardous material (i.e., one having the same shipping name and identification number) may retain a single copy of the shipping paper, instead of a copy for each shipment made, if the carrier also retains a record of each shipment made, to include shipping name, identification number, quantity transported, and date of shipment.

§172.202 Description of hazardous material on shipping papers.

(a) **The shipping description of a hazardous material** on the shipping paper must include:

(1) *The proper shipping name* prescribed for the material in column 2 of the §172.101 table;

(2) *The hazard class or division* prescribed for the material as shown in column 3 of the §172.101 table (class names or subsidiary hazard class or division number may be entered following the numerical hazard class, or following the basic description). The hazard class need not be included for the entry "Combustible liquid, n.o.s.";

(3) *The identification number* prescribed for the material as shown in column 4 of the §172.101 table;

(4) *The packing group* in Roman numerals, as designated for the hazardous material in Column 5 of the §172.101 Table. Class 1 (explosives) materials, self-reactive substances, organic peroxides and entries that are not assigned a packing group are excepted from this requirement. The packing group may be preceded by the letters "PG" (for example, "PG II"); and

(5) *Except for empty packagings (see* §173.29 of this subchapter), cylinders for Class 2 (compressed gases) materials, and bulk packagings, the total quantity (by net or gross mass, capacity, or as otherwise appropriate), including the unit of measurement, of the hazardous material covered by the description (e.g., "800 lbs", "55 gal.", "3629 kg", or "208 L"). For cylinders for Class 2 (compressed gases) materials and bulk packagings, some indication of total quantity must be shown (e.g., "10 cylinders" or "1 cargo tank").

(b) **Except as provided in this subpart,** the basic description specified in paragraphs (a) (1), (2), (3) and (4) of this section must be shown in sequence with no additional information interspersed. For example: "Gasoline, 3, UN 1203, PG II".

(c) **The total quantity of the material covered by one description** must appear before or after, or both before and after, the description required and authorized by this subpart. The type of packaging and destination marks may be entered in any appropriate manner before or after the basic description. Abbreviations may be used to express units of measurement and types of packagings.

(d) **Technical and chemical group names may be entered** in parentheses between the proper shipping name and hazard class or following the basic description. An appropriate modifier, such as "contains" or "containing," and/or the percentage of the technical constituent may also be used. For example: "Flammable liquids, n.o.s. (contains Xylene and Benzene), 3, UN 1993, II".

(e) **Except for those materials in the UN Recommendations,** the ICAO Technical Instructions, or the IMDG Code (see §171.7 of this subchapter), a material that is not a hazardous material according to this subchapter may not be offered for transportation or transported when its description on a shipping paper includes a hazard class or an identification number specified in the §172.101 Table.

§172.203 Additional description requirements.

(a) **Exemptions.** Each shipping paper issued in connection with a shipment made under an exemption must bear the notation "DOT-E" followed by the exemption number assigned and so located that the notation is clearly associated with the description to which the exemption applies.

(b) **Limited quantities.** The description for a material offered for transportation as "limited quantity," as authorized by this subchapter, must include the words "Limited Quantity" or "Ltd Qty" following the basic description.

(c) **Hazardous substances.**

(1) *Except for Class 7 (radioactive) materials* described in accordance with paragraph (d) of this section, if the proper shipping name for a material that is a hazardous substance does not identify the hazardous substance by name, the name of the hazardous substance must be entered in parentheses in association with the basic description. If the material contains two or more hazardous substances, at least two hazardous substances, including the two with the lowest reportable quantities (RQs), must be identified. For a hazardous waste, the waste code (e.g., D001), if appropriate, may be used to identify the hazardous substance.

(2) *The letters "RQ"* shall be entered on the shipping paper either before or after, the basic description required by §172.202 for each hazardous substance (see definition in §171.8 of this subchapter). For example: "RQ, Allyl alcohol, 6.1, UN 1098, I"; or "Environmentally hazardous substance, solid, n.o.s., 9, UN 3077, III, RQ (Adipic acid)".

(d) **Radioactive material.** The description for a shipment of a Class 7 (radioactive) material must include the following additional entries as appropriate:

(1) *The words* "RADIOACTIVE MATERIAL" unless these words are contained in the proper shipping name.

(2) *The name* of each radionuclide in the Class 7 (radioactive) material that is listed in §173.435 of this subchapter. For mixtures of radionuclides, the radionuclides that must be shown must be determined in accordance with §173.433(f) of this subchapter. Abbreviations, e.g., "^{99} Mo", are authorized.

(3) *A description* of the physical and chemical form of the material, if the material is not in special form (generic chemical description is acceptable for chemical form).

(4) *The activity* contained in each package of the shipment in terms of the appropriate SI units (e.g., Becquerel, Terabecquerel, etc.) or in terms of the appropriate SI units followed by the customary units (e.g., Curies, millicuries, etc.). Abbreviations are authorized. Except for plutonium-238, plutonium-239, and plutonium-241, the weight in grams or kilograms of fissile radionuclides may be inserted instead of activity units. For plutonium-238, plutonium-239, and plutonium-241 the weight in grams or kilograms of fissile radionuclides may be inserted in addition to the activity units. For the shipment of a package containing a highway route controlled quantity of Class 7 (radioactive) materials (see §173.403 of this subchapter) the words "Highway route controlled quantity" must be entered in association with the basic description.

(5) *The category* of label applied to each package in the shipment. For example: "RADIOACTIVE WHITE-I."

(6) *The transport index* assigned to each package in the shipment bearing RADIOACTIVE YELLOW-II or RADIOACTIVE YELLOW-III labels.

(7) *For a shipment of fissile Class 7(radioactive) materials:*

(i) *The words* "Fissile Excepted" if the package is excepted pursuant to §173.453 of this subchapter;

(ii) *For a fissile material,* controlled shipment, the additional notation: "Warning — Fissile material, controlled shipment. Do not load more than * * * packages per vehicle." (Asterisks to be replaced by appropriate number.) "In loading and storage areas, keep at least 6 m (20 feet) from other packages bearing radioactive labels"; and

(iii) *If a fissile material,* controlled shipment is to be transported by water, the supplementary notation must also include the following statement: "For shipment by water, only one fissile material, controlled shipment is permitted in each hold."

(8) *For a package* approved by the U.S. Department of Energy (DOE) or U.S. Nuclear Regulatory Commission (USNRC), a notation of the package identification marking as prescribed in the applicable DOE or USNRC approval. (See §173.471 of the subchapter.)

(9) *For an export shipment* or a shipment in a foreign made package, a notation of the package identification marking as prescribed in the applicable International Atomic Energy Agency (IAEA) Certificate of Competent Authority which has been issued for the package. (See §173.473 of the subchapter.)

(10) *For a shipment* required by this subchapter to be consigned as exclusive use:

(i) *An indication that the shipment is consigned as exclusive use; or*

(ii) *If all the descriptions* on the shipping paper are consigned as exclusive use, then the statement "Exclusive Use Shipment" may be entered only once on the shipping paper in a clearly visible location.

(11) *For a shipment* of low specific activity material or surface contaminated objects, the appropriate group notation of LSA-I, LSA-II, LSA-III, SCO-I, or SCO-II, unless the group notation is contained in the proper shipping name as described in the §172.101 Table.

(e) **Empty packagings.**

(1) *The description* on the shipping paper for a packaging containing the residue of a hazardous material may include the words "RESIDUE: Last Contained * * *" in association with the basic description of the hazardous material last contained in the packaging.

(2) *The description* on the shipping paper for a tank car containing the residue of a hazardous material must include the phrase, "RESIDUE: LAST CONTAINED * * *" before the basic description.

(f) **Transportation by air.** When a package containing a hazardous material is offered for transportation by air and this subchapter prohibits its transportation aboard passenger-carrying aircraft, the words "Cargo aircraft only" must be entered after the basic description.

(g) **Transportation by rail.**

(1) *A shipping paper* prepared by a rail carrier for a rail car, freight container, transport vehicle or portable tank that contains hazardous materials must include the reporting mark and number when displayed on the rail car, freight container, transport vehicle or portable tank.

(2) *The shipping paper* for each DOT-113 tank car containing a Division 2.1 material or its residue must contain an appropriate notation, such as "DOT 113", and the statement "Do not hump or cut off car while in motion."

(3) *When shipments* of elevated temperature materials are transported under the exception permitted in §173.247(h)(3) of this subchapter, the shipping paper must contain an appropriate notation, such as "Maximum operating speed 15 mph.".

(h) **Transportation by highway.** Following the basic description for a hazardous material in a Specification MC 330 or MC 331 cargo tank, there must be entered for —

(1) *Anhydrous ammonia.*

(i) *The words* "0.2 PERCENT WATER" to indicate the suitability for shipping anhydrous ammonia in a cargo tank made of quenched and tempered steel as authorized by §173.315(a), Note 14 of this subchapter, or

(ii) *The words* "NOT FOR Q and T TANKS" when the anhydrous ammonia does not contain 0.2 percent or more water by weight.

(2) *Liquefied petroleum gas.*

(i) *The word* "NONCORROSIVE" or "NONCOR" to indicate the suitability for shipping "Noncorrosive" liquefied petroleum gas in a cargo tank made of quenched and tempered steel as authorized by §173.315(a), Note 15 of this subchapter, or

(ii) *The words* "NOT FOR Q and T TANKS" for grades of liquefied petroleum gas other than "Noncorrosive".

(i) **Transportation by water.** Each shipment by water must have the following additional shipping paper entries:

(1) *Identification* of the type of packagings such as barrels, drums, cylinders, and boxes.

(2) *The number* of each type of package including those in a freight container or on a pallet.

(3) *The gross mass* of each type of package or the individual gross mass of each package.

(4) *The name of the shipper.*

(5) *Minimum flash point* if 61 °C or below (in °C closed cup (c.c.) in association with the basic description.

(6) *Subsidiary hazards* not communicated in the proper shipping name shown either following the hazard class or division in parentheses, or in association with the basic description.

(j) **[Reserved]**

(k) **Technical names for "n.o.s."** and other generic descriptions. Unless otherwise excepted, if a material is described on a shipping paper by one of the proper shipping names identified by the letter "G" in column (1) of the §172.101 Table, the technical name of the hazardous material must be entered in parentheses in association with the basic description. For example "Corrosive liquid, n.o.s., (Octanoyl chloride), 8, UN 1760, II", or "Corrosive liquid, n.o.s., 8, UN 1760, II (contains Octanoyl chloride)". The word "contains" may be used in association with the technical name, if appropriate. For organic peroxides which may qualify for more than one generic listing depending on concentration, the technical name must include the actual concentration being shipped or the concentration range for the appropriate generic listing. For example, "Organic peroxide type B, solid, 5.2, UN 3102 (dibenzoyl peroxide, 52-100%)" or "Organic peroxide type E, solid, 5.2, UN 3108 (dibenzoyl peroxide, paste, 52%)". Shipping descriptions for toxic materials that meet the criteria of Division 6.1, PG I or II (as specified in §173.132(a) of this subchapter) or Division 2.3 (as specified in §173.115(c) of this subchapter) and are identified by the letter "G" in column (1) of the §172.101 Table, must have the technical name of the toxic constituent entered in parentheses in association with the basic description.

(1) *If a hazardous material* is a mixture or solution of two or more hazardous materials, the technical names of at least two components most predominately contributing to the hazards of the mixture or solution must be entered on the shipping paper as required by paragraph (k) of this section. For example, "Flammable liquid, corrosive, n.o.s., 3, UN 2924, II (contains Methanol, Potassium hydroxide)".

(2) *The provisions of this paragraph do not apply —*

(i) *To a material* that is a hazardous waste and described using the proper shipping name "Hazardous waste, liquid or solid, n.o.s.", classed as a miscellaneous Class 9, provided the EPA hazardous waste number is included on the shipping paper in association with the basic description, or provided the material is described in accordance with the provisions of §172.203(c) of this part.

(ii) *To a material* for which the hazard class is to be determined by testing under the criteria in §172.101(c)(11).

(iii) *If the n.o.s. description* for the material (other than a mixture of hazardous materials of different classes meeting the definitions of more than one hazard class) contains the name of the chemical element or group which is primarily responsible for the material being included in the hazard class indicated.

(iv) *If the n.o.s. description* for the material (which is a mixture of hazardous materials of different classes meeting the definition of more than one hazard class) contains the name of the chemical element or group responsible for the material meeting the definition of one of these classes. In such cases, only the technical name of the component that is not appropriately identified in the n.o.s. description shall be entered in parentheses.

(l) **Marine pollutants.**

(1) *If the proper shipping name* for a material which is a marine pollutant does not identify by name the component which makes the material a marine pollutant, the name of that component must appear in parentheses in association with the basic description. Where two or more components which make a material a marine pollutant are present, the names of at least two of the components most predominantly contributing to the marine pollutant designation must appear in parentheses in association with the basic description.

(2) *The words* "Marine Pollutant" shall be entered in association with the basic description for a material which is a marine pollutant.

(3) *Except for transportation by vessel,* marine pollutants subject to the provisions of 49 CFR 130.11 are excepted from the requirements of paragraph (l) of this section if a phrase indicating the material is an oil is placed in association with the basic description.

(m) **Poisonous materials.** Notwithstanding the hazard class to which a material is assigned —

(1) *If a liquid or solid material* in a package meets the definition of a Division 6.1, Packing Group I or II, according to this subchapter, and the fact that it is a poison is not disclosed in the shipping name or class entry, the word "Poison" or "Toxic" shall be entered on the shipping paper in association with the shipping description.

(2) *For materials* which are poisonous by inhalation (see §171.8 of this subchapter), the words "Poison-Inhalation Hazard" or "Toxic-Inhalation Hazard" and the words "Zone A", "Zone B", "Zone C", or "Zone D", for gases or "Zone A" or "Zone B" for liquids, as appropriate, shall be entered on the shipping paper immediately following the shipping description. The word "Poison" or "Toxic" need not be repeated if it otherwise appears in the shipping description.

(n) **Elevated temperature materials.** If a liquid material in a package meets the definition of an elevated temperature material in §171.8 of this subchapter, and the fact that it is an elevated temperature material is not disclosed in the proper shipping name (for example, when the words "Molten" or "Elevated temperature" are part of the proper shipping name), the word "HOT" must immediately precede the proper shipping name of the material on the shipping paper.

(o) **Organic peroxides and self-reactive materials.** The description on a shipping paper for a Division 4.1 (self-reactive) material or a Division 5.2 (organic peroxide) material must include the following additional information, as appropriate:

(1) *If notification* or competent authority approval is required, the shipping paper must contain a statement of approval of the classification and conditions of transport.

(2) *For Division 4.1* (self-reactive) and Division 5.2 (organic peroxide) materials that require temperature control during transport, the control and emergency temperature must be included on the shipping paper.

(3) *The word "SAMPLE"* must be included in association with the basic description when a sample of a Division 4.1 (self-reactive) material (see §173.224(c)(3) of this subchapter) or Division 5.2 (organic peroxide) material (see §173.225(c)(2) of this subchapter) is offered for transportation or transported.

§172.204 Shipper's certification.

(a) **General.** Except as provided in paragraphs (b) and (c) of this section, each person who offers a hazardous material for transportation shall certify that the material is offered for transportation in accordance with this subchapter by printing (manually or mechanically) on the shipping paper containing the required shipping description the certification contained in paragraph (a)(1) of this section or the certification (declaration) containing the language contained in paragraph (a)(2) of this section.

(1) *"This is to certify* that the above-named materials are properly classified, described, packaged, marked and labeled, and are in proper condition for transportation according to the applicable regulations of the Department of Transportation."

NOTE: In line one of the certification the words "herein-named" may be substituted for the words "above-named".

(2) *"I hereby declare* that the contents of this consignment are fully and accurately described above by the proper shipping name, and are classified, packaged, marked and labelled/placarded, and are in all respects in proper condition for transport according to applicable international and national governmental regulations."

(b) **Exceptions.**

(1) *Except for a hazardous waste,* no certification is required for a hazardous material offered for transportation by motor vehicle and transported:

(i) *In a cargo tank supplied by the carrier, or*

(ii) *By the shipper* as a private carrier except for a hazardous material that is to be reshipped or transferred from one carrier to another.

(2) *No certification* is required for the return of an empty tank car which previously contained a hazardous material and which has not been cleaned or purged.

(c) **Transportation by air —**

(1) *General.* Certification containing the following language may be used in place of the certification required by paragraph (a) of this section:

I hereby certify that the contents of this consignment are fully and accurately described above by proper shipping name and are classified, packaged, marked and labeled, and in proper condition for carriage by air according to applicable national governmental regulations.

Note to Paragraph (c)(1): In the certification, the word "packed" may be used instead of the word "packaged" until October 1, 2010.

(2) *Certificate in duplicate.* Each person who offers a hazardous material to an aircraft operator for transportation by air shall provide two copies of the certification required in this section. (See §175.30 of this subchapter.)

(3) *Passenger and cargo aircraft.* Each person who offers for transportation by air a hazardous material authorized for air transportation shall add to the certification required in this section the following statement:

This shipment is within the limitations prescribed for passenger aircraft/cargo aircraft only (delete nonapplicable).

(4) *Radioactive material.* Each person who offers any radioactive material for transportation aboard a passenger-carrying aircraft shall sign (mechanically or manually) a printed certificate stating that the shipment contains radioactive material intended for use in, or incident to, research, or medical diagnosis or treatment.

(d) **Signature.** The certifications required by paragraph (a) or (c) of this section:

(1) *Must be legibly signed* by a principal, officer, partner, or employee of the shipper or his agent; and

(2) *May be legibly signed* manually, by typewriter, or by other mechanical means.

§172.205 Hazardous waste manifest.

(a) **No person may offer, transport, transfer, or deliver** a hazardous waste (waste) unless an EPA Form 8700-22 and 8700-22A (when necessary) hazardous waste manifest (manifest) is prepared in accordance with 40 CFR 262.20 and is signed, carried, and given as required of that person by this section.

(b) **The shipper (generator) shall prepare the manifest** in accordance with 40 CFR part 262.

(c) **The original copy of the manifest** must be dated by, and bear the handwritten signature of, the person representing:

(1) *The shipper (generator)* of the waste at the time it is offered for transportation, and

(2) *The initial carrier accepting the waste for transportation.*

(d) **A copy of the manifest must be dated by,** and bear the handwritten signature of the person representing:

(1) *Each subsequent carrier* accepting the waste for transportation, at the time of acceptance, and

(2) *The designated facility receiving the waste, upon receipt.*

(e) **A copy of the manifest bearing all required dates** and signatures must be:

(1) *Given to a person* representing each carrier accepting the waste for transportation,

(2) *Carried during transportation* in the same manner as required by this subchapter for shipping papers,

(3) *Given to a person* representing the designated facility receiving the waste,

(4) *Returned to the shipper* (generator) by the carrier that transported the waste from the United States to a foreign destination with a notation of the date of departure from the United States, and

(5) *Retained by the shipper* (generator) and by the initial and each subsequent carrier for three years from the date the waste was accepted by the initial carrier. Each retained copy must bear all required signatures and dates up to and including those entered by the next person who received the waste.

(f) **Transportation by rail.** Notwithstanding the requirements of paragraphs (d) and (e) of this section, the following requirements apply:

(1) *When accepting* hazardous waste from a non-rail transporter, the initial rail transporter must:

(i) *Sign and date* the manifest acknowledging acceptance of the hazardous waste;

(ii) *Return a signed copy of the manifest to the non-rail transporter;*

(iii) *Forward at least three copies of the manifest to:*

[A] The next non-rail transporter, if any;

[B] The designated facility, if the shipment is delivered to that facility by rail; or

[C] The last rail transporter designated to handle the waste in the United States; and

(iv) *Retain one copy* of the manifest and rail shipping paper in accordance with 40 CFR 263.22.

(2) *Rail transporters* must ensure that a shipping paper containing all the information required on the manifest (excluding the EPA identification numbers, generator certification and signatures) and, for exports, an EPA Acknowledgment of Consent accompanies the hazardous waste at all times. Intermediate rail transporters are not required to sign either the manifest or shipping paper.

(3) *When delivering* hazardous waste to the designated facility, a rail transporter must:

(i) *Obtain the date of delivery* and handwritten signature of the owner or operator of the designated facility on the manifest or the shipping paper (if the manifest has not been received by the facility); and

(ii) *Retain a copy* of the manifest or signed shipping paper in accordance with 40 CFR 263.22.

(4) *When delivering* hazardous waste to a non-rail transporter, a rail transporter must:

(i) *Obtain the date of delivery* and the handwritten signature of the next non-rail transporter on the manifest; and

(ii) *Retain a copy of the manifest in accordance with 40 CFR 263.22.*

(5) *Before accepting* hazardous waste from a rail transporter, a non-rail transporter must sign and date the manifest and provide a copy to the rail transporter.

(g) **The person delivering a hazardous waste** to an initial rail carrier shall send a copy of the manifest, dated and signed by a representative of the rail carrier, to the person representing the designated facility.

(h) **A hazardous waste manifest required by 40 CFR part 262,** containing all of the information required by this subpart, may be used as the shipping paper required by this subpart.

Subpart D - Marking

§172.300 Applicability.

(a) **Each person who offers a hazardous material** for transportation shall mark each package, freight container, and transport vehicle containing the hazardous material in the manner required by this subpart.

(b) **When assigned the function by this subpart,** each carrier that transports a hazardous material shall mark each package, freight container, and transport vehicle containing the hazardous material in the manner required by this subpart.

§172.301 General marking requirements for non-bulk packagings.

(a) **Proper shipping name and identification number.**

(1) *Except as otherwise provided* by this subchapter, each person who offers for transportation a hazardous material in a non-bulk packaging shall mark the package with the proper shipping name and identification number (preceded by "UN" or "NA", as appropriate) for the material as shown in the §172.101 table. Identification numbers are not required on packages which contain only limited quantities, as defined in §171.8 of this subchapter, or ORM-D materials.

(2) *The proper shipping name* for a hazardous waste (as defined in §171.8 of this subchapter) is not required to include the word "waste" if the package bears the EPA marking prescribed by 40 CFR 262.32.

(3) *Large quantities* of a single hazardous material in non-bulk packages. A transport vehicle or freight container containing only a single hazardous material in non-bulk packages must be marked, on each side and each end as specified in the §172.332 or §172.336, with the identification number specified for the hazardous material in the §172.101 Table, subject to the following provisions and limitations:

(i) *Each package* is marked with the same proper shipping name and identification number;

(ii) *The aggregate gross weight* of the hazardous material is 4,000 kg (8,820 pounds) or more;

(iii) *All of the hazardous material is loaded at one loading facility;*

(iv) *The transport vehicle* or freight container contains no other material, hazardous or otherwise; and

(v) *The identification number* marking requirement of this paragraph (a)(3) does not apply to Class 1, Class 7, or to non-bulk packagings for which identification numbers are not required.

(b) **Technical names.** In addition to the marking required by paragraph (a) of this section, each non-bulk packaging containing hazardous materials subject to the provisions of §172.203(k) of this part shall be marked with the technical name in parentheses in association with the proper shipping name in accordance with the requirements and exceptions specified for display of technical descriptions on shipping papers in §172.203(k) of this part.

(c) **Exemption packagings.** The outside of each package authorized by an exemption shall be plainly and durably marked "DOT-E" followed by the exemption number assigned.

(d) **Consignee's or consignor's name and address.** Each person who offers for transportation a hazardous material in a non-bulk package shall mark that package with the name and address of the consignor or consignee except when the package is —

(1) *Transported by highway only* and will not be transferred from one motor carrier to another; or

(2) *Part of a carload lot,* truckload lot or freight container load, and the entire contents of the rail car, truck or freight container are shipped from one consignor to one consignee.

(e) **Previously marked packagings.** A package which has been previously marked as required for the material it contains and on which the marking remains legible, need not be remarked. (For empty packagings, see §173.29 of this subchapter.)

§172.302 General marking requirements for bulk packagings.

(a) **Identification numbers.** Except as otherwise provided in this subpart, no person may offer for transportation or transport a hazardous material in a bulk packaging unless the packaging is marked as required by §172.332 with the identification number specified for the material in the §172.101 table —

(1) *On each side and each end,* if the packaging has a capacity of 3,785 L (1,000 gallons) or more;

(2) *On two opposing sides,* if the packaging has a capacity of less than 3,785 L (1,000 gallons); or

(3) *For cylinders* permanently installed on a tube trailer motor vehicle, on each side and each end of the motor vehicle.

(b) **Size of markings.** Except as otherwise provided, markings required by this subpart on bulk packagings must —

(1) *Have a width* of at least 6.0 mm (0.24 inch) and a height of at least 100 mm (3.9 inches) for rail cars;

(2) *Have a width* of at least 4.0 mm (0.16 inch) and a height of at least 25 mm (one inch) for portable tanks with capacities of less than 3,785 L (1,000 gallons) and IBCs; and

(3) *Have a width* of at least 6.0 mm (0.24 inch) and a height of at least 50 mm (2.0 inches) for cargo tanks and other bulk packagings.

(c) **Exemption packagings.** The outside of each bulk package used under the terms of an exemption shall be plainly and durably marked "DOT-E" followed by the exemption number assigned.

(d) **Each bulk packaging marked with a proper shipping name,** common name or identification number as required by this subpart must remain marked when it is emptied unless it is —

(1) *Sufficiently cleaned* of residue and purged of vapors to remove any potential hazard; or

(2) *Refilled,* with a material requiring different markings or no markings, to such an extent that any residue remaining in the packaging is no longer hazardous.

(e) **Additional requirements for marking portable tanks,** cargo tanks, tank cars, multi-unit tank car tanks, and other bulk packagings are prescribed in §§172.326, 172.328, 172.330, and 172.331, respectively, of this subpart.

(f) **A bulk packaging marked prior to October 1, 1991,** in conformance to the regulations of this subchapter in effect on September 30, 1991, need not be remarked if the key words of the proper shipping name are identical to those currently specified in the §172.101 table. For example, a tank car marked "ANHYDROUS AMMONIA" need not be remarked "ANHYDROUS AMMONIA, LIQUEFIED".

(g) **A rail car, freight container, truck body or trailer** in which the lading has been fumigated with any hazardous material, or is undergoing fumigation, must be marked as specified in §173.9 of this subchapter.

§172.303 Prohibited marking.

(a) **No person may offer for transportation** or transport a package which is marked with the proper shipping name or identification number of a hazardous material unless the package contains the identified hazardous material or its residue.

(b) **This section does not apply to —**

(1) *Transportation of a package* in a transport vehicle or freight container if the package is not visible during transportation and is loaded by the shipper and unloaded by the shipper or consignee.

(2) *Markings on a package* which are securely covered in transportation.

(3) *The marking of a shipping name* on a package when the name describes a material not regulated under this subchapter.

§172.304 Marking requirements.

(a) **The marking required in this subpart —**

(1) *Must be durable,* in English and printed on or affixed to the surface of a package or on a label, tag, or sign.

(2) *Must be displayed on a background of sharply contrasting color;*

(3) *Must be unobscured by labels or attachments; and*

(4) *Must be located* away from any other marking (such as advertising) that could substantially reduce its effectiveness.

(b) **[Reserved]**

§172.306 [Reserved]

§172.308 Authorized abbreviations.

(a) **Abbreviations may not be used** in a proper shipping name marking except as authorized in this section.

(b) **The abbreviation "ORM" may be used** in place of the words "Other Regulated Material."

(c) **Abbreviations which appear as authorized descriptions** in column 2 of the §172.101 table (e.g., "TNT" and "PCB") are authorized.

§172.310 Class 7 (radioactive) materials.

In addition to any other markings required by this subpart, each package containing Class 7 (radioactive) materials must be marked as follows:

(a) **Each package with a gross mass** greater than 50 kg (110 pounds) must have its gross mass marked on the outside of the package.

(b) **Each packaging must be marked** on the outside of the package, in letters at least 13 mm (0.5 inch) high, with the words "TYPE A" or "TYPE B" as appropriate. A packaging which does not conform to Type A or Type B requirements may not be so marked.

(c) **Each Type B, Type B(U) or Type B(M) packaging** must be marked on the outside of the package with a radiation symbol that conforms to the requirements of appendix B to part 172.

(d) **Each package destined for export shipment** must also be marked "USA" in conjunction with the specification marking, or other package certificate identification. (See §§173.471, 173.472, and 173.473 of this subchapter).

§172.312 Liquid hazardous materials in non-bulk packagings.

(a) **Except as provided in this section,** each non-bulk combination package having inner packagings containing liquid hazardous materials must be:

(1) *Packed with closures upward, and*

(2) *Legibly marked,* with package orientation markings that conform pictorially to the illustration shown in this paragraph, on two opposite vertical sides of the package with the arrows pointing in the correct upright direction. Depicting a rectangular border around the arrows is optional.

Package orientation

(b) **Arrows for purposes other than indicating** proper package orientation may not be displayed on a package containing a liquid hazardous material.

(c) **The requirements of paragraph (a) of this section** do not apply to —

(1) *A non-bulk package with inner packagings which are cylinders.*

(2) *Except when* offered or intended for transportation by aircraft, packages containing flammable liquids in inner packagings of 1 L or less prepared in accordance with §173.150 (b) or (c) of this subchapter.

(3) *When offered* or intended for transportation by aircraft, packages containing flammable liquids in inner packagings of 120 mL (4 fluid oz.) or less prepared in accordance with §173.150 (b) or (c) of this subchapter when packed with sufficient absorption material between the inner and outer packagings to completely absorb the liquid contents.

(4) *Liquids contained in manufactured articles* (e.g., alcohol or mercury in thermometers) which are leak-tight in all orientations.

(5) *A non-bulk package with hermetically-sealed inner packagings.*

§172.313 Poisonous hazardous materials.

In addition to any other markings required by this subpart:

(a) **A material poisonous by inhalation** (see §171.8 of this subchapter) shall be marked "Inhalation Hazard" in association with the required labels or placards, as appropriate, and shipping name when required. The marking must be on two opposing sides of a bulk packaging. (See §172.302(b) of this subpart for size of markings on bulk packages.) When the words "Inhalation Hazard" appear on the label, as prescribed in §§172.416 and 172.429, or placard, as prescribed in §§172.540 and 172.555, the "Inhalation Hazard" marking is not required on the package.

(b) **Each non-bulk plastic outer packaging used** as a single or composite packaging for materials meeting the definition of Division 6.1 (in §173.132 of this subchapter) shall be permanently marked, by embossment or other durable means, with the word "POISON" in letters at least 6.3 mm (0.25 inch) in height. Additional text or symbols related to hazard warning may be included in the marking. The marking shall be located within 150 mm (6 inches) of the closure of the packaging.

(c) **A transport vehicle or freight container** containing a material poisonous by inhalation in non-bulk packages shall be marked, on each side and each end as specified in §172.332 or §172.336, with the identification number specified for the hazardous material in the §172.101 table, subject to the following provisions and limitations:

(1) *The material is in Hazard Zone A or B;*

(2) *The transport vehicle* or freight container is loaded at one facility with 1,000 kg (2,205 pounds) or more aggregate gross weight of the material in non-bulk packages marked with the same proper shipping name and identification number; and

(3) *If the transport vehicle* or freight container contains more than one material meeting the provisions of this paragraph (c), it shall be marked with the identification number for one material, determined as follows:

(i) *For different materials* in the same hazard zone, with the identification number of the material having the greatest aggregate gross weight; and

(ii) *For different materials* in both Hazard Zones A and B, with the identification number for the Hazard Zone A material.

(d) **For a packaging containing a Division 6.1 PG III material,** "PG III" may be marked adjacent to the POISON label. (See §172.405(c).)

§172.316 Packagings containing materials classed as ORM-D.

(a) **Each non-bulk packaging containing a material** classed as ORM-D must be marked on at least one side or end with the ORM-D designation immediately following or below the proper shipping name of the material. The ORM designation must be placed within a rectangle that is approximately 6.3 mm (0.25 inches) larger on each side than the designation. The designation for ORM-D must be:

(1) *ORM-D-AIR* for an ORM-D that is prepared for air shipment and packaged in accordance with the provisions of §173.27 of this subchapter.

(2) *ORM-D* for an ORM-D other than as described in paragraph (a)(1) of this section.

(b) **When the ORM-D marking including** the proper shipping name can not be affixed on the package surface, it may be on an attached tag.

(c) **The marking ORM-D is the certification** by the person offering the packaging for transportation that the material is properly described, classed, packaged, marked and labeled (when appropriate) and in proper condition for transportation according to the applicable regulations of this subchapter. This form of certification does not preclude the requirement for a certificate on a shipping paper when required by subpart C of this part.

§172.320 Explosive hazardous materials.

(a) **Except as otherwise provided** in paragraphs (b), (c), (d) and (e) of this section, each package containing a Class 1 material must be marked with the EX-number for each substance, article or device contained therein.

(b) **Except for fireworks approved** in accordance with §173.56(j) of this subchapter, a package of Class 1 materials may be marked, in lieu of the EX-number required by paragraph (a) of this section, with a national stock number issued by the Department of Defense or identifying information, such as a product code required by regulations for commercial explosives specified in 27 CFR part 55, if the national stock number or identifying information can be specifically associated with the EX-number assigned.

(c) **When more than five different Class 1 materials** are packed in the same package, the package may be marked with only five of the EX-numbers, national stock numbers, product codes, or combination thereof.

(d) **The requirements of this section do not apply** if the EX-number, product code or national stock number of each explosive item described under a proper shipping description is shown in association with the shipping description required by §172.202(a) of this part. Product codes and national stock numbers must be traceable to the specific EX-number assigned by the Associate Administrator.

(e) **The requirements of this section do not apply** to the following Class 1 materials:

(1) *Those being shipped* to a testing agency in accordance with §173.56(d) of this subchapter;

(2) *Those being shipped* in accordance with §173.56(e) of this subchapter, for the purposes of developmental testing;

(3) *Those which meet* the requirements of §173.56(h) of this subchapter and therefore are not subject to the approval process of §173.56 of this subchapter;

(4) *Until October 1, 1993,* those which are shipped under §171.19 of this subchapter; and

(5) *Those that are transported* in accordance with §173.56(c)(2) of this subchapter and, therefore, are covered by a national security classification currently in effect.

§172.322 Marine pollutants.

(a) **For vessel transportation of each non-bulk packaging** that contains a marine pollutant —

(1) *If the proper shipping name* for a material which is a marine pollutant does not identify by name the component which makes the material a marine pollutant, the name of that component must be marked on the package in parentheses in association with the marked proper shipping name. Where two or more components which make a material a marine pollutant are present, the names of at least two of the components most predominantly contributing to the marine pollutant designation must appear in parentheses in association with the marked proper shipping name; and

(2) *The MARINE POLLUTANT mark* shall be placed in association with the hazard warning labels required by subpart E of this part or, in the absence of any labels, in association with the marked proper shipping name.

(b) **A bulk packaging that contains a marine pollutant must —**

(1) *Be marked* with the MARINE POLLUTANT mark on at least two opposing sides or two ends other than the bottom if the packaging has a capacity of less than 3,785 L (1,000 gallons). The mark must be visible from the direction it faces. The mark may be displayed in black lettering on a square-on-point configuration having the same outside dimensions as a placard; or

(2) *Be marked* on each end and each side with the MARINE POLLUTANT mark if the packaging has a capacity of 3,785 L (1,000 gallons) or more. The mark must be visible from the direction it faces. The mark may be displayed in black lettering on a square-on-point configuration having the same outside dimensions as a placard.

(c) **A transport vehicle or freight container** that contains a package subject to the marking requirements of paragraph (a) or (b) of this section must be marked with the MARINE POLLUTANT mark. The mark must appear on each side and each end of the transport vehicle or freight container, and must be visible from the direction it faces. This requirement may be met by the marking displayed on a freight container or portable tank loaded on a motor vehicle or rail car. This mark may be displayed in black lettering on a white square-on-point configuration having the same outside dimensions as a placard.

(d) **The MARINE POLLUTANT mark is not required —**

(1) *On a combination package* containing a severe marine pollutant (see appendix B to §172.101), in inner packagings each of which contains:

(i) *0.5 L (17 ounces) or less net capacity for liquids; or*

(ii) *500 g (17.6 ounces) or less net capacity for solids.*

(2) *On a combination packaging* containing a marine pollutant, other than a severe marine pollutant, in inner packagings each of which contains:

(i) *5 L (1.3 gallons) or less net capacity for liquids; or*

(ii) *5 kg (11 pounds) or less net capacity for solids.*

(3) *Except for transportation* by vessel, on a bulk packaging, freight container or transport vehicle that bears a label or placard specified in subparts E or F of this part.

(e) **MARINE POLLUTANT mark.** The MARINE POLLUTANT mark must conform to the following:

(1) *Except for size,* the MARINE POLLUTANT mark must appear as follows:

(2) *The symbol, letters and border* must be black and the background white, or the symbol, letters, border and background must be of contrasting color to the surface to which the mark is affixed. Each side of the mark must be —

(i) *At least 100 mm (3.9 inches) for marks applied to:*

[A] Non-bulk packagings, except in the case of packagings which, because of their size, can only bear smaller marks; or

[B] Bulk packagings with a capacity of less than 3785 L (1,000 gallons); or

(ii) *At least 250 mm* (9.8 inches) for marks applied to all other bulk packagings.

§172.323 Infectious substances.

(a) **In addition to other requirements of this subpart,** after September 30, 2003, a bulk packaging containing a regulated medical waste, as defined in §173.134(a)(5) of this subchapter, must be marked with a BIOHAZARD marking conforming to 29 CFR 1910.1030(g)(1)(i) —

(1) *On two opposing sides* or two ends other than the bottom if the packaging has a capacity of less than 3,785 L (1,000 gallons). The BIOHAZARD marking must measure at least 152.4 mm (6 inches) on each side and must be visible from the direction it faces.

(2) *On each end* and each side if the packaging has a capacity of 3,785 L (1,000 gallons) or more. The BIOHAZARD marking must measure at least 152.4 mm (6 inches) on each side and must be visible from the direction it faces.

(b) **For a bulk packaging contained in or on** a transport vehicle or freight container, if the BIOHAZARD marking on the bulk packaging is not visible, the transport vehicle or freight container must be marked as required by paragraph (a) of this section on each side and each end.

(c) **The background color for the BIOHAZARD marking** required by paragraph (a) of this section must be orange and the symbol and letters must be black. Except for size the BIOHAZARD marking must appear as follows:

(d) **The BIOHAZARD marking required by paragraph (a)** of this section must be displayed on a background of contrasting color. It may be displayed on a plain white square-on-point configuration having the same outside dimensions as a placard, as specified in §172.519(c) of this part.

§172.324 Hazardous substances in non-bulk packagings.

For each non-bulk package that contains a hazardous substance —

(a) **Except for packages of radioactive material** labeled in accordance with §172.403, if the proper shipping name of a material that is a hazardous substance does not identify the hazardous substance by name, the name of the hazardous substance must be marked on the package, in parentheses, in association with the proper shipping name. If the material contains two or more hazardous substances, at least two hazardous substances, including the two with the lowest reportable quantities (RQs), must be identified. For a hazardous waste, the waste code (e.g., D001), if appropriate, may be used to identify the hazardous substance.

(b) **The letters "RQ" shall be marked** on the package in association with the proper shipping name.

§172.325 Elevated temperature materials.

(a) **Except as provided in paragraph (b) of this section,** a bulk packaging containing an elevated temperature material must be marked on two opposing sides with the word "HOT" in black or white Gothic lettering on a contrasting background. The marking must be displayed on the packaging itself or in black lettering on a plain white square-on-point configuration having the same outside dimensions as a placard. (See §172.302(b) for size of markings on bulk packagings.)

(b) **Bulk packagings containing molten aluminum** or molten sulfur must be marked "MOLTEN ALUMINUM" or "MOLTEN SULFUR", respectively, in the same manner as prescribed in paragraph (a) of this section.

(c) **If the identification number is displayed** on a white-square-on-point display configuration, as prescribed in §172.336(b), the word "HOT" may be displayed in the upper corner of the same white-square-on-point display configuration. The word "HOT" must be in black letters having a height of at least 50 mm (2.0 inches). Except for size, these markings shall be as illustrated for an Elevated temperature material, liquid, n.o.s.:

§172.326 Portable tanks.

(a) **Shipping name.** No person may offer for transportation or transport a portable tank containing a hazardous material unless it is legibly marked on two opposing sides with the proper shipping name specified for the material in the §172.101 table.

(b) **Owner's name.** The name of the owner or of the lessee, if applicable, must be displayed on a portable tank that contains a hazardous material.

(c) **Identification numbers.**

(1) *If the identification number markings* required by §172.302(a) are not visible, a transport vehicle or freight container used to transport a portable tank containing a hazardous material must be marked on each side and each end as required by §172.332 with the identification number specified for the material in the §172.101 table.

(2) *Each person* who offers a portable tank containing a hazardous material to a motor carrier, for transportation in a transport vehicle or freight container, shall provide the motor carrier with the required identification numbers on placards, orange panels, or the white square-on-point configuration, as appropriate, for each side and each end of the transport vehicle or freight container from which identification numbers on the portable tank are not visible.

§172.328 Cargo tanks.

(a) **Providing and affixing identification numbers.** Unless a cargo tank is already marked with the identification numbers required by this subpart, the identification numbers must be provided or affixed as follows:

(1) *A person* who offers a hazardous material to a motor carrier for transportation in a cargo tank shall provide the motor carrier the identification numbers on placards or shall affix orange panels containing the required identification numbers, prior to or at the time the material is offered for transportation.

(2) *A person* who offers a cargo tank containing a hazardous material for transportation shall affix the required identification numbers on panels or placards prior to or at the time the cargo tank is offered for transportation.

(3) *For a cargo tank* transported on or in a transport vehicle or freight container, if the identification number marking on the cargo tank required by §172.302(a) would not normally be visible during transportation —

(i) *The transport vehicle* or freight container must be marked as required by §172.332 on each side and each end with the identification number specified for the material in the §172.101 table; and

(ii) *When the cargo tank* is permanently installed within an enclosed cargo body of the transport vehicle or freight container, the identification number marking required by §172.302(a) need only be displayed on each side and end of a cargo tank that is visible when the cargo tank is accessed.

(b) **Required markings: Gases.** Except for certain nurse tanks which must be marked as specified in §173.315(m) of this subchapter, each cargo tank transporting a Class 2 material subject to this subchapter must be marked, in lettering no less than 50 mm (2.0 inches), on each side and each end with —

(1) *The proper shipping name* specified for the gas in the §172.101 table; or

(2) *An appropriate* common name for the material (e.g., "Refrigerant Gas").

(c) **QT/NQT markings.** Each MC 330 and MC 331 cargo tank must be marked near the specification plate, in letters no less than 50 mm (2.0 inches) in height, with —

(1) *"QT",* if the cargo tank is constructed of quenched and tempered steel; or

(2) *"NQT",* if the cargo tank is constructed of other than quenched and tempered steel.

FEDERAL REGISTER UPDATES

In the April 18, 2003 Federal Register, §172.328 paragraph (d) was added, effective October 1, 2003.

(d) **After October 3, 2005,** each on-vehicle manually-activated remote shutoff device for closure of the internal self-closing stop valve must be identified by marking "Emergency Shutoff" in letters at least 0.75 inches in height, in a color that contrasts with its background, and located in an area immediately adjacent to the means of closure.

§172.330 Tank cars and multi-unit tank car tanks.

(a) **Shipping name and identification number.** No person may offer for transportation or transport a hazardous material —

(1) *In a tank car unless the following conditions are met:*

(i) *The tank car* must be marked on each side and each end as required by §172.302 with the identification number specified for the material in the §172.101 table; and

(ii) *A tank car* containing any of the following materials must be marked on each side with the key words of the proper shipping name specified for the material in the §172.101 table, or with a common name authorized for the material in this subchapter (e.g., "Refrigerant Gas"):

Acrolein, stabilized
Ammonia, anhydrous, liquefied
Ammonia solutions (more than 50% ammonia)
Bromine or Bromine solutions
Bromine chloride
Chloroprene, stabilized
Dispersant gas or Refrigerant gas (as defined in §173.115 of this subchapter)
Division 2.1 materials
Division 2.2 materials (in Class DOT 107 tank cars only)
Division 2.3 materials
Formic acid
Hydrocyanic acid, aqueous solutions
Hydrofluoric acid, solution
Hydrogen cyanide, stabilized (less than 3% water)
Hydrogen fluoride, anhydrous
Hydrogen peroxide, aqueous solutions (greater than 20% hydrogen peroxide)
Hydrogen peroxide, stabilized
Hydrogen peroxide and peroxyacetic acid mixtures
Nitric acid (other than red fuming)
Phosphorus, amorphous
Phosphorus, white dry or Phosphorus, white, under water or Phosphorus white, in solution, or Phosphorus, yellow dry or Phosphorus, yellow, under water or Phosphorus, yellow, in solution
Phosphorus white, molten
Potassium nitrate and sodium nitrate mixtures
Potassium permanganate
Sulfur trioxide, stabilized
Sulfur trioxide, uninhibited

(2) *In a multi-unit tank car tank,* unless the tank is marked on two opposing sides, in letters and numerals no less than 50 mm (2.0 inches) high —

(i) *With the proper shipping name* specified for the material in the §172.101 table or with a common name authorized for the material in this subchapter (e.g., "Refrigerant Gas"); and

(ii) *With the identification number* specified for the material in the §172.101 table, unless marked in accordance with §§172.302(a) and 172.332 of this subpart.

(b) **A motor vehicle or rail car** used to transport a multi-unit tank car tank containing a hazardous material must be marked on each side and each end, as required by §172.332, with the identification number specified for the material in the §172.101 table.

§172.331 Bulk packagings other than portable tanks, cargo tanks, tank cars and multi-unit tank car tanks.

(a) **Each person who offers a hazardous material** to a motor carrier for transportation in a bulk packaging shall provide the motor carrier with the required identification numbers on placards or plain white square-on-point display configurations, as authorized, or shall affix orange panels containing the required identification numbers to the packaging prior to or at the time the material is offered for transportation, unless the packaging is already marked with the identification number as required by this subchapter.

(b) **Each person who offers a bulk packaging** containing a hazardous material for transportation shall affix to the packaging the required identification numbers on orange panels, square-on-point configurations or placards, as appropriate, prior to, or at the time the packaging is offered for transportation unless it is already marked with identification numbers as required by this subchapter.

(c) **For a bulk packaging contained in or on** a transport vehicle or freight container, if the identification number marking on the bulk packaging (e.g., an IBC) required by §172.302(a) not visible, the transport vehicle or freight container must be marked as required by §172.332 on each side and each end with the identification number specified for the material in the §172.101 table.

§172.332 Identification number markings.

(a) **General.** When required by §172.301, §172.302, §172.313, §172.326, §172.328, §172.330, or §172.331, identification number markings must be displayed on orange panels or placards as specified in this section, or on white square-on-point configurations as prescribed in §172.336(b).

(b) **Orange panels.** Display of an identification number on an orange panel shall be in conformance with the following:

(1) *The orange panel* must be 160 mm (6.3 inches) high by 400 mm (15.7 inches) wide with a 15 mm (0.6 inches) black outer border. The identification number shall be displayed in 100 mm (3.9 inches) black Helvetica Medium numerals on the orange panel. Measurements may vary from those specified plus or minus 5 mm (0.2 inches).

(2) *The orange panel* may be made of any durable material prescribed for placards in §172.519, and shall be of the orange color specified for labels or placards in appendix A to this part.

(3) *The name and hazard class* of a material may be shown in the upper left border of the orange panel in letters not more than 18 points high.

(4) *Except for size and color,* the orange panel and identification numbers shall be as illustrated for Liquefied petroleum gas:

1075

(c) **Placards.** Display of an identification number on a hazard warning placard shall be in conformance with the following:

(1) *The identification number* shall be displayed across the center area of the placard in 88 mm (3.5 inches) black Alpine Gothic or Alternate Gothic No. 3 numerals on a white background 100 mm (3.9 inches) high and approximately 215 mm (8.5 inches) wide and may be outlined with a solid or dotted line border.

(2) *The top of the 100 mm* (3.9 inches) high white background shall be approximately 40 mm (1.6 inches) above the placard horizontal center line.

(3) *An identification number* may be displayed only on a placard corresponding to the primary hazard class of the hazardous material.

(4) *For a COMBUSTIBLE placard* used to display an identification number, the entire background below the white background for the identification number must be white during transportation by rail and may be white during transportation by highway.

(5) *The name* of the hazardous material and the hazard class may be shown in letters not more than 18 points high immediately within the upper border of the space on the placard bearing the identification number of the material.

(6) *If an identification number* is placed over the word(s) on a placard, the word(s) should be substantially covered to maximize the effectiveness of the identification number.

(d) **Except for size and color,** the display of an identification number on a placard shall be as illustrated for Acetone:

§172.334 Identification numbers; prohibited display.

(a) **No person may display an identification number** on a RADIOACTIVE, EXPLOSIVES 1.1, 1.2, 1.3, 1.4, 1.5 or 1.6, DANGEROUS, or subsidiary hazard placard.

(b) **No person may display an identification number** on a placard, orange panel or white square-on-point display configuration unless —

(1) *The identification number is specified for the material in §172.101;*

(2) *The identification number* is displayed on the placard, orange panel or white square-on-point configuration authorized by §172.332 or §172.336(b), as appropriate, and any placard used for display of the identification number corresponds to the hazard class of the material specified in §172.504;

(3) *Except as provided* under §172.336 (c)(4) or (c)(5), the package, freight container, or transport vehicle on which the number is displayed contains the hazardous material associated with that identification number in §172.101.

(c) **Except as required by §172.332(c)(4)** for a combustible liquid, the identification number of a material may be displayed only on the placards required by the tables in §172.504.

(d) **Except as provided in §172.336,** a placard bearing an identification number may not be used to meet the requirements of subpart F of this part unless it is the correct identification number for all hazardous materials of the same class in the transport vehicle or freight container on which it is displayed.

(e) **Except as specified in §172.338,** an identification number may not be displayed on an orange panel on a cargo tank unless affixed to the cargo tank by the person offering the hazardous material for transportation in the cargo tank.

(f) **If a placard is required by §172.504,** an identification number may not be displayed on an orange panel unless it is displayed in proximity to the placard.

(g) **No person shall add any color, number, letter,** symbol, or word other than as specified in this subchapter, to any identification number marking display which is required or authorized by this subchapter.

§172.336 Identification numbers; special provisions.

(a) **When not required or prohibited by this subpart,** identification numbers may be displayed on a transport vehicle or a freight container in the manner prescribed by this subpart.

(b) **Identification numbers, when required,** must be displayed on either orange panels (see §172.332(b)) or on a plain white square-on-point display configuration having the same outside dimensions as a placard. In addition, for materials in hazard classes for which placards are specified and identification number displays are required, but for which identification numbers may not be displayed on the placards authorized for the material (see §172.334(a)), identification numbers must be displayed on orange panels or on the plain white square-on-point display configuration in association with the required placards. An identification number displayed on a white square-on-point display configuration is not considered to be a placard.

(1) *The 100 mm* (3.9 inch) by 215 mm (8.5 inches) area containing the identification number shall be located as prescribed by §172.332 (c)(1) and (c)(2) and may be outlined with a solid or dotted line border.

(2) *[Reserved]*

(c) Identification numbers are not required:

(1) *On the ends* of a portable tank, cargo tank or tank car having more than one compartment if hazardous materials having different identification numbers are being transported therein. In such a circumstance, the identification numbers on the sides of the tank shall be displayed in the same sequence as the compartments containing the materials they identify.

(2) *On a cargo tank* containing only gasoline, if the cargo tank is marked "Gasoline" on each side and rear in letters no less than 50 mm (2 inches) high, or is placarded in accordance with §172.542(c).

(3) *On a cargo tank* containing only fuel oil, if the cargo tank is marked "Fuel Oil" on each side and rear in letters no less than 50 mm (2 inches) high, or is placarded in accordance with §172.544(c).

(4) *For each* of the different liquid petroleum distillate fuels, including gasoline and gasohol in a compartmented cargo tank or tank car, if the identification number is displayed for the distillate fuel having the lowest flash point.

(5) *For each* of the different liquid petroleum distillate fuels, including gasoline and gasohol transported in a cargo tank, if the identification number is displayed for the liquid petroleum distillate fuel having the lowest flash point.

(6) *On nurse tanks* meeting the provisions of §173.315(m) of this subchapter.

§172.338 Replacement of identification numbers.

If more than one of the identification number markings on placards, orange panels, or white square-on-point display configurations that are required to be displayed are lost, damaged or destroyed during transportation, the carrier shall replace all the missing or damaged identification numbers as soon as practicable. However, in such a case, the numbers may be entered by hand on the appropriate placard, orange panel or white square-on-point display configuration providing the correct identification numbers are entered legibly using an indelible marking material. When entered by hand, the identification numbers must be located in the white display area specified in §172.332. This section does not preclude required compliance with the placarding requirements of subpart F of this subchapter.

Subpart E - Labeling

§172.400 General labeling requirements.

(a) Except as specified in §172.400a, each person who offers for transportation or transports a hazardous material in any of the following packages or containment devices, shall label the package or containment device with labels specified for the material in the §172.101 table and in this subpart:

(1) *A non-bulk package;*

(2) *A bulk packaging,* other than a cargo tank, portable tank, or tank car, with a volumetric capacity of less than 18 m^3 (640 cubic feet), unless placarded in accordance with subpart F of this part;

(3) *A portable tank* of less than 3785 L (1000 gallons) capacity, unless placarded in accordance with subpart F of this part;

(4) *A DOT Specification* 106 or 110 multi-unit tank car tank, unless placarded in accordance with subpart F of this part; and

(5) *An overpack,* freight container or unit load device, of less than 18 m^3 (640 cubic feet), which contains a package for which labels are required, unless placarded or marked in accordance with §172.512 of this part.

(b) Labeling is required for a hazardous material which meets one or more hazard class definitions, in accordance with column 6 of the §172.101 table and the following table:

Hazard class or division	Label name	Label design or section reference
1.1	EXPLOSIVES 1.1	172.411
1.2	EXPLOSIVES 1.2	172.411
1.3	EXPLOSIVES 1.3	172.411
1.4	EXPLOSIVES 1.4	172.411
1.5	EXPLOSIVES 1.5	172.411
1.6	EXPLOSIVES 1.6	172.411
2.1	FLAMMABLE GAS	172.417
2.2	NONFLAMMABLE GAS	172.415
2.3	POISON GAS	172.416
3 (flammable liquid) Combustible liquid	FLAMMABLE LIQUID (none)	172.419
4.1	FLAMMABLE SOLID	172.420
4.2	SPONTANEOUSLY COMBUSTIBLE	172.422
4.3	DANGEROUS WHEN WET	172.423
5.1	OXIDIZER	172.426
5.2	ORGANIC PEROXIDE	172.427
6.1 (inhalation hazard, Zone A or B)	POISON INHALATION HAZARD	172.429
6.1 (other than inhalation hazard, Zone A or B)	POISON	172.430
6.2	INFECTIOUS SUBSTANCE[1]	172.432
7 (see §172.403)	RADIOACTIVE WHITE-I	172.436
7	RADIOACTIVE YELLOW-II	172.438
7	RADIOACTIVE YELLOW-III	172.440
7 (empty packages, see §173.428 of this subchapter)	EMPTY	172.450
8	CORROSIVE	172.442
9	CLASS 9	172.446

1. The ETIOLOGIC AGENT label specified in regulations of the Department of Health and Human Services at 42 CFR 72.3 may apply to packages of infectious substances.

§172.400a Exceptions from labeling.

(a) Notwithstanding the provisions of §172.400, a label is not required on —

(1) *A cylinder,* or a Dewar flask conforming to §173.320 of this subchapter containing a Division 2.1 or Division 2.2 gas that is —

(i) *Not poisonous;*

(ii) *Carried by a private or contract motor carrier;*

(iii) *Not overpacked; and*

(iv) *Durably and legibly marked* in accordance with CGA Pamphlet C-7, appendix A.

(2) *A package or unit* of military explosives (including ammunition) shipped by or on behalf of the DOD when in —

(i) *Freight containerload,* carload or truckload shipments, if loaded and unloaded by the shipper or DOD; or

(ii) *Unitized or palletized* break-bulk shipments by cargo vessel under charter to DOD if at least one required label is displayed on each unitized or palletized load.

(3) *A package* containing a hazardous material other than ammunition that is —

(i) *Loaded and unloaded* under the supervision of DOD personnel, and

(ii) *Escorted by DOD personnel in a separate vehicle.*

(4) *A compressed gas cylinder* permanently mounted in or on a transport vehicle.

(5) *A freight container, aircraft unit load device or portable tank, which —*

(i) *Is placarded in accordance with subpart F of this part, or*

(ii) *Conforms to paragraph (a)(3) or (b)(3) of §172.512.*

(6) *An overpack* or unit load device in or on which labels representative of each hazardous material in the overpack or unit load device are visible.

(7) *A package* of low specific activity radioactive material and surface contaminated objects, when transported under §173.427(a)(6)(vi) of this subchapter.

(b) **Certain exceptions to labeling requirements** are provided for small quantities and limited quantities in applicable sections in part 173 of this subchapter.

(c) **Notwithstanding the provisions of §172.402(a),** a subsidiary hazard label is not required on a package containing a Class 8 (corrosive) material which has a subsidiary hazard of Division 6.1 (poisonous) if the toxicity of the material is based solely on the corrosive destruction of tissue rather than systemic poisoning.

(d) **A package containing a material** poisonous by inhalation (see §171.8 of this subchapter) in a closed transport vehicle or freight container may be excepted from the POISON INHALATION HAZARD or POISON GAS label or placard, under the conditions set forth in §§171.12 and 171.12a of this subchapter.

§172.401 Prohibited labeling.

(a) **Except as otherwise provided in this section,** no person may offer for transportation and no carrier may transport a package bearing a label specified in this subpart unless:

(1) *The package contains a material that is a hazardous material, and*

(2) *The label* represents a hazard of the hazardous material in the package.

(b) **No person may offer for transportation** and no carrier may transport a package bearing any marking or label which by its color, design, or shape could be confused with or conflict with a label prescribed by this part.

(c) **The restrictions in paragraphs (a) and (b) of this section,** do not apply to packages labeled in conformance with:

(1) *The UN Recommendations (see §171.7 of this subchapter);*

(2) *The IMDG Code (see §171.7 of this subchapter);*

(3) *The ICAO Technical Instructions (see §171.7 of this subchapter);*

(4) *The TDG Regulations (see §171.7 of this subchapter).*

(d) **The provisions of paragraph (a) of this section** do not apply to a packaging bearing a label if that packaging is:

(1) *Unused or cleaned and purged of all residue;*

(2) *Transported in a transport vehicle* or freight container in such a manner that the packaging is not visible during transportation; and

(3) *Loaded by the shipper and unloaded by the shipper or consignee.*

§172.402 Additional labeling requirements.

(a) **Subsidiary hazard labels.** Each package containing a hazardous material —

(1) *Shall be labeled* with primary and subsidiary hazard labels as specified in column 6 of the §172.101 table (unless excepted in paragraph (a)(2) of this section); and

(2) *For other than* Class 1 or Class 2 materials (for subsidiary labeling requirements for Class 1 or Class 2 materials see paragraph (e) or paragraphs (f) and (g), respectively, of this section), if not already labeled under paragraph (a)(1) of this section, shall be labeled with subsidiary hazard labels in accordance with the following table:

Subsidiary Hazard Labels

Subsidiary hazard level (packing group)	Subsidiary Hazard (Class or Division)						
	3	4.1	4.2	4.3	5.1	6.1	8
I	X	***	***	X	X	X	X
II	X	X	X	X	X	X	X
III	*	X	X	X	X	X	X

X — Required for all modes.

* — Required for all modes, except for a material with a flash point at or above 38 °C (100 °F) transported by rail or highway.

** — Reserved

*** — Impossible as subsidiary hazard.

(b) **Display of hazard class on labels.** The appropriate hazard class or division number must be displayed in the lower corner of a primary hazard label and a subsidiary hazard label. A subsidiary label meeting the specifications of this section which were in effect on September 30, 2001, such as, a label without the hazard class or division number displayed in the lower corner of the label) may continue to be used as a subsidiary label in domestic transportation by rail or highway until October 1, 2005, provided the color tolerances are maintained and are in accordance with the display requirements in this subchapter.

(c) **Cargo Aircraft Only label.** Each person who offers for transportation or transports by aircraft a package containing a hazardous material which is authorized on cargo aircraft only shall label the package with a CARGO AIRCRAFT ONLY label specified in §172.448 of this subpart.

(d) **Class 7 (Radioactive) Materials.** Except as otherwise provided in this paragraph, each package containing a Class 7 material that also meets the definition of one or more additional hazard classes must be labeled as a Class 7 material as required by §172.403 of this subpart and for each additional hazard. A subsidiary hazard label is not required on a package containing a Class 7 material that conforms to criteria specified in §173.4 of this subchapter, except §173.4(a)(1)(iv) of this subchapter.

(e) **Class 1 (Explosive) Materials.** In addition to the label specified in column 6 of the §172.101 table, each package of Class 1 material that also meets the definition for:

(1) *Division 6.1,* Packing Groups I or II, shall be labeled POISON or POISON INHALATION HAZARD, as appropriate.

(2) *Class 7,* shall be labeled in accordance with §172.403 of this subpart.

(f) **Division 2.2 materials.** In addition to the label specified in column 6 of the §172.101 table, each package of Division 2.2 material that also meets the definition for an oxidizing gas (see §171.8 of this subchapter) must be labeled OXIDIZER.

(g) **Division 2.3 materials.** In addition to the label specified in column 6 of the §172.101 table, each package of Division 2.3 material that also meets the definition for:

(1) *Division 2.1, must be labeled Flammable Gas;*

(2) *Division 5.1, must be labeled Oxidizer; and*

(3) *Class 8, must be labeled Corrosive.*

§172.403 Class 7 (radioactive) material.

(a) **Unless excepted from labeling by §§173.421 through 173.427** of this subchapter, each package of radioactive material must be labeled as provided in this section.

(b) **The proper label to affix to a package** of Class 7 (radioactive) material is based on the radiation level at the surface of the package and the transport index. The proper category of label must be determined in accordance with paragraph (c) of this section. The label to be applied must be the highest category required for any of the two determining conditions for the package. RADIOACTIVE WHITE-I is the lowest category and RADIOACTIVE YELLOW-III is the highest. For example, a package with a transport index of 0.8 and a maximum surface radiation level of 0.6 millisievert (60 millirems) per hour must bear a RADIOACTIVE YELLOW-III label.

(c) **Category of label to be applied** to Class 7 (radioactive) materials packages:

Transport index	Maximum radiation level at any point on the external surface	Label category[1]
0[2]	Less than or equal to 0.005 mSv/h (0.5 mrem/h)	WHITE-I
More than 0 but not more than 1	Greater than 0.005 mSv/h (0.5 mrem/h) but less than or equal to 0.5 mSv/h (50 mrem/h)	YELLOW-II
More than 1 but not more than 10	Greater than 0.5 mSv/h (50 mrem/h) but less than or equal to 2 mSv/h (200 mrem/h)	YELLOW-III
More than 10	Greater than 2 mSv/h (200 mrem/h) but less than or equal to 10 mSv/h (1,000 mrem/h)	YELLOW-III (Must be shipped under exclusive use provisions; see 173.441(b) of this subchapter.)

1. Any package containing a "highway route controlled quantity" (§173.403 of this subchapter) must be labelled as RADIOACTIVE YELLOW-III.

2. If the measured TI is not greater than 0.05, the value may be considered to be zero.

(d) **EMPTY label.** See §173.428(d) of this subchapter for EMPTY labeling requirements.

(e) **[Reserved]**

(f) **Each package required by this section** to be labeled with a RADIOACTIVE label must have two of these labels, affixed to opposite sides of the package. (See §172.406(e)(3) for freight container label requirements).

(g) **The following applicable items of information** must be entered in the blank spaces on the RADIOACTIVE label by legible printing (manual or mechanical), using a durable weather resistant means of marking:

(1) *Contents.* The name of the radionuclides as taken from the listing of radionuclides in §173.435 of this subchapter (symbols

which conform to established radiation protection terminology are authorized, i.e., \99\Mo, \60\Co, etc.). For mixtures of radionuclides, with consideration of space available on the label, the radionuclides that must be shown must be determined in accordance with §173.433(f) of this subchapter.

(2) *Activity.* Activity units must be expressed in appropriate SI units (e.g., Becquerels (Bq), Terabecquerels (Tbq), etc.) or in both appropriate SI units and appropriate customary units (Curies (Ci), MilliCuries (mCi) microCuries (uCi), etc.). Abbreviations are authorized. Except for plutonium-238, plutonium-239, and plutonium-241, the weight in grams or kilograms of fissile radionuclides may be inserted instead of activity units. For plutonium-238, plutonium-239, and plutonium-241, the weight in grams or kilograms of fissile radionuclides may be inserted in addition to the activity units.

(3) *Transport index.* (See §173.403 of this subchapter.)

§172.404 Labels for mixed and consolidated packaging.

(a) Mixed packaging. When hazardous materials having different hazard classes are packed within the same packaging, or within the same outside container or overpack as described in §173.25 and authorized by §173.21 of this subchapter, the packaging, outside container or overpack must be labeled as required for each class of hazardous material contained therein.

(b) Consolidated packaging. When two or more packages containing compatible hazardous material (see §173.21 of this subchapter) are placed within the same outside container or overpack, the outside container or overpack must be labeled as required for each class of hazardous material contained therein.

§172.405 Authorized label modifications.

(a) For Classes 1, 2, 3, 4, 5, 6, and 8, text indicating a hazard (for example FLAMMABLE LIQUID) is not required on a primary or subsidiary label.

(b) For a package containing Oxygen, compressed, or Oxygen, refrigerated liquid, the OXIDIZER label specified in §172.426 of this subpart, modified to display the word "OXYGEN" instead of "OXIDIZER", and the class number "2" instead of "5.1", may be used in place of the NON-FLAMMABLE GAS and OXIDIZER labels. Notwithstanding the provisions of paragraph (a) of this section, the word "OXYGEN" must appear on the label.

(c) For a package containing a Division 6.1, Packing Group III material, the POISON label specified in §172.430 may be modified to display the text "PG III" instead of "POISON" or "TOXIC" below the mid line of the label. Also see §172.313(d).

§172.406 Placement of labels.

(a) General.

(1) *Except as provided* in paragraphs (b) and (e) of this section, each label required by this subpart must —

(i) *Be printed on* or affixed to a surface (other than the bottom) of the package or containment device containing the hazardous material; and

(ii) *Be located on* the same surface of the package and near the proper shipping name marking, if the package dimensions are adequate.

(2) *Except as provided* in paragraph (e) of this section, duplicate labeling is not required on a package or containment device (such as to satisfy redundant labeling requirements).

(b) Exceptions. A label may be printed on or placed on a securely affixed tag, or may be affixed by other suitable means to:

(1) *A package* that contains no radioactive material and which has dimensions less than those of the required label;

(2) *A cylinder; and*

(3) *A package* which has such an irregular surface that a label cannot be satisfactorily affixed.

(c) Placement of multiple labels. When primary and subsidiary hazard labels are required, they must be displayed next to each other. Placement conforms to this requirement if labels are within 150 mm (6 inches) of one another.

(d) Contrast with background. Each label must be printed on or affixed to a background of contrasting color, or must have a dotted or solid line outer border.

(e) Duplicate labeling. Generally, only one of each different required label must be displayed on a package. However, duplicate labels must be displayed on at least two sides or two ends (other than the bottom) of —

(1) *Each package* or overpack having a volume of 1.8 m^3 (64 cubic feet) or more;

(2) *Each non-bulk package containing a radioactive material;*

(3) *Each DOT* 106 or 110 multi-unit tank car tank. Labels must be displayed on each end;

(4) *Each portable tank of less than 3,785 L (1000 gallons) capacity; and*

(5) *Each freight container* or aircraft unit load device having a volume of 1.8 m^3 (64 cubic feet) or more, but less than 18 m^3 (640 cubic feet). One of each required label must be displayed on or near the closure.

(f) Visibility. A label must be clearly visible and may not be obscured by markings or attachments.

§172.407 Label specifications.

(a) Durability. Each label, whether printed on or affixed to a package, must be durable and weather resistant. A label on a package must be able to withstand, without deterioration or a substantial change in color, a 30-day exposure to conditions incident to transportation that reasonably could be expected to be encountered by the labeled package.

(b) Design.

(1) *Except for size and color,* the printing, inner border, and symbol on each label must be as shown in §§172.411 through 172.448 of this subpart, as appropriate.

(2) *The dotted line border* shown on each label is not part of the label specification, except when used as an alternative for the solid line outer border to meet the requirements of §172.406(d) of this subpart.

(c) Size.

(1) *Each diamond (square-on-point) label* prescribed in this subpart must be at least 100 mm (3.9 inches) on each side with each side having a solid line inner border 5.0 to 6.3 mm (0.2 to 0.25 inches) from the edge.

(2) *The CARGO AIRCRAFT ONLY label* must be a rectangle measuring at least 110 mm (4.3 inches) in height by 120 mm (4.7 inches) in width. The word "DANGER" must be shown in letters measuring at least 12.7 mm (0.5 inches) in height.

(3) *Except as otherwise provided* in this subpart, the hazard class number, or division number, as appropriate, must be at least 6.3 mm (0.25 inches) and not greater than 12.7 mm (0.5 inches).

(4) *When text indicating* a hazard is displayed on a label, the label name must be shown in letters measuring at least 7.6 mm (0.3 inches) in height. For SPONTANEOUSLY COMBUSTIBLE or DANGEROUS WHEN WET labels, the words "Spontaneously" and "When Wet" must be shown in letters measuring at least 5.1 mm (0.2 inches) in height.

(5) *The symbol* on each label must be proportionate in size to that shown in the appropriate section of this subpart.

(d) Color.

(1) *The background color* on each label must be as prescribed in §§172.411 through 172.448 of this subpart, as appropriate.

(2) *The symbol,* text, numbers, and border must be shown in black on a label except that —

(i) *White may be used* on a label with a one color background of green, red or blue; and

(ii) *White must be used* for the text and class number for the CORROSIVE label.

(3) *Black and any color* on a label must be able to withstand, without substantial change, a 72-hour fadeometer test (for a description of equipment designed for this purpose, see ASTM G 23-69 (1975) or ASTM G 26-70).

(4) (i) *A color on a label,* upon visual examination, must fall within the color tolerances —

[A] Displayed on color charts conforming to the technical specifications for charts set forth in table 1 or 2 in appendix A to this part; or

[B] For labels printed on packaging surfaces, specified in table 3 in appendix A to this part.

(ii) *Color charts* conforming to appendix A to this part are on display in Office of Hazardous Materials Safety, Office of Hazardous Materials Standards, Room 8422, Nassif Building, 400 Seventh Street, SW., Washington DC 20590-0001.

(5) *The specified label color* must extend to the edge of the label in the area designated on each label except the CORROSIVE, RADIOACTIVE YELLOW-II AND RADIOACTIVE YELLOW-III labels on which the color must extend only to the inner border.

(e) Form identification. A label may contain form identification information, including the name of its maker, provided that information is printed outside the solid line inner border in no larger than 10-point type.

(f) Exceptions. Except for materials poisonous by inhalation (See §171.8 of this subchapter), a label conforming to specifications in the UN Recommendations may be used in place of a corresponding label that conforms to the requirements of this subpart.

(g) Trefoil symbol. The trefoil symbol on the RADIOACTIVE WHITE-I, RADIOACTIVE YELLOW-II, and RADIOACTIVE YELLOW-III labels must meet the appropriate specifications in appendix B of this part.

§172.411 EXPLOSIVE 1.1, 1.2, 1.3, 1.4, 1.5 and 1.6 labels.

(a) Except for size and color, the EXPLOSIVE 1.1, EXPLOSIVE 1.2 and EXPLOSIVE 1.3 labels must be as follows:

(b) In addition to complying with §172.407, the background color on the EXPLOSIVE 1.1, EXPLOSIVE 1.2 and EXPLOSIVE 1.3 labels must be orange. The "**" shall be replaced with the appropriate division number and compatibility group. The compatibility group letter must be the same size as the division number and must be shown as a capitalized Roman letter.

(c) Except for size and color, the EXPLOSIVE 1.4, EXPLOSIVE 1.5 and EXPLOSIVE 1.6 labels must be as follows:

EXPLOSIVE 1.4:

EXPLOSIVE 1.5:

EXPLOSIVE 1.6:

(d) In addition to complying with §172.407, the background color on the EXPLOSIVE 1.4, EXPLOSIVE 1.5, EXPLOSIVE 1.6 and EXPLOSIVE subsidiary label must be orange. The "*" shall be replaced with the appropriate compatibility group. The compatibility group letter must be shown as a capitalized Roman letter. Division numerals must measure at least 30 mm (1.2 inches) in height and at least 5 mm (0.2 inches) in width.

§172.415 NON-FLAMMABLE GAS label.

(a) Except for size and color, the NON-FLAMMABLE GAS label must be as follows:

(b) In addition to complying with §172.407, the background color on the NON-FLAMMABLE GAS label must be green.

§172.416 POISON GAS label.

(a) **Except for size and color,** the POISON GAS label must be as follows:

(b) **In addition to complying with §172.407,** the background on the POISON GAS label and the symbol must be white. The background of the upper diamond must be black and the lower point of the upper diamond must be 14 mm (0.54 inches) above the horizontal center line.

§172.417 FLAMMABLE GAS label.

(a) **Except for size and color,** the FLAMMABLE GAS label must be as follows:

(b) **In addition to complying with §172.407,** the background color on the FLAMMABLE GAS label must be red.

§172.419 FLAMMABLE LIQUID label.

(a) **Except for size and color,** the FLAMMABLE LIQUID label must be as follows:

(b) **In addition to complying with §172.407,** the background color on the FLAMMABLE LIQUID label must be red.

§172.420 FLAMMABLE SOLID label.

(a) **Except for size and color,** the FLAMMABLE SOLID label must be as follows:

(b) **In addition to complying with §172.407,** the background on the FLAMMABLE SOLID label must be white with vertical red stripes equally spaced on each side of a red stripe placed in the center of the label. The red vertical stripes must be spaced so that, visually, they appear equal in width to the white spaces between them. The symbol (flame) and text (when used) must be overprinted. The text "FLAMMABLE SOLID" may be placed in a white rectangle.

§172.422 SPONTANEOUSLY COMBUSTIBLE label.

(a) **Except for size and color,** the SPONTANEOUSLY COMBUSTIBLE label must be as follows:

(b) **In addition to complying with §172.407,** the background color on the lower half of the SPONTANEOUSLY COMBUSTIBLE label must be red and the upper half must be white.

§172.423 DANGEROUS WHEN WET label.

(a) **Except for size and color,** the DANGEROUS WHEN WET label must be as follows:

(b) **In addition to complying with §172.407,** the background color on the DANGEROUS WHEN WET label must be blue.

§172.426 OXIDIZER label.

(a) **Except for size and color,** the OXIDIZER label must be as follows:

(b) **In addition to complying with §172.407,** the background color on the OXIDIZER label must be yellow.

§172.427 ORGANIC PEROXIDE label.

(a) **Except for size and color,** the ORGANIC PEROXIDE label must be as follows:

(b) **In addition to complying with §172.407,** the background color on the ORGANIC PEROXIDE label must be yellow.

§172.429 POISON INHALATION HAZARD label.

(a) **Except for size and color,** the POISON INHALATION HAZARD label must be as follows:

(b) **In addition to complying with §172.407,** the background on the POISON INHALATION HAZARD label and the symbol must be white. The background of the upper diamond must be black and the lower point of the upper diamond must be 14 mm (0.54 inches) above the horizontal center line.

§172.430 POISON label.

(a) **Except for size and color, the POISON label must be as follows:**

(b) **In addition to complying with §172.407,** the background on the POISON label must be white. The word "TOXIC" may be used in lieu of the word "POISON".

§172.431 [Reserved]

§172.432 INFECTIOUS SUBSTANCE label.

(a) **Except for size and color,** the INFECTIOUS SUBSTANCE label must be as follows:

(b) **In addition to complying with §172.407,** the background on the INFECTIOUS SUBSTANCE label must be white.

§172.436 RADIOACTIVE WHITE-I label.

(a) **Except for size and color,** the RADIOACTIVE WHITE-I label must be as follows:

(b) **In addition to complying with §172.407,** the background on the RADIOACTIVE WHITE-I label must be white. The printing and symbol must be black, except for the "I" which must be red.

172 Table, Special Provisions, Communications, and More

§172.438 RADIOACTIVE YELLOW-II label.

(a) **Except for size and color,** the RADIOACTIVE YELLOW-II label must be as follows:

(b) **In addition to complying with §172.407,** the background color on the RADIOACTIVE YELLOW-II label must be yellow in the top half and white in the lower half. The printing and symbol must be black, except for the "II" which must be red.

§172.440 RADIOACTIVE YELLOW-III label.

(a) **Except for size and color,** the RADIOACTIVE YELLOW-III label must be as follows:

(b) **In addition to complying with §172.407,** the background color on the RADIOACTIVE YELLOW-III label must be yellow in the top half and white in the lower half. The printing and symbol must be black, except for the "III" which must be red.

§172.442 CORROSIVE label.

(a) **Except for size and color,** the CORROSIVE label must be as follows:

(b) **In addition to complying with §172.407,** the background on the CORROSIVE label must be white in the top half and black in the lower half.

§172.444 [Reserved]

§172.446 CLASS 9 label.

(a) **Except for size and color,** the "CLASS 9" (miscellaneous hazardous materials) label must be as follows:

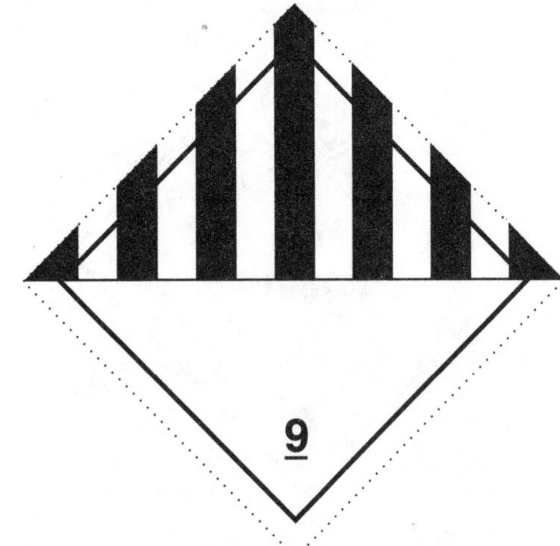

(b) **In addition to complying with §172.407,** the background on the CLASS 9 label must be white with seven black vertical stripes on the top half. The black vertical stripes must be spaced, so that, visually, they appear equal in width to the six white spaces between them. The lower half of the label must be white with the class number "9" underlined and centered at the bottom.

§172.448 CARGO AIRCRAFT ONLY label.

(a) Except for size and color, the CARGO AIRCRAFT ONLY label must be as follows:

(b) The CARGO AIRCRAFT ONLY label must be black on an orange background.

§172.450 EMPTY label.

(a) Each EMPTY label, except for size, must be as follows:

(1) *Each side must be* at least 6 inches (152 mm.) with each letter at least 1 inch (25.4 mm.) in height.
(2) *The label must be white with black printing.*

(b) [Reserved]

Subpart F - Placarding

§172.500 Applicability of placarding requirements.

(a) Each person who offers for transportation or transports any hazardous material subject to this subchapter shall comply with the applicable placarding requirements of this subpart.

(b) This subpart does not apply to —

(1) *Infectious substances;*
(2) *Hazardous materials classed as ORM-D;*
(3) *Hazardous materials* authorized by this subchapter to be offered for transportation as Limited Quantities when identified as such on shipping papers in accordance with §172.203(b);
(4) *Hazardous materials* prepared in accordance with §173.13 of this subchapter;
(5) *Hazardous materials* which are packaged as small quantities under the provisions of §173.4 of this subchapter; and
(6) *Combustible liquids in non-bulk packagings.*

§172.502 Prohibited and permissive placarding.

(a) Prohibited placarding. Except as provided in paragraph (b) of this section, no person may affix or display on a packaging, freight container, unit load device, motor vehicle or rail car —

(1) *Any placard described in this subpart unless —*
(i) *The material being offered or transported is a hazardous material;*
(ii) *The placard* represents a hazard of the hazardous material being offered or transported; and
(iii) *Any placarding conforms to the requirements of this subpart.*
(2) *Any sign,* advertisement, slogan (such as "Drive Safely"), or device that, by its color, design, shape or content, could be confused with any placard prescribed in this subpart.

(b) Exceptions.

(1) *The restrictions* in paragraph (a) of this section do not apply to a bulk packaging, freight container, unit load device, transport vehicle or rail car which is placarded in conformance with TDG Regulations, the IMDG Code or the UN Recommendations (see §171.7 of this subchapter).
(2) *The restrictions* of paragraph (a) of this section do not apply to the display of a BIOHHAZARD marking, a "HOT" marking, or an identification number on a white square-on-point configuration in accordance with §§172.323(c), 172.325(c), or 172.336(b) of this part, respectively.
(3) *The restrictions* in paragraph (a)(2) of this section do not apply until October 1, 2001 to a safety sign or safety slogan (e.g., "Drive Safely" or "Drive Carefully"), which was permanently marked on a transport vehicle, bulk packaging, or freight container on or before August 21, 1997.

(c) Permissive placarding. Placards may be displayed for a hazardous material, even when not required, if the placarding otherwise conforms to the requirements of this subpart.

§172.503 Identification number display on placards.

For procedures and limitations pertaining to the display of identification numbers on placards, see §172.334.

§172.504 General placarding requirements.

(a) General. Except as otherwise provided in this subchapter, each bulk packaging, freight container, unit load device, transport vehicle or rail car containing any quantity of a hazardous material must be placarded on each side and each end with the type of placards specified in tables 1 and 2 of this section and in accordance with other placarding requirements of this subpart, including the specifications for the placards named in the tables and described in detail in §§172.519 through 172.560.

(b) DANGEROUS placard. A freight container, unit load device, transport vehicle, or rail car which contains non-bulk packages with two or more categories of hazardous materials that require different placards specified in table 2 of paragraph (e) of this section may be placarded with a DANGEROUS placard instead of the separate placarding specified for each of the materials in table 2 of paragraph (e) of this section. However, when 1,000 kg (2,205 pounds) aggregate gross weight or more of one category of material is loaded therein at one loading facility on a freight container, unit load device, transport vehicle, or rail car, the placard specified in table 2 of paragraph (e) of this section for that category must be applied.

(c) Exception for less than 454 kg (1,001 pounds). Except for bulk packagings and hazardous materials subject to §172.505, when hazardous materials covered by table 2 of this section are transported by highway or rail, placards are not required on —

(1) *A transport vehicle* or freight container which contains less than 454 kg (1001 pounds) aggregate gross weight of hazardous materials covered by table 2 of paragraph (e) of this section; or
(2) *A rail car* loaded with transport vehicles or freight containers, none of which is required to be placarded. The exceptions provided in paragraph (c) of this section do not prohibit the display of placards in the manner prescribed in this subpart, if not otherwise prohibited (see §172.502), on transport vehicles or freight containers which are not required to be placarded.

(d) Exception for empty non-bulk packages. A non-bulk packaging that contains only the residue of a hazardous material covered by table 2 of paragraph (e) of this section need not be included in determining placarding requirements.

(e) Placarding tables. Placards are specified for hazardous materials in accordance with the following tables:

Table 1

Category of material (Hazard class or division number and additional description, as appropriate)	Placard name	Placard design section reference (§)
1.1	EXPLOSIVES 1.1	172.522
1.2	EXPLOSIVES 1.2	172.522
1.3	EXPLOSIVES 1.3	172.522
2.3	POISON GAS	172.540
4.3	DANGEROUS WHEN WET	172.548
5.2 (Organic peroxide, Type B, liquid or solid, temperature controlled)	ORGANIC PEROXIDE	172.552
6.1 (inhalation hazard, Zone A or B)	POISON INHALATION HAZARD	172.555
7 (Radioactive Yellow III label only)	RADIOACTIVE[1]	172.556

1. RADIOACTIVE placard also required for exclusive use shipments of low specific activity material and surface contaminated objects transported in accordance with §173.427(a) of this subchapter.

Table 2

Category of material (Hazard class or division number and additional description, as appropriate)	Placard name	Placard design section reference (§)
1.4	EXPLOSIVES 1.4	172.523
1.5	EXPLOSIVES 1.5	172.524
1.6	EXPLOSIVES 1.6	172.525
2.1	FLAMMABLE GAS	172.532
2.2	NON-FLAMMABLE GAS	172.528
3	FLAMMABLE	172.542
Combustible liquid	COMBUSTIBLE	172.544
4.1	FLAMMABLE SOLID	172.546
4.2	SPONTANEOUSLY COMBUSTIBLE	172.547
5.1	OXIDIZER	172.550
5.2 (Other than organic peroxide, Type B, liquid or solid, temperature controlled)	ORGANIC PEROXIDE	172.552
6.1 (other than inhalation hazard, Zone A or B)	POISON	172.554
6.2	(None)	
8	CORROSIVE	172.558
9	Class 9 (see §172.504(f)(9))	172.560
ORM-D	(None)	

(f) Additional placarding exceptions.

(1) *When more than one* division placard is required for Class 1 materials on a transport vehicle, rail car, freight container or unit load device, only the placard representing the lowest division number must be displayed.

(2) *A FLAMMABLE placard* may be used in place of a COMBUSTIBLE placard on —

(i) *A cargo tank or portable tank.*

(ii) *A compartmented tank car* which contains both flammable and combustible liquids.

(3) *A NON-FLAMMABLE GAS placard* is not required on a transport vehicle which contains non-flammable gas if the transport vehicle also contains flammable gas or oxygen and it is placarded with FLAMMABLE GAS or OXYGEN placards, as required.

(4) *OXIDIZER placards* are not required for Division 5.1 materials on freight containers, unit load devices, transport vehicles or rail cars which also contain Division 1.1 or 1.2 materials and which are placarded with EXPLOSIVES 1.1 or 1.2 placards, as required.

(5) *For transportation* by transport vehicle or rail car only, an OXIDIZER placard is not required for Division 5.1 materials on a transport vehicle, rail car or freight container which also contains Division 1.5 explosives and is placarded with EXPLOSIVES 1.5 placards, as required.

(6) *The EXPLOSIVE 1.4 placard* is not required for those Division 1.4 Compatibility Group S (1.4S) materials that are not required to be labeled 1.4S.

(7) *For domestic transportation of oxygen,* compressed or oxygen, refrigerated liquid, the OXYGEN placard in §172.530 of this subpart may be used in place of a NON-FLAMMABLE GAS placard.

(8) *For domestic transportation,* a POISON INHALATION HAZARD placard is not required on a transport vehicle or freight container that is already placarded with the POISON GAS placard.

(9) *For domestic transportation,* a Class 9 placard is not required. A bulk packaging containing a Class 9 material must be marked with the appropriate identification number displayed on a Class 9 placard, an orange panel or a white-square-on-point display configuration as required by subpart D of this part.

(10) *For Division 6.* 1, PG III materials, a POISON placard may be modified to display the text "PG III" below the mid line of the placard.

(11) *For domestic transportation,* a POISON placard is not required on a transport vehicle or freight container required to display a POISON INHALATION HAZARD or POISON GAS placard.

(g) For shipments of Class 1 (explosive) materials by aircraft or vessel, the applicable compatibility group letter must be displayed on the placards required by this section. When more than one compatibility group placard is required for Class 1 materials, only one placard is required to be displayed as follows:

(1) *Explosive articles* of compatibility groups C, D or E may be placarded displaying compatibility group E.

(2) *Explosive articles* of compatibility groups C, D, E or N may be placarded displaying compatibility group D.

(3) *Explosive substances* of compatibility groups C and D may be placarded displaying compatibility group D.

(4) *Explosive articles* of compatibility groups C, D, E or G, except for fireworks, may be placarded displaying compatibility group E.

§172.505 Placarding for subsidiary hazards.

(a) Each transport vehicle, freight container, portable tank, unit load device, or rail car that contains a poisonous material subject to the "Poison Inhalation Hazard" shipping description of §172.203(m)(2) must be placarded with a POISON INHALATION HAZARD or POISON GAS placard, as appropriate, on each side and each end, in addition to any other placard required for that material in §172.504. Duplication of the POISON INHALATION HAZARD or POISON GAS placard is not required.

(b) In addition to the RADIOACTIVE placard which may be required by §172.504(e) of this subpart, each transport vehicle, portable tank or freight container that contains 454 kg (1001 pounds) or more gross weight of fissile or low specific activity uranium hexafluoride shall be placarded with a CORROSIVE placard on each side and each end.

(c) Each transport vehicle, portable tank, freight container or unit load device that contains a material which has a subsidiary hazard of being dangerous when wet, as defined in §173.124 of this subchapter, shall be placarded with DANGEROUS WHEN WET placards, on each side and each end, in addition to the placards required by §172.504.

(d) Hazardous materials that possess secondary hazards may exhibit subsidiary placards that correspond to the placards described in this part, even when not required by this part (see also §172.519(b) (4) of this subpart).

§172.506 Providing and affixing placards: Highway.

(a) Each person offering a motor carrier a hazardous material for transportation by highway shall provide to the motor carrier the required placards for the material being offered prior to or at the same time the material is offered for transportation, unless the carrier's motor vehicle is already placarded for the material as required by this subpart.

(1) *No motor carrier* may transport a hazardous material in a motor vehicle, unless the placards required for the hazardous material are affixed thereto as required by this subpart.

(2) *[Reserved]*

(b) [Reserved]

§172.507 Special placarding provisions: Highway.

(a) Each motor vehicle used to transport a package of highway route controlled quantity Class 7 (radioactive) materials (see §173.403 of this subchapter) must have the required RADIOACTIVE warning placard placed on a square background as described in §172.527.

(b) A nurse tank, meeting the provisions of §173.315(m) of this subchapter, is not required to be placarded on an end containing valves, fittings, regulators or gauges when those appurtenances prevent the markings and placard from being properly placed and visible.

§172.508 Placarding and affixing placards: Rail.

(a) Each person offering a hazardous material for transportation by rail shall affix to the rail car containing the material, the placards specified by this subpart. Placards displayed on motor vehicles, transport containers, or portable tanks may be used to satisfy this requirement, if the placards otherwise conform to the provisions of this subpart.

(b) No rail carrier may accept a rail car containing a hazardous material for transportation unless the placards for the hazardous material are affixed thereto as required by this subpart.

§172.510 Special placarding provisions: Rail.

(a) White square background. The following must have the specified placards placed on a white square background, as described in §172.527:

(1) *Division 1.1 and 1.2* (explosive) materials which require EXPLOSIVES 1.1 or EXPLOSIVES 1.2 placards affixed to the rail car;

(2) *Materials classed* in Division 2.3 Hazard Zone A or 6.1 Packing Group I Hazard Zone A which require POISON GAS or POISON placards affixed to the rail car, including tank cars containing only a residue of the material; and

(3) *Class DOT 113 tank cars* used to transport a Division 2.1 (flammable gas) material, including tank cars containing only a residue of the material.

(b) Chemical ammunition. Each rail car containing Division 1.1 or 1.2 (explosive) ammunition which also meets the definition of a material poisonous by inhalation (see §171.8 of this subchapter) must be placarded EXPLOSIVES 1.1 or EXPLOSIVES 1.2 and POISON GAS or POISON INHALATION HAZARD.

§172.512 Freight containers and aircraft unit load devices.

(a) Capacity of 640 cubic feet or more. Each person who offers for transportation, and each person who loads and transports, a hazardous material in a freight container or aircraft unit load device having a capacity of 640 cubic feet or more shall affix to the freight container or aircraft unit load device the placards specified for the material in accordance with §172.504. However:

(1) *The placarding exception* provided in §172.504(c) applies to motor vehicles transporting freight containers and aircraft unit load devices,

(2) *The placarding exception* provided in §172.504(c) applies to each freight container and aircraft unit load device being transported for delivery to a consignee immediately following an air or water shipment, and,

(3) *Placarding is not required* on a freight container or aircraft unit load device if it is only transported by air and is identified as containing a hazardous material in the manner provided in part 5, chapter 2, section 2.7, of the ICAO Technical Instructions (see §171.7 of this subchapter).

(b) Capacity less than 18 m^3 (640 cubic feet). Each person who offers for transportation by air, and each person who loads and transports by air, a hazardous material in a freight container or aircraft unit load device having a capacity of less than 18 m^3 (640 cubic feet) shall affix one placard of the type specified by paragraph (a) of this section unless the freight container or aircraft unit load device:

(1) *Is labeled* in accordance with subpart E of this part, including §172.406(e);

(2) *Contains radioactive materials* requiring the Radioactive Yellow III label and is placarded with one Radioactive placard and is labeled in accordance with subpart E of this part, including §172.406(e); or,

(3) *Is identified* as containing a hazardous material in the manner provided in part 5, chapter 2, section 2.7, of the ICAO Technical Instructions.

When hazardous materials are offered for transportation, not involving air transportation, in a freight container having a capacity of less than 640 cubic feet the freight container need not be placarded. However, if not placarded it must be labeled in accordance with subpart E of this part.

(c) Notwithstanding paragraphs (a) and (b) of this section, packages containing hazardous materials, other than ORM-D, offered for transportation by air in freight containers are subject to the inspection requirements of §175.30 of this chapter.

§172.514 Bulk packagings.

(a) Except as provided in paragraph (c) of this section, each person who offers for transportation a bulk packaging which contains a hazardous material, shall affix the placards specified for the material in §§172.504 and 172.505.

(b) Each bulk packaging that is required to be placarded when it contains a hazardous material, must remain placarded when it is emptied, unless it is —

(1) *Sufficiently cleaned* of residue and purged of vapors to remove any potential hazard; or

(2) *Refilled, with a material* requiring different placards or no placards, to such an extent that any residue remaining in the packaging is no longer hazardous.

(c) Exceptions. The following packagings may be placarded on only two opposite sides or, alternatively, may be labeled instead of placarded in accordance with subpart E of this part:

(1) *A portable tank* having a capacity of less than 3,785 L (1000 gallons);

(2) *A DOT 106 or 110 multi-unit tank car tank;*

(3) *A bulk packaging* other than a portable tank, cargo tank, or tank car (e.g., a bulk bag or box) with a volumetric capacity of less than 18 m^3 (640 cubic feet); and

(4) *An IBC.*

§172.516 Visibility and display of placards.

(a) Each placard on a motor vehicle and each placard on a rail car must be clearly visible from the direction it faces, except from the direction of another transport vehicle or rail car to which the motor vehicle or rail car is coupled. This requirement may be met by the placards displayed on the freight containers or portable tanks loaded on a motor vehicle or rail car.

(b) The required placarding of the front of a motor vehicle may be on the front of a truck-tractor instead of or in addition to the placarding on the front of the cargo body to which a truck-tractor is attached.

(c) Each placard on a transport vehicle, bulk packaging, freight container or aircraft unit load device must —

(1) *Be securely attached* or affixed thereto or placed in a holder thereon. (See appendix C to this part.);

(2) *Be located* clear of appurtenances and devices such as ladders, pipes, doors, and tarpaulins;

(3) *So far as practicable,* be located so that dirt or water is not directed to it from the wheels of the transport vehicle;

(4) *Be located* away from any marking (such as advertising) that could substantially reduce its effectiveness, and in any case at least 3 inches (76.0 mm.) away from such marking;

(5) *Have the words* or identification number (when authorized) printed on it displayed horizontally, reading from left to right;

(6) *Be maintained* by the carrier in a condition so that the format, legibility, color, and visibility of the placard will not be substantially reduced due to damage, deterioration, or obscurement by dirt or other matter;

(7) *Be affixed* to a background of contrasting color, or must have a dotted or solid line outer border which contrasts with the background color.

(d) Recommended specifications for a placard holder are set forth in appendix C of this part. Except for a placard holder similar to that contained in appendix C to this part, the means used to attach a placard may not obscure any part of its surface other than the borders.

(e) A placard or placard holder may be hinged provided the required format, color, and legibility of the placard are maintained.

§172.519 General specifications for placards.

(a) Strength and durability. Placards must conform to the following:

(1) *A placard* may be made of any plastic, metal or other material capable of withstanding, without deterioration or a substantial reduction in effectiveness, a 30-day exposure to open weather conditions.

(2) *A placard* made of tagboard must be at least equal to that designated commercially as white tagboard. Tagboard must have a weight of at least 80 kg (176 pounds) per ream of 610 by 910 mm (24 by 36-inch) sheets, waterproofing materials included. In addition, each placard made of tagboard must be able to pass a 414 kPa (60 p.s.i.) Mullen test.

(3) *Reflective or retroreflective materials* may be used on a placard if the prescribed colors, strength and durability are maintained.

(b) Design.

(1) *Except as provided* in §172.332 of this part, each placard must be as described in this subpart, and except for size and color, the printing, inner border and symbol must be as shown in §§172.521 through 172.560 of this subpart, as appropriate.

(2) *The dotted line border* shown on each placard is not part of the placard specification. However, a dotted or solid line outer border may be used when needed to indicate the full size of a placard that is part of a larger format or is on a background of a noncontrasting color.

(3) *For other than Class 7* or the DANGEROUS placard, text indicating a hazard (for example, "FLAMMABLE") is not required. Text may be omitted from the OXYGEN placard only if the specific identification number is displayed on the placard.

(4) *For a placard* corresponding to the primary or subsidiary hazard class of a material, the hazard class or division number must be displayed in the lower corner of the placard. However, a permanently affixed subsidiary placard meeting the specifications of this section which were in effect on October 1, 2001, (such as, a placard without the hazard class or division number displayed in the lower corner of the placard) and which was installed prior to October 1, 2001, may continue to be used as a subsidiary placard in domestic transportation by rail or highway, provided the color tolerances are maintained and are in accordance with the display requirements in this subchapter. Stocks of non-permanently affixed subsidiary placards in compliance with the requirements in effect on September 30, 2001, may continue to be used in domestic transportation by rail or highway until October 1, 2005, or until current stocks are depleted, whichever occurs first.

(c) Size.

(1) *Each placard* prescribed in this subpart must measure at least 273 mm (10.8 inches) on each side and must have a solid line inner border approximately 12.7 mm (0.5 inches) from each edge.

(2) *Except as otherwise provided* in this subpart, the hazard class or division number, as appropriate, must be shown in numerals measuring at least 41 mm (1.6 inches) in height.

(3) *Except as otherwise provided* in this subpart, when text indicating a hazard is displayed on a placard, the printing must be in letters measuring at least 41 mm (1.6 inches) in height.

(d) **Color.**

(1) *The background color,* symbol, text, numerals and inner border on a placard must be as specified in §§172.521 through 172.560 of this subpart, as appropriate.

(2) *Black and any color* on a placard must be able to withstand, without substantial change —

(i) *A 72-hour fadeometer test* (for a description of equipment designed for this purpose, see ASTM G 23-69 or ASTM G 26-70); and

(ii) *A 30-day exposure to open weather.*

(3) *Upon visual examination,* a color on a placard must fall within the color tolerances displayed on the appropriate Hazardous Materials Label and Placard Color Tolerance Chart (see §172.407(d)(4)).

(4) *The placard color* must extend to the inner border and may extend to the edge of the placard in the area designated on each placard except the color on the CORROSIVE and RADIOACTIVE placards (black and yellow, respectively) must extend only to the inner border.

(e) **Form identification.** A placard may contain form identification information, including the name of its maker, provided that information is printed outside of the solid line inner border in no larger than 10-point type.

(f) **Exceptions.** When hazardous materials are offered for transportation or transported under the provisions of §§171.11, 171.12, or 171.12a of this subchapter, a placard conforming to the specifications in the ICAO Technical Instructions, the IMDG Code, or the TDG Regulations, respectively, may be used in place of a corresponding placard that conforms to the requirements of this subpart, except that a bulk packaging, transport vehicle, or freight container containing a material poisonous by inhalation (see §171.8 of this subchapter) must be placarded in accordance with this subpart (see §§171.12(b)(8), 171.12(e) and 171.12a(b)(5) of this subchapter).

(g) **Trefoil symbol.** The trefoil symbol on the RADIOACTIVE placard must meet the appropriate specification in appendix B of this part.

§172.521 DANGEROUS placard.

(a) **Except for size and color,** the DANGEROUS placard must be as follows:

(b) **In addition to meeting the requirements of §172.519,** and appendix B to this part, the DANGEROUS placard must have a red upper and lower triangle. The placard center area and 1/2-inch (12.7 mm.) border must be white. The inscription must be black with the 1/8-inch (3.2 mm.) border marker in the white area at each end of the inscription red.

§172.522 EXPLOSIVES 1.1, EXPLOSIVES 1.2 and EXPLOSIVES 1.3 placards.

(a) **Except for size and color,** the EXPLOSIVES 1.1, EXPLOSIVES 1.2 and EXPLOSIVES 1.3 placards must be as follows:

(b) **In addition to complying with §172.519 of this subpart,** the background color on the EXPLOSIVES 1.1, EXPLOSIVES 1.2, and EXPLOSIVES 1.3 placards must be orange. The "*" shall be replaced with the appropriate division number and, when required, appropriate compatibility group letter. The symbol, text, numerals and inner border must be black.

§172.523 EXPLOSIVES 1.4 placard.

(a) **Except for size and color,** the EXPLOSIVES 1.4 placard must be as follows:

(b) **In addition to complying with §172.519 of this subpart,** the background color on the EXPLOSIVES 1.4 placard must be orange. The "*" shall be replaced, when required, with the appropriate compatibility group letter. The division numeral, 1.4, must measure at least 64 mm (2.5 inches) in height. The text, numerals and inner border must be black.

§172.524 EXPLOSIVES 1.5 placard.

(a) **Except for size and color,** the EXPLOSIVES 1.5 placard must be as follows:

(b) **In addition to complying with the §172.519 of this subpart,** the background color on EXPLOSIVES 1.5 placard must be orange. The "*" shall be replaced, when required, with the appropriate compatibility group letter. The division numeral, 1.5, must measure at least 64 mm (2.5 inches) in height. The text, numerals and inner border must be black.

§172.525 EXPLOSIVES 1.6 placard.

(a) **Except for size and color,** the EXPLOSIVES 1.6 placard must be as follows:

(b) **In addition to complying with §172.519 of this subpart,** the background color on the EXPLOSIVES 1.6 placard must be orange. The "*" shall be replaced, when required, with the appropriate compatibility group letter. The division numeral, 1.6, must measure at least 64 mm (2.5 inches) in height. The text, numerals and inner border must be black.

§172.526 [Reserved]

§172.527 Background requirements for certain placards.

(a) **Except for size and color,** the square background required by §172.510(a) for certain placards on rail cars, and §172.507 for placards on motor vehicles containing a package of highway route controlled quantity radioactive materials, must be as follows:

(b) **In addition to meeting the requirements of §172.519** for minimum durability and strength, the square background must consist of a white square measuring 14 1/4 inches (362.0 mm.) on each side surrounded by a black border extending to 15 1/4 inches (387.0 mm.) on each side.

§172.528 NON-FLAMMABLE GAS placard.

(a) **Except for size and color,** the NON-FLAMMABLE GAS placard must be as follows:

(b) **In addition to complying with §172.519,** the background color on the NON-FLAMMABLE GAS placard must be green. The letters in both words must be at least 38 mm (1.5 inches) high. The symbol, text, class number and inner border must be white.

§172.530 OXYGEN placard.

(a) **Except for size and color,** the OXYGEN placard must be as follows:

(b) **In addition to complying with §172.519 of this subpart,** the background color on the OXYGEN placard must be yellow. The symbol, text, class number and inner border must be black.

§172.532 FLAMMABLE GAS placard.

(a) **Except for size and color,** the FLAMMABLE GAS placard must be as follows:

(b) **In addition to complying with §172.519,** the background color on the FLAMMABLE GAS placard must be red. The symbol, text, class number and inner border must be white.

§172.536 [Reserved]

§172.540 POISON GAS placard.

(a) **Except for size and color,** the POISON GAS placard must be as follows:

(b) **In addition to complying with §172.519,** the background on the POISON GAS placard and the symbol must be white. The background of the upper diamond must be black and the lower point of the upper diamond must be 65 mm (2 5/8 inches) above the horizontal center line. The text, class number, and inner border must be black.

§172.542 FLAMMABLE placard.

(a) **Except for size and color,** the FLAMMABLE placard must be as follows:

(b) **In addition to complying with §172.519,** the background color on the FLAMMABLE placard must be red. The symbol, text, class number and inner border must be white.

(c) **The word "GASOLINE" may be used** in place of the word "FLAMMABLE" on a placard that is displayed on a cargo tank or a portable tank being used to transport gasoline by highway. The word "GASOLINE" must be shown in white.

§172.544 COMBUSTIBLE placard.

(a) **Except for size and color,** the COMBUSTIBLE placard must be as follows:

(b) **In addition to complying with §172.519,** the background color on the COMBUSTIBLE placard must be red. The symbol, text, class number and inner border must be white. On a COMBUSTIBLE placard with a white bottom as prescribed by §172.332(c)(4), the class number must be red or black.

(c) **The words "FUEL OIL" may be used** in place of the word "COMBUSTIBLE" on a placard that is displayed on a cargo tank or portable tank being used to transport by highway fuel oil that is not classed as a flammable liquid. The words "FUEL OIL" must be white.

§172.546 FLAMMABLE SOLID placard.

(a) **Except for size and color,** the FLAMMABLE SOLID placard must be as follows:

(b) **In addition to complying with §172.519,** the background on the FLAMMABLE SOLID placard must be white with seven vertical red stripes. The stripes must be equally spaced, with one red stripe placed in the center of the label. Each red stripe and each white space between two red stripes must be 25 mm (1.0 inches) wide. The letters in the word "SOLID" must be at least 38.1 mm (1.5 inches) high. The symbol, text, class number and inner border must be black.

§172.547 SPONTANEOUSLY COMBUSTIBLE placard.

(a) **Except for size and color,** the SPONTANEOUSLY COMBUSTIBLE placard must be as follows:

(b) **In addition to complying with §172.519,** the background color on the SPONTANEOUSLY COMBUSTIBLE placard must be red in the lower half and white in upper half. The letters in the word "SPONTANEOUSLY" must be at least 12 mm (0.5 inch) high. The symbol, text, class number and inner border must be black.

§172.548 DANGEROUS WHEN WET placard.

(a) **Except for size and color,** the DANGEROUS WHEN WET placard must be as follows:

(b) **In addition to complying with §172.519,** the background color on the DANGEROUS WHEN WET placard must be blue. The letters in the words "WHEN WET" must be at least 25 mm (1.0 inches) high. The symbol, text, class number and inner border must be white.

§172.550 OXIDIZER placard.

(a) **Except for size and color,** the OXIDIZER placard must be as follows:

(b) **In addition to complying with §172.519,** the background color on the OXIDIZER placard must be yellow. The symbol, text, division number and inner border must be black.

§172.552 ORGANIC PEROXIDE placard.

(a) **Except for size and color,** the ORGANIC PEROXIDE placard must be as follows:

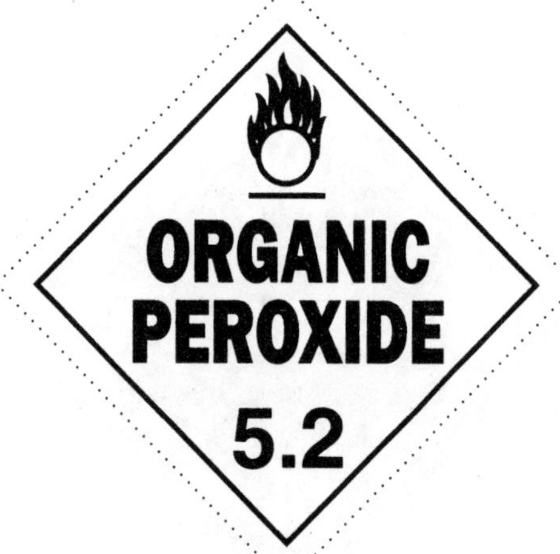

(b) **In addition to complying with §172.519,** the background color on the ORGANIC PEROXIDE placard must be yellow. The symbol, text, division number and inner border must be black.

§172.553 [Reserved]

§172.554 POISON placard.

(a) **Except for size and color,** the POISON placard must be as follows:

(b) **In addition to complying with §172.519,** the background on the POISON placard must be white. The symbol, text, class number and inner border must be black. The word "TOXIC" may be used in lieu of the word "POISON".

§172.555 POISON INHALATION HAZARD placard.

(a) **Except for size and color,** the POISON INHALATION HAZARD placard must be as follows:

(b) **In addition to complying with §172.519,** the background on the POISON INHALATION HAZARD placard and the symbol must be white. The background of the upper diamond must be black and the lower point of the upper diamond must be 65 mm (2 5/8 inches) above the horizontal center line. The text, class number, and inner border must be black.

§172.556 RADIOACTIVE placard.

(a) **Except for size and color,** the RADIOACTIVE placard must be as follows:

(b) **In addition to complying with §172.519,** the background color on the RADIOACTIVE placard must be white in the lower portion with a yellow triangle in the upper portion. The base of the yellow triangle must be 29 mm 5 mm (1.1 inches 0.2 inches) above the placard horizontal center line. The symbol, text, class number and inner border must be black.

§172.558 CORROSIVE placard.

(a) **Except for size and color,** the CORROSIVE placard must be as follows:

(b) **In addition to complying with §172.519,** the background color on the CORROSIVE placard must be black in the lower portion with a white triangle in the upper portion. The base of the white triangle must be 38 mm 5 mm (1.5 inches 0.2 inches) above the placard horizontal center line. The text and class number must be white. The symbol and inner border must be black.

§172.560 CLASS 9 placard.

(a) **Except for size and color,** the CLASS 9 (miscellaneous hazardous materials) placard must be as follows:

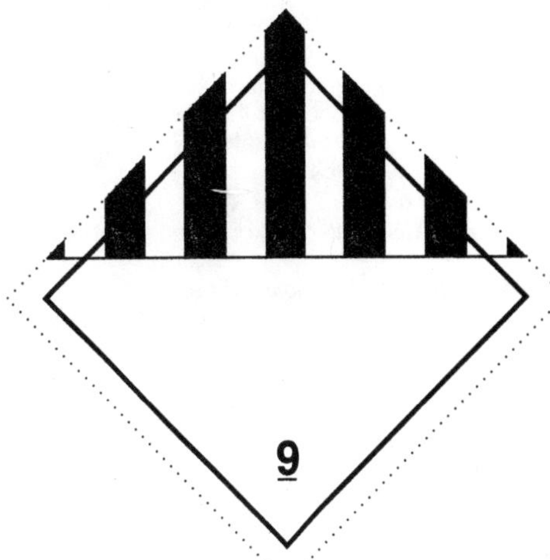

(b) **In addition to conformance with §172.519,** the background on the CLASS 9 placard must be white with seven black vertical stripes on the top half extending from the top of the placard to one inch above the horizontal centerline. The black vertical stripes must be spaced so that, visually, they appear equal in width to the six white spaces between them. The space below the vertical lines must be white with the class number 9 underlined and centered at the bottom.

Subpart G - Emergency Response Information

§172.600 Applicability and general requirements.

(a) **Scope.** Except as provided in paragraph (d) of this section, this subpart prescribes requirements for providing and maintaining emergency response information during transportation and at facilities where hazardous materials are loaded for transportation, stored incidental to transportation or otherwise handled during any phase of transportation.

(b) **Applicability.** This subpart applies to persons who offer for transportation, accept for transportation, transfer or otherwise handle hazardous materials during transportation.

(c) **General requirements.** No person to whom this subpart applies may offer for transportation, accept for transportation, transfer, store or otherwise handle during transportation a hazardous material unless:

(1) *Emergency response information* conforming to this subpart is immediately available for use at all times the hazardous material is present; and

(2) *Emergency response information,* including the emergency response telephone number, required by this subpart is immediately available to any person who, as a representative of a Federal, State or local government agency, responds to an incident involving a hazardous material, or is conducting an investigation which involves a hazardous material.

(d) **Exceptions.** The requirements of this subpart do not apply to hazardous material which is excepted from the shipping paper requirements of this subchapter or a material properly classified as an ORM-D.

§172.602 Emergency response information.

(a) Information required. For purposes of this subpart, the term "emergency response information" means information that can be used in the mitigation of an incident involving hazardous materials and, as a minimum, must contain the following information:

(1) *The basic description and technical name* of the hazardous material as required by §§172.202 and 172.203(k), the ICAO Technical Instructions, the IMDG Code, or the TDG Regulations, as appropriate (see §171.7 of this subchapter);

(2) *Immediate hazards to health;*

(3) *Risks of fire or explosion;*

(4) *Immediate precautions* to be taken in the event of an accident or incident;

(5) *Immediate methods for handling fires;*

(6) *Initial methods* for handling spills or leaks in the absence of fire; and

(7) *Preliminary first aid measures.*

(b) Form of information. The information required for a hazardous material by paragraph (a) of this section must be:

(1) *Printed legibly in English;*

(2) *Available for use* away from the package containing the hazardous material; and

(3) *Presented* —

(i) *On a shipping paper;*

(ii) *In a document,* other than a shipping paper, that includes both the basic description and technical name of the hazardous material as required by §§172.202 and 172.203(k), the ICAO Technical Instructions, the IMDG Code, or the TDG Regulations, as appropriate, and the emergency response information required by this subpart (e.g., a material safety data sheet); or

(iii) *Related to the information* on a shipping paper, a written notification to pilot-in-command, or a dangerous cargo manifest, in a separate document (e.g., an emergency response guidance document), in a manner that cross-references the description of the hazardous material on the shipping paper with the emergency response information contained in the document. Aboard aircraft, the ICAO "Emergency Response Guidance for Aircraft Incidents Involving Dangerous Goods" and, aboard vessels, the IMO "Emergency Procedures for Ships Carrying Dangerous Goods", or equivalent documents, may be used to satisfy the requirements of this section for a separate document.

(c) Maintenance of information. Emergency response information shall be maintained as follows:

(1) *Carriers.* Each carrier who transports a hazardous material shall maintain the information specified in paragraph (a) of this section and §172.606 of this part in the same manner as prescribed for shipping papers, except that the information must be maintained in the same manner aboard aircraft as the notification of pilot-in-command, and aboard vessels in the same manner as the dangerous cargo manifest. This information must be immediately accessible to train crew personnel, drivers of motor vehicles, flight crew members, and bridge personnel on vessels for use in the event of incidents involving hazardous materials.

(2) *Facility operators.* Each operator of a facility where a hazardous material is received, stored or handled during transportation, shall maintain the information required by paragraph (a) of this section whenever the hazardous material is present. This information must be in a location that is immediately accessible to facility personnel in the event of an incident involving the hazardous material.

§172.604 Emergency response telephone number.

(a) A person who offers a hazardous material for transportation must provide an emergency response telephone number, including the area code or international access code, for use in the event of an emergency involving the hazardous material. The telephone number must be —

(1) *Monitored at all times* the hazardous material is in transportation, including storage incidental to transportation;

(2) *The number of a person* who is either knowledgeable of the hazardous material being shipped and has comprehensive emergency response and incident mitigation information for that material, or has immediate access to a person who possesses such knowledge and information; and

(3) *Entered on a shipping paper, as follows:*

(i) *Immediately following* the description of the hazardous material required by subpart C of this part; or

(ii) *Entered once* on the shipping paper in a clearly visible location. This provision may be used only if the telephone number applies to each hazardous material entered on the shipping paper, and if it is indicated that the telephone number is for emergency response information (for example: "EMERGENCY CONTACT: * * *).

(b) The telephone number required by paragraph (a) of this section must be the number of the person offering the hazardous material for transportation or the number of an agency or organization capable of, and accepting responsibility for, providing the detailed information concerning the hazardous material. A person offering a hazardous material for transportation who lists the telephone number of an agency or organization shall ensure that agency or organization has received current information on the material, as required by paragraph (a)(2) of this section before it is offered for transportation.

(c) The requirements of this section do not apply to —

(1) *Hazardous materials* that are offered for transportation under the provisions applicable to limited quantities; and

(2) *Materials properly described under the following shipping names:*

Battery powered equipment
Battery powered vehicle
Carbon dioxide, solid
Castor bean
Castor flake
Castor meal
Castor pomace
Consumer commodity
Dry ice
Engines, internal combustion
Fish meal, stabilized
Fish scrap, stabilized
Refrigerating machine
Vehicle, flammable gas powered
Vehicle, flammable liquid powered
Wheelchair, electric

§172.606 Carrier information contact.

(a) Each carrier who transports or accepts for transportation a hazardous material for which a shipping paper is required shall instruct the operator of a motor vehicle, train, aircraft, or vessel to contact the carrier (e.g., by telephone or mobile radio) in the event of an incident involving the hazardous material.

(b) For transportation by highway, if a transport vehicle, (e.g., a semi-trailer or freight container-on-chassis) contains hazardous material for which a shipping paper is required and the vehicle is separated from its motive power and parked at a location other than a facility operated by the consignor or consignee or a facility (e.g., a carrier's terminal or a marine terminal) subject to the provisions of §172.602(c)(2), the carrier shall —

(1) *Mark the transport vehicle* with the telephone number of the motor carrier on the front exterior near the brake hose and electrical connections or on a label, tag, or sign attached to the vehicle at the brake hose or electrical connection; or

(2) *Have the shipping paper* and emergency response information readily available on the transport vehicle.

(c) The requirements specified in paragraph (b) of this section do not apply to an unattended motor vehicle separated from its motive power when the motor vehicle is marked on an orange panel, a placard, or a plain white square-on-point configuration with the identification number of each hazardous material loaded therein, and the marking or placard is visible on the outside of the motor vehicle.

Subpart H - Training

§172.700 Purpose and scope.

(a) Purpose. This subpart prescribes requirements for training hazmat employees.

(b) Scope. Training as used in this subpart means a systematic program that ensures a hazmat employee has familiarity with the general provisions of this subchapter, is able to recognize and identify hazardous materials, has knowledge of specific requirements of this subchapter applicable to functions performed by the employee, and has knowledge of emergency response information, self-protection measures and accident prevention methods and procedures (see §172.704).

(c) Modal-specific training requirements. Additional training requirements for the individual modes of transportation are prescribed in parts 174, 175, 176, and 177 of this subchapter.

§172.701 Federal-State relationship.

This subpart and the parts referenced in §172.700(c) prescribe minimum training requirements for the transportation of hazardous materials. For motor vehicle drivers, however, a State may impose more stringent training requirements only if those requirements —

(a) **Do not conflict with the training requirements** in this subpart and in part 177 of this subchapter; and

(b) **Apply only to drivers domiciled in that State.**

§172.702 Applicability and responsibility for training and testing.

(a) **A hazmat employer shall ensure that each** of its hazmat employees is trained in accordance with the requirements prescribed in this subpart.

(b) **Except as provided in §172.704(c)(1),** a hazmat employee who performs any function subject to the requirements of this subchapter may not perform that function unless instructed in the requirements of this subchapter that apply to that function. It is the duty of each hazmat employer to comply with the applicable requirements of this subchapter and to thoroughly instruct each hazmat employee in relation thereto.

(c) **Training may be provided by the hazmat employer** or other public or private sources.

(d) **A hazmat employer shall ensure that each** of its hazmat employees is tested by appropriate means on the training subjects covered in §172.704.

§172.704 Training requirements.

(a) **Hazmat employee training must include the following:**

(1) *General awareness/familiarization training.* Each hazmat employee shall be provided general awareness/familiarization training designed to provide familiarity with the requirements of this subchapter, and to enable the employee to recognize and identify hazardous materials consistent with the hazard communication standards of this subchapter.

(2) *Function-specific training.*

(i) *Each hazmat employee* shall be provided function-specific training concerning requirements of this subchapter, or exemptions issued under subchapter A of this chapter, which are specifically applicable to the functions the employee performs.

(ii) *As an alternative* to function-specific training on the requirements of this subchapter, training relating to the requirements of the ICAO Technical Instructions and the IMDG Code may be provided to the extent such training addresses functions authorized by §§171.11 and 171.12 of this subchapter.

(3) *Safety training.* Each hazmat employee shall receive safety training concerning —

(i) *Emergency response information* required by subpart G of part 172;

(ii) *Measures to protect* the employee from the hazards associated with hazardous materials to which they may be exposed in the work place, including specific measures the hazmat employer has implemented to protect employees from exposure; and

(iii) *Methods and procedures* for avoiding accidents, such as the proper procedures for handling packages containing hazardous materials.

(4) *Security awareness training.* No later than the date of the first scheduled recurrent training after March 25, 2003, and in no case later than March 24, 2006, each hazmat employee must receive training that provides an awareness of security risks associated with hazardous materials transportation and methods designed to enhance transportation security. This training must also include a component covering how to recognize and respond to possible security threats. After March 25, 2003, new hazmat employees must receive the security awareness training required by this paragraph within 90 days after employment.

(5) *In-depth security training.* By December 22, 2003, each hazmat employee of a person required to have a security plan in accordance with subpart I of this part must be trained concerning the security plan and its implementation. Security training must include company security objectives, specific security procedures, employee responsibilities, actions to take in the event of a security breach, and the organizational security structure.

(b) **OSHA, EPA, and other training.** Training conducted by employers to comply with the hazard communication programs required by the Occupational Safety and Health Administration of the Department of Labor (29 CFR 1910.120 or 1910.1200) or the Environmental Protection Agency (40 CFR 311.1), or training conducted by employers to comply with security training programs required by other Federal or international agencies, may be used to satisfy the training requirements in paragraph (a) of this section to the extent that such training addresses the training components specified in paragraph (a) of this section.

(c) **Initial and recurrent training —**

(1) *Initial training.* A new hazmat employee, or a hazmat employee who changes job functions may perform those functions prior to the completion of training provided —

(i) *The employee* performs those functions under the direct supervision of a properly trained and knowledgeable hazmat employee; and

(ii) *The training* is completed within 90 days after employment or a change in job function.

(2) *Recurrent training.* A hazmat employee shall receive the training required by this subpart at least once every three years.

(3) *Relevant Training.* Relevant training received from a previous employer or other source may be used to satisfy the requirements of this subpart provided a current record of training is obtained from hazmat employees' previous employer.

(4) *Compliance.* Each hazmat employer is responsible for compliance with the requirements of this subchapter regardless of whether the training required by this subpart has been completed.

(d) **Recordkeeping.** A record of current training, inclusive of the preceding three years, in accordance with this section shall be created and retained by each hazmat employer for as long as that employee is employed by that employer as a hazmat employee and for 90 days thereafter. The record shall include:

(1) *The hazmat employee's name;*

(2) *The most recent* training completion date of the hazmat employee's training;

(3) *A description,* copy, or the location of the training materials used to meet the requirements in paragraph (a) of this section;

(4) *The name and address of the person providing the training; and*

(5) *Certification* that the hazmat employee has been trained and tested, as required by this subpart.

(e) **Limitation.** A hazmat employee who repairs, modifies, reconditions, or tests packagings as qualified for use in the transportation of hazardous materials, and who does not perform any other function subject to the requirements of this subchapter, is not subject to the safety training requirement of paragraph (a)(3) of this section.

Subpart I - Security Plans

§172.800 Purpose and applicability.

(a) **Purpose.** This subpart prescribes requirements for development and implementation of plans to address security risks related to the transportation of hazardous materials in commerce.

(b) **Applicability.** By September 25, 2003, each person who offers for transportation in commerce or transports in commerce one or more of the following hazardous materials must develop and adhere to a security plan for hazardous materials that conforms to the requirements of this subpart:

(1) *A highway route-controlled quantity* of a Class 7 (radioactive) material, as defined in §173.403 of this subchapter, in a motor vehicle, rail car, or freight container;

(2) *More than 25 kg (55 pounds)* of a Division 1.1, 1.2, or 1.3 (explosive) material in a motor vehicle, rail car, or freight container;

(3) *More than one L (1.06 qt) per package* of a material poisonous by inhalation, as defined in §171.8 of this subchapter, that meets the criteria for Hazard Zone A, as specified in §§173.116(a) or 173.133(a) of this subchapter;

(4) *A shipment of a quantity of hazardous materials* in a bulk packaging having a capacity equal to or greater than 13,248 L (3,500 gallons) for liquids or gases or more than 13.24 cubic meters (468 cubic feet) for solids;

(5) *A shipment in other than a bulk packaging* of 2,268 kg (5,000 pounds) gross weight or more of one class of hazardous materials for which placarding of a vehicle, rail car, or freight container is required for that class under the provisions of subpart F of this part;

(6) *A select agent or toxin* regulated by the Centers for Disease Control and Prevention under 42 CFR part 73; or

(7) *A quantity of hazardous material* that requires placarding under the provisions of Subpart F of this part.

§172.802 Components of a security plan.

(a) **The security plan must include an assessment** of possible transportation security risks for shipments of the hazardous materials listed in §172.800 and appropriate measures to address the assessed risks. Specific measures put into place by the plan may vary commensurate with the level of threat at a particular time. At a minimum, a security plan must include the following elements:

(1) *Personnel security.* Measures to confirm information provided by job applicants hired for positions that involve access to and handling of the hazardous materials covered by the security plan. Such confirmation system must be consistent with applicable Federal and State laws and requirements concerning employment practices and individual privacy.

(2) *Unauthorized access.* Measures to address the assessed risk that unauthorized persons may gain access to the hazardous materials covered by the security plan or transport conveyances being prepared for transportation of the hazardous materials covered by the security plan.

(3) *En route security.* Measures to address the assessed security risks of shipments of hazardous materials covered by the security plan en route from origin to destination, including shipments stored incidental to movement.

(b) **The security plan must be in writing** and must be retained for as long as it remains in effect. Copies of the security plan, or portions thereof, must be available to the employees who are responsible for implementing it, consistent with personnel security clearance or background investigation restrictions and a demonstrated need to know. The security plan must be revised and updated as necessary to reflect changing circumstances. When the security plan is updated or revised, all copies of the plan must be maintained as of the date of the most recent revision.

§172.804 Relationship to other Federal requirements.

To avoid unnecessary duplication of security requirements, security plans that conform to regulations, standards, protocols, or guidelines issued by other Federal agencies, international organizations, or industry organizations may be used to satisfy the requirements in this subpart, provided such security plans address the requirements specified in this subpart.

Appendix A to Part 172

Office of Hazardous Materials Transportation color tolerance charts and tables.

The following are Munsell notations and Commission Internationale de L'Eclairage (CIE) coordinates which describe the Office of Hazardous Materials Transportation Label and Placard Color Tolerance Charts in tables 1 and 2, and the CIE coordinates for the color tolerances specified in table 3. Central colors and tolerances described in table 2 approximate those described in table 1 while allowing for differences in production methods and materials used to manufacture labels and placards surfaced with printing inks. Primarily, the color charts based on table 1 are for label or placard colors applied as opaque coatings such as paint, enamel or plastic, whereas color charts based on table 2 are intended for use with labels and placards surfaced only with inks.

For labels printed directly on packaging surfaces, table 3 may be used, although compliance with either table 1 or table 2 is sufficient. However, if visual reference indicates that the colors of labels printed directly on package surfaces are outside the table 1 or 2 tolerances, a spectrophotometer or other instrumentation may be required to insure compliance with table 3.

Table 1 - Specifications for Color Tolerance Charts for Use With Labels and Placards Surfaced With Paint, Lacquer, Enamel, Plastic, Other Opaque Coatings, or Ink [1]

Color	Munsell notations	CIE data for source C		
		Y	x	y
Red:				
Central color	7.5R 4.0/14	12.00	.5959	.3269
Orange	8.5R 4.0/14	12.00	.6037	.3389
Purple and vivid	6.5R 4.0/14	12.00	.5869	.3184
Grayish	7.5R 4.0/12	12.00	.5603	.3321
Vivid	7.5R 4.0/16	12.00	.6260	.3192
Light	7.5R 4.5/14	15.57	.5775	.3320
Dark	7.5R 3.5/14	09.00	.6226	.3141
Orange:				
Central color	5.OYR 6.0/15	30.05	.5510	.4214
Yellow and Grayish	6.25YR 6.0/15	30.05	.5452	.4329
Red and vivid	3.75YR 6.0/15	30.05	.5552	.4091
Grayish	5.OYR 6.0/13	30.05	.5311	.4154
Vivid	5.OYR 6.0/16	30.05	.5597	.4239
Light	5.OYR 6.5/15	36.20	.5427	.4206
Dark	5.OYR 5.5/15	24.58	.5606	.4218
Yellow:				
Central color	5.OY 8.0/12	59.10	.4562	.4788
Green	6.5Y 8.0/12	59.10	.4498	.4865
Orange and vivid	3.5Y 8.0/12	59.10	.4632	.4669
Grayish	5.OY 8.0/10	59.10	.4376	.4601
Vivid	5.OY 8.0/14	59.10	.4699	.4920
Light	5.OY 8.5/12	68.40	.4508	.4754
Dark	5.OY 7.5/12	50.68	.4620	.4823
Green:				
Central color	7.5G 4.0/9	12.00	.2111	.4121
Bluish	0.5BG 4.0/9	12.00	.1974	.3809
Green-yellow	5.0G 4.0/9	12.00	.2237	.4399
Grayish A	7.5G 4.0/7	12.00	.2350	.3922
Grayish B[2]	7.5G 4.0/6	12.00	.2467	.3822
Vivid	7.5G 4.0/11	12.00	.1848	.4319
Light	7.5G 4.5/9	15.57	.2204	.4060
Dark	7.5G 3.5/9	09.00	.2027	.4163
Blue:				
Central color	2.5PB 3.5/10	09.00	.1691	.1744
Purple	4.5PB 3.5/10	09.00	.1796	.1711
Green and vivid	10.0B 3.5/10	09.00	.1557	.1815
Grayish	2.5PB 3.5/8	09.00	.1888	.1964
Vivid	2.5PB 3.5/12	09.00	.1516	.1547
Light	2.5PB 4.0/10	12.00	.1805	.1888
Dark	2.5PB 3.0/10	06.55	.1576	.1600
Purple:				
Central color	10.0P 4.5/10	15.57	.3307	.2245
Reddish purple	2.5RP 4.5/10	15.57	.3584	.2377
Blue purple	7.5P 4.5/10	15.57	.3068	.2145
Reddish gray	10.0P 4.5/8	15.57	.3280	.2391
Gray[2]	10.0P 4.5/6.5	15.57	.3254	.2519
Vivid	10.0P 4.5/12	15.57	.3333	.2101
Light	10.0P 5.0/10	19.77	.3308	.2328
Dark	10.0P 4.0/10	12.00	.3306	.2162

1. Maximum chroma is not limited.
2. For the colors green and purple, the minimum saturation (chroma) limits for porcelain enamel on metal are lower than for most other surface coatings. Therefore, the minimum chroma limits of these two colors as displayed on the Charts for comparison to porcelain enamel on metal is low, as shown for green (grayish B) and purple (gray).

NOTE: CIE=Commission Internationale de L'Eclairage.

Table 2 - Specifications for Color Tolerance Charts for Use With Labels and Placards Surfaced With Ink

Color/series	Munsell notation	CIE data for source C		
		Y	x	y
Red:				
Central series:				
Central color	6.8R 4.47/12.8	15.34	.5510	.3286
Grayish	7.2R 4.72/12.2	17.37	.5368	.3348
Purple	6.4R 4.49/12.7	15.52	.5442	.3258
Purple and vivid	6.1R 4.33/13.1	14.25	.5529	.3209
Vivid	6.7R 4.29/13.2	13.99	.5617	.3253
Orange	7.3R 4.47/12.8	15.34	.5572	.3331
Orange and grayish	7.65R 4.70/12.4	17.20	.5438	.3382
Light series:				
Light	7.0R 4.72/13.2	17.32	.5511	.3322
Light and orange	7.4R 4.96/12.6	19.38	.5365	.3382
Light and purple	6.6R 4.79/12.9	17.94	.5397	.3289
Dark series:				
Dark A	6.7R 4.19/12.5	13.30	.5566	.3265
Dark B	7.0R 4.25/12.35	13.72	.5522	.3294
Dark and purple	7.5R 4.23/12.4	13.58	.5577	.3329
Orange:				
Central series:				
Central color	5.0YR 6.10/12.15	31.27	.5193	.4117
Yellow and grayish A	5.8YR 6.22/11.7	32.69	.5114	.4155
Yellow and grayish B	6.1YR 6.26/11.85	33.20	.5109	.4190
Vivid	5.1YR 6.07/12.3	30.86	.5226	.4134
Red and vivid A	3.9YR 5.87/12.75	28.53	.5318	.4038
Red and vivid B	3.6YR 5.91/12.6	29.05	.5291	.4021
Grayish	4.9YR 6.10/11.9	31.22	.5170	.4089
Light series:				
Light and vivid A	5.8YR 6.78/12.7	39.94	.5120	.4177
Light and yellow	6.0YR 6.80/12.8	40.20	.5135	.4198
Light and vivid B	4.9YR 6.60/12.9	37.47	.5216	.4126
Dark series:				
Dark and yellow	5.8YR 5.98/11.0	29.87	.5052	.4132
Dark A	5.1YR 5.80/11.1	27.80	.5127	.4094
Dark B	5.0YR 5.80/11.0	27.67	.5109	.4068

Table 2 - Specifications for Color Tolerance Charts for Use With Labels and Placards Surfaced With Ink

Color/series	Munsell notation	CIE data for source C		
		Y	x	y
Yellow:				
Central series:				
Central color	4.3Y 7.87/10.3	56.81	.4445	.4589
Vivid A	4.5Y 7.82/10.8	55.92	.4503	.4658
Vivid B	3.3Y 7.72/11.35	54.24	.4612	.4624
Vivid and orange	3.2Y 7.72/10.8	54.25	.4576	.4572
Grayish A	4.1Y 7.95/9.7	58.18	.4380	.4516
Grayish B	5.1Y 8.06/9.05	60.12	.4272	.4508
Green-yellow	5.2Y 7.97/9.9	58.53	.4356	.4605
Light series:				
Light	5.4Y 8.59/10.5	70.19	.4351	.4628
Light and green-yellow	5.4Y 8.56/11.2	69.59	.4414	.4692
Light and vivid	4.4Y 8.45/11.4	67.42	.4490	.4662
Dark series:				
Dark and green-yellow	4.4Y 7.57/9.7	51.82	.4423	.4562
Dark and orange A	3.4Y 7.39/10.4	48.86	.4584	.4590
Dark and orange B	3.5Y 7.41/10.0	49.20	.4517	.4544
Green:				
Central series:				
Central color	9.75G 4.26/7.75	13.80	.2214	.3791
Grayish	10G 4.46/7.5	15.25	.2263	.3742
Blue A	1.4BG 4.20/7.4	13.36	.2151	.3625
Blue B	1.0BG 4.09/7.75	12.60	.2109	.3685
Vivid	8.4G 4.09/8.05	12.59	.2183	.3954
Vivid green-yellow	7.0G 4.23/8.0	13.54	.2292	.4045
Green-yellow	7.85G 4.46/7.7	15.23	.2313	.3914
Light series:				
Light and vivid	9.5G 4.45/8.8	15.21	.2141	.3863
Light and blue	0.2BG 4.31/8.8	14.12	.2069	.3814
Light and green-yellow	8.3G 4.29/9.05	14.01	.2119	.4006
Dark series:				
Dark and green-yellow	7.1G 4.08/7.1	12.55	.2354	.3972
Dark and grayish	9.5G 4.11/6.9	12.70	.2282	.3764
Dark	8.5G 3.97/7.2	11.78	.2269	.3874
Blue:				
Central series:				
Central color	3.5PB 3.94/9.7	11.58	.1885	.1911
Green and grayish A	2.0PB 4.35/8.7	14.41	.1962	.2099
Green and grayish B	1.7PB 4.22/9.0	13.50	.1898	.2053
Vivid	2.9PB 3.81/9.7	10.78	.1814	.1852
Purple and vivid A	4.7PB 3.53/10.0	9.15	.1817	.1727
Purple and vivid B	5.0PB 3.71/9.9	10.20	.1888	.1788
Grayish	3.75PB 4.03/9.1	12.17	.1943	.1961
Light series:				
Light and green A	1.7PB 4.32/9.2	14.22	.1904	.2056
Light and green B	1.5PB 4.11/9.6	12.72	.1815	.1971
Light and vivid	3.2PB 3.95/10.05	11.70	.1831	.1868
Dark series:				
Dark and grayish	3.9PB 4.01/8.7	12.04	.1982	.1992
Dark and purple A	4.8PB 3.67/9.3	9.95	.1918	.1831
Dark and purple B	5.2PB 3.80/9.05	10.76	.1985	.1885
Purple:				
Central series:				
Central color	9.5P 4.71/11.3	17.25	.3274	.2165
Red	1.0RP 5.31/10.8	22.70	.3404	.2354
Red and vivid A	1.4RP 5.00/11.9	19.78	.3500	.2274
Red and vivid B	0.2RP 4.39/12.5	14.70	.3365	.2059
Vivid	8.0P 4.04/12.0	12.23	.3098	.1916
Blue	7.0P 4.39/10.8	14.71	.3007	.2037
Grayish	8.8P 5.00/10.3	19.73	.3191	.2251
Light series:				
Light and red A	0.85RP 5.56/11.1	25.18	.3387	.2356
Light and red B	1.1RP 5.27/12.3	22.27	.3460	.2276
Light and vivid	9.2P 4.94/11.95	19.24	.3247	.2163
Dark series:				
Dark and grayish	9.6P 4.70/10.9	17.19	.3283	.2204
Dark and vivid	8.4P 4.05/11.6	12.35	.3144	.1970
Dark and blue	7.5P 4.32/10.5	14.19	.3059	.2078

Table 3 - Specification for Colors for Use With Labels Printed on Packagings Surfaces

CIE data for source C	Red	Orange	Yellow	Green	Blue	Purple
x	.424	.460	.417	.228	.200	.377
y	.306	.370	.392	.354	.175	.205
x	.571	.543	.490	.310	.255	.377
y	.306	.400	.442	.354	.250	.284
x	.424	.445	.390	.228	.177	.342
y	.350	.395	.430	.403	.194	.205
x	.571	.504	.440	.310	.230	.342
y	.350	.430	.492	.403	.267	.284
Y (high)	23.0	41.6	72.6	20.6	15.9	21.2
Y (low)	7.7	19.5	29.1	7.4	6.5	8.2

Appendix B to Part 172

Trefoil symbol.

1. **Except as provided in paragraph 2 of this appendix,** the trefoil symbol required for RADIOACTIVE labels and placards and required to be marked on certain packages of Class 7 materials must conform to the design and size requirements of this appendix.
2. **RADIOACTIVE labels and placards that were printed** prior to April 1, 1996, in conformance with the requirements of this subchapter in effect on March 30, 1996, may continue to be used.

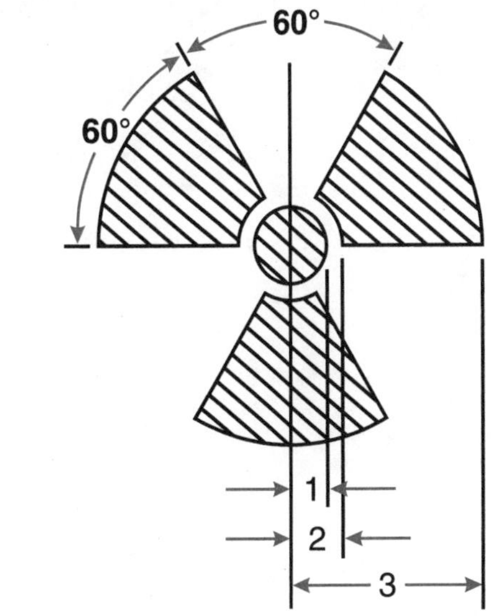

1=Radius of Circle —
Minimum dimensions
4 mm (0.16 inch) for markings and labels
12.5 mm (0.5 inch) for placards
2=1 1/2 Radii
3=5 radii for markings and labels
4 1/2 radii for placards.

Appendix C to Part 172

Dimensional specifications for recommended placard holder.

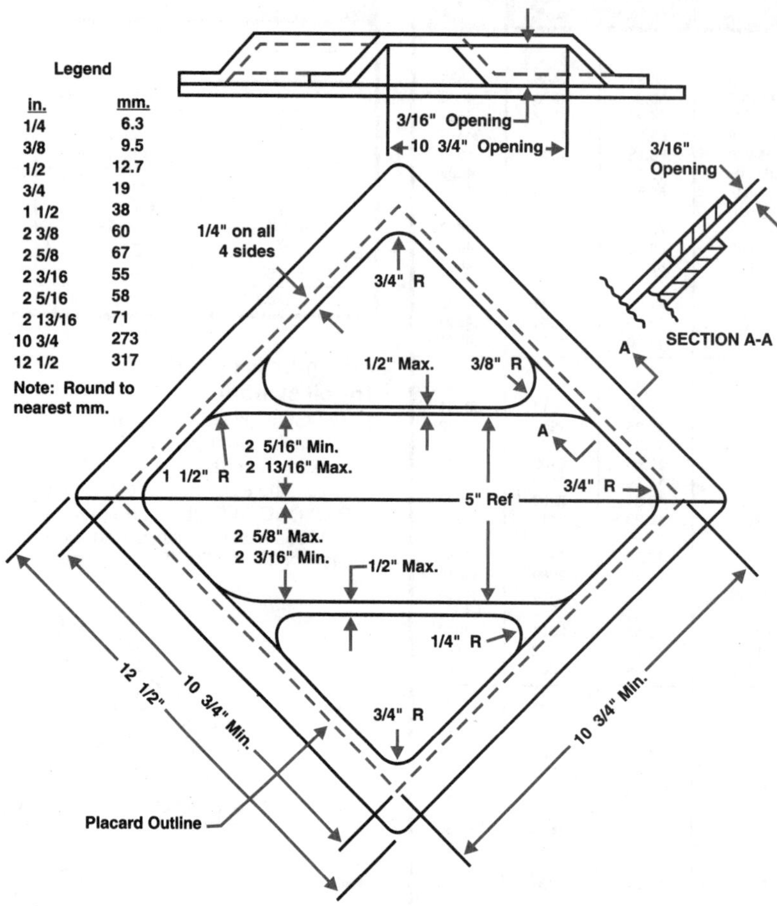

Part 173 - Shippers — General Requirements for Shipments and Packagings

Subpart A - General

§173.1 Purpose and scope.

(a) This part includes:

(1) *Definitions of hazardous materials for transportation purposes;*

(2) *Requirements to be observed* in preparing hazardous materials for shipment by air, highway, rail, or water, or any combination thereof; and

(3) *Inspection, testing,* and retesting responsibilities for persons who retest, recondition, maintain, repair and rebuild containers used or intended for use in the transportation of hazardous materials.

(b) A shipment of hazardous materials that is not prepared in accordance with this subchapter may not be offered for transportation by air, highway, rail, or water. It is the responsibility of each hazmat employer subject to the requirements of this subchapter to ensure that each hazmat employee is trained in accordance with the requirements prescribed in this subchapter. It is the duty of each person who offers hazardous materials for transportation to instruct each of his officers, agents, and employees having any responsibility for preparing hazardous materials for shipment as to applicable regulations in this subchapter.

(c) When a person other than the person preparing a hazardous material for shipment performs a function required by this part, that person shall perform the function in accordance with this part.

(d) In general, the Hazardous Materials Regulations (HMR) contained in this subchapter are based on the UN Recommendations and are consistent with international regulations issued by the International Civil Aviation Organization (ICAO Technical Instructions) and the International Maritime Organization (IMDG Code). However, the HMR are not consistent in all respects with the UN Recommendations, the ICAO Technical Instructions or the IMDG Code, and compliance with the HMR will not guarantee acceptance by regulatory bodies outside of the United States.

§173.2 Hazardous materials classes and index to hazard class definitions.

The hazard class of a hazardous material is indicated either by its class (or division) number, its class name, or by the letters "ORM-D". The following table lists class numbers, division numbers, class or division names and those sections of this subchapter which contain definitions for classifying hazardous materials, including forbidden materials.

Class No.	Division No. (if any)	Name of class or division	49 CFR reference for definitions
None	.....	Forbidden materials	173.21
None	.....	Forbidden explosives	173.54
1	1.1	Explosives (with a mass explosion hazard)	173.50
1	1.2	Explosives (with a projection hazard)	173.50
1	1.3	Explosives (with predominately a fire hazard)	173.50
1	1.4	Explosives (with no significant blast hazard)	173.50
1	1.5	Very insensitive explosives; blasting agents	173.50
1	1.6	Extremely insensitive detonating substances	173.50
2	2.1	Flammable gas	173.115
2	2.2	Non-flammable compressed gas	173.115
2	2.3	Poisonous gas	173.115
3	.....	Flammable and combustible liquid	173.120
4	4.1	Flammable solid	173.124
4	4.2	Spontaneously combustible material	173.124
4	4.3	Dangerous when wet material	173.124
5	5.1	Oxidizer	173.127
5	5.2	Organic peroxide	173.128
6	6.1	Poisonous materials	173.132
6	6.2	Infectious substance (Etiologic agent)	173.134
7	.....	Radioactive material	173.403
8	.....	Corrosive material	173.136
9	.....	Miscellaneous hazardous material	173.140
None	.....	Other regulated material: ORM-D	173.144

§173.2a Classification of a material having more than one hazard.

(a) **Classification of a material having** more than one hazard. Except as provided in paragraph (c) of this section, a material not specifically listed in the §172.101 table that meets the definition of more than one hazard class or division as defined in this part, shall be classed according to the highest applicable hazard class of the following hazard classes, which are listed in descending order of hazard:

(1) *Class 7 (radioactive materials, other than limited quantities).*

(2) *Division 2.3 (poisonous gases).*

(3) *Division 2.1 (flammable gases).*

(4) *Division 2.2 (nonflammable gases).*

(5) *Division 6.1 (poisonous liquids),* Packing Group I, poisonous-by-inhalation only.

(6) *A material* that meets the definition of a pyrophoric material in §173.124(b)(1) of this subchapter (Division 4.2).

(7) *A material* that meets the definition of a self-reactive material in §173.124(a)(2) of this subchapter (Division 4.1).

(8) *Class 3 (flammable liquids),* Class 8 (corrosive materials), Division 4.1 (flammable solids), Division 4.2 (spontaneously combustible materials), Division 4.3 (dangerous when wet materials), Division 5.1 (oxidizers) or Division 6.1 (poisonous liquids or solids other than Packing Group I, poisonous-by-inhalation). The hazard class and packing group for a material meeting more than one of these hazards shall be determined using the precedence table in paragraph (b) of this section.

(9) *Combustible liquids.*

(10) *Class 9 (miscellaneous hazardous materials).*

(b) **Precedence of hazard table for Classes 3 and 8** and Divisions 4.1, 4.2, 4.3, 5.1 and 6.1. The following table ranks those materials that meet the definition of Classes 3 and 8 and Divisions 4.1, 4.2, 4.3, 5.1 and 6.1:

Precedence of Hazard Table
[Hazard class and packing group]

	4.2	4.3	5.1 I[1]	5.1 II[1]	5.1 III[1]	6.1, I dermal	6.1, I oral	6.1 II	6.1 III	8, I liquid	8, I solid	8, II liquid	8, II solid	8, III liquid	8, III solid
3 I[2]	.....	.....	.....	.....	.....	3	3	3	3	3	([3])	3	([3])	3	([3])
3 II[2]	.....	.....	.....	.....	.....	3	3	3	3	8	([3])	3	([3])	3	([3])
3 III[2]	.....	.....	.....	.....	.....	6.1	6.1	6.1	3[4]	8	([3])	8	([3])	3	([3])
4.1 II[2]	4.2	4.3	5.1	4.1	4.1	6.1	6.1	4.1	4.1	([3])	8	([3])	4.1	([3])	4.1
4.1 III[2]	4.2	4.3	5.1	4.1	4.1	6.1	6.1	6.1	4.1	([3])	8	([3])	8	([3])	4.1
4.2 II	.....	4.3	5.1	4.2	4.2	6.1	6.1	4.2	4.2	8	8	4.2	4.2	4.2	4.2
4.2 III	.....	4.3	5.1	5.1	4.2	6.1	6.1	6.1	4.2	8	8	8	8	4.2	4.2
4.3 I	.....	.....	5.1	4.3	4.3	6.1	4.3	4.3	4.3	4.3	4.3	4.3	4.3	4.3	4.3
4.3 II	.....	.....	5.1	4.3	4.3	6.1	4.3	4.3	4.3	8	8	4.3	4.3	4.3	4.3
4.3 III	.....	.....	5.1	5.1	4.3	6.1	6.1	6.1	4.3	8	8	8	8	4.3	4.3
5.1 I[1]	.....	.....	.....	.....	.....	5.1	5.1	5.1	5.1	5.1	5.1	5.1	5.1	5.1	5.1
5.1 II[1]	.....	.....	.....	.....	.....	6.1	5.1	5.1	5.1	8	8	5.1	5.1	5.1	5.1
5.1 III[1]	.....	.....	.....	.....	.....	6.1	6.1	6.1	5.1	8	8	8	8	5.1	5.1
6.1 I, Dermal	.....	.....	.....	.....	.....	.....	.....	.....	.....	8	6.1	6.1	6.1	6.1	6.1
6.1 I, Oral	.....	.....	.....	.....	.....	.....	.....	.....	.....	8	6.1	6.1	6.1	6.1	6.1
6.1 II, Inhalation	.....	.....	.....	.....	.....	.....	.....	.....	.....	8	6.1	6.1	6.1	6.1	6.1
6.1 II, Dermal	.....	.....	.....	.....	.....	.....	.....	.....	.....	8	6.1	8	6.1	6.1	6.1
6.1 II, Oral	.....	.....	.....	.....	.....	.....	.....	.....	.....	8	8	8	6.1	6.1	6.1
6.1 III	.....	.....	.....	.....	.....	.....	.....	.....	.....	8	8	8	8	8	8

1. See §173.127.
2. Materials of Division 4.1 other than self-reactive substances and solid desensitized explosives, and materials of Class 3 other than liquid desensitized explosives.
3. Denotes an impossible combination.
4. For pesticides only, where a material has the hazards of Class 3, Packing Group III, and Division 6.1, Packing Group III, the primary hazard is Division 6.1, Packing Group III.

NOTE 1: The most stringent packing group assigned to a hazard of the material takes precedence over other packing groups; for example, a material meeting Class 3 PG II and Division 6.1 PG I (oral toxicity) is classified as Class 3 PG I.

NOTE 2: A material which meets the definition of Class 8 and has an inhalation toxicity by dusts and mists which meets criteria for Packing Group I specified in §173.133(a)(1) must be classed as Division 6.1 if the oral or dermal toxicity meets criteria for Packing Group I or II. If the oral or dermal toxicity meets criteria for Packing Group III or less, the material must be classed as Class 8.

(c) **The following materials are not subject** to the provisions of paragraph (a) of this section because of their unique properties:

(1) *A Class 1 (explosive) material* that meets any other hazard class or division as defined in this part shall be assigned a division in Class 1. Class 1 materials shall be classed and approved in accordance with §173.56 of this part;

(2) *A Division 5.2 (organic peroxide) material* that meets the definition of any other hazard class or division as defined in this part, shall be classed as Division 5.2;

(3) *A Division 6.2 (infectious substance) material* that also meets the definition of another hazard class or division, other than Class 7, or that also is a limited quantity Class 7 material, shall be classed as Division 6.2;

(4) *A material* that meets the definition of a wetted explosive in §173.124(a)(1) of this subchapter (Division 4.1). Wetted explosives are either specifically listed in the §172.101 table or are approved by the Associate Administrator (see §173.124(a)(1) of this subchapter); and

(5) *A limited quantity* of a Class 7 (radioactive) material that meets the definition for more than one hazard class or division shall be classed in accordance with §173.423.

§173.3 Packaging and exceptions.

(a) **The packaging of hazardous materials** for transportation by air, highway, rail, or water must be as specified in this part. Methods of manufacture, packing, and storage of hazardous materials, that affect safety in transportation, must be open to inspection by a duly authorized representative of the initial carrier or of the Department. Methods of manufacture and related functions necessary for completion of a DOT specification or U.N. standard packaging must be open to inspection by a representative of the Department.

(b) **The regulations setting forth packaging requirements** for a specific material apply to all modes of transportation unless otherwise stated, or unless exceptions from packaging requirements are authorized.

(c) **Salvage drums.** Packages of hazardous materials that are damaged, defective, or found leaking and hazardous materials that have spilled or leaked may be placed in a metal or plastic removable head salvage drum that is compatible with the lading and shipped for repackaging or disposal under the following conditions:

(1) *Except as provided* in paragraph (c)(7) of this section, the drum must be a UN 1A2, 1B2, 1N2 or 1H2 tested and marked for Packing Group III or higher performance standards for liquids or solids and a leakproofness test of 20 kPa (3 psig). Alternatively, a drum manufactured and marked prior to October 1, 1993 as a salvage drum, in accordance with the provisions of this section in effect on September 30, 1991, is authorized. Capacity of the drum may not exceed 450 L (119 gallons).

(2) *Each drum* shall be provided when necessary with sufficient cushioning and absorption material to prevent excessive movement of the damaged package and to eliminate the presence of any free liquid at the time the salvage drum is closed. All cushioning and absorbent material used in the drum must be compatible with the hazardous material.

(3) *Each salvage packaging* must be marked with the proper shipping name of the hazardous material inside the packaging and the name and address of the consignee. In addition, the packaging must be marked "SALVAGE" or "SALVAGE DRUM".

(4) *Each drum shall be labeled as prescribed for the respective material.*

(5) *The shipper* shall prepare shipping papers in accordance with subpart C of part 172 of this subchapter.

(6) *The overpack requirements* of §173.25 do not apply to drums used in accordance with this paragraph.

(7) *A salvage packaging* marked "T" in accordance with applicable provisions in the UN Recommendations may be used.

§173.4 Small quantity exceptions.

(a) **Small quantities of Class 3, Division 4.1, Division 4.2** (PG II and III), Division 4.3 (PG II and III), Division 5.1, Division 5.2, Division 6.1, Class 7, Class 8, and Class 9 materials that also meet the definition of one or more of these hazard classes, are not subject to any other requirements of this subchapter when —

(1) *The maximum quantity* of material per inner receptacle or article is limited to —

(i) *Thirty (30) mL* (1 ounce) for authorized liquids, other than Division 6.1, Packing Group I, Hazard Zone A or B materials;

(ii) *Thirty (30) g (1 ounce) for authorized solid materials;*

(iii) *One (1) g* (0.04 ounce) for authorized materials meeting the definition of a Division 6.1, Packing Group I, Hazard Zone A or B material; and

(iv) *An activity level* not exceeding that specified in §§173.421, 173.424, 173.425 or 173.426, as appropriate, for a package containing a Class 7 (radioactive) material.

(2) *With the exception* of temperature sensing devices, each inner receptacle:

(i) *Is not liquid-full at 55 °C (131 °F), and*

(ii) *Is constructed* of plastic having a minimum thickness of no less than 0.2 mm (0.008 inch), or earthenware, glass, or metal;

(3) *Each inner receptacle* with a removable closure has its closure held securely in place with wire, tape, or other positive means;

(4) *Unless equivalent* cushioning and absorbent material surrounds the inside packaging, each inner receptacle is securely packed in an inside packaging with cushioning and absorbent material that:

(i) *Will not react chemically with the material, and*

(ii) *Is capable* of absorbing the entire contents (if a liquid) of the receptacle;

(5) *The inside packaging* is securely packed in a strong outside packaging;

(6) *The completed package,* as demonstrated by prototype testing, is capable of sustaining —

(i) *Each of the following* free drops made from a height of 1.8 m (5.9 feet) directly onto a solid unyielding surface without breakage or leakage from any inner receptacle and without a substantial reduction in the effectiveness of the package:

[A] One drop flat on bottom;

[B] One drop flat on top;

[C] One drop flat on the long side;

[D] One drop flat on the short side; and

[E] One drop on a corner at the junction of three intersecting edges; and

(ii) *A compressive load* as specified in §178.606(c) of this subchapter.

Note to Paragraph (a)(6): Each of the tests in paragraph (a)(6) of this section may be performed on a different but identical package; i.e., all tests need not be performed on the same package.

(7) *Placement of the material* in the package or packing different materials in the package does not result in a violation of §173.21;

(8) *The gross mass* of the completed package does not exceed 29 kg (64 pounds);

(9) *The package* is not opened or otherwise altered until it is no longer in commerce; and

(10) *The shipper* certifies conformance with this section by marking the outside of the package with the statement "This package conforms to 49 CFR 173.4" or, alternatively, until October 1, 2001, with the statement "This package conforms to the conditions and limitations specified in 49 CFR 173.4."

(b) **A package containing a Class 7 (radioactive) material** also must conform to the requirements of §173.421(a)(1) through (a)(5) or §173.424(a) through (g), as appropriate.

(c) **Packages which contain a Class 2, Division 4.2 (PG I),** or Division 4.3 (PG I) material conforming to paragraphs (a)(1) through (a)(10) of this section may be offered for transportation or transported if specifically approved by the Associate Administrator.

§173.5 Agricultural operations.

(a) **For other than a Class 2 material,** the transportation of an agricultural product over local roads between fields of the same farm is excepted from the requirements of this subchapter. A Class 2 material transported over local roads between fields of the same farm is excepted from subparts G and H of part 172 of this subchapter. In either instance, transportation of the hazardous material is subject to the following conditions:

(1) *It is transported* by a farmer who is an intrastate private motor carrier; and

(2) *The movement* of the agricultural product conforms to requirements of the State in which it is transported and is specifically authorized by a State statute or regulation in effect before October 1, 1998.

(b) **The transportation of an agricultural product** to or from a farm, within 150 miles of the farm, is excepted from the requirements in subparts G and H of part 172 of this subchapter and from the specific packaging requirements of this subchapter when:

(1) *It is transported* by a farmer who is an intrastate private motor carrier;

(2) *The total amount* of agricultural product being transported on a single vehicle does not exceed:

(i) *7,300 kg (16,094 lbs.)* of ammonium nitrate fertilizer properly classed as Division 5.1, PG III, in a bulk packaging, or

(ii) *1900 L (502 gallons)* for liquids or gases, or 2,300 kg (5,070 lbs.) for solids, of any other agricultural product;

(3) *The movement and packaging* of the agricultural product conform to the requirements of the State in which it is transported and are specifically authorized by a State statute or regulation in effect before October 1, 1998; and

(4) *Each person* having any responsibility for transporting the agricultural product or preparing the agricultural product for shipment has been instructed in the applicable requirements of this subchapter.

(c) **Formulated liquid agricultural products** in specification packagings of 220 L (58 gallons) capacity, or less, with closures manifolded to a closed mixing system and equipped with positive dry disconnect devices may be transported by a private motor carrier between a final distribution point and an ultimate point of application or for loading aboard an airplane for aerial application.

(d) **See §173.315(m) pertaining to nurse tanks of anhydrous ammonia.**

(e) **See §173.6 pertaining to materials of trade.**

§173.5a Oilfield service vehicles.

Notwithstanding §173.29 of this subchapter, a cargo tank mounted on a transport vehicle used in oilfield servicing operations is not subject to the specification requirements of this subchapter if —

(a) **The cargo tank and equipment contains** only residual amounts (i.e., it is emptied so far as practicable) of a flammable liquid alone or in combination with water,

(b) **No flame producing device is operated during transportation, and**

(c) **The proper shipping name is preceded** by "Residual" on the shipping paper for each movement on a public highway.

§173.6 Materials of trade exceptions.

When transported by motor vehicle in conformance with this section, a material of trade (see §171.8 of this subchapter) is not subject to any other requirements of this subchapter besides those set forth or referenced in this section.

(a) **Materials and amounts.** A material of trade is limited to the following:

(1) *A Class 3, 8, 9,* Division 4.1, 5.1, 5.2, 6.1, or ORM-D material contained in a packaging having a gross mass or capacity not over —

(i) *0.5 kg (1 pound) or 0.5 L (1 pint) for a Packing Group I material;*

(ii) *30 kg (66 pounds)* or 30 L (8 gallons) for a Packing Group II, Packing Group III, or ORM-D material;

(iii) *1500 L (400 gallons)* for a diluted mixture, not to exceed 2 percent concentration, of a Class 9 material.

(2) *A Division 2.1 or 2.2 material* in a cylinder with a gross weight not over 100 kg (220 pounds), or a permanently mounted tank manufactured to ASME standards of not more than 70 gallon water capacity for a non-liquefied Division 2.2 material with no subsidiary hazard.

(3) *A Division 4.3 material* in Packing Group II or III contained in a packaging having a gross capacity not exceeding 30 mL (1 ounce).

(4) *A Division 6.2 material,* other than a Risk Group 4 material, that is a diagnostic specimen, biological product, or regulated medical waste. The material must be contained in a combination packaging. For liquids, the inner packaging must be leak tight, and the outer packaging must contain sufficient absorbent material to absorb the entire contents of the inner packaging. For sharps, the inner packaging must be constructed of a rigid material resistant to punctures and leaks. For all Division 6.2 materials, the outer packaging must be a strong, tight packaging securely closed and secured against movement.

(i) *For a diagnostic specimen* or biological product, combination packagings must conform to the following capacity limitations:

[A] One or more inner packagings where the gross mass or capacity of each inner packaging does not exceed 0.5 kg (1.1 pound), or 0.5 L (17 ounces), and an outer packaging having a gross mass or capacity not exceeding 4 kg (8.8 pounds) or 4 L (1 gallon); or

[B] A single inner packaging with a gross mass or capacity not exceeding 16 kg (35.2 pounds) or 16 L (4.2 gallons) in a single outer packaging.

(ii) *For a regulated medical waste,* a combination packaging must consist of one or more inner packagings having a gross mass or capacity not exceeding 4 kg (8.8 pounds) or 4 L (1 gallon), and an outer packaging having a gross mass or capacity not exceeding 16 kg (35.2 pounds) or 16 L (4.2 gallons).

(5) *This section* does not apply to a hazardous material that is self-reactive (see §173.124), poisonous by inhalation (see §173.133), or a hazardous waste.

(b) **Packaging.**

(1) *Packagings must be* leak tight for liquids and gases, sift proof for solids, and be securely closed, secured against movement, and protected against damage.

(2) *Each material* must be packaged in the manufacturer's original packaging, or a packaging of equal or greater strength and integrity.

(3) *Outer packagings* are not required for receptacles (e.g., cans and bottles) that are secured against movement in cages, carts, bins, boxes or compartments.

(4) *For gasoline,* a packaging must be made of metal or plastic and conform to the requirements of this subchapter or to the requirements of the Occupational Safety and Health Administration of the Department of Labor contained in 29 CFR 1910.106(d)(2) or 1926.152(a)(1).

(5) *A cylinder* or other pressure vessel containing a Division 2.1 or 2.2 material must conform to packaging, qualification, maintenance, and use requirements of this subchapter, except that outer packagings are not required. Manifolding of cylinders is authorized provided all valves are tightly closed.

(c) **Hazard communication.**

(1) *A non-bulk packaging* other than a cylinder (including a receptacle transported without an outer packaging) must be marked with a common name or proper shipping name to identify the material it contains, including the letters "RQ" if it contains a reportable quantity of a hazardous substance.

(2) *A bulk packaging* containing a diluted mixture of a Class 9 material must be marked on two opposing sides with the four-digit identification number of the material. The identification number must be displayed on placards, orange panels or, alternatively, a white square-on-point configuration having the same outside dimensions as a placard (at least 273 mm (10.8 inches) on a side), in the manner specified in §172.332 (b) and (c) of this subchapter.

(3) *A DOT specification cylinder* (except DOT specification 39) must be marked and labeled as prescribed in this subchapter. Each DOT-39 cylinder must display the markings specified in 178.65(i).

(4) *The operator* of a motor vehicle that contains a material of trade must be informed of the presence of the hazardous material (including whether the package contains a reportable quantity) and must be informed of the requirements of this section.

(d) **Aggregate gross weight.** Except for a material of trade authorized by paragraph (a)(1)(iii) of this section, the aggregate gross weight of all materials of trade on a motor vehicle may not exceed 200 kg (440 pounds).

(e) **Other exceptions.** A material of trade may be transported on a motor vehicle under the provisions of this section with other hazardous materials without affecting its eligibility for exceptions provided by this section.

§173.7 U.S. Government material.

(a) **Hazardous materials offered for transportation** by, for, or to the Department of Defense (DOD) of the U.S. Government, including commercial shipments pursuant to a DOD contract, must be packaged in accordance with the regulations in this subchapter or in packagings of equal or greater strength and efficiency as certified by DOD in accordance with the procedures prescribed by "Performance Oriented Packaging of Hazardous Material, DLAR 4145.41/AR 700-143/AFR 71-5/NAVSUPINST 4030.55/MCO 4030.40." Hazardous materials offered for transportation by DOD under this provision may be reshipped by any shipper to any consignee provided the original packaging has not been damaged or altered in any manner.

(1) *Hazardous materials* sold by the DOD in packagings that are not marked in accordance with the requirements of this subchapter may be shipped from DOD installations if the DOD certifies in writing that the packagings are equal to or greater in strength and efficiency than the packaging prescribed in this subchapter. The shipper shall obtain such a certification in

duplicate for each shipment. He shall give one copy to the originating carrier and retain the other for no less than 1 year.

(2) *[Reserved]*

(b) **Shipments of hazardous materials,** made by or under the direction or supervision of the U.S. Department of Energy (DOE) or the Department of Defense (DOD), for the purpose of national security, and which are escorted by personnel specifically designated by or under the authority of those agencies, are not subject to the requirements of this subchapter. For transportation by a motor vehicle or a rail car, the escorts must be in a separate transport vehicle from the transport vehicle carrying the hazardous materials that are excepted by this paragraph. A document certifying that the shipment is for the purpose of national security must be in the possession of the person in charge of providing security during transportation.

(c) **Shipments of explosive samples,** not exceeding 1 g net weight, offered by and consigned to the Bureau of Alcohol, Tobacco and Firearms (ATF) of the Department of the Treasury are not otherwise subject to the regulations in parts 110-189 of this subchapter when placed in a specifically designed multi-unit assembly packed in a strong outside packaging. The packaging must be of a type accepted by ATF as capable of precluding a propagation of any explosion outside the packaging. The second component from the outside of the packaging must be marked or tagged to indicate the presence of an explosive.

(d) **Notwithstanding the requirements of §§173.416 and 173.417** of this subchapter, packagings made by or under the direction of the U.S. Department of Energy may be used for the transportation of Class 7 materials when evaluated, approved, and certified by the Department of Energy against packaging standards equivalent to those specified in 10 CFR part 71. Packages shipped in accordance with this paragraph shall be marked and otherwise prepared for shipment in a manner equivalent to that required by this subchapter for packagings approved by the Nuclear Regulatory Commission.

(e) **Class 1 (explosive) materials owned** by the Department of Defense and packaged prior to January 1, 1990, in accordance with the requirements of this subchapter in effect at that time, are excepted from the marking and labeling requirements of part 172 of this subchapter and the packaging and package marking requirements of part 178 of this subchapter, provided the packagings have maintained their integrity and the explosive material is declared as "government-owned goods packaged prior to January 1, 1990" on the shipping papers. In addition, packages of these materials owned by the Department of Defense that are marked and labeled in conformance with the requirements of the HMR that were in effect at the time they were originally marked and labeled are excepted from the current marking and labeling requirements.

§173.8 Exceptions for non-specification packagings used in intrastate transportation.

(a) **Non-specification bulk packagings.** Notwithstanding requirements for specification packagings in subpart F of this part and parts 178 and 180 of this subchapter, a non-specification bulk packaging may be used for transportation of a hazardous material by an intrastate motor carrier until July 1, 2000, in accordance with the provisions of paragraph (d) of this section.

(b) **Non-specification cargo tanks for petroleum products.** Notwithstanding requirements for specification packagings in subpart F of this part and parts 178 and 180 of this subchapter, a non-specification cargo tank motor vehicle having a capacity of less than 13,250 L (3,500 gallons) may be used by an intrastate motor carrier for transportation of a flammable liquid petroleum product in accordance with the provisions of paragraph (d) of this section.

(c) **Permanently secured non-bulk tanks for petroleum products.** Notwithstanding requirements for specification packagings in subpart F of this part 173 and parts 178 and 180 of this subchapter, a non-specification metal tank permanently secured to a transport vehicle and protected against leakage or damage in the event of a turnover, having a capacity of less than 450 L (119 gallons), may be used by an intrastate motor carrier for transportation of a flammable liquid petroleum product in accordance with the provisions of paragraph (d) of this section.

(d) **Additional requirements.** A packaging used under the provisions of paragraphs (a), (b) or (c) of this section must —

(1) *Be operated* by an intrastate motor carrier and in use as a packaging for hazardous material before October 1, 1998;

(2) *Be operated* in conformance with the requirements of the State in which it is authorized;

(3) *Be specifically authorized* by a State statute or regulation in effect before October 1, 1998, for use as a packaging for the hazardous material being transported;

(4) *Be offered* for transportation and transported in conformance with all other applicable requirements of this subchapter;

(5) *Not be used* to transport a flammable cryogenic liquid, hazardous substance, hazardous waste, or a marine pollutant (except for gasoline); and

(6) *On and after July 1, 2000,* for a tank authorized under paragraph (b) or (c) of this section, conform to all requirements in part 180 (except for §180.405(g)) of this subchapter in the same manner as required for a DOT specification MC 306 cargo tank motor vehicle.

§173.9 Transport vehicles or freight containers containing lading which has been fumigated.

(a) **For the purpose of this section,** not including 49 CFR part 387, a rail car, freight container, truck body, or trailer in which the lading has been fumigated with any material, or is undergoing fumigation, is a package containing a hazardous material, unless the transport vehicle or freight container has been sufficiently aerated so that it does not pose an unreasonable risk to health and safety.

(b) **No person may offer for transportation or transport** a rail car, freight container, truck body, or trailer in which the lading has been fumigated or treated with any material, or is undergoing fumigation, unless the FUMIGANT marking specified in paragraph (c) of this section is prominently displayed so that it can be seen by any person attempting to enter the interior of the transport vehicle or freight container. For domestic transportation, a hazard warning label authorized by EPA under 40 CFR part 156 may be used as an alternative to the FUMIGANT marking.

(c) **FUMIGANT marking.**

(1) *The FUMIGANT marking* must consist of red letters on a white background that is at least 30 cm (11.8 inches) wide and at least 25 cm (9.8 inches) high. Except for size and color, the FUMIGANT marking must be as follows:

DANGER

THIS UNIT IS UNDER FUMIGATION

WITH *__________ APPLIED ON

Date ____________

Time ____________

DO NOT ENTER

(2) *The "*" shall be replaced with the technical name of the fumigant.*

(d) **No person may affix or display on a rail car,** freight container, truck body, or trailer (a package) the FUMIGANT marking specified in paragraph (c) of this section, unless the lading has been fumigated or is undergoing fumigation.

(e) **The FUMIGANT marking required by paragraph (b)** of this section must remain on the rail car, freight container, truck body, or trailer until:

(1) *The fumigated lading is unloaded; and*

(2) *The transport vehicle or freight container* has undergone sufficient aeration to assure that it does not pose an unreasonable risk to health and safety.

(f) **For international shipments, transport documents** must indicate the date of fumigation, type and amount of fumigant used, and instructions for disposal of any residual fumigant, including fumigation devices.

(g) **Any person subject to the requirements of this section,** solely due to the fumigated lading, must be informed of the requirements of this section and the safety precautions necessary to protect themselves and others in the event of an incident or accident involving the fumigated lading.

(h) **Any person who offers for transportation** or transports a rail car, freight container, truck body or trailer that is subject to this subchapter solely because of the hazardous materials designation specified in paragraph (a) of this section is not subject to any other requirements of this subchapter.

§173.10 Tank car shipments.

(a) **Tank cars containing any 2.1 material** (including a cryogenic liquid) or Class 3 material with a flash point below 38 °C (100 °F), except liquid road asphalt or tar, may not be offered for transportation unless originally consigned or subsequently reconsigned to parties having private-siding (see Note 1 of this section) or to parties using railroad siding facilities which have been equipped for piping the liquid from tank cars to permanent storage tanks of sufficient capacity to receive contents of car.

(b) **A tank car containing any Class 2 material** must not be offered for transportation unless the car is consigned for delivery (see paragraph (c) of this section) and unloading on a private track (see Note 1 of this section) except that where no private track is available, delivery and unloading on carrier tracks is permitted provided the following conditions are complied with:

(1) *Any tank car* of DOT-106A or 110A type (see §§179.300 and 179.301 of this subchapter) may be offered for transportation and the loaded unit tanks may be removed from car frame on carrier tracks, provided the shipper has obtained from the delivering carrier and filed with originating carrier, written permission (see Note 2 of this section) for such removal. The consignee must furnish adequately safe mechanical hoist, obtained from the carrier if desirable, by which the tanks shall be lifted from the car and deposited directly upon vehicles furnished by the consignee for immediate removal from carrier property or tanks must be lifted by adequately safe mechanical hoist from car directly to vessels for further transportation.

(c) **Any tank car of other than DOT-106A or 110A type** (see §§179.300 and 179.301 of this subchapter), containing anhydrous ammonia, liquefied hydrocarbon or liquefied petroleum gas, and having interior pipes of liquid and gas discharge valves equipped with check valves, may be consigned for delivery and unloading on carrier tracks, if the lading is piped directly from the car to permanent storage tanks of sufficient capacity to receive the entire contents of the car. Such cars may also be consigned for storage on a private track or on a carrier track when designated by the carrier for such storage.

(d) **For cars of the DOT-106A or 110A type** (see §§179.300 and 179.301 of this subchapter), the tanks must be placed in position and attached to the car structure by the shipper.

(e) **Class 3 materials with a flash point** below 38 °C (100 °F) and Division 2.1 materials (including a cryogenic liquid) may not be loaded into tank cars on carrier property from tank trucks or drums.

NOTE 1: For this purpose, a private track is a track outside of carrier's right-of-way, yard, and terminals, and of which the carrier does not own either the rails, ties, roadbed or right-of-way; or a track or portion of a track which is devoted to the purpose of its user, either by lease or written agreement; in which case the lease or written agreement will be considered as equivalent to ownership.

NOTE 2: Carriers should give permission for the unloading of these containers on carrier tracks only where no private siding is available within reasonable trucking distance of final destination. The danger involved is the release of compressed gases due to accidental damage to container in handling. The exposure to this danger decreases directly with the isolation of the unloading point.

§173.12 Exceptions for shipment of waste materials.

(a) **Open head drums.** If a hazardous material that is a hazardous waste is required by this subchapter to be shipped in a closed head drum (i.e., a drum with a 7.0 cm (3 inches) or less bung opening) and the hazardous waste contains solids or semisolids that make its placement in a closed head drum impracticable, an equivalent (except for closure) open head drum may be used for the hazardous waste.

(b) **Lab packs.**

(1) *Waste materials* classed as Class or Division 3, 4.1, 4.2, 4.3, 5.1, 6.1, 8, or 9 are excepted from the specification packaging requirements of this subchapter for combination packagings if packaged in accordance with this paragraph and transported for disposal or recovery by highway only. In addition, a generic description from the §172.101 table may be used in place of specific chemical names, when two or more chemically compatible waste materials in the same hazard class are packaged in the same outside packaging.

(2) *Additional packaging requirements are as follows:*

(i) *The outer packaging* must be a UN 1A2 or UN 1B2 metal drum, a UN 1D plywood drum, a UN 1G fiber drum or a UN 1H2 plastic drum tested and marked at least for the Packing Group III performance level for liquids or solids;

(ii) *The inner packagings* must be either glass, not exceeding 4 L (1 gallon) rated capacity, or metal or plastic, not exceeding 20 L (5.3 gallons) rated capacity;

(iii) *Each outer packaging* may contain only one class of hazardous material;

(iv) *Inner packagings* containing liquid must be surrounded by a chemically compatible absorbent material in sufficient quantity to absorb the total liquid contents; and

(v) *Gross weight* of the complete package may not exceed 205 kg (452 lbs).

(3) *Prohibited materials.* The following materials may not be packaged or described under the provisions of this paragraph (b): a material poisonous by inhalation, a Division 6.1 Packing Group I material, a Division 4.2 Packing Group I material, chloric acid and oleum (fuming sulfuric acid).

(c) **Reuse of packagings.** A previously used packaging may be reused for the shipment of hazardous waste to designated facilities, not subject to the reconditioning and reuse provisions contained in §173.28 and part 178 of this subchapter, under the following conditions:

(1) *Except as authorized* by this paragraph, the waste must be packaged in accordance with this part and offered for transportation in accordance with the requirements of this subchapter.

(2) *Transportation is performed by highway only.*

(3) *A package* is not offered for transportation less than 24 hours after it is finally closed for transportation, and each package is inspected for leakage and is found to be free from leaks immediately prior to being offered for transportation.

(4) *Each package* is loaded by the shipper and unloaded by the consignee, unless the motor carrier is a private or contract carrier.

(5) *The packaging* may be used only once under this paragraph and may not be used again for shipment of hazardous materials except in accordance with §173.28.

(d) **Technical names for n.o.s. descriptions.** The requirements for the inclusion of technical names for n.o.s. descriptions on shipping papers and package markings, §§172.203 and 172.301 of this subchapter, respectively, do not apply to packages prepared in accordance with paragraph (b) of this section, except that packages containing materials meeting the definition of a hazardous substance must be described as required in §172.203 of this subchapter and marked as required in §172.324 of this subchapter.

§173.13 Exceptions for Class 3, Divisions 4.1, 4.2, 4.3, 5.1, 6.1, and Classes 8 and 9 materials.

(a) **A Class 3, 8 or 9, or Division 4.1, 4.2, 4.3, 5.1, or 6.1 material** is excepted from the labeling (except for the CARGO AIRCRAFT ONLY label) and placarding requirements of this subchapter if prepared for transportation in accordance with the requirements of this section. A material that meets the definition of a material poisonous by inhalation may not be offered for transportation or transported under provisions of this section.

(b) **A hazardous material conforming to requirements** of this section may be transported by motor vehicle, rail car, or cargo-only aircraft. Only hazardous materials permitted to be transported aboard a cargo-only aircraft by column (9B) of the Hazardous Materials Table in §172.101 of this subchapter are authorized for transport aboard cargo-only aircraft pursuant to the provisions of this section.

(c) **A hazardous material permitted by paragraph (a)** of this section must be packaged as follows:

(1) *For liquids:*

(i) *The hazardous material* must be placed in a tightly closed glass, plastic or metal inner packaging with a maximum capacity not exceeding 1.2 L. Sufficient outage must be provided such that the inner packaging will not become liquid full at 55 °C (130 °F). The net quantity (measured at 20 °C (68 °F)) of liquid in any inner packaging may not exceed 1 L.

(ii) *The inner packaging* must be placed in a hermetically-sealed barrier bag which is impervious to the lading, and then wrapped in a non-reactive absorbent material in sufficient quantity to completely absorb the contents of the inner packaging, and placed in a snugly fitting, metal can.

(iii) *The metal can* must be securely closed. For liquids that are in Division 4.2 or 4.3, the metal can must be hermetically sealed. For Division 4.2 materials in Packing Group I, the metal can must be tested in accordance with part 178 of this subchapter at the Packing Group I performance level.

(iv) *The metal can* must be placed in a fiberboard box that is placed in a hermetically-sealed barrier bag which is impervious to the lading.

(v) *The intermediate packaging* must be placed inside a securely closed, outer packaging conforming to §173.201.

(vi) *Not more than* four intermediate packagings are permitted in an outer packaging.

(2) *For solids:*

(i) *The hazardous material* must be placed in a tightly closed glass, plastic or metal inner packaging. The net quantity of material in any inner packaging may not exceed 2.85 kg (6.25 pounds).

(ii) *The inner packaging* must be placed in a hermetically-sealed barrier bag which is impervious to the lading.

(iii) *The barrier bag* and its contents must be placed in a fiberboard box that is placed in a hermetically-sealed barrier bag which is impervious to the lading.

(iv) *The intermediate packaging* must be placed inside an outer packaging conforming to §173.211.

(v) *Not more than* four intermediate packagings are permitted in an outer packaging.

(d) **The outside of the package must be marked,** in association with the proper shipping name, with the statement: "This package conforms to 49 CFR 173.13."

Subpart B - Preparation of Hazardous Materials for Transportation

§173.21 Forbidden materials and packages.

Unless otherwise provided in this subchapter, the offering for transportation or transportation of the following is forbidden:

(a) **Materials that are designated "Forbidden"** in Column 3 of the §172.101 table.

(b) **Forbidden explosives as defined in §173.54 of this part.**

(c) **Electrical devices which are likely to create sparks** or generate a dangerous quantity of heat, unless packaged in a manner which precludes such an occurrence.

(d) **For carriage by aircraft, any package** which has a magnetic field of more than 0.00525 gauss measured at 4.5 m (15 feet) from any surface of the package.

(e) **A material in the same packaging, freight container,** or overpack with another material, the mixing of which is likely to cause a dangerous evolution of heat, or flammable or poisonous gases or vapors, or to produce corrosive materials.

(f) **A package containing a material which is likely** to decompose with a self-accelerated decomposition temperature (SADT) of 50 °C (122 °F) or less, or polymerize at a temperature of 54 °C (130 °F) or less with an evolution of a dangerous quantity of heat or gas when decomposing or polymerizing, unless the material is stabilized or inhibited in a manner to preclude such evolution. The SADT may be determined by any of the test methods described in Part II of the UN Manual of Tests and Criteria (see §171.7 of this subchapter).

(1) *A package* meeting the criteria of paragraph (f) of this section may be required to be shipped under controlled temperature conditions. The control temperature and emergency temperature for a package shall be as specified in the table in this paragraph based upon the SADT of the material. The control temperature is the temperature above which a package of the material may not be offered for transportation or transported. The emergency temperature is the temperature at which, due to imminent danger, emergency measures must be initiated.

§173.21 Table - Method of Determining Control and Emergency Temperature

SADT[1]	Control temperatures	Emergency temperature
SADT ≤ 20 °C (68 °F)	20 °C (36 °F) below SADT	10 °C (18 °F) below SADT
20 °C (68 °F) < SADT ≤ 35 °C (95 °F)	15 °C (27 °F) below SADT	10 °C (18 °F) below SADT
35 °C (95 °F) < SADT ≤ 50 °C (122 °F)	10 °C (18 °F) below SADT	5 °C (9 °F) below SADT
50 °C (122 °F) < SADT	([2])	([2])

1. Self-accelerating decomposition temperature.
2. Temperature control not required.

(2) *For self-reactive materials* listed in §173.224(b) table control and emergency temperatures, where required are shown in Columns 5 and 6, respectively. For organic peroxides listed in The Organic Peroxides Table in §173.225 control and emergency temperatures, where required, are shown in Columns 7a and 7b, respectively.

(3) *Refrigeration may be used* as a means of stabilization only when approved by the Associate Administrator. For status of approvals previously issued by the Bureau of Explosives, see §171.19 of this subchapter. Methods of stabilization approved by the Associate Administrator are as follows:

(i) *For highway transportation:*

[A] A material meeting the criteria of this paragraph (f) may be transported only in a transport vehicle, freight container, or motor vehicle equipped with a mechanical refrigeration unit, or loaded with a consumable refrigerant, capable of maintaining the inside temperature of the hazardous material at or below the control temperature required for the material during transportation.

[B] Each package containing a material meeting the criteria of this paragraph (f) must be loaded and maintained at or below the control temperature required for the material. The temperature of the material must be determined by appropriate means and entered on a written record at the time the packaging is loaded.

[C] The vehicle operator shall monitor the inside temperature of the transport vehicle, freight container, or motor vehicle and enter that temperature on a written record at the time the package is loaded and thereafter at intervals not exceeding two hours. Alternatively, a transport vehicle, freight container, or motor vehicle may be equipped with a visible or audible warning device that activates when the inside temperature of the transport vehicle, freight container, or motor vehicle exceeds the control temperature required for the material. The warning device must be readily visible or audible, as appropriate, from the vehicle operator's seat in the vehicle.

[D] The carrier shall advise the vehicle operator of the emergency temperature for the material, and provide the vehicle operator with written procedures that must be followed to assure maintenance of the control temperature inside the transport vehicle, freight container, or motor vehicle. The written procedures must include instructions for the vehicle operator on actions to take if the inside temperature exceeds the control temperature and approaches or reaches the emergency temperature for the material. In addition, the written temperature-control procedures must identify enroute points where the consumable refrigerant may be procured, or where repairs to, or replacement of, the mechanical refrigeration unit may be accomplished.

[E] The vehicle operator shall maintain the written temperature-control procedures, and the written record of temperature measurements specified in paragraph (f)(3)(i)(C) of this section, if applicable, in the same manner as specified in §177.817 of this subchapter for shipping papers.

[F] If the control temperature is maintained by use of a consumable refrigerant (e.g., dry ice or liquid nitrogen), the quantity of consumable refrigerant must be sufficient to maintain the control temperature for twice the average transit time under normal conditions of transportation.

[G] A material that has a control temperature of 40 °C (104 °F) or higher may be transported by common carrier. A material that has a control temperature below 40 °C (104 °F) must be transported by a private or contract carrier.

(ii) *For transportation by vessel,* shipments are authorized in accordance with the control-temperature requirements of Section 21 of the General Introduction of the IMDG Code (see §171.7 of this subchapter).

(g) **Packages which give off a flammable gas or vapor,** released from a material not otherwise subject to this subchapter, likely to create a flammable mixture with air in a transport vehicle.

(h) **Packages containing materials** (other than those classed as explosive) which will detonate in a fire.

(1) *For purposes* of this paragraph, "detonate" means an explosion in which the shock wave travels through the material at a speed greater than the speed of sound.

(2) *When tests* are required to evaluate the performance of a package under the provisions of this paragraph, the testing must be done or approved by one of the agencies specified in §173.56.

(i) **A package containing a cigarette lighter,** or other similar device, equipped with an ignition element and containing fuel; except that a cigarette lighter or similar device subject to this paragraph may be shipped if the design of the device and its inner packaging has been examined by the Bureau of Explosives and specifically approved by the Associate Administrator. The examination of cigarette lighters and similar devices containing gaseous fuel will include scrutiny for compliance with §173.308 of this part. For the status of approvals previously issued by the Bureau of Explosives, see §171.19 of this subchapter.

(j) **An organic peroxide of the "ketone peroxide" category** which contains more than 9 percent available oxygen as calculated using the equation in §173.128(a)(4)(ii). The category, ketone peroxide, includes, but is not limited to:

Acetyl acetone peroxide
Cyclohexanone peroxide(s)
Diacetone alcohol peroxides
Methylcyclohexanone peroxide(s)
Methyl ethyl ketone peroxide(s)
Methyl isobutyl ketone peroxide(s)

(k) **Notwithstanding any other provision of this subchapter,** including §§171.11 and 175.10(a)(2) of this subchapter, an oxygen generator (chemical) as cargo on a passenger-carrying aircraft. This prohibition does not apply to an oxygen generator for medical or personal use of a passenger that meets the requirements of §175.10(a)(7) of this subchapter.

§173.22 Shipper's responsibility.

(a) **Except as otherwise provided in this part,** a person may offer a hazardous material for transportation in a packaging or container required by this part only in accordance with the following:

(1) *The person* shall class and describe the hazardous material in accordance with parts 172 and 173 of this subchapter, and

(2) *The person* shall determine that the packaging or container is an authorized packaging, including part 173 requirements, and that it has been manufactured, assembled, and marked in accordance with:

(i) *Section 173.7(a) and parts 173, 178, or 179 of this subchapter;*

(ii) *A specification* of the Department in effect at the date of manufacture of the packaging or container;

(iii) *National or international regulations* based on the UN Recommendations, as authorized in §173.24(d)(2);

(iv) *An approval issued under this subchapter; or*

(v) *An exemption issued under subchapter A of this chapter.*

(3) *In making* the determination under paragraph (a)(2) of this section, the person may accept:

(i) *Except for the marking* on the bottom of a metal or plastic drum with a capacity over 100 L which has been reconditioned, remanufactured or otherwise converted, the manufacturer's certification, specification, approval, or exemption marking (see §§178.2 and 179.1 of this subchapter); or

(ii) *With respect* to cargo tanks provided by a carrier, the manufacturer's identification plate or a written certification of specification or exemption provided by the carrier.

(4) *For a DOT specification* or UN standard packaging subject to the requirements of part 178 of this subchapter, a person shall perform all functions necessary to bring that package into compliance with part 178 of this subchapter, as identified by the packaging manufacturer or subsequent distributor, in accordance with §178.2 of this subchapter.

(b) **[Reserved]**

(c) **Prior to each shipment of fissile radioactive materials,** and Type B or highway route controlled quantity packages of radioactive materials (see §173.403), the shipper shall notify the consignee of the dates of shipment and expected arrival. The shipper shall also notify each consignee of any special loading/unloading instructions prior to his first shipment. For any shipment of irradiated reactor fuel, the shipper shall provide physical protection in compliance with a plan established under:

(1) *Requirements prescribed* by the U.S. Nuclear Regulatory Commission, or

(2) *Equivalent requirements* approved by the Associate Administrator, RSPA.

§173.22a Use of packagings authorized under exemptions.

(a) **Except as provided in paragraph (b) of this section,** no person may offer a hazardous material for transportation in a packaging the use of which is dependent upon an exemption issued under subpart B of part 107 of this title, unless that person is the holder of or a party to the exemption.

(b) **If an exemption authorizes the use of a packaging** for the shipment or transportation of a hazardous material by any person or class of persons other than or in addition to the holder of the exemption, that person or a member of that class of persons may use the packaging for the purposes authorized in the exemption subject to the terms specified therein. However, no person may use a packaging under the authority of this paragraph unless he maintains a copy of the exemption at each facility where the packaging is being used in connection with the shipment or transportation of the hazardous material concerned. Copies of exemptions may be obtained from the Associate Administrator for Hazardous Materials Safety, U.S. Department of Transportation, Washington, DC 20590-0001, Attention: RSPA Records Center.

(c) **When an exemption issued to a person** who offers a hazardous material contains requirements that apply to a carrier of the hazardous material, the offeror shall furnish a copy of the exemption to the carrier before or at the time a shipment is tendered.

§173.23 Previously authorized packaging.

(a) **When the regulations specify a packaging** with a specification marking prefix of "DOT," a packaging marked prior to January 1, 1970, with the prefix of "ICC" may be used in its place if the packaging otherwise conforms to applicable specification requirements.

(b) **[Reserved]**

(c) **After July 2, 1982, a seamless aluminum cylinder** manufactured in conformance with and for use under DOT special permit (SP) or exemption (E) 6498, 7042, 8107, 8364 or 8422 may be continued in use if marked before or at the time of the next retest with either the specification identification "3AL" immediately above the special permit or exemption number, or the DOT mark (e.g., DOT 3AL 1800) in proximity to the special permit or exemption marking.

(d) **Cylinders (spheres) manufactured and marked** under DOT special permit (SP) or exemption (E) 6616 prior to January 1, 1983, may be continued in use if marked before or at the time of the next retest with the specification identification "4BA" near the special permit or exemption marking.

(e) **After October 1, 1984, cylinders manufactured** for use under special permit (SP) or exemption (E) 6668 or 8404 may be continued in use, and must be marked "DOT-4LXXXYY" (XXX to be replaced by the service pressure, YY to be replaced by the letters "AL", if applicable) in compliance with Specification 4L (§178.57 of this subchapter) on or before January 1, 1986. The "DOT-4LXXXYY" must appear in proximity to other required special permit or exemption markings.

(f) **An MC 331 cargo tank motor vehicle must conform** to structural integrity requirements in §178.337-3 or to corresponding requirements in effect at the time of manufacture.

(g) **A non-bulk packaging manufactured, tested, marked,** and certified on or before September 30, 1996, in accordance with the applicable provisions of subparts L and M of part 178 of this subchapter in effect on September 30, 1995, may be used as authorized by this subchapter if the packaging conforms to all requirements applicable at the time of manufacture. In addition, such a packaging may be reused as authorized by §173.28 without a nominal thickness marking, if it conforms to the minimum thickness criteria prescribed in §173.28(b)(4).

§173.24 General requirements for packagings and packages.

(a) **Applicability.** Except as otherwise provided in this subchapter, the provisions of this section apply to —

(1) *Bulk and non-bulk packagings;*

(2) *New packagings and packagings which are reused; and*

(3) *Specification and non-specification packagings.*

(b) **Each package used for the shipment** of hazardous materials under this subchapter shall be designed, constructed, maintained, filled, its contents so limited, and closed, so that under conditions normally incident to transportation —

(1) *Except as otherwise provided* in this subchapter, there will be no identifiable (without the use of instruments) release of hazardous materials to the environment;

(2) *The effectiveness* of the package will not be substantially reduced; for example, impact resistance, strength, packaging compatibility, etc. must be maintained for the minimum and maximum temperatures encountered during transportation;

(3) *There will be* no mixture of gases or vapors in the package which could, through any credible spontaneous increase of heat or pressure, significantly reduce the effectiveness of the packaging.

(c) **Authorized packagings.** A packaging is authorized for a hazardous material only if —

(1) *The packaging* is prescribed or permitted for the hazardous material in a packaging section specified for that material in Column 8 of the §172.101 table and conforms to applicable requirements in the special provisions of Column 7 of the §172.101 table and, for specification packagings (but not including UN standard packagings manufactured outside the United States), the specification requirements in parts 178 and 179 of this subchapter; or

(2) *The packaging* is permitted under, and conforms to, provisions contained in §§171.11, 171.12, 171.12a, 173.3, 173.4, 173.5, 173.7, 173.27, or 176.11 of this subchapter.

(d) Specification packagings and UN standard packagings manufactured outside the U.S. —

(1) *Specification packagings.* A specification packaging, including a UN standard packaging manufactured in the United States, must conform in all details to the applicable specification or standard in part 178 or part 179 of this subchapter.

(2) *UN standard packagings* manufactured outside the United States. A UN standard packaging manufactured outside the United States, in accordance with national or international regulations based on the UN Recommendations (see §171.7 of this subchapter), may be imported and used and is considered to be an authorized packaging under the provisions of paragraph (c)(1) of this section, subject to the following conditions and limitations:

(i) *The packaging* fully conforms to applicable provisions in the UN Recommendations and the requirements of this subpart, including reuse provisions;

(ii) *The packaging* is capable of passing the prescribed tests in part 178 of this subchapter applicable to that standard; and

(iii) *The competent authority* of the country of manufacture provides reciprocal treatment for UN standard packagings manufactured in the U.S.

(e) Compatibility.

(1) *Even though* certain packagings are specified in this part, it is, nevertheless, the responsibility of the person offering a hazardous material for transportation to ensure that such packagings are compatible with their lading. This particularly applies to corrosivity, permeability, softening, premature aging and embrittlement.

(2) *Packaging materials* and contents must be such that there will be no significant chemical or galvanic reaction between the materials and contents of the package.

(3) *Plastic packagings and receptacles.*

(i) *Plastic used* in packagings and receptacles must be of a type compatible with the lading and may not be permeable to an extent that a hazardous condition is likely to occur during transportation, handling or refilling.

(ii) *Each plastic* packaging or receptacle which is used for liquid hazardous materials must be capable of withstanding without failure the procedure specified in appendix B of this part ("Procedure for Testing Chemical Compatibility and Rate of Permeation in Plastic Packagings and Receptacles"). The procedure specified in appendix B of this part must be performed on each plastic packaging or receptacle used for Packing Group I materials. The maximum rate of permeation of hazardous lading through or into the plastic packaging or receptacles may not exceed 0.5 percent for materials meeting the definition of a Division 6.1 material according to §173.132 and 2.0 percent for other hazardous materials, when subjected to a temperature no lower than —

[A] 18 °C (64 °F) for 180 days in accordance with Test Method 1 in appendix B of this part;

[B] 50 °C (122 °F) for 28 days in accordance with Test Method 2 in appendix B of this part; or

[C] 60 °C (140 °F) for 14 days in accordance with Test Method 3 in appendix B of this part.

(iii) *Alternative procedures* or rates of permeation are permitted if they yield a level of safety equivalent to or greater than that provided by paragraph (e)(3)(ii) of this section and are specifically approved by the Associate Administrator.

(4) *Mixed contents.* Hazardous materials may not be packed or mixed together in the same outer packaging with other hazardous or non-hazardous materials if such materials are capable of reacting dangerously with each other and causing —

(i) *Combustion or dangerous evolution of heat;*

(ii) *Evolution of flammable, poisonous, or asphyxiant gases; or*

(iii) *Formation of unstable or corrosive materials.*

(5) *Packagings used* for solids, which may become liquid at temperatures likely to be encountered during transportation, must be capable of containing the hazardous material in the liquid state.

(f) Closures.

(1) *Closures on packagings* shall be so designed and closed that under conditions (including the effects of temperature and vibration) normally incident to transportation —

(i) *Except as provided* in paragraph (g) of this section, there is no identifiable release of hazardous materials to the environment from the opening to which the closure is applied; and

(ii) *The closure is secure and leakproof.*

(2) *Except as otherwise provided* in this subchapter, a closure (including gaskets or other closure components, if any) used on a specification packaging must conform to all applicable requirements of the specification.

(g) Venting. Venting of packagings, to reduce internal pressure which may develop by the evolution of gas from the contents, is permitted only when —

(1) *Transportation by aircraft is not involved;*

(2) *Except as otherwise provided* in this subchapter, the evolved gases are not poisonous, likely to create a flammable mixture with air or be an asphyxiant under normal conditions of transportation;

(3) *The packaging* is designed so as to preclude an unintentional release of hazardous materials from the receptacle; and

(4) *For shipments* in bulk packagings, venting is authorized for the specific hazardous material by a special provision in the §172.101 table or by the applicable bulk packaging specification in part 178 of this subchapter.

(h) Outage and filling limits —

(1) *General.* When filling packagings and receptacles for liquids, sufficient ullage (outage) must be left to ensure that neither leakage nor permanent distortion of the packaging or receptacle will occur as a result of an expansion of the liquid caused by temperatures likely to be encountered during transportation. Requirements for outage and filling limits for non-bulk and bulk packagings are specified in §§173.24a(d) and 173.24b(a), respectively.

(2) *Compressed gases and cryogenic liquids.* Filling limits for compressed gases and cryogenic liquids are specified in §§173.301 through 173.306 for cylinders and §§173.314 through 173.319 for bulk packagings.

(i) Air transportation. Packages offered or intended for transportation by aircraft must conform to the general requirements for transportation by aircraft in §173.27, except as provided in §171.11 of this subchapter.

§173.24a Additional general requirements for non-bulk packagings and packages.

(a) Packaging design. Except as provided in §172.312 of this subchapter:

(1) *Inner packaging closures.* A combination packaging containing liquid hazardous materials must be packed so that closures on inner packagings are upright.

(2) *Friction.* The nature and thickness of the outer packaging must be such that friction during transportation is not likely to generate an amount of heat sufficient to alter dangerously the chemical stability of the contents.

(3) *Securing and cushioning.* Inner packagings of combination packagings must be so packed, secured and cushioned to prevent their breakage or leakage and to control their movement within the outer packaging under conditions normally incident to transportation. Cushioning material must not be capable of reacting dangerously with the contents of the inner packagings or having its protective properties significantly weakened in the event of leakage.

(4) *Metallic devices.* Nails, staples and other metallic devices shall not protrude into the interior of the outer packaging in such a manner as to be likely to damage inner packagings or receptacles.

(5) *Vibration.* Each non-bulk package must be capable of withstanding, without rupture or leakage, the vibration test procedure specified in §178.608 of this subchapter.

(b) Non-bulk packaging filling limits.

(1) *A single or composite* non-bulk packaging may be filled with a liquid hazardous material only when the specific gravity of the material does not exceed that marked on the packaging, or a specific gravity of 1.2 if not marked, except as follows:

(i) *A Packing Group I packaging* may be used for a Packing Group II material with a specific gravity not exceeding the greater of 1.8, or 1.5 times the specific gravity marked on the packaging, provided all the performance criteria can still be met with the higher specific gravity material;

(ii) *A Packing Group I packaging* may be used for a Packing Group III material with a specific gravity not exceeding the greater of 2.7, or 2.25 times the specific gravity marked on the packaging, provided all the performance criteria can still be met with the higher specific gravity material; and

(iii) *A Packing Group II packaging* may be used for a Packing Group III material with a specific gravity not exceeding the greater of 1.8, or 1.5 times the specific gravity marked on the packaging, provided all the performance criteria can still be met with the higher specific gravity material.

(2) *Except as otherwise provided* in this section, a non-bulk packaging may not be filled with a hazardous material to a gross mass greater than the maximum gross mass marked on the packaging.

(3) *A single or composite* non-bulk packaging which is tested and marked for liquid hazardous materials may be filled with a solid hazardous material to a gross mass, in kilograms, not exceeding the rated capacity of the packaging in liters, multiplied by the specific gravity marked on the packaging, or 1.2 if not marked. In addition:

(i) *A single or composite non-bulk packaging* which is tested and marked for Packing Group I liquid hazardous materials may be filled with a solid Packing Group II hazardous material to a gross mass, in kilograms, not exceeding the rated capacity of the packaging in liters, multiplied by 1.5, multiplied by the specific gravity marked on the packaging, or 1.2 if not marked.

(ii) *A single or composite* non-bulk packaging which is tested and marked for Packing Group I liquid hazardous materials may be filled with a solid Packing Group III hazardous material to a gross mass, in kilograms, not exceeding the rated capacity of the packaging in liters, multiplied by 2.25, multiplied by the specific gravity marked on the packaging, or 1.2 if not marked.

(iii) *A single or composite* non-bulk packaging which is tested and marked for Packing Group II liquid hazardous materials may be filled with a solid Packing Group III hazardous material to a gross mass, in kilograms, not exceeding the rated capacity of the packaging in liters, multiplied by 1.5, multiplied by the specific gravity marked on the packaging, or 1.2 if not marked.

(4) *Packagings tested* as prescribed in §178.605 of this subchapter and marked with the hydrostatic test pressure as prescribed in §178.503(a)(5) of this subchapter may be used for liquids only when the vapor pressure of the liquid conforms to one of the following:

(i) *The vapor pressure* must be such that the total pressure in the packaging (i.e., the vapor pressure of the liquid plus the partial pressure of air or other inert gases, less 100 kPa (15 psia)) at 55 °C (131 °F), determined on the basis of a maximum degree of filling in accordance with paragraph (d) of this section and a filling temperature of 15 °C (59 °F)), will not exceed two-thirds of the marked test pressure;

(ii) *The vapor pressure* at 50 °C (122 °F) must be less than four-sevenths of the sum of the marked test pressure plus 100 kPa (15 psia); or

(iii) *The vapor pressure* at 55 °C (131 °F) must be less than two-thirds of the sum of the marked test pressure plus 100 kPa (15 psia).

(5) *No hazardous material* may remain on the outside of a package after filling.

(c) Mixed contents.

(1) *An outer non-bulk packaging* may contain more than one hazardous material only when —

(i) *The inner and outer packagings* used for each hazardous material conform to the relevant packaging sections of this part applicable to that hazardous material;

(ii) *The package* as prepared for shipment meets the performance tests prescribed in part 178 of this subchapter for the packing group indicating the highest order of hazard for the hazardous materials contained in the package;

(iii) *Corrosive materials* (except ORM-D) in bottles are further packed in securely closed inner receptacles before packing in outer packagings; and

(iv) *For transportation* by aircraft, the total net quantity does not exceed the lowest permitted maximum net quantity per package as shown in Column 9a or 9b, as appropriate, of the §172.101 table. The permitted maximum net quantity must be calculated in kilograms if a package contains both a liquid and a solid.

(2) *A packaging* containing inner packagings of Division 6.2 materials may not contain other hazardous materials, except dry ice.

(d) Liquids must not completely fill a receptacle at a temperature of 55 °C (131 °F) or less.

§173.24b Additional general requirements for bulk packagings.

(a) Outage and filling limits.

(1) *Except as otherwise provided* in this subchapter, liquids and liquefied gases must be so loaded that the outage is at least five percent for materials poisonous by inhalation, or at least one percent for all other materials, of the total capacity of a cargo tank, portable tank, tank car (including dome capacity), multi-unit tank car tank, or any compartment thereof, at the following reference temperatures —

(i) *46 °C (115 °F) for a noninsulated tank;*

(ii) *43 °C (110 °F)* for a tank car having a thermal protection system, incorporating a metal jacket that provides an overall thermal conductance at 15.5 °C (60 °F) of no more than 10.22 kilojoules per hour per square meter per degree Celsius (0.5 Btu per hour/per square foot/per degree F) temperature differential; or

(iii) *41 °C (105 °F) for an insulated tank.*

(2) *Hazardous materials* may not be loaded into the dome of a tank car. If the dome of the tank car does not provide sufficient outage, vacant space must be left in the shell to provide the required outage.

(b) Equivalent steel. For the purposes of this section, the reference stainless steel is stainless steel with a guaranteed minimum tensile strength of 51.7 deka newtons per square millimeter (75,000 psi) and a guaranteed elongation of 40 percent or greater. Where the regulations permit steel other than stainless steel to be used in place of a specified stainless steel (for example, as in §172.102 of this subchapter, special provision B30), the minimum thickness for the steel must be obtained from one of the following formulas, as appropriate:

Formula for metric units

$$e_1 = (12.74e_0) / (Rm_1\ A_1)^{1/3}$$

Formula for nonmetric units

$$e_1 = (144.2e_0) / (Rm_1\ A_1)^{1/3}$$

Where:

e_0 = Required thickness of the reference stainless steel in mm or inches respectively;

e_1 = Equivalent thickness of the steel used in mm or inches respectively;

Rm_1 = Specified minimum tensile strength of the steel used in dekanewtons per square millimeter or pounds per square inch respectively; and

A_1 = Specified minimum percentage elongation of the steel used multiplied by 100 (for example, 20 percent times 100 equals 20). Elongation values used must be determined from a 50 mm or 2 inch test specimen.

(c) Air pressure in excess of ambient atmospheric pressure may not be used to load or unload any lading which may create an air-enriched mixture within the flammability range of the lading in the vapor space of the tank.

(d) A bulk packaging may not be loaded with a hazardous material that:

(1) *Is at a temperature* outside of the packaging's design temperature range; or

(2) *Except as otherwise provided* in this subchapter, exceeds the maximum weight of lading marked on the specification plate.

(e) UN portable tanks.

(1) *A UN portable tank* manufactured in the United States must conform in all details to the applicable requirements in parts 172, 173, 178 and 180 of this subchapter.

(2) *UN portable tanks* manufactured outside the United States. A UN portable tank manufactured outside the United States, in accordance with national or international regulations based on the UN Recommendations on the Transport of Dangerous Goods which is an authorized packaging under §173.24 of this subchapter, may be filled, offered and transported in the United States, if the §172.101 Table of this subchapter authorizes the hazardous material for transportation in the UN portable tank and it conforms to the applicable T codes, and tank provision codes, or other special provisions assigned to the hazardous material in Column (7) of the Table when manufactured in a country other than the United States. In addition, the portable tank must —

(i) *Conform to* applicable provisions in the UN Recommendations on the Transport of Dangerous Goods (see §171.7 of this subchapter) and the requirements of this subpart;

(ii) *Be capable* of passing the prescribed tests and inspections in part 180 of this subchapter applicable to the UN portable tank specification;

(iii) *Be designed and manufactured* according to the ASME Code (see §171.7 of this subchapter) or a pressure vessel design code approved by the Associate Administrator;

(iv) *Be approved* by the Associate Administrator when the portable tank is designed and constructed under the provisions of an alternative arrangement (see §178.274(a)(2) of this subchapter); and

(v) *The competent authority* of the country of manufacture must provide reciprocal treatment for UN portable tanks manufactured in the United States.

§173.25 Authorized packagings and overpacks.

(a) **Authorized packages containing hazardous materials** may be offered for transportation in an overpack as defined in §171.8 of this subchapter, if all of the following conditions are met:

(1) *The package* meets the requirements of §§173.21 and 173.24 of this subchapter.

(2) *The overpack* is marked with the proper shipping name and identification number, and labeled as required by this subchapter for each hazardous material contained therein unless markings and labels representative of each hazardous material in the overpack are visible.

(3) *Each package* subject to the orientation marking requirements of §172.312 of this subchapter is packed in the overpack with its filling holes up and the overpack is marked with package orientation marking arrows on two opposite vertical sides of the overpack with the arrows pointing in the correct direction of orientation.

(4) *The overpack* is marked with a statement indicating that the inside (inner) packages comply with prescribed specifications when specification packagings are required, unless specification markings on the inside packages are visible.

(5) *Packages containing* Class 8 (corrosive) materials in Packing Group I or Division 5.1 (oxidizing) materials in Packing Group I may not be overpacked with any other materials.

(b) **Shrink-wrapped or stretch-wrapped trays** may be used as outer packagings for inner packagings prepared in accordance with the limited quantity provisions or consumer commodity provisions of this subchapter, provided that —

(1) *Inner packagings* are not fragile, liable to break or be easily punctured, such as those made of glass, porcelain, stoneware or certain plastics; and

(2) *Each complete package* does not exceed 20 kg (44 lbs) gross weight.

(c) **Hazardous materials which are required** to be labeled POISON may be transported in the same motor vehicle with material that is marked or known to be foodstuffs, feed or any edible material intended for consumption by humans or animals provided the hazardous material is marked, labeled, and packaged in accordance with this subchapter, conforms to the requirements of paragraph (a) of this section and is overpacked as specified in §177.841(e) of this subchapter or in an overpack which is a UN 1A2, 1B2, or 1N2 drum tested and marked for a Packing Group II or higher performance level.

§173.26 Quantity limitations.

When quantity limitations do not appear in the packaging requirements of this subchapter, the permitted gross weight or capacity authorized for a packaging is as shown in the packaging specification or standard in part 178 or 179, as applicable, of this subchapter.

§173.27 General requirements for transportation by aircraft.

(a) **The requirements of this section are in addition** to the requirements in §173.24 and apply to packages offered or intended for transportation aboard aircraft. Notwithstanding any Packing Group III performance level specified in Column 5 of the §172.101 table, the required performance level for packages containing Class 4, 5, or 8 materials, when offered or intended for transportation aboard aircraft, is at the Packing Group II performance level, unless otherwise excepted from performance requirements in subpart E of this part.

(b) **Packages authorized on board aircraft.**

(1) *When Column 9a* of the §172.101 table indicates that a material is "Forbidden", that material may not be offered for transportation or transported aboard passenger-carrying aircraft.

(2) *When Column 9b* of the §172.101 table indicates that a material is "Forbidden", that material may not be offered for transportation or transported aboard aircraft.

(3) *The maximum quantity* of hazardous material in a package that may be offered for transportation or transported aboard a passenger-carrying aircraft or cargo aircraft may not exceed that quantity prescribed for the material in Column 9a or 9b, respectively, of the §172.101 table.

(4) *A package* containing a hazardous material which is authorized aboard cargo aircraft but not aboard passenger aircraft must be labeled with the CARGO AIRCRAFT ONLY label required by §172.402(c) of this subchapter and may not be offered for transportation or transported aboard passenger-carrying aircraft.

(c) **Pressure requirements.**

(1) *Packagings must be* designed and constructed to prevent leakage that may be caused by changes in altitude and temperature during transportation aboard aircraft.

(2) *Packagings for which* retention of liquid is a basic function must be capable of withstanding without leakage the greater of —

(i) *An internal pressure* which produces a gauge pressure of not less than 75 kPa (11 psig) for liquids in Packing Group III of Class 3 or Division 6.1; or 95 kPa (14 psig) for other liquids; or

(ii) *A pressure* related to the vapor pressure of the liquid to be conveyed, determined by one of the following:

[A] The total gauge pressure measured in the receptacle (i.e., the vapor pressure of the material and the partial pressure of air or other inert gases, less 100 kPa (15 psia)) at 55 °C (131 °F), multiplied by a safety factor of 1.5; determined on the basis of a filling temperature of 15 °C (59 °F) and a degree of filling such that the receptacle is not completely liquid full at a temperature of 55 °C (131 °F) or less;

[B] 1.75 times the vapor pressure at 50 °C (122 °F) less 100 kPa (15 psia); or

[C] 1.5 times the vapor pressure at 55 °C (131 °F) less 100 kPa (15 psia).

(3) *Notwithstanding the provisions of paragraph (c)(2) of this section* —

(i) *Hazardous materials* may be contained in an inner packaging which does not itself meet the pressure requirement provided that the inner packaging is packed within a supplementary packaging which does meet the pressure requirement and other applicable packaging requirements of this subchapter.

(ii) *Packagings* which are subject to the hydrostatic pressure test and marking requirements of §§178.605 and 178.503(a)(5), respectively, of this subchapter must have a marked test pressure of not less than 250 kPa (36 psig) for liquids in Packing Group I, 80 kPa (12 psig) for liquids in Packing Group III of Class 3 or Division 6.1, and 100 kPa (15 psig) for other liquids.

(d) **Closures.** Stoppers, corks or other such friction-type closures must be held securely, tightly and effectively in place by positive means. Each screw-type closure on any packaging must be secured to prevent closure from loosening due to vibration or substantial change in temperature.

(e) **Absorbent materials.** Except as otherwise provided in this subchapter, liquids in Packing Group I or II of Class 3, 4, 5, 6, or 8, when in glass or earthenware inner packagings, must be packaged using material capable of absorbing and not likely to react dangerously with the liquid. Absorbent material is not required if the inner packagings are so protected that breakage of them and leakage of their contents from the outer packaging is not likely to occur under normal conditions of transportation and is not required for packagings containing liquids in Packing Group II for transport aboard cargo aircraft only. Where absorbent material is required and an outer packaging is not liquid-tight, a means of containing the liquid in the event of leakage must be used in the form of a leakproof liner, plastic bag or other equally efficient means of containment. Where absorbent material is required, the quantity and disposition of it in each outer packaging must be as follows:

(1) *For packagings* containing liquids in Packing Group I offered for transportation or transported aboard passenger-carrying aircraft, each packaging must contain sufficient absorbent material to absorb the contents of all inner packagings containing such liquids;

(2) *For packagings* containing liquids in Packing Group I offered for transportation or transported aboard cargo aircraft only and packagings containing liquids in Packing Group II offered for transportation or transported aboard passenger aircraft, each package must contain sufficient absorbent material to absorb the contents of any one of the inner packagings containing such liquids and, where they are of different sizes and quantities, sufficient absorbent material to absorb the contents of the inner packaging containing the greatest quantity of liquid.

(f) **Combination packagings.** Unless otherwise specified in this part, or in §171.11 of this subchapter, when combination packagings are offered for transportation aboard aircraft, inner packagings must conform to the quantity limitations set forth in table 1 of this paragraph for transport aboard passenger-carrying aircraft and table 2 of this paragraph for transport aboard cargo aircraft only, as follows:

Table 1 - Maximum Net Capacity of Inner Packaging for Transportation on Passenger-Carrying Aircraft

Maximum net quantity per package from Column 9a of the §172.101 table	Maximum authorized net capacity of each inner packaging	
	Glass, earthenware or fiber inner packagings	Metal or plastic inner packagings
Liquids:		
Not greater than 0.5L	0.5L	0.5L
Greater than 0.5L, not greater than 1L	0.5L	1L
Greater than 1L, not greater than 5L	1L	5L
Greater than 5L, not greater than 60L	2.5L	10L
Greater than 60L, not greater than 220L	5L	25L
Greater than 220L	No limit	No limit
Solids:		
Not greater than 5 kg	0.5 kg	1 kg
Greater than 5 kg, not greater than 25 kg	1 kg	2.5 kg
Greater than 25 kg, not greater than 200 kg	5 kg	10 kg
Greater than 200 kg	No limit	No limit

Table 2 - Maximum Net Capacity of Inner Packaging for Transportation on Cargo Aircraft

Maximum net quantity per package from Column 9b of the §172.101 table	Maximum authorized net capacity of each inner packaging	
	Glass, earthenware or fiber inner packagings	Metal or plastic inner packagings
Liquids:		
Not greater than 2.5L	1L	1L
Greater than 2.5L, not greater than 30L	2.5L	2.5L
Greater than 30L, not greater than 60L	5L	10L
Greater than 60L, not greater than 220L	5L	25L
Greater than 220L	No limit	No limit
Solids:		
Not greater than 15 kg	1 kg	2.5 kg
Greater than 15 kg, not greater than 50 kg	2.5 kg	5 kg
Greater than 50 kg, not greater than 200 kg	5 kg	10 kg
Greater than 200 kg	No limit	No limit

(g) Cylinders. For any cylinder containing hazardous materials and incorporating valves, sufficient protection must be provided to prevent operation of, and damage to, the valves during transportation, by one of the following methods:

(1) *By equipping* each cylinder with securely attached valve caps or protective headrings; or

(2) *By boxing or crating the cylinder.*

(h) Tank cars and cargo tanks. Any tank car or cargo tank containing a hazardous material may not be transported aboard aircraft.

§173.28 Reuse, reconditioning, and remanufacture of packagings.

(a) General. Packagings and receptacles used more than once must be in such condition, including closure devices and cushioning materials, that they conform in all respects to the prescribed requirements of this subchapter. Before reuse, each packaging must be inspected and may not be reused unless free from incompatible residue, rupture, or other damage which reduces its structural integrity.

(b) Reuse of non-bulk packaging. A non-bulk packaging used more than once must conform to the following provisions and limitations:

(1) *A non-bulk packaging* which, upon inspection, shows evidence of a reduction in integrity may not be reused unless it is reconditioned in accordance with paragraph (c) of this section.

(2) *Before reuse,* packagings subject to the leakproofness test with air prescribed in §178.604 of this subchapter shall be —

(i) *Retested without failure* in accordance with §178.604 of this subchapter using an internal air pressure (gauge) of at least 48 kPa (7.0 psig) for Packing Group I and 20 kPa (3.0 psig) for Packing Group II and Packing Group III; and

(ii) *Marked with the letter "L",* with the name and address or symbol of the person conducting the test, and the last two digits of the year the test was conducted. Symbols, if used, must be registered with the Associate Administrator.

(3) *Packagings made* of paper, plastic film, or textile are not authorized for reuse;

(4) *Metal and plastic* drums and jerricans used as single packagings or the outer packagings of composite packagings are authorized for reuse only when they are marked in a permanent manner (e.g., embossed) in mm with the nominal (for metal packagings) or minimum (for plastic packagings) thickness of the packaging material, as required by §178.503(a)(9) of this subchapter, and —

(i) *Except as provided* in paragraph (b)(4)(ii) of this section, conform to the following minimum thickness criteria:

Maximum capacity not over	Minimum thickness of packaging material	
	Metal drum or jerrican	Plastic drum or jerrican
20 L	0.63 mm (0.025 inch)	1.1 mm (0.043 inch)
30 L	0.73 mm (0.029 inch)	1.1 mm (0.043 inch)
40 L	0.73 mm (0.029 inch)	1.8 mm (0.071 inch)
60 L	0.92 mm (0.036 inch)	1.8 mm (0.071 inch)
120 L	0.92 mm (0.036 inch)	2.2 mm (0.087 inch)
220 L	0.92 mm (0.036 inch)[1]	2.2 mm (0.087 inch)
450 L	1.77 mm (0.070 inch)	5.0 mm (0.197 inch)

1. Metal drums or jerricans with a minimum thickness of 0.82 mm body and 1.09 mm heads which are manufactured and marked prior to January 1, 1997 may be reused. Metal drums or jerricans manufactured and marked on or after January 1, 1997, and intended for reuse, must be constructed with a minimum thickness of 0.82 mm body and 1.11 mm heads.

(ii) *For stainless steel* drums and jerricans, conform to a minimum wall thickness as determined by the following equivalence formula:

Formula for Metric Units

$$e_1 = \frac{21.4 \text{ x } e_0}{\sqrt[3]{Rm_1 \text{ x } A_1}}$$

Formula for U.S. Standard Units

$$e_1 = \frac{21.4 \text{ x } e_0}{\sqrt[3]{(Rm_1 \text{ x } A_1)/145}}$$

Where:

e_1 = required equivalent wall thickness of the metal to be used (in mm or, for U.S. Standard units, use inches).

e_0 = required minimum wall thickness for the reference steel (in mm or, for U.S. Standard units, use inches).

Rm_1 = guaranteed minimum tensile strength of the metal to be used (in N/mm^2 or for U.S. Standard units, use psi).

A_1 = guaranteed minimum elongation (as a percentage) of the metal to be used on fracture under tensile stress (see paragraph (c)(1) of this section).

(5) *Plastic inner receptacles* of composite packagings must have a minimum thickness of 1.0 mm (0.039 inch).

(6) *A previously used* non-bulk packaging may be reused for the shipment of hazardous waste, not subject to the reconditioning and reuse provisions of this section, in accordance with §173.12(c).

(7) *Notwithstanding the provisions* of paragraph (b)(2) of this section, a packaging otherwise authorized for reuse may be reused without being leakproofness tested with air provided the packaging —

(i) *Is refilled* with a material which is compatible with the previous lading:

(ii) *Is refilled and offered for transportation by the original filler;*

(iii) *Is transported* in a transport vehicle or freight container under the exclusive use of the refiller of the packaging; and

(iv) *Is constructed of* —

[A] Stainless steel, monel or nickel with a thickness not less than one and one-half times the minimum thickness prescribed in paragraph (b)(4) of this section;

[B] Plastic, provided the packaging is not refilled for reuse on a date more than five years from the date of manufacture marked on the packaging in accordance with §178.503(a)(6) of this subchapter; or

[C] Another material or thickness when approved under the conditions established by the Associate Administrator for reuse without retesting.

(c) Reconditioning of non-bulk packaging.

(1) *For the purpose of this subchapter, reconditioning of metal drums is:*

(i) *Cleaning to base material* of construction, with all former contents, internal and external corrosion, and any external coatings and labels removed;

(ii) *Restoring to original* shape and contour, with chimes (if any) straightened and sealed, and all non-integral gaskets replaced: and

(iii) *Inspecting after cleaning but before painting,* Packagings that have visible pitting, significant reduction in material thickness, metal fatigue, damaged threads or closures, or other significant defects, must be rejected.

(2) *For the purpose* of this subchapter, reconditioning of a non-bulk packaging other than a metal drum or a UN 1H1 plastic drum includes:

(i) *Removal of all former contents,* external coatings and labels, and cleaning to the original materials of construction;

(ii) *Inspection after cleaning* with rejection of packagings with visible damage such as tears, creases or cracks, or damaged threads or closures, or other significant defects;

(iii) *Replacement of all* non-integral gaskets and closure devices with new or refurbished parts, and cushioning and cushioning materials; and components including gaskets, closure devices and cushioning and cushioning material. (For a UN 1H1 plastic drum, replacing a removable gasket or closure device with another of the same design and material that provides equivalent performance does not constitute reconditioning); and

(iv) *Ensuring that the packagings* are restored to a condition that conforms in all respects with the prescribed requirements of this subchapter.

(3) *A person* who reconditions a packaging manufactured and marked under the provisions of subpart L of part 178 of this subchapter, shall mark that packaging as required by §178.503(c) and (d) of this subchapter. The marking is the certification of the reconditioner that the packaging conforms to the standard for which it is marked and that all functions performed by the reconditioner which are prescribed by this subchapter have been performed in compliance with this subchapter.

(4) *The markings* applied by the reconditioner may be different from those applied by the manufacturer at the time of original manufacture, but may not identify a greater performance capability than that for which the original design type had been tested (for example, the reconditioner may mark a drum which was originally marked as 1A1/Y1.8 as 1A1/Y1.2 or 1A1/Z2.0).

(5) *Packagings* which have significant defects which cannot be repaired may not be reused.

(d) Remanufacture of non-bulk packagings. For the purpose of this subchapter, remanufacture is the conversion of a non-specification, non-bulk packaging to a DOT specification or U.N. standard, the conversion of a packaging meeting one specification or standard to another specification or standard (for example, conversion of 1A1 non-removable head drums to 1A2 removable head drums) or the replacement of integral structural packaging components (such as non-removable heads on drums). A person who remanufactures a non-bulk packaging to conform to a specification or standard in part 178 of this subchapter is subject to the requirements of part 178 of this subchapter as a manufacturer.

(e) Non-reusable containers. A packaging marked as NRC according to the DOT specification or UN standard requirements of part 178 of this subchapter may be reused for the shipment of any material not required by this subchapter to be shipped in a DOT specification or UN standard packaging.

(f) A Division 6.2 packaging to be reused must be disinfected prior to reuse by any means effective for neutralizing the infectious substance the packaging previously contained. A secondary packaging or outer packaging conforming to the requirements of §173.196 or §173.199 need not be disinfected prior to reuse if no leakage from the primary receptacle has occurred.

§173.29 Empty packagings.

(a) General. Except as otherwise provided in this section, an empty packaging containing only the residue of a hazardous material shall be offered for transportation and transported in the same manner as when it previously contained a greater quantity of that hazardous material.

(b) Notwithstanding the requirements of paragraph (a) of this section, an empty packaging is not subject to any other requirements of this subchapter if it conforms to the following provisions:

(1) *Any hazardous material* shipping name and identification number markings, any hazard warning labels or placards, and any other markings indicating that the material is hazardous (e.g., RQ, INHALATION HAZARD) are removed, obliterated, or securely covered in transportation. This provision does not apply to transportation in a transport vehicle or a freight container if the packaging is not visible in transportation and the packaging is loaded by the shipper and unloaded by the shipper or consignee;

(2) *The packaging* —

(i) *Is unused;*

(ii) *Is sufficiently cleaned* of residue and purged of vapors to remove any potential hazard;

(iii) *Is refilled* with a material which is not hazardous to such an extent that any residue remaining in the packaging no longer poses a hazard; or

(iv) *Contains only the residue of* —

[A] An ORM-D material; or

[B] A Division 2.2 non-flammable gas, other than ammonia, anhydrous, and with no subsidiary hazard, at an absolute pressure less than 280 kPa (40.6 psia); at 20 °C (68 °F); and

(3) *Any material* contained in the packaging does not meet the definitions in §171.8 of this subchapter for a hazardous substance, a hazardous waste, or a marine pollutant.

(c) A non-bulk packaging containing only the residue of a hazardous material covered by table 2 of §172.504 of this subchapter —

(1) *Does not have to be included* in determining the applicability of the placarding requirements of subpart F of part 172 of this subchapter; and

(2) *Is not subject* to the shipping paper requirements of this subchapter when collected and transported by a contract or private carrier for reconditioning, remanufacture or reuse.

(d) Notwithstanding the stowage requirements in Column 10a of the §172.101 table for transportation by vessel, an empty drum or cylinder may be stowed on deck or under deck.

(e) Specific provisions for describing an empty packaging on a shipping paper appear in §172.203(e) of this subchapter.

(f) [Reserved]

(g) A package which contains a residue of an elevated temperature material may remain marked in the same manner as when it contained a greater quantity of the material even though it no longer meets the definition in §171.8 of this subchapter for an elevated temperature material.

§173.30 Loading and unloading of transport vehicles.

A person who loads or unloads hazardous materials into or from a transport vehicle or vessel shall comply with the applicable loading and unloading requirements of parts 174, 175, 176, and 177 of this subchapter.

§173.31 Use of tank cars.

(a) General.

(1) *No person* may offer a hazardous material for transportation in a tank car unless the tank car meets the applicable specification and packaging requirements of this subchapter or, when this subchapter authorizes the use of an non-DOT specification tank car, the applicable specification to which the tank was constructed.

(2) *Tank cars and appurtenances* may be used for the transportation of any commodity for which they are authorized in this part and specified on the certificate of construction (AAR Form 4-2 or by addendum on Form R-1). See §179.5 of this subchapter. Transfer of a tank car from one specified service on its certificate of construction to another may be made only by the owner or with the owner's authorization. A tank car proposed for a commodity service other than specified on its certificate of construction must be approved for such service by the AAR's Tank Car Committee.

(3) *No person* may fill a tank car overdue for periodic inspection with a hazardous material and then offer it for transportation. Any tank car marked as meeting a DOT specification and any non-specification tank car transporting a hazardous material must have a periodic inspection and test conforming to subpart F of part 180 of this subchapter.

(4) *No railroad tank car,* regardless of its construction date, may be used for the transportation in commerce of any hazardous material unless the air brake equipment support attachments of such tank car conform to the standards for attachments set forth in §§179.100-16 and 179.200-19 of this subchapter.

(5) *No railroad tank car,* regardless of its construction date, may be used for the transportation in commerce of any hazardous material with a self-energized manway located below the liquid level of the lading.

(6) *Unless otherwise specifically provided in this part:*

(i) *When the tank car delimiter is an "A,"* offerors may also use tank cars with a delimiter "S," "J" or "T".

(ii) *When the tank car delimiter is an "S,"* offerors may also use tank cars with a delimiter "J" or "T".

(iii) *When a tank car delimiter is a "T"* offerors may also use tank cars with a delimiter of "J".

(iv) *When a tank car delimiter is a "J",* offerors may not use a tank car with any other delimiter.

(b) Safety systems —

(1) *Coupler vertical restraint.* Each tank car conforming to a DOT specification and any other tank car used for transportation of a hazardous material must be equipped with a coupler vertical restraint system that meets the requirements of §179.14 of this subchapter.

(2) *Pressure relief devices.*

(i) *Pressure relief devices* on tank cars must conform to part 179 of this subchapter.

(ii) *Except for shipments* of chloroprene, stabilized, in class DOT 115 tank cars, single-unit tank cars used for materials meeting the definition for Division 6.1 liquid, Packing Group I or II, Class 2 materials, or Class 3 or 4 liquids, must have reclosing pressure relief devices. However, a tank car built before January 1, 1991, and equipped with a non-closing pressure relief device may be used to transport a Division 6.1 or Class 4 liquid if the liquid is not poisonous by inhalation. Unless otherwise specifically provided in this subchapter, rupture discs may not have any perforated holes to allow for venting.

(3) *Tank-head puncture-resistance requirements.* The following tank cars must have a tank-head puncture-resistance system that conforms to the requirements in §179.16 of this subchapter, or to the corresponding requirements in effect at the time of installation:

(i) *Tank cars transporting a Class 2 material.*

(ii) *Tank cars* constructed from aluminum or nickel plate that are used to transport hazardous material.

(iii) *Except as provided* in paragraph (b)(3)(iv) of this section, those tank cars specified in paragraphs (b)(3)(i) and (ii) of this section not requiring a tank-head puncture resistance system prior to July 1, 1996, must have a tank-head puncture resistance system installed no later than July 1, 2006.

(iv) *Class DOT* 105A tank cars built prior to September 1, 1981, having a tank capacity less than 70 kl (18,500 gallons), and used to transport a Division 2.1 (flammable gas) material, must have a tank-head puncture-resistant system installed no later than July 1, 2001.

(4) *Thermal protection requirements.* The following tank cars must have thermal protection that conforms to the requirements of §179.18 of this subchapter:

(i) *Tank cars* transporting a Class 2 material, except for a class 106, 107A, 110, and 113 tank car. A tank car equipped with a thermal protection system conforming to §179.18 of this subchapter, or that has an insulation system having an overall thermal conductance of no more than 0.613 kilojoules per hour, per square meter, per degree Celsius temperature differential (0.03 B.t.u. per square foot, per hour, per degree Fahrenheit temperature differential), conforms to this requirement.

(ii) *A tank car* transporting a Class 2 material that was not required to have thermal protection prior to July 1, 1996, must be equipped with thermal protection no later than July 1, 2006.

(5) *Bottom-discontinuity* protection requirements. No person may offer for transportation a hazardous material in a tank car with bottom discontinuity protection unless the tank car has bottom-discontinuity protection that conforms to the requirements of E9.00 and E10.00 of the AAR Specifications for Tank Cars. Tank cars not requiring bottom-discontinuity protection under the terms of appendix Y of the AAR Specifications for Tank Cars as of July 1, 1996, must conform to these requirements no later than July 1, 2006. Tank cars modified before July 1, 1996, may conform to the bottom-discontinuity protection requirements of appendix Y of the 1992 edition of the AAR Specifications for Tank Cars.

(6) *Scheduling of modifications and progress reporting.* The date of conformance for the continued use of tank cars subject to paragraphs (b)(3), (b)(4), (b)(5), (e)(2), and (f) of this section and §§173.314(j) and 173.323(c)(1) is subject to the following conditions and limitations.

(i) *Each tank car owner* shall modify, reassign, retire, or remove at least 50 percent of their in-service tank car fleet within the first half of the compliance period and the remainder of their in-service tank car fleet during the second half of the compliance period.

(ii) *By October 1 of each year,* each owner of a tank car subject to this paragraph (b)(6) shall submit to the Federal Railroad Administration, Hazardous Materials Division, Office of Safety Assurance and Compliance, 1120 Vermont Avenue, Mail Stop 25, Washington, DC 20590, a progress report that shows the total number of in-service tank cars that need head protection, thermal protection, or bottom-discontinuity protection; the number of new or different tank cars acquired to replace those tank cars required to be upgraded to a higher service pressure; and the total number of tank cars modified, reassigned, acquired, retired, or removed from service the previous year.

(c) Tank car test pressure. A tank car used for the transportation of a hazardous material must have a tank test pressure equal to or greater than the greatest of the following:

(1) *Except for shipments* of carbon dioxide, anhydrous hydrogen chloride, vinyl fluoride, ethylene, or hydrogen, 133 percent of the sum of lading vapor pressure at the reference temperature of 46 °C (115 °F) for non-insulated tank cars or 41 °C (105 °F) for insulated tank cars plus static head, plus gas padding pressure in the vacant space of a tank car;

(2) *133 percent* of the maximum loading or unloading pressure, whichever is greater;

(3) *20.7 Bar* (300 psig) for materials that are poisonous by inhalation (see §173.31(e)(2)(ii) for compliance dates);

(4) *The minimum pressure* prescribed by the specification in part 179 of this subchapter; or

(5) *The minimum test pressure* prescribed for the specific hazardous material in the applicable packaging section in subpart F or G of this part.

(d) Examination before shipping.

(1) *No person* may offer for transportation a tank car containing a hazardous material or a residue of a hazardous material unless that person determines that the tank car is in proper condition and safe for transportation. As a minimum, each person offering a tank car for transportation must perform an external visual inspection that includes:

(i) *Except where* insulation or a thermal protection system precludes an inspection, the tank shell and heads for abrasion, corrosion, cracks, dents, distortions, defects in welds, or any other condition that makes the tank car unsafe for transportation;

(ii) *The piping, valves, fittings, and gaskets* for corrosion, damage, or any other condition that makes the tank car unsafe for transportation;

(iii) *For missing or loose* bolts, nuts, or elements that make the tank car unsafe for transportation;

(iv) *All closures* on tank cars and determine that the closures and all fastenings securing them are properly tightened in place by the use of a bar, wrench, or other suitable tool;

(v) *Protective housings for proper securement;*

(vi) *The pressure relief device,* including a careful inspection of the rupture disc in non-reclosing pressure relief devices, for corrosion or damage that may alter the intended operation of the device;

(vii) *Each tell-tale indicator* after filling and prior to transportation to ensure the integrity of the rupture disc;

(viii) *The external* thermal protection system, tank-head puncture resistance system, coupler vertical restraint system, and bottom discontinuity protection for conditions that make the tank car unsafe for transportation;

(ix) *The required markings on the tank car for legibility; and*

(x) *The periodic* inspection date markings to ensure that the inspection and test intervals are within the prescribed intervals.

(2) *Closures on tank cars* are required, in accordance with this subchapter, to be designed and closed so that under conditions normally incident to transportation, including the effects of temperature and vibration, there will be no identifiable release of a hazardous material to the environment. In any action brought to enforce this section, the lack of securement of any closure to a tool-tight condition, detected at any point, will establish a rebuttable presumption that a proper inspection was not performed by the offeror of the car. That presumption may be rebutted by any evidence indicating that the lack of securement resulted from a specific cause not within the control of the offeror.

(e) Special requirements for materials poisonous by inhalation —

(1) *Interior heater coils.* Tank cars used for materials poisonous by inhalation may not have interior heater coils.

(2) *Tank car specifications.* A tank car used for a material poisonous by inhalation must have a tank test pressure of 20.7 Bar (300

psig) or greater, head protection, and a metal jacket (e.g., DOT 105S300W), except that —

(i) *A higher test pressure* is required if otherwise specified in this subchapter; and

(ii) *Other than as provided* in paragraph (b)(6) of this section, a tank car which does not conform to the requirements of this paragraph (e)(2), and was authorized for the material poisonous by inhalation under the regulations in effect on June 30, 1996, may continue in use until July 1, 2006.

(f) **Special requirements for hazardous substances.**

(1) *A tank car* used for a hazardous substance listed in paragraph (f)(2) of this section must have a tank test pressure of at least 13.8 Bar (200 psig), head protection and a metal jacket, except that —

(i) *No metal jacket is required if* —

[A] The tank test pressure is 23.4 Bar (340 psig) or higher; or

[B] The tank shell and heads are manufactured from AAR steel specification TC-128, normalized;

(ii) *A higher test pressure* is required if otherwise specified in this subchapter; and

(iii) *Other than* as provided in paragraph (b)(6) of this section, a tank car which does not conform to the requirements of this paragraph (f)(1), and was authorized for a hazardous substance under the regulations in effect on June 30, 1996, may continue in use until July 1, 2006.

(2) *List of hazardous substances.* Hazardous substances for which the provisions of this paragraph (f) apply are as follows:

Aldrin
Allyl chloride
alpha-BHC
beta-BHC
delta-BHC
gamma-BHC
Bis(2-chloroethyl) ether
Bromoform
Carbon tetrachloride
Chlordane
p-Chloroaniline
Chlorobenzene
Chlorobenzilate
p-Chloro-m-cresol
2-Chloroethyl vinyl ether
Chloroform
2-Chloronapthalene
o-Chlorophenol
3-Chloropropionitrile
DDE
DDT
1,2-Dibromo-3-chloropropane
m-Dichlorobenzene
o-Dichlorobenzene
p-Dichlorobenzene
3,3'-Dichlorobenzidine
1,4-Dichloro-2-butene
1,1-Dichloroethane
1,2-Dichloroethane
1,1-Dichloroethylene
Dichloroisopropyl ether
Dichloromethane @
2,4-Dichlorophenol
2,6-Dichlorophenol
1,2-Dichloropropane
1,3-Dichloropropene
Dieldrin
alpha-Endosulfan
beta-Endosulfan
Endrin
Endrin aldehyde
Heptachlor
Heptachlor epoxide
Hexachlorobenzene
Hexachlorobutadiene
Hexachloroethane
Hexachlorophene
Hexachloropropene
Isodrin
Kepone
Methoxychlor
4,4'-Methylenebis(2-chloroaniline)
Methylene bromide
Pentachlorobenzene
Pentachloroethane
Pentachloronitrobenzene (PCNB)
Pentachlorophenol
Polychlorinated biphenyls (PCBs)
Pronamide
Silvex (2,4,5-TP)
2,4,5-T
TDE
1,2,4,5-Tetrachlorobenzene
2,3,7,8-Tetrachlorodibenzo-p-dioxin (TCDD)
Tetrachloroethane
Tetrachloroethylene
2,3,4,6-Tetrachlorophenol
Toxaphene
1,2,4-Trichlorobenzene
1,1,1-Trichloroethane
1,1,2-Trichloroethane
Trichloroethylene
2,4,5-Trichlorophenol
2,4,6-Trichlorophenol
Tris(2,3-dibromopropyl) phosphate

§173.32 Requirements for the use of portable tanks.

(a) **General requirements.** No person may offer a hazardous material for transportation in a portable tank except as authorized by this subchapter.

(1) *Except as otherwise provided* in this subpart, no person may use a portable tank for the transportation of a hazardous material unless it meets the requirements of this subchapter.

(2) *No person* may fill and offer for transportation a portable tank when the prescribed periodic test or inspection under subpart G of part 180 of this subchapter has become due until the test or inspection has been successfully completed. This requirement does not apply to any portable tank filled prior to the test or inspection due date.

(3) *When a portable tank* is used as a cargo tank motor vehicle, it must conform to all the requirements prescribed for cargo tank motor vehicles. (See §173.33.)

(b) **Substitute packagings.** A particular Specification portable tank may be substituted for another portable tank as follows:

(1) *An IM or UN portable tank* may be used whenever an IM or UN portable tank having less stringent requirements is authorized provided the portable tank meets or exceeds the requirements for pressure-relief devices, bottom outlets and any other special provisions specified in §172.102(c)(7)(vi) of this subchapter.

(2) *Where a Specification* IM101 or IM102 portable tank is prescribed, a UN portable tank or Specification 51 portable tank otherwise conforming to the special commodity requirements of §172.102(c)(7) of this subchapter for the material to be transported may be used.

(3) *A DOT Specification* 51 portable tank may be used whenever a DOT Specification 56, 57, or 60 portable tank is authorized. A DOT Specification 60 portable tank may be used whenever a DOT Specification 56 or 57 portable tank is authorized. A higher integrity tank used instead of a specified portable tank must meet the same design profile; for example, a DOT Specification 51 portable tank must be lined if used instead of a lined DOT Specification 60 portable tank.

(c) **Grandfather provisions for portable tanks** —

(1) *Continued use* of Specification 56 and 57 portable tanks. Continued use of an existing portable tank constructed to DOT Specification 56 or 57 is authorized only for a portable tank constructed before October 1, 1996. A stainless steel portable tank internally lined with polyethylene that was constructed on or before October 1, 1996, and that meets all requirements of DOT Specification 57 except for being equipped with a polypropylene discharge ball valve and polypropylene secondary discharge opening closure, may be marked as a Specification 57 portable tank and used in accordance with the provisions of this section.

(2) *A DOT Specification 51,* IM 101, or IM 102 portable tank may not be manufactured after January 1, 2003; however, such tanks may continue to be used for the transportation of a hazardous material provided they meet the requirements of this subchapter, including the specification requirements and the requirements of this subchapter for the transportation of the particular hazardous material according to the T codes in effect on September 30, 2001 or the new T codes in §172.102(c)(7)(i) (see 171.14(d)(4) for transitional provisions applicable to T

codes), and provided it conforms to the periodic inspection and tests specified for the particular portable tank in subpart G of part 180 of this subchapter. After January 1, 2003, all newly manufactured portable tanks must conform to the requirements for the design, construction and approval of UN portable tanks as specified in §§178.273, 178.274, 178.275, 178.276, 178.277 and part 180, subpart G, of this subchapter.

(3) *A DOT Specification* portable tank manufactured prior to January 1, 1992 that is equipped with a non-reclosing pressure relief device may continue in service for the hazardous materials for which it is authorized. Except for a DOT Specification 56 or 57 portable tank, a DOT Specification portable tank manufactured after January 1, 1992, used for materials meeting the definition for Division 6.1 liquids, Packing Group I or II, Class 2 gases, or Class 3 or 4 liquids, must be equipped with a reclosing pressure relief valve having adequately sized venting capacity unless otherwise specified in this subchapter (see §§178.275(f)(4) and 178.277 of this subchapter).

(4) *Any portable tank container* constructed prior to May 15, 1950, complying with the requirements of either the ASME Code for Unfired Pressure Vessels, 1946 Edition, or the API ASME Code for Unfired Pressure Vessels, 1943 Edition (see §171.7 of this subchapter), may be used for the transportation of liquefied compressed gas, provided it fulfills all the requirements of the part and specifications for the particular gas or gases to be transported. Such portable tanks must be marked "ICC Specification 51X" on the plate required by the specification, except as modified by any or all of the following:

(i) *Portable tanks* designed and constructed in accordance with Pars. U-68, U-69, or U-201 of the ASME Code (see §171.7 of this subchapter) may be used. Portable tanks designed and constructed in accordance with Par. U-68 or Par. U-69 may be re-rated at a working pressure 25 percent in excess of the design pressure for which the portable tank was originally constructed. If the portable tank is re-rated, the re-rated pressure must be marked on the plate as follows: "Re-rated working pressure — psig".

Note to Paragraph (c)(4)(i): For purposes of setting safety relief valves, pressure control valves, establishing retest pressure and maximum and minimum design pressures, the re-rated working pressure must be considered as the equivalent of the design pressure as defined in the specification.

(ii) *Loading and unloading* accessories, valves, piping, fittings, safety and gauging devices, do not have to comply with the requirements for the particular location on the portable tank.

(5) *Any ICC Specification* 50 portable tank fulfilling the requirements of that specification may be continued in service for transportation of a liquefied petroleum gas if it is retested every five years in accordance with the requirements in §180.605 of this subchapter. Use of existing portable tanks is authorized. New construction is not authorized.

(d) **Determination of an authorized portable tank.** Prior to filling and offering a portable tank for transportation, the shipper must ensure that the portable tank conforms to the authorized specification and meets the applicable requirements in this subchapter for the hazardous material. The shipper must ensure that the MAWP, design pressure or test pressure of the portable tank, as applicable, is appropriate for the hazardous material being transported. Determination of the applicable pressure must take into account the maximum pressure used to load or unload the hazardous material, the vapor pressure, static head and surge pressures of the hazardous material and the temperatures that the hazardous material will experience during transportation.

(e) **External inspection prior to filling.** Each portable tank must be given a complete external inspection prior to filling. Any unsafe condition must be corrected prior to its being filled and offered for transportation. The external inspection shall include a visual inspection of:

(1) *The shell,* piping, valves and other appurtenances for corroded areas, dents, defects in welds and other defects such as missing, damaged, or leaking gaskets;

(2) *All flanged connections* or blank flanges for missing or loose nuts and bolts;

(3) *All emergency devices* for corrosion, distortion, or any damage or defect that could prevent their normal operation;

(4) *All required markings on the tank for legibility; and*

(5) *Any device* for tightening manhole covers to ensure such devices are operative and adequate to prevent leakage at the manhole cover.

(f) **Loading requirements.**

(1) *A hazardous material* may not be loaded into a portable tank if the hazardous material would:

(i) *Damage the portable tank;*

(ii) *React with the portable tank; or*

(iii) *Otherwise compromise its product retention capability.*

(2) *A hazardous material* may not be loaded in a DOT Specification 51, DOT Specification 60, an IM or UN portable tank unless the portable tank has a pressure relief device that provides total relieving capacity meeting the requirements of this subchapter.

(3) *Except during a pressure test,* a portable tank may not be subjected to a pressure greater than its marked maximum allowable working pressure or, when appropriate, its marked design pressure.

(4) *A portable tank* may not be loaded to a gross mass greater than the maximum allowable gross mass specified on its identification plate.

(5) *Except for* a non-flowable solid or a liquid with a viscosity of 2,680 centistokes (millimeters squared per second) or greater at 20 °C (68 °F), an IM or UN portable tank, or compartment thereof, having a volume greater than 7,500 L (1,980 gallons) may not be loaded to a filling density of more than 20% and less than 80% by volume. This filling restriction does not apply if a portable tank is divided by partitions or surge plates into compartments of not more than 7,500 L (1,980 gallons) capacity; this portable tank must not be offered for transportation in an ullage condition liable to produce an unacceptable hydraulic force due to surge.

(6) *The outage* for a portable tank may not be less than 2% at a temperature of 50 °C (122 °F) unless otherwise specified in this subchapter. For UN portable tanks, the applicable maximum filling limits apply as specified according to the assigned TP codes in Column (7) of the §172.101 Table of this subchapter except when transported domestically.

(7) *Each tell-tale indicator* or pressure gauge located in the space between a frangible disc and a safety relief valve mounted in series must be checked after the tank is filled and prior to transportation to ensure that the frangible disc is leak free. Any leakage through the frangible disc must be corrected prior to offering the tank for transportation.

(8) *During filling,* the temperature of the hazardous materials shall not exceed the limits of the design temperature range of the portable tank.

(9) *The maximum mass* of liquefied compressed gas per liter (gallon) of shell capacity (kg/L or lbs./gal.) may not exceed the density of the liquefied compressed gas at 50 °C (122 °F). The portable tank must not be liquid full at 60 °C (140 °F).

(g) **Additional requirements for specific modal transport.** In addition to other applicable requirements, the following apply:

(1) *A portable tank* containing a hazardous material may not be loaded on to a highway or rail transport vehicle unless loaded entirely within the horizontal outline thereof, without overhang or projection of any part of the tank assembly. In addition, for unloading a portable tank, see §177.834(i)(2) of this subchapter.

(2) *An IM or UN* portable tank used for the transportation of flammable liquids by rail may not be fitted with non-reclosing pressure relief devices except in series with reclosing pressure relief valves.

(3) *A portable tank* or Specification 106A or 110A multi-unit tank car containing a hazardous material may not be offered for transportation aboard a passenger vessel unless:

(i) *The vessel* is operating under a change to its character of vessel certification as defined in §171.8 of this subchapter; and

(ii) *The material* is permitted to be transported aboard a passenger vessel in the §172.101 Table of this subchapter.

(h) **Additional general commodity-specific requirements.** In addition to other applicable requirements, the following requirements apply:

(1) *Each uninsulated* portable tank used for the transportation of a liquefied compressed gas must have an exterior surface finish that is significantly reflective, such as a light-reflecting color if painted, or a bright reflective metal or other material if unpainted.

(2) *If a hazardous material* is being transported in a molten state, the portable tank must be thermally insulated with suitable insulation material of sufficient thickness that the overall thermal conductance is not more than 0.080 Btu per hour per square foot per degree Fahrenheit differential.

(i) **Additional requirements for portable tanks** other than IM specification and UN portable tanks.

(1) *The bursting strength* of any piping and fittings must be at least four times the design pressure of the tank, and at least four times the pressure to which, in any instance, it may be subjected in service by the action of a pump or other device (not including safety relief valves) that may subject piping to pressures greater than the design pressure of the tank.

(2) *Pipe joints must be threaded, welded or flanged.* If threaded pipe is used, the pipe and pipe fittings must not be lighter than Sched-

ule 80 weight. Where copper tubing is permitted, joints must be brazed or be of equally strong metal union type. The melting point of brazing material may not be lower than 1,000 °F (537.8 °C). The method of joining tubing must not decrease the strength of the tubing such as by the cutting of threads.

(3) *Non-malleable metals* may not be used in the construction of valves or fittings.

(4) *Suitable provision* must be made in every case to allow for expansion, contraction, jarring and vibration of all pipe. Slip joints may not be used for this purpose.

(5) *Piping and fittings* must be grouped in the smallest practicable space and must be protected from damage as required by the specification.

(6) *All piping,* valves and fittings on every portable tank must be leakage tested with gas or air after installation and proved tight at not less than the design pressure of the portable tank on which they are used. In the event of replacement, all such piping, valves, or fittings must be tested in accordance with the requirements of this section before the portable tank is returned to transportation service. The requirements of this section apply to all hoses used on portable tanks, except that hoses may be tested either before or after installation on the portable tank.

(7) *All materials* used in the construction of portable tanks and their appurtenances may not be subject to destructive attack by the contents of the portable tank.

(8) *No aluminum, copper, silver, zinc* nor their alloys may be used. Brazed joints may not be used. All parts of a portable tank and its appurtenances used for anhydrous ammonia must be steel.

(9) *Each outlet* of a portable tank used for the transportation of non-refrigerated liquefied compressed gases, except carbon dioxide, must be provided with a suitable automatic excess-flow valve (see definition in §178.337-1(g) of this subchapter). The valve must be located inside the portable tank or at a point outside the portable tank where the line enters or leaves the portable tank. The valve seat must be located inside the portable tank or may be located within a welded flange or its companion flange, or within a nozzle or within a coupling. The installation must be made in such a manner as to reasonably assure that any undue strain which causes failure requiring functioning of the valve shall cause failure in such a manner that it will not impair the operation of the valve.

(i) *A safety device connection* or liquid level gauging device that is constructed so that the outward flow of the tank contents will not exceed that passed by an opening of 0.1397 cm (0.0550 inches) is not required to be equipped with excess-flow valves.

(ii) *An excess-flow valve* must close automatically if the flow reaches the rated flow of gas or liquid specified by the original valve manufacturer when piping mounted directly on the valve is sheared off before the first valve, pump, or fitting downstream from the excess flow valve.

(iii) *An excess-flow valve* may be designed with a by-pass, not to exceed a 0.1016 cm (0.040 inches) diameter opening to allow equalization of pressure.

(iv) *Filling and discharge lines* must be provided with manually operated shut-off valves located as close to the tank as practical. Unless this valve is manually operable at the valve, the line must also have a manual shut-off valve. The use of "Stop-Check" valves to satisfy with one valve the requirements of this section is forbidden. For portable tanks used for refrigerated liquefied gases, a "stop check" valve may be used on the vapor side of the pressure buildup circuit.

(10) *Each portable tank* used for carbon dioxide or nitrous oxide must be lagged with a suitable insulation material of such thickness that the overall thermal conductance is not more than 0.08 Btu per square foot per degree Fahrenheit differential in temperature per hour. The conductance must be determined at 60 °Fahrenheit. Insulation material used on portable tanks for nitrous oxide must be noncombustible.

(11) *Refrigerating or heating coils* must be installed in portable tanks used for carbon dioxide and nitrous oxide. Such coils must be tested externally to at least the same pressure as the test pressure of the portable tank. The coils must also be tested internally to at least twice the working pressure of the heating or refrigerating system to be used, but in no case less than the test pressure of the portable tank. Such coils must be securely anchored. In the event of leakage, the refrigerant or heating medium to be circulated through the coil or coils must have no adverse chemical reaction with the portable tank or its contents.

(12) *Excess flow valves* are not required for portable tanks used for the transport of refrigerated liquefied gases.

FEDERAL REGISTER UPDATES

In the May 30, 2003 Federal Register, §173.32 was revised, effective June 30, 2003.

(g) [1]

(1) *A portable tank* containing a hazardous material may not be loaded onto a highway or rail transport vehicle unless loaded entirely within the horizontal outline of the vehicle, without overhang or projection of any part of the tank assembly. [2]

(h) [3]

(3) *No person may offer* a liquid hazardous material of Class 3, PG I or II, or PG III with a flash point of less than 100 °F (38 °C); Division 5.1, PG I or II; or Division 6.1, PG I or II, in an IM or UN portable tank that is equipped with a bottom outlet as authorized in Column (7) of the §172.101 Table of this subchapter by assignment of a T Code in the appropriate proper shipping name entry, for unloading to a facility while it remains on a transport vehicle with the power unit attached unless — [4]

(i) *The tank outlets conform to §178.275(d)(3) of this subchapter; or*

(ii) *The facility* at which the IM or UN portable tank is to be unloaded conforms to the requirements in §177.834(o) of this subchapter.

1. Paragraph (g) is the same as before.
2. Paragraph (g)(1) was revised.
3. Paragraph (h) is the same as before.
4. Paragraph (h)(3) was added.

§173.33 Hazardous materials in cargo tank motor vehicles.

(a) General requirements.

(1) *No person* may offer or accept a hazardous material for transportation in a cargo tank motor vehicle except as authorized by this subchapter.

(2) *Two or more materials* may not be loaded or accepted for transportation in the same cargo tank motor vehicle if, as a result of any mixture of the materials, an unsafe condition would occur, such as an explosion, fire, excessive increase in pressure or heat, or the release of toxic vapors.

(3) *No person* may fill and offer for transportation a specification cargo tank motor vehicle for which the prescribed periodic retest or reinspection under subpart E of part 180 of this subchapter is past due until the retest or inspection has been successfully completed. This requirement does not apply to a cargo tank supplied by a motor carrier who is other than the person offering the hazardous material for transportation (see §180.407(a)(1) of this subchapter), or to any cargo tank filled prior to the retest or inspection due date.

(b) Loading requirements.

(1) *A hazardous material* may not be loaded in a cargo tank if during transportation any part of the tank in contact with the hazardous material lading would have a dangerous reaction with the hazardous material.

(2) *A cargo tank* may not be loaded with a hazardous material that will have an adverse effect on the tank's integrity or —

(i) *May combine chemically* with any residue or contaminants in the tank to produce an explosion, fire, excessive increase in pressure, release of toxic vapors or other unsafe condition.

(ii) - (iii) *[Reserved]*

(iv) *May severely corrode* or react with the tank material at any concentration and temperature that will exist during transportation.

(v) *Is prohibited by §173.21 or §173.24 of this subchapter.*

(3) *Air pressure* in excess of ambient atmospheric pressure may not be used to load or unload any lading which may create an air-enriched mixture within the flammability range of the lading in the vapor space of the tank.

(4) *To prevent* cargo tank rupture in a loading or unloading accident, the loading or unloading rate used must be less than or equal to that indicated on the cargo tank specification plate, except as specified in §173.318(b)(6). If no loading or unloading rate is marked on the specification plate, the loading or unloading rate and pressure used must be limited such that the pressure in the tank may not exceed 130% of the MAWP.

(c) Maximum Lading Pressure.

(1) *Prior to loading and offering* a cargo tank motor vehicle for transportation with material that requires the use of a specification cargo tank, the person must confirm that the cargo tank motor vehicle conforms to the specification required for the lading and that the MAWP of the cargo tank is greater than or equal to the largest pressure obtained under the following conditions:

(i) *For compressed gases* and certain refrigerated liquids that are not cryogenic liquids, the pressure prescribed in §173.315 of this subchapter.

(ii) *For cryogenic liquids,* the pressure prescribed in §173.318 of this subchapter.

(iii) *For liquid hazardous materials* loaded in DOT specification cargo tanks equipped with a 1 psig normal vent, the sum of the tank static head plus 1 psig. In addition, for hazardous materials loaded in these cargo tanks, the vapor pressure of the lading at 115 °F must be not greater than 1 psig, except for gasoline transported in accordance with Special Provision B33 in §172.102(c)(3) of this subchapter.

(iv) *For liquid hazardous materials* not covered in paragraph (c)(1)(i), (ii), or (iii) of this section, the sum of the vapor pressure of the lading at 115 °F, plus the tank static head exerted by the lading, plus any pressure exerted by the gas padding, including air in the ullage space or dome.

(v) *The pressure* prescribed in subpart B, D, E, F, G, or H of this part, as applicable.

(vi) *The maximum pressure in the tank during loading or unloading.*

(2) *Any Specification* MC 300, MC 301, MC 302, MC 303, MC 305, MC 306 or MC 312, cargo tank motor vehicle with no marked design pressure or marked with a design pressure of 3 psig or less may be used for an authorized lading where the pressure derived from §173.33(c)(1) is less than or equal to 3 psig. After December 31, 1990, a cargo tank may not be loaded and offered for transportation unless marked or remarked with an MAWP or design pressure in accordance with 49 CFR 180.405(k).

(3) *Any Specification* MC 310 or MC 311 cargo tank motor vehicle may be used for an authorized lading where the pressure derived from §173.33(c)(1) is less than or equal to the MAWP or MWP, respectively, as marked on the specification plate.

(4) *Any cargo tank* marked or certified before August 31, 1995, marked with a design pressure rather than an MAWP may be used for an authorized lading where the largest pressure derived from §173.33(c)(1) is less than or equal to the design pressure marked on the cargo tank.

(5) *Any material* that meets the definition of a Division 6.1, Packing Group I or II (poisonous liquid) material must be loaded in a cargo tank motor vehicle having a MAWP of 25 psig or greater.

(d) **Relief system.**

(1) *Non-reclosing* pressure relief devices are not authorized in any cargo tank except when in series with a reclosing pressure relief device. However, a cargo tank marked or certified before August 31, 1995 which is fitted with non-reclosing pressure relief devices may continue to be used in any hazardous material service for which it is authorized. The requirements in this paragraph do not apply to MC 330, MC 331 and MC 338 cargo tanks.

(2) *Each cargo tank* motor vehicle used to transport a liquid hazardous material with a gas pad must have a pressure relief system that provides the venting capacity prescribed in §178.345-10(e) of this subchapter. The requirements in this paragraph do not apply to MC 330, MC 331 and MC 338 cargo tanks.

(3) *A cargo tank* motor vehicle made to a specification listed in column 1 may have pressure relief devices or outlets conforming to the applicable specification to which the tank was constructed, or the pressure relief devices or outlets may be modified to meet the applicable requirement for the specification listed in column 2 without changing the markings on the tank specification plate. The venting capacity requirements of the original DOT cargo tank specification must be met whenever a pressure relief valve is modified.

Column 1	Column 2
MC 300, MC 301, MC 302, MC 303, MC 305	MC 306 or DOT 406
MC 306	DOT 406
MC 304	MC 307 or DOT 407
MC 307	DOT 407
MC 310, MC 311	MC 312 or DOT 412
MC 312	DOT 412
MC 330	MC 331

(e) **Retention of hazardous materials in product piping** during transportation. DOT specification cargo tanks used for the transportation of any material that is a Division 6.1 (poisonous liquid) material, oxidizer liquid, liquid organic peroxide or corrosive liquid (corrosive to skin only) may not be transported with hazardous materials lading retained in the piping, unless the cargo tank motor vehicle is equipped with bottom damage protection devices meeting the requirements of §178.337-10 or §178.345-8(b) of this subchapter, or the accident damage protection requirements of the specification under which it was manufactured. This requirement does not apply to a residue which remains after the piping is drained. A sacrificial device (see §178.345-1 of this subchapter) may not be used to satisfy the accident damage protection requirements of this paragraph.

(f) **An MC 331 type cargo tank may be used** where MC 306, MC 307, MC 312, DOT 406, DOT 407 or DOT 412 type cargo tanks are authorized. An MC 307, MC 312, DOT 407 or DOT 412 type cargo tank may be used where MC 306 or DOT 406 type cargo tanks are authorized. A higher integrity tank used instead of a specified tank must meet the same design profile (for example, an MC 331 cargo tank must be lined if used in place of a lined MC 312 cargo tank.)

(g) **Unless otherwise specified,** where MC 307, MC 312, DOT 407 or DOT 412 cargo tanks are authorized, minimum tank design pressure is 172.4 kPa (25 psig) for any Packing Group I or Packing Group II liquid lading that meets more than one hazard class definition.

(h) **Each liquid or vapor discharge opening** in an MC 330 or MC 331 cargo tank and each liquid filling and liquid discharge line in an MC 338 cargo tank must be provided with a remotely controlled internal self-closing stop valve, except when an MC 330 or MC 331 cargo tank is marked and used exclusively to transport carbon dioxide, or except when an MC 338 is used to transport argon, carbon dioxide, helium, krypton, neon, nitrogen, and xenon. However, if the cargo tank motor vehicle was certified before January 1, 1995, this requirement is applicable only when an MC 330 or MC 331 cargo tank is used to transport a flammable liquid, flammable gas, hydrogen chloride (refrigerated liquid), or anhydrous ammonia; or when an MC 338 cargo tank is used to transport flammable ladings.

FEDERAL REGISTER UPDATES

In the April 18, 2003 Federal Register, §173.33 was revised, effective October 1, 2003.

(c) [1]

(6) *Substitute packagings.* Unless otherwise specified, where MC 307, MC 312, DOT 407 or DOT 412 cargo tanks are authorized, minimum tank design pressure is 172.4 kPa (25 psig) for any Packing Group I or Packing Group II liquid lading that meets more than one hazard class definition. [2]

(g) **Remote control of self-closing stop valves** — MC 330, MC 331 and MC 338 cargo tanks. Each liquid or vapor discharge opening in an MC 330 or MC 331 cargo tank and each liquid filling and liquid discharge line in an MC 338 cargo tank must be provided with a remotely controlled internal self-closing stop valve, except when an MC 330 or MC 331 cargo tank is marked and used exclusively to transport carbon dioxide, or except when an MC 338 is used to transport argon, carbon dioxide, helium, krypton, neon, nitrogen, and xenon. However, if the cargo tank motor vehicle was certified before January 1, 1995, this requirement is applicable only when an MC 330 or MC 331 cargo tank is used to transport a flammable liquid, flammable gas, hydrogen chloride (refrigerated liquid), or anhydrous ammonia; or when an MC 338 cargo tank is used to transport flammable ladings. [3]

1. Paragraph (c) is the same as before.
2. Paragraph (g) was redesignated as paragraph (c)(6), and the paragraph heading for new paragraph (c)(6) was added.
3. Paragraph (h) was redesignated as paragraph (g), and the paragraph heading for new paragraph (g) was added.

§173.34 [Reserved]

§173.35 Hazardous materials in IBCs.

(a) **No person may offer or accept a hazardous material** for transportation in an IBC except as authorized by this subchapter. Each IBC used for the transportation of hazardous materials must conform to the requirements of its specification and regulations for the transportation of the particular commodity. A specification IBC, for which the prescribed periodic retest or inspection under subpart D of part 180 of this subchapter is past due, may not be filled and offered for transportation until the retest or inspection have been successfully completed. This requirement does not apply to any IBC filled prior to the retest or inspection due date.

(b) **Initial use and reuse of IBCs.** An IBC other than a multiwall paper IBC (13M1 and 13M2) may be reused. If an inner liner is required, the inner liner must be replaced before each reuse. Before an IBC is filled and offered for transportation, the IBC and its service equipment must be given an external visual inspection, by the person filling the IBC, to ensure that:

(1) *The IBC* is free from corrosion, contamination, cracks, cuts, or other damage which would render it unable to pass the prescribed design type test to which it is certified and marked; and

(2) *The IBC* is marked in accordance with requirements in §178.703 of this subchapter. Additional marking allowed for each design type may be present. Required markings that are missing, damaged or difficult to read must be restored or returned to original condition.

(c) **A metal IBC, or a part thereof,** subject to thinning by mechanical abrasion or corrosion due to the lading, must be protected by providing a suitable increase in thickness of material, a lining or some other suitable method of protection. Increased thickness for corrosion or abrasion protection must be added to the wall thickness specified in §178.705(c)(1)(iv) of this subchapter.

(d) Notwithstanding requirements in §173.24b of this subpart, when filling an IBC with liquids, sufficient ullage must be left to ensure that, at the mean bulk temperature of 50 °C (122 °F), the IBC is not filled to more than 98 percent of its water capacity.

(e) Where two or more closure systems are fitted in series, the system nearest to the hazardous material being carried must be closed first.

(f) During transportation —

(1) *No hazardous material may remain on the outside of the IBC; and*

(2) *Each IBC* must be securely fastened to or contained within the transport unit.

(g) Each IBC used for transportation of solids which may become liquid at temperatures likely to be encountered during transportation must also be capable of containing the substance in the liquid state.

(h) Liquid hazardous materials may only be offered for transportation in a metal, rigid plastic, or composite IBC that is appropriately resistant to an increase of internal pressure likely to develop during transportation.

(1) *A rigid plastic or composite IBC* may only be filled with a liquid having a vapor pressure less than or equal to the greater of the following two values: the first value is determined from any of the methods in paragraphs (h)(1) (i), (ii) or (iii) of this section. The second value is determined by the method in paragraph (h)(1)(iv) of this section.

(i) *The gauge pressure* (pressure in the IBC above ambient atmospheric pressure) measured in the IBC at 55 °C (131 °F). This gauge pressure must not exceed two-thirds of the marked test pressure and must be determined after the IBC was filled and closed at 15 °C (60 °F) to less than or equal to 98 percent of its capacity.

(ii) *The absolute pressure* (vapor pressure of the hazardous material plus atmospheric pressure) in the IBC at 50 °C (122 °F). This absolute pressure must not exceed four-sevenths of the sum of the marked test pressure and 100 kPa (14.5 psia).

(iii) *The absolute pressure* (vapor pressure of the hazardous material plus atmospheric pressure) in the IBC at 55 °C (131 °F). This absolute pressure must not exceed two-thirds of the sum of the marked test pressure and 100 kPa (14.5 psia).

(iv) *Twice the static pressure of the substance,* measured at the bottom of the IBC. This value must not be less than twice the static pressure of water.

(2) *Gauge pressure* (pressure in the IBC above ambient atmospheric pressure) in metal IBC must not exceed 110 kPa (16 psig) at 50 °C (122 °F) or 130 kPa (18.9 psig) at 55 °C (131 °F).

(i) The requirements in this section do not apply to DOT-56 or -57 portable tanks.

(j) No IBC may be filled with a Packing Group I liquid. Rigid plastic, composite, flexible, wooden or fiberboard IBC used to transport Packing Group I solid materials may not exceed 1.5 cubic meters (53 cubic feet) capacity. For Packing Group I solids, a metal IBC may not exceed 3 cubic meters (106 cubic feet) capacity.

(k) When an IBC is used for the transportation of liquids with a flash point of 60.5 °C (141 °F) (closed cup) or lower, or powders with the potential for dust explosion, measures must be taken during product loading and unloading to prevent a dangerous electrostatic discharge.

(l) IBC filling limits.

(1) *Except as provided in this section,* an IBC may not be filled with a hazardous material in excess of the maximum gross mass marked on that container.

(2) *An IBC which is tested and marked* for Packing Group II liquid materials may be filled with a Packing Group III liquid material to a gross mass not exceeding 1.5 times the maximum gross mass marked on that container, if all the performance criteria can still be met at the higher gross mass.

(3) *An IBC which is tested and marked* for liquid hazardous materials may be filled with a solid hazardous material to a gross mass not exceeding the maximum gross mass marked on that container. In addition, an IBC intended for the transport of liquids which is tested and marked for Packing Group II liquid materials may be filled with a Packing Group III solid hazardous material to a gross mass not exceeding the marked maximum gross mass multiplied by 1.5 if all the performance criteria can still be met at the higher gross mass.

(4) *An IBC which is tested and marked* for Packing Group I solid materials may be filled with a Packing Group II solid material to a gross mass not exceeding the maximum gross mass marked on that container, multiplied by 1.5, if all the performance criteria can be met at the higher gross mass; or a Packing Group III solid material to a gross mass not exceeding the maximum gross mass marked on the IBC, multiplied by 2.25, if all the performance criteria can be met at the higher gross mass. An IBC which is tested and marked for Packing Group II solid materials may be filled with a Packing Group III solid material to a gross mass not exceeding the maximum gross mass marked on the IBC, multiplied by 1.5.

§173.40 General packaging requirements for toxic materials packaged in cylinders.

When this section is referenced for a Hazard Zone A or B hazardous material elsewhere in this subchapter, the requirements in this section are applicable to cylinders used for that material.

(a) Authorized cylinders.

(1) *A cylinder* must conform to one of the specifications for cylinders in subpart C of part 178 of this subchapter, except that specification 8, 8AL, and 39 cylinders are not authorized.

(2) *After September 30, 2002,* DOT 3AL cylinders made of aluminum alloy 6351-T6 may not be filled and offered for transportation or transported with a Division 2.3 Hazard Zone A material, a Division 6.1 Hazard Zone A material, or any liquid meeting the definition of Division 6.1 and the criteria for Packing Group I Hazard Zone A, as specified in §173.133. If it is otherwise serviceable and conforms to the regulations in effect on September 30, 2002, a DOT 3AL cylinder made of aluminum alloy 6351-T6 and filled before October 1, 2002, may be transported for reprocessing or disposal of the cylinder's contents until April 1, 2003.

(b) Outage and pressure requirements. The pressure at 55 °C (131 °F) of Hazard Zone A and, after December 31, 2003, Hazard Zone B materials may not exceed the service pressure of the cylinder. Sufficient outage must be provided so that the cylinder will not be liquid full at 55 °C (131 °F).

(c) Closures. Each cylinder containing a Hazard Zone A material must be closed with a plug or valve conforming to the following:

(1) *Each plug or valve* must have a taper-threaded connection directly to the cylinder and be capable of withstanding the test pressure of the cylinder without damage or leakage.

(2) *Each valve* must be of the packless type with non-perforated diaphragm, except that, for corrosive materials, a valve may be of the packed type with an assembly made gas-tight by means of a seal cap with gasketed joint attached to the valve body or the cylinder to prevent loss of material through or past the packing.

(3) *Each valve outlet* must be sealed by a threaded cap or threaded solid plug and inert gasketing material.

(4) *The materials* of construction for the cylinder, valves, plugs, outlet caps, luting, and gaskets must be compatible with each other and with the lading.

(d) Additional handling protection. Each cylinder or cylinder overpack combination offered for transportation containing a Division 2.3 or 6.1 Hazard Zone A or B material must conform to the valve damage protection performance requirements of this section. In addition to the requirements of this section, overpacks must conform to the overpack provisions of §173.25.

(1) *Each cylinder* with a wall thickness at any point of less than 2.03 mm (0.08 inch) and each cylinder that does not have fitted valve protection must be overpacked in a box. The box must conform to overpack provisions in §173.25. Box and valve protection must be of sufficient strength to protect all parts of the cylinder and valve, if any, from deformation and breakage resulting from a drop of 2.0 m (7 ft) or more onto a non-yielding surface, such as concrete or steel, impacting at an orientation most likely to cause damage. "Deformation" means a cylinder or valve that is bent, distorted, mangled, misshapen, twisted, warped, or in a similar condition.

(2) *Each cylinder* with a valve must be equipped with a protective metal cap, other valve protection device, or an overpack which is sufficient to protect the valve from breakage or leakage resulting from a drop of 2.0 m (7 ft) onto a non-yielding surface, such as concrete or steel. Impact must be at an orientation most likely to cause damage.

(e) Interconnection. Cylinders may not be manifolded or interconnected.

Subpart C - Definitions, Classification, and Packaging for Class 1

§173.50 Class 1 — Definitions.

(a) **Explosive.** For the purpose of this subchapter, an explosive means any substance or article, including a device, which is designed to function by explosion (i.e., an extremely rapid release of gas and heat) or which, by chemical reaction within itself, is able to function in a similar manner even if not designed to function by explosion, unless the substance or article is otherwise classed under the provision of this subchapter.

(b) **Explosives in Class 1 are divided into six divisions as follows:**

(1) **Division 1.1** consists of explosives that have a mass explosion hazard. A mass explosion is one which affects almost the entire load instantaneously.

(2) **Division 1.2** consists of explosives that have a projection hazard but not a mass explosion hazard.

(3) **Division 1.3** consists of explosives that have a fire hazard and either a minor blast hazard or a minor projection hazard or both, but not a mass explosion hazard.

(4) **Division 1.4** consists of explosives that present a minor explosion hazard. The explosive effects are largely confined to the package and no projection of fragments of appreciable size or range is to be expected. An external fire must not cause virtually instantaneous explosion of almost the entire contents of the package.

(5) **Division 1.5**[1] consists of very insensitive explosives. This division is comprised of substances which have a mass explosion hazard but are so insensitive that there is very little probability of initiation or of transition from burning to detonation under normal conditions of transport.

(6) **Division 1.6**[2] consists of extremely insensitive articles which do not have a mass explosive hazard. This division is comprised of articles which contain only extremely insensitive detonating substances and which demonstrate a negligible probability of accidental initiation or propagation.

§173.51 Authorization to offer and transport explosives.

(a) **Unless otherwise provided in this subpart,** no person may offer for transportation or transport an explosive, unless it has been tested and classed and approved by the Associate Administrator (§173.56).

(b) **Reports of explosives approved by** the Department of Defense or the Department of Energy must be filed with, and receive acknowledgement in writing by, the Associate Administrator prior to such explosives being offered for transportation.

§173.52 Classification codes and compatibility groups of explosives.

(a) **The classification code for an explosive,** which is assigned by the Associate Administrator in accordance with this subpart, consists of the division number followed by the compatibility group letter. Compatibility group letters are used to specify the controls for the transportation, and storage related thereto, of explosives and to prevent an increase in hazard that might result if certain types of explosives were stored or transported together. Transportation compatibility requirements for carriers are prescribed in §§174.81, 175.78. 176.83 and 177.848 of this subchapter for transportation by rail, air, vessel, and public highway, respectively, and storage incidental thereto.

(b) **Compatibility groups and classification codes** for the various types of explosives are set forth in the following tables. Table 1 sets forth compatibility groups and classification codes for substances and articles described in the first column of table 1. Table 2 shows the number of classification codes that are possible within each explosive division. Altogether, there are 35 possible classification codes for explosives.

1. The probability of transition from burning to detonation is greater when large quantities are transported in a vessel.
2. The risk from articles of Division 1.6 is limited to the explosion of a single article.

Table 1 - Classification Codes

Description of substances or article to be classified	Compatibility group	Classification code
Primary explosive substance	A	1.1A
Article containing a primary explosive substance and not containing two or more effective protective features. Some articles, such as detonators for blasting, detonator assemblies for blasting and primers, cap-type, are included, even though they do not contain primary explosives	B	1.1B 1.2B 1.4B
Propellant explosive substance or other deflagrating explosive substance or article containing such explosive substance	C	1.1C 1.2C 1.3C 1.4C
Secondary detonating explosive substance or black powder or article containing a secondary detonating explosive substance, in each case without means of initiation and without a propelling charge, or article containing a primary explosive substance and containing two or more effective protective features	D	1.1D 1.2D 1.4D 1.5D
Article containing a secondary detonating explosive substance, without means of initiation, with a propelling charge (other than one containing flammable liquid or gel or hypergolic liquid)	E	1.1E 1.2E 1.4E
Article containing a secondary detonating explosive substance with its means of initiation, with a propelling charge (other than one containing flammable liquid or gel or hypergolic liquid) or without a propelling charge	F	1.1F 1.2F 1.3F 1.4F
Pyrotechnic substance or article containing a pyrotechnic substance, or article containing both an explosive substance and an illuminating, incendiary, tear-producing or smoke-producing substance (other than a water-activated article or one containing white phosphorus, phosphide or flammable liquid or gel or hypergolic liquid)	G	1.1G 1.2G 1.3G 1.4G
Article containing both an explosive substance and white phosphorus	H	1.2H 1.3H
Article containing both an explosive substance and flammable liquid or gel	J	1.1J 1.2J 1.3J
Article containing both an explosive substance and a toxic chemical agent	K	1.2K 1.3K
Explosive substance or article containing an explosive substance and presenting a special risk (e.g., due to water-activation or presence of hybergolic liquids, phosphides or pyrophoric substances) needing isolation of each type	L	1.1L 1.2L 1.3L
Articles containing only extremely insensitive detonating substances	N	1.6N
Substance or article so packed or designed that any hazardous effects arising from accidental functioning are limited to the extent that they do not significantly hinder or prohibit fire fighting or other emergency response efforts in the immediate vicinity of the package	S	1.4S

Table 2 - Scheme of Classification of Explosives, Combination of Hazard Division With Compatibility Group

Hazard division	Compatibility group													
	A	B	C	D	E	F	G	H	J	K	L	N	S	A-S
1.1	1.1A	1.1B	1.1C	1.1D	1.1E	1.1F	1.1G		1.1J		1.1L			9
1.2		1.2B	1.2C	1.2D	1.2E	1.2F	1.2G	1.2H	1.2J	1.2K	1.2L			10
1.3			1.3C			1.3F	1.3G	1.3H	1.3J	1.3K	1.3L			7
1.4		1.4B	1.4C	1.4D	1.4E	1.4F	1.4G						1.4S	7
1.5				1.5D										1
1.6												1.6N		1
1.6	1	3	4	4	3	4	4	2	3	2	3	1	1	35

§173.53 Provisions for using old classifications of explosives.

Where the classification system in effect prior to January 1, 1991, is referenced in State or local laws, ordinances or regulations not pertaining to the transportation of hazardous materials, the following table may be used to compare old and new hazard class names:

Current classification	Class name prior to Jan. 1, 1991
Division 1.1	Class A explosives
Division 1.2	Class A or Class B explosives
Division 1 3	Class B explosive
Division 1.4	Class C explosives
Division 1.5	Blasting agents
Division 1.6	No applicable hazard class

§173.54 Forbidden explosives.

Unless otherwise provided in this subchapter, the following explosives shall not be offered for transportation or transported:

(a) **An explosive that has not been approved** in accordance with §173.56 of this subpart.

(b) **An explosive mixture or device containing a chlorate** and also containing:

(1) *An ammonium salt,* including a substituted ammonium or quaternary ammonium salt; or

(2) *An acidic substance,* including a salt of a weak base and a strong acid.

(c) **A leaking or damaged package of explosives.**

(d) **Propellants that are unstable, condemned or deteriorated.**

(e) **Nitroglycerin, diethylene glycol dinitrate,** or any other liquid explosives not specifically authorized by this subchapter.

(f) **A loaded firearm (except as provided in 49 CFR 1544.219).**

(g) **Fireworks that combine an explosive and a detonator.**

(h) **Fireworks containing yellow or white phosphorus.**

(i) **A toy torpedo, the maximum outside dimension** of which exceeds 23 mm (0.906 inch), or a toy torpedo containing a mixture of potassium chlorate, black antimony (antimony sulfide), and sulfur, if the weight of the explosive material in the device exceeds 0.26 g (0.01 ounce).

(j) **Explosives specifically forbidden in the §172.101 table** of this subchapter.

(k) **Explosives not meeting the acceptance criteria** specified in §173.57 of this subchapter.

(l) **An explosive article with its means of initiation** or ignition installed, unless approved in accordance with §173.56.

§173.55 [Reserved]

§173.56 New explosives — definition and procedures for classification and approval.

(a) **Definition of new explosive.** For the purposes of this subchapter a new explosive means an explosive produced by a person who:

(1) *Has not previously produced that explosive; or*

(2) *Has previously produced* that explosive but has made a change in the formulation, design or process so as to alter any of the properties of the explosive. An explosive will not be considered a "new explosive" if an agency listed in paragraph (b) of this section has determined, and confirmed in writing to the Associate Administrator, that there are no significant differences in hazard characteristics from the explosive previously approved.

(b) **Examination, classing and approval.** Except as provided in paragraph (j) of this section, no person may offer a new explosive for transportation unless that person has specified to the examining agency the ranges of composition of ingredients and compounds, showing the intended manufacturing tolerances in the composition of substances or design of articles which will be allowed in that material or device, and unless it has been examined, classed and approved as follows:

(1) *Except for an explosive* made by or under the direction or supervision of the Department of Defense (DOD) or the Department of Energy (DOE), a new explosive must be examined and assigned a recommended shipping description, division and compatibility group, based on the tests and criteria prescribed in §§173.52, 173.57 and 173.58. The person requesting approval of the new explosive must submit to the Associate Administrator a report of the examination and assignment of a recommended shipping description, division, and compatibility group. If the Associate Administrator finds the approval request meets the regulatory criteria, the new explosive will be approved in writing and assigned an EX number. The examination must be performed by a person who is approved by the Associate Administrator under the provisions of subpart H of part 107 of this chapter and who —

(i) *Has* (directly, or through an employee involved in the examination) at least ten years of experience in the examination, testing and evaluation of explosives;

(ii) *Does not manufacture or market explosives,* and is not controlled by or financially dependent on any entity that manufactures or markets explosives, and whose work with respect to explosives is limited to examination, testing and evaluation; and

(iii) *Is a resident of the United States.*

(2) *A new explosive* made by or under the direction or supervision of a component of the DOD may be examined, classed, and concurred in by:

(i) *U.S. Army Technical Center* for Explosives Safety (SMCAC-EST), Naval Sea Systems Command (SEA-9934), or Air Force Safety Agency (SEW), when approved by the Chairman, DOD Explosives Board, in accordance with the Department of Defense Explosives Hazard Classification Procedures (TB 700-2); or

(ii) *The agencies* and procedures specified in paragraph (b)(1) of this section.

(3) *A new explosive* made by or under the direction or supervision of the Department of Energy (DOE) may be —

(i) *Examined by the DOE* in accordance with the Explosives Hazard Classification Procedures (TB 700-2), and must be classed and approved by DOE; or

(ii) *Examined, classed, and approved* in accordance with paragraph (b)(1) of this section.

(4) *For a material* shipped under the description of "ammonium nitrate-fuel oil mixture (ANFO)", the only test required for classification purposes is the Cap Sensitivity Test (Test Method 5(a) prescribed in the Explosive Test Manual). The test must be performed by an agency listed in paragraph (b)(1), (b)(2), or (b)(3) of this section, the manufacturer, or the shipper. A copy of the test report must be submitted to the Associate Administrator before the material is offered for transportation, and a copy of the test report must be retained by the shipper for as long as that material is shipped. At a minimum, the test report must contain the name and address of the person or organization conducting the test, date of the test, quantitative description of the mixture. including prill size and porosity, and a description of the test results.

(c) **Filing DOD or DOE approval report.** DOD or DOE must file a copy of each approval, accompanied by supporting laboratory data, with the Associate Administrator and receive acknowledgement in writing before offering the new explosive for transportation, unless the new explosive is:

(1) *Being transported under paragraph (d) or (e) of this section; or*

(2) *Covered by a national security classification currently in effect.*

(d) **Transportation of explosive samples for examination.** Notwithstanding the requirements of paragraph (b) of this section with regard to the transportation of a new explosive that has not been approved, a person may offer a sample of a new explosive for transportation, by railroad, highway, or vessel from the place where it was produced to an agency identified in paragraph (b) of this section, for examination if —

(1) *The new explosive* has been assigned a tentative shipping description and class in writing by the testing agency;

(2) *The new explosive* is packaged as required by this part according to the tentative description and class assigned, unless otherwise specified in writing by the testing agency; and,

(3) *The package* is labeled as required by this subchapter and the following is marked on the package:

(i) *The words "SAMPLE FOR LABORATORY EXAMINATION";*

(ii) *The net weight of the new explosive; and*

(iii) *The tentative shipping name and identification number.*

(e) **Transportation of unapproved explosives** for developmental testing. Notwithstanding the requirements of paragraph (b) of this section, the owner of a new explosive that has not been examined or approved may transport that new explosive from the place where it was produced to an explosives testing range if —

(1) *It is not a primary* (a 1.1A initiating) explosive or a forbidden explosive according to this subchapter;

(2) *It is described as* a Division 1.1 explosive (substance or article) and is packed, marked, labeled, described on shipping papers and is otherwise offered for transportation in conformance with the requirements of this subchapter applicable to Division 1.1;

(3) *It is transported* in a motor vehicle operated by the owner of the explosive; and

(4) *It is accompanied* by a person, in addition to the operator of the motor vehicle, who is qualified by training and experience to handle the explosive.

(f) **Notwithstanding the requirements of paragraphs (b) and (d)** of this section, the Associate Administrator may approve a new explosive on the basis of an approval issued for the explosive by the competent authority of a foreign government, or when examination of the explosive by a person approved by the Associate Administrator is impracticable, on the basis of reports of tests conducted by disinterested third parties, or may approve the transportation of an explosives sample for the purpose of examination by a person approved by the Associate Administrator.

(g) **Notwithstanding the requirements of paragraph (b)** of this section, an explosive may be transported under §§171.11, 171.12, 171.12a or 176.11 of this subchapter without the approval of the Associate Administrator if the Associate Administrator has acknowledged, in writing, the acceptability of an approval issued by the competent authority of a foreign government pursuant to the provisions of the UN Recommendations, the ICAO Technical Instructions, the IMDG Code, or other national or international regulations based on the UN Recommendations. In such a case, a copy of the foreign competent authority approval, and a copy of the written acknowledgement of its acceptance must accompany each shipment of that explosive.

(h) **The requirements of this section do not apply** to cartridges, small arms which are:

(1) *Not a forbidden explosive under §173.54 of this subchapter;*

(2) *Ammunition for rifle, pistol, or shotgun;*

(3) *Ammunition with inert projectile or blank ammunition; and*

(4) *Ammunition not exceeding* 50 caliber for rifle or pistol cartridges or 8 gauge for shotgun shells. Cartridges, small arms meeting the criteria of this paragraph (h) may be assigned a classification code of 1.4S by the manufacturer.

(i) **If experience or other data indicate that the hazard** of a material or a device containing an explosive composition is greater or less than indicated according to the definition and criteria specified in §§173.50, 173.56, and 173.58 of this subchapter, the Associate Administrator may specify a classification or except the material or device from the requirements of this subchapter.

(j) **Fireworks.** Notwithstanding the requirements of paragraph (b) of this section, Division 1.3 and 1.4 fireworks may be classed and approved by the Associate Administrator without prior examination and offered for transportation if the following conditions are met:

(1) *The fireworks* are manufactured in accordance with the applicable requirements in APA Standard 87-1;

(2) *A thermal stability test* is conducted on the device by the BOE, the BOM, or the manufacturer. The test must be performed by maintaining the device, or a representative prototype of a large device such as a display shell, at a temperature of 75 °C (167 °F) for 48 consecutive hours. When a device contains more than one component, those components which could be in physical contact with each other in the finished device must be placed in contact with each other during the thermal stability test; and

(3) *The manufacturer* applies in writing to the Associate Administrator following the applicable requirements in APA Standard 87-1, and is notified in writing by the Associate Administrator that the fireworks have been classed, approved, and assigned an EX-number. Each application must be complete, including all relevant background data and copies of all applicable drawings, test results, and any other pertinent information on each device for which approval is being requested. The manufacturer must sign the application and certify that the device for which approval is requested conforms to APA Standard 87-1 and that the descriptions and technical information contained in the application are complete and accurate. If the application is denied, the manufacturer will be notified in writing of the reasons for the denial. The Associate Administrator may require that the fireworks be examined by an agency listed in paragraph (b)(1) of this section.

§173.57 Acceptance criteria for new explosives.

(a) **Unless otherwise excepted,** an explosive substance must be subjected to the Drop Weight Impact Sensitivity Test (Test Method 3(a)(i)), the Friction Sensitivity Test (Test Method 3(b)(iii)), the Thermal Stability Test (Test Method 3(c)) at 75 °C (167 °F) and the Small-Scale Burning Test (Test Method 3(d)(i)), each as described in the Explosive Test Manual (UN Recommendations on the Transport of Dangerous Goods, Manual of Tests and Criteria (see §171.7 of this subchapter)). A substance is forbidden for transportation if any one of the following occurs:

(1) *For a liquid,* failure to pass the test criteria when tested in the Drop Weight Impact Sensitivity Test apparatus for liquids;

(2) *For a solid,* failure to pass the test criteria when tested in the Drop Weight Impact Sensitivity Test apparatus for solids;

(3) *The substance* has a friction sensitiveness equal to or greater than that of dry pentaerythrite tetranitrate (PETN) when tested in the Friction Sensitivity Test;

(4) *The substance* fails to pass the test criteria specified in the Thermal Stability Test at 75 °C (167 °F); or

(5) *Explosion occurs when tested in the Small-Scale Burning Test.*

(b) **An explosive article, packaged or unpackaged,** or a packaged explosive substance must be subjected to the Thermal Stability Test for Articles and Packaged Articles (Test method 4(a)(i)) and the Twelve Meter Drop Test (Test Method 4(b)(ii)), when appropriate, in the Explosive Test Manual. An article or packaged substance is forbidden for transportation if evidence of thermal instability or excessive impact sensitivity is found in those tests according to the criteria and methods of assessing results prescribed therein.

(c) **Dynamite (explosive, blasting, type A)** is forbidden for transportation if any of the following occurs:

(1) *It does not have* uniformly mixed with the absorbent material a satisfactory antacid in a quantity sufficient to have the acid neutralizing power of an amount of magnesium carbonate equal to one percent of the nitroglycerin or other liquid explosive ingredient;

(2) *During the centrifuge test* (Test Method D-2, in appendix D to this part) or the compression test (Test Method D-3 in appendix D to this part), a non-gelatin dynamite loses more than 3 percent by weight of the liquid explosive or a gelatin dynamite loses more than 10 percent by weight of the liquid explosive; or

(3) *During the leakage test* (Test Method D-1 in appendix D to this part), there is any loss of liquid.

§173.58 Assignment of class and division for new explosives.

(a) **Division 1.1., 1.2., 1.3., and 1.4 explosives.** In addition to the test prescribed in §173.57 of this subchapter, a substance or article in these divisions must be subjected to Test Methods 6(a), 6(b), and 6(c), as described in the UN Manual of Tests and Criteria, for assignment to an appropriate division. The criteria for assignment of class and division are as follows:

(1) *Division 1.1 if the major hazard is mass explosion;*

(2) *Division 1.2 if the major hazard is dangerous projections;*

(3) *Division 1.3* if the major hazard is radiant heat or violent burning, or both, but there is no blast or projection hazard;

(4) *Division 1.4* if there is a small hazard with no mass explosion and no projection of fragments of appreciable size or range;

(5) *Division 1.4* Compatibility Group S (1.4S) if the hazardous effects are confined within the package or the blast and projection effects do not significantly hinder emergency response efforts; or

(6) *Not in the explosive class* if the substance or article does not have significant explosive hazard or if the effects of explosion are completely confined within the article.

(b) **Division 1.5 explosive.** Except for ANFO, a substance that has been examined in accordance with the provisions §173.57(a) of this subchapter, must be subjected to the following additional tests: Cap Sensitivity Test, Princess Incendiary Spark Test, DDT Test, and External Fire Test, each as described in the Explosive Test Manual. A material may not be classed as a Division 1.5 explosive if any of the following occurs:

(1) *Detonation occurs in the Cap Sensitivity Test* (Test Method 5(a));

(2) *Detonation occurs in the DDT Test* (Test Method 5(b)(ii));

(3) *An explosion,* evidenced by a loud noise and projection of fragments, occurs in the External Fire Test (Test Method 5(c), or

(4) *Ignition or explosion* occurs in the Princess Incendiary Spark Test (Test Method 5(d)).

(c) **Division 1.6 explosive.**

(1) *In order to be classed* as a 1.6 explosive, an article must pass all of the following tests, as prescribed in the Explosive Test Manual:

(i) *The 1.6 Article External Fire Test;*

(ii) *The 1.6 Article Slow Cook-off Test;*

(iii) *The 1.6 Article Propagation Test; and*

(iv) *The 1.6 Article Bullet Impact Test.*

(2) *A substance intended* for use as the explosive load in an article of Division 1.6 must be an extremely insensitive detonating substance (EIDS). In order to determine if a substance is an EIDS, it must be subjected to the tests in paragraphs (c)(2)(i) through

(c)(2)(x) of this section, which are described in the Explosive Test Manual. The substance must be tested in the form (i.e., composition, granulation, density, etc.) in which it is to be used in the article. A substance is not an EIDS if it fails any of the following tests:

(i) *The Drop Weight Impact Sensitivity Test;*
(ii) *The Friction Sensitivity Test;*
(iii) *The Thermal Sensitivity Test at 75°C (167°F);*
(iv) *The Small Scale Burning Test;*
(v) *The EIDS Cap Test;*
(vi) *The EIDS Gap Test;*
(vii) *The Susan Test;*
(viii) *The EIDS Bullet Impact Test;*
(ix) *The EIDS External Fire Test; and*
(x) *The EIDS Slow Cook-off Test.*

(d) **The Associate Administrator may waive or modify** certain test(s) identified in §§173.57 and 173.58 of this subchapter, or require additional testing, if appropriate. In addition, the Associate Administrator may limit the quantity of explosive in a device.

(e) **Each explosive is assigned a compatibility group letter** by the Associate Administrator based on the criteria prescribed in §173.52(b) of this subchapter.

§173.59 Description of terms for explosives.

For the purpose of this subchapter, a description of the following terms is provided for information only. They must not be used for purposes of classification or to replace proper shipping names prescribed in §172.101 of this subchapter.

Ammonium-nitrate — fuel oil mixture (ANFO). A blasting explosive containing no essential ingredients other than prilled ammonium nitrate and fuel oil.

Ammunition. Generic term related mainly to articles of military application consisting of all types of bombs, grenades, rockets, mines, projectiles and other similar devices or contrivances.

Ammunition, illuminating, with or without burster, expelling charge or propelling charge. Ammunition designed to produce a single source of intense light for lighting up an area. The term includes illuminating cartridges, grenades and projectiles, and illuminating and target identification bombs. The term excludes the following articles which are listed separately: cartridges, signal; signal devices; hand signals; distress flares, aerial and flares, surface.

Ammunition, incendiary. Ammunition containing an incendiary substance which may be a solid, liquid or gel including white phosphorus. Except when the composition is an explosive per se, it also contains one or more of the following: a propelling charge with primer and igniter charge, or a fuze with burster or expelling charge. The term includes: Ammunition, incendiary, liquid or gel, with burster, expelling charge or propelling charge; Ammunition, incendiary with or without burster, expelling charge or propelling charge; and Ammunition, incendiary, white phosphorus, with burster, expelling charge or propelling charge.

Ammunition, practice. Ammunition without a main bursting charge, containing a burster or expelling charge. Normally it also contains a fuze and propelling charge. The term excludes the following article which is listed separately: Grenades, practice.

Ammunition, proof. Ammunition containing pyrotechnic substance, used to test the performance or strength of new ammunition, weapon component or assemblies.

Ammunition, smoke. Ammunition containing a smoke-producing substance such as chlorosulphonic acid mixture (CSAM), titanium tetrachloride (FM), white phosphorus, or smoke-producing substance whose composition is based on hexachlorothannol (HC) or red phosphorus. Except when the substance is an explosive per se, the ammunition also contains one or more of the following: a propelling charge with primer and igniter charge, or a fuze with burster or expelling charge. The term includes: Ammunition, smoke, with or without burster, expelling charge or propelling charge; Ammunition, smoke, white phosphorus with burster, expelling charge or propelling charge.

Ammunition, tear-producing with burster, expelling charge or propelling charge. Ammunition containing tear-producing substance. It may also contain one or more of the following: a pyrotechnic substance, a propelling charge with primer and igniter charge, or a fuze with burster or expelling charge.

Ammunition, toxic. Ammunition containing toxic agent. It may also contain one or more of the following: a pyrotechnic substance, a propelling charge with primer and igniter charge, or a fuze with burster or expelling charge.

Articles, explosive, extremely insensitive (Articles, EEI). Articles that contain only extremely insensitive detonating substances and which demonstrate a negligible probability of accidental initiation or propagation under normal conditions of transport and which have passed Test Series 7.

Articles, pyrophoric. Articles which contain a pyrophoric substance (capable of spontaneous ignition when exposed to air) and an explosive substance or component. The term excludes articles containing white phosphorus.

Articles, pyrotechnic for technical purposes. Articles which contain pyrotechnic substances and are used for technical purposes, such as heat generation, gas generation, theatrical effects, etc. The term excludes the following articles which are listed separately: all ammunition; cartridges, signal; cutters, cable, explosive; fireworks; flares, aerial; flares, surface; release devices, explosives; rivets, explosive; signal devices, hand; signals, distress; signals, railway track, explosive; and signals, smoke.

Black powder (gunpowder). Substance consisting of an intimate mixture of charcoal or other carbon and either potassium or sodium nitrate, and sulphur. It may be meal, granular, compressed, or pelletized.

Bombs. Explosive articles which are dropped from aircraft. They may contain a flammable liquid with bursting charge, a photo-flash composition or bursting charge. The term excludes torpedoes (aerial) and includes bombs, photo-flash; bombs with bursting charge; bombs with flammable liquids, with bursting charge.

Boosters. Articles consisting of a charge of detonating explosive without means of initiation. They are used to increase the initiating power of detonators or detonating cord.

Bursters, explosive. Articles consisting of a small charge of explosive to open projectiles or other ammunition in order to disperse their contents.

Cartridges, blank. Articles which consist of a cartridge case with a center or rim fire primer and a confined charge of smokeless or black powder, but no projectile. Used in training, saluting, or in starter pistols, etc.

Cartridges, flash. Articles consisting of a casing, a primer and flash powder, all assembled in one piece for firing.

Cartridges for weapons.

(1) *Fixed (assembled)* or semi-fixed (partially assembled) ammunition designed to be fired from weapons. Each cartridge includes all the components necessary to function the weapon once. The name and description should be used for military small arms cartridges that cannot be described as cartridges, small arms. Separate loading ammunition is included under this name and description when the propelling charge and projectile are packed together (see also Cartridges, blank).

(2) *Incendiary, smoke, toxic,* and tear-producing cartridges are described under ammunition, incendiary, etc.

Cartridges for weapons, inert projectile. Ammunition consisting of a casing with propelling charge and a solid or empty projectile.

Cartridges, oil well. Articles consisting of a casing of thin fiber, metal or other material containing only propellant explosive. The term excludes charges, shaped, commercial.

Cartridges, power device. Articles designed to accomplish mechanical actions. They consist of a casing with a charge of deflagrating explosive and a means of ignition. The gaseous products of the deflagration produce inflation, linear or rotary motion; activate diaphragms, valves or switches, or project fastening devices or extinguishing agents.

Cartridges, signal. Articles designed to fire colored flares or other signals from signal pistols or devices.

Cartridges, small arms. Ammunition consisting of a cartridge case fitted with a center or rim fire primer and containing both a propelling charge and solid projectile(s). They are designed to be fired in weapons of caliber not larger than 19.1 mm. Shotgun cartridges of any caliber are included in this description. The term excludes: Cartridges, small arms, blank, and some military small arms cartridges listed under Cartridges for weapons, inert projectile.

Cases, cartridge, empty with primer. Articles consisting of a cartridge case made from metal, plastics or other non-flammable materials, in which only the explosive component is the primer.

Cases, combustible, empty, without primer. Articles consisting of cartridge cases made partly or entirely from nitrocellulose.

Charges, bursting. Articles consisting of a charge of detonating explosive such as hexolite, octolite, or plastics-bonded explosive designed to produce effect by blast or fragmentation.

Charges, demolition. Articles consisting of a charge of detonating explosive in a casing of fiberboard, plastics, metal or other material. The term excludes articles identified as bombs, mines, etc.

Charges, depth. Articles consisting of a charge of detonating explosive contained in a drum or projectile. They are designed to detonate under water.

Charges, expelling. A charge of deflagrating explosive designed to eject the payload from the parent article without damage.

Charges, explosive, without detonator. Articles consisting of a charge of detonating explosive without means of initiation, used for explosive welding, joining, forming, and other processes.

Charges, propelling. Articles consisting of propellant charge in any physical form, with or without a casing, for use in cannon or for reducing drag for projectiles or as a component of rocket motors.

Charges, propelling for cannon. Articles consisting of a propellant charge in any physical form, with or without a casing, for use in a cannon.

Charges, shaped, without detonator. Articles consisting of a casing containing a charge of detonating explosive with a cavity lined with rigid material, without means of initiation. They are designed to produce a powerful, penetrating jet effect.

Charges, shaped, flexible, linear. Articles consisting of a V-shaped core of a detonating explosive clad by a flexible metal sheath.

Charges, supplementary, explosive. Articles consisting of a small removable booster used in the cavity of a projectile between the fuze and the bursting charge.

Components, explosive train, n.o.s. Articles containing an explosive designed to transmit a detonation or deflagration within an explosive train.

Contrivance, water-activated with burster, expelling charge or propelling charge. Articles whose functioning depends of physico-chemical reaction of their contents with water.

Cord, detonating, flexible. Articles consisting of a core of detonating explosive enclosed in spun fabric with plastics or other covering.

Cord (fuse) detonating, metal clad. Articles consisting of a core of detonating explosive clad by a soft metal tube with or without protective covering. When the core contains a sufficiently small quantity of explosive, the words "mild effect" are added.

Cord igniter. Articles consisting of textile yarns covered with black powder or another fast-burning pyrotechnic composition and a flexible protective covering, or consisting of a core of black powder surrounded by a flexible woven fabric. It burns progressively along its length with an external flame and is used to transmit ignition from a device to a charge or primer.

Cutters, cable, explosive. Articles consisting of a knife-edged device which is driven by a small charge of deflagrating explosive into an anvil.

Detonator assemblies, non-electric, for blasting. Non-electric detonators assembled with and activated by such means as safety fuse, shock tube, flash tube, or detonating cord. They may be of instantaneous design or incorporate delay elements. Detonating relays incorporating detonating cord are included. Other detonating relays are included in Detonators, nonelectric.

Detonators. Articles consisting of a small metal or plastic tube containing explosives such as lead azide, PETN, or combinations of explosives. They are designed to start a detonation train. They may be constructed to detonate instantaneously, or may contain a delay element. They may contain no more than 10 g of total explosives weight, excluding ignition and delay charges, per unit. The term includes: detonators for ammunition; detonators for blasting, both electric and non-electric; and detonating relays without flexible detonating cord.

Dynamite. A detonating explosive containing a liquid explosive ingredient (generally nitroglycerin, similar organic nitrate esters, or both) that is uniformly mixed with an absorbent material, such as wood pulp, and usually contains materials such as nitrocellulose, sodium and ammonium nitrate.

Entire load and total contents. The phrase means such a substantial portion of the material explodes that the practical hazard should be assessed by assuming simultaneous explosion of the whole of the explosive content of the load or package.

Explode. The term indicates those explosive effects capable of endangering life and property through blast, heat, and projection of missiles. It encompasses both deflagration and detonation.

Explosion of the total contents. The phrase is used in testing a single article or package or a small stack of articles or packages.

Explosive, blasting. Detonating explosive substances used in mining, construction, and similar tasks. Blasting explosives are assigned to one of five types. In addition to the ingredients listed below for each type, blasting explosives may also contain inert components, such as kieselguhr, and other minor ingredients, such as coloring agents and stabilizers.

Explosive, blasting, type A. Substances consisting of liquid organic nitrates, such as nitroglycerin, or a mixture of such ingredients with one or more of the following: nitrocellulose, ammonium nitrate or other inorganic nitrates, aromatic nitro-derivatives, or combustible materials, such as wood-meal and aluminum powder. Such explosives must be in powdery, gelatinous, plastic or elastic form. The term includes dynamite, blasting gelatine and gelatine dynamites.

Explosive, blasting, type B. Substances consisting of a mixture of ammonium nitrate or other inorganic nitrates with an explosive, such as trinitrotoluene, with or without other substances, such as wood-meal or aluminum powder, or a mixture of ammonium nitrate or other inorganic nitrates with other combustible substances which are not explosive ingredients. Such explosives may not contain nitroglycerin, similar liquid organic nitrates, or chlorates.

Explosive, blasting, type C. Substances consisting of a mixture of either potassium or sodium chlorate or potassium, sodium or ammonium perchlorate with organic nitro-derivatives or combustible materials, such as wood-meal or aluminum powder, or a hydrocarbon. Such explosives must not contain nitroglycerin or any similar liquid organic nitrate.

Explosive, blasting, type D. Substances consisting of a mixture of organic nitrate compounds and combustible materials, such as hydrocarbons and aluminum powder. Such explosives must not contain nitroglycerin, any similar liquid organic nitrate, chlorate or ammonium-nitrate. The term generally includes plastic explosives.

Explosive, blasting, type E. Substances consisting of water as an essential ingredient and high proportions of ammonium nitrate or other oxidizer, some or all of which are in solution. The other constituents may include nitro-derivatives, such as trinitrotoluene, hydrocarbons or aluminum powder. The term includes: explosives, emulsion; explosives, slurry; and explosives, watergel.

Explosive, deflagrating. A substance, e.g., propellant, which reacts by deflagration rather than detonation when ignited and used in its normal manner.

Explosive, detonating. A substance which reacts by detonation rather than deflagration when initiated and used in its normal manner.

Explosive, extremely insensitive detonating substance (EIDS). A substance which, although capable of sustaining a detonation, has demonstrated through tests that it is so insensitive that there is very little probability of accidental initiation.

Explosive, primary. Explosive substance which is manufactured with a view to producing a practical effect by explosion, is very sensitive to heat, impact, or friction, and even in very small quantities, detonates. The major primary explosives are mercury fulminate, lead azide, and lead styphnate.

Explosive, secondary. An explosive substance which is relatively insensitive (when compared to primary explosives) and is usually initiated by primary explosives with or without the aid of boosters or supplementary charges. Such an explosive may react as a deflagrating or as a detonating explosive.

Fireworks. Pyrotechnic articles designed for entertainment.

Flares. Articles containing pyrotechnic substances which are designed to illuminate, identify, signal, or warn. The term includes: flares, aerial and flares, surface.

Flash powder. Pyrotechnic substance which, when ignited, produces an intense light.

Fracturing devices, explosive, for oil wells, without detonators. Articles consisting of a charge of detonating explosive contained in a casing without the means of initiation. They are used to fracture the rock around a drill shaft to assist the flow of crude oil from the rock.

Fuse/Fuze. Although these two words have a common origin (French fusee, fusil) and are sometimes considered to be different spellings, it is useful to maintain the convention that fuse refers to a cord-like igniting device, whereas fuze refers to a device used in ammunition which incorporates mechanical, electrical, chemical, or hydrostatic components to initiate a train by deflagration or detonation.

Fuse, igniter. Articles consisting of a metal tube with a core of deflagrating explosives.

Fuse, instantaneous, non-detonating (Quickmatch). Article consisting of cotton yarns impregnated with fine black powder. It burns with an external flame and is used in ignition trains for fireworks, etc.

Fuse, safety. Article consisting of a core of fine-grained black powder surrounded by a flexible woven fabric with one or more protective outer coverings. When ignited, it burns at a predetermined rate without any explosive effect.

Fuzes. Articles designed to start a detonation or deflagration in ammunition. They incorporate mechanical, electrical, chemical, or hydrostatic components and generally protective features. The term includes: Fuzes, detonating; fuzes detonating with protective features; and fuzes igniting.

Grenades, hand or rifle. Articles which are designed to be thrown by hand or to be projected by rifle. The term includes: grenades, hand or rifle, with bursting charge; and grenades, practice, hand or rifle. The term excludes: grenades, smoke.

Igniters. Articles containing one or more explosive substance used to start deflagration of an explosive train. They may be actuated chemically, electrically, or mechanically. The term excludes: cord, igniter; fuse, igniter; fuse, instantaneous, non-detonating; fuze, igniting; lighters, fuse, instantaneous, non-detonating; fuzes, igniting; lighters, fuse; primers, cap type; and primers, tubular.

Ignition, means of. A general term used in connection with the method employed to ignite a deflagrating train of explosive or pyrotechnic substances (for example: a primer for propelling charge, an igniter for a rocket motor or an igniting fuze).

Initiation, means of.

(1) *A device* intended to cause the detonation of an explosive (for example: detonator, detonator for ammunition, or detonating fuze).

(2) *The term* with its own means of initiation means that the contrivance has its normal initiating device assembled to it and this device is considered to present a significant risk during transport but not one great enough to be unacceptable. The term does not apply, however, to a contrivance packed together with its means of initiation, provided the device is packaged so as to eliminate the risk of causing detonation of the contrivance in the event of functioning of the initiating device. The initiating device can even be assembled in the contrivance provided there are protective features ensuring that the device is very unlikely to cause detonation of the contrivance under conditions which are associated with transport.

(3) *For the purposes of classification,* any means of initiation without two effective protective features should be regarded as Compatibility Group B; an article with its own means of initiation, without two effective protective features, is Compatibility Group F. A means of initiation which itself possesses two effective protective features is Compatibility Group D, and an article with its own means of initiation which possesses two effective features is Compatibility Group D or E. A means of initiation, adjudged as having two effective protective features, must be approved by the Associate Administrator. A common and effective way of achieving the necessary degree of protection is to use a means of initiation which incorporates two or more independent safety features.

Jet perforating guns, charged, oil well, without detonator. Articles consisting of a steel tube or metallic strip, into which are inserted shaped charges connected by detonating cord, without means of initiation.

Lighters, fuse. Articles of various design actuated by friction, percussion, or electricity and used to ignite safety fuse.

Mass explosion. Explosion which affects almost the entire load virtually instantaneously.

Mines. Articles consisting normally of metal or composition receptacles and bursting charge. They are designed to be operated by the passage of ships, vehicles, or personnel. The term includes Bangalore torpedoes.

Powder cake (powder paste). Substance consisting of nitrocellulose impregnated with not more than 60 percent of nitroglycerin or other liquid organic nitrates or a mixture of these.

Powder, smokeless. Substance based on nitrocellulose used as propellant. The term includes propellants with a single base (nitrocellulose (NC) alone), those with a double base (such as NC and nitroglycerin (NG)) and those with a triple base (such as NC/NG/nitroguanidine). Cast pressed or bag-charges of smokeless powder are listed under charges, propelling and charges, propelling for cannon.

Primers, cap type. Articles consisting of a metal or plastic cap containing a small amount of primary explosive mixture that is readily ignited by impact. They serve as igniting elements in small arms cartridges and in percussion primers for propelling charges.

Primers, tubular. Articles consisting of a primer for ignition and an auxiliary charge of deflagrating explosive, such as black powder, used to ignite the propelling charge in a cartridge case for cannon, etc.

Projectiles. Articles, such as a shell or bullet, which are projected from a cannon or other artillery gun, rifle, or other small arm. They may be inert, with or without tracer, or may contain a burster, expelling charge or bursting charge. The term includes: projectiles, inert, with tracer; projectiles, with burster or expelling charge; and projectiles, with bursting charge.

Propellant, liquid. Substances consisting of a deflagrating liquid explosive, used for propulsion.

Propellant, solid. Substances consisting of a deflagrating solid explosive, used for propulsion.

Propellants. Deflagrating explosives used for propulsion or for reducing the drag of projectiles.

Release devices, explosive. Articles consisting of a small charge of explosive with means of initiation. They sever rods or links to release equipment quickly.

Rocket motors. Articles consisting of a solid, liquid, or hypergolic propellant contained in a cylinder fitted with one or more nozzles. They are designed to propel a rocket or guided missile. The term includes: rocket motors; rocket motors with hypergolic liquids with or without an expelling charge; and rocket motors, liquid fuelled.

Rockets. Articles containing a rocket motor and a payload which may be an explosive warhead or other device. The term includes: guided missiles; rockets, line-throwing; rockets, liquid fuelled, with bursting charge; rockets, with bursting charge; rockets, with expelling charge; and rockets, with inert head.

Signals. Articles consisting of pyrotechnic substances designed to produce signals by means of sound, flame, or smoke or any combination thereof. The term includes: signal devices, hand; signals, distress ship; signals, railway track, explosive; signals, smoke.

Sounding devices, explosive. Articles consisting of a charge of detonating explosive. They are dropped from ships and function when they reach a predetermined depth or the sea bed.

Substance, explosive, very insensitive (Substance, EVI) N.O.S. Substances which present a mass explosive hazard but which are so insensitive that there is very little probability of initiation, or of transition from burning to detonation under normal conditions of transport and which have passed test series 5.

Torpedoes. Articles containing an explosive or non-explosive propulsion system and designed to be propelled through water. They may contain an inert head or warhead. The term includes: torpedoes, liquid fuelled, with inert head; torpedoes, liquid fuelled, with or without bursting charge; and torpedoes, with bursting charge.

Tracers for ammunition. Sealed articles containing pyrotechnic substances, designed to reveal the trajectory of a projectile.

Warheads. Articles containing detonating explosives, designed to be fitted to a rocket, guided missile, or torpedo. They may contain a burster or expelling charge or bursting charge. The term includes: warhead rocket with bursting charge; and warheads, torpedo, with bursting charge.

§173.60 General packaging requirements for explosives.

(a) **Unless otherwise provided in this subpart** and in §173.7(a), packaging used for Class 1 (explosives) materials must meet Packing Group II requirements. Each packaging used for an explosive must be capable of meeting the test requirements of subpart M of part 178 of this subchapter, at the specified level of performance, and the applicable general packaging requirements of paragraph (b) of this section.

(b) **The general requirements for packaging** of explosives are as follows:

(1) *Nails, staples, and other closure devices,* made of metal, having no protective covering may not penetrate to the inside of the outer packaging unless the inner packaging adequately protects the explosive against contact with the metal.

(2) *The closure device* of containers for liquid explosives must provide double protection against leakage, such as a screw cap secured in place with tape.

(3) *Inner packagings,* fittings, and cushioning materials, and the placing of explosive substances or articles in packages, must be such that the explosive substance is prevented from becoming loose in the outer packaging during transportation. Metallic components of articles must be prevented from making contact with metal packagings. Articles containing explosive substances not enclosed in an outer casing must be separated from each other in order to prevent friction and impact. Padding, trays, partitioning in the inner or outer packaging, molded plastics or receptacles may be used for this purpose.

(4) *When the packaging* includes water that could freeze during transportation, a sufficient amount of anti-freeze, such as denatured ethyl alcohol, must be added to the water to prevent freezing. If the anti-freeze creates a fire hazard, it may not be used. When a percentage of water in the substance is specified, the combined weight of water and anti-freeze may be substituted.

(5) *If an article* is fitted with its own means of ignition or initiation, it must be effectively protected from accidental actuation during normal conditions of transportation.

(6) *The entry* of explosive substances into the recesses of double-seamed metal packagings must be prevented.

(7) *The closure device* of a metal drum must include a suitable gasket; if the closure device includes metal-to-metal screw-threads, the ingress of explosive substances into the threading must be prevented.

(8) *Whenever loose* explosive substances or the explosive substance of an uncased or partly cased article may come into contact with the inner surface of metal packagings (1A2, 1B2, 4A, 4B and metal receptacles), the metal packaging should be provided with an inner liner or coating.

(9) *Packagings must be made* of materials compatible with, and impermeable to, the explosives contained in the package, so that neither interaction between the explosives and the packaging materials, nor leakage, causes the explosive to become unsafe in transportation, or the hazard division or compatibility group to change (see §173.24(e)(2)).

(10) *An explosive article* containing an electrical means of initiation that is sensitive to external electromagnetic radiation, must have its means of initiation effectively protected from electromagnetic radiation sources (for example, radar or radio transmitters) through either design of the packaging or of the article, or both.

(11) *Plastic packagings* may not be able to generate or accumulate sufficient static electricity to cause the packaged explosive substances or articles to initiate, ignite or inadvertently function. Metal packagings must be compatible with the explosive substance they contain.

(12) *Explosive substances* may not be packed in inner or outer packagings where the differences in internal and external pressures, due to thermal or other effects, could cause an explosion or rupture of the package.

(13) *Packagings for water soluble substances* must be water resistant. Packagings for desensitized or phlegmatized substances must be closed to prevent changes in concentration during transport. When containing less alcohol, water, or phlegmatizer than specified in its proper shipping description, the substance is a "forbidden" material.

(14) *Large and robust explosives articles,* normally intended for military use, without their means of initiation or with their means of initiation containing at least two effective protective features, may be carried unpackaged provided that a negative result was obtained in Test Series 4 of the UN Manual of Tests and Criteria on an unpackaged article. When such articles have propelling charges or are self-propelled, their ignition systems shall be protected against stimuli encountered during normal conditions of transport. Such unpackaged articles may be fixed to cradles or contained in crates or other suitable handling, storage or launching devices in such a way that they will not become loose during normal conditions of transport and are in accordance with DOD-approved procedures.

§173.61 Mixed packaging requirements.

(a) **An explosive may not be packed** in the same outside packaging with any other material that could, under normal conditions of transportation, adversely affect the explosive or its packaging unless packaged by DOD or DOE in accordance with §173.7(a).

(b) **Hardware necessary for assembly of explosive articles** at the point-of-use may be packed in the same outside packaging with the explosive articles. The hardware must be securely packed in a separate inside packaging. Sufficient cushioning materials must be used to ensure that all inside packagings are securely packed in the outside packaging.

(c) **The following explosives may not be packed together** with other Class 1 explosives: UN 0029, UN 0030, UN 0073, UN 0106, UN 0107, UN 0255, UN 0257, UN 0267, UN 0360, UN 0361, UN 0364, UN 0365, UN 0366, UN 0367, UN 0408, UN 0409, UN 0410, UN 0455, UN 0456, and NA 0350. These explosives may be mix-packed with each other in accordance with the compatibility requirements prescribed in paragraph (e).

(d) **Division 1.1 and 1.2 explosives** may not be packed with the following explosives: UN 0333, UN 0334, UN 0335, UN 0336, and UN 0337.

(e) **Except as prescribed in paragraphs (c) and (d) of this section,** different explosives may be packed in one outside packaging in accordance with the following compatibility requirements:

(1) *Explosives of the same compatibility group* and same division number may be packed together.

(2) *Explosives of the same compatibility group* or authorized combination of compatibility group but different division number may be packed together, provided that the whole package is treated as though its entire contents were comprised of the lower division number. For example, a mixed package of Division 1.2 explosives and Division 1.4 explosives, compatibility group D, must be treated as 1.2D explosives. However, when 1.5D explosives are packed together with 1.2D explosives, the whole package must be treated as 1.1D explosives.

(3) *Explosives of compatibility group S* may be packaged together with explosives of any other compatibility group except A or L, and the combined package may be treated as belonging to any of the packaged compatibility groups except S.

(4) *Explosives of compatibility group L* shall only be packed with an identical explosive.

(5) *Explosives articles* of compatibility groups C, D, or E may be packed together and the entire package shall be treated as belonging to compatibility group E.

(6) *Explosives articles* of compatibility groups C, D, E, or N may be packed together and the entire package shall be treated as belonging to compatibility group D.

(7) *Explosives substances* of compatibility groups C and D may be packaged together and the entire package shall be treated as belonging to compatibility group D.

(8) *Explosive articles* of compatibility group G, except for fireworks and articles requiring special packaging, may be packaged together with explosive articles of compatibility groups C, D or E and the combined package shall be treated as belonging to compatibility group E.

§173.62 Specific packaging requirements for explosives.

(a) **Except as provided in §173.7 of this subchapter,** when the §172.101 Table specifies that an explosive must be packaged in accordance with this section, only packagings which conform to the provisions of paragraphs (b) and (c) of this section or §173.7(e) of this subchapter and the applicable requirements in §§173.60 and 173.61 may be used unless otherwise approved by the Associate Administrator.

(b) **Explosives Table.** The Explosives Table specifies the Packing Instructions assigned to each explosive. Explosives are identified in the first column in numerical sequence by their identification number (ID#), which is listed in column 4 of the §172.101 table, of this subchapter. The second column of the Explosives Table specifies the Packing Instruction (PI) which must be used for packaging the explosive. The Explosives Packing Method Table in paragraph (c) of this section defines the methods of packaging. The Packing Instructions are identified using a 3 digit designation. The Packing Instruction prefixed by the letters "US" is particular to the United States and not found in applicable international regulations.

Explosives Table

ID#	PI
UN0004	112
UN0005	130
UN0006	130
UN0007	130
UN0009	130
UN0010	130
UN0012	130
UN0014	130
UN0015	130
UN0016	130
UN0018	130
UN0019	130
UN0020	101
UN0021	101
UN0027	113
UN0028	113
UN0029	131
UN0030	131
UN0033	130
UN0034	130
UN0035	130
UN0037	130
UN0038	130
UN0039	130
UN0042	132
UN0043	133
UN0044	133

Explosives Table

ID#	PI
UN0048	130
UN0049	135
UN0050	135
UN0054	135
UN0055	136
UN0056	130
UN0059	137
UN0060	132
UN0065	139
UN0066	140
UN0070	134
UN0072	112(a)
UN0073	133
UN0074	110(a) or 110(b)
UN0075	115
UN0076	112
UN0077	114(a) or 114(b)
UN0078	112
UN0079	112(b) or 112(c)
UN0081	116
UN0082	116 or 117
UN0083	116
UN0084	116
UN0092	135
UN0093	135
UN0094	113
UN0099	134
UN0101	140
UN0102	139
UN0103	140
UN0104	139
UN0105	140
UN0106	141
UN0107	141
UN0110	141
UN0113	110(a) or 110(b)
UN0114	110(a) or 110(b)
UN0118	112
UN0121	142
UN0124	US1
UN0129	110(a) or 110(b)
UN0130	110(a) or 110(b)
UN0131	142
UN0132	114(b)
UN0133	112(a)
UN0135	110(a) or 110(b)
UN0136	130
UN0137	130
UN0138	130
UN0143	115
UN0144	115
UN0146	112
UN0147	112(b)
UN0150	112(a) or 112(b)
UN0151	112
UN0153	112(b) or 112(c)
UN0154	112
UN0155	112(b) or 112(c)
UN0159	111
UN0160	114(b)
UN0161	114(b)

Explosives Table

ID#	PI
UN0167	130
UN0168	130
UN0169	130
UN0171	130
UN0173	134
UN0174	134
UN0180	130
UN0181	130
UN0182	130
UN0183	130
UN0186	130
UN0190	101
UN0191	135
UN0192	135
UN0193	135
UN0194	135
UN0195	135
UN0196	135
UN0197	135
UN0204	134
UN0207	112(b) or 112(c)
UN0208	112(b) or 112(c)
UN0209	112
UN0212	133
UN0213	112(b) or 112(c)
UN0214	112
UN0215	112
UN0216	112(b) or 112(c)
UN0217	112(b) or 112(c)
UN0218	112(b) or 112(c)
UN0219	112
UN0220	112
UN0221	130
UN0222	112(b) or 112(c)
UN0224	110(a) or 110(b)
UN0225	133
UN0226	112(a)
UN0234	114(a) or 114(b)
UN0235	114(a) or 114(b)
UN0236	114(a) or 114(b)
UN0237	138
UN0238	130
UN0240	130
UN0241	116 or 117
UN0242	130
UN0243	130
UN0244	130
UN0245	130
UN0246	130
UN0247	101
UN0248	144
UN0249	144
UN0250	101
UN0254	130
UN0255	131
UN0257	141
UN0266	112
UN0267	131
UN0268	133
UN0271	143
UN0272	143

Explosives Table

ID#	PI
UN0275	134
UN0276	134
UN0277	134
UN0278	134
UN0279	130
UN0280	130
UN0281	130
UN0282	112
UN0283	132
UN0284	141
UN0285	141
UN0286	130
UN0287	130
UN0288	138
UN0289	139
UN0290	139
UN0291	130
UN0292	141
UN0293	141
UN0294	130
UN0295	130
UN0296	134
UN0297	130
UN0299	130
UN0300	130
UN0301	130
UN0303	130
UN0305	113
UN0306	133
UN0312	135
UN0313	135
UN0314	142
UN0315	142
UN0316	141
UN0317	141
UN0318	141
UN0319	133
UN0320	133
UN0321	130
UN0322	101
UN0323	134
UN0324	130
UN0325	142
UN0326	130
UN0327	130
UN0328	130
UN0329	130
UN0330	130
UN0331	116 or 117
UN0332	116 or 117
UN0333	135
UN0334	135
UN0335	135
UN0336	135
UN0337	135
UN0338	130
UN0339	130
UN0340	112(a) or 112(b)
UN0341	112(b)
UN0342	114(a)
UN0343	111

Explosives Table

ID#	PI
UN0344	130
UN0345	130
UN0346	130
UN0347	130
UN0348	130
UN0349	101
UN0350	101
UN0351	101
UN0352	101
UN0353	101
UN0354	101
UN0355	101
UN0356	101
UN0357	101
UN0358	101
UN0359	101
UN0360	131
UN0361	131
UN0362	130
UN0363	130
UN0364	133
UN0365	133
UN0366	133
UN0367	141
UN0368	141
UN0369	130
UN0370	130
UN0371	130
UN0372	141
UN0373	135
UN0374	134
UN0375	134
UN0376	133
UN0377	133
UN0378	133
UN0379	136
UN0380	101
UN0381	134
UN0382	101
UN0383	101
UN0384	101
UN0385	112(b) or 112(c)
UN0386	112(b) or 112(c)
UN0387	112(b) or 112(c)
UN0388	112(b) or 112(c)
UN0389	112(b) or 112(c)
UN0390	112(b) or 112(c)
UN0391	112(a)
UN0392	112(b) or 112(c)
UN0393	112(b)
UN0394	112(a)
UN0395	101
UN0396	101
UN0397	101
UN0398	101
UN0399	101
UN0400	101
UN0401	112
UN0402	112(b) or 112(c)
UN0403	135
UN0404	135

Explosives Table

ID#	PI
UN0405	135
UN0406	114(b)
UN0407	114(b)
UN0408	141
UN0409	141
UN0410	141
UN0411	112(b) or 112(c)
UN0412	130
UN0413	130
UN0414	130
UN0415	143
UN0417	130
UN0418	135
UN0419	135
UN0420	135
UN0421	135
UN0424	130
UN0425	130
UN0426	130
UN0427	130
UN0428	135
UN0429	135
UN0430	135
UN0431	135
UN0432	135
UN0433	111
UN0434	130
UN0435	130
UN0436	130
UN0437	130
UN0438	130
UN0439	137
UN0440	137
UN0441	137
UN0442	137
UN0443	137
UN0444	137
UN0445	137
UN0446	136
UN0447	136
UN0448	114(b)
UN0449	101
UN0450	101
UN0451	130
UN0452	141
UN0453	130
UN0454	142
UN0455	131
UN0456	131
UN0457	130
UN0458	130
UN0459	130
UN0460	130
UN0461	101
UN0462	101
UN0463	101
UN0464	101
UN0465	101
UN0466	101
UN0467	101

Explosives Table

ID#	PI
UN0468	101
UN0469	101
UN0470	101
UN0471	101
UN0472	101
UN0473	101
UN0474	101
UN0475	101
UN0476	101
UN0477	101
UN0478	101
UN0479	101
UN0480	101
UN0481	101
UN0482	101
UN0483	112(b) or 112(c)
UN0484	112(b) or 112(c)
UN0486	101
UN0487	135
UN0488	130
UN0489	112(b) or 112(c)
UN0490	112(b) or 112(c)
UN0491	143
UN0492	135
UN0493	135
UN0494	US1
UN0495	115
UN0496	112(b) or 112(c)
UN0497	115
UN0498	114(b)
UN0499	114(b)
UN0500	131
UN0502	130
UN0504	112(c)
NA0124	US1
NA0276	134
NA0323	134
NA0331	116 or 117
NA0337	135
NA0349	133
NA0494	US1

(c) **Explosives Packing Instruction Table.** Explosives must be packaged in accordance with the following table:

(1) *The first column lists,* in alphanumeric sequence, the packing methods prescribed for explosives in the Explosives Table of paragraph (b) of this section.

(2) *The second column* specifies the inner packagings that are required. If inner packagings are not required, a notation of "Not necessary" appears in the column. The term "Not necessary" means that a suitable inner packaging may be used but is not required.

(3) *The third column* specifies the intermediate packagings that are required. If intermediate packagings are not required, a notation of "Not necessary" appears in the column. The term "Not necessary" means that a suitable intermediate packaging may be used but is not required.

(4) *The fourth column* specifies the outer packagings which are required. If inner packagings and/or intermediate packagings are specified in the second and third columns, then the packaging specified in the fourth column must be used as the outer packaging of a combination packaging; otherwise it may be used as a single packaging.

(5) *Packing Instruction 101* may be used for any explosive substance or article if an equivalent level of safety is shown to be maintained subject to the approval of the Associate Administrator.

Table of Packing Methods

Packing instruction	Inner packagings	Intermediate packagings	Outer packagings
101 PARTICULAR PACKING REQUIREMENTS OR EXCEPTIONS: 1. Samples of new or existing explosive substances or articles may be transported as directed by the Associate Administrator for purposes including: testing, classification, research and development, quality control, or as a commercial sample. Explosive samples which are wetted or desensitized must be limited to 25 kg. Explosive samples which are not wetted or desensitized must be limited to 10 kg in small packages as specified by the Associate Administrator for Hazardous Materials Safety	This Packing Instruction may be used as an alternative to a specifically assigned packing method with the approval of the Associate Administrator prior to transportation. When this packing instruction is used, the following must be marked on the shipping documents: "Packaging approved by the competent authority of the United States of America (USA)"		
110(a) PARTICULAR PACKING REQUIREMENTS OR EXCEPTIONS: 1. The Intermediate packagings must be filled with water saturated material such as an anti-freeze solution or wetted cushioning 2. Outer packagings must be filled with water saturated material such as an anti-freeze solution or wetted cushioning. Outer packagings must be constructed and sealed to prevent evaporation of the wetting solution, except when 0224 is being carried dry	Bags plastics textile, plastic coated or lined rubber textile, rubberized textile	Bags plastics textile, plastic coated or lined rubber textile, rubberized Receptacles plastics metal	Drums steel, removable head (1A2) plastics, removable head (1H2)
110(b) PARTICULAR PACKING REQUIREMENTS OR EXCEPTIONS: For UN 0074, 0113, 0114, 0129, 0130, 0135 and 0224, the following conditions must be satisfied: a. inner packagings must not contain more than 50 g of explosive substance (quantity corresponding to dry substance); b. each inner packaging must be separated from other inner packagings by dividing partitions; and c. the outer packaging must not be partitioned with more than 25 compartments	Bags rubber, conductive plastics, conductive Receptacles metal wood rubber, conductive plastics, conductive	Dividing partitions metal wood plastics fibreboard	Boxes natural wood, sift-proof wall (4C2) plywood (4D) reconstituted wood (4F)
111 PARTICULAR PACKING REQUIREMENTS OR EXCEPTIONS: For UN 0159, inner packagings are not required when metal (1A2 or 1B2) or plastics (1H2) drums are used as outer packagings	Bags paper, waterproofed plastics textile, rubberized Sheets plastics textile, rubberized	Not necessary	Boxes steel (4A) aluminium (4B) natural wood, ordinary (4C1) natural wood, sift proof (4C2) plywood (4D) reconstituted wood (4F) fibreboard (4G) plastics, expanded (4H1) plastics, solid (4H2) Drums steel, removable head (1A2) aluminum, removable head (1B2) plywood (1D) fibreboard (1G) plastics, removable head (1H2)
112(a) This packing instruction applies to wetted solids PARTICULAR PACKING REQUIREMENTS OR EXCEPTIONS: 1. For UN Nos. 0004, 0076, 0078, 0154, 0219 and 0394, packagings must be lead free 2. Intermediate packagings are not required if leakproof drums are used as the outer packaging 3. For UN 0072 and UN 0226, intermediate packagings are not required	Bags paper, multiwall, water resistant plastics textile textile, rubberized woven plastics Receptacles metal plastics	Bags plastics textile, plastic coated or lined Receptacles metal plastics	Boxes steel (4A) aluminium (4B) natural wood, ordinary (4C1) natural wood, sift proof (4C2) plywood (4D) reconstituted wood (4F) fibreboard (4G) plastics, expanded (4H1) plastics, solid (4H2) Drums steel, removable head (1A2) aluminium, removable head (1B2) plywood (1D) fibre (1G) plastics, removable head (1H2)
112(b) This packing instruction applies to dry solids other than powders PARTICULAR PACKING REQUIREMENTS OR EXCEPTIONS: 1. For UN 0004, 0076, 0078, 0154, 0216, 0219 and 0386, packagings must be lead free 2. For UN 0209, bags, sift-proof (5H2) are recommended for flake or prilled TNT in the dry state and a maximum net mass of 30 kg 3. For UN 0222 and UN 0223, inner packagings are not required	Bags paper, Kraft paper, multiwall, water resistant plastics textile textile, rubberized plastics woven plastics	Bags (for UN 0150 only) plastics textile, plastic coated or lined	Bags woven plastics sift-proof (5H2/3) plastics, film (5H4) textile, sift-proof (5L2) textile, water resistant (5L3) paper, multiwall, water resistant (5M2) Boxes steel (4A) aluminium (4B) natural wood, ordinary (4C1) natural wood, sift proof (4C2) plywood (4D) reconstituted wood (4F) fibreboard (4G) plastics, expanded (4H1) plastics, solid (4H2) Drums steel, removable head (1A2) aluminium, removable head (1B2) plywood (1D) fibre (1G) plastics, removable head (1H2)

Table of Packing Methods

Packing instruction	Inner packagings	Intermediate packagings	Outer packagings
112(c) This packing instruction applies to solid dry powders PARTICULAR PACKING REQUIREMENTS OR EXCEPTIONS: 1. For UN 0004, 0076, 0078, 0154, 0216, 0219 and 0386, packagings must be lead free 2. For UN 0209, bags, sift-proof (5H2) are recommended for flake or prilled TNT in the dry state. Bags must not exceed a maximum net mass of 30 kg 3. Inner packagings are not required if drums are used as the outer packaging 4. At least one of the packagings must be sift-proof	Bags paper, multiwall, water resistant plastics woven plastics Receptacles fibreboard metal plastics wood	Bags paper, multiwall, water resistant with inner lining plastics Receptacles metal plastics	Boxes steel (4A) natural wood, aluminum (4B) ordinary (4C1) natural wood, sift proof (4C2) plywood (4D) reconstituted wood (4F) fibreboard (4G) plastics, solid (4H2) Drums plastics, removable head (1H2) steel, removable head (1A2) aluminium, removable head (1B2) plywood (1D) fibre (1G)
113 PARTICULAR PACKING REQUIREMENTS OR EXCEPTIONS: 1. For UN 0094 and UN 0305, no more than 50 g of substance must be packed in an inner packaging 2. For UN 0027, inner packagings are not necessary when drums are used as the outer packaging 3. At least one of the packagings must be sift-proof 4. Sheets must only be used for UN 0028	Bags paper plastics textile, rubberized Receptacles fibreboard metal plastics wood Sheets paper, kraft paper, waxed	Not necessary	Boxes steel (4A) aluminum (4B) natural wood, ordinary (4C1) natural wood, sift-proof walls (4C2) plywood (4D) reconstituted wood (4F) fibreboard (4G) plastics, solid (4H2) Drums plastics, removable head (1H2) steel, removable head (1A2) aluminium, removable head (1B2) plywood (1D) fibre (1G)
114(a) This packing instruction applies to wetted solids PARTICULAR PACKING REQUIREMENTS OR EXCEPTIONS: 1. For UN 0077, 0234, 0235 and 0236, packagings must be lead free 2. For UN 0342, inner packagings are not required when metal (1A2 or 1B2) or plastics (1H2) drums are used as outer packagings 3. Intermediate packagings are not required if leakproof removable head drums are used as the outer packaging	Bags plastics textile woven plastics Receptacles metal plastics	Bags plastics textile, plastic coated or lined Receptacles metal plastics	Boxes steel (4A) natural wood, ordinary (4C1) natural wood, sift proof walls (4C2) plywood (4D) reconstituted wood (4F) fibreboard (4G) plastics, solid (4H2) Drums steel, removable head (1A2) aluminium, removable head (1B2) plywood (1D) fibre (1G) plastics, removable head (1H2)
114(b) This packing instruction applies to dry solids PARTICULAR PACKING REQUIREMENTS OR EXCEPTIONS: 1. For UN 0077, 0132, 0234, 0235 and 0236, packagings must be lead free 2. For UN 0160 and UN 0161, when metal drums (1A2 or 1B2) are used as the outer packaging, metal packagings must be so constructed that the risk of explosion, by reason of increased internal pressure from internal or external causes is prevented 3. For UN 0160 and UN 0161, inner packagings are not required if drums are used as the outer packaging	Bags paper, kraft plastics textile, sift-proof woven plastics, sift-proof Receptacles fibreboard metal paper plastics woven plastics, sift-proof	Not necessary	Boxes natural wood, ordinary (4C1) natural wood, sift proof walls (4C2) plywood (4D) reconstituted wood (4F) fibreboard (4G) Drums steel, removable head (1A2) aluminium, removable head (1B2) plywood (1D) fibre (1G) plastics, removable head (1H2)
115 PARTICULAR PACKING REQUIREMENTS OR EXCEPTIONS: 1. For liquid explosives, inner packagings must be surrounded with non-combustible absorbent cushioning material in sufficient quantity to absorb the entire liquid content. Metal receptacles should be cushioned from each other. The net mass of explosive per package may not exceed 30 kg when boxes are used as outer packaging. The net volume of explosive in each package other than boxes must not exceed 120 litres 2. For UN 0075, 0143, 0495 and 0497 when boxes are used as the outer packaging, inner packagings must have taped screw cap closures and be not more than 5 litres capacity each. A composite packaging consisting of a plastic receptacle in a metal drum (6HA1) may be used in lieu of combination packagings. Liquid substances must not freeze at temperatures above -15 °C (+5 °F) 3. For UN 0144, intermediate packagings are not necessary	Receptacles metal plastics	Bags plastics in metal receptacles Drums metal	Boxes natural wood, ordinary (4C1) natural wood, sift proof walls (4C2) plywood (4D) reconstituted wood (4F) fibreboard (4G) Drums plastics, removable head (1H2) steel, removable head (1A2) aluminium, removable head (1B2) plywood (1D) fibre (1G) Specification MC-200 containers may be used for transport by motor vehicle

Table of Packing Methods

Packing instruction	Inner packagings	Intermediate packagings	Outer packagings
116 PARTICULAR PACKING REQUIREMENTS OR EXCEPTIONS: 1. For UN 0082, 0241, 0331 and 0332, inner packagings are not necessary if leakproof removable head drums are used as the outer packaging 2. For UN 0082, 0241, 0331 and 0332, inner packagings are not required when the explosive is contained in a material impervious to liquid 3. For UN 0081, inner packagings are not required when contained in rigid plastic which is impervious to nitric esters 4. For UN 0331, inner packagings are not required when bags (5H2), (5H3) or (5H4) are used as outer packagings 5. Bags (5H2 or 5H3) must be used only for UN 0082, 0241, 0331 and 0332 6. For UN 0081, bags must not be used as outer packagings	Bags paper, water and oil resistant plastics textile, plastic coated or lined woven plastics, sift-proof Receptacles fibreboard, water resistant metal plastics wood, sift-proof Sheets paper, water resistant paper, waxed plastics	Not necessary	Bags woven plastics (5H1/2/3) paper, mulitwall, water resistant (5M2) plastics, film (5H4) textile, sift-proof (5L2) textile, water resistant (5L3) Boxes steel (4A) aluminium (4B) wood, natural, ordinary (4C1) natural wood, sift proof walls (4C2) plywood (4D) reconstituted wood (4F) fibreboard (4G) plastics, solid (4H2) Drums steel, removable head (1A2) aluminium, removable head (1B2) plywood (1D) fibre (1G) plastics, removable head (1H2) Jerricans steel, removable head (3A2) plastics, removable head (3H2)
117 PARTICULAR PACKING REQUIREMENTS OR EXCEPTIONS: 1. This packing instruction may only be used for explosives of 0082 when they are mixtures of ammonium nitrate or other inorganic nitrates with other combustible substances which are not explosive ingredients. Such explosives must not contain nitroglycerin, similar liquid organic nitrates, liquid or solid nitrocarbons, or chlorates 2. This packing instruction may only be used for explosives of UN 0241 which consist of water as an essential ingredient and high proportions of ammonium nitrate or other oxidizers, some or all of which are in solution. The other constituents may include hydrocarbons or aluminium powder, but must not include nitro-derivatives such as trinitrotoluene 3. Metal IBCs must not be used for UN 0082 and 0241 4. Flexible IBCs may only be used for solids	Not necessary	Not necessary	IBCs metal (11A), (11B), (11N), (21A), (21B), (21N), (31A), (31B), (31N). flexible (13H2), (13H3), (13H4), (13L2), (13L3), (13L4), (13M2). rigid plastics (11H1), (11H2), (21H1), (21H2), (31H1), (31H2). composite (11HZ1), (11HZ2), (21HZ1), (21HZ2), (31HZ1), (31HZ2)
130 PARTICULAR PACKING REQUIREMENTS OR EXCEPTIONS: 1. The following applies to UN 0006, 0009, 0010, 0015, 0016, 0018, 0019, 0034, 0035, 0038, 0039, 0048, 0056, 0137, 0138, 0168, 0169, 0171, 0181, 0182, 0183, 0186, 0221, 0238, 0243, 0244, 0245, 0246, 0254, 0280, 0281, 0286, 0287, 0297, 0299, 0300, 0301, 0303, 0321, 0328, 0329, 0344, 0345 0346, 0347, 0362, 0363, 0370, 0412, 0424, 0425, 0434, 0435, 0436, 0437, 0438, 0451, 0459 and 0488. Large and robust explosives articles, normally intended for military use, without their means of initiation or with their means of initiation containing at least two effective protective features, may be carried unpackaged. When such articles have propelling charges or are self-propelled, their ignition systems must be protected against stimuli encountered during normal conditions of transport. A negative result in Test Series 4 on an unpackaged article indicates that the article can be considered for transport unpackaged. Such unpackaged articles may be fixed to cradles or contained in crates or other suitable handling devices	Not necessary	Not necessary	Boxes steel (4A) aluminium (4B) wood natural, ordinary (4C1) natural wood, sift proof walls (4C2) plywood (4D) reconstituted wood (4F) fibreboard (4G) plastics, expanded (4H1) plastics, solid (4H2) Drums steel, removable head (1A2) aluminium, removable head (1B2) plywood (1D) fibre (1G) plastics, removable head (1H2)
131 PARTICULAR PACKING REQUIREMENTS OR EXCEPTIONS: 1. For UN 0029, 0267 and 0455, bags and reels may not be used as inner packagings 2. For UN 0030, 0255 and 0456, inner packagings are not required when detonators are packed in pasteboard tubes, or when their leg wires are wound on spools with the caps either placed inside the spool or securely taped to the wire on the spool, so as to restrict freedom of movement of the caps and to protect them from impact forces 3. For UN 0360, 0361 and 0500, detonators are not required to be attached to the safety fuse, metal-clad mild detonating cord, detonating cord, or shock tube. Inner packagings are not required if the packing configuration restricts freedom of movement of the caps and protects them from impact forces	Bags paper plastics Receptacles fibreboard metal plastics wood Reels	Not necessary	Boxes steel (4A) aluminium (4B) wood, natural, ordinary (4C1) natural wood, sift proof walls (4C2) plywood (4D) reconstituted wood (4F) fibreboard (4G) Drums steel, removable head (1A2) aluminium, removable head (1B2) plywood (1D) fibre (1G) plastics, removable head (1H2)
132(a)	Not necessary	Not necessary	Boxes steel (4A) aluminium (4B) wood, natural, ordinary (4C1) wood, natural, sift proof walls (4C2) plywood (4D) reconstituted wood (4F) fibreboard (4G) plastics, solid (4H2)
132(b)	Receptacles fibreboard metal plastics Sheets paper plastics	Not necessary	Boxes steel (4A) aluminium (4B) wood, natural, ordinary (4C1) wood, natural, sift proof walls (4C2) plywood (4D) reconstituted wood (4F) fibreboard (4G) plastics, solid (4H2)

Table of Packing Methods

Packing instruction	Inner packagings	Intermediate packagings	Outer packagings
133 PARTICULAR PACKING REQUIREMENTS OR EXCEPTIONS: 1. For UN 0043, 0212, 0225, 0268 and 0306 trays are not authorized as inner packagings	Receptacles Intermediate packagings are only required when trays are used as inner packagings fibreboard metal plastics wood Trays, fitted with dividing partitions fibreboard plastics wood	Receptacles fibreboard metal plastics wood	Boxes steel (4A) aluminium (4B) wood, natural, ordinary (4C1) wood, natural, sift proof walls (4C2) plywood (4D) reconstituted wood (4F) fibreboard (4G) plastics, solid (4H2)
134	Bags water resistant Receptacles fibreboard metal plastics wood Sheets fibreboard, corru-gated Tubes fibreboard	Not necessary	Boxes steel (4A) aluminium (4B) wood, natural, ordinary (4C1) wood, natural, sift proof walls (4C2) plywood (4D) reconstituted wood (4F) fibreboard (4G) plastics, solid (4H2) Drums fiberboard (1G) plastics, removable head (1H2) steel, removable head (1A2) aluminium, removable head (1B2) plywood (1D)
135	Bags paper plastics Receptacles fibreboard metal plastics wood Sheets paper plastics	Not necessary	Boxes steel (4A) aluminium (4B) wood, natural, ordinary (4C1) wood, natural, sift proof walls (4C2) plywood (4D) reconstituted wood (4F) fibreboard (4G) plastics, expanded (4H1) plastics, solid (4H2) Drums steel, removable head (1A2) aluminium, removable head (1B2) plywood (1D) fibre (1G) plastics, removable head (1H2)
136	Bags plastics textile Boxes fibreboard plastics wood Dividing partitions in the outer packagings	Not necessary	Boxes steel (4A) aluminium (4B) wood, natural, ordinary (4C1) wood, natural, sift proof walls (4C2) plywood (4D) reconstituted wood (4F) fibreboard (4G) plastics, solid (4H2) Drums steel, removable head (1A2) aluminium, removable head (1B2) plywood (1D) fibre (1G) plastics, removable head (1H2)
137 PARTICULAR PACKING REQUIREMENTS OR EXCEPTIONS: For UN 0059, 0439, 0440 and 0441, when the shaped charges are packed singly, the conical cavity must face downwards and the package marked "THIS SIDE UP". When the shaped charges are packed in pairs, the conical cavities must face inwards to minimize the jetting effect in the event of accidental initiation	Bags plastics Boxes fibreboard Tubes fibreboard metal plastics Dividing partitions in the outer packagings	Not necessary	Boxes steel (4A) aluminium (4B) wood, natural, ordinary (4C1) wood, natural, sift proof walls (4C2) plywood (4D) reconstituted wood (4F) fibreboard (4G)
138 PARTICULAR PACKING REQUIREMENTS OR EXCEPTIONS: If the ends of the articles are sealed, inner packagings are not necessary	Bags plastics	Not necessary	Boxes steel (4A) aluminium (4B) wood, natural, ordinary (4C1) wood, natural, sift proof walls (4C2) plywood (4D) reconstituted wood (4F) fibreboard (4G) plastics, solid (4H2) Drums fiberboard (1G) plastics, removable head (1H2) steel, removable head (1A2) aluminium, removable head (1B2)

Table of Packing Methods

Packing instruction	Inner packagings	Intermediate packagings	Outer packagings
139 PARTICULAR PACKING REQUIREMENTS OR EXCEPTIONS: 1. For UN 0065, 0102, 0104, 0289 and 0290, the ends of the detonating cord must be sealed, for example, by a plug firmly fixed so that the explosive cannot escape. The ends of CORD DETONATING flexible must be fastened securely 2. For UN 0065 and UN 0289, inner packagings are not required when they are fastened securely in coils	Bags plastics Receptacles fibreboard metal plastics wood Reels Sheets paper plastics	Not necessary	Boxes steel (4A) aluminium (4B) wood, natural, ordinary (4C1) wood, natural, sift proof walls (4C2) plywood (4D) reconstituted wood (4F) fibreboard (4G) plastics, solid (4H2) Drums steel, removable head (1A2) aluminium, removable head (1B2) plywood (1D) fibre (1G) plastics, removable head (1H2)
140 PARTICULAR PACKING REQUIREMENTS OR EXCEPTIONS: 1. If the ends of UN 0105 are sealed, no inner packagings are required 2. For UN 0101, the packaging must be sift-proof except when the fuse is covered by a paper tube and both ends of the tube are covered with removable caps 3. For UN 0101, steel or aluminium boxes or drums must not be used	Bags plastics Reels Sheets paper, kraft plastics	Not necessary	Boxes steel (4A) aluminium (4B) wood, natural, ordinary (4C1) wood, natural, sift proof walls (4C2) plywood (4D) reconstituted wood (4F) fibreboard (4G) plastics, solid (4H2) Drums plastics, removable head (1H2) steel, removable head (1A2) aluminium, removable head (1B2) plywood (1D) fibre (1G)
141	Receptacles fibreboard metal plastics wood Trays, fitted with dividing partitions plastics wood Dividing partitions in the outer packagings	Not necessary	Boxes steel (4A) aluminium (4B) wood, natural, ordinary (4C1) wood, natural, sift proof walls (4C2) plywood (4D) reconstituted wood (4F) fibreboard (4G) plastics, solid (4H2) Drums steel, removable head (1A2) aluminium, removable head (1B2) plywood (1D) fibre (1G) plastics, removable head (1H2)
142	Bags paper plastics Receptacles fibreboard metal plastics wood Sheets paper Trays, fitted with dividing partitions plastics	Not necessary	Boxes steel (4A) aluminium (4B) wood, natural, ordinary (4C1) wood, natural, sift proof walls (4C2) plywood (4D) reconstituted wood (4F) fibreboard (4G) plastics, solid (4H2) Drums steel, removable head (1A2) aluminium, removable head (1B2) plywood (1D) fibre (1G) plastics, removable head (1H2)
143 PARTICULAR PACKING REQUIREMENTS OR EXCEPTIONS: 1. For UN 0271, 0272, 0415 and 0491 when metal packagings are used, metal packagings must be so constructed that the risk of explosion, by reason of increase in internal pressure from internal or external causes is prevented 2. Composite packagings (6HH2) (plastic receptacle with outer solid box) may be used in lieu of combination packagings	Bag paper, kraft plastics textile textile, rubberized Receptacles fibreboard metal plastics Trays, fitted with dividing partitions plastics wood	Not necessary	Boxes steel (4A) aluminum (4B) wood, natural, ordinary (4C1) wood, natural, sift proof walls (4C2) plywood (4D) reconstituted wood (4F) fibreboard (4G) plastics, solid (4H2) Drums steel, removable head (1A2) aluminium, removable head (1B2) plywood (1D) fibre (1G) plastics, removable head (1H2)

Table of Packing Methods

Packing instruction	Inner packagings	Intermediate packagings	Outer packagings
144 PARTICULAR PACKING REQUIREMENTS OR EXCEPTIONS: For UN 0248 and UN 0249, packagings must be protected against the ingress of water. When CONTRIVANCES, WATER ACTIVATED are transported unpackaged, they must be provided with at least two independent protective features which prevent the ingress of water	Receptacles fibreboard metal plastics Dividing partitions in the outer packagings	Not necessary	Boxes Drums steel, removable head (1A2) aluminium, removable head (1B2) plastics, removable head (1H2) plywood (1D) 2steel (4A) aluminum (4B) wood, natural, ordinary (4C1) with metal liner plywood (4D) with metal liner reconstituted wood (4F) with metal liner plastics, expanded (4H1) plastics, solid (4H2)

US 1

1. A jet perforating gun, charged, oil well may be transported under the following conditions:
   a. Initiation devices carried on the same motor vehicle or offshore supply vessel must be segregated; each kind from every other kind, and from any gun, tool or other supplies, unless approved in accordance with §173.56. Segregated initiation devices must be carried in a container having individual pockets for each such device or in a fully enclosed steel container lined with a non-sparking material. No more than two segregated initiation devices per gun may be carried on the same motor vehicle.
   b. Each shaped charge affixed to the gun may not contain more than 112 g (4 ounces) of explosives.
   c. Each shaped charge if not completely enclosed in glass or metal, must be fully protected by a metal cover after installation in the gun.
   d. A jet perforating gun classed as 1.1D or 1.4D may be transported by highway by private or contract carriers engaged in oil well operations.
      (i) A motor vehicle transporting a gun must have specially built racks or carrying cases designed and constructed so that the gun is securely held in place during transportation and is not subject to damage by contact, one to the other or any other article or material carried in the vehicle; and.
      (ii) The assembled gun packed on the vehicle may not extend beyond the body of the motor vehicle.
   e. A jet perforating gun classed as 1.4D may be transported by a private offshore supply vessel only when the gun is carried in a motor vehicle as specified in paragraph (d) of this packing method or on offshore well tool pallets provided that:.
      (i) All the conditions specified in paragraphs (a), (b), and (c) of this packing method are met;
      (ii) The total explosive contents do not exceed 90.8 kg (200 pounds) per tool pallet;
      (iii) Each cargo vessel compartment may contain up to 90.8 kg (200 pounds) of explosive content if the segregation requirements in §176.83(b) of this subchapter are met; and
      (iv) When more than one vehicle or tool pallet is stowed "on deck" a minimum horizontal separation of 3 m (9.8 feet) must be provided.

§173.63 Packaging exceptions.

(a) **Cord, detonating (UN 0065),** having an explosive content not exceeding 6.5 g (0.23 ounces) per 30 centimeter length (one linear foot) may be offered for transportation domestically and transported as Cord, detonating (UN 0289), Division 1.4 Compatibility Group D (1.4D) explosives, if the gross weight of all packages containing Cord, detonating (UN 0065), does not exceed 45 kg (99 pounds) per:

(1) *Transport vehicle, freight container, or cargo-only aircraft;*

(2) *Off-shore down-hole tool pallet carried on an off-shore supply vessel;*

(3) *Cargo compartment of a cargo vessel; or*

(4) *Passenger-carrying aircraft* used to transport personnel to remote work sites, such as offshore drilling units.

(b) **Cartridges, small arms, and cartridges power devices.**

(1) *Cartridges, small arms,* and cartridges power devices (which are used to project fastening devices) which have been classed as a Division 1.4S explosive may be reclassed, offered for transportation, and transported as ORM-D material when packaged in accordance with paragraph (b)(2) of this section; such transportation is excepted from the requirements of subparts E (Labeling) and F (Placarding) of part 172 of this subchapter. Cartridges, small arms, and cartridges power devices that may be shipped as ORM-D material is limited to:

(i) *Ammunition for rifle, pistol or shotgun;*

(ii) *Ammunition with inert projectiles or blank ammunition;*

(iii) *Ammunition having* no tear gas, incendiary, or detonating explosive projectiles;

(iv) *Ammunition not exceeding* 12.7 mm (50 caliber or 0.5 inch) for rifle or pistol, cartridges or 8 gauge for shotshells; and

(v) *Cartridges, power devices* which are used to project fastening devices.

(2) *Packaging for cartridges,* small arms, and cartridges power devices as ORM-D material must be as follows:

(i) *Ammunition must be packed* in inside boxes, or in partitions which fit snugly in the outside packaging, or in metal clips;

(ii) *Primers must be protected from accidental initiation;*

(iii) *Inside boxes,* partitions or metal clips must be packed in securely-closed strong outside packagings;

(iv) *Maximum gross weight* is limited to 30 kg (66 pounds) per package; and

(v) *Cartridges, power devices* which are used to project fastening devices and 22 caliber rim-fire cartridges may be packaged loose in strong outside packagings.

(c) - (e) **[Reserved]**

(f) **Detonators containing no more than 1 g explosive** (excluding ignition and delay charges) that are electric blasting caps with leg wires 4 feet long or longer, delay connectors in plastic sheaths, or blasting caps with empty plastic tubing 12 feet long or longer may be packed as follows in which case they are excepted from the packaging requirements of §173.62:

(1) *No more than 50 detonators in one inner packaging;*

(2) *IME Standard 22* container or compartment is used as the outer packaging;

(3) *No more than 1000 detonators in one outer packaging; and*

(4) *No material* may be loaded on top of the IME Standard 22 container and no material may be loaded against the outside door of the IME Standard 22 compartment.

(g) **Detonators that are classed as 1.4B or 1.4S** and contain no more than 1 g of explosive (excluding ignition and delay charges) may be packed as follows in which case they are excepted from the packaging requirements of §173.62:

(1) *No more than 50 detonators in one inner packaging;*

(2) *IME Standard 22 container is used as the outer packaging;*

(3) *No more than 1000 detonators in one outer packaging; and*

(4) *Each inner packaging* is marked "I.4B Detonators" or "1.4S Detonators", as appropriate.

Subpart D - Definitions, Classification, Packing Group Assignments and Exceptions for Hazardous Materials Other Than Class 1 and Class 7

§173.115 Class 2, Divisions 2.1, 2.2, and 2.3 — Definitions.

(a) **Division 2.1 (Flammable gas).** For the purpose of this subchapter, a flammable gas (Division 2.1) means any material which is a gas at 20 °C (68 °F) or less and 101.3 kPa (14.7 psia) of pressure (a material which has a boiling point of 20 °C (68 °F) or less at 101.3 kPa (14.7 psia)) which —

(1) *Is ignitable* at 101.3 kPa (14.7 psia) when in a mixture of 13 percent or less by volume with air; or

(2) *Has a flammable range* at 101.3 kPa (14.7 psia) with air of at least 12 percent regardless of the lower limit.

Except for aerosols, the limits specified in paragraphs (a)(1) and (a)(2) of this section shall be determined at 101.3 kPa (14.7 psi) of pressure and a temperature of 20 °C (68 °F) in accordance with ASTM E681-85, Standard Test Method for Concentration Limits of Flammability of Chemicals or other equivalent method approved by the Associate Administrator. The flammability of aerosols is determined by the tests specified in §173.306(i) of this part.

(b) **Division 2.2 (non-flammable, nonpoisonous compressed gas — including compressed gas, liquefied gas, pressurized cryo-**

genic gas, compressed gas in solution, asphyxiant gas and oxidizing gas). For the purpose of this subchapter, a non-flammable, nonpoisonous compressed gas (Division 2.2) means any material (or mixture) which —

(1) *Exerts in the packaging* an absolute pressure of 280 kPa (40.6 psia) or greater at 20 °C (68 °F), and

(2) *Does not meet the definition of Division 2.1 or 2.3.*

(c) **Division 2.3 (Gas poisonous by inhalation).** For the purpose of this subchapter, a gas poisonous by inhalation (Division 2.3) means a material which is a gas at 20 °C (68 °F) or less and a pressure of 101.3 kPa (14.7 psia) (a material which has a boiling point of 20 °C (68 °F) or less at 101.3 kPa (14.7 psia)) and which —

(1) *Is known to be* so toxic to humans as to pose a hazard to health during transportation, or

(2) *In the absence* of adequate data on human toxicity, is presumed to be toxic to humans because when tested on laboratory animals it has an LC_{50} value of not more than 5000 mL/m^3 (see §173.116(a) of this subpart for assignment of Hazard Zones A, B, C or D). LC_{50} values for mixtures may be determined using the formula in §173.133(b)(1)(i) or CGA Pamphlet P-20 (incorporated by reference; see §171.7 of this subchapter).

(d) **Non-liquefied compressed gas.** A non-liquefied compressed gas means a gas, other than in solution, which in a packaging under the charged pressure is entirely gaseous at a temperature of 20 °C (68 °F).

(e) **Liquefied compressed gas.** A liquefied compressed gas means a gas which in a packaging under the charged pressure, is partially liquid at a temperature of 20 °C (68 °F).

(f) **Compressed gas in solution.** A compressed gas in solution is a non-liquefied compressed gas which is dissolved in a solvent.

(g) **Cryogenic liquid.** A cryogenic liquid means a refrigerated liquefied gas having a boiling point colder than -90 °C (-130 °F) at 101.3 kPa (14.7 psia) absolute. A material meeting this definition is subject to requirements of this subchapter without regard to whether it meets the definition of a non-flammable, non-poisonous compressed gas in paragraph (b) of this section.

(h) **Flammable range.** The term flammable range means the difference between the minimum and maximum volume percentages of the material in air that forms a flammable mixture.

(i) **Service pressure.** The term service pressure means the authorized pressure marking on the packaging. For example, for a cylinder marked "DOT 3A1800", the service pressure is 12410 kPa (1800 psig).

(j) **Refrigerant gas or Dispersant gas.** The terms Refrigerant gas and Dispersant gas apply to all nonpoisonous refrigerant gases; dispersant gases (fluorocarbons) listed in §172.101 of this subchapter and §§173.304, 173.314(c), 173.315(a), and 173.315(h) and mixtures thereof; and any other compressed gas having a vapor pressure not exceeding 260 psia at 54 °C(130 °F), used only as a refrigerant, dispersant, or blowing agent.

§173.116 Class 2 — Assignment of hazard zone.

(a) **The hazard zone of a Class 2, Division 2.3 material** is assigned in Column 7 of the §172.101 Table. There are no hazard zones for Divisions 2.1 and 2.2. When the §172.101 Table provides more than one hazard zone for a Division 2.3 material, or indicates that the hazard zone be determined on the basis of the grouping criteria for Division 2.3, the hazard zone shall be determined by applying the following criteria:

Hazard zone	Inhalation toxicity
A	LC_{50} less than or equal to 200 ppm
B	LC_{50} greater than 200 ppm and less than or equal to 1000 ppm
C	LC_{50} greater than 1000 ppm and less than or equal to 3000 ppm
D	LC_{50} greater than 3000 ppm or less than or equal to 5000 ppm

(b) **The criteria specified in paragraph (a) of this section** are represented graphically in §173.133, Figure 1.

§§173.117-173.119 [Reserved]

§173.120 Class 3 — Definitions.

(a) **Flammable liquid.** For the purpose of this subchapter, a flammable liquid (Class 3) means a liquid having a flash point of not more than 60.5 °C (141 °F), or any material in a liquid phase with a flash point at or above 37.8 °C (100 °F) that is intentionally heated and offered for transportation or transported at or above its flash point in a bulk packaging, with the following exceptions:

(1) *Any liquid meeting one of the definitions specified in §173.115.*

(2) *Any mixture* having one or more components with a flash point of 60.5 °C (141 °F) or higher, that make up at least 99 percent of the total volume of the mixture, if the mixture is not offered for transportation or transported at or above its flash point.

(3) *Any liquid* with a flash point greater than 35 °C (95 °F) which does not sustain combustion according to ASTM 4206 or the procedure in appendix H of this part.

(4) *Any liquid* with a flash point greater than 35 °C (95 °F) and with a fire point greater than 100 °C (212 °F) according to ISO 2592.

(5) *Any liquid* with a flash point greater than 35 °C (95 °F) which is in a water-miscible solution with a water content of more than 90 percent by mass.

(b) **Combustible liquid.**

(1) *For the purpose of this subchapter,* a combustible liquid means any liquid that does not meet the definition of any other hazard class specified in this subchapter and has a flash point above 60.5 °C (141 °F) and below 93 °C (200 °F).

(2) *A flammable liquid* with a flash point at or above 38 °C (100 °F) that does not meet the definition of any other hazard class may be reclassed as a combustible liquid. This provision does not apply to transportation by vessel or aircraft, except where other means of transportation is impracticable. An elevated temperature material that meets the definition of a Class 3 material because it is intentionally heated and offered for transportation or transported at or above its flash point may not be reclassed as a combustible liquid.

(3) *A combustible liquid* which does not sustain combustion is not subject to the requirements of this subchapter as a combustible liquid. Either the test method specified in ASTM 4206 or the procedure in appendix H of this part may be used to determine if a material sustains combustion when heated under test conditions and exposed to an external source of flame.

(c) **Flash point.**

(1) *Flash point* means the minimum temperature at which a liquid gives off vapor within a test vessel in sufficient concentration to form an ignitable mixture with air near the surface of the liquid. It shall be determined as follows:

(i) *For a homogeneous,* single-phase, liquid having a viscosity less than 45 S.U.S. at 38 °C (100 °F) that does not form a surface film while under test, one of the following test procedures shall be used:

[A] Standard Method of Test for Flash Point by Tag Closed Tester, (ASTM D 56);

[B] Standard Methods of Test for Flash Point of Liquids by Setaflash Closed Tester, (ASTM D 3278); or

[C] Standard Test Methods for Flash Point by Small Scale Closed Tester, (ASTM D 3828).

(ii) *For a liquid* other than one meeting all of the criteria of paragraph (c)(1)(i) of this section, one of the following test procedures shall be used:

[A] Standard Method of Test for Flash Point by Pensky — Martens Closed Tester, (ASTM D 93). For cutback asphalt, use Method B of ASTM D 93 or alternate tests authorized in this standard; or

[B] Standard Methods of Test for Flash Point of Liquids by Setaflash Closed Tester (ASTM D 3278).

(2) *For a liquid* that is a mixture of compounds that have different volatility and flash points, its flash point shall be determined as specified in paragraph (c)(1) of this section, on the material in the form in which it is to be shipped. If it is determined by this test that the flash point is higher than -7 °C (20 °F) a second test shall be made as follows: a portion of the mixture shall be placed in an open beaker (or similar container) of such dimensions that the height of the liquid can be adjusted so that the ratio of the volume of the liquid to the exposed surface area is 6 to one. The liquid shall be allowed to evaporate under ambient pressure and temperature (20 to 25 °C (68 to 77 °F)) for a period of 4 hours or until 10 percent by volume has evaporated, whichever comes first. A flash point is then run on a portion of the liquid remaining in the evaporation container and the lower of the two flash points shall be the flash point of the material.

(3) *For flash point* determinations by Setaflash closed tester, the glass syringe specified need not be used as the method of measurement of the test sample if a minimum quantity of 2 mL (0.1 ounce) is assured in the test cup.

(d) **If experience or other data indicate** that the hazard of a material is greater or less than indicated by the criteria specified in paragraphs (a) and (b) of this section, the Associate Administrator may revise the classification or make the material subject or not subject to the requirements of parts 170-189 of this subchapter.

§173.121 Class 3 — Assignment of packing group.

(a) **The packing group of a Class 3 material** is as assigned in column 5 of the §172.101 table. When the §172.101 table provides more than one packing group for a hazardous material, the packing group shall be determined by applying the following criteria:

Packing group	Flash point (closed-cup)	Initial boiling point
I	......	≤ 35 °C (95 °F)
II	< 23 °C (73 °F)	> 35 °C (95 °F)
III	≥ 23 °C, ≤ 60.5 °C (≥ 73 °F, ≤ 141 °F)	> 35 °C (95 °F)

(b) **Criteria for inclusion of viscous Class 3 materials** in Packing Group III.

(1) *Viscous Class 3 materials* in Packing Group II with a flash point of less than 23 °C (73 °F) may be grouped in Packing Group III provided that —

(i) *Less than 3 percent* of the clear solvent layer separates in the solvent separation test;

(ii) *The mixture* does not contain any substances with a primary or a subsidiary risk of Division 6.1 or Class 8;

(iii) *The capacity* of the packaging is not more than 30 L (7.9 gallons); and

(iv) *The viscosity and flash point* are in accordance with the following table:

Flow time t in seconds	Jet diameter in mm	Flash point c.c.
2 < t ≤ 60	4	above 17 °C (62.6 °F)
60 < t ≤ 100	4	above 10 °C (50 °F)
20 < t ≤ 32	6	above 5 °C (41 °F)
32 < t ≤ 44	6	above -1 °C (31.2 °F)
44 < t ≤ 100	6	above -5 °C (23 °F)
100 < t	6	-5 °C (23 °F) and below

(2) *The methods* by which the tests referred to in paragraph (b)(1) of this section shall be performed are as follows:

(i) *Viscosity test.* The flow time in seconds is determined at 23 °C (73.4 °F) using the ISO standard cup with a 4 mm (0.16 inch) jet (ISO 2431:1984). Where the flow time exceeds 100 seconds, a further test is carried out using the ISO standard cup with a 6 mm (0.24 inch) jet.

(ii) *Solvent Separation Test.* This test is carried out at 23 °C (73 °F) using a 100.0 mL(3 ounces) measuring cylinder of the stoppered type of approximately 25.0 cm (9.8 inches) total height and of a uniform internal diameter of approximately 30 mm (1.2 inches) over the calibrated section. The sample should be stirred to obtain a uniform consistency, and poured in up to the 100 mL (3 ounces) mark. The stopper should be inserted and the cylinder left standing undisturbed for 24 hours. After 24 hours, the height of the upper separated layer should be measured and the percentage of this layer as compared with the total height of the sample calculated.

§173.124 Class 4, Divisions 4.1, 4.2 and 4.3 — Definitions.

(a) **Division 4.1 (Flammable Solid).** For the purposes of this subchapter, flammable solid (Division 4.1) means any of the following three types of materials:

(1) **Desensitized explosives** that —

(i) *When dry* are Explosives of Class 1 other than those of compatibility group A, which are wetted with sufficient water, alcohol, or plasticizer to suppress explosive properties; and

(ii) *Are specifically authorized* by name either in the §172.101 Table or have been assigned a shipping name and hazard class by the Associate Administrator under the provisions of —

[A] An exemption issued under subchapter A of this chapter; or

[B] An approval issued under §173.56(i) of this part.

(2) (i) **Self-reactive materials** are materials that are thermally unstable and that can undergo a strongly exothermic decomposition even without participation of oxygen (air). A material is excluded from this definition if any of the following applies:

[A] The material meets the definition of an explosive as prescribed in subpart C of this part, in which case it must be classed as an explosive;

[B] The material is forbidden from being offered for transportation according to §172.101 of this subchapter or §173.21;

[C] The material meets the definition of an oxidizer or organic peroxide as prescribed in subpart D of this part, in which case it must be so classed;

[D] The material meets one of the following conditions:

[1] Its heat of decomposition is less than 300 J/g; or

[2] Its self-accelerating decomposition temperature (SADT) is greater than 75 °C (167 °F) for a 50 kg package; or

[E] The Associate Administrator has determined that the material does not present a hazard which is associated with a Division 4.1 material.

(ii) **Generic types.** Division 4.1 self-reactive materials are assigned to a generic system consisting of seven types. A self-reactive substance identified by technical name in the Self-Reactive Materials Table in §173.224 is assigned to a generic type in accordance with that table. Self-reactive materials not identified in the Self-Reactive Materials Table in §173.224 are assigned to generic types under the procedures of paragraph (a)(2)(iii) of this section.

[A] **Type A.** Self-reactive material type A is a self-reactive material which, as packaged for transportation, can detonate or deflagrate rapidly. Transportation of type A self-reactive material is forbidden.

[B] **Type B.** Self-reactive material type B is a self-reactive material which, as packaged for transportation, neither detonates nor deflagrates rapidly, but is liable to undergo a thermal explosion in a package.

[C] **Type C.** Self-reactive material type C is a self-reactive material which, as packaged for transportation, neither detonates nor deflagrates rapidly and cannot undergo a thermal explosion.

[D] **Type D.** Self-reactive material type D is a self-reactive material which —

[1] Detonates partially, does not deflagrate rapidly and shows no violent effect when heated under confinement;

[2] Does not detonate at all, deflagrates slowly and shows no violent effect when heated under confinement; or

[3] Does not detonate or deflagrate at all and shows a medium effect when heated under confinement.

[E] **Type E.** Self-reactive material type E is a self-reactive material which, in laboratory testing, neither detonates nor deflagrates at all and shows only a low or no effect when heated under confinement.

[F] **Type F.** Self-reactive material type F is a self-reactive material which, in laboratory testing, neither detonates in the cavitated state nor deflagrates at all and shows only a low or no effect when heated under confinement as well as low or no explosive power.

[G] **Type G.** Self-reactive material type G is a self-reactive material which, in laboratory testing, does not detonate in the cavitated state, will not deflagrate at all, shows no effect when heated under confinement, nor shows any explosive power. A type G self-reactive material is not subject to the requirements of this subchapter for self-reactive material of Division 4.1 provided that it is thermally stable (self-accelerating decomposition temperature is 50 °C (122 °F) or higher for a 50 kg (110 pounds) package). A self-reactive material meeting all characteristics of type G except thermal stability is classed as a type F self-reactive, temperature control material.

(iii) *Procedures for assigning* a self-reactive material to a generic type. A self-reactive material must be assigned to a generic type based on —

[A] Its physical state (i.e. liquid or solid), in accordance with the definition of liquid and solid in §171.8 of this subchapter;

[B] A determination as to its control temperature and emergency temperature, if any, under the provisions of §173.21(f);

[C] Performance of the self-reactive material under the test procedures specified in the UN Recommendations on the Transport of Dangerous Goods, Tests and Criteria (see §171.7 of this subchapter) and the provisions of paragraph (a)(2)(iii) of this section; and

[D] Except for a self-reactive material which is identified by technical name in the Self-Reactive Materials Table in §173.224(b) or a self-reactive material which may be shipped as a sample under the provisions of §173.224, the self-reactive material is approved in writing by the Associate Administrator. The person requesting approval shall submit to the Associate Administrator the tentative shipping description and generic type and —

[1] All relevant data concerning physical state, temperature controls, and tests results; or

[2] An approval issued for the self-reactive material by the competent authority of a foreign government.

(iv) *Tests.* The generic type for a self-reactive material must be determined using the testing protocol from Figure 14.2 (Flow Chart for Assigning Self-Reactive Substances to Division 4.1) from the UN Recommendations on the Transport of Dangerous Goods, Tests and Criteria.

(3) **Readily combustible solids** are materials that —

(i) *Are solids* which may cause a fire through friction, such as matches;

(ii) *Show a burning rate* faster than 2.2 mm (0.087 inches) per second when tested in accordance with UN Manual of Tests and Criteria; or

(iii) *Any metal powders* that can be ignited and react over the whole length of a sample in 10 minutes or less, when tested in accordance with UN Manual of Tests and Criteria.

(b) **Division 4.2 (Spontaneously Combustible Material).** For the purposes of this subchapter, spontaneously combustible material (Division 4.2) means —

(1) *A pyrophoric material.* A pyrophoric material is a liquid or solid that, even in small quantities and without an external ignition source, can ignite within five (5) minutes after coming in contact with air when tested according to UN Manual of Tests and Criteria.

(2) *A self-heating material.* A self-heating material is a material that, when in contact with air and without an energy supply, is liable to self-heat. A material of this type which exhibits spontaneous ignition or if the temperature of the sample exceeds 200 °C (392 °F) during the 24-hour test period when tested in accordance with UN Manual of Tests and Criteria, is classed as a Division 4.2 material.

(c) **Division 4.3 (Dangerous when wet material).** For the purposes of this chapter, dangerous when wet material (Division 4.3) means a material that, by contact with water, is liable to become spontaneously flammable or to give off flammable or toxic gas at a rate greater than 1 L per kilogram of the material, per hour, when tested in accordance with UN Manual of Tests and Criteria.

§173.125 Class 4 — Assignment of packing group.

(a) **The packing group of a Class 4 material** is assigned in column (5) of the §172.101 table. When the §172.101 table provides more than one packing group for a hazardous material, the packing group shall be determined on the basis of test results following test methods given in the UN Manual of Tests and Criteria and by applying the appropriate criteria given in this section.

(b) **Packing group criteria for readily combustible materials** of Division 4.1 are as follows:

(1) *Powdered, granular or pasty materials* must be classified in Division 4.1 when the time of burning of one or more of the test runs, in accordance with the UN Manual of Tests and Criteria, is less than 45 seconds or the rate of burning is more than 2.2 mm/s. Powders of metals or metal alloys must be classified in Division 4.1 when they can be ignited and the reaction spreads over the whole length of the sample in 10 minutes or less.

(2) *Packing group criteria* for readily combustible materials of Division 4.1 are assigned as follows:

(i) *For readily combustible solids* (other than metal powders), Packing Group II if the burning time is less than 45 seconds and the flame passes the wetted zone. Packing Group II must be assigned to powders of metal or metal alloys if the zone of reaction spreads over the whole length of the sample in 5 minutes or less.

(ii) *For readily combustible solids* (other than metal powders), Packing Group III must be assigned if the burning rate time is less than 45 seconds and the wetted zone stops the flame propagation for at least 4 minutes. Packing Group III must be assigned to metal powders if the reaction spreads over the whole length of the sample in more than 5 minutes but not more than 10 minutes.

(c) **Packing group criteria for Division 4.2 materials is as follows:**

(1) *Pyrophoric liquids and solids* of Division 4.2 are assigned to Packing Group I.

(2) *A self-heating material is assigned to —*

(i) *Packing Group II,* if the material gives a positive test result when tested with a 25 mm cube size sample at 140 °C; or

(ii) *Packing Group III, if —*

[A] A positive test result is obtained in a test using a 100 mm sample cube at 140 °C and a negative test result is obtained in a test using a 25 mm sample cube at 140 °C and the substance is transported in packagings with a volume of more than 3 cubic meters; or

[B] A positive test result is obtained in a test using a 100 mm sample cube at 120 °C and a negative result is obtained in a test using a 25 mm sample cube at 140 °C and the substance is transported in packagings with a volume of more than 450 L; or

[C] A positive result is obtained in a test using a 100 mm sample cube at 100 °C and a negative result is obtained in a test using a 25 mm sample cube at 140 °C and the substance is transported in packagings with a volume of less than 450 L.

(d) **A Division 4.3 dangerous when wet material is assigned to —**

(1) *Packing Group I,* if the material reacts vigorously with water at ambient temperatures and demonstrates a tendency for the gas produced to ignite spontaneously, or which reacts readily with water at ambient temperatures such that the rate of evolution of flammable gases is equal or greater than 10 L per kilogram of material over any one minute;

(2) *Packing Group II,* if the material reacts readily with water at ambient temperatures such that the maximum rate of evolution of flammable gases is equal to or greater than 20 L per kilogram of material per hour, and which does not meet the criteria for Packing Group I; or

(3) *Packing Group III,* if the material reacts slowly with water at ambient temperatures such that the maximum rate of evolution of flammable gases is greater than 1 L per kilogram of material per hour, and which does not meet the criteria for Packing Group I or II.

§173.127 Class 5, Division 5.1 — Definition and assignment of packing groups.

(a) **Definition.** For the purpose of this subchapter, oxidizer (Division 5.1) means a material that may, generally by yielding oxygen, cause or enhance the combustion of other materials.

(1) *A solid material* is classed as a Division 5.1 material if, when tested in accordance with the UN Manual of Tests and Criteria, its mean burning time is less than or equal to the burning time of a 3:7 potassium bromate/cellulose mixture.

(2) *A liquid material* is classed as a Division 5.1 material if, when tested in accordance with the UN Manual of Tests and Criteria, it spontaneously ignites or its mean time for a pressure rise from 690 kPa to 2070 kPa gauge is less then the time of a 1:1 nitric acid (65 percent)/cellulose mixture.

(b) **Assignment of packing groups.**

(1) *The packing group* of a Division 5.1 material which is a solid shall be assigned using the following criteria:

(i) *Packing Group I,* for any material which, in either concentration tested, exhibits a mean burning time less than the mean burning time of a 3:2 potassium bromate/cellulose mixture.

(ii) *Packing Group II,* for any material which, in either concentration tested, exhibits a mean burning time less than or equal to the mean burning time of a 2:3 potassium bromate/cellulose mixture and the criteria for Packing Group I are not met.

(iii) *Packing Group III,* for any material which, in either concentration tested, exhibits a mean burning time less than or equal to the mean burning time of a 3:7 potassium bromate/cellulose mixture and the criteria for Packing Group I and II are not met.

(2) *The packing group* of a Division 5.1 material which is a liquid shall be assigned using the following criteria:

(i) *Packing Group I for:*

[A] Any material which spontaneously ignites when mixed with cellulose in a 1:1 ratio; or

[B] Any material which exhibits a mean pressure rise time less than the pressure rise time of a 1:1 perchloric acid (50 percent)/cellulose mixture.

(ii) *Packing Group II,* any material which exhibits a mean pressure rise time less than or equal to the pressure rise time of a 1:1 aqueous sodium chlorate solution (40 percent)/cellulose mixture and the criteria for Packing Group I are not met.

(iii) *Packing Group III,* any material which exhibits a mean pressure rise time less than or equal to the pressure rise time of a 1:1 nitric acid (65 percent)/cellulose mixture and the criteria for Packing Group I and II are not met.

§173.128 Class 5, Division 5.2 — Definitions and types.

(a) **Definitions.** For the purposes of this subchapter, organic peroxide (Division 5.2) means any organic compound containing oxygen (O) in the bivalent -O-O- structure and which may be considered a derivative of hydrogen peroxide, where one or more of the hydrogen atoms have been replaced by organic radicals, unless any of the following paragraphs applies:

(1) *The material* meets the definition of an explosive as prescribed in subpart C of this part, in which case it must be classed as an explosive;

(2) *The material* is forbidden from being offered for transportation according to §172.101 of this subchapter or §173.21;

(3) *The Associate Administrator* has determined that the material does not present a hazard which is associated with a Division 5.2 material; or

(4) *The material meets one of the following conditions:*

(i) *For materials* containing no more than 1.0 percent hydrogen peroxide, the available oxygen, as calculated using the equation in paragraph (a)(4)(ii) of this section, is not more than 1.0 percent, or

(ii) *For materials* containing more than 1.0 percent but not more than 7.0 percent hydrogen peroxide, the available oxygen, content (Oa) is not more than 0.5 percent, when determined using the equation:

$$O_a = 16 \times \sum_{i=1}^{k} \frac{n_i c_i}{m_i}$$

where, for a material containing k species of organic peroxides:
n_i = number of -O-O- groups per molecule of the i th species
c_i = concentration (mass percent) of the i th species
m_i = molecular mass of the i th species

(b) **Generic types.** Division 5.2 organic peroxides are assigned to a generic system which consists of seven types. An organic peroxide identified by technical name in the Organic Peroxides Table in §173.225 is assigned to a generic type in accordance with that table. Organic peroxides not identified in the Organic Peroxides table are assigned to generic types under the procedures of paragraph (c) of this section.

(1) *Type A.* Organic peroxide type A is an organic peroxide which can detonate or deflagrate rapidly as packaged for transport. Transportation of type A organic peroxides is forbidden.

(2) *Type B.* Organic peroxide type B is an organic peroxide which, as packaged for transport, neither detonates nor deflagrates rapidly, but can undergo a thermal explosion.

(3) *Type C.* Organic peroxide type C is an organic peroxide which, as packaged for transport, neither detonates nor deflagrates rapidly and cannot undergo a thermal explosion.

(4) *Type D.* Organic peroxide type D is an organic peroxide which —

(i) *Detonates only partially,* but does not deflagrate rapidly and is not affected by heat when confined;

(ii) *Does not detonate,* deflagrates slowly, and shows no violent effect if heated when confined; or

(iii) *Does not detonate or deflagrate,* and shows a medium effect when heated under confinement.

(5) *Type E.* Organic peroxide type E is an organic peroxide which neither detonates nor deflagrates and shows low, or no, effect when heated under confinement.

(6) *Type F.* Organic peroxide type F is an organic peroxide which will not detonate in a cavitated state, does not deflagrate, shows only a low, or no, effect if heated when confined, and has low, or no, explosive power.

(7) *Type G.* Organic peroxide type G is an organic peroxide which will not detonate in a cavitated state, will not deflagrate at all, shows no effect when heated under confinement, and shows no explosive power. A type G organic peroxide is not subject to the requirements of this subchapter for organic peroxides of Division 5.2 provided that it is thermally stable (self-accelerating decomposition temperature is 50 °C (122 °F) or higher for a 50 kg (110 pounds) package). An organic peroxide meeting all characteristics of type G except thermal stability and requiring temperature control is classed as a type F, temperature control organic peroxide.

(c) **Procedure for assigning an organic peroxide** to a generic type. An organic peroxide shall be assigned to a generic type based on —

(1) *Its physical state* (i.e., liquid or solid), in accordance with the definitions for liquid and solid in §171.8 of this subchapter;

(2) *A determination* as to its control temperature and emergency temperature, if any, under the provisions of §173.21(f); and

(3) *Performance of the organic peroxide* under the test procedures specified in the UN Manual of Tests and Criteria, and the provisions of paragraph (d) of this section.

(d) **Approvals.**

(1) *An organic peroxide* must be approved, in writing, by the Associate Administrator, before being offered for transportation or transported, including assignment of a generic type and shipping description, except for —

(i) *An organic peroxide* which is identified by technical name in the Organic Peroxides Table in §173.225(b);

(ii) *A mixture* of organic peroxides prepared according to §173.225 (c); or

(iii) *An organic peroxide* which may be shipped as a sample under the provisions of §173.225(c).

(2) *A person* applying for an approval must submit all relevant data concerning physical state, temperature controls, and tests results or an approval issued for the organic peroxide by the competent authority of a foreign government.

(e) **Tests.** The generic type for an organic peroxide shall be determined using the testing protocol from Figure 20.1(a) (Classification and Flow Chart Scheme for Organic Peroxides) from the UN Manual of Tests and Criteria (see §171.7 of this subchapter).

§173.129 Class 5, Division 5.2 — Assignment of packing group.

All Division 5.2 materials are assigned to Packing Group II in column 5 of the §172.101 table.

§173.132 Class 6, Division 6.1 — Definitions.

(a) **For the purpose of this subchapter, poisonous material** (Division 6.1) means a material, other than a gas, which is known to be so toxic to humans as to afford a hazard to health during transportation, or which, in the absence of adequate data on human toxicity:

(1) *Is presumed* to be toxic to humans because it falls within any one of the following categories when tested on laboratory animals (whenever possible, animal test data that has been reported in the chemical literature should be used):

(i) *Oral Toxicity.* A liquid with an LD_{50} for acute oral toxicity of not more than 500 mg/kg or a solid with an LD_{50} for acute oral toxicity of not more than 200 mg/kg.

(ii) *Dermal Toxicity.* A material with an LD_{50} for acute dermal toxicity of not more than 1000 mg/kg.

(iii) *Inhalation Toxicity.*

[A] A dust or mist with an LC_{50} for acute toxicity on inhalation of not more than 10 mg/L; or

[B] A material with a saturated vapor concentration in air at 20 °C (68 °F) greater than or equal to one-fifth of the LC_{50} for acute toxicity on inhalation of vapors and with an LC_{50} for acute toxicity on inhalation of vapors of not more than 5000 mL/mm^3; or

(2) *Is an irritating material,* with properties similar to tear gas, which causes extreme irritation, especially in confined spaces.

(b) **For the purposes of this subchapter —**

(1) **LD_{50} for acute oral toxicity** means that dose of the material administered to both male and female young adult albino rats which causes death within 14 days in half the animals tested. The number of animals tested must be sufficient to give statistically valid results and be in conformity with good pharmacological practices. The result is expressed in mg/kg body mass.

(2) **LD_{50} for acute dermal toxicity** means that dose of the material which, administered by continuous contact for 24 hours with the shaved intact skin (avoiding abrading) of an albino rabbit, causes death within 14 days in half of the animals tested. The number of animals tested must be sufficient to give statistically valid results and be in conformity with good pharmacological practices. The result is expressed in mg/kg body mass.

(3) **LC_{50} for acute toxicity on inhalation** means that concentration of vapor, mist, or dust which, administered by continuous inhalation for one hour to both male and female young adult albino rats, causes death within 14 days in half of the animals tested. If the material is administered to the animals as a dust or mist, more than 90 percent of the particles available for inhalation in the test must have a diameter of 10 microns or less if it is reasonably foreseeable that such concentrations could be encountered by a human during transport. The result is expressed in mg/L of air for dusts and mists or in mL/m^3 of air (parts per million) for vapors. See §173.133(b) for LC_{50} determination for mixtures and for limit tests.

(i) *When provisions* of this subchapter require the use of the LC_{50} for acute toxicity on inhalation of dusts and mists based on a one-hour exposure and such data is not available, the LC_{50} for acute toxicity on inhalation based on a four-hour exposure may be multiplied by four and the product substituted for the one-hour LC_{50} for acute toxicity on inhalation.

(ii) *When the provisions* of this subchapter require the use of the LC_{50} for acute toxicity on inhalation of vapors based on a one-hour exposure and such data is not available, the LC_{50} for acute toxicity on inhalation based on a four-hour exposure may be multiplied by two and the product substituted for the one-hour LC_{50} for acute toxicity on inhalation.

(iii) *A solid substance* should be tested if at least 10 percent of its total mass is likely to be dust in a respirable range, e.g. the aerodynamic diameter of that particle-fraction is 10 microns or less. A liquid substance should be tested if a mist is likely to be generated in a leakage of the transport containment. In carrying out the test both for solid and liquid substances, more than 90% (by mass) of a specimen prepared for inhalation toxicity testing must be in the respirable range as defined in this paragraph (b)(3)(iii).

(c) **For purposes of classifying and assigning** packing groups to mixtures possessing oral or dermal toxicity hazards according to the criteria in §173.133(a)(1), it is necessary to determine the acute LD_{50} of the mixture. If a mixture contains more than one active constituent, one of the following methods may be used to determine the oral or dermal LD_{50} of the mixture:

(1) *Obtain reliable* acute oral and dermal toxicity data on the actual mixture to be transported;

(2) *If reliable,* accurate data is not available, classify the formulation according to the most hazardous constituent of the mixture as if that constituent were present in the same concentration as the total concentration of all active constituents; or

(3) *If reliable, accurate data is not available, apply the formula:*

$$\frac{C_A}{T_A} + \frac{C_B}{T_B} + \frac{C_Z}{T_Z} = \frac{100}{T_M}$$

Where:

C = the % concentration of constituent A, B ... Z in the mixture;

T = the oral LD_{50} values of constituent A, B ... Z;

T_M = the oral LD_{50} value of the mixture.

Note to formula in paragraph (c)(3): This formula also may be used for dermal toxicities provided that this information is available on the same species for all constituents. The use of this formula does not take into account any potentiation or protective phenomena.

(d) **The foregoing categories shall not apply** if the Associate Administrator has determined that the physical characteristics of the material or its probable hazards to humans as shown by documented experience indicate that the material will not cause serious sickness or death.

§173.133 Assignment of packing group and hazard zones for Division 6.1 materials.

(a) **The packing group of Division 6.1 materials** shall be as assigned in column 5 of the §172.101 table. When the §172.101 table provides more than one packing group or hazard zone for a hazardous material, the packing group and hazard zone shall be determined by applying the following criteria:

(1) *The packing group assignment* for routes of administration other than inhalation of vapors shall be in accordance with the following table:

Packing Group	Oral toxicity LD_{50} (mg/kg)	Dermal toxicity LD_{50} (mg/kg)	Inhalation toxicity by dusts and mists LC_{50} (mg/L)
I	≤ 5	≤ 40	≤ 0.5
II	$> 5, \leq 50$	$> 40, \leq 200$	$> 0.5, \leq 2$
III	solids: $> 50, \leq 200$; liquids: $> 50, \leq 500$;	$> 200, \leq 1000$	$> 2, \leq 10$

(2) (i) *The packing group* and hazard zone assignments for liquids (see §173.115(c) of this subpart for gases) based on inhalation of vapors shall be in accordance with the following table:

Packing Group	Vapor concentration and toxicity
I (Hazard Zone A)	$V \geq 500\ LC_{50}$ and $LC_{50} \leq 200$ mL/m^3
I (Hazard Zone B)	$V \geq 10\ LC_{50}$; $LC_{50} \leq 1000$ mL/m^3; and the criteria for Packing Group I, Hazard Zone A, are not met
II	$V \geq LC_{50}$; $LC_{50} \leq 3000$ mL/m^3; and the criteria for Packing Group I, are not met
III	$V \geq .2\ LC_{50}$; $LC_{50} \leq 5000$ mL/m^3; and the criteria for Packing Groups I and II, are not met

NOTE 1: V is the saturated vapor concentration in air of the material in mL/m^3 at 20 °C and standard atmospheric pressure.

NOTE 2: A liquid in Division 6.1 meeting criteria for Packing Group I, Hazard Zones A or B stated in paragraph (a)(2) of this section is a material poisonous by inhalation subject to the additional hazard communication requirements in §§172.203(m)(2), 172.313 and table 1 of §172.504(e) of this subchapter.

(ii) *These criteria are represented graphically in Figure 1:*

Figure 1

Inhalation Toxicity: Packing Group and Hazard Zone Borderlines

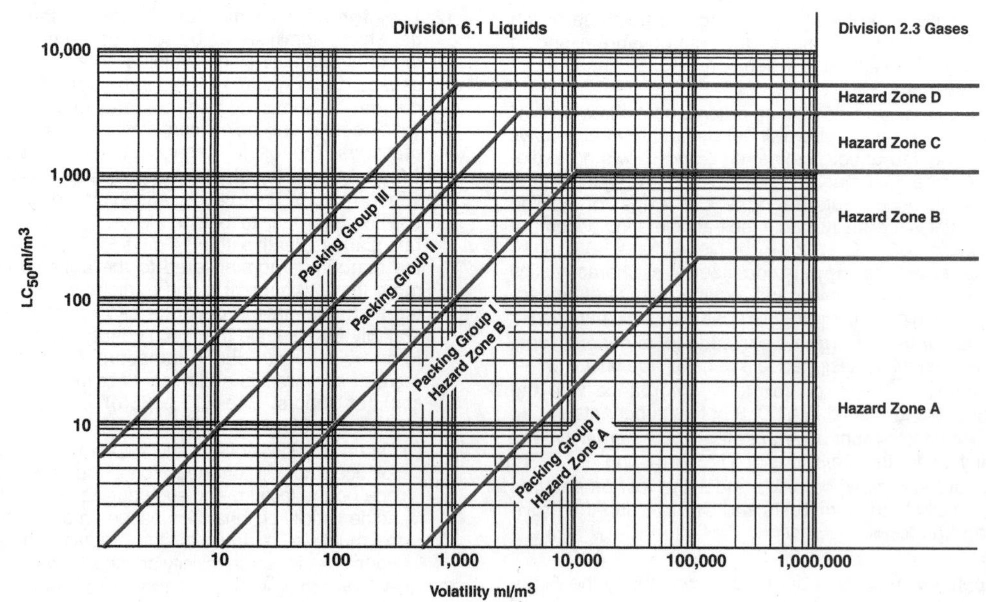

(3) *When the packing group* determined by applying these criteria is different for two or more (oral, dermal or inhalation) routes of administration, the packing group assigned to the material shall be that indicated for the highest degree of toxicity for any of the routes of administration.

(4) *Notwithstanding* the provisions of this paragraph, the packing group and hazard zone of a tear gas substance is as assigned in column 5 of the §172.101 table.

(b) **The packing group and hazard zone** for Division 6.1 mixtures that are poisonous (toxic) by inhalation may be determined by one of the following methods:

(1) *Where LC_{50} data* is available on each of the poisonous (toxic) substances comprising the mixture —

(i) *The LC_{50} of the mixture is estimated using the formula:*

$$LC50\ (\text{mixture}) = \frac{1}{\sum_{i=1}^{n} \frac{f_i}{LC50_i}}$$

where

f_i = mole fraction of the ith component substance of the liquid.

LC_{50i} = mean lethal concentration of the ith component substance in mL/m^3

(ii) The volatility of each component substance is estimated using the formula:

$$V_i = P_i \times \frac{10^6}{101.3}\ mL/m^3$$

Where:

P_i = partial pressure of the ith component substance in kPa at 20 °C and one atmospheric pressure. Pi may be calculated according to Raoult's Law using appropriate activity coefficients. Where activity coefficients are not available, the coefficient may be assumed to be 1.0.

(iii) *The ratio* of the volatility to the LC_{50} is calculated using the formula:

$$R = \sum_{i=1}^{n} \frac{V_i}{L_{c50i}}$$

(iv) *Using the calculated values* LC_{50} (mixture) and R, the packing group for the mixture is determined as follows:

Packing Group (hazard zone)	Ratio of volatility and LC_{50}
I (Hazard Zone A)	$R \geq 500$ and LC_{50} (mixture) $\leq 200\ mL/m^3$
I (Hazard Zone B)	$R \geq 10$ LC_{50} (mixture) $\leq 1000\ mL/m^3$; and the criteria for Packing Group I, Hazard Zone A, are not met
II	$R \geq 1$ and LC_{50} (mixture) $\leq 3000\ mL/m^3$; and the criteria for Packing Group I, Hazard Zones A and B, are not met
III	$R \geq 1/5$ and LC_{50} (mixture) $\leq 5000\ mL/m^3$; and the criteria for Packing Group I, Hazard Zones A and B, and Packing Group II are not met

(2) *In the absence* of LC_{50} data on the poisonous (toxic) constituent substances, the mixture may be assigned a packing group and hazard zone based on the following simplified threshold toxicity tests. When these threshold tests are used, the most restrictive packing group and hazard zone must be determined and used for the transportation of the mixture.

(i) *A mixture* is assigned to Packing Group I, Hazard Zone A only if both the following criteria are met:

[A] A sample of the liquid mixture is vaporized and diluted with air to create a test atmosphere of 200 mL/m^3 vaporized mixture in air. Ten albino rats (five male and five female) are exposed to the test atmosphere as determined by an analytical method appropriate for the material being classified for one hour and observed for fourteen days. If five or more of the animals die within the fourteen-day observation period, the mixture is presumed to have an LC_{50} equal to or less than 200 mL/m^3.

[B] A sample of the vapor in equilibrium with the liquid mixture is diluted with 499 equal volumes of air to form a test atmosphere. Ten albino rats (five male and five female) are exposed to the test atmosphere for one hour and observed for fourteen days. If five or more of the animals die within the fourteen-day observation period, the mixture is presumed to have a volatility equal to or greater than 500 times the mixture LC_{50}.

(ii) *A mixture* is assigned to Packing Group I, Hazard Zone B only if both the following criteria are met, and the mixture does not meet the criteria for Packing Group I, Hazard Zone A:

[A] A sample of the liquid mixture is vaporized and diluted with air to create a test atmosphere of 1000 mL/m^3 vaporized mixture in air. Ten albino rats (five male and five female) are exposed to the test atmosphere for one hour and observed for fourteen days. If five or more of the animals die within the fourteen-day observation period, the mixture is presumed to have an LC_{50} equal to or less than 1000 mL/m^3.

[B] A sample of the vapor in equilibrium with the liquid mixture is diluted with 9 equal volumes of air to form a test atmosphere. Ten albino rats (five male and five female) are exposed to the test atmosphere for one hour and observed for fourteen days. If five or more of the animals die within the fourteen-day observation period, the mixture is presumed to have a volatility equal to or greater than 10 times the mixture LC_{50}.

(iii) *A mixture* is assigned to Packing Group II only if both the following criteria are met, and the mixture does not meet the criteria for Packing Group I (Hazard Zones A or B):

[A] A sample of the liquid mixture is vaporized and diluted with air to create a test atmosphere of 3000 mL/m^3 vaporized mixture in air. Ten albino rats (five male and five female) are exposed to the test atmosphere for one hour and observed for fourteen days. If five or more of the animals die within the fourteen-day observation period, the mixture is presumed to have an LC_{50} equal to or less than 3000 mL/m^3.

[B] A sample of the vapor in equilibrium with the liquid mixture is used to form a test atmosphere. Ten albino rats (five male and five female) are exposed to the test atmosphere for one hour and observed for fourteen days. If five or more of the animals die within the fourteen-day observation period, the mixture is presumed to have a volatility equal to or greater than the mixture LC_{50}.

(iv) *A mixture* is assigned to Packing Group III only if both the following criteria are met, and the mixture does not meet the criteria for Packing Groups I (Hazard Zones A or B) or Packing Group II (Hazard Zone C):

[A] A sample of the liquid mixture is vaporized and diluted with air to create a test atmosphere of 5000 mL/m^3 vaporized mixture in air. Ten albino rats (five male and five female) are exposed to the test atmosphere for one hour and observed for fourteen days. If five or more of the animals die within the fourteen-day observation period, the mixture is presumed to have an LC_{50} equal to or less than 5000 mL/m^3.

[B] The vapor pressure of the liquid mixture is measured and if the vapor concentration is equal to or greater than 1000 mL/m^3, the mixture is presumed to have a volatility equal to or greater than 1/5 the mixture LC_{50}.

§173.134 Class 6, Division 6.2 — Definitions and exceptions.

(a) **Definitions and classification criteria.** For purposes of this subchapter, the following definitions and classification criteria apply:

(1) **Division 6.2 (infectious substance)** means a material known to contain or suspected of containing a pathogen. A pathogen is a virus or micro-organism (including its viruses, plasmids, or other genetic elements, if any) or a proteinaceous infectious particle (prion) that has the potential to cause disease in humans or animals. A Division 6.2 material must be assigned to a risk group in accordance with this paragraph (a). Assignment to a risk group is based on known medical condition and history of the source patient or animal, endemic local conditions, symptoms of the source patient or animal, or professional judgement concerning individual circumstances of the source patient or animal. Infectious substances are subject to applicable requirements in 42 CFR Part 72 — Interstate Shipment of Etiologic Agents.

(2) **Biological product** means a virus, therapeutic serum, toxin, antitoxin, vaccine, blood, blood component or derivative, allergenic product, or analogous product used in the prevention, diagnosis, treatment, or cure of diseases in humans or animals. A biological product includes a material manufactured and distributed in accordance with one of the following provisions: 9 CFR part 102 (Licenses for Biological Products); 9 CFR part 103 (Experimental Products, Distribution, and Evaluation of Biological Products Prior to Licensing); 9 CFR part 104 (Permits for Biological Products); 21 CFR part 312 (Investigational New Drug Application); 21 CFR part

314 (Applications for FDA Approval to Market a New Drug); 21 CFR parts 600 to 680 (Biologics); or 21 CFR part 812 (Investigational Device Exemptions). A biological product known to contain or suspected of containing a pathogen in Risk Group 2, 3, or 4 must be classed as Division 6.2, described as an infectious substance, and assigned to UN 2814 or UN 2900, as appropriate, unless otherwise excepted.

(3) **Cultures and stocks** means a material prepared and maintained for growth and storage and containing a Risk Group 2, 3 or 4 infectious substance.

(4) **Diagnostic specimen** means any human or animal material, including excreta, secreta, blood and its components, tissue, and tissue fluids being transported for diagnostic or investigational purposes, but excluding live infected humans or animals. A diagnostic specimen is not assigned a UN identification number unless the source patient or animal has or may have a serious human or animal disease from a Risk Group 4 pathogen, in which case it must be classed as Division 6.2, described as an infectious substance, and assigned to UN 2814 or UN 2900, as appropriate. Assignment to UN 2814 or UN 2900 is based on known medical condition and history of the patient or animal, endemic local conditions, symptoms of the source patient or animal, or professional judgement concerning individual circumstances of the source patient or animal.

(5) **Regulated medical waste** means a waste or reusable material known to contain or suspected of containing an infectious substance in Risk Group 2 or 3 and generated in the diagnosis, treatment, or immunization of human beings or animals; research on the diagnosis, treatment or immunization of human beings or animals; or the production or testing of biological products. Regulated medical waste containing an infectious substance in Risk Group 4 must be classed as Division 6.2, described as an infectious substance, and assigned to UN 2814 or UN 2900, as appropriate.

(6) **Risk group** means a ranking of a micro-organism's ability to cause injury through disease. A risk group is defined by criteria developed by the World Health Organization (WHO) based on the severity of the disease caused by the organism, the mode and relative ease of transmission, the degree of risk to both an individual and a community, and the reversibility of the disease through the availability of known and effective preventative agents and treatment. There is no relationship between a risk group and a packing group. The criteria for each risk group according to the level of risk are as follows:

Risk Group Table

Risk group	Pathogen	Risk to individuals	Risk to the community
4	A pathogen that usually causes serious human or animal disease and that can be readily transmitted from one individual to another, directly or indirectly, and for which effective treatments and preventive measures are not usually available.	High	High
3	A pathogen that usually causes serious human or animal disease but does not ordinarily spread from one infected individual to another, and for which effective treatments and preventive measures are available.	High	Low
2	A pathogen that can cause human or animal disease but is unlikely to be a serious hazard, and, while capable of causing serious infection on exposure, for which there are effective treatments and preventive measures available and the risk of spread of infection is limited.	Moderate	Low
1	A micro-organism that is unlikely to cause human or animal disease. A material containing only such micro-organisms is not subject to the requirements of this subchapter.	None or very low	None or very low

(7) **Sharps** means any object contaminated with a pathogen or that may become contaminated with a pathogen through handling or during transportation and also capable of cutting or penetrating skin or a packaging material. Sharps includes needles, syringes, scalpels, broken glass, culture slides, culture dishes, broken capillary tubes, broken rigid plastic, and exposed ends of dental wires.

(8) **Toxin** means a Division 6.1 material from a plant, animal, or bacterial source. A toxin containing an infectious substance or a toxin contained in an infectious substance must be classed as Division 6.2, described as an infectious substance, and assigned to UN 2814 or UN 2900, as appropriate.

(9) **Used health care product** means a medical, diagnostic, or research device or piece of equipment, or a personal care product used by consumers, medical professionals, or pharmaceutical providers that does not meet the definition of a diagnostic specimen, biological product, or regulated medical waste, is contaminated with potentially infectious body fluids or materials, and is not decontaminated or disinfected to remove or mitigate the infectious hazard prior to transportation.

(b) **Exceptions.** The following are not subject to the requirements of this subchapter as Division 6.2 materials:

(1) *A biological product* known to contain or suspected of containing a micro-organism in Risk Group 1, or that does not contain a pathogen.

(2) *A diagnostic specimen* known to contain or suspected of containing a micro-organism in Risk Group 1, or that does not contain a pathogen, or a diagnostic specimen in which the pathogen has been neutralized or inactivated so it cannot cause disease when exposure to it occurs.

(3) *A biological product,* including an experimental product or component of a product, subject to Federal approval, permit, or licensing requirements, such as those required by the Food and Drug Administration of the Department of Health and Human Services or the U.S. Department of Agriculture.

(4) *Blood collected* for the purpose of blood transfusion or the preparation of blood products; blood products; tissues or organs intended for use in transplant operations; and human cell, tissues, and cellular and tissue-based products regulated under authority of the Public Health Service Act and/or the Food, Drug, and Cosmetic Act.

(5) *Blood collected* for the purpose of blood transfusion or the preparation of blood products and sent for testing as part of the collection process, except where the person collecting the blood has reason to believe it contains an infectious substance, in which case the test sample must be shipped in accordance with §173.199.

(6) *A diagnostic specimen* or biological product when transported by a private or contract carrier in a motor vehicle used exclusively to transport diagnostic specimens or biological products. Medical or clinical equipment and laboratory products may be transported aboard the same vehicle provided they are properly packaged and secured against exposure or contamination. If a diagnostic specimen or biological product meets the definition of regulated medical waste in paragraph (a)(5) of this section, it must be offered for transportation and transported in conformance with the appropriate requirements for regulated medical waste.

(7) *Laundry or medical equipment* conforming to the regulations of the Occupational Safety and Health Administration of the Department of Labor in 29 CFR 1910.1030. This exception includes medical equipment intended for use, cleaning, or refurbishment, such as reusable surgical equipment, or equipment used for testing where the components within which the equipment is contained essentially function as packaging. This exception does not apply to medical equipment being transported for disposal.

(8) *A material,* including waste, that previously contained an infectious substance that has been treated by steam sterilization, chemical disinfection, or other appropriate method, so it no longer meets the definition of an infectious substance.

(9) *A living person.*

(10) *Any waste* or recyclable material, other than regulated medical waste, including —

(i) *Garbage and trash* derived from hotels, motels, and households, including but not limited to single and multiple residences;

(ii) *Sanitary waste or sewage;*

(iii) *Sewage sludge or compost;*

(iv) *Animal waste* generated in animal husbandry or food production; or

(v) *Medical waste* generated from households and transported in accordance with applicable state, local, or tribal requirements.

(11) *Corpses, remains,* and anatomical parts intended for interment, cremation, or medical research at a college, hospital, or laboratory.

(12) *Forensic material* transported on behalf of a U.S. Government, state, local or Indian tribal government agency, except that —

(i) *Forensic material* known or suspected to contain a Risk Group 2 or 3 infectious substance must be shipped in a packaging conforming to the provisions of §173.24.

(ii) *Forensic material* known or suspected to contain a Risk Group 4 infectious substance or an infectious substance listed as a select agent in 42 CFR Part 72 must be transported in packaging capable of meeting the test standards in §178.609 of this subchapter. The secondary packaging must be marked with a BIOHAZARD symbol conforming to specifications in 29 CFR 1910.1030(g)(1)(i). An itemized list of contents must be enclosed between the secondary packaging and the outer packaging.

(13) *Environmental microbiological samples,* such as a sample of dust from a ventilation system or mold from a wallboard, collected to evaluate occupational and residential exposure risks.

(14) *Agricultural products* and food as defined in the Federal Food, Drug, and Cosmetics Act.

(c) **Exceptions for regulated medical waste.** The following provisions apply to the transportation of regulated medical waste:

(1) *A regulated medical waste* transported by a private or contract carrier is excepted from —

(i) *The requirement* for an "INFECTIOUS SUBSTANCE" label if the outer packaging is marked with a "BIOHAZARD" marking in accordance with 29 CFR 1910.1030; and

(ii) *For other than* a waste culture or stock of an infectious substance, the specific packaging requirements of this section if packaged in a rigid non-bulk packaging conforming to the general packaging requirements of §§173.24 and 173.24a and packaging requirements specified in 29 CFR 1910.1030.

(2) *A waste culture* or stock of a Risk Group 2 or 3 infectious substance may be offered for transportation and transported as a regulated medical waste when it is packaged in a rigid non-bulk packaging conforming to the general packaging requirements of §§173.24 and 173.24a and packaging requirements specified in 29 CFR 1910.1030 and transported by a private or contract carrier using a vehicle dedicated to the transportation of regulated medical waste. Medical or clinical equipment and laboratory products may be transported aboard the same vehicle provided they are properly packaged and secured against exposure or contamination.

(d) **If an item listed in paragraph (b) or (c) of this section** meets the definition of another hazard class or if it is a hazardous substance, hazardous waste, or marine pollutant, it must be offered for transportation and transported in accordance with applicable requirements of this subchapter.

§173.136 Class 8 — Definitions.

(a) **For the purpose of this subchapter,** "corrosive material" (Class 8) means a liquid or solid that causes full thickness destruction of human skin at the site of contact within a specified period of time. A liquid that has a severe corrosion rate on steel or aluminum based on the criteria in §173.137(c)(2) is also a corrosive material.

(b) **If human experience or other data indicate** that the hazard of a material is greater or less than indicated by the results of the tests specified in paragraph (a) of this section, RSPA may revise its classification or make the determination that the material is not subject to the requirements of this subchapter.

(c) **Skin corrosion test data produced** no later than September 30, 1995, using the procedures of part 173, appendix A, in effect on September 30, 1995 (see 49 CFR part 173, appendix A, revised as of October 1, 1994) for appropriate exposure times may be used for classification and assignment of packing group for Class 8 materials corrosive to skin.

§173.137 Class 8 — Assignment of packing group.

The packing group of Class 8 material is indicated in column 5 of the §172.101 table. When the §172.101 table provides more than one packing group for a Class 8 material, the packing group must be determined using data obtained from tests conducted in accordance with the 1992 OECD Guideline for Testing of Chemicals, Number 404 "Acute Dermal Irritation/Corrosion" as follows:

(a) **Packing Group I.** Materials that cause full thickness destruction of intact skin tissue within an observation period of up to 60 minutes starting after the exposure time of three minutes or less.

(b) **Packing Group II.** Materials other than those meeting Packing Group I criteria that cause full thickness destruction of intact skin tissue within an observation period of up to 14 days starting after the exposure time of more than three minutes but not more than 60 minutes.

(c) **Packing Group III.** Materials, other than those meeting Packing Group I or II criteria —

(1) *That cause* full thickness destruction of intact skin tissue within an observation period of up to 14 days starting after the exposure time of more than 60 minutes but not more than 4 hours; or

(2) *That do not cause* full thickness destruction of intact skin tissue but exhibit a corrosion rate on steel or aluminum surfaces exceeding 6.25 mm (0.25 inch) a year at a test temperature of 55 °C (130 °F). For the purpose of testing steel P3 (ISO 9328-1) or a similar type, and for testing aluminum, non-clad types 7075-T6 or AZ5GU-T6 should be used. An acceptable test is described in ASTM G 31-72 (Reapproved 1995).

§173.140 Class 9 — Definitions.

For the purposes of this subchapter, miscellaneous hazardous material (Class 9) means a material which presents a hazard during transportation but which does not meet the definition of any other hazard class. This class includes:

(a) **Any material which has an anesthetic, noxious** or other similar property which could cause extreme annoyance or discomfort to a flight crew member so as to prevent the correct performance of assigned duties; or

(b) **Any material that meets the definition in §171.8** of this subchapter for an elevated temperature material, a hazardous substance, a hazardous waste, or a marine pollutant.

§173.141 Class 9 — Assignment of packing group.

The packing group of a Class 9 material is as indicated in column 5 of the §172.101 table.

§173.144 Other Regulated Materials (ORM) — Definitions.

For the purpose of this subchapter, "ORM-D material" means a material such as a consumer commodity, which, although otherwise subject to the regulations of this subchapter, presents a limited hazard during transportation due to its form, quantity and packaging. It must be a material for which exceptions are provided in the §172.101 table. Each ORM-D material and category of ORM-D material is listed in the §172.101 table.

§173.145 Other Regulated Materials — Assignment of packing group.

Packing groups are not assigned to ORM-D materials.

§173.150 Exceptions for Class 3 (flammable) and combustible liquids.

(a) **General.** Exceptions for hazardous materials shipments in the following paragraphs are permitted only if this section is referenced for the specific hazardous material in the §172.101 table of this subchapter and the material does not meet the definition of another hazard class except Division 6.1, Packing Group III or Class 8, Packing Group III.

(b) **Limited quantities.** Limited quantities of flammable liquids (Class 3) and combustible liquids are excepted from labeling requirements, unless offered for transportation or transported by aircraft, and the specification packaging requirements of this subchapter when packaged in combination packagings according to this paragraph. In addition, shipments of limited quantities are not subject to subpart F (Placarding) of part 172 of this subchapter. Each package must conform to the packaging requirements of subpart B of this part and may not exceed 30 kg (66 pounds) gross weight. The following combination packagings are authorized:

(1) *For flammable liquids* in Packing Group I, inner packagings not over 0.5 L (0.1 gallon) net capacity each, packed in strong outer packagings;

(2) *For flammable liquids* in Packing Group II, inner packagings not over 1.0 L (0.3 gallon) net capacity each, packed in strong outer packaging; and

(3) *For flammable liquids* in Packing Group III and combustible liquids, inner packagings not over 5.0 L (1.3 gallons) net capacity each, packed in strong outer packagings.

(c) **Consumer commodities.** A limited quantity which conforms to the provisions of paragraph (b) of this section and is a "consumer commodity" as defined in §171.8 of this subchapter, may be renamed "Consumer commodity" and reclassed as ORM-D material. In addition to the exceptions provided by paragraph (b) of this section, shipments of ORM-D materials are not subject to the shipping paper requirements of subpart C of part 172 of this subchapter, unless the material meets the definition of a hazardous substance, hazardous waste, marine pollutant, or are offered for transportation and transported by aircraft, and are eligible for the exceptions provided in §173.156.

(d) **Alcoholic beverages.** An alcoholic beverage (wine and distilled spirits as defined in 27 CFR 4.10 and 5.11) is not subject to the requirements of this subchapter if it —

(1) *Contains 24 percent or less alcohol by volume;*

(2) *Is in an inner packaging* of 5 L (1.3 gallons) or less, and for transportation on passenger-carrying aircraft conforms to §175.10(a)(17) of this subchapter as checked or carry-on baggage; or

(3) *Is a Packing Group III* alcoholic beverage in a packaging of 250 L (66 gallons) or less, unless transported by air.

(e) **Aqueous solutions of alcohol.** An aqueous solution containing 24 percent or less alcohol by volume and no other hazardous material —

(1) *May be reclassed as a combustible liquid.*

(2) *Is not subject* to the requirements of this subchapter if it contains no less than 50 percent water.

(f) **Combustible liquids.**

(1) *A flammable liquid* with a flash point at or above 38 °C (100 °F) that does not meet the definition of any other hazard class may be reclassed as a combustible liquid. This provision does not apply to transportation by vessel or aircraft, except where other means of transportation is impracticable.

(2) *The requirements* in this subchapter do not apply to a material classed as a combustible liquid in a non-bulk packaging unless the combustible liquid is a hazardous substance, a hazardous waste, or a marine pollutant.

(3) *A combustible liquid* that is in a bulk packaging or a combustible liquid that is a hazardous substance, a hazardous waste, or a marine pollutant is not subject to the requirements of this subchapter except those pertaining to:

(i) *Shipping papers,* waybills, switching orders, and hazardous waste manifests;

(ii) *Marking of packages;*

(iii) *Display of identification numbers on bulk packages;*

(iv) *For bulk packagings only,* placarding requirements of subpart F of part 172 of this subchapter;

(v) *Carriage aboard* aircraft and vessels (for packaging requirements for transport by vessel, see §176.340 of this subchapter);

(vi) *Reporting incidents* as prescribed by §§171.15 and 171.16 of this subchapter;

(vii) *Packaging requirements* of subpart B of this part and, in addition, non-bulk packagings must conform with requirements of §173.203; and

(viii) *The requirements* of §§173.1, 173.21, 173.24, 173.24a, 173.24b, 174.1, 177.804, 177.817, 177.834(j), and 177.837(d) of this subchapter.

(4) *A combustible liquid* that is not a hazardous substance, a hazardous waste, or a marine pollutant is not subject to the requirements of this subchapter if it is a mixture of one or more components that —

(i) *Has a flash point at or above 93 °C (200 °F),*

(ii) *Comprises at least 99 percent of the volume of the mixture, and*

(iii) *Is not offered* for transportation or transported as a liquid at a temperature at or above its flash point.

FEDERAL REGISTER UPDATES

In the April 18, 2003 Federal Register, §173.150 was revised, effective October 1, 2003.

(f) [1]

(3) [2]

(vii) *Packaging requirements* of subpart B of this part and, in addition, non-bulk packagings must conform to the requirements of §173.203; [3]

(viii) *The requirements* of §§173.1, 174.1, 177.804, 177.817, and 177.834 of this subchapter, except §177.834(i)(3); and [4]

(ix) *The training requirements of subpart H of part 172 of this subchapter.* [5]

1. Paragraph (f) is the same as before.
2. Paragraph (f)(3) is the same as before.
3. Paragraph (f)(3)(vii) was revised.
4. Paragraph (f)(3)(viii) was revised.
5. Paragraph (f)(3)(ix) was added.

§173.151 Exceptions for Class 4.

(a) **General.** Exceptions for hazardous materials shipments in the following paragraphs are permitted only if this section is referenced for the specific hazardous material in the §172.101 table of this subchapter.

(b) **Limited quantities of Division 4.1 flammable solids.** Limited quantities of flammable solids (Division 4.1) in Packing Groups II and III are excepted from labeling, unless offered for transportation or transported by aircraft, and the specification packaging requirements of this subchapter when packaged in combination packagings according to this paragraph. In addition, shipments of limited quantities are not subject to subpart F (Placarding) of part 172 of this subchapter. Each package must conform to the packaging requirements of subpart B of this part and may not exceed 30 kg (66 pounds) gross weight. The following combination packagings are authorized:

(1) *For flammable solids* in Packing Group II, inner packagings not over 1.0 kg (2.2 pounds) net capacity each, packed in strong outer packagings; and

(2) *For flammable solids* in Packing Group III, inner packagings not over 5.0 kg (11 pounds) net capacity each, packed in strong outer packagings.

(c) **Consumer commodities.** A limited quantity which conforms to the provisions of paragraph (b) of this section, and charcoal briquettes in packagings not exceeding 30 kg (66 pounds) gross weight, may be renamed "Consumer commodity" and reclassed as ORM-D material, if the material is a "consumer commodity" as defined in §171.8 of this subchapter. In addition to the exceptions provided by paragraph (b) of this section, shipments are not subject to the shipping paper requirements of subpart C of part 172 of this subchapter, unless the material meets the definition of a hazardous substance, a hazardous waste, or a marine pollutant or unless offered for transportation or transported by aircraft, and are eligible for the exceptions provided in §173.156.

(d) **Limited quantities of Division 4.3** (dangerous when wet) material. Limited quantities of Division 4.3 (dangerous when wet) solids in Packing Groups II and III are excepted from labeling, unless offered for transportation or transported by aircraft, and the specification packaging requirements of this subchapter when packaged in combination packagings according to this paragraph. In addition, shipments of limited quantities are not subject to subpart F (Placarding) of part 172 of this subchapter. Each package must conform to the packaging requirements of subpart B of this part and may not exceed 30 kg (66 pounds) gross weight. The following combination packagings are authorized:

(1) *For Division 4.3 solids* in Packing Group II, inner packagings not over 0.5 kg (1.1 pound) net capacity each, packed in strong outer packagings; and

(2) *For Division 4.3 solids* in Packing Group III, inner packagings not over 1 kg (2.2 pounds) net capacity each, packed in strong outer packagings.

§173.152 Exceptions for Division 5.1 (oxidizers) and Division 5.2 (organic peroxides).

(a) **General.** Exceptions for hazardous materials shipments in the following paragraphs are permitted only if this section is referenced for the specific hazardous material in the §172.101 table of this subchapter.

(b) **Limited quantities.** Limited quantities of oxidizers (Division 5.1) in Packing Groups II and III and organic peroxides (Division 5.2) are excepted from labeling, unless offered or intended for transportation by aircraft, and the specification packaging requirements of this subchapter when packaged in combination packagings according to this paragraph. In addition, shipments of these limited quantities are not subject to subpart F of part 172 (Placarding) of this subchapter. Each package must conform to the packaging requirements of subpart B of this part and may not exceed 30 kg (66 pounds) gross weight. The following combination packagings are authorized:

(1) *For oxidizers* in Packing Group II, inner packagings not over 1.0 L (0.3 gallon) net capacity each for liquids or not over 1.0 kg (2.2 pounds) net capacity each for solids, packed in strong outer packagings.

(2) *For oxidizers* in Packing Group III, inner packagings not over 4.0 L (1 gallon) net capacity each for liquids or not over 5.0 kg (11 pounds) net capacity each for solids, packed in strong outer packagings.

(3) *For organic peroxides* which do not require temperature control during transportation —

(i) *For Type D, E, or F* organic peroxides, inner packagings not over 125 mL (4.22 ounces) net capacity each for liquids or 500 g (17.64 ounces) net capacity for solids, packed in strong outer packagings.

(ii) *For Type B or C* organic peroxides, inner packagings not over 25 mL (0.845 ounces) net capacity each for liquids or 100 g (3.528 ounces) net capacity for solids, packed in strong outer packagings.

(4) *For polyester resin kits* consisting of a base material component (Class 3, Packing Group II or III) and an activator component (Type C, D, E, or F organic peroxide which does not require temperature control) —

(i) *The organic peroxide component* must be packed in inner packagings not over 125 mL (4.22 ounces) net capacity each for liquids or 500 g (17.64 ounces) net capacity each for solids;

(ii) *The flammable liquid component* must be packed in inner packagings not over 1.0 L (0.3 gallons) net capacity each for Packing Group II liquids or 5.0 L (1.3 gallons) net capacity each for Packing Group III liquids; and

(iii) *The flammable liquid component* and the organic peroxide component may be packed in the same strong outer packaging provided they will not interact dangerously in the event of leakage.

(c) **Consumer commodities.** A limited quantity which conforms to the provisions of paragraph (b) of this section and is a "consumer commodity" as defined in §171.8 of this subchapter, may be renamed "Consumer commodity" and reclassed as ORM-D material. In addition to the exceptions provided by paragraph (b) of this section, shipments are not subject to the shipping paper requirements of subpart C of part 172 of this subchapter, unless the material meets the definition of a hazardous substance, a hazardous waste, or a marine pollutant or unless offered for transportation or transported by aircraft, and are eligible for the exceptions provided in §173.156.

§173.153 Exceptions for Division 6.1 (poisonous materials).

(a) **General.** Exceptions for hazardous materials shipments in the following paragraphs are permitted only if this section is referenced for the specific hazardous material in the §172.101 table of this subchapter.

(b) **Limited quantities of Division 6.1 materials.** Limited quantities of poisonous materials (Division 6.1) in Packing Group III are excepted from the specification packaging requirements of this subchapter when packaged in combination packagings according to this paragraph. In addition, shipments of these limited quantities are not subject to subpart F of part 172 (Placarding) of this subchapter. Each package must conform to the packaging requirements of subpart B of this part and may not exceed 30 kg (66 pounds) gross weight. The following combination packagings are authorized:

(1) *For poisonous liquids,* inner packagings not over 4.0 L (1 gallon) net capacity each, packed in strong outer packagings; and

(2) *For poisonous solids,* inner packagings not over 5.0 kg (11 pounds) net capacity each, packed in strong outer packagings.

(c) **Consumer commodities.** The following provisions apply to consumer commodities:

(1) *A limited quantity* which conforms to the provisions of paragraph (b) of this section and is a "consumer commodity" as defined in §171.8 of this subchapter, may be renamed "Consumer commodity" and reclassed as ORM-D material.

(2) *A poisonous material* which is a drug or medicine and is a "consumer commodity" as defined in §171.8 of this subchapter, may be renamed "Consumer commodity" and reclassed as ORM-D material if packaged in a combination packaging not exceeding 30 kg (66 pounds) with inner packagings not over 250 mL (8 ounces) net capacity for liquids or 250 g (8.8 ounces) net capacity for solids packed in strong outer packagings. Each package must conform to the packaging requirements of subpart B of this part.

(3) *Packages of ORM-D material* are excepted from the specification packaging requirements of this subchapter and from the labeling requirements of subpart E of part 172 of this subchapter. Shipments of ORM-D material are eligible for the exceptions provided in §173.156 and in paragraph (b) of this section and are not subject to the shipping paper requirements of subpart C of part 172 of this subchapter, unless the material meets the definition of a hazardous substance, a hazardous waste, or a marine pollutant or unless offered for transportation or transported by aircraft.

§173.154 Exceptions for Class 8 (corrosive materials).

(a) **General.** Exceptions for hazardous materials shipments in the following paragraphs are permitted only if this section is referenced for the specific hazardous material in the §172.101 table of this subchapter.

(b) **Limited quantities.** Limited quantities of corrosive materials (Class 8) in Packing Groups II and III are excepted from labeling, unless offered or intended for transportation by aircraft, and the specification packaging requirements of this subchapter when packaged in combination packagings according to this paragraph. In addition, shipments of these limited quantities are not subject to subpart F (Placarding) of part 172 of this subchapter. Each package must conform to the packaging requirements of subpart B of this part and may not exceed 30 kg (66 pounds) gross weight. The following combination packagings are authorized:

(1) *For corrosive materials* in Packing Group II, in inner packagings not over 1.0 L (0.3 gallon) net capacity each for liquids or not over 1.0 kg (2.2 pounds) net capacity each for solids, packed in strong outer packagings.

(2) *For corrosive materials* in Packing Group III, in inner packagings not over 4.0 L (1 gallon) net capacity each for liquids or not over 5.0 kg (11 pounds) net capacity each for solids, packed in strong outer packagings.

(c) **Consumer commodities.** A limited quantity which conforms to the provisions of paragraph (b) of this section and is a "consumer commodity" as defined in §171.8 of this subchapter may be renamed "Consumer commodity" and reclassed as ORM-D material. In addition to the exceptions provided by paragraph (b) of this section, shipments of ORM-D materials are not subject to the shipping paper requirements of subpart C of part 172 of this subchapter, unless the material meets the definition of a hazardous substance, a hazardous waste, or a marine pollutant or unless offered or intended for transportation by aircraft, and are eligible for the exceptions provided in §173.156.

(d) **Materials corrosive to aluminum or steel only.** Except for a hazardous substance, a hazardous waste, or a marine pollutant, a material classed as a Class 8, Packing Group III, material solely because of its corrosive effect —

(1) *On aluminum* is not subject to any other requirements of this subchapter when transported by motor vehicle or rail car in a packaging constructed of materials that will not react dangerously with or be degraded by the corrosive material; or

(2) *On steel* is not subject to any other requirements of this subchapter when transported by motor vehicle or rail car in a bulk packaging constructed of materials that will not react dangerously with or be degraded by the corrosive material.

§173.155 Exceptions for Class 9 (miscellaneous hazardous materials).

(a) **General.** Exceptions for hazardous materials shipments in the following paragraphs are permitted only if this section is referenced for the specific hazardous material in the §172.101 table of this subchapter.

(b) **Limited quantities.** Limited quantities of miscellaneous hazardous materials (Class 9) are excepted from labeling, unless offered or intended for transportation by aircraft, and the specification packaging requirements of this subchapter when packaged in combination packagings according to this paragraph. In addition, shipments of these limited quantities are not subject to subpart F (Placarding) of part 172 of this subchapter. Each package must conform to the packaging requirements of subpart B of this part and may not exceed 30 kg (66 pounds) gross weight. The following combination packagings are authorized:

(1) *For liquids,* inner packagings not over 5.0 L (1.3 gallons) net capacity each. packed in strong outer packagings.

(2) *For solids,* inner packagings not over 5.0 kg (11 pounds) net capacity each, packed in strong outer packagings.

(c) **Consumer commodities.** A limited quantity which conforms to the provisions of paragraph (b) of this section and is a "consumer commodity" as defined in §171.8 of this subchapter, may be renamed "Consumer commodity" and reclassed as ORM-D material. In addition to the exceptions provided by paragraph (b) of this section, shipments of ORM-D materials are not subject to the shipping paper requirements of subpart C of part 172 of this subchapter, unless the material meets the definition of a hazardous substance, a hazardous waste, or a marine pollutant or unless offered for transportation or transported by aircraft, and are eligible for the exceptions provided in §173.156.

§173.156 Exceptions for ORM materials.

(a) **Exceptions for hazardous materials shipments** in the following paragraphs are permitted only if this section is referenced for the specific hazardous material in the §172.101 table or in a packaging section in this part.

(b) **ORM-D.** Packagings for ORM-D materials are specified according to hazard class in §§173.150 through 173.155 and in §173.306. In addition to other exceptions specified for ORM-D materials in this part:

(1) *Strong outer packagings* as specified in this part, marking requirements specified in subpart D of part 172 of this subchapter, and the 30 kg (66 pounds) gross weight limitation are not required for materials classed as ORM-D when —

(i) *Unitized in cages, carts, boxes or similar overpacks;*

(ii) *Offered for transportation or transported by:*

[A] Rail;

[B] Private or contract motor carrier; or

[C] Common carrier in a vehicle under exclusive use for such service; and

(iii) *Transported to* or from a manufacturer, a distribution center, or a retail outlet, or transported to a disposal facility from one offeror.

(2) *The 30 kg (66 pounds)* gross weight limitation does not apply to materials classed as ORM-D when offered for transportation, or transported, by highway or rail between a manufacturer, a distribution center, and a retail outlet provided —

(i) *Inner packagings* conform to the quantity limits for inner packagings specified in §§173.150(b), 173.152(b), 173.154(b), 173.155(b) and 173.306 (a) and (b), as appropriate;

(ii) *The inner packagings* are packed into corrugated fiberboard trays to prevent them from moving freely;

(iii) *The trays* are placed in a fiberboard box which is banded and secured to a wooden pallet by metal, fabric, or plastic straps, to form a single palletized unit;

(iv) *The package* conforms to the general packaging requirements of subpart B of this part;

(v) *The maximum* net quantity of hazardous material permitted on one palletized unit is 250 kg (550 pounds); and

(vi) *The package* is properly marked in accordance with §172.316 of this subchapter.

Subpart E - Non-bulk Packaging for Haz. Materials Other Than Class 1 and Class 7

§173.158 Nitric acid.

(a) **Nitric acid exceeding 40 percent concentration** may not be packaged with any other material.

(b) **Nitric acid in any concentration which does not contain** sulfuric acid or hydrochloric acid as impurities, when offered for transportation or transported by rail, highway, or water shall be packaged in specification containers as follows:

(1) *1A1 stainless steel drums* are authorized, subject to the following limitations:

(i) *Stainless steel used* in drums must conform to the following thicknesses:

Nominal (marked) capacity (in liters) of 1A1 drum	Minimum thickness (in mm) of stainless steel
55	0.9
115	1.2
210	1.5
450	2.0

(ii) *Drums weighing* less than 85 percent of their original tare weight may not be used.

(iii) *Type 304* or other grades of equivalent corrosion-resistant steels in the as-welded condition are permissible for nitric acid concentrations up to and including 78 percent.

(iv) *For all concentrations* of nitric acid, the following are permissible:

[A] Type 304 heat-treated (quenched in water at 1040 °C (1900 °F)),

[B] Stabilized Type 347 in the as-welded condition,

[C] Stabilized Type 347 stress-relieved (845-900 °C (1550-1650 °F)),

[D] Stabilized Type 347 heat-treated (quenched in water at 1040 °C (1900 °F)), or

[E] Other grades of equivalent corrosion resistance.

(v) *All parts of drum* exposed to lading must be capable of withstanding the corrosive effect of nitric acid to the extent that 65 percent boiling nitric acid does not penetrate the metal more than 0.0381 mm (0.002 inches) per month. (ASTM A 262-68 may be used for a suitable corrosion test procedure.)

(vi) *In addition* to marking required by §178.503 of this subchapter, the following marks, in lettering of at least 12.7 mm (0.5 inch) height, must be placed on drums used to transport nitric acid:

[A] The type of steel used in body and head sheets as identified by American Iron and Steel Institute type number, and, in addition, the letters "HT" following the steel designation on containers subject to stress relieving or heat treatment during manufacture.

[B] The thickness in mm of metal in thinnest part. When the thickness of metal in the body differs from that in the head, both must be indicated with slanting line between and with the gauge of the body indicated first.

[C] Original tare weight in kilograms, preceded by the letters "TW." An example of the markings required by paragraphs (b)(1)(vi) (A), (B), and (C) of this section is "304HT/1.9/2.7/TW55."

(2) *4H1 expanded plastics* outer packagings with glass inner receptacles of not greater than 2.5 L (0.66 gallon) capacity each. No more than four 2.5 L (0.66 gallon) inner receptacles may be packed in one outer packaging.

(c) **Nitric acid of 80 percent or greater concentration** which does not contain sulfuric acid or hydrochloric acid as impurities, when offered for transportation or transported by rail, highway, or water may be packaged in 1B1 aluminum drums.

(d) **Nitric acid of 90 percent or greater concentration,** when offered for transportation or transported by rail, highway, or water may be packaged as follows:

(1) *In 4C1, 4C2, 4D or 4F* wooden boxes with inner packagings consisting of glass bottles further individually overpacked in tightly closed metal packagings. Glass bottles must be of 2.5 L (0.66 gallon) or less capacity and cushioned with a non-reactive, absorbent material within the metal packagings.

(2) *In combination packagings* with 1A2, 1B2, 1D, 1G, 1H2, 3H2 or 4G outer packagings with inner glass packagings of 2.5 L (0.66 gallons) or less capacity cushioned with a non-reactive, absorbent material and packed within a tightly closed intermediate packaging of metal or plastic.

(e) **Nitric acid of less than 90 percent concentration,** when offered for transportation or transported by rail, highway, or water may be packaged in 4G fiberboard boxes or 4C1, 4C2, 4D or 4F wooden boxes with inside glass packagings of not over 2.5 L (0.66 gallon) capacity each.

(f) **Nitric acid of 70 percent or less concentration,** when offered for transportation or transported by rail, highway, or water, may be packaged as follows:

(1) *In composite packagings* 6PA1, 6PA2, 6PB1, 6PB2, 6PC, 6PD1, 6PH1, or 6PH2. 6HH1 and 6HA1 composite packaging with plastic inner receptacles meeting the compatibility requirements §173.24(e) (e.g., PFA Teflon) are authorized.

(2) *In 4H1 expanded plastic boxes* with inner glass packagings of not over 2.5 L (0.66 gallon) each.

(3) *In combination packagings* with 1A2, 1B2, 1D, 1G, 1H2, 3H2, 4C1, 4C2, 4D, 4F or 4G outer packagings and plastic inner packagings not over 2.5 L (0.66 gallon) capacity further individually overpacked in tightly closed metal packagings.

(g) **Nitric acid of more than 70 percent concentration,** when offered for transportation or transported by cargo aircraft only, must be packaged in combination packagings with 1A2, 1B2, 1D, 1G, 1H2, 3H2, 4C1, 4C2, 4D, 4F or 4G outer packagings with glass or earthenware inner packagings of not over 1 L (0.3 gallon) or glass ampoules of not over 0.5 L (0.1 gallon).

(h) **Nitric acid of less than 70 percent concentration,** when offered for transportation in cargo aircraft only must be packaged in combination packagings with 1A2, 1B2, 1D, 1G, 1H2, 3H2, 4C1, 4C2, 4D, 4F or 4G outer packagings with inner packagings of —

(1) *Glass or earthenware not over 2.5 L (0.66 gallon) capacity;*

(2) *Plastic not over 2.5 L* (0.66 gallon) capacity further individually overpacked in tightly closed metal packagings; or

(3) *Glass ampoule not over 0.5 L (0.1 gallon) capacity.*

§173.159 Batteries, wet.

(a) **Electric storage batteries,** containing electrolyte acid or alkaline corrosive battery fluid, must be completely protected so that short circuits will be prevented; they may not be packed with other materials except as provided in paragraphs (g) and (h) of this section and in §§173.220 and 173.222.

(b) **The following specification packagings are authorized** for batteries packed without other materials:

(1) *4C1, 4C2, 4D, or 4F wooden boxes.*

(2) *4G fiberboard boxes.*

(3) *1D plywood drums.*

(4) *1G fiber drums.*

(5) *1H2 and 3H2 plastic drums and jerricans.*

(6) *4H2 plastic boxes.*

(c) **The following non-specification packagings** are authorized for batteries packed without other materials:

(1) *Electric storage batteries* protected against short circuits and firmly secured to skids or pallets capable of withstanding the shocks normally incident to transportation, are authorized for transportation by rail, highway, or water. The height of the completed unit must not exceed 1 1/2 times the width of the skid or pallet. The unit must be capable of withstanding, without damage, a superimposed weight equal to two times the weight of the unit or, if the weight of the unit exceeds 907 kg (2000 pounds), a superimposed weight of 1814 kg (4000 pounds). Battery terminals must not be relied upon to support any part of the superimposed weight.

(2) *Electric storage batteries* weighing 225 kg (500 pounds) or more, consisting of carriers' equipment, may be shipped by rail when mounted on suitable skids and protected against short circuits. Such shipments may not be offered in interchange service.

(3) *One to three batteries* not over 11.3 kg (25 pounds) each, packed in outer boxes. The maximum authorized gross weight is 34 kg (75 pounds).

(4) *Not more than* four batteries not over 7 kg (15 pounds) each, packed in strong outer fiberboard or wooden boxes. Batteries must be securely cushioned and packed to prevent short circuits. The maximum authorized gross weight is 30 kg (65 pounds).

(5) *Not more than* five batteries not over 4.5 kg (10 pounds) each, packed in strong outer fiberboard or wooden boxes. Batteries must be securely cushioned and packed to prevent short circuits. The maximum authorized gross weight is 30 kg (65 pounds).

(6) *Single batteries* not exceeding 34 kg (75 pounds) each, packed in 5-sided slip covers or in completely closed fiberboard boxes. Slip covers and boxes must be of solid or double-faced corrugated fiberboard of at least 91 kg (200 pounds) Mullen test strength. The slip cover or fiberboard box must fit snugly and provide inside top clearance of at least 1.3 cm (0.5 inch) above battery terminals and filler caps with reinforcement in place. Assembled for shipment, the bottom edges of the slipcover must come to within 2.5 cm (1 inch) of the bottom of the battery. The completed package (battery and box or slip cover) must be capable of withstanding a top-to-bottom compression test of at least 225 kg (500 pounds) without damage to battery terminals, cell covers or filler caps.

(7) *Single batteries* exceeding 34 kg (75 pounds) each may be packed in completely closed fiberboard boxes. Boxes must be of double-wall corrugated fiberboard of at least 181 kg (400 pounds) test, or solid fiberboard testing at least 181 kg (400 pounds); a box may have hand holes in its ends provided that the handholes will not materially weaken the box. Sides and ends of the box must have cushioning between the battery and walls of the box; combined thickness of cushioning material and walls of the box must not be less than 1.3 cm (0.5 inch); and cushioning must be excelsior pads, corrugated fiberboard, or other suitable cushioning material. The bottom of the battery must be protected by a minimum of one excelsior or double-wall corrugated fiberboard pad. The top of the battery must be protected by a wood frame, corrugated trays or scored sheets of corrugated fiberboard having minimum test of 91 kg (200 pounds), or other equally effective cushioning material. Top protection must bear evenly on connectors and/or edges of the battery cover to facilitate stacking of batteries. No more than one battery may be placed in one box. The maximum authorized gross weight is 91 kg (200 pounds).

(d) **A nonspillable wet electric storage battery** is excepted from all other requirements of this subchapter under the following conditions:

(1) *The battery* must be protected against short circuits and securely packaged;

(2) *For batteries* manufactured after September 30, 1995, the battery and the outer packaging must be plainly and durably marked "NONSPILLABLE" or "NONSPILLABLE BATTERY"; and

(3) *The battery* must be capable of withstanding the following two tests, without leakage of battery fluid from the battery:

(i) *Vibration test.* The battery must be rigidly clamped to the platform of a vibration machine, and a simple harmonic motion having an amplitude of 0.8 mm (0.03 inches), with a 1.6 mm (0.063 inches) maximum total excursion must be applied. The frequency must be varied at the rate of 1 Hz/min between the limits of 10 Hz to 55 Hz. The entire range of frequencies and return must be traversed in 955 minutes for each mounting position (direction of vibrator) of the battery. The battery must be tested in three mutually perpendicular positions (to include testing with fill openings and vents, if any, in an inverted position) for equal time periods.

(ii) *Pressure differential test.* Following the vibration test, the battery must be stored for six hours at 24 °C ± 4 °C (75 °F ± 7 °F) while subjected to a pressure differential of at least 88 kPa (13 psig). The battery must be tested in three mutually perpendicular positions (to include testing with fill openings and vents, if any, in an inverted position) for at least six hours in each position.

(e) **Electric storage batteries containing electrolyte** or corrosive battery fluid are not subject to the requirements of this subchapter for transportation by highway or rail if all of the following requirements are met:

(1) *No other hazardous materials* may be transported in the same vehicle;

(2) *The batteries* must be loaded or braced so as to prevent damage and short circuits in transit;

(3) *Any other material* loaded in the same vehicle must be blocked, braced, or otherwise secured to prevent contact with or damage to the batteries; and

(4) *The transport vehicle* may not carry material shipped by any person other than the shipper of the batteries.

(f) **Electric storage batteries,** containing electrolyte or corrosive battery fluid in a coil from which it is injected into the battery cells by a gas generator and initiator assembled with the battery, and which are nonspillable under the criteria of paragraph (d) of this section, are excepted from other requirements of this subchapter when examined by the Bureau of Explosives and approved by the Associate Administrator.

(g) **Electrolyte, acid, or alkaline corrosive battery fluid,** packed with storage batteries wet or dry, must be packed in one of the following specification packagings:

(1) *In 4C1, 4C2, 4D, or 4F* wooden boxes with inner receptacles of glass, not over 4.0 L (1 gallon) each with not over 8.0 L (2 gallons) total in each outside container. Inside containers must be well-cushioned and separated from batteries by a strong solid wooden partition. The completed package must conform to Packing Group III requirements.

(2) *Electrolyte, acid,* or alkaline corrosive battery fluid included with storage batteries and filling kits may be packed in strong rigid outer packagings when shipments are made by, for, or to the Departments of the Army, Navy, or Air Force of the United States. Packagings must conform to military specifications. The electrolyte, acid, or alkaline corrosive battery fluid must be packed in polyethylene bottles of not over 1.0 L (0.3 gallon) capacity each. Not more than 24 bottles, securely separated from storage batteries and kits, may be offered for transportation or transported in each package.

(3) *In 4G fiberboard boxes* with not more than 12 inside packagings of polyethylene or other material resistant to the lading, each not over 2.0 L (0.5 gallon) capacity each. Completed packages must conform to Packing Group III requirements. Inner packagings must be adequately separated from the storage battery. The maximum authorized gross weight is 29 kg (64 pounds). These packages are not authorized for transportation by aircraft.

(h) **Dry storage batteries or battery charger devices** may be packaged in 4G fiberboard boxes with inner receptacles containing battery fluid. Completed packagings must conform to Packing Group III requirements. Not more than 12 inner receptacles may be packed in one outer box. The maximum authorized gross weight is 34 kg (75 pounds).

§173.160 Bombs, smoke, non-explosive (corrosive).

Bombs, smoke, non-explosive may be shipped provided they are without ignition elements, bursting charges, detonating fuses or other explosive components. They must be packaged in wooden (4C1, 4C2), plywood (4D) or reconstituted wood (4F) boxes, or plywood drums (1D), which meet Packing Group II requirements.

§173.161 Chemical kits.

(a) **Except as otherwise provided,** chemical kits must be packed, marked, and labeled as prescribed by this subchapter for the specific corrosive materials contained therein.

(b) **Chemical kits containing limited quantities** of corrosive liquids in inner receptacles of not over 177 mL (6 fluid ounces) capacity each are excepted from labeling (except when offered for transportation or transported by air) and the specification packaging requirements of this subchapter if all of the following requirements are met:

(1) *The kit may contain* only corrosive liquids for which packaging exceptions are provided in the §172.101 table.

(2) *This kit must be* a strong wooden or metal outer packaging, or must be packed in a strong wooden or metal packaging.

(3) *The corrosive liquids* must be cushioned with sufficient absorbent material to completely absorb the contents of the individual containers, and must be protected from damage by other materials in the kit.

(4) *The contents of the kit* must be of a nature and packed so there will be no possibility of the mixture of contents causing dangerous evolution of heat or gas.

In addition, chemical kits meeting these requirements are not subject to subpart F of part 172 of this subchapter (Placarding), to part 174 (Carriage by rail) of this subchapter except §174.24 (Shipping papers), and to part 177 (Carriage by highway) of this subchapter except §177.817 (Shipping papers).

(c) **Except as provided in paragraph (b) of this section,** chemical kits must be packed in 4G fiberboard boxes with inner glass receptacles of not over 1 L (0.3 gallon) capacity each, securely cushioned and separated from other inside containers. The contents of the kit must be of such a nature and so packed that there will be no possibility of the mixture of contents causing dangerous evolution of heat or gas.

§173.162 Gallium.

(a) **Except when packaged in cylinders or steel flasks,** gallium must be packaged in packagings which meet the requirements of part 178 of this subchapter at the Packing Group I performance level for transportation by aircraft, and at the Packing Group III performance level for transport by highway, rail or vessel, as follows:

(1) *In combination packagings* intended to contain liquids consisting of glass, earthenware or rigid plastic inner packagings with a maximum net mass of 15 kg (33 pounds) each. The inner packagings must be packed in wood boxes (4C1, 4C2, 4D, 4F), fiberboard boxes (4G), plastic boxes (4H1, 4H2), fiber drums (1G) or removable head steel and plastic drums or jerricans (1A2, 1H2, 3A2 or 3H2) with sufficient cushioning materials to prevent breakage. Either the inner packagings or the outer packagings must have an inner liner that is leakproof or bags of strong leakproof and puncture-resistant material impervious to the contents and completely surrounding the contents to prevent it from escaping from the package, irrespective of its position.

(2) *In packagings* intended to contain liquids consisting of semi-rigid plastic inner packagings of not more than 2.5 kg (5.5 pounds) net capacity each, individually enclosed in a sealed, leak-tight bag of strong puncture-resistant material. The sealed bags must be packed in wooden (4C1, 4C2), plywood (4D), reconstituted wood (4F), fiberboard (4G) or plastic (4H1, 4H2) boxes or in fiber (1G) or steel (1A2) drums, which are lined with leak-tight, puncture-resistant material. Bags and liner material must be chemically resistant to gallium.

(3) *Cylinders and steel flasks with vaulted bottoms are also authorized.*

(b) **When it is necessary to transport gallium** at low temperatures in order to maintain it in a completely solid state, the above packagings may be overpacked in a strong, water-resistant outer packaging which contains dry ice or other means of refrigeration. If a refrigerant is used, all of the above materials used in the packaging of gallium must be chemically and physically resistant to the refrigerant and must have impact resistance at the low temperatures of the refrigerant employed. If dry ice is used, the outer packaging must permit the release of carbon dioxide gas.

(c) **Manufactured articles or apparatuses,** each containing not more than 100 mg (0.0035 ounce) of gallium and packaged so that the quantity of gallium per package does not exceed 1 g (0.35 ounce) are not subject to the requirements of this subchapter.

§173.163 Hydrogen fluoride.

Hydrogen fluoride (hydrofluoric acid, anhydrous) must be packaged in a specification 3, 3A, 3AA, 3B, 3BN, 3E, or 4A cylinder; or a specification 4B, 4BA, or 4BW cylinder if the cylinder is not brazed. Filling density may not exceed 85 percent of the cylinder's water weight capacity. In place of the periodic volumetric expansion test, cylinders used in exclusive service may be given a complete external visual inspection in conformance with part 180, subpart C, of this subchapter, at the time such periodic requalification becomes due. Cylinders removed from hydrogen fluoride service must be condemned in accordance with §180.205 of this subchapter and, at the direction of the owner, the cylinder may be rendered incapable of holding pressure.

§173.164 Mercury (metallic and articles containing mercury).

(a) **For transportation by aircraft,** mercury must be packaged in packagings which meet the requirements of part 178 of this subchapter at the Packing Group I performance level, as follows:

(1) *In inner packagings* of earthenware, glass or plastic containing not more than 3.5 kg (7.7 pounds) of mercury, or inner packagings which are glass ampoules containing not more than 0.5 kg (1.1 pounds) of mercury, or iron or steel quicksilver flasks containing not more than 35 kg (77 pounds) of mercury. The inner packagings or flasks must be packed in steel drums (1A2), steel jerricans (3A2), wooden boxes (4C1), (4C2), plywood boxes (4D), reconstituted wood boxes (4F), fiberboard boxes (4G), plastic boxes (4H2), plywood drums (1D) or fiber drums (1G).

(2) *Packagings must meet* the requirements of Part 178 of this subchapter at the Packing Group I performance level.

(3) *When inner packagings* of earthenware, glass or plastic are used, they must be packed in the outer packaging with sufficient cushioning material to prevent breakage.

(4) *Either the inner packagings* or the outer packagings must have inner linings or bags of strong leakproof and puncture-resistant material impervious to mercury, completely surrounding the contents, so that the escape of mercury will be prevented irrespective of the position of the package.

(b) **Manufactured articles or apparatuses,** each containing not more than 100 mg (0.0035 ounce) of mercury and packaged so that the quantity of mercury per package does not exceed 1 g (0.035 ounce) are not subject to the requirements of this subchapter.

(c) **Manufactured articles or apparatuses containing mercury** are excepted from the specification packaging requirements of this subchapter when packaged as follows:

(1) *Manufactured articles* or apparatuses of which metallic mercury is a component part, such as manometers, pumps, thermometers, switches, etc. (for electron tubes, mercury vapor tubes and similar tubes, see paragraph (c)(3) of this section), must be in strong outer packagings, having sealed inner liners or bags of strong leakproof and puncture-resistant material impervious to mercury, which will prevent the escape of mercury from the package irrespective of its position. Mercury switches and relays are excepted from these packaging requirements, if they are totally enclosed, leakproof and in sealed metal or plastic units.

(2) *Thermometers, switches and relays,* each containing a total quantity of not more than 15 g (0.53 ounces) of mercury, are excepted from the requirements of this subchapter if installed as an integral part of a machine or apparatus and so fitted that shock of impact damage, leading to leakage of mercury, is unlikely to occur under conditions normally incident to transport.

(3) *Electron tubes,* mercury vapor tubes and similar tubes must be packaged as follows:

(i) *Tubes which are packed* in strong outer packagings with all seams and joints sealed with self-adhesive, pressure-sensitive tape which will prevent the escape of mercury from the package, are authorized up to a total net quantity of 450 g (15.9 ounces) of mercury per package;

(ii) *Tubes with more than 450 g* (15.9 ounces) of mercury are authorized only when packed in strong outer packagings, having sealed inner liners or bags of strong leakproof and puncture-resistant material impervious to mercury which will prevent escape of mercury from the package irrespective of its position;

(iii) *Tubes which do not contain* more than 5 g (0.2 ounce) of mercury each and which are packed in the manufacturer's original packagings, are authorized up to a total net quantity of 30 g (1.1 ounces) of mercury per package;

(iv) *Tubes which are* completely jacketed in sealed leakproof metal cases are authorized in the manufacturer's original packagings.

(4) *A person* offering for transportation electron tubes, mercury vapor tubes, and similar tubes shall indicate the quantity of mercury therein on the shipping paper.

(5) *Mercurial barometers* conforming to paragraph (c)(1) of this section, which are loaded and unloaded from an aircraft under the supervision of, and accompanied in flight by, a National Weather Service official or similar United States agency official, are excepted from any other requirements of this subchapter.

(d) **For transportation by other than aircraft,** mercury must be packaged —

(1) *In any packaging* which meets the requirements of part 178 of this subchapter at the Packing Group III performance level; or

(2) *In non-specification reusable metal packagings.*

(e) **Except for a hazardous substance** or a hazardous waste or for transportation by aircraft or vessel, packages containing less than 0.45 kg (1.0 pound) net weight of mercury are not subject to the requirements of this subchapter.

§173.166 Air bag inflators, air bag modules, and seat-belt pre-tensioners.

(a) **Definitions.** An **air bag inflator** (consisting of a casing containing an igniter, a booster material, a gas generant and, in some cases, a pressure vessel (cylinder)) is a gas generator used to inflate an air bag in a supplemental restraint system in a motor vehicle. An **air bag module** is the air bag inflator plus an inflatable bag assembly. A **seat-belt pre-tensioner** contains similar hazardous materials and is used in the operation of a seat-belt restraining system in a motor vehicle.

(b) **Classification.** An air bag inflator, air bag module, or seat-belt pre-tensioner may be classed as Class 9 (UN3268) or Division 2.2 (UN3353) if it meets the following requirements —

(1) *The manufacturer* has submitted each design type air bag inflator or seat-belt pre-tensioner to a person approved by the Associate Administrator for examination and testing. The submission must contain a detailed description of the inflator or pre-tensioner (or, if more than a single inflator or pre-tensioner is involved, the maximum parameters of each particular inflator or pre-tensioner design type for which approval is sought) and details on the complete package.

(2) *Samples of the inflator* or pre-tensioner, packaged as for transport, have been subjected to test series 6(c) of the UN Recom-

mendations on the Transport of Dangerous Goods, Manual of Tests and Criteria (see §171.7 of this subchapter), with no explosion of the device, no fragmentation of device casings, and no projection hazard or thermal effect which would significantly hinder fire-fighting or other emergency response efforts in the immediate vicinity.

(3) *The manufacturer submits an application, including —*

(i) *The test results* and report recommending the shipping description and classification for each device or design type; or

(ii) *An approved classification* issued by the competent authority of a foreign government, to the Associate Administrator, and is notified in writing by the Associate Administrator that the device has been classed as Class 9 or Division 2.2 and approved for transportation.

(4) *No approval applications* are required for air bag modules containing an approved air bag inflator.

(5) *Air bag inflators* or seat belt pre-tensioners previously reclassed from Class 1 to Division 4.1 under the terms of an exemption may be reclassed as Class 9 materials without further testing.

(c) EX numbers. When offered for transportation, the shipping paper must contain the EX number or product code for each approved inflator or pre-tensioner in association with the basic description required by §172.202(a) of this subchapter. Product codes must be traceable to the specific EX number assigned to the inflator, module or pre-tensioner by the Associate Administrator. Marking the EX number or product code on the outside package is not required. This paragraph (c) does not apply to a device classed as Division 2.2.

(d) Exceptions.

(1) *An air bag module* or seat-belt pretensioner that has been approved by the Associate Administrator and is installed in a motor vehicle or in completed vehicle components, such as steering columns or door panels, is not subject to the requirements of this subchapter.

(2) *An air bag module,* containing an inflator that has previously been examined and approved for transportation as a Division 4.1 material, is not required to be submitted for examination or approval.

(3) *Shipments for recycling.* When offered for domestic transportation by highway, rail freight, cargo vessel or cargo aircraft only, a serviceable air bag module or seat-belt pretensioner removed from a motor vehicle that was manufactured as required for use in the United States may be offered for transportation and transported without compliance with the shipping paper requirement prescribed in paragraph (c) of this section. However, the word "Recycled" must be entered on the shipping paper immediately after the basic description prescribed in §172.202 of this subchapter. No more than one device is authorized in the packaging prescribed in paragraph (e)(1), (2) or (3) of this section. The device must be cushioned and secured within the package to prevent movement during transportation.

(e) Packagings. The following packagings at the Packing Group III performance level are authorized for Class 9 devices:

(1) *1A2, 1B2, 1G or 1H2 drums.*

(2) *3A2 or 3H2 jerricans.*

(3) *4C1, 4C2, 4D, 4F, 4G or 4H2 boxes.*

(4) *Reusable high strength* plastic or metal containers or dedicated handling devices are authorized for shipment of air bag inflators, air bag modules, and seat-belt pretensioners from a manufacturing facility to the assembly facility, subject to the following conditions:

(i) *The gross weight* of the container or handling device may not exceed 1000 kg (2205 pounds). The container or handling device structure must provide adequate support to allow them to be stacked at least three high with no damage to the containers or devices.

(ii) *If not completely enclosed* by design, the container or handling device must be covered with plastic, fiberboard, or metal. The covering must be secured to the container by banding or other comparable methods.

(iii) *Internal dunnage* must be sufficient to prevent movement of the devices within the container.

(f) Labeling. Notwithstanding the provisions of §172.402 of this subchapter, each package or handling device must display a CLASS 9 or NON-FLAMMABLE GAS label. Additional labeling is not required when the package contains no hazardous materials other than the devices.

§173.170 Black powder for small arms.

Black powder for small arms that has been classed in Division 1.1 may be reclassed as a Division 4.1 material, for domestic transportation by motor vehicle, rail freight, and cargo vessel only, subject to the following conditions:

(a) The powder must be examined and approved for Division 1.1 and Division 4.1 classification in accordance with §§173.56 and 173.58;

(b) The total quantity of black powder in one motor vehicle, rail car, or freight container may not exceed 45.4 kg (100 pounds) net mass, and no more than four freight containers may be on board one cargo vessel;

(c) The black powder must be packed in inner metal or heavy wall conductive plastic receptacles not over 454 g (16 ounces) net capacity each, with no more than 25 cans in one outer UN 4G fiberboard box. The inner packagings must be arranged and protected so as to prevent simultaneous ignition of the contents. The complete package must be of the same type which has been examined as required in §173.56;

(d) Each completed package must be marked "BLACK POWDER FOR SMALL ARMS" and "NA 0027"; and

(e) Each package must bear the FLAMMABLE SOLID label.

§173.171 Smokeless powder for small arms.

Smokeless powder for small arms which has been classed in Division 1.3 may be reclassed in Division 4.1, for transportation by motor vehicle, rail car, vessel, or cargo-only aircraft, subject to the following conditions:

(a) The powder must be examined and approved for a Division 1.3 and Division 4.1 classification in accordance with §§173.56 and 173.58 of this part.

(b) The total quantity of smokeless powder may not exceed 45.4 kg (100 pounds) net mass in:

(1) *One rail car, motor vehicle, or cargo-only aircraft; or*

(2) *One freight container* on a vessel, not to exceed four freight containers per vessel.

(c) Only combination packagings with inner packagings not exceeding 3.6 kg (8 pounds) net mass are authorized. Inner packagings must be arranged and protected so as to prevent simultaneous ignition of the contents. The complete package must be of the same type which has been examined as required in §173.56 of this part.

(d) Inside packages that have been examined and approved by the Associate Administrator may be packaged in UN 4G fiberboard boxes meeting the Packing Group I performance level, provided all inside containers are packed to prevent movement and the net weight of smokeless powder in any one box does not exceed 7.3 kg (16 pounds).

§173.172 Aircraft hydraulic power unit fuel tank.

Aircraft hydraulic power unit fuel tanks containing a mixture of anhydrous hydrazine and monomethyl hydrazine (M86 fuel) and designed for installation as complete units in aircraft are excepted from the specification packaging requirements of this subchapter when they conform to either of the following conditions:

(a) The unit must consist of an aluminum pressure vessel made from tubing and having welded heads. Primary containment of the fuel within this vessel must consist of a welded aluminum bladder having a maximum internal volume of 46 L (12 gallons). The outer vessel must have a minimum design gauge pressure of 1,275 kPa (185 psig) and a minimum burst gauge pressure of 2,755 kPa (400 psig). Each vessel must be leak-checked during manufacture and before shipment and must be found leakproof. The complete inner unit must be securely packed in non-combustible cushioning material, such as vermiculite, in a strong outer tightly closed metal packaging which will adequately protect all fittings. Maximum quantity of fuel per unit and package is 42 L (11 gallons); or

(b) The unit must consist of an aluminum pressure vessel. Primary containment of the fuel within this vessel must consist of a welded hermetically sealed fuel compartment with an elastomeric bladder having a maximum internal volume of 46 L (12 gallons). The pressure vessel must have a minimum design gauge pressure of 5,170 kPa (750 psig). Each vessel must be leak-checked during manufacture and before shipment and must be securely packed in non-combustible cushioning material, such as vermiculite, in a strong outer tightly closed metal packaging which will adequately protect all fittings. Maximum quantity of fuel per unit and package is 42 L (11 gallons).

§173.173 Paint, paint-related material, adhesives, ink and resins.

(a) **When the §172.101 table specifies** that a hazardous material be packaged under this section, the following requirements apply. Except as otherwise provided in this part, the description "Paint" is the proper shipping name for paint, lacquer, enamel, stain, shellac, varnish, liquid aluminum, liquid bronze, liquid gold, liquid wood filler, and liquid lacquer base. The description "Paint-related material" is the proper shipping name for a paint thinning, drying, reducing or removing compound. However, if a more specific description is listed in the §172.101 table of this subchapter, that description must be used.

(b) **Paint, paint-related material, adhesives,** ink and resins must be packaged as follows:

(1) *As prescribed* in §173.202 of this part if it is a Packing Group II material or §173.203 of this part if it is a Packing Group III material; or

(2) *In inner glass packagings* of not over 1 L (0.3 gallon) capacity each or inner metal packagings of not over 5 L (1 gallon) each, packed in a strong outer packaging. Packages must conform to the packaging requirements of subpart B of this part but need not conform to the requirements of part 178 of this subchapter.

§173.174 Refrigerating machines.

A refrigerating machine assembled for shipment and containing 7 kg (15 pounds) or less of a flammable liquid for its operation in a strong, tight receptacle is excepted from labeling (except when offered for transportation or transported by air) and the specification packaging requirements of this subchapter. In addition. shipments are not subject to subpart F of part 172 of this subchapter (Placarding), to part 174 of this subchapter (Carriage by rail) except §174.24 (Shipping papers) and to part 177 (Carriage by highway) of this subchapter except §177.817 (Shipping papers).

§173.181 Pyrophoric materials (liquids).

When the §172.101 table specifies that a hazardous material be packaged under this section, only the following non-bulk packagings are authorized:

(a) **Specification steel or nickel cylinders prescribed** for any compressed gas except acetylene having a minimum design pressure of 1206 kPa (175 psig). Cylinders with valves must be:

(1) *Equipped with* steel valve protection caps or collars, unless overpacked; or

(2) *Overpacked in a wooden box* (4C1, 4C2, 4D or 4F); fiberboard box (4G), or plastic box (4H1 or 4H2). Cylinders must be secured to prevent movement in the box and, when offered for transportation or transported, must be so loaded that pressure relief devices remain in the vapor space of the cylinder. (See §177.838(h) of this subchapter.)

(b) **Wooden boxes (4C1, 4C2, 4D, or 4F)** or fiberboard boxes (4G) enclosing not more than four strong, tight metal cans with inner receptacles of glass or metal, not over 1 L (0.3 gallon) capacity each, having positive screwcap closures adequately gasketed. Inner packagings must be cushioned on all sides with dry, absorbent, incombustible material in a quantity sufficient to absorb the entire contents. The strong, tight metal cans must be closed by positive means, not by friction.

(c) **Steel drums (1A2) or fiber drums (1G)** not exceeding 220 L (58 gallons) capacity each with strong tight inner metal cans not over 4.0 L (1 gallon) capacity each, closed by positive means, not friction.

(1) *Inner packagings* must have no opening exceeding 25 mm (1 inch) diameter and must be surrounded with noncombustible cushioning material.

(2) *Net quantity* of pyrophoric liquids may not exceed two-thirds of the rated capacity of the outer drum. For example, a 220 L (58 gallons) outer drum may contain no more than 147 L (39 gallons) of pyrophoric liquids.

(3) *Each layer* of inner containers must be separated by a metal plate separator in addition to cushioning material.

§173.182 Barium azide — 50 percent or more water wet.

Barium azide — 50 percent or more water wet, must be packed in wooden boxes (4C1, 4C2, 4D, or 4F) or fiber drums (1G) with inner glass packagings not over 0.5 kg (1.1 pounds) capacity each. Packagings must have rubber stoppers wire tied for securement. If transportation is to take place when and where freezing weather is possible, a suitable antifreeze solution must be used to prevent freezing. Each packaging must conform to the requirements of part 178 of this subchapter at the Packing Group I performance level.

§173.183 Nitrocellulose base film.

Films, nitrocellulose base, must be packaged in packagings conforming to the requirements of part 178 of this subchapter at the Packing Group III performance level, as follows:

(a) **In steel drums (1A2), aluminum drums (1B2),** steel jerricans (3A2), wooden (4C1, 4C2), plywood (4D) or reconstituted wood (4F) boxes or plywood drums (1D) with each reel in a tightly closed metal can, polypropylene canister, or strong cardboard or fiberboard inner packaging with cover held in place by adhesive tape or paper; or

(b) **In fiberboard (4G) boxes or fiber drums (1G)** with a single tightly closed metal can, polypropylene canister, or strong cardboard or fiberboard inner packaging with cover held in place by adhesive tape or paper; authorized only for not over 600 m (1969 feet) of film.

§173.184 Highway or rail fusee.

(a) **A fusee is a device designed to burn at a controlled rate** and to produce visual effects for signaling purposes. The composition of the fusee must be such that the fusee will not ignite spontaneously or undergo marked decomposition when subjected to a temperature of 75 °C (167 °F) for 48 consecutive hours.

(b) **Fusees (highway and railway) must be packaged** in steel drums (1A2), steel jerricans (3A2), wooden (4C1, 4C2), plywood (4D) or reconstituted wood (4F) boxes or in fiberboard boxes (4G), plywood (1D) or fiber (1G) drums. If the fusees are equipped with spikes packagings must have reinforced ends to prevent penetration of spikes through the outer packagings; packages must be capable of passing drop test requirements (§178.603 of this subchapter), including at least one drop with spike in a downward position, and other requirements of part 178 of this subchapter, at the Packing Group II performance level.

§173.185 Lithium batteries and cells.

(a) **Except as otherwise provided in this subpart,** a lithium cell or battery is authorized for transportation only if it conforms to the provisions of this section. For the purposes of this subchapter, "lithium content" means the mass of lithium in the anode of a lithium metal or lithium alloy cell, except in the case of a lithium ion cell where the "equivalent lithium content" in grams is calculated to be 0.3 times the rated capacity in ampere-hours. The lithium-equivalent content of a battery equals the sum of the grams of lithium-equivalent content contained in the component cells of the battery.

(b) **Exceptions.** Cells and batteries are not subject to the requirements of this subchapter if they meet the following requirements:

(1) *Each cell* with a liquid cathode may contain not more than 0.5 g of lithium content. Each cell with a solid cathode may contain not more than 1.0 g of lithium content. Each lithium ion cell may contain not more than 1.5 g of equivalent lithium content;

(2) *Each battery* with a liquid cathode may contain an aggregate quantity of not more than 1.0 g of lithium content. Each battery with a solid cathode may contain an aggregate quantity of not more than 2.0 g of lithium content. Each lithium-ion battery may contain an aggregate quantity of not more than 8.0 grams of equivalent lithium content;

(3) *Each cell or battery* containing a liquid cathode must be hermetically sealed;

(4) *Cells and batteries* must be packed in such a way so as to prevent short circuits and must be packed in strong packagings, except when installed in equipment; and

(5) *If when fully charged,* the aggregate lithium content of the anodes in a liquid cathode battery is more than 0.5 g, or the aggregate lithium content of the anodes in a solid cathode battery is more than 1.0 g, then the battery may not contain a liquid or gas that is a hazardous material according to this subchapter unless the liquid or gas, if free, would be completely absorbed or neutralized by other materials in the battery.

(c) **Additional exceptions.** Cells and batteries also are not subject to this subchapter if they meet the following requirements:

(1) *The lithium content* of the anode of each cell, when fully charged, is not more than 5 g;

(2) *The aggregate lithium content* of the anodes of each battery, when fully charged, is not more than 25 g;

(3) *Each cell or battery* is of the type proven to be non-dangerous by testing in accordance with tests in the UN Manual of Tests and Criteria (see §171.7 of this subchapter). Such testing must be carried out on each type of cell or battery prior to the initial transport of that type; and

(4) *Cells and batteries* are designed or packed in such a way as to prevent short circuits under conditions normally encountered in transportation.

(d) **Cells and batteries and equipment containing** cells and batteries which were first transported prior to January 1, 1995, and were assigned to Class 9 on the basis of the requirements of this subchapter in effect on October 1, 1993, may continue to be transported in accordance with the applicable requirements in effect on October 1, 1993.

(e) **Cells and batteries may be transported** as items of Class 9 if they meet the requirements in paragraphs (e)(1) through (e)(7) of this section:

(1) *Each cell and battery* must be equipped with an effective means of preventing external short circuits.

(2) *Each cell and battery* must incorporate a safety venting device or be designed in a manner that will preclude a violent rupture under conditions normally incidental to transportation.

(3) *Batteries containing* cells or series of cells connected in parallel must be equipped with effective means, (such as diodes, fuses, etc.) as necessary to prevent dangerous reverse current flow.

(4) *Cells and batteries* must be packed in inner packagings in such a manner as to effectively prevent short circuits and to prevent movement which could lead to short circuits.

(5) *Cells and batteries* must be packaged in packagings conforming to the requirements of part 178 of this subchapter at the Packing Group II performance level: Inner packagings must be packed within metal boxes (4A or 4B), wooden boxes (4C1, 4C2, 4D or 4F), fiberboard boxes (4G), solid plastic boxes (4H2), fiber drums (1G), metal drums (1A2 or 1B2), plywood drums (1D), plastic jerricans (3H2), or metal jerricans (3A2 or 3B2).

(6) *Each cell or battery* must be of the type proven to meet the lithium battery requirements in the UN Manual of Tests and Criteria (see §171.7 of this subchapter).

(7) *Except as provided* in paragraph (h) of this section, cells or batteries may not be offered for transportation or transported if any cell has been discharged to the extent that the open circuit voltage is less than two volts or is less than 2/3 of the voltage of the fully charged cell, whichever is less.

(f) **Equipment containing or packed with cells and batteries** meeting the requirements of paragraph (b) or (c) of this section is excepted from all other requirements of this subchapter.

(g) **Equipment containing or packed with cells and batteries** may be transported as items of Class 9 if the batteries and cells meet all requirements of paragraph (e) of this section and are packaged as follows:

(1) *Equipment containing* cells and batteries must be packed in a strong outer packaging that is waterproof or has a waterproof liner, unless the equipment is made waterproof by nature of its construction. The equipment must be secured within the outer packaging and be packed as to effectively prevent movement, short circuits, and accidental operation during transport; and

(2) *Cells and batteries* packed with equipment must be packed in inner packagings conforming to (e)(5) of this section in such a manner as to effectively prevent movement and short circuits.

(h) **Cells and batteries, for disposal,** may be offered for transportation or transported to a permitted storage facility and disposal site by motor vehicle when they meet the following requirements:

(1) *Be equipped* with an effective means of preventing external short circuits; and

(2) *Be packed* in a strong outer packaging conforming to the requirements of §§173.24 and 173.24a. The packaging need not conform to performance requirements of part 178 of this subchapter.

(i) **Cells and batteries and equipment containing** or packed with cells and batteries which do not comply with the provisions of this section may be transported only if they are approved by the Associate Administrator.

(j) **For testing purposes, when not contained** in equipment, cells and batteries may be offered for transportation or transported by highway as items of Class 9. Packaging must conform with paragraph (e)(5) of this section.

§173.186 Matches.

(a) **Matches must be of a type** which will not ignite spontaneously or undergo marked decomposition when subjected for 8 consecutive hours to a temperature of 93 °C (200 °F).

(b) **Definitions.**

(1) **Fusee matches** are matches the heads of which are prepared with a friction-sensitive igniter composition and a pyrotechnic composition which burns with little or no flame, but with intense heat.

(2) **Safety matches** are matches combined with or attached to the box, book or card that can be ignited by friction only on a prepared surface.

(3) **Strike anywhere matches** are matches that can be ignited by friction on a solid surface.

(4) **Wax "Vesta" matches** are matches that can be ignited by friction either on a prepared surface or on a solid surface.

(c) **Safety matches and wax "Vesta" matches** must be tightly packed in securely closed inner packagings to prevent accidental ignition under conditions normally incident to transportation, and further packed in outer fiberboard, wooden, or other equivalent-type packagings. These matches in outer packagings not exceeding 23 kg (50 pounds) gross weight are not subject to any other requirement (except marking) of this subchapter. These matches may be packed in the same outer packaging with materials not subject to this subchapter.

(d) **Strike-anywhere matches may not be packed** in the same outer packaging with any material other than safety matches or wax "Vesta" matches, which must be packed in separate inner packagings.

(e) **Packagings.** Strike-anywhere matches must be tightly packed in securely closed chipboard, fiberboard, wooden, or metal inner packagings to prevent accidental ignition under conditions normally incident to transportation. Each inner packaging may contain no more than 700 strike-anywhere matches and must be packed in outer steel drums (1A2), aluminum drums (1B2), steel jerricans (3A2), wooden (4C1, 4C2), plywood (4D), reconstituted wood (4F) or fiberboard (4G) boxes, plywood (1D) or fiber (1G) drums. Gross weight of fiberboard boxes (4G) must not exceed 27 kg (60 pounds). Gross weight of other outer packagings must not exceed 45 kg (100 pounds).

§173.187 Pyrophoric solids, metals or alloys, n.o.s.

Packagings for pyrophoric solids, metals, or alloys, n.o.s. must conform to the requirements of part 178 of this subchapter at the packing group performance level specified in the §172.101 table. These materials must be packaged as follows:

(a) **In wooden boxes (4C1, 4C2, 4D, or 4F)** with inner metal receptacles which have a positive (not friction) means of closure and contain not more than 15 kg (33 pounds) each.

(b) **In steel drums (1A1 or 1A2)** with a gross mass not exceeding 150 kg (331 pounds) per drum.

(c) **In fiberboard boxes (4G) with inner metal receptacles** which have a positive (not friction) means of closure and contain not more than 7.5 kg (17 pounds) each.

(d) **In fiber drums (1G) with inner metal receptacles** which have a positive (not friction) means of closure and contain not more than 15 kg (33 pounds) each.

(e) **In plywood drums (1D) with inner metal receptacles** which have a positive (not friction) means of closure and contain not more than 15 kg (33 pounds) each.

§173.188 White or yellow phosphorus.

Phosphorus, white or yellow, when offered for transportation or transported by rail, highway, or water, must be packaged in water or dry in packagings conforming to the requirements of part 178 of this subchapter at the Packing Group I performance level, as follows:

(a) **When placed in water, it must be packaged** in specification packagings as follows:

(1) *Wooden boxes (4C1, 4C2, 4D, or 4F) with:*

(i) *Inner hermetically sealed* (soldered) metal cans, enclosed in other hermetically sealed (soldered) metal cans, or

(ii) *Inner water-tight metal cans* containing not over 0.5 kg (1 pound) of phosphorus with screw-top closures; or

(2) *Steel drums (1A1)* not over 250 L (66 gallons) capacity each or steel drums (1A2) not over 115 L (30 gallons) capacity each.

(b) **When dry, it must be cast solid and shipped** in packagings as follows:

(1) *Steel drums (1A2) not over 115 L (30 gallons) capacity each, or*

(2) *In projectiles or bombs* when shipped by, for, or to the Departments of the Army, Navy, or Air Force of the United States Government, without bursting elements.

§173.189 Batteries containing sodium or cells containing sodium.

(a) **Batteries and cells may not contain** any hazardous material other than sodium, sulfur or polysulfides. Cells not forming a component of a completed battery may not be offered for transportation at a temperature at which any liquid sodium is present in the cell. Batteries may only be offered for transportation, or transported, at a temperature at which any liquid sodium present in the battery conforms to the conditions prescribed in paragraph (d) of this section.

(b) **Cells must consist of hermetically sealed metal casings** which fully enclose the hazardous materials and which are so constructed and closed as to prevent the release of the hazardous materials under normal conditions of transport. Cells must be placed in suitable outer packagings with sufficient cushioning material to prevent contact between cells and between cells and the internal surfaces of the outer packaging, and to ensure that no dangerous movement of the cells within the outer packaging occurs in transport. Cells must be packaged in 1A2, 1B2, 1D, 1G, 1H2, 4C1, 4C2, 4D, 4F, 4G or 4H2 outer packagings which meet the requirements of part 178 of this subchapter at the Packing Group II performance level.

(c) **Batteries must consist of cells secured within,** and fully enclosed by a metal casing so constructed and closed as to prevent the release of the hazardous materials under normal conditions of transport. Batteries may be offered for transportation, and transported, unpacked or in protective packagings that are not subject to the requirements of part 178 of this subchapter.

(d) **Batteries containing any liquid sodium may not be offered** for transportation, or transported, by aircraft. Batteries containing liquid sodium may be transported by motor vehicle, rail car or vessel under the following conditions:

(1) *Batteries must be equipped* with an effective means of preventing external short circuits, such as by providing complete electrical insulation of battery terminals or other external electrical connectors. Battery terminals or other electrical connectors penetrating the heat insulation fitted in battery casings must be provided with thermal insulation sufficient to prevent the temperature of the exposed surfaces of such devices from exceeding 55 °C (130 °F).

(2) *No battery may be offered* for transportation if the temperature at any point on the external surface of the battery exceeds 55 °C (130 °F).

(3) *If any external* source of heating is used during transportation to maintain sodium in batteries in a molten state, means must be provided to ensure that the internal temperature of the battery does not reach or exceed 400 °C (752 °F).

(4) *When loaded in a transport vehicle or freight container:*

(i) *Batteries must be secured* so as to prevent significant movement within the transport vehicle or freight container under conditions normally incident to transportation;

(ii) *Adequate ventilation* and/or separation between batteries must be provided to ensure that the temperature at any point on the external surface of the battery casing will not exceed 240 °C (464 °F) during transportation; and

(iii) *No other hazardous materials,* with the exception of cells containing sodium, may be loaded in the same transport vehicle or freight container. Batteries must be separated from all other freight by a distance of not less than 0.5 m (1.6 feet).

(e) **Batteries containing sodium or cells containing sodium,** when installed as part of a motor vehicle, are not subject to the requirements of this subchapter.

§173.192 Packaging for certain toxic gases in Hazard Zone A.

When §172.101 of this subchapter specifies a toxic material must be packaged under this section, only specification cylinders are authorized, as follows:

(a) **Specification 3A1800, 3AA1800, 3AL1800, or 3E1800 cylinders,** under the following conditions:

(1) *Specification 3A,* 3AA, or 3AL cylinders may not exceed 57 kg (125 lb) water capacity (nominal).

(2) *Specification 3AL cylinders* may only be offered for transportation or transported by highway and rail.

(b) **Packagings must conform to the requirements of §173.40.**

(c) **For cylinders used for phosgene:**

(1) *The filling density may not exceed 125 percent;*

(2) *A cylinder* may not contain more than 68 kg (150 lb) of phosgene; and

(3) *Each cylinder* containing phosgene must be tested for leakage before it is offered for transportation or transported and must show no leakage. The leakage test must consist of immersing the cylinder and valve, without the protective cap attached, in a bath of water at a temperature of approximately 66 °C (150 °F) for at least 30 minutes, during which time frequent examinations must be made to note any escape of gas. The valve of the cylinder may not be loosened after this test. Suitable safeguards must be provided to protect personnel and facilities should failure occur during the test. As an alternative, each cylinder containing phosgene may be tested for leakage by a method approved in writing by the Associate Administrator.

§173.193 Bromoacetone, methyl bromide, chloropicrin and methyl bromide or methyl chloride mixtures, etc.

(a) **Bromoacetone must be packaged as follows** in wooden boxes (4C1, 4C2, 4D or 4F) with inner glass receptacles or tubes in hermetically sealed metal receptacles in corrugated fiberboard cartons. Bottles may not contain over 500 g (17.6 ounces) of liquid each and must be cushioned in cans with at least 12.7 mm (0.5 inch) of absorbent material. Total amount of liquid in the outer box must not exceed 11 kg (24 pounds). Packagings must conform to the requirements of part 178 of this subchapter at the Packing Group I performance level.

(b) **Bromoacetone, methyl bromide, chloropicrin** and methyl bromide mixtures, chloropicrin and methyl chloride mixtures, and chloropicrin mixtures charged with non-flammable, non-liquefied compressed gas must be packed in Specification 3A, 3AA, 3B, 3C, 3E, 4A, 4B, 4BA, 4BW, or 4C cylinders having not over 113 kg (250 pounds) water capacity (nominal). This capacity does not apply to shipments of methyl bromide.

(c) **Methyl bromide mixtures containing up to 2% chloropicrin** must be packaged in 4G fiberboard boxes with inside metal cans containing not over one pound each, or inside metal cans with a minimum wall thickness of 0.007 inch containing not over 1 3/4 pounds each. The one-pound can must be capable of withstanding an internal pressure of 130 psig without leakage or permanent distortion. Vapor pressure of the contents must not exceed 130 psig at 55 °C (130 °F). The 1 3/4-pound can must be capable of withstanding an internal pressure of 140 psig without leakage or permanent distortion. Vapor pressure of the contents must not exceed 140 psig at 55 °C (130 °F). Cans must not be liquid full at 130 °F Cans must be constructed of tinplate or lined with suitable material and must have concave or pressure ends.

(d) **Cylinders, except those containing methyl bromide,** must conform to §173.40 of this part.

§173.194 Gas identification sets.

Gas identification sets containing poisonous material must be packaged in packagings conforming to the requirements of part 178 of this subchapter at the Packing Group I performance level, as follows:

(a) **In glass inner receptacles, hermetically sealed,** of not over 40 mL (1.4 fluid ounces) each. Each glass inner receptacle must in turn be placed in a sealed fiberboard receptacle, cushioned with absorbent material. Not more than 12 fiberboard receptacles must in turn be placed in a 4G fiberboard box. No more than four boxes, well-cushioned, may in turn be placed in a steel cylinder. The cylinder must have a wall thickness of at least 3.7 mm (0.146 inch) and must have a hermetically sealed steel closure.

(b) **When the poisonous material is absorbed** in a medium such as activated charcoal or silical gel, gas identification sets may be shipped as follows:

(1) *If the poisonous material* does not exceed 5 mL (0.2 fluid ounce) if a liquid or 5 g (0.2 ounce) if a solid, it may be packed in glass inner receptacles of not over 120 mL (4.1 fluid ounces) each. Each glass receptacle, cushioned with absorbent material must be packed in a hermetically sealed metal can of not less than 0.30 mm (0.012 inch) wall thickness. Metal cans, surrounded on all sides by at least 25 mm (1 inch) of dry sawdust, must be packed in 4C1, 4C2, 4D or 4F wooden boxes. Not more than 100 mL (3.4 fluid ounces) or 100 g (3.5 ounces) of poisonous materials may be packed in one outer wooden box.

(2) *If the poisonous material* does not exceed 5 mL (0.2 fluid ounce) if a liquid or 20 g (0.7 ounce) if a solid, it may be packed in glass inner receptacles with screw-top closures of not less than 60 mL (2 ounces), hermetically sealed. Twelve bottles containing poisonous material, not to exceed 100 mL (3.4 ounces) or 100 g (3.5 ounces), or both, may be placed in a plastic carrying case, each glass receptacle surrounded by absorbent cushioning and each separated from the other by sponge rubber partitions. The plastic carrying case must be placed in a tightly fitting fiberboard box which in turn must be placed in a tightly fitting 4C1, 4C2, 4D or 4F wooden box.

§173.195 Hydrogen cyanide, anhydrous, stabilized (hydrocyanic acid, aqueous solution).

(a) **Hydrogen cyanide, anhydrous, stabilized,** must be packed in specification cylinders as follows:

(1) *As prescribed in §173.192, or*

(2) *Specification 3A480,* 3A480X, 3AA480, or 3A1800 metal cylinders of not over 126 kg (278 pounds) water capacity (nominal). Shipments in 3AL cylinders are authorized only when transported by highway and rail.

(b) **Cylinders may not be charged** with more than 0.27 kg (0.6 pound) of liquid per 0.45 kg (1 pound) water capacity of cylinder. Each filled cylinder must be tested for leakage before being offered for transportation or transported and must show absolutely no leakage; this test must consist of passing a piece of Guignard's sodium picrate paper over the closure of the cylinder, without the protection cap attached, to detect any escape of hydrogen cyanide from the cylinder. Other equally efficient test methods may be used in place of sodium picrate paper.

(c) **Packagings for hydrogen cyanide must conform to §173.40.**

§173.196 Infectious substances.

(a) **Division 6.2 packaging.** A Division 6.2 packaging must meet the test standards of §178.609 of this subchapter and must be marked in conformance with §178.503(f) of this subchapter. Division 6.2 packaging is a triple packaging consisting of the following components:

(1) *A watertight primary receptacle.*

(2) *A watertight secondary packaging.* If multiple fragile primary receptacles are placed in a single secondary packaging, they must be wrapped individually to prevent contact between them.

(3) *An outer packaging* of adequate strength for its capacity, mass and intended use. The outer packaging must measure at least 100 mm (3.9 inches) at its smallest overall external dimension.

(4) *For a liquid infectious substance,* an absorbent material placed between the primary receptacle and the secondary packaging. The absorbent material must be sufficient to absorb the entire contents of all primary receptacles.

(5) *An itemized list* of contents enclosed between the secondary packaging and the outer packaging.

(6) *The primary receptacle* or secondary packaging used for infectious substances must be capable of withstanding, without leakage, an internal pressure producing a pressure differential of not less than 95 kPa (0.95 bar, 14 psi).

(7) *The primary receptacle* or secondary packaging used for infectious substances must be capable of withstanding without leakage temperatures in the range of -40 °C to +55 °C (-40 °F to +131 °F).

(b) **Additional requirements for packaging** infectious substances. Infectious substances must be packaged according to the following requirements depending on the physical state and other characteristics of the material:

(1) *Infectious lyophilized* (freeze-dried) substances. Primary receptacles must be flame-sealed glass ampules or rubber-stopped glass vials fitted with metal seals.

(2) *Liquid or solid infectious substances —*

(i) *Infectious substances* shipped at ambient temperatures or higher. Authorized primary receptacles are those of glass, metal, or plastic. Positive means of ensuring a leakproof seal must be provided, such as heat seal, skirted stopper, or metal crimp seal. If screw caps are used, they must be secured by positive means, such as with adhesive tape.

(ii) *Infectious substances* shipped refrigerated or frozen (ice, prefrozen packs, dry ice). Ice or dry ice must be placed outside the secondary packagings or in an overpack with one or more complete packages marked in accordance with §178.503 of this subchapter. Interior supports must be provided to secure the secondary packagings in the original position after the ice or dry ice has dissipated. If ice is used, the outside packaging must be leakproof. If dry ice is used, the outside packaging must permit the release of carbon dioxide gas and otherwise meet the provisions in §173.217. The primary receptacle and the secondary packaging must maintain their integrity at the temperature of the refrigerant used as well as the temperatures and pressures of air transport to which they could be subjected if refrigeration were lost.

(iii) *Infectious substances* shipped in liquid nitrogen. Primary receptacles capable of withstanding very low temperatures must be used. Secondary packaging must withstand very low temperatures and in most cases will need to be fitted over individual primary receptacles. The primary receptacle and the secondary packaging must maintain their integrity at the temperature of the liquid nitrogen as well as the temperatures and pressures of air transport to which they could be subjected if refrigeration were to be lost. Refrigerated liquid nitrogen packagings must be metal vacuum insulated vessels or flasks (also called "dry shippers") vented to the atmosphere to prevent any increase in pressure within the packaging. The use of safety relief valves, check valves, frangible discs, or similar devices in the vent lines is prohibited. Fill and discharge openings must be protected against the entry of foreign materials that might cause an increase in the internal pressure. The package orientation markings specified in §172.312(a) of this subchapter must be marked on the packaging. The packaging must be designed to prevent the release of any refrigerated liquid nitrogen irrespective of the packaging orientation.

(c) **Live animals may not be used to transport** infectious substances unless such substances cannot be sent by any other means. An animal containing or contaminated with an infectious substance must be transported under terms and conditions approved by the Associate Administrator for Hazardous Materials Safety.

(d) **Body parts, organs or whole bodies** meeting the definition of Division 6.2 material must be packaged as follows:

(1) *In Division 6.2 packaging,* as specified in paragraphs (a) and (b) of this section; or

(2) *In packaging meeting the requirements of §173.197.*

§173.197 Regulated medical waste.

(a) **General provisions.** Non-bulk packagings, large packagings, and bulk outer packagings used for the transportation of regulated medical waste must be rigid containers meeting the provisions of subpart B of this part.

(b) **Non-bulk packagings.** Except as otherwise provided in §173.134 of this subpart, non-bulk packagings for regulated medical waste must be DOT specification packagings conforming to the requirements of Part 178 of this subchapter at the Packing Group II performance level. A non-bulk packaging must be puncture-resistant for sharps and sharps with residual fluid as demonstrated by conducting the performance tests in Part 178, Subpart M, of this subchapter on packagings containing materials representative of the sharps and fluids (such as sterile sharps) intended to be transported in the packagings.

(c) **Large Packagings.** Large Packagings constructed, tested, and marked in accordance with the requirements of the UN Recommendations and conforming to other requirements of this paragraph (c) may be used for the transportation of regulated medical waste, provided the waste is contained in inner packagings conforming to the requirements of paragraph (e) of this section. Each Large Packaging design must be capable of meeting the vibration test specified in §178.819 of this subchapter. Each Large Packaging is subject to the periodic design requalification requirements for intermediate bulk containers in §178.801(e) of this subchapter and to the proof of compliance requirements of §178.801(j) and record retention requirements of §178.801(l) of this subchapter. Inner packagings used for liquids must be rigid.

(1) *Authorized packagings.* Only the following Large Packagings are authorized for the transportation of liquid or solid regulated medical waste:

(i) *Metal: 50A, 50B, or 50N.*

(ii) *Rigid plastic: 50H.*

(2) *Additional requirements.* Each Large Packaging used to transport liquid regulated medical waste must contain absorbent material in sufficient quantity and appropriate location to absorb the entire amount of liquid present in the event of an unintentional release of contents. Each Large Packaging design intended for the transportation of sharps containers must be puncture resistant and capable of retaining liquids. The design must also be tested and certified as meeting the performance tests specified for intermediate bulk containers intended for the transportation of liquids in subpart O of part 178 of this subchapter.

(d) **Non-specification bulk packaging.** A wheeled cart (Cart) or bulk outer packaging (BOP) is authorized as an outer packaging for the transportation of regulated medical waste in accordance with the provisions of this paragraph (d).

(1) *General requirements.* The following requirements apply to the transportation of regulated medical waste in Carts or BOPs:

(i) *Regulated medical waste* in each Cart or BOP must be contained in non-bulk inner packagings conforming to paragraph (e) of this section.

(ii) *Each Cart or BOP* must have smooth, non-porous interior surfaces free of cracks, crevices, and other defects that could damage plastic film inner packagings or impede disinfection operations.

(iii) *Except as otherwise provided* in this paragraph (d), each Cart or BOP must be used exclusively for the transportation of regulated medical waste. Prior to reuse, each Cart or BOP must be disinfected by any means effective for neutralizing the infectious substance the packaging previously contained.

(iv) *Untreated cultures* and stocks of infectious substances containing Risk Group 4 materials may not be transported in a Cart or BOP.

(v) *Division 6.1* toxic waste or Class 7 radioactive waste, with the exception of chemotherapeutic waste, may not be transported in a Cart or BOP.

(vi) *Division 6.1* or Class 7 chemotherapeutic waste; untreated stocks and cultures of infectious substances containing Risk Group 2 or 3 pathogenic organisms; unabsorbed liquids; and sharps containers may be transported in a Cart or BOP only if packaged in rigid non-bulk packagings conforming to paragraph (a) of this section.

(2) *Wheeled cart (Cart).* A Cart is authorized as an outer packaging for the transportation of regulated medical waste if it conforms to the following requirements:

(i) *Each Cart* must consist of a solid, one-piece body with a nominal volume not exceeding 1,655 L (437 gallons).

(ii) *Each Cart* must be constructed of metal, rigid plastic, or fiberglass fitted with a lid to prevent leakage during transport.

(iii) *Each Cart* must be capable of meeting the requirements of §178.603 (drop test), as specified for solids at the Packing Group II performance level.

(iv) *Inner packagings* must be placed into a Cart and restrained in such a manner as to minimize the risk of breakage.

(3) *Bulk outer packaging (BOP).* A BOP is authorized as an outer packaging for regulated medical waste if it conforms to the following requirements:

(i) *Each BOP* must be constructed of metal or fiberglass and have a capacity of at least 3.5 cubic meters (123.6 cubic feet) and not more than 45 cubic meters (1,590 cubic feet).

(ii) *Each BOP* must have bottom and side joints of fully welded or seamless construction and a rigid, weatherproof top to prevent the intrusion of water (e.g., rain or snow).

(iii) *Each opening* in a BOP must be fitted with a closure to prevent the intrusion of water or the release of any liquid during all loading, unloading, and transportation operations.

(iv) *In the upright position,* each BOP must be leakproof and able to contain a liquid quantity of at least 300 liters (79.2 gallons) with closures open.

(v) *Inner packagings* must be placed in a BOP in such a manner as to minimize the risk of breakage. Rigid inner packagings may not be placed in the same BOP with plastic film bag inner packagings unless separated from each other by rigid barriers or dividers to prevent damage to the packagings caused by load shifting during normal conditions of transportation.

(vi) *Division 6.1* or Class 7 chemotherapeutic waste, untreated cultures and stocks of infectious substances containing Risk Group 2 or 3 pathogenic organisms, unabsorbed liquids, and sharps may be transported in a BOP only if separated and secured as provided by paragraph (d)(3)(v) of this section.

(e) **Inner packagings authorized for Large Packagings,** Carts, and BOPs. After September 30, 2003, inner packagings must be durably marked or tagged with the name and location (city and state) of the offeror, except when the entire contents of the Large Packaging, Cart, or BOP originates at a single location and is delivered to a single location.

(1) *Solids.* A plastic film bag is authorized as an inner packaging for solid regulated medical waste transported in.a Cart, Large Packaging, or BOP. Waste material containing absorbed liquid may be packaged as a solid in a plastic film bag if the bag contains sufficient absorbent material to absorb and retain all liquid during transportation.

(i) *The film bag* may not exceed a volume of 175 L (46 gallons). The film bag must be marked and certified by its manufacturer as having passed the tests prescribed for tear resistance in ASTM D 1709-01, Standard Test Methods for Impact Resistance of Plastic Film by the Free-Falling Dart Method (see §171.7 of this subchapter), and for impact resistance in ASTM D 1922-00a, Standard Test Method for Propagation Tear Resistance of Plastic Film and Thin Sheeting by Pendulum Method (see §171.7 of this subchapter). The film bag must meet an impact resistance of 165 grams and a tearing resistance of 480 grams in both the parallel and perpendicular planes with respect to the length of the bag.

(ii) *The plastic film bag* must be closed with a minimum of entrapped air to prevent leakage in transportation. The bag must be capable of being held in an inverted position with the closed end at the bottom for a period of 5 minutes without leakage.

(iii) *When used* as an inner packaging for Carts or BOPs, a plastic film bag may not weigh more than 10 kg (22 lbs.) when filled.

(2) *Liquids.* Liquid regulated medical waste transported in a Large Packaging, Cart, or BOP must be packaged in a rigid inner packaging conforming to the requirements of paragraph (a) of this section. Liquid materials are not authorized for transportation in inner packagings having a capacity greater than 19 L (5 gallons).

(3) *Sharps.* Sharps transported in a Large Packaging, Cart, or BOP must be packaged in a puncture-resistant inner packaging (sharps container). Each sharps container exceeding 76 L (20 gallons) in volume must be capable of passing the performance tests in §178.601 of this subchapter at the Packing Group II performance level. A sharps container may be reused only if it conforms to the following criteria:

(i) *The sharps container* is specifically approved and certified by the U.S. Food and Drug Administration as a medical device for reuse.

(ii) *The sharps container must be permanently marked for reuse.*

(iii) *The sharps container* must be disinfected prior to reuse by any means effective for the infectious substance the container previously contained.

(iv) *The sharps container* must have a capacity greater than 7.57 L (2 gallons) and not greater than 151.42 L (40 gallons) in volume.

§173.198 Nickel carbonyl.

(a) **Nickel carbonyl must be packed in specification steel** or nickel cylinders as prescribed for any compressed gas except acetylene. A cylinder used exclusively for nickel carbonyl may be given a complete external visual inspection instead of the pressure test required by §180.205 of this subchapter. Visual inspection must be in accordance with CGA Pamphlet C-6 (incorporated by reference; see §171.7 of this subchapter).

(b) **Packagings for nickel carbonyl must conform to §173.40.**

§173.199 Diagnostic specimens and used health care products.

(a) **Diagnostic specimens.** Except as provided in this paragraph (a), diagnostic specimens are excepted from all other requirements of this subchapter when offered for transportation or transported in accordance with this section. Diagnostic specimens offered for transportation or transported by aircraft under the provisions of this section are subject to the incident reporting requirements in §§171.15 and 171.16 of this subchapter. A diagnostic specimen meeting the definition of a hazard class other than Division 6.2 must be offered for transportation or transported in accordance with applicable requirements of this subchapter.

(1) *Diagnostic specimens* must be packaged in a triple packaging, consisting of a primary receptacle, a secondary packaging, and an outer packaging.

(2) *Primary receptacles* must be packed in secondary packaging in such a way that, under normal conditions of transport, they cannot break, be punctured, or leak their contents into the secondary packaging.

(3) *Secondary packagings* must be secured in outer packagings with suitable cushioning material such that any leakage of the contents will not impair the protective properties of the cushioning material or the outer packaging.

(4) *The completed package* must be capable of successfully passing the drop test in §178.603 of this subchapter at a drop height of at least 1.2 meters (3.9 feet). The outer packaging must be clearly and durably marked with the words "Diagnostic Specimen."

(b) **Liquid diagnostic specimens.** Liquid diagnostic specimens must be packaged in conformance with the following provisions:

(1) *The primary receptacle* must be leakproof with a volumetric capacity of not more than 500 mL (16.9 ounces).

(2) *Absorbent material* must be placed between the primary receptacle and secondary packaging. If several fragile primary receptacles are placed in a single secondary packaging, they must be individually wrapped or separated so as to prevent contact between them. The absorbent material must be of sufficient quantity to absorb the entire contents of the primary receptacles.

(3) *The secondary packaging must be leakproof.*

(4) *For shipments by aircraft,* the primary receptacle or the secondary packaging must be capable of withstanding without leakage an internal pressure producing a pressure differential of not less than 95 kPa (0.95 bar, 14 psi).

(5) *The outer packaging may not exceed 4 L (1 gallon) capacity.*

(c) **Solid diagnostic specimens.** Solid diagnostic specimens must be packaged in a triple packaging, consisting of a primary receptacle, secondary packaging, and outer packaging, conforming to the following provisions:

(1) *The primary receptacle* must be siftproof with a capacity of not more than 500 g (1.1 pounds).

(2) *If several fragile* primary receptacles are placed in a single secondary packaging, they must be individually wrapped or separated so as to prevent contact between them.

(3) *The secondary packaging must be leakproof.*

(4) *The outer packaging may not exceed 4 kg (8.8 pounds) capacity.*

(d) **Used health care products.** A used health care product being returned to the manufacturer or the manufacturer's designee is excepted from the requirements of this subchapter when offered for transportation or transported in accordance with this section. For purposes of this section, a health care product is used when it has been removed from its original inner packaging. Used health care products contaminated with or suspected of contamination with a Risk Group 4 infectious substance may not be transported under the provisions of this section.

(1) *Each used* health care product must be drained of free liquid to the extent practicable and placed in a watertight primary container designed and constructed to assure that it remains intact under conditions normally incident to transportation. For a used health care product capable of cutting or penetrating skin or packaging material, the primary container must be capable of retaining the product without puncture of the packaging under normal conditions of transport. Each primary container must be marked with a BIOHAZARD marking conforming to 29 CFR 1910.1030(g)(1)(i).

(2) *Each primary container* must be placed inside a watertight secondary container designed and constructed to assure that it remains intact under conditions normally incident to transportation. The secondary container must be marked with a BIOHAZARD marking conforming to 29 CFR 1910.1030(g)(1)(i).

(3) *The secondary container* must be placed inside an outer packaging with sufficient cushioning material to prevent movement between the secondary container and the outer packaging. An itemized list of the contents of the primary container and information concerning possible contamination with a Division 6.2 material, including its possible location on the product, must be placed between the secondary container and the outside packaging.

(e) **Training.** Each person who offers or transports a diagnostic specimen or used health care product under the provisions of this section must know about the requirements of this section.

§173.201 Non-bulk packagings for liquid hazardous materials in Packing Group I.

(a) **When §172.101 of this subchapter** specifies that a liquid hazardous material be packaged under this section, only non-bulk packagings prescribed in this section may be used for its transportation. Each packaging must conform to the general packaging requirements of subpart B of part 173, to the requirements of part 178 of this subchapter at the Packing Group I performance level, and to the requirements of the special provisions of column 7 of the §172.101 table.

(b) **The following combination packagings are authorized:**

Outer packagings:

Steel drum: 1A1 or 1A2
Aluminum drum: 1B1 or 1B2
Metal drum other than steel or aluminum: 1N1 or 1N2
Plywood drum: 1D
Fiber drum: 1G
Plastic drum: 1H1 or 1H2
Steel jerrican: 3A1 or 3A2
Plastic jerrican: 3H1 or 3H2
Aluminum jerrican: 3B1 or 3B2
Steel box: 4A
Aluminum box: 4B
Natural wood box: 4C1 or 4C2
Plywood box: 4D
Reconstituted wood box: 4F
Fiberboard box: 4G
Expanded plastic box: 4H1
Solid plastic box: 4H2

Inner packagings:

Glass or earthenware receptacles
Plastic receptacles
Metal receptacles
Glass ampoules

(c) **Except for transportation by passenger aircraft,** the following single packagings are authorized:

Steel drum: 1A1 or 1A2
Aluminum drum: 1B1 or 1B2
Metal drum other than steel, or aluminum: 1N1 or 1N2
Plastic drum: 1H1 or 1H2
Steel jerrican: 3A1 or 3A2
Plastic jerrican: 3H1 or 3H2
Aluminum jerrican: 3B1 or 3B2
Plastic receptacle in steel, aluminum, fiber or plastic drum: 6HA1, 6HB1, 6HG1, 6HH1
Plastic receptacle in steel, aluminum, wooden, plywood or fiberboard box: 6HA2, 6HB2, 6HC, 6HD2 or 6HG2
Glass, porcelain or stoneware in steel, aluminum or fiber drum: 6PA1, 6PB1 or 6PG1
Glass, porcelain or stoneware in steel, aluminum, wooden or fiberboard box: 6PA2, 6PB2, 6PC or 6PG2
Glass, porcelain or stoneware in solid or expanded plastic packaging: 6PH1 or 6PH2
Cylinders, specification, as prescribed for any compressed gas, except for Specifications 8 and 3HT

§173.202 Non-bulk packagings for liquid hazardous materials in Packing Group II.

(a) **When §172.101 of this subchapter** specifies that a liquid hazardous material be packaged under this section, only non-bulk packagings prescribed in this section may be used for its transportation. Each packaging must conform to the general packaging requirements of subpart B of part 173, to the requirements of part 178 of this subchapter at the Packing Group I or II performance level (unless otherwise excepted), and to the particular requirements of the special provisions of column 7 of the §172.101 table.

(b) **The following combination packagings are authorized:**

Outer packagings:

Steel drum: 1A1 or 1A2
Aluminum drum: 1B1 or 1B2
Metal drum other than steel or aluminum: 1N1 or 1N2
Plywood drum: 1D
Fiber drum: 1G
Plastic drum: 1H1 or 1H2
Wooden barrel: 2C2
Steel jerrican: 3A1 or 3A2
Plastic jerrican: 3H1 or 3H2
Aluminum jerrican: 3B1 or 3B2
Steel box: 4A
Aluminum box: 4B
Natural wood box: 4C1 or 4C2
Plywood box: 4D
Reconstituted wood box: 4F
Fiberboard box: 4G
Expanded plastic box: 4H1
Solid plastic box: 4H2

Inner packagings:

Glass or earthenware receptacles
Plastic receptacles
Metal receptacles
Glass ampoules

(c) **Except for transportation by passenger aircraft,** the following single packagings are authorized:

Steel drum: 1A1 or 1A2
Aluminum drum: 1B1 or 1B2
Metal drum other than steel or aluminum: 1N1 or 1N2
Plastic drum: 1H1 or 1H2
Fiber drum: 1G (with liner)
Wooden barrel: 2C1
Steel jerrican: 3A1 or 3A2
Plastic jerrican: 3H1 or 3H2
Aluminum jerrican: 3B1 or 3B2
Plastic receptacle in steel, aluminum, fiber or plastic drum: 6HA1, 6HB1, 6HG1 or 6HH1
Plastic receptacle in steel, aluminum, wooden, plywood or fiberboard box: 6HA2, 6HB2, 6HC, 6HD2 or 6HG2
Glass, porcelain or stoneware in steel, aluminum or fiber drum: 6PA1, 6PB1 or 6PG1
Glass, porcelain or stoneware in steel, aluminum, wooden or fiberboard box: 6PA2, 6PB2, 6PC or 6PG2
Glass, porcelain or stoneware in solid or expanded plastic packaging: 6PH1 or 6PH2
Plastic receptacle in plywood drum: 6HD1

Glass, porcelain or stoneware in plywood drum or wickerwork hamper: 6PDI or 6PD2

Cylinders, specification, as prescribed for any compressed gas, except for Specifications 8 and 3HT

§173.203 Non-bulk packagings for liquid hazardous materials in Packing Group III.

(a) **When §172.101 of this subchapter** specifies that a liquid hazardous material be packaged under this section, only non-bulk packagings prescribed in this section may be used for its transportation. Each packaging must conform to the general packaging requirements of subpart B of part 173, to the requirements of part 178 of this subchapter at the Packing Group I, II or III performance level, and to the requirements of the special provisions of column 7 of the §172.101 table.

(b) **The following combination packagings are authorized:**

Outer packagings:

Steel drum: 1A1 or 1A2
Aluminum drum: 1B1 or 1B2
Metal drum other than steel or aluminum: 1N1 or 1N2
Plywood drum: 1D
Fiber drum: 1G
Plastic drum: 1H1 or 1H2
Wooden barrel: 2C2
Steel jerrican: 3A1 or 3A2
Plastic jerrican: 3H1 or 3H2
Aluminum jerrican: 3B1 or 3B2
Steel box: 4A
Aluminum box: 4B
Natural wood box: 4C1 or 4C2
Plywood box: 4D
Reconstituted wood box: 4F
Fiberboard box: 4G
Expanded plastic box: 4H1
Solid plastic box: 4H2

Inner packagings:

Glass or earthenware receptacles
Plastic receptacles
Metal receptacles
Glass ampoules

(c) **The following single packagings are authorized:**

Steel drum: 1A1 or 1A2
Aluminum drum: 1B1 or 1B2
Metal drum other than steel or aluminum: 1N1
Plastic drum: 1H1 or 1H2
Fiber drum: 1G (with liner)
Wooden barrel: 2C1
Steel jerrican: 3A1 or 3A2
Plastic jerrican: 3H1 or 3H2
Aluminum jerrican: 3B1 or 3B2
Plastic receptacle in steel, aluminum, fiber or plastic drum: 6HA1, 6HB1, 6HG1 or 6HH1
Plastic receptacle in steel, aluminum, wooden, plywood or fiberboard box: 6HA2, 6HB2, 6HC, 6HD2 or 6HG2
Glass, porcelain or stoneware in steel, aluminum or fiber drum: 6PA1, 6PB1, or 6PG1
Glass, porcelain or stoneware in steel, aluminum, wooden or fiberboard box: 6PA2, 6PB2, 6PC or 6PG2
Glass, porcelain or stoneware in solid or expanded plastic packaging: 6PH1 or 6PH2
Plastic receptacle in plywood drum: 6HD1
Glass, porcelain or stoneware in plywood drum or wickerwork hamper: 6PD1 or 6PD2
Cylinders, as prescribed for any compressed gas, except for Specifications 8 and 3HT

§173.204 Non-bulk, non-specification packagings for certain hazardous materials.

When §172.101 of this subchapter specifies that a liquid or solid hazardous material be packaged under this section, any appropriate non-bulk packaging which conforms to the general packaging requirements of subpart B of part 173 may be used for its transportation. Packagings need not conform to the requirements of part 178 of this subchapter.

§173.205 Specification cylinders for liquid hazardous materials.

When §172.101 of this subchapter specifies that a hazardous material be packaged under this section, any specification cylinder, except those specified for acetylene, is authorized. Cylinders used for poisonous materials (Division 6.1 or 2.3) must conform to the requirements of §173.40.

§173.211 Non-bulk packagings for solid hazardous materials in Packing Group I.

(a) **When §172.101 of this subchapter** specifies that a solid hazardous material be packaged under this section, only non-bulk packagings prescribed in this section may be used for its transportation. Each package must conform to the general packaging requirements of subpart B of part 173, to the requirements of part 178 of this subchapter at the Packing Group I performance level, and to the requirements of the special provisions of column 7 of the §172.101 table.

(b) **The following combination packagings are authorized:**

Outer packagings:

Steel drum: 1A1 or 1A2
Aluminum drum: 1B1 or 1B2
Metal drum other than steel or aluminum: 1N1 or 1N2
Plywood drum: 1D
Fiber drum: 1G
Plastic drum: 1H1 or 1H2
Wooden barrel: 2C2
Steel jerrican: 3A1 or 3A2
Plastic jerrican: 3H1 or 3H2
Aluminum jerrican: 3B1 or 3B2
Steel box: 4A
Aluminum box: 4B
Natural wood box: 4C1 or 4C2
Plywood box: 4D
Reconstituted wood box: 4F
Fiberboard box: 4G
Solid plastic box: 4H2

Inner packagings:

Glass or earthenware receptacles
Plastic receptacles
Metal receptacles
Glass ampoules

(c) **Except for transportation by passenger aircraft,** the following single packagings are authorized:

Steel drum: 1A1 or 1A2
Aluminum drum: 1B1 or 1B2
Metal drum other than steel or aluminum: 1N1 or 1N2
Plastic drum: 1H1 or 1H2
Fiber drum: 1G
Steel jerrican: 3A1 or 3A2
Plastic jerrican: 3H1 or 3H2
Aluminum jerrican: 3B1 or 3B2
Steel box with liner: 4A
Aluminum box with liner: 4B
Natural wood box, sift proof: 4C2
Plastic receptacle in steel, aluminum, plywood, fiber or plastic drum: 6HA1, 6HB1, 6HD1, 6HG1 or 6HH1
Plastic receptacle in steel, aluminum, wooden, plywood or fiberboard box: 6HA2, 6HB2, 6HC, 6HD2 or 6HG2
Glass, porcelain or stoneware in steel, aluminum, plywood or fiber drum: 6PA1, 6PB1, 6PD1 or 6PG1
Glass, porcelain or stoneware in steel, aluminum, wooden or fiberboard box: 6PA2, 6PB2, 6PC or 6PG2
Glass, porcelain or stoneware in expanded or solid plastic packaging: 6PH1 or 6PH2

§173.212 Non-bulk packagings for solid hazardous materials in Packing Group II.

(a) **When §172.101 of this subchapter** specifies that a solid hazardous material be packaged under this section, only non-bulk packagings prescribed in this section may be used for its transportation. Each package must conform to the general packaging requirements of subpart B of part 173, to the requirements of part 178 of this subchapter at the Packing Group I or II performance level, and to the requirements of the special provisions of column 7 of the §172.101 table.

(b) The following combination packagings are authorized:

Outer packagings:
Steel drum: 1A1 or 1A2
Aluminum drum: 1B1 or 1B2
Metal drum other than steel or aluminum: 1N1 or 1N2
Plywood drum: 1D
Fiber drum: 1G
Plastic drum: 1H1 or 1H2
Wooden barrel: 2C2
Steel jerrican: 3A1 or 3A2
Plastic jerrican: 3H1 or 3H2
Aluminum jerrican: 3B1 or 3B2
Steel box: 4A
Aluminum box: 4B
Natural wood box: 4C1 or 4C2
Plywood box: 4D
Reconstituted wood box: 4F
Fiberboard box: 4G
Solid plastic box: 4H2

Inner packagings:
Glass or earthenware receptacles
Plastic receptacles
Metal receptacles
Glass ampoules

(c) Except for transportation by passenger aircraft, the following single packagings are authorized:
Steel drum: 1A1 or 1A2
Aluminum drum: 1B1 or 1B2
Plywood drum: 1D
Plastic drum: 1H1 or 1H2
Fiber drum: 1G
Metal drum other than steel or aluminum: 1N1 or 1N2
Wooden barrel: 2C1 or 2C2
Steel jerrican: 3A1 or 3A2
Plastic jerrican: 3H1 or 3H2
Aluminum jerrican: 3B1 or 3B2
Steel box: 4A
Steel box with liner: 4A
Aluminum box: 4B
Aluminum box with liner: 4B
Natural wood box: 4C1
Natural wood box, sift proof: 4C2
Plywood box: 4D
Reconstituted wood box: 4F
Fiberboard box: 4G
Expanded plastic box: 4H1
Solid plastic box: 4H2
Bag, woven plastic: 5H1, 5H2 or 5H3
Bag, plastic film: 5H4
Bag, textile: 5L1, 5L2 or 5L3
Bag, paper, multiwall, water resistant: 5M2
Plastic receptacle in steel, aluminum, plywood, fiber or plastic drum: 6HA1, 6HB1, 6HD1, 6HG1 or 6HH1
Plastic receptacle in steel aluminum, wood, plywood or fiberboard box: 6HA2, 6HB2, 6HC, 6HD2 or 6HG2
Glass, porcelain or stoneware in steel, aluminum, plywood or fiber drum: 6PA1, 6PB1, 6PD1 or 6PG1
Glass, porcelain or stoneware in steel, aluminum, wooden or fiberboard box: 6PA2, 6PB2, 6PC or 6PG2
Glass, porcelain or stoneware in expanded or solid plastic packaging: 6PH1 or 6PH2

§173.213 Non-bulk packagings for solid hazardous materials in Packing Group III.

(a) When §172.101 of this subchapter specifies that a solid hazardous material be packaged under this section, only non-bulk packagings prescribed in this section may be used for its transportation. Each package must conform to the general packaging requirements of subpart B of part 173, to the requirements of part 178 of this subchapter at the Packing Group I, II or III performance level, and to the requirements of the special provisions of column 7 of the §172.101 table.

(b) The following combination packagings are authorized:

Outer packagings:
Steel drum: 1A1 or 1A2
Aluminum drum: 1B1 or 1B2
Metal drum other than steel or aluminum: 1N1 or 1N2
Plywood drum: 1D
Fiber drum: 1G
Plastic drum: 1H1 or 1H2
Wooden barrel: 2C2
Steel jerrican: 3A1 or 3A2
Plastic jerrican: 3H1 or 3H2
Aluminum jerrican: 3B1 or 3B2
Steel box: 4A
Aluminum box: 4B
Natural wood box: 4C1 or 4C2
Plywood box: 4D
Reconstituted wood box: 4F
Fiberboard box: 4G
Solid plastic box: 4H2

Inner packagings:
Glass or earthenware receptacles
Plastic receptacles
Metal receptacles
Glass ampoules

(c) The following single packagings are authorized:
Steel drum: 1A1 or 1A2
Aluminum drum: 1B1 or 1B2
Plywood drum: 1D
Fiber drum: 1G
Plastic drum: 1H1 or 1H2
Metal drum other than steel or aluminum: 1N1 or 1N2
Wooden barrel: 2C1 or 2C2
Steel jerrican: 3A1 or 3A2
Plastic jerrican: 3H1 or 3H2
Aluminum jerrican: 3B1 or 3B2
Steel box with liner: 4A
Steel box: 4A
Aluminum box with liner: 4B
Natural wood box: 4C1
Natural wood box, sift proof: 4C2
Plywood box: 4D
Reconstituted wood box: 4F
Fiberboard box: 4G
Expanded plastic box: 4H1
Solid plastic box: 4H2
Bag, woven plastic: 5H1, 5H2 or 5H3
Bag, plastic film: 5H4
Bag, textile: 5L1, 5L2 or 5L3
Bag, paper, multiwall, water resistant: 5M2
Plastic receptacle in steel, aluminum, plywood, fiber or plastic drum: 6HA1, 6HB1, 6HD1, 6HG1 or 6HH1
Plastic receptacle in steel, aluminum, wooden, plywood or fiberboard box: 6HA2, 6HB2, 6HC, 6HD2 or 6HG2
Glass, porcelain or stoneware in steel, aluminum, plywood or fiber drum: 6PA1, 6PB1, 6PD1 or 6PG1
Glass, porcelain or stoneware in steel, aluminum, wooden or fiberboard box: 6PA2, 6PB2, 6PC or 6PG2
Glass, porcelain or stoneware in expanded or solid plastic packaging: 6PH1 or 6PH2

§173.214 Packagings which require approval by the Associate Administrator.

When §172.101 of this subchapter specifies that a hazardous material be packaged under this section, packagings and method of shipment must be approved by the Associate Administrator prior to the first shipment.

§173.216 Asbestos, blue, brown or white.

(a) Asbestos, blue, brown or white, includes each of the following hydrated mineral silicates: chrysolite, crocidolite, amosite, anthophyllite asbestos, tremolite asbestos, actinolite asbestos, and every product containing any of these materials.

(b) Asbestos which is immersed or fixed in a natural or artificial binder material (such as cement, plastic, asphalt, resins or mineral ore), and manufactured products containing asbestos are not subject to the requirements of this subchapter.

(c) Packagings for asbestos must conform to the general packaging requirements of subpart B of this part but need not conform to the requirements of part 178 of this subchapter. Asbestos must be offered for transportation and transported in —

(1) *Rigid, leaktight packagings,* such as metal, plastic or fiber drums, portable tanks, hopper-type rail cars, or hopper-type motor vehicles;

(2) *Bags or other* non-rigid packagings in closed freight containers, motor vehicles, or rail cars that are loaded by and for the exclusive use of the consignor and unloaded by the consignee;

(3) *Bags or other* non-rigid packagings which are dust and sift-proof. When transported by other than private carrier by highway, such packagings containing asbestos must be palletized and unitized by methods such as shrink-wrapping in plastic film or wrapping in fiberboard secured by strapping. Pallets need not be used during transportation by vessel for loads with slings that are unitized by methods such as shrink-wrapping, if the slings adequately and evenly support the loads and the unitizing method prevents shifting of the bags or other non-rigid packagings during conditions normally incident to transportation; or

(4) *Bags or other* non-rigid packagings which are dust and sift-proof in strong outside fiberboard or wooden boxes.

§173.217 Carbon dioxide, solid (dry ice).

(a) **Carbon dioxide, solid (dry ice),** when offered for transportation or transported by aircraft or water, must be packed in packagings designed and constructed to permit the release of carbon dioxide gas to prevent a build-up of pressure that could rupture the packagings. Packagings must conform to the general packaging requirements of subpart B of this part but need not conform to the requirements of part 178 of this subchapter. For each shipment by air exceeding 2.3 kg (5 lbs) per package, advance arrangements must be made between the shipper and each carrier.

(b) **Railroad cars and motor vehicles containing** solid carbon dioxide, when accepted for transportation on board ocean vessels, must be conspicuously marked on two sides "WARNING CO2 SOLID (DRY ICE)."

(c) **Other packagings containing solid carbon dioxide,** when offered or accepted for transportation on board ocean vessels, must be marked "CARBON DIOXIDE, SOLID — DO NOT STOW BELOW DECKS."

(d) **Not more than 200 kg (441 pounds)** of solid carbon dioxide may be transported in any one cargo compartment or bin on any aircraft except by specific and special written arrangement between the shipper and the aircraft operator.

(e) **Carbon dioxide, solid (dry ice)** is excepted from the shipping paper and certification requirements of this subchapter if the requirements of paragraphs (a) and (d) of this section are complied with and the package is marked "Carbon dioxide, solid" or "Dry ice" and marked with an indication that the material being refrigerated is used for diagnostic or treatment purposes (e.g., frozen medical specimens).

§173.218 Fish meal or fish scrap.

(a) **Except as provided in paragraph (b) of this section,** fish meal or fish scrap, containing at least 6 percent but not more than 12 percent water, is authorized for transportation by water only when packaged as follows:

(1) *Burlap (jute) bag;*

(2) *Multi-wall paper bag;*

(3) *Polyethylene-lined burlap or paper bag;*

(4) *Cargo tank;*

(5) *Portable tank;*

(6) *Rail car; or*

(7) *Freight container.*

(b) **Fish meal or fish scrap may not be offered** for transportation if the temperature of the material exceeds 49 °C (120 °F).

(c) **When fish scrap or fish meal is offered for transportation** by vessel in bulk in freight containers, the fish meal must contain at least 100 ppm of anti-oxident (ethoxyquin) at the time of shipment.

§173.219 Life-saving appliances.

(a) **A life-saving appliance, self-inflating or non-self-inflating,** containing small quantities of hazardous materials which are required as part of the life-saving appliance must conform to the requirements of this section. Packagings must conform to the general packaging requirements of subpart B of this part but need not conform to the requirements of part 178 of this subchapter.

(b) **Hazardous materials therein must be packaged as follows:**

(1) *Nonflammable compressed gases* must be packaged in cylinders in accordance with the requirements of this subchapter;

(2) *Smoke and illumination* signal flares must be in plastic or fiberboard receptacles;

(3) *Strike-anywhere matches* must be cushioned to prevent movement or friction in a cylindrical metal or composition receptacle with a screw-type closure;

(4) *Flammable liquids* must be in strong inner packagings in a repair kit; and

(5) *Limited quantities* of other hazardous materials are permitted if packaged in accordance with the requirements of this subchapter.

(c) **Materials therein not subject to the requirements** of this subchapter which are an integral part of the life-saving appliance must be packaged in a strong fiberglass kit case which is overpacked in a waterproof fiberboard packaging, or be packaged in other strong outer packagings.

§173.220 Internal combustion engines, self-propelled vehicles, mechanical equipment containing internal combustion engines, and battery powered vehicles or equipment.

(a) **Applicability.** An internal combustion engine, self-propelled vehicle, mechanized equipment containing an internal combustion engine, or a battery powered vehicle or equipment is subject to the requirements of this subchapter when transported as cargo on a transport vehicle, vessel, or aircraft if —

(1) *The engine or fuel tank* contains a liquid or gaseous fuel. An engine may be considered as not containing fuel when the fuel tank, engine components, and fuel lines have been completely drained, sufficiently cleaned of residue, and purged of vapors to remove any potential hazard and the engine when held in any orientation will not release any liquid fuel;

(2) *It is equipped* with a wet electric storage battery other than a non-spillable battery; or

(3) *Except as provided* in paragraph (d)(1) of this section, it contains other hazardous materials subject to the requirements of this subchapter.

(b) **Requirements.** Unless otherwise excepted in paragraph (b)(4) of this section, vehicles, engines and equipment are subject to the following requirements:

(1) *Flammable liquid fuel.* A fuel tank containing a flammable liquid fuel must be drained and securely closed, except that up to 500 mL (17 ounces) of residual fuel may remain in the tank, engine components, or fuel lines provided they are securely closed to prevent leakage of fuel during transportation. Self-propelled vehicles containing diesel fuel are excepted from the requirement to drain the fuel tanks, provided that sufficient ullage space has been left inside the tank to allow fuel expansion without leakage, and the tank caps are securely closed.

(2) *Flammable liquefied* or compressed gas fuel. Fuel tanks and fuel systems containing flammable liquefied or compressed gas fuel must be securely closed. For transportation by water, the requirements of §§176.78(k) and 176.905 of this subchapter apply. For transportation by air, the fuel tank and fuel system must be emptied and securely closed or must be removed, packaged and transported in accordance the requirements of this subchapter.

(3) *Truck bodies or trailers on flat* cars — flammable liquid or gas powered. Truck bodies or trailers with automatic heating or refrigerating equipment of the flammable liquid type may be shipped with fuel tanks filled and equipment operating or inoperative, when used for the transportation of other freight and loaded on flat cars as part of a joint rail and highway movement, provided the equipment and fuel supply conform to the requirements of §177.834(l) of this subchapter.

(4) *Modal exceptions.* Quantities of flammable liquid fuel greater than 500 mL (17 ounces) may remain in self-propelled vehicles and mechanical equipment only under the following conditions:

(i) *For transportation* by motor vehicle or rail car, the fuel tanks must be securely closed.

(ii) *For transportation by vessel,* the shipment must conform to §176.905 of this subchapter.

(iii) *For transportation by aircraft* designed or modified for vehicle ferry operations, the shipment must conform to §175.305 of this subchapter.

(c) **Wet battery powered or installed.** Wet batteries must be securely installed and fastened in an upright position. Batteries must be protected against short circuits and leakage or removed and packaged separately under §173.159. Battery powered vehicles, machinery or equipment including battery powered wheelchairs and mobility aids are excepted from the requirements of this subchapter when transported by rail, highway or vessel.

(d) **Other hazardous materials.**

(1) *Items of equipment* containing hazardous materials, fire extinguishers, compressed gas accumulators, safety devices and other

hazardous materials which are integral components of the motor vehicle, engine or mechanical equipment and are necessary for the operation of the vehicle, engine or equipment, or for the safety of its operator or passengers must be securely installed in the motor vehicle, engine or mechanical equipment. Such items are not otherwise subject to the requirements of this subchapter.

(2) *Other hazardous materials* must be packaged and transported in accordance with the requirements of this subchapter.

(e) **Exceptions.** Except as provided in paragraph (d)(2) of this section, shipments made under the provisions of this section —

(1) *Are not subject* to any other requirements of this subchapter, for transportation by motor vehicle or rail car; and

(2) *Are not subject* to the requirements of subparts D, E and F (marking, labeling and placarding, respectively) of part 172 of this subchapter or §172.604 of this subchapter (emergency response telephone number) for transportation by vessel or aircraft. For transportation by aircraft, all other applicable requirements of this subchapter, including shipping papers, emergency response information, notification of pilot-in-command, general packaging requirements, and the requirements specified in §173.27 must be met. For transportation by vessel, additional exceptions are specified in §176.905 of this subchapter.

§173.221 Polymeric beads, expandable and Plastic molding compound.

(a) **Non-bulk shipments of Polymeric beads** (or granules), expandable, evolving flammable vapor and Plastic molding compound in dough, sheet or extruded rope form, evolving flammable vapor must be packed in: wooden (4C1 or 4C2), plywood (4D), fiberboard (4G), reconstituted wood (4F) boxes, plywood drums (1D) or fiber drums (1G) with sealed inner plastic liners; in vapor tight metal or plastic drums (1A1, 1A2, 1B1, 1B2, 1H1 or 1H2); or packed in non-specification packagings when transported in dedicated vehicles or freight containers. The packagings need not conform to the requirements for package testing in part 178 of this subchapter, but must be capable of containing any evolving gases from the contents during normal conditions of transportation.

(b) **Bulk shipments of Polymeric beads** (or granules), expandable, evolving flammable vapor or Plastic molding compounds in dough, sheet or extruded rope, evolving flammable vapor may be packed in non-specification bulk packagings. Except for transportation by highway and rail, bulk packagings must be capable of containing any gases evolving from the contents during normal conditions of transportation.

§173.222 Dangerous goods in equipment, machinery, or apparatus.

Hazardous materials in machinery or apparatus are excepted from the specification packaging requirements of this subchapter when packaged according to this section. Hazardous materials in machinery or apparatus must be packaged in strong outer packagings, unless the receptacles containing the hazardous materials are afforded adequate protection by the construction of the machinery or apparatus. Each package must conform to the packaging requirements of subpart B of this part, except for the requirements in §§173.24(a)(1) and 173.27(e), and the following requirements:

(a) **If the equipment, machinery, or apparatus** contains more than one hazardous material, the materials must not be capable of reacting dangerously together.

(b) **The nature of the containment must be as follows —**

(1) *Damage to the receptacles* containing the hazardous materials during transport is unlikely. However, in the event of damage to the receptacles containing the hazardous materials, no leakage of the hazardous materials from the equipment, machinery or apparatus is possible. A leakproof liner may be used to satisfy this requirement.

(2) *Receptacles containing* hazardous materials must be secured and cushioned so as to prevent their breakage or leakage and so as to control their movement within the equipment, machinery or apparatus during normal conditions of transportation. Cushioning material must not react dangerously with the content of the receptacles. Any leakage of the contents must not substantially impair the protective properties of the cushioning material.

(3) *Receptacles for gases,* their contents and filling densities must conform to the applicable requirements of this subchapter, unless otherwise approved by the Associate Administrator.

(c) **The total net quantity of hazardous materials** contained in one item of equipment, machinery or apparatus must not exceed the following:

(1) *1 kg (2.2 pounds) in the case of solids;*

(2) *0.5 L (0.3 gallons) in the case of liquids;*

(3) *0.5 kg (1.1 pounds) in the case of Division 2.2 gases; and*

(4) *A total quantity* of not more than the aggregate of that permitted in paragraphs (c)(1) through (c)(3) of this section, for each category of material in the package, when a package contains hazardous materials in two or more of the categories in paragraphs (c)(1) through (c)(3) of this section.

(d) **When a package contains hazardous materials** in two or more of the categories listed in paragraphs (c)(1) through (c)(3) of this section, the total quantity required by §172.202(c) of this subchapter to be entered on the shipping paper, must be the aggregate quantity of all hazardous materials, expressed as net mass.

§173.224 Packaging and control and emergency temperatures for self-reactive materials.

(a) **General.** When the §172.101 table of this subchapter specifies that a Division 4.1 material be packaged in accordance with this section, only packagings which conform to the provisions of this section may be used. Each packaging must conform to the general packaging requirements of subpart B of this part and the applicable requirements of part 178 of this subchapter. Non-bulk packagings must meet Packing Group II performance levels. To avoid unnecessary confinement, metallic non-bulk packagings meeting Packing Group I are not authorized. Self-reactive materials which require temperature control are subject to the provisions of §173.21(f). Packagings required to bear a Class 1 subsidiary label must conform to §§173.60 through 173.62.

(b) **Self-Reactive Materials Table.** The Self-Reactive Materials Table specifies, by technical name, those self-reactive materials that are authorized for transportation and not subject to the approval provisions of §173.124(a)(2)(iii). A self-reactive material identified by technical name in the following table is authorized for transportation only if it conforms to all applicable provisions of the table. The column headings of the Self-Reactive Materials Table are as follows:

(1) *Technical name.* Column 1 specifies the technical name.

(2) *ID number.* Column 2 specifies the identification number which is used to identify the proper shipping name in the §172.101 table.

(3) *Concentration of self-reactive material.* Column 3 specifies the concentration (percent) limitations, if any, in mixtures or solutions for the self-reactive material. Limitations are given as minimums, maximums, or a range, as appropriate. A range includes the lower and upper limits (i.e., "53-100" means from, and including, 53 percent to, and including 100 percent).

(4) *Packing method.* Column 4 specifies the highest packing method which is authorized for the self-reactive material. A packing method corresponding to a smaller package size may be used, but a packing method corresponding to a larger package size may not be used. The Table of Packing Methods in §173.225(d) defines the packing methods. Bulk packagings are authorized as specified in §173.225(d) for Type F self-reactive substances. Additional bulk packagings are authorized if approved by the Associate Administrator.

(5) *Control temperature.* Column 5 specifies the control temperature in °C. Temperatures are specified only when temperature controls are required (see §173.21(f)).

(6) *Emergency temperature.* Column 6 specifies the emergency temperature in °C. Temperatures are specified only when temperature controls are required (see §173.21(f)).

(7) *Notes.* Column 7 specifies other applicable provisions, as set forth in notes following the table.

Self-Reactive Materials Table

Self-reactive substance (1)	Identification No. (2)	Concentration — (%) (3)	Packing method (4)	Control temperature — (°C) (5)	Emergency temperature (6)	Notes (7)
Azodicarbonamide formulation type B, temperature controlled	3232	< 100	OP5			1
Azodicarbonamide formulation type C	3224	< 100	OP6			
Azodicarbonamide formulation type C, temperature controlled	3234	< 100	OP6			1
Azodicarbonamide formulation type D	3226	< 100	OP7			
Azodicarbonamide formulation type D, temperature controlled	3236	< 100	OP7			1
2,2'-Azodi(2,4-dimethyl-4-methoxyvaleronitrile)	3236	100	OP7	-5	+5	
2,2'-Azodi(2,4-dimethylvaleronitrile)	3236	100	OP7	+10	+15	
2,2'-Azodi(ethyl 2-methylpropionate)	3235	100	OP7	+20	+25	
1,1-Azodi(hexahydrobenzonitrile)	3226	100	OP7			
2,2-Azodi(isobutyronitrile)	3234	100	OP6	+40	+45	
2,2'-Azodi(isobutyronitrile) as a water based paste	3224	≤ 50%	OP6			
2,2-Azodi(2-methylbutyronitrile)	3236	100	OP7	+35	+40	
Benzene-1,3-disulphohydrazide, as a paste	3226	52	OP7			
Benzene sulphohydrazide	3226	100	OP7			
4-(Benzyl(ethyl)amino)-3-ethoxybenzenediazonium zinc chloride	3226	100	OP7			
4-(Benzyl(methyl)amino)-3-ethoxybenzenediazonium zinc chloride	3236	100	OP7	+40	+45	
3-Chloro-4-diethylaminobenzenediazonium zinc chloride	3226	100	OP7			
2-Diazo-1-Naphthol-4-sulphochloride	3222	100	OP5			
2-Diazo-1-Naphthol-5-sulphochloride	3222	100	OP5			
2,5-Diethoxy-4-morpholinobenzenediazonium zinc chloride	3236	67-100	OP7	+35	+40	
2,5-Diethoxy-4-morpholinobenzenediazonium zinc chloride	3236	66	OP7	+40	+45	
2,5-Diethoxy-4-morpholinobenzenediazonium tetrafluoroborate	3236	100	OP7	+30	+35	
2,5-Diethoxy-4-(phenylsulphonyl)benzenediazonium zinc chloride	3236	67	OP7	+40	+45	
Diethylene glycol bis(allyl carbonate) + Diisopropylperoxydicarbonate	3237	≥ 88 + ≤ 12	OP8	-10	0	
2,5-Dimethoxy-4-(4-methylphenylsulphony)benzenediazonium zinc chloride	3236	79	OP7	+40	+45	
4-Dimethylamino-6-(2-dimethylaminoethoxy)toluene-2-diazonium zinc chloride	3236	100	OP7	+40	+45	
N,N'-Dinitroso-N, N'-dimethyl-terephthalamide, as a paste	3224	72	OP6			
N,N'-Dinitrosopentamethylenetetramine	3224	82	OP6			2
Diphenyloxide-4,4'-disulphohydrazide	3226	100	OP7			
4-Dipropylaminobenzenediazonium zinc chloride	3226	100	OP7			
2-(N,N-Ethoxycarbonylphenylamino)-3-methoxy-4-(N-methyl-N-cyclohexylamino) benzenediazonium zinc chloride	3236	63-92	OP7	+40	+45	
2-(N,N-Ethoxycarbonylphenylamino)-3-methoxy-4-(N-methyl-N-cyclohexylamino) benzenediazonium zinc chloride	3236	62	OP7	+35	+40	
N-Formyl-2-(nitromethylene)-1,3-perhydrothiazine	3236	100	OP7	+45	+50	
2-(2-Hydroxyethoxy)-1-(pyrrolidin-1-yl) benzene-4-diazonium zinc chloride	3236	100	OP7	+45	+50	
3-(2-Hydroxyethoxy)-4-(pyrrolidin-1-yl) benzenediazonium zinc chloride	3236	100	OP7	+40	+45	
2-(N,N-Methylaminoethylcarbonyl)-4-(3,4-dimethyl-phenylsulphonyl) benzene diazonium zinc chloride	3236	96	OP7	+45	+50	
4-Methylbenzenesulphonylhydrazide	3226	100	OP7			
3-Methyl-4-(pyrrolidin-1-yl) benzenediazonium tetrafluoroborate	3234	95	OP6	+45	+50	
4-Nitrosophenol	3236	100	OP7	+35	+40	
Self-reactive liquid, sample	3223		OP2			3
Self-reactive liquid, sample, temperature control	3233		OP2			3
Self-reactive solid, sample	3224		OP2			3
Self-reactive solid, sample, temperature control	3234		OP2			3
Sodium 2-diazo-1-naphthol-4-sulphonate	3226	100	OP7			
Sodium 2-diazo-1-naphthol-5-sulphonate	3226	100	OP7			
Tetramine palladium (II) nitrate	3234	100	OP6	+30	+35	

NOTES:
1. The emergency and control temperatures must be determined in accordance with §173.21(f).
2. With a compatible diluent having a boiling point of not less than 150 °C.
3. Samples may only be offered for transportation under the provisions of paragraph(c)(3) of this section.

(c) New self-reactive materials, formulations and samples.

(1) *Except as provided* for samples in paragraph (c)(3) of this section, no person may offer, accept for transportation, or transport a self-reactive material which is not identified by technical name in the Self-Reactive Materials Table of this section, or a formulation of one or more self-reactive materials which are identified by technical name in the table, unless the self-reactive material is assigned a generic type and shipping description and is approved by the Associate Administrator under the provisions of §173.124(a)(2)(iii).

(2) *Except as provided* by an approval issued under §173.124(a)(2)(iii), intermediate bulk and bulk packagings are not authorized.

(3) *Samples.* Samples of new self-reactive materials or new formulations of self-reactive materials identified in the Self-Reactive Materials Table in paragraph (b) of this section, for which complete test data are not available, and which are to be transported for further testing or product evaluation, may be assigned an appropriate shipping description for Self-reactive materials Type C, packaged and offered for transportation under the following conditions:

(i) *Data available* to the person offering the material for transportation must indicate that the sample would pose a level of hazard no greater than that of a self-reactive material Type B and that the control temperature, if any, is sufficiently low to prevent any dangerous decomposition and sufficiently high to prevent any dangerous phase separation;

(ii) *The sample* must be packaged in accordance with packing method OP2;

(iii) *Packages of* the self-reactive material may be offered for transportation and transported in a quantity not to exceed 10 kg (22 pounds) per transport vehicle; and

(iv) *One of the following shipping descriptions must be assigned:*

[A] Self-reactive, liquid, type C, 4.1, UN3223.

[B] Self-reactive, solid, type C, 4.1, UN3224.

[C] Self-reactive, liquid, type C, temperature controlled, 4.1, UN3233.

[D] Self-reactive, solid, type C, temperature controlled, 4.1, UN3234.

§173.225 Packaging requirements and other provisions for organic peroxides.

(a) General. When the §172.101 table specifies that an organic peroxide be packaged under this section, the organic peroxide must be packaged and offered for transportation in accordance with the provisions of this section. Each packaging must conform to the general requirements of subpart B of part 173 and to the applicable requirements of part 178 of this subchapter. Non-bulk packagings must meet Packing Group II performance levels. To avoid unnecessary confinement, metallic non-bulk packagings meeting Packing Group I are not authorized. No used material, other than production residues or regrind from the same production process, may be used in plastic packagings. Organic peroxides which require temperature control are subject to the provisions of §173.21(f).

(b) Organic peroxides table. The following Organic Peroxides Table specifies, by technical name, those organic peroxides that are authorized for transportation and not subject to the approval provisions of §173.128 of this part. An organic peroxide identified by technical name in the following table is authorized for transportation only if it conforms to all applicable provisions of the table. For an organic peroxide not identified in the table by technical name or a formulation of identified organic peroxides, the provisions of paragraph (c) of §173.128 apply. The column headings of the Organic Peroxides Table are as follows:

(1) *Technical name.* The first column specifies the technical name.

(2) *ID number.* The second column specifies the identification (ID) number which is used to identify the proper shipping name in the §172.101 table. The word "EXEMPT" appearing in the column denotes that the material is not regulated as an organic peroxide.

(3) *Concentration of organic peroxide.* The third column specifies concentration (mass percent) limitations, if any, in mixtures or solutions for the organic peroxide. Limitations are given as minimums, maximums, or a range, as appropriate. A range includes the lower and upper limits (i.e., "53-100" means from, and including, 53 percent to, and including 100 percent). See introductory paragraph of §172.203(k) of this subchapter for additional description requirements for an organic peroxide that may qualify for more than one generic listing, depending on its concentration.

(4) *Concentration of diluents.* The fourth column specifies the type and concentration (mass percent) of diluent or inert solid, when required. Other types and concentrations of diluents may be authorized if approved by the Associate Administrator.

(i) *The required* mass percent of "Diluent type A" is specified in column 4a. A diluent type A is an organic liquid that does not detrimentally affect the thermal stability or increase the hazard of the organic peroxide and with a boiling point not less than 150 °C at atmospheric pressure. Type A diluents may be used for desensitizing all organic peroxides.

(ii) *The required* mass percent of "Diluent type B" is specified in column 4b. A diluent type B is an organic liquid which is compatible with the organic peroxide and which has a boiling point, at atmospheric pressure, of less than 150 °C (302 °F) but at least 60 °C (140 °F), and a flash point greater than 5 °C (41 °F). Type B diluents may be used for desensitizing all organic peroxides provided that the boiling point is at least 60 °C (140 °F) above the SADT of the peroxide in a 50 kg (110 lbs) package. A type A diluent may be used to replace a type B diluent in equal concentration.

(iii) *The required* mass percent of "Inert solid" is specified in column 4c. An inert solid is a solid that does not detrimentally affect the thermal stability or increase the hazard of the organic peroxide.

(5) *Concentration of water.* Column 5 specifies, in mass percent, the minimum amount of water, if any, which must be in formulation.

(6) *Packing method.* Column 6 specifies the highest packing method (largest packaging capacity) authorized for the organic peroxide. Lower numbered packing methods (smaller packaging capacities) are also authorized. For example, if OP3 is specified, then OP2 and OP1 are also authorized. When an IBC or bulk packaging is authorized and meets the requirements of paragraph (e) of this section, lower control temperatures than those specified for non-bulk packagings are required. The Table of Packing Methods in paragraph (d) of this section defines the non-bulk packing methods.

(7) *Temperatures.* Column 7a specifies the control temperature. Column 7b specifies the emergency temperature. Temperatures are specified only when temperature controls are required. (See §173.21(f)).

(8) *Notes.* Column 8 specifies other applicable provisions, as set forth in notes following the table.

Organic Peroxide Table

Technical name	ID number	Concentration (mass %)	Diluent (mass %)			Water (mass %)	Packing method	Temperature (°C)		Notes
			A	B	I			Control	Emergency	
(1)	(2)	(3)	(4a)	(4b)	(4c)	(5)	(6)	(7a)	(7b)	(8)
Acetyl acetone peroxide	UN3105	≤ 42	≥ 48			≥ 8	OP7			2
Acetyl acetone peroxide [as a paste]	UN3106	≤ 32					OP7			21
Acetyl benzoyl peroxide	UN3105	≤ 45	≥ 55				OP7			
Acetyl cyclohexanesulfonyl peroxide	UN3112	≤ 82				≥ 12	OP4	-10	0	
Acetyl cyclohexanesulfonyl peroxide	UN3115	≤ 32		≥ 68			OP7	-10	0	
tert-Amyl hydroperoxide	UN3107	≤ 88	≥ 6			≥ 6	OP8			
tert-Amyl peroxyacetate	UN3107	≤ 62	≥ 38				OP8			
tert-Amyl peroxybenzoate	UN3103	≤ 100					OP5			
tert-Amyl peroxy-2-ethylhexanoate	UN3115	≤ 100					OP7	+20	+25	
tert-Amyl peroxy-2-ethylhexyl carbonate	UN3105	≤ 100					OP7			
tert-Amyl peroxyneodecanoate	UN3115	≤ 77		≥ 23			OP7	0	+10	
tert-Amyl peroxypivalate	UN3113	≤ 77		≥ 23			OP5	+10	+15	

Organic Peroxide Table

Technical name	ID number	Concen- tration (mass %)	Diluent (mass %)			Water (mass %)	Packing method	Temperature (°C)		Notes
			A	B	I			Control	Emer- gency	
(1)	(2)	(3)	(4a)	(4b)	(4c)	(5)	(6)	(7a)	(7b)	(8)
tert-Amylperoxy-3,5,5-trimethylhexanoate	UN3101	≤ 100					OP5			
tert-Butyl cumyl peroxide	UN3105	>42-100					OP7			1, 9
tert-Butyl cumyl peroxide	UN3106	≤ 42			≥ 58		OP7			1, 9
n-Butyl-4,4-di-(tert-butylperoxy)valerate	UN3103	>52-100					OP5			
n-Butyl-4,4-di-(tert-butylperoxy)valerate	UN3106	≤ 52			≥ 48		OP7			
n-Butyl-4,4-di-(tert-butylperoxy)valerate	UN3108	≤ 42			≥ 58		OP8			
tert-Butyl hydroperoxide	UN3103	>79-90				≥ 10	OP5			13
tert-Butyl hydroperoxide	UN3105	≤ 80	≥ 20				OP7			4, 13
tert-Butyl hydroperoxide	UN3107	≤ 79				> 14	OP8			13, 16
tert-Butyl hydroperoxide	UN3109	≤ 72				≥ 28	OP8			13
tert-Butyl hydroperoxide [and] Di-tert-butylperoxide	UN3103	< 82 + > 9				≥ 7	OP5			13
tert-Butyl monoperoxymaleate	UN3102	>52-100					OP5			
tert-Butyl monoperoxymaleate	UN3103	≤ 52	≥ 48				OP6			
tert-Butyl monoperoxymaleate	UN3108	≤ 52			≥ 48		OP8			
tert-Butyl monoperoxymaleate [as a paste]	UN3108	≤ 52					OP8			
tert-Butyl monoperoxymaleate [as a paste]	UN3110	≤ 42					OP8			
tert-Butyl monoperoxyphthalate	UN3102	≤ 100					OP5			
tert-Butyl peroxyacetate	UN3101	>52-77	≥ 23				OP5			
tert-Butyl peroxyacetate	UN3103	>32-52	≥ 48				OP6			
tert-Butyl peroxyacetate	UN3109	≤ 32	≥ 68				OP8			
tert-Butyl peroxyacetate	UN3119	≤ 32		≥ 68			Bulk	+30	+35	
tert-Butyl peroxyacetate	UN3109	≤ 22		≥ 78			OP8			14
tert-Butyl peroxybenzoate	UN3103	>77-100	≤ 23				OP5			
tert-Butyl peroxybenzoate	UN3105	>52-77	≥ 23				OP7			1
tert-Butyl peroxybenzoate	UN3106	≤ 52			≤ 48		OP7			
tert-Butyl peroxybutyl fumarate	UN3105	≤ 52	≥ 48				OP7			
tert-Butyl peroxycrotonate	UN3105	≤ 77	≥ 23				OP7			
tert-Butyl peroxydiethylacetate	UN3113	≤ 100					OP5	+20	+25	
tert-Butyl peroxydiethylacetate [and] tert-Butyl peroxybenzoate	UN3105	≤ 33 + ≤ 33	≥ 33				OP7			
tert-Butyl peroxy-2-ethylhexanoate	UN3113	>52-100					OP6	+20	+25	
tert-Butyl peroxy-2-ethylhexanoate	UN3117	>32-52		≥ 48			OP8	+30	+35	
tert-Butyl peroxy-2-ethylhexanoate	UN3118	≤ 52			≥ 48		OP8	+20	+25	
tert-Butyl peroxy-2-ethylhexanoate	UN3119	≤ 32		≥ 68			OP8	+40	+45	
tert-Butyl peroxy-2-ethylhexanoate	UN3119	≤ 32		≥ 68			IBC	+30	+35	
tert-Butyl peroxy-2-ethylhexanoate	UN3119	≤ 32		≥ 68			Bulk	+15	+20	14
tert-Butyl peroxyneodecanoate [as a stable dispersion in water]	UN3117	≤ 52					OP8	0	+10	
tert-Butyl peroxyneodecanoate [as a stable dispersion in water]	UN3119	≤ 42					IBC	-5	+5	
tert-Butyl peroxy-2-ethylhexanoate [and] 2,2-di-(tert-Butylperoxy) butane	UN3115	≤ 31 + ≤ 36		≥33			OP7	+35	+40	
tert-Butyl peroxy-2-ethylhexanoate [and] 2,2-di-(tert-Butylperoxy) butane	UN3106	≤ 12 + ≤ 14	≥ 14		≥ 60		OP7			
tert-Butyl peroxy-2-ethylhexylcarbonate	UN3105	≤ 100					OP7			
tert-Butyl peroxyisobutyrate	UN3111	>52-77		≥ 23			OP5	+15	+20	
tert-Butyl peroxyisobutyrate	UN3115	≤ 52		≥ 48			OP7	+15	+20	
tert-Butylperoxy isopropylcarbonate	UN3103	≤ 77	≥ 23				OP5			
1-(2-tert-Butylperoxy isopropyl)-3-isopropenylbenzene	UN3105	≤ 77	≥ 23				OP7			
1-(2-tert-Butylperoxy isopropyl)-3-isopropenylbenzene	UN3108	≤ 42			≥ 58		OP8			
tert-Butyl peroxy-2-methylbenzoate	UN3103	≤ 100					OP5			
tert-Butyl peroxyneodecanoate	UN3115	>77-100					OP7	-5	+5	
tert-Butyl peroxyneodecanoate	UN3115	≤ 77		≥ 23			OP7	0	+10	
tert-Butyl peroxyneodecanoate [as a stable dispersion in water (frozen)]	UN3118	≤ 42					OP8	0	+10	
tert-Butyl peroxyneodecanoate	UN3119	≤ 32	≥ 68				IBC	0	+10	
tert-Butyl peroxyneoheptanoate	UN3115	≤ 77	≥ 23				OP7	0	+10	
3-tert-Butylperoxy-3-phenylphthalide	UN3106	≤ 100					OP7			
tert-Butyl peroxypivalate	UN3113	>67-77	≥ 23				OP5	0	+10	
tert-Butyl peroxypivalate	UN3115	≤ 67		≥ 33			OP7	0	+10	
tert-Butyl peroxypivalate	UN3119	≤ 27		≥ 73			Bulk	+5	+10	14
tert-Butyl peroxypivalate	UN3119	≤ 27		≥ 73			OP8	+30	+35	
tert-Butyl peroxypivalate	UN3119	≤ 27		≥ 73			IBC	+10	+15	

Organic Peroxide Table

Technical name	ID number	Concen-tration (mass %)	Diluent (mass %)			Water (mass %)	Packing method	Temperature (°C)		Notes
			A	B	I			Control	Emer-gency	
(1)	(2)	(3)	(4a)	(4b)	(4c)	(5)	(6)	(7a)	(7b)	(8)
tert-Butylperoxy stearylcarbonate	UN3106	≤ 100					OP7			
tert-Butyl peroxy-3,5,5-trimethylhexanoate	UN3105	>32-100					OP7			
tert-Butyl peroxy-3,5,5-trimethylhexanoate	UN3109	≤ 32	≥ 68				OP8			
tert-Butyl peroxy-3,5,5-trimethylhexanoate	UN3119	≤ 32		≥ 68			Bulk	+35	+40	14
3-Chloroperoxybenzoic acid	UN3102	>57-86			≥ 14		OP1			
3-Chloroperoxybenzoic acid	UN3106	≤ 77			≥ 6	≥ 17	OP7			
3-Chloroperoxybenzoic acid	UN3106	≤ 57			≥ 3	≥ 40	OP7			
Cumyl hydroperoxide	UN3107	>90-98	≤ 10				OP8			13
Cumyl hydroperoxide	UN3109	≤ 90	≥ 10				OP8			13, 15
Cumyl peroxyneodecanoate	UN3115	≤ 77		≥ 23			OP7	-10	0	
Cumyl peroxyneoheptanoate	UN3115	≤ 77	≥ 23				OP7	-10	0	
Cumyl peroxyneodecanoate [as a stable dispersion in water]	UN3119	≤ 52					OP8	-10	0	
Cumyl peroxyneodecanoate [as a stable dispersion in water]	UN3119	≤ 52					IBC	-15	-5	
Cumyl peroxypivalate	UN3115	≤ 77		≥ 23			OP7	-5	+5	
Cyclohexanone peroxide(s)	UN3104	≤ 91				≥ 9	OP6			13
Cyclohexanone peroxide(s)	UN3105	≤ 72	≥ 28				OP7			5
Cyclohexanone peroxide(s) [as a paste]	UN3106	≤ 72					OP7			5, 21
Cyclohexanone peroxide(s)	Exempt	≤ 32			≥ 68		Exempt			
Diacetone alcohol peroxides	UN3115	≤ 57		≥ 26		≥ 8	OP7	+40	+45	5
Diacetyl peroxide	UN3115	≤ 27		≥ 73			OP7	+20	+25	8,13
Di-tert-amyl peroxide	UN3107	≤ 100					OP8			
1,1-Di-(tert-amylperoxy)cyclohexane	UN3103	≤ 82	≥ 18				OP6			
Dibenzoyl peroxide	UN3102	>51-100			≤ 48		OP2			3
Dibenzoyl peroxide	UN3102	>77-94				≥ 6	OP4			3
Dibenzoyl peroxide	UN3104	≤ 77				≥ 23	OP6			
Dibenzoyl peroxide	UN3106	≤ 62			≥ 28	≥ 10	OP7			
Dibenzoyl peroxide [as a paste]	UN3106	>52-62					OP7			21
Dibenzoyl peroxide [as a paste]	UN3108	≤ 56.5				≥ 15	OP8			
Dibenzoyl peroxide	UN3106	>35-52			≥ 48		OP7			
Dibenzoyl peroxide [as a paste]	UN3108	≤ 52					OP8			21
Dibenzoyl peroxide	UN3107	>36-42	≥ 18			≤ 40	OP8			
Dibenzoyl peroxide	UN3107	>36-42	≥ 58				OP8			
Dibenzoyl peroxide [as a stable dispersion in water]	UN3109	≤ 42					OP8			
Dibenzoyl peroxide	Exempt	≤ 35			≥ 65		Exempt			
Dibenzyl peroxydicarbonate	UN3112	≤ 87				≥ 13	OP5	+25	+30	
Di-(4-tert-butylcyclohexyl) peroxydicarbonate	UN3114	≤ 100					OP6	+30	+35	
Di-(4-tert-butylcyclohexyl) peroxydicarbonate [as a stable dispersion in water]	UN3119	≤ 42					OP8	+30	+35	
Di-tert-butyl peroxide	UN3107	>32-100					OP8			
Di-tert-butyl peroxide	UN3109	≤ 52		≥ 48			OP8			24
Di-tert-butyl peroxyazelate	UN3105	≤ 52	≥ 48				OP7			
2,2-Di-(tert-butylperoxy) butane	UN3103	≤ 52	≥ 48				OP6			
1,1-Di-(tert-butylperoxy) cyclohexane	UN3101	>80-100					OP5			
1,1-Di-(tert-butylperoxy) cyclohexane	UN3103	>52-80	≥ 20				OP5			
1,1-Di-(tert-butylperoxy) cyclohexane	UN3105	≤ 52	≥ 48				OP7			
1,1-Di-(tert-butylperoxy) cyclohexane	UN3106	≤ 42	≥ 13		≥ 45		OP7			
1,1-Di-(tert-butylperoxy) cyclohexane	UN3109	≤ 42	≥ 58				OP8			
1,1-Di-(tert-butylperoxy) cyclohexane	UN3107	≤ 27	≥ 36				OP8			22
1,1-Di-(tert-butylperoxy) cyclohexane	UN3109	≤ 25	≥ 25	≥ 50			OP8			
1,1-Di-(tert-butylperoxy) cyclohexane	UN3109	≤ 13	≥ 13	≥ 74			OP8			
Di-n-butyl peroxydicarbonate	UN3115	>27-52		≥ 48			OP7	-15	-5	
Di-n-butyl peroxydicarbonate [as a stable dispersion in water (frozen)]	UN3118	≤ 42					OP8	-15	-5	
Di-n-butyl peroxydicarbonate	UN3117	≤ 27		≥ 73			OP8	-10	0	
Di-sec-butyl peroxydicarbonate	UN3113	>52-100					OP4	-20	-10	6
Di-sec-butyl peroxydicarbonate	UN3115	≤ 52		≥ 48			OP7	-15	-5	
Di-(2-tert-butylperoxyisopropyl) benzene(s)	UN3106	>42-100			≤ 57		OP7			1, 9
Di-(2-tert-butylperoxyisopropyl) benzene(s)	Exempt	≤ 42			≥ 58		Exempt			
Di-(tert-butylperoxy) phthalate	UN3105	>42-52	≥ 48				OP7			

Organic Peroxide Table

Technical name	ID number	Concentration (mass %)	Diluent (mass %)			Water (mass %)	Packing method	Temperature (°C)		Notes
			A	B	I			Control	Emergency	
(1)	(2)	(3)	(4a)	(4b)	(4c)	(5)	(6)	(7a)	(7b)	(8)
Di-(tert-butylperoxy) phthalate [as a paste]	UN3106	≤ 52					OP7			21
Di-(tert-butylperoxy) phthalate	UN3107	≤ 42	≥ 58				OP8			
2,2-Di-(tert-butylperoxy) propane	UN3105	≤ 52	≥ 48				OP7			
2,2-Di-(tert-butylperoxy) propane	UN3106	≤ 42	≥ 13		≥ 45		OP7			
1,1-Di-(tert-butylperoxy)-3,3,5-trimethylcyclohexane	UN3101	>90-100					OP5			
1,1-Di-(tert-butylperoxy)-3,3,5-trimethylcyclohexane	UN3103	>57-90	≥ 10				OP5			
1,1-Di-(tert-butylperoxy)-3,3,5-trimethylcyclohexane	UN3105	≤ 77		≥ 23			OP7			
1,1-Di-(tert-butylperoxy)-3,3,5-trimethylcyclohexane	UN3106	≤ 57			≥ 43		OP7			
1,1-Di-(tert-butylperoxy)-3,3,5-trimethylcyclohexane	UN3107	≤ 57	≥ 43				OP8			
1,1-Di-(tert-butylperoxy)-3,3,5-trimethylcyclohexane	UN3107	≤ 32	≥ 26	≥ 42			OP8			
Dicetyl peroxydicarbonate	UN3116	≤ 100					OP7	+30	+35	
Dicetyl peroxydicarbonate [as a stable dispersion in water]	UN3119	≤ 42					OP8	+30	+35	
Di-4-chlorobenzoyl peroxide	UN3102	≤ 77				≥ 23	OP5			
Di-4-chlorobenzoyl peroxide [as a paste]	UN3106	≤ 52					OP7			21
Di-4-chlorobenzoyl peroxide	Exempt	≤ 32			≥ 68		Exempt			
Dicumyl peroxide	UN3109	>52-100		≤ 48			OP8			9, 11
Dicumyl peroxide	UN3110	>52-100			≤ 48		OP8			9, 11
Dicumyl peroxide	Exempt	≤ 52	≥ 48				Exempt			
Dicumyl peroxide	Exempt	≤ 52			≥ 48		Exempt			
Dicyclohexyl peroxydicarbonate	UN3112	>91-100					OP3	+5	+10	
Dicyclohexyl peroxydicarbonate	UN3114	≤ 91				≥ 9	OP5	+5	+10	
Didecanoyl peroxide	UN3114	≤ 100					OP6	+30	+35	
2,2-Di-(4,4-di(tert-butylperoxy) cyclohexyl) propane	UN3106	≤ 42			≥ 58		OP7			
2,2-Di-(4,4-di(tert-butylperoxy) cyclohexyl) propane	UN3107	≤ 25		≥ 75			OP8			
Di-2,4-dichlorobenzoyl peroxide	UN3102	≤ 77				≥ 23	OP5			
Di-2,4-dichlorobenzoyl peroxide [as a paste with silicone oil]	UN3106	≤ 52					OP7			
Di-(2-ethylhexyl) peroxydicarbonate	UN3113	>77-100					OP5	-20	-10	
2,2-Di-(4,4-di-(tert-butylperoxy cyclohexyl) propane	UN3107	≤ 22		≥ 78			OP8			
Di-(2-ethylhexyl) peroydicarbonate [as a stable dispersion in water]	UN3119	≤ 52					IBC	-20	-10	
Di-(2-ethoxyethyl) peroxydicarbonate	UN3115	≤ 52		≥ 48			OP7	-10	0	
Di-(2-ethylhexyl) peroxydicarbonate	UN3115	≤ 77		≥ 23			OP7	-15	-5	
Di-(2-ethylhexyl) peroxydicarbonate [as a stable dispersion in water]	UN3117	≤ 62					OP8	-15	-5	
Di-(2-ethylhexyl) peroxydicarbonate [as a stable dispersion in water]	UN3119	≤ 52					OP8	-15	-5	
Di-(2-ethylhexyl) peroxydicarbonate [as a stable dispersion in water (frozen)]	UN3118	≤ 42					OP8	-15	-5	
Diethyl peroxydicarbonate	UN3115	≤ 27	≥ 73				OP7	-10	0	
2,2-Dihydroperoxypropane	UN3102	≤ 27			≥ 73		OP5			
Di-(1-hydroxycyclohexyl) peroxide	UN3106	≤ 100					OP7			
Diisobutyryl peroxide	UN3111	>32-52		≥ 48			OP5	-20	-10	
Diisobutyryl peroxide	UN3115	≤ 32		≥ 68			OP7	-20	-10	
Diisopropylbenzene dihydroperoxide	UN3106	≤ 82	≥ 5			≥ 5	OP7			17
Diisopropyl peroxydicarbonate	UN3112	>52-100					OP2	-15	-5	
Diisopropyl peroxydicarbonate	UN3115	≤ 52		≥ 48			OP7	-20	-10	
Diisotridecyl peroxydicarbonate	UN3115	≤ 100					OP7	-10	0	
Dilauroyl peroxide	UN3106	≤ 100					OP7			
Dilauroyl peroxide [as a stable dispersion in water]	UN3109	≤ 42					OP8			
Di-(2-methylbenzoyl) peroxide	UN3112	≤ 87				≥ 13	OP5	+30	+35	
Di-(3-methoxybutyl) peroxydicarbonate	UN3115	≤ 52		≥ 48			OP7	-5	+5	
Di-(3-methylbenzoyl) peroxide + Benzoyl (3-methylbenzoyl) peroxide + Dibenzoyl peroxide	UN3115	≤ 20 + ≤ 18 + ≤ 4		≥ 58			OP7	+35	+40	
Di-(4-methylbenzoyl) peroxide [as a paste with silicone oil]	UN3106	≤ 52					OP7			
2,5-Dimethyl-2,5-di-(benzoylperoxy) hexane	UN3102	>82-100					OP5			
2,5-Dimethyl-2,5-di-(benzoylperoxy) hexane	UN3104	≤ 82				≥ 18	OP5			
2,5-Dimethyl-2,5-di-(benzoylperoxy) hexane	UN3106	≤ 82			≥ 18		OP7			
2,5-Dimethyl-2,5-di-(tert-butylperoxy) hexane	UN3105	>52-100					OP7			
2,5-Dimethyl-2,5-di-(tert-butylperoxy) hexyne-3	UN3101	>87-100					OP5			
2,5-Dimethyl-2,5-di-(tert-butylperoxy) hexyne-3	UN3103	>52-86	≥ 14				OP5			
2,5-Dimethyl-2,5-di-(tert-butylperoxy) hexane	UN3106	≤ 52			≥ 48		OP7			

Organic Peroxide Table

Technical name	ID number	Concentration (mass %)	Diluent (mass %)			Water (mass %)	Packing method	Temperature (°C)		Notes
			A	B	I			Control	Emergency	
(1)	(2)	(3)	(4a)	(4b)	(4c)	(5)	(6)	(7a)	(7b)	(8)
2,5-Dimethyl-2,5-di-(tert-butylperoxy) hexane	UN3109	≤ 52	≥ 48				OP8			
2,5-Dimethyl-2,5-di-(tert-butylperoxy) hexyne-3	UN3106	≤ 52			≥ 48		OP7			
2,5-Dimethyl-2,5-di-(tert-butylperoxy) hexane [as a paste]	UN3108	≤ 47					OP8			
2,5 Dimethyl 2,5 di-2-ethylhexanoylperoxy hexane	UN3113	≤ 100					OP5	+20	+25	
2,5-Dimethyl-2,5-di-(tert-butylperoxy) hexane	UN3108	≤ 77			≥ 23		OP8			
2,5-Dimethyl-2,5-di-(tert-butylperoxy) hexyne-3	UN3101	>86-100					OP5			
2,5-Dimethyl-2,5-dihydroperoxyhexane	UN3104	≤ 82				≥ 18	OP7			
2,5-Dimethyl-2,5-di-(3,5,5-trimethylhexanoylperoxy) hexane	UN3105	≤ 77	≥ 23				OP7			
1,1-Dimethyl-3-hydroxybutylperoxyneoheptanoate	UN3117	≤ 52	≥ 48				OP8	+0	+10	
Dimyristyl peroxydicarbonate	UN3116	≤ 100					OP7	+20	+25	
Dimyristyl peroxydicarbonate [as a stable dispersion in water]	UN3119	≤ 42					OP8	+20	+25	
Dimyristyl peroxydicarbonate [as a stable dispersion in water]	UN3119	≤ 42					IBC	+15	+20	
Di-(2-neodecanoylperoxyisopropyl) benzene	UN3115	≤ 52	≥ 48				OP7	-10	0	
Di-n-nonanoyl peroxide	UN3116	≤ 100					OP7	0	+10	
Di-n-octanoyl peroxide	UN3114	≤ 100					OP5	+10	+15	
Diperoxy azelaic acid	UN3116	≤ 27			≥ 73		OP7	+35	+40	
Diperoxy dodecane diacid	UN3116	>13-42			≥ 58		OP7	+40	+45	
Diperoxy dodecane diacid	Exempt	≤ 13			≥ 87		Exempt			
Di-(2-phenoxyethyl) peroxydicarbonate	UN3102	>85-100					OP5			
Di-(2-phenoxyethyl)peroxydicarbonate	UN3106	≤ 85				≥ 15	OP7			
Dipropionyl peroxide	UN3117	≤ 27		≥ 73			OP8	+15	+20	
Di-n-propyl peroxydicarbonate	UN3113	≤ 100					OP3	-25	-15	
Di-n-propyl peroxydicarbonate	UN3113	≤ 77		≥ 23			OP5	-20	-10	
Distearyl peroxydicarbonate	UN3106	≤ 87			≥ 13		OP7			
Disuccinic acid peroxide	UN3102	>72-100					OP4			18
Disuccinic acid peroxide	UN3116	≤ 72				≥ 28	OP7	+10	+15	
Di-(3,5,5-trimethyl-1,2-dioxolanyl-3) peroxide [as a paste]	UN3116	≤ 52					OP7	+30	+35	21
Di-(3,5,5-trimethylhexanoyl) peroxide	UN3115	>38-82	≥ 18				OP7	0	+10	
Di-(3,5,5-trimethylhexanoyl) peroxide [as a stable dispersion in water]	UN3117	≤ 52					OP8	+10	+15	
Di-(3,5,5-trimethylhexanoyl) peroxide	UN3119	≤ 38	≥ 62				OP8	+20	+25	
Di-(3,5,5-trimethylhexanoyl) peroxide	UN3119	≤ 38	≥ 62				IBC	+10	+15	
Ethyl 3,3-di-(tert-amylperoxy) butyrate	UN3105	≤ 67	≥ 33				OP7			
Ethyl 3,3-di-(tert-butylperoxy) butyrate	UN3103	>77-100					OP5			
Ethyl 3,3-di-(tert-butylperoxy) butyrate	UN3105	≤ 77	≥ 23				OP7			
Ethyl 3,3-di-(tert-butylperoxy) butyrate	UN3106	≤ 52			≥ 48		OP7			
3,3,6,6,9,9-Hexamethyl-1,2,4,5-tetraoxacyclononane	UN3102	>52-100					OP4			
3,3,6,6,9,9-Hexamethyl-1,2,4,5-tetraoxacyclononane	UN3105	≤ 52	≥ 48				OP7			
3,3,6,6,9,9-Hexamethyl-1,2,4,5-tetraoxacyclononane	UN3106	≤ 52			≥ 48		OP7			
tert-Hexyl peroxyneodecanoate	UN3115	≤ 71	≥ 29				OP7	0	+10	
tert-Hexyl peroxypivalate	UN3115	≤ 72		≥ 28			OP7	+10	+15	
Isopropylcumyl hydroperoxide	UN3109	≤ 72	≥ 28				OP8			13ROW ≤
p-Menthyl hydroperoxide	UN3105	> 72-100					OP7			13
p-Menthyl hydroperoxide	UN3109	≤ 72	≥ 28				OP8			25
Methylcyclohexanone peroxide(s)	UN3115	≤ 67		≥ 33			OP7	+35	+40	
Methyl ethyl ketone peroxide(s)	UN3101	≤ 52	≥ 48				OP5			5, 13
Methyl ethyl ketone peroxide(s)	UN3105	≤ 45	≥ 55				OP7			5
Methyl ethyl ketone peroxide(s)	UN3105	≤ 37	≥ 55			≥ 8	OP7			5
Methyl ethyl ketone peroxide(s)	UN3107	≤ 40	≥ 60				OP8			5
Methyl isobutyl ketone peroxide(s)	UN3105	≤ 62	≥ 19				OP7			5, 23
Organic peroxide, liquid, sample	UN3103						OP2			12
Organic peroxide, liquid, sample, temperature controlled	UN3113						OP2			12
Organic peroxide, solid, sample	UN3104						OP2			12
Organic peroxide, solid, sample, temperature controlled	UN3114						OP2			12
Peracetic acid with not more than 20% hydrogen peroxide	Exempt	≤ 6				≥ 60	Exempt			
Peracetic acid with not more than 26% hydrogen peroxide	UN3109	≤ 17				≥ 27	OP8			13
Peracetic acid with 7% hydrogen peroxide	UN3107	≤ 36				≥ 15	OP8			13
Peroxyacetic acid, type D, stabilized	UN3105	≤ 43					OP7			13, 20

Organic Peroxide Table

Technical name	ID number	Concentration (mass %)	Diluent (mass %)			Water (mass %)	Packing method	Temperature (°C)		Notes
			A	B	I			Control	Emergency	
(1)	(2)	(3)	(4a)	(4b)	(4c)	(5)	(6)	(7a)	(7b)	(8)
Peroxyacetic acid, type E, stabilized	UN3107	≤ 43					OP8			13, 20
Peroxyacetic acid, type F, stabilized	UN3109	≤ 43					OP8			13, 20
Pinanyl hydroperoxide	UN3105	56-100					OP7			13
Pinanyl hydroperoxide	UN3109	< 56	>44				OP8			
Tetrahydronaphthyl hydroperoxide	UN3106	≤ 100					OP7			
1,1,3,3-Tetramethylbutyl hydroperoxide	UN3105	≤ 100					OP7			
1,1,3,3-Tetramethylbutylperoxy-2-ethylhexanoate	UN3115	≤ 100					OP7	+20	+25	
1,1,3,3-Tetramethylbutyl peroxyneodecanoate	UN3115	≤ 72		≥ 28			OP7	-5	+5	
1,1,3,3-Tetramethylbutyl peroxyneodecanoate [as a stable dispersion in water]	UN3119	≤ 52					IBC	-5	+5	
1,1,3,3-Tetramethylbutyl peroxy phenoxyacetate	UN3115	≤ 37		≥ 63			OP7	-10	0	
3,6,9-Triethyl-3,6,9-trimethyl-1,4,7-triperoxonane	UN3105	≤ 42	≥ 58				OP7			26

NOTES:
1. For domestic shipments, OP8 is authorized.
2. Available oxygen must be < 4.7 percent.
3. For concentrations < 80 percent OP5 is allowed. For concentrations of at least 80 percent but < 85 percent, OP4 is allowed. For concentrations of at least 85 percent, maximum package size is OP2.
4. The diluent may be replaced by di-tert-butyl peroxide.
5. Available oxygen must be ≤ 9 percent.
6. For domestic shipments, OP5 is authorized.
7. [Reserved]
8. Only non-metallic packagings are authorized.
9. For domestic shipments, this material may be transported in bulk packagings under the provisions of paragraph (e)(3)(ii) of this section.
10. [Reserved]
11. Up to 2000 kg per container authorized.
12. Samples may only be offered for transportation under the provisions of paragraph (c)(2) of this section.
13. "Corrosive" subsidiary risk label is required.
14. This material may be transported in bulk packagings under the provisions of paragraph (e) of this section.
15. No "Corrosive" subsidiary risk label is required for concentrations below 80%.
16. With < 6% di-tert-butyl peroxide.
17. With ≥ 8% 1-isopropylhydroperoxy-4-isopropylhydroxybenzene.
18. Addition of water to this organic peroxide will decrease its thermal stability.
19. [Reserved]
20. Mixtures with hydrogen peroxide, water and acid(s).
21. With diluent type A, with or without water.
22. With >36 percent, by mass, ethylbenzene.
23. With >19 percent, by mass, methyl isobutyl ketone.
24. Diluent type b with boiling point >100 C.
25. No "Corrosive" subsidiary risk label is required for concentrations below 56%.
26. Available oxygen must be ≤ 7.6%.

(c) New organic peroxides, formulations and samples.

(1) *Except as provided* for samples in paragraph (c)(2) of this section, no person may offer for transportation an organic peroxide which is not identified by technical name in the Organic Peroxides Table of this section, or a formulation of one or more organic peroxides which are identified by technical name in that table, unless the organic peroxide is assigned a generic type and shipping description and is approved by the Associate Administrator under the provisions of §173.128(c) of this subchapter.

(2) *Samples.* Samples of new organic peroxides or new formulations of organic peroxides identified in the Organic Peroxides Table in paragraph (b) of this section, for which complete test data are not available, and which are to be transported for further testing or product evaluation, may be assigned an appropriate shipping description for organic peroxide Type C, packaged and offered for transportation, under the following conditions:

(i) *Data available* to the person offering the material for transportation must indicate that the sample would pose a level of hazard no greater than that of an organic peroxide Type B and that the control temperature, if any, is sufficiently low to prevent any dangerous decomposition and sufficiently high to prevent any dangerous phase separation;

(ii) *The sample* must be packaged in accordance with packing method OP2, for a liquid or solid, respectively;

(iii) *Packages of the organic peroxide* may be offered for transportation and transported in a quantity not to exceed 10 kg (22 pounds) per transport vehicle; and

(iv) *One of the following shipping descriptions must be assigned:*

[A] Organic peroxide Type C, liquid, 5.2, UN 3103;

[B] Organic peroxide Type C, solid, 5.2, UN 3104;

[C] Organic peroxide Type C, liquid, temperature controlled, 5.2, UN 3113; or

[D] Organic peroxide Type C, solid, temperature controlled, 5.2, UN 3114.

(3) *Mixtures.* Mixtures of organic peroxides individually identified in the Organic Peroxides Table in paragraph (b) of this section may be classified as the same type of organic peroxide as that of the most dangerous component and be transported under the conditions for transportation given for this type. If the stable components form a thermally less stable mixture, the SADT of the mixture must be determined and the new control and emergency temperature derived under the provisions of §173.21(f).

(d) Packing Method Table. Packagings for organic peroxides and self-reactive substances are listed in the Maximum Quantity per Packing Method Table. The packing methods are designated OP1 to OP8. The quantities specified for each packing method represent the maximum that is authorized.

(1) *The following types of packagings are authorized:*

(i) *Drums: 1A1, 1A2, 1B1, 1B2, 1D, 1G, 1H1, 1H2;*

(ii) *Jerricans: 3A1, 3A2, 3B1, 3B2, 3H1, 3H2;*

(iii) *Boxes: 4C1, 4C2, 4D, 4F, 4G, 4H1, 4H2, 4A, 4B; or*

(iv) *Composite packagings* with a plastic inner receptacle: 6HA1, 6HA2, 6HB1, 6HB2, 6HC, 6HD1, 6HD2, 6HG1, 6HG2, 6HH1, 6HH2.

(2) *Metal packaging* (including inner packagings of combination packagings and outer packagings of combination or composite packagings) are used only for packing methods OP7 and OP8.

(3) *In combination packagings,* glass receptacles are used only as inner packagings with a maximum content of 0.5 kg or 0.5 L.

(4) *The maximum quantity* per packaging or package for Packing Methods OP1-OP8 must be as follows:

Maximum Quantity Per Packaging/Package for Packing Methods OP1 to OP8

Maximum quantity	Packing method							
	OP1	OP2[1]	OP3	OP4[1]	OP5	OP6	OP7	OP8
Solids and combination packagings (liquid and solid) (kg)	0.5	0.5/10	5	5/25	25	50	50	[2]200
Liquids (L)	0.5		5		30	60	60	[3]225

1. If two values are given, the first applies to the maximum net mass per inner packaging and the second to the maximum net mass of the complete package.
2. 60 kg for jerricans and 100 kg for boxes.
3. 60 L for jerricans.

(e) Bulk packagings for organic peroxides. The following bulk packagings are authorized:

(1) *Rail cars.* Class DOT 103, 104, 105, 109, 111, 112, 114, 115, or 120 fusion-weld tank car tank are authorized. DOT 103W, 111A60F1 and 111A60W1 tank car tanks must have bottom outlets effectively sealed from inside. Gauging devices are required on DOT 103W tank car tanks. Riveted tank car tanks are not authorized.

(2) *Cargo tanks.* Specification MC 307, MC 310, MC 311, MC 312, DOT 407, and DOT 412 cargo tank motor vehicles with a tank design pressure of at least 172 kPa (25 psig) are authorized.

(3) *Portable tanks.* The following requirements apply to portable tanks intended for the transport of Type F organic peroxides or Type F self-reactive substances. DOT 51, 57, IM 101 portable tanks, and UN portable tanks that conform to the requirements of T23 (see §172.102(c)(7) of this subchapter), when T23 is specified in Column (7) of the §171.101 Table of this subchapter for the Type F organic peroxide or Type F self-reactive substance. Type F organic peroxide or self-reactive substance formulations other than those indicated in T23 may be transported in portable tanks if approved by the Associate Administrator. The following conditions also apply:

(i) *The portable tank* must be designed for a test pressure of at least 0.4 MPa (4 bar).

(ii) *Portable tanks must be fitted with temperature-sensing devices.*

(iii) *Portable tanks* must be fitted with pressure relief devices and emergency-relief devices. Vacuum-relief devices may also be used. Pressure relief devices must operate at pressures determined according to both the properties of the hazardous material and the construction characteristics of the portable tank. Fusible elements are not allowed in the shell.

(iv) *The pressure relief devices* must consist of reclosing devices fitted to prevent significant build-up within the portable tank of the decomposition products and vapors released at a temperature of 50 °C (122 °F). The capacity and start-to-discharge pressure of the relief devices must be in accordance with the applicable requirements of this subchapter specified for the portable tank. The start-to-discharge pressure must in no case be such that liquid would escape from the pressure relief devices if the portable tank were overturned.

(v) *[A] The emergency-relief devices* may be of the reclosing or frangible types, or a combination of the two, designed to vent all the decomposition products and vapors evolved during a period of not less than one hour of complete fire engulfment as calculated by the following formula:

$$q=70961\ F\ A^{0.82}$$

Where:
q = heat absorption (W)
A = wetted area (m^2)
F = insulation factor (-)

[B] Insulation factor (F) in the formula in paragraph (e)(3)(v)[A] of this section equals 1 for non-insulated vessels and for insulated vessels F is calculated using the following formula:

$$F = \frac{U(923-T_{PO})}{47032}$$

Where:
U = K/L = heat transfer coefficient of the insulation ($W{\bullet}m^{-2}{\bullet}K^{-1}$); where K = heat conductivity of insulation layer ($W{\bullet}m^{-1}{\bullet}K^{-1}$), and L = thickness of insulation layer (m).
T_{PO} = temperature of material at relieving conditions (K).

(vi) *The start-to-discharge pressure* of emergency-relief devices must be higher than that specified for the pressure relief devices in paragraph (e)(3)(iv) of this section. The emergency-relief devices must be sized and designed in such a way that the maximum pressure in the shell never exceeds the test pressure of the portable tank.

Note to Paragraph (e)(3)(vi): An example of a method to determine the size of emergency-relief devices is given in Appendix 5 of the UN Manual of Tests and Criteria (incorporated by reference, see §171.7 of this subchapter).

(vii) *For insulated portable tanks,* the capacity and setting of emergency-relief devices must be determined assuming a loss of insulation from 1 percent of the surface area.

(viii) *Vacuum-relief devices* and reclosing devices on portable tanks used for flammable hazardous materials must be provided with flame arresters. Any reduction of the relief capacity caused by the flame arrester must be taken into account and the appropriate relief capacity must be provided.

(ix) *Service equipment* such as devices and external piping must be designed and constructed so that no hazardous material remains in them after filling the portable tank.

(x) *Portable tanks* may be either insulated or protected by a sunshield. If the SADT of the hazardous material in the portable tank is 55 °C (131 °F) or less, the portable tank must be completely insulated. The outer surface must be finished in white or bright metal.

(xi) *The degree of filling must not exceed 90% at 15 °C (59 °F).*

(xii) *DOT 57 metal portable tanks* are authorized only for tert-butyl cumyl peroxide, di-(2-tert-butylperoxyisopropyl-benzene(s), dicumyl peroxide and mixtures of two or more of these peroxides. DOT 57 portable tanks must conform to the venting requirements of paragraph (e)(5) of this section. These portable tanks are not subject to the requirements of paragraphs (e)(3)(ii) and (e)(3)(iv) of this section.

(4) *For tertiary butyl hydroperoxide (TBHP),* each tank car, cargo tank or portable tank must contain 7.6 cm (3.0 inches) low density polyethylene (PE) saddles having a melt index of at least 0.2 grams per 10 minutes (ASTM D1238, condition E) as part of the lading, with a ratio of PE to TBHP over a range of 0.008 to 0.012 by mass. Alternatively, plastic or metal containers equipped with fusible plugs having a melting point between 69 °C (156 °F) and 71 °C (160 °F) and filled with a sufficient quantity of water to dilute the TBHP to 65 percent or less by mass may be used. The PE saddles must be visually inspected after each trip and, at a minimum, once every 12 months, and replaced when discoloration, fracture, severe deformation, or other indication of change is noted.

(5) *IBCs.* IBCs are authorized subject to the conditions and limitations of this section provided the IBC type is authorized according to IB52 (see §172.102(c)(4) of this subchapter), as applicable, and the IBC conforms to the requirements in subpart O of part 178 of this subchapter at the Packing Group II performance level. The following additional requirements also apply:

(i) *IBCs shall be provided* with a device to allow venting during transportation. The inlet to the pressure relief device shall be sited in the vapor space of the IBC under maximum filling conditions during transportation.

(ii) *To prevent explosive rupture* of metal IBCs or composite IBCs with complete metal casing, the emergency-relief devices shall be designed to vent all the decomposition products and vapors evolved during self-accelerating decomposition or during a period of not less than one hour of complete fire-engulfment as calculated by the formula in paragraph (e)(3)(v) of this section. The control and emergency temperatures specified in IB52 are based on a non-insulated IBC.

§173.226 Materials poisonous by inhalation, Division 6.1, Packing Group I, Hazard Zone A.

Division 6.1, Packing Group I, materials that are poisonous by inhalation and that fall within the boundaries of Hazard Zone A in the graph found in §173.133 must be packed in non-bulk packagings in accordance with the following paragraphs:

(a) In seamless specification cylinders conforming to the requirements of §173.40. However, a welded cylinder filled before October 1, 2002, may be transported for reprocessing or disposal of the cylinder's contents until December 31, 2003.

(b) In 1A1, 1B1, 1H1, 1N1, or 6HA1 drums further packed in a 1A2 or 1H2 drum. Both inner and outer drums must conform to the performance test requirements of subpart M of part 178 of this subchapter at the Packing Group I performance level. The outer drum must have a minimum thickness of 1.35 mm (0.053 inch) for a 1A2 outer drum or 6.30 mm (0.248 inch) for a 1H2 outer drum. Outer 1A2 and 1H2 drums must withstand a hydrostatic test pressure of 100 kPa (15 psig). Capacity of the inner drum may not exceed 220 L (58 gallons). In addition, the inner drum must —

(1) *Be capable* of satisfactorily withstanding the hydrostatic pressure test in §178.605 of this subchapter at a test pressure of 550 kPa (80 psig);

(2) *Satisfactorily withstand* the leakproofness test in §178.604 of this subchapter using an internal air pressure of at least twice the vapor pressure at 55 °C (131 °F) of the material to be packaged;

(3) *Have screw-type closures that are* —

(i) *Closed and tightened* to a torque prescribed by the closure manufacturer, using a device that is capable of measuring torque;

(ii) *Physically held in place* by any means capable of preventing back-off or loosening of the closure by impact or vibration during transportation; and

(iii) *Provided with a cap seal* that is properly applied in accordance with the cap seal manufacturer's recommendations and is capable of withstanding an internal pressure of at least 100 kPa (15 psig).

(4) *Have a minimum thickness as follows:*
(i) *If the capacity* of the inner drum is less than or equal to 120 L (32 gallons), the minimum thickness of the inner drum is —
[A] For a 1A1 or 1N1 drum, 1.3 mm (0.051 inch);
[B] For a 1B1 drum, 3.9 mm (0.154 inch);
[C] For a 1H1 drum, 3.16 mm (0.124 inch); and
[D] For a 6HA1 drum, the plastic inner container shall be 1.58 mm (0.0622 inch) and the outer steel drum shall be 0.96 mm (0.0378 inch).
(ii) *If the capacity* of the inner drum is greater than 120 L (32 gallons), the thickness of the inner drum is —
[A] For a 1A1 or 1N1 drum, 1.7 mm (0.067 inch);
[B] For a 1B1 drum, 4.7 mm (0.185 inch);
[C] For a 1H1 drum, 3.16 mm (0.124 inch); and
[D] For a 6HA1 drum, the plastic inner container shall be 1.58 mm (0.0622 inch) and the outer steel drum shall be 1.08 mm (0.043 inch); and
(5) *Be isolated* from the outer drum by a shock-mitigating, non-reactive material.
(c) **In combination packagings,** consisting of an inner packaging system and an outer packaging, as follows:
(1) *Outer packagings:*
Steel drum: 1A2
Aluminum drum: 1B2
Metal drum, other than steel or aluminum: 1N2
Plywood drum: 1D
Fiber drum: 1G
Plastic drum: 1H2
Wooden barrel: 2C2
Steel jerrican: 3A2
Plastic jerrican: 3H2
Aluminum jerrican: 3B2
Steel box: 4A
Aluminum box: 4B
Natural wood box: 4C1 or 4C2
Plywood box: 4D
Reconstituted wood box: 4F
Fiberboard box: 4G
Expanded plastic box: 4H2
Solid plastic box: 4H2
(2) *Inner packaging system.* The inner packaging system consists of two packagings: an impact-resistant receptacle of glass, earthenware, plastic or metal securely cushioned with a non-reactive, absorbent material and packed within a leak-tight packaging of metal or plastic. This combination packaging in turn is packed within the outer packaging. Capacity of each inner receptacle may not exceed 4 L (1 gallon). An inner receptacle that has a closure must have a closure which is physically held in place by any means capable of preventing back-off or loosening of the closure by impact or vibration during transportation. Both the inner packaging system and the outer packaging must conform to the performance test requirements of subpart M of part 178 of this subchapter, at the Packaging Group I performance level. The inner packaging system must meet these tests without the benefit of the outer packaging. The total amount of liquid contained in the outer packaging may not exceed 16 L (4 gallons).

§173.227 Materials poisonous by inhalation. Division 6.1, Packing Group I, Hazard Zone B.

Division 6.1, Packing Group I, materials that are poisonous by inhalation and that fall within the boundaries of Hazard Zone B in the graph found in §173.133 shall be packed in non-bulk packagings which conform to the performance test requirements of subpart M of part 178 of this subchapter, at the Packing Group I performance level. The following packagings are authorized:
(a) **In packagings as authorized in §173.226** and seamless and welded specification cylinders conforming to the requirements of §173.40.
(b) **1A1, 1B1, 1N1 or 1H1 drum or 6HA1 composite** further packed in a 1A2 or 1H2 drum. Both the inner and outer drums must conform to the performance test requirements of subpart M of part 178 of this subchapter at the Packing Group I performance level. The outer drum must have a minimum thickness of 1.35 mm (0.053 inches) for a 1A2 outer drum or 6.30 mm (0.248 inches) for a 1H2 outer drum. Outer 1A2 and 1H2 drums must withstand a hydrostatic test pressure of 100 kPa (15 psig). In addition, the inner drum must —
(1) *Satisfactorily withstand* the leakproofness test in §178.604 of this subchapter using an internal air pressure of at least two times the vapor pressure at 55 °C (131 °F) of the material to be packaged;
(2) *Have screw closures that are —*
(i) *Closed and tightened* to a torque prescribed by the closure manufacturer, using a device that is capable of measuring torque;
(ii) *Physically held in place* by any means capable of preventing back-off or loosening of the closure by impact or vibration during transportation; and
(iii) *Provided with a cap seal* that is properly applied in accordance with the cap seal manufacturer's recommendations and is capable of withstanding an internal pressure of at least 100 kPa (15 psig).
(3) *Have a minimum thickness as follows:*
(i) *If the capacity* of the inner drum is less than or equal to 30 L (7.9 gallons), the minimum thickness of the inner drum is:
[A] For a 1A1 drum, 0.69 mm (0.027 inch);
[B] For a 1B1 drum, 2.79 mm (0.110 inch);
[C] For a 1H1 drum, 1.14 mm (0.045 inch); and
[D] For a 6HA1 drum, the plastic inner container shall be 1.58 mm (0.0625 inch), the outer steel drum shall be 0.70 mm (0.027 inch).
(ii) *If the capacity* of the inner drum is greater than 30 L (7.9 gallons) but less than or equal to 120 L (32 gallons), the minimum thickness of the inner drum is —
[A] For a 1A1 drum, 1.08 mm (.043 inch);
[B] For a 1B1 drum, 3.9 mm (0.154 inch);
[C] For a 1H1 drum, 3.16 mm (0.124 inch); and
[D] For a 6HA1 drum, the plastic inner container shall be 1.58 mm (0.0625 inch) and the outer steel drum shall be 0.96 mm (0.0378 inches).
(iii) *If the capacity* of the inner drum is greater than 120 L (31.7 gallons), the thickness of the inner drum is —
[A] For a 1A1 or 1N1 drum, 1.35 mm (0.053 inches);
[B] For a 1B1 drum, 4.7 mm (0.185 inches);
[C] For a 1H1 drum, 3.16 mm (0.124 inches); and
[D] For a 6HA1 drum, the plastic inner container shall be 1.58 mm (0.0625 inch) and the outer steel drum shall be 1.08 mm (0.043 inch).
(4) *Be isolated* from the outer drum by a shock-mitigating, non-reactive material; and
(5) *Have a capacity not greater than 220 L (58 gallons).*
(c) **1A1, 1B1, 1H1, 1N1 or 6HA1 drums** described in paragraph (b) of this section may be used without being further packed in a 1A2 or 1H2 drum if the shipper loads the material, blocks and braces the drums within the transport vehicle and seals the transport vehicle used. Drums may not be stacked (double decked) within the transport vehicle. Shipments must be from one origin to one destination only without any intermediate pickup or delivery.

§173.228 Bromine pentafluoride or bromine trifluoride.

The following packagings are authorized for bromine pentafluoride and bromine trifluoride:
(a) **Specification 3A150, 3AA150, 3B240, 3BN150,** 4B240, 4BA240, 4BW240 and 3E1800 cylinders. No cylinder may be equipped with a pressure relief device.
(b) **A material in Hazard Zone A must be transported** in a seamless specification cylinder conforming to the requirements of §173.40. However, a welded cylinder filled before October 1, 2002, in accordance with the requirements of this subchapter in effect at the time of filling, may be transported for reprocessing or disposal of the cylinder's contents until December 31, 2003. No cylinder may be equipped with a pressure relief device.

§173.229 Chloric acid solution or chlorine dioxide hydrate, frozen.

When the §172.101 table specifies that a hazardous material be packaged in accordance with this section, only 4G fiberboard boxes, with inner packagings of polyethylene or other suitable material, are authorized. Fiberboard boxes must be reinforced and insulated and sufficient dry ice must be used to maintain the hydrate or acid in a frozen state during transportation. Each packaging must conform to the general packaging requirements of subpart B of part 173, and to the requirements of part 178 of this subchapter at the Packing Group I performance level. Transportation is authorized only by private or contract carrier by motor vehicle.

Subpart F - Bulk Packaging for Hazardous Materials Other Than Class 1 and Class 7

§173.240 Bulk packaging for certain low hazard solid materials.

When §172.101 of this subchapter specifies that a hazardous material be packaged under this section, only the following bulk packagings are authorized, subject to the requirements of subparts A and B of part 173 of this subchapter and the special provisions specified in column 7 of the §172.101 table.
(a) **Rail cars:** Class DOT 103, 104, 105, 109, 111, 112, 114, 115, or 120 tank car tanks; Class 106 or 110 multi-unit tank car tanks; and

metal non-DOT specification, sift-proof tank car tanks and sift-proof closed cars.

(b) Motor vehicles: Specification MC 300, MC 301, MC 302, MC 303, MC 304, MC 305, MC 306, MC 307, MC 310, MC 311, MC 312, MC 330, MC 331, DOT 406, DOT 407, and DOT 412 cargo tank motor vehicles; non-DOT specification, sift-proof cargo tank motor vehicles; and sift-proof closed vehicles.

(c) Portable tanks and closed bulk bins. DOT 51, 56, 57 and 60 portable tanks; IMO type 1, 2 and 5, and IM 101 and IM 102 portable tanks; UN portable tanks; marine portable tanks conforming to 46 CFR part 64; and sift-proof non-DOT Specification portable tanks and closed bulk bins are authorized.

(d) IBCs. IBCs are authorized subject to the conditions and limitations of this section provided the IBC type is authorized according to the IBC packaging code specified for the specific hazardous material in Column (7) of the §172.101 Table of this subchapter and the IBC conforms to the requirements in subpart O of part 178 of this subchapter at the Packing Group performance level as specified in Column (5) of the §172.101 Table of this subchapter for the material being transported.

(1) *IBCs may not be used for the following hazardous materials:*

(i) *Packing Group I liquids; and*

(ii) *Packing Group I solids* that may become liquid during transportation.

(2) *The following IBCs* may not be used for Packing Group II and III solids that may become liquid during transportation:

(i) *Wooden: 11C, 11D and 11F;*

(ii) *Fiberboard: 11G;*

(iii) *Flexible:* 13H1, 13H2, 13H3, 13H4, 13H5, 13L1, 13L2, 13L3, 13L4, 13M1 and 13M2; and

(iv) *Composite: 11HZ2 and 21HZ2.*

§173.241 Bulk packagings for certain low hazard liquid and solid materials.

When §172.101 of this subchapter specifies that a hazardous material be packaged under this section, only the following bulk packagings are authorized, subject to the requirements of subparts A and B of part 173 of this subchapter and the special provisions specified in column 7 of the §172.101 table.

(a) Rail cars: Class DOT 103, 104, 105, 109, 111, 112, 114, 115, or 120 tank car tanks; Class 106 or 110 multi-unit tank car tanks and AAR Class 203W, 206W, and 211W tank car tanks.

(b) Cargo tanks: DOT specification MC 300, MC 301, MC 302, MC 303, MC 304, MC 305, MC 306, MC 307, MC 310, MC 311, MC 312, MC 330, MC 331, DOT 406, DOT 407, and DOT 412 cargo tank motor vehicles; and non-DOT specification cargo tank motor vehicles suitable for transport of liquids.

(c) Portable tanks. DOT Specification 51, 56, 57 and 60 portable tanks; IMO type 1, 2 and 5, and IM 101 and IM 102 portable tanks; UN portable tanks; marine portable tanks conforming to 46 CFR part 64; and non-DOT Specification portable tanks suitable for transport of liquids are authorized.

(d) IBCs. IB7s are authorized subject to the conditions and limitations of this section provided the IBC type is authorized according to the IBC packaging code specified for the specific hazardous material in Column (7) of the §172.101 Table of this subchapter and the IBC conforms to the requirements in subpart O of part 178 of this subchapter at the Packing Group performance level as specified in Column (5) of the §172.101 Table for the material being transported.

(1) *IBCs may not be used for the following hazardous materials:*

(i) *Packing Group I liquids; and*

(ii) *Packing Group I solids* that may become liquid during transportation.

(2) *The following IBCs* may not be used for Packing Group II and III solids that may become liquid during transportation:

(i) *Wooden: 11C, 11D and 11F;*

(ii) *Fiberboard: 11G;*

(iii) *Flexible:* 13H1, 13H2, 13H3, 13H4, 13H5, 13L1, 13L2, 13L3, 13L4, 13M1 and 13M2; and

(iv) *Composite: 11HZ2 and 21HZ2.*

§173.242 Bulk packagings for certain medium hazard liquids and solids, including solids with dual hazards.

When §172.101 of this subchapter specifies that a hazardous material be packaged under this section, only the following bulk packagings are authorized, subject to the requirements of subparts A and B of part 173 of this subchapter and the special provisions specified in column 7 of the §172.101 table.

(a) Rail cars: Class DOT 103, 104, 105, 109, 111, 112, 114, 115, or 120 tank car tanks; Class 106 or 110 multi-unit tank car tanks and AAR Class 206W tank car tanks.

(b) Cargo tanks: Specification MC 300, MC 301, MC 302, MC 303, MC 304, MC 305, MC 306, MC 307, MC 310, MC 311, MC 312, MC 330, MC 331, DOT 406, DOT 407, and DOT 412 cargo tank motor vehicles. Cargo tanks used to transport Class 3, Packing Group I or II, or Packing Group III with a flash point of less than 38 °C (100 °F); Class 6, Packing Group I or II; and Class 8, Packing Group I or II materials must conform to the following special requirements:

(1) *Pressure relief system:* Except as provided by §173.33(d), each cargo tank must be equipped with a pressure relief system meeting the requirements of §178.346-3 or §178.347-4 of this subchapter. However, pressure relief devices on MC 310, MC 311 and MC 312 cargo tanks must meet the requirements for a Specification MC 307 cargo tank (except for Class 8, Packing Group I and II). Pressure relief devices on MC 330 and MC 331 cargo tanks must meet the requirement in §178.337-9 of this subchapter.

(2) *Bottom outlets:* DOT 406, DOT 407 and DOT 412 must be equipped with stop-valves meeting the requirements of §178.345-11 of this subchapter; MC 304, MC 307, MC 310, MC 311, and MC 312 cargo tanks must be equipped with stop-valves capable of being remotely closed within 30 seconds of actuation by manual or mechanic means and (except for Class 8, Packing Group I and II) by a closure activated at a temperature not over 121 °C (250 °F); MC 330 and MC 331 cargo tanks must be equipped with internal self-closing stop-valves meeting the requirements in §178.337-11 of this subchapter.

(c) Portable tanks. DOT Specification 51, 56, 57 and 60 portable tanks; Specification IM 101, IM 102, and UN portable tanks when a T Code is specified in Column (7) of the §172.101 Hazardous Materials Table for a specific hazardous material; and marine portable tanks conforming to 46 CFR part 64 are authorized. DOT Specification 57 portable tanks used for the transport by vessel of Class 3, Packaging Group II materials must conform to the following:

(1) *Minimum design pressure.* Each tank must have a minimum design pressure of 62 kPa (9 psig);

(2) *Pressure relief devices.* Each tank must be equipped with at least one pressure relief device, such as a spring-loaded valve or fusible plug, conforming to the following:

(i) *Each pressure relief device* must communicate with the vapor space of the tank when the tank is in a normal transportation attitude. Shutoff valves may not be installed between the tank opening and any pressure relief device. Pressure relief devices must be mounted, shielded, or drained to prevent the accumulation of any material that could impair the operation or discharge capability of the device;

(ii) *Frangible devices are not authorized;*

(iii) *No pressure relief device* may open at less than 34.4 kPa (5 psig);

(iv) *If a fusible device* is used for relieving pressure, the device must have a minimum area of 1.25 square inches. The device must function at a temperature between 104 °C and 149 °C (220 °F and 300 °F) and at a pressure less than the design test pressure of the tank, unless this latter function is accomplished by a separate device; and

(v) *No relief device* may be used which would release flammable vapors under normal conditions of transportation (temperature up to and including 54 °C (130 °F)); and

(3) *Venting capacity.* The minimum venting capacity for pressure activated vents must be 6,000 cubic feet of free air per hour (measured at 101.3 kPa (14.7 psi) and 15.6 °C (60 °F)) at not more than 34.4 kPa (5 psi). The total emergency venting capacity (cu. ft./hr.) of each portable tank must be at least that determined from the following table:

Total surface area square feet[1,2]	Cubic feet free air per hour
20	15,800
30	23,700
40	31,600
50	39,500
60	47,400
70	55,300
80	63,300
90	71,200
100	79,100
120	94,900
140	110,700
160	126,500

1. Interpolate for intermediate sizes.
2. Surface area excludes area of legs.

173 Shippers — Gen. Requirements for Shipments and Packagings

(d) **IBCs.** IBCs are authorized subject to the conditions and limitations of this section provided the IBC type is authorized according to the IBC packaging code specified for the specific hazardous material in Column (7) of the §172.101 Table of this subchapter and the IBC conforms to the requirements in subpart O of part 178 of this subchapter at the Packing Group performance level as specified in Column (5) of the §172.101 Table of this subchapter for the material being transported.

(1) *IBCs may not be used for the following hazardous materials:*

(i) *Packing Group I liquids; and*

(ii) *Packing Group I solids* that may become liquid during transportation.

(2) *The following IBCs* may not be used for Packing Group II and III solids that may become liquid during transportation:

(i) *Wooden: 11C, 11D and 11F;*

(ii) *Fiberboard: 11G;*

(iii) *Flexible:* 13H1, 13H2, 13H3, 13H4, 13H5, 13L1, 13L2, 13L3, 13L4, 13M1 and 13M2; and

(iv) *Composite: 11HZ2 and 21HZ2.*

FEDERAL REGISTER UPDATES

In the May 30, 2003 Federal Register, §173.242 was revised, effective June 30, 2003.

(c) [1]

(4) *Unless provided by §173.32(h)(3),* an IM 101, 102 or UN portable tank with a bottom outlet and used to transport a liquid hazardous material that is a Class 3, PG I or II, or PG III with a flash point of less than 38 °C (100 °F); Division 5.1 PG I or II; or Division 6.1, PG I or II, must have internal valves conforming to §178.275(d)(3) of this subchapter. [2]

1. Paragraph (c) is the same as before.
2. Paragraph (c)(4) was added.

§173.243 Bulk packaging for certain high hazard liquids and dual hazard materials which pose a moderate hazard.

When §172.101 of this subchapter specifies that a hazardous material be packaged under this section, only the following bulk packagings are authorized, subject to the requirements of subparts A and B of part 173 of this subchapter and the special provisions specified in column 7 of the §172.101 table.

(a) **Rail cars.** Class DOT 103, 104, 105, 109, 111, 112, 114, 115, or 120 fusion-welded tank car tanks; and Class 106 or 110 multi-unit tank car tanks.

(b) **Cargo tanks.** Specification MC 304, MC 307, MC 330, MC 331 cargo tank motor vehicles; and MC 310, MC 311, MC 312, DOT 407, and DOT 412 cargo tank motor vehicles with tank design pressure of at least 172.4 kPa (25 psig). Cargo tanks used to transport Class 3 or Division 6.1 materials, or Class 8, Packing Group I or II materials must conform to the following special requirements:

(1) *Pressure relief system:* Except as provided by §173.33(d), each cargo tank must be equipped with a pressure relief system meeting the requirements of §178.346-3 or 178.347-4 of this subchapter. However, pressure relief devices on MC 310, MC 311 and MC 312 cargo tanks must meet the requirements for a Specification MC 307 cargo tank (except for Class 8, Packing Group I and II). Pressure relief devices on MC 330 and MC 331 cargo tanks must meet the requirement in §178.337-9 of this subchapter.

(2) *Bottom outlets:* DOT 407 and DOT 412 cargo tanks must be equipped with stop-valves meeting the requirements of §178.345-11 of this subchapter; MC 304, MC 307, MC 310, MC 311, and MC 312 cargo tanks must be equipped with stop-valves capable of being remotely closed within 30 seconds of actuation by manual or mechanic means and (except for Class 8, Packing Group I and II) by a closure activated at a temperature not over 121 °C (250 °F); MC 330 and MC 331 cargo tanks must be equipped with internal self-closing stop-valves meeting the requirements in §178.337-11 of this subchapter.

(c) **Portable tanks.** DOT Specification 51 and 60 portable tanks; UN portable tanks and IM 101 and IM 102 portable tanks when a T code is specified in Column (7) of the §172.101 Table of this subchapter for a specific hazardous material; and marine portable tanks conforming to 46 CFR part 64 with design pressure of at least 172.4 kPa (25 psig) are authorized.

(d) **IBCs.** IBCs are authorized subject to the conditions and limitations of this section provided the IBC type is authorized according to the IBC packaging code specified for the specific hazardous material in Column (7) of the §172.101 Table of this subchapter and the IBC conforms to the requirements in subpart O of part 178 of this subchapter at the Packing Group performance level as specified in Column (5) of the §172.101 Table of this subchapter for the material being transported.

(1) *IBCs may not be used for the following hazardous materials:*

(i) *Packing Group I liquids; and*

(ii) *Packing Group I solids* that may become liquid during transportation.

(2) *The following IBCs* may not be used for Packing Group II and III solids that may become liquid during transportation:

(i) *Wooden: 11C, 11D and 11F;*

(ii) *Fiberboard: 11G;*

(iii) *Flexible:* 13H1, 13H2, 13H3, 13H4, 13H5, 13L1, 13L2, 13L3, 13L4, 13M1 and 13M2; and

(iv) *Composite: 11HZ2 and 21HZ2.*

(e) **A dual hazard material may be packaged** in accordance with §173.242 if:

(1) *The subsidiary hazard* is Class 3 with a flash point greater than 38 °C (100 °F); or

(2) *The subsidiary hazard is Division 6.1, Packing Group III; or*

(3) *The subsidiary hazard is Class 8, Packaging Group, III.*

FEDERAL REGISTER UPDATES

In the May 30, 2003 Federal Register, a second sentence was added to §173.243(c), effective June 30, 2003.

(c) **Portable tanks.** DOT Specification 51 and 60 portable tanks; UN portable tanks and IM 101 and IM 102 portable tanks when a T code is specified in Column (7) of the §172.101 Table of this subchapter for a specific hazardous material; and marine portable tanks conforming to 46 CFR part 64 with design pressure of at least 172.4 kPa (25 psig) are authorized. Unless provided by §173.32(h)(3), an IM 101, 102 or UN portable tank, with a bottom outlet, used to transport a liquid hazardous material that is a Class 3, PG I or II, or PG III with a flash point of less than 38 °C (100 °F); Division 5.1, PG I or II; or Division 6.1, PG I or II, must have internal valves conforming to §178.275(d)(3) of this subchapter.

§173.244 Bulk packaging for certain pyrophoric liquids (Division 4.2), dangerous when wet (Division 4.3) materials, and poisonous liquids with inhalation hazards (Division 6.1).

When §172.101 of this subchapter specifies that a hazardous material be packaged under this section, only the following bulk packagings are authorized, subject to the requirements of subparts A and B of part 173 of this subchapter and the special provisions specified in column 7 of the §172.101 table.

(a) **Rail cars:** Class DOT 105, 109, 112, 114, or 120 fusion-welded tank car tanks; and Class 106 or 110 multi-unit tank car tanks.

(b) **Cargo tanks:** Specifications MC 330 and MC 331 cargo tank motor vehicles and, except for Division 4.2 materials, MC 312 and DOT 412 cargo tank motor vehicles.

(c) **Portable tanks:** DOT 51 portable tanks.

§173.245 Bulk packaging for extremely hazardous materials such as poisonous gases (Division 2.3).

When §172.101 of this subchapter specifies that a hazardous material be packaged under this section, only the following bulk packagings are authorized, subject to the requirements of subparts A and B of part 173 of this subchapter and the special provisions specified in column 7 of the §172.101 table.

(a) **Tank car tanks and multi-unit tank car tanks,** when approved by the Associate Administrator.

(b) **Cargo tank motor vehicles and portable tanks,** when approved by the Associate Administrator.

§173.247 Bulk packaging for certain elevated temperature materials.

When §172.101 of this subchapter specifies that a hazardous material be packaged under this section, only the following bulk packagings are authorized, subject to the requirements of subparts A and B of part 173 of this subchapter and the special provisions in column 7 of the §172.101 table. On or after October 1, 1993, authorized packagings must meet all requirements in paragraph (g) of this section, unless otherwise excepted.

(a) **Rail cars:** Class DOT 103, 104, 105, 109, 111, 112, 114, 115, or 120 tank car tanks; Class DOT 106, 110 multi-unit tank car tanks; AAR Class 203W, 206W, 211W tank car tanks; and non-DOT specification tank car tanks equivalent in structural design and accident damage resistance to specification packagings.

(b) **Cargo tanks:** Specification MC 300, MC 301, MC 302, MC 303, MC 304, MC 305, MC 306, MC 307, MC 310, MC 311, MC 312, MC 330, MC 331 cargo tank motor vehicles; DOT 406, DOT 407, DOT 412 cargo tank motor vehicles; and non-DOT specification cargo tank motor vehicles equivalent in structural design and accident damage resistance to specification packagings. A non-DOT specification cargo tank motor vehicle constructed of carbon steel which is in elevated temperature material service is excepted from §178.345-7(d)(5) of this subchapter.

(c) **Portable tanks.** DOT Specification 51, 56, 57 and 60 portable tanks; IM 101 and IM 102 portable tanks; UN portable tanks; marine portable tanks conforming to 46 CFR part 64; metal IBCs and non-specification portable tanks equivalent in structural design and accident damage resistance to specification packagings are authorized.

(d) **Crucibles:** Nonspecification crucibles designed and constructed such that the stress in the packaging does not exceed one fourth (0.25) of the ultimate strength of the packaging material at any temperature within the design temperature range. Stress is determined under a load equal to the sum of the static or working pressure in combination with the loads developed from accelerations and decelerations incident to normal transportation. For highway transportation, these forces are assumed to be "1.7g" vertical, "0.75g" longitudinal, and "0.4g" transverse, in reference to the axes of the transport vehicle. Each accelerative or decelerative load may be considered separately.

(e) **Kettles:** A kettle, for the purpose of this section, is a bulk packaging (portable tank or cargo tank) having a capacity not greater than 5678 L (1500 gallons) with an integral heating apparatus used for melting various bituminous products such as asphalt. Kettles used for the transport of asphalt or bitumen are subject to the following requirements:

(1) *Low stability kettles.* Kettles with a ratio of track-width to fully loaded center of gravity (CG) height less than 2.5 must meet all requirements of paragraph (g) of this section (track-width is the distance measured between the outer edge of the kettle tires; CG height is measured perpendicular from the road surface).

(2) *High stability kettles.*

(i) *Kettles with a total capacity* of less than 2650 L (700 gallons) and a ratio of track-width to fully loaded CG height of 2.5 or more are excepted from all requirements of paragraph (g)(2) of this section and the rollover protection requirements of paragraph (g)(6) of this section, if closures meet the requirements of paragraph (e)(2)(iii) of this section.

(ii) *Kettles with a total capacity* of 2650 L (700 gallons) or more and a ratio of track-width to fully loaded CG height of 2.5 or more are excepted from the "substantially leak tight" requirements of paragraph (g)(2) of this section and the rollover protection requirements of paragraph (g)(6) of this section if closures meet the requirements of paragraph (e)(2)(iii) of this section.

(iii) *Closures must be* securely closed during transportation. Closures also must be designed to prevent opening and the expulsion of lading in a rollover accident.

(f) **Other bulk packagings:** Bulk packagings, other than those specified in paragraphs (a) through (e) of this section, which are used for the transport of elevated temperature materials, must conform to all requirements of paragraph (g) of this section on or after October 1, 1993.

(g) **General requirements.** Bulk packagings authorized or used for transport of elevated temperature materials must conform to the following requirements:

(1) *Pressure and vacuum control equipment.* When pressure or vacuum control equipment is required on a packaging authorized in this section, such equipment must be of a self-reclosing design, must prevent package rupture or collapse due to pressure, must prevent significant release of lading due to packaging overturn or splashing or surging during normal transport conditions, and may be external to the packaging.

(i) *Pressure control equipment* is not required if pressure in the packaging would increase less than 10 percent as a result of heating the lading from the lowest design operating temperature to a temperature likely to be encountered if the packaging were engulfed in a fire. When pressure control equipment is required, it must prevent rupture of the packaging from heating, including fire engulfment.

(ii) *Vacuum control equipment* is not required if the packaging is designed to withstand an external pressure of 100 kPa (14.5 psig) or if pressure in the packaging would decrease less than 10 percent as a result of the lading cooling from the highest design operating temperature to the lowest temperature incurred in transport. When vacuum control equipment is required, it must prevent collapse of the packaging from a cooling-induced pressure differential.

(iii) *When the regulations* require a reclosing pressure relief device, the lading must not render the devices inoperable (i.e. from clogging, freezing, or fouling). If the lading affects the proper operation of the device, the packaging must have:

[A] A safety relief device incorporating a frangible disc or a permanent opening, each having a maximum effective area of 22 cm^2 (3.4 $in.^2$), for transportation by highway;

[B] For transportation of asphalt by highway, a safety relief device incorporating a frangible disc or a permanent opening, each having a maximum effective area of 48 cm^2 (7.4 in^2); or

[C] For transportation by rail, a non-reclosing pressure relief device incorporating a rupture disc conforming to the requirements of §179.15 of this subchapter.

(iv) *Reclosing pressure relief devices,* rupture discs or permanent openings must not allow the release of lading during normal transportation conditions (i.e., due to splashing or surging).

(2) *Closures.* All openings, except permanent vent openings authorized in paragraph (g)(1)(iii) of this section, must be securely closed during transportation. Packagings must be substantially leak-tight so as not to allow any more than dripping or trickling of a non-continuous flow when overturned. Closures must be designed and constructed to withstand, without exceeding the yield strength of the packaging, twice the static loading produced by the lading in any packaging orientation and at all operating temperatures.

(3) *Strength.* Each packaging must be designed and constructed to withstand, without exceeding the yield strength of the packaging, twice the static loading produced by the lading in any orientation and at all operating temperatures.

(4) *Compatibility.* The packaging and lading must be compatible over the entire operating temperature range.

(5) *Markings.* In addition to any other markings required by this subchapter, each packaging must be durably marked in a place readily accessible for inspection in characters at least 4.8 mm (3/16 inch) with the manufacturer's name, date of manufacture, design temperature range, and maximum product weight (or "load limit" for tank cars) or volumetric capacity.

(6) *Accident damage protection.* For transportation by highway, external loading and unloading valves and closures must be protected from impact damage resulting from collision or overturn. Spraying equipment and the road oil application portion of a packaging are excepted from this requirement.

(7) *New construction.* Specification packagings that are being manufactured for the transport of elevated temperature materials must be authorized for current construction.

(h) **Exceptions —**

(1) *General.* Packagings manufactured for elevated temperature materials service prior to October 1, 1993, which are not in full compliance with the requirements in paragraph (g) of this section, may continue in service if they meet the applicable requirements of subparts A and B of this part and meet the closure requirements in paragraph (g)(2) of this section by March 30, 1995.

(2) *Kettles.* Kettles in service prior to October 1, 1993, which are used to transport asphalt or bitumen, are excepted from specific provisions of this section as follows:

(i) *Kettles with a total capacity* of less than 2650 L (700 gallons), which are not in full compliance with the requirements of paragraph (g) of this section, may continue in elevated temperature material service if they meet the applicable requirements of subparts A and B of this part and if, after March 30, 1995, closures are secured during transport to resist opening in an overturn.

(ii) *Kettles with a total capacity* of 2650 L (700 gallons) or more, which are not in full compliance with the requirements of paragraph (g) of this section, may continue in elevated temperature material service if they meet the applicable requirements of subparts A and B of this part and if, after March 30, 1995, closures are secured during transport to resist opening in an overturn and no opening exceeds 46 cm^2 (7.1 in^2).

(3) *Molten metals and molten glass.* This section does not apply to packagings used for transportation of molten metals and molten glass by rail when movement is restricted to operating speeds less than 15 miles per hour. (See §172.203(g)(3) of this subchapter for shipping paper requirements.)

(4) *Solid elevated temperature materials.* A material which meets the definition of a solid elevated temperature material is excepted from all requirements of this subchapter except §172.325 of this subchapter.

§173.249 Bromine.

When §172.101 of this subchapter specifies that a hazardous material be packaged under this section, only the following bulk packagings are authorized, subject to the requirements of subparts A and B of part 173 of this subchapter and the special provisions specified in column 7 of the §172.101 table.

(a) **Class DOT 105A300W or 105A500W tank cars.** Class 105A500W tank cars may be equipped with manway cover plates, pressure relief valves, vent valves, and loading/unloading valves that are required on Class 105A-300W tank cars. Tank cars must conform with paragraphs (d) through (f) of this section.

(b) **Specification MC 310, MC 311, MC 312** or DOT 412 cargo tank motor vehicles conforming with paragraphs (d) through (f) of this section. The total quantity in one tank may not be less than 88 percent nor more than 96 percent of the volume of the tank. Cargo tanks in bromine service built prior to August 31, 1991 may continue in service under the requirements contained in §173.252(a)(4) of this part in effect on September 30, 1991.

(c) **Specification IM 101 portable tanks** conforming with paragraphs (d) through (f) of this section. The total quantity in one tank may not be less than 88 percent nor more than 92 percent of the volume of the tank.

(d) **The tank must be made from nickel-clad** or lead-lined steel plate. Nickel cladding or lead lining must be on the inside of the tank. Nickel cladding must comprise at least 20 percent of the required minimum total thickness. Nickel cladding must conform to ASTM Specification B162-69. Lead lining must be at least 4.763 mm (0.188 inch) thick. All tank equipment and appurtenances in contact with the lading must be lined or made from metal not subject to deterioration by contact with lading.

(e) **Maximum filling density is 300 percent** of the tank's water capacity. Minimum filling density is 287 percent of the tank's water capacity. Maximum water capacity is 9,253 kg (20,400 pounds) for DOT 105A300W tank cars. Maximum quantity of lading in DOT 105A300W tank cars is 27,216 kg (60,000 pounds). Maximum water capacity is 16,964 kg (37,400 pounds) for DOT 105A500W tank cars and DOT 105A500W tank cars equipped as described in paragraph (a) of this section. Maximum quantity of lading in DOT 105A500W tank cars is 49,895 kg (110,000 pounds).

(f) **Tank shell and head thickness for cargo tank motor vehicles** and portable tanks must be at least 9.5 mm (0.375 inch) excluding lead lining.

Subpart G - Gases; Preparation and Packaging

§173.300 [Reserved]

§173.301 General requirements for shipment of compressed gases in cylinders and spherical pressure vessels.

(a) **General qualifications for use of cylinders.** As used in this subpart, filled or charged means an introduction or presence of a hazardous material in a cylinder. A Class 2 material (gas) offered for transportation in a cylinder must be prepared in accordance with this section and §§173.301a through 173.305, as applicable.

(1) *Compressed gases* must be in metal cylinders and containers built in accordance with the DOT and ICC specifications, as shown in this paragraph (a)(1), in effect at the time of manufacture, and requalified and marked as required by the specification and the regulation for requalification, if applicable:

Packagings
2P
2Q
ICC-3[1]*COM019*
3A
3AA
3AL
3AX
3A480X
3AAX
3B
3BN
3E
3HT
3T
4AA480
4B
4B240ET
4BA
4BW
4D
4DA
4DS
4E
4L
8
8AL
39

1. Use of existing cylinders is authorized. New construction is not authorized.

(2) *A cylinder* must be filled in accordance with this part. Before each filling of a cylinder, the person filling the cylinder must visually inspect the outside of the cylinder. A cylinder that has a crack or leak, is bulged, has a defective valve or a leaking or defective pressure relief device, or bears evidence of physical abuse, fire or heat damage, or detrimental rusting or corrosion, may not be filled and offered for transportation. A cylinder may be repaired and requalified only as prescribed in subpart C of part 180 of this subchapter.

(3) *Pressure relief devices* must be tested for leaks before a filled cylinder is shipped from the cylinder filling plant. It is expressly forbidden to repair a leaking fusible plug device where the leak is through the fusible metal or between the fusible metal and the opening in the plug body, except by removal and replacement of the pressure relief device.

(4) *A cylinder* that previously contained a Class 8 material must be requalified in accordance with §180.205(e) of this subchapter.

(5) *When a cylinder* with a marked pressure limit is prescribed, another cylinder made under the same specification but with a higher marked pressure limit is authorized. For example, a cylinder marked "DOT-4B500" may be used when "DOT-4B300" is specified.

(6) *No person* may fill a cylinder overdue for periodic requalification with a hazardous material and then offer it for transportation. The prohibition against offering a cylinder for transportation that is overdue for periodic requalification does not apply to a cylinder filled prior to the requalification due date.

(7) *A cylinder* with an authorized service life may not be offered for transportation in commerce after its authorized service life has expired. However, a cylinder in transportation or a cylinder filled prior to the expiration of its authorized service life may be transported for reprocessing or disposal of the cylinder's contents. After emptying, the cylinder must be condemned in accordance with §180.205 of this subchapter.

(8) *The pressure* of the hazardous material at 55 °C (131 °F) may not exceed 5/4 of the service pressure of the cylinder. Sufficient outage must be provided so the cylinder will not be liquid full at 55 °C (131 °F).

(9) *Specification 2P, 2Q, 3E, 3HT,* spherical 4BA, 4D, 4DA, 4DS, and 39 cylinders must be shipped in strong outer packagings. The strong outer packaging must conform to paragraph (h) of this section and to §173.25.

(b) **Cylinder markings.** Required markings on a cylinder must be legible and must meet the applicable requirements of subpart C of part 180 of this subchapter. Additional information may be marked on the cylinder provided it does not affect the required markings prescribed in the applicable cylinder specification.

(c) **Toxic gases and mixtures.** Cylinders containing toxic gases and toxic gas mixtures meeting the criteria of Division 2.3 Hazard Zone A or B must conform to the requirements of §173.40 and CGA Pamphlets S-1.1 and S-7 (incorporated by reference; see §171.7 of this subchapter). A DOT 39 cylinder may not be used for toxic gases or toxic gas mixtures meeting the criteria for Division 2.3, Hazard Zone A or B.

(d) **Gases capable of combining chemically.** A filled cylinder may not contain any gas or material capable of combining chemically with the cylinder's contents or with the cylinder's material of construction, so as to endanger the cylinder's serviceability. After September 30, 2002, DOT 3AL cylinders made of aluminum alloy 6351-T6 may not be filled and offered for transportation with pyrophoric gases; however, if it is otherwise serviceable and conforms to the regulations in effect on September 30, 2002, a DOT 3AL cylinder made of aluminum alloy 6351-T6 and filled before October 1, 2002, may be transported for reprocessing or disposal of the cylinder's contents until April 1, 2003.

(e) **Ownership of cylinder.** A cylinder filled with a hazardous material may not be offered for transportation unless it was filled by the owner of the cylinder or with the owner's consent.

(f) **Pressure relief device systems.**

(1) *Except as provided* in paragraphs (f)(5) and (f)(6) of this section, a cylinder filled with a gas and offered for transportation must be equipped with one or more pressure relief devices sized and selected as to type, location, and quantity, and tested in accordance with CGA Pamphlets S-1.1 (incorporated by reference; see §171.7 of this subchapter; compliance with paragraph 9.1.1.1 of CGA Pamphlet S-1.1 is not required) and S-7 (incorporated by reference; see §171.7 of this subchapter). The pressure relief device must be capable of preventing rupture of the normally filled cylinder when subjected to a fire test conducted in accordance with CGA Pamphlet C-14 (incorporated by reference; see §171.7 of this subchapter), or, in the case of an acetylene cylinder, CGA Pamphlet C-12 (incorporated by reference; see §171.7 of this subchapter).

(2) *After December 31, 2003,* a pressure relief device, when installed, must be in communication with the vapor space of a cylinder containing a Division 2.1 (flammable gas) material.

(3) *For a specification* 3, 3A, 3AA, 3AL, 3AX, 3AXX, 3B, 3BN, or 3T cylinder filled with gases in other than Division 2.2, beginning with the first requalification due after December 31, 2003, the burst pressure of a CG-1, CG-4, or CG-5 pressure relief device must be at test pressure with a tolerance of plus zero to minus 10%. An additional 5% tolerance is allowed when a combined rupture disk is placed inside a holder. This requirement does not apply if a CG-2, CG-3 or CG-9 thermally activated relief device or a CG-7 reclosing pressure valve is used on the cylinder.

(4) *A pressure relief device* is required on a DOT 39 cylinder regardless of cylinder size or filled pressure. A DOT 39 cylinder used for liquefied Division 2.1 materials must be equipped with a metal pressure relief device. Fusible pressure relief devices are not authorized on a DOT 39 cylinder containing a liquefied gas.

(5) *A pressure relief device is not required on —*

(i) *A cylinder* 305 mm (12 inches) or less in length, exclusive of neck, and 114 mm (4.5 inches) or less in outside diameter, except when the cylinder is filled with a liquefied gas for which this part requires a service pressure of 1800 psig or higher or a nonliquefied gas to a pressure of 1800 psig or higher at 21 °C (70 °F);

(ii) *A cylinder* with a water capacity of less than 454 kg (1000 lbs) filled with a nonliquefied gas to a pressure of 300 psig or less at 21 °C (70 °F), except for a DOT 39 cylinder or a cylinder used for acetylene in solution; or

(iii) *A cylinder* containing a Class 3 or a Class 8 material without pressurization, unless otherwise specified for the hazardous material.

(6) *A pressure relief device* is prohibited on a cylinder filled with a Division 2.3 or 6.1 material in Hazard Zone A.

(g) Manifolding cylinders in transportation.

(1) *Cylinder manifolding* is authorized only under conditions prescribed in this paragraph (g). Manifolded cylinders must be supported and held together as a unit by structurally adequate means. Except for Division 2.2 materials, each cylinder must be equipped with an individual shutoff valve that must be tightly closed while in transit. Manifold branch lines must be sufficiently flexible to prevent damage to the valves that otherwise might result from the use of rigid branch lines. Each cylinder must be individually equipped with a pressure relief device as required in paragraph (f) of this section, except that pressure relief devices on manifolded horizontal cylinders that are mounted on a motor vehicle or framework may be selected as to type, location, and quantity according to the lowest marked pressure limit of an individual cylinder in the manifolded unit. The pressure relief devices selected for the manifolded unit must have been tested in accordance with CGA pamphlets S-1.1 and S-7 (incorporated by reference; see §171.7 of this subchapter). Pressure relief devices on manifolded horizontal cylinders filled with a compressed gas must be arranged to discharge unobstructed to the open air. In addition, for Division 2.1 (flammable gas) material, the PRDs must be arranged to discharge upward to prevent any escaping gas from contacting personnel or any adjacent cylinders. Valves and pressure relief devices on manifolded cylinders filled with a compressed gas must be protected from damage by framing, a cabinet, or other method. Manifolding is authorized for cylinders containing the following gases:

(i) *Nonliquefied (permanent)* compressed gases authorized by §173.302.

(ii) *Liquefied compressed gases* authorized by §173.304. Each manifolded cylinder containing a liquefied compressed gas must be separately filled and means must be provided to ensure no interchange of cylinder contents can occur during transportation.

(iii) *Acetylene as authorized by §173.303.*

(2) *For the checking* of tare weights or replacing solvent, the cylinder must be removed from the manifold. This requirement is not intended to prohibit filling acetylene cylinders while manifolded.

(h) Cylinder valve protection.

(1) *A cylinder* used to transport a hazardous material must meet the requirements specified in this paragraph (h). The following cylinders are not subject to the cylinder valve protection requirements in this paragraph (h):

(i) *A cylinder* containing only a Division 2.2 material without a Division 5.1 subsidiary hazard;

(ii) *A cylinder containing a Class 8 liquid corrosive only to metal;*

(iii) *A cylinder* with a water capacity of 4.8 liters (293 in^3) or less containing oxygen, compressed;

(iv) *A cylinder containing oxygen, refrigerated liquid (cryogenic liquid);*

(v) *A Medical E cylinder* with a water capacity of 4.9 liters (300 in^3) or less;

(vi) *A fire extinguisher; or*

(vii) *A "B" style cylinder* with a capacity of 40 ft^3 (1.13 m^3) or an "MC" style cylinder with a capacity of 10 ft^3 (0.28^3) containing acetylene.

(2) *For cylinders* manufactured before October 1, 2007, a cylinder must have its valves protected by one of the following methods:

(i) *By equipping* the cylinder with securely attached metal caps of sufficient strength to protect valves from damage during transportation;

(ii) *By boxing or crating* the cylinders so as to protect valves from damage during transportation;

(iii) *By constructing* the cylinder so that the valve is recessed into the cylinder or otherwise protected to the extent that it will not be subjected to a blow when the container is dropped onto a flat surface; or

(iv) *By loading the cylinders* in an upright position and securely bracing the cylinders in rail cars or motor vehicles, when loaded by the consignor and unloaded by the consignee.

(3) *For cylinders* manufactured on or after October 1, 2007, each cylinder valve assembly must be of sufficient strength or protected such that no leakage occurs when a cylinder with the valve installed is dropped 1.8 m (6 ft.) or more onto a non-yielding surface, such as concrete or steel, impacting the valve assembly or protection device at an orientation most likely to cause damage. The cylinder valve assembly protection may be provided by any method meeting the performance requirement in this paragraph (h)(3). Examples include:

(i) *Equipping the cylinder with a securely attached metal cap.*

(ii) *Packaging the cylinder* in a box, crate, or other strong outside packaging conforming to the requirements of §173.25.

(iii) *Constructing the cylinder* such that the valve is recessed into the cylinder or otherwise protected.

(i) Cylinders mounted on motor vehicles or in frames. Seamless DOT specification cylinders longer than 2 m (6.5 feet) are authorized for transportation only when horizontally mounted on a motor vehicle or in an ISO framework or other framework of equivalent structural integrity. Cylinders may not be transported by rail in container on freight car (COFC) or trailer on flat car (TOFC) service except under conditions approved by the Associate Administrator for Safety, Federal Railroad Administration. The cylinder must be configured as follows:

(1) *Each cylinder* must be fixed at one end of the vehicle or framework with provision for thermal expansion at the opposite end attachment;

(2) *The valve* and pressure relief device protective structure must be sufficiently strong to withstand a force equal to twice the weight of the cylinder and framework assembly with a safety factor of four, based on the ultimate strength of the material used; and

(3) *The pressure relief device* must be arranged to discharge unobstructed to the open air. In addition, for Division 2.1 (flammable gas) material, the pressure relief devices must be arranged to discharge upward to prevent any escaping gas from contacting personnel or any adjacent cylinders.

(j) Non-specification cylinders in domestic use. Except as provided in paragraphs (k) and (l) of this section, a filled non-DOT specification cylinder, other than a DOT exemption cylinder or a cylinder used as a fire extinguisher in conformance with §173.309, may not be offered for transportation or transported to, from, or within the United States.

(k) Importation of foreign cylinders for discharge within a single port area. A cylinder manufactured to other than a DOT specification and certified as being in conformance with the transportation regulations of another country may be authorized, upon written request to and approval by the Associate Administrator, for transportation within a single port area, provided —

(1) *The cylinder is transported in a closed freight container;*

(2) *The cylinder* is certified by the importer to provide a level of safety at least equivalent to that required by the regulations in this subchapter for a comparable DOT specification cylinder; and

(3) *The cylinder* is not refilled for export unless in compliance with paragraph (l) of this section.

(l) Filling of foreign cylinders for export. A cylinder not manufactured, inspected, tested and marked in accordance with part 178 of this subchapter, or a cylinder manufactured to other than a DOT specification or exemption, may be filled with a gas in the United States and offered for transportation and transported for export, if the following conditions are met:

(1) *The cylinder* has been requalified and marked with the month and year of requalification in accordance with subpart C of part

180 of this subchapter, or has been requalified as authorized by the Associate Administrator.

(2) *The maximum* filling density and service pressure for each cylinder conform to the requirements of this part for the gas involved.

(3) *The bill of lading* or other shipping paper identifies the cylinder and includes the following certification: "This cylinder has (These cylinders have) been qualified, as required, and filled in accordance with the DOT requirements for export."

(m) **Canadian cylinders in domestic use.** A Canadian Transport Commission (CTC) specification cylinder manufactured, originally marked and approved in accordance with the CTC regulations and in full conformance with the Canadian Transport of Dangerous Goods (TDG) Regulations is authorized for the transportation of a hazardous material to, from or within the United States under the following conditions:

(1) *The CTC specification* corresponds with a DOT specification and the cylinder markings are the same as those specified in this subchapter except that they were originally marked with the letters "CTC" in place of "DOT";

(2) *The cylinder has been requalified* under a program authorized by the Canadian TDG regulations or requalified in accordance with the requirements in §180.205 within the prescribed requalification period provided for the corresponding DOT specification;

(3) *When the regulations* authorize a cylinder for a specific hazardous material with a specification marking prefix of "DOT", a cylinder marked "CTC" which otherwise bears the same markings that would be required of the specified "DOT" cylinder may be used; and

(4) *Transport of the cylinder* and the material it contains is in all other respects in conformance with the requirements of this subchapter (e.g. valve protection, filling requirements, operational requirements, etc.).

(n) **Metal attachments.** Metal attachments to cylinders must have rounded or chamfered corners, or be otherwise protected, so as to prevent the likelihood of causing puncture or damage to other hazardous materials packages. This requirement applies to anything temporarily or permanently attached to the cylinder, such as metal skids.

§173.301a Additional general requirements for shipment of specification cylinders.

(a) **General.** The requirements in this section are in addition to the requirements in §173.301 and apply to the shipment of gases in specification cylinders.

(b) **Authorized cylinders not marked with a service pressure.** For authorized cylinders not marked with a service pressure, the service pressure is designated as follows:

Specification marking	Service Pressure psig
3	1800
3E	1800
8	250

(c) **Cylinder pressure at 21 °C (70 °F).** The pressure in a cylinder at 21 °C (70 °F) may not exceed the service pressure for which the cylinder is marked or designated, except as provided in §173.302a(b). For certain liquefied gases, the pressure at 21 °C (70 °F) must be lower than the marked service pressure to avoid having a pressure at a temperature of 55 °C (131 °F) that is greater than permitted.

(d) **Cylinder pressure at 55 °C (131 °F).** The pressure in a cylinder at 55 °C (131 °F) may not exceed 5/4 times the service pressure, except:

(1) *For a cylinder* filled with acetylene, liquefied nitrous oxide, or carbon dioxide.

(2) *For a cylinder* filled in accordance with §173.302a(b), the pressure in the cylinder at 55 °C (131 °F) may not exceed 5/4 times the filling pressure.

(3) *The pressure* at 55 °C (131 °F) of Hazard Zone A and, after December 31, 2003, Hazard Zone B materials, may not exceed the service pressure of the cylinder. Sufficient outage must be provided so that the cylinder will not be liquid full at 55 °C (131 °F).

(e) **Grandfather clause.** A cylinder in domestic use prior to the date on which the specification for the cylinder was first made effective may be used if the cylinder has been properly tested and otherwise conforms to the requirements applicable to the gas with which it is charged.

§173.301b [Reserved]

§173.302 Filling of cylinders with nonliquefied (permanent) compressed gases.

(a) **General requirements.** A cylinder filled with a nonliquefied compressed gas (except gas in solution) must be offered for transportation in accordance with the requirements of this section and §§173.301, 173.301a, 173.302a, and 173.305, as applicable. Where more than one section applies to a cylinder, the most restrictive requirements must be followed.

(b) **Aluminum cylinders in oxygen service.** Each aluminum cylinder filled with oxygen must meet all of the following conditions:

(1) *Metallic portions* of a valve that may come into contact with the oxygen in the cylinder must be constructed of brass or stainless steel.

(2) *Each cylinder opening must be configured with straight threads only.*

(3) *Each cylinder* must be cleaned in accordance with the requirements of Federal Specification RR-C-901C, paragraphs 3.3.1 and 3.3.2 (incorporated by reference; see §171.7 of this subchapter). Cleaning agents equivalent to those specified in RR-C-901C may be used provided they do not react with oxygen. One cylinder selected at random from a group of 200 or fewer and cleaned at the same time must be tested for oil contamination in accordance with Specification RR-C-901C, paragraph 4.4.2.2 (incorporated by reference; see §171.7 of this subchapter), and meet the specified standard of cleanliness.

(4) *The pressure in each cylinder* may not exceed 3000 psig at 21 °C (70 °F).

(c) **Notwithstanding the provisions of §173.24(b)(1),** an authorized cylinder containing oxygen continuously fed to tanks containing live fish may be offered for transportation and transported.

(d) **Shipment of Division 2.1 materials in aluminum cylinders** is authorized for transportation only by motor vehicle, rail car, or cargo-only aircraft.

§173.302a Additional requirements for shipment of nonliquefied (permanent) compressed gases in specification cylinders.

(a) **Detailed filling requirements.** Nonliquefied compressed gases (except gas in solution) for which filling requirements are not specifically prescribed in §173.304a must be shipped subject to the requirements in this section and §§173.301, 173.301a, 173.302, and 173.305 in specification cylinders, as follows:

(1) *DOT 3, 3A, 3AA, 3AL, 3B, 3E, 4B, 4BA and 4BW cylinders.*

(2) *DOT 3HT cylinders.* These cylinders are authorized for aircraft use only and only for nonflammable gases. They have a maximum service life of 24 years from the date of manufacture. The cylinders must be equipped with frangible disc type pressure relief devices that meet the requirements of §173.301(f). Each frangible disc must have a rated bursting pressure not exceeding 90 percent of the minimum required test pressure of the cylinder. Discs with fusible metal backing are not permitted. Specification 3HT cylinders may be offered for transportation only when packed in strong outer packagings conforming to the requirements of §173.25.

(3) *For a DOT 39 cylinder* filled with a Division 2.1 material, the internal volume of the cylinder may not exceed 1.23 L (75 in^3).

(4) *DOT 3AX, 3AAX,* and 3T cylinders are authorized for Division 2.1 and 2.2 materials and for carbon monoxide. DOT 3T cylinders are not authorized for hydrogen. When used in methane service, the methane must be a nonliquefied gas with a minimum purity of 98.0 percent methane and commercially free of corroding components.

(5) *Aluminum cylinders* manufactured in conformance with specifications DOT 39 and 3AL are authorized for oxygen only under the conditions specified in §173.302(b).

(b) **Special filling limits** for DOT 3A, 3AX, 3AA, 3AAX, and 3T cylinders. A DOT 3A, 3AX, 3AA, 3AAX, and 3T cylinder may be filled with a compressed gas, other than a liquefied, dissolved, Division 2.1, or Division 2.3 gas, to a pressure 10 percent in excess of its marked service pressure, provided:

(1) *The cylinder* is equipped with a frangible disc pressure relief device (without fusible metal backing) having a bursting pressure not exceeding the minimum prescribed test pressure.

(2) *The cylinder's* elastic expansion was determined at the time of the last test or retest by the water jacket method.

(3) *Either the average* wall stress or the maximum wall stress does not exceed the wall stress limitation shown in the following table:

Type of steel	Average wallstress limitation	Maximum wallstress limitation
I. Plain carbon steels over 0.35 carbon and medium manganese steels	53,000	58,000
II. Steels of analysis and heat-treatment specified in spec. 3AA	67,000	73,000
III. Steel of analysis and heat treatment specified in spec. DOT-3T	87,000	94,000
IV. Plain carbon steels less than 0.35 carbon made prior to 1920	45,000	48,000

(i) *[A] The average wall stress* shall be computed from the elastic expansion data using the following formula:

S = 1.7EE / KV - 0.4P

Where:

S = wall stress, pounds per square inch;

EE = elastic expansion (total less permanent) in cubic centimeters;

K = factor x 10^{-7} experimentally determined for the particular type of cylinder being tested or derived in accordance with CGA Pamphlet C-5;

V = internal volume in cubic centimeter (1 cubic inch = 16.387 cubic centimeters);

P = test pressure, pounds per square inch.

[B] The formula in paragraph (b)(3)(i)(A) of this section is derived from the formula in paragraph (b)(3)(ii) of this section and the following:

EE = $(PKVD^2) / (D^2 - d^2)$

(ii) *The maximum wall stress must be computed from the formula:*

S = $(P(1.3D^2 + 0.4d^2)) / (D^2 - d^2)$

Where:

S = wall stress, pounds per square inch;

P = test pressure, pounds per square inch;

D = outside diameter, inches;

d = D - 2t, where t=minimum wall thickness determined by a suitable method.

(iii) *Compliance with average wall stress limitation* may be determined by computing the elastic expansion rejection limit in accordance with CGA Pamphlet C-5 (incorporated by reference; see §171.7 of this subchapter), by reference to data tabulated in CGA Pamphlet C-5, or by the manufacturer's marked elastic expansion rejection limit (REE) on the cylinder.

(4) *An external and internal visual examination* made at the time of test or retest shows the cylinder to be free from excessive corrosion, pitting, or dangerous defects.

(5) *A plus sign (+)* is added following the test date marking on the cylinder to indicate compliance with paragraphs (b) (2), (b)(3), and (b)(4) of this section.

(c) **Carbon monoxide.** Carbon monoxide must be offered in a DOT 3, 3A, 3AX, 3AA, 3AAX, 3AL, 3E, or 3T cylinder having a minimum service pressure of 1800 psig. The pressure in a steel cylinder may not exceed 1000 psig at 21 °C (70 °F), except that if the gas is dry and sulfur free, the cylinder may be filled to 5/6 of the cylinder's service pressure or 2000 psig, whichever is less. A DOT 3AL cylinder may be filled to its marked service pressure. A DOT 3AL cylinder is authorized only when transported by motor vehicle, rail car, or cargo-only aircraft.

(d) **Diborane and diborane mixtures.** Diborane and diborane mixed with compatible compressed gas must be offered in a DOT 3AA1800 cylinder. The maximum filling density of the diborane may not exceed 7 percent. Diborane mixed with compatible compressed gas may not have a pressure exceeding the service pressure of the cylinder if complete decomposition of the diborane occurs. Cylinder valve assemblies must be protected in accordance with §173.301(h).

§173.302b [Reserved]

§173.303 Charging of cylinders with compressed gas in solution (acetylene).

(a) **Cylinder, filler and solvent requirements.** (Refer to applicable parts of Specification 8 and 8AL). Acetylene gas must be shipped in Specification 8 or 8AL (§178.59 or §178.60 of this subchapter) cylinders. The cylinders shall consist of metal shells filled with a porous material, and this material must be charged with a suitable solvent. The cylinders containing the porous material and solvent, shall be tested with satisfactory results in accordance with CGA Pamphlet C-12. Representative samples of cylinders charged with acetylene shall be tested with satisfactory results in accordance with CGA Pamphlet C-12.

(1) *The specific gravity* of acetone solvent in acetylene cylinders must be 0.796 or over at 15.5 °C (59.9 °F).

(2) *The amount of solvent* added in the refilling operation must not cause the tare weight of the cylinder to exceed its marked tare weight. The tare weight includes the weight of the cylinder shell, porous filling, valve, safety relief devices and solvent, but without removable cap.

(b) **Filling limits.** The pressure in cylinders containing acetylene gas must not exceed 250 psig at 70 °F, and in case the cylinders are marked for a lower allowable charging pressure, at 70 °F, then that pressure must not be exceeded.

(c) **Data requirements on filler and solvent.** Cylinders containing acetylene gas must not be shipped unless they were charged by or with the consent of the owner, and by a person, firm, or company having possession of complete information as to the nature of the porous filling, the kind and quantity of solvent in the cylinders, and the meaning of such markings on the cylinders as are prescribed by the Department's regulations and specifications applying to containers for the transportation of acetylene gas.

(d) **Verification of container pressure.**

(1) *Each day,* the pressure in a container representative of that day's compression must be checked by the charging plant after the container has cooled to a settled temperature and a record of this test kept for at least 30 days.

(e) **Prefill requirements.** Before each filling of an acetylene cylinder, the person filling the cylinder must visually inspect the outside of the cylinder in accordance with the prefill requirements contained in CGA Pamphlet C-13, Section 3.

§173.304 Filling of cylinders with liquefied compressed gases.

(a) **General requirements.** Liquefied compressed gases (except gas in solution) must be shipped in accordance with the requirements in this section and in §§173.301, 173.301a, 173.304a, and 173.305.

(1) *A DOT 3AL cylinder* may not be used for any material with a primary or subsidiary hazard of Class 8.

(2) *Shipments of* Division 2.1 materials in aluminum cylinders are authorized only when transported by motor vehicle, rail car, or cargo-only aircraft.

(b) **Filling limits.** Except for carbon dioxide; 1,1-Difluoroethylene (R-1132A); nitrous oxide; and vinyl fluoride, inhibited, the liquid portion of a liquefied gas may not completely fill the packaging at any temperature up to and including 55 °C (131 °F). The liquid portion of vinyl fluoride, inhibited, may completely fill the cylinder at 55 °C (131 °F) provided the pressure at the critical temperature does not exceed 1.25 times the service pressure of the cylinder.

(c) **Mixture of compressed gas and other material.** A mixture of compressed gas must be shipped in accordance with §173.305.

(d) **Refrigerant and dispersant gases.** Nontoxic and nonflammable refrigerant or dispersant gases must be offered for transportation in cylinders prescribed in §173.304a, or in DOT 2P and 2Q containers (§§178.33, 178.33a of this subchapter). DOT 2P and 2Q containers must be packaged in a strong wooden or fiberboard box of such design as to protect valves from damage or accidental functioning under conditions incident to transportation. Pressure in the inside metal containers may not exceed 87 psia at 21 °C (70 °F). Each completed metal container filled for shipment must be heated until its contents reach a minimum temperature of 55 °C (131 °F) without evidence of leakage, distortion, or other defect. Each outside package must be plainly marked "INSIDE CONTAINERS COMPLY WITH PRESCRIBED SPECIFICATIONS".

(e) **Engine starting fluid.** Engine starting fluid containing a flammable compressed gas or gases must be shipped in a cylinder as prescribed in §173.304a or as follows:

(1) *Inside non-refillable* metal containers having a capacity not greater than 500 mL (32 in^3). The containers must be packaged in strong, tight outer packagings. The pressure in the container may not exceed 145 psia at 54 °C (130 °F). If the pressure exceeds 145 psia at 54 °C (130 °F), a DOT 2P container must be used. In either case, the metal container must be capable of withstanding, without bursting, a pressure of 1.5 times the pressure of the contents at 54 °C (130 °F). The liquid content of the material and gas may not completely fill the container at 54 °C (130 °F). Each container filled for shipment must have been heated until its contents reach a minimum temperature of 54 °C (130 °F), without evidence of leakage, distortion, or other defect. Each outside shipping container must be plainly marked, "INSIDE CONTAINERS COMPLY WITH PRESCRIBED SPECIFICATIONS".

(2) *[Reserved]*

§173.304a Additional requirements for shipment of liquefied compressed gases in specification cylinders.

(a) **Detailed filling requirements.** Liquefied gases (except gas in solution) must be offered for transportation, subject to the requirements in this section and §§173.301 and 173.304, in specification cylinders, as follows:

(1) *DOT 3, 3A, 3AA,* 3AL, 3B, 3BN, 3E, 4B, 4BA, 4B240ET, 4BW, 4E, 39, except that no DOT 4E or 39 packaging may be filled and shipped with a mixture containing a pyrophoric liquid, carbon bisulfide (disulfide), ethyl chloride, ethylene oxide, nickel carbonyl, spirits of nitroglycerin, or toxic material (Division 6.1 or 2.3), unless specifically authorized in this part.

(2) *For the gases named,* the following requirements apply (for cryogenic liquids, see §173.316):

Kind of gas	Maximum permitted filling density (percent) (see Note 1)	Packaging marked as shown in this column or of the same type with higher service pressure must be used, except as provided in §§173.301(l),173.301a(e), and 180.205(a) (see notes following table)
Anhydrous ammonia	54	DOT-4; DOT-3A480; DOT-3AA480; DOT-3A480X; DOT-4A480; DOT-4AA480;DOT-3; DOT-3E1800; DOT-3AL480
Bromotrifluoromethane (R-13B1 or H-1301)	124	DOT-3A400; DOT-3AA400; DOT-3B400; DOT-4A400; DOT-4AA480; DOT-4B400; DOT-4BA400; DOT-4BW400; DOT-3E1800; DOT-39; DOT-3AL40
Carbon dioxide (see Notes 4, 7, and 8)	68	DOT-3A1800; DOT-3AX1800; DOT-3AA1800; DOT-3AAX1800; DOT-3; DOT-3E1800; DOT-3T1800; DOT-3HT2000; DOT-39; DOT-3AL1800
Carbon dioxide, refrigerated liquid (see paragraph (e) of this section)		DOT-4L
Chlorine (see Note 2)	125	DOT-3A480; DOT-3AA480; DOT-3; DOT-3BN480; DOT-3E1800
Chlorodifluroethane or 1-Chloro-1, 1-difluoroethane (R-142b)	100	DOT-3A150; DOT-3AA150; DOT-3B150; DOT-4B150; DOT-4BA225; DOT-4BW225; DOT-3E1800; DOT-39; DOT-3AL150
Chlorodifluoromethane (R-22) (see Note 8)	105	DOT-3A240; DOT-3AA240; DOT-3B240; DOT-4B240; DOT-4BA240; DOT-4BW240; DOT-4B240ET; DOT-4E240; DOT-39; DOT-41; DOT-3E1800; DOT-3AL240
Chloropentafluorethane (R-115)	110	DOT-3A225; DOT-3AA225; DOT-3B225; DOT-4A225; DOT-4BA225; DOT-4B225; DOT-4BW225; DOT-3E1800; DOT-39; DOT-3AL225
Chlorotrifluoromethane (R-13) (see Note 8)	100	DOT-3A1800; DOT-3AA1800; DOT-3; DOT-3E1800; DOT-39; DOT-3AL1800
Cyclopropane (see Note 8)	55	DOT-3A225; DOT-3A480X; DOT-3AA225; DOT-3B225; DOT-4A225; DOT-4AA480; DOT-4B225; DOT-4BA225; DOT-4BW225; DOT-4B240ET; DOT-3; DOT-3E1800; DOT-39; DOT-3AL225
Dichlorodifluoromethane (R-12) (see Note 8)	119	DOT-3A225; DOT-3AA225; DOT-3B225; DOT-4A225; DOT-4B225; DOT-4BA225; DOT-4BW225; DOT-4B240ET; DOT-4E225; DOT-9; DOT-39; DOT-41; DOT-3E1800; DOT-3AL225
Dichlorodifluoromethane and difluoroethane mixture (constant boiling mixture) (R-500) (see Note 8)	Not liquid full at 131 °F	DOT-3A240; DOT-3AA240; DOT-3B240; DOT-3E1800; DOT-4A240; DOT-4B240; DOT-4BA240; DOT-4BW240; DOT-4E240; DOT-9; DOT-39
1,1- Difluoroethane (R-152a) (see Note 8)	79	DOT-3A150; DOT-3AA150; DOT-3B150; DOT-4B150; DOT-4BA225; DOT-4BW225; DOT-3E1800; DOT-3AL150
1,1-Difluoroethylene (R-1132A)	73	DOT-3A2200; DOT-3AA2200; DOT-3AX2200; DOT-3AAX2200; DOT-3T2200; DOT-39
Dimethylamine, anhydrous	59	DOT-3A150; DOT-3AA150; DOT-3B150; DOT-4B150; DOT-4BA225; DOT-4BW225; ICC-3E1800
Ethane (see Note 8)	35.8	DOT-3A1800; DOT-3AX1800; DOT-3AA1800; DOT-3AAX1800; DOT-3; DOT-3E1800; DOT-3T1800; DOT-39; DOT-3AL1800
Ethane (see Note 8)	36.8	DOT-3A2000; DOT-3AX2000; DOT-3AA2000; DOT-3AAX2000; DOT-3T2000; DOT-39; DOT-3AL2000
Ethylene (see Note 8)	31.0	DOT-3A1800; DOT-3AX1800; DOT-3AA1800; DOT-3AAX1800; DOT-3; DOT-3E1800; DOT-3T1800; DOT-39; DOT-3AL1800
Ethylene (see Note 8)	32.5	DOT-3A2000; DOT-3AX2000; DOT-3AA2000; DOT-3AAX2000; DOT-3T2000; DOT-39; DOT-3AL2000
Ethylene (see Note 8)	35.5	DOT-3A2400; DOT-3AX2400; DOT-3AA2400; DOT-3AAX2400; DOT-3T2400; DOT-39; DOT-3AL2400
Hydrogen chloride, anhydrous	65	DOT-3A1800; DOT-3AA1800; DOT-3AX1800; DOT-3AAX1800; DOT-3; DOT-3T1800; DOT-3E1800
Hydrogen sulfide (see Notes 10 and 14)	62.5	DOT-3A480; DOT-3AA480; DOT-3B480; DOT-4A480; DOT-4B480; DOT-4BA480; DOT-4BW480; DOT-3E1800; DOT-3AL480
Insecticide, gases liquefied (see Notes 8 and 12)	Not liquid full at 131 °F	DOT-3A300; DOT-3AA300; DOT-3B300; DOT-4B300; DOT-4BA300; DOT-4BW300; DOT-9; DOT-40; DOT-41; DOT-3E1800
Liquefied nonflammable gases, other than classified flammable, corrosive, toxic & mixtures or solution thereof filled w/nitrogen, carbon dioxide, or air (see Notes 7 and 8)	Not liquid full at 131 °F	Specification packaging authorized in paragraph (a)(1) of this section and DOT-3HT; DOT-4D; DOT-4DA; DOT-4DS
Methyl acetylene-propadiene, mixtures, stabilized DOT-3A240; (see Note 5)	Not liquid full at 131 °F	DOT-4B240 without brazed seams; DOT-4BA240 without brazed seams; DOT-3A240; DOT-3AA240; DOT-3B240; DOT-3E1800; DOT-4BW240; DOT-4E240; DOT-4B240ET; DOT-4; DOT-41; DOT-3AL240
Methyl chloride	84	DOT-3A225; DOT-3AA225; DOT-3B225; DOT-4A225; DOT-4B225; DOT-4BA225; DOT-4BW225; DOT-3; DOT-4; DOT-38; DOT-3E1800; DOT-4B240ET. Cylinders complying with DOT-3A150; DOT-3B150; DOT-4A150; and DOT-4B150 manufactured prior to Dec. 7, 1936 are also authorized.
Methyl mercaptan	80	DOT-3A240; DOT-3AA240; DOT-3B240; DOT-4B240; DOT-4B240ET; DOT-3E1800; DOT-4BA240; DOT-4BW240
Nitrosyl chloride	110	DOT-3BN400 only
Nitrous oxide (see Notes 7, 8, and 11)	68	DOT-3A1800; DOT-3AX1800; DOT-3AA1800; DOT-3AAX1800; DOT-3; DOT-3E1800; DOT-3T1800; DOT-3HT2000; DOT-39; DOT-3AL1800
Nitrous oxide, refrigerated liquid (see paragraph (e) of this section).		DOT-4L
Refrigerant gas, n.o.s. or Dispersant gas, n.o.s. (see Notes 8 and 13)	Not liquid full at 130 °F	DOT-3A240; DOT-3AA240; DOT-3B240; DOT-3E1800; DOT-4A240; DOT-4B240; DOT-4BA240; DOT-4BW240; DOT-4E240; DOT-9; DOT-39; DOT-3AL240
Sulfur dioxide (see Note 8)	125	DOT-3A225; DOT-3AA225; DOT-3B225; DOT-4A225; DOT-4B225; DOT-4BA225; DOT-4BW225; DOT-4B240ET; DOT-3; DOT-4; DOT-38; DOT-39; DOT-3E1800; DOT-3AL225
Sulfur hexafluoride	120	DOT-3A1000; DOT-3AA1000; DOT-AAX2400; DOT-3; DOT-3AL1000; DOT-3E1800; DOT-3T1800
Sulfuryl fluoride	106	DOT-3A480; DOT-3AA480; DOT-3E1800; DOT-4B480; DOT-4BA480; DOT-4BW480
Tetrafluoroethylene, stabilized	90	DOT-3A1200; DOT-3AA1200; DOT-3E1800
Trifluorochloroethylene, stabilized	115	DOT-3A300; DOT-3AA300; DOT-3B300; DOT-4A300; DOT-4B300; DOT-4BA300; DOT-4BW300; DOT-3E1800
Trimethylamine, anhydrous	57	DOT-3A150; DOT-3AA150; DOT-3B150; DOT-4B150; DOT-4BA225; DOT-4BW225; DOT-3E1800
Vinyl chloride (see Note 5)	84	DOT-4B150 without brazed seams; DOT-4BA225 without brazed seams; DOT-4BW225; DOT-3A150; DOT-3AA150; DOT-3E1800; DOT-3AL150
Vinyl fluoride, stabilized	62	DOT-3A1800; DOT-3AA1800; DOT-3E1800; DOT-3AL1800

Kind of gas	Maximum permitted filling density (percent) (see Note 1)	Packaging marked as shown in this column or of the same type with higher service pressure must be used, except as provided in §§173.301(l),173.301a(e), and 180.205(a) (see notes following table)
Vinyl methyl ether, stabilized (see Note 5)	68	DOT-4B150, without brazed seams; DOT-4BA225 without brazed seams; DOT-4BW225; DOT-3A150; DOT-3AA150; DOT-3B1800; DOT-3E1800

NOTE 1: "Filling density" means the percent ratio of the weight of gas in a packaging to the weight of water that the container will hold at 16 °C (60 °F). (1 lb of water = 27.737 in^3 at 60 °F).
NOTE 2: Cylinders purchased after Oct. 1, 1944, for the transportation of chlorine must contain no aperture other than that provided in the neck of the cylinder for attachment of a valve equipped with an approved pressure relief device. Cylinders purchased after Nov. 1, 1935, and filled with chlorine may not contain over 68.04 kg (150 lb) of gas.
NOTE 3: [Reserved]
NOTE 4: Special carbon dioxide mining devices containing a heating element and filled with not over 2.72 kg (6 lb) of carbon dioxide may be filled to a density of not over 85 percent, provided the cylinder is made of steel with a calculated bursting pressure in excess of 39000 psig, fitted with a frangible disc that will operate at not over 57 percent of that pressure, and is able to withstand a drop of 10 feet when striking crosswise on a steel rail while under a pressure of at least 3000 psig. Such devices must be shipped in strong boxes or must be wrapped in heavy burlap and bound by 12-gauge wire with the wire completely covered by friction tape. Wrapping must be applied so as not to interfere with the functioning of the frangible disc pressure relief device. Shipments must be described as "liquefied carbon dioxide gas (mining device)" and marked, labeled, and certified as prescribed for liquefied carbon dioxide.
NOTE 5: All parts of valve and pressure relief devices in contact with contents of cylinders must be of a metal or other material, suitably treated if necessary, that will not cause formation of any acetylides.
NOTE 6: [Reserved]
NOTE 7: Specification 3HT cylinders for aircraft use only, having a maximum service life of 24 years. Authorized only for nonflammable gases. Cylinders must be equipped with pressure relief devices of the frangible disc type that meet the requirements of §173.301(f). Each frangible disc must have a rated bursting pressure that does not exceed 90 percent of the minimum required test pressure of the cylinder. Discs with fusible metal backing are not permitted. Cylinders may be shipped only when packed in strong outside packagings.
NOTE 8: See §173.301(a)(8).
NOTE 9: [Reserved]
NOTE 10: Each valve outlet must be sealed by a threaded cap or a threaded solid plug.
NOTE 11: Must meet the valve and cleaning requirements in §173.302(b).
NOTE 12: For an insecticide gas that is nontoxic and nonflammable, see §173.305(c).
NOTE 13: For a refrigerant or dispersant gas that is nontoxic and nonflammable, see §173.304(d).
NOTE 14: The use of DOT specification cylinder with a marked service pressure of 480 psi is authorized until December 31, 2003.

(b) [Reserved]

(c) Verification of content in cylinder. Except as noted in paragraph (d)(4) of this section, the amount of liquefied gas filled into a cylinder must be by weight or, when the gas is lower in pressure than required for liquefaction, a pressure-temperature chart for the specific gas may be used to ensure that the service pressure at 55 °C (131 °F) will not exceed 5/4 of the service pressure at 21 °C (70 °F). The weight of liquefied gas filled into the cylinder also must be checked, after disconnecting the cylinder from the filling line, by the use of an accurate scale.

(d) Requirements for liquefied petroleum gas.

(1) *Filling density limits are as follows:*

Minimum specific gravity of the liquid material at 60 °F	Maximum the filling density in percent of the water-weight capacity of the cylinder
0.271 to 0.289	26
0.290 to 0.306	27
0.307 to 0.322	28
0.323 to 0.338	29
0.339 to 0.354	30
0.355 to 0.371	31
0.372 to 0.398	32
0.399 to 0.425	33
0.426 to 0.440	34
0.441 to 0.452	35
0.453 to 0.462	36
0.463 to 0.472	37
0.473 to 0.480	38
0.481 to 0.488	39
0.489 to 0.495	40
0.496 to 0.503	41
0.504 to 0.510	42
0.511 to 0.519	43
0.520 to 0.527	44
0.528 to 0.536	45
0.537 to 0.544	46
0.545 to 0.552	47
0.553 to 0.560	48
0.561 to 0.568	49
0.569 to 0.576	50
0.577 to 0.584	51
0.585 to 0.592	52
0.593 to 0.600	53
0.601 to 0.608	54
0.609 to 0.617	55
0.618 to 0.626	56
0.627 to 0.634	57

(2) *Subject to §173.301a(d),* any filling density percentage prescribed in this section is authorized to be increased by a factor of 2 for liquefied petroleum gas in DOT 3 cylinders or in DOT 3A cylinders marked for 1800 psig, or higher, service pressure.

(3) *Liquefied petroleum gas* must be shipped in specification cylinders as follows:

(i) *DOT 3, 3A, 3AA,* 3B, 3E, 3AL, 4B, 4BA, 4B240ET, 4BW, 4E, or 39 cylinders. Shipments of flammable gases in DOT 3AL cylinders are authorized only when transported by motor vehicle, rail car, or cargo-only aircraft.

(ii) *Additional containers* may be used within the limits of quantity and pressure as follows:

Type of container	Maximum capacity (cubic inches)	Maximum filling pressure (p.s.i.g.)
DOT-2P or DOT-2Q (see Note 1)	31.83	45 psig at 70 °F and 105 psig at 130 °F (see Note 2)
DOT-2P or DOT-2Q (see Note 1)	31.83	35 psig at 70 °F and 100 psig at 130 °F

NOTE 1: Containers must be packed in strong wooden or fiber boxes of such design as to protect valves from damage or accidental functioning under conditions normally incident to transportation. Each completed container filled for shipment must have been heated until its contents reach a temperature of 54 °C (130 °F), without evidence of leakage, distortion, or other defect. Each outside shipping container must be plainly marked "INSIDE CONTAINERS COMPLY WITH PRESCRIBED SPECIFICATIONS."

NOTE 2: A container must be equipped with a pressure relief device that will prevent rupture of the container and dangerous projection of a closing device when exposed to fire.

(4) *Verification of content.* A cylinder with a water capacity of 90.72 kg (200 lb) or more and for use with a liquefied petroleum gas with a specific gravity of 0.504 or greater at 16 °C (60 °F) may have the quantity of its contents determined by using a fixed length dip tube gauging device. The length of the dip tube must be such that when a liquefied petroleum gas, with a specific volume of 0.03051 cu. ft./lb. at a temperature of 40 °F, is filled into the container, the liquid just reaches the bottom of the tube. The weight of this liquid may not exceed 42 percent of the water capacity of the container, which must be stamped on the cylinder. The length of the dip tube, expressed in inches carried out to one decimal place and prefixed with the letters "DT", must be stamped on the container and on the exterior of removable type dip tube. For the purpose of this requirement, the marked length must be expressed as the distance measured along the axis of a straight tube from the top of the boss through which the tube is inserted to the proper level of the liquid in the container. The length of each dip tube must be checked when installed by weighing each container after filling except when installed in groups of substantially identical containers, in which case one of each 25 containers must be weighed. The quantity of liquefied gas in each container must be checked by means of the dip tube after disconnecting from the filling line. The outlet from the dip tube may not be larger than 0.1016 centimeters (0.040 inch; No. 54 drill bit size orifice). A container representative of each day's filling at each filling plant must have its contents checked by weighing after disconnecting from the filling line.

(e) Carbon dioxide, refrigerated liquid or nitrous oxide, refrigerated liquid.

(1) *The following provisions* apply to carbon dioxide, refrigerated liquid, and nitrous oxide, refrigerated liquid:

(i) *DOT 4L cylinders* conforming to the provisions of this paragraph are authorized.

(ii) *Each cylinder* must be protected with at least one pressure relief device and at least one frangible disc conforming to §173.301(f) and paragraph (a)(2) of this section. The relieving capacity of the pressure relief device system must be equal to or greater than that calculated by the applicable formula in paragraph 5.9 of CGA Pamphlet S-1.1 (incorporated by reference; see §171.7 of this subchapter).

(iii) *The temperature* and pressure of the gas at the time the shipment is offered for transportation may not exceed -18 °C (0 °F) and 290 psig for carbon dioxide and -15.6 °C (+4 °F) and 290 psig for nitrous oxide. Maximum time in transit may not exceed 120 hours.

(2) *The following* pressure relief device settings, design service temperatures and filling densities apply:

Pressure relief device setting maximum start — to discharge gauge pressure in psig	Maximum permitted filling density (percent by weight)	
	Carbon dioxide, refrigerated liquid	Nitrous oxide, refrigerated liquid
105 psig	108	104
170 psig	105	101
230 psig	104	99
295 psig	102	97
360 psig	100	95
450 psig	98	83
540 psig	92	87
625 psig	86	80
Design service temperature °C (°F)	-196 °C (-320 °F)	-196 °C (-320 °F)

§173.304b [Reserved]

§173.305 Charging of cylinders with a mixture of compressed gas and other material.

(a) **Detailed requirements.** A mixture of a compressed gas and any other material must be shipped as a compressed gas if the mixture is a compressed gas as designated in §173.115 and when not in violation of §173.301(a).

(b) **Filling limits.** (See §173.301.) For mixtures, the liquid portion of the liquefied compressed gas at 131 °F plus any additional liquid or solid must not completely fill the container.

(c) **Nonpoisonous and nonflammable mixtures.** Mixtures containing compressed gas or gases including insecticides, which mixtures are nonpoisonous and nonflammable under this part must be shipped in cylinders as prescribed in §173.304(a) or as follows:

(1) *Specification 2P* (§178.33 of this subchapter). Inside metal containers equipped with safety relief devices of a type examined by the Bureau of Explosives and approved by the Associate Administrator, and packed in strong wooden or fiber boxes of such design as to protect valves from damage or accidental functioning under conditions incident to transportation. Pressure in the container may not exceed 85 psia at 70 °F. Each completed metal container filled for shipment must be heated until content reaches a minimum temperature of 130 °F, without evidence of leakage, distortion or other defect. Each outside shipping container must be plainly marked "INSIDE CONTAINERS COMPLY WITH PRESCRIBED SPECIFICATIONS."

(2) *[Reserved]*

(d) **Poisonous mixtures.** A mixture containing any poisonous material (Division 6.1 or 2.3) in such proportions that the mixture would be classed as poisonous under §173.115 or §173.132 must be shipped in packagings as authorized for these poisonous materials.

§173.306 Limited quantities of compressed gases.

(a) **Limited quantities of compressed gases** for which exceptions are permitted as noted by reference to this section in §172.101 of this subchapter are excepted from labeling (except when offered for transportation by air) and, unless required as a condition of the exception, specification packaging requirements of this subchapter when packed in accordance with the following paragraphs. In addition, shipments are not subject to subpart F of part 172 of this subchapter, to part 174 of this subchapter except §174.24 and to part 177 of this subchapter except §177.817. Each package may not exceed 30 kg (66 pounds) gross weight.

(1) *When in containers* of not more than 4 fluid ounces capacity (7.22 cubic inches or less) except cigarette lighters. Special exceptions for shipment of certain compressed gases in the ORM-D class are provided in paragraph (h) of this section.

(2) *When in metal containers* filled with a material that is not classed as a hazardous material to not more than 90 percent of capacity at 70 °F and then charged with nonflammable, nonliquefied gas. Each container must be tested to three times the pressure at 70 °F and, when refilled, be retested to three times the pressure of the gas at 70 °F. Also, one of the following conditions must be met:

(i) *Container is not over* 1 quart capacity and charged to not more than 170 psig at 70 °F and must be packed in a strong outside packaging, or

(ii) *Container is not over* 30 gallons capacity and charged to not more than 75 psig at 70 °F.

(3) *When in a metal container* for the sole purpose of expelling a nonpoisonous (other than a Division 6.1 Packing Group III material) liquid, paste or powder, provided all of the following conditions are met. Special exceptions for shipment of aerosols in the ORM-D class are provided in paragraph (h) of this section.

(i) *Capacity must not exceed 1 L(61.0 cubic inches).*

(ii) *Pressure in the container* must not exceed 180 psig at 130 °F. If the pressure exceeds 140 psig at 130 °F, but does not exceed 160 psig at 130 °F, a specification DOT 2P (§178.33 of this subchapter) inside metal container must be used; if the pressure exceeds 160 psig at 130 °F, a specification DOT 2Q (§178.33a of this subchapter) inside metal container must be used. In any event, the metal container must be capable of withstanding without bursting a pressure of one and one-half times the equilibrium pressure of the content at 130 °F.

(iii) *Liquid content* of the material and gas must not completely fill the container at 130 °F.

(iv) *The container must be packed in strong outside packagings.*

(v) *Each container* must be subjected to a test performed in a hot water bath; the temperature of the bath and the duration of the test must be such that the internal pressure reaches that which would be reached at 55 °C (131 °F) (50 °C (122 °F) if the liquid phase does not exceed 95% of the capacity of the container at 50 °C (122 °F)). If the contents are sensitive to heat, the temperature of the bath must be set at between 20 °C (68 °F) and 30 °C (86 °F) but, in addition, one container in 2,000 must be tested at the higher temperature. No leakage or permanent deformation of a container may occur.

(vi) *Each outside packaging* must be marked "INSIDE CONTAINERS COMPLY WITH PRESCRIBED REGULATIONS."

(4) *Gas samples must be transported under the following conditions:*

(i) *A gas sample* may only be transported as non-pressurized gas when its pressure corresponding to ambient atmospheric pressure in the container is not more than 105 kPa absolute (15.22 psia).

(ii) *Non-pressurized gases,* toxic (or toxic and flammable) must be packed in hermetically sealed glass or metal inner packagings of not more than one L (0.3 gallons) overpacked in a strong outer packaging.

(iii) *Non-pressurized gases,* flammable must be packed in hermetically-sealed glass or metal inner packagings of not more than 5 L (1.3 gallons) and overpacked in a strong outer packaging.

(b) **Exceptions for foodstuffs, soap, biologicals,** electronic tubes, and audible fire alarm systems. Limited quantities of compressed gases, (except Division 2.3 gases) for which exceptions are provided as indicated by reference to this section in §172.101 of this subchapter, when in accordance with one of the following paragraphs are excepted from labeling (except when offered for transportation by air) and the specification packaging requirements of this subchapter. In addition, shipments are not subject to subpart F of part 172 of this subchapter, to part 174 of this subchapter except §174.24 and to part 177 of this subchapter, except §177.817. Special exceptions for shipment of certain compressed gases in the ORM-D class are provided in paragraph (h) of this section.

(1) *Foodstuffs or soaps* in a nonrefillable metal container not exceeding 1 L (61.0 cubic inches), with soluble or emulsified compressed gas, provided the pressure in the container does not exceed 140 p.s.i.g. at 130 °F. The metal container must be capable of withstanding without bursting a pressure of one and one-half times the equilibrium pressure of the content at 130 °F.

(i) *Containers must be packed in strong outside packagings.*

(ii) *Liquid content* of the material and the gas must not completely fill the container at 130 °F.

(iii) *Each outside packaging* must be marked "INSIDE CONTAINERS COMPLY WITH PRESCRIBED REGULATIONS."

(2) *Cream in refillable* metal receptacles with soluble or emulsified compressed gas. Containers must be of such design that they will hold pressure without permanent deformation up to 375 psig and must be equipped with a device designed so as to

release pressure without bursting of the container or dangerous projection of its parts at higher pressures. This exception applies to shipments offered for transportation by refrigerated motor vehicles only.

(3) *Nonrefillable metal containers* charged with a Division 6.1 Packing Group III or nonflammable solution containing biological products or a medical preparation which could be deteriorated by heat, and compressed gas or gases. The capacity of each container may not exceed 35 cubic inches (19.3 fluid ounces). The pressure in the container may not exceed 140 psig at 130 °F, and the liquid content of the product and gas must not completely fill the containers at 130 °F. One completed container out of each lot of 500 or less, filled for shipment, must be heated, until the pressure in the container is equivalent to equilibrium pressure of the content at 130 °F. There must be no evidence of leakage, distortion, or other defect. Container must be packed in strong outside packagings.

(4) *Electronic tubes,* each having a volume of not more than 30 cubic inches and charged with gas to a pressure of not more than 35 psig and packed in strong outside packagings.

(5) *Audible fire alarm systems* powered by a compressed gas contained in an inside metal container when shipped under the following conditions:

(i) *Each inside container* must have contents which are not flammable, poisonous, or corrosive as defined under this part,

(ii) *Each inside container* may not have a capacity exceeding 35 cubic inches (19.3 fluid ounces),

(iii) *Each inside container* may not have a pressure exceeding 70 psig at 70 °F and the liquid portion of the gas may not completely fill the inside container at 130 °F, and

(iv) *Each nonrefillable* inside container must be designed and fabricated with a burst pressure of not less than four times its charged pressure at 130 °F. Each refillable inside container must be designed and fabricated with a burst pressure of not less than five times its charged pressure at 130 °F.

(c) - (d) [Reserved]

(e) Refrigerating machines.

(1) *New (unused)* refrigerating machines or components thereof are excepted from the specification packaging requirements of this part if they meet the following conditions. In addition, shipments are not subject to subpart F of part 172 of this subchapter, to part 174 of this subchapter except §174.24 and to part 177 of this subchapter except §177.817.

(i) *Each pressure vessel* may not contain more than 5,000 pounds of Group A1 refrigerant as classified in ANSI/ASHRAE Standard 15 or not more than 50 pounds of refrigerant other than Group A1.

(ii) *Machines or components* having two or more charged vessels may not contain an aggregate of more than 2,000 pounds of Group I refrigerant or more than 100 pounds of refrigerant other than Group I.

(iii) *Each pressure vessel* must be equipped with a safety device meeting the requirements of ANSI/ASHRAE 15.

(iv) *Each pressure vessel* must be equipped with a shut-off valve at each opening except openings used for safety devices and with no other connection. These valves must be closed prior to and during transportation.

(v) *Pressure vessels* must be manufactured, inspected and tested in accordance with ANSI/ASHRAE 15, or when over 6 inches internal diameter, in accordance with the ASME Code.

(vi) *All parts* subject to refrigerant pressure during shipment must be tested in accordance with ANSI/ASHRAE 15.

(vii) *The liquid portion* of the refrigerant, if any, may not completely fill any pressure vessel at 130 °F.

(viii) *The amount* of refrigerant, if liquefied, may not exceed the filling density prescribed in §173.304.

(f) Accumulators. The following applies to accumulators, which are hydraulic accumulators containing nonliquefied, nonflammable gas, and nonflammable liquids or pneumatic accumulators containing nonliquefied, nonflammable gas, fabricated from materials which will not fragment upon rupture.

(1) *Accumulators installed* in motor vehicles, construction equipment, and assembled machinery and designed and fabricated with a burst pressure of not less than five times their charged pressure at 70 °F, when shipped, are not subject to the requirements of this subchapter.

(2) *Accumulators charged* with limited quantities of compressed gas to not more than 200 p.s.i.g. at 70 °F are excepted from labeling (except when offered for transportation by air) and the specification packaging requirements of this subchapter when shipped under the following conditions. In addition, shipments are not subject to subpart F of part 172 of this subchapter, to part 174 of this subchapter except §174.24 and to part 177 of this subchapter except §177.817.

(i) *Each accumulator must be shipped as an inside packaging,*

(ii) *Each accumulator* may not have a gas space exceeding 2,500 cubic inches under stored pressure, and

(iii) *Each accumulator* must be tested, without evidence of failure or damage, to at least three times its charged pressure of 70 °F, but not less than 120 p.s.i. before initial shipment and before each refilling and reshipment.

(3) *Accumulators with* a charging pressure exceeding 200 p.s.i.g. at 70 °F are excepted from labeling (except when offered for transportation by air) and the specification packaging requirements of this subchapter when shipped under the following conditions:

(i) *Each accumulator* must be in compliance with the requirements stated in paragraph (f)(2), (i), (ii), and (iii) of this section, and

(ii) *Each accumulator* must be designed and fabricated with a burst pressure of not less than five times its charged pressure at 70 °F when shipped.

(4) *Accumulators intended* to function as shock absorbers, struts, gas springs, pneumatic springs or other impact or energy-absorbing devices are not subject to the requirements of this subchapter provided each:

(i) *Has a gas space capacity* not exceeding 1.6 L and a charge pressure not exceeding 280 bar, where the product of the capacity expressed in liters and charge pressure expressed in bars does not exceed 80 (for example, 0.5 L gas space and 160 bar charge pressure);

(ii) *Has a minimum burst pressure* of 4 times the charge pressure at 20 °C for products not exceeding 0.5 L gas space capacity and 5 times the charge pressure for products greater than 0.5 L gas space capacity;

(iii) *Design type* has been subjected to a fire test demonstrating that the article relieves its pressure by means of a fire degradable seal or other pressure relief device, such that the article will not fragment and that the article does not rocket; and

(iv) *Accumulators must be manufactured* under a written quality assurance program which monitors parameters controlling burst strength, burst mode and performance in a fire situation as specified in paragraphs (f)(4)(i) through (f)(4)(iii) of this section. A copy of the quality assurance program must be maintained at each facility at which the accumulators are manufactured.

(5) *Accumulators not conforming* to the provisions of paragraphs (f)(1) through (f) (4) of this section, may only be transported subject to the approval of the Associate Administrator.

(g) Water pump system tank. Water pump system tanks charged with compressed air or limited quantities of nitrogen to not over 40 psig for single-trip shipment to installation sites are excepted from labeling (transportation by air not authorized) and the specification packaging requirements of this subchapter when shipped under the following conditions. In addition, shipments are not subject to subpart F of this subchapter, to part 174 of this subchapter except §174.24 and part 177 except §177.817.

(1) *The tank must be* of steel, welded with heads concave to pressure, having a rated water capacity not exceeding 120 gallons and with outside diameter not exceeding 24 inches. Safety relief devices not required.

(2) *The tank must be* pneumatically tested to 100 psig. Test pressure must be permanently marked on the tank.

(3) *The stress at prescribed pressure must* not exceed 20,000 psi using formula:

$S = Pd / 2t$

Where:

S = wall stress in psi:

P = prescribed pressure for the tank of at least 3 times charged pressure at 70 °F or 100 psig, whichever is greater;

d = inside diameter in inches;

t = minimum wall thickness, in inches.

(4) *The burst pressure* must be at least 6 times the charge pressure at 70 °F.

(5) *Each tank* must be overpacked in a strong outer packaging in accordance with §173.301(h).

(h) A limited quantity which conforms to the provisions of paragraph (a)(1), (a)(3), or (b) of this section and is a "consumer commodity" as defined in §171.8 of this subchapter, may be renamed "consumer commodity" and reclassed as ORM-D material. Each package may not exceed 30 kg (66 pounds) gross weight. In addition to the exceptions provided by paragraphs (a) and (b) of this section —

(1) *Outside packagings* are not required to be marked "INSIDE CONTAINERS COMPLY WITH PRESCRIBED REGULATIONS";

(2) *Shipments of ORM-D materials* are not subject to the shipping paper requirements of subpart C of part 172 of this subchapter, unless the material meets the definition of a hazardous substance, a hazardous waste, or a marine pollutant or unless offered for transportation or transported by aircraft; and
(3) *Shipments of ORM-D materials* are eligible for the exceptions provided in §173.156.

(i) **An aerosol is flammable if a positive test result** is obtained using any of the following test methods:
(1) *Using the Bureau of Explosives'* Flame Projection Apparatus, the flame projects more than 18 inches beyond the ignition source with valve opened fully, or the flame flashes back and burns at the valve with any degree of valve opening.
(2) *Using the Bureau of Explosives'* Open Drum Apparatus, there is any significant propagation of flame away from the ignition source.
(3) *Using the Bureau of Explosives'* Closed Drum Apparatus, there is any explosion of the vapor-air mixture in the drum.

§173.307 Exceptions for compressed gases.

(a) **The following materials are not subject** to the requirements of this subchapter:
(1) *Carbonated beverages.*
(2) *Except as provided* in §175.10(a)(2) of this subchapter, tires when inflated to pressures not greater than their rated inflation pressures.
(3) *Balls used for sports.*
(4) *Refrigerating machines,* including dehumidifiers and air conditioners, and components thereof, such as precharged tubing containing:
(i) *12 kg (25 pounds) or less of a non-flammable, non-toxic gas;*
(ii) *12 L (3 gallons) or less of ammonia solution (UN2672);*
(iii) *Except when offered* or transported by air, 12 kg (25 pounds) or less of a flammable, non-toxic gas;
(iv) *Except when offered* or transported by air or vessel, 20 kg (44 pounds) or less of a Group A1 refrigerant specified in ANSI/ASHRAE Standard 15; or
(v) *100 g (4 ounces) or less of a flammable, non-toxic liquefied gas.*

(b) **[Reserved]**

§173.308 Cigarette lighter or other similar device charged with fuel.

(a) **In addition to the requirements of §173.21(i),** a cigarette lighter or other similar device charged with a flammable gas must be shipped as follows:
(1) *No more than 70 mL* (2.3 fluid ounces) of liquefied gas may be loaded into each device;
(2) *The liquid portion* of the gas may not exceed 85 percent of the volumetric capacity of each fluid chamber at 15 °C (59 °F);
(3) *Each device,* including closures, must be capable of withstanding without leakage or rupture an internal pressure of at least two times the vapor pressure of the fuel at 55 °C (131 °F); and
(4) *Devices must be* overpacked in packaging that is designed or arranged to prevent movement of the device itself.

(b) **When no more than 1,500 devices** covered by this section are transported in one motor vehicle by highway, the requirements of subparts C through H of part 172 of this subchapter, and part 177 of this subchapter do not apply. However, no person may offer for transportation or transport the devices or prepare the devices for shipment unless that person has been specifically informed of the requirements of this section. The outer packaging, as specified in Special Provision N10 of §172.102(c)(5) of this subchapter, must be plainly and durably marked with the required proper shipping name specified in §172.101 of this subchapter, or the words "CIGARETTE LIGHTERS" and the number of devices contained in the package.

(c) **For transportation by water in a closed transport vehicle** or a closed freight container, the following warning must be affixed to the access doors:
WARNING — MAY CONTAIN EXPLOSIVE MIXTURES WITH AIR — KEEP IGNITION SOURCES AWAY WHEN OPENING.
The warning must be on a contrasting background and must be readily legible from a distance of 8 m (26 feet).

§173.309 Fire extinguishers.

(a) **Fire extinguishers charged with a limited quantity** of compressed gas to not more than 1660 kPa (241 psig) at 21 °C (70 °F) are excepted from labeling (except when offered for transportation by air) and the specification packaging requirements of this subchapter when shipped under the following conditions. In addition, shipments are not subject to subpart F of part 172 of this subchapter, to part 174 of this subchapter except §174.24 or to part 177 of this subchapter except §177.817.
(1) *Each fire extinguisher* must have contents which are nonflammable, non-poisonous, and noncorrosive as defined under this subchapter.
(2) *Each fire extinguisher must be shipped as an inner packaging.*
(3) *Nonspecification cylinders* are authorized subject to the following conditions:
(i) *The internal volume* of each cylinder may not exceed 18 L (1,100 cubic inches). For fire extinguishers not exceeding 900 mL (55 cubic inches) capacity, the liquid portion of the gas plus any additional liquid or solid must not completely fill the container at 55 °C (130 °F). Fire extinguishers exceeding 900 mL (55 cubic inches) capacity may not contain any liquefied compressed gas;
(ii) *Each fire extinguisher* manufactured on and after January 1, 1976, must be designed and fabricated with a burst pressure of not less than six times its charged pressure at 21 °C (70 °F) when shipped;
(iii) *Each fire extinguisher* must be tested, without evidence of failure or damage, to at least three times its charged pressure at 21 °C (70 °F) but not less than 825 kPa (120 psig) before initial shipment, and must be marked to indicate the year of the test (within 90 days of the actual date of the original test) and with the words "MEETS DOT REQUIREMENTS." This marking is considered a certification that the fire extinguisher is manufactured in accordance with the requirements of this section. The words "This extinguisher meets all requirements of 49 CFR 173.306" may be displayed on fire extinguishers manufactured prior to January 1, 1976; and
(iv) *For any subsequent shipment,* each fire extinguisher must be in compliance with the retest requirements of the Occupational Safety and Health Administration Regulations of the Department of Labor, 29 CFR 1910.157(e).
(4) *Specification 2P or 2Q* (§§178.33 and 178.33a of this subchapter) inner nonrefillable metal packagings are authorized for use as fire extinguishers subject to the following conditions:
(i) *The liquid portion* of the gas plus any additional liquid or solid may not completely fill the packaging at 55 °C (130 °F);
(ii) *Pressure in the packaging* shall not exceed 1250 kPa (181 psig) at 55 °C (130 °F). If the pressure exceeds 920 kPa (141 psig) at 55 °C (130 °F), but does not exceed 1100 kPa (160 psig) at 55 °C (130 °F), a specification DOT 2P inner metal packaging must be used; if the pressure exceeds 1100 kPa (160 psig) at 55 °C (130 °F), a specification DOT 2Q inner metal packaging must be used. The metal packaging must be capable of withstanding, without bursting, a pressure of one and one-half times the equilibrium pressure of the contents at 55 °C (130 °F); and
(iii) *Each completed inner packaging* filled for shipment must have been heated until the pressure in the container is equivalent to the equilibrium pressure of the contents at 55 °C (130 °F) without evidence of leakage, distortion, or other defect.

(b) **Specification 3A, 3AA, 3E, 3AL, 4B, 4BA,** 4B240ET or 4BW (§§178.36, 178.37, 178.42, 178.46, 178.50, 178.51, 178.55 and 178.61 of this subchapter) cylinders are authorized for use as fire extinguishers.

§173.314 Compressed gases in tank cars and multi-unit tank cars.

(a) **Definitions.** For definitions of compressed gases, see §173.115.

(b) **General requirements.**
(1) *Tank car tanks* containing compressed gases must not be shipped unless they were loaded by or with the consent of the owner thereof.
(2) *Tank car tanks* must not contain gases capable of combining chemically and must not be loaded with any gas which combines chemically with the gas previously loaded therein, until all residue has been removed and interior of tank thoroughly cleaned.
(3) *For tanks* of the DOT-106A and 110A class, the tanks must be placed in position and attached to car structure by the shipper.
(4) *Wherever the word* "approved" is used in this part of the regulations, it means approval by the Association of American Railroads Committee on Tank Cars as prescribed in §179.3 of this subchapter.
(5) *Each tank car* used for the transportation of anhydrous ammonia or any material that meets the criteria of Division 2.1 or 2.3 must have gaskets for manway cover plates and for mounting of fittings designed (for temperature, application, media, pressure, and size) to create a positive seal so that, under conditions normally incident to transportation, there will not be an identifiable release of the material to the environment. The use of sealants to install gaskets is prohibited.

(c) Authorized gases, filling limits for tank cars. A compressed gas in a tank car or a multi-unit tank car must be offered for transportation in accordance with §173.31 and this section. The named gases must be loaded and offered for transportation in accordance with the following table:

Proper shipping name	Outage and filling limits (see Note 1)	Authorized tank car class
Ammonia, anhydrous, or ammonia solutions > 50 percent ammonia	Notes 2, 10	105, 112, 114, 120
	Note 3	106
Ammonia solutions with > 35 percent, but ≤ 50 percent ammonia by mass	Note 3	105, 109, 112, 114, 120
Argon, compressed	Note 4	107
Boron trichloride	Note 3	105, 106
Carbon dioxide, refrigerated liquid	Note 5	105
Chlorine	Note 6	105
	125	106
Chlorine trifluoride	Note 3	106, 110
Chlorine pentafluoride	Note 3	106, 110
Dimethyl ether	Note 3	105, 106, 110, 112, 114, 120
Dimethylamine, anhydrous	Note 3	105, 106, 112
Dinitrogen tetroxide, inhibited	Note 3	105, 106, 110
Division 2.1 materials not specifically identified in this table	Notes 9, 10	105, 106, 110, 112, 114, 120
Division 2.2 materials not specifically identified in this table	Note 3	105, 106, 109, 110, 112, 114, 120
Division 2.3 Zone A materials not specifically identified in this table	None	See §173.245
Division 2.3 Zone B materials not specifically identified in this table	Note 3	105, 106, 110, 112, 114, 120
Division 2.3 Zone C materials not specifically identified in this table	Note 3	105, 106, 110, 112, 114, 120
Division 2.3 Zone D materials not specifically identified in this table	Note 3	105, 106, 109, 110, 112, 114, 120
Ethylamine	Note 3	105, 106, 110, 112, 114, 120
Helium, compressed	Note 4	107
Hydrogen	Note 4	107
Hydrogen chloride, refrigerated liquid	Note 7	105
Hydrogen sulphide, liquified	68	106
Methyl bromide	Note 3	105, 106
Methyl chloride	Note 3	105, 106, 112
Methyl mercaptan	Note 3	105, 106
Methylamine, anhydrous	Note 3	105, 106, 112
Nitrogen, compressed	Note 4	107
Nitrosyl chloride	124	105
	110	106
Nitrous oxide, refrigerated liquid	Note 5	105
Oxygen, compressed	Note 4	107
Phosgene	Note 3	106
Sulfur dioxide, liquified	125	105, 106, 110
Sulfuryl fluoride	120	105
Vinyl fluoride, stabilized	Note 8	105

NOTES:

1. The percent filling density for liquefied gases is hereby defined as the percent ratio of the mass of gas in the tank to the mass of water that the tank will hold. For determining the water capacity of the tank in kilograms, the mass of 1 L of water at 15.5 °C in air is 1 kg. (the mass of one gallon of water at 60 °F in air is 8.32828 pounds).
2. The liquefied gas must be loaded so that the outage is at least two percent of the total capacity of the tank at the reference temperature of 46 °C (115 °F) for a noninsulated tank; 43 °C (110 °F) for a tank having a thermal protection system incorporating a metal jacket that provides an overall thermal conductance at 15.5 °C (60 °F) of no more than 10.22 kilojoules per hour per square meter per degree Celsius (0.5 Btu per hour/per square foot/ per degree F) temperature differential; and 41 °C (105 °F) for an insulated tank having an insulation system incorporating a metal jacket that provides an overall thermal conductance at 15.5 °C (60 °F) of no more than 1.5333 kilojoules per hour per square meter per degree Celsius (0.075 Btu per hour/per square foot/per degree F) temperature differential.
3. The requirements of §173.24b(a) apply.
4. The gas pressure at 54.44 °C (130 °F) in any non-insulated tank car may not exceed 7/10 of the marked test pressure, except that a tank may be charged with helium to a pressure 10 percent in excess of the marked maximum gas pressure at 54.44 °C (130 °F) of each tank.
5. The liquid portion of the gas at -17.77 °C (0 °F) must not completely fill the tank.
6. The maximum permitted filling density is 125 percent. The quantity of chlorine loaded into a single unit-tank car may not be loaded in excess of the normal lading weights nor in excess of 81.65 Mg (90 tons).
7. 89 percent maximum to 80.1 percent minimum at a test pressure of 6.2 Bar (90 psig).
8. 59.6 percent maximum to 53.6 percent minimum at a test pressure of 7.2 Bar (105 psig).
9. For a liquefied petroleum gas, the liquefied gas must be loaded so that the outage is at least one percent of the total capacity of the tank at the reference temperature of 46 °C (115 °F) for a noninsulated tank; 43 °C (110 °F) for a tank having a thermal protection system incorporating a metal jacket that provides an overall thermal conductance at 15.5 °C (60 °F) of no more than 10.22 kilojoules per hour per square meter per degree Celsius (0.5 Btu per hour/per square foot/per degree F) temperature differential; and 41 °C (105 °F) for an insulated tank having an insulation system incorporating a metal jacket that provides an overall thermal conductance at 15.5 °C (60 °F) of no more than 1.5333 kilojoules per hour per square meter per degree Celsius (0.075 Btu per hour/per square foot/per degree F) temperature differential.
10. For liquefied petroleum gas and anhydrous ammonia, during the months of November through March (winter), the following reference temperatures may be used: 38 °C (100 °F) for a noninsulated tank; 32 °C (90 °F) for a tank having a thermal protection system incorporating a metal jacket that provides an overall thermal conductance at 15.5 °C (60 °F) of no more than 10.22 kilojoules per hour per square meter per degree Celsius (0.5 Btu per hour/per square foot/per degree F) temperature differential; and 29 °C (85 °F) for an insulated tank having an insulation system incorporating a metal jacket and insulation that provides an overall thermal conductance at 15.5 °C (60 °F) of no more than 1.5333 kilojoules per hour per square meter per degree Celsius (0.075 Btu per hour/per square foot/per degree F) temperature differential. The winter reference temperatures may only be used for a tank car shipped directly to a consumer for unloading and not stored in transit. The offeror of the tank must inform each customer that the tank car was filled based on winter reference temperatures. The tank must be unloaded as soon as possible after March in order to retain the specified outage and to prevent a release of hazardous material which might occur due to the tank car becoming liquid full at higher temperatures.

(d) [Reserved]

(e) Verification of content. The amount of liquefied gas loaded into each tank may be determined either by measurement or calculation of the weight. If by measurement, the weight must be checked after disconnecting the loading line by the use of proper scales. If by calculation, the weight of liquefied petroleum gas, methylacetylene propadiene, stabilized, dimethylamine, methylamine anhydrous, or trimethylamine may be calculated using the outage tables supplied by the tank car owners and the specific gravities as determined at the plant, and this computation must be checked by determination of specific gravity of product after loading. Carriers may verify calculated weights by use of proper scales. The use of a fixed tube gauge device is authorized for determining the weight of methyl mercaptan in Specification 105A300W tanks instead of weighing.

(f) [Reserved]

(g) Special requirements for hydrogen chloride, refrigerated liquid, and vinyl fluoride,stabilized.

(1) *The shipper* shall notify the Bureau of Explosives whenever a car is not received by the consignee within 20 days from the date of shipment.

(2) *A tank car* containing hydrogen chloride, refrigerated liquid must have the auxiliary valve on the pressure relief device closed during transportation.

(3) *See §179.102-17 of this subchapter for additional requirements.*

(4) *Tank cars* containing hydrogen chloride, refrigerated liquid, must be unloaded to such an extent that any residue remaining in the tank at a reference temperature of 32 °C (90 °F) will not actuate the reclosing pressure relief device.

(h) - (i) [Reserved]

(j) Special requirements for materials having a primary or secondary Division 2.1 (flammable gas) hazard. For single unit tank cars, interior pipes of loading and unloading valves, sampling devices, and gauging devices with an opening for the passage of the lading exceeding 1.52 mm (0.060 inch) diameter must be equipped with excess flow valves. For single unit tank cars constructed before January 1, 1972, gauging devices must conform to this paragraph by no later than July 1, 2006. The protective housing cover must be provided with an opening, with a weatherproof cover, above each pressure relief valve that is concentric with the discharge of the pressure relief valve and that has an area at least equal to the valve outlet area. Class DOT 109 tank cars and tank cars manufactured from aluminum or nickel plate are not authorized.

(k) Special requirements for chlorine. Tank cars built after September 30, 1991, must have an insulation system consisting of 5.08 cm (2 inches) glass fiber placed over 5.08 cm (2 inches) of ceramic fiber. Tank cars must have excess flow valves on the interior pipes of liquid discharge valves. Tank cars constructed to a DOT 105A500W specification may be marked as a DOT 105A300W specification with the size and type of safety relief valves required by the marked specification.

(l) Special requirements for hydrogen sulphide. Each multi-unit tank car must be equipped with adequate pressure relief devices of the fusible plug type having a yield temperature not over 76.66 °C (170 °F), and not less than 69.44 °C (157 °F). Each device must be resistant to extrusion of the fusible alloy and leak tight at 55 °C (130 °F). A threaded solid plug must seal each valve outlet. In addition, a metal cover must protect all valves.

(m) **Special requirements for nitrosyl chloride.** Single unit tank cars and their associated service equipment, such as venting, loading and unloading valves, and safety relief valves, must be made of metal or clad with a material that is not subject to rapid deterioration by the lading. Multi-unit tank car tanks must be nickel-clad and have safety relief devices incorporating a fusible plug having a yield temperature of 79.44 °C (175 °F). Safety relief devices must be vapor tight at 54.44 °C (130 °F).

(n) **Special requirements for hydrogen.** Each tank car must be equipped with one or more pressure relief devices. The discharge outlet for each pressure relief device must be connected to a manifold having a non-obstructed discharge area of at least 1.5 times the total discharge area of the pressure relief devices connected to the manifold. All manifolds must be connected to a single common header having a non-obstructed discharge pointing upward and extending above the top of the car. The header and the header outlet must each have a non-obstructed discharge area at least equal to the total discharge area of the manifolds connected to the header. The header outlet must be equipped with an ignition device that will instantly ignite any hydrogen discharged through the pressure relief device.

(o) **Special requirements for carbon dioxide,** refrigerated liquid and nitrous oxide, refrigerated liquid. Each tank car must have an insulation system so that the thermal conductance is not more than 0.613 kilojoules per hour, per square meter, per degree Celsius (0.03 B.t.u. per square foot per hour, per degree Fahrenheit) temperature differential. Each tank car must be equipped with one reclosing pressure relief valve having a start-to-discharge pressure not to exceed 75 percent of the tank test pressure and one non-reclosing pressure relief valve having a rupture disc design to burst at a pressure less than the tank test pressure. The discharge capacity of each pressure relief device must be sufficient to prevent building up of pressure in the tank in excess of 82.5 percent of the test pressure of the tank. Tanks must be equipped with two regulating valves set to open at a pressure not to exceed 24.1 Bar (350 psi) on DOT 105A500W tanks and at a pressure not to exceed 27.6 Bar (400 psi) on DOT 105A600W tanks. Each regulating valve and pressure relief device must have its final discharge piped to the outside of the protective housing.

§173.315 Compressed gases in cargo tanks and portable tanks.

(a) **Liquefied compressed gases that are transported** in UN portable tanks must be loaded and offered for transportation in accordance with portable tank provision T50 in §172.102 of this subchapter. A liquefied compressed gas offered for transportation in a cargo tank motor vehicle or a portable tank must be prepared in accordance with this section, §173.32, §173.33 and subpart E or subpart G of part 180 of this subchapter, as applicable. For cryogenic liquids, see §173.318. For marking requirements, see §§172.326 and 172.328 of this subchapter. Except for UN portable tanks, a liquefied compressed gas must be loaded and offered for transportation in accordance with the following table:

Kind of gas	Maximum permitted filling density		Specification container required	
	Percent by weight (see Note 1)	Percent by volume (see par. (f) of this section)	Type (see Note 2)	Minimum design pressure (psig)
Ammonia, anhydrous or Ammonia solutions with greater than 50 percent ammonia (see Notes 14 and 17)	56	82; see Note 5	DOT-51, MC-330, MC-331; see Notes 12 and 17	265; see Note 17
Ammonia solutions with more than 35 percent but not more than 50 percent ammonia	See par. (c) of this section	See Note 7	DOT-51, MC-330, MC-331; see Note 12	100; see par. (c) of this section
Bromotrifluoromethane (R-13B1 or H-1301) (see Note 9);	133	See Note 7	DOT-51, MC-330, MC-331	365
Butadiene, stabilized	See par. (b) of this section	See par. (b) of this section	DOT-51, MC-330, MC-331	100
Carbon dioxide, refrigerated liquid	See par. (c)(1) of this section	95	do	200; see Note 3
Chlorine	125	See Note 7	DOT-51, MC-330, MC-331	225; see Notes 4 and 8
Chlorodifluoroethane (R-142b) (1-Chloro 1,1-difluoroethane) (see Note 9)	100	See Note 7	DOT-51, MC-330, MC-331	100
Chlorodifluoromethane (R-22) (see Note 9)	105	See Note 7	DOT-51, MC-330, MC-331	250
Chloropentafluoroethane (R-115) (see Note 9)	See par. (c) of this section	See Note 7	DOT-51, MC-330, MC-331	See par. (c) of this section
Chlorotrifluoromethane (R-13) (see Note 9)	See par. (c) of this section	See Note 7	DOT-51, MC-330, MC-331	See par. (c) of this section
Dichlorodifluoromethane (R-12) (see Note 9)	119	See Note 7	DOT-51, MC-330, MC-331	150
Difluoroethane (R-152a) (see Note 9)	79	See Note 7	DOT-51, MC-330, MC-331	150
Dimethyl ether (see Note 16)	59	do	do	200
Dimethylamine, anhydrous	59	See Note 7	DOT-51, MC-330, MC-331	150
Division 2.1, materials not specifically provided for in this table	See par. (c) of this section	See Note 7	DOT-51, MC-330, MC-331	See Note 18
Division 2.2, materials not specifically provided for in this table	See par. (c) of this section	See Note 7	DOT-51, MC-330, MC-331	See Note 19
Division 2.3, Hazard Zone A, materials not specifically provided for in this table	See par. (c) of this section	See Note 7	DOT-51, MC-330, MC-331; see Note 23	See Note 20
Division 2.3, Hazard Zone B, materials not specifically provided for in this table	See par. (c) of this section	See Note 7	DOT-51, MC-330, MC-331; see Note 23	See Note 20
Division 2.3, Hazard Zone C, materials not specifically provided for in this table	See par. (c) of this section	See Note 7	DOT-51, MC-330, MC-331; see Note 24	See Note 21
Division 2.3, Hazard Zone D, materials not specifically provided for in this table	See par. (c) of this section	See Note 7	DOT-51, MC-330, MC-331; see Note 25	See Note 22
Ethane, refrigerated liquid		See par. (c) of this section	MC-331, MC-338	100; see Note 11
Ethane-propane mixture, refrigerated liquid		See par. (c) of this section	MC-331, MC-338	275; see Note 11
Hexafluoropropylene	110	See Note 7	DOT-51, MC-330, MC-331	250
Hydrogen chloride, refrigerated liquid	103.0 91.6 86.7	See Note 7 do do	MC-331, MC-338 do do	100; see Note 11 300; see Note 11 450; see Note 11
Liquefied petroleum gas (see Note 15)	See par. (b) of this section	See par. (b) of this section	DOT-51, MC-330, MC-331; see Note 26	See par. (c) of this section

Kind of gas	Maximum permitted filling density		Specification container required	
	Percent by weight (see Note 1)	Percent by volume (see par. (f) of this section)	Type (see Note 2)	Minimum design pressure (psig)
Methylacetylene-propadiene, stabilized (see Note 13)	53	90	DOT-51, MC-330, MC-331	200
Methylamine, anhydrous	60	See Note 7	DOT-51, MC-330, MC-331	
Methyl chloride	84	88.5	do	150
Methyl chloride (optional portable tank 2,000 pounds water capacity, fusible plug)	do	See Note 6	DOT-51	225
Methyl mercaptan	80	90	DOT-51, MC-330, MC-331; see Note 23	100
Nitrous oxide, refrigerated liquid	See par. (c)(1) of this section	95	DOT-51, MC-330, MC-331	200; see Note 3
Refrigerant gas, n.o.s. or Dispersant gas, n.o.s. (see Note 9)	See par. (c) of this section	See Note 7	DOT-51, MC-330, MC-331	See par. (c) of this section
Sulfur dioxide (tanks not over 1,200 gallons water capacity)	125	87.5	DOT-51, MC-330, MC-331; see Note 24	150; see Note 4
Sulfur dioxide (tanks over 1,200 gallons water capacity)	125	87.5	DOT-51, MC-330, MC-331; see Note 24	125; see Note 4
Sulfur dioxide (optional portable tank 1,000-2,000 pounds water capacity, fusible plug)	125	See Note 6	DOT-51; see Note 24	225
Trimethylamine, anhydrous	57	See Note 7	DOT-51, MC-330, MC-331	150
Vinyl chloride	84 (see Note 13)	See Note 7	MC-330, MC-331	150
Vinyl fluoride, stabilized	66	do	do	250; see Note 11
Vinyl methyl ether	68	See Notes 7 and 13	do	100

NOTE 1: Maximum filling density for liquefied gases is hereby defined as the percent ratio of the weight of gas in the tank to the weight of water that the tank will hold. For determining the water capacity of the tank in pounds, the weight of a gallon (231 cubic inches) of water at 60 °F in air shall be 8.32828 pounds.

NOTE 2: See §173.32 for authority to use other portable tanks and for manifolding cargo tanks, see paragraph (q) of this section. Specifications MC 330 cargo tanks may be painted as specified for MC 331 cargo tanks.

NOTE 3: If cargo tanks and portable tank containers for carbon dioxide, refrigerated liquid and nitrous oxide, refrigerated liquid are designed to conform to the requirements of the ASME Code for Low Temperature Operation, the design pressure may be reduced to 100 p.s.i.g. or the controlled pressure, whichever is greater.

NOTE 4: Material must be steel. Packagings must have a corrosion allowance of 20 percent or 0.10 inch, whichever is less, added to the metal thickness. The minimum wall thickness for chlorine packagings is 0.300 inch for stainless steel or 0.625 inch for carbon steel, including corrosion allowance.

NOTE 5: Unlagged cargo tanks and portable tank containers for liquid anhydrous ammonia may be filled to 87.5 percent by volume provided the temperature of the anhydrous ammonia being loaded into such tanks is determined to be not lower than 30 °F or provided the filling of such tanks is stopped at the first indication of frost or ice formation on the outside surface of the tank and is not resumed until such frost or ice has disappeared.

NOTE 6: Tanks equipped with fusible plugs must be filled by weight.

NOTE 7: Tanks must be filled by weight.

NOTE 8: Chlorine packagings may be shipped only if the contents are to be unloaded at one unloading point.

NOTE 9: This gas may be transported in authorized cargo tanks and portable tanks marked "DISPERSANT GAS," or "REFRIGERANT GAS."

NOTE 10: [Reserved]

NOTE 11: MC-330, MC-331 and MC-338 cargo tanks must be insulated. Cargo tanks must meet all the following requirements. Each tank must have a design service temperature of minus 100 °F, or no warmer than the boiling point at one atmosphere of the hazardous material to be shipped therein, whichever is colder, and must conform to the low-temperature requirements of the ASME Code. When the normal travel time is 24 hours or less, the tank's holding time as loaded must be at least twice the normal travel time. When the normal travel time exceeds 24 hours, the tank's holding time as loaded must be at least 24 hours greater than the normal travel time. The holding time is the elapsed time from loading until venting occurs under equilibrium conditions. The cargo tank must have an outer jacket made of steel when the cargo tank is used to transport a flammable gas.

NOTE 12: No aluminum, copper, silver, zinc or an alloy of any of these metals shall be used in packaging construction where it comes into contact with the lading.

NOTE 13: All parts of valves and safety devices in contact with contents of tank must be of a metal or other material suitably treated if necessary, which will not cause formation of any acetylides.

NOTE 14: Specifications MC 330 and MC 331 cargo tanks constructed of other than quenched and tempered steel "(NQT)" are authorized for all grades of anhydrous ammonia. Specifications MC 330 and MC 331 cargo tanks constructed of quenched and tempered steel "(QT)" (see marking requirements of §172.328(c) of this subchapter) are authorized for anhydrous ammonia having a minimum water content of 0.2 percent by weight. Any tank being placed in anhydrous ammonia service or a tank which has been in other service or has been opened for inspection, test, or repair, must be cleaned of the previous product and must be purged of air before loading. See §172.203(h) of this subchapter for special shipping paper requirements.

NOTE 15: Specifications MC 330 and MC 331 cargo tanks constructed of other than quenched and tempered steel (NQT) are authorized for all grades of liquefied petroleum gases. Only grades of liquefied petroleum gases determined to be "noncorrosive" are authorized in Specification MC 330 and MC 331 cargo tanks constructed of quenched and tempered steel (QT). "Noncorrosive" means the corrosiveness of the gas does not exceed the limitations for classification 1 of the ASTM Copper Strip Classifications when tested in accordance with ASTM D1838-64, "Copper Strip Corrosion by Liquefied Petroleum (LP) Gases." (For (QT) and (NQT) marking requirements see §172.328(c) of this subchapter. For special shipping paper requirements, see §172.203(h) of this subchapter.)

NOTE 16: Openings, inlets, and outlets on MC 330 and MC 331 cargo tanks must conform to §178.337-8(a) of this subchapter. MC 330 and MC 331 cargo tanks must be equipped with emergency discharge control equipment as specified in §178.337-11(a) of this subchapter.

NOTE 17: A Specification MC-330 or MC-331 cargo tank or a nonspecification cargo tank meeting, and marked in conformance with, the edition of the ASME Code in effect when it was fabricated, may be used for the transportation of anhydrous ammonia if it:

(1) Has a minimum design pressure not lower than 250 psig;

(2) Was manufactured in conformance with the ASME Code prior to January 1, 1981, according to its ASME name plate and manufacturer's data report;

(3) Is painted white or aluminum;

(4) Complies with NOTE 12 of this paragraph;

(5) Has been inspected and tested in accordance with subpart E of part 180 of this subchapter as specified for MC 331 cargo tanks.

(6) Was used to transport anhydrous ammonia prior to January 1, 1981;

(7) Is operated exclusively in intrastate commerce (including its operation by a motor carrier otherwise engaged in interstate commerce) in a state where its operation was permitted by the laws of that State (not including the incorporation of this subchapter) prior to January 1, 1981; and

(8) Is operated in conformance with all other requirements of this subchapter.

NOTE 18: The minimum packaging design pressure must not be less than the vapor pressure at the reference temperature of the lading plus one percent or 173.4 kPa (25 psig), whichever is less.

NOTE 19: The minimum packaging design pressure must not be less than the vapor pressure at the reference temperature of the lading.

NOTE 20: The minimum packaging design pressure must not be less than 1.5 times the vapor pressure of the lading at 46 °C (115 °F).

NOTE 21: The minimum packaging design pressure must not be less than 1.3 times the vapor pressure of the lading at 46 °C (115 °F).

NOTE 22: The minimum packaging design pressure must not be less than 1.1 times the vapor pressure of the lading at 46 °C (115 °F).

NOTE 23: Packagings must be made of stainless steel except that steel other than stainless steel may be used in accordance with the provisions of §173.24b(b) of this part. Thickness of stainless steel for shell and heads must be the greater of 7.62 mm (0.300 inch) or the thickness required for the packaging at its minimum design pressure.

NOTE 24: Packagings must be made of stainless steel except that steel other than stainless steel may be used in accordance with the provisions of §173.24b(b) of this part. Thickness of stainless steel for shell and heads must be the greater of 6.35 mm (0.250 inch) or the thickness required for the packaging at its minimum design pressure. For sulphur dioxide, this Note does not apply until October 1, 1994.

NOTE 25: Packagings must be made of stainless steel except that steel other than stainless steel may be used in accordance with the provisions of §173.24b(b) of this part. Thickness for shell and heads must be as calculated for the packaging at its minimum design pressure.

NOTE 26: Non-specification cargo tanks may be used for the transportation of liquefied petroleum gas, subject to the conditions prescribed in paragraph (k) of this section.

(b) Maximum permitted filling densities for cargo and portable tank containers for transportation of butadiene, stabilized, and liquefied petroleum gas are as follows:

Maximum specific gravity of the liquid material at 60 °F	Maximum permitted filling density in percent of the water-weight capacity of the tanks (percent) See Note 1	
	1200 gallons or less	Over 1200 gallons
0.473 to 0.480	38	41
0.481 to 0.488	39	42
0.489 to 0.495	40	43
0.496 to 0.503	41	44
0.504 to 0.510	42	45
0.511 to 0.519	43	46
0.520 to 0.527	44	47
0.528 to 0.536	45	48
0.537 to 0.544	46	49
0.545 to 0.552	47	50
0.553 to 0.560	48	51
0.561 to 0.568	49	52
0.569 to 0.576	50	53
0.577 to 0.584	51	54
0.585 to 0.592	52	55
0.593 to 0.600	53	56
0.601 to 0.608	54	57
0.609 to 0.617	55	58
0.618 to 0.626	56	59
0.627 and over	57	60

NOTE 1: Filling is permitted by volume provided the same filling density is used as permitted by weight, except when using fixed length dip tube or other fixed maximum liquid level indicators (paragraph (f) of this section), in which case the maximum permitted filling density shall not exceed 97 percent of the maximum permitted filling density by weight contained in the table.

(1) *Odorization.* All liquefied petroleum gas shall be effectively odorized as required in Note 2 of this paragraph to indicate positively, by a distinctive odor, the presence of gas down to a concentration in air of not over one-fifth the lower limit of combustibility: Provided, however, That odorization is not required if harmful in the use or further processing of the liquefied petroleum gas, or if odorization will serve no useful purpose as a warning agent in such use or further processing.

NOTE 1: The lower limits of combustibility of the more commonly used liquefied petroleum gases are: Propane, 2.15 percent; butane, 1.55 percent. These figures represent volumetric percentages of gas-air mixtures in each case.

NOTE 2: The use of 1.0 pound of ethyl mercaptan, 1.0 pound of thiophane, or 1.4 pounds of amyl mercaptan per 10,000 gallons of liquefied petroleum gas shall be considered sufficient to meet the requirements of §173.315(b)(1). This note does not exclude the use of any other odorant in sufficient quantity to meet the requirements of §173.315(b)(1).

(c) Except as otherwise provided, the loading of a liquefied gas into a cargo tank or portable tank shall be determined by weight or by a suitable liquid level gauging device. The vapor pressure (psig) at 115 °F must not exceed the design pressure of the cargo tank or portable tank container. The outage and filling limits for liquefied gases must be as prescribed in §173.24b of this part, except that this requirement does not apply to:

(1) *A tank* containing carbon dioxide, refrigerated liquid or nitrous oxide, refrigerated liquid. Such tank is required to be equipped with suitable pressure control valves and may not be filled to a level exceeding 95 percent of the volumetric capacity of the tank.

(2) *A tank* containing ethane, refrigerated liquid; ethane-propane mixture, refrigerated liquid; or hydrogen chloride, refrigerated liquid. Such tank must be filled to allow at least two percent outage below the inlet of the pressure relief valve or pressure control valve under conditions of incipient opening, with the tank in a level attitude.

(d) If the loading of cargo tanks and portable tank containers with liquefied gases is to be determined by weight, the gross weight shall be checked after the filling line is disconnected in each instance. The gross weight shall be calculated from the tank capacity and tare weight set forth on the metal plate required by the specification, and the maximum filling density permitted for the material being loaded into the tank as set forth in the table, paragraph (a) of this section.

(e) If the loading of cargo tanks and portable tank containers with liquefied gases is to be determined by adjustable liquid level device, each tank and each compartment thereof shall have a thermometer well, so that the internal liquid temperature can easily be determined, and the amount of liquid in the tank shall be corrected to a 60 °F basis. Liquid levels shall not exceed a level corresponding to the maximum filling density permitted for the material being loaded into the tank as set forth in the table in paragraph (a) of this section.

(f) When the loading of cargo tanks and portable tank containers with liquefied gases is determined only by fixed length dip tube or other fixed maximum liquid level indicator, the device shall be arranged to function at a level not to exceed the maximum permitted volume prescribed by the table, paragraph (a) of this section. Loading shall be stopped when the device functions.

(g) Containers, the liquid level of which has been determined by means of a fixed length dip tube gauging device, shall not be acceptable for stowage as cargo on vessels in commerce subject to the jurisdiction of the United States Coast Guard. Nothing contained in this section shall be so construed as to prohibit the transportation on car floats or car ferries of motor vehicles laden with containers nor cargo tanks the liquid level of either of which has been determined by means of fixed length dip tube devices.

(h) Each cargo tank and portable tank, except a tank filled by weight, must be equipped with one or more of the gauging devices described in the following table which indicate accurately the maximum permitted liquid level. Additional gauging devices may be installed but may not be used as primary controls for filling of cargo tanks and portable tanks. Gauge glasses are not permitted on any cargo tank or portable tank. Primary gauging devices used on cargo tanks of less than 3500 gallons water capacity are exempt from the longitudinal location requirements specified in paragraphs (h)(2) and (3) of this section provided: The tank length does not exceed three times the tank diameter; and the cargo tank is unloaded within 24 hours after each filling of the tank.

Kind of gas	Gaging device permitted for filling purposes
Anhydrous ammonia	Rotary tube; adjustable slip tube; fixed length dip tube
Anhydrous dimethylamine	None
Anhydrous monomethylamine	Do
Anhydrous trimethylamine	Do
Aqua ammonia solution containing anhydrous ammonia	Rotary tube; adjustable slip tube; fixed length dip tube
Butadiene, stabilized	Do
Carbon dioxide, refrigerated liquid	Do
Chlorine	None
Dichlorodifluoromethane	Do
Difluoroethane	Do
Difluoromonochloroethane	Do
Dimethyl ether	Do
Ethane, refrigerated liquid	Rotary tube; adjustable slip tube; fixed length dip tube
Ethane-propane mixture, refrigerated liquid	Do
Hexafluoropropylene	None
Hydrogen chloride, refrigerated liquid	Do
Liquefied petroleum gases	Rotary tube; adjustable slip tube; fixed length dip tube
Methyl chloride	Fixed length dip tube
Methyl mercaptan	Rotary tube; adjustable slip tube; fixed length dip tube
Monochlorodifluoromethane	None
Nitrous oxide, refrigerated liquid	Rotary tube; adjustable slip tube; fixed length dip tube
Methylacetylenepropadiene, stabilized	Do
Refrigerant gas, n.o.s. or Dispersant gas, n.o.s.	None
Sulfur dioxide	Fixed length dip tube
Vinyl chloride	None
Vinyl fluoride, inhibited	Do

(1) *The design pressure* of the liquid level gauging devices shall be at least equal to the design pressure of the tank.

(2) *If the primary* gauging device is adjustable, it must be capable of adjustment so that the end of the tube will be in the location specified in paragraph (h)(3) of this section for at least one of the ladings to be transported, at the filling level corresponding to an average loading temperature. Exterior means must be provided to indicate this adjustment. The gauging device must be legibly and permanently marked in increments not exceeding 20 Fahrenheit degrees (or not exceeding 25 p.s.i.g. on tanks for carbon dioxide, refrigerated liquid or nitrous oxide, refrigerated liquid), to indicate the maximum levels to which the tank may be filled with liquid at temperatures above 20 °F. However, if it is not practicable to so mark the gauging device, this information must be legibly and permanently marked on a plate affixed to the tank adjacent to the gauging device.

(3) *A dip tube* gauging device consists of a pipe or tube with a valve at its outer end with its intake limited by an orifice not larger than 0.060 inch in diameter. If a fixed length dip tube is used, the intake must be located midway of the tank both longitudinally and laterally and at maximum permitted filling level. In tanks for liquefied petroleum gases, the intake must be located at the level reached by the lading when the tank is loaded to maximum filling density at 40 °F.

(4) *Except on a tank* used exclusively for the transportation of carbon dioxide, refrigerated liquid or nitrous oxide, refrigerated liquid, each opening for a pressure gauge must be restricted at or inside the tank by an orifice no larger than 0.060 inch in diameter. For carbon dioxide, refrigerated liquid or nitrous oxide, refrigerated liquid service, the pressure gauge need only be used during the filling operation.

(i) **Each tank must be provided with one or more** pressure relief devices which, unless otherwise specified in this part, must be of the spring-loaded type. Each valve must be arranged to discharge upward and unobstructed to the outside of the protective housing to prevent any impingement of escaping gas upon the tank. For each chlorine tank the protective housing must be in compliance with the requirements set forth in the applicable specification.

(1) *The safety relief valves* on each tank must meet the following conditions:

(i) *The total relieving capacity,* as determined by the flow formulas contained in Section 5 of CGA Pamphlet S-1.2, must be sufficient to prevent a maximum pressure in the tank of more than 120 percent of the design pressure;

(ii) *The flow capacity* rating, testing and marking must be in accordance with Sections 5, 6 and 7 of CGA Pamphlet S-1.2.

(iii) *For an insulated tank,* the required relieving capacity of the relief devices must be the same as for an uninsulated tank, unless the insulation will remain in place and will be effective under fire conditions. In this case, except for UN portable tanks, each insulated tank must be covered by a sheet metal jacket of not less than 16 gauge thickness. For UN portable tanks where the relieving capacity of the valves has been reduced on the basis of the insulation system, the insulation system must remain effective at all temperatures less than 649 °C (1200.2 °F) and be jacketed with a material having a melting point of 700 °C (1292.0 °F) or greater.

(iv) *An MC 330 cargo tank* that has relief valves sized by Fetterly's formula dated November 27, 1928, may be continued in service.

(2) *Each safety relief valve* must be arranged to minimize the possibility of tampering. If the pressure setting or adjustment is external to the valve, the safety relief valve must be provided with means for sealing the adjustment and it must be sealed.

(3) *Each safety relief valve* on a portable tank, other than a UN portable tank, must be set to start-to-discharge at pressure no higher than 110% of the tank design pressure and no lower than the design pressure specified in paragraph (a) of this section for the gas transported. For UN portable tanks used for liquefied compressed gases and constructed in accordance with the requirements of §178.276 of this subchapter, the pressure relief device(s) must conform to §178.276(e) of this subchapter.

(4) *Except for UN portable tanks,* each safety relief valve must be plainly and permanently marked with the pressure in p.s.i.g. at which it is set to discharge, with the actual rate of discharge of the device in cubic feet per minute of the gas or of air at 60 °F (15.6 °C) and 14.7 p.s.i.a., and with the manufacturer's name or trade name and catalog number. The start-to-discharge valve marking must be visible after the valve is installed. The rated discharge capacity of the device must be determined at a pressure of 120% of the design pressure of the tank. For UN portable tanks, each pressure relief device must be clearly and permanently marked as specified in §178.274(f)(1) of this subchapter.

(5) *Each safety relief valve* must have direct communication with the vapor space in the tank.

(6) *Each connection* to a safety relief valve must be of sufficient size to provide the required rate of discharge through the safety relief valve.

(7) *[Reserved]*

(8) *Each pressure relief* valve outlet must be provided with a protective device to prevent the entrance and accumulation of dirt and water. This device must not impede flow through the valve. Pressure relief devices must be designed to prevent the entry of foreign matter, the leakage of liquid and the development of any dangerous excess pressure.

(9) *On tanks* for carbon dioxide, refrigerated liquid or nitrous oxide, refrigerated liquid each safety relief device must be installed and located so that the cooling effect of the contents will not prevent the effective operation of the device. In addition to the required safety relief valves, these tanks may be equipped with one or more pressure controlling devices.

(10) *Each tank* for carbon dioxide, refrigerated liquid also may be equipped with one or more non-reclosing pressure relief devices set to function at a pressure not over two times nor less than 1.5 times the design pressure of the tank.

(11) *Each portion* of connected liquid piping or hose that can be closed at both ends must be provided with a safety relief valve without an intervening shut-off valve to prevent excessive hydrostatic pressure that could burst the piping or hose.

(12) *Subject to conditions* of paragraph (a) of this section for the methyl chloride and sulfur dioxide optional portable tanks, one or more fusible plugs examined by the Bureau of Explosives and approved by the Associate Administrator may be used on these tanks in place of safety relief valves of the spring-loaded type. The fusible plug or plugs must be in accordance with CGA Pamphlet S-1.2, to prevent a pressure rise in the tank of more than 120 percent of the design pressure. If the tank is over 30 inches long, each end must have the total specified safety discharge area.

(13) *A safety relief valve* on a chlorine cargo tank must conform to one of the following standards of The Chlorine Institute, Inc.: Type 1 1/2 JQ225, Dwg. H51970, dated October 7, 1968; or Type 1 1/2 JQ225, Dwg. H50155, Revision A, dated April 28, 1969.

(j) **Storage containers for liquefied petroleum gas** for permanent installation on consumer premises may be shipped by private motor carrier only under the following conditions:

(1) *Each container* must be constructed in compliance with the requirements of the ASME Code (containers built in compliance with earlier editions starting with 1943 are authorized) and must be marked to indicate compliance in the manner specified by the respective Code.

(2) *Each container* must be equipped with safety devices in compliance with the requirements for safety devices on containers as specified in NFPA Pamphlet No. 58.

(3) *The containers* shall be so braced or otherwise secured on the vehicle as to prevent relative motion while in transit. Valves or other fittings shall be adequately protected against damage during transportation. (See §177.834(g) of this subchapter.)

(4) *Except as provided* in paragraph (j)(5) of this section, containers shall not be shipped when charged with liquefied petroleum gas to more than 5 percent of their water capacity.

(5) *Storage containers* of less than 1,042 pounds water capacity (125 gallons) may be shipped when charged with liquefied petroleum gas in compliance with DOT filling density.

(k) **A nonspecification cargo tank meeting,** and marked in conformance with, the edition of the ASME Code in effect when it was fabricated may be used for the transportation of liquefied petroleum gas provided it meets all of the following conditions:

(1) *It must have a minimum design pressure no lower than 250 psig.*

(2) *It must have a capacity of 13,247.5 L (3,500 water gallons) or less.*

(3) *It must have been manufactured* in conformance with the ASME Code prior to January 1, 1981, according to its ASME name plate and manufacturer's data report.

(4) *It must conform* to applicable provisions of NFPA Pamphlet 58, except to the extent that provisions of Pamphlet 58 are inconsistent with requirements in parts 178 and 180 of this subchapter.

(5) *It must be* inspected, tested, and equipped in accordance with subpart E of part 180 of this subchapter as specified for MC 331 cargo tank motor vehicles.

(6) *Except as provided* in this paragraph (k), it must be operated exclusively in intrastate commerce, including its operation by a motor carrier otherwise engaged in interstate commerce, in a state where its operation was permitted by law (not including the incorporation of this subchapter) prior to January 1, 1981. A cargo tank motor vehicle operating under authority of this section may cross state lines to travel to and from a qualified assembly, repair, maintenance, or requalification facility. The cargo tank need not be cleaned and purged, but it may not contain liquefied petroleum gas in excess of five percent of the water capacity of the cargo tank. If the vehicle engine is supplied fuel from the cargo tank, enough fuel in excess of five percent of the cargo tank's water capacity may be carried for the trip to or from the facility.

(7) *It must have been used* to transport liquefied petroleum gas prior to January 1, 1981.

(8) *It must be operated* in conformance with all other requirements of this subchapter.

(l) Anhydrous ammonia must not be offered for transportation or transported in specification MC 330 and MC 331 cargo tanks constructed of quenched and tempered ("QT") steel except as provided in this paragraph.

(1) *The ammonia* must have a minimum water content of 0.2 percent by weight. Any addition of water must be made using steam condensate, deionized, or distilled water.

(2) *Except as otherwise provided* in this paragraph, each person offering for transportation or transporting anhydrous ammonia shall perform a periodic analysis for prescribed water content in the ammonia. The analysis must be performed:

(i) *From a sample* of the ammonia in storage taken at least once every 7 days, or each time ammonia is added to the storage tanks, whichever is less frequent; or

(ii) *At the time* the cargo tanks are loaded, then a sample of the ammonia taken from at least one loaded cargo tank out of each 10 loads, or from one cargo tank every 24 hours, whichever is less frequent; or

(iii) *At the same frequency* as described in paragraph (l)(2)(ii) of this section, from a sample taken from the loading line to the cargo tank.

(3) *If water is added at the time of loading:*

(i) *The sample* for analysis must be taken from a point in the loading line between the water injection equipment and the cargo tank; and

(ii) *Positive provisions* must be made to assure water injection equipment is operating.

(4) *If water injection equipment* becomes inoperative, suitable corrective maintenance must be performed after which a sample from the first loaded cargo tank must be analyzed for prescribed water content.

(5) *The analysis method* for water content must be as prescribed in CGA Pamphlet G-2.2, titled "Tentative Standard Method for Determining Minimum of 0.2 per cent water in Anhydrous Ammonia," 1975 edition.

(6) *Records indicating* the results of the analysis taken, as required by this paragraph, must be retained for 2 years and must be open to inspection by a representative of the Department.

(7) *Each person* receiving anhydrous ammonia containing 0.2 per cent water by weight may offer for transportation or transport that ammonia without performing the prescribed analysis for water content provided:

(i) *The ammonia received* was certified as containing 0.2 percent water as prescribed in §§172.203(h)(l)(i) and 177.817(a) of this subchapter; and

(ii) *The amount of water* in the ammonia has not been reduced by any means.

(m) A cargo tank (commonly known as a nurse tank and considered an implement of husbandry) transporting anhydrous ammonia, and operated by a private carrier exclusively for agricultural purposes does not have to meet the specification requirements of part 178 of this subchapter if it:

(1) *Has a minimum* design pressure of 250 psig and meets the requirements of the edition of the ASME code in effect at the time it was manufactured and is marked accordingly;

(2) *Is equipped* with safety relief valves meeting the requirements of CGA pamphlet S1.2;

(3) *Is painted white or aluminum;*

(4) *Has capacity of 3,000 gallons or less;*

(5) *Is loaded to a filling density no greater than 56 percent;*

(6) *Is securely mounted on a farm wagon; and*

(7) *Is in conformance* with the requirements of part 172 of this subchapter except that shipping papers are not required; and it need not be marked or placarded on one end if that end contains valves, fittings, regulators or gauges when those appurtenances prevent the markings and placard from being properly placed and visible.

(n) Emergency discharge control for cargo tank motor vehicles in liquefied compressed gas service.

(1) *Required emergency* discharge control equipment. Each cargo tank motor vehicle in liquefied compressed gas service must have an emergency discharge control capability as specified in the following table:

§173.315(n)(1)(*)	Material	Delivery service	Required emergency discharge control capability
(i)	Division 2.2 materials with no subsidiary hazard, excluding anhydrous ammonia	All	None
(ii)	Division 2.3 materials	All	Paragraph (n)(2) of this section
(iii)	Division 2.2 materials with a subsidiary hazard, Division 2.1 materials, and anhydrous ammonia	Other than metered delivery service	Paragraph (n)(2) of this section
(iv)	Division 2.2 materials with a subsidiary hazard, Division 2.1 materials, and anhydrous ammonia in a cargo tank motor vehicle with a capacity of 13,247.5 L (3,500 water gallons) or less	Metered delivery service	Paragraph (n)(3) of this section
(v)	Division 2.2 materials with a subsidiary hazard, Division 2.1 materials, and anhydrous ammonia in a cargo tank motor vehicle with a capacity greater than 13,247.5 L (3,500 water gallons).	Metered delivery service	Paragraph (n)(3) of this section, and, for obstructed view deliveries where permitted by §177.840(p) of this subchapter, paragraph (n)(2) or (n)(4) of this section

(2) *Cargo tank motor vehicles* in other than metered delivery service. A cargo tank motor vehicle in other than metered delivery service must have a means to automatically shut off the flow of product without the need for human intervention within 20 seconds of an unintentional release caused by a complete separation of a liquid delivery hose (passive shut-down capability).

(i) *Designed flow* of product through a bypass in the valve is acceptable when authorized by this subchapter.

(ii) *The design* for the means to automatically shut off product flow must be certified by a Design Certifying Engineer. The certification must consider any specifications of the original component manufacturer and must explain how the passive means to shut off the flow of product operates. It must also outline the parameters (e.g., temperature, pressure, types of product) within which the passive means to shut off the flow of product is designed to operate. All components of the discharge system that are integral to the design must be included in the certification. A copy of the design certification must be provided to the owner of the cargo tank motor vehicle on which the equipment will be installed.

(iii) *Installation must be performed* under the supervision of a Registered Inspector unless the equipment is installed and removed as part of regular operation (e.g., a hose). The Registered Inspector must certify that the equipment is installed and tested, if it is possible to do so without damaging the equipment, in accordance with the Design Certifying Engineer's certification. The Registered Inspector must provide the certification to the owner of the cargo tank motor vehicle.

(3) *Cargo tank motor vehicles* in metered delivery service. When required by the table in paragraph (n)(1) of this section, a cargo tank motor vehicle must have an off-truck remote means to close the internal self-closing stop valve and shut off all motive and auxiliary power equipment upon activation by a qualified person attending the unloading of the cargo tank motor vehicle (off-truck remote shut-off). It must function reliably at a distance of 45.72 m (150 feet). The off-truck remote shut-off activation device must not be capable of reopening the internal self-closing stop valve after emergency activation.

(i) *The emergency* discharge control equipment must be installed under the supervision of a Registered Inspector. Each wireless transmitter/receiver must be tested to demonstrate that it will close the internal self-closing stop valve and shut off all motive and auxiliary power equipment at a distance of 91.44 m (300 feet) under optimum conditions. Emergency discharge control equipment that does not employ a wireless transmitter/receiver must be tested to demonstrate its functioning at the maximum length of the delivery hose.

(ii) *The Registered Inspector* must certify that the remote control equipment is installed in accordance with the original component manufacturer's specifications and is tested in accordance with paragraph (n)(3)(i) of this section. The Registered Inspector must provide the owner of the cargo tank motor vehicle with this certification.

(4) *Query systems.* When a transmitter/receiver system is used to satisfy the requirements of paragraph (n)(1)(v) of this section, it must close the internal self-closing stop valve and shut off all motive and auxiliary power equipment unless the qualified person attending the unloading operation prevents it from doing so at least once every five minutes. Testing and certification must be as specified in paragraph (n)(3) of this section.

(5) *Compliance dates.*

(i) *Each specification* MC 331 cargo tank motor vehicle with a certificate of construction issued two or more years after July 1, 1999, must have an appropriate emergency discharge control capability as specified in this paragraph (n).

(ii) *No MC 330, MC 331,* or nonspecification cargo tank motor vehicle authorized under paragraph (k) of this section may be operated unless it has an appropriate emergency discharge control capability as specified in this paragraph (n) no later than the date of its first scheduled pressure retest required after July 1, 2001. No MC 330, MC 331 or nonspecification cargo tank motor vehicle authorized under paragraph (k) of this section may be operated after July 1, 2006, unless it has been equipped with emergency discharge control equipment as specified in this paragraph (n).

(iii) *No MC 330 or MC 331* cargo tank motor vehicle with a capacity over 13,247 L (3,500 gallons) used in metered delivery service may be operated unless it has an appropriate discharge control capability as specified in this paragraph (n) no later than July 1, 2003, or the date of its first scheduled pressure retest required after July 1, 2001, whichever is earlier.

(o) **Chlorine cargo tank motor vehicles.** Each cargo tank motor vehicle used for the transportation of chlorine must meet the requirements in the following:

(1) *Any hose,* piping, or tubing used for loading or unloading that is mounted or carried on the motor vehicle may not be attached to any valve and must be capped at all ends to prevent the entry of moisture, except at the time of loading or unloading. Except at the time of loading and unloading, the pipe connection of each angle valve must be closed with a screw plug which is chained or otherwise fastened to prevent misplacement.

(2) *Each chlorine* cargo tank motor vehicle angle valve must be tested to be leak free at not less than 225 psig using dry air or inert gas before installation and thereafter every 2 years when performing the required periodic retest in §180.407(c) of this subchapter. Prior to each loading, the cargo tank motor vehicle must be inspected and the angle valves and gasketed joints must be examined and tested at a pressure of not less than 50 psig to determine that they are not leaking and are in proper condition for transportation. Any leaks must be corrected before the cargo tank motor vehicle is offered for transportation.

(3) *Excess flow valves* on the cargo tank motor vehicle must meet the requirements of paragraph (n) of this section.

(p) **Fusible elements.** Each MC 330, MC 331, or nonspecification cargo tank authorized under paragraph (k) of this section must have a thermal means of closure for each internal self-closing stop valve as specified in §178.337-8(a)(4) of this subchapter.

(q) **Manifolding is authorized for cargo tanks** containing anhydrous ammonia provided each individual cargo tank is equipped with a pressure relief device or valves and gauging devices as required by paragraphs (h) and (i) of this section. Each valve must be tightly closed while the cargo tank is in transit. Each cargo tank must be filled separately.

§173.316 Cryogenic liquids in cylinders.

(a) **General requirements.**

(1) *A cylinder* may not be loaded with a cryogenic liquid colder than the design service temperature of the packaging.

(2) *A cylinder* may not be loaded with any material which may combine chemically with any residue in the packaging to produce an unsafe condition.

(3) *The jacket* covering the insulation on a cylinder used to transport any flammable cryogenic liquid must be made of steel.

(4) *A valve or fitting* made of aluminum with internal rubbing or abrading aluminum parts that may come in contact with oxygen in the cryogenic liquid form may not be installed on any cylinder used to transport oxygen, cryogenic liquid unless the parts are anodized in accordance with ASTM Standard B 580 (incorporated by reference, see §171.7 of this subchapter).

(5) *An aluminum valve,* pipe or fitting may not be installed on any cylinder used to transport any flammable cryogenic liquid.

(6) *Each cylinder* must be provided with one or more pressure relief devices, which must be installed and maintained in compliance with the requirements of this subchapter.

(7) *Each pressure relief device* must be installed and located so that the cooling effect of the contents during venting will not prevent effective operation of the device.

(8) *The maximum weight* of the contents in a cylinder with a design service temperature colder than -320 °F may not exceed the design weight marked on the cylinder (see §178.35 of this subchapter).

(b) **Pressure control systems.** Each cylinder containing a cryogenic liquid must have a pressure control system that conforms to §173.34(d) and is designed and installed so that it will prevent the cylinder from becoming liquid full.

(c) **Specification cylinder requirements and filling limits.** Specification DOT-4L cylinders (§178.57 of this subchapter) are authorized for the transportation of cryogenic liquids when carried in the vertical position as follows:

(1) *For purposes of this section,* "filling density," except for hydrogen, is defined as the percent ratio of the weight of lading in the packaging to the weight of water that the packaging will hold at 60 °F (1 lb. of water = 27.737 cubic inches at 60 °F).

(2) *The cryogenic liquids* of argon, nitrogen, oxygen, helium and neon must be loaded and shipped in accordance with the following table:

Pressure control valve setting (maximum start-to-discharge pressure psig)	Maximum permitted filling density (percent by weight)					
	Air	Argon	Nitrogen	Oxygen	Helium	Neon
45	82.5	133	76	108	12.5	109
75	80.3	130	74	105	12.5	104
105	78.4	127	72	103	12.5	100
170	76.2	122	70	100	12.5	92
230	75.1	119	69	98	12.5	85
295	73.3	115	68	96	12.5	77
360	70.7	113	65	93	12.5	....
450	65.9	111	61	91	12.5	....
540	62.9	107	58	88	12.5	....
625	60.1	104	55	86	12.5	....
Design service temperature (°F)	-320	-320	-320	-320	-452	-411

(3) *Hydrogen* (minimum 95 percent parahydrogen) must be loaded and shipped as follows:

Column 1	Column 2
Design service temperature	-423 °F or colder
Maximum permitted filling density, based on cylinder capacity at -423 °F (see Note 1)	6.7 percent
The pressure control valve must be designed and set to limit the pressure in the cylinder to not more than	17 psig

NOTE 1: The filling density for hydrogen, cryogenic liquid is defined as the percent ratio of the weight of lading in a packaging to the weight of water that the packaging will hold at minus 423 °F. The volume of the packaging at minus 423 °F is determined in cubic inches. The volume is converted to pounds of water (1 lb. of water = 27.737 cubic inches).

(i) *Each cylinder* must be constructed, insulated and maintained so that during transportation the total rate of venting shall not exceed 30 SCF of hydrogen per hour.

(ii) *In addition* to the marking requirements in §178.35 of this subchapter, the total rate of venting in SCF per hour (SCFH) shall be marked on the top head or valve protection band in letters at least one-half inch high as follows: "VENT

RATE**SCFH" (with the asterisks replaced by the number representing the total rate of venting, in SCF per hour).

(iii) *Carriage by highway* is subject to the conditions specified in §177.840(a) of this subchapter.

(d) **Mixtures of cryogenic liquid.** Where charging requirements are not specifically prescribed in paragraph (c) of this section, the cryogenic liquid must be shipped in packagings and under conditions approved by the Associate Administrator.

§173.318 Cryogenic liquids in cargo tanks.

(a) **General requirements.**

(1) *A cargo tank* may not be loaded with a cryogenic liquid colder than the design service temperature of the packaging.

(2) *A cargo tank* may not be loaded with any material that may combine chemically with any residue in the packaging to produce an unsafe condition (see §178.338-15).

(3) *The jacket* covering the insulation on a tank used to transport a cryogenic liquid must be made of steel if the cryogenic liquid:

(i) *Is to be transported by vessel* (see §176.76(g) of this subchapter); or

(ii) *Is oxygen or a flammable material.*

(4) *A valve or fitting* made of aluminum with internal rubbing or abrading aluminum parts that may come in contact with oxygen in the cryogenic liquid form may not be installed on any cargo tank used to transport oxygen, cryogenic liquid unless the parts are anodized in accordance with ASTM Standard B 580 (incorporated by reference, see §171.7 of this subchapter).

(5) *An aluminum valve, pipe or fitting,* external to the jacket that retains lading during transportation may not be installed on any cargo tank used to transport oxygen, cryogenic liquid or any flammable cryogenic liquid.

(6) *A cargo tank* used to transport oxygen, cryogenic liquid must be provided with a manhole (see §178.338-6 of this subchapter).

(b) **Pressure relief systems and pressure control valves —**

(1) *Types of pressure relief systems —*

(i) *Tanks in oxygen* and flammable cryogenic liquid service. Except as otherwise provided in this paragraph, each tank in oxygen and flammable cryogenic liquid service must be protected by two independent pressure relief systems which are not connected in series, namely:

[A] A primary system of one or more pressure relief valves; and

[B] A secondary system of one of more frangible discs or pressure relief valves. For a tank in carbon monoxide service, the secondary system must be pressure relief valves only.

(ii) *Tanks in helium and atmospheric gas* (except oxygen) cryogenic liquid service. For a tank used in helium and atmospheric gas (except oxygen) cryogenic liquid service, the tank must be protected by at least one pressure relief system consisting of:

[A] One or more pressure relief valves; or

[B] A combination of one or more pressure relief valves and one or more frangible discs.

(2) *Capacities of pressure relief systems —*

(i) *Tanks in oxygen* or flammable cryogenic liquid service. For tanks in oxygen or flammable cryogenic liquid service, the primary system and the secondary system of pressure relief devices must each have a flow capacity equal to or greater than that calculated by the applicable formula in paragraph 5.3.2 or paragraph 5.3.3 of CGA Pamphlet S-1.2. In addition:

[A] The primary pressure relief system must have a total flow capacity at a pressure not exceeding 120 percent of the tank's design pressure.

[B] The secondary pressure relief system must have a total flow capacity at a pressure not exceeding 150 percent of the tank's design pressure.

[C] The flow capacity and rating must be verified and marked by the manufacturer of the device in accordance with CGA Pamphlet S-1.2.

(ii) *Tanks in helium and atmospheric gas* (except oxygen) cryogenic liquid service. For tanks in helium and atmospheric gas (except oxygen) cryogenic liquid service, the pressure relief system must have a flow capacity equal to or greater than that calculated by the applicable formula in paragraphs 5.3.2 or 5.3.3 of CGA Pamphlet S-1.2. If the pressure relief system consists of a combination of pressure relief valves and frangible discs, the pressure relief valves must have a total venting capacity equal to or greater than that calculated by the applicable formula in paragraph 4.1.10.1.1 of CGA Pamphlet S-1.2. The pressure relief system must have this total flow capacity at a pressure not exceeding 150 percent of the tank's design pressure. The flow capacity and rating must be verified and marked by the manufacturer of the device in accordance with CGA Pamphlet S-1.2.

(3) *Type and construction of pressure relief devices.*

(i) *Each pressure relief device* must be designed and constructed for a pressure equal to or exceeding the tank's design pressure at the coldest temperature reasonably expected to be encountered.

(ii) *Pressure relief devices* must be either spring-loaded pressure relief valves or frangible discs. Pressure relief valves must be of a type that automatically open and close at predetermined pressures.

(4) *Setting of pressure relief devices.*

(i) *On a tank* used in oxygen or flammable cryogenic liquid service, the pressure relief devices must perform as follows.

[A] Each pressure relief valve in the primary relief system must be set-to-discharge at a pressure no higher than 110 percent of the tank's design pressure.

[B] Each pressure relief device in the secondary pressure relief system must be designed to commence functioning at a pressure no lower than 130 percent and no higher than 150 percent of the tank's design pressure.

(ii) *On a tank* used in helium and atmospheric gas (except oxygen) cryogenic liquid service, the pressure relief devices in the pressure relief system must be designed to commence functioning at no higher than 150 percent of the tank's design pressure.

(5) *Optional pressure relief devices* and pressure control valves. In addition to the required pressure relief devices, a cargo tank in cryogenic liquid (except carbon monoxide) service may be equipped with one or both of the following:

(i) *One or more* pressure control valves set at a pressure below the tank's design pressure.

(ii) *One or more* frangible discs set to function at a pressure not less than one and one-half times or more than two times the tank's design pressure.

(6) *Maximum filling rate.*

(i) *For a tank* used in oxygen and flammable cryogenic liquid service, the maximum rate at which the tank is filled must not exceed the liquid flow capacity of the primary pressure relief system rated at a pressure not exceeding 120 percent of the tank's design pressure.

(ii) *On a tank* used in helium and atmospheric gas (except oxygen) cryogenic liquid service, the maximum rate at which the tank is filled must not exceed the liquid flow capacity of the pressure relief valves rated at 150 percent of the tank's design pressure.

(7) *Arrangement and location of pressure relief devices.*

(i) *The discharge* from any pressure relief system must be directed upward and be unobstructed to the outside of the protective housing in such a manner as to prevent impingement of gas upon the jacket or any structural part of the vehicle.

(ii) *Each pressure relief valve* must be arranged or protected to prevent the accumulation of foreign material between the relief valve and the atmospheric discharge opening in any relief piping. The arrangement must not impede flow through the device.

(iii) *Each pressure relief valve* must be designed and located to minimize the possibility of tampering. If the pressure setting or adjustment is external to the valve, the valve adjustment must be sealed.

(iv) *Each pressure relief device* must have direct communication with the vapor space of the tank at the midlength of the top centerline.

(v) *Each pressure relief device* must be installed and located so that the cooling effect of the contents during venting will not prevent the effective operation of the device.

(8) *Connections.*

(i) *Each connection* to a pressure relief device must be of sufficient size to allow the required rate of discharge through the pressure relief device. The inlet connection must be not less than one-half inch nominal pipe size.

(ii) *A shut-off valve* may be installed in a pressure relief system only when the required relief capacity is provided at all times.

(9) *Pressure relief devices* for piping hose and vacuum-insulated jackets.

(i) *Each portion* of connected liquid piping or hose that can be closed at both ends must be provided with either a hydrostatic pressure relief valve without an intervening shut-off valve, or a check valve permitting flow from the pipe or hose into the tank. If used, the relief valve must be located so as to prevent its discharge from impinging on the tank, piping, or operating personnel.

(ii) *On a vacuum-insulated* cargo tank the jacket must be protected by a suitable relief device to release internal pressure. The discharge area of this device must be at least 0.00024 square inch per pound of water capacity of the tank. This relief device must function at a pressure not exceeding the internal design pressure of the jacket, calculated in accordance with the ASME Code, or 25 psig, whichever is less.

(10) *Tank inlet,* outlet, pressure relief device and pressure control valve markings.

(i) *Each tank inlet and outlet,* except pressure relief devices and pressure control valves, must be permanently marked to indicate whether it communicates with "vapor" or "liquid" when the tank is filled to the maximum permitted filling density.

(ii) *Each pressure relief valve* must be plainly and permanently marked with the pressure, in psig, at which it is set-to-discharge, the discharge rate of the device in SCF per minute (SCFM) of free air, and the manufacturer's name or trade name and catalog number. The marked set-to-discharge pressure valve must be visible with the valve in its installed position. The rated discharge capacity of the device must be determined at a pressure of 120 percent of the design pressure of the tank.

(iii) *Each pressure control valve* must be plainly and permanently marked with the pressure, in psig, at which it is set-to-discharge.

(c) **Weight of lading requirements.** The weight of a cryogenic liquid in the tank must be determined by weighing or by the use of a liquid level gauging device authorized in §178.338-14(a) of this subchapter, and may not exceed the lesser of:

(1) *The weight* of lading in the tank, based on the water capacity stamped on the nameplate (§178.338-18(a)(4) of this subchapter) and the appropriate maximum permitted filling density specified in paragraph (f) of this section; or

(2) *The maximum weight* of lading for which the cargo tank was designed, as marked on the specification plate (see §178.338-18(b) of this subchapter).

(d) **Outage.** Except for a cargo tank containing helium, cryogenic liquid, a cargo tank offered for transportation must have an outage of at least two percent below the inlet of the pressure relief device or pressure control valve, under conditions of incipient opening, with the tank in a level attitude.

(e) **Temperature.** A flammable cryogenic liquid in a cargo tank at the start of travel must be at a temperature sufficiently cold that the pressure setting of the pressure control valve or the required pressure relief valve, whichever is lower, will not be reached in less time than the marked rated holding time for the cryogenic liquid (see paragraph (g)(3) of this section and §178.338-9(b) of this subchapter).

(f) **Specification MC-338 (§178.338 of this subchapter)** cargo tanks are authorized for the shipment of the following cryogenic liquids subject to the following additional requirements:

(1) *For purposes of this section,* "filling density" is defined as the percent ratio of the weight of lading in the tank to the weight of water that the tank will hold at the design service temperature (one pound of water = 27.737 cubic inches at 60 °F, or one gallon of water = 231 cubic inches at 60 °F and weighs 8.32828 pounds).

(2) *Air, argon,* helium, nitrogen, and oxygen, cryogenic liquids must be loaded and shipped in accordance with the following table:

Maximum set-to-discharge pressure (psig)	Maximum permitted filling density (percent by weight)				
	Air	Argon	Helium	Nitrogen	Oxygen
26			12.5		
30	80.3	129	12.5	74	105
40	79.2		12.5		
50	78.0		12.5		
55	77.3	125	12.5	71	102
60	76.9		12.5		
80	75.3		12.5		
85	75.1	121	12.5		99
100	73.0		12.5		
105	73.7		12.5	67	
120	72.2		12.5		
140	71.4		12.5		
145	70.9	115	12.5	64	94
180	68.3		12.5		
200	67.3	110	12.5	61	91
250	63.3	106	12.5	57	87
275	62.3	105	12.5	56	86
325	59.4	101		53	83
Design service temperature	-320 °F	-320 °F	-452 °F	-320 °F	-320 °F

(3) *Carbon monoxide, hydrogen* (minimum 95 percent para-hydrogen), ethylene, and methane or natural gas, cryogenic liquids must be loaded and shipped in accordance with the following table:

Maximum set-to-discharge pressure (psig)	Maximum permitted filling density (percent by weight)			
	Carbon monoxide	Ethylene	Hydrogen	Methane or Natural Gas
13			6.6	
15	75.0		6.6	40.5
17	74.0		6.6	
20		53.5		40.0
25	73.0			
30	72.0	52.7	6.3	39.1
35				
40		52.0		38.6
45	71.5			
50		51.4	6.0	38.2
55				
60		50.8		
70		50.2	5.7	37.5
90		49.2		
95				
100		48.4	5.4	36.6
115		48.2		
125			5.0	
150			4.5	
175	62.5	45.8		
285	56.0			
Design service temperature	-320 °F	-155 °F	-423 °F	-260 °F

(4) *Mixtures of cryogenic liquid.* Where charging requirements are not specifically prescribed in this paragraph (f), the cryogenic liquid must be shipped in packagings and under conditions approved by the Associate Administrator.

(g) **One-way travel time; marking.** The jacket of a cargo tank to be used to transport a flammable cryogenic liquid must be marked on its right side near the front, in letters and numbers at least two inches high, "One-Way-Travel-Time ____ hrs.", with the blank filled in with a number indicating the one-way travel time (OWTT), in hours, of the cargo tank for the flammable cryogenic liquid to be transported. A cargo tank that is partially unloaded at one or more locations must have additional marking "One-Way-Travel-Time ____ hrs. ____ psig to ____ psig at ____ percent filling density," with the second blank filled in with the pressure existing after partial unloading and the third blank filled in with the set-to-discharge pressure of the control valve or pressure relief valve, and the fourth blank with the filling density following partial unloading. Multiple OWTT markings for different pressure levels are permitted. The abbreviation "OWTT" may be used in place of the words "One-way-travel-time" in the marking required by this paragraph.

(1) *OWTT is based* on the marked rated holding time (MRHT) of the cargo tank for the cryogenic liquid to be transported in the cargo tank. If the MRHT for the flammable cryogenic liquid is not displayed on or adjacent to the specification plate, this MRHT may be derived.

(2) *The MRHT is converted to OWTT, in hours, as follows:*

(i) *For a tank with an MRHT of 72 hours or less,*
OWTT = (MRHT - 24) / 2

(ii) *For a tank with an MRHT greater than 72 hours,*
OWTT = MRHT - 48

(3) *Each cargo tank* motor vehicle used to transport a flammable cryogenic liquid must be examined after each shipment to determine its actual holding time. The record required by §177.840(h) of this subchapter may be used for this determination. If the examination indicates that the actual holding time of the cargo tank, after adjustment to reflect an average ambient temperature of 85 °F, is less than 90 percent of the marked rated holding time (MRHT) for the cryogenic liquid marked on the specification plate or adjacent thereto (see §178.338-18(b) of this subchapter), the tank may not be refilled with any flammable cryogenic liquid until it is restored to its marked rated holding time value or it is re-marked with the actual marked rated holding time determined by this examination. If the name of the flammable cryogenic liquid that was transported and its marked rated holding time is not displayed on or adjacent to the specification plate, this requirement may be met by deriving the MRHT of the cargo tank for that flammable cryogenic liquid and comparing that derived MRHT with the actual holding time after adjustment.

§173.319 Cryogenic liquids in tank cars.

(a) General requirements.

(1) *A tank car* containing a flammable cryogenic liquid may not be shipped unless it was loaded by, or with the consent of, the owner of the tank car.

(2) *The amount* of flammable cryogenic liquid loaded into a tank car must be determined, either by direct measurement or by calculation based on weight, to verify that the tank has not been filled to a level in excess of the limits specified in paragraph (d)(2) of this section. The weight of any flammable cryogenic liquid loaded, except hydrogen, must be checked by use of scales after disconnecting the loading line.

(3) *Whenever a tank car* containing any flammable cryogenic lading is not received by the consignee within 20 days from the date of shipment, the shipper of the lading shall notify the Bureau of Explosives.

(4) *A tank car may not be loaded with any flammable cryogenic liquid:*

(i) *That may combine* chemically with any residue in the tank to produce an unsafe condition,

(ii) *That is colder than the design service temperature of the tank,*

(iii) *If the average* daily pressure rise in the tank exceeded 3 psig during the prior shipment,

(iv) *Unless it is marked* with the name of contents, in accordance with §172.330 of this subchapter.

(b) When a tank car containing a flammable cryogenic liquid is offered for transportation:

(1) *At least* 0.5 percent outage must be provided below the inlet of the pressure relief or pressure control valve at the start-to-discharge pressure setting of the valve, with the tank car in a level attitude, and

(2) *The absolute pressure* in the annular space must be less than 75 microns of mercury.

(c) Temperature. A flammable cryogenic liquid must be loaded into a tank car at such a temperature that the average daily pressure rise during transportation will not exceed 3 psig (see paragraph (a)(4)(iii) of this section).

(d) A Class DOT-113 tank car is authorized for the shipment of the following cryogenic liquids subject to the following additional requirements:

(1) *For purposes of this section,* "filling density" is defined as the percent ratio of the weight of lading in the tank to the weight of water that the tank will hold at the design service temperature (one pound of water = 27.737 cubic inches at 60 °F, or one gallon of water = 231 cubic inches at 60 °F and weighs 8.32828 pounds).

(2) *Ethylene, and hydrogen* (minimum 95 percent parahydrogen), cryogenic liquids must be loaded and shipped in accordance with the following table:

Pressure Control Valve Setting or Relief Valve Setting

Maximum start-to-discharge pressure (psig)	Maximum permitted filling density (percent by weight)			
	Ethylene	Ethylene	Ethlyene	Hydrogen
17				6.60
45	52.8			
75		51.1.	51.1	
Maximum pressure when offered for transportation	10 psig	10 psig	20 psig	
Design service temperature	- 260 °F	- 260 °F	- 155 °F	- 423 °F
Specification (see §180.507(b)(3) of this subchapter)	113D60W 113C60W	113C120W	113D120W	113A175W 113A60W

(e) Special requirements for class DOT 113 tank cars —

(1) *A class DOT-113 tank car* need not be periodically pressure tested; however, each shipment must be monitored to determine the average daily pressure rise in the tank car. If the average daily pressure rise during any shipment exceeds 0.2 Bar (3 psig) per day, the tank must be tested for thermal integrity prior to any subsequent shipment.

(2) *Thermal integrity test.* When required by paragraph (e)(1) of this section, either of the following thermal integrity tests may be used:

(i) *Pressure rise test.* The pressure rise in the tank may not exceed 0.34 Bar (5 psig) in 24 hours. When the pressure rise test is performed, the absolute pressure in the annular space of the loaded tank car may not exceed 75 microns of mercury at the beginning of the test and may not increase more than 25 microns during the 24-hour period; or

(ii) *Calculated heat transfer rate test.* The insulation system must be performance tested as prescribed in §179.400-4 of this subchapter. When the calculated heat transfer rate test is performed, the absolute pressure in the annular space of the loaded tank car may not exceed 75 microns of mercury at the beginning of the test and may not increase more than 25 microns during the 24-hour period. The calculated heat transfer rate in 24 hours may not exceed:

[A] 120 percent of the appropriate standard heat transfer rate specified in §179.401-1 of this subchapter, for DOT-113A60W and DOT-113C120W tank cars;

[B] 122.808 joules (0.1164 Btu/day/lb.) of inner tank car water capacity, for DOT-113A175W tank cars;

[C] 345.215 joules (0.3272 Btu/day/lb.) of inner tank car water capacity, for DOT-113C60W and 113D60W tank cars; or

[D] 500.09 joules (0.4740 Btu/day/lb.) of inner tank car water capacity, for DOT-113D120W tank cars.

(3) *A tank car* that fails a test prescribed in paragraph (e)(2) of this section must be removed from hazardous materials service. A tank car removed from hazardous materials service because it failed a test prescribed in paragraph (e)(2) of this section may not be used to transport a hazardous material unless the tank car conforms to all applicable requirements of this subchapter.

(4) *Each rupture disc* must be replaced every 12 months, and the replacement date must be marked on the car near the pressure relief valve information.

(5) *Pressure relief valves* and alternate pressure relief valves must be tested every five years. The start-to-discharge pressure and vapor tight pressure requirements for the pressure relief valves must be as specified in §179.401-1 of this subchapter. The alternate pressure relief device values specified in §179.401-1 of this subchapter for a DOT-113C120W tank car apply to a DOT-113D120W tank car.

§173.320 Cryogenic liquids; exceptions.

(a) Atmospheric gases and helium, cryogenic liquids, in Dewar flasks, insulated cylinders, insulated portable tanks, insulated cargo tanks, and insulated tank cars, designed and constructed so that the pressure in such packagings will not exceed 25.3 psig under ambient temperature conditions during transportation are not subject to the requirements of this subchapter when transported by motor vehicle or railcar except as specified in paragraphs (a)(1), (a)(2), and (a)(3) of this section.

(1) *Sections 171.15 and 171.16* of this subchapter pertaining to the reporting of incidents, not including a release that is the result of venting through a pressure control valve, or the neck of the Dewar flask.

(2) *Subparts A, B, C, and D* of part 172, (§§174.24 for rail and 177.817 for highway) and in addition, part 172 in its entirety for oxygen.

(3) *Subparts A and B* of part 173, and §§174.1 and 177.800, 177.804, and 177.823 of this subchapter.

(b) The requirements of this subchapter do not apply to atmospheric gases and helium:

(1) *During loading and unloading operations* (pressure rises may exceed 25.3 psig); or

(2) *When used* in operation of a process system; such as a refrigeration system (pressure may exceed 25.3 psig).

(c) For transportation aboard aircraft, see the ICAO Technical Instructions, Packing Instruction 202 and the packaging specifications in part 6, Chapter 5. (See §171.7 of this subchapter for ICAO Technical Instructions.)

§173.321 Ethylamine.

Ethylamine must be packaged as follows:

(a) In 1A1 drums which meet Packing Group I performance level requirements.

(b) In specification cylinders as prescribed for any compressed gas except acetylene.

§173.322 Ethyl chloride.

Ethyl chloride must be packaged in any of the following single or combination non-bulk packagings which meet Packing Group I performance level requirements:

(a) **In 4C1, 4C2, 4D or 4F wooden boxes** with glass, earthenware, or metal inner receptacles not over 500 g (17.6 ounces) capacity each;

(b) **In 4G fiberboard boxes with glass, earthenware,** or metal inner receptacles not over 500 g (17.6 ounces) capacity each. Outer packagings may not exceed 30 kg (66 pounds) gross weight;

(c) **In 1A1 drums of not over 100 L (26 gallons) capacity each; or**

(d) **In specification cylinders as prescribed** for any compressed gas except acetylene.

§173.323 Ethylene oxide.

(a) **For packaging ethylene oxide in non-bulk packagings,** silver mercury or any of its alloys or copper may not be used in any part of a packaging, valve, or other packaging appurtenance if that part, during normal conditions of transportation, may come in contact with ethylene oxide liquid or vapor. Copper alloys may be used only where gas mixtures do not contain free acetylene at any concentration that will form copper acetylene. All packaging and gaskets must be constructed of materials which are compatible with ethylene oxide and do not lower the auto-ignition temperature of ethylene oxide.

(b) **Ethylene oxide must be packaged in one of the following:**

(1) *In 4G fiberboard boxes* with inner glass ampoules or vials. Total quantity of ethylene oxide may not exceed 100 grams (3.5 ounces) per package. The completed package must be capable of passing Packing Group I performance tests.

(2) *In 4G fiberboard boxes* constructed with top and bottom pads and perimeter liner. Inner packagings must be aluminum receptacles of no more than 135 g (4.8 ounces) capacity cushioned with incombustible material. No more than 12 receptacles may be packed in one box, and no more than 10 boxes may be overpacked under the provisions of §173.25 of this part. Each completed package must be capable of passing Packing Group I performance tests.

(3) *In 4C1, 4C2, 4D or 4F* wooden boxes or 4G fiberboard boxes with inner metal receptacles of no more than 340 g (12 ounces) capacity. The metal receptacle must be capable of withstanding no less than a 1241.1 kPa (180 psig) burst pressure. No more than 12 receptacles may be packed in one box, and each receptacle may not be liquid full below 82 °C (180 °F). Each inner receptacle must be insulated and equipped with a relief device of the fusible plug type with yield temperature of 69 °C to 77 °C (156 °F to 171 °F). The capacity of relief device and insulation must be such that the charged receptacle will not explode when tested by the method described in CGA Pamphlet C-14 or other equivalent method. Each completed package must be capable of passing all Packing Group I performance tests.

(4) *In specification cylinders,* as authorized for any compressed gas except acetylene. Pressurizing valves and insulation are required for cylinders over 4 L (1 gallon) capacity. Eductor tubes must be provided for cylinders over 19 L (5 gallons) capacity. Cylinders must be seamless or welded steel (not brazed) with a nominal capacity of no more than 115 L (30 gallons) and may not be liquid full below 82 °C (180 °F). Before each refilling, each cylinder must be tested for leakage at no less than 103.4 kPa (15 psig) pressure. In addition, each cylinder must be equipped with a fusible type relief device with yield temperature of 69 °C to 77 °C (157 °F to 170 °F). The capacity of the relief device and the effectiveness of the insulation must be such that the charged cylinder will not explode when tested by the method described in CGA Pamphlet C-14 or other equivalent method.

(5) *In 1A1 steel drums* of no more than 231 L (61 gallons) and meeting Packing Group I performance standards. The drum must be lagged, of all welded construction with the inner shell having a minimum thickness of 1.7 mm (0.068 inches) and the outer shell having a minimum thickness of 2.4 mm (0.095 inches). Drums must be capable of withstanding a hydrostatic test pressure of 690 kPa (100 psig). Lagging must be of sufficient thickness so that the drum, when filled with ethylene oxide and equipped with the required pressure relief device, will not rupture when exposed to fire. The drum may not be liquid full below 85 °C (185 °F), and must be marked "THIS END UP" on the top head. Before each refilling, each drum must be tested for leakage at no less than 103 kPa (15 psig) pressure. Each drum must be equipped with a fusible type relief device with yield temperature of 69 °C to 77 °C (157 °F to 170 °F), and the capacity of the relief device must be such that the filled drum is capable of passing, without rupture, the test method described in CGA Pamphlet C-14 or other equivalent method.

(c) **When §172.101 of this subchapter specifies** that a hazardous material be packaged under this section, only the following bulk packagings are authorized, subject to the requirements of subparts A and B of this part, the special provisions specified in column 7 of the §172.101 table, and paragraphs (d) through (j) of this section:

(1) *Tank cars.* Class DOT 105J tank cars: Notwithstanding the requirements of §173.31(c), each tank car must have a tank test pressure of at least 20.7 Bar (300 psig) no later than July 1, 2006.

(2) *Cargo tanks.* Specification MC 330 and MC 331 cargo tank motor vehicles.

(3) *Portable tanks. DOT 51 portable tanks.*

(d) **The pressure relief devices must be set** to function at 517 kPa (75 psig). Portable tanks fitted with non-reclosing devices made and in use prior to December 31, 1987, may continue to be used in ethylene oxide service.

(e) **In determining outage, consideration must be given** to the lading temperature and solubility of inert gas padding in ethylene oxide as well as the partial pressure exerted by the gas padding.

(f) **Each tank, loaded or empty, must be padded** with dry nitrogen or other suitable inert gas of sufficient quantity to render the vapor space of the tank nonflammable up to 41 °C (105 °F). The gas used for padding must be free of impurities which may cause the ethylene oxide to polymerize, decompose or undergo other violent chemical reaction.

(g) **Copper, silver, mercury, magnesium or their alloys** may not be used in any part of the tank or appurtenances that are normally in contact with the lading.

(h) **Neoprene, natural rubber and asbestos gaskets** are prohibited. All packing and gaskets must be made of materials which do not react with or lower the autoignition temperature of the lading.

(i) **Each tank must be insulated with cork** (at least 10 cm (4 inches) thick), or mineral wool, fiberglass or other suitable insulation material of sufficient thickness so that the thermal conductance at 16 °C (60 °F) is not more than 0.075 Btu per hour per square foot per degree F. temperature differential. Portable tanks made and in use prior to December 31, 1987 equipped with fusible plugs instead of a pressure relief valve or rupture disc, must have sufficient insulation so that the tank as filled for shipment will not rupture in a fire. The insulation on portable tanks or cargo tank motor vehicles must be protected with a steel jacket at least 2.54 mm (0.100 inch) thick, or as required by the specification.

(j) **Tank car tanks built after December 30, 1971** must be equipped with a thermometer well.

§173.334 Organic phosphates mixed with compressed gas.

Hexaethyl tetraphosphate, parathion, tetraethyl dithio pyrophosphate, tetraethyl pyrophosphate, or other Division 6.1 organic phosphates (including a compound or mixture), may be mixed with a non-flammable compressed gas. This mixture may not contain more than 20 percent by weight of organic phosphate and must be packaged in DOT 3A240, 3AA240, 3B240, 4A240, 4B240, 4BA240, or 4BW240 cylinders meeting all of the following requirements:

(a) **Each cylinder may be filled with not more than** 5 kg (11.0 lb) of the mixture, to a maximum filling density of not more than 80 percent of the water capacity.

(b) **No cylinder may be equipped with an education tube** or a fusible plug.

(c) **No cylinder may be equipped with any valve** unless the valve is a type approved by the Associate Administrator.

(d) **Cylinders must be overpacked in a box, crate,** or other strong outside packaging conforming to the requirements of §173.25 and arranged to protect each valve or other closing device from damage. Except as provided in paragraph (e) of this section, no more than four cylinders may be packed in a strong outside packaging. Each strong outside packaging with its closing device protection must be sufficiently strong to protect all parts of each cylinder from deformation or leakage if the completed package is dropped 1.8 m (6 feet) onto a non-yielding surface, such as concrete or steel, impacting at the packaging's weakest point.

(e) **Cylinders may be packed in strong wooden boxes** with valves or other closing devices protected from damage, with not more than twelve cylinders in one outside wooden box. An outer fiberboard box may be used when not more than four such cylinders are to be shipped in one packaging. Valves must be adequately protected. Box and valve protection must be of sufficient strength to protect all parts of inner packagings and valves from deformation or breakage resulting from a drop of at least 1.8 m (6 feet) onto a non-yielding surface, such as concrete or steel, impacting at the weakest point.

§173.335 Gas generator assemblies.

Gas generator assemblies (aircraft) containing liquefied non-flammable, non-toxic gas and a solid propellant cartridge must be packaged as follows:

(a) **The gas must be packaged in specification steel cylinders** authorized for any compressed gas except acetylene not exceeding 10.5 L (2.8 gallons) internal volume and having a minimum design burst pressure of 19,700 kPa (2,857 psig);

(b) **Fittings must be protected against damage** under conditions normal incident to transport, any trigger must be fitted with a safety locking pin, and a non-propulsive plug must be installed on the discharge tube; and

(c) **Each complete unit must be individually** and tightly packed to prevent movement in wooden boxes (4C1 or 4C2), plywood boxes (4D), reconstituted wood boxes (4F), fiberboard boxes (4G), or plastic boxes, (4H1and 4H2) of Packing Group II performance level, or in the original manufacturer's transit box.

§173.336 Nitrogen dioxide, liquefied, or dinitrogen tetroxide, liquefied.

Nitrogen dioxide, liquefied, or dinitrogen tetroxide, liquefied, must be packaged in specification cylinders as prescribed in §173.192. Specification cylinders prescribed in §173.192 with valve removed are authorized. Each valve opening must be closed by means of a solid metal plug with tapered thread properly luted to prevent leakage. Transportation in DOT 3AL cylinders is authorized only by highway or rail. Each cylinder must be cleaned in compliance with the requirements of Federal Specification RR-C-901C, paragraphs 3.3.1 and 3.3.2 (incorporated by reference; see §171.7 of this subchapter). Cleaning agents equivalent to those specified in RR-C-901C may be used; however, any cleaning agent must not be capable of reacting with oxygen. One cylinder selected at random from a group of 200 or fewer and cleaned at the same time must be tested for oil contamination in accordance with Specification RR-C-901C, paragraphs 4.4.2.2 (incorporated by reference; see §171.7 of this subchapter) and meet the standard of cleanliness specified therein.

§173.337 Nitric oxide.

Nitric oxide must be packed in DOT 3A1800, 3AA1800, 3E1800, or 3AL1800 cylinders conforming to the requirements of §173.40. Cylinders must be equipped with a stainless steel valve and valve seat that will not deteriorate if in contact with nitric oxide or nitrogen dioxide. Cylinders or valves may not be equipped with pressure relief devices of any type. In addition —

(a) **Transportation in DOT 3AL or 3ALM cylinders** is authorized only by highway or rail.

(b) **Each cylinder must be cleaned in compliance with** the requirements of Federal Specification RR-C-901C, paragraphs 3.3.1 and 3.3.2 (incorporated by reference; see §171.7 of this subchapter). Cleaning agents equivalent to those specified in Federal Specification RR-C-901C may be used; however, any cleaning agent must not be capable of reacting with oxygen. One cylinder selected at random from a group of 200 or fewer and cleaned at the same time must be tested for oil contamination in accordance with Federal Specification RR-C-901C paragraph 4.4.2.2 (incorporated by reference; see §171.7 of this subchapter) and meet the standard of cleanliness specified therein.

§173.338 Tungsten hexafluoride.

Tungsten hexafluoride must be packed in specification 3A, 3AA, 3BN, or 3E (§§178.36, 178.37, 178.39, 178.42 of this subchapter) cylinders. Cylinders must be equipped with a valve protection cap or be packed in a strong outside container complying with the provisions of §173.40. Outlets of any valves must be capped or plugged. As an alternative, the cylinder opening may be closed by the use of a metal plug. Specification 3E cylinders must be shipped in an overpack that complies with the provisions of §173.40.

§173.340 Tear gas devices.

(a) **Packagings for tear gas devices must be approved** prior to initial transportation by the Associate Administrator.

(b) **Tear gas devices may not be assembled with,** or packed in the same packaging with, mechanically- or manually-operated firing, igniting, bursting, or other functioning elements unless of a type and design which has been approved by the Associate Administrator.

(c) **Tear gas grenades, tear gas candles, and similar devices** must be packaged in one of the following packagings conforming to the requirements of part 178 of this subchapter at the Packing Group II performance level:

(1) *In UN 4C1, 4C2, 4D, or 4F* metal-strapped wooden boxes. Functioning elements not assembled in grenades or devices must be in a separate compartment of these boxes, or in inner or separate outer boxes, UN 4C1, 4C2, 4D, or 4F, and must be so packed and cushioned that they may not come in contact with each other or with the walls of the box during transportation. Not more than 50 tear gas devices and 50 functioning elements must be packed in one box, and the gross weight of the outer box may not exceed 35 kg (77 pounds).

(2) *In a UN 1A2 metal drum.* Functioning elements must be packed in a separate inner packaging or compartment. Not more than 24 tear gas devices and 24 functioning elements must be packed in one outer drum, and the gross weight of the drum may not exceed 35 kg (77 pounds).

(3) *In a UN 4G fiberboard box* with inside tear gas devices meeting Specifications 2P or 2Q. Each inside packaging must be placed in fiberboard tubes fitted with metal ends or a fiber box with suitable padding. Not more than 30 inner packagings must be packed in one outer box, and the gross weight of the outer box may not exceed 16 kg (35 pounds).

(4) *In other packagings* of a type or design which has been approved by the Associate Administrator.

(d) **Tear gas devices may be shipped** completely assembled when offered by or consigned to the U.S. Department of Defense, provided the functioning elements are so packed that they cannot accidentally function. Outer packagings must be UN 4C1, 4C2, 4D, or 4F metal-strapped wooden boxes.

Subpart H [Reserved]

Subpart I - Class 7 (Radioactive) Materials

§173.401 Scope.

(a) **This subpart sets forth requirements for the packaging** and transportation of Class 7 (radioactive) materials by offerors and carriers subject to this subchapter. The requirements prescribed in this subpart are in addition to, not in place of, other requirements set forth in this subchapter for Class 7 (radioactive) materials and those of the Nuclear Regulatory Commission in 10 CFR part 71.

(b) **This subpart does not apply to:**

(1) *Class 7 (radioactive) materials* produced, used, transported, or stored within an establishment other than during the course of transportation, including storage in transportation.

(2) *Class 7 (radioactive) materials* contained in a medical device, such as a heart pacemaker, which is implanted in a human being or live animal.

(3) *Class 7 (radioactive) materials* that have been injected into, ingested by, or are otherwise placed into, and are still in, human beings or live animals.

§173.403 Definitions.

For purposes of this subpart —

A_1 means the maximum activity of special form Class 7 (radioactive) material permitted in a Type A package.

A_2 means the maximum activity of Class 7 (radioactive) material, other than special form, LSA or SCO, permitted in a Type A package. These values are either listed in §173.435 or derived in accordance with the procedure prescribed in §173.433.

Class 7 (radioactive) material. See the definition of Radioactive material in this section.

Closed transport vehicle means a transport vehicle or conveyance equipped with a securely attached exterior enclosure that during normal transportation restricts the access of unauthorized persons to the cargo space containing the Class 7 (radioactive) materials. The enclosure may be either temporary or permanent, and in the case of packaged materials may be of the "see-through" type, and must limit access from top, sides, and bottom.

Containment system means the assembly of components of the packaging intended to retain the radioactive contents during transportation.

Conveyance means:

(1) *For transport by public highway or rail:* any transport vehicle or large freight container;

(2) *For transport by water:* any vessel, or any hold, compartment, or defined deck area of a vessel including any transport vehicle on board the vessel; and

(3) *For transport by aircraft, any aircraft.*

Design means the description of a special form Class 7 (radioactive) material, a package, packaging, or LSA-III, that enables those items to be fully identified. The description may include specifications, engineering drawings, reports showing compliance with regulatory requirements, and other relevant documentation.

Exclusive use (also referred to in other regulations as "sole use" or "full load") means sole use by a single consignor of a conveyance for which all initial, intermediate, and final loading and unloading are carried out in accordance with the direction of the consignor or consignee. The consignor and the carrier must ensure that any loading or unloading is performed by personnel having radiological training and resources appropriate for safe handling of the consignment. The consignor must issue specific instructions in writing, for maintenance of exclusive use shipment controls, and include them with the shipping paper information provided to the carrier by the consignor.

Fissile material means plutonium-238, plutonium-239, plutonium-241, uranium-233, uranium-235, or any combination of these radionuclides. The definition does not apply to unirradiated natural uranium and depleted uranium, and natural uranium or depleted uranium that has been irradiated in a thermal reactor. Certain additional exceptions are provided in §173.453.

Fissile material, controlled shipment means any shipment that contains one or more packages that have been assigned, in accordance with §173.457, nuclear criticality control transport indices greater than 10.

Freight container means a reusable container having a volume of 1.81 cubic meters (64 cubic feet) or more, designed and constructed to permit its being lifted with its contents intact and intended primarily for containment of packages in unit form during transportation. A "small freight container" is one which has either one outer dimension less than 1.5 m (4.9 feet) or an internal volume of not more than 3.0 cubic meters (106 cubic feet). All other freight containers are designated as "large freight containers."

Highway route controlled quantity means a quantity within a single package which exceeds:

(1) *3,000 times the A_1 value* of the radionuclides as specified in §173.435 for special form Class 7 (radioactive) material;

(2) *3,000 times the A_2 value* of the radionuclides as specified in §173.435 for normal form Class 7 (radioactive) material; or

(3) *1,000 TBq* (27,000 Ci), whichever is least.

Limited quantity of Class 7 (radioactive) material means a quantity of Class 7 (radioactive) material not exceeding the materials package limits specified in §173.425 and conforming with requirements specified in §173.421.

Low Specific Activity (LSA) material means Class 7 (radioactive) material with limited specific activity which satisfies the descriptions and limits set forth below. Shielding materials surrounding the LSA material may not be considered in determining the estimated average specific activity of the package contents. LSA material must be in one of three groups:

(1) *LSA-I.*

(i) *Ores containing* only naturally occurring radionuclides (e.g., uranium, thorium) and uranium or thorium concentrates of such ores; or

(ii) *Solid unirradiated* natural uranium or depleted uranium or natural thorium or their solid or liquid compounds or mixtures; or

(iii) *Class 7 (radioactive) material,* other than fissile material, for which the A_2 value is unlimited; or

(iv) *Mill tailings,* contaminated earth, concrete, rubble, other debris, and activated material in which the Class 7 (radioactive) material is essentially uniformly distributed and the average specific activity does not exceed $10^{-6}A_2g$.

(2) *LSA-II.*

(i) *Water with tritium concentration up to 0.8 TBq/L (20.0 Ci/liter); or*

(ii) *Material in which* the Class 7 (radioactive) material is distributed throughout and the average specific activity does not exceed $10^{-4}A_2g$ for solids and gases, and $10^{-5}A_2g$ for liquids.

(3) *LSA-III.* Solids (e.g., consolidated wastes, activated materials) that meet the requirements of §173.468 and which:

(i) *The Class 7 (radioactive) material* is distributed throughout a solid or a collection of solid objects, or is essentially uniformly distributed in a solid compact binding agent (such as concrete, bitumen, ceramic, etc.); and

(ii) *The Class 7 (radioactive) material* is relatively insoluble, or it is intrinsically contained in a relatively insoluble material, so that, even under loss of packaging, the loss of Class 7 (radioactive) material per package by leaching when placed in water for seven days would not exceed 0.1 A_2; and

(iii) *The average specific activity* of the solid does not exceed 2 x $10^{-3}A_2g$.

Low toxicity alpha emitters are:

(1) *Natural uranium, depleted uranium, and natural thorium;*

(2) *Ores, concentrates or tailings* containing uranium-235, uranium-238, thorium-232, thorium-228 and thorium-230; or

(3) *Alpha emitters with a half-life of less than 10 days.*

Maximum normal operating pressure means the maximum gauge pressure that would develop in a receptacle in a period of one year, in the absence of venting or cooling, under the heat conditions specified in 10 CFR 71.71(c)(1).

Multilateral approval means approval of a package or shipment by the relevant competent authority of the country of origin and of each country through or into which the package or shipment is to be transported. This definition does not include approval from a country over which Class 7 (radioactive) materials are carried in aircraft, if there is no scheduled stop in that country.

Natural thorium means thorium with the naturally occurring distribution of thorium isotopes (essentially 100 percent by weight of thorium-232).

Non-fixed radioactive contamination means radioactive contamination that can be readily removed from a surface by wiping with an absorbent material. Non-fixed (removable) radioactive contamination is not significant if it does not exceed the limits specified in §173.443.

Normal form Class 7 (radioactive) material means Class 7 (radioactive) material which has not been demonstrated to qualify as "special form Class 7 (radioactive) material."

Package means, for Class 7 (radioactive) materials, the packaging together with its radioactive contents as presented for transport.

(1) Excepted package means a packaging together with its excepted Class 7 (radioactive) materials as specified in §§173.421-173.426 and 173.428.

(2) Type A package means a packaging that, together with its radioactive contents limited to A_1 or A_2 as appropriate, meets the requirements of §§173.410 and 173.412 and is designed to retain the integrity of containment and shielding required by this part under normal conditions of transport as demonstrated by the tests set forth in §173.465 or §173.466, as appropriate. A Type A package does not require Competent Authority Approval.

(3) Type B package means a Type B packaging that, together with its radioactive contents, is designed to retain the integrity of containment and shielding required by this part when subjected to the normal conditions of transport and hypothetical accident test conditions set forth in 10 CFR part 71.

(i) Type B(U) package means a Type B packaging that, together with its radioactive contents, for international shipments requires unilateral approval only of the package design and of any stowage provisions that may be necessary for heat dissipation.

(ii) Type B(M) package means a Type B packaging, together with its radioactive contents, that for international shipments requires multilateral approval of the package design, and may require approval of the conditions of shipment. Type B(M) packages are those Type B package designs which have a maximum normal operating pressure of more than 700 kilopascals per square centimeter (100 pounds per square inch) gauge or a relief device which would allow the release of Class 7 (radioactive) material to the environment under the hypothetical accident conditions specified in 10 CFR part 71.

(4) Industrial package means a packaging that, together with its low specific activity (LSA) material or surface contaminated object (SCO) contents, meets the requirements of §§173.410 and 173.411. Industrial packages are categorized in §173.411 as either:

(i) *"Industrial package Type 1 (IP-1)";*

(ii) *"Industrial package Type 2 (IP-2)"; or*

(iii) *"Industrial package Type 3 (IP-3)".*

Packaging means, for Class 7 (radioactive) materials, the assembly of components necessary to ensure compliance with the packaging requirements of this subpart. It may consist of one or more receptacles, absorbent materials, spacing structures, thermal insulation, radiation shielding, service equipment for filling, emptying, venting and pressure relief, and devices for cooling or absorbing mechanical shocks. The conveyance, tie-down system, and auxiliary equipment may sometimes be designated as part of the packaging.

Radiation level means the radiation dose-equivalent rate expressed in millisievert(s) per hour or mSv/h (millirem(s) per hour or mrem/

h). Neutron flux densities may be converted into radiation levels according to table 1:

Table 1 - Neutron Fluence Rates To Be Regarded as Equivalent to a Radiation Level of 0.01 mSv/h (1 mrem/h)[1]

Energy of neutron	Flux density equivalent to 0.01 mSv/h (1 mrem/h) neutrons per square centimeter per second (n/cm^2/s)
Thermal (2.510E-8)MeV	272.0
1 keV	272.0
10 keV	281.0
100 keV	47.0
500 keV	11.0
1 MeV	7.5
5 MeV	6.4
10 MeV	6.7

1. Flux densities equivalent for energies between those listed in this table may be obtained by linear interpolation.

Radioactive contents means a Class 7 (radioactive) material, together with any contaminated liquids or gases within the package.

Radioactive instrument or article means any manufactured instrument or article such as an instrument, clock, electronic tube or apparatus, or similar instrument or article having Class 7 (radioactive) material in gaseous or non-dispersible solid form as a component part.

Radioactive material means any material having a specific activity greater than 70 Bq per gram (0.002 microcurie per gram) (see definition of "specific activity").

Special form Class 7 (radioactive) material means Class 7 (radioactive) material which satisfies the following conditions:

(1) *It is either* a single solid piece or is contained in a sealed capsule that can be opened only by destroying the capsule;

(2) *The piece or capsule* has at least one dimension not less than 5 mm (0.2 inch); and

(3) *It satisfies* the test requirements of §173.469. Special form encapsulations designed in accordance with the requirements of §173.389(g) in effect on June 30, 1983 (see 49 CFR part 173, revised as of October 1, 1982), and constructed prior to July 1, 1985 and special form encapsulations designed in accordance with the requirements of §173.403 in effect on March 31, 1996 (see 49 CFR part 173, revised as of October 1, 1995), and constructed prior to April 1, 1997, may continue to be used. Any other special form encapsulation must meet the requirements of this paragraph.

Specific activity of a radionuclide means the activity of the radionuclide per unit mass of that nuclide. The specific activity of a material in which the radionuclide is essentially uniformly distributed is the activity per unit mass of the material.

Surface Contaminated Object (SCO) means a solid object which is not itself radioactive but which has Class 7 (radioactive) material distributed on any of its surfaces. SCO must be in one of two groups with surface activity not exceeding the following limits:

(1) *SCO-I: A solid object on which:*

(i) *The non-fixed contamination* on the accessible surface averaged over 300 cm^2 (or the area of the surface if less than 300 cm^2) does not exceed 4 Bq/cm^2 (10^{-4} microcurie/cm^2) for beta and gamma and low toxicity alpha emitters, or 0.4 Bq/cm^2 (10^{-5} microcurie/cm^2) for alpha emitters;

(ii) *The fixed contamination* on the accessible surface averaged over 300 cm^2 (or the area of the surface if less than 300 cm^2) does not exceed 4 x 10^4 Bq/cm^2 (1.0 microcurie/cm^2) for beta and gamma and low toxicity alpha emitters, or 4 x 10^3 Bq/cm^2 (0.1 microcurie/cm^2) for all other alpha emitters; and

(iii) *The non-fixed contamination* plus the fixed contamination on the inaccessible surface averaged over 300 cm^2 (or the area of the surface if less than 300 cm^2) does not exceed 4 x 10^4 Bq/cm^2 (1 microcurie/cm^2) for beta and gamma and low toxicity alpha emitters, or 4 x 10^3 Bq/cm^2 (0.1 microcurie/cm^2) for all other alpha emitters.

(2) *SCO-II:* A solid object on which the limits for SCO-I are exceeded and on which:

(i) *The non-fixed contamination* on the accessible surface averaged over 300 cm^2 (or the area of the surface if less than 300 cm^2) does not exceed 400 Bq/cm^2 (10^{-2} microcurie/cm^2) for beta and gamma and low toxicity alpha emitters or 40 Bq/cm^2 (10^{-3} microcurie/cm^2) for all other alpha emitters;

(ii) *The fixed contamination* on the accessible surface averaged over 300 cm^2 (or the area of the surface if less than 300 cm^2) does not exceed 8 x 10^5 Bq/cm^2 (20 microcurie/cm^2) for beta and gamma and low toxicity alpha emitters, or 8 x 10^4 Bq/cm^2 (2 microcuries/cm^2) for all other alpha emitters; and

(iii) *The non-fixed contamination* plus the fixed contamination on the inaccessible surface averaged over 300 cm^2 (or the area of the surface if less than 300 cm^2) does not exceed 8 x 10^5 Bq/cm^2 (20 microcuries/cm^2) for beta and gamma and low toxicity alpha emitters, or 8 x 10^4 Bq/cm^2 (2 microcuries/cm^2) for all other alpha emitters.

Transport index (TI) means the dimensionless number (rounded up to the next tenth) placed on the label of a package to designate the degree of control to be exercised by the carrier during transportation. The transport index is determined as follows:

(1) *For nonfissile material packages,* the number determined by multiplying the maximum radiation level in milliSievert(s) per hour at 1 m (3.3 feet) from the external surface of the package by 100 (equivalent to the maximum radiation level in millirem per hour at 1 m (3.3 feet)); or

(2) *For fissile material packages,* the number determined by multiplying the maximum radiation level in milliSievert per hour at 1 m (3.3 feet) from any external surface of the package by 100 (equivalent to the maximum radiation level in millirem per hour at 1 m (3.3 feet)) or, for criticality control purposes, the number obtained by dividing 50 by the allowable number of packages which may be transported together, whichever number is larger.

Type A quantity means a quantity of Class 7 (radioactive) material, the aggregate radioactivity which does not exceed A_1 for special form Class 7 (radioactive) material or A_2 for normal form Class 7 (radioactive) material, where A_1 and A_2 values are given in §173.435 or are determined in accordance with §173.433.

Type B quantity means a quantity of material greater than a Type A quantity.

Unilateral approval means approval of a package solely by the competent authority of the country of origin.

Unirradiated thorium means thorium containing not more than 10^{-7} grams uranium-233 per gram of thorium-232. Unirradiated uranium means uranium containing not more than 10^{-6} grams plutonium per gram of uranium-235 and a fission product activity of not more than 9 MBq (0.24 millicuries) of fission products per gram of uranium-235.

Uranium — natural, depleted or enriched means the following:

(1) **Natural uranium** means uranium with the naturally occurring distribution of uranium isotopes (approximately 0.711 weight percent uranium-235, and the remainder essentially uranium-238).

(2) **Depleted uranium** means uranium containing less uranium-235 than the naturally occurring distribution of uranium isotopes.

(3) **Enriched uranium** means uranium containing more uranium-235 than the naturally occurring distribution of uranium isotopes.

§173.410 General design requirements.

In addition to the requirements of subparts A and B of this part, each package used for the shipment of Class 7 (radioactive) materials must be designed so that —

(a) **The package can be easily handled and properly secured** in or on a conveyance during transport.

(b) **Each lifting attachment that is a structural part** of the package must be designed with a minimum safety factor of three against yielding when used to lift the package in the intended manner, and it must be designed so that failure of any lifting attachment under excessive load would not impair the ability of the package to meet other requirements of this subpart. Any other structural part of the package which could be used to lift the package must be capable of being rendered inoperable for lifting the package during transport or must be designed with strength equivalent to that required for lifting attachments.

(c) **The external surface, as far as practicable,** will be free from protruding features and will be easily decontaminated.

(d) **The outer layer of packaging will avoid,** as far as practicable, pockets or crevices where water might collect.

(e) **Each feature that is added to the package** will not reduce the safety of the package.

(f) **The package will be capable of withstanding** the effects of any acceleration, vibration or vibration resonance that may arise under normal conditions of transport without any deterioration in the effectiveness of the closing devices on the various receptacles or in the integrity of the package as a whole and without loosening or unintentionally releasing the nuts, bolts, or other securing devices even after repeated use (see §§173.24, 173.24a, and 173.24b).

(g) **The materials of construction of the packaging** and any components or structure will be physically and chemically compatible with each other and with the package contents. The behavior of the packaging and the package contents under irradiation will be taken into account.

(h) **All valves through which the package contents** could escape will be protected against unauthorized operation.

(i) **For transport by air** —

(1) *The temperature* of the accessible surfaces of the package will not exceed 50 °C (122 °F) at an ambient temperature of 38 °C (100 °F) with no account taken for insulation;

(2) *The integrity of containment* will not be impaired if the package is exposed to ambient temperatures ranging from -40 °C (-40 °F) to +55 °C (131 °F); and

(3) *Packages containing liquid contents* will be capable of withstanding, without leakage, an internal pressure that produces a pressure differential of not less than 95 kPa (13.8 lb/in^2).

§173.411 Industrial packagings.

(a) **General.** Each industrial packaging must comply with the requirements of this section which specifies packaging tests, and record retention applicable to Industrial Packaging Type 1 (IP-1), Industrial Packaging Type 2 (IP-2), and Industrial Packaging Type 3 (IP-3).

(b) **Industrial packaging certification and tests.**

(1) *Each IP-1* must meet the general design requirements prescribed in §173.410.

(2) *Each IP-2* must meet the general design requirements prescribed in §173.410 and when subjected to the tests specified in §173.465 (c) and (d) or evaluated against these tests by any of the methods authorized by §173.461(a), must prevent:

(i) *Loss or dispersal of the radioactive contents; and*

(ii) *A significant increase* in the radiation levels recorded or calculated at the external surfaces for the condition before the test.

(3) *Each IP-3 packaging* must meet the requirements for an IP-1 and an IP-2, and must meet the requirements specified in §173.412(a) through §173.412(j).

(4) *Each specification* IM 101 or IM 102 portable tank (§§178.270, 178.271, 178.272 of this subchapter) that is certified as meeting the requirements for an IP-2 or IP-3 must:

(i) *Satisfy the requirements for IP-2 or IP-3, respectively;*

(ii) *Be capable* of withstanding a test pressure of 265 kPa (37.1 psig) gauge;

(iii) *Be designed* so that any added shielding is capable of withstanding the static and dynamic stresses resulting from normal handling and normal conditions of transport; and

(iv) *Be designed* so that loss of shielding will not result in a significant increase in the radiation levels recorded at the external surfaces.

(5) *Each freight container* that is certified as meeting the requirements of IP-2 or IP-3, must —

(i) *Satisfy the requirements for IP-2 or IP-3, respectively;*

(ii) *Be designed* to conform to the requirements of ISO 1496-3-1995(E), "Series 1 Freight Containers — Specifications and Testing — Part 3: Tank Containers for Liquids, Gases and Pressurized Dry Bulk";

(iii) *Be designed* so that loss of shielding will not result in a significant increase in the radiation levels recorded at the external surfaces if they are subjected to the tests specified in ISO 1496/1-1995(E); and

(iv) *For international transportation,* have a safety approval plate in conformance with 49 CFR 451.21 through 451.25.

(c) **Except for IP-1 packagings,** each offeror of an industrial package must maintain on file for at least one year after the latest shipment, and shall provide to the Associate Administrator on request, complete documentation of tests and an engineering evaluation or comparative data showing that the construction methods, packaging design, and materials of construction comply with that specification.

§173.412 Additional design requirements for Type A packages.

In addition to meeting the general design requirements prescribed in §173.410, each Type A packaging must be designed so that —

(a) **The outside of the packaging incorporates a feature,** such as a seal, that is not readily breakable, and that, while intact, is evidence that the package has not been opened. In the case of packages shipped in closed transport vehicles in exclusive use, the cargo compartment, instead of the individual packages, may be sealed.

(b) **The smallest external dimension of the package** is not less than 10 cm (4 inches).

(c) **Containment and shielding is maintained** during transportation and storage in a temperature range of -40 °C (-40 °F) to 70 °C (158 °F). Special attention shall be given to liquid contents and to the potential degradation of the packaging materials within the temperature range.

(d) **The packaging must include a containment system** securely closed by a positive fastening device that cannot be opened unintentionally or by pressure that may arise within the package during normal transport. Special form Class 7 (radioactive) material, as demonstrated in accordance with §173.469, may be considered as a component of the containment system. If the containment system forms a separate unit of the package, it must be securely closed by a positive fastening device that is independent of any other part of the package.

(e) **For each component of the containment system** account is taken, where applicable, of radiolytic decomposition of materials and the generation of gas by chemical reaction and radiolysis.

(f) **The containment system will retain** its radioactive contents under the reduction of ambient pressure to 25 kPa (3.6 psi).

(g) **Each valve, other than a pressure relief device,** is provided with an enclosure to retain any leakage.

(h) **Any radiation shield that encloses a component** of the packaging specified as part of the containment system will prevent the unintentional escape of that component from the shield.

(i) **Failure of any tie-down attachment** that is a structural part of the packaging, under both normal and accident conditions, must not impair the ability of the package to meet other requirements of this subpart.

(j) **When evaluated against the performance requirements** of this section and the tests specified in §173.465 or using any of the methods authorized by §173.461(a), the packaging will prevent —

(1) *Loss or dispersal of the radioactive contents; and*

(2) *A significant increase* in the radiation levels recorded or calculated at the external surfaces for the condition before the test.

(k) **Each packaging designed for liquids will** —

(1) *Be designed* to provide for ullage to accommodate variations in temperature of the contents, dynamic effects and filling dynamics;

(2) *Meet the conditions* prescribed in paragraph (j) of this section when subjected to the tests specified in §173.466 or evaluated against these tests by any of the methods authorized by §173.461(a); and

(3) *Either* —

(i) *Have sufficient* suitable absorbent material to absorb twice the volume of the liquid contents. The absorbent material must be compatible with the package contents and suitably positioned to contact the liquid in the event of leakage; or

(ii) *Have a containment system* composed of primary inner and secondary outer containment components designed to assure retention of the liquid contents within the secondary outer component in the event that the primary inner component leaks.

(l) **Each package designed for gases,** other than tritium not exceeding 40 TBq (1000Ci) or noble gases not exceeding the A_2 value appropriate for the noble gas, will be able to prevent loss or dispersal of contents when the package is subjected to the tests prescribed in §173.466 or evaluated against these tests by any of the methods authorized by §173.461(a).

§173.413 Requirements for Type B packages.

Except as provided in §173.416, each Type B(U) or Type B(M) package must be designed and constructed to meet the applicable requirements specified in 10 CFR part 71.

§173.415 Authorized Type A packages.

The following packages are authorized for shipment if they do not contain quantities exceeding A_1 or A_2 as appropriate:

(a) **DOT Specification 7A (§178.350 of this subchapter)** Type A general packaging. Each offeror of a Specification 7A package must maintain on file for at least one year after the latest shipment, and shall provide to DOT on request, complete documentation of tests and an engineering evaluation or comparative data showing that the construction methods, packaging design, and materials of construction comply with that specification. Use of Specification 7A packagings designed in accordance with the requirements of §178.350 of this subchapter in effect on June 30, 1983 (see 49 CFR part 178 revised as of October 1, 1982), is not authorized after April 1, 1997.

(b) **Any other Type A packaging that also meets** the applicable standards for fissile materials in 10 CFR part 71 and is used in accordance with §173.471.

(c) **Any Type B, Type B(U) or Type B(M) packaging** authorized pursuant to §173.416.

(d) **Any foreign-made packaging that meets the standards** in IAEA "Safety Series No. 6" (incorporated by reference, see §171.7 of this subchapter) and bears the marking "Type A" and was used for the import of Class 7 (radioactive) materials. Such packagings may be subsequently used for domestic and export shipments of Class 7 (radioactive) materials provided the offeror obtains the applicable documentation of tests and engineering evaluations and maintains the documentation on file in accordance with paragraph (a) of this section. These packagings must conform with requirements of the country of origin (as indicated by the packaging marking) and the IAEA regulations applicable to Type A packagings.

§173.416 Authorized Type B packages.

Each of the following packages is authorized for shipment of quantities exceeding A_1 or A_2, as appropriate:

(a) **Any Type B, Type B(U) or Type B(M) packaging** that meets the applicable requirements of 10 CFR part 71 and that has been approved by the U.S. Nuclear Regulatory Commission may be shipped pursuant to §173.471.

(b) **Any Type B, B(U) or B(M) packaging** that meets the applicable requirements of the regulations of the International Atomic Energy Agency (IAEA) in its "Regulations for the Safe Transport of Radioactive Materials, Safety Series No. 6" (incorporated by reference, see §171.7 of this subchapter) and for which the foreign competent authority certificate has been revalidated by DOT pursuant to §173.473. These packagings are authorized only for export and import shipments.

(c) **DOT Specification 6M (§178.354 of this subchapter)** metal packaging, only for solid or gaseous Class 7 (radioactive) materials that will not undergo pressure-generating decomposition at temperatures up to 121 °C (250 °F) and that do not generate more than 10 watts of radioactive decay heat.

(d) **For contents in other than special form;** DOT Specification 20WC (§178.362 of this subchapter), wooden protective jacket, when used with a single, snug-fitting inner DOT Specification 2R (§178.360 of this subchapter). For liquid contents, the inner packaging must conform to §173.412(j) and (k).

(e) **For contents in special form only;** DOT Specification 20WC (§178.362 of this subchapter), wooden protective jacket, with a single snug-fitting inner Type A packaging that has a metal outer wall and conforms to §178.350 of this subchapter. Radioactive decay heat may not exceed 100 watts.

(f) **For contents in special form only;** DOT Specification 21WC (§178.364 of this subchapter), wooden protective overpack, with a single inner DOT Specification 2R (§178.360 of this subchapter). Contents must be loaded within the inner packaging in such a manner as to prevent loose movement during transportation. The inner packaging must be securely positioned and centered within the overpack so that there will be no significant displacement of the inner packaging if the overpack containing it is subjected to the 9 m (30 feet) drop test described in 10 CFR part 71.

§173.417 Authorized fissile materials packages.

(a) **Except as provided in §173.453,** fissile materials containing not more than A_1 or A_2 as appropriate, must be packaged in one of the following packagings:

(1) *DOT Specification 6L* (§178.352 of this subchapter), metal packaging, for materials prescribed in paragraph (b)(1) of this section.

(2) *DOT Specification 6M* (§178.354 of this subchapter), metal packaging, for materials prescribed in paragraph (b)(2) of this section.

(3) *Any packaging* listed in §173.415, limited to the Class 7 (radioactive) materials specified in 10 CFR part 71, subpart C.

(4) *Any other* Type A or Type B, Type B(U), or Type B(M) packaging for fissile Class 7 (radioactive) materials that also meets the applicable standards for fissile materials in 10 CFR part 71.

(5) *Any other* Type A or Type B, Type B(U), or Type B(M) packaging that also meets the applicable requirements for fissile material packaging in Section V of the International Atomic Energy Agency "Regulations for the Safe Transport of Radioactive Materials, Safety Series No. 6" (incorporated by reference, see §171.7 of this subchapter), and for which the foreign competent authority certificate has been revalidated by the U.S. Competent Authority, in accordance with §173.473. These packages are authorized only for export and import shipments.

(6) *A 55-gallon 1A2 steel drum,* meeting the applicable packaging testing requirements of subpart M of part 178 of this subchapter at the packing group I performance level, subject to the following conditions:

(i) *The quantity* may not exceed 350 grams of uranium-235 in any non-pyrophoric form, enriched to any degree in the uranium-235 isotope;

(ii) *Each drum* must have a minimum 18 gauge body and bottom head and 16 gauge removable top head with one or more corrugations in the cover near the periphery;

(iii) *Closure must conform to §178.352 of this subchapter;*

(iv) *At least* four equally spaced 12 mm (0.5 inch) diameter vent holes must be provided on the sides of the drum near the top, each covered with weatherproof tape; or equivalent device;

(v) *Appropriate primary,* inner containment of the contents and sufficient packaging material, such as plastic or metal jars or cans, must be provided such that Specification 7A (§178.350 of this subchapter) provisions are satisfied by the inner packaging;

(vi) *Each inner container* must be capable of venting if subjected to the thermal test described in 10 CFR part 71;

(vii) *Liquid contents* must be packaged in accordance with §173.412 (j) and (k); and

(viii) *The maximum weight* of contents, including internal packaging, may not exceed 91 kg (200 pounds) with fissile material content limited as shown in table 2:

Table 2 - Fissile Material Content and Transport Index for UN1A2 Package

Maximum quantity and minimum transport index		Maximum No. of packages transported as a fissile material controlled shipment
U-235 per package (grams)	Minimum transport index per package	
350	1.8	72
300	1.0	129
250	0.5	256
200	0.3	500
150	0.1	500
100	0.1	500
50	(1)	(2)

1. Transport index is limited by the external radiation levels.
2. Maximum number is limited by the total transport index.

(7) *Any metal cylinder* that meets the requirements of §173.415 and §178.350 of this subchapter for Specification 7A Type A packaging may be used for the transport of residual "heels" of enriched solid uranium hexafluoride without a protective overpack in accordance with table 3, as follows:

Table 3 - Allowable Content of Uranium Hexafluoride (UF_6) "Heels" in a Specification 7A Cylinder

Maximum cylinder diameter		Cylinder volume		Maximum uranium-235 enrichment (weight percent)	Maximum "Heel" weight per cylinder			
					UF6		Uranium-235	
Cm	Inches	Liters	Cubic feet		kg	lb	kg	lb
12.7	5	8.8	0.311	100.0	0.045	0.1	0.031	0.07
20.3	8	39.0	1.359	12.5	0.227	0.5	0.019	0.04
30.5	12	68.0	2.410	5.0	0.454	1.0	0.015	0.03
76.0	30	725.0	25.64	5.0	11.3	25.0	0.383	0.84
122.0	48	3,084.0	[1]108.9	4.5	22.7	50.0	0.690	1.52
122.0	48	4,041.0	[2]142.7	4.5	22.7	50.0	0.690	1.52

1. 10 ton.
2. 14 ton.

(8) *DOT Specification* 20PF-1, 20PF-2, or 20PF-3 (§178.356 of this subchapter), or Specification 21PF-1A, 21PF-1B, or 21PF-2 (§178.358 of this subchapter) phenolic-foam insulated overpack with snug fitting inner metal cylinders, meeting all requirements of §§173.24, 173.410, 173.412, and 173.420 and the following:

(i) *Handling procedures* and packaging criteria must be in accordance with DOE Report ORO-651 or ANSI N14.1 (incorporated by reference, see §171.7 of this subchapter).

(ii) *Quantities of uranium hexafluoride* are authorized as shown in table 6 of this section, with each package assigned a minimum transport index as also shown.

(b) **Fissile Class 7 (radioactive) materials** with radioactive content exceeding A_1 or A_2 must be packaged in one of the following packagings:

(1) *DOT Specification 6L* (§178.352 of this subchapter), metal packaging. These packages may contain only uranium-235, plutonium-239, or plutonium-241, as metal, oxide, or compounds that do not decompose at temperatures up to 149 °C (300 °F). Radioactive decay heat output may not exceed 5 watts. Class 7 (radioactive) materials in normal form must be packaged in one or more tightly sealed metal or polyethylene bottles within a DOT Specification 2R (§178.360 of this subchapter) containment vessel. Authorized contents are limited in accordance with table 4, as follows:

Table 4 - Authorized Contents in Kilograms (kg) and Conditions for Specification 6L Packages

Uranium-235		Plutonium (Plutonium solutions are not authorized)		Minimum fissile transport index	Maximum No. of packages transported as a fissile material control shipment
H/X≤3[1]	3 H/X≤10	H/X≤10	10≤H/X≤20		
14	[2]3.6	2.5	2.4	1.3	80
				1.8	50

1. H/X is the ratio of hydrogen to fissile atoms in their inner containment with all sources of hydrogen in the containment considered.
2. Volume not to exceed 3.6 L.

(2) *DOT Specification 6M* (§178.354 of this subchapter), metal packaging. These packages must contain only solid Class 7 (radioactive) materials that will not decompose at temperatures up to 121 °C (250 °F). Radioactive decay heat output may not exceed 10 watts. Class 7 (radioactive) materials in other than special form must be packaged in one or more tightly sealed metal cans or polyethylene bottles within a DOT Specification 2R (§178.360 of this subchapter) containment vessel.

(i) *For fissile material* with a criticality TI equal to 0.0, packages are limited to the following amounts of fissile Class 7 (radioactive) materials: 1.6 kg of uranium-235; 0.9 kg of plutonium (except that due to the 10-watt thermal decay heat limitation, the limit for plutonium-238 is 0.02 kg); and 0.5 kg of uranium-233. The maximum ratio of hydrogen to fissile material may not exceed three, including all of the sources of hydrogen within the DOT Specification 2R containment vessel.

(ii) *Maximum quantities* of fissile material and other restrictions for materials with a criticality TI of greater than 0.0 are given in table 5. The minimum transport index to be assigned per package and, for fissile material, controlled shipments, the allowable number of similar packages per conveyance and per transport vehicle are shown in table 5. Where a maximum ratio of hydrogen to fissile material is specified in table 5, only the hydrogen interspersed with the fissile material must be considered. For a uranium-233 shipment, the maximum inside diameter of the inner containment vessel may not exceed 12.1 cm (4.75 inches). Where necessary, a tight-fitting steel insert must be used to reduce a larger diameter inner containment vessel specified in §178.354 of this subchapter to the 12.1 cm (4.75 inch) limit. Table 5 is as follows:

Table 5 - Authorized Contents for Specification 6M Packages[1]

Uranium-233 [5]			Uranium-235 [4, 7]			Plutonium [2, 3, 4]			Minimum transport index	Maximum No. of packages transported as a fissile material control shipment
Metal or alloy	Compounds		Metal or alloy	Compounds		Metal or alloy	Compounds			
H/X=0[8]	H/X=0	H/X≤3	H/X=0	H/X=0	H/X≤3	H/X=0	H/X=0	H/X≤3		
0.5	0.5	0.5	1.6	1.6	1.6	[9]0.9	[9]0.9	[9]0.9	0	N/A
3.6	4.4	2.9	7.2	7.6	5.3	3.1	4.1	3.4	0.1	1,250
[6]4.2	5.2	3.5	8.7	9.6	6.4	3.4	4.5	4.1	0.2	625
[6]5.2	6.8	4.5	11.2	13.9	8.3	4.2		4.5	0.5	250
			13.5	16.0	10.1	4.5			1.0	125
				26.0	16.1				5.0	25
				32.0	19.5				10.0	12

1. Quantity in kg.
2. Minimum percentage of plutonium-240 is 5 weight percent.
3. 4.5 kg limitation of plutonium due to watt decay heat limitation.
4. For a mixture of uranium-235 and plutonium an equal amount of uranium-235 may be substituted for any portion of the plutonium authorized.
5. Maximum inside diameter of specification 2R containment vessel not to exceed 12.1 cm (4.75 inches) (see paragraph (b)(2)(ii) of this section).
6. Granulated or powdered metal with any particle less than 6.4 mm (0.25 inch) in the smallest dimension is not authorized.
7. Except for material with a criticality TI of 0.0, the maximum permitted uranium-235 enrichment is 93.5 percent.
8. H/X is the ratio of hydrogen to fissile atoms in the inner containment.
9. For Pu-238, the limit is 0.02 kg because of the 10 watt thermal decay heat limitation.

(3) *Type B,* or Type B(U), or B(M) packaging that meets the standards for packaging of fissile materials in 10 CFR part 71, and is approved by the U.S. Nuclear Regulatory Commission and used in accordance with §173.471.

(4) *Type B,* B(U), or B(M) packaging that meets the applicable requirements for fissile Class 7 (radioactive) materials in Section V of the IAEA "Regulations for the Safe Transport of Radioactive Materials, Safety Series No. 6" (incorporated by reference, see §171.7 of this subchapter), and for which the foreign competent authority certificate has been revalidated by the U.S. Competent Authority in accordance with §173.473. These packagings are authorized only for import and export shipments.

(5) *DOT Specifications* 20PF-1, 20PF-2, or 20PF-3 (§178.356 of this subchapter), or DOT Specifications 21PF-1A or 21PF-1B (§178.358 of this subchapter) phenolic-foam insulated overpack with snug fitting inner metal cylinders, meeting all requirements of §§173.24, 173.410, and 173.412, and the following:

(i) *Handling procedures* and packaging criteria must be in accordance with DOE Report ORO-651 or ANSI N14.1; and

(ii) *Quantities of uranium hexafluoride* are authorized as shown in table 6, with each package assigned a minimum transport index as also shown:

Table 6 - Authorized Quantities of Uranium Hexafluoride

Protective overpack specification number	Maximum inner cylinder diameter		Maximum weight of UF6 contents		Maximum U-235 enrichment (weight/ percent)	Minimum transport index
	Cm	Inches	Kilo-grams	Pounds		
20PF-1	12.7	5	25	55	100.0	0.1
20PF-2	20.3	8	116	255	12.5	0.4
20PF-3	30.5	12	209	460	5.0	1.1
21PF-1A[1] or 21PF-1B[1]	[2]76.0	[2]30	2,250	4,950	5.0	5.0
21PF-1A[1] or 21PF-1B[1]	[3]76.0	[3]30	2,282	5,020	5.0	5.0
21PF-2[1]	[2]76.0	[2]30	2,250	4,950	5.0	5.0
21PF-2[1]	[3]76.0	[3]30	2,282	5,020	5.0	5.0

1. For 76 cm (30 in) cylinders, the maximum H/U atomic ratio is 0.088.
2. Model 30A inner cylinder (reference ORO-651).
3. Model 30B inner cylinder (reference ORO-651).

§173.418 Authorized packages — pyrophoric Class 7 (radioactive) materials.

Pyrophoric Class 7 (radioactive) materials, as referenced in the §172.101 table of this subchapter, in quantities not exceeding A_2 per package must be transported in DOT Specification 7A packagings constructed of materials that will not react with, nor be decomposed by, the contents. Contents of the package must be —

(a) **In solid form and must not be fissile unless excepted by §173.453;**

(b) **Contained in sealed and corrosion resistant receptacles** with positive closures (friction or slip-fit covers or stoppers are not authorized);

(c) **Free of water and contaminants** that would increase the reactivity of the material; and

(d) **Inerted to prevent self-ignition during transport by either —**

(1) *Mixing with large volumes* of inerting materials, such as graphite, dry sand, or other suitable inerting material, or blended into a matrix of hardened concrete; or

(2) *Filling the innermost receptacle* with an appropriate inert gas or liquid.

§173.419 Authorized packages — oxidizing Class 7 (radioactive) materials.

(a) **An oxidizing Class 7 (radioactive) material,** as referenced in the §172.101 table of this subchapter, is authorized in quantities not exceeding an A_2 per package, in a DOT Specification 7A package provided that —

(1) *The contents are:*

(i) *Not fissile;*

(ii) *Packed in* inside packagings of glass, metal or compatible plastic; and

(iii) *Cushioned with* a material that will not react with the contents; and

(2) *The outside packaging is made of wood, metal, or plastic.*

(b) **The package must be capable** of meeting the applicable test requirements of §173.465 without leakage of contents.

(c) **For shipment by air,** the maximum quantity in any package may not exceed 11.3 kg (25 pounds).

§173.420 Uranium hexafluoride (fissile, fissile excepted and non-fissile).

(a) **In addition to any other applicable requirements** of this subchapter, uranium hexafluoride, fissile, fissile excepted or non-fissile, must be offered for transportation as follows:

(1) *Before initial filling* and during periodic inspection and test, packagings must be cleaned in accordance with American National Standard N14.1.

(2) *Packagings must be* designed, fabricated, inspected, tested and marked in accordance with —

(i) *American National Standard N14.1* (2001, 1995, 1990, 1987, 1982, 1971) (incorporated by reference, see §171.7 of this subchapter) in effect at the time the packaging was manufactured;

(ii) *Specifications for* Class DOT-106A multi-unit tank car tanks (§§179.300 and 179.301 of this subchapter); or

(iii) *Section VIII,* Division I of the ASME Code (incorporated by reference, see §171.7 of this subchapter), provided the packaging —

[A] Was manufactured on or before June 30, 1987;

[B] Conforms to the edition of the ASME Code in effect at the time the packaging was manufactured;

[C] Is used within its original design limitations; and

[D] Has shell and head thicknesses that have not decreased below the minimum value specified in the following table:

Packaging model	Minimum thickness; millimeters (inches)
1S, 2S	1.58 (0.062)
5A, 5B, 8A	3.17 (0.125)
12A, 12B	4.76 (0.187)
30B	7.93 (0.312)
48A, F, X, and Y	12.70 (0.500)
48T, O, OM, OM Allied, HX, H, AND G	6.35 (0.250)

(3) *Uranium hexafluoride must be in solid form.*

(4) *The volume* of solid uranium hexafluoride, except solid depleted uranium hexafluoride, at 20 °C (68 °F) may not exceed 61% of the certified volumetric capacity of the packaging. The volume of solid depleted uranium hexafluoride at 20 °C (68 °F) may not exceed 62% of the certified volumetric capacity of the packaging.

(5) *The pressure* in the package at 20 °C (68 °F) must be less than 101.3 kPa (14.8 psia).

(b) **Packagings for uranium hexafluoride** must be periodically inspected, tested, marked and otherwise conform with the latest incorporated edition of ANSI N14.1 (incorporated by reference, see §171.7 of this subchapter).

(c) **Each repair to a packaging for uranium hexafluoride** must be performed in accordance with the latest incorporated edition of ANSI N14.1 (incorporated by reference, see §171.7 of this subchapter).

§173.421 Excepted packages for limited quantities of Class 7 (radioactive) materials.

(a) **A Class 7 (radioactive) material whose activity** per package does not exceed the limits specified in §173.425 and its packaging are excepted from the specification packaging, marking, labeling and, if not a hazardous substance or hazardous waste, the shipping paper and certification requirements of this subchapter and requirements of this subpart if:

(1) *Each package meets the general design requirements of §173.410;*

(2) *The radiation level* at any point on the external surface of the package does not exceed 0.005 mSv/hour (0.5 mrem/hour);

(3) *The nonfixed (removable)* radioactive surface contamination on the external surface of the package does not exceed the limits specified in §173.443(a);

(4) *The outside* of the inner packaging or, if there is no inner packaging, the outside of the packaging itself bears the marking "Radioactive";

(5) *Except as provided* in §173.426, the package does not contain more than 15 grams of uranium-235; and

(6) *The material* is otherwise prepared for shipment as specified in accordance with §173.422.

(b) **A limited quantity of Class 7 (radioactive) material** that is a hazardous substance or a hazardous waste, is not subject to the provisions in §172.203(d) or §172.204(c)(4) of this subchapter.

§173.422 Additional requirements for excepted packages containing Class 7 (radioactive) materials.

(a) **Except for materials subject to the shipping paper** requirements of subpart C of part 172 of this subchapter, excepted packages prepared for shipment under the provisions of §173.421, §173.424, §173.426, or §173.428 must be certified as being acceptable for transportation by having a notice enclosed in or on the package, included with the packing list, or otherwise forwarded with the package. This notice must include the name of the consignor or consignee and one of the following statements, as appropriate:

(1) *"This package conforms* to the conditions and limitations specified in 49 CFR 173.421 for radioactive material, excepted package-limited quantity of material, UN2910";

(2) *"This package conforms* to the conditions and limitations specified in 49 CFR 173.424 for radioactive material, excepted package-instruments or articles, UN2910";

(3) *"This package conforms* to the conditions and limitations specified in 49 CFR 173.426 for radioactive material, excepted package-articles manufactured from natural or depleted uranium, or natural thorium, UN2910"; or

(4) *"This package conforms* to the conditions and limitations specified in 49 CFR 173.428 for radioactive material, excepted package-empty package, UN2910."

(b) **An excepted package of Class 7 (radioactive) material** that is classed as Class 7 and is prepared for shipment under the provisions of §173.421, §173.423, §173.424, §173.426, or §173.428 is not subject to the requirements of this subchapter, except for —

(1) *Sections 171.15,* 171.16, 174.750 and 176.710 of this subchapter, pertaining to the reporting of incidents and decontamination, when transported by a mode other than air;

(2) *Sections 171.15,* 171.16, and 175.700(b) of this subchapter pertaining to the reporting of incidents and decontamination when transported by aircraft; and

(3) *The training requirements* of subpart H of part 172 of this subchapter and, for materials that meet the definition of a hazardous substance or a hazardous waste, the shipping paper requirements of subpart C of part 172 of this subchapter.

§173.423 Requirements for multiple hazard limited quantity Class 7 (radioactive) materials.

(a) **Except as provided in §173.4,** when a limited quantity radioactive material meets the definition of another hazard class or division, it must be —

(1) *Classed for the additional hazard;*

(2) *Packaged to conform* with the requirements specified in §173.421 (a)(1) through (a)(5) or §173.424(a) through (g), as appropriate; and

(3) *Offered for transportation* in accordance with the requirements applicable to the hazard for which it is classed.

(b) **A limited quantity Class 7 (radioactive) material** which is classed other than Class 7 in accordance with this subchapter is excepted from the requirements of §§173.422(a), 172.203(d), and 172.204(c)(4) of this subchapter if the entry "Limited quantity radioactive material" appears on the shipping paper in association with the basic description.

§173.424 Excepted packages for radioactive instruments and articles.

A radioactive instrument or article and its packaging is excepted from the specification packaging, shipping paper and certification, marking and labeling requirements of this subchapter and requirements of this subpart, if:

(a) **Each package meets the general design requirements of §173.410;**

(b) **The activity of the instrument or article** does not exceed the relevant limit listed in table 7 in §173.425;

(c) **The total activity per package does not exceed** the relevant limit listed in table 7 in §173.425;

(d) **The radiation level at 10 cm (4 in) from any point** on the external surface of any unpackaged instrument or article does not exceed 0.1 mSv/hour (10 mrem/hour);

(e) **The radiation level at any point on the external surface** of a package bearing the article or instrument does not exceed 0.005 mSv/hour (0.5 mrem/hour), or, for exclusive use domestic shipments, 0.02 mSv (2 mrem/hour);

(f) **The nonfixed (removable) radioactive surface contamination** on the external surface of the package does not exceed the limits specified in §173.443(a);

(g) **Except as provided in §173.426,** the package does not contain more than 15 grams of uranium-235; and

(h) **The package is otherwise prepared for shipment** as specified in §173.422.

§173.425 Table of activity limits — excepted quantities and articles.

The limits applicable to instruments, articles, and limited quantities subject to exceptions under §§173.421 and 173.424 are set forth in table 7 as follows:

Table 7 - Activity Limits for Limited Quantities, Instruments, and Articles

Nature of contents	Instruments and articles: Limits for each instrument or article[1]	Instruments and articles: Package limits[1]	Limited quantity package limits[1]
Solids:			
Special form	10^{-2} A_1	A_1	10^{-3} A_1
Normal form	10^{-2} A_2	A_2	10^{-3} A_2
Liquids:			
Tritiated water:			
<0.0037 TBq/L (0.1 Ci/L)			37 TBq (1,000 Ci)
0.0037 TBq to 0.037 TBq/L (0.1 Ci to 1.0 Ci/L)			3.7 TBq (100 Ci)
>0.037 TBq/L (1.0 Ci/L)			0.037 TBq (1.0 Ci)
Other Liquids	10^{-3} A_2	10^{-1} A_2	10^{-4} A_2
Gases:			
Tritium[2]	2 x 10^{-2} A_2	2 x 10^{-1} A_2	2 x 10^{-2} A_2
Special form	10^{-3} A_1	10^{-2} A_1	10^{-3} A_1
Normal form	10^{-3} A_2	10^{-2} A_2	10^{-3} A_2

1. For mixtures of radionuclides see §173.433(d).
2. These values also apply to tritium in activated luminous paint and tritium adsorbed on solid carriers.

§173.426 Excepted packages for articles containing natural uranium or thorium.

A manufactured article in which the sole Class 7 (radioactive) material content is natural or unirradiated depleted uranium or natural thorium and its packaging is excepted from the specification packaging, shipping paper and certification, marking, and labeling requirements of this subchapter and requirements of this subpart if:

(a) **Each package meets the general design requirements of §173.410;**

(b) **The outer surface of the uranium or thorium** is enclosed in an inactive sheath made of metal or other durable protective material;

(c) **The conditions specified in §173.421(a) (2), (3) and (4)** are met; and

(d) **The article is otherwise prepared for shipment** as specified in §173.422.

§173.427 Transport requirements for low specific activity (LSA) Class 7 (radioactive) materials and surface contaminated objects (SCO).

(a) **In addition to other applicable requirements** specified in this subchapter, low specific activity (LSA) materials and surface contaminated objects (SCO), unless excepted by paragraph (d) of this section, must be packaged in accordance with paragraph (b) or (c) of this section and must be transported in accordance with the following conditions:

(1) *The external dose rate* must not exceed an external radiation level of 10 mSv/h (1 rem/h) at 3 m from the unshielded material;

(2) *The quantity* of LSA and SCO material in any single conveyance must not exceed the limits specified in table 9;

(3) *LSA material and SCO* that are or contain fissile material must meet the applicable requirements of §§173.453, 173.457, 173.459 and 173.467;

(4) *Packages must meet* the contamination control limits specified in §173.443;

(5) *External radiation levels must comply with §173.441; and*

(6) *For LSA material and SCO* required by this section to be consigned as exclusive use:

(i) *Shipments must be loaded* by the consignor and unloaded by the consignee from the conveyance or freight container in which originally loaded;

(ii) *There must be* no loose Class 7 (radioactive) material in the conveyance, however, when the conveyance is the packaging there must be no leakage of Class 7 (radioactive) material from the conveyance;

(iii) *Packages must be braced* so as to prevent shifting of lading under conditions normally incident to transportation;

(iv) *Specific instructions* for maintenance of exclusive use shipment controls must be provided by the offeror to the carrier. Such instructions must be included with the shipping paper information;

(v) *Except for shipments* of unconcentrated uranium or thorium ores, the transport vehicle must be placarded in accordance with subpart F of part 172 of this subchapter;

(vi) *For domestic transportation only,* packages are excepted from the marking and labeling requirements of this subchapter. However, the exterior of each nonbulk package must be stenciled or otherwise marked "Radioactive — LSA" or "Radioactive — SCO", as appropriate, and nonbulk packages that contain a hazardous substance must also be stenciled or otherwise marked with the letters "RQ" in association with the above description; and

(vii) *Except when transported* in an industrial package in accordance with table 8, transportation by aircraft is prohibited.

(b) Except as provided in paragraph (c) of this section, LSA material and SCO must be packaged as follows:

(1) *In an industrial package* (IP-1, IP-2 or IP-3; §173.411), subject to the limitations of table 8;

(2) *For domestic transportation only,* in a DOT Specification 7A (§178.350 of this subchapter) Type A package. The requirements of §173.412 (a), (b), (c) and (k) do not apply;

(3) *For domestic transportation only,* in a strong, tight package that prevents leakage of the radioactive content under normal conditions of transport. In addition to the requirements of paragraph (a) of this section, the following requirements must be met:

(i) *The shipment must be exclusive use;*

(ii) *The quantity* of Class 7 (radioactive) material in each packaging may not exceed an A_2 quantity;

(4) *For domestic transportation only,* in a packaging that complies with the provisions of 10 CFR 71.52, and is transported in exclusive use; or

(5) *Any Type B,* B(U) or B(M) packaging authorized pursuant to §173.416.

(c) LSA-I and SCO-I (see §173.403), unless packaged in accordance with paragraph (b) of this section, must be packaged in bulk packagings in accordance with this paragraph. The shipment must be, in addition to complying with the applicable requirements of paragraph (a) of this section, exclusive use:

(1) *Solids.* Packages must be strong tight packagings, meeting the requirements of subpart B of this part. The requirements of §173.410 do not apply.

(2) *Liquids.* Liquids must be transported in the following packagings:

(i) *Specification 103CW,* 111A60W7 (§§179.200 and 179.201 of this subchapter) tank cars. Bottom openings in tanks are prohibited; or

(ii) *Specification MC 310,* MC 311, MC 312, MC 331 or DOT 412 (§178.348 or §178.337 of this subchapter) cargo tank motor vehicles. Bottom outlets are not authorized. Trailer-on-flat-car service is not authorized.

(d) Except for transportation by aircraft, LSA material and SCO that conform to the provisions specified in 10 CFR 20.2005 are excepted from all requirements of this subchapter pertaining to Class 7 (radioactive) materials when offered for transportation for disposal or recovery. A material which meets the definition of another hazard class is subject to the provisions of this subchapter relating to that hazard class.

(e) LSA and SCO that exceed the packaging limits in this section must be packaged in accordance with 10 CFR part 71.

(f) Tables 8 and 9 are as follows:

Table 8 - Industrial Package Integrity Requirements for LSA Material and SCO

Contents	Industrial packaging type	
	Exclusive use shipment	Nonexclusive use shipment
LSA-I:		
Solid	IP-1	IP-1
Liquid	IP-1	IP-2
LSA-II:		
Solid	IP-2	IP-2
Liquid and gas	IP-2	IP-3
LSA-III	IP-2	IP-3
SCO-I	IP-1	IP-1
SCO-II	IP-2	IP-2

Table 9 - Conveyance Activity Limits for LSA Material and SCO

Nature of material	Activity limit for conveyances
LSA-I	No limit
LSA-II and LSA-III; noncombustible solids	No limit
LSA-II and LSA-III; Combustible solids and all liquids and gases	100 A_2
SCO	100 A_2

§173.428 Empty Class 7 (radioactive) materials packaging.

A packaging which previously contained Class 7 (radioactive) materials and has been emptied of contents as far as practical, is excepted from the shipping paper, certification, and marking requirements of this subchapter, and from requirements of this chapter, provided that —

(a) The packaging meets the requirements of §173.421(a) (2), (3), and (5) of this subpart;

(b) The packaging is in unimpaired condition and is securely closed so that there will be no leakage of Class 7 (radioactive) material under conditions normally incident to transportation;

(c) Internal contamination does not exceed 100 times the limits in §173.443(a);

(d) Any labels previously applied in conformance with subpart E of part 172 of this subchapter are removed, obliterated, or covered and the "Empty" label prescribed in §172.450 of this subchapter is affixed to the packaging; and

(e) The packaging is prepared for shipment as specified in §173.422.

§173.431 Activity limits for Type A and Type B packages.

(a) Except for LSA material and SCO, a Type A package may not contain a quantity of Class 7 (radioactive) materials greater than A_1 for special form Class 7 (radioactive) material or A_2 for normal form Class 7 (radioactive) material as listed in §173.435, or, for Class 7 (radioactive) materials not listed in §173.435, as determined in accordance with §173.433.

(b) The limits on activity contained in a Type B, Type B(U), or Type B(M) package are those prescribed in §§173.416 and 173.417, or in the applicable approval certificate under §§173.471, 173.472 or 173.473.

§173.433 Requirements for determining A_1 and A_2 values for radionuclides and for the listing of radionuclides on shipping papers and labels.

(a) Values of A_1 and A_2 for individual radionuclides that are the basis for many activity limits elsewhere in this subchapter are given in the table in §173.435.

(b) For individual radionuclides whose identities are known, but which are not listed in the table in §173.435, the determination of the values of A_1 and A_2 requires approval from the Associate Administrator except that the values of A_1 and A_2 in table 10 may be used without obtaining approval from Associate Administrator.

(c) In calculating A_1 and A_2 values for a radionuclide not listed in the table in §173.435, a single radioactive decay chain in which the radionuclides are present in their naturally-occurring proportions, and in which no daughter nuclide has a half life either longer than 10 days or longer than that of the parent nuclide, will be considered as a single radionuclide, and the activity to be taken into account and the A_1 or A_2 value to be applied will be those corresponding to the parent nuclide of that chain. Otherwise, the parent and daughter nuclides will be considered as a mixture of different nuclides.

(d) Mixtures of radionuclides whose identities and respective activities are known, must conform to the following conditions:

(1) *For special form Class 7 (radioactive) material:*

$$\sum_i \frac{B(i)}{A_1(i)} \quad \textbf{less than or equal to 1}$$

Where B(i) is the activity of radionuclide i and $A_1(i)$ is the A_1 value for radionuclide i; or

(2) *For other forms of Class 7 (radioactive) material, either —*

$$\sum_i \frac{B(i)}{A_2(i)} \quad \textbf{less than or equal to 1}$$

Where B(i) is the activity of radionuclide i and $A_2(i)$ is the A_2 value for radionuclide i;

or

$$A_2 \text{ for mixture} = \frac{1}{\sum_i \frac{f(i)}{A_2(i)}}$$

where f(i) is the fraction of activity of nuclide i in the mixture and $A_2(i)$ is the appropriate A_2 value for nuclide i.

(e) When the identity of each nuclide is known but the individual activities of some of the radionuclides are not known, the radionuclides may be grouped and the lowest A_1 or A_2 value, as appropriate, for the radionuclides in each group may be used in applying the formulas in paragraph (d) of this section. Groups may be based on the total alpha activity and the total beta/gamma activity when these are known, using the lowest A_1 or A_2 values for the alpha emitters or beta/gamma emitters, respectively.

(f) Shipping papers and labeling.

(1) *For mixtures of radionuclides,* the radionuclides (n) that must be shown on shipping papers and labels in accordance with §§172.203 and 172.403 of this subchapter, respectively, must be determined on the basis of the following formula:

$$\sum_{i=1}^{n} \frac{a_{(i)}}{A_{(i)}} \geq 0.95 \sum_{i=1}^{n+m} \frac{a_{(i)}}{A_{(i)}}$$

Where n + m represents all the radionuclides in the mixture, m are the radionuclides that do not need to be considered, ai is the activity of radionuclide i in the mixture, and Ai is the A_1 or A_2 value, as appropriate for radionuclide i.

(g) Table 10 is as follows:

Table 10 - General Values for A_1 and A_2

Contents	A_1		A_2	
	(TBq)	(Ci)	(TBq)	(Ci)
Only beta or gamma emitting nuclides are known to be present	0.2	5	0.02	0.5
Alpha emitting nuclides are known to be present or no relevant data are available	0.10	2.70	2×10^{-5}	5.41×10^{-4}

§173.434 Activity-mass relationships for uranium and natural thorium.

The table of activity-mass relationships for uranium and natural thorium are as follows:

Thorium and uranium enrichment[1] (Wt% 235 U present)	Specific activity			
	TBq/gram	Grams/Tbq	Ci/gram	Grams/Ci
0.45 (depleted)	1.9×10^{-8}	5.4×10^{7}	5.0×10^{-7}	2.0×10^{6}
0.72 (natural)	2.6×10^{-8}	3.8×10^{7}	7.1×10^{-7}	1.4×10^{6}
1.0	2.8×10^{-8}	3.6×10^{7}	7.6×10^{-7}	1.3×10^{6}
1.5	3.7×10^{-8}	2.7×10^{7}	1.0×10^{-6}	1.0×10^{6}
5.0	1.0×10^{-7}	1.0×10^{7}	2.7×10^{-6}	3.7×10^{5}
10.0	1.8×10^{-7}	5.6×10^{6}	4.8×10^{-6}	2.1×10^{5}
20.0	3.7×10^{-7}	2.7×10^{6}	1.0×10^{-5}	1.0×10^{5}
35.0	7.4×10^{-7}	1.4×10^{6}	2.0×10^{-5}	5.0×10^{4}
50.0	9.3×10^{-7}	1.1×10^{6}	2.5×10^{-5}	4.0×10^{4}
90.0	2.1×10^{-6}	4.7×10^{5}	5.8×10^{-5}	1.7×10^{4}
93.0	2.6×10^{-6}	3.9×10^{5}	7.0×10^{-5}	1.4×10^{4}
95.0	3.4×10^{-6}	3.0×10^{5}	9.1×10^{-5}	1.1×10^{4}
Natural thorium	8.1×10^{-9}	1.2×10^{8}	2.2×10^{-7}	4.6×10^{6}

1. The figures for uranium include representative values for the activity of uranium-234 which is concentrated during the enrichment process. The activity for thorium includes the equilibrium concentration of thorium-228.

§173.435 Table of A_1 and A_2 values for radionuclides.

The table of A_1 and A_2 values for radionuclides is as follows:

Symbol of radionuclide	Element and atomic number	A_1(TBq)	A_1(Ci)	A_2(TBq)	A_2(Ci)	Specific activity	
						(TBq/g)	(Ci/g)
Ac-225	Actinium(89)	0.6	16.2	1×10^{-2}	0.270	2.1×10^{3}	5.8×10^{4}
Ac-227		40	1080	2×10^{-5}	5.41×10^{-4}	2.7	7.2×10^{1}
Ac-228		0.6	16.2	0.4	10.8	8.4×10^{4}	2.2×10^{6}
Ag-105	Silver(47)	2	54.1	2	54.1	1.1×10^{3}	3.0×10^{4}
Ag-108m		0.6	16.2	0.6	16.2	9.7×10^{-1}	2.6×10^{1}
Ag-110m		0.4	10.8	0.4	10.8	1.8×10^{2}	4.7×10^{3}
Ag-111		0.6	16.2	0.5	13.5	5.8×10^{3}	1.6×10^{5}
Al-26	Aluminum(13)	0.4	10.8	0.4	10.8	7.0×10^{-4}	1.9×10^{-2}
Am-241	Americium(95)	2	54.1	2×10^{-4}	5.41×10^{-3}	1.3×10^{-1}	3.4
Am-242m		2	54.1	2×10^{-4}	5.41×10^{-3}	3.6×10^{-1}	1.0×10^{1}
Am-243		2	54.1	2×10^{-4}	5.41×10^{-3}	7.4×10^{-3}	2.0×10^{-1}
Ar-37	Argon(18)	40	1080	40	1080	3.7×10^{3}	9.9×10^{4}
Ar-39		20	541	20	541	1.3	3.4×10^{1}
Ar-41		0.6	16.2	0.6	16.2	1.5×10^{6}	4.2×10^{7}
Ar-42		0.2	5.41	0.2	5.41	9.6	2.6×10^{2}
As-72	Arsenic(33)	0.2	5.41	0.2	5.41	6.2×10^{4}	1.7×10^{6}
As-73		40	1080	40	1080	8.2×10^{2}	2.2×10^{4}
As-74		1	27.0	0.5	13.5	3.7×10^{3}	9.9×10^{4}
As-76		0.2	5.41	0.2	5.41	5.8×10^{4}	1.6×10^{6}
As-77		20	541	0.5	13.5	3.9×10^{4}	1.0×10^{6}
At-211	Astatine(85)	30	811	2	54.1	7.6×10^{4}	2.1×10^{6}
Au-193	Gold(79)	6	162	6	162	3.4×10^{4}	9.2×10^{5}
Au-194		1	27.0	1	27.0	1.5×10^{4}	4.1×10^{5}
Au-195		10	270	10	270	1.4×10^{2}	3.7×10^{3}
Au-196		2	54.1	2	54.1	4.0×10^{3}	1.1×10^{5}
Au-198		3	81.1	0.5	13.5	9.0×10^{3}	2.4×10^{5}
Au-199		10	270	0.9	24.3	7.7×10^{3}	2.1×10^{5}
Ba-131	Barium(56)	2	54.1	2	54.1	3.1×10^{3}	8.4×10^{4}
Ba-133m		10	270	0.9	24.3	2.2×10^{4}	6.1×10^{5}
Ba-133		3	81.1	3	81.1	9.4	2.6×10^{2}
Ba-140		0.4	10.8	0.4	10.8	2.7×10^{3}	7.3×10^{4}

Symbol of radionuclide	Element and atomic number	A_1(TBq)	A_1(Ci)	A_2(TBq)	A_2(Ci)	Specific activity	
						(TBq/g)	(Ci/g)
Be-7	Beryllium(4)	20	541	20	541	1.3×10^{4}	3.5×10^{5}
Be-10		20	541	0.5	13.5	8.3×10^{-4}	2.2×10^{-2}
Bi-205	Bismuth(83)	0.6	16.2	0.6	16.2	1.5×10^{3}	4.2×10^{4}
Bi-206		0.3	8.11	0.3	8.11	3.8×10^{3}	1.0×10^{5}
Bi-207		0.7	18.9	0.7	18.9	1.9	5.2×10^{1}
Bi-210m		0.3	8.11	3×10^{-2}	0.811	2.1×10^{-5}	5.7×10^{-4}
Bi-210		0.6	16.2	0.5	13.5	4.6×10^{3}	1.2×10^{5}
Bi-212		0.3	8.11	0.3	8.11	5.4×10^{5}	1.5×10^{7}
Bk-247	Berkelium(97)	2	54.1	2×10^{-4}	5.41×10^{-3}	3.8×10^{-2}	1.0
Bk-249		40	1080	8×10^{-2}	2.16	6.1×10^{1}	1.6×10^{3}
Br-76	Bromine(35)	0.3	8.11	0.3	8.11	9.4×10^{4}	2.5×10^{6}
Br-77		3	81.1	3	81.1	2.6×10^{4}	7.1×10^{5}
Br-82		0.4	10.8	0.4	10.8	4.0×10^{4}	1.1×10^{6}
C-11	Carbon(6)	1	27	0.5	13.5	3.1×10^{7}	8.4×10^{8}
C-14		40	1080	2	54.1	1.6×10^{-1}	4.5
Ca-41	Calcium(20)	40	1080	40	1080	3.1×10^{-3}	8.5×10^{-2}
Ca-45		40	1080	0.9	24.3	6.6×10^{2}	1.8×10^{4}
Ca-47		0.9	24.3	0.5	13.5	2.3×10^{4}	6.1×10^{5}
Cd-109	Cadmium(48)	40	1080	1	27.0	9.6×10^{1}	2.6×10^{3}
Cd-113m		20	541	9×10^{-2}	2.43	8.3×10^{4}	2.2×10^{2}
Cd-115m		0.3	8.11	0.3	8.11	9.4×10^{2}	2.5×10^{4}
Cd-115		4	108	0.5	13.5	1.9×10^{4}	5.1×10^{5}
Ce-139	Cerium(58)	6	162	6	162	2.5×10^{26}	$.8 \times 10^{3}$
Ce-141		10	270	0.5	13.5	1.1×10^{3}	2.8×10^{4}
Ce-143		0.6	16.2	0.5	13.5	2.5×10^{4}	6.6×10^{5}
Ce-144		0.2	5.41	0.2	5.41	1.2×10^{2}	3.2×10^{3}
Cf-248	Californium (98)	30	811	3×10^{-3}	8.11×10^{-2}	5.8×10^{1}	1.6×10^{3}
Cf-249		2	54.1	2×10^{-4}	5.41×10^{-3}	1.5×10^{-1}	4.1
Cf-250		5	135	5×10^{-4}	1.35×10^{-2}	4.0	1.1×10^{2}
Cf-251		2	54.1	2×10^{-4}	5.41×10^{-3}	5.9×10^{-2}	1.6
Cf-252		0.1	2.70	1×10^{-3}	2.70×10^{-2}	2.0×10^{1}	5.4×10^{2}
Cf-253		40	1080	6×10^{-2}	1.62	1.1×10^{3}	2.9×10^{4}
Cf-254		3×10^{-3}	8.11×10^{-2}	6×10^{-4}	1.62×10^{-2}	3.1×10^{2}	8.5×10^{3}
Cl-36	Chlorine (17)	20	541	0.5	13.5	1.2×10^{-3}	3.3×10^{-2}
Cl-38		0.2	5.41	0.2	5.41	4.9×10^{6}	1.3×10^{8}
Cm-240	Curium(96)	40	1080	2×10^{-2}	0.541	7.5×10^{2}	2.0×10^{4}
Cm-241		2	54.1	0.9	24.3	6.1×10^{2}	1.7×10^{4}
Cm-242		40	1080	1×10^{-2}	0.270	1.2×10^{2}	3.3×10^{3}
Cm-243		3	81.1	3×10^{-4}	8.11×10^{-3}	1.9	5.2×10^{1}
Cm-244		4	108	4×10^{-4}	1.08×10^{-2}	3.0	8.1×10^{1}
Cm-245		2	54.1	2×10^{-4}	5.41×10^{-3}	6.4×10^{-3}	1.7×10^{-1}
Cm-246		2	54.1	2×10^{-4}	5.41×10^{-3}	1.1×10^{-2}	3.1×10^{-1}
Cm-247		2	54.1	2×10^{-4}	5.41×10^{-3}	3.4×10^{-6}	9.3×10^{-5}
Cm-248		4×10^{-2}	1.08	5×10^{-5}	1.35×10^{-3}	1.6×10^{-4}	4.2×10^{-3}
Co-55	Cobalt(27)	0.5	13.5	0.5	13.5	1.1×10^{5}	3.1×10^{6}
Co-56		0.3	8.11	0.3	8.11	1.1×10^{3}	3.0×10^{4}
Co-57		8	216	8	216	3.1×10^{2}	8.4×10^{3}
Co-58m		40	1080	40	1080	2.2×10^{5}	5.9×10^{6}
Co-58		1	27.0	1	27.0	1.2×10^{3}	3.2×10^{4}
Co-60		0.4	10.8	0.4	10.8	4.2×10^{1}	1.1×10^{3}
Cr-51	Chromium(24)	30	811	30	811	3.4×10^{3}	9.2×10^{4}
Cs-129	Cesium(55)	4	108	4	108	2.8×10^{4}	7.6×10^{5}
Cs-131		40	1080	40	1080	3.8×10^{3}	1.0×10^{5}
Cs-132		1	27.0	1	27.0	5.7×10^{3}	1.5×10^{5}
Cs-134m		40	1080	9	243	3.0×10^{5}	8.0×10^{6}
Cs-134		0.6	16.2	0.5	13.5	4.8×10^{1}	1.3×10^{3}
Cs-135		40	1080	0.9	24.3	4.3×10^{-5}	1.2×10^{-3}
Cs-136		0.5	13.5	0.5	13.5	2.7×10^{3}	7.3×10^{4}
Cs-137		2	54.1	0.5	13.5	3.2	8.7×10^{1}
Cu-64	Copper(29)	5	135	0.9	24.3	1.4×10^{5}	3.9×10^{6}
Cu-67		9	243	0.9	24.3	2.8×10^{4}	7.6×10^{5}

Symbol of radionuclide	Element and atomic number	A_1(TBq)	A_1(Ci)	A_2(TBq)	A_2(Ci)	Specific activity	
						(TBq/g)	(Ci/g)
Dy-159	Dysprosium(66)	20	541	20	541	2.1×10^{2}	5.7×10^{3}
Dy-165		0.6	16.2	0.5	13.5	3.0×10^{5}	8.2×10^{6}
Dy-166		0.3	8.11	0.3	8.11	8.6×10^{3}	2.3×10^{5}
Er-169	Erbium(68)	40	1080	0.9	24.3	3.1×10^{3}	8.3×10^{4}
Er-171		0.6	16.2	0.5	13.5	9.0×10^{4}	2.4×10^{6}
Es-253	Einsteinium(99)[a]	200	5400	2.1×10^{-2}	5.4×100^{-1}		
Es-254		30	811	3×10^{-3}	8.11×10^{-2}		
Es-254m		0.6	16.2	0.4	10.8		
Es-255							
Eu-147	Europium(63)	2	54.1	2	54.1	1.4×10^{3}	3.7×10^{4}
Eu-148		0.5	13.5	0.5	13.5	6.0×10^{2}	1.6×10^{4}
Eu-149		20	541	20	541	3.5×10^{2}	9.4×10^{3}
Eu-150		0.7	18.9	0.7	18.9	6.1×10^{4}	1.6×10^{6}
Eu-152m		0.6	16.2	0.5	13.5	8.2×10^{4}	2.2×10^{6}
Eu-152		0.9	24.3	0.9	24.3	6.5	1.8×10^{2}
Eu-154		0.8	21.6	0.5	13.5	9.8	2.6×10^{2}
Eu-155		20	541	2	54.1	1.8×10^{1}	4.9×10^{2}
Eu-156		0.6	16.2	0.5	13.5	2.0×10^{3}	5.5×10^{4}
F-18	Fluorine(9)	1	27.0	0.5	13.5	3.5×10^{6}	9.5×10^{7}
Fe-52	Iron(26)	0.2	5.41	0.2	5.41	2.7×10^{5}	7.3×10^{6}
Fe-55		40	1080	40	1080	8.8×10^{1}	2.4×10^{3}
Fe-59		0.8	21.6	0.8	21.6	1.8×10^{3}	5.0×10^{4}
Fe-60		40	1080	0.2	5.41	7.4×10^{-4}	2.0×10^{-2}
Fm-255	Fermium(100)[b]	40	1080	0.8	21.6		
Fm-257		10	270	8×10^{-3}	21.6×10^{-1}		
Ga-67	Gallium(31)	6	162	6	162	2.2×10^{4}	6.0×10^{5}
Ga-68		0.3	8.11	0.3	8.11	1.5×10^{6}	4.1×10^{7}
Ga-72		0.4	10.8	0.4	10.8	1.1×10^{5}	3.1×10^{6}
Gd-146	Gadolinium(64)	0.4	10.8	0.4	10.8	6.9×10^{2}	1.9×10^{4}
Gd-148		3	81.1	3×10^{-4}	8.11×10^{-3}	1.2	3.2×10^{1}
Gd-153		10	270	5	135	1.3×10^{2}	3.5×10^{3}
Gd-159		4	108	0.5	13.5	3.9×10^{4}	1.1×10^{6}
Ge-68	Germanium(32)	0.3	8.11	0.3	8.11	2.6×10^{2}	7.1×10^{3}
Ge-71		40	1080	40	1080	5.8×10^{3}	1.6×10^{5}
Ge-77		0.3	8.11	0.3	8.11	1.3×10^{5}	3.6×10^{6}
H-3	Hydrogen(1) See T-Tritium						
Hf-172	Hafnium(72)	0.5	13.5	0.3	8.11	4.1×10^{1}	1.1×10^{3}
Hf-175		3	81.1	3	81.1	3.9×10^{2}	1.1×10^{4}
Hf-181		2	54.1	0.9	24.3	6.3×10^{2}	1.7×10^{4}
Hf-182		4	108	3×10^{-2}	0.811	8.1×10^{-6}	2.2×10^{-4}
Hg-194	Mercury(80)	1	27.0	1	27.0	1.3×10^{-1}	3.5
Hg-195m		5	135	5	135	1.5×10^{4}	4.0×10^{5}
Hg-197m		10	270	0.9	24.3	2.5×10^{4}	6.7×10^{5}
Hg-197		10	270	10	270	9.2×10^{3}	2.5×10^{5}
Hg-203		4	108	0.9	24.3	5.1×10^{2}	1.4×10^{4}
Ho-163	Holmium(67)	40	1080	40	1080	2.7	7.6×10^{1}
Ho-166m		0.6	16.2	0.3	8.11	6.6×10^{-2}	1.8
Ho-166		0.3	8.11	0.3	8.11	2.6×10^{4}	7.0×10^{5}
I-123	Iodine(53)	6	162	6	162	7.1×10^{4}	1.9×10^{6}
I-124		0.9	24.3	0.9	24.3	9.3×10^{3}	2.5×10^{5}
I-125		20	541	2	54.1	6.4×10^{2}	1.7×10^{4}
I-126		2	54.1	0.9	24.3	2.9×10^{3}	8.0×10^{4}
I-129		Unlimited	Unlimited	Unlimited	Unlimited	6.5×10^{-6}	1.8×10^{-4}
I-131		3	81.1	0.5	13.5	4.6×10^{3}	1.2×10^{5}
I-132		0.4	10.8	0.4	10.8	3.8×10^{5}	1.0×10^{7}
I-133		0.6	16.2	0.5	13.5	4.2×10^{4}	1.1×10^{6}
I-134		0.3	8.11	0.3	8.11	9.9×10^{5}	2.7×10^{7}
I-135		0.6	16.2	0.5	13.5	1.3×10^{5}	3.5×10^{6}
In-111	Indium(49)	2	54.1	2	54.1	1.5×10^{4}	4.2×10^{5}
In-113m		4	108	4	108	6.2×10^{5}	1.7×10^{7}
In-114m		0.3	8.11	0.3	8.11	8.6×10^{2}	2.3×10^{4}

Symbol of radionuclide	Element and atomic number	A_1(TBq)	A_1(Ci)	A_2(TBq)	A_2(Ci)	Specific activity	
						(TBq/g)	(Ci/g)
In-115m		6	162	0.9	24.3	2.2×10^5	6.1×10^6
Ir-189	Iridium(77)	10	270	10	270	1.9×10^3	5.2×10^4
Ir-190		0.7	18.9	0.7	18.9	2.3×10^3	6.2×10^4
Ir-192		1	27.0	0.5	13.5	3.4×10^2	9.2×10^3
Ir-193m		10	270	10	270	2.4×10^3	6.4×10^4
Ir-194		0.2	5.41	0.2	5.41	3.1×10^4	8.4×10^5
K-40	Potassium(19)	0.6	16.2	0.6	16.2	2.4×10^{-7}	6.4×10^{-6}
K-42		0.2	5.41	0.2	5.41	2.2×10^5	6.0×10^6
K-43		1.0	27.0	0.5	13.5	1.2×10^5	3.3×10^6
Kr-81	Krypton(36)	40	1080	40	1080	7.8×10^{-4}	2.1×10^{-2}
Kr-85m		6	162	6	162	3.0×10^5	8.2×10^6
Kr-85		20	541	10	270	1.5×10^1	3.9×10^2
Kr-87		0.2	5.41	0.2	5.41	1.0×10^6	2.8×10^7
La-137	Lanthanum(57)	40	1080	2	54.1	1.6×10^{-3}	4.4×10^{-2}
La-140		0.4	10.8	0.4	10.8	2.1×10^4	5.6×10^5
Lu-172	Lutetium(71)	0.5	13.5	0.5	13.5	4.2×10^3	1.1×10^5
Lu-173		8	216	8	216	5.6×10^1	1.5×10^3
Lu-174m		20	541	8	216	2.0×10^2	5.3×10^3
Lu-74		8	216	4	108	2.3×10^1	6.2×10^2
Lu-177		30	811	0.9	24.3	4.1×10^3	1.1×10^5
MFP		(see §173.433)		(see §173.433)			
Mg-28	Magnesium(12)	0.2	5.41	0.2	5.41	2.0×10^5	5.4×10^6
Mn-52	Manganese(25)	0.3	8.11	0.3	8.11	1.6×10^4	4.4×10^5
Mn-53		Unlimited	Unlimited	Unlimited	Unlimited	6.8×10^{-5}	1.8×10^{-3}
Mn-54		1	27.0	1	27.0	2.9×10^2	7.7×10^3
Mn-56		0.2	5.41	0.2	5.41	8.0×10^5	2.2×10^7
Mo-93	Molybdenum(42)	40	1080	7	189	4.1×10^{-2}	1.1
Mo-99		0.6	16.2	0.5	13.5^c	1.8×10^4	4.8×10^5
N-13	Nitrogen(7)	0.6	16.2	0.5	13.5	5.4×10^7	1.5×10^9
Na-22	Sodium(11)	0.5	13.5	0.5	13.5	2.3×10^2	6.3×10^3
Na-24		0.2	5.41	0.2	5.41	3.2×10^5	8.7×10^6
Nb-92m	Niobium(41)	0.7	18.9	0.7	18.9	5.2×10^3	1.4×10^5
Nb-93m		40	1080	6	162	8.8	2.4×10^2
Nb-94		0.6	16.2	0.6	16.2	6.9×10^{-3}	1.9×10^{-1}
Nb-95		1	27.0	1	27.0	1.5×10^3	3.9×10^4
Nb-97		0.6	16.2	0.5	13.5	9.9×10^5	2.7×10^7
Nd-147	Neodymium(60)	4	108	0.5	13.5	3.0×10^3	8.1×10^4
Nd-149		0.6	16.2	0.5	13.5	4.5×10^5	1.2×10^7
Ni-59	Nickel(28)	40	1080	40	1080	3.0×10^{-3}	8.0×10^{-2}
Ni-63		40	1080	30	811	2.1	5.7×10^1
Ni-65		0.3	8.11	0.3	8.11	7.1×10^5	1.9×10^7
Np-235	Neptunium(93)	40	1080	40	1080	5.2×10^1	1.4×10^3
Np-236		7	189	1×10^{-3}	2.70×10^{-2}	4.7×10^{-4}	1.3×10^{-2}
Np-237		2	54.1	2×10^{-4}	5.41×10^{-3}	2.6×10^{-5}	7.1×10^{-4}
Np-239		6	162	0.5	13.5	8.6×10^3	2.3×10^5
Os-185	Osmium(76)	1	27.0	1	27.0	2.8×10^2	7.5×10^3
Os-191m		40	1080	40	1080	4.6×10^4	1.3×10^6
Os-191		10	270	0.9	24.3	1.6×10^3	4.4×10^4
Os-193		0.6	16.2	0.5	13.5	2.0×10^4	5.3×10^5
Os-194		0.2	5.41	0.2	5.41	1.1×10^1	3.1×10^2
P-32	Phosphorus(15)	0.3	8.11	0.3	8.11	1.1×10^4	2.9×10^5
P-33		40	1080	0.9	24.3	5.8×10^3	1.6×10^5
Pa-230	Protactinium(91)	2	54.1	0.1	2.70	1.2×10^3	3.3×10^4
Pa-231		0.6	16.2	6×10^{-5}	1.62×10^{-3}	1.7×10^{-3}	4.7×10^{-2}
Pa-233		5	135	0.9	24.3	7.7×10^2	2.1×10^4
Pb-201	Lead(82)	1	27.0	1	27.0	6.2×10^4	1.7×10^6
Pb-202		40	1080	2	54.1	1.2×10^{-4}	3.4×10^{-3}
Pb-203		3	81.1	3	81.1	1.1×10^4	3.0×10^5
Pb-205		Unlimited	Unlimited	Unlimited	Unlimited	4.5×10^{-6}	1.2×10^{-4}
Pb-210		0.6	16.2	9×10^{-3}	0.243	2.8	7.6×10^1
Pb-212		0.3	8.11	0.3	8.11	5.1×10^4	1.4×10^6

Symbol of radionuclide	Element and atomic number	A_1(TBq)	A_1(Ci)	A_2(TBq)	A_2(Ci)	Specific activity	
						(TBq/g)	(Ci/g)
Pd-103	Palladium(46)	40	1080	40	1080	2.8×10^{3}	7.5×10^{4}
Pd-107		Unlimited	Unlimited	Unlimited	Unlimited	1.9×10^{-5}	5.1×10^{-4}
Pd-109		0.6	16.2	0.5	13.5	7.9×10^{4}	2.1×10^{6}
Pm-143	Promethium(61)	3	81.1	3	81.1	1.3×10^{2}	3.4×10^{3}
Pm-144		0.6	16.2	0.6	16.2	9.2×10^{1}	2.5×10^{3}
Pm-145		30	811	7	189	5.2	1.4×10^{2}
Pm-147		40	1080	0.9	24.3	3.4×10^{1}	9.3×10^{2}
Pm-148m		0.5	13.5	0.5	13.5	7.9×10^{2}	2.1×10^{4}
Pm-149		0.6	16.2	0.5	13.5	1.5×10^{4}	4.0×10^{5}
Pm-151		3	81.1	0.5	13.5	2.7×10^{4}	7.3×10^{5}
Po-208	Polonium(84)	40	1080	2×10^{-2}	0.541	2.2×10^{1}	5.9×10^{2}
Po-209		40	1080	2×10^{-2}	0.541	6.2×10^{-1}	1.7×10^{1}
Po-210		40	1080	2×10^{-2}	0.541	1.7×10^{2}	4.5×10^{3}
Pr-142	Praseodymium (59)	0.2	5.41	0.2	5.41	4.3×10^{4}	1.2×10^{6}
Pr-143		4	108	0.5	13.5	2.5×10^{3}	6.7×10^{4}
Pt-188	Platinum(78)	0.6	16.2	0.6	16.2	2.5×10^{3}	6.8×10^{4}
Pt-191		3	81.1	3	81.1	8.7×10^{3}	2.4×10^{5}
Pt-193m		40	1080	9	243	5.8×10^{3}	1.6×10^{5}
Pt-193		40	1080	40	1080	1.4	3.7×10^{1}
Pt-195m		10	270	2	54.1	6.2×10^{3}	1.7×10^{5}
Pt-197m		10	270	0.9	24.3	3.7×10^{5}	1.0×10^{7}
Pt-197		20	541	0.5	13.5	3.2×10^{4}	8.7×10^{5}
Pu-236	Plutonium(94)	7	189	7×10^{-4}	1.89×10^{-2}	2.0×10^{1}	5.3×10^{2}
Pu-237		20	541	20	541	4.5×10^{2}	1.2×10^{4}
Pu-238		2	54.1	2×10^{-4}	5.41×10^{-3}	6.3×10^{-1}	1.7×10^{1}
Pu-239		2	54.1	2×10^{-4}	5.41×10^{-3}	2.3×10^{-3}	6.2×10^{-2}
Pu-240		2	54.1	2×10^{-4}	5.41×10^{-3}	8.4×10^{-3}	2.3×10^{-1}
Pu-241		40	1080	1×10^{-2}	0.270	3.8	1.0×10^{2}
Pu-242		2	54.1	2×10^{-4}	5.41×10^{-3}	1.5×10^{-4}	3.9×10^{-3}
Pu-244		0.3	8.11	2×10^{-4}	5.41×10^{-3}	6.7×10^{-7}	1.8×10^{-5}
Ra-223	Radium(88)	0.6	16.2	3×10^{-2}	0.811	1.9×10^{3}	5.1×10^{4}
Ra-224		0.3	8.11	6×10^{-2}	1.62	5.9×10^{3}	1.6×10^{5}
Ra-225		0.6	16.2	2×10^{-2}	0.541	1.5×10^{3}	3.9×10^{4}
Ra-226		0.3	8.11	2×10^{-2}	0.541	3.7×10^{-2}	1.0
Ra-228		0.6	16.2	4×10^{-2}	1.08	1.0×10^{1}	2.7×10^{2}
Rb-81	Rubidium(37)	2	54.1	0.9	24.3	3.1×10^{5}	8.4×10^{6}
Rb-83		2	54.1	2	54.1	6.8×10^{2}	1.8×10^{4}
Rb-84		1	27.0	0.9	24.3	1.8×10^{3}	4.7×10^{4}
Rb-86		0.3	8.11	0.3	8.11	3.0×10^{3}	8.1×10^{4}
Rb-87		Unlimited	Unlimited	Unlimited	Unlimited	3.2×10^{-9}	8.6×10^{-8}
Rb (natural)		Unlimited	Unlimited	Unlimited	Unlimited	6.7×10^{6}	1.8×10^{8}
Re-183	Rhenium(75)	5	135	5	135	3.8×10^{2}	1.0×10^{4}
Re-184m		3	81.1	3	81.1	1.6×10^{2}	4.3×10^{3}
Re-184		1	27.0	1	27.0	6.9×10^{2}	1.9×10^{4}
Re-186		4	108	0.5	13.5	6.9×10^{3}	1.9×10^{5}
Re-187		Unlimited	Unlimited	Unlimited	Unlimited	1.4×10^{-9}	3.8×10^{-8}
Re-188		0.2	5.41	0.2	5.41	3.6×10^{4}	9.8×10^{5}
Re-189		4	108	0.5	13.5	2.5×10^{4}	6.8×10^{5}
Re (natural)		Unlimited	Unlimited	Unlimited	Unlimited	———	2.4×10^{8}
Rh-99	Rhodium(45)	2	54.1	2	54.1	3.0×10^{3}	8.2×10^{4}
Rh-101		4	108	4	108	4.1×10^{1}	1.1×10^{3}
Rh-102m		2	54.1	0.9	24.3	2.3×10^{2}	6.2×10^{3}
Rh-102		0.5	13.5	0.5	13.5	4.5×10^{1}	1.2×10^{3}
Rh-103m		40	1080	40	1080	1.2×10^{6}	3.3×10^{7}
Rh-105		10	270	0.9	24.3	3.1×10^{4}	8.4×10^{5}
Rn-222	Radon(86)	0.2	5.41	4×10^{-3}	0.108	5.7×10^{3}	1.5×10^{5}
Ru-97	Ruthenium(44)	4	108	4	108	1.7×10^{4}	4.6×10^{5}
Ru-103		2	54.1	0.9	24.3	1.2×10^{3}	3.2×10^{4}
Ru-105		0.6	16.2	0.5	13.5	2.5×10^{5}	6.7×10^{6}
Ru-106		0.2	5.41	0.2	5.41	1.2×10^{2}	3.3×10^{3}
S-35	Sulfur(16)	40	1080	2	54.1	1.6×10^{3}	4.3×10^{4}

Symbol of radionuclide	Element and atomic number	A_1(TBq)	A_1(Ci)	A_2(TBq)	A_2(Ci)	Specific activity	
						(TBq/g)	(Ci/g)
Sb-122	Antimony(51)	0.3	8.11	0.3	8.11	1.5×10^{4}	4.0×10^{5}
Sb-124		0.6	16.2	0.5	13.5	6.5×10^{2}	1.7×10^{4}
Sb-125		2	54.1	0.9	24.3	3.9×10^{1}	1.0×10^{3}
Sb-126		0.4	10.8	0.4	10.8	3.1×10^{3}	8.4×10^{4}
Sc-44	Scandium(21)	0.5	13.5	0.5	13.5	6.7×10^{5}	1.8×10^{7}
Sc-46		0.5	13.5	0.5	13.5	1.3×10^{3}	3.4×10^{4}
Sc-47		9	243	0.9	24.3	3.1×10^{4}	8.3×10^{5}
Sc-48		0.3	8.11	0.3	8.11	5.5×10^{4}	1.5×10^{6}
Se-75	Selenium(34)	3	81.1	3	81.1	5.4×10^{2}	1.5×10^{4}
Se-79		40	1080	2	54.1	2.6×10^{-3}	7.0×10^{-2}
Si-31	Silicon(14)	0.6	16.2	0.5	13.5	1.4×10^{6}	3.9×10^{7}
Si-32		40	1080	0.2	5.41	3.9	1.1×10^{2}
Sm-145	Samarium(62)	20	541	20	541	9.8×10^{1}	2.610 ^{3}
Sm-147		Unlimited	Unlimited	Unlimited	Unlimited	8.5×10^{-10}	2.3×10^{-8}
Sm-151		40	1080	4	108	9.7×10^{-1}	2.6×10^{1}
Sm-153		4	108	0.5	13.5	1.6×10^{4}	4.4×10^{5}
Sn-113	Tin(50)	4	108	4	108	3.7×10^{2}	1.0×10^{4}
Sn-117m		6	162	2	54.1	3.0×10^{3}	8.2×10^{4}
Sn-119m		40	1080	40	1080	1.4×10^{2}	3.7×10^{3}
Sn-121m		40	1080	0.9	24.3	2.0	5.4×10^{1}
Sn-123		0.6	16.2	0.5	13.5	3.0×10^{2}	8.2×10^{3}
Sn-125		0.2	5.41	0.2	5.41	4.0×10^{3}	1.1×10^{5}
Sn-126		0.3	8.11	0.3	8.11	1.0×10^{-3}	2.8×10^{-2}
Sr-82	Strontium(38)	0.2	5.41	0.2	5.41	2.3×10^{3}	6.2×10^{4}
Sr-85m		5	135	5	135	1.2×10^{6}	3.3×10^{7}
Sr-85		2	54.1	2	54.1	8.8×10^{2}	2.4×10^{4}
Sr-87m		3	81.1	3	81.1	4.8×10^{5}	1.3×10^{7}
Sr-89		0.6	16.2	0.5	13.5	1.1×10^{3}	2.9×10^{4}
Sr-90		0.2	5.41	0.1	2.70	5.1	1.4×10^{2}
Sr-91		0.3	8.11	0.3	8.11	1.3×10^{5}	3.6×10^{6}
Sr-92		0.8	21.6	0.5	13.5	4.7×10^{5}	1.3×10^{7}
T	Tritium(1)	40	1080	40	1080	3.6×10^{2}	9.7×10^{3}
Ta-178	Tantalum(73)	1	27.0	1	27.0	4.2×10^{6}	1.1×10^{8}
Ta-179		30	811	30	811	4.1×10^{1}	1.1×10^{3}
Ta-182		0.8	21.6	0.5	13.5	2.3×10^{2}	6.2×10^{3}
Tb-157	Terbium(65)	40	1080	10	270	5.6×10^{-1}	1.5×10^{1}
Tb-158		1	27.0	0.7	18.0	5.6×10^{-1}	1.5×10^{1}
Tb-160		0.9	24.3	0.5	13.5	4.2×10^{2}	1.1×10^{4}
Tc-95m	Technetium(43)	2	54.1	2	54.1	8.3×10^{2}	2.2×10^{4}
Tc-96m		0.4	10.8	0.4	10.8	1.4×10^{6}	3.8×10^{7}
Tc-96		0.4	10.8	0.4	10.8	1.2×10^{4}	3.2×10^{5}
Tc-97m		40	1080	40	1080	5.6×10^{2}	1.5×10^{4}
Tc-97		Unlimited	Unlimited	Unlimited	Unlimited	5.2×10^{-5}	1.4×10^{-3}
Tc-98		0.7	18.9	0.7	18.9	3.2×10^{-5}	8.7×10^{-4}
Tc-99m		8	216	8	216	1.9×10^{5}	5.3×10^{6}
Tc-99		40	1080	0.9	24.3	6.3×10^{-4}	1.7×10^{-2}
Te-118	Tellurium(52)	0.2	5.41	0.2	5.41	6.8×10^{3}	1.8×10^{5}
Te-121m		5	135	5	135	2.6×10^{2}	7.0×10^{3}
Te-121		2	54.1	2	54.1	2.4×10^{3}	6.4×10^{4}
Te-123m		7	189	7	189	3.3×10^{2}	8.9×10^{3}
Te-125m		30	811	9	243	6.7×10^{2}	1.8×10^{4}
Te-127m		20	541	0.5	13.5	3.5×10^{2}	9.4×10^{3}
Te-127		20	541	0.5	13.5	9.8×10^{4}	2.6×10^{6}
Te-129m		0.6	16.2	0.5	13.5	1.1×10^{3}	3.0×10^{4}
Te-129		0.6	16.2	0.5	13.5	7.7×10^{5}	2.1×10^{7}
Te-131m		0.7	18.9	0.5	13.5	3.0×10^{4}	8.0×10^{5}
Te-132		0.4	10.8	0.4	10.8	1.1×10^{4}	3.0×10^{5}
Th-227	Thorium(90)	9	243	1×10^{-2}	0.270	1.1×10^{3}	3.1×10^{4}
Th-228		0.3	8.11	4×10^{-4}	1.08×10^{-2}	3.0×10^{1}	8.2×10^{2}
Th-229		0.3	8.11	3×10^{-5}	8.11×10^{-4}	7.9×10^{-3}	2.1×10^{-1}
Th-230		2	54.1	2×10^{-4}	5.41×10^{-3}	7.6×10^{-4}	2.1×10^{-2}

Symbol of radionuclide	Element and atomic number	A_1(TBq)	A_1(Ci)	A_2(TBq)	A_2(Ci)	Specific activity	
						(TBq/g)	(Ci/g)
Th-231		40	1080	0.9	24.3	2.0×10^4	5.3×10^5
Th-232		Unlimited	Unlimited	Unlimited	Unlimited	4.0×10^{-9}	1.1×10^{-7}
Th-234		0.2	5.41	0.2	5.41	8.6×10^2	2.3×10^4
Th (natural)		Unlimited	Unlimited	Unlimited	Unlimited	8.1×10^{-9}	2.2×10^{-7}
Ti-44	Titanium(22)	0.5	13.5	0.2	5.41	6.4	1.7×10^2
Tl-200	Thallium(81.1)	0.8	21.6	0.8	21.6	2.2×10^4	6.0×10^5
Tl-201		10	270	10	270	7.9×10^3	2.1×10^5
Tl-202		2	54.1	2	54.1	2.0×10^3	5.3×10^4
Tl-204		4	108	0.5	13.5	1.7×10^1	4.6×10^2
Tm-167	Thulium(69)	7	189	7	189	3.1×10^3	8.5×10^4
Tm-168		0.8	21.6	0.8	21.6	3.1×10^2	8.3×10^3
Tm-170		4	108	0.5	13.5	2.2×10^2	6.0×10^3
Tm-171		40	1080	10	270	4.0×10^1	1.1×10^3
U-230	Uranium(92)	40	1080	1×10^{-2}	0.270	1.0×10^3	2.7×10^4
U-232		3	81.1	3×10^{-4}	8.11×10^{-3}	8.3×10^{-1}	2.2×10^1
U-233		10	270	1×10^{-3}	2.70×10^{-2}	3.6×10^{-4}	9.7×10^{-3}
U-234		10	270	1×10^{-3}	2.70×10^{-2}	2.3×10^{-4}	6.2×10^{-3}
U-235		Unlimited	Unlimited	Unlimited	Unlimited	8.0×10^{-8}	2.2×10^{-6}
U-236		10	270	1×10^{-3}	2.70×10^{-2}	2.4×10^{-6}	6.5×10^{-5}
U-238		Unlimited	Unlimited	Unlimited	Unlimited	1.2×10^{-8}	3.4×10^{-7}
U (natural)		Unlimited	Unlimited	Unlimited	Unlimited	2.6×10^{-8}	7.1×10^{-7}
U (enriched 5% or less)		Unlimited	Unlimited	Unlimited	Unlimited	———	(see §173.434)
U (enriched more than 5%)		10	270	1×10^{-3}	2.70×10^{-2}	———	(see §173.434)
U (depleted)		Unlimited	Unlimited	Unlimited	Unlimited	———	(see §173.434)
V-48	Vanadium(23)	0.3	8.11	0.3	8.11	6.3×10^3	1.7×10^5
V-49		40	1080	40	1080	3.0×10^2	8.1×10^3
W-178	Tungsten(74)	1	27.0	1	27.0	1.3×10^{-3}	3.4×10^4
W-181		30	811	30	811	2.2×10^2	6.0×10^3
W-185		40	1080	0.9	24.3	3.5×10^2	9.4×10^3
W-187		2	54.1	0.5	13.5	2.6×10^4	7.0×10^5
W-188		0.2	5.41	0.2	5.41	3.7×10^2	1.0×10^4
Xe-122	Xenon(54)	0.2	5.41	0.2	5.41	4.8×10^4	1.3×10^6
Xe-123		0.2	5.41	0.2	5.41	4.4×10^5	1.2×10^7
Xe-127		4	108	4	108	1.0×10^3	2.8×10^4
Xe-131m		40	1080	40	1080	3.1×10^3	8.4×10^4
Xe-133		20	541	20	541	6.9×10^3	1.9×10^5
Xe-135		4	108	4	108	9.5×10^4	2.6×10^6
Y-87	Yttrium(39)	2	54.1	2	54.1	1.7×10^4	4.5×10^5
Y-88		0.4	10.8	0.4	10.8	5.2×10^2	1.4×10^4
Y-90		0.2	5.41	0.2	5.41	2.0×10^4	5.4×10^5
Y-91m		2	54.1	2	54.1	1.5×10^6	4.2×10^7
Y-91		0.3	8.11	0.3	8.11	9.1×10^2	2.5×10^4
Y-92		0.2	5.41	0.2	5.41	3.6×10^5	9.6×10^6
Y-93		0.2	5.41	0.2	5.41	1.2×10^5	3.3×10^6
Yb-169	Ytterbium(70)	3	81.1	3	81.1	8.9×10^2	2.4×10^4
Yb-175		30	811	0.9	24.3	6.6×10^3	1.8×10^5
Zn-65	Zinc(30)	2	54.1	2	54.1	3.0×10^2	8.2×10^3
Zn-69m		2	54.1	0.5	13.5	1.2×10^5	3.3×10^6
Zn-69		4	108	0.5	13.5	1.8×10^6	4.9×10^7
Zr-88	Zirconium(40)	3	81.1	3	81.1	6.6×10^2	1.8×10^4
Zr-93		40	1080	0.2	5.41	9.3×10^{-5}	2.5×10^{-3}
Zr-95		1	27.0	0.9	24.3	7.9×10^2	2.1×10^4
Zr-97		0.3	8.11	0.3	8.11	7.1×10^4	1.9×10^6

a. International shipments of Einsteinium require multilateral approval of A_1 and A_2 values.
b. International shipments of Fermium require multilateral approval of A_1 and A_2 values.
c. 20 Ci for Mo^{99} for domestic use.
MFP: For mixed fission products, use formula for mixtures or table 10 in §173.433.
NOTE: The activity per gram of radionuclide quantities are technical information that might not provide a direct relationship between the activity and total mass of material contained in a package.

§173.441 Radiation level limitations.

(a) Except as provided in paragraph (b) of this section, each package of Class 7 (radioactive) materials offered for transportation must be designed and prepared for shipment, so that under conditions normally incident to transportation, the radiation level does not exceed 2 mSv/hour (200 mrem/hour) at any point on the external surface of the package, and the transport index does not exceed 10.

(b) A package which exceeds the radiation level limits specified in paragraph (a) of this section must be transported by exclusive use shipment, and the radiation levels for such shipment may not exceed the following during transportation:

(1) *2 mSv/h (200 mrem/h)* on the external surface of the package unless the following conditions are met, in which case the limit is 10 mSv/h (1000 mrem/h):

(i) *The shipment is made in a closed transport vehicle;*

(ii) *The package* is secured within the vehicle so that its position remains fixed during transportation; and

(iii) *There are* no loading or unloading operations between the beginning and end of the transportation;

(2) *2 mSv/h (200 mrem/h)* at any point on the outer surfaces of the vehicle, including the top and underside of the vehicle; or in the case of a flat-bed style vehicle, at any point on the vertical planes projected from the outer edges of the vehicle, on the upper surface of the load or enclosure if used, and on the lower external surface of the vehicle;

(3) *0.1 mSv/h (10 mrem/h)* at any point 2 m (6.6 feet) from the outer lateral surfaces of the vehicle (excluding the top and underside of the vehicle); or in the case of a flat-bed style vehicle, at any point 2 m (6.6 feet) from the vertical planes projected by the outer edges of the vehicle (excluding the top and underside of the vehicle); and

(4) *0.02 mSv/h (2 mrem/h)* in any normally occupied space, except that this provision does not apply to carriers if they operate under the provisions of a State or federally regulated radiation protection program and if personnel under their control who are in such an occupied space wear radiation dosimetry devices.

(c) For shipments made under the provisions of paragraph (b) of this section, the offeror shall provide specific written instructions for maintenance of the exclusive use shipment controls to the carrier. The instructions must be included with the shipping paper information. The instructions must be sufficient so that, when followed, they will cause the carrier to avoid actions that will unnecessarily delay delivery or unnecessarily result in increased radiation levels or radiation exposures to transport workers or members of the general public.

(d) Packages exceeding the radiation level or transport index prescribed in paragraph (a) of this section may not be transported by aircraft.

§173.442 Thermal limitations.

A package of Class 7 (radioactive) material must be designed, constructed, and loaded so that —

(a) The heat generated within the package by the radioactive contents will not, during conditions normally incident to transport, affect the integrity of the package; and

(b) The temperature of the accessible external surfaces of the loaded package will not, assuming still air in the shade at an ambient temperature of 38 °C (100 °F), exceed either —

(1) *50 °C (122 °F) in other than an exclusive use shipment; or*

(2) *85 °C (185 °F) in an exclusive use shipment.*

§173.443 Contamination control.

(a) The level of non-fixed (removable) radioactive contamination on the external surfaces of each package offered for transport must be kept as low as reasonably achievable. The level of non-fixed radioactive contamination may not exceed the limits set forth in table 11 and must be determined by either:

(1) *Wiping an area* of 300 square cm of the surface concerned with an absorbent material, using moderate pressure, and measuring the activity on the wiping material. Sufficient measurements must be taken in the most appropriate locations to yield a representative assessment of the non-fixed contamination levels. The amount of radioactivity measured on any single wiping material, when averaged over the surface wiped, may not exceed the limits set forth in table 11 at any time during transport; or

(2) *Using other methods* of assessment of equal or greater efficiency, in which case the efficiency of the method used must be taken into account and the non-fixed contamination on the external surfaces of the package may not exceed ten times the limits set forth in table 11, as follows:

Table 11 - Non-Fixed External Radioactive Contamination-Wipe Limits

Contaminant	Maximum permissible limits		
	Bq/cm^2	uCi/cm^2	dpm/cm^2
Beta and gamma emitters and low toxicity alpha emitters	0.4	10^{-5}	22
All other alpha emitting radionuclides	0.04	10^{-6}	2.2

(b) Except as provided in paragraph (d) of this section, in the case of packages transported as exclusive use shipments by rail or public highway only, the removable (non-fixed) radioactive contamination on any package at any time during transport may not exceed ten times the levels prescribed in paragraph (a) of this section. The levels at the beginning of transport may not exceed the levels prescribed in paragraph (a) of this section.

(c) Except as provided in paragraph (d) of this section, each transport vehicle used for transporting Class 7 (radioactive) materials as an exclusive use shipment that utilizes the provisions of paragraph (b) of this section must be surveyed with appropriate radiation detection instruments after each use. A vehicle may not be returned to service until the radiation dose rate at each accessible surface is 0.005 mSv per hour (0.5 mrem per hour) or less, and there is no significant removable (non-fixed) radioactive surface contamination as specified in paragraph (a) of this section.

(d) Paragraphs (b) and (c) of this section do not apply to any closed transport vehicle used solely for the transportation by highway or rail of Class 7 (radioactive) material packages with contamination levels that do not exceed 10 times the levels prescribed in paragraph (a) of this section if —

(1) *A survey* of the interior surfaces of the empty vehicle shows that the radiation dose rate at any point does not exceed 0.1 mSv per hour (10 mrem per hour) at the surface or 0.02 mSv per hour (2 mrem per hour) at 1 m (3.3 feet) from the surface;

(2) *Each vehicle* is stenciled with the words "For Radioactive Materials Use Only" in letters at least 76 millimeters (3 inches) high in a conspicuous place on both sides of the exterior of the vehicle; and

(3) *Each vehicle is kept closed except for loading or unloading.*

§173.447 Storage incident to transportation — general requirements.

The following requirements apply to temporary storage during the course of transportation but not to Nuclear Regulatory Commission or Agreement State-licensed facilities or U.S. Government-owned or contracted facilities.

(a) The number of packages bearing RADIOACTIVE YELLOW-II or RADIOACTIVE YELLOW-III labels stored in any one storage area, such as a transit area, terminal building, storeroom, waterfront pier, or assembly yard, must be limited so that the sum of the transport indexes in any individual group of packages does not exceed 50. Groups of these packages must be stored so as to maintain a spacing of at least 6 m (20 feet) from other groups of packages containing Class 7 (radioactive) materials.

(b) Mixing of different kinds of Class 7 (radioactive) materials packages that include fissile materials packages is authorized only in accordance with §173.459.

§173.448 General transportation requirements.

(a) Each shipment of Class 7 (radioactive) materials must be secured to prevent shifting during normal transportation conditions.

(b) Except as provided in §§174.81, 176.83, and 177.848 of this subchapter, or as otherwise required by the competent authority in the applicable certificate, a package of Class 7 (radioactive) materials may be carried among packaged general cargo without special stowage provisions, if —

(1) *The heat output* in watts does not exceed 0.1 times the minimum package dimension in cm; or

(2) *The average surface* heat flux of the package does not exceed 15 watts per square meter and the immediately surrounding cargo is not in sacks or bags or otherwise in a form that would seriously impede air circulation for heat removal.

(c) Packages bearing labels prescribed in §172.403 of this subchapter may not be carried in compartments occupied by passengers, except in those compartments exclusively reserved for couriers accompanying those packages.

(d) Mixing of different kinds of packages that include fissile packages is authorized only in accordance with §173.459.

(e) No person shall offer for transportation or transport aboard a passenger-carrying aircraft any single package with a transport index greater than 3.0 or an overpack with a transport index greater than 3.0.

(f) **No person shall offer for transportation or transport** aboard a passenger-carrying aircraft any Class 7 (radioactive) material unless that material is intended for use in, or incident to, research, medical diagnosis or treatment.

(g) **If an overpack is used to consolidate** individual packages of Class 7 (radioactive) materials, the packages must comply with the packaging, marking, and labeling requirements of this subchapter, and the following:

(1) *The overpack* must be labeled as prescribed in §172.403 of this subchapter, except as follows:

(i) *The "contents" entry* on the label may state "mixed" unless each inside package contains the same radionuclide(s);

(ii) *The "activity" entry* on the label must be determined by adding together the number of Becquerels (curies) of the Class 7 (radioactive) materials packages contained therein;

(iii) *For a non-rigid overpack,* the required label together with required package markings must be affixed to the overpack by means of a securely attached, durable tag. The transport index must be determined by adding together the transport indexes of the Class 7 (radioactive) materials packages contained therein; and

(iv) *For a rigid overpack,* the transport index must be determined by:

[A] Adding together the transport indexes of the Class 7 (radioactive) materials packages contained in the overpack; or

[B] Except for fissile Class 7 (radioactive) materials, direct measurements as prescribed in §173.403 for transport index, taken by the person initially offering the packages contained within the overpack for shipment.

(2) *The overpack* must be marked as prescribed in subpart D of part 172 of this subchapter and §173.25(a).

(3) *The transport index* of the overpack may not exceed 3.0 for passenger-carrying aircraft shipments, or 10.0 for cargo-aircraft only shipments.

§173.453 Fissile materials — exceptions.

The requirements of §§173.457 and 173.459 do not apply to:

(a) **A package containing 15 g or less of fissile radionuclides.** If the material is transported in bulk, the quantity limitation applies to the conveyance.

(b) **A package containing homogeneous solutions or mixtures where:**

(1) *The minimum ratio* of the number of hydrogen atoms to the number of atoms of fissile radionuclides (H/X) is 5200;

(2) *The maximum concentration* of fissile radionuclides is 5 g per liter; and

(3) *The maximum mass* of fissile radionuclides in the package is 500 g, except that for a mixture in which the total mass of plutonium and uranium-233 does not exceed 1% of the mass of uranium-235, the limit is 800 g of uranium-235. If the material is transported in bulk, the quantity limitations apply to the conveyance.

(c) **A package containing uranium enriched in uranium-235** to a maximum of 1% by mass, and mixed with a total plutonium and uranium-233 content of up to 1% of the mass of uranium-235, if the fissile radionuclides are distributed homogeneously throughout the package contents, and do not form a lattice arrangement within the package.

(d) **A package containing not more than 5 g** of fissile radionuclides in any 10 L volume, provided that the material is contained in packages that will maintain the limitation on fissile radionuclide distribution during normal conditions of transport.

(e) **A package containing 1 kg or less** of plutonium of which 20% or less by mass may consist of plutonium-239, plutonium-241, or any combination of those radionuclides.

(f) **A package containing liquid solutions of uranyl nitrate** enriched in uranium-235 to a maximum of 2% by mass, with total plutonium and uranium-233 content not exceeding 0.1% of the mass of uranium-235 with a nitrogen-to-uranium atomic ratio (N/U) of 2.

§173.457 Transportation of fissile material, controlled shipments — specific requirements.

Shipments of fissile material packages that have been assigned a transport index of greater than 10 for criticality control purposes in accordance with 10 CFR 71.59 must meet the requirements of this section and §173.441(a) or (b).

(a) **For fissile material, controlled shipments,** the offeror or carrier, as appropriate, must incorporate transportation controls which:

(1) *Provide nuclear criticality safety;*

(2) *Protect against* loading, storing, or transporting that shipment with any other fissile material; and

(3) *Include in the shipping papers* the description required by §172.203 (d) of this subchapter.

(b) **Fissile material, controlled shipments must be transported:**

(1) *In an exclusive use conveyance;*

(2) *Except for shipments* by aircraft, in a conveyance with an escort having the capability, equipment, authority, and instructions to provide administrative controls necessary to assure compliance with this section;

(3) *In a conveyance* containing no other packages of any Class 7 (radioactive) material required to bear one of the labels prescribed in §172.403 of this subchapter. Specific arrangements must be made between the offeror and the carrier, with instructions to that effect issued with the shipping papers; or

(4) *Under any other procedure* approved by the Associate Administrator in accordance with part 107 of this subchapter.

§173.459 Mixing of fissile material packages.

(a) **Mixing of fissile material packages with other types** of Class 7 (radioactive) materials is authorized only if the transport index of any single package does not exceed 10 and the total transport index in any conveyance or storage location does not exceed 50.

(b) **Fissile packages may be shipped** with an external radiation level greater than 0.1 mSv/hr (10 mrem per hour) at 1 m (3.3 feet), and combined with other packages of the same or different designs in a fissile material, controlled shipment, under the conditions prescribed in §173.457, if:

(1) *Each package* in the shipment has been assigned a transport index for criticality control purposes in accordance with the 10 CFR 71.59;

(2) *The nuclear* criticality control transport index does not exceed 10 for any single package;

(3) *The total* nuclear criticality control transport index does not exceed 100 for all packages in the shipment; and

(4) *Except as provided* in §176.704(e) of this subchapter, the shipment is not transported by vessel.

(c) **A fissile material, controlled shipment of packages** may be combined with other packages of the same or different design when each package has been assigned a nuclear criticality control transport index in accordance with 10 CFR 71.59, and may be combined with other fissile packages into a fissile material, controlled shipment under the conditions prescribed in §173.457, if:

(1) *The nuclear* criticality control transport index which has been assigned in the package approval does not exceed 50 for any single package;

(2) *The total* nuclear criticality control transport index for all packages in the shipment does not exceed 100; and

(3) *Except as provided* in §176.704(e) of this subchapter, the shipment is not transported by vessel.

§173.461 Demonstration of compliance with tests.

(a) **Compliance with the design requirements** in §173.412 and the test requirements in §§173.465 through 173.469 must be shown by any of the methods prescribed in this paragraph, or by a combination of these methods appropriate for the particular feature being evaluated:

(1) *Performance of tests* with prototypes or samples of the specimens representing LSA-III, special form Class 7 (radioactive) material, or packaging, in which case the contents of the packaging for the test must simulate as closely as practicable the expected range of physical properties of the radioactive contents or packaging to be tested, must be prepared as normally presented for transport. The use of non-radioactive substitute contents is encouraged provided that the results of the testing take into account the radioactive characteristics of the contents for which the package is being tested;

(2) *Reference to a previous,* satisfactory demonstration of compliance of a sufficiently similar nature;

(3) *Performance of tests* with models of appropriate scale incorporating those features that are significant with respect to the item under investigation, when engineering experience has shown results of those tests to be suitable for design purposes. When a scale model is used, the need for adjusting certain test parameters, such as the penetrator diameter or the compressive load, must be taken into account; or

(4) *Calculations or reasoned evaluation,* using reliable and conservative procedures and parameters.

(b) **With respect to the initial conditions** for the tests under §§173.465 through 173.469, except for the water immersion tests, compliance must be based upon the assumption that the package is in equilibrium at an ambient temperature of 38 °C (100 °F).

§173.462 Preparation of specimens for testing.

(a) **Each specimen (i.e., sample, prototype or scale model)** must be examined before testing to identify and record faults or damage, including:

(1) *Divergence from the specifications or drawings;*

(2) *Defects in construction;*

(3) *Corrosion or other deterioration; and*

(4) *Distortion of features.*

(b) **Any deviation found under paragraph** (a) of this section from the specified design must be corrected or appropriately taken into account in the subsequent evaluation.

(c) **The containment system of the packaging** must be clearly specified.

(d) **The external features of the specimen** must be clearly identified so that reference may be made to any part of it.

§173.465 Type A packaging tests.

(a) **The packaging, with contents, must be capable** of withstanding the water spray, free drop, stacking and penetration tests prescribed in this section. One prototype may be used for all tests if the requirements of paragraph (b) of this section are met.

(b) **Water spray test.** The water spray test must precede each test or test sequence prescribed in this section. The water spray test must simulate exposure to rainfall of approximately 5 cm (2 inches) per hour for at least one hour. The time interval between the end of the water spray test and the beginning of the next test must be such that the water has soaked in to the maximum extent without appreciable drying of the exterior of the specimen. In the absence of evidence to the contrary, this interval may be assumed to be two hours if the water spray is applied from four different directions simultaneously. However, no time interval may elapse if the water spray is applied from each of the four directions consecutively.

(c) **Free drop test.** The specimen must drop onto the target so as to suffer maximum damage to the safety features being tested, and:

(1) *The height of the drop measured* from the lowest point of the specimen to the upper surface of the target may not be less than the distance specified in table 12, for the applicable package mass. The target must be as specified in §173.465(c)(5). Table 12 is as follows:

Table 12 - Free Drop Distance for Testing Packages to Normal Conditions of Transport

Packaging mass	Free drop distance	
Kilograms (pounds)	Meters	(Feet)
< Mass 5,000 (11,000)	1.2	(4)
5,000 (11,000) Mass to 10,000 (22,000)	0.9	(3)
10,000 (22,000) Mass to 15,000 (33,000)	0.6	(2)
> 15,000 (33,000) Mass	0.3	(1)

(2) *For packages* containing fissile material, the free drop test specified in paragraph (c)(1) of this section must be preceded by a free drop from a height of 0.3 m (1 foot) on each corner, or in the case of cylindrical packages, onto each of the quarters of each rim.

(3) *For fiberboard or wood* rectangular packages with a mass of 50 kg (110 pounds) or less, a separate specimen must be subjected to a free drop onto each corner from a height of 0.3 m (1 foot).

(4) *For cylindrical fiberboard packages* with a mass of 100 kg (220 pounds) or less, a separate specimen must be subjected to a free drop onto each of the quarters of each rim from a height of 0.3 m (1 foot).

(5) *The target* for the free drop test must be a flat, horizontal surface of such mass and rigidity that any increase in its resistance to displacement or deformation upon impact by the specimen would not significantly increase the damage to the specimen.

(d) **Stacking test.**

(1) *The specimen* must be subjected for a period of at least 24 hours to a compressive load equivalent to the greater of the following:

(i) *Five times the mass of the actual package; or*

(ii) *The equivalent* of 13 kilopascals (1.9 psi) multiplied by the vertically projected area of the package.

(2) *The compressive load* must be applied uniformly to two opposite sides of the specimen, one of which must be the base on which the package would normally rest.

(e) **Penetration test.** For the penetration test, the specimen must be placed on a rigid, flat, horizontal surface that will not move significantly while the test is being performed.

(1) *A bar* of 3.2 cm (1.25 inches) in diameter with a hemispherical end and a mass of 6 kg (13.2 pounds) must be dropped and directed to fall with its longitudinal axis vertical, onto the center of the weakest part of the specimen, so that, if it penetrates far enough, it will hit the containment system. The bar may not be significantly deformed by the test; and

(2) *The height* of the drop of the bar measured from its lower end to the intended point of impact on the upper surface of the specimen must be 1 m (3.3 feet) or greater.

§173.466 Additional tests for Type A packagings designed for liquids and gases.

(a) **In addition to the tests prescribed in §173.465,** Type A packagings designed for liquids and gases must be capable of withstanding the following tests:

(1) *Free drop test.* The packaging specimen must drop onto the target so as to suffer the maximum damage to its containment. The height of the drop measured from the lowest part of the packaging specimen to the upper surface of the target must be 9 m (30 feet) or greater. The target must be as specified in §173.465(c)(5).

(2) *Penetration test.* The specimen must be subjected to the test specified in §173.465(e) except that the height of the drop must be 1.7 m (5.5 feet).

(b) **[Reserved]**

§173.467 Tests for demonstrating the ability of Type B and fissile materials packagings to withstand accident conditions in transportation.

Each Type B packaging or packaging for fissile material must meet the test requirements prescribed in 10 CFR part 71 for ability to withstand accident conditions in transportation.

§173.468 Test for LSA-III material.

(a) **LSA-III Class 7 (radioactive) material must meet** the test requirement of paragraph (b) of this section. Any differences between the material to be transported and the test material must be taken into account in determining whether the test requirements have been met.

(b) **Test method.**

(1) *The specimen* representing no less than the entire contents of the package must be immersed for 7 days in water at ambient temperature.

(2) *The volume of water* to be used in the test must be sufficient to ensure that at the end of the test period the free volume of the unabsorbed and unreacted water remaining will be at least 10% of the volume of the specimen itself.

(3) *The water* must have an initial pH of 6-8 and a maximum conductivity of 10 micromho/cm at 20 °C (68 °F).

(4) *The total activity* of the free volume of water must be measured following the 7 day immersion test and must not exceed 0.1 A_2.

§173.469 Tests for special form Class 7 (radioactive) materials.

(a) **Special form Class 7 (radioactive) materials** must meet the test requirements of paragraph (b) of this section. Each solid Class 7 (radioactive) material or capsule specimen to be tested must be manufactured or fabricated so that it is representative of the actual solid material or capsule that will be transported with the proposed radioactive content duplicated as closely as practicable. Any differences between the material to be transported and the test material, such as the use of non-radioactive contents, must be taken into account in determining whether the test requirements have been met. The following additional conditions apply:

(1) *A different specimen may be used for each of the tests;*

(2) *The specimen* may not break or shatter when subjected to the impact, percussion, or bending tests;

(3) *The specimen* may not melt or disperse when subjected to the heat test; and

(4) *After each test,* leaktightness or indispersibility of the specimen must be determined by —

(i) *A method* no less sensitive than the leaching assessment prescribed in paragraph (c) of this section. For a capsule resistant to corrosion by water, and which has an internal void volume greater than 0.1 milliliter, an alternative to the leaching assessment is a demonstration of leaktightness of 10^{-4} torr-1/s (1.3×10^{-4} atm-cm^3/s) based on air at 25 °C (77 °F) and one atmosphere differential pressure for solid radioactive content, or 10^{-6} torr-1/s (1.3×10^{-6} atm-cm^3/s) for liquid or gaseous radioactive content; or

(ii) *A specimen* that comprises or simulates Class 7 (radioactive) material contained in a sealed capsule need not be subjected to the leaktightness procedure specified in this section provided it is alternatively subjected to any of the tests prescribed in ISO/TR4826-1979(E), "Sealed Radioactive Sources Leak Test Methods."

(b) Test methods.

(1) *Impact Test.* The specimen must fall onto the target from a height of 9 m (30 feet) or greater. The target must be as specified in §173.465(c)(5).

(2) *Percussion Test.*

(i) *The specimen* must be placed on a sheet of lead that is supported by a smooth solid surface, and struck by the flat face of a steel billet so as to produce an impact equivalent to that resulting from a free drop of 1.4 kg (3 pounds) through 1 m (3.3 feet).

(ii) *The flat face* of the billet must be 2.5 cm (1 inch) in diameter with the edges rounded off to a radius of 3 mm ± 0.3 mm (0.12 inch ± 0.012 inch).

(iii) *The lead* must be of hardness number 3.5 to 4.5 on the Vickers scale and thickness 2.5 cm (1 inch) or greater, and must cover an area greater than that covered by the specimen.

(iv) *A fresh surface of lead must be used for each impact.*

(v) *The billet* must strike the specimen so as to cause maximum damage.

(3) *Bending test.*

(i) *This test* applies only to long, slender sources with a length of 10 cm (4 inches) or greater and a length to width ratio of 10 or greater.

(ii) *The specimen* must be rigidly clamped in a horizontal position so that one half of its length protrudes from the face of the clamp.

(iii) *The orientation* of the specimen must be such that the specimen will suffer maximum damage when its free end is struck by the flat face of a steel billet.

(iv) *The billet* must strike the specimen so as to produce an impact equivalent to that resulting from a free vertical drop of 1.4 kg (3 pounds) through 1 m (3.3 feet).

(v) *The flat face* of the billet must be 2.5 cm (1 inch) in diameter with the edges rounded off to a radius of 3 mm ± 0.3 mm (.12 inch ± 0.012 inch).

(4) *Heat test.* The specimen must be heated in air to a temperature of not less than 800 °C (1475 °F), held at that temperature for a period of 10 minutes, and then allowed to cool.

(c) Leaching assessment methods.

(1) *For indispersible solid material —*

(i) *The specimen* must be immersed for seven days in water at ambient temperature. The water must have a pH range of 6 to 8 and a maximum conductivity of 10 micromho per centimeter at 20 °C (68 °F).

(ii) *The water* with specimen must then be heated to a temperature of 50 °C ± 5 °(122 °F ± 9 °) and maintained at this temperature for four hours.

(iii) *The activity of the water must then be determined.*

(iv) *The specimen* must then be stored for at least seven days in still air of relative humidity not less than 90 percent at 30 °C (86 °F).

(v) *The specimen* must then be immersed in water under the same conditions as in paragraph (c)(1)(i) of this section, and the water with specimen must be heated to 50 C ± 5 °(122 °F ± 9 °) and maintained at that temperature for four hours.

(vi) *The activity* of the water must then be determined. The activities determined in paragraph (c)(1)(iii) of this section and this paragraph, (c)(1)(vi), may not exceed 2 kilobecquerels (0.05 microcurie).

(2) *For encapsulated material —*

(i) *The specimen* must be immersed in water at ambient temperature. The water must have a pH of 6-8 and a maximum conductivity of 10 micromho per centimeter.

(ii) *The water* and specimen must be heated to a temperature of 50 °C ± 5°(122 °F ± 9°) and maintained at this temperature for four hours.

(iii) *The activity of the water must then be determined.*

(iv) *The specimen* must then be stored for at least seven days in still air at a temperature of 30 °C (86 °F) or greater.

(v) *The process* in paragraphs (c)(2)(i), (c)(2)(ii), and (c)(2)(iii) of this section must be repeated.

(vi) *The activity* determined in paragraph (c)(2)(iii) of this section may not exceed 2 kilobecquerels (0.05 microcurie).

(d) A specimen that comprises or simulates Class 7 (radioactive) material contained in a sealed capsule need not be subjected to —

(1) *The impact test* and the percussion test of this section provided that the specimen is alternatively subjected to the Class 4 impact test prescribed in ISO 2919-1980(e), "Sealed Radioactive Sources-Classification" (see §171.7 of this subchapter); and

(2) *The heat test* of this section, provided the specimen is alternatively subjected to the Class 6 temperature test specified in the International Organization for Standardization document ISO 2919-1980(e), "Sealed Radioactive Sources-Classification." (see §171.7 of this subchapter)

§173.471 Requirements for U.S. Nuclear Regulatory Commission approved packages.

In addition to the applicable requirements of the U.S. Nuclear Regulatory Commission (USNRC) and other requirements of this subchapter, any offeror of a Type B, Type B(U), Type B(M), or fissile material package that has been approved by the USNRC in accordance with 10 CFR part 71 must also comply with the following requirements:

(a) The offeror shall be registered with the USNRC as a party to the packaging approval, and make the shipment in compliance with the terms of the packaging approval;

(b) The outside of each package must be durably and legibly marked with the package identification marking indicated in the USNRC packaging approval;

(c) Each shipping paper related to the shipment of the package must bear the package identification marking indicated in the USNRC packaging approval;

(d) Before export shipment of the package, the offeror shall obtain a U.S. Competent Authority Certificate for that package design, or if one has already been issued, the offeror shall register in writing (including a description of the quality assurance program required by 10 CFR Part 71) with the U.S. Competent Authority as a user of the certificate. (Note: The person who originally applies for a U.S. Competent Authority Certificate will be registered automatically.) The registration request must be sent to the Associate Administrator for Hazardous Materials Safety (DHM-23), Department of Transportation, 400 Seventh Street, SW., Washington DC 20590-0001. Alternatively, the application with any attached supporting documentation in an appropriate format may be submitted by facsimile (fax) to (202) 366-3753 or (202) 366-3650, or by electronic mail (e-mail) to "ramcert@rspa.dot.gov." Upon registration, the offeror will be furnished with a copy of the certificate. The offeror shall then submit a copy of the U.S. Competent Authority Certificate applying to that package design to the national competent authority of each country into or through which the package will be transported, unless the offeror has documentary evidence that a copy has already been furnished; and

(e) Each request for a U.S. Competent Authority Certificate as required by the IAEA regulations must be submitted in writing to the Associate Administrator. The request must be in triplicate and include copies of the applicable USNRC packaging approval, USNRC Quality Assurance Program approval number, and a reproducible 22 cm x 30 cm (8.5" x 11") drawing showing the make-up of the package. The request and accompanying documentation must be sent to the Associate Administrator for Hazardous Materials Safety (DHM-23), Department of Transportation, 400 Seventh Street, SW., Washington DC 20590-0001. Alternatively, the application with any attached supporting documentation in an appropriate format may be submitted by facsimile (fax) to (202) 366-3753 or (202) 366-3650, or by electronic mail (e-mail) to "ramcert@rspa.dot.gov." Each request is considered in the order in which it is received. To allow sufficient time for consideration, requests must be received at least 90 days before the requested effective date.

§173.472 Requirements for exporting DOT Specification Type B and fissile packages.

(a) Any offeror who exports a DOT Specification Type B or fissile material package authorized by §173.416 or §173.417 shall comply with paragraphs (b) through (f) of this section.

(b) The shipment must be made in accordance with the conditions of the U.S. Certificate of Competent Authority.

(c) The outside of each package must be durably and legibly marked with the package identification marking indicated in the U.S. Competent Authority Certificate.

(d) Each shipping paper related to the shipment of the package must bear the package identification marking indicated in the U.S. Competent Authority Certificate.

(e) Before export of the package, the offeror shall obtain a U.S. Competent Authority Certificate for that package design, or if one has already been issued, the offeror shall register in writing (including a description of the quality assurance program required by 10 CFR Part 71, subpart H, or 49 CFR 173.474 and 173.475) with the U.S. Competent Authority as a user of the certificate. Upon registration, the offeror will be furnished with a copy of the certificate. The offeror shall then submit a copy of the U.S. Competent Authority Certificate applying to that package design to the national competent authority of each country into or through which the package will be transported, unless the offeror has documentary evidence that a copy has already been furnished.

(f) **Each request for a U.S. Competent Authority Certificate** as required by the IAEA regulations must be submitted in writing to the Associate Administrator. The request must be in triplicate and must include a description of the quality assurance program required by 10 CFR part 71, subpart H, or 49 CFR 173.474 and 173.475, and a reproducible 22 cm x 30 cm (8.5" x 11") drawing showing the make-up of the package. A copy of the USNRC quality assurance program approval will satisfy the requirement for describing the quality assurance program. The request and accompanying documentation may be sent by mail or other delivery service. Alternatively, the request with any attached supporting documentation submitted in an appropriate format may be sent by facsimile (fax) to (202) 366-3753 or (202) 366-3650, or by electronic mail (e-mail) to "ramcert@rspa.dot.gov." Each request is considered in the order in which it is received. To allow sufficient time for consideration, requests must be received at least 90 days before the requested effective date.

§173.473 Requirements for foreign-made packages.

In addition to other applicable requirements of this subchapter, each offeror of a foreign-made Type B, Type B(U), Type B(M), or fissile material package for which a Competent Authority Certificate is required by IAEA's "Regulations for the Safe Transport of Radioactive Materials, Safety Series No. 6," shall also comply with the following requirements:

(a) **Prior to the shipment of such a package** of Class 7 (radioactive) materials into or from the U.S., the offeror shall —

(1) *Have the foreign* competent authority certificate revalidated by the U.S. Competent Authority, unless this has been done previously. Each request for revalidation must be submitted to the Associate Administrator. The request must be in triplicate, contain all the information required by Section VII of the IAEA regulations in Safety Series No. 6 (incorporated by reference, see §171.7 of this subchapter), and include a copy in English of the foreign competent authority certificate. Alternatively, the request with any attached supporting documentation submitted in an appropriate format may be sent by facsimile (fax) to (202) 366-3753 or (202) 366-3650, or by electronic mail to "ramcert@rspa.dot.gov." Each request is considered in the order in which it is received.

To allow sufficient time for consideration, requests must be received at least 90 days before the requested effective date;

(2) *Register in writing* with the U.S. Competent Authority as a user of the package covered by the foreign competent authority certificate and its U.S. revalidation. Alternatively, the registration request with any attached supporting documentation submitted in an appropriate format may be sent by facsimile (fax) to (202) 366-3753 or (202) 366-3650, or by electronic mail (e-mail) to "ramcert@rspa.dot.gov." If the offeror is requesting the revalidation, registration is automatic; and

(3) *Supply to the carrier,* upon request, the applicable competent authority certificates. However, the competent authority certificates are not required to accompany the packages to which they apply.

(b) **The outside of each package must be** durably and legibly marked with the competent authority identification marking indicated on the Competent Authority Certificate and revalidation.

(c) **Each shipping paper for a shipment** of Class 7 (radioactive) materials must bear a notation of the package identification marking indicated on the competent authority certificate or revalidation.

(d) **All requirements of the foreign** competent authority certificate and the U.S. Competent Authority revalidation must be fulfilled.

§173.474 Quality control for construction of packaging.

Prior to the first use of any packaging for the shipment of Class 7 (radioactive) material, the offeror shall determine that —

(a) **The packaging meets the quality** of design and construction requirements as specified in this subchapter; and

(b) **The effectiveness of the shielding,** containment and, when required, the heat transfer characteristics of the package, are within the limits specified for the package design.

§173.475 Quality control requirements prior to each shipment of Class 7 (radioactive) materials.

Before each shipment of any Class 7 (radioactive) materials package, the offeror must ensure, by examination or appropriate tests, that —

(a) **The packaging is proper for the contents to be shipped;**

(b) **The packaging is in unimpaired physical condition,** except for superficial marks;

(c) **Each closure device of the packaging,** including any required gasket, is properly installed, secured, and free of defects;

(d) **For fissile material, each moderator and neutron absorber,** if required, is present and in proper condition;

(e) **Each special instruction for filling, closing,** and preparation of the packaging for shipment has been followed;

(f) **Each closure, valve, or other opening** of the containment system through which the radioactive content might escape is properly closed and sealed;

(g) **Each packaging containing liquid in excess** of an A_2 quantity and intended for air shipment has been tested to show that it will not leak under an ambient atmospheric pressure of not more than 25 kPa, absolute (3.6 psia). The test must be conducted on the entire containment system, or on any receptacle or vessel within the containment system, to determine compliance with this requirement;

(h) **The internal pressure of the containment system** will not exceed the design pressure during transportation; and

(i) **External radiation and contamination levels** are within the allowable limits specified in this subchapter.

§173.476 Approval of special form Class 7 (radioactive) materials.

(a) **Each offeror of special form Class 7** (radioactive) materials must maintain on file for at least one year after the latest shipment, and provide to the Associate Administrator on request, a complete safety analysis, including documentation of any tests, demonstrating that the special form material meets the requirements of §173.469. An IAEA Certificate of Competent Authority issued for the special form material may be used to satisfy this requirement.

(b) **Prior to the first export shipment** of a special form Class 7 (radioactive) material from the United States, each offeror shall obtain a U.S. Competent Authority Certificate for the specific material. For special form material manufactured outside the United States, an IAEA Certificate of Competent Authority from the country of origin may be used to meet this requirement.

(c) **Each request for a U.S. Competent Authority Certificate** as required by the IAEA regulations must be submitted in writing, in triplicate, by mail or other delivery service to the Associate Administrator. Alternatively, the request with any attached supporting documentation submitted in an appropriate format may be sent by facsimile (fax) to (202) 366-3753 or (202) 366-3650, or by electronic mail (e-mail) to "ramcert@rspa.dot.gov". Each request is considered in the order in which it is received. To allow sufficient time for consideration, requests must be received at least 90 days before the requested effective date. Each petition for a U.S. Competent Authority Certificate must include the following information:

(1) *A detailed description* of the material, or if a capsule, a detailed description of the contents. Particular reference must be made to both physical and chemical states;

(2) *A detailed statement* of the capsule design and dimensions, including complete engineering drawings [22cm x 30cm (8 1/2 inches x 11 inches)] and schedules of material, and methods of construction;

(3) *A statement* of the tests that have been made and their results; or evidence based on calculative methods to show that the material is able to pass the tests; or other evidence that the special form Class 7 (radioactive) material complies with §173.469; and

(4) *For the original request* for a Competent Authority Certificate, evidence of a quality assurance program.

(d) **Paragraphs (a) and (b) of this section** do not apply in those cases where A_1 equals A_2 and the material is not required to be described on the shipping papers as "Radioactive Material, Special Form, n.o.s."

Subparts J-O [Reserved]

Appendix A to Part 173 [Reserved]

Appendix B to Part 173

Procedure for testing chemical compatibility and rate of permeation in plastic packaging and receptacles.

1. **The purpose of this procedure is to determine** the chemical compatibility and permeability of liquid hazardous materials packaged in plastic packaging and receptacles. Alternatives for this procedure are permitted as specified in §173.24(e)(3)(iii) of this subchapter.
2. **Compatibility and rate of permeation are determined** by subjecting full size plastic containers (or smaller containers as permitted in paragraph 4 of this appendix) and hazardous material lading to one of the following combinations of time and temperature:
   a. *Test Method 1:* 180 days at a temperature no lower than 18 °C (64 °F).
   b. *Test Method 2:* 28 days at a temperature no lower than 50 °C (122 °F).
   c. *Test Method 3:* 14 days at a temperature no lower than 60 °C (140 °F).

3. **Regardless of which test method is used,** at least three sample containers shall be tested for each combination of hazardous material and size and design of container. Fill containers to rated capacity with the specific hazardous material (at the concentration to be transported) and close as for shipment. For the first and last 24 hours of storage under the selected test method, place the containers with closures downward, except that containers fitted with a vent are so placed on each occasion for five minutes only.
4. **For testing under Test Method 2 or 3 in those instances** where it is not practicable to use full size containers, smaller containers may be used. The small container shall be manufactured by the same process as the larger container (for example, using the same method of molding and processing temperatures) and be made of identical resins, pigments and additives.
5. **Determine filled container weight or net weight** of contents both before and after storage under the selected test method. Rate of permeation is determined from loss of hazardous materials contents, during the conduct of the test, expressed as a percentage of the original weight.
6. **After storage under the selected test method,** the container shall be drained, rinsed, filled to rated capacity with water and, with filled container at ambient temperature, dropped from a height determined in accordance with §178.603(e) of this subchapter onto a rigid non-resilient, flat and horizontal surface.
7. **Each of the following constitute test failure:**
   a. *Visible evidence* of permanent deformation due to vapor pressure build-up or collapse of walls, deterioration, swelling, crazing, cracking, excessive corrosion, oxidization, embrittlement, leakage, rupture or other defects likely to cause premature failure or a hazardous condition.
   b. *For materials* meeting the definition of a poison according to this subchapter, a rate of permeation in excess of 0.5% determined over the test period. For all other hazardous materials, a rate of permeation in excess of 2.0% determined over the test period.

Appendix C to Part 173

Procedure for base-level vibration testing.

Base-level vibration testing shall be conducted as follows:

1. **Three sample packagings, selected at random,** must be filled and closed as for shipment. A non-hazardous material may be used in place of the hazardous material if it has essentially the same physical characteristics.
2. **The three packages must be placed** on a vibrating platform that has a vertical double-amplitude (peak-to-peak displacement) of one inch. The packages should be constrained horizontally to prevent them from falling off the platform, but must be left free to move vertically, bounce and rotate.
3. **The test must be performed continuously for one hour** at a frequency that causes each package to be raised from the vibrating platform to such a degree that a piece of material of approximately 1.6 mm (0.063 inch) thickness (such as steel strapping or paperboard) can be passed between the bottom of any package and the platform.
4. **Immediately following the period of vibration,** each package shall be removed from the platform, turned on its side and observed for any evidence of leakage.
5. **Rupture or leakage from any of the packages** constitutes failure of the test.

Appendix D to Part 173

Test methods for dynamite (explosive, blasting, Type A).

1. **Test method D-1 — Leakage Test**
   A wooden stick, 114 mm (4.5 inches) long and 4.8 mm (0.2 inch) inch in diameter, with a sharpened end is used to punch 5 holes in one end of the wrapper of a dynamite cartridge. A cork stopper is placed on the bottom of a glass volumetric cylinder. The dynamite cartridge is placed, perforated end down, resting on the cork stopper in the cylinder. The entire assembly is placed in an oven at 38 °C (100 °F) for 48 hours and then examined visually for evidence of leakage.
2. **Test method D-2 — Centrifugal Exudation Test**
   The test apparatus consists of a glass tube, 135 mm (5.3 inches) long and one inch in diameter, with both ends open, and is assembled in the following manner:
   (a) *Close the bottom* with a plastic plug of diameter equal to the inner diameter of the glass tube;
   (b) *Place a small amount of absorbent cotton on top of the plug;*
   (c) *Place a plastic disk* that matches the inner diameter to the glass tube and has seven small perforations on top of the cotton; and
   (d) *Place 10 g* (0.35 ounce) of the dynamite sample on top of the disk. The assembled glass tube is then placed in a hand-operated centrifuge and spun for one minute at 600 rpm (revolutions per minute). The dynamite sample is then removed from the glass tube and weighed to determine the percent of weight loss.
3. **Test method D-3 — Compression Exudation Test**
   The entire apparatus for this test is shown in Figure 1 of this appendix. The test is conducted using the following procedures:
   (a) *A glass tube,* 135 mm (5.3 inches) long and one inch in diameter, is held on a wooden base;
   (b) *A small amount*of absorbent cotton is placed into the bottom of the glass tube;
   (c) *Ten g (0.35 ounce)* of dynamite sample are placed on top of the cotton in the glass tube;
   (d) *A small amount* of absorbent cotton is placed on top of the dynamite sample;
   (e) *A plastic disk* that matches the inner diameter of the glass tube and has seven small perforations is placed on top of the cotton;
   (f) *A plastic plug* matching the inner diameter of the glass tube is then placed on top of the disk;
   (g) *The glass tube assembly* is placed under the compression rod, and compression is applied by means of the weight on the metal lever rod. The sample is compressed for one minute; and
   (h) *The dynamite sample* is then removed from the glass tube and weighed to determine the percent of weight loss.

FIGURE 1
COMPRESSION APPARATUS

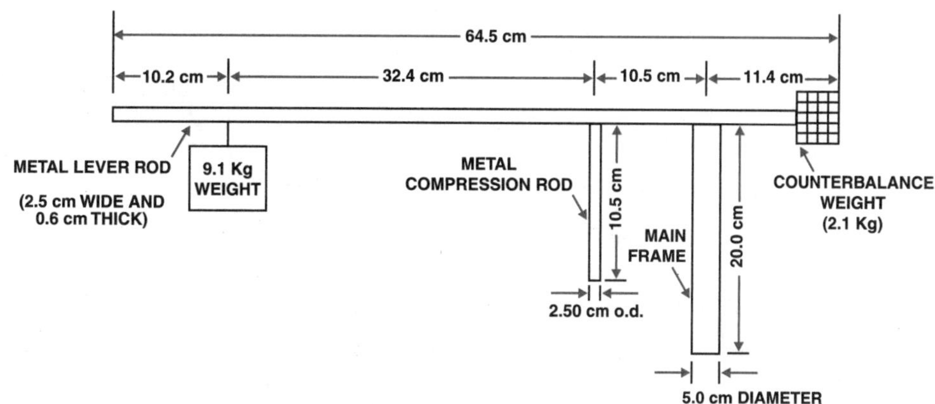

Appendixes E-G to Part 173
[Reserved]

Appendix H to Part 173
Method of testing for sustained combustibility.

1. **Method**
The method describes a procedure for determining if the material when heated under the test conditions and exposed to an external source of flame applied in a standard manner sustains combustion.

2. **Principle of the method**
A metal block with a concave depression (test portion well) is heated to a specified temperature. A specified volume of the material under test is transferred to the well, and its ability to sustain combustion is noted after application and subsequent removal of a standard flame under specified conditions.

3. **Apparatus**
A combustibility tester consisting of a block of aluminum alloy or other corrosion-resistant metal of high thermal conductivity is used. The block has a concave well and a pocket drilled to take a thermometer. A small gas jet assembly on a swivel is attached to the block. The handle and gas inlet for the gas jet may be fitted at any convenient angle to the gas jet. A suitable apparatus is shown in Figure 5.1 of the UN Recommendations, and the essential dimensions are given in Figures 5.1 and 5.2 of the UN Recommendations. The following equipment is needed:
   (a) *Gauge, for checking* that the height of the center of the gas jet above the top of the test portion well is 2.2 mm (see Figure 5.1);
   (b) *Thermometer, mercury in glass,* for horizontal operation, with a sensitivity not less than 1 mm/°C, or other measuring device of equivalent sensitivity permitting reading at 0.5 °C intervals. When in position in the block, the thermometer bulb must be surrounded with thermally conducting thermoplastic compound;
   (c) *Hotplate, fitted with* a temperature-control device. (Other types of apparatus with suitable temperature-control facilities may be employed to heat the metal block);
   (d) *Stopwatch, or other suitable timing device;*
   (e) *Syringe, capable of delivering 2 mL to an accuracy of 0.1 mL; and*
   (f) *Fuel source, butane test fuel.*

4. **Sampling**
The sample must be representative of the material to be tested and must be supplied and kept in a tightly closed container prior to test. Because of the possibility of loss of volatile constituents, the sample must receive only the minimum treatment necessary to ensure its homogeneity. After removing each test portion, the sample container must be immediately closed tightly to ensure that no volatile components escape from the container; if this closure is incomplete, an entirely new sample must be taken.

5. **Procedure**
Carry out the determination in triplicate.
WARNING — Do not carry out the test in a small confined area (for example a glove box) because of the hazard of explosions.
   (a) *It is essential* that the apparatus be set up in a completely draft-free area (see warning) and in the absence of strong light to facilitate observation of flash, flame, etc.
   (b) *Place the metal block* on the hotplate or heat the metal block by other suitable means so that its temperature, as indicated by the thermometer placed in the metal block, is maintained at the specified temperature within a tolerance of 1 °C. For the appropriate test temperature, see paragraph 5.(h) of this appendix. Correct this temperature for the difference in barometric pressure from the standard atmospheric pressure (101.3 kPa) by raising the test temperature for a higher pressure or lowering the test temperature for a lower pressure by 1.0 °C for each 4 kPa difference. Ensure that the top of the metal block is exactly horizontal. Use the gauge to check that the jet is 2.2 mm above the top of the well when in the test position.
   (c) *Light the butane test fuel* with the jet away from the test position (i.e. in the "off" position, away from the well). Adjust the size of the flame so that it is 8 mm to 9 mm high and approximately 5 mm wide.
   (d) *Using the syringe,* take from the sample container at least 2 mL of the sample and rapidly transfer a test portion of 2 mL 0.1 mL to the well of the combustibility tester and immediately start the timing device.
   (e) *After a heating time* of 60 seconds (s), by which time the test portion is deemed to have reached its equilibrium temperature, and if the test fluid has not ignited, swing the test flame into the test position over the edge of the pool of liquid. Maintain it in this position for 15 s and then return it to the "off" position while observing the behavior of the test portion. The test flame must remain lighted throughout the test.
   (f) *For each test observe and record:*
      (i) *whether there is* ignition and sustained combustion or flashing, or neither, of the test portion before the test flame is moved into the test position;
      (ii) *whether the test portion* ignites while the test flame is in the test position, and, if so, how long combustion is sustained after the test flame is returned to the "off" position.
   (g) *If sustained* combustion interpreted in accordance with paragraph 6. of this appendix is not found, repeat the complete procedure with new test portions, but with a heating time of 30 s.
   (h) *If sustained* combustion interpreted in accordance with paragraph 6. of this appendix is not found at a test temperature of 60.5 °C (141 °F), repeat the complete procedure with new test portions, but at a test temperature of 75 °C (167 °F). In the case of a material which has a flash point above 60.5 °C (141 °F) and below 93 °C (200 °F), if sustained combustion interpreted in accordance with paragraph 6. of this appendix is not found at a test temperature of 5 °C (9 °F) above its flash point, repeat the complete procedure with new test portions, but at a test temperature of 20 °C (36 °F) above its flash point.

6. **Interpretation of observations**
The material must be assessed either as not sustaining combustion or as sustaining combustion. Sustained combustion must be reported at either of the heating times if one of the following occurs with either of the test portions:
   (a) *When the test flame* is in the "off" position, the test portion ignites and sustains combustion;
   (b) *The test portion* ignites while the test flame is in the test position for 15 s, and sustains combustion for more than 15 s after the test flame has been returned to the "off" position.

Note to paragraph 6 of this appendix: Intermittent flashing may not be interpreted as sustained combustion. Normally, at the end of 15 s, the combustion has either clearly ceased or continues. In cases of doubt, the material must be deemed to sustain combustion.

Part 174 - Carriage by Rail

Subpart A - General Requirements

§174.1 Purpose and scope.

This part prescribes requirements in addition to those contained in parts 171, 172, 173, and 179 of this subchapter, to be observed with respect to the transportation of hazardous materials in or on rail cars.

§174.3 Unacceptable hazardous materials shipments.

No person may accept for transportation or transport by rail any shipment of hazardous material that is not in conformance with the requirements of this subchapter.

§174.5 Carrier's materials and supplies.

This subchapter applies to the transportation of a carrier's materials and supplies moving by rail, except that the shipper's certification is not required when these materials and supplies are being transported by the carrier who owns them. The requirements of this subchapter do not apply to railway torpedoes or fusees when carried in engines or rail cars. Railway torpedoes must be in closed metal boxes when not in use.

§174.9 Inspection and acceptance.

At each location where a hazardous material is accepted for transportation or placed in a train, the carrier shall inspect each rail car containing the hazardous material, at ground level, for required markings, labels, placards, securement of closures and leakage. This inspection may be performed in conjunction with inspections required under parts 215 and 232 of this title.

§174.14 Movements to be expedited.

(a) **A carrier must forward each shipment** of hazardous materials promptly and within 48 hours (Saturdays, Sundays, and holidays excluded), after acceptance at the originating point or receipt at any yard, transfer station, or interchange point, except that where biweekly or weekly service only is performed, a shipment of hazardous materials must be forwarded on the first available train.

(b) **A tank car loaded with any Division 2.1** (flammable gas), Division 2.3 (poisonous gas) or Class 3 (flammable liquid) material, may not be received and held at any point, subject to forwarding orders, so as to defeat the purpose of this section or of §174.204 of this subchapter.

§174.16 Removal and disposition of hazardous materials at destination.

(a) **Delivery at non-agency stations.** A shipment of Class 1 (explosive) materials may not be unloaded at non-agency stations unless the consignee is there to receive it or unless properly locked and secure storage facilities are provided at that point for its protection. If delivery cannot be so made, the shipment must be taken to next or nearest agency station for delivery.

(b) **Delivery at agency stations.** A carrier shall require the consignee of each shipment of hazardous materials to remove the shipment from carrier's property within 48 hours (exclusive of Saturdays, Sundays, and holidays) after notice of arrival has been sent or given. If not so removed, the carrier shall immediately dispose of the shipments as follows:

(1) *Division 1.1 or 1.2 (explosive) materials:* If safe storage is available, by storage at the owner's expense; if safe storage is not available, by return to the shipper, sale, or destruction under supervision of a competent person; or if safety requires, by destruction under supervision of a competent person.

(2) *Hazardous materials,* except Division 1.1 or 1.2 (explosive) materials, in carload shipments: By storage on the carrier's property; by storage on other than the carrier's property, if safe storage on the carrier's property is not available; or by sale at expiration of 15 calendar days after notice of arrival has been sent or given to the consignee, provided the consignor has been notified of the non-delivery at the expiration of a 48-hour period and orders for disposition have not been received.

(3) *Hazardous materials,* except Division 1.1 or 1.2 (Class A explosive) materials, in less-than-carload shipments: By return to the shipper if notice of non-delivery was requested and given the consignor as prescribed by the carrier's tariff, and orders for return to shipper have been received; by storage on the carrier's property; by storage on other than the carrier's property, if safe storage on carrier's property is not available; or by sale at expiration of 15 calendar days after notice of arrival has been sent or given to the consignee, provided the consignor has been notified of non-delivery at expiration of a 48-hour period and orders for disposition have not been received.

§174.20 Local or carrier restrictions.

(a) **When local conditions make the acceptance,** transportation, or delivery of hazardous materials unusually hazardous, local restrictions may be imposed by the carrier.

(b) **Each carrier must report to the Bureau of Explosives** for publication the full information as to any restrictions which it imposes against the acceptance, delivery, or transportation of hazardous materials, over any portion of its lines under this section.

Subpart B - General Operating Requirements

§174.24 Shipping papers.

(a) **A person may not accept a hazardous material** for transportation or transport a hazardous material by rail unless that person receives a shipping paper prepared in accordance with part 172 of this subchapter, unless the material is excepted from shipping paper requirements under this subchapter. Only an initial carrier within the United States must receive and retain a copy of the shipper's certification as required by §172.204 of this subchapter. This section does not apply to a material that is excepted from shipping paper requirements by this subchapter.

(b) **Each person receiving a shipping paper** required by this section must retain a copy or an electronic image thereof, that is accessible at or through its principal place of business and must make the shipping paper available, upon request, to an authorized official of a Federal, State, or local government agency at reasonable times and locations. For a hazardous waste, each shipping paper copy must be retained for three years after the material is accepted by the initial carrier. For all other hazardous materials, each shipping paper copy must be retained for 375 days after the material is accepted by the initial carrier. Each shipping paper copy must include the date of acceptance by the initial carrier. The date on the shipping paper may be the date a shipper notifies the rail carrier that a shipment is ready for transportation, as indicated on the waybill or bill of lading, as an alternative to the date the shipment is picked up, or accepted, by the carrier.

§174.26 Notice to train crews.

(a) **The train crew must have a document that reflects** the current position in the train of each rail car containing a hazardous material. The train crew must update the document to indicate changes in the placement of a rail car within the train. For example, the train crew may update the document by handwriting on it or by appending or attaching another document to it.

(b) **A member of the crew of a train transporting** a hazardous material must have a copy of a document for the hazardous material being transported showing the information required by part 172 of this subchapter.

§174.50 Nonconforming or leaking packages.

A leaking non-bulk package may not be forwarded until repaired, reconditioned, or overpacked in accordance with §173.3 of this subchapter. Except as otherwise provided in this section, a bulk packaging that no longer conforms to this subchapter may not be forwarded by rail unless repaired or approved for movement by the Associate Administrator for Safety, Federal Railroad Administration. Notification and approval must be in writing, or through telephonic or electronic means, with subsequent written confirmation provided within two weeks. For the applicable address and telephone number, see §107.117(d)(4) of this chapter. A leaking bulk package containing a hazardous material may be moved without repair or approval only so far as necessary to reduce or to eliminate an immediate threat or harm to human health or to the environment when it is determined its movement would provide greater safety than allowing the package to remain in place. In the case of a liquid leak, measures must be taken to prevent the spread of liquid.

Subpart C - General Handling and Loading Requirements

§174.55 General requirements.

(a) **Each package containing a hazardous material** being transported by rail in a freight container or transport vehicle must be loaded so that it cannot fall or slide and must be safeguarded in such a manner that other freight cannot fall onto or slide into it under conditions normally incident to transportation. When this protection cannot be provided by using other freight, it must be provided by blocking and bracing. For examples of blocking and bracing in freight containers and transport vehicles, see Bureau of Explosives Pamphlet Nos. 6 and 6C.

(b) Each package containing a hazardous material bearing package orientation markings prescribed in §172.312 of this subchapter must be loaded within a transport vehicle or freight container to remain in the correct position indicated by those markings during transportation.

(c) The doors of a freight container or transport vehicle may not be used to secure a load that includes a package containing a hazardous material unless the doors meet the design strength requirements of Specification M-930 (for freight containers) and M-931 (for trailers) in the AAR's Manual of Standards and Recommended Practices and the load is also within the limits of the design strength requirements for the doors.

§174.57 Cleaning cars.

All hazardous material which has leaked from a package in any rail car or on other railroad property must be carefully removed.

§174.59 Marking and placarding of rail cars.

No person may transport a rail car carrying hazardous materials unless it is marked and placarded as required by this subchapter. Placards and car certificates lost in transit must be replaced at the next inspection point, and those not required must be removed at the next terminal where the train is classified. For Canadian shipments, required placards lost in transit, must be replaced either by those required by part 172 of this subchapter or by those authorized under §171.12a.

§174.61 Transport vehicles and freight containers on flat cars.

(a) A transport vehicle, freight container, or package containing a hazardous material must be designed and loaded so that it will not become damaged to an extent that would affect its integrity under conditions normally incident to transportation. Each unit must be secured on a flatcar so that it cannot permanently change position during transit. Packages of hazardous materials contained therein must be loaded and braced as provided by §§174.101, 174.112, 174.115 and 174.55. Placards must be applied when prescribed by part 172 of this subchapter and part 174.

(b) Except as specified in §173.21, a truck body, trailer, or freight container equipped with heating or refrigerating equipment which has fuel or any article classed as a hazardous material may be loaded and transported on a flat car as part of a joint rail highway movement. The heating or refrigerating equipment is considered to be a part of the truck body or trailer and is not subject to any other requirements of this subchapter. The truck body, trailer, or freight container must be secured on the flatcar so that it cannot change position during transit.

§174.63 Portable tanks, IM portable tanks, IBCs, cargo tanks, and multi-unit tank car tanks.

(a) A carrier may not transport a bulk packaging (e.g., portable tank, IM portable tank, IBC, cargo tank, or multi-unit tank car tank) containing a hazardous material in container-on-flatcar (COFC) or trailer-on-flatcar (TOFC) service except as authorized by this section or unless approved for transportation by the Associate Administrator for Safety, FRA.

(b) A bulk packaging containing a hazardous material (including IM 101 and IM 102 when appropriate according to dimensions and weight distribution) may be transported inside a fully closed transport vehicle or fully closed freight container provided it is properly secured with a restraint system that will prevent it from changing position, sliding into other packages, or contacting the side or end walls (including doors) under conditions normally incident to transportation.

(c) When not transported in conformance with and subject to paragraph (b) of this section, a bulk packaging may be transported in COFC service or TOFC service subject to the following conditions as applicable:

(1) *The bulk packaging* contains a material packaged in accordance with §173.240, 173.241, 173.242, or 173.243 of this subchapter;

(2) *The tank and flatcar* conform to requirements in AAR 600 of the AAR Specifications for Tank Cars, Specification M-1002, entitled "Specifications for Acceptability of Tank Containers";

(3) *For TOFC service,* the trailer chassis conforms to requirements in paragraphs 3, 4, 5, and 6 of AAR Specification M-943 "Container Chassis For TOFC Service" of the AAR specification for "Specially Equipped Freight Car and Intermodal Equipment";

(4) *For COFC service,* the container support and securement systems conform to requirements in Specification M-952 "Intermodal Container Support and Securement Systems for Freight Cars", of the AAR specification for "Specially Equipped Freight Car and Intermodal Equipment";

(5) *If transported in a well car —*

(i) *The tank* is not in a double-stacked configuration (i.e., no freight container or portable tank is placed above or below the tank); and

(ii) *The tank* is transported in the well with its outlet valve facing outward towards the end of the well and away from any adjacent tank or container; and

(6) *All securement fittings* shall be fully engaged and in the locked position, provided; however, if the tank is transported in a well car, it must be loaded into a well appropriate for the length of the container and any void filling device present must be secured in its designed appropriate position.

(d) An approval in effect on February 28, 1991 for the transportation of portable tanks or IM portable tanks in TOFC or COFC service expires on the date stated in the approval letter or June 15, 1995, whichever is later.

(e) A carrier may not transport a cargo tank or multi-unit tank car tank containing a hazardous material in TOFC or COFC service unless approved for such service by the Associate Administrator for Safety, FRA. However, in the event of an accident or incident, no such approval is necessary for the transportation of a cargo tank containing a hazardous material in TOFC service under the following condition(s):

(1) *There is an emergency need* for the cargo tank in order to mitigate the consequences of an incident; and

(2) *Movement of the cargo tank* is limited to transportation necessary for emergency purposes.

§174.67 Tank car unloading.

(a) In unloading tank cars, the following rules must be observed (see subpart F of this part for gases):

(1) *Unloading operations* must be performed only by reliable persons properly instructed in unloading hazardous materials and made responsible for careful compliance with this part.

(2) *Brakes must be set and wheels blocked on all cars being unloaded.*

(3) *Caution signs* must be so placed on the track or cars to give necessary warning to persons approaching the cars from the open end of a siding and must be left up until after the cars are unloaded and disconnected from the discharge connection. The signs must be of metal or other comparable material, at least 30 cm (12 inches) high by 38 cm (15 inches) wide in size, and bear the words, "STOP — Tank Car Connected", or "STOP — Men at Work", the word "STOP" being in letters at least 10 cm (3.9 inches) high and the other words in letters at least 5 cm (2 inches) high. The letters must be white on a blue background.

(4) *Before a manhole cover* or outlet valve cap is removed from a tank car, the car must be relieved of all interior pressure by cooling the tank with water or by venting the tank by raising the safety valve or opening the dome vent at short intervals. However, if venting to relieve pressure will cause a dangerous amount of vapor to collect outside the car, venting and unloading must be deferred until the pressure is reduced by allowing the car to stand overnight or otherwise cooling the contents. These precautions are not necessary when the car is equipped with a manhole cover which hinges inward or with an inner manhole cover which does not have to be removed to unload the car, and when pressure is relieved by piping vapor into a condenser or storage tank.

(b) After the pressure is released, the seal must be broken and the manhole cover removed as follows:

(1) *Screw type.* The cover must be loosened by placing a bar between the manhole cover lug and knob. After two complete turns, so that vent openings are exposed, the operation must be stopped, and if there is any sound of escaping vapor, the cover must be screwed down tightly and the interior pressure relieved as prescribed in paragraph (a)(4) of this section, before again attempting to remove the cover.

(2) *Hinged and bolted type.* All nuts must be unscrewed one complete turn, after which same precautions as prescribed for screw type cover must be observed.

(3) *Interior type.* All dirt and cinders must be carefully removed from around the cover before the yoke is unscrewed.

(c) When the car is unloaded through a bottom outlet valve, the manhole cover must be adjusted as follows:

(1) *Screw type.* The cover must be put in place, but not entirely screwed down, so that air may enter the tank through the vent holes in threaded flange of the cover.

(2) *Hinged and bolted type.* A non-metallic block must be placed under one edge of the cover.

(3) *Interior type.* The screw must be tightened up in the yoke so that the cover is brought up within one-half inch of the closed position.

(d) **When unloading through the bottom outlet** of a car equipped with an interior manhole type cover, and in each case where unloading is done through the manhole (unless a special cover with a safety vent opening and a tight connection for the discharge outlet is used), the manhole must be protected by asbestos or metal covers against the entrance of sparks or other sources of ignition of vapor, or by being covered and surrounded with wet burlap or similar cloth material. The burlap or other cloth must be kept damp by the replacement or the application of water as needed.

(e) **Seals or other substances must not be thrown** into the tank and the contents may not be spilled over the car or tank.

(f) **The valve rod handle or control in the dome** must be operated several times to see that outlet valve in bottom of tank is on its seat before valve cap is removed.

(g) **The valve cap, or the reducer when a large outlet** is to be used, must be removed with a suitable wrench after the set screws are loosened and a pail must be placed in position to catch any liquid that may be in the outlet chamber. If the valve cap or reducer does not unscrew easily, it may be tapped lightly with a mallet or wooden block in an upward direction. If leakage shows upon starting the removal, the cap or reducer may not be entirely unscrewed. Sufficient threads must be left engaged and sufficient time allowed to permit controlled escape of any accumulation of liquid in the outlet chamber. If the leakage stops or the rate of leakage diminishes materially, the cap or reducer may be entirely removed. If the initial rate of leakage continues, further efforts must be made to seat the outlet valve (see paragraph (f) of this section). If this fails, the cap or reducer must be screwed up tight and the tank must be unloaded through the dome. If upon removal of the outlet cap the outlet chamber is found to be blocked with frozen liquid or any other matter, the cap must be replaced immediately and a careful examination must be made to determine whether the outlet casting has been cracked. If the obstruction is not frozen liquid, the car must be unloaded through the dome. If the obstruction is frozen liquid and no crack has been found in the outlet casting, the car may, if circumstances require it, be unloaded from the bottom by removing the cap and attaching unloading connections immediately. Before opening the valve inside the tank car, steam must be applied to the outside of the outlet casting or wrap casting with burlap or other rags and hot water must be applied to melt the frozen liquid.

(h) **Unloading connections must be securely attached** to unloading pipes on the dome or to the bottom discharge outlets before any discharge valves are opened.

(i) **Tank cars may not be allowed to stand** with unloading connections attached after unloading is completed. Throughout the entire period of unloading, and while car is connected to unloading device, the car must be attended by the unloader.

(j) **If necessary to discontinue unloading a tank car** for any reason, all unloading connections must be disconnected. All valves must first be tightly closed, and the closures of all other openings securely applied.

(k) **As soon as a tank car is completely unloaded,** all valves must be made tight by the use of a bar, wrench or other suitable tool, the unloading connections must be removed and all other closures made tight.

(l) **Railroad defect cards may not be removed.**

(m) **If oil or gasoline has been spilled on the ground** around connections, it must be covered with fresh, dry sand or dirt.

(n) **All tools and implements used in connection** with unloading must be kept free of oil, dirt, and grit.

§174.81 Segregation of hazardous materials.

(a) **This section applies to materials which meet** one or more of the hazard classes defined in this subchapter and are in packages which are required to be labeled or placarded under the provisions of part 172 of this subchapter.

(b) **When a rail car is to be transported by vessel,** other than a ferry vessel, hazardous materials on or within that rail car must be stowed and segregated in accordance with §176.83(b) of this subchapter.

(c) **In addition to the provisions of paragraph (d)** of this section, cyanides or cyanide mixtures may not be loaded or stored with acids.

(d) **Hazardous materials may not be loaded,** transported, or stored together, except as provided in this section, and in accordance with the following table:

Segregation Table for Hazardous Materials

Class or Division		Notes	1.1, 1.2	1.3	1.4	1.5	1.6	2.1	2.2	2.3 gas Zone A	2.3 gas Zone B	3	4.1	4.2	4.3	5.1	5.2	6.1 liquids PG I Zone A	7	8 liquids only
Explosives	1.1 and 1.2	A	*	*	*	*	*	X	X	X	X	X	X	X	X	X	X	X	X	X
Explosives	1.3		*	*	*	*	*	X		X	X	X		X	X	X	X	X		X
Explosives	1.4		*	*	*	*	*	O		O	O	O		O				O		O
Very insensitive explosives	1.5	A	*	*	*	*	*	X	X	X	X	X	X	X	X	X	X	X	X	X
Extremely insensitive explosives	1.6		*	*	*	*	*													
Flammable gases	2.1		X	X	O	X				X	O							O	O	
Non-toxic, non-flammable gases	2.2		X			X														
Poisonous gas Zone A	2.3		X	X	O	X		X				X	X	X	X	X	X			X
Poisonous gas Zone B	2.3		X	X	O	X		O				O	O	O	O	O	O			O
Flammable liquids	3		X	X	O	X				X	O					O		X		
Flammable solids	4.1		X			X				X	O							X		O
Spontaneously combustible materials	4.2		X	X	O	X				X	O							X		X
Dangerous when wet materials	4.3		X	X		X				X	O							X		O
Oxidizers	5.1	A	X	X		X				X	O	O						X		O
Organic peroxides	5.2		X	X		X				X	O							X		O
Poisonous liquids PG I Zone A	6.1		X	X	O	X		O				X	X	X	X	X	X			X
Radioactive materials	7		X			X		O												
Corrosive liquids	8		X	X	O	X				X	O		O	X	O	O	O	X		

174

Carriage by Rail

(e) Instructions for using the segregation table for hazardous materials in paragraph (d) of this section are as follows:

(1) *The absence* of any hazard class or division, or a blank space in the table indicates that no restrictions apply.

(2) *The letter "X"* in the table indicates that these materials may not be loaded, transported, or stored together in the same rail car or storage facility during the course of transportation.

(3) *The letter "O"* in the table indicates that these materials may not be loaded, transported, or stored together in the same rail car or storage facility during the course of transportation unless separated in a manner that, in the event of leakage from packages under conditions normally incident to transportation, commingling of hazardous materials would not occur. Notwithstanding the methods of separation employed, Class 8 (corrosive) liquids may not be loaded above or adjacent to Class 4 (flammable) or Class 5 (oxidizing) materials; except that shippers may load carload shipments of such materials together when it is known that the mixture of contents would not cause a fire or a dangerous evolution of heat or gas.

(4) *The "*" in the table* indicates that segregation among different Class 1 (explosive) materials is governed by the compatibility table in paragraph (f) of this section.

(5) *The note "A"* in the second column of the table means that, notwithstanding the requirements of the letter "X", ammonium nitrate fertilizer may be loaded or stored with Division 1.1 (explosive) or Division 1.5 materials.

(6) *When the §172.101 table* or §172.402 of this subchapter requires a package to bear a subsidiary hazard label, segregation appropriate to the subsidiary hazard must be applied when that segregation is more restrictive than that required by the primary hazard. However, hazardous materials of the same class may be loaded and transported together without regard to segregation required by any secondary hazard if the materials are not capable of reacting dangerously with each other and causing combustion or dangerous evolution of heat, evolution of flammable, poisonous, or asphyxiant gases, or formation of corrosive or unstable materials.

(f) Class 1 (explosive) materials may not be loaded, transported, or stored together, except as provided in this section, and in accordance with the following table:

Compatibility Table For Class 1 (Explosive) Materials

Compatibility group	A	B	C	D	E	F	G	H	J	K	L	N	S
A		X	X	X	X	X	X	X	X	X	X	X	X
B	X		X	4	X	X	X	X	X	X	X	X	4/5
C	X	X		2	2	X	6	X	X	X	X	3	4/5
D	X	4	2		2	X	6	X	X	X	X	3	4/5
E	X	X	2	2		X	6	X	X	X	X	3	4/5
F	X	X	X	X	X		X	X	X	X	X	X	4/5
G	X	X	6	6	6	X		X	X	X	X	X	4/5
H	X	X	X	X	X	X	X		X	X	X	X	4/5
J	X	X	X	X	X	X	X	X		X	X	X	4/5
K	X	X	X	X	X	X	X	X	X		X	X	4/5
L	X	X	X	X	X	X	X	X	X	X	1	X	X
N	X	X	3	3	3	X	X	X	X	X	X		4/5
S	X	4/5	4/5	4/5	4/5	4/5	4/5	4/5	4/5	4/5	X	4/5	

(g) Instructions for using the compatibility table for Class 1 (explosive) materials in paragraph (f) of this section are as follows:

(1) *A blank space in the table indicates that no restrictions apply.*

(2) *The letter "X"* in the table indicates that explosives of different compatibility groups may not be carried on the same rail car, unless packed in separate freight containers (e.g., two or more freight containers mounted upon the same rail car).

(3) *The numbers in the table mean the following:*

(i) *"1" means* explosives from compatibility group L may only be carried on the same rail car with an identical explosive.

(ii) *"2" means* any combination of explosives from compatibility group C, D, or E is assigned to compatibility group E.

(iii) *"3" means* any combination of explosives from compatibility group C, D, or E with those in compatibility group N is assigned to compatibility group D.

(iv) *"4" means* detonators and detonating primers, Division 1.4S (explosives), may not be loaded in the same car with Division 1.1 and 1.2 (explosive) materials.

(v) *"5" means* Division 1.4S fireworks may not be loaded in the same car with Division 1.1 or 1.2 (explosive) materials.

(vi) *"6" means* explosive articles in compatibility group G, other than fireworks and those requiring special stowage, may be loaded and transported with articles of compatibility groups C, D and E, provided no explosive substances are carried in the same rail car.

(h) Except as provided in paragraph (i) of this section, explosives of the same compatibility group but of different divisions may be transported together provided that the whole shipment is transported as though its entire contents were of the lower numerical division (i.e., Division 1.1 being lower than Division 1.2). For example, a mixed shipment of Division 1.2 (explosive) materials and Division 1.4 (explosive) materials, compatibility group D, must be transported as Division 1.2 (explosive) materials.

(i) When Division 1.5 materials, compatibility group D are transported in the same freight container as Division 1.2 (explosive) materials, compatibility group D, the shipment must be transported as Division 1.1 (explosive) materials, compatibility group D.

Subpart D - Handling of Placarded Rail Cars, Transport Vehicles and Freight Containers

§174.82 General requirements for the handling of placarded rail cars, transport vehicles, freight containers, and bulk packages.

(a) Unless otherwise specified, this subpart does not apply to the handling of rail cars, transport vehicles, freight containers, or bulk packagings, which contain Division 1.6, combustible liquids, Division 6.1 PG III materials, Class 9 materials, or ORM-D materials.

(b) A placarded rail car, transport vehicle, freight container, or bulk package may not be transported in a passenger train.

§174.83 Switching placarded rail cars, transport vehicles, freight containers, and bulk packagings.

(a) In switching operations where the use of hand brakes is necessary —

(1) *It must be determined by trial* whether a loaded, placarded car, or a car occupied by a rider in a draft containing a placarded car, has its hand brakes in proper working condition before it is cut off;

(2) *A loaded, placarded tank car* or a draft which includes a loaded placarded tank car may not be cut off until the preceding rail car clears the ladder track; and

(3) *A loaded, placarded tank car* or a draft which includes a loaded placarded tank car must clear the ladder track before another rail car is allowed to follow.

(b) Any loaded rail car placarded for a Division 1.1 or Division 1.2 explosive, a Division 2.3 Hazard Zone A gas or a Division 6.1 PG I Hazard Zone A material, or a Class DOT 113 tank car displaying a Division 2.1 (flammable gas) placard, including a Class DOT 113 tank car containing only a residue of a Division 2.1 material, may not be:

(1) *Cut off while in motion;*

(2) *Coupled into* with more force than is necessary to complete the coupling; or

(3) *Struck by any car moving under its own momentum.*

(c) A placarded flatcar, or a flatcar carrying a placarded transport vehicle, freight container, or bulk packaging under this subchapter may not be cut off while in motion.

(d) No rail car moving under its own momentum may be permitted to strike any placarded flatcar or any flatcar carrying a placarded transport vehicle, freight container, or bulk packaging.

(e) No placarded flatcar or any flatcar carrying a placarded transport vehicle, freight container, or bulk packaging may be coupled into with more force than is necessary to complete the coupling.

(f) When transporting a rail car, transport vehicle, or freight container placarded for Division 1.1 or 1.2 (explosive) materials in a terminal, yard, or on a side track or siding, the placarded rail car must be separated from the engine by at least one non-placarded rail car and must be placed in a location so that it will be safe from danger of fire. A rail car, transport vehicle, or freight container placarded for Division 1.1 or 1.2 (explosive) materials may not be placed under a bridge or overhead crossing, or in or alongside a passenger shed or station, except during transfer operations.

§174.84 Position in train of loaded placarded rail cars, transport vehicles, freight containers or bulk packagings when accompanied by guards or technical escorts.

A rail car placarded in Division 1.1 or 1.2 (explosive); Division 2.3 (Hazard Zone A; poisonous gas); or Division 6.1 (PG I, Hazard Zone A; poisonous liquid) in a moving or standing train must be next to and ahead of any car occupied by the guards or technical escorts accompanying the placarded rail car. However, if a rail car occupied by the guards or technical escorts has temperature control equipment in operation, it must be the fourth car behind any car requiring Division 1.1 or 1.2 (explosive) placards.

§174.85 Position in train of placarded cars, transport vehicles, freight containers, and bulk packagings.

(a) **Except as provided in paragraphs (b) and (c)** of this section, the position in a train of each loaded placarded car, transport vehicle, freight container, and bulk packaging must conform to the provisions of this section.

(b) **A car placarded "RADIOACTIVE" must comply** with train positioning requirements of paragraph (d) of this section and must be separated from a locomotive, occupied caboose, or carload of undeveloped film by at least one non-placarded car.

(c) **A tank car containing the residue** of a hazardous material must be separated from a locomotive or occupied caboose by at least one rail car other than a placarded tank car.

(d) **Position of rail cars in a train.** In the following table:

Position in Train of Placarded Cars Transporting Hazardous Materials

RESTRICTIONS	Placard Group 1	Placard Group 2		Placard Group 3		Placard Group 4
	Rail Car	Tank Car	Rail Car	Tank Car	Rail Car	Rail Car
1. When train length permits, placarded car may not be nearer than the sixth car from the engine or occupied caboose	X	X		X		
2. When train length does not permit, placarded car must be placed near the middle of the train, but not nearer than the second car from an engine or occupied caboose	X	X		X		
3. A placarded car may not be placed next to an open-top car when any of the lading in the open top car protrudes beyond the car ends, or if the lading shifted, would protrude beyond the car ends	X	X		X		
4. A placarded car may not be placed next to a loaded flat car, except closed TOFC/COFC equipment, auto carriers, and other specially equipped cars with tie-down devices for securing vehicles. Permanent bulk head flat cars are considered the same as open-top cars	X	X		X		
5. A placarded car may not be placed next to any transport vehicle or freight container having an internal combustion engine or an open-flame device in operation	X	X		X		
6. Placarded cars may not be placed next to each other based on the following:						
Placard Group 1		X	X	X	X	X
Placard Group 2	X			X	X	X
Placard Group 3	X	X	X			X
Placard Group 4	X	X	X	X	X	

PLACARD GROUP:

Group 1 — Divisions 1.1 and 1.2 (explosive) materials.

Group 2 — Divisions 1.3, 1.4, 1.5 (explosive), Class 2 (compressed gas; other than Div 2.3, PG I, Zone A), Class 3 (flammable liquid), Class 4 (flammable solid), Class 5 (oxidizing), Class 6 (poisonous liquid; other than Div 6.1, PG I, Zone A), and Class 8 (corrosive) materials.

Group 3 — Divisions 2.3 (Zone A; poisonous gas) and 6.1 (PG I, Zone A; poisonous liquid) materials.

Group 4 — Class 7 (radioactive) materials.

(1) *Where an "X"* appears at the intersection of a Placard Group column and a Restriction row, the corresponding restriction applies.

(2) *"Rail Car" means a car other than a tank car.*

(3) *For purposes of this subpart,* each unit of an articulated intermodal rail car shall be considered as one car.

§174.86 Maximum allowable operating speed.

For molten metals and molten glass shipped in packagings other than those prescribed in §173.247 of this subchapter, the maximum allowable operating speed may not exceed 15 mph for shipments by rail.

Subpart E - Class I (Explosive) Materials

§174.101 Loading Class 1 (explosive) materials.

(a) **Boxes containing Division 1.1 or 1.2 (explosive) materials** must be loaded so that the ends of wooden boxes will not bear against sides of any fiberboard boxes and so that the ends of any box will not cause a pressure point on a small area of another box.

(b) **Explosive bombs, unfuzed projectiles,** rocket ammunition and rocket motors, Division 1.1, 1.2, or 1.3 (explosive) materials, which are not packed in wooden boxes, or large metal packages of incendiary bombs, each weighing 226 kg (500 pounds) or more, may be loaded in stock cars or in flat bottom gondola cars only if they are adequately braced. Boxed bombs, rocket ammunition and rocket motors, Division 1.1, 1.2, or 1.3 (explosive) materials, which due to their size cannot be loaded in closed cars, may be loaded in open-top cars or on flatcars, provided they are protected from the weather and accidental ignition.

(c) **Boxes of Division 1.1 or 1.2 (explosive) materials** packed in long cartridges, bags, or sift-proof liners, and containing no liquid explosive ingredient, may be loaded on their sides or ends.

(d) **Division 1.1 or 1.2 (explosive) materials** may not be loaded higher than any permanent car lining unless additional lining is provided as high as the lading.

(e) **When the lading of a car includes** any Class 1 (explosive) materials, the weight of the lading must be distributed insofar as possible to equalize the weight on each side of the car and over the trucks.

(f) **Except when boxed, metal kegs containing** Class 1 (explosive) materials must be loaded on their sides with their ends toward the ends of the car. Packages of Class 1 (explosive) materials may not be placed in the space opposite the doors unless the doorways are boarded on the inside as high as the lading. This paragraph does not apply to palletized packages if they are braced so they cannot fall or slide into the doorways during transportation.

(g) **Wooden kegs, fiber kegs, barrels, and drums** must be loaded on their sides or ends, to best suit the conditions.

(h) **Packages containing any Division 1. 1 or 1.2** (explosive) materials for (see §174.104), detonators, detonator assemblies, or boosters with detonators must be securely blocked and braced to prevent the packages from changing position, falling to the floor, or sliding into each other, under conditions normally incident to transportation. Class 1 (explosive) materials must be loaded so as to avoid transfer at stations. For recommended methods of blocking and bracing, see Bureau of Explosives Pamphlets No. 6 and 6A. Heavy packages or containers must be trucked, rolled, or moved by skids, fork trucks, or other handling devices and may not be dropped from trucks, platforms, or cars. Planks for rolling trucks from platforms to cars must have beveled ends. Loading platforms and the shoes of each workman must be free from grit. All possible precautions must be taken against fire. Class 1 (explosive) materials must be kept in a safe place and inaccessible to unauthorized persons while being held by a carrier for loading or delivery.

(i) **To prevent delays of local freight trains,** when there are shipments of Class 1 (explosive) materials for different destinations loaded in a "peddler car" or "way car" the shipment for each destination must be stayed separately.

(j) **Forwarding and transfer stations for Class 1** (explosive) materials must be provided with the necessary materials for staying.

(k) **Shippers must furnish the material** for staying packages of Class 1 (explosive) materials loaded by them.

(l) **Division 1.1 or 1.2 (explosive) materials** may not be loaded, transported, or stored in a rail car equipped with any type of lighted heater or open-flame device, or electric devices having exposed heating coils, or in a rail car equipped with any apparatus or mechanism utilizing an internal combustion engine in its operation.

(m) **[Reserved]**

(n) **A container car or freight container** on a flatcar or a gondola car other than a drop-bottom car, when properly loaded, blocked, and braced to prevent change of position under conditions normally incident to transportation, may be used to transport any Division 1.1 or 1.2 (explosive) material except black powder packed in metal containers. A freight container must be designed, constructed, and maintained so as to be weather tight and capable of preventing the entrance of sparks. In addition:

(1) *A freight container* must be of such design and so braced as to show no evidence of failure of the container or the bracing when

subjected to impact from each end of at least 13 km (8.1 miles) per hour. Its efficiency shall be determined by actual test, using dummy loads equal in weight and general character to material to be shipped.

(2) *A container car or car* which is loaded with freight containers must be placarded with the Class 1 (explosive) materials placards as required by subpart F of part 172 of this subchapter and with properly executed car certificates as required by §174.104.

(3) *Lading must be* so loaded, blocked, and braced within the freight container that it will not change position under impact from each end of at least 13 km (8.1 miles) per hour.

(o) **Division 1.1, 1.2, or 1.3 (explosive) materials** may be loaded and transported in a tight closed truck body or trailer on a flatcar. Wooden boxed bombs, rocket ammunition, and rocket motors, Division 1.1, 1.2, or 1.3 (explosive) materials, which due to their size cannot be loaded in tight, closed truck bodies or trailers, may be loaded in or on open-top truck bodies or trailers. However, they must be protected against accidental ignition. In addition:

(1) *Each truck body or trailer* must meet the requirements of part 177 of this subchapter, applicable to shipments of Class 1 (explosive) materials by motor vehicle.

(2) *Each truck body or trailer* must be so secured on the rail car so that it will not permanently change position or show evidence of failure or impending failure of the method of securing the truck body or trailer under impact from each end of at least 13 km (8.1 miles) per hour. Its efficiency shall be determined by actual test, using dummy loads equal in weight and general character to the material to be shipped. For recommended methods of blocking and bracing, see Bureau of Explosives Pamphlet 6C.

(3) *Lading must be* so loaded, blocked, and braced within or on the truck body or trailer that it will not change position under impact from each end of at least 13 km (8.1 miles) per hour. For recommended methods of blocking and bracing see Bureau of Explosives Pamphlet 6C.

(4) *Each rail car* containing Class 1 (explosive) materials and each rail car loaded with truck bodies, trailers or containers containing Class 1 (explosive) materials must be placarded with Class 1 (explosive) materials placards as required by subpart F of part 172 of this subchapter and with properly executed car certificates as required by §174.104.

(5) *Each fuel tank* of a heater or refrigerating machinery on the truck bodies or trailers must be drained and all automatic heating or refrigerating machinery must be made inoperative by disconnection of the automatic controls or the source of power for their operations.

§174.102 Forbidden mixed loading and storage.

(a) **Division 1.1 or 1.2 (explosive) materials** and initiating or priming explosives may not be transported together in the same rail car. Additionally, they may not be transported or loaded in the same rail car or stored on carrier property with charged electric storage batteries or with any hazardous material for which a NONFLAMMABLE GAS, FLAMMABLE GAS, FLAMMABLE LIQUID, FLAMMABLE SOLID, OXIDIZER, ORGANIC PEROXIDE, RADIOACTIVE or CORROSIVE label is required.

(b) **Class 1 (explosive) materials may not be loaded** together or with other hazardous materials, except as provided in §174.81. See §174.104 for loading shipments of Class 1 (explosive) materials or any other material in a placarded and certified car containing a shipment of Division 1.1 or 1.2 (explosive) materials.

§174.103 Disposition of damaged or astray shipments.

(a) **Packages of Class 1 (explosive) materials** found damaged or broken in transit may be repaired when practicable and not dangerous. A broken box of Division 1.1 or 1.2 (explosive) materials that cannot be repaired must be reinforced by stout wrapping paper and twine, placed in another strong box and surrounded by dry, fine sawdust or dry and clean cotton waste or elastic wads made from dry newspapers. A ruptured can or keg must be sealed and enclosed in a strong cloth bag of good quality and boxed. Damaged packages thus protected and properly marked may be forwarded. The box and waybill must be marked to indicate that it has been repacked.

(b) **Care must be exercised in repacking** damaged containers so that no spark is produced by contact of metal or other hard surfaces which could ignite loose particles of explosive compositions that may be strewn on car floors or freight. In addition, the car floors must be thoroughly swept, and washed with a plentiful supply of water. Iron-wheel trucks, metal hammers, or other metal tools that may produce sparks may not be used. Metal tools must be limited to those made of brass, bronze, or copper.

(c) **Each package of Class 1 (explosive) materials** showing evidence of leakage of liquid ingredients must:

(1) *Be refused if leakage is discovered before acceptance;*

(2) *Be disposed of* to a person who is competent and willing to remove them from the carrier's property, if the leakage is discovered while the shipment is in transit; or

(3) *Be removed immediately* by consignee, if the leakage is discovered at the shipment's destination.

(d) **When the disposition required by paragraph (c)** of this section cannot be made, the leaking package must be packed in other boxes large enough to permit enclosure and the leaking boxes must be surrounded by at least 5 cm (2 inches) of dry, fine sawdust or dry and clean cotton waste, and be stored in a station magazine or other safe place until the arrival of an inspector of the Bureau of Explosives, or other authorized person, to superintend the destruction or disposition of the condemned material.

(e) **If careful inspection shows that an astray shipment** of Class 1 (explosive) materials is in proper condition for safe transportation, it must be forwarded immediately to its destination if known, or returned to the shipper by the most practicable route.

(f) **When a package in an astray shipment** is not in proper condition for safe transportation (see paragraphs (a), (c), and (d) of this section), or when the name and address of the consignee and the shipper are unknown, disposition must be made as prescribed by paragraphs (c) and (d) of this section.

§174.104 Division 1.1 or 1.2 (explosive) materials; car selection, preparation, inspection, and certification.

(a) **Except as provided in §174.101 (b), (n), and (o),** Division 1.1 or 1.2 (explosive) materials being transported by rail may be transported only in a certified and properly placarded closed car of not less than 36,300 kg (80,028 pounds) capacity, with steel underframes and friction draft gear or cushioned underframe, except that on a narrow-gauge railroad they may be transported in a car of less capacity as long as the car of greatest capacity and strength available is used.

(b) **Each rail car used for transporting Division 1.1 or 1.2** (explosive) materials must meet the following requirements as applicable:

(1) *The car* must be equipped with air brakes, hand brakes, and roller bearings which are in condition for service.

(2) *The car* may not have any holes or cracks in the roof, sides, ends, or doors through which sparks may enter, or unprotected decayed spots which may hold sparks and start a fire.

(3) *The roof* of the car must be carefully inspected from the outside for decayed spots, especially under or near the running board, and such spots must be covered or repaired to prevent their holding fire from sparks. A car with a roof generally decayed, even if tight, may not be used.

(4) *The doors* must close tightly so that sparks cannot get in at the joints, and, if necessary to achieve this degree of tightness, the doors must be stripped. The stripping should be placed on the inside and fastened to the door frames where it will form a shoulder against which the closed doors are pressed by means of wedges or cleats in door shoes or keepers. The openings under the doors should be similarly closed. The hasp fastenings must be examined with the doors closed and fastened, and the doors must be cleated when necessary to prevent them from shifting. When the car is opened for any reason, the wedges or cleats must be replaced before car containing Class 1 (explosive) materials is permitted to proceed.

(5) *The roller bearings* and the trucks must be carefully examined and put in such condition as to reduce to a minimum the danger of hotboxes or other failure necessitating the setting out of the car before reaching its destination.

(6) *The car* must be carefully swept out before it is loaded. For less-than-carload shipments the space in which the packages are to be loaded must be carefully swept. If evidence of a potential hazardous residue is apparent after the floor has been swept, the carrier must either decontaminate the car or provide a suitable substitute car.

(7) *Any holes* in the floor or lining must be repaired and special care taken that there are no projecting nails or bolts or exposed pieces of metal which may work loose or produce holes in packages of Class 1 (explosive) materials during transit. Protruding nails in the floor or lining which have worked loose must be drawn, and if necessary for the purpose of fastening the floor or lining, new nails must be driven through other parts thereof.

(8) *Metal floor plates* must be completely covered with wood, plywood, or fiber or composition sheets of adequate thickness and strength to prevent contact of the floor plates with the packages

of Class 1 (explosive) materials under conditions incident to transportation, except that the covering of metal floor plates is not necessary for carload shipments loaded by the Department of Defense provided the Class 1 (explosive) materials are of such nature that they are not liable to leakage of dust, powder, or vapor which might become the cause of an explosion.

(9) *If the car* is equipped with automobile loading devices, it may not be used unless the loading device is securely attached to the roof of the car with fastenings supplementing those already provided and so fixed that it cannot fall.

(10) *The car* must be equipped with high-friction composition brake shoes (except metal deck flat cars used for COFC/TOFC service may be equipped with high phosphorus cast iron brake-shoes) and brake rigging designed for this type of brake shoe. Each brake shoe on the car must be at least 1 cm (0.4 inch) thick, and in safe and suitable condition for service.

(11) *The car* must have either a metal subfloor with no combustible material exposed beneath the car, or metal spark shields extending from center sill to side sills and from end sills to at least 30 cm (12 inches) beyond the extreme treads of the inside wheels of each truck, which are tightly fitted against the subfloor so that there is no vacant space or combustible material exposed. The metal subfloor or spark shields may not have an accumulation of oil, grease, or other debris which could support combustion.

(c) **Before Division 1.1 or 1.2 (explosive) materials** may be loaded into a rail car, the car must have been inspected and certified to be in compliance with the requirements of paragraph (b) of this section by a qualified person designated under §215.11 of this title. The certification shall be made in Car Certificate No. 1 on the form prescribed in paragraph (f) of this section.

(d) **If the carrier furnishes the car to a shipper** for loading Division 1.1 or 1.2 (explosive) materials, the shipper or his authorized employee shall, before commencing the loading of the car, inspect the interior thereof, and after loading certify to the proper condition of the car and the loading. This certification shall be made on the first signature line in Car Certificate No. 2 on the form prescribed in paragraph (f) of this section. In addition, the finished load must be inspected and certified to be in compliance with the requirements of this part by a qualified person designated under §215.11 of this title before the car goes forward. This certification shall be made on the second signature line in Car Certificate No. 2 on the form prescribed in paragraph (f) of this section. If the loading is performed by the carrier, Car Certificate No. 2 may only be signed by a qualified person designated under §215.11 of this title.

(e) **If a trailer or container containing** Division 1.1 or 1.2 (explosive) materials is loaded on a flatcar, the loading and securing of the load on the car must be supervised by a representative of the shipper or carrier. The certification shall be made in Car Certificate No. 3 on the form prescribed in paragraph (f) of this section.

(f) **Each car certificate for use in connection with** the inspection of rail cars for the carriage of Division 1.1 or 1.2 (explosive) materials shall be printed on strong tag board measuring 18 by 18 cm (7.1 by 7.1 inches) or 15 by 20 cm (5.9 by 7.9 inches). It must be duly executed in triplicate by the carrier, and by the shipper if he loads the shipments. The original must be filed by the carrier at the forwarding station in a separate file and the other two must be attached to the car, one to each outer side on a fixed placard board or as otherwise provided.

________________________________Railroad

CAR CERTIFICATE

No. 1 ______________ Station__________________________
19__.

I hereby certify that I have this day personally examined Car Number ______ and that the car is in condition for service and complies with the FRA Freight Car Safety Standards (49 CFR part 215) and with the requirements for freight cars used to transport explosives prescribed by the DOT Hazardous Materials Regulation (49 CFR part 174).

Qualified Person Designated Under 49 CFR 215.11

No. 2 ______________ Station__________________________
19__.

I have this day personally examined the above car and hereby certify that the explosives in or on this car, or in or on vehicles or in containers have been loaded and braced; that placards have been applied, according to the regulations prescribed by the Department of Transportation; and that the doors of cars so equipped fit or have been stripped so that sparks cannot enter.

Shipper or his authorized agent

Qualified Person Designated Under 49 CFR 215.11

No. 3 ______________ Station__________________________
19__.

I hereby certify that I have this day personally supervised the loading of the vehicles or containers on and their securement to the above car.

Shipper or railway employee inspecting loading and securement

NOTE 1: A shipper must decline to use a car not in proper condition.
NOTE 2: All certificates, where applicable, must be signed.
NOTE 3: Car certificates remaining on hand as of the effective date of these regulations may be used until stocks are exhausted but not after July 1, 1977.

§174.105 Routing shipments, Division 1.1 or 1.2 (explosive) materials.

Before a shipment of Division 1.1 or 1.2 (explosive) materials destined to a point beyond the lines of the initial carrier is accepted from the shipper, the initial carrier shall ascertain that the shipment can go forward by the route designated. To avoid delays en route, the initial carrier must be in possession of full rate information before forwarding the shipment.

§174.106 "Order-Notify" or "C.O.D." shipments, Division 1.1 or 1.2 (explosive) materials.

(a) **A carrier may not accept for transportation** Division 1.1 or 1.2 (explosive) materials, detonators, or detonating primers in any quantity when consigned to "order-notify" or "C.O.D.", except on a through bill of lading to a place outside the United States.

(b) **A carrier may not accept for transportation** Division 1.1 or 1.2 (explosive) materials, detonators, or detonating primers which the shipper consigns to himself unless the shipper has a resident representative to receive them at the delivery point.

(c) **A carrier may not accept Division 1.1 or 1.2** (explosive) materials for transportation subject to "stop-off privileges en route for partial loading or unloading."

§174.110 Car magazine.

When specially authorized by the carrier, Division 1.1 or 1.2 (explosive) materials in quantity not exceeding 68 kg (150 pounds) may be carried in construction or repair cars if the packages of Class 1 (explosive) materials are placed in a "magazine" box made of sound lumber not less than 2.5 cm (0.98 inch) thick, covered on the exterior with metal, and provided with strong handles. The box must be plainly stenciled on the top, sides, and ends, in letters not less than 5 cm (2 inches) high, "EXPLOSIVES — DANGEROUS — HANDLE CAREFULLY". The box must be provided with strong hinges and with a lock for keeping it securely closed. Vacant space in the box must be filled with a cushioning material such as sawdust or excelsior, and the box must be properly stayed to prevent movement within the car. The car must be placarded with EXPLOSIVES 1.1 or 1.2 (EXPLOSIVES A) placards when the magazine contains Division 1.1 or 1.2 (explosive) materials.

§174.112 Loading Division 1.3 materials and Division 1.2 (explosive) materials (Also see §174.101).

(a) **Division 1.3 materials and Division 1.2** (explosive) materials may not be loaded, transported or stored in a rail car equipped with any type of lighted heater or open-flame device, or in a rail car equipped with any apparatus or mechanism utilizing an internal combustion engine in its operation.

(b) **Except as provided in §174.101(b), (n), or (o)** Division 1.3 materials and Division 1.2 (explosive) materials must be transported in a closed car or container car which is in good condition, and into which sparks cannot enter. The car does not require the car certificates prescribed in §174.104(c) through (f). If the doors are not tight, they must be stripped to prevent the entrance of sparks. Wood floored cars must be equipped with spark shields (see §174.104). Packages of Division 1.3 materials and Division 1.2 (explosive) materials must be blocked and braced to prevent their movement and possible damage due to movement of other freight during transportation. For recommended methods of blocking and bracing see Bureau of Explosives Pamphlet No. 6.

(c) **Division 1.3 materials and Division 1.2** (explosive) materials may not be transported in a truck body, trailer, or container on a flatcar unless:

(1) *The truck body, trailer, or container is closed and tight;*

(2) *All automatic* heating or refrigerating machinery with which the truck body, trailer, or container is equipped is inoperative; and

(3) *Packages of* Division 1.3 materials and Division 1.2 (explosive) materials are blocked and braced within the truck body, trailer, or container to prevent their movement and possible damage

due to movement of other freight during transportation (ends, sidewalls, or doors of the truck body, trailer, or container may not be relied on to prevent the shifting of heavy loads). For recommended methods of blocking and bracing see Bureau of Explosives Pamphlet No. 6C. See §174.101(o).

§174.114 Record to be made of change of seals on "Cars loaded with Division 1.1 or 1.2 (explosive) materials".

When a car seal is changed on a car requiring "EXPLOSIVES 1.1 or EXPLOSIVES 1.2 (EXPLOSIVES A) placards" while en route or before delivery to a consignee, a record of the change showing the following information must be made on or attached to the waybill or other form of memorandum which must accompany the car to its destination:

Railroad Place Date

Car Initials Car Number Number or description of seal broken

Number or description of seal used to reseal car_______________

Reasons for opening car_______________

Condition of load_______________

Name and occupation of person opening car_______________

§174.115 Loading Division 1.4 (explosive) materials.

(a) **Division 1.4 (explosive) materials may be loaded** into any closed car in good condition, or into any container car in good condition. Car certificates are not required. Packages of Division 1.4 (explosive) materials must be blocked and braced to prevent their movement and possible damage due to movement of other freight during transportation. For methods of recommended loading and bracing see Bureau of Explosives Pamphlet No. 6.

(b) **Division 1.4 (explosive) materials may not be transported** in a truck body, trailer, or container on a flatcar unless:

(1) *The truck body, trailer, or container is closed and tight;*

(2) *All automatic* heating or refrigerating machinery with which the truck body, trailer, or container is equipped is inoperative; and

(3) *Packages of Division 1.4* (explosive) materials are blocked and braced within the truck body, trailer, or container to prevent their movement and possible damage due to movement of other freight during transportation. Ends, side walls, or doors of the truck body, trailer, or container may not be relied on to prevent shifting of heavy loads. For recommended methods of blocking and bracing see Bureau of Explosives Pamphlet No. 6C.

Subpart F - Detailed Requirements for Class 2 (Gases) Materials

§174.200 Special handling requirements.

(a) **Division 2.1 (flammable gas) materials** may not be loaded, transported, or stored in a rail car equipped with any type of lighted heater or open-flame device, or in a rail car equipped with any apparatus or mechanism utilizing an internal combustion engine in its operation.

(b) **Division 2.1 (flammable gas) materials** may not be loaded in a truck body or trailer equipped with any type of lighted heater or any automatic heating or refrigerating apparatus when such truck bodies or trailers are loaded on flatcars except as provided in paragraph (c) of this section.

(c) **Heating or refrigeration apparatus may be operated** on a motor vehicle loaded on a flatcar when the motor vehicle is loaded with Division 2.1 (flammable gas) materials only if:

(1) *The lading space* is not equipped with any electrical apparatus that is not non-sparking or explosion-proof;

(2) *There is no combustion apparatus in the lading space;*

(3) *There is no connection* for the return of air from the lading space to any combustion apparatus; and

(4) *The heating system* conforms to §393.77 of this title and does not heat any part of the lading over 54 °C (129 °F).

§174.201 Class 2 (gases) material cylinders.

(a) **Except as provided in paragraphs (b) and (c)** of this section, cylinders containing Class 2 (gases) materials being transported in a rail car must be:

(1) *Securely lashed* in an upright position so as to prevent their overturning;

(2) *Loaded into racks securely attached to the car;*

(3) *Packed in boxes* or crates of such dimensions as to prevent their overturning; or

(4) *Loaded in a horizontal position.*

(b) **Specification DOT-4L (§178.57 of this subchapter)** cylinders being transported in a rail car must be loaded in an upright position and be securely braced.

(c) **Cylinders containing Class 2 (gases) materials** may be transported in stock cars, gondola cars and flat cars. However, they may not be transported in hopper bottom cars.

§174.204 Tank car delivery of gases, including cryogenic liquids.

(a) **A tank car containing Class 2 (gases) material** may not be unloaded unless it is consigned for delivery and unloaded on a private track (see §171.8 of this subchapter). However, if a private track is not available, it may be delivered and unloaded on carrier tracks subject to the following conditions:

(1) *A tank car* of DOT-106A or 110A type (§179.300 or §179.301 of this subchapter) may not be delivered and the loaded unit tanks may not be removed from the car frame on carrier tracks. However, a carrier may give permission for the unloading of these containers on carrier tracks only if a private siding is not available within a reasonable trucking distance of the final destination. In addition, before the car is accepted for transportation, the shipper must obtain from the delivering carrier and file with the originating carrier, written permission for the removal and the consignee must furnish an adequately strong mechanical hoist by which the tanks can be lifted from the car and deposited directly upon vehicles furnished by the consignee for immediate removal from carrier property.

(2) *The following tank cars* may not be delivered and unloaded on carrier tracks unless the lading is piped directly from the car to permanent storage tanks of sufficient capacity to receive the entire contents of the car; however, such cars may be stored on a private track (see §171.8 of this subchapter) or on carrier tracks designated by the carrier for such storage:

(i) *A tank car* containing Division 2.1 (flammable gas) material that is a cryogenic liquid; or

(ii) *A tank car,* except for a DOT-106A or 110A multi-unit tank car tank (§179.300 or §179.301 of this subchapter), containing anhydrous ammonia; hydrogen chloride, refrigerated liquid; hydrocarbon gas, liquefied; or liquefied petroleum gas; and having interior pipes for liquid and gas discharge valves equipped with check valves.

(b) **[Reserved]**

§174.290 Materials extremely poisonous by inhalation shipped by, for, or to the Department of Defense.

(a) **General.** The provisions of this section apply only to materials extremely poisonous by inhalation which are Division 2.3 materials in Hazard Zone A and Division 6.1 materials in Hazard Zone A, as defined in §173.133(a)(2) of this subchapter. Such materials when shipped by, for, or to the Department of Defense may be transported by rail only if loaded and handled in accordance with the requirements of this section.

(b) **A Division 2.3 Hazard Zone A** or a Division 6.1 Hazard Zone A material extremely poisonous by inhalation may be transported in:

(1) *UN 1N1 or UN 1N2* metal drums or equivalent military specification metal drums, by boxcar, gondola car (flat bottom), or stock car in carload lots. See §§174.55 and 174.600 for blocking, bracing, and stowage requirements;

(2) *Tanks which are authorized* under this subchapter for a Hazard Zone A material extremely poisonous by inhalation, Specification DOT 106A (§§179.300 and 179.301 of this subchapter), mounted on or secured to a multi-unit car or gondola car (flat bottom) in carload lots only;

(3) *Bombs, by boxcar,* or gondola car (flat bottom) in carload lots only; or

(4) *Projectiles or ammunition* for cannon with gas filled projectiles, by boxcar in carload or less-than-carload lots.

(c) **Each shipment of one or more carloads** of a material extremely poisonous by inhalation, as described in paragraph (b) of this section, must be accompanied by a Department of Defense qualified escort supplied with equipment to handle leaks and other packaging failures which could result in escape of the material. The escort shall remain with the shipment during the entire time that it is in the custody of the carrier and in the event of leakage or escape of material, shall make repairs and perform decontamination as necessary.

(d) **When a material extremely poisonous by inhalation** is transported in a tank, the tank must be securely mounted on a rail car especially provided for it or on a gondola car prepared with substantial wooden frames and blocks.

(e) **Bombs, projectiles, and cannon ammunition** being transported by rail must be loaded, blocked and braced as shown in Bureau of Explosives Pamphlet No. 6A, or Department of Defense specifications. When a shipment is loaded in a gondola car it must be securely blocked and braced and not loaded higher than the sides of the car.

(f) **When a material extremely poisonous by inhalation** is transported in drums with filling holes in the heads, they must be loaded on their bottoms. They may be loaded in rows, lengthwise of the car and any space between the sides of the car and the nearest row of drums must be "filled in" with wooden boards or lumber nailed to sides of the car sufficient in length and width to contact both hoops of drums, or they may be loaded across the car in staggered stacks of which the number of drums in alternate stacks is reduced by one drum. All drums in stacks following the first stack loaded in the end of the car must be placed tightly into the angle of the space formed by the sidewalls of the drum in the preceding stack. Any space between the sides of the car and the drums in stacks having the greater number of drums must be filled in with wooden boards or lumber nailed to sides of the car sufficient in length and width to contact both hoops of the drums.

(g) **When a material extremely poisonous by inhalation** is transported in drums with filling holes in the sides, they must be loaded on their sides with the filling holes up. They must be loaded lengthwise of the car in rows and any space between the sides of the car and the nearest row of drums must be filled in with wooden boards or lumber nailed to sides of the car sufficient in length and width to contact both hoops of the drums.

(h) **When a material extremely poisonous by inhalation** is transported in drums in a boxcar, they must be loaded from ends of the car toward the space between the car doors, and there braced by center gates and wedges. See Sketch 1, Bureau of Explosives Pamphlet No. 6.

(i) **The doorways of a boxcar in which a material** poisonous by inhalation is being transported must be protected by one of the methods prescribed in Sketch 1, Bureau of Explosives Pamphlet No. 6A.

Subpart G - Detailed Requirements for Class 3 (Flammable Liquid) Materials

§174.300 Special handling requirements.

(a) **Class 3 (flammable liquid) materials may not be** loaded, transported, or stored in a rail car equipped with any type of lighted heater or open-flame device, or in a rail car equipped with any apparatus or mechanism utilizing an internal combustion engine in its operation.

(b) **A truck body or trailer which is loaded** with a Class 3 (flammable liquid) materials and equipped with a lighted heater or any automatic heating or refrigerating apparatus may not be loaded on a flatcar except as provided in paragraph (c) of this section.

(c) **Heating or refrigeration apparatus on a motor vehicle** loaded with Class 3 (flammable liquid) materials may be operated while the motor vehicle is loaded on a flatcar only if:

(1) *The lading space* is not equipped with any electrical apparatus that is not non-sparking or explosion-proof;

(2) *There is no combustion apparatus in the lading space;*

(3) *There is no connection* for the return of air from the lading space to any combustion apparatus; and

(4) *The heating system* conforms to §393.77 of this title and does not heat any part of the lading over 54 °C (129 °F).

(d) **Metal barrels or drums containing Class 3** (flammable liquid) materials may be transported in a steel gondola or flatcar or in a stock car. However, they may not be transported in a hopper bottom car.

§174.304 Class 3 (flammable liquid) materials in tank cars.

A tank car containing a Class 3 (flammable liquid) material, other than liquid road asphalt or tar, may not be transported by rail unless it is originally consigned or subsequently reconsigned to a party having a private track on which it is to be delivered and unloaded (see §171.8 of this subchapter) or to a party using railroad siding facilities which are equipped for piping the liquid from the tank car to permanent storage tanks of sufficient capacity to receive the entire contents of the car.

Subparts H-I [Reserved]

Subpart J - Detailed Requirements for Division 6.1 (Poisonous) Materials

§174.600 Special handling requirements for materials extremely poisonous by inhalation.

A tank car containing a material extremely poisonous by inhalation which is a Division 2.3 material in Hazard Zone A or a Division 6.1 material in Hazard Zone A, as defined in §173.133(a)(2) of this subchapter, may not be transported by rail unless it is originally consigned or subsequently reconsigned to a party having a private track on which it is to be delivered and unloaded (see §171.8 of this subchapter) or to a party using railroad siding facilities which are equipped for piping the liquid or gas from the tank car to permanent storage tanks or sufficient capacity to receive the entire contents of the car. See the requirements in §174.290 for materials extremely poisonous by inhalation which are shipped by, for, or to the Department of Defense.

§174.615 Cleaning cars.

(a) **[Reserved]**

(b) **After Division 6.1 (poisonous) materials** are unloaded from a rail car, that car must be thoroughly cleaned unless the car is used exclusively in the carriage of Division 6.1 (poisonous) materials.

§174.680 Division 6.1 (poisonous) materials with foodstuffs.

(a) **Except as provided in paragraph (b) of this section,** a carrier may not transport any package bearing a POISON or POISON INHALATION HAZARD label in the same car with any material marked as, or known to be, a foodstuff, feed or any other edible material intended for consumption by humans or animals.

(b) **A carrier must separate any package** bearing a POISON label displaying the text "PG III," or bearing a "PG III" mark adjacent to the POISON label, from materials marked as or known to be foodstuffs, feed or any other edible materials intended for consumption by humans or animals, as required in §174.81(e)(3) for classes identified with the letter "O" in the Segregation Table for Hazardous Materials.

Subpart K - Detailed Requirements for Class 7 (Radioactive) Materials

§174.700 Special handling requirements for Class 7 (radioactive) materials.

(a) **Each rail shipment of low specific activity materials** or surface contaminated objects as defined in §173.403 of this subchapter must be loaded so as to avoid spillage and scattering of loose material. Loading restrictions are prescribed in §173.427 of this subchapter.

(b) **The number of packages of Class 7 (radioactive)** materials that may be transported by rail car or stored at any single location is limited to a total transport index number (as defined in §173.403 of this subchapter) of not more than 50. This provision does not apply to exclusive use shipments as described in §§173.403, 173.427, 173.441, and 173.457 of this subchapter.

(c) **Each package of Class 7 (radioactive)** material bearing RADIOACTIVE YELLOW-II or RADIOACTIVE YELLOW-III labels may not be placed closer than 0.9 m (3 feet) to an area (or dividing partition between areas) which may be continuously occupied by any passenger, rail employee, or shipment of one or more animals, nor closer than 4.5 m (15 feet) to any package containing undeveloped film (if so marked). If more than one package of Class 7 (radioactive) materials is present, the distance must be computed from the table below on the basis of the total transport index number (determined by adding together the transport index numbers on the labels of the individual packages) of packages in the rail car or storage area:

Total transport index	Minimum separation distance to nearest undeveloped film		Minimum distance to area of persons or minimum distance from dividing partition of a combination car	
	Meters	Feet	Meters	Feet
None	0	0	0	0
0.1 to 10.0	4.5	15	0.9	3
10.1 to 20.0	6.7	22	1.2	4
20.1 to 30.0	7.7	29	1.5	5
30.1 to 40.0	10	33	1.8	6
40.1 to 50.0	10.9	36	2.1	7

NOTE: The distance in this table must be measured from the nearest point on the nearest packages of Class 7 (radioactive) materials.

(d) **Each fissile material, controlled shipment** must be transported in accordance with one of the methods prescribed in §173.457 of this subchapter. The transport controls must be adequate to assure that no fissile material, controlled shipment is transported in the same transport vehicle with any other fissile Class 7 (radioactive) material shipment. In loading and storage areas, each fissile material, controlled shipment must be segregated by a distance of at least 6 m (20 feet) from other packages required to bear one of the "radioactive" labels described in part 172 of this subchapter.

(e) **A person shall not remain unnecessarily** in, on or near a transport vehicle containing Class 7 (radioactive) materials.

(f) **In the case of packages shipped** under the exclusive use provisions of §173.441(b) of this subchapter for packages with external radiation levels in excess of 2 mSv per hour (200 mrem per hour) at the package surface —

(1) *The transport vehicle* must meet the requirements for a closed transport vehicle (§173.403 of this subchapter);

(2) *Each package* must be secured so that its position within the transport vehicle remains fixed under conditions normally incident to transportation; and

(3) *The radiation level* may not exceed 0.02 mSv per hour (2 mrem per hour) in any normally occupied position in the transport vehicle or adjacent rail car.

§174.715 Cleanliness of transport vehicles after use.

(a) **Each transport vehicle used for transporting** Class 7 (radioactive) materials as exclusive use, as defined in §173.403 of this subchapter, must be surveyed with appropriate radiation detection instruments after each use. A transport vehicle may not be returned to service until the radiation dose rate at any accessible surface is 0.005 mSv per hour (0.5 mrem per hour) or less, and there is no significant removable radioactive surface contamination, as defined in §173.443 of this subchapter.

(b) **This section does not apply to any transport vehicle** used solely for transporting Class 7 (radioactive) materials if a survey of the interior surface shows that the radiation dose rate does not exceed 0.1 mSv per hour (10 mrem per hour) at the interior surface or 0.02 mSv per hour (2 mrem per hour) at 1 m (3.3 feet) from any interior surface. The transport vehicle must be stenciled with the words "FOR RADIOACTIVE MATERIALS USE ONLY" in lettering at least 7.6 cm (3 inches) high in a conspicuous place on both sides of the exterior of the transport vehicle, and it must be kept closed at all times other than during loading and unloading.

§174.750 Incidents involving leakage.

(a) **In addition to the incident reporting requirements** of §§171.15 and 171.16 of this subchapter, the carrier shall also notify the offeror at the earliest practicable moment following any incident in which there has been breakage, spillage, or suspected radioactive contamination involving Class 7 (radioactive) materials shipments. Transport vehicles, buildings, areas, or equipment in which Class 7 (radioactive) materials have been spilled may not be again placed in service or routinely occupied until the radiation dose rate at every accessible surface is less than 0.005 mSv per hour (0.5 mrem per hour) and there is no significant removable radioactive surface contamination (see §173.443 of this subchapter).

(b) **The package or materials should be segregated** as far as practicable from personnel contact. If radiological advice or assistance is needed, the U.S. Department of Energy (DOE) should also be notified. In case of obvious leakage, or if it appears likely that the inside container may have been damaged, care should be taken to avoid inhalation, ingestion, or contact with the Class 7 (radioactive) material. Any loose Class 7 (radioactive) materials should be left in a segregated area and held pending disposal instructions, from qualified persons.

Part 175 - Carriage by Aircraft

Subpart A - General Information and Regulations

§175.1 Purpose and scope.

This part prescribes requirements, in addition to those contained in parts 171, 172 and 173 of this subchapter, applicable to aircraft operators transporting hazardous materials aboard (including attached to or suspended from) aircraft.

§175.3 Unacceptable hazardous materials shipments.

Hazardous materials that are not prepared for shipment in accordance with this subchapter may not be accepted for transportation or transported aboard an aircraft.

§175.5 Applicability.

(a) **This part applies to the acceptance** for transportation, loading and transportation of hazardous materials in any aircraft in the United States and in aircraft of United States registry anywhere in air commerce. This part does not apply to:

(1) *Aircraft owned and operated* by a government when not engaged in carrying persons or property for commercial purposes;

(2) *Aircraft which are not owned* by a government nor engaged in carrying persons or property for commercial purposes but which are under the exclusive direction and control of a government for a period of not less than 90 days as specified in a written contract or lease. An aircraft is under the exclusive direction and control of a government when the government exercises responsibility for:

(i) *Approving crew members* and determining that they are qualified to operate the aircraft;

(ii) *Determining the airworthiness* and directing maintenance of the aircraft; and

(iii) *Dispatching the aircraft,* including the times of departure, airports to be used, and type and amount of cargo to be carried;

(3) *Aircraft of United States registry* under lease to and operated by foreign nationals outside the United States if:

(i) *Hazardous materials* forbidden aboard aircraft by §172.101 of this subchapter are not carried on the aircraft; and

(ii) *Other hazardous materials* are carried in accordance with the regulations of the State (nation) of the aircraft operator.

§175.10 Exceptions.

(a) **This subchapter does not apply to:**

(1) *Aviation fuel and oil in tanks* that are in compliance with the installation provisions of 14 CFR, chapter 1.

(2) *Hazardous materials* required aboard an aircraft in accordance with the applicable airworthiness requirements and operating regulations. Unless otherwise approved by the Associate Administrator, items of replacement for such hazardous materials must be transported in accordance with this subchapter except that —

(i) *In place* of the required packagings, packagings specially designed for the transport of aircraft spares and supplies may be used, provided such packagings provide at least an equivalent level of protection to those that would be required by this subchapter;

(ii) *Aircraft batteries* are not subject to quantity limitations such as those provided in §172.101 or §175.75(a) of this subchapter; and,

(iii) *A tire assembly* with a serviceable tire is not subject to the provisions of this subchapter provided the tire is not inflated to a gauge pressure exceeding the maximum rated pressure for that tire.

(3) *Hazardous materials* loaded and carried in hoppers or tanks of aircraft certificated for use in aerial seeding, dusting, spraying, fertilizing, crop improvement, or pest control, to be dispensed during such an operation.

(4) *The following hazardous materials* when carried by a passenger or crew member for personal use in conformance with the following conditions:

(i) *Non-radioactive* medicinal and toilet articles (including aerosols) may be carried in checked or carry-on baggage;

(ii) *One self-defense spray* (see §171.8 of this subchapter), not exceeding 118 mL (4 fluid ounces) by volume, that incorporates a positive means to prevent accidental discharge may be carried in checked baggage only;

(iii) *Other aerosols* in Division 2.2 with no subsidiary risk may be carried in checked baggage only; and

(iv) *The aggregate quantity* of hazardous materials carried by the person may not exceed 2 kg (70 ounces) by mass or 2 L (68 fluid ounces) by volume and the capacity of each container may not exceed 0.5 kg (18 ounces) by mass or 470 mL (16 fluid ounces) by volume.

(5) *Small-arms ammunition* for personal use carried by a crewmember or passenger in his baggage (excluding carry-on baggage) if securely packed in fiber, wood or metal boxes, or other packagings specifically designed to carry small amounts of ammunition. This paragraph does not apply to persons traveling under the provisions of 14 CFR 1544.219.

(6) *[Reserved]*

(7) *Oxygen, or any hazardous material* used for the generation of oxygen, for medical use by a passenger, which is furnished by the aircraft operator in accordance with 14 CFR 121.574 or 135.91. For purposes of this paragraph, an aircraft operator that is not a certificate holder under 14 CFR part 121 or part 135, may apply this exception in conformance with 14 CFR 121.574 or 135.91 in the same manner as required for a certificate holder.

(8) *Human beings and animals* with an implanted medical device, such as a heart pacemaker, that contains Class 7 (radioactive) materials or with radio-pharmaceuticals that have been injected or ingested.

(9) *Smoke grenades,* flares, or similar devices carried only for use during a sport parachute jumping activity.

(10) *Safety matches* or a lighter intended for use by an individual when carried on one's person. However, lighters containing unabsorbed liquid fuel (other than liquefied gas), lighter fuel, and lighter refills are not permitted on one's person or in checked or carry-on baggage.

(11) *Smoke grenades,* flares, and pyrotechnic devices affixed to aircraft carrying no person other than a required flight crewmember during any flight conducted at and as a part of a scheduled air show or exhibition of aeronautical skill. The affixed installation accommodating the smoke grenades, flares, or pyrotechnic devices on the aircraft must be approved by the FAA for its intended use.

(12) *Hazardous materials* which are loaded and carried on or in cargo aircraft only, and which are to be dispensed or expended during flight for weather control, enviromental restoration or protection, forest preservation and protection, flood control, avalanche control purposes, or routine quality control testing of special fireworks manufactured for the Department of Defense, when the following requirements are met:

(i) *Operations may not be* conducted over densely populated areas, in a congested airway, or near any airport where air carrier passenger operations are conducted.

(ii) *Each operator* shall prepare and keep current a manual containing operational guidelines and handling procedures, for the use and guidance of flight, maintenance, and ground personnel concerned in the dispensing or expending of hazardous materials. The manual must be approved by the FAA Civil Aviation Security Office responsible for the operator's overall aviation security program or the FAA Civil Aviation Security Office in the region where the operator is located. The manual must be approved by the FAA Civil Aviation Security Field Office responsible for reviewing the operator's hazardous materials program or the FAA Civil Aviation Security Field Office in the region where the operator is located. Each operation must be conducted in accordance with the manual.

(iii) *No person* other than a required flight crewmember, FAA inspector, or person necessary for handling or dispensing the hazardous material may be carried on the aircraft.

(iv) *The operator* of the aircraft must have advance permission from the owner of any airport to be used for the dispensing or expending operation.

(v) *When dynamite* and blasting caps are carried for avalanche control flights, the explosives must be handled by, and at all times be under the control of, a qualified blaster. When required by State or local authority, the blaster must be licensed and the State or local authority must be identified in writing to the FAA Civil Aviation Security Field Office responsible for reviewing the operator's hazardous materials program or the FAA Civil Aviation Security Field Office in the region where the operator is located.

(vi) *When special fireworks* aerial illuminating flares, manufactured specifically for the DOD, are carried for in-flight routine quality control testing, the fireworks must be handled by, and at all times be under the control of, a qualified person who has been trained in accordance with a program approved by the local FAA Civil Aviation Security Field Office. The aircraft must be specially modified to conduct the testing operation and must be specifically approved for such operations by the local FAA Civil Aviation Security Field Office before the flight.

(13) *Carbon dioxide, solid (dry ice) when:*

(i) *In quantities* not exceeding 2.3 kg (5.07 pounds) per package packed as prescribed by §173.217 of this subchapter and used as a refrigerant for the contents of the package. The package must be marked with the name of the contents being cooled, the net weight of the dry ice or an indication that the net weight is 2.3 kg (5.07 pounds) or less, and also marked "Carbon Dioxide, Solid" or "Dry Ice";

(ii) *Intended for use* in food and beverage service aboard aircraft; or

(iii) *In quantities* not exceeding 2 kg (4.4 pounds) per passenger when used to pack perishables in carry-on baggage provided the package permits the release of carbon dioxide gas.

(14) *A transport incubator unit* necessary to protect life or an organ preservation unit necessary to protect human organs provided:

(i) *The compressed gas* used to operate the unit is in an authorized DOT specification cylinder and is marked, labeled, filled and maintained as prescribed by this subchapter;

(ii) *Each battery* used in the operation of the unit is of the non-spillable type;

(iii) *The unit* is constructed so that valves, fittings, and gauges are protected from damage;

(iv) *The pilot* in command is advised when the unit is on board, and when it is intended for use;

(v) *The unit is accompanied by a person qualified to operate it;*

(vi) *The unit* is secured in the aircraft in a manner so as not to restrict access to or use of any required emergency or regular exit or of the aisle in the passenger compartment; and,

(vii) *Smoking within 3 m (10 feet) of the unit is prohibited.*

(15) *Alcoholic beverages,* perfumes, colognes, and liquefied gas lighters that have been examined by the Bureau of Explosives (B of E) and approved by the Associate Administrator, carried aboard a passenger-carrying aircraft by the operator for use or sale on the aircraft.

(16) *Perfumes and colognes,* purchased through duty-free sales, carried by passengers or crew in carry-on baggage.

(17) *Alcoholic beverages containing:*

(i) *Not more than 24% alcohol by volume; or*

(ii) *More than 24%* and not more than 70% alcohol by volume when in retail packagings not exceeding 5 liters (1.3 gallons) carried by a crew member or passenger in checked or carry-on baggage, with a total net quantity per person of 5 liters (1.3 gallons) for such beverages.

(18) *Carbon dioxide gas cylinders* worn by passengers for the operation of mechanical limbs and spare cylinders of a similar size for the same purpose in sufficient quantities to ensure an adequate supply for the duration of the journey.

(19) *A wheelchair* or other battery-powered mobility aid equipped with a nonspillable battery, when carried as checked baggage, provided that —

(i) *The battery* meets the provisions of §173.159(d) for nonspillable batteries;

(ii) *Visual inspection* including, where necessary, removal of the battery, reveals no obvious defects (however, removal of the battery from the housing should be performed by qualified airline personnel only);

(iii) *The battery* is disconnected and terminals are insulated to prevent short circuits; and

(iv) *The battery* is securely attached to the wheelchair or mobility aid, is removed and placed in a strong, rigid packaging that is marked "NONSPILLABLE BATTERY" (unless fully enclosed in a rigid housing that is properly marked), or is handled in accordance with paragraph (a)(20)(iv) of this section.

(20) *A wheelchair* or other battery-powered mobility aid equipped with a spillable battery, when carried as checked baggage, provided that —

(i) *Visual inspection* including, where necessary, removal of the battery, reveals no obvious defects (however, removal of the battery from the housing should be performed by qualified airline personnel only);

(ii) *The battery is disconnected* and terminals are insulated to prevent short circuits;

(iii) *The pilot-in-command is advised,* either orally or in writing, prior to departure, as to the location of the battery aboard the aircraft; and

(iv) *The wheelchair* or mobility aid is loaded, stowed, secured and unloaded in an upright position or the battery is removed, the wheelchair or mobility aid is carried as checked baggage without further restriction, and the removed battery is carried in a strong, rigid packaging under the following conditions:

[A] *The packaging* must be leak-tight and impervious to battery fluid. An inner liner may be used to satisfy this requirement if there is absorbent material placed inside of the liner and the liner has a leakproof closure;

[B] *The battery* must be protected against short circuits, secured upright in the packaging, and be packaged with enough compatible absorbent material to completely absorb liquid contents in the event of rupture of the battery; and

[C] *The packaging* must be labeled with a CORROSIVE label, marked to indicate proper orientation, and marked with the words "Battery, wet, with wheelchair."

(21) *Hair curlers* containing hydrocarbon gas, no more than one per passenger or crew member, provided that the safety cover is securely fitted over the heating element. Gas refills for such curlers are not permitted in checked or carry-on baggage.

(22) *A mercurial barometer* or thermometer carried as carry-on-baggage only, by a representative of a government weather bureau or similar official agency, provided that individual advises the operator of the presence of the barometer or thermometer in his baggage. The barometer or thermometer must be packaged in a strong outer packaging having sealed inner liner or bag of strong, leak proof and puncture-resistant material impervious to mercury, which will prevent the escape of mercury from the package irrespective of its position. The pilot-in-command must be informed of the presence of any such barometer or thermometer by the operator of the aircraft.

(23) *With the approval* of the operator of the aircraft and as carry-on baggage, electrically powered heat-producing articles (e.g., battery-operated equipment, such as underwater torches and soldering equipment), which, if accidentally activated, will generate extreme heat and can cause fire. The heat-producing component, or the energy source, must be removed so as to prevent unintentional functioning during transport.

(24) *[Reserved]*

(25) *With approval* of the aircraft operator, one small carbon dioxide cylinder fitted into a self-inflating life-jacket, plus one spare cartridge, may be carried by a passenger or crew member in checked or carry-on baggage.

(26) *A small* medical or clinical mercury thermometer for personal use, when carried in protective cases by passengers or crew members.

(b) A cylinder containing medical-use compressed oxygen, owned or leased by an aircraft operator or offered for transportation by a passenger needing it for personal medical use at destination, may be carried in the cabin of a passenger-carrying aircraft in accordance with the following provisions:

(1) *No more than six cylinders* belonging to the aircraft operator and, in addition, no more than one cylinder per passenger needing the oxygen at destination, may be transported in the cabin of the aircraft under the provisions of this paragraph (b);

(2) *The rated capacity* of each cylinder may not exceed 850 L(30 cubic feet);

(3) *Each cylinder* and its overpack or outer packaging (see Special Provision A52 in §172.102 of this subchapter) must conform to the provisions of this subchapter;

(4) *The aircraft operator* shall securely stow the cylinder in its overpack or outer packaging in the cabin of the aircraft and shall notify the pilot-in-command as specified in §175.33 of this part; and

(5) *Shipments under this paragraph (b) are not subject to —*

(i) *Subpart C* and, for passengers only, subpart H of part 172 of this subchapter;

(ii) *Section 173.25(a)(4) of this subchapter.*

(iii) *Section 175.85(i).*

§175.20 Compliance and training.

(a) **Unless this subchapter specifically provides** that another person shall perform a particular duty, each operator shall comply with all applicable requirements in parts 106, 171, 172, and 175 of this chapter and shall ensure each of its hazmat employees receive training in relation thereto. (See also 14 CFR 121.135, 121.401, 121.433a, 135.323, 135.327 and 135.333.)

(b) **A carrier may not transport a hazardous material** by aircraft unless each of its hazmat employees involved in that transportation is trained as required by subpart H of part 172 of this subchapter.

§175.25 Notification at air passenger facilities of hazardous materials restrictions.

(a) **Each aircraft operator who engages** in for-hire transportation of passengers shall display notices of the requirements applicable to the carriage of hazardous materials aboard aircraft, and the penalties for failure to comply with those requirements. Each notice must be legible, and be prominently displayed so that it can be seen by passengers in locations where the aircraft operator issues tickets, checks baggage, and maintains aircraft boarding areas.

(1) *At a minimum,* each notice must communicate the following information:

Federal law forbids the carriage of hazardous materials aboard aircraft in your luggage or on your person.

A violation can result in five years' imprisonment and penalties of $250,000 or more (49 U.S.C. 5124).

Hazardous materials include explosives, compressed gases, flammable liquids and solids, oxidizers, poisons, corrosives and radioactive materials.

Examples: Paints, lighter fluid, fireworks, tear gases, oxygen bottles, and radio-pharmaceuticals.

There are special exceptions for small quantities (up to 70 ounces total) of medicinal and toilet articles carried in your luggage and certain smoking materials carried on your person.

For further information contact your airline representative.

(2) *The information* contained in paragraph (a)(1) of this section must be printed:

(i) *In legible English* and may, in addition to English, be displayed in other languages; and

(ii) *In lettering* of at least 1 cm (0.4 inch) in height for the first paragraph and 4.0 mm (0.16 inch) in height for the other paragraphs; and

(iii) *On a background of contrasting color.*

(3) *Size and color* of the notice are optional. Additional information, examples, or illustrations, if not inconsistent with the required information, may be included.

(4) *Notwithstanding the requirements* of paragraph (a)(1) of this section, a notice with the wording "A violation can result in penalties of up to $25,000 and five years' imprisonment. (49 U.S.C. 1809)" may be used through December 31, 2001.

(b) **[Reserved]**

§175.26 Notification at cargo facilities of hazardous materials requirements.

(a) **After September 30, 1994, each person who engages** in the acceptance or transport of cargo for transportation by aircraft shall display notices, at each facility where cargo is accepted, to persons offering such cargo of the requirements applicable to the carriage of hazardous materials aboard aircraft, and the penalties for failure to comply with those requirements. Each notice must be legible, and be prominently displayed so that it can be seen. At a minimum, each notice must communicate the following information:

(1) *Cargo containing* hazardous materials (dangerous goods) for transportation by aircraft must be offered in accordance with the Federal Hazardous Materials Regulations (49 CFR parts 171-180).

(2) *A violation* can result in five years' imprisonment and penalties of $250,000 or more (49 U.S.C. 5124).

(3) *Hazardous materials* (dangerous goods) include explosives, compressed gases, flammable liquids and solids, oxidizers, poisons, corrosives and radioactive materials.

(4) *Notwithstanding the requirements* of paragraph (a)(2) of this section, a notice with the wording "A violation can result in penalties of up to $25,000 and five years' imprisonment (49 U.S.C. 1809)" may be used through December 31, 2001.

(b) **The information contained in paragraph (a)** of this section must be printed:

(1) *Legibly in English,* and, where cargo is accepted outside of the United States, in the language of the host country; and

(2) *On a background of contrasting color.*

(c) **Size and color of the notice are optional.** Additional information, examples, or illustrations, if not inconsistent with required information, may be included.

(d) **Exceptions:** Display of a notice required by paragraph (a) of this section is not required at:

(1) *An unattended location* (e.g., a drop box) provided a general notice advising customers of a prohibition on shipments of hazardous materials through that location is prominently displayed; or

(2) *A customer's facility* where hazardous materials packages are accepted by a carrier.

§175.30 Accepting and inspecting shipments.

(a) **No person may accept a hazardous material** for transportation aboard an aircraft unless the hazardous material is:

(1) *Authorized,* and is within the quantity limitations specified for carriage aboard aircraft according to §172.101 of this subchapter or as otherwise specifically provided by this subchapter.

(2) *Described and certified* on a shipping paper prepared in duplicate in accordance with part 172 of this subchapter or as authorized by §171.11 of this subchapter. Each person receiving a shipping paper required by this section must retain a copy or an electronic image thereof, that is accessible at or through its principal place of business and must make the shipping paper available, upon request, to an authorized official of a federal, state, or local government agency at reasonable times and locations.

For a hazardous waste, each shipping paper copy must be retained for three years after the material is accepted by the initial carrier. For all other hazardous materials, each shipping paper copy must be retained for 375 days after the material is accepted by the carrier. Each shipping paper copy must include the date of acceptance by the carrier. The date on the shipping paper may be the date a shipper notifies the air carrier that a shipment is ready for transportation, as indicated on the airbill or bill of lading, as an alternative to the date the shipment is picked up or accepted by the carrier. Only an initial carrier must receive and retain a copy of the shipper's certification, as required by §172.204 of this subchapter.

(3) *Labeled and marked* in accordance with subparts D and E of part 172 or as authorized in §171.11 of this subchapter, and placarded (when required) in accordance with subpart F of part 172 of this subchapter; and,

(4) *Labeled with* a "CARGO AIRCRAFT ONLY" label (see §172.448 of this subchapter) if the material as presented is not permitted aboard passenger-carrying aircraft.

(b) **Except as provided in paragraph (d) of this section,** no person may carry a hazardous material in a package, outside container, or overpack aboard an aircraft unless the package, outside container, or overpack is inspected by the operator of the aircraft immediately before placing it:

(1) *Aboard the aircraft; or,*

(2) *In a unit load device or on a pallet prior to loading aboard the aircraft.*

(c) **A hazardous material may only be carried aboard** an aircraft if, based on the inspection prescribed in paragraph (b) of this section, the operator determines that the package, outside container, or overpack containing the hazardous material:

(1) *Has no holes,* leakage or other indication that its integrity has been compromised; and

(2) *For Class 7* (radioactive) materials, does not have a broken seal, except that packages contained in overpacks need not be inspected for seal integrity.

(d) **The requirements of paragraphs (b) and (c)** of this section do not apply to:

(1) *An ORM-D material* packed in a freight container and offered for transportation by one consignor; or

(2) *Dry ice (carbon dioxide, solid).*

(e) **An overpack containing packages of hazardous materials** may be accepted only if the operator has taken all reasonable steps to establish that:

(1) *The overpack* does not contain a package bearing the "CARGO AIRCRAFT ONLY" label unless —

(i) *The overpack* affords clear visibility of and easy access to the package; or

(ii) *The package* contains a material which may be carried inaccessibly under the provisions of §175.85(c)(1); or

(iii) *Not more than one package is overpacked.*

(2) *The proper* shipping names, identification numbers, labels and special handling instructions appearing on the inside packages are clearly visible or reproduced on the outside of the overpack, and

(3) *Has determined* that a statement to the effect that the inside packages comply with the prescribed specifications appears on the outside of the overpack, when specification packagings are prescribed.

§175.31 Reports of discrepancies.

(a) **Each person who discovers a discrepancy,** as defined in paragraph (b) of this section, relative to the shipment of a hazardous material following its acceptance for transportation aboard an aircraft shall, as soon as practicable, notify the nearest FAA Civil Aviation Security Office by telephone and shall provide the following information:
  (1) *Name and telephone number* of the person reporting the discrepancy.
  (2) *Name of the aircraft operator.*
  (3) *Specific location of the shipment concerned.*
  (4) *Name of the shipper.*
  (5) *Nature of discrepancy.*

(b) **Discrepancies which must be reported** under paragraph (a) of this section are those involving hazardous materials which are improperly described, certified, labeled, marked, or packaged, in a manner not ascertainable when accepted under the provisions of §175.30(a) of this subchapter, including:
  (1) *Packages which are found to contain hazardous materials:*
    (i) *Other than as described or certified on shipping papers;*
    (ii) *In quantities exceeding authorized limits;*
    (iii) *In inside containers* which are not authorized or have improper closures;
    (iv) *In inside containers not oriented as shown by package markings;*
    (v) *With insufficient* or improper absorption materials, when required; or
  (2) *Packages or baggage* which are found to contain hazardous materials subsequent to their being offered and accepted as other than hazardous materials.

§175.33 Notification of pilot-in-command.

(a) **Except as provided in §175.10,** when a hazardous material subject to the provisions of this subchapter is carried in an aircraft, the operator of the aircraft must provide the pilot-in-command with accurate and legible written information as early as practicable before departure of the aircraft, which specifies at least the following:
  (1) *The proper* shipping name, hazard class and identification number of the material as specified in §172.101 of this subchapter or the ICAO Technical Instructions. In the case of Class 1 material, the compatibility group letter also must be shown. If a hazardous material is described by the proper shipping name, hazard class, and identification number appearing in:
    (i) *Section 172.101 of this subchapter,* any additional description requirements provided in §§172.202 and 172.203 of this subchapter must also be shown in the notification.
    (ii) *The ICAO Technical Instructions,* any additional information required to be shown on shipping papers by §171.11 of this subchapter must also be shown in the notification.
  (2) *The total number of packages;*
  (3) *The net quantity* or gross weight, as applicable, for each package except those containing Class 7 (radioactive) materials and those for which there is no limit imposed on the maximum net quantity per package;
  (4) *The location of the packages aboard the aircraft;*
  (5) *Confirmation* that no damaged or leaking packages have been loaded on the aircraft;
  (6) *For Class 7* (radioactive) materials, the number of packages, overpacks or freight containers their category, transport index (if applicable), and their location aboard the aircraft;
  (7) *Confirmation that the package* must be carried on cargo aircraft only if its transportation aboard passenger-carrying aircraft is forbidden; and
  (8) *An indication,* when applicable, that a hazardous material is being carried under terms of an exemption.

(b) **A copy of the written notification to pilot-in-command** shall be readily available to the pilot-in-command during flight. Emergency response information required by subpart G of part 172 of this subchapter must be maintained in the same manner as the written notification to pilot-in-command during transport of the hazardous material aboard the aircraft.

FEDERAL REGISTER UPDATES

In the March 25, 2003 Federal Register, §175.33 was revised, effective October 1, 2003.

(a) [1]
  (1) *The proper* shipping name, hazard class, and identification number of the material, including any remaining aboard from prior stops, as specified in §172.101 of this subchapter or the ICAO Technical Instructions. In the case of Class 1 materials, the compatibility group letter also must be shown. If a hazardous material is described by the proper shipping name, hazard class, and identification number appearing in: [2]
  (7) *The date of the flight;* [3, 4]
  (8) *The telephone number* of a person not aboard the aircraft from whom the information contained in the notification of pilot-in-command can be obtained. The aircraft operator must ensure the telephone number is monitored at all times the aircraft is in flight. The telephone number is not required to be placed on the notification of pilot-in-command if the phone number is in a location in the cockpit available and known to the flight crew.

(c) **The aircraft operator must retain** at the airport of departure or the operator's principal place of business a copy of each notification of pilot-in-command, an electronic image thereof, or the information contained therein for 90 days. Except as provided in paragraph (d) of this section, the aircraft operator must make this information available, upon request, to an authorized official of a Federal, State, or local government agency at reasonable times and locations.

(d) **The aircraft operator must have the information required** to be retained under paragraph (c) of this section readily accessible at the airport of departure and the intended airport of arrival for the duration of the flight leg and, upon request, must make the information immediately available, in an accurate and legible format, to any representative of a Federal, State, or local government agency (including an emergency responder) who is responding to an incident involving the flight.

1. Paragraph (a) is the same as before.
2. Paragraph (a)(1) introductory text was revised.
3. Paragraphs (a)(7) and (a)(8) were redesignated as paragraphs (a)(9) and (a)(10).
4. New paragraphs (a)(7), (a)(8), (c), and (d) were added.

§175.35 Shipping papers aboard aircraft.

(a) **A copy of the shipping papers required by §175.30(a)(2)** must accompany the shipment it covers during transportation aboard an aircraft.

(b) **The documents required by paragraph (a) of this section** and §175.33 may be combined into one document if it is given to the pilot-in-command before departure of the aircraft.

§175.40 Keeping and replacement of labels.

(a) **Aircraft operators who engage in the transportation** of hazardous materials must keep an adequate supply of the labels specified in subpart E of part 172 of this subchapter, on hand at each location where shipments are loaded aboard aircraft.

(b) **Lost or detached labels for packages** of hazardous materials must be replaced in accordance with the information provided on the shipping papers.

Subpart B - Loading, Unloading, and Handling

§175.75 Quantity limitations aboard aircraft.

(a) **Except as provided in §175.85(c)(3),** no person may carry on an aircraft:
  (1) *A hazardous material except as permitted by this subchapter;*
  (2) *More than 25 kg* (55 pounds) net weight of hazardous material (and in addition thereto, 75 kg (165 pounds) net weight of Division 2.2 (non-flammable compressed gas) materials permitted to be carried aboard passenger-carrying aircraft:
    (i) *In an inaccessible cargo compartment,*
    (ii) *In any freight container* within an accessible cargo compartment, or
    (iii) *In any accessible* cargo compartment in a cargo aircraft only in a manner that makes it inaccessible unless in a freight container;
  (3) *Packages containing* Class 7 (radioactive) materials when their combined transport index number (determined by adding together the transport index numbers shown on the labels of the individual packages and/or overpacks):
    (i) *In passenger carrying aircraft,* exceeds 50.0 or, for any single package, exceeds 3.0, or
    (ii) *In cargo aircraft only,* exceeds 200.00 (for fissile Class 7 (radioactive) materials, see §175.702(b)(2)(iv)) or, for any single package, exceeds 10.0.

(b) **No limitation applies to the number of packages** of Class 9 (miscellaneous hazardous) materials, or ORM-D materials aboard an aircraft.

§175.78 Stowage compatibility of cargo.

(a) **For stowage on an aircraft, in a cargo facility,** or in any other area at an airport designated for the stowage of hazardous materials, packages containing hazardous materials which might react dangerously with one another may not be placed next to each other or in a position that would allow a dangerous interaction in the event of leakage.

(b) **As a minimum, the segregation instructions** prescribed in the following Segregation Table must be followed to maintain acceptable segregation between packages containing hazardous materials with different hazards. The Segregation Table instructions apply whether or not the class or division is the primary or subsidiary risk. The Segregation Table follows:

Segregation Table

Hazard label	Class or division							
	1	2	3	4.2	4.3	5.1	5.2	8
1	Note 1	Note 2	Note 2	Note 2	Note 2	Note 2	Note 2	Note 2
2	Note 2	....	....	....	....	....	....	....
3	Note 2	....	....	....	....	X	....	....
4.2	Note 2	....	....	....	....	X	....	....
4.3	Note 2	....	....	....	....	....	....	X
5.1	Note 2	....	X	X	....	....	....	....
5.2	Note 2	....	....	....	....	....	....	....
8	Note 2	....	....	....	X	....	....	....

(c) **Instructions for using the Segregation Table are as follows:**

(1) *The dots* at the intersection of a row and column indicate that no restrictions apply.

(2) *The letter "X"* at the intersection of a row and column indicates that packages containing these classes of hazardous materials may not be stowed next to or in contact with each other, or in a position which would allow interaction in the event of leakage of the contents.

(3) *Note 1.* "Note 1" at the intersection of a row and column means the following:

(i) *For explosives in compatibility groups A through K and N —*

[A] Packages bearing the same compatibility group letter and the same division number may be stowed together.

[B] Explosives of the same compatibility group, but different divisions may be stowed together provided the whole shipment is treated as belonging to the division having the smaller number. However, when explosives of Division 1.5 Compatibility Group D are stowed together with explosives of Division 1.2 Compatibility Group D, the whole shipment must be treated as Division 1.1, Compatibility Group D.

[C] Packages bearing different compatibility group letters may not be stowed together whether or not they belong to the same division, except as provided in paragraphs (c)(3)(ii) and (iii) of this section.

(ii) *Explosives in Compatibility Group L* may not be stowed with explosives in other compatibility groups. They may only be stowed with the same type of explosives in Compatibility Group L.

(iii) *Explosives of Division 1.4,* Compatibility Group S, may be stowed with explosives of all compatibility groups except for Compatibility Groups A and L.

(iv) *Other than explosives* of Division 1.4, Compatibility Group S (see paragraph (c)(3)(iii) of this section), and Compatibility Groups C, D and E that may be stowed together, explosives that do not belong in the same compatibility group may not be stowed together.

[A] Any combination of substances in Compatibility Groups C and D must be assigned to the most appropriate compatibility group shown in the §172.101 Table of this subchapter.

[B] Explosives in Compatibility Group N may be stowed together with explosives in Compatibility Groups C, D or E when the combination is assigned Compatibility Group D.

(4) *Note 2.* "Note 2" at the intersection of a row and column means that other than explosives of Division 1.4, Compatibility Group S, explosives may not be stowed together with that class.

(5) *Packages containing* hazardous materials with multiple hazards in the class or divisions, which require segregation in accordance with the Segregation Table need not be segregated from other packages bearing the same UN number.

(6) *A package labeled* "BLASTING AGENT" may not be stowed next to or in a position that will allow contact with a package of special fireworks or railway torpedoes.

§175.79 Orientation of cargo.

(a) **A package containing hazardous materials** marked "THIS SIDE UP" or "THIS END UP", or with arrows to indicate the proper orientation of the package, must be stored and loaded aboard an aircraft in accordance with such markings.

(b) **A package containing liquid hazardous materials** not marked as indicated in paragraph (a) of this section, must be stored and loaded with closures up (other than side closures in addition to top closures).

§175.81 Securing of packages containing hazardous materials.

(a) **Packages containing hazardous materials** must be secured in an aircraft in a manner that will prevent any movement in flight which would result in damage to or change in the orientation of the packages.

(b) **Packages containing Class 7 (radioactive) materials** must be secured in a manner that insures that the separation requirements of §§175.701 and 175.702 will be maintained at all times during flight.

§175.85 Cargo location.

(a) **Except as provided in §175.10, no person may carry** a hazardous material subject to the requirements of this subchapter in the cabin of a passenger-carrying aircraft or on the flight deck of any aircraft. Hazardous materials may be carried in a main deck cargo compartment of a passenger aircraft provided that the compartment is inaccessible to passengers and that it meets all certification requirements for a Class B aircraft cargo compartment in 14 CFR 25.857(b) or for a Class C aircraft cargo compartment in 14 CFR 25.857(c).

(b) **Each package containing a hazardous material** acceptable only for cargo aircraft must be loaded in such a manner that a crew member or other authorized person can see, handle and when size and weight permit, separate such packages from other cargo during flight.

(c) **Notwithstanding the provisions of paragraph (b) of this section:**

(1) *When packages* of the following hazardous materials are carried on cargo aircraft only, they may be carried in a location which is inaccessible to a crewmember during flight and are not subject to the weight limitation specified in paragraph (a)(2) of §175.75 of this subchapter.

(i) *Class 7 (radioactive) materials,*

(ii) *Division 6.1 (poisonous) materials* (except those labeled FLAMMABLE),

(iii) *Materials in Division 6.2* (etiologic or infectious substances),

(iv) *Class 3 (flammable liquid) materials* with a flash point above 23 °C (73 °F) that do not meet the definition of another hazardous class,

(v) *Class 9 (miscellaneous hazardous) materials,* and ORM-D materials.

(2) *When packages* of hazardous materials acceptable for cargo-only or passenger-carrying aircraft are carried on cargo aircraft only where other means of transportation are impracticable or not available, packages may be carried in accordance with procedures approved in writing by the FAA Air Transportation Security Field Office responsible for the operator's overall aviation security program or the FAA Air Transportation Security Division in the region where the operator is located.

(3) *When packages* of hazardous materials acceptable for cargo-only or passenger-carrying aircraft are carried on small, single pilot, cargo aircraft only being used where other means of transportation are impracticable or not available, they may be carried without quantity limitation as specified in §175.75 in a location that is not accessible to the pilot if:

(i) *No person* other than the pilot, an FAA inspector, the shipper or consignee of the material or a representative of the shipper or consignee so designated in writing, or a person necessary for handling the material is carried on the aircraft;

(ii) *The pilot* is provided with written instructions on characteristics and proper handling of the materials; and

(iii) *Whenever a change of pilots occurs* while the material is on board, the new pilot is briefed under a hand-to-hand signature service provided by the operator of the aircraft.

(d) **[Reserved]**

(e) **No person may carry a material** subject to the requirements of this subchapter that is acceptable for carriage in a passenger-carrying aircraft (other than magnetized materials) unless it is located in the aircraft in a place that is inaccessible to persons other than crew-members.

(f) **Paragraphs (a) and (e) of this section** do not apply to a person operating an aircraft under §175.310 which, because of its size and configuration, makes it impossible for that person to comply.

(g) **No person may load magnetized material** (which might cause an erroneous magnetic compass reading) on an aircraft, in the vicinity of a magnetic compass, or compass master unit, that is a part of the instrument equipment of the aircraft, in a manner that affects its operation. If this requirement cannot be met, a special aircraft swing and compass calibration may be made.

(h) **Compressed oxygen, when properly labeled** Oxidizer or Oxygen, may be loaded and transported as provided in paragraph (i) of this section. No person may load or transport any other package containing a hazardous material for which an OXIDIZER label is required under this subchapter in an inaccessible cargo compartment that does not have a fire or smoke detection system and a fire suppression system.

(i) **In addition to the quantity limitations** prescribed in §175.75, cylinders of compressed oxygen must be stowed in accordance with the following:

(1) *No more than* a combined total of six cylinders of compressed oxygen may be stowed on an aircraft in the inaccessible aircraft cargo compartment(s) that do not have fire or smoke detection systems and fire suppression systems.

(2) *When loaded* into a passenger-carrying aircraft or in an inaccessible cargo location on a cargo-only aircraft, cylinders of compressed oxygen must be stowed horizontally on the floor or as close as practicable to the floor of the cargo compartment or unit load device. This provision does not apply to cylinders stowed in the cabin of the aircraft in accordance with §175.10(b).

(3) *When transported* in a Class B aircraft cargo compartment (see 14 CFR 25.857(b)) or its equivalent (i.e., an accessible cargo compartment equipped with a fire or smoke detection system but not a fire suppression system), cylinders of compressed oxygen must be loaded in a manner that a crew member can see, handle and, when size and weight permit, separate the cylinders from other cargo during flight. No more than six cylinders of compressed oxygen and, in addition, one cylinder of medical-use compressed oxygen per passenger needing oxygen at destination — with a rated capacity of 850 L (30 cubic feet) or less of oxygen — may be carried in a Class B aircraft cargo compartment or its equivalent.

§175.88 Inspection of unit load devices.

A unit load device may not be loaded on an aircraft unless the device has been inspected and found to be free from any evidence of leakage from, or damage to, any package containing hazardous materials.

§175.90 Damaged shipments.

(a) **Packages or overpacks containing hazardous materials** must be inspected for damage or leakage after being unloaded from an aircraft. When packages or overpacks containing hazardous materials are carried in a unit load device, the area where the unit load device was stowed must be inspected for evidence of leakage or contamination immediately upon removal of the unit load device from the aircraft, and the packages or overpacks inspected for evidence of damage or leakage when the unit load device is unloaded. In the event of leakage or suspected leakage, the compartment in which the package, overpack, or unit load device was carried must be inspected for contamination and any dangerous level of contamination removed.

(b) **Except as provided for in §175.700,** the operator of an aircraft shall remove from the aircraft any package subject to this subchapter that appears to be damaged or leaking. In the case of a package which appears to be leaking, the operator must insure that the remainder of the packages in the same shipment are in proper condition for transport aboard the aircraft and that no other package has been contaminated.

(c) **No person shall place a package that is damaged** or appears to be damaged or leaking aboard an aircraft subject to this part.

(d) **If a package containing a material in Division 6.2** (etiologic or infectious substance) is found to be damaged or leaking, the person finding the package shall:

(1) *Avoid handling the package or keep handling to a minimum;*

(2) *Inspect packages* adjacent to the leaking package for contamination and withhold from further transportation any contaminated packages until it is ascertained that they can be safely transported;

(3) *Comply with* the reporting requirement of §171.15 of this subchapter; and

(4) *Notify the consignor or consignee.*

Subpart C - Specific Regulations Applicable According to Classification of Material

§175.305 Self-propelled vehicles.

(a) **Self-propelled vehicles are exempt from** the drainage requirements of §173.220 of this subchapter when carried in aircraft designed or modified for vehicle ferry operations and when all of the following conditions are met:

(1) *Authorization for* this type of operation has been given by the appropriate authority in the government of the country in which the aircraft is registered;

(2) *Each vehicle is secured in an upright position;*

(3) *Each fuel tank* is filled in a manner and only to a degree that will preclude spillage of fuel during loading, unloading, and transportation; and

(4) *Each area or compartment* in which a self-propelled vehicle is being transported is suitably ventilated to prevent the accumulation of fuel vapors.

(b) **[Reserved]**

§175.310 Transportation of flammable liquid fuel in small, passenger-carrying aircraft.

A small aircraft or helicopter operated entirely within the State of Alaska or into a remote area elsewhere in the United States may carry, in other than scheduled passenger operations, not more than 76 L(20 gallons) of flammable liquid fuel, if:

(a) **Transportation by air is the only practical means** of providing suitable fuel;

(b) **The flight is necessary to meet the needs of a passenger;**

(c) **The fuel is carried in metal containers that are either:**

(1) *In strong* tight metal containers of not more than 20 L (5.3 gallons) capacity, each packed inside a UN 4G fiberboard box or each packed inside a UN 4C1 wooden box, or in the case of a small aircraft in Alaska, each packed inside a wooden box of at least 1.3 cm (0.51 inch) thickness;

(2) *Airtight, leakproof,* inside containers of not more than 40 L (11 gallons) capacity and of at least 28-gauge metal, each packed inside a UN 4C1 wooden box or, in the case of a small aircraft in Alaska, each packed inside a wooden box of at least 1.3 cm (0. 51 inch) thickness;

(3) *UN 1A1 steel drums* of not more than 20 L (5.3 gallons) capacity; or

(4) *Fuel tanks* attached to flammable liquid fuel powered equipment under the following conditions:

(i) *Each piece of equipment is secured in an upright position;*

(ii) *Each fuel tank* is filled in a manner that will preclude spillage of fuel during loading, unloading, and transportation; and

(d) **In the case of a helicopter,** the fuel is carried on external cargo racks;

(e) **Each area or compartment in which the fuel is loaded** is suitably ventilated to prevent the accumulation of fuel vapors;

(f) **Before each flight, the pilot-in-command:**

(1) *Informs each passenger* of the location of the fuel and the hazards involved; and

(2) *Prohibits smoking,* lighting matches, the carrying of any lighted cigar, pipe, cigarette or flame, and the use of anything that might cause an open flame or spark, while loading or unloading or in flight; and

(g) **Fuel is transferred to the fuel tanks** only while the aircraft is on the surface.

§175.320 Cargo aircraft only; only means of transportation.

(a) **Notwithstanding §172.101 of this subchapter,** when means of transportation other than air are impracticable or not available, hazardous materials listed in the following table may be carried on a cargo aircraft only, subject to the conditions stated in the table and in paragraph (b) of this section and, when appropriate, paragraph (c) of this section:

Material	Class	Conditions
Detonators, detonator assemblies and boosters with detonators	Division 1.1 or 1.2 explosives	Permitted only when no other hazardous material is aboard the aircraft.
Detonators, detonator assemblies and boosters with detonators	Division 1.4 explosives	With the exception of Division 1.1 or 1.2 Detonators, detonator assemblies and boosters with detonators, permitted only when there are no Division 1.1 or 1.2 (Class A) explosives aboard aircraft.
Fuel, aviation, turbine engine; methyl alcohol; or toluene	Class 3 (flammable liquid)	Permitted in metal drums authorized for Packing Group I or II liquid hazardous materials having rated capacities of 220 L (58.1 gallons) or less. May not be transported in the same aircraft with Class 1 (explosives), Class 5 (oxidizer), or Class 8 (corrosive) materials. Permitted in installed tanks each having a capacity of more than 450 L (118.9 gallons) subject to the conditions specified in paragraph (c) of this section.
Gasoline	Class 3 (flammable liquid)	Permitted in metal drum having rated capacities of 220 L (58.1 gallons) or less. May not be transported in the same aircraft with materials classed as Class 1 (explosive), Class 5 (oxidizer), or Class 8 (corrosive) materials. Permitted in installed tanks each having a capacity of 450 L (118.9 gallons). Subject to the conditions specified in paragraph (c) of this section.

Material	Class	Conditions
High explosives	Class 1 (explosive) materials	Limited to Class 1 (explosive) materials to be used for blasting. Permitted only when no other cargo is aboard the aircraft or when being transported in the same aircraft with an authorized shipment of any one or more of any of the following materials to be used for blasting: Ammonium nitrate-fuel oil mixtures. Explosive, blasting, TYPE A,B,C,D,and E (Div. 1.1D or 1.5D), or Agent, blasting, TYPE B (Div. 1.5D); Substances, explosive, very insensitive, n.o.s., or Substances, EVI, n.o.s. (Div. 1.5D); Articles, explosive, extremely insensitive or Articles, EEI (Div.1.6N). Detonating cord. Propellant explosive (solid) (Division 1.3) (water gels only) Propellant explosive (liquid) (Division 1.3) (water gels only)
Oil n.o.s.; petroleum oil or petroleum oil, n.o.s.	Class 3 (flammable liquid)	Permitted in metal drums having rated capacities of 220 L (58.1 gallons) or less. May not be transported in the same aircraft with materials classed as Class 1 (explosive), Class 5 (oxidizer), or Class 8 (corrosive) materials. Permitted in installed tanks each having a capacity of 450 L (118.9 gallons). Subject to the conditions specified in paragraph (c) of this section.
Combustible liquid n.o.s.	Class 3 (combustible liquid)	Permitted in installed tanks each having a capacity of more than 450 L (118.9 gallons) subject to the conditions specified in paragraph (c) of this section.

(b) The following conditions apply to the carriage of hazardous materials performed under the authority of this section:

(1) *No person* other than a required flight crewmember, an FAA inspector, the shipper or consignee of the material or a representative of the shipper or consignee so designated in writing, or a person necessary for handling the material may be carried on the aircraft.

(2) *The operator* of the aircraft must have advance permission from the owner or operator of each manned airport where the material is to be loaded or unloaded or where the aircraft is to land while the material is on board. When the destination is changed after departure because of weather or other unforeseen circumstances, permission from the owner or operator of the alternate airport should be obtained as soon as practicable before landing.

(3) *At any airport* where the airport owner or operator or authorized representative thereof has designated a location for loading or unloading the material concerned, the material may not be loaded or unloaded at any other location.

(4) *If the material concerned* can create destructive forces or have lethal or injurious effects over an appreciable area as a result of an accident involving the aircraft or the material, the loading and unloading of the aircraft and its operation in takeoff, en route, and in landing must be conducted at a safe distance from heavily populated areas and from any place of human abode or assembly.

(5) *If the aircraft* is being operated by a holder of a certificate issued under 14 CFR part 121, part 133 or part 135, operations must be conducted in accordance with conditions and limitations specified in the certificate holder's operations specifications or operations manual accepted by the FAA. If the aircraft is being operated under 14 CFR part 91, operations must be conducted in accordance with an operations plan accepted and acknowledged in writing by the Civil Aviation Security Office serving the operator's location or the place where the material is to be loaded.

(6) *Each pilot* of the aircraft must be provided written instructions stating the conditions and limitations of the operation being conducted and the name of the airport official[s] granting the advance permission required by the first sentence of paragraph (b)(2) of this section.

(7) *The aircraft* and the loading arrangement to be used must be approved for safe carriage of the particular materials concerned by the FAA Civil Aviation Security Office responsible for the operator's overall aviation security program or the appropriate FAA Civil Aviation Security Office serving the place where the material is to be loaded.

(8) *When Division 1.1 or 1.2* (explosive) materials are carried aboard cargo aircraft only under the provisions of this section, the aircraft operator shall take all possible action to insure that routes over heavily populated areas are avoided commensurate with considerations of flight safety. During the approach and landing phase, the aircraft operator shall request appropriate vectors when under radar control to avoid heavily populated areas.

(9) *During loading and unloading,* no person may smoke, carry a lighted cigarette, cigar, or pipe, or operate any device capable of causing an open flame or spark within 15 m (50 feet) of the aircraft.

(10) *If the movement* involves international transportation, permission for the shipment may also be required from the appropriate authorities of the countries of origin, destination, transit and overflight prior to departure.

(c) The following additional conditions apply to the carriage of Class 3 (flammable) and combustible liquid materials in tanks each having a capacity of more than 420 liters (111 gallons) under the authority of this section:

(1) *The tanks* and their associated piping and equipment and the installation thereof must have been approved for the material to be transported by the appropriate FAA Regional Office.

(2) *In the case* of an aircraft being operated by a certificate holder, the operator shall list the aircraft and the approval information in its operating specifications. If the aircraft is being operated by other than a certificate holder, a copy of the FAA Regional Office approval required by this section must be carried on the aircraft.

(3) *The crew* of the aircraft must be thoroughly briefed on the operation of the particular bulk tank system being used.

(4) *During loading and unloading* and thereafter until any remaining fumes within the aircraft are dissipated:

(i) *Only those* electrically operated bulk tank shutoff valves that have been approved under a supplemental type certificate may be electrically operated.

(ii) *No engine* or electrical equipment, avionic equipment, or auxiliary power units may be operated, except position lights in the steady position and equipment required by approved loading or unloading procedures, as set forth in the operator's operations manual, or for operators that are not certificate holders, as set forth in a written statement.

(iii) *No person* may fill a container, other than an approved bulk tank, with a Class 3 (flammable and combustible liquid) materials or discharge a Class 3 (flammable and combustible liquid) materials from a container, other than an approved bulk tank, while that container is inside or within 15 m (50 feet) of the aircraft.

(iv) *When filling* an approved bulk tank by hose from inside the aircraft, the doors and hatches must be fully open to insure proper ventilation.

(v) *Static ground wires* must be connected between the storage tank or fueler and the aircraft, and between the aircraft and a positive ground device.

§175.630 Special requirements for Division 6.1 (poisonous) material and Division 6.2 (infectious substance) material.

(a) A hazardous material bearing a POISON, POISON INHALATION HAZARD, or INFECTIOUS SUBSTANCE label may not be carried in the same compartment of an aircraft with material which is marked as or known to be a foodstuff, feed, or any other edible material intended for consumption by humans or animals unless either the Division 6.1 (poisonous) material or material in Division 6.2 (infectious substance) and the foodstuff, feed, or other edible material are loaded in separate unit load devices which, when stowed on the aircraft, are not adjacent to each other, or the Division 6.1 (poisonous) material or material in Division 6.2 (infectious substance) are loaded in one closed unit load device and the foodstuff, feed or other material is loaded in another closed unit load device.

(b) No person may operate an aircraft that has been used to transport any package bearing a POISON or POISON INHALATION HAZARD label unless, upon removal of such package, the area in the aircraft in which it was carried is visually inspected for evidence of leakage, spillage, or other contamination. All contamination discovered must be either isolated or removed from the aircraft. The operation of an aircraft contaminated with such Division 6.1 (poisonous) materials is considered to be the carriage of poisonous materials under paragraph (a) of this section.

§175.700 Special limitations and requirements for Class 7 (radioactive) materials.

(a) In addition to other requirements, no person may carry in a passenger-carrying aircraft any package required to be labeled in accordance with §172.403 of this subchapter with a Radioactive Yellow-II or Radioactive Yellow-III label unless:

(1) *For a package* required to be labeled Radioactive Yellow-III, the transport index does not exceed 3.0;

(2) *The package* is carried on the floor of the cargo compartment, or freight container; and

(3) *The package* is carried in the aircraft in accordance with §§175.701 and 175.703(c).

(b) **In addition to the reporting requirements of §171.15** of this subchapter, the carrier shall also notify the offeror at the earliest practicable moment following any incident in which there has been breakage, spillage, or suspected radioactive contamination involving Class 7 (radioactive) materials shipments. Aircraft in which Class 7 (radioactive) materials have been spilled may not again be placed in service or routinely occupied until the radiation dose rate at every accessible surface is less than 0.005 mSv per hour (0.5 mrem per hour) and there is no significant removable radioactive surface contamination as determined in accordance with §173.443 of this subchapter. When contamination is present or suspected, the package and/or materials it has touched must be segregated as far as practicable from personnel contact until appropriate radiological advice or assistance is obtained. The Regional Office of the U.S. Department of Energy or appropriate State or local radiological authorities can provide advice or assistance, and should be notified in cases of obvious leakage, or if it appears likely that the inside container may have been damaged. For personnel safety, the carrier shall take care to avoid possible inhalation, ingestion, or contact by any person with Class 7 (radioactive) materials that may have leaked or spilled from its package. Any loose Class 7 (radioactive) materials and associated packaging materials must be left in a segregated area pending disposal instructions from responsible radiological authorities.

(c) **Except as provided in §§173.4, 173.422 and 173.423** of this subchapter, no person shall carry any Class 7 (radioactive) materials aboard a passenger carrying aircraft unless that material is intended for use in, or incident to research, medical diagnosis or treatment.

(d) **Type B(M) packages may not be offered or accepted** for transportation, nor transported, on passenger-carrying aircraft.

§175.701 Separation distance requirements for packages containing Class 7 (radioactive) materials in passenger-carrying aircraft.

(a) **General.** No person may carry in a passenger-carrying aircraft any package required by §172.403 of this subchapter to be labeled Radioactive Yellow-II, or Radioactive Yellow-III unless the package is placed in the aircraft in accordance with the minimum separation distances prescribed in paragraph (b) or (c) of this section.

(b) **Separation distances.**

(1) *Except as provided* in paragraph (c) of this section, the minimum separation distances prescribed in paragraphs (b)(2) and (b)(3) of this section are determined by measuring the shortest distance between the surfaces of the Class 7 (radioactive) materials package and the surfaces bounding the space occupied by passengers or animals. If more than one package of Class 7 (radioactive) materials is placed in a passenger-carrying aircraft, the minimum separation distance for these packages shall be determined in accordance with paragraphs (b)(2) and (b)(3) of this section on the basis of the sum of the transport index numbers of the individual packages or overpacks.

(2) *The following table* prescribes minimum separation distances that must be maintained in passenger-carrying aircraft between Class 7 (radioactive) materials labeled Radioactive Yellow-II or Radioactive Yellow-III and passengers and crew:

Transport index or sum of transport indexes of all packages in the aircraft or predesignated area	Minimum separation distances	
	Centimeters	Inches
0.1 to 1.0	30	12
1.1 to 2.0	50	20
2.1 to 3.0	70	28
3.1 to 4.0	85	34
4.1 to 5.0	100	40
5.1 to 6.0	115	46
6.1 to 7.0	130	52
7.1 to 8.0	145	57
8.1 to 9.0	155	61
9.1 to 10.0	165	65
10.1 to 11.0	175	69
11.1 to 12.0	185	73
12.1 to 13.0	195	77
13.1 to 14.0	205	81
14.1 to 15.0	215	85
15.1 to 16.0	225	89
16.1 to 17.0	235	93
17.1 to 18.0	245	97
18.1 to 20.0	260	102
20.1 to 25.0	290	114
25.1 to 30.0	320	126
30.1 to 35.0	350	138
35.1 to 40.0	375	148
40.1 to 45.0	400	157
45.1 to 50.0	425	167

(3) *Class 7 (radioactive) materials* in packages, overpacks or freight containers labeled Radioactive Yellow-II or Radioactive Yellow-III must be separated from live animals by a distance of at least 0.5 m (20 inches) for journeys not exceeding 24 hours, and by a distance of at least 1.0 m (39 inches) for journeys longer than 24 hours.

(c) **Predesignated areas.** A package required by §172.403 of this subchapter to be labeled Radioactive Yellow-II or Radioactive Yellow-III may be carried in a passenger-carrying aircraft in accordance with a system of predesignated areas established by the aircraft operator. Each aircraft operator that elects to use a system of predesignated areas shall submit a detailed description of the proposed system to the Associate Administrator for approval prior to implementation of the system. A proposed system of predesignated areas is approved if the Associate Administrator determines that it is designed to assure that:

(1) *The packages* can be placed in each predesignated area in accordance with the minimum separation distances prescribed in paragraph (b)(2) of this section; and

(2) *The predesignated areas* are separated from each other by minimum distance equal to at least four times the distances required by paragraphs (b)(1) and (b)(2) of this section for the predesignated area containing packages with the largest sum of transport indexes.

§175.702 Requirements for carriage of packages containing Class 7 (radioactive) materials in a cargo aircraft only.

(a) **As used in this section,** the term "group of packages" means packages that are separated from each other in an aircraft by a distance of 6 m (20 feet) or less.

(b) **No person may carry in a cargo aircraft** only any package required by §172.403 of this subchapter to be labeled Radioactive Yellow-II or Radioactive Yellow-III unless:

(1) *The total transport index* for all of the packages does not exceed 50.0 and the package is carried in accordance with §175.701(a); or

(2) *The total transport index for all of the packages exceeds 50.0 and:*

(i) *The separation distance* between the surfaces of the Class 7 (radioactive) materials packages, overpacks or freight containers and any space occupied by —

[A] Humans is at least 9 m (30 feet); and

[B] Live animals is at least 0.5 m (20 inches) for journeys not exceeding 24 hours and at least 1.0 m (39 inches) for journeys longer than 24 hours;

(ii) *The transport index* for any group of packages does not exceed 50.0; and

(iii) *Each group of packages* is separated from every other group in the aircraft by not less than 6 m (20 feet), measured from the outer surface of each group; and

(iv) *The total transport index* for all packages containing fissile Class 7 (radioactive) materials does not exceed 50.0.

§175.703 Other special requirements for the acceptance and carriage of packages containing Class 7 (radioactive) materials.

(a) **No person may carry in an aircraft any package** of Class 7 (radioactive) materials required by §172.403 of this subchapter to be labeled Radioactive Yellow-II or Radioactive Yellow-III closer than the distances shown in the following table to any package marked as containing undeveloped film:

Transport index	Minimum separation distance to nearest undeveloped film for various times of transit									
	Up to 2 hours		2 to 4 hours		4 to 8 hours		8 to 12 hours		Over 12 hours	
	Meters	Feet	Meters	Feet	Meters	Feet	Meters	Feet	Meters	Feet
0.1 to 1.0	0.3	1	0.6	2	0.9	3	1.2	4	1.5	5
1.1 to 5.0	0.9	3	1.2	4	1.8	6	2.4	8	3.3	11
5.1 to 10.0	1.2	4	1.8	6	2.7	9	3.3	11	4.5	15
10.1 to 20.0	1.5	5	2.4	8	3.6	12	4.8	16	6.6	22
20.1 to 30.0	2.1	7	3.0	10	4.5	15	6.0	20	8.7	29
30.1 to 40.0	2.4	8	3.3	11	5.1	17	6.6	22	9.9	33
40.1 to 50.0	2.7	9	3.6	12	5.7	19	7.2	24	10.8	36

(b) **No person may accept for carriage in an aircraft** packages of Class 7 (radioactive) materials, other than limited quantities, contained in a rigid or non-rigid overpack, including a fiberboard box or plastic bag, unless they have been prepared for shipment in accordance with §173.448(g) of this subchapter.

(c) **No person shall carry in an aircraft** a fissile material controlled shipment (as defined in §173.403 of this subchapter), except —

(1) *In a cargo aircraft* only which has been assigned for the exclusive use of the shipper for the specific shipment of fissile Class 7 (radioactive) material. Instructions for the exclusive use must be developed by the shipper and carrier, and the instructions issued with the shipping papers; or

(2) *In an aircraft* in which there are no other packages required to bear a radioactive label as prescribed in §172.403 of this subchapter. Specific arrangements must be made between the shipper and carrier, with instructions to that effect issued with the shipping papers.

(d) **No person shall offer or accept for transportation,** or transport, by air —

(1) *Vented Type B(M) packages,* packages which require external cooling by an ancillary cooling system or packages subject to operational controls during transport; or

(2) *Liquid pyrophoric Class 7 (radioactive) materials.*

(e) **Packages with radiation levels at the package surface** or a transport index in excess of the limits specified in §173.441(a) of this subchapter may not be transported by aircraft except under special arrangements approved by RSPA.

§175.704 Plutonium shipments.

Shipments of plutonium by air which are subject to 10 CFR 71.88(a)(4) must comply with the following:

(a) **A plutonium package weighing less than 40 kg (88 lbs)** and having its height and diameter both less than 50 cm (19.7 in), must be stowed aboard the aircraft on the main deck or the lower cargo compartment in the aft-most location that is possible for cargo of its size and weight. No other type of cargo may be stowed aft of a plutonium package.

(b) **A plutonium package must be secured and restrained** to prevent shifting under normal transport. A plutonium package weighing 40 kg (88 lbs) or more must be securely cradled and tied down to the main deck of the aircraft such that the tied down system is capable of providing package restraint against the following inertial forces acting separately relative to the deck of the aircraft: Upward, 2g; Forward, 9g; Sideward, 1.5g; Downward, 4.5g.

(c) **A plutonium package weighing less than 40 kg (88 lbs),** and having its height and diameter both less than 50 cm (19.7 in), may not be transported aboard an aircraft carrying other cargo required to bear an "Explosive A" or an "Explosive 1.1" label. Any other plutonium package may not be transported aboard an aircraft carrying other cargo bearing any of the following hazardous material labels: Explosive A; Explosive B; Explosive C; Explosive 1.1, 1.2, 1.3, 1.4, 1.5 or 1.6; Spontaneously Combustible; Dangerous When Wet; Organic Peroxide; Non-Flammable Gas; Flammable Liquid; Flammable Solid; Flammable Gas; Oxidizer; or Corrosive.

§175.705 Inspection of aircraft for contamination by Class 7 (radioactive) materials.

(a) **Aircraft used routinely for the carriage of Class 7** (radioactive) materials shall be periodically checked for radioactive contamination. The frequency of checks shall be related to the likelihood of contamination and the extent to which Class 7 (radioactive) materials are carried.

(b) **An aircraft must be taken out of service** if the level of contamination exceeds that provided in §175.700(b).

Notes

Part 176 - Carriage by Vessel

Subpart A - General

§176.1 Purpose and scope.

This part prescribes requirements in addition to those contained in parts 171, 172, and 173 of this subchapter to be observed with respect to the transportation of hazardous materials by vessel.

§176.2 Definitions.

As used in this part —

Cantline means the v-shaped groove between two abutting, parallel horizontal cylinders.

Cargo net means a net made of fiber or wire used to provide convenience in handling loose or packaged cargo to and from a vessel.

Clear of living quarters means that the hazardous material must be located so that in the event of release of the material, leakage or vapors will not penetrate accommodations, machinery spaces or other work areas by means of entrances or other openings in bulkheads or ventilation ducts.

Closed freight container means a freight container which totally encloses its contents by permanent structures. A freight container formed partly by a tarpaulin, plastic sheet, or similar material is not a closed freight container.

Commandant (G-MSO), USCG means the Chief, Office of Operating and Environmental Standards, United States Coast Guard, Washington, DC 20593-0001.

Compartment means any space on a vessel that is enclosed by the vessel's decks and its sides or permanent steel bulkheads.

CSC safety approval plate means the safety approval plate specified in Annex I of the International Convention for Safe Containers (1972) and conforming to the specifications in 49 CFR 451.23 and 451.25. The plate is evidence that a freight container was designed, constructed, and tested under international rules incorporated into U.S. regulations in 49 CFR parts 450 through 453. The plate is found in the door area of the container.

Deck structure means a structure of substantial weight and size located on the weather deck of a vessel and integral with the deck. This term includes superstructures, deck houses, mast houses, and bridge structures.

Draft means a load or combination of loads capable of being hoisted into or out of a vessel in a single lift.

Dunnage means lumber of not less than 25 mm (0.98 inch) commercial thickness or equivalent material laid over or against structures such as tank tops, decks, bulkheads, frames, plating, or ladders, or used for filling voids or fitting around cargo, to prevent damage during transportation.

Explosives anchorage means an anchorage so designated under 33 CFR part 110, subpart B.

Explosive article means an article or device which contains one or more explosive substances. Individual explosive articles are identified in the schedules for Class I (explosive) articles found in the IMDG Code (see §171.7 of this subchapter).

Explosives handling facility means —

(1) *A "designated waterfront facility"* designated under 33 CFR part 126 when loading, handling, and unloading Class 1 (explosives) materials; or

(2) *A facility* for loading, unloading, and handling military Class 1 (explosives) materials which is operated or controlled by an agency of the Department of Defense.

Explosive substance means a solid or liquid material, or a mixture of materials, which is in itself capable by chemical reaction of producing gas at such a temperature and pressure and at such a speed as to cause damage to its surroundings. Individual explosive substances are identified in the schedules for Class 1 (explosive) substances in the IMDG Code.

Handling means the operation of loading and unloading a vessel; transfer to, from, or within a vessel, and any ancillary operations.

Hold means a compartment below deck that is used exclusively for the carriage of cargo.

In containers or the like means in any clean, substantial, weatherproof box structure which can be secured to the vessel's structure, including a portable magazine or a closed transport unit. Whenever this stowage is specified, stowage in deckhouses, mast lockers and oversized weatherproof packages (overpacks) is also acceptable.

Incompatible materials means two materials whose stowage together may result in undue hazards in the case of leakage, spillage, or other accident.

INF cargo means packaged irradiated nuclear fuel, plutonium or high-level radioactive wastes as those terms are defined in the "International Code for the Safe Carriage of Packaged Irradiated Nuclear Fuel, Plutonium and High-Level Radioactive Wastes on Board Ships' (INF Code) (contained in IMDG Code, incorporated by reference, see §171.7 of this subchapter).

Landing mat means a shock absorbing pad used in loading Class 1 (explosive) materials on vessels.

Machinery Spaces of Category A are those spaces, and trunks to such spaces, which contain:

(1) *Internal combustion machinery used for main propulsion:*

(2) *Internal combustion machinery* used for purposes other than main propulsion where such machinery has in the aggregate a total power output of not less than 375 kw; or

(3) *any oil-fired boiler or fuel unit.*

Magazine means an enclosure designed to protect certain goods of Class 1 (explosive) materials from damage by other cargo and adverse weather conditions during loading, unloading, and when in transit; and to prevent unauthorized access. A magazine may be a fixed structure in the vessel, a closed freight container, a closed transport vehicle, or a portable magazine.

Master of the Vessel, as used in this part, includes the person in charge of an unmanned vessel or barge.

Open freight container means a freight container that does not totally enclose its contents by permanent structures.

Overstowed means a package or container is stowed directly on top of another. However, with regard to Class 1 (explosive) stowage, such goods may themselves be stacked to a safe level but other goods should not be stowed directly on top of them.

Pallet means a portable platform for stowing, handling, and moving cargo.

Palletized unit means packages or unpackaged objects stacked on a pallet, banded and secured to the pallet by metal, fabric, or plastic straps for the purpose of handling as a single unit.

Pie plate means a round, oval, or hexagonal pallet without sideboards, used in conjunction with a cargo net to handle loose cargo on board a vessel.

Portable magazine means a strong, closed, prefabricated, steel or wooden, closed box or container, other than a freight container, designed and used to handle Class 1 (explosive) materials either by hand or mechanical means.

Readily combustible material means a material which may or may not be classed as a hazardous material but which is easily ignited and supports combustion. Examples of readily combustible materials include wood, paper, straw, vegetable fibers, products made from such materials, coal, lubricants, and oils. This definition does not apply to packaging material or dunnage.

Responsible person means a person empowered by the master of the vessel to make all decisions relating to his or her specific task, and having the necessary knowledge and experience for that purpose.

Safe working load means the maximum gross weight that cargo handling equipment is approved to lift.

Skilled person means a person having the knowledge and experience to perform a certain duty.

Skipboard means a square or rectangular pallet without sideboards, usually used in conjunction with a cargo net to handle loose cargo on board a vessel.

Splice as used in §176.172 of this part, means any repair of a freight container main structural member which replaces material, other than complete replacement of the member.

Transport unit means a transport vehicle or a freight container. A closed transport unit means a transport unit in which the contents are totally enclosed by permanent structures. An open transport unit means a transport unit which is not a closed transport unit. Transport units with fabric sides or tops are not closed transport units for the purposes of this part.

Tray means a type of pallet constructed to specific dimensions for handling a particular load.

§176.3 Unacceptable hazardous materials shipments.

(a) **A carrier may not transport by vessel** any shipment of a hazardous material that is not prepared for transportation in accordance with parts 172 and 173 of this subchapter.

(b) **A carrier may not transport by vessel** any explosive or explosive composition described in §173.54 of this subchapter.

§176.4 Port security and safety regulations.

(a) **Each carrier, master, agent, and charterer** of a vessel and all other persons engaged in handling hazardous materials on board vessels shall comply with the applicable provisions of 33 CFR parts 6, 109, 110, 125, 126, and 160.

(b) **Division 1.1 and 1.2 (explosive) materials** may only be loaded on and unloaded from a vessel at —

(1) *A facility of particular hazard as defined in 33 CFR 126.05(b);*

(2) *An explosives anchorage listed in 33 CFR part 110; or*

(3) *A facility operated or controlled by the Department of Defense.*

(c) **With the concurrence of the COTP,** Division 1.1 and 1.2 (explosive) materials may be loaded on or unloaded from a vessel in any location acceptable to the COTP.

§176.5 Application to vessels.

(a) **Except as provided in paragraph (b) of this section,** this subchapter applies to each domestic or foreign vessel when in the navigable waters of the United States, regardless of its character, tonnage, size, or service, and whether self-propelled or not, whether arriving or departing, underway, moored, anchored, aground, or while in dry dock.

(b) **This subchapter does not apply to:**

(1) *A public vessel not engaged in commercial service;*

(2) *A vessel* constructed or converted for the principal purpose of carrying flammable or combustible liquid cargo in bulk in its own tanks, when only carrying these liquid cargoes;

(3) *A vessel* of 15 gross tons or smaller when not engaged in carrying passengers for hire;

(4) *A vessel used exclusively for pleasure;*

(5) *A vessel of 500 gross tons or smaller when engaged in fisheries;*

(6) *A tug or towing vessel,* except when towing another vessel having Class 1 (explosive) materials, Class 3 (flammable liquids), or Division 2.1 (flammable gas) materials, in which case the owner/operator of the tug or towing vessel shall make such provisions to guard against and extinguish fire as the Coast Guard may prescribe;

(7) *A cable vessel,* dredge, elevator vessel, fireboat, icebreaker, pile driver, pilot boat, welding vessel, salvage vessel, or wrecking vessel; or

(8) *A foreign vessel* transiting the territorial sea of the United States without entering the internal waters of the United States, if all hazardous materials being carried on board are being carried in accordance with the requirements of the IMDG Code (see §171.7 of this subchapter).

(c) **[Reserved]**

(d) **Except for transportation in bulk packagings** (as defined in §171.8 of this subchapter), the bulk carriage of hazardous materials by water is governed by 46 CFR chapter I, subchapters D, I, N and O.

FEDERAL REGISTER UPDATES

An Interim Final Rule was published In the May 5, 2003 Federal Register, adding §176.7.

§176.7 Documentation for vessel personnel.
Each owner, operator, master, agent, person in charge, and charterer must ensure that vessel personnel required to have a license, certificate of registry, or merchant mariner's document by 46 CFR parts 10 and 12 possess a license, certificate or document, as appropriate.

§176.9 "Order-Notify" or "C.O.D." shipments.

A carrier may not transport Division 1.1 or 1.2 (explosive) materials, detonators, or boosters with detonators which are:

(a) **Consigned to "order-notify" or "C.O.D.",** except on a through bill of lading to a place outside the United States; or

(b) **Consigned by the shipper to himself** unless he has a resident representative to receive the shipment at the port of discharge.

§176.11 Exceptions.

(a) **A hazardous material may be offered and accepted** for transport by vessel when in conformance with the IMDG Code (see §171.7 of this subchapter), subject to the conditions and limitations set forth in §171.12 of this subchapter. The requirements of §§176.83, 176.84, and 176.112 through 176.174 are not applicable to shipments of Class 1 (explosive) materials made in accordance with the IMDG Code. A hazardous material which conforms to the provisions of this paragraph (a) is not subject to the requirement specified in §172.201(d) of this subchapter for an emergency response telephone number, when transportation of the hazardous material originates and terminates outside the United States and the hazardous material —

(1) *Is not offloaded from the vessel; or*

(2) *Is offloaded* between ocean vessels at a U.S. port facility without being transported by public highway.

(b) **Canadian shipments and packages may be transported** by vessel if they are transported in accordance with this subchapter. (See §171.12a of this subchapter.)

(c) **The requirements of this subchapter governing** the transportation of combustible liquids do not apply to the transportation of combustible liquids in non-bulk (see definitions in §171.8 of this subchapter) packages on board vessels.

(d) **Transport vehicles, containing hazardous materials** loaded in accordance with specific requirements of this subchapter applicable to such vehicles, may be transported on board a ferry vessel or carfloat, subject to the applicable requirements specified in §§176.76, 176.100, and subpart E of this part.

(e) **Hazardous materials classed and shipped as ORM-D** are not subject to the requirements of this part unless they are offered for transportation as hazardous wastes.

(f) **Paragraph (a) of this section does not apply** to hazardous materials, including certain hazardous wastes and hazardous substances as defined in §171.8 of this subchapter, which are not subject to the requirements of the IMDG Code.

(g) **The requirements of this subchapter do not apply** to atmospheric gases used in a refrigeration system.

§176.13 Responsibility for compliance and training.

(a) **Unless this subchapter specifically provides** that another person shall perform a particular duty, each carrier shall perform the duties specified and comply with all applicable requirements in this part and shall ensure its hazmat employees receive training in relation thereto.

(b) **A carrier may not transport a hazardous material** by vessel unless each of its hazmat employees involved in that transportation is trained as required by subpart H of part 172 of this subchapter.

(c) **The record of training required by §172.704(d)** of this subchapter for a crewmember who is a hazmat employee subject to the training requirements of this subchapter must be kept on board the vessel while the crewmember is in service on board the vessel.

§176.15 Enforcement.

(a) **An enforcement officer of the U.S. Coast Guard** may at any time and at any place, within the jurisdiction of the United States, board any vessel for the purpose of enforcement of this subchapter and inspect any shipment of hazardous materials as defined in this subchapter.

(b) **[Reserved]**

§176.18 Assignment and certification.

(a) **The National Cargo Bureau, Inc., is authorized** to assist the Coast Guard in administering this subchapter with respect to the following:

(1) *Inspection of vessels for suitability for loading hazardous materials;*

(2) *Examination of stowage of hazardous materials;*

(3) *Making recommendations* for stowage requirements of hazardous materials cargo; and

(4) *Issuance of certificates* of loading setting forth that the stowage of hazardous materials is in accordance with the requirements of this subchapter.

(b) **A certificate of loading issued by** the National Cargo Bureau, Inc., may be accepted by the Coast Guard as prima facie evidence that the cargo is stowed in conformity with the requirements of this subchapter.

Subpart B - General Operating Requirements

§176.24 Shipping papers.

(a) **A person may not accept a hazardous material** for transportation or transport a hazardous material by vessel unless that person has received a shipping paper prepared in accordance with part 172 of this subchapter, or as authorized by §171.12 of this subchapter, unless the material is excepted from shipping paper requirements under this subchapter.

(b) **Each person receiving a shipping paper** required by this section must retain a copy or an electronic image thereof, that is accessible at or through its principal place of business and must make the shipping paper available, upon request, to an authorized official of a Federal, State, or local government agency at reasonable times and locations. For a hazardous waste, each shipping paper copy must be retained for three years after the material is accepted by the initial carrier. For all other hazardous materials, each shipping paper copy must be retained for 375 days after the material is accepted by the carrier. Each shipping paper copy must include the date of acceptance by the carrier. The date on the shipping paper may be the date a shipper presents a booking for carriage with the carrier as an alternative to the date the shipment is picked up, accepted, or loaded on the vessel by the carrier.

§176.27 Certificate.

(a) **A carrier may not transport a hazardous material** by vessel unless he has received a certificate prepared in accordance with §172.204 of this subchapter.

(b) **In the case of an import or export shipment** of hazardous materials which will not be transported by rail, highway, or air, the shipper may certify on the bill of lading or other shipping paper that the hazardous material is properly classed, described, marked, packaged, and labeled according to part 172 of this subchapter or in accordance with the requirements of the IMDG Code (see §171.7 of this subchapter). See §171.12 of this subchapter.

(c)(1) *A person* responsible for packing or loading a freight container or transport vehicle containing hazardous materials for transportation by a manned vessel in ocean or coastwise service, must provide the vessel operator, at the time the shipment is offered for transportation by vessel, with a signed container packing certificate stating, at a minimum, that —

(i) *The freight container* or transport unit is serviceable for the materials loaded therein, contains no incompatible goods, and is properly marked, labeled or placarded, as applicable; and

(ii) *When the freight container* or transport unit contains packages, those packages have been inspected prior to loading, are properly marked, labeled or placarded, as applicable; are not damaged; and are properly secured.

(2) *The certification* may appear on a shipping paper or on a separate document as a statement such as "It is declared that the packing of the container has been carried out in accordance with the provisions of 49 CFR 176.27(c)".

§176.30 Dangerous cargo manifest.

(a) **The carrier, its agents, and any person** designated for this purpose by the carrier or agents shall prepare a dangerous cargo manifest, list, or stowage plan. This document may not include a material which is not subject to the requirements of 49 CFR or the IMDG Code (see §171.7 of this subchapter). This document must be kept in a designated holder on or near the vessel's bridge. It must contain the following information:

(1) *Name of vessel and official number.* (If the vessel has no official number, the international radio call sign must be substituted.);

(2) *Nationality of vessel;*

(3) *Shipping name and identification number* of each hazardous material on board as listed in §172.101 of this subchapter or as listed in the IMDG Code and an emergency response telephone number as prescribed in subpart G of part 172 of this subchapter.

(4) *The number and description of packages* (barrels, drums, cylinders, boxes, etc.) and gross weight for each type of packaging;

(5) *Classification of the hazardous material in accordance with either:*

(i) *The Hazardous Materials Table, the §172.101 table; or*

(ii) *The IMDG Code.*

(6) *Any additional description required by §172.203 of this subchapter.*

(7) *Stowage location of the hazardous material on board the vessel.*

(8) *In the case* of a vessel used for the storage of explosives or other hazardous materials, the following additional information is required:

(i) *Name and address of vessel's owner;*

(ii) *Location of vessel's mooring;*

(iii) *Name of person in charge of vessel;*

(iv) *Name and address of the owner of the cargo; and*

(v) *A complete record,* by time intervals of one week, of all receipts and disbursements of hazardous materials. The name and address of the consignor must be shown against all receipts and the name and address of the consignee against all deliveries.

(b) **The hazardous material information** on the dangerous cargo manifest must be the same as the information furnished by the shipper on the shipping order or other shipping paper, except that the IMO "correct technical name" and the IMO class may be indicated on the manifest as provided in paragraphs (a)(3) and (a)(5) of this section. The person who supervises the preparation of the manifest, list, or stowage plan shall ensure that the information is correctly transcribed, and shall certify to the truth and accuracy of this information to the best of his knowledge and belief by his signature and notation of the date prepared.

(c) **The carrier and its agents shall insure that the master,** or a licensed deck officer designated by the master and attached to the vessel, or in the case of a barge, the person in charge of the barge, acknowledges the correctness of the dangerous cargo manifest, list or stowage plan by his signature.

(d) **For barges, manned or unmanned,** the requirements of this section apply except for the following:

(1) *In the case of a manned barge,* the person in charge of the barge shall prepare the dangerous cargo manifest.

(2) *In the case of an unmanned barge,* the person responsible for loading the barge is responsible for the preparation of a dangerous cargo manifest, list, or stowage plan and must designate an individual for that purpose.

(3) *For all barges, manned or unmanned,* the dangerous cargo manifest must be on board the barge in a readily accessible location and a copy must be furnished to the person in charge of the towing vessel.

(e) **Each carrier who transports or stores** hazardous materials on a vessel shall retain a copy of the dangerous cargo manifest, list, or stowage plan for at least one year, and shall make that document available for inspection in accordance with §176.36(b) of this subchapter.

§176.31 Exemptions.

If a hazardous material is being transported by vessel under the authority of an exemption and a copy of the exemption is required to be on board the vessel, it must be kept with the dangerous cargo manifest.

§176.36 Preservation of records.

(a) **When this part requires shipping orders,** manifest, cargo lists, stowage plans, reports, or any other papers, documents or similar records to be prepared, the carrier shall preserve them or copies of them in his place of business or office in the United States for a period of one year after their preparation.

(b) **Any record required to be preserved must be** made available upon request to an authorized representative of the Department.

§176.39 Inspection of cargo.

(a) **Manned vessels.** The carrier, its agents, and any person designated for this purpose by the carrier or agents shall cause an inspection of each hold or compartment containing hazardous materials to be made after stowage is complete, and at least once every 24 hours thereafter, weather permitting, in order to ensure that the cargo is in a safe condition and that no damage caused by shifting, spontaneous heating, leaking, sifting, wetting, or other cause has been sustained by the vessel or its cargo since loading and stowage. However, freight containers or individual barges need not be opened. A vessel's holds equipped with smoke or fire detecting systems having an automatic monitoring capability need not be inspected except after stowage is complete and after periods of heavy weather. The carrier, its agents, and any person designated for this purpose by the carrier or agents shall cause an entry to be made in the vessel's deck log book for each inspection of the stowage of hazardous materials performed.

(b) **Unmanned and magazine vessels.** An inspection of the cargo must be made after stowage has been completed to ensure that stowage has been accomplished properly and that there are no visible signs of damage to any packages or evidence of heating, leaking, or sifting. This inspection must be made by the individual who is responsible to the carrier and who is in charge of loading and stowing the cargo on the unmanned vessels or the individual in charge in the case of a magazine vessel.

(c) **The carrier, its agents, and any person** designated for this purpose by the carrier or agents of each ocean-going vessel carrying hazardous material shall, immediately prior to entering a port in the United States, cause an inspection of that cargo to be made.

(d) **When inspecting a cargo of hazardous materials** capable of evolving flammable vapors, any artificial means of illumination must be of an explosion-proof type.

§176.45 Emergency situations.

(a) **When an accident occurs on board a vessel** involving hazardous materials, and the safety of the vessel, its passengers or crew are endangered, the master shall adopt such procedures as will, in his judgment, provide maximum safety for the vessel, its passengers, and its crew. When the accident results in damaged packages or the emergency use of unauthorized packagings, these packages may not be offered to any forwarding carrier for transportation. The master shall notify the nearest Captain of the Port, U.S. Coast Guard, and request instructions for disposition of the packages.

(b) **Hazardous materials may be jettisoned** only if the master believes this action necessary to prevent or substantially reduce a hazard to human life or reduce a substantial hazard to property.

§176.48 Situation requiring report.

(a) **When a fire or other hazardous condition exists** on a vessel transporting hazardous materials, the master shall notify the nearest Captain of the Port as soon as possible and shall comply with any instructions given by the Captain of the Port.

(b) **When an incident occurs during transportation** in which a hazardous material is involved, a report may be required (see §§171.15 and 171.16 of this subchapter).

(c) **If a package, portable tank, freight container,** highway or railroad vehicle containing hazardous materials is jettisoned or lost, the master shall notify the nearest Captain of the Port as soon as possible of the location, quantity, and type of the material.

§176.50 Acceptance of damaged or leaking packages.

A carrier may not transport by vessel any package that is so damaged as to permit the escape of its contents, that appears to have leaked, or that gives evidence of failure to properly contain the contents unless it is restored or repaired to the satisfaction of the master of the vessel. A package containing radioactive materials (other than low specific activity materials) may not be repaired or restored.

§176.52 Rejections of shipments in violation.

(a) **A carrier may not knowingly transport by vessel** any hazardous material offered under a false or deceptive name, marking, invoice, shipping paper or other declaration, or without the shipper furnishing written information about the true nature of the material at the time of delivery.

(b) **If a shipment in violation is found in transit,** the master of the vessel shall adopt procedures which in his judgment provide maximum safety to the vessel, its passengers and its crew and which are in compliance with §176.45. If the vessel is in port, the material may not be delivered to any party, and the master shall immediately notify the nearest Captain of the Port and request instructions for disposition of the material.

§176.54 Repairs involving welding, burning, and power-actuated tools and appliances.

(a) **Except as provided in paragraph (b) of this section,** repairs or work involving welding or burning, or the use of power-actuated tools or appliances which may produce intense heat may not be undertaken on any vessel having on board explosives or other hazardous materials as cargo.

(b) **Paragraph (a) of this section does not apply if:**

(1) *The repairs or work* are approved by the COTP under 33 CFR 126.15(c); or

(2) *Emergency repairs* to the vessel's main propelling or boiler plant or auxiliaries are necessary for the safety of the vessel. If such repairs are performed, the master of the vessel must immediately notify the nearest COTP.

Subpart C - General Handling and Stowage

§176.57 Supervision of handling and stowage.

(a) **Hazardous materials may be handled or stowed** on board a vessel only under the direction and observation of a responsible person assigned this duty.

(b) **For a vessel engaged in coastwise voyages,** or on rivers, bays, sounds or lakes, including the Great Lakes when the voyage is not foreign-going, the responsible person may be an employee of the carrier and assigned this duty by the carrier, or a licensed officer attached to the vessel and assigned by the master of the vessel.

(c) **For a domestic vessel engaged in a foreign-going** or intercoastal voyage, the responsible person must be an officer possessing an unexpired license issued by the USCG and assigned this duty by the master of the vessel.

(d) **For a foreign vessel, the responsible person** must be an officer of the vessel assigned this duty by the master of the vessel.

§176.58 Preparation of the vessel.

(a) **Each hold or compartment in which hazardous materials** are to be stowed must be free of all debris before the hazardous materials are stowed. Bilges must be examined and all residue of previous cargo removed.

(b) **All decks, gangways, hatches, and cargo ports** over or through which hazardous materials must be passed or handled in loading or unloading must be free of all loose materials before cargo handling operations begin.

(c) **No debris that creates a fire hazard or a hazardous condition** for persons engaged in handling hazardous materials may be on the weather deck of a vessel during loading or unloading operations.

(d) **Hatch beams and hatch covers may not be stowed** in a location that would interfere with cargo handling.

§176.60 "No Smoking" signs.

When smoking is prohibited during the loading, stowing, storing, transportation, or unloading of hazardous materials by this part, the carrier and the master of the vessel are jointly responsible for posting "NO SMOKING" signs in conspicuous locations.

§176.63 Stowage locations.

(a) **The table in §172.101 of this subchapter** specifies generally the locations authorized for stowage of the various hazardous materials on board vessels. This part prescribes additional requirements with respect to the stowage of specific hazardous materials in addition to those authorized in §172.101 of this subchapter. This section sets forth the basic physical requirements for the authorized locations.

(b) **To qualify as "on deck" stowage,** the location must be on the weather deck. If it is in a house on the weather deck, it must have a permanent structural opening to the atmosphere, such as a door, hatch, companionway or manhole, and must be vented to the atmosphere. It may not have any structural opening to any living quarters, cargo, or other compartment unless the opening has means for being closed off and secured. Any deck house containing living quarters, a steering engine, a refrigerating unit, a refrigerated stowage box, or a heating unit may not be used unless that area is isolated from the cargo stowage area by a permanent, and tight metallic bulkhead. Stowage in a shelter or 'tween deck is not considered to be "on deck". A barge which is vented to the atmosphere and is stowed on deck on a barge-carrying ship is considered to be "on deck". When an entry in §172.101 of this subchapter requires "on-deck" stowage and is qualified by the requirement "shade from radiant heat", the stowage must be protected from the direct rays of the sun by means of structural erections or awnings except that such protection is not required for shipment in portable tanks.

(c) **To qualify as "under deck" stowage,** the location must be in a hold or compartment below the weather deck capable of being ventilated and allotted entirely to the carriage of cargo. It must be bounded by permanent steel decks and bulkheads or the shell of the vessel. The deck openings must have means for effectively closing the hold or compartment against the weather, and in the case of superimposed holds, for effectively closing off each hold. A hold or compartment containing a crew passage formed by battens or by mesh or wire screen bulkhead may not be used for the stowage of any hazardous material unless a watchman is provided for this area.

(d) **To qualify as "under deck away from heat",** the location must be under deck and have built-in means for ventilation. If it is subject to heat from any artificial source, it only qualifies for the stowage of those hazardous materials for which "under deck" stowage is authorized.

(e) **Closed cargo transport unit, for the purpose** of stowage of Class 1 (explosive) materials on board a vessel, means a clean, substantial, weatherproof box structure which can be secured to the ship's structure and includes a closed freight container, a closed vehicle, a closed rail wagon or a portable magazine. When this stowage is specified, stowage in small compartments such as deckhouses and mast lockers or oversized weatherproof packages (overpacks) are acceptable alternatives. The floor of any closed cargo transport unit or compartment shall be constructed of wood, close boarded or arranged so that goods are stowed on sparred gratings, wooden pallets or dunnage. Provided that the necessary additional specifications are met, a closed cargo transport unit may be used for Class 1 (explosive) magazine stowage type "A," "B" or "C," but not as a portable magazine.

§176.65 Alternative stowage procedures.

When a hazardous material is to be loaded on board a vessel and it is shown to the satisfaction of the Coast Guard Captain of the Port for the place where the vessel is being loaded that it is impracticable to comply with a stowage location requirement specified in the §172.101 table of this subchapter or a segregation, handling or stowage requirement specified in this part, the Captain of the Port may authorize in writing the use of an alternative stowage location or method of segregation, handling or stowage subject to such conditions as he finds will insure a level of safety at least equal to that afforded by the regulatory requirement concerned.

§176.69 General stowage requirements for hazardous materials.

(a) **Hazardous materials (except as provided** in paragraph (c) of this section and Class 9 (miscellaneous hazardous) materials) must be stowed in a manner that will facilitate inspection during the voyage, their removal from a potentially dangerous situation, and the removal of packages in case of fire.

(b) **Each package marked in accordance with §172.312(a)(2)** of this subchapter must be stowed as to remain in the position indicated during transportation.

(c) **If a vessel designed for and carrying hazardous materials** in freight containers or a vessel designed for and carrying hazardous materials in barges is equipped with a fixed fire extinguishing and fire detection system, the freight containers or barges need not be stowed in the manner required by paragraph (a) of this section. When freight containers or barges containing hazardous materials are stowed on deck, they need not be stowed in the manner required by paragraph (a) of this section if fire fighting equipment capable of reaching and piercing the freight container or barge is on board the vessel.

(d) **Packages of hazardous materials must be** secured and dunnaged to prevent movement in any direction. Vertical restraints are not required if the shape of the package and the stuffing pattern preclude shifting of the load.

(e) **Packages of hazardous materials must be** braced and dunnaged so that they are not likely to be pierced by the dunnage or crushed by a superimposed load.

§176.70 Stowage requirements for marine pollutants.

(a) **Marine pollutants must be properly stowed** and secured to minimize the hazards to the marine environment without impairing the safety of the ship and the persons on board.

(b) **Where stowage is permitted "on deck or under deck"**, under deck stowage is preferred except when a weather deck provides equivalent protection.

(c) **Where stowage "on deck only" is required**, preference should be given to stowage on well-protected decks or to stowage inboard in sheltered areas of exposed decks.

§176.72 Handling of break-bulk hazardous materials.

(a) **A metal bale hook may not be used for handling** any package of hazardous materials.

(b) **The use of equipment designed to lift or move cargo** by means of pressure exerted on the packages may not be used for handling any package of hazardous materials if the device can damage the package or the package is not designed to be moved in that manner.

(c) **Pallets, slings, cargo nets and other related equipment** used in loading packages of hazardous materials must give adequate support to the packages. The packages must be contained so that they are not able to fall during loading.

§176.74 On deck stowage of break-bulk hazardous materials.

(a) **Packages containing hazardous materials** must be secured by enclosing in boxes, cribs or cradles and proper lashing by use of wire rope, strapping or other means, including shoring and bracing, or both. Lashing of deck cargo is permitted if eye pads are used to attach the lashings. Lashings may not be secured to guard rails. Bulky articles must be shored.

(b) **A packaging susceptible to weather or water damage** must be protected so that it will not be exposed to the weather or to sea water.

(c) **Not more than fifty percent of the total open deck area** should be used for stowage of hazardous materials (except Class 9 (miscellaneous hazardous material) materials.

(d) **Fireplugs, hoses, sounding pipes, and access** to these must be free and clear of all cargo.

(e) **Crew and passenger spaces and areas set aside** for the crew's use may not be used to stow any hazardous material.

(f) **A hazardous material may not be stowed** within a horizontal distance of 25 feet of an operating or embarkation point of a lifeboat.

(g) **Hazardous materials must be stowed to permit** safe access to the crew's quarters and to all parts of the deck required in navigation and necessary working of the vessel.

(h) **When runways for use of the crew are built** over stowed hazardous materials, they must be constructed and fitted with rails and lifelines so as to afford complete protection to the crew when in use.

§176.76 Transport vehicles, freight containers, and portable tanks containing hazardous materials.

(a) **Except as provided in paragraphs (b) through (f)** of this section, hazardous materials authorized to be transported by vessel may be carried on board a vessel in a transport vehicle or freight container, subject to the following conditions (see additional requirements concerning the transport of Class 1 (explosive) materials in §§176.168 through 176.172 of this subchapter):

(1) *The material* must be in proper condition for transportation according to the requirements of this subchapter;

(2) *All packages* in the transport vehicle or freight container must be secured to prevent movement in any direction. Vertical restraint is not required if the shape of the packages, loading pattern, and horizontal restraint preclude vertical movement of the load within the freight container or transport vehicle;

(3) *Bulkheads made of dunnage* which extend to the level of the cargo must be provided unless the packages are stowed flush with the sides or ends;

(4) *Dunnage must be secured to the floor* when the cargo consists of dense materials or heavy packages;

(5) *Each package* marked in accordance with §172.312(a)(2) of this subchapter must be stowed as marked;

(6) *Any slack spaces between packages must be filled with dunnage;*

(7) *The weight in a container* must be distributed throughout as evenly as possible and the maximum permissible weight must not be exceeded;

(8) *Adjacent levels* of baggaged and baled cargo must be stowed in alternate directions so that each tier binds the tier above and below it;

(9) *[Reserved]*

(10) *The lading* must be contained entirely within the freight container or vehicle body without overhang or projection except that oversized machinery such as tractors or vehicles with batteries attached may overhang or project outside the intermodal container provided all of that portion of the lading that consists of hazardous materials is contained entirely within the freight container. No open-bed container or vehicle is permitted to carry hazardous materials unless it is equipped with a means of properly securing the lading.

(b) **A transport vehicle containing hazardous materials** may be carried only on board a trailership, trainship, ferry vessel or car float.

(c) **[Reserved]**

(d) **A transport vehicle or freight container** equipped with heating or refrigeration equipment may be operated on board a vessel. However, the equipment may not be operated in any hold or compartment in which any flammable liquid or gas is stowed. Any heating or air conditioning equipment having a fuel tank containing a flammable liquid or gas may be stowed only "on deck". Equipment electrically powered and designed to operate within an environment containing flammable vapors may be operated below deck in a hold or compartment containing a flammable liquid or gas.

(e) **A transport vehicle, loaded with any hazardous material** which is required to be stowed "on deck" by §172.101 of this subchapter, may be stowed one deck below the weather deck when transported on a trainship or trailership which is unable to provide "on deck" stowage because of the vessel's design. Otherwise, the transport vehicle or container must be transported "on deck."

(f) **A hazardous material may be carried on board** a vessel in a portable tank subject to the following conditions:

(1) *Small passenger vessels* of 100 gross tons, or less, may carry a hazardous material in a portable tank only when 16 or less passengers are on board and only when specifically authorized by the Officer-in-Charge, Marine Inspection, by endorsement of the vessel's Certificate of Inspection.

(2) *Portable tanks* containing flammable liquids or gases, combustible liquids with flashpoints below 141 °F that are insoluble in water, or organic peroxides, spontaneously combustible materials, or water reactive materials must be stowed on deck irrespective of the stowage authorized in §172.101 of this subchapter. Portable tanks containing hazardous materials not restricted to on deck stowage by the previous sentence must be stowed in accordance with the requirements specified in §172.101 of this subchapter.

(3) *Aluminum, magnesium, and their alloys* are specifically prohibited as materials of construction of portable tanks.

(g) **Cryogenic liquids.** For shipment of cryogenic liquids on board a vessel the packaging must be designed and filled so that:

(1) *Any cryogenic liquid* being transported in a cargo tank, regardless of the pressure in the package, must be contained in a steel jacketed Specification MC-338 (§178.338 of this subchapter) insulated cargo tank.

(2) *Any valve or fitting* with moving or abrading parts that may come in contact with any cryogenic liquid may not be made of aluminum.

(3) *For a flammable cryogenic liquid* being transported in a cargo tank, the elapsed time between the loading of the cargo tank and the subsequent unloading of the cargo tank at its final destination may not exceed the marked rated holding time (MRHT) of the cargo tank for the cryogenic liquid being transported, which must be displayed on or adjacent to the specification plate.

(4) *Portable tanks,* cargo tanks, and tank cars containing cryogenic liquids must be stowed "on deck" regardless of the stowage

authorized in §172.101 of this subchapter. Cargo tanks or tank cars containing cryogenic liquids may be stowed one deck below the weather deck when transported on a trailership or trainship that is unable to provide "on deck" stowage because of the vessel's design. Tank cars must be Class DOT-113 or AAR-204W tank cars.

(h) **A fumigated transport unit may only be transported** on board a vessel subject to the following conditions and limitations:

(1) *The fumigated transport unit* may be placed on board a vessel only if at least 24 hours have elapsed since the unit was last fumigated;

(2) *The fumigated transport unit* is accompanied by a document showing the date of fumigation and the type and amount of fumigant used;

(3) *Prior to loading,* the master is informed of the intended placement of the fumigated transport unit on board the vessel and the information provided on the accompanying document;

(4) *Equipment that is capable* of detecting the fumigant and instructions for the equipment's use is provided on the vessel;

(5) *The fumigated transport unit* must be stowed at least 5 m from any opening to accommodation spaces;

(6) *Fumigated transport units* may only be transported on deck on vessels carrying more than 25 passengers; and

(7) *Fumigants may not be added* to transport units while on board a vessel.

(i) **Containers packed or loaded with flammable gases** or liquids having a flash point of 23 °C or less and carried on deck must be stowed "away from" possible sources of ignition.

§176.77 Stowage of barges containing hazardous materials on board barge-carrying vessels.

(a) **A barge which contains hazardous materials** may be transported on board a barge-carrying vessel if it is stowed in accordance with the requirements of this section.

(b) **A barge which contains hazardous materials** for which only "on deck" stowage is authorized must be stowed above the weather deck and be vented to the atmosphere.

(c) **A barge which contains hazardous materials** for which both "on deck" and "below deck" storage is authorized may be stowed above or below the weather deck.

§176.78 Use of power-operated industrial trucks on board vessels.

(a) **Power Operated trucks.** A power-operated truck (including a power-operated tractor, forklift, or other specialized truck used for cargo handling) may not be used on board a vessel in a space containing a hazardous material unless the truck conforms to the requirements of this section. The COTP may suspend or prohibit the use of cargo handling vehicles or equipment when that use constitutes a safety hazard.

(b) **Each truck must have a specific designation** of Underwriter's Laboratories or Factory Mutual Laboratories. Any repair or alteration to a truck must be equivalent to that required on the original designation.

(c) **Description of designations.** The recognized testing laboratory type designations are as follows:

(1) *An "E" designated unit* is an electrically-powered unit that has minimum acceptable safeguards against inherent fire hazards.

(2) *An "EE" designated unit* is an electrically-powered unit that has, in addition to all the requirements for the "E" unit, the electric motor and all other electrical equipment completely enclosed.

(3) *An "EX" designated unit* is an electrically-powered unit that differs from the "E" and "EE" unit in that the electrical fittings and equipment are so designed, constructed, and assembled that the unit may be used in certain atmospheres containing flammable vapors or dusts.

(4) *A "G" designated unit* is a gasoline-powered unit having minimum acceptable safeguards against inherent fire hazards.

(5) *A "GS" designated unit* is a gasoline-powered unit that is provided with additional safeguards to the exhaust, fuel, and electrical systems.

(6) *An "LP" designated unit* is similar to a "G" unit except that it is powered by liquefied petroleum gas instead of gasoline.

(7) *An "LPS" designated unit* is a unit similar to a "GS" unit except that liquefied petroleum gas is used for fuel instead of gasoline.

(8) *A "D" designated unit* is a unit similar to a "G" unit except that it is powered by a diesel engine instead of a gasoline engine.

(9) *A "DS" designated unit* is a unit powered by a diesel engine provided with additional safeguards to the exhaust, fuel, and electrical systems.

(d) **Class 1 (explosive) materials.** No power-operated truck may be used to handle Class 1 (explosive) materials or other cargo in an area near Class 1 (explosive) materials on board a vessel except:

(1) *A power-operated truck designated EE or EX.*

(2) *A power-operated truck* designated LPS, GS, D, or DS may be used under conditions acceptable to the COTP.

(e) **Other hazardous materials.**

(1) *Only an* "EX", "EE", "GS", "LPA", or "DS" truck may be used in a hold or compartment containing Division 2.1 (flammable gas) materials, Class 3 (flammable liquids), Class 4 (flammable solids) materials, or Class 5 (oxidizers or organic peroxides) materials, cottons or other vegetable fibers, or bulk sulfur.

(2) *Only a designated truck* may be used to handle any other hazardous material not covered in paragraph (d) or (e)(1) of this section.

(f) **Minimum safety features.** In addition to the construction and design safety features required, each truck must have at least the following minimum safety features:

(1) *The truck must be equipped* with a warning horn, whistle, gong, or other device that may be heard clearly above normal shipboard noises.

(2) *When the truck operation* may expose the operator to danger from a falling object, the truck must be equipped with a driver's overhead guard. When the overall height of the truck with forks in the lowered position is limited by head room the overhead guard may be omitted. This overhead guard is only intended to offer protection from impact of small packages, boxes, bagged material, or similar hazards.

(3) *A forklift truck* used to handle small objects or unstable loads must be equipped with a load backrest extension having height, width, and strength sufficient to prevent any load, or part of it, from falling toward the mast when the mast is in a position of maximum backward tilt. The load backrest extension must be constructed in a manner that does not interfere with good visibility.

(4) *The forks* on a fork lift truck must be secured to the carriage so as to prevent any unintentional lifting of the toe which could create a hazard. The forks may not display permanent deformation when subjected to a test load of three times the rated capacity.

(5) *Each fork extension* or other attachment must be secured to prevent unintentional lifting or displacement on primary forks.

(6) *Tires extending* beyond the confines of the truck shall be provided with a guard to prevent the tires from throwing particles at the operator.

(7) *Unless the steering mechanism* is a type that prevents road reactions from causing the steering handwheel to spin, a mushroom type steering knob must be used to engage the palm of the operator's hand, or the steering mechanism must be arranged in some other manner to prevent injury. The knob must be mounted within the perimeter of the wheel.

(8) *All steering controls* must be confined within the clearance of the truck or guarded so that movement of the controls will not result in injury to the operator when passing stanchions, obstructions or other.

(g) **Special operating conditions.**

(1) *A truck* may not be used on board a vessel unless prior notification of its use is given to the master or senior deck officer on board.

(2) *Before a truck* is operated on board a vessel, it must be in a safe operating condition as determined by the master or senior deck officer on board.

(3) *Any truck* that emits sparks or flames from the exhaust system must immediately be removed from service and may not be returned to service until the cause of these sparks or flames has been eliminated.

(4)-(5) *[Reserved]*

(6) *All truck motors* must be shut off immediately when a breakage or leakage of packages containing flammable liquids or gases, flammable solids, oxidizers, or organic peroxides occurs or is discovered.

(7) *The rated capacity of the truck* must be posted on the truck at all times in a conspicuous place. This capacity may not be exceeded.

(8) *At least* one Coast Guard approved marine type size 1 Type B, or UL approved 5BC portable fire extinguisher, or its approved equivalent, must be affixed to the truck in a readily accessible position or must be kept in close proximity, available for immediate use.

(9) *The vessel's fire fighting equipment,* both fixed (where installed) and portable, must be kept ready for immediate use in the vicinity of the space being worked.

(h) **Refueling.**

(1) *A truck using gasoline as fuel* may not be refueled in the hold or on the weather deck of a vessel unless a portable non-spilling fuel handling system of not over five gallons capacity is used. Gasoline may not be transferred to a portable non-spilling fuel handling device on board the vessel.

(2) *A truck using liquefied petroleum gas as fuel* may not be refueled in the hold or on the weather deck of a vessel unless it is fitted

with a removable tank and the hand-operated shutoff valve of the depleted tank is closed. In addition, the motor must be run until it stalls from lack of fuel and then the hand-operated shut off valve closed before the quick disconnect fitting to the fuel tank is disconnected.

(3) *A truck using diesel oil as fuel* may not be refueled on the weather deck or in the hold of a vessel unless a portable container of not over a five gallon capacity is used. A truck may be refueled or a portable container may be refilled from a larger container of diesel fuel on the weather deck of a vessel if a suitable pump is used for the transfer operation and a drip pan of adequate size is used to prevent any dripping of fuel on the deck.

(4) *Refueling must be performed* under the direct supervision of an experienced and responsible person specifically designated for this duty by the person in charge of the loading or unloading of the vessel.

(5) *Refueling may not be undertaken* with less than two persons specifically assigned and present for the complete operation, at least one of whom must be experienced in using the portable fire extinguishers required in the fuel area.

(6) *At least* one Coast Guard approved marine type size 1 Type B or UL approved 5BC portable fire extinguisher or its approved equivalent, must be provided in the fueling area. This is in addition to the extinguisher required by paragraph (g)(8) of this section.

(7) *The location* for refueling trucks must be designated by the master or senior deck officer on board the vessel. "NO SMOKING" signs must be conspicuously posted in the area.

(8) *The location* designated for refueling must be adequately ventilated to insure against accumulation of any hazardous concentration of vapors.

(9) *Before any truck* in a hold is refueled or before any fuel handling device or unmounted liquefied petroleum gas cylinder is placed in a hold, the motors of all trucks in the same hold must be stopped.

(10) *All fuel handling devices* and unmounted liquefied petroleum gas containers must be removed from a hold before any truck motor is started and the trucks are placed in operation in that hold.

(i) **Replacing batteries.** Batteries for electrically powered trucks and for the ignition systems of internal combustion powered trucks may be changed in the hold of a vessel subject to the following conditions:

(1) *Only suitable handling equipment may be employed.*

(2) *Adequate precautions* must be taken to avoid damage to the battery, short circuiting of the battery, and spillage of the electrolyte.

(j) **Charging of batteries.** Batteries of industrial trucks may be recharged in a hold of a vessel subject to the following conditions:

(1) *The batteries* must be housed in a suitable, ventilated, portable metal container with a suitable outlet at the top for connection of a portable air hose, or must be placed directly beneath a suitable outlet at the top for connection of a portable air hose. The air hose must be permanently connected to an exhaust duct leading to the open deck and terminate in a gooseneck or other suitable weather head. If natural ventilation is not practicable or adequate, mechanical means of exhaust must be employed in conjunction with the duct. The air outlet on the battery container must be equipped with an interlock switch so arranged that the charging of the battery cannot take place unless the air hose is properly connected to the box.

(2) *If mechanical ventilation is used,* an additional interlock must be provided between the fan and the charging circuit so that the fan must be in operation in order to complete the charging circuit for operation. It is preferable that this interlock switch be of a centrifugal type driven by the fan shaft.

(3) *The hold may not contain any hazardous materials.*

(4) *The charging facilities* may be part of the truck equipment or may be separate from the truck and located inside or outside the cargo hold. The power supply or charging circuit (whichever method is used) must be connected to the truck by a portable plug connection of the break-away type. This portable plug must be so engaged with the truck battery charging outlet that any movement of the truck away from the charging station will break the connection between the plug and receptacle without exposing any live parts to contact with a conducting surface or object and without the plug falling to the deck where it may become subject to damage.

(5) *All unmounted batteries* must be suitably protected or removed from an area in the hold of the vessel before any truck is operated in that area.

(k) **Stowage of power-operated industrial trucks** on board a vessel. Trucks stowed on board a vessel must meet vessel stowage requirements in §176.905.

(l) **Packaging and stowage of fuel on board a vessel.** Division 2.1 (flammable gas) materials and flammable liquids used as fuel for industrial trucks must be packaged and stowed as authorized in 46 CFR 147.60 or 46 CFR 147.45, respectively.

Subpart D - General Segregation Requirements

§176.80 Applicability.

(a) **This subpart sets forth segregation requirements** in addition to any segregation requirements set forth elsewhere in this subchapter.

(b) **Hazardous materials in limited quantities** when loaded in transport vehicles and freight containers, are excepted from the segregation requirements of this subpart and any additional segregation specified in this subchapter for transportation by vessel.

§176.83 Segregation.

(a) **General.**

(1) *The requirements* of this section apply to all cargo spaces on deck or under deck of all types of vessels, and to all cargo transport units.

(2) *Segregation is obtained* by maintaining certain distances between incompatible hazardous materials or by requiring the presence of one or more steel bulkheads or decks between them or a combination thereof. Intervening spaces between such hazardous materials may be filled with other cargo which is not incompatible with the hazardous materials.

(3) *The general requirements* for segregation between the various classes of dangerous goods are shown in the segregation table. In addition to these general requirements, there may be a need to segregate a particular material from other materials which would contribute to its hazard. Such segregation requirements are indicated by code numbers in Column 10B of the §172.101 Table.

(4) *Segregation is not required* between hazardous materials of different classes which comprise the same substance but vary only in their water content (e.g., sodium sulphide in Division 4.2 or Class 8).

(5) *Whenever hazardous materials* are stowed together, whether or not in a transport unit, the segregation of such hazardous materials from others must always be in accordance with the most restrictive requirements for any of the hazardous materials concerned.

(6) *When the §172.101 Table* or §172.402 requires packages to bear a subsidiary hazard label or labels, the segregation appropriate to the subsidiary hazards must be applied when that segregation is more restrictive than that required by the primary hazard. For the purposes of this paragraph, the segregation requirements corresponding to an explosive subsidiary hazard are — except for organic peroxides which are those corresponding to Division 1.3 — those for Division 1.4 (explosive) materials.

(7) *Where, for the purposes* of segregation, terms such as "away from" a particular hazard class are used in the §172.101 Table, the segregation requirement applies to:

(i) *All hazardous materials within the hazard class; and*

(ii) *All hazardous materials* for which a secondary hazard label of that class is required.

(8) *Notwithstanding the requirements* of paragraphs (a)(6) and (a)(7) of this section, hazardous materials of the same class may be stowed together without regard to segregation required by secondary hazards (subsidiary risk label(s)), provided the substances do not react dangerously with each other and cause:

(i) *Combustion and/or evolution of considerable heat;*

(ii) *Evolution of flammable, toxic or asphyxiant gases;*

(iii) *The formation of corrosive substances; or*

(iv) *The formation of unstable substances.*

(9) *Stowage in a shelter-'tween deck cargo* space is not considered to be "on deck" stowage.

(10) *Where the code* in column (10B) of the §172.101 Table specifies that "Segregation as for..." applies, the segregation requirements applicable to that class in the §176.83(b) General Segregation Table must be applied. However, for the purposes of paragraph (a)(8) of this section, which permits substances of the same class to be stowed together provided they do not react dangerously with each other, the segregation requirements of the class as represented by the primary hazard class in the §172.101 Table entry must be applied.

(b) **General Segregation Table.** The following table sets forth the general requirements for segregation between the various classes of hazardous materials. The properties of materials within each class may vary greatly and may require greater segregation than is reflected in this table. If the §172.101 Table sets forth particular requirements for segregation, they take precedence over these general requirements.

Table 176.83(b) - General Segregation Requirements for Hazardous Materials
[Segregation must also take account of a single secondary hazard label, as required by paragraph (a)(6) of this section.]

Class	1.1 1.2 1.5	1.3	1.4 1.6	2.1	2.2	2.3	3	4.1	4.2	4.3	5.1	5.2	6.1	6.2	7	8	9
Explosives, 1.1, 1.2, 1.5	(*)	(*)	(*)	4	2	2	4	4	4	4	4	4	2	4	2	4	X
Explosives, 1.3	(*)	(*)	(*)	4	2	2	4	3	3	4	4	4	2	4	2	2	X
Explosives, 1.4, 1.6	(*)	(*)	(*)	2	1	1	2	2	2	2	2	2	X	4	2	2	X
Flammable gases 2.1	4	4	2	X	X	X	2	1	2	X	2	2	X	4	2	1	X
Non-toxic, non-flammable gases 2.2	2	2	1	X	X	X	1	X	1	X	X	1	X	2	1	X	X
Poisonous gases 2.3	2	2	1	X	X	X	2	X	2	X	X	2	X	2	1	X	X
Flammable liquids 3	4	4	2	2	1	2	X	X	2	1	2	2	X	3	2	X	X
Flammable solids 4.1	4	3	2	1	X	X	X	X	1	X	1	2	X	3	2	1	X
Spontaneously combustible substances 4.2	4	3	2	2	1	2	2	1	X	1	2	2	1	3	2	1	X
Substances which are dangerous when wet 4.3	4	4	2	X	X	X	1	X	1	X	2	2	X	2	2	1	X
Oxidizing substances 5.1	4	4	2	2	X	X	2	1	2	2	X	2	1	3	1	2	X
Organic peroxides 5.2	4	4	2	2	1	2	2	2	2	2	2	X	1	3	2	2	X
Poisons 6.1	2	2	X	X	X	X	X	X	1	X	1	1	X	1	X	X	X
Infectious substances 6.2	4	4	4	4	2	2	3	3	3	2	3	3	1	X	3	3	X
Radioactive materials 7	2	2	2	2	1	1	2	2	2	2	1	2	X	3	X	2	X
Corrosives 8	4	2	2	1	X	X	X	1	1	1	2	2	X	3	2	X	X
Miscellaneous dangerous substances 9	X	X	X	X	X	X	X	X	X	X	X	X	X	X	X	X	X

Numbers and symbols relate to the following terms as defined in this section:
1 — "Away from."
2 — "Separated from."
3 — "Separated by a complete compartment or hold from."
4 — "Separated longitudinally by an intervening complete compartment or hold from."
X — The segregation, if any, is shown in the §172.101 table.
* — See §176.144 of this part for segregation within Class 1.

(c) **Segregation requirements for breakbulk cargo.**

(1) *The requirements of this paragraph* apply to the segregation of packages containing hazardous materials and stowed as breakbulk cargo;

(2) *Definition of the segregation terms:*

(i) **Legend:**

[A] Package containing incompatible goods.

[B] Reference package.

[C] Deck resistant to fire and liquid.

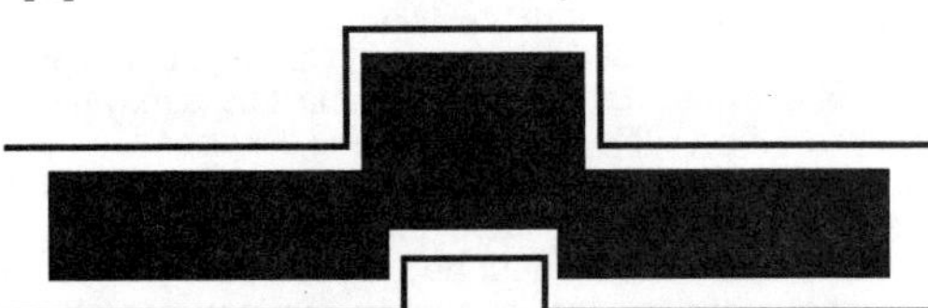

NOTE: Full vertical lines represent transverse bulkheads between compartments or holds resistant to fire and liquid.

(ii) **Away from:** Effectively segregated so that the incompatible materials cannot interact dangerously in the event of an accident but may be carried in the same compartment or hold or on deck provided a minimum horizontal separation of 3 m (10 feet) projected vertically is obtained.

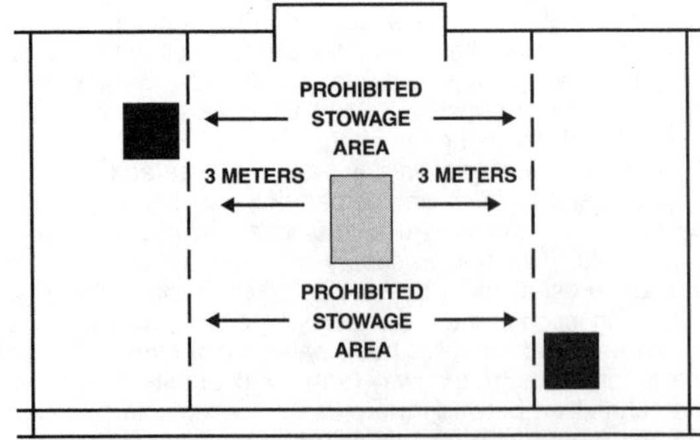

(iii) **Separated From.** In different compartments or holds when stowed under deck. If the intervening deck is resistant to fire and liquid, a vertical separation (i.e., in different compartments) is acceptable as equivalent to this segregation. For "on deck" stowage, this segregation means a separation by a distance of at least 6 m (20 feet) horizontally.

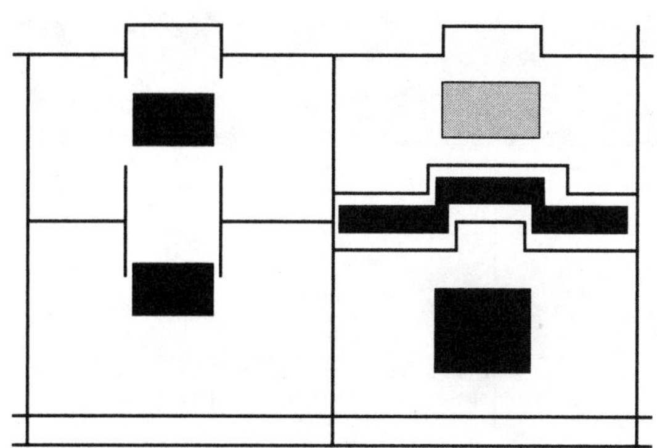

(iv) **Separated by a complete compartment or hold from:** Either a vertical or horizontal separation. If the intervening decks are not resistant to fire and liquid, then only a longitudinal separation (i.e., by a intervening complete compartment or hold) is acceptable. For "on deck" stowage, this segregation means a separation by a distance of at least 12 m (39 feet) horizontally. The same distance must be applied if one package is stowed "on deck", and the other one in an upper compartment.

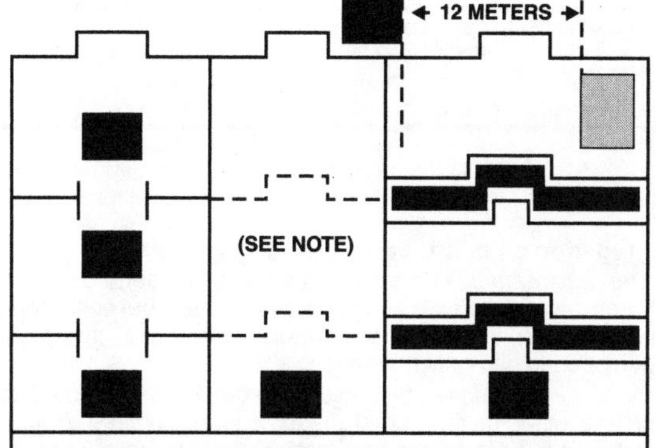

NOTE: One of the two decks must be resistant to fire and liquid.

(v) **Separated longitudinally by an intervening complete compartment or hold from:** Vertical separation alone does not meet this requirement. Between a package "under deck" and one "on deck" a minimum distance of 24 m (79 feet) including a complete compartment must be maintained longitudinally. For "on deck" stowage, this segregation means a separation by a distance of at least 24 m (79 feet) longitudinally.

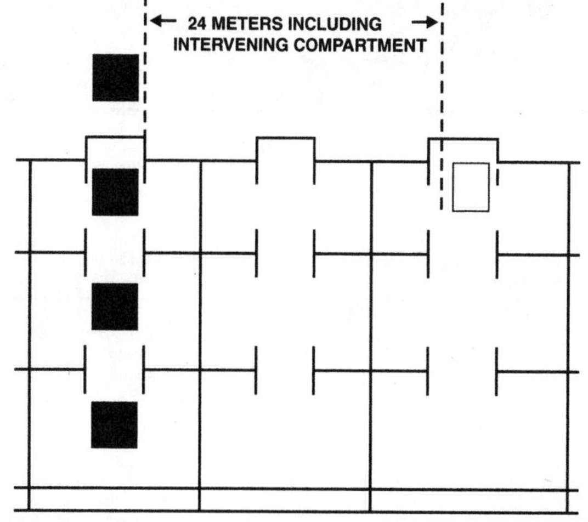

(d) **Segregation in transport units:** Two hazardous materials for which any segregation is required may not be stowed in the same transport unit.

(e) **Segregation of hazardous materials stowed** as breakbulk cargo from those packed in transport units:

(1) *Hazardous materials* stowed as breakbulk cargo must be segregated from materials packed in open transport units in accordance with paragraph (c) of this section.

(2) *Hazardous materials* stowed as breakbulk cargo must be segregated from materials packed in closed transport units in accordance with paragraph (c) of this section, except that:

(i) *Where "away from"* is required, no segregation between packages and the closed transport units is required; and

(ii) *Where "separated from"* is required, the segregation between the packages and the closed transport units may be the same as for "away from".

(f) **Segregation of containers on board container vessels:**

(1) *This paragraph* applies to the segregation of freight containers which are carried on board container vessels, or on other types of vessels provided these cargo spaces are properly fitted for permanent stowage of freight containers during transport.

(2) *For container vessels* which have cargo spaces used for breakbulk cargo or any other method of stowage, the appropriate paragraph of this section applies to the relevant cargo space.

(3) *Segregation Table:* Table §176.83(f) sets forth the general requirements for segregation between freight containers on board container vessels.

(4) *In table §176.83(f),* a container space means a distance of not less than 6 m (20 feet) fore and aft or not less than 2.5 m (8 feet) athwartship.

Table 176.83(f) - Segregation of Containers on Board Container Ships

Segregation requirement	Vertical			Horizontal						
	Closed versus closed	Closed versus open	Open versus open		Closed versus closed		Closed versus open		Open versus open	
					On deck	Under deck	On deck	Under deck	On deck	Under deck
1. "Away from"	One on top of the other permitted	Open on top of closed permitted	Not in the same vertical line unless segregated by a deck	Fore and aft	No restriction	No restriction	No restriction	No restriction	One container space	One container space or one bulkhead
		Otherwise as for open versus open		Athwartships	No restriction	No restriction	No restriction	No restriction	One container space	One container space
2. "Separated from"	Not in the same vertical line unless segregated by a deck	As for open versus open	Not in the same vertical line unless segregated by a deck	Fore and aft	One container space	One container space or one bulkhead	One container space	One container space or one bulkhead	One container space	One bulkhead
				Athwartships	One container space	One container space	One container space	Two container spaces	Two container spaces	One bulkhead
3. "Separated by a complete compartment or hold from"	Not in the same vertical line unless segregated by a deck	As for open versus open	Not in the same vertical line unless segregated by a deck	Fore and aft	One container space	One bulkhead	One container space	One bulkhead	Two container spaces	Two bulkheads
				Athwartships	Two container spaces	One bulkhead	Two container spaces	One bulkhead	Three container spaces	Two bulkheads
4. "Separated longitudinally by an intervening complete compartment or hold from"	Prohibited			Fore and aft	Four container spaces	One bulkhead and four container spaces*	Four container spaces	Two bulkheads	Four container spaces	Two bulkheads
				Athwartships	Prohibited	Prohibited	Prohibited	Prohibited	Prohibited	Prohibited

* Containers not less than 6 m (20 feet) from intervening bulkhead.
NOTE: All bulkheads and decks must be resistant to fire and liquid.

(g) Segregation of transport units on board trailerships:

(1) *The requirements* of this paragraph apply to the segregation of transport units which are carried on board trailerships or in "roll-on/roll-off" cargo spaces.

(2) *For trailerships* which have spaces suitable for breakbulk cargo, containers, or any other method of stowage, the appropriate paragraph of this section applies to the relevant cargo space.

(3) *Segregation Table.* Table §176.83(g) sets forth the general requirements for segregation between transport units on board trailerships.

Table 176.83(g) - Segregation of Transport Units on Board Trailerships and Trainships

Segregation requirement		Closed versus closed		Closed versus open		Open versus open	
		On deck	Under deck	On deck	Under deck	On deck	Under deck
1. "Away from"	Fore and aft	No restriction	No restriction	No restriction	No restriction	At least 3 m	At least 3 m
	Athwartships	No restriction	No restriction	No restriction	No restriction	At least 3 m	At least 3 m
2. "Separated from"	Fore and aft	At least 6 m	At least 6 m or one bulkhead	At least 6 m	At least 6 m or one bulkhead	At least 6 m	At least 12 m or one bulkhead
	Athwartships	At least 3 m	At least 3 m or one bulkhead	At least 3 m	At least 6 m or one bulkhead	At least 6 m	At least 12 m or one bulkhead
3. "Separated by a complete compartment or hold from"	Fore and aft	At least 12 m	At least 24 m + deck	At least 24 m	At least 24 m + deck	At least 36 m	Two decks or two bulkheads
	Athwartships	At least 12 m	At least 24 m + deck	At least 24 m	At least 24 m + deck	At least 36 m	Prohibited
4. "Separated longitudinally by an intervening complete compartment or hold from"	Fore and aft	At least 36 m	Two bulkheads or at least 36 m + two decks	At least 36 m	At least 48 m including two bulkheads	At least 48 m	Prohibited
	Athwartships	Prohibited	Prohibited	Prohibited	Prohibited	Prohibited	Prohibited

NOTE: All bulkheads and decks must be resistant to fire and liquid.

(h) Segregation on board barge carrying vessels:

(1) *The requirements* of this section apply to the segregation in shipborne barges as well as to the segregation between shipborne barges carried on board vessels specially designed and equipped to carry such barges.

(2) *On barge-carrying vessels* which incorporate other stowage spaces or any other method of stowage, barges containing hazardous materials must be segregated from hazardous materials not stowed in barges as prescribed in paragraphs (b) and (j) of this section.

(i) Segregation in shipborne barges: Hazardous materials transported in shipborne barges must be segregated as prescribed in paragraphs (a), (b), and (c) of this section.

(j) Segregation between shipborne barges on barge-carrying vessels:

(1) *When a shipborne barge* is loaded with two or more hazardous materials with different requirements for segregation, the most stringent applicable segregation requirement must be applied.

(2) *"Away from" and "separated from"* require no segregation between shipborne barges.

(3) *For barge-carrying vessels* with vertical holds, "Separated by a complete compartment or hold from" means that separate holds are required. On barge-carrying vessels having horizontal barge levels, separate barge levels are required and the barges may not be in the same vertical line.

(4) *"Separated longitudinally* by an intervening complete compartment or hold from" means, for barge-carrying vessels with vertical holds, that separation by an intervening hold or engine room is required. On barge-carrying vessels having horizontal barge levels, separate barge levels and a longitudinal separation by at least two intervening barge spaces are required.

(k) Segregation requirements for ferry vessels: A ferry vessel (when operating either as a passenger or cargo vessel) that cannot provide the separation required in this section may carry incompatible hazardous materials in separate transport vehicles if they are stowed to give the maximum possible separation.

§176.84 Other requirements for stowage and segregation for cargo vessels and passenger vessels.

(a) **General.** When column 10B of the §172.101 Table refers to a numbered or alpha-numeric stowage provision for water shipments, the meaning and requirements of that provision are as set forth in this section. Terms in quotation marks are defined in §176.83.

(b) **Table of provisions:**

Code	Provisions
1	[Reserved]
2	Temperature controlled material.
3	Do not stow with high explosives.
4	Stow "Separated from" liquid organic materials.
5	Stow "Separated from" powdered metals and their compounds.
6	Emergency temperature material.
7	[Reserved]
8	Glass carboys not permitted on passenger vessels.
9	Glass carboys not permitted under deck.
10	Glass bottles not permitted under deck.
11	Keep away from heat and open flame.
12	Keep as cool as reasonably practicable.
13	Keep as dry as reasonably practicable.
14	For metal drums, stowage permitted under deck on cargo vessels.
15	May be stowed in portable magazine or metal locker.
16	No other cargo may be stowed in the same hold with this material.
17	Segregation same as for flammable gases but "away from" dangerous when wet.
18	Prohibited on any vessel carrying explosives (except explosives in Division 1.4, Compatibility group S).
19	Protect from sparks and open flames.
20	Segregation same as for corrosives.
21	Segregation same as for flammable liquids.
22	Segregation same as for flammable liquids if flash point below 61 °C (142 °F).
23	Segregation same as for flammable liquids if flash point between 23 °C (73 °F) and 61 °C (142 °F).
24	Segregation same as for flammable solids.
25	Shade from radiant heat.
26	Stow "away from" acids.
27	Stow "away from" alkaline compounds.
28	Stow "away from" flammable liquids.
29	Stow "away from" ammonium compounds.
30	Stow "away from" animal or vegetable oils.
31	Stow "away from" combustible materials.
32	Stow "away from" copper, its alloys and its salts.
33	Stow "away from" fluorides.
34	Stow "away from" foodstuffs.
35	Stow "away from" all odor-absorbing cargo.
36	Stow "away from" heavy metals and their compounds.
37	Stow "away from" hydrazine.
38	Stow "away from" all other corrosives.
39	Stow "away from" liquid halogenated hydrocarbons.
40	Stow "clear of living quarters".
41	Stow "away from" mercury and its compounds.
42	Stow "away from" nitric acids and perchloric acids not exceeding 50 percent acid by weight.
43	Stow "away from" organic materials.
44	Stow "away from" oxidizers.
45	Stow "away from" permanganates.
46	Stow "away from" powdered metals.
47	Stow "away from" sodium compounds.
48	Stow "away from" sources of heat.
49	Stow "away from" corrosives.
50	Stow "away from" sources of heat where temperatures in excess of 55 °C (131 °F) for a period of 24 hours or more will be encountered.
51	Stow "separated from" acetylene.
52	Stow "separated from" acids.
53	Stow "separated from" alkaline compounds.
54	Stow "separated from" animal or vegetable oils.
55	Stow "separated from" ammonia.
56	Stow "separated from" ammonium compounds.
57	Stow "separated from" chlorine.
58	Stow "separated from" cyanides.
59	Stow "separated from" combustible materials.
60	Stow "separated from" chlorates, chlorites, hypochlorites, nitrites, perchlorates, permanganates, and metallic powders.
61	Stow "separated from" corrosive materials.
62	Stow "separated from" diborane.
63	Stow "separated from" diethylene triamine.
64	Stow "separated from" explosives.
65	Stow "separated from" flammable substances.
66	Stow "separated from" flammable solids.
67	Stow "separated from" halides.
68	Stow "separated from" hydrogen.
69	Stow "separated from" hydrogen peroxide.
70	Stow "separated from" mercury salts.
71	Stow "separated from" nitric acid.
72	Stow "separated from" nitrogen compounds.
73	Stow "separated from" chlorates.
74	Stow "separated from" oxidizers.
75	Stow "separated from" permanganates.
76	Stow "separated by a complete compartment or hold from" organic peroxides.
77	Stow "separated longitudinally by a complete compartment or hold from" explosives.
78	Stow "separated longitudinally by an intervening complete compartment or hold from" explosives.
79	The maximum net quantity in one package for this material shipped aboard a passenger vessel is limited to 22.7 kg (50 pounds).
80	Toy torpedoes must not be packed with other special fireworks.
81	Under deck stowage permitted only if an indicating substance such as chloropicrin has been added.
82	Under deck stowage is permitted only if containing not more than 36 percent by weight of hydrazine.
83	[Reserved]
84	Under deck stowage must be in well-ventilated space.
85	Under deck stowage must be in mechanically ventilated space.
86	Stow "separated by a complete compartment or hold from" explosives Division 1.3.
87	Stow "separated from" Class 1 (explosives) except Division 1.4.
88	Stow "separated by a complete compartment or hold from" Class 1 (explosives) except Division 1.4.
89	Segregation same as for oxidizers.
90	Stow "separated from" radioactive materials.
91	Stow "separated from" flammable liquids.
92	Stow "separated from" powdered materials.
93	Stow not accessible to unauthorized persons on passenger vessels.
94	Plastic jerricans and plastic drums not permitted under deck.
95	Stow "separated from" foodstuffs.
96	Glass carboys not permitted under deck on passenger vessels.
97	Stow "away from" azides.
98	Stow "away from" all flammable materials.
99	Only new metal drums permitted on passenger vessels.
100	Stow "away from" flammable solids.
101	Stow "separated from" iron oxide.
102	Stow "separated from" all odor absorbing cargoes.
103	Only to be loaded under dry weather conditions.
104	Stow "separated from" bromine.
105	As approved by the Competent Authority of the country concerned.
106	Stow "separated from" powdered metal.
107	Stow "separated from" peroxides and superoxides.
108	The transport temperature should be indicated on the tank.
109	Label as a flammable liquid if flash point is 61 °C (142 °F) or below.
110	Packaging Group II if concentration does not exceed 70 percent acid.
111	If concentration exceeds 50 percent acid, notes 66, 74, 89, and 90 apply.

Code	Provisions
112	Packaging Group II for concentrations not less that 50 percent and Packaging Group III for concentrations less than 50 percent.
113	Packaging Group II if concentrations does not exceed 60 percent acid.
114	Corrosive subsidiary risk label required unless concentration is less than 80 percent.
115	If packaged in glass or earthenware inner packagings in wooden or fiberboard outer packagings, the maximum quantity on any vessel is 500 kg (equivalent to 450 L).
116	In a cargo space capable of being opened up in an emergency. The possible need to open hatches in case of fire to provide maximum ventilation and to apply water in an emergency and the consequent risk to the stability of the ship through flooding of the cargo space should be considered before loading.
117	In a clean cargo space capable of being opened up in an emergency. In the case of bagged fertilizer in freight containers, it is sufficient if in the case of an emergency, the cargo is accessible through free approaches (hatch entries) and mechanical ventilation enables the master to exhaust any gases or fumes resulting from decomposition. The possible need to open hatches in case of fire to provide maximum ventilation and to apply water in an emergency and the consequent risk to the stability of the ship through flooding of the cargo space should be considered before loading.
118	Stowage — Category D, Category E freight containers and pallet boxes only. Ventilation may be required. The possible need to open hatches in a case of fire to provide maximum ventilation and to supply water in an emergency, and the consequent risk to the stability of the ship through flooding of the cargo space, should be considered before loading.
119	Double strip stowage recommended.
120	Provide good surface and through ventilation.
121	Packaging group III when the flash point of the flammable liquid is 23 °C (73 °F) or above.
122	Stow "separated from" infectious substances.
123	Stow "away from" infectious substances.
M1 — M6	[Reserved]

(c) **Provisions for the stowage of Class 1 (explosive) materials:**

(1) *Explosive substances* and explosive articles must be stowed in accordance with Column (10A) and Column (10B) of the 172.101 Table of this subchapter.

(2) *The following notes* in column 10B of the §172.101 Table apply to the transport of Class 1 (explosive) materials by vessel:

Notes	Provisions
5E	Stow "away from" lead and its compounds.
7E	Stowage category "04" for projectiles or cartridges for guns, cannons or mortars; Stowage category "08" for other types.
8E	When under deck, special stowage is required.
14E	On deck, cargo transport unit must be steel.
15E	On deck, cargo transport unit must be leakproof.
17E	On deck stowage is recommended.
19E	Stow "away from" Explosive, blasting, type C, UN0083 which contain chlorates or perchlorates.
20E	Stowage category "03" for projectiles or cartridges for guns, cannons or mortars; Stowage category "07" for other types; magazines must be of steel construction that prevents leakage.
21E	Cargo space ventilation must be carefully controlled to avoid excessive condensation.
22E	When containing chlorates or perchlorates, stow "away from" explosives containing ammonium nitrate or other ammonium salts.
23E	Segregate from other Class 1 (explosive) materials in the same manner as is required for flammable liquids.
26E	Stowage category "13" and, for on deck stowage, non-metallic lining of closed cargo transport unit is required when not in effectively sealed, sift-proof packages; Stowage category "10" permitted when in effectively sealed, sift-proof packages.
27E	For closed cargo transport units, a non-metallic lining is required.

Subpart E - Special Requirements for Transport Vehicles Loaded With Hazardous Materials and Transported on Board Ferry Vessels

§176.88 Applicability.

The requirements in this subpart are applicable to transport vehicles containing hazardous materials being transported on board ferry vessels and are in addition to any prescribed elsewhere in this subchapter. Vessels in a service similar to a ferry service, but not over a designated ferry route, may be treated as a ferry vessel for the purpose of this subpart if approved in writing by the District Commander.

§176.89 Control of transport vehicles.

(a) **A transport vehicle containing hazardous materials** may be transported on board a ferry vessel, subject to the following conditions:

(1) *The operator* or person in charge of the vehicle shall deliver to the vessel's representative a copy of the shipping papers and certificate required by §§176.24 and 176.27;

(2) *The vehicle* shall be placed at the location indicated by the vessel's representative;

(3) *The parking brakes* of the vehicle shall be set securely to prevent movement;

(4) *The motor* of a highway vehicle shall be shut off and not restarted until the vessel has completed its voyage and docked;

(5) *All vehicle lights* shall be cut off and not relighted until the vessel has completed its voyage and docked;

(6) *The operator of a highway vehicle shall remain with the vehicle;*

(7) *No repairs* or adjustments must be made to the vehicle while it is on the vessel;

(8) *No hazardous materials are to be released from the vehicle; and*

(9) *Any instructions* given by the vessel's representative during the voyage, and during "roll on" and "roll off" operations must be observed.

(b) **Smoking by any person in or around a vehicle is prohibited.**

§176.90 Private automobiles.

A private automobile which is carrying any Class 1 (explosive) material (except permitted fireworks or small arms ammunition) may not be transported on a passenger-carrying ferry vessel unless the Class 1 (explosive) material is in compliance with packaging, labeling, marking, and certification requirements of this subchapter. Permitted fireworks and small arms ammunition may be carried without the required packaging, labeling, marking, or certification if they are in tight containers.

§176.91 Motorboats.

A motorboat may be transported on board a ferry vessel with gasoline in the tank and two other containers not exceeding 23 L (six gallons) capacity each if they are in the motorboat, closed, and in good condition.

§176.92 Cylinders laden in vehicles.

Any cylinder of Class 2 (compressed gas) material which is required to have a valve protection cap fitted in place may be transported on board a ferry vessel without having the valve protection cap in place when it is laden in a transport vehicle and is not removed from the vehicle while on the vessel.

§176.93 Vehicles having refrigerating or heating equipment.

(a) **A transport vehicle fitted with refrigerating** or heating equipment using a flammable liquid or Division 2.1 (flammable gas) material, or diesel oil as fuel, may be transported on a ferry vessel. However, the refrigerating or heating equipment may not be operated while the vehicle is on the vessel, unless the equipment complies with the following requirements:

(1) *The installation* is rigidly mounted and free of any movement other than normal vibration in operation;

(2) *An easily accessible* shutoff control is fitted to the fuel and electrical supply of the refrigerating or heating equipment; and

(3) *The fuel storage tank,* the fuel lines, the carburetor and any other fuel devices are tight and show no signs of leakage.

(b) **If the vehicle operator desires to operate** the refrigerating or heating equipment while on the vessel and the equipment is not fitted with automatic starting and stopping devices, it must be started before the vehicle is taken on board. It may continue in operation while the vehicle is on the vessel, but if the motor stops it may not be restarted.

(c) **In the case of a ferry vessel on a voyage** exceeding 30 minutes' duration, stowage must be provided for transport vehicles having refrigerating or heating equipment operated by internal combustion engines which will permit ready diffusion of exhaust gases to the open air. Passenger vehicles may not be stowed in a position adjacent to vehicles operating internal combustion motors which expose the occupants of the passenger vehicles to excessive concentrations of exhaust fumes from such motors.

(d) **A transport vehicle containing solid carbon dioxide** as a refrigerant may be transported on a ferry vessel only if it is stowed in a well ventilated location.

Subpart F - Special Requirements for Barges

§176.95 Applicability.

The requirements prescribed in this subpart are applicable to the transportation of packaged hazardous materials on board barges. The requirements prescribed elsewhere in this subchapter for vessels similarly apply, except as provided in this subpart, to the transportation of packaged hazardous materials on board barges.

§176.96 Materials of construction.

Barges used to transport hazardous materials must be constructed of steel.

§176.97 Prohibition of dump scows.

Dump scows are barges having cargo carrying compartments of the hopper type and fitted with a bottom dump or a side dump. This type of barge is prohibited from the carriage of any class of hazardous material.

§176.98 Stowage of hazardous materials on board barges.

A material for which "on deck" stowage only is required by column (10) of the Hazardous Materials Table (§172.101 of this subchapter) may be stowed "under deck" on unmanned barges.

§176.99 Permit requirements for certain hazardous materials.

The permits required by §§176.100 and 176.415 for loading, unloading, and handling Divisions 1.1 and 1.2 (explosives) materials, Division 1.5 materials, ammonium nitrate and certain ammonium nitrate mixtures and fertilizers must be obtained before these materials may be loaded on, unloaded from, or handled on board a barge or barge-carrying vessel. However, a barge loaded with these materials being placed on, removed from, or handled on board a barge-carrying vessel is not subject to these permit requirements.

Subpart G - Detailed Requirements for Class 1 (Explosive) Materials

§176.100 Permit for Divisions 1.1 and 1.2 (explosive) materials.

Before Divisions 1.1 and 1.2 (explosive) materials may be discharged from, loaded on, handled or restowed on board a vessel at any place in the United States, the carrier must obtain a permit from the COTP in accordance with the procedures in 33 CFR 126.19. Exceptions to this permit requirement may be authorized by the COTP.

§176.102 Supervisory detail.

(a) Except as provided in paragraph (c) of this section, the COTP may assign a USCG supervisory detail to any vessel to supervise the loading, handling or unloading of Class 1 (explosive) materials.

(b) The owner, agent, charterer, master or person in charge of the vessel, and all persons engaged in the handling, loading, unloading, and stowage of Class 1 (explosive) materials shall obey all orders that are given by the officer in charge of the supervisory detail.

(c) If Class 1 (explosive) materials are loaded onto or unloaded from a vessel at a facility operated or controlled by the Department of Defense, the Commanding Officer of that facility may decline the USCG supervisory detail. Whenever the supervisory detail is declined, the Commanding Officer of the facility shall ensure compliance with the regulations in this part.

§176.104 Loading and unloading Class 1 (explosive) materials.

(a) Packages of Class 1 (explosive) materials may not be thrown, dropped, rolled, dragged, or slid over each other or over a deck.

(b) When Class 1 (explosive) materials are stowed in a hold below one in which any cargo is being handled, the hatch in the deck dividing the two holds must have all covers securely in place.

(c) Drafts of Class 1 (explosive) materials must be handled in accordance with the following:

(1) *A draft* may not be raised, lowered, or stopped by sudden application of power or brake.

(2) *A draft* may not be released by tripping or freeing one side of the cargo-handling equipment and tumbling the Class 1 (explosive) materials off.

(3) *All drafts,* beams, shackles, bridles, slings, and hoods must be manually freed before the winch takes control.

(4) *Slings may not be* dragged from under a draft by winching except for the topmost layer in the hold when power removal is the only practical method and when the cargo cannot be toppled.

(5) *Handles or brackets* on packages in a draft may not be used for slinging purposes.

(d) A combination woven rope and wire sling or a sling that is formed by use of an open hook may not be used in handling Class 1 (explosive) materials.

(e) Only a safety hook or a hook that has been closed by wire may be used in handling drafts of Class 1 (explosive) materials.

(f) Wire rope or wire rope assemblies, including splices and fittings, used in handling Class 1 (explosive) materials must be unpainted and kept bare to permit inspection of their safe working condition. A mechanical end fitting (pressed fitting) may be used in place of a eye splice, if the efficiency of the mechanical end fitting is at least equal to the efficiency of an eye splice prepared as prescribed in 29 CFR 1918.51(c)(1).

(g) Packages of Division 1.1 and 1.2 materials that are not part of a palletized unit must be loaded and unloaded from a vessel using a chute, conveyor or a mechanical hoist and a pallet, skipboard, tray or pie plate fitted with a cargo net or sideboards.

(h) Packages of Division 1.1 and 1.2 (explosive) materials must be loaded or unloaded in accordance with the following:

(1) *A cargo net* with a pallet, skipboard, tray, or pie plate, must be loaded so that no more than a minimum displacement of packages occurs when it is lifted.

(2) *A cargo net* must completely encompass the bottom and sides of the draft. The mesh of the cargo net must be of a size and strength that will prevent a package in the draft from passing through the net.

(3) *When a tray* is used in handling packages, no package may extend more than one-third its vertical dimension above the sideboard of the tray.

(i) A landing mat must be used when a draft of nonpalletized Division 1.1 or 1.2 (explosive) materials is deposited on deck. The landing mat must have dimensions of at least l m (3 feet) wide, 2 m (7 feet) long, and 10 cm (3.9 inches) thick, and be made of woven hemp, sisal, or similar fiber, or foam rubber, polyurethane or similar resilient material.

(j) In addition to the other requirements of this section, packages of Division 1.1 and 1.2 (explosive) materials must be handled in accordance with the following:

(1) *Packages may not be loaded or unloaded* through a hatch at the same time that other cargo is being handled in any hold served by that hatch.

(2) *Packages may not be loaded or unloaded* from the same hatch by using two pieces of cargo equipment unless the equipment is positioned at the forward and aft ends of the hatch.

(3) *Packages may not be lifted over any hazardous materials.*

(4) *The height* of any structure, equipment, or load on a deck over which packages must be lifted may not be higher than the hatch coaming or bulwark, or 1 m (3 feet), whichever is greater.

(k) Unpackaged explosive devices may not be handled by their lifting lugs or suspension lugs.

(l) A chute may not be used when loading or unloading Class 1 (explosive) materials in compatibility group A or B.

§176.108 Supervision of Class 1 (explosive) materials during loading, unloading, handling, and stowage.

(a) During the loading, unloading, handling and stowage of Class 1 (explosive) materials, a responsible person shall be in constant attendance during the entire operation to direct the loading, unloading, handling and stowage of Class 1 (explosive) materials, including the preparation of the holds. The responsible person must be aware of the hazards involved and the steps to be taken in an emergency, and must maintain sufficient contact with the master to ensure proper steps are taken in an emergency.

(b) Each person involved in the handling of Class 1 (explosive) materials on a vessel shall obey the orders of the responsible person.

(c) The responsible person must inspect all cargo-handling equipment to determine that it is in safe operating condition before it is used to handle Class 1 (explosive) materials.

Stowage

§176.112 Applicability.

The provisions of §§176.116(e), 176,118, and 176.120 of this subpart do not apply to Division 1.4 (explosive) materials, compatibility group S. Such materials may be stowed together with all other Class 1 (explosive) materials except those of compatibility group A or L. They must be segregated from other hazardous materials in accordance with table 176.83(b) of this part.

§176.116 General stowage conditions for Class 1 (explosive) materials.

(a) Heat and sources of ignition:

(1) *Class 1 (explosive) materials* must be stowed in a cool part of the ship and must be kept as cool as practicable while on board. Stowage must be well away from all sources of heat, including steam pipes, heating coils, sparks, and flame.

(2) *Except where* the consignment of Class 1 (explosive) materials consists only of explosive articles, the wearing of shoes or boots with unprotected metal nails, heels, or tips of any kind is prohibited.

(b) Wetness:

(1) *Spaces where Class 1 (explosive) materials* are stowed below deck must be dry. In the event of the contents of packages being affected by water when on board immediate advice must be sought from the shippers; pending this advice handling of the packages must be avoided.

(2) *Bilges and bilge sections* must be examined and any residue of previous cargo removed before Class 1 materials (explosive) are loaded onto the vessel.

(c) Security: All compartments, magazines, and transport units containing Class 1 (explosive) materials must be locked or suitably secured in order to prevent unauthorized access.

(d) Secure stowage: Class 1 (explosive) materials must be securely stowed to prevent movement in transit; where necessary, precautions must be taken to prevent cargo sliding down between the frames at the ship's sides.

(e) Separation from accommodation spaces and machinery spaces:

(1) *Class 1 (explosive) materials* must be stowed as far away as practicable from any accommodation spaces or any machinery space and may not be stowed directly above or below such a space. The requirements in paragraphs (e)(2) through (e)(4) of this section are minimum requirements in addition to the applicable requirements of 46 CFR chapter I. Where the requirements of this subpart are less stringent than those of 46 CFR chapter I, the 46 CFR chapter I requirements must be satisfied for ships to which they are applicable.

(2) *There must be* a permanent A Class steel bulkhead between any accommodation space and any compartment containing Class 1 (explosive) materials. Division 1.1, 1.2, 1.3, or 1.5 materials may not be stowed within 3 m (10 feet) of this bulkhead; in the decks immediately above or below an accommodation space they must be stowed at least 3 m (10 feet) from the line of this bulkhead projected vertically.

(3) *There must be* a permanent A Class steel bulkhead between a compartment containing Class 1 (explosive) materials and any machinery space. Class 1 (explosive) materials, except those in Division 1.4 (explosive), may not be stowed within 3 m (10 feet) of this bulkhead; and in the decks above or below the machinery space they must be stowed at least 3 m (10 feet) from the line of this bulkhead projected vertically. In addition to this separation, there must be insulation to Class A60 standard as defined in 46 CFR 72.05-10(a)(1) if the machinery space is one of Category 'A' unless the only Class 1 (explosive) materials carried are in Division 1.4S (explosive).

(4) *Where Class 1 (explosive) materials* are stowed away from bulkheads bounding any accommodation space or machinery space, the intervening space may be filled with cargo that is not readily combustible.

§176.118 Electrical requirement.

(a) Electrical equipment and cables installed in compartments in which Class 1 (explosive) materials are stowed which do not need to be energized during the voyage must be isolated from the supply so that no part of the circuit within the compartment is energized. The method of isolation may be by withdrawal of fuses, opening of switches or circuit breakers, or disconnection from bus bars. The means, or access to the means, of disconnection/reconnection must be secured by a locked padlock under the control of a responsible person.

(b) Electrical equipment and cables in a cargo space in which Class 1 (explosive) materials are stowed which are energized during the voyage for the safe operation of the ship must meet the requirements of subchapter J of 46 CFR chapter I. Before Class 1 (explosive) materials are loaded aboard a vessel, all cables must be tested by a skilled person to ensure that they are safe and to determine satisfactory grounding, insulation resistance, and continuity of the cable cores, metal sheathing or armoring.

(c) All Class 1 (explosive) materials must be stowed in a safe position relative to electrical equipment and cables. Additional physical protection must be provided where necessary to minimize possible damage to the electrical equipment or cables, especially during loading and unloading.

(d) Cable joints in the compartments must be enclosed in metal-clad junction boxes.

(e) All lighting equipment and cables must be of the fixed type, and must meet the relevant inspection, test, and installation standards of 46 CFR chapter I, subchapter J.

§176.120 Lightning protection.

A lightning conductor grounded to the sea must be provided on any mast or similar structure on a vessel on which Class 1 (explosive) materials are stowed unless effective electrical bonding is provided between the sea and the mast or structure from its extremity and throughout to the main body of the hull structure. (Steel masts in ships of all welded construction comply with this requirement).

§176.122 Stowage arrangements under deck.

When stowed under deck, Class 1 (explosive) materials must be in conformance with one of the stowage arrangements described in §§176.124 through 176.136 of this subpart.

§176.124 Ordinary stowage.

(a) Ordinary stowage is authorized for most explosive articles carried by vessel. The exceptions are those for which this subpart prescribes "magazine" or "special" stowage.

(b) Class 1 (explosive) materials requiring ordinary stowage must be stowed in accordance with §176.116 of this subpart.

§176.128 Magazine stowage, general.

(a) Magazine stowage is sub-divided into three different types of magazines designated by the letters A, B, and C. A magazine may be a fixed structure in the vessel, a closed freight container, or a portable magazine unit. Freight containers, portable magazines, and vehicles must be properly secured in position. Magazines may be positioned in any part of the vessel conforming to the general stowage conditions for Class 1 (explosive) materials, except magazines which are fixed structures must be constructed in a location in which their doors, where fitted, are easily accessible.

(b) Magazine stowage is required for all explosive substances, except "Explosive Substances, n.o.s." in compatibility groups G, L, or S. Magazine stowage type A is required for those substances which must be kept clear of steelwork. All other explosive substances must be given magazine stowage type B, except those in compatibility group A for which magazine stowage type C is prescribed.

(c) Magazine stowage type B is required for Charges, propelling, for cannon, UN 0279, UN 0414, and UN 0242; and Charges, supplementary, explosive, UN 0600, in compatibility group C or D. Magazine stowage type C is required for detonators and similar articles in divisions and compatibility group 1.1B and 1.2B (explosive).

§176.130 Magazine stowage Type A.

(a) In addition to protecting the Class 1 (explosive) materials and preventing unauthorized access, magazine stowage type A guards against friction between any spilled contents of packages and the vessel's sides and bulkheads.

(b) Class 1 (explosive) materials requiring magazine stowage type A must be stowed in a magazine which is tightly sheathed with wood on its inner sides and floor.

(c) When utilized as part of the magazine structure, the vessel's sides and bulkheads must be clean, free from rust or scale, and protected by battening or sweatboards spaced not more than 150 mm (6 inches) apart. All stanchions and other unprotected structural members must be similarly clean and battened. The underside of the deck above the magazine must be clean and free of rust and scale, but need not be battened.

(d) The top of the stow within the magazine must be at least 30 cm (12 inches) from the underside of the deck above.

(e) A type A magazine constructed in the square of a cargo space may not be loaded from the top.

(f) When other Class 1 (explosive) materials are stowed with Class 1 (explosive) materials for which magazine stowage type A is required, they or their packagings may have no exposed external parts made of ferrous metal or aluminum alloy.

§176.132 Magazine stowage Type B.

(a) **Magazine stowage type B is the same** as magazine stowage type A as prescribed in §176.130 of this part, except:

(1) *The floor* need not be tightly sheathed with wood but must be sparred or protected by wooden pallets or dunnage; and

(2) *Battening of* the vessel's sides, bulkheads, and stanchions is not required.

(b) **A compartment may be used for magazine stowage** type B without a magazine structure provided that:

(1) *The Class 1* (explosive) materials are stowed on wooden gratings, pallets, or dunnage, directly on the deck and not on other cargo;

(2) *Other cargo* stowed in the same compartment is not readily combustible material; and

(3) *The position* of the stowage is such that there is direct access to the hatchway.

(c) **Class 1 (explosive) materials and other cargo** in the same compartment must be secured to eliminate the possibility of significant movement. Where an entire deck is used as a magazine, the stowage must be so arranged that the Class 1 (explosive) materials stowed therein will be removed from the ship before working any cargo in any decks above or below the space in the same hatch.

§176.133 Magazine stowage Type C.

The construction requirements for magazine stowage type C are the same as for magazine stowage Type B as prescribed in §176.132 of this part, except that the magazine must be located as near as practicable to the centerline of the vessel and must not be closer to the vessel's side than a distance equal to one-eighth of the vessel's beam or 2.5 m (8.2 feet), whichever is less.

§176.134 Vehicles.

Closed vehicles may be used to transport Class 1 (explosive) materials requiring magazine stowage when carried by vessel if they meet the requirements of the appropriate magazine stowage type. See §176.168 of this subpart for additional requirements relating to the transport of Class 1 (explosive) materials in vehicles.

§176.136 Special stowage.

(a) **Special stowage is required for certain articles** presenting both explosive and chemical hazards, such as smoke or lachrymatory (compatibility group G or H), toxic (compatibility group K), or substances and articles which present a special risk (compatibility group L). Except as permitted in paragraph (c) of this section, Class 1 (explosive) materials requiring special stowage must be stowed on deck unless such stowage is impracticable and the COTP authorizes special stowage below deck.

(b) **Class 1 (explosive) materials for which** special stowage is required must be stowed as far away as practicable from living accommodation, and working areas, and may not be overstowed. Steel portable magazines and freight containers in which such Class 1 (explosive) materials are stowed may not be located closer to the vessel's side than a distance equal to one-eighth of the vessel's beam or 2.5 m (8.2 feet), whichever is less.

(c) **Explosive articles having UN number,** UN 0015, UN 0016, UN 0018, UN 0019, UN 0301, or UN 0303 may be given ordinary stowage in a lower hold or 'tween deck. Other Class 1 (explosive) materials in compatibility groups G and H may be in open stowage out to the ship's side on a floodable lower hold or deep tank in such a position that other cargo cannot be contaminated by leakage; in all other cases such Class 1 (explosive) materials must be stowed in steel portable magazines or in freight containers. If a freight container is used for this purpose, the floor of the freight container must be leakproof; for example, an all-metal container may be used and a fillet of cement or other material worked across the bottom of the door opening.

(d) **Class 1 (explosive) materials stowed** in one compartment may not be of more than one compatibility group, except the COTP may allow Class 1 (explosive) materials of compatibility groups G and H in separate steel portable magazines to be stowed in the same compartment, not less than 3 m (10 feet) apart.

(e) **Class 1 (explosive) materials in compatibility groups** K and L must be stowed in a steel magazine regardless of the stowage position in the vessel.

§176.137 Portable magazine.

(a) **Each portable magazine used for the stowage** of Class 1 (explosive) materials on board vessels must meet the following requirements:

(1) *It must be weather-tight,* constructed of wood or metal lined with wood at least 2 cm (0.787 inch) thick, and with a capacity of no more than 3.1 cubic m (110 cubic feet).

(2) *All inner surfaces* must be smooth and free of any protruding nails, screws or other projections.

(3) *If constructed of wood,* a portable magazine must be framed of nominal 5 cm x 10 cm (2 x 4 inch) lumber, and sheathed with nominal 20 mm (0.787 inch) thick boards or plywood.

(4) *When constructed of metal,* the metal must be not less than 3.2 mm (0.126 inch) thick.

(5) *Runners, bearers, or skids* must be provided to elevate the magazine at least 10 cm (3.9 inches) from the deck. Padeyes, ring bolts, or other suitable means must be provided for securing.

(6) *If the portable magazine* has a door or hinged cover, the door or cover must have a strong hasp and padlock or equally effective means of securing.

(7) *The portable magazine* must be marked on its top and four sides, in letters at least 8 cm (3 inches) high, as follows: EXPLOSIVES — HANDLE CAREFULLY — KEEP LIGHTS AND FIRE AWAY.

(b) **A portable magazine which meets the requirements** for a type 2 or type 3 magazine under 27 CFR part 55 subpart K may be used for the stowage of Class 1 (explosive) materials on board vessels.

(c) **A portable magazine with a capacity** exceeding 3.1 m^3 (110 cubic feet) may be used for the stowage of Class 1 (explosive) materials under such construction, handling, and stowage requirements as the COTP approves.

§176.138 Deck stowage.

(a) **Class 1 (explosive) materials stowed on deck** must be carried as close to the vessel's centerline as practicable.

(b) **Class 1 (explosive) materials may not be stowed** within a horizontal distance of 6 m (20 feet) from any fire, machinery exhaust, galley uptake, locker used for combustible stores, or other potential sources of ignition. They must be clear of walkways and cargo working areas, fire hydrants, steam pipes, and means of access; away from all other facilities necessary for the safe working of the vessel, and not less than a horizontal distance of 8 m (26 feet) from the bridge, accommodation areas, and lifesaving appliances.

(c) **Where vessels are fitted with container fastening** arrangements, freight containers containing Class 1 (explosive) materials may be overstowed by containers of compatible Class 1 (explosive) materials or non-hazardous cargo. Where vessels are not fitted with container fastening arrangements, freight containers loaded with Class 1 (explosive) materials may be stowed only on the bottom tier of the stowage.

Segregation

§176.140 Segregation from other classes of hazardous materials.

(a) **Class 1 (explosive) materials must be segregated** from other packaged hazardous materials in accordance with §176.83.

(b) **Class 1 (explosive) materials must be segregated** from bulk solid dangerous cargoes in accordance with the General Introduction to the IMDG Code. Notwithstanding §176.83(b), ammonium nitrate and sodium nitrate may be stowed together with blasting explosives, except those containing chlorates, provided the mixed stowage is treated as blasting explosives (see §176.410(e)).

§176.142 Hazardous materials of extreme flammability.

(a) **Except as allowed by paragraph (b) of this section,** certain hazardous materials of extreme flammability may not be transported in a vessel carrying Class 1 (explosive) materials. This prohibition applies to the following liquid hazardous materials:

Carbon disulfide	UN1131	Class 3
Diethylzinc	UN1366	Division 4.2
Dimethylzinc	UN1370	Division 4.2
Magnesium alkyls	UN3053	Division 4.2
Methyl phosphonous dichloride, pyrophoric liquid	NA2845	Division 6.1
Nickel carbonyl	UN1259	Division 6.1
Pyrophoric liquid, inorganic, n.o.s.	UN3194	Division 4.2
Pyrophoric liquids, organic, n.o.s.	UN2845	Division 4.2
Pyrophoric organometallic compound, water-reactive, n.o.s.	UN3203	Division 4.2

(b) **The hazardous materials listed in paragraph (a)** of this section may be transported in a vessel carrying the following Class 1 (explosive) materials as cargo:

(1) *Division 1.4 (explosive) materials, compatibility group S.*

(2) *Explosive articles* having the following proper shipping names and identification numbers (see column (4) of the §172.101 table) if designed for lifesaving purposes and their total net explosive mass (weight) does not exceed 50 kg (110 lbs) per vessel:

(i) *ARTICLES, PYROTECHNIC:* UN Nos. 0428, 0429, 0430, 0431.

(ii) *CARTRIDGES, FLASH:* UN Nos. 0049, 0050.

(iii) *CARTRIDGES, SIGNAL:* UN Nos. 0054, 0312.

(iv) *SIGNAL DEVICES, HAND:* UN No. 0191.

(v) *SIGNALS, DISTRESS:* UN Nos. 0194, 0195.

(vi) *SIGNALS, SMOKE:* UN Nos. 0196, 0197, 0313.

(3) *Class 1 (explosive) materials* in compatibility groups C, D, and E if the total net explosive mass (weight) does not exceed 10 kg (22 pounds) per vessel.

(4) *Explosive articles* in compatibility group G, except fireworks and Class 1 (explosive) materials requiring special stowage if the total net explosive mass (weight) does not exceed 10 kg (22 pounds) per vessel.

(c) **When a vessel carrying Class 1 (explosive) materials** allowed under paragraph (b) of this section also carries a hazardous material of extreme flammability, that hazardous material must be stowed in a part of the vessel as remote as practicable from the Class 1 (explosive) materials.

§176.144 Segregation of Class 1 (explosive) materials.

(a) **Except as provided in §176.145 of this subpart,** Class 1 (explosive) materials may be stowed within the same compartment, magazine, portable magazine, or transport unit as indicated in table 176.144(a).

Table 176.144(a) - Authorized Mixed Stowage for Explosives
[An "X" indicates that explosives in the two different compatibility groups reflected by the location of the "X" may not be stowed in the same compartment, portable magazine, or transport unit]

Compatibility groups	A	B	C	D	E	F	G	H	J	K	L	N	S
A		X	X	X	X	X	X	X	X	X	X	X	X
B	X		X	X	X	X	X	X	X	X	X	X	
C	X	X				X	1	X	X	X	X		
D	X	X				X	1	X	X	X	X		
E	X	X				X	1	X	X	X	X		
F	X	X	X	X	X		X	X	X	X	X	X	
G	X	X	1	1	1	X		X	X	X	X	X	
H	X	X	X	X	X	X	X		X	X	X	X	
J	X	X	X	X	X	X	X	X		X	X	X	
K	X	X	X	X	X	X	X	X	X		X	X	
L	X	X	X	X	X	X	X	X	X	X	2	X	X
N	X	X				X	X	X	X	X	X		
S	X										X		

NOTES:

1. Explosive articles in compatibility group G, other than fireworks and those requiring special stowage, may be stowed with articles of compatibility groups C, D, and E, provided no explosive substances are carried in the same compartment, portable magazine or transport unit.
2. Explosives in compatibility group L may only be stowed in the same compartment, magazine or transport unit with identical explosives within compatibility group L.

(b) **Where Class 1 (explosive) materials** of different compatibility groups are allowed to be stowed in the same compartment, magazine, portable magazine, or transport unit, the stowage arrangements must conform to the most stringent requirements for the entire load.

(c) **Where a mixed load of Class 1 (explosive) materials** of different hazard divisions and/or stowage arrangements is carried within a compartment, magazine, or transport unit, the entire load must be treated as belonging to the hazard division having the greatest hazard. (For example, if a load of Division 1.1 (explosive) materials is mixed with Division 1.3 (explosive) materials, the load is treated as a Division 1.1 (explosive) material as defined in §173.50(b) of this subchapter and the stowage must conform to the most stringent requirements for the entire load).

(d) **If some of the Class 1 (explosive) materials** in a stowage mixture require magazine stowage, Class 1 (explosive) materials requiring ordinary stowage may be stowed in the same magazine. When the magazine is used for substances requiring Type A stowage, the other Class 1 (explosive) materials stowed therein must have no exposed parts of any ferrous metal or aluminum alloy, unless separated by a partition.

(e) **Segregation on deck:** When Class 1 (explosive) materials in different compatibility groups are carried on deck, they must be stored not less than 6 m (20 feet) apart unless they are allowed under table 176.144(a) to be stowed in the same compartment, magazine, or transport unit.

(f) **On a barge used to transfer Class 1 (explosive) materials** from a waterfront facility to a vessel at an explosives anchorage (or from the vessel to the water front facility), if compliance with paragraph (e) of this section is not practicable, a sandbag barrier at least 0.6 m (2 feet) in thickness may be substituted for the 6 m (20 feet) separation.

§176.145 Segregation in single hold vessels.

(a) **On board a vessel having a single cargo hold,** Class 1 (explosive) materials in hazard division/compatibility group 1.1B and 1.2B may be stowed in the same compartment with substances of compatibility group D, provided:

(1) *The net explosive weight* of the compatibility group B explosive does not exceed 50 kg (110 pounds); and

(2) *The compatibility group B* explosive materials are stowed in a steel portable magazine that is stowed at least 6 m (20 feet) from the compatibility group D substances.

(b) **Division/compatibility group 1.4B** (explosive) materials may be stowed in the same compartment with substances of compatibility group D provided the Class 1 (explosive) materials of different compatibility groups are separated by either a distance of at least 6 m (20 feet) or by a steel partition.

§176.146 Segregation from non-hazardous materials.

(a) **Except as required by paragraphs (b) and (c)** of this section, Class 1 (explosive) materials need not be segregated from other cargo of a non-dangerous nature.

(b) **Mail, baggage, and personal and household effects** may not be stowed in the same compartment as, or in compartments immediately above or below, Class 1 (explosive) materials other than those in compatibility group S.

(c) **Where Class 1 (explosive) materials are stowed** against an intervening bulkhead, any mail on the other side of the bulkhead must be stowed away from it.

(d) **In order to avoid contamination:**

(1) *An explosive substance* or article which has a secondary POISON hazard label must be stowed "separated from" all foodstuffs, except when such materials are stowed in separate closed transport units, the requirements for "away from" segregation apply.

(2) *An explosive substance* or article which has a secondary CORROSIVE hazard label must be stowed "away from" foodstuffs.

Precautions During Loading and Unloading

§176.148 Artificial lighting.

Electric lights, except arc lights, are the only form of artificial lighting permitted when loading and unloading Class 1 (explosive) materials.

§176.150 Radio and radar.

(a) **Except as provided in paragraph (b) of this section,** when Class 1 (explosive) materials (other than explosive articles in Division 1.4 [explosive] or any explosive substance) are loaded, unloaded, or handled, the responsible person must ensure that all sources of electromagnetic radiation such as radio and radar transmitters are deenergized by opening the main switches controlling the sources and tagging them to warn that the devices are not to be energized until loading or unloading has ceased.

(b) **During the loading or unloading of all explosive articles** (except those in Division 1.4 [explosive]), no radio or radar transmitter may be used within 50 m (164 feet) of such articles except for VHF transmitters the power output of which does not exceed 25 watts and of which no part of the antenna system is within 2 m (7 feet) of the Class 1 (explosive) materials.

(c) **Explosive articles which are sensitive** to electromagnetic radiation from external sources must be stowed at a safe distance from the vessel's radio cabin, receiving and transmitting apparatus radio antenna or lead-in, and radar installation, with due regard to the character of the vessel and the degree of screening-off of the explosive articles.

§176.154 Fueling (bunkering).

(a) **Class 1 (explosive) materials, except those** in compatibility group S, may not be loaded or unloaded when fueling (bunkering) is in progress except with the prior authorization of the COTP, and under conditions prescribed by that officer.

(b) **Vessels containing Class 1 (explosive) materials** may not be fueled (bunkered) with the hatches open unless authorized by the COTP.

§176.156 Defective packages.

(a) **No leaking, broken, or otherwise defective package** containing Class 1 (explosive) materials, including packages which have been adversely affected by moisture, may be accepted for shipment. The master or person in charge of a vessel on which there is a defective package containing Class 1 (explosive) materials must seek advice from the shipper concerning withdrawal, repair, or replacement. No repair of damaged or defective package containing Class 1 (explosive) materials may be performed on board a vessel.

(b) **No Class 1 (explosive) material,** which for any reason has deteriorated or undergone a change of condition that increases the hazard attendant upon its conveyance or handling, may be moved in the port area, except as directed by the COTP.

(c) **If any package of Class 1 (explosive) materials,** or seal of a package of Class 1 (explosive) materials, appears to be damaged, that package must be set aside for examination and repair or otherwise legally disposed of as directed by the shipper.

(d) **If any Class 1 (explosive) materials are spilled** or released from a package, the responsible person must ensure that an appropriate emergency response is undertaken in accordance with the emergency response information required under §172.602 of this subchapter. The master of the vessel must report each incident involving spillage or release of Class 1 (explosive) materials to the COTP as soon as practicable.

§176.160 Protection against weather.

Any person loading or unloading packages containing Class 1 (explosive) materials shall take adequate measures to prevent these packages from becoming wet.

§176.162 Security.

A responsible person must be present at all times when the hatches of spaces containing Class 1 (explosive) materials are open. No unauthorized person may be permitted to access spaces in which Class 1 (explosive) materials are stowed. Magazines must be secured against unauthorized entry when loading has been completed, or when loading or unloading is stopped. Packages containing Class 1 (explosive) materials may not be opened on board ship.

§176.164 Fire precautions and firefighting.

(a) **Matches, lighters, fire, and other ignition sources** are prohibited on and near any vessel on which Class 1 (explosive) materials are being loaded, unloaded, or handled except in places designated by the master or the COTP.

(b) **A fire hose of sufficient length to reach every part** of the loading area with an effective stream of water must be laid and connected to the water main, ready for immediate use.

(c) **No repair work may be carried out** in a cargo space containing Class 1 (explosive) materials other than those of Division 1.4 (explosive). No welding, burning, cutting, or riveting operations involving the use of fire, flame, spark, or arc-producing equipment may be conducted on board except in an emergency; and, if in port, with the consent of the COTP.

(d) **Each compartment, including a closed vehicle deck space,** which contains Class 1 (explosive) materials must be provided with a fixed fire extinguishing system. Each adjacent cargo compartment either must be protected by a fixed fire extinguishing installation or must be accessible for firefighting operations.

(e) **A vessel must have two sets of breathing apparatus** and a power-operated fire pump, which, together with its source of power and sea connections, must be located outside the machinery space.

Passenger Vehicles

§176.166 Transport of Class 1 (explosive) materials on passenger vessels.

(a) **Only the following Class 1 (explosive) materials** may be transported as cargo on passenger vessels:

(1) *Division 1.4 (explosive) materials, compatibility group S.*

(2) *Explosive articles* designed for lifesaving purposes as identified in §176.142(b)(2), if the total net explosive mass (weight) does not exceed 50 kg (110 pounds).

(3) *Class 1 (explosive) materials* in compatibility groups C, D, and E, if the total net explosive mass (weight) does not exceed 10 kg (22 pounds) per vessel.

(4) *Articles in compatibility group G* other than those requiring special stowage, if the total net explosive mass (weight) does not exceed 10 kg (22 pounds) per vessel.

(5) *Articles in compatibility group B,* if the total net explosive mass (weight) does not exceed 5 kg (11 pounds).

(b) **Class 1 (explosive) materials which may be carried** on passenger vessels are identified in column (10) of the §172.101 table. They must be stowed in accordance with table 176.166(b).

Table 176.166(b) - Stowage Arrangements in Passenger Vessels

Class/ Division	Samples, explosive	Goods, N.O.S. Class 1	Goods shipped under a specific proper shipping name — Compatibility group												
			A	B	C	D	E	F	G	H	J	K	L	N	S
1.1	d	d	c	e	e	e	e	c	e	--	c	--	c	--	--
1.2	d	d	--	e	e	e	e	c	e	c	c	c	c	--	--
1.3	d	d	--	--	e	e	--	c	e	c	c	c	c	--	--
1.4	d	d	--	b	b	b	b	c	b	--	--	--	--	--	a
1.5	d	d	--	--	--	e	--	--	--	--	--	--	--	--	--
1.6	d	d	--	--	--	--	--	--	--	--	--	--	--	e	--

a — As for cargo ships, on deck or under deck.
b — As for cargo ships, on deck or under deck, in portable magazines only.
c — Prohibited.
d — As specified by the Associate Administrator, or the competent authority of the country in which the Class 1 (explosive) materials are loaded on the vessel.
e — In containers or the like, on deck only.

(c) **Notwithstanding the provisions of paragraph (a)** of this section, a combination of the substances and articles listed in paragraphs (a)(1) through (a)(5) of this section may be transported on the same passenger vessel provided the total net explosive mass (weight) of the combination of Class 1 (explosive) materials carried does not exceed the smallest quantity specified for any one of the substances or articles in the combination.

Transport Units and Shipborne Barges

§176.168 Transport of Class 1 (explosive) materials in vehicle spaces.

(a) **All transport vehicles and cargo must be properly secured.**

(b) **All transport vehicles used for the carriage** of Class 1 (explosive) materials must be structurally serviceable as defined in §176.172(a)(2).

(c) **Vehicles used to transport Class 1 explosive) materials** must conform to the requirements in §§177.834 and 177.835 of this subchapter.

(d) **Class 1 (explosive) materials which require** special stowage must be transported in transport vehicles approved for the purpose by the Associate Administrator except that Class 1 (explosive) materials in compatibility group G or H may be carried in steel portable magazines or freight containers. Closed transport vehicles may be used as magazines; transport vehicles of other types may be used to transport Class 1 (explosive) materials which require ordinary stowage.

(e) **Class 1 (explosive) materials of different compatibility groups** may not be stowed in the same vehicle except as allowed in §176.144 of this subpart.

(f) **Vehicles containing different Class 1** (explosive) materials require no segregation from each other, except that these materials may be carried together under the provisions of §176.144 of this subchapter. In all other instances, the vehicles must be "separated from" one another.

(g) **All transport vehicles used for the transport** of Class 1 (explosive) materials must have lashing arrangements for securing the vehicle on the ship and preventing the movement of the vehicle on its springs during the sea passage.

(h) **Where a portable magazine or closed freight container** is carried on a chassis, twist locks or other suitable securing arrangements must be provided and made secure.

§176.170 Transport of Class 1 (explosive) materials in freight containers.

(a) **When Class 1 (explosive) materials are stowed** in a freight container, the freight container, for the purposes of this subpart, may be regarded as a magazine but not as a separate compartment.

(b) **Freight containers exceeding 6 m (20 feet) in length** may not carry more than 5000 kg (11,023 pounds) net explosive weight of explosive substances, except explosive substances in Division 1.4.

(c) **Freight containers used to transport Class 1** (explosive) materials for which magazine stowage type A is required must have a floor consisting of tightly fitted wooden boards, plywood or equivalent non-metallic material, and a non-metallic lining.

(d) **Class 1 (explosive) materials of different compatibility groups** may not be stowed within the same freight container except as allowed in §176.144 of this subpart.

(e) **On vessels, other than specially fitted** container ships, freight containers containing Class 1 (explosive) materials must be stowed only in the lowest tier.

(f) **Freight containers carrying different Class 1** (explosive) materials require no segregation from each other, if the provisions of §176.144 of this subpart allow the Class 1 (explosive) materials to be carried together in the same compartment. In all other instances, the containers must be "separated from" one another in accordance with §176.83(f) of this part.

(g) **Freight containers carrying Class 1 (explosive) materials** may not be handled on board a vessel with fork lift trucks unless approved by the COTP. This does not preclude the use of front-loading trucks using side-frame lifting equipment.

§176.172 Structural serviceability of freight containers and vehicles carrying Class 1 (explosive) materials on ships.

(a) **A freight container may not be offered** for the carriage of Class 1 (explosive) materials unless the container is structurally serviceable as evidenced by a current CSC (International Convention for Safe Containers) approval plate and verified by a detailed visual examination as follows:

(1) *Before a freight container* or transport vehicle is packed with Class 1 (explosive) materials, it must be visually examined by the shipper to ensure it is structurally serviceable, free of any residue of previous cargo, and its interior walls and floors are free from protrusions.

(2) **Structurally serviceable** means the freight container or the vehicle cannot have major defects in its structural components, such as top and bottom side rails, top and bottom end rails, door sill and header, floor cross members, corner posts, and corner fittings in a freight container. Major defects include —

(i) *Dents or bends* in the structural members greater than 19 mm (0.75 inch) in depth, regardless of length;

(ii) *Cracks or breaks in structural members;*

(iii) *More than one splice* or an improper splice (such as a lapped splice) in top or bottom end rails or door headers;

(iv) *More than two splices in any one top or bottom side rail;*

(v) *Any splice in a door sill or corner post;*

(vi) *Door hinges and hardware* that are seized, twisted, broken, missing, or otherwise inoperative;

(vii) *Gaskets and seals that do not seal; or*

(viii) *For freight containers,* any distortion of the overall configuration great enough to prevent proper alignment of handling equipment, mounting and securing chassis or vehicle, or insertion into ships' cells.

(3) *In addition,* deterioration of any component of the freight container or vehicle, regardless of the material of construction, such as rusted-out metal in sidewalls or disintegrated fiberglass, is prohibited. Normal wear, however, including oxidation (rust), slight dents and scratches, and other damage that does not affect serviceability or the weather-tight integrity of the units, is not prohibited.

(b) **As used in paragraph (a) of this section,** splice means any repair of a freight container main structural member which replaces material, except complete replacement of the member.

(c) **All shipments of Class 1 (explosive) materials** except those in Division 1.4 (explosive) must be accompanied by a statement, which may appear on the shipping paper, certifying that the freight container or the vehicle is structurally serviceable as defined in paragraph (a)(2) of this section.

§176.174 Transport of Class 1 (explosive) materials in shipborne barges.

(a) **Fixed magazines may be built within a shipboard barge.** Portable magazines and freight containers may be used as magazines with a barge.

(b) **Shipborne barges may be used for the carriage** of all types of Class 1 (explosive) materials. When carrying Class 1 (explosive) materials requiring special stowage, the following requirements apply:

(1) *Class 1 (explosive) materials* in compatibility group G or H must be stowed in steel portable magazines or freight containers.

(2) *Class 1 (explosive) materials* in compatibility group K or L must be stowed in steel portable magazines.

(c) **Class 1 (explosive) materials of different compatibility groups** may not be stowed within the same shipborne barge unless under §176.144(b) of this subpart they are authorized to be stowed in the same compartment.

Handling Class 1 (Explosive) Materials in Port

§176.176 Signals.

When Class 1 (explosive) materials are being loaded, handled, or unloaded on a vessel, the vessel must exhibit the following signals:

(a) **By day, flag "B" (Bravo) of the international code of signals; and**

(b) **By night, an all-round fixed red light.**

§176.178 Mooring lines.

(a) **All lines used in mooring the vessel** must be of sufficient strength, type, and number for the size of the vessel and local conditions.

(b) **While the vessel is moored or anchored** in a port area, towing wires of adequate size and length must be properly secured to mooring bits at the bow and stern ready for immediate use with the towing eyes passed outboard and kept at about water level.

(c) **The mooring arrangements must be such** that the vessel can be released quickly in an emergency.

§176.180 Watchkeeping.

Whenever Class 1 (explosive) materials are on board a vessel in port, there must be sufficient crew on board to maintain a proper watch and to operate the propulsion and firefighting equipment in case of an emergency.

§176.182 Conditions for handling on board ship.

(a) **Weather conditions.** Class 1 (explosive) materials may not be handled in weather conditions which may seriously increase the hazards presented by the Class 1 (explosive) materials. During electrical storms, cargo operations must be halted and all hatches containing Class 1 (explosive) materials must be closed.

(b) **Darkness.** Class 1 (explosive) materials may not be handled on board a vessel during the hours of darkness unless prior consent has been obtained from the COTP.

(c) **Lighting.** The area where Class 1 (explosive) materials are handled, or where preparations are being made to handle Class 1 (explosive) materials, must be illuminated with lighting that is sufficient to safely perform the handling operation.

(d) **Protective equipment.**

(1) *A sufficient quantity* of appropriate protective equipment must be provided for the personnel involved in handling Class 1 (explosive) materials.

(2) *The protective equipment* must provide adequate protection against the hazards specific to the Class 1 (explosive) materials handled.

(e) **Intoxicated persons.** No person under the influence of alcohol or drugs to such an extent that the person's judgment or behavior is impaired may participate in any operation involving the handling of Class 1 (explosive) materials. The master of the vessel must keep any such person clear of any areas where Class 1 (explosive) materials are being handled.

(f) **Smoking.**

(1) *Smoking is prohibited on the vessel* while Class 1 (explosive) materials are being handled or stowed except in places designated by the master of the vessel.

(2) *Conspicuous notices* prohibiting smoking must be posted and clearly visible at all locations where Class 1 (explosive) materials are handled or stored.

(g) **All hatches and cargo ports opening** into a compartment in which Class 1 (explosive) materials are stowed must be kept closed except during loading and unloading of the compartment. After loading, hatches must be securely closed.

§176.184 Class 1 (explosive) materials of Compatibility Group L.

Class 1 (explosive) materials in compatibility group L may not be handled in a port area without the special permission of, and subject to any special precautions required by, the COTP.

§176.190 Departure of vessel.

When loading of Class 1 (explosive) materials is completed, the vessel must depart from the port area as soon as is reasonably practicable.

§176.192 Cargo handling equipment for freight containers carrying Class 1 (explosive) materials.

(a) **Except in an emergency, only cargo handling equipment** that has been specifically designed or modified for the handling of freight containers may be used to load, unload, or handle freight containers containing Division 1.1 or 1.2 (explosive) materials.

(b) **The gross weight of a freight container** containing Class 1 (explosive) materials may not exceed the safe working load of the cargo handling equipment by which it is handled.

Magazine Vessels

§176.194 Stowage of Class 1 (explosive) materials on magazine vessels.

(a) **General.** The requirements of this section are applicable to magazine vessels and are in addition to any other requirements in this subchapter.

(b) **Type vessel authorized.** A single deck vessel with or without a house on deck is the only type vessel that may be used as a magazine vessel. A magazine vessel may not be moved while Class 1 (explosive) materials are on board.

(c) **Location of explosives.** Division 1.1, 1.2, or 1.3 (explosive) materials, in excess of 2268 kg (5000 pounds), stored in any magazine vessel must be stowed below deck. No Class 1 (explosive) materials may be stowed on deck unless the vessel is fitted with a deck house having a stowage area which meets the requirements in this subpart for the stowage of Class 1 (explosive) materials. Detonators, detonator assemblies and boosters with detonators, Division 1.1 (explosive) may not be stored on the same magazine vessel with other Division 1.1, 1.2. and 1.3 (explosive) materials.

(d) **Class 1 (explosive) materials storage spaces.** Any compartment on a magazine vessel used for the stowage of Class 1 (explosive) materials must be completely sealed with wood so as to provide a smooth interior surface. Each metal stanchion in the compartment must be boxed in the same manner. An overhead ceiling is not required when the overdeck is weather tight. All nail and bolt heads must be countersunk and any exposed metal must be covered with wood.

(e) **Initiating explosives, detonators and boosters** with detonators. No explosive substance in Division 1.1, compatibility group A may be stowed in the same compartment with any other Class 1 (explosive) materials when there are explosive substances in Division 1.1 or 1.2 (explosive) on the same magazine vessel. Detonators, detonator assemblies and boosters with detonators must be stowed at least 8 m (26 feet) from any bulkhead forming a boundary of a compartment containing any other Class 1 (explosive) materials.

(f) **Dry storage spaces.** A magazine vessel having a dry storage space capable of being used for any purpose whatsoever must have a cofferdam at least 61 cm (24 inches) wide fitted between the dry storage space and each adjacent compartment containing Class 1 (explosive) materials. The cofferdam must be constructed of wood or steel, formed by two tight athwartship bulkheads extending from the skin of the vessel to the overdeck. If the cofferdam extends to the weather deck, a watertight hatch must be fitted in the deck to provide access to the cofferdam.

(g) **Lighting.** Non-sparking, battery-powered, self-contained electric lanterns or non-sparking hand flashlights are the only means of artificial light authorized.

(h) **Living quarters.** Living quarters must be fitted on the inside with a non-combustible material approved by the Commandant, USCG. Bracketed ship's lamps are the only lighting fixtures authorized to be used in the living quarters. Any stove used for heating or cooking must be securely fastened and may not be mounted closer than 15 cm (5.9 inches) to the deck or sides of the house. Any smoke pipe for the stove which passes through the roof of the house must be kept at least 8 cm (3 inches) away from any woodwork. Each smoke pipe must be protected by a layer of non-combustible material approved by the Commandant, USCG, an air space of at least 2.54 cm (1 inch), and a metal collar of at least 1.5 mm (0.059 inch) sheet secured only on the weather side of the roof. There may be no opening from any living quarters into any stowage compartment.

(i) **Storage of other hazardous materials.** Magazine vessels having Class 1 (explosive) materials on board may not be used for the storage of any other hazardous material.

(j) **Magazine vessel's stores.** Hazardous materials used as stores on board any magazine vessel must comply with the requirements of 46 CFR part 147.

(k) **Matches.** Safety matches requiring a prepared surface for ignition are the only type of matches authorized to be possessed or used on board a magazine vessel. They must be kept in a metal box or can with a metal cover and stored in the custodian's living quarters.

(l) **Firearms.** Firearms and ammunition (other than cargo) are not permitted on board a magazine vessel.

(m) **Fire extinguishing equipment.** No Class 1 (explosive) materials may be loaded or stowed in, unloaded from, or handled on any magazine vessel unless four fire extinguishers that meet the requirements for Type A Size II or Type B Size III in 46 CFR part 95, subpart 95.50 are near and accessible to the magazines.

(n) **Supervision.** A magazine vessel containing Class 1 (explosive) materials must be continuously attended by a custodian employed for that purpose by the vessel's owner.

(o) **Unauthorized persons on magazine vessels.** The custodian of a magazine vessel shall prevent unauthorized persons from coming on board unless it is necessary to abate a hazard to human life or a substantial hazard to property.

(p) **Repacking of Class 1 (explosive) materials on board.** No Class 1 (explosive) materials may be repacked on board a magazine vessel. Broken or damaged packages must be handled in accordance with the requirements of §176.156. Packages requiring an emergency response must be handled in accordance with the emergency response information required under §172.602 of this subchapter.

(q) **Work boat.** Each magazine vessel must be equipped with a work boat.

(r) **Life preservers.** One approved personal flotation device must be available for each person employed on a magazine vessel.

(s) **Fenders.** Each magazine vessel must be fitted with fenders in sufficient number and size to prevent any vessel tieing up alongside from coming in contact with the hull.

Subpart H - Detailed Requirements for Class 2 (Compressed Gas) Materials

§176.200 General stowage requirements.

(a) **Each package of Class 2 (compressed gas) material** being transported by vessel must be prevented from making direct contact with the vessel's deck, side, or bulwark by dunnage, shoring, or other effective means.

(b) **When cylinders of Class 2 (compressed gas) materials** being transported by vessel are stowed in a horizontal position, each tier must be stowed in the cantlines of the tier below it, and the valves on cylinders in adjacent tiers must be at alternate ends of the stow. Each tier may be stepped back and the ends alternated in order to clear the flange. Lashing must be provided to prevent any movement.

(c) **When cylinders of Class 2 (compressed gas) materials** being transported by vessel are stowed in a vertical position they must be stowed upright in a block and cribbed or boxed in with suitable dunnage. The box or crib must be dunnaged at least 10 cm (3.9 inches) off any metal deck. The cylinders in the box or crib must be braced to prevent any movement. The box or crib must be securely chocked and lashed to prevent any movement.

(d) **Any package containing Division 2.3 (poison gas) materials** must be stowed separate from all foodstuffs.

(e) **Class 2 (compressed gas) materials** may not be stowed "on deck" over a hold or compartment containing coal.

(f) **Class 2 (compressed gas) material** must be kept as cool as practicable and be stowed away from all sources of heat and ignition.

§176.205 Under deck stowage requirements.

(a) **When a Class 2 (compressed gas) material** is stowed below deck, it must be stowed in a mechanically ventilated cargo space with no source of artificial heat and clear of living quarters. No bulkhead or deck of that hold or compartment may be a common boundary with any boiler room, engine room, coal bunker, galley or boiler room uptake.

(b) **When Division 2.1 (flammable gas) materials** are stowed below deck, they must be stowed in a hold or compartment which complies with paragraph (a) of this section and the following requirements:

(1) *Each hold or compartment must be ventilated.*

(2) *Each hold or compartment* must be equipped with an overhead water sprinkler system or fixed fire extinguishing system.

(3) *Each electrical power line* in the hold or compartment must be protected by a strong metal covering to prevent crushing by cargo being stowed against it.

(4) *Except when fitted* with electrical fixtures of the explosion-proof type, each electrical circuit serving the hold or compartment must be disconnected from all sources of power. No circuit may be energized until the Division 2.1 (flammable gas) cargo and any vapors have been removed from the hold or compartment. Explosion-proof portable lighting may be used if the source of power is from electrical outlets outside the hold or compartment and above the weather deck.

(5) *Any opening* in a common bulkhead of an adjacent hold or compartment must be securely closed off and made gas-tight, unless the adjacent hold or compartment is also used for the stowage of Division 2.1 (flammable gas) materials.

(6) *Full and efficient hatch covers must be used.* Tarpaulins, if fitted, must be protected by dunnaging before overstowing with any cargo. Each tarpaulin must be in one piece and free of rents, tears, and holes.

(7) *A fire screen* must be fitted at the weather end of each vent duct leading from the hold or compartment. The fire screen must completely cover the open area. It must consist of two layers of corrosion-resistant metal wire of 20 x 20 mesh or finer, spaced not less than 1 cm (0.4 inch) or more than 4 cm (1.6 inches) apart. The screen may be removable if means for securing it in place when in service are provided.

(8) *The hold or compartment* may not be fitted with any gooseneck type vent trunk head.

(9) *Any electrical apparatus* located in the hold or compartment must be capable of being disconnected from its power source by a positive means located outside the hold or compartment.

§176.210 On deck stowage requirements.

Cylinders of Class 2 (compressed gas) materials being transported by vessel must be protected from radiant heat, including the direct rays of the sun, by structural erections or awnings. A tarpaulin covering the cylinders is not acceptable if it comes in contact with them.

§176.220 Smoking or open flame and posting of warning signs.

(a) **Smoking or the use of open flame is prohibited** in any hold or compartment containing a Division 2.1 (flammable gas) material, near any Division 2.1 (flammable gas) material stowed on deck, or near any ventilator leading to a hold containing this material.

(b) **A sign carrying the legend:**

FLAMMABLE VAPORS
KEEP LIGHTS AND FIRE AWAY
NO SMOKING

---

must be conspicuously posted at each approach to an "on deck" Division 2.1 (flammable gas) material stowage area and near each cargo hold ventilator leading to a hold containing this material. The sign must be painted on a white background using red letters. The letters may not be less than 8 cm (3 inches) high.

§176.225 Stowage of chlorine.

Chlorine (UN 1017) must be stowed separate from copper or brass leaf sheets and from finely divided organic material.

§176.230 Stowage of Division 2.1 (flammable gas) materials.

Division 2.1 (flammable gas) materials transported in Specification 106A or 110A multi-unit car tanks must be stowed on deck only, and must be shaded from radiant heat.

Subpart I - Detailed Requirements for Class 3 (Flammable) and Combustible Liquid Materials

§176.305 General stowage requirements.

(a) **A Class 3 (flammable) or combustible liquid** must be kept as cool as reasonably practicable and be stowed away from all sources of heat and ignition.

(b) **Except as otherwise provided in §176.76(g)**, a package containing a Class 3 (flammable) liquid and equipped with a vent or safety relief device must be stowed "on deck" only.

(c) **The following requirements apply to each** hold or compartment in which any Class 3 (flammable) or combustible liquids are being transported:

(1) *The hold or compartment* must be ventilated except that the stowage of non-bulk packages of Class 3 (flammable) liquids with a flash point above 23 °C (73 °F) (see 49 CFR 171.8 definitions) may be in non-ventilated holds.

(2) *Stowage of a Class 3* (flammable) or combustible liquid within 6 m (20 feet) of a bulkhead which forms a boundary or deck of a boiler room, engine room, coal bunker, galley, or boiler room uptake is not permitted. If the amount of the liquid to be stowed in a hold will not permit compliance with the requirement for a 6 m (20 foot) separation, less separation distance is authorized if at least one of the following conditions exists:

(i) *The bulkhead or deck* is covered with at least 8 cm (3 inches) of insulation on the entire area subject to heat;

(ii) *A temporary wooden bulkhead* at least 5 cm (2 inches) thick is constructed in the hold at least 8 cm (3 inches) off an engine room or 15 cm (5.9 inches) off a boiler room bulkhead, covering the entire area of the bulkhead that is subject to heat, and the space between the permanent bulkhead and the temporary wooden bulkhead is filled with mineral wool or equivalent bulk noncombustible insulating material; or

(iii) *A temporary wooden bulkhead* is constructed of at least 2.5 cm (1 inch) thick tongue and groove sheathing, located 1 m (3 feet) from the boiler room or engine room bulkhead, and filled with sand to a height of 2 m (7 feet) above the tank top, or, if the cargo compartment is located between decks, 1 m (3 feet) of sand.

(3) *Combustible liquids* may not be stowed in a hold within 6 m (20 feet) of a common bulkhead with the engine room unless the means of vessel propulsion is internal combustion engines.

(4) *Each cargo opening* in a bulkhead of an adjacent hold must be securely closed off and made gas-tight, unless the adjacent hold is also used for the stowage of a Class 3 (flammable) or combustible liquid.

(d) **In addition to the requirements specified** in paragraph (b) of this section, the following requirements apply to each hold or compartment in which a Class 3 (flammable) liquid is transported:

(1) *Full and effective hatch covers* must be used. Tarpaulins, if fitted, must be protected by dunnaging before overstowing with any cargo. Each tarpaulin must be in one piece and free of rents, tears, and holes;

(2) *If Class 3 (flammable) liquids* in excess of 1016 kg (2240 pounds) are stowed under deck in any one hold or compartment, a fire screen must be fitted at the weather end of each vent duct leading from that hold or compartment. The fire screen must completely cover the open area. It must consist of two layers of corrosion-resistant metal wire of 20 x 20 mesh or finer, spaced not less than 1 cm (0.4 inch) or more than 4 cm (1.6 inches) apart. The screen may be removable only if means for securing it in place when in service are provided;

(3) *Each electrical power line* in the hold or compartment must be protected by a strong metal covering to prevent crushing by cargo being stowed against it;

(4) *Except when fitted* with explosion-proof type electrical fixtures, each electrical circuit serving the hold or compartment must be disconnected from all sources of power from a point outside the hold or compartment containing flammable liquids. No circuit may be energized until the flammable liquids and any vapors have been removed from the hold or compartment. Explosion-proof type portable lighting may be used if the source of power is from electrical outlets outside the hold or compartment and above the weather deck; and

(5) *A Class 3 (flammable) liquid* in excess of 1016 kg (2240 pounds) may not be transported in any hold or compartment that is fitted with a gooseneck type of vent head.

(e) **On a passenger vessel, each hold or compartment** used to transport a Class 3 (flammable) liquid must be equipped with an overhead water sprinkler system or fixed fire-extinguishing system.

(f) **On a passenger vessel, each hold or compartment** used to transport Class 3 (flammable) liquids under a passenger space must have an overdeck of an A-60 type construction (see 46 CFR 72.05-10(c)(1)) or equivalent or have its underside covered with at least 8 cm (3 inches) of noncombustible insulation.

(g) **No Class 3 (flammable) liquid in a drum or wooden case,** having inside packagings of more than 1 L (0.3 gallon) capacity each, may be stowed as a beam filler. A wooden barrel, a wooden box or a fiberboard box, with any Class 3 (flammable) liquid material in inside packagings of not more than 1 L (0.3 gallon) capacity each, may only be stowed as a beam filler if it is possible to stow and observe any "THIS SIDE UP" marking.

§176.315 Fire protection requirements.

(a) **For each 79,500 L (21,000 U.S. gallons)** or part thereof of any Class 3 (flammable) or combustible liquid being transported on board a vessel in a portable tank, rail tank car, or a motor vehicle cargo tank, there must be provided at least one B-V semiportable foam (152 L/40 gallon capacity) (see 46 CFR 95.50), dry chemical (45.4 kg (100 pounds) minimum capacity) or equivalent fire extinguisher, or a fire hose fitted with an approved portable mechanical foam nozzle with pick-up tube and two 19 L (5 gallon) cans of foam liquid concentrate. Each foam system must be suitable for use with each Class 3 (flammable) or combustible liquid for which it is required. Each fire extinguisher must be accessible to the tank it is intended to cover.

(b) **The fire hose at each fire hydrant in the vicinity** of Class 3 (flammable) and combustible liquids stowage areas must be fitted with an approved combination solid stream and water spray nozzle.

(c) **The pressure must be maintained in the vessel's fire mains** during the loading and unloading of any Class 3 (flammable) or combustible liquids.

(d) **Two 7 kg (15-pound) capacity hand portable dry chemical** or two portable 10 L (2.6 gallons) foam-type extinguishers must be accessible to any packaged Class 3 (flammable) or combustible liquid and suitable for use with the lading.

(e) **The requirements of this section do not apply** to portable tanks and their contents authorized under 46 CFR part 98 or 46 CFR part 64.

§176.320 Use of hand flashlights.

Each hand flashlight used on deck near or in any hold or compartment containing a Class 3 (flammable) liquid, must be suitable for use in hazardous locations where fire or explosion hazards may exist.

§176.325 Smoking or open flame and posting of warning signs.

(a) **Smoking or the use of open flame is prohibited** in any hold or compartment containing a Class 3 (flammable) or combustible liquid, near any Class 3 (flammable) or combustible liquid stowed on deck, or near any ventilator leading to a hold containing such material.

(b) **A sign carrying the legend:**

FLAMMABLE VAPORS
KEEP LIGHTS AND FIRE AWAY
NO SMOKING

---

must be conspicuously posted at each approach to a Class 3 (flammable) or combustible liquid stowed "on deck" and near each cargo hold ventilator leading to a hold or compartment containing this material. This sign must be painted on a white background using red letters. The letters may not be less than 8 cm (3 inches) high.

§176.340 Combustible liquids in portable tanks.

Combustible liquids, having a flash point of 38 °C (100 °F) or higher, may be transported by vessel only in one of the portable tanks as specified below:

(a) **Portable tanks authorized in §173.241 of this subchapter.**

(b) **In nonspecification portable tanks,** subject to the following conditions:

(1) *Each portable tank* must conform to a DOT specification 57 portable tank, except as otherwise provided in this paragraph;

(2) *The rated capacity* of the tank may not exceed 4,542 L (1,200 gallons), and the rated gross weight may not exceed 13,608 kg (30,000 pounds);

(3) *The vibration test need not be performed;*

(4) *When the total surface area* of the tank exceeds 14.9 square meters (160 square feet), the total emergency venting capacity must be determined in accordance with table I in §178.345-10 of this subchapter;

(5) *In place* of a specification identification marking, the tank must be marked, on two sides in letters at least 5 cm (2 inches) high on contrasting background: "FOR COMBUSTIBLE LIQUIDS ONLY" and "49 CFR 176.340". This latter marking constitutes certification by the person offering the combustible liquid materials for transportation that the portable tank conforms to this paragraph;

(6) *Each tank must be made of steel;*

(7) *The design pressure* of the tank must be not less than 62 kPa (9 psig);

(8) *No pressure relief device may open at less than 34.4 kPa (5 psig);*

(9) *Each tank* must be retested and marked at least once every 2 years in accordance with the requirements applicable to a DOT specification 57 portable tank in §180.605 of this subchapter; and

(10) *Each tank* must conform to the provisions of §173.24 of this subchapter and paragraphs 180.605(b) and (j) of this subchapter.

(c) **Portable tanks approved by the Commandant (G-MSO), USCG.**

Subpart J - Detailed Requirements for Class 4 (Flammable Solids), Class 5 (Oxidizers and Organic Peroxides), and Division 1.5 Materials

§176.400 Stowage of Division 1.5, Class 4 (flammable solids) and Class 5 (oxidizers and organic peroxides) materials.

(a) **Class 4 (flammable solid) material and Division 5.2** (organic peroxide) material must be kept as cool as reasonably practicable and be stowed away from all sources of heat and ignition.

(b) **Division 5.2 (organic peroxide) material** must be stowed away from living quarters or access to them. Division 5.2 (organic peroxide) material not requiring temperature control should be protected from radiant heat, which includes direct rays of the sun, and stowed in a cool, well-ventilated area.

(c) **No Division 1.5 or Class 5** (oxidizers and organic peroxides) material being transported by vessel may be stowed in the same hold or compartment with any readily combustible material such as a combustible liquid, a textile product, or with a finely divided substance, such as an organic powder.

(d) **No Division 1.5 or Class 5** (oxidizers and organic peroxides) material being transported by vessel may be stowed in a hold or compartment containing sulfur in bulk, or in any hold or compartment above, below, or adjacent to one containing sulfur in bulk.

§176.405 Stowage of charcoal.

(a) **Before stowing charcoal Division 4.2 (flammable solid),** UN 1361, NA 1361, or UN 1362 on a vessel for transportation, the hold or compartment in which it is to be stowed must be swept as clean as practicable. All residue of any former cargo, including especially a petroleum product, a vegetable or animal oil, nitrate, or sulfur, must be removed.

(b) **Charcoal packed in bags and offered** for transportation on board a vessel in a quantity over 1016 kg (2240 pounds) must be loaded so that the bags are laid horizontally and stacked with space for efficient air circulation. If the bags are not compactly filled and closed to avoid free space within, vertical and horizontal dunnage strips must be laid between the bags. Space for ventilating must be maintained near bulkheads, the shell of the vessel, the deck, and the overhead. No more than 40,600 kg (89,508 pounds) of charcoal may be stowed in a hold or compartment when other stowage space is available. If the unavailability of hold or compartment space requires the stowage of a larger amount, the arrangement of the stow for ventilation must be adjusted to ensure a sufficient venting effect.

(c) **Any loose material from bags broken during loading** must be removed. Broken bags may be repacked or have the closures repaired and the repaired bags restowed.

(d) **Charcoal "screenings" packed in bags must be stowed** to provide spaces for air circulation between tiers regardless of the quantity stowed.

§176.410 Division 1.5 materials, ammonium nitrate and ammonium nitrate mixtures.

(a) **This section prescribes requirements to be observed** with respect to transportation of each of the following hazardous materials by vessel:

(1) *Explosives, blasting,* type E, and Explosives, blasting, type B, Division 1.5 compatibility group D, UN 0331 and UN 0332.

(2) *Ammonium nitrate fertilizer, Division 5.1 (oxidizer), UN 1942.*

(3) *Ammonium nitrate fertilizer, Division 5.1 (oxidizer), UN 2068.*

(4) *Ammonium nitrate fertilizer, Division 5.1 (oxidizer), UN 2067.*

(5) *Ammonium nitrate fertilizer,* Division 5.1 (oxidizer), UN 2069 or NA 2072.

(6) *Ammonium nitrate fertilizer, Division 5.1 (oxidizer), UN 2070.*

(b) **This section does not apply to** Ammonium nitrate fertilizer, Class 9, UN 2071 or to any non-acidic ammonium nitrate mixed fertilizer containing 13 percent or less ammonium nitrate, less than 5 percent organic material, and no other oxidizing material, and which does not meet the criteria for any other hazard set forth in part 173 of this subchapter.

(c) **When Division 1.5 compatibility group D materials,** ammonium nitrate, or any of the ammonium nitrate fertilizers listed in paragraph (a) of this section are transported by vessel:

(1) *They must be stowed* well away from any steam pipe, electric circuit, or other source of heat;

(2) *Smoking is prohibited* except in designated areas away from the material and "No-Smoking" signs must be posted in accordance with §176.60;

(3) *Fire hoses* must be connected, laid out, and tested before loading or unloading commences; and

(4) *A fire watch* must be posted in the hold or compartment where the material is being loaded or unloaded.

(d) **When any of the hazardous materials** listed in paragraph (a) of this section is transported in bags by vessel:

(1) *The requirements specified* in paragraph (c) of this section must be complied with;

(2) *The temperature of the bagged material* may not exceed 54 °C (130 °F);

(3) *Minimum dunnage and sweatboards* must be used to prevent any friction or abrasion of bags, and to allow for the circulation of air and access of water in the event of fire;

(4) *The bags* must be stowed from side to side, out to the sweatboards;

(5) *A space* of 46 cm (18 inches) must be provided between any transverse bulkhead and the bags;

(6) *The bags* must be stowed so as to provide a 46 cm (18 inch) athwartship trench along the centerline of the compartment, continuous from top to bottom;

(7) *The bags* must be stowed so as to provide a 46 cm (18 inch) amidship trench running fore and aft from bulkhead to bulkhead;

(8) *The bags* may not be stowed less than 46 cm (18 inches) from any overhead deck beam;

(9) *The bags* must be stowed so as to provide vent flues 36 cm (14 inches) square at each corner of the hatch continuous from top to bottom;

(10) *Trenching must be accomplished* by alternating the direction of the bags in each tier (bulkheading); and

(11) *The bags* must be blocked and braced as necessary to prevent shifting of the bagged cargo adjacent to any trench area.

(e) **Notwithstanding §176.83(b) of this part,** ammonium nitrate and ammonium nitrate fertilizers classed as Division 5.1 (oxidizers) materials, may be stowed in the same hold, compartment, magazine, or freight container with Class 1 materials (explosive), except those containing chlorates, in accordance with the segregation and separation requirements of §176.144 of this part applying to Explosives, blasting, type B, and Explosives, blasting, type E, Division 1.5 compatibility group D.

(f) **No mixture containing ammonium nitrate** and any ingredient which would accelerate the decomposition of ammonium nitrate under conditions incident to transportation may be transported by vessel.

§176.415 Permit requirements for Division 1.5, ammonium nitrates, and certain ammonium nitrate fertilizers.

(a) **Except as provided in paragraph (b) of this section,** before any of the following material is loaded on or unloaded from a vessel at any waterfront facility, the owner/operator must obtain written permission from the nearest COTP:

(1) *Ammonium nitrate UN 1942,* ammonium nitrate fertilizers containing more than 60 percent ammonium nitrate, ammonium nitrate fertilizer, Division 5.1 (oxidizer) UN 2070, or Division 1.5 compatibility group D materials packaged in a paper bag, burlap bag, or other nonrigid combustible packaging, or any rigid packaging with combustible inside packagings.

(2) *Any other ammonium nitrate* or ammonium nitrate fertilizer not listed in §176.410 (a) or (b) except ammonium nitrate fertilizer, Class 9, UN 2071.

(b) **Any of the following may be loaded on or unloaded** from a vessel at any waterfront facility without a permit:

(1) *Ammonium nitrate fertilizer,* Division 5.1 (oxidizer) UN 1942, in a rigid packaging with noncombustible inside packaging.

(2) *Ammonium nitrate fertilizer,* Division 5.1 (oxidizer) UN 2067, if the nearest COTP is notified at least 24 hours in advance of any loading or unloading in excess of 454 kg (1,000 pounds).

(3) *Ammonium nitrate fertilizer, n.o.s.,* Division 5.1 (oxidizer) NA 2072, containing 40 percent or more fine calcium carbonate or dolomite.

(4) *Non-acidic* ammonium nitrate fertilizer, n.o.s., Division 5.1 (oxidizer) UN 2072, containing less than 5 percent organic material and 60 percent or less ammonium nitrate.

(5) *Division 1.5* compatibility group D material in a rigid packaging with non-combustible inside packaging.

(6) *Ammonium nitrate fertilizer, Class 9, UN 2071.*

(c) **Before a permit may be issued,** the following requirements must be met in addition to any others the COTP may impose:

(1) *If the material* is ammonium nitrate fertilizer, Division 5.1 (oxidizer), UN2070; or Explosives, blasting, type E, Division 1.5 compatibility group D, UN0332 in combustible packaging or in a rigid packaging with combustible inside packaging, it must be loaded or unloaded at a facility remote from populous areas or high value or high hazard industrial facilities so that in the event of fire or explosion loss of lives and property may be minimized;

(2) *If the material* is an ammonium nitrate fertilizer, Division 5.1 (oxidizer), UN2070, containing more than 60 percent ammonium nitrate; or ammonium nitrate fertilizer, Division 5.1 (oxidizer), UN2070 in rigid packagings with combustible inside packagings, it must be loaded or unloaded at a facility removed from congested areas or high value or high hazard industrial facilities;

(3) *Each facility* at which the material is to be loaded or unloaded must conform with the requirements of the port security and local regulations and must have an abundance of water readily available for fire fighting;

(4) *Each facility* at which the material is to be loaded or unloaded must be located so that each vessel to be loaded or unloaded has an unrestricted passage to open water. Each vessel must be moored bow to seaward, and must be maintained in a mobile status during loading, unloading, or handling operations by the presence of tugs or the readiness of engines. Each vessel must have two wire towing hawsers, each having an eye splice, lowered to the water's edge, one at the bow and the other at the stern; and

(5) *If the material* is ammonium nitrate fertilizer, Division 5.1 (oxidizer), UN2070; an ammonium nitrate fertilizer, Division 5.1 (oxidizer) containing more than 60 percent ammonium nitrate; or a Division 1.5 compatibility group D material in non-rigid combustible packaging and loaded in freight containers or transport vehicles, it may be loaded or unloaded at a non-isolated facility provided that facility is approved by the COTP.

Subpart K [Reserved]

Subpart L - Detailed Requirements for Division 2.3 (Poisonous Gas) and Division 6.1 (Poisonous) Materials

§176.600 General stowage requirements.

(a) **Each package required to have** a POISON GAS, POISON INHALATION HAZARD, or POISON label, being transported on a vessel, must be stowed clear of living quarters and any ventilation ducts serving living quarters and separated from foodstuffs, except when the hazardous materials and the foodstuffs are in different closed transport units.

(b) **Each package required to have** both a POISON GAS label and a FLAMMABLE GAS label thereon must be segregated as a Division 2.1 (flammable gas) material.

(c) **Each package bearing a POISON label** displaying the text "PG III" or bearing a "PG III" mark adjacent to the poison label must be stowed away from foodstuffs.

(d) **Each package of Division 2.3 (poisonous gas) material** or Division 6.1 (poison) material which also bears a FLAMMABLE LIQUID or FLAMMABLE GAS label must be stowed in a mechanically ventilated space, kept as cool as reasonably practicable, and be stowed away from all sources of heat and ignition.

§176.605 Care following leakage or sifting of Division 2.3 (poisonous gas) and Division 6.1 (poisonous) materials.

A hold or compartment containing a package of a Division 2.3 (poisonous gas) or Division 6.1 (poisonous) material which has leaked or sifted must be thoroughly cleaned and decontaminated after the cargo is unloaded and before the hold or compartment is used for the stowage of any other cargo.

Subpart M - Detailed Requirements for Radioactive Materials

§176.700 General stowage requirements.

(a) [Reserved]

(b) **A package of radioactive materials** which in still air has a surface temperature more than 5 °C (9 °F) above the ambient air may not be overstowed with any other cargo. If the package is stowed under deck, the hold or compartment in which it is stowed must be ventilated.

(c) **Each fissile material, controlled shipment** must be stowed in a separate hold, compartment, or defined deck area and be separated by a distance of at least 6 m (20 feet) from all other RADIOACTIVE YELLOW-II or YELLOW-III labeled packages.

(d) **For a shipment of radioactive materials** requiring supplemental operational procedures, the shipper must furnish the master or person in charge of the vessel a copy of the necessary operational instructions.

(e) **A person may not remain unnecessarily** in a hold, or compartment, or in the immediate vicinity of any package on deck, containing radioactive materials.

(The information collection requirements in paragraph (d) were approved by the Office of Management and Budget under control numbers 2137-0534, 2137-0535 and 2137-0536)

§176.704 Requirements relating to transport indexes.

(a) **The sum of the transport indexes for all packages** of Class 7 (radioactive) materials on board a vessel may not exceed the limits specified in table III.

(b) **For packages in freight containers, the radiation level** may not exceed 2 mSv per hour (200 mrem per hour) at any point on the surface and 0.1 mSv per hour (10 mrem per hour) at 2 m (6.6 feet) from the outside surface of the freight container.

(c) **The limitations specified in table III do not apply** to consignments of LSA materials if the packages are marked "RADIOACTIVE LSA" and no fissile Class 7 (radioactive) materials are included in the shipment.

(d) **Each group of fissile packages must be separated** from other Class 7 (radioactive) material by a distance of at least 6 m (20 feet) at all times.

(e) **The limitations specified in paragraphs (a) through (c)** of this section do not apply when the entire vessel is reserved or chartered for use by a single offeror under exclusive use conditions if —

(1) *The number* of fissile packages of Class 7 (radioactive) materials aboard the vessel does not exceed the amount authorized in §§173.457 and 173.459 of this subchapter; and

(2) *The entire shipment operation* is approved by the Associate Administrator in advance.

(f) **Table III is as follows:**

Table III - TI Limits for Freight Containers and Conveyances

Type of freight container or conveyance	Limit on total sum of transport indexes in a single freight container or aboard a conveyance			
	Not under exclusive use		Under exclusive use	
	Non-fissile material	Fissile material	Non-fissile material	Fissile material[a]
Freight container — Small	50	50	N/A	N/A
Freight container — Large	50	50	No limit	100[b]
Vessel[c]:				
1. Hold, compartment or defined deck area:				
Packages, overpacks, small freight containers	50	50	No limit	100[b]
Large freight containers	200[d]	50	No limit	100[b]
2. Total vessel:				
Packages, etc.	200[d]	200[d]	No limit[e]	200[e]
Large freight containers	No limit[d]	No limit[d]	No limit	No limit[d]

[a] Provided that transport is direct from the consignor to the consignee without any intermediate in-transit storage, where the total TI exceed 50.

[b] In cases in which the total TI is greater than 50, the consignment must be so handled and stowed so that it is always separated from any package, overpack, portable tank or freight container carrying Class 7 (radioactive) materials by at least 6 m (20 feet).

[c] For vessels the requirements given in 1 and 2 must be fulfilled.

[d] Provided that the packages, overpacks, portable tanks or freight containers, as applicable, are stowed so that the total sum of the TI's in any group does not exceed 50, and that each group is handled and stowed so that the groups are separate from each other by at least 6 m (20 feet).

[e] Packages or overpacks carried in or on a transport vehicle which are offered for transport under the provisions of §173.441(b) of this subchapter may be transported by vessel provided that they are not removed from the vehicle at anytime while on board the vessel.

§176.708 Segregation distance table.

(a) **Table IV applies to the stowage of packages** of Class 7 (radioactive) materials on board a vessel with regard to transport index numbers which are shown on the labels of individual packages.

(b) **RADIOACTIVE YELLOW-II or YELLOW-III** labeled packages may not be stowed any closer to living accommodations, regularly occupied working spaces, spaces that may be continually occupied by any person (except those spaces exclusively reserved for couriers specifically authorized to accompany such packages), or undeveloped film than the distances specified in TABLE IV.

(c) **Where only one consignment of a Class 7** (radioactive) material is to be loaded on board a vessel under exclusive use conditions, the appropriate segregation distance may be established by demonstrating that the direct measurement of the radiation level at regularly occupied working spaces and living quarters is less than 7.5 microsieverts per hour (0.75 mrem per hour).

(d) **More than one consignment may be loaded** on board a vessel with the appropriate segregation distance established by demonstrating that direct measurement of the radiation level at regularly occupied working spaces and living quarters is less than 7.5 microSieverts per hour (0.75 mrem per hour), provided that:

(1) *The vessel* has been chartered for the exclusive use of a competent person specialized in the carriage of Class 7 (radioactive) material; and

(2) *Stowage arrangements* have been predetermined for the entire voyage, including any Class 7 (radioactive) material to be loaded at ports of call enroute.

(e) **The radiation level must be measured** by a responsible person skilled in the use of monitoring instruments.

(f) **Table IV is as follows:**

Table IV

Sum of transport indexes of the packages	Minimum distance in feet from living accommodation or regularly occupied working space		Minimum distance in feet from undeveloped film and plates																							
			1 day voyage			2 day voyage			4 day voyage			10 day voyage			20 day voyage			30 day voyage			40 day voyage			50 day voyage		
	Cargo thickness in feet (unit density)																									
	Nil	3	Nil	3	6	Nil	3	6	Nil	3	6	Nil	3	6	Nil	3	6	Nil	3	6	Nil	3	6	Nil	3	6
0.1 to 0.5	5	X	6	X	X	8	X	X	11	X	X	17	4	X	25	6	X	30	7	X	35	8	X	39	9	X
0.6 to 1	6	X	8	X	X	11	X	X	16	4	X	25	6	X	35	8	X	42	10	X	50	12	X	55	13	X
1.1 to 2	9	X	11	X	X	16	4	X	22	5	X	35	8	X	50	12	X	61	14	X	70	17	X	78	19	X
2.1 to 3	10	X	14	X	X	19	5	X	27	6	X	42	10	X	61	14	X	74	18	X	86	20	X	96	23	X
3.1 to 5	13	X	17	4	X	25	6	X	35	8	X	55	13	X	78	19	X	96	23	X	110	26	X	124	29	7
5.1 to 10	19	4	25	6	X	35	8	X	50	12	X	78	19	X	110	26	X	135	33	8	155	37	9	175	42	10
10.1 to 20	26	6	35	8	X	50	12	X	69	17	X	110	26	X	155	37	9	190	46	11	220	53	13	250	59	14
20.1 to 30	32	8	43	10	X	61	14	X	85	20	X	135	32	8	190	45	11	235	56	13	270	65	16	305	72	17
30.1 to 50	42	10	55	13	X	78	19	X	110	26	X	175	42	10	245	58	14	300	73	17	350	84	20	390	94	22
50.1 to 100	59	14	78	19	X	110	26	X	155	37	9	245	59	14	350	82	20	430	105	24	515	118	28	550	130	32
100.1 to 150	72	17	96	23	X	135	32	8	190	46	11	300	72	17	425	100	24	525	125	30	600	145	35	(7)	165	39
150.1 to 200	84	20	110	26	X	155	37	9	200	53	13	350	84	20	490	115	28	600	140	35	(7)	165	40	(7)	190	45
200.1 to 300	105	24	135	32	X	190	46	11	270	64	15	425	105	25	600	145	35	(7)	180	42	(7)	205	49	(7)	230	55
300.1 to 400	120	28	160	37	9	220	53	13	310	75	18	500	120	28	(7)	165	40	(7)	205	49	(7)	235	57	(7)	265	63

NOTE:

(1) X — indicates that thickness of screening cargo is sufficient without any additional segregation distance.

(2) By using 6 feet of intervening unit density cargo for persons and 10 feet for film and plates, no distance shielding is necessary for any length of voyage specified.

(3) Using 1 steel bulkhead or steel deck — multiply segregation distance by 0.8. Using 2 steel bulkheads or steel decks — multiply segregation distance by 0.64.

(4) "Cargo of Unit Density" means cargo stowed at a density of 1 ton (long) per 36 cubic feet; where the density is less than this the depth of cargo specified must be increased in proportion.

(5) "Minimum distance" means the least in any direction whether vertical or horizontal from the outer surface of the nearest package.

(6) The total consignment on board at any time must not exceed transport indexes totalling 200 except if carried under the provisions of §176.704(f). The figures below the double line of the table should be used in such a contingency.

(7) Not to be carried unless screening by other cargo and bulkheads can be arranged in accordance with the other columns.

§176.710 Care following leakage or sifting of radioactive materials.

(a) **In case of fire, collision, or breakage** involving any shipment of radioactive materials, other than materials of low specific activity, the radioactive materials must be segregated from unnecessary contact with personnel. In case of obvious leakage, or if the inside container appears to be damaged, the stowage area (hold, compartment, or deck area) containing this cargo must be isolated as much as possible to prevent radioactive material from entering any person's body through contact, inhalation, or ingestion. No person may handle the material or remain in the vicinity unless supervised by a qualified person.

(b) **A hold or compartment in which leakage** of radioactive materials has occurred may not be used for other cargo until it is decontaminated in accordance with the requirements of §176.715.

(c) **For reporting requirements, see §171.15 of this subchapter.**

§176.715 Contamination control.

Each hold, compartment, or deck area used for the transportation of low specific activity or surface contaminated object Class 7 (radioactive) materials under exclusive use conditions must be surveyed with appropriate radiation detection instruments after each use. Such holds, compartments, and deck areas may not be used again until the radiation dose rate at every accessible surface is less than 5 microSieverts per hour (0.5 mrem per hour), and the removable (non-fixed) radioactive surface contamination is not greater than the limits prescribed in §173.443 of this subchapter.

§176.720 Requirements for carriage of INF cargo in international transportation.

A vessel carrying INF cargo (see §176.2, under INF cargo definition) in international transportation must meet the requirements of the INF Code (contained in IMDG Code, 2000 edition, see §171.7 of this subchapter) in addition to all other applicable requirements of this subchapter.

Subpart N - Detailed Requirements for Class 8 (Corrosive Materials) Materials

§176.800 General stowage requirements.

(a) **Each package required to have a Class 8** (corrosive) label thereon being transported on a vessel must be stowed clear of living quarters, and away from foodstuffs and cargo of an organic nature.

(b) **A package of Class 8 (corrosive material) material** may not be stowed over any readily combustible material.

(c) **Glass carboys containing Class 8** (corrosive material) material may not be stowed on board any vessel, other than a barge, more than two tiers high unless each carboy is boxed or crated with neck protection extending to the sides of the carboy box. This protective construction must be strong enough to permit stacking one on top of the other.

(d) **A Class 8 (corrosive material) material** may not be stowed over a hold or compartment containing cotton unless the deck is of steel and the hatch is fitted with a tight coaming. In addition, the deck must be tight against leakage and the Class 8 (corrosive material) material may not be stowed over the square of the hatch.

(e) **Each package of Class 8 (corrosive material)** which also bears a FLAMMABLE LIQUID label must be stowed away from all sources of heat and ignition.

§176.805 On deck stowage.

When break bulk Class 8 (corrosive materials) materials being transported on a vessel are stowed on deck:

(a) **Provisions must be made for leakage** from any package to drain away from other cargo into an overboard scupper or freeing port. The drainage may not enter an enclosed drainage system other than a direct overboard scupper. If this stowage is not practical, sufficient clean dry sand must be placed under and around the lower tier of packages to absorb any leakage.

(b) **Dunnage must be provided on the deck** and arranged so that any leakage will be apparent.

(c) **Any leakage that occurs must be washed down,** using liberal quantities of water.

Subpart O - Detailed Requirements for Cotton & Vegetable Fibers, Motor Vehicles & Asbestos

§176.900 Packaging and stowage of cotton and vegetable fibers; general.

(a) **Cotton, Class 9, NA 1365, Cotton, wet, Division 4.2,** UN 1365, and other vegetable fibers, Division 4.1, being transported on a vessel must be securely baled and bound. Each bale of cotton or vegetable fibers must be covered with bagging on at least three-fourths of its surface, including both ends. Cut cotton linters may be accepted for transportation by vessel when baled and covered with bagging on the soft sides only if the bale is compressed to a density of at least 512 kg/m^3 (32 pounds per cubic foot) and it is bound with at least six bands per bale. Any poorly compressed bale or any bale having damaged bindings may not be transported by vessel.

(b) **Each bale of Cotton, wet, Division 4.2, UN 1365** must be stowed separately from any bales of dry cotton or vegetable fibers, in a 'tween deck space, and not overstowed. Any bale of cotton or vegetable fibers which is saturated with water may not be transported by vessel.

(c) **Bales of cotton or vegetable fibers** showing contact with oil or grease may not be accepted for transportation by vessel.

(d) **Cotton or vegetable fibers must be** stowed in a hold or compartment in accordance with the following requirements:

(1) *All traces* of oil or residue in the hold or compartment must be removed;

(2) *A recently painted* hold or compartment may not be used unless it is thoroughly dry;

(3) *Each ventilation cowl* serving the hold or compartment must be fitted with a spark screen;

(4) *When a bulkhead* of the hold or compartment is common with a boiler room, engine room, coal bunker, or galley and subjected to heat, a wooden bulkhead must be erected between the bulkhead and any cotton or vegetable fibers. This wooden bulkhead must be at least 15 cm (6 inches) from a boiler room bulkhead, and at least 5 cm (2 inches) from an engine room, coal bunker, or galley bulkhead;

(5) *Each 'tween deck hatch* must be closed with hatch covers, tarpaulins, and dunnage; however, metal hatch covers which are sealed by other means to provide equivalent protection may be used;

(6) *Each hold or compartment* must be equipped with a carbon dioxide or overhead water sprinkler system or other approved fixed extinguishing system. Before loading, the extinguishing system must be examined to ensure that it is in good working condition; and

(7) *Each hold or compartment* must be clear of all debris and swept as clean as practicable before loading.

(e) **Naked lights or any fire likely to produce sparks** are not permitted on the vessel, dock area, or on any lighters alongside a vessel during loading or unloading of cotton or vegetable fibers.

(f) **Upon completion of stowage,** each opening must be completely closed. Where required, tarpaulins must be fitted and secured in place to provide a tight hold. During a period of temporary stoppage of loading or unloading, a hatch may be left open. However, during that period, a fire watch, designated by the master or officer-in-charge, must be stationed in the hold or compartment in which the cotton or vegetable fibers are stowed.

(g) **At least one fire hose must be connected** while cotton or vegetable fibers are being loaded or unloaded. Each fire pump must be operated before any loading or unloading. Pressure must be maintained on each fire main during the loading and the fire hose laid out ready for immediate use. Portable fire extinguishers must be placed to be readily available. The fire hose, fire pumps, and fire extinguishers may be the vessel's equipment or shore equipment.

(h) **Smoking is not permitted on a vessel** during the loading or unloading of cotton or vegetable fibers except at those times and in those places designated by the master. "NO SMOKING" signs must be conspicuously posted in appropriate places, and the responsible person in charge of the loading or unloading (see §176.57 of this part) must ensure that they are observed.

(i) **Cotton or vegetable fibers may be stowed** in the same hold over bulk sulfur if the sulfur has been trimmed and leveled and the hold is thoroughly cleaned of sulfur dust. A tight floor of two layers of 2.54 cm (1 inch) crossed clean dunnage boards must be laid on the sulfur before cotton or vegetable fibers are stowed. These substances may be stowed alongside each other in the same hold if they are separated by a tight dustproof wood bulkhead.

(j) **Cotton or vegetable fibers may not be stowed** in a 'tween deck hold over bulk sulfur in a lower hold unless the 'tween deck hold has been thoroughly cleaned of all sulfur dust and the 'tween deck hatch covers are in place and covered with tarpaulins and dunnage.

§176.901 Stowage of cotton or vegetable fibers with rosin or pitch.

(a) **Unless impracticable, cotton or vegetable fibers** being transported on a vessel may not be stowed in the same hold or compartment with rosin or pitch being transported on the same vessel.

(b) **When separate stowage is impracticable,** the cotton or vegetable fibers may be stowed in the same hold or compartment with rosin or pitch if they are separated by clean dunnage or a cargo of a non-combustible nature. When such stowage within the same hold or compartment involves large amounts of cotton or fibers or of rosin or pitch, the rosin or pitch must be floored off with at least two layers of 2.54 cm (1 inch) dunnaging and the cotton or vegetable fibers stowed above.

§176.903 Stowage of cotton or vegetable fibers with coal.

Cotton or vegetable fibers being transported on a vessel may not be stowed in the same hold with coal. They may be stowed in adjacent holds if the holds are separated by a tight steel bulkhead and the cotton or vegetable fibers are dunnaged at least 5 cm (2 inches) off the bulkhead. Cotton or vegetable fibers may be stowed in a hold above or below one in which coal is stowed if there is a tight steel intervening deck and all hatch covers are in place and covered with tarpaulins.

§176.905 Motor vehicles or mechanical equipment powered by internal combustion engines.

(a) **A motor vehicle or any mechanized equipment** powered by an internal combustion engine is subject to the following requirements when carried as cargo on a vessel:

(1) *Before being loaded on a vessel,* each motor vehicle or mechanical equipment must be inspected for fuel leaks and identifiable faults in the electrical system that could result in short circuit or other unintended electrical source of ignition. A motor vehicle or mechanical equipment showing any signs of leakage or electrical fault may not be transported.

(2) *The fuel tank* of a motor vehicle or mechanical equipment powered by liquid fuel may not be more than one-fourth full.

(3) *Whenever possible,* each vehicle or mechanical equipment must be stowed to allow for its inspection during transit.

(4) *Motor vehicles* or mechanical equipment may be refueled when necessary in the hold of a vessel in accordance with §176.78.

(5) *When a motor vehicle* or mechanical equipment with fuel in its tanks is stowed in a closed freight container, a warning, displayed on a contrasting background and readily legible from a distance of 8 m (26 feet), must be affixed to the access doors to read as follows:

WARNING — MAY CONTAIN EXPLOSIVE MIXTURES WITH AIR — KEEP IGNITION SOURCES AWAY WHEN OPENING

(6) *A motor vehicle* or mechanical equipment's ignition key may not be in the ignition while the vehicle or mechanical equipment is stowed aboard a vessel.

(b) **All equipment used for handling vehicles** or mechanical equipment must be designed so that the fuel tank and fuel system of the vehicle or mechanical equipment are protected from stress that might cause rupture or other damage incident to handling.

(c) **Two hand-held, portable, dry chemical fire extinguishers** of at least 4.5 kg (10 pounds) capacity each must be separately located in an accessible location in each hold or compartment in which any motor vehicle or mechanical equipment is stowed.

(d) **"NO SMOKING" signs must be conspicuously posted** at each access opening to the hold or compartment.

(e) **Each portable electrical light, including a flashlight,** used in the stowage area must be an approved, explosion-proof type. All electrical connections for any portable light must be made to outlets outside the space in which any vehicle or mechanical equipment is stowed.

(f) **Each hold or compartment must be ventilated and fitted** with an overhead water sprinkler system or fixed fire extinguishing system.

(g) **Each hold or compartment must be equipped** with a smoke or fire detection system capable of alerting personnel on the bridge.

(h) **All electrical equipment in the hold or compartment** other than fixed explosion-proof lighting must be disconnected from its power source at a location outside the hold or compartment during the handling and transportation of any vehicle or mechanical equipment. Where the disconnecting means is a switch or circuit breaker, it must be locked in the open position until all vehicles have been removed.

(i) **Exceptions.** A motor vehicle or mechanical equipment is excepted from the requirements of this subchapter if the following requirements are met:

(1) *The motor vehicle* or mechanical equipment has an internal combustion engine using liquid fuel that has a flash point less than

38 °C (100 °F), the fuel tank is empty, and the engine is run until it stalls for lack of fuel;

(2) *The motor vehicle* or mechanical equipment has an internal combustion engine using liquid fuel that has a flash point of 38 °C (100 °F) or higher, the fuel tank contains 418 L (110 gallons) of fuel or less, and there are no fuel leaks in any portion of the fuel system;

(3) *The motor vehicle* or mechanical equipment is stowed in a hold or compartment designated by the administration of the country in which the vessel is registered to be specially suited for vehicles. See 46 CFR 70.10-44 and 90.10-38 for U.S. vessels;

(4) *The motor vehicle* or mechanical equipment is electrically powered by wet electric storage batteries; or

(5) *The motor vehicle* or mechanical equipment is equipped with liquefied petroleum gas or other compressed gas fuel tanks, the tanks are completely emptied of liquid and the positive pressure in the tank does not exceed 2 bar (29 psig), the line from the fuel tank to the regulator and the regulator itself is drained of all trace of (liquid) gas, and the fuel shut-off valve is closed.

(j) Except as provided in §173.220(d) of this subchapter, the provisions of this subchapter do not apply to items of equipment such as fire extinguishers, compressed gas accumulators, airbag inflators and the like which are installed in the motor vehicle or mechanical equipment if they are necessary for the operation of the vehicle or equipment, or for the safety of its operator or passengers.

Part 177 - Carriage by Public Highway

Subpart A - General Information and Regulations

§177.800 Purpose and scope of this part and responsibility for compliance and training.

(a) **Purpose and scope.** This part prescribes requirements, in addition to those contained in parts 171, 172, 173, 178 and 180 of this subchapter, that are applicable to the acceptance and transportation of hazardous materials by private, common, or contract carriers by motor vehicle.

(b) **Responsibility for compliance.** Unless this subchapter specifically provides that another person shall perform a particular duty, each carrier, including a connecting carrier, shall perform the duties specified and comply with all applicable requirements in this part and shall ensure its hazmat employees receive training in relation thereto.

(c) **Responsibility for training.** A carrier may not transport a hazardous material by motor vehicle unless each of its hazmat employees involved in that transportation is trained as required by this part and subpart H of part 172 of this subchapter.

(d) **No unnecessary delay in movement of shipments.** All shipments of hazardous materials must be transported without unnecessary delay, from and including the time of commencement of the loading of the hazardous material until its final unloading at destination.

§177.801 Unacceptable hazardous materials shipments.

No person may accept for transportation or transport by motor vehicle a forbidden material or hazardous material that is not prepared in accordance with the requirements of this subchapter.

§177.802 Inspection.

Records, equipment, packagings and containers under the control of a motor carrier, insofar as they affect safety in transportation of hazardous materials by motor vehicle, must be made available for examination and inspection by a duly authorized representative of the Department.

§177.804 Compliance with Federal Motor Carrier Safety Regulations.

Motor carriers and other persons subject to this part shall comply with 49 CFR parts 390 through 397 (excluding §§397.3 and 397.9) to the extent those regulations apply.

FEDERAL REGISTER UPDATES

An Interim Final Rule was published In the May 5, 2003 Federal Register, revising §177.804.

§177.804 Compliance with Federal Motor Carrier Safety Regulations.
Motor carriers and other persons subject to this part must comply with 49 CFR part 383 and 49 CFR parts 390 through 397 (excluding §§397.3 and 397.9) to the extent those regulations apply.

§177.810 Vehicular tunnels.

Except as regards Class 7 (radioactive) materials, nothing contained in parts 170-189 of this subchapter shall be so construed as to nullify or supersede regulations established and published under authority of State statute or municipal ordinance regarding the kind, character, or quantity of any hazardous material permitted by such regulations to be transported through any urban vehicular tunnel used for mass transportation.

§177.816 Driver training.

(a) **In addition to the training requirements of §177.800,** no carrier may transport, or cause to be transported, a hazardous material unless each hazmat employee who will operate a motor vehicle has been trained in the applicable requirements of 49 CFR parts 390 through 397 and the procedures necessary for the safe operation of that motor vehicle. Driver training shall include the following subjects:

(1) *Pre-trip safety inspection;*

(2) *Use of vehicle controls and equipment,* including operation of emergency equipment;

(3) *Operation of vehicle,* including turning, backing, braking, parking, handling, and vehicle characteristics including those that affect vehicle stability, such as effects of braking and curves, effects of speed on vehicle control, dangers associated with maneuvering through curves, dangers associated with weather or road conditions that a driver may experience (e.g., blizzards, mountainous terrain, high winds), and high center of gravity;

(4) *Procedures* for maneuvering tunnels, bridges, and railroad crossings;

(5) *Requirements pertaining* to attendance of vehicles, parking, smoking, routing, and incident reporting; and

(6) *Loading and unloading of materials, including —*

(i) *Compatibility and segregation of cargo in a mixed load;*

(ii) *Package handling methods; and*

(iii) *Load securement.*

(b) **Specialized requirements for cargo tanks** and portable tanks. In addition to the training requirement of paragraph (a) of this section, each person who operates a cargo tank or a vehicle with a portable tank with a capacity of 1,000 gallons or more must receive training applicable to the requirements of this subchapter and have the appropriate State-issued commercial driver's license required by 49 CFR part 383. Specialized training shall include the following:

(1) *Operation of* emergency control features of the cargo tank or portable tank;

(2) *Special vehicle handling characteristics,* including: high center of gravity, fluid-load subject to surge, effects of fluid-load surge on braking, characteristic differences in stability among baffled, unbaffled, and multi-compartmented tanks; and effects of partial loads on vehicle stability;

(3) *Loading and unloading procedures;*

(4) *The properties and hazards of the material transported; and*

(5) *Retest and inspection requirements for cargo tanks.*

(c) **The training required by paragraphs (a) and (b)** of this section may be satisfied by compliance with the current requirements for a Commercial Driver's License (CDL) with a tank vehicle or hazardous materials endorsement.

(d) **Training required by paragraph (b) of this section** must conform to the requirements of §172.704 of this subchapter with respect to frequency and recordkeeping.

§177.817 Shipping papers.

(a) **General requirements.** A person may not accept a hazardous material for transportation or transport a hazardous material by highway unless that person has received a shipping paper prepared in accordance with part 172 of this subchapter, unless the material is excepted from shipping paper requirements under this subchapter. A carrier may not transport a hazardous material unless it is accompanied by a shipping paper prepared in accordance with part 172 of this subchapter.

(b) **Shipper certification.** An initial carrier may not accept a hazardous material offered for transportation unless the shipping paper describing the material includes a shipper's certification which meets the requirements in §172.204 of this subchapter. Except for a hazardous waste, the certification is not required for shipments to be transported entirely by private carriage and for bulk shipments to be transported in a cargo tank supplied by the carrier.

(c) **Requirements when interlining with carriers by rail.** A motor carrier shall mark on the shipping paper required by this section, if it offers or delivers a freight container or transport vehicle to a rail carrier for further transportation:

(1) *A description of the freight container or transport vehicle; and*

(2) *The kind of placard* affixed to the freight container or transport vehicle.

(d) **This subpart does not apply to a material** that is excepted from shipping paper requirements as specified in §172.200 of this subchapter.

(e) **Shipping paper accessibility — accident or inspection.** A driver of a motor vehicle containing hazardous material, and each carrier using such a vehicle, shall ensure that the shipping paper required by this section is readily available to, and recognizable by, authorities in the event of accident or inspection. Specifically, the driver and the carrier shall:

(1) *Clearly distinguish the shipping paper,* if it is carried with other shipping papers or other papers of any kind, by either distinctively tabbing it or by having it appear first; and

(2) *Store the shipping paper as follows:*

(i) *When the driver is at the vehicle's controls,* the shipping paper shall be:

[A] Within his immediate reach while he is restrained by the lap belt; and

[B] either readily visible to a person entering the driver's compartment or in a holder which is mounted to the inside of the door on the driver's side of the vehicle.

(ii) *When the driver* is not at the vehicle's controls, the shipping paper shall be:

[A] In a holder which is mounted to the inside of the door on the driver's side of the vehicle; or

[B] on the driver's seat in the vehicle.

(f) Retention of shipping papers. Each person receiving a shipping paper required by this section must retain a copy or an electronic image thereof, that is accessible at or through its principal place of business and must make the shipping paper available, upon request, to an authorized official of a Federal, State, or local government agency at reasonable times and locations. For a hazardous waste, the shipping paper copy must be retained for three years after the material is accepted by the initial carrier. For all other hazardous materials, the shipping paper copy must be retained for 375 days after the material is accepted by the carrier. Each shipping paper copy must include the date of acceptance by the carrier. A motor carrier (as defined in §390.5 of Subchapter B of Chapter III of Subtitle B) that uses a shipping paper without change for multiple shipments of a single hazardous material (i.e., one having the same shipping name and identification number) may retain a single copy of the shipping paper, instead of a copy for each shipment made, if the carrier also retains a record of each shipment made, to include shipping name, identification number, quantity transported, and date of shipment.

FEDERAL REGISTER UPDATES

In the April 18, 2003 Federal Register, §177.817(a) was revised, effective October 1, 2003.

(a) General requirements. A person may not accept a hazardous material for transportation or transport a hazardous material by highway unless that person has received a shipping paper prepared in accordance with part 172 of this subchapter or the material is excepted from shipping paper requirements under this subchapter. A subsequent carrier may not transport a hazardous material unless it is accompanied by a shipping paper prepared in accordance with part 172 of this subchapter, except for §172.204, which is not required.

§177.823 Movement of motor vehicles in emergency situations.

(a) A carrier may not move a transport vehicle containing a hazardous material unless the vehicle is marked and placarded in accordance with part 172 or as authorized in §171.12a of this subchapter, or unless, in an emergency:

(1) *The vehicle* is escorted by a representative of a state or local government;

(2) *The carrier has permission from the Department; or*

(3) *Movement of* the transport vehicle is necessary to protect life or property.

(b) Disposition of contents of cargo tank when unsafe to continue. In the event of a leak in a cargo tank of such a character as to make further transportation unsafe, the leaking vehicle should be removed from the traveled portion of the highway and every available means employed for the safe disposal of the leaking material by preventing, so far as practicable, its spread over a wide area, such as by digging trenches to drain to a hole or depression in the ground, diverting the liquid away from streams or sewers if possible, or catching the liquid in containers if practicable. Smoking, and any other source of ignition, in the vicinity of a leaking cargo tank is not permitted.

(c) Movement of leaking cargo tanks. A leaking cargo tank may be transported only the minimum distance necessary to reach a place where the contents of the tank or compartment may be disposed of safely. Every available means must be utilized to prevent the leakage or spillage of the liquid upon the highway.

Subpart B - Loading and Unloading

§177.834 General requirements.

NOTE: For prohibited loading and storage of hazardous materials, see §177.848.

(a) Packages secured in a vehicle. Any tank, barrel, drum, cylinder, or other packaging not permanently attached to a motor vehicle and containing any Class 2 (gases), Class 3 (flammable liquid), Division 6.1 (poisonous), Division 6.2 (infectious substance), Class 7 (radioactive), or Class 8 (corrosive) material must be secured against movement within the vehicle on which it is being transported, under conditions normally incident to transportation.

(b) [Reserved]

(c) No smoking while loading or unloading. Smoking on or about any motor vehicle while loading or unloading any Class 1 (explosive), Class 3 (flammable liquid), Class 4 (flammable solid), Class 5 (oxidizing), or Division 2.1 (flammable gas) materials is forbidden.

(d) Keep fire away, loading and unloading. Extreme care shall be taken in the loading or unloading of any Class 1 (explosive), Class 3 (flammable liquid), Class 4 (flammable solid), Class 5 (oxidizing), or Division 2.1 (flammable gas) materials into or from any motor vehicle to keep fire away and to prevent persons in the vicinity from smoking, lighting matches, or carrying any flame or lighted cigar, pipe, or cigarette.

(e) Handbrake set while loading and unloading. No hazardous material shall be loaded into or on, or unloaded from, any motor vehicle unless the handbrake be securely set and all other reasonable precautions be taken to prevent motion of the motor vehicle during such loading or unloading process.

(f) Use of tools, loading and unloading. No tools which are likely to damage the effectiveness of the closure of any package or other container, or likely adversely to affect such package or container, shall be used for the loading or unloading of any Class 1 (explosive) material or other dangerous article.

(g) Prevent relative motion between containers. Containers of Class 1 (explosive), Class 2 (gases), Class 3 (flammable liquid), Class 4 (flammable solid), Class 5 (oxidizing), Division 6.1 (poisonous), Division 6.2 (infectious substance), or Class 8 (corrosive) materials must be so braced as to prevent motion thereof relative to the vehicle while in transit. Containers having valves or other fittings must be loaded to minimize the likelihood of damage thereto during transportation.

(h) Precautions concerning containers in transit; fueling road units. Reasonable care should be taken to prevent undue rise in temperature of containers and their contents during transit. There must be no tampering with such container or the contents thereof nor any discharge of the contents of any container between point of origin and point of billed destination. Discharge of contents of any container, other than a cargo tank or IM portable tank, must not be made prior to removal from the motor vehicle. Nothing contained in this paragraph shall be so construed as to prohibit the fueling of machinery or vehicles used in road construction or maintenance.

(i) Attendance requirements.

(1) *Loading.* A cargo tank must be attended by a qualified person at all times when it is being loaded. The person who is responsible for loading the cargo tank is also responsible for ensuring that it is so attended.

(2) *Unloading.* A motor carrier who transports hazardous materials by a cargo tank must ensure that the cargo tank is attended by a qualified person at all times during unloading. However, the carrier's obligation to ensure attendance during unloading ceases when:

(i) *The carrier's obligation for transporting the materials is fulfilled;*

(ii) *The cargo tank* has been placed upon the consignee's premises; and

(iii) *The motive power* has been removed from the cargo tank and removed from the premises.

(3) *Except for unloading operations* subject to §§177.837(d), 177.840(p), and 177.840(q), a qualified person "attends" the loading or unloading of a cargo tank if, throughout the process, he is alert and is within 7.62 m (25 feet) of the cargo tank. The qualified person attending the unloading of a cargo tank must have an unobstructed view of the cargo tank and delivery hose to the maximum extent practicable during the unloading operation.

(4) *A person is "qualified"* if he has been made aware of the nature of the hazardous material which is to be loaded or unloaded, he has been instructed on the procedures to be followed in emergencies, he is authorized to move the cargo tank, and he has the means to do so.

(j) Manholes and valves closed. A person may not drive a cargo tank and a motor carrier may not permit a person to drive a cargo tank motor vehicle containing a hazardous material regardless of quantity unless:

(1) *All manhole closures are closed and secured; and*

(2) *All valves* and other closures in liquid discharge systems are closed and free of leaks.

(k) [Reserved]

(l) Use of cargo heaters when transporting certain hazardous material. Transportation includes loading, carrying, and unloading.

(1) *When transporting Class 1 (explosive) materials.* A motor vehicle equipped with a cargo heater of any type may transport Class 1 (explosive) materials only if the cargo heater is rendered inoperable by: (i) Draining or removing the cargo heater fuel tank; and (ii) disconnecting the heater's power source.

(2) *When transporting certain flammable material —*

(i) *Use of combustion cargo heaters.* A motor vehicle equipped with a combustion cargo heater may be used to transport Class 3 (flammable liquid) or Division 2.1 (flammable gas) materials only if each of the following requirements are met:

[A] It is a catalytic heater.

[B] The heater's surface temperature cannot exceed 54 °C (130 °F) — either on a thermostatically controlled heater or on a heater without thermostatic control when the outside or ambient temperature is 16 °C (61 °F) or less.

[C] The heater is not ignited in a loaded vehicle.

[D] There is no flame, either on the catalyst or anywhere in the heater.

[E] The manufacturer has certified that the heater meets the requirements under paragraph (l)(2)(i) of this section by permanently marking the heater "MEETS DOT REQUIREMENTS FOR CATALYTIC HEATERS USED WITH FLAMMABLE LIQUID AND GAS."

[F] The heater is also marked "DO NOT LOAD INTO OR USE IN CARGO COMPARTMENTS CONTAINING FLAMMABLE LIQUID OR GAS IF FLAME IS VISIBLE ON CATALYST OR IN HEATER."

[G] Heater requirements under §393.77 of this title are complied with.

(ii) *Effective date* for combustion heater requirements. The requirements under paragraph (l)(2)(i) of this section govern as follows:

[A] Use of a heater manufactured after November 14, 1975, is governed by every requirement under (l)(2)(i) of this section;

[B] Use of a heater manufactured before November 15, 1975, is governed only by the requirements under (l)(2)(i) (A), (C), (D), (F) and (G) of this section until October 1, 1976; and

[C] Use of any heater after September 30, 1976, is governed by every requirement under paragraph (l)(2)(i) of this section.

(iii) *Restrictions on automatic* cargo-space-heating temperature control devices. Restrictions on these devices have two dimensions: Restrictions upon use and restrictions which apply when the device must not be used.

[A] Use restrictions. An automatic cargo-space-heating temperature control device may be used when transporting Class 3 (flammable liquid) or Division 2.1 (flammable gas) materials only if each of the following requirements is met:

[1] Electrical apparatus in the cargo compartment is non-sparking or explosion proof.

[2] There is no combustion apparatus in the cargo compartment.

[3] There is no connection for return of air from the cargo compartment to the combustion apparatus.

[4] The heating system will not heat any part of the cargo to more than 54 °C (129 °F).

[5] Heater requirements under §393.77 of this title are complied with.

[B] Protection against use. Class 3 (flammable liquid) or Division 2.1 (flammable gas) materials may be transported by a vehicle, which is equipped with an automatic cargo-space-heating temperature control device that does not meet each requirement of paragraph (l)(2)(iii)(A) of this section, only if the device is first rendered inoperable, as follows:

[1] Each cargo heater fuel tank, if other than LPG, must be emptied or removed.

[2] Each LPG fuel tank for automatic temperature control equipment must have its discharge valve closed and its fuel feed line disconnected.

(m) Tanks constructed and maintained in compliance with Spec. 106A or 110A (§§179.300, 179.301 of this subchapter) that are authorized for the shipment of hazardous materials by highway in part 173 of this subchapter must be carried in accordance with the following requirements:

(1) *Tanks must be* securely chocked or clamped on vehicles to prevent any shifting.

(2) *Equipment suitable* for handling a tank must be provided at any point where a tank is to be loaded upon or removed from a vehicle.

(3) *No more than* two cargo carrying vehicles may be in the same combination of vehicles.

(4) *Compliance with* §§174.200 and 174.204 of this subchapter for combination rail freight, highway shipments and for trailer-on-flat-car service is required.

(n) Specification 56, 57, IM 101, and IM 102 portable tanks, when loaded, may not be stacked on each other nor placed under other freight during transportation by motor vehicle.

(o) Unloading of IM portable tanks. An IM portable tank may be unloaded while remaining on a transport vehicle with the power unit attached if the tank meets the outlet requirements in §178.345-11 of this subchapter and the tank is attended by a qualified person during the unloading in accordance with the requirements in paragraph (i) of this section.

FEDERAL REGISTER UPDATES

In the April 18, 2003 Federal Register, the introductory text in §177.834(j) was revised, effective October 1, 2003.

(j) Except for a cargo tank conforming to §173.29(b)(2) of this subchapter, a person may not drive a cargo tank motor vehicle containing a hazardous material regardless of quantity unless:

FEDERAL REGISTER UPDATES

In the May 30, 2003 Federal Register, §177.834(o) was revised, effective June 30, 2003.

(o) Unloading of IM and UN portable tanks. No person may unload an IM or UN portable tank while it remains on a transport vehicle with the motive power unit attached except under the following conditions:

(1) *The unloading operation* must be attended by a qualified person in accordance with the requirements in paragraph (i) of this section. The person performing unloading functions must be trained in handling emergencies that may occur during the unloading operation.

(2) *Prior to unloading,* the operator of the vehicle on which the portable tank is transported must ascertain that the conditions of this paragraph (o) are met.

(3) *An IM or UN portable tank* equipped with a bottom outlet as authorized in Column (7) of the §172.101 Table of this subchapter by assignment of a T Code in the appropriate proper shipping name entry, and that contains a liquid hazardous material of Class 3, PG I or II, or PG III with a flash point of less than 100 °F (38 °C); Division 5.1, PG I or II; or Division 6.1, PG I or II, must conform to the outlet requirements in §178.275(d)(3) of this subchapter; or, until October 1, 2004, be unloaded only at a facility conforming to the following —

(i) *The applicable fire suppression requirements* in 29 CFR 1910.106(e), (f), (g), (h), and (i);

(ii) *The emergency shutdown requirements* in 29 CFR 1910.119(f), 1910.120(q) and 1910.38(a);

(iii) *The emergency response planning requirements* in 29 CFR part 1910 and 40 CFR part 68;

(iv) *An emergency* discharge control procedure applicable to unloading operations, including instructions on handling emergencies that may occur during the unloading operation; and

(v) *Public access to the unloading area* must be controlled in a manner ensuring no public access during unloading.

(4) *Alternatively,* conformance to equivalent or more stringent non-federal requirements is authorized in place of paragraphs (o)(3)(i) through (o)(3)(iv) of this section.

§177.835 Class 1 (explosive) materials.

(See also §177.834 (a) to (j).)

(a) Engine stopped. No Class 1 (explosive) materials shall be loaded into or on or be unloaded from any motor vehicle with the engine running.

(b) Care in loading, unloading, or other handling of Class 1 (explosive) materials. No bale hooks or other metal tools shall be used for the loading, unloading, or other handling of Class 1 (explosive) materials, nor shall any package or other container of Class 1 (explosive) materials, except barrels or kegs, be rolled. No packages of Class 1 (explosive) materials shall be thrown or dropped during process of loading or unloading or handling of Class 1 (explosive) materials. Special care shall be exercised to the end that packages or other containers containing Class 1 (explosive) materials shall not catch fire from sparks or hot gases from the exhaust tailpipe.

(1) *Whenever tarpaulins* are used for covering Class 1 (explosive) materials, they shall be secured by means of rope, wire, or other equally efficient tie downs. Class 1 (explosive) materials placards or markings required by §177.823 shall be secured, in the appropriate locations, directly to the equipment transporting the Class 1 (explosive) materials. If the vehicle is provided with placard boards, the placards must be applied to these boards.

(2) *[Reserved]*

(c) Class 1 (explosive) materials on vehicles in combination. Division 1.1 or 1.2 (explosive) materials may not be loaded into or carried on any vehicle or a combination of vehicles if:

(1) *More than two cargo carrying vehicles are in the combination;*

(2) *Any full trailer* in the combination has a wheel base of less than 184 inches;

(3) *Any vehicle* in the combination is a cargo tank which is required to be marked or placarded under §177.823; or

(4) *The other vehicle in the combination contains any:*

(i) *Substances, explosive, n.o.s.,* Division 1.1A (explosive) material (Initiating explosive),

(ii) *Packages of Class 7 (radioactive) materials* bearing "Yellow III" labels,

177 Carriage by Public Highway

(iii) *Division 2.3 (poisonous gas)* or Division 6.1 (poisonous) materials, or

(iv) *Hazardous materials* in a portable tank or a DOT specification 106A or 110A tank.

(d) **[Reserved]**

(e) **No sharp projections inside body of vehicles.** No motor vehicle transporting any kind of Class 1 (explosive) material shall have on the interior of the body in which the Class 1 (explosive) materials are contained, any inwardly projecting bolts, screws, nails, or other inwardly projecting parts likely to produce damage to any package or container of Class 1 (explosive) materials during the loading or unloading process or in transit.

(f) **Class 1 (explosive) materials vehicles,** floors tight and lined. Motor vehicles transporting Division 1.1, 1.2, or 1.3 (explosive) materials shall have tight floors; shall have that portion of the interior in contact with the load lined with either non-metallic material or non-ferrous metals, except that the lining is not required for truck load shipments loaded by the Departments of the Army, Navy or Air Force of the United States Government provided the Class 1 (explosive) materials are of such nature that they are not liable to leakage of dust, powder, or vapor which might become the cause of an explosion. The interior of the cargo space must be in good condition so that there will not be any likelihood of containers being damaged by exposed bolts, nuts, broken side panels or floor boards, or any similar projections.

(g) **No detonator assembly or booster with detonator** may be transported on the same motor vehicle with any Division 1.1, 1.2 or 1.3 material (except other detonator assemblies, boosters with detonators or detonators), detonating cord Division 1.4 material or Division 1.5 material. No detonator may be transported on the same motor vehicle with any Division 1.1, 1.2 or 1.3 material (except other detonators, detonator assemblies or boosters with detonators), detonating cord Division 1.4 material or Division 1.5 material unless —

(1) *It is packed* in a specification MC 201 (§178.318 of this subchapter) container; or

(2) *The package* conforms with requirements prescribed in §173.63 of this subchapter, and its use is restricted to instances when —

(i) *There is no* Division 1.1, 1.2, 1.3 or 1.5 material loaded on the motor vehicle; and

(ii) *A separation* of 61 cm (24 inches) is maintained between each package of detonators and each package of detonating cord; or

(3) *It is packed and loaded* in accordance with a method approved by the Department. One method approved by the Department requires that —

(i) *The detonators* are in packagings as prescribed in §173.63 of this subchapter which in turn are loaded into suitable containers or separate compartments; and

(ii) *That both* the detonators and the container or compartment meet the requirements of the Institute of Makers of Explosives' Safety Library Publication No. 22 (incorporated by reference, see §171.7 of this subchapter).

(h) **Lading within body or covered tailgate closed.** Except as provided in paragraph (g) of this section, dealing with the transportation of liquid nitroglycerin, desensitized liquid nitroglycerin or diethylene glycol dinitrate, all of that portion of the lading of any motor vehicle which consists of Class 1 (explosive) materials shall be contained entirely within the body of the motor vehicle or within the horizontal outline thereof, without overhang or projection of any part of the load and if such motor vehicle has a tailboard or tailgate, it shall be closed and secured in place during such transportation. Every motor vehicle transporting Class 1 (explosive) materials must either have a closed body or have the body thereof covered with a tarpaulin, and in either event care must be taken to protect the load from moisture and sparks, except that subject to other provisions of these regulations, Class 1 (explosive) materials other than black powder may be transported on flat-bed vehicles if the explosive portion of the load on each vehicle is packed in fire and water resistant containers or covered with a fire and water resistant tarpaulin.

(i) **Class 1 (explosive) materials to be protected** against damage by other lading. No motor vehicle transporting any Class 1 (explosive) material may transport as a part of its load any metal or other articles or materials likely to damage such Class 1 (explosive) material or any package in which it is contained, unless the different parts of such load be so segregated or secured in place in or on the motor vehicle and separated by bulkheads or other suitable means as to prevent such damage.

(j) **Transfer of Class 1 (explosive) materials en route.** No Division 1.1, 1.2, or 1.3 (explosive) material shall be transferred from one container to another, or from one motor vehicle to another vehicle, or from another vehicle to a motor vehicle, on any public highway, street, or road, except in case of emergency. In such cases red electric lanterns, red emergency reflectors or red flags shall be set out in the manner prescribed for disabled or stopped motor vehicles. (See Motor Carrier Safety Regulations, part 392 of this title.) In any event, all practicable means, in addition to these hereinbefore prescribed, shall be taken to protect and warn other users of the highway against the hazard involved in any such transfer or against the hazard occasioned by the emergency making such transfer necessary.

§177.837 Class 3 (flammable liquid) materials.

(See also §177.834 (a) to (j).)

(a) **Engine stopped.** Unless the engine of a cargo tank motor vehicle is to be used for the operation of a pump, no Class 3 material shall be loaded into, or on, or unloaded from any cargo tank motor vehicle while the engine is running.

(b) **Bonding and grounding containers** other than cargo tanks prior to and during transfer of lading. For containers which are not in metallic contact with each other, either metallic bonds or ground conductors shall be provided for the neutralization of possible static charges prior to and during transfers of Class 3 (flammable liquid) materials between such containers. Such bonding shall be made by first connecting an electric conductor to the container to be filled and subsequently connecting the conductor to the container from which the liquid is to come, and not in any other order. To provide against ignition of vapors by discharge of static electricity, the latter connection shall be made at a point well removed from the opening from which the Class 3 (flammable liquid) material is to be discharged.

(c) **Bonding and grounding cargo tanks** before and during transfer of lading.

(1) *When a cargo tank* is loaded through an open filling hole, one end of a bond wire shall be connected to the stationary system piping or integrally connected steel framing, and the other end to the shell of the cargo tank to provide a continuous electrical connection. (If bonding is to the framing, it is essential that piping and framing be electrically interconnected.) This connection must be made before any filling hole is opened, and must remain in place until after the last filling hole has been closed. Additional bond wires are not needed around All-Metal flexible or swivel joints, but are required for nonmetallic flexible connections in the stationary system piping. When a cargo tank is unloaded by a suction-piping system through an open filling hole of the cargo tank, electrical continuity shall be maintained from cargo tank to receiving tank.

(2) *When a cargo tank* is loaded or unloaded through a vapor-tight (not open hole) top or bottom connection, so that there is no release of vapor at a point where a spark could occur, bonding or grounding is not required. Contact of the closed connection must be made before flow starts and must not be broken until after the flow is completed.

(3) *Bonding or grounding* is not required when a cargo tank is unloaded through a nonvapor-tight connection into a stationary tank provided the metallic filling connection is maintained in contact with the filling hole.

(d) **Unloading combustible liquids.** For a cargo tank unloading a material meeting the definition for combustible liquid in §173.150(f) of this subchapter, the qualified person attending the unloading operation must remain within 45.72 meters (150 feet) of the cargo tank and 7.62 meters (25 feet) of the delivery hose and must observe both the cargo tank and the receiving container at least once every five minutes during unloading operations that take more than five minutes to complete.

§177.838 Class 4 (flammable solid) materials, Class 5 (oxidizing) materials, and Division 4.2 (pyroforic liquid) materials.

(See also §177.834 (a) to (j).)

(a) **Lading within body or covered;** tailgate closed; pick-up and delivery. All of that portion of the lading of any motor vehicle transporting Class 4 (flammable solid) or Class 5 (oxidizing) materials shall be contained entirely within the body of the motor vehicle and shall be covered by such body, by tarpaulins, or other suitable means, and if such motor vehicle has a tailboard or tailgate, it shall be closed and secured in place during such transportation: Provided, however, That the provisions of this paragraph need not apply to "pick-up and delivery" motor vehicles when such motor vehicles are used in no other transportation than in and about cities, towns, or villages. Shipment in water-tight bulk containers need not be covered by a tarpaulin or other means.

(b) **Articles to be kept dry.** Special care shall be taken in the loading of any motor vehicle with Class 4 (flammable solid) or Class 5 (oxidizing) materials which are likely to become hazardous to transport when wet, to keep them from being wetted during the loading process and to keep them dry during transit. Special care shall also be taken in the loading of any motor vehicle with Class 4 (flammable solid) or Class 5 (oxidizing) materials, which are likely to become more hazardous to transport by wetting, to keep them from being wetted during the loading process and to keep them dry during transit. Examples of such dangerous materials are charcoal screenings, ground, crushed, or pulverized charcoal, and lump charcoal.

(c) **Lading ventilation, precautions against** spontaneous combustion. Whenever a motor carrier has knowledge concerning the hazards of spontaneous combustion or heating of any article to be loaded on a motor vehicle, such article shall be so loaded as to afford sufficient ventilation of the load to provide reasonable assurance against fire from this cause; and in such a case the motor vehicle shall be unloaded as soon as practicable after reaching its destination. Charcoal screenings, or ground, crushed, granulated, or pulverized charcoal, in bags, shall be so loaded that the bags are laid horizontally in the motor vehicle, and so piled that there will be spaces for effective air circulation, which spaces shall not be less than 10 cm (3.9 inches) wide; and air spaces shall be maintained between rows of bags. Bags shall not be piled closer than 15 cm (5.9 inches) from the top of any motor vehicle with a closed body.

(d)-(e) **[Reserved]**

(f) **Nitrates, except ammonium nitrate** having organic coating, must be loaded in closed or open type motor vehicles, which must be swept clean and be free of any projections capable of injuring bags when so packaged. When shipped in open type motor vehicles, the lading must be suitably covered. Ammonium nitrate having organic coating must not be loaded in all-metal vehicles, other than those made of aluminum or aluminum alloys of the closed type.

(g) **A motor vehicle may only contain 45.4 kg** (100 pounds) or less net mass of material described as "Smokeless powder for small arms, Division 4.1".

(h) **Division 4.2 (pyrophoric liquid) materials** in cylinders. Cylinders containing Division 4.2 (pyrophoric liquid) materials, unless packed in a strong box or case and secured therein to protect valves, must be loaded with all valves and safety relief devices in the vapor space. All cylinders must be secured so that no shifting occurs in transit.

§177.839 Class 8 (corrosive) materials.

(See also §177.834 (a) to (j).)

(a) **Nitric acid.** No packaging of nitric acid of 50 percent or greater concentration may be loaded above any packaging containing any other kind of material.

(b) **Storage batteries.** All storage batteries containing any electrolyte must be so loaded, if loaded with other lading, that all such batteries will be protected against other lading falling onto or against them, and adequate means must be provided in all cases for the protection and insulation of battery terminals against short circuits.

§177.840 Class 2 (gases) materials.

(See also §177.834 (a) to (j).)

(a) **Floors or platforms essentially flat.** Cylinders containing Class 2 (gases) materials shall not be loaded onto any part of the floor or platform of any motor vehicle which is not essentially flat; cylinders containing Class 2 (gases) materials may be loaded onto any motor vehicle not having a floor or platform only if such motor vehicle be equipped with suitable racks having adequate means for securing such cylinders in place therein. Nothing contained in this section shall be so construed as to prohibit the loading of such cylinders on any motor vehicle having a floor or platform and racks as hereinbefore described.

(1) *Cylinders.* Cylinders containing Class 2 gases must be securely restrained in an upright or horizontal position, loaded in racks, or packed in boxes or crates to prevent the cylinders from being shifted, overturned or ejected from the motor vehicle under normal transportation conditions. However, after December 31, 2003, a pressure relief device, when installed, must be in communication with the vapor space of a cylinder containing a Division 2.1 (flammable gas) material.

(2) *Cylinders for hydrogen,* cryogenic liquid. A Specification DOT-4L cylinder containing hydrogen, cryogenic liquid may only be transported on a motor vehicle as follows:

(i) *The vehicle* must have an open body equipped with a suitable rack or support having a means to hold the cylinder upright when subjected to an acceleration of 2 "g" in any horizontal direction;

(ii) *The combined total* of the hydrogen venting rates, as marked, on the cylinders transported on one motor vehicle may not exceed 60 SCF per hour;

(iii) *The vehicle may not enter a tunnel; and*

(iv) *Highway transportation* is limited to private and contract carriage and to direct movement from point of origin to destination.

(b) **Portable tank containers containing Class 2** (gases) materials shall be loaded on motor vehicles only as follows:

(1) *Onto a flat floor or platform of a motor vehicle.*

(2) *Onto a suitable frame of a motor vehicle.*

(3) *In either such case,* such containers shall be safely and securely blocked or held down to prevent movement relative to each other or to the supporting structure when in transit, particularly during sudden starts and stops and changes of direction of the vehicle.

(4) *Requirements of* paragraphs (1) and (2) of this paragraph (b) shall not be construed as prohibiting stacking of containers provided the provisions of paragraph (3) of this paragraph (b) are fully complied with.

(c) **[Reserved]**

(d) **Engine to be stopped in cargo tank motor vehicles,** except for transfer pump. No Division 2.1 (flammable gas) material shall be loaded into or on or unloaded from any cargo tank motor vehicles with the engine running unless the engine is used for the operation of the transfer pump of the vehicle. Unless the delivery hose is equipped with a shut-off valve at its discharge end, the engine of the motor vehicle shall be stopped at the finish of such loading or unloading operation while the filling or discharge connections are disconnected.

(e) **Chlorine cargo tank motor vehicles shall be shipped** only when equipped:

(1) *With a gas mask* of a type approved by the The National Institute of Occupational Safety and Health (NIOSH) Pittsburgh Research Center, U.S. Department of Health and Human Services for chlorine service; and

(2) *With an emergency kit* for controlling leaks in fittings on the dome cover plate.

(f) **A cargo tank motor vehicle used for transportation** of chlorine may not be moved, coupled or uncoupled, when any loading or unloading connections are attached to the vehicle, nor may it be left without the power unit attached unless the vehicle is chocked or equivalent means are provided to prevent motion. For additional requirements, see §173.315(o) of this subchapter.

(g) **Each liquid discharge valve on a cargo tank** motor vehicle, other than an engine fuel line valve, must be closed during transportation except during loading and unloading.

(h) **The driver of a motor vehicle transporting** a Division 2.1 (flammable gas) material that is a cryogenic liquid in a package exceeding 450 L (119 gallons) of water capacity shall avoid unnecessary delays during transportation. If unforeseen conditions cause an excessive pressure rise, the driver shall manually vent the tank at a remote and safe location. For each shipment, the driver shall make a written record of the cargo tank pressure and ambient (outside) temperature:

(1) *At the start of each trip,*

(2) *Immediately before and after any manual venting,*

(3) *At least once every five hours, and*

(4) *At the destination point.*

(i) **No person may transport a Division 2.1** (flammable gas) material that is a cryogenic liquid in a cargo tank motor vehicle unless the pressure of the lading is equal to or less than that used to determine the marked rated holding time (MRHT) and the one-way travel time (OWTT), marked on the cargo tank in conformance with §173.318(g) of this subchapter, is equal to or greater than the elapsed time between the start and termination of travel. This prohibition does not apply if, prior to expiration of the OWTT, the cargo tank is brought to full equilibration as specified in paragraph (j) of this section.

(j) **Full equilibration of a cargo tank** transporting a Division 2.1 (flammable gas) material that is a cryogenic liquid may only be done at a facility that loads or unloads a Division 2.1 (flammable gas) material that is a cryogenic liquid and must be performed and verified as follows:

(1) *The temperature* and pressure of the liquid must be reduced by a manually controlled release of vapor; and

(2) *The pressure* in the cargo tank must be measured at least ten minutes after the manual release is terminated.

(k) **A carrier of carbon monoxide,** cryogenic liquid must provide each driver with a self-contained air breathing apparatus that is approved by the National Institute of Occupational Safety and Health; for example, Mine Safety Appliance Co., Model 401, catalog number 461704.

(l) **Operating procedure.** Each operator of a cargo tank motor vehicle that is subject to the emergency discharge control requirements in §173.315(n) of this subchapter must carry on or within the cargo tank motor vehicle written emergency discharge control procedures for all delivery operations. The procedures must describe the cargo tank motor vehicle's emergency discharge control features and, for a passive shut-down capability, the parameters within which they are designed to function. The procedures must describe the process to be followed if a facility-provided hose is used for unloading when the cargo tank motor vehicle has a specially equipped delivery hose assembly to meet the requirements of §173.315(n)(2) of this subchapter.

(m) **Cargo tank motor vehicle safety check.** Before unloading from a cargo tank motor vehicle containing a liquefied compressed gas, the qualified person performing the function must check those components of the discharge system, including delivery hose assemblies and piping, that are readily observed during the normal course of unloading to assure that they are of sound quality, without obvious defects detectable through visual observation and audio awareness, and that connections are secure. This check must be made after the pressure in the discharge system has reached at least equilibrium with the pressure in the cargo tank. Operators need not use instruments or take extraordinary actions to check components not readily visible. No operator may unload liquefied compressed gases from a cargo tank motor vehicle with a delivery hose assembly found to have any condition identified in §180.416(g)(1) of this subchapter or with piping systems found to have any condition identified in §180.416(g)(2) of this subchapter.

(n) **Emergency shut down.** If there is an unintentional release of product to the environment during unloading of a liquefied compressed gas, the qualified person unloading the cargo tank motor vehicle must promptly shut the internal self-closing stop valve or other primary means of closure and shut down all motive and auxiliary power equipment.

(o) **Daily test of off-truck remote shut-off activation device.** For a cargo tank motor vehicle equipped with an off-truck remote means to close the internal self-closing stop valve and shut off all motive and auxiliary power equipment, an operator must successfully test the activation device within 18 hours prior to the first delivery of each day. For a wireless transmitter/receiver, the person conducting the test must be at least 45.72 m (150 feet) from the cargo tank and may have the cargo tank in his line of sight.

(p) **Unloading procedures for liquefied petroleum gas** and anhydrous ammonia in metered delivery service. An operator must use the following procedures for unloading liquefied petroleum gas or anhydrous ammonia from a cargo tank motor vehicle in metered delivery service:

(1) *For a cargo tank* with a capacity of 13,247.5 L (3,500 water gallons) or less, excluding delivery hose and piping, the qualified person attending the unloading operation must remain within 45.72 meters (150 feet) of the cargo tank and 7.62 meters (25 feet) of the delivery hose and must observe both the cargo tank and the receiving container at least once every five minutes when the internal self-closing stop valve is open during unloading operations that take more than five minutes to complete.

(2) *For a cargo tank* with a capacity greater than 13,247.5 L (3,500 water gallons), excluding delivery hose and piping, the qualified person attending the unloading operation must remain within 45.72 m (150 feet) of the cargo tank and 7.62 m (25 feet) of the delivery hose when the internal self-closing stop valve is open.

(i) *Except as provided* in paragraph (p)(2)(ii) of this section, the qualified person attending the unloading operation must have an unobstructed view of the cargo tank and delivery hose to the maximum extent practicable, except during short periods when it is necessary to activate controls or monitor the receiving container.

(ii) *For deliveries* where the qualified person attending the unloading operation cannot maintain an unobstructed view of the cargo tank, when the internal self-closing stop valve is open, the qualified person must observe both the cargo tank and the receiving container at least once every five minutes during unloading operations that take more than five minutes to complete. In addition, by the compliance dates specified in §§173.315(n)(5) and 180.405(m)(3) of this subchapter, the cargo tank motor vehicle must have an emergency discharge control capability that meets the requirements of §173.315(n)(2) or §173.315(n)(4) of this subchapter.

(q) **Unloading procedures for liquefied petroleum gas** and anhydrous ammonia in other than metered delivery service. An operator must use the following procedures for unloading liquefied petroleum gas or anhydrous ammonia from a cargo tank motor vehicle in other than metered delivery service:

(1) *The qualified person* attending the unloading operation must remain within 7.62 m (25 feet) of the cargo tank when the internal self-closing stop valve is open.

(2) *The qualified person* attending the unloading operation must have an unobstructed view of the cargo tank and delivery hose to the maximum extent practicable, except during short periods when it is necessary to activate controls or monitor the receiving container.

(r) **Unloading using facility-provided hoses.** A cargo tank motor vehicle equipped with a specially designed delivery hose assembly to meet the requirements of §173.315(n)(2) of this subchapter may be unloaded using a delivery hose assembly provided by the receiving facility under the following conditions:

(1) *The qualified person* monitoring unloading must visually examine the facility hose assembly for obvious defects prior to its use in the unloading operation.

(2) *The qualified person* monitoring unloading must remain within arm's reach of the mechanical means of closure for the internal self-closing stop valve when the internal self-closing stop valve is open except for short periods when it is necessary to activate controls or monitor the receiving container. For chlorine cargo tank motor vehicles, the qualified person must remain within arm's reach of a means to stop the flow of product except for short periods when it is necessary to activate controls or monitor the receiving container.

(3) *If the facility hose* is equipped with a passive means to shut off the flow of product that conforms to and is maintained to the performance standard in §173.315(n)(2) of this subchapter, the qualified person may attend the unloading operation in accordance with the attendance requirements prescribed for the material being unloaded in §177.834 of this section.

(s) **Off-truck remote shut-off activation device.** For a cargo tank motor vehicle with an off-truck remote control shut-off capability as required by §§173.315(n)(3) or (n)(4) of this subchapter, the qualified person attending the unloading operation must be in possession of the activation device at all times during the unloading process. This requirement does not apply if the activation device is part of a system that will shut off the unloading operation without human intervention in the event of a leak or separation in the hose.

(t) **Unloading without appropriate emergency discharge** control equipment. Until a cargo tank motor vehicle is equipped with emergency discharge control equipment in conformance with §§173.315(n)(2) and 180.405(m)(1) of this subchapter, the qualified person attending the unloading operation must remain within arm's reach of a means to close the internal self-closing stop valve when the internal self-closing stop valve is open except during short periods when the qualified person must activate controls or monitor the receiving container. For chlorine cargo tank motor vehicles unloaded after December 31, 1999, the qualified person must remain within arm's reach of a means to stop the flow of product except for short periods when it is necessary to activate controls or monitor the receiving container.

(u) **Unloading of chlorine cargo tank motor vehicles.** After July 1, 2001, unloading of chlorine from a cargo tank motor vehicle must be performed in compliance with Section 3 of Pamphlet 57, Emergency Shut-off Systems for Bulk Transfer of Chlorine, of the Chlorine Institute.

(Approved by the Office of Management and Budget under control number 2137-0542)

§177.841 Division 6.1 (poisonous) and Division 2.3 (poisonous gas) materials.

(See also §177.834 (a) to (j).)

(a) **Arsenical compounds in bulk.** Care shall be exercised in the loading and unloading of "arsenical dust", "arsenic trioxide", and "sodium arsenate", allowable to be loaded into sift-proof, steel hopper-type or dump-type motor-vehicle bodies equipped with water-proof, dust-proof covers well secured in place on all openings, to accomplish such loading with the minimum spread of such compounds into the atmosphere by all means that are practicable; and no such loading or unloading shall be done near or adjacent to any place where there are or are likely to be, during the loading or unloading process assemblages of persons other than those engaged in the loading or unloading process, or upon any public highway or in any public place. Before any motor vehicle may be used for transporting any other articles, all detectable traces of arsenical materials must be removed therefrom by flushing with water, or by other appropriate method, and the marking removed.

(b) **[Reserved]**

(c) Division 2.3 (poisonous gas) or Division 6.1 (poisonous) materials. The transportation of a Division 2.3 (poisonous gas) or Division 6.1 (poisonous) material is not permitted if there is any interconnection between packagings.

(d) [Reserved]

(e) A motor carrier may not transport a package:

(1) *Except as provided* in paragraph (e)(3) of this section, bearing or required to bear a POISON or POISON INHALATION HAZARD label in the same motor vehicle with material that is marked as or known to be a foodstuffs, feed or edible material intended for consumption by humans or animals unless the poisonous material is packaged in accordance with this subchapter and is:

(i) *Overpacked in a metal drum* as specified in §173.25(c) of this subchapter; or

(ii) *Loaded into a closed* unit load device and the foodstuffs, feed, or other edible material are loaded into another closed unit load device;

(2) *Bearing or required* to bear a POISON, POISON GAS or POISON INHALATION HAZARD label in the driver's compartment (including a sleeper berth) of a motor vehicle; or

(3) *Bearing a POISON label* displaying the text "PG III," or bearing a "PG III" mark adjacent to the POISON label, with materials marked as, or known to be, foodstuffs, feed or any other edible material intended for consumption by humans or animals, unless the package containing the Division 6.1, Packing Group III material is separated in a manner that, in the event of leakage from packages under conditions normally incident to transportation, commingling of hazardous materials with foodstuffs, feed or any other edible material would not occur.

§177.842 Class 7 (radioactive) material.

(a) The number of packages of Class 7 (radioactive) materials in any transport vehicle or in any single group in any storage location must be limited so that the total transport index number does not exceed 50. The total transport index of a group of packages and overpacks is determined by adding together the transport index number on the labels on the individual packages and overpacks in the group. This provision does not apply to exclusive use shipments described in §§173.441(b), 173.457, and 173.427 of this subchapter.

(b) Packages of Class 7 (radioactive) material bearing "RADIOACTIVE YELLOW-II" or "RADIOACTIVE YELLOW-III" labels may not be placed in a transport vehicle, storage location or in any other place closer than the distances shown in the following table to any area which may be continuously occupied by any passenger, employee, or animal, nor closer than the distances shown in the table to any package containing undeveloped film (if so marked), and must conform to the following conditions:

(1) *If more than one* of these packages is present, the distance must be computed from the following table on the basis of the total transport index number determined by adding together the transport index number on the labels on the individual packages and overpacks in the vehicle or storeroom.

(2) *Where more than one* group of packages is present in any single storage location, a single group may not have a total transport index greater than 50. Each group of packages must be handled and stowed not closer than 6 m (20 feet) (measured edge to edge) to any other group. The following table is to be used in accordance with the provisions of paragraph (b) of this section:

Total transport index	Minimum separation distance in meters (feet) to nearest undeveloped film in various times of transit					Minimum distance in meters (feet) to area of persons, or minimum distance in meters (feet) from dividing partition of cargo compartments
	Up to 2 hours	2-4 hours	4-8 hours	8-12 hours	Over 12 hours	
None	0.0 (0)	0.0 (0)	0.0 (0)	0.0 (0)	0.0 (0)	0.0 (0)
0.1 to 1.0	0.3 (1)	0.6 (2)	0.9 (3)	1.2 (4)	1.5 (5)	0.3 (1)
1.1 to 5.0	0.9 (3)	1.2 (4)	1.8 (6)	2.4 (8)	3.4 (11)	0.6 (2)
5.1 to 10.0	1.2 (4)	1.8 (6)	2.7 (9)	3.4 (11)	4.6 (15)	0.9 (3)
10.1 to 20.0	1.5 (5)	2.4 (8)	3.7 (12)	4.9 (16)	6.7 (22)	1.2 (4)
20.1 to 30.0	2.1 (7)	3.0 (10)	4.6 (15)	6.1 (20)	8.8 (29)	1.5 (5)
30.1 to 40.0	2.4 (8)	3.4 (11)	5.2 (17)	6.7 (22)	10.1 (33)	1.8 (6)
40.1 to 50.0	2.7 (9)	3.7 (12)	5.8 (19)	7.3 (24)	11.0 (36)	2.1 (7)

NOTE: The distance in this table must be measured from the nearest point on the nearest packages of Class 7 (radioactive) material.

(c) Shipments of low specific activity materials and surface contaminated objects, as defined in §173.403 of this subchapter, must be loaded so as to avoid spillage and scattering of loose materials. Loading restrictions are set forth in §173.427 of this subchapter.

(d) Packages must be so blocked and braced that they cannot change position during conditions normally incident to transportation.

(e) Persons should not remain unnecessarily in a vehicle containing Class 7 (radioactive) materials.

(f) Each fissile material, controlled shipment (as defined in §173.403 of this subchapter) must be transported in accordance with one of the methods prescribed in §173.457 of this subchapter. The transport controls must be adequate to assure that no fissile material, controlled shipment is transported in the same transport vehicle with any other fissile Class 7 (radioactive) material shipment. In loading and storage areas each fissile material, controlled shipment must be segregated by a distance of at least 6 m (20 feet) from any other package required to bear one of the "Radioactive" labels described in §172.403 of this subchapter.

(g) For shipments transported under exclusive use conditions the radiation dose rate may not exceed 0.02 mSv per hour (2 mrem per hour) in any position normally occupied in the motor vehicle. For shipments transported as exclusive use under the provisions of §173.441(b) of this subchapter for packages with external radiation levels in excess of 2 mSv (200 mrem per hour) at the package surface, the motor vehicle must meet the requirements of a closed transport vehicle (§173.403 of this subchapter). The total transport index for packages containing fissile material may not exceed 100.

§177.843 Contamination of vehicles.

(a) Each motor vehicle used for transporting Class 7 (radioactive) materials under exclusive use conditions in accordance with §173.427(b)(3) or (c) or §173.443(c) of this subchapter must be surveyed with radiation detection instruments after each use. A vehicle may not be returned to service until the radiation dose rate at every accessible surface is 0.005 mSv per hour (0.5 mrem per hour) or less and the removable (non-fixed) radioactive surface contamination is not greater than the level prescribed in §173.443(a) of this subchapter.

(b) This section does not apply to any vehicle used solely for transporting Class 7 (radioactive) material if a survey of the interior surface shows that the radiation dose rate does not exceed 0.1 mSv per hour (10 mrem per hour) at the interior surface or 0.02 mSv per hour (2 mrem per hour) at 1 meter (3.3 feet) from any interior surface. These vehicles must be stenciled with the words "For Radioactive Materials Use Only" in lettering at least 7.6 cm (3 inches) high in a conspicuous place, on both sides of the exterior of the vehicle. These vehicles must be kept closed at all times other than loading and unloading.

(c) In case of fire, accident, breakage, or unusual delay involving shipments of Class 7 (radioactive) material, see §§171.15, 171.16 and 177.854 of this subchapter.

(d) Each transport vehicle used to transport Division 6.2 materials must be disinfected prior to reuse if a Division 6.2 material is released from its packaging during transportation. Disinfection may be by any means effective for neutralizing the material released.

Subpart C - Segregation and Separation Chart of Hazardous Materials

§177.848 Segregation of hazardous materials.

(a) This section applies to materials which meet one or more of the hazard classes defined in this subchapter and are:

(1) *In packages* which require labels in accordance with part 172 of this subchapter;

(2) *In a compartment* within a multi-compartmented cargo tank subject to the restrictions in §173.33 of this subchapter; or

(3) *In a portable tank loaded in a transport vehicle or freight container.*

(b) When a transport vehicle is to be transported by vessel, other than a ferry vessel, hazardous materials on or within that vehicle must be stowed and segregated in accordance with §176.83(b) of this subchapter.

(c) In addition to the provisions of paragraph (d) of this section, cyanides or cyanide mixtures may not be loaded or stored with acids if a mixture of the materials would generate hydrogen cyanide.

(d) Hazardous materials may not be loaded, transported, or stored together, except as provided in this section, and in accordance with the following table:

Segregation Table for Hazardous Materials

Class or division		Notes	1.1 1.2	1.3	1.4	1.5	1.6	2.1	2.2	2.3 gas Zone A	2.3 gas Zone B	3	4.1	4.2	4.3	5.1	5.2	6.1 liquids PG I zone A	7	8 liquids only
Explosives	1.1 and 1.2	A	*	*	*	*	*	X	X	X	X	X	X	X	X	X	X	X	X	X
Explosives	1.3		*	*	*	*	*	X		X	X	X		X	X	X	X	X		X
Explosives	1.4		*	*	*	*	*	O		O	O	O		O				O		O
Very insensitive explosives	1.5	A	*	*	*	*	*	X	X	X	X	X	X	X	X	X	X	X	X	X
Extremely insensitive explosives	1.6		*	*	*	*	*													
Flammable gases	2.1		X	X	O	X				X	O							O	O	
Non-toxic, non-flammable gases	2.2		X			X														
Poisonous gas Zone A	2.3		X	X	O	X		X				X	X	X	X	X	X			X
Poisonous gas Zone B	2.3		X	X	O	X		O				O	O	O	O	O	O			O
Flammable liquids	3		X	X	O	X				X	O					O		X		
Flammable solids	4.1		X			X				X	O							X		O
Spontaneously combustible materials	4.2		X	X	O	X				X	O							X		X
Dangerous when wet materials	4.3		X	X		X				X	O							X		O
Oxidizers	5.1	A	X	X		X				X	O	O						X		O
Organic peroxides	5.2		X	X		X				X	O							X		O
Poisonous liquids PG I Zone A	6.1		X	X	O	X		O				X	X	X	X	X	X			X
Radioactive material	7		X			X		O												
Corrosive liquids	8		X	X	O	X				X	O		O	X	O	O	O	X		

(e) **Instructions for using the segregation table** for hazardous materials are as follows:

(1) *The absence* of any hazard class or division or a blank space in the table indicates that no restrictions apply.

(2) *The letter "X"* in the table indicates that these materials may not be loaded, transported, or stored together in the same transport vehicle or storage facility during the course of transportation.

(3) *The letter "O"* in the table indicates that these materials may not be loaded, transported, or stored together in the same transport vehicle or storage facility during the course of transportation unless separated in a manner that, in the event of leakage from packages under conditions normally incident to transportation, commingling of hazardous materials would not occur. Notwithstanding the methods of separation employed, Class 8 (corrosive) liquids may not be loaded above or adjacent to Class 4 (flammable) or Class 5 (oxidizing) materials; except that shippers may load truckload shipments of such materials together when it is known that the mixture of contents would not cause a fire or a dangerous evolution of heat or gas.

(4) *The "*"* in the table indicates that segregation among different Class 1 (explosive) materials is governed by the compatibility table in paragraph (f) of this section.

(5) *The note "A"* in the second column of the table means that, notwithstanding the requirements of the letter "X", ammonium nitrate (UN 1942) and ammonium nitrate fertilizer may be loaded or stored with Division 1.1 (explosive) or Division 1.5 materials.

(6) *When the §172.101 table* or §172.402 of this subchapter requires a package to bear a subsidiary hazard label, segregation appropriate to the subsidiary hazard must be applied when that segregation is more restrictive than that required by the primary hazard. However, hazardous materials of the same class may be stowed together without regard to segregation required for any secondary hazard if the materials are not capable of reacting dangerously with each other and causing combustion or dangerous evolution of heat, evolution of flammable, poisonous, or asphyxiant gases, or formation of corrosive or unstable materials.

(f) **Class 1 (explosive) materials shall not be** loaded, transported, or stored together, except as provided in this section, and in accordance with the following table:

Compatibility Table For Class 1 (Explosive) Materials

Compatibility group	A	B	C	D	E	F	G	H	J	K	L	N	S
A		X	X	X	X	X	X	X	X	X	X	X	X
B	X		X	$X_{(4)}$	X	X	X	X	X	X	X	X	4/5
C	X	X		2	2	X	6	X	X	X	X	3	4/5
D	X	$X_{(4)}$	2		2	X	6	X	X	X	X	3	4/5
E	X	X	2	2		X	6	X	X	X	X	3	4/5
F	X	X	X	X	X		X	X	X	X	X	X	4/5
G	X	X	6	6	6	X		X	X	X	X	X	4/5
H	X	X	X	X	X	X	X		X	X	X	X	4/5
J	X	X	X	X	X	X	X	X		X	X	X	4/5
K	X	X	X	X	X	X	X	X	X		X	X	4/5
L	X	X	X	X	X	X	X	X	X	X	1	X	X
N	X	X	3	3	3	X	X	X	X	X	X		4/5
S	X	4/5	4/5	4/5	4/5	4/5	4/5	4/5	4/5	4/5	X	4/5	

(g) **Instructions for using the compatibility table** for Class 1 (explosive) materials are as follows:

(1) *A blank space in the table indicates that no restrictions apply.*

(2) *The letter "X"* in the table indicates that explosives of different compatibility groups may not be carried on the same transport vehicle.

(3) *The numbers in the table mean the following:*

(i) *"1" means* an explosive from compatibility group L shall only be carried on the same transport vehicle with an identical explosive.

(ii) *"2" means* any combination of explosives from compatibility groups C, D, or E is assigned to compatibility group E.

(iii) *"3" means* any combination of explosives from compatibility groups C, D, or E with those in compatibility group N is assigned to compatibility group D.

(iv) *"4" means see §177.835(g) when transporting detonators.*

(v) *"5" means* Division 1.4S fireworks may not be loaded on the same transport vehicle with Division 1.1 or 1.2 (explosive) materials.

(vi) *"6" means* explosive articles in compatibility group G, other than fireworks and those requiring special handling, may be loaded, transported and stored with other explosive articles of compatibility groups C, D and E, provided that explosive substances (such as those not contained in articles) are not carried in the same vehicle.

(h) **Except as provided in paragraph (i)** of this section, explosives of the same compatibility group but of different divisions may be transported together provided that the whole shipment is transported as though its entire contents were of the lower numerical division (i.e., Division 1.1 being lower than Division 1.2). For example, a mixed shipment of Division 1.2 (explosive) materials and Division 1.4 (explosive) materials, both of compatibility group D, must be transported as Division 1.2 (explosive) materials.

(i) **When Division 1.5 materials, compatibility group D,** are transported in the same freight container as Division 1.2 (explosive) materials, compatibility group D, the shipment must be transported as Division 1.1 (explosive) materials, compatibility group D.

Subpart D - Vehicles and Shipments in Transit; Accidents

§177.854 Disabled vehicles and broken or leaking packages; repairs.

(a) **Care of lading, hazardous materials.** Whenever for any cause other than necessary traffic stops any motor vehicle transporting any hazardous material is stopped upon the traveled portion of any highway or shoulder thereof, special care shall be taken to guard the vehicle and its load or to take such steps as may be necessary to provide against hazard. Special effort shall be made to remove the motor vehicle to a place where the hazards of the materials being transported may be provided against. See §§392.22, 392.24, and 392.25 of this title for warning devices required to be displayed on the highway.

(b) **Disposition of containers found broken or leaking** in transit. When leaks occur in packages or containers during the course of transportation, subsequent to initial loading, disposition of such package or container shall be made by the safest practical means afforded under paragraphs (c), (d), and (e) of this section.

(c) **Repairing or overpacking packages.**

(1) *Packages may be repaired* when safe and practicable, such repairing to be in accordance with the best and safest practice known and available.

(2) *Packages of hazardous materials* that are damaged or found leaking during transportation, and hazardous materials that have spilled or leaked during transportation, may be forwarded to destination or returned to the shipper in a salvage drum in accordance with the requirements of §173.3(c) of this subchapter.

(d) **Transportation of repaired packages.** Any package repaired in accordance with the requirements of paragraph (c)(1) of this section may be transported to the nearest place at which it may safely be disposed of only in compliance with the following requirements:

(1) *The package must be safe for transportation.*

(2) *The repair* of the package must be adequate to prevent contamination of or hazardous admixture with other lading transported on the same motor vehicle therewith.

(3) *If the carrier* is not himself the shipper, the consignee's name and address must be plainly marked on the repaired package.

(e) **Disposition of unsafe broken packages.** In the event any leaking package or container cannot be safely and adequately repaired for transportation or transported, it shall be stored pending proper disposition in the safest and most expeditious manner possible.

(f) **Stopped vehicles; other dangerous articles.** Whenever any motor vehicle transporting Class 3 (flammable liquid), Class 4 (flammable solid), Class 5 (oxidizing), Class 8 (corrosive), Class 2 (gases), or Division 6.1 (poisonous) materials, is stopped for any cause other than necessary traffic stops upon the traveled portion of any highway, or a shoulder next thereto, the following requirements shall be complied with during the period of such stop:

(1) *For motor vehicles* other than cargo tank motor vehicles used for the transportation of Class 3 (flammable liquid) or Division 2.1 (flammable gas) materials and not transporting Division 1.1, 1.2, or 1.3 (explosive) materials, warning devices must be set out in the manner prescribed by §392.22 of this title.

(2) *For cargo tanks* used for the transportation of Class 3 (flammable liquid) or Division 2.1 (flammable gas) materials, whether loaded or empty, and vehicles transporting Division 1.1, 1.2, or 1.3 (explosive) materials, warning devices must be set out in the manner prescribed by §392.25 of this title.

(g) **Repair and maintenance of vehicles containing** certain hazardous materials —

(1) *General.* No person may use heat, flame or spark producing devices to repair or maintain the cargo or fuel containment system of a motor vehicle required to be placarded, other than COMBUSTIBLE, in accordance with subpart F of part 172 of this subchapter. As used in this section, "containment system" includes all vehicle components intended physically to contain cargo or fuel during loading or filling, transport, or unloading.

(2) *Repair and maintenance* inside a building. No person may perform repair or maintenance on a motor vehicle subject to paragraph (g)(1) of this section inside a building unless:

(i) *The motor vehicle's* cargo and fuel containment systems are closed (except as necessary to maintain or repair the vehicle's motor) and do not show any indication of leakage;

(ii) *A means is provided,* and a person capable to operate the motor vehicle is available, to immediately remove the motor vehicle if necessary in an emergency;

(iii) *The motor vehicle* is removed from the enclosed area upon completion of repair or maintenance work; and

(iv) *For motor vehicles* loaded with Division 1.1, 1.2, or 1.3 (explosive), Class 3 (flammable liquid), or Division 2.1 (flammable gas) materials, all sources of spark, flame or glowing heat within the area of enclosure (including any heating system drawing air therefrom) are extinguished, made inoperable or rendered explosion-proof by a suitable method. Exception: Electrical equipment on the vehicle, necessary to accomplish the maintenance function, may remain operational.

(h) **No repair with flame unless gas-free.** No repair of a cargo tank used for the transportation of any Class 3 (flammable liquid) or Division 6.1 (poisonous liquid) material, or any compartment thereof, or of any container for fuel of whatever nature, may be repaired by any method employing a flame, arc, or other means of welding, unless the tank or compartment shall first have been made gas-free.

Subpart E - Regulations Applying to Hazardous Material on Motor Vehicles Carrying Passengers for Hire

§177.870 Regulations for passenger carrying vehicles.

(a) **Vehicles transporting passengers and property.** In addition to the regulations in parts 170-189 of this subchapter the following requirements shall apply to vehicles transporting passengers and property.

(b) **No Class 1 (explosive) materials** or other hazardous materials on passenger-carrying vehicles, exceptions. No hazardous materials except small-arms ammunition, emergency shipments of drugs, chemicals and hospital supplies, and the accompanying munitions of war of the Departments of the Army, Navy, and Air Force of the United States Government, are authorized by parts 170-189 of this subchapter to be transported on motor vehicles carrying passengers for hire where other practicable means of transportation is available.

(c) **Class 1 (explosive) materials in passenger-carrying** space forbidden. No Class 1 (explosive) material, except small-arms ammunition, may be carried in the passenger-carrying space of any motor vehicle transporting passengers for hire.

(d) **Hazardous materials on passenger carrying vehicles; quantity.** Where no other practicable means of transportation is available the following articles in the quantities as shown may be transported in motor vehicles carrying passengers for hire in a space other than that provided for passengers: Not to exceed 45 kg (99 pounds) gross weight of any or all of the kinds of Class 1 (explosive) materials permitted to be transported by passenger-carrying aircraft or rail car may be transported on a motor vehicle transporting passengers: Provided, however, That samples of Class 1 (explosive) materials for laboratory examination, not to exceed two samples, or a total of no more than 100 detonators, Division 1.4 (explosive) materials at one time in a single motor vehicle, may be transported in a motor vehicle transporting passengers.

(e) **Articles other than Class 1 (explosive) materials** on passenger-carrying vehicles. The gross weight of any given class of hazard-

177

Carriage by Public Highway

ous material other than Class 1 (explosive) materials shall not exceed 45 kg (99 pounds), and the aggregate weight of all such other dangerous articles shall not exceed 225 kg (496 pounds). This provision does not apply to nontoxic, nonflammable refrigerants, when such refrigerant is for servicing operations of a motor carrier on whose motor vehicles the refrigerant is used. A cylinder secured against movement while in transit and not exceeding 113 kg (250 pounds) gross weight may be transported.

(f) **Division 6.1 (poisonous) or Division 2.3** (poisonous gas) materials on passenger-carrying vehicles. No motor carrier may transport any extremely dangerous Division 6.1 (poisonous) or Division 2.3 (poisonous gas) material, or any paranitroaniline, in any amount, in or on any bus while engaged in the transportation of passengers; or any less dangerous Division 6.1 (poisonous) material, which is other than a liquid, in any amount exceeding an aggregate of 45 kg (99 pounds) gross weight in or on any such bus.

(g) **Class 7 (radioactive) materials.** In addition to the limitations prescribed in paragraphs (b) and (e) of this section, no person may transport any Class 7 (radioactive) material requiring labels under §§172.436, 172.438, and 172.440 of this subchapter in or on any motor vehicle carrying passengers for hire except where no other practicable means of transportation is available. Packages of Class 7 (radioactive) materials must be stored only in the trunk or baggage compartment of the vehicle, and must not be stored in any compartment occupied by persons. Packages of Class 7 (radioactive) materials must be handled and placed in the vehicle as prescribed in §177.842.

Part 178 - Specifications for Packagings

§178.1 Purpose and scope.

This part prescribes the manufacturing and testing specifications for packaging and containers used for the transportation of hazardous materials in commerce.

§178.2 Applicability and responsibility.

(a) **Applicability.**

(1) *The requirements of this part apply to packagings manufactured—*

(i) *To a DOT specification,* regardless of country of manufacture; or

(ii) *To a UN standard,* for packagings manufactured within the United States. For UN standard packagings manufactured outside the United States, see §173.24(d)(2) of this subchapter. For UN standard packagings for which standards are not prescribed in this part, see §178.3(b).

(2) *A manufacturer* of a packaging subject to the requirements of this part is primarily responsible for compliance with the requirements of this part. However, any person who performs a function prescribed in this part shall perform that function in accordance with this part.

(b) **Specification markings.** When this part requires that a packaging be marked with a DOT specification or UN standard marking, marking of the packaging with the appropriate DOT or UN markings is the certification that —

(1) *Except as otherwise provided in this section,* all requirements of the DOT specification or UN standard, including performance tests, are met; and

(2) *All functions* performed by, or on behalf of, the person whose name or symbol appears as part of the marking conform to requirements specified in this part.

(c) **Notification.** Except as specifically provided in §§178.337-18 and 178.345-10 of this part, the manufacturer or other person certifying compliance with the requirements of this part, and each subsequent distributor of that packaging shall —

(1) *Notify in writing* each person to whom that packaging is transferred —

(i) *Of all requirements in this part not met at the time of transfer, and*

(ii) *Of the type and dimensions* of any closures, including gaskets, needed to satisfy performance test requirements.

(2) *Retain copies* of each written notification for at least one year from date of issuance; and

(3) *Make copies* of all written notifications available for inspection by a representative of the Department.

(d) **Except as provided in paragraph (c) of this section,** a packaging not conforming to the applicable specifications or standards in this part may not be marked to indicate such conformance.

(e) **Definitions.** For the purpose of this part —

Manufacturer means the person whose name and address or symbol appears as part of the specification markings required by this part or, for a packaging marked with the symbol of an approval agency, the person on whose behalf the approval agency certifies the packaging.

Specification markings mean the packaging identification markings required by this part including, where applicable, the name and address or symbol of the packaging manufacturer or approval agency.

(f) **No packaging may be manufactured or marked** to a packaging specification that was in effect on September 30, 1991, and that was removed from this part 178 by a rule published in the Federal Register on December 21, 1990 and effective October 1, 1991.

§178.3 Marking of packagings.

(a) **Each packaging represented as manufactured** to a DOT specification or a UN standard must be marked on a non-removable component of the packaging with specification markings conforming to the applicable specification, and with the following:

(1) *In an unobstructed area,* with letters, and numerals identifying the standards or specification (e.g. UN 1A1, DOT 4B240ET, etc.).

(2) *Unless otherwise specified in this part,* with the name and address or symbol of the packaging manufacturer or, where specifically authorized, the symbol of the approval agency certifying compliance with a UN standard. Symbols, if used, must be registered with the Associate Administrator. Duplicative symbols are not authorized.

(3) *The markings* must be stamped, embossed, burned, printed or otherwise marked on the packaging to provide adequate accessibility, permanency, contrast, and legibility so as to be readily apparent and understood.

(4) *Unless otherwise specified,* letters and numerals must be at least 12.0 mm (0.47 inches) in height except that for packagings of less than or equal to 30 L (7.9 gallons) capacity for liquids or 30 kg (66 pounds) capacity for solids the height must be at least 6.0 mm (0.2 inches). For packagings having a capacity of 5 L (1 gallon) or 5 kg (11 pounds) or less, letters and numerals must be of an appropriate size.

(5) *For packages* with a gross mass of more than 30 kg (66 pounds), the markings or a duplicate thereof must appear on the top or on a side of the packaging.

(b) **A UN standard packaging for which the UN standard** is set forth in this part may be marked with the United Nations symbol and other specification markings only if it fully conforms to the requirements of this part. A UN standard packaging for which the UN standard is not set forth in this part may be marked with the United Nations symbol and other specification markings for that standard as provided in the ICAO Technical Instructions or the IMDG Code subject to the following conditions:

(1) *The U.S. manufacturer* must establish that the packaging conforms to the applicable provisions of the ICAO Technical Instructions or the IMDG Code, respectively.

(2) *If an indication* of the name of the manufacturer or other identification of the packaging as specified by the competent authority is required, the name and address or symbol of the manufacturer or the approval agency certifying compliance with the UN standard must be entered. Symbols, if used, must be registered with the Associate Administrator.

(3) *The letters "USA"* must be used to indicate the State authorizing the allocation of the specification marks if the packaging is manufactured in the United States.

(c) **Where a packaging conforms to more than one** UN standard or DOT specification, the packaging may bear more than one marking, provided the packaging meets all the requirements of each standard or specification. Where more than one marking appears on a packaging, each marking must appear in its entirety.

(d) **No person may mark or otherwise certify** a packaging or container as meeting the requirements of a manufacturing exemption unless that person is the holder of or a party to that exemption, an agent of the holder or party for the purpose of marking or certification, or a third party tester.

Subpart A [Reserved]

Subpart B - Specifications for Inside Containers, and Linings

§178.33 Specification 2P; inner nonrefillable metal receptacles.

§178.33-1 Compliance.

(a) **Required in all details.**

(b) **[Reserved]**

§178.33-2 Type and size.

(a) **Single-trip inside containers.** Must be seamless, or with seams, welded, soldered, brazed, double seamed, or swedged.

(b) **The maximum capacity of containers** in this class shall not exceed one liter (61.0 cubic inches). The maximum inside diameter shall not exceed 3 inches.

§178.33-3 Inspection.

(a) **By competent inspector.**

(b) **[Reserved]**

§178.33-4 Duties of inspector.

(a) **To inspect material and completed containers** and witness tests, and to reject defective materials or containers.

(b) **[Reserved]**

§178.33-5 Material.

(a) **Uniform quality steel plate such as black plate,** electrotin plate, hot dipped tin plate, tern plate or other commercially accepted can making plate; or nonferrous metal of uniform drawing quality.

(b) **Material with seams, cracks, laminations** or other injurious defects not authorized.

§178.33-6 Manufacture.

(a) By appliances and methods that will assure uniformity of completed containers; dirt and scale to be removed as necessary; no defect acceptable that is likely to weaken the finished container appreciably; reasonably smooth and uniform surface finish required.

(b) Seams when used must be as follows:

(1) *Circumferential seams:* By welding, swedging, brazing, soldering, or double seaming.

(2) *Side seams:* By welding, brazing, or soldering.

(c) Ends: The ends shall be of pressure design.

§178.33-7 Wall thickness.

(a) The minimum wall thickness for any container shall be 0.007 inch.

(b) [Reserved]

§178.33-8 Tests.

(a) One out of each lot of 25,000 containers or less, successively produced per day shall be pressure tested to destruction and must not burst below 240 psig gauge pressure. The container tested shall be complete with end assembled.

(b) Each such 25,000 containers or less, successively produced per day, shall constitute a lot and if the test container shall fail, the lot shall be rejected or ten additional containers may be selected at random and subjected to the test under which failure occurred. These containers shall be complete with ends assembled. Should any of the ten containers thus tested fail, the entire lot must be rejected. All containers constituting a lot shall be of like material, size, design construction, finish, and quality.

§178.33-9 Marking.

(a) By means of printing, lithographing, embossing, or stamping, each container must be marked to show:

(1) *DOT-2P.*

(2) *Name or symbol* of person making the mark specified in paragraph (a)(1) of this section. Symbol, if used, must be registered with the Associate Administrator.

(b) [Reserved]

§178.33a Specification 2Q; inner nonrefillable metal receptacles.

§178.33a-1 Compliance.

(a) Required in all details.

(b) [Reserved]

§178.33a-2 Type and size.

(a) Single-trip inside containers. Must be seamless, or with seams welded, soldered, brazed, double seamed, or swedged.

(b) The maximum capacity of containers in this class shall not exceed 1 L (61.0 cubic inches). The maximum inside diameter shall not exceed 3 inches.

§178.33a-3 Inspection.

(a) By competent inspector.

(b) [Reserved]

§178.33a-4 Duties of inspector.

(a) To inspect material and completed containers and witness tests, and to reject defective materials or containers.

(b) [Reserved]

§178.33a-5 Material.

(a) Uniform quality steel plate such as black plate, electrotin plate, hot dipped tinplate, ternplate or other commercially accepted can making plate; or nonferrous metal of uniform drawing quality.

(b) Material with seams, cracks, laminations or other injurious defects not authorized.

§178.33a-6 Manufacture.

(a) By appliances and methods that will assure uniformity of completed containers; dirt and scale to be removed as necessary; no defect acceptable that is likely to weaken the finished container appreciably; reasonably smooth and uniform surface finish required.

(b) Seams when used must be as follows:

(1) *Circumferential seams.* By welding, swedging, brazing, soldering, or double seaming.

(2) *Side seams.* By welding, brazing or soldering.

(c) Ends. The ends shall be of pressure design.

§178.33a-7 Wall thickness.

(a) The minimum wall thickness for any container shall be 0.008 inch.

(b) [Reserved]

§178.33a-8 Tests.

(a) One out of each lot of 25,000 containers or less, successively produced per day, shall be pressure tested to destruction and must not burst below 270 psig gauge pressure. The container tested shall be complete with end assembled.

(b) Each such 25,000 containers or less, successively produced per day, shall constitute a lot and if the test container shall fail, the lot shall be rejected or ten additional containers may be selected at random and subjected to the test under which failure occurred. These containers shall be complete with ends assembled. Should any of the ten containers thus tested fail, the entire lot must be rejected. All containers constituting a lot shall be of like material, size, design, construction, finish and quality.

§178.33a-9 Marking.

(a) By means of printing, lithographing, embossing, or stamping, each container must be marked to show:

(1) *DOT-2Q.*

(2) *Name or symbol* of person making the mark specified in paragraph (a)(1) of this section. Symbol, if used, must be registered with the Associate Administrator.

(b) [Reserved]

Subpart C - Specifications for Cylinders

§178.35 General requirements for specification cylinders.

(a) Compliance. Compliance with the requirements of this subpart is required in all details.

(b) Inspections and analyses. Chemical analyses and tests required by this subchapter must be made within the United States, unless otherwise approved in writing by the Associate Administrator, in accordance with subpart I of part 107 of this chapter. Inspections and verification must be performed by —

(1) *An independent inspection agency* approved in writing by the Associate Administrator, in accordance with subpart I of part 107 of this chapter; or

(2) *For DOT Specifications* 3B, 3BN, 3E, 4B, 4BA, 4D (water capacity less than 1,100 cubic inches), 4B240ET, 4AA480, 4L, 8, 8AL, 4BW, 39 (marked service pressure 900 p.s.i.g. or lower) and 4E manufactured in the United States, a competent inspector of the manufacturer.

(c) Duties of inspector. The inspector shall determine that each cylinder made is in conformance with the applicable specification. Except as otherwise specified in the applicable specification, the inspector shall perform the following:

(1) *Inspect all material* and reject any not meeting applicable requirements. For cylinders made by the billet-piercing process, billets must be inspected and shown to be free from pipe, cracks, excessive segregation and other injurious defects after parting or, when applicable, after nick and cold break.

(2) *Verify the material* of construction meets the requirements of the applicable specification by —

(i) *Making a chemical analysis of each heat of material;*

(ii) *Obtaining a certified chemical analysis* from the material manufacturer for each heat of material (a ladle analysis is acceptable); or

(iii) *If an analysis* is not provided for each heat of material by the material manufacturer, by making a check analysis of a sample from each coil, sheet, or tube.

(3) *Verify compliance of cylinders with the applicable specification by —*

(i) *Verifying identification of material is proper;*

(ii) *Inspecting the inside of the cylinder before closing in ends;*

(iii) *Verifying that the heat treatment is proper;*

(iv) *Obtaining samples* for all tests and check chemical analyses (NOTE: Recommended locations for test specimens taken from welded cylinders are depicted in Figures 1 through 5 in Appendix C to this subpart for the specific construction design.);

(v) *Witnessing all tests;*

(vi) *Verify threads by gauge;*

(vii) *Reporting volumetric capacity* and tare weight (see report form) and minimum thickness of wall noted; and

(viii) *Verifying that each cylinder* is marked in accordance with the applicable specification.

(4) *Furnish complete test reports* required by this subpart to the maker of the cylinder and, upon request, to the purchaser. The test report must be retained by the inspector for fifteen years from the original test date of the cylinder.

(d) **Defects and attachments.** Cylinders must conform to the following:

(1) *A cylinder* may not be constructed of material with seams, cracks or laminations, or other injurious defects.

(2) *Metal attachments* to cylinders must have rounded or chamfered corners or must be protected in such a manner as to prevent the likelihood of causing puncture or damage to other hazardous materials packages. This requirement applies to anything temporarily or permanently attached to the cylinder, such as metal skids.

(e) **Safety devices.** Pressure relief devices and protection for valves, safety devices, and other connections, if applied, must be as required or authorized by the appropriate specification, and as required in §173.301 of this subchapter.

(f) **Markings.** Markings on a DOT Specification cylinder must conform to applicable requirements.

(1) *Each cylinder must be marked with the following information:*

(i) *The DOT specification marking* must appear first, followed immediately by the service pressure. For example, DOT-3A1800.

(ii) *The serial number* must be placed just below or immediately following the DOT specification marking.

(iii) *A symbol (letters)* must be placed just below, immediately before or following the serial number. Other variations in sequence of markings are authorized only when necessitated by a lack of space. The symbol and numbers must be those of the manufacturer. The symbol must be registered with the Associate Administrator; duplications are not authorized.

(iv) *The inspector's official mark* and date of test (such as 5-95 for May 1995) must be placed near the serial number. This information must be placed so that dates of subsequent tests can be easily added. An example of the markings prescribed in this paragraph (f)(1) is as follows:

DOT-3A1800
1234
XY
AB 5-95

Or:

DOT-3A1800-1234-XY
AB 5-95

Where:
DOT-3A = specification number
1800 = service pressure
1234 = serial number
XY = symbol of manufacturer
AB = inspector's mark
5-95 = date of test

(2) *Additional required marking* must be applied to the cylinder as follows:

(i) *The word "spun" or "plug"* must be placed near the DOT specification marking when an end closure in the finished cylinder has been welded by the spinning process, or effected by plugging.

(ii) *As prescribed* in specification 3HT (§178.44) or 3T (§178.45), if applicable.

(3) *Marking exceptions.* A DOT 3E cylinder is not required to be marked with an inspector's mark or a serial number.

(4) *Unless otherwise specified* in the applicable specification, the markings on each cylinder must be stamped plainly and permanently on the shoulder, top head, or neck.

(5) *The size* of each marking must be at least 0.25 inch or as space permits.

(6) *Other markings* are authorized provided they are made in low stress areas other than the side wall and are not of a size and depth that will create harmful stress concentrations. Such marks may not conflict with any DOT required markings.

(g) **Inspector's report.** Each inspector shall prepare a report containing, at a minimum, the applicable information listed in CGA Pamphlet C-11 or, until October 1, 1997, in accordance with the applicable test report requirements of this subchapter in effect on September 30, 1996. Any additional information or markings that are required by the applicable specification must be shown on the test report. The signature of the inspector on the reports certifies that the processes of manufacture and heat treatment of cylinders were observed and found satisfactory.

(h) **Report retention.** The manufacturer of the cylinders shall retain the reports required by this subpart for 15 years from the original test date of the cylinder.

§178.36 Specification 3A and 3AX seamless steel cylinders.

(a) **Type size and service pressure.** In addition to the requirements of §178.35, cylinders must conform to the following:

(1) *A DOT-3A cylinder* is a seamless steel cylinder with a water capacity (nominal) not over 1,000 pounds and a service pressure of at least 150 psig.

(2) *A DOT-3AX* is a seamless stainless steel cylinder with a water capacity not less than 1,000 pounds and a service pressure of at least 500 psig, conforming to the following requirements:

(i) *Assuming the cylinder* is to be supported horizontally at its two ends only and to be uniformly loaded over its entire length consisting of the weight per unit of length of the straight cylindrical portion filled with water and compressed to the specified test pressure; the sum of two times the maximum tensile stress in the bottom fibers due to bending, plus that in the same fibers (longitudinal stress), due to hydrostatic test may not exceed 80 percent of the minimum yield strength of the steel at such maximum stress. Wall thickness must be increased when necessary to meet the requirement.

(ii) *To calculate* the maximum longitudinal tensile stress due to bending, the following formula must be used:

$S = Mc / I$

(iii) *To calculate* the maximum longitudinal tensile stress due to hydrostatic test pressure, the following formula must be used:

$S = A_1 P / A_2$

Where:
S = tensile stress — p.s.i.;
M = bending moment-inch pounds — $(wl^2) / 8$;
w = weight per inch of cylinder filled with water;
l = length of cylinder-inches;
c = radius (D) / (2) of cylinder-inches;
I = moment of inertia — $0.04909 (D^4 - d^4)$ inches fourth;
D = outside diameter-inches;
d = inside diameter-inches;
A_1 = internal area in cross section of cylinder-square inches;
A_2 = area of metal in cross section of cylinder-square inches;
P = hydrostatic test pressure-psig.

(b) **Steel.** Open-hearth or electric steel of uniform quality must be used. Content percent may not exceed the following: Carbon, 0.55; phosphorous, 0.045; sulphur, 0.050.

(c) **Identification of material.** Material must be identified by any suitable method, except that plates and billets for hot-drawn cylinders must be marked with the heat number.

(d) **Manufacture.** Cylinders must be manufactured using equipment and processes adequate to ensure that each cylinder produced conforms to the requirements of this subpart. No fissure or other defect is permitted that is likely to weaken the finished cylinder appreciably. A reasonably smooth and uniform surface finish is required. If not originally free from such defects, the surface may be machined or otherwise treated to eliminate these defects. The thickness of the bottoms of cylinders welded or formed by spinning is, under no condition, to be less than two times the minimum wall thickness of the cylindrical shell; such bottom thicknesses must be measured within an area bounded by a line representing the points of contact between the cylinder and floor when the cylinder is in a vertical position.

(e) **Welding or brazing.** Welding or brazing for any purpose whatsoever is prohibited except as follows:

(1) *Welding or brazing* is authorized for the attachment of neckrings and footrings which are non-pressure parts and only to the tops and bottoms of cylinders having a service pressure of 500 psig or less. Cylinders, neckrings, and footrings must be made of weldable steel, the carbon content of which may not exceed 0.25 percent except in the case of 4130X steel which may be used with proper welding procedures.

(2) *As permitted in paragraph (d) of this section.*

(3) *Cylinders used solely* in anhydrous ammonia service may have a 1/2 inch diameter bar welded within their concave bottoms.

(f) **Wall thickness.** For cylinders with service pressure less than 900 pounds, the wall stress may not exceed 24,000 psig. A minimum wall thickness of 0.100 inch is required for any cylinder over 5 inches outside diameter. Wall stress calculation must be made by using the following formula:

$S = [P(1.3D^2 + 0.4d^2)] / (D^2 - d^2)$

Where:
S = wall stress in psi;
P = minimum test pressure prescribed for water jacket test or 450 psig whichever is the greater;
D = outside diameter in inches;
d = inside diameter in inches.

(g) Heat treatment. The completed cylinder must be uniformly and properly heat-treated prior to tests.

(h) Openings in cylinders and connections (valves, fuse plugs, etc.) for those openings. Threads are required on openings.

(1) *Threads must be clean cut, even, without checks, and to gauge.*

(2) *Taper threads,* when used, must be of length not less than as specified for American Standard taper pipe threads.

(3) *Straight threads* having at least 6 engaged threads are authorized. Straight threads must have a tight fit and calculated shear strength of at least 10 times the test pressure of the cylinder. Gaskets, adequate to prevent leakage, are required.

(i) Hydrostatic test. Each cylinder must successfully withstand a hydrostatic test, as follows:

(1) *The test* must be by water-jacket, or other suitable methods, operated so as to obtain accurate data. The pressure gauge must permit reading to an accuracy of 1 percent. The expansion gauge must permit reading of total expansion to an accuracy of either 1 percent or 0.1 cubic centimeter.

(2) *Pressure must be maintained* for at least 30 seconds and sufficiently longer to ensure complete expansion. Any internal pressure applied after heat-treatment and previous to the official test may not exceed 90 percent of the test pressure. If, due to failure of the test apparatus the test pressure cannot be maintained the test may be repeated at a pressure increased by 10 percent or 100 psig, whichever is the lower.

(3) *Permanent, volumetric expansion* may not exceed 10 percent of the total volumetric expansion at test pressure.

(4) *Each cylinder must be tested to at least 5/3 times service pressure.*

(j) Flattening test. A flattening test must be performed on one cylinder taken at random out of each lot of 200 or less, by placing the cylinder between wedge shaped knife edges having a 60° included angle, rounded to 1/2-inch radius. The longitudinal axis of the cylinder must be at a 90-degree angle to knife edges during the test. For lots of 30 or less, flattening tests are authorized to be made on a ring at least 8 inches long cut from each cylinder and subjected to same heat treatment as the finished cylinder.

(k) Physical test. A physical test must be conducted to determine yield strength, tensile strength, elongation, and reduction of area of material as follows:

(1) *The test* is required on 2 specimens cut from 1 cylinder taken at random out of each lot of 200 or less. For lots of 30 or less, physical tests are authorized to be made on a ring at least 8 inches long cut from each cylinder and subjected to same heat treatment as the finished cylinder.

(2) *Specimens must conform to the following:*

(i) *Gauge length* of 8 inches with a width of not over 1 1/2 inches, a gauge length of 2 inches with a width of not over 1 1/2 inches, or a gauge length of at least 24 times thickness with width not over 6 times thickness is authorized when cylinder wall is not over 3/16 inch thick.

(ii) *The specimen,* exclusive of grip ends, may not be flattened. Grip ends may be flattened to within 1 inch of each end of the reduced section.

(iii) *When size of cylinder* does not permit securing straight specimens, the specimens may be taken in any location or direction and may be straightened or flattened cold, by pressure only, not by blows. When specimens are so taken and prepared, the inspector's report must show in connection with record of physical tests detailed information in regard to such specimens.

(iv) *Heating of a specimen for any purpose is not authorized.*

(3) *The yield strength in tension* must be the stress corresponding to a permanent strain of 0.2 percent of the gauge length. The following conditions apply:

(i) *The yield strength* must be determined by either the "offset" method or the "extension under load" method as prescribed in ASTM E 8 (incorporated by reference; see §171.7 of this subchapter).

(ii) *In using the "extension under load" method,* the total strain (or "extension under load") corresponding to the stress at which the 0.2-percent permanent strain occurs may be determined with sufficient accuracy by calculating the elastic extension of the gauge length under appropriate load and adding thereto 0.2 percent of the gauge length. Elastic extension calculations must be based on an elastic modulus of 30,000,000. In the event of controversy the entire stress-strain diagram must be plotted and the yield strength determined from the 0.2 percent offset.

(iii) *For the purpose of strain measurement,* the initial strain must be set while the specimen is under a stress of 12,000 psig and the strain indicator reading must be set at the calculated corresponding strain.

(iv) *Cross-head speed* of the testing machine may not exceed 1/8 inch per minute during yield strength determination.

(l) Acceptable results for physical and flattening tests. Either of the following is an acceptable result:

(1) *An elongation* at least 40 percent for a 2-inch gauge length or at least 20 percent in other cases and yield strength not over 73 percent of tensile strength. In this instance, the flattening test is not required.

(2) *An elongation* at least 20 percent for a 2-inch gauge length or 10 percent in other cases and a yield strength not over 73 percent of tensile strength. In this instance, the flattening test is required, without cracking, to 6 times the wall thickness.

(m) Leakage test. All spun cylinders and plugged cylinders must be tested for leakage by gas or air pressure after the bottom has been cleaned and is free from all moisture subject to the following conditions and limitations:

(1) *Pressure, approximately* the same as but no less than service pressure, must be applied to one side of the finished bottom over an area of at least 1/16 of the total area of the bottom but not less than 3/4 inch in diameter, including the closure, for at least 1 minute, during which time the other side of the bottom exposed to pressure must be covered with water and closely examined for indications of leakage. Except as provided in paragraph (n) of this section, a cylinder that is leaking must be rejected.

(2) *A spun cylinder* is one in which an end closure in the finished cylinder has been welded by the spinning process.

(3) *A plugged cylinder* is one in which a permanent closure in the bottom of a finished cylinder has been effected by a plug.

(4) *As a safety precaution,* if the manufacturer elects to make this test before the hydrostatic test, the manufacturer should design the test apparatus so that the pressure is applied to the smallest area practicable, around the point of closure, and so as to use the smallest possible volume of air or gas.

(n) Rejected cylinders. Reheat treatment is authorized for rejected cylinders. Subsequent thereto, cylinders must pass all prescribed tests to be acceptable. Repair by welding or spinning is not authorized. Spun cylinders rejected under the provisions of paragraph (m) of this section may be removed from the spun cylinder category by drilling to remove defective material, tapping and plugging.

§178.37 Specification 3AA and 3AAX seamless steel cylinders.

(a) Type, size and service pressure. In addition to the requirements of §178.35, cylinders must conform to the following:

(1) *A DOT-3AA cylinder* is a seamless steel cylinder with a water capacity (nominal) of not over 1,000 pounds and a service pressure of at least 150 psig.

(2) *A DOT-3AAX cylinder* is a seamless steel cylinder with a water capacity of not less than 1,000 pounds and a service pressure of at least 500 psig, conforming to the following requirements:

(i) *Assuming the cylinder* is to be supported horizontally at its two ends only and to be uniformly loaded over its entire length consisting of the weight per unit of length of the straight cylindrical portion filled with water and compressed to the specified test pressure; the sum of two times the maximum tensile stress in the bottom fibers due to bending, plus that in the same fibers (longitudinal stress), due to hydrostatic test pressure may not exceed 80 percent of the minimum yield strength of the steel at such maximum stress. Wall thickness must be increased when necessary to meet the requirement.

(ii) *To calculate* the maximum tensile stress due to bending, the following formula must be used:

$S = Mc / I$

(iii) *To calculate* the maximum longitudinal tensile stress due to hydrostatic test pressure, the following formula must be used:

$S = A^1 P / A^2$

Where:

S = tensile stress — p.s.i.;

M = bending moment-inch pounds — $(wl^2) / 8$;

w = weight per inch of cylinder filled with water;

l = length of cylinder-inches;

c = radius (D) / (2) of cylinder-inches;

I = moment of inertia — $0.04909 (D^4 - d^4)$ inches fourth;

D = outside diameter-inches;

d = inside diameter-inches;

A^1 = internal area in cross section of cylinder-square inches;

A^2 = area of metal in cross section of cylinder-square inches;
P = hydrostatic test pressure-psig.

(b) **Authorized steel.** Open-hearth, basic oxygen, or electric steel of uniform quality must be used. A heat of steel made under the specifications in table 1 of this paragraph (b), check chemical analysis of which is slightly out of the specified range, is acceptable, if satisfactory in all other respects, provided the tolerances shown in table 2 of this paragraph (b) are not exceeded. When a carbon-boron steel is used, a hardenability test must be performed on the first and last ingot of each heat of steel. The results of this test must be recorded on the Record of Chemical Analysis of Material for Cylinders required by §178.35. This hardness test must be made 5/16-inch from the quenched end of the Jominy quench bar and the hardness must be at least Rc 33 and no more than Rc 53. The following chemical analyses are authorized:

Table 1 - Authorized Materials

Designation	4130X (percent)[1]	NE-8630 (percent)[1]	9115 (percent)[1]	9125 (percent)[1]	Carbon-boron (percent)	Intermediate manganese (percent)
Carbon	0.25/0.35	0.28/0.33	0.10/0.20	0.20/0.30	0.27-0.37	0.40 max
Manganese	0.40/0.90	0.70/0.90	0.50/0.75	0.50/0.75	0.80-1.40	1.35/1.65
Phosphorus	0.04 max	0.04 max	0.04 max	0.04 max	0.035 max	0.04 max
Sulfur	0.05 max	0.04 max	0.04 max	0.04 max	0.045 max	0.05 max
Silicon	0.15/0.35	0.20/0.35	0.60/0.90	0.60/0.90	0.3 max	0.10/0.30
Chromium	0.80/1.10	0.40/0.60	0.50/0.65	0.50/0.65		
Molybdenum	0.15/0.25	0.15/0.25				
Zirconium			0.05/0.15	0.05/0.15		
Nickel		0.40/0.70				
Boron					0.0005/ 0.003	

1. This designation may not be restrictive and the commercial steel is limited in analysis as shown in this table.

Table 2 - Check Analysis Tolerances

Element	Limit or maximum specified (percent)	Tolerance (percent) over the maximum limit or under the minimum limit	
		Under minimum limit	Over maximum limit
Carbon	To 0.15 incl	0.02	0.03
	Over 0.15 to 0.40 incl	.03	.04
Manganese	To 0.60 incl	.03	.03
	Over 0.60 to 1.15 incl	0.04	0.04
	Over 1.15 to 2.50 incl	0.05	0.05
Phosphorus[1]	All ranges		.01
Sulphur	All ranges		.01
Silicon	To 0.30 incl	.02	.03
	Over 0.30 to 1.00 incl	.05	.05
Nickel	To 1.00 incl	.03	.03
Chromium	To 0.90 incl	.03	.03
	0.90 to 2.90 incl	.05	.05
Molybdenum	To 0.20 incl	.01	.01
	Over 0.20 to 0.40	.02	.02
Zirconium	All ranges	.01	.05

1. Rephosphorized steels not subject to check analysis for phosphorus.

(c) **Identification of material.** Material must be identified by any suitable method except that plates and billets for hot-drawn cylinders must be marked with the heat number.

(d) **Manufacture.** Cylinders must be manufactured using equipment and processes adequate to ensure that each cylinder produced conforms to the requirements of this subpart. No fissure or other defects is permitted that is likely to weaken the finished cylinder appreciably. A reasonably smooth and uniform surface finish is required. If not originally free from such defects, the surface may be machined or otherwise treated to eliminate these defects. The thickness of the bottoms of cylinders welded or formed by spinning is, under no condition, to be less than two times the minimum wall thickness of the cylindrical shell; such bottom thicknesses must be measured within an area bounded by a line representing the points of contact between the cylinder and floor when the cylinder is in a vertical position.

(e) **Welding or brazing.** Welding or brazing for any purpose whatsoever is prohibited except as follows:

(1) *Welding or brazing* is authorized for the attachment of neckrings and footrings which are non-pressure parts, and only to the tops and bottoms of cylinders having a service pressure of 500 psig or less. Cylinders, neckrings, and footrings must be made of weldable steel, the carbon content of which may not exceed 0.25 percent except in the case of 4130X steel which may be used with proper welding procedure.

(2) *As permitted in paragraph (d) of this section.*

(f) **Wall thickness.** The thickness of each cylinder must conform to the following:

(1) *For cylinders* with a service pressure of less than 900 psig, the wall stress may not exceed 24,000 psi. A minimum wall thickness of 0.100 inch is required for any cylinder with an outside diameter of over 5 inches.

(2) *For cylinders* with service pressure of 900 psig or more the minimum wall must be such that the wall stress at the minimum specified test pressure may not exceed 67 percent of the minimum tensile strength of the steel as determined from the physical tests required in paragraphs (k) and (l) of this section and must be not over 70,000 psi.

(3) *Calculation must be made by the formula:*

$S = [P(1.3D^2 + 0.4d^2)] / (D^2 - d^2)$

Where:

S = wall stress in psi;

P = minimum test pressure prescribed for water jacket test or 450 psig whichever is the greater;

D = outside diameter in inches;

d = inside diameter in inches.

(g) **Heat treatment.** The completed cylinders must be uniformly and properly heat treated prior to tests. Heat treatment of cylinders of the authorized analyses must be as follows:

(1) *All cylinders* must be quenched by oil, or other suitable medium except as provided in paragraph (g)(5) of this section.

(2) *The steel temperature* on quenching must be that recommended for the steel analysis, but may not exceed 1750 °F.

(3) *All steels* must be tempered at a temperature most suitable for that steel.

(4) *The minimum* tempering temperature may not be less than 1000 °F except as noted in paragraph (g)(6) of this section.

(5) *Steel 4130X* may be normalized at a temperature of 1650 °F instead of being quenched and cylinders so normalized need not be tempered.

(6) *Intermediate manganese steels* may be tempered at temperatures not less than 1150 °F, and after heat treating each cylinder must be submitted to a magnetic test to detect the presence of quenching cracks. Cracked cylinders must be rejected and destroyed.

(7) *Except as otherwise provided* in paragraph (g)(6) of this section, all cylinders, if water quenched or quenched with a liquid producing a cooling rate in excess of 80 percent of the cooling rate of water, must be inspected by the magnetic particle, dye penetrant or ultrasonic method to detect the presence of quenching cracks. Any cylinder designed to the requirements for specification 3AA and found to have a quenching crack must be rejected and may not be requalified. Cylinders designed to the requirements for specification 3AAX and found to have cracks must have cracks removed to sound metal by mechanical means. Such specification 3AAX cylinders will be acceptable if the repaired area is subsequently examined to assure no defect, and it is determined that design thickness requirements are met.

(h) **Openings in cylinders and connections** (valves, fuse plugs, etc.) for those openings. Threads are required on openings.

(1) *Threads must be clean cut, even, without checks, and to gauge.*

(2) *Taper threads,* when used, must be of a length not less than as specified for American Standard taper pipe threads.

(3) *Straight threads* having at least 6 engaged threads are authorized. Straight threads must have a tight fit and a calculated shear strength of at least 10 times the test pressure of the cylinder. Gaskets, adequate to prevent leakage, are required.

(i) **Hydrostatic test.** Each cylinder must successfully withstand a hydrostatic test as follows:

(1) *The test* must be by water-jacket, or other suitable method, operated so as to obtain accurate data. The pressure gauge must

permit reading to an accuracy of 1 percent. The expansion gauge must permit reading of total expansion to an accuracy of either 1 percent or 0.1 cubic centimeter.

(2) *Pressure must be maintained* for at least 30 seconds and sufficiently longer to ensure complete expansion. Any internal pressure applied after heat-treatment and previous to the official test may not exceed 90 percent of the test pressure. If, due to failure of the test apparatus, the test pressure cannot be maintained, the test may be repeated at a pressure increased by 10 percent or 100 psig, whichever is the lower.

(3) *Permanent volumetric expansion* may not exceed 10 percent of total volumetric expansion at test pressure.

(4) *Each cylinder* must be tested to at least 5/3 times the service pressure.

(j) **Flattening test.** A flattening test must be performed on one cylinder taken at random out of each lot of 200 or less, by placing the cylinder between wedge shaped knife edges having a 60° included angle, rounded to 1/2-inch radius. The longitudinal axis of the cylinder must be at a 90-degree angle to knife edges during the test. For lots of 30 or less, flattening tests are authorized to be made on a ring at least 8 inches long cut from each cylinder and subjected to same heat treatment as the finished cylinder.

(k) **Physical test.** A physical test must be conducted to determine yield strength, tensile strength, elongation, and reduction of area of material as follows:

(1) *The test* is required on 2 specimens cut from 1 cylinder taken at random out of each lot of 200 or less. For lots of 30 or less, physical tests are authorized to be made on a ring at least 8 inches long cut from each cylinder and subjected to the same heat treatment as the finished cylinder.

(2) *Specimens must conform to the following:*

(i) *Gauge length* of 8 inches with a width of not over 1 1/2 inches, a gauge length of 2 inches with a width of not over 1 1/2 inches, or a gauge length of at least 24 times the thickness with width not over 6 times thickness when the thickness of the cylinder wall is not over 3/16 inch.

(ii) *The specimen,* exclusive of grip ends, may not be flattened. Grip ends may be flattened to within 1 inch of each end of the reduced section.

(iii) *When size of cylinder* does not permit securing straight specimens, the specimens may be taken in any location or direction and may be straightened or flattened cold, by pressure only, not by blows. When specimens are so taken and prepared, the inspector's report must show in connection with record of physical tests detailed information in regard to such specimens.

(iv) *Heating of a specimen for any purpose is not authorized.*

(3) *The yield strength* in tension must be the stress corresponding to a permanent strain of 0.2 percent of the gauge length. The following conditions apply:

(i) *The yield strength* must be determined by either the "offset" method or the "extension under load" method as prescribed in ASTM E 8 (incorporated by reference; see §171.7 of this subchapter).

(ii) *In using* the "extension under load" method, the total strain (or "extension under load") corresponding to the stress at which the 0.2 percent permanent strain occurs may be determined with sufficient accuracy by calculating the elastic extension of the gauge length under appropriate load and adding thereto 0.2 percent of the gauge length. Elastic extension calculations must be based on an elastic modulus of 30,000,000. In the event of controversy, the entire stress-strain diagram must be plotted and the yield strength determined from the 0.2 percent offset.

(iii) *For the purpose* of strain measurement, the initial strain must be set while the specimen is under a stress of 12,000 psi, the strain indicator reading being set at the calculated corresponding strain.

(iv) *Cross-head speed* of the testing machine may not exceed 1/8 inch per minute during yield strength determination.

(l) **Acceptable results for physical and flattening tests.** An acceptable result for physical and flattening tests is elongation at least 20 percent for 2 inches of gauge length or at least 10 percent in other cases. Flattening is required, without cracking, to 6 times the wall thickness of the cylinder.

(m) **Leakage test.** All spun cylinders and plugged cylinders must be tested for leakage by gas or air pressure after the bottom has been cleaned and is free from all moisture. Pressure, approximately the same as but no less than the service pressure, must be applied to one side of the finished bottom over an area of at least 1/16 of the total area of the bottom but not less than 3/4 inch in diameter, including the closure, for at least one minute, during which time the other side of the bottom exposed to pressure must be covered with water and closely examined for indications of leakage. Except as provided in paragraph (n) of this section, a cylinder must be rejected if there is any leaking.

(1) *A spun cylinder* is one in which an end closure in the finished cylinder has been welded by the spinning process.

(2) *A plugged cylinder* is one in which a permanent closure in the bottom of a finished cylinder has been effected by a plug.

(3) *As a safety precaution,* if the manufacturer elects to make this test before the hydrostatic test, the manufacturer should design the test apparatus so that the pressure is applied to the smallest area practicable, around the point of closure, and so as to use the smallest possible volume of air or gas.

(n) **Rejected cylinders.** Reheat treatment is authorized for rejected cylinders. Subsequent thereto, cylinders must pass all prescribed tests to be acceptable. Repair by welding or spinning is not authorized. Spun cylinders rejected under the provision of paragraph (m) of this section may be removed from the spun cylinder category by drilling to remove defective material, tapping and plugging.

§178.38 Specification 3B seamless steel cylinders.

(a) **Type, size, and service pressure.** A DOT 3B cylinder is seamless steel cylinder with a water capacity (nominal) of not over 1,000 pounds and a service pressure of at least 150 to not over 500 psig.

(b) **Steel.** Open-hearth or electric steel of uniform quality must be used. Content percent may not exceed the following: carbon, 0.55; phosphorus, 0.045; sulphur, 0.050.

(c) **Identification of material.** Material must be identified by any suitable method except that plates and billets for hot-drawn cylinders must be marked with the heat number.

(d) **Manufacture.** Cylinders must be manufactured using equipment and processes adequate to ensure that each cylinder produced conforms to the requirements of this subpart. No fissure or other defect is permitted that is likely to weaken the finished cylinder appreciably. A reasonably smooth and uniform surface finish is required. If not originally free from such defects, the surface may be machined or otherwise treated to eliminate these defects. The thickness of the bottoms of cylinders welded or formed by spinning is, under no condition, to be less than two times the minimum wall thickness of the cylindrical shell; such bottom thicknesses to be measured within an area bounded by a line representing the points of contact between the cylinder and floor when the cylinder is in a vertical position.

(e) **Welding or brazing.** Welding or brazing for any purpose whatsoever is prohibited except as follows:

(1) *Welding or brazing* is authorized for the attachment of neckrings and footrings which are non-pressure parts, and only to the tops and bottoms of cylinders having a service pressure of 500 psig or less. Cylinders, neckrings, and footrings must be made of weldable steel, carbon content of which may not exceed 0.25 percent except in the case of 4130X steel which may be used with proper welding procedure.

(2) *As permitted in paragraph (d) of this section.*

(f) **Wall thickness.** The wall stress may not exceed 24,000 psi. The minimum wall thickness is 0.090 inch for any cylinder with an outside diameter of 6 inches. Calculation must be made by the following formula:

$S = [P(1.3D^2 + 0.4d^2)] / (D^2 - d^2)$

Where:

S = wall stress in psi;

P = at least two times service pressure or 450 psig, whichever is the greater;

D = outside diameter in inches;

d = inside diameter in inches.

(g) **Heat treatment.** The completed cylinders must be uniformly and properly heat-treated prior to tests.

(h) **Openings in cylinders and connections** (valves, fuse plugs, etc.) for those openings. Threads, conforming to the following, are required on all openings:

(1) *Threads must be clean cut, even, without checks, and to gauge.*

(2) *Taper threads* when used, must be of a length not less than as specified for American Standard taper pipe threads.

(3) *Straight threads* having at least 4 engaged threads are authorized. Straight threads must have a tight fit, and calculated shear strength at least 10 times the test pressure of the cylinder. Gaskets, adequate to prevent leakage, are required.

(i) **Hydrostatic test.** Cylinders must successfully withstand a hydrostatic test, as follows:

(1) *The test* must be by water-jacket, or other suitable method, operated so as to obtain accurate data. The pressure gauge must permit reading to an accuracy of 1 percent. The expansion gauge must permit reading of total expansion to an accuracy either of 1 percent or 0.1 cubic centimeter.

(2) *Pressure must be maintained* for at least 30 seconds and sufficiently longer to insure complete expansion. Any internal pressure applied after heat-treatment and previous to the official test may not exceed 90 percent of the test pressure. If, due to failure of the test apparatus, the test pressure cannot be maintained, the test may be repeated at a pressure increased by 10 percent or 100 psig, whichever is the lower.

(3) *Permanent volumetric expansion* may not exceed 10 percent of total volumetric expansion at test pressure.

(4) *Cylinders must be tested as follows:*

(i) *Each cylinder; to at least 2 times service pressure; or*

(ii) *1 cylinder* out of each lot of 200 or less; to at least 3 times service pressure. Others must be examined under pressure of 2 times service pressure and show no defect.

(j) **Flattening test.** A flattening test must be performed on one cylinder taken at random out of each lot of 200 or less, by placing the cylinder between wedge shaped knife edges having a 60° included angle, rounded to 1/2-inch radius. The longitudinal axis of the cylinder must be at a 90-degree angle to knife edges during the test. For lots of 30 or less, flattening tests are authorized to be made on a ring at least 8 inches long cut from each cylinder and subjected to same heat treatment as the finished cylinder.

(k) **Physical test.** A physical test must be conducted to determine yield strength, tensile strength, elongation, and reduction of area of material, as follows:

(1) *The test* is required on 2 specimens cut from 1 cylinder taken at random out of each lot of 200 or less. For lots of 30 or less, physical tests are authorized to be made on a ring at least 8 inches long cut from each cylinder and subjected to same heat treatment as the finished cylinder.

(2) *Specimens must conform to the following:*

(i) *Gauge length* of 8 inches with a width of not over 1 1/2 inches; or a gauge length of 2 inches with a width of not over 1 1/2 inches; or a gauge length at least 24 times the thickness with a width not over 6 times thickness is authorized when a cylinder wall is not over 3/16 inch thick.

(ii) *The specimen,* exclusive of grip ends, may not be flattened. Grip ends may be flattened to within one inch of each end of the reduced section.

(iii) *When size of cylinder* does not permit securing straight specimens, the specimens may be taken in any location or direction and may be straightened or flattened cold, by pressure only, not by blows. When specimens are so taken and prepared, the inspector's report must show in connection with record of physical tests detailed information in regard to such specimens.

(iv) *Heating of a specimen for any purpose is not authorized.*

(3) *The yield strength* in tension must be the stress corresponding to a permanent strain of 0.2 percent of the gauge length. The following conditions apply:

(i) *The yield strength* must be determined by either the "offset" method or the "extension under load" method as prescribed in ASTM E 8 (incorporated by reference; see §171.7 of this subchapter).

(ii) *In using* the "extension under load" method, the total strain (or "extension under load") corresponding to the stress at which the 0.2 percent permanent strain occurs may be determined with sufficient accuracy by calculating the elastic extension of the gauge length under appropriate load and adding thereto 0.2 percent of the gauge length. Elastic extension calculations must be based on an elastic modulus of 30,000,000. In the event of controversy, the entire stress-strain diagram must be plotted and the yield strength determined from the 0.2 percent offset.

(iii) *For the purpose* of strain measurement, the initial strain must be set while the specimen is under a stress of 12,000 psi, and the strain indicator reading being set at the calculated corresponding strain.

(iv) *Cross-head speed* of the testing machine may not exceed 1/8 inch per minute during yield strength determination.

(l) **Acceptable results for physical and flattening tests.** Either of the following is an acceptable result:

(1) *An elongation* of at least 40 percent for a 2-inch gauge length or at least 20 percent in other cases and yield strength not over 73 percent of tensile strength. In this instance, the flattening test is not required.

(2) *An elongation* of at least 20 percent for a 2-inch gauge length or 10 percent in other cases and yield strength not over 73 percent of tensile strength. Flattening is required, without cracking, to 6 times the wall thickness.

(m) **Leakage test.** All spun cylinders and plugged cylinders must be tested for leakage by gas or air pressure after the bottom has been cleaned and is free from all moisture, subject to the following conditions and limitations:

(1) *Pressure, approximately* the same as but no less than service pressure, must be applied to one side of the finished bottom over an area of at least 1/16 of the total area of the bottom but not less than 3/4 inch in diameter, including the closure, for at least one minute, during which time the other side of the bottom exposed to pressure must be covered with water and closely examined for indications of leakage. Except as provided in paragraph (n) of this section, a cylinder must be rejected if there is any leaking.

(2) *A spun cylinder* is one in which an end closure in the finished cylinder has been welded by the spinning process.

(3) *A plugged cylinder* is one in which a permanent closure in the bottom of a finished cylinder has been effected by a plug.

(4) *As a safety precaution,* if the manufacturer elects to make this test before the hydrostatic test, he should design his apparatus so that the pressure is applied to the smallest area practicable, around the point of closure, and so as to use the smallest possible volume of air or gas.

(n) **Rejected cylinders.** Reheat treatment of rejected cylinders is authorized. Subsequent thereto, cylinders must pass all prescribed tests to be acceptable. Repair by welding or spinning is not authorized. Spun cylinders rejected under the provisions of paragraph (m) of this section may be removed from the spun cylinder category by drilling to remove defective material, tapping and plugging.

(o) **Marking.** Markings may be stamped into the sidewalls of cylinders having a service pressure of 150 psig if all of the following conditions are met:

(1) *Wall stress at test pressure may not exceed 24,000 psi.*

(2) *Minimum wall thickness must be not less than 0.090 inch.*

(3) *Depth of stamping* must be no greater than 15 percent of the minimum wall thickness, but may not exceed 0.015 inch.

(4) *Maximum outside diameter of cylinder may not exceed 5 inches.*

(5) *Carbon content* of cylinder may not exceed 0.25 percent. If the carbon content exceeds 0.25 percent, the complete cylinder must be normalized after stamping.

(6) *Stamping must be adjacent to the top head.*

§178.39 Specification 3BN seamless nickel cylinders.

(a) **Type, size and service pressure.** A DOT 3BN cylinder is a seamless nickel cylinder with a water capacity (nominal) not over 125 pounds water capacity (nominal) and a service pressure at least 150 to not over 500 psig.

(b) **Nickel.** The percentage of nickel plus cobalt must be at least 99.0 percent.

(c) **Identification of material.** The material must be identified by any suitable method except that plates and billets for hot-drawn cylinders must be marked with the heat number.

(d) **Manufacture.** Cylinders must be manufactured using equipment and processes adequate to ensure that each cylinder produced conforms to the requirements of this subpart. No defect is permitted that is likely to weaken the finished cylinder appreciably. A reasonably smooth and uniform surface finish is required. Cylinders closed in by spinning process are not authorized.

(e) **Welding or brazing.** Welding or brazing for any purpose whatsoever is prohibited except that welding is authorized for the attachment of neckrings and footrings which are nonpressure parts, and only to the tops and bottoms of cylinders. Neckrings and footrings must be of weldable material, the carbon content of which may not exceed 0.25 percent. Nickel welding rod must be used.

(f) **Wall thickness.** The wall stress may not exceed 15,000 psi. A minimum wall thickness of 0.100 inch is required for any cylinder over 5 inches in outside diameter. Wall stress calculation must be made by using the following formula:

$S = [P(1.3D^2 + 0.4d^2)] / (D^2 - d^2)$

Where:

S = wall stress in psi;

P = Minimum test pressure prescribed for water jacket test or 450 psig whichever is greatest;

D = outside diameter in inches;

d = inside diameter in inches.

(g) Heat treatment. The completed cylinders must be uniformly and properly heat-treated prior to tests.

(h) Openings in cylinders and connections (valves, fuse plugs, etc.) for those openings. Threads conforming to the following are required on openings:

(1) *Threads must be clean cut, even, without checks, and to gauge.*

(2) *Taper threads,* when used, to be of length not less than as specified for American Standard taper pipe threads.

(3) *Straight threads* having at least 6 engaged threads are authorized. Straight threads must have a tight fit and a calculated shear strength of at least 10 times the test pressure of the cylinder. Gaskets, adequate to prevent leakage, are required.

(i) Hydrostatic test. Each cylinder must successfully withstand a hydrostatic test, as follows:

(1) *The test* must be by water-jacket, or other suitable method, operated so as to obtain accurate data. The pressure gauge must permit reading to an accuracy of 1 percent. The expansion gauge must permit reading of total expansion to an accuracy either of 1 percent or 0.1 cubic centimeter.

(2) *Pressure must be maintained* for at least 30 seconds and sufficiently longer to ensure complete expansion. Any internal pressure applied after heat-treatment and previous to the official test may not exceed 90 percent of the test pressure. If, due to failure of the test apparatus, the test pressure cannot be maintained, the test may be repeated at a pressure increased by 10 percent or 100 psig, whichever is the lower.

(3) *Permanent volumetric expansion* may not exceed 10 percent of total volumetric expansion at test pressure.

(4) *Each cylinder must be tested to at least 2 times service pressure.*

(j) Flattening test. A flattening test must be performed on one cylinder taken at random out of each lot of 200 or less, by placing the cylinder between wedge shaped knife edges having a 60° included angle, rounded to 1/2-inch radius. The longitudinal axis of the cylinder must be at a 90-degree angle to knife edges during the test. For lots of 30 or less, flattening tests are authorized to be made on a ring at least 8 inches long cut from each cylinder and subjected to same heat treatment as the finished cylinder.

(k) Physical test. A physical test must be conducted to determine yield strength, tensile strength, elongation, and reduction of area of material, as follows:

(1) *The test* is required on 2 specimens cut from 1 cylinder taken at random out of each lot of 200 or less. For lots of 30 or less, physical tests are authorized to be made on a ring at least 8 inches long cut from each cylinder and subjected to same heat treatment as the finished cylinder.

(2) *Specimens must conform to the following:*

(i) *A gauge length* of 8 inches with a width of not over 1 1/2 inches, a gauge length of 2 inches with a width of not over 1 1/2 inches, or a gauge length of at least 24 times the thickness with a width not over 6 times thickness is authorized when a cylinder wall is not over 3/16 inch thick.

(ii) *The specimen,* exclusive of grip ends, may not be flattened. Grip ends may be flattened to within one inch of each end of the reduced section.

(iii) *When size* of cylinder does not permit securing straight specimens, the specimens may be taken in any location or direction and may be straightened or flattened cold, by pressure only, not by blows. When specimens are so taken and prepared, the inspector's report must show in connection with record of physical tests detailed information in regard to such specimens.

(iv) *Heating of a specimen for any purpose is not authorized.*

(3) *The yield strength* in tension must be the stress corresponding to a permanent strain of 0.2 percent of the gauge length. The following conditions apply:

(i) *The yield strength* must be determined by either the "offset" method or the "extension under load" method as prescribed in ASTM E 8 (incorporated by reference; see §171.7 of this subchapter).

(ii) *In using* the "extension under load" method, the total strain (or "extension under load") corresponding to the stress at which the 0.2 percent permanent strain occurs may be determined with sufficient accuracy by calculating the elastic extension of the gauge length under appropriate load and adding thereto 0.2 percent of the gauge length. Elastic extension calculations must be based on an elastic modulus of 30,000,000. In the event of controversy, the entire stress-strain diagram must be plotted and the yield strength determined from the 0.2 percent offset.

(iii) *For the purpose of strain measurement,* the initial strain must be set while the specimen is under a stress of 12,000 psi, and the strain indicator reading must be set at the calculated corresponding strain.

(iv) *Cross-head speed* of the testing machine may not exceed 1/8 inch per minute during yield strength determination.

(l) Acceptable results for physical and flattening tests. Either of the following is an acceptable result:

(1) *An elongation* of at least 40 percent for a 2 inch gauge length or at least 20 percent in other cases and yield point not over 50 percent of tensile strength. In this instance, the flattening test is not required.

(2) *An elongation* of at least 20 percent for a 2 inch gauge length or 10 percent in other cases and a yield point not over 50 percent of tensile strength. Flattening is required, without cracking, to 6 times the wall thickness.

(m) Rejected cylinders. Reheat treatment is authorized for rejected cylinders. Subsequent thereto, cylinders must pass all prescribed tests to be acceptable. Repair by welding is not authorized.

§178.42 Specification 3E seamless steel cylinders.

(a) Type, size, and service pressure. A DOT 3E cylinder is a seamless steel cylinder with an outside diameter not greater than 2 inches nominal, a length less than 2 feet and a service pressure of 1,800 psig.

(b) Steel. Open-hearth or electric steel of uniform quality must be used. Content percent may not exceed the following: Carbon, 0.55; phosphorus, 0.045; sulphur, 0.050.

(c) Identification of steel. Materials must be identified by any suitable method.

(d) Manufacture. Cylinders must be manufactured by best appliances and methods. No defect is permitted that is likely to weaken the finished cylinder appreciably. A reasonably smooth and uniform surface finish is required. The thickness of the spun bottom is, under no condition, to be less than two times the minimum wall thickness of the cylindrical shell; such bottom thickness must be measured within an area bounded by a line representing the points of contact between the cylinder and floor when the cylinder is in a vertical position.

(e) Openings in cylinders and connections (valves, fuse plugs, etc.) for those openings. Threads conforming to the following are required on openings.

(1) *Threads must be clean cut, even, without checks, and to gauge.*

(2) *Taper threads,* when used, must be of length not less than as specified for American Standard taper pipe threads.

(3) *Straight threads* having at least 4 engaged threads are authorized. Straight threads must have a tight fit and a calculated shear strength of at least 10 times the test pressure of the cylinder. Gaskets, adequate to prevent leakage, are required.

(f) Hydrostatic test. Cylinders must be tested as follows:

(1) *One cylinder* out of each lot of 500 or less must be subjected to a hydrostatic pressure of 6,000 psig or higher.

(2) *The cylinder* referred to in paragraph (f)(1) of this section must burst at a pressure higher than 6,000 psig without fragmenting or otherwise showing lack of ductility, or must hold a pressure of 12,000 psig for 30 seconds without bursting. In which case, it must be subjected to a flattening test without cracking to six times wall thickness between knife edges, wedge shaped 60 degree angle, rounded out to a 1/2 inch radius. The inspector's report must be suitably changed to show results of latter alternate and flattening test.

(3) *Other cylinders* must be examined under pressure of at least 3,000 psig and not to exceed 4,500 psig and show no defect. Cylinders tested at a pressure in excess of 3,600 psig must burst at a pressure higher than 7,500 psig when tested as specified in paragraph (f)(2) of this section. The pressure must be maintained for at least 30 seconds and sufficiently longer to ensure complete examination.

(g) Leakage test. All spun cylinders and plugged cylinders must be tested for leakage by gas or air pressure after the bottom has been cleaned and is free from all moisture subject to the following conditions and limitations:

(1) *A pressure,* approximately the same as but not less than the service pressure, must be applied to one side of the finished bottom over an area of at least 1/16 of the total area of the bottom but not less than 3/4 inch in diameter, including the closure, for at least one minute, during which time the other side of the bottom exposed to pressure must be covered with water and closely examined for indications of leakage. Accept as provided in paragraph (h) of this section, a cylinder must be rejected if there is any leakage.

(2) *A spun cylinder* is one in which an end closure in the finished cylinder has been welded by the spinning process.

(3) *A plugged cylinder* is one in which a permanent closure in the bottom of a finished cylinder has been effected by a plug.

(4) *As a safety precaution,* if the manufacturer elects to make this test before the hydrostatic test, the manufacturer shall design the test apparatus so that the pressure is applied to the smallest area practicable, around the point of closure, and so as to use the smallest possible volume of air or gas.

(h) **Rejected cylinders.** Reheat treatment is authorized for rejected cylinders. Subsequent thereto, cylinders must pass all prescribed tests to be acceptable. Repair by welding or spinning is not authorized. Spun cylinders rejected under the provisions of paragraph (g) of this section may be removed from the spun cylinder category by drilling to remove defective material, tapping and plugging.

(i) **Marking.** Markings required by §178.35 must be stamped plainly and permanently on the shoulder, top head, neck or sidewall of each cylinder.

§178.44 Specification 3HT seamless steel cylinders for aircraft use.

(a) **Type, size and service pressure.** A DOT 3HT cylinder is a seamless steel cylinder with a water capacity (nominal) of not over 150 pounds and a service pressure of at least 900 psig.

(b) **Authorized steel.** Open hearth or electric furnace steel of uniform quality must be used. A heat of steel made under the specifications listed in table 1 in this paragraph (b), check chemical analysis of which is slightly out of the specified range, is acceptable, if satisfactory in all other respects, provided the tolerances shown in table 2 in this paragraph (b) are not exceeded. Grain size 6 or finer according to ASTM E 112. Steel of the following chemical analysis is authorized:

Table 1 - Authorized Materials

Designation	AISI 4130 (percent)
Carbon	0.28/0.33
Manganese	0.40/0.60
Phosphorus	0.040 maximum
Sulfur	0.040 maximum
Silicon	0.15/0.35
Chromium	0.80/1.10
Molybdenum	0.15/0.25

Table 2 - Check Analysis Tolerances

Element	Limit or maximum specified (percent)	Tolerance (percent) over the maximum limit or under the minimum limit	
		Under minimum limit	Over maximum limit
Carbon	Over 0.15 to 0.40 incl	.03	.04
Manganese	To 0.60 incl	.03	.03
Phosphorus[1]	All ranges		.01
Sulphur	All ranges		.01
Silicon	To 0.30 incl	.02	.03
	Over 0.30 to 1.00 incl	.05	.05
Chromium	To 0.90 incl	.03	.03
	Over 0.90 to 2.10 incl	.05	.05
Molybdenum	To 0.20 incl	.01	.01
	Over 0.20 to 0.40 incl	.02	.02

1. Rephosphorized steels not subject to check analysis for phosphorus.

(c) **Identification of material.** Material must be identified by any suitable method. Steel stamping of heat identifications may not be made in any area which will eventually become the side wall of the cylinder. Depth of stamping may not encroach upon the minimum prescribed wall thickness of the cylinder.

(d) **Manufacture.** Cylinders must be manufactured using equipment and processes adequate to ensure that each cylinder produced conforms to the requirements of this subpart. No fissure or other defect is permitted that is likely to weaken the finished container appreciably. The general surface finish may not exceed a roughness of 250 RMS. Individual irregularities such as draw marks, scratches, pits, etc., should be held to a minimum consistent with good high stress pressure vessel manufacturing practices. If the cylinder is not originally free of such defects or does not meet the finish requirements, the surface may be machined or otherwise treated to eliminate these defects. The point of closure of cylinders closed by spinning may not be less than two times the prescribed wall thickness of the cylindrical shell. The cylinder end contour must be hemispherical or ellipsoidal with a ratio of major-to-minor axis not exceeding two to one and with the concave side to pressure.

(e) **Welding or brazing.** Welding or brazing for any purpose whatsoever is prohibited, except that welding by spinning is permitted to close the bottom of spun cylinders. Machining or grinding to produce proper surface finish at point of closure is required.

(f) **Wall thickness.**

(1) *Minimum wall thickness* for any cylinder must be 0.050 inch. The minimum wall thickness must be such that the wall stress at the minimum specified test pressure may not exceed 75 percent of the minimum tensile strength of the steel as determined from the physical tests required in paragraph (m) of this section and may not be over 105,000 psi.

(2) *Calculations must be made by the formula:*

$$S = [P(1.3D^2 + 0.4d^2)] / (D^2 - d^2)$$

Where:

S = Wall stress in psi;

P = Minimum test pressure prescribed for water jacket test;

D = Outside diameter in inches;

d = Inside diameter in inches.

(3) *Wall thickness* of hemispherical bottoms only permitted to 90 percent of minimum wall thickness of cylinder sidewall but may not be less than 0.050 inch. In all other cases, thickness to be no less than prescribed minimum wall.

(g) **Heat treatment.** The completed cylinders must be uniformly and properly heated prior to tests. Heat treatment of the cylinders of the authorized analysis must be as follows:

(1) *All cylinders must be quenched by oil, or other suitable medium.*

(2) *The steel temperature* on quenching must be that recommended for the steel analysis, but may not exceed 1750 °F.

(3) *The steel* must be tempered at a temperature most suitable for the particular steel analysis but not less than 850 °F.

(4) *All cylinders* must be inspected by the magnetic particle or dye penetrant method to detect the presence of quenching cracks. Any cylinder found to have a quenching crack must be rejected and may not be requalified.

(h) **Openings in cylinders and connections** (valves, fuse plugs, etc.) for those openings. Threads conforming to the following are required on openings:

(1) *Threads must be clean cut, even, without cracks, and to gauge.*

(2) *Taper threads,* when used, must be of length not less than as specified for National Gas Tapered Thread (NGT) as required by American Standard Compressed Gas Cylinder Valve Outlet and Inlet Connections.

(3) *Straight threads* having at least 6 engaged threads are authorized. Straight threads must have a tight fit and a calculated shear stress of at least 10 times the test pressure of the cylinder. Gaskets, adequate to prevent leakage, are required.

(i) **Hydrostatic test.** Each cylinder must withstand a hydrostatic test, as follows:

(1) *The test* must be by water-jacket, or other suitable method, operated so as to obtain accurate data. Pressure gauge must permit reading to an accuracy of 1 percent. The expansion gauge must permit reading of total expansion to an accuracy either of 1 percent of 0.1 cubic centimeter.

(2) *Pressure must be maintained* for at least 30 seconds and sufficiently longer to ensure complete expansion. Any internal pressure applied after heat treatment and previous to the official test may not exceed 90 percent of the test pressure. If, due to failure of the test apparatus, the test pressure cannot be maintained, the test may be repeated at a pressure increased by 10 percent or 100 psig, which ever is the lower.

(3) *Permanent volumetric expansion* may not exceed 10 percent of total volumetric expansion at test pressure.

(4) *Each cylinder must be tested to at least 5/3 times service pressure.*

(j) **Cycling tests.** Prior to the initial shipment of any specific cylinder design, cyclic pressurization tests must have been performed on at least three representative samples without failure as follows:

(1) *Pressurization must be performed* hydrostatically between approximately zero psig and the service pressure at a rate not in excess of 10 cycles per minute. Adequate recording instrumentation must be provided if equipment is to be left unattended for periods of time.

(2) *Tests prescribed* in paragraph (j)(1) of this section must be repeated on one random sample out of each lot of cylinders. The cylinder may then be subjected to a burst test.

(3) *A lot is defined* as a group of cylinders fabricated from the same heat of steel, manufactured by the same process and heat treated in the same equipment under the same conditions of time, temperature, and atmosphere, and may not exceed a quantity of 200 cylinders.

(4) *All cylinders used in cycling tests* must be destroyed.

(k) **Burst test.** One cylinder taken at random out of each lot of cylinders must be hydrostatically tested to destruction.

(l) **Flattening test.** A flattening test must be performed on one cylinder taken at random out of each lot of 200 or less, by placing the cylinder between wedge shaped knife edges having a 60° included angle, rounded to 1/2-inch radius. The longitudinal axis of the cylinder must be at a 90-degree angle to knife edges during the test. For lots of 30 or less, flattening tests are authorized to be made on a ring at least 8 inches long cut from each cylinder and subjected to same heat treatment as the finished cylinder.

(m) **Physical tests.** A physical test must be conducted to determine yield strength, tensile strength, elongation, and reduction of area of material, as follows:

(1) *Test is required* on 2 specimens cut from 1 cylinder taken at random out of each lot of cylinders.

(2) *Specimens must conform to the following:*

(i) *A gauge length* of at least 24 times the thickness with a width not over six times the thickness. The specimen, exclusive of grip ends, may not be flattened. Grip ends may be flattened to within one inch of each end of the reduced section. When size of cylinder does not permit securing straight specimens, the specimens may be taken in any location or direction and may be straightened or flattened cold by pressure only, not by blows. When specimens are so taken and prepared, the inspector's report must show in connection with the record of physical tests detailed information in regard to such specimens.

(ii) *Heating of a specimen for any purpose is not authorized.*

(3) *The yield strength* in tension must be the stress corresponding to a permanent strain of 0.2 percent of the gauge length.

(i) *The yield strength* must be determined by either the "offset" method or the "extension under load" method as prescribed in ASTM E 8 (incorporated by reference; see §171.7 of this subchapter).

(ii) *In using the "extension under load" method,* the total strain (or "extension under load") corresponding to the stress at which the 0.2 percent permanent strain occurs may be determined with sufficient accuracy by calculating the elastic extension of the gauge length under appropriate load and adding thereto 0.2 percent of the gauge length. Elastic extension calculations must be based on an elastic modulus of 30,000,000. In the event of controversy, the entire stress-strain diagram must be plotted and the yield strength determined from the 0.2 percent offset.

(iii) *For the purpose of strain measurement,* the initial strain must be set while the specimen is under a stress of 12,000 psi, the strain indicator reading being set at the calculated corresponding strain.

(iv) *Cross-head speed* of the testing machine may not exceed 1/8 inch per minute during yield strength determination.

(n) **Magnetic particle inspection.** Inspection must be performed on the inside of each container before closing and externally on each finished container after heat treatment. Evidence of discontinuities, which in the opinion of a qualified inspector may appreciably weaken or decrease the durability of the cylinder, must be cause for rejection.

(o) **Leakage test.** All spun cylinders and plugged cylinders must be tested for leakage by dry gas or dry air pressure after the bottom has been cleaned and is free from all moisture, subject to the following conditions and limitations:

(1) *Pressure, approximately the same as* but not less than service pressure, must be applied to one side of the finished bottom over an area of at least 1/16 of the total area of the bottom but not less than 3/4 inch in diameter, including the closure, for at least one minute, during which time the other side of the bottom exposed to pressure must be covered with water and closely examined for indications of leakage. Except as provided in paragraph (q) of this section, a cylinder must be rejected if there is leakage.

(2) *A spun cylinder* is one in which an end closure in the finished cylinder has been welded by the spinning process.

(3) *A plugged cylinder* is one in which a permanent closure in the bottom of a finished cylinder has been affected by a plug.

(4) *As a safety precaution,* if the manufacturer elects to make this test before the hydrostatic test, the manufacturer should design the test apparatus so that the pressure is applied to the smallest area practicable, around the point of closure, and so as to use the smallest possible volume of air or gas.

(p) **Acceptable results of tests.** Results of the flattening test, physical tests, burst test, and cycling test must conform to the following:

(1) *Flattening required* without cracking to ten times the wall thickness of the cylinder.

(2) *Physical tests:*

(i) *An elongation* of at least 6 percent for a gauge length of 24 times the wall thickness.

(ii) *The tensile strength may not exceed 165,000 p.s.i.*

(3) *The burst pressure must be at least 4/3 times the test pressure.*

(4) *Cycling-at least 10,000 pressurizations.*

(q) **Rejected cylinders.** Reheat treatment is authorized for rejected cylinders. Subsequent thereto, cylinders must pass all prescribed tests to be acceptable. Repair by welding or spinning is not authorized. For each cylinder subjected to reheat treatment during original manufacture, sidewall measurements must be made to verify that the minimum sidewall thickness meets specification requirements after the final heat treatment.

(r) **Marking.**

(1) *Cylinders must be marked* by low stress type steel stamping in an area and to a depth which will insure that the wall thickness measured from the root of the stamping to the interior surface is equal to or greater than the minimum prescribed wall thickness. Stamping must be permanent and legible. Stamping on side wall not authorized.

(2) *The rejection elastic expansion (REE),* in cubic cm (cc), must be marked on the cylinder near the date of test. The REE for a cylinder is 1.05 times its original elastic expansion.

(3) *Name plates are authorized,* provided that they can be permanently and securely attached to the cylinder. Attachment by either brazing or welding is not permitted. Attachment by soldering is permitted provided steel temperature does not exceed 500 ^{o}F.

(s) **Inspector's report.** In addition to the requirements of §178.35, the inspector's report must indicate the rejection elastic expansion (REE), in cubic cm (cc).

§178.45 Specification 3T seamless steel cylinder.

(a) **Type, size, and service pressure.** A DOT 3T cylinder is a seamless steel cylinder with a minimum water capacity of 1,000 pounds and a minimum service pressure of 1,800 psig. Each cylinder must have integrally formed heads concave to pressure at both ends. The inside head shape must be hemispherical, ellipsoidal in which the major axis is two times the minor axis, or a dished shape falling within these two limits. Permanent closures formed by spinning are prohibited.

(b) **Material, steel.** Only open hearth, basic oxygen, or electric furnace process steel of uniform quality is authorized. The steel analysis must conform to the following:

Analysis Tolerances

Element	Ladle analysis	Check analysis	
		Under	Over
Carbon	0.35 to 0.50	0.03	0.04
Manganese	0.75 to 1.05	0.04	0.04
Phosphorus (max)	0.035		0.01
Sulphur (max)	0.04		0.01
Silicon	0.15 to 0.35	0.02	0.03
Chromium	0.80 to 1.15	0.05	0.05
Molybdenum	0.15 to 0.25	0.02	0.02

(1) *A heat of steel* made under the specifications in the table in this paragraph (b), the ladle analysis of which is slightly out of the specified range, is acceptable if satisfactory in all other aspects. However, the check analysis tolerances shown in the table in this paragraph (b) may not be exceeded except as approved by the Department.

(2) *Material with* seams, cracks, laminations, or other injurious defects is not permitted.

(3) *Material used must be identified by any suitable method.*

(c) **Manufacture.** General manufacturing requirements are as follows:

(1) *Surface finish must be uniform and reasonably smooth.*

(2) *Inside surfaces must be clean, dry, and free of loose particles.*

(3) *No defect* of any kind is permitted if it is likely to weaken a finished cylinder.

(4) *If the cylinder surface* is not originally free from the defects, the surface may be machined or otherwise treated to eliminate these defects provided the minimum wall thickness is maintained.

(5) *Welding or brazing on a cylinder is not permitted.*

(d) **Wall thickness.** The minimum wall thickness must be such that the wall stress at the minimum specified test pressure does not exceed 67 percent of the minimum tensile strength of the steel as determined by the physical tests required in paragraphs (j) and (k) of this section. A wall stress of more than 90,500 p.s.i. is not permitted. The minimum wall thickness for any cylinder may not be less than 0.225 inch.

(1) *Calculation of the stress* for cylinders must be made by the following formula:

$S = [P(1.3D^2 + 0.4d^2)] / (D^2 - d^2)$

Where:

S = Wall stress in psi;

P = Minimum test pressure, at least 5/3 service pressure;

D = Outside diameter in inches;

d = Inside diameter in inches.

(2) *Each cylinder* must meet the following additional requirement which assumes a cylinder horizontally supported at its two ends and uniformly loaded over its entire length. This load consists of the weight per inch of length of the straight cylindrical portion filled with water compressed to the specified test pressure. The wall thickness must be increased when necessary to meet this additional requirement:

(i) *The sum* of two times the maximum tensile stress in the bottom fibers due to bending (see paragraph (d)(2)(ii) of this section), plus the maximum tensile stress in the same fibers due to hydrostatic testing (see paragraph (d)(2)(iii) of this section) may not exceed 80 percent of the minimum yield strength of the steel at this maximum stress.

(ii) *The following formula* must be used to calculate the maximum tensile stress due to bending:

$S = Mc / I$

Where:

S = Tensile stress in psi;

M = Bending moment in inch-pounds ($wl^2 / 8$);

I = Moment of inertia — 0.04909 ($D^4 - d^4$) in inches fourth;

c = Radius (D / 2) of cylinder in inches;

w = Weight per inch of cylinder filled with water;

l = Length of cylinder in inches;

D = Outside diameter in inches;

d = Inside diameter in inches.

(iii) *The following formula* must be used to calculate the maximum longitudinal tensile stress due to hydrostatic test pressure:

$S = A_1 P / A_2$

Where:

S = Tensile stress in psi;

A_1 = Internal area in cross section of cylinder in square inches;

P = Hydrostatic test pressure-psig;

A_2 = Area of metal in cross section of cylinder in square inches.

(e) **Heat treatment.** Each completed cylinder must be uniformly and properly heat treated prior to testing, as follows:

(1) *Each cylinder* must be heated and held at the proper temperature for at least one hour per inch of thickness based on the maximum thickness of the cylinder and then quenched in a suitable liquid medium having a cooling rate not in excess of 80 percent of water. The steel temperature on quenching must be that recommended for the steel analysis, but it must never exceed 1750 °F.

(2) *After quenching,* each cylinder must be reheated to a temperature below the transformation range but not less than 1050 °F, and must be held at this temperature for at least one hour per inch of thickness based on the maximum thickness of the cylinder. Each cylinder must then be cooled under conditions recommended for the steel.

(f) **Openings.** Openings in cylinders must comply with the following:

(1) *Openings are permitted on heads only.*

(2) *The size* of any centered opening in a head may not exceed one half the outside diameter of the cylinder.

(3) *Openings in a head* must have ligaments between openings of at least three times the average of their hole diameter. No off-center opening may exceed 2.625 inches in diameter.

(4) *All openings must be circular.*

(5) *All openings must be threaded.* Threads must be in compliance with the following:

(i) *Each thread* must be clean cut, even, without any checks, and to gauge.

(ii) *Taper threads,* when used, must be the American Standard Pipe thread (NPT) type and must be in compliance with the requirements of NBS Handbook H-28, Part II, Section VII.

(iii) *Taper threads* conforming to National Gas Taper thread (NGT) standards must be in compliance with the requirements of NBS Handbook H-28, Part II, Sections VII and IX.

(iv) *Straight threads* conforming with National Gas Straight thread (NGS) standards are authorized. These threads must be in compliance with the requirements of NBS Handbook H-28, Part II, Sections VII and IX.

(g) **Hydrostatic test.** Each cylinder must be tested at an internal pressure by the water jacket method or other suitable method, conforming to the following requirements:

(1) *The testing apparatus* must be operated in a manner that will obtain accurate data. Any pressure gauge used must permit reading to an accuracy of one percent. Any expansion gauge used must permit reading of the total expansion to an accuracy of one percent.

(2) *Any internal pressure* applied to the cylinder after heat treatment and before the official test may not exceed 90 percent of the test pressure.

(3) *The pressure* must be maintained sufficiently long to assure complete expansion of the cylinder. In no case may the pressure be held less than 30 seconds.

(4) *If, due to failure* of the test apparatus, the required test pressure cannot be maintained, the test must be repeated at a pressure increased by 10 percent or 100 psig, whichever is lower or, the cylinder must be reheat treated.

(5) *Permanent volumetric expansion* of the cylinder may not exceed 10 percent of its total volumetric expansion at the required test pressure.

(6) *Each cylinder* must be tested to at least 5/3 times its service pressure.

(h) **Ultrasonic examination.** After the hydrostatic test, the cylindrical section of each vessel must be examined in accordance with ASTM Standard E 213 (incorporated by reference; see §171.7 of this subchapter). The equipment used must be calibrated to detect a notch equal to five percent of the design minimum wall thickness. Any discontinuity indication greater than that produced by the five percent notch must be cause for rejection of the cylinder, unless the discontinuity is repaired within the requirements of this specification.

(i) **Basic requirements for tension and Charpy impact tests.** Cylinders must be subjected to a tension and Charpy impact as follows:

(1) *When the cylinders* are heat treated in a batch furnace, two tension specimens and three Charpy impact specimens must be tested from one of the cylinders or a test ring from each batch. The lot size represented by these tests may not exceed 200 cylinders.

(2) *When the cylinders* are heat treated in a continuous furnace, two tension specimens and three Charpy impact specimens must be tested from one of the cylinders or a test ring from each four hours or less of production. However, in no case may a test lot based on this production period exceed 200 cylinders.

(3) *Each specimen* for the tension and Charpy impact tests must be taken from the side wall of a cylinder or from a ring which has been heat treated with the finished cylinders of which the specimens must be representative. The axis of the specimens must be parallel to the axis of the cylinder. Each cylinder or ring specimen for test must be of the same diameter, thickness, and metal as the finished cylinders they represent. A test ring must be at least 24 inches long with ends covered during the heat treatment process so as to simulate the heat treatment process of the finished cylinders it represents.

(4) *A test cylinder or test ring* need represent only one of the heats in a furnace batch provided the other heats in the batch have previ-

ously been tested and have passed the tests and that such tests do not represent more than 200 cylinders from any one heat.

(5) *The test results* must conform to the requirements specified in paragraphs (j) and (k) of this section.

(6) *When the test results* do not conform to the requirements specified, the cylinders represented by the tests may be reheat treated and the tests repeated. Paragraph (i)(5) of this section applies to any retesting.

(j) **Basic conditions for acceptable physical testing.** The following criteria must be followed to obtain acceptable physical test results:

(1) *Each tension specimen* must have a gauge length of two inches with a width not exceeding one and one-half inches. Except for the grip ends, the specimen may not be flattened. The grip ends may be flattened to within one inch of each end of the reduced section.

(2) *A specimen* may not be heated after heat treatment specified in paragraph (d) of this section.

(3) *The yield strength in tension* must be the stress corresponding to a permanent strain of 0.2 percent of the gage length.

(i) *This yield strength* must be determined by the "offset" method or the "extension under load" method described in ASTM E 8 (incorporated by reference; see §171.7 of this subchapter).

(ii) *For the "extension under load" method,* the total strain (or extension under load) corresponding to the stress at which the 0.2 percent permanent strain occurs may be determined with sufficient accuracy by calculating the elastic extension of the gage length under appropriate load and adding thereto 0.2 percent of the gage length. Elastic extension calculations must be based on an elastic modulus of 30,000,000. However, when the degree of accuracy of this method is questionable the entire stress-strain diagram must be plotted and the yield strength determined from the 0.2 percent offset.

(iii) *For the purpose* of strain measurement, the initial strain must be set with the specimen under a stress of 12,000 p.s.i. and the strain indicator reading set at the calculated corresponding strain.

(iv) *The cross-head speed* of the testing machine may not exceed 1/8 inch per minute during the determination of yield strength.

(4) *Each impact specimen* must be Charpy V-notch type size 10 mm x 10 mm taken in accordance with paragraph 11 of ASTM Standard A-333-67. When a reduced size specimen is used, it must be the largest size obtainable.

(k) **Acceptable physical test results.** Results of physical tests must conform to the following:

(1) *The tensile strength may not exceed 155,000 p.s.i.*

(2) *The elongation* must be at least 16 percent for a two-inch gage length.

(3) *The Charpy* V-notch impact properties for the three impact specimens which must be tested at 0 °F may not be less than the values shown as follows:

Size of specimen (mm)	Average value for acceptance (3 specimens)	Minimum value (1 specimen only of the 3)
10.0 x 10.0	25.0 ft. lbs.	20.0 ft. lbs.
10.0 x 7.5	21.0 ft. lbs.	17.0 ft. lbs.
10.0 x 5.0	17.0 ft. lbs.	14.0 ft. lbs.

(4) *After the final heat treatment,* each vessel must be hardness tested on the cylindrical section. The tensile strength equivalent of the hardness number obtained may not be more than 165,000 p.s.i. (Rc 36). When the result of a hardness test exceeds the maximum permitted, two or more retests may be made; however, the hardness number obtained in each retest may not exceed the maximum permitted.

(l) **Rejected cylinders.** Reheat treatment is authorized for rejected cylinders. However, each reheat treated cylinder must subsequently pass all the prescribed tests. Repair by welding is not authorized.

(m) **Markings.** Marking must be done by stamping into the metal of the cylinder. All markings must be legible and located on a shoulder.

(n) **Inspector's report.** In addition to the requirements of §178.35, the inspector's report for the physical test report, must indicate the average value for three specimens and the minimum value for one specimen for each lot number.

§178.46 Specification 3AL seamless aluminum cylinders.

(a) **Size and service pressure.** A DOT 3AL cylinder is a seamless aluminum cylinder with a maximum water capacity of 1000 pounds and minimum service pressure of 150 psig.

(b) **Authorized material and identification of material.** The material of construction must meet the following conditions:

(1) *Starting stock must be cast stock or traceable to cast stock.*

(2) *Material with seams,* cracks, laminations, or other defects likely to weaken the finished cylinder may not be used.

(3) *Material must be identified* by a suitable method that will identify the alloy, the aluminum producer's cast number, the solution heat treat batch number and the lot number.

(4) *The material must be of uniform quality.* Only the following heat treatable aluminum alloys in table 1 and 2 are permitted as follows:

Table 1 - Heat or Cast Analysis for Aluminum; Similar to "Aluminum Association"[1] Alloy 6061 [Chemical Analysis in Weight Percent][2]

Si min/max	Fe max	Cu min/max	Mn max	Mg min/max	Cr min/max	Zn max	Ti max	Pb max	Bi max	Other each max	Other total max	A1
0.4/0.8	0.7	0.15/0.4	0.15	0.8/1.2	0.4/0.35	0.25	0.15	0.005	0.005	0.05	0.15	Bal.

1. The "Aluminum Association" refers to "Aluminum Standards and Data 1993," published by the Aluminum Association Inc.
2. Except for "Pb" and "Bi," the chemical composition corresponds with that of Table 1 of ASTM B221 for Aluminum Association alloy 6061.

Table 2 - Mechanical Property Limits

Alloy and temper	Tensile strength — PSI		Elongation — percent minimum for 2" or 4D[1] size specimen
	Ultimate — minimum	Yield — minimum	
6061-T6	38,000	35,000	[2]14

1. "D" represents specimen diameters. When the cylinder wall is greater than 3/16-inch thick, a retest without reheat treatment using the 4D size specimen is authorized if the test using the 2 inch size specimen fails to meet elongation requirements.
2. When cylinder wall is not over 3/16-inch thick, 10 percent elongation is authorized when using a 24t x 6t size test specimen.

(5) *All starting stock* must be 100 percent ultrasonically inspected, along the length at right angles to the central axis from two positions at 90° to one another. The equipment and continuous scanning procedure must be capable of detecting and rejecting internal defects such as cracks which have an ultrasonic response greater than that of a calibration block with a 5/64-inch diameter flat bottomed hole.

(6) *Cast stock* must have uniform equiaxed grain structure not to exceed 500 microns maximum.

(7) *Any starting stock* not complying with the provisions of paragraphs (b)(1) through (b)(6) of this section must be rejected.

(c) **Manufacture.** Cylinders must be manufactured in accordance with the following requirements:

(1) *Cylinder shells* must be manufactured by the backward extrusion method and have a cleanliness level adequate to ensure proper inspection. No fissure or other defect is acceptable that is likely to weaken the finished cylinder below the design strength requirements. A reasonably smooth and uniform surface finish is required. If not originally free from such defects, the surface may be machined or otherwise conditioned to eliminate these defects.

(2) *Thickness of the cylinder base* may not be less than the prescribed minimum wall thickness of the cylindrical shell. The cylinder base must have a basic torispherical, hemispherical, or ellipsoidal interior base configuration where the dish radius is no greater than 1.2 times the inside diameter of the shell. The knuckle radius may not be less than 12 percent of the inside diameter of the shell. The interior base contour may deviate from the true torispherical, hemispherical or ellipsoidal configuration provided that —

(i) *Any areas of deviation* are accompanied by an increase in base thickness;

(ii) *All radii of merging surfaces* are equal to or greater than the knuckle radius;

(iii) *Each design* has been qualified by successfully passing the cycling tests in this paragraph (c); and

(iv) *Detailed specifications* of the base design are available to the inspector.

(3) *For free standing cylinders,* the base thickness must be at least two times the minimum wall thickness along the line of contact between the cylinder base and the floor when the cylinders are in the vertical position.

(4) *Welding or brazing is prohibited.*

(5) *Each new design* and any significant change to any acceptable design must be qualified for production by testing prototype samples as follows:

(i) *Three samples* must be subjected to 100,000 pressure reversal cycles between zero and service pressure or 10,000 pressure reversal cycles between zero and test pressure, at a rate not in excess of 10 cycles per minute without failure.

(ii) *Three samples* must be pressurized to destruction and failure may not occur at less than 2.5 times the marked cylinder service pressure. Each cylinder must remain in one piece. Failure must initiate in the cylinder sidewall in a longitudinal direction. Rate of pressurization may not exceed 200 psig per second.

(6) *In this specification* "significant change" means a 10 percent or greater change in cylinder wall thickness, service pressure, or diameter; a 30 percent or greater change in water capacity or base thickness; any change in material; over 100 percent increase in size of openings; or any change in the number of openings.

(d) **Wall thickness.** The minimum wall thickness must be such that the wall stress at the minimum specified test pressure will not exceed 80 percent of the minimum yield strength nor exceed 67 percent of the minimum ultimate tensile strength as verified by physical tests in paragraph (i) of this section. The minimum wall thickness for any cylinder with an outside diameter greater than 5 inches must be 0.125 inch. Calculations must be made by the following formula:

$S = [P(1.3D^2 + 0.4d^2)] / (D^2 - d^2)$

Where:

S = Wall stress in psi;

P = Prescribed minimum test pressure in psig (see paragraph (g) of this section);

D = Outside diameter in inches; and

d = Inside diameter in inches.

(e) **Openings.** Openings must comply with the following requirements:

(1) *Openings are permitted in heads only.*

(2) *The size* of any centered opening in a head may not exceed one-half the outside diameter of the cylinder.

(3) *Other openings are permitted in the head of a cylinder if:*

(i) *Each opening* does not exceed 2.625 inches in diameter, or one-half the outside diameter of the cylinder; whichever is less;

(ii) *Each opening is separated from each other by a ligament; and*

(iii) *Each ligament* which separates two openings must be at least three times the average of the diameters of the two openings.

(4) *All openings must be circular.*

(5) *All openings* must be threaded. Threads must comply with the following:

(i) *Each thread* must be clean cut, even, without checks, and to gauge.

(ii) *Taper threads,* when used, must conform to one of the following:

[A] American Standard Pipe Thread (NPT) type, conforming to the requirements of Federal Standard H-28, Section 7;

[B] National Gas Taper Thread (NGT) type, conforming to the requirements of Federal Standard H-28, Sections 7 and 9; or

[C] Other taper threads conforming to other standards may be used provided the length is not less than that specified for NPT threads.

(iii) *Straight threads,* when used, must conform to one of the following:

[A] National Gas Straight Thread (NGS) type, conforming to the requirements of Federal Standard H-28, Sections 7 and 9;

[B] Unified Thread (UN) type, conforming to the requirements of Federal Standard H-28, Section 2;

[C] Controlled Radius Root Thread (UN) type, conforming to the requirements of Federal Standard H-28, Section 4; or

[D] Other straight threads conforming to other recognized standards may be used provided that the requirements in paragraph (e)(5)(iv) of this section are met.

(iv) *All straight threads* must have at least 6 engaged threads, a tight fit, and a factor of safety in shear of at least 10 at the test pressure of the cylinder. Shear stress must be calculated by using the appropriate thread shear area in accordance with Federal Standard H-28, Appendix A5, Section 3.

(f) **Heat treatment.** Prior to any test, all cylinders must be subjected to a solution heat treatment and aging treatment appropriate for the aluminum alloy used.

(g) **Hydrostatic test.** Each cylinder must be subjected to an internal test pressure using the water jacket equipment and method or other suitable equipment and method and comply with the following requirements:

(1) *The testing apparatus* must be operated in a manner so as to obtain accurate data. The pressure gauge used must permit reading to an accuracy of one percent. The expansion gauge must permit reading the total expansion to an accuracy of either one percent or 0.1 cubic centimeter.

(2) *The test pressure* must be maintained for a sufficient period of time to assure complete expansion of the cylinder. In no case may the pressure be held less than 30 seconds. If, due to failure of the test apparatus, the required test pressure cannot be maintained, the test may be repeated at a pressure increased by 10 percent or 100 psig, whichever is lower. If the test apparatus again fails to maintain the test pressure, the cylinder being tested must be rejected. Any internal pressure applied to the cylinder before any official test may not exceed 90 percent of the test pressure.

(3) *The minimum test pressure is the greatest of the following:*

(i) *450 psig regardless of service pressure;*

(ii) *Two times* the service pressure for cylinders having service pressure less than 500 psig; or

(iii) *Five-thirds times* the service pressure for cylinders having a service pressure of at least 500 psig.

(4) *Permanent volumetric expansion* may not exceed 10 percent of total volumetric expansion at test pressure.

(h) **Flattening test.** One cylinder taken at random out of each lot must be subjected to a flattening test as follows:

(1) *The test* must be between knife edges, wedge shaped, having a 60° included angle, and rounded in accordance with the following table. The longitudinal axis of the cylinder must be at an angle 90° to the knife edges during the test. The flattening test table is as follows:

Table 3 - Flattening Test Table

Cylinder wall thickness in inches	Radius in inches
Under .150	.500
.150 to .249	.875
.250 to .349	1.500
.350 to .449	2.125
.450 to .549	2.750
.550 to .649	3.500
.650 to .749	4.125

(2) *An alternate bend test* in accordance with ASTM E 290 using a mandrel diameter not more than 6 times the wall thickness is authorized to qualify lots that fail the flattening test of this section without reheat treatment. If used, this test must be performed on two samples from one cylinder taken at random out of each lot of 200 cylinders or less.

(3) *Each test cylinder* must withstand flattening to nine times the wall thickness without cracking. When the alternate bend test is used, the test specimens must remain uncracked when bent inward around a mandrel in the direction of curvature of the cylinder wall until the interior edges are at a distance apart not greater than the diameter of the mandrel.

(i) **Mechanical properties test.** Two test specimens cut from one cylinder representing each lot of 200 cylinders or less must be subjected to the mechanical properties test, as follows:

(1) *The results of the test* must conform to at least the minimum acceptable mechanical property limits for aluminum alloys as specified in paragraph (b) of this section.

(2) *Specimens must be* 4D bar or gauge length 2 inches with width not over 1 1/2 inch taken in the direction of extrusion approximately 180° from each other; provided that gauge length at least 24 times thickness with width not over 6 times thickness is authorized, when cylinder wall is not over 3/16 inch thick. The specimen, exclusive of grip ends, may not be flattened. Grip ends may be flattened to within one inch of each end of the reduced section. When the size of the cylinder does not permit securing straight specimens, the specimens may be taken in any location or direction and may be straightened or flattened cold by pressure only, not by blows. When such specimens are used, the inspector's report must show that the specimens were so taken and prepared. Heating of specimens for any purpose is forbidden.

(3) *The yield strength* in tension must be the stress corresponding to a permanent strain of 0.2 percent of the gauge length.

(i) *The yield strength* must be determined by either the "offset" method or the "extension under load" method as prescribed in ASTM Standard B-557.

(ii) *In using the "extension under load" method,* the total strain (or "extension under load") corresponding to the stress at which the 0.2 percent permanent strain occurs may be determined with sufficient accuracy by calculating the elastic extension of the gauge length under appropriate load and adding thereto 0.2 percent of the gauge length. Elastic extension calculations must be based on an elastic modulus of 10,000,000 psi. In the event of controversy, the entire stress-strain diagram must be plotted and the yield strength determined from the 0.2 percent offset.

(iii) *For the purpose* of strain measurement, the initial strain must be set while the specimen is under a stress of 6,000 psi, the strain indicator reading being set at the calculated corresponding strain.

(iv) *Cross-head speed* of the testing machine may not exceed 1/8 inch per minute during yield strength determination.

(j) **Rejected cylinder.** Reheat treatment of rejected cylinders is authorized one time. Subsequent thereto, cylinders must pass all prescribed tests to be acceptable.

(k) **Duties of inspector.** In addition to the requirements of §178.35, the inspector shall:

(1) *Verify compliance* with the provisions of paragraph (b) of this section by:

(i) *Performing or witnessing* the performance of the chemical analyses on each melt or cast lot or other unit of starting material; or

(ii) *Obtaining a certified chemical analysis* from the material or cylinder manufacturer for each melt, or cast of material; or

(iii) *Obtaining a certified check analysis* on one cylinder out of each lot of 200 cylinders or less, if a certificate containing data to indicate compliance with the material specification is obtained.

(2) *The inspector* shall verify ultrasonic inspection of all material by inspection or by obtaining the material producer's certificate of ultrasonic inspection. Ultrasonic inspection must be performed or verified as having been performed in accordance with paragraph (c) of this section.

(3) *The inspector* must also determine that each cylinder complies with this specification by:

(i) *Selecting the samples* for check analyses performed by other than the material producer;

(ii) *Verifying that* the prescribed minimum thickness was met by measuring or witnessing the measurement of the wall thickness; and

(iii) *Verifying that the identification of material is proper.*

(4) *Prior to initial production of any* design or design change, verify that the design qualification tests prescribed in paragraph (c)(6) of this section have been performed with acceptable results.

(l) **Definitions.**

(1) *In this specification,* a "lot" means a group of cylinders successively produced having the same:

(i) *Size and configuration;*

(ii) *Specified material of construction;*

(iii) *Process of manufacture and heat treatment;*

(iv) *Equipment of manufacture and heat treatment; and*

(v) *Conditions of time,* temperature and atmosphere during heat treatment.

(2) *In no case* may the lot size exceed 200 cylinders, but any cylinder processed for use in the required destructive physical testing need not be counted as being one of the 200.

(m) **Inspector's report.** In addition to the information required by §178.35, the record of chemical analyses must also include the alloy designation, and applicable information on iron, titanium, zinc, magnesium and any other applicable element used in the construction of the cylinder.

§178.47 Specification 4DS welded stainless steel cylinders for aircraft use.

(a) **Type, size, and service pressure.** A DOT 4DS cylinder is either a welded stainless steel sphere (two seamless hemispheres) or circumferentially welded cylinder both with a water capacity of not over 100 pounds and a service pressure of at least 500 but not over 900 psig.

(b) **Steel.** Types 304, 321 and 347 stainless steel are authorized with proper welding procedure. A heat of steel made under the specifications in table 1 in this paragraph (b), check chemical analysis of which is slightly out of the specified range, is acceptable, if satisfactory in all other respects, provided the tolerances shown in table 2 in this paragraph (b) are not exceeded, except as approved by Associate Administrator. The following chemical analyses are authorized:

Table 1 - Authorized Materials

	Stainless steels		
	304 (percent)	321 (percent)	347 (percent)
Carbon (max)	0.08	0.08	0.08
Manganese (max)	2.00	2.00	2.00
Phosphorus (max)	.030	.030	.030
Sulphur (max)	.030	.030	.030
Silicon (max)	.75	.75	.75
Nickel	8.0/11.0	9.0/13.0	9.0/13.0
Chromium	18.0/20.0	17.0/20.0	17.0/20.0
Molybdenum			
Titanium		(1)	
Columbium			(2)

1. Titanium may not be more than 5C and not more than 0.60%.
2. Columbium may not be less than 10C and not more than 1.0%.

Table 2 - Check Analysis Tolerances

Element	Limit or maximum specified (percent)	Tolerance (percent) over the maximum limit or under the minimum limit	
		Under minimum limit	Over maximum limit
Carbon	To 0.15 incl	0.01	0.01
Manganese	Over 1.15 to 2.50 incl	0.05	0.05
Phosphorus[1]	All ranges		.01
Sulphur	All ranges		.01
Silicon	Over 0.30 to 1.00 incl	.05	.05
Nickel	Over 5.30 to 10.00 incl	.10	.10
	Over 10.00 to 14.00 incl	.15	.15
Chromium	Over 15.00 to 20.00 incl	.20	.20
Titanium	All ranges	.05	.05
Columbium	All ranges	.05	.05

1. Rephosphorized steels not subject to check analysis for phosphorus.

(c) **Identification of material.** Materials must be identified by any suitable method.

(d) **Manufacture.** Cylinders must be manufactured using equipment and processes adequate to ensure that each cylinder produced conforms to the requirements of this subpart. No defect is permitted that is likely to weaken the finished cylinder appreciably, a reasonably smooth and uniform surface finish is required. No abrupt change in wall thickness is permitted. Welding procedures and operators must be qualified in accordance with CGA Pamphlet C-3 (incorporated by reference; see §171.7 of this subchapter). All seams of the sphere or cylinder must be fusion welded. Seams must be of the butt type and means must be provided for accomplishing complete penetration of the joint.

(e) **Attachments.** Attachments to the container are authorized by fusion welding provided that such attachments are made of weldable stainless steel in accordance with paragraph (b) of this section.

(f) **Wall thickness.** The minimum wall thickness must be such that the wall stress at the minimum specified test pressure may not be over 60,000 psig. A minimum wall thickness of 0.040 inch is required for any diameter container. Calculations must be made by the following formulas:

(1) *Calculation for sphere must be made by the formula:*

$S = PD / 4tE$

Where:

S = Wall stress in psi;

P = Test pressure prescribed for water jacket test, i.e., at least two times service pressure, in psig;

D = Outside diameter in inches;

t = Minimum wall thickness in inches;

E = 0.85 (provides 85 percent weld efficiency factor which must be applied in the girth weld area and heat zones which zone must extend a distance of 6 times wall thickness from center of weld);

E = 1.0 (for all other areas).

(2) *Calculation for a cylinder must be made by the formula:*

$S = [P(1.3D^2 + 0.4d^2)] / (D^2 - d^2)$

Where:

S = Wall stress in psi;

P = Test pressure prescribed for water jacket test, i.e., at least two times service pressure, in psig;

D = Outside diameter in inches;

d = Inside diameter in inches.

(g) **Heat treatment.** The seamless hemispheres and cylinders may be stress relieved or annealed for forming. Welded container must be stress relieved at a temperature of 775 °F $\pm$ 25° after process treatment and before hydrostatic test.

(h) **Openings in container.** Openings must comply with the following:

(1) *Each opening* in the container must be provided with a fitting, boss or pad of weldable stainless steel securely attached to the container by fusion welding.

(2) *Attachments to a fitting,* boss, or pad must be adequate to prevent leakage. Threads must comply with the following:

(i) *Threads must be* clean cut, even, without checks, and tapped to gauge.

(ii) *Taper threads* to be of length not less than as specified for American Standard taper pipe threads.

(iii) *Straight threads* having at least 4 engaged threads, to have tight fit and calculated shear strength at least 10 times the test pressure of the container; gaskets required, adequate to prevent leakage.

(i) **Process treatment.** Each container must be hydraulically pressurized in a water jacket to at least 100 percent, but not more than 110 percent, of the test pressure and maintained at this pressure for a minimum of 3 minutes. Total and permanent expansion must be recorded and included in the inspector's report.

(j) **Hydrostatic test.** Each cylinder must successfully withstand a hydrostatic test as follows:

(1) *The test* must be by water-jacket, operated so as to obtain accurate data. The pressure gauge must permit reading to an accuracy of 1 percent. The expansion gauge must permit reading of total expansion to an accuracy either of 1 percent or 0.1 cubic centimeter.

(2) *Pressure must be maintained* for at least 30 seconds and sufficiently longer to ensure complete expansion. If, due to failure of the test apparatus, the test pressure cannot be maintained, the test may be repeated at a pressure increased by 10 percent or 100 psig, whichever is the lower.

(3) *Permanent volumetric expansion* may not exceed 10 percent of total volumetric expansion at test pressure.

(4) *Each container must be tested to at least 2 times service pressure.*

(5) *Container must then be inspected.* Any wall thickness lower than that required by paragraph (f) of this section must be cause for rejection. Bulges and cracks must be cause for rejection. Welded joint defects exceeding requirements of paragraph (k) of this section must be cause for rejection.

(k) **Radiographic inspection.** Radiographic inspection is required on all welded joints which are subjected to internal pressure, except that at the discretion of the disinterested inspector, openings less than 25 percent of the container diameter need not be subjected to radiographic inspection. Evidence of any defects likely to seriously weaken the container is cause for rejection. Radiographic inspection must be performed subsequent to the hydrostatic test.

(l) **Burst test.** One container taken at random out of 200 or less must be hydrostatically tested to destruction. Rupture pressure must be included as part of the inspector's report.

(m) **Flattening test.** A flattening test must be performed as follows:

(1) *For spheres* the test must be at the weld between parallel steel plates on a press with welded seam at right angles to the plates. Test one sphere taken at random out of each lot of 200 or less after the hydrostatic test. Any projecting appurtenances may be cut off (by mechanical means only) prior to crushing.

(2) *For cylinders* the test must be between knife edges, wedge shaped, 60° angle, rounded to 1/2-inch radius. Test one cylinder taken at random out of each lot of 200 or less, after the hydrostatic test.

(n) **Acceptable results for flattening and burst tests.** Acceptable results for flattening and burst tests are as follows:

(1) *Flattening required* to 50 percent of the original outside diameter without cracking.

(2) *Burst pressure must be at least 3 times the service pressure.*

(o) **Rejected containers.** Repair of welded seams by welding prior to process treatment is authorized. Subsequent thereto, containers must be heat treated and pass all prescribed tests.

(p) **Duties of inspector.** In addition to the requirements of §178.35, the inspector must verify that all tests are conducted at temperatures between 60 °F and 90 °F.

(q) **Marking.** Markings must be stamped plainly and permanently on a permanent attachment or on a metal nameplate permanently secured to the container by means other than soft solder.

§178.50 Specification 4B welded or brazed steel cylinders.

(a) **Type, size, and service pressure.** A DOT 4B is a welded or brazed steel cylinder with longitudinal seams that are forged lap-welded or brazed and with water capacity (nominal) not over 1,000 pounds and a service pressure of at least 150 but not over 500 psig. Cylinders closed in by spinning process are not authorized.

(b) **Steel.** Open-hearth, electric or basic oxygen process steel of uniform quality must be used. Content percent may not exceed the following: Carbon, 0.25; phosphorus, 0.045; sulphur, 0.050.

(c) **Identification of material.** Material must be identified by any suitable method except that plates and billets for hotdrawn cylinders must be marked with the heat number.

(d) **Manufacture.** Cylinders must be manufactured using equipment and processes adequate to ensure that each cylinder produced conforms to the requirements of this subpart. No defect is permitted that is likely to weaken the finished cylinder appreciably. A reasonably smooth and uniform surface finish is required. Exposed bottom welds on cylinders over 18 inches long must be protected by footrings. Welding procedures and operators must be qualified in accordance with CGA Pamphlet C-3 (incorporated by reference; see §171.7 of this subchapter). Seams must be made as follows:

(1) *Welded or brazed circumferential seams.* Heads attached by brazing must have a driving fit with the shell, unless the shell is crimped, swedged, or curled over the skirt or flange of the head, and be thoroughly brazed until complete penetration by the brazing material of the brazed joint is secured. Depth of brazing from end of shell must be at least four times the thickness of shell metal.

(2) *Longitudinal seams in shells.* Longitudinal seams must be forged lap welded, by copper brazing, by copper alloy brazing, or by silver alloy brazing. Copper alloy composition must be: Copper, 95 percent minimum; Silicon, 1.5 percent to 3.85 percent; Manganese, 0.25 percent to 1.10 percent. The melting point of the silver alloy brazing material must be in excess of 1000 °F. When brazed, the plate edge must be lapped at least eight times the thickness of plate, laps being held in position, substantially metal to metal, by riveting or electric spot-welding; brazing must be done by using a suitable flux and by placing brazing material on one side of seam and applying heat until this material shows uniformly along the seam of the other side.

(e) **Welding or brazing.** Only the attachment of neckrings, footrings, handles, bosses, pads, and valve protection rings to the tops and bottoms of cylinders by welding or brazing is authorized. Such attachments and the portion of the container to which they are attached must be made of weldable steel, the carbon content of which may not exceed 0.25 percent except in the case of 4130X steel which may be used with proper welding procedure.

(f) **Wall thickness.** The wall thickness of the cylinder must comply with the following requirements:

(1) *For cylinders* with outside diameters over 6 inches the minimum wall thickness must be 0.090 inch. In any case, the minimum wall thickness must be such that calculated wall stress at minimum test pressure (paragraph (i)(4) of this section) may not exceed the following values:

(i) *24,000 psi for cylinders without longitudinal seam.*

(ii) *22,800 psig* for cylinders having copper brazed or silver alloy brazed longitudinal seam.

(iii) *18,000 psi* for cylinders having forged lapped welded longitudinal seam.

(2) *Calculation must be made by the formula:*

$S = [P(1.3D^2 + 0.4d^2)] / (D^2 - d^2)$

Where:

S = wall stress in psi;

P = minimum test pressure prescribed for water jacket test or 450 psig whichever is the greater;

D = outside diameter in inches;

d = inside diameter in inches.

(g) **Heat treatment.** Cylinder body and heads, formed by drawing or pressing, must be uniformly and properly heat treated prior to tests.

(h) **Opening in cylinders.** Openings in cylinders must conform to the following:

(1) *Each opening in cylinders,* except those for safety devices, must be provided with a fitting, boss, or pad, securely attached to cylinder by brazing or by welding or by threads. Fitting, boss, or pad must be of steel suitable for the method of attachment employed, and which need not be identified or verified as to analysis except that if attachment is by welding, carbon content may not exceed 0.25 percent. If threads are used, they must comply with the following:

(i) *Threads must be* clean cut, even without checks, and tapped to gauge.

(ii) *Taper threads* to be of length not less than as specified for American Standard taper pipe threads.

(iii) *Straight threads,* having at least 4 engaged threads, to have tight fit and calculated shear strength at least 10 times the test pressure of the cylinder; gaskets required, adequate to prevent leakage.

(iv) *A brass fitting* may be brazed to the steel boss or flange on cylinders used as component parts of hand fire extinguishers.

(2) *The closure* of a fitting, boss, or pad must be adequate to prevent leakage.

(i) **Hydrostatic test.** Cylinders must withstand a hydrostatic test as follows:

(1) *The test* must be by water-jacket, or other suitable method, operated so as to obtain accurate data. The pressure gauge must permit reading to an accuracy of 1 percent. The expansion gauge must permit reading of total expansion to an accuracy either of 1 percent or 0.1 cubic centimeter.

(2) *Pressure must be maintained* for at least 30 seconds and sufficiently longer to ensure complete expansion. Any internal pressure applied after heat-treatment and previous to the official test may not exceed 90 percent of the test pressure. If, due to failure of the test apparatus, the test pressure cannot be maintained, the test may be repeated at a pressure increased by 10 percent or 100 psig, whichever is the lower.

(3) *Permanent volumetric expansion* may not exceed 10 percent of total volumetric expansion at test pressure.

(4) *Cylinders must be tested as follows:*

(i) *At least one cylinder* selected at random out of each lot of 200 or less must be tested as outlined in paragraphs (i)(1), (i)(2), and (i)(3) of this section to at least two times service pressure.

(ii) *All cylinders* not tested as outlined in paragraph (i)(4)(i) of this section must be examined under pressure of at least two times service pressure and show no defect.

(j) **Flattening test.** After the hydrostatic test, a flattening test must be performed on one cylinder taken at random out or each lot of 200 or less, by placing the cylinder between wedge shaped knife edges having a 60° included angle, rounded to 1/2-inch radius. The longitudinal axis of the cylinder must be at a 90-degree angle to knife edges during the test. For lots of 30 or less, flattening tests are authorized to be made on a ring at least 8 inches long cut from each cylinder and subjected to same heat treatment as the finished cylinder.

(k) **Physical test.** A physical test must be conducted to determine yield strength, tensile strength, elongation, and reduction of area of material as follows:

(1) *The test* is required on 2 specimens cut from 1 cylinder, or part thereof heat-treated as required, taken at random out of each lot of 200 or less. For lots of 30 or less, physical tests are authorized to be made on a ring at least 8 inches long cut from each cylinder and subjected to same heat treatment as the finished cylinder.

(2) *Specimens must conform to the following:*

(i) *A gauge length* of 8 inches with a width of not over 1 1/2 inches, a gauge length of 2 inches with a width of not over 1 1/2 inches, or a gauge length at least 24 times the thickness with a width not over 6 times the thickness is authorized when a cylinder wall is not over 3/16 inch thick.

(ii) *The specimen,* exclusive of grip ends, may not be flattened. Grip ends may be flattened to within one inch of each end of the reduced section.

(iii) *When size of cylinder* does not permit securing straight specimens, the specimens may be taken in any location or direction and may be straightened or flattened cold, by pressure only, not by blows. When specimens are so taken and prepared, the inspector's report must show in connection with record of physical tests detailed information in regard to such specimens.

(iv) *Heating of a specimen for any purpose is not authorized.*

(3) *The yield strength in tension* must be the stress corresponding to a permanent strain of 0.2 percent of the gauge length. The following conditions apply:

(i) *The yield strength* must be determined by either the "offset" method or the "extension under load" method as prescribed in ASTM E 8 (incorporated by reference; see §171.7 of this subchapter).

(ii) *In using the "extension under load" method,* the total strain (or "extension under load") corresponding to the stress at which the 0.2 percent permanent strain occurs may be determined with sufficient accuracy by calculating the elastic extension of the gauge length under appropriate load and adding thereto 0.2 percent of the gauge length. Elastic extension calculations must be based on an elastic modulus of 30,000,000. In the event of controversy, the entire stress-strain diagram must be plotted and the yield strength determined from the 0.2 percent offset.

(iii) *For the purpose* of strain measurement, the initial strain must be set while the specimen is under a stress of 12,000 psi, and strain indicator reading must be set at the calculated corresponding strain.

(iv) *Cross-head speed* of the testing machine may not exceed 1/8 inch per minute during yield strength determination.

(l) **Acceptable results for physical and flattening tests.** Either of the following is an acceptable result:

(1) *An elongation* of at least 40 percent for a 2-inch gauge length or at least 20 percent in other cases and yield strength not over 73

percent of tensile strength. In this instance, a flattening test is not required.

(2) *When cylinders are constructed* of lap welded pipe, flattening test is required, without cracking, to 6 times the wall thickness. In such case, the rings (crop ends) cut from each end of pipe, must be tested with the weld 45° or less from the point of greatest stress. If a ring fails, another from the same end of pipe may be tested.

(m) **Rejected cylinders.** Reheat treatment is authorized for rejected cylinder. Subsequent thereto, cylinders must pass all prescribed tests to be acceptable. Repair of brazed seams by brazing and welded seams by welding is authorized.

(n) **Markings.** Markings must be stamped plainly and permanently in any of the following locations on the cylinder:

(1) *On shoulders* and top heads when they are not less than 0.087-inch thick.

(2) *On side wall* adjacent to top head for side walls which are not less than 0.090 inch thick.

(3) *On a cylindrical portion* of the shell which extends beyond the recessed bottom of the cylinder, constituting an integral and non-pressure part of the cylinder.

(4) *On a metal plate* attached to the top of the cylinder or permanent part thereof; sufficient space must be left on the plate to provide for stamping at least six retest dates; the plate must be at least 1/16-inch thick and must be attached by welding, or by brazing. The brazing rod must melt at a temperature of 1100 °F. Welding or brazing must be along all the edges of the plate.

(5) *On the neck,* neckring, valve boss, valve protection sleeve, or similar part permanently attached to the top of the cylinder.

(6) *On the footring* permanently attached to the cylinder, provided the water capacity of the cylinder does not exceed 25 pounds.

§178.51 Specification 4BA welded or brazed steel cylinders.

(a) **Type, size, and service pressure.** A DOT 4BA cylinder is a cylinder, either spherical or cylindrical in shape, with a water capacity of 1,000 pounds or less and a service pressure of at least 225 and not over 500 psig. Closures made by the spinning process are not authorized.

(1) *Spherical type cylinders* must be made from two seamless hemispheres joined by the welding of one circumferential seam.

(2) *Cylindrical type cylinders* must be of circumferentially welded or brazed construction.

(b) **Steel.** The steel used in the construction of the cylinder must be as specified in table 1 of appendix A to this part.

(c) **Identification of material.** Material must be identified by any suitable method except that plates and billets for hotdrawn cylinders must be marked with the heat number.

(d) **Manufacture.** Cylinders must be manufactured using equipment and processes adequate to ensure that each cylinder produced conforms to the requirements of this subpart. No defect is permitted that is likely to weaken the finished cylinder appreciably. A reasonably smooth and uniform surface finish is required. Exposed bottom welds on cylinders over 18 inches long must be protected by footrings.

(1) *Seams must be made as follows:*

(i) *Minimum thickness* of heads and bottoms must be not less than 90 percent of the required thickness of the side wall.

(ii) *Circumferential seams* must be made by welding or by brazing. Heads must be attached by brazing and must have a driving fit with the shell, unless the shell is crimped, swedged or curled over the skirt or flange of the head and must be thoroughly brazed until complete penetration by the brazing material of the brazed joint is secured. Depth of brazing from end of the shell must be at least four times the thickness of shell metal.

(iii) *Longitudinal seams* in shells must be made by copper brazing, copper alloy brazing, or by silver alloy brazing. Copper alloy composition must be: Copper 95 percent minimum, Silicon 1.5 percent to 3.85 percent, Manganese 0.25 percent to 1.10 percent. The melting point of the silver alloy brazing material must be in excess of 1,000 °F. The plate edge must be lapped at least eight times the thickness of plate, laps being held in position, substantially metal to metal, by riveting or by electric spot-welding. Brazing must be done by using a suitable flux and by placing brazing material on one side of seam and applying heat until this material shows uniformly along the seam of the other side. Strength of longitudinal seam: Copper brazed longitudinal seam must have strength at least 3/2 times the strength of the steel wall.

(2) *Welding procedures* and operators must be qualified in accordance with CGA Pamphlet C-3 (incorporated by reference; see §171.7 of this subchapter).

(e) **Welding and brazing.** Only the welding or brazing of neckrings, footrings, handles, bosses, pads, and valve protection rings to the tops and bottoms of cylinders is authorized. Provided that such attachments and the portion of the container to which they are attached are made of weldable steel, the carbon content of which may not exceed 0.25 percent except in the case of 4130 x steel which may be used with proper welding procedure.

(f) **Wall thickness.** The minimum wall thickness of the cylinder must meet the following conditions:

(1) *For any cylinder* with an outside diameter of greater than 6 inches, the minimum wall thickness is 0.078 inch. In any case the minimum wall thickness must be such that the calculated wall stress at the minimum test pressure may not exceed the lesser value of any of the following:

(i) *The value shown* in table 1 of appendix A to this part, for the particular material under consideration;

(ii) *One-half of the minimum* tensile strength of the material determined as required in paragraph (j) of this section;

(iii) *35,000 psi; or*

(iv) *Further provided* that wall stress for cylinders having copper brazed longitudinal seams may not exceed 95 percent of any of the above values. Measured wall thickness may not include galvanizing or other protective coating.

(2) *Cylinders that are cylindrical in shape* must have the wall stress calculated by the formula:

$S = [P(1.3D^2 + 0.4d^2)] / (D^2 - d^2)$

Where:

S = wall stress in psi;

P = minimum test pressure prescribed for water jacket test;

D = outside diameter in inches;

d = inside diameter in inches.

(3) *Cylinders that are* spherical in shape must have the wall stress calculated by the formula:

$S = PD / 4tE$

Where:

S = wall stress in psi;

P = minimum test pressure prescribed for water jacket test;

D = outside diameter in inches;

t = minimum wall thickness in inches;

E = 0.85 (provides 85 percent weld efficiency factor which must be applied in the girth weld area and heat affected zones which zone must extend a distance of 6 times wall thickness from center line of weld);

E = 1.0 (for all other areas).

(4) *For a cylinder* with a wall thickness less than 0.100 inch, the ratio of tangential length to outside diameter may not exceed 4.1.

(g) **Heat treatment.** Cylinders must be heat treated in accordance with the following requirements:

(1) *Each cylinder* must be uniformly and properly heat treated prior to test by the applicable method shown in table 1 of appendix A to this part. Heat treatment must be accomplished after all forming and welding operations, except that when brazed joints are used, heat treatment must follow any forming and welding operations, but may be done before, during or after the brazing operations.

(2) *Heat treatment* is not required after the welding or brazing of weldable low carbon parts to attachments of similar material which have been previously welded or brazed to the top or bottom of cylinders and properly heat treated, provided such subsequent welding or brazing does not produce a temperature in excess of 400 °F in any part of the top or bottom material.

(h) **Openings in cylinders.** Openings in cylinders must comply with the following requirements:

(1) *Any opening must be placed on other than a cylindrical surface.*

(2) *Each opening* in a spherical type cylinder must be provided with a fitting, boss, or pad of weldable steel securely attached to the container by fusion welding.

(3) *Each opening* in a cylindrical type cylinder must be provided with a fitting, boss, or pad, securely attached to container by brazing or by welding.

(4) *If threads are used, they must comply with the following:*

(i) *Threads must be* clean-cut, even, without checks and tapped to gauge.

(ii) *Taper threads* must be of a length not less than that specified for American Standard taper pipe threads.

(iii) *Straight threads,* having at least 4 engaged threads, must have a tight fit and a calculated shear strength of at least 10 times the test pressure of the cylinder. Gaskets, adequate to prevent leakage, are required.

(i) **Hydrostatic test.** Each cylinder must successfully withstand a hydrostatic test, as follows:

(1) *The test* must be by water jacket, or other suitable method, operated so as to obtain accurate data. A pressure gauge must permit reading to an accuracy of 1 percent. An expansion gauge must permit reading of total expansion to an accuracy of either 1 percent or 0.1 cubic centimeter.

(2) *Pressure must be maintained* for at least 30 seconds and sufficiently longer to ensure complete expansion. Any internal pressure applied after heat treatment and previous to the official test may not exceed 90 percent of the test pressure.

(3) *Permanent volumetric expansion* may not exceed 10 percent of the total volumetric expansion at test pressure.

(4) *Cylinders must be tested as follows:*

(i) *At least one cylinder* selected at random out of each lot of 200 or less must be tested as outlined in paragraphs (i)(1), (i)(2), and (i)(3) of this section to at least two times service pressure.

(ii) *All cylinders* not tested as outlined in paragraph (i)(4)(i) of this section must be examined under pressure of at least two times service pressure and show no defect.

(j) **Physical test.** A physical test must be conducted to determine yield strength, tensile strength, elongation, and reduction of area of material, as follows:

(1) *The test is required* on 2 specimens cut from one cylinder or part thereof having passed the hydrostatic test and heat-treated as required, taken at random out of each lot of 200 or less. Physical tests for spheres are required on 2 specimens cut from flat representative sample plates of the same heat taken at random from the steel used to produce the spheres. This flat steel from which 2 specimens are to be cut must receive the same heat treatment as the spheres themselves. Sample plates must be taken from each lot of 200 or less spheres.

(2) *Specimens must conform to the following:*

(i) *A gauge length* of 8 inches with a width not over 1 1/2 inches, or a gauge length of 2 inches with a width not over 1 1/2 inches, or a gauge length at least 24 times the thickness with a width not over 6 times the thickness is authorized when a cylinder wall is not over 3/16 inch thick.

(ii) *The specimen,* exclusive of grip ends, may not be flattened. Grip ends may be flattened to within one inch of each end of the reduced section.

(iii) *When size* of the cylinder does not permit securing straight specimens, the specimens may be taken in any location or direction and may be straightened or flattened cold, by pressure only, not by blows. When specimens are so taken and prepared, the inspector's report must show in connection with record of physical tests detailed information in regard to such specimens.

(iv) *Heating of a specimen for any purpose is not authorized.*

(3) *The yield strength* in tension must be the stress corresponding to a permanent strain of 0.2 percent of the gauge length. The following conditions apply:

(i) *The yield strength* must be determined by either the "offset" method or the "extension under load" method as prescribed in ASTM E 8 (incorporated by reference; see §171.7 of this subchapter).

(ii) *In using the "extension under load" method,* the total strain (or "extension under load"), corresponding to the stress at which the 0.2 percent permanent strain occurs may be determined with sufficient accuracy by calculating the elastic extension of the gauge length under appropriate load and adding thereto 0.2 percent of the gauge length. Elastic extension calculations must be based on an elastic modulus of 30,000,000. In the event of controversy, the entire stress-strain diagram must be plotted and the yield strength determined from the 0.2 percent offset.

(iii) *For the purpose of strain measurement,* the initial strain reference must be set while the specimen is under a stress of 12,000 psi, and the strain indicator reading must be set at the calculated corresponding strain.

(iv) *Cross-head speed* of the testing machine may not exceed 1/8 inch per minute during yield strength determination.

(k) **Elongation.** Physical test specimens must show at least a 40 percent elongation for a 2-inch gauge length or at least 20 percent in other cases. Except that these elongation percentages may be reduced numerically by 2 for 2-inch specimens, and by 1 in other cases, for each 7,500 psi increment of tensile strength above 50,000 psi to a maximum of four such increments.

(l) **Tests of welds.** Except for brazed seams, welds must be tested as follows:

(1) *Tensile test.* A specimen must be cut from one cylinder of each lot of 200 or less, or welded test plate. The welded test plate must be of one of the heats in the lot of 200 or less which it represents, in the same condition and approximately the same thickness as the cylinder wall except that in no case must it be of a lesser thickness than that required for a quarter size Charpy impact specimen. The weld must be made by the same procedures and subjected to the same heat treatment as the major weld on the cylinder. The specimen must be taken from across the major seam and must be prepared and tested in accordance with and must meet the requirements of CGA Pamphlet C-3 (incorporated by reference; see §171.7 of this subchapter). Should this specimen fail to meet the requirements, specimens may be taken from two additional cylinders or welded test plates from the same lot and tested. If either of the latter specimens fail to meet the requirements, the entire lot represented must be rejected.

(2) *Guided bend test.* A root bend test specimen must be cut from the cylinder or welded test plate, used for the tensile test specified in paragraph (l)(1) of this section. Specimens must be taken from across the major seam and must be prepared and tested in accordance with and must meet the requirements of CGA Pamphlet C-3 (incorporated by reference; see §171.7 of this subchapter).

(3) *Alternate guided-bend test.* This test may be used and must be as required by CGA Pamphlet C-3 (incorporated by reference; see §171.7 of this subchapter). The specimen must be bent until the elongation at the outer surface, adjacent to the root of the weld, between the lightly scribed gage lines a to b, must be at least 20 percent, except that this percentage may be reduced for steels having a tensile strength in excess of 50,000 psig, as provided in paragraph (k) of this section.

(m) **Rejected cylinders.** Reheat treatment is authorized for rejected cylinders. Subsequent thereto, cylinders must pass all prescribed tests to be acceptable. Repair of brazed seams by brazing and welded seams by welding is authorized.

(n) **Markings.** Markings must be stamped plainly and permanently in one of the following locations on the cylinder:

(1) *On shoulders and top heads not less than 0.087 inch thick.*

(2) *On side wall* adjacent to top head for side walls not less than 0.090 inch thick.

(3) *On a cylindrical portion* of the shell which extends beyond the recessed bottom of the cylinder constituting an integral and non-pressure part of the cylinder.

(4) *On a plate* attached to the top of the cylinder or permanent part thereof; sufficient space must be left on the plate to provide for stamping at least six retest dates; the plate must be at least 1/16 inch thick and must be attached by welding, or by brazing at a temperature of at least 1100 °F, throughout all edges of the plate.

(5) *On the neck,* neckring, valve boss, valve protection sleeve, or similar part permanently attached to the top of the cylinder.

(6) *On the footring* permanently attached to the cylinder, provided the water capacity of the cylinder does not exceed 25 pounds.

§178.53 Specification 4D welded steel cylinders for aircraft use.

(a) **Type, size, and service pressure.** A DOT 4D cylinder is a welded steel sphere (two seamless hemispheres) or circumferentially welded cylinder (two seamless drawn shells) with a water capacity not over 100 pounds and a service pressure of at least 300 but not over 500 psig. Cylinders closed in by spinning process are not authorized.

(b) **Steel.** Open-hearth or electric steel of uniform and weldable quality must be used. Content may not exceed the following: Carbon, 0.25; phosphorus, 0.045; sulphur, 0.050, except that the following steels commercially known as 4130X and Type 304, 316, 321, and 347 stainless steels may be used with proper welding procedure. A heat of steel made under table 1 in this paragraph (b), check chemical analysis of which is slightly out of the specified range, is acceptable, if satisfactory in all other respects, provided the tolerances shown in table 2 in this paragraph (b) are not exceeded, except as approved by the Associate Administrator. The following chemical analyses are authorized:

Table 1 - 4130X Steel

4130X	Percent
Carbon	0.25/0.35
Manganese	0.40/0.60
Phosphorus	0.04 max
Sulphur	0.05 max
Silicon	0.15/0.35
Chromium	0.80/1.10
Molybdenum	0.15/0.25
Zirconium	None
Nickel	None

Table 2 - Authorized Stainless Steels

	Stainless steels			
	304 (percent)	316 (percent)	321 (percent)	347 (percent)
Carbon (max)	0.08	0.08	0.08	0.08
Manganese (max)	2.00	2.00	2.00	2.00
Phosphorus (max)	.030	.045	.030	.030
Sulphur (max)	.030	.030	.030	.030
Silicon (max)	.75	1.00	.75	.75
Nickel	8.0/11.0	10.0/14.0	9.0/13.0	9.0/13.0
Chromium	18.0/20.0	16.0/18.0	17.0/20.0	17.0/20.0
Molybdenum		2.0/3.0		
Titanium			(1)	
Columbium				(2)

1. Titanium may not be less than 5C and not more than 0.60%.
2. Columbium may not be less than 10C and not more than 1.0%.

Table 3 - Check Analysis Tolerances

Element	Limit or maximum specified (percent)	Tolerance (percent) over the maximum limit or under the minimum limit	
		Under minimum limit	Over maximum limit
Carbon	To 0.15 incl	0.01	0.01
	Over 0.15 to 0.40 incl	.03	.04
Manganese	To 0.60 incl	.03	.03
	Over 1.15 to 2.50 incl	.05	.05
Phosphorus[1]	All ranges		.01
Sulphur	All ranges		.01
Silicon	To 0.30 incl	.02	.03
	Over 0.30 to 1.00 incl	.05	.05
Nickel	Over 5.30 to 10.00 incl	.10	.10
	Over 10.00 to 14.00 incl	.15	.15
Chromium	To 0.90 incl	.03	.03
	Over 0.90 to 2.10 incl	.05	.05
	Over 15.00 to 20.00 incl	.20	.20
Molybdenum	To 0.20 incl	.01	.01
	Over 0.20 to 0.40 incl	.02	.02
	Over 1.75 to 3.0 incl	.10	.10
Titanium	All ranges	.05	.05
Columbium	All ranges	.05	.05

1. Rephosphorized steels not subject to check analysis for phosphorus.

(c) **Identification of material.** Material must be identified by any suitable method except that plates and billets for hotdrawn cylinders must be marked with the heat number.

(d) **Manufacture.** Cylinders must be manufactured using equipment and processes adequate to ensure that each cylinder produced conforms to the requirements of this subpart. No defect is permitted that is likely to weaken the finished container appreciably. A reasonably smooth and uniform surface finish is required. Welding procedures and operators must be qualified in accordance with CGA Pamphlet C-3 (incorporated by reference; see §171.7 of this subchapter).

(e) **Wall thickness.** The wall stress at the minimum test pressure may not exceed 24,000 psi, except where steels commercially known as 4130X, types 304, 316, 321, and 347 stainless steels are used, stress at the test pressures may not exceed 37,000 psi. The minimum wall thickness for any container having a capacity of 1,100 cubic inches or less is 0.04 inch. The minimum wall thickness for any container having a capacity in excess of 1,100 cubic inches is 0.095 inch. Calculations must be done by the following:

(1) *Calculation for a "sphere" must be made by the formula:*

$S = PD / 4tE$

Where:

S = wall stress in psi;

P = test pressure prescribed for water jacket test, i.e., at least two times service pressure, in psig;

D = outside diameter in inches;

t = minimum wall thickness in inches;

E = 0.85 (provides 85 percent weld efficiency factor which must be applied in the girth weld area and heat affected zones which zone must extend a distance of 6 times wall thickness from center line of weld);

E = 1.0 (for all other areas).

(2) *Calculation for a cylinder must be made by the formula:*

$S = [P(1.3D^2 + 0.4d^2)] / (D^2 - d^{T12})$

Where:

S = wall stress in psi;

P = test pressure prescribed for water jacket test, i.e., at least two times service pressure, in psig;

D = outside diameter in inches;

d = inside diameter in inches.

(f) **Heat treatment.** The completed cylinders must be uniformly and properly heat-treated prior to tests.

(g) **Openings in container.** Openings in cylinders must comply with the following:

(1) *Each opening in the container,* except those for safety devices, must be provided with a fitting, boss, or pad, securely attached to the container by brazing or by welding or by threads. If threads are used, they must comply with the following:

(i) *Threads must be* clean cut, even, without checks, and tapped to gauge.

(ii) *Taper threads* must be of a length not less than that specified for American Standard taper pipe threads.

(iii) *Straight threads,* having at least 4 engaged threads, must have a tight fit and calculated shear strength of at least 10 times the test pressure of the container. Gaskets, adequate to prevent leakage, are required.

(2) *Closure of a fitting,* boss, or pad must be adequate to prevent leakage.

(h) **Hydrostatic test.** Each cylinder must successfully withstand a hydrostatic test, as follows:

(1) *The test* must be by water-jacket, or other suitable method, operated so as to obtain accurate data. A pressure gauge must permit a reading to an accuracy of 1 percent. An expansion gauge must permit reading of total expansion to an accuracy of either 1 percent or 0.1 cubic centimeter.

(2) *Pressure must be maintained* for at least 30 seconds and sufficiently longer to ensure complete expansion. Any internal pressure applied after heat-treatment and previous to the official test may not exceed 90 percent of the test pressure. If, due to failure of the test apparatus, the test pressure cannot be maintained, the test may be repeated at a pressure increased by 10 percent or 100 psig, whichever is the lower.

(3) *Permanent volumetric expansion* may not exceed 10 percent of the total volumetric expansion at test pressure.

(4) *Containers must be tested as follows:*

(i) *Each container to at least 2 times service pressure; or*

(ii) *One container* out of each lot of 200 or less to at least 3 times service pressure. Others must be examined under pressure of 2 times service pressure and show no defects.

(i) **Flattening test for spheres and cylinders.** Spheres and cylinders must be subjected to a flattening test as follows:

(1) *One sphere* taken at random out of each lot of 200 or less must be subjected to a flattening test as follows:

(i) *The test must be performed after the hydrostatic test.*

(ii) *The test* must be between parallel steel plates on a press with a welded seam at right angles to the plates. Any projecting appurtenances may be cut off (by mechanical means only) prior to crushing.

(2) *One cylinder* taken at random out of each lot of 200 or less must be subjected to a flattening test, as follows:

(i) *The test must be performed after the hydrostatic test.*

(ii) *The test* must be between knife edges, wedge shaped, 60° angle, rounded to 1/2 inch radius. For lots of 30 or less, physical tests are authorized to be made on a ring at least 8 inches long cut from each cylinder and subjected to the same heat treatment as the finished cylinder.

(j) **Physical test and specimens for spheres and cylinders.** Spheres and cylinders must be subjected to a physical test as follows:

(1) *Physical test* for spheres are required on 2 specimens cut from a flat representative sample plate of the same heat taken at random from the steel used to produce the sphere. This flat steel from which the 2 specimens are to be cut must receive the same heat-treatment as the spheres themselves. Sample plates must be taken for each lot of 200 or less spheres.

(2) *Specimens for spheres* must have a gauge length 2 inches with a width not over 1 1/2 inches, or a gauge length at least 24 times the thickness with a width not over 6 times the thickness is authorized when a wall is not over 3/16 inch thick.

(3) *Physical test* for cylinders is required on 2 specimens cut from 1 cylinder taken at random out of each lot of 200 or less. For lots of 30 or less, physical tests are authorized to be made on a ring at least 8 inches long cut from each cylinder and subjected to the same heat treatment as the finished cylinder.

(4) *Specimens for cylinders must conform to the following:*

(i) *A gauge length* of 8 inches with a width not over 1 1/2 inches, or a gauge length of 2 inches with a width not over 1 1/2 inches, or a gauge length at least 24 times the thickness with a width not over 6 times the thickness is authorized when a cylinder wall is not over 3/16 inch thick.

(ii) *The specimen,* exclusive of grip ends, may not be flattened. Grip ends may be flattened to within 1 inch of each end of the reduced section. Heating of the specimen for any purpose is not authorized.

(5) *The yield strength* in tension must be the stress corresponding to a permanent strain of 0.2 percent of the gauge length. The following conditions apply:

(i) *The yield strength* must be determined by either the "offset" method or the "extension under load" method as prescribed in ASTM Standard E 8 (incorporated by reference; see §171.7 of this subchapter).

(ii) *In using the "extension under load" method,* the total strain (or "extension under load") corresponding to the stress at which the 0.2 percent permanent strain occurs may be determined with sufficient accuracy by calculating the elastic extension of the gauge length under appropriate load and adding thereto 0.2 percent of the gauge length. Elastic extension calculations must be based on an elastic modulus of 30,000,000. In the event of controversy, the entire stress-strain diagram must be plotted and the yield strength determined from the 0.2 percent offset.

(iii) *For the purpose of strain measurement,* the initial strain must be set while the specimen is under a stress of 12,000 psi and the strain indicator reading being set at the calculated corresponding strain.

(iv) *Cross-head speed* of the testing machine may not exceed 1/8 inch per minute during yield strength determination.

(k) **Acceptable results for physical and flattening tests.** Either of the following is an acceptable result:

(1) *An elongation* of at least 40 percent for a 2 inch gauge length or at least 20 percent in other cases and yield strength not over 73 percent of tensile strength. In this instance, the flattening test is not required.

(2) *An elongation* of at least 20 percent for a 2 inch gauge length or 10 percent in other cases. Flattening is required to 50 percent of the original outside diameter without cracking.

(l) **Rejected cylinders.** Reheat-treatment is authorized for rejected cylinders. Subsequent thereto, containers must pass all prescribed tests to be acceptable. Repair of welded seams by welding prior to reheat-treatment is authorized.

(m) **Marking.** Marking on each container by stamping plainly and permanently are only authorized where the metal is at least 0.09 inch thick, or on a metal nameplate permanently secured to the container by means other than soft solder, or by means that would not reduce the wall thickness.

§178.55 Specification 4B240ET welded or brazed cylinders.

(a) **Type, spinning process, size and service pressure.** A DOT 4B240ET cylinder is a brazed type cylinder made from electric resistance welded tubing. The maximum water capacity of this cylinder is 12 pounds or 333 cubic inches and the service must be 240 psig. The maximum outside diameter of the shell must be five inches and maximum length of the shell is 21 inches. Cylinders closed in by a spinning process are authorized.

(b) **Steel.** Open-hearth, basic oxygen, or electric steel of uniform quality must be used. Plain carbon steel content may not exceed the following: Carbon, 0.25; phosphorus, 0.045; sulfur, 0.050. The addition of other elements for alloying effect is prohibited.

(c) **Identification of material.** Material must be identified by any suitable method.

(d) **Manufacture.** Cylinders must be manufactured using equipment and processes adequate to ensure that each cylinder produced conforms to the requirements of this subpart. No defect is permitted that is likely to weaken the finished cylinder appreciably. A reasonably smooth and uniform surface finish is required. Heads may be attached to shells by lap brazing or may be formed integrally. The thickness of the bottom of cylinders welded or formed by spinning is, under no condition, to be less than two times the minimum wall thickness of the cylindrical shell. Such bottom thicknesses must be measured within an area bounded by a line representing the points of contact between the cylinder and the floor when the cylinder is in a vertical position. Seams must conform to the following:

(1) *Circumferential seams* must be by brazing only. Heads must be attached to shells by the lap brazing method and must overlap not less than four times the wall thickness. Brazing material must have a melting point of not less than 1000 °F. Heads must have a driving fit with the shell unless the shell is crimped, swedged, or curled over the skirt or flange of the head and be thoroughly brazed until complete penetration of the joint by the brazing material is secured. Brazed joints may be repaired by brazing.

(2) *Longitudinal seams* in shell must be by electric resistance welded joints only. No repairs to longitudinal joints is permitted.

(3) *Welding procedures* and operators must be qualified in accordance with CGA Pamphlet C-3.

(e) **Welding or brazing.** Only the attachment, by welding or brazing, to the tops and bottoms of cylinders of neckrings, footrings, handles, bosses, pads, and valve protection rings is authorized. Provided that such attachments and the portion of the container to which they are attached are made of weldable steel, the carbon content of which may not exceed 0.25 percent.

(f) **Wall thickness.** The wall stress must be at least two times the service pressure and may not exceed 18,000 psi. The minimum wall thickness is 0.044 inch. Calculation must be made by the following formula:

$S = [P(1.3D^2 + 0.4d^2)] / (D^2 - d^2)$

Where:

S = wall stress in psig;

P = 2 times service pressure;

D = outside diameter in inches;

d = inside diameter in inches.

(g) **Heat treatment.** Heads formed by drawing or pressing must be uniformly and properly heat treated prior to tests. Cylinders with integral formed heads or bases must be subjected to a normalizing operation. Normalizing and brazing operations may be combined, provided the operation is carried out at a temperature in excess of the upper critical temperature of the steel.

(h) **Openings in cylinders.** Openings in cylinders must comply with the following:

(1) *Each opening* in cylinders, except those for safety devices, must be provided with a fitting, boss, or pad, securely attached to the cylinder by brazing or by welding or by threads. A fitting, boss, or pad must be of steel suitable for the method of attachment employed, and which need not be identified or verified as to analysis, except that if attachment is by welding, carbon content may not exceed 0.25 percent. If threads are used, they must comply with the following:

(i) *Threads must be* clean cut, even without checks, and tapped to gauge.

(ii) *Taper threads* to be of length not less than as specified for American Standard taper pipe threads.

(iii) *Straight threads,* having at least 4 engaged threads, to have tight fit and calculated shear strength at least 10 times the test pressure of the cylinder; gaskets required, adequate to prevent leakage.

(2) *Closure of a fitting, boss, or pad* must be adequate to prevent leakage.

(i) **Hydrostatic test.** Each cylinder must successfully withstand a hydrostatic test as follows:

(1) *The test must be by water-jacket,* or other suitable method, operated so as to obtain accurate data. The pressure gauge must permit reading to an accuracy of 1 percent. The expansion gauge must permit reading of total expansion to an accuracy of either 1 percent or 0.1 cubic centimeter.

(2) *Pressure must be maintained* for at least 30 seconds and sufficiently longer to ensure complete expansion. Any internal pressure applied after heat-treatment and previous to the official test may not exceed 90 percent of the test pressure. If, due to failure of the test apparatus, the test pressure cannot be maintained, the test may be repeated at a pressure increased by 10 percent or 100 psig, whichever is the lower.

(3) *Permanent volumetric expansion* may not exceed 10 percent of total volumetric expansion at test pressure.

(4) *Cylinders must be tested as follows:*

(i) *At least one cylinder* selected at random out of each lot of 200 or less must be tested as outlined in paragraphs (i)(1), (i)(2), and (i)(3) of this section to at least two times service pressure.

(ii) *All cylinders* not tested as outlined in paragraph (i)(4)(i) of this section must be examined under pressure of at least two times service pressure and show no defect.

(5) *Each 1000 cylinders or less* successively produced each day must constitute a lot. One cylinder must be selected from each lot and hydrostatically tested to destruction. If this cylinder bursts below five times the service pressure, then two additional cylinders must be selected and subjected to this test. If either of these cylinders fails by bursting below five times the service pressure then the entire lot must be rejected. All cylinders constituting a lot must be of identical size, construction heat-treatment, finish, and quality.

(j) **Flattening test.** Following the hydrostatic test, one cylinder taken at random out of each lot of 200 or less, must be subjected to a flattening test that is between knife edges, wedge shaped, 60° angle, rounded to 1/2 inch radius.

(k) **Physical test.** A physical test must be conducted to determine yield strength, tensile strength, elongation, and reduction of area of material, as follows:

(1) *The test* is required on 2 specimens cut from 1 cylinder, or part thereof heat-treated as required, taken at random out of each lot of 200 or less in the case of cylinders of capacity greater than 86 cubic inches and out of each lot of 500 or less for cylinders having a capacity of 86 cubic inches or less.

(2) *Specimens must conform to the following:*

(i) *A gauge length* of 8 inches with a width not over 1 1/2 inches, a gauge length of 2 inches with a width not over 1 1/2 inches, or a gauge length at least 24 times the thickness with a width not over 6 times the thickness is authorized when a cylinder wall is not over 3/16 inch thick.

(ii) *The specimen,* exclusive of grip ends, may not be flattened. Grip ends may be flattened to within one inch of each end of the reduced section.

(iii) *When size* of cylinder does not permit securing straight specimens, the specimens may be taken in any location or direction and may be straightened or flattened cold by pressure only, not by blows. When specimens are so taken and prepared, the inspector's report must show in connection with record of physical tests detailed information in regard to such specimens.

(iv) *Heating of a specimen for any purpose is not authorized.*

(3) *The yield strength* in tension must be the stress corresponding to a permanent strain of 0.2 percent of the gauge length. The following conditions apply:

(i) *The yield strength* must be determined by either the "offset" method or the "extension under load" method as prescribed in ASTM E 8 (incorporated by reference; see §171.7 of this subchapter).

(ii) *In using the "extension under load" method,* the total strain (or "extension under load") corresponding to the stress at which the 0.2 percent permanent strain occurs may be determined with sufficient accuracy by calculating the elastic extension of the gauge length under appropriate load and adding thereto 0.2 percent of the gauge length. Elastic extension calculations must be based on an elastic modulus of 30,000,000. In the event of controversy, the entire stress-strain diagram must be plotted and the yield strength determined from the 0.2 percent offset.

(iii) *For the purpose of strain measurement,* the initial strain must be set while the specimen is under a stress of 12,000 psi and the strain indicator reading being set at the calculated corresponding strain.

(iv) *Cross-head speed* of the testing machine may not exceed 1/8 inch per minute during yield strength determination.

(l) **Acceptable results for physical and flattening tests.** Acceptable results for the physical and flattening tests are an elongation of at least 40 percent for a 2 inch gauge length or at least 20 percent in other cases and a yield strength not over 73 percent of tensile strength. In this instance the flattening test is required, without cracking, to six times the wall thickness with a weld 90° from the direction of the applied load. Two rings cut from the ends of length of pipe used in production of a lot may be used for the flattening test provided the rings accompany the lot which they represent in all thermal processing operations. At least one of the rings must pass the flattening test.

(m) **Leakage test.** All spun cylinders and plugged cylinders must be tested for leakage by gas or air pressure after the bottom has been cleaned and is free from all moisture, subject to the following conditions:

(1) *Pressure, approximately the same as* but no less than service pressure, must be applied to one side of the finished bottom over an area of at least 1/16 of the total area of the bottom but not less than 3/4 inch in diameter, including the closure, for at least 1 minute, during which time the other side of the bottom exposed to pressure must be covered with water and closely examined for indications of leakage. Except as provided in paragraph (n) of this section, cylinders which are leaking must be rejected.

(2) *A spun cylinder* is one in which an end closure in the finished cylinder has been welded by the spinning process.

(3) *A plugged cylinder* is one in which a permanent closure in the bottom of a finished cylinder has been effected by a plug.

(4) *As a safety precaution,* if the manufacturer elects to make this test before the hydrostatic test, he should design his apparatus so that the pressure is applied to the smallest area practicable, around the point of closure, and so as to use the smallest possible volume of air or gas.

(n) **Rejected cylinders.** Repairs of rejected cylinders is authorized. Cylinders that are leaking must be rejected, except that:

(1) *Spun cylinders* rejected under the provisions of paragraph (m) of this section may be removed from the spun cylinder category by drilling to remove defective material, tapping, and plugging.

(2) *Brazed joints may be rebrazed.*

(3) *Subsequent to the operations* noted in paragraphs (n)(1) and (n)(2) of this section, acceptable cylinders must pass all prescribed tests.

(o) **Marking.** Markings on each cylinder must be by stamping plainly and permanently on shoulder, top head, neck or valve protection collar which is permanently attached to the cylinders and forming an integral part thereof, provided that cylinders not less than 0.090 inch thick may be stamped on the side wall adjacent to top head.

§178.56 Specification 4AA480 welded steel cylinders.

(a) **Type, size, and service pressure.** A DOT 4AA480 cylinder is a welded steel cylinder having a water capacity (nominal) not over 1,000 pounds water capacity and a service pressure of 480 psig. Closures welded by spinning process not permitted.

(b) **Steel.** The limiting chemical composition of steel authorized by this specification must be as shown in table I of appendix A to this part.

(c) **Identification of material.** Material must be identified by any suitable method except that plates and billets for hotdrawn cylinders must be marked with the heat number.

(d) **Manufacture.** Cylinders must be manufactured using equipment and processes adequate to ensure that each cylinder produced conforms to the requirements of this subpart. No defect is permitted that is likely to weaken the finished cylinder appreciably. A reasonably smooth and uniform surface finish is required. Exposed bottom welds on cylinders over 18 inches long must be protected by footrings. Minimum thickness of heads and bottoms may not be less than 90 percent of the required thickness of the side wall. Seams must be made as follows:

(1) *Circumferential seams must be welded. Brazing is not authorized.*

(2) *Longitudinal seams are not permitted.*

(3) *Welding procedures and operators* must be qualified in accordance with CGA Pamphlet C-3.

(e) **Welding.** Only the welding of neckrings, footrings, bosses, pads, and valve protection rings to the tops and bottoms of cylinders is authorized. Provided that such attachments are made of weldable steel, the carbon content of which does not exceed 0.25 percent.

(f) Wall thickness. The wall thickness of the cylinder must conform to the following:

(1) *For cylinders* with an outside diameter over 5 inches, the minimum wall thickness is 0.078 inch. In any case, the minimum wall thickness must be such that the calculated wall stress at the minimum test pressure (in paragraph (i) of this section) may not exceed the lesser value of either of the following:

(i) *One-half of the minimum* tensile strength of the material determined as required in paragraph (j) of this section; or

(ii) *35,000 psi.*

(2) *Calculation must be made by the formula:*

$S = [P(1.3D^2 + 0.4d^2)] / (D^2 - d^2)$

Where:

S = wall stress in psi;

P = minimum test pressure prescribed for water jacket test;

D = outside diameter in inches;

d = inside diameter in inches.

(3) *The ratio* of tangential length to outside diameter may not exceed 4.0 for cylinders with a wall thickness less than 0.100 inch.

(g) Heat treatment. Each cylinder must be uniformly and properly heat treated prior to tests. Any suitable heat treatment in excess of 1100 °F is authorized except that liquid quenching is not permitted. Heat treatment must be accomplished after all forming and welding operations. Heat treatment is not required after welding weldable low carbon parts to attachments of similar material which have been previously welded to the top or bottom of cylinders and properly heat treated, provided such subsequent welding does not produce a temperature in excess of 400 °F, in any part of the top or bottom material.

(h) Openings in cylinders. Openings in cylinders must conform to the following:

(1) *All openings must be in the heads or bases.*

(2) *Each opening in the cylinder,* except those for safety devices, must be provided with a fitting boss, or pad, securely attached to the cylinder by welding or by threads. If threads are used they must comply with the following:

(i) *Threads must be* clean-cut, even without checks and cut to gauge.

(ii) *Taper threads* to be of length not less than as specified for American Standard taper pipe threads.

(iii) *Straight threads* having at least 6 engaged threads, must have a tight fit and a calculated shear strength at least 10 times the test pressure of the cylinder. Gaskets, adequate to prevent leakage, are required.

(3) *Closure of a fitting,* boss or pad must be adequate to prevent leakage.

(i) Hydrostatic test. Each cylinder must successfully withstand a hydrostatic test as follows:

(1) *The test* must be by water jacket, or other suitable method, operated so as to obtain accurate data. The pressure gauge must permit reading to an accuracy of 1 percent. The expansion gauge must permit reading of total expansion to an accuracy of either 1 percent or 0.1 cubic centimeter.

(2) *Pressure must be maintained* for at least 30 seconds or sufficiently longer to assure complete expansion. Any internal pressure applied after heat-treatment and before the official test may not exceed 90 percent of the test pressure. If, due to failure of test apparatus, the test pressure cannot be maintained, the test may be repeated at a pressure increased by 10 percent or 100 psig, whichever is lower.

(3) *Permanent volumetric expansion* may not exceed 10 percent of the total volumetric expansion at test pressure.

(4) *Cylinders must be tested as follows:*

(i) *At least one cylinder* selected at random out of each lot of 200 or less must be tested as described in paragraphs (i)(1), (i)(2), and (i)(3) of this section, to at least two times service pressure. If a selected cylinder fails, then two additional specimens must be selected at random from the same lot and subjected to the prescribed test. If either of these fails the test, then each cylinder in that lot must be so tested; and

(ii) *Each cylinder* not tested as prescribed in paragraph (i)(4)(i) of this section must be examined under pressure of at least two times service pressure and must show no defect. A cylinder showing a defect must be rejected unless it may be requalified under paragraph (m) of this section.

(j) Physical test. A physical test must be conducted to determine yield strength, tensile strength, elongation, and reduction of area of material, as follows:

(1) *The test is required* on 2 specimens cut from one cylinder having passed the hydrostatic test, or part thereof heat-treated as required, taken at random out of each lot of 200 or less.

(2) *Specimens must conform to the following:*

(i) *A gauge length* of 8 inches with a width not over 1 1/2 inches, a gauge length of 2 inches with a width not over 1 1/2 inches, or a gauge length at least 24 times the thickness with a width not over 6 times thickness is authorized when the cylinder wall is not over 3/16 inch thick.

(ii) *The specimen,* exclusive of grip ends, may not be flattened. Grip ends may be flattened to within one inch of each end of the reduced section.

(iii) *When size of cylinder* does not permit securing straight specimens, the specimens may be taken in any location or direction and may be straightened or flattened cold, by pressure only, not by blows. When specimens are so taken and prepared, the inspector's report must show in connection with record of physical tests detailed information in regard to such specimens.

(iv) *Heating of a specimen for any purpose is not authorized.*

(3) *The yield strength* in tension must be the stress corresponding to a permanent strain of 0.2 percent of the gauge length. The following conditions apply:

(i) *The yield strength* must be determined by either the "offset" method or the "extension under load" method as prescribed in ASTM E 8 (incorporated by reference; see §171.7 of this subchapter).

(ii) *In using the "extension under load" method,* the total strain (or "extension under load"), corresponding to the stress at which the 0.2 percent permanent strain occurs may be determined with sufficient accuracy by calculating the elastic extension of the gauge length under appropriate load and adding thereto 0.2 percent of the gauge length. Elastic extension calculations must be based on an elastic modulus of 30,000,000. In the event of controversy, the entire stress-strain diagram must be plotted and the yield strength determined from the 0.2 percent offset.

(iii) *For the purpose of strain measurement,* the initial strain reference must be set while the specimen is under a stress of 12,000 psi and the strain indicator reading being set at the calculated corresponding strain.

(iv) *Cross-head speed* of the testing machine may not exceed 1/8 inch per minute during yield strength determination.

(k) Elongation. Physical test specimens must show at least a 40 percent elongation for 2-inch gauge lengths or at least a 20 percent elongation in other cases. Except that these elongation percentages may be reduced numerically by 2 for 2-inch specimens and by 1 in other cases for each 7,500 psi increment of tensile strength above 50,000 psi to a maximum of four such increments.

(l) Tests of welds. Welds must be tested as follows:

(1) *Tensile test.* A specimen must be cut from one cylinder of each lot of 200 or less, or a welded test plate. The welded test plate must be of one of the heats in the lot of 200 or less which it represents, in the same condition and approximately the same thickness as the cylinder wall except that it may not be of a lesser thickness than that required for a quarter size Charpy impact specimen. The weld must be made by the same procedures and subjected to the same heat treatment as the major weld on the cylinder. The specimens must be taken across the major seam and must be prepared and tested in accordance with and must meet the requirements of CGA Pamphlet C-3 (incorporated by reference; see §171.7 of this subchapter). Should this specimen fail to meet the requirements, specimens may be taken from two additional cylinders or welded test plates from the same lot and tested. If either of the latter specimens fail to meet the requirements, the entire lot represented must be rejected.

(2) *Guided bend test.* A root bend test specimen must be cut from the cylinder or a welded test plate, used for the tensile test specified in paragraph (l)(1) of this section. Specimens must be taken from across the major seam and must be prepared and tested in accordance with and must meet the requirements of CGA Pamphlet C-3 (incorporated by reference; see §171.7 of this subchapter).

(3) *Alternate guided-bend test.* This test may be used and must be as required by CGA Pamphlet C-3 (incorporated by reference; see §171.7 of this subchapter). The specimen must be bent until the elongation at the outer surface, adjacent to the root of the weld, between the lightly scribed gage lines-a to b, is at least 20 percent, except that this percentage may be reduced for steels having a tensile strength in excess of 50,000 psi, as provided in paragraph (k) of this section.

(m) Rejected cylinders. Reheat treatment of rejected cylinders is authorized. Subsequent thereto, cylinders must pass all prescribed tests to be acceptable. Repair of welded seams by welding is authorized.

(n) **Markings.** Markings must be stamped plainly and permanently in one of the following locations on the cylinder:

(1) *On shoulders and top heads not less than 0.087 inch thick.*

(2) *On neck,* valve boss, valve protection sleeve, or similar part permanently attached to top end of cylinder.

(3) *On a plate* attached to the top of the cylinder or permanent part thereof: sufficient space must be left on the plate to provide for stamping at least six retest dates: the plate must be at least 1/16 inch thick and must be attached by welding or by brazing at a temperature of at least 1100 °F, throughout all edges of the plate.

(4) *Variations in location* of markings authorized only when necessitated by lack of space.

§178.57 Specification 4L welded insulated cylinders.

(a) **Type, size, service pressure, and design service temperature.** A DOT 4L cylinder is a fusion welded insulated cylinder with a water capacity (nominal) not over 1,000 pounds water capacity and a service pressure of at least 40 but not greater than 500 psig conforming to the following requirements:

(1) *For liquefied hydrogen service,* the cylinders must be designed to stand on end, with the axis of the cylindrical portion vertical.

(2) *The design service temperature* is the coldest temperature for which a cylinder is suitable. The required design service temperatures for each cryogenic liquid is as follows:

Cryogenic liquid	Design service temperature
Argon	- 320 °F or colder
Helium	- 452 °F or colder
Hydrogen	- 423 °F or colder
Neon	- 411 °F or colder
Nitrogen	- 320 °F or colder
Oxygen	- 320 °F or colder

(b) **Material.** Material use in the construction of this specification must conform to the following:

(1) *Inner containment vessel (cylinder).* Designations and limiting chemical compositions of steel authorized by this specification must be as shown in table 1 in paragraph (o) of this section.

(2) *Outer jacket.* Steel or aluminum may be used subject to the requirements of paragraph (o)(2) of this section.

(c) **Identification of material.** Material must be identified by any suitable method.

(d) **Manufacture.** Cylinders must be manufactured using equipment and processes adequate to ensure that each cylinder produced conforms to the requirements of this subpart and to the following requirements:

(1) *No defect* is permitted that is likely to weaken the finished cylinder appreciably. A reasonably smooth and uniform surface finish is required. The shell portion must be a reasonably true cylinder.

(2) *The heads* must be seamless, concave side to the pressure, hemispherical or ellipsoidal in shape with the major diameter not more than twice the minor diameter. Minimum thickness of heads may not be less than 90 percent of the required thickness of the sidewall. The heads must be reasonably true to shape, have no abrupt shape changes, and the skirts must be reasonably true to round.

(3) *The surface* of the cylinder must be insulated. The insulating material must be fire resistant. The insulation on non-evacuated jackets must be covered with a steel jacket not less than 0.060-inch thick or an aluminum jacket not less than 0.070 inch thick, so constructed that moisture cannot come in contact with the insulating material. If a vacuum is maintained in the insulation space, the evacuated jacket must be designed for a minimum collapsing pressure of 30 psig differential whether made of steel or aluminum. The construction must be such that the total heat transfer, from the atmosphere at ambient temperature to the contents of the cylinder, will not exceed 0.0005 Btu per hour, per Fahrenheit degree differential in temperature, per pound of water capacity of the cylinder. For hydrogen, cryogenic liquid service, the total heat transfer, with a temperature differential of 520 Fahrenheit degrees, may not exceed that required to vent 30 SCF of hydrogen gas per hour.

(4) *For a cylinder* having a design service temperature colder than minus 320 °F, a calculation of the maximum weight of contents must be made and that weight must be marked on the cylinder as prescribed in §178.35.

(5) *Welding procedures and operators* must be qualified in accordance with CGA Pamphlet C-3 (incorporated by reference; see §171.7 of this subchapter). In addition, an impact test of the weld must be performed in accordance with paragraph (l) of this section as part of the qualification of each welding procedure and operator.

(e) **Welding.** Welding of the cylinder must be as follows:

(1) *All seams of the cylinder* must be fusion welded. A means must be provided for accomplishing complete penetration of the joint. Only butt or joggle butt joints for the cylinder seams are authorized. All joints in the cylinder must have reasonably true alignment.

(2) *All attachments* to the sidewalls and heads of the cylinder must be by fusion welding and must be of a weldable material complying with the impact requirements of paragraph (l) of this section.

(3) *For welding the cylinder,* each procedure and operator must be qualified in accordance with the sections of CGA Pamphlet C-3 (incorporated by reference; see §171.7 of this subchapter) that apply. In addition, impact tests of the weld must be performed in accordance with paragraph (l) of this section as part of the qualification of each welding procedure and operator.

(4) *Brazing, soldering, and threading* are permitted only for joints not made directly to the cylinder body. Threads must comply with the requirements of paragraph (h) of this section.

(f) **Wall thickness.** The minimum wall thickness of the cylinder must be such that the calculated wall stress at the minimum required test pressure may not exceed the least value of the following:

(1) *45,000 psi.*

(2) *One-half of the minimum tensile strength* across the welded seam determined in paragraph (l) of this section.

(3) *One-half of the minimum tensile strength* of the base metal determined as required in paragraph (j) of this section.

(4) *The yield strength* of the base metal determined as required in paragraph (l) of this section.

(5) *Further provided* that wall stress for cylinders having longitudinal seams may not exceed 85 percent of the above value, whichever applies.

(6) *Calculation must be made by the following formula:*

$S = [P(1.3D^2 + 0.4d^2)] / (D^2 - d^2)$

Where:

S = wall stress in pounds psi;

P = minimum test pressure prescribed for pressure test in psig;

D = outside diameter in inches;

d = inside diameter in inches.

(g) **Heat treatment.** Heat treatment is not permitted.

(h) **Openings in cylinder.** Openings in cylinders must conform to the following:

(1) *Openings are permitted in heads only.* They must be circular and may not exceed 3 inches in diameter or one third of the cylinder diameter, whichever is less. Each opening in the cylinder must be provided with a fitting, boss or pad, either integral with, or securely attached to, the cylinder body by fusion welding. Attachments to a fitting, boss or pad may be made by welding, brazing, mechanical attachment, or threading.

(2) *Threads must comply with the following:*

(i) *Threads must be* clean-cut, even, without checks and cut to gauge.

(ii) *Taper threads* to be of a length not less than that specified for NPT.

(iii) *Straight threads* must have at least 4 engaged threads, tight fit and calculated shear strength at least 10 times the test pressure of the cylinder. Gaskets, which prevent leakage and are inert to the hazardous material, are required.

(i) **Pressure test.** Each cylinder, before insulating and jacketing, must be examined under a pressure of at least 2 times the service pressure maintained for at least 30 seconds without evidence of leakage, visible distortion or other defect. The pressure gauge must permit reading to an accuracy of 1 percent.

(j) **Physical test.** A physical test must be conducted to determine yield strength, tensile strength, and elongation as follows:

(1) *The test* is required on 2 specimens selected from material of each heat and in the same condition as that in the completed cylinder.

(2) *Specimens must conform to the following:*

(i) *A gauge length* of 8 inches with a width not over 1 1/2 inches, a gauge length of 2 inches with width not over 1 1/2 inches, or a gauge length at least 24 times thickness with a width not over 6 times thickness (authorized when cylinder wall is not over 1/16 inch thick).

(ii) *The specimen,* exclusive of grip ends, may not be flattened. Grip ends may be flattened to within one inch of each end of the reduced section.

(iii) *When size of the cylinder* does not permit securing straight specimens, the specimens may be taken in any location or direction and may be straightened or flattened cold by pressure only, not by blows. When specimens are so taken and prepared, the inspector's report must show in connection with record of physical tests detailed information in regard to such specimens.

(iv) *Heating of a specimen for any purpose is not authorized.*

(3) *The yield strength* in tension must be the stress corresponding to a permanent strain of 0.2 percent of the gauge length. The following conditions apply:

(i) *The yield strength* must be determined by either the "offset" method or the "extension under load" method as prescribed in ASTM E 8 (incorporated by reference; see §171.7 of this subchapter).

(ii) *In using the "extension under load" method,* the total strain (or "extension under load"), corresponding to the stress at which the 0.2 percent permanent strain occurs may be determined with sufficient accuracy by calculating the elastic expansion of the gauge length under appropriate load and adding thereto 0.2 percent of the gauge length. Elastic extension calculations must be based on the elastic modulus of the material used. In the event of controversy, the entire stress-strain diagram must be plotted and the yield strength determined from the 0.2 percent offset.

(iii) *For the purpose of strain measurement,* the initial strain reference must be set while the specimen is under a stress of 12,000 psi and the strain indicator reading being set at the calculated corresponding strain.

(iv) *Cross-head speed* of the testing machine may not exceed 1/8 inch per minute during yield strength determination.

(k) Acceptable results for physical tests. Physical properties must meet the limits specified in paragraph (o)(1), table 1, of this section, for the particular steel in the annealed condition. The specimens must show at least a 20 percent elongation for a 2-inch gage length. Except that the percentage may be reduced numerically by 2 for each 7,500 psi increment of tensile strength above 100,000 psi to a maximum of 5 such increments. Yield strength and tensile strength must meet the requirements of paragraph (o)(1), table 1, of this section.

(l) Tests of welds. Welds must be tested as follows:

(1) *Tensile test.* A specimen must be cut from one cylinder of each lot of 200 or less, or welded test plate. The welded test plate must be of one of the heats in the lot of 200 or less which it represents, in the same condition and approximately the same thickness as the cylinder wall except that it may not be of a lesser thickness than that required for a quarter size Charpy impact specimen. The weld must be made by the same procedures and subjected to the same heat treatment as the major weld on the cylinder. The specimen must be taken across the major seam and must be prepared and tested in accordance with and must meet the requirements of CGA Pamphlet C-3 (incorporated by reference; see §171.7 of this subchapter). Should this specimen fail to meet the requirements, specimens may be taken from two additional cylinders or welded test plates from the same lot and tested. If either of the latter specimens fails to meet the requirements, the entire lot represented must be rejected.

(2) *Guided bend test.* A "root" bend test specimen must be cut from the cylinder or welded test plate, used for the tensile test specified in paragraph (l)(1) of this section and from any other seam or equivalent welded test plate if the seam is welded by a procedure different from that used for the major seam. Specimens must be taken across the particular seam being tested and must be prepared and tested in accordance with and must meet the requirements of CGA Pamphlet C-3 (incorporated by reference; see §171.7 of this subchapter).

(3) *Alternate guided-bend test.* This test may be used and must be as specified in CGA Pamphlet C-3 (incorporated by reference; see §171.7 of this subchapter). The specimen must be bent until the elongation at the outer surface, adjacent to the root of the weld, between the lightly scribed gage lines a to b, is at least 20 percent, except that this percentage may be reduced for steels having a tensile strength in excess of 100,000 psig, as provided in paragraph (c) of this section.

(4) *Impact tests.* One set of three impact test specimens (for each test) must be prepared and tested for determining the impact properties of the deposited weld metal —

(i) *As part of the qualification of the welding procedure.*

(ii) *As part of the qualification of the operators.*

(iii) *For each "heat" of welding rodor wire used.*

(iv) *For each 1,000 feet* of weld made with the same heat of welding rod or wire.

(v) *All impact test specimens* must be of the charpy type, keyhole or milled U-notch, and must conform in all respects to Figure 3 of ASTM E 23 (incorporated by reference; see §171.7 of this subchapter). Each set of impact specimens must be taken across the weld and have the notch located in the weld metal. When the cylinder material thickness is 2.5 mm or thicker, impact specimens must be cut from a cylinder or welded test plate used for the tensile or bend test specimens. The dimension along the axis of the notch must be reduced to the largest possible of 10 mm, 7.5 mm, 5 mm or 2.5 mm, depending upon cylinder thickness. When the material in the cylinder or welded test plate is not of sufficient thickness to prepare 2.5 mm impact test specimens, 2.5 mm specimens must be prepared from a welded test plate made from 1/8 inch thick material meeting the requirements specified in paragraph (o)(1), table 1, of this section and having a carbon analysis of .05 minimum, but not necessarily from one of the heats used in the lot of cylinders. The test piece must be welded by the same welding procedure as used on the particular cylinder seam being qualified and must be subjected to the same heat treatment.

(vi) *Impact test specimens* must be cooled to the design service temperature. The apparatus for testing the specimens must conform to the requirements of ASTM Standard E 23 (incorporated by reference; see §171.7 of this subchapter). The test piece, as well as the handling tongs, must be cooled for a length of time sufficient to reach the service temperature. The temperature of the cooling device must be maintained within a range of plus or minus 3 °F. The specimen must be quickly transferred from the cooling device to the anvil of the testing machine and broken within a time lapse of not more than six seconds.

(vii) *The impact properties* of each set of impact specimens may not be less than the values in the following table:

Size of specimen	Minimum impact value required for avg. of each set of three specimens (ft.-lb.)	Minimum impact value permitted on one only of a set of three (ft.-lb.)
10 mm x 10 mm	15	10
10 mm x 7.5 mm	12.5	8.5
10 mm x 5 mm	10	7.0
10 mm x 2.5 mm	5	3.5

(viii) *When the average value* of the three specimens equals or exceeds the minimum value permitted for a single specimen and the value for more than one specimen is below the required average value, or when the value for one specimen is below the minimum value permitted for a single specimen, a retest of three additional specimens must be made. The value of each of these retest specimens must equal or exceed the required average value. When an erratic result is caused by a defective specimen, or there is uncertainty in test procedure, a retest is authorized.

(m) Radiographic examination. Cylinders must be subject to a radiographic examination as follows:

(1) *The techniques and acceptability* of radiographic inspection must conform to the standards set forth in CGA Pamphlet C-3 (incorporated by reference; see §171.7 of this subchapter).

(2) *One finished longitudinal seam* must be selected at random from each lot of 100 or less successively produced and be radiographed throughout its entire length. Should the radiographic examination fail to meet the requirements of paragraph (m)(1) of this section, two additional seams of the same lot must be examined, and if either of these fail to meet the requirements of (m)(1) of this section, only those passing are acceptable.

(n) Rejected cylinders. Reheat treatment of rejected cylinders is authorized. Subsequent thereto, cylinders must pass all prescribed tests to be acceptable. Welds may be repaired by suitable methods of fusion welding.

(o) **Authorized materials of construction.** Authorized materials of construction are as follows:

(1) *Inner containment vessel (cylinder).* Electric furnace steel of uniform quality must be used. Chemical analysis must conform to ASTM A 240/A 240M (incorporated by reference; see §171.7 of this subchapter), Type 304 Stainless Steel. A heat of steel made under table 1 and table 2 in this paragraph (o)(1) is acceptable, even though its check chemical analysis is slightly out of the specified range, if it is satisfactory in all other respects, provided the tolerances shown in table 3 in this paragraph (o)(1) are not exceeded. The following chemical analyses and physical properties are authorized:

Table 1 - Authorized Materials

Designation	Chemical analysis, limits in percent
Carbon[1]	0.08 max
Manganese	2.00 max
Phosphorus	0.045 max
Sulphur	0.030 max
Silicon	1.00 max
Nickel	8.00-10.50
Chromium	18.00-20.00
Molybdenum	None
Titanium	None
Columbium	None

1. The carbon analysis must be reported to the nearest hundredth of one percent.

Table 2 - Physical Properties

	Physical properties (annealed)
Tensile strength, p.s.i. (minimum)	75,000
Yield strength, p.s.i. (minimum)	30,000
Elongation in 2 inches (minimum) percent	30.0
Elongation other permissible gauge lengths (minimum) percent	15.0

Table 3 - Check Analysis Tolerances

Element	Limit or specified range (percent)	Tolerance over the maximum limit or under the minimum limit
Carbon	To 0.030, incl	0.005
	Over 0.30 to 0.20, incl	0.01
Manganese	To 1.00 incl	.03
	Over 1.00 to 3.00, incl	0.04
Phosphorus[1]	To 0.040, incl	0.005
	Over 0.040 to 0.020 incl	0.010
Sulphur	To .40 incl	0.005
Silicon	To 1.00, incl	0.05
Nickel	Over 5.00 to 10.00, incl	0.10
	Over 10.00 to 20.00, incl	0.15
Chromium	Over 15.00 to 20.00, incl	0.20

1. Rephosphorized steels not subject to check analysis for phosphorus.

(2) *Outer jacket.*

(i) *Nonflammable cryogenic liquids.* Cylinders intended for use in the transportation of nonflammable cryogenic liquid must have an outer jacket made of steel or aluminum.

(ii) *Flammable cryogenic liquids.* Cylinders intended for use in the transportation of flammable cryogenic liquid must have an outer jacket made of steel.

(p) **Markings.**

(1) *Markings must be stamped* plainly and permanently on shoulder or top head of jacket or on a permanently attached plate or head protective ring.

(2) *The letters "ST",* followed by the design service temperature (for example, ST-423F), must be marked on cylinders having a design service temperature of colder than minus 320 °F only. Location to be just below the DOT mark.

(3) *The maximum weight of contents,* in pounds (for example, "Max. Content 51 #"), must be marked on cylinders having a design service temperature colder than minus 320 °F only. Location to be near symbol.

(4) *Special orientation instructions* must be marked on the cylinder (for example, THIS END UP), if the cylinder is used in an orientation other than vertical with openings at the top of the cylinder.

(5) *If the jacket of the cylinder* is constructed of aluminum, the letters "AL" must be marked after the service pressure marking. Example: DOT-4L150 AL.

(6) *Except for serial number* and jacket material designation, each marking prescribed in this paragraph (p) must be duplicated on each cylinder by any suitable means.

(q) **Inspector's report.** In addition to the information required by §178.35, the inspector's reports must contain information on:

(1) *The jacket material and insulation type;*

(2) *The design service temperature (°F); and*

(3) *The impact test results, on a lot basis.*

§178.58 Specification 4DA welded steel cylinders for aircraft use.

(a) **Type, size, and service pressure.** A DOT 4DA is a welded steel sphere (two seamless hemispheres) or a circumferentially welded cylinder (two seamless drawn shells) with a water capacity not over 100 pounds and a service pressure of at least 500 but not over 900 psig.

(b) **Steel.** Open-hearth or electric steel of uniform quality must be used. A heat of steel made under table 1 in this paragraph (b), check chemical analysis of which is slightly out of the specified range, is acceptable, if satisfactory in all other respects, provided the tolerances shown in table 2 in this paragraph (b) are not exceeded except as approved by the Associate Administrator. The following chemical analyses are authorized:

Table 1 - Authorized Materials

4130	Percent
Carbon	0.28/0.33
Manganese	0.40/0.60
Phosphorus	0.040 max
Sulfur	0.040 max
Silicon	0.15/0.35
Chromium	0.80/1.10
Molybdenum	0.15/0.25

Table 2 - Check Analysis Tolerances

Element	Limit or maximum specified (percent)	Tolerance (percent) over the maximum limit or under the minimum limit	
		Under minimum limit	Over maximum limit
Carbon	Over 0.15 to 0.40 incl	.03	.04
Manganese	To 0.60 incl	.03	.03
Phosphorus[1]	All ranges		.01
Sulphur	All ranges		.01
Silicon	To 0.30 incl Over 0.30 to 1.00 incl	.02 .05	.03 .05
Chromium	To 0.90 incl Over 0.90 to 2.10 incl	.03 .05	.03 .05
Molybdenum	To 0.20 incl Over 0.20 to 0.40, incl	.01 .02	.01 .02

1. Rephosphorized steels not subject to check analysis for phosphorus.

(c) **Identification of material.** Materials must be identified by any suitable method except that plates and billets for hot-drawn containers must be marked with the heat number.

(d) **Manufacture.** Cylinders must be manufactured in accordance with the following requirements:

(1) *By best appliances and methods.* No defect is acceptable that is likely to weaken the finished container appreciably. A reasonably smooth and uniform surface finish is required. No abrupt change in wall thickness is permitted. Welding procedures and operators must be qualified in accordance with CGA Pamphlet C-3 (incorporated by reference; see §171.7 of this subchapter).

(2) *All seams* of the sphere or cylinders must be fusion welded. Seams must be of the butt or joggle butt type and means must be provided for accomplishing complete penetration of the joint.

(e) Welding. Attachments to the container are authorized by fusion welding provided that such attachments are made of weldable steel, the carbon content of which may not exceed 0.25 percent except in the case of 4130 steel.

(f) Wall thickness. The minimum wall thickness must be such that the wall stress at the minimum specified test pressure may not exceed 67 percent of the minimum tensile strength of the steel as determined from the physical and burst tests required and may not be over 70,000 p.s.i. For any diameter container, the minimum wall thickness is 0.040 inch. Calculations must be made by the formulas in (f)(1) or (f)(2) of this section:

(1) *Calculation for a sphere must be made by the following formula:*

$S = PD / 4tE$

Where:

S = wall stress in pounds psi;

P = test pressure prescribed for water jacket test, i.e., at least 2 times service pressure, in psig;

D = outside diameter in inches;

t = minimum wall thickness in inches;

E = 0.85 (provides 85 percent weld efficiency factor which must be applied in the girth weld area and heat affected zones which zone must extend a distance of 6 times wall thickness from center line of weld);

E = 1.0 (for all other areas).

(2) *Calculation for a cylinder must be made by the following formula:*

$S = [P(1.3D^2 + 0.4d^2)] / (D^2 - d^2)$

Where:

S = wall stress in pounds psi;

P = test pressure prescribed for water jacket test, i.e., at least 2 times service pressure, in psig;

D = outside diameter in inches;

d = inside diameter in inches.

(g) Heat treatment. The completed containers must be uniformly and properly heat-treated prior to tests. Heat-treatment of containers of the authorized analysis must be as follows:

(1) *All containers* must be quenched by oil, or other suitable medium except as provided in paragraph (g)(4) of this section.

(2) *The steel temperature* on quenching must be that recommended for the steel analysis, but may not exceed 1,750 °F.

(3) *The steel* must be tempered at the temperature most suitable for the analysis except that in no case shall the tempering temperature be less than 1,000 °F.

(4) *The steel* may be normalized at a temperature of 1,650 °F instead of being quenched, and containers so normalized need not be tempered.

(5) *All cylinders,* if water quenched or quenched with a liquid producing a cooling rate in excess of 80 percent of the cooling rate of water, must be inspected by the magnetic particle or dye penetrant method to detect the presence of quenching cracks. Any cylinder found to have a quench crack must be rejected and may not be requalified.

(h) Openings in container. Openings in the container must comply with the following requirements:

(1) *Each opening in the container* must be provided with a fitting, boss, or pad of weldable steel securely attached to the container by fusion welding.

(2) *Attachments to a fitting, boss, or pad* must be adequate to prevent leakage. Threads must comply with the following:

(i) *Threads must be* clean cut, even, without checks, and tapped to gauge.

(ii) *Taper threads* to be of length not less than as specified for American Standard taper pipe threads.

(iii) *Straight threads,* having at least 4 engaged threads, to have tight fit and calculated shear strength at least 10 times the test pressure of the container; gaskets required, adequate to prevent leakage.

(i) Hydrostatic test. Each cylinder must successfully withstand a hydrostatic test as follows:

(1) *The test* must be by water-jacket, or other suitable method, operated so as to obtain accurate data. The pressure gauge must permit reading to an accuracy of 1 percent. The expansion gauge must permit reading of total expansion to accuracy either of 1 percent or 0.1 cubic centimeter.

(2) *Pressure must be maintained* for at least 30 seconds and sufficiently longer to ensure complete expansion. Any internal pressure applied after heat-treatment and previous to the official test may not exceed 90 percent of the test pressure. If, due to failure of the test apparatus, the test pressure cannot be maintained, the test may be repeated at a pressure increased by 10 percent or 100 psig, whichever is the lower.

(3) *Permanent volumetric expansion* may not exceed 10 percent of total volumetric expansion at test pressure.

(4) *Each container* must be tested to at least 2 times service pressure.

(j) Burst test. One container taken at random out of 200 or less must be hydrostatically tested to destruction. The rupture pressure must be included as part of the inspector's report.

(k) Flattening test. Spheres and cylinders must be subjected to a flattening test as follows:

(1) *Flattening test for spheres.* One sphere taken at random out of each lot of 200 or less must be subjected to a flattening test as follows:

(i) *The test must be performed after the hydrostatic test.*

(ii) *The test* must be at the weld between the parallel steel plates on a press with a welded seam, at right angles to the plates. Any projecting appurtenances may be cut off (by mechanical means only) prior to crushing.

(2) *Flattening test for cylinders.* One cylinder taken at random out of each lot of 200 or less, must be subjected to a flattening test as follows:

(i) *The test must be performed after the hydrostatic test.*

(ii) *The test cylinder* must be placed between wedge-shaped knife edges having a 60° angle, rounded to a 1/2-inch radius.

(l) Radiographic inspection. Radiographic examinations is required on all welded joints which are subjected to internal pressure, except that at the discretion of the disinterested inspector, openings less than 25 percent of the sphere diameter need not be subjected to radiographic inspection. Evidence of any defects likely to seriously weaken the container must be cause for rejection.

(m) Physical test and specimens for spheres and cylinders. Spheres and cylinders must be subjected to a physical test as follows:

(1) *A physical test* for a sphere is required on 2 specimens cut from a flat representative sample plate of the same heat taken at random from the steel used to produce the sphere. This flat steel from which the 2 specimens are to be cut must receive the same heat-treatment as the spheres themselves. Sample plates to be taken for each lot of 200 or less spheres.

(2) *Specimens for spheres* have a gauge length of 2 inches with a width not over 1 1/2 inches, or a gauge length at least 24 times thickness with a width not over 6 times thickness is authorized when wall of sphere is not over 3/16 inch thick.

(3) *A physical test* for cylinders is required on 2 specimens cut from 1 cylinder taken at random out of each lot of 200 or less.

(4) *Specimens for cylinder must conform to the following:*

(i) *A gauge length* of 8 inches with a width not over 1 1/2 inches, a gauge length of 2 inches with a width not over 1 1/2 inches, a gauge length at least 24 times thickness with a width not over 6 times thickness is authorized when a cylinder wall is not over 3/16 inch thick.

(ii) *The specimen,* exclusive of grip ends, may not be flattened. Grip ends may be flattened to within 1 inch of each end of the reduced section.

(iii) *Heating of a specimen for any purpose is not authorized.*

(5) *The yield strength* in tension must be the stress corresponding to a permanent strain of 0.2 percent of the gauge length. The following conditions apply:

(i) *The yield strength* must be determined by either the "offset" method or the "extension under load" method as prescribed in ASTM E 8 (incorporated by reference; see §171.7 of this subchapter).

(ii) *In using the "extension under load" method,* the total strain (or "extension under load") corresponding to the stress at which the 0.2 percent permanent strain occurs may be determined with sufficient accuracy by calculating the elastic extension of the gauge length under appropriate load and adding thereto 0.2 percent of the gauge length. Elastic extension calculations must be based on an elastic modulus of 30,000,000. In the event of controversy, the entire stress-strain diagram must be plotted and the yield strength determined from the 0.2 percent offset.

(iii) *For the purpose of strain measurement,* the initial strain must be set while the specimen is under a stress of 12,000 psi and the strain indicator reading being set at the calculated corresponding strain.

(iv) *Cross-head speed* of the testing machine may not exceed 1/8 inch per minute during yield strength determination.

(n) **Acceptable results for physical, flattening, and burst tests.** The following are acceptable results of the physical, flattening and burst test:

(1) *Elongation must be* at least 20 percent for a 2-inch gauge length or 10 percent in other cases.

(2) *Flattening is required* to 50 percent of the original outside diameter without cracking.

(3) *Burst pressure must be at least 3 times service pressure.*

(o) **Rejected containers.** Reheat-treatment of rejected cylinders is authorized. Subsequent thereto, containers must pass all prescribed tests to be acceptable. Repair of welded seams by welding prior to reheat-treatment is authorized.

(p) **Marking.** Markings on each container must be stamped plainly and permanently on a permanent attachment or on a metal name-plate permanently secured to the container by means other than soft solder.

§178.59 Specification 8 steel cylinders with porous fillings for acetylene.

(a) **Type and service pressure.** A DOT 8 cylinder is a seamless cylinder with a service pressure of 250 psig. The following steel is authorized:

(1) *A longitudinal seam if forge lap welded;*

(2) *Attachment of heads* by welding or by brazing by dipping process; or

(3) *A welded* circumferential body seam if the cylinder has no longitudinal seam.

(b) **Steel.** Open-hearth, electric or basic oxygen process steel of uniform quality must be used. Content percent may not exceed the following: Carbon, 0.25; phosphorus, 0.045; sulphur, 0.050.

(c) **Identification of steel.** Materials must be identified by any suitable method except that plates and billets for hot-drawn cylinders must be marked with the heat number.

(d) **Manufacture.** Cylinders must be manufactured using equipment and processes adequate to ensure that each cylinder produced conforms to the requirements of this subpart. No defect is acceptable that is likely to weaken the finished cylinder appreciably. A reasonably smooth and uniform surface finish is required. Welding procedures and operators must be qualified in accordance with CGA Pamphlet C-3 (incorporated by reference; see §171.7 of this subchapter).

(e) **Exposed bottom welds.** Exposed bottom welds on cylinders over 18 inches long must be protected by footrings.

(f) **Heat treatment.** Body and heads formed by drawing or pressing must be uniformly and properly heat treated prior to tests.

(g) **Openings.** Openings in the cylinders must comply with the following:

(1) *Standard taper pipe threads are required;*

(2) *Length may not be* less than as specified for American Standard pipe threads; tapped to gauge; clean cut, even, and without checks.

(h) **Hydrostatic test.** Each cylinder must successfully withstand a hydrostatic test as follows:

(1) *The test* must be by water-jacket, or other suitable method, operated so as to obtain accurate data. The pressure gauge must permit reading to an accuracy of 1 percent. The expansion gauge must permit reading of total expansion to an accuracy of either 1 percent or 0.1 cubic centimeter.

(2) *Pressure must be maintained* for at least 30 seconds and sufficiently longer to ensure complete expansion. Any internal pressure applied after heat-treatment and previous to the official test may not exceed 90 percent of the test pressure.

(3) *Permanent volumetric expansion* may not exceed 10 percent of total volumetric expansion at test pressure.

(4) *One cylinder* out of each lot of 200 or less must be hydrostatically tested to at least 750 psig. Cylinders not so tested must be examined under pressure of between 500 and 600 psig and show no defect. If hydrostatically tested cylinder fails, each cylinder in the lot may be hydrostatically tested and those passing are acceptable.

(i) **Leakage test.** Cylinders with bottoms closed in by spinning must be subjected to a leakage test by setting the interior air or gas pressure to not less than the service pressure. Cylinders which leak must be rejected.

(j) **Physical test.** A physical test must be conducted as follows:

(1) *The test is required* on 2 specimens cut longitudinally from 1 cylinder or part thereof taken at random out of each lot of 200 or less, after heat treatment.

(2) *Specimens must conform* to a gauge length of 8 inches with a width not over 1 1/2 inches, a gauge length of 2 inches with width not over 1 1/2, or a gauge length at least 24 times thickness with a width not over 6 times thickness is authorized when a cylinder wall is not over 3/16 inch thick.

(3) *The yield strength* in tension must be the stress corresponding to a permanent strain of 0.2 percent of the gauge length. The following conditions apply:

(i) *The yield strength* must be determined by either the "offset" method or the "extension under load" method as prescribed in ASTM E 8 (incorporated by reference; see §171.7 of this subchapter).

(ii) *In using the "extension under load" method,* the total strain (or "extension under load") corresponding to the stress at which the 0.2 percent permanent strain occurs may be determined with sufficient accuracy by calculating the elastic extension of the gauge length under appropriate load and adding thereto 0.2 percent of the gauge length. Elastic extension calculations must be based on an elastic modulus of 30,000,000. In the event of controversy, the entire stress-strain diagram must be plotted and the yield strength determined from the 0.2 offset.

(iii) *For the purpose of strain measurement,* the initial strain must be set while the specimen is under a stress of 12,000 psi and the strain indicator reading being set at the calculated corresponding strain.

(iv) *Cross-head speed* of the testing machine may not exceed 1/8 inch per minute during yield strength determination.

(4) *Yield strength* may not exceed 73 percent of tensile strength. Elongation must be at least 40 percent in 2 inch or 20 percent in other cases.

(k) **Rejected cylinders.** Reheat treatment of rejected cylinder is authorized. Subsequent thereto, cylinders must pass all prescribed tests to be acceptable. Repair by welding is authorized.

(l) **Porous filling.**

(1) *Cylinders must be filled* with a porous material in accordance with the following:

(i) *The porous material* may not disintegrate or sag when wet with solvent or when subjected to normal service;

(ii) *The porous filling material* must be uniform in quality and free of voids, except that a well drilled into the filling material beneath the valve is authorized if the well is filled with a material of such type that the functions of the filling material are not impaired;

(iii) *Overall shrinkage* of the filling material is authorized if the total clearance between the cylinder shell and filling material, after solvent has been added, does not exceed 1/2 of 1 percent of the respective diameter or length, but not to exceed 1/8 inch, measured diametrically and longitudinally;

(iv) *The clearance may not impair the functions of the filling material;*

(v) *The installed filling material* must meet the requirements of CGA Pamphlet C-12; and

(vi) *Porosity of filling material* may not exceed 80 percent except that filling material with a porosity of up to 92 percent may be used when tested with satisfactory results in accordance with CGA Pamphlet C-12.

(2) *When the porosity* of each cylinder is not known, a cylinder taken at random from a lot of 200 or less must be tested for porosity. If the test cylinder fails, each cylinder in the lot may be tested individually and those cylinders that pass the test are acceptable.

(3) *For filling* that is molded and dried before insertion in cylinders, porosity test may be made on a sample block taken at random from material to be used.

(4) *The porosity* of the filling material must be determined. The amount of solvent at 70 ^{o}F for a cylinder:

(i) *Having shell volumetric capacity* above 20 pounds water capacity (nominal) may not exceed the following:

Percent porosity of filler	Maximum acetone solvent percent shell capacity by volume
90 to 92	43.4
87 to 90	42.0
83 to 87	40.0
80 to 83	38.6
75 to 80	36.2
70 to 75	33.8
65 to 70	31.4

(ii) *Having volumetric capacity* of 20 pounds or less water capacity (nominal), may not exceed the following:

Percent porosity of filler	Maximum acetone solvent percent shell capacity by volume
90 to 92	41.8
83 to 90	38.5
80 to 83	37.1
75 to 80	34.8
70 to 75	32.5
65 to 70	30.2

(m) **Tare weight.** The tare weight is the combined weight of the cylinder proper, porous filling, valve, and solvent, without removable cap.

(n) **Duties of inspector.** In addition to the requirements of §178.35, the inspector is required to —

(1) *Certify chemical analyses* of steel used, signed by manufacturer thereof; also verify by, check analyses of samples taken from each heat or from 1 out of each lot of 200 or less, plates, shells, or tubes used.

(2) *Verify compliance* of cylinder shells with all shell requirements; inspect inside before closing in both ends; verify heat treatment as proper; obtain all samples for all tests and for check analyses; witness all tests; verify threads by gauge; report volumetric capacity and minimum thickness of wall noted.

(3) *Prepare report* on manufacture of steel shells in form prescribed in §178.35. Furnish one copy to manufacturer and three copies to the company that is to complete the cylinders.

(4) *Determine porosity* of filling and tare weights; verify compliance of marking with prescribed requirements; obtain necessary copies of steel shell reports; and furnish complete reports required by this specification to the person who has completed the manufacture of the cylinders and, upon request, to the purchaser. The test reports must be retained by the inspector for fifteen years from the original test date of the cylinder.

(o) **Marking.**

(1) *Marking on each cylinder* must be stamped plainly and permanently on or near the shoulder, top head, neck or valve protection collar which is permanently attached to the cylinder and forming integral part thereof.

(2) *Tare weight of cylinder,* in pounds and ounces, must be marked on the cylinder.

(3) *Cylinders, not completed,* when delivered must each be marked for identification of each lot of 200 or less.

§178.60 Specification 8AL steel cylinders with porous fillings for acetylene.

(a) **Type and service pressure.** A DOT 8AL cylinder is a seamless steel cylinder with a service pressure of 250 psig. However, the attachment of heads by welding or by brazing by dipping process and a welded circumferential body seam is authorized. Longitudinal seams are not authorized.

(b) **Authorized steel.** The authorized steel is as specified in table I of appendix A to this part.

(c) **Identification of steel.** Material must be identified by any suitable method except that plates and billets for hot-drawn cylinders must be marked with heat number.

(d) **Manufacture.** Cylinders must be manufactured using equipment and processes adequate to ensure that each cylinder produced conforms to the requirements of this subpart. No defect is permitted that is likely to weaken the finished cylinder appreciably. A reasonably smooth and uniform surface finish is required. Welding procedures and operators must be qualified in accordance with CGA Pamphlet C-3 (incorporated by reference; see §171.7 of this subchapter).

(e) **Footrings.** Exposed bottom welds on cylinders over 18 inches long must be protected by footrings.

(f) **Welding or brazing.** Welding or brazing for any purpose whatsoever is prohibited except as follows:

(1) *The attachment* to the tops or bottoms of cylinders of neckrings, footrings, handlers, bosses, pads, and valve protecting rings is authorized provided that such attachments and the portion of the container to which they are attached are made of weldable steel, the carbon content of which may not exceed 0.25 percent.

(2) *Heat treatment* is not required after welding or brazing weldable low carbon parts to attachments, specified in paragraph (f)(1) of this section, of similar material which have been previously welded or brazed to the top or bottom of cylinders and properly heat treated, provided such subsequent welding or brazing does not produce a temperature in excess of 400 °F in any part of the top or bottom material.

(g) **Wall thickness;** wall stress. The wall thickness/wall stress of the cylinder must conform to the following:

(1) *The calculated wall stress* at 750 psi may not exceed 35,000 psi, or one-half of the minimum ultimate strength of the steel as determined in paragraph (l) of this section, whichever value is the smaller. The measured wall thickness may not include galvanizing or other protective coating.

(i) *Calculation of wall stress must be made by the formula:*

$S = [P(1.3D^2 + 0.4d^2)] / (D^2 - d^2)$

Where:

S = wall stress in pounds psi;

P = 750 psig (minimum test pressure);

D = outside diameter in inches;

d = inside diameter in inches.

(ii) *Either D or d* must be calculated from the relation D = d + 2t, where t = minimum wall thickness.

(2) *Cylinders with* a wall thickness less than 0.100 inch, the ratio of straight side wall length to outside diameter may not exceed 3.5.

(3) *For cylinders* having outside diameter over 5 inches, the minimum wall thickness must be 0.087 inch.

(h) **Heat treatment.** Each cylinder must be uniformly and properly heat treated, prior to tests, by any suitable method in excess of 1100 °F. Heat treatment must be accomplished after all forming and welding operations, except that when brazed joints are used, heat treatment must follow any forming and welding operations but may be done before, during, or after the brazing operations. Liquid quenching is not authorized.

(i) **Openings.** Standard taper pipe threads required in all openings. The length of the opening may not be less than as specified for American Standard pipe threads; tapped to gauge; clean cut, even, and without checks.

(j) **Hydrostatic test.** Each cylinder must successfully withstand a hydrostatic test as follows:

(1) *The test must be by water-jacket,* or other suitable method, operated so as to obtain accurate data. The pressure gauge must permit reading to an accuracy of 1 percent. The expansion gauge must permit reading of total expansion to an accuracy of either 1 percent or 0.1 cubic centimeter.

(2) *Pressure must be maintained* for at least 30 seconds and sufficiently longer to ensure complete expansion. Any internal pressure applied after heat-treatment and previous to the official test may not exceed 90 percent of the test pressure.

(3) *Permanent volumetric expansion* may not exceed 10 percent of total volumetric expansion at test pressure.

(4) *One cylinder* out of each lot of 200 or less must be hydrostatically tested to at least 750 psig. Cylinders not so tested must be examined under pressure of between 500 and 600 psig and show no defect. If a hydrostatically tested cylinder fails, each cylinder in the lot may be hydrostatically tested and those passing are acceptable.

(k) **Leakage test.** Cylinders with bottoms closed in by spinning must be leakage tested by setting the interior air or gas pressure at not less than the service pressure. Any cylinder that leaks must be rejected.

(l) **Physical test.** A physical test must be conducted as follows:

(1) *The test* is required on 2 specimens cut longitudinally from 1 cylinder or part thereof taken at random out of each lot of 200 or less, after heat treatment.

(2) *Specimens must conform* to a gauge length of 8 inches with a width not over 1 1/2 inches, a gauge length 2 inches with a width not over 1 1/2 inches, or a gauge length at least 24 times thickness with a width not over 6 times thickness is authorized when a cylinder wall is not over 3/16 inch thick.

(3) *The yield strength* in tension must be the stress corresponding to a permanent strain of 0.2 percent of the gauge length. The following conditions apply:

(i) *The yield strength* must be determined by either the "offset" method or the "extension under load" method as prescribed in ASTM E 8 (incorporated by reference; see §171.7 of this subchapter).

(ii) *In using the "extension under load" method,* the total strain (or "extension under load") corresponding to the stress at which the 0.2 percent permanent strain occurs may be determined with sufficient accuracy by calculating the elastic extension of the gauge length under appropriate load and adding thereto 0.2 percent of the gauge length. Elastic extension calculations must be based on an elastic modulus of 30,000,000. In the event of controversy, the entire stress-strain diagram must be plotted and the yield strength determined from the 0.2 offset.

(iii) *For the purpose* of strain measurement, the initial strain must be set while the specimen is under a stress of 12,000 psi, the strain indicator reading being set at the calculated corresponding strain.

(iv) *Cross-head speed* of the testing machine may not exceed 1/8 inch per minute during yield strength determination.

(m) **Elongation.** Physical test specimens must show at least a 40 percent elongation for a 2 inch gauge length or at least a 20 percent elongation in other cases. Except that these elongation percentages may be reduced numerically by 2 for 2 inch specimens and 1 in other cases for each 7,500 psi increment of tensile strength above 50,000 psi to a maximum of four such increments.

(n) **Weld tests.** Specimens taken across the circumferentially welded seam must be cut from one cylinder taken at random from each lot of 200 or less cylinders after heat treatment and must pass satisfactorily the following tests:

(1) *Tensile test.* A specimen must be cut from one cylinder of each lot of 200 or less, or welded test plate. The specimen must be taken from across the major seam and must be prepared and tested in accordance with and must meet the requirements of CGA Pamphlet C-3 (incorporated by reference; see §171.7 of this subchapter). Should this specimen fail to meet the requirements, specimens may be taken from two additional cylinders or welded test plates from the same lot and tested. If either of the latter specimens fail to meet the requirements, the entire lot represented must be rejected.

(2) *Guided bend test.* A root bend test specimen must be cut from the cylinder or welded test plate, used for the tensile test specified in paragraph (n)(1) of this section. Specimens must be prepared and tested in accordance with and must meet the requirements of CGA Pamphlet C-3 (incorporated by reference; see §171.7 of this subchapter).

(3) *Alternate guided-bend test.* This test may be used and must be as required by CGA Pamphlet C-3 (incorporated by reference; see §171.7 of this subchapter). The specimen must be bent until the elongation at the outer surface, adjacent to the root of the weld, between the lightly scribed gage lines-a to b, must be at least 20 percent, except that this percentage may be reduced for steels having a tensile strength in excess of 50,000 psi, as provided in paragraph (m) of this section.

(o) **Rejected cylinders.** Reheat treatment of rejected cylinders is authorized. Subsequent thereto, cylinders must pass all prescribed tests to be acceptable. Repair by welding is authorized.

(p) **Porous filling.**

(1) *Cylinders must be filled* with a porous material in accordance with the following:

(i) *The porous material* may not disintegrate or sag when wet with solvent or when subjected to normal service;

(ii) *The filling material* must be uniform in quality and free of voids, except that a well drilled into the filling material beneath the valve is authorized if the well is filled with a material of such type that the functions of the filling material are not impaired;

(iii) *Overall shrinkage* of the filling material is authorized if the total clearance between the cylinder shell and filling material, after solvent has been added, does not exceed 1/2 of 1 percent of the respective diameter or length but not to exceed 1/8 inch, measured diametrically and longitudinally;

(iv) *The clearance may not impair the functions of the filling material;*

(v) *The installed filling material* must meet the requirements of CGA Pamphlet C-12; and

(vi) *Porosity of filling material* may not exceed 80 percent except that filling material with a porosity of up to 92 percent may be used when tested with satisfactory results in accordance with CGA Pamphlet C-12.

(2) *When the porosity* of each cylinder is not known, a cylinder taken at random from a lot of 200 or less must be tested for porosity. If the test cylinder fails, each cylinder in the lot may be tested individually and those cylinders that pass the test are acceptable.

(3) *For filling* that is molded and dried before insertion in cylinders, porosity test may be made on sample block taken at random from material to be used.

(4) *The porosity* of the filling material must be determined; the amount of solvent at 70 °F for a cylinder:

(i) *Having shell volumetric capacity* above 20 pounds water capacity (nominal) may not exceed the following:

Percent porosity of filler	Maximum acetone solvent percent shell capacity by volume
90 to 92	43.4
87 to 90	42.0
83 to 87	40.0
80 to 83	38.6
75 to 80	36.2
70 to 75	33.8
65 to 70	31.4

(ii) *Having volumetric capacity* of 20 pounds or less water capacity (nominal), may not exceed the following:

Percent porosity of filler	Maximum acetone solvent percent shell capacity by volume
90 to 92	41.8
83 to 90	38.5
80 to 83	37.1
75 to 80	34.8
70 to 75	32.5
65 to 70	30.2

(q) **Tare weight.** The tare weight is the combined weight of the cylinder proper, porous filling, valve, and solvent, but without removable cap.

(r) **Duties of inspector.** In addition to the requirements of §178.35, the inspector shall —

(1) *Certify chemical analyses of steel used,* signed by manufacturer thereof; also verify by check analyses, of samples taken from each heat or from 1 out of each lot of 200 or less plates, shells, or tubes used.

(2) *Verify compliance of cylinder shells* with all shell requirements, inspect inside before closing in both ends, verify heat treatment as proper; obtain all samples for all tests and for check analyses, witness all tests; verify threads by gauge, report volumetric capacity and minimum thickness of wall noted.

(3) *Report percentage* of each specified alloying element in the steel. Prepare report on manufacture of steel shells in form prescribed in §178.35. Furnish one copy to manufacturer and three copies to the company that is to complete the cylinders.

(4) *Determine porosity* of filling and tare weights; verify compliance of marking with prescribed requirements; obtain necessary copies of steel shell reports prescribed in paragraph (b) of this section; and furnish complete test reports required by this specification to the person who has completed the manufacturer of the cylinders and, upon request, to the purchaser. The test reports must be retained by the inspector for fifteen years from the original test date of the cylinder.

(s) **Marking.**

(1) *Tare weight of cylinder,* in pounds and ounces, must be marked on the cylinder.

(2) *Cylinders, not completed,* when delivered must each be marked for identification of each lot of 200 or less.

(3) *Markings must be stamped* plainly and permanently in locations in accordance with the following:

(i) *On shoulders and top heads not less than 0.087 inch thick; or*

(ii) *On neck,* valve boss, valve protection sleeve, or similar part permanently attached to the top end of cylinder; or

(iii) *On a plate of ferrous material* attached to the top of the cylinder or permanent part thereof; the plate must be at least 1/16 inch thick, and must be attached by welding, or by brazing at a temperature of at least 1,100 °F throughout all edges of the plate. Sufficient space must be left on the plate to provide for stamping at least four (4) retest dates.

§178.61 Specification 4BW welded steel cylinders with electric-arc welded longitudinal seam.

(a) **Type, size and service pressure.** A DOT 4BW cylinder is a welded type steel cylinder with a longitudinal electric-arc welded seam, a water capacity (nominal) not over 1,000 pounds and a service pressure at least 225 and not over 500 psig gauge. Cylinders closed in by spinning process are not authorized.

(b) Authorized steel. Steel used in the construction of the cylinder must conform to the following:

(1) *The body* of the cylinder must be constructed of steel conforming to the limits specified in table 1 of appendix A to this part.

(2) *Material for heads* must meet the requirements of paragraph (a) of this section or be open hearth, electric or basic oxygen carbon steel of uniform quality. Content percent may not exceed the following: Carbon 0.25, Manganese 0.60, Phosphorus 0.045, Sulfur 0.050. Heads must be hemispherical or ellipsoidal in shape with a maximum ratio of 2.1. If low carbon steel is used, the thickness of such heads must be determined by using a maximum wall stress of 24,000 p.s.i. in the formula described in paragraph (f)(4) of this section.

(c) Identification of material. Material must be identified by any suitable method.

(d) Manufacture. Cylinders must be manufactured using equipment and processes adequate to ensure that each cylinder produced conforms to the requirements of this subpart and the following:

(1) *No defect* is permitted that is likely to weaken the finished cylinder appreciably. A reasonably smooth and uniform surface is required. Exposed bottom welds on cylinders over 18 inches long must be protected by footrings. Minimum thickness of heads may not be less than 90 percent of the required thickness of the sidewall. Heads must be concave to pressure.

(2) *Circumferential seams* must be by electric-arc welding. Joints must be butt with one member offset (joggle butt) or lap with minimum overlap of at least four times nominal sheet thickness.

(3) *Longitudinal seams in shells must conform to the following:*

(i) *Longitudinal electric-arc welded seams* must be of the butt welded type. Welds must be made by a machine process including automatic feed and welding guidance mechanisms. Longitudinal seams must have complete joint penetration, and must be free from undercuts, overlaps or abrupt ridges or valleys. Misalignment of mating butt edges may not exceed 1/6 of nominal sheet thickness or 1/32 inch whichever is less. All joints with nominal sheet thickness up to and including 1/8 inch must be tightly butted. When nominal sheet thickness is greater than 1/8 inch, the joint must be gapped with maximum distance equal to one-half the nominal sheet thickness or 1/32 inch whichever is less. Joint design, preparation and fit-up must be such that requirements of this paragraph (d) are satisfied.

(ii) *Maximum joint efficiency* must be 1.0 when each seam is radiographed completely. Maximum joint efficiency must be 0.90 when one cylinder from each lot of 50 consecutively welded cylinders is spot radiographed. In addition, one out of the first five cylinders welded following a shut down of welding operations exceeding four hours must be spot radiographed. Spot radiographs, when required, must be made of a finished welded cylinder and must include the girth weld for 2 inches in both directions from the intersection of the longitudinal and girth welds and include at least 6 inches of the longitudinal weld. Maximum joint efficacy of 0.75 must be permissible without radiography.

(4) *Welding procedures and operators* must be qualified in accordance with CGA Pamphlet C-3 (incorporated by reference; see §171.7 of this subchapter).

(e) Welding of attachments. The attachment to the tops and bottoms only of cylinders by welding of neckrings, footrings, handles, bosses, pads and valve protection rings is authorized provided that such attachments and the portion of the container to which they are attached are made of weldable steel, the carbon content of which may not exceed 0.25 percent.

(f) Wall thickness. For outside diameters over 6 inches the minimum wall thickness must be 0.078 inch. For a cylinder with a wall thickness less than 0.100 inch, the ratio of tangential length to outside diameter may not exceed 4 to1 (4:1). In any case the minimum wall thickness must be such that the wall stress calculated by the formula listed in paragraph (f)(4) of this section may not exceed the lesser value of any of the following:

(1) *The value referenced* in paragraph (b) of this section for the particular material under consideration.

(2) *One-half of the minimum* tensile strength of the material determined as required in paragraph (j) of this section.

(3) *35,000 psi.*

(4) *Stress must be calculated by the following formula:*

$S = [2P(1.3D^2 + 0.4d^2)] / [E(D^2 - d^2)]$

Where:

S = wall stress, psi;

P = service pressure, psig;

D = outside diameter, inches;

d = inside diameter, inches;

E = joint efficiency of the longitudinal seam (from paragraph (d) of this section).

(g) Heat treatment. Each cylinder must be uniformly and properly heat treated prior to test by the applicable method referenced in paragraph (b) of this section. Heat treatment must be accomplished after all forming and welding operations. Heat treatment is not required after welding or brazing of weldable low carbon parts to attachments of similar material which have been previously welded to the top or bottom of cylinders and properly heat treated, provided such subsequent welding or brazing does not produce a temperature in excess of 400 °F in any part of the top or bottom material.

(h) Openings in cylinders. Openings in the cylinder must conform to the following:

(1) *All openings must be in the heads or bases.*

(2) *Openings in cylinders* must be provided with adequate fittings, bosses, or pads, integral with or securely attached to the cylinder by welding.

(3) *Threads must comply with the following:*

(i) *Threads must be clean cut and to gauge.*

(ii) *Taper threads* must be of length not less than as specified for American Standard Taper Pipe threads.

(iii) *Straight threads,* having at least 4 engaged threads, to have tight fit and calculated shear strength at least 10 times the test pressure of the cylinder; gaskets required, adequate to prevent leakage.

(4) *Closure of fittings,* boss or pads must be adequate to prevent leakage.

(i) Hydrostatic test. Cylinders must withstand a hydrostatic test, as follows:

(1) *The test* must be by water-jacket, or other suitable method, operated so as to obtain accurate data. The pressure gauge must permit readings to an accuracy of 1 percent. The expansion gauge must permit readings of total volumetric expansion to an accuracy either of 1 percent or 0.1 cubic centimeter.

(2) *Pressure must be maintained* for at least 30 seconds and sufficiently longer to ensure complete expansion. Any internal pressure applied after heat treatment and previous to the official test may not exceed 90 percent of the test pressure.

(3) *Permanent volumetric expansion* may not exceed 10 percent of the total volumetric expansion at test pressure.

(4) *Cylinders must be tested as follows:*

(i) *At least 1 cylinder* selected at random out of each lot of 200 or less must be tested as outlined in paragraphs (i)(1), (i)(2), and (i)(3) of this section to at least two times service pressure.

(ii) *All cylinders* not tested as outlined in paragraph (i)(4)(i) of this section must be examined under pressure of at least two times service pressure and show no defect.

(5) *One finished cylinder* selected at random out of each lot of 500 or less successively produced must be hydrostatically tested to 4 times service pressure without bursting.

(j) Physical tests. Cylinders must be subjected to a physical test as follows:

(1) *Specimens must be taken* from one cylinder after heat treatment and chosen at random from each lot of 200 or less, as follows:

(i) *Body specimen.* One specimen must be taken longitudinally from the body section at least 90 degrees away from the weld.

(ii) *Head specimen.* One specimen must be taken from either head on a cylinder when both heads are made of the same material. However, if the two heads are made of differing materials, a specimen must be taken from each head.

(iii) *If due to welded attachments* on the top head there is insufficient surface from which to take a specimen, it may be taken from a representative head of the same heat treatment as the test cylinder.

(2) *Specimens must conform to the following:*

(i) *A gauge length* of 8 inches with a width not over 1 1/2 inches, a gauge length of 2 inches with a width not over 1 1/2 inches, or a gauge length at least 24 times thickness with a width not over 6 times thickness is authorized when a cylinder wall is not over 3/16 inch thick.

(ii) *The specimen,* exclusive of grip ends, may not be flattened. Grip ends may be flattened to within 1 inch of each end of the reduced section.

(iii) *When size* of the cylinder does not permit securing straight specimens, the specimens may be taken in any location or direction and may be straightened or flattened cold, by pressure only, not by blows when specimens are so taken and prepared, the inspector's report must show in connection with record of physical tests detailed information in regard to such specimens.

(iv) *Heating of a specimen for any purpose is not authorized.*

(3) *The yield strength in tension* must be the stress corresponding to a permanent strain of 0.2 percent of the gauge length. The following conditions apply:

(i) *The yield strength* must be determined by either the "offset" method or the "extension under load" method as prescribed in ASTM E 8 (incorporated by reference; see §171.7 of this subchapter).

(ii) *In using the "extension under load" method,* the total strain (or "extension under load"), corresponding to the stress at which the 0.2-percent permanent strain occurs may be determined with sufficient accuracy by calculating the elastic extension of the gauge length under appropriate load and adding thereto 0.2 percent of the gauge length. Elastic extension calculations must be based on an elastic modulus of 30,000,000. In the event of controversy, the entire stress-strain diagram must be plotted and the yield strength determined from the 0.2-percent offset.

(iii) *For the purpose of strain measurement,* the initial strain reference must be set while the specimen is under a stress of 12,000 psi and the strain indicator reading being set at the calculated corresponding strain.

(iv) *Cross-head speed* of the testing machine may not exceed 1/8 inch per minute during yield strength determination.

(k) **Elongation.** Physical test specimens must show at least a 40 percent elongation for a 2-inch gauge length or at least a 20 percent elongation in other cases. Except that these elongation percentages may be reduced numerically by 2 for 2-inch specimens and by 1 in other cases for each 7,500 psi increment of tensile strength above 50,000 psi to a maximum of four increments.

(l) **Tests of welds.** Welds must be subjected to the following tests:

(1) *Tensile test.* A specimen must be cut from one cylinder of each lot of 200 or less. The specimen must be taken from across the longitudinal seam and must be prepared and tested in accordance with and must meet the requirements of CGA Pamphlet C-3 (incorporated by reference; see §171.7 of this subchapter).

(2) *Guided bend test.* A root test specimen must be cut from the cylinder used for the tensile test specified in paragraph (l)(1) of this section. Specimens must be taken from across the longitudinal seam and must be prepared and tested in accordance with and must meet the requirements of CGA Pamphlet C-3 (incorporated by reference; see §171.7 of this subchapter).

(3) *Alternate guided bend test.* This test may be used and must be as required by CGA Pamphlet C-3 (incorporated by reference; see §171.7 of this subchapter). The specimen must be bent until the elongation at the outer surface, adjacent to the root of the weld, between the lightly scribed gauge lines a to b, must be at least 20 percent, except that this percentage may be reduced for steels having a tensile strength in excess of 50,000 psi, as provided in paragraph (k) of this section.

(m) **Radiographic examination.** Welds of the cylinders must be subjected to a radiographic examination as follows:

(1) *Radiographic inspection* must conform to the techniques and acceptability criteria set forth in CGA Pamphlet C-3 (incorporated by reference; see §171.7 of this subchapter). When fluoroscopic inspection is used, permanent film records need not be retained.

(2) *Should spot radiographic examination* fail to meet the requirements of paragraph (m)(1) of this section, two additional welds from the same lot of 50 cylinders or less must be examined, and if either of these fail to meet the requirements, each cylinder must be examined as previously outlined; only those passing are acceptable.

(n) **Rejected cylinders.**

(1) *Unless otherwise stated,* if a sample cylinder or specimen taken from a lot of cylinders fails the prescribed test, then two additional specimens must be selected from the same lot and subjected to the prescribed test. If either of these fails the test, then the entire lot must be rejected.

(2) *Reheat treatment* of rejected cylinders is authorized. Subsequent thereto, cylinders must pass all prescribed tests to be acceptable. Repair of welded seams by welding is authorized provided that all defective metal is cut away and the joint is rewelded as prescribed for original welded joints.

(o) **Markings.** Markings must be stamped plainly and permanently in any of the following locations on the cylinder:

(1) *On shoulders and top heads* when they are not less than 0.087-inch thick.

(2) *On a metal plate* attached to the top of the cylinder or permanent part thereof; sufficient space must be left on the plate to provide for stamping at least six retest dates; the plate must be at least 1/16-inch thick and must be attached by welding, or by brazing. The brazing rod is to melt at a temperature of 1100 °F Welding or brazing must be along all the edges of the plate.

(3) *On the neck,* valve boss, valve protection sleeve, or similar part permanently attached to the top of the cylinder.

(4) *On the footring* permanently attached to the cylinder, provided the water capacity of the cylinder does not exceed 25 pounds.

(p) **Inspector's report.** In addition to the information required by §178.35, the inspector's report must indicate the type and amount of radiography.

§178.65 Specification 39 non-reusable (non-refillable) cylinders.

(a) **Type, size, service pressure, and test pressure.** A DOT 39 cylinder is a seamless, welded, or brazed cylinder with a service pressure not to exceed 80 percent of the test pressure. Spherical pressure vessels are authorized and covered by references to cylinders in this specification.

(1) *Size limitation.* Maximum water capacity may not exceed: (i) 55 pounds (1,526 cubic inches) for a service pressure of 500 p.s.i.g. or less, and (ii) 10 pounds (277 cubic inches) for a service pressure in excess of 500 p.s.i.g.

(2) *Test pressure.* The minimum test pressure is the maximum pressure of contents at 130 °F or 180 p.s.i.g. whichever is greater.

(3) *Pressure of contents.* The term "pressure of contents" as used in this specification means the total pressure of all the materials to be shipped in the cylinder.

(b) **Material; steel or aluminum.** The cylinder must be constructed of either steel or aluminum conforming to the following requirements:

(1) *Steel.*

(i) *The steel analysis must conform to the following:*

	Ladle analysis	Check analysis
Carbon, maximum percent	0.12	0.15
Phosphorus, maximum percent	.04	.05
Sulfur, maximum percent	.05	.06

(ii) *For a cylinder* made of seamless steel tubing with integrally formed ends, hot drawn, and finished, content percent for the following may not exceed: Carbon, 0.55; phosphorous, 0.045; sulfur, 0.050.

(iii) *For non-heat treated* welded steel cylinders, adequately killed deep drawing quality steel is required.

(iv) *Longitudinal or helical* welded cylinders are not authorized for service pressures in excess of 500 p.s.i.g.

(2) *Aluminum.* Aluminum is not authorized for service pressures in excess of 500 p.s.i.g. The analysis of the aluminum must conform to the Aluminum Association standard for alloys 1060, 1100, 1170, 3003, 5052, 5086, 5154, 6061, and 6063 as specified in its publication entitled "Aluminum Standards and Data".

(3) *Material with seams,* cracks, laminations, or other injurious defects not permitted.

(4) *Material used must be identified by any suitable method.*

(c) **Manufacture.**

(1) *General manufacturing requirements are as follows:*

(i) *The surface finish must be uniform and reasonably smooth.*

(ii) *Inside surfaces must be clean, dry, and free of loose particles.*

(iii) *No defect* of any kind is permitted if it is likely to weaken a finished cylinder.

(2) *Requirements for seams:*

(i) *Brazing is not authorized on aluminum cylinders.*

(ii) *Brazing material* must have a melting point of not lower than 1,000 °F.

(iii) *Brazed seams* must be assembled with proper fit to ensure complete penetration of the brazing material throughout the brazed joint.

(iv) *Minimum width of brazed joints* must be at least four times the thickness of the shell wall.

(v) *Brazed seams* must have design strength equal to or greater than 1.5 times the minimum strength of the shell wall.

(vi) *Welded seams* must be properly aligned and welded by a method that provides clean, uniform joints with adequate penetration.

(vii) *Welded joints* must have a strength equal to or greater than the minimum strength of the shell material in the finished cylinder.

(3) *Attachments to the cylinder* are permitted by any means which will not be detrimental to the integrity of the cylinder. Welding or brazing of attachments to the cylinder must be completed prior to all pressure tests.

(4) *Welding procedures and operators* must be qualified in accordance with CGA Pamphlet C-3 (incorporated by reference; see §171.7 of this subchapter).

(d) Wall thickness. The minimum wall thickness must be such that the wall stress at test pressure does not exceed the yield strength of the material of the finished cylinder wall. Calculations must be made by the following formulas:

(1) *Calculation of the stress* for cylinders must be made by the following formula:

$S = [P(1.3D^2 + 0.4d^2)] / (D^2 - d^2)$

Where:

S = Wall stress, in psi;

P = Test pressure in psig;

D = Outside diameter, in inches;

d = Inside diameter, in inches.

(2) *Calculation of the stress* for spheres must be made by the following formula:

$S = PD / 4t$

Where:

S = Wall stress, in psi;

P = Test pressure in psig;

D = Outside diameter, in inches;

t = Minimum wall thickness, in inches.

(e) Openings and attachments. Openings and attachments must conform to the following:

(1) *Openings and attachments are permitted on heads only.*

(2) *All openings* and their reinforcements must be within an imaginary circle, concentric to the axis of the cylinder. The diameter of the circle may not exceed 80 percent of the outside diameter of the cylinder. The plane of the circle must be parallel to the plane of a circumferential weld and normal to the long axis of the cylinder.

(3) *Unless a head* has adequate thickness, each opening must be reinforced by a securely attached fitting, boss, pad, collar, or other suitable means.

(4) *Material used* for welded openings and attachments must be of weldable quality and compatible with the material of the cylinder.

(f) Pressure tests.

(1) *Each cylinder* must be tested at an internal pressure of at least the test pressure and must be held at that pressure for at least 30 seconds.

(i) *The leakage test* must be conducted by submersion under water or by some other method that will be equally sensitive.

(ii) *If the cylinder leaks,* evidences visible distortion, or any other defect, while under test, it must be rejected (see paragraph (h) of this section).

(2) *One cylinder* taken from the beginning of each lot, and one from each 1,000 or less successively produced within the lot thereafter, must be hydrostatically tested to destruction. The entire lot must be rejected (see paragraph (h) of this section) if:

(i) *A failure occurs* at a gage pressure less than 2.0 times the test pressure;

(ii) *A failure initiates* in a braze or a weld or the heat affected zone thereof;

(iii) *A failure* is other than in the sidewall of a cylinder longitudinal with its long axis; or

(iv) *In a sphere,* a failure occurs in any opening, reinforcement, or at a point of attachment.

(3) *A "lot" is defined* as the quantity of cylinders successively produced per production shift (not exceeding 10 hours) having identical size, design, construction, material, heat treatment, finish, and quality.

(g) Flattening test. One cylinder must be taken from the beginning of production of each lot (as defined in paragraph (f)(3) of this section) and subjected to a flattening test as follows:

(1) *The flattening test* must be made on a cylinder that has been tested at test pressure.

(2) *A ring taken* from a cylinder may be flattened as an alternative to a test on a complete cylinder. The test ring may not include the heat affected zone or any weld. However, for a sphere, the test ring may include the circumferential weld if it is located at a 45 degree angle to the ring, 5 degrees.

(3) *The flattening* must be between 60 degrees included-angle, wedge shaped knife edges, rounded to a 0.5 inch radius.

(4) *Cylinders and test rings* may not crack when flattened so that their outer surfaces are not more than six times wall thickness apart when made of steel or not more than ten times wall thickness apart when made of aluminum.

(5) *If any cylinder* or ring cracks when subjected to the specified flattening test, the lot of cylinders represented by the test must be rejected (see paragraph (h) of this section).

(h) Rejected cylinders. Rejected cylinders must conform to the following requirements:

(1) *If the cause for rejection* of a lot is determinable, and if by test or inspection defective cylinders are eliminated from the lot, the remaining cylinders must be qualified as a new lot under paragraphs (f) and (g) of this section.

(2) *Repairs to welds are permitted.* Following repair, a cylinder must pass the pressure test specified in paragraph (f) of this section.

(3) *If a cylinder* made from seamless steel tubing fails the flattening test described in paragraph (g) of this section, suitable uniform heat treatment must be used on each cylinder in the lot. All prescribed tests must be performed subsequent to this heat treatment.

(i) Markings.

(1) *The markings* required by this section must be durable and waterproof. The requirements of §178.35(h) do not apply to this section.

(2) *Required markings are as follows:*

(i) *DOT-39.*

(ii) *NRC.*

(iii) *The service pressure.*

(iv) *The test pressure.*

(v) *The registration number (M****) of the manufacturer.*

(vi) *The lot number.*

(vii) *The date* of manufacture if the lot number does not establish the date of manufacture.

(viii) *With one of the following statements:*

[A] For cylinders manufactured prior to October 1, 1996: "Federal law forbids transportation if refilled-penalty up to $25,000 fine and 5 years imprisonment (49 U.S.C. 1809)" or "Federal law forbids transportation if refilled-penalty up to $500,000 fine and 5 years imprisonment (49 U.S.C. 5124)."

[B] For cylinders manufactured on or after October 1, 1996: "Federal law forbids transportation if refilled-penalty up to $500,000 fine and 5 years imprisonment (49 U.S.C. 5124)."

(3) *The markings* required by paragraphs (i)(2)(i) through (i)(2)(v) of this section must be in numbers and letters at least 1/8-inch high and displayed sequentially. For example: DOT-39 NRC 250/500 M1001.

(4) *No person* may mark any cylinder with the specification identification "DOT-39" unless it was manufactured in compliance with the requirements of this section and its manufacturer has a registration number (M****) from the Associate Administrator.

§178.68 Specification 4E welded aluminum cylinders.

(a) Type, size and service pressure. A DOT 4E cylinder is a welded aluminum cylinder with a water capacity (nominal) of not over 1,000 pounds and a service pressure of at least 225 to not over 500 psig. The cylinder must be constructed of not more than two seamless drawn shells with no more than one circumferential weld. The circumferential weld may not be closer to the point of tangency of the cylindrical portion with the shoulder than 20 times the cylinder wall thickness. Cylinders or shells closed in by spinning process and cylinders with longitudinal seams are not authorized.

(b) Authorized material. The cylinder must be constructed of aluminum of uniform quality. The following chemical analyses are authorized:

Table 1 - Authorized Materials

Designation	Chemical analysis — limits in percent 5154[1]
Iron plus silicon	0.45 maximum
Copper	0.10 maximum
Manganese	0.10 maximum
Magnesium	3.10/3.90
Chromium	0.15/0.35
Zinc	0.20 maximum
Titanium	0.20 maximum
Others, each	0.05 maximum
Others, total	0.15 maximum
Aluminum	remainder

1. Analysis must regularly be made only for the elements specifically mentioned in this table. If, however, the presence of other elements is indicated in the course of routine analysis, further analysis should be made to determine conformance with the limits specified for other elements.

(c) **Identification.** Material must be identified by any suitable method that will identify the alloy and manufacturer's lot number.

(d) **Manufacture.** Cylinders must be manufactured using equipment and processes adequate to ensure that each cylinder produced conforms to the requirements of this subpart. No defect is permitted that is likely to weaken the finished cylinder appreciably. A reasonably smooth and uniform surface finish is required. All welding must be by the gas shielded arc process.

(e) **Welding.** The attachment to the tops and bottoms only of cylinders by welding of neckrings or flanges, footrings, handles, bosses and pads and valve protection rings is authorized. However, such attachments and the portion of the cylinder to which it is attached must be made of weldable aluminum alloys.

(f) **Wall thickness.** The wall thickness of the cylinder must conform to the following:

(1) *The minimum wall thickness* of the cylinder must be 0.140 inch. In any case, the minimum wall thickness must be such that calculated wall stress at twice service pressure may not exceed the lesser value of either of the following:

(i) *20,000 psi.*

(ii) *One-half of the minimum* tensile strength of the material as required in paragraph (j) of this section.

(2) *Calculation must be made by the following formula:*

$S = [P(1.3D^2 + 0.4d^2)] / (D^2 - d^2)$

Where:

S = wall stress in psi;

P = minimum test pressure prescribed for water jacket test;

D = outside diameter in inches;

d = inside diameter in inches.

(3) *Minimum thickness* of heads and bottoms may not be less than the minimum required thickness of the side wall.

(g) **Opening in cylinder.** Openings in cylinders must conform to the following:

(1) *All openings must be in the heads or bases.*

(2) *Each opening in cylinders,* except those for safety devices, must be provided with a fitting, boss, or pad, securely attached to cylinder by welding by inert gas shielded arc process or by threads. If threads are used, they must comply with the following:

(i) *Threads must be* clean-cut, even, without checks and cut to gauge.

(ii) *Taper threads* to be of length not less than as specified for American Standard taper pipe threads.

(iii) *Straight threads,* having at least 4 engaged threads, to have tight fit and calculated shear strength at least 10 times the test pressure of the cylinder; gaskets required, adequate to prevent leakage.

(3) *Closure of a fitting,* boss, or pad must be adequate to prevent leakage.

(h) **Hydrostatic test.** Each cylinder must successfully withstand a hydrostatic test, as follows:

(1) *The test* must be by water jacket, or other suitable method, operated so as to obtain accurate data. The pressure gauge must permit reading to an accuracy of 1 percent. The expansion gauge must permit a reading of the total expansion to an accuracy either of 1 percent or 0.1 cubic centimeter.

(2) *Pressure of 2 times* service pressure must be maintained for at least 30 seconds and sufficiently longer to insure complete expansion. Any internal pressure applied previous to the official test may not exceed 90 percent of the test pressure. If, due to failure of the test apparatus, the test pressure cannot be maintained, the test may be repeated at a pressure increased by 10 percent over the pressure otherwise specified.

(3) *Permanent volumetric expansion* may not exceed 12 percent of total volumetric expansion at test pressure.

(4) *Cylinders having* a calculated wall stress of 18,000 psi or less at test pressure may be tested as follows:

(i) *At least one cylinder* selected at random out of each lot of 200 or less must be tested in accordance with paragraphs (h)(1), (h)(2), and (h)(3) of this section.

(ii) *All cylinders* not tested as provided in paragraph (h)(4)(i) of this section must be examined under pressure of at least 2 times service pressure and show no defect.

(5) *One finished cylinder* selected at random out of each lot of 1,000 or less must be hydrostatically tested to 4 times the service pressure without bursting. Inability to meet this requirement must result in rejection of the lot.

(i) **Flattening test.** After hydrostatic testing, a flattening test is required on one section of a cylinder, taken at random out of each lot of 200 or less as follows:

(1) *If the weld* is not at midlength of the cylinder, the test section must be no less in width than 30 times the cylinder wall thickness. The weld must be in the center of the section. Weld reinforcement must be removed by machining or grinding so that the weld is flush with the exterior of the parent metal. There must be no evidence of cracking in the sample when it is flattened between flat plates to no more than 6 times the wall thickness.

(2) *If the weld* is at midlength of the cylinder, the test may be made as specified in paragraph (i)(1)(i) of this section or must be made between wedge shaped knife edges (60° angle) rounded to a 1/2 inch radius. There must be no evidence of cracking in the sample when it is flattened to no more than 6 times the wall thickness.

(j) **Physical test.** A physical test must be conducted to determine yield strength, tensile strength, elongation, and reduction of area of material as follows:

(1) *The test* is required on 2 specimens cut from one cylinder or part thereof taken at random out of each lot of 200 or less.

(2) *Specimens must conform to the following:*

(i) *A gauge length* of 8 inches with a width not over 1 1/2 inches, a gauge length of 2 inches with a width not over 1 1/2 inches.

(ii) *The specimen,* exclusive of grip ends, may not be flattened. Grip ends may be flattened to within 1 inch of each end of the reduced section.

(iii) *When size of cylinder* does not permit securing straight specimens, the specimens may be taken in any location or direction and may be straightened or flattened cold, by pressure only, not by blows; when specimens are so taken and prepared, the inspector's report must show in connection with record of physical test detailed information in regard to such specimens.

(iv) *Heating of a specimen for any purpose is not authorized.*

(3) *The yield strength* in tension must be the stress corresponding to a permanent strain of 0.2 percent of the gauge length. The following conditions apply:

(i) *The yield strength* must be determined by the "offset" method as prescribed in ASTM E 8 (incorporated by reference; see §171.7 of this subchapter).

(ii) *Cross-head speed* of the testing machine may not exceed 1/8 inch per minute during yield strength determination.

(k) **Acceptable results for physical tests.** An acceptable result of the physical test requires an elongation to at least 7 percent and yield strength not over 80 percent of tensile strength.

(l) **Weld tests.** Welds of the cylinder are required to successfully pass the following tests:

(1) *Reduced section tensile test.* A specimen must be cut from the cylinder used for the physical tests specified in paragraph (j) of this section. The specimen must be taken from across the seam, edges must be parallel for a distance of approximately 2 inches on either side of the weld. The specimen must be fractured in tension. The apparent breaking stress calculated on the minimum wall thickness must be at least equal to 2 times the stress calculated under paragraph (f)(2) of this section, and in addition must have an actual breaking stress of at least 30,000 psi. Should this specimen fail to meet the requirements, specimens may be taken from 2 additional cylinders from the same lot and tested. If either of the latter specimens fails to meet requirements, the entire lot represented must be rejected.

(2) *Guided bend test.* A bend test specimen must be cut from the cylinder used for the physical tests specified in paragraph (j) of this section. Specimen must be taken across the seam, must be 1 1/2 inches wide, edges must be parallel and rounded with a file, and back-up strip, if used, must be removed by machining. The specimen must be bent to refusal in the guided bend test jig illustrated in paragraph 6.10 of CGA Pamphlet C-3 (incorporated by reference; see §171.7 of this subchapter). The root of the weld (inside surface of the cylinder) must be located away from the ram of the jig. No specimen must show a crack or other open defect exceeding 1/8 inch in any direction upon completion of the test. Should this specimen fail to meet the requirements, specimens may be taken from each of 2 additional cylinders from the same lot and tested. If either of the latter specimens fail to meet requirements, the entire lot represented must be rejected.

(m) **Rejected cylinders.** Repair of welded seams is authorized. Acceptable cylinders must pass all prescribed tests.

(n) **Inspector's report.** In addition to the information required by §178.35, the record of chemical analyses must also include applicable information on iron, titanium, zinc, and magnesium used in the construction of the cylinder.

Appendix A to Subpart C of Part 178

Illustrations: Cylinder tensile sample.

The following figures illustrate the recommended locations for test specimens taken from welded cylinders:

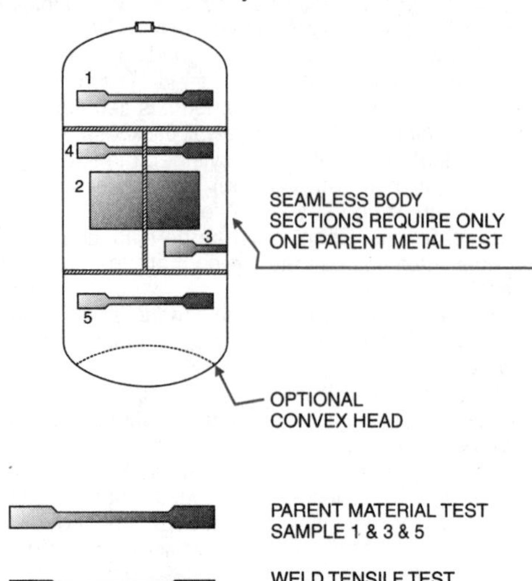

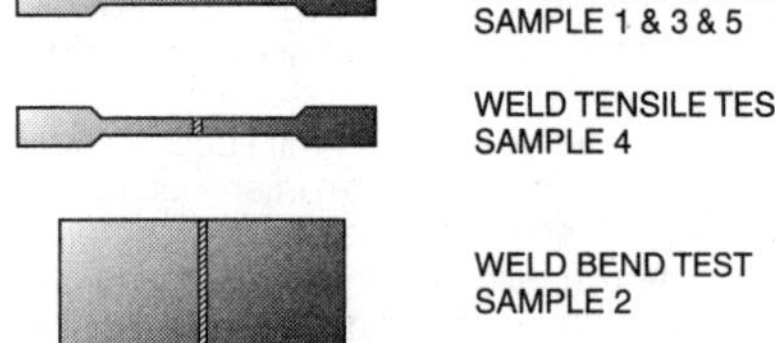

THIS FIGURE ILLUSTRATES THE PROPER TENSILE LOCATION FOR A 3 PIECE CYLINDER WITH THE HEADS HAVING STRAIGHT SIDEWALLS.

Figure #1

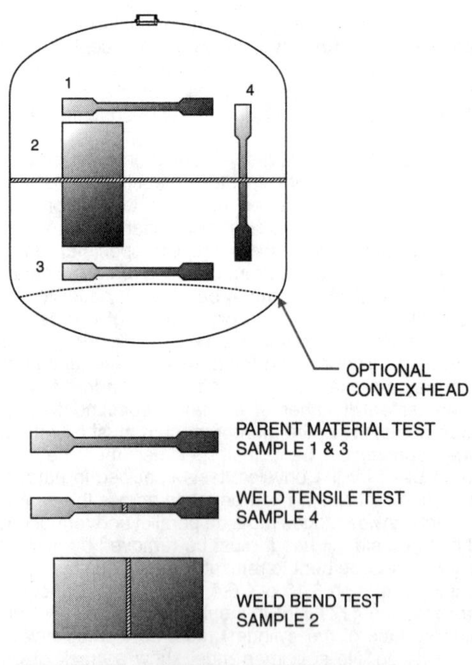

THIS FIGURE ILLUSTRATES THE PROPER TENSILE LOCATION FOR A 2 PIECE CYLINDER WITH THE HEADS HAVING STRAIGHT SIDEWALLS.

Figure #2

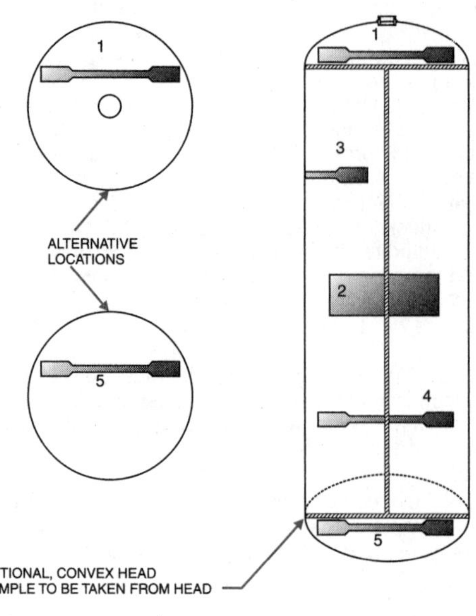

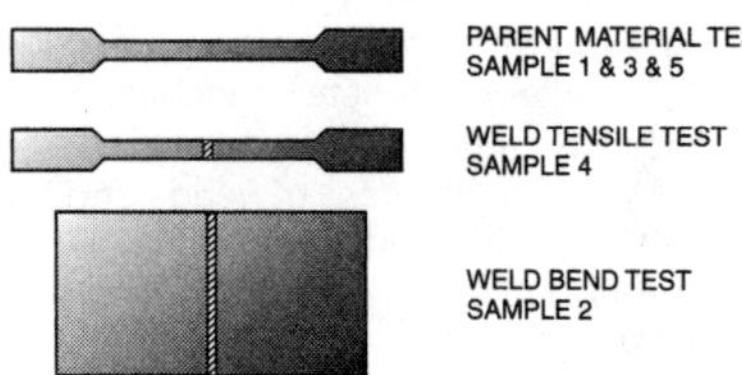

THIS FIGURE ILLUSTRATES THE PROPER TENSILE LOCATION FOR A 2 PIECE CYLINDER THAT HAS DEEP DRAWN HEADS.

Figure #3

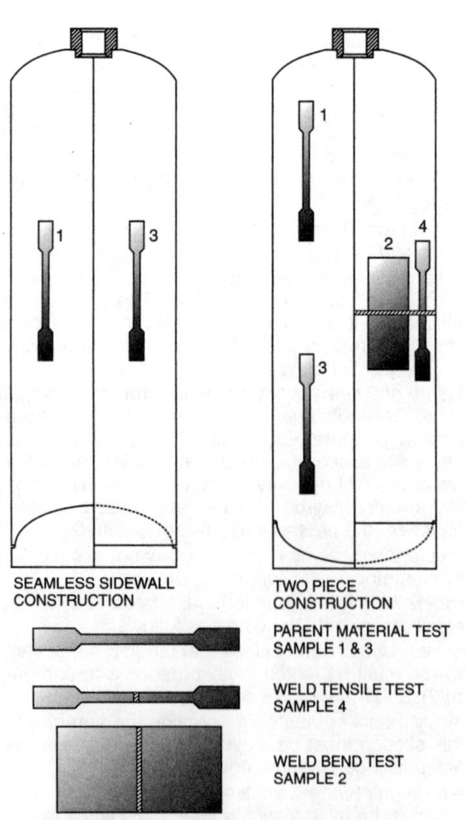

THIS FIGURE ILLUSTRATES THE PROPER TENSILE LOCATION FOR A 2 PIECE CYLINDER THAT HAS DEEP DRAWN HEADS.

Figure #4

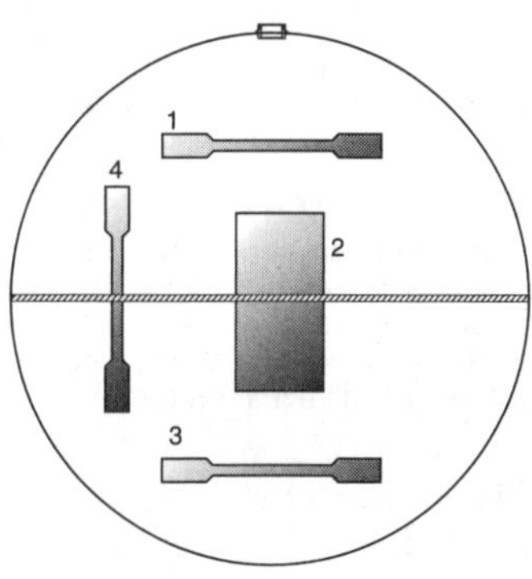

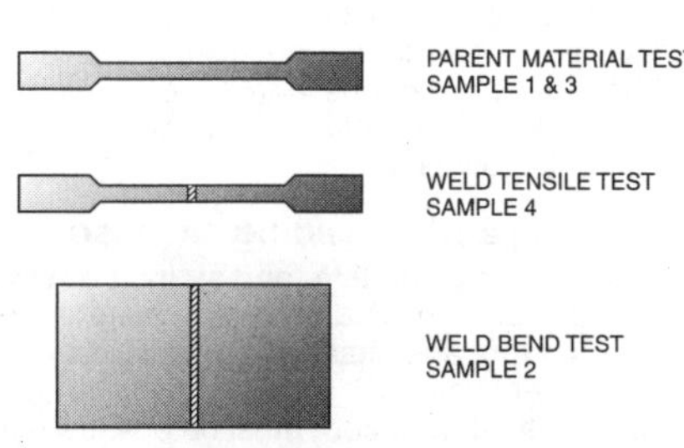

THIS FIGURE ILLUSTRATES THE PROPER TENSILE LOCATION FOR A 2 PIECE CYLINDER.

Figure #5

Subparts D-G [Reserved]

Subpart H - Specifications for Portable Tanks

§178.245 Specification 51; steel portable tanks.

§178.245-1 Requirements for design and construction.

(a) **Tanks must be seamless or welded steel construction** or combination of both and have a water capacity in excess of 454 kg (1,000 pounds). Tanks must be designed, constructed, certified and stamped in accordance with the ASME Code.

(b) **Tanks must be postweld heat treated** and radiographed as prescribed in the ASME Code except that each tank constructed in accordance with part UHT of the ASME Code must be postweld heat treated. Where postweld heat treatment is required, the tank must be treated as a unit after completion of all the welds in and/or to the shell and heads. The method must be as prescribed in the ASME Code. Welded attachments to pads may be made after postweld heat treatment is made. A tank used for anhydrous ammonia must be postweld heat treated. The postweld heat treatment must be as prescribed in the ASME Code, but in no event at less than 1050 °F tank metal temperature. Additionally, tanks constructed in accordance with part UHT of the ASME Code must conform to the following requirements:

(1) *Welding procedure* and welder performance tests must be made annually in accordance with section IX of the ASME Code. In addition to the essential variables named therein, the following must be considered to be essential variables: number of passes, thickness of plate, heat input per pass, and manufacturer's identification of rod and flux. The number of passes, thickness of plate and heat input per pass may not vary more than 25 percent from the procedure qualification. Records of the qualification must be retained for at least 5 years by the tank manufacturer and made available to duly identified representatives of the Department of Transportation or the owner of the tank.

(2) *Impact tests* must be made on a lot basis. A lot is defined as 100 tons or less of the same heat and having a thickness variation no greater than plus or minus 25 percent. The minimum impact required for full-sized specimens shall be 20 foot-pounds (or 10 foot-pounds for half-sized specimens) at 0 °F Charpy V-Notch in both the longitudinal and transverse direction. If the lot test does not pass this requirement, individual plates may be accepted if they individually meet this impact requirement.

(c) **Except as provided in paragraph (d) of this section,** all openings in the tank shall be grouped in one location, either at the top of the tank or at one end of the tank.

(d) **The following openings may be installed** at locations other than on the top or end of the tank:

(1) *The openings* for liquid level gauging devices, pressure gauges, or for safety devices, may be installed separately at the other location or in the side of the shell;

(2) *One plugged opening* of 2-inch National Pipe Thread or less provided for maintenance purposes may be located elsewhere;

(3) *An opening* of 3-inch National Pipe Size or less may be provided at another location, when necessary, to facilitate installation of condensing coils; or

(4) *Filling and discharge connections* may be installed below the normal liquid level of the tank if the tank design conforms to the following requirements:

(i) *The tank* must be permanently mounted in a full framework for containerized transport. For each tank design, a prototype tank, must fulfill the requirements of parts 450 through 453 of this title for compliance with the requirements of Annex II of the International Convention for Safe Containers.

(ii) *Each filling and discharge connection* must be equipped with an internal self-closing stop-valve capable of closing within 30 seconds of actuation. Each internal self-closing stop-valve must be protected by a shear section or sacrificial device located outboard of the valve. The shear section or sacrificial device must break at no more than 70 percent of the load that would cause failure of the internal self-closing stop-valve.

(iii) *Each internal self-closing stop-valve* must be provided with remote means of automatic closure, both thermal and mechanical. The thermal means of automatic closure must actuate at a temperature of not over 250 °F.

(e) **Each uninsulated tank used for the transportation** of compressed gas, as defined in §173.300 of this subchapter, must have an exterior surface finish that is significantly reflective, such as a light reflecting color if painted, or a bright reflective metal or other material if unpainted.

§178.245-2 Material.

(a) **All material used for the construction** of the tank and appurtenances shall be suitable for use with the commodity to be transported therein.

(b) **A material of thickness less than 3/16 inch** shall not be used for the shells and heads.

§178.245-3 Design pressure.

(a) **The design pressure of a tank authorized** under this specification shall be not less than the vapor pressure of the commodity contained therein at 115 °F, or as prescribed for a particular commodity by part 173 of this chapter, except that in no case shall the design pressure of any container be less than 100 psig or more than 500 psig. When corrosion factor is prescribed by these regulations, the wall thickness of the tank calculated in accordance with the "Code" (see §178.245-1(a)) shall be increased by 20 percent or 0.10 inch, whichever is less.

NOTE 1: The term design pressure as used in this specification is identical to the term MAWP as used in the "Code" (see §178.245-1(a)).

(b) [Reserved]

§178.245-4 Tank mountings.

(a) **Tanks shall be designed and fabricated** with mountings to provide a secure base in transit. "Skids" or similar devices shall be deemed to comply with this requirement.

(b) **All tank mountings such as skids, fastenings,** brackets, cradles, lifting lugs, etc., intended to carry loadings shall be permanently secured to tanks in accordance with the requirements of the Code under which the tanks were fabricated and shall be designed to withstand static loadings in any direction equal to twice the weight of the tank and attachments when filled with the lading using a safety factor of not less than four, based on the ultimate strength of the material to be used. The specific gravity used in determining the static loadings shall be shown on the marking required by §178.245-6(a) and on the report required by §178.245-7(a).

(c) **Lifting lugs or hold-down lugs may be added** to either the tank or tank mountings. If lifting lugs and hold-down lugs are added directly to the tank, they shall be secured to doubling plates welded to the tank and located at points of support, except that lifting lugs or hold-down lugs with integral bases serving as doubling plates may be welded directly to the tank. Each lifting lug and hold-down lug shall be designed to withstand static loadings in any direction equal to twice the weight of the tank and attachments when filled with the lading using a safety factor of not less than four, based on the ultimate strength of the material to be used.

(d) **All tank mountings shall be designed** so as to prevent the concentration of excessive loads on the tank shell.

(e) **A DOT 51 portable tank that meets the definition** of "container" in §450.3(a)(2) of this title must meet the requirements of parts 450 through 453 of this title, in addition to the requirements of this subchapter.

§178.245-5 Protection of valves and accessories.

(a) **All valves, fittings, accessories, safety devices,** gaging devices, and the like shall be adequately protected against mechanical damage.

(b) **The protective device or housing shall conform** to the requirements under which the tanks are fabricated with respect to design and construction, and shall be designed to withstand static loadings in any direction equal to twice the weight of the tank and attachments when filled with the lading using a safety factor of not less than four, based on the ultimate strength of the material to be used.

(c) **Requirements concerning types of valves, retesting,** and qualification of portable tanks contained in §§173.32 and 173.315 of this chapter must be observed.

§178.245-6 Name plate.

(a) **In addition to the markings required by the Code** (see §178.245-1(a)) under which tanks were constructed, they shall have permanently affixed, in close proximity to the ASME "U" stamp certification, a metal plate. This plate shall be permanently affixed by means of soldering, brazing, or welding around its complete perimeter. Neither the plate itself nor the means of attachment to the tank shall be subject to destructive attack by the contents of tank. Upon such plate shall be plainly marked by stamping, embossing, or other means of forming letters into or onto the metal plate itself the following information in characters at least 1/8-inch high:

Manufacturer's name ________________

Serial No. ____________ Owner's serial No. ____________

D.O.T. Specification No. ________________

Water capacity (pounds) ________________

Tare weight (pounds) ________________

Design pressure (psig) ________________

Design specific gravity ________________

Original test date ________________

Tank retested at ____________ (psig) on: ____________

(b) **All tank outlets and inlets,** except safety relief valves, shall be marked to designate whether they communicate with vapor or liquid when the tank is filled to the maximum permitted filling density.

§178.245-7 Report.

(a) **A copy of the manufacturer's data report** required by the Code (See §178.245-1(a)) under which the tank is fabricated shall be furnished to the owner for each new tank.

(b) **[Reserved]**

§§178.251-178.253-5 [Reserved]

§178.255 Specification 60; steel portable tanks.

§178.255-1 General requirements.

(a) **Tanks must be of fusion welded construction,** cylindrical in shape with seamless heads concave to the pressure. Tank shells may be of seamless construction.

(b) **Tanks must be designed and constructed** in accordance with and fulfill all the requirements of the ASME Code.

(c) **Tanks including all permanent attachments** must be postweld heat treated as a unit.

(d) **Requirements concerning types of valves,** retesting, and qualification of portable tanks contained in §§173.32 and 173.315 of this chapter must be observed.

§178.255-2 Material.

(a) **Material used in the tank must** be steel of good weldable quality and conform with the requirements of the ASME Code.

(b) **The minimum thickness of metal,** exclusive of lining material, for shell and heads of tanks shall be as follows:

Tank capacity	Minimum thickness (inch)
Not more than 1,200 gallons	1/4
Over 1,200 to 1,800 gallons	5/16
Over 1,800 gallons	3/8

§178.255-3 Expansion domes.

(a) **Expansion domes, if applied,** must have a minimum capacity of one percent of the combined capacity of the tank and dome.

(b) **[Reserved]**

§178.255-4 Closures for manholes and domes.

(a) **The manhole cover shall be designed** to provide a secure closure of the manhole. All covers, not hinged to the tanks, shall be attached to the outside of the dome by at least 1/8 inch chain or its equivalent. Closures shall be made tight against leakage of vapor and liquid by use of gaskets of suitable material.

(b) **[Reserved]**

§178.255-5 Bottom discharge outlets.

(a) **Bottom discharge outlets prohibited,** except on tanks used for shipments of sludge acid and alkaline corrosive liquids.

(b) **If installed, bottom outlets or bottom washout chambers** shall be of metal not subject to rapid deterioration by the lading, and each shall be provided with a valve or plug at its upper end and liquid-tight closure at it lower end. Each valve or plug shall be designed to insure against unseating due to stresses or shocks incident to transportation. Bottom outlets shall be adequately protected against handling damage and outlet equipment must not extend to within less than one inch of the bottom bearing surface of the skids or tank mounting.

§178.255-6 Loading and unloading accessories.

(a) **When installed, gauging, loading, and air inlet devices,** including their valves, shall be provided with adequate means for their secure closure; and means shall also be provided for the closing of pipe connections of valves.

(b) **Interior heater coils, if installed,** must be of extra heavy pipe and so constructed that breaking off of exterior connections will not cause leakage of tanks.

§178.255-7 Protection of valves and accessories.

(a) **All valves, fittings, accessories, safety devices,** gauging devices, and the like shall be adequately protected against mechanical damage by a housing closed with a cover plate.

(b) **Protective housing shall comply with the requirements** under which the tanks are fabricated with respect to design and construction, and shall be designed with a minimum factor of safety of four to withstand loadings in any direction equal to two times the weight of the tank and attachments when filled with water.

§178.255-8 Safety devices.

(a) **See §173.315(i) of this subchapter.**

(b) **[Reserved]**

§178.255-9 Compartments.

(a) **When the interior of the tank is divided** into compartments, each compartment shall be designed, constructed and tested as a separate tank. Thickness of shell and compartment heads shall be determined on the basis of total tank capacity.

(b) **[Reserved]**

§178.255-10 Lining.

(a) **If a lining is required, the material used** for lining the tank shall be homogeneous, nonporous, imperforate when applied, not less elastic than the metal of the tank proper. It shall be of substantially uniform thickness, not less than 1/32 inch thick if metallic, and not less than 1/16 inch thick if nonmetallic, and shall be directly bonded or attached by other equally satisfactory means. Rubber lining shall be not less than 3/16 inch thick. Joints and seams in the lining shall be made by fusing the material together or by other equally satisfactory means. The interior of the tank shall be free from scale, oxidation, moisture and all foreign matter during the lining operation.

(b) **[Reserved]**

§178.255-11 Tank mountings.

(a) **Tanks shall be designed and fabricated** with mountings to provide a secure base in transit. "Skids" or similar devices shall be deemed to comply with this requirement.

(b) **All tank mountings such as skids, fastenings,** brackets, cradles, lifting lugs, etc., intended to carry loadings shall be permanently secured to tanks in accordance with the requirements under which the tanks are fabricated, and shall be designed with a factor of safety of four, and built to withstand loadings in any direction equal to two times the weight of the tanks and attachments when filled to the maximum permissible loaded weight.

(c) **Lifting lugs or side hold-down lugs shall be provided** on the tank mountings in a manner suitable for attaching lifting gear and hold-down devices. Lifting lugs and hold-down lugs welded directly to the tank shall be of the pad-eye type. Doubling plates welded to the tank and located at the points of support shall be deemed to comply with this requirement.

(d) **All tank mountings shall be so designed** as to prevent the concentration of excessive loads on the tank shell.

§178.255-12 Pressure test.

(a) **Each completed portable tank prior to application** of lining shall be tested before being put into transportation service by completely filling the tank with water or other liquid having a similar viscosity, the temperature of which shall not exceed 100 °F during the test, and applying a pressure of 60 psig. The tank shall be capable of holding the prescribed pressure for at least 10 minutes without leakage, evidence of impending failure, or failure. All closures shall be in place while the test is made and the pressure shall be gauged at the top of the tank. Safety devices and/or vents shall be plugged during this test.

(b) [Reserved]

§178.255-13 Repair of tanks.

(a) **Tanks failing to meet the test may be repaired and retested,** provided that repairs are made in complete compliance with the requirements of this specification.

(b) [Reserved]

§178.255-14 Marking.

(a) **In addition to marking required by** the American Society of Mechanical Engineers Code, every tank shall bear permanent marks at least 1/8-inch high stamped into the metal near the center of one of the tank heads or stamped into a plate permanently attached to the tank by means of brazing or welding or other suitable means as follows:

Manufacturer's name ________________ Serial No.________

DOT specification ______________________________

Nominal capacity ______________________ (gallons)

Tare weight __________________________ (pounds)

Date of manufacture ____________________________

(b) [Reserved]

§178.255-15 Report.

(a) **A copy of the manufacturer's data report** required by the Code (See §178.245-1(a)) under which the tank is fabricated must be furnished to the owner for each new tank.

Place ______________________________________

Date _______________________________________

Portable tank

Manufactured for ______________________________

Company Location _____________________________

Manufactured by _______________________________

Company Location _____________________________

Consigned to __________________________________

Company Location _____________________________

Size ______ feet outside diameter by ______ long.

Marks on tank as prescribed by §178.255-14 of this specification are as follows:

Manufacturer's name ____________________________

Serial number _________________________________

Owner's serial number ___________________________

DOT specification ______________________________

ASME Code Symbol (par U-201) ____________________

Date of manufacture _____________________________

Nominal capacity _____________ gallons.

It is hereby certified that this tank is in complete compliance with the requirements of DOT specification No. 60.

(Signed) ____________________________________

Manufacturer or owner

(b) [Reserved]

§178.270 Specification IM 101 and IM 102 steel portable tanks; general design and construction requirements.

§178.270-1 Specification requirements for IM 101 and IM 102 steel portable tanks.

(a) **Each IM portable tank must meet the requirements** of this section in addition to the requirements of §178.271 (IM 101) or §178.272 (IM 102). These requirements apply to IM portable tanks of diameters no greater than 2438 mm (96 inches) that are designed to carry liquids having a vapor pressure of less than 2.97 bar-absolute (43 psia) at a temperature of 50 °C (122 °F).

(b) [Reserved]

§178.270-2 General.

(a) **Each tank, including attachments** and service and structural equipment, must be designed to withstand, without loss of contents, the maximum internal pressure that can be anticipated to result from the contents and the static and dynamic stresses incurred in normal handling and transportation.

(b) **For the purpose of this subchapter** MAWP is the maximum pressure that an IM portable tank may experience during any normal operation (including loading and unloading). The only exception to this limitation is hydrostatic testing.

(c) **Each portable tank must have a cross-sectional design** that is capable of being stress analyzed either mathematically or by the experimental method contained in UG-101 of the ASME Code, or other method acceptable to the Associate Administrator.

(d) **Each portable tank must be designed** so that the center of gravity of the filled tank is approximately centered within the points of attachment for lifting devices.

(e) **When credit is taken for insulation to reduce** the required emergency venting capacity of safety relief devices, the insulation must be jacketed or otherwise protected from the accumulation of moisture or foreign matter that would decrease its efficiency or corrode the tank.

(f) **Each portable tank that has a lining** must have a lining material that meets the following requirements:

(1) *The material used to line the tank must be —*

(i) *Substantially immune* to attack by the hazardous material transported;

(ii) *Homogeneous;*

(iii) *Nonporous;*

(iv) *Imperforated when applied;*

(v) *At least as elastic as the material of the tank shell; and*

(vi) *Have thermal-expansion characteristics* compatible with the tank shell.

(2) *The lining of the tank, tank fitting and piping must be —*

(i) *Attached by bonding or other satisfactory means;*

(ii) *Continuous; and*

(iii) *Extended around the face of any flange.*

(3) *Joints and seams* in the lining must be made by fusing the material together or by other equally effective means.

§178.270-3 Materials of construction.

(a) **Each portable tank must be constructed** of carbon or alloy steels. Materials included in part UHT of the ASME Code or equivalent materials are not authorized. Any materials used in the tank shell must conform to a recognized national standard and must be suitable for the external environments in which the tank will be carried. The minimum elongation for any material must be 20 percent or greater.

(b) **The maximum stress allowed for a material** shall be determined using one of the following methods:

(1) *1.5 times* the specified values for the material at 93 °C (200 °F) in Section VIII, Division 1 of the ASME Code;

(2) *Derived by test* for the actual yield and tensile strengths at 93 °C (200 °F) for the actual group of plates used to fabricate the tank using the methods described in §178.270-3(d); or

(3) *Derived from* the minimum yield and tensile strengths at 93 °C (200 °F) specified by the national standard to which the material is manufactured using the methods described in §178.270-3(d).

(c) **Maximum allowable stress values,** derived for an actual group of plates, that are based on actual tensile and yield strengths of the material at 93 °C (200 °F) shall not be greater than 120 percent of the specified minimum yield and tensile strength specified in the national standard to which the material is manufactured.

(d) **The maximum allowable stress values must** be derived from the following criteria:

(1) *For austenitic steels;*

(i) *When the yield strength* is determined using the 0.2 percent offset, 93.75 percent of the yield strength.

(ii) *When the yield strength* is determined using the 1.0 percent offset, 75 percent of the yield strength.

(2) *For carbon and low alloy steels,* the yield strength is determined using the 0.2 percent offset. The maximum allowable stress value is the lower of 93.75 percent of the yield strength or 37.5 percent of the tensile strength.

(e) **For purposes of these specifications,** tensile strength, yield strength and elongation must be determined using a specimen having a gauge length:

$L_0 = 5.65(S_0)^{1/2}$

Where:

L_0 = the gauge length of the specimen — millimeters (inches); and

S_0 = the cross sectional area of the specimen — square millimeters (square inches).

Tensile tests and analysis of results must be in accordance with "ISO 82 Steels-Tensile Testing." The yield strength in tension shall be the stress corresponding to a permanent strain of 0.2 percent of the gauge length, except that for high alloy austenitic steels the yield strength shall be the stress corresponding to a permanent strain of 0.2 or 1.0 percent of the gauge length as appropriate. The elongation must be at least 20 percent.

(f) **If maximum allowable stress values or minimum tank** wall thicknesses are based on the actual yield strength, the actual tensile strength, or the actual elongation for the material used to fabricate the tank, the test records or certification of test results by the material producer or tank manufacturer must be approved by the approval agency, retained by the tank manufacturer for a period not less than 15 years, and made available to any duly identified representative of the Department or the owner of the tank.

§178.270-4 Structural integrity.

(a) **Maximum stress values.** The maximum calculated stress value in a tank at the Test Pressure must be less than or equal to that specified for the material of construction at 93 °C (200 °F) in §178.270-3 of this part.

(b) **Tank shell loadings.** Tank shells, heads, and their fastenings shall be designed to prevent stresses in excess of two thirds those specified in §178.270-3 of this part. The design calculations must include the forces imposed by each of the following loads:

(1) *An internal pressure* equal to the MAWP less 1 bar (14.5 psig) in combination with the simultaneously applied loadings of 3W vertically downward, 2W longitudinally, and 1W laterally acting through the center of the tank (W is the maximum permissible weight of the loaded tank and its attachments), and the requirements of paragraphs (b) (4), (5) and (6) of this section;

(2) *An internal pressure* equal to the MAWP less 1 bar (14.5 psig), in combination with the simultaneously applied loadings of 1W vertically upward, 2W longitudinally, and 1W laterally acting through the center of the tank (W is the maximum permissible weight of the loaded tank and its attachment), and the requirements of paragraphs (b) (4), (5) and (6) of this section;

(3) *The load* on the tank head resulting from an internal pressure equal to the MAWP, less 1 bar (14.5 psig), in combination with the dynamic pressure resulting from a longitudinal deceleration of 2 "g", and the requirements of paragraphs (b) (4), (5) and (6) of this section;

(4) *Loads resulting* from any discontinuities between tank shell and heads;

(5) *Superimposed loads* such as operating equipment, insulation, linings and piping; and

(6) *Reactions of supporting lugs and saddles or other supports.*

(c) **The shell thickness used in calculating** the resulting stress levels in a tank shall be exclusive of any corrosion allowance.

§178.270-5 Minimum thickness of shells and heads.

(a) **For the purposes of this section,** mild steel is steel with a guaranteed minimum tensile strength of 37 decanewtons per square millimeter (53,650 p.s.i.) and a guaranteed elongation of 27 percent or greater.

(b) **Except as otherwise provided in this subchapter,** the shell and heads of each portable tank constructed of reference mild steel:

(1) *With a maximum* cross-sectional dimension of 1.8 m (5.9 feet) or less, shall be at least 5 mm (0.197 inches) thick; or,

(2) *With a maximum* cross-sectional dimension exceeding 1.8 m (5.9 feet), shall be at least 6.35 mm (0.250 inches) thick.

(c) **The minimum thickness of the shell and heads** of each portable tank constructed of a steel other than the reference mild steel, shall be obtained from the following formula:

Formula for metric units

$e_1 = (10e_0) / (Rm_1\ A_1)^{1/3}$

Formula for nonmetric units

$e_1 = (112.3e_0) / (Rm_1\ A_1)^{1/3}$

Where:

e_0 = Required thickness of the reference steel from §178.270-5(b) — millimeters (inches);

e_1 = Equivalent thickness of the steel used — millimeters (inches);

Rm_1 = Specified minimum tensile strength of the steel used — decanewtons per square millimeter (p.s.i.); and

A_1 = Specified minimum percentage elongation of the steel used — percent times 100 (i.e., if 20% use 20.0).

(d) **When other than the standard minimum thickness** for the reference mild steel is specified for a tank in this subchapter, the specified minimum shell and head thickness must be at least equal to the larger of the thicknesses calculated from the formula given in §178.270-5(c) and the following formula:

Formula for metric units

$e_1 = (10e_0\ d_1) / 1.8(Rm_1\ A_1)^{1/3}$

Formula for metric units

$e_1 = (112.3e_0\ d_1) / 5.9(Rm_1\ A_1)^{1/3}$

Where:

e_1 = Equivalent thickness of the steel used — millimeters (inches);

e_0 = The specified minimum shell and head thickness of the reference mild steel specified in the IM Tank Table — millimeters (inches);

d_1 = Actual outside diameter of the tank — m (feet);

Rm_1 = Specified minimum tensile strength of the steel used — decanewtons per square millimeter (p.s.i.); and

A_1 = Specified minimum percentage elongation of the steel used — percent times 100 (i.e., if 20% use 20.0).

NOTE: For paragraphs (c) and (d) of this section the actual values for the tensile strength and percent elongation for the steel, as determined through tests on specimens from the group of plates to be used in the fabrication of the tank, may be substituted for the specified minimum values in the calculation prescribed in this paragraph (See §178.270-3 of this part). Test records or certification of test results by the material producer or tank manufacturer must be retained by the tank manufacturer for a period not less than 15 years and must be made available to the Department or the owner of the tank.

§178.270-6 Tank supports, frameworks and lifting attachments.

(a) **Each portable tank must be constructed** with a permanent support structure that provides a secure base in transport. Skids, frameworks, cradles, or similar devices are acceptable. The calculated stress in tank supports, frameworks, and lifting attachments must not exceed 80 percent of the specified minimum yield strength of the material of construction under the applicable loading conditions specified in §178.270-4(b).

(b) **An IM portable tank that meets the definition** of "container" in §450.3(a)(3) must meet the requirements of parts 450 through 453 of this title, in addition to the requirements of this subchapter.

§178.270-7 Joints in tank shells.

Joints in tank shells must be made by fusion welding. Such joints and their efficiencies must be as required by the ASME Code. Weld procedures and welder performance must be ASME Code qualified or must be qualified by the approval agency in accordance with the procedures in the ASME Code, Section IX, Welding and Brazing Qualifications. A record of each qualification must be retained by the manufacturer for the period prescribed in ASME Code, Section VIII, Pressure Vessels, and must be made available to any duly identified representative of the Department and the owner of the tank.

§178.270-8 Protection of valves and accessories.

Each valve, fitting, accessory, safety device, gauging device, and other appurtenance shall be adequately protected against mechanical damage.

§178.270-9 Inspection openings.

Each portable tank must be fitted with a manhole or other inspection opening sited above the maximum liquid level to allow for complete internal inspection and adequate access for maintenance and repair of the interior. Each portable tank with a capacity of more than 1894 L (500 gallons) must be fitted with an elliptical or round manhole at least 279 x 381 mm (11 x 15 inches), or 254 x 405 mm (10 x 16 inches), or with a circular manhole at least 381 mm (15 inches) in diameter. Any inspection opening and closure must be designed and reinforced as required by the ASME Code.

§178.270-10 External design pressure.

(a) **Each portable tank not fitted with vacuum relief devices** must be designed to withstand a positive external pressure differential of at least 0.4 bar (6 psig).

(b) **Each portable tank fitted with vacuum relief devices** must be designed to withstand a positive external pressure differential not less than the set pressure of the vacuum relief device and in any case at least 0.21 bar (3 psig).

§178.270-11 Pressure and vacuum relief devices.

(a) **Relief devices required.** Each portable tank, or each independent compartment of a portable tank, must be fitted with pressure relief devices in accordance with the following:

(1) *Each portable tank,* or each independent compartment of a portable tank, with a capacity of more than 1893 L (500 gallons), must be provided with a primary spring-loaded pressure relief device, and, in addition, may have one or more emergency pressure relief devices that may be a spring-loaded pressure relief valve, a rupture disc or fusible element in parallel with the primary pressure relief device.

(2) *Each portable tank,* or each independent compartment of a portable tank, with a capacity of 1893 L (500 gallons) or less, must be fitted with a primary pressure relief device that may either be a non-reclosing device or a spring-loaded pressure relief valve.

(3) *If a non-reclosing device* is inserted in series with a required pressure relief valve, the space between them must have a suitable tell-tale indicator to permit detection, prior to and during shipment, of disc rupture, pinholing, or leakage which could cause a malfunction of the pressure relief system. The frangible disc must rupture at a tank pressure within the range specified in paragraph (c)(1) of this section.

(b) **Location and construction of relief devices.**

(1) *Pressure relief devices* must be spring-loaded valves, rupture discs, or fusible elements. Vacuum relief devices must be capable of reclosing in any attitude. Each pressure relief device inlet must be situated in the vapor space of the tank. The discharge from any device must be unrestricted and directed to prevent impingement upon the tank shell or structural framework. Protective devices which deflect the flow of vapor are permissible provided the required vent capacity is maintained. Pressure and vacuum relief devices including their inlets must be sited on the top of the tank in a position as near as possible to the longitudinal and transversal center of the tank within the following limitation:

(i) *Longitudinally on the tank* within 107 cm (3 1/2 feet) or 1/6 the tank length, whichever is less, from the top center of the tank; and

(ii) *Transversally within 12 degrees of the tank top.*

(2) *Except for a relief device* installed in a piping system, each relief device must provide unrestricted venting under all conditions. Each pressure relief system, including any piping, must provide a venting capacity at least equal to the venting capacity specified in §178.270-11(d) for the tank on which the system is installed.

(3) *Fusible elements,* when installed, must not be protected from direct communication with external heat sources.

(4) *Spring-loaded pressure relief valves* must be constructed in a manner to prevent unauthorized adjustment of the relief setting.

(c) **Pressure settings of relief devices —**

(1) *Primary pressure relief devices.* The primary relief device required by paragraph (a) of this section must be set to function in the range of —

(i) *No less than* 67 percent and no greater than 83 percent of test pressure for tanks hydrostatically tested under §178.270-13(a) of this subpart at a gauge pressure below 455 kPa (66 psig). Spring-loaded pressure relief valves must close after discharge at a pressure not less than 80 percent of start-to-discharge pressure.

(ii) *No less than* 67 percent and no greater than 74 percent of test pressure for tanks hydrostatically tested under §178.270-13(a) of this subpart at a gauge pressure of 455 kPa (66 psig) or higher. Spring-loaded pressure relief valves must close after discharge at a pressure not less than 90 percent of start-to-discharge pressure.

(2) *Emergency pressure relief devices.* Each rupture disc, other than one used as a primary relief device in accordance with paragraph (b)(2) of this section, must be designed to burst at a pressure greater than 83 percent of and less than or equal to tank hydrostatic test pressure. Each spring-loaded pressure relief device must be set to operate at no less than 83 percent of hydrostatic test pressure and be fully open at test pressure.

(3) *Fusible elements.* Fusible elements must have a nominal yield temperature greater than the highest tank operating temperature and less than or equal to 121 °C (250 °F). The pressure developed in the tank at the fusible element yield temperature must be below the test pressure of the tank.

(4) *Vacuum relief devices.* Vacuum relief devices, when used, must be designed to provide total containment of product under normal and accident conditions and must be set to open at a nominal external overpressure of not less than 0.21 bar (3 psig) but not greater than the external pressure for which the tank is designed. Each vacuum relief device must have a minimum cross sectional flow area of 2.84 cm ^{2} (0.44 square inches).

(d) **Venting capacity of pressure relief devices —**

(1) *Pressure relief valves (spring-loaded).* Each pressure relief valve must have a minimum vent capacity of at least 170 standard cubic meters per hour (SCMH) (6,000 standard cubic feet per hour (SCFH)). The minimum total pressure relief valve vent capacity for each tank shall be 340 SCMH (12,000 SCFH) per 32.5m^2 (350 square feet) of exposed tank area, but in any case at least 340 SCMH (12,000 SCFH).

(2) *Total tank vent capacity.* The total vent capacity of all pressure relief devices installed on each portable tank must be sufficient with all devices operating to limit the pressure in the tank to less than or equal to the test pressure. Except as provided in paragraph (d)(3) or (d)(4) of this section, the total vent capacity must be at least equal to that shown in the following table:

Table I - Minimum Total Vent Capacity
[Metric units table in cubic meters of air per hour at atmospheric pressure and 15 °C]

Exposed area square meters	Cubic meters free air per hour	Exposed area square meters	Cubic meters free air per hour
2	841	37.5	9.306
3	1,172	40	9,810
4	1,485	42.5	10,308
5	1,783	45	10,806
6	2,069	47.5	11,392
7	2,348	50	11,778
8	2,621	52.5	12,258
9	2,821	55	12,732
10	3,146	57.5	13,206
12	3,655	60	13,674
14	4,146	62.5	14,142
16	4,625	65	14,604
18	5,092	67.5	15,066
20	5,556	70	15,516
22.5	6,120	75	16,422
25	6,672	80	17,316
27.5	7,212	85	18,198
30	7,746	90	19,074
32.5	8,268	95	19,938
35	8,790	100	20,790

[Nonmetric units in cubic feet of air per hour at atmospheric pressure and 59 °F]

Exposed area square feet	Cubic feet free air per hour	Exposed area square feet	Cubic feet free air per hour
20	27,600	275	237,000
30	38,500	300	256,000
40	48,600	350	289,500
50	58,600	400	322,100
60	67,700	450	355,900
70	77,000	500	391,000
80	85,500	550	417,500
90	94,800	600	450,000
100	104,000	650	479,000
120	121,000	700	512,000
140	136,200	750	540,000
160	152,100	800	569,000
180	168,200	850	597,000
200	184,000	900	621,000
225	199,000	950	656,000
250	219,500	1,000	686,000

NOTE: Interpolate for intermediate sizes.

(3) *Notwithstanding the minimum* total vent capacity shown in table I, of paragraph (d)(2), a tank in dedicated service may have a lesser total vent capacity provided the approval certificate required by §178.273(b)(7) specifies the hazardous materials for which the tank is suitable. The lesser total vent capacity must be determined in accordance with the following formula:

Formula for metric units

$Q = 5{,}660{,}000\ A^{0.82}\ (ZT)^{0.5} / (LC)(M^{0.5})$

Formula for nonmetric units

$Q = 37{,}980{,}000\ A^{0.82}\ (ZT)^{0.5} / (LC)(M^{0.5})$

Where:

Q = The total required venting capacity, in cubic meters of air per hour at standard conditions of 15.6 °C and 1 atm (cubic feet of air per hour at standard conditions of 60 °F and 14.7 psia);

T = The absolute temperature of the vapor at the venting conditions — degrees Kelvin (°C+273) [degrees Rankine (°F+460)];

A = The exposed surface area of tank shell — square meters (square feet);

L = The latent heat of vaporization of the lading — calories per gram (BTU/lb);

Z = The compressibiliy factor for the vapor (if this factor is unknown, let Z equal 1.0);

M = The molecular weight of vapor;

C = A constant derived from (K), the ratio of specific heats of the vapor. If (K) is unknown, let C = 315.

$C = 520[K(2/(K+1))\ [^{(K+1)/(K-1)}]]1/2$

Where:

$K = C_p / C_v$

C_p = The specific heat at constant pressure, in calories per gram degree centigrade (BTU/lb °F); and

C_v = The specific heat at constant volume, in calories per gram degree centigrade (BTU/lb °F).

(4) *The required* total venting capacity determined by using table I or paragraph (d)(3) of this section may be reduced for insulated tanks to Q_t by the following formula:

$Q_t = FQ_1$

Where:

Q_t = The total required venting capacity of the insulated tank;

Q_1 = The total venting capacity required for an uninsulated tank according to table I or paragraph (d)(3) of this section;

F = A coefficient with a value greater than or equal to 0.25 according to the following formula:

Formula for metric units

$F = 8U(649-t) / 93.5 \times 10^6$

Formula for nonmetric units

$F = 8U(1200-t) / 34{,}500$

Where:

U = The thermal conductance of the insulation system taken at 38 °C (100 °F), in gram calories per hour square meter °C (BTU per hour square feet °F); and

t = The actual temperature of the substance at loading, in °C (°F).

(5) *Insulation systems,* used for the purpose of reducing the venting capacity, must be approved by the approval agency. In all cases, insulation systems approved for this purpose must:

(i) *Remain effective* at all temperatures up to 649 °C (1200 °F); and

(ii) *Be jacketed* with a material having a melting point of 649 °C (1200 °F) or greater.

(6) *The flow capacity rating* of any pressure relief device must be certified by the manufacturer to be in accordance with the applicable provisions of the ASME Code with the following exceptions:

(i) *The ASME Code stamp is not required; and*

(ii) *The flow capacity* certification test for spring loaded pressure relief valves may be conducted at a pressure not to exceed 120% of the set pressure provided the stamped flow capacity rating is not greater than 83% of the average capacity of the valves tested.

(e) **Markings on pressure and vacuum relief devices.** The following information shall be plainly displayed on each pressure relief device:

(1) *The pressure* or, when appropriate, the temperature at which the device is set to function;

(2) *Except for vacuum relief devices,* the rated flow capacity of air discharged per minute at 15 °C (59 °F) and atmospheric pressure, at:

(i) *The set pressure for rupture discs;*

(ii) *No greater* than 20% above the start-to-discharge pressure for spring-loaded relief devices; or

(iii) *The fusing temperature for fusible elements.*

(3) *The manufacturer's name and catalog number; and*

(4) *The allowable tolerances* at the start-to-discharge pressure and the allowable tolerances at the discharge temperature.

§178.270-12 Valves, nozzles, piping, and gauging devices.

(a) **All tank nozzles, except those provided** for filling and discharge connections below the normal liquid level of the tank, relief devices, thermometer wells, and inspection openings, must be fitted with manually operated stop valves located as near the shell as practicable either internal or external to the shell. Each filling and discharge connection located below the normal liquid level of the tank must be equipped with an internal discharge valve. A tank nozzle installed in the vapor space to provide a filling or cleaning opening, which is closed by a blank flange or other suitable means, need not be provided with a manually operated stop valve. A tank nozzle installed for a thermometer well or inspection opening need not be provided with a manually operated stop valve.

(b) **Each valve must be designed and constructed** to a rated pressure not less than the MAWP of the tank. Each stop valve with a screwed spindle must be closed by a clockwise motion of the handwheel. All valves must be constructed to prevent unintentional opening.

(c) **Each internal discharge valve shall be self-closing,** located inside the tank, within the welded flange or within its companion flange.

(d) **A shear section must be located outboard** of each internal discharge valve seat and within 10.2 cm (4 inches) of the vessel. The shear section must break under strain without affecting the product retention capabilities of the tank and any attachments.

(e) **All piping must be of suitable material.** Welded joints must be used wherever practicable. The bursting strength of all piping and pipe fittings must be at least 4 times the MAWP of the tank. Piping must be supported in such a manner as to prevent damage due to thermal stresses, jarring or vibration.

(f) **All nozzles and tank shell penetrations for nozzles** shall be designed and constructed in accordance with the ASME Code.

(g) **Glass liquid level gauges, or gauges** of other easily destructible material, which are in direct communication with the contents of the tank are prohibited.

§178.270-13 Testing.

(a) **Hydrostatic test.** Each portable tank and all piping, valves, and other attachments which are subject to the pressure of the contents of the tank, except pressure relief devices, must be hydrostatically tested by completely filling the tank (including domes, if any) with water or other liquid having a similar density and viscosity and applying a pressure of at least 150 percent of the MAWP. The pressure shall be maintained for at least 10 minutes. While under pressure, the tank shall be inspected for leakage, undue distortion, or other conditions which indicate weakness or which might render the tank unsafe for transportation service. Failure to successfully meet the test criteria shall be deemed evidence of failure to meet the requirements of this specification. Tanks failing to pass the test shall be suitably repaired and must successfully pass the prescribed tests prior to use for transporting any hazardous material.

(b) **Testing of internal coils.** Internal coils, if installed, must be hydrostatically tested to an internal pressure of 13.8 bar (200 psig) or 150 percent of the rated pressure of the coils, whichever is greater.

(c) **Tank container qualification test.** For each tank design, a prototype tank, using a framework for containerized transport, must fulfill the requirements of parts 450-453 of this title for compliance with the requirements of Annex II of the International Convention for Safe Containers. In addition, the following tests must be completed without leakage or deformation that would render the tank unsuitable for use:

(1) *Longitudinal inertia.* The tank loaded to its maximum gross weight must be positioned with its longitudinal axis vertical. It shall be held in this position for five minutes by support at the lower end of the base structure providing vertical and lateral restraint and by support at the upper end of the base structure providing lateral restraint only.

(2) *Lateral inertia.* The tank loaded to its maximum gross weight must be positioned for five minutes with its transverse axis vertical. It shall be held in this position for five minutes by support at the lower side of the base structure providing vertical and lateral restraint and by support at the upper side of the base structure providing lateral restraint only.

(d) **Approval of smaller tanks of the same design.** Design approval must include the prototype testing of at least one tank of each design and each size; however, a set of tests made on a tank of one size may serve for the approval of smaller tanks with equal or lesser diameter and length) made of the same material and thickness by the same fabrication technique and with identical supports and equivalent closures and other appurtenances.

(e) **Pressure and vacuum relief devices.** Each spring loaded relief device must be tested for the accuracy of the setting prior to installation on a tank and must be effectively sealed to maintain the required setting.

§178.270-14 Marking of tanks.

(a) **General.** Each tank must bear a corrosion resistant metal identification plate that is permanently attached to the portable tank and readily accessible for inspection. The information required in paragraph (b), and, when appropriate, paragraph (c) of this section must be stamped, embossed or otherwise marked by an equally durable method on the plate in characters at least 3 mm (0.118 inches) high. The plate must not be painted.

(b) **Required information.** At least the following information must appear on the metal identification plate for each tank:

(1) *US DOT Specification number.*

(2) *Country of manufacture.*

(3) *Manufacturer's name.*

(4) *Date of manufacture.*

(5) *Manufacturer's serial number.*

(6) *Identification of USA/DOT approval agency and approval number.*

(7) *MAWP, in bar or psig.*

(8) *Test pressure, in bar or psig.*

(9) *Total measured water capacity at 20 °C (68 °F), in liters or gallons.*

(10) *Maximum allowable gross weight, in kg or lbs.*

(11) *Equivalent minimum shell thickness in mild steel, in mm or inches.*

(12) *Tank material and specification number.*

(13) *Metallurgical design temperature range, in °C or °F.*

(c) **Additional information.** The following additional information must appear on the metal identification plate when applicable:

(1) *Lining material.*

(2) *Heating coil MAWP in bar and psig.*

(3) *Corrosion allowance, in mm or in.*

(d) **In addition to the markings required above,** each tank used in international transport must have a Safety Approval Plate containing the information required in §§451.21 through 451.25 of this title.

(e) **Nothing in this section shall be deemed to preclude** the display of other pertinent information on the required metal identification plate.

§178.271 Specification IM 101 steel portable tanks.

§178.271-1 General requirements.

(a) **Specification IM 101 portable tanks must conform** to the general design and construction requirements in §178.270 of this subpart in addition to the specific design requirements contained in this section.

(b) **The MAWP of each tank shall be** equal to or greater than 1.75 bar (25.4 psig) and less than 6.8 bar (100 psig).

(c) **Each tank shall be designed and constructed** in accordance with the requirements of Section VIII, Division 1, of the ASME Code except as limited or modified in this section or in §178.270 of this subpart. ASME certification or stamp is not required.

§178.272 Specification IM 102 steel portable tanks.

§178.272-1 General requirements.

(a) **Specification IM 102 portable tanks must conform** to the general design and construction requirements in §178.270 of this subpart in addition to the specific design requirements contained in this section.

(b) **The MAWP of each tank shall be less than** 1.75 bar (25.4 psig) but at least 1.0 bar (14.5 psig).

(c) **Each tank shall be designed and constructed** in accordance with the requirements of Section VIII, Division 1, of the ASME Code except as limited or modified in this section or in §178.270 of this subpart. ASME certification or stamp is not required.

§178.272-2 Minimum thickness of shells and heads.

(a) **The approval agency may authorize** a minimum thickness less than that required by §178.270-5 of this subpart where additional protection against tank puncture provides equal integrity.

(b) **The shell and head thickness of a tank must be at least:**

(1) *3.18 mm (0.125 inches)* for a tank with a maximum cross-sectional dimension of 1.8 m (5.9 feet) or less; or

(2) *4 mm (0.157 inches)* for a tank constructed of the reference mild steel having a maximum cross-sectional dimension exceeding 1.8 m (5.9 feet). For tanks having a maximum cross-sectional dimension exceeding 1.8 m (5.9 feet) constructed of other steels, an equivalent head and shell thickness calculated in accordance with §178.270-5(c) of this subpart may be used, subject to an absolute minimum of 3.18 mm (0.125 inches).

(c) **The following additional puncture protection systems** are authorized:

(1) *An overall external structural protection,* such as a jacket, which is rigidly secured to the tank with a layer of cushioning material installed between the external structural protection and the tank; or

(2) *A complete framework* surrounding the tank including both longitudinal and transverse structural members.

§178.273 Approval of Specification IM portable tanks and UN portable tanks.

(a) **Application for approval.**

(1) *An owner or manufacturer* of a portable tank shall apply for approval to a designated approval agency authorized to approve the portable tank in accordance with the procedures in subpart E, part 107 of this subchapter.

(2) *Each application for approval must contain the following information:*

(i) *Two complete copies* of all engineering drawings, calculations, and test data necessary to ensure that the design meets the relevant specification.

(ii) *The manufacturer's serial number* that will be assigned to each portable tank.

(iii) *A statement* as to whether the design type has been examined by any approval agency previously and judged unacceptable. Affirmative statements must be documented with the name of the approval agency, reason for nonacceptance, and the nature of modifications made to the design type.

(b) **Action by approval agency.** The approval agency must perform the following activities:

(1) *Review the application* for approval to determine whether it is complete and conforms with the requirements of paragraph (a) of this section. If an application is incomplete, it will be returned to the applicant with an explanation as to why the application is incomplete.

(2) *Review all drawings and calculations* to ensure that the design is in compliance with all requirements of the relevant specification. If the application is approved, one set of the approved drawings, calculations, and test data shall be returned to the applicant. The second (inspector's copy) set of approved drawings, calculations, and test data shall be retained by the

approval agency. Maintain drawings and approval records for as long as the portable tank remains in service. The drawings and records must be provided to the Department of Transportation (DOT) upon request.

(3) *Witness all tests* required for the approval of the portable tank specified in this section and part 180, subpart G of this subchapter.

(4) *Ensure, through appropriate inspection* that each portable tank is fabricated in all respects in conformance with the approved drawings, calculations, and test data.

(5) *Determine and ensure* that the portable tank is suitable for its intended use and that it conforms to the requirements of this subchapter.

(6) *For UN portable tanks* intended for non-refrigerated and refrigerated liquefied gases and Division 6.1 liquids which meet the inhalation toxicity criteria (Zone A or B) as defined in §173.132 of this subchapter, or that are designated as toxic by inhalation materials in the §172.101 Table of this subchapter, the approval agency must ensure that:

(i) *The portable tank* has been constructed in accordance with the ASME Code, Section VIII, Division 1 (see §171.7 of this subchapter). ASME Code, Section VIII, Division 2 (see §171.7 of this subchapter) or other design codes may be used if approved by the Associate Administrator (see §178.274(b)(1));

(ii) *All applicable provisions* of the design and construction have been met to the satisfaction of the designated approval agency in accordance with the rules established in the ASME Code and that the portable tank meets the requirements of the ASME Code and all the applicable requirements specified in this subchapter;

(iii) *The inspector* has carried out all the inspections specified by the rules established in the ASME Code; and

(iv) *The portable tank* is marked with a U stamp code symbol under the authority of the authorized independent inspector.

(7) *Upon successful completion* of all requirements of this subpart, the approval agency must:

(i) *Apply its name,* identifying mark or identifying number, and the date upon which the approval was issued, to the metal identification marking plate attached to the portable tank. Any approvals for UN portable tanks authorizing design or construction alternatives (Alternate Arrangements) approved by the Associate Administrator (see §178.274(a)(2)) must be indicated on the plate as specified in §178.274(i).

(ii) *Issue an approval certificate* for each portable tank or, in the case of a series of identical portable tanks manufactured to a single design type, for each series of portable tanks. The approval certificate must include all the information required to be displayed on the required metal identification plate required by §178.270-14 of this subchapter for IM portable tanks, §178.245-6 for Specification 51 steel portable tanks, or §178.274(i) for UN portable tanks. The approval certificate must certify that the approval agency designated to approve the portable tank has approved the portable tank in accordance with the procedures in subpart E of part 107 of this subchapter and that the portable tank is suitable for its intended purpose and meets the requirements of this subchapter. When a series of portable tanks is manufactured without change in the design type, the certificate may be valid for the entire series of portable tanks representing a single design type. For UN portable tanks, the certificate must refer to the prototype test report, the hazardous material or group of hazardous materials allowed to be transported, the materials of construction of the shell and lining (when applicable) and an approval number. The approval number must consist of the distinguishing sign or mark of the country ("USA" for the United States of America) where the approval was granted and a registration number.

(iii) *Retain a copy of each approval certificate.*

(8) *For UN portable tanks,* the approval certificate must also include the following:

(i) *The results* of the applicable framework and rail impact test specified in part 180, subpart G, of this subchapter; and

(ii) *The results* of the initial inspection and test in §178.274(j) of this subchapter.

(9) *The approval agency* shall be independent from the manufacturer. The approval agency and the authorized inspector may be the same entity.

(c) Manufacturers' responsibilities. The manufacturer is responsible for compliance with the applicable specifications for the design and construction of portable tanks. In addition to responsibility for compliance, manufacturers are responsible for ensuring that the contracted approval agency and authorized inspector, if applicable, are qualified, reputable and competent. The manufacturer of a portable tank shall —

(1) *Comply with* all the applicable requirements of the ASME Code (see §171.7 of this subchapter) and of this subpart including, but not limited to, ensuring that the quality control, design calculations and required tests are performed and that all aspects of the portable tank meet the applicable requirements.

(2) *Obtain and use* a designated approval agency, if applicable, and obtain and use a DOT-designated approval agency to approve the design, construction and certification of the portable tank.

(3) *Provide a statement* in the manufacturers' data report certifying that each portable tank that is manufactured complies with the relevant specification and all the applicable requirements of this subchapter.

(4) *Maintain records* of the qualification of portable tanks for at least 5 years and provide copies to the approval agency, the owner or lessee of the tank. Upon request, provide these records to a representative of DOT.

(d) Denial of application for approval. If an approval agency finds that a portable tank cannot be approved for any reason, it shall notify the applicant in writing and shall provide the applicant with the reasons for which the approval is denied. A copy of the notification letter shall be provided to the Associate Administrator. An applicant aggrieved by a decision of an approval agency may appeal the decision in writing, within 90 days of receipt, to the Associate Administrator.

(e) Modifications to approved portable tanks.

(1) *Prior to modification* of any approved portable tank which may affect conformance and the safe use of an IM or UN portable tank, which may involve a change to the design type or which may affect its ability to retain the hazardous material in transportation, the person desiring to make such modification shall inform the approval agency that issued the initial approval of the portable tank (or if unavailable another approval agency) of the nature of the modification and request approval of the modification. The person desiring to modify the tank must supply the approval agency with three sets of all revised drawings, calculations, and test data relative to the intended modification.

(2) *A statement* as to whether the intended modification has been examined and determined to be unacceptable by any approval agency. The written statement must include the name of the approving agency, the reason for nonacceptance, and the nature of changes made to the modification since its original rejection.

(3) *The approval agency* shall review the request for modification, and if it is determined that the proposed modification is in full compliance with the relevant DOT specification, including a UN portable tank, the request shall be approved and the approval agency shall perform the following activities:

(i) *Return one set* of the approved revised drawings, calculations, and test data to the applicant. The second and third sets of the approved revised drawings, calculations, and data shall be retained by the approval agency as required in §107.404(a)(3) of this subchapter.

(ii) *Ensure through* appropriate inspection that all modifications conform to the revised drawings, calculations, and test data.

(iii) *Determine the extent* to which retesting of the modified tank is necessary based on the nature of the proposed modification, and ensure that all required retests are satisfactorily performed.

(iv) *If modification* to an approved tank alters any information on the approval certificate, issue a new approval certificate for the modified tank and ensure that any necessary changes are made to the metal identification plate. A copy of each newly issued approval certificate shall be retained by the approval agency and by the owner of each portable tank.

(4) *If the approval agency* determines that the proposed modification is not in compliance with the relevant DOT specification, the approval agency shall deny the request in accordance with paragraph (d) of this section.

(f) Termination of Approval Certificate.

(1) *The Associate Administrator* may terminate an approval issued under this section if he determines that —

(i) *Information upon which* the approval was based is fraudulent or substantially erroneous; or

(ii) *Termination of the approval* is necessary to adequately protect against risks to life and property; or

(iii) *The approval* was not issued by the approval agency in good faith; or

(iv) *The portable tank does not meet the specification.*

(2) *Before an approval is terminated,* the Associate Administrator gives the interested party(ies):

(i) *Written notice* of the facts or conduct believed to warrant the termination;

(ii) *Opportunity to submit oral and written evidence; and*

(iii) *Opportunity to demonstrate* or achieve compliance with the applicable requirements.

(3) *If the Associate Administrator* determines that a certificate of approval must be terminated to preclude a significant and imminent adverse affect on public safety, he may terminate the certificate immediately. In such circumstances, the opportunities of paragraphs (f)(2) (ii) and (iii) of this section need not be provided prior to termination of the approval, but shall be provided as soon as practicable thereafter.

§178.274 Specifications for UN portable tanks.

(a) General.

(1) *Each UN portable tank* must meet the requirements of this section. In addition to the requirements of this section, requirements specific to UN portable tanks used for liquid and solid hazardous materials, non-refrigerated liquefied gases and refrigerated liquefied gases are provided in §§178.275, 178.276 and 178.277, respectively. Requirements for approval, maintenance, inspection, testing and use are provided in §178.273 and part 180, subpart G, of this subchapter. Any portable tank which meets the definition of a "container" within the terms of the International Convention for Safe Containers (CSC) must meet the requirements of the CSC as amended and 49 CFR parts 450 through 453 and must have a CSC safety approval plate.

(2) *In recognition* of scientific and technological advances, the technical requirements applicable to UN portable tanks may be varied if approved by the Associate Administrator and the portable tank is shown to provide a level of safety equal to or exceeding the requirements of this subchapter. Portable tanks approved to alternative technical requirements must be marked "Alternative Arrangement" as specified in paragraph (i) of this section.

(3) *Definitions.* The following definitions apply for the purposes of design and construction of UN portable tanks under this subpart:

Alternate Arrangement portable tank means a UN portable tank that has been approved to alternative technical requirements or testing methods other than those specified for UN portable tanks in part 178 or part 180 of this subchapter.

Approval agency means the designated approval agency authorized to approve the portable tank in accordance with the procedures in subpart E of part 107 of this subchapter.

Design pressure is defined according to the hazardous materials intended to be transported in the portable tank. See §§178.275, 178.276 and 178.277, as applicable.

Design type means a portable tank or series of portable tanks made of materials of the same material specifications and thicknesses, manufactured by a single manufacturer, using the same fabrication techniques (for example, welding procedures) and made with equivalent structural equipment, closures, and service equipment.

Fine grain steel means steel which has a ferritic grain size of 6 or finer when determined in accordance with ASTM E 112-96 (see §171.7 of this subchapter).

Fusible element means a non-reclosing pressure relief device that is thermally activated and that provides protection against excessive pressure buildup in the portable tank developed by exposure to heat, such as from a fire (see §178.275(g)).

Jacket means the outer insulation cover or cladding which may be part of the insulation system.

Leakage test means a test using gas to subject the shell and its service equipment to an internal pressure.

Maximum allowable working pressure (MAWP) is defined according to the hazardous materials intended to be transported in the portable tank. See §§178.275, 178.276 and 178.277, as applicable.

Maximum permissible gross mass (MPGM) means the sum of the tare mass of the portable tank and the heaviest hazardous material authorized for transportation.

Mild steel means a steel with a guaranteed minimum tensile strength of 360 N/mm^2 to 440 N/mm^2 and a guaranteed minimum elongation at fracture as specified in paragraph (c)(10) of this section.

Offshore portable tank means a portable tank specially designed for repeated use in the transportation of hazardous materials to, from and between offshore facilities. An offshore portable tank is designed and constructed in accordance with the Guidelines for the Approval of Containers Handled in Open Seas specified in the IMDG Code (see §171.7 of this subchapter).

Reference steel means a steel with a tensile strength of 370 N/mm^2 and an elongation at fracture of 27%.

Service equipment means measuring instruments and filling, discharge, venting, safety, heating, cooling and insulating devices.

Shell means the part of the portable tank which retains the hazardous materials intended for transportation, including openings and closures, but does not include service equipment or external structural equipment.

Structural equipment means the reinforcing, fastening, protective and stabilizing members external to the shell.

Test pressure means the maximum gauge pressure at the top of the shell during the hydraulic pressure test equal to not less than 1.5 times the design pressure for liquids and 1.3 for liquefied compressed gases and refrigerated liquefied gases. In some instances a pneumatic test is authorized as an alternative to the hydraulic test. The minimum test pressures for portable tanks intended for specific liquid and solid hazardous materials are specified in the applicable portable tank T codes (such as T1-T23) assigned to these hazardous materials in the §172.101 Table of this subchapter.

(b) General design and construction requirements.

(1) *The design temperature range* for the shell must be -40 °C to 50 °C (-40 °F to 122 °F) for hazardous materials transported under normal conditions of transportation, except for portable tanks used for refrigerated liquefied gases where the minimum design temperature must not be higher than the lowest (coldest) temperature (for example, service temperature) of the contents during filling, discharge or transportation. For hazardous materials handled under elevated temperature conditions, the design temperature must not be less than the maximum temperature of the hazardous material during filling, discharge or transportation. More severe design temperatures must be considered for portable tanks subjected to severe climatic conditions (for example, portable tanks transported in arctic regions). Shells must be designed and constructed in accordance with the requirements of the ASME Code, Section VIII, Division 1 (see §171.7 of this subchapter), except as limited or modified in this subchapter. For portable tanks used for liquid or solid hazardous materials, a design code other than the ASME Code may be used if approved by the Associate Administrator. Portable tanks used for non-refrigerated and refrigerated liquified compressed gases require an ASME certification and U stamp. Shells must be made of metallic materials suitable for forming. Non-metallic materials may be used for the attachments and supports between the shell and jacket, provided their material properties at the minimum and maximum design temperatures are proven to be sufficient. For welded shells, only a material whose weldability has been fully demonstrated may be used. Welds must be of high quality and conform to a level of integrity at least equivalent to the welding requirements specified in Section VIII of the ASME Code for the welding of pressure vessels. When the manufacturing process or the materials make it necessary, the shells must be suitably heat-treated to guarantee adequate toughness in the weld and in the heat-affected zones. In choosing the material, the design temperature range must be taken into account with respect to risk of brittle fracture, stress corrosion cracking, resistance to impact, and suitability for the hazardous materials intended for transportation in the portable tank. When fine grain steel is used, the guaranteed value of the yield strength must be not more than 460 N/mm^2 and the guaranteed value of the upper limit of the tensile strength must be not more than 725 N/mm^2 according to the material specification. Aluminum may not be used as a construction material for the shells of portable tanks intended for the transport of non-refrigerated liquefied gases. For portable tanks intended for the transport of liquid or solid hazardous materials, aluminum may only be used as a construction material for portable tank shells if approved by the Associate Administrator. Portable tank materials must be suitable for the external environment where they will be transported, taking into account the determined design temperature range. Portable tanks shall be designed to withstand, without loss of contents, at least the internal pressure due to the contents and the static, dynamic and thermal loads during normal conditions of handling and transportation. The design must take into account the effects of fatigue, caused by repeated application of these loads through the expected life of the portable tank.

(2) *Portable tank shells, fittings, and pipework* shall be constructed from materials that are:

(i) *Compatible with the hazardous materials* intended to be transported; or

(ii) *Properly passivated or neutralized* by chemical reaction, if applicable; or

(iii) *For portable tanks* used for liquid and solid materials, lined with corrosion-resistant material directly bonded to the shell or attached by equivalent means.

(3) *Gaskets and seals* shall be made of materials that are compatible with the hazardous materials intended to be transported.

(4) *When shells are lined,* the lining must be compatible with the hazardous materials intended to be transported, homogeneous, non-porous, free from perforations, sufficiently elastic and compatible with the thermal expansion characteristics of the shell. The lining of every shell, shell fittings and piping must be continuous and must extend around the face of any flange. Where external fittings are welded to the tank, the lining must be continuous through the fitting and around the face of external flanges. Joints and seams in the lining must be made by fusing the material together or by other equally effective means.

(5) *Contact between dissimilar metals* which could result in damage by galvanic action must be prevented by appropriate measures.

(6) *The construction materials* of the portable tank, including any devices, gaskets, linings and accessories, must not adversely affect or react with the hazardous materials intended to be transported in the portable tank.

(7) *Portable tanks* must be designed and constructed with supports that provide a secure base during transportation and with suitable lifting and tie-down attachments.

(c) Design criteria.

(1) *Portable tanks* and their fastenings must, under the maximum permissible loads and maximum permissible working pressures, be capable of absorbing the following separately applied static forces (for calculation purposes, acceleration due to gravity (g) = 9.81m/s^2):

(i) *In the direction of travel:* 2g (twice the MPGM multiplied by the acceleration due to gravity);

(ii) *Horizontally at right angles* to the direction of travel: 1g (the MPGM multiplied by the acceleration due to gravity);

(iii) *Vertically upwards:* 1g (the MPGM multiplied by the acceleration due to gravity); and

(iv) *Vertically downwards:* 2g (twice the MPGM multiplied by the acceleration due to gravity).

(2) *Under each of the forces* specified in paragraph (c)(1) of this section, the safety factor must be as follows:

(i) *For metals* having a clearly defined yield point, a design margin of 1.5 in relation to the guaranteed yield strength; or

(ii) *For metals* with no clearly defined yield point, a design margin of 1.5 in relation to the guaranteed 0.2% proof strength and, for austenitic steels, the 1% proof strength.

(3) *The values* of yield strength or proof strength must be the values according to recognized material standards. When austenitic steels are used, the specified minimum values of yield strength or proof strength according to the material standards may be increased by up to 15% for portable tanks used for liquid and solid hazardous materials, other than toxic by inhalation liquids meeting the criteria of Hazard Zone A or Hazard Zone B (see §173.133 of this subchapter), when these greater values are attested in the material inspection certificate.

(4) *Portable tanks* must be capable of being electrically grounded to prevent dangerous electrostatic discharge when they are used for Class 2 flammable gases or Class 3 flammable liquids, including elevated temperature materials transported at or above their flash point.

(5) *For shells* of portable tanks used for liquefied compressed gases, the shell must consist of a circular cross section. Shells must be of a design capable of being stress-analyzed mathematically or experimentally by resistance strain gauges as specified in UG-101, Section VIII of the ASME Code (see §171.7 of this subchapter), or other methods approved by the Associate Administrator.

(6) *Shells must be* designed and constructed to withstand a hydraulic test pressure of not less than 1.5 times the design pressure for portable tanks used for liquids and 1.3 times the design pressure for portable tanks used for liquefied compressed gases. Specific requirements are provided for each hazardous material in the applicable T Code or portable tank special provision specified in the §172.101 Table of this subchapter. The minimum shell thickness requirements must also be taken into account.

(7) *For metals* exhibiting a clearly defined yield point or characterized by a guaranteed proof strength (0.2% proof strength, generally, or 1% proof strength for austenitic steels), the primary membrane stress (sigma) in the shell must not exceed 0.75 Re or 0.50 Rm, whichever is lower, at the test pressure, where:

Re = yield strength in N/mm^2, or 0.2% proof strength or, for austenitic steels, 1% proof strength;

Rm = minimum tensile strength in N/mm^2.

(8) *The values* of Re and Rm to be used must be the specified minimum values according to recognized material standards. When austenitic steels are used, the specified minimum values for Re and Rm according to the material standards may be increased by up to 15% when greater values are attested in the material inspection certificate.

(9) *Steels which have* a Re/Rm ratio of more than 0.85 are not allowed for the construction of welded shells. The values of Re and Rm to be used in determining this ratio must be the values specified in the material inspection certificate.

(10) *Steels used* in the construction of shells must have an elongation at fracture, in percentage, of not less than 10,000/Rm with an absolute minimum of 16% for fine grain steels and 20% for other steels.

(11) *For the purpose* of determining actual values for materials for sheet metal, the axis of the tensile test specimen must be at right angles (transversely) to the direction of rolling. The permanent elongation at fracture must be measured on test specimens of rectangular cross sections in accordance with ISO 6892 (see §171.7 of this subchapter), using a 50 mm gauge length.

(d) Minimum shell thickness.

(1) *The minimum shell thickness* must be the greatest thickness of the following:

(i) *the minimum thickness* determined in accordance with the requirements of paragraphs (d)(2) through (d)(7) of this section;

(ii) *the minimum thickness* determined in accordance with Section VIII of the ASME Code (see §171.7 of this subchapter) or other approved pressure vessel code; or

(iii) *the minimum thickness* specified in the applicable T code or portable tank special provision indicated for each hazardous material in the §172.101 Table of this subchapter.

(2) *Shells* (cylindrical portions, heads and manhole covers) not more than 1.80 m in diameter may not be less than 5 mm thick in the reference steel or of equivalent thickness in the metal to be used. Shells more than 1.80 m in diameter may not be less than 6 mm (0.2 inches) thick in the reference steel or of equivalent thickness in the metal to be used. For portable tanks used only for the transportation of powdered or granular solid hazardous materials of Packing Group II or III, the minimum thickness requirement may be reduced to 5 mm in the reference steel or of equivalent thickness in the metal to be used regardless of the shell diameter. For vacuum-insulated tanks, the aggregate thickness of the jacket and the shell must correspond to the minimum thickness prescribed in this paragraph, with the thickness of the shell itself not less than the minimum thickness prescribed in paragraph (d)(3) of this section.

(3) *When additional protection* against shell damage is provided in the case of portable tanks used for liquid and solid hazardous materials requiring test pressures less than 2.65 bar (265.0 kPa), subject to certain limitations specified in the UN Recommendations (see §171.7 of this subchapter), the Associate Administrator may approve a reduced minimum shell thickness.

(4) *The cylindrical portions,* heads and manhole covers of all shells must not be less than 3 mm (0.1 inch) thick regardless of the material of construction, except for portable tanks used for liquefied compressed gases where the cylindrical portions, ends (heads) and manhole covers of all shells must not be less than 4 mm (0.2 inch) thick regardless of the material of construction.

(5) *When steel is used,* that has characteristics other than that of reference steel, the equivalent thickness of the shell and heads must be determined according to the following formula:

$$e_1 = \frac{21.4 e_0 d_1}{1.8m \sqrt[3]{Rm_1 \times A_1}}$$

Where:

e_1 = required equivalent thickness (in mm) of the metal to be used;

e_0 = minimum thickness (in mm) of the reference steel specified in the applicable T code or portable tank special provision indicated for each material in the §172.101 Table of this subchapter;

d_1 = 1.8m, unless the formula is used to determine the equivalent minimum thickness for a portable tank shell that is required to have a minimum thickness of 8mm or 10mm according to the applicable T code indicated in the §172.101 Table of this subchapter. When reference steel thicknesses of 8mm or 10mm are specified, d1 is equal to the actual diameter of the shell but not less than 1.8m;

Rm_1 = guaranteed minimum tensile strength (in N/mm^2) of the metal to be used;

A_1 = guaranteed minimum elongation at fracture (in %) of the metal to be used according to recognized material standards.

(6) *The wall* and all parts of the shell may not have a thickness less than that prescribed in paragraphs (d)(2), (d)(3) and (d)(4) of this section. This thickness must be exclusive of any corrosion allowance.

(7) *There must be* no sudden change of plate thickness at the attachment of the heads to the cylindrical portion of the shell.

(e) Service equipment.

(1) *Service equipment* must be arranged so that it is protected against the risk of mechanical damage by external forces during handling and transportation. When the connections between the frame and the shell allow relative movement between the sub-assemblies, the equipment must be fastened to allow such movement without risk of damage to any working part. The external discharge fittings (pipe sockets, shut-off devices) and the internal stop-valve and its seating must be protected against mechanical damage by external forces (for example, by using shear sections). Each internal self-closing stop-valve must be protected by a shear section or sacrificial device located outboard of the valve. The shear section or sacrificial device must break at no more than 70% of the load that would cause failure of the internal self-closing stop valve. The filling and discharge devices (including flanges or threaded plugs) and any protective caps must be capable of being secured against unintended opening.

(2) *Each filling* or discharge opening of a portable tank must be clearly marked to indicate its function.

(3) *Each stop-valve* or other means of closure must be designed and constructed to a rated pressure not less than the MAWP of the shell taking into account the temperatures expected during transport. All stop-valves with screwed spindles must close by a clockwise motion of the handwheel. For other stop-valves, the position (open and closed) and direction of closure must be clearly indicated. All stop-valves must be designed to prevent unintentional opening.

(4) *Piping must be* designed, constructed and installed to avoid the risk of damage due to thermal expansion and contraction, mechanical shock and vibration. All piping must be of a suitable metallic material. Welded pipe joints must be used wherever possible.

(5) *Joints in copper tubing* must be brazed or have an equally strong metal union. The melting point of brazing materials must be no lower than 525 ^{o}C (977 ^{o}F). The joints must not decrease the strength of the tubing, such as may happen when cutting threads. Brazed joints are not authorized for portable tanks intended for refrigerated liquefied gases.

(6) *The burst pressure* of all piping and pipe fittings must be greater than the highest of four times the MAWP of the shell or four times the pressure to which it may be subjected in service by the action of a pump or other device (except pressure relief devices).

(7) *Ductile metals* must be used in the construction of valves and accessories.

(f) Pressure relief devices.

(1) *Marking of pressure relief devices.* Every pressure relief device must be clearly and permanently marked with the following:

(i) *the pressure* (in bar or kPa) or temperature for fusible elements (in ^{o}C) at which it is set to discharge;

(ii) *the allowable tolerance* at the discharge pressure for reclosing devices;

(iii) *the reference temperature* corresponding to the rated pressure for frangible discs;

(iv) *the allowable temperature tolerance for fusible elements;*

(v) *the rated flow capacity* of the device in standard cubic meters of air per second (m^3/s) determined according to ISO 4126-1 (see §171.7 of this subchapter); and

(vi) *when practicable,* the device must show the manufacturer's name and product number.

(2) *Connections to pressure relief devices.* Connections to pressure relief devices must be of sufficient size to enable the required discharge to pass unrestricted to the safety device. No stop-valve may be installed between the shell and the pressure relief devices except where duplicate devices are provided for maintenance or other reasons and the stop-valves serving the devices actually in use are locked open or the stop-valves are interlocked so that at least one of the devices is always in use. There must be no obstruction in an opening leading to a vent or pressure relief device which might restrict or cut-off the flow from the shell to that device. Vents or pipes from the pressure relief device outlets, when used, must deliver the relieved vapor or liquid to the atmosphere in conditions of minimum back-pressure on the relieving devices.

(3) *Location of pressure relief devices.*

(i) *Each pressure relief device inlet* must be situated on top of the shell in a position as near the longitudinal and transverse center of the shell as reasonably practicable. All pressure relief device inlets must, under maximum filling conditions, be situated in the vapor space of the shell and the devices must be so arranged as to ensure that any escaping vapor is not restricted in any manner. For flammable hazardous materials, the escaping vapor must be directed away from the shell in such a manner that it cannot impinge upon the shell. For refrigerated liquefied gases, the escaping vapor must be directed away from the tank and in such a manner that it cannot impinge upon the tank. Protective devices which deflect the flow of vapor are permissible provided the required relief-device capacity is not reduced.

(ii) *Provisions must be implemented* to prevent unauthorized persons from access to the pressure relief devices and to protect the devices from damage caused by the portable tank overturning.

(g) Gauging devices. Unless a portable tank is intended to be filled by weight, it must be equipped with one or more gauging devices. Glass level-gauges and gauges made of other fragile material, which are in direct communication with the contents of the tank are prohibited. A connection for a vacuum gauge must be provided in the jacket of a vacuum-insulated portable tank.

(h) Portable tank supports, frameworks, lifting and tie-down attachments.

(1) *Portable tanks* must be designed and constructed with a support structure to provide a secure base during transport. The forces and safety factors specified in paragraphs (c)(1) and (c)(2) of this section, respectively, must be taken into account in this aspect of the design. Skids, frameworks, cradles or other similar structures are acceptable.

(2) *The combined stresses* caused by portable tank mountings (for example, cradles, framework, etc.) and portable tank lifting and tie-down attachments must not cause stress that would damage the shell in a manner that would compromise its lading retention capability. Permanent lifting and tie-down attachments must be fitted to all portable tanks. Preferably they should be fitted to the portable tank supports but may be secured to reinforcing plates located on the shell at the points of support. Each portable tank must be designed so that the center of gravity of the filled tank is approximately centered within the points of attachment for lifting devices.

(3) *In the design of supports and frameworks,* the effects of environmental corrosion must be taken into account.

(4) *Forklift pockets* must be capable of being closed off. The means of closing forklift pockets must be a permanent part of the framework or permanently attached to the framework. Single compartment portable tanks with a length less than 3.65 m (12 ft.) need not have forklift pockets that are capable of being closed off provided that:

(i) *The shell,* including all the fittings, are well protected from being hit by the forklift blades; and

(ii) *The distance* between forklift pockets (measured from the center of each pocket) is at least half of the maximum length of the portable tank.

(5) *During transport,* portable tanks must be adequately protected against damage to the shell, and service equipment resulting from lateral and longitudinal impact and overturning, or the shell and service equipment must be constructed to withstand the forces resulting from impact or overturning. External fittings must be protected so as to preclude the release of the shell contents upon impact or overturning of the portable tank on its fittings. Examples of protection include:

(i) *Protection against lateral impact* which may consist of longitudinal bars protecting the shell on both sides at the level of the median line;

(ii) *Protection of the portable tank* against overturning which may consist of reinforcement rings or bars fixed across the frame;

(iii) *Protection against rear impact* which may consist of a bumper or frame;

(iv) *Protection of the shell* against damage from impact or overturning by use of an ISO frame in accordance with ISO 1496-3 (see §171.7 of this subchapter); and

(v) *Protection of the portable tank* from impact or damage that may result from overturning by an insulation jacket.

(i) **Marking.**

(1) *Every portable tank* must be fitted with a corrosion resistant metal plate permanently attached to the portable tank in a conspicuous place and readily accessible for inspection. When the plate cannot be permanently attached to the shell, the shell must be marked with at least the information required by Section VIII of the ASME Code (see §171.7 of this subchapter). At a minimum, the following information must be marked on the plate by stamping or by any other equivalent method:

Country of manufacture

U N

Approval Country

Approval Number

Alternative Arrangements (see §178.247(a)(2)) "AA"

Manufacturer's name or mark

Manufacturer's serial number

Approval Agency (Authorized body for the design approval)

Owner's registration number

Year of manufacture

Pressure vessel code to which the shell is designed

Test pressure________bar gauge

MAWP________bar gauge

External design pressure (not required for portable tanks used for refrigerated liquefied gases)________bar gauge

Design temperature range________ °C to________ °C (For portable tanks used for refrigerated liquefied gases, the minimum design temperature must be marked.)

Water capacity at 20 °C/________liters

Water capacity of each compartment at 20 °C________liters

Initial pressure test date and witness identification

MAWP for heating/cooling system________bar gauge

Shell material(s) and material standard reference(s)

Equivalent thickness in reference steel________mm

Lining material (when applicable)

Date and type of most recent periodic test(s)

Month________Year_______Test pressure________bar gauge

Stamp of approval agency that performed or witnessed the most recent test

For portable tanks used for refrigerated liquefied gases:

Either "thermally insulated" or "vacuum insulated"________.

Effectiveness of the insulation system (heat influx)______Watts (W)

Reference holding time________days or hours and initial pressure________bar/kPa gauge and degree of filling________in kg for each refrigerated liquefied gas permitted for transportation

(2) *The following information* must be marked either on the portable tank itself or on a metal plate firmly secured to the portable tank:

Name of the operator

Name of hazardous materials being transported and maximum mean bulk temperature (except for refrigerated liquefied gases, the name and temperature are only required when the maximum mean bulk temperature is higher than 50 °C)

Maximum permissible gross mass (MPGM)________kg

Unladen (tare) mass________kg

Note to Paragraph (i)(2): For the identification of the hazardous materials being transported refer to part 172 of this subchapter.

(3) *If a portable tank* is designed and approved for open seas operations, such as offshore oil exploration, in accordance with the IMDG Code, the words "OFFSHORE PORTABLE TANK" must be marked on the identification plate.

(j) **Initial inspection and test.** The initial inspection and test of a portable tank must include the following:

(1) *A check of the design characteristics.*

(2) *An internal* and external examination of the portable tank and its fittings, taking into account the hazardous materials to be transported. For UN portable tanks used for refrigerated liquefied gases, a pressure test using an inert gas may be conducted instead of a hydrostatic test. An internal inspection is not required for a portable tank used for the dedicated transportation of refrigerated liquefied gases that are not filled with an inspection opening.

(3) *A pressure test as specified in paragraph (i) of this section.*

(4) *A leakage test.*

(5) *A test* of the satisfactory operation of all service equipment including pressure relief devices must also be performed. When the shell and its fittings have been pressure-tested separately, they must be subjected to a leakage test after reassembly. All welds, subject to full stress level in the shell, must be inspected during the initial test by radiographic, ultrasonic, or another suitable non-destructive test method. This does not apply to the jacket.

(6) *A UN portable tank* that meets the definition of "container" in the CSC (see 49 CFR 450.3(a)(2)) must be subjected to an impact test using a prototype representing each design type. The prototype portable tank must be shown to be capable of absorbing the forces resulting from an impact not less than 4 times (4 g) the maximum permissable gross mass of the fully loaded portable tank at a duration typical of the mechanical shocks experienced in rail transportation. A listing of standards describing methods acceptable for performing the impact test are provided in the UN Recommendations (see §171.7 of this subchapter). UN portable tanks used for the dedicated transportation of "Helium, refrigerated liquid," UN1963 and "Hydrogen, refrigerated liquid," UN1966 that are marked "NOT FOR RAIL TRANSPORT" in letters of a minimum height of 20 cm (8 inches) on at least two sides of the portable tank are excepted from the 4 g impact test.

(7) *The following tests* must be completed on a portable tank or a series of portable tanks designed and constructed to a single design type that is also a CSC container without leakage or deformation that would render the portable tank unsafe for transportation and use:

(i) *Longitudinal inertia.* The portable tank loaded to its maximum gross weight must be positioned with its longitudinal axis vertical. It shall be held in this position for five minutes by support at the lower end of the base structure providing vertical and lateral restraint and by support at the upper end of the base structure providing lateral restraint only.

(ii) *Lateral inertia.* The portable tank loaded to its maximum gross weight must be positioned for five minutes with its transverse axis vertical. It shall be held in this position for five minutes by support at the lower side of the base structure providing vertical and lateral restraint and by support at the upper side of the base structure providing lateral restraint only.

§178.275 Specification for UN Portable Tanks intended for the transportation of liquid and solid hazardous materials.

(a) **In addition to the requirements of §178.274,** this section sets forth definitions and requirements that apply to UN portable tanks intended for the transportation of liquid and solid hazardous materials.

(b) **Definitions and requirements —**

(1) **Design pressure** means the pressure to be used in calculations required by the recognized pressure vessel code. The design pressure must not be less than the highest of the following pressures:

(i) *The maximum* effective gauge pressure allowed in the shell during filling or discharge; or

(ii) *The sum of —*

[A] The absolute vapor pressure (in bar) of the hazardous material at 65 °C, minus 1 bar (149 °F, minus 100 kPa);

[B] The partial pressure (in bar) of air or other gases in the ullage space, resulting from their compression during filling without pressure relief by a maximum ullage temperature of 65 °C (149 °F) and a liquid expansion due to an increase in mean bulk temperature of 35 °C (95 °F); and

[C] A head pressure determined on the basis of the forces specified in §178.274(c) of this subchapter, but not less than 0.35 bar (35 kPa).

(2) **Maximum allowable working pressure (MAWP)** means a pressure that must not be less than the highest of the following pressures measured at the top of the shell while in operating position:

(i) *The maximum* effective gauge pressure allowed in the shell during filling or discharge; or

(ii) *The maximum* effective gauge pressure to which the shell is designed which must be not less than the design pressure.

(c) **Service equipment.**

(1) *In addition* to the requirements specified in §178.274, for service equipment, all openings in the shell, intended for filling or discharging the portable tank must be fitted with a manually operated stop-valve located as close to the shell as reasonably practicable. Other openings, except for openings leading to venting or pressure relief devices, must be equipped with either a stop-valve or another suitable means of closure located as close to the shell as reasonably practicable.

(2) *All portable tanks* must be fitted with a manhole or other inspection openings of a suitable size to allow for internal inspection and adequate access for maintenance and repair of the interior. Compartmented portable tanks must have a manhole or other inspection openings for each compartment.

(3) *For insulated portable tanks,* top fittings must be surrounded by a spill collection reservoir with suitable drains.

(4) *Piping must be* designed, constructed and installed to avoid the risk of damage due to thermal expansion and contraction, mechanical shock and vibration. All piping must be of a suitable metallic material. Welded pipe joints must be used wherever possible.

(d) **Bottom openings.**

(1) *Certain hazardous materials* may not be transported in portable tanks with bottom openings. When the applicable T code or portable tank special provision, as referenced for materials in the §172.101 Table of this subchapter, specifies that bottom openings are prohibited, there must be no openings below the liquid level of the shell when it is filled to its maximum permissible filling limit. When an existing opening is closed, it must be accomplished by internally and externally welding one plate to the shell.

(2) *Bottom discharge outlets* for portable tanks carrying certain solid, crystallizable or highly viscous hazardous materials must be equipped with at least two serially fitted and mutually independent shut-off devices. Use of only two shut-off devices is only authorized when this paragraph is referenced in the applicable T Code indicated for each hazardous material in the §172.101 Table of this subchapter. The design of the equipment must be to the satisfaction of the approval agency and must include:

(i) *An external stop-valve* fitted as close to the shell as reasonably practicable; and

(ii) *A liquid tight* closure at the end of the discharge pipe, which may be a bolted blank flange or a screw cap.

(3) *Except as provided* in paragraph (c)(2) of this section, every bottom discharge outlet must be equipped with three serially fitted and mutually independent shut-off devices. The design of the equipment must include:

(i) *A self-closing internal stop-valve,* which is a stop-valve within the shell or within a welded flange or its companion flange, such that:

[A] The control devices for the operation of the valve are designed to prevent any unintended opening through impact or other inadvertent act;

[B] The valve is operable from above or below;

[C] If possible, the setting of the valve (open or closed) must be capable of being verified from the ground;

[D] Except for portable tanks having a capacity less than 1,000 liters (264.2 gallons), it must be possible to close the valve from an accessible position on the portable tank that is remote from the valve itself within 30 seconds of actuation; and

[E] The valve must continue to be effective in the event of damage to the external device for controlling the operation of the valve;

(ii) *An external stop-valve* fitted as close to the shell as reasonably practicable;

(iii) *A liquid tight closure* at the end of the discharge pipe, which may be a bolted blank flange or a screw cap; and

(iv) *For portable tanks* used for the transportation of liquid materials that are flammable, pyrophoric, oxidizing or toxic, the remote means of closure must be capable of thermal activation. The thermal means of activation must activate at a temperature of not more than 121 °C (250 °F).

(e) **Pressure relief devices.** All portable tanks must be fitted with at least one pressure relief device. All relief devices must be designed, constructed and marked in accordance with the requirements of this subchapter.

(f) **Vacuum-relief devices.**

(1) *A shell* which is to be equipped with a vacuum-relief device must be designed to withstand, without permanent deformation, an external pressure of not less than 0.21 bar (21.0 kPa). The vacuum-relief device must be set to relieve at a vacuum setting not greater than -0.21 bar (-21.0 kPa) unless the shell is designed for a higher external over pressure, in which case the vacuum-relief pressure of the device to be fitted must not be greater than the tank design vacuum pressure. A shell that is not fitted with a vacuum-relief device must be designed to withstand, without permanent deformation, an external pressure of not less than 0.4 bar (40.0 kPa).

(2) *Vacuum-relief devices* used on portable tanks intended for the transportation of hazardous materials meeting the criteria of Class 3, including elevated temperature hazardous materials transported at or above their flash point, must prevent the immediate passage of flame into the shell or the portable tank must have a shell capable of withstanding, without leakage, an internal explosion resulting from the passage of flame into the shell.

(g) **Pressure relief devices.**

(1) *Each portable tank* with a capacity not less than 1,900 liters (501.9 gallons) and every independent compartment of a portable tank with a similar capacity, must be provided with one or more pressure relief devices of the reclosing type. Such portable tanks may, in addition, have a frangible disc or fusible element in parallel with the reclosing devices, except when the applicable T code assigned to a hazardous material requires that the frangible disc precede the pressure relief device, according to paragraph (g)(3) of this section, or when no bottom openings are allowed. The pressure relief devices must have sufficient capacity to prevent rupture of the shell due to over pressurization or vacuum resulting from filling, discharging, heating of the contents or fire.

(2) *Pressure relief devices* must be designed to prevent the entry of foreign matter, the leakage of liquid and the development of any dangerous excess pressure.

(3) *When required* for certain hazardous materials by the applicable T code or portable tank special provision specified for a hazardous material in the §172.101 Table of this subchapter, portable tanks must have a pressure relief device consistent with the requirements of this subchapter. Except for a portable tank in dedicated service that is fitted with an approved relief device constructed of materials compatible with the hazardous material, the relief device system must include a frangible disc preceding (such as, between the lading and the reclosing pressure relief device) a reclosing pressure relief device. A pressure gauge or suitable tell-tale indicator for the detection of disc rupture, pin-holing or leakage must be provided in the space between the frangible disc and the pressure relief device to allow the portable tank operator to check to determine if the disc is leak free. The frangible disc must rupture at a nominal pressure 10% above the start-to-discharge pressure of the reclosable pressure relief device.

(4) *Every portable tank* with a capacity less than 1,900 liters (501.9 gallons) must be fitted with a pressure relief device which, except as provided in paragraph (g)(3) of this section, may be a frangible disc when this disc is set to rupture at a nominal pressure equal to the test pressure at any temperature within the design temperature range.

(5) *When the shell* is fitted for pressure discharge, a suitable pressure relief device must provide the inlet line to the portable tank and set to operate at a pressure not higher than the MAWP of the shell, and a stop-valve must be fitted as close to the shell as practicable to minimize the potential for damage.

(6) *Setting of pressure relief devices.*

(i) *Pressure relief devices* must operate only in conditions of excessive rise in temperature. The shell must not be subject to undue fluctuations of pressure during normal conditions of transportation.

(ii) *The required pressure relief device* must be set to start to discharge at a nominal pressure of five-sixths of the test pressure for shells having a test pressure of not more than 4.5 bar (450 kPa) and 110% of two-thirds of the test pressure for shells having a test pressure of more than 4.5 bar (450 kPa). A self-closing relief device must close at a pressure not more than 10% below the pressure at which the discharge starts. The device must remain closed at all lower pressures. This requirement does not prevent the use of vacuum-relief or combination pressure relief and vacuum-relief devices.

(h) **Fusible elements.** Fusible elements must operate at a temperature between 110 °C (230 °F) and 149 °C (300.2 °F) provided that the pressure in the shell at the fusing temperature will not exceed the test pressure. They must be placed at the top of the shell with their inlets in the vapor space and in no case may they be shielded from external heat. Fusible elements must not be utilized on portable tanks with a test pressure which exceeds 2.65 bar (265.0 kPa). Fusible elements used on portable tanks intended for the transport of elevated temperature hazardous materials must be designed to operate at a temperature higher than the maximum temperature that will be experienced during transport and must be designed to the satisfaction of the approval agency.

(i) **Capacity of pressure relief devices.**

(1) *The reclosing pressure relief device* required by paragraph (g)(1) of this section must have a minimum cross sectional flow area equivalent to an orifice of 31.75 mm (1.3 inches) diameter. Vacuum-relief devices, when used, must have a cross sectional flow area not less than 284 mm^2 (11.2 $inches^2$).

(2) *Under conditions* of complete fire engulfment of the portable tank, the combined delivery capacity of the relief devices must be sufficient to limit the pressure in the shell to 20% above the start-to-discharge pressure specified in paragraph (g)(6) of this section. Emergency pressure relief devices may be used to achieve the full relief capacity prescribed. The total required capacity of the relief devices may be determined using the formula in paragraph (i)(2)(i)(A) of this section or the table in paragraph (i)(2)(iii) of this section.

(i) ***[A]*** *To determine* the total required capacity of the relief devices, which must be regarded as being the sum of the individual capacities of all the contributing devices, the following formula must be used:

$$Q = 12.4\frac{FA^{0.82}}{LC}\sqrt{\frac{ZT}{M}}$$

Where:

Q = minimum required rate of discharge in cubic meters of air per second (m^3/s) at standard conditions: 1 bar and 0 °C (273 K);

F = for uninsulated shells: 1; for insulated shells: U(649-t)/13.6 but in no case is less than 0.25 where: U = thermal conductance of the insulation, in $kW{\cdot}m^{-2}\,K^{-1}$, at 38 °C; and t = actual temperature of the hazardous material during filling (in °C) or when this temperature is unknown, let t = 15 °C. The value of F given in this paragraph (i)(2)(i)(A) for insulated shells may only be used if the insulation is in conformance with paragraph (i)(2)(iv) of this section;

A = total external surface area of shell in square meters;

Z = the gas compressibility factor in the accumulating condition (when this factor is unknown, let Z equal 1.0);

T = absolute temperature in Kelvin (deg . C + 273) above the pressure relief devices in the accumulating condition;

L = the latent heat of vaporization of the liquid, in kJ/kg, in the accumulating condition;

M = molecular weight of the hazardous material.

[B] *The constant C,* as shown in the formula in paragraph (i)(2)(i)(A) of this section, is derived from one of the following formula as a function of the ratio k of specific heats:

$$k = \frac{c_p}{c_v}$$

Where:

c_p is the specific heat at constant pressure; and
c_v is the specific heat at constant volume.

[C] *When k >1:*

$$C = \sqrt{k\left(\frac{2}{k+1}\right)^{\frac{k+1}{k-1}}}$$

[D] *When k = 1 or k is unknown,* a value of 0.607 may be used for the constant C. C may also be taken from the following table:

C Constant Value Table

k	C	k	C	k	C
1.00	0.607	1.26	0.660	1.52	0.704
1.02	0.611	1.28	0.664	1.54	0.707
1.04	0.615	1.30	0.667	1.56	0.710
1.06	0.620	1.32	0.671	1.58	0.713
1.08	0.624	1.34	0.674	1.60	0.716
1.10	0.628	1.36	0.678	1.62	0.719
1.12	0.633	1.38	0.681	1.64	0.722
1.14	0.637	1.40	0.685	1.66	0.725
1.16	0.641	1.42	0.688	1.68	0.728
1.18	0.645	1.44	0.691	1.70	0.731
1.20	0.649	1.46	0.695	2.00	0.770
1.22	0.652	1.48	0.698	2.20	0.793
1.24	0.656	1.50	0.701		

(ii) *As an alternative* to the formula in paragraph (i)(2)(i)(A) of this section, relief devices for shells used for transporting liquids may be sized in accordance with the table in paragraph (i)(2)(iii) of this section. The table in paragraph (i)(2)(iii) of this section assumes an insulation value of F = 1 and must be adjusted accordingly when the shell is insulated. Other values used in determining the table in paragraph (i)(2)(iii) of this section are: L = 334.94 kJ/kg; M = 86.7; T = 394 K; Z = 1; and C = 0.607.

(iii) *Minimum emergency vent capacity,* Q, in cubic meters per air per second at 1 bar and 0 °C (273 K) shown in the following table:

Minimum Emergency Vent Capacity [Q Values]

A Exposed area (square meters)	Q (Cubic meters of air per second)	A Exposed area (square meters)	Q (Cubic meters of air per second)
2	0.230	37.5	2.539
3	0.320	40	2.677
4	0.405	42.5	2.814
5	0.487	45	2.949
6	0.565	47.5	3.082
7	0.641	50	3.215
8	0.715	52.5	3.346
9	0.788	55	3.476
10	0.859	57.5	3.605
12	0.998	60	3.733
14	1.132	62.5	3.860
16	1.263	65	3.987
18	1.391	67.5	4.112
20	1.517	70	4.236
22.5	1.670	75	4.483
25	1.821	80	4.726
27.5	1.969	85	4.967
30	2.115	90	5.206
32.5	2.258	95	5.442
35	2.400	100	5.676

(iv) *Insulation systems,* used for the purpose of reducing venting capacity, must be specifically approved by the approval agency. In all cases, insulation systems approved for this purpose must —

[A] *Remain effective* at all temperatures up to 649 °C (1200.2 °F); and

[B] *Be jacketed* with a material having a melting point of 700 °C (1292 °F) or greater.

(j) Approval, inspection and testing. Approval procedures for UN portable tanks are specified in §178.273. Inspection and testing requirements are specified in §180.605 of this subchapter.

FEDERAL REGISTER UPDATES

In the May 30, 2003 Federal Register, §178.275 was revised, effective June 30, 2003.

(d) [1]

(3) [2]

(iv) *For UN portable tanks,* with bottom outlets, used for the transportation of liquid hazardous materials that are Class 3, PG I or II, or PG III with a flash point of less than 100 °F (38 °C); Division 5.1, PG I or II; or Division 6.1, PG I or II, the remote means of closure must be capable of thermal activation. The thermal means of activation must activate at a temperature of not more than 250 °F (121 °C). [3]

1. Paragraph (d) is the same as before.
2. Paragraph (d)(3) is the same as before.
3. Paragraph (d)(3)(iv) was revised.

§178.276 Requirements for the design, construction, inspection and testing of portable tanks intended for the transportation of non-refrigerated liquefied compressed gases.

(a) In addition to the requirements of §178.274 applicable to UN portable tanks, the following requirements apply to UN portable tanks used for non-refrigerated liquefied compressed gases. In addition to the definitions in §178.274, the following definitions apply:

(1) Design pressure means the pressure to be used in calculations required by the ASME Code, Section VIII (see §171.7 of this subchapter). The design pressure must be not less than the highest of the following pressures:

(i) *The maximum* effective gauge pressure allowed in the shell during filling or discharge; or

(ii) *The sum of:*

[A] *The maximum* effective gauge pressure to which the shell is designed as defined in this paragraph under "MAWP"; and

[B] A head pressure determined on the basis of the dynamic forces specified in paragraph (h) of this section, but not less than 0.35 bar (35 kPa).

(2) **Design reference temperature** means the temperature at which the vapor pressure of the contents is determined for the purpose of calculating the MAWP. The value for each portable tank type is as follows:

(i) *Shell with a diameter* of 1.5 meters (4.9 ft.) or less: 65 °C (149 °F); or

(ii) *Shell with a diameter of more than 1.5 meters (4.9 ft.):*

[A] Without insulation or sun shield: 60 °C (140 °F);

[B] With sun shield: 55 °C (131 °F); and

[C] With insulation: 50 °C (122 °F).

(3) **Filling density** means the average mass of liquefied compressed gas per liter of shell capacity (kg/l).

(4) **Maximum allowable working pressure (MAWP)** means a pressure that must be not less than the highest of the following pressures measured at the top of the shell while in operating position, but in no case less than 7 bar (700 kPa):

(i) *The maximum* effective gauge pressure allowed in the shell during filling or discharge; or

(ii) *The maximum* effective gauge pressure to which the shell is designed, which must be:

[A] Not less than the pressure specified for each liquefied compressed gas listed in portable tank special provision T50; and

[B] Not less than the sum of:

[1] The absolute vapor pressure (in bar) of the liquefied compressed gas at the design reference temperature minus 1 bar; and

[2] The partial pressure (in bar) of air or other gases in the ullage space which is determined by the design reference temperature and the liquid phase expansion due to the increase of the mean bulk temperature of tr-tf (tf = filling temperature, usually 15 °C, tr = 50 °C maximum mean bulk temperature).

(b) **General design and construction requirements.**

(1) *Shells must be* of seamless or welded steel construction, or combination of both, and have a water capacity greater than 450 liters (118.9 gallons). Shells must be designed, constructed, certified and stamped in accordance with the ASME Code, Section VIII (see §171.7 of this subchapter).

(2) *Portable tanks* must be postweld heat-treated and radiographed as prescribed in Section VIII of the ASME Code, except that each portable tank constructed in accordance with part UHT of the ASME Code must be postweld heat-treated. Where postweld heat treatment is required, the portable tank must be treated as a unit after completion of all the welds in and/or to the shell and heads. The method must be as prescribed in the ASME Code. Welded attachments to pads may be made after postweld heat treatment is made. A portable tank used for anhydrous ammonia must be postweld heat-treated. The postweld heat treatment must be as prescribed in the ASME Code, but in no event at less than 1050 °F tank metal temperature. Additionally, portable tanks constructed in accordance with part UHT of the ASME Code must conform to the following requirements:

(i) *Welding procedure* and welder performance tests must be made annually in accordance with Section IX of the ASME Code (see §171.7 of this subchapter). In addition to the essential variables named therein, the following must be considered to be essential variables: number of passes, thickness of plate, heat input per pass, and manufacturer's identification of rod and flux. The number of passes, thickness of plate and heat input per pass may not vary more than 25 percent from the qualified procedure. Records of the qualification must be retained for at least 5 years by the portable tank manufacturer or his designated agent and, upon request, made available to a representative of the Department of Transportation or the owner of the tank.

(ii) *Impact tests* must be made on a lot basis. A lot is defined as 100 tons or less of the same heat and having a thickness variation no greater than plus or minus 25 percent. The minimum impact required for full-sized specimens shall be 20 foot-pounds (or 10 foot-pounds for half-sized specimens) at 0 °F (-17.8 °F) Charpy V-Notch in both the longitudinal and transverse direction. If the lot test does not pass this requirement, individual plates may be accepted if they individually meet this impact requirement.

(3) *When the shells* intended for the transportation of non-refrigerated liquefied compressed gases are equipped with thermal insulation, a device must be provided to prevent any dangerous pressure from developing in the insulating layer in the event of a leak, when the protective covering is closed it must be gas tight. The thermal insulation must not inhibit access to the fittings and discharge devices. In addition, the thermal insulation systems must satisfy the following requirements:

(i) *consist of a shield* covering not less than the upper third, but not more than the upper half of the surface of the shell, and separated from the shell by an air space of approximately 40 mm (1.7 inches) across; or

(ii) *consist of a complete* cladding of insulating materials. The insulation must be of adequate thickness and constructed to prevent the ingress of moisture and damage to the insulation. The insulation and cladding must have a thermal conductance of not more than 0.67 ($W{\cdot}m^{-2}{\cdot}K^{-1}$) under normal conditions of transportation.

(c) **Service equipment.**

(1) *Each opening* with a diameter of more than 1.5 mm (0.1 inch) in the shell of a portable tank, except openings for pressure-relief devices, inspection openings and closed bleed holes, must be fitted with at least three mutually independent shut-off devices in series: the first being an internal stop-valve, excess flow valve, integral excess flow valve, or excess flow feature (see §178.337-1(g)), the second being an external stop-valve and the third being a blank flange, thread cap, plug or equivalent tight liquid closure device.

(2) *When a portable tank* is fitted with an excess flow valve, the excess flow valve must be so fitted that its seating is inside the shell or inside a welded flange or, when fitted externally, its mountings must be designed so that in the event of impact it maintains its effectiveness. The excess flow valves must be selected and fitted so as to close automatically when the rated flow, specified by the manufacturer, is reached. Connections and accessories leading to or from such a valve must have a capacity for a flow more than the excess flow valve's rated flow.

(3) *For filling and discharge openings* that are located below the liquid level, the first shut-off device must be an internal stop-valve and the second must be a stop-valve placed in an accessible position on each discharge and filling pipe.

(4) *For filling and discharge openings* located below the liquid level of portable tanks intended for the transportation of flammable and/or toxic liquefied compressed gases, the internal stop-valve must be a self-closing safety device that fully closes automatically during filling or discharge in the event of fire engulfment. The device shall fully close within 30 seconds of actuation and the thermal means of closure must actuate at a temperature of not more than 121 °C (250 °F). Except for portable tanks having a capacity less than 1,000 liters (264.2 gallons), this device must be operable by remote control.

(5) *In addition to filling,* discharge and gas pressure equalizing orifices, shells may have openings in which gauges, thermometers and manometers can be fitted. Connections for such instruments must be made by suitable welded nozzles or pockets and may not be connected by screwed connections through the shell.

(6) *All portable tanks* must be fitted with manholes or other inspection openings of suitable size to allow for internal inspection and adequate access for maintenance and repair of the interior.

(7) *Inlets and discharge outlets* on chlorine portable tanks. The inlet and discharge outlets on portable tanks used to transport chlorine must meet the requirements of §178.337-1(c)(2) and must be fitted with an internal excess flow valve. In addition to the internal excess flow valve, the inlet and discharge outlets must be equipped with an external stop valve (angle valve). Excess flow valves must conform to the standards of The Chlorine Institute, Inc. (see §171.7 of this subchapter) as follows:

(i) *A valve* conforming to Drawing 101-7, dated July 1993, must be installed under each liquid angle valve.

(ii) *A valve* conforming to Drawing 106-6, dated July 1993, must be installed under each gas angle valve. For portable tanks used to transport non-refrigerated liquefied gases.

(8) *External fittings* must be grouped together as close as reasonably practicable. The following openings may be installed at locations other than on the top or end of the tank:

(i) *The openings* for liquid level gauging devices, pressure gauges, or for safety devices, may be installed separately at the other location or in the side of the shell;

(ii) *One plugged opening* of 2-inch National Pipe Thread or less provided for maintenance purposes may be located elsewhere;

(iii) *An opening* of 3-inch National Pipe Size or less may be provided at another location, when necessary, to facilitate installation of condensing coils.

(9) *Filling and discharge connections* are not required to be grouped and may be installed below the normal liquid level of the tank if:

(i) *The portable tank* is permanently mounted in a full framework for containerized transport;

(ii) *For each portable tank design,* a prototype portable tank, meets the requirements of parts 450 through 453 of this title for compliance with the requirements of Annex II of the International Convention for Safe Containers; and

(iii) *Each filling and discharge outlet* meets the requirements of paragraph (c)(4) of this section.

(d) Bottom openings. Bottom openings are prohibited on portable tanks when the portable tank special provision T50 in §172.102(c)(7) of this subchapter indicates that bottom openings are not allowed. In this case, there may be no openings located below the liquid level of the shell when it is filled to its maximum permissible filling limit.

(e) Pressure relief devices.

(1) *Portable tanks* must be provided with one or more reclosing pressure relief devices. The pressure relief devices must open automatically at a pressure not less than the MAWP and be fully open at a pressure equal to 110% of the MAWP. These devices must, after discharge, close at a pressure not less than 10% below the pressure at which discharge starts and must remain closed at all lower pressures. The pressure relief devices must be of a type that will resist dynamic forces including liquid surge. A frangible disc may only be used in series with a reclosing pressure relief device.

(2) *Pressure relief devices* must be designed to prevent the entry of foreign matter, the leakage of gas and the development of any dangerous excess pressure.

(3) *A portable tank* intended for the transportation of certain liquefied compressed gases identified in portable tank special provision T50 in §172.102 of this subchapter must have a pressure relief device which conforms to the requirements of this subchapter. Unless a portable tank, in dedicated service, is fitted with a relief device constructed of materials compatible with the hazardous material, the relief device must be comprised of a frangible disc preceded by a reclosing device. The space between the frangible disc and the device must be provided with a pressure gauge or a suitable tell-tale indicator. This arrangement must facilitate the detection of disc rupture, pinholing or leakage which could cause a malfunction of the pressure relief device. The frangible disc must rupture at a nominal pressure 10% above the start-to-discharge pressure of the relief device.

(4) *In the case* of portable tanks used for more than one gas, the pressure relief devices must open at a pressure indicated in paragraph (e)(1) of this section for the gas having the highest maximum allowable pressure of the gases allowed to be transported in the portable tank.

(f) Capacity of relief devices. The combined delivery capacity of the relief devices must be sufficient so that, in the event of total fire engulfment, the pressure inside the shell cannot exceed 120% of the MAWP. Reclosing relief devices must be used to achieve the full relief capacity prescribed. In the case of portable tanks used for more than gas, the combined delivery capacity of the pressure relief devices must be taken for the liquefied compressed gas which requires the highest delivery capacity of the liquefied compressed gases allowed to be transported in the portable tank. The total required capacity of the relief devices must be determined according to the requirements in §178.275(h). These requirements apply only to liquefied compressed gases which have critical temperatures well above the temperature at the accumulating condition. For gases which have critical temperatures near or below the temperature at the accumulating condition, the calculation of the pressure relief device delivery capacity must consider the additional thermodynamic properties of the gas (for example, CGA S-1.2-1980 (see §171.7 of this subchapter).

§178.277 Requirements for the design, construction, inspection and testing of portable tanks intended for the transportation of refrigerated liquefied gases.

(a) In addition to the requirements of §178.274 applicable to UN portable tanks, the following requirements and definitions apply to UN portable tanks used for refrigerated liquefied gases:

Design pressure. For the purpose of this section the term "design pressure" is consistent with the definition for design pressure in the ASME Code, Section VIII (see §171.7 of this subchapter).

Holding time is the time, as determined by testing, that will elapse from loading until the pressure of the contents, under equilibrium conditions, reaches the lowest set pressure of the pressure limiting device(s) (for example, pressure control valve or pressure relief device). Holding time must be determined as specified in §178.338-9.

Maximum allowable working pressure (MAWP) means the maximum effective gauge pressure permissible at the top of the shell of a loaded portable tank in its operating position including the highest effective pressure during filling and discharge.

Minimum design temperature means the temperature which is used for the design and construction of the shell not higher than the lowest (coldest) service temperature of the contents during normal conditions of filling, discharge and transportation.

Shell means the part of the portable tank which retains the refrigerated liquefied gas intended for transport, including openings and their closures, but does not include service equipment or external structural equipment.

Tank means a construction which normally consists of either:

(1) *A jacket* and one or more inner shells where the space between the shell(s) and the jacket is exhausted of air (vacuum insulation) and may incorporate a thermal insulation system; or

(2) *A jacket* and an inner shell with an intermediate layer of solid thermally insulating material (for example, solid foam).

(b) General design and construction requirements.

(1) *Portable tanks* must be of seamless or welded steel construction and have a water capacity of more than 450 liters (118.9 gallons). Portable tanks must be designed, constructed, certified and stamped in accordance with Section VIII of the ASME Code (see §171.7 of this subchapter).

(2) *Portable tanks* must be postweld heat treated and radiographed as prescribed in the ASME Code except that each tank constructed in accordance with part UHT of the ASME Code must be postweld heat treated. Where postweld heat treatment is required, the tank must be treated as a unit after completion of all the welds to the shell and heads. The method must be as prescribed in the ASME Code. Welded attachments to pads may be made after postweld heat treatment is made. The postweld heat treatment must be as prescribed in Section VIII of the ASME Code, but in no event at less than 1050 °F tank metal temperature.

(3) *Welding procedure* and welder performance tests must be made annually in accordance with Section IX of the ASME Code (see §171.7 of this subchapter). In addition to the essential variables named in the ASME Code, the following must be considered as essential variables: number of passes, thickness of plate, heat input per pass, and the specified rod and flux. The number of passes, thickness of plate and heat input per pass may not vary more than 25% from the procedure qualification. Records of the qualification must be retained for at least 5 years by the portable tank manufacturer and made available to the approval agency and the owner of the portable tank as specified in §178.273.

(4) *Shells and jackets* must be made of metallic materials suitable for forming. Jackets must be made of steel. Non-metallic materials may be used for the attachments and supports between the shell and jacket, provided their material properties at the minimum design temperature are proven to be sufficient. In choosing the material, the minimum design temperature must be taken into account with respect to risk of brittle fracture, to hydrogen embrittlement, to stress corrosion cracking and to resistance to impact.

(5) *Any part* of a portable tank, including fittings, gaskets and pipework, which can be expected normally to come into contact with the refrigerated liquefied gas transported must be compatible with that refrigerated liquefied gas.

(6) *The thermal insulation system* must include a complete covering of the shell with effective insulating materials. External insulation must be protected by a jacket so as to prevent the ingress of moisture and other damage under normal transport conditions.

(7) *When a jacket* is so closed as to be gas-tight, a device must be provided to prevent any dangerous pressure from developing in the insulation space.

(8) *Materials which may react* with oxygen or oxygen enriched atmospheres in a dangerous manner may not be used in portable tanks intended for the transport of refrigerated liquefied gases having a boiling point below minus 182 °C at atmospheric pressure in locations with the thermal insulation where there is a risk of contact with oxygen or with oxygen enriched fluid.

(9) *Insulating materials* must not deteriorate to an extent that the effectiveness of the insulation system, as determined in accordance with paragraph (b)(11) of this section, would be reduced in service.

(10) *A reference holding time* must be determined for each refrigerated liquefied gas intended for transport in a portable tank. The reference holding time must be determined by testing in accordance with the requirements of §178.338-9, considering the following factors:

(i) *The effectiveness* of the insulation system, determined in accordance with paragraph (b)(11) of this section;

(ii) *The lowest set pressure of the pressure limiting device;*

(iii) *The initial filling conditions;*

(iv) *An assumed ambient temperature of 30 °C (86 °F);*

(v) *The physical properties* of the individual refrigerated liquefied gas intended to be transported.

(11) *The effectiveness* of the insulation system (heat influx in watts) may be determined by type testing the portable tank in accordance with a procedure specified in §178.338-9(c) or by using the holding time test in §178.338-9(b). This test must consist of either:

(i) *A constant pressure test* (for example, at atmospheric pressure) when the loss of refrigerated liquefied gas is measured over a period of time; or

(ii) *A closed system test* when the rise in pressure in the shell is measured over a period of time.

(12) *When performing* the constant pressure test, variations in atmospheric pressure must be taken into account. When performing either test, corrections must be made for any variation of the ambient temperature from the assumed ambient temperature reference value of 30 °C (86 °F).

(13) *The jacket* of a vacuum-insulated double-wall tank must have either an external design pressure not less than 100 kPa (1 bar) gauge pressure calculated in accordance with the ASME Code or a calculated critical collapsing pressure of not less than 200 kPa (2 bar) gauge pressure. Internal and external reinforcements may be included in calculating the ability of the jacket to resist the external pressure.

Note to Paragraph (b): For the determination of the actual holding time, as indicated by paragraphs (b)(10), (11), (12), and (13), before each journey, refer to §178.338-9(b).

(c) **Design criteria.** For shells with vacuum insulation, the test pressure must not be less than 1.3 times the sum of the MAWP and 100 kPa (1 bar). In no case may the test pressure be less than 300 kPa (3 bar) gauge pressure.

(d) **Service equipment.**

(1) *Each filling and discharge opening* in portable tanks used for the transport of flammable refrigerated liquefied gases must be fitted with at least three mutually independent shut-off devices in series: the first being a stop-valve situated as close as reasonably practicable to the jacket, the second being a stop-valve and the third being a blank flange or equivalent device. The shut-off device closest to the jacket must be a self-closing device, which is capable of being closed from an accessible position on the portable tank that is remote from the valve within 30 seconds of actuation. This device must actuate at a temperature of not more than 121 °C (250 °F).

(2) *Each filling and discharge opening* in portable tanks used for the transport of non-flammable refrigerated liquefied gases must be fitted with at least two mutually independent shut-off devices in series: the first being a stop-valve situated as close as reasonably practicable to the jacket and the second a blank flange or equivalent device.

(3) *For sections of piping* which can be closed at both ends and where liquid product can be trapped, a method of automatic pressure relief must be provided to prevent excess pressure build-up within the piping.

(4) *Each filling and discharge opening* on a portable tank must be clearly marked to indicate its function.

(5) *When pressure-building units* are used, the liquid and vapor connections to that unit must be provided with a valve as close to the jacket as reasonably practicable to prevent the loss of contents in case of damage to the pressure-building unit. A check valve may be used for this purpose if it is located on the vapor side of the pressure build-up coil.

(6) *The materials* of construction of valves and accessories must have satisfactory properties at the lowest operating temperature of the portable tank.

(7) *Vacuum insulated* portable tanks are not required to have an inspection opening.

(e) **Pressure relief devices.**

(1) *Every shell* must be provided with not less than two independent reclosing pressure relief devices. The pressure relief devices must open automatically at a pressure not less than the MAWP and be fully open at a pressure equal to 110% of the MAWP. These devices must, after discharge, close at a pressure not lower than 10% below the pressure at which discharge starts and must remain closed at all lower pressures. The pressure relief devices must be of the type that will resist dynamic forces including surge.

(2) *Except for portable tanks* used for oxygen, portable tanks for non-flammable refrigerated liquefied gases (except oxygen) and hydrogen may in addition have frangible discs in parallel with the reclosing devices as specified in paragraphs (e)(4)(ii) and (e)(4)(iii) of this section.

(3) *Pressure relief devices* must be designed to prevent the entry of foreign matter, the leakage of gas and the development of any dangerous excess pressure.

(4) *Capacity and setting of pressure relief devices.*

(i) *In the case* of the loss of vacuum in a vacuum-insulated tank or of loss of 20% of the insulation of a portable tank insulated with solid materials, the combined capacity of all pressure relief devices installed must be sufficient so that the pressure (including accumulation) inside the shell does not exceed 120% of the MAWP.

(ii) *For non-flammable* refrigerated liquefied gases (except oxygen) and hydrogen, this capacity may be achieved by the use of frangible discs in parallel with the required safety-relief devices. Frangible discs must rupture at nominal pressure equal to the test pressure of the shell.

(iii) *Under the circumstances* described in paragraphs (e)(4)(i) and (e)(4)(ii) of this section, together with complete fire engulfment, the combined capacity of all pressure relief devices installed must be sufficient to limit the pressure in the shell to the test pressure.

(iv) *The required capacity* of the relief devices must be calculated in accordance with CGA Pamphlet S-1.2 (see §171.7 of this subchapter).

Subpart I [Reserved]

Subpart J - Specifications for Containers for Motor Vehicle Transportation

§178.318 Specification MC 201; container for detonators and percussion caps.

§178.318-1 Scope.

(a) **This specification pertains to a container to be used** for the transportation of detonators and percussion caps in connection with the transportation of liquid nitroglycerin, desensitized liquid nitroglycerin or diethylene glycol dinitrate, where any or all of such types of caps may be used for the detonation of liquid nitroglycerin, desentitized liquid nitroglycerin or diethylene glycol dinitrate in blasting operations. This specification is not intended to take the place of any shipping or packing requirements of this Department where the caps in question are themselves articles of commerce.

(b) **[Reserved]**

§178.318-2 Container.

(a) **Every container for detonators and percussion caps** coming within the scope of this specification shall be constructed entirely of hard rubber, phenolresinous or other resinous material, or other nonmetallic, nonsparking material, except that metal parts may be used in such locations as not in any event to come in contact with any of the caps. Space shall be provided so that each detonator of whatever nature may be inserted in an individual cell in the body of the container, into which each such cap shall snugly fit. There shall be provided no more than twenty (20) such cellular spaces. Space may be provided into which a plurality of percussion caps may be carried, provided that such space may be closed with a screw cap, and further provided that each or any such space is entirely separate from any space provided for any detonator. Each cellular space into which a detonator is to be inserted and carried shall be capable of being covered by a rotary cover so arranged as to expose not more than one cell at any time, and capable of rotation to such a place that all cells will be covered at the same time, at which place means shall be provided to lock the cover in place. Means shall be provided to lock in place the cover for the cells provided for the carrying of detonators. The requirement that not more than one cell be exposed at one time need not apply in the case of detonators, although spaces for such caps and detonators shall be separate. Sufficient annular space shall be provided inside the cover for such detonators that, when the cover is closed, there will be sufficient space to accommodate the wires customarily attached to such caps. If the material is of such a nature as to require treatment to prevent the absorption of moisture, such treatment shall be applied as shall be necessary in order to provide against the penetration of water by permeation. A suitable carrying handle shall be provided, except for which handle no part of the container may project beyond the exterior of the body.

(b) **Exhibited in plates I and II are line drawings** of a container for detonators and percussion caps, illustrative of the requirements set forth in §178.318-2(a). These plates shall not be construed as a part of this specification.

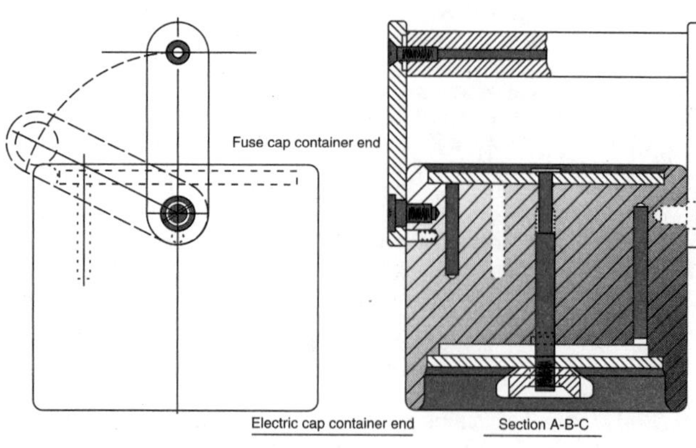

BLASTING CAP CONTAINER
PLATE 1

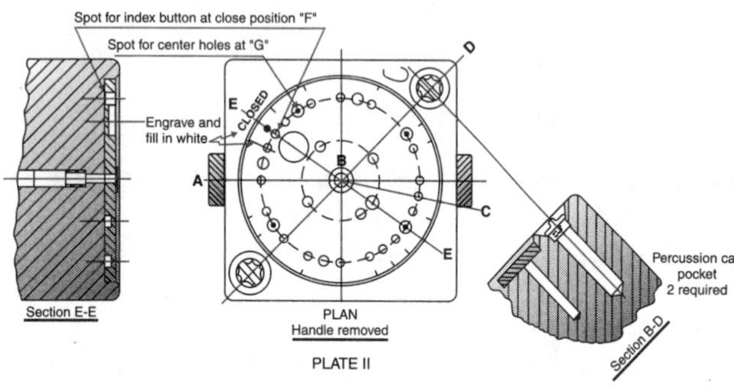

PLATE II

§178.318-3 Marking.

Each container must be marked as prescribed in §178.2(b).

§178.320 General requirements applicable to all DOT-specification cargo tank motor vehicles.

(a) **Definitions.** For the purposes of this subpart,

Cargo tank, as defined in §171.8 of this subchapter, means a bulk packaging which:

(1) *Is a tank intended primarily* for the carriage of liquids or gases (including appurtenances, reinforcements, fittings, and closures). (For definition of "tank", see §178.345-1(c), §178.337-1, or §178.338-1, as applicable);

(2) *Is permanently attached to* or forms a part of a motor vehicle but which, by reason of its size, construction or attachment to a motor vehicle is loaded or unloaded without being removed from the motor vehicle; and

(3) *Is not fabricated* under a specification for cylinders, portable tanks, tank cars, or multi-unit tank car tanks.

Cargo tank motor vehicle, as defined in §171.8 of this subchapter, means a motor vehicle with one or more cargo tanks permanently attached to or forming an integral part of the motor vehicle.

Cargo tank wall means those parts of the cargo tank which make up the primary lading retention structure including shell, bulkheads, and fittings which, when closed during transportation of lading, yields the minimum volume of the cargo tank assembly.

Design type means one or more cargo tanks which are made —

(1) *To the same specification;*

(2) *By the same manufacturer;*

(3) *To the same* engineering drawings and calculations, except for minor variations in piping which do not affect the lading retention capability of the cargo tank;

(4) *Of the same materials of construction;*

(5) *To the same cross-sectional dimensions;*

(6) *To a length varying by no more than five percent;*

(7) *With the volume* varying by no more than five percent (due to a change in length only); and

(8) *For the purposes of §178.338 only, with the same insulation system.*

Manufacturer means any person engaged in the manufacture of a DOT specification cargo tank, cargo tank motor vehicle or cargo tank equipment which forms part of the cargo tank wall. This term includes attaching a cargo tank to a motor vehicle or to a motor vehicle suspension component which involves welding on the cargo tank wall. A manufacturer shall register with the Department in accordance with subpart F of part 107 in subchapter A of this chapter.

(b) **Design certification.**

(1) *Each cargo tank design type* shall be certified in conformance with the specification requirements by a Design Certifying Engineer registered in accordance with subpart F of part 107.

(2) *The Design Certifying Engineer* shall furnish to the manufacturer a certificate to indicate compliance with the specification requirements. The certificate must include the sketches, drawings, and calculations used for certification. Each certificate, including sketches, drawings, and calculations, shall be signed by the Design Certifying Engineer.

(3) *The manufacturer* shall retain the design certificate at his principal place of business for as long as he manufactures DOT specification cargo tanks.

(c) **Exceptions to the ASME Code.** Unless otherwise specified, when exceptions are provided in this subpart from compliance with certain paragraphs of the ASME Code, compliance with those paragraphs is not prohibited.

FEDERAL REGISTER UPDATES

In the April 18, 2003 Federal Register, §178.320 was revised, effective October 1, 2003.

(a) **Definitions.** For the purpose of this subchapter: [1]

Appurtenance means any attachment to a cargo tank that has no lading retention or containment function and provides no structural support to the cargo tank.

Baffle means a non-liquid-tight transverse partition device that deflects, checks or regulates fluid motion in a tank.

Bulkhead means a liquid-tight transverse closure at the ends of or between cargo tanks.

Cargo tank means a bulk packaging that:

(1) *Is a tank intended primarily* for the carriage of liquids or gases and includes appurtenances, reinforcements, fittings and closures (for tank, see §§178.345-1(c), 178.337-1, or 178.338-1, as applicable);

(2) *Is permanently attached to* or forms a part of a motor vehicle, or is not permanently attached to a motor vehicle but that, by reason of its size, construction or attachment to a motor vehicle is loaded or unloaded without being removed from the motor vehicle; and

(3) *Is not fabricated* under a specification for cylinders, intermediate bulk containers, multi-unit tank car tanks, portable tanks, or tank cars.

Cargo tank motor vehicle means a motor vehicle with one or more cargo tanks permanently attached to or forming an integral part of the motor vehicle.

Cargo tank wall means those parts of the cargo tank that make up the primary lading retention structure, including shell, bulkheads, and fittings and, when closed, yield the minimum volume of the cargo tank assembly.

Charging line means a hose, tube, pipe, or a similar device used to pressurize a tank with material other than the lading.

Companion flange means one of two mating flanges where the flange faces are in contact or separated only by a thin leak-sealing gasket and are secured to one another by bolts or clamps.

Connecting structure means the structure joining two cargo tanks.

Constructed and certified in accordance with the ASME Code means a cargo tank is constructed and stamped in accordance with the ASME Code, and is inspected and certified by an Authorized Inspector.

Constructed in accordance with the ASME Code means a cargo tank is constructed in accordance with the ASME Code with authorized exceptions (see §§178.346, 178.347, and 178.348) and is inspected and certified by a Registered Inspector.

Design type means one or more cargo tanks that are made —

(1) *To the same specification;*

(2) *By the same manufacturer;*

(3) *To the same* engineering drawings and calculations, except for minor variations in piping that do not affect the lading retention capability of the cargo tank;

(4) *Of the same materials of construction;*

(5) *To the same cross-sectional dimensions;*

(6) *To a length varying by no more than 5 percent;*

(7) *With the volume* varying by no more than 5 percent (due to a change in length only); and

(8) *For the purposes of §178.338 only, with the same insulation system.*

External self-closing stop valve means a self-closing stop valve designed so that the self-stored energy source is located outside the cargo tank and the welded flange.

Extreme dynamic loading means the maximum loading a cargo tank motor vehicle may experience during its expected life, excluding accident loadings resulting from an accident, such as overturn or collision.

Flange means the structural ring for guiding or attachment of a pipe or fitting with another flange (companion flange), pipe, fitting or other attachment.

Inspection pressure means the pressure used to determine leak tightness of the cargo tank when testing with pneumatic pressure.

Internal self-closing stop valve means a self-closing stop valve designed so that the self-stored energy source is located inside the cargo tank or cargo tank sump, or within the welded flange, and the valve seat is located within the cargo tank or within one inch of the external face of the welded flange or sump of the cargo tank.

Lading means the hazardous material contained in a cargo tank.

Loading/unloading connection means the fitting in the loading/unloading line farthest from the loading/unloading outlet to which the loading/unloading hose, pipe, or device is attached.

(continued on next page)

(continued from previous page)

Loading/unloading outlet means a cargo tank outlet used for normal loading/unloading operations.

Loading/unloading stop valve means the stop valve farthest from the cargo tank loading/unloading outlet to which the loading/unloading connection is attached.

Maximum allowable working pressure or **MAWP** means the maximum pressure allowed at the top of the tank in its normal operating position. The MAWP must be calculated as prescribed in Section VIII, Division 1 of the ASME Code (incorporated by reference; see §171.7 of this subchapter). In use, the MAWP must be greater than or equal to the maximum lading pressure conditions prescribed in §173.33 of this subchapter for each material transported.

Maximum lading pressure. See §173.33(c).

Minimum thickness means the minimum required shell and head (and baffle and bulkhead when used as tank reinforcement) thickness needed to meet the specification. The minimum thickness is the greatest of the following values:

(1) (i) *For MC 330, MC 331,* and MC 338 cargo tanks, the specified minimum thickness found the applicable specification(s); or

(ii) *For DOT 406, DOT 407* and DOT 412 cargo tanks, the specified minimum thickness found in Tables I and II of the applicable specification(s); or

(iii) *For MC 300, MC 301, MC 302,* MC 303, MC 304, MC 305, MC 306, MC 307, MC 310, MC 311, and MC 312 cargo tanks, the in-service minimum thickness prescribed in Tables I and II of §180.407(i)(5) of this subchapter, for the minimum thickness specified by Tables I and II of the applicable specification(s); or

(2) *The thickness necessary* to meet with the structural integrity and accident damage requirements of the applicable specification(s); or

(3) *The thickness as computed per the ASME Code requirements (if applicable).*

Multi-specification cargo tank motor vehicle means a cargo tank motor vehicle equipped with two or more cargo tanks fabricated to more than one cargo tank specification.

Normal operating loading means the loading a cargo tank motor vehicle may be expected to experience routinely in operation.

Nozzle means a subassembly consisting of a pipe or tubular section with or without a welded or forged flange on one end.

Outlet means any opening in the shell or head of a cargo tank, (including the means for attaching a closure), except that the following are not outlets: a threaded opening securely closed during transportation with a threaded plug or a threaded cap, a flanged opening securely closed during transportation with a bolted or welded blank flange, a manhole, a gauging device, a thermometer well, or a pressure relief device.

Outlet stop valve means the stop valve at a cargo tank loading or unloading outlet.

Pipe coupling means a fitting with internal threads on both ends.

Rear bumper means the structure designed to prevent a vehicle or object from under-riding the rear of another motor vehicle. See §393.86 of this title.

Rear-end tank protection device means the structure designed to protect a cargo tank and any lading retention piping or devices in case of a rear end collision.

Sacrificial device means an element, such as a shear section, designed to fail under a load in order to prevent damage to any lading retention part or device. The device must break under strain at no more than 70 percent of the strength of the weakest piping element between the cargo tank and the sacrificial device. Operation of the sacrificial device must leave the remaining piping and its attachment to the cargo tank intact and capable of retaining lading.

Self-closing stop valve means a stop valve held in the closed position by means of self-stored energy, that opens only by application of an external force and that closes when the external force is removed.

Shear section means a sacrificial device fabricated in such a manner as to abruptly reduce the wall thickness of the adjacent piping or valve material by at least 30 percent.

Shell means the circumferential portion of a cargo tank defined by the basic design radius or radii excluding the bulkheads.

Stop valve means a valve that stops the flow of lading.

Sump means a protrusion from the bottom of a cargo tank shell designed to facilitate complete loading and unloading of lading.

Tank means a container, consisting of a shell and heads, that forms a pressure tight vessel having openings designed to accept pressure tight fittings or closures, but excludes any appurtenances, reinforcements, fittings, or closures.

Test pressure means the pressure to which a tank is subjected to determine structural integrity.

Toughness of material means the capability of a material to absorb energy represented by the area under a stress strain curve (indicating the energy absorbed per unit volume of the material) up to the point of rupture.

Vacuum cargo tank means a cargo tank that is loaded by reducing the pressure in the cargo tank to below atmospheric pressure.

Variable specification cargo tank means a cargo tank that is constructed in accordance with one specification, but that may be altered to meet another specification by changing relief device, closures, lading discharge devices, and other lading retention devices.

Void means the space between tank heads or bulkheads and a connecting structure.

Welded flange means a flange attached to the tank by a weld joining the tank shell to the cylindrical outer surface of the flange, or by a fillet weld joining the tank shell to a flange shaped to fit the shell contour.

(b)[2]

(1) *Each cargo tank* or cargo tank motor vehicle design type and each accident damage protection device design must be certified to be in conformance with the specification requirements by a Design Certifying Engineer who is registered in accordance with subpart F of part 107 of this title.[3]

1. Paragraph (a) was revised.
2. Paragraph (b) is the same as before.
3. Paragraph (b)(1) was revised.

§178.337 Specification MC 331; cargo tank motor vehicle primarily for transportation of compressed gases as defined in subpart G of part 173 of this subchapter.

§178.337-1 General requirements.

(a) ASME Code construction. Tanks must be —

(1) *Seamless or welded construction, or a combination of both;*

(2) *Designed and constructed in accordance with the ASME Code;*

(3) *Made of steel or aluminum;* however, if aluminum is used, the cargo tank must be insulated and the hazardous material to be transported must be compatible with the aluminum (see §§178.337-1(e)(2), 173.315(a) table, and 178.337-2(a)(1) of this subchapter); and

(4) *Covered with a steel jacket* if the cargo tank is insulated and used to transport a flammable gas (see §173.315(a) table Note 11 of this subchapter).

(b) Design pressure. The design pressure of a cargo tank authorized under this specification shall be not less than the vapor pressure of the commodity contained therein at 115 °F or as prescribed for a particular commodity in §173.315(a) of this subchapter, except that in no case shall the design pressure of any cargo tank be less than 100 p.s.i.g. nor more than 500 p.s.i.g.

NOTE 1: The term design pressure as used in this specification, is identical to the term MAWP as used in the ASME Code.

(c) Openings.

(1) *Excess pressure relief valves* shall be located in the top of the cargo tank or heads.

(2) *A chlorine cargo tank* shall have only one opening. That opening shall be in the top of the cargo tank and shall be fitted with a nozzle that meets the following requirements:

(i) *On a cargo tank* manufactured on or before December 31, 1974, the nozzle shall be protected by a dome cover plate which conforms to either the standard of The Chlorine Institute, Inc., Dwg. 103-3, dated January 23, 1958, or to the standard specified in paragraph (c) (2) (ii) of this section.

(ii) *On a cargo tank* manufactured on or after January 1, 1975, the nozzle shall be protected by a manway cover which conforms to the standard of The Chlorine Institute, Inc., Dwg. 103-4, dated September 1, 1971.

(d) Reflective design. Every uninsulated cargo tank permanently attached to a cargo tank motor vehicle shall, unless covered with a jacket made of aluminum, stainless steel, or other bright nontarnishing metal, be painted a white, aluminum or similar reflecting color on the upper two-thirds of area of the cargo tank.

(e) Insulation.

(1) *Each cargo tank* required to be insulated must conform with the use and performance requirements contained in §§173.315(a) table and 178.337-1 (a)(3) and (e)(2) of this subchapter.

(2) *Each cargo tank* intended for chlorine; carbon dioxide, refrigerated liquid; or nitrous oxide, refrigerated liquid service must have suitable insulation of such thickness that the overall thermal conductance is not more than 0.08 Btu per square foot per °F differential per hour. The conductance must be determined at 60 °F. Insulation material used on cargo tanks for nitrous oxide, refrigerated liquid must be noncombustible. Insulating material used on cargo tanks for chlorine must be corkboard or polyurethane foam, with a minimum thickness of 4 inches, or 2 inches minimum thickness of ceramic fiber/fiberglass of 4 pounds per cubic foot minimum density covered by 2 inches minimum thickness of fiber.

(f) Postweld heat treatment. Postweld heat treatment must be as prescribed in the ASME Code except that each cargo tank constructed in accordance with Part UHT of the ASME Code must be postweld heat treated. Each chlorine cargo tank must be fully radiographed and postweld heat treated in accordance with the provisions of the ASME Code under which it is constructed. Where postweld heat treatment is required, the cargo tank must be treated as a unit after completion of all the welds in and/or to the shells and heads. The method must be as prescribed in the ASME Code. Welded attachments to pads may be made after postweld heat treatment. A cargo tank used for anhydrous ammonia must be postweld heat treated. The postweld heat treatment must be as prescribed in the ASME Code, but in no event at less than 1050 °F cargo tank metal temperature.

(g) Definitions. The following definitions apply to §§178.337-1 through 178.337-18:

Emergency discharge control means the ability to stop a cargo tank unloading operation in the event of an unintentional release. Emergency discharge control can utilize passive or off-truck remote means to stop the unloading operation. A passive means of emergency discharge control automatically shuts off the flow of product without the need for human intervention within 20 seconds of an unintentional release caused by a complete separation of the liquid delivery hose. An off-truck remote means of emergency discharge control permits a qualified person attending the unloading operation to close the cargo tank's internal self-closing stop valve and shut off all motive and auxiliary power equipment at a distance from the cargo tank motor vehicle.

Excess flow valve, integral excess flow valve, or excess flow feature means a component that will close automatically if the flow rate of a gas or liquid through the component reaches or exceeds the rated flow of gas or liquid specified by the original valve manufacturer when piping mounted directly on the valve is sheared off before the first valve, pump, or fitting downstream from the valve.

Internal self-closing stop valve means a primary shut off valve installed in a product discharge outlet of a cargo tank and designed to be kept closed by self-stored energy.

Primary discharge control system means a primary shut-off installed at a product discharge outlet of a cargo tank consisting of an internal self-closing stop valve that may include an integral excess flow valve or an excess flow feature, together with linkages that must be installed between the valve and remote actuator to provide manual and thermal on-truck remote means of closure.

§178.337-2 Material.

(a) General.

(1) *All material* used for construction of the cargo tank and appurtenances must be suitable for use with the commodities to be transported therein and must conform to the requirements of the ASME Code and/or requirements of the American Society for Testing and Materials in all respects.

(2) *Impact tests* are required on steel used in the fabrication of each cargo tank constructed in accordance with part UHT of the ASME Code. The tests must be made on a lot basis. A lot is defined as 100 tons or less of the same heat treatment processing lot having a thickness variation no greater than plus or minus 25 percent. The minimum impact required for full size specimens must be 20 foot-pounds in the longitudinal direction at -30 °F, Charpy V-Notch and 15 foot-pounds in the transverse direction at -30 °F, Charpy V-Notch. The required values for subsize specimens must be reduced in direct proportion to the cross-sectional area of the specimen beneath the notch. If a lot does not meet this requirement, individual plates may be accepted if they individually meet this requirement.

(3) *The fabricator* shall record the heat, and slab numbers, and the certified Charpy impact values, where required, of each plate used in each cargo tank on a sketch showing the location of each plate in the shell and heads of the cargo tank. Copies of each sketch shall be provided to the owner and retained for at least five years by the fabricator and made available to duly identified representatives of the Department of Transportation.

(4) *The direction* of final rolling of the shell material shall be the circumferential orientation of the cargo tank shell.

(b) For a chlorine cargo tank. Plates, the manway nozzle, and anchorage shall be made of carbon steel which meets the following requirements:

(1) *For a cargo tank manufactured on or before December 31, 1974 —*

(i) *Material shall conform* to ASTM Specification A-300-58, titled "Steel Plates for Pressure Vessels for Service at Low Temperatures";

(ii) *Material shall be Class 1, Grade A, flange or firebox quality;*

(iii) *Plate impact test specimens,* as required under paragraph (a) of this section, shall be of the Charpy keyhole notch type; and

(iv) *Plate impact test specimens* shall meet the impact test requirements in paragraph (a) of this section in both the longitudinal and transverse directions of rolling at a temperature of minus 45.5 C. (-50 °F).

(2) *For a cargo tank manufactured on or after January 1, 1975 —*

(i) *Material shall conform* to ASTM Specification A-612-72a, Grade B or A 516, Grade 65 or 70;

(ii) *Material shall meet* the Charpy V-notch test requirements of ASTM Specification A 20; and

(iii) *Plate impact test specimens* shall meet the impact test requirements in paragraph (a) of this section in both the longitudinal and transverse directions of rolling at a temperature of minus 40 °C (-40 °F).

(c) A cargo tank in anhydrous ammonia service must be constructed of steel. The use of copper, silver, zinc or their alloys is prohibited. Baffles made from aluminum may be used only if joined to the cargo tank by a process not requiring postweld heat treatment of the cargo tank.

§178.337-3 Structural integrity.

(a) General requirements and acceptance criteria.

(1) *Except as provided* in paragraph (d) of this section, the maximum calculated design stress at any point in the cargo tank may not exceed the maximum allowable stress value prescribed in Section VIII of the ASME Code, or 25 percent of the tensile strength of the material used.

(2) *The relevant physical properties* of the materials used in each cargo tank may be established either by a certified test report from the material manufacturer or by testing in conformance with a recognized national standard. In either case, the ultimate tensile strength of the material used in the design may not exceed 120 percent of the ultimate tensile strength specified in either the ASME Code or the ASTM standard to which the material is manufactured.

(3) *The maximum design stress* at any point in the cargo tank must be calculated separately for the loading conditions described in paragraphs (b), (c), and (d) of this section. Alternate test or analytical methods, or a combination thereof, may be used in place of the procedures described in paragraphs (b), (c), and (d) of this section, if the methods are accurate and verifiable.

(4) *Corrosion allowance material* may not be included to satisfy any of the design calculation requirements of this section.

(b) The static design and construction of each cargo tank must be in accordance with section VIII of the ASME Code. The cargo tank design must include calculation of stresses generated by design pressure, the weight of lading, the weight of structure supported by the cargo tank wall, and the effect of temperature gradients resulting from lading and ambient temperature extremes. When dissimilar materials are used, their thermal coefficients must be used in calculation of thermal stresses. Stress concentrations in tension, bending and torsion which occur at pads, cradles, or other supports must be considered in accordance with appendix G of the ASME Code.

(c) Shell design. Shell stresses resulting from static or dynamic loadings, or combinations thereof, are not uniform throughout the cargo tank motor vehicle. The vertical, longitudinal, and lateral normal operating loadings can occur simultaneously and must be combined. The vertical, longitudinal and lateral extreme dynamic loadings occur separately and need not be combined.

(1) *Normal operating loadings.* The following procedure addresses stress in the tank shell resulting from normal operating loadings. The effective stress (the maximum principal stress at any point) must be determined by the following formula:

$$S = 0.5(S_y + S_x) \pm [0.25(S_y - S_x)^2 + S_s^2]^{0.5}$$

Where:

(i) *S* = effective stress at any given point under the combination of static and normal operating loadings that can occur at the same time, in psi.

(ii) S_y = circumferential stress generated by the MAWP and external pressure, when applicable, plus static head, in psi.

(iii) S_x = The following net longitudinal stress generated by the following static and normal operating loading conditions, in psi:

[A] The longitudinal stresses resulting from the MAWP and external pressure, when applicable, plus static head, in combination with the bending stress generated by the static weight of the fully loaded cargo tank motor vehicle, all structural elements, equipment and appurtenances supported by the cargo tank wall;

[B] The tensile or compressive stress resulting from normal operating longitudinal acceleration or deceleration. In each case, the forces applied must be 0.35 times the vertical reaction at the suspension assembly, applied at the road surface, and as transmitted to the cargo tank wall through the suspension assembly of a trailer during deceleration; or the horizontal pivot of the truck tractor or converter dolly fifth wheel, or the drawbar hinge on the fixed dolly during acceleration; or anchoring and support members of a truck during acceleration and deceleration, as applicable. The vertical reaction must be calculated based on the static weight of the fully loaded cargo tank motor vehicle, all structural elements, equipment and appurtenances supported by the cargo tank wall. The following loadings must be included:

[1] The axial load generated by a decelerative force;

[2] The bending moment generated by a decelerative force;

[3] The axial load generated by an accelerative force; and

[4] The bending moment generated by an accelerative force; and

[C] The tensile or compressive stress generated by the bending moment resulting from normal operating vertical accelerative force equal to 0.35 times the vertical reaction at the suspension assembly of a trailer; or the horizontal pivot of the upper coupler (fifth wheel) or turntable; or anchoring and support members of a truck, as applicable. The vertical reaction must be calculated based on the static weight of the fully loaded cargo tank motor vehicle, all structural elements, equipment and appurtenances supported by the cargo tank wall.

(iv) S_s = The following shear stresses generated by the following static and normal operating loading conditions, in psi:

[A] The static shear stress resulting from the vertical reaction at the suspension assembly of a trailer, and the horizontal pivot of the upper coupler (fifth wheel) or turntable; or anchoring and support members of a truck, as applicable. The vertical reaction must be calculated based on the static weight of the fully loaded cargo tank motor vehicle, all structural elements, equipment and appurtenances supported by the cargo tank wall;

[B] The vertical shear stress generated by a normal operating accelerative force equal to 0.35 times the vertical reaction at the suspension assembly of a trailer; or the horizontal pivot of the upper coupler (fifth wheel) or turntable; or anchoring and support members of a truck, as applicable. The vertical reaction must be calculated based on the static weight of the fully loaded cargo tank motor vehicle, all structural elements, equipment and appurtenances supported by the cargo tank wall;

[C] The lateral shear stress generated by a normal operating lateral accelerative force equal to 0.2 times the vertical reaction at each suspension assembly of a trailer, applied at the road surface, and as transmitted to the cargo tank wall through the suspension assembly of a trailer, and the horizontal pivot of the upper coupler (fifth wheel) or turntable; or anchoring and support members of a truck, as applicable. The vertical reaction must be calculated based on the static weight of the fully loaded cargo tank motor vehicle, all structural elements, equipment and appurtenances supported by the cargo tank wall; and

[D] The torsional shear stress generated by the same lateral forces as described in paragraph (c)(1)(iv)(C) of this section.

(2) *Extreme dynamic loadings.* The following procedure addresses stress in the tank shell resulting from extreme dynamic loadings. The effective stress (the maximum principal stress at any point) must be determined by the following formula:

$S = 0.5(S_y + S_x) \pm [0.25(S_y - S_x)^2 + S_s^2]^{0.5}$

Where:

(i) *S* = effective stress at any given point under a combination of static and extreme dynamic loadings that can occur at the same time, in psi.

(ii) S_y = circumferential stress generated by MAWP and external pressure, when applicable, plus static head, in psi.

(iii) S_x = the following net longitudinal stress generated by the following static and extreme dynamic loading conditions, in psi:

[A] The longitudinal stresses resulting from the MAWP and external pressure, when applicable, plus static head, in combination with the bending stress generated by the static weight of the fully loaded cargo tank motor vehicle, all structural elements, equipment and appurtenances supported by the tank wall;

[B] The tensile or compressive stress resulting from extreme longitudinal acceleration or deceleration. In each case the forces applied must be 0.7 times the vertical reaction at the suspension assembly, applied at the road surface, and as transmitted to the cargo tank wall through the suspension assembly of a trailer during deceleration; or the horizontal pivot of the truck tractor or converter dolly fifth wheel, or the drawbar hinge on the fixed dolly during acceleration; or the anchoring and support members of a truck during acceleration and deceleration, as applicable. The vertical reaction must be calculated based on the static weight of the fully loaded cargo tank motor vehicle, all structural elements, equipment and appurtenances supported by the cargo tank wall. The following loadings must be included:

[1] The axial load generated by a decelerative force;

[2] The bending moment generated by a decelerative force;

[3] The axial load generated by an accelerative force; and

[4] The bending moment generated by an accelerative force; and

[C] The tensile or compressive stress generated by the bending moment resulting from an extreme vertical accelerative force equal to 0.7 times the vertical reaction at the suspension assembly of a trailer, and the horizontal pivot of the upper coupler (fifth wheel) or turntable; or the anchoring and support members of a truck, as applicable. The vertical reaction must be calculated based on the static weight of the fully loaded cargo tank motor vehicle, all structural elements, equipment and appurtenances supported by the cargo tank wall.

(iv) S_s = The following shear stresses generated by static and extreme dynamic loading conditions, in psi:

[A] The static shear stress resulting from the vertical reaction at the suspension assembly of a trailer, and the horizontal pivot of the upper coupler (fifth wheel) or turntable; or anchoring and support members of a truck, as applicable. The vertical reaction must be calculated based on the static weight of the fully loaded cargo tank motor vehicle, all structural elements, equipment and appurtenances supported by the cargo tank wall;

[B] The vertical shear stress generated by an extreme vertical accelerative force equal to 0.7 times the vertical reaction at the suspension assembly of a trailer, and the horizontal pivot of the upper coupler (fifth wheel) or turntable; or anchoring and support members of a truck, as applicable. The vertical reaction must be calculated based on the static weight of the fully loaded cargo tank motor vehicle, all structural elements, equipment and appurtenances supported by the cargo tank wall;

[C] The lateral shear stress generated by an extreme lateral accelerative force equal to 0.4 times the vertical reaction at the suspension assembly of a trailer, applied at the road surface, and as transmitted to the cargo tank wall through the suspension assembly of a trailer, and the horizontal pivot of the upper coupler (fifth wheel) or turntable; or anchoring and support members of a truck, as applicable. The vertical reaction must be calculated based on the static weight of the fully loaded cargo tank motor vehicle, all structural elements, equipment and appurtenances supported by the cargo tank wall; and

[D] The torsional shear stress generated by the same lateral forces as described in paragraph (c)(2)(iv)(C) of this section.

(d) In order to account for stresses due to impact in an accident, the design calculations for the cargo tank shell and heads must include the load resulting from the design pressure in combination with the dynamic pressure resulting from a longitudinal deceleration of "2g". For this loading condition the stress value used may not exceed the lesser of the yield strength or 75 percent of the ultimate tensile strength of the material of construction. For cargo tanks constructed of stainless steel the maximum design stress may not exceed 75 percent of the ultimate tensile strength of the type steel used.

(e) The minimum metal thickness for the shell and heads must be 4.75 mm (0.187 inch) for steel and 6.86 mm (0.270 inch) for aluminum, except for chlorine and sulfur dioxide tanks. For a cargo tank used in chlorine or sulfur dioxide service, the cargo tank must be made of steel. A corrosion allowance of 20 percent or 2.54 mm (0.10 inch), whichever is less, must be added to the thickness otherwise required for sulfur dioxide and chlorine tank material. In chlorine cargo tanks, the wall thickness must be at least 1.59 cm (0.625 inch), including corrosion allowance.

(f) Where a cargo tank support is attached to any part of the cargo tank wall, the stresses imposed on the cargo tank wall must meet the requirements in paragraph (a) of this section.

(g) The design, construction, and installation of an appurtenance to the cargo tank must be such that, in the event of its damage or failure, the lading retention integrity of the cargo tank will not be adversely affected.

(1) *A lightweight attachment,* such as a conduit clip, brakeline clip or placard holder, must be constructed of a material of lesser strength than the cargo tank wall material and may not be more than 72 percent of the thickness of the material to which it is attached. The attachment may be secured directly to the cargo tank wall if the device is designed and installed in such a manner that, if damaged, it will not affect the lading retention integrity of the cargo tank. The lightweight attachment must be secured to the cargo tank wall by continuous weld or in such a manner as to preclude formation of pockets, which may become sites for incipient corrosion. Attachments meeting the requirements of this paragraph are not authorized for cargo tanks constructed under part UHT of the ASME Code.

(2) *Except as prescribed* in §178.337-3(g)(1), the welding of any appurtenance of the cargo tank wall must be made by attachment of a mounting pad, so that there will be no adverse effect upon the lading retention integrity of the cargo tank if any force is applied to the appurtenance, from any direction. The thickness of the mounting pad may not be less than that of the shell or head to which it is attached, and not more than 1.5 times the shell or head thickness. However, a pad with a minimum thickness of 6.35 mm (0.250 inch) may be used when the shell or head thickness is over 6.35 mm (0.250 inch). If weep holes or tell-tale holes are used, the pad must be drilled or punched at its lowest point before it is welded. Each pad must:

(i) *Extend at least 5.08 cm (2 inches)* in each direction from any point of attachment of an appurtenance;

(ii) *Have rounded corners,* or otherwise be shaped in a manner to minimize stress concentrations on the shell or head; and

(iii) *Be attached* by a continuous weld around the pad, except for a small gap at the lowest point for draining, using filler material conforming to the recommendations of the manufacturer of the head or shell material.

FEDERAL REGISTER UPDATES

In the April 18, 2003 Federal Register, §178.337-3 was revised, effective October 1, 2003.

(b) Static design and construction. [1]

(1) *The static design and construction* of each cargo tank must be in accordance with Section VIII, Division 1 of the ASME Code (incorporated by reference; see §171.7 of thus subchapter). The cargo tank design must include calculation of stresses generated by design pressure, the weight of lading, the weight of structure supported by the cargo tank wall, and the effect of temperature gradients resulting from lading and ambient temperature extremes. When dissimilar materials are used, their thermal coefficients must be used in calculation of thermal stresses.

(2) *Stress concentrations* in tension, bending, and torsion that occur at pads, cradles, or supports must be considered in accordance with Appendix G of Section VIII, Division 1 of the ASME Code.

(e) The minimum metal thickness for the shell and heads on tanks with a design pressure of 100 psig or more must be 4.75 mm (0.187 inch) for steel and 6.86 mm (0.270 inch) for aluminum, except for chlorine and sulfur dioxide tanks. In all cases, the minimum thickness of the tank shell and head shall be determined using structural design requirements in Section VIII of the ASME Code or 25% of the tensile strength of the material used. For a cargo tank used in chlorine or sulfur dioxide service, the cargo tank must be made of steel. A corrosion allowance of 20 percent or 2.54 mm (0.10 inch), whichever is less, must be added to the thickness otherwise required for sulfur dioxide and chlorine tank material. In chlorine cargo tanks, the wall thickness must be at least 1.59 cm (0.625 inch), including corrosion allowance. [2]

(g) The design, construction, and installation of an attachment, appurtenance to the cargo tank, structural support member between the cargo tank and the vehicle or suspension component, or accident protection device must conform to the following requirements: [3]

(1) *Structural members,* the suspension sub-frame, accident protection structures, and external circumferential reinforcement devices must be used as sites for attachment of appurtenances and other accessories to the cargo tank, when practicable.

(2) *A lightweight attachment* to the cargo tank wall such as a conduit clip, brake line clip, skirting structure, lamp mounting bracket, or placard holder must be of a construction having lesser strength than the cargo tank wall materials and may not be more than 72 percent of the thickness of the material to which it is attached. The lightweight attachment may be secured directly to the cargo tank wall if the device is designed and installed in such a manner that, if damaged, it will not affect the lading retention integrity of the tank. A lightweight attachment must be secured to the cargo tank shell or head by a continuous weld or in such a manner as to preclude formation of pockets which may become sites for corrosion. Attachments meeting the requirements of this paragraph are not authorized for cargo tanks constructed under part UHT, Section VIII, Division 1 of the ASME Code.

(3) *Except as prescribed* in paragraphs (g)(1) and (g)(2) of this section, the welding of any appurtenance to the cargo tank wall must be made by attachment of a mounting pad so that there will be no adverse effect upon the lading retention integrity of the cargo tank if any force less than that prescribed in paragraph (b)(1) of this section is applied from any direction. The thickness of the mounting pad may not be less than that of the shell wall or head wall to which it is attached, and not more than 1.5 times the shell or head thickness. However, a pad with a minimum thickness of 0.25 inch may be used when the shell or head thickness is over 0.25 inch. If weep holes or tell-tale holes are used, the pad must be drilled or punched at the lowest point before it is welded to the tank. Each pad must —

(i) *Be fabricated* from material determined to be suitable for welding to both the cargo tank material and the material of the appurtenance or structural support member; a Design Certifying Engineer must make this determination considering chemical and physical properties of the materials and must specify filler material conforming to the requirements of the ASME Code (incorporated by reference; see §171.7 of this subchapter).

(ii) *Be preformed to an inside radius* no greater than the outside radius of the cargo tank at the attachment location.

(iii) *Extend at least 2 inches* in each direction from any point of attachment of an appurtenance or structural support member. This dimension may be measured from the center of the attached structural member.

(iv) *Have rounded corners,* or otherwise be shaped in a manner to minimize stress concentrations on the shell or head.

(v) *Be attached by continuous fillet welding.* Any fillet weld discontinuity may only be for the purpose of preventing an intersection between the fillet weld and a tank or jacket seam weld.

1. Paragraph (b) was revised.
2. Paragraph (e) was revised.
3. Paragraph (g) was revised.

§178.337-4 Joints.

(a) Joints shall be as required by the ASME Code, with all undercutting in shell and head material repaired as specified therein.

(b) Welding procedure and welder performance must be in accordance with Section IX of the ASME Code. In addition to the essential variables named therein, the following must be considered as essential variables: Number of passes; thickness of plate; heat input per pass; and manufacturer's identification of rod and flux. When fabrication is done in accordance with part UHT of the ASME Code, filler material containing more than 0.08 percent vanadium must not be used. The number of passes, thickness of plate, and heat input per pass may not vary more than 25 percent from the procedure or welder qualifications. Records of the qualifications must be retained for at least 5 years by the cargo tank manufacturer and must be made available to duly identified representatives of the Department and the owner of the cargo tank.

(c) All longitudinal shell welds shall be located in the upper half of the cargo tank.

(d) Edge preparation of shell and head components may be by machine heat processes, provided such surfaces are remelted in the subsequent welding process. Where there will be no subsequent remelting of the prepared surface as in a tapered section, the final 0.050 inch of material shall be removed by mechanical means.

(e) The maximum tolerance for misalignment and butting up shall be in accordance with the ASME Code.

(f) Substructures shall be properly fitted before attachment, and the welding sequence shall be such as to minimize stresses due to shrinkage of welds.

§178.337-5 Bulkheads, baffles and ring stiffeners.

(a) Not a specification requirement.

(b) [Reserved]

§178.337-6 Closure for manhole.

(a) Each cargo tank marked or certified after April 21, 1994, must be provided with a manhole conforming to paragraph UG-46(g)(1) and other applicable requirements of the ASME Code, except that a cargo tank constructed of NQT steel having a capacity of 3500 water gallons or less may be provided with an inspection opening conforming to paragraph UG-46 and other applicable requirements of the ASME Code instead of a manhole.

(b) The manhole assembly of cargo tanks constructed after June 30, 1979, may not be located on the front head of the cargo tank.

§178.337-7 Overturn protection.

(a) See §178.337-10.

(b) [Reserved]

§178.337-8 Openings, inlets, and outlets.

(a) General. The requirements in this paragraph (a) apply to MC 331 cargo tanks except for those used to transport chlorine. The requirements for inlets and outlets on chlorine cargo tanks are in paragraph (b) of this section.

(1) *An opening* must be provided on each cargo tank used for the transportation of liquefied materials to permit complete drainage.

(2) *Except for* gauging devices, thermometer wells, pressure relief valves, manhole openings, product inlet openings, and product discharge openings, each opening in a cargo tank must be closed with a plug, cap, or bolted flange.

(3) *Except as provided* in paragraph (b) of this section, each product inlet opening, including vapor return lines, must be fitted with a back flow check valve or an internal self-closing stop valve located inside the cargo tank or inside a welded nozzle that is an integral part of the cargo tank. The valve seat must be located inside the cargo tank or within 2.54 cm (one inch) of the external face of the welded flange. Damage to parts exterior to the cargo tank or mating flange must not prevent effective seating of the valve. All parts of a valve inside a cargo tank or welded flange must be made of material that will not corrode or deteriorate in the presence of the lading.

(4) *Except as provided* in paragraphs (a)(5), (b), and (c) of this section, each liquid or vapor discharge outlet must be fitted with a primary discharge control system as defined in §178.337-1(g). Thermal remote operators must activate at a temperature of 121.11 °C (250 °F) or less. Linkages between closures and remote operators must be corrosion resistant and effective in all types of environmental conditions incident to discharging of product.

(i) *On a cargo tank* over 13,247.5 L (3,500 gallons) water capacity, thermal and mechanical means of remote closure must be installed at the ends of the cargo tank in at least two diagonally opposite locations. If the loading/unloading connection at the cargo tank is not in the general vicinity of one of the two locations specified in the first sentence of this paragraph (a)(4)(i), additional means of thermal remote closure must be installed so that heat from a fire in the loading/unloading connection area or the discharge pump will activate the primary discharge control system. The loading/unloading connection area is where hoses or hose reels are connected to the permanent metal piping.

(ii) *On a cargo tank* of 13,247.5 L (3,500 gallons) water capacity or less, a thermal means of remote closure must be installed at or near the internal self-closing stop valve. A mechanical means of remote closure must be installed on the end of the cargo tank furthest away from the loading/unloading connection area. The loading/unloading connection area is where hoses or hose reels are connected to the permanent metal piping. Linkages between closures and remote operators must be corrosion resistant and effective in all types of environmental conditions incident to discharge of product.

(iii) *All parts* of a valve inside a cargo tank or within a welded flange must be made of material that will not corrode or deteriorate in the presence of the lading.

(iv) *An excess flow valve,* integral excess flow valve, or excess flow feature must close if the flow reaches the rated flow of a gas or liquid specified by the original valve manufacturer when piping mounted directly on the valve is sheared off before the first valve, pump, or fitting downstream from the excess flow valve, integral excess flow valve, or excess flow feature.

(v) *An integral excess flow valve* or the excess flow feature of an internal self-closing stop valve may be designed with a bypass, not to exceed 0.1016 cm (0.040 inch) diameter opening, to allow equalization of pressure.

(vi) *The internal self-closing stop valve* must be designed so that the self-stored energy source and the valve seat are located inside the cargo tank or within 2.54 cm (one inch) of the external face of the welded flange. Damage to parts exterior to the cargo tank or mating flange must not prevent effective seating of the valve.

(5) *A primary discharge control system is not required on the following:*

(i) *A vapor* or liquid discharge opening of less than 1 1/4 NPT equipped with an excess flow valve together with a manually operated external stop valve in place of an internal self-closing stop valve.

(ii) *An engine fuel line* on a truck-mounted cargo tank of not more than 3/4 NPT equipped with a valve having an integral excess flow valve or excess flow feature.

(iii) *A cargo tank motor vehicle* certified before January 1, 1995, unless intended for use to transport a flammable liquid, flammable gas, hydrogen chloride, refrigerated liquid, or anhydrous ammonia.

(6) *In addition* to the internal self-closing stop valve, each filling and discharge line must be fitted with a stop valve located in the line between the internal self-closing stop valve and the hose connection. A back flow check valve or excess flow valve may not be used to satisfy this requirement.

(7) *An excess flow valve* may be designed with a bypass, not to exceed a 0.1016 centimeter (0.040 inch) diameter opening, to allow equalization of pressure.

(b) **Inlets and discharge outlets on chlorine tanks.** The inlet and discharge outlets on a cargo tank used to transport chlorine must meet the requirements of §178.337-1(c)(2) and must be fitted with an internal excess flow valve. In addition to the internal excess flow valve, the inlet and discharge outlets must be equipped with an external stop valve (angle valve). Excess flow valves must conform to the standards of The Chlorine Institute, Inc., as follows:

(1) *A valve* conforming to Drawing 101-7, dated July 1993, must be installed under each liquid angle valve.

(2) *A valve* conforming to Drawing 106-6, dated July 1993, must be installed under each gas angle valve.

(c) **Discharge outlets on carbon dioxide,** refrigerated liquid, cargo tanks. A discharge outlet on a cargo tank used to transport carbon dioxide, refrigerated liquid is not required to be fitted with an internal self-closing stop valve.

FEDERAL REGISTER UPDATES

In the April 18, 2003 Federal Register, §178.337-8 was revised, effective October 1, 2003.

(a) [1]

(5) [2]

(iii) *A cargo tank motor vehicle* used to transport refrigerated liquids such as argon, carbon dioxide, helium, krypton, neon, nitrogen, and xenon, or mixtures thereof. [3]

1. Paragraph (a) is the same as before.
2. Paragraph (a)(5) is the same as before.
3. Paragraph (a)(5)(iii) was revised.

§178.337-9 Pressure relief devices, piping, valves, hoses, and fittings.

(a) **Pressure relief devices.**

(1) *See §173.315(i) of this subchapter.*

(2) *On cargo tanks* for carbon dioxide or nitrous oxide see §173.315 (i) (9) and (10) of this subchapter.

(3) *Each valve* must be designed, constructed, and marked for a rated pressure not less than the cargo tank design pressure at the temperature expected to be encountered.

(b) **Piping, valves, hose, and fittings.**

(1) *The burst pressure* of all piping, pipe fittings, hose and other pressure parts, except for pump seals and pressure relief devices, must be at least 4 times the design pressure of the cargo tank. Additionally, the burst pressure may not be less than 4 times any higher pressure to which each pipe, pipe fitting, hose or other pressure part may be subjected to in service. For chlorine service, see paragraph (b)(7) of this section.

(2) *Pipe joints* must be threaded, welded or flanged. If threaded pipe is used, the pipe and fittings must be Schedule 80 weight or heavier. Malleable metals must be used in the construction of valves and fittings. Where copper tubing is permitted, joints shall be brazed or be of equally strong metal union type. The melting point of the brazing material may not be lower than 1000 °F. The method of joining tubing must not reduce the strength of the tubing, such as by the cutting of threads.

(3) *Each hose coupling* must be designed for a pressure of at least 120 percent of the hose design pressure and so that there will be no leakage when connected.

(4) *Piping must be* protected from damage due to thermal expansion and contraction, jarring, and vibration. Slip joints are not authorized for this purpose.

(5) *Piping and fittings* must be grouped in the smallest practicable space and protected from damage as required by §178.337-10.

(6) *Cargo tank* manufacturers and fabricators must demonstrate that all piping, valves, and fittings on a cargo tank are free from leaks. To meet this requirement, the piping, valves, and fittings must be tested after installation at not less than 80 percent of the design pressure marked on the cargo tank.

(7) *A hose assembler must:*

(i) *Permanently mark* each hose assembly with a unique identification number.

(ii) *Demonstrate that* each hose assembly is free from leaks by performing the tests and inspections in §180.416(f) of this subchapter.

(iii) *Mark each hose assembly* with the month and year of its original pressure test.

(8) *Chlorine cargo tanks.* Angle valves on cargo tanks intended for chlorine service must conform to Drawing 104-8, dated July 1993, in the standards of The Chlorine Institute. Before installation, each angle valve must be tested for leakage at not less than 225 psig using dry air or inert gas.

(c) **Marking inlets and outlets.** Except for gauging devices, thermometer wells, and pressure relief valves, each cargo tank inlet and outlet must be marked "liquid" or "vapor" to designate whether it communicates with liquid or vapor when the cargo tank is filled to the maximum permitted filling density. A filling line that communicates with vapor may be marked "spray-fill" instead of "vapor."

(d) **Refrigeration and heating coils.**

(1) *Refrigeration and heating coils* must be securely anchored with provisions for thermal expansion. The coils must be pressure tested externally to at least the cargo tank test pressure, and

internally to either the tank test pressure or twice the working pressure of the heating/refrigeration system, whichever is higher. A cargo tank may not be placed in service if any leakage occurs or other evidence of damage is found. The refrigerant or heating medium to be circulated through the coils must not be capable of causing any adverse chemical reaction with the cargo tank lading in the event of leakage. The unit furnishing refrigeration may be mounted on the motor vehicle.

(2) *Where any liquid* susceptible to freezing, or the vapor of any such liquid, is used for heating or refrigeration, the heating or refrigeration system shall be arranged to permit complete drainage.

FEDERAL REGISTER UPDATES

In the April 18, 2003 Federal Register, §178.337-9 was revised, effective October 1, 2003.

(b) [1]

(2) *Pipe joints* must be threaded, welded, or flanged. If threaded pipe is used, the pipe and fittings must be Schedule 80 weight or heavier. Except for sacrificial devices, malleable steel, stainless steel, or ductile iron must be used in the construction of primary valves and fittings used in liquid filling or vapor equalization; however, stainless steel may not be used for internal components such as shutoff discs and springs. Where copper tubing is permitted, joints must be brazed or be of equally strong metal union type. The melting point of the brazing material may not be lower than 538 °C (1000 °F). The method of joining tubing may not reduce the strength of the tubing. [2]

(5) *[Reserved]* [3]

1. Paragraph (b) is the same as before.
2. Paragraph (b)(2) was revised.
3. Paragraph (b)(5) was removed and reserved.

§178.337-10 Protection of fittings.

(a) **All valves, fittings, safety relief devices,** and other accessories to the tank proper shall be protected in accordance with paragraph (b) of this section against such damage as could be caused by collision with other vehicles or objects, jackknifing and overturning. In addition, safety relief valves shall be so protected that in the event of overturn of the vehicle on to a hard surface, their opening will not be prevented and their discharge will not be restricted.

(b) **The protective devices or housing must be designed** to withstand static loading in any direction equal to twice the weight of the tank and attachments when filled with the lading, using a safety factor of not less than four, based on the ultimate strength of the material to be used, without damage to the fittings protected, and must be made of metal at least 3/16-inch thick.

(c) **For chlorine tanks.** There shall be a protective housing and manway cover to permit the use of standard emergency kits for controlling leaks in fittings on the dome cover plate. The housing and manway cover must conform to the Chlorine Institute's standards as follows:

(1) *Tanks manufactured on or before December 31, 1974:* Dwg. 137-1, dated November 7, 1962, or Dwg. 137-2, dated September 1, 1971.

(2) *Tanks manufactured on or after January 1, 1975:* Dwg. 137-2, dated September 1, 1971.

(d) **Each cargo tank shall be provided** with at least one rear bumper designed to protect the tank and piping in the event of a rear end collision and minimize the possibility of any part of the colliding vehicle striking the tank. The design shall be such as to transmit the force of a rear end collision in a horizontal line to the chassis of the vehicle. The bumper shall be designed to withstand the impact of the fully loaded vehicle with a deceleration of 2 "g", using a safety factor of four based on the ultimate strength of the bumper material. The bumpers shall conform dimensionally to §393.86, chapter III of this title.

FEDERAL REGISTER UPDATES

In the April 18, 2003 Federal Register, §178.337-10 was revised, effective October 1, 2003.

§178.337-10 Accident damage protection. [1]

(c) **Rear-end tank protection.** Rear-end tank protection devices must: [2]

(1) *Consist of* at least one rear bumper designed to protect the cargo tank and piping in the event of a rear end collision. The bumper design must transmit the force of the collision directly to the chassis of the vehicle. The rear bumper and its attachments to the chassis must be designed to withstand a load equal to twice the weight of the loaded cargo tank and attachments, using a safety factor of four based on the tensile strength of the materials used, with such load being applied horizontally and parallel to the major axis of the cargo tank. The rear bumper dimensions must meet the requirements of §393.86 of this title and extend vertically to a height adequate to protect all valves and fittings located at the rear of the cargo tank from damage that could result in loss of lading; or

(2) *Conform to the requirements of §178.345-8.*

(d) **Chlorine tanks.** A chlorine tank must be equipped with a protective housing and a manway cover to permit the use of standard emergency kits for controlling leaks in fittings on the dome cover plate. The housing and manway cover must conform to the Chlorine Institute's standards as follows:

(1) *Tanks manufactured on or before December 31, 1974:* Dwg. 137-1, dated November 7, 1962, or Dwg. 137-2, dated September 1, 1971.

(2) *Tanks manufactured on or after January 1, 1975:* Dwg. 137-2, dated September 1, 1971.

(e) **Piping and fittings.** Piping and fittings must be grouped in the smallest practicable space and protected from damage as required in this section.

(f) **Shear section.** Shear sections or sacrificial devices are required on the following attachments:

(1) *A section that will break* under undue strain must be provided adjacent to or outboard of each valve specified in §178.337-8(a)(3) and (4).

(2) *Internal self-closing stop valves,* excess flow valves and check valves must be protected by a shear section or other sacrificial device. The sacrificial device must be located in the piping system outboard of the stop valve and within the accident damage protection to prevent any accidental loss of lading. The device must break at no more than 70 percent of the load that would be required to cause the failure of the protected lading retention device, part or cargo tank wall. The failure of the sacrificial device must leave the protected lading retention device and its attachment to the cargo tank wall intact and capable of retaining product.

1. The section heading was revised.
2. Paragraphs (c) and (d) were revised, and paragraphs (e) and (f) were added.

§178.337-11 Emergency discharge control.

(a) **Emergency discharge control equipment.** Emergency discharge control equipment must be installed in a liquid discharge line as specified by product and service in §173.315(n) of this subchapter. The performance and certification requirements for emergency discharge control equipment are specified in §173.315(n) of this subchapter and are not a part of the cargo tank motor vehicle certification made under this specification.

(b) **Engine fuel lines.** On a truck-mounted cargo tank, emergency discharge control equipment is not required on an engine fuel line of not more than 3/4 NPT equipped with a valve having an integral excess flow valve or excess flow feature.

§178.337-12 Shear section.

(a) **Design or installation of valves** specified in §178.337-8(a)(2) shall provide adjacent to and outboard of such valves a section which will break under undue strain.

(b) **[Reserved]**

FEDERAL REGISTER UPDATES

In the April 18, 2003 Federal Register, §178.337-12 was removed and reserved, effective October 1, 2003.

§178.337-12 [Removed and reserved]

§178.337-13 Supporting and anchoring.

(a) **A cargo tank that is not permanently attached to** or integral with a vehicle chassis must be secured by turnbuckles or equally efficient securing devices for drawing the cargo tank down tight on the frame. Anchors, stops, or other means must be provided to prevent relative motion between the cargo tank and the vehicle chassis when the vehicle is in operation.

(b) **A cargo tank motor vehicle designed and constructed** so that the cargo tank constitutes in whole or in part the stress member used in place of a frame must have the cargo tank supported by external cradles. A cargo tank mounted on a frame must be supported by external cradles or longitudinal members. The cradles, where used, must subtend at least 120 degrees of the shell circumference. The design calculations for the supports must include beam stress, shear stress, torsion stress, bending moment, and acceleration stress, for the loaded cargo tank motor vehicle as a unit, using a factor of safety of 4, based on the ultimate strength of the material and on a 2 "g" longitudinal and lateral loading and 3 times the static weight in vertical loading (see appendix G of the ASME Code).

(c) **Where any cargo tank support is attached to** any part of a cargo tank head, the stresses imposed upon the head shall be provided for as required in paragraph (b) of this section.

(d) **No cargo tank support or bumper** may be welded directly to the cargo tank. All supports and bumpers shall be attached by means of pads of the same material as the cargo tank. The pad thickness shall be no less than 1/4 inch, or the thickness of the shell material if less, and no greater than the shell material. Each pad shall extend at least 4 times its thickness, in each direction, beyond the weld attaching the support or bumper. Each pad shall be preformed to an inside radius no greater than the outside radius of the cargo tank at the place of attachment. Each pad corner shall be rounded to a radius at least one-fourth the width of the pad, and no greater than one-half the width of the pad. Weep holes and telltale holes, if used shall be drilled or punched before the pads are attached to the cargo tank. Each pad shall be attached to the cargo tank by continuous fillet welding using filler material having properties conforming to the recommendations of the maker of the shell and head material.

FEDERAL REGISTER UPDATES

In the April 18, 2003 Federal Register, §178.337-13 was revised, effective October 1, 2003.

§178.337-13 **Supporting and anchoring.**

(a) **A cargo tank that is not permanently attached to** or integral with a vehicle chassis must be secured by the use of restraining devices designed to prevent relative motion between the cargo tank and the vehicle chassis when the vehicle is in operation. Such restraining devices must be readily accessible for inspection and maintenance.

(b) **On a cargo tank motor vehicle designed and constructed** so that the cargo tank constitutes in whole or in part the structural member used in place of a motor vehicle frame, the cargo tank must be supported by external cradles. A cargo tank mounted on a motor vehicle frame must be supported by external cradles or longitudinal members. Where used, the cradles must subtend at least 120 degrees of the shell circumference.

(c) **The design calculations of the support elements** must satisfy the requirements of §178.337-3, (a), (b), (c), and (d).

(d) **Where any cargo tank support is attached to** any part of a cargo tank head, the stresses imposed upon the head must be provided for as required in paragraph (c) of this section.

§178.337-14 Gauging devices.

(a) **Liquid level gauging devices.** See §173.315(h) of this subchapter.

(b) **Pressure gauges.**

(1) *See §173.315(h) of this subchapter.*

(2) *Each cargo tank* used in carbon dioxide, refrigerated liquid or nitrous oxide, refrigerated liquid service must be provided with a suitable pressure gauge. A shut-off valve must be installed between the pressure gauge and the cargo tank.

(c) **Orifices.** See §173.315(h) (3) and (4) of this subchapter.

§178.337-15 Pumps and compressors.

(a) **Liquid pumps or gas compressors, if used,** must be of suitable design, adequately protected against breakage by collision, and kept in good condition. They may be driven by motor vehicle power take-off or other mechanical, electrical, or hydraulic means. Unless they are of the centrifugal type, they shall be equipped with suitable pressure actuated by-pass valves permitting flow from discharge to suction or to the cargo tank.

(b) **A liquid chlorine pump may not be installed** on a cargo tank intended for the transportation of chlorine.

§178.337-16 Testing.

(a) **Inspection and tests.** Inspection of materials of construction of the cargo tank and its appurtenances and original test and inspection of the finished cargo tank and its appurtenances must be as required by the ASME Code and as further required by this specification except that for cargo tanks constructed in accordance with part UHT of the ASME Code the original test pressure must be at least twice the cargo tank design pressure.

(b) **Weld testing and inspection.**

(1) *Each cargo tank* constructed in accordance with part UHT of the ASME Code must be subjected, after postweld heat treatment and hydrostatic tests, to a wet fluorescent magnetic particle inspection to be made on all welds in or on the cargo tank shell and heads both inside and out. The method of inspection must conform to Appendix VI of the ASME Code, paragraph UA-70 through UA-72 except that permanent magnets shall not be used.

(2) *On cargo tanks* of over 3,500 gallons water capacity other than those described in paragraph (b)(1) of this section unless fully radiographed, a test must be made of all welds in or on the shell and heads both inside and outside by either the wet fluorescent magnetic particle method conforming to appendix VI of the ASME Code, liquid dye penetrant method, or ultrasonic testing in accordance with appendix U of the ASME Code. Permanent magnets must not be used to perform the magnetic particle inspection.

(c) **All defects found shall be repaired,** the cargo tanks shall then again be postweld heat treated, if such heat treatment was previously performed, and the repaired areas shall again be tested.

§178.337-17 Marking.

(a) **Metal identification plate.** Each cargo tank built after July 1, 1985 shall have a corrosion resistant metal plate permanently affixed by brazing or welding around its perimeter, on the left side (on the right side prior to July 1, 1985) near the front, in a place readily accessible for inspection. It must be maintained in a legible condition. On multi-cargo tank motor vehicles plates shall be attached to each cargo tank at the front in a place readily accessible for inspection. Each insulated cargo tank shall have an additional plate, as described, affixed to the jacket in the location specified. Neither the plate itself nor the means of attachment to the cargo tank or jacket may be subject to attack by the cargo tank contents. If the plate is attached directly to the cargo tank by welding it shall be welded thereto before the cargo tank is postweld heat treated. The plate shall be plainly marked by stamping, embossing, or other means of forming letters into the metal of the plate, with the following information in addition to that required by the ASME Code, in characters at least 3/8 inch high:

Vehicle manufacturer.

Vehicle manufacturer's serial number.

D.O.T. specification number MC-331.

Vessel material specification number.

Water capacity in pounds (see NOTE 1).

Original test date.

NOTE 1: See §173.315(a) of this chapter regarding water capacity.

(b) **Each cargo tank must also be marked** as required by §172.328 of this subchapter.

FEDERAL REGISTER UPDATES

In the April 18, 2003 Federal Register, §178.337-17 was revised, effective October 1, 2003.

§178.337-17 **Marking.**

(a) **General.** Each cargo tank certified after October 1, 2004 must have a corrosion-resistant metal name plate (ASME Plate) and specification plate permanently attached to the cargo tank by brazing, welding, or other suitable means on the left side near the front, in a place accessible for inspection. If the specification plate is attached directly to the cargo tank wall by welding, it must be welded to the tank before the cargo tank is postweld heat treated.

(1) *The plates must be legibly marked* by stamping, embossing, or other means of forming letters into the metal of the plate, with the information required in paragraphs (b) and (c) of this section, in addition to that required by the ASME Code, in characters at least 3/16 inch high (parenthetical abbreviations may be used). All plates must be maintained in a legible condition.

(2) *Each insulated cargo tank* must have additional plates, as described, attached to the jacket in the location specified unless the specification plate is attached to the chassis and has the information required in paragraphs (b) and (c) of this section.

(3) *The information required* for both the name and specification plate may be displayed on a single plate. If the information required by this section is displayed on a plate required by the ASME, the information need not be repeated on the name and specification plates.

(4) *The specification plate* may be attached to the cargo tank motor vehicle chassis rail by brazing, welding, or other suitable means on the left side near the front head, in a place accessible for inspection. If the specification plate is attached to the chassis rail, then the cargo tank serial number assigned by the cargo tank manufacturer must be included on the plate.

(b) **Name plate.** The following information must be marked on the name plate in accordance with this section:

(1) *DOT-specification number MC 331 (DOT MC 331).*

(2) *Original test date (Orig, Test Date).*

(3) *MAWP in psig.*

(4) *Cargo tank test pressure (Test P), in psig.*

(5) *Cargo tank design temperature (Design Temp. Range)* ____ °F to ____ °F.

(6) *Nominal capacity (Water Cap.), in pounds.*

(7) *Maximum design density of lading* (Max. Lading density), in pounds per gallon.

(8) *Material specification number-shell* (Shell matl, yyy * * *), where "yyy" is replaced by the alloy designation and "* * *" is replaced by the alloy type.

(9) *Material specification number-heads* (Head matl. Yyy * * *), where "yyy" is replaced by the alloy designation and "* * *" by the alloy type.

NOTE: When the shell and heads materials are the same thickness, they may be combined, (Shell & head matl, yyy * * *).

(10) *Weld material (Weld matl.).*

(11) *Minimum Thickness-shell* (Min. Shell-thick), in inches. When minimum shell thicknesses are not the same for different areas, show (top ___, side ___, bottom ___, in inches).

(12) *Minimum thickness-heads (Min heads thick.), in inches.*

(13) *Manufactured thickness-shell (Mfd. Shell thick.),* top ___, side ___, bottom ___, in inches. (Required when additional thickness is provided for corrosion allowance.)

(14) *Manufactured thickness-heads* (Mfd. Heads thick.), in inches. (Required when additional thickness is provided for corrosion allowance.)

(15) *Exposed surface area, in square feet.*

(c) **Specification plate.** The following information must be marked on the specification plate in accordance with this section:

(1) *Cargo tank motor vehicle manufacturer (CTMV mfr.).*

(2) *Cargo tank motor vehicle certification date (CTMV cert. date).*

(3) *Cargo tank manufacturer (CT mfr.).*

(4) *Cargo tank date of manufacture (CT date of mfr.), month and year.*

(continued on next page)

(continued from previous page)

(5) *Maximum weight of lading (Max. Payload), in pounds*
(6) *Maximum loading rate in gallons per minute (Max. Load rate, GPM).*
(7) *Maximum unloading rate in gallons per minute* (Max Unload rate, GPM).
(8) *Lining materials (Lining), if applicable.*
(9) *Heating system design pressure (Heating sys, press.), in psig, if applicable.*
(10) *Heating system design temperature (Heating sys, temp.), in °F, if applicable.*
(11) *Cargo tank serial number,* assigned by cargo tank manufacturer (CT serial), if applicable.

NOTE 1 to paragraph (c): See 173.315(a) of this chapter regarding water capacity.
NOTE 2 to paragraph (c): When the shell and head materials are the same thickness, they may be combined (Shell & head matl, yyy * * *).

(d) The design weight of lading used in determining the loading in §§178.337(3)(b), 178.337-10(b) and (c), and 178.337-13(a) and (b) must be shown as the maximum weight of lading marking required by paragraph (c) of this section.

§178.337-18 Certification.

(a) At or before the time of delivery, the cargo tank motor vehicle manufacturer must supply and the owner must obtain, a cargo tank motor vehicle manufacturer's data report as required by the ASME Code, and a certificate stating that the completed cargo tank motor vehicle conforms in all respects to Specification MC 331 and the ASME Code. The registration numbers of the manufacturer, the Design Certifying Engineer, and the Registered Inspector, as appropriate, must appear on the certificates (see subpart F, part 107 in subchapter A of this chapter).

(1) *For each design type,* the certificate must be signed by a responsible official of the manufacturer and a Design Certifying Engineer; and

(2) *For each cargo tank motor vehicle,* the certificate must be signed by a responsible official of the manufacturer and a Registered Inspector.

(3) *The certificate* must state whether or not it includes certification that all valves, piping, and protective devices conform to the requirements of the specification. If it does not so certify, the installer of any such valve, piping, or device shall supply and the owner shall obtain a certificate asserting complete compliance with these specifications for such devices. The certificate, or certificates, will include sufficient sketches, drawings, and other information to indicate the location, make, model, and size of each valve and the arrangement of all piping associated with the cargo tank.

(4) *The certificate* must contain a statement indicating whether or not the cargo tank was postweld heat treated for anhydrous ammonia as specified in §178.337-1(f).

(b) The owner shall retain the copy of the data report and certificates and related papers in his files throughout his ownership of the cargo tank motor vehicle and for at least one year thereafter; and in the event of change in ownership, retention by the prior owner of nonfading photographically reproduced copies will be deemed to satisfy this requirement. Each motor carrier using the cargo tank motor vehicle, if not the owner thereof, shall obtain a copy of the data report and certificate and retain them in his files during the time he uses the cargo tank motor vehicle and for at least one year thereafter.

FEDERAL REGISTER UPDATES

In the April 18, 2003 Federal Register, §178.337-18 was revised, effective October 1, 2003.

(a) [1]

(3) *When a cargo tank motor vehicle* is manufactured in two or more stages, each manufacturer who performs a manufacturing function or portion thereof on the incomplete cargo tank motor vehicle must provide to the succeeding manufacturer, at or before the time of delivery, a certificate that states the function performed by the manufacturer, including any certificates received from previous manufacturers, Registered Inspectors, and Design Certifying Engineers. [2]

(4) *Specification shortages.* When a cargo tank motor vehicle is manufactured in two or more stages, the manufacturer of the cargo tank must attach the name plate and specification plate as required by §178.337-17(a) and (b) without the original date of certification stamped on the specification plate. Prior manufacturers must list the specification requirements that are not completed on the Certificate of Compliance. When the cargo tank motor vehicle is brought into full compliance with the applicable specification, the cargo tank motor vehicle manufacturer must have a Registered Inspector stamp the date of certification on the specification plate and issue a Certificate of Compliance to the owner of the cargo tank motor vehicle. The Certificate of Compliance must list the actions taken to bring the cargo tank motor vehicle into full compliance. In addition, the certificate must include the date of certification and the person (manufacturer, carrier or repair organization) accomplishing compliance.

1. Paragraph (a) is the same as before.
2. Paragraphs (a)(3) and (a)(4) were redesignated as paragraphs (a)(5) and (a)(6) respectively, and new paragraphs (a)(3) and (a)(4) were added.

§178.338 Specification MC-338; insulated cargo tank motor vehicle.

§178.338-1 General requirements.

(a) For the purposes of this section —

(1) **Design pressure** means the "MAWP" as used in the ASME Code, and is the gauge pressure at the top of the tank.

(2) **Design service temperature** means the coldest temperature for which the tank is suitable (see §§173.318 (a)(1) and (f) of this subchapter).

(b) Each cargo tank must consist of a suitably supported welded inner vessel enclosed within an outer shell or jacket, with insulation between the inner vessel and outer shell or jacket, and having piping, valves, supports and other appurtenances as specified in this subchapter. For the purpose of this specification, tank means inner vessel and jacket means either the outer shell or insulation cover.

(c) Each tank must be designed and constructed to meet the requirements of the ASME Code.

(1) *The design pressure* of the tank must be at least 25.3 psig but not more than 500 psig. To determine the required thicknesses of the parts of the tank, the static head of the lading shall be added to the design pressure. If the jacket is evacuated, the tank must be designed for a pressure of 14.7 psi, plus the lading static head, higher than its design pressure. The jacket must be designed in accordance with paragraph (e) or (f) of this section, as appropriate.

(2) *The design service temperature* of the tank, piping and valves may not be warmer than the liquefaction temperature at one atmosphere of the lading to be transported (see §§173.318 (a)(1) and (f) of this subchapter).

(3) *Design and construction details* of the tank interior may not allow collection and retention of cleaning materials or contaminants. To preclude the entrapment of foreign material, the design and construction of the tank must allow washing of all interior surfaces by the normal surging of the lading during transportation.

(d) The exterior surface of the tank must be insulated with a material compatible with the lading.

(1) *Each cargo tank* must have an insulation system that will prevent the tank pressure from exceeding the pressure relief valve set pressure within the specified holding time when the tank is loaded with the specific cryogenic liquid at the design conditions of —

(i) *The specified* temperature and pressure of the cryogenic liquid, and

(ii) *The exposure* of the filled cargo tank to an average ambient temperature of 85 °F.

(2) *For a cargo tank* used to transport oxygen, the insulation may not sustain combustion in a 99.5 percent oxygen atmosphere at atmospheric pressure when contacted with a continuously heated glowing platinum wire. The cargo tank must be marked in accordance with §178.338-18(b)(7).

(3) *Each vacuum-insulated cargo tank* must be provided with a connection for a vacuum gauge to indicate the absolute pressure within the insulation space.

(e) The insulation must be completely covered by a metal jacket. The jacket or the insulation must be so constructed and sealed as to prevent moisture from coming into contact with the insulation (see §173.318(a)(3) of this subchapter). Minimum metal thicknesses are as follows:

Type metal	Jacket evacuated		Jacket not evacuated	
	Gauge	Inches	Gauge	Inches
Stainless steel	18	0.0428	22	0.0269
Low carbon mild steel	12	0.0946	14	0.0677
Aluminum		0.125		0.1000

(f) An evacuated jacket must be in compliance with the following requirements:

(1) *The jacket* must be designed to sustain a minimum critical collapsing pressure of 30 psig.

(2) *If the jacket* also supports additional loads, such as the weight of the tank and lading, the combined stress, computed according to the formula in §178.338-3(b), may not exceed 25 percent of the minimum specified tensile strength.

§178.338-2 Material.

(a) **All material used in the construction of a tank** and its appurtenances that may come in contact with the lading must be compatible with the lading to be transported. All material used for tank pressure parts must conform to the requirements of the ASME Code. All material used for evacuated jacket pressure parts must conform to the chemistry and steelmaking practices of one of the material specifications of Section II of the ASME Code or the following ASTM Specifications: A 242, A 441, A 514, A 572, A 588, A 606, A 607, A 633, A 715.

(b) **All tie-rods, mountings, and other appurtenances** within the jacket and all piping, fittings and valves must be of material suitable for use at the lowest temperature to be encountered.

(c) **Impact tests are required on all tank materials,** except aluminum, and must be performed using the procedure prescribed in the ASME Code.

(d) **The direction of final rolling of the shell material** must be the circumferential orientation of the tank shell.

(e) **Each tank constructed in accordance with part UHT** of the ASME Code must be postweld heat treated as a unit after completion of all welds to the shell and heads. Other tanks must be postweld heat treated as required by the ASME Code. For all tanks the method must be as prescribed in the ASME Code. Welded attachments to pads may be made after postweld heat treatment.

(f) **The fabricator shall record the heat and slab numbers** and the certified Charpy impact values of each plate used in the tank on a sketch showing the location of each plate in the shell and heads of the tank. A copy of the sketch must be provided to the owner of the cargo tank and a copy must be retained by the fabricator for at least five years and made available, upon request, to any duly identified representative of the Department.

FEDERAL REGISTER UPDATES

In the April 18, 2003 Federal Register, §178.338-2(c) was revised, effective October 1, 2003.

(c) **Impact tests are required on all tank materials,** except materials that are excepted from impact testing by the ASME Code, and must be performed using the procedure prescribed in the ASME Code (incorporated by reference; see §171.7 of this subchapter).

§178.338-3 Structural integrity.

(a) **General requirements and acceptance criteria.**

(1) *Except as permitted* in paragraph (d) of this section, the maximum calculated design stress at any point in the tank may not exceed the lesser of the maximum allowable stress value prescribed in section VIII of the ASME Code, or 25 percent of the tensile strength of the material used.

(2) *The relevant physical properties* of the materials used in each tank may be established either by a certified test report from the material manufacturer or by testing in conformance with a recognized national standard. In either case, the ultimate tensile strength of the material used in the design may not exceed 120 percent of the minimum ultimate tensile strength specified in either the ASME Code or the ASTM standard to which the material is manufactured.

(3) *The maximum design stress* at any point in the tank must be calculated separately for the loading conditions described in paragraphs (b), (c), and (d) of this section. Alternate test or analytical methods, or a combination thereof, may be used in lieu of the procedures described in paragraphs (b), (c), and (d) of this section, if the methods are accurate and verifiable.

(4) *Corrosion allowance material* may not be included to satisfy any of the design calculation requirements of this section.

(b) **The static design and construction** of each tank must be in accordance with section VIII of the ASME Code. The tank design must include calculation of stresses due to design pressure, the weight of lading, the weight of structures supported by the tank wall, and the effect of temperature gradients resulting from lading and ambient temperature extremes. When dissimilar materials are used, their thermal coefficients must be used in calculation of the thermal stresses. Stress concentrations in tension, bending and torsion which occur at pads, cradles, or other supports must be considered in accordance with appendix G of the ASME Code.

(c) **Stresses resulting from static and dynamic loadings,** or a combination thereof, are not uniform throughout the cargo tank motor vehicle. The following is a simplified procedure for calculating the effective stress in the tank resulting from static and dynamic loadings. The effective stress (the maximum principal stress at any point) must be determined by the following formula:

$$S = 0.5 (S_y + S_x) \pm (0.25(S_y - S_x)^2 + S_s^2)^{0.5}$$

Where:

(1) S = effective stress at any given point under the most severe combination of static and dynamic loadings that can occur at the same time, in psi.

(2) S_y = circumferential stress generated by internal and external pressure when applicable, in psi.

(3) S_x = the net longitudinal stress, in psi, generated by the following loading conditions:

(i) *The longitudinal tensile stress generated by internal pressure;*

(ii) *The tensile or compressive stress* generated by the axial load resulting from a decelerative force applied independently to each suspension assembly at the road surface using applicable static loadings specified in §178.338-13 (b) and (c);

(iii) *The tensile or compressive stress* generated by the bending moment resulting from a decelerative force applied independently to each suspension assembly at the road surface using applicable static loadings specified in §178.338-13 (b) and (c);

(iv) *The tensile or compressive stress* generated by the axial load resulting from an accelerative force applied to the horizontal pivot of the fifth wheel supporting the vehicle using applicable static loadings specified in §178.338-13 (b) and (c);

(v) *The tensile or compressive stress* generated by the bending moment resulting from an accelerative force applied to the horizontal pivot of the fifth wheel supporting the vehicle using applicable static loadings specified in §178.338-13 (b) and (c); and

(vi) *The tensile or compressive stress* generated by a bending moment produced by a vertical force using applicable static loadings specified in §178.338-13 (b) and (c).

(4) S_s = The following shear stresses that apply, in psi,: The vectorial sum of the applicable shear stresses in the plane under consideration, including direct shear generated by the static vertical loading; direct lateral and torsional shear generated by a lateral accelerative force applied at the road surface, using applicable static loads specified in §178.338-13 (b) and (c)

(d) **In order to account for stresses due to impact** in an accident, the design calculations for the tank shell and heads must include the load resulting from the design pressure in combination with the dynamic pressure resulting from a longitudinal deceleration of "2g". For this loading condition the stress value used may not exceed the lesser of the yield strength or 75 percent of the ultimate tensile strength of the material of construction. For a cargo tank constructed of stainless steel, the maximum design stress may not exceed 75 percent of the ultimate tensile strength of the type steel used.

(e) **The minimum thickness of the shell or heads** of the tank must be 0.187 inch for steel and 0.270 inch for aluminum. However, the minimum thickness for steel may be 0.110 inches provided the cargo tank is:

(1) *Vacuum insulated, or*

(2) *Double walled* with a load bearing jacket designed to carry a proportionate amount of structural loads prescribed in this section.

(f) **Where a tank support is attached to any part** of the tank wall, the stresses imposed on the tank wall must meet the requirements in paragraph (a) of this section.

(g) **The design, construction, and installation** of an appurtenance to the cargo tank or jacket must be such that, in the event of its damage or failure, the lading retention integrity of the tank will not be adversely affected.

(1) *A lightweight attachment,* such as a conduit clip, brakeline clip or placard holder, must be constructed of a material of lesser strength than the cargo tank wall or jacket material and may not be more than 72 percent of the thickness of the material to which it is attached. The attachment may be secured directly to the cargo tank wall or jacket if the device is designed and installed in such a manner that, if damaged, it will not affect the lading retention integrity of the tank. The lightweight attachment must be secured to the cargo tank wall or jacket by continuous weld or in such a manner as to preclude formation of pockets, which may become sites for incipient corrosion. Attachments conforming with this paragraph are not authorized for cargo tanks constructed under part UHT of the ASME Code.

(2) *Except as prescribed in §178.338-3(g)(1),* the welding of any appurtenance to the cargo tank wall or jacket must be made by attachment of a mounting pad, so that there will be no adverse affect upon the lading retention integrity of the tank if any force is applied to the appurtenance, from any direction. The thickness of the mounting pad may not be less than that of the shell or head to which it is attached, and not more than 1.5 times the shell or head thickness. However, a pad with a minimum thickness of 0.187 inch may be used when the shell or head thickness is over 0.187 inch. If weep

holes or tell tale holes are used, the pad must be drilled or punched at its lowest point before it is welded. Each pad must —

(i) *Extend at least 2 inches* in each direction from any point of attachment of an appurtenance;

(ii) *Be attached* by a continuous weld around the pad except for a small gap at the lowest point for draining.

FEDERAL REGISTER UPDATES

In the April 18, 2003 Federal Register, §178.338-3 was revised, effective October 1, 2003.

(b) Static design and construction. [1]

(1) *The static design and construction* of each tank must be in accordance with Appendix G of Section VII, Division 1 of the ASME Code (incorporated by reference; see §171.7 of this subchapter). The tank design must include calculation of stress due to the design pressure, the weight of lading, the weight of structures supported by the tank wall, and the effect of temperature gradients resulting from lading and ambient temperature extremes. When dissimilar materials are used, their thermal coefficients must be used in calculation of the thermal stresses.

(2) *Stress concentrations* in tension, bending, and torsion which occur at pads, cradles, or other supports must be considered in accordance with Appendix G of Section VII, Division 1 of the ASME Code.

(g) The design, construction and installation of an attachment, appurtenance to the cargo tank or structural support member between the cargo tank and the vehicle or suspension component or accident protection device must conform to the following requirements: [2]

(1) *Structural members,* the suspension subframe, accident protection structures and external circumferential reinforcement devices must be used as sites for attachment of appurtenances and other accessories to the cargo tank, when practicable.

(2) *A lightweight attachment* to the cargo tank wall such as a conduit clip, brakeline clip, skirting structure, lamp mounting bracket, or placard holder must be of a construction having lesser strength than the cargo tank wall materials and may not be more than 72 percent of the thickness of the material to which it is attached. The lightweight attachment may be secured directly to the cargo tank wall if the device is designed and installed in such a manner that, if damaged, it will not affect the lading retention integrity of the tank. A lightweight attachment must be secured to the cargo tank shell or head by a continuous weld or in such a manner as to preclude formation of pockets that may become sites for corrosion. Attachments meeting the requirements of this paragraph are not authorized for cargo tanks constructed under part UHT, Section VIII, Division 1 of the ASME Code.

(3) *Except as prescribed* in paragraphs (g)(1) and (g)(2) of this section, the welding of any appurtenance the cargo tank wall must be made by attachment of a mounting pad so that there will be no adverse effect upon the lading retention integrity of the cargo tank if any force less than that prescribed in paragraph (b)(1) of this section is applied from any direction. The thickness of the mounting pad may not be less than that of the shell or head to which it is attached, and not more than 1.5 times the shell or head thickness. However, a pad with a minimum thickness of 0.187 inch may be used when the shell or head thickness is over 0.187 inch. If weep holes or tell-tale holes are used, the pad must be drilled or punched at the lowest point before it is welded to the tank. Each pad must:

(i) *Be fabricated from material* determined to be suitable for welding to both the cargo tank material and the material of the appurtenance or structural support member; a Design Certifying Engineer must make this determination considering chemical and physical properties of the materials and must specify filler material conforming to the requirements of the ASME Code (incorporated by reference; see §171.7 of this subchapter).

(ii) *Be preformed to an inside radius* no greater than the outside radius of the cargo tank at the attachment location.

(iii) *Extend at least 2 inches* in each direction from any point of attachment of an appurtenance or structural support member. This dimension may be measured from the center of the attached structural member.

(iv) *Have rounded corners,* or otherwise be shaped in a manner to minimize stress concentrations on the shell or head.

(v) *Be attached by continuous fillet welding.* Any fillet weld discontinuity may only be for the purpose of preventing an intersection between the fillet weld and a tank or jacket seam weld.

1. Paragraph (b) was revised.
2. Paragraph (g) was revised.

§178.338-4 Joints.

(a) All joints in the tank, and in the jacket if evacuated, must be as prescribed in the ASME Code, except that a butt weld with one plate edge offset is not authorized.

(b) Welding procedure and welder performance tests must be made in accordance with Section IX of the ASME Code. Records of the qualification must be retained by the tank manufacturer for at least five years and must be made available, upon request, to any duly identified representative of the Department, or the owner of the cargo tank.

(c) All longitudinal welds in tanks and load bearing jackets must be located so as not to intersect nozzles or supports other than load rings and stiffening rings.

(d) Substructures must be properly fitted before attachment and the welding sequence must minimize stresses due to shrinkage of welds.

(e) Filler material containing more than 0.05 percent vanadium may not be used with quenched and tempered steel.

(f) All tank nozzle-to-shell and nozzle-to-head welds must be full penetration welds.

(Approved by the Office of Management and Budget under control number 2137-0017)

§178.338-5 Stiffening rings.

(a) A tank is not required to be provided with stiffening rings, except as prescribed in the ASME Code.

(b) If a jacket is evacuated, it must be constructed in compliance with §178.338-1(f). Stiffening rings may be used to meet these requirements.

§178.338-6 Manholes.

(a) Each tank in oxygen service must be provided with a manhole as prescribed in the ASME Code.

(b) Each tank having a manhole must be provided with a means of entrance and exit through the jacket, or the jacket must be marked to indicate the manway location on the tank.

(c) A manhole with a bolted closure may not be located on the front head of the tank.

§178.338-7 Openings.

(a) The inlet to the liquid product discharge opening of each tank intended for flammable ladings must be at the bottom centerline of the tank.

(b) If the leakage of a single valve, except a pressure relief valve, pressure control valve, full trycock or gas phase manual vent valve, would permit loss of flammable material, an additional closure that is leak tight at the tank design pressure must be provided outboard of such valve.

§178.338-8 Pressure relief devices, piping, valves, and fittings.

(a) Pressure relief devices. Each tank pressure relief device must be designed, constructed, and marked in accordance with §173.318(b) of this subchapter.

(b) Piping, valves, and fittings.

(1) *The burst pressure* of all piping, pipe fittings, hoses and other pressure parts, except for pump seals and pressure relief devices, must be at least 4 times the design pressure of the tank. Additionally, the burst pressure may not be less than 4 times any higher pressure to which each pipe, pipe fitting, hose or other pressure part may be subjected to in service.

(2) *Pipe joints* must be threaded, welded or flanged. If threaded pipe is used, the pipe and fittings must be Schedule 80 weight or heavier. Malleable metals must be used in the construction of valves and fittings. Where copper tubing is permitted, joints shall be brazed or be of equally strong metal union type. The melting point of the brazing materials may not be lower than 1000 °F. The method of joining tubing may not reduce the strength of the tubing, such as by the cutting of threads.

(3) *Each hose coupling* must be designed for a pressure of at least 120 percent of the hose design pressure and so that there will be no leakage when connected.

(4) *Piping must be* protected from damage due to thermal expansion and contraction, jarring, and vibration. Slip joints are not authorized for this purpose.

(5) *All piping, valves and fittings* on a cargo tank must be proved free from leaks. This requirement is met when such piping, valves, and fittings have been tested after installation with gas or air and proved leak tight at not less than the design pressure marked on the cargo tank. This requirement is applicable to all hoses used in a cargo tank, except that hose may be tested before or after installation on the tank.

(6) *Each valve* must be suitable for the tank design pressure at the tank design service temperature.

(7) *All fittings* must be rated for the maximum tank pressure and suitable for the coldest temperature to which they will be subjected in actual service.

(8) *All piping, valves, and fittings* must be grouped in the smallest practicable space and protected from damage as required by §178.338-10.

(9) *When a pressure-building coil* is used on a tank designed to handle oxygen or flammable ladings, the vapor connection to that coil must be provided with a valve or check valve as close to the tank shell as practicable to prevent the loss of vapor from the tank in case of damage to the coil. The liquid connection to that coil must also be provided with a valve.

§178.338-9 Holding time.

(a) "Holding time" is the time, as determined by testing, that will elapse from loading until the pressure of the contents, under equilibrium conditions, reaches the level of the lowest pressure control valve or pressure relief valve setting.

(b) Holding time test.

(1) *The test* to determine holding time must be performed by charging the tank with a cryogenic liquid having a boiling point, at a pressure of one atmosphere, absolute, no lower than the design service temperature of the tank. The tank must be charged to its maximum permitted filling density with that liquid and stabilized to the lowest practical pressure, which must be equal to or less than the pressure to be used for loading. The cargo tank together with its contents must then be exposed to ambient temperature.

(2) *The tank pressure* and ambient temperature must be recorded at 3-hour intervals until the pressure level of the contents reaches the set-to-discharge pressure of the pressure control valve or pressure relief valve with the lowest setting. This total time lapse in hours represents the measured holding time at the actual average ambient temperature. This measured holding time for the test cryogenic liquid must be adjusted to an equivalent holding time for each cryogenic liquid that is to be identified on or adjacent to the specification plate, at an average ambient temperature of 85 °F. This is the rated holding time (RHT). The marked rated holding time (MRHT) displayed on or adjacent to the specification plate (see §178.338-18(b)(9)) may not exceed this RHT.

(c) Optional test regimen.

(1) *If more than one* cargo tank is made to the same design, only one cargo tank must be subjected to the full holding time test at the time of manufacture. However, each subsequent cargo tank made to the same design must be performance tested during its first trip. The holding time determined in this test may not be less than 90 percent of the marked rated holding time. This test must be performed in accordance with §§173.318(g)(3) and 177.840(h) of this subchapter, regardless of the classification of the cryogenic liquid.

(2) *Same design.* The term "same design" as used in this section means cargo tanks made to the same design type. See §178.320(a)(3) for definition of "design type".

(3) *For a cargo tank* used in nonflammable cryogenic liquid service, in place of the holding time tests prescribed in paragraph (b) of this section, the marked rated holding time (MRHT) may be determined as follows:

(i) *While the cargo tank is stationary,* the heat transfer rate must be determined by measuring the normal evaporation rate (NER) of the test cryogenic liquid (preferably the lading, where feasible) maintained at approximately one atmosphere. The calculated heat transfer rate must be determined from:

$q = [n(\Delta h)(85-t_1)] / [t_s - t_f]$

Where:

q = calculated heat transfer rate to cargo tank with lading, Btu/hr

n = normal evaporation rate (NER), which is the rate of evaporation, determined by the test of a test cryogenic liquid in a cargo tank maintained at a pressure of approximately one atmosphere, absolute, lb/hr

Δh = latent heat of vaporization of test fluid at test pressure, Btu/lb

t_s = average temperature of outer shell during test, °F

t_1 = equilibrium temperature of lading at maximum loading pressure, °F

t_f = equilibrium temperature of test fluid at one atmosphere, °F

(ii) *The rated holding time (RHT) must be calculated as follows:*

$RHT = [(U_2 - U_1) W] / q$

Where:

RHT = rated holding time, in hours

U_1 and U_2 = internal energy for the combined liquid and vapor lading at the pressure offered for transportation, and the set pressure of the applicable pressure control valve or pressure relief valve, respectively, Btu/lb

W = total weight of the combined liquid and vapor lading in the cargo tank, pounds

q = calculated heat transfer rate to cargo tank with lading, Btu/hr

(iii) *The MRHT* (see §178.338-18(b)(9) of this subchapter) may not exceed the RHT.

§178.338-10 Collision damage protection.

(a) All valves, fittings, pressure relief devices and other accessories to the tank proper, which are not isolated from the tank by closed intervening shut-off valves or check valves, must be installed within the motor vehicle framework or within a suitable collision resistant guard or housing, and appropriate ventilation must be provided. Each pressure relief device must be protected so that in the event of the upset of the vehicle onto a hard surface, the device's opening will not be prevented and its discharge will not be restricted.

(b) Each protective device or housing, and its attachment to the vehicle structure, must be designed to withstand static loading in any direction that it may be loaded as a result of front, rear, side, or sideswipe collision, or the overturn of the vehicle. The static loading shall equal twice the loaded weight of the tank and attachments. A safety factor of four, based on the tensile strength of the material, shall be used. The protective device or the housing must be made of steel at least 3/16-inch thick, or other material of equivalent strength.

(c) Each tank motor vehicle must be provided with at least one rear bumper designed to protect the cargo tank and piping in the event of a rear end collision. The bumper design must transmit the force of the collision directly to the chasis of the vehicle. The rear bumper and its attachments to the chasis must be designed to withstand a load equal to twice the weight of the loaded cargo tank and attachments, using a safety factor of four based on the tensile strength of the materials used, with such load being applied horizontally and parallel to the major axis of the cargo tank, or within 30 horizontal degrees thereof. The rear bumper dimensions must meet the requirements of §393.86 of this title and extend vertically to a height adequate to protect all valves and fittings located at the rear of the cargo tank from damage that could result in loss of lading.

(d) Every part of the loaded cargo tank, and any associated valve, pipe, enclosure, or protective device or structure (exclusive of wheel assemblies), must be at least 14 inches above level ground.

FEDERAL REGISTER UPDATES

In the April 18, 2003 Federal Register, §178.338-10 was revised, effective October 1, 2003.

§178.338-10 Accident damage protection. [1]

(c) Rear-end tank protection. Rear-end tank protections devices must: [2]

(1) *Consist of at least one rear bumper* designed to protect the cargo tank and piping in the event of a rear-end collision. The rear-end tank protection device design must transmit the force of the collision directly to the chassis of the vehicle. The rear-end tank protection device and its attachments to the chassis must be designed to withstand a load equal to twice the weight of the loaded cargo tank and attachments, using a safety factor of four based on the tensile strength of the materials used, with such load being applied horizontally and parallel to the major axis of the cargo tank. The rear-end tank protection device dimensions must meet the requirements of §393.86 of this title and extend vertically to a height adequate to protect all valves and fittings located at the rear of the cargo tank from damage that could result in loss of lading; or

(2) *Conform to the requirements of §178.345-8.*

1. The section heading was revised.
2. Paragraph (c) was revised.

§178.338-11 Discharge control devices.

(a) Excess-flow valves are not required.

(b) Each liquid filling and liquid discharge line must be provided with a shut-off valve located as close to the tank as practicable. Unless this valve is manually operable at the valve, the line must also have a manual shut-off valve.

(c) Except for a cargo tank used to transport the following refrigerated liquids: argon, carbon dioxide, helium, krypton, neon, nitrogen, and xenon; each liquid filling and liquid discharge line must be provided with a remotely controlled self-closing shut-off valve. This requirement does not apply to a cargo tank motor vehicle certified before January 1, 1995, unless intended for use to transport flammable ladings. If pressure from a reservoir or from an engine driven pump or compressor is used to open this valve, the control must be of fail-safe design, spring-biased to stop the admission of such pressure. If the jacket is not evacuated, the seat of the valve must be inside the tank, in the opening nozzle or flange, or in a companion flange bolted to the nozzle. If the jacket is evacuated, the remotely controlled valve must be located as close to the tank as practicable.

(1) *On a cargo tank* with a capacity in excess of 3,500 gallons of water, each remotely controlled shut-off valve must be provided with remote means of automatic closure, both mechanical and thermal, installed at the ends of the cargo tank in at least two diagonally opposite locations. The thermal means shall consist of fusible elements actuated at a temperature not exceeding 250 °F., or equivalent devices. One means may be used to close more than one remotely controlled valve.

(2) *On a cargo tank* with a capacity of 3,500 gallons of water or less, each remotely controlled shut-off valve must be provided with at least one remote control station on the end of the cargo tank opposite the main control station. The remote control station must contain a manual means of closure. In addition, it may contain fusible elements actuated at a temperature not exceeding 250 °F., or equivalent devices. One means may be used to close more than one remotely controlled valve.

FEDERAL REGISTER UPDATES

In the April 18, 2003 Federal Register, §178.338-11(c) was revised, effective October 1, 2003.

(c) **Except for a cargo tank that is used to transport** argon, carbon dioxide, helium, krypton, neon, nitrogen, xenon, or mixtures thereof, each liquid filling and liquid discharge line must be provided with an on-vehicle remotely controlled self-closing shutoff valve.

(1) *If pressure from a reservoir* or from an engine-driven pump or compressor is used to open this valve, the control must be of fail-safe design and spring-biased to stop the admission of such pressure into the cargo tank. If the jacket is not evacuated, the seat of the valve must be inside the tank, in the opening nozzle or flange, or in a companion flange bolted to the nozzle. If the jacket is evacuated, the remotely controlled valve must be located as close to the tank as practicable.

(2) *Each remotely controlled shut off valve* must be provided with on-vehicle remote means of automatic closure, both mechanical and thermal. One means may be used to close more than one remotely controlled valve. Cable linkage between closures and remote operators must be corrosion resistant and effective in all types of environment and weather. The thermal means must consist of fusible elements actuated at a temperature not exceeding 121 °C (250 °F), or equivalent devices. The loading/unloading connection area is where hoses are connected to the permanent metal piping. The number and location of remote operators and thermal devices shall be as follows:

(i) *On a cargo tank motor vehicle* over 3,500 gallons water capacity, remote means of automatic closure must be installed at the ends of the cargo tank in at least two diagonally opposite locations. If the loading/unloading connection at the cargo tank is not in the general vicinity of one of these locations, at least one additional thermal device must be installed so that heat from a fire in the loading/unloading connection area will activate the emergency control system.

(ii) *On a cargo tank motor vehicle* of 3,500 gallons water capacity or less, at least one remote means of automatic closure must be installed on the end of the cargo tank farthest away from the loading/ unloading connection area. At least one thermal device must be installed so that heat from a fire in the loading/unloading connection area will activate the emergency control system.

§178.338-12 Shear section.

Unless the valve is located in a rear cabinet forward of and protected by the bumper (see §178.338-10(c)), the design and installation of each valve, damage to which could result in loss of liquid or vapor, must incorporate a shear section or breakage groove adjacent to, and outboard of, the valve. The shear section or breakage groove must yield or break under strain without damage to the valve that would allow the loss of liquid or vapor. The protection specified in §178.338-10 is not a substitute for a shear section or breakage groove.

§178.338-13 Supports and anchoring.

(a) **All attachments of supports and bumpers** to tanks and to load-bearing jackets must be made by means of pads of material similar to that of the tank or jacket, by load rings, or by bosses designed or gusseted to distribute the load. The pad must be at least 1/4-inch thick, or as thick as the tank or jacket material, if less, but shall in no case be thicker than the tank or jacket material. Each pad must extend at least four times its thickness, in each direction, beyond the weld attaching the support or bumper. Each pad must be preformed to an inside radius no greater than the outside radius of the tank or jacket at the place of attachment. Each pad corner must be rounded to a radius at least one-fourth the width of the pad and no greater than one-half the width of the pad. If weep holes or telltale holes are used, they must be drilled or punched before the pads are attached. Each pad must be attached to the tank or jacket by continuous fillet welding using filler material having properties conforming to the recommendations of the manufacturer of the tank or jacket material. Any fillet weld discontinuity may only be for the purpose of preventing an intersection between the fillet weld and a tank or jacket seam weld.

(b) **A tank motor vehicle constructed so that** the cargo tank constitutes in whole or in part the structural member used in place of a motor vehicle frame must have the tank or the jacket supported by external cradles or by load rings. A cargo tank mounted on a motor vehicle frame must have the tank or jacket supported by external cradles, load rings, or longitudinal members. If cradles are used, they must subtend at least 120 degrees of the cargo tank circumference. The design calculations for the supports and load bearing tank or jacket, and the support attachments must include beam stress, shear stress, torsion stress, bending moment, and acceleration stress for the loaded vehicle as a unit, using a safety factor of four, based on the tensile strength of the material, and static loadings that take into consideration the weight of the cargo tank and its attachments when filled to the design weight of the lading (see appendix G of the ASME Code). The effects of fatigue must also be considered in the calculations. Minimum static loadings must be as follows:

(1) *For a vacuum-insulated cargo tank —*
- (i) *Vertically downward of 2;*
- (ii) *Vertically upward of 2;*
- (iii) *Longitudinally of 2; and*
- (iv) *Laterally of 2.*

(2) *For a nonvacuum-insulated cargo tank —*
- (i) *Vertically downward of 3;*
- (ii) *Vertically upward of 2;*
- (iii) *Longitudinally of 2; and*
- (iv) *Laterally of 2.*

(c) **When a loaded tank is supported** within the vacuum jacket by structural members, the design calculations for the tank and its structural members must be based on a safety factor of four and the tensile strength of the material at ambient temperature. The enhanced tensile strength of the material at actual operating temperature may be substituted for the tensile strength at ambient temperature to the extent recognized in the ASME Code for static loadings. Static loadings must take into consideration the weight of the tank and the structural members when the tank is filled to the design weight of lading (see appendix G of the ASME Code). When load rings in the jacket are used for supporting the tank, they must be designed to carry the fully loaded tank at the specified static loadings, plus external pressure. Minimum static loadings must be as follows:

(1) *Vertically downward of 2;*
(2) *Vertically upward of 1 1/2;*
(3) *Longitudinally of 1 1/2; and,*
(4) *Laterally of 1 1/2.*

FEDERAL REGISTER UPDATES

In the April 18, 2003 Federal Register, §178.338-13 was revised, effective October 1, 2003.

§178.338-13 **Supporting and anchoring.**

(a) **On a cargo tank motor vehicle designed and constructed** so that the cargo tank constitutes in whole or in part the structural member used in place of a motor vehicle frame, the cargo tank or the jacket must be supported by external cradles or by load rings. For a cargo tank mounted on a motor vehicle frame, the tank or jacket must be supported by external cradles, load rings, or longitudinal members. If cradles are used, they must subtend at least 120 degrees of the cargo tank circumference. The design calculations for the supports and load-bearing tank or jacket, and the support attachments must include beam stress, shear stress, torsion stress, bending moment, and acceleration stress for the loaded vehicle as a unit, using a safety factor of four, based on the tensile strength of the material, and static loading that uses the weight of the cargo tank and its attachments when filled to the design weight of the lading (see Appendix G of Section VIII, Division 1 of the ASME Code), multiplied by the following factors. The effects of fatigue must also be considered in the calculations. Minimum static loadings must be as follows:

(1) *For a vacuum-insulated cargo tank —*
- (i) *Vertically downward of 2;*
- (ii) *Vertically upward of 2;*
- (iii) *Longitudinally of 2; and*
- (iv) *Laterally of 2.*

(2) *For any other insulated cargo tank —*
- (i) *Vertically downward of 3;*
- (ii) *Vertically upward of 2;*
- (iii) *Longitudinally of 2; and*
- (iv) *Laterally of 2.*

(b) **When a loaded tank is supported** within the vacuum jacket by structural members, the design calculations for the tank and its structural members must be based on a safety factor of four and the tensile strength of the material at ambient temperature. The enhanced tensile strength of the material at actual operating temperature may be substituted for the tensile strength at ambient temperature to the extent recognized in the ASME Code for static loadings. Static loadings must take into consideration the weight of the tank and the structural members when the tank is filled to the design weight of lading (see Appendix G of Section VIII, Division 1 of the ASME Code), multiplied by the following factors. When load rings in the jacket are used for supporting the tank, they must be designed to carry the fully loaded tank at the specified static loadings, and external pressure. Minimum static loadings must be as follows:

(1) *Vertically downward of 2;*
(2) *Vertically upward of 1 1/2;*
(3) *Longitudinally of 1 1/2; and,*
(4) *Laterally of 1 1/2.*

§178.338-14 Gauging devices.

(a) Liquid level gauging devices.

(1) *Unless a cargo tank* is intended to be filled by weight, it must be equipped with one or more gauging devices, which accurately indicate the maximum permitted liquid level at the loading pressure, in order to provide a minimum of two percent outage below the inlet of the pressure control valve or pressure relief valve at the condition of incipient opening of that valve. A fixed-length dip tube, a fixed trycock line, or a differential pressure liquid level gauge must be used as the primary control for filling. Other gauging devices, except gauge glasses, may be used, but not as the primary control for filling.

(2) *The design pressure* of each liquid level gauging device must be at least that of the tank.

(3) *If a fixed length* dip tube or trycock line gauging device is used, it must consist of a pipe or tube of small diameter equipped with a valve at or near the jacket and extending into the cargo tank to a specified filling height. The fixed height at which the tube ends in the cargo tank must be such that the device will function when the liquid reaches the maximum level permitted in loading.

(4) *The liquid level* gauging device used as a primary control for filling must be designed and installed to accurately indicate the maximum filling level at the point midway of the tank both longitudinally and laterally.

(b) Pressure gauges. Each cargo tank must be provided with a suitable pressure gauge indicating the lading pressure and located on the front of the jacket so it can be read by the driver in the rear view mirror. Each gauge must have a reference mark at the cargo tank design pressure or the set pressure of the pressure relief valve or pressure control valve, whichever is lowest.

(c) Orifices. All openings for dip tube gauging devices and pressure gauges in flammable cryogenic liquid service must be restricted at or inside the jacket by orifices no larger than 0.060-inch diameter. Trycock lines, if provided, may not be greater than 1/2-inch nominal pipe size.

§178.338-15 Cleanliness.

A cargo tank constructed for oxygen service must be thoroughly cleaned to remove all foreign material in accordance with CGA Pamphlet G-4.1. All loose particles from fabrication, such as weld beads, dirt, grinding wheel debris, and other loose materials, must be removed prior to the final closure of the manhole of the tank. Chemical or solvent cleaning with a material compatible with the intending lading must be performed to remove any contaminants likely to react with the lading.

§178.338-16 Inspection and testing.

(a) General. The material of construction of a tank and its appurtenances must be inspected for conformance to the ASME Code. The tank must be subjected to either a hydrostatic or pneumatic test. The test pressure must be one and one-half times the sum of the design pressure, plus static head of lading, plus 14.7 psi if subjected to external vacuum, except that for tanks constructed in accordance with Part UHT of the ASME Code the test pressure must be twice the design pressure.

(b) Additional requirements for pneumatic test. A pneumatic test may be used in place of the hydrostatic test. Due regard for protection of all personnel should be taken because of the potential hazard involved in a pneumatic test. The pneumatic test pressure in the tank must be reached by gradually increasing the pressure to one-half of the test pressure. Thereafter, the test pressure must be increased in steps of approximately one-tenth of the test pressure until the required test pressure has been reached. Then the pressure must be reduced to a value equal to four-fifths of the test pressure and held for a sufficient time to permit inspection of the cargo tank for leaks.

(c) Weld inspection. All tank shell or head welds subject to pressure shall be radiographed in accordance with the ASME Code. A tank which has been subjected to inspection by the magnetic particle method, the liquid penetrant method, or any method involving a material deposit on the interior tank surface, must be cleaned to remove any such residue by scrubbing or equally effective means, and all such residue and cleaning solution must be removed from the tank prior to final closure of the tank.

(d) Defect repair. All cracks and other defects must be repaired as prescribed by the ASME Code. The welder and the welding procedure must be qualified in accordance with the ASME Code. After repair, the tank must again be postweld heat-treated, if such heat treatment was previously performed, and the repaired areas must be retested.

(e) Verification must be made of the interior cleanliness of a tank constructed for oxygen service by means that assure that all contaminants that are likely to react with the lading have been removed as required by §178.338-15.

§178.338-17 Pumps and compressors.

(a) Liquid pumps and gas compressors, if used, must be of suitable design, adequately protected against breakage by collision, and kept in good condition. They may be driven by motor vehicle power take-off or other mechanical, electrical, or hydraulic means. Unless they are of the centrifugal type, they shall be equipped with suitable pressure actuated by-pass valves permitting flow from discharge to suction to the tank.

(b) A valve or fitting made of aluminum with internal rubbing or abrading aluminum parts that may come in contact with oxygen, cryogenic liquid, may not be installed on any cargo tank used to transport oxygen, cryogenic liquid, unless the parts are anodized in accordance with ASTM Standard B 580 (incorporated by reference, see §171.7 of this subchapter).

§178.338-18 Marking.

(a) Nameplate. Each tank built after July 1, 1985 shall have a corrosion resistant metal plate permanently affixed by brazing or welding around its perimeter, on the left side (on the right side prior to July 1, 1985) near the front. If this nameplate is attached by welding, it must be welded before the tank is postweld heat-treated. The nameplate must be plainly marked by stamping, embossing, or other means of forming letters into the metal of the plate, in characters at least 3/8-inches high. The following information, in addition to that required by the ASME Code, must be included (parenthetical abbreviations may be used):

(1) *DOT Specification number MC-338 (DOT MC-338);*

(2) *Material specification number (Mat. Spec. No.);*

(3) *Maximum density of lading* for which the tank is designed (Max. Dens. of Lading);

(4) *Water capacity,* in pounds net at 60 °F, with the tank at its coldest operating temperature, after deduction for the volume above the inlet to the pressure relief device or pressure control valve, structural members, baffles, piping, and other appurtenances inside the tank (W. Cap.); and

(5) *Original test date (Orig. Test Date);*

(b) Specification plate. Each tank built after July 1, 1985 shall have an additional plate, in the form specified in paragraph (a) of this section. It must be welded, brazed, or riveted to the jacket on the left side (on the right side prior to July 1, 1985) near the front, or at the control station, in a position readily legible to operating personnel. It must be marked with the information specified in paragraph (a) of this section and in addition, in characters at least 3/8-inches high, the following (parenthetical abbreviations may be used):

(1) *Vehicle manufacturer (Veh. Mfr.);*

(2) *Manufacturer's vehicle serial number (Veh. No.);*

(3) *Lining material, if any (Lining);*

(4) *Date of manufacture (Date of Mfr.);*

(5) *Certificate date (Cert. Date);*

(6) *Design service temperature (Design Serv. Temp.);*

(7) *"Insulation for Oxygen Service"* or "Not Authorized for Oxygen Service," as appropriate;

(8) *Maximum weight of lading* for which the cargo tank is designed, in pounds (Max. Net Wt. ___ lbs.);

(9) *Marked rated holding time* for at least one cryogenic liquid, in hours, and the name of that cryogenic liquid (MRHT ___ hrs, name of cryogenic liquid). MRHT markings for additional cryogenic liquids may be displayed on or adjacent to the specification plate.

(c) The design weight of lading used in determining the loading in §§178.338-3(b), 178.338-10 (b) and (c), and 178.338-13 (b) and (c) must be shown as the maximum weight of lading marking required by paragraph (b) of this section.

FEDERAL REGISTER UPDATES

In the April 18, 2003 Federal Register, §178.338-18 was revised, effective October 1, 2003.

§178.338-18 Marking.

(a) General. Each cargo tank certified after October 1, 2004 must have a corrosion-resistant metal name plate (ASME Plate) and specification plate permanently attached to the cargo tank by brazing, welding, or other suitable means on the left side near the front, in a place accessible for inspection. If the specification plate is attached directly to the cargo tank wall by welding, it must be welded to the tank before the cargo tank is postweld heat treated.

(continued on next page)

(continued from previous page)

(1) *The plates must be legibly marked* by stamping, embossing, or other means of forming letters into the metal of the plate, with the information required in paragraphs (b) and (c) of this section, in addition to that required by the ASME Code (incorporated by reference; see §171.7 of this subchapter), in characters at least 3/16 inch high (parenthetical abbreviations may be used). All plates must be maintained in a legible condition.

(2) *Each insulated cargo tank* must have additional plates, as described, attached to the jacket in the location specified unless the specification plate is attached to the chassis and has the information required in paragraphs (b) and (c) of this section.

(3) *The information required* for both the name and specification plate may be displayed on a single plate. If the information required by this section is displayed on a plate required by the ASME Code, the information need not be repeated on the name and specification plates.

(4) *The specification plate* may be attached to the cargo tank motor vehicle chassis rail by brazing, welding, or other suitable means on the left side near the front head, in a place accessible for inspection. If the specification plate is attached to the chassis rail, then the cargo tank serial number assigned by the cargo tank manufacturer must be included on the plate.

(b) **Name plate.** The following information must be marked on the name plate in accordance with this section:

(1) *DOT-specification number MC 338 (DOT MC 338).*

(2) *Original test date (Orig, Test Date).*

(3) *MAWP in psig.*

(4) *Cargo tank test pressure (Test P), in psig.*

(5) *Cargo tank design temperature* (Design Temp. Range) ____ °F to ____ °F.

(6) *Nominal capacity (Water Cap.), in pounds.*

(7) *Maximum design density of lading* (Max. Lading density), in pounds per gallon.

(8) *Material specification number — shell* (Shell matl, yyy * * *), where "yyy" is replaced by the alloy designation and "* * *" is replaced by the alloy type.

(9) *Material specification number — heads* (Head matl. yyy * * *), where "yyy" is replaced by the alloy designation and "* * *" by the alloy type. Note: When the shell and heads materials are the same thickness, they may be combined, (Shell & head matl, yyy * * *).

(10) *Weld material (Weld matl.).*

(11) *Minimum Thickness-shell* (Min. Shell-thick), in inches. When minimum shell thicknesses are not the same for different areas, show (top ___, side ___, bottom ___, in inches).

(12) *Minimum thickness-heads (Min heads thick.), in inches.*

(13) *Manufactured thickness-shell* (Mfd. Shell thick.), top ___, side ___, bottom ___, in inches. (Required when additional thickness is provided for corrosion allowance.)

(14) *Manufactured thickness-heads* (Mfd. Heads thick.), in inches. (Required when additional thickness is provided for corrosion allowance.)

(15) *Exposed surface area, in square feet.*

(c) **Specification plate.** The following information must be marked on the specification plate in accordance with this section:

(1) *Cargo tank motor vehicle manufacturer (CTMV mfr.).*

(2) *Cargo tank motor vehicle certification date (CTMV cert. date).*

(3) *Cargo tank manufacturer (CT mfr.).*

(4) *Cargo tank date of manufacture (CT date of mfr.), month and year.*

(5) *Maximum weight of lading (Max. Payload), in pounds.*

(6) *Maximum loading rate in gallons per minute (Max. Load rate, GPM).*

(7) *Maximum unloading rate in gallons per minute (Max Unload rate).*

(8) *Lining materials (Lining), if applicable.*

(9) *"Insulated for oxygen service"* or "Not insulated for oxygen service" as appropriate.

(10) *Marked rated holding time* for at least one cryogenic liquid, in hours, and the name of that cryogenic liquid (MRHT ___ hrs, name of cryogenic liquid). Marked rated holding marking for additional cryogenic liquids may be displayed on or adjacent to the specification plate.

(11) *Cargo tank serial number (CT serial),* as assigned by cargo tank manufacturer, if applicable.

NOTE 1 to paragraph (c): See §173.315(a) of this chapter regarding water capacity.

NOTE 2 to paragraph (c): When the shell and head materials are the same thickness, they may be combined (Shell & head matl, yyy***).

(d) **The design weight of lading used in determining** the loading in §§178.338-3(b), 178.338-10(b) and (c), and 178.338-13(b) and (c) must be shown as the maximum weight of lading marking required by paragraph (c) of this section.

§178.338-19 Certification.

(a) **At or before the time of delivery,** the manufacturer of a cargo tank motor vehicle shall furnish to the owner of the completed vehicle the following:

(1) *The tank manufacturer's* data report as required by the ASME Code, and a certificate bearing the manufacturer's vehicle serial number stating that the completed cargo tank motor vehicle conforms to all applicable requirements of Specification MC 338, including the ASME Code in effect on the date (month, year) of certification. The registration numbers of the manufacturer, the Design Certifying Engineer, and the Registered Inspector, as appropriate, must appear on the certificates (See subpart F, part 107 in subchapter B of this chapter).

(i) *For each design type,* the certificate must be signed by a responsible official of the manufacturer and a Design Certifying Engineer; and

(ii) *For each cargo tank motor vehicle,* the certificate must be signed by a responsible official of the manufacturer and a Design Certifying Engineer;

(2) *A photograph,* pencil rub, or other facsimile of the plates required by paragraphs (a) and (b) of §178.338-18.

(b) **In the case of a cargo tank vehicle** manufactured in two or more stages, each manufacturer who performs a manufacturing operation on the incomplete vehicle or portion thereof shall furnish to the succeeding manufacturer, at or before the time of delivery, a certificate covering the particular operation performed by that manufacturer, and any certificates received from previous manufacturers, Registered Inspectors, and Design Certifying Engineers. The certificates must include sufficient sketches, drawings, and other information to indicate the location, make, model and size of each valve and the arrangement of all piping associated with the tank. Each certificate must be signed by an official of the manufacturing firm responsible for the portion of the complete cargo tank vehicle represented thereby, such as basic tank fabrication, insulation, jacket, or piping. The final manufacturer shall furnish the owner with all certificates, as well as the documents required by paragraph (a) of this section.

(c) **The owner shall retain the data report, certificates,** and related papers throughout his ownership of the cargo tank. In the event of change of ownership, the prior owner shall retain non-fading photographically reproduced copies of these documents for at least one year. Each operator using the cargo tank vehicle, if not the owner thereof, shall obtain a copy of the data report and the certificate or certificates and retain them during the time he uses the cargo tank and for at least one year thereafter.

§§178.340-178.343 [Reserved]

§178.345 General design and construction requirements applicable to Specification DOT 406 (§178.346), DOT 407 (§178.347), and DOT 412 (§178.348) cargo tank motor vehicles.

§178.345-1 General requirements.

(a) **Specification DOT 406, DOT 407 and DOT 412** cargo tank motor vehicles must conform to the requirements of this section in addition to the requirements of the applicable specification contained in §§178.346, 178.347 or 178.348.

(b) **All specification requirements are minimum requirements.**

(c) **Definitions.** The following terms apply to §§178.345, 178.346, 178.347 and 178.348.

Appurtenance means any cargo tank accessory attachment that has no lading retention or containment function and provides no structural support to the cargo tank.

Baffle means a non-liquid-tight transverse partition device that deflects, checks or regulates fluid motion in a tank.

Bulkhead means a liquid-tight transverse closure at the ends of or between cargo tanks.

Charging line means a hose, tube, pipe, or similar device used to pressurize a tank with material other than the lading.

Companion flange means one of two mating flanges where the flange faces are in contact or separated only by a thin leak sealing gasket and are secured to one another by bolts or clamps.

Connecting structure means the structure joining two cargo tanks.

Constructed and certified in conformance with the ASME Code means the cargo tank is constructed and stamped in accordance with the ASME Code, and is inspected and certified by an Authorized Inspector.

Constructed in accordance with the ASME Code means the cargo tank is constructed in accordance with the ASME Code with the authorized exceptions (see §§178.346, 178.347, and 178.348) and is inspected and certified by a Registered Inspector.

External self-closing stop-valve means a self-closing stop-valve designed so that the self-stored energy source is located outside the cargo tank and the welded flange.

Extreme dynamic loading means the maximum single-acting loading a cargo tank motor vehicle may experience during its expected life, excluding accident loadings.

Flange means the structural ring for guiding or attachment of a pipe or fitting with another flange (companion flange), pipe, fitting or other attachment.

Inspection pressure means the pressure used to determine leak tightness of the cargo tank when testing with pneumatic pressure.

Internal self-closing stop-valve means a self-closing stop-valve designed so that the self-stored energy source is located inside the cargo tank or cargo tank sump, or within the welded flange, and the valve seat is located within the cargo tank or within one inch of the external face of the welded flange or sump of the cargo tank.

Lading means the hazardous material contained in a cargo tank.

Loading/unloading connection means the fitting in the loading/unloading line farthest from the loading/unloading outlet to which the loading/unloading hose or device is attached.

Loading/unloading outlet means the cargo tank outlet used for normal loading/unloading operations.

Loading/unloading stop-valve means the stop valve farthest from the cargo tank loading/unloading outlet to which the loading/unloading connection is attached.

MAWP. See §178.345-1(k).

Multi-specification cargo tank motor vehicle means a cargo tank motor vehicle equipped with two or more cargo tanks fabricated to more than one cargo tank specification.

Normal operating loading means the loading a cargo tank motor vehicle may be expected to experience routinely in operation.

Nozzle means the subassembly consisting of a pipe or tubular section with or without a welded or forged flange on one end.

Outlet means any opening in the shell or head of a cargo tank, (including the means for attaching a closure), except that the following are not outlets: A threaded opening securely closed during transportation with a threaded plug or a threaded cap, a flanged opening securely closed during transportation with a bolted or welded blank flange, a manhole, or gauging devices, thermometer wells, and safety relief devices.

Outlet stop-valve means the stop-valve at the cargo tank loading/unloading outlet.

Pipe coupling means a fitting with internal threads on both ends.

Rear bumper means the structure designed to prevent a vehicle or object from under-riding the rear of a motor vehicle. See §393.86 of this title.

Rear-end tank protection device means the structure designed to protect a cargo tank and any lading retention piping or devices in case of a rear end collision.

Sacrificial Device means an element, such as a shear section, designed to fail under load in order to prevent damage to any lading retention part or device. The device must break under strain at no more than 70 percent of the strength of the weakest piping element between the cargo tank and the sacrificial device. Operation of the sacrificial device must leave the remaining piping and its attachment to the cargo tank intact and capable of retaining lading.

Self-closing stop-valve means a stop-valve held in the closed position by means of self-stored energy, which opens only by application of an external force and which closes when the external force is removed.

Shear section means a sacrificial device fabricated in such a manner as to abruptly reduce the wall thickness of the adjacent piping or valve material by at least 30 percent.

Shell means the circumferential portion of a cargo tank defined by the basic design radius or radii excluding the closing heads.

Stop-valve means a valve that stops the flow of lading.

Sump means a protrusion from the bottom of a cargo tank shell designed to facilitate complete loading and unloading of lading.

Tank means a container, consisting of a shell and heads, that forms a pressure tight vessel having openings designed to accept pressure tight fittings or closures, but excludes any appurtenances, reinforcements, fittings, or closures.

Test pressure means the pressure to which a tank is subjected to determine pressure integrity.

Toughness of material means the capability of a material to absorb the energy represented by the area under the stress strain curve (indicating the energy absorbed per unit volume of the material) up to the point of rupture.

Vacuum cargo tank means a cargo tank that is loaded by reducing the pressure in the cargo tank to below atmospheric pressure.

Variable specification cargo tank means a cargo tank that is constructed in accordance with one specification, but which may be altered to meet another specification by changing relief device, closures, lading discharge devices, and other lading retention devices.

Void means the space between tank heads or bulkheads and a connecting structure.

Welded flange means a flange attached to the tank by a weld joining the tank shell to the cylindrical outer surface of the flange, or by a fillet weld joining the tank shell to a flange shaped to fit the shell contour.

(d) **A manufacturer of a cargo tank must hold** a current ASME certificate of authorization and must be registered with the Department in accordance with part 107, subpart F of this chapter.

(e) **All construction must be certified** by an Authorized Inspector or by a Registered Inspector as applicable to the cargo tank.

(f) **Each cargo tank must be designed and constructed** in conformance with the requirements of the applicable cargo tank specification. Each DOT 412 cargo tank with a MAWP greater than 15 psig, and each DOT 407 cargo tank with a MAWP greater than 35 psig must be "constructed and certified in conformance with the ASME Code" except as limited or modified by the applicable cargo tank specification. Other cargo tanks must be "constructed in accordance with the ASME Code", except as limited or modified by the applicable cargo tank specification.

(g) **Requirements relating to parts and accessories** on motor vehicles, which are contained in part 393 of the Federal Motor Carrier Safety Regulations of this title, are incorporated into these specifications.

(h) **Any additional requirements prescribed in part 173** of this subchapter that pertain to the transportation of a specific lading are incorporated into these specifications.

(i) **Cargo tank motor vehicle composed of multiple cargo tanks.**

(1) *A cargo tank motor vehicle* composed of more than one cargo tank may be constructed with the cargo tanks made to the same specification or to different specifications. Each cargo tank must conform in all respects with the specification for which it is certified.

(2) *The strength* of the connecting structure joining multiple cargo tanks in a cargo tank motor vehicle must meet the structural design requirements in §178.345-3. Any void within the connecting structure must be vented to the atmosphere and have a drain located on the bottom centerline. Each drain must be accessible and must be kept open at all times. The drain in any void within the connecting structure of a carbon steel, self-supporting cargo tank may be either a single drain of at least 1.0 inch diameter, or two or more drains of at least 0.5 inch diameter, 6.0 inches apart, one of which is located on the bottom centerline.

(j) **Variable specification cargo tank.** A cargo tank that may be physically altered to conform to another cargo tank specification must have the required physical alterations to convert from one specification to another clearly indicated on the variable specification plate.

(k) **MAWP.** The MAWP for each cargo tank must be greater than or equal to the largest of the following (the MAWP derived is the pressure to be used as prescribed in the ASME Code in the design of the tank):

(1) *The pressure prescribed for the lading in part 173;*

(2) *Vapor pressure* of the most volatile lading, at 115 °F (expressed in psig), plus the maximum static pressure exerted by the lading at the maximum lading density, plus any pressure exerted by a gas padding (including air in the ullage space or dome), if used; or

(3) *The maximum pressure in the tank during loading or unloading.*

FEDERAL REGISTER UPDATES

In the April 18, 2003 Federal Register, §178.345-1 was revised, effective October 1, 2003.

(c) **Definitions.** See §178.320(a) for the definition of certain terms used in §§178.345, 178.346, 178.347 and 178.348. [1]

(k) **[Removed]** [2]

1. Paragraph (c) was revised.
2. Paragraph (k) was removed.

§178.345-2 Material and material thickness.

(a) **All material for shell, heads, bulkheads, and baffles** must conform to section II, parts A and B, of the ASME Code except as follows:

(1) *The following steels* are also authorized for cargo tanks "constructed in accordance with the ASME Code".

ASTM A 569
ASTM A 570
ASTM A 572
ASTM A 607
ASTM A 622
ASTM A 656
ASTM A 715

(2) *Aluminum alloys* suitable for fusion welding and conforming with the 0, H32 or H34 tempers of one of the following ASTM specifications may be used for cargo tanks "constructed in accordance with the ASME Code":

ASTM B-209 Alloy 5052
ASTM B-209 Alloy 5086
ASTM B-209 Alloy 5154
ASTM B-209 Alloy 5254
ASTM B-209 Alloy 5454
ASTM B-209 Alloy 5652

All heads, bulkheads and baffles must be of 0 temper (annealed) or stronger tempers. All shell materials shall be of H 32 or H 34 tempers except that the lower ultimate strength tempers may be used if the minimum shell thicknesses in the tables are increased in inverse proportion to the lesser ultimate strength.

(b) Minimum thickness. The minimum thickness for the shell and heads must be such that the maximum stress levels specified in §178.345-3 of this subpart are not exceeded. In no case may the shell or head thickness be less than that specified in the applicable specification.

(c) Corrosion or abrasion protection. When required by 49 CFR part 173 for a particular lading, a cargo tank or a part thereof, subject to thinning by corrosion or mechanical abrasion due to the lading, must be protected by providing the tank or part of the tank with a suitable increase in thickness of material, a lining or some other suitable method of protection.

(1) *Corrosion allowance.* Material added for corrosion allowance need not be of uniform thickness if different rates of attack can reasonably be expected for various areas of the cargo tank.

(2) *Lining.* Lining material must consist of a nonporous, homogeneous material not less elastic than the parent metal and substantially immune to attack by the lading. The lining material must be bonded or attached by other appropriate means to the cargo tank wall and must be imperforate when applied. Any joint or seam in the lining must be made by fusing the materials together, or by other satisfactory means.

FEDERAL REGISTER UPDATES

In the April 18, 2003 Federal Register, §178.345-2(b) was revised, effective October 1, 2003.

(b) Minimum thickness. The minimum thickness for the shell and heads (or baffles and bulkheads when used as tank reinforcement) must be no less than that determined under criteria for minimum thickness specified in §178.320(a).

§178.345-3 Structural integrity.

(a) General requirements and acceptance criteria.

(1) *The maximum calculated design stress* at any point in the cargo tank wall may not exceed the maximum allowable stress value prescribed in section VIII of the ASME Code, or 25 percent of the tensile strength of the material used at design conditions.

(2) *The relevant physical properties* of the materials used in each cargo tank may be established either by a certified test report from the material manufacturer or by testing in conformance with a recognized national standard. In either case, the ultimate tensile strength of the material used in the design may not exceed 120 percent of the minimum ultimate tensile strength specified in either the ASME Code or the ASTM standard to which the material is manufactured.

(3) *The maximum design stress* at any point in the cargo tank must be calculated separately for the loading conditions described in paragraphs (b) and (c) of this section. Alternate test or analytical methods, or a combination thereof, may be used in place of the procedures described in paragraphs (b) and (c) of this section, if the methods are accurate and verifiable.

(4) *Corrosion allowance material* may not be included to satisfy any of the design calculation requirements of this section.

(b) ASME Code design and construction. The static design and construction of each cargo tank must be in accordance with Section VIII, Division 1 of the ASME Code. The cargo tank design must include calculation of stresses generated by the MAWP, the weight of the lading, the weight of structures supported by the cargo tank wall and the effect of temperature gradients resulting from lading and ambient temperature extremes. When dissimilar materials are used, their thermal coefficients must be used in the calculation of thermal stresses.

(1) *Stress concentrations* in tension, bending and torsion which occur at pads, cradles, or other supports must be considered in accordance with Appendix G of Section VIII, Division 1 of the ASME Code.

(2) *Longitudinal compressive* buckling stress for ASME certified vessels must be calculated using paragraph UG-23(b), Section VIII, Division 1 of the ASME Code. For cargo tanks not required to be certified in accordance with the ASME Code, compressive buckling stress may be calculated using alternative analysis methods which are accurate and verifiable. When alternative methods are used calculations must include both the static loads described in this paragraph and the dynamic loads described in paragraph (c) of this section.

(c) Shell design. Shell stresses resulting from static or dynamic loadings, or combinations thereof, are not uniform throughout the cargo tank motor vehicle. The vertical, longitudinal, and lateral normal operating loadings can occur simultaneously and must be combined. The vertical, longitudinal and lateral extreme dynamic loadings occur separately and need not be combined.

(1) *Normal operating loadings.* The following procedure addresses stress in the cargo tank shell resulting from normal operating loadings. The effective stress (the maximum principal stress at any point) must be determined by the following formula:

$S = 0.5(S_y + S_x) \pm [0.25(S_y - S_x)^2 + S_s^2]^{0.5}$

Where:

(i) S = effective stress at any given point under the combination of static and normal operating loadings that can occur at the same time, in psi.

(ii) S_y = circumferential stress generated by the MAWP and external pressure, when applicable, plus static head, in psi.

(iii) S_x = The following net longitudinal stress generated by the following static and normal operating loading conditions, in psi:

[A] The longitudinal stresses resulting from the MAWP and external pressure, when applicable, plus static head, in combination with the bending stress generated by the static weight of the fully loaded cargo tank motor vehicle, all structural elements, equipment and appurtenances supported by the cargo tank wall;

[B] The tensile or compressive stress resulting from normal operating longitudinal acceleration or deceleration. In each case, the forces applied must be 0.35 times the vertical reaction at the suspension assembly, applied at the road surface, and as transmitted to the cargo tank wall through the suspension assembly of a trailer during deceleration; or the horizontal pivot of the truck tractor or converter dolly fifth wheel, or the drawbar hinge on the fixed dolly during acceleration; or anchoring and support members of a truck during acceleration and deceleration, as applicable. The vertical reaction must be calculated based on the static weight of the fully loaded cargo tank motor vehicle, all structural elements, equipment and appurtenances supported by the cargo tank wall. The following loadings must be included:

[1] The axial load generated by a decelerative force;

[2] The bending moment generated by a decelerative force;

[3] The axial load generated by an accelerative force; and

[4] The bending moment generated by an accelerative force; and

[C] The tensile or compressive stress generated by the bending moment resulting from normal operating vertical accelerative force equal to 0.35 times the vertical reaction at the suspension assembly of a trailer; or the horizontal pivot of the upper coupler (fifth wheel) or turntable; or anchoring and support members of a truck, as applicable. The vertical reaction must be calculated based on the static weight of the fully loaded cargo tank motor vehicle, all structural elements, equipment and appurtenances supported by the cargo tank wall.

(iv) S_s = The following shear stresses generated by the following static and normal operating loading conditions, in psi:

[A] The static shear stress resulting from the vertical reaction at the suspension assembly of a trailer, and the horizontal pivot of the upper coupler (fifth wheel) or turntable; or anchoring and support members of a truck, as applicable. The vertical reaction must be calculated based on the static weight of the fully loaded cargo tank motor vehicle, all structural elements, equipment and appurtenances supported by the cargo tank wall;

[B] The vertical shear stress generated by a normal operating accelerative force equal to 0.35 times the vertical reaction at the suspension assembly of a trailer; or the horizontal pivot of the upper coupler (fifth wheel) or turntable; or anchoring and support members of a truck, as applicable. The vertical reaction must be calculated based on the static weight of the fully loaded cargo tank motor vehicle, all structural elements, equipment and appurtenances supported by the cargo tank wall;

[C] The lateral shear stress generated by a normal operating lateral accelerative force equal to 0.2 times the vertical reaction at each suspension assembly of a trailer, applied at the road surface, and as transmitted to the cargo tank wall through the suspension assembly of a trailer, and the horizontal pivot of the upper coupler (fifth wheel) or turntable; or anchoring and support members of a truck, as applicable. The vertical reaction must be calculated based on the static weight of the fully loaded cargo tank motor vehicle, all structural elements, equipment and appurtenances supported by the cargo tank wall; and

[D] The torsional shear stress generated by the same lateral forces as described in paragraph (c)(1)(iv)(C) of this section.

(2) *Extreme dynamic loadings.* The following procedure addresses stress in the cargo tank shell resulting from extreme dynamic loadings. The effective stress (the maximum principal stress at any point) must be determined by the following formula:

$S = 0.5(S_y + S_x) \pm [0.25(S_y - S_x)^2 + S_s^2]^{0.5}$

Where:

(i) *S* = effective stress at any given point under a combination of static and extreme dynamic loadings that can occur at the same time, in psi.

(ii) S_y = circumferential stress generated by MAWP and external pressure, when applicable, plus static head, in psi.

(iii) S_x = the following net longitudinal stress generated by the following static and extreme dynamic loading conditions, in psi:

[A] The longitudinal stresses resulting from the MAWP and external pressure, when applicable, plus static head, in combination with the bending stress generated by the static weight of the fully loaded cargo tank motor vehicle, all structural elements, equipment and appurtenances supported by the tank wall;

[B] The tensile or compressive stress resulting from extreme longitudinal acceleration or deceleration. In each case the forces applied must be 0.7 times the vertical reaction at the suspension assembly, applied at the road surface, and as transmitted to the cargo tank wall through the suspension assembly of a trailer during deceleration; or the horizontal pivot of the truck tractor or converter dolly fifth wheel, or the drawbar hinge on the fixed dolly during acceleration; or the anchoring and support members of a truck during acceleration and deceleration, as applicable. The vertical reaction must be calculated based on the static weight of the fully loaded cargo tank motor vehicle, all structural elements, equipment and appurtenances supported by the cargo tank wall. The following loadings must be included:

[1] The axial load generated by a decelerative force;

[2] The bending moment generated by a decelerative force;

[3] The axial load generated by an accelerative force; and

[4] The bending moment generated by an accelerative force; and

[C] The tensile or compressive stress generated by the bending moment resulting from an extreme vertical accelerative force equal to 0.7 times the vertical reaction at the suspension assembly of a trailer, and the horizontal pivot of the upper coupler (fifth wheel) or turntable; or the anchoring and support members of a truck, as applicable. The vertical reaction must be calculated based on the static weight of the fully loaded cargo tank motor vehicle, all structural elements, equipment and appurtenances supported by the cargo tank wall.

(iv) S_s = The following shear stresses generated by static and extreme dynamic loading conditions, in psi:

[A] The static shear stress resulting from the vertical reaction at the suspension assembly of a trailer, and the horizontal pivot of the upper coupler (fifth wheel) or turntable; or anchoring and support members of a truck, as applicable. The vertical reaction must be calculated based on the static weight of the fully loaded cargo tank motor vehicle, all structural elements, equipment and appurtenances supported by the cargo tank wall;

[B] The vertical shear stress generated by an extreme vertical accelerative force equal to 0.7 times the vertical reaction at the suspension assembly of a trailer, and the horizontal pivot of the upper coupler (fifth wheel) or turntable; or anchoring and support members of a truck, as applicable. The vertical reaction must be calculated based on the static weight of the fully loaded cargo tank motor vehicle, all structural elements, equipment and appurtenances supported by the cargo tank wall;

[C] The lateral shear stress generated by an extreme lateral accelerative force equal to 0.4 times the vertical reaction at the suspension assembly of a trailer, applied at the road surface, and as transmitted to the cargo tank wall through the suspension assembly of a trailer, and the horizontal pivot of the upper coupler (fifth wheel) or turntable; or anchoring and support members of a truck, as applicable. The vertical reaction must be calculated based on the static weight of the fully loaded cargo tank motor vehicle, all structural elements, equipment and appurtenances supported by the cargo tank wall; and

[D] The torsional shear stress generated by the same lateral forces as described in paragraph (c)(2)(iv)(C) of this section.

(d) **In no case may the minimum thickness** of the cargo tank shells and heads be less than that prescribed in §178.346-2, §178.347-2, or §178.348-2, as applicable.

(e) **For a cargo tank mounted on a frame** or built with integral structural supports, the calculation of effective stresses for the loading conditions in paragraph (c) of this section may include the structural contribution of the frame or the integral structural supports.

(f) **The design, construction, and installation** of an appurtenance to the cargo tank must conform to the following requirements:

(1) *Structural members,* the suspension subframe, accident protection and external rings must be used as sites for attachment of appurtenances and other accessories to the cargo tank, when practicable.

(2) *A lightweight attachment* to the cargo tank wall, such as a conduit clip, brakeline clip, skirting structure, lamp mounting bracket, or placard holder, must be of a construction having lesser strength than the cargo tank wall materials and may not be more than 72 percent of the thickness of the material to which it is attached. The lightweight attachment may be secured directly to the cargo tank wall if the device is designed and installed in such a manner that, if damaged, it will not affect the lading retention integrity of the tank. A lightweight attachment must be secured to the cargo tank shell or head by continuous weld or in such a manner as to preclude formation of pockets, which may become sites for incipient corrosion.

(3) *Except as prescribed* in paragraphs (f)(1) and (f)(2) of this section, the welding of any appurtenance to the cargo tank wall must be made by attachment of a mounting pad, so that there will be no adverse effect upon the lading retention integrity of the cargo tank if any force less than that prescribed in §178.345-8(b)(1) of this subchapter is applied from any direction. The thickness of the mounting pad may not be less than that of the shell or head to which it is attached, and not more than 1.5 times the shell or head thickness. However, a pad with a minimum thickness of 0.187 inch may be used when the shell or head thickness is over 0.187 inch. If weep holes or tell-tale holes are used, the pad must be drilled or punched at its lowest point before it is welded. Each pad must —

(i) *Extend at least 2 inches* in each direction from any point of attachment of an appurtenance;

(ii) *Have rounded corners,* or otherwise be shaped in a manner to minimize stress concentrations on the shell or head; and

(iii) *Be attached by a continuous weld* around the pad except for a small gap at the lowest point for draining.

FEDERAL REGISTER UPDATES

In the April 18, 2003 Federal Register, §178.345-3 was revised, effective October 1, 2003.

(b) [1]

(3) *Cargo tank designers and manufacturers* must consider all of the conditions specified in §173.33(c) of this subchapter when matching a cargo tank's performance characteristic to the characteristic of each lading transported. [2]

(f) **The design, construction, and installation** of an attachment, appurtenance to a cargo tank, structural support member between the cargo tank and the vehicle or suspension component must conform to the following requirements: [3]

(1) *Structural members,* the suspension sub-frame, accident protection structures and external circumferential reinforcement devices must be used as sites for attachment of appurtenances and other accessories to the cargo tank, when practicable.

(2) *A lightweight attachment* to a cargo tank wall such as a conduit clip, brake line clip, skirting structure, lamp mounting bracket, or placard holder must be of a construction having lesser strength than the cargo tank wall materials and may not be more than 72 percent of the thickness of the material to which it is attached. The lightweight attachment may be secured directly to the cargo tank wall if the device is designed and installed in such a manner that, if damaged, it will not affect the lading retention integrity of the tank. A lightweight attachment must be secured to the cargo tank shell or head by continuous weld or in such a manner as to preclude formation of pockets which may become sites for corrosion.

(3) *Except as prescribed* in paragraphs (f)(1) and (f)(2) of this section, the welding of any appurtenance to the cargo tank wall must be made by attachment of a mounting pad so that there will be no adverse effect upon the lading retention integrity of the cargo tank if any force less than that prescribed in paragraph (b)(1) of this section is applied from any direction. The thickness of the mounting pad may not be less than that of the shell or head to which it is attached, and not more than 1.5 times the shell or head thickness. However, a pad with a minimum thickness of 0.187 inch may be used when the shell or head thickness is over 0.187 inch. If weep holes or tell-tale holes are used, the pad must be drilled or punched at the lowest point before it is welded to the tank.

(continued on next page)

(continued from previous page)

Each pad must:

(i) *Be fabricated* from material determined to be suitable for welding to both the cargo tank material and the material of the appurtenance or structural support member; a Design Certifying Engineer must make this determination considering chemical and physical properties of the materials and must specify filler material conforming to the requirements of the ASME Code (incorporated by reference; see §171.7 of this subchapter).

(ii) *Be preformed to an inside radius* no greater than the outside radius of the cargo tank at the attachment location.

(iii) *Extend at least 2 inches* in each direction from any point of attachment of an appurtenance or structural support member. This dimension may be measured from the center of the structural member attached.

(iv) *Have rounded corners,* or otherwise be shaped in a manner to minimize stress concentrations on the shell or head.

(v) *Be attached by continuous fillet welding.* Any fillet weld discontinuity may only be for the purpose of preventing an intersection between the fillet weld and the tank or jacket seam weld.

1. Paragraph (b) is the same as before.
2. Paragraph (b)(3) was added.
3. Paragraph (f) was revised.

§178.345-4 Joints.

(a) **All joints between the cargo tank shell, heads,** baffles, baffle attaching rings, and bulkheads must be welded in conformance with the ASME Code welding procedures.

(b) **Where practical all welds must be easily accessible for inspection.**

§178.345-5 Manhole assemblies.

(a) **Each cargo tank with capacity greater** than 400 gallons must be accessible through a manhole at least 15 inches in diameter.

(b) **Each manhole, fill opening and washout assembly** must be structurally capable of withstanding, without leakage or permanent deformation that would affect its structural integrity, a static internal fluid pressure of at least 36 psig, or cargo tank test pressure, whichever is greater. The manhole assembly manufacturer shall verify compliance with this requirement by hydrostatically testing at least one percent (or one manhole closure, whichever is greater) of all manhole closures of each type produced each 3 months, as follows:

(1) *The manhole,* fill opening, or washout assembly must be tested with the venting devices blocked. Any leakage or deformation that would affect the product retention capability of the assembly shall constitute a failure.

(2) *If the manhole,* fill opening, or washout assembly tested fails, then five more covers from the same lot must be tested. If one of these five covers fails, then all covers in the lot from which the tested covers were selected are to be 100% tested or rejected for service.

(c) **Each manhole, filler and washout cover** must be fitted with a safety device that prevents the cover from opening fully when internal pressure is present.

(d) **Each manhole and fill cover must be secured** with fastenings that will prevent opening of the covers as a result of vibration under normal transportation conditions or shock impact due to a rollover accident on the roadway or shoulder where the fill cover is not struck by a substantial obstacle.

(e) **Each manhole cover must be permanently marked** by stamping or other means with:

(1) *Manufacturer's name;*

(2) *Test pressure ____ psig;*

(3) *A statement* certifying that the manhole cover meets the requirements in §178.345-5.

(f) **All fittings and devices mounted on a manhole cover,** coming in contact with the lading, must withstand the same static internal fluid pressure and contain the same permanent compliance markings as that required for the manhole cover. The fitting or device manufacturer shall verify compliance using the same test procedure and frequency of testing as specified in §178.345-5(b).

FEDERAL REGISTER UPDATES

In the April 18, 2003 Federal Register, the introductory text to §178.345-5(e) was revised, effective October 1, 2003.

(e) **On cargo tank motor vehicles** manufactured after October 1, 2004, each manhole assembly must be permanently marked on the outside by stamping or other means in a location visible without opening the manhole assembly or fill opening, with:

§178.345-6 Supports and anchoring.

(a) **A cargo tank with a frame not integral** to the cargo tank must have the tank secured by restraining devices to eliminate any motion between the tank and frame that may abrade the tank shell due to the stopping, starting, or turning of the cargo tank motor vehicle. The design calculations of the support elements must include the stresses indicated in §178.345-3(b) and as generated by the loads described in §178.345-3(c). Such restraining devices must be readily accessible for inspection and maintenance, except that insulation and jacketing are permitted to cover the restraining devices.

(b) **A cargo tank designed and constructed** so that it constitutes, in whole or in part, the structural member used in lieu of a frame must be supported in such a manner that the resulting stress levels in the cargo tank do not exceed those specified in §178.345-3(a). The design calculations of the support elements must include the stresses indicated in §178.345-3(b) and as generated by the loads described in §178.345-3(c).

§178.345-7 Circumferential reinforcements.

(a) **A cargo tank with a shell thickness** of less than 3/8 inch must be circumferentially reinforced with bulkheads, baffles, ring stiffeners, or any combination thereof, in addition to the cargo tank heads.

(1) *Circumferential reinforcement* must be located so that the thickness and tensile strength of the shell material in combination with the frame and reinforcement produces structural integrity at least equal to that prescribed in §178.345-3 and in such a manner that the maximum unreinforced portion of the shell does not exceed 60 inches. For cargo tanks designed to be loaded by vacuum, spacing of circumferential reinforcement may exceed 60 inches provided the maximum unreinforced portion of the shell conforms with the requirements of Section VIII, Division 1 of the ASME Code.

(2) *Where circumferential joints* are made between conical shell sections, or between conical and cylindrical shell sections, and the angle between adjacent sections is less than 160 degrees, circumferential reinforcement must be located within one inch of the shell joint, unless otherwise reinforced with structural members capable of maintaining shell stress levels authorized in §178.345-3. When the joint is formed by the large ends of adjacent conical shell sections, or by the large end of a conical shell and a cylindrical shell section, this angle is measured inside the shell; when the joint is formed by the small end of a conical shell section and a cylindrical shell section, it is measured outside the shell.

(b) **Except for doubler plates and knuckle pads,** no reinforcement may cover any circumferential joint.

(c) **When a baffle or baffle attachment ring is used** as a circumferential reinforcement member, it must produce structural integrity at least equal to that prescribed in §178.345-3 and must be circumferentially welded to the cargo tank shell. The welded portion may not be less than 50 percent of the total circumference of the cargo tank and the length of any unwelded space on the joint may not exceed 40 times the shell thickness unless reinforced external to the cargo tank.

(d) **When a ring stiffener is used** as a circumferential reinforcement member, whether internal or external, reinforcement must be continuous around the circumference of the cargo tank shell and must be in accordance with the following:

(1) *The section modulus about the neutral* axis of the ring section parallel to the shell must be at least equal to that derived from the applicable formula:

I/C = 0.00027WL, for MS, HSLA and SS;

or

I/C = 0.000467WL, for aluminum alloys;

Where:

I/C = Section modulus in inches^3

W = Tank width, or diameter, inches

L = Spacing of ring stiffener, inches; i.e., the maximum longitudinal distance from the midpoint of the unsupported shell on one side of the ring stiffener to the midpoint of the unsupported shell on the opposite side of the ring stiffener.

(2) *If a ring stiffener* is welded to the cargo tank shell, a portion of the shell may be considered as part of the ring section for purposes of computing the ring section modulus. This portion of the shell may be used provided at least 50 percent of the total circumference of the cargo tank is welded and the length of any unwelded space on the joint does not exceed 40 times the shell thickness. The maximum portion of the shell to be used in these calculations is as follows:

Number of circumferential ring stiffener-to-shell welds	J[1]	Shell section
1		20t
2	Less than 20t	20t+J
2	20t or more	40t

1. where:
t = Shell thickness, inches;
J = Longitudinal distance between parallel circumferential ring stiffener-to-shell welds.

(3) *When used* to meet the vacuum requirements of this section, ring stiffeners must be as prescribed in the ASME Code.

(4) *If configuration* of internal or external ring stiffener encloses an air space, this air space must be arranged for venting and be equipped with drainage facilities which must be kept operative at all times.

(5) *Hat shaped* or open channel ring stiffeners which prevent visual inspection of the cargo tank shell are prohibited on cargo tank motor vehicles constructed of carbon steel.

§178.345-8 Accident damage protection.

(a) **General.** Each cargo tank motor vehicle must be designed and constructed in accordance with the requirements of this section and the applicable individual specification to minimize the potential for the loss of lading due to an accident.

(1) *Any dome,* sump, or washout cover plate projecting from the cargo tank wall that retains lading in any tank orientation, must be as strong and tough as the cargo tank wall and have a thickness at least equal to that specified by the appropriate cargo tank specification. Any such projection located in the lower 1/3 of the tank circumference (or cross section perimeter for non-circular cargo tanks) that extends more than half its diameter at the point of attachment to the tank or more than 4 inches from the cargo tank wall, or located in the upper 2/3 of the tank circumference (or cross section perimeter for non-circular cargo tanks) that extends more than 1/4 its diameter or more than 2 inches from the point of attachment to the tank must have accident damage protection devices that are:

(i) *As specified in this section;*

(ii) *125 percent* as strong as the otherwise required accident damage protection device; or

(iii) *Attached to the cargo tank* in accordance with the requirements of paragraph (a)(3) of this section.

(2) *Outlets, valves, closures,* piping, or any devices that if damaged in an accident could result in a loss of lading from the cargo tank must be protected by accident damage protection devices as specified in this section.

(3) *Accident damage protection devices* attached to the wall of a cargo tank must be able to withstand or deflect away from the cargo tank the loads specified in this section. They must be designed, constructed and installed so as to maximize the distribution of loads to the cargo tank wall and to minimize the possibility of adversely affecting the lading retention integrity of the cargo tank. Accident induced stresses resulting from the appropriate accident damage protection device requirements in combination with the stresses from the cargo tank operating at the MAWP may not result in a cargo tank wall stress greater than the ultimate strength of the material of construction using a safety factor of 1.3. Deformation of the protection device is acceptable provided the devices being protected are not damaged when loads specified in this section are applied.

(4) *Any piping* that extends beyond an accident damage protection device must be equipped with a stop-valve and a sacrificial device such as a shear section. The sacrificial device must be located in the piping system outboard of the stop-valve and within the accident damage protection device to prevent any accidental loss of lading. The device must break at no more than 70 percent of the load that would be required to cause the failure of the protected lading retention device, part or cargo tank wall. The failure of the sacrificial device must leave the protected lading retention device and its attachment to the cargo tank wall intact and capable of retaining product.

(5) *Minimum road clearance.* The minimum allowable road clearance of any cargo tank motor vehicle component or protection device located between any two adjacent axles on a vehicle or vehicle combination must be at least one-half inch for each foot separating such axles, and in no case less than 12 inches.

(b) **Each outlet, projection or piping located** in the lower 1/3 of the cargo tank circumference (or cross section perimeter for non-circular cargo tanks) that could be damaged in an accident that may result in the loss of lading must be protected by a bottom damage protection device, except as provided by paragraph (a)(1) of this section and §173.33(e) of this subchapter. Outlets, projections and piping may be grouped or clustered together and protected by a single protection device.

(1) *Any bottom damage protection device* must be able to withstand a force of 155,000 pounds (based on the ultimate strength of the material) from the front, side, or rear, uniformly distributed over each surface of the device, over an area not to exceed 6 square feet, and a width not to exceed 6 feet. Suspension components and structural mounting members may be used to provide all, or part, of this protection. The device must extend no less than 6 inches beyond any component that may contain lading in transit.

(2) *A lading discharge opening* equipped with an internal self-closing stop-valve need not conform to paragraph (b)(1) of this section provided it is protected so as to reasonably assure against the accidental loss of lading. This protection must be provided by a sacrificial device located outboard of each internal self-closing stop-valve and within 4 inches of the major radius of the cargo tank shell or within 4 inches of a sump, but in no case more than 8 inches from the major radius of the tank shell. The device must break at no more than 70 percent of the load that would be required to cause the failure of the protected lading retention device, part or cargo tank wall. The failure of the sacrificial device must leave the protected lading retention device or part and its attachment to the cargo tank wall intact and capable of retaining product.

(c) **Each closure for openings,** including but not limited to the manhole, filling or inspection openings, and each valve, fitting, pressure relief device, vapor recovery stop valve or lading retaining fitting located in the upper 2/3 of a cargo tank circumference (or cross section perimeter for non-circular tanks) must be protected by being located within or between adjacent rollover damage protection devices, or by being 125 percent of the strength that would be provided by the otherwise required damage protection device.

(1) *A rollover damage protection device* on a cargo tank motor vehicle must be designed and installed to withstand loads equal to twice the weight of the loaded cargo tank motor vehicle applied as follows: normal to the cargo tank shell (perpendicular to the cargo tank surface); and tangential (perpendicular to the normal load) from any direction. The stresses shall not exceed the ultimate strength of the material of construction. These design loads may be considered to be uniformly distributed and independently applied. If more than one rollover protection device is used, each device must be capable of carrying its proportionate share of the required loads and in each case at least one-fourth the total tangential load. The design must be proven capable of carrying the required loads by calculations, tests or a combination of tests and calculations.

(2) *A rollover damage protection device* that would otherwise allow the accumulation of liquid on the top of the cargo tank, must be provided with a drain that directs the liquid to a safe point of discharge away from any structural component of the cargo tank motor vehicle.

(d) **Rear-end protection.** Each cargo tank motor vehicle must be provided with a rear-end protection device to protect the cargo tank and piping in the event of a rear-end collision and reduce the likelihood of damage which could result in the loss of lading. The rear-end tank protection device must conform to the following requirements (Nothing in this paragraph shall be construed to relieve a manufacturer of responsibility for complying with the requirements of §393.86 of this title):

(1) *The rear-end cargo tank protection device* must be designed so that it can deflect at least 6 inches horizontally forward with no contact between any part of the cargo tank motor vehicle which contains lading during transit and with any part of the rear-end protection device, or with a vertical plane passing through the outboard surface of the protection device.

(2) *The dimensions* of the rear-end cargo tank protection device shall conform to the following:

(i) *The bottom surface* of the rear-end protection device must be at least 4 inches below the lower surface of any part at the rear of the cargo tank motor vehicle which contains lading during transit and not more than 60 inches from the ground when the vehicle is empty.

(ii) *The maximum width* of a notch, indentation, or separation between sections of a rear-end cargo tank protection device may not exceed 24 inches. A notched, indented, or separated rear-end protection device may be used only when the piping at the rear of the cargo tank is equipped with a sacrificial device outboard of a shut-off valve.

(iii) *The widest part* of the motor vehicle at the rear may not extend more than 18 inches beyond the outermost ends of the device or (if separated) devices on either side of the vehicle.

(3) *The structure* of the rear-end protection device and its attachment to the vehicle must be designed to satisfy the conditions specified in paragraph (d)(1) of this section when subjected to an impact of the cargo tank motor vehicle at rated payload, at a deceleration of 2 "g". Such impact must be considered as being uniformly applied in the horizontal plane at an angle of 10 degrees or less to the longitudinal axis of the vehicle.

(e) **Longitudinal deceleration protection.** In order to account for stresses due to longitudinal impact in an accident, the cargo tank shell and heads must be able to withstand the load resulting from the design pressure in combination with the dynamic pressure resulting from a longitudinal deceleration of 2 "g". For this loading condition, the allowable stress value used may not exceed the ultimate strength of the material of construction using a safety factor of 1.3. Performance testing, analytical methods, or a combination thereof, may be used to prove this capability provided the methods are accurate and verifiable. For cargo tanks with internal baffles, the decelerative force may be reduced by 0.25 "g" for each baffle assembly, but in no case may the total reduction in decelerative force exceed 1.0 "g".

FEDERAL REGISTER UPDATES

In the April 18, 2003 Federal Register, §178.345-8 was revised, effective October 1, 2003.

(a) [1]

(5) *Minimum road clearance.* The minimum road clearance of any cargo tank motor vehicle component or protection device located between any two adjacent axles on a vehicle or vehicle combination must be at least one-half inch for each foot separating the component or device from the nearest axle of the adjacent pair, but in no case less than twelve (12) inches, except that the minimum road clearance for landing gear or other attachments within ten (10) feet of an axle must be no less than ten (10) inches. These measurements must be calculated at the gross vehicle weight rating of the cargo tank motor vehicle. [2]

(d) **Rear-end tank protection.** Each cargo tank motor vehicle must be provided with a rear-end tank protection device to protect the cargo tank and piping in the event of a rear-end collision and reduce the likelihood of damage that could result in the loss of lading. Nothing in this paragraph relieves the manufacturer of responsibility for complying with the requirements of §393.86 of this title and, if applicable, paragraph (b) of this section. The rear-end tank protection device must conform to the following requirements: [3]

1. Paragraph (a) is the same as before.
2. Paragraph (a)(5) was revised.
3. Paragraph (d) introductory text was revised.

§178.345-9 Pumps, piping, hoses and connections.

(a) **Suitable means must be provided** during loading or unloading operations to ensure that pressure within a cargo tank does not exceed test pressure.

(b) **Each hose, piping, stop-valve,** lading retention fitting and closure must be designed for a bursting pressure of the greater of 100 psig or four times the MAWP.

(c) **Each hose coupling must be designed** for a bursting pressure of the greater of 120 psig or 4.8 times the MAWP of the cargo tank, and must be designed so that there will be no leakage when connected.

(d) **Suitable provision must be made to allow for** and prevent damage due to expansion, contraction, jarring, and vibration. Slip joints may not be used for this purpose in the lading retention system.

(e) **Any heating device, when installed,** must be so constructed that the breaking of its external connections will not cause leakage of the cargo tank lading.

(f) **Any gauging, loading or charging device,** including associated valves, must be provided with an adequate means of secure closure to prevent leakage.

(g) **The attachment and construction of each loading/unloading** or charging line must be of sufficient strength, or be protected by a sacrificial device, such that any load applied by loading/unloading or charging lines connected to the cargo tank cannot cause damage resulting in loss of lading from the cargo tank.

(h) **Use of a nonmetallic pipe, valve or connection** that is not as strong and heat resistant as the cargo tank material is authorized only if such attachment is located outboard of the lading retention system.

§178.345-10 Pressure relief.

(a) **Each cargo tank must be equipped** to relieve pressure and vacuum conditions in conformance with this section and the applicable individual specification. The pressure and vacuum relief system must be designed to operate and have sufficient capacity to prevent cargo tank rupture or collapse due to over-pressurization or vacuum resulting from loading, unloading, or from heating and cooling of lading.

(b) **Type and construction of relief systems and devices.**

(1) *Each cargo tank* must be provided with a primary pressure relief system consisting of one or more reclosing pressure relief valves. A secondary pressure relief system consisting of another pressure relief valve in parallel with the primary pressure relief system may be used to augment the total venting capacity of the cargo tank. Non-reclosing pressure relief devices are not authorized in any cargo tank except when in series with a reclosing pressure relief device. Gravity actuated reclosing valves are not authorized on any cargo tank.

(2) *When provided* by §173.33(c)(1)(iii) of this subchapter, cargo tanks may be equipped with a normal vent. Such vents must be set to open at not less than 1 psig and must be designed to prevent loss of lading through the device in case of vehicle overturn.

(3) *Each pressure relief system* must be designed to withstand dynamic pressure surges in excess of the design set pressure as specified in paragraphs (b)(3) (i) and (ii) of this section. Set pressure is a function of MAWP as set forth in paragraph (d) of this section.

(i) *Each pressure relief device* must be able to withstand dynamic pressure surge reaching 30 psig above the design set pressure and sustained above the set pressure for at least 60 milliseconds with a total volume of liquid released not exceeding one gallon before the relief device recloses to a leak-tight condition. This requirement must be met regardless of vehicle orientation. This capability must be demonstrated by testing. An acceptable test procedure is outlined in TTMA RP No. 81— "Performance of Spring Loaded Pressure Relief Valves on MC 306, MC 307, and MC 312 Tanks," May 24, 1989 edition.

(ii) *After August 31, 1995,* each pressure relief device must be able to withstand a dynamic pressure surge reaching 30 psig above the design set pressure and sustained above the design set pressure for at least 60 milliseconds with a total volume of liquid released not exceeding 1 L before the relief valve recloses to a leak-tight condition. This requirement must be met regardless of vehicle orientation. This capability must be demonstrated by testing. TTMA RP No. 81, cited in paragraph (b)(3)(i) of this section, is an acceptable test procedure.

(4) *Each reclosing pressure relief valve* must be constructed and installed in such a manner as to prevent unauthorized adjustment of the relief valve setting.

(5) *No shut-off valve or other device* that could prevent venting through the pressure relief system may be installed in a pressure relief system.

(6) *The pressure relief system* must be mounted, shielded and drainable so as to minimize the accumulation of material that could impair the operation or discharge capability of the system by freezing, corrosion or blockage.

(c) **Location of relief devices.** Each pressure relief device must communicate with the vapor space above the lading as near as practicable to the center of the vapor space. For example, on a cargo tank designed to operate in a level attitude, the device should be positioned at the horizontal and transverse center of the cargo tank; on cargo tanks sloped to the rear, the device should be located in the forward half of the cargo tank. The discharge from any device must be unrestricted. Protective devices which deflect the flow of vapor are permissible provided the required vent capacity is maintained.

(d) **Settings of pressure relief system.** The set pressure of the pressure relief system is the pressure at which it starts to open, allowing discharge.

(1) *Primary pressure relief system.* The set pressure of each primary relief valve must be no less than 120 percent of the MAWP, and no more than 132 percent of the MAWP. The valve must reclose at not less than 108 percent of the MAWP and remain closed at lower pressures.

(2) *Secondary pressure relief system.* The set pressure of each pressure relief valve used as a secondary relief device must be not less than 120 percent of the MAWP.

(e) **Venting capacity of pressure relief systems.** The pressure relief system (primary and secondary, including piping) must have sufficient venting capacity to limit the cargo tank internal pressure to not more than the cargo tank test pressure. The total venting capacity, rated at not more than the cargo tank test pressure, must be at least that specified in table I, except as provided in §178.348-4.

Table I - Minimum Emergency Vent Capacity
[In cubic feet free air/hour at 60 °F and 1 atm.]

Exposed area in square feet	Cubic feet free air per hour
20	15,800
30	23,700
40	31,600
50	39,500
60	47,400
70	55,300
80	63,300
90	71,200
100	79,100
120	94,900
140	110,700
160	126,500
180	142,300
200	158,100
225	191,300
250	203,100
275	214,300
300	225,100
350	245,700
400	265,000
450	283,200
500	300,600
550	317,300
600	333,300
650	348,800
700	363,700
750	378,200
800	392,200
850	405,900
900	419,300
950	432,300
1,000	445,000

NOTE 1: Interpolate for intermediate sizes.

(1) *Primary pressure relief system.* Unless otherwise specified in the applicable individual specification, the primary relief system must have a minimum venting capacity of 12,000 SCFH per 350 square feet of exposed cargo tank area, but in any case at least one fourth the required total venting capacity for the cargo tank.

(2) *Secondary pressure relief system.* If the primary pressure relief system does not provide the required total venting capacity, additional capacity must be provided by a secondary pressure relief system.

(f) **Certification of pressure relief devices.** The manufacturer of any pressure relief device, including valves, frangible (rupture) disks, vacuum vents and combination devices must certify that the device model was designed and tested in accordance with this section and the appropriate cargo tank specification. The certificate must contain sufficient information to describe the device and its performance. The certificate must be signed by a responsible official of the manufacturer who approved the flow capacity certification.

(g) **Rated flow capacity certification test.** Each pressure relief device model must be successfully flow capacity certification tested prior to first use. Devices having one design, size and set pressure are considered to be one model. The testing requirements are as follows:

(1) *At least 3 devices* of each specific model must be tested for flow capacity at a pressure not greater than the test pressure of the cargo tank. For a device model to be certified, the capacities of the devices tested must fall within a range of plus or minus 5 percent of the average for the devices tested.

(2) *The rated flow capacity* of a device model may not be greater than 90 percent of the average value for the devices tested.

(3) *The rated flow capacity* derived for each device model must be certified by a responsible official of the device manufacturer.

(h) **Marking of pressure relief devices.** Each pressure relief device must be permanently marked with the following:

(1) *Manufacturer's name;*

(2) *Model number;*

(3) *Set pressure, in psig; and*

(4) *Rated flow capacity, in SCFH at the rating pressure, in psig.*

FEDERAL REGISTER UPDATES

In the April 18, 2003 Federal Register, §178.345-10 was revised, effective October 1, 2003.

(a) **Each cargo tank must be equipped** to relieve pressure and vacuum conditions in conformance with this section and the applicable individual specification. The pressure and vacuum relief system must be designed to operate and have sufficient capacity to prevent cargo tank rupture or collapse due to over-pressurization or vacuum resulting from loading, unloading, or from heating and cooling of lading. Pressure relief systems are not required to conform to the ASME Code.[1]

(b) [2]

(3) [3]

(i) *Each pressure relief device* must be able to withstand dynamic pressure surge reaching 30 psig above the design set pressure and sustained above the set pressure for at least 60 milliseconds with a total volume of liquid released not exceeding one gallon before the relief device recloses to a leak-tight condition. This requirement must be met regardless of vehicle orientation. This capability must be demonstrated by testing. An acceptable method is outlined in TTMA RP No. 81-97 "Performance of Spring Loaded Pressure Relief Valves on MC 306, MC 307, MC 312, DOT 406, DOT 407, and DOT 412 Tanks" (incorporated by reference; see §171.7 of this subchapter).[4]

1. Paragraph (a) was revised.
2. Paragraph (b) is the same as before.
3. Paragraph (b)(3) is the same as before.
4. The last sentence of (b)(3)(i) was revised.

§178.345-11 Tank outlets.

(a) **General.** As used in this section, "loading/unloading outlet" means any opening in the cargo tank wall used for loading or unloading of lading, as distinguished from outlets such as manhole covers, vents, vapor recovery devices, and similar closures. Cargo tank outlets, closures and associated piping must be protected in accordance with §178.345-8.

(b) **Each cargo tank loading/unloading outlet** must be equipped with an internal self-closing stop-valve, or alternatively, with an external stop-valve located as close as practicable to the cargo tank wall. Each cargo tank loading/unloading outlet must be in accordance with the following provisions:

(1) *Each loading/unloading outlet* must be fitted with a self-closing system capable of closing all such outlets in an emergency within 30 seconds of actuation. During normal operations the outlets may be closed manually. The self-closing system must be designed according to the following:

(i) *Each self-closing system* must include a remotely actuated means of closure located more than 10 feet from the loading/unloading outlet where vehicle length allows, or on the end of the cargo tank farthest away from the loading/unloading outlet. The actuating mechanism must be corrosion-resistant and effective in all types of environment and weather.

(ii) *If the actuating system* is accidentally damaged or sheared off during transportation, each loading/unloading outlet must remain securely closed and capable of retaining lading.

(iii) *When required* by part 173 of this subchapter for materials which are flammable, pyrophoric, oxidizing, or Division 6.1 (poisonous liquid) materials, the remote means of closure must be capable of thermal activation. The means by which the self-closing system is thermally activated must be located as close as practicable to the primary loading/unloading connection and must actuate the system at a temperature not over 250 °F. In addition, outlets on these cargo tanks must be capable of being remotely closed manually or mechanically.

(2) *Bottom loading outlets* which discharge lading into the cargo tank through fixed internal piping above the maximum liquid level of the cargo tank need not be equipped with a self-closing system.

(c) **Any loading/unloading outlet extending beyond** an internal self-closing stop-valve, or beyond the innermost external stop-valve which is part of a self-closing system, must be fitted with another stop-valve or other leak-tight closure at the end of such connection.

(d) **Each cargo tank outlet that is not** a loading/unloading outlet must be equipped with a stop-valve or other leak-tight closure located as close as practicable to the cargo tank outlet. Any connection extending beyond this closure must be fitted with another stop-valve or other leak-tight closure at the end of such connection.

§178.345-12 Gauging devices.

Each cargo tank, except a cargo tank intended to be filled by weight, must be equipped with a gauging device that indicates the maximum permitted liquid level to within 0.5 percent of the nominal capacity as measured by volume or liquid level. Gauge glasses are not permitted.

§178.345-13 Pressure and leakage tests.

(a) **Each cargo tank must be pressure and leakage tested** in accordance with this section.

(b) **Pressure test.** Each cargo tank or cargo tank compartment must be tested hydrostatically or pneumatically. Each cargo tank of a multi-cargo tank motor vehicle must be tested with the adjacent cargo tanks empty and at atmospheric pressure. Each closure, except pressure relief devices and loading/unloading venting devices rated at less than the prescribed test pressure, must be in place during the test. If the venting device is not removed during the test, such device must be rendered inoperative by a clamp, plug or other equally effective restraining device, which may not prevent the detection of leaks, or damage the device. Restraining devices must be removed immediately after the test is completed.

(1) *Hydrostatic method.* Each cargo tank, including its domes, must be filled with water or other liquid having similar viscosity, the temperature of which may not exceed 100 °F. The cargo tank must then be pressurized as prescribed in the applicable specification. The pressure must be gauged at the top of the cargo tank. The prescribed test pressure must be maintained for at least 10 minutes during which time the cargo tank must be inspected for leakage, bulging, or other defect.

(2) *Pneumatic method.* A pneumatic test may be used in place of the hydrostatic test. However, pneumatic pressure testing may involve higher risk than hydrostatic testing. Therefore, suitable safeguards must be provided to protect personnel and facilities should failure occur during the test. The cargo tank must be pressurized with air or an inert gas. Test pressure must be reached gradually by increasing the pressure to one half of test pressure. Thereafter, the pressure must be increased in steps of approximately one tenth of the test pressure until test pressure is reached. Test pressure must be held for at least 5 minutes. The pressure must then be reduced to the inspection pressure which must be maintained while the entire cargo tank surface is inspected for leakage and other sign of defects. The inspection method must consist of coating all joints and fittings with a solution of soap and water or other equally sensitive method.

(c) **Leakage test.** The cargo tank with all its accessories in place and operable must be leak tested at not less than 80 percent of tank's MAWP with the pressure maintained for at least 5 minutes.

(d) **Any cargo tank that leaks, bulges or shows** any other sign of defect must be rejected. Rejected cargo tanks must be suitably repaired and retested successfully prior to being returned to service. The retest after any repair must use the same method of test under which the cargo tank was originally rejected.

FEDERAL REGISTER UPDATES

In the April 18, 2003 Federal Register, §178.345-13(a) was revised, effective October 1, 2003.

(a) **Each cargo tank must be pressure and leakage tested** in accordance with this section and §§178.346-5, 178.347-5, or 178.348-5.

§178.345-14 Marking.

(a) **General.** The manufacturer shall certify that each cargo tank motor vehicle has been designed, constructed and tested in accordance with the applicable Specification DOT 406, DOT 407 or DOT 412 (§§178.345, 178.346, 178.347, 178.348) cargo tank requirements, and when applicable, with the ASME Code. The certification shall be accomplished by marking the cargo tank as prescribed in paragraphs (b) and (c) of this section, and by preparing the certificate prescribed in §178.345-15. Metal plates prescribed by paragraphs (b), (c), (d) and (e) of this section, must be permanently attached to the cargo tank or its integral supporting structure, by brazing, welding or other suitable means. These plates must be affixed on the left side of the vehicle near the front of the cargo tank (or the frontmost cargo tank of a multi-cargo tank motor vehicle), in a place readily accessible for inspection. The plates must be permanently and plainly marked in English by stamping, embossing or other means in characters at least 3/16 inch high. The information required by paragraphs (b) and (c) of this section may be combined on one specification plate.

(b) **Nameplate.** Each cargo tank must have a corrosion resistant nameplate permanently attached to it. The following information, in addition to any applicable information required by the ASME Code, must be marked on the tank nameplate (parenthetical abbreviations may be used):

(1) *DOT Specification number* DOT XXX (DOT XXX), where "XXX" is replaced with the applicable specification number.

(2) *Original test date, month and year (Orig. Test Date).*

(3) *Tank MAWP in psig.*

(4) *Cargo tank test pressure (Test P), in psig.*

(5) *Cargo tank design* temperature range (Design temp. range),__ °F to __ °F.

(6) *Nominal capacity (Water cap.), in gallons.*

(7) *Maximum design* density of lading (Max. lading density), in pounds per gallon.

(8) *Material specification number — shell* (Shell matl, yyy***), where "yyy" is replaced by the alloy designation and "***" by the alloy type.

(9) *Material specification number — heads* (Head matl, yyy***), where "yyy" is replaced by the alloy designation and "***" by the alloy type.

NOTE: When the shell and heads materials are the same thickness, they may be combined, (Shell&head matl, yyy***).

(10) *Weld material (Weld matl.).*

(11) *Minimum thickness — shell* (Min. shell-thick), in inches. When minimum shell thicknesses are not the same for different areas, show (top __, side __, bottom __, in inches).

(12) *Minimum thickness — heads (Min. heads thick.), in inches.*

(13) *Manufactured thickness — shell* (Mfd. shell thick.), top __, side __, bottom __, in inches. (Required when additional thickness is provided for corrosion allowance.)

(14) *Manufactured thickness — heads* (Mfd. heads thick.), in inches. (Required when additional thickness is provided for corrosion allowance.)

(15) *Exposed surface area, in square feet.*

(c) **Specification plate.** Each cargo tank motor vehicle must have an additional corrosion resistant metal specification plate attached to it. The specification plate must contain the following information (parenthetical abbreviations may be used):

(1) *Cargo tank motor vehicle manufacturer (CTMV mfr.).*

(2) *Cargo tank motor vehicle certification date* (CTMV cert. date), if different from the cargo tank certification date.

(3) *Cargo tank manufacturer (CT mfr.).*

(4) *Cargo tank date of manufacture (CT date of mfr.), month and year.*

(5) *Maximum weight of lading (Max. payload), in pounds.*

(6) *Maximum loading rate* in gallons per minute (Max. load rate, GPM) at maximum loading pressure ____ psig.

(7) *Maximum unloading rate* in gallons per minute (Max. unload rate, GPM), at maximum unloading pressure ____ psig.

(8) *Lining material (Lining), if applicable.*

(9) *Heating system design pressure* (Heating sys. press.), in psig, if applicable.

(10) *Heating system design temperature* (Heating sys. temp.), in °F, if applicable.

(d) **Multi-cargo tank motor vehicle.** For a multi-cargo tank motor vehicle having all its cargo tanks not separated by any void, the information required by paragraphs (b) and (c) of this section may be combined on one specification plate. When separated by a void, each cargo tank must have an individual nameplate as required in paragraph (b) of this section, unless all cargo tanks are made by the same manufacturer with the same materials, manufactured thickness, minimum thickness and to the same specification. The cargo tank motor vehicle may have a combined nameplate and specification plate. When only one plate is used, the plate must be visible and not covered by insulation. The required information must be listed on the plate from front to rear in the order of the corresponding cargo tank location.

(e) **Variable specification cargo tank.** Each variable specification cargo tank must have a corrosion resistant metal variable specification plate attached to it. The mounting of this variable specification plate must be such that only the plate identifying the applicable specification under which the tank is being operated is legible.

(1) *The following information* must be included (parenthetical abbreviations are authorized):

Specification DOT XXX (DOT XXX), where "XXX" is replaced with the applicable specification number.

Equipment required	Required rating[1]
Pressure relief devices:	
Pressure actuated type	______
Frangible type	______
Lading discharge devices	______
Top	______
Bottom	______
Pressure unloading fitting	______
Closures:	
Manhole	______
Fill openings	______
Discharge openings	______

1. Required rating — to meet the applicable specification.

(2) *If no change* of information in the specification plate is required, the letters "NC" must follow the rating required. If the cargo tank is not so equipped, the word "None" must be inserted.

(3) *Those parts* to be changed or added must be stamped with the appropriate MC or DOT Specification markings.

(4) *The alterations* that must be made in order for the tank to be modified from one specification to another must be clearly indicated on the manufacturer's certificate and on the variable specification plate.

FEDERAL REGISTER UPDATES

In the April 18, 2003 Federal Register, §178.345-14 was revised, effective October 1, 2003.

(b) [1]

(1) *DOT-specification number* DOT XXX (DOT XXX) where "XXX" is replaced with the applicable specification number. For cargo tanks having a variable specification plate, the DOT-specification number is replaced with the words "See variable specification plate." [2]

(c) [3]

(1) *Cargo tank motor vehicle manufacturer (CTMV mfr.).* [4]
(2) *Cargo tank motor vehicle certification date* (CTMV cert. date), if different from the cargo tank certification date.
(3) *Cargo tank manufacturer (CT mfr.).*
(4) *Cargo tank date of manufacture (CT date if mfr.), month and year.*
(5) *Maximum weight of lading (Max. Payload), in pounds.*
(6) *Maximum loading rate in gallons per minute (Max. Load rate, GPM).*
(7) *Maximum unloading rate in gallons per minute (Max Unload rate).*
(8) *Lining material (Lining), if applicable.*
(9) *Heating system design pressure* (Heating sys. press.), in psig, if applicable.
(10) *Heating system design temperature* (Heating sys. temp.), in °F, if applicable.

1. Paragraph (b) is the same as before.
2. Paragraph (b)(1) was revised.
3. Paragraph (c) is the same as before.
4. Paragraphs (c)(1)-(10) were revised.

§178.345-15 Certification.

(a) **At or before the time of delivery,** the manufacturer of a cargo tank motor vehicle must provide certification documents to the owner of the cargo tank motor vehicle. The registration numbers of the manufacturer, the Design Certifying Engineer, and the Registered Inspector, as appropriate, must appear on the certificates (see subpart F, part 107 in subchapter A of this chapter).

(b) **The manufacturer of a cargo tank motor vehicle** made to any of these specifications must provide:

(1) *For each design type,* a certificate signed by a responsible official of the manufacturer and a Design Certifying Engineer certifying that the cargo tank motor vehicle design meets the applicable specification; and

(2) *For each ASME cargo tank,* a cargo tank manufacturer's data report as required by the ASME Code. For each cargo tank motor vehicle, a certificate signed by a responsible official of the manufacturer and a Registered Inspector certifying that the cargo tank motor vehicle is constructed, tested and completed in conformance with the applicable specification.

(c) **The manufacturer of a variable specification** cargo tank motor vehicle must provide:

(1) *For each design type,* a certificate signed by a responsible official of the manufacturer and a Design Certifying Engineer certifying that the cargo tank motor vehicle design meets the applicable specifications; and

(2) *For each variable* specification cargo tank motor vehicle, a certificate signed by a responsible official of the manufacturer and a Registered Inspector certifying that the cargo tank motor vehicle is constructed, tested and completed in conformance with the applicable specifications. The certificate must include all the information required and marked on the variable specification plate.

(d) **In the case of a cargo tank motor vehicle** manufactured in two or more stages, each manufacturer who performs a manufacturing operation on the incomplete vehicle or portion thereof shall provide to the succeeding manufacturer, at or before the time of delivery, a certificate covering the particular operation performed by that manufacturer, including any certificates received from previous manufacturers, Registered Inspectors, and Design Certifying Engineers. Each certificate must indicate the portion of the complete cargo tank motor vehicle represented thereby, such as basic cargo tank fabrication, insulation, jacket, lining, or piping. The final manufacturer shall provide all applicable certificates to the owner.

(e) **Specification shortages.** If a cargo tank is manufactured which does not meet all applicable specification requirements, thereby requiring subsequent manufacturing involving the installation of additional components, parts, appurtenances or accessories, the cargo tank manufacturer may affix the name plate and specification plate, as required by §178.345-14 (b) and (c), without the original date of certification stamped on the specification plate. The manufacturer shall state the specification requirements not complied with on the manufacturer's Certificate of Compliance. When the cargo tank is brought into full compliance with the applicable specification, the Registered Inspector shall stamp the date of compliance on the specification plate. The Registered Inspector shall issue a Certificate of Compliance stating details of the particular operations performed on the cargo tank, and the date and person (manufacturer, carrier, or repair organization) accomplishing the compliance.

§178.346 Specification DOT 406; cargo tank motor vehicle.

§178.346-1 General requirements.

(a) **Each Specification DOT 406 cargo tank motor vehicle** must meet the general design and construction requirements in §178.345, in addition to the specific requirements contained in this section.

(b) **MAWP:** The MAWP of each cargo tank must be no lower than 2.65 psig and no higher than 4 psig.

(c) **Vacuum loaded cargo tanks must not be constructed** to this specification.

(d) **Each cargo tank must be "constructed in accordance** with the ASME Code" except as modified herein:

(1) *The recordkeeping requirements* contained in the ASME Code Section VIII, Division I do not apply. Parts UG-90 thru 94 of Section VIII, Division I do not apply. Inspection and certification must be made by an inspector registered in accordance with subpart F of part 107.

(2) *Loadings must be as prescribed in §178.345-3.*

(3) *The knuckle radius* of flanged heads must be at least three times the material thickness, and in no case less than 0.5 inch. Stuffed (inserted) heads may be attached to the shell by a fillet weld. The knuckle radius and dish radius versus diameter limitations of UG-32 do not apply. Shell sections of cargo tanks designed with a non-circular cross section need not be given a preliminary curvature, as prescribed in UG-79(b).

(4) *Marking, certification,* data reports, and nameplates must be as prescribed in §§178.345-14 and 178.345-15.

(5) *Manhole closure assemblies* must conform to §§178.345-5 and 178.346-5.

(6) *Pressure relief devices must be as prescribed in §178.345-10.*

(7) *The hydrostatic or pneumatic test* must be as prescribed in §178.345-13.

(8) *The following paragraphs* in parts UG and UW of the ASME Code, Section VIII, Division I do not apply: UG-11, UG-12, UG-22(g), UG-32(e), UG-34, UG-35, UG-44, UG-76, UG-77, UG-80, UG-81, UG-96, UG-97, UW-13(b)(2), UW-13.1(f) and the dimensional requirements found in Figure UW-13.1.

(9) *Single full fillet lap joints* without plug welds may be used for arc or gas welded longitudinal seams without radiographic examination under the following conditions:

(i) *For a truck-mounted cargo tank,* no more than two such joints may be used on the top half of the tank and no more than two joints may be used on the bottom half. They may not be located farther from the top and bottom centerline than 16 percent of the shell's circumference.

(ii) *For a self-supporting cargo tank,* no more than two such joints may be used on the top of the tank. They may not be located farther from the top centerline than 12.5 percent of the shell's circumference.

(iii) *Compliance test.* Two test specimens of the material to be used in the manufacture of a cargo tank must be tested to failure in tension. The test specimens must be of the same thicknesses and joint configuration as the cargo tank, and joined by the same welding procedures. The test specimens may represent all the tanks that are made of the same materials and welding procedures, have the same joint configuration, and are made in the same facility within 6 months after the tests are completed. Before welding, the fit-up of the joints on the test specimens must represent production conditions that would result in the least joint strength. Evidence of joint fit-up and test results must be retained at the manufacturers' facility.

(iv) *Weld joint efficiency.* The lower value of stress at failure attained in the two tensile test specimens shall be used to compute the efficiency of the joint as follows: Determine the failure ratio by dividing the stress at failure by the mechanical properties of the adjacent metal; this value, when multiplied by 0.75, is the design weld joint efficiency.

(10) *The requirements* of paragraph UW-9(d), of Section VIII, Division 1, ASME Code do not apply.

FEDERAL REGISTER UPDATES

In the April 18, 2003 Federal Register, §178.346-1 was revised, effective October 1, 2003.

(d) [1]

(6) Pressure relief devices must be as prescribed in §178.346-3. [2]

(7) The hydrostatic or pneumatic test must be as prescribed in §178.346-5. [3]

1. Paragraph (d) is the same as before.
2. In paragraph (d)(6), the reference to "§178.345-10" was revised to read " §178.346-3."
3. In paragraph (d)(7), the reference to "§178.345-13" was revised to read "§178.346-5."

§178.346-2 Material and thickness of material.

The type and thickness of material for DOT 406 cargo tank motor vehicles must conform to §178.345-2 of this part, but may in no case be less than that indicated in tables I and II below.

Table I - Minimum Thickness of Heads (or Bulkheads and Baffles When Used as Tank Reinforcement) Using Mild Steel (MS), High Strength Low Alloy Steel (HSLA), Austenitic Stainless Steel (SS) or Aluminum (AL) — Expressed in Decimals of an Inch After Forming

Material	Volume capacity in gallons per inch of length								
	14 or less			Over 14 to 23			Over 23		
	MS	HSLA SS	AL	MS	HSLA SS	AL	MS	HSLA SS	AL
Thickness	.100	.100	.160	.115	.115	.173	.129	.129	.187

Table II - Minimum Thickness of Shell Using Mild Steel (MS), High Strength Low Alloy Steel (HSLA), Austenitic Stainless Steel (SS) or Aluminum (AL) — Expressed in Decimals of an Inch After Forming[1]

Cargo tank motor vehicle rated capacity (gallons)	MS	SS/HSLA	AL
More than 0 to at least 4,500	0.100	0.100	0.151
More than 4,500 to at least 8,000	0.115	0.100	0.160
More than 8,000 to at least 14,000	0.129	0.129	0.173
More than 14,000	0.143	0.143	0.187

1. Maximum distance between bulkheads, baffles, or ring stiffeners shall not exceed 60 inches.

FEDERAL REGISTER UPDATES

In the April 18, 2003 Federal Register, §178.346-2 was revised, effective October 1, 2003.

The type and thickness of material for DOT 406 specification cargo tanks must conform to §178.345-2, but in no case may the thickness be less than that determined by the minimum thickness requirements in §178.320(a). The following Tables I and II identify the specified minimum thickness values to be employed in that determination. [1]

Table I - Specified Minimum Thickness of Heads (or Bulkheads and Baffles When Used as Tank Reinforcement) Using Mild Steel (MS), High Strength Low Alloy Steel (HSLA), Austenitic Stainless Steel (SS), or Aluminum (AL) — Expressed in Decimals of an Inch After Forming [2]

Table II - Specified Minimum Thickness of Shell Using Mild Steel (MS), High Strength Low Alloy Steel (HSLA), Austenitic Stainless Steel (SS), or Aluminum (AL) — Expressed in Decimals of an Inch After Forming [3]

1. The introductory text was revised.
2. The title to Table I was revised.
3. The title to Table II was revised.

§178.346-3 Pressure relief.

(a) **Each cargo tank must be equipped** with a pressure relief system in accordance with §178.345-10 and this section.

(b) **Type and construction.** In addition to the pressure relief devices required in §178.345-10:

(1) *Each cargo tank* must be equipped with one or more vacuum relief devices;

(2) *When intended for use* only for lading meeting the requirements of §173.33(c)(1)(iii) of this subchapter, the cargo tank may be equipped with a normal vent. Such vents must be set to open at not less than 1 psig and must be designed to prevent loss of lading through the device in case of vehicle upset; and

(3) *Notwithstanding the requirements* in §178.345-10(b), after August 31, 1996, each pressure relief valve must be able to withstand a dynamic pressure surge reaching 30 psig above the design set pressure and sustained above the set pressure for at least 60 milliseconds with a total volume of liquid released not exceeding 1 L before the relief valve recloses to a leak-tight condition. This requirement must be met regardless of vehicle orientation. This capability must be demonstrated by testing. TTMA RP No. 81, cited at §178.345-10(b)(3)(i), is an acceptable test procedure.

(c) **Pressure settings of relief valves.**

(1) *Notwithstanding the requirements* in §178.345-10(d), the set pressure of each primary relief valve must be not less than 110 percent of the MAWP or 3.3 psig, whichever is greater, and not more than 138 percent of the MAWP. The valve must close at not less than the MAWP and remain closed at lower pressures.

(2) *Each vacuum relief device* must be set to open at no more than 6 ounces vacuum.

(d) **Venting capacities.**

(1) *Notwithstanding the requirements* in §178.345-10 (e) and (g), the primary pressure relief valve must have a venting capacity of at least 6,000 SCFH, rated at not greater than 125 percent of the tank test pressure and not greater than 3 psig above the MAWP. The venting capacity required in §178.345-10(e) may be rated at these same pressures.

(2) *Each vacuum relief system* must have sufficient capacity to limit the vacuum to 1 psig.

(3) *If pressure loading or unloading devices* are provided, the relief system must have adequate vapor and liquid capacity to limit the tank pressure to the cargo tank test pressure at maximum loading or unloading rate. The maximum loading and unloading rates must be included on the metal specification plate.

§178.346-4 Outlets.

(a) **All outlets on each tank must conform** to §178.345-11 and this section.

(b) **External self-closing stop-valves are not authorized** as an alternative to internal self-closing stop-valves on loading/unloading outlets.

§178.346-5 Pressure and leakage tests.

(a) **Each cargo tank must be tested** in accordance with §178.345-13 and this section.

(b) **Pressure test. Test pressure must be as follows:**

(1) *Using the hydrostatic test method,* the test pressure must be the greater of 5.0 psig or 1.5 times the cargo tank MAWP.

(2) *Using the pneumatic test method,* the test pressure must be the greater of 5.0 psig or 1.5 times the cargo tank MAWP, and the inspection pressure must be the cargo tank MAWP.

(c) **Leakage test.** Cargo tanks equipped with vapor collection equipment may be leakage tested in accordance with the Environmental Protection Agency's "Method 27 — Determination of Vapor Tightness of Gasoline Delivery Tank Using Pressure-Vacuum Test," as set forth in 40 CFR part 60, appendix A. Acceptance criteria are found at 40 CFR 60.501 and 60.601.

FEDERAL REGISTER UPDATES

In the April 18, 2003 Federal Register, §178.346-5(c) was revised, effective October 1, 2003.

(c) **Leakage test.** A cargo tank used to transport a petroleum distillate fuel that is equipped with vapor recovery equipment may be leakage tested in accordance with 40 CFR 63.425(e). To satisfy the leakage test requirements of this paragraph, the test specified in 40 CFR 63.425(e)(1) must be conducted using air. The hydrostatic test alternative permitted under Appendix A to 40 CFR Part 60 ("Method 27— Determination of Vapor Tightness of Gasoline Delivery Tank Using Pressure-Vacuum Test") may not be used to satisfy the leakage test requirements of this paragraph. A cargo tank tested in accordance with 40 CFR 63.425(e) may be marked as specified in §180.415 of this subchapter.

§178.347 Specification DOT 407; cargo tank motor vehicle.

§178.347-1 General requirements.

(a) **Each specification DOT 407 cargo tank** motor vehicle must conform to the general design and construction requirements in §178.345 in addition to the specific requirements contained in this section.

(b) **Each tank must be of a circular cross-section** and have an MAWP of at least 25 psig.

(c) **Any cargo tank built to this specification** with a MAWP greater than 35 psig and each tank designed to be loaded by vacuum must be "constructed and certified in accordance with the ASME Code". The external design pressure for a cargo tank loaded by vacuum must be at least 15 psig.

(d) **Each cargo tank built to this specification** with a MAWP greater than 35 psig and each tank designed to be loaded by vacuum must be constructed and certified in conformance with the ASME Code (incorporated by reference; see §171.7 of this subchapter). The external design pressure for a cargo tank loaded by vacuum must be at least 15 psi.

(1) *The recordkeeping requirements* contained in the ASME Code, Section VIII, Division I, do not apply. The inspection requirements of parts UG-90 thru 94 do not apply. Inspection and certification must be made by an inspector registered in accordance with subpart F of part 107.

(2) *Loadings must be as prescribed in §178.345-3.*

(3) *The knuckle radius* of flanged heads must be at least three times the material thickness, and in no case less than 0.5 inch. Stuffed (inserted) heads may be attached to the shell by a fillet weld. The knuckle radius and dish radius versus diameter limitations of UG-32 do not apply for cargo tank motor vehicles with a MAWP of 35 psig or less.

(4) *Marking, certification,* data reports and nameplates must be as prescribed in §§178.345-14 and 178.345-15.

(5) *Manhole closure assemblies* must conform to §§178.345-5 and 178.347-5.

(6) *Pressure relief devices must be as prescribed in §178.345-10.*

(7) *The hydrostatic or pneumatic test* must be as prescribed in §178.345-13.

(8) *The following paragraphs* in parts UG and UW of the ASME Code, Section VIII, Division I do not apply: UG-11, UG-12, UG-22(g), UG-32(e), UG-34, UG-35, UG-44, UG-76, UG-77, UG-80, UG-81, UG-96, UG-97, UW-13(b)(2), UW-13.1(f), and the dimensional requirements found in Figure UW-13.1.

FEDERAL REGISTER UPDATES

In the April 18, 2003 Federal Register, §178.347-1 was revised, effective October 1, 2003.

(c) **Any cargo tank built to this specification** with a MAWP greater than 35 psig and each tank designed to be loaded by vacuum must be constructed and certified in conformance with the ASME Code (incorporated by reference; see §171.7 of this subchapter). The external design pressure for a cargo tank loaded by vacuum must be at least 15 psi. [1]

(d) [2]

(5) *Manhole closure assemblies must conform to §178.347-3.* [3]

(6) *Pressure relief devices must be as prescribed in §178.347-4.* [4]

(7) *The hydrostatic or pneumatic test must be as prescribed in §178.347-5.* [5]

(9) *The strength of a weld seam* in a bulkhead that has not been radiographically examined shall be 0.85 of the strength of the bulkhead under the following conditions: [6]

(i) *The welded seam must be a full penetration butt weld.*

(ii) *No more than one seam may be used per bulkhead.*

(iii) *The welded seam* must be completed before forming the dish radius and knuckle radius.

(iv) *Compliance test:* Two test specimens of materials representative of those to be used in the manufacture of a cargo tank bulkhead must be tested to failure in tension. The test specimen must be of the same thickness and joined by the same welding procedure. The test specimens may represent all the tanks that are made in the same facility within 6 months after the tests are completed. Before welding, the fit-up of the joints on the test specimens must represent production conditions that would result in the least joint strength. Evidence of joint fit-up and test results must be retained at the manufacturers' facility for at least 5 years.

(v) *Acceptance criteria:* The ratio of the actual tensile stress at failure to the actual tensile strength of the adjacent material of all samples of a test lot must be greater than 0.85.

1. Paragraph (c) was revised.
2. Paragraph (d) is the same as before.
3. In paragraph (d)(5), the reference to "§§178.345-5 and 178.347-5" was revised to read "§178.347-3".
4. In paragraph (d)(6), the reference to "§178.345-10" was revised to read "§178.347-4".
5. In paragraph (d)(7), the reference to "§178.345-13" was revised to read "§178.347-5".
6. Paragraph (d)(9) was added.

§178.347-2 Material and thickness of material.

(a) **The type and thickness of material** for DOT 407 specification cargo tanks must conform to §178.345-2 and this section. In no case may the thickness be less than that indicated in Tables I and II below.

Table I - Minimum Thickness of Heads (or Bulkheads and Baffles When Used as Tank Reinforcement) Using Mild Steel (MS), High Strength Low Alloy Steel (HSLA), Austenitic Stainless Steel (SS) or Aluminum (AL) — Expressed in Decimals of an Inch After Forming

Volume capacity in gallons per inch	10 or less	Over 10 to 14	Over 14 to 18	Over 18 to 22	Over 22 to 26	Over 26 to 30	Over 30
Thickness (MS)	0.100	0.100	0.115	0.129	0.129	0.143	0.156
Thickness (HSLA)	0.100	0.100	0.115	0.129	0.129	0.143	0.156
Thickness (SS)	0.100	0.100	0.115	0.129	0.129	0.143	0.156
Thickness (AL)	0.160	0.160	0.173	0.187	0.194	0.216	0.237

Table II - Minimum Thickness of Shell Using Mild Steel (MS), High Strength Low Alloy Steel (HSLA), Austenitic Stainless Steel (SS) or Aluminum (AL) — Expressed in Decimals of an Inch After Forming

Volume capacity in gallons per inch	10 or less	Over 10 to 14	Over 14 to 18	Over 18 to 22	Over 22 to 26	Over 26 to 30	Over 30
Thickness (MS)	0.100	0.100	0.115	0.129	0.129	0.143	0.156
Thickness (HSLA)	0.100	0.100	0.115	0.129	0.129	0.143	0.156
Thickness (SS)	0.100	0.100	0.115	0.129	0.129	0.143	0.156
Thickness (AL)	0.151	0.151	0.160	0.173	0.194	0.216	0.237

(b) [Reserved]

FEDERAL REGISTER UPDATES

In the April 18, 2003 Federal Register, §178.347-2 was revised, effective October 1, 2003.

(a) **The type and thickness of material** for DOT 407 specification cargo tanks must conform to §178.345-2, but in no case may the thickness be less than that determined by the minimum thickness requirements in §178.320(a). Tables I and II identify the specified minimum thickness values to be employed in that the determination: [1]

Table I - Specified Minimum Thickness of Heads (or Bulkheads and Baffles When Used as Tank Reinforcement) Using Mild Steel (MS), High Strength Low Alloy Steel (HSLA), Austenitic Stainless Steel (SS), or Aluminum (AL) — Expressed in Decimals of an Inch After Forming [2]

Table II - Specified Minimum Thickness of Shell Using Mild Steel (MS), High Strength Low Alloy Steel (HSLA), Austenitic Stainless Steel (SS), or Aluminum (AL) — Expressed in Decimals of an Inch After Forming [3]

1. Paragraph (a) was revised.
2. The title to Table I was revised.
3. The title to Table II was revised.

§178.347-3 Manhole assemblies.

Each manhole assembly must conform to §178.345-5, except that each manhole assembly must be capable of withstanding internal fluid pressures of 40 psig or test pressure of the tank, whichever is greater.

§178.347-4 Pressure relief.

(a) **Each cargo tank must be equipped with** a pressure and vacuum relief system in accordance with §178.345-10 and this section.

(b) **Type and Construction.** Vacuum relief devices are not required for cargo tanks designed to be loaded by vacuum or built to withstand full vacuum.

(c) **Pressure settings of relief valves.** The setting of pressure relief valves must be in accordance with §178.345-10(d).

(d) **Venting capacities.**

(1) *The vacuum relief system* must limit the vacuum to less than 80 percent of the design vacuum capability of the cargo tank.

(2) *If pressure loading* or unloading devices are provided, the relief system must have adequate vapor and liquid capacity to limit the tank pressure to the cargo tank test pressure at maximum loading or unloading rate. The maximum loading or unloading rate must be included on the metal specification plate.

§178.347-5 Pressure and leakage test.

(a) Each cargo tank must be tested in accordance with §178.345-13 and this section.

(b) Pressure test. Test pressure must be as follows:

(1) *Using the hydrostatic test method,* the test pressure must be at least 40 psig or 1.5 times tank MAWP, whichever is greater.

(2) *Using the pneumatic test method,* the test pressure must be 40 psig or 1.5 times tank MAWP, whichever is greater, and the inspection pressure is tank MAWP.

§178.348 Specification DOT 412; cargo tank motor vehicle.

§178.348-1 General requirements.

(a) Each specification DOT 412 cargo tank motor vehicle must conform to the general design and construction requirements in §178.345 in addition to the specific requirements of this section.

(b) The MAWP of each cargo tank must be at least 5 psig.

(c) The MAWP for each cargo tank designed to be loaded by vacuum must be at least 25 psig internal and 15 psig external.

(d) Each cargo tank having a MAWP greater than 15 psig must be of circular cross-section.

(e) Each cargo tank having a —

(1) *MAWP greater* than 15 psig must be "constructed and certified in conformance with the ASME Code"; or

(2) *MAWP of 15 psig* or less must be "constructed in accordance with the ASME Code," except as modified herein:

(i) *The recordkeeping requirements* contained in the ASME Code, Section VIII, Division I, do not apply. Parts UG-90 thru 94 of Section VIII, Division I do not apply. Inspection and certification must be made by an inspector registered in accordance with subpart F of part 107.

(ii) *Loadings must be as prescribed in §178.345-3.*

(iii) *The knuckle radius* of flanged heads must be at least three times the material thickness, and in no case less than 0.5 inch. Stuffed (inserted) heads may be attached to the shell by a fillet weld. The knuckle radius and dish radius versus diameter limitations of UG-32 do not apply for cargo tank motor vehicles with a MAWP of 15 psig or less. Shell sections of cargo tanks designed with a non-circular cross section need not be given a preliminary curvature, as prescribed in UG-79(b).

(iv) *Marking, certification,* data reports, and nameplates must be as prescribed in §§178.345-14 and 178.345-15.

(v) *Manhole closure assemblies* must conform to §§178.345-5 and 178.348-5.

(vi) *Pressure relief devices must be as prescribed in §178.345-10.*

(vii) *The hydrostatic* or pneumatic test must be as prescribed in §178.345-13.

(viii) *The following paragraphs* in parts UG and UW of the ASME Code, Section VIII, Division I do not apply: UG-11, UG-12, UG-22(g), UG-32(e), UG-34, UG-35, UG-44, UG-76, UG-77, UG-80, UG-81, UG-96, UG-97, UW-13(b)(2), UW-13.1(f), and the dimensional requirements found in Figure UW-13.1.

FEDERAL REGISTER UPDATES

In the April 18, 2003 Federal Register, §178.348-1 was revised, effective October 1, 2003.

(e) [1]

(2) [2]

(v) *Manhole closure assemblies must conform to §§178.345-5.* [3]

(vi) *Pressure relief devices must be as prescribed in §178.348-4.* [4]

(vii) *The hydrostatic* or pneumatic test must be as prescribed in §178.348-5. [5]

1. Paragraph (e) is the same as before.
2. Paragraph (e)(2) is the same as before.
3. In paragraph (e)(2)(v), the reference to "§§178.345-5 and 178.348-5" was revised to read "§178.345-5".
4. In paragraph (e)(2)(vi), the reference to "§178.345-10" was revised to read "§178.348-4".
5. In paragraph (e)(2)(vii), the reference to "§178.345-13" was revised to read "§178.348-5".

§178.348-2 Material and thickness of material.

(a) The type and thickness of material for DOT 412 cargo tanks must conform to §178.345-2 of this part, but in no case may the thickness be less than that indicated in tables I and II below.

Table I - Minimum Thickness of Heads (or Bulkheads and Baffles When Used as Tank Reinforcement) Using Mild Steel (MS), High Strength Low Alloy Steel (HSLA), Austenitic Stainless Steel (SS) or Aluminum (AL) — Expressed in Decimals of an Inch After Forming

Volume capacity (gallons per inch)	10 or less				Over 10 to 14				Over 14 to 18			18 and over		
Lading density at 60 °F in pounds per gallon	10 lbs and less	Over 10 to 13 lbs	Over 13 to 16 lbs	Over 16 lbs	10 lbs and less	Over 10 to 13 lbs	Over 13 to 16 lbs	Over 16 lbs	10 lbs and less	Over 10 to 13 lbs	Over 13 to 16 lbs	10 lbs and less	Over 10 to 13 lbs	Over 13 to 16 lbs
Thickness (inch), steel	.100	.129	.157	.187	.129	.157	.187	.250	.157	.250	.250	.157	.250	.312
Thickness (inch), aluminum	.144	.187	.227	.270	.187	.227	.270	.360	.227	.360	.360	.227	.360	.450

Table II - Minimum Thickness of Shell Using Mild Steel (MS), High Strength Low Alloy Steel (HSLA) or Austenitic Stainless Steel (SS) or Aluminum (AL) — Expressed in Decimals of an Inch After Forming

Volume capacity (gallons per inch)	10 or less				Over 10 to 14				Over 14 to 18			18 and over		
Lading density at 60 °F in pounds per gallon	10 lbs and less	Over 10 to 13 lbs	Over 13 to 16 lbs	Over 16 lbs	10 lbs and less	Over 10 to 13 lbs	Over 13 to 16 lbs	Over 16 lbs	10 lbs and less	Over 10 to 13 lbs	Over 13 to 16 lbs	10 lbs and less	Over 10 to 13 lbs	Over 13 to 16 lbs
Thickness (steel): Distances between heads (and bulkheads baffles and ring stiffeners when used as tank reinforcement):														
36 in. or less	.100	.129	.157	.187	.100	.129	.157	.187	.100	.129	.157	.129	.157	.187
Over 36 in. to 54 inches	.100	.129	.157	.187	.100	.129	.157	.187	.129	.157	.187	.157	.250	.250
Over 54 in. to 60 inches	.100	.129	.157	.187	.129	.157	.187	.250	.157	.250	.250	.187	.250	.312
Thickness (aluminum): Distances between heads (and bulkheads baffles and ring stiffeners when used as tank reinforcement):														
36 in. or less	.144	.187	.227	.270	.144	.187	.227	.270	.144	.187	.227	.187	.227	.270
Over 36 in. to 54 inches	.144	.187	.227	.270	.144	.187	.227	.270	.187	.227	.270	.157	.360	.360
Over 54 in. to 60 inches	.144	.187	.227	.270	.187	.227	.270	.360	.227	.360	.360	.270	.360	.450

(b) [Reserved]

FEDERAL REGISTER UPDATES

In the April 18, 2003 Federal Register, §178.348-2 was revised, effective October 1, 2003.

(a) **The type and thickness of material** for DOT 412 specification cargo tanks must conform to §178.345-2, but in no case may the thickness be less than that determined by the minimum thickness requirements in §178.320(a). The following Tables I and II identify the "Specified Minimum Thickness" values to be employed in that determination.[1]

Table I - Specified Minimum Thickness of Heads (or Bulkheads and Baffles When Used as Tank Reinforcement) Using Mild Steel (MS), High Strength Low Alloy Steel (HSLA), Austenitic Stainless Steel (SS), or Aluminum (AL) — Expressed in Decimals of an Inch After Forming[2]

Table II - Specified Minimum Thickness of Shell Using Mild Steel (MS), High Strength Low Alloy Steel (HSLA), Austenitic Stainless Steel (SS), or Aluminum (AL) — Expressed in Decimals of an Inch After Forming[3]

1. Paragraph (a) was revised.
2. The title to Table I was revised.
3. The title to Table II was revised.

§178.348-3 Pumps, piping, hoses and connections.

Each pump and all piping, hoses and connections on each cargo tank motor vehicle must conform to §178.345-9, except that the use of nonmetallic pipes, valves, or connections are authorized on DOT 412 cargo tanks.

§178.348-4 Pressure relief.

(a) **Each cargo tank must be equipped** with a pressure and vacuum relief system in accordance with §178.345-10 and this section.

(b) **Type and construction.** Vacuum relief devices are not required for cargo tanks designed to be loaded by vacuum or built to withstand full vacuum.

(c) **Pressure settings of relief valves.** The setting of the pressure relief devices must be in accordance with §178.345-10(d), except as provided in paragraph (d)(3) of this section.

(d) **Venting capacities.**

(1) *The vacuum relief system* must limit the vacuum to less than 80 percent of the design vacuum capability of the cargo tank.

(2) *If pressure loading or unloading devices* are provided, the pressure relief system must have adequate vapor and liquid capacity to limit tank pressure to the cargo tank test pressure at the maximum loading or unloading rate. The maximum loading and unloading rates must be included on the metal specification plate.

(3) *Cargo tanks* used in dedicated service for materials classed as corrosive material, with no secondary hazard, may have a total venting capacity which is less than required by §178.345-10(e). The minimum total venting capacity for these cargo tanks must be determined in accordance with the formula contained in §178.270-11(d)(3). Use of the approximate values given for the formula in §178.270-11(d)(3) is acceptable.

§178.348-5 Pressure and leakage test.

(a) **Each cargo tank must be tested** in accordance with §178.345-13 and this section.

(b) **Pressure test. Test pressure must be as follows:**

(1) *Using the hydrostatic test method,* the test pressure must be at least 1.5 times MAWP.

(2) *Using the pneumatic test method,* the test pressure must be at least 1.5 times tank MAWP, and the inspection pressure is tank MAWP.

Subpart K - Specifications for Packagings for Class 7 (Radioactive) Materials

§178.350 Specification 7A; general packaging, Type A.

(a) **Each packaging must meet all applicable requirements** of subpart B of part 173 of this subchapter and be designed and constructed so that it meets the requirements of §§173.403, 173.410, 173.412, 173.415 and 173.465 of this subchapter for Type A packaging.

(b) **Each Specification 7A packaging must be marked** on the outside "USA DOT 7A Type A" and "Radioactive Material."

§178.352 Specification 6L; metal packaging.

§178.352-1 General requirements.

Each packaging must meet the applicable requirements of §173.24 of this subchapter.

§178.352-2 Rated capacity.

(a) **Rated capacity as marked (see §178.352-6).** Not less than 55 gallons nor more than 110 gallons for the outer steel drum. Not more than 17.74 L for the inner vessel.

(b) **The authorized maximum gross weight of the package** is 160 kg (350 pounds) for sizes not over 210 L (55 gallons) or 220 kg (480 pounds) for sizes over 210 L (55 gallons) but not over 420 L (110 gallons).

§178.352-3 General construction requirements.

(a) **The outer shell must be of straight sided steel,** with welded body seams and at least 18-gauge body and bottom head sheets, and 14-gauge removable head sheets (unless there are one or more corrugations in the cover near the periphery, in which case 16-gauge is authorized). The shell may be either a single sheet of steel or may be fabricated by welding together two appropriate lengths of 210 L (55-gallon) drums, such as a DOT Specification 6J or 17H, with rolled or swedged in hoops as prescribed for either of those specifications. The head must be convex (crowned), not extending beyond the level of the chime, with a minimum convexity of 1 cm (3/8-inch). The inside diameter of the shell must be at least 57 cm (22.5 inches).

(b) **Inner containment vessel must conform** to specification 2R (except that cast iron is not authorized), with a maximum usable inside dimension of 13.3 cm (5.25 inches) maximum height of 127 cm (50 inches) (with caps in place) and minimum wall thickness of 6 mm (0.25 inch).

(c) **Inner containment vessel must be fixed** within the outer shell by one of the following types of centering devices:

(1) *At least 8 steel rod spacers,* of at least 6 mm (0.25-inch) diameter (for packages of 210 L (55-gallon) capacity) or 1 cm of (0.375-inch) diameter (for packages with greater than 210 L (55-gallon) capacity) cold rolled steel, welded to the vessel at each end by minimum 5 cm (2-inch) continuous weld. Each rod must be welded to the vessel at radial positions not exceeding 45 degrees as not to interfere with closure of the inner vessel. Each spacer rod must extend at least 5.6 cm (2.25 inches) beyond the inner vessel at each end, then radially to the wall of the outer drum (to provide a springlike snug fit) and along the entire length of the wall of the outer drum. For a packaging of more than 210 L (55-gallon) capacity, each spacer rod must be braced by welding a 6 millimeter (0.25-inch) by 5 cm (2-inch) steel plate to the spacer rod and the pipe with a continuous weld at each joint, the joints being located approximately half way along the length of the drum. For containers manufactured prior to March 31, 1975, this requirement is effective December 31, 1975.

(2) *At least three steel "spiders,"* not more than 24 inches apart, with each spider having at least four legs. Each leg must be constructed of materials having dimensions not less than those listed in this paragraph, welded by continuous weld at each joint to inner and outer steel bands of at least 1/4-inch by 1-inch steel. The inner steel band must be welded to the inner vessel by at least six 2-inch welds on both edges of the band. The outer steel band must be welded to the outer drum by at least six 2-inch welds on both edges of the top outer band, such that the inner vessel is at least 2 1/4 inches from the top and bottom of the drum. Authorized construction materials are:

(i) *2.5 cm* (1 inch) by 2.5 cm (1 inch) by 6 mm (1/4-inch) steel angle iron.

(ii) *3 cm* (1 1/4 inches) by 3 cm (1 1/4 inches) by 5 mm (3/16-inch) steel angle iron.

(iii) *2.5 cm (1 inch) schedule 40 steel pipe.*

(iv) *1 1/2-inch* diameter solid steel rods, with only two such spiders required instead of three.

(3) *There must not be* less than 2 spacer mechanisms for a packaging of 210 L (55-gallon) capacity nor less than 3 spacer mechanisms for a packaging greater than 210 L (55-gallon) capacity. Each spacer mechanism must consist of not less than 6 steel angles, pipe, or rod radial supports of at least 2.7 square cm (0.42 square inch) cross-section. Each radial support must be welded at one end to the containment vessel by a continuous weld or to an inner steel band of at least 6 mm (1/4-inch) by 2.5 cm (1 inch) by a continuous weld at radial positions not exceeding 60 degrees from the center of the package. The inner band, when used, must be welded to the inner containment vessel by at least 6 equally spaced 5 cm (2-inch) welds on each edge of the band. The opposite end of the radial support must be welded by a continuous weld to an outer steel band of at least 6 mm (1/4-inch) by 2.5 cm (1 inch). The outer steel band must be welded to the outer shell by at least 6 equally spaced welds on each edge of the top band, such that the inner vessel is fixed at least 5.7 cm (2.25 inches) from the top and bottom of the drum. The spacer mechanism must be welded as specified near each end

of the containment vessel so as not to interfere with the vessel closure. For a packaging greater than 210 L (55-gallon) capacity, the additional spacer mechanism must be located at approximately midpoint along the length of the inner vessel.

(d) **The void between the inner containment vessel** and the outer shell must be completely filled with bagged or tamped vermiculite (expanded mica), with a density of at least 0.072 g/cc (4.5 pounds per cubic foot). Loose, untamped vermiculite is not authorized.

§178.352-4 Welding.

Welding must be of material having a melting point in excess of 800 °C (1475 °F) (except that for packages constructed prior to March 31, 1975, this temperature may be 540 °C (1000 °F)), with a joint efficiency of at least 0.85. This requirement applies to welding used in adding spacer rods to comply with §178.352-3(c)(1).

§178.352-5 Closure.

(a) **The outer drum closure must be at least** a 12-gauge bolted ring with drop forged lugs, one of which is threaded, and having at least a 1.6 centimeter (5/8-inch) diameter steel bolt and a lock nut, or equivalent device.

(b) **The closure device must have a means** for the attachment of a tamper-proof lock wire and seal, or equivalent.

§178.352-6 Markings.

(a) **Markings on each container,** by die stamping on a metal plate attached to the outside of the outer container by spot welding, or other equally efficient method, in letters and figures of at least one-fourth inch in height, as follows:

(1) *"DOT-6L".*

(2) *"FISSILE RADIOACTIVE MATERIAL."*

(3) *Name or symbol* of person making the marks specified in paragraph (a) (1) of this section. Symbol, if used, must be registered with the Associate Administrator.

(4) *Gauge of metal* of the outer steel drum in the thinnest part, rated capacity of the outer steel drum in gallons, and the year of manufacture of the assembled package (e.g., 18-110-68). When the gauge of the metal in the drum wall differs from that in the head, both must be indicated with a slanting line between, and with the gauge of the body indicated first (e.g., 18/16-110-68 for 18-gauge body and 16-gauge head).

(b) [Reserved]

§178.354 Specification 6M; metal packaging.

§178.354-1 General requirements.

(a) **Each package must meet the applicable** requirements of §173.24 of this chapter.

(b) [Reserved]

§178.354-2 Rated capacity.

(a) **Rated capacity as marked (see §178.354-5).** Not less than 10 gallons nor more than 110 gallons for the outer steel drum. Not less than 1.24 L for the inner containment vessel.

(b) [Reserved]

§178.354-3 General construction requirements.

(a) **The outer shell must be of straight-sided steel,** with welded body seams, and may be either a single sheet of steel, or may be fabricated by welding together two appropriate lengths of drums with each length to contain 3 swedged or rolled rolling hoops as prescribed for either of these specifications. A removable head for a packaging of 210 L (55 gallons) or larger volume must have one or more corrugations in the cover near the periphery. For a packaging exceeding 57 L (15 gallons) volume, the head must be crowned (convexed), not extending beyond the level of the chime, with a minimum convexity of 1 cm (3/8-inch).

(1) *The maximum authorized gross weight,* metal thickness, and minimum end insulation thickness for the marked volume is as follows:

Marked capacity		Maximum authorized gross weight		Minimum thickness of uncoated sheets and heads (gauge)	Minimum thickness of end insulation	Cm
Gallons not over	Liters	Pounds	Kilograms		Inches	
15	57	160	73	20	1.88	4.7
30	114	480	219	18	3.75	9.5
55	210	640	292	16	3.75	9.5
110	420	640	292	16	3.75	9.5

(2) *Each drum* must have at least four 1.2 centimeter (0.5-inch) diameter vents near the top, each covered with a weatherproof tape or fusible plug; or equivalent device. A layer of porous refractory fiber may be placed behind the pressure-relief vent holes.

(b) **Inner containment vessel must conform** to specification 2R or equivalent (cast iron or brass are prohibited), with maximum usable inside diameter of 13.3 cm (5.25 inches), minimum usable inside diameter of 10 cm (4 inches), and minimum height of 15 cm (6 inches).

(c) **Inner containment vessel must be fixed** within the outer shell by one of the following types of solid centering media, with the sides of the inner vessel protected by at least 9.5 cm (3.75 inches) of insulation media, and the ends with at least the thickness as prescribed in paragraph (a)(1) of this section.

(1) *Machined discs and rings* made of solid industrial cane fiberboard having a density of at least 0.24 g/cc (15 pounds per cubic foot) fitted such that the radial clearances between the fiberboard, inner vessel, and shell do not exceed 6 mm (1/4-inch); or

(2) *Hardwood or plywood* at least 1.2 centimeter (1/2-inch) thick, having a density of at least 0.45 g/cc (28 pounds per cubic foot). There must be no gap or direct heat path from the shell to the inner vessel.

(d) **Any radiation shielding material used** must be placed within the inner containment vessel or must be protected in all directions by at least the thickness of the thermal insulating material prescribed in paragraph (a) of this section.

(e) **For a packaging having an authorized gross weight** in excess of 219 kg (480 pounds), a steel bearing plate, at least 6 mm (0.25-inch) thick or a plywood disc, at least 2.5 cm (1-inch) thick, and at least 25 cm (10 inches) in diameter must be provided at both ends and adjacent to the specification 2R inner containment vessel, to provide additional load-bearing surface against the insulation-centering medium.

§178.354-4 Closure.

(a) **The outer drum closure must be** at least 16-gauge bolt-type locking ring having at least a 5/16-inch steel bolt for drum sizes not over 15 gallons, or a 12-gauge bolted ring with drop-forged lugs, one of which is threaded, and a 5/8-inch steel bolt for drum sizes over 15 gallons. Each bolt must be provided with a lock nut or equivalent device.

(b) **The closure device must have means** for the attachment of a tamper-proof lock wire and seal, or equivalent.

§178.354-5 Markings.

(a) **Marking must be as prescribed in §178.3.**

(b) **Marking on the outside of each package** must be as follows: "DOT-6M Type B," "Radioactive Materials," or "Fissile Radioactive Materials," as appropriate; and the gauge of metal of the outer drum in the thinnest part, rated capacity of the outer drum in gallons, and year of manufacture (for example, 18-30-69). When the gauge of the metal in the drum wall differs from that in the head, both must be indicated with a slanting line between, and with the gauge of the body indicated first (e.g., 18/16-55-69 for 18-gauge body and 16-gauge head).

§178.356 Specification 20PF phenolic-foam insulated, metal overpack.

§178.356-1 General requirements.

(a) **Each overpack must meet all of the applicable requirements** of §173.24 of this subchapter.

(b) **The maximum gross weight of the package,** including the inner cylinder and its contents, must not exceed the following:

(1) *Specification 20PF-1 — 138 kg (300 pounds).*

(2) *Specification 20PF-2 — 320 kg (700 pounds).*

(3) *Specification 20PF-3 — 455 kg (1000 pounds).*

(c) **The general configuration of the overpack** must be a right cylinder, consisting of an insulated base section, a steel liner lid, and an insulated top section. The inner liner and outer shell must be at least 16-gauge and 18-gauge steel, respectively, with the intervening cavity filled with a molded-in-place, fire-resistant, phenolic-foam insulation interspersed with wooden members for bracing and support Wood pieces must be securely attached to both the liner and shell. No hole is permitted in the liner. Each joint between sections must be stepped a minimum of 5 cm (2 inches) and gaps between mating surfaces must not exceed 5 mm (0.2 inch). Gaps between foam surface of top section and liner lid must not exceed 1 cm (0.4 inch) or 5 cm (2 inches) where taper is required for mold stripping. For the specification 20PF-1, the top section may consist of a plug of foam insulation and a steel cover. The liner and shell closures must each be gasketed against moisture penetration.

The liner must have a bolted flange closure. Shell closure must conform to paragraph (d) of this section.

(d) **Drums over 5 gallons capacity must be closed** by means of 12-gauge bolted ring with drop forged lugs, one of which is threaded, and having 3/8 inch bolt and nut for drums not over 30 gallons capacity and 5/8 inch bolt and nut for drums over 30 gallons capacity. Five gallon drums must be of lug type closure with cover having at least 16 lugs.

(e) **Drawings in CAPE-1662, which include bills of material,** are a part of this specification.

§178.356-2 Materials of construction and other requirements.

(a) **Phenolic foam insulation must be fire-resistant** and fabricated in accordance with USDOE Material and Equipment Specification SP-9, Rev. 1 and Supplement, which is a part of this specification. (Note: Packagings manufactured under USAEC Specification SP-9 and Rev. 1 thereto are authorized for continued manufacture and use.) A 5.4-inch (13.7 cm) minimum thickness of foam must be provided over the entire liner except:

(1) *Where wood spacers replace the foam; or*

(2) *At protrusions* of liner or shell, such as flanges, baffles, etc., where minimum insulation thickness is 9 cm (3.5 inches); or

(3) *Where alternate top section* (specification 20PF-1) is used. Foam must not interfere with proper seating of screws in inner liner flange assembly. Average density of insulation must be 0.13 g/cc (8 pounds per cubic foot (pcf)) minimum for bottom section and 0.16 g/cc (10 pcf) minimum for top section, except 0.1 g/cc (6.5 pcf) for the specification 20PF-1 top section.

(b) **Gaskets must be as follows:**

(1) *Inner liner flange* — Neoprene rubber of 30 to 60 type A durometer hardness or other equivalent gasket material which is compatible with the specific contents.

(2) *Outer shell* — Synthetic rubber conforming to MIL-R-6855 (available from the Naval Publications Forms Center, 5801 Tabor Avenue, Philadelphia, Pennsylvania 19120) class 2, grade 60.

(3) *Support and pressure pads* for inner liner top and bottom must be sponge rubber or equivalent.

(c) **Alternate top section (specification 20PF-1 only).** Average insulation density must be 0.16 g/cc (10 pcf minimum). Thickness of plug must be 11 cm (4.3 inches) minimum, except thickness may be reduced to 10 cm (4 inches) to clear bolt heads. A flush mounted top lifting device must be securely fastened to a wood block encapsulated by the foam.

(d) **Vent holes 5 mm (0.2-inch) diameter** must be drilled in the outer shell to provide pressure relief during the insulation foaming and in the event of a fire. These holes, which must be drilled in all areas of the shell which mate with the foam insulation, must be spaced in accordance with CAPE-1662.

(e) **Welding must be by a fusion welding process** in accordance with American Welding Society Codes B-3.0 and D-1.0. Body seams and joints for the liner or shell must be continuous welds.

(f) **Waterproofing.** Each screw hole in the outer shell must be sealed with appropriate resin-type sealing material, or equivalent, during installation of the screw. All exposed foam surfaces, including any vent hole, must be sealed with waterproofing material as prescribed in USDOE Material and Equipment Specification SP-9, Rev. 1 and Supplement, or equivalent.

§178.356-3 Tests.

(a) **Leakage test — Each inner liner assembly must be tested** for leakage prior to installation. Seam welds of the liner must be covered for a distance of at least 15 cm (6 inches) on either side of the seam with soapsuds, heavy oil, or equivalent material, and interior air pressure applied to at least 776 mm Hg (15 p.s.i.g.) above atmospheric pressure must be held for at least 30 seconds. Liners failing to pass this test may not be used until repairs are made, and retests successfully passed.

(b) **[Reserved]**

§178.356-4 Required markings.

(a) **Marking must be as prescribed in §178.3.**

(b) **Marking on the outside of each overpack must be as follows:**

(1) *"USA-DOT-20PF-1" or "-2,"* as appropriate, and if the entire liner is made of stainless steel, additional marking such as "3041-SS" to indicate the type of stainless steel used.

(2) *"TARE WT: xxx lbs."* where xxx is the tare weight of the assembled overpack without the inner container.

(3) *Year of manufacture.*

§178.356-5 Typical assembly detail.

(a) **Specifications 20PF-1.**

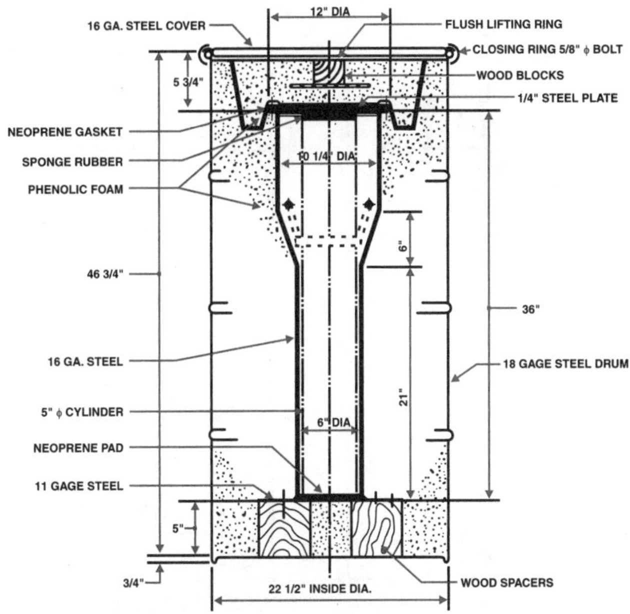

(b) **Specification 20PF-2.**

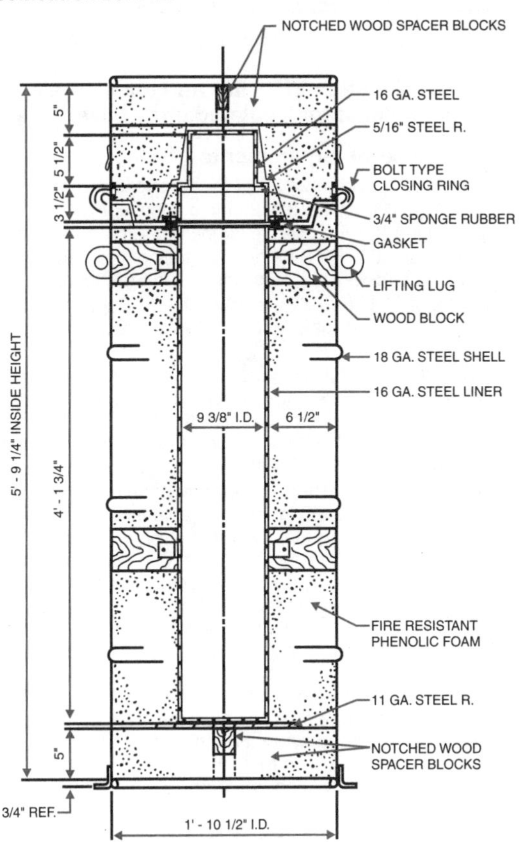

178 Specifications for Packagings

(c) Specification 20PF-3.

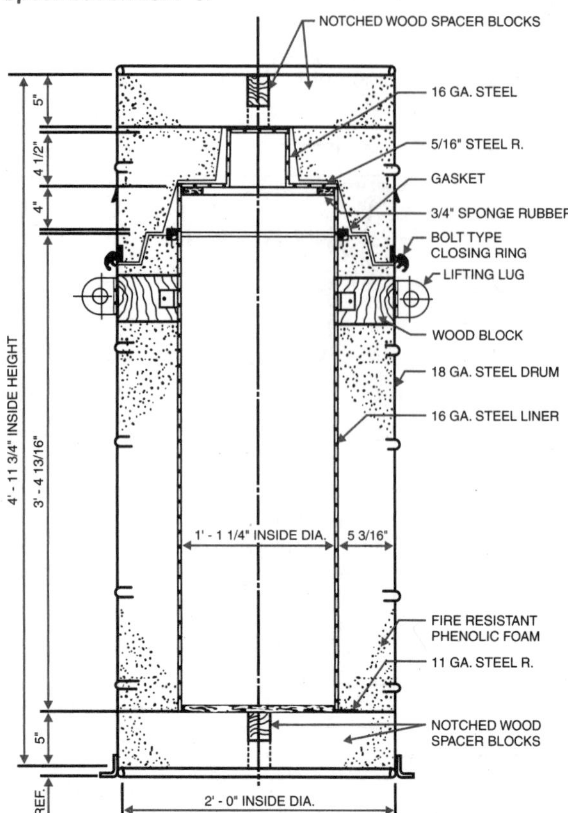

§178.358 Specification 21PF fire and shock resistant, phenolic-foam insulated, metal overpack.

§178.358-1 General requirements.

(a) **Each overpack must meet all of the applicable requirements** of §§173.24, 173.411, and 173.412 of this subchapter.

(1) *Specification 21PF-1* overpacks includes the series of 21PF-1, 21PF-1A, and 21PF-1B models. Details of the three models are included in CAPE-1662, Revision 1 and Supplement 1.

(2) *Drawings in CAPE-1662,* Revision 1 and Supplement 1, which include bills of materials, and K/SS-471, are a part of this specification.

(b) **Each overpack is authorized for use** in applications where the maximum gross weight of the package, including the inner container and contents does not exceed 3725 kg (8200 pounds), (horizontally-loaded specification 21 PF-1 unit), or 3900 kg (8600 pounds), (end-loaded specification 21 PF-2 unit).

(c) **The general configuration of the overpack** must be a right cylinder, consisting of a steel inner liner (at least 16-gauge) and steel outer shell (at least 14-gauge) with the intervening cavity filled with a molded-in-place, fire-resistant, phenolic foam insulation and interspersed wooden members for bracing and support. Two specific configurations are authorized; a horizontal loading unit (specification 21PF-1) consisting of insulated base and top sections jointed in a longitudinal peripheral closure joint; or an end-loading unit (specification 21PF-2), consisting of an insulated main section, a steel plate liner lid, and an insulated end cap. For either type each joint between sections must be stepped at least 1.8 cm (0.75-inch) and gaps between mating surfaces may not exceed 5 mm (0.2-inch). Bolted closures, which must each be gasketed against moisture penetration, must be in accordance with CAPE-1662. Each bolt must be equipped with a locking device to prevent loosening from vibration. Outer steel bracing and support framework must be attached to the shell to facilitate normal handling.

(d) **Specification 21PF-1 overpacks in use** or under construction before April 1, 1989, must be modified to Specification 21PF-1A before April 1, 1991. All new construction to Specification 21PF-1 beginning after March 31, 1989, must meet Specification 21PF-1B. Use of unmodified 21PF-1 overpacks after March 31, 1991, is prohibited.

§178.358-2 Materials of construction and other requirements.

(a) **Phenolic foam insulation must be fire resistant** and fabricated in accordance with USDOE Material and Equipment Specification SP-9, Rev. 1 and Supplement, which is a part of this specification. (Note: Packagings manufactured under USAEC Specification SP-9, and Rev. 1 thereto are authorized for continued manufacture and use.) A 5.5-inch (14 cm) minimum thickness of foam must be provided over the entire liner except where:

(1) *Wood spacers replace the foam material; or*

(2) *At protrusions* of liner or shell, such as flanges, baffles, etc., where the minimum thickness of foam, wood, or a combination of these is 10 cm (4 inches).

(3) *Solid wood* or laminated wood solidly glued may be used to replace the foam between liner and shell (i.e., in ends of overpack). In this case, minimum wood thickness is 10 cm (4 inches). Average density of insulation must be 0.1g/cc (6.75 pounds per cubic foot (pcf)) minimum, except that 0.13 g/cc (8 pcf) is required in the removable end cap of the specification 21PF-2, which must have a minimum foam thickness of 12.7 cm (5 inches).

(b) **Gaskets for inner liner, outer shell,** or where otherwise specified in CAPE-1662, Revision 1, must be as specified in CAPE-1662, Revision 1.

(c) **Support and pressure pads for the inner liner** must be of neoprene, sponge rubber, or equivalent.

(d) **Fire-retardant (intumescent) paint must be applied** to any wood blocking which is located at any joint in the shell.

(e) **Vent holes 5 mm (0.2-inch) diameter** must be drilled in the outer shell to provide pressure relief during the insulation foaming and in the event of a fire. These holes, which must be drilled in all areas of the shell which made with the foam insulation, must be spaced in accordance with CAPE-1662.

(f) **Welding must be by a fusion process** in accordance with the American Welding Society Code. Body seams and joints for the liner and shell must be continuous welds.

(g) **Waterproofing.** Each screw hole in the outer shell must be sealed with appropriate resin-type sealing material, or equivalent, during installation of the screw. All exposed foam surfaces, including any vent hole, must be sealed with either:

(1) *Waterproofing material* as prescribed in USDOE Material and Equipment Specification SP-9, Rev. 1 and Supplement, or

(2) *As specified in CAPE-1662, Revision 1.*

§178.358-3 Modification of Specification 21PF-1 overpacks.

(a) **Each Specification 21PF-1 overpack for which** construction began or was completed before April 1, 1989, in conformance with drawing E-S-31536-J, Revision 11, of CAPE-1662 must be modified in conformance with drawing S1E-31536-J1-D of CAPE-1662, Revision 1, Supplement 1, before April 1, 1991.

(b) **Each such existing Specification 21PF-1 overpack** must be dried and weighed in accordance with the following procedures:

(1) *Drill out or otherwise clean* the plug material from the vent holes originally provided for foam expansion. See drawing S1E-31536-J1-D of CAPE-1662, Revision 1, Supplement 1, for locations.

(2) *Weigh each packaging element* (top and bottom halves) separately to an accuracy of 2.3 kg (5 pounds) and record the weights. If this measured weight exceeds the initially measured weight at the time of fabrication by 11.3 kg (25 pounds) (indicating a significant retained water content), the packaging element must be dried.

(3) *Place overpack element in drying oven;* maintain temperature between 87.8-98.9 $^{\circ}$C (190 $^{\circ}$and 210 $^{\circ}$F) for a minimum of 72 hours. The oven should have a provision for air exchange or other means of removing moisture driven from the foam structure.

(4) *Drying may be discontinued* after 72 hours if the weight of the packaging element does not exceed the initially measured tare weight of that element at the time of fabrication by more than 11.3 kg (25 pounds). If the weight of the packaging element exceeds the initial fabricated weight (indicating a significant remaining water content) by more than 11.3 kg (25 pounds), drying must be continued until the weight differential is not higher than 11.3 kg (25 pounds), or until the rate of weight loss is less than 1.1 kg (2.5 pounds) per day.

(5) *As an alternate moisture measurement,* a calibrated moisture meter reading for 20 percent maximum water content may be used to indicate an end point in the drying cycle (see details in report "Renovation of DOT Specification 21PF-1 Protective Shipping Packages," Report No. K-2057, Revision 1, November 21, 1986, available from the USDOE and part of USDOE Report No. K/SS-471).

(6) *Following drying,* each overpack element (top and bottom halves) must be weighed and the weight in both pounds and kilograms must be engraved on the identification plate required by §178.358-5(c).

(c) **After modification as provided for herein,** each Specification 21PF-1 overpack must be marked "USA-DOT-21PF-1A". See the marking requirements of §178.358-5.

§178.358-4 Construction of Specification 21PF-1B overpacks.

(a) **Each Specification 21PF-1 overpack for which** construction began after March 31, 1989, must meet the requirements of Specification 21PF-1B, in conformance with drawings E-S-31536-J-P, and S1E-31536-J2-B of CAPE-1662, Revision 1, Supplement 1.

(b) **With the exception of the closure nuts and bolts,** all metal parts of the Specification 21PF-1B must be of stainless steel as shown on the drawings referred to in paragraph (a) of this section.

§178.358-5 Required markings.

(a) **Markings must be as prescribed in §178.3.**

(b) **Specification marking on the outside of each overpack** must be as follows: "USA-DOT-21PF-1", "1A", "1B", or "2", as appropriate.

(1) *For Specifications 21PF-1 and 21PF-2 only,* if the inner shell is constructed of stainless steel, additional marking such as "304L-SS" are to be marked on the outside of the overpack to indicate the type of stainless steel used.

(2) *For Specification 21PF-1 and 21PF-2 only,* "TARE WT: * * * lbs. (* * * kg)" where * * * is the tare weight in pounds and kilograms, respectively, of the assembled overpack without the inner product container.

(3) *For Specification 21PF-1A and 21PF-1B only:* "TARE WT. of Cover: * * * lbs (* * * kg) TARE WT. of BOTTOM: * * * lbs (* * * kg)" where * * * is the tare weight in pounds and kilograms, respectively, of the separate halves of the overpack without the inner product container. For Specification 21PF-1A overpacks, the previous tare weight must be changed to reflect the modified tare weight value or must be covered or removed.

(4) *Year of manufacture* followed by the year of modification, if applicable.

(5) *The name or symbol* of maker or party certifying compliance with specification requirements. A symbol, if used, must be registered with the Associate Administrator.

(c) **For Specification 21PF-1A and -1B only,** the markings required by this section must be affixed to each overpack by inscription upon a metal identification plate 11 inches wide x 15 inches long (28 cm x 38 cm), fabricated of 16 to 20 gauge stainless steel sheet, ASTM A 240/A 240M (incorporated by reference; see §171.1 of this subchapter), Type 304L.

§178.358-6 Typical assembly detail.

(a) **Specification 21PF-1 (horizontal loading overpack).**

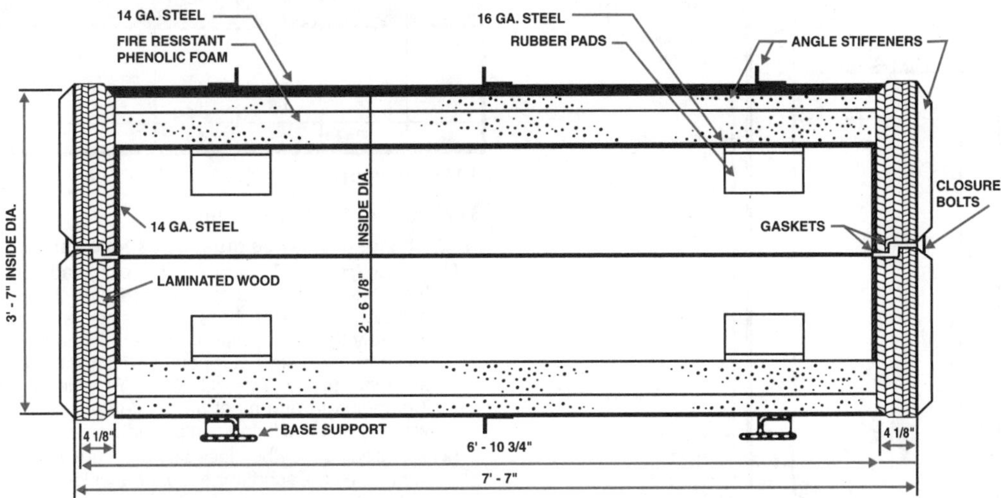

(b) **Specification 21PF-1A and 21PF-1B (horizontal loading overpack).**

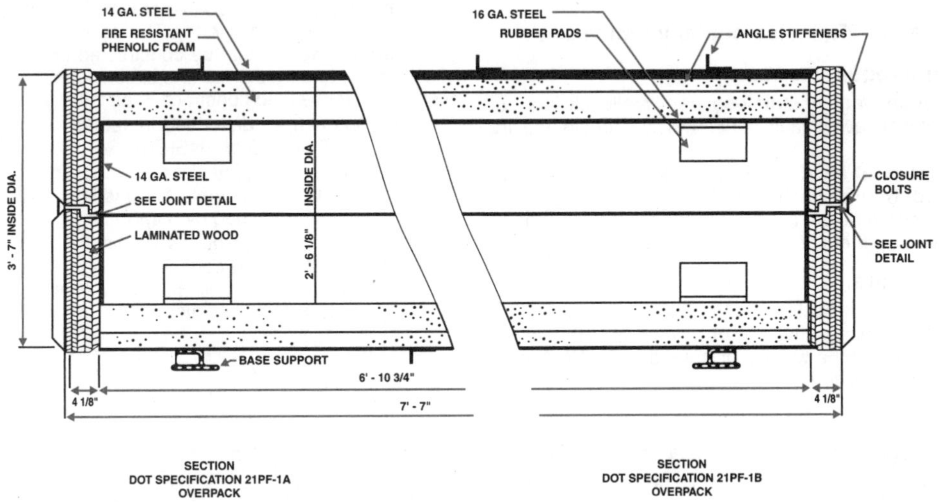

SECTION
DOT SPECIFICATION 21PF-1A
OVERPACK

SECTION
DOT SPECIFICATION 21PF-1B
OVERPACK

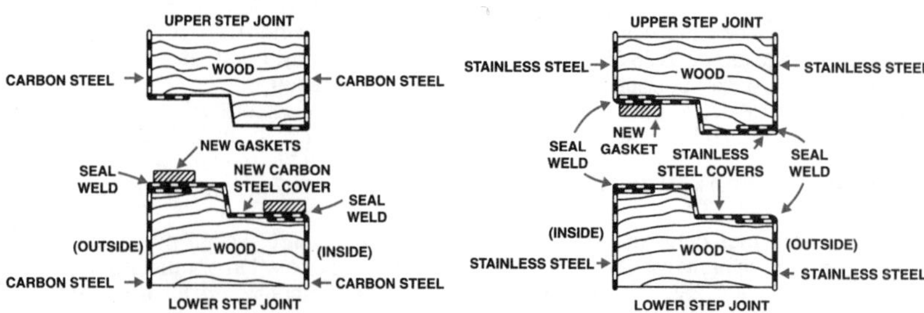

JOINT DETAIL
DOT SPECIFICATION 21PF-1A
OVERPACK

JOINT DETAIL
DOT SPECIFICATION 21PF-1B
OVERPACK

(c) Specification 21PF-2 (end loading overpack).

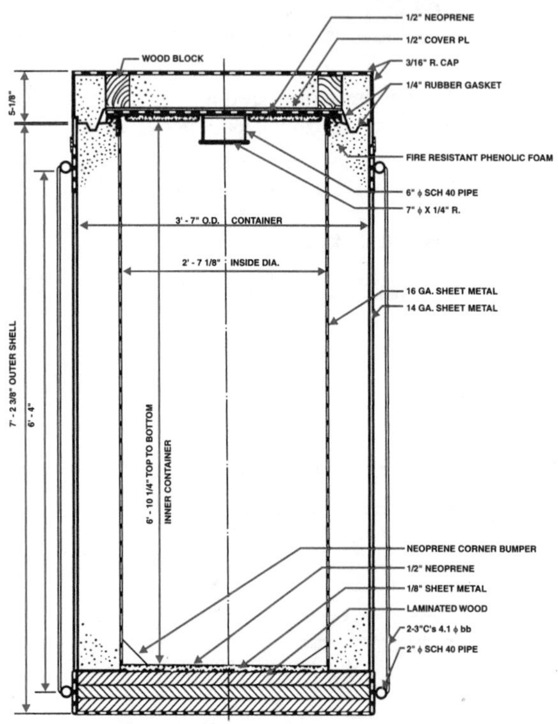

§178.360 Specification 2R; inside containment vessel.

§178.360-1 General requirements.

(a) **Each vessel must be made of stainless steel,** malleable iron, or brass, or other material having equivalent physical strength and fire resistance.

(b) **Each vessel must meet all of the applicable requirements** of §173.24 (c) and (d) of this subchapter. Letters and numerals at least 6 mm (1/4-inch) in height are authorized for the marking of a vessel not exceeding 5 cm (2 inches) inside diameter.

§178.360-2 Manufacture.

The ends of the vessel must be fitted with screw-type closures or flanges (see §178.360-4), except that one or both ends of the vessel may be permanently closed by a welded or brazed plate. Welded or brazed side seams are authorized.

§178.360-3 Dimensions.

(a) **The inside diameter of the vessel may not exceed** 30 cm (12 inches) exclusive of flanges for handling or fastening devices and must have wall thickness and length in accordance with the following:

Inside diameter maximum		Threaded closure		Wall thickness minimum — Flanged closure	Length maximum	
Inches	Cm	Inches	Mm		Inches	Cm
2	5	3/32	2.5	Not less than that prescribed for schedule 40 pipe	16	41
6	15	1/8	3.2		72	183
12	30	1/4	6.5		72	183

(b) [Reserved]

§178.360-4 Closure devices.

(a) **Each closure device must be as follows:**

(1) *Screw-type cap or plug;* number of threads per inch must not be less than United States standard pipe threads and must have sufficient length of thread to engage at least 5 threads when securely tightened. Pipe threads must be luted with an appropriate non-hardening compound which must be capable of withstanding up to 149 °C (300 °F) without loss of efficiency. Tightening torque must be adequate to maintain leak tightness with the specific luting compound.

(2) *An opening* may be closed by a securely bolted flange and leak-tight gasket. Each flange must be welded or brazed to the body of the 2R vessel per (ANSI) Standard B16.5 or (AWWA) Standard C207-55, section 10. A torque wrench must be used in securing the flange with a corresponding torque of no more than twice the force necessary to seal the selected gasket. Gasket material must be capable of withstanding up to 149 °C (300 °F) without loss of efficiency. The flange, whether of ferrous or non-ferrous metal, must be constructed from the same metal as the vessel and must meet the dimensional and fabrication specifications for welded construction as follows:

(i) *Pipe flanges* described in Tables 13, 14, 16, 17, 19, 20, 22, 23, 25 and 26 of ANSI B16.5.

(ii) *For nominal pipe sizes,* 6, 8, 10, and 12 inches, AWWA Standard C207-55, Table 1, class B, may be used in place of the tables prescribed by paragraph (a)(2)(i) of this section.

(iii) *Sizes under 6 inches,* nominal pipe size, the following table with the same configuration as illustrated in AWWA C207-55, Table 1, class B, may be used in place of paragraph (a)(2)(i) of this section.

Nominal pipe size		Flange O.D.		Number of bolts	Bolt circle diameter		Diameter of bolts		Flange thickness	
Inches	Cm	Inches	Cm		Inches	Cm	Inches	Cm	Inches	Cm
2	5	6	15	4	4 3/4	11.8	1/2	1.2	5/8	1.6
2 1/2	6.2	7	17.5	4	5 1/2	13.8	1/2		5/8	
3	7.5	7 1/2	18.8	4	6	15	1/2		5/8	
3 1/2	8.8	8 1/2	21.3	8	7	17.5	1/2		5/8	
4	10	9	22.5	8	7 1/2	18.8	1/2		5/8	
5	12.6	10	25.4	8	8 1/2	21.3	1/2		5/8	

(iv) *Cast iron flanges prohibited.*

(b) [Reserved]

§178.362 Specification 20WC wooden protective jacket.

§178.362-1 General requirements.

(a) Each jacket must meet the applicable requirements of §173.24 of this subchapter.

(b) Maximum gross weight of the jacket plus the contents may not exceed the following:

(1) *Specification 20WC-1:* 225 kg (500 pounds).
(2) *Specification 20WC-2:* 225 kg (500 pounds).
(3) *Specification 20WC-3:* 455 kg (1000 pounds).
(4) *Specification 20WC-4:* 910 kg (2000 pounds).
(5) *Specification 20WC-5:* 1820 kg (4000 pounds).
(6) *Specification 20WC-6:* 2730 kg (6000 pounds).

§178.362-2 Materials of construction.

(a) The general configuration of the wooden protective jacket must be a hollow cylindrical shell constructed of one-piece discs and rings of plywood or solid hardwood reinforced with steel rods.

(1) *The specification 20WC-2* must be additionally completely encased, snugly fit, within an 18-gauge steel shell. The steel shell must be provided with at least four 6 millimeter (0.25-inch) diameter vent holes. Each hole must be covered with durable weatherproof tape, or equivalent device.

(2) *The specification 20WC-6 jacket* must be additionally completely encased, snugly-fit, within a 12-gauge steel shell. The steel shell must be provided with at least twelve 1.2 cm (0.5-inch) diameter vent holes, located in 3 rows of 4 holes each, spaced at 90 degree intervals near the top, middle, and bottom of the drum. Each hole must be covered with durable weatherproof tape, or equivalent device.

(b) Plywood must be exterior-grade, void-free, Douglas fir (or equivalent) not more than 2.5 cm (1 inch) thick. Solid hardwood is authorized for specification 20WC-2 only.

(c) Discs and rings must be glued together with a strong, shock-resistant adhesive, such as either of the following:

(1) *Asorcinol-formaldehyde adhesive,* which has been bonded under both heat and pressure; or

(2) *A polyvinyl-acetate emulsion,* which has been reinforced with cement-coated nails. The nails must be randomly spaced and must be at least 2.5 times as long as the minimum thickness of the plywood discs or rings.

(d) Full-length steel rods are required for reinforcement and lid closure.

(1) *The minimum* number of rods and the minimum rod diameter are as shown in the following table:

Specification	Minimum number or rods	Minimum rod diameter	
		Inches	Mm
20WC-1	6	0.25	6.0
20WC-2	6	.25	6.0
20WC-3	12	.375	9.5
20WC-4	16	.375	9.5
20WC-5	16	.50	12.0
20WC-6	16	.50	12.0

(2) *For specifications 20WC-1 and 20WC-2,* steel rods must be equally spaced around the circumference to the rings and discs, midway between the O.D. and I.D. of the rings. For specifications 20WC-3 and 20WC-4, bolts may be staggered alternately in two rows, at ±1.2 cm (0.5-inch) from the line midway between the O.D. and I.D. of the rings. For specifications 20WC-5 and 20WC-6, bolts may be staggered alternately in two rows at ±2.5 cm (1 inch) from the line midway between the O.D. and I.D. of the rings.

(3) *Rod ends* must be threaded and secured with lock nuts and steel washers, or equivalent device, to provide at least a 2.5 cm (1 inch) diameter bearing surface on each end. Ends of the rods must terminate 1.4 cm (0.75-inch) below the surface of the plywood for specifications 20WC-1 and 20WC-2. For specifications 20WC-3, 20WC-4, 20WC-5 and 20WC-6, the ends of the rods must terminate 3.7 cm (1.5 inches) below the surface of the plywood, and that portion of each end disc which extends beyond the rod ends must be further held in place with lag screws at least 10 cm (4 inches) long.

(e) Thickness of wooden shell:

(1) *Specification 20WC-1:* At least 10 cm (4 inches) thick.

(2) *Specification 20WC-2:* At least 7.5 cm (3 inches) thick.

(3) *Specification 20WC-3:* At least 13 cm (5 inches) thick for the jacket wall, and at least 15 cm (6 inches) thick for the end discs. In addition, at least 3 plywood chines, 5 cm (2 inches) wide and protruding 5 cm (2 inches) beyond the outer surfaces, must be located at each end and midway along the length of the jacket.

(4) *Specification 20WC-4:* At least 15 cm (6 inches) thick for the jacket wall, and at least 15 cm (6 inches) thick for the end discs. In addition, at least 3 plywood chines, 5 cm (2 inches) wide and protruding 5 cm (2 inches) beyond the outer surfaces, must be located at each end and midway along the length of the jacket.

(5) *Specifications 20WC-5 and 20WC-6:* At least 15 cm (6 inches) thick for the jacket wall, and at least 20 cm (8 inches) thick for the end discs. In addition, at least 5 plywood chimes, 5 cm (2 inches) wide and protruding 5 cm (2 inches) beyond the outer surfaces, must be located at each end and equally spaced along the length of the jacket.

§178.362-3 Closure.

(a) Closure for the wooden protective jacket is provided by the steel reinforcing rods. The end cap (lid) must fit tightly to the body of the jacket to prevent a heat path to the inside of the jacket. The lid joint for specifications 20WC-3, 20WC-4, 20WC-5, and 20WC-6, may not be coplanar with the end of the inner containment vessel.

(b) Specifications 20WC-2 and 20WC-6. Locking ring closure, if used, must conform to §178.354-4. Flanged closure, if used, must have at least 8 steel bolts (at least 6 mm (0.25-inch) diameter for 20WC-2 or 1.2 cm (0.50-inch) diameter for 20WC-6) and lock nuts (or equivalent device), spaced not more than 13 cm (5 inches) between centers.

§178.362-4 Tests.

Prior to each use, each jacket must be visually inspected for defects such as improper bonding, cracking, corrosion of steel rods, and improperly fitting closure lid, or other manufacturing defects. Particular attention must be given to any separation of the plywood discs and rings which would provide a heat path to the inside of the jacket.

§178.362-5 Painting.

Each jacket (other than 20WC-2 and 20WC-6) must be completely painted with a high quality exterior weather resistant paint.

§178.362-6 Marking.

(a) Each jacket must be marked on the external surface as follows: "USA-DOT 20WC-( ) TYPE B." The appropriate numeral must be inserted in the marking to indicate the appropriate specification 20WC category: e.g., "20WC-2."

(b) Each jacket must also be marked with the name or symbol of person making the marks specified in paragraph (a) of this section. Symbol, if used, must be registered with the Associate Administrator.

§178.362-7 Typical assembly sketches.

(a) Spec. 20WC-2.

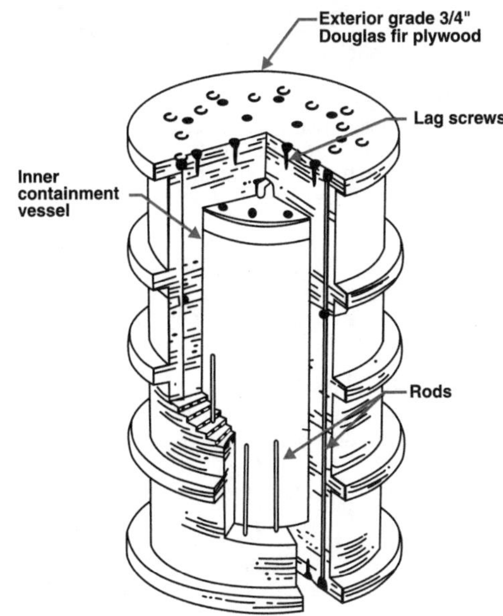

(b) Spec. 20WC-5.

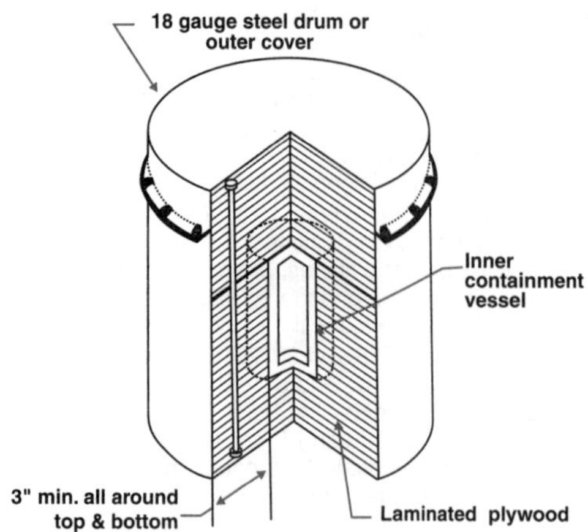

§178.364 Specification 21WC wooden-steel protective overpack.

§178.364-1 General requirements.

(a) Each jacket must meet all the applicable requirements of §173.24 of this subchapter.

(b) The maximum authorized gross weight of the overpack, including its inner container and contents may not exceed 1360 kg (3000 pounds).

§178.364-2 Materials of construction and other requirements.

(a) The general configuration of the protective overpack must be a combination of two nested plywood boxes, each 2.5 cm (1 inch) thick, nested within a third wooden box of nominal 5 cm (2-inch) thickness solid hardwood. The three nested boxes must be enclosed within a welded framework 10 cement-coated nails spaced on nominally 1 centimeter (3/8-inch) thick by 8-10 cm (3-4 inches) wide. All outer surfaces of each box must be coated with intumescent paint.

(b) Plywood must be exterior-grade, void-free, Douglas fir, or equivalent, at least 2.5 cm (1 inch) thick. Solid hardwood must be maple, or equivalent.

(c) All box joints and interior surfaces must be glued with a strong, shock-resistant adhesive such as polyvinylacetate emulsion, or equivalent.

(d) All hardwood joints must be mitered, or equivalent, reinforced with No. 10 cement-coated nails space on nominal 15 cm (6-inch) centers.

(e) All plywood joints must be butt-type, or equivalent, reinforced with No. 10 cement-coated nails spaced on nominal 15 cm (6-inch) centers.

(f) The angles and strapping of the metal frame must be spaced such that separation distances do not exceed 15 cm (6 inches).

(g) The lid must be of the same material as the box and fabricated in such a manner that closure forms a mitered joint with the hardwood box and 2 stepped-joints with the plywood boxes.

§178.364-3 Closure.

Closure for the protective overpack must be provided by at least 4 mild steel hinges formed from minimum 2.5 cm (1 inch) x 5 mm (3/16 inch) bar stock. Hinge pins must be minimum 6 mm (1/4 inch) diameter by 13.3 cm (5 1/4 inches) long mild steel rod drilled at both ends for cotter pins.

§178.364-4 Tests.

Prior to each use, each overpack must be visually inspected for defects such as wood checking or splintering weld cracking, corrosion of steel parts, improper joint bonding, or improperly fitting closure lid.

§178.364-5 Required marking.

(a) Marking must be as prescribed in §178.3.

(b) Marking on the outside of each overpack must include the following:

(1) *"USA-DOT 21WC" and "TYPE B" as appropriate.*

(2) *[Reserved]*

§178.364-6 Typical assembly detail.

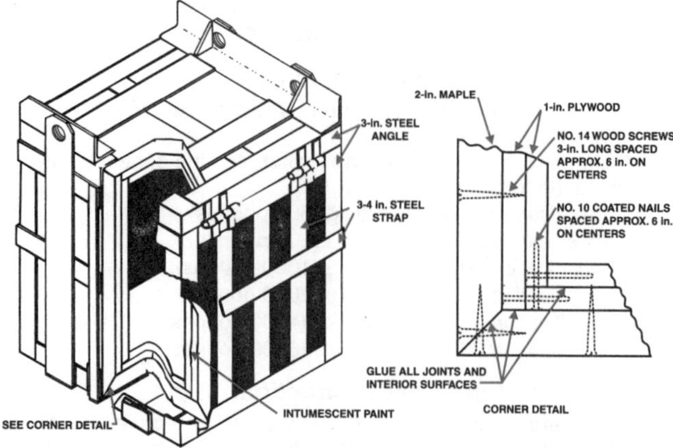

RADIOISOTOPES SHIPPING CASK FIRE AND IMPACT SHIELD

Subpart L - Non-bulk Performance-oriented Packaging Standards

§178.500 Purpose, scope and definitions.

(a) This subpart prescribes certain requirements for non-bulk packagings for hazardous materials. Standards for these packagings are based on the UN Recommendations.

(b) Terms used in this subpart are defined in §171.8 of this subchapter.

§178.502 Identification codes for packagings.

(a) Identification codes for designating kinds of packagings consist of the following:

(1) *A numeral indicating the kind of packaging, as follows:*

(i) *"1" means a drum.*

(ii) *"2" means a wooden barrel.*

(iii) *"3" means a jerrican.*

(iv) *"4" means a box.*

(v) *"5" means a bag.*

(vi) *"6" means a composite packaging.*

(vii) *"7" means a pressure receptacle.*

(2) *A capital letter indicating the material of construction, as follows:*

(i) *"A" means steel (all types and surface treatments).*

(ii) *"B" means aluminum.*

(iii) *"C" means natural wood.*

(iv) *"D" means plywood.*

(v) *"F" means reconstituted wood.*

(vi) *"G" means fiberboard.*

(vii) *"H" means plastic.*

(viii) *"L" means textile.*

(ix) *"M" means paper, multi-wall.*

(x) *"N" means metal (other than steel or aluminum).*

(xi) *"P" means glass, porcelain or stoneware.*

(3) *A numeral indicating* the category of packaging within the kind to which the packaging belongs. For example, for steel drums ("1A"), "1" indicates a non-removable head drum (i.e., "1A1") and "2" indicates a removable head drum (i.e., "1A2").

(b) For composite packagings, two capital letters are used in sequence in the second position of the code, the first indicating the material of the inner receptacle and the second, that of the outer packaging. For example, a plastic receptacle in a steel drum is designated "6HA1".

(c) For combination packagings, only the code number for the outer packaging is used.

(d) Identification codes are set forth in the standards for packagings in §§178.504 through 178.523 of this subpart.

§178.503 Marking of packagings.

(a) A manufacturer must mark every packaging that is represented as manufactured to meet a UN standard with the marks specified in this section. The markings must be durable, legible and placed in a location and of such a size relative to the packaging as to be readily visible, as specified in §178.3(a). Except as otherwise provided in this section, every reusable packaging liable to undergo a reconditioning process which might obliterate the packaging marks must bear the marks specified in paragraphs (a)(1) through (a)(6) and (a)(9) of this section in a permanent form (e.g. embossed) able to withstand the reconditioning process. A marking may be applied in a single line or in multiple lines provided the correct sequence is used. As illustrated by the examples in paragraph (e) of this section, the following information must be presented in the correct sequence. Slash marks should be used to separate this information. A packaging conforming to a UN standard must be marked as follows:

(1) *The United Nations symbol* as illustrated in paragraph (e)(1) of this section (for embossed metal receptacles, the letters UN may be applied in place of the symbol);

(2) *A packaging identification code* designating the type of packaging, the material of construction and, when appropriate, the category of packaging under §§178.504 through 178.523 of this subpart within the type to which the packaging belongs. The letter "V" must follow the packaging identification code on packagings tested in accordance with §178.601(g)(2); for example, "4GV". The letter "W" must follow the packaging identification code on packagings when required by an approval under the provisions of §178.601(h) of this part;

(3) *A letter identifying* the performance standard under which the packaging design type has been successfully tested, as follows:

(i) *X — for packagings meeting Packing Group I, II and III tests;*

(ii) *Y — for packagings meeting Packing Group II and III tests; or*

(iii) *Z — for packagings only meeting Packing Group III tests;*

(4) *A designation* of the specific gravity or mass for which the packaging design type has been tested, as follows:

(i) *For packagings* without inner packagings intended to contain liquids, the designation shall be the specific gravity rounded down to the first decimal but may be omitted when the specific gravity does not exceed 1.2; and

(ii) *For packagings* intended to contain solids or inner packagings, the designation shall be the maximum gross mass in kilograms;

(5) (i) *For single and composite packagings* intended to contain liquids, the test pressure in kilopascals rounded down to the nearest 10 kPa of the hydrostatic pressure test that the packaging design type has successfully passed;

(ii) *For packagings* intended to contain solids or inner packagings, the letter "S";

(6) *The last two digits* of the year of manufacture. Packagings of types 1H and 3H shall also be marked with the month of manufacture in any appropriate manner; this may be marked on the packaging in a different place from the remainder of the markings;

(7) *The state authorizing allocation of the mark.* The letters "USA" indicate that the packaging is manufactured and marked in the United States in compliance with the provisions of this subchapter;

(8) *The name and address* or symbol of the manufacturer or the approval agency certifying compliance with subpart L and subpart M of this part. Symbols, if used, must be registered with the Associate Administrator;

(9) *For metal or plastic drums* or jerricans intended for reuse or reconditioning as single packagings or the outer packagings of a composite packaging, the thickness of the packaging material, expressed in mm (rounded to the nearest 0.1 mm), as follows:

(i) *Metal drums or jerricans* must be marked with the nominal thickness of the metal used in the body. The marked nominal thickness must not exceed the minimum thickness of the steel used by more than the thickness tolerance stated in ISO Standard 3574. (See appendix C of this part.) The unit of measure is not required to be marked. When the nominal thickness of either head of a metal drum is thinner than that of the body, the nominal thickness of the top head, body, and bottom head must be marked (eg., "1.0-1.2-1.0" or "0.9-1.0-1.0").

(ii) *Plastic drums or jerricans* must be marked with the minimum thickness of the packaging material. Minimum thicknesses of plastic must be as determined in accordance with §173.28(b)(4). The unit of measure is not required to be marked;

(10) *In addition* to the markings prescribed in paragraphs (a)(1) through (a)(9) of this section, every new metal drum having a capacity greater than 100 L must bear the marks described in paragraphs (a)(1) through (a)(6), and (a)(9)(i) of this section, in a permanent form, on the bottom. The markings on the top head or side of these packagings need not be permanent, and need not include the thickness mark described in paragraph (a)(9) of this section. This marking indicates a drum's characteristics at the time it was manufactured, and the information in paragraphs (a)(1) through (a)(6) of this section that is marked on the top head or side must be the same as the information in paragraphs (a)(1) through (a)(6) of this section permanently marked by the original manufacturer on the bottom of the drum; and

(11) *Rated capacity* of the packaging expressed in liters may be marked.

(b) For a packaging with a removable head, the markings may not be applied only to the removable head.

(c) Marking of reconditioned packagings.

(1) *If a packaging is reconditioned,* it shall be marked by the reconditioner near the marks required in paragraphs (a)(1) through (6) of this section with the following additional information:

(i) *The name* of the country in which the reconditioning was performed (in the United States, use the letters "USA");

(ii) *The name and address* or symbol of the reconditioner. Symbols, if used, must be registered with the Associate Administrator;

(iii) *The last two digits of the year of reconditioning;*

(iv) *The letter "R"; and*

(v) *For every packaging* successfully passing a leakproofness test, the additional letter "L".

(2) *When, after reconditioning,* the markings required by paragraph (a)(1) through (a)(5) of this section no longer appear on the top head or the side of the metal drum, the reconditioner must apply them in a durable form followed by the markings in paragraph (c)(1) of this section. These markings may identify a different performance capability than that for which the original design type had been tested and marked, but may not identify a greater performance capability. The markings applied in accordance with this paragraph may be different from those which are permanently marked on the bottom of a drum in accordance with paragraph (a)(10) of this section.

(d) Marking of remanufactured packagings. For remanufactured metal drums, if there is no change to the packaging type and no replacement or removal of integral structural components, the required markings need not be permanent (e.g., embossed). Every other remanufactured drum must bear the marks required in paragraphs (a)(1) through (a)(6) of this section in a permanent form (e.g., embossed) on the top head or side. If the metal thickness marking required in paragraph (a)(9)(i) of this section does not appear on the bottom of the drum, or if it is no longer valid, the remanufacturer also must mark this information in permanent form.

(e) The following are examples of symbols and required markings:

(1) *The United Nations symbol is:*

(2) *Examples of markings for a new packaging are as follows:*

(i) *For a fiberboard box designed to contain an inner packaging:*

(as in §178.503 (a)(1) through (a)(9) of this subpart).

(ii) *For a steel drum designed to contain liquids:*

(as in §178.503 (a)(1) through (a)(10) of this subpart).

(iii) *For a steel drum to transport solids or inner packagings:*

§178.503 (a)(1) through (a)(8) of this subpart).

(3) *Examples of markings for reconditioned packagings are as follows:*

(as in §178.503(c)(1)).

(f) **A manufacturer must mark every UN specification package** represented as manufactured to meet the requirements of §178.609 for packaging of infectious substances with the marks specified in this section. The markings must be durable, legible, and must be readily visible, as specified in §178.3(a). An infectious substance packaging that successfully passes the tests conforming to the UN standard must be marked as follows:

(1) *The United Nations symbol* as illustrated in paragraph (e) of this section.

(2) *The code* designating the type of packaging and material of construction according to the identification codes for packagings specified in §178.502.

(3) *The text "CLASS 6.2".*

(4) *The last two digits of the year of manufacture of the packaging.*

(5) *The country* authorizing the allocation of the mark. The letters "USA" indicate the packaging is manufactured and marked in the United States in compliance with the provisions of this subchapter.

(6) *The name and address* or symbol of the manufacturer or the approval agency certifying compliance with subparts L and M of this part. Symbols, if used, must be registered with the Associate Administrator for Hazardous Materials Safety.

(7) *For packagings* meeting the requirements of §178.609(i)(3), the letter "U" must be inserted immediately following the marking designating the type of packaging and material required in paragraph (f)(2) of this section.

§178.504 Standards for steel drums.

(a) **The following are identification codes for steel drums:**

(1) *1A1 for a non-removable head steel drum; and*

(2) *1A2 for a removable head steel drum.*

(b) **Construction requirements for steel drums are as follows:**

(1) *Body and heads* must be constructed of steel sheet of suitable type and adequate thickness in relation to the capacity and intended use of the drum. Minimum thickness and marking requirements in §§173.28(b)(4) and 178.503(a)(9) of this subchapter apply to drums intended for reuse.

(2) *Body seams* must be welded on drums designed to contain more than 40 L (11 gallons) of liquids. Body seams must be mechanically seamed or welded on drums intended to contain only solids or 40 L (11 gallons) or less of liquids.

(3) *Chimes must be* mechanically seamed or welded. Separate reinforcing rings may be applied.

(4) *The body* of a drum of a capacity greater than 60 L (16 gallons) may have at least two expanded rolling hoops or two separate rolling hoops. If there are separate rolling hoops, they must be fitted tightly on the body and so secured that they cannot shift. Rolling hoops may not be spot-welded.

(5) *Openings for filling, emptying and venting* in the bodies or heads of non-removable head (1A1) drums may not exceed 7.0 cm (3 inches) in diameter. Drums with larger openings are considered to be of the removable head type (1A2). Closures for openings in the bodies and heads of drums must be so designed and applied that they will remain secure and leakproof under normal conditions of transport. Closure flanges may be mechanically seamed or welded in place. Gaskets or other sealing elements must be used with closures unless the closure is inherently leakproof.

(6) *Closure devices* for removable head drums must be so designed and applied that they will remain secure and drums will remain leakproof under normal conditions of transport. Gaskets or other sealing elements must be used with all removable heads.

(7) *If materials* used for body, heads, closures, and fittings are not in themselves compatible with the contents to be transported, suitable internal protective coatings or treatments must be applied. These coatings or treatments must retain their protective properties under normal conditions of transport.

(8) *Maximum capacity of drum:* 450 L (119 gallons).

(9) *Maximum net mass:* 400 kg (882 pounds).

§178.505 Standards for aluminum drums.

(a) **The following are the identification codes for aluminum drums:**

(1) *1B1 for a non-removable head aluminum drum; and*

(2) *1B2 for a removable head aluminum drum.*

(b) **Construction requirements for aluminum drums are as follows:**

(1) *Body and heads* must be constructed of aluminum at least 99 percent pure or an aluminum base alloy. Material must be of suitable type and adequate thickness in relation to the capacity and the intended use of the drum. Minimum thickness and marking requirements in §§173.28(b)(4) and 178.503(a)(9) of this subchapter apply to drums intended for reuse.

(2) *All seams must be welded.* Chime seams, if any, must be reinforced by the application of separate reinforcing rings.

(3) *The body* of a drum of a capacity greater than 60 L (16 gallons) may have at least two expanded rolling hoops or two separate rolling hoops. If there are separate rolling hoops, the hoops must be fitted tightly on the body and so secured that they cannot shift. Rolling hoops may not be spot-welded.

(4) *Openings for filling, emptying, or venting* in the bodies or heads of non-removable head (1B1) drums may not exceed 7.0 cm (3 inches) in diameter. Drums with larger openings are considered to be of the removable head type (1B2). Closures for openings in the bodies and heads of drums must be so designed and applied that they will remain secure and leakproof under normal conditions of transport. Closure flanges may be welded in place so that the weld provides a leakproof seam. Gaskets or other sealing elements must be used with closures unless the closure is inherently leakproof.

(5) *Closure devices* for removable head drums must be so designed and applied that they remain secure and drums remain leakproof under normal conditions of transport. Gaskets or other sealing elements must be used with all removable heads.

(6) *Maximum capacity of drum:* 450 L (119 gallons).

(7) *Maximum net mass:* 400 kg (882 pounds).

§178.506 Standards for metal drums other than steel or aluminum.

(a) **The following are the identification codes** for metal drums other than steel or aluminum:

(1) *1N1 for a non-removable head metal drum; and*

(2) *1N2 for a removable head metal drum.*

(b) **Construction requirements for metal drums** other than steel or aluminum are as follows:

(1) *Body and heads* must be constructed of metal (other than steel or aluminum) of suitable type and adequate thickness in relation to the capacity and the intended use of the drum. Minimum thickness and marking requirements in §§173.28(b)(4) and 178.503(a)(9) of this subchapter apply to drums intended for reuse.

(2) *All seams must be welded.* Chime seams, if any, must be reinforced by the application of separate reinforcing rings.

(3) *The body* of a drum of a capacity greater than 60 L (16 gallons) may have at least two expanded rolling hoops or two separate rolling hoops. If there are separate rolling hoops, the hoops must be fitted tightly on the body and so secured that they cannot shift. Rolling hoops may not be spot-welded.

(4) *Openings for filling, emptying, or venting* in the bodies or heads of non-removable head (1N1) drums may not exceed 7.0 cm (3 inches) in diameter. Drums with larger openings are considered to be of the removable head type (1N2). Closures for openings in the bodies and heads of drums must be so designed and applied that they will remain secure and leakproof under normal conditions of transport. Closure flanges may be welded in place so that the weld provides a leakproof seam. Gaskets or other sealing elements must be used with closures unless the closure is inherently leakproof.

(5) *Closure devices* for removable head drums must be so designed and applied that they remain secure and drums remain leakproof under normal conditions of transport. Gaskets or other sealing elements must be used with all removable heads.

(6) *Maximum capacity of drum:* 450 L (119 gallons).

(7) *Maximum net mass:* 400 kg (882 pounds).

§178.507 Standards for plywood drums.

(a) The identification code for a plywood drum is 1D.

(b) Construction requirements for plywood drums are as follows:

(1) *The wood used* must be well-seasoned, commercially dry and free from any defect likely to lessen the effectiveness of the drum for the purpose intended. A material other than plywood, of at least equivalent strength and durability, may be used for the manufacture of the heads.

(2) *At least two-ply plywood* must be used for the body and at least three-ply plywood for the heads; the plies must be firmly glued together, with their grains crosswise.

(3) *The body and heads* of the drum and their joints must be of a design appropriate to the capacity of the drum and its intended use.

(4) *In order to prevent* sifting of the contents, lids must be lined with kraft paper or some other equivalent material which must be securely fastened to the lid and extend to the outside along its full circumference.

(5) *Maximum capacity of drum:* 250 L (66 gallons).

(6) *Maximum net mass:* 400 kg (882 pounds).

§178.508 Standards for fiber drums.

(a) The identification code for a fiber drum is 1G.

(b) Construction requirements for fiber drums are as follows:

(1) *The body* of the drum must be constructed of multiple plies of heavy paper or fiberboard (without corrugations) firmly glued or laminated together and may include one or more protective layers of bitumen, waxed kraft paper, metal foil, plastic material, or similar materials.

(2) *Heads must be* of natural wood, fiberboard, metal, plywood, plastics, or other suitable material and may include one or more protective layers of bitumen, waxed kraft paper, metal foil, plastic material, or similar material.

(3) *The body and heads* of the drum and their joints must be of a design appropriate to the capacity and intended use of the drum.

(4) *The assembled packaging* must be sufficiently water-resistant so as not to delaminate under normal conditions of transport.

(5) *Maximum capacity of drum:* 450 L (119 gallons).

(6) *Maximum net mass:* 400 kg (882 pounds).

§178.509 Standards for plastic drums and jerricans.

(a) The following are identification codes for plastic drums and jerricans:

(1) *1H1 for a non-removable head plastic drum;*

(2) *1H2 for a removable head plastic drum;*

(3) *3H1 for a non-removable head jerrican; and*

(4) *3H2 for a removable head jerrican.*

(b) Construction requirements for plastic drums and jerricans are as follows:

(1) *The packaging* must be manufactured from suitable plastic material and be of adequate strength in relation to its capacity and intended use. No used material other than production residues or regrind from the same manufacturing process may be used unless approved by the Associate Administrator. The packaging must be adequately resistant to aging and to degradation caused either by the substance contained or by ultra-violet radiation. Any permeation of the substance contained may not constitute a danger under normal conditions of transport.

(2) *If protection* against ultra-violet radiation is required, it must be provided by the addition of carbon black or other suitable pigments or inhibitors. These additives must be compatible with the contents and remain effective throughout the life of the packaging. Where use is made of carbon black, pigments or inhibitors other than those used in the manufacture of the design type, retesting may be omitted if the carbon black content does not exceed 2 percent by mass or if the pigment content does not exceed 3 percent by mass; the content of inhibitors of ultra-violet radiation is not limited.

(3) *Additives serving purposes* other than protection against ultra-violet radiation may be included in the composition of the plastic material provided they do not adversely affect the chemical and physical properties of the packaging material.

(4) *The wall thickness* at every point of the packaging must be appropriate to its capacity and its intended use, taking into account the stresses to which each point is liable to be exposed. Minimum thickness and marking requirements in §§173.28(b)(4) and 178.503(a)(9) of this subchapter apply to drums intended for reuse.

(5) *Openings for filling, emptying and venting* in the bodies or heads of non-removable head (1H1) drums and jerricans (3H1) may not exceed 7.0 cm (3 inches) in diameter. Drums and jerricans with larger openings are considered to be of the removable head type (1H2 and 3H2). Closures for openings in the bodies or heads of drums and jerricans must be so designed and applied that they remain secure and leakproof under normal conditions of transport. Gaskets or other sealing elements must be used with closures unless the closure is inherently leakproof.

(6) *Closure devices* for removable head drums and jerricans must be so designed and applied that they remain secure and leakproof under normal conditions of transport. Gaskets must be used with all removable heads unless the drum or jerrican design is such that when the removable head is properly secured, the drum or jerrican is inherently leakproof.

(7) *Maximum capacity of drums and jerricans:* 1H1, 1H2: 450 L (119 gallons); 3H1, 3H2: 60 L (16 gallons).

(8) *Maximum net mass:* 1H1, 1H2: 400 kg (882 pounds); 3H1, 3H2: 120 kg (265 pounds).

§178.510 Standards for wooden barrels.

(a) The following are identification codes for wooden barrels:

(1) *2C1 for a bung type wooden barrel; and*

(2) *2C2 for a slack type (removable head) wooden barrel.*

(b) Construction requirements for wooden barrels are as follows:

(1) *The wood used* must be of good quality, straight-grained, well-seasoned and free from knots, bark, rotten wood, sapwood or other defects likely to lessen the effectiveness of the barrel for the purpose intended.

(2) *The body and heads* must be of a design appropriate to the capacity and intended use of the barrel.

(3) *Staves and heads* must be sawn or cleft with the grain so that no annual ring extends over more than half the thickness of a stave or head.

(4) *Barrel hoops* must be of steel or iron of good quality. The hoops of 2C2 barrels may be of a suitable hardwood.

(5) *For wooden barrels 2C1,* the diameter of the bung-hole may not exceed half the width of the stave in which it is placed.

(6) *For wooden barrels 2C2, heads must fit tightly into crozes.*

(7) *Maximum capacity of barrel:* 250 L (66 gallons).

(8) *Maximum net mass:* 400 kg (882 pounds).

§178.511 Standards for aluminum and steel jerricans.

(a) The following are identification codes for aluminum and steel jerricans:

(1) *3A1 for a non-removable head steel jerrican;*

(2) *3A2 for a removable head steel jerrican;*

(3) *3B1 for a non-removable head aluminum jerrican; and*

(4) *3B2 for a removable head aluminum jerrican.*

(b) Construction requirements for aluminum and steel jerricans are as follows:

(1) *For steel jerricans* the body and heads must be constructed of steel sheet of suitable type and adequate thickness in relation to the capacity of the jerrican and its intended use. Minimum thickness and marking requirements in §§173.28(b)(4) and 178.503(a)(9) of this subchapter apply to jerricans intended for reuse.

(2) *For aluminum jerricans* the body and heads must be constructed of aluminum at least 99% pure or of an aluminum base alloy. Material must be of a type and of adequate thickness in relation to the capacity of the jerrican and to its intended use.

(3) *Chimes of all jerricans* must be mechanically seamed or welded. Body seams of jerricans intended to carry more than 40 L (11 gallons) of liquid must be welded. Body seams of jerricans intended to carry 40 L (11 gallons) or less must be mechanically seamed or welded.

(4) *Openings in jerricans* (3A1) may not exceed 7.0 cm (3 inches) in diameter. Jerricans with larger openings are considered to be of the removable head type. Closures must be so designed that they remain secure and leakproof under normal conditions of transport. Gaskets or other sealing elements must be used with closures, unless the closure is inherently leakproof.

(5) *If materials used* for body, heads, closures and fittings are not in themselves compatible with the contents to be transported, suitable internal protective coatings or treatments must be applied. These coatings or treatments must retain their protective properties under normal conditions of transport.

(6) *Maximum capacity of jerrican:* 60 L (16 gallons).

(7) *Maximum net mass:* 120 kg (265 pounds).

§178.512 Standards for steel or aluminum boxes.

(a) The following are identification codes for steel or aluminum boxes:

(1) *4A for a steel box; and*

(2) *4B for an aluminum box.*

(b) Construction requirements for steel or aluminum boxes are as follows:

(1) *The strength* of the metal and the construction of the box must be appropriate to the capacity and intended use of the box.

(2) *Boxes must be lined* with fiberboard or felt packing pieces or must have an inner liner or coating of suitable material in accordance with subpart C of part 173 of this subchapter. If a double seamed metal liner is used, steps must be taken to prevent the ingress of materials, particularly explosives, into the recesses of the seams.

(3) *Closures may be* of any suitable type, and must remain secure under normal conditions of transport.

(4) *Maximum net mass:* 400 kg (882 pounds).

§178.513 Standards for boxes of natural wood.

(a) The following are the identification codes for boxes of natural wood:

(1) *4C1 for an ordinary box; and*

(2) *4C2 for a box with sift-proof walls.*

(b) Construction requirements for boxes of natural wood are as follows:

(1) *The wood used* must be well-seasoned, commercially dry and free from defects that would materially lessen the strength of any part of the box. The strength of the material used and the method of construction must be appropriate to the capacity and intended use of the box. The tops and bottoms may be made of water-resistant reconstituted wood such as hard board, particle board or other suitable type.

(2) *Fastenings must be* resistant to vibration experienced under normal conditions of transportation. End grain nailing must be avoided whenever practicable. Joints which are likely to be highly stressed must be made using clenched or annular ring nails or equivalent fastenings.

(3) *Each part* of the 4C2 box must be one piece or equivalent. Parts are considered equivalent to one piece when one of the following methods of glued assembly is used: Linderman joint, tongue and groove joint, ship lap or rabbet joint, or butt joint with at least two corrugated metal fasteners at each joint.

(4) *Maximum net mass:* 400 kg (882 pounds).

§178.514 Standards for plywood boxes.

(a) The identification code for a plywood box is 4D.

(b) Construction requirements for plywood boxes are as follows:

(1) *Plywood used* must be at least 3 ply. It shall be made from well-seasoned rotary cut, sliced or sawn veneer, commercially dry and free from defects that would materially lessen the strength of the box. The strength of the material used and the method of construction must be appropriate to the capacity and intended use of the box. All adjacent plies must be glued with water-resistant adhesive. Other suitable materials may be used together with plywood in the construction of boxes. Boxes must be nailed or secured to corner posts or ends or assembled with other equally suitable devices.

(2) *Maximum net mass:* 400 kg (882 pounds).

§178.515 Standards for reconstituted wood boxes.

(a) The identification code for a reconstituted wood box is 4F.

(b) Construction requirements for reconstituted wood boxes are as follows:

(1) *The walls of boxes* must be made of water-resistant, reconstituted wood such as hardboard, particle board, or other suitable type. The strength of the material used and the method of construction must be appropriate to the capacity of the boxes and their intended use.

(2) *Other parts of the box may be made of other suitable materials.*

(3) *Boxes must be securely assembled by means of suitable devices.*

(4) *Maximum net mass:* 400 kg (882 pounds).

§178.516 Standards for fiberboard boxes.

(a) The identification code for a fiberboard box is 4G.

(b) Construction requirements for fiberboard boxes are as follows:

(1) *Strong, solid or double-faced* corrugated fiberboard (single or multi-wall) must be used, appropriate to the capacity and intended use of the box. The water resistance of the outer surface must be such that the increase in mass, as determined in a test carried out over a period of 30 minutes by the Cobb method of determining water absorption, is not greater than 155 g per square meter (0.0316 pounds per square foot) — see ISO International Standard 535. Fiberboard must have proper bending qualities. Fiberboard must be cut, creased without cutting through any thickness of fiberboard, and slotted so as to permit assembly without cracking, surface breaks, or undue bending. The fluting of corrugated fiberboard must be firmly glued to the facings.

(2) *The ends of boxes* may have a wooden frame or be entirely of wood or other suitable material. Reinforcements of wooden battens or other suitable material may be used.

(3) *Manufacturing joints.*

(i) *Manufacturing joints in the bodies of boxes must be —*

[A] Taped;

[B] Lapped and glued; or

[C] Lapped and stitched with metal staples.

(ii) *Lapped joints must have an appropriate overlap.*

(4) *Where closing* is effected by gluing or taping, a water resistant adhesive must be used.

(5) *Boxes must be designed so as to provide a snug fit to the contents.*

(6) *Maximum net mass:* 400 kg (882 pounds).

§178.517 Standards for plastic boxes.

(a) The following are identification codes for plastic boxes:

(1) *4H1 for an expanded plastic box; and*

(2) *4H2 for a solid plastic box.*

(b) Construction requirements for plastic boxes are as follows:

(1) *The box* must be manufactured from suitable plastic material and be of adequate strength in relation to its capacity and intended use. The box must be adequately resistant to aging and to degradation caused either by the substance contained or by ultra-violet radiation.

(2) *An expanded plastic box* must consist of two parts made of a molded expanded plastic material: a bottom section containing cavities for the inner receptacles, and a top section covering and interlocking with the bottom section. The top and bottom sections must be so designed that the inner receptacles fit snugly. The closure cap for any inner receptacle may not be in contact with the inside of the top section of the box.

(3) *For transportation,* an expanded plastic box must be closed with a self-adhesive tape having sufficient tensile strength to prevent the box from opening. The adhesive tape must be weather-resistant and its adhesive compatible with the expanded plastic material of the box. Other closing devices at least equally effective may be used.

(4) *For solid plastic boxes,* protection against ultra-violet radiation, if required, must be provided by the addition of carbon black or other suitable pigments or inhibitors. These additives must be compatible with the contents and remain effective throughout the life of the box. Where use is made of carbon black pigment or inhibitors other than those used in the manufacture of the tested design type, retesting may be waived if the carbon black content does not exceed 2 percent by mass or if the pigment content does not exceed 3 percent by mass; the content of inhibitors of ultra-violet radiation is not limited.

(5) *Additives serving purposes* other than protection against ultra-violet radiation may be included in the composition of the plastic material if they do not adversely affect the material of the box. Addition of these additives does not change the design type.

(6) *Solid plastic boxes* must have closure devices made of a suitable material of adequate strength and so designed as to prevent the box from unintentionally opening.

(7) *Maximum net mass 4H1:* 60 kg (132 pounds); 4H2: 400 kg (882 pounds).

§178.518 Standards for woven plastic bags.

(a) The following are identification codes for woven plastic bags:

(1) *5H1 for an unlined or non-coated woven plastic bag;*

(2) *5H2 for a sift-proof woven plastic bag; and*

(3) *5H3 for a water-resistant woven plastic bag.*

(b) Construction requirements for woven plastic fabric bags are as follows:

(1) *Bags must be made* from stretched tapes or monofilaments of a suitable plastic material. The strength of the material used and the construction of the bag must be appropriate to the capacity and intended use of the bag.

(2) *If the fabric is woven flat,* the bags must be made by sewing or some other method ensuring closure of the bottom and one side. If the fabric is tubular, the bag must be closed by sewing, weaving, or some other equally strong method of closure.
(3) *Bags, sift-proof, 5H2* must be made sift-proof by appropriate means such as use of paper or a plastic film bonded to the inner surface of the bag or one or more separate inner liners made of paper or plastic material.
(4) *Bags, water-resistant, 5H3:* To prevent the entry of moisture, the bag must be made waterproof by appropriate means, such as separate inner liners of water-resistant paper (e.g., waxed kraft paper, double-tarred kraft paper or plastic-coated kraft paper), or plastic film bonded to the inner or outer surface of the bag, or one or more inner plastic liners.
(5) *Maximum net mass:* 50 kg (110 pounds).

§178.519 Standards for plastic film bags.

(a) The identification code for a plastic film bag is 5H4.
(b) Construction requirements for plastic film bags are as follows:
(1) *Bags must be made* of a suitable plastic material. The strength of the material used and the construction of the bag must be appropriate to the capacity and the intended use of the bag. Joints and closures must be capable of withstanding pressures and impacts liable to occur under normal conditions of transportation.
(2) *Maximum net mass:* 50 kg (110 pounds).

§178.520 Standards for textile bags.

(a) The following are identification codes for textile bags:
(1) *5L1 for an unlined or non-coated textile bag;*
(2) *5L2 for a sift-proof textile bag; and*
(3) *5L3 for a water-resistant textile bag.*
(b) Construction requirements for textile bags are as follows:
(1) *The textiles used* must be of good quality. The strength of the fabric and the construction of the bag must be appropriate to the capacity and intended use of the bag.
(2) *Bags, sift-proof, 5L2:* The bag must be made sift-proof, by appropriate means, such as by the use of paper bonded to the inner surface of the bag by a water-resistant adhesive such as bitumen, plastic film bonded to the inner surface of the bag, or one or more inner liners made of paper or plastic material.
(3) *Bags, water-resistant, 5L3:* To prevent entry of moisture, the bag must be made waterproof by appropriate means, such as by the use of separate inner liners of water-resistant paper (e.g., waxed kraft paper, tarred paper, or plastic-coated kraft paper), or plastic film bonded to the inner surface of the bag, or one or more inner liners made of plastic material or metalized film or foil.
(4) *Maximum net mass:* 50 kg (110 pounds).

§178.521 Standards for paper bags.

(a) The following are identification codes for paper bags:
(1) *5M1 for a multi-wall paper bag; and*
(2) *5M2 for a multi-wall water-resistant paper bag.*
(b) Construction requirements for paper bags are as follows:
(1) *Bags must be made* of a suitable kraft paper, or of an equivalent paper with at least three plies. The strength of the paper and the construction of the bag must be appropriate to the capacity and intended use of the bag. Seams and closures must be sift-proof.
(2) *Paper bags 5M2:* To prevent the entry of moisture, a bag of four plies or more must be made waterproof by the use of either a water-resistant ply as one of the two outermost plies or a water-resistant barrier made of a suitable protective material between the two outermost plies. A 5M2 bag of three plies must be made waterproof by the use of a water-resistant ply as the outermost ply. When there is danger of the lading reacting with moisture, or when it is packed damp, a waterproof ply or barrier, such as double-tarred kraft paper, plastics-coated kraft paper, plastics film bonded to the inner surface of the bag, or one or more inner plastics liners, must also be placed next to the substance. Seams and closures must be waterproof.
(3) *Maximum net mass:* 50 kg (110 pounds).

§178.522 Standards for composite packagings with inner plastic receptacles.

(a) The following are the identification codes for composite packagings with inner plastic receptacles:
(1) *6HA1 for a plastic receptacle within a protective steel drum;*
(2) *6HA2 for a plastic receptacle within a protective steel crate or box;*
(3) *6HB1 for a plastic receptacle within a protective aluminum drum;*
(4) *6HB2 for a plastic receptacle* within a protective aluminum crate or box;
(5) *6HC for a plastic receptacle within a protective wooden box;*
(6) *6HD1 for a plastic receptacle within a protective plywood drum;*
(7) *6HD2 for a plastic receptacle within a protective plywood box;*
(8) *6HG1 for a plastic receptacle within a protective fiber drum;*
(9) *6HG2 for a plastic receptacle within a protective fiberboard box;*
(10) *6HH1 for a plastic receptacle* within a protective plastic drum; and
(11) *6HH2 for a plastic receptacle within a protective plastic box.*
(b) Construction requirements for composite packagings with inner receptacles of plastic are as follows:
(1) *Inner receptacles* must be constructed under the applicable construction requirements prescribed in §178.509(b) (1) through (7) of this subpart.
(2) *The inner plastic receptacle* must fit snugly inside the outer packaging, which must be free of any projections which may abrade the plastic material.
(3) *Outer packagings must be constructed as follows:*
(i) *6HA1 or 6HB1:* Protective packaging must conform to the requirements for steel drums in §178.504(b) of this subpart, or aluminum drums in §178.505(b) of this subpart.
(ii) *6HA2 or 6HB2:* Protective packagings with steel or aluminum crate must conform to the requirements for steel or aluminum boxes found in §178.512(b) of this subpart.
(iii) *6HC protective packaging* must conform to the requirements for wooden boxes in §178.513(b) of this subpart.
(iv) *6HD1:* Protective packaging must conform to the requirements for plywood drums, in §178.507(b) of this subpart.
(v) *6HD2:* Protective packaging must conform to the requirements of plywood boxes, in §178.514(b) of this subpart.
(vi) *6HG1:* Protective packaging must conform to the requirements for fiber drums, in §178.508(b) of this subpart.
(vii) *6HG2:* protective packaging must conform to the requirements for fiberboard boxes, in §178.516(b) of this subpart.
(viii) *6HH1:* Protective packaging must conform to the requirements for plastic drums, in §178.509(b).
(ix) *6HH2:* Protective packaging must conform to the requirements for plastic boxes, in §178.517(b).
(4) *Maximum capacity* of inner receptacles is as follows: 6HA1, 6HB1, 6HD1, 6HG1, 6HH1 — 250 L (66 gallons); 6HA2, 6HB2, 6HC, 6HD2, 6HG2, 6HH2 — 60 L (16 gallons).
(5) *Maximum net mass is as follows:* 6HA1, 6HB1, 6HD1, 6HG1, 6HH1 — 400kg (882 pounds); 6HB2, 6HC, 6HD2, 6HG2, 6HH2 — 75 kg (165 pounds).

§178.523 Standards for composite packagings with inner glass, porcelain, or stoneware receptacles.

(a) The following are identification codes for composite packagings with inner receptacles of glass, porcelain, or stoneware:
(1) *6PA1 for* glass, porcelain, or stoneware receptacles within a protective steel drum;
(2) *6PA2 for* glass, porcelain, or stoneware receptacles within a protective steel crate or box;
(3) *6PB1 for* glass, porcelain, or stoneware receptacles within a protective aluminum drum;
(4) *6PB2 for* glass, porcelain, or stoneware receptacles within a protective aluminum crate or box;
(5) *6PC for* glass, porcelain, or stoneware receptacles within a protective wooden box;
(6) *6PD1 for* glass, porcelain, or stoneware receptacles within a protective plywood drum;
(7) *6PD2 for* glass, porcelain, or stoneware receptacles within a protective wickerwork hamper;
(8) *6PG1 for* glass, porcelain, or stoneware receptacles within a protective fiber drum;
(9) *6PG2 for* glass, porcelain, or stoneware receptacles within a protective fiberboard box;
(10) *6PH1 for* glass, porcelain, or stoneware receptacles within a protective expanded plastic packaging; and
(11) *6PH2 for* glass, porcelain, or stoneware receptacles within a protective solid plastic packaging.
(b) Construction requirements for composite packagings with inner receptacles of glass, porcelain, or stoneware are as follows:
(1) *Inner receptacles must conform to the following requirements:*
(i) *Receptacles must be* of suitable form (cylindrical or pear-shaped), be made of good quality materials free from any defect that could impair their strength, and be firmly secured in the outer packaging.

(ii) *Any part* of a closure likely to come into contact with the contents of the receptacle must be resistant to those contents. Closures must be fitted so as to be leakproof and secured to prevent any loosening during transportation. Vented closures must conform to §173.24(f) of this subchapter.

(2) *Protective packagings must conform to the following requirements:*

(i) *For receptacles* with protective steel drum 6PAl, the drum must comply with §178.504(b) of this subpart. However, the removable lid required for this type of packaging may be in the form of a cap.

(ii) *For receptacles* with protective packaging of steel crate or steel box 6PA2, the protective packaging must conform to the following:

[A] Section 178.512(b) of this subpart.

[B] In the case of cylindrical receptacles, the protective packaging must, when upright, rise above the receptacle and its closure; and

[C] If the protective crate surrounds a pear-shaped receptacle and is of matching shape, the protective packaging must be fitted with a protective cover (cap).

(iii) *For receptacles* with protective aluminum drum 6PB1, the requirements of §178.505(b) of this subpart apply to the protective packaging.

(iv) *For receptacles* with protective aluminum box or crate 6PB2, the requirements of §178.512(b) of this subpart apply to the protective packaging.

(v) *For receptacles* with protective wooden box 6PC, the requirements of §178.513(b) of this subpart apply to the protective packaging.

(vi) *For receptacles* with protective plywood drum 6PD1, the requirements of §178.507(b) of this subpart apply to the protective packaging.

(vii) *For receptacles* with protective wickerwork hamper 6PD2, the wickerwork hamper must be properly made with material of good quality. The hamper must be fitted with a protective cover (cap) so as to prevent damage to the receptacle.

(viii) *For receptacles* with protective fiber drum 6PG1, the drum must conform to the requirements of §178.508(b) of this subpart.

(ix) *For receptacles* with protective fiberboard box 6PG2, the requirements of §178.516(b) of this subpart apply to the protective packaging.

(x) *For receptacles* with protective solid plastic or expanded plastic packaging 6PH1 or 6PH2, the requirements of §178.517(b) of this subpart apply to the protective packaging. Solid protective plastic packaging must be manufactured from high-density polyethylene from some other comparable plastic material. The removable lid required for this type of packaging may be a cap.

(3) *Quantity limitations are as follows:*

(i) *Maximum net capacity for packaging for liquids:* 60 L (16 gallons).

(ii) *Maximum net mass for packagings for solids:* 75 kg (165 pounds).

Subpart M - Testing of Non-bulk Packagings and Packages

§178.600 Purpose and scope.

This subpart prescribes certain testing requirements for performance-oriented packagings identified in subpart L of this part.

§178.601 General requirements.

(a) **General.** The test procedures prescribed in this subpart are intended to ensure that packages containing hazardous materials can withstand normal conditions of transportation and are considered minimum requirements. Each packaging must be manufactured and assembled so as to be capable of successfully passing the prescribed tests and of conforming to the requirements of §173.24 of this subchapter at all times while in transportation.

(b) **Responsibility.** It is the responsibility of the packaging manufacturer to assure that each package is capable of passing the prescribed tests. To the extent that a package assembly function, including final closure, is performed by the person who offers a hazardous material for transportation, that person is responsible for performing the function in accordance with §§173.22 and 178.2 of this subchapter.

(c) **Definitions.** For the purpose of this subpart:

(1) **Design qualification testing** is the performance of the tests prescribed in §178.603, §178.604, §178.605, §178.606, §178.607, §178.608, or §178.609, as applicable, for each new or different packaging, at the start of production of that packaging.

(2) **Periodic retesting** is the performance of the drop, leakproofness, hydrostatic pressure, and stacking tests, as applicable, as prescribed in §178.603, §178.604, §178.605, or §178.606, respectively, at the frequency specified in paragraph (e) of this section. For infectious substances packagings required to meet the requirements of §178.609, periodic retesting is the performance of the tests specified in §178.609 at the frequency specified in paragraph (e) of this section.

(3) **Production testing** is the performance of the leakproofness test prescribed in §178.604 of this subpart on each single or composite packaging intended to contain a liquid.

(4) **A different packaging** is one that differs (i.e. is not identical) from a previously produced packaging in structural design, size, material of construction, wall thickness or manner of construction but does not include:

(i) *A packaging which differs only in surface treatment;*

(ii) *A combination packaging* which differs only in that the outer packaging has been successfully tested with different inner packagings. A variety of such inner packagings may be assembled in this outer packaging without further testing;

(iii) *A plastic packaging* which differs only with regard to additives which conform to §178.509(b)(3) or §178.517(b) (4) or (5) of this part;

(iv) *A combination packaging* with inner packagings conforming to the provisions of paragraph (g) of this section;

(v) *Packagings which differ* from the design type only in their lesser design height; or

(vi) *For a steel drum,* variations in design elements which do not constitute a different design type under the provisions of paragraph (g)(8) of this section.

(d) **Design qualification testing.** The packaging manufacturer shall achieve successful test results for the design qualification testing at the start of production of each new or different packaging.

(e) **Periodic retesting.** The packaging manufacturer must achieve successful test results for the periodic retesting at intervals established by the manufacturer of sufficient frequency to ensure that each packaging produced by the manufacturer is capable of passing the design qualification tests. Changes in retest frequency are subject to the approval of the Associate Administrator for Hazardous Materials Safety. For single or composite packagings, the periodic retests must be conducted at least once every 12 months. For combination packagings, the periodic retests must be conducted at least once every 24 months. For infectious substances packagings, the periodic retests must be conducted at least once every 24 months.

(f) **Test samples.** The manufacturer shall conduct the design qualification and periodic tests prescribed in this subpart using random samples of packagings, in the numbers specified in the appropriate test section. In addition, the leakproofness test, when required, shall be performed on each packaging produced by the manufacturer, and each packaging prior to reuse under §173.28 of this subchapter, by the reconditioner.

(g) **Selective testing.** The selective testing of packagings that differ only in minor respects from a tested type is permitted as described in this section. For air transport, packagings must comply with §173.27(c)(1) and (c)(2) of this subchapter.

(1) *Selective testing of combination packagings.* Variation 1. Variations are permitted in inner packagings of a tested combination package, without further testing of the package, provided an equivalent level of performance is maintained, as follows:

(i) *Inner packagings* of equivalent or smaller size may be used provided —

[A] The inner packagings are of similar design to the tested inner packagings (i.e. shape — round, rectangular, etc.);

[B] The material of construction of the inner packagings (glass, plastic, metal, etc.) offers resistance to impact and stacking forces equal to or greater than that of the originally tested inner packaging;

[C] The inner packagings have the same or smaller openings and the closure is of similar design (e.g., screw cap, friction lid, etc.);

[D] Sufficient additional cushioning material is used to take up void spaces and to prevent significant movement of the inner packagings;

[E] Inner packagings are oriented within the outer packaging in the same manner as in the tested package; and,

[F] The gross mass of the package does not exceed that originally tested.

(ii) *A lesser number* of the tested inner packagings, or of the alternative types of inner packagings identified in paragraph (g)(1)(i) of this section, may be used provided sufficient cushioning is added to fill void space(s) and to prevent significant movement of the inner packagings.

(2) *Selective testing of combination packagings.* Variation 2. Articles or inner packagings of any type, for solids or liquids, may be assembled and transported without testing in an outer packaging under the following conditions:

(i) *The outer packaging* must have been successfully tested in accordance with §178.603 with fragile (e.g. glass) inner packagings containing liquids at the Packing Group I drop height;

(ii) *The total* combined gross mass of inner packagings may not exceed one-half the gross mass of inner packagings used for the drop test;

(iii) *The thickness* of cushioning material between inner packagings and between inner packagings and the outside of the packaging may not be reduced below the corresponding thickness in the originally tested packaging; and when a single inner packaging was used in the original test, the thickness of cushioning between inner packagings may not be less than the thickness of cushioning between the outside of the packaging and the inner packaging in the original test. When either fewer or smaller inner packagings are used (as compared to the inner packagings used in the drop test), sufficient additional cushioning material must be used to take up void spaces.

(iv) *The outer packaging* must have successfully passed the stacking test set forth in §178.606 of this subpart when empty, i.e., without either inner packagings or cushioning materials. The total mass of identical packages must be based on the combined mass of inner packagings used for the drop test;

(v) *Inner packagings* containing liquids must be completely surrounded with a sufficient quantity of absorbent material to absorb the entire liquid contents of the inner packagings;

(vi) *When the outer packaging* is intended to contain inner packagings for liquids and is not leakproof, or is intended to contain inner packagings for solids and is not siftproof, a means of containing any liquid or solid contents in the event of leakage must be provided in the form of a leakproof liner, plastic bag, or other equally efficient means of containment. For packagings containing liquids, the absorbent material required in paragraph (g)(2)(v) of this section must be placed inside the means of containing liquid contents; and

(vii) *Packagings must be marked* in accordance with §178.503 of this part as having been tested to Packing Group I performance for combination packagings. The marked maximum gross mass may not exceed the sum of the mass of the outer packaging plus one half the mass of the filled inner packagings of the tested combination packaging. In addition, the marking required by §178.503(a)(2) of this part must include the letter "V".

(3) *Variation 3.* Packagings other than combination packagings which are produced with reductions in external dimensions (i.e., length, width or diameter) of up to 25 percent of the dimensions of a tested packaging may be used without further testing provided an equivalent level of performance is maintained. The packagings must, in all other respects (including wall thicknesses), be identical to the tested design-type. The marked gross mass (when required) must be reduced in proportion to the reduction in volume.

(4) *Variation 4.* Variations are permitted in outer packagings of a tested design-type combination packaging, without further testing, provided an equivalent level of performance is maintained, as follows:

(i) *Each external dimension* (length, width and height) is less than or equal to the corresponding dimension of the tested design-type;

(ii) *The structural design* of the tested outer packaging (i.e. methods of construction, materials of construction, strength characteristics of materials of construction, method of closure and material thicknesses) is maintained;

(iii) *The inner packagings* are identical to the inner packagings used in the tested design type except that their size and mass may be less; and they are oriented within the outer packaging in the same manner as in the tested packaging;

(iv) *The same type* or design of absorbent materials, cushioning materials and any other components necessary to contain and protect inner packagings, as used in the tested design type, are maintained. The thickness of cushioning material between inner packagings and between inner packagings and the outside of the packaging may not be less than the thicknesses in the tested design type packaging; and

(v) *Sufficient additional cushioning material* is used to take up void spaces and to prevent significant movement of the inner packagings. An outer packaging qualifying for use in transport in accordance with all of the above conditions may also be used without testing to transport inner packagings substituted for the originally tested inner packagings in accordance with the conditions set out in Variation 1 in paragraph (g)(1) of this section.

(5) *Variation 5.* Single packagings (i.e., non-bulk packagings other than combination packagings), that differ from a tested design type only to the extent that the closure device or gasketing differs from that used in the originally tested design type, may be used without further testing, provided an equivalent level of performance is maintained, subject to the following conditions (the qualifying tests):

(i) *A packaging* with the replacement closure devices or gasketing must successfully pass the drop test specified in §178.603 in the orientation which most severely tests the integrity of the closure or gasket;

(ii) *When intended* to contain liquids, a packaging with the replacement closure devices or gasketing must successfully pass the leakproofness test specified in §178.604, the hydrostatic pressure test specified in §178.605, and the stacking test specified in §178.606.

Replacement closures and gasketings qualified under the above test requirements are authorized without additional testing for packagings described in paragraph (g)(3) of this section. Replacement closures and gasketings qualified under the above test requirements also are authorized without additional testing for different tested design types packagings of the same type as the originally tested packaging, provided the original design type tests are more severe or comparable to tests which would otherwise be conducted on the packaging with the replacement closures or gasketings. (For example: The packaging used in the qualifying tests has a lesser packaging wall thickness than the packaging with replacement closure devices or gasketing; the gross mass of the packaging used in the qualifying drop test equals or exceeds the mass for which the packaging with replacement closure devices or gasketing was tested; the packaging used in the qualifying drop test was dropped from the same or greater height than the height from which the packaging with replacement closure devices or gasketing was dropped in design type tests; and the specific gravity of the substance used in the qualifying drop test was the same or greater than the specific gravity of the liquid used in the design type tests of the packaging with replacement closure devices or gasketing.)

(6) *The provisions* in Variations 1, 2, and 4 in paragraphs (g)(1), (2) and (4) of this section for combination packagings may be applied to packagings containing articles, where the provisions for inner packagings are applied analogously to the articles. In this case, inner packagings need not comply with §173.27(c)(1) and (c)(2) of this subchapter.

(7) *Approval of selective testing.* In addition to the provisions of §178.601(g)(1) through (g)(6) of this subpart, the Associate Administrator may approve the selective testing of packagings that differ only in minor respects from a tested type.

(8) *For a steel drum* with a capacity greater than 50 L (13 gallons) manufactured from low carbon, cold-rolled sheet steel meeting ASTM designations A366/A366M or A568/A568M, variations in elements other than the following design elements are considered minor and do not constitute a different drum design type, or "different packaging" as defined in paragraph (c) of this section for which design qualification testing and periodic retesting are required. Minor variations authorized without further testing include changes in the identity of the supplier of component material made to the same specifications, or the original manufacturer of a DOT specification or UN standard drum to be remanufactured. A change in any one or more of the following design elements constitutes a different drum design type:

(i) *The packaging type* and category of the original drum and the remanufactured drum, i.e., 1A1 or 1A2;

(ii) *The style, (i.e., straight-sided or tapered);*

(iii) *Except as provided* in paragraph (g)(3) of this section, the rated (marked) capacity and outside dimensions;

(iv) *The physical state* for which the packaging was originally approved (e.g., tested for solids or liquids);

(v) *An increase* in the marked level of performance of the original drum (i.e., to a higher packing group, hydrostatic test pressure, or specific gravity to which the packaging has been tested);

(vi) *Type of side seam welding;*

(vii) *Type of steel;*

(viii) *An increase* greater than 10% or any decrease in the steel thickness of the head, body, or bottom;

(ix) *End seam type, (e.g., triple or double seam);*

(x) *A reduction* in the number of rolling hoops which equal or exceed the diameter over the chimes;

(xi) *The location,* type or size, and material of closures (other than the cover of UN 1A2 drums); and

(xii) *For UN 1A2 drums:*

[A] Gasket material (e.g., plastic), or properties affecting the performance of the gasket;

[B] Configuration or dimensions of the gasket;

[C] Closure ring style including bolt size, (e.g., square or round back, 0.625" bolt); and

[D] Closure ring thickness.

(h) Approval of equivalent packagings. A packaging having specifications different from those in §§178.504-178.523 of this part, or which is tested using methods or test intervals, other than those specified in subpart M of this part, may be used if approved by the Associate Administrator. Such packagings must be shown to be equally effective, and testing methods used must be equivalent.

(i) Proof of compliance. Notwithstanding the periodic retest intervals specified in paragraph (e) of this section, the Associate Administrator may at any time require demonstration of compliance by a manufacturer, through testing in accordance with this subpart, that packagings meet the requirements of this subpart. As required by the Associate Administrator, the manufacturer shall either —

(1) *Conduct performance tests,* or have tests conducted by an independent testing facility, in accordance with this subpart; or

(2) *Supply packagings,* in quantities sufficient to conduct tests in accordance with this subpart, to the Associate Administrator or a designated representative of the Associate Administrator.

(j) Coatings. If an inner treatment or coating of a packaging is required for safety reasons, the manufacturer shall design the packaging so that the treatment or coating retains its protective properties even after withstanding the tests prescribed by this subpart.

(k) Number of test samples. Provided the validity of the test results is not affected and with the approval of the Associate Administrator, several tests may be performed on one sample.

(l) Record retention. Following each design qualification test and each periodic retest on a packaging, a test report must be prepared. The test report must be maintained at each location where the packaging is manufactured and each location where the design qualification tests are conducted, for as long as the packaging is produced and for at least two years thereafter, and at each location where the periodic retests are conducted until such tests are successfully performed again and a new test report produced. In addition, a copy of the test report must be maintained by a person certifying compliance with this part. The test report must be made available to a user of a packaging or a representative of the Department upon request. The test report, at a minimum, must contain the following information:

(1) *Name and address of test facility;*

(2) *Name and address of applicant (where appropriate);*

(3) *A unique test report identification;*

(4) *Date of the test report;*

(5) *Manufacturer of the packaging;*

(6) *Description of the packaging design type* (e.g. dimensions, materials, closures, thickness, etc.), including methods of manufacture (e.g. blow molding) and which may include drawing(s) and/or photograph(s);

(7) *Maximum capacity;*

(8) *Characteristics of test contents,* e.g. viscosity and relative density for liquids and particle size for solids;

(9) *Test descriptions and results; and*

(10) *Signed with the name and title of signatory.*

§178.602 Preparation of packagings and packages for testing.

(a) Except as otherwise provided in this subchapter, each packaging and package must be closed in preparation for testing and tests must be carried out in the same manner as if prepared for transportation, including inner packagings in the case of combination packagings.

(b) For the drop and stacking test, inner and single-unit receptacles must be filled to not less than 95 percent of maximum capacity (see §171.8 of this subchapter) in the case of solids and not less than 98 percent of maximum capacity in the case of liquids. The material to be transported in the packagings may be replaced by a non-hazardous material, except for chemical compatibility testing or where this would invalidate the results of the tests.

(c) If the material to be transported is replaced for test purposes by a non-hazardous material, the material used must be of the same or higher specific gravity as the material to be carried, and its other physical properties (grain, size, viscosity) which might influence the results of the required tests must correspond as closely as possible to those of the hazardous material to be transported. Water may also be used for the liquid drop test under the conditions specified in §178.603(e) of this subpart. It is permissible to use additives, such as bags of lead shot, to achieve the requisite total package mass, so long as they are placed so that the test results are not affected.

(d) Paper or fiberboard packagings must be conditioned for at least 24 hours immediately prior to testing in an atmosphere maintained —

(1) *At 50 percent* ± 2 percent relative humidity, and at a temperature of 23 °C ± 2 °C (73 °F ± 4 °F). Average values should fall within these limits. Short-term fluctuations and measurement limitations may cause individual measurements to vary by up to 5 percent relative humidity without significant impairment of test reproducibility;

(2) *At 65 percent* ± 2 percent relative humidity, and at a temperature of 20 °C ± 2 °C (68 °F ± 4 °F), or 27 °C ± 2 °C (81 °F ± 4 °F). Average values should fall within these limits. Short-term fluctuations and measurement limitations may cause individual measurements to vary by up to 5 percent relative humidity without significant impairment of test reproducibility; or

(3) *For testing* at periodic intervals only (i.e., other than initial design qualification testing), at ambient conditions.

(e) Except as otherwise provided, each packaging must be closed in preparation for testing in the same manner as if prepared for actual shipment. All closures must be installed using proper techniques and torques.

(f) Bung-type barrels made of natural wood must be left filled with water for at least 24 hours before the tests.

§178.603 Drop test.

(a) General. The drop test must be conducted for the qualification of all packaging design types and performed periodically as specified in §178.601(e). For other than flat drops, the center of gravity of the test packaging must be vertically over the point of impact. Where more than one orientation is possible for a given drop test, the orientation most likely to result in failure of the packaging must be used. The number of drops required and the packages' orientations are as follows:

Packaging	No. of tests (samples)	Drop orientation of samples
Steel drums, Aluminum drums, Metal drums (other than steel or aluminum), Steel Jerricans, Plywood drums, Wooden barrels, Fiber drums, Plastic drums and Jerricans, Composite packagings which are in the shape of a drum.	Six — (three for each drop).	First drop (using three samples): The package must strike the target diagonally on the chime or, if the packaging has no chime, on a circumferential seam or an edge. Second drop (using the other three samples): The package must strike the target on the weakest part not tested by the first drop, for example a closure or, for some 7 cylindrical drums, the welded longitudinal seam of the drum body.
Boxes of natural wood, Plywood boxes, Reconstituted wood boxes, Fiberboard boxes, Plastic boxes, Steel or aluminum boxes, Composite packagings which are in the shape of a box.	Five — (one for each drop).	First drop: Flat on the bottom (using the first sample). Second drop: Flat on the top (using the second sample). Third drop: Flat on the long side (using the third sample). Fourth drop: Flat on the short side (using the fourth sample). Fifth drop: On a corner (using the fifth sample).
Bags — single-ply with a side seam.	Three — (three drops per bag).	First drop: Flat on a wide face (using all three samples). Second drop: Flat on a narrow face (using all three samples). Third drop: On an end of the bag (using all three samples).
Bags — single-ply without a side seam, or multi-ply.	Three — (two drops per bag).	First drop: Flat on a wide face (using all three samples). Second drop: On an end of the bag (using all three samples).

(b) Exceptions. For testing of single or composite packagings constructed of stainless steel, nickel, or monel at periodic intervals only (i.e., other than design qualification testing), the drop test may be conducted with two samples, one sample each for the two drop orientations. These samples may have been previously used for the hydrostatic pressure or stacking test. Exceptions for the number of steel and aluminum packaging samples used for conducting the drop test are subject to the approval of the Associate Administrator.

(c) **Special preparation of test samples for the drop test.** Testing of plastic drums, plastic jerricans, plastic boxes other than expanded polystyrene boxes, composite packagings (plastic material), and combination packagings with plastic inner packagings other than plastic bags intended to contain solids or articles must be carried out when the temperature of the test sample and its contents has been reduced to -18 °C (0 °F) or lower. Test liquids shall be kept in the liquid state, if necessary, by the addition of anti-freeze. Test samples prepared in this way are not required to be conditioned in accordance with §178.602(d).

(d) **Target.** The target must be a rigid, non-resilient, flat and horizontal surface.

(e) **Drop height.** Drop heights, measured as the vertical distance from the target to the lowest point on the package, must be equal to or greater than the drop height determined as follows:

(1) *For solids and liquids,* if the test is performed with the solid or liquid to be transported or with a non-hazardous material having essentially the same physical characteristic, the drop height must be determined according to packing group, as follows:

(i) *Packing Group I:* 1.8 m (5.9 feet).

(ii) *Packing Group II:* 1.2 m (3.9 feet).

(iii) *Packing Group III:* 0.8 m (2.6 feet).

(2) *For liquids, if the test is performed with water* —

(i) *Where the materials* to be carried have a specific gravity not exceeding 1.2, drop height must be determined according to packing group, as follows:

[A] Packing Group I: 1.8 m (5.9 feet).

[B] Packing Group II: 1.2 m (3.9 feet).

[C] Packing Group III: 0.8 m (2.6 feet).

(ii) *Where the materials* to be transported have a specific gravity exceeding 1.2, the drop height must be calculated on the basis of the specific gravity (SG) of the material to be carried, rounded up to the first decimal, as follows:

[A] Packing Group I: SG x 1.5 m (4.9 feet).

[B] Packing Group II: SG x 1.0 m (3.3 feet).

[C] Packing Group III: SG x 0.67 m (2.2 feet).

(f) **Criteria for passing the test.** A package is considered to successfully pass the drop tests if for each sample tested —

(1) *For packagings containing liquid,* each packaging does not leak when equilibrium has been reached between the internal and external pressures, except for inner packagings of combination packagings when it is not necessary that the pressures be equalized;

(2) *For removable head drums for solids,* the entire contents are retained by an inner packaging (e.g., a plastic bag) even if the closure on the top head of the drum is no longer sift-proof;

(3) *For a bag,* neither the outermost ply nor an outer packaging exhibits any damage likely to adversely affect safety during transport;

(4) *For a composite or combination packaging,* there is no damage to the outer packaging likely to adversely affect safety during transport, and there is no leakage of the filling substance from the inner packaging;

(5) *Any discharge* from a closure is slight and ceases immediately after impact with no further leakage; and

(6) *No rupture* is permitted in packagings for materials in Class 1 which would permit spillage of loose explosive substances or articles from the outer packaging.

§178.604 Leakproofness test.

(a) **General.** The leakproofness test must be performed with compressed air or other suitable gases on all packagings intended to contain liquids, except that:

(1) *The inner receptacle* of a composite packaging may be tested without the outer packaging provided the test results are not affected; and

(2) *This test* is not required for inner packagings of combination packagings.

(b) **Number of packagings to be tested** —

(1) *Production testing.* All packagings subject to the provisions of this section must be tested and must pass the leakproofness test:

(i) *Before they are first used in transportation; and*

(ii) *Prior to reuse,* when authorized for reuse by §173.28 of this subchapter.

(2) *Design qualification and periodic testing.* Three samples of each different packaging must be tested and must pass the leakproofness test. Exceptions for the number of samples used in conducting the leakproofness test are subject to the approval of the Associate Administrator.

(c) **Special preparation** —

(1) *For design qualification and periodic testing,* packagings must be tested with closures in place. For production testing, packagings need not have their closures in place. Removable heads need not be installed during production testing.

(2) *For testing with closures in place,* vented closures must either be replaced by similar non-vented closures or the vent must be sealed.

(d) **Test method.** The packaging must be restrained under water while an internal air pressure is applied; the method of restraint must not affect the results of the test. The test must be conducted, for other than production testing, for a minimum time of five minutes. Other methods, at least equally effective, may be used in accordance with appendix B of this part.

(e) **Pressure applied.** An internal air pressure (gauge) must be applied to the packaging as indicated for the following packing groups:

(1) *Packing Group I:* Not less than 30 kPa (4 psi).

(2) *Packing Group II:* Not less than 20 kPa (3 psi).

(3) *Packing Group III:* Not less than 20 kPa (3 psi).

(f) **Criteria for passing the test.** A packaging passes the test if there is no leakage of air from the packaging.

§178.605 Hydrostatic pressure test.

(a) **General.** The hydrostatic pressure test must be conducted for the qualification of all metal, plastic, and composite packaging design types intended to contain liquids and be performed periodically as specified in §178.601(e). This test is not required for inner packagings of combination packagings. For internal pressure requirements for inner packagings of combination packagings intended for transportation by aircraft, see §173.27(c) of this subchapter.

(b) **Number of test samples.** Three test samples are required for each different packaging. For packagings constructed of stainless steel, monel, or nickel, only one sample is required for periodic retesting of packagings. Exceptions for the number of aluminum and steel sample packagings used in conducting the hydrostatic pressure test are subject to the approval of the Associate Administrator.

(c) **Special preparation of receptacles for testings.** Vented closures must either be replaced by similar non-vented closures or the vent must be sealed.

(d) **Test method and pressure to be applied.** Metal packagings and composite packagings other than plastic (e.g., glass, porcelain or stoneware), including their closures, must be subjected to the test pressure for 5 minutes. Plastic packagings and composite packagings (plastic material), including their closures, must be subjected to the test pressure for 30 minutes. This pressure is the one to be marked as required in §178.503(a)(5) of this part. The receptacles must be supported in a manner that does not invalidate the test. The test pressure must be applied continuously and evenly, and it must be kept constant throughout the test period. The hydraulic pressure (gauge) applied, taken at the top of the receptacle, and determined by any one of the following methods must be:

(1) *Not less than* the total gauge pressure measured in the packaging (i.e., the vapor pressure of the filling material and the partial pressure of the air or other inert gas minus 100 kPa (15 psi)) at 55 °C (131 °F), multiplied by a safety factor of 1.5. This total gauge pressure must be determined on the basis of a maximum degree of filling in accordance with §173.24a(d) of this subchapter and a filling temperature of 15 °C (59 °F);

(2) *Not less than* 1.75 times the vapor pressure at 50 °C (122 °F) of the material to be transported minus 100 kPa (15 psi) but with a minimum test pressure of 100 kPa (15 psig); or

(3) *Not less than* 1.5 times the vapor pressure at 55 °C (131 °F) of the material to be transported minus 100 kPa (15 psi), but with a minimum test pressure of 100 kPa (15 psig). Packagings intended to contain hazardous materials of Packing Group I must be tested to a minimum test pressure of 250 kPa (36 psig).

(e) **Criteria for passing the test.** A package passes the hydrostatic test if, for each test sample, there is no leakage of liquid from the package.

§178.606 Stacking test.

(a) **General.** All packaging design types other than bags must be subjected to a stacking test.

(b) **Number of test samples.** Three test samples are required for each different packaging. For periodic retesting of packagings constructed of stainless steel, monel, or nickel, only one test sample is required. Exceptions for the number of aluminum and steel sample packagings used in conducting the stacking test are subject to the approval of the Associate Administrator. Notwithstanding the provisions of §178.602(a) of this subpart, combination packagings may be subjected to the stacking test without their inner packagings, except where this would invalidate the results of the test.

(c) **Test method —**

(1) *Design qualification testing.* The test sample must be subjected to a force applied to the top surface of the test sample equivalent to the total weight of identical packages which might be stacked on it during transport; where the contents of the test sample are non-hazardous liquids with specific gravities different from that of the liquid to be transported, the force must be calculated based on the specific gravity that will be marked on the packaging. The minimum height of the stack, including the test sample, must be 3.0 m (10 feet). The duration of the test must be 24 hours, except that plastic drums, jerricans, and composite packagings 6HH intended for liquids shall be subjected to the stacking test for a period of 28 days at a temperature of not less than 40 °C (104 °F). Alternative test methods which yield equivalent results may be used if approved by the Associate Administrator. In guided load tests, stacking stability must be assessed after completion of the test by placing two filled packagings of the same type on the test sample. The stacked packages must maintain their position for one hour. Plastic packagings must be cooled to ambient temperature before this stacking stability assessment.

(2) *Periodic retesting.* The test sample must be tested in accordance with:

(i) *Section 178.606(c)(1) of this subpart; or*

(ii) *The packaging may be tested* using a dynamic compression testing machine. The test must be conducted at room temperature on an empty, unsealed packaging. The test sample must be centered on the bottom platen of the testing machine. The top platen must be lowered until it comes in contact with the test sample. Compression must be applied end to end. The speed of the compression tester must be one-half inch plus or minus one-fourth inch per minute. An initial preload of 50 pounds must be applied to ensure a definite contact between the test sample and the platens. The distance between the platens at this time must be recorded as zero deformation. The force A to then be applied must be calculated using the formula:

Liquids: A = (n - 1) [w + (s x v x 8.3 x .98)] x 1.5;

Solids: A = (n - 1) [w + (s x v x 8.3 x .95)] x 1.5

Where:

A = applied load in pounds

n = minimum number of containers that, when stacked, reach a height of 3 m

s = specific gravity of lading

w = maximum weight of one empty container in pounds

v = actual capacity of container (rated capacity + outage) in gallons

And:

8.3 corresponds to the weight in pounds of 1.0 gallon of water.

1.5 is a compensation factor that converts the static load of the stacking test into a load suitable for dynamic compression testing.

(d) **Criteria for passing the test.** No test sample may leak. In composite packagings or combination packagings, there must be no leakage of the filling substance from the inner receptacle, or inner packaging. No test sample may show any deterioration which could adversely affect transportation safety or any distortion likely to reduce its strength, cause instability in stacks of packages, or cause damage to inner packagings likely to reduce safety in transportation. For the dynamic compression test, a container passes the test if, after application of the required load, there is no buckling of the sidewalls sufficient to cause damage to its expected contents; in no case may the maximum deflection exceed one inch.

§178.607 Cooperage test for bung-type wooden barrels.

(a) **Number of samples.** One barrel is required for each different packaging.

(b) **Method of testing.** Remove all hoops above the bilge of an empty barrel at least two days old.

(c) **Criteria for passing the test.** A packaging passes the cooperage test only if the diameter of the cross-section of the upper part of the barrel does not increase by more than 10 percent.

§178.608 Vibration standard.

(a) **Each packaging must be capable of withstanding,** without rupture or leakage, the vibration test procedure outlined in this section.

(b) **Test method.**

(1) *Three sample packagings,* selected at random, must be filled and closed as for shipment.

(2) *The three samples* must be placed on a vibrating platform that has a vertical or rotary double-amplitude (peak-to-peak displacement) of one inch. The packages should be constrained horizontally to prevent them from falling off the platform, but must be left free to move vertically, bounce and rotate.

(3) *The test* must be performed for one hour at a frequency that causes the package to be raised from the vibrating platform to such a degree that a piece of material of approximately 1.6 mm (0.063 inch) thickness (such as steel strapping or paperboard) can be passed between the bottom of any package and the platform.

(4) *Immediately following* the period of vibration, each package must be removed from the platform, turned on its side and observed for any evidence of leakage.

(5) *Other methods,* at least equally effective, may be used, if approved by the Associate Administrator.

(c) **Criteria for passing the test.** A packaging passes the vibration test if there is no rupture or leakage from any of the packages. No test sample should show any deterioration which could adversely affect transportation safety or any distortion liable to reduce packaging strength.

§178.609 Test requirements for packagings for infectious substances.

(a) **Samples of each packaging must be prepared** for testing as described in paragraph (b) of this section and then subjected to the tests in paragraphs (d) through (i) of this section.

(b) **Samples of each packaging must be prepared** as for transport except that a liquid or solid infectious substance should be replaced by water or, where conditioning at -18 °C (0 °F) is specified, by water/antifreeze. Each primary receptacle must be filled to 98 percent capacity. Packagings for live animals should be tested with the live animal being replaced by an appropriate dummy of similar mass.

(c) **Packagings prepared as for transport must be subjected** to the tests in Table I of this paragraph (c), which, for test purposes, categorizes packagings according to their material characteristics. For outer packagings, the headings in Table I relate to fiberboard or similar materials whose performance may be rapidly affected by moisture; plastics that may embrittle at low temperature; and other materials, such as metal, for which performance is not significantly affected by moisture or temperature. Where a primary receptacle and a secondary packaging of an inner packaging are made of different materials, the material of the primary receptacle determines the appropriate test. In instances where a primary receptacle is made of more than one material, the material most likely to be damaged determines the appropriate test.

Table I - Tests Required

Material of					Tests required				
Outer packaging			Inner packaging		Refer to para. (d)				Refer to para. (h)
Fiberboard	Plastics	Other	Plastics	Other	(d)	(e)	(f)	(g)	
X			X			X	X	When dry ice is used	X
X				X		X			X
	X		X				X		X
	X			X			X		X
		X	X				X		X
		X		X	X				X

(d) **Samples must be subjected to free-fall drops** onto a rigid, non-resilient, flat, horizontal surface from a height of 9 m (30 feet). The drops must be performed as follows:

(1) *Where the samples* are in the shape of a box, five must be dropped in sequence:

(i) *Flat on the base;*

(ii) *Flat on the top;*

(iii) *Flat on the longest side;*

(iv) *Flat on the shortest side; and*

(v) *On a corner.*

(2) *Where the samples* are in the shape of a drum, three must be dropped in sequence:

(i) *Diagonally on the top chime,* with the center of gravity directly above the point of impact;

(ii) *Diagonally on the base chime; and*

(iii) *Flat on the side.*

(3) *While the sample* should be released in the required orientation, it is accepted that for aerodynamic reasons the impact may not take place in that orientation.

(4) *Following the appropriate drop sequence,* there must be no leakage from the primary receptacle(s) which should remain protected by absorbent material in the secondary packaging.

(e) **The samples must be subjected to a water spray** to simulate exposure to rainfall of approximately 50 mm (2 inches) per hour for at least one hour. They must then be subjected to the test described in paragraph (d) of this section.

(f) **The sample must be conditioned in an atmosphere** of -18 °C (0 °F) or less for a period of at least 24 hours and within 15 minutes of removal from that atmosphere be subjected to the test described in paragraph (d) of this section. Where the sample contains dry ice, the conditioning period may be reduced to 4 hours.

(g) **Where packaging is intended to contain dry ice,** a test additional to that specified in paragraph (d) or (e) or (f) of this section must be carried out. One sample must be stored so that all the dry ice dissipates and then be subjected to the test described in paragraph (d) of this section.

(h) **Packagings with a gross mass of 7 kg** (15 pounds) or less should be subjected to the tests described in paragraph (h)(1) of this section and packagings with a gross mass exceeding 7 kg (15 pounds) to the tests in paragraph (h)(2) of this section.

(1) *Samples must be placed* on a level, hard surface. A cylindrical steel rod with a mass of at least 7 kg (15 pounds), a diameter not exceeding 38 mm (1.5 inches), and, at the impact end edges, a radius not exceeding 6 mm (0.2 inches), must be dropped in a vertical free fall from a height of 1 m (3 feet), measured from the impact end of the sample's impact surface. One sample must be placed on its base. A second sample must be placed in an orientation perpendicular to that used for the first. In each instance, the steel rod must be aimed to impact the primary receptacle(s). For a successful test, there must be no leakage from the primary receptacle(s) following each impact.

(2) *Samples must be dropped* onto the end of a cylindrical steel rod. The rod must be set vertically in a level, hard surface. It must have a diameter of 38 mm (1.5 inches) and a radius not exceeding 6 mm (0.2 inches) at the edges of the upper end. The rod must protrude from the surface a distance at least equal to that between the primary receptacle(s) and the outer surface of the outer packaging with a minimum of 200 mm (7.9 inches). One sample must be dropped in a vertical free fall from a height of 1 m (3 feet), measured from the top of the steel rod. A second sample must be dropped from the same height in an orientation perpendicular to that used for the first. In each instance, the packaging must be oriented so the steel rod will impact the primary receptacle(s). For a successful test, there must be no leakage from the primary receptacle(s) following each impact.

(i) **Variations.** The following variations in the primary receptacles placed within the secondary packaging are allowed without additional testing of the completed package. An equivalent level of performance must be maintained.

(1) *Variation 1.* Primary receptacles of equivalent or smaller size as compared to the tested primary receptacles may be used provided they meet all of the following conditions:

(i) *The primary receptacles* are of similar design to the tested primary receptacle (e.g., shape: round, rectangular, etc.).

(ii) *The material* of construction of the primary receptacle (glass, plastics, metal, etc.) offers resistance to impact and a stacking force equal to or greater than that of the originally tested primary receptacle.

(iii) *The primary receptacles* have the same or smaller openings and the closure is of similar design (e.g., screw cap, friction lid, etc.).

(iv) *Sufficient additional cushioning material* is used to fill void spaces and to prevent significant movement of the primary receptacles.

(v) *Primary receptacles* are oriented within the intermediate packaging in the same manner as in the tested package.

(2) *Variation 2.* A lesser number of the tested primary receptacles, or of the alternative types of primary receptacles identified in paragraph (i)(1) of this section, may be used provided sufficient cushioning is added to fill the void space(s) and to prevent significant movement of the primary receptacles.

(3) *Variation 3.* Primary receptacles of any type may be placed within a secondary packaging and shipped without testing in the outer packaging provided all of the following conditions are met:

(i) *The secondary and outer packaging combination* must be successfully tested in accordance with paragraphs (a) through (h) of this section with fragile (e.g., glass) inner receptacles.

(ii) *The total combined gross weight* of inner receptacles may not exceed one-half the gross weight of inner receptacles used for the drop test in paragraph (d) of this section.

(iii) *The thickness of cushioning material* between inner receptacles and between inner receptacles and the outside of the secondary packaging may not be reduced below the corresponding thicknesses in the originally tested packaging. If a single inner receptacle was used in the original test, the thickness of cushioning between the inner receptacles must be no less than the thickness of cushioning between the outside of the secondary packaging and the inner receptacle in the original test. When either fewer or smaller inner receptacles are used (as compared to the inner receptacles used in the drop test), sufficient additional cushioning material must be used to fill the void.

(iv) *The outer packaging* must pass the stacking test in §178.606 while empty. The total weight of identical packages must be based on the combined mass of inner receptacles used in the drop test in paragraph (d) of this section.

(v) *For inner receptacles containing liquids,* an adequate quantity of absorbent material must be present to absorb the entire liquid contents of the inner receptacles.

(vi) *If the outer packaging* is intended to contain inner receptacles for liquids and is not leakproof, or is intended to contain inner receptacles for solids and is not sift proof, a means of containing any liquid or solid contents in the event of leakage must be provided. This can be a leakproof liner, plastic bag, or other equally effective means of containment.

(vii) *In addition,* the marking required in §178.503(f) of this subchapter must be followed by the letter "U".

Subpart N - IBC Performance-oriented Standards

§178.700 Purpose, scope, and definitions.

(a) **This subpart prescribes requirements applying** to IBCs intended for the transportation of hazardous materials. Standards for these packagings are based on the UN Recommendations.

(b) **Terms used in this subpart are defined** in §171.8 of this subchapter and in paragraph (c) of this section.

(c) **The following definitions pertain to the IBC standards** in this subpart.

(1) **Body** means the receptacle proper (including openings and their closures, but not including service equipment), that has a volumetric capacity of not more than three cubic meters (3,000 L, 793 gallons, or 106 cubic feet) and not less than 0.45 cubic meters (450 L, 119 gallons, or 15.9 cubic feet) or a maximum net mass of not less than 400 kg (882) pounds.

(2) **Service equipment** means filling and discharge, pressure relief, safety, heating and heat-insulating devices and measuring instruments.

(3) **Structural equipment** means the reinforcing, fastening, handling, protective or stabilizing members of the body or stacking load bearing structural members (such as metal cages).

(4) **Maximum permissible gross mass** means the mass of the body, its service equipment, structural equipment and the maximum net mass (see §171.8 of this subchapter).

§178.702 IBC codes.

(a) **Intermediate bulk container code designations consist of:** two numerals specified in paragraph (a)(1) of this section; followed by the capital letter(s) specified in paragraph (a)(2) of this section; followed, when specified in an individual section, by a numeral indicating the category of intermediate bulk container.

(1) *IBC code number designations are as follows:*

Type	For solids, discharged		For liquids
	by gravity	Under pressure of more than 10 kPa (1.45 psig)	
Rigid	11	21	31
Flexible	13		

(2) *Intermediate bulk container* code letter designations are as follows:
"A" means steel (all types and surface treatments).
"B" means aluminum.
"C" means natural wood.
"D" means plywood.
"F" means reconstituted wood.
"G" means fiberboard.
"H" means plastic.
"L" means textile.
"M" means paper, multiwall.
"N" means metal (other than steel or aluminum).

(b) **For composite IBCs, two capital letters are used** in sequence following the numeral indicating IBC design type. The first letter indicates the material of the IBC inner receptacle. The second letter indicates the material of the outer IBC. For example, 31HA1 is a composite IBC with a plastic inner receptacle and a steel outer packaging.

§178.703 Marking of IBCs.

(a) **The manufacturer shall:**

(1) *Mark every IBC* in a durable and clearly visible manner. The marking may be applied in a single line or in multiple lines provided the correct sequence is followed with the information required by this section in letters, numerals and symbols of at least 12 mm in height. This minimum marking size applies only to IBCs manufactured after October 1, 2001). The following information is required in the sequence presented:

(i) *The United Nations symbol* as illustrated in §178.503(e)(1). For metal IBCs on which the marking is stamped or embossed, the capital letters `UN' may be applied instead of the symbol.

(ii) *The code number* designating IBC design type according to §178.702(a). The letter "W" must follow the IBC design type identification code on an IBC when the IBC differs from the requirements in subpart N of this part, or is tested using methods other than those specified in this subpart, and is approved by the Associate Administrator in accordance with the provisions in §178.801(i).

(iii) *A capital letter* identifying the performance standard under which the design type has been successfully tested, as follows:

[A] X — for IBCs meeting Packing Group I, II and III tests;
[B] Y — for IBCs meeting Packing Group II and III tests; and
[C] Z — for IBCs meeting only Packing Group III tests.

(iv) *The month* (designated numerically) and year (last two digits) of manufacture.

(v) *The country* authorizing the allocation of the mark. The letters "USA" indicate that the IBC is manufactured and marked in the United States in compliance with the provisions of this subchapter.

(vi) *The name* and address or symbol of the manufacturer or the approval agency certifying compliance with subparts N and O of this part. Symbols, if used, must be registered with the Associate Administrator.

(vii) *The stacking test load* in kilograms (kg). For IBCs not designed for stacking, the figure "0" must be shown.

(viii) *The maximum* permissible gross mass or, for flexible IBCs, the maximum net mass, in kg.

(2) *The following are examples of symbols and required markings:*

(i) *For a metal IBC* containing solids discharged by gravity made from steel:

11A/Y/02 92/USA/ABC/5500/1500

(ii) *For a flexible IBC* containing solids discharged by gravity and made from woven plastic with a liner:

13H3/Z/03 92/USA/ABC/0/1500

(iii) *For a rigid plastic IBC* containing liquids, made from plastic with structural equipment withstanding the stack load and with a manufacturer's symbol in place of the manufacturer's name and address:

31H1/Y/04 93/USA/M9399/10800/1200

(iv) *For a composite IBC* containing liquids, with a rigid plastic inner receptacle and an outer steel body and with the symbol of a DOT approved third-party test laboratory:

31HA1/Y/05 93/USA/+ZT1235/10800/1200

(b) **Additional marking.** In addition to markings required in paragraph (a) of this section, each IBC must be marked as follows in a place near the markings required in paragraph (a) of this section that is readily accessible for inspection. Where units of measure are used, the metric unit indicated (e.g., 450 L) must also appear.

(1) *For each* rigid plastic and composite IBC, the following markings must be included:

(i) *Rated capacity in L of water at 20 °C (68 °F);*
(ii) *Tare mass in kilograms;*
(iii) *Gauge test pressure in kPa;*
(iv) *Date of last leakproofness test,* if applicable (month and year); and
(v) *Date of last inspection (month and year).*

(2) *For each metal IBC,* the following markings must be included on a metal corrosion-resistant plate:

(i) *Rated capacity in L of water at 20 °C (68 °F);*
(ii) *Tare mass in kilograms;*
(iii) *Date of last leakproofness test, if applicable (month and year);*
(iv) *Date of last inspection (month and year);*
(v) *Maximum loading/discharge pressure, in kPa, if applicable;*
(vi) *Body material and its minimum thickness in mm; and*
(vii) *Serial number assigned by the manufacturer.*

(3) *Markings required* by paragraph (b)(1) or (b)(2) of this section may be preceded by the narrative description of the marking, e.g. "Tare Mass: * * *" where the "* * *" are replaced with the tare mass in kilograms of the IBC.

(4) *For each* fiberboard and wooden IBC, the tare mass in kg must be shown.

(5) *Each flexible IBC* may be marked with a pictogram displaying recommended lifting methods.

(6) *For each composite IBC,* the inner receptacle must be marked with at least the following information:

(i) *The code number* designating the IBC design type, the name and address or symbol of the manufacturer, the date of manufacture and the country authorizing the allocation of the mark as specified in paragraph (a) of this section;

(ii) *When a composite IBC* is designed in such a manner that the outer casing is intended to be dismantled for transport when empty (such as, for the return of the IBC for reuse to the original consignor), each of the parts intended to be detached when so dismantled must be marked with the month and year of manufacture and the name or symbol of the manufacturer.

§178.704 General IBC standards.

(a) **Each IBC must be resistant to, or protected from,** deterioration due to exposure to the external environment. IBCs intended for solid hazardous materials must be sift-proof and water-resistant.

(b) **All service equipment must be so positioned or protected** as to minimize potential loss of contents resulting from damage during IBC handling and transportation.

(c) **Each IBC, including attachments,** and service and structural equipment, must be designed to withstand, without loss of hazardous materials, the internal pressure of the contents and the stresses of normal handling and transport. An IBC intended for stacking must be designed for stacking. Any lifting or securing features of an IBC must be of sufficient strength to withstand the normal conditions of handling and transportation without gross distortion or failure and must be positioned so as to cause no undue stress in any part of the IBC.

(d) **An IBC consisting of a packaging within a framework** must be so constructed that:
(1) *The body is not damaged by the framework;*
(2) *The body is retained within the framework at all times; and*
(3) *The service and structural equipment* are fixed in such a way that they cannot be damaged if the connections between body and frame allow relative expansion or movement.
(e) **Bottom discharge valves must be secured** in the closed position and the discharge system suitably protected from damage. Valves having lever closures must be secured against accidental opening. The open or closed position of each valve must be readily apparent. For each IBC containing a liquid, a secondary means of sealing the discharge aperture must also be provided, e.g., by a blank flange or equivalent device.
(f) **IBC design types must be constructed** in such a way as to be bottom-lifted or top-lifted as specified in §§178.811 and 178.812.

§178.705 Standards for metal IBCs.

(a) **The provisions in this section apply to metal IBCs** intended to contain liquids and solids. Metal IBC types are designated:
(1) *11A, 11B, 11N or solids that are loaded or discharged by gravity.*
(2) *21A, 21B, 21N* for solids that are loaded or discharged at a gauge pressure greater than 10 kPa (1.45 psig).
(3) *31A, 31B, 31N for liquids or solids.*
(b) **Definitions for metal IBCs:**
(1) **Metal IBC** means an IBC with a metal body, together with appropriate service and structural equipment.
(2) **Protected** means providing the IBC body with additional external protection against impact and abrasion. For example, a multi-layer (sandwich) or double wall construction or a frame with a metal lattice-work casing.
(c) **Construction requirements for metal IBCs are as follows:**
(1) *Body.* The body must be made of ductile metal materials. Welds must be made so as to maintain design type integrity of the receptacle under conditions normally incident to transportation.
(i) *The use* of dissimilar metals must not result in deterioration that could affect the integrity of the body.
(ii) *Aluminum IBCs* intended to contain flammable liquids must have no movable parts, such as covers and closures, made of unprotected steel liable to rust, which might cause a dangerous reaction from friction or percussive contact with the aluminum.
(iii) *Metals used* in fabricating the body of a metal IBC must meet the following requirements:
[A] For steel, the percentage elongation at fracture must not be less than 10,000/Rm with a minimum of 20 percent; where Rm = minimum tensile strength of the steel to be used, in N/mm^2; if U.S. Standard units of psi are used for tensile strength then the ratio becomes 10,000 x (145/Rm).
[B] For aluminum, the percentage elongation at fracture must not be less than 10,000/(6Rm) with an absolute minimum of eight percent; if U.S. Standard units of psi are used for tensile strength then the ratio becomes 10,000 x 145 / (6Rm).
[C] Specimens used to determine the elongation at fracture must be taken transversely to the direction of rolling and be so secured that:
Lo = 5d
or
Lo = 5.65 $\sqrt{A}$
Where:
Lo = gauge length of the specimen before the test
d = diameter
A = cross-sectional area of test specimen
(iv) *Minimum wall thickness:*
[A] For a reference steel having a product of Rm X Ao = 10,000, where Ao is the minimum elongation (as a percentage) of the reference steel to be used on fracture under tensile stress, (Rm X Ao = 10,000 X 145; if tensile strength is in U.S. Standard units of pounds per square inch) the wall thickness must not be less than:

Capacity (C) in liters[1]	Wall thickness (T) in mm			
	Types 11A, 11B, 11N	Types 21A, 21B, 21N, 31A, 31B, 31N		
		Unprotected	Protected	Unprotected
C ≤ 1000	2.0	1.5	2.5	2.0
1000 < C ≤ 2000	T=C/2000 + 1.5	T=C/2000 + 1.0	T=C/2000 + 2.0	T=C/2000 + 1.5
2000 < C ≤ 3000	T=C/2000 + 1.5	T=C/2000 + 1.0	T=C/1000 + 1.0	T=C/2000 + 1.5

1. Where: gallons = liters X 0.264.

[B] For metals other than the reference steel described in paragraph (c)(1)(iii)(A) of this section, the minimum wall thickness is the greater of 1.5 mm (0.059 inches) or as determined by use of the following equivalence formula:

Formula for Metric Units

$$e_1 = \frac{21.4 \text{ x } e_0}{\sqrt[3]{Rm_1 \text{ x } A_1}}$$

Formula for U.S. Standard Units

$$e_1 = \frac{21.4 \text{ x } e_0}{\sqrt[3]{(Rm_1 \text{ x } A_1)/145}}$$

Where:
e_1 = required equivalent wall thickness of the metal to be used (in mm or if e_0 is in inches, use formula for U.S. Standard units).
e_0 = required minimum wall thickness for the reference steel (in mm or if e_0 is in inches, use formula for U.S. Standard units).
Rm_1 = guaranteed minimum tensile strength of the metal to be used (in N/mm^2 or for U.S. Standard units, use psi).
A_1 = minimum elongation (as a percentage) of the metal to be used on fracture under tensile stress (see paragraph (c)(1) of this section).
[C] For purposes of the calculation described in paragraph (c)(1)(iv)(B) of this section, the guaranteed minimum tensile strength of the metal to be used (Rm1) must be the minimum value according to material standards. However, for austenitic (stainless) steels, the specified minimum value for Rm, according to the material standards, may be increased by up to 15% when a greater value is provided in the material inspection certificate. When no material standard exists for the material in question, the value of Rm must be the minimum value indicated in the material inspection certificate.
(2) *Pressure relief.* The following pressure relief requirements apply to IBCs intended for liquids:
(i) *IBCs must be* capable of releasing a sufficient amount of vapor in the event of fire engulfment to ensure that no rupture of the body will occur due to pressure build-up. This can be achieved by spring-loaded or non-reclosing pressure relief devices or by other means of construction.
(ii) *The start-to-discharge pressure* may not be higher than 65 kPa (9 psig) and no lower than the vapor pressure of the hazardous material plus the partial pressure of the air or other inert gases, measured in the IBC at 55 °C (131 °F), determined on the basis of a maximum degree of filling as specified in §173.35(d) of this subchapter. This does not apply to fusible devices unless such devices are the only source of pressure relief for the IBC. Pressure relief devices must be fitted in the vapor space.

§178.706 Standards for rigid plastic IBCs.

(a) **The provisions in this section apply** to rigid plastic IBCs intended to contain solids or liquids. Rigid plastic IBC types are designated:
(1) *11H1 fitted* with structural equipment designed to withstand the whole load when IBCs are stacked, for solids which are loaded or discharged by gravity.
(2) *11H2 freestanding,* for solids which are loaded or discharged by gravity.
(3) *21H1 fitted* with structural equipment designed to withstand the whole load when IBCs are stacked, for solids which are loaded or discharged under pressure.
(4) *21H2 freestanding,* for solids which are loaded or discharged under pressure.
(5) *31H1 fitted* with structural equipment designed to withstand the whole load when IBCs are stacked, for liquids.
(6) *31H2 freestanding, for liquids.*
(b) **Rigid plastic IBCs consist of a rigid plastic body,** which may have structural equipment, together with appropriate service equipment.
(c) **Rigid plastic IBCs must be manufactured** from plastic material of known specifications and be of a strength relative to its capacity and to the service it is required to perform. In addition to conform-

ance to §173.24 of this subchapter, plastic materials must be resistant to aging and to degradation caused by ultraviolet radiation.

(1) *If protection* against ultraviolet radiation is necessary, it must be provided by the addition of a pigment or inhibiter such as carbon black. These additives must be compatible with the contents and remain effective throughout the life of the IBC body. Where use is made of carbon black, pigments or inhibitors, other than those used in the manufacture of the tested design type, retesting may be omitted if changes in the carbon black content, the pigment content or the inhibitor content do not adversely affect the physical properties of the material of construction.

(2) *Additives may be included* in the composition of the plastic material to improve the resistance to aging or to serve other purposes, provided they do not adversely affect the physical or chemical properties of the material of construction.

(3) *No used material* other than production residues or regrind from the same manufacturing process may be used in the manufacture of rigid plastic IBCs.

(4) *Rigid plastic IBCs* intended for the transportation of liquids must be capable of releasing a sufficient amount of vapor to prevent the body of the IBC from rupturing if it is subjected to an internal pressure in excess of that for which it was hydraulically tested. This may be achieved by spring-loaded or non-reclosing pressure relief devices or by other means of construction.

§178.707 Standards for composite IBCs.

(a) **The provisions in this section apply** to composite IBCs intended to contain solids and liquids. To complete the marking codes listed below, the letter "Z" must be replaced by a capital letter in accordance with §178.702(a)(2) to indicate the material used for the outer packaging. Composite IBC types are designated:

(1) *11HZ1 Composite IBCs* with a rigid plastic inner receptacle for solids loaded or discharged by gravity.

(2) *11HZ2 Composite IBCs* with a flexible plastic inner receptacle for solids loaded or discharged by gravity.

(3) *21HZ1 Composite IBCs* with a rigid plastic inner receptacle for solids loaded or discharged under pressure.

(4) *21HZ2 Composite IBCs* with a flexible plastic inner receptacle for solids loaded or discharged under pressure.

(5) *31HZ1 Composite IBCs* with a rigid plastic inner receptacle for liquids.

(6) *31HZ2 Composite IBCs* with a flexible plastic inner receptacle for liquids.

(b) **Definitions for composite IBC types:**

(1) A **composite IBC** is an IBC which consists of a rigid outer packaging enclosing a plastic inner receptacle together with any service or other structural equipment. The outer packaging of a composite IBC is designed to bear the entire stacking load. The inner receptacle and outer packaging form an integral packaging and are filled, stored, transported, and emptied as a unit.

(2) The term **plastic** means polymeric materials (i.e., plastic or rubber).

(3) A **"rigid" inner receptacle** is an inner receptacle which retains its general shape when empty without closures in place and without benefit of the outer casing. Any inner receptacle that is not "rigid" is considered to be "flexible."

(c) **Construction requirements for composite IBCs** with plastic inner receptacles are as follows:

(1) *The outer packaging* must consist of rigid material formed so as to protect the inner receptacle from physical damage during handling and transportation, but is not required to perform the secondary containment function. It includes the base pallet where appropriate. The inner receptacle is not intended to perform a containment function without the outer packaging.

(2) *A composite IBC* with a fully enclosing outer packaging must be designed to permit assessment of the integrity of the inner container following the leakproofness and hydraulic tests. The outer packaging of 31HZ2 composite IBCs must enclose the inner receptacles on all sides.

(3) *The inner receptacle* must be manufactured from plastic material of known specifications and be of a strength relative to its capacity and to the service it is required to perform. In addition to conformance with the requirements of §173.24 of this subchapter, the material must be resistant to aging and to degradation caused by ultraviolet radiation. The inner receptacle of 31HZ2 composite IBCs must consist of at least three plies of film.

(i) *If necessary,* protection against ultraviolet radiation must be provided by the addition of pigments or inhibitors such as carbon black. These additives must be compatible with the contents and remain effective throughout the life of the inner receptacle. Where use is made of carbon black, pigments, or inhibitors, other than those used in the manufacture of the tested design type, retesting may be omitted if the carbon black content, the pigment content, or the inhibitor content do not adversely affect the physical properties of the material of construction.

(ii) *Additives may be included* in the composition of the plastic material of the inner receptacle to improve resistance to aging, provided they do not adversely affect the physical or chemical properties of the material.

(iii) *No used material* other than production residues or regrind from the same manufacturing process may be used in the manufacture of inner receptacles.

(iv) *Composite INCs* intended for the transportation of liquids must be capable of releasing a sufficient amount of vapor to prevent the body of the IBC from rupturing if it is subjected to an internal pressure in excess of that for which it was hydraulically tested. This may be achieved by spring-loaded or non-reclosing pressure relief devices or by other means of construction.

(4) *The strength* of the construction material comprising the outer packaging and the manner of construction must be appropriate to the capacity of the composite IBC and its intended use. The outer packaging must be free of any projection that might damage the inner receptacle.

(i) *Outer packagings* of natural wood must be constructed of well seasoned wood that is commercially dry and free from defects that would materially lessen the strength of any part of the outer packaging. The tops and bottoms may be made of water-resistant reconstituted wood such as hardboard or particle board. Materials other than natural wood may be used for construction of structural equipment of the outer packaging.

(ii) *Outer packagings* of plywood must be made of well-seasoned, rotary cut, sliced, or sawn veneer, commercially dry and free from defects that would materially lessen the strength of the casing. All adjacent plies must be glued with water-resistant adhesive. Materials other than plywood may be used for construction of structural equipment of the outer packaging. Outer packagings must be firmly nailed or secured to corner posts or ends or be assembled by equally suitable devices.

(iii) *Outer packagings* of reconstituted wood must be constructed of water-resistant reconstituted wood such as hardboard or particle board. Materials other than reconstituted wood may be used for the construction of structural equipment of reconstituted wood outer packaging.

(iv) *Fiberboard outer packagings* must be constructed of strong, solid, or double-faced corrugated fiberboard (single or multiwall).

[A] *Water resistance* of the outer surface must be such that the increase in mass, as determined in a test carried out over a period of 30 minutes by the Cobb method of determining water absorption, is not greater than 155 grams per square meter (0.0316 pounds per square foot — see ISO International Standard 535-1976 (E)). Fiberboard must have proper bending qualities. Fiberboard must be cut, creased without cutting through any thickness of fiberboard, and slotted so as to permit assembly without cracking, surface breaks, or undue bending. The fluting of corrugated fiberboard must be firmly glued to the facings.

[B] *The ends* of fiberboard outer packagings may have a wooden frame or be constructed entirely of wood. Wooden battens may be used for reinforcements.

[C] *Manufacturers' joints* in the bodies of outer packagings must be taped, lapped and glued, or lapped and stitched with metal staples.

[D] *Lapped joints must have an appropriate overlap.*

[E] *Where closing* is effected by gluing or taping, a water-resistant adhesive must be used.

[F] *All closures must be sift-proof.*

(v) *Outer packagings* of plastic materials must be constructed in accordance with the relevant provisions of paragraph (c)(3) of this section.

(5) *Any integral* pallet base forming part of an IBC, or any detachable pallet, must be suitable for the mechanical handling of an IBC filled to its maximum permissible gross mass.

(i) *The pallet* or integral base must be designed to avoid protrusions that may cause damage to the IBC in handling.

(ii) *The outer packaging* must be secured to any detachable pallet to ensure stability in handling and transportation. Where a detachable pallet is used, its top surface must be free from sharp protrusions that might damage the IBC.

(iii) *Strengthening devices,* such as timber supports to increase stacking performance, may be used but must be external to the inner receptacle.

(iv) *The load-bearing surfaces* of IBCs intended for stacking must be designed to distribute loads in a stable manner. An IBC intended for stacking must be designed so that loads are not supported by the inner receptacle.

(6) *Intermediate IBCs* of type 31HZ2 must be limited to a capacity of not more than 1,250 L.

§178.708 Standards for fiberboard IBCs.

(a) **The provisions of this section apply** to fiberboard IBCs intended to contain solids that are loaded or discharged by gravity. Fiberboard IBCs are designated: 11G.

(b) **Definitions for fiberboard IBC types:**

(1) **Fiberboard IBCs** consist of a fiberboard body with or without separate top and bottom caps, appropriate service and structural equipment, and if necessary an inner liner (but no inner packaging).

(2) **Liner** means a separate tube or bag, including the closures of its openings, inserted in the body but not forming an integral part of it.

(c) **Construction requirements for fiberboard IBCs are as follows:**

(1) *Top lifting devices are prohibited in fiberboard IBCs.*

(2) *Fiberboard IBCs* must be constructed of strong, solid or double-faced corrugated fiberboard (single or multiwall) that is appropriate to the capacity of the outer packaging and its intended use. Water resistance of the outer surface must be such that the increase in mass, as determined in a test carried out over a period of 30 minutes by the Cobb method of determining water absorption, is not greater than 155 grams per square meter (0.0316 pounds per square foot see ISO 535-1976(E)). Fiberboard must have proper bending qualities. Fiberboard must be cut, creased without cutting through any thickness of fiberboard, and slotted so as to permit assembly without cracking, surface breaks, or undue bending. The fluting of corrugated fiberboard must be firmly glued to the facings.

(i) *The walls,* including top and bottom, must have a minimum puncture resistance of 15 Joules (11 foot-pounds of energy) measured according to ISO 3036, incorporated by reference in §171.7 of this subchapter.

(ii) *Manufacturers' joints* in the bodies of IBCs must be made with an appropriate overlap and be taped, glued, stitched with metal staples or fastened by other means at least equally effective. Where joints are made by gluing or taping, a water-resistant adhesive must be used. Metal staples must pass completely through all pieces to be fastened and be formed or protected so that any inner liner cannot be abraded or punctured by them.

(3) *The strength* of the material used and the construction of the liner must be appropriate to the capacity of the IBC and the intended use. Joints and closures must be sift-proof and capable of withstanding pressures and impacts liable to occur under normal conditions of handling and transport.

(4) *Any integral* pallet base forming part of an IBC, or any detachable pallet, must be suitable for the mechanical handling of an IBC filled to its maximum permissible gross mass.

(i) *The pallet* or integral base must be designed to avoid protrusions that may cause damage to the IBC in handling.

(ii) *The outer packaging* must be secured to any detachable pallet to ensure stability in handling and transport. Where a detachable pallet is used, its top surface must be free from sharp protrusions that might damage the IBC.

(iii) *Strengthening devices,* such as timber supports to increase stacking performance, may be used but must be external to the inner liner.

(iv) *The load-bearing surfaces* of IBCs intended for stacking must be designed to distribute loads in a stable manner.

§178.709 Standards for wooden IBCs.

(a) **The provisions in this section apply to wooden IBCs** intended to contain solids that are loaded or discharged by gravity. Wooden IBC types are designated:

(1) *11C Natural wood with inner liner.*

(2) *11D Plywood with inner liner.*

(3) *11F Reconstituted wood with inner liner.*

(b) **Definitions for wooden IBCs:**

(1) **Wooden IBCs** consist of a rigid or collapsible wooden body together with an inner liner (but no inner packaging) and appropriate service and structural equipment.

(2) **Liner** means a separate tube or bag, including the closures of its openings, inserted in the body but not forming an integral part of it.

(c) **Construction requirements for wooden IBCs are as follows:**

(1) *Top lifting devices are prohibited in wooden IBCs.*

(2) *The strength* of the materials used and the method of construction must be appropriate to the capacity and intended use of the IBC.

(i) *Natural wood* used in the construction of an IBC must be well-seasoned, commercially dry, and free from defects that would materially lessen the strength of any part of the IBC. Each IBC part must consist of uncut wood or a piece equivalent in strength and integrity. IBC parts are equivalent to one piece when a suitable method of glued assembly is used (i.e., a Lindermann joint, tongue and groove joint, ship lap or rabbet joint, or butt joint with at least two corrugated metal fasteners at each joint, or when other methods at least equally effective are used). Materials other than natural wood may be used for the construction of structural equipment of the outer packaging.

(ii) *Plywood used* in construction of bodies must be at least 3-ply. Plywood must be made of well-seasoned, rotary-cut, sliced or sawn veneer, commercially dry, and free from defects that would materially lessen the strength of the body. All adjacent plies must be glued with water-resistant adhesive. Materials other than plywood may be used for the construction of structural equipment of the outer packaging.

(iii) *Reconstituted wood* used in construction of bodies must be water resistant reconstituted wood such as hardboard or particle board. Materials other than reconstituted wood may be used for the construction of structural equipment of the outer packaging.

(iv) *Wooden IBCs* must be firmly nailed or secured to corner posts or ends or be assembled by similar devices.

(3) *The strength* of the material used and the construction of the liner must be appropriate to the capacity of the IBC and its intended use. Joints and closures must be sift-proof and capable of withstanding pressures and impacts liable to occur under normal conditions of handling and transportation.

(4) *Any integral pallet base* forming part of an IBC, or any detachable pallet, must be suitable for the mechanical handling of an IBC filled to its maximum permissible gross mass.

(i) *The pallet or integral base* must be designed to avoid protrusions that may cause damage to the IBC in handling.

(ii) *The outer packaging* must be secured to any detachable pallet to ensure stability in handling and transportation. Where a detachable pallet is used, its top surface must be free from sharp protrusions that might damage the IBC.

(iii) *Strengthening devices,* such as timber supports to increase stacking performance, may be used but must be external to the inner liner.

(iv) *The load-bearing surfaces* of IBCs intended for stacking must be designed to distribute loads in a stable manner.

§178.710 Standards for flexible IBCs.

(a) **The provisions of this section apply to flexible IBCs** intended to contain solid hazardous materials. Flexible IBC types are designated:

(1) *13H1 woven plastic without coating or liner.*

(2) *13H2 woven plastic, coated.*

(3) *13H3 woven plastic with liner.*

(4) *13H4 woven plastic, coated and with liner.*

(5) *13H5 plastic film.*

(6) *13L1 textile without coating or liner.*

(7) *13L2 textile, coated.*

(8) *13L3 textile with liner.*

(9) *13L4 textile, coated and with liner.*

(10) *13M1 paper, multiwall.*

(11) *13M2 paper, multiwall, water resistant.*

(b) **Definitions for flexible IBCs:**

(1) **Flexible IBCs** consist of a body constructed of film, woven plastic, woven fabric, paper, or combination thereof, together with any appropriate service equipment and handling devices, and if necessary, an inner coating or liner.

(2) **Woven plastic** means a material made from stretched tapes or monofilaments.

(3) **Handling device** means any sling, loop, eye, or frame attached to the body of the IBC or formed from a continuation of the IBC body material.

(c) **Construction requirements for flexible IBCs are as follows:**

(1) *The strength* of the material and the construction of the flexible IBC must be appropriate to its capacity and its intended use.

(2) *All materials* used in the construction of flexible IBCs of types 13M1 and 13M2 must, after complete immersion in water for not less than 24 hours, retain at least 85 percent of the tensile strength as measured originally on the material conditioned to equilibrium at 67 percent relative humidity or less.

(3) *Seams must be* stitched or formed by heat sealing, gluing or any equivalent method. All stitched seam-ends must be secured.

(4) *In addition* to conformance with the requirements of §173.24 of this subchapter, flexible IBCs must be resistant to aging and degradation caused by ultraviolet radiation.

(5) *For plastic flexible IBCs,* if necessary, protection against ultraviolet radiation must be provided by the addition of pigments or inhibitors such as carbon black. These additives must be compatible with the contents and remain effective throughout the life of the container. Where use is made of carbon black, pigments, or inhibitors, other than those used in the manufacture of the tested design type, retesting may be omitted if the carbon black content, the pigment content or the inhibitor content does not adversely affect the physical properties of the material of construction. Additives may be included in the composition of the plastic material to improve resistance to aging, provided they do not adversely affect the physical or chemical properties of the material.

(6) *No used material* other than production residues or regrind from the same manufacturing process may be used in the manufacture of plastic flexible IBCs. This does not preclude the re-use of component parts such as fittings and pallet bases, provided such components have not in any way been damaged in previous use.

(7) *When flexible IBCs are filled,* the ratio of height to width may not be more than 2:1.

Subpart O - Testing of IBCs

§178.800 Purpose and scope.

This subpart prescribes certain testing requirements for IBCs identified in subpart N of this part.

§178.801 General requirements.

(a) **General.** The test procedures prescribed in this subpart are intended to ensure that IBCs containing hazardous materials can withstand normal conditions of transportation and are considered minimum requirements. Each packaging must be manufactured and assembled so as to be capable of successfully passing the prescribed tests and of conforming to the requirements of §173.24 of this subchapter at all times while in transportation.

(b) **Responsibility.** It is the responsibility of the IBC manufacturer to assure that each IBC is capable of passing the prescribed tests. To the extent that an IBC assembly function, including final closure, is performed by the person who offers a hazardous material for transportation, that person is responsible for performing the function in accordance with §§173.22 and 178.2 of this subchapter.

(c) **Definitions.** For the purpose of this subpart:

(1) **IBC design type** refers to IBC which does not differ in structural design, size, material of construction, wall thickness, manner of construction and representative service equipment.

(2) **Design qualification testing** is the performance of the drop, leakproofness, hydrostatic pressure, stacking, bottom-lift or top-lift, tear, topple, righting and vibration tests, as applicable, prescribed in this subpart, for each different IBC design type, at the start of production of that packaging.

(3) **Periodic design requalification test** is the performance of the applicable tests specified in paragraph (c)(2) of this section on an IBC design type, in order to requalify the design for continued production at the frequency specified in paragraph (e) of this section.

(4) **Production inspection** is the inspection that must initially be conducted on each newly manufactured IBC.

(5) **Production testing** is the performance of the leakproofness test in accordance with paragraph (f) of this section on each IBC intended to contain solids discharged by pressure or intended to contain liquids.

(6) **Periodic retest and inspection** is performance of the applicable test and inspections on each IBC at the frequency specified in §180.352 of this subchapter.

(7) **Different IBC design type** is one that differs from a previously qualified IBC design type in structural design, size, material of construction, wall thickness, or manner of construction, but does not include:

(i) *A packaging which differs in surface treatment;*

(ii) *A rigid plastic IBC* or composite IBC which differs with regard to additives used to comply with §§178.706(c), 178.707(c) or 178.710(c);

(iii) *A packaging* which differs only in its lesser external dimensions (i.e., height, width, length) provided materials of construction and material thicknesses or fabric weight remain the same;

(iv) *A packaging which differs in service equipment.*

(d) **Design qualification testing.** The packaging manufacturer shall achieve successful test results for the design qualification testing at the start of production of each new or different IBC design type. The service equipment selected for this design qualification testing shall be representative of the type of service equipment that will be fitted to any finished IBC body under the design. Application of the certification mark by the manufacturer shall constitute certification that the IBC design type passed the prescribed tests in this subpart.

(e) **Periodic design requalification testing.**

(1) *Periodic design requalification* must be conducted on each qualified IBC design type if the manufacturer is to maintain authorization for continued production. The IBC manufacturer shall achieve successful test results for the periodic design requalification at sufficient frequency to ensure each packaging produced by the manufacturer is capable of passing the design qualification tests. Design requalification tests must be conducted at least once every 12 months.

(2) *Changes in the frequency* of design requalification testing specified in paragraph (e)(1) of this section are authorized if approved by the Associate Administrator. These requests must be based on:

(i) *Detailed quality assurance programs* that assure that proposed decreases in test frequency maintain the integrity of originally tested IBC design types; and

(ii) *Demonstrations that each* IBC produced is capable of withstanding higher standards (e.g., increased drop height, hydrostatic pressure, wall thickness, fabric weight).

(f) **Production testing and inspection.**

(1) *Production testing* consists of the leakproofness test prescribed in §178.813 of this subpart and must be performed on each IBC intended to contain solids discharged by pressure or intended to contain liquids. For this test:

(i) *The IBC need not have its closures fitted.*

(ii) *The inner receptacle* of a composite IBC may be tested without the outer IBC body, provided the test results are not affected.

(2) *Applicable inspection requirements* in §180.352 of this subchapter must be performed on each IBC initially after production.

(g) **Test samples.** The IBC manufacturer shall conduct the design qualification and periodic design requalification tests prescribed in this subpart using random samples of IBCs, according to the appropriate test section.

(h) **Selective testing of IBCs.** Variation of a tested IBC design type is permitted without further testing, provided selective testing demonstrates an equivalent or greater level of safety than the design type tested and which has been approved by the Associate Administrator.

(i) **Approval of equivalent packagings.** An IBC which differs from the standards in subpart N of this part, or which is tested using methods other than those specified in this subpart, may be used if approved by the Associate Administrator. Such IBCs must be shown to be equally effective, and testing methods used must be equivalent. A large packaging, as defined in §171.8 of this subchapter, may be used if approved by the Associate Administrator. The large packaging must conform to the construction standards, performance testing and packaging marking requirements specified in the UN Recommendations.

(j) **Proof of compliance.** Notwithstanding the periodic design requalification testing intervals specified in paragraph (e) of this section, the Associate Administrator, or a designated representative, may at any time require demonstration of compliance by a manufacturer, through testing in accordance with this subpart, that packagings meet the requirements of this subpart. As required by the Associate Administrator, or a designated representative, the manufacturer shall either:

(1) *Conduct performance tests* or have tests conducted by an independent testing facility, in accordance with this subpart; or

(2) *Make a sample IBC* available to the Associate Administrator, or a designated representative, for testing in accordance with this subpart.

(k) **Coatings.** If an inner treatment or coating of an IBC is required for safety reasons, the manufacturer shall design the IBC so that the treatment or coating retains its protective properties even after withstanding the tests prescribed by this subpart.

(l) **Record retention.**

(1) *The person* who certifies an IBC design type shall keep records of design qualification tests for each IBC design type and for each periodic design requalification as specified in this part. These records must be maintained at each location where the IBC is manufactured and at each location where design qualification and periodic design requalification testing is performed. These records must be maintained for as long as IBCs are manufactured in accordance with each qualified design type and for at least 2.5 years thereafter. These records must include the following information: name and address of test facility; name and address of the person certifying the IBC; a unique test report identification; date of test report; manufacturer of the IBC; description of the IBC design type (e.g., dimensions, materials, closures, thickness, representative service equipment, etc.); maximum IBC capacity; characteristics of test contents; test descriptions and results (including drop heights, hydrostatic pressures, tear propagation length, etc.). Each test report must be signed with the name of the person conducting the test, and name of the person responsible for testing.

(2) *The person* who certifies each IBC must make all records of design qualification tests and periodic design requalification tests available for inspection by a representative of the Department upon request.

§178.802 Preparation of fiberboard IBCs for testing.

(a) **Fiberboard IBCs and composite IBCs** with fiberboard outer packagings must be conditioned for at least 24 hours in an atmosphere maintained:

(1) *At 50 percent* ± 2 percent relative humidity, and at a temperature of 23 °± 2 °C (73 °F ± 4 °F); or

(2) *At 65 percent* ± 2 percent relative humidity, and at a temperature of 20 °± 2 °C (68 °F ± 4 °F), or 27 °C ± 2 °C (81 °F ± 4 °F).

(b) **Average values for temperature and humidity** must fall within the limits in paragraph (a) of this section. Short-term fluctuations and measurement limitations may cause individual measurements to vary by up to 5 percent relative humidity without significant impairment of test reproducibility.

(c) **For purposes of periodic design requalification only,** fiberboard IBCs or composite IBCs with fiberboard outer packagings may be at ambient conditions.

§178.803 Testing and certification of IBCs.

Tests required for the certification of each IBC design type are specified in the following table. The letter X indicates that one IBC (except where noted) of each design type must be subjected to the tests in the order presented:

Performance test	IBC type					
	Metal IBCs	Rigid plastic IBCs	Composite IBCs	Fiberboard IBCs	Wooden IBCs	Flexible IBCs
Vibration	[6] X	[6] X	[6] X	[6] X	[6] X	[1.5] X
Bottom lift	[2] X	X	X	X	X	
Top lift	[2] X	[2] X	[2] X			[2,5] X
Stacking	[7] X	[7] X	[7] X	[7] X	[7] X	[5] X
Leakproofness	[3] X	[3] X	[3] X			
Hydrostatic	[3] X	[3] X	[3] X			
Drop	[4] X	[4] X	[4] X	[4] X	[4] X	[5] X
Topple						[5] X
Righting						[2,5] X
Tear						[5] X

1. Flexible IBCs must be capable of withstanding the vibration test.
2. This test must be performed only if IBCs are designed to be handled this way. For metal IBCs, at least one of the bottom lift or top lift tests must be performed.
3. The leakproofness and hydrostatic pressure tests are required only for IBCs intended to contain liquids or intended to contain solids loaded or discharged under pressure.
4. Another IBC of the same design type may be used for the drop test set forth in §178.810 of this subchapter.
5. Another different flexible IBC of the same design type may be used for each test.
6. The vibration test may be performed in another order for IBCs manufactured and tested under provisions of an exemption before October 1, 1994 and for non-DOT specification portable tanks tested before October 1, 1994, intended for export.
7. This test must be performed only if the IBC is designed to be stacked.

§178.810 Drop test.

(a) **General.** The drop test must be conducted for the qualification of all IBC design types and performed periodically as specified in §178.801(e) of this subpart.

(b) **Special preparation for the drop test.**

(1) *Metal, rigid plastic, and composite IBCs* intended to contain solids must be filled to not less than 95 percent of their capacity, or if intended to contain liquids, to not less than 98 percent of their capacity. Pressure relief devices must be removed and their apertures plugged or rendered inoperative.

(2) *Fiberboard, wooden, and flexible IBCs* must be filled with a solid material to not less than 95 percent of their capacity.

(3) *Rigid plastic IBCs and composite IBCs* with plastic inner receptacles must be conditioned for testing by reducing the temperature of the packaging and its contents to -18 °C (0 °F) or lower. Test liquids must be kept in the liquid state. Anti-freeze should be used, if necessary.

(c) **Test method.** Samples of all IBC design types must be dropped onto a rigid, non-resilient, smooth, flat and horizontal surface. The point of impact must be the most vulnerable part of the base of the IBC being tested. Following the drop, the IBC must be restored to the upright position for observation.

(d) **Drop height.**

(1) *For all IBCs, drop heights are specified as follows:*

(i) *Packing Group I:* 1.8 m (5.9 feet).

(ii) *Packing Group II:* 1.2 m (3.9 feet).

(iii) *Packing Group III:* 0.8 m (2.6 feet).

(2) *Drop tests* are to be performed with the solid or liquid to be transported or with a non-hazardous material having essentially the same physical characteristics.

(3) *The specific gravity and viscosity* of a substituted non-hazardous material used in the drop test for liquids must be similar to the hazardous material intended for transportation. Water also may be used for the liquid drop test under the following conditions:

(i) *Where the substances* to be carried have a specific gravity not exceeding 1.2, the drop heights must be those specified in paragraph (d)(1) of this section for each IBC design type; and

(ii) *Where the substances* to be carried have a specific gravity exceeding 1.2, the drop heights must be as follows:

[A] Packing Group I: SG x 1.5 m (4.9 feet).

[B] Packing Group II: SG x 1.0 m (3.3 feet).

[C] Packing Group III: SG x 0.67 m (2.2 feet).

(e) **Criteria for passing the test.** For all IBC design types there may be no loss of contents. A slight discharge from a closure upon impact is not considered to be a failure of the IBC provided that no further leakage occurs. A slight discharge (e.g., from closures or stitch holes) upon impact is not considered a failure of the flexible IBC provided that no further leakage occurs after the IBC has been raised clear of the ground.

§178.811 Bottom lift test.

(a) **General.** The bottom lift test must be conducted for the qualification of all IBC design types designed to be lifted from the base.

(b) **Special preparation for the bottom lift test.** The IBC must be loaded to 1.25 times its maximum permissible gross mass, the load being evenly distributed.

(c) **Test method.** All IBC design types must be raised and lowered twice by a lift truck with the forks centrally positioned and spaced at three quarters of the dimension of the side of entry (unless the points of entry are fixed). The forks must penetrate to three quarters of the direction of entry. The test must be repeated from each possible direction of entry.

(d) **Criteria for passing the test.** For all IBC design types designed to be lifted from the base, there may be no permanent deformation which renders the IBC unsafe for transportation and no loss of contents.

§178.812 Top lift test.

(a) **General.** The top lift test must be conducted for the qualification of all IBC design types designed to be lifted from the top or, for flexible IBCs, from the side.

(b) **Special preparation for the top lift test.**

(1) *Metal, rigid plastic,* and composite IBC design types must be loaded to twice the maximum permissible gross mass.

(2) *Flexible IBC design types* must be filled to six times the maximum net mass, the load being evenly distributed.

(c) **Test method.**

(1) *A metal or flexible IBC* must be lifted in the manner for which it is designed until clear of the floor and maintained in that position for a period of five minutes.

(2) *Rigid plastic and composite IBC design types must be:*

(i) *Lifted by each pair* of diagonally opposite lifting devices, so that the hoisting forces are applied vertically, for a period of five minutes; and

(ii) *Lifted by each pair* of diagonally opposite lifting devices, so that the hoisting forces are applied towards the center at 45° to the vertical, for a period of five minutes.

(3) *If not tested* as indicated in paragraph (c)(1) of this section, a flexible IBC design type must be tested as follows:

(i) *Fill the flexible IBC* to 95% full with a material representative of the product to be shipped.

(ii) *Suspend the flexible IBC by its lifting devices.*

(iii) *Apply a constant downward force* through a specially designed platen. The platen will be a minimum of 60% and a maximum of 80% of the cross sectional surface area of the flexible IBC.

(iv) *The combination* of the mass of the filled flexible IBC and the force applied through the platen must be a minimum of six times the maximum net mass of the flexible IBC. The test must be conducted for a period of five minutes.

(v) *Other equally effective methods* of top lift testing and preparation may be used with approval of the Associate Administrator.

(d) **Criteria for passing the test.** For all IBC design types designed to be lifted from the top, there may be no permanent deformation which renders the IBC, including the base pallets when applicable, unsafe for transportation, and no loss of contents.

§178.813 Leakproofness test.

(a) **General.** The leakproofness test must be conducted for the qualification of all IBC design types and on all production units intended to contain solids that are loaded or discharged under pressure or intended to contain liquids.

(b) **Special preparation for the leakproofness test.** Vented closures must either be replaced by similar non-vented closures or the vent must be sealed. For metal IBC design types, the initial test must be carried out before the fitting of any thermal insulation equipment. The inner receptacle of a composite IBC may be tested without the outer packaging provided the test results are not affected.

(c) **Test method and pressure applied.** The leakproofness test must be carried out for a suitable length of time using air at a gauge pressure of not less than 20 kPa (2.9 psig). Leakproofness of IBC design types must be determined by coating the seams and joints with a heavy oil, a soap solution and water, or other methods suitable for the purpose of detecting leaks. Other methods, if at least equally effective, may be used in accordance with appendix B of this part, or if approved by the Associate Administrator, as provided in §178.801(i)).

(d) **Criterion for passing the test.** For all IBC design types intended to contain solids that are loaded or discharged under pressure or intended to contain liquids, there may be no leakage of air from the IBC.

§178.814 Hydrostatic pressure test.

(a) **General.** The hydrostatic pressure test must be conducted for the qualification of all metal, rigid plastic, and composite IBC design types intended to contain solids that are loaded or discharged under pressure or intended to contain liquids.

(b) **Special preparation for the hydrostatic pressure test.** For metal IBCs, the test must be carried out before the fitting of any thermal insulation equipment. For all IBCs, pressure relief devices and vented closures must be removed and their apertures plugged or rendered inoperative.

(c) **Test method.** Hydrostatic gauge pressure must be measured at the top of the IBC. The test must be carried out for a period of at least 10 minutes applying a hydrostatic gauge pressure not less than that indicated in paragraph (d) of this section. The IBCs may not be mechanically restrained during the test.

(d) **Hydrostatic gauge pressure applied.**

(1) *For metal* IBC design types 31A, 31B, 31N: 65 kPa gauge pressure (9.4 psig).

(2) *For metal* IBC design types 21A, 21B, 21N, 31A, 31B, 31N: 200 kPa (29 psig). For metal IBC design types 31A, 31B and 31N, the tests in paragraphs (d)(1) and (d)(2) of this section must be conducted consecutively.

(3) *For metal* IBCs design types 21A, 21B, and 21N, for Packing Group I solids: 250 kPa (36 psig) gauge pressure.

(4) *For rigid plastic* IBC design types 21H1 and 21H2 and composite IBC design types 21HZ1 and 21HZ2: 75 kPa (11 psig).

(5) *For rigid plastic* IBC design types 31H1 and 31H2 and composite IBC design types 31HZ1 and 31HZ2: whichever is the greater of:

(i) *The pressure determined by any one of the following methods:*

[A] The gauge pressure (pressure in the IBC above ambient atmospheric pressure) measured in the IBC at 55 °C (131 °F) multiplied by a safety factor of 1.5. This pressure must be determined on the basis of the IBC being filled and closed to no more than 98 percent capacity at 15 °C (60 °F);

[B] If absolute pressure (vapor pressure of the hazardous material plus atmospheric pressure) is used, 1.5 multiplied by the vapor pressure of the hazardous material at 55 °C (131 °F) minus 100 kPa (14.5 psi). If this method is chosen, the hydrostatic test pressure applied must be at least 100 kPa gauge pressure (14.5 psig); or

[C] If absolute pressure (vapor pressure of the hazardous material plus atmospheric pressure) is used, 1.75 multiplied by the vapor pressure of the hazardous material at 50 °C (122 °F) minus 100 kPa (14.5 psi). If this method is chosen, the hydrostatic test pressure applied must be at least 100 kPa gauge pressure (14.5 psig); or

(ii) *Twice the greater of:*

[A] The static pressure of the hazardous material on the bottom of the IBC filled to 98 percent capacity; or

[B] The static pressure of water on the bottom of the IBC filled to 98 percent capacity.

(e) **Criteria for passing the test(s).**

(1) *For metal IBCs,* subjected to the 65 kPa (9.4 psig) test pressure specified in paragraph (d)(1) of this section, there may be no leakage or permanent deformation that would make the IBC unsafe for transportation.

(2) *For metal IBCs* intended to contain liquids, when subjected to the 200 kPa (29 psig) and the 250 kPa (36 psig) test pressures specified in paragraphs (d)(2) and (d)(3) of this section, respectively, there may be no leakage.

(3) *For rigid plastic* IBC types 21H1, 21H2, 31H1, and 31H2, and composite IBC types 21HZ1, 21HZ2, 31HZ1, and 31HZ2, there may be no leakage and no permanent deformation which renders the IBC unsafe for transportation.

§178.815 Stacking test.

(a) **General.** The stacking test must be conducted for the qualification of all IBC design types intended to be stacked.

(b) **Special preparation for the stacking test.**

(1) *All IBCs* except flexible IBC design types must be loaded to their maximum permissible gross mass.

(2) *The flexible IBC* must be filled to not less than 95 percent of its capacity and to its maximum net mass, with the load being evenly distributed.

(c) **Test method.**

(1) *All IBCs* must be placed on their base on level, hard ground and subjected to a uniformly distributed superimposed test load for a period of at least five minutes (see paragraph (d) of this section).

(2) *Fiberboard, wooden, and composite IBCs* with outer packagings constructed of other than plastic materials must be subjected to the test for 24 hours.

(3) *Rigid plastic* IBC types and composite IBC types with plastic outer packagings (11HH1, 11HH2, 21HH1, 21HH2, 31HH1 and 31HH2) which bear the stacking load must be subjected to the test for 28 days at 40 °C (104 °F).

(4) *For all IBCs,* the load must be applied by one of the following methods:

(i) *One or more IBCs* of the same type loaded to their maximum permissible gross mass and stacked on the test IBC;

(ii) *The calculated* superimposed test load weight loaded on either a flat plate or a reproduction of the base of the IBC, which is stacked on the test IBC; or

(iii) *The packaging* may be tested using a dynamic compression testing machine. The test must be conducted at room temperature on an empty, unsealed packaging. The test sample must be centered on the bottom platen of the testing machine. The top platen must be lowered until it comes in contact with the test sample. Compression must be applied end to end. The speed of the compression tester must be one-half inch plus or minus one-fourth inch per minute. An initial preload of 50 pounds must be applied to ensure a definite contact between the test sample and the platens. The distance between the platens at this time must be recorded as zero deformation. The force "A" to then be applied must be calculated using the applicable formula:

Liquids: A = (n-1) [w+ (s x v x 8.3 x .98)] x 1.5;

or

Solids: A = (n-1) [w+ (s x v x 8.3 x .95)] x 1.5

Where:

A = applied load in pounds

n = minimum number of containers that, when stacked, reach a height of 3 m

s = specific gravity of lading

w = maximum weight of one empty container in pounds

v = actual capacity of container (rated capacity + outage) in gallons

And:

8.3 corresponds to the weight in pounds of 1.0 gallon of water.

1.5 is a compensation factor that converts the static load of the stacking test into a load suitable for dynamic compression testing.

(d) **Calculation of superimposed test load.** For all IBCs, the load to be placed on the IBC must be 1.8 times the combined maximum permissible gross mass of the number of similar IBCs that may be stacked on top of the IBC during transportation.

(e) **Criteria for passing the test.**

(1) *For metal, rigid plastic, and composite IBCs* there may be no permanent deformation which renders the IBC unsafe for transportation and no loss of contents.

(2) *For fiberboard and wooden IBCs* there may be no loss of contents and no permanent deformation which renders the whole IBC, including the base pallet, unsafe for transportation.

(3) *For flexible IBCs,* there may be no deterioration which renders the IBC unsafe for transportation and no loss of contents.

§178.816 Topple test.

(a) **General.** The topple test must be conducted for the qualification of all flexible IBC design types.

(b) **Special preparation for the topple test.** The flexible IBC must be filled to not less than 95 percent of its capacity and to its maximum net mass, with the load being evenly distributed.

(c) **Test method.** A flexible IBC must be toppled onto any part of its top upon a rigid, non-resilient, smooth, flat, and horizontal surface.

(d) **Topple height.** For all flexible IBCs, the topple height is specified as follows:

(1) *Packing Group I:* 1.8 m (5.9 feet).

(2) *Packing Group II:* 1.2 m (3.9 feet).

(3) *Packing Group III:* 0.8 m (2.6 feet).

(e) **Criteria for passing the test.** For all flexible IBCs, there may be no loss of contents. A slight discharge (e.g., from closures or stitch holes) upon impact is not considered to be a failure, provided no further leakage occurs.

§178.817 Righting test.

(a) **General.** The righting test must be conducted for the qualification of all flexible IBCs designed to be lifted from the top or side.

(b) **Special preparation for the righting test.** The flexible IBC must be filled to not less than 95 percent of its capacity and to its maximum net mass, with the load being evenly distributed.

(c) **Test method.** The flexible IBC, lying on its side, must be lifted at a speed of at least 0.1 m/second (0.33 ft/s) to an upright position, clear of the floor, by one lifting device, or by two lifting devices when four are provided.

(d) **Criterion for passing the test.** For all flexible IBCs, there may be no damage to the IBC or its lifting devices which renders the IBC unsafe for transportation or handling.

§178.818 Tear test.

(a) **General.** The tear test must be conducted for the qualification of all flexible IBC design types.

(b) **Special preparation for the tear test.** The flexible IBC must be filled to not less than 95 percent of its capacity and to its maximum net mass, the load being evenly distributed.

(c) **Test method.** Once the IBC is placed on the ground, a 100-mm (4-inch) knife score, completely penetrating the wall of a wide face, is made at a 45° angle to the principal axis of the IBC, halfway between the bottom surface and the top level of the contents. The IBC must then be subjected to a uniformly distributed superimposed load equivalent to twice the maximum net mass. The load must be applied for at least five minutes. An IBC which is designed to be lifted from the top or the side must, after removal of the superimposed load, be lifted clear of the floor and maintained in that position for a period of five minutes.

(d) **Criterion for passing the test.** The IBC passes the tear test if the cut does not propagate more than 25 percent of its original length.

§178.819 Vibration test.

(a) **General.** The vibration test must be conducted for the qualification of all rigid IBC design types. Flexible IBC design types must be capable of withstanding the vibration test.

(b) **Test method.**

(1) *A sample IBC,* selected at random, must be filled and closed as for shipment.

(2) *The sample IBC* must be placed on a vibrating platform that has a vertical double-amplitude (peak-to-peak displacement) of one inch. The IBC must be constrained horizontally to prevent it from falling off the platform, but must be left free to move vertically and bounce.

(3) *The test* must be performed for one hour at a frequency that causes the package to be raised from the vibrating platform to such a degree that a piece of material of approximately 1.6-mm (0.063-inch) thickness (such as steel strapping or paperboard) can be passed between the bottom of the IBC and the platform. Other methods at least equally effective may be used (see §178.801(i)).

(c) **Criteria for passing the test.** An IBC passes the vibration test if there is no rupture or leakage.

Appendix A to Part 178
Specifications for steel.

Table 1

[Open-hearth, basic oxygen, or electric steel of uniform quality. The following chemical composition limits are based on ladle analysis:]

Designation	Chemical composition, percent-ladle analysis		
	Grade 1[1]	Grade 2[1,2]	Grade 3[2,4,5]
Carbon	0.10/0.20	0.24 maximum	0.22 maximum
Manganese	1.10/1.60	0.50/1.00	1.25 maximum
Phosphorus, maximum	0.04	0.04	0.045[6]
Sulfur, maximum	0.05	0.05	0.05
Silicon	0.15/0.30	0.30 maximum	
Copper, maximum	0.40		
Columbium		0.01/0.04	
Heat treatment authorized	([3])	([3])	([3])
Maximum stress (p.s.i.)	35,000	35,000	35,000

1. Addition of other elements to obtain alloying effect is not authorized.
2. Ferritic grain size 6 or finer according to ASTM E112-63.
3. Any suitable heat treatment in excess of 1,100 ^{o}F, except that liquid quenching is not permitted.
4. Other alloying elements may be added and shall be reported.
5. For compositions with a maximum carbon content of 0.15 percent of ladle analysis, the maximum limit for manganese on ladle analysis may be 1.40 percent.
6. Rephosphorized Grade 3 steels containing no more than 0.15 percent phosphorus are permitted if carbon content does not exceed 0.15 percent and manganese does not exceed 1 percent.

Check Analysis Tolerances

[A heat of steel made under any of the above grades, the ladle analysis of which is slightly out of the specified range is acceptable if the check analysis is within the following variations:]

Element	Limit or maximum specified (percent)	Tolerance (percent) over the maximum limit or under the minimum limit	
		Under minimum limit	Over maximum limit
Carbon	To 0.15 inclusive	0.02	0.03
	Over 0.15 to 0.40 inclusive	0.03	0.04
Manganese	To 0.60 inclusive	0.03	0.03
	Over 0.60 to 1.15 inclusive	0.04	0.04
	Over 1.15 to 2.50 inclusive	0.05	0.05
Phosphorus[7]	All ranges		0.01
Sulfur	All ranges		0.01
Silicon	To 0.30 inclusive	0.02	0.03
	Over 0.30 to 1.00 inclusive	0.05	0.05
Copper	To 1.00 inclusive	0.03	0.03
	Over 1.00 to 2.00 inclusive	0.05	0.05
Nickel	To 1.00 inclusive	0.03	0.03
	Over 1.00 to 2.00 inclusive	0.05	0.05
Chromium	To 0.90 inclusive	0.03	0.03
	Over 0.90 to 2.10 inclusive	0.05	0.05
Molybdenum	To 0.20 inclusive	0.01	0.01
	Over 0.20 to 0.40 inclusive	0.02	0.02
Zirconium	All ranges	0.01	0.05
Columbium	To 0.04 inclusive	0.005	0.01
Aluminum	Over 0.10 to 0.20 inclusive	0.04	0.04
	Over 0.20 to 0.30 inclusive	0.05	0.05

7. Rephosphorized steels not subject to check analysis for phosphorus.

Appendix B to Part 178
Alternative leakproofness test methods.

In addition to the method prescribed in §178.604 of this subchapter, the following leakproofness test methods are authorized:

(1) *Helium test.* The packaging must be filled with at least 1 L inert helium gas, air tight closed, and placed in a testing chamber. The testing chamber must be evacuated down to a pressure of 5 kPa which equals an over-pressure inside the packaging of 95 kPa. The air in the testing chamber must be analyzed for traces of helium gas by means of a mass spectrograph. The test must be conducted for a period of time sufficient to evacuate the chamber and to determine if there is leakage into or out of the packaging. If helium gas is detected, the leaking packaging must be automatically separated from non-leaking drums and the leaking area determined according to the method prescribed in §178.604(d) of this subchapter. A packaging passes the test if there is no leakage of helium.

(2) *Pressure differential test.* The packaging shall be restrained while either pressure or a vacuum is applied internally. The packaging must be pressurized to the pressure required by §178.604(e) of this subchapter for the appropriate packing group. The method of restraint must not affect the results of the test. The test must be conducted for a period of time sufficient to appropriately pressurize or evacuate the interior of the packaging and to determine if there is leakage into or out of the packaging. A packaging passes the pressure differential test if there is no change in measured internal pressure.

(3) *Solution over seams.* The packaging must be restrained while an internal air pressure is applied; the method of restraint may not affect the results of the test. The exterior surface of all seams and welds must be coated with a solution of soap suds or a water and oil mixture. The test must be conducted for a period of time sufficient to pressurize the interior of the packaging to the specified air pressure and to determine if there is leakage of air from the packaging. A packaging passes the test if there is no leakage of air from the packaging.

(4) *Solution over partial seams test.* For other than design qualification testing, the following test may be used for metal drums: The packaging must be restrained while an internal air pressure of 48 kPa (7.0 psig) is applied; the method of restraint may not affect the results of the test. The packaging must be coated with a soap solution over the entire side seam and a distance of not less than eight inches on each side of the side seam along the chime seam(s). The test must be conducted for a period of time sufficient to pressurize the interior of the packaging to the specified air pressure and to determine if there is leakage of air from the packaging. A packaging passes the test if there is no leakage of air from the packaging. Chime cuts must be made on the initial drum at the beginning of each production run and on the initial drum after any adjustment to the chime seamer. Chime cuts must be maintained on file in date order for not less than six months and be made available to a representative of the Department of Transportation on request.

Appendix C to Part 178
Nominal and minimum thicknesses of steel drums and jerricans.

For each listed packaging capacity, the following table compares the ISO Standard 3574 nominal thickness with the corresponding ISO Standard 3574 minimum thickness.

Maximum capacity (L)	ISO nominal (mm)	Corresponding ISO minimum (mm)
20	0.7	0.63
30	0.8	0.73
40	0.8	0.73
60	1.0	0.92
120	1.0	0.92
220	1.0	0.92
450	1.9	1.77

Part 179 - Specifications for Tank Cars

Subpart A - Introduction, Approvals and Reports

§179.1 General.

(a) This part prescribes the specifications for tanks that are to be mounted on or form part of a tank car and which are used for the transportation of hazardous materials in commerce.

(b) Except as provided in paragraph (c) of this section, tanks to which this part is applicable, must be built to the specifications prescribed in this part.

(c) Tanks built to specifications predating those in this part may continue in use as provided in §180.507 of this subchapter.

(d) Any person who performs a function prescribed in this part, shall perform that function in accordance with this part.

(e) When this part requires a tank to be marked with a DOT specification (for example, DOT-105A100W), compliance with that requirement is the responsibility of the tank builder. Marking the tank with the DOT specification shall be understood to certify compliance by the builder that the functions performed by the builder, as prescribed in this part, have been performed in compliance with this part.

(f) The tank builder should inform each person to whom that tank is transferred of any specification requirements which have not been met at time of transfer.

§179.2 Definitions and abbreviations.

(a) The following apply in part 179:

(1) **AAR** means Association of American Railroads.

(2) **Approved** means approval by the AAR Tank Car Committee.

(3) **ASTM** means American Society for Testing and Materials.

(4) *[Reserved]*

(5) *Definitions in part 173 of this chapter also apply.*

(6) **F** means degrees Fahrenheit.

(7) **NGT** means National Gas Taper Threads.

(8) **NPT** means American Standard Taper Pipe Thread.

(9) *[Reserved]*

(10) **Tank car facility** means an entity that manufactures, repairs, inspects, tests, qualifies, or maintains a tank car to ensure that the tank car conforms to this part and subpart F of part 180 of this subchapter, that alters the certificate of construction of the tank car, that ensures the continuing qualification of a tank car by performing a function prescribed in parts 179 or 180 of this subchapter, or that makes any representation indicating compliance with one or more of the requirements of parts 179 or 180 of this subchapter.

(11) **Tanks** means tank car tanks.

(b) [Reserved]

§179.3 Procedure for securing approval.

(a) Application for approval of designs, materials and construction, conversion or alteration of tank car tanks under these specifications, complete with detailed prints, must be submitted in prescribed form to the Executive Director — Tank Car Safety, AAR, for consideration by its Tank Car Committee and other appropriate committees. Approval or rejections of applications based on appropriate committee action will be issued by the executive director.

(b) When, in the opinion of the Committee, such tanks or equipment therefor are in compliance with effective regulations and specifications of the Department, the application will be approved.

(c) When, in the opinion of the Committee, such tanks or equipment therefor are not in compliance with effective regulations and specifications of the Department, the Committee may recommend service trials to determine the merits of a change in specifications. Such service trials may be authorized by the Department under the terms of exemptions.

§179.4 Changes in specifications for tank cars.

(a) Proposed changes in or additions to specifications for tanks must be submitted to the Executive Director — Tank Car Safety, AAR, for consideration by its Tank Car Committee. An application for construction of tanks to any new specification may be submitted with proposed specification. Construction should not be started until the specification has been approved or an exemption has been issued. When proposing a new specification, the applicant shall furnish information to justify a new specification. This data should include the properties of the lading and the method of loading and unloading.

(b) The Tank Car Committee will review the proposed specifications at its earliest convenience and report its recommendations through the Executive Director — Tank Car Safety to the Department. The recommendation will be considered by the Department in determining appropriate action.

§179.5 Certificate of construction.

(a) Before a tank car is placed in service, the party assembling the completed car shall furnish a Certificate of Construction, Form AAR 4-2 to the owner, the Department, and the Executive Director — Tank Car Safety, AAR, certifying that the tank, equipment, and car fully conforms to all requirements of the specification.

(b) When cars or tanks are covered in one application and are identical in all details are built in series, one certificate will suffice for each series when submitted to the Executive Director — Tank Car Safety, AAR. One copy of the Certificate of Construction must be furnished to the Department for each car number of consecutively numbered group or groups covered by the original application.

(c) If the owner elects to furnish the appurtenances such as valves and safety devices, the owner shall furnish to the Bureau of Explosives, and to the Secretary, Mechanical Division, AAR, a report in prescribed form, certifying that the appurtenances comply with all the requirements of the specifications.

(d) When cars or tanks which are covered on one application and are identical in all details are built in series, one certificate shall suffice for each series when submitted to the Secretary. One copy of the Certificate of Construction must be furnished to the Bureau of Explosives for each car number of consecutively numbered group or groups covered by the original application.

§179.6 Repairs and alterations.

For procedure to be followed in making repairs or alterations, see appendix R of the AAR Specifications for Tank Cars.

§179.7 Quality assurance program.

(a) At a minimum, each tank car facility shall have a quality assurance program, approved by AAR, that —

(1) *Ensures the finished product* conforms to the requirements of the applicable specification and regulations of this subchapter;

(2) *Has the means* to detect any nonconformity in the manufacturing, repair, inspection, testing, and qualification or maintenance program of the tank car; and

(3) *Prevents non-conformities from recurring.*

(b) At a minimum, the quality assurance program must have the following elements

(1) *Statement of authority* and responsibility for those persons in charge of the quality assurance program.

(2) *An organizational chart* showing the interrelationship between managers, engineers, purchasing, construction, inspection, testing, and quality control personnel.

(3) *Procedures to ensure* that the latest applicable drawings, design calculations, specifications, and instructions are used in manufacture, inspection, testing, and repair.

(4) *Procedures to ensure* that the fabrication and construction materials received are properly identified and documented.

(5) *A description* of the manufacturing, repair, inspection, testing, and qualification or maintenance program, including the acceptance criteria, so that an inspector can identify the characteristics of the tank car and the elements to inspect, examine, and test at each point.

(6) *Monitoring and control* of processes and product characteristics during production.

(7) *Procedures for correction of nonconformities.*

(8) *Provisions indicating* that the requirements of the AAR Specifications for Tank Cars, Specification M-1002, apply.

(9) *Qualification requirements* of personnel performing non-destructive inspections and tests.

(10) *Procedures for* evaluating the inspection and test technique employed, including the accessibility of the area and the sensitivity and reliability of the inspection and test technique and minimum detectable crack length.

(11) *Procedures for* the periodic calibration and measurement of inspection and test equipment.

(12) *A system* for the maintenance of records, inspections, tests, and the interpretation of inspection and test results.

(c) Each tank car facility shall ensure that only personnel qualified for each non-destructive inspection and test perform that particular operation.

(d) **Each tank car facility shall provide** written procedures to its employees to ensure that the work on the tank car conforms to the specification, AAR approval, and owner's acceptance criteria.

(e) **Each tank car facility shall train its employees** in accordance with subpart H of part 172 of this subchapter on the program and procedures specified in paragraph (b) of this section to ensure quality.

(f) **Date of conformance.** After July 1, 1998, no tank car facility may manufacture, repair, inspect, test, qualify or maintain tank cars subject to requirements of this subchapter, unless it is operating in conformance with a quality assurance program and written procedures required by paragraphs (a) and (b) of this section.

Subpart B - General Design Requirements

§179.10 Tank mounting.

(a) **The manner in which tanks are attached** to the car structure shall be approved. The use of rivets to secure anchors to tanks prohibited.

(b) **[Reserved]**

§179.11 Welding certification.

(a) **Welding procedures, welders and fabricators shall be approved.**

(b) **[Reserved]**

§179.12 Interior heater systems.

(a) **Interior heater systems shall be of approved design** and materials. If a tank is divided into compartments, a separate system shall be provided for each compartment.

(b) **Each interior heater system shall be hydrostatically tested** at not less than 13.79 bar (200 psig) and shall hold the pressure for 10 minutes without leakage or evidence of distress.

§179.13 Tank car capacity and gross weight limitation.

Tank cars built after November 30, 1970, must not exceed 34,500 gallons capacity or 263,000 pounds gross weight on rail. Existing tank cars may not be converted to exceed 34,500 gallons capacity or 263,000 pounds gross weight on rail.

§179.14 Coupler vertical restraint system.

(a) **Performance standard.** Each tank car shall be equipped with couplers capable of sustaining, without disengagement or material failure, vertical loads of at least 200,000 pounds (90,718.5 kg) applied in upward and downward directions in combination with buff loads of 2,000 pounds (907.2 kg), when coupled to cars which may or may not be equipped with couplers having this vertical restraint capability.

(b) **Test verification.** Except as provided in paragraph (d) of this section, compliance with the requirements of paragraph (a) of this section shall be achieved by verification testing of the coupler vertical restraint system in accordance with paragraph (c) of this section.

(c) **Coupler vertical restraint tests.** A coupler vertical restraint system shall be tested under the following conditions:

(1) *The test coupler* shall be tested with a mating coupler (or simulated coupler) having only frictional vertical force resistance at the mating interface; or a mating coupler (or simulated coupler) having the capabilities described in paragraph (a) of this section;

(2) *The testing apparatus* shall simulate the vertical coupler performance at the mating interface and may not interfere with coupler failure or otherwise inhibit failure due to force applications and reactions; and

(3) *The test shall be conducted as follows:*

(i) *A minimum* of 200,000 pounds (90,718.5 kg) vertical downward load shall be applied continuously for at least 5 minutes to the test coupler head simultaneously with the application of a nominal 2,000 pounds (907.2 kg) buff load;

(ii) *The procedures* prescribed in paragraph (c)(3)(i) of this section, shall be repeated with a minimum vertical upward load of 200,000 pounds (90,718.5 kg); and

(iii) *A minimum* of three consecutive successful tests shall be performed for each load combination prescribed in paragraphs (c)(3) (i) and (ii) of this section. A test is successful when a vertical disengagement or material failure does not occur during the application of any of the loads prescribed in this paragraph.

(d) **Authorized couplers.** As an alternative to the test verifications in paragraph (c) of this section, the following couplers are authorized:

(1) *E double shelf couplers* designated by the Association of American Railroads' Catalog Nos., SE60CHT, SE60CC, SE60CHTE, SE60CE, SE60DC, SE60DE, SE67CC, SE67CE, SE67BHT, SE67BC, SE67BHTE, SE67BE, SE68BHT, SE68BC, SE68BHTE, SE68BE, SE69AHTE, and SE69AE.

(2) *F double shelf couplers* designated by the Association of American Railroads' Catalog Nos., SF70CHT, SF70CC, SF70CHTE, SF70CE, SF73AC, SF73AE, SF73AHT, SF73AHTE, SF79CHT, SF79CC, SF79CHTE, and SF79CE.

§179.15 Pressure relief devices.

Except for DOT Class 106, 107, 110, and 113 tank cars, tanks must have a pressure relief device, made of material compatible with the lading, that conforms to the following requirements:

(a) **Performance standard.** Each tank must have a pressure relief device, made of material compatible with the lading having sufficient flow capacity to prevent pressure build-up in the tank to no more than the flow rating pressure of the pressure relief device in fire conditions as defined in Appendix A of the Association of American Railroads Specifications for Tank Cars.

(b) **Settings for reclosing pressure relief devices.**

(1) *Except as provided* in paragraph (b)(2) of this section, a reclosing pressure relief valve must have a minimum start-to-discharge pressure equal to the sum of the static head and gas padding pressure and the lading vapor pressure at the following reference temperatures:

(i) *46 °C (115 °F) for noninsulated tanks;*

(ii) *43 °C* (110 °F) for tanks having a thermal protection system incorporating a metal jacket that provides an overall thermal conductance at 15.5 °C (60 °F) of no more than 10.22 kilojoules per hour per square meter per degree Celsius (0.5 Btu per hour/per square foot/per degree F) temperature differential; and

(iii) *41 °C (105 °F) for insulated tanks.*

(2) (i) *The start-to-discharge pressure* of a pressure relief device may not be lower than 5.17 Bar (75 psig) or exceed 33 percent of the minimum tank burst pressure.

(ii) *Tanks built* prior to October 1, 1997 having a minimum tank burst pressure of 34.47 Bar (500 psig) or less may be equipped with a reclosing pressure relief valve having a start-to-discharge pressure of not less than 14.5 percent of the minimum tank burst pressure but no more than 33 percent of the minimum tank burst pressure.

(3) *The vapor tight pressure* of a reclosing pressure relief valve must be at least 80 percent of the start-to-discharge pressure.

(4) *The flow rating pressure* must be 110 percent of the start-to-discharge pressure for tanks having a minimum tank burst pressure greater than 34.47 Bar (500 psig) and from 110 percent to 130 percent for tanks having a minimum tank burst pressure less than or equal to 34.47 Bar (500 psig).

(5) *The tolerance* for a reclosing pressure relief valve is 3 psi for valves with a start-to-discharge pressure of 6.89 Bar (100 psig) or less and 3 percent for valves with a start-to-discharge pressure greater than 6.89 Bar (100 psig).

(c) **Flow capacity of pressure relief devices.** The total flow capacity of each reclosing and nonreclosing pressure relief device must conform to Appendix A of the Association of American Railroads Specifications for Tank Cars.

(d) **Flow capacity tests.** The manufacturer of any reclosing or nonreclosing pressure relief device must design and test the device in accordance with Appendix A of the Association of American Railroads Specifications for Tank Cars.

(e) **Combination pressure relief systems.** A non-reclosing pressure relief device may be used in series with a reclosing pressure relief valve. The pressure relief valve must be located outboard of the non-reclosing pressure relief device.

(1) *When a breaking pin device* is used in combination with a reclosing pressure relief valve, the breaking pin must be designed to fail at the start-to-discharge pressure specified in paragraph (b) of this section, and the reclosing pressure relief valve must be designed to discharge at not greater than 95 percent of the start-to-discharge pressure.

(2) *When a rupture disc* is used in combination with a reclosing pressure relief valve, the rupture disc must be designed to burst at the pressure specified in paragraph (b) of this section, and the reclosing pressure relief valve must be designed to discharge at not greater than 95 percent of the pressure. A device must be installed to detect any accumulation of pressure between the rupture disc and the reclosing pressure relief valve. The detection device must be a needle valve, trycock, or tell-tale indicator. The detection device must be closed during transportation.

(3) *The vapor tight pressure* and the start-to-discharge tolerance is based on the discharge setting of the reclosing pressure relief device.

(f) **Nonreclosing pressure relief device.** In addition to paragraphs (a), (b)(4), (c), and (d) of this section, a nonreclosing pressure relief device must conform to the following requirements:

(1) *A non-reclosing* pressure relief device must incorporate a rupture disc designed to burst at a pressure equal to the greater of 100% of the tank test pressure, or 33% of the tank burst pressure.

(2) *The approach channel* and the discharge channel may not reduce the required minimum flow capacity of the pressure relief device.

(3) *The non-reclosing* pressure relief device must be designed to prevent interchange with other fittings installed on the tank car, must have a structure that encloses and clamps the rupture disc in position (preventing any distortion or damage to the rupture disc when properly applied), and must have a cover, with suitable means of preventing misplacement, designed to direct any discharge of the lading downward.

(4) *The non-reclosing* pressure relief device must be closed with a rupture disc that is compatible with the lading and manufactured in accordance with Appendix A of the AAR Specifications for Tank Cars. The tolerance for a rupture disc is +0 to -15 percent of the burst pressure marked on the disc.

(g) **Location of relief devices.** Each pressure relief device must communicate with the vapor space above the lading as near as practicable on the longitudinal center line and center of the tank.

(h) **Marking of pressure relief devices.** Each pressure relief device and rupture disc must be permanently marked in accordance with the Appendix A of the Association of American Railroads Specifications for Tank Cars.

§179.16 Tank-head puncture-resistance systems.

(a) **Performance standard.** When the regulations in this subchapter require a tank-head puncture-resistance system, the system shall be capable of sustaining, without any loss of lading, coupler-to-tank-head impacts at relative car speeds of 29 km/hour (18 mph) when:

(1) *The weight of the impact car is at least 119,295 kg (263,000 pounds);*

(2) *The impacted tank car* is coupled to one or more backup cars that have a total weight of at least 217,724 kg (480,000 pounds) and the hand brake is applied on the last "backup" car; and

(3) *The impacted tank car is pressurized to at least 6.9 Bar (100 psig).*

(b) **Verification by testing.** Compliance with the requirements of paragraph (a) of this section shall be verified by full-scale testing according to appendix A of this part.

(c) **Alternative compliance by other than testing.** As an alternative to requirements prescribed in paragraph (b) of this section, compliance with the requirements of paragraph (a) of this section may be met by installing full-head protection (shields) or full tank-head jackets on each end of the tank car conforming to the following:

(1) *The full-head protection* (shields) or full tank-head jackets must be at least 1.27 cm (0.5 inch) thick, shaped to the contour of the tank head and made from steel having a tensile strength greater than 379.21 N/mm^2 (55,000 psi).

(2) *The design* and test requirements of the full-head protection (shields) or full tank-head jackets must meet the impact test requirements of Section 5.3 of the AAR Specifications for Tank Cars.

(3) *The workmanship* must meet the requirements of Section C, Part II, Chapter 5 of the AAR Specifications for Design, Fabrication, and Construction of Freight Cars.

§179.18 Thermal protection systems.

(a) **Performance standard.** When the regulations in this subchapter require thermal protection on a tank car, the tank car must have sufficient thermal resistance so that there will be no release of any lading within the tank car, except release through the pressure release device, when subjected to:

(1) *A pool fire for 100 minutes; and*

(2) *A torch fire for 30 minutes.*

(b) **Thermal analysis.**

(1) *Compliance with* the requirements of paragraph (a) of this section shall be verified by analyzing the fire effects on the entire surface of the tank car. The analysis must consider the fire effects on and heat flux through tank discontinuities, protective housings, underframes, metal jackets, insulation, and thermal protection. A complete record of each analysis shall be made, retained, and upon request, made available for inspection and copying by an authorized representative of the Department. The procedures outlined in "Temperatures, Pressures, and Liquid Levels of Tank Cars Engulfed in Fires," DOT/FRA/OR&D-84/08.11, (1984), Federal Railroad Administration, Washington, DC (available from the National Technical Information Service, Springfield, VA) shall be deemed acceptable for analyzing the fire effects on the entire surface of the tank car.

(2) *When the analysis* shows the thermal resistance of the tank car does not conform to paragraph (a) of this section, the thermal resistance of the tank car must be increased by using a system listed by the Department under paragraph (c) of this section or by testing a new or untried system and verifying it according to appendix B of this part.

(c) **Systems that no longer require test verification.** The Department maintains a list of thermal protection systems that comply with the requirements of appendix B of this part and that no longer require test verification. Information necessary to equip tank cars with one of these systems is available in the RSPA Records Center, Research and Special Programs Administration, 400 Seventh Street, SW., Washington, DC 20590-0001.

§179.20 Service equipment; protection systems.

If an applicable tank car specification authorizes location of filling or discharge connections in the bottom shell, the connections must be designed, constructed, and protected according to paragraphs E9.00 and E10.00 of the AAR Specifications for Tank Cars, M-1002.

§179.22 Marking.

In addition to any other marking requirement in this subchapter, the following marking requirements apply:

(a) **Each tank car must be marked** according to the requirements in Appendix C of the AAR Specifications for Tank Cars.

(b) **Each tank car that requires** a tank-head puncture-resistance system must have the letter "S" substituted for the letter "A" in the specification marking.

(c) **Each tank car that requires** a tank-head puncture-resistance system, a thermal protection system, and a metal jacket must have the letter "J" substituted for the letter "A" or "S" in the specification marking.

(d) **Each tank car that requires** a tank-head puncture-resistance system, a thermal protection system, and no metal jacket must have the letter "T" substituted for the letter "A" or "S" in the specification marking.

Subpart C - Specifications for Pressure Tank Car Tanks (Classes DOT-105, 109, 112, 114 and 120)

§179.100 General specifications applicable to pressure tank car tanks.

§179.100-1 Tanks built under these specifications shall comply with the requirements of §§179.100, 179.101 and when applicable, §§179.102 and 179.103.

§179.100-3 Type.

(a) **Tanks built under this specification shall be** fusion-welded with heads designed convex outward. Except as provided in §179.103 they shall be circular in cross section, shall be provided with a manway nozzle on top of the tank of sufficient size to permit access to the interior, a manway cover to provide for the mounting of all valves, measuring and sampling devices, and a protective housing. Other openings in the tank are prohibited, except as provided in part 173 of this chapter, §§179.100-14, 179.101-1, 179.102 or §179.103.

(b) **[Reserved]**

§179.100-4 Insulation.

(a) **If insulation is applied, the tank shell** and manway nozzle must be insulated with an approved material. The entire insulation must be covered with a metal jacket of a thickness not less than 11 gauge (0.1196 inch) nominal (Manufacturers' Standard Gauge) and flashed around all openings so as to be weather-tight. The exterior surface of a carbon steel tank, and the inside surface of a carbon steel jacket must be given a protective coating.

(b) **If insulation is a specification requirement,** it shall be of sufficient thickness so that the thermal conductance at 60 °F is not more than 0.075 Btu per hour, per square foot, per degree F temperature differential. If exterior heaters are attached to tank, the thickness of the insulation over each heater element may be reduced to one-half that required for the shell.

§179.100-6 Thickness of plates.

(a) **The wall thickness after forming of the tank shell** and heads must not be less than that specified in §179.101, nor that calculated by the following formula:

t = Pd / 2SE

Where:

d = Inside diameter in inches;

E = 1.0 welded joint efficiency; except for heads with seams=0.9;

P = Minimum required bursting pressure in p.s.i.;

S = Minimum tensile strength of plate material in p.s.i., as prescribed in §179.100-7;

t = Minimum thickness of plate in inches after forming.

(b) **If plates are clad with material having** tensile strength properties at least equal to the base plate, the cladding may be considered a part of the base plate when determining thickness. If cladding material does not have tensile strength at least equal to the base plate, the base plate alone shall meet the thickness requirement.

(c) **When aluminum plate is used,** the minimum width of bottom sheet of tank shall be 60 inches, measured on the arc, but in all cases the width shall be sufficient to bring the entire width of the longitudinal welded joint, including welds, above the bolster.

§179.100-7 Materials.

(a) **Steel plate:** Steel plate materials used to fabricate tank shell and manway nozzle must comply with one of the following specifications with the indicated minimum tensile strength and elongation in the welded condition. The maximum allowable carbon content must be 0.31 percent when the individual specification allows carbon greater than this amount. The plates may be clad with other approved materials.

Specifications	Minimum tensile strength (p.s.i.) welded condition[1]	Minimum elongation in 2 inches (percent) welded condition (longitudinal)
AAR TC128, Gr. B	81,000	19
ASTM A 302, Gr. B	80,000	20
ASTM A 516	70,000	20
ASTM A 537, Class 1	70,000	23

1. Maximum stresses to be used in calculations.

(b) **Aluminum alloy plate:** Aluminum alloy plate material used to fabricate tank shell and manway nozzle must be suitable for fusion welding and must comply with one of the following specifications with its indicated minimum tensile strength and elongation in the welded condition.

Specifications	Minimum tensile strength (p.s.i.) 0 temper, welded condition[3,4]	Minimum elongation in 2 inches (percent) 0 temper, welded condition (longitudinal)
ASTM B 209, Alloy 5052[1]	25,000	18
ASTM B 209, Alloy 5083[2]	38,000	16
ASTM B 209, Alloy 5086[1]	35,000	14
ASTM B 209, Alloy 5154[1]	30,000	18
ASTM B 209, Alloy 5254[1]	30,000	18
ASTM B 209, Alloy 5454[1]	31,000	18
ASTM B 209, Alloy 5652[1]	25,000	18

1. For fabrication, the parent plate material may be 0, H112, or H32 temper, but design calculations must be based on minimum tensile strength shown.
2. 0 temper only.
3. Weld filler metal 5556 must not be used.
4. Maximum stress to be used in calculations.

(c) **High alloy steel plate.**

(1) *High alloy steel plate must conform to the following specifications:*

Specifications	Minimum tensile strength (p.s.i.) welded condition[1]	Minimum elongation in 2 inches (percent) weld metal (longitudinal)
ASTM A 240/ASTM A 240M (incorporated by reference, see §171.7 of this subchapter), Type 304L	70,000	30
ASTM A 240/ASTM A 240M (incorporated by reference, see §171.7 of this subchapter), Type 316L	70,000	30

1. Maximum stresses to be used in calculations.

(2) (i) *High alloy steels* used to fabricate tank must be tested in accordance with the following procedures in ASTM Specification A262 titled, "Standard Practices for Detecting Susceptibility to Intergranular Attack in Austenitic Stainless Steel," and must exhibit corrosion rates not exceeding the following:

Test procedures	Material	Corrosion rate i.p.m.
Practice B	Types 304L and 316L	0.0040
Practice C	Type 304L	0.0020

(ii) *Type 304L and 316L* test specimens must be given a sensitizing treatment prior to testing.

(d) **All attachments welded to tank shell** must be of approved material which is suitable for welding to the tank.

§179.100-8 Tank heads.

(a) **The tank head shape shall be an ellipsoid** of revolution in which the major axis shall equal the diameter of the shell adjacent to the head and the minor axis shall be one-half the major axis.

(b) **Each tank head made from steel which is required** to be "fine grain" by the material specification, which is hot formed at a temperature exceeding 1700 °F, must be normalized after forming by heating to a temperature between 1550° and 1700 °F, by holding at that temperature for at least 1 hour per inch of thickness (30-minute minimum), and then by cooling in air. If the material specification requires quenching and tempering, the treatment specified in that specification must be used instead of the one specified above.

§179.100-9 Welding.

(a) **All joints shall be fusion-welded in compliance** with the requirements of AAR Specifications for Tank Cars, appendix W. Welding procedures, welders and fabricators shall be approved.

(b) **[Reserved]**

§179.100-10 Postweld heat treatment.

(a) **After welding is complete, steel tanks** and all attachments welded thereto must be postweld heat treated as a unit in compliance with the requirements of AAR Specifications for Tank Cars, appendix W.

(b) **For aluminum tanks, postweld heat treatment is prohibited.**

(c) **Tank and welded attachments,** fabricated from ASTM A 240/ASTM A 240M (incorporated by reference, see §171.7 of this subchapter), Type 304L or Type 316L materials do not require postweld heat treatment, but these materials do require a corrosion resistance test as specified in §179.100-7(c)(2).

§179.100-12 Manway nozzle, cover, and protective housing.

(a) **Manway nozzles must be of approved design** of forged or rolled steel for steel tanks or of fabricated aluminum alloy for aluminum tanks, with access opening at least 18 inches inside diameter, or at least 14 inches by 18 inches around or oval. Nozzle must be welded to the tank and the opening reinforced in an approved manner in compliance with the requirements of AAR Specifications for Tank Cars, appendix E, Figure E10.

(b) **Manway cover shall be machined to approved dimensions** and be of forged or rolled carbon or alloy steel, rolled aluminum alloy or nickel when required by the lading. Minimum thickness is listed in §179.101. Manway cover shall be attached to manway nozzle by through or stud bolts not entering tank, except as provided in §179.103-2(a).

(c) **Except as provided in §179.103,** protective housing of cast, forged or fabricated approved materials must be bolted to manway cover with not less than twenty 3/4-inch studs. The shearing value of the bolts attaching protective housing to manway cover must not exceed 70 percent of the shearing value of bolts attaching manway cover to manway nozzle. Housing must have steel sidewalls not less than three-fourths inch in thickness and must be equipped with a metal cover not less than one-fourth inch in thickness that can be securely closed. Housing cover must have suitable stop to prevent cover striking loading and unloading connections and be hinged on one side only with approved riveted pin or rod with nuts and cotters. Openings in wall of housing must be equipped with screw plugs or other closures.

§179.100-13 Venting, loading and unloading valves, measuring and sampling devices.

(a) **Venting, loading and unloading valves** must be of approved design, made of metal not subject to rapid deterioration by the lading, and must withstand the tank test pressure without leakage. The valves shall be bolted to seatings on the manway cover, except as provided in §179.103. Valve outlets shall be closed with approved screw plugs or other closures fastened to prevent misplacement.

(b) **The interior pipes of the loading and unloading valves** shall be anchored and, except as prescribed in §179.102 or §179.103, may be equipped with excess flow valves of approved design.

(c) **Gauging device, sampling valve and thermometer well** are not specification requirements. When used, they shall be of approved design, made of metal not subject to rapid deterioration by the lading, and shall withstand the tank test pressure without leakage. Interior pipes of the gauging device and sampling valve, except as prescribed in §179.102 or §179.103, may be equipped with excess flow valves of approved design. Interior pipe of the thermometer well shall be anchored in an approved manner to prevent breakage due to vibration. The thermometer well shall be closed by an approved valve attached close to the manway cover, or other approved location, and closed by a screw plug. Other approved arrangements that permit testing thermometer well for leaks without complete removal of the closure may be used.

(d) **An excess flow valve as referred to in this specification,** is a device which closes automatically against the outward flow of the contents of the tank in case the external closure valve is broken off or removed during transit. Excess flow valves may be designed with a by-pass to allow the equalization of pressures.

(e) **Bottom of tank shell may be equipped** with a sump or siphon bowl, or both, welded or pressed into the shell. Such sumps or siphon bowls, if applied, are not limited in size and must be made of cast, forged or fabricated metal. Each sump or siphon bowl must be of good welding quality in conjunction with the metal of the tank shell. When the sump or siphon bowl is pressed in the bottom of the tank shell, the wall thickness of the pressed section must not be less than that specified for the shell. The section of a circular cross section tank to which a sump or siphon bowl is attached need not comply with the out-of-roundness requirement specified in AAR Specifications for Tank Cars, appendix W, W14.06. Any portion of a sump or siphon bowl not forming a part of cylinder of revolution must have walls of such thickness and be so reinforced that the stresses in the walls caused by a given internal pressure are no greater than the circumferential stress which would exist under the same internal pressure in the wall of a tank of circular cross section designed in accordance with §179.100-6(a). In no case less than that specified in §179.101-1.

§179.100-14 Bottom outlets.

(a) **Bottom outlets for discharge of lading is prohibited,** except as provided in §179.103-3. If indicated in §179.101, tank may be equipped with a bottom washout of approved construction. If applied, bottom washout shall be in accordance with the following requirements;

(1) *The extreme projection* of the bottom washout equipment may not be more than that allowed by appendix E of the AAR Specifications for Tank Cars.

(2) *Bottom washout* shall be of cast, forged or fabricated metal and shall be fusion-welded to the tank. It shall be of good weldable quality in conjunction with metal of tank.

(3) *If the bottom washout nozzle extends* 6 inches or more from shell of tank, a V-shaped breakage groove shall be cut (not cast) in the upper part of the outlet nozzle at a point immediately below the lowest part of the inside closure seat or plug. In no case may the nozzle wall thickness at the root of the "V" be more than 1/4-inch. Where the nozzle is not a single piece, provision shall be made for the equivalent of the breakage groove. The nozzle must be of a thickness to insure that accidental breakage will occur at or below the "V" groove or its equivalent. On cars without continuous center sills, the breakage groove or its equivalent may not be more than 15 inches below the tank shell. On cars with continuous center sills, the breakage groove or its equivalent must be above the bottom of the center sill construction.

(4) *The closure plug and seat* shall be readily accessible or removable for repairs.

(5) *The closure of the washout nozzle* must be equipped with a 3/4-inch solid screw plug. Plug must be attached by at least a 1/4-inch chain.

(6) *Joints between closures and their seats* may be gasketed with suitable material.

(b) **[Reserved]**

§179.100-16 Attachments.

(a) **Reinforcing pads must be used between external brackets** and shells if the attachment welds exceed 6 linear inches of 1/4-inch fillet or equivalent weld per bracket or bracket leg. When reinforcing pads are used, they must not be less than one-fourth inch in thickness, have each corner rounded to a 1-inch minimum radius, and be attached to the tank by continuous fillet welds except for venting provisions. The ultimate shear strength of the bracket-to-reinforcing pad weld must not exceed 85 percent of the ultimate shear strength of the reinforcing pad-to-tank weld.

(b) **Attachments not otherwise specified shall be applied** by approved means.

§179.100-17 Closures for openings.

(a) **Closures shall be of approved design** and made of metal not subject to rapid deterioration by the lading. Plugs, if used, shall be solid, with NPT threads, and shall be of a length which will screw at least six threads inside the face of fitting or tank.

(b) **[Reserved]**

§179.100-18 Tests of tanks.

(a) **Each tank shall be tested by completely filling** tank and manway nozzle with water or other liquid having similar viscosity, at a temperature which shall not exceed 100 °F during the test; and applying the pressure prescribed in §179.101. The tank shall hold the prescribed pressure for at least 10 minutes without leakage or evidence of distress.

(b) **Insulated tanks shall be tested before insulation is applied.**

(c) **Caulking of welded joints to stop leaks** developed during the foregoing test is prohibited. Repairs in welded joints shall be made as prescribed in AAR Specifications for Tank Cars, appendix W (see §171.7 of this subchapter).

(d) **Testing of exterior heaters is not a specification requirement.**

§179.100-19 Tests of safety relief valves.

(a) **Each valve shall be tested by air or gas** for compliance with §179.15 before being put into service.

(b) **[Reserved]**

§179.100-20 Stamping.

(a) **To certify that the tank complies with** all specification requirements, each tank shall be plainly and permanently stamped in letters and figures at least 3/8 inch high into the metal near the center of both outside heads as follows:

	Examples of required stamping
Specification	DOT-105A100W
Material	ASTM A 516
Cladding material (if any)	ASTM A240-304 Clad
Tank builder's initials	ABC
Date of original test	00-0000
Car assembler (if other than tanker builder)	DEF

(b) **[Reserved]**

§179.101 Individual specification requirements applicable to pressure tank car tanks.

Editorial Note: At 66 FR 45186, Aug. 28, 2001, an amendment published amending a table in §179.101. No text or table appears in §179.101.

§179.101-1 Individual specification requirements.

In addition to §179.100, the individual specification requirements are as follows:

DOT specification	Insulation	Bursting pressure (psig)	Minimum plate thickness (inches)	Test pressure (psig)	Manway cover thickness	Bottom outlet	Bottom washout	Reference (179.***)
105A100ALW	Yes	500	5/8	100	[2] 2 1/2	No	No	
105A200ALW	Yes	500	5/8	200	[2] 2 1/2	No	No	
105A300ALW	Yes	750	5/8	300	[2] 2 5/8	No	No	
105A100W	Yes	500	[3] 9/16	100	2 1/4	No	No	
105A200W	Yes	500	[3] 9/16	200	2 1/4	No	No	
105A300W	Yes	750	[1] 11/16	300	[7] 2 1/4	No	No	
105A400W	Yes	1,000	[1] 11/16	400	[7] 2 1/4	No	No	
105A500W	Yes	1,250	[1] 11/16	500	2 1/4	No	No	102-1, 102-2
105A600W	Yes	1,500	[1] 11/16	600	2 1/4	No	No	102-4, 102-17
109A100ALW	Optional	500	5/8	100	[2] 2 1/2	No	Optional	
109A200ALW	Optional	500	5/8	200	[2] 2 1/2	No	Optional	
109A300ALW	Optional	750	5/8	300	[2] 2 5/8	No	Optional	
109A300W	Optional	500	[1] 11/16	300	2 1/4	No	Optional	
112A200W	Optional[4]	500	[3,5] 9/16	200	2 1/4	No	No	
112A340W	Optional[4]	850	[1] 11/16	340	2 1/4	No	No	
112A400W	Optional[4]	1,000	[1] 11/16	400	2 1/4	No	No	
112A500W	Optional[4]	1,250	[1] 11/16	500	2 1/4	No	No	
114A340W	Optional[4]	850	[1] 11/16	340	([6])	Optional	Optional	103
114A400W	Optional[4]	1,000	[1] 11/16	400	([6])	Optional	Optional	103
120A200ALW	Yes	500	5/8	200	[2] 2 1/2	Optional	Optional	103
120A100W	Yes	500	[3] 9/16	100	2 1/4	Optional	Optional	103
120A200W	Yes	500	[3] 9/16	200	2 1/4	Optional	Optional	103
120A300W	Yes	750	[1] 11/16	300	2 1/4	Optional	Optional	103
120A400W	Yes	1,000	[1] 11/16	400	2 1/4	Optional	Optional	103
120A500W	Yes	1,250	[1] 11/16	500	2 1/4	Optional	Optional	103

1. When steel of 65,000 to 81,000 p.s.i. minimum tensile strength is used, the thickness of plates shall be not less than 5/8 inch, and when steel of 81,000 p.s.i. minimum tensile strength is used, the minimum thickness of plate shall be not less than 9/16 inch.
2. When approved material other than aluminum alloys are used, the thickness shall be not less than 2 1/4 inches.
3. When steel of 65,000 p.s.i. minimum tensile strength is used, minimum thickness of plates shall be not less than 1/2 inch.
4. Tank cars not equipped with a thermal protection or an insulation system used for the transportation of a Class 2 (compressed gas) material must have at least the upper two-thirds of the exterior of the tank, including manway nozzle and all appurtenances in contact with this area, finished with a reflective coat of white paint.
5. For inside diameter of 87 inches or less, the thickness of plates shall be not less than 1/2 inch.
6. See AAR specifications for tank cars, Appendix E, E4.01 and §179.103-2.
7. When the use of nickel is required by the lading, the thickness shall not be less than two inches.

§179.102 Special commodity requirements for pressure tank car tanks.

(a) In addition to §§179.100 and 179.101, the following requirements are applicable:

(b) [Reserved]

§179.102-1 Carbon dioxide, refrigerated liquid.

(a) Tank cars used to transport carbon dioxide, refrigerated liquid must comply with the following special requirements:

(1) *All plates* for tank, manway nozzle and anchorage of tanks must be made of carbon steel complying with ASTM Specification A 516, Grades 55, 60, 65, or 70, or AAR Specification TC128-78, Grade B. The ASTM A516 plate must also meet the Charpy V-Notch test requirements of ASTM A20-79b (see table 16) in the longitudinal direction of rolling. The TC128 plate must also meet the Charpy V-Notch energy absorption requirements of 15 ft-lb minimum average for 3 specimens and 10 ft-lb minimum for one specimen at minus 50 °F in the longitudinal direction of rolling in accord with ASTM Specification A 370. Production-welded test plates prepared as required by W4.00 of AAR Specifications for Tank Cars, appendix W, must include impact test specimens of weld metal and heat-affected zone. As an alternate, anchor legs may be fabricated of stainless steel, ASTM A 240/ASTM A 240M (incorporated by reference, see §171.7 of this subchapter), Types 304, 304L, 316 or 316L for which impact tests are not required.

(2)-(6) *[Reserved]*

(b) [Reserved]

§179.102-2 Chlorine.

(a) Each tank car used to transport chlorine must comply with all of the following:

(1) *Tanks must be* fabricated from carbon steel complying with ASTM Specification A 516, Grade 70, or AAR Specification TC-128, Grade A or B.

(2)-(3) *[Reserved]*

(b) [Reserved]

§179.102-4 Vinyl fluoride, inhibited.

Each tank used to transport vinyl fluoride, stabilized, must comply with the following special requirements:

(a) All plates for the tank must be fabricated of material listed in paragraph (a)(2) of this section, and appurtenances must be fabricated of material listed in paragraph (a)(1) or (a)(2) of this section.

(1) *Stainless steel,* ASTM A 240/ASTM A 240M (incorporated by reference, see §171.7 of this subchapter), Type 304, 304L, 316 or 316L, in which case impact tests are not required; or

(2) *Steel complying* with ASTM Specification A516; Grade 70; ASTM Specification A537, Class 1; or AAR Specification TC128, Grade B, in which case impact tests must be performed as follows:

(i) *ASTM Specification* A516 and A537 material must meet the Charpy V-notch test requirements, in longitudinal direction of rolling, of ASTM Specification A20.

(ii) *AAR Specification TC128 material must meet* the Charpy V-notch test requirements, in longitudinal direction of rolling, of 15 ft.-lb. minimum average for 3 specimens, with a 10 ft.-lb. minimum for any one specimen, at minus 50 °F or colder, in accordance with ASTM Specification A 370.

(iii) *Production welded test plates must* —

[A] Be prepared in accordance with AAR Specifications for Tank Cars, appendix W, W4.00;

[B] Include impact specimens of weld metal and heat affected zone prepared and tested in accordance with AAR Specifications for Tank Cars, appendix W, W9.00; and

[C] Meet the same impact requirements as the plate material.

(b) Insulation must be of approved material.

(c) Excess flow valves must be installed under all liquid and vapor valves, except safety relief valves.

(d) A thermometer well may be installed.

(e) Only an approved gaging device may be installed.

(f) A pressure gage may be installed.

(g) **Aluminum, copper, silver, zinc, or an alloy** containing any of these metals may not be used in the tank construction, or in fittings in contact with the lading.

(h) **The jacket must be stenciled,** adjacent to the water capacity stencil, MINIMUM OPERATING TEMPERATURE __ °F.

(i) **The tank car and insulation must be designed** to prevent the vapor pressure of the lading from increasing from the pressure at the maximum allowable filling density to the start-to-discharge pressure of the reclosing pressure relief valve within 30 days, at an ambient temperature of 90 °F.

§179.102-17 Hydrogen chloride, refrigerated liquid.

Each tank car used to transport hydrogen chloride, refrigerated liquid must comply with the following special requirements:

(a) **The tank car must comply with** Specification DOT-105J600W and be designed for loading at minus 50 °F or colder.

(b) **All plates for the tank must be fabricated** of material listed in paragraph (b)(2) of this section, and appurtenances must be fabricated of material listed in paragraph (b)(1) or (b)(2) of this section.

(1) *Stainless steel,* ASTM A 240/ASTM A 240M (incorporated by reference, see §171.7 of this subchapter), Type 304, 304L, 316, or 316L, in which case impact tests are not required; or

(2) *Steel complying* with ASTM Specification A516, Grade 70; ASTM Specification A537, Class 1; or AAR Specification TC128, Grade B, in which case impact tests must be performed as follows:

(i) *ASTM Specification* A516 and A537 material must meet the Charpy V-notch test requirements, in longitudinal direction of rolling, of ASTM Specification A20.

(ii) *AAR Specification* TC128 material must meet the Charpy V-notch test requirements, in longitudinal direction of rolling of 15 ft.-lb. minimum average for 3 specimens, with a 10 ft.-lb. minimum for any one specimen, at minus 50 °F or colder, in accordance with ASTM Specification A 370.

(iii) *Production welded test plates must —*

[A] Be prepared in accordance with AAR Specifications for Tank Cars, appendix W, W4.00;

[B] include impact test specimens of weld metal and heat affected zone prepared and tested in accordance with AAR Specifications for Tank Cars, appendix W, W9.00; and

[C] meet the same impact requirements as the plate material.

(c) **Insulation must be of approved material.**

(d) **Pressure relief valves must be trimmed** with monel or other approved material and equipped with a rupture disc of silver, polytetrafluoroethylene coated monel, or tantalum. Each pressure relief device shall have the space between the rupture disc and the valve vented with a suitable auxiliary valve. The discharge from each pressure relief valve must be directed outside the protective housing.

(e) **Loading and unloading valves must be trimmed** with Hastelloy B or C, monel, or other approved material, and identified as "Vapor" or "Liquid". Excess flow valves must be installed under all liquid and vapor valves, except safety relief valves.

(f) **A thermometer well may be installed.**

(g) **Only an approved gaging device may be installed.**

(h) **A sump must be installed in the bottom of the tank** under the liquid pipes.

(i) **All gaskets must be made of, or coated with,** polytetrafluoroethylene or other approved material.

(j) **The tank car tank may be equipped with** exterior cooling coils on top of the tank car shell.

(k) **The jacket must be stenciled, adjacent to the water capacity stencil,** MINIMUM OPERATING TEMPERATURE __ °F.

(l) **The tank car and insulation must be designed** to prevent the pressure of the lading from increasing from the pressure at the maximum allowable filling density to the start-to-discharge pressure of the pressure relief valve within 30 days, at an ambient temperature of 90 °F.

§179.103 Special requirements for class 114A * * * tank car tanks.

(a) **In addition to the applicable requirements** of §§179.100 and 179.101 the following requirements shall be complied with:

(b) **[Reserved]**

§179.103-1 Type.

(a) **Tanks built under this section may be** of any approved cross section.

(b) **Any portion of the tank shell not circular** in cross section shall have walls of such thickness and be so reinforced that the stresses in the walls caused by a given internal pressure are no greater than the circumferential stresses which would exist under the same internal pressure in the wall of a tank of circular cross section designed in accordance with paragraphs §179.100-6 (a) and (b), but in no case shall the wall thickness be less than that specified in §179.101.

(c) **[Reserved]**

(d) **Valves and fittings need not be mounted on the manway cover.**

(e) **One opening may be provided in each head** for use in purging the tank interior.

§179.103-2 Manway cover.

(a) **The manway cover must be an approved design.**

(b) **If no valves or measuring and sampling devices** are mounted on manway cover, no protective housing is required.

§179.103-3 Venting, loading and unloading valves, measuring and sampling devices.

(a) **Venting, loading and unloading valves,** measuring and sampling devices, when used, shall be attached to a nozzle or nozzles on the tank shell or heads.

(b) **These valves and appurtenances must be grouped** in one location and, except as provided in §179.103-5, must be equipped with a protective housing with cover, or may be recessed into tank shell with cover. An additional set grouped in another location may be provided. Protective housing with cover, when used, must have steel sidewalls not less than three-fourths inch in thickness and a metal cover not less than one-fourth inch in thickness that can be securely closed. Underframe sills are an acceptable alternate to the protective housing cover, provided the arrangement is of approved design. For fittings recessed into tank shell, protective cover must be metal and not less than one-fourth inch in thickness.

(c) **When tank car is used to transport** liquefied flammable gases, the interior pipes of the loading, unloading, and sampling valves must be equipped with excess flow valves of approved design except when quick closing internal valves of approved design are used. When the interior pipe of the gaging device provides a means for the passage of lading from the interior to the exterior of the tank, it must be equipped with an excess flow valve of approved design or with an orifice not exceeding 0.060 inch.

§179.103-4 Safety relief devices and pressure regulators.

(a) **Safety relief devices and pressure regulators** must be located on top of the tank near the center of the car on a nozzle, mounting plate or recess in the shell. Through or stud bolts, if used, must not enter the tank.

(b) **Metal guard of approved design must be provided** to protect safety relief devices and pressure regulators from damage.

§179.103-5 Bottom outlets.

(a) **In addition to or in place of the venting,** loading and unloading valves, measuring and sampling devices as prescribed in §179.103-3, tanks may be equipped with approved bottom outlet valves. If applied, bottom outlet valves must meet the following requirements:

(1) *On cars with center sills,* a ball valve may be welded to the outside bottom of the tank or mounted on a pad or nozzle with a tongue and groove or male and female flange attachment, but in no case shall the breakage groove or equivalent extend below the bottom flange of the center sill. On cars without continuous center sills, a ball valve may be welded to the outside bottom of the tank or mounted with a tongue and groove or male and female flange attachment on a pad attached to the outside bottom of the tank. The mounting pad must have a maximum thickness of 2 1/2 inches measured on the longitudinal centerline of the tank. The valve operating mechanism must be provided with a suitable locking arrangement to insure positive closure during transit.

(2) *When internal bottom outlet valve* is used in liquefied flammable gas service, the outlet of the valve must be equipped with an excess flow valve of approved design, except when a quick-closing internal valve of approved design is used. Protective housing is not required.

(3) *Bottom outlet* must be equipped with a liquid tight closure at its lower end.

(b) **Bottom outlet equipment must be of approved design** and must meet the following requirements:

(1) *The extreme projection* of the bottom outlet equipment may not be more than allowed by appendix E of the AAR Specifications for Tank Cars. All bottom outlet reducers and closures and their

attachments shall be secured to car by at least 3/8-inch chain, or its equivalent, except that bottom outlet closure plugs may be attached by 1/4-inch chain. When the bottom outlet closure is of the combination cap and valve type, the pipe connection to the valve shall be closed by a plug, cap, or approved quick coupling device. The bottom outlet equipment should include only the valve, reducers and closures that are necessary for the attachment of unloading fixtures. The permanent attachment of supplementary exterior fittings must be approved by the AAR Committee on Tank Cars.

(2) *To provide* for the attachment of unloading connections, the discharge end of the bottom outlet nozzle or reducer, the valve body of the exterior valve, or some fixed attachment thereto, shall be provided with one of the following arrangements or an approved modification thereof. (See appendix E. Fig. E17 of the AAR Specifications for Tank Cars for illustrations of some of the possible arrangements.)

(i) *A bolted flange* closure arrangement including a minimum 1-inch NPT pipe plug (see Fig. E17.1) or including an auxiliary valve with a threaded closure.

(ii) *A threaded* cap closure arrangement including a minimum 1-inch NPT pipe plug (see Fig. E17.2) or including an auxiliary valve with a threaded closure.

(iii) *A quick-coupling device* using a threaded plug closure of at least 1-inch NPT or having a threaded cap closure with a minimum 1-inch NPT pipe plug (see Fig. E17.3 through E17.5). A minimum 1-inch auxiliary test valve with a threaded closure may be substituted for the 1-inch pipe plug (see Fig E17.6). If the threaded cap closure does not have a pipe plug or integral auxiliary test valve, a minimum 1-inch NPT pipe plug shall be installed in the outlet nozzle above the closure (see Fig. E17.7).

(iv) *A two-piece* quick-coupling device using a clamped dust cap must include an in-line auxiliary valve, either integral with the quick-coupling device or located between the primary bottom outlet valve and the quick-coupling device. The quick-coupling device closure dust cap or outlet nozzle shall be fitted with a minimum 1-inch NPT closure (see Fig. E17.8 and E17.9).

(3) *The valve operating mechanism* must be provided with a suitable locking arrangement to insure positive closure during transit.

(4) *If the outlet nozzle* extends 6 inches or more from shell of tank, a V-shaped breakage groove shall be cut (not cast) in the upper part to the outlet nozzle at a point immediately below the lowest part of value closest to the tank. In no case may the nozzle wall thickness at the roof of the "V" be more than 1/4-inch. On cars without continuous center sills, the breakage groove or its equivalent may not be more than 15 inches below the tank shell. On cars with continuous center sills, the breakage groove or its equivalent must be above the bottom of the center sill construction.

(5) *The valve body* must be of a thickness which will insure that accidental breakage of the outlet nozzle will occur at or below the "V" groove, or its equivalent, and will not cause distortion of the valve seat or valve.

Subpart D - Specifications for Non-pressure Tank Car Tanks (Classes DOT-103, 104, 111AF, 111AW, and 115AW)

§179.200 General specifications applicable to non-pressure tank car tanks (Classes DOT-103, 104, and 111).

§179.200-1 Tank built under these specifications must meet the requirements of §§179.200, and 179.201.

§179.200-3 Type.

Tank built under these specifications must be circular in cross section, with formed heads designed convex outward. When specified in §179.201-1, the tank must have at least one manway or one expansion dome with manway, and such other external projections as are prescribed herein. When the tank is divided into compartments, each compartment must be treated as a separate tank.

§179.200-4 Insulation.

(a) **If insulation is applied, the tank shell and expansion dome** when used must be insulated with an approved material. The entire insulation must be covered with a metal jacket of a thickness not less than 11 gauge (0.1196 inch) nominal (Manufacturer's Standard Gauge) and flashed around all openings so as to be weather tight. The exterior surface of a carbon steel tank and the inside surface of a carbon steel jacket must be given a protection coating.

(b) **If insulation is a specification requirement,** it shall be of sufficient thickness so that the thermal conductance at 60 °F is not more than 0.225 Btu per hour, per square foot, per degree F temperature differential, unless otherwise provided in §179.201-1. If exterior heaters are attached to tank, the thickness of the insulation over each heater element may be reduced to one-half that required for the shell.

§179.200-6 Thickness of plates.

(a) **The wall thickness after forming** of the tank shell, dome shell, and of 2:1 ellipsoidal heads must be not less than specified in §179.201-1, nor that calculated by the following formula:

$$t = \frac{Pd}{2SE}$$

Where:

d = Inside diameter in inches;

E = 0.9 Welded joint efficiency; except E=1.0 for seamless heads;

P = Minimum required bursting pressure in psig;

S = Minimum tensile strength of plate material in p.s.i. as prescribed in §179.200-7;

t = Minimum thickness of plate in inches after forming.

(b) **The wall thickness after forming** of 3:1 ellipsoidal heads must be not less than specified in §179.201-1, nor that calculated by the following formula:

$$t = \frac{Pd}{2SE} \times 1.83$$

Where:

d = Inside diameter in inches;

E = 0.9 Welded joint efficiency; except E=1.0 for seamless heads;

P = Minimum required bursting pressure in psig;

S = Minimum tensile strength of plate material in p.s.i. as prescribed in §179.200-7;

t = Minimum thickness of plate in inches after forming.

(c) **The wall thickness after forming** of a flanged and dished head must be not less than specified in §179.201-1, nor that calculated by the following formula:

$$t = \frac{5PL}{6SE}$$

Where:

E = 0.9 Welded joint efficiency; except E=1.0 for seamless heads;

L = Main inside radius to which head is dished, measured on concave side in inches;

P = Minimum required bursting pressure in psig;

S = Minimum tensile strength of plate material in p.s.i. as prescribed in §179.200-7;

t = Minimum thickness of plate in inches after forming.

(d) **If plates are clad with material having** tensile strength properties at least equal to the base plate, the cladding may be considered a part of the base plate when determining thickness. If cladding material does not have tensile strength at least equal to the base plate, the base plate alone must meet the thickness requirements.

(e) **For a tank constructed of longitudinal sections,** the minimum width of bottom sheet of the tank must be 60 inches measured on the arc, but in all cases the width must be sufficient to bring the entire width of the longitudinal welded joint, including welds, above the bolster.

(f) **For a tank built of one piece cylindrical sections,** the thickness specified for bottom sheet must apply to the entire cylindrical section.

(g) **See §179.200-9 for thickness requirements** for a compartmented tank.

§179.200-7 Materials.

(a) **Plate material used to fabricate the tank** and, when used, expansion dome or manway nozzle material, must meet one of the following specifications with the indicated minimum tensile strength and elongation in the welded condition.

(b) **Carbon steel plate:** The maximum allowable carbon content must be 0.31 percent when the individual specification allows carbon content greater than this amount. The plates may be clad with other approved materials:

Specifications	Minimum tensile strength (p.s.i.) welded condition[1]	Minimum elongation in 2 inches (percent) weld metal (longitudinal)
AAR TC 128, Gr. B	81,000	19
ASTM A 516, Gr. 70	70,000	20

1. Maximum stresses to be used in calculations.

(c) **Aluminum alloy plate:** Aluminum alloy plate must be suitable for welding and comply with one of the following specifications:

Specifications	Minimum tensile strength (p.s.i.) welded condition[3,4]	Minimum elongation in 2 inches (percent) 0 temper, weld metal (longitudinal)
ASTM B 209, Alloy 5052[1]	25,000	18
ASTM B 209, Alloy 5083[2]	38,000	16
ASTM B 209, Alloy 5086[1]	35,000	14
ASTM B 209, Alloy 5154[1]	30,000	18
ASTM B 209, Alloy 5254[1]	30,000	18
ASTM B 209, Alloy 5454[1]	31,000	18
ASTM B 209, Alloy 5652[1]	25,000	18

1. For fabrication, the parent plate material may be 0, H112, or H32 temper, but design calculations must be based on minimum tensile strength shown.
2. 0 temper only.
3. Weld filler metal 5556 must not be used.
4. Maximum stresses to be used in calculations.

(d) **High alloy steel plate:** High alloy steel plate must comply with one of the following specifications:

Specifications	Minimum tensile strength (p.s.i.) welded condition[1]	Minimum elongation in 2 inches (percent) weld metal (longitudinal)
ASTM A 240/ASTM A 240M (incorporated by reference, see §171.7 of this subchapter), Type 304	75,000	30
ASTM A 240/ASTM A 240M (incorporated by reference, see §171.7 of this subchapter), Type 304L	70,000	30
ASTM A 240/ASTM A 240M (incorporated by reference, see §171.7 of this subchapter), Type 316	75,000	30
ASTM A 240/ASTM A 240M (incorporated by reference, see §171.7 of this subchapter), Type 316L	70,000	30

1. Maximum stresses to be used in calculations.
2. High alloy steel materials used to fabricate tank and expansion dome, when used, must be tested in accordance with Practice A of ASTM Specification A 262 titled, "Standard Practices for Detecting Susceptibility to Intergranular Attack in Austenitic Stainless Steels." If the specimen does not pass Practice A, Practice B or C must be used and the corrosion rates may not exceed the following:

Test procedure	Material	Corrosion rate i.p.m.
Practice B	Types 304, 304L, 316, and 316L	0.0040
Practice C	Type 304L	0.0020

Type 304L and Type 316L test specimens must be given a sensitizing treatment prior to testing. (A typical sensitizing treatment is 1 hour at 1250 F.)

(e) **Nickel plate:** Nickel plate must comply with the following specification:

Specifications	Minimum tensile strength (p.s.i.) welded condition[1]	Minimum elongation in 2 inches (percent) weld metal (longitudinal)
ASTM B 162[2]	40,000	20

1. Maximum stresses to be used in calculations.
2. When used as cladding for carbon steel plate, low-carbon nickel is required.

(f) **Manganese-molybdenum steel plate:** Manganese-molybdenum steel plate must be suitable for fusion welding and comply with the following specification:

Specifications	Minimum tensile strength (p.s.i.) welded condition[1]	Minimum elongation in 2 inches (percent) weld metal (longitudinal)
ASTM A 302, Gr. B	80,000	20

1. Maximum stresses to be used in calculations.

(g) **All parts and items of construction in contact** with the lading must be made of material compatible with plate material and not subject to rapid deterioration by the lading, or be coated or lined with suitable corrosion resistant material.

(h) **All external projections which may be in contact** with the lading and all castings, forgings, or fabrications used for fittings or attachments to tank and expansion dome, when used, in contact with lading must be made of material to an approved specification. See AAR Specifications for Tank Cars, appendix M, M4.05 (See §171.7 of this subchapter) for approved material specifications for castings for fittings.

§179.200-8 Tank heads.

(a) **All external tank heads must be an ellipsoid** of revolution in which the major axis must equal the diameter of the shell and the minor axis must be one-half the major axis.

(b) **Internal compartment tank heads may be** 2:1 ellipsoidal, 3:1 ellipsoidal, or flanged and dished to thicknesses as specified in §179.200-6. Flanged and dished heads must have main inside radius not exceeding 10 feet, and inside knuckle radius must not be less than 3 3/4 inches for steel, alloy steel, or nickel tanks, and not less than 5 inches for aluminum alloy tanks.

§179.200-9 Compartment tanks.

(a) **When a tank is divided into compartments,** by inserting interior heads, interior heads must be inserted in accordance with AAR Specifications for Tank Cars, appendix E, E7.00, and must comply with the requirements specified in §179.201-1. Voids between compartment heads must be provided with at least one tapped drain hole at their lowest point, and a tapped hole at the top of the tank. Top hole must be closed, and the bottom hole may be closed, with not less than 3/4 inch nor more than 1 1/2-inches solid pipe plugs having NPT threads.

(b) **When the tank is divided into compartments** by constructing each compartment as a separate tank, these tanks shall be joined together by a cylinder made of plate, having a thickness not less than that required for the tank shell and applied to the outside surface of tank head flanges. The cylinder shall fit the straight flange portion of the compartment tank head tightly. The cylinder shall contact the head flange for a distance of at least two times the plate thickness, or a minimum of 1 inch, whichever is greater. The cylinder shall be joined to the head flange by a full fillet weld. Distance from head seam to cylinder shall not be less than 1 1/2 inches or three times the plate thickness, whichever is greater. Voids created by the space between heads of tanks joined together to form a compartment tank shall be provided with a tapped drain hole at their lowest point and a tapped hole at top of tank. The top hole shall be closed and the bottom hole may be closed with solid pipe plugs not less than 3/4 inch nor more than 1 1/2 inches having NPT threads.

§179.200-10 Welding.

(a) **All joints shall be fusion-welded in compliance** with the requirements of AAR Specifications for Tank Cars, appendix W. Welding procedures, welders and fabricators shall be approved.

(b) **Welding is not permitted on or to ductile iron** or malleable iron fittings.

§179.200-11 Postweld heat treatment.

After welding is complete, postweld heat treatment must be in compliance with the requirements of AAR Specifications for Tank Cars, appendix W, when specified in §179.201-1.

§179.200-13 Manway ring or flange, pressure relief device flange, bottom outlet nozzle flange, bottom washout nozzle flange and other attachments and openings.

(a) **These attachments shall be fusion welded** to the tank and reinforced in an approved manner in compliance with the requirements of appendix E, figure 10, of the AAR Specifications for Tank Cars.

(b) **The opening in the manway ring must be at least** 16 inches in diameter except that acid resistant lined manways must be at least 18 inches in diameter before lining.

(c) **The manway ring or flange, shall be made** of cast, forged or fabricated metal. The metal of the dome, tank, or nozzle must be compatible with the manway ring or flange, so that they may be welded together.

(d) **The openings for the manway or other fittings** shall be reinforced in an approved manner.

§179.200-14 Expansion capacity.

(a) **Tanks shall have expansion capacity as prescribed** in this subchapter. This capacity shall be provided in the tank for Class DOT-111A cars, or in a dome for Class DOT-103 and 104 type cars.

(b) **For tank cars having an expansion dome,** the expansion capacity is the total capacity of the tank and dome combined. The capacity of the dome shall be measured from the inside top of shell of tank to the inside top of dome or bottom of any vent pipe projecting inside of dome, except that when a pressure relief device is applied to side of dome, the effective capacity of the dome shall be measured from top of the pressure relief device opening inside of dome to inside top of shell of tank.

(c) **The opening in the tank shell within the dome** shall be at least 29 inches in diameter. When the opening in the tank shell exceeds 30 inches in diameter, the opening shall be reinforced in an approved manner. This additional reinforcement may be accomplished by the use of a dome opening of the flued-type as shown in appendix E, Figure E 10C of the AAR Specifications for Tank Cars or by the use of reinforcing as outlined in Appendix E, E3.04 and Figures E10K and E10L. When the opening in the tank shell is less than the inside diameter of the dome, and the dome pocket is not closed off in an approved manner, dome pocket drain holes shall be provided in the tank shell with nipples projecting inside the tank at least 1 inch.

(d) **The dome head shall be of approved contour** and shall be designed for pressure on concave side.

(e) **Aluminum alloy domes:**

(1) *The dome shell thickness* shall be calculated by the formula in §179.200-6(a).

(2) *The dome head* may be an ellipsoid of revolution in which the major axis shall be equal to the diameter of the dome shell and the minor axis shall be one-half the major axis. The thickness in this case shall be determined by using formula in §179.200-6(a).

(3) *The dome head,* if dished, must be dished to a radius not exceeding 96 inches. Thickness of dished dome head must be calculated by the formula in §179.200-6(c).

(4) *Tank shell* shall be reinforced by the addition of a plate equal to or greater than shell in thickness and the cross sectional area shall exceed metal removed for dome opening, or tank shell shall be reinforced by a seamless saddle plate equal to or greater than shell in thickness and butt welded to tank shell. The reinforcing saddle plate shall be provided with a fluid opening having a vertical flange of the diameter of the dome for butt welding shell of dome to the flange. The reinforcing saddle plate shall extend about the dome a distance measured along shell of tank at least equal to the extension at top of tank. Other approved designs may be used.

(f) **For thickness of carbon or alloy steel domes, see §179.201-2.**

§179.200-15 Closures for manways.

(a) **Manway covers must be of approved type.**

(b) **Manway covers shall be designed to provide** a secure closure of the manway.

(c) **Manway covers must be of approved** cast, forged, or fabricated metals. Malleable iron, if used, must comply with ASTM A47-68, Grade 35018. Cast iron manway covers must not be used.

(d) **All joints between manway covers and their seats** shall be made tight against leakage of vapor and liquid by use of gaskets of suitable material.

(e) **For other manway cover requirements, see §179.201-1.**

§179.200-16 Gauging devices, top loading and unloading devices, venting and air inlet devices.

(a) **When installed, these devices shall be** of an approved design which will prevent interchange with any other fixture, and be tightly closed. Unloading pipes shall be securely anchored within the tank. Each tank or compartment may be equipped with one separate air connection.

(b) **When the characteristics of the commodity** for which the car is authorized are such that these devices must be equipped with valves or fittings to permit the loading and unloading of the contents, these devices, including valves, shall be of an approved design, and be provided with a protective housing except when plug or ball type valves with operating handles removed are used. Provision shall be made for closing pipe connections of valves.

(c) **A tank may be equipped with a vacuum relief valve** of an approved design. Protective housing is not required.

(d) **When using a visual gauging device on a car** with a hinged manway cover, an outage scale visible through the manway opening shall be provided. If loading devices are applied to permit tank loading with cover closed, a telltale pipe may be provided. Telltale pipe shall be capable of determining that required outage is provided. Pipe shall be equipped with 1/4 inch minimum NPT control valve mounted outside tank and enclosed within a housing. Other approved devices may be used in lieu of outage scale or telltale pipe.

(e) **Bottom of tank shell may be equipped** with a sump or siphon bowl, or both, welded or pressed into the shell. Such sumps or siphon bowls, if applied are not limited in size and must be made of cast, forged, or fabricated metal. Each sump or siphon bowl must be of good welding quality in conjunction with the metal of the tank shell. When sump or siphon bowl is pressed in the bottom of the tank shell, the wall thickness of the pressed section must not be less than that specified for the shell. The section of a circular cross section tank to which a sump or siphon bowl is attached need not comply with the out-of-roundness requirement specified in appendix W, W14.06, of the AAR Specifications for Tank Cars. Any portion of a sump or siphon bowl not forming a part of a cylinder of revolution must have walls of such thickness and be so reinforced that the stresses in the walls caused by a given internal pressure are not greater than the circumferential stress which would exist under the same internal pressure in the wall of a tank of circular cross section designed in accordance with §179.200-6 (a) and (d). In no case shall the wall thickness be less than that specified in §179.201-1(a).

(f) **When top loading and discharge devices,** or venting and air inlet devices are installed with exposed piping to a removed location, shutoff valves must be applied directly to reinforcing pads or nozzles at their communication through the tank shell, and must be enclosed in a protective housing with provision for a seal. The piping must include breakage grooves, and suitable bracing. Relief valves must be applied to liquid lines for protection in case lading is trapped. Provision must be made to insure closure of the valves while the car is in transit.

(g) **Protective housing, when required,** must be fabricated of approved material and have cover and sidewalls not less than 0.119 inch in thickness.

§179.200-17 Bottom outlets.

(a) **If indicated in §179.201-1, tank may be equipped** with bottom outlet. Bottom outlet, if applied, must comply with the following requirements:

(1) *The extreme projection* of the bottom outlet equipment may not be more than that allowed by appendix E of the AAR Specifications for Tank Cars. All bottom outlet reducers and closures and their attachments shall be secured to the car by at least 3/8-inch chain, or its equivalent, except that the bottom outlet closure plugs may be attached by 1/4-inch chain. When the bottom outlet closure is of the combination cap and valve type, the pipe connection to the valve shall be closed by a plug, cap, or approved quick coupling device. The bottom outlet equipment should include only the valve, reducers and closures that are necessary for the attachment of unloading fixtures. The permanent attachment of supplementary exterior fittings shall be approved by the AAR Committee on Tank Cars.

(2) *Bottom outlet* must be of approved construction, and be provided with a liquid-tight closure at its lower end.

(3) *On cars with center sills,* a ball valve may be welded to the outside bottom of the tank or mounted on a pad or nozzle with a tongue and groove or male and female flange attachment. In no case shall the breakage groove or equivalent extend below the bottom flange of the center sill. On cars without continuous center sills, a ball valve may be welded to the outside bottom of the tank

or mounted with a tongue and groove or male and female flange attachment on a pad attached to the outside bottom of the tank. The mounting pad must have a maximum thickness of 2 1/2 inches measured on the longitudinal centerline of the tank. The valve operating mechanism must be provided with a suitable locking arrangement to insure positive closure during transit.

(4) *The valve operating mechanism* for valves applied to the interior of the tank, and outlet nozzle construction, must insure against the unseating of the valve due to stresses or shocks incident to transportation.

(5) *Bottom outlet nozzle* of interior valves and the valve body of exterior valves, must be of cast, fabricated, or forged metal. If welded to tank, they must be of good weldable quality in conjunction with metal of tank.

(6) *To provide* for the attachment of unloading connections, the discharge end of the bottom outlet nozzle or reducer, the valve body of the exterior valve, or some fixed attachment thereto, shall be provided with one of the following arrangements or an approved modification thereof. (See appendix E. Fig. E17 of the AAR Specifications for Tank Cars for illustrations of some of the possible arrangements.)

(i) *A bolted flange* closure arrangement including a minimum 1-inch NPT pipe plug (see Fig. E17.1) or including an auxiliary valve with a threaded closure.

(ii) *A threaded cap* closure arrangement including a minimum 1-inch NPT pipe plug (see Fig. E17.2) or including an auxiliary valve with a threaded closure.

(iii) *A quick-coupling device* using a threaded plug closure of at least 1-inch NPT or having a threaded cap closure with a minimum 1-inch NPT pipe plug (see Fig. E17.3 through E17.5). A minimum 1-inch auxiliary test valve with a threaded closure may be substituted for the 1-inch pipe plug (see Fig. E17.6). If the threaded cap closure does not have a pipe plug or integral auxiliary test valve, a minimum 1-inch NPT pipe plug shall be installed in the outlet nozzle above the closure (see Fig. E17.7).

(iv) *A two-piece* quick-coupling device using a clamped dust cap must include an in-line auxiliary valve, either integral with the quick-coupling device or located between the primary bottom outlet valve and the quick-coupling device. The quick-coupling device closure dust cap or outlet nozzle shall be fitted with a minimum 1-inch NPT closure (see Fig. E17.8 and E17.9).

(7) *If the outlet nozzle* extends 6 inches or more from the shell of the tank, a V-shaped breakage groove shall be cut (not cast) in the upper part of the outlet nozzle at a point immediately below the lowest part of valve closest to the tank. In no case may the nozzle wall thickness at the root of the "V" be more than 1/4 inch. The outlet nozzle on interior valves or the valve body on exterior valves may be steam jacketed, in which case the breakage groove or its equivalent must be below the steam chamber but above the bottom of center sill construction. If the outlet nozzle is not a single piece, or if exterior valves are applied, provisions shall be made for the equivalent of the breakage groove. On cars without continuous center sills, the breakage groove or its equivalent must be no more than 15 inches below the tank shell. On cars with continuous center sills, the breakage groove or its equivalent must be above the bottom of the center sill construction.

(8) *The flange* on the outlet nozzle or the valve body of exterior valves must be of a thickness which will prevent distortion of the valve seat or valve by any change in contour of the shell resulting from expansion of lading, or other causes, and which will insure that accidental breakage of the outlet nozzle will occur at or below the "V" groove, or its equivalent.

(9) *The valve* must have no wings or stem projecting below the "V" groove or its equivalent. The valve and seat must be readily accessible or removable for repairs, including grinding.

(10) *The valve operating mechanism* on interior valves must have means for compensating for variation in the vertical diameter of the tank produced by expansion, weight of the liquid contents, or other causes, and may operate from the interior of the tank, but in the event the rod is carried through the dome, or tank shell, leakage must be prevented by packing in stuffing box or other suitable seals and a cap.

(b) **If indicated in §179.201-1, tank may be equipped** with bottom washout of approved construction. If applied, bottom washout shall be in accordance with the following requirements:

(1) *The extreme projection* of the bottom washout equipment may not be more than that allowed by appendix E of the AAR Specifications for Tank Cars.

(2) *Bottom washout* shall be of cast, forged or fabricated metal. If welded to tank, they shall be of good weldable quality in conjunction with metal of tank.

(3) *If the washout nozzle* extends 6 inches or more from the shell of the tank, a V-shaped breakage groove shall be cut (not cast) in the upper part of the nozzle at a point immediately below the lowest part of the inside closure seat or plug. In no case may the nozzle wall thickness at the root of the "V" be more than 1/4 inch. Where the nozzle is not a single piece, provisions shall be made for the equivalent of the breakage groove. The nozzle must be of a thickness to insure that accidental breakage will occur at or below the "V" groove or its equivalent. On cars without continuous center sills, the breakage groove or its equivalent may not be more than 15 inches below the outer shell. On cars with continuous center sills, the breakage groove or its equivalent must be above the bottom of the center sill construction.

(4) *The closure plug and seat* must be readily accessible or removable for repairs, including grinding.

(5) *The closure* of the washout nozzle must be equipped with a 3/4-inch solid screw plug. Plug must be attached by at least a 1/4-inch chain.

(6) *Joints between* closures and their seats may be gasketed with suitable material.

§179.200-19 Reinforcements, when used, and appurtenances not otherwise specified.

(a) **All attachments to tank and dome shall be applied** by approved means. Rivets if used shall be caulked inside and outside.

(b) **Reinforcing pads must be used between** external brackets and shells if the attachment welds exceed 6 lineal inches of 1/4-inch fillet or equivalent weld per bracket or bracket leg. When reinforcing pads are used, they must not be less than one-fourth inch in thickness, have each corner rounded to a 1 inch minimum radius, and be attached to the tank by continuous fillet welds except for venting provisions. The ultimate shear strength of the bracket to reinforcing pad weld must not exceed 85 percent of the ultimate shear strength of the reinforcing pad to tank weld.

§179.200-21 Closures for openings.

(a) **All plugs shall be solid, with NPT threads,** and shall be of a length which will screw at least 6 threads inside the face of fitting or tank. Plugs, when inserted from the outside of tank heads, shall have the letter "S" at least 3/8 inch in size stamped with steel stamp or cast on the outside surface to indicate the plug is solid.

(b) **[Reserved]**

§179.200-22 Test of tanks.

(a) **Each tank shall be tested by completely filling** the tank and dome or nozzles with water, or other liquid having similar viscosity, of a temperature which shall not exceed 100 °F during the test; and applying the pressure prescribed in §179.201-1. Tank shall hold the prescribed pressure for at least 10 minutes without leakage or evidence of distress. All rivets and closures, except safety relief valves or safety vents, shall be in place when test is made.

(b) **Insulated tanks shall be tested before insulation is applied.**

(c) **Rubber-lined tanks shall be tested before rubber lining is applied.**

(d) **Caulking of welded joints to stop leaks** developed during the foregoing tests is prohibited. Repairs in welded joints shall be made as prescribed in AAR Specifications for Tank Cars, appendix W.

§179.200-23 Tests of safety relief valves.

(a) **Each valve shall be tested by air or gas** for compliance with §179.15 before being put into service.

(b) **[Reserved]**

§179.200-24 Stamping.

(a) To certify that the tank complies with all specification requirements, each tank shall be plainly and permanently stamped in letters and figures at least 3/8 inch high into the metal near the center of both outside heads as follows:

	Examples of required stamping
Specification	DOT-103-W
Material	ASTM A 516-GR 70
Cladding material (if any)	ASTM A240-304 Clad
Tank builder's initials	ABC
Date of original test	00-0000
Car assembler (if other than tanker builder)	DEF

(b) On Class DOT-111 tank cars, the last numeral of the specification number may be omitted from the stamping; for example, DOT-111A100W.

§179.201 Individual specification requirements applicable to non-pressure tank car tanks.

§179.201-1 Individual specification requirements.

In addition to §179.200, the individual specification requirements are as follows:

DOT Specification[1]	Insulation	Bursting pressure (psig)	Minimum plate thickness (inches)	Test pressure (psig)	Bottom outlet	Bottom washout	Reference (179.201-***)
103A-ALW	Optional	240	1/2	60	No	Optional	
103AW	Optional	240	179.201-2	60	No	Optional	
103ALW	Optional	240	1/2	60	Optional	Optional	6(a)
103ANW	Optional	240	179.201-2	60	No	Optional	6(d)
103BW	Optional	240	179.201-2	60	No	No	6(b), 3
103CW	Optional	240	179.201-2	60	No	No	6(c), 4, 5
103DW	Optional	240	179.201-2	60	Optional	Optional	6(a), 6(c), 4, 5
103EW	Optional	240	179.201-2	60	No	Optional	6(c), 4, 5
103W	Optional	240	179.201-2	60	Optional	Optional	6(a)
104W	Yes	240	179.201-2	60	Optional	Optional	6(a)
111A60ALW1	Optional	240	1/2	60	Optional	Optional	6(a)
111A60ALW2	Optional	240	1/2	60	No	Optional	
111A60W1	Optional	240	7/16	60	Optional	Optional	6(a)
111A60W2	Optional	240	7/16	60	No	Optional	
111A60W5	Optional	240	7/16	60	No	No	3, 6(b)
111A60W6	Optional	240	7/16	60	Optional	Optional	4, 5, 6(a), 6(c)
111A60W7	Optional	240	7/16	60	No	No	4, 5, 6(a)
111A100ALW1	Optional	500	5/8	100	Optional	Optional	6(a)
111A100ALW2	Optional	500	5/8	100	No	Optional	
111A100W1	Optional	500	7/16	100	Optional	Optional	6(a)
111A100W2	Optional	500	7/16	100	No	Optional	
111A100W3	Yes	500	7/16	100	Optional	Optional	6(a)
111A100W4	Yes (see 179.201-11)	500	7/16	100	No	No	6(a), 8, 10
111A100W5	Optional	500	7/16	100	No	No	3
111A100W6	Optional	500	7/16	100	Optional	Optional	4, 5, 6(a) and 6(c)
111A100W7	Optional	500	7/16	100	No	No	4, 5, 6(c)

1. Tanks marked "ALW" are constructed from aluminum alloy plate; "AN" nickel plate; "CW," "DW," "EW," "W6," and "W7" high alloy steel or manganese-molybdenum steel plate; and those marked "BW" or "W5" must have an interior lining that conforms to §179.201-3.

§179.201-2 Minimum plate thickness.

(a) The minimum plate thickness, after forming, must be as follows:

Inside diameter of tanks	Bottom sheets	Shell sheets	Expansion dome sheets	2:1 ellipsoidal heads	3:1 ellipsoidal and dished tank heads	Expansion dome heads	Interior compartment heads
	Inches						
60 inches or under	7/16	1/4	5/16	7/16	1/2	5/16	5/16
Over 60 to 78 inches	7/16	5/16	5/16	7/16	1/2	5/16	5/16
Over 78 to 96 inches	1/2[1]	3/8	5/16	7/16	1/2	5/16	3/8
Over 96 to 112 inches	1/2[1]	7/16	5/16	7/16	9/16	5/16	7/16
Over 112 to 122 inches	1/2	1/2	5/16	1/2	5/8	5/16	1/2

1. May be reduced to 7/16 inch when approved steels having tensile strength of 65,000 psi or higher are used.

(b) [Reserved]

§179.201-3 Lined tanks.

(a) Rubber-lined tanks.

(1) *Each tank* or each compartment thereof must be lined with acid-resistant rubber or other approved rubber compound vulcanized or bonded directly to the metal tank, to provide a nonporous laminated lining, at least 5/32-inch thick, except overall rivets and seams formed by riveted attachments in the lining must be double thickness. The rubber lining must overlap at least 1 1/2 inches at all edges which must be straight and be beveled to an angle of approximately 45°, or butted edges of lining must be sealed with a 3-inch minimum strip of lining having 45° beveled edges.

(2) *As an alternate method,* the lining may be joined with a skived butt seam then capped with a separate strip of lining 3 inches wide having 45° beveled edges. An additional rubber reinforcing pad at least 4 1/2 feet square and at least 1/2-inch thick must be applied by vulcanizing to the lining on bottom of tank directly under the manway opening. The edges of the rubber pad must be beveled to an angle of approximately 45°. An opening in this pad for sump is permitted. No lining must be under tension when applied except due to conformation over rivet heads. Interior of tank must be free from scale, oxidation, moisture, and all foreign matter during the lining operation.

(3) *Other approved lining materials* may be used provided the material is resistant to the corrosive or solvent action of the lading in the liquid or gas phase and is suitable for the service temperatures.

(b) Before a tank car tank is lined with rubber, or other rubber compound, a report certifying that the tank and its equipment have been brought into compliance with spec. DOT-103B, 103BW, 111A60W5, or 111A100W5 must be furnished by car owner to the party who is to apply the lining. A copy of this report in approved form, certifying that tank has been lined in compliance with all requirements of one of the above specifications, must be furnished by party lining tank to car owner. Reports of the latest lining application must be retained by the car owner until the next relining has been accomplished and recorded.

(c) All rivet heads on inside of tank must be buttonhead, or similar shape, and of uniform size. The under surface of heads must be driven tight against the plate. All plates, castings and rivet heads on the inside of the tank must be calked. All projecting edges of plates, castings and rivet heads on the inside of the tank must be rounded and free from fins and other irregular projections. Castings must be free from porosity.

(d) All surfaces of attachments or fittings and their closures exposed to the lading must be covered with at least 1/8-inch acid resistant material. Attachments made of metal not affected by the lading need not be covered with rubber or other acid resistant material.

(e) Hard rubber or polyvinyl chloride may be used for pressure retaining parts of safety vents provided the material is resistant to the corrosive or solvent action of the lading in the liquid or gas phase and is suitable for the service temperatures.

(f) Polyvinyl chloride lined tanks. Tank car tanks or each compartment thereof may be lined with elastomeric polyvinyl chloride having a minimum lining thickness of three thirty-seconds inch.

(g) Polyurethane lined tanks. Tank car tanks or each compartment thereof may be lined with elastomeric polyurethane having a minimum lining thickness of one-sixteenth inch.

§179.201-4 Material.

All fittings, tubes, and castings and all projections and their closures, except for protective housing, must also meet the requirements specified in ASTM Specification A 262, except that when preparing the specimen for testing the carburized surface may be finished by grinding or machining.

§179.201-5 Postweld heat treatment and corrosion resistance.

(a) Tanks and attachments welded directly thereto must be postweld heat treated as a unit at the proper temperature except as indicated below. Tanks and attachments welded directly thereto fabricated from ASTM A 240/ASTM A 240M (incorporated by reference, see §171.7 of this subchapter), Type 430A, Type 304 and Type 316 materials must be postweld heat treated as a unit and must be tested to demonstrate that they possess the corrosion resistance specified in §179.200-7(d), Footnote 2. Tanks and attachments welded directly thereto, fabricated from ASTM A 240/ASTM A 240M (incorporated by reference, see §171.7 of this subchapter), Type 304L or Type 316L materials are not required to be postweld heat treated.

(b) Tanks and attachments welded directly thereto, fabricated from ASTM A 240/ASTM A 240M (incorporated by reference, see §171.7 of this subchapter) Type 304L and Type 316 materials must be tested to demonstrate that they possess the corrosion resistance specified in §179.200-7(d), Footnote 2.

§179.201-6 Manways and manway closures.

(a) The manway cover for spec. DOT 103ALW, 103DW, 103W, 104W, 111A60-ALW1, 111A60W1, 111A100ALW1, 111A-100W1, 111A100W3, or 111A100W6 must be designed to make it impossible to remove the cover while the interior of the tank is subjected to pressure.

(b) The manway cover for spec. DOT 103BW, 11A60W5, or 111A100W5 must be made of a suitable metal. The top, bottom and edge of manway cover must be acid resistant material covered as prescribed in §179.201-3. Through-bolt holes must be lined with acid resistant material at least one-eighth inch in thickness. Cover made of metal not affected by the lading need not be acid resistant material covered.

(c) The manway ring and cover for spec. DOT-103CW, 103DW, 103EW, 111360W7, or 11A100W6 must be made of the metal and have the same inspection procedures specified in AAR Specifications for Tanks Cars Appendix M, M3.03.

(d) The manway ring for DOT-103 ANW must be made of cast, forged or fabricated nickel and be a good weldable quality in conjunction with the metal of the dome. Manway cover must be made of nickel.

§179.201-8 Sampling device and thermometer well.

(a) Sampling valve and thermometer well are not specification requirements. When used, they must be of approved design, made of metal not subject to rapid deterioration by lading, and must withstand a pressure of 100 psig without leakage. Interior pipes of the sampling valve must be equipped with excess flow valves of an approved design. Interior pipe of thermometer well must be closed by an approved valve attached close to fitting where it passes through the tank and closed by a screw plug. Other approved arrangements that permit testing thermometer well for leaks without complete removal of the closure may be used.

(b) [Reserved]

§179.201-9 Gauging device.

A gauging device of an approved design must be applied to permit determining the liquid level of the lading. The gauging device must be made of materials not subject to rapid deterioration by the lading. When the interior pipe of the gauging device provides a means for passage of the lading from the interior to the exterior of the tank, it must be equipped with an excess flow valve of an approved design. If the opening for passage of lading through the gauging device is not more than 0.060 inch diameter an excess flow valve is not required. The gauging device must be provided with a protective housing.

§179.201-10 Water capacity marking.

(a) **Water capacity of the tank in pounds** stamped plainly and permanently in letters and figures at least 3/8 inch high into the metal of the tank immediately below the stamped marks specified in §179.200-24(a). This mark shall also be stenciled on the jacket immediately below the dome platform and directly behind or within 3 feet of the right or left side of the ladder, or ladders, if there is a ladder on each side of the tank, in letters and figures at least 1 1/2 inches high as follows:

WATER CAPACITY
000000 Pounds

(b) **[Reserved]**

§179.201-11 Insulation.

(a) **Insulation shall be of sufficient thickness** so that the thermal conductance at 60 °F is not more than 0.075 Btu per hour, per square foot, per degree F temperature differential.

(b) **[Reserved]**

§§179.202-179.202-22 [Reserved]

§179.220 General specifications applicable to nonpressure tank car tanks consisting of an inner container supported within an outer shell (class DOT-115).

§179.220-1 Tanks built under these specifications must meet the requirements of §§179.220 and 179.221.

§179.220-3 Type.

(a) **Tanks built under these specifications must consist** of an inner container, a support system for the inner container, and an outer shell.

(b) **The inner container must be a fusion welded tank** of circular cross section with formed heads designed convex outward and must have a manway on top of the tank as prescribed herein. When the inner container is divided into compartments, each compartment must be considered a separate container.

(c) **The outer shell must be a fusion welded tank** with formed heads designed convex outward.

§179.220-4 Insulation.

The annular space between the inner container and the outer shell must contain an approved insulation material.

§179.220-6 Thickness of plates.

(a) **The wall thickness, after forming** of the inner container shell and 2:1 ellipsoidal heads must be not less than specified in §179.221-1, or not less than that calculated by the following formula:

$$t = \frac{Pd}{2SE}$$

Where:

d = Inside diameter in inches;

E = 0.9 welded joint efficiency; except E=1.0 for seamless heads;

P = Minimum required bursting pressure in psig;

S = Minimum tensile strength of plate material in p.s.i. as prescribed in AAR Specifications for Tank Cars, appendix M, Table M1;

t = Minimum thickness of plate in inches after forming.

(b) **The wall thickness after forming** of the inner container heads, if flanged and dished, must be not less than specified in §179.221-1, or not less than that calculated by the following formula:

$$t = \frac{5PL}{6SE}$$

Where:

E = 0.9 welded joint efficiency; except E=1.0 for seamless heads;

L = Main inside radius to which head is dished, measured on concave side in inches;

P = Minimum required bursting pressure in psig;

S = Minimum tensile strength of plate material in p.s.i. as prescribed in AAR Specifications for Tank Cars, appendix M., Table M1;

t = Minimum thickness of plate in inches after forming.

(c) **The wall thickness after forming** of the cylindrical section and heads of the outer shell must be not less than seven-sixteenths of an inch.

(d) **See §179.220-9 for plate thickness requirements** for inner container when divided into compartments.

§179.220-7 Materials.

(a) **The plate material used to fabricate** the inner container and nozzles must meet one of the following specifications and with the indicated minimum tensile strength and elongation in the welded condition.

(b) **Carbon steel plate:** The maximum allowable carbon content must be 0.31 percent when the individual specification allows carbon content greater than this amount. The plates may be clad with other approved materials.

Specifications	Minimum tensile strength (p.s.i.) welded condition[1]	Minimum elongation in 2 inches (percent) weld metal (longitudinal)
AAR TC 128, Gr. B	81,000	19
ASTM A 516, Gr. 70	70,000	20

1. Maximum stresses to be used in calculations.

(c) **Aluminum alloy plate:** Aluminum alloy plate must be suitable for welding and comply with one of the following specifications:

Specifications	Minimum tensile strength (p.s.i.) welded condition[3,4]	Minimum elongation in 2 inches (percent) weld metal (longitudinal)
ASTM B 209, Alloy 5052[1]	25,000	18
ASTM B 209, Alloy 5083[2]	38,000	16
ASTM B 209, Alloy 5086[1]	35,000	14
ASTM B 209, Alloy 5154[1]	30,000	18
ASTM B 209, Alloy 5254[1]	30,000	18
ASTM B 209, Alloy 5454[1]	31,000	18
ASTM B 209, Alloy 5652[1]	25,000	18

1. For fabrication, the parent plate material may be 0 H112, or H32 temper, but design calculations must be based on the minimum tensile strength shown.
2. 0 temper only.
3. Weld filler metal 5556 must not be used.
4. Maximum stresses to be used in calculations.

(d) **High alloy steel plate:** High alloy steel plate must comply with one of the following specifications:

Specifications	Minimum tensile strength (p.s.i.) welded condition[1]	Minimum elongation in 2 inches (percent) weld metal (longitudinal)
ASTM A 240/ASTM A 240M (incorporated by reference, see §171.7 of this subchapter), Type 304	75,000	30
ASTM A 240/ASTM A 240M (incorporated by reference, see §171.7 of this subchapter), Type 304L	70,000	30
ASTM A 240/ASTM A 240M (incorporated by reference, see §171.7 of this subchapter), Type 316	74,000	30
ASTM A 240/ASTM A 240M (incorporated by reference, see §171.7 of this subchapter), Type 316L	70,000	30

1. Maximum stresses to be used in calculations.

(e) **Manganese-molybdenum steel plate:** Manganese-molybdenum steel plate must be suitable for fusion welding and must comply with the following specification:

Specifications	Minimum tensile strength (p.s.i.) welded condition[1]	Minimum elongation in 2 inches (percent) weld metal (longitudinal)
ASTM A 302, Gr. B	80,000	20

1. Maximum stresses to be used in calculations.

(f) **Plate materials used to fabricate** the outer shell and heads must be those listed in paragraphs (b), (c), (d), or (e) of this section. The maximum allowable carbon content must be 0.31 percent when the individual specification allows carbon content greater than this amount. The plates may be clad with other approved materials.

(g) **All appurtenances on the inner container** in contact with the lading must be made of approved material compatible with the plate material of the inner container. These appurtenances must not be subject to rapid deterioration by the lading, or must be coated or lined with suitable corrosion resistant material. See AAR Specifications for Tank Cars, appendix M, M4.05 for approved material specifications for castings for fittings.

§179.220-8 Tank heads.

(a) **Tank heads of the inner container,** inner container compartments and outer shell must be of approved contour, and may be flanged and dished or ellipsoidal for pressure on concave side.

(b) **Flanged and dished heads must have** main inside radius not exceeding 10 feet and inside knuckle radius must be not less than 3 3/4 inches for steel and alloy steel tanks nor less than 5 inches for aluminum alloy tanks.

(c) **Ellipsoidal heads must be an ellipsoid** of revolution in which the major axis must equal the diameter of the shell and the minor axis must be one-half the major axis.

§179.220-9 Compartment tanks.

(a) **The inner container may be divided into compartments** by inserting interior heads, or by fabricating each compartment as a separate container and joining with a cylinder, or by fabricating each compartment as a separate tank without a joining cylinder. Each compartment must be capable of withstanding, without evidence of yielding or leakage, the required test pressure applied in each compartment separately, or in any combination of compartments.

(b) **When the inner container is divided into compartments** by fabricating each compartment as a separate container and joining with a cylinder, the cylinder must have a plate thickness not less than that required for the inner container shell and must be applied to the outside surface of the straight flange portion of the container head. The cylinder must fit the straight flange tightly for a distance of at least two times the plate thickness, or 1 inch, whichever is greater and must be joined to the straight flange by a full fillet weld. Distance from fillet weld seam to container head seam must be not less than 1 1/2 inches or three times the plate thickness, whichever is greater.

§179.220-10 Welding.

(a) **All joints must be fusion-welded in compliance** with AAR Specifications for Tank Cars, appendix W. Welding procedures, welders, and fabricators shall be approved.

(b) **Radioscopy of the outer shell is not a specification requirement.**

(c) **Welding is not permitted on or to ductile iron** or malleable iron fittings.

§179.220-11 Postweld heat treatment.

(a) **Postweld heat treatment of the inner container** is not a specification requirement.

(b) **Postweld heat treatment of the cylindrical portions** of the outer shell to which the anchorage or draft sills are attached must comply with AAR Specifications for Tank Cars, appendix W.

(c) **When cold formed heads are used on the outer shell** they must be heat treated before welding to shell if postweld heat treatment is not practicable due to assembly procedures.

§179.220-13 Inner container manway nozzle and cover.

(a) **Inner container manway nozzle must be** of approved design with access opening at least 18 inches inside diameter, or at least 14 inches by 18 inches obround or oval.

(b) **Manway covers must be of approved type.** Design must provide a secure closure of the manway and must make it impossible to remove the cover while the tank interior is under pressure.

(c) **All joints between manway covers and their seats** must be made tight against leakage of vapor and liquid by use of suitable gaskets.

(d) **Manway covers must be cast, forged, or fabricated metal** complying with subsection §179.220-7(g) of this section.

(e) **A seal must be provided between** the inner container manway nozzle and the opening in the outer shell.

§179.220-14 Openings in the tanks.

Openings in the inner container and the outer shell must be reinforced in compliance with AAR Specifications for Tank Cars, appendix E. In determining the required reinforcement area for openings in the outer shell, t shall be one-fourth inch.

§179.220-15 Support system for inner container.

(a) **The inner container must be supported** within the outer shell by a support system of adequate strength and ductility at its operating temperature to support the inner container when filled with liquid lading to any level. The support system must be designed to support, without yielding, impact loads producing accelerations of the following magnitudes and directions when the inner container is loaded so that the car is at its rail load limit, and the car is equipped with a conventional AAR Specification M-901 draft gear.

Longitudinal........7G
Transverse........3G
Vertical........3G

(b) **The longitudinal acceleration may be reduced to 3G** where a cushioning device of approved design, which has been tested to demonstrate its ability to limit body forces to 400,000 pounds maximum at a 10 miles per hour impact, is used between the coupler and the tank structure. The support system must be of approved design and the inner container must be thermally isolated from the outer shell to the best practical extent. The inner container and outer shell must be permanently bonded to each other electrically either by the support system used, piping, or by a separate electrical connection of approved design.

§179.220-16 Expansion capacity.

Expansion capacity must be provided in the shell of the inner container as prescribed in §179.221-1.

§179.220-17 Gauging devices, top loading and unloading devices, venting and air inlet devices.

(a) **When installed, each device must be** of approved design which will prevent interchange with any other fixture and must be tightly closed. Each unloading pipe must be securely anchored within the inner container. Each inner container or compartment thereof may be equipped with one separate air connection.

(b) **When the characteristics of the commodity** for which the car is authorized require these devices to be equipped with valves or fittings to permit the loading and unloading of the contents, these devices including valves, shall be provided with a protective housing except when plug or ball-type valves with operating handles removed are used. Provision must be made for closing pipe connections of valves.

(c) **Inner container may be equipped** with a vacuum relief valve of approved design. Protective housing is not required.

(d) **When a gauging device is required in §179.221-1,** an outage scale visible through the manway opening must be provided. If loading devices are applied to permit tank loading with cover closed, a telltale pipe may be provided. The telltail pipe must be capable of determining that required outage is provided. The pipe must be equipped with 1/4-inch maximum, NPT control valve mounted outside tank and enclosed within a protective housing. Other approved devices may be used in place of an outage scale or a telltale pipe.

(e) **The bottom of the tank shell may be equipped** with a sump or siphon bowl, or both, welded or pressed into the shell. These sumps or siphon bowls, if applied, are not limited in size and must be made of cast, forged, or fabricated metal. Each sump or siphon bowl must be of good welding quality in conjunction with the metal of the tank shell. When the sump or siphon bowl is pressed in the bottom of the tank shell, the wall thickness of the pressed section must not be less than that specified for the shell. The section of a circular cross section tank to which a sump or siphon bowl is attached need not comply with the out-of-roundness requirement specified in appendix W, W14.06 of the AAR Specifications for Tank Cars. Any portion of a sump or siphon bowl not forming a part of a cylinder of revolution must have walls of such thickness and must be so reinforced that the stresses in the walls caused by a given internal pressure are not greater than the circumferential stress which would exist under the same internal pressure in the wall of a tank of circular cross section designed in accordance with §§179.220-6(a) and 179.220-9. In no case shall the wall thickness be less than that specified in §179.221-1(a).

(f) **Protective housing, when required,** must be of approved material and must have cover and sidewalls not less than 0.119 inch in thickness.

§179.220-18 Bottom outlets.

(a) **The inner container may be equipped** with a bottom outlet of approved design and an opening provided in the outer shell of its access. If applied, the bottom outlet must comply with the following requirements:

(1) *The extreme projection* of the bottom outlet equipment may not be more than that allowed by appendix E of the AAR Specifications for Tank Cars. All bottom outlet reducers and closures and their attachments shall be secured to car by at least 3/8-inch chain, or its equivalent, except that bottom outlet closure plugs may be attached by 1/4-inch chain. When the bottom outlet closure is of the combination cap and valve type, the pipe connection to the valve shall be closed by a plug, or cap. The bottom outlet equipment should include only the valve, reducers and

closures that are necessary for the attachment of unloading fixtures. The permanent attachment of supplementary exterior fittings shall be approved by the AAR Committee on Tank Cars.

(2) *Each bottom outlet* must be provided with a liquid tight closure at its lower end.

(3) *The valve and its operating mechanism* must be applied to the outside bottom of the inner container. The valve operating mechanism must be provided with a suitable locking arrangement to insure positive closure during transportation.

(4) *Valve outlet nozzle* and valve body must be of cast, fabricated or forged metal. If welded to inner container, they must be of good weldable quality in conjunction with metal of tank.

(5) *To provide* for the attachment of unloading connections, the bottom of the main portion of the outlet nozzle or valve body, or some fixed attachment thereto, must be provided with threaded cap closure arrangement or bolted flange closure arrangement having minimum 1-inch threaded pipe plug.

(6) *If outlet nozzle and its closure* extends below the bottom of the outer shell, a V-shaped breakage groove shall be cut (not cast) in the upper part of the outlet nozzle at a point immediately below the lowest part of the valve closest to the tank. In no case may the nozzle wall thickness at the root of the "V" be more than 1/4-inch. The outlet nozzle or the valve body may be steam jacketed, in which case the breakage groove or its equivalent must be below the steam chamber but above the bottom of the center sill construction. If the outlet nozzle is not a single piece or its exterior valves are applied, provision shall be made for the equivalent of the breakage groove. On cars without continuous center sills, the breakage groove or its equivalent may not be more than 15 inches below the outer shell. On cars with continuous center sills, the breakage groove or its equivalent must be above the bottom of the center sill construction.

(7) *The valve body* must be of a thickness which will prevent distortion of the valve seat or valve by any change in contour of the shell resulting from expansion of lading, or other causes, and which will insure that accidental breakage of the outlet nozzle will occur at or below the "V" groove, or its equivalent.

(8) *The valve* must have no wings or stem projection below the "V" groove or its equivalent. The valve and seat must be readily accessible or removable for repairs, including grinding.

(b) **Inner container may be equipped** with bottom washout of approved design. If applied, bottom washout must comply with the following requirements:

(1) *The extreme projection* of the bottom washout equipment may not be more than that allowed by appendix E of the AAR Specifications for Tank Cars.

(2) *Bottom washout* must be of cast, forged or fabricated metals. If it is welded to the inner container, it must be of good weldable quality in conjunction with metal of tank.

(3) *If washout nozzle* extends below the bottom of the outer shell, a V-shaped breakage groove shall be cut (not cast) in the upper part of the nozzle at a point immediately below the lowest part of the inside closure seat or plug. In no case may the nozzle wall thickness at the root of the "V" be more than 1/4-inch. Where the nozzle is not a single piece, provisions shall be made for the equivalent of the breakage groove. The nozzle must be of a thickness to insure that accidental breakage will occur at or below the "V" groove or its equivalent. On cars without a continuous center sill, the breakage groove or its equivalent may not be more than 15 inches below the outer shell. On cars with continuous center sills, the breakage groove or its equivalent must be above the bottom of the center sill construction.

(4) *The closure plug and seat* must be readily accessible or removable for repairs.

(5) *The closure* of the washout nozzle must be equipped with a 3/4-inch solid screw plug. Plug must be attached by at least a 1/4-inch chain.

(6) *Joints between* closures and their seats may be gasketed with suitable material.

§179.220-20 Reinforcements, when used, and appurtenances not otherwise specified.

All attachments to inner container and outer shell must be applied by approved means.

§179.220-22 Closure for openings.

(a) **All plugs must be solid, with NPT threads,** and must be of a length which will screw at least six threads inside the face of fitting or tank. Plugs, when inserted from the outside of the outer shell tank heads, must have the letter "S" at least three-eighths inch in size stamped with steel stamp or cast on the outside surface to indicate the plug is solid.

(b) **Openings in the outer shell used during construction** for installation must be closed in an approved manner.

§179.220-23 Test of tanks.

(a) **Each inner container or compartment must be tested** hydrostatically to the pressure specified in §179.221-1. The temperature of the pressurizing medium must not exceed 100 °F during the test. The container must hold the prescribed pressure for at least 10 minutes without leakage or evidence of distress. Safety relief devices must not be in place when the test is made.

(b) **The inner container must be pressure tested** before installation within the outer shell. Items which, because of assembly sequence, must be welded to inner container after its installation within outer shell must have their attachment welds thoroughly inspected by a nondestructive dye penetrant method or its equivalent.

(c) **Pressure testing of outer shell is not a specification requirement.**

§179.220-24 Tests of pressure relief valves.

Each safety relief valve must be tested by air or gas for compliance with §179.15 before being put into service.

§179.220-25 Stamping.

To certify that the tank complies with all specification requirements, each outer shell must be plainly and permanently stamped in letters and figures at least 3/8-inch high into the metal near the center of both outside heads as follows:

	Examples of required stamping
Specifications	DOT-115A60W6
Inner container:	
Material	ASTM A240-316L
Shell thickness	Shell 0.167 in
Head thickness	Head 0.150 in
Tank builders initials	ABC
Date of original test	00-0000
Outer shell:	
Material	ASTM A285-C
Tank builders initials	WYZ
Car assembler (if other than inner container or outer shell builders)	DEF

§179.220-26 Stenciling.

(a) **The outer shell, or the jacket if the outer shell** is insulated, must be stenciled in compliance with AAR Specifications for Tank Cars, appendix C.

(b) **Stenciling must be applied on both sides** of the outer shell or jacket near the center in letters and figures at least 1 1/2 inches high to indicate the safe upper temperature limit, if applicable, for the inner tank, insulation, and the support system.

§179.221 Individual specification requirements applicable to tank car tanks consisting of an inner container supported within an outer shell.

§179.221-1 Individual specification requirements.

In addition to §179.220, the individual specification requirements are as follows:

DOT specification	Insulation	Bursting pressure (psig)	Minimum plate thickness (inches)	Test pressure (psig)	Bottom outlet	Bottom washout	Reference (179.221-***)
115A60ALW	Yes	240	3/16	60	Optional	Optional	
115A60W1	Yes	240	1/8	60	Optional	Optional	1
115A60W6	Yes	240	1/8	60	Optional	Optional	1

Subpart E - Specifications for Multi-unit Tank Car Tanks (Classes DOT-106A and 110AW)

§179.300 General specifications applicable to multi-unit tank car tanks designed to be removed from car structure for filling and emptying (Classes DOT-106A and 110AW).

§179.300-1 Tanks built under these specifications shall meet the requirements of §179.300, §179.301 and when applicable, §179.302.

§179.300-3 Type and general requirements.

(a) Tanks built under this specification shall be cylindrical, circular in cross section, and shall have heads of approved design. All openings shall be located in the heads.

(b) Each tank shall have a water capacity of at least 1500 pounds and not more than 2600 pounds.

(c) For tanks made in foreign countries, a chemical analysis of materials and all tests as specified shall be carried out within the limits of the United States under the supervision of a competent and impartial inspector.

§179.300-4 Insulation.

(a) Tanks shall not be insulated.

(b) [Reserved]

§179.300-6 Thickness of plates.

(a) For class DOT-110A tanks, the wall thickness after forming of the cylindrical portion of the tank must not be less than that specified in §179.301 nor that calculated by the following formula:

$$t = \frac{Pd}{2SE}$$

Where:

d = inside diameter in inches;

E = 1.0 welded joint efficiency;

P = minimum required bursting pressure in psig;

S = minimum tensile strength of plate material in p.s.i. as prescribed in §179.300-7;

t = minimum thickness of plate material in inches after forming.

(b) For class DOT-106A tanks, the wall thickness of the cylindrical portion of the tank shall not be less than that specified in §179.301 and shall be such that at the tank test pressure the maximum fiber stress in the wall of the tank will not exceed 15,750 p.s.i. as calculated by the following formula:

$s = [p(1.3D^2 + 0.4d^2)] / (D^2 - d^2)$

Where:

d = inside diameter in inches;

D = outside diameter in inches;

p = tank test pressure in psig;

s = wall stress in psig.

(c) If plates are clad with material having tensile strength at least equal to the base plate, the cladding may be considered a part of the base plate when determining the thickness. If cladding material does not have tensile strength at least equal to the base plate, the base plate alone shall meet the thickness requirements.

§179.300-7 Materials.

(a) Steel plate material used to fabricate tanks must conform with the following specifications with the indicated minimum tensile strength and elongation in the welded condition. However, the maximum allowable carbon content for carbon steel must not exceed 0.31 percent, although the individual ASTM specification may allow for a greater amount of carbon. The plates may be clad with other approved materials:

Specifications	Tensile strength (psi) welded condition[1] (minimum)	Elongation in 2 inches (percent) welded condition[1] (longitudinal) (minimum)
ASTM A 240 type 304	75,000	25
ASTM A 240 type 304L	70,000	25
ASTM A 240 type 316	75,000	25
ASTM A 240 type 316L	70,000	25
ASTM A 240 type 321	75,000	25
ASTM A285 Gr. A	45,000	29
ASTM A285 Gr. B	50,000	20
ASTM A285 Gr. C	55,000	20
ASTM A515 Gr. 65	65,000	20
ASTM A515 Gr. 70	70,000	20
ASTM A516 Gr. 70	70,000	20

1. Maximum stresses to be used in calculations.

(b) [Reserved]

(c) All plates must have their heat number and the name or brand of the manufacturer legibly stamped on them at the rolling mill.

§179.300-8 Tank heads.

(a) Class DOT-110A tanks shall have fusion-welded heads formed concave to pressure. Heads for fusion welding shall be an ellipsoid of revolution 2:1 ratio of major to minor axis. They shall be one piece, hot formed in one heat so as to provide a straight flange at least 1 1/2 inches long. The thickness shall not be less than that calculated by the following formula:

$$t = \frac{Pd}{2SE}$$

where symbols are as defined in §179.300-6(a).

(b) Class DOT-106A tanks must have forged-welded heads, formed convex to pressure. Heads for forge welding must be torispherical with an inside radius not greater than the inside diameter of the shell. They must be one piece, hot formed in one heat so as to provide a straight flange at least 4 inches long. They must have snug drive fit into the shell for forge welding. The wall thickness after forming must be sufficient to meet the test requirements of §179.300-16 and to provide for adequate threading of openings.

§179.300-9 Welding.

(a) Longitudinal joints must be fusion welded. Head-to-shell joints must be forge welded on class DOT-106A tanks and fusion welded on class DOT-110A tanks. Welding procedures, welders and fabricators must be approved in accordance with AAR Specifications for Tank Cars, appendix W.

(b) Fusion-welded joints must be in compliance with the requirements of AAR Specifications for Tank Cars, appendix W, except that circumferential welds in tanks less than 36 inches inside diameter need not be radiotaped.

(c) Forge-welded joints shall be thoroughly hammered or rolled to insure sound welds. The flanges of the heads shall be forge lap-welded to the shell and then crimped inwardly toward the center line at least one inch on the radius. Welding and crimping must be accomplished in one heat.

§179.300-10 Postweld heat treatment.

After welding is complete, steel tanks and all attachments welded thereto, must be postweld heat treated as a unit in compliance with the requirements of AAR Specifications for Tank Cars, appendix W.

§179.300-12 Protection of fittings.

(a) **Tanks shall be of such design as will afford** maximum protection to any fittings or attachment to the head including the housing referred to in §179.300-12(b). Tank ends shall slope or curve inward toward the axis so that the diameter at each end is at least 2 inches less than the maximum diameter.

(b) **Loading and unloading valves shall be protected** by a detachable protective housing of approved design which shall not project beyond the end of the tank and shall be securely fastened to the tank head. Safety relief devices shall not be covered by the housing.

§179.300-13 Venting, loading and unloading valves.

(a) **Valves shall be of approved type,** made of metal not subject to rapid deterioration by lading, and shall withstand tank test pressure without leakage. The valves shall be screwed directly into or attached by other approved methods to one tank head. Provision shall be made for closing outlet connections of the valves.

(b) **Threads for openings shall be National Gas Taper Threads** (NGT) tapped to gage, clean cut, even and without checks.

§179.300-14 Attachments not otherwise specified.

Siphon pipes and their couplings on the inside of the tank head and lugs on the outside of the tank head for attaching the valve protective housing must be fusion-welded in place prior to postweld heat treatment. All other fixtures and appurtenances, except as specifically provided for, are prohibited.

§179.300-15 Pressure relief devices.

(a) **Unless prohibited in part 173 of this chapter,** tanks shall be equipped with one or more safety relief devices of approved type, made of metal not subject to rapid deterioration by the lading and screwed directly into tank heads or attached to tank heads by other approved methods. The total discharge capacity shall be sufficient to prevent building up pressure in tank in excess of 82.5 percent of the tank test pressure. When safety relief devices of the fusible plug type are used, the required discharge capacity shall be available in each head. See AAR Specifications for Tank Cars, appendix A, for formula for calculating discharge capacity.

(b) **Threads for openings shall be** National Gas Taper Threads (NGT) tapped to gage, clean cut, even and without checks.

(c) **Pressure relief devices shall be set** for start-to-discharge and rupture discs shall burst at a pressure not exceeding that specified in §179.301.

(d) **Fusible plugs shall function at a temperature** not exceeding 175 °F and shall be vapor-tight at a temperature of not less than 130 °F.

§179.300-16 Tests of tanks.

(a) **After postweld heat treatment, tanks shall be** subjected to hydrostatic expansion test in a water jacket, or by other approved methods. No tank shall have been subjected previously to internal pressure within 100 pounds of the test pressure. Each tank shall be tested to the pressure prescribed in §179.301. Pressure shall be maintained for 30 seconds and sufficiently longer to insure complete expansion of tank. Pressure gage shall permit reading to accuracy of one percent. Expansion gage shall permit reading of total expansion to accuracy of one percent. Expansion shall be recorded in cubic cm.

(1) *No leaks* shall appear and permanent volumetric expansion shall not exceed 10 percent of total volumetric expansion at test pressure.

(2) *[Reserved]*

(b) **After all fittings have been installed,** each tank shall be subjected to interior air pressure test of at least 100 psig under conditions favorable to detection of any leakage. No leaks shall appear.

(c) **Repairs of leaks detected in manufacture** or in foregoing tests shall be made by the same process as employed in manufacture of tank. Caulking, soldering, or similar repairing is prohibited.

§179.300-17 Tests of pressure relief devices.

(a) **Each valve shall be tested by air or gas** before being put into service. The valve shall open and be vapor-tight at the pressure prescribed in §179.301.

(b) **Rupture discs of non-reclosing pressure relief devices** must be tested as prescribed in Appendix A, A5.03 of the AAR Manual of Standards and Recommended Practices, Section C — Part III, Specifications for Tank Cars, Specification M-1002, January 1996 (see §171.7 of this subchapter).

(c) **For pressure relief devices of the fusible plug type,** a sample of the plug used shall function at the temperatures prescribed in §179.300-15.

(d) **The start-to-discharge and vapor-tight pressures** shall not be affected by any auxiliary closure or other combination.

§179.300-18 Stamping.

(a) **To certify that the tank complies with all** specification requirements, each tank shall be plainly and permanently stamped in letters and figures 3/8 inch high into the metal of valve end chime as follows:

(1) *DOT Specification number.*

(2) *Material and cladding material* if any (immediately below the specification number).

(3) *Owner's or builder's* identifying symbol and serial number (immediately below the material identification). The symbol shall be registered with the Bureau of Explosives, duplications are not authorized.

(4) *Inspector's official mark* (immediately below the owner's or builder's symbol).

(5) *Date of original tank test* (month and year, such as 1-64 for January 1964). This should be so placed that dates of subsequent tests may easily be added thereto.

(6) *Water capacity — 0000 pounds.*

(b) **A copy of the above stamping in letters and figures** of the prescribed size stamped on a brass plate secured to one of the tank heads is authorized.

§179.300-19 Inspection.

(a) **Tank shall be inspected within** the United States and Canada by a competent and impartial inspector acceptable to the Bureau of Explosives. For tanks made outside the United States and Canada, the specified inspection shall be made within the United States.

(b) **The inspector shall carefully inspect all plates** from which tanks are to be made and secure records certifying that plates comply with the specification. Plates which do not comply with §179.300-7 shall be rejected.

(c) **The inspector shall make such inspection** as may be necessary to see that all the requirements of this specification, including markings, are fully complied with; shall see that the finished tanks are properly stress relieved and tested.

(d) **The inspector shall stamp his official mark** on each accepted tank as required in §179.300-18, and render the report required in §179.300-20.

§179.300-20 Reports.

(a) **Before a tank is placed in service,** the inspector shall furnish to the builder, tank owner, Bureau of Explosives and the Secretary, Mechanical Division, Association of American Railroads, a report in approved form certifying that the tank and its equipment comply with all the requirements of this specification.

(b) **For builder's Certificate of Construction, see §179.5 (b), (c), and (d).**

§179.301 Individual specification requirements for multi-unit tank car tanks.

(a) **In addition to §179.300 the individual** specification requirements are as follows:

DOT specification	106A500-X	106A800-X	110A500-W	110A600-W	110A800-W	110A1000-W
Minimum required bursting pressure, psig	(1)	(1)	1250	1500	2000	2500
Minimum thickness shell, inches	13/32	11/16	11/32	3/8	15/32	19/32
Test pressure, psig (see §179.300-16)	500	800	500	600	800	1000
Safety relief devices, psig (see §179.300-15)						
Start-to-discharge, or burst maximum, p.s.i.	375	600	375	450	600	700
Vapor-tight, minimum psig	300	480	300	360	480	650

1. None specified.

(b) [Reserved]

§179.302 [Reserved]

Subpart F - Specification for Cryogenic Liquid Tank Car Tanks & Seamless Steel Tanks (Classes DOT-113 and 107A)

§179.400 General specification applicable to cryogenic liquid tank car tanks.

§179.400-1 General.

A tank built to this specification must comply with §§179.400 and 179.401.

§179.400-3 Type.

(a) A tank built to this specification must —

(1) *Consist of an inner tank* of circular cross section supported essentially concentric within an outer jacket of circular cross section, with the out of roundness of both the inner tank and outer jacket limited in accordance with Section VIII, Division I, Paragraph UG-80 of the ASME Code;

(2) *Have the annular space* evacuated after filling the annular space with an approved insulating material;

(3) *Have the inner tank heads designed concave to pressure; and*

(4) *Have the outer jacket heads designed convex to pressure.*

(b) The tank must be equipped with piping systems for vapor venting and transfer of lading, and with pressure relief devices, controls, gages and valves, as prescribed herein.

§179.400-4 Insulation system and performance standard.

(a) For the purposes of this specification —

(1) **Standard Heat Transfer Rate (SHTR),** expressed in Btu/day/lb of water capacity, means the rate of heat transfer used for determining the satisfactory performance of the insulation system of a cryogenic tank car tank in cryogenic liquid service (see §179.401-1 table).

(2) **Test cryogenic liquid** means the cryogenic liquid, which may be different from the lading intended to be shipped in the tank, being used during the performance tests of the insulation system.

(3) **Normal evaporation rate (NER),** expressed in lbs. (of the cryogenic liquid)/day, means the rate of evaporation, determined by test of a test cryogenic liquid in a tank maintained at a pressure of approximately one atmosphere, absolute. This determination of the NER is the NER test.

(4) **Stabilization period** means the elapsed time after a tank car tank is filled with the test cryogenic liquid until the NER has stabilized, or 24 hours has passed, whichever is greater.

(5) **Calculated heat transfer rate.** The calculated heat transfer rate (CHTR) is determined by the use of test data obtained during the NER test in the formula:

$q = [N(\Delta h)(90-t_l)] / [V(8.32828)(t_s - t_f)]$

Where:

q = CHTR, in Btu/day/lb., of water capacity;

N = NER, determined by NER test, in lbs./day;

Δh = latent heat of vaporization of the test cryogenic liquid at the NER test pressure of approximately one atmosphere, absolute, in Btu/lb.;

90 = ambient temperature at 90 °F;

V = gross water volume at 60 °F of the inner tank, in gallons;

t_l = equilibrium temperature of intended lading at maximum shipping pressure, in °F;

8.32828 = constant for converting gallons of water at 60 °F to lbs. of water at 60 °F, in lbs./gallon;

t_s = average temperature of outer jacket, determined by averaging jacket temperatures at various locations on the jacket at regular intervals during the NER test, in °F;

t_f = equilibrium temperature of the test cryogenic liquid at the NER test pressure of approximately, one atmosphere, absolute, in °F.

(b) DOT-113A60W tank cars must —

(1) *Be filled* with hydrogen, cryogenic liquid to the maximum permitted fill density specified in §173.319(d)(2) table of this subchapter prior to performing the NER test; and

(2) *Have a CHTR* equal to or less than the SHTR specified in §179.401-1 table for a DOT-113A60W tank car.

(c) DOT-113C120W tank cars must —

(1) *Be filled* with ethylene, cryogenic liquid to the maximum permitted fill density specified in §173.319(d)(2) table of this subchapter prior to performing the NER test, or be filled with nitrogen, cryogenic liquid to 90 percent of the volumetric capacity of the inner tank prior to performing the NER test; and

(2) *Have a CHTR* equal to or less than 75 percent of the SHTR specified in §179.401-1 table for a DOT-113C120W tank car.

(d) Insulating materials must be approved.

(e) If the insulation consists of a powder having a tendency to settle, the entire top of the cylindrical portion of the inner tank must be insulated with a layer of glass fiber insulation at least one-inch nominal thickness, or equivalent, suitably held in position and covering an area extending 25 degrees to each side of the top center line of the inner tank.

(f) The outer jacket must be provided with fittings to permit effective evacuation of the annular space between the outer jacket and the inner tank.

(g) A device to measure the absolute pressure in the annular space must be provided. The device must be portable with an easily accessible connection or permanently positioned where it is readily visible to the operator.

§179.400-5 Materials.

(a) Stainless steel of ASTM A 240/ASTM A 240M (incorporated by reference, see §171.7 of this subchapter), Type 304 or 304L must be used for the inner tank and its appurtenances, as specified in AAR Specifications for Tank Cars, appendix M, and must be —

(1) *In the annealed condition* prior to fabrication, forming and fusion welding;

(2) *Suitable for use at the temperature of the lading; and*

(3) *Compatible with the lading.*

(b) Any steel casting, steel forging, steel structural shape or carbon steel plate used to fabricate the outer jacket or heads must be as specified in AAR Specifications for Tank Cars, appendix M.

(c) Impact tests must be —

(1) *Conducted in accordance* with AAR Specifications for Tank Cars, appendix W, W9.01;

(2) *Performed on longitudinal specimens of the material;*

(3) *Conducted at the tank design service temperature or colder; and*

(4) *Performed on* test plate welds and materials used for inner tanks and appurtenances and which will be subjected to cryogenic temperatures.

(d) Impact test values must be equal to or greater than those specified in AAR Specifications for Tank Cars, appendix W. The report of impact tests must include the test values and lateral expansion data.

§179.400-6 Bursting and buckling pressure.

(a) [Reserved]

(b) The outer jacket of the required evacuated insulation system must be designed in accordance with §179.400-8(d) and in addition must comply with the design loads specified in Section 6.2 of the AAR Specifications for Tank Cars. The designs and calculations must provide for the loadings transferred to the outer jacket through the support system.

§179.400-7 Tank heads.

(a) Tank heads of the inner tank and outer jacket must be flanged and dished, or ellipsoidal.

(b) Flanged and dished heads must have —

(1) *A main inside dish radius* not greater than the outside diameter of the straight flange;

(2) *An inside knuckle radius* of not less than 6 percent of the outside diameter of the straight flange; and

(3) *An inside knuckle radius* of at least three times the head thickness.

§179.400-8 Thickness of plates.

(a) The minimum wall thickness, after forming, of the inner shell and any 2:1 ellipsoidal head for the inner tank must be that specified in §179.401-1, or that calculated by the following formula, whichever is greater:

$t = Pd / 2SE$

Where:

t = minimum thickness of plate, after forming, in inches;

P = minimum required bursting pressure in psig;

d = inside diameter, in inches;

S = minimum tensile strength of the plate material, as prescribed in AAR Specifications for Tank Cars, appendix M, table M1, in psi;

E = 0.9, a factor representing the efficiency of welded joints, except that for seamless heads, E = 1.0.

(b) **The minimum wall thickness,** after forming, of any 3:1 ellipsoidal head for the inner tank must be that specified in §179.401-1, or that calculated by the following formula, whichever is greater:

$t = 1.83 Pd / 2SE$

Where:

t = minimum thickness of plate, after forming, in inches;

P = minimum required bursting pressure in psig;

d = inside diameter, in inches;

S = minimum tensile strength of the plate material, as prescribed in AAR Specifications for Tank Cars, Appendix M, Table M1, in psi;

E = 0.9, a factor representing the efficiency of welded joints, except that for seamless heads, E=1.0.

(c) **The minimum wall thickness,** after forming, of a flanged and dished head for the inner tank must be that specified in §179.401-1, or that calculated by the following formula, whichever is greater:

$t = [PL(3 + \sqrt{(L/r)})] / (8SE)$

Where:

t = minimum thickness of plate, after forming, in inches;

P = minimum required bursting pressure in psig;

L = main inside radius of dished head, in inches;

r = inside knuckle radius, in inches;

S = minimum tensile strength of plate material, as prescribed in AAR Specifications for Tank Cars, appendix M, table M1, in psi;

E = 0.9, a factor representing the efficiency of welded joints, except that for seamless heads, E = 1.0.

(d) **The minimum wall thickness,** after forming, of the outer jacket shell may not be less than 7/16 inch. The minimum wall thickness, after forming, of the outer jacket heads may not be less than 1/2 inch and they must be made from steel specified in §179.16(c). The annular space is to be evacuated, and the cylindrical portion of the outer jacket between heads, or between stiffening rings if used, must be designed to withstand an external pressure of 37.5 psig (critical collapsing pressure), as determined by the following formula:

$P_c = [2.6E(t/D)^{2.5}] / [(L/D) - 0.45(t/D)^{0.5}]$

Where:

P_c = Critical collapsing pressure (37.5 psig minimum) in psig;

E = modulus of elasticity of jacket material, in psi;

t = minimum thickness of jacket material, after forming, in inches;

D = outside diameter of jacket, in inches;

L = distance between stiffening ring centers in inches. (The heads may be considered as stiffening rings located 1/3 of the head depth from the head tangent line.)

§179.400-9 Stiffening rings.

(a) **If stiffening rings are used in designing** the cylindrical portion of the outer jacket for external pressure, they must be attached to the jacket by means of fillet welds. Outside stiffening ring attachment welds must be continuous on each side of the ring. Inside stiffening ring attachment welds may be intermittent welds on each side of the ring with the total length of weld on each side not less than one-third of the circumference of the tank. The maximum space between welds may not exceed eight times the outer jacket wall thickness.

(b) **A portion of the outer jacket may be included** when calculating the moment of inertia of the ring. The effective width of jacket plate on each side of the attachment of the stiffening ring is given by the following formula:

$W = 0.78(Rt)^{0.5}$

Where:

W = width of jacket effective on each side of the stiffening ring, in inches;

R = outside radius of the outer jacket, in inches;

t = plate thickness of the outer jacket, after forming, in inches.

(c) **Where a stiffening ring is used that consists** of a closed section having two webs attached to the outer jacket, the jacket plate between the webs may be included up to the limit of twice the value of "W", as defined in paragraph (b) of this section. The outer flange of the closed section, if not a steel structural shape, is subject to the same limitations with "W" based on the "R" and "t" values of the flange. Where two separate members such as two angles, are located less than "2W" apart they may be treated as a single stiffening ring member. (The maximum length of plate which may be considered effective is 4W.) The closed section between an external ring and the outer jacket must be provided with a drain opening.

(d) **The stiffening ring must have a moment of inertia** large enough to support the critical collapsing pressure, as determined by either of the following formulas:

$I = [0.035D^3 LP_c] / E$,

or

$I' = [0.046D^3 LP_c] / E$

Where:

I = required moment of inertia of stiffening ring about the centroidal axis parallel to the vessel axis, in inches to the fourth power;

I' = required moment of inertia of combined section of stiffening ring and effective width of jacket plate about the centroidal axis parallel to the vessel axis, in inches to the fourth power;

D = outside diameter of the outer jacket, in inches;

L = one-half of the distance from the centerline of the stiffening ring to the next line of support on one side, plus one-half of the distance from the centerline to the next line of support on the other side of stiffening ring. Both distances are measured parallel to the axis of the vessel, in inches. (A line of support is:

(1) A stiffening ring which meets the requirements of this paragraph, or

(2) A circumferential line of a head at one-third the depth of the head from the tangent line);

P_c = critical collapsing pressure (37.5 psig minimum) in psig;

E = modulus of elasticity of stiffening ring material, in psi.

(e) **Where loads are applied to the outer jacket** or to stiffening rings from the system used to support the inner tank within the outer jacket, additional stiffening rings, or an increased moment of inertia of the stiffening rings designed for the external pressure, must be provided to carry the support loads.

§179.400-10 Sump or siphon bowl.

A sump or siphon bowl may be in the bottom of the inner tank shell if —

(a) **It is formed directly into the inner tank shell,** or is formed and welded to the inner tank shell and is of weldable quality metal that is compatible with the inner tank shell;

(b) **The stress in any orientation under any condition** does not exceed the circumferential stress in the inner tank shell; and

(c) **The wall thickness is not less than that specified in §179.401-1.**

§179.400-11 Welding.

(a) **Except for closure of openings and a maximum** of two circumferential closing joints in the cylindrical portion of the outer jacket, each joint of an inner tank and the outer jacket must be a fusion double welded butt joint.

(b) **The closure for openings and the circumferential** closing joints in the cylindrical portion of the outer jacket, including head to shell joints, may be a single welded butt joint using a backing strip on the inside of the joint.

(c) **Each joint must be welded in accordance with** the requirements of AAR Specifications for Tank Cars, appendix W.

(d) **Each welding procedure, welder, and fabricator must be approved.**

§179.400-12 Postweld heat treatment.

(a) **Postweld heat treatment of the inner tank is not required.**

(b) **The cylindrical portion of the outer jacket,** with the exception of the circumferential closing seams, must be postweld heat treated as prescribed in AAR Specifications for Tank Cars, appendix W. Any item to be welded to this portion of the outer jacket must be attached before postweld heat treatment. Welds securing the following need not be postweld heat treated when it is not practical due to final assembly procedures:

(1) *the inner tank support system to the outer jacket,*

(2) *connections at piping penetrations,*

(3) *closures for access openings, and*

(4) *circumferential closing joints of head to shell joints.*

(c) **When cold formed heads are used on** the outer jacket they must be heat treated before welding to the jacket shell if postweld heat treatment is not practical due to assembly procedures.

§179.400-13 Support system for inner tank.

(a) **The inner tank must be supported** within the outer jacket by a support system of approved design. The system and its areas of attachment to the outer jacket must have adequate strength and ductility at operating temperatures to support the inner tank when filled with the lading to any level incident to transportation.

(b) **The support system must be designed to support,** without yielding, impact loads producing accelerations of the following magnitudes and directions when the inner tank is fully loaded and the car is equipped with a conventional draft gear:

Longitudinal..7"g"
Transverse..3"g"
Vertical..3"g"

The longitudinal acceleration may be reduced to 3"g" where a cushioning device of approved design, which has been tested to demonstrate its ability to limit body forces to 400,000 pounds maximum at 10 miles per hour, is used between the coupler and the tank structure.

(c) **The inner tank and outer jacket** must be permanently bonded to each other electrically, by either the support system, piping, or a separate electrical connection of approved design.

§179.400-14 Cleaning of inner tank.

The interior of the inner tank and all connecting lines must be thoroughly cleaned and dried prior to use. Proper precautions must be taken to avoid contamination of the system after cleaning.

§179.400-15 Radioscopy.

Each longitudinal and circumferential joint of the inner tank, and each longitudinal and circumferential double welded butt joint of the outer jacket, must be examined along its entire length in accordance with the requirements of AAR Specifications for Tank Cars, appendix W.

§179.400-16 Access to inner tank.

(a) **The inner tank must be provided** with a means of access having a minimum inside diameter of 16 inches. Reinforcement of the access opening must be made of the same material used in the inner tank. The access closure must be of an approved material and design.

(b) **If a welded closure is used, it must be designed** to allow it to be reopened by grinding or chipping and to be closed again by rewelding, preferably without a need for new parts. A cutting torch may not be used.

§179.400-17 Inner tank piping.

(a) **Product lines.** The piping system for vapor and liquid phase transfer and venting must be made for material compatible with the product and having satisfactory properties at the lading temperature. The outlets of all vapor phase and liquid phase lines must be located so that accidental discharge from these lines will not impinge on any metal of the outer jacket, car structures, trucks or safety appliances. Suitable provision must be made to allow for thermal expansion and contraction.

(1) *Loading and unloading line.* A liquid phase transfer line must be provided and it must have a manually operated shut-off valve located as close as practicable to the outer jacket, plus a secondary closure that is liquid and gas tight. This secondary closure must permit any trapped pressure to bleed off before the closure can be removed completely. A vapor trap must be incorporated in the line and located as close as practicable to the inner tank. On a DOT-113A60W tank car, any loading and unloading line must be vacuum jacketed between the outer jacket and the shut-off valve and the shut-off valve must also be vacuum jacketed.

(2) *Vapor phase line.* A vapor phase line must connect to the inner tank and must be of sufficient size to permit the pressure relief devices specified in §179.400-20 and connected to this line to operate at their design capacity without excessive pressure build-up in the tank. The vapor phase line must have a manually operated shut-off valve located as close as practicable to the outer jacket, plus a secondary closure that is liquid and gas tight. This secondary closure must permit any trapped pressure to bleed off before the closure can be removed completely.

(3) *Vapor phase blowdown line.* A blowdown line must be provided. It must be attached to the vapor phase line specified in paragraph (a)(2) of this section, upstream of the shut-off valve in that line. A by-pass line with a manually operated shut-off valve must be provided to permit reduction of the inner tank pressure when the vapor phase line is connected to a closed system. The discharge from this line must be outside the housing and must be directed upward and away from operating personnel.

(b) **Any pressure building system provided** for the purpose of pressurizing the vapor space of the inner tank to facilitate unloading the liquid lading must be approved.

§179.400-18 Test of inner tank.

(a) **After all items to be welded to the inner tank** have been welded in place, the inner tank must be pressure tested at the test pressure prescribed in §179.401-1. The temperature of the pressurizing medium may not exceed 100 °F during the test. The inner tank must hold the prescribed pressure for a period of not less than ten minutes without leakage or distortion. In a pneumatic test, due regard for the protection of all personnel should be taken because of the potential hazard involved. After a hydrostatic test the container and piping must be emptied of all water and purged of all water vapor.

(b) **Caulking of welded joints to stop leaks** developed during the test is prohibited. Repairs to welded joints must be made as prescribed in AAR Specifications for Tank Cars, appendix W.

§179.400-19 Valves and gages.

(a) **Valves.** Manually operated shut-off valves and control valves must be provided wherever needed for control of vapor phase pressure, vapor phase venting, liquid transfer and liquid flow rates. All valves must be made from approved materials compatible with the lading and having satisfactory properties at the lading temperature.

(1) *Liquid control valves must be of extended stem design.*

(2) *Packing, if used,* must be satisfactory for use in contact with the lading and of approved materials that will effectively seal the valve stem without causing difficulty of operation.

(3) *Each control valve* and shut-off valve must be readily operable. These valves must be mounted so that their operation will not transmit excessive forces to the piping system.

(b) **Gages.** Gages, except portable units, must be securely mounted within suitable protective housings. A liquid level gage and a vapor phase pressure gage must be provided as follows:

(1) *Liquid level gage.*

(i) *A gage of approved design* to indicate the quantity of liquefied lading within the inner tank, mounted where it will be readily visible to an operator during transfer operations or storage, or a portable gage with a readily accessible connection, or

(ii) *A fixed length dip tube,* with a manually operated shut-off valve located as close as practicable to the outer jacket. The dip tube must indicate the maximum liquid level for the allowable filling density. The inner end of the dip tube must be located on the longitudinal centerline of the inner tank and within four feet of the transverse centerline of the inner tank.

(2) *Vapor phase pressure gage.* A vapor phase pressure gage of approved design, with a manually operated shut-off valve located as close as practicable to the outer jacket. The gage must indicate the vapor pressure within the inner tank and must be mounted where it will be readily visible to an operator. An additional fitting for use of a test gage must be provided.

§179.400-20 Pressure relief devices.

(a) **The tank must be provided with pressure relief devices** for the protection of the tank assembly and piping system. The discharge from these devices must be directed away from operating personnel, principal load bearing members of the outer jacket, car structure, trucks and safety appliances. Vent or weep holes in pressure relief devices are prohibited. All main pressure relief devices must discharge to the outside of the protective housings in which they are located, except that this requirement does not apply to pressure relief valves installed to protect isolated sections of lines between the final valve and end closure.

(b) **Materials.** Materials used in pressure relief devices must be suitable for use at the temperature of the lading and otherwise compatible with the lading in both the liquid and vapor phases.

(c) **Inner tank.** Pressure relief devices for the inner tank must be attached to vapor phase piping and mounted so as to remain at ambient temperature prior to operation. The inner tank must be equipped with one or more pressure relief valves and one or more safety vents (except as noted in paragraph (c)(3)(iv) of this section), and installed without an intervening shut-off valve (except as noted in paragraph (c)(3)(iii) of this section). Additional requirements are as follows:

(1) *Safety vent.* The safety vent shall function at the pressure specified in §179.401-1. The safety vent must be flow rated in accordance with the applicable provisions of AAR Specifications for Tank Cars, appendix A, and provide sufficient capacity to meet the requirements of AAR Specifications for Tanks Cars, appendix A, A8.07(a).

(2) *Pressure relief valve.* The pressure relief valve must:

(i) *be set* to start-to-discharge at the pressure specified in §179.401-1, and

(ii) *meet the requirements* of AAR Specifications for Tank Cars, appendix A, A8.07(b).

(3) *Installation of safety vent and pressure relief valve.*

(i) *Inlet piping.*

[A] The opening through all piping and fittings between the inner tank and its pressure relief devices must have a cross-sectional area at least equal to that of the pressure relief device inlet, and the flow characteristics of this upstream system must be such that the pressure drop

will not adversely affect the relieving capacity or the proper operation of the pressure relief device.

[B] When the required relief capacity is met by the use of multiple pressure relief device placed on one connection, the inlet internal cross-sectional area of this connection must be sufficient to provide the required flow capacity for the proper operation of the pressure relief device system.

(ii) *Outlet piping.*

[A] The opening through the discharge lines must have a cross-sectional area at least equal to that of the pressure relief device outlet and may not reduce the relieving capacity below that required to properly protect the inner tank.

[B] When the required relieving capacity is met by use of multiple pressure relief devices placed on a common discharge manifold, the manifold outlet internal cross-sectional area must be at least equal to the combined outlet areas of the pressure relief devices.

(iii) *Duplicate pressure relief devices* may be used when an approved 3-way selector valve is installed to provide for relief through either duplicate pressure relief device. The 3-way valve must be included in the mounting prescribed by AAR Specifications for Tank Cars, appendix A, A6.02(g), when conducting the flow capacity test on the safety vent prescribed by AAR Specifications for Tank Cars, appendix A, A6.01. Flow capacity tests must be performed with the 3-way valve at both of the extreme positions as well as at the mid-position and the flow capacity must be in accordance with AAR Specifications for Tank Cars, appendix A, A8.07(a).

(iv) *An alternate pressure relief valve,* set as required in §179.401-1, may be used in lieu of the safety vent, provided it meets the flow capacity prescribed in AAR Specifications for Tank Cars, appendix A at a flow rating pressure of 110 percent of its start-to-discharge pressure. Installation must —

[A] Prevent moisture accumulation at the seat by providing drainage away from that area,

[B] Permit periodic drainage of the vent piping, and

[C] Prevent accumulation of foreign material in the vent system.

(4) *Evaporation control.* The routine release of vaporized lading may be controlled with a pressure controlling and mixing device, except that a pressure controlling and mixing device is required on each DOT-113A60W car. Any pressure controlling and mixing device must —

(i) *Be set* to start-to-discharge at a pressure not greater than that specified in §179.401-1;

(ii) *Have sufficient capacity* to limit the pressure within the inner tank to that pressure specified in §179.401-1, when the discharge is equal to twice the normal venting rate during transportation, with normal vacuum and the outer shell at 130 °F; and

(iii) *Prevent the discharge* of a gas mixture exceeding 50% of the lower flammability limit to the atmosphere under normal conditions of storage or transportation.

(5) *Safety interlock.* If a safety interlock is provided for the purpose of allowing transfer of lading at a pressure higher than the pressure control valve setting but less than the pressure relief valve setting, the design must be such that the safety interlock will not affect the discharge path of the pressure relief value or safety vent at any time. The safety interlock must automatically provide an unrestricted discharge path for the pressure control device at all times when the tank car is in transport service.

(d) **Outer jacket.** The outer jacket must be provided with a suitable system to prevent buildup of annular space pressure in excess of 16 psig or the external pressure for which the inner tank was designed, whichever is less. The total relief area provided by the system must be a minimum of 25 square inches, and means must be provided to prevent clogging of any system opening, as well as to ensure adequate communication to all areas of the insulation space. If a safety vent is a part of the system, it must be designed to prevent distortion of the rupture disc when the annular space is evacuated.

(e) **Piping system.** Where a piping circuit can be isolated by closing a valve, means for pressure relief must be provided.

§179.400-21 Test of pressure relief valves.

Each valve must be tested with air or gas for compliance with §179.401-1 before being put into service.

§179.400-22 Protective housings.

Each valve, gage, closure and pressure relief device, with the exception of secondary relief valves for the protection of isolated piping, must be enclosed within a protective housing. The protective housing must be adequate to protect the enclosed components from direct solar radiation, mud, sand, adverse environmental exposure and mechanical damage incident to normal operation of the tank car. It must be designed to provide reasonable access to the enclosed components for operation, inspection and maintenance and so that vapor concentrations cannot build up to a dangerous level inside the housing in the event of valve leakage or pressure relief valve operation. All equipment within the protective housing must be operable by personnel wearing heavy gloves and must incorporate provisions for locks or seals. A protective housing and its cover must be constructed of metal not less than 0.119 inch thick.

§179.400-23 Operating instructions.

All valves and gages must be clearly identified with corrosion-resistant nameplates. A plate of corrosion-resistant material bearing precautionary instructions for the safe operation of the equipment during storage and transfer operations must be securely mounted so as to be readily visible to an operator. The instruction plate must be mounted in each housing containing operating equipment and controls for product handling. These instructions must include a diagram of the tank and its piping system with the various gages, control valves and pressure relief devices clearly identified and located.

§179.400-24 Stamping.

(a) **A tank that complies with all** specification requirements must have the following information plainly and permanently stamped into the metal near the center of the head of the outer jacket at the "B" end of the car, in letters and figures at least 3/8-inch high, in the following order:

	Examples of required stamping
Specification	DOT-113A60W
Design service temperature	Minus 423 °F
Inner tank	Inner Tank
Material	ASTM A240-304
Shell thickness	Shell 3/16 inch
Head thickness	Head 3/16 inch
Inside diameter	ID 107 inch
Inner tank builder's initials	ABC
Date of original test (month and year) and initials of person conducting original test	00-0000GHK
Water capacity	00000 lbs
Outer jacket	Outer jacket
Material	ASTM A515-70
Outer jacket builder's initials	DEF
Car assembler's initials (if other than inner tank or outer jacket builder)	XYZ

(b) **Any stamping on the shell or heads** of the inner tank is prohibited.

(c) **In lieu of the stamping required by paragraph (a)** of this section, the specified markings may be incorporated on a data plate of corrosion-resistant metal, fillet welded in place on the head of the outer jacket at the "B" end of the car.

§179.400-25 Stenciling.

Each tank car must be stenciled in compliance with the provisions of the AAR Specifications for Tank Cars, appendix C. The stenciling must also include the following:

(a) **The date on which the rupture disc was last replaced** and the initials of the person making the replacement, on the outer jacket in letters and figures at least 1 1/2 inches high.

(b) **The design service temperature and maximum lading weight,** in letters and figures at least 1 1/2 inches high adjacent to the hazardous material stencil.

(c) **The water capacity, in pounds net at 60 °F,** with the tank at its coldest operating temperature, after deduction for the volume above the inlet to the pressure relief device or pressure control valve, structural members, baffles, piping, and other appurtenances inside the tank, in letters and figures at least 1 1/2 inches high.

(d) **Both sides of the tank car, in letters** at least 1 1/2 inches high, with the statement "Do Not Hump or Cut Off While in Motion."

(e) **The outer jacket,** below the tank classification stencil, in letters at least 1 1/2 inches high, with the statement, "vacuum jacketed."

§179.401 Individual specification requirements applicable to inner tanks for cryogenic liquid tank car tanks.

§179.401-1 Individual specification requirements.

In addition to §179.400, the individual specification requirements for the inner tank and its appurtenances are as follows:

DOT specification	113A60W	113C120W
Design service temperature, °F	-423	-260
Material	§179.400-5	§179.400-5
Impact test (weld and plate material)	§179.400-5(c)	§179.400-5(c)
Impact test values	§179.400-5(d)	§179.400-5(d)
Standard heat transfer rate (Btu per day per lb. of water capacity, max.) (see §179.400-4)	0.097	0.4121
Bursting pressure, min. psig	240	300
Minimum plate thickness shell, inches (see §179.400-7(a))	3/16	3/16
Minimum head thickness, inches (see §179.400-8 (a), (b), and (c))	3/16	3/16
Test pressure, psig (see §179.400-16)	60	120
Safety vent bursting pressure, max. psig	60	120
Pressure relief valve start-to-discharge pressure, psig (± 3 psi)	30	75
Pressure relief valve vapor tight pressure, min. psig	24	60
Pressure relief valve flow rating pressure, max. psig	40	85
Alternate pressure relief valve start to-discharge pressure, psig (± 3 psi)		90
Alternate pressure relief valve vapor tight pressure, min. psig		72
Alternate pressure relief valve flow rating pressure, max. psig		100
Pressure control valve Start-to-vent, max. psig (see §179.400-20(c)(4))	17	Not required
Relief device discharge restrictions	§179.400-20	179.400-20
Transfer line insulation	§179.400-17	Not required

§179.500 Specification DOT-107A * * * * seamless steel tank car tanks.

§179.500-1 Tanks built under these specifications shall meet the requirements of §179.500.

§179.500-3 Type and general requirements.

(a) **Tanks built under this specification shall be** hollow forged or drawn in one piece. Forged tanks shall be machined inside and outside before ends are necked-down and, after necking-down, the ends shall be machined to size on the ends and outside diameter. Machining not necessary on inside or outside of seamless steel tubing, but required on ends after necking-down.

(b) **For tanks made in foreign countries,** chemical analysis of material and all tests as specified must be carried out within the limits of the United States under supervision of a competent and disinterested inspector; in addition to which, provisions in §179.500-18 (b) and (c) shall be carried out at the point of manufacture by a recognized inspection bureau with principal office in the United States.

(c) **The term "marked end" and "marked test pressure"** used throughout this specification are defined as follows:

(1) **Marked end** is that end of the tank on which marks prescribed in §179.500-17 are stamped.

(2) **Marked test pressure** is that pressure in psig which is indicated by the figures substituted for the **** in the marking DOT-107A **** stamped on the marked end of tank.

(d) **The gas pressure at 130 °F in the tank** shall not exceed 7/10 of the marked test pressure of the tank.

§179.500-4 Thickness of wall.

(a) **Minimum thickness of wall of each finished tank** shall be such that at a pressure equal to 7/10 of the marked test pressure of the tank, the calculated fiber stress in psi at inner wall of tank multiplied by 3.0 will not exceed the tensile strength of any specimen taken from the tank and tested as prescribed in §179.500-7(b). Minimum wall thickness shall be 1/4 inch.

(b) **Calculations to determine the maximum marked** test pressure permitted to be marked on the tank shall be made by the formula:
$P = [10S(D^2 - d^2)] / [7(D^2 + d^2)]$

Where:
P = Maximum marked test pressure permitted;
S = U / 3.0
Where:
U = Tensile strength of that specimen which shows the lower tensile strength of the two specimens taken from the tank and tested as prescribed in §179.500-7(b).
3 = Factor of safety.
$(D^2 - d^2 / (D^2 + d^2)$ = The smaller value obtained for this factor by the operations specified in §179.500-4(c).

(c) **Measure at one end,** in a plane perpendicular to the longitudinal axis of the tank and at least 18 inches from that end before necking-down:

d = Maximum inside diameter (inches) for the location under consideration; to be determined by direct measurement to an accuracy of 0.05 inch.

t = Minimum thickness of wall for the location under consideration; to be determined by direct measurement to an accuracy of 0.001 inch.

Take D = d + 2t.

Calculate the value of $(D^2 - d^2) / (D^2 + d^2)$

(1) *Make similar measurements* and calculation for a corresponding location at the other end of the tank.

(2) *Use the smaller result obtained,* from the foregoing, in making calculations prescribed in paragraph (b) of this section.

§179.500-5 Material.

(a) **Tanks shall be made from open-hearth or electric steel** of uniform quality. Material shall be free from seams, cracks, laminations, or other defects injurious to finished tank. If not free from such defects, the surface may be machined or ground to eliminate these defects. Forgings and seamless tubing for bodies of tanks shall be stamped with heat numbers.

(b) **Steel (see Note 1) must conform** to the following requirements as to chemical composition:

Designation	Class I (percent)	Class II (percent)	Class III (percent)
Carbon, maximum	0.50	0.50	0.53
Manganese, maximum	1.65	1.65	1.85
Phosphorus, maximum	.05	.05	.05
Sulphur, maximum	.06	.05	.05
Silicon, maximum	.35	.30	.37
Molybdenum, maximum		.25	.30
Chromium, maximum		.30	.30
Sum of manganese and carbon not over	2.10	2.10	

NOTE 1: Alternate steel containing other alloying elements may be used if approved.

(1) *For instructions* as to the obtaining and checking of chemical analysis, see §179.500-18(b)(3).

(2) *[Reserved]*

§179.500-6 Heat treatment.

(a) **Each necked-down tank shall be uniformly heat treated.** Heat treatment shall consist of annealing or normalizing and tempering for Class I, Class II and Class III steel or oil quenching and tempering for Class III steel. Tempering temperatures shall not be less than 1000 °F. Heat treatment of alternate steels shall be approved. All scale shall be removed from outside of tank to an extent sufficient to allow proper inspection.

(b) **To check uniformity of heat treatment,** Brinnel hardness tests shall be made at 18 inch intervals on the entire longitudinal axis. The hardness shall not vary more than 35 points in the length of the tank. No hardness tests need be taken within 12 inches from point of head to shell tangency.

(c) **A magnetic particle inspection shall be performed** after heat treatment on all tanks subjected to a quench and temper treatment to detect the presence of quenching cracks. Cracks shall be removed to sound metal by grinding and the surface exposed shall be blended smoothly into the surrounding area. A wall thickness check shall then be made of the affected area by ultrasonic equipment or other suitable means acceptable to the inspector and if the remaining wall thickness is less than the minimum recorded thickness as determined by §179.500-4(b) it shall be used for making the calculation prescribed in paragraph (b) of this section.

§179.500-7 Physical tests.

(a) **Physical tests shall be made on two test specimens** 0.505 inch in diameter within 2-inch gauge length, taken 180 degrees apart, one from each ring section cut from each end of each forged or drawn tube before necking-down, or one from each prolongation at each end of each necked-down tank. These test specimen ring sections or prolongations shall be heat treated, with the necked-down tank which they represent. The width of the test specimen ring section must be at least its wall thickness. Only when diameters and wall thickness will not permit removal of 0.505 by 2-inch tensile test bar, laid in the transverse direction, may test bar cut in the longitudinal direction be substituted. When the thickness will not permit obtaining a 0.505 specimen, then the largest diameter specimen obtainable in the longitudinal direction shall be used. Specimens shall have bright surface and a reduced section. When 0.505 specimen is not used the gauge length shall be a ratio of 4 to 1 length to diameter.

(b) **Elastic limit as determined by extensometer,** shall not exceed 70 percent of tensile strength for class I steel or 85 percent of tensile strength for class II and class III steel. Determination shall be made at cross head speed of not more than 0.125 inch per minute with an extensometer reading to 0.0002 inch. The extensometer shall be read at increments of stress not exceeding 5,000 psi. The stress at which the strain first exceeds

stress (psi) / 30,000,000 (psi) +0.005 (inches per inch)

shall be recorded as the elastic limit.

(1) *Elongation shall be* at least 18 percent and reduction of area at least 35 percent.

NOTE 1: Upon approval, the ratio of elastic limit to ultimate strength may be raised to permit use of special alloy steels of definite composition that will give equal or better physical properties than steels herein specified.

(2) *[Reserved]*

§179.500-8 Openings in tanks.

(a) **Each end shall be closed by a cover made of forged steel.** Covers shall be secured to ends of tank by through bolts or studs not entering interior of tank. Covers shall be of a thickness sufficient to meet test requirements of §179.500-12 and to compensate for the openings closed by attachments prescribed herein.

(1) *It is also provided* that each end may be closed by internal threading to accommodate an approved fitting. The internal threads as well as the threads on fittings for these openings shall be clean cut, even, without checks, and tapped to gauge. Taper threads are required and shall be of a length not less than as specified for American Standard taper pipe threads. External threading of an approved type shall be permissible on the internal threaded ends.

(b) **Joints between covers and ends and between** cover and attachments shall be of approved form and made tight against vapor or liquid leakage by means of a confined gasket of suitable material.

§179.500-10 Protective housing.

(a) **Safety devices, and loading and unloading valves** on tanks shall be protected from accidental damage by approved metal housing, arranged so it may be readily opened to permit inspection and adjustment of safety relief devices and valves, and securely locked in closed position. Housing shall be provided with opening having an opening equal to twice the total discharge area of pressure relief device enclosed.

(b) [Reserved]

§179.500-11 Loading and unloading valves.

(a) **Loading and unloading valve or valves** shall be mounted on the cover or threaded into the marked end of tank. These valves shall be of approved type, made of metal not subject to rapid deterioration by lading or in service, and shall withstand without leakage a pressure equal to the marked test pressure of tank. Provision shall be made for closing service outlet of valves.

(b) [Reserved]

§179.500-12 Pressure relief devices.

(a) **Tank shall be equipped with one or more** pressure relief devices of approved type and discharge area, mounted on the cover or threaded into the non-marked end of the tank. If fittings are mounted on a cover, they shall be of the flanged type, made of metal not subject to rapid deterioration by lading or in service. Total flow capacity shall be such that, with tank filled with air at pressure equal to 70 percent of the marked test pressure of tank, flow capacity will be sufficient to reduce air pressure to 30 percent of the marked test pressure within 3 minutes after pressure relief device opens.

(b) **Safety relief devices shall open at pressure** not exceeding the marked test pressure of tank and not less than 7/10 of marked test pressure. (For tolerance for safety relief valves, see §179.500-16(a).)

(c) **Cars used for the transportation of flammable gases** shall have the safety devices equipped with an approved ignition device.

§179.500-13 Fixtures.

(a) **Attachments, other than those mounted** on tank covers or serving as threaded closures for the ends of the tank, are prohibited.

(b) [Reserved]

§179.500-14 Test of tanks.

(a) **After heat-treatment, tanks shall be subjected** to hydrostatic tests in a water jacket, or by other accurate method, operated so as to obtain reliable data. No tank shall have been subjected previously to internal pressure greater than 90 percent of the marked test pressure. Each tank shall be tested to a pressure at least equal to the marked test pressure of the tank. Pressure shall be maintained for 30 seconds, and sufficiently longer to insure complete expansion of tank. Pressure gauge shall permit reading to accuracy of one percent. Expansion gauge shall permit reading of total expansion to accuracy of one percent. Expansion shall be recorded in cubic cm.

(b) **No leaks shall appear and permanent** volumetric expansion shall not exceed 10 percent of the total volumetric expansion at test pressure.

§179.500-15 Handling of tanks failing in tests.

(a) **Tanks rejected for failure in any of the tests** prescribed may be reheat-treated, and will be acceptable if subsequent to reheat-treatment they are subjected to and pass all of the tests.

(b) [Reserved]

§179.500-16 Tests of pressure relief devices.

(a) **Pressure relief valves shall be tested** by air or gas before being put into service. Valve shall open at pressure not exceeding the marked test pressure of tank and shall be vapor-tight at 80 percent of the marked test pressure. These limiting pressures shall not be affected by any auxiliary closure or other combination.

(b) **For pressure relief devices that incorporate** a rupture disc, samples of the discs used shall burst at a pressure not exceeding the marked test pressure of tank and not less than 7/10 of marked test pressure.

§179.500-17 Marking.

(a) **Each tank shall be plainly and permanently marked,** thus certifying that tank complies with all requirements of this specification. These marks shall be stamped into the metal of necked-down section of tank at marked end, in letters and figures at least 1/4 inch high, as follows:

(1) *Spec. DOT-107A * * * *,* the * * * * to be replaced by figures indicating marked test pressure of the tank. This pressure shall not exceed the calculated maximum marked test pressure permitted, as determined by the formula in §179.500-4(b).

(2) *Serial number* immediately below the stamped mark specified in paragraph (a)(1) of this section.

(3) *Inspector's official mark* immediately below the stamped mark specified in paragraph (a)(1) of this section.

(4) *Name, mark* (other than trademark), or initials of company or person for whose use tank is being made, which shall be recorded with the Bureau of Explosives.

(5) *Date* (such as 1-01, for January 2001) of tank test, so placed that dates of subsequent tests may easily be added.

(6) *Date* (such as 1-01, for January 2001) of latest test of pressure relief device or of the rupture disc, required only when tank is used for transportation of flammable gases.

(b) [Reserved]

§179.500-18 Inspection and reports.

(a) **Before a tank car is placed in service,** the party assembling the completed car shall furnish to car owner, Bureau of Explosives, and the Secretary, Mechanical Division, Association of American Railroads, a report in proper form certifying that tanks and their equipment comply with all the requirements of this specification and including information as to serial numbers, dates of tests, and ownership marks on tanks mounted on car structure.

(b) **Purchaser of tanks shall provide for** inspection by a competent inspector as follows:

(1) *Inspector shall carefully inspect* all material and reject that not complying with §179.500-5.

(2) *Inspector shall stamp* his official mark on each forging or seamless tube accepted by him for use in making tanks, and shall verify proper application of heat number to such material by occasional inspections at steel manufacturer's plant.

(3) *Inspector shall obtain* certified chemical analysis of each heat of material.

(4) *Inspector shall make* inspection of inside surface of tanks before necking-down, to insure that no seams, cracks, laminations, or other defects exist.

(5) *Inspector shall fully verify* compliance with specification, verify heat treatment of tank as proper; obtain samples for all tests and check chemical analyses; witness all tests; and report minimum thickness of tank wall, maximum inside diameter, and calculated value of D, for each end of each tank as prescribed in §179.500-4(c).

(6) *Inspector shall stamp* his official mark on each accepted tank immediately below serial number, and make certified report (see paragraph (c) of this section) to builder, to company or person for whose use tanks are being made, to builder of car structure on which tanks are to be mounted, to the Bureau of Explosives, and to the Secretary, Mechanical Division, Association of American Railroads.

(c) Inspector's report required herein shall be in the following form:

(Place) ____________________

(Date) ____________________

STEEL TANKS

It is hereby certified that drawings were submitted for these tanks under AAR Application for Approval ____________ and approved by the AAR Committee on Tank Cars under date of ___/___/___.

Built for ____________________ Company

Location at ____________________

Built by ____________________ Company

Location at ____________________

Consigned to ____________________ Company

Location at ____________________

Quantity ____________________

Length (inches) ________

Outside diameter (inches) ________

Marks stamped into tank as required in §179.500-17 are:

DOT-107A* * * *

Note 1: The marked test pressure substituted for the * * * * on each tank is shown on Record of General Data on Tanks attached hereto.

Serial numbers ____________ to ____________ inclusive

Inspector's mark ____________________

Owner's mark ____________________

Test date ____________________

Water capacity (see Record of Hydrostatic Tests).

Tare weights (yes or no) (see Record of Hydrostatic Tests).

These tanks were made by process of ____________________

Steel used was identified as indicated by the attached list showing the serial number of each tank, followed by the heat number.

Steel used was verified as to chemical analysis and record thereof is attached hereto. Heat numbers were stamped into metal. All material was inspected and each tank was inspected both before and after closing in ends; all material accepted was found free from seams, cracks, laminations, and other defects which might prove injurious to strength of tank. Processes of manufacture and heat-treatment of tanks were witnessed and found to be efficient and satisfactory.

Before necking-down ends, each tank was measured at each location prescribed in §179.500-4(c) and minimum wall thickness in inches at each location was recorded; maximum inside diameter in inches at each location was recorded; value of D in inches at each location was calculated and recorded; maximum fiber stress in wall at location showing larger value for

$(D^2+d^2)/(D^2-d^2)$

was calculated for 7/10 the marked test pressure and recorded. Calculations were made by the formula:

$S=[0.7P(D^2-d^2)/(D^2+d^2)]$

Hydrostatic tests, tensile test of material, and other tests as prescribed in this specification, were made in the presence of the inspector, and all material and tanks accepted were found to be in compliance with the requirements of this specification. Records thereof are attached hereto.

I hereby certify that all of these tanks proved satisfactory in every way and comply with the requirements of Department of Transportation Specification No. 107A * * * *.

(Inspector)

(Signed) ____________________

(Place) ____________________

(Date) ____________________

RECORD OF CHEMICAL ANALYSIS OF STEEL FOR TANKS

Numbered ____________ to ____________ inclusive

Size ____ inches outside diameter by ____ inches long

Built by ____________________ Company

For ____________________ Company

Heat No.	Tanks represented (Serial Nos.)	Chemical Analysis							
		C	Mn	P	S	Si	Ni	Cr	Mo

These analyses were made by

(Signed) ____________________

* Full-size forms available free of charge at www.dotcfr.com.

(Place) ____________________

(Date) ____________________

RECORD OF CHEMICAL ANALYSIS OF STEEL IN TANKS

Numbered ____________ to ____________ inclusive

Size ____ inches outside by ____ inches long

Built by ____________________ Company

For ____________________ Company

Heat No.	Tanks represented by test (Serial Nos.)	Elastic limit (psi)	Tensile strength (psi)	Elongation (percent in 2 inches)	Reduction of area (percent)

(Signed) ____________________

(Place) ____________________

(Date) ____________________

RECORD OF HYDROSTATIC TESTS ON TANKS

Numbered ____________ to ____________ inclusive

Size ____ inches outside by ____ inches long

Built by ____________________ Company

For ____________________ Company

Serial Nos. of tank	Actual test pressure (psig)	Total expansion (cubic cm)	Permanent expansion (cubic cm)	Percent ratio of permanent expansion to total expansion[1]	Tare weight (pounds)[2]	Capacity in pounds of water at 60 °F

[1] If tests are made by method involving measurement of amount of liquid forced into tank by test pressure, then the basic data on which calculations are made, such as pump factors, temperature of liquid, coefficient of compressibility of liquid, etc., must also be given.

[2] Do not include protective housing, but state whether with or without valves.

(Signed) ____________________

(Place) ____________________

(Date) ____________________

RECORD OF GENERAL DATA ON TANKS

Numbered ____________ to ____________ inclusive

Built by ____________________ Company

For ____________________ Company

Data obtained as prescribed in §179.500-4(c)							Larger value of the factor D^2+d^2/D^2-d^2	(S) Calculated fiber stress in psi at 7/10 marked test pressure	Marked test pressure in psig stamped in tank	Minimum tensile strength of material in psi recorded
Marked end of tank				Other end of tank						
Serial No. of tank	(t) Min. thickness of wall in inches	(d) Max. inside diameter in inches	(D) Calculated value of D in inches = d + 2t	(t) Minimum thickness of wall in inches	(d) Max. inside diameter in inches	(D) calculated value of D in inches=d + 2t				

(Signed) ____________________

179 Specifications for Tank Cars

Appendix A to Part 179
Procedures for tank-head puncture-resistance test.

1. **This test procedure is designed to verify** the integrity of new or untried tank-head puncture-resistance systems and to test for system survivability after coupler-to-tank-head impacts at relative speeds of 29 km/hour (18 mph). Tank-head puncture-resistance is a function of one or more of the following: Head thickness, jacket thickness, insulation thickness, and material of construction.
2. **Tank-head puncture-resistance test.** A tank-head puncture-resistance system must be tested under the following conditions:
   a. *The ram car used* must weigh at least 119,295 kg (263,000 pounds), be equipped with a coupler, and duplicate the condition of a conventional draft sill including the draft yoke and draft gear. The coupler must protrude from the end of the ram car so that it is the leading location of perpendicular contact with the impacted test car.
   b. *The impacted test car* must be loaded with water at six percent outage with internal pressure of at least 6.9 Bar (100 psig) and coupled to one or more "backup" cars which have a total weight of 217,724 kg (480,000 pounds) with hand brakes applied on the last "backup" car.
   c. *At least two separate tests* must be conducted with the coupler on the vertical centerline of the ram car. One test must be conducted with the coupler at a height of 53.3 cm (21 inches), plus-or-minus 2.5 cm (1 inch), above the top of the sill; the other test must be conducted with the coupler height at 79 cm (31 inches), plus-or-minus 2.5 cm (1 inch), above the top of the sill. If the combined thickness of the tank head and any additional shielding material is less than the combined thickness on the vertical centerline of the car, a third test must be conducted with the coupler positioned so as to strike the thinnest point of the tank head.
3. **One of the following test conditions must be applied:**

Minimum weight of attached ram cars in kg (pounds)	Minimum velocity of impact in km/hour (mph)	Restrictions
119,295 (263,000)	29 (18)	One ram car only
155,582 (343,000)	25.5 (16)	One ram car or one car plus one rigidly attached car
311,164 (686,000)	22.5 (14)	One ram car plus one or more rigidly attached cars

4. **A test is successful if there is no visible leak** from the standing tank car for at least one hour after impact.

Appendix B to Part 179
Procedures for simulated pool and torch-fire testing.

1. **This test procedure is designed to measure** the thermal effects of new or untried thermal protection systems and to test for system survivability when exposed to a 100-minute pool fire and a 30-minute torch fire.
2. **Simulated pool fire test.**
   a. *A pool-fire environment must be simulated in the following manner:*
      (1) *The source* of the simulated pool fire must be hydrocarbon fuel with a flame temperature of 871 °C (1,600 °F), ±37.8 °C (100 °F), throughout the duration of the test.
      (2) *A square bare plate* with thermal properties equivalent to the material of construction of the tank car must be used. The plate dimensions must be not less than one foot by one foot by nominal 1.6 cm (0.625 inch) thick. The bare plate must be instrumented with not less than nine thermocouples to record the thermal response of the bare plate. The thermocouples must be attached to the surface not exposed to the simulated pool fire and must be divided into nine equal squares with a thermocouple placed in the center of each square.
      (3) *The pool-fire simulator* must be constructed in a manner that results in total flame engulfment of the front surface of the bare plate. The apex of the flame must be directed at the center of the plate.
      (4) *The bare plate holder* must be constructed in such a manner that the only heat transfer to the back side of the bare plate is by heat conduction through the plate and not by other heat paths.
      (5) *Before the bare plate* is exposed to the simulated pool fire, none of the temperature recording devices may indicate a plate temperature in excess of 37.8 °C (100 °F) nor less than 0 °C (32 °F).
      (6) *A minimum* of two thermocouple devices must indicate 427 °C (800 °F) after 13 minutes, plus-or-minus one minute, of simulated pool-fire exposure.
   b. *A thermal protection system* must be tested in the simulated pool-fire environment described in paragraph 2a of this appendix in the following manner:
      (1) *The thermal protection system* must cover one side of a bare plate as described in paragraph 2a(2) of this appendix.
      (2) *The non-protected side* of the bare plate must be instrumented with not less than nine thermocouples placed as described in paragraph 2a(2) of this appendix to record the thermal response of the plate.
      (3) *Before exposure* to the pool-fire simulation, none of the thermocouples on the thermal protection system configuration may indicate a plate temperature in excess of 37.8 °C (100 °F) nor less than 0 °C (32 °F).
      (4) *The entire surface* of the thermal protection system must be exposed to the simulated pool fire.
      (5) *A pool-fire simulation test* must run for a minimum of 100 minutes. The thermal protection system must retard the heat flow to the plate so that none of the thermocouples on the non-protected side of the plate indicate a plate temperature in excess of 427 °C (800 °F).
      (6) *A minimum* of three consecutive successful simulation fire tests must be performed for each thermal protection system.
3. **Simulated torch fire test.**
   a. *A torch-fire environment must be simulated in the following manner:*
      (1) *The source* of the simulated torch must be a hydrocarbon fuel with a flame temperature of 1,204 °C (2,200 °F), plus-or-minus 37.8 °C (100 °F), throughout the duration of the test. Furthermore, torch velocities must be 64.4 km/h ± 16 km/h (40 mph ± 10 mph) throughout the duration of the test.
      (2) *A square bare plate* with thermal properties equivalent to the material of construction of the tank car must be used. The plate dimensions must be at least four feet by four feet by nominal 1.6 cm (0.625 inch) thick. The bare plate must be instrumented with not less than nine thermocouples to record the thermal response of the plate. The thermocouples must be attached to the surface not exposed to the simulated torch and must be divided into nine equal squares with a thermocouple placed in the center of each square.
      (3) *The bare plate holder* must be constructed in such a manner that the only heat transfer to the back side of the plate is by heat conduction through the plate and not by other heat paths. The apex of the flame must be directed at the center of the plate.
      (4) *Before exposure* to the simulated torch, none of the temperature recording devices may indicate a plate temperature in excess of 37.8 °C (100 °F) or less than 0 °C (32 °F).
      (5) *A minimum* of two thermocouples must indicate 427 °C (800 °F) in four minutes, plus-or-minus 30 seconds, of torch simulation exposure.
   b. *A thermal protection system* must be tested in the simulated torch-fire environment described in paragraph 3a of this appendix in the following manner:
      (1) *The thermal protection system* must cover one side of the bare plate identical to that used to simulate a torch fire under paragraph 3a(2) of this appendix.
      (2) *The back* of the bare plate must be instrumented with not less than nine thermocouples placed as described in paragraph 3a(2) of this appendix to record the thermal response of the material.
      (3) *Before exposure* to the simulated torch, none of the thermocouples on the back side of the thermal protection system configuration may indicate a plate temperature in excess of 37.8 °C (100 °F) nor less than 0 °C (32 °F).
      (4) *The entire outside surface* of the thermal protection system must be exposed to the simulated torch-fire environment.
      (5) *A torch-simulation test* must be run for a minimum of 30 minutes. The thermal protection system must retard the heat flow to the plate so that none of the thermocouples on the backside of the bare plate indicate a plate temperature in excess of 427 °C (800 °F).
      (6) *A minimum* of two consecutive successful torch-simulation tests must be performed for each thermal protection system.

Part 180 - Continuing Qualification and Maintenance of Packagings

Subpart A - General

§180.1 Purpose and scope.

This part prescribes requirements pertaining to the maintenance, reconditioning, repair, inspection and testing of packagings, and any other function having an effect on the continuing qualification and use of a packaging under the requirements of this subchapter.

§180.2 Applicability.

(a) **Any person who performs a function** prescribed in this part shall perform that function in accordance with this part.

(b) **Any person who performs a function** prescribed in this part is considered subject to the regulations of this subchapter when that person —

(1) *Makes any representation* indicating compliance with one or more of the requirements of this part; or

(2) *Reintroduces into commerce* a packaging that bears markings indicating compliance with this part.

§180.3 General requirements.

(a) **No person may represent, mark, certify, sell, or offer** a packaging or container as meeting the requirements of this part, or an exemption pertaining to this part issued under subchapter A of this chapter, whether or not the packaging or container is intended to be used for the transportation of a hazardous material, unless it is marked, maintained, reconditioned, repaired, or retested, as appropriate, in accordance with this part, an approval issued thereunder, or an exemption issued under subchapter A of this chapter.

(b) **The representations, markings, and certifications** subject to the prohibitions of paragraph (a) of this section include:

(1) *Identifications that include the letters "DOT", "MC", "ICC", or "UN";*

(2) *Exemption, approval, and registration numbers* that include the letters "DOT";

(3) *Test dates* displayed in association with specification, registration, approval, or exemption markings indicating conformance to a test or retest requirement of this subchapter, an approval issued thereunder, or an exemption issued under subchapter A of this chapter;

(4) *Documents indicating* conformance to the testing, inspection, maintenance or other continuing qualification requirements of this part; and

(5) *Sales literature,* including advertising, indicating that the packaging or container represented therein conforms to requirements contained in subchapter A or C of this chapter.

Subpart B [Reserved]

Subpart C - Qualification, Maintenance, and Use of Cylinders

§180.201 Applicability.

This subpart prescribes requirements, in addition to those contained in parts 107, 171, 172, 173, and 178 of this chapter, applicable to any person responsible for the continuing qualification, maintenance, or periodic requalification of DOT specification and exemption cylinders.

§180.203 Definitions.

In addition to the definitions contained in §171.8 of this subchapter, the following definitions apply to this subpart:

Commercially free of corrosive components means a hazardous material having a dew point at or below minus 46.7 °C (minus 52 °F) at 101kPa (1 atmosphere) and free of components that will adversely react with the cylinder (e.g. chemical stress corrosion).

Condemn means a determination that a cylinder is unserviceable for the continued transportation of hazardous materials in commerce and that the cylinder may not be restored by repair, rebuilding, requalification, or any other procedure.

Defect means an imperfection requiring removal of a cylinder from service.

Elastic expansion means a temporary increase in a cylinder's volume, due to application of pressure, that is lost when pressure is released (elastic expansion = total expansion minus permanent expansion).

Filled or **charged** means an introduction or presence of a hazardous material in a cylinder.

Non-corrosive service means a hazardous material that, in the presence of moisture, is not corrosive to the materials of construction of a cylinder (including valve, pressure relief device, etc.).

Over-heated means a condition in which the temperature of any portion of an aluminum cylinder has reached 176 °C (350 °F) or higher, or in which the temperature of any portion of a steel or nickel cylinder has reached 343 °C (650 °F) or higher.

Permanent expansion means a permanent increase in a cylinder's volume after the test pressure is released.

Proof pressure test means a pressure test by interior pressurization without the determination of a cylinder's expansion.

Rebuild means the replacement of a pressure part (e.g. a wall, head, or pressure fitting) by welding.

Rejected cylinder means a cylinder that cannot be used for the transportation of a hazardous material in commerce without repair, rebuilding, and requalification.

Repair means a procedure for correction of a rejected cylinder that may involve welding.

Requalification means the completion of a visual inspection and/or the test(s) required to be performed on a cylinder to determine its suitability for continued service.

Requalification identification number or RIN means a code assigned by DOT to uniquely identify a cylinder requalification, repair, or rebuilding facility.

Test pressure means the pressure used for the requalification of a cylinder.

Total expansion means the total increase in a cylinder's volume due to application of the test pressure.

Visual inspection means an internal or external visual examination, or both, performed as part of the cylinder requalification process.

Volumetric expansion test means a pressure test to determine the total and permanent expansion of a cylinder at a given pressure. The volumetric expansion test is conducted using the water jacket or direct expansion methods:

(1) **Water jacket method** means a volumetric expansion test to determine a cylinder's total and permanent expansion by measuring the difference between the volume of water the cylinder externally displaces at test pressure and the volume of water the cylinder externally displaces at ambient pressure.

(2) **Direct expansion method** means a volumetric expansion test to calculate a cylinder's total and permanent expansion by measuring the amount of water forced into a cylinder at test pressure, adjusted for the compressibility of water, as a means of determining the expansion.

§180.205 General requirements for requalification of cylinders.

(a) **General.** Each cylinder used for the transportation of hazardous materials must be an authorized packaging. To qualify as an authorized packaging, each cylinder must conform to this subpart, the applicable requirements specified in part 173 of this subchapter, and the applicable requirements of subpart C of part 178 of this subchapter.

(b) **Persons performing requalification functions.** No person may represent that a repair or requalification of a cylinder has been performed in accordance with the requirements in this subchapter unless that person holds a current approval issued under the procedural requirements prescribed in subpart I of part 107 of this chapter. No person may mark a cylinder with a RIN and a requalification date or otherwise represent that a DOT specification or exemption cylinder has been requalified unless all applicable requirements of this subpart have been met. A person who requalifies cylinders must maintain the records prescribed in §180.215 at each location at which it inspects, tests, or marks cylinders.

(c) **Periodic requalification of cylinders.** Each cylinder bearing a DOT specification marking must be requalified and marked as specified in the Requalification Table in this subpart. Each cylinder bearing a DOT exemption number must be requalified and marked in conformance with this section and the terms of the applicable exemption. No cylinder may be filled with a hazardous material and offered for transportation in commerce unless that cylinder has been successfully requalified and marked in accordance with this subpart. A cylinder may be requalified at any time during or before the month and year that the requalification is due. However, a cylinder filled before the requalification becomes due may remain in service until it is emptied. A cylinder with a specified service life may not be refilled and offered for transportation after its authorized service life has expired.

(1) *Each cylinder* that is requalified in accordance with the requirements specified in this section must be marked in accordance with §180.213.

(2) *Each cylinder that fails requalification must be:*
(i) *Rejected and may be requalified in accordance with §180.211; or*
(ii) *Condemned in accordance with paragraph (i) of this section.*
(3) *For DOT specification cylinders,* the marked service pressure may be changed upon approval of the Associate Administrator and in accordance with written procedures specified in the approval.
(4) *For a specification* 3, 3A, 3AA, 3AL, 3AX, 3AXX, 3B, 3BN, or 3T cylinder filled with gases in other than Division 2.2, from the first requalification due on or after December 31, 2003, the burst pressure of a CG-1, CG-4, or CG-5 pressure relief device must be at test pressure with a tolerance of plus zero to minus 10%. An additional 5% tolerance is allowed when a combined rupture disc is placed inside a holder. This requirement does not apply if a CG-2, CG-3 or CG-9 thermally activated relief device or a CG-7 reclosing pressure valve is used on the cylinder.

(d) **Conditions requiring test and inspection of cylinders.** Without regard to any other periodic requalification requirements, a cylinder must be tested and inspected in accordance with this section prior to further use if —
(1) *The cylinder* shows evidence of dents, corrosion, cracked or abraded areas, leakage, thermal damage, or any other condition that might render it unsafe for use in transportation;
(2) *The cylinder* has been in an accident and has been damaged to an extent that may adversely affect its lading retention capability;
(3) *The cylinder* shows evidence of or is known to have been overheated; or
(4) *The Associate Administrator* determines that the cylinder may be in an unsafe condition.

(e) **Cylinders containing Class 8 (corrosive) liquids.** A cylinder previously containing a Class 8 (corrosive) liquid may not be used to transport a Class 2 material in commerce unless the cylinder is —
(1) *Visually inspected,* internally and externally, in accordance with paragraph (f) of this section and the inspection is recorded as prescribed in §180.215;
(2) *Requalified in accordance with this section,* regardless of the date of the previous requalification;
(3) *Marked in accordance with §180.213; and*
(4) *Decontaminated to remove* all significant residue or impregnation of the Class 8 material.

(f) **Visual inspection.** Except as otherwise provided in this subpart, each time a cylinder is pressure tested, it must be given an internal and external visual inspection.
(1) *The visual inspection* must be performed in accordance with the following CGA Pamphlets: C-6 for steel and nickel cylinders (incorporated by reference; see §171.7 of this subchapter); C-6.1 for seamless aluminum cylinders (incorporated by reference; see §171.7 of this subchapter); C-6.2 for fiber reinforced composite exemption cylinders (incorporated by reference; see §171.7 of this subchapter); C-6.3 for low pressure aluminum cylinders (incorporated by reference; see §171.7 of this subchapter); C-8 for DOT 3HT cylinders (incorporated by reference; see §171.7 of this subchapter); and C-13 for DOT 8 series cylinders (incorporated by reference; see §171.7 of this subchapter).
(2) *For each cylinder* with a coating or attachments that would inhibit inspection of the cylinder, the coating or attachments must be removed before performing the visual inspection.
(3) *Each cylinder* subject to visual inspection must be approved, rejected, or condemned according to the criteria in the applicable CGA pamphlet.
(4) *In addition* to other requirements prescribed in this paragraph (f), a specification or exemption cylinder made of aluminum alloy 6351- T6 must be inspected for evidence of sustained load cracking (SLC) in the neck and shoulder area.

(g) **Pressure test.**
(1) *Unless otherwise provided,* each cylinder required to be retested under this subpart must be retested by means suitable for measuring the expansion of the cylinder under pressure. Bands and other removable attachments must be loosened or removed before testing so that the cylinder is free to expand in all directions.
(2) *The pressure indicating device* of the testing apparatus must permit reading of pressures to within 1% of the minimum prescribed test pressure of each cylinder tested, except that for an analog device, interpolation to 1/2 of the marked gauge divisions is acceptable. The expansion-indicating device of the testing apparatus must also permit incremental reading of the cylinder expansion to 1% of the total expansion of each cylinder tested or 0.1 cc, whichever is larger. Midpoint visual interpolation is permitted.
(3) *Each day before retesting,* the retester shall confirm, by using a calibrated cylinder or other method authorized in writing by the Associate Administrator, that:
(i) *The pressure-indicating device,* as part of the retest apparatus, is accurate within ±1.0% of the prescribed test pressure of any cylinder tested that day. The pressure indicating device, itself, must be certified as having an accuracy of ±0.5%, or better, of its full range, and must permit readings of pressure from 90%-110% of the minimum prescribed test pressure of the cylinder to be tested. The accuracy of the pressure indicating device within the test system can be demonstrated at any point within 500 psig of the actual test pressure for test pressures at or above 3000 psig, or 10% of the actual test pressure for test pressures below 3000 psig.
(ii) *The expansion-indicating device,* as part of the retest apparatus, gives a stable reading of expansion and is accurate to ±1.0% of the total expansion of any cylinder tested or 0.1 cc, whichever is larger. The expansion-indicating device itself must have an accuracy of ±0.5%, or better, of its full scale.
(4) *The test equipment* must be verified to be accurate within ±1.0% of the calibrated cylinder's pressure and corresponding expansion values. This may be accomplished by bringing the pressure to a value shown on the calibration certificate for the calibrated cylinder used and verifying that the resulting total expansion is within ±1.0% of the total expansion shown on the calibration certificate. Alternatively, calibration may be demonstrated by bringing the total expansion to a known value on the calibration certificate for the calibrated cylinder used and verifying that the resulting pressure is within ±1.0% of the pressure shown on the calibration certificate. The calibrated cylinder must show no permanent expansion. The retester must demonstrate calibration in conformance with this paragraph (g) to an authorized inspector on any day that it retests cylinders. A retester must maintain calibrated cylinder certificates in conformance with §180.215(b)(4).
(5) *Minimum test pressure* must be maintained for at least 30 seconds, and as long as necessary for complete expansion of the cylinder. A system check may be performed at or below 90% of test pressure prior to the retest. In the case of a malfunction of the test equipment, the test may be repeated at a pressure increased by 10% or 100 psig, whichever is less. This paragraph (g) does not authorize retest of a cylinder otherwise required to be condemned under paragraph (i) of this section.

(h) **Cylinder rejection.** A cylinder must be rejected when, after a visual inspection, it meets a condition for rejection under the visual inspection requirements of paragraph (f) of this section.
(1) *Except as provided* in paragraphs (h)(3) and (h)(4) of this section, a cylinder that is rejected may not be marked as meeting the requirements of this section.
(2) *The requalifier* must notify the cylinder owner, in writing, that the cylinder has been rejected.
(3) *Unless the cylinder* is requalified in conformance with requirements in §180.211, it may not be filled with a hazardous material and offered for transportation in commerce where use of a specification packaging is required.
(4) *A rejected cylinder* with a service pressure of less than 900 psig may be requalified and marked if the cylinder is repaired or rebuilt and subsequently inspected and tested in conformance with —
(i) *The visual inspection requirements* of paragraph (f) of this section;
(ii) *Part 178 of this subchapter and this part;*
(iii) *Any exemption* covering the manufacture, requalification, and/or use of that cylinder; and
(iv) *Any approval required under §180.211.*

(i) **Cylinder condemnation.**
(1) *A cylinder must be condemned when —*
(i) *The cylinder* meets a condition for condemnation under the visual inspection requirements of paragraph (f) of this section.
(ii) *The cylinder leaks through its wall.*
(iii) *Evidence of cracking* exists to the extent that the cylinder is likely to be weakened appreciably.
(iv) *For a DOT specification cylinder,* other than a DOT 4E aluminum cylinder or an exemption cylinder, permanent expansion exceeds 10 percent of total expansion.
(v) *For a DOT 3HT cylinder —*
[A] The pressure test yields an elastic expansion exceeding the marked rejection elastic expansion (REE) value.
[B] The cylinder shows evidence of denting or bulging.
[C] The cylinder bears a manufacture or an original test date older than twenty-four years or after 4380 pressurizations, whichever occurs first. If a cylinder is refilled, on average, more than once every other day, an accurate

record of the number of rechargings must be maintained by the cylinder owner or the owner's agent.

(vi) *For a DOT 4E* aluminum cylinder, permanent expansion exceeds 12 percent of total expansion.

(vii) *For a DOT exemption cylinder,* permanent expansion exceeds the limit in the applicable exemption, or the cylinder meets another criterion for condemnation in the applicable exemption.

(viii) *For an aluminum* or an aluminum-lined composite exemption cylinder, the cylinder is known to have been or shows evidence of having been over-heated.

(2) *When a cylinder must be condemned,* the requalifier must stamp a series of X's over the DOT specification number and the marked pressure or stamp "CONDEMNED" on the shoulder, top head, or neck using a steel stamp. Alternatively, at the direction of the owner, the requalifier may render the cylinder incapable of holding pressure. In addition, the requalifier must notify the cylinder owner, in writing, that the cylinder is condemned and may not be filled with hazardous material and offered for transportation in commerce where use of a specification packaging is required.

(3) *No person may remove or obliterate the "CONDEMNED" marking.*

§180.207 [Reserved]

§180.209 Requirements for requalification of specification cylinders.

(a) Periodic qualification of cylinders.

(1) *Each specification cylinder* that becomes due for periodic requalification, as specified in the following table, must be requalified and marked in conformance with the requirements of this subpart. Requalification records must be maintained in accordance with §180.215. Table 1 follows:

Table 1 - Requalification of Cylinders[1]

Specification under which cylinder was made	Minimum test pressure (psig)[2]	Requalification period (years)
DOT 3	3000 psig	5
DOT 3A, 3AA	5/3 times service pressure, except noncorrosive service (see §180.209(g))	5, 10, or 12 (see §180.209(b), (f), (h), and (j)
DOT 3AL	5/3 times service pressure	5 or 12 (see §180.209(j))
DOT 3AX, 3AAX	5/3 times service pressure	5
3B, 3BN	2 times service pressure (see §180.209(g))	5 or 10 (see §180.209(f))
3E	Test not required	
3HT	5/3 times service pressure	3 (see §§180.209(k) and 180.213(c))
3T	5/3 times service pressure	5
4AA480	2 times service pressure (see 180.209(g))	5 or 10 (see §180.209(h))
4B, 4BA, 4BW, 4B-240ET	2 times service pressure, except non-corrosive service (see §180.209(g))	5, 10, or 12 (see §180.209(e), (f), and (j))
4D, 4DA, 4DS	2 times service	5
DOT 4E	2 times service pressure, except non-corrosive (see §180.209(g))	5
4L	Test not required	
8, 8AL		10 or 20 (see §180.209(i))
Exemption cylinder	See current exemption	See current exemption
Foreign cylinder (see §173.301(j) of this subchapter for restrictions on use)	As marked on cylinder, but not less than 5/3 of any service or working pressure marking	5 (see §§180.209(l) and 180.213(d)(2))

1. Any cylinder not exceeding 2 inches outside diameter and less than 2 feet in length is excepted from volumetric expansion test.
2. For cylinders not marked with a service pressure, see §173.301a(b) of this subchapter.

(b) DOT 3A or 3AA cylinders.

(1) *A cylinder* conforming to specification DOT 3A or 3AA with a water capacity of 56.7 kg (125 lb) or less that is removed from any cluster, bank, group, rack, or vehicle each time it is filled, may be requalified every ten years instead of every five years, provided the cylinder conforms to all of the following conditions:

(i) *The cylinder was manufactured after December 31, 1945.*

(ii) *The cylinder* is used exclusively for air; argon; cyclopropane; ethylene; helium; hydrogen; krypton; neon; nitrogen; nitrous oxide; oxygen; sulfur hexafluoride; xenon; chlorinated hydrocarbons, fluorinated hydrocarbons, liquefied hydrocarbons, and mixtures thereof that are commercially free from corroding components; permitted mixtures of these gases (see §173.301(d) of this subchapter); and permitted mixtures of these gases with up to 30 percent by volume of carbon dioxide, provided the gas has a dew point at or below minus (52 °F) at 1 atmosphere.

(iii) *Before each refill,* the cylinder is removed from any cluster, bank, group, rack or vehicle and passes the hammer test specified in CGA Pamphlet C-6 (incorporated by reference; see §171.7 of this subchapter).

(iv) *The cylinder* is dried immediately after hydrostatic testing to remove all traces of water.

(v) *The cylinder is not used for underwater breathing.*

(vi) *Each cylinder* is stamped with a five-pointed star at least one-fourth of an inch high immediately following the test date.

(2) *If, since the last* required requalification, a cylinder has not been used exclusively for the gases specifically identified in paragraph (b)(1)(ii) of this section, but currently conforms with all other provisions of paragraph (b)(1) of this section, it may be requalified every 10 years instead of every five years, provided it is first requalified and examined as prescribed by §173.302a(b) (2), (3) and (4) of this subchapter.

(3) *Except as specified* in paragraph (b)(2) of this section, if a cylinder, marked with a star, is filled with a compressed gas other than as specified in paragraph (b)(1)(ii) of this section, the star following the most recent test date must be obliterated. The cylinder must be requalified five years from the marked test date, or prior to the first filling with a compressed gas, if the required five-year requalification period has passed.

(c) **DOT 4-series cylinders.** A DOT 4-series cylinder, except a 4L cylinder, that at any time shows evidence of a leak or of internal or external corrosion, denting, bulging or rough usage to the extent that it is likely to be weakened appreciably, or that has lost five percent or more of its official tare weight must be requalified before being refilled and offered for transportation. (Refer to CGA Pamphlet C-6 or C-6.3, as applicable, regarding cylinder weakening.) After testing, the actual tare weight must be recorded as the new tare weight.

(d) **Cylinders 5.44 kg (12 lb) or less** with service pressures of 300 psig or less. A cylinder of 5.44 (12 lb) or less water capacity authorized for service pressure of 300 psig or less must be given a complete external visual inspection at the time periodic requalification becomes due. External visual inspection must be in accordance with CGA Pamphlet C-6 or C-6.1 (incorporated by reference; see §171.7 of this subchapter). The cylinder may be proof pressure tested. The test is successful if the cylinder, when examined under test pressure, does not display a defect described in §180.205(i)(1) (ii) or (iii). Upon successful completion of the test and inspection, the cylinder must be marked in accordance with §180.213.

(e) **Proof pressure test.** A cylinder made in conformance with specifications DOT 4B, 4BA, 4BW, or 4E used exclusively for: liquefied petroleum gas that meets the detail requirement limits in Table I of ASTM D 1835, "Standard Specification for Liquefied Petroleum (LP) Gases" (incorporated by reference; see §171.7 of this subchapter) or an equivalent standard containing the same limits; anhydrous dimethylamine; anhydrous methylamine; anhydrous trimethylamine; methyl chloride; methylacetylene-propadiene stabilized; or dichlorodifluoromethane, difluoroethane, difluorochloroethane, chlorodifluoromethane, chlorotetrafluoroethane, trifluorochloroethylene, or mixture thereof, or mixtures of one or more with trichlorofluoromethane; and commercially free from corroding components and protected externally by a suitable corrosion-resistant coating (such as galvanizing or painting) may be requalified by volumetric expansion testing every 12 years instead of every five years. As an alternative, the cylinder may be subjected to a proof pressure test at least two times the marked service pressure, but this latter type of test must be repeated every seven years after expiration of the first 12-year period. When subjected to a proof pressure test, the cylinder must be carefully examined under test pressure and removed from service if a leak or defect is found.

(f) **Poisonous materials.** A cylinder conforming to specification DOT 3A, 3AA, 3B, 4BA, or 4BW having a service pressure of 300 psig or less and used exclusively for methyl bromide, liquid; mixtures of methyl bromide and ethylene dibromide, liquid; mixtures of methyl bromide and chlorpicrin, liquid; mixtures of methyl bromide and petroleum solvents, liquid; or methyl bromide and nonflammable, nonliquefied compressed gas mixtures, liquid; commercially free of corroding components, and protected externally by a suitable corrosion resistant coating (such as galvanizing or painting) and internally by a suitable corrosion resistant lining (such as galvanizing) may be tested every 10 years instead of every five years, provided a visual internal and external examination of the cylinder is conducted every five years in accordance with CGA Pamphlet C-6 (incorporated by reference; see §171.7 of this subchapter). The cylinder must be examined at each filling, and rejected if a dent, corroded area, leak or other condition indicates possible weakness.

(g) **Visual inspections.** A cylinder conforming to a specification listed in the table in this paragraph and used exclusively in the service indicated may, instead of a periodic hydrostatic test, be given a complete external visual inspection at the time periodic requalification becomes due. External visual inspection must be in accordance with CGA Pamphlet C-6 or C-6.3, as applicable (incorporated by reference; see §171.7 of this subchapter). When this inspection is used instead of hydrostatic pressure testing, subsequent inspections are required at five-year intervals after the first inspection. After September 30, 2003, inspections must be made only by persons holding a current RIN and the results recorded and maintained in accordance with §180.215. Records must include: date of inspection (month and year); DOT specification number; cylinder identification (registered symbol and serial number, date of manufacture, and owner); type of cylinder protective coating (including statement as to need of refinishing or recoating); conditions checked (e.g., leakage, corrosion, gouges, dents or digs in shell or heads, broken or damaged footring or protective ring or fire damage); disposition of cylinder (returned to service, returned to cylinder manufacturer for repairs or condemned). A cylinder passing requalification by the external visual inspection must be marked in accordance with §180.213. Specification cylinders must be in exclusive service as shown in the following table:

Cylinders conforming to —	Used exclusively for —
DOT 3A, DOT 3AA, DOT 3A480X, DOT 4AA480	Anhydrous ammonia of at least 99.95% purity
DOT 3A, DOT 3AA, DOT 3A480X, DOT 3B, DOT 4B, DOT 4BA, DOT 4BW	Butadiene, inhibited, that is commercially free from corroding components
DOT 3A, DOT 3A480X, DOT 3AA, DOT 3B, DOT 4AA480, DOT 4B, DOT 4BA, DOT 4BW	Cyclopropane that is commercially free from corroding components
DOT 3A, DOT 3AA, DOT 3A480X, DOT 4B, DOT 4BA, DOT 4BW, DOT 4E	Chlorinated hydrocarbons and mixtures thereof that are commercially free from corroding components.
DOT 3A, DOT 3AA, DOT 3A480X, DOT 4B, DOT 4BA, DOT 4BW, DOT 4E	Fluorinated hydrocarbons and mixtures thereof that are commercially free from corroding components
DOT 3A, DOT 3AA, DOT 3A480X, DOT 3B, DOT 4B, DOT 4BA, DOT 4BW, DOT 4E	Liquefied hydrocarbon gas that is commercially free from corroding components
DOT 3A, DOT 3AA, DOT 3A480X, DOT 3B, DOT 4B, DOT 4BA, DOT 4BW, DOT 4E	Liquefied petroleum gas that meets the detail requirements limits in Table 1 of ASTM 1835, Standard Specification for Liquefied Petroleum (LP) Gases (incorporated by reference; see §171.7 of this subchapter) or an equivalent standard containing the same limits.
DOT 3A, DOT 3AA, DOT 3B, DOT 4B, DOT 4BA, DOT 4BW, DOT 4E	Methylacetylene-propadiene, stabilized, that is commercially free from corroding components
DOT 3A, DOT 3AA, DOT 3B, DOT 4B, DOT 4BA, DOT 4BW	Anhydrous mono, di,trimethylamines that are commercially free from corroding components
DOT 4B240, DOT 4BW240	Ethyleneimine, stabilized.

(h) **Cylinders containing anhydrous ammonia.** A cylinder conforming to specification DOT 3A, 3A480X, or 4AA480 used exclusively for anhydrous ammonia, commercially free from corroding components, and protected externally by a suitable corrosion-resistant coating (such as paint) may be requalified every 10 years instead of every five years.

(i) **Requalification of DOT-8 series cylinders.**

(1) *Each owner* of a DOT-8 series cylinder used to transport acetylene must have the cylinder shell and the porous filler requalified in accordance with CGA Pamphlet C-13 (incorporated by reference; see §171.7 of this subchapter). Requalification must be performed in accordance with the following schedule:

Date of cylinder manufacture	Shell (visual inspection) requalification		Porous filler requalification	
	Initial	Subsequent	Initial	Subsequent
Before January 1, 1991	Before January 1, 2001	10 years	Before January 1, 2011	Not required
On or after January 1, 1991	10 years[1]	10 years	3 to 20 years[2]	Not required

1. Years from date of cylinder manufacture.
2. For a cylinder manufactured on or after January 1, 1991, requalification of the porous filler must be performed no sooner than 3 years, and no later than 20 years, from the date of manufacture.

(2) *Unless requalified and marked* in accordance with CGA Pamphlet C-13 (incorporated by reference; see §171.7 of this subchapter) before October 1, 1994, an acetylene cylinder must be requalified by a person who holds a current RIN.

(3) *If a cylinder valve is replaced,* a cylinder valve of the same weight must be used or the tare weight of the cylinder must be adjusted to compensate for valve weight differential.

(4) *The person* performing a visual inspection or requalification must record the results as specified in §180.215.

(5) *The person* performing a visual inspection or requalification must mark the cylinder as specified in §180.213.

(j) **Cylinder used as a fire extinguisher.** Only a DOT specification cylinder used as a fire extinguisher and meeting Special Provision 18 in §172.102(c)(1) of this subchapter may be requalified in accordance with this paragraph (j).

(1) *A DOT* 4B, 4BA, 4B240ET or 4BW cylinder may be tested as follows:

(i) *For a cylinder* with a water capacity of 5.44 kg (12 lb) or less, by volumetric expansion test using the water jacket method or by proof pressure test. A requalification must be performed by the end of 12 years after the original test date and at 12-year intervals thereafter.

(ii) *For a cylinder having a water capacity over 5.44 kg (12 lb)* —

[A] By proof pressure test. A requalification must be performed by the end of 12 years after the original test date and at 7-year intervals; or

[B] By volumetric expansion test using the water jacket method. A requalification must be performed 12 years after the original test date and at 12-year intervals thereafter.

(2) *A DOT 3A,* 3AA, or 3AL cylinder must be requalified by volumetric expansion test using the water jacket method. A requalification must be performed 12 years after the original test date and at 12-year intervals thereafter.

(k) **3HT cylinders.** In addition to the other requirements of this section, a cylinder marked DOT-3HT must be requalified in accordance with CGA Pamphlet C-8.

(l) **Requalification of foreign cylinders filled for export.** A cylinder manufactured outside the United States, other than as provided in §171.12a of this subchapter, that has not been manufactured, inspected, tested and marked in accordance with part 178 of this subchapter may be filled with compressed gas in the United States, and shipped solely for export if it meets the following requirements, in addition to other requirements of this subchapter:

(1) *It has been* inspected, tested and marked (with only the month and year of test) in conformance with the procedures and requirements of this subpart or the Associate Administrator has authorized the filling company to fill foreign cylinders under an alternative method of qualification; and

(2) *It is offered* for transportation in conformance with the requirements of §173.301(l) of this subchapter.

§180.211 Repair, rebuilding, and reheat treatment of DOT-4 series specification cylinders.

(a) **General requirements for repair and rebuilding.** Any repair or rebuilding of a DOT 4-series cylinder must be performed by a person holding an approval as specified in §107.805 of this chapter. A person performing a rebuild function is considered a manufacturer subject to the requirements of §178.2(a)(2) and subpart C of part 178 of this subchapter. The person performing a repair, rebuild, or reheat treatment must record the test results as specified in §180.215. Each cylinder that is successfully repaired or rebuilt must be marked in accordance with §180.213.

(b) **General repair requirements.** Each repair of a DOT 4-series cylinder must be made in accordance with the following conditions:

(1) *The repair and the inspection* of the work performed must be made in accordance with the requirements of the cylinder specification.

(2) *The person* performing the repair must use the procedure, equipment, and filler metal or brazing material as authorized by the approval issued under §107.805 of this chapter.

(3) *Welding and brazing* must be performed on an area free from contaminants.

(4) *A weld defect,* such as porosity in a pressure retaining seam, must be completely removed before re-welding. Puddling may be used to remove a weld defect only by the tungsten inert gas shielded arc process.

(5) *After removal* of a non-pressure attachment and before its replacement, the cylinder must be given a visual inspection in accordance with §180.205(f).

(6) *Reheat treatment* of DOT 4B, 4BA or 4BW specification cylinders after replacement of non-pressure attachments is not required when the total weld material does not exceed 20.3 cm (8 inches). Individual welds must be at least 7.6 cm (3 inches) apart.

(7) *After repair* of a DOT 4B, 4BA or 4BW cylinder, the weld area must be leak tested at the service pressure of the cylinder.

(8) *Repair of weld defects must be free of cracks.*

(9) *When a non-pressure attachment* with the original cylinder specification markings is replaced, all markings must be transferred to the attachment on the repaired cylinder.

(10) *Walls, heads or bottoms* of cylinders with defects or leaks in base metal may not be repaired, but may be replaced as provided for in paragraph (d) of this section.

(c) Additional repair requirements for 4L cylinders.

(1) *Repairs to* a DOT 4L cylinder must be performed in accordance with paragraphs (a) and (b) of this section and are limited to the following:

(i) *The removal* of either end of the insulation jacket to permit access to the cylinder, piping system, or neck tube.

(ii) *The replacement of the neck tube.* At least a 13 mm (0.51 inch) piece of the original neck tube must be protruding above the cylinder's top end. The original weld attaching the neck tube to the cylinder must be sound and the replacement neck tube must be welded to this remaining piece of the original neck tube.

(iii) *The replacement* of material such as, but not limited to, the insulating material and the piping system within the insulation space is authorized. The replacement material must be equivalent to that used at the time of original manufacture.

(iv) *Other welding procedures* that are permitted by CGA Pamphlet C-3 (incorporated by reference; see §171.7 of this subchapter), and not excluded by the definition of "rebuild," are authorized.

(2) *After repair, the cylinder must be —*

(i) *Pressure tested* in accordance with the specifications under which the cylinder was originally manufactured;

(ii) *Leak tested* before and after assembly of the insulation jacket using a mass spectrometer detection system; and

(iii) *Tested for heat conductivity requirements.*

(d) General rebuilding requirements.

(1) *The rebuilding* of a DOT 4-series cylinder must be made in accordance with the following requirements:

(i) *The person* rebuilding the cylinder must use the procedures and equipment as authorized by the approval issued under §107.805 of this chapter.

(ii) *After removal* of a non-pressure component and before replacement of any non-pressure component, the cylinder must be visually inspected in accordance with CGA Pamphlet C-6 (incorporated by reference; see §171.7 of this subchapter).

(iii) *The rebuilder* may rebuild a DOT 4B, 4BA or 4BW cylinder having a water capacity of 9.07 kg (20 lb) or greater by replacing a head of the cylinder using a circumferential joint. When this weld joint is located at other than an original welded joint, a notation of this modification must be shown on the Manufacturer's Report of Rebuilding in §180.215(c)(2). The weld joint must be on the cylindrical section of the cylinder.

(iv) *Any welding* and the inspection of the rebuilt cylinder must be in accordance with the requirements of the applicable cylinder specification and the following requirements:

[A] *Rebuilding of any cylinder* involving a joint subject to internal pressure may only be performed by fusion welding;

[B] *Welding must be performed* on an area free from contaminants; and

[C] *A weld defect,* such as porosity in a pressure retaining seam, must be completely removed before re-welding. Puddling may be used to remove a weld defect only by using the tungsten inert gas shielded arc process.

(2) *Any rebuilt cylinder must be —*

(i) *Heat treated in accordance with paragraph (f) of this section;*

(ii) *Subjected to* a volumetric expansion test on each cylinder. The results of the tests must conform to the applicable cylinder specification;

(iii) *Inspected and have* test data reviewed to determine conformance with the applicable cylinder specification; and

(iv) *Made of material* conforming to the specification. Determination of conformance shall include chemical analysis, verification, inspection and tensile testing of the replaced part. Tensile tests must be performed on the replaced part after heat treatment by lots defined in the applicable specification.

(3) *For each rebuilt cylinder,* an inspector's report must be prepared to include the information listed in §180.215(d).

(4) *Rebuilding a cylinder with brazed seams is prohibited.*

(5) *When an end* with the original cylinder specification markings is replaced, all markings must be transferred to the rebuilt cylinder.

(e) Additional rebuilding requirements for DOT 4L cylinders.

(1) *The rebuilding* of a DOT 4L cylinder must be performed in accordance with paragraph (d) of this section. Rebuilding of a DOT 4L cylinder is:

(i) *Substituting or adding* material in the insulation space not identical to that used in the original manufacture of that cylinder;

(ii) *Making a weld repair* not to exceed 150 mm (5.9 inches) in length on the longitudinal seam of the cylinder or 300 mm (11.8 inches) in length on a circumferential weld joint of the cylinder; or

(iii) *Replacing the outer jacket.*

(2) *Reheat treatment of cylinders is prohibited.*

(3) *After rebuilding,* each inner containment vessel must be proof pressure tested at 2 times its service pressure. Each completed assembly must be leak-tested using a mass spectrometer detection system.

(f) Reheat treatment.

(1) *Prior to reheat treatment,* each cylinder must be given a visual inspection, internally and externally, in accordance with §180.205(f).

(2) *Cylinders must be segregated* in lots for reheat treatment. The reheat treatment and visual inspection must be performed in accordance with the specification for the cylinders except as provided in paragraph (f)(4) of this section.

(3) *After reheat treatment,* each cylinder in the lot must be subjected to a volumetric expansion test and meet the acceptance criteria in the applicable specification or be scrapped.

(4) *After all welding and heat treatment,* a test of the new weld must be performed as required by the original specification. The test results must be recorded in accordance with §180.215.

§180.213 Requalification markings.

(a) General. Each cylinder requalified in accordance with this subpart with acceptable results must be marked as specified in this section. Required specification markings may not be altered or removed.

(b) Placement of markings. Each cylinder must be plainly and permanently marked on the metal of the cylinder as permitted by the applicable specification. Unless authorized by the cylinder specification, marking on the cylinder sidewall is prohibited.

(1) *Requalification and required* specification markings must be legible so as to be readily visible at all times. Illegible specification markings may be remarked on the cylinder as provided by the original specification. Requalification markings may be placed on any portion of the upper end of the cylinder excluding the sidewall, as provided in this section. Requalification and required specification markings that are illegible may be reproduced on a metal plate and attached as provided by the original specification.

(2) *Previous requalification markings* may not be obliterated, except that, when the space originally provided for requalification dates becomes filled, additional dates may be added as follows:

(i) *All preceding* requalification dates may be removed by peening provided that —

[A] *Permission is obtained from the cylinder owner;*

[B] *The minimum wall thickness* is maintained in accordance with manufacturing specifications for the cylinder; and

[C] *The original manufacturing test date is not removed.*

(ii) *When the cylinder* is fitted with a footring, additional dates may be marked on the external surface of the footring.

(c) Requalification marking method. The depth of requalification markings may not be greater than specified in the applicable specification. The markings must be made by stamping, engraving, scribing or other method that produces a legible, durable mark.

(1) *A cylinder* used as a fire extinguisher (§180.209(j)) may be marked by using a pressure sensitive label.

(2) *For a DOT 3HT cylinder,* the test date and RIN must be applied by low-stress steel stamps to a depth no greater than that prescribed at the time of manufacture. Stamping on the sidewall is not authorized.

(d) Requalification markings. Each cylinder that has successfully passed requalification must be marked with the RIN set in a square pattern, between the month and year of the requalification date. The first character of the RIN must appear in the upper left corner of the square pattern; the second in the upper right; the third in the lower right, and the fourth in the lower left. Example: A cylinder requalified in September 1998, and approved by a person who has been issued RIN "A123", would be marked plainly and permanently into the metal of the cylinder in accordance with location requirements of the cylinder specification or on a metal plate permanently secured to the cylinder in accordance with paragraph (b) of this section. An example of the markings prescribed in this paragraph (d) is as follows:

A1
9 98 X
32

Where:
"9" is the month of requalification,
"A123" is the RIN,
"98" is the year of requalification, and
"X" represents the symbols described in paragraphs (f)(2) through (f)(7) of this section.

(1) *Upon a written request,* variation from the marking requirement may be approved by the Associate Administrator.

(2) *Exception.* A cylinder subject to the requirements of §173.301(l) of this subchapter may not be marked with a RIN.

(e) **Size of markings.** The size of the markings must be at least 6.35 mm (1/4 in.) high, except RIN characters must be at least 3.18 mm (1/8 in.) high.

(f) **Marking illustrations.** Examples of required requalification markings for DOT specification and exemption cylinders are illustrated as follows:

(1) *For designation* of the 5-year volumetric expansion test, 10-year volumetric expansion test for cylinders conforming to §180.209(f) and (h), or 12-year volumetric expansion test for fire extinguishers conforming to §173.309(b) of this subchapter and cylinders conforming to §180.209(e) and §180.209(g), the marking is as illustrated in paragraph (d) of this section.

(2) *For designation* of the 10-year volumetric expansion test for cylinders conforming to §180.209(b), the marking is as illustrated in paragraph (d) of this section, except that the "X" is replaced with a five-point star.

(3) *For designation* of special filling limits up to 10% in excess of the marked service pressure for cylinders conforming to §173.302a(b) of this subchapter, the marking is as illustrated in paragraph (d) of this section, except that the "X" is replaced with a plus sign "+".

(4) *For designation* of the proof pressure test, the marking is as illustrated in paragraph (d) of this section, except that the "X" is replaced with the letter "S".

(5) *For designation* of the 5-year external visual inspection for cylinders conforming to §180.209(g), the marking is as illustrated in paragraph (d) of this section, except that the "X" is replaced with the letter "E".

(6) *For designation* of DOT 8 series cylinder shell requalification only, the marking is as illustrated in paragraph (d) of this section, except that the "X" is replaced with the letter "S".

(7) *For designation* of DOT 8 series cylinder shell and porous filler requalification, the marking is as illustrated in paragraph (d) of this section, except that the "X" is replaced with the letters "FS".

§180.215 Reporting and record retention requirements.

(a) **Facility records.** A person who requalifies, repairs or rebuilds cylinders must maintain the following records where the requalification is performed:

(1) *Current RIN issuance letter;*

(2) *If the RIN* has expired and renewal is pending, a copy of the renewal request;

(3) *Copies of notifications* to Associate Administrator required under §107.805 of this chapter;

(4) *Current copies* of those portions of this subchapter applicable to its cylinder requalification and marking activities at that location;

(5) *Current copies* of all exemptions governing exemption cylinders requalified or marked by the requalifier at that location; and

(6) *The information* contained in each applicable CGA or ASTM standard incorporated by reference in §171.7 of this subchapter applicable to the requalifier's activities. This information must be the same as contained in the edition incorporated by reference in §171.7 of this subchapter.

(b) **Requalification records.** Daily records of visual inspection, pressure test, and ultrasonic examination if permitted under an exemption, as applicable, must be maintained by the person who performs the requalification until either the expiration of the requalification period or until the cylinder is again requalified, whichever occurs first. A single date may be used for each test sheet, provided each test on the sheet was conducted on that date. Ditto marks or a solid vertical line may be used to indicate repetition of the preceding entry for the following entries only: date; actual dimensions; manufacturer's name or symbol, if present; owner's name or symbol, if present; and test operator. Blank spaces may not be used to indicate repetition of a prior entry. The records must include the following information:

(1) *Calibration test records.* For each test to demonstrate calibration, the date; serial number of the calibrated cylinder; calibration test pressure; total, elastic and permanent expansions; and legible identification of test operator. The test operator must be able to demonstrate that the results of the daily calibration verification correspond to the hydrostatic tests performed on that day. The daily verification of calibration(s) may be recorded on the same sheets as, and with, test records for that date.

(2) *Pressure test and visual inspection records.* The date of requalification; serial number; DOT specification or exemption number; marked pressure; actual dimensions; manufacturer's name or symbol; owner's name or symbol, if present; result of visual inspection; actual test pressure; total, elastic and permanent expansions; percent permanent expansion; disposition, with reason for any repeated test, rejection or condemnation; and legible identification of test operator. For each cylinder marked pursuant to §173.302a(b)(5) of this subchapter, the test sheet must indicate the method by which any average or maximum wall stress was computed. Records must be kept for all completed, as well as unsuccessful tests. The entry for a second test after a failure to hold test pressure must indicate the date of the earlier test.

(3) *Wall stress.* Calculations of average and maximum wall stress pursuant to §173.302a(b)(3) of this subchapter, if performed.

(4) *Calibration certificates.* The most recent certificate of calibration must be maintained for each calibrated cylinder.

(c) **Repair, rebuilding or reheat treatment records.**

(1) *Records covering* welding or brazing repairs, rebuilding or reheat treating shall be retained for a minimum of fifteen years by the approved facility.

(2) *A record of rebuilding,* in accordance with §180.211(d), must be completed for each cylinder rebuilt. The record must be clear, legible, and contain the following information:

(i) *Name and address* of test facility, date of test report, and name of original manufacturer;

(ii) *Marks stamped* on cylinder to include specification number, service pressure, serial number, symbol of manufacturer, inspector's mark, and other marks, if any;

(iii) *Cylinder outside diameter and length in inches;*

(iv) *Rebuild process (welded, brazed, type seams, etc.);*

(v) *Description of assembly* and any attachments replaced (e.g., neckrings, footrings);

(vi) *Chemical analysis* of material for the cylinder, including seat and Code No., type of analysis (ladle, check), chemical components (Carbon (C), Phosphorous (P), Sulfur (S), Silicon (Si), Manganese (Mn), Nickel (Ni), Chromium (Cr), Molybdenum (Mo), Copper (Cu), Aluminum (Al), Zinc (Zn)), material manufacturer, name of person performing the analysis, results of physical tests of material for cylinder (yield strength (psi), tensile strength (psi), elongation percentage (inches), reduction in area percentage, weld bend, tensile bend, name of inspector);

(vii) *Results of proof pressure test* on cylinder, including test method, test pressure, total expansion, permanent expansion, elastic expansion, percent permanent expansion (permanent expansion may not exceed ten percent (10%) of total expansion), and volumetric capacity (volumetric capacity of a rebuilt cylinder must be within $\pm$3% of the calculated capacity);

(viii) *Each report* must include the following certification statement: "I certify that this rebuilt cylinder is accurately represented by the data above and conforms to all of the requirements in Subchapter C of Chapter I of Title 49 of the Code of Federal Regulations.". The certification must be signed by the rebuild technician and principal, officer, or partner of the rebuild facility.

Subpart D - Qualification and Maintenance of IBCs

§180.350 Applicability.

This subpart prescribes requirements, in addition to those contained in parts 107, 171, 172, 173, and 178 of this chapter, applicable to any person responsible for the continuing qualification, maintenance, or periodic retesting of an IBC.

§180.351 Qualification of IBCs.

(a) **General.** Each IBC used for the transportation of hazardous materials must be an authorized packaging.

(b) **IBC specifications.** To qualify as an authorized packaging, each IBC must conform to this subpart, the applicable requirements specified in part 173 of this subchapter, and the applicable requirements of subparts N and O of part 178 of this subchapter.

§180.352 Requirements for retest and inspection of IBCs.

(a) **General.** Each IBC constructed in accordance with a UN standard for which a test or inspection specified in paragraphs (b)(1), (b)(2) and (b)(3) of this section is required may not be filled and offered for transportation or transported until the test or inspection has been successfully completed. This paragraph does not apply to any IBC filled prior to the test or inspection due date. The requirements in this section do not apply to DOT 56 and 57 portable tanks.

(b) **Test and inspections for metal, rigid plastic,** and composite IBCs. Each IBC is subject to the following test and inspections:

(1) *Each IBC* intended to contain solids that are loaded or discharged under pressure or intended to contain liquids must be tested in accordance with the leakproofness test prescribed in §178.813 of this subchapter every 2.5 years, starting from the date of manufacture or the date of a repair conforming to paragraph (d)(1) of this section.

(2) *An external visual inspection* must be conducted initially after production and every 2.5 years starting from the date of manufacture or the date of a repair conforming to paragraph (d)(1) of this section to ensure that:

(i) *The IBC* is marked in accordance with requirements in §178.703 of this subchapter. Missing or damaged markings, or markings difficult to read must be restored or returned to original condition.

(ii) *Service equipment* is fully functional and free from damage which may cause failure. Missing, broken, or damaged parts must be repaired or replaced.

(iii) *The IBC* is capable of withstanding the applicable design qualification tests. The IBC must be externally inspected for cracks, warpage, corrosion or any other damage which might render the IBC unsafe for transportation. An IBC found with such defects must be removed from service or repaired in accordance with paragraph (d) of this section. The inner receptacle of a composite IBC must be removed from the outer IBC body for inspection unless the inner receptacle is bonded to the outer body or unless the outer body is constructed in such a way (e.g., a welded or riveted cage) that removal of the inner receptacle is not possible without impairing the integrity of the outer body. Defective inner receptacles must be replaced in accordance with paragraph (d) of this section or the entire IBC must be removed from service. For metal IBCs, thermal insulation must be removed to the extent necessary for proper examination of the IBC body.

(3) *Each metal,* rigid plastic and composite IBC must be internally inspected at least every five years to ensure that the IBC is free from damage and to ensure that the IBC is capable of withstanding the applicable design qualification tests.

(i) *The IBC* must be internally inspected for cracks, warpage, and corrosion or any other defect that might render the IBC unsafe for transportation. An IBC found with such defects must be removed from hazardous materials service until restored to the original design type of the IBC.

(ii) *Metal IBCs* must be inspected to ensure the minimum wall thickness requirements in §178.705(c)(1)(iv) of this subchapter are met. Metal IBCs not conforming to minimum wall thickness requirements must be removed from hazardous materials service.

(c) **Visual inspection for flexible, fiberboard, or wooden IBCs.** Each IBC must be visually inspected prior to first use and permitted reuse, by the person who places hazardous materials in the IBC, to ensure that:

(1) *The IBC* is marked in accordance with requirements in §178.703 of this subchapter. Additional marking allowed for each design type may be present. Required markings that are missing, damaged or difficult to read must be restored or returned to original condition.

(2) *Proper construction and design specifications have been met.*

(i) *Each flexible IBC must be inspected to ensure that:*

[A] Lifting straps if used, are securely fastened to the IBC in accordance with the design type.

[B] Seams are free from defects in stitching, heat sealing or gluing which would render the IBC unsafe for transportation of hazardous materials. All stitched seam-ends must be secure.

[C] Fabric used to construct the IBC is free from cuts, tears and punctures. Additionally, fabric must be free from scoring which may render the IBC unsafe for transport.

(ii) *Each fiberboard IBC must be inspected to ensure that:*

[A] Fluting or corrugated fiberboard is firmly glued to facings.

[B] Seams are creased and free from scoring, cuts, and scratches.

[C] Joints are appropriately overlapped and glued, stitched, taped or stapled as prescribed by the design. Where staples are used, the joints must be inspected for protruding staple-ends which could puncture or abrade the inner liner. All such ends must be protected before the IBC is authorized for hazardous materials service.

(iii) *Each wooden IBC must be inspected to ensure that:*

[A] End joints are secured in the manner prescribed by the design.

[B] IBC walls are free from defects in wood. Inner protrusions which could puncture or abrade the liner must be covered.

(d) **Requirements applicable to repair of IBCs.**

(1) *Except for flexible and fiberboard IBCs* and the bodies of rigid plastic and composite IBCs, damaged IBCs may be repaired and the inner receptacles of composite packagings may be replaced and returned to service provided:

(i) *The repaired IBC* conforms to the original design type and is capable of withstanding the applicable design qualification tests;

(ii) *An IBC* intended to contain liquids or solids that are loaded or discharged under pressure is subjected to a leakproofness test as specified in §178.813 of this subchapter and is marked with the date of the test; and

(iii) *The IBC* is subjected to the internal and external inspection requirements as specified in paragraph (b) of this section.

(2) *Except for flexible and fiberboard IBCs,* the structural equipment of an IBC may be repaired and returned to service provided:

(i) *The repaired IBC* conforms to the original design type and is capable of withstanding the applicable design qualification tests; and

(ii) *The IBC* is subjected to the internal and external inspection requirements as specified in paragraph (b) of this section.

(3) *Service equipment may be replaced provided:*

(i) *The repaired IBC* conforms to the original design type and is capable of withstanding the applicable design qualification tests;

(ii) *The IBC* is subjected to the external visual inspection requirements as specified in paragraph (b) of this section; and

(iii) *The proper functioning* and leak tightness of the service equipment, if applicable, is verified.

(e) **Retest date.** The date of the most recent periodic retest must be marked as provided in §178.703(b) of this subchapter.

(f) **Record retention.** The IBC owner or lessee shall keep records of periodic retests and initial and periodic inspections. Records must include design types and packaging specifications, test and inspection dates, name and address of test and inspection facilities, names or name of any persons conducting tests or inspections, and test or inspection specifics and results. Records must be kept for each packaging at each location where periodic tests are conducted, until such tests are successfully performed again or for at least 2.5 years from the date of the last test. These records must be made available for inspection by a representative of the Department on request.

Subpart E - Qualification and Maintenance of Cargo Tanks

§180.401 Applicability.

This subpart prescribes requirements, in addition to those contained in parts 107, 171, 172, 173 and 178 of this subchapter, applicable to any person responsible for the continuing qualification, maintenance or periodic testing of a cargo tank.

§180.403 Definitions.

In addition to the definitions contained in §§171.8, 178.320(a) and 178.345-1 of this subchapter, the following definitions apply to this subpart:

Corrosive to the tank/valve means a lading meets the criteria for corrosivity specified in §173.136 of this subchapter, for the material of construction of the tank or valve; or the lading has been shown through experience to be corrosive to the tank or valve.

Delivery hose assembly means a liquid delivery hose and its attached couplings.

Modification means any change to the original design and construction of a cargo tank or a cargo tank motor vehicle that affects its structural integrity or lading retention capability including changes to equipment certified as part of an emergency discharge control system required by §173.315(n)(2) of this subchapter. Any modification that involves welding on the cargo tank wall must also meet all requirements for "Repair" as defined in this section. Excluded from this category are the following:

(1) *A change to motor vehicle equipment* such as lights, truck or tractor power train components, steering and brake systems, and suspension parts, and changes to appurtenances, such as fender attachments, lighting brackets, ladder brackets; and

(2) *Replacement of components* such as valves, vents, and fittings with a component of a similar design and of the same size.

Owner means the person who owns a cargo tank motor vehicle used for the transportation of hazardous materials, or that person's authorized agent.

Piping system means any component of a cargo tank delivery system, other than a delivery hose assembly, that contains product during loading or unloading.

Rebarrelling means replacing more than 50 percent of the combined shell and head material of a cargo tank.

Repair means any welding on a cargo tank wall done to return a cargo tank or a cargo tank motor vehicle to its original design and construction specification, or to a condition prescribed for a later equivalent specification in effect at the time of the repair. Excluded from this category are the following:

(1) *A change to motor vehicle equipment* such as lights, truck or tractor power train components, steering and brake systems, and suspension parts, and changes to appurtenances, such as fender attachments, lighting brackets, ladder brackets; and

(2) *Replacement of components* such as valves, vents, and fittings with a component of a similar design and of the same size.

(3) *Replacement of an appurtenance by welding to a mounting pad.*

Replacement of a barrel means to replace the existing tank on a motor vehicle chassis with an unused (new) tank. For the definition of tank, see §178.345-1(c), §178.337-1, or §178.338-1 of this subchapter, as applicable.

Stretching means any change in length, width or diameter of the cargo tank, or any change to a cargo tank motor vehicle's undercarriage that may affect the cargo tank's structural integrity.

FEDERAL REGISTER UPDATES

In the April 18, 2003 Federal Register, §180.403 was revised, effective October 1, 2003.

Corroded or **abraded** means any visible reduction in the material thickness of the cargo tank wall or valve due to pitting, flaking, gouging, or chemical reaction to the material surface that effects the safety or serviceability of the cargo tank. The term does not include cosmetic or minor surface degradation that does not effect the safety or serviceability of the cargo tank. [1]

Corrosive to the tank or valve means that the lading has been shown through experience or test data to reduce the thickness of the material of construction of the tank wall or valve. [1]

1. The definition for "Corrosive to the tank/valve" was removed and new definitions for "Corroded or abraded" and "Corrosive to the tank or valve" were added.

§180.405 Qualification of cargo tanks.

(a) **General.** Unless otherwise provided in this subpart, each cargo tank used for the transportation of hazardous material must be an authorized packaging.

(b) **Cargo tank specifications.** To qualify as an authorized packaging, each cargo tank must conform to this subpart, the applicable requirements specified in part 173 of this subchapter for the specific lading and, where a DOT specification cargo tank is required, an applicable specification in effect on the date the initial construction began: MC 300, MC 301, MC 302, MC 303, MC 304, MC 305, MC 306, MC 307, MC 310, MC 311, MC 312, MC 330, MC 331, MC 338, DOT 406, DOT 407, or DOT 412 (§178.337, §178.338, §178.345, §178.346, §178.347, §178.348 of this subchapter). However, no cargo tank may be marked or certified after August 31, 1995, to the applicable MC 306, MC 307, MC 312, MC 331 or MC 338 specification in effect on December 30, 1990.

(c) **Cargo tank specifications no longer authorized for construction.**

(1) *A cargo tank* made to a specification listed in column 1 of table 1 or table 2 of this paragraph (c)(1) may be used when authorized in this part, provided —

(i) *The cargo tank* initial construction began on or before the date listed in table 1, column 2, as follows:

Table 1

Column 1	Column 2
MC 300	Sept. 2, 1967
MC 301	June 12, 1961
MC 302, MC 303, MC 304, MC 305, MC 310, MC 311	Sept. 2, 1967
MC 330	May 15, 1967

(ii) *The cargo tank* was marked or certified before the date listed in table 2, column 2, as follows:

Table 2

Column 1	Column 2
MC 306, MC 307, MC 312	Sept. 1, 1995

(2) *A cargo tank* of a specification listed in paragraph (c)(1) of this section may have its pressure relief devices and outlets modified as follows:

(i) *A Specification* MC 300, MC 301, MC 302, MC 303, or MC 305 cargo tank, to conform with a Specification MC 306 or DOT 406 cargo tank (See §§178.346-3 and 178.346-4 of this subchapter).

(ii) *A Specification* MC 306 cargo tank to conform to a Specification DOT 406 cargo tank (See §§178.346-3 and 178.346-4 of this subchapter).

(iii) *A Specification* MC 304 cargo tank, to conform with a Specification MC 307 or DOT 407 cargo tank (See §§178.347-4 and 178.345-11 of this subchapter).

(iv) *A Specification* MC 307 cargo tank, to conform with a Specification DOT 407 cargo tank (See §§178.347-4 and 178.345-11 of this subchapter).

(v) *A Specification* MC 310 or MC 311 cargo tank, to conform with a Specification MC 312 or DOT 412 cargo tank (See §§178.348-4 and 178.345-11 of this subchapter).

(vi) *A Specification* MC 312 cargo tank, to conform with a Specification DOT 412 cargo tank (See §§178.348-4 and 178.345-11 of this subchapter).

(vii) *A Specification* MC 330 cargo tank, to conform with a Specification MC 331 cargo tank, except as specifically required by §173.315 of this subchapter (see §§178.337-8 and 178.337-9 of this subchapter).

(d) **MC 338 cargo tank.** The owner of a cargo tank that conforms to and was used under the terms of an exemption issued before October 1, 1984, that authorizes the transportation of a cryogenic liquid shall remove the exemption number stenciled on the cargo tank and stamp the specification plate (or a plate placed adjacent to the specification plate) "DOT MC 338" followed by the exemption number, for example, "DOT MC 338-E * * * *". (Asterisks to be replaced by the exemption number). The cargo tank must be remarked prior to the expiration date of the exemption. During the period the cargo tank is in service, the owner of a cargo tank that is remarked in this manner must retain at its principal place of business a copy of the last exemption in effect. No new construction of cargo tanks pursuant to such exemption is authorized.

(1) *The holding time* must be determined, as required in §178.338-9 of this subchapter, on each cargo tank or on at least one cargo tank of each design. Any subsequent cargo tank manufactured to the same design type (see §178.320), if not individually tested, must have the optional test regimen performed during the first shipment (see §178.338-9 (b) and (c) of this subchapter).

(2) *The holding time* determined by test for one authorized cryogenic liquid may be used as the basis for establishing the holding time for other authorized cryogenic liquids.

(e) **MC 331 cargo tanks.** The owner of a MC 331 (§178.337 of this subchapter) cargo tank that conforms to and was used under an exemption issued before October 1, 1984, that authorizes the transportation of ethane, refrigerated liquid; ethane-propane mixture, refrigerated liquid; or hydrogen chloride, refrigerated liquid shall remove the exemption number stenciled on the cargo tank and stamp the exemption number on the specification plate (or a plate placed adjacent to the specification plate), immediately after the DOT Specification, for example, "DOT MC 331-E * * * *". (Asterisks to be replaced by the exemption number.) The cargo tank must be remarked prior to the expiration date of the exemption. During the period the cargo tank is in service, the owner of a cargo tank that is remarked in this manner must retain at the owner's principal place of business a copy of the last exemption in effect.

(f) **MC 306, MC 307, MC 312 cargo tanks.** Either a Registered Inspector or a Design Certifying Engineer and the owner of a MC 306, MC 307 or MC 312 cargo tank motor vehicle constructed in accordance with and used under an exemption issued before December 31, 1990, that authorizes a condition specified in this paragraph shall examine the cargo tank motor vehicle and its design to determine if it meets the requirements of the applicable MC 306, MC 307 or MC 312 specification in effect at the time of manufacture, except as specified herein.

(1) *A cargo tank motor vehicle* constructed after August 1, 1981, or the date specified in the applicable exemption, in conformance with the following conditions that apply, may be remarked and certified in accordance with paragraphs (f) (5) and (6) of this section:

(i) *A vacuum-loaded cargo tank* must have an ASME Code stamped specification plate marked with a minimum internal design pressure of 25 psig, and be designed for a minimum external design pressure of 15 psig.

(ii) *An outlet equipped* with a self-closing system which includes an external stop-valve must have the stop valve and associated piping protected within the vehicle's rear-end tank protection device, vehicle frame or an equally adequate accident damage protection device (See §178.345-8 of this subchapter.) The self-closing system (See §178.345-11 of this subchapter) must be equipped with a remotely actuated means of closure as follows:

[A] For a cargo tank used in other than corrosive service, the remote means of closure must be activated for closure by manual or mechanical means and, in case of fire, by an automatic heat activated means.

[B] For a cargo tank used in corrosive service, the remote means of closure may be actuated by manual or mechanical means only.

(iii) *A cargo tank* having an unreinforced portion of the shell exceeding 60 inches must have the circumferential reinforcement located so that the thickness and tensile strength of shell material in combination with the frame and circumferential reinforcement produces a structural integrity at least equal to that prescribed in §178.345-3 of this subchapter or the specification in effect at time of manufacture.

(iv) *A cargo tank* having a projection from the tank shell or head that may contain lading in any tank position is authorized, provided such projection is as strong as the tank shell or head and is located within the motor vehicle's rear-end tank protection or other appropriate accident damage protection device.

(v) *A cargo tank* may be constructed of nickel, titanium, or other ASME sheet or plate materials in accordance with an exemption.

(2) *A vacuum-loaded cargo tank* constructed after August 1, 1981, or the date specified in the applicable exemption, in conformance with paragraph (f)(1) of this section, except that an outlet equipped with an external valve which is not part of a self-closing system:

(i) *Must be equipped* with a self-closing system prior to September 1, 1993.

(ii) *May be remarked and certified* in accordance with paragraphs (f)(5) and (6) of this section after the cargo tank motor vehicle has been equipped with the self-closing system.

(3) *A vacuum-loaded cargo tank* constructed prior to August 1, 1981, in conformance with paragraph (f)(1) of this section, except for paragraph (f)(1)(i), may be remarked and certified in accordance with paragraphs (f) (5) and (6) of this section.

(4) *A vacuum-loaded cargo tank* constructed prior to August 1, 1981, in conformance with paragraph (f)(1) of this section, except for paragraph (f)(1)(i) of this section, and except that an outlet is equipped with an external valve which is not part of a self-closing system:

(i) *Must be equipped* with a self-closing system prior to September 1, 1993.

(ii) *May be remarked* and certified in accordance with paragraphs (f)(5) and (6) of this section after the cargo tank motor vehicle has been equipped with the self-closing system.

(5) *The owner of a cargo tank* for which a determination has been made that the cargo tank is in conformance with paragraph (f) (1), (2), (3), or (4) of this section shall complete a written certification, in English, signed by the owner and containing at least the following information:

(i) *A statement* certifying that each cargo tank conforms to §180.405 (f) (1), (2), (3), or (4);

(ii) *The applicable* DOT exemption number, the applicable specification number and the owner's and manufacturer's serial number for the cargo tank;

(iii) *A statement* setting forth any modifications made to bring the cargo tank into conformance with §180.405(f)(1), (2), (3), or (4), or the applicable specification;

(iv) *A statement* identifying the person certifying the cargo tank and the date of certification.

(6) *The owner* of a certified cargo tank shall remove the exemption number stenciled on the cargo tank and shall durably mark the specification plate (or a plate placed adjacent to the specification plate) "MC +++-E ****####" (where "+++" is to be replaced by the applicable specification number, "* * * *" by the exemption number and "# # # #" by the alloy.)

(7) *A cargo tank* remarked and certified in conformance with this paragraph (f) is excepted from the provisions of §180.405(c).

(8) *During the period* the cargo tank is in service, and for one year thereafter, the owner of a cargo tank that is certified and remarked in this manner must retain on file at its principal place of business a copy of the certificate and the last exemption in effect.

(g) Cargo tank manhole assemblies.

(1) *MC 306, MC 307, and MC 312* cargo tanks marked or certified after December 30, 1990, and DOT 406, DOT 407, and DOT 412 cargo tank motor vehicles must be equipped with manhole assemblies conforming with §178.345-5 of this subchapter.

(2) *On or before* August 31, 1995, each owner of a cargo tank marked or certified before December 31, 1990, authorized for the transportation of a hazardous material, must have the cargo tank equipped with manhole assemblies conforming with §178.345-5, except for the dimensional requirements in §178.345-5(a), the hydrostatic testing requirements in §178.345-5(b), and the marking requirements in §178.345-5(e) of this subchapter. A manhole assembly meeting one of the following provisions is considered to be in compliance with this paragraph:

(i) *Manhole assemblies* on MC 300, MC 301, MC 302, MC 303, MC 305, MC 306, MC 310, MC 311 and MC 312 cargo tanks which are marked or certified in writing as conforming to §178.345-5 of this subchapter or TTMA RP No. 61, or are tested and certified in accordance with TTMA TB No. 107.

(ii) *Manhole assemblies on MC 304 and MC 307 cargo tanks.*

(iii) *Manhole assemblies* on MC 310, MC 311, and MC 312 cargo tanks with a test pressure of 36 psig or greater.

(3) *The owner* of five or more DOT specification cargo tanks requiring retrofit or certification of the manhole closure must retrofit or certify at least 20 percent of the affected cargo tanks each year beginning in 1991 until all affected manhole closures on cargo tanks have been retrofitted or certified. The owner of fewer than 5 DOT specification cargo tanks has until August 31, 1995 to retrofit or certify the manhole closures.

(h) Pressure relief system. Properly functioning reclosing pressure relief valves and frangible or fusible vents need not be replaced. However, replacement of reclosing pressure relief valves on MC-specification cargo tanks is authorized subject to the following requirements:

(1) *Until August 31, 1998,* the owner of a cargo tank may replace a reclosing pressure relief device with a device which is in compliance with the requirements for pressure relief devices in effect at the time the cargo tank specification became superseded. If the pressure relief device is installed as an integral part of a manhole cover assembly, the manhole cover must comply with the requirements of paragraph (g) of this section.

(2) *After August 31, 1998,* replacement for any reclosing pressure relief valve must be capable of reseating to a leak-tight condition after a pressure surge, and the volume of lading released may not exceed 1 L. Specific performance requirements for these pressure relief valves are set forth in §178.345-10(b)(3) of this subchapter.

(3) *As provided* in paragraph (c)(2) of this section, the owner of a cargo tank may elect to modify reclosing pressure relief devices to more recent cargo tank specifications. However, replacement devices constructed to the requirements of §178.345-10 of this subchapter must provide the minimum venting capacity required by the original specification to which the cargo tank was designed and constructed.

(i) Flammable cryogenic liquids. Each cargo tank used to transport a flammable cryogenic liquid must be examined after each shipment to determine its actual holding time (See §173.318(g)(3) of this subchapter.)

(j) Withdrawal of certification. A specification cargo tank that for any reason no longer meets the applicable specification may not be used to transport hazardous materials unless the cargo tank is repaired and retested in accordance with §§180.413 and 180.407 prior to being returned to hazardous materials service. If the cargo tank is not in conformance with the applicable specification requirements, the specification plate on the cargo tank must be removed, obliterated or securely covered. The details of the conditions necessitating withdrawal of the certification must be recorded and signed on the written certificate for that cargo tank. The vehicle owner shall retain the certificate for at least 1 year after withdrawal of the certification.

(k) DOT specification cargo tank with no marked design pressure or a marked design pressure of less than 3 psig. The owner of an MC 300, MC 301, MC 302, MC 303, MC 305, MC 306 or MC 312 cargo tank, which has a pressure relief system set at 3 psig, may mark or remark the cargo tank with an MAWP or design pressure of not greater than 3 psig.

(l) MC 300, MC 301, MC 302, MC 303, MC 305, MC 306 cargo tank — Rear accident damage protection.

(1) *Notwithstanding the requirements* in §180.405(b), the applicable specification requirement for a rear bumper or rear-end tank protection device on MC 300, MC 301, MC 302, MC 303, MC 305, and MC 306 cargo tanks does not apply to a cargo tank truck (power unit) until July 1, 1992, if the cargo tank truck —

(i) *Was manufactured before July 1, 1989;*

(ii) *Is used to transport gasoline* or any other petroleum distillate product; and

(iii) *Is operated* in combination with a cargo tank full trailer. However, an empty cargo tank truck, without a cargo tank full trailer attached, may be operated without the required rear bumper or rear-end tank protection device on a one-time basis while being transported to a repair facility for installation of a rear bumper or rear-end protection device.

(2) *Each cargo tank* shall be provided with a rear accident damage protection device to protect the tank and piping in the event of a rear-end collision and reduce the likelihood of damage which could result in the loss of lading. The rear-end protection device must be in the form of a rear-end tank protection device meeting the requirements of §178.345-8(d) or a rear bumper meeting the following:

(i) *The bumper* shall be located at least 6 inches to the rear of any vehicle component used for loading or unloading or that may contain lading while the vehicle is in transit.

(ii) *The dimensions* of the bumper shall conform to §393.86 of this title.

(iii) *The structure* of the bumper shall be designed to withstand, without leakage of lading, the impact of the vehicle with rated payload, at a deceleration of 2 "g" using a safety factor of two based on the ultimate strength of the bumper material. Such impact shall be considered uniformly distributed and applied horizontally (parallel to the ground) from any direction at an angle not exceeding 30 degrees to the longitudinal axis of the vehicle.

(m) **Specification MC 330, MC 331 cargo tank motor vehicles,** and nonspecification cargo tank motor vehicles conforming to §173.315(k) of this subchapter, intended for use in the transportation of liquefied compressed gases.

(1) *No later* than the date of its first scheduled pressure test after July 1, 2001, each specification MC 330 and MC 331 cargo tank motor vehicle, and each nonspecification cargo tank motor vehicle conforming to §173.315(k) of this subchapter, marked and certified before July 1, 2001, that is used to transport a Division 2.1 material, a Division 2.2 material with a subsidiary hazard, a Division 2.3 material, or anhydrous ammonia must have an emergency discharge control capability as specified in §173.315(n) of this subchapter. Each passive shut-off system installed prior to July 1, 2001, must be certified by a Design Certifying Engineer that it meets the requirements of §173.315(n)(2) of this subchapter.

(2) *The requirement* in paragraph (m)(1) of this section does not apply to a cargo tank equal to or less than 13,247.5 L (3,500 gallons) water capacity transporting in metered delivery service a Division 2.1 material, a Division 2.2 material with a subsidiary hazard, or anhydrous ammonia equipped with an off-truck remote shut-off device that was installed prior to July 1, 2000. The device must be capable of stopping the transfer of lading by operation of a transmitter carried by a qualified person attending unloading of the cargo tank. The device is subject to the requirement in §177.840(o) of this subchapter for a daily test at 45.72 meters (150 feet).

(3) *Each specification* MC 330 and MC 331 cargo tank in metered delivery service of greater than 13,247.5 L (3,500 gallons) water capacity transporting a Division 2.1 material, a Division 2.2 material with a subsidiary hazard, or anhydrous ammonia, marked and certified before July 1, 1999, must have an emergency discharge control capability as specified in §§173.315(n) and 177.840 of this subchapter no later than the date of its first scheduled pressure test after July 1, 2001, or July 1, 2003, whichever is earlier.

(n) **Thermal activation.** No later than the date of its first scheduled leakage test after July 1, 1999, each specification MC 330 or MC 331 cargo tank motor vehicle and each nonspecification cargo tank motor vehicle conforming to §173.315(k) of this subchapter, marked and certified before July 1, 1999, that is used to transport a liquefied compressed gas, other than carbon dioxide and chlorine, that has a water capacity of 13,247.5 L (3,500 gallons) or less must be equipped with a means of thermal activation for the internal self-closing stop valve as specified in §178.337-8(a)(4) of this subchapter.

FEDERAL REGISTER UPDATES

In the April 18, 2003 Federal Register, §180.405 was revised, effective October 1, 2003.

(b) **Cargo tank specifications.** [1]

(1) *To qualify as an authorized packaging,* each cargo tank must conform to this subpart, the applicable requirements specified in part 173 of this subchapter for the specific lading, and where a DOT specification cargo tank is required, an applicable specification in effect on the date initial construction began: MC 300, MC 301, MC 302, MC 303, MC 304, MC 305, MC 306, MC 307, MC 310, MC 311, MC 312, MC 330, MC 331, MC 338, DOT 406, DOT 407, or DOT 412 (§§178.337, 178.338, 178.345, 178.346, 178.347, 178.348 of this subchapter). However, except as provided in paragraphs (b)(2), (d), (e), (f)(5), and (f)(6) of this section, no cargo tank may be marked or certified after August 31, 1995, to the applicable MC 306, MC 307, MC 312, MC 331, or MC 338 specification in effect on December 30, 1990.

(2) *Exception.* A cargo tank originally manufactured to the MC 306, MC 307, or MC 312 specification that has not been stretched, rebarrelled, or modified may be re-certified to the original specification provided:

(i) *Sufficient records* are available verifying the cargo tank was originally manufactured to the specification;

(ii) *A Design Certifying Engineer* or Registered Inspector verifies the cargo tank conforms to all applicable requirements of the original specification and furnishes to the owner written documentation which verifies the tank complies with the original structural design requirements in effect at the time the tank was originally constructed;

(iii) *The cargo tank* meets all applicable tests and inspections required by §180.407(c); and

(iv) *The cargo tank* is re-certified to the original specification in accordance with the reporting and record retention provisions of §180.417. The certification documents required by §180.417(a)(3) must include both the date the cargo tank was originally certified to the specification, and the date it was re-certified. The specification plate on the cargo tank or cargo tank motor vehicle must display the date the cargo tank was originally certified to the specification.

(g) [2]

(2) [3]

(i) *Manhole assemblies* on MC 300, MC 301, MC 302, MC 303, MC 305, MC 306, MC 310, MC 311, and MC 312 cargo tanks that are marked or certified in writing as conforming to §178.345-5 of this subchapter or TTMA RP No. 61-98 (incorporated by reference; see §171.7 of this subchapter), or are tested and certified in accordance with TTMA TB No. 107 (incorporated by reference; see §171.7 of this subchapter). [4]

(3) *[Reserved]* [5]

(k) **DOT-specification cargo tank** with no marked design pressure or a marked design pressure of less than 3 psig. The owner of an MC 300, MC 301, MC 302, MC 303, MC 305, MC 306, or MC 312 cargo tank with a pressure relief system set at 3 psig, must mark or remark the cargo tank with an MAWP or design pressure of not less than 3 psig. [6]

(l) [7]

(2) [8]

(iii) *The structure* of the bumper must be designed in accordance with §178.345-8(d)(3) of this subchapter. [9]

(o) **On-truck remote control** of self-closing stop valves — MC 330, MC 331, and MC 338. On or before October 2, 2006 — [10]

(1) *Each owner* of an MC 330 or MC 331 cargo tank motor vehicle marked or certified before January 1, 1995, must equip the cargo tank with an on-vehicle remote means of closure of the internal self-closing stop valve in conformance with §178.337-8(a)(4) of this subchapter. This requirement does not apply to cargo tanks used only for carbon dioxide and marked "For carbon dioxide only" or intended for use in chlorine service only.

(2) *Each owner* of an MC 338 cargo tank motor vehicle marked or certified before January 1, 1995, must equip each remotely controlled shutoff valve with an on-vehicle remote means of automatic closure in conformance with §178.338-11(c) of this subchapter. This requirement does not apply to cargo tanks used for the transportation of argon, carbon dioxide, helium, krypton, neon, nitrogen, or xenon, or mixtures thereof.

1. Paragraph (b) was revised.
2. Paragraph (g) is the same as before.
3. Paragraph (g)(2) is the same as before.
4. Paragraph (g)(2)(i) was revised.
5. Paragraph (g)(3) was removed and reserved.
6. Paragraph (k) was revised.
7. Paragraph (l) is the same as before.
8. Paragraph (l)(2) is the same as before.
9. Paragraph (l)(2)(iii) was revised.
10. Paragraph (o) was added.

§180.407 Requirements for test and inspection of specification cargo tanks.

(a) **General.**

(1) *A cargo tank* constructed in accordance with a DOT specification for which a test or inspection specified in this section has become due, may not be filled and offered for transportation or transported until the test or inspection has been successfully completed. This paragraph does not apply to any cargo tank filled prior to the test or inspection due date.

(2) *Except during a pressure test* or during loading or unloading, a cargo tank may not be subjected to a pressure greater than its design pressure or MAWP.

(3) *A person witnessing or performing* a test or inspection specified in this section must meet the minimum qualifications prescribed in §180.409.

(4) *Each cargo tank* must be evaluated in accordance with the acceptable results of tests and inspections prescribed in §180.411.

(5) *Each cargo tank* which has successfully passed a test or inspection specified in this section must be marked in accordance with §180.415.

(6) *A cargo tank which fails a prescribed test or inspection must:*

(i) *Be repaired and retested in accordance with §180.413; or*

(ii) *Be removed* from hazardous materials service and the specification plate removed, obliterated or covered in a secure manner.

(b) **Conditions requiring test and inspection of cargo tanks.** Without regard to any other test or inspection requirements, a specification cargo tank must be tested and inspected in accordance with this section prior to further use if:

(1) *The cargo tank shows evidence* of bad dents, corroded or abraded areas, leakage, or any other condition that might render it unsafe for transportation service.

(2) *The cargo tank has been in an accident* and has been damaged to an extent that may adversely affect its lading retention capability.

(3) *The cargo tank has been* out of hazardous materials transportation service for a period of one year or more. Each cargo tank that has been out of hazardous materials transportation service for a period of one year or more must be pressure tested in accordance with §180.407(g) prior to further use.

(4) *The cargo tank has been modified* from its original design specification.

(5) *The Department so requires* based on the existence of probable cause that the cargo tank is in an unsafe operating condition.

(c) **Periodic test and inspection.** Each specification cargo tank must be tested and inspected as specified in the following table by an inspector meeting the qualifications in §180.409.

Compliance Dates - Inspections and Test Under §180.407(c)

Test or inspection (cargo tank specification, configuration, and service)	Date by which first test must be completed[1]	Interval period after first test
External Visual Inspection:		
All cargo tanks designed to be loaded by vacuum with full opening rear heads	September 1, 1991	6 months
All other cargo tanks	September 1, 1991	1 year
Internal Visual Inspection:		
All insulated cargo tanks, except MC 330, MC 331, MC 338	September 1, 1991	1 year
All cargo tanks transporting lading corrosive to the tank	September 1, 1991	1 year
All other cargo tanks, except MC 338	September 1, 1995	5 years
Lining Inspection:		
All lined cargo tanks transporting lading corrosive to the tank	September 1, 1991	1 year
Leakage Test:		
MC 330 and MC 331 cargo tanks in chlorine service	September 1, 1991	2 years
All other cargo tanks except MC 338	September 1, 1991	1 year
Pressure Test:		
(Hydrostatic or pneumatic)[2,3]		
All cargo tanks which are insulated with no manhole or insulated and lined, except MC 338	September 1, 1991	1 year
All cargo tanks designed to be loaded by vacuum with full opening rear heads	September 1, 1992	2 years
MC 330 and MC 331 cargo tanks in chlorine service	September 1, 1992	2 years
All other cargo tanks	September 1, 1995	5 years
Thickness Test:		
All unlined cargo tanks transporting material corrosive to the tank, except MC 338	September 1, 1992	2 years

1. If a cargo tank is subject to an applicable inspection or test requirement under the regulations in effect on December 30, 1990, and the due date (as specified by a requirement in effect on December 30, 1990) for completing the required inspection or test occurs before the compliance date listed in table I, the earlier date applies.
2. Pressure testing is not required for MC 330 and MC 331 cargo tanks in dedicated sodium metal service.
3. Pressure testing is not required for uninsulated lined cargo tanks, with a design pressure or MAWP 15 psig or less, which receive an external visual inspection and lining inspection at least once each year.

(d) External visual inspection and testing.

(1) *Where insulation precludes* external visual inspection, the cargo tank, other than an MC 330 or MC 331 cargo tank, must be given a visual internal inspection in accordance with §180.407(e). The tank must be hydrostatically or pneumatically tested in accordance with §180.407(c) and (g) where:

(i) *Visual inspection is precluded by internal lining or coating, or*

(ii) *The cargo tank is not equipped* with a manhole or inspection opening.

(2) *The external visual inspection and testing* must include as a minimum the following:

(i) *The tank shell and heads* must be inspected for corroded or abraded areas, dents, distortions, defects in welds and any other conditions, including leakage, that might render the tank unsafe for transportation service;

(ii) *The piping, valves, and gaskets* must be carefully inspected for corroded areas, defects in welds, and other conditions, including leakage, that might render the tank unsafe for transportation service;

(iii) *All devices for tightening manhole covers* must be operative and there must be no evidence of leakage at manhole covers or gaskets;

(iv) *All emergency devices and valves* including self-closing stop valves, excess flow valves and remote closure devices must be free from corrosion, distortion, erosion and any external damage that will prevent safe operation. Remote closure devices and self-closing stop valves must be functioned to demonstrate proper operation;

(v) *Missing bolts, nuts* and fusible links or elements must be replaced, and loose bolts and nuts must be tightened;

(vi) *All markings on the cargo tank* required by parts 172, 178 and 180 of this subchapter must be legible;

(vii) *[Reserved]*

(viii) *All major appurtenances* and structural attachments on the cargo tank including, but not limited to, suspension system attachments, connecting structures, and those elements of the upper coupler (fifth wheel) assembly that can be inspected without dismantling the upper coupler (fifth wheel) assembly must be inspected for any corrosion or damage which might prevent safe operation;

(ix) *For cargo tanks* transporting lading corrosive to the tank, areas covered by the upper coupler (fifth wheel) assembly must be inspected at least once in each two year period for corroded and abraded areas, dents, distortions, defects in welds, and any other condition that might render the tank unsafe for transportation service. The upper coupler (fifth wheel) assembly must be removed from the cargo tank for this inspection.

(3) *All reclosing pressure relief valves* must be externally inspected for any corrosion or damage which might prevent safe operation. All reclosing pressure relief valves on cargo tanks carrying lading corrosive to the valve must be removed from the cargo tank for inspection and testing. Each reclosing pressure relief valve required to be removed and tested must open at the required set pressure and reseat to a leak-tight condition at 90 percent of the set-to-discharge pressure or the pressure prescribed for the applicable cargo tank specification.

(4) *Corroded or abraded areas* of the cargo tank wall must be thickness tested in accordance with the procedures set forth in paragraphs (i)(2), (i)(3), (i)(5) and (i)(6) of this section.

(5) *The gaskets on any full opening rear head must be:*

(i) *Visually inspected for cracks or splits* caused by weather or wear; and

(ii) *Replaced if cuts or cracks* which are likely to cause leakage, or are of a depth one-half inch or more, are found.

(6) *The inspector must record the results* of the external visual examination as specified in §180.417(b).

(e) Internal visual inspection.

(1) *When the cargo tank* is not equipped with a manhole or inspection opening, or the cargo tank design precludes an internal inspection, the tank shall be hydrostatically or pneumatically tested in accordance with 180.407(c) and (g).

(2) *The internal visual inspection* must include as a minimum the following:

(i) *The tank shell and heads* must be inspected for corroded and abraded areas, dents, distortions, defects in welds, and any other condition that might render the tank unsafe for transportation service.

(ii) *Tank liners must be inspected as specified in §180.407(f).*

(3) *Corroded or abraded areas* of the cargo tank wall must be thickness tested in accordance with paragraphs (i)(2), (i)(3), (i)(5) and (i)(6) of this section.

(4) *The inspector must record the results* of the internal visual inspection as specified in §180.417(b).

(f) Lining inspection. The integrity of the lining on all lined cargo tanks, when lining is required by this subchapter, must be verified at least once each year as follows:

(1) *Rubber (elastomeric) lining must be tested for holes as follows:*

(i) *Equipment must consist of:*

[A] *A high frequency spark tester* capable of producing sufficient voltage to ensure proper calibration;

[B] *A probe with an "L" shaped* 2.4 mm (0.09 inch) diameter wire with up to a 30.5 cm (12-inch) bottom leg (end bent to a 12.7 mm (0.5 inch) radius), or equally sensitive probe; and

[C] *A steel calibration coupon* 30.5 cm x 30.5 cm (12 inches x 12 inches) covered with the same material and thickness as that to be tested. The material on the coupon shall have a test hole to the metal substrate made by puncturing the material with a 22 gauge hypodermic needle or comparable piercing tool.

(ii) *The probe must be passed* over the surface of the calibration coupon in a constant uninterrupted manner until the hole is found. The hole is detected by the white or light blue spark formed. (A sound lining causes a dark blue or purple spark.) The voltage must be adjusted to the lowest setting that will produce a minimum 12.7 mm (0.5 inch) spark measured from the top of the lining to the probe. To assure that the setting on the probe has not changed, the spark tester must be calibrated periodically using the test calibration coupon, and the same power source, probe, and cable length.

(iii) *After calibration,* the probe must be passed over the lining in an uninterrupted stroke.

(iv) *Holes that are found* must be repaired using equipment and procedures prescribed by the lining manufacturer or lining installer.

(2) *Linings made of other than rubber* (elastomeric material) must be tested using equipment and procedures prescribed by the lining manufacturer or lining installer.

(3) *Degraded or defective areas* of the cargo tank liner must be removed and the cargo tank wall below the defect must be inspected. Corroded areas of the tank wall must be thickness tested in accordance with paragraphs (i)(2), (i)(3), (i)(5) and (i)(6) of this section.

(4) *The inspector must record the results* of the lining inspection as specified in §180.417(b).

(g) Pressure test. All components of the cargo tank wall, as defined in §178.320(a) of this subchapter, must be pressure tested as prescribed by this paragraph.

(1) *Test Procedure —*

(i) *As part of the pressure test,* the inspector must perform an external and internal visual inspection, except that on an MC 338 cargo tank, or a cargo tank not equipped with a manhole or inspection opening, an internal inspection is not required.

(ii) *All reclosing pressure relief valves must be:*

[A] *Removed from the cargo tank* for inspection and testing. Each reclosing pressure relief valve must open at the required set pressure and reseat to a leak-tight condition at 90 percent of the set-to- discharge pressure or the pressure prescribed for the applicable cargo tank specification; or,

[B] *Replaced.*

(iii) *Except for cargo tanks* carrying lading corrosive to the tank, areas covered by the upper coupler (fifth wheel) assembly must be inspected for corroded and abraded areas, dents, distortions, defects in welds, and any other condition that might render the tank unsafe for transportation service. The upper coupler (fifth wheel) assembly must be removed from the cargo tank for this inspection.

(iv) *Each cargo tank must be tested* hydrostatically or pneumatically to the internal pressure specified in the following table:

Specification	Test pressure
MC 300, 301, 302, 303, 305, 306	20.7 kPa (3 psig) or design pressure, whichever is greater.
MC 304, 307	275.8 kPa (40 psig) or 1.5 times the design pressure, whichever is greater.
MC 310, 311, 312	20.7 kPa (3 psig) or 1.5 times the design pressure, whichever is greater.
MC 330, 331	1.5 times either the MAWP or the re-rated pressure, whichever is applicable.
MC 338	1.25 times either the MAWP or the re-rated pressure, whichever is applicable.
DOT 406	34.5 kPa (5 psig) or 1.5 times the MAWP, whichever is greater.
DOT 407	275.8 kPa (40 psig) or 1.5 times the MAWP, whichever is greater.
DOT 412	1.5 times the MAWP.

(v) *Each owner of 5 or more* MC 300, MC 301, MC 302, MC 303, MC 304, MC 305, MC 306, MC 307, MC 310, MC 311, or MC 312 cargo tanks must pressure test at least 20 percent of the cargo tanks in his ownership each year beginning in 1991. The owner of fewer than five MC specification cargo tanks has until August 31, 1995, to pressure test these units.

(vi) *Each cargo tank* of a multi-tank cargo tank motor vehicle must be tested with the adjacent cargo tanks empty and at atmospheric pressure.

(vii) *All closures except pressure relief devices* must be in place during the test. All prescribed loading and unloading venting devices rated at less than test pressure may be removed during the test. If retained, the devices must be rendered inoperative by clamps, plugs, or other equally effective restraining devices. Restraining devices may not prevent detection of leaks or damage the venting devices and must be removed immediately after the test is completed.

(viii) *Hydrostatic test method.* Each cargo tank, including its domes, must be filled with water or other liquid having similar viscosity, at a temperature not exceeding 100 °F. The cargo tank must then be pressurized to not less than the pressure specified in paragraph (g)(1)(iv) of this section. The cargo tank, including its closures, must hold the prescribed test pressure for at least 10 minutes during which time it shall be inspected for leakage, bulging or any other defect.

(ix) *Pneumatic test method.* Pneumatic testing may involve higher risk than hydrostatic testing. Therefore, suitable safeguards must be provided to protect personnel and facilities should failure occur during the test. The cargo tank must be pressurized with air or an inert gas. The pneumatic test pressure in the cargo tank must be reached by gradually increasing the pressure to one-half of the test pressure. Thereafter, the pressure must be increased in steps of approximately one-tenth of the test pressure until the required test pressure has been reached. The test pressure must be held for at least 5 minutes. The pressure must then be reduced to the MAWP, which must be maintained during the time the entire cargo tank surface is inspected. During the inspection, a suitable method must be used for detecting the existence of leaks. This method must consist either of coating the entire surface of all joints under pressure with a solution of soap and water, or using other equally sensitive methods.

(2) *When testing an insulated cargo tank,* the insulation and jacketing need not be removed unless it is otherwise impossible to reach test pressure and maintain a condition of pressure equilibrium after test pressure is reached, or the vacuum integrity cannot be maintained in the insulation space. If an MC 338 cargo tank used for the transportation of a flammable gas or oxygen, refrigerated liquid is opened for any reason, the cleanliness must be verified prior to closure using the procedures contained in §178.338-15 of this subchapter.

(3) *Each MC 330 and MC 331 cargo tank* constructed of quenched and tempered steel (Part UHT of the ASME Code), or constructed of other than quenched and tempered steel but without postweld heat treatment, used for the transportation of anhydrous ammonia, or any other hazardous materials that may cause corrosion stress cracking, must be internally inspected by the wet fluorescent magnetic particle method immediately prior to and in conjunction with the performance of the pressure test prescribed in this section. Each MC 330 and MC 331 cargo tank constructed of quenched and tempered steel (Part UHT of the ASME Code) used for the transportation of liquefied petroleum gas must be internally inspected by the wet fluorescent magnetic particle method immediately prior to and in conjunction with the performance of the pressure test prescribed in this section. The wet fluorescent magnetic particle inspection must be in accordance with Section V of the ASME Code and CGA Technical Bulletin TB-2. This paragraph does not apply to cargo tanks that do not have manholes. (See §180.417(c) for reporting requirements.)

(4) *All pressure bearing portions* of a cargo tank heating system employing a medium such as, but not limited to, steam or hot water for heating the lading must be hydrostatically pressure tested at least once every 5 years. The test pressure must be at least 1.5 times the heating system design pressure and must be maintained for five minutes. A heating system employing flues for heating the lading must be tested to ensure against lading leakage into the flues or into the atmosphere.

(5) *Exceptions.*

(i) *Pressure testing is not required* for MC 330 and MC 331 cargo tanks in dedicated sodium metal service.

(ii) *Pressure testing is not required* for uninsulated lined cargo tanks, with a design pressure or MAWP of 15 psig or less, which receive an external visual inspection and a lining inspection at least once each year.

(6) *Acceptance criteria.* A cargo tank that leaks, fails to retain test pressure or pneumatic inspection pressure, shows distortion, excessive permanent expansion, or other evidence of weakness that might render the cargo tank unsafe for transportation service, may not be returned to service, except as follows: A cargo tank with a heating system which does not hold pressure may remain in service as an unheated cargo tank if:

(i) *The heating system* remains in place and is structurally sound and no lading may leak into the heating system, and

(ii) *The specification plate* heating system information is changed to indicate that the cargo tank has no working heating system.

(7) *The inspector must record the results* of the pressure test as specified in §180.417(b).

(h) Leakage test.

(1) *Each cargo tank* must be tested for leaks in accordance with §180.407(c). The leakage test must include product piping with all valves and accessories in place and operative, except that any venting devices set to discharge at less than the leakage test pressure must be removed or rendered inoperative during the test. Test pressure must be maintained at least 5 minutes. Suitable safeguards must be provided to protect personnel should a failure occur. MC 330 and MC 331 cargo tanks may be leakage tested with the hazardous materials contained in the tank during the test. Leakage test pressure must be not less than 80 percent of the tank design pressure or MAWP, whichever is marked on the certification or specification plate, except as follows:

(i) *A cargo tank with an MAWP* of 690 kPa (100 psig) or more may be leakage tested at its maximum normal operating pressure provided it is in dedicated service or services; or

(ii) *An MC 330 or MC 331 cargo tank* in dedicated liquified petroleum gas service may be leakage tested at not less than 414 kPa (60 psig).

(iii) *An operator* of a specification MC 330 or MC 331 cargo tank, and a nonspecification cargo tank authorized under §173.315(k) of this subchapter, equipped with a meter may check leak tightness of the internal self-closing stop valve by conducting a meter creep test. (See appendix B to this part.)

(2) *Cargo tanks equipped* with vapor collection equipment may be leakage tested in accordance with the Environmental Protection Agency's "Method 27 — Determination of Vapor Tightness of Gasoline Delivery Tank Using Pressure-Vacuum Test," as set forth in 40 CFR part 60, appendix A. Acceptance criteria are found at 40 CFR 60.501.

(3) *A cargo tank* that fails to retain leakage test pressure may not be returned to service as a specification cargo tank, except under conditions specified in §180.411(d).

(4) *After July 1, 2000,* Registered Inspectors of specification MC 330 and MC 331 cargo tanks, and nonspecification cargo tanks authorized under §173.315(k) of this subchapter must visually inspect the delivery hose assembly and piping system while the assembly is under leakage test pressure utilizing the rejection criteria listed in §180.416(g). Delivery hose assemblies not permanently attached to the cargo tank motor vehicle may be inspected separately from the cargo tank motor vehicle. In addition to a written record of the inspection prepared in accordance with §180.417(b), the Registered Inspector conducting the test must note the hose identification number, the date of the test, and the condition of the hose assembly and piping system tested.

(5) *The inspector must record the results* of the leakage test as specified in §180.417(b).

(i) Thickness testing.

(1) *The shell and head thickness* of all unlined cargo tanks used for the transportation of materials corrosive to the tank must be measured at least once every 2 years, except that cargo tanks measuring less than the sum of the minimum prescribed thickness, plus one-fifth of the original corrosion allowance, must be tested annually.

(2) *Measurements must be made* using a device capable of accurately measuring thickness to within ± 0.002 of an inch.

(3) *Any person performing thickness testing* must be trained in the proper use of the thickness testing device used in accordance with the manufacturer's instruction.

(4) *Thickness testing* must be performed in the following areas of the cargo tank wall, as a minimum:

(i) *Areas of the tank shell and heads* and shell and head area around any piping that retains lading;

(ii) *Areas of high shell stress* such as the bottom center of the tank;
(iii) *Areas near openings;*
(iv) *Areas around weld joints;*
(v) *Areas around shell reinforcements;*
(vi) *Areas around appurtenance attachments;*
(vii) *Areas near upper coupler (fifth wheel) assembly attachments;*
(viii) *Areas near* suspension system attachments and connecting structures;
(ix) *Known thin areas* in the tank shell and nominal liquid level lines; and
(x) *Connecting structures* joining multiple cargo tanks of carbon steel in a self-supporting cargo tank motor vehicle.

(5) *Minimum thicknesses* for MC 300, MC 301, MC 302, MC 303, MC 304, MC 305, MC 306, MC 307, MC 310, MC 311, and MC 312 cargo tanks are shown in the tables below. The columns headed "Specified Manufactured Thickness" tabulate the minimum values required for new construction, generally found in Tables I and II of each specification. "In-Service Minimum Thicknesses" are based on 90 percent of the manufactured thickness as specified in the DOT specification, rounded to three places.

Table I - Minimum Thickness for MC 300, MC 303, MC 304, MC 306, MC 307, MC 310, MC 311 and MC 312 Specification Cargo Tanks Constructed of Steel and Steel Alloys

Specified manufactured thickness (US gauge or inches)	Nominal decimal equivalent for reference (inches)	In-service minimum thickness (inches)
19	0.0418	0.038
18	0.0478	0.043
17	0.0538	0.048
16	0.0598	0.054
15	0.0673	0.061
14	0.0747	0.067
13	0.0897	0.081
12	0.1046	0.094
11	0.1196	0.108
10	0.1345	0.121
9	0.1495	0.135
8	0.1644	0.148
7	0.1793	0.161
3/16	0.1875	0.169
1/4	0.2500	0.225
5/16	0.3125	0.281
3/8	0.3750	0.338

Table II - Minimum Thickness for MC 301, MC 302, MC 304, MC 305, MC 306, MC 307, MC 311 and MC 312 Specification Cargo Tanks Constructed of Aluminum and Aluminum Alloys

Specified manufactured thickness (inches)	In-service minimum thickness (inches)
0.078	0.070
0.087	0.078
0.096	0.086
0.109	0.098
0.130	0.117
0.141	0.127
0.151	0.136
0.172	0.155
0.173	0.156
0.194	0.175
0.216	0.194
0.237	0.213
0.270	0.243
0.360	0.324
0.450	0.405
0.540	0.486

(6) *An owner of a cargo tank* that no longer conforms with the minimum thickness prescribed for the maximum lading density marked on the specification plate may use the cargo tank to carry lading of lower density under the following conditions:
(i) *A Design Certifying Engineer must certify* that the cargo tank design and thickness is appropriate for the lower density lading, by issuance of a new manufacturer's certificate, and
(ii) *The tank's nameplate* must be changed to reflect the new service limits (maximum density of lading).

(7) *An owner of a cargo tank* that no longer conforms with the minimum thickness prescribed for the specification may not return the cargo tank to hazardous materials service. The tank's specification plate must be removed, obliterated or covered in a secure manner.

(8) *The inspector must record* the results of the thickness test as specified in §180.417(b).

FEDERAL REGISTER UPDATES

In the April 18, 2003 Federal Register, §180.407 was revised, effective October 1, 2003. The following changes were made:

(a) Paragraphs (b)(4) and (g)(1)(v) were removed and reserved.
(b) Paragraphs (d)(4), (d)(5), and (d)(6) were redesignated as (d)(5), (d)(6), and (d)(7) respectively.
(c) Paragraphs (a)(2), (b)(1), (b)(2), (c), (d)(1), (g)(1)(ii), (g)(1)(iv) introductory text, (g)(4), (h)(1) introductory text, (h)(2), (i)(5) introductory text, titles and column headings to Tables I and II in (i)(5), and (i)(6) were revised.
(d) In the table in paragraph (c), the entry under "Internal Visual Inspection" for "All insulated cargo tanks, except MC 330, MC 331, MC 338" was revised and a New Note 4 to the table was added.
(e) Paragraphs (d) introductory text, (d)(4), (h) introductory text, (h)(1)(iv), (h)(1)(v), (i)(9), and (i)(10) were added.

For your convenience, the new §180.407 is listed below and on the following pages.

§180.407 **Requirements for test and inspection of specification cargo tanks.**

(a) General.
(1) *A cargo tank* constructed in accordance with a DOT specification for which a test or inspection specified in this section has become due, may not be filled and offered for transportation or transported until the test or inspection has been successfully completed. This paragraph does not apply to any cargo tank filled prior to the test or inspection due date.
(2) *Except during a pressure test,* a cargo tank may not be subjected to a pressure greater than its design pressure or MAWP.
(3) *A person witnessing or performing* a test or inspection specified in this section must meet the minimum qualifications prescribed in §180.409.
(4) *Each cargo tank* must be evaluated in accordance with the acceptable results of tests and inspections prescribed in §180.411.
(5) *Each cargo tank* which has successfully passed a test or inspection specified in this section must be marked in accordance with §180.415.
(6) *A cargo tank which fails a prescribed test or inspection must:*
(i) *Be repaired and retested in accordance with §180.413; or*
(ii) *Be removed* from hazardous materials service and the specification plate removed, obliterated or covered in a secure manner.

(b) **Conditions requiring test and inspection of cargo tanks.** Without regard to any other test or inspection requirements, a specification cargo tank must be tested and inspected in accordance with this section prior to further use if:
(1) *The cargo tank shows evidence* of dents, cuts, gouges, corroded or abraded areas, leakage, or any other condition that might render it unsafe for hazardous materials service. At a minimum, any area of a cargo tank showing evidence of dents, cuts, digs, gouges, or corroded or abraded areas must be thickness tested in accordance with the procedures set forth in paragraphs (i)(2), (i)(3), (i)(5), and (i)(6) of this section and evaluated in accordance with the criteria prescribed in §180.411. Any signs of leakage must be repaired in accordance with §180.413. The suitability of any repair affecting the structural integrity of the cargo tank must be determined either by the testing required in the applicable manufacturing specification or in paragraph (g)(1)(iv) of this section.
(2) *The cargo tank has sustained damage* to an extent that may adversely affect its lading retention capability. A damaged cargo tank must be pressure tested in accordance with the procedures set forth in paragraph (g) of this section.
(3) *The cargo tank* has been out of hazardous materials transportation service for a period of one year or more. Each cargo tank that has been out of hazardous materials transportation service for a period of one year or more must be pressure tested in accordance with §180.407(g) prior to further use.
(4) *[Reserved]*
(5) *The Department* so requires based on the existence of probable cause that the cargo tank is in an unsafe operating condition.

(c) **Periodic test and inspection.** Each specification cargo tank must be tested and inspected as specified in the following table by an inspector meeting the qualifications in §180.409. The retest date shall be determined from the specified interval identified in the following table from the most recent inspection or the CTMV certification date.

Compliance Dates - Inspections and Test Under §180.407(c)

Test or inspection (cargo tank specification, configuration, and service)	Date by which first test must be completed[1]	Interval period after first test
External Visual Inspection:		
All cargo tanks designed to be loaded by vacuum with full opening rear heads	September 1, 1991	6 months
All other cargo tanks	September 1, 1991	1 year
Internal Visual Inspection:		
All insulated cargo tanks, except MC 330, MC 331, MC 338[4]	September 1, 1991	1 year
All cargo tanks transporting lading corrosive to the tank	September 1, 1991	1 year
All other cargo tanks, except MC 338	September 1, 1995	5 years
Lining Inspection:		
All lined cargo tanks transporting lading corrosive to the tank	September 1, 1991	1 year
Leakage Test:		
MC 330 and MC 331 cargo tanks in chlorine service	September 1, 1991	2 years
All other cargo tanks except MC 338	September 1, 1991	1 year
Pressure Test:		
(Hydrostatic or pneumatic)[2,3]		
All cargo tanks which are insulated with no manhole or insulated and lined, except MC 338	September 1, 1991	1 year
All cargo tanks designed to be loaded by vacuum with full opening rear heads	September 1, 1992	2 years
MC 330 and MC 331 cargo tanks in chlorine service	September 1, 1992	2 years
All other cargo tanks	September 1, 1995	5 years
Thickness Test:		
All unlined cargo tanks transporting material corrosive to the tank, except MC 338	September 1, 1992	2 years

1. If a cargo tank is subject to an applicable inspection or test requirement under the regulations in effect on December 30, 1990, and the due date (as specified by a requirement in effect on December 30, 1990) for completing the required inspection or test occurs before the compliance date listed in table I, the earlier date applies.
2. Pressure testing is not required for MC 330 and MC 331 cargo tanks in dedicated sodium metal service.
3. Pressure testing is not required for uninsulated lined cargo tanks, with a design pressure or MAWP 15 psig or less, which receive an external visual inspection and lining inspection at least once each year.
4. Insulated cargo tanks equipped with manholes or inspection openings may perform either an internal visual inspection in conjunction with the external visual inspection or a hydrostatic or pneumatic pressure-test of the cargo tank.

(d) External visual inspection and testing. The following applies to the external visual inspection and testing of cargo tanks:

(1) *Where insulation precludes* a complete external visual inspection as required by paragraphs (d)(2) through (d)(6) of this section, the cargo tank also must be given an internal visual inspection in accordance with paragraph (e) of this section. If external visual inspection is precluded because any part of the cargo tank wall is externally lined, coated, or designed to prevent an external visual inspection, those areas of the cargo tank must be internally inspected. If internal visual inspection is precluded because the cargo tank is lined, coated, or designed so as to prevent access for internal inspection, the tank must be hydrostatically or pneumatically tested in accordance with paragraph (g)(1)(iv) of this section. Those items able to be externally inspected must be externally inspected and noted in the inspection report.

(2) [1]

(3) [1]

(4) *Ring stiffeners or other appurtenances,* installed on cargo tanks constructed of mild steel or high-strength, low-alloy steel, that create air cavities adjacent to the tank shell that do not allow for external visual inspection must be thickness tested in accordance with paragraphs (i)(2) and (i)(3) of this section, at least once every 2 years. At least four symmetrically distributed readings must be taken to establish an average thickness for the ring stiffener or appurtenance. If any thickness reading is less than the average thickness by more than 10%, thickness testing in accordance with paragraphs (i)(2) and (i)(3) of this section must be conducted from the inside of the cargo tank on the area of the tank wall covered by the appurtenance or ring stiffener.

(5) *Corroded or abraded areas* of the cargo tank wall must be thickness tested in accordance with the procedures set forth in paragraphs (i)(2), (i)(3), (i)(5) and (i)(6) of this section.

(6) *The gaskets on any full opening rear head must be:*

(i) *Visually inspected* for cracks or splits caused by weather or wear; and

(ii) *Replaced if* cuts or cracks which are likely to cause leakage, or are of a depth one-half inch or more, are found.

(7) *The inspector* must record the results of the external visual examination as specified in §180.417(b).

(e) [2]

(f) [3]

(g) Pressure test. All components of the cargo tank wall, as defined in §178.320(a) of this subchapter, must be pressure tested as prescribed by this paragraph.

(1) *Test Procedure —*

(i) *As part of the pressure test,* the inspector must perform an external and internal visual inspection, except that on an MC 338 cargo tank, or a cargo tank not equipped with a manhole or inspection opening, an internal inspection is not required.

(ii) *All self-closing pressure relief valves,* including emergency relief vents and normal vents, must be removed from the cargo tank for inspection and testing.

[A] Each self-closing pressure relief valve that is an emergency relief vent must open at the required set pressure and seat to a leak-tight condition at 90 percent of the set-to-discharge pressure or the pressure prescribed for the applicable cargo tank specification.

[B] Normal vents (1 psig vents) must be tested according to the testing criteria established by the valve manufacturer.

[C] Self-closing pressure relief devices not tested or failing the tests in this paragraph (g)(1)(ii) must be repaired or replaced.

(iii) *Except for cargo tanks* carrying lading corrosive to the tank, areas covered by the upper coupler (fifth wheel) assembly must be inspected for corroded and abraded areas, dents, distortions, defects in welds, and any other condition that might render the tank unsafe for transportation service. The upper coupler (fifth wheel) assembly must be removed from the cargo tank for this inspection.

(iv) *Each cargo tank* must be tested hydrostatically or pneumatically to the internal pressure specified in the following table. At no time during the pressure test may a cargo tank be subject to pressures that exceed those identified in the following table:[4]

(v) *[Reserved]* [5]

(4) *All pressure bearing portions* of a cargo tank heating system employing a medium such as, but not limited to, steam or hot water for heating the lading must be hydrostatically pressure tested at least once every 5 years. The test pressure must be at least the maximum system design operating pressure and must be maintained for five minutes. A heating system employing flues for heating the lading must be tested to ensure against lading leakage into the flues or into the atmosphere.

(5) *Exceptions.*

(i) *Pressure testing* is not required for MC 330 and MC 331 cargo tanks in dedicated sodium metal service.

(ii) *Pressure testing* is not required for uninsulated lined cargo tanks, with a design pressure or MAWP of 15 psig or less, which receive an external visual inspection and a lining inspection at least once each year.

(6) *Acceptance criteria.* A cargo tank that leaks, fails to retain test pressure or pneumatic inspection pressure, shows distortion, excessive permanent expansion, or other evidence of weakness that might render the cargo tank unsafe for transportation service, may not be returned to service, except as follows: A cargo tank with a heating system which does not hold pressure may remain in service as an unheated cargo tank if:

(i) *The heating system* remains in place and is structurally sound and no lading may leak into the heating system, and

(ii) *The specification plate* heating system information is changed to indicate that the cargo tank has no working heating system.

(7) *The inspector* must record the results of the pressure test as specified in §180.417(b).

(h) Leakage test. The following requirements apply to cargo tanks requiring a leakage test:

(1) *Each cargo tank* must be tested for leaks in accordance with paragraph (c) of this section. The leakage test must include testing product piping with all valves and accessories in place and operative, except that any venting devices set to discharge at less than the leakage test pressure must be removed or rendered inoperative during the test. All internal or external self-closing stop valves must be tested for leak tightness. Each cargo tank of a multi-cargo tank motor vehicle must be tested with adjacent cargo tanks empty and at atmospheric pressure. Test pressure must be maintained for at least 5 minutes. Cargo tanks in liquefied compressed gas service must be externally inspected for leaks during the leakage test. Suitable safeguards must be provided to protect personnel should a failure occur. Cargo tanks may be leakage tested with hazardous materials contained in the cargo tank during the test. Leakage test pressure must be no less than 80% of MAWP marked on the specification plate except as follows:

(i) *A cargo tank* with an MAWP of 690 kPa (100 psig) or more may be leakage tested at its maximum normal operating pressure provided it is in dedicated service or services; or

(ii) *An MC 330 or MC 331* cargo tank in dedicated liquified petroleum gas service may be leakage tested at not less than 414 kPa (60 psig).

(iii) *An operator* of a specification MC 330 or MC 331 cargo tank, and a nonspecification cargo tank authorized under §173.315(k) of this subchapter, equipped with a meter may check leak tightness of the internal self-closing stop valve by conducting a meter creep test. (See appendix B to this part.)

(iv) *An MC 330 or MC 331 cargo tank* in dedicated service for anhydrous ammonia may be leakage tested at not less than 414 kPa (60 psig).

(v) *A non-specification cargo tank* required by §173.8(d) of this subchapter to be leakage tested, must be leakage tested at not less than 16.6 kPa (2.4 psig), or as specified in paragraph (h)(2) of this section.

(2) *Cargo tanks* used to transport petroleum distillate fuels that are equipped with vapor collection equipment may be leak tested in accordance with the Environmental Protection Agency's "Method 27 — Determination of Vapor Tightness of Gasoline Delivery Tank Using Pressure-Vacuum Test," as set forth in Appendix A to 40 CFR part 60. Test methods and procedures and maximum allowable pressure and vacuum changes are in 40 CFR 63.425(e)(1). The hydrostatic test alternative, using liquid in Environmental Protection Agency's "Method 27 — Determination of Vapor Tightness of Gasoline Delivery Tank Using Pressure-Vacuum Test," may not be used to satisfy the leak testing requirements of this paragraph. The test must be conducted using air.

(3) [6]

(i) [7]

(5) *Minimum thicknesses* for MC 300, MC 301, MC 302, MC 303, MC 304, MC 305, MC 306, MC 307, MC 310, MC 311, and MC 312 cargo tanks are determined based on the definition of minimum thickness found in §178.320(a) of this subchapter. The following Tables I and II identify the "In-Service Minimum Thickness" values to be used to determine the minimum thickness for the referenced cargo tanks. The column headed "Minimum Manufactured Thickness" indicates the minimum values required for new construction of DOT 400 series cargo tanks, found in Tables I and II of §§178.346-2, 178.347-2, and 178.348-2 of this subchapter. In-Service Minimum Thicknesses for MC 300, MC 301, MC 302, MC 303, MC 304, MC 305, MC 306, MC 307, MC 310, MC 311, and MC 312 cargo tanks are based on 90 percent of the manufactured thickness specified in the DOT specification, rounded to three places. [8]

Table I - In-Service Minimum Thickness for MC 300, MC 303, MC 304, MC 306, MC 307, MC 310, MC 311, and MC 312 Specification Cargo Tank Constructed of Steel and Steel Alloys

Minimum manufactured thickness (US gauge or inches)	Nominal decimal equivalent for (inches)	In-service minimum thickness reference (inches)

Table II - In-Service Minimum Thickness for MC 301, MC 302, MC 304, MC 305, MC 306, MC 307, MC 311, and MC 312 Specification Cargo Tanks Constructed of Aluminum and Aluminum Alloys

Minimum manufactured thickness	In-service minimum thickness (inches)

(6) *An owner of a cargo tank* that no longer conforms to the minimum thickness prescribed for the design as manufactured may use the cargo tank to transport authorized materials at reduced maximum weight of lading or reduced maximum working pressure, or combinations thereof, provided the following conditions are met:

(i) *A Design Certifying Engineer* must certify that the cargo tank design and thickness are appropriate for the reduced loading conditions by issuance of a revised manufacturer's certificate, and

(ii) *The cargo tank motor vehicle's nameplate* must reflect the revised service limits.

(7) *An owner* of a cargo tank that no longer conforms with the minimum thickness prescribed for the specification may not return the cargo tank to hazardous materials service. The tank's specification plate must be removed, obliterated or covered in a secure manner.

(8) *The inspector* must record the results of the thickness test as specified in §180.417(b).

(9) *For MC 331 cargo tanks* constructed before October 1, 2003, minimum thickness shall be determined by the thickness indicated on the U1A form minus any corrosion allowance. For MC 331 cargo tanks constructed after October 1, 2003, the minimum thickness will be the value indicated on the specification plate. If no corrosion allowance is indicated on the U1A form then the thickness of the tank shall be the thickness of the material of construction indicated on the UIA form with no corrosion allowance.

(10) *For 400-series cargo tanks,* minimum thickness is calculated according to tables in each applicable section of this subchapter for that specification: §178.346-2 for DOT 406 cargo tanks, §178.347-2 for DOT 407 cargo tanks, and §178.348-2 for DOT 412 cargo tanks.

1. Paragraphs (d)(2) and (d)(3) are the same as before.
2. Paragraph (e) is the same as before.
3. Paragraph (f) is the same as before.
4. The table in (g)(1)(iv) is the same as before.
5. The table in (g)(1)(vi) through (g)(3) is the same as before.
6. Paragraphs (h)(3) through (i)(4)(x) are the same as before.
7. Paragraph (i)(1)-(4) is the same as before.
8. The titles and column headings to Tables I and II in (i)(5) were revised.

§180.409 Minimum qualifications for inspectors and testers.

(a) Except as otherwise provided in this section, any person performing or witnessing the inspections and tests specified in §180.407(c) must —

(1) *Be registered* with the Department in accordance with part 107, subpart F of this chapter, and

(2) *Be familiar with* DOT specification cargo tanks and must be trained and experienced in use of the inspection and testing equipment needed.

(b) A person who only performs annual external visual inspections and leakage tests on a cargo tank motor vehicle, owned or operated by that person, with a capacity of less than 13,250 L (3,500 gallons) used exclusively for flammable liquid petroleum fuels, is not required to meet the educational and years of experience requirements set forth in the definition of "Registered Inspector" in §171.8 of this subchapter. Although not required to meet the educational and years of experience requirements, a person who performs visual inspections or leakage tests or signs the inspection reports must have the knowledge and ability to perform such inspections and tests and must perform them as required by this subchapter, and must register with the Department as required by subpart F of part 107 of this chapter.

(c) A person who performs only annual external visual inspections and leakage tests on a permanently mounted non-bulk tank, owned or operated by that person, for petroleum products as authorized by §173.8(c) of this subchapter, is not required to be registered in accordance with subpart F of part 107 of this chapter. In addition the person who signs the inspection report required by §180.417(b) of this subpart for such non-bulk tanks is not required to be registered. Although not required to register, a person who performs visual inspections or leakage tests or signs the inspection reports must have the knowledge and ability to perform such inspections and tests and must perform them as required by this subchapter.

(d) A motor carrier or cargo tank owner who meets the requirements of paragraph (a) of this section may use an employee who is not a Registered Inspector to perform a portion of the pressure retest required by §180.407(g). External and internal visual inspections must be accomplished by a Registered Inspector, but the hydrostatic or pneumatic pressure test, as set forth in §180.407(g)(1)(viii) and (ix), respectively, may be done by an employee who is not a Registered Inspector provided that —

(1) *The employee* is familiar with the cargo tank and is trained and experienced in the use of the inspection and testing equipment used;

(2) *The employer* submits certification that such employee meets the qualification requirements to the Associate Administrator, Attn: (DHM-32), Research and Special Programs Administration, Department of Transportation, 400 Seventh Street, SW., Washington, DC 20590; and

(3) *The employer* retains a copy of the tester's qualifications with the documents required by §180.417(b).

FEDERAL REGISTER UPDATES

In the April 18, 2003 Federal Register, §180.409 was revised, effective October 1, 2003.

(a) [1]

(1) *Be registered* with the Federal Motor Carrier Safety Administration in accordance with part 107, subpart F of this chapter, [2]

(2) *Be familiar with* DOT-specification cargo tanks and trained and experienced in use of the inspection and testing equipment needed, and [2]

(3) *Have the training and experience* required to meet the definition of "Registered Inspector" in §171.8 of this chapter. [3]

1. Paragraph (a) is the same as before.
2. Paragraphs (a)(1) and (a)(2) were revised.
3. Paragraph (a)(3) was added.

§180.411 Acceptable results of tests and inspections.

(a) Corroded or abraded areas. The minimum thickness may not be less than that prescribed in the applicable specification.

(b) Dents, cuts, digs and gouges. (See CGA Pamphlet C-6 for evaluation procedures.)

(1) *For dents* at welds or that include a weld, the maximum allowable depth is 1/2 inch. For dents away from welds, the maximum allowable depth is 1/10 of the greatest dimension of the dent, but in no case may the depth exceed one inch.

(2) *The minimum thickness* remaining beneath a cut, dig, or gouge may not be less than that prescribed in the applicable specification.

(c) Weld or structural defects. Any cargo tank with a weld defect such as a crack, pinhole, or incomplete fusion, or a structural defect must be taken out of hazardous materials service until repaired.

(d) Leakage. All sources of leakage must be properly repaired prior to returning a tank to hazardous materials service.

(e) Relief valves. Any pressure relief valve that fails to open and reclose at the prescribed pressure must be repaired or replaced.

(f) Liner integrity. Any defect shown by the test must be properly repaired.

(g) Pressure test. Any tank that fails to meet the acceptance criteria found in the individual specification that applies must be properly repaired.

§180.413 Repair, modification, stretching, or rebarrelling of cargo tanks.

(a) **General.** For purposes of this section, "stretching" is not considered a "modification" and "rebarrelling" is not considered a "repair." Any repair, modification, stretching, or rebarrelling of a cargo tank must be performed in conformance with the requirements of this section.

(b) **Repair—**

(1) *Non-ASME Code stamped cargo tanks.* Any work involving repair on an MC 300, MC 301, MC 302, MC 303, MC 304, MC 305, MC 306, MC 307, MC 310, MC 311, or MC 312 cargo tank that is not ASME Code stamped must be performed by:

(i) *A cargo tank manufacturer* holding a valid ASME Certificate of Authorization for the use of the ASME "U" stamp and registered with DOT; or

(ii) *A repair facility* holding a valid National Board Certificate of Authorization for the use of the National Board "R" stamp and registered with DOT.

(2) *ASME Code stamped cargo tanks.* Any work involving repair on any ASME Code stamped cargo tank must be performed by a repair facility holding a valid National Board Certificate of Authorization for the use of the National Board "R" stamp and registered in accordance with subpart F of part 107 of subchapter B of this chapter.

(3) *The following provisions apply to cargo tank repairs:*

(i) *DOT 406,* DOT 407, and DOT 412 cargo tanks must be repaired in accordance with the specification requirements in effect either at the time of manufacture or at the time of repair;

(ii) *MC 300,* MC 301, MC 302, MC 303, MC 305, and MC 306 cargo tanks must be repaired in accordance with either the original specification or with the DOT 406 specification in effect at the time of repair;

(iii) *MC 304 and MC 307 cargo tanks* must be repaired in accordance with either the original specification or with the DOT 407 specification in effect at the time of repair;

(iv) *MC 310,* MC 311, and MC 312 cargo tanks must be repaired in accordance with either the original specification or with the DOT 412 specification in effect at the time of the repair;

(v) *MC 338 cargo tanks* must be repaired in accordance with the specification requirements in effect either at the time of manufacture or at the time of repair; and

(vi) *MC 330 and MC 331 cargo tanks* must be repaired in accordance with the repair procedures described in CGA Technical Bulletin TB-2 and the National Board Inspection Code — Provisions for Repair of Pressure Vessels. Each cargo tank having cracks or other defects requiring welded repairs must meet all of the requirements of §178.337-16 of this subchapter (in effect at the time of the repair), except that postweld heat treatment after minor weld repairs is not required. When any repair is made of defects revealed by the wet fluorescent magnetic particle inspection, including those by grinding, the affected area of the cargo tank must again be examined by the wet fluorescent magnetic particle method after hydrostatic testing to assure that all defects have been removed.

(4) *Prior to any repair work,* the cargo tank must be emptied of any hazardous material lading. Cargo tanks containing flammable or toxic lading must be purged.

(5) *Any repair of a cargo tank* involving welding on the shell or head must be certified by a Registered Inspector. Any repair of an ASME Code "U" stamped cargo tank must be in accordance with the National Board Inspection Code.

(6) *The suitability* of any repair affecting the structural integrity of the cargo tank must be determined by the testing required either in the applicable manufacturing specification, or in §180.407(g)(1)(iv).

(c) **Maintenance or replacement of piping,** valves, hoses or fittings. In the event of repair, maintenance or replacement, any piping, valve, or fitting must be properly installed in accordance with the provisions of the applicable specification before the cargo tank is returned to hazardous materials service. After maintenance or replacement which does not involve welding on the cargo tank wall, the repaired piping, valves or fittings, the replaced segment of the piping must be leak tested. After repair or replacement of piping, valves or fittings which involves welding on the cargo tank wall, the entire cargo tank, including the repaired or replaced piping, valve or fitting, must be pressure tested in accordance with the applicable specification. Hoses permanently attached to the cargo tank must be tested either before or after installation.

(d) **Modification, stretching, or rebarrelling.** Modification, stretching or rebarrelling of a cargo tank must conform to the following provisions:

(1) *Non-ASME Code stamped cargo tanks.* If the modification, stretching, or rebarrelling will result in a design type change, then it must be approved by a Design Certifying Engineer. Any work involving modification, stretching, or rebarrelling on an MC 300, MC 301, MC 302, MC 303, MC 304, MC 305, MC 306, MC 307, MC 310, MC 311, or MC 312 cargo tank that is not ASME stamped must be performed by:

(i) *A cargo tank manufacturer* holding a valid ASME Certificate of Authorization for the use of the ASME "U" stamp and registered with DOT; or

(ii) *A repair facility* holding a valid National Board Certificate of Authorization for the use of the National Board "R" stamp and registered with DOT.

(2) *ASME Code stamped cargo tanks.* The modification, stretching, or rebarrelling on any ASME Code stamped cargo tank must be performed by a repair facility holding a valid National Board Certificate of Authorization for the use of the National Board "R" stamp and registered in accordance with subpart F of part 107 of subchapter B of this chapter. If the modification, stretching, or rebarrelling will result in a design type change, then it must be approved by a Design Certifying Engineer.

(3) *Except as provided* in paragraph (d)(3)(v) in this section, all new material and equipment, and equipment affected by modification, stretching or rebarrelling must meet the requirements of the specification in effect at the time such work is performed, and must meet the applicable structural integrity requirements (§§178.337-3, 178.338-3, or 178.345-3 of this subchapter). The work must conform to the requirements of the applicable specification as follows:

(i) *For specification MC 300,* MC 301, MC 302, MC 303, MC 305 and MC 306 cargo tanks, the provisions of either specification MC 306 or DOT 406 until August 31, 1995 and, thereafter to specification DOT 406 only;

(ii) *For specification MC 304 and MC 307* cargo tanks, the provisions of either specification MC 307 or DOT 407 until August 31, 1995 and, thereafter to specification DOT 407 only;

(iii) *For specification MC 310,* MC 311, and MC 312 cargo tanks, the provisions of either specification MC 312 or DOT 412 until August 31, 1995 and, thereafter to specification DOT 412 only;

(iv) *For specification MC 330 cargo tanks,* the provisions of specification MC 331; and

(v) *For Specification MC 338 cargo tanks,* the provisions of specification MC 338. However, structural modifications to MC 338 cargo tanks authorized under §180.405(d) may conform to applicable provisions of the ASME Code instead of specification MC 338, provided the structural integrity of the modified cargo tank is at least equivalent to that of the original cargo tank.

(4) *The person performing the modification,* stretching, or rebarrelling must:

(i) *Have knowledge* of the original design concept, particularly with respect to structural design analysis, material and welding procedures;

(ii) *Assure compliance* with the rebuilt cargo tank's structural integrity, venting, and accident damage protection requirements;

(iii) *Assure compliance* with all applicable Federal Motor Carrier Safety Regulations for any newly installed safety equipment;

(iv) *Perform all retest procedures* on each cargo tank in accordance with the applicable specification and §180.407;

(v) *Change the existing specification plate* to reflect the cargo tank as modified, stretched or rebarrelled. This must include the name of the person doing the work, his DOT registration number, date, retest information, etc. A supplemental specification plate may be installed immediately adjacent to the existing plate(s), or the existing specification plate may be removed and replaced with a new plate; and

(vi) *On a variable specification cargo tank,* install a supplemental or new variable specification plate, and replace the specification listed on the original specification plate with the words "see variable specification plate".

(5) *The design* of the modified, stretched, or rebarrelled cargo tank must be approved by a Design Certifying Engineer registered in accordance with subpart F of part 107 of subchapter B of this chapter. The Design Certifying Engineer must certify that the modified, stretched, or rebarrelled cargo tank meets the structural integrity requirements of the applicable specification. The person performing the modifying, stretching or rebarrelling and a Registered Inspector must certify that the cargo tank is in compliance with this section and the applicable specification by issuing a supplemental manufacturer's certificate. The registra-

tion number of the Registered Inspector and the person performing the modification, stretching, or rebarrelling must be entered on the certificate. When a cargo tank is rebarrelled, it must be designed, constructed and certified in accordance with a cargo tank specification currently authorized for construction in part 178 of this subchapter.

(6) *If the mounting* of the cargo tank on the cargo tank motor vehicle involves welding on the cargo tank head or shell, then the mounting must be performed as follows:

(i) *Non-ASME Code stamped cargo tanks.* For a non-ASME Code stamped cargo tank —

[A] By a cargo tank manufacturer holding an ASME "U" stamp, registered with DOT, and under the direction of a Design Certifying Engineer; or

[B] By a repair facility holding an ASME "U" stamp or a National Board "R" stamp, registered with DOT, and under the direction of a Design Certifying Engineer.

(ii) *ASME Code stamped cargo tank.* For an ASME Code stamped cargo tank, by a repair facility holding a National Board "R" stamp, registered in accordance with subpart F of part 107 of subchapter B of this chapter, and approved by a Design Certifying Engineer.

(7) *If the mounting* of a cargo tank on a cargo tank motor vehicle does not involve welding on the cargo tank head or shell, or a change or modification of the methods of attachment, then the mounting shall be in accordance with the original specification or with the specification in effect at the time of the mounting. If the mounting involves any change or modification of the methods of attachment, then the mounting must be approved by a Design Certifying Engineer.

(8) *Prior to* any modification, stretching, or rebarrelling a cargo tank must be emptied of any hazardous material lading. Cargo tanks containing flammable or toxic lading must be purged.

(9) *Any modification, stretching, or rebarrelling* on the cargo tank involving welding on the shell or head must be certified by a Registered Inspector. Any repair of an ASME Code "U" stamped cargo tank must be in accordance with the National Board Inspection Code.

(10) *The suitability* of any modification affecting the structural integrity of the cargo tank, with respect to pressure, must be determined by the testing required either in the applicable manufacturing specification, or in §180.407(g)(1)(iv).

(e) Records. Each owner of a cargo tank must retain at its principal place of business all records of repair, modification, stretching, or rebarrelling made to each cargo tank during the time the cargo tank is in service and for one year thereafter. Copies of these records must be retained by a motor carrier, who is not the owner of the cargo tank, at its principal place of business during the period the cargo tank is in the carrier's service. The seller of a specification cargo tank shall provide the purchaser a copy of the cargo tank Certificate of Compliance, and all repair, inspection and test reports upon sale as an MC or DOT cargo tank.

FEDERAL REGISTER UPDATES

In the April 18, 2003 Federal Register, §180.413 was revised, effective October 1, 2003.

§180.413 Repair, modification, stretching, rebarrelling, or mounting of specification cargo tanks.

(a) General. Any repair, modification, stretching, rebarrelling, or mounting of a cargo tank must be performed in conformance with the requirements of this section.

(1) *Except as otherwise provided in this section,* each repair, modification, stretching, or rebarrelling of a specification cargo tank must be performed by a repair facility holding a valid National Board Certificate of Authorization for use of the National Board "R" stamp and must be made in accordance with the edition of the National Board Inspection Code in effect at the time the work is performed.

(i) *Repairs, modifications,* stretchings, and rebarrellings performed on non-ASME stamped specification cargo tanks may be performed by:

[A] A cargo tank manufacturer holding a valid ASME Certificate of Authorization for the use of the ASME "U" stamp using the quality control procedures used to obtain the Certificate of Authorization; or

[B] A repair facility holding a valid National Board Certificate of Authorization for use of the National Board "R" stamp using the quality control procedures used to obtain the Certificate of Authorization.

(ii) *A repair, modification,* stretching, or rebarrelling of a non-ASME stamped cargo tank may be done without certification by an Authorized Inspector, completion of the R-1 form, or being stamped with the "R" stamp.

(2) *Prior to each* repair, modification, stretching, rebarrelling, or mounting, the cargo tank motor vehicle must be emptied of any hazardous material lading. In addition, cargo tank motor vehicles used to transport flammable or toxic lading must be sufficiently cleaned of residue and purged of vapors so any potential hazard is removed, including void spaces between double bulkheads, piping and vapor recovery systems.

(3) *Each person performing* a repair, modification, stretching, rebarrelling or mounting of a DOT specification cargo tank must be registered in accordance with subpart F of part 107 of this chapter.

(b) Repair. The suitability of each repair affecting the structural integrity or lading retention capability of the cargo tank must be determined by the testing required either in the applicable manufacturing specification or in §180.407(g)(1)(iv). Each repair of a cargo tank involving welding on the shell or head must be certified by a Registered Inspector. The following provisions apply to specific cargo tank repairs:

(1) *DOT 406, DOT 407, and DOT 412 cargo tanks* must be repaired in accordance with the specification requirements in effect at the time of repair;

(2) *MC 300, MC 301, MC 302,* MC 303, MC 305, and MC 306 cargo tanks must be repaired in accordance with either the most recent revision of the original specification or with the DOT 406 specification in effect at the time of repair;

(3) *MC 304 and MC 307 cargo tanks* must be repaired in accordance with either the most recent revision of the original specification or with the DOT 407 specification in effect at the time of repair;

(4) *MC 310, MC 311, and MC 312 cargo tanks* must be repaired in accordance with either the most recent revision of the original specification or with the DOT 412 specification in effect at the time of repair;

(5) *MC 338 cargo tanks* must be repaired in accordance with the specification requirements in effect at the time of repair; and

(6) *MC 330 and MC 331 cargo tanks* must be repaired in accordance with the repair procedures described in CGA Technical Bulletin TB-2 and the National Board Inspection Code (see §171.1 of this subchapter). Each cargo tank having cracks or other defects requiring welded repairs must meet all inspection, test, and heat treatment requirements in §178.337-16 of this subchapter in effect at the time of the repair, except that postweld heat treatment after minor weld repairs is not required. When a repair is made of defects revealed by the wet fluorescent magnetic particle inspection, including those repaired by grinding, the affected area of the cargo tank must again be examined by the wet fluorescent magnetic particle method after hydrostatic testing to assure that all defects have been removed.

(c) Maintenance or replacement of piping, valves, hoses, or fittings. After each repair, maintenance or replacement of a pipe, valve, hose, or fitting on a cargo tank, that component must be installed in accordance with the provisions of the applicable specification before the cargo tank is returned to service.

(1) *After maintenance or replacement* that does not involve welding on the cargo tank wall, the repaired or replaced piping, valve, hose or fitting must be tested for leaks. This requirement is met when the piping, valve, hose or fitting is tested after installation at not less than 80 percent of the design pressure marked on the cargo tank. A hose may be tested before or after installation on the cargo tank.

(2) *After repair or replacement* of piping, valves, or fittings that involves welding on the cargo tank wall, the cargo tank must be pressure tested in accordance with the applicable manufacturing specification or §180.407(g)(1)(iv). In addition, the affected piping, valve, or fitting must be tested in accordance with paragraph (c)(1) of this section.

(3) *Hoses on cargo tanks* in dedicated liquefied compressed gas, except carbon dioxide, service are excepted from these testing requirements, but must be tested in accordance with §180.416(f).

(d) Modification, stretching, or rebarrelling. Modification, stretching or rebarrelling of a cargo tank motor vehicle must conform to the following provisions:

(1) *The design* of the modified, stretched, or rebarrelled cargo tank motor vehicle must be certified in writing by a Design Certifying Engineer as meeting the structural integrity and accident damage protection requirements of the applicable specification.

(2) *Except as provided* in paragraph (d)(2)(v) of this section, all new material and equipment affected by modification, stretching, or rebarrelling must meet the requirements of the specification in effect at the time such work is performed, and all applicable structural integrity requirements (§178.337-3, §178.338-3, or §178.345-3 of this subchapter). The work must conform to the requirements of the applicable specification as follows:

(i) *For specification* MC 300, MC 301, MC 302, MC 303, MC 305 and MC 306 cargo tanks, the provisions of either specification MC 306 or DOT 406 until August 31, 1995 and, thereafter to specification DOT 406 only;

(ii) *For specification* MC 304 and MC 307 cargo tanks, the provisions of either specification MC 307 or DOT 407 until August 31, 1995 and, thereafter to specification DOT 407 only;

(iii) *For specification* MC 310, MC 311, and MC 312 cargo tanks, the provisions of either specification MC 312 or DOT 412 until August 31, 1995 and, thereafter to specification DOT 412 only;

(iv) *For specification* MC 330 cargo tanks, the provisions of specification MC 331; and

(v) *For specification* MC 338 cargo tanks, the provisions of specification MC 338. However, structural modifications to MC 338 cargo tanks authorized under §180.405(d) may conform to applicable provisions of the ASME Code instead of specification MC 338, provided the structural integrity of the modified cargo tank is at least equivalent to that of the original cargo tank.

(3) *The person performing* the modification, stretching, or rebarrelling must:

(i) *Have knowledge* of the original design concept, particularly with respect to structural design analysis, material and welding procedures.

(ii) *Assure compliance* of the rebuilt cargo tank's structural integrity, venting, and accident damage protection with the applicable specification requirements.

(iii) *Assure compliance* with all applicable Federal Motor Carrier Safety Regulations for all newly installed safety equipment.

(iv) *Assure the suitability* of each modification, stretching and rebarrelling that affects the lading retention capability of the cargo tank by performing the tests required in the applicable specification or §180.407(g)(1)(iv).

(continued on next page)

(continued from previous page)

(v) *Any modification* that changes information displayed on the specification plate requires the installation of a supplemental specification plate, nameplate, or both containing the information that reflects the cargo tank as modified, stretched or rebarrelled. The plate must include the name of the person or facility doing the work, DOT registration number, date work is completed, retest information, and any other information that differs from the original plate. The supplemental plates must be installed immediately adjacent to the existing plate or plates.

(vi) *On a variable specification cargo tank,* install a supplemental or new variable specification plate, and replace the specification listed on the original specification plate with the words "see variable specification plate."

(4) *A Registered Inspector* must certify that the modified, stretched, or rebarrelled cargo tank conforms to the requirements of this section and the applicable specification by issuing a supplemental certificate of compliance. The registration number of the Registered Inspector must be entered on the certificate.

(e) **Mounting of cargo tanks.** Mounting a cargo tank on a cargo tank motor vehicle must be:

(1) *Performed as required* by paragraph (d)(2) of this section and certified by a Design Certifying Engineer if the mounting of a cargo tank on a motor vehicle chassis involves welding on the cargo tank head or shell or any change or modification of the methods of attachment; or

(2) *In accordance* with the original specification for attachment to the chassis or the specification for attachment to the chassis in effect at the time of the mounting, and performed under the supervision of a Registered Inspector if the mounting of a cargo tank on a motor vehicle chassis does not involve welding on the cargo tank head or shell or a change or modification of the methods of attachment.

(f) **Records.** Each owner of a cargo tank motor vehicle must retain at the owner's principal place of business all records of repair, modification, stretching, or rebarrelling, including notation of any tests conducted to verify the suitability of the repair, modification, stretching, or rebarrelling made to each cargo tank during the time the cargo tank motor vehicle is in service and for one year thereafter. Copies of these records must be retained by a motor carrier, if not the owner of the cargo tank motor vehicle, at its principal place of business during the period the cargo tank motor vehicle is in the carrier's service.

§180.415 Test and inspection markings.

(a) **Each cargo tank successfully completing the test** and inspection requirements contained in §180.407 must be marked as specified in this section.

(b) **Each cargo tank must be durably and legibly marked,** in English, with the date (month and year) and the type of test or inspection performed. The date must be readily identifiable with the applicable test or inspection. The marking must be in letters and numbers at least 32 mm (1.25 inches) high, on the tank shell near the specification plate or anywhere on the front head. The type of test or inspection may be abbreviated as follows: V for external visual inspection and test; I for internal visual inspection; P for pressure test; L for lining inspection, K for leakage test; and T for thickness test. For example, the markings "10-95 P, V, L" would indicate that in October 1995 the cargo tank received and passed the prescribed pressure test, external visual inspection and test, and the lining inspection.

(c) **For a cargo tank motor vehicle composed** of multiple cargo tanks constructed to the same specification, which are tested and inspected at the same time, one set of test and inspection markings may be used to satisfy the requirements of this section. For a cargo tank motor vehicle composed of multiple cargo tanks constructed to different specifications, which are tested and inspected at different intervals, the test and inspection markings must appear in the order of the cargo tank's corresponding location, from front to rear.

FEDERAL REGISTER UPDATES

In the April 18, 2003 Federal Register, §180.415(b) was revised, effective October 1, 2003.

(b) **Each cargo tank must be durably and legibly marked,** in English, with the date (month and year) and the type of test or inspection performed, subject to the following provisions:

(1) *The date must be readily identifiable with the applicable test or inspection.*

(2) *The markings must be in letters and numbers* at least 32 mm (1.25 inches) high, near the specification plate or anywhere on the front head.

(3) *The type of test or inspection may be abbreviated as follows:*

(i) *V for external visual inspection and test;*

(ii) *I for internal visual inspection;*

(iii) *P for pressure test;*

(iv) *L for lining inspection;*

(v) *T for thickness test; and*

(vi) *K for leakage test* for a cargo tank tested under §180.407, except §180.407(h)(2); and

(vii) *K-EPA27 for a cargo tank* tested under §180.407(h)(2) after October 1, 2004.

Examples to paragraph (b). The markings "10-99 P, V, L" represent that in October 1999, a cargo tank passed the prescribed pressure test, external visual inspection and test, and the lining inspection. The markings "2-00 K-EPA" represent that in February 2000, a cargo tank passed the leakage test under §180.407(h)(2). The markings "2-00 K, K-EPA" represent that in February 2000, a cargo tank passed the leakage test under both §180.407(h)(1) and under EPA Method 27 under §180.407(h)(2).

§180.416 Discharge system inspection and maintenance program for cargo tanks transporting liquefied compressed gases.

(a) **Applicability.** This section is applicable to an operator using specification MC 330, MC 331, and nonspecification cargo tanks authorized under §173.315(k) of this subchapter for transportation of liquefied compressed gases other than carbon dioxide. Paragraphs (b), (c), (d)(1), (d)(5), (e), (f), and (g)(1) of this section, applicable to delivery hose assemblies, apply only to hose assemblies installed or carried on the cargo tank.

(b) **Hose identification.** By July 1, 2000, the operator must assure that each delivery hose assembly is permanently marked with a unique identification number and maximum working pressure.

(c) **Post-delivery hose check.** After each unloading, the operator must visually check that portion of the delivery hose assembly deployed during the unloading.

(d) **Monthly inspections and tests.**

(1) *The operator must visually inspect* each delivery hose assembly at least once each calendar month the delivery hose assembly is in service.

(2) *The operator must visually inspect* the piping system at least once each calendar month the cargo tank is in service. The inspection must include fusible elements and all components of the piping system, including bolts, connections, and seals.

(3) *At least once each calendar month* a cargo tank is in service, the operator must actuate all emergency discharge control devices designed to close the internal self-closing stop valve to assure that all linkages operate as designed. appendix A to this part outlines acceptable procedures that may be used for this test.

(4) *The operator of a cargo tank* must check the internal self-closing stop valve in the liquid discharge opening for leakage through the valve at least once each calendar month the cargo tank is in service. On cargo tanks equipped with a meter, the meter creep test as outlined in appendix B to this part or a test providing equivalent accuracy is acceptable. For cargo tanks that are not equipped with a meter, appendix B to this part outlines one acceptable method that may be used to check internal self-closing stop valves for closure.

(5) *After July 1, 2000,* the operator must note each inspection in a record. That record must include the inspection date, the name of the person performing the inspection, the hose assembly identification number, the company name, the date the hose was assembled and tested, and an indication that the delivery hose assembly and piping system passed or failed the tests and inspections. A copy of each test and inspection record must be retained by the operator at its principal place of business or where the vehicle is housed or maintained until the next test of the same type is successfully completed.

(e) **Annual hose leakage test.** The owner of a delivery hose assembly that is not permanently attached to a cargo tank motor vehicle must ensure that the hose assembly is annually tested in accordance with §180.407(h)(4).

(f) **New or repaired delivery hose assemblies.** Each operator of a cargo tank must ensure each new and repaired delivery hose assembly is tested at a minimum of 120 percent of the hose maximum working pressure.

(1) *The operator* must visually examine the delivery hose assembly while it is under pressure.

(2) *Upon successful completion* of the pressure test and inspection, the operator must assure that the delivery hose assembly is permanently marked with the month and year of the test.

(3) *After July 1, 2000,* the operator must complete a record documenting the test and inspection, including the date, the signature of the inspector, the hose owner, the hose identification number, the date of original delivery hose assembly and test, notes of any defects observed and repairs made, and an indication that the delivery hose assembly passed or failed the tests and inspections. A copy of each test and inspection record must be retained by the operator at its principal place of business or where the vehicle is housed or maintained until the next test of the same type is successfully completed.

(g) **Rejection criteria.**

(1) *No operator* may use a delivery hose assembly determined to have any condition identified below for unloading liquefied compressed gases. An operator may remove and replace damaged sections or correct defects discovered. Repaired hose assemblies may be placed back in service if retested successfully in accordance with paragraph (f) of this section.

(i) *Damage to the hose cover that exposes the reinforcement.*

(ii) *Wire braid reinforcement* that has been kinked or flattened so as to permanently deform the wire braid.

(iii) *Soft spots* when not under pressure, bulging under pressure, or loose outer covering.
(iv) *Damaged, slipping, or excessively worn hose couplings.*
(v) *Loose or missing* bolts or fastenings on bolted hose coupling assemblies.

(2) *No operator* may use a cargo tank with a piping system found to have any condition identified in this paragraph (g)(2) for unloading liquefied compressed gases.
(i) *Any external leak identifiable without the use of instruments.*
(ii) *Bolts that are loose, missing, or severely corroded.*
(iii) *Manual stop valves that will not actuate.*
(iv) *Rubber hose flexible connectors* with any condition outlined in paragraph (g)(1) of this section.
(v) *Stainless steel flexible connectors* with damaged reinforcement braid.
(vi) *Internal self-closing stop valves* that fail to close or that permit leakage through the valve detectable without the use of instruments.
(vii) *Pipes or joints that are severely corroded.*

§180.417 Reporting and record retention requirements.

(a) Vehicle certification.

(1) *Each owner* of a specification cargo tank must retain the manufacturer's certificate, the manufacturer's ASME U1A data report, where applicable, and related papers certifying that the specification cargo tank identified in the documents was manufactured and tested in accordance with the applicable specification. This would include any certification of emergency discharge control systems required by §173.315(n) of this subchapter or §180.405(m). The owner must retain the documents throughout his ownership of the specification cargo tank and for one year thereafter. In the event of a change in ownership, the prior owner must retain non-fading photo copies of these documents for one year.

(2) *Each motor carrier* who uses a specification cargo tank motor vehicle must obtain a copy of the manufacturer's certificate and related papers or the alternative report authorized by paragraph (a)(3)(i) or (ii) of this section and retain the documents as specified in this paragraph (a)(2). A motor carrier who is not the owner of a cargo tank motor vehicle must also retain a copy of the vehicle certification report for as long as the cargo tank motor vehicle is used by that carrier and for one year thereafter. The information required by this section must be maintained at the company's principal place of business or at the location where the vehicle is housed or maintained. The provisions of this section do not apply to a motor carrier who leases a cargo tank for less than 30 days.

(3) *DOT Specification* cargo tanks manufactured before September 1, 1995 —
(i) *Non-ASME Code stamped cargo tanks.* If an owner does not have a manufacturer's certificate for a cargo tank and he wishes to certify it as a specification cargo tank, the owner must perform appropriate tests and inspections, under the direct supervision of a Registered Inspector, to determine if the cargo tank conforms with the applicable specification. Both the owner and the Registered Inspector must certify that the cargo tank fully conforms to the applicable specification. The owner must retain the certificate, as specified in this section.
(ii) *ASME Code Stamped cargo tanks.* If the owner does not have the manufacturer's certificate required by the specification and the manufacturer's data report required by the ASME, the owner may contact the National Board for a copy of the manufacturer's data report, if the cargo tank was registered with the National Board, or copy the information contained on the cargo tank's identification and ASME Code plates. Additionally, both the owner and the Registered Inspector must certify that the cargo tank fully conforms to the specification. The owner must retain such documents, as specified in this section.

(b) Test or inspection reporting. Each cargo tank which is tested or reinspected as specified in §180.407 must have a written report, in English, prepared in accordance with this paragraph.

(1) *The test or inspection report must include the following:*
(i) *Type of test or inspection* performed and a listing of all items either tested or inspected (a checklist is acceptable);
(ii) *Owner's and manufacturer's serial numbers;*
(iii) *DOT Specification;*
(iv) *Test Date (Month and year);*
(v) *Location of defects found and method used to repair each defect;*
(vi) *Name and address* of person performing the test, the DOT registration number of the facility or the person performing the test;
(vii) *Disposition statement,* such as "Cargo tank returned to service" or "Cargo tank withdrawn from service"; and
(viii) *DOT registration number* of the inspector, and dated signature of inspector and owner.

(2) *The owner and the motor carrier,* if not the owner, must each retain a copy of the test and inspection reports until the next test or inspection of the same type is successfully completed. This requirement does not apply to a motor carrier leasing a cargo tank for less than 30 days.

(c) Additional requirements for Specification MC 330 and MC 331 cargo tanks.

(1) *After completion* of the pressure test specified in §180.407(g)(3), each motor carrier operating a Specification MC 330 or MC 331 cargo tank in anhydrous ammonia, liquefied petroleum gas, or any other service that may cause stress corrosion cracking, must make a written report containing the following information:
(i) *Carrier's name,* address of principal place of business, and telephone number;
(ii) *Complete identification* plate data required by Specification MC 330 or MC 331, including data required by ASME Code;
(iii) *Carrier's equipment number;*
(iv) *A statement* indicating whether or not the tank was stress relieved after fabrication;
(v) *Name and address* of the person performing the test and the date of the test;
(vi) *A statement* of the nature and severity of any defects found. In particular, information must be furnished to indicate the location of defects detected, such as in weld, heat-affected zone, the liquid phase, the vapor phase, or the head-to-shell seam. If no defect or damage was discovered, that fact must be reported;
(vii) *A statement* indicating the methods employed to make repairs, who made the repairs, and the date they were completed. Also, a statement of whether or not the tank was stress relieved after repairs and, if so, whether full or local stress relieving was performed;
(viii) *A statement* of the disposition of the cargo tank, such as "cargo tank scrapped" or "cargo tank returned to service"; and
(ix) *A statement* of whether or not the cargo tank is used in anhydrous ammonia, liquefied petroleum gas, or any other service that may cause stress corrosion cracking. Also, if the cargo tank has been used in anhydrous ammonia service since the last report, a statement indicating whether each shipment of ammonia was certified by its shipper as containing 0.2 percent water by weight.

(2) *A copy of the report* must be retained by the carrier at its principal place of business during the period the cargo tank is in the carrier's service and for one year thereafter. Upon a written request to, and with the approval of, the Field Administrator, Regional Service Center, Federal Motor Carrier Safety Administration for the region in which a motor carrier has its principal place of business, the carrier may maintain the reports at a regional or terminal office.

(3) *The requirement* in paragraph (c)(1) of this section does not apply to a motor carrier leasing a cargo tank for less than 30 days.

(d) Supplying reports. Each carrier offering a DOT Specification cargo tank for sale or lease must make available for inspection a copy of the most recent report made under this section to each purchaser or lessee. Copies of such reports must be provided to the purchaser, or the lessee if the cargo tank is leased for more than 30 days.

FEDERAL REGISTER UPDATES

In the April 18, 2003 Federal Register, §180.417 was revised, effective October 1, 2003.

(b) Test or inspection reporting. Each person performing a test or inspection as specified in §180.407 must prepare a written report, in English, in accordance with this paragraph. [1]

(1) *Each test or inspection report* must include the following information:
(i) *Owner's and manufacturer's unique serial number* for the cargo tank;
(ii) *Name of cargo tank manufacturer;*
(iii) *Cargo tank DOT or MC specification number;*
(iv) *MAWP of the cargo tank;*
(v) *Minimum thickness of the cargo tank shell and heads;*
(vi) *Indication of whether* the cargo tank is lined, insulated, or both; and
(vii) *Indication of special service of the cargo tank* (e.g., transports material corrosive to the tank, dedicated service, etc.)

(2) *Each test or inspection report* must include the following specific information as appropriate for each individual type of test or inspection:
(i) *Type of test or inspection performed;*
(ii) *Date of test or inspection (month and year);*
(iii) *Listing of all items tested or inspected,* including information about pressure relief devices that are removed, inspected and tested or replaced, when applicable (type of device, set to discharge pressure, pressure at which device opened, pressure at which device re-seated, and a statement of disposition of the device (e.g., reinstalled, repaired, or replaced)); information regarding the inspection of upper coupler assemblies, when applicable (visually examined in place, or removed for examination); and, information regarding leakage and pressure testing, when applicable (pneumatic or hydrostatic testing method, identification of the fluid used for the test, test pressure, and holding time of test);

(continued on next page)

(continued from previous page)

(iv) *Location of defects found and method of repair;*
(v) *ASME or National Board* number of person performing repairs, if applicable;
(vi) *Name and address of person performing test;*
(vii) *Registration number of the facility or person performing the test;*
(viii) *Continued qualification statement,* such as Acargo tank meets the requirements of the DOT-specification identified on this report" or "cargo tank fails to meet the requirements of the DOT-specification identified on this report";
(ix) *DOT registration number of the registered inspector; and*
(x) *Dated signature* of the registered inspector and the cargo tank owner.

(3) *The owner and the motor carrier,* if not the owner, must each retain a copy of the test and inspection reports until the next test or inspection of the same type is successfully completed. This requirement does not apply to a motor carrier leasing a cargo tank for fewer than 30 days.

(d) **Supplying certificates and reports.** Each person offering a DOT-specification cargo tank for sale or lease must provide the purchaser or lessee a copy of the cargo tank certificate of compliance, records of repair, modification, stretching, or rebarrelling; and the most recent inspection and test reports made under this section. Copies of such reports must be provided to the lessee if the cargo tank is leased for more than 30 days.[2]

1. Paragraph (b) was revised.
2. Paragraph (d) was revised.

Subpart F - Qualification and Maintenance of Tank Cars

§180.501 Applicability.

(a) **This subpart prescribes requirements,** in addition to those contained in parts 107, 171, 172, 173, and 179 of this subchapter, applicable to any person who manufactures, fabricates, marks, maintains, repairs, inspects, or services tank cars to ensure continuing qualification.

(b) **Any person who performs a function prescribed** in this part shall perform that function in accordance with this part.

§180.503 Definitions.

The definitions contained in §§171.8 and 179.2 of this subchapter apply.

§180.505 Quality assurance program.

The quality assurance program requirements of §179.7 of this subchapter apply.

§180.507 Qualification of tank cars.

(a) **Each tank car marked as meeting a "DOT" specification** or any other tank car used for the transportation of a hazardous material must meet the requirements of this subchapter or the applicable specification to which the tank was constructed.

(b) **Tank car specifications no longer authorized for construction.**

(1) *Tank cars* prescribed in the following table are authorized for service provided they conform to all applicable safety requirements of this subchapter:

Specification prescribed in the current regulations	Other specifications permitted	Notes
105A200W	105A100W	1
105A200ALW	105A100ALW	1
105A300W	ICC-105, 105A300	
105A400W	105A400	
105A500W	105A500	
105A600W	105A600	
106A500X	ICC-27, BE-27, 106A500	
106A800X	106A800	
107A * * * *		2

NOTE 1: Tanks built as Specification DOT 105A100W or DOT 105A100ALW may be altered and converted to DOT 105A200W and DOT 105A200ALW, respectively.

NOTE 2: The test pressures of tanks built in the United States between January 1, 1941 and December 31, 1955, may be increased to conform to Specification 107A. Original and revised test pressure markings must be indicated and may be shown on the tank or on a plate attached to the bulkhead of the car. Tanks built before 1941 are not authorized.

(2) *For each tank car* conforming to and used under an exemption issued before October 1, 1984, which authorized the transportation of a cryogenic liquid in a tank car, the owner or operator shall remove the exemption number stenciled on the tank car and stamp the tank car with the appropriate Class DOT-113 specification followed by the applicable exemption number. For example: DOT-113D60W-E * * * * (asterisks to be replaced by the exemption number). The owner or operator marking a tank car in this manner shall retain on file a copy of the last exemption in effect during the period the tank car is in service. No person may modify a tank car marked under this paragraph unless the modification is in compliance with an applicable requirement or provision of this subchapter.

(3) *Specification DOT-113A175W,* DOT-113C60W, DOT-113D60W, and DOT-113D120W tank cars may continue in use, but new construction is not authorized.

(4) *Class DOT* 105A and 105S tank cars used to transport hydrogen chloride, refrigerated liquid under the terms of DOT-E 3992 may continue in service, but new construction is not authorized.

§180.509 Requirements for inspection and test of specification tank cars.

(a) **General.**

(1) *Each tank car facility* shall evaluate a tank car according to the requirements specified in §180.511.

(2) *Each tank car* that successfully passes a periodic inspection and test must be marked as prescribed in §180.515.

(3) *A written report* as specified in §180.517(b) must be prepared for each tank car that is inspected and tested under this section.

(b) **Conditions requiring inspection and test of tank cars.** Without regard to any other periodic inspection and test requirements, a tank car must have an appropriate inspection and test according to the type of defect and the type of maintenance or repair performed if:

(1) *The tank car* shows evidence of abrasion, corrosion, cracks, dents, distortions, defects in welds, or any other condition that makes the tank car unsafe for transportation. An exaple is if maintenance is performed to replace a fitting, then only a leakage pressure test needs to be performed.

(2) *The tank car* was in an accident and damaged to an extent that may adversely affect its capability to retain its contents.

(3) *The tank bears evidence of damage caused by fire.*

(4) *The Associate Administrator* for Safety, FRA, requires it based on the existence of probable cause that a tank car or a class or design of tank cars may be in an unsafe operating condition.

(c) **Frequency of inspection and tests.** Each tank car shall have an inspection and test according to the requirements of this paragraph.

(1) *For Class 107* tank cars and tank cars of riveted construction, the tank car must have a hydrostatic pressure test and visual inspection conforming to the requirements in effect prior to July 1, 1996, for the tank specification.

(2) *For Class DOT 113 tank cars, see §173.319(e) of this subchapter.*

(3) *For fusion welded tank cars,* each tank car must have an inspection and test in accordance with paragraphs (d) through (k) of this section.

(i) *For cars* transporting materials not corrosive to the tank, every 10 years for the tank and service equipment (i.e., filling and discharge, venting, safety, heating, and measuring devices).

(ii) *For non-lined* or non-coated tank cars transporting materials corrosive to the tank, an interval based on the following formula, but in no case shall the interval exceed 10 years for the tank and 5 years for service equipment:

$$i = \frac{t_1 - t_2}{r}$$

Where:
i is the inspection and test interval.
t_1 is the actual thickness.
t_2 is the allowable minimum thickness under paragraph (g) of this section.
r is the corrosion rate per year.

(iii) *For lined or coated tank cars* transporting a material corrosive to the tank, every 10 years for the tank, 5 years for the service equipment.

[A] When a lining or coating is applied to protect the tank shell from the lading, the owner of the lining or coating shall determine the periodic inspection interval, test technique, and acceptance criteria for the lining or coating. The owner must maintain at its principal place of business all supporting documentation used to make such a determination, such as the lining or coating manufacturer's recommended inspection interval, test technique, and acceptance criteria. The supporting documentation must be made available to FRA upon request.

[B] The owner of the lining or coating shall provide the periodic inspection interval, test technique, and acceptance criteria for the lining or coating to the person responsible for qualifying the lining and coating.

(d) Visual inspection. At a minimum, each tank car facility must visually inspect the tank externally and internally as follows:

(1) *An internal inspection* of the tank shell and heads for abrasion, corrosion, cracks, dents, distortions, defects in welds, or any other condition that makes the tank car unsafe for transportation, and except in the areas where insulation or a thermal protection system precludes it, an external inspection of the tank shell and heads for abrasion, corrosion, cracks, dents, distortions, defects in welds, or any other condition that makes the tank car unsafe for transportation;

(2) *An inspection* of the piping, valves, fittings, and gaskets for indications of corrosion and other conditions that make the tank car unsafe for transportation;

(3) *An inspection* for missing or loose bolts, nuts, or elements that make the tank car unsafe for transportation;

(4) *An inspection* of all closures on the tank car for proper securement in a tool tight condition and an inspection of the protective housings for proper securement;

(5) *An inspection* of excess flow valves having threaded seats for tightness; and

(6) *An inspection of the required markings on the tank car for legibility.*

(e) Structural integrity inspections and tests. At a minimum, each tank car facility shall inspect the tank car for structural integrity as specified in this section. The structural integrity inspection and test shall include all transverse fillet welds greater than 0.64 cm (0.25 inch) within 121.92 cm (4 feet) of the bottom longitudinal center line; the termination of longitudinal fillet welds greater than 0.64 cm (0.25 inch) within 121.92 cm (4 feet) of the bottom longitudinal center line; and all tank shell butt welds within 60.96 cm (2 feet) of the bottom longitudinal center line by one or more of the following inspection and test methods to determine that the welds are in proper condition:

(1) *Dye penetrant test;*

(2) *Radiography test;*

(3) *Magnetic particle test;*

(4) *Ultrasonic test; or*

(5) *Optically-aided visual inspection* (e.g., magnifiers, fiberscopes, borescopes, and machine vision technology).

(f) Thickness tests.

(1) *Each tank car facility* shall measure the thickness of the tank car shell, heads, sumps, domes, and nozzles on each tank car by using a device capable of accurately measuring the thickness to within 0.05 mm (±0.002 inch).

(2) *After repairs,* alterations, conversions or modifications of a tank car that result in a reduction to the tank car shell thickness, the tank car facility shall measure the thickness of the tank car shell in the area of reduced shell thickness to ensure that the shell thickness conforms to paragraph (g) of this section.

(g) Service life shell thickness allowance.

(1) *A tank car* found with a shell thickness below the required minimum thickness after forming for its specification, as stated in part 179 of this subchapter, may continue in service if:

(i) *Construction of* the tank car shell and heads is from carbon steel, stainless steel, aluminum, nickel, or manganese-molybdenum steel; and

(ii) *Any reduction* in the required minimum thickness of the tank shell or head is not more than that provided in the following table:

Allowable Shell Thickness Reductions

Damage type	Class DOT 103, 104, 111, and 115 tank cars		Class DOT 105, 109, 112, and 114 tank cars	
	Top shell and tank head	Bottom shell	Top shell and tank head	Bottom shell
Corrosion	3.17 mm (0.125 inch)	1.58 mm (0.063 inch)	0.79 mm (0.031 inch)	0.79 mm (0.031 inch)
Corrosion and mechanical	3.17 mm (0.125 inch)	1.58 mm (0.063 inch)	0.79 mm (0.031 inch)	0.79 mm (0.031 inch)
Corrosion, local	4.76 mm (0.188 inch)	3.17 mm (0.125 inch)	1.58 mm (0.063 inch)	1.58 mm (0.063 inch)
Mechanical, local	3.17 mm (0.125 inch)	1.58 mm (0.063 inch)	1.58 mm (0.063 inch)	1.58 mm (0.063 inch)
Corrosion and mechanical, local	4.76 mm (0.188 inch)	3.17 mm (0.125 inch)	1.58 mm (0.063 inch)	1.58 mm (0.063 inch)

NOTES:

1. The perimeter for a local reduction may not exceed a 60.96 cm (24 inch) perimeter. Local reductions in the top shell must be separated from other reductions in the top shell by at least 40.64 cm (16 inches). The cumulative perimeter for local reductions in the bottom shell may not exceed 182.88 cm (72 inches).
2. Any reduction in the tank car shell may not affect the structural strength of the tank car so that the tank car shell no longer conforms to Section 6.2 of the AAR Specifications for Tank Cars.
3. Any reduction applies only to the outer shell for Class DOT 115 tank cars.
4. For Class DOT 103 and 104 tank cars, the inside diameter may not exceed 243.84 cm (96 inches).

(h) Safety system inspections. At a minimum, each tank car facility must inspect:

(1) *Tank car* thermal protection systems, tank head puncture resistance systems, coupler vertical restraint systems, and systems used to protect discontinuities (i.e., skid protection and protective housings) to ensure their integrity.

(2) *Reclosing pressure relief devices by:*

(i) *Removing the reclosing* pressure relief device from the tank car for inspection; and

(ii) *Testing the reclosing* pressure relief device with air or another gas to ensure that it conforms to the start-to-discharge pressure for the specification or hazardous material in this subchapter.

(i) Lining and coating inspection and test. When this subchapter requires a lining or coating, at a minimum, each tank car facility must inspect the lining or coating installed on the tank car according to the inspection interval test technique, and acceptance criteria established by the owner of the lining or coating in accordance with paragraph (c)(3)(iii) of this section.

(j) Leakage pressure test.

(1) *After reassembly* of a tank car or service equipment, a tank car facility must perform a leak test on the tank or service equipment to detect leakage, if any, between manway covers, cover plates, and service equipment. The test may be conducted with the hazardous material in the tank. When the test pressure exceeds the start-to-discharge or burst pressure of a pressure relief device, the device must be rendered inoperative. The written procedures and test method for leak testing must ensure for the sensitivity and reliability of the test method and for the serviceability of components to prevent premature failure.

(2) *Interior heater systems* must be tested hydrostatically at 13.87 Bar (200 psig) and must show no signs of leakage.

(k) Alternative inspection and test procedures. In lieu of the other requirements of this section, a person may use an alternative inspection and test procedure or interval based on a damage-tolerance fatigue evaluation (that includes a determination of the probable locations and modes of damage due to fatigue, corrosion, or accidental damage), when the evaluation is examined by the Association of American Railroads Tank Car Committee and approved by the Associate Administrator for Safety, FRA.

(1) *Inspection and test* compliance date for tank cars. After July 1, 2000, each tank car with a metal jacket or with a thermal protection system shall have an inspection and test conforming to this section no later than the date the tank car requires a periodic hydrostatic pressure test (i.e., the marked due date on the tank car for the hydrostatic test).

(2) *After July 1, 1998,* each tank car without a metal jacket shall have an inspection and test conforming to this section no later than the date the tank car requires a periodic hydrostatic pressure test (i.e., the marked due date on the tank car for the hydrostatic test).

(3) *For tank cars* on a 20-year periodic hydrostatic pressure test interval (i.e., Class DOT 103W, 104W, 111A60W1, 111A100W1, and 111A100W3 tank cars), the next inspection and test date is the midpoint between the compliance date in paragraph (l)(1) or (2) of this section and the remaining years until the tank would have had a hydrostatic pressure test.

§180.511 Acceptable results of inspections and tests.

Provided it conforms with other applicable requirements of this subchapter, a tank car is qualified for use if it successfully passes the following inspections and tests conducted in accordance with this subpart:

(a) Visual inspection. A tank car successfully passes the visual inspection when the inspection shows no structural defect that may cause leakage from or failure of the tank before the next inspection and test interval.

(b) Structural integrity inspection and test. A tank car successfully passes the structural integrity inspection and test when it shows no structural defect that may initiate cracks or propagate cracks and cause failure of the tank before the next inspection and test interval.

(c) Service life shell thickness. A tank car successfully passes the service life shell thickness inspection when the tank shell and heads show no thickness reduction below that allowed in §180.509(g).

(d) Safety system inspection. A tank car successfully passes the safety system inspection when each thermal protection system, tank head puncture resistance system, coupler vertical restraint system, and system used to protect discontinuities (e.g., breakage grooves on bottom outlets and protective housings) on the tank car conform to this subchapter.

(e) Lining and coating inspection. A tank car successfully passes the lining and coating inspection and test when the lining or coating conforms to the owner's acceptance criteria.

(f) Leakage pressure test. A tank car successfully passes the leakage pressure test when all product piping, fittings and closures show no indication of leakage.

(g) Hydrostatic test. A Class 107 tank car or a riveted tank car successfully passes the hydrostatic test when it shows no leakage, distortion, excessive permanent expansion, or other evidence of weakness that might render the tank car unsafe for transportation service.

§180.513 Repairs, alterations, conversions, and modifications.

(a) In order to repair tank cars, the tank car facility must comply with the requirements of appendix R of the AAR Specifications for Tank Cars.

(b) Unless the exterior tank car shell or interior tank car jacket has a protective coating, after a repair that requires the complete removal of the tank car jacket, the exterior tank car shell and the interior tank car jacket must have a protective coating applied to prevent the deterioration of the tank shell and tank jacket.

§180.515 Markings.

(a) When a tank car passes the required inspection and test with acceptable results, the tank car facility shall mark the date of the inspection and test and the due date of the next inspection and test on the tank car in accordance with appendix C of the AAR Specifications for Tank Cars. When a tank car facility performs multiple inspection and test at the same time, one date may be used to satisfy the requirements of this section. One date also may be shown when multiple inspection and test have the same due date.

(b) Pressure converted tank cars must have the new specification and conversion date permanently marked in letters and figures at least 0.95 cm (0.375 inch) high on the outside of the manway nozzle or the edge of the manway nozzle flange on the left side of the car. The marking may have the last numeral of the specification number omitted (e.g., "DOT 111A100W" instead of "DOT 111A100W1").

(c) When pressure tested within six months of installation and protected from deterioration, the test date marking of a reclosing pressure relief device is the installation date on the tank car.

§180.517 Reporting and record retention requirements.

(a) Certification and representation. Each owner of a specification tank car shall retain the certificate of construction (AAR Form 4-2) and related papers certifying that the manufacture of the specification tank car identified in the documents is in accordance with the applicable specification. The owner shall retain the documents throughout the period of ownership of the specification tank car and for one year thereafter. Upon a change of ownership, the requirements of Section 1.3.15 of the AAR Specifications for Tank Cars apply.

(b) Inspection and test reporting. Each tank car that is inspected as specified in §180.509 must have a written report, in English, prepared according to this paragraph. The owner must retain a copy of the inspection and test reports until successfully completing the next inspection and test of the same type. The inspection and test report must include the following:

(1) *Type of inspection and test performed (a checklist is acceptable);*

(2) *The results of each inspection and test performed;*

(3) *Owner's reporting mark;*

(4) *DOT Specification;*

(5) *Inspection and test date (month and year);*

(6) *Location and description* of defects found and method used to repair each defect;

(7) *The name and address* of the tank car facility and the signature of inspector.

§180.519 Periodic retest and inspection of tank cars other than single-unit tank car tanks.

(a) General. Unless otherwise provided in this subpart, tanks designed to be removed from cars for filling and emptying and tanks built to a Class DOT 107A specification and their safety relief devices must be retested periodically as specified in Retest Table 1 of paragraph (b)(5) of this section. Retests may be made at any time during the calendar year the retest falls due.

(b) Pressure test.

(1) *Each tank* must be subjected to the specified hydrostatic pressure and its permanent expansion determined. Pressure must be maintained for 30 seconds and for as long as necessary to secure complete expansion of the tank. Before testing, the pressure gauge must be shown to be accurate within 1 percent at test measure. The expansion gauge must be shown to be accurate, at test pressure, to within 1 percent. Expansion must be recorded in cubic cm. Permanent volumetric expansion may not exceed 10 percent of total volumetric expansion at test pressure and the tank must not leak or show evidence of distress.

(2) *Each tank,* except tanks built to specification DOT 107A, must also be subjected to interior air pressure test of at least 100 psig under conditions favorable to detection of any leakage. No leaks may appear.

(3) *Safety relief valves* must be retested by air or gas, must start-to-discharge at or below the prescribed pressure and must be vapor tight at or above the prescribed pressure.

(4) *Rupture discs* and fusible plugs must be removed from the tank and visually inspected.

(5) *Tanks must be retested* as specified in Retest Table 1 of this paragraph (b)(5), and before returning to service after repairs involving welding or heat treatment:

Retest Table 1

Specification	Retest interval — years		Minimum Retest pressure — psig		Pressure relief valve pressure — psig	
	Tank	Pressure relief devices [d]	Tank hydrostatic expansion [c]	Tank air test	Start-to-discharge	Vapor tight
DOT 27	5	2	500	100	375	300
106A500	5	2	500	100	375	300
106A500X	5	2	500	100	375	300
106A800	5	2	800	100	600	480
106A800X	5	2	800	100	600	480
106A800NCI	5	2	800	100	600	480
107A * * * *	[d]5	[a]2	([b])	None	None	None
110A500-W	5	2	500	100	375	300
110A600-W	5	2	600	100	500	360
110A800-W	5	2	800	100	600	480
110A1000-W	5	2	1,000	100	750	600
BE-27	5	2	500	100	375	300

NOTES:

[a] If DOT 107A * * * * tanks are used for transportation of flammable gases, one rupture disc from each car must be burst at the interval prescribed. The sample disc must burst at a pressure not exceeding the marked test pressure of the tank and not less than 70 percent of the marked test pressure. If the sample disc does not burst within the prescribed limits, all discs on the car must be replaced.

[b] The hydrostatic expansion test pressure must at least equal the marked test pressure.

[c] See §180.519(b)(1).

[d] Safety relief valves of the spring-loaded type on tanks used exclusively for fluorinated hydrocarbons and mixtures thereof which are free from corroding components may be retested every 5 years.

(6) *The month and year of test,* followed by a "V" if visually inspected as described in paragraph (c) of this section, must be plainly and permanently stamped into the metal of one head or chime of each tank with successful test results; for example, 01-90 for January 1990. On DOT 107A**** tanks, the date must be stamped into the metal of the marked end, except that if all tanks mounted on a car have been tested, the date may be stamped into the metal of a plate permanently applied to the bulkhead on the "A" end of the car. Dates of previous tests and all prescribed markings must be kept legible.

(c) **Visual inspection.** Tanks of Class DOT 106A and DOT 110A-W specifications (§§179.300 and 179.301 of this subchapter) used exclusively for transporting fluorinated hydrocarbons and mixtures thereof, and that are free from corroding components, may be given a periodic complete internal and external visual inspection in place of the periodic hydrostatic retest. Visual inspections shall be made only by competent persons. The tank must be accepted or rejected in accordance with the criteria in CGA Pamphlet C-6.

(d) **Written records.** The results of the pressure test and visual inspection must be recorded on a suitable data sheet. Completed copies of these reports must be retained by the owner and by the person performing the pressure test and visual inspection as long as the tank is in service. The information to be recorded and checked on these data sheets are: Date of test and inspection; DOT specification number; tank identification (registered symbol and serial number, date of manufacture and ownership symbol); type of protective coating (painted, etc., and statement as to need for refinishing or recoating); conditions checked (leakage, corrosion, gouges, dents or digs, broken or damaged chime or protective ring, fire, fire damage, internal condition); test pressure; results of tests; and disposition of tank (returned to service, returned to manufacturer for repair, or scrapped); and identification of the person conducting the retest or inspection.

Subpart G - Qualification and Maintenance of Portable Tanks

§180.601 Applicability.

This subpart prescribes requirements, in addition to those contained in parts 107, 171, 172, 173, and 178 of this subchapter, applicable to any person responsible for the continuing qualification, maintenance or periodic retesting of a portable tank.

§180.603 Qualification of portable tanks.

(a) **Each portable tank used for the transportation** of hazardous materials must be an authorized packaging.

(b) **To qualify as an authorized packaging,** each portable tank must conform to the requirements of this subchapter and the applicable design specification to which the portable tank was constructed.

(c) **The following portable tanks are authorized** for use provided they conform to all applicable safety requirements of this subchapter: 51, 56, 57, 60, IM 101, IM 102 and UN portable tanks.

(d) **A portable tank that also meets the definition** of "container" in 49 CFR 450.3(a)(3) must conform to the requirements in parts 450 through 453 of this title for compliance with Annex II of the Convention for Safe Containers (CSC).

(e) **Exemption portable tanks based on DOT 51 portable tanks.** The owner of a portable tank constructed in accordance with and used under an exemption issued prior to August 31, 1996, which was in conformance with the requirements for Specification DOT 51 portable tanks with the exception of the location of fill and discharge outlets, shall examine the portable tank and its design to determine if it meets the outletrequirements in effect on October 1, 1996. If the owner determines that the portable tank is in compliance with all requirements of the DOT 51 specification, the exemption number stenciled on the portable tank shall be removed and the specification plate (or a plate placed adjacent to the specification plate) shall be durably marked "DOT 51-E*****" (where ***** is to be replaced by the exemption number). During the period the portable tank is in service, and for one year thereafter, the owner of the portable tank must retain on file, at its principal place of business, a copy of the last exemption in effect.

§180.605 Requirements for periodic testing, inspection, and repair of portable tanks.

(a) **A portable tank constructed in accordance** with a DOT specification for which a test or inspection specified in this subpart has become due, must be tested or inspected prior to being returned for transportation.

(b) **Conditions requiring test and inspection** of portable tanks. Without regard to any other test or inspection requirements, a Specification or UN portable tank must be tested and inspected in accordance with this section prior to further use if any of the following conditions exist:

(1) *The portable tank* shows evidence of dents, corroded or abraded areas, leakage, or any other condition that might render it unsafe for transportation service.

(2) *The portable tank* has been in an accident and has been damaged to an extent that may adversely affect its ability to retain the hazardous material.

(3) *The portable tank* has been out of hazardous materials transportation service for a period of one year or more.

(4) *The portable tank* has been modified from its original design specification.

(5) *The portable tank* is in an unsafe operating condition based on the existence of probable cause.

(c) **Schedule for periodic inspections and tests.** Each Specification portable tank must be tested and inspected in accordance with the following schedule:

(1) *Each IM or UN portable tank* must be given an initial inspection and test before being placed into service, a periodic inspection and test at least once every 5 years, and an intermediate periodic inspection and test at least every 2.5 years following the initial inspection and the last 5 year periodic inspection and test.

(2) *Each Specification 51* portable tank must be given a periodic inspection and test at least once every five years.

(3) *Each Specification 56 or 57* portable tank must be given a periodic inspection and test at least once every 2.5 years.

(4) *Each Specification 60* portable tank must be given a periodic inspection and test at the end of the first 4-year period after the original test; at least once every 2 years thereafter up to a total of 12 years of service; and at least once annually thereafter. Retesting is not required on a rubber-lined tank except before each relining.

(d) **Intermediate periodic inspection and test.** For IM and UN portable tanks the intermediate 2.5 year periodic inspection and test must include at least an internal and external examination of the portable tank and its fittings taking into account the hazardous materials intended to be transported; a leakage test; and a test of the satisfactory operation of all service equipment. Sheathing, thermal insulation, etc. need only be removed to the extent required for reliable appraisal of the condition of the portable tank. For portable tanks intended for the transportation of a single hazardous material, the internal examination may be waived if it is leakage tested in accordance with the procedures in paragraph (h) of this section prior to each filling, or if approved by the Associate Administrator. Portable tanks used for dedicated transportation of refrigerated liquefied gases that are not fitted with inspection openings are excepted from the internal inspection requirement.

(e) **Periodic inspection and test.** The 5 year periodic inspection and test must include an internal and external examination and, unless excepted, a pressure test as specified in this section. Sheathing, thermal insulation, etc. need only to be removed to the extent required for reliable appraisal of the condition of the portable tank. Except for DOT Specification 56 and 57 portable tanks, reclosing pressure relief devices must be removed from the tank and tested separately unless they can be tested while installed on the portable tank. For portable tanks where the shell and equipment have been pressure-tested separately, after assembly they must be subjected together to a leakage test and effectively tested and inspected for corrosion. Portable tanks used for the transportation of refrigerated, liquefied gases are excepted from the requirement for internal inspection and the hydraulic pressure test during the 5-year periodic inspection and test, if the portable tanks were pressure tested to a minimum test pressure of 1.3 times the design pressure using an inert gas as prescribed in §178.338-16(a) and (b) of this subchapter before putting the portable tank into service initially and after any exceptional inspections and tests specified in paragraph (f) of this section.

(f) **Exceptional inspection and test.** The exceptional inspection and test is necessary when a portable tank shows evidence of damaged or corroded areas, or leakage, or other conditions that indicate a deficiency that could affect the integrity of the portable tank. The extent of the exceptional inspection and test must depend on the amount of damage or deterioration of the portable tank. It must include at least the inspection and a pressure test according to paragraph (e) of this section. Pressure relief devices need not be tested or replaced unless there is reason to believe the relief devices have been affected by the damage or deterioration.

(g) **Internal and external examination.** The internal and external examinations must ensure that:

(1) *The shell* is inspected for pitting, corrosion, or abrasions, dents, distortions, defects in welds or any other conditions, including leakage, that might render the portable tank unsafe for transportation;

(2) *The piping, valves, and gaskets* are inspected for corroded areas, defects, and other conditions, including leakage, that might render the portable tank unsafe for filling, discharge or transportation;

(3) *Devices for tightening* manhole covers are operative and there is no leakage at manhole covers or gaskets;

(4) *Missing or loose* bolts or nuts on any flanged connection or blank flange are replaced or tightened;

(5) *All emergency devices and valves* are free from corrosion, distortion and any damage or defect that could prevent their normal operation. Remote closure devices and self-closing stop-valves must be operated to demonstrate proper operation;

(6) *Required markings* on the portable tank are legible and in accordance with the applicable requirements; and

(7) *The framework,* the supports and the arrangements for lifting the portable tank are in satisfactory condition.

(h) **Pressure test procedures for specification 51, 57, 60,** IM or UN portable tanks.

(1) *Each Specification 57* portable tank must be leak tested by a minimum sustained air pressure of at least 3 psig applied to the entire tank. Each Specification 51 or 56 portable tank must be tested by a minimum pressure (air or hydrostatic) of at least 2 psig or at least one and one-half times the design pressure (maximum allowable working pressure, or re-rated pressure) of the tank, whichever is greater. The leakage test for portable tanks used for refrigerated liquefied gas must be performed at 90% of MAWP. Leakage tests for all other portable tanks must be at a pressure of at least 25% of MAWP. During each air pressure test, the entire surface of all joints under pressure must be coated with or immersed in a solution of soap and water, heavy oil, or other material suitable for the purpose of detecting leaks. The pressure must be held for a period of time sufficiently long to assure detection of leaks, but in no case less than five minutes. During the air or hydrostatic test, relief devices may be removed, but all the closure fittings must be in place and the relief device openings plugged. Lagging need not be removed from a lagged tank if it is possible to maintain the required test pressure at constant temperature with the tank disconnected from the source of pressure.

(2) *Each Specification 60* portable tank must be retested by completely filling the tank with water or other liquid having a similar viscosity, the temperature of the liquid must not exceed 37.7 °C (100 °F) during the test, and applying a pressure of 60 psig. The portable tank must be capable of holding the prescribed pressure for at least 10 minutes without leakage, evidence of impending failure, or failure. All closures shall be in place while the test is made and the pressure shall be gauged at the top of the tank. Safety devices and/or vents shall be plugged during this test.

(3) *Each Specification IM or UN* portable tank, except for UN portable tanks used for non-refrigerated and refrigerated liquefied gases, and all piping, valves and accessories, except pressure relief devices, must be hydrostatically tested with water, or other liquid of similar density and viscosity, to a pressure not less than 150% of its maximum allowable working pressure. UN portable tanks used for the transportation of non-refrigerated liquefied gases must be hydrostatically tested with water, or other liquid of similar density and viscosity, to a pressure not less than 130% of its maximum allowable working pressure. UN portable tanks used for the transportation of refrigerated liquefied gases may be tested hydrostatically or pneumatically using an inert gas to a pressure not less than 1.3 times the design pressure. For pneumatic testing, due regard for protection of all personnel must be taken because of the potential hazard involved in such a test. The pneumatic test pressure in the portable tank must be reached by gradually increasing the pressure to one-half of the test pressure. Thereafter, the test pressure must be increased in steps of approximately one-tenth of the test pressure until the required test pressure has been reached. The pressure must then be reduced to a value equal to four-fifths of the test pressure and held for a sufficient time to permit inspection of the portable tank for leaks. The minimum test pressure for a portable tank is determined on the basis of the hazardous materials that are intended to be transported in the portable tanks. For liquid, solid and non-refrigerated liquefied gases, the minimum test pressure for specific hazardous materials are specified in the applicable T Codes assigned to a particular hazardous material in the §172.101 Table of this subchapter. While under pressure the tank shall be inspected for leakage, distortion, or any other condition which might render the tank unsafe for service. A portable tank fails to meet the requirements of the pressure test if, during the test, there is permanent distortion of the tank exceeding that permitted by the applicable specification; if there is any leakage; or if there are any deficiencies that would render the portable tank unsafe for transportation. Any portable tank that fails must be rejected and may not be used again for the transportation of a hazardous material unless the tank is adequately repaired, and, thereafter, a successful test is conducted in accordance with the requirements of this paragraph. An approval agency shall witness the hydrostatic or pneumatic test. Any damage or deficiency that might render the portable tank unsafe for service shall be repaired to the satisfaction of the witnessing approval agency. The repaired tank must be retested to the original pressure test requirements. Upon successful completion of the hydrostatic or pneumatic test, as applicable, the witnessing approval agency shall apply its name, identifying mark or identifying number in accordance with paragraph (k) of this section.

(i) **Rejection criteria.** When evidence of any unsafe condition is discovered, the portable tank may not be returned to service until it has been repaired and the pressure test is repeated and passed.

(j) **Repair.** The repair of a portable tank is authorized, provided such repairs are made in accordance with the requirements prescribed in the specification for the tank's original design and construction. In addition to any other provisions of the specification, no portable tank may be repaired so as to cause leakage or cracks or so as to increase the likelihood of leakage or cracks near areas of stress concentration due to cooling metal shrinkage in welding operations, sharp fillets, reversal of stresses, or otherwise. No field welding may be done except to non-pressure parts. Any cutting, burning or welding operations on the shell of an IM or UN portable tank must be done with the approval of the approval agency and be done in accordance with the requirements of this subchapter, taking into account the pressure vessel code used for the construction of the shell. A pressure test to the original test pressure must be performed after the work is completed.

(k) **Inspection and test markings.** Each IM or UN portable tank must be durably and legibly marked, in English, with the date (month and year) of the last pressure test, the identification markings of the approval agency witnessing the test, when required, and the date of the last visual inspection. The marking must be placed on or near the metal identification plate, in letters not less than 3 mm (0.118 inches) high when on the metal identification plate, and 12 mm (0.5 inches) high when on the portable tank.

(l) **Record retention.** The owner of each portable tank or his authorized agent shall retain a written record of the date and results of all required inspections and tests, including an ASME manufacturer's date report, if applicable, and the name and address of the person performing the inspection or test, in accordance with the applicable specification. The manufacturer's data report, including a certificate(s) signed by the manufacturer, and the authorized design approval agency, as applicable, indicating compliance with the applicable specification of the portable tank, must be retained in the files of the owner, or his authorized agent, during the time that such portable tank is used for such service, except for Specifications 56 and 57 portable tanks.

Appendix A to Part 180

Internal self-closing stop valve emergency closure test for liquefied compressed gases.

1. **In performing this test, all internal** self-closing stop valves must be opened. Each emergency discharge control remote actuator (on-truck and off-truck) must be operated to ensure that each internal self-closing stop valve's lever, piston, or other valve indicator has moved to the closed position.
2. **On pump-actuated pressure differential internal valves,** the three-way toggle valve handle or its cable attachment must be activated to verify that the toggle handle moves to the closed position.

Appendix B to Part 180

Acceptable internal self-closing stop valve leakage tests for cargo tanks transporting liquefied compressed gases.

For internal self-closing stop valve leakage testing, leakage is defined as any leakage through the internal self-closing valve or to the atmosphere that is detectable when the valve is in the closed position. On some valves this will require the closure of the pressure by-pass port.

(a) Meter Creep Test.

1. *An operator* of a cargo tank equipped with a calibrated meter may check the internal self-closing stop valve for leakage through the valve seat using the meter as a flow measurement indicator. The test is initiated by starting the delivery process or returning product to the cargo tank through the delivery system. This may be performed at an idle. After the flow is established, the operator closes the internal self-closing stop valve and monitors the meter flow. The meter flow must stop within 30 seconds with no meter creep within 5 seconds after the meter stops.
2. *On pump-actuated* pressure differential internal self-closing stop valves, the valve must be closed with the remote actuator to assure that it is functioning. On other types of internal self-closing stop valves, the valve(s) may be closed using either the normal valve control or the discharge control system (e.g., remote).
3. *Rejection criteria:* Any detectable meter creep within the first five seconds after initial meter stoppage.

(b) Internal Self-Closing Stop Valve Test.

An operator of a cargo tank that is not equipped with a meter may check the internal self-closing stop valve(s) for leakage as follows:

1. *The internal self-closing stop valve must be in the closed position.*
2. *All of the material* in the downstream piping must be evacuated, and the piping must be returned to atmospheric temperature and pressure.
3. *The outlet must be monitored for 30 seconds for detectable leakage.*
4. *Rejection criteria.* Any detectable leakage is considered unacceptable.

Hazardous Materials Registration Program and Forms[1]

Must YOU Register?

Registering As An Offeror or Transporter of Hazardous Materials

U.S. Department of Transportation
Hazardous Materials Registration Program
Instructions & Form DOT F 5800.2
For Registration Year 2003-2004

This information outlines registration requirements applicable to persons who offer or transport hazardous materials in commerce. You should read the section titled "Who Must Register" to determine whether your company must comply. If your company generates hazardous waste, please read the section titled "Requirements for Hazardous Waste Generators" to determine whether your company is required to register.

• Fees Reduced Effective with the 2003-2004 Registration Year

The following changes became effective with the 2003-2004 registration year (July 1, 2003, through June 30, 2004). These changes were established by Final Rules published in the *Federal Register* on September 16, 2002, and January 9, 2003.

- The annual registration fee for the 2003-2004 registration year has been reduced to $150 for each person meeting the Small Business Administration's size standard for a small business and for not-for-profit organizations, and to $300 for all other persons. The fees will remain at this level through the 2005-2006 registration year. The fees have been reduced for these years in order to eliminate an unexpected balance in the special U.S. Treasury account established to contain the fees paid to support the Hazardous Materials Emergency Preparedness Grants Program. Assuming that the unexpended balance will have been eliminated in these three years, in 2006-2007 the registration fees have been set at $275 for persons meeting the SBA size standard for a small business and for not-for-profit organizations, and at $1,000 for all other registrants. The annual fees for registration years 1992-1993 through 2002-2003 remain at the previously established amounts. A complete table of fees is supplied in the section titled "Registration Fee Table."
- A new fee category for not-for-profit organizations has been established. A not-for-profit organization is an organization exempt from taxation under 26 U.S.C. 501(a).
- RSPA also adopted the Small Business Administration's use of the North American Industry Classification System (NAICS) codes to determine whether a registrant meets the SBA's size standard for a small business. Starting in registration year 2003-2004, registrants are to supply the NAICS code that represents the major business activity of the registrant.

You may register by using one of the following methods:

- Register through the Internet as explained in the section titled "Registering Through the Internet."
- Complete form DOT F 5800.2 (revised 3/03) and mail it with payment of the appropriate fee to the address given on the printed form.
- Register by telephone through the expedited procedures described in the section titled "Expedited Registration."

Please also note:

- **Changes effective July 1, 2000.** We made several changes to the registration requirements beginning with the 2000-2001 registration year. One of these changes expanded the requirement to register to any person that offers or transports a quantity of hazardous materials (including hazardous waste) that requires placarding. Many persons who were not required to register before July 1, 2000, are now required to register.
- **Prior years.** The Hazardous Materials Registration Program has been in effect since the 1992-1993 registration year. Your company must register for prior years if (1) it engaged in activities that required registration during those years, and (2) it failed to register. See "If You Have Failed To Register For Past Years."
- **Each "person" must register.** The Hazardous Materials Registration requirements apply to a "person," which includes each separate corporation, partnership, or association, as well as a sole proprietorship. Registration is not required for each vehicle that you operate or for each facility or terminal operated by a single "person." See the discussion of "Person" in the section titled "Who Must Register?".
- **Mailings.** If you received this in the mail, we sent it to you because your company is currently registered in the Hazardous Materials Registration Program or appears on one or more of several lists of companies as an offeror or transporter of hazardous materials (including hazardous wastes). These lists were collected primarily from offices within the U.S. Department of Transportation. While inclusion in any of our source lists is not an absolute indication that you are required to register, it does indicate that you may be subject to the registration requirements.

  In most years we make "follow-up" mailings several weeks after this information packet is first mailed out, to remind people of the registration requirements. For both the initial and follow-up mailings we try to remove duplicate address records from the lists we use. However, when working with lists from different sources, it is not always possible to eliminate multiple entries, especially when a single company appears in different lists under slightly different names or with different addresses. Consequently, this packet may have been sent more than once to a single company or "person." We regret any inconvenience this may cause.

Registration Phone Numbers
Hazardous Materials Registration Program

Form and Instructions	(617) 494-2545
Automated Fax-on-Demand Service for Brochure and Form (request document 700)	(800) 467-4922
Four Weeks and No Certificate?	(617) 494-2545
Registration Information and Answers	(202) 366-4109
General Hazardous Materials Information — Hazardous Materials Information Center	(800) 467-4922
Expedited Registration	(800) 942-6990
Verify U.S. DOT ID Number (FMCSA/OMC)	call the FMCSA local office
SBA Size and NAICS Code Questions (SBA)	(202) 205-6618
Copy of Relevant Regulations (49 CFR Parts 100 to 185)	(202) 512-1800

• Background and Uses of the Fee

Under the federal hazardous material transportation law (49 U.S.C. 5101 et seq.), certain offerors and transporters of hazardous materials, including hazardous waste, are required to file a registration statement with the U.S. Department of Transportation and to pay an annual fee. This program began in 1992 and is administered by the Associate Administrator for Hazardous Materials Safety, Research and Special Programs Administration (RSPA). The registration regulations are found at 49 CFR 107.601-107.620.

The fee provides funds for grants distributed to states and Indian tribes for hazardous materials emergency response planning and training through the Hazardous Materials Emergency Preparedness Grants Program. For use in FY 2003, 50 states, the District of Columbia, five territories, and ten Indian tribes received grant awards totaling $12.8 million. These grants support planning and training of emergency personnel to respond to incidents involving hazardous materials. Grants are used to train, in part, approximately 140,000 emergency responders each year. In addition, $1.5 million in grants have been made to the International Association of Fire Fighters to support its hazardous materials instructor train-the-trainer program. The fees are also used to publish the *Emergency Response Guidebook*. **Your fee is helping communities prepare for a spill, accident or other hazardous materials emergency that may occur.**

1. The information that follows is taken from the 2003-2004 registration year instruction brochure and registration form published by the U.S. Department of Transportation, Research and Special Programs Administration.

Hazardous Materials Emergency Preparedness (HMEP)
Grants Made for Use in Fiscal Year 2003

State/Territory	Amount	State/Territory	Amount	State/Territory	Amount
Alabama	$236,183	Minnesota	$262,068	Virginia	$243,051
Alaska	$82,560	Mississippi	$177,883	Washington	$206,220
Arizona	$183,283	Missouri	$266,548	West Virginia	$140,570
Arkansas	$158,959	Montana	$118,746	Wisconsin	$260,053
California	$964,316	Nebraska	$183,399	Wyoming	$94,237
Colorado	$181,716	Nevada	$123,594	American Samoa	$66,207
Connecticut	$145,112	New Hampshire	$106,013	Guam	$67,353
Delaware	$91,223	New Jersey	$289,579	Northern Mariana Islands	$65,973
District of Columbia	$73,484	New Mexico	$150,123	Puerto Rico	$126,417
Florida	$453,407	New York	$470,968	US Virgin Islands	$66,984
Georgia	$300,494	North Carolina	$316,260	**American Indian Tribes**	**Amount**
Hawaii	$88,920	North Dakota	$137,298	Fallon Paiute-Shoshone Tribe, NV	$22,485
Idaho	$113,259	Ohio	$510,751	Inter Tribal Council, AZ	$160,000
Illinois	$612,982	Oklahoma	$188,028	Menominee Indian Tribe, WI	$19,254
Indiana	$302,514	Oregon	$175,178	MS Band of Choctaw Indians, MS	$16,150
Iowa	$204,938	Pennsylvania	$404,762	Pueblo of Acoma, NM	$26,735
Kansas	$230,885	Rhode Island	$92,480	Pueblo of Laguna, NM	$31,788
Kentucky	$182,148	South Carolina	$190,616	Pyramid Lake Paiute Tribe, NV	$43,278
Louisiana	$204,058	South Dakota	$126,980	Reno Sparks Indian Colony, NV	$18,923
Maine	$107,242	Tennessee	$249,996	St. Regis Mohawk Tribe, NY	$24,200
Maryland	$186,902	Texas	$668,460	Salish & Kootenai Tribes, MT	$10,000
Massachusetts	$214,283	Utah	$145,957		
Michigan	$331,393	Vermont	$84,172	**Grand Total**	**$12,799,998**

• Who Must Register?

Each person[1] as defined by the federal hazardous material transportation law that engages in any of the activities requiring registration must register. See the discussion of person below for exceptions to the requirement.

Activities Requiring Registration:

A person who, between July 1 of a year and June 30 of the following year, offers or transports in commerce any of the following categories of hazardous materials (including hazardous wastes) must register with RSPA for that twelve-month period (Note: the letters identifying each of the following sections represents the "category" of activity used on the Registration Statement):

A. A highway route controlled quantity of a Class 7 (radioactive) material, as defined in 49 CFR 173.403.

B. More than 25 kilograms (55 pounds) of a Division 1.1, 1.2, or 1.3 (explosive) material (see 49 CFR 173.50) in a motor vehicle, rail car, or freight container.

C. More than one liter (1.06 quarts) per package of a "material extremely toxic by inhalation" (that is, a "material poisonous by inhalation," as defined in 49 CFR 171.8, that meets the criteria for "hazard zone A" as specified in 49 CFR 173.116(a) for gases or 173.133(a) for liquids).

D. A hazardous material (including hazardous wastes) in a bulk packaging having a capacity equal to or greater than 13,248 liters (3,500 gallons) for liquids or gases or more than 13.24 cubic meters (468 cubic feet) for solids. Please note that under this provision persons who offer or transport hazardous materials that do not require placarding (that is, Class 9 materials) in a bulk packaging with a capacity greater than 3,500 gallons or 468 cubic feet, must register.

E. A shipment in other than a bulk packaging of 2,268 kilograms (5,000 pounds) gross weight or more of one class of hazardous materials (including hazardous wastes) for which placarding of a vehicle, rail car, or freight container is required for that class.

F. A quantity of hazardous material that requires placarding. The offering and transporting of hazardous materials by farmers in direct support of their farming operations are excepted from this category of activities requiring registration. See the section "Requirements for Farmers" below.

Since the beginning of the program in 1992, activities in Categories A through E have required registration by law. Category F was added by regulation beginning with the 2000-2001 registration year.

Person:

A person is defined by federal hazardous material transportation law as including an individual, firm, copartnership, corporation, company, association, joint-stock association, including any trustee, receiver, assignee, or similar representative thereof, or government, Indian tribe, or agency or instrumentality of any government or Indian tribe when it offers hazardous materials for transportation in commerce or transports hazardous materials to further a commercial enterprise. However, the following are specifically excepted by statute or regulation from the registration requirements:

A. Agencies of the federal government.

B. Agencies of states.

C. Agencies of political subdivisions of states.

D. Employees of those agencies listed in [A], [B], or [C] with respect to their official duties.

E. Hazmat employees, including the owner-operator of a motor vehicle that transports hazardous materials in commerce if that vehicle, at the time of those activities, is leased to a registered motor carrier under a 30-day or longer lease as prescribed in 49 CFR Part 376 or an equivalent contractual relationship.

F. Persons domiciled outside the United States whose only activity involving the transportation of hazardous materials within the United States is to offer hazardous materials for transportation in commerce from locations outside the United States, if the country in which they are domiciled does not impose registration or a fee upon U.S. companies for offering hazardous materials into that country. However, persons domiciled outside the United States must register if they transport the types and quantities of hazardous materials that require registration within the United States.

G. Farmers who offer or transport only hazardous materials that are used in direct support of their farming operations **and** who are not engaged in activities included in 49 CFR 107.601(a)(1) through (a)(5), that is, Categories A through E described in "Activities Requiring Registration" above. See "Requirements for Farmers" below.

1. Underlined words are defined on the following pages.

Clarifications:

The registration requirement applies to all persons who (1) engage in interstate, intrastate, or foreign commerce; (2) engage in any of the activities discussed in "Activities Requiring Registration" above; and (3) are not specifically excepted from the requirement.

Each person who acts as an intermediary in the transportation of hazardous materials, such as a freight forwarder or agent, is subject to the registration requirements if that person performs or contracts to perform any of the functions of an offeror of hazardous materials.

Each U.S. company engaged in a specified hazardous materials activity that is (1) incorporated separately from a parent company, (2) under the majority stock ownership of another company, or (3) a wholly owned or controlled subsidiary of another company, is required to register even when the parent company is also subject to registration.

You must also register if you engage in any of the activities discussed in "Activities Requiring Registration" above, and are:

1. A merchant vessel carrier transporting, transiting, or transhipping hazardous materials within 12 miles of the U.S. coast; or
2. A federal, state, or local government contractor.

Requirements for Farmers:

1. If you are a farmer who offers or transports only hazardous materials that (a) are used in direct support of your farming activities **and** (b) are not included in Categories A through E of "Activities Requiring Registration" above, you are not required to register.
2. If you are a farmer who offers or transports hazardous materials that require placarding that are **not** in direct support of your farming operation, you must register and pay the appropriate registration fee. For example, a farmer who offers or transports home heating fuel for commercial purposes in quantities requiring placarding must register.
3. If you are a farmer who offers or transports for any purpose any of the hazardous materials included in Categories A through E of "Activities Requiring Registration" above, you must register and pay the appropriate registration fee. For example, if you transport 55 lbs or more of a Division 1.1 explosive, even if the explosive is to be used in direct support of your farming operations, you must register.

Requirements for Hazardous Waste Generators:

Hazardous waste generators are subject to the registration requirement if they offer or transport hazardous wastes in the quantities that require registration. All hazardous wastes subject to the Hazardous Waste Manifest Requirements of the U.S. Environmental Protection Agency are hazardous materials. In July 2000 the number of hazardous waste generators required to register significantly increased when the regulations were revised to require registration of all persons who offer or transport a quantity of hazardous materials that requires placarding.

Any person who performs any of the activities of an offeror, which include signing the shipping paper (hazardous waste manifest), for a quantity that requires placarding must register. Depending on the type of packaging (container) and the amount of waste being removed at one time, even generators of relatively small quantities of hazardous waste may be subject to the registration requirement.

A hazardous waste generator must register if it:

1. offers or transports any amount of a waste other than Division 6.2 or Class 9 materials (which do not require placarding) in bulk packagings (for example, a cargo tank, a tank car, or a bulk transport vehicle); or
2. offers or transports any amount of a Division 6.2 or Class 9 material in bulk packagings with capacities equal to or greater than 3,500 gallons or 468 cubic feet; or
3. offers or transports hazardous waste in other than bulk packagings (any container with a capacity of less than 119 gallons, for example, a 55 gallon drum) if a single shipment contains 1,000 pounds or more of one or more classes of hazardous waste that require placarding. Please note that it is the amount of material being removed from a site in non-bulk packagings at one time that triggers the registration requirement for the generator, not the amount of material that is contained in total on the truck, part of which may have been shipped by another hazardous waste generator.

Placarding:

Placarding requirements are found in 49 CFR Part 172, Subpart F. The requirements are summarized as follows:

1. Except for Division 6.2 and Class 9 materials, any quantity of a hazardous material offered for transportation or transported in a **bulk packaging** requires placarding.
2. For materials offered for transportation or transported in a **non-bulk packaging**, the quantity that requires placarding depends on whether the material is in a class or division included in Table 1 or Table 2 below:

Table 1 (Placard any quantity)

Hazard Class or Division	Placard Name
1.1	EXPLOSIVES 1.1
1.2	EXPLOSIVES 1.2
1.3	EXPLOSIVES 1.3
2.3	POISON GAS
4.3	DANGEROUS WHEN WET
5.2 (Organic peroxide, Type B, liquid or solid, temperature controlled)	ORGANIC PEROXIDE
6.1 (Inhalation Hazard, Zone A or B)	POISON INHALATION HAZARD
7 (Radioactive Yellow III label only)	RADIOACTIVE

Table 2 (Placard when the aggregate quantity of hazardous materials is 1,001 pounds or more)

Hazard Class or Division	Placard Name
1.4	EXPLOSIVES 1.4
1.5	EXPLOSIVES 1.5
1.6	EXPLOSIVES 1.6
2.1	FLAMMABLE GAS
2.2	NON-FLAMMABLE GAS
3	FLAMMABLE
Combustible Liquid	COMBUSTIBLE
4.1	FLAMMABLE SOLID
4.2	SPONTANEOUSLY COMBUSTIBLE
5.1	OXIDIZER
5.2 (Other than organic peroxide, Type B, liquid or solid, temperature controlled)	ORGANIC PEROXIDE
6.1 (PG I or II, other than Zone A or B inhalation hazard)	POISON
6.1 (PG III)	KEEP AWAY FROM FOOD
6.2 (Infectious substance)	NONE
8	CORROSIVE
9	CLASS 9 (placard not required for domestic transportation)
ORM-D	NONE

NOTE: Infectious substances, hazardous materials classed as ORM-D, hazardous materials authorized to be offered for transportation as Limited Quantities when identified as such on shipping papers, hazardous materials prepared in accordance with 49 CFR 173.13, hazardous materials which are packaged as small quantities under the provisions of 49 CFR 173.4, combustible liquids in non-bulk packagings (see 49 CFR 172.500(b)), and materials offered or transported under the "materials of trade" exception (see 49 CFR 173.6) are excepted from the placarding requirements.

• Definitions

Bulk Packaging:

A bulk packaging is a packaging, other than a vessel or a barge, with (1) a maximum capacity greater than 450 liters (119 gallons) as a receptacle for a liquid; (2) a maximum net mass greater than 400 kilograms (882 pounds) and a maximum capacity greater than 450 liters (119 gallons) as a receptacle for a solid; or (3) a water capacity greater than 454 kilograms (1000 pounds) as a receptacle for a gas (see 49 CFR 171.8).

The extension of the registration requirement to any placarded shipment basically over-rides activities that require registration in categories D and E. Hazardous materials (particularly Class 9 hazardous wastes) that do **not** require placarding but **are** transported in bulk packagings with capacities greater than 3,500 gallons or 468 cubic feet require registration under category D. However, shipments of hazardous materials that do **not** require placarding (for example, Class 9 materials), placed in bulk packagings with capacities **less than** 3,500 gallons or 468 cubic feet, do **not** require registration.

It is important to note that the use of bulk packagings requires registration no matter how small the quantity of hazardous materials actually offered or transported. For example, persons who have hazardous waste picked up in tank trucks, and persons who return unpurged tank trucks or rail tank cars from which they have unloaded hazardous materials so that the tanks still contain residues of hazardous materials when returned, must register under the provisions of Category F (or Category D if the material is a Division 6.2 or Class 9 material).

Calendar Year:

Although the registration year extends from July 1 of a year through June 30 of the following year, a calendar year is used to report activity in item 7 of the registration statement, "Prior-Year Survey Information." This calendar year is the twelve-month period (January 1 through December 31) immediately preceding the beginning date of the registration year (or years) for which you are filing the registration statement. You are asked to supply information on your activities in calendar year 2002 on the statement submitted for 2003-2004 (or 2003-2005, or 2003-2006). The use of the preceding calendar year in reporting activity provides a definite and verifiable (rather than speculative) basis for this section of the form.

Farmer:

The term "farmer" means a person engaged in the production or raising of crops, poultry, or livestock (49 CFR 171.8).

Highway Route Controlled Quantity:

The criteria for determining whether a shipment of radioactive material is a "highway route controlled quantity" are found in 49 CFR 173.403, which further references 49 CFR 173.435. Please note that any shipment of a "highway route controlled quantity" of a radioactive material, whether by highway, rail, air, or water, subjects the offeror and carrier to the registration requirement.

If you think you are an offeror or carrier of highway route controlled quantities, please review the defining criteria carefully. Shipments of highway route controlled quantities must be specifically identified as such by the offeror on the shipping papers (see 49 CFR 172.203(d)(4)).

Modes:

The four modes of transportation that are covered under the Hazardous Materials Regulations, including the registration requirement, are highway, rail, air, and water. Highway transportation includes all interstate, intrastate, and foreign shipments that meet the registration criteria and are not specifically excepted by regulation. Water transportation does not include hazardous materials loaded or carried on board a vessel without benefit of containers or labels and received and handled by the vessel carrier without mark or count. This type of shipment, for which the vessel becomes the container, such as LNG or oil tanker vessels, falls under the authority of the U.S. Coast Guard, now part of the Department of Homeland Security.

Not-for-Profit Organization:

A Not-for-Profit Organization is an organization exempt from taxation under 26 U.S.C. 501(a). This category of registrant was first established for the 2003-2004 registration year. Not-for-profit organizations registering for years before 2003-2004 must pay the fee appropriate to the SBA size category (small or not-small) according to the SBA size standard established for the NAICS code of its primary business activity.

Offeror:

An offeror is a person who ships hazardous materials in commerce, or a person who acts as an intermediary in the transportation of hazardous materials (such as a freight forwarder or agent) if the intermediary performs any of the functions of an offeror of hazardous materials. Functions of an offeror, besides shipping, include, but are not limited to: selecting the packaging for a regulated hazardous material, physically transferring a hazardous material to a carrier, determining the hazard class of a hazardous material, preparing shipping papers, reviewing shipping papers to verify compliance with the hazardous materials regulations or their international equivalents, signing hazardous materials certifications on shipping papers, placing hazardous materials markings or placards on vehicles or packages, and providing placards to a carrier.

A formal interpretation of the terms "offeror" and "transporter" as related to the registration requirements was published in the *Federal Register* on October 28, 1992, pages 48739 - 48741. Further clarification of the term "offeror" was supplied in the Final Rule published in the *Federal Register* on February 14, 2000, page 7304.

In item 7 of the registration statement, you are asked to indicate whether you operated as a "Shipper," "Carrier," or "Other" during the calendar year preceding the beginning of the registration year. Persons who act as intermediaries should mark "Other" (marking "Shipper" or "Carrier" as well, if appropriate).

Shipment:

The term "shipment" as used in the registration regulations means the offering or loading of hazardous material at one loading facility using one transport vehicle, or the transport of that transport vehicle (see 49 CFR 107.601(c)).

Small Business:

A person is a "small business" if its size does not exceed the size standard established by the U.S. Small Business Administration (SBA) in 13 CFR 121 for the primary commercial activity of the person (company).

Since the 2000-2001 registration year, the amount of the annual registration fee has depended on whether the registering company meets the Small Business Administration's (SBA) size standard for a small business. The SBA assigns a size standard, which is expressed, with a few exceptions, either as the number of employees or as the gross annual receipts of the company, for each industry group. In registration years 2000-2001, 2001-2002, and 2002-2003, we used the SBA's size standard assigned to the Standard Industrial Classification (SIC) code for each industry group identified in the SIC system. In a rulemaking published in the *Federal Register* on September 16, 2002, (67 FR 58343) RSPA adopted the SBA's use of the North American Industry Classification System (NAICS) codes as the basis for establishing size standards. Beginning with the 2003-2004 registration year, and for any registration statement filed after May 1, 2003, you are to report the NAICS code that represents the major business activity of the registering company and use this code to determine whether your company qualifies as a small business.

A representative list of the NAICS code, the corresponding SIC code(s), and the current size standard for some common hazardous materials industry groups is given in the section titled "Selected Small Business Administration Size Standards by NAICS Industry Codes." If your industry group is not included in this list, see the complete list of size standards by NAICS code at the SBA Internet site at:

http://www.sba.gov/size/sizetable2002.html

The NAICS system was revised by the Office of Management and Budget effective January 1, 2002 (referred to as NAICS 2002), which was adopted by the SBA effective October 1, 2002. Because some sections of the previous version of the NAICS system were significantly revised in NAICS 2002, you may want to verify that the NAICS code you report to us is the correct code.

If you do not know your company's NAICS code, the SBA provides a search engine of the NAICS and SIC systems at:

https://eweb1.sba.gov/naics/dsp_naicssearch2.cfm

At this site you can search for a NAICS code, a SIC code, or the description (example: enter "ethyl alcohol" or "trucking"). The site displays the NAICS description, NAICS number, SBA size standard, and the corresponding SIC codes. Because the NAICS system is more detailed than the SIC system, more than one NAICS code may be represented on the list if you search by the description or your SIC number. You will need to determine which description and NAICS code best reflects your primary business. In some cases, you may need to enter additional words in the "description" box to narrow the range of selections.

If you need to see the full descriptions of NAICS industry groups, the Bureau of the Census provides a search tool of the NAICS 2002 system at:

http://www.census.gov/epcd/naics02/

You can enter a NAICS number or a keyword in the search box. Clicking on the NAICS 2002 code in the results page will display the full NAICS description. Once you determine which NAICS code is appropriate to your major business activity, you will need to go to the SBA size standard site to find the size standard appropriate for the NAICS code.

The SBA Office of Size Standards Internet site at:

http://www.sba.gov/size/

provides other useful information on the SBA size standards. You may also call the SBA Office of Size Standards at 202-205-6618 for assistance in determining your company's industry group and its size standard.

With a few exceptions, the size standard is either the number of employees or the gross annual receipts. The number of **employees** is defined by SBA as being the average number of employees (including all individuals employed on a full-time, part-time, temporary, or other basis) employed during the pay periods in the preceding twelve months. See 13 CFR 121.106 for the applicable SBA definition.

Gross annual receipts is defined by SBA at 13 CFR 121.104. "Receipts" generally means "total income" (or in the case of a sole proprietorship, "gross income") plus the "cost of goods sold" as these terms are defined or reported on Internal Revenue Service (IRS) federal tax returns. The term, however, excludes net capital gains or losses, taxes collected for and remitted to a taxing authority if included in gross or total income, and proceeds from the transactions between a concern and its domestic or foreign affiliates (if also excluded from gross or total income on a consolidated return filed with the IRS). If your company has been in business for three or more years, the "annual receipts" is the receipts over its last three completed fiscal years divided by three. For companies in existence less than three years, the "annual receipts" is calculated by taking the receipts for the period the company has been in business divided by the number of weeks in business, multiplied by 52.

Whether annual receipts or number of employees is the size standard established for your industry group, you should consider the receipts or number of employees for the person required to register to determine whether your company must pay the fee for a "Small Business" or "Not a Small Business." The person required to register may pay the fee appropriate for a small business even though it may be part of an "entity" (which includes affiliates) that the SBA does not consider a small business concern for its purposes.

The SBA periodically adjusts its size standards to reflect changes in industry characteristics. When the SBA adopted the NAICS system in place of the SIC system in October 2000, a significant number of size standards were adjusted. If you are registering for the 2000-2001 year, you may use the SBA size standards for SIC codes as of September 30, 2000, to determine whether your company qualified as a small business for that registration year. A table of these standards is provided at the SBA Internet site at:

http://www.sbaonline.sba.gov/regulations/siccodes/

For all years after 2000-2001, we recommend that you use the current size standards by NAICS code. Almost all revisions to the size standards increase the number of employees or annual receipts that a company may have in order to qualify as a small business. If you are registering for 2001-2002 or 2002-2003 and feel that using the SBA size standards in effect during the year or years for which you are registering would be to your advantage, you may do so, but neither SBA nor RSPA maintains helps for determining the size standards in effect for these years. You are responsible for demonstrating that the size standard you use is correct for previous years.

Transportation:

Transportation means the movement of property and any loading, unloading, or storage incidental to the movement (49 U.S.C. 5102(12)).

• Registration Deadline

The completed 2003-2004 registration statement and payment must be submitted before July 1, 2003, or before engaging in any of the activities requiring registration, whichever is later. If you submit your registration statement by mail, we suggest that you submit it at least four weeks in advance of the date you will need the registration certificate in order to allow sufficient time for the registration to be processed and the certificate produced and mailed to you. If you need to obtain a registration number immediately, see the instructions for "Registering Through the Internet" or "Expedited Registration."

• Recordkeeping Requirements

Copies of the registration statement and the certificate of registration must be kept for three years at your principal place of business and must be available for inspection. Motor carriers and vessel operators must also have on board a copy of the current certificate of registration, or another document bearing the current year's registration number identified as the "U.S. DOT Hazmat Reg. No." Every truck or truck tractor or vessel you use for the transportation of a hazardous material that meets the registration criteria must have this proof of registration on board.

• State Registrations

Some states have hazardous materials registration or permitting programs that may also apply to you. Registration with RSPA does not replace state requirements.

• Use The Proper Registration Statement

Because of the changes in the registration requirements in 2003, you must use a Registration Statement with a "revised" date of 3/03. All forms with earlier revision dates will be returned to you unprocessed and will therefore delay your registration. A copy of the Registration Statement, Form DOT F 5800.2 (Revised 3/03), is supplied in this Addendum. You may use this form to register for years prior to 2003-2004, but for years before 2000-2001, the NAICS code, the indication of business size, and Category F of the Prior Year Survey need not be supplied. For years between 2000-2001 and 2002-2003 you do not need to supply the not-for-profit status information and may supply the SIC (Standard Industrial Classification) code that represents the major industrial activity of your company in place of the NAICS code.

• Penalties For Failure To Register

The requirement to register with DOT is based on a federal law. The enforcement of this requirement is conducted cooperatively by federal, state, and local agencies. Federal, state, or local officials may impose penalties for failing to register or failing to meet the recordkeeping requirements.

• Registering As A Non-Resident

If you are not a resident of the United States, you must designate a permanent U.S. resident to serve as "agent for service of process" in accordance with 49 CFR 107.7. The name and address of your agent must be attached to the statement.

• Sources Of Information

For Copies of this Brochure and Registration Forms:

- Download copies from the RSPA Registration Internet Home Page at http://hazmat.dot.gov/register.htm.
- Dial RSPA's automated Fax-on-Demand service at 1-800-467-4922. Press "2" and follow the instructions to request document number 700.
- E-mail your request to REGISTER@rspa.dot.gov.
- Call 617-494-2545 or 202-366-4109.

For Questions on the Registration Program Requirements:

- Call the Registration Program office at 202-366-4109.
- E-mail questions to REGISTER@rspa.dot.gov.

For Questions About the Hazardous Materials Regulations:

- Call the Hazardous Materials Information Center at 1-800-467-4922.

For Questions About the SBA Size Standards:

- See the complete listing of size standards by NAICS code at http://www.sba.gov/size/sizetable2002.html.
- Visit the SBA Office of Size Standards Internet site at http://www.sba.gov/size/.
- Call the SBA Office of Size Standards at 202-205-6618.

For Information on the NAICS 2002 Codes:

- See the U.S. Bureau of the Census site at http://www.census.gov/epcd/naics02/.

For Information on the HMEP Grants Program:

- Visit the HMEP Grants Internet site at http://hazmat.dot.gov/hmep.htm.
- Call the Grants Program office at 202-366-0001.

For the Status of your Registration Submission:

- Call 617-494-2545.

For Expedited Registration:

- Call 1-800-942-6990.

Registering Through the Internet:

- Register through the Internet at http://hazmat.dot.gov/register.htm as explained in the section titled "Registering Through the Internet."
- If you need assistance or encounter problems with the Internet registration process, call 202-366-4484.

For Copies of the Hazardous Materials Program Regulations:

- Contact the Superintendent of Documents, Government Printing Office, Washington, DC 20402; telephone 202-512-1800. Ask for Title 49 of the Code of Federal Regulations, Parts 100 to 185.
- Access the Code of Federal Regulations through the Internet at http://www.access.gpo.gov/nara/cfr or http://hazmat.dot.gov/rules.htm.

To Obtain a U.S. DOT ID Number:

- Call the local Federal Motor Carrier Safety Administration's Office of Motor Carriers (usually in your state capitol). See the list of FMCSA field offices at http://www.fmcsa.dot.gov/contactus/fieldoffs.shtm.
- The application for a US DOT or MC/MX number can be filed electronically at http://www.safersys.org/FMCSAReg.shtml.

For Information About Hazardous Materials Safety:

- The Office of Hazardous Materials Safety's Internet homepage contains extensive information on the transportation of hazardous materials. Please visit our site at http://hazmat.dot.gov.

If You Have Failed To Register For Past Years. . .

If you engaged in any of the hazardous materials activities described in 49 CFR 107.601(a)(1) through (a)(5), that is, those listed on the statement as categories A through E, in registration years before 2000-2001, or if you engaged in any of the activities described in 49 CFR 107.601(a)(1) through (a)(6), that is, those listed on the statement as categories A through F, in registration year 2000-2001, 2001-2002, or 2002-2003 but did not register, you must do so now. There are eleven prior registration years:

1992-93 (September 16, 1992, to June 30, 1993);

1993-94 (July 1, 1993, to June 30, 1994);

1994-95 (July 1, 1994, to June 30, 1995);

1995-96 (July 1, 1995, to June 30, 1996);

1996-97 (July 1, 1996, to June 30, 1997);

1997-98 (July 1, 1997, to June 30, 1998);

1998-99 (July 1, 1998, to June 30, 1999);

1999-2000 (July 1, 1999, to June 30, 2000);

2000-2001 (July 1, 2000, to June 30, 2001);

2001-2002 (July 1, 2001, to June 30, 2002); and

2002-2003 (July 1, 2002, to June 30, 2003).

You must file a registration statement and pay the appropriate fee for each year for which you need to register. For registration years **1992-1993 through 1999-2000**, the fee is $300 per year and is not dependent on the SBA size criteria. For these years, you must submit a **separate** statement for each of the years for which you are registering. Multiple year statements are not accepted for registration years 1992-1993 through 1999-2000. For registration year **2000-2001 or 2001-2002 or 2002-2003**, the fee is $300 if you meet the SBA criteria for a small business or $2,000 if you do not meet the SBA criteria for a small business. See the definition of Small Business for further information on the size standards for these years. You may combine registrations for 2000-2001 and later years to a maximum of three consecutive registration years on a single registration statement. A complete table of possible registration periods and the appropriate fees is given in the section titled "Registration Fee Table." Be careful to enter the proper registration years at the top of the statement and pay the proper fees for one, two, or three years. You may copy and use the form supplied in this Addendum to register for any previous year.

Complete the "Activities" and "States" sections of item 7 of the registration statement to reflect the type of activities you conducted and the states in which you conducted them during the calendar year preceding the beginning of the registration year for which the statement is being filed. For example, if you are filing for the 2002-2003 registration year, report the activities you engaged in, and the states in which you offered or transported hazardous materials, between January 1 and December 31, 2001.

If you are registering for a year between 1992-1993 and 1999-2000, you do not need to supply the NAICS code, the business category information (Item 5), or Category F of Item 7 (Prior Year Survey). If you are registering for a year before 2003-2004 you do not need to supply the not-for-profit status information.

Two Letter State Abbreviations

State	Abbr.	State	Abbr.	State	Abbr.
Alabama	AL	Kentucky	KY	Ohio	OH
Alaska	AK	Louisiana	LA	Oklahoma	OK
American Samoa	AS	Maine	ME	Oregon	OR
Arizona	AZ	Maryland	MD	Pennsylvania	PA
Arkansas	AR	Massachusetts	MA	Puerto Rico	PR
California	CA	Michigan	MI	Rhode Island	RI
Colorado	CO	Minnesota	MN	South Carolina	SC
Connecticut	CT	Mississippi	MS	South Dakota	SD
Delaware	DE	Missouri	MO	Tennessee	TN
Dist. Columbia	DC	Montana	MT	Texas	TX
Florida	FL	Nebraska	NE	Utah	UT
Georgia	GA	Nevada	NV	Vermont	VT
Guam	GU	New Hampshire	NH	Virgin Islands	VI
Hawaii	HI	New Jersey	NJ	Virginia	VA
Idaho	ID	New Mexico	NM	Washington	WA
Illinois	IL	New York	NY	West Virginia	WV
Indiana	IN	North Carolina	NC	Wisconsin	WI
Iowa	IA	North Dakota	ND	Wyoming	WY
Kansas	KS	N. Mariana Is.	MP		

Registration Instructions

You may register for one, two, or three registration years beginning July 1, 2003, through the submission of a single registration statement and the payment of the appropriate fees. You may register for the one-year period **2003-2004** (July 1, 2003, through June 30, 2004), OR for the two-year period **2003-2005** (July 1, 2003, through June 30, 2005), OR for the three-year period **2003-2006** (July 1, 2003, through June 30, 2006). You may complete a registration statement (DOT Form F 5800.2 Revised 03/03), and send the statement with payment to the U.S. Department of Transportation at the address shown on the back of the form, or you may register through the Internet by following the directions in the section titled "Registering Through the Internet." You may use this form or the Internet service to register for previous years. See the instructions for "If You Have Failed to Register For Past Years" and for Internet registration.

Register before July 1, 2003, or before engaging in any of the activities requiring registration,[1] whichever is later. You must have the DOT certificate and registration number before you offer or transport hazardous materials. Allow four weeks after mailing your completed registration statement and payment to receive your certificate. You will receive a new registration number for each properly completed registration statement you submit.

The instructions for completing the registration statement form begin on this page and continue on the following page. You may find it useful to read through the instructions and the statement before completing it. Please fill in the top block before starting item 1.

Top Block

- Fill in the appropriate registration year or years. You may enter "2003-2004" (for one year), "2003-2005" (for two years) or "2003-2006" (for three years). If you are registering for a past year, please see the instructions in the box titled "If You Have Failed To Register For Past Years. . .".
- Check the kind of registration you are making:

  Initial Registration means you are registering for the first time. Since you have no registration number yet, leave the space for "Current Registration #" blank.

  Renewal of Registration means you have registered in one or more previous years; please enter your most recently issued registration number as the "Current Registration #."

  Amendment to Registration means you are updating information currently on file (which you must do if your name or principal place of business changes during the year). If you need instructions only for making this kind of change, skip to the box below.

  Expedited Follow-up means you already made an expedited registration by phone and are providing follow-up data to that transaction. Enter the temporary registration number you received over the phone as the "Current Registration #." **If you check Expedited Follow-up, please turn to the section titled "Expedited Follow-Up" for special instructions on completing this form.**

Amending Your Registration

You must amend your registration statement within 30 days if there is a change in your company's name or principal place of business. You may submit an amendment through the Internet (see in the section titled "Registering Through the Internet") at http://hazmat.dot.gov/register.htm or by following these directions:

Check "Amendment to Registration" on the top block of the registration statement, enter the "Current Registration #," record the new name or address in items 1 and 2, and complete and sign item 8, CERTIFICATION OF INFORMATION. You need not fill in any other sections.

Attach a copy of the original certificate of registration to the amended form. Send the amendment to the Atlanta, Georgia, address printed on the form.

There is no additional fee for filing an amendment whether done by mail or through the Internet.

1. Underlined words are defined in the sections titled "Who Must Register?" and "Definitions."

Identifying Information

1 and 2. Name and Address of Registrant: Enter your business name and address. If your company is operating under a "Doing Business As" (DBA) name, you may use whichever of the names is most appropriate for your business. A certificate of registration displaying this name, and any necessary correspondence, will be mailed to the address entered here. If we have provided you with a preprinted label and no corrections are necessary, you may use that label to supply this information.

3. Registrant's US DOT ID Number, MC/MX Number, or Reporting Railroad Alphabetic Code: If you have any of these identifiers, enter them. If you do not have any of these identifiers, leave these spaces blank. To verify or obtain a U.S. DOT ID number or MC/MX number (formerly the ICC number), see the Federal Motor Carrier Safety Administration's Internet site at:

http://www.safersys.org/FMCSAReg.shtml

4. Mode(s) Used to Transport Hazardous Materials: Check all the ways you moved hazardous materials during the calendar year ending last December. If you are a carrier, mark only the mode(s) you used to transport hazardous materials. If you are a shipper or other offeror, check all modes used to transport shipments offered by your company.

Registration Fees and Payment Information

5. Business Category:

a. *NAICS Code:* Enter the six-digit North American Industry Classification System (NAICS) code that best describes the primary business activity (industry group) of your company.

b. *SBA Size:* Indicate whether your company meets the U.S. Small Business Administration's size standard for a small business for the appropriate industry group. See the definition of small business and the resources for help in the section titled "Definitions." Apply the specified size standard (either the number of employees or the gross annual receipts) to the registering person.

c. *Not-for-Profit Organization:* Also indicate whether you are a not-for-profit organization. A not-for-profit organization is an organization exempt from taxation under 26 U.S.C. 501(a).

6. Fees:

2003-2004, 2003-2005, or 2003-2006: The fee structure for registration year 2003-2004 and following have been reduced by a Final Rule published on January 9, 2003, in the *Federal Register.*

If your company meets the SBA size standard for a small business, or is a not-for-profit organization, the fee for a single year (2003-2004) is $150, for two years (2003-2005) is $275, and for three years (2003-2006) it is $400.

If your company does not meet the SBA criteria for a small business and is not a not-for-profit organization, the fee for one year (2003-2004) is $300, for two years (2003-2005) is $575, and for three years (2003-2006) is $850.

If your company does not meet the SBA criteria for a small business, is not a not-for-profit organization, and is submitting an Expedited Follow-Up for the 2003-2004 registration year, the remaining fee is $150.

2000-2001, 2001-2002, or 2002-2003: If you are registering for the 2000-2001, 2001-2002, or 2002-2003 registration year, the fee is $300 for small businesses and $2,000 for not-small businesses. To determine whether your company qualifies for the small business fee, see the discussion of Size Standards under the definition of Small Business in the section titled "Definitions."

1992-1993 through 1999-2000: If you are registering for a year prior to 2000-2001, the fee is $300 for all businesses. You must submit a separate statement for each of these years for which you are required to register.

All possible registration periods, business categories, and the appropriate fees are provided in the **Registration Fee Table**.

Enter the amount due for this particular statement in the place provided for "Total Amount Due for this Registration." If you are paying by credit or debit card, this is the amount you are authorizing us to charge to your account.

Payment Options:

a. Enclose a check or money order, identified as Hazmat Registration Fee, and drawn on a U.S. bank in U.S. funds, payable to "U.S. Department of Transportation" OR

b. Pay by VISA, MasterCard, American Express, or Discover by completing the credit/debit card payment block on the form. You may use a debit card for this payment only if your debit card displays a VISA or MasterCard logo.

Registration and full fee payment are required of any person engaging in any of the specified activities at any time during the registration year. The fee is not prorated for registrations submitted after July 1.

You may submit one check in payment for multiple registration statements. If you send a single check for multiple statements, please enter the amount due for each particular statement in the appropriate place on the statement.

Be sure to send the payment with the statement(s). **Statements without payments and checks unaccompanied by statements will be returned to you and will significantly delay the processing of your registration.**

Hazardous Materials Activities:

Prior-Year Survey Information

7. Use this part of the form to record your hazardous materials activities during the calendar year ending last December 31. Even if you engaged in none of the hazardous materials activities described here last year, but you intend to do so this year, you must register and pay the appropriate fee (mark category G).

Item 7 defines six categories of hazardous materials activities that require registration. Mark each category that your company engaged in during the last completed calendar year. Shipments of materials included in Categories A, B, C, D, or E should not also be included in Category F, even though in most instances such shipments require placarding. For instance, if your only hazardous materials activity is carrying more than 55 lbs. of Division 1.1 explosives, you should mark only Category B — not B and F. If, however, your only activity is shipping hazardous materials in quantities that require placarding that are not included in Categories A through E, mark only Category F. If you carry both shipments of more than 55 lbs. of Division 1.1 explosives and shipments of hazardous materials not included in Categories A through E, not in bulk packagings, of more than 1,000 lbs. but less than 5,000 lbs., you would mark both Categories B and F. If you are registering for a year prior to 2000-2001, you do not need to mark Category F even if you engaged in that activity during the applicable preceding calendar year. Activity in Category F requires registration only beginning with Registration Year 2000-2001.

For each of the categories A, B, C, D, E, or F, that you marked, also tell us for each one:

(1) *Shipper, Carrier, Other:* Whether you handled the hazardous materials as a shipper, carrier, or "other." Check as many as apply. "Other" refers to activities other than those of the "shipper" or "carrier" in which any of the functions of an offeror or carrier are performed. See the definition of offeror in the section titled "Definitions."

(2) *States:* Which states you operated in with respect to this hazardous material. Circle the abbreviation for each state or territory in which you did business in hazardous materials. If you checked "carrier," circle all states in which you operated as a carrier of that category of hazardous material. If you checked "shipper" or "other," circle only those states from which you offered hazardous materials — you need not indicate states to which or through which the materials were transported. Registrants operating in all of the "lower 48" states may circle "48 Contiguous States." (This excludes Alaska, Hawaii, the District of Columbia, and our five territories, which must be circled individually, if appropriate.) A list of the states and territories and their abbreviations is provided in the section titled "Two Letter State Abbreviations."

Remember, if you did not engage last year in any of the activities described in categories A through F, check category G.

Certification of Information

8. Your signature in item 8 certifies that the information on this form is true, accurate, and complete. BE ADVISED that false statements may violate the law (18 U.S.C. 1001). Complete this part with the signer's name, telephone number, title, and the date the certification is signed. The individual who signs this certification should be an appropriate representative of the registrant. Correspondence regarding registration, including the certificate of registration and next year's form and instructions, will be addressed to this individual.

MAILING INSTRUCTIONS

Mail your completed registration form (one copy) and payment together to:

U.S. Department of Transportation

Hazardous Materials Registration

P.O. Box 740188

Atlanta, GA 30374-0188

Do not send them to Washington, D.C. Be sure to mail form and payment **together**.

Be careful to use a mail service that delivers to P.O. Box addresses. (The Atlanta address is a post office box and many services cannot deliver to P.O. Boxes.)

Allow four weeks to receive your certificate of registration.

Expedited Registration

If you need to register for 2003-2004 more quickly than the normal procedures provide and you are not able to register over the Internet (see below), you may do so by telephone with credit or debit card payment of an initial $200 fee, which includes an additional $50 expedited registration fee. A debit card can be used only if it displays a VISA or MasterCard logo. For registrants that meet the SBA size standard for a small business or are not-for-profit organizations, this $200 fee will be accepted as full payment of a single-year registration for the 2003-2004 registration year. For registrants that do not meet the SBA size standard for a small business and are not not-for-profit organizations, payment of an additional $150 must be made as part of the follow-up procedures (for a full payment of $350, which includes a $50 expedited registration fee). You may register only for registration year 2003-2004 through the expedited procedures. You will be provided with a temporary registration number, which can be used for 45 days to prove compliance with the registration requirement. To obtain a registration number promptly, you may also register over the Internet (see below). No additional processing fee is required for registration over the Internet.

To register by telephone, please do the following:

1. Call 800-942-6990 or 617-494-2545 for service 24 hours a day, 7 days a week. Be ready to provide your company name, the mailing address of the principal place of business, and valid VISA, Mastercard, American Express, or Discover information. Your credit or debit card account will be billed for $200 and payment will be confirmed while you are on the phone.
2. A DOT registration specialist will provide a temporary registration number over the phone, which is good for proving compliance for 45 days from the date of your call. DOT will mail a temporary registration letter that serves as proof of payment of the fee, along with a copy of the registration statement for you to complete. You must complete the statement and return it to the address given in the letter within 10 days of receiving the registration package. Follow the special instructions for "Expedited Follow-Up" below and given in the letter. If your company meets the SBA size standard for a small business or is a not-for-profit organization, do not resubmit credit or debit card information or send another payment. If your company does not meet the SBA size standard for a small business and is not a not-for-profit organization, you must either submit credit/debit card information or enclose a check or money order for $150 to complete the payment of the appropriate fee.
3. A certificate of registration with the current registration number will be sent to you. Use this number to replace the temporary number given to you over the phone.

Because the expedited procedures allow only single-year registrations (for 2003-2004), and involve the later payment of the remaining $150 fee if your company does not meet the SBA size standard for a small business or is not a not-for-profit organization, we suggest that registration through the Internet may be a more convenient means of obtaining a registration number immediately.

Registering Through the Internet

You may register over the Internet at http://hazmat.dot.gov/register.htm. A link provided at "To Register On-Line Click Here" takes you to the Department's e-commerce site, Do It Yourself. Your Internet browser must support 128-bit encryption to use this service. Assistance in checking your browser version and encryption level and upgrading to the 128-bit encryption versions is provided. Click on "HAZMAT Registration Applications" in the right-hand column. The next page is the registration options page, which allows you to choose "Initial HAZMAT Registration" or "Renewal of HAZMAT Registration" under "**Registration for years 2000-2001 and later**" or "**Registration for years 1999-2000 and prior**" and also offers "**Registration Amendment**" and "**Hazmat Company Lookup**" (at the bottom of the page). Because of the changes in the registration requirements and fees beginning with the 2000-2001 registration year and revised again for the 2003-2004 registration year, please be very careful to select either "Initial HAZMAT Registration" or "Renewal of HAZMAT Registration" under the proper registration years heading. Help in filing your registration through the Internet is provided at the top of the application form pages.

There is no additional charge for registering over the Internet, and at the end of the session, after payment has been made electronically, you will receive a registration number and be able to print a registration certificate. We recommend this process, especially if you are in immediate need of a registration number.

If you have questions about registering through the Internet or need assistance, please call 202-366-4484.

Expedited Follow-Up

SPECIAL INSTRUCTIONS FOR COMPLETING EXPEDITED REGISTRATION

[For Those Who Have Made Expedited Registration By Phone And Have Paid The $200 Initial Expedited Registration Fee]

FOLLOW THESE INSTRUCTIONS CAREFULLY TO AVOID DELAY

1. Check "Expedited Follow-up" in the top block and enter your temporary registration number in the space for "Current Registration #."
2. Complete items 1 through 8. In item 6 enter "0" for the "Total Amount Due for this Registration" if your company meets the SBA size standard for a small business or is a not-for-profit organization, or "$150" if your company does not meet the SBA size standard for a small business and is not a not-for-profit organization. If the "Total Amount Due for this Registration" is $0, do not resubmit credit or debit card information.
3. Send the completed statement and any necessary payment to DOT at the address in Cambridge, MA, given in the temporary registration letter.
4. Include a copy of the temporary registration letter with this submission as proof of payment of the initial $200 fee.

DOT will mail a certificate of registration with your current registration number for the year as confirmation that your registration process is complete. Use this number to replace the temporary number for all subsequent purposes.

You must respond within 10 days of receipt of the temporary registration letter.

Registration Fee Table

As amended by the Final Rule of January 9, 2003

For registration years 1992-1993 through 1999-2000, the annual registration fee is $300 for all registrants. Starting with the 2000-2001 registration year, the amount of the fee depends on whether or not the registrant meets the SBA size standard for a small business. Also starting in registration year 2000-2001 a registrant may submit a single registration statement for a one, two, or three year period.

A Final Rule published in the Federal Register on January 9, 2003, reduces the fees for registration years beginning with 2003-2004. In the table below, the fees for all registration periods that include one or more of these years reflect the reductions. A new fee category for "not-for-profit organizations" was also established by this Final Rule. A "not-for-profit organization" is an organization exempt from taxation under 26 U.S.C. 501(a). For multiple year registrations that include both 2002-2003 and 2003-2004, the "Small Business/Non-Profit" column is to be used by a not-for-profit organization that, for 2002-2003, meets the SBA small business size standard for the NAICS code that describes the primary business activity of the organization; the "Not-Small Business/Non-Profit" column is to be used by a not-for-profit organization that, for 2002-2003, does not meet the SBA small business size standard.

Registrants whose SBA business size changed within a period for which a multiple-year registration could otherwise be submitted are advised to register for the years in which they qualified as a small business separately from the years for which they do not qualify as a small business.

All fee amounts include the appropriate processing fee.

Registration Period	Small Business	Small Business/ Non-Profit	Not-Small Business	Not-Small Business/ Non-Profit
1992-1993 through 1999-2000 the annual fee is $300 for all registrants				
2000-2001 (1 year)	$300	-	$2,000	-
2000-2002 (2 years)	$575	-	$3,975	-
2000-2003 (3 years)	$850	-	$5,950	-
2001-2002 (1 year)	$300	-	$2,000	-
2001-2003 (2 years)	$575	-	$3,975	-
2001-2004 (3 years)	$700	$700	$4,250	$4,100
2002-2003 (1 year)	$300	-	$2,000	-
2002-2004 (2 years)	$425	$425	$2,275	$2,125
2003-2005 (3 years)	$550	$550	$2,550	$2,250
	Small Business	**All Non-Profit**	**Not-Small Business**	
2003-2004 (1 year)	$150	$150	$300	-
2003-2005 (2 years)	$275	$275	$575	-
2003-2006 (3 years)	$400	$400	$850	-
Expedited Registration Follow-up Payment for Not-Small Business for 2003-2004 is $150				

Selected Small Business Administration Size Standards by NAICS Industry Codes

NOTE: *If your primary industry group does not appear below, check the SBA Internet site at* http://www.sba.gov/size/sizetable2002.html *for the complete listing of codes and size standards.*

NAICS	NAICS U.S. Industry Title	SIC	Size Standards in Number of Employees or Millions of Dollars
Sector 21 - Mining	**Subsector 211 - Oil and Gas Extraction**		
211111	Crude Petroleum and Natural Gas Extraction	1311	500
Sector 23 - Construction	**Subsector 237 - Heavy and Civil Engineering Construction**		
237310	Highway, Street and Bridge Construction	1611, 1622, 1721, 1799	$28.5
Sectors 31-33 - Manufacturing	**Subsector 325 - Chemical Manufacturing**		
325110	Petrochemical Manufacturing	2865, 2869	1,000
325120	Industrial Gas Manufacturing	2813, 2869	1,000
325188	All Other Basic Inorganic Chemical Manufacturing	2819, 2869	1,000
325193	Ethyl Alcohol Manufacturing	2869	1,000
325199	All Other Basic Organic Chemical Manufacturing	2869, 2899	1,000
325510	Paint and Coating Manufacturing	2851, 2899	500
325998	All Other Miscellaneous Chemical Product and Preparation Manufacturing	2819, 2899, 3952, 3999, 7389	500
	Subsector 332 - Fabricated Metal Product Manufacturing		
332813	Electroplating, Plating, Polishing, Anodizing, and Coloring	3399, 3471	500
Sector 42 - Wholesale Trade	**Subsector 424 - Merchant Wholesalers, Nondurable Goods**		
424510	Grain and Field Bean Merchant Wholesalers	5153	100
424690	Other Chemical and Allied Products Merchant Wholesalers	5169	100
424710	Petroleum Bulk Stations and Terminals	5171	100
424720	Petroleum and Petroleum Products Merchant Wholesalers (except Bulk Stations and Terminals)	5172	100
424910	Farm Supplies Merchant Wholesalers	5181, 5182	100
Sectors 44-45 - Retail Trade	**Subsector 447 - Gasoline Stations**		
447110	Gasoline Stations with Convenience Stores	5411, 5541	$23.0
447190	Other Gasoline Stations	5541	$7.5
	Subsector 454 - Nonstore Retailers		
454311	Heating Oil Dealers	5171, 5983	$10.5
454312	Liquefied Petroleum Gas (Bottled Gas) Dealers	5171, 5984	$6.0
454319	Other Fuel Dealers	5989	$6.0
Sectors 48-49 - Transportation	**Subsector 482 - Rail Transportation**		
482111	Line-haul Railroads	4011	1,500
482112	Short Line Railroads	4013	500
	Subsector 484 - Truck Transportation		
484110	General Freight Trucking, Local	4212, 4214	$21.5
484121	General Freight Trucking, Long-Distance, Truckload	4213	$21.5
484122	General Freight Trucking, Long-Distance, Less than Truckload	4213	$21.5
484220	Specialized Freight (except Used Goods) Trucking, Local	4212, 4214	$21.5
484230	Specialized Freight (except Used Goods) Trucking, Long-Distance	4213	$21.5
	Subsector 488 - Support Activities for Transportation		
488210	Support Activities for Rail Transportation	4013, 4741, 4789	$6.0
488510	Freight Transportation Arrangement	4731, 4213, 4214, 4226	$6.0
	Except Non-Vessel Owning Common Carriers and Household Goods Forwarders	4731	$21.5[1]
	Subsector 493 - Warehousing and Storage		
493110	General Warehousing and Storage	4225, 4226	$21.5
Sector 56 - Administrative Support	**Subsector 562 - Waste Management and Remediation Services**		
562111	Solid Waste Collection	4212	$10.5
562112	Hazardous Waste Collection	4212	$10.5
562119	Other Waste Collection	4212	$10.5
562211	Hazardous Waste Treatment and Disposal	4953	$10.5
562212	Solid Waste Landfill	4953	$10.5
562213	Solid Waste Combustors and Incinerators	4953	$10.5
562219	Other Nonhazardous Waste Treatment and Disposal	4953	$10.5

Notes: Size standards effective 10/1/02.

[1] NAICS code 488510 - As measured by total revenues, but excluding funds received in trust for an unaffiliated third party, such as bookings or sales subject to commissions. The commissions received are included as revenue.

Page 1 of 2 Exempted from Paperwork Reduction Act by 49 U.S.C. 5108(i)

U. S. DEPARTMENT OF TRANSPORTATION
HAZARDOUS MATERIALS REGISTRATION STATEMENT
REGISTRATION YEAR 20_____ - 20_____

(Please Type or Print all Responses)

Initial Registration ____ Renewal of Registration ____ Amendment to Registration _____ Expedited Follow-up ____

Current Registration # _ _ _ _ _ _ _ _ _ _ _ _ _ _ _ _

1. Registrant ____
(Company Name)

(Place pre-printed label here if provided and if name and address are correct. Otherwise, provide correct information.)

2. Mailing Address of Principal Place of Business

Street or P.O. Box ______________________________ City ______________

County ______________ State _ _ Zip Code _ _ _ _ _ - _ _ _ _ Country ______________

3. Registrant's US DOT ID Number, MC/MX Number, or Reporting Railroad Alphabetic Code (if applicable)

US DOT ID #______________ MC/MX #______________ Railroad Alphabetic Code __________

4. Mode(s) Used to Transport Hazardous Materials: Highway ____ Rail ____ Water ____ Air ____

5. Business Category (determined by answering a-c):

a) North American Industrial Classification System (NAICS) Code for Primary Commercial Activity:

(enter one six-digit code): _ _ _ _ _ _

b) Using the SBA size standard for the NAICS code entered above, mark one: ____Small Business as defined by SBA

____Not an SBA Small Business

c) Not-For-Profit Organization (under 26 U.S.C. 501(a)): Yes ____ No ____

6. Registration Fees

See Registration Fee Table. All fees include the appropriate processing fee.

Total Amount Due for this Registration:____________________

Make check or money order in U.S. funds, drawn on a U.S. bank, and payable to "U.S. Department of Transportation," and identified as payment for the "Hazmat Registration Fee."

Method of Payment (check one)

Check ___ Money Order ___ Credit/Debit* Card: *VISA* ___ *MasterCard* ___ *American Express* ___ *Discover* ___

* For Debit Card payments, see "Payment Options" under the section titled "Registration Instructions."

Credit/Debit Card Users Please Provide the Following Information:

Card Number: | | | | | | | | | | | | | | | | | Expiration Date: | | | | | (MO YR)

Name as it appears on the card ______________________________

Authorized Signature ______________________________

Cardholder acknowledges ordering goods or services in the amount of the total shown hereon and agrees to perform the obligations set forth in the Cardholder's agreement with the issuer. Card statement will list this payment as "US DOT Hazmat Regis."

NOTE: If a **Small Business** or **Not-For-Profit Organization** completing an expedited registration, **do not** resubmit card information here.

Form DOT F 5800.2 (Revised 3/03) Supercedes all previous versions. THIS FORM MAY BE REPRODUCED

7. Prior-Year Survey Information. Mark all categories and activities engaged in during the previous calendar year (e.g., 2002 for the 2003-2004 Registration Year) and the state(s) in which you operated (see instructions).

A. ____ Offered or transported in commerce a highway route controlled quantity of a Class 7 (radioactive) material.

1. Shipper ____ 2. Carrier ____ 3. Other (Freight Forwarder, Agent, etc.) ____

AL AR AZ CA CO CT DE FL GA ID IL IN IA KS KY LA MA MD ME MI MN
MO MS MT NC ND NE NH NJ NM NV NY OH OK OR PA RI SC SD TN TX UT
VT VA WA WV WI WY 48 Contiguous States AK AS DC GU HI MP PR VI

B. ____ Offered or transported in commerce more than 25 kilograms (55 pounds) of a Division 1.1, 1.2, or 1.3 (explosive) material in a motor vehicle, rail car, or freight container.

1. Shipper ____ 2. Carrier ____ 3. Other (Freight Forwarder, Agent, etc.) ____

AL AR AZ CA CO CT DE FL GA ID IL IN IA KS KY LA MA MD ME MI MN
MO MS MT NC ND NE NH NJ NM NV NY OH OK OR PA RI SC SD TN TX UT
VT VA WA WV WI WY 48 Contiguous States AK AS DC GU HI MP PR VI

C. ____ Offered or transported in commerce more than 1 liter (1.06 quarts) per package of a material extremely toxic by inhalation (materials poisonous by inhalation that meet one of the defining criteria for Hazard Zone A).

1. Shipper ____ 2. Carrier ____ 3. Other (Freight Forwarder, Agent, etc.) ____

AL AR AZ CA CO CT DE FL GA ID IL IN IA KS KY LA MA MD ME MI MN
MO MS MT NC ND NE NH NJ NM NV NY OH OK OR PA RI SC SD TN TX UT
VT VA WA WV WI WY 48 Contiguous States AK AS DC GU HI MP PR VI

D. ____ Offered or transported in commerce a hazardous material (including a hazardous waste) in a bulk packaging (see 49 CFR 171.8) having a capacity equal to or greater than 13,248 liters (3,500 gallons) for liquids or gases or more than 13.24 cubic meters (468 cubic feet) for solids.

1. Shipper ____ 2. Carrier ____ 3. Other (Freight Forwarder, Agent, etc.) ____

AL AR AZ CA CO CT DE FL GA ID IL IN IA KS KY LA MA MD ME MI MN
MO MS MT NC ND NE NH NJ NM NV NY OH OK OR PA RI SC SD TN TX UT
VT VA WA WV WI WY 48 Contiguous States AK AS DC GU HI MP PR VI

E. ____ Offered or transported in commerce a shipment, in other than a bulk packaging, of 2,268 kilograms (5,000 pounds) gross weight or more of one class of hazardous material (including a hazardous waste) for which placarding of a vehicle, rail car, or freight container is required.

1. Shipper ____ 2. Carrier ____ 3. Other (Freight Forwarder, Agent, etc.) ____

AL AR AZ CA CO CT DE FL GA ID IL IN IA KS KY LA MA MD ME MI MN
MO MS MT NC ND NE NH NJ NM NV NY OH OK OR PA RI SC SD TN TX UT
VT VA WA WV WI WY 48 Contiguous States AK AS DC GU HI MP PR VI

F. ____ Offered or transported in commerce a shipment of a quantity of hazardous material (including a hazardous waste) that requires placarding of the bulk packaging, freight container, unit load device, transport vehicle, or rail car, other than those included in A through E above. Activities performed by farmers are generally excepted. See 49 CFR 107.601(b).

1. Shipper ____ 2. Carrier ____ 3. Other (Freight Forwarder, Agent, etc.) ____

AL AR AZ CA CO CT DE FL GA ID IL IN IA KS KY LA MA MD ME MI MN
MO MS MT NC ND NE NH NJ NM NV NY OH OK OR PA RI SC SD TN TX UT
VT VA WA WV WI WY 48 Contiguous States AK AS DC GU HI MP PR VI

G. ____ Did not engage in any of the activities listed in A through F during the previous calendar year.

8. Certification of Information. I certify that, to the best of my knowledge, the above information is true, accurate, and complete.

Certifier's Name ______________________________ Date ______________
(Print the signer's name)

Title ______________________________ Phone (_ _ _)_ _ _ - _ _ _ _

Certifier's Signature ______________________________

FALSE STATEMENTS MAY VIOLATE 18 U.S.C. 1001.

MAIL COMPLETED FORM WITH PAYMENT TO :

U.S. Department of Transportation
Hazardous Materials Registration
P.O. Box 740188
Atlanta, GA 30374-0188

Please retain a copy of this form for your records.

U.S. Department
of Transportation

Research and
Special Programs
Administration

Guide for Preparing Hazardous Materials Incidents Reports

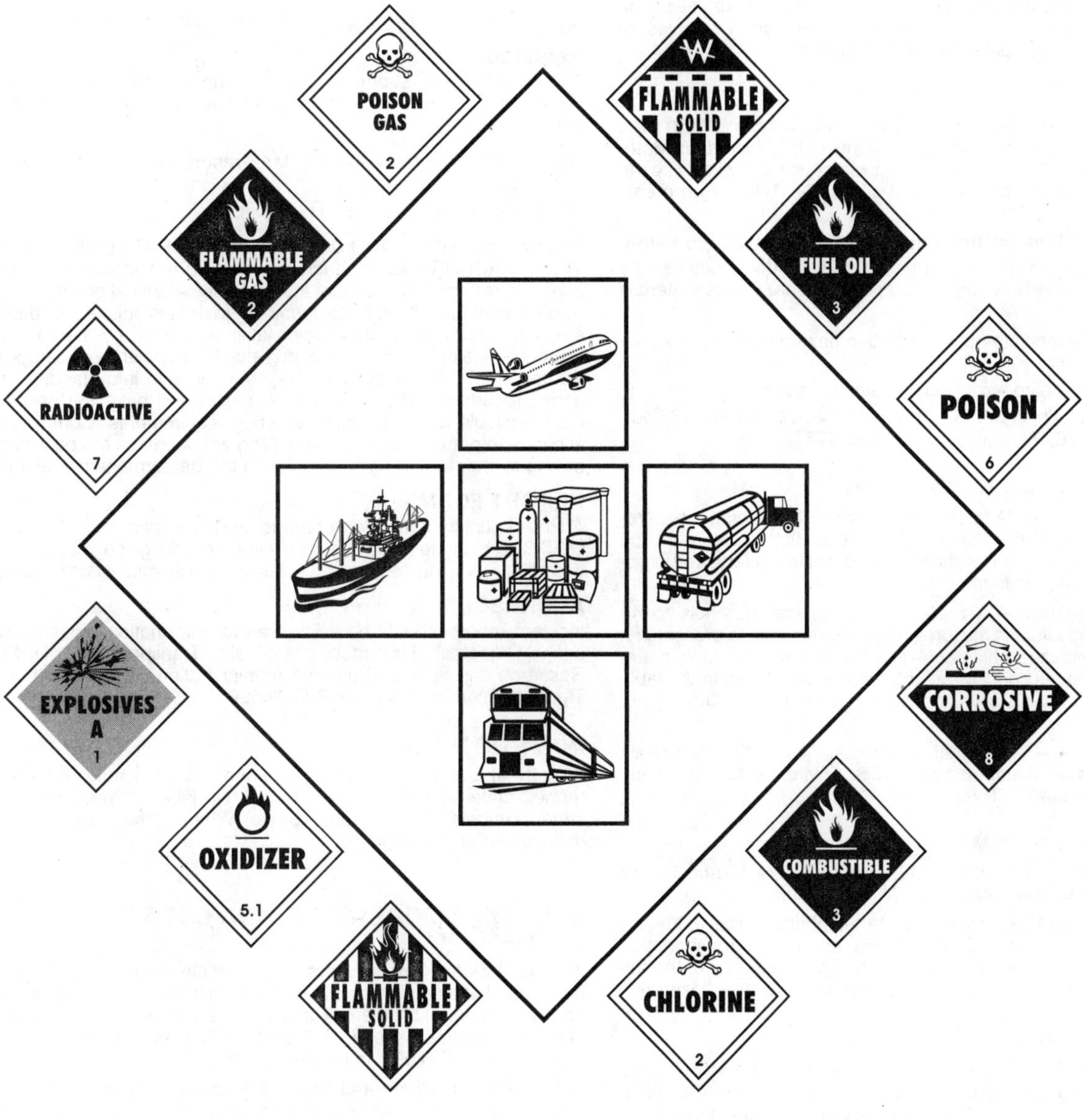

Revised January 1990
Supersedes Previous Edition

Guide for Preparing Hazardous Materials Incident Reports

NOTE: PUBLIC REPORTING BURDEN FOR THIS COLLECTION OF INFORMATION IS ESTIMATED TO AVERAGE 1 HOUR PER RESPONSE, INCLUDING THE TIME FOR REVIEWING INSTRUCTIONS, SEARCHING EXISTING DATA SOURCES, GATHERING AND MAINTAINING THE DATA NEEDED, AND COMPLETING AND REVIEWING THE COLLECTION OF INFORMATION. SEND COMMENTS REGARDING THIS BURDEN ESTIMATE OR ANY OTHER ASPECT OF THIS COLLECTION OF INFORMATION, INCLUDING SUGGESTIONS FOR REDUCING THIS BURDEN, TO INFORMATION SYSTEMS MANAGER, OFFICE OF HAZARDOUS MATERIALS TRANSPORTATION, DHM-63, RESEARCH AND SPECIAL PROGRAMS ADMINISTRATION, U.S. DEPARTMENT OF TRANSPORTATION, WASHINGTON, DC 20590; AND TO THE OFFICE OF INFORMATION AND REGULATORY AFFAIRS, OFFICE OF MANAGEMENT AND BUDGET, WASHINGTON, DC 20503.

PURPOSE

This guide is meant to assist carriers in accurately completing the MANDATORY Hazardous Materials Incident Report. Examples of required information are given for each section.

OVERVIEW

The Hazardous Materials Incident Reporting System (HMIS) was established in 1971 to meet the requirements of the Hazardous Materials Control Act of 1970. This reporting system now complies with the Hazardous Materials Transportation Act of 1974 (Title I, Public Law 93-633).

Title 49 Code of Federal Regulations (49 CFR), Transportation, Parts 100 to 179 (governing the transport of hazardous materials by rail, air, water, and highway) requires reporting of hazardous materials incidents:

- Sec. 171.15 Immediate notice of certain hazardous materials incidents
- Sec. 171.16 Detailed hazardous materials incident reports
- Specific regulations for: Rail (Sec. 174.45), Air (Sec. 175.45), Water (Sec. 176.48), and Highway (Sec. 177.807).

DEFINITIONS (see 49 CFR 171.8)

Hazardous Material — "A substance or material, including a hazardous substance" (listed in 49 CFR 172.101, 172.102) determined to be "capable of posing an unreasonable risk to health, safety, and property when transported in commerce."

Hazardous Substance — A material listed in the Appendix to 49 CFR 172.101, including its mixtures and solutions, that is present in a quantity in one package which equals or exceeds its reportable quantity (RQ) and when its concentration by weight (as shown in the table in 49 CFR 171.8) equals or exceeds the RQ of any constituent pure material.

Hazardous Waste — "Any material that is subject to the Hazardous Waste Manifest Requirements of the U.S. Environmental Protection Agency specified in 40 CFR Part 262."

REPORTING SYSTEM

The reporting system required by 49 CFR Secs. 171.15 and 171.16 has two parts: Telephone Notice and Written Report.

1. TELEPHONE NOTICE: An immediate telephone notice (800-424-8802) is required whenever, during the course of transportation (including loading, unloading, and temporary storage), one of the following circumstances occurs as the direct result of the hazardous material:

- A person is killed or hospitalized, or
- Estimated carrier and/or property damage exceeds $50,000, or
- Evacuation of the general public occurs lasting one or more hours, or
- One or more major transportation arteries or facilities are closed or shutdown for one hour or more, or
- The operational flight plan or routine of an aircraft is altered.

An immediate telephonic notice also is required whenever, during the course of transportation (including loading, unloading, and temporary storage), any of the following events occur:

- Fire, breakage, spillage, or suspected radioactive contamination occurs involving the shipment of radioactive materials.
- Fire, breakage, spillage, or suspected contamination occurs involving the shipment of etiological agents.
- The carrier judges that the situation should be reported even though it does not meet the above criteria.

2. WRITTEN REPORT: A detailed written report is required for all incidents for which a telephone notice has been made. The written report is ***also required*** whenever there is ***any unintentional release of a hazardous material during transportation*** (including loading, unloading, and temporary storage related to transportation). This includes all hazardous substances with a hazard class that is different from the hazard class ORM-E. For hazardous substances with the hazard class ORM-E, a written report is required for any release of the substance in a quantity equal to or greater than its reportable quantity (RQ). This reporting requirement also applies to the release of ***any quantity of hazardous waste*** discharged during transportation. A copy of this report shall be retained for a period of two years at the carrier's principal place of business or at such other place as approved and authorized in writing by an agency of the Department of Transportation (DOT). (See 49 CFR Sections 171.15 and 171.16 for details).

HAZARDOUS MATERIALS INCIDENT REPORT

Required:

The carrier MUST submit to the DOT the original and one copy of Form DOT F 5800.1 within thirty (30) days of the date of discovery of the incident.

Optional: Any interested party MAY report the incident using Form DOT F 5800.1.

NOTE: Please type or legibly print the report.

Accuracy: VERIFY AND DOUBLE CHECK THAT YOUR INFORMATION IS ACCURATE. Although the required information is generally available at the time of the incident, some investigation may be needed to obtain all the facts pertaining to deaths, injuries, or damage amounts. Much of the information also is needed by the carrier for insurance claims, damage claims, etc. Carriers are encouraged to incorporate DOT incident reporting requirements into standard company procedures. Thus, a carrier company will have the necessary data available to comply with reporting requirements. Complete and accurate information at the time of filing will decrease the possibility of having to supply missing information to the Department at a later date.

REPORT FORMS

A limited supply of the report form is available upon written request to DOT. The blank form on the back pages of this guide may be reproduced. Larger quantities may be obtained from several industry sources.

ADDRESS

Incident reports should be addressed to: Information Systems Manager, Office of Hazardous Materials Transportation, DHM-63, Research and Special Programs Administration, U.S. Department of Transportation, Washington, D.C. 20590.

INSTRUCTIONS

FILL IN ALL BLANKS. Use "N/A" when not applicable. If there are "none," state "NONE," "No markings," "No label," "No symbols," "No serial numbers," etc., as appropriate. When "Other" applies, briefly describe what "Other" is.

SECTION I: MODE, DATE, AND LOCATION OF INCIDENT

Item 1: Mark the box that best describes the mode of transportation being used at time of the incident. If the incident occurred during temporary storage, mark the box that best describes the mode of transportation that was last used. If the "OTHER" field is marked, include a description of "OTHER" in the space provided.

Item 2: Enter the date and time the incident occurred. If the actual date and time are not known, give the date and time of discovery. Use military time for the incident time (e.g. "1430" for 2:30 p.m., or "0845" for 8:45 a.m.).

Item 3: Enter the geographic location of the incident. If the actual location of the incident is not known, give the location of discovery. The location includes the city, county, state, and route or street where the incident occurred. For incidents occurring at airports, include the name of the airport in the ROUTE/STREET field. ***DO NOT*** include such information as "on trailer 376" or "between New York and Chicago."

Example: A highway transport of hazardous materials experienced a release of material at 2:30 p.m. on October 17, 1989 in the town of Belvoir, Fairfax County, Virginia while on U.S. Route 1.

I. MODE, DATE, AND LOCATION OF INCIDENT					
1. MODE OF TRANSPORTATION:	☐ AIR	☒ HIGHWAY	☐ RAIL	☐ WATER	☐ OTHER ______
2. DATE AND TIME OF INCIDENT (Use Military Time, e.g. 8:30am = 0830, noon = 1200, 6pm = 1800, midnight = 2400).		Date: 10 / 17 / 1989		TIME: 1430	
3. LOCATION OF INCIDENT (Include airport name in ROUTE/STREET if incident occurs at an airport.)					
CITY: Belvoir			STATE: Virginia		
COUNTY: Fairfax			ROUTE/STREET: US Route 1		

SECTION II: DESCRIPTION OF CARRIER, COMPANY, OR INDIVIDUAL REPORTING

Item 4: Fill in the complete company name. Do not use abbreviations. If you are not the carrier involved in the incident, indicate your connection with the incident (e.g. "J & J Chemicals - Consignee") ***AND*** identify the carrier.

Item 5: Enter the main office address of the company, ***NOT*** the address of the terminal at which the report is being prepared. The address should include the street address or post office box, city, state, and zip code.

Item 6: Specify the carrier's OMC Motor Carrier Census Number, Reporting Railroad Alphabetic Mode, Merchant Vessel ID Number, or other Reporting Code or Number. Highway carriers without a census number are urged to contact the Office of Motor Carrier Safety for their state.

Example: To comply with the regulations, the carrier, ABC Trucking Company of 1492 Columbus Avenue, Richmond, Virginia, is completing a DOT F 5800.1 form to report a recent hazardous material release. ABC Trucking's Motor Carrier Census Number is "MC 654321."

II. DESCRIPTION OF CARRIER, COMPANY, OR INDIVIDUAL REPORTING	
4. FULL NAME ABC Trucking Company	5. ADDRESS (Principal place of business) 1492 Columbus Avenue Richmond, VA 23021
6. LIST YOUR OMC MOTOR CARRIER CENSUS NUMBER, REPORTING RAILROAD ALPHABETIC CODE, MERCHANT VESSEL NAME AND ID NUMBER OR OTHER REPORTING CODE OR NUMBER. MC 654321	

SECTION III: SHIPMENT INFORMATION

Item 7: Enter the shipper's complete name and the address of the shipper's headquarters or principal place of business (e.g. "Scientific Div. - AHS" is not a complete name. It should read "Scientific Division American Hotel Supply"). The address should include the street address or post office box, city, state, and zip code.

Item 8: Enter the consignee's complete name and the address of the consignee's headquarters or principal place of business. See Item 7.

Item 9: Enter the complete shipment origin address when different from the shipper's address. The address should include the street address or post office box, city, state, and zip code.

Item 10: Enter the complete shipment designation address when different from the consignee's address. The address should include the street address or post office box, city, state, and zip code.

Item 11: Specify both the type of shipping paper and its identification number.

Example: The shipment is being sent from the Scientific Division American Hotel Supply of 1101 South Peachtree Street, Atlanta, Georgia, to J & J Chemicals of 1506 Wayne Street, Alexandria, Virginia. J & J Chemicals' headquarter address is 9801 Sluice Parkway, Newark, New Jersey. The carrier's pro number on the shipping paper is "98765."

III. SHIPMENT INFORMATION (From Shipping Paper or Packaging)	
7. SHIPPER NAME AND ADDRESS (Principal place of business) Scientific Division - American Hotel Supply 1101 South Peachtree Street Atlanta, GA 30303	8. CONSIGNEE NAME AND ADDRESS (Principal place of business) J & J Chemicals 9801 Sluice Parkway Newark, NJ 07101
9. ORIGIN ADDRESS (If different from Shipper address) N/A	10. DESTINATION ADDRESS (If different from Consignee address) 1506 Wayne Street Alexandria, VA 22301
11. SHIPPING PAPER/WAYBILL IDENTIFICATION NO. Carrier's PRO 98765	

SECTION IV: HAZARDOUS MATERIAL SPILLED

Item 12: Enter the proper shipping name of the hazardous material. This name ***MUST*** be one of the entries in column 2 of the commodity list of the DOT Hazardous Materials Table (49 CFR Sec. 172.101 or 172.102). The proper shipping name is the part that is ***NOT*** in italics.

Item 13: Fill in the chemical or trade name for the commodity if it differs from the proper shipping name.

Item 14: Enter the hazard class of the commodity as shown in column 3 of the Hazardous Materials Table (e.g. "Flammable Liquid", "Corrosive Material").

Item 15: Include the identification number of the commodity as found in column 3A of the Hazardous Materials Table (e.g. "UN 1090").

Item 16: Mark the box which signifies whether or not the material is a hazardous substance.

Item 17: Mark the box which signifies whether or not the RQ (Reportable Quantity) was met.

Example: 45 gallons of the hazardous material acetone was spilled. Acetone is a proper shipping name as well as a chemical name. Acetone is listed as a flammable liquid and is identified as UN 1090 in the Hazardous Materials Table. Acetone is also a hazardous substance that, in terms of the quantity spilled, has not met its RQ.

IV. HAZARDOUS MATERIAL(S) SPILLED (NOTE: REFERENCE 49 CFR SECTION 172.101.)			
12. PROPER SHIPPING NAME	13. CHEMICAL/TRADE NAME	14. HAZARD CLASS	15. IDENTIFICATION NUMBER (e.g. UN 2764, NA 2020)
Acetone	N/A	Flammable Liquid	UN 1090
16. IS MATERIAL A HAZARDOUS SUBSTANCE? ☒ YES ☐ NO		17. WAS THE RQ MET? ☐ YES ☒ NO	

SECTION V: CONSEQUENCES OF SPILL

Item 18: Enter the estimated quantity of the hazardous material released. Include the unit of measurement. This Item ***MUST NOT*** be left blank.

Item 19: Include only the number of fatalities ***RESULTING FROM THE HAZARDOUS MATERIALS INVOLVED.***

Item 20: Include only the number of injuries requiring hospitalization ***RESULTING FROM THE HAZARDOUS MATERIALS INVOLVED.***

Item 21: Include only the number of injuries ***NOT*** requiring hospitalization ***RESULTING FROM THE HAZARDOUS MATERIALS INVOLVED.***

Note for Items 19-21: If the cause of a casualty can be traced back and attributed in any part to the hazardous material, the casualty ***IS*** to be recorded. If all casualties ***were NOT attributed to the release of a hazardous material***, then enter "NONE."

Example for Items 19-21: A driver injured in a vehicle accident in which he was not physically affected by the hazardous material ***IS NOT*** recorded as an injury.

Item 22: Enter the estimated number of persons evacuated during the incident. If there was no evacuation, enter "NONE."

Item 23: Enter the estimated dollar amount of loss, property damage, decontamination, or clean-up, ***RESULTING FROM THE HAZARDOUS MATERIALS INVOLVED.*** Round off to the nearest dollar. If the category does not apply, enter "N/A." These items ***MUST NOT*** be left blank.

- **Item 23A:** Value of product loss
- **Item 23B:** Carrier damage
- **Item 23C:** Public or Private property damage
- **Item 23D:** Decontamination or Clean-up costs
- **Item 23E:** Other costs

Item 24: Mark all the boxes that describe the consequences of the incident. If the "OTHER" field is marked, include a description of "OTHER" in the space provided.

NOTE: The entry "Material Entered Waterway/Sewer" includes all sizes of waterways and drainage systems (e.g. storm drains, drainage ditches, streams, canals, lakes).

Example: 45 gallons of the acetone was spilled. There were no fatalities or injuries requiring hospitalization. One Highway Patrolman had some of the liquid splash on his hand. He received first aid at the scene. No people were evacuated. Estimates for the dollar amount of loss and damages are $90 of product loss and $100 for cleanup. The material was confined within the trailer.

V. CONSEQUENCES OF INCIDENT, DUE TO THE HAZARDOUS MATERIAL				
18. ESTIMATED QUANTITY HAZARDOUS MATERIAL RELEASED (Include units of measurement): 45 Gallons		19. FATALITIES: None	20. HOSPITALIZED INJURIES: None	21. NON-HOSPITALIZED INJURIES: 1
22. NUMBER OF PEOPLE EVACUATED: None				
23. ESTIMATED DOLLAR AMOUNT OF LOSS AND/OR PROPERTY DAMAGE, INCLUDING COST OF DECONTAMINATION OR CLEANUP (Round off in dollars)				
A. PRODUCT LOSS	B. CARRIER DAMAGE	C. PUBLIC/PRIVATE PROPERTY DAMAGE	D. DECONTAMINATION/ CLEANUP	E. OTHER
$90.00	N/A	N/A	$100.00	N/A
24. CONSEQUENCES ASSOCIATED WITH THE INCIDENT: ☒ SPILLAGE ☐ FIRE ☐ EXPLOSION ☐ VAPOR (GAS) DISPERSION ☐ ENVIRONMENTAL DAMAGE ☐ MATERIAL ENTERED WATERWAY/SEWER ☐ NONE ☐ OTHER ______				

SECTION VI: TRANSPORT ENVIRONMENT

Item 25: Indicate all the types of vehicles involved in the incident. If the "OTHER" field is marked, include a description of "OTHER" in the space provided.

NOTE: "RAIL CAR" includes rail box cars, flat cars, and hopper cars.

Item 26: Mark the box that best describes the transportation phase during which the incident occurred or was discovered.

Item 27: Mark the box that best describes the land use at the incident site.

Item 28: Mark the box that best describes the type of community surrounding the incident site.

Item 29: Mark the box which signifies whether or not the incident was caused by a vehicular accident or derailment. If "YES," answer items 29A through 29C when they apply. Enter item 29A for ***all modes of transport***. Items 29B and 29C apply only to the highway transport mode.

- **Item 29A:** Enter the estimated speed of the vehicle carrying hazardous material at the time of the accident. If the vehicle carrying the hazardous material was not moving at the time of the accident, enter "zero" or "0."
- **Item 29B:** Select the type of highway on which the accident occurred.

NOTE: "Divided/Limited Access" highways include any highway where the opposite lanes are separated by any type of median.

- **Item 29C:** Indicate the number of highway lanes present at the accident site. If "Divided/Limited Access" was marked in Item 29B, the ***number of lanes in the direction of travel*** is to be indicated. If "Undivided" is marked in Item 25B, the ***total number of highway lanes*** is to be indicated.

Example: The release occurred while the van trailer carrying the hazardous material was en route to its destination. The land surrounding the release site is a commercial center in a suburban area. The release was caused by a vehicle accident between the van trailer and a passenger car. The van trailer was traveling at 25 mph at the time of the accident. Route 1 at the scene of the accident is a divided highway with 2 lanes in each direction.

VI. TRANSPORT ENVIRONMENT			
25. INDICATE TYPE(S) OF VEHICLE(S) INVOLVED: ☐ TANK CAR ☐ RAIL CAR ☐ TOFC/COFC ☐ CARGO TANK ☐ AIRCRAFT ☒ VAN TRUCK/TRAILER ☐ BARGE ☐ FLAT BED TRUCK/TRAILER ☐ SHIP ☐ OTHER ______			
26. TRANSPORTATION PHASE DURING WHICH INCIDENT OCCURRED OR WAS DISCOVERED: ☒ EN ROUTE BETWEEN ORIGIN/DESTINATION ☐ LOADING ☐ UNLOADING ☐ TEMPORARY STORAGE/TERMINAL			
27. LAND USE AT INCIDENT SITE: ☐ INDUSTRIAL ☒ COMMERCIAL ☐ RESIDENTIAL ☐ AGRICULTURAL ☐ UNDEVELOPED			
28. COMMUNITY TYPE AT SITE: ☐ URBAN ☒ SUBURBAN ☐ RURAL			
29. WAS THE SPILL THE RESULT OF A VEHICLE ACCIDENT/DERAILMENT? IF YES AND APPLICABLE, ANSWER PARTS A THRU C. ☒ YES ☐ NO			
A. ESTIMATED SPEED: 25 mph	B. HIGHWAY TYPE: ☒ DIVIDED/LIMITED ACCESS ☐ UNDIVIDED	C. TOTAL NUMBER OF LANES: ☐ ONE ☒ TWO ☐ THREE ☐ FOUR OR MORE	SPACE FOR DOT USE ONLY

SECTION VII: PACKAGING INFORMATION

Columns A, B, and C are to be used to report details of (1) an ***overpacked package*** consisting of up to ***three layers*** of packaging material (i.e. bottles inside bags inside boxes), or up to (2) three ***different types*** of packages from which hazardous materials escaped, (3) three packages of the ***same type*** but of ***different sizes***, (4) three packages of the ***same type and size*** but made by three ***different manufacturers***, (5) three packages of the ***same type and size*** but containing ***different hazardous materials***, or (6) any combination of the above descriptions.

If more columns are needed, attach a separate sheet to the report.

Item 30: Enter the type of packaging involved in the incident (e.g. steel drums, fiberboard box, tank car, cargo tank). If the package is overpacked, label column A "Inner" for the innermost package, column B "Middle" or "Outer" for the next outer package, and column C "Outer" for the outermost package.

Item 31: Indicate the capacity of the packaging. Specify units of measure used (e.g. pounds, gallons).

Item 32: Enter the number of similar packages which failed in the same manner or for which failure was caused by a common source (e.g. if out of a shipment of 12 17H drums, 1 released hazardous material, the reporter would enter "1" for this item).

Item 33: Indicate the total number of similar packages in the shipment (e.g. if out of a shipment of 12 17H drums, 1 released hazardous material, the reporter would enter "12" for this item).

Example for items 30-33: 2 glass bottles out of 4 glass bottles in a carton were broken. If there were 10 such cartons in the shipment, then the report should state that hazardous materials escaped from ***2 bottles*** out of ***40 bottles*** in the shipment and from ***1 carton*** out of ***10 cartons***. There should be no doubt that the 40 bottles were the inner containers of 10 outer containers in one shipment.

Item 34: Show ***all*** of the specification identification markings on the package. (e.g. "12B" ***is not*** the complete marking for a DOT fiberboard box, it should be "DOT 12B40" or "DOT 12B60." Canadian packages may be prefixed with "CTC" as in "CTC 3AA500" while packages made to United Nations standards may be prefixed with "UN" as in "UN 1A1.") If the package bears no specification marking, enter "NONE" in the space. This field ***MUST NOT*** be left blank.

Item 35: Include any additional markings related to identifying the package (e.g. Drums are usually embossed with the gauge of the metal, capacity in gallons and year of manufacture as in "18/16-55-70." A UN 4G fiberboard box may have additional markings such as "Y1.4/150/87"). If no additional markings are found, enter "NONE."

Item 36: Enter the name and address (city and state) of the packaging manufacturer. Include initials, abbreviations, symbols, and combinations of letters and symbols.

Item 37: Indicate the serial number of a cylinder, cargo tank, tank car, or portable tank. The serial number of a cylinder appears just below the cylinder neck. A tank car serial number might be similar to "GATX 98765."

Item 38: Enter the label or placard information found on the package (e.g. "Flammable Liquid" or "Corrosive"). If no label or placard is present, state "NONE."

Item 39: If the package is reconditioned or requalified show the following:

- **Item 39A:** the ***symbols and registration numbers*** (e.g. "DOT R 1000").
- **Item 39B:** the date of the last test or inspection for containers that require testing.

Item 40: Include any Exemption, Special Permit, Approval, or Competent Authority Number(s) applicable to the shipment or packaging (e.g. "DOT-E 7052," "CTC-E 9898," "EX 98789").

Example: The shipment was made up of 12 steel drums with plastic liners. Each drum contained 55 gallons of acetone and was labeled "Flammable Liquid." Only 1 drum was damaged and failed. The specification number was "DOT 2SL" for the liner and "DOT 17H" for the drum. The liner was also marked "55-12-81" while the drum has "STC 18/16-55-80" marked on it. The manufacturing symbol on the liner is "AAA" while the drum has "FUBAR." The drums are reconditioned and registered as "DOT R1000" and last tested in February 1985.

VII. PACKAGING INFORMATION: If the package is overpacked (consists of several packages, e.g. glass jars within a fiberboard box), begin with Column A for information on the innermost package.	A (Inner)	B (Outer)	C
30. TYPE OF PACKAGING, INCLUDING INNER RECEPTACLES (e.g. Steel drum, tank car)	Plastic Liner	Steel Drum	
31. CAPACITY OR WEIGHT PER UNIT PACKAGE (e.g. 55 gallons, 65 lbs.)	55 Gallons	55 Gallons	
32. NUMBER OF PACKAGES OF SAME TYPE WHICH FAILED IN IDENTICAL MANNER	1	1	
33. NUMBER OF PACKAGES OF SAME TYPE IN SHIPMENT	12	12	
34. PACKAGE SPECIFICATION IDENTIFICATION (e.g. DOT 17E, DOT 105A100, UN 1A1 or none)	DOT 2SL	DOT 17H	
35. ANY OTHER PACKAGING MARKINGS (e.g. STC, 18/16-55-88, Y1.4/150/87)	55-12-81	STC 18/16-55-80	
36. NAME AND ADDRESS, SYMBOL OR REGISTRATION NUMBER OF PACKAGING MANUFACTURER	AAA - Toledo, OH	FUBAR - Flint, MI	
37. SERIAL NUMBER OF CYLINDERS, PORTABLE TANKS, CARGO TANKS, TANK CARS	N/A	N/A	
38. TYPE OF LABELING OR PLACARDING APPLIED	None	Flammable Liquid	
39. IF RECONDITIONED OR REQUALIFIED — A. REGISTRATION NUMBER OR SYMBOL	N/A	DOT R1000	
39. IF RECONDITIONED OR REQUALIFIED — B. DATE OF LAST TEST OR INSPECTION	N/A	2/85	
40. EXEMPTION/APPROVAL/COMPETENT AUTHORITY NUMBER, IF APPLICABLE (e.g. DOT E1012)	N/A	N/A	

SECTION VIII: DESCRIPTION OF PACKAGING FAILURE

Items 41 through 45: Check all the applicable boxes for the packages that failed. Mark the boxes under columns A, B, and C to report information about the packages reported in the corresponding columns A, B, and C in Section VII. If the "OTHER" field is marked, include a description of "OTHER" in the space provided.

Item 41: Action contributing to the package failure.

Item 42: Object causing the failure.

Item 43: How the package failed.

Item 44: Package area that failed.

Item 45: What failed on the package.

Example: Improper blocking resulted in the drum being struck by other freight during the vehicle collision. The drum was crushed and punctured with its liner along the center chime.

VIII. DESCRIPTION OF PACKAGING FAILURE: Check all applicable boxes for the package(s) identified above.

41. ACTION CONTRIBUTING TO PACKAGING FAILURE

	A	B	C			A	B	C	
a.	☒	☒	☐	TRANSPORT VEHICLE COLLISION	j.	☐	☐	☐	CORROSION
b.	☐	☐	☐	TRANSPORT VEHICLE OVERTURN	k.	☐	☐	☐	METAL FATIGUE
c.	☐	☐	☐	OVERLOADING/OVERFILLING	l.	☐	☐	☐	FRICTION/RUBBING
d.	☐	☐	☐	LOOSE FITTINGS, VALVES	m.	☐	☐	☐	FIRE/HEAT
e.	☐	☐	☐	DEFECTIVE FITTINGS, VALVES	n.	☐	☐	☐	FREEZING
f.	☐	☐	☐	DROPPED	o.	☐	☐	☐	VENTING
g.	☒	☒	☐	STRUCK/RAMMED	p.	☐	☐	☐	VANDALISM
h.	☐	☐	☐	IMPROPER LOADING	q.	☐	☐	☐	INCOMPATIBLE MATERIALS
i.	☐	☒	☐	IMPROPER BLOCKING	r.	☐	☐	☐	OTHER ________

42. OBJECT CAUSING FAILURE

	A	B	C	
a.	☒	☒	☐	OTHER FREIGHT
b.	☐	☐	☐	FORKLIFT
c.	☐	☐	☐	NAIL/PROTRUSION
d.	☐	☐	☐	OTHER TRANSPORT VEHICLE
e.	☐	☐	☐	WATER/OTHER LIQUID
f.	☐	☐	☐	GROUND/FLOOR/ROADWAY
g.	☐	☐	☐	ROADSIDE OBSTACLE
h.	☐	☐	☐	NONE
i.	☐	☐	☐	OTHER ________

43. HOW PACKAGE(S) FAILED

	A	B	C	
a.	☒	☒	☐	PUNCTURED
b.	☐	☐	☐	CRACKED
c.	☐	☐	☐	BURST/INTERNAL PRESSURE
d.	☐	☐	☐	RIPPED
e.	☐	☒	☐	CRUSHED
f.	☐	☐	☐	RUBBED/ABRADED
g.	☐	☐	☐	RUPTURED
h.	☐	☐	☐	OTHER ________

44. PACKAGE AREA THAT FAILED

	A	B	C	
a.	☐	☐	☐	END, FORWARD
b.	☐	☐	☐	END, REAR
c.	☐	☐	☐	SIDE, RIGHT
d.	☐	☐	☐	SIDE, LEFT
e.	☐	☐	☐	TOP
f.	☐	☐	☐	BOTTOM
g.	☒	☒	☐	CENTER
h.	☐	☐	☐	OTHER ________

45. WHAT FAILED ON PACKAGE(S)

	A	B	C	
a.	☒	☐	☐	BASIC PACKAGE MATERIAL
b.	☐	☐	☐	FITTING/VALVE
c.	☐	☐	☐	CLOSURE
d.	☐	☒	☐	CHIME
e.	☐	☐	☐	WELD/SEAM
f.	☐	☐	☐	HOSE/PIPING
g.	☐	☒	☐	INNER LINER
h.	☐	☐	☐	OTHER ________

SECTION IX: DESCRIPTION OF EVENTS

Describe the sequence of events that led to the incident. Include actions taken at time of discovery and actions taken to prevent future incidents. If a vehicle or its freight was contaminated, include the method of decontamination and the disposal of the vehicle or freight. Estimate the quantity of hazardous substance or waste removed from the scene, include the name and address of the receiving facility, and describe the disposal of any unremoved substance or waste (see 49 CFR 171.16(a)(2)). Photographs and diagrams should be submitted when necessary to clarify the events. Continue description on additional sheets if space is needed.

ATTACH a copy of the ***HAZARDOUS WASTE MANIFEST*** for all incidents involving hazardous waste (see 49 CFR 171.16(a)(1)).

Item 46: Print or type the name of person responsible for preparing the report.

Item 47: Signature of the person responsible for preparing the report.

Item 48: Title of the person responsible for preparing the report.

Item 49: Phone number, including area code, of the person responsible for preparing the report.

Item 50: Date the report was signed.

Example: Since acetone is a hazardous substance, the description of events must include an estimate of the quantity of acetone removed from the scene, as well as, the name and address of the receiving facility. Mr. A. Smythe, Traffic Safety Coordinator for ABC Trucking, was responsible for preparing this report.

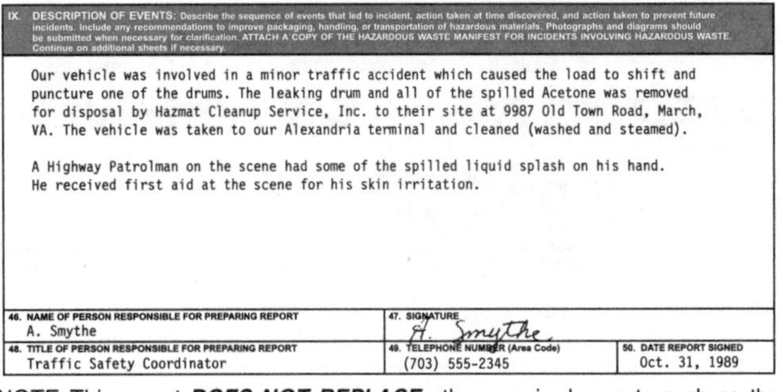

IX. DESCRIPTION OF EVENTS: Describe the sequence of events that led to incident, action taken at time discovered, and action taken to prevent future incidents. Include any recommendations to improve packaging, handling, or transportation of hazardous materials. Photographs and diagrams should be submitted when necessary for clarification. ATTACH A COPY OF THE HAZARDOUS WASTE MANIFEST FOR INCIDENTS INVOLVING HAZARDOUS WASTE. Continue on additional sheets if necessary.

Our vehicle was involved in a minor traffic accident which caused the load to shift and puncture one of the drums. The leaking drum and all of the spilled Acetone was removed for disposal by Hazmat Cleanup Service, Inc. to their site at 9987 Old Town Road, March, VA. The vehicle was taken to our Alexandria terminal and cleaned (washed and steamed).

A Highway Patrolman on the scene had some of the spilled liquid splash on his hand. He received first aid at the scene for his skin irritation.

46. NAME OF PERSON RESPONSIBLE FOR PREPARING REPORT	47. SIGNATURE	
A. Smythe	A. Smythe	
48. TITLE OF PERSON RESPONSIBLE FOR PREPARING REPORT	**49. TELEPHONE NUMBER (Area Code)**	**50. DATE REPORT SIGNED**
Traffic Safety Coordinator	(703) 555-2345	Oct. 31, 1989

NOTE: This report ***DOES NOT REPLACE*** other required reports such as the accident report MCS-50 required by the Federal Highway Administration.

Department of Transportation
Hazardous Materials Incident Report

REQUIREMENTS: The regulations requiring reporting of hazardous materials incidents are contained in the Code of Federal Regulations (CFR), Title 49 Parts 100-179 (governing the transport of hazardous materials by rail, air, water, and highway). Failure to comply with the reporting requirements contained therein can result in a civil penalty.

A *Guide for Preparing the Hazardous Materials Incident Report* is available from the Information Systems Manager, Office of Hazardous Materials Transportation, DHM-63, Research and Special Programs Administration, U.S. Department of Transportation, Washington, DC 20590.

PUBLIC REPORTING BURDEN FOR THIS COLLECTION OF INFORMATION IS ESTIMATED TO AVERAGE 1 HOUR PER RESPONSE, INCLUDING THE TIME FOR REVIEWING INSTRUCTIONS, SEARCHING EXISTING DATA SOURCES, GATHERING AND MAINTAINING THE DATA NEEDED, AND COMPLETING AND REVIEWING THE COLLECTION OF INFORMATION. SEND COMMENTS REGARDING THIS BURDEN ESTIMATE OR ANY OTHER ASPECT OF THIS COLLECTION OF INFORMATION, INCLUDING SUGGESTIONS FOR REDUCING THIS BURDEN, TO INFORMATION SYSTEMS MANAGER, OFFICE OF HAZARDOUS MATERIALS TRANSPORTATION, DHM-63, RESEARCH AND SPECIAL PROGRAMS ADMINISTRATION, U.S. DEPARTMENT OF TRANSPORTATION, WASHINGTON, DC 20590; AND TO THE OFFICE OF INFORMATION AND REGULATORY AFFAIRS, OFFICE OF MANAGEMENT AND BUDGET, WASHINGTON, DC 20503.

* U.S. G.P.O.:1994-301-717:80635

DEPARTMENT OF TRANSPORTATION
HAZARDOUS MATERIALS INCIDENT REPORT

Form Approved OMB No. 2137-0039

INSTRUCTIONS: Submit this report in duplicate to the Information Systems Manager, Office of Hazardous Materials Transportation, DHM-63, Research and Special Programs Administration, U.S. Department of Transportation, Washington, D.C. 20590. If space provided for any item is inadequate, complete that item under Section IX, keying to the entry number being completed. Copies of this form, in limited quantities, may be obtained from the Information Systems Manager, Office of Hazardous Materials Transportation. Additional copies in this prescribed format may be reproduced and used, if on the same size and kind of paper.

I. MODE, DATE, AND LOCATION OF INCIDENT

1. MODE OF TRANSPORTATION: ☐ AIR ☐ HIGHWAY ☐ RAIL ☐ WATER ☐ OTHER ______

2. DATE AND TIME OF INCIDENT (Use Military Time, e.g. 8:30am = 0830, noon = 1200, 6pm = 1800, midnight = 2400). Date: ____/____/____ TIME: ______

3. LOCATION OF INCIDENT (Include airport name in ROUTE/STREET if incident occurs at an airport.)

CITY: ______ STATE: ______

COUNTY: ______ ROUTE/STREET: ______

II. DESCRIPTION OF CARRIER, COMPANY, OR INDIVIDUAL REPORTING

4. FULL NAME

5. ADDRESS (Principal place of business)

6. LIST YOUR OMC MOTOR CARRIER CENSUS NUMBER, REPORTING RAILROAD ALPHABETIC CODE, MERCHANT VESSEL NAME AND ID NUMBER OR OTHER REPORTING CODE OR NUMBER.

III. SHIPMENT INFORMATION (From Shipping Paper or Packaging)

7. SHIPPER NAME AND ADDRESS (Principal place of business)

8. CONSIGNEE NAME AND ADDRESS (Principal place of business)

9. ORIGIN ADDRESS (If different from Shipper address)

10. DESTINATION ADDRESS (If different from Consignee address)

11. SHIPPING PAPER/WAYBILL IDENTIFICATION NO.

IV. HAZARDOUS MATERIAL(S) SPILLED (NOTE: REFERENCE 49 CFR SECTION 172.101.)

12. PROPER SHIPPING NAME

13. CHEMICAL/TRADE NAME

14. HAZARD CLASS

15. IDENTIFICATION NUMBER (e.g. UN 2764, NA 2020)

16. IS MATERIAL A HAZARDOUS SUBSTANCE? ☐ YES ☐ NO

17. WAS THE RQ MET? ☐ YES ☐ NO

V. CONSEQUENCES OF INCIDENT, DUE TO THE HAZARDOUS MATERIAL.

18. ESTIMATED QUANTITY HAZARDOUS MATERIAL RELEASED (Include units of measurement)

19. FATALITIES

20. HOSPITALIZED INJURIES

21. NON-HOSPITALIZED INJURIES

22. NUMBER OF PEOPLE EVACUATED

23. ESTIMATED DOLLAR AMOUNT OF LOSS AND/OR PROPERTY DAMAGE, INCLUDING COST OF DECONTAMINATION OR CLEANUP (Round off in dollars)

A. PRODUCT LOSS	B. CARRIER DAMAGE	C. PUBLIC/PRIVATE PROPERTY DAMAGE	D. DECONTAMINATION/ CLEANUP	E. OTHER

24. CONSEQUENCES ASSOCIATED WITH THE INCIDENT: ☐ VAPOR (GAS) DISPERSION ☐ MATERIAL ENTERED WATERWAY/SEWER ☐ SPILLAGE ☐ FIRE ☐ EXPLOSION ☐ ENVIRONMENTAL DAMAGE ☐ NONE ☐ OTHER ______

VI. TRANSPORT ENVIRONMENT

25. INDICATE TYPE(S) OF VEHICLE(S) INVOLVED: ☐ CARGO TANK ☐ VAN TRUCK/TRAILER ☐ FLAT BED TRUCK/TRAILER ☐ TANK CAR ☐ RAIL CAR ☐ TOFC/COFC ☐ AIRCRAFT ☐ BARGE ☐ SHIP ☐ OTHER ______

26. TRANSPORTATION PHASE DURING WHICH INCIDENT OCCURRED OR WAS DISCOVERED: ☐ EN ROUTE BETWEEN ORIGIN/DESTINATION ☐ LOADING ☐ UNLOADING ☐ TEMPORARY STORAGE/TERMINAL

27. LAND USE AT INCIDENT SITE: ☐ INDUSTRIAL ☐ COMMERCIAL ☐ RESIDENTIAL ☐ AGRICULTURAL ☐ UNDEVELOPED

28. COMMUNITY TYPE AT SITE: ☐ URBAN ☐ SUBURBAN ☐ RURAL

29. WAS THE SPILL THE RESULT OF A VEHICLE ACCIDENT/DERAILMENT? IF YES AND APPLICABLE, ANSWER PARTS A THRU C. ☐ YES ☐ NO

A. ESTIMATED SPEED:	B. HIGHWAY TYPE:	C. TOTAL NUMBER OF LANES:	SPACE FOR DOT USE ONLY
	☐ DIVIDED/LIMITED ACCESS ☐ UNDIVIDED	☐ ONE ☐ THREE ☐ TWO ☐ FOUR OR MORE	

FORM DOT F 5800.1 (Rev. 6/89) Supersedes DOT F 5800.1 (10/70) (9/1/76) THIS FORM MAY BE REPRODUCED

VII. PACKAGING INFORMATION: If the package is overpacked (consists of several packages, e.g. glass jars within a fiberboard box), begin with Column A for information on the innermost package.

ITEM		A	B	C
30. TYPE OF PACKAGING, INCLUDING INNER RECEPTACLES (e.g. Steel drum, tank car)				
31. CAPACITY OR WEIGHT PER UNIT PACKAGE (e.g. 55 gallons, 65 lbs.)				
32. NUMBER OF PACKAGES OF SAME TYPE WHICH FAILED IN IDENTICAL MANNER				
33. NUMBER OF PACKAGES OF SAME TYPE IN SHIPMENT				
34. PACKAGE SPECIFICATION IDENTIFICATION (e.g. DOT 17E, DOT 105A100, UN 1A1 or none)				
35. ANY OTHER PACKAGING MARKINGS (e.g. STC, 18/16-55-88, Y1.4/150/87)				
36. NAME AND ADDRESS, SYMBOL OR REGISTRATION NUMBER OF PACKAGING MANUFACTURER				
37. SERIAL NUMBER OF CYLINDERS, PORTABLE TANKS, CARGO TANKS, TANK CARS				
38. TYPE OF LABELING OR PLACARDING APPLIED				
39. IF RECONDITIONED OR REQUALIFIED	A. REGISTRATION NUMBER OR SYMBOL			
	B. DATE OF LAST TEST OR INSPECTION			
40. EXEMPTION/APPROVAL/COMPETENT AUTHORITY NUMBER, IF APPLICABLE (e.g. DOT E1012)				

VIII. DESCRIPTION OF PACKAGING FAILURE: Check all applicable boxes for the package(s) identified above.

41. ACTION CONTRIBUTING TO PACKAGING FAILURE

	A	B	C	
a.	☐	☐	☐	TRANSPORT VEHICLE COLLISION
b.	☐	☐	☐	TRANSPORT VEHICLE OVERTURN
c.	☐	☐	☐	OVERLOADING/OVERFILLING
d.	☐	☐	☐	LOOSE FITTINGS, VALVES
e.	☐	☐	☐	DEFECTIVE FITTINGS, VALVES
f.	☐	☐	☐	DROPPED
g.	☐	☐	☐	STRUCK/RAMMED
h.	☐	☐	☐	IMPROPER LOADING
i.	☐	☐	☐	IMPROPER BLOCKING
j.	☐	☐	☐	CORROSION
k.	☐	☐	☐	METAL FATIGUE
l.	☐	☐	☐	FRICTION/RUBBING
m.	☐	☐	☐	FIRE/HEAT
n.	☐	☐	☐	FREEZING
o.	☐	☐	☐	VENTING
p.	☐	☐	☐	VANDALISM
q.	☐	☐	☐	INCOMPATIBLE MATERIALS
r.	☐	☐	☐	OTHER ____________

42. OBJECT CAUSING FAILURE

	A	B	C	
a.	☐	☐	☐	OTHER FREIGHT
b.	☐	☐	☐	FORKLIFT
c.	☐	☐	☐	NAIL/PROTRUSION
d.	☐	☐	☐	OTHER TRANSPORT VEHICLE
e.	☐	☐	☐	WATER/OTHER LIQUID
f.	☐	☐	☐	GROUND/FLOOR/ROADWAY
g.	☐	☐	☐	ROADSIDE OBSTACLE
h.	☐	☐	☐	NONE
i.	☐	☐	☐	OTHER ____________

43. HOW PACKAGE(S) FAILED

	A	B	C	
a.	☐	☐	☐	PUNCTURED
b.	☐	☐	☐	CRACKED
c.	☐	☐	☐	BURST/INTERNAL PRESSURE
d.	☐	☐	☐	RIPPED
e.	☐	☐	☐	CRUSHED
f.	☐	☐	☐	RUBBED/ABRADED
g.	☐	☐	☐	RUPTURED
h.	☐	☐	☐	OTHER ____________

44. PACKAGE AREA THAT FAILED

	A	B	C	
a.	☐	☐	☐	END, FORWARD
b.	☐	☐	☐	END, REAR
c.	☐	☐	☐	SIDE, RIGHT
d.	☐	☐	☐	SIDE, LEFT
e.	☐	☐	☐	TOP
f.	☐	☐	☐	BOTTOM
g.	☐	☐	☐	CENTER
h.	☐	☐	☐	OTHER ____________

45. WHAT FAILED ON PACKAGE(S)

	A	B	C	
a.	☐	☐	☐	BASIC PACKAGE MATERIAL
b.	☐	☐	☐	FITTING/VALVE
c.	☐	☐	☐	CLOSURE
d.	☐	☐	☐	CHIME
e.	☐	☐	☐	WELD/SEAM
f.	☐	☐	☐	HOSE/PIPING
g.	☐	☐	☐	INNER LINER
h.	☐	☐	☐	OTHER ____________

IX. DESCRIPTION OF EVENTS: Describe the sequence of events that led to incident, action taken at time discovered, and action taken to prevent future incidents. Include any recommendations to improve packaging, handling, or transportation of hazardous materials. Photographs and diagrams should be submitted when necessary for clarification. ATTACH A COPY OF THE HAZARDOUS WASTE MANIFEST FOR INCIDENTS INVOLVING HAZARDOUS WASTE. Continue on additional sheets if necessary.

46. NAME OF PERSON RESPONSIBLE FOR PREPARING REPORT	47. SIGNATURE	
48. TITLE OF PERSON RESPONSIBLE FOR PREPARING REPORT	49. TELEPHONE NUMBER (Area Code)	50. DATE REPORT SIGNED

Enhancing Security of Hazardous Materials Shipments Against Acts of Terrorism or Sabotage Using RSPA's Risk Management Self-Evaluation Framework (RMSEF)

January 2002

Revision 1

This template or overlay for the Risk Management Self-Evaluation Framework applies the methodology to the issue of security. It is a tool and not a regulatory requirement. Its use, like that of the basic framework, is voluntary.

We would appreciate feedback on your experiences using this template and suggestions for improvement. Comments should be provided to the U.S. Department of Transportation's Research and Special Programs Administration, Office of Hazardous Materials Technology, DHM-20, 400 7th Street, S.W., Washington, DC 20590 or by accessing our website at http://hazmat.dot.gov/risk.htm.

RMSEF SECURITY TEMPLATE

Enhancing Security of Hazardous Materials Shipments Against Acts of Terrorism or Sabotage Using RSPA's Risk Management Self-Evaluation Framework (RMSEF)

I. RMSEF and Hazardous Materials Transportation Security

Given the heightened specter of terrorism, the security of hazardous materials (hazmat) shipments has become a priority for carriers, shippers, consignees, emergency responders, and government officials. The existing hazmat transportation process, including personnel, procedures, and facilities/equipment needs to be reexamined with a security focus. Addressing such security concerns should be part of an overall strategy to manage the risk of hazardous materials during transportation. Now an existing tool from the Research and Special Programs Administration's (RSPA) Office of Hazardous Materials Safety (OHMS) can be used by carriers, shippers, consignees, emergency responders, and government officials to enhance security and safeguard shipments of hazardous materials against terrorist attacks or sabotage. The Risk Management Self-Evaluation Framework (RMSEF) is a voluntary tool that helps evaluate and manage the risks associated with transporting hazardous materials in a proactive manner. A company or organization knows what works best for itself; RMSEF provides a structured way of assessing risk and helping hone practical, common-sense knowledge to reduce risks even further. RMSEF is applicable to all transportation modes and is flexible enough to provide the framework needed to evaluate and mitigate security risks.

II. RMSEF Principles Applied to Managing Security Risk

RMSEF outlines the following fundamental principles that are critical for successfully managing risk. As tailored to security, the principles include:

- Obtaining **commitment** to reducing security risks on the part of both managers and workers.
- Promoting a "risk reduction **culture** with a security focus" in day-to-day operations.
- **Partnering** with all parties involved in securing the hazardous materials transport chain.
- **Prioritizing** security risks so that resources can be allocated effectively.
- Taking **action** to reduce the security risks that have been identified.
- Striving for **continuous improvement**.
- **Communicating** with all parties to ensure each knows its role and is aware of relevant security risk information.

III. RMSEF's Stepwise Process Applied to Security Risk

Once the groundwork for risk management is laid by instilling the principles throughout a particular organization, RMSEF provides a systematic "stepwise process" to assess and reduce risks. The stepwise process is based on other risk management efforts and was developed through a collaborative effort between government, industry, and the public.

These steps of the RMSEF (see flowchart exhibit) are sufficiently general that the framework can be customized to address a variety of risk management issues and achieve measurable improvements. It is adaptable by shippers and carriers to systematically help in securing their hazardous materials shipments against acts of terrorism or sabotage.

Other methods for assessing and addressing security risk have been developed by government or private industry in specialized circumstances; however, none have a general focus on hazardous materials transportation. These methods differ in the source of their creation, the number of steps, and the scope of their activities. However, they share many steps common to the RMSEF (see Attachment 1). The following gives practical suggestions for ways in which each step of the RMSEF can be applied to protecting hazardous materials shipments from terrorist activity or sabotage. As shown in the exhibit below, management commitment and adequate documentation are essential to the risk management process.

Step 1: Scoping

Security considerations can cut across the entire hazmat transportation process. However, to effectively focus an effort on security risk, a company should generally characterize its hazmat transportation operations, and then make initial decisions as to which transportation activities should have more security scrutiny. The initial decisions could be made based on company perceptions regarding the greatest security risks or based on previous threats. For example, a shipper may decide that all of its hazardous materials shipments are vulnerable to terrorist attacks or sabotage, or perhaps it may narrow the focus to select chemicals with specific hazard potential (e.g., toxic gases). Similarly, a carrier may decide that its rail operations are more vulnerable to attack than its highway shipments. In light of concerns regarding the fraudulent use of Commercial Drivers' Licenses (CDLs) and hazardous materials endorsements, companies may wish to focus on their potential new employee screening process. Defining the scope of the activities to be considered in terms of security also includes identifying other partners (e.g., shipper, container manufacturer, local emergency response, law enforcement personnel, consignees) that are interested in the security of the company's hazardous materials transportation processes.

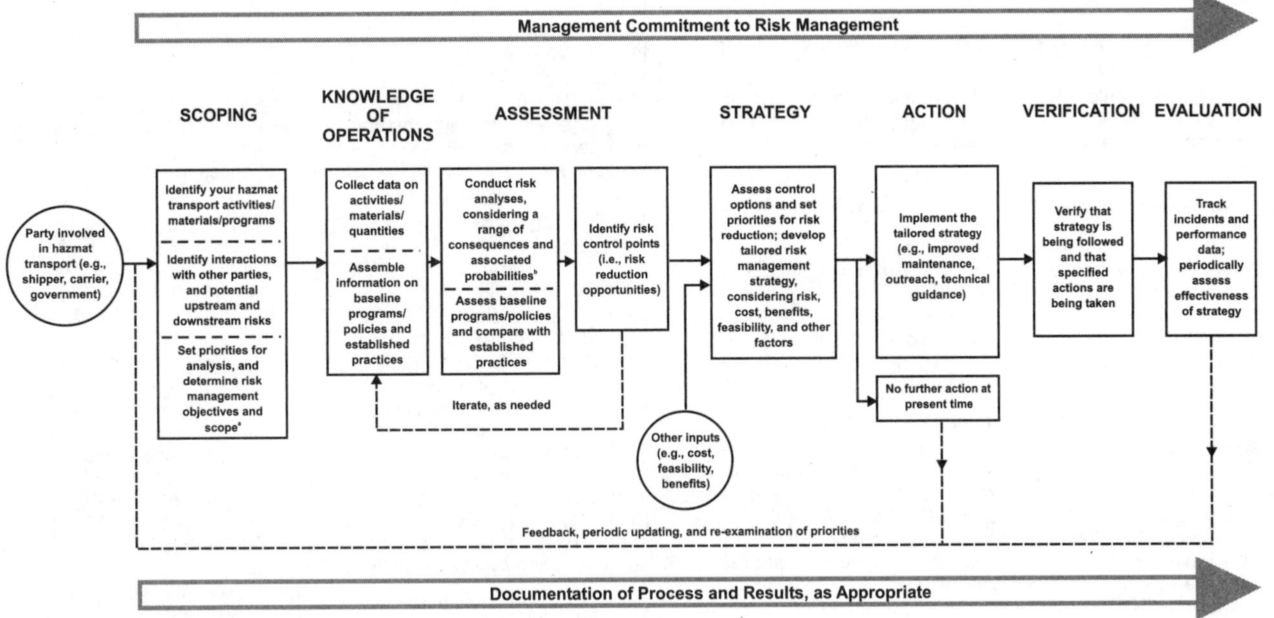

[a] Scope can vary from extremely broad, such as addressing an organization's entire hazardous materials operations, to very specific, such as targeted to a single material or transport route or to the type of risk (e.g., security).

[b] Analyses can be qualitative and quantitative, and are usually both.

Step 2: Knowledge of Operations

The next step of the RMSEF involves collecting detailed information about the hazmat transportation operations/decisions that will be examined for security risks. A company should describe the quantities of hazmat transported, who handles the materials, the routes used, and where and when they are handled. Additionally, a company should describe the existing security activities associated with these hazmat transportation operations. It is important to include security activities that were originally designed for security (e.g., fencing) as well as activities considered originally for safety or risk management (e.g., chlorine valve cap), but now have a security value. The inventory of information should cover security issues with personnel (e.g., background checks, licensing, training), security procedures and plans, and security of facilities and equipment. Current safety and risk regulations (e.g., parking restrictions) that have security impacts are also important to list. In determining the security activities to describe, a company may want to ask how are loads secured? Is there a forum for employees to constructively air grievances? Is there certainty that drivers actively follow the company's security guidelines? What are the chief causes of transportation-related accidents at the company? Have any threats previously been received by any company offices? Are there any trends that can be identified (e.g., regions or trailer types with a higher frequency of theft)? Having knowledge of existing security measures and transportation operations also enables a company to compare security measures with the industry and with recommendations by the government.

Step 3: Assessment

This assessment step involves analysis of a company's operations and characterization of the nature and magnitude of the security risks. The assessment does not have to be costly or complex, but can begin simply and progress in complexity as needed. It can simply involve reporting the impressions of experienced company staff, brainstorming, or conducting a survey by a diverse team composed of staff from various operations (e.g., risk managers, drivers, tank car vendors), or conducting more formal and rigorous hazard assessment techniques (e.g., use of risk matrices and scoring or ranking systems, fault tree analysis, or hazops). In any case, the goal is the same. A key element of this step is to identify points in the hazmat transportation chain where security risk exists, but where actions can be taken to reduce the security risk. These points are called risk control points. These risk control points can vary widely, including everything from changing driver training curricula, to increasing emphasis on load safety, to rethinking routing procedures or adding to existing emergency response protocols.

When selecting security risk control points, the following areas may require special attention:

- *Personnel backgrounds* (e.g., employment history and verification of citizenship or immigration status);
- *Hazardous materials and package control* (e.g., adequate lighting, locks, and security systems);
- *En route security* (e.g., avoidance of tunnels, high population centers);
- *Technical innovations* (e.g., appropriate access control systems, use of satellite tracking and surveillance systems);
- *Management prerogatives* (e.g., fingerprinting applicants during employment process);
- *Communications* (e.g., use of cell phones to reach all key personnel as well as risk communications for public and immediate reporting of suspicious activity or thefts to appropriate authorities);
- *Emergency Response* (e.g., adequacy of training and resources for response to terrorist type incidents); and
- *Readjustment based upon current conditions* (e.g., heightened security after initial terrorist attacks or in accordance with threat levels that may have been established by appropriate authorities).

Step 4: Strategy

The heart of a strategy to address security risks is to develop a security action plan. The plan prioritizes the security risk control points based on the degree of vulnerability and potential impact. The plan also outlines potential preventive and control actions based on the ability to reduce risk and the resources available. For example, if a company has a high turnover rate, it may decide to review employee rosters to ensure that comprehensive background checks have been performed on all individuals with particular scrutiny being applied to employees who have links to countries identified as supporting terrorist activities. Badges or personnel identification cards may be required for access to areas containing hazardous materials. Guard forces or fences at rail yards may be increased. Routing may be changed to avoid high population areas or to enable hazardous materials shipments to be delivered more rapidly. New locking mechanisms may be installed for fifth wheels so that trailers are less likely to be stolen, or electronic engine controls may be adjusted to require an entry code in addition to a key.

Additionally, the plan should have a schedule, assigned responsibilities and, most importantly, management commitment. The plan should be summarized in a written document.

Step 5: Action

This step involves implementation of the written plan developed in Step 4.

Step 6: Verification

After implementing the written plan, a monitoring protocol should be established to ensure that activities are proceeding according to plan. For example, third party inspectors (government or industry) can be requested to perform an independent evaluation of a company's vulnerability to terrorist attacks or sabotage. Any security breaches discovered during this evaluation would then need to be promptly addressed.

Step 7: Evaluation

This step determines if the goals established for reducing security risk for hazardous materials transportation are being met. To measure progress, a company needs to have relevant, cost-effective performance indicators. For example, logs tracking the incidence of theft or property damage can be monitored to determine whether significant improvements have resulted from implementation of the selected risk management strategies. Trade associations such as the National Tank Truck Carriers (NTTC) often assemble information on safety-related performance indicators that can be made available to their member companies. With set performance indicators, progress in meeting the goals and strategies can then be compared with performance indicators used by other companies in similar fields. Periodic reviews and assessment of existing plans should be scheduled.

IV. Specific Reference Information for Security of Hazardous Materials Transportation

Below is a list of reference materials that can be used to flesh out the RMSEF and tailor it more specifically to a company's needs. This is by no means an exhaustive list of the information available on this topic and interested individuals are encouraged to investigate additional resources. Suggested references are as follows:

- DOT's Hazardous Materials Safety Webpage: Provides the latest government alerts on terrorism. The website address is http://hazmat.dot.gov. Information on the RMSEF's development, structure, and testing can be found at http://hazmat.dot.gov/rmsef.htm.
- Federal Motor Carrier Safety Administration Security Talking. Security talking points can be found at the DOT Federal Motor Carrier Safety Administration Website www.fmcsa.dot.gov/hazmatsecure.htm. The topics include general security information, personnel security, hazardous materials and package controls, en route security, technical innovations, management prerogatives, communications, and readjustment based upon current conditions.
- American Chemistry Council Webpage: Provides guidance on transportation security and guidelines on site security for chemical plants. The website address is http://www.americanchemistry.com.
- Transportation Research Board Security Webpage: Provides links to documents and other information on the following topics: general transportation security, aviation security, surface transportation security, seaport/maritime security, and general national security webstes. The website address is http://www4.trb.org/trb/homepage.nsf/web/security.
- National Safety Council Webpage: Presents general safety information, including a document entitled "Effective Emergency Response Plans: Anticipate the worst, prepare for the best results." The website address is www.nsc.org/issues/emerg/99esc.htm.
- National Cargo Security Council Webpage: Provides theft prevention information, including a list of cargo security links and the document *Guidelines for Cargo Security & Loss Control: How to maximize cargo security on land, air & sea*, edited by Lou Tyska, CPP. The website address is www.cargosecurity.com.
- American Society for Industrial Security Webpage: Includes security information for industrial facilities, as well as a document entitled *Cargo Theft Prevention: A handbook for logistics security* by Louis A. Tyska, CPP, and Lawrence J. Fennelly. The website address is www.asisonline.org.
- American Trucking Associations (ATA) Webpage: Provides a host of information on government security warnings, security tips, and other guidance. Available documents include *Guidelines for Loss Prevention: Physical security in motor carrier freight terminals* and *Security and the Driver*, both authored by the Safety & Loss Prevention Management Council. The ATA website address is www.truckline.com. In addition, ATA hosts CargoTIPS, an interactive cargo theft information processing system available at www.cargotips.org.
- Agency for Toxic Substances and Disease Registry (ATSDR) Webpage: Provides information on general hazardous materials emergency response as well as strategies for mitigating and preventing terrorism involving industrial chemicals. The website address is http://cisat1.isciii.es/.
- U.S. Environmental Protection Agency (EPA)'s Counter-Terrorism Webpage: Provides publications, links, and alerts related to EPA's role in counter-terrorism. EPA's recommendations on chemical accident prevention and site security can be found at http://www.epa.gov/ceppo/pubs/secale.pdf. The website address is http://www.epa.gov/ceppo/cntr-ter.html.
- Department of Defense (DoD) Guidance on Security and Transportation. Although these DoD guidances are written specifically to ensure the security of nuclear, chemical, or conventional weapons during transportation, many of the practices are easily applicable to the transportation of other high-value loads, including hazardous materials loads. 1) Physical Security of Sensitive Conventional Arms, Ammunition, and Explosives (DoD 5100.76-M); 2) DoD Nuclear Weapons Transportation Manual (DoD 4540.5-M); and 3) Physical Security Program (DoD 5200.8-R). The website address is http://www.dtic.mil/whs/directives.
- National Institute of Justice and Sandia National Laboratories: Provides information on security, terrorism, and assessment methodologies. The website addresses are http://www.ojp.usdoj.gov/nij and http://www.sandia.gov, respectively.

Attachment 1

Other Security Methodologies

- **Chemical Facility Vulnerability Assessment Methodology**

  This methodology was developed by the National Institute of Justice in partnership with the U.S. Department of Energy's Sandia National Laboratories, with the cooperation and assistance of chemical industry representatives. It is a tool for assessing the potential security risks at chemical facilities, focusing on terrorist or criminal actions that could have significant national impact or could cause the airborne release of hazardous chemicals resulting in deaths and contamination. The assessment methodology contains twelve-steps that similar in many ways to those in RMSEF. A priority ranking matrix helps determine risk levels and suggest adoption of features to address vulnerabilities when these levels are too high.
- **Assessment of Vulnerability to Attacks on the Physical Surface Transportation Infrastructure or on the Surface Transportation Information Systems and Network**

  The National Research Council was directed by Congress to establish research and development priorities for "defending against, mitigating the consequences of, or assisting in the investigation of attacks on the physical surface transportation infrastructure or on the surface transportation information systems and network." The methodology used to assess the vulnerability of these transportation assets consists of nine steps, which are primarily focused around the scoping, knowledge of operations, strategy, and assessment steps of the RMSEF.
- **ATSDR 10-Step Procedure for Protecting Against Chemical Terrorism**

  The Agency for Toxic Substances and Disease Registry (ATSDR) developed a risk management methodology to "assist local public health and safety officials in analyzing, mitigating and preventing [chemical terrorism]." This procedure consists of ten steps, mainly focused on the RMSEF's scoping, strategy, and action steps.
- **Transportation Loss Prevention & Security Council Security Survey**

  Unlike the security risk management protocols described above, this procedure is intended for use by individual companies wishing to enhance the physical security of their property. This security survey consists of five elements similar to the RMSEF's scoping, knowledge of operations, and strategy steps.

INFECTIOUS SUBSTANCES

What You Need to Know

U.S. Department of Transportation
Research and Special Programs Administration
Hazardous Materials Safety

To obtain general hazardous materials transportation information, call the:

INFO-LINE
1-800-HMR49-22
(1-800-467-4922)

In the Washington, DC metro area, the number is (202) 366-4488.

NOTE:

This pamphlet highlights rules and exceptions. It does not take the place of the published regulations.

Department of Transportation Regulations for Infectious Substances and Regulated Medical Waste

The safe transportation of hazardous materials is a matter of concern to the public, Congress, and Federal, state and local officials. To ensure public safety and minimize risks posed by hazardous materials in transportation, Congress requires the Secretary of Transportation to prescribe regulations for safe transportation of hazardous materials.

The Research and Special Programs Administration is the agency within the Department of Transportation responsible for developing and issuing the hazardous materials regulations (HMR; 49 CFR Parts 171-180). The HMR govern the classification, hazard communication, and packaging of hazardous materials for transportation.

Infectious substances, including regulated medical waste, are one class (Division 6.2) of hazardous materials regulated under the HMR. An infectious substance may not be offered for transportation or transported in interstate or foreign commerce by rail, water, air, or highway, unless the requirements of the HMR are met.

Definitions
(49 CFR 173.134)

An **infectious substance** is a viable microorganism, or its toxin, that causes or may cause disease in humans or animals. It includes agents listed in 42 CFR 72.3 of the regulations of the Department of Health and Human Services and any other agent that causes or may cause severe, disabling or fatal disease.

A **regulated medical waste** is a waste, or reusable material, that contains an infectious substance and is generated in the diagnosis, treatment, or research of humans or animals. This definition does not include discarded cultures or stocks.

A **biological product** is a material prepared and manufactured in accordance with certain regulations of the Department of Agriculture or the Department of Health and Human Services.

A **diagnostic specimen** is any human or animal material being shipped for purposes of diagnosis. It includes but is not limited to excreta, secreta, blood, blood components, tissue, and tissue fluids.

Hazard Communication
(see the applicable Subpart of 49 CFR Part 172)

Each offeror of a Division 6.2 material must: describe the material on shipping papers (Subpart C); mark (Subpart D) and label (Subpart E) the package; and provide emergency response information (Subpart G).

Additional Requirements

Training (Subpart H of 49 CFR Part 172)

- All hazmat employees
- General awareness, function specific, and safety
- Test and maintain record
- Retrain every 2 years

Incident Reporting (49 CFR 171.15)

- Any infectious substance spill, contact Center for Disease Control - CDC (1-800-232-0124)
- Other reportable hazardous material, contact the Department of Transportation's National Response Center - NRC (1-800-424-8802)

PACKAGING

Infectious Substances Packaging
(49 CFR 173.196)

- Watertight primary & secondary inner containers
- Primary <u>or</u> secondary inner containers capable of withstanding internal pressure of 95 kpa at -40° F. to 131° F.
- Outer packaging - smallest external dimension at least 100 mm (3.9 in)
- Capable of passing:
  - 9 m (30 ft) drop test
  - Penetration test
  - Vibration standard

A typical infectious substance packaging configuration (closures not shown):

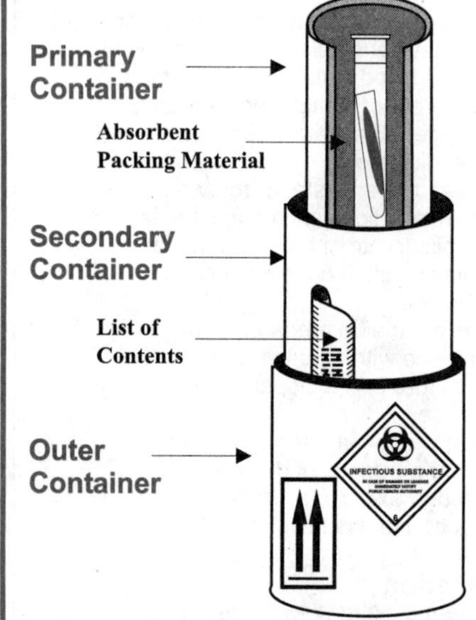

Exceptions
(49 CFR 173.134)

Regulated medical waste transported by a private or contract carrier is excepted from packaging and labeling requirements if:

- Packaged in rigid, non-bulk packagings conforming to general packaging requirements of §§173.24 and 173.24a, and
- Packaged and marked with the "BIOHAZARD" marking in accordance with the Department of Labor regulations in 29 CFR 1910.1030.

Diagnostic specimens and Biological products are not subject to the HMR, except when transported as regulated medical waste.

Certain wastes may not be subject to the HMR (see 49 CFR 173.134).

Regulated Medical Waste Packaging
(49 CFR 173.197)

- Non-bulk max capacity = 450 L (119 gal) or less
- Non-bulk max net mass = 400 kg (882 lbs) or less
- Meets UN Packing Group II,
- Rigid,
- Leak resistant,
- Impervious to moisture,
- Of sufficient strength to prevent tearing or bursting under normal conditions of use and handling,
- Sealed to prevent leakage during transport,
- Puncture resistant for sharps,
- Break-resistant, and
- Tightly lidded or stoppered for fluids in quantities greater than 20 cc.

A typical regulated medical waste packaging configuration:

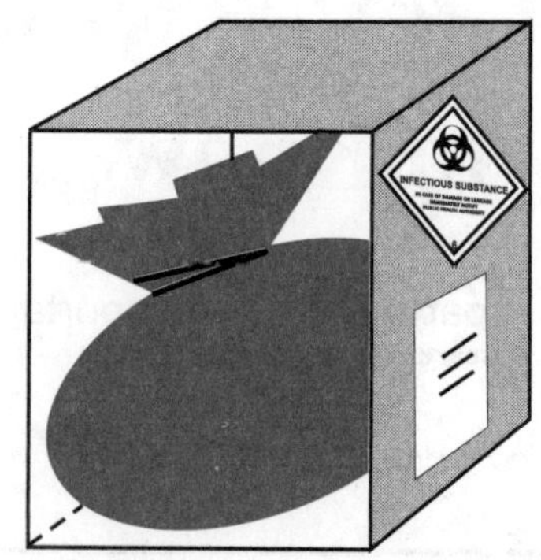

Where can I learn more?

Visit RSPA's Hazmat Safety Homepage on the Internet to view the HMR, copies of the latest rulemakings, exemptions, clarifications of the regulations, hazmat publications and training schedules.

http://hazmat.dot.gov

Download or print related brochures for Materials of Trade and Intrastate Operations.

US Department of Transportation
Research and Special Programs Administration
400 Seventh St., SW, DHM-50
Washington, DC 20590

E-Mail: Training@rspa.dot.gov

Hazardous Materials
INFO-LINE

(800) HMR49-22
(800) 467-4922

What Hazardous Materials Regulations Apply to Agricultural Transportation?

U.S. Department of Transportation

The Hazardous Materials Regulations (HMR) set forth requirements that you must follow if you ship or transport a hazardous material in the course of your business. The HMR tell you:

- how to classify and package a hazardous material;
- how the package must be marked and labeled;
- how to complete a shipping paper;
- how to provide emergency response information that must accompany a hazardous material shipment;
- whether the vehicle in which a hazardous material shipment is being transported must be placarded and the specific placards that must be used; and
- about training requirements for persons who transport hazardous materials or prepare hazardous materials for shipment.

The HMR are published in Title 49, Code of Federal Regulations (49 CFR) Parts 171-180.

Many fertilizers, pesticides, soil amendments, and fuels used in farming are hazardous materials. If you transport a hazardous material on a public road in the course of your business, the HMR apply to you. Until October 1, 1998, the HMR apply directly to persons who ship or transport materials between states (interstate), but all States have adopted the HMR requirements (with some exceptions). After October 1, 1998, the HMR apply to transportation within a single state (intrastate).

What Exceptions Apply Specifically to Farmers?

Section 173.5 of the HMR contains exceptions for farmers when they transport agricultural products between fields of their own farm or to or from their farm.

Exceptions apply to "agricultural products"

Agricultural products are defined as hazardous materials used to support farming operations, such as a fertilizer, pesticide, soil amendment or fuel, but limited to materials that are:

- flammable and non-flammable gases (Class 2)
- flammable or combustible liquids (Class 3)
- corrosive materials (Class 8)
- miscellaneous hazardous materials (Class 9)
- oxidizers (Division 5.1)
- poisons (Division 6.1), or
- consumer commodities (ORM-D).

Transporting Agricultural Products between Fields of Your Own Farm?

If you are a farmer transporting agricultural products other than gases (Class 2) between fields of the same farm using local roads, you need not comply with any of the requirements in the HMR. The agricultural products must be for use on your own farm. Your state must authorize these exceptions by law or regulation, and you must comply with all state requirements.

NOTE: *Gases (Class 2) such as liquefied petroleum gas (LPG) or anhydrous ammonia are not within this exception. However, other exceptions for LPG and anhydrous ammonia allowing the use of non-specification cargo tanks are provided in § 173.315(k) and 173.315(m) of the HMR.*

Transporting Agricultural Products To or From Your Farm?

If you are a farmer transporting agricultural products to or from a farm, within 150 miles of the farm, you must comply with hazard communication (such as shipping papers and placarding) and incident reporting requirements of the HMR. However, you need not comply with the emergency response and training requirements in the HMR. Your state may also authorize a different packaging than required by the HMR. In all cases, your state must authorize these exceptions by law or regulation, and you must comply with all state requirements.

You may use this exception only if:

- you are transporting no more than 502 gallons (1,900 L) of aliquid or gas agricultural product or 5,070 pounds (2,300 kg) of a solid agricultural product;
- you are transporting no more thanl6,094 pounds (7,300 kg) of ammonium nitrate fertilizer in a bulk container and the ammonium nitrate is an oxidizer, Packing Group III; and
- you are a farmer who is an intrastate private motor carrier.

NOTE: *Packaged hazardous materials purchased from a retailer should be in packages that meet the HMR requirements. The retailer is responsible for providing shipping papers and placards when these are required.*

What Other Exceptions May Apply to Farmers?

For anhydrous ammonia in nurse tanks, see § 173.315(m) of the HMR.

For flammable liquid petroleum products in cargo tanks or permanently mounted smaller tanks, see § 173.8 of the HMR.

For formulated liquid agricultural products manifolded to closed mixing systems, see § 173.5(c) of the HMR.

For "materials of trade" exceptions, see § 173.6 of the HMR and the separate Materials of Trade pamphlet.

Where can I learn more?

Visit RSPA's Hazmat Safety Homepage on the Internet to view the HMR, copies of the latest rulemakings, exemptions, clarifications of the regulations, hazmat publications and training schedules.

http://hazmat.dot.gov

Download or print the following brochures on HM-200's special provisions for Materials of Trade and Agricultural Operations.

US Department of Transportation
Research and Special Programs Administration
400 Seventh St., SW, DHM-50
Washington, DC 20590

E-Mail: Training@rspa.dot.gov

Do you transport
Hazardous Materials
by motor vehicle solely in
***intra**state commerce?*

If so, effective
October 1, 1998
you must comply with the Federal
Hazardous Materials Regulations

Our society relies on many different chemical products such as fertilizers, pesticides, explosives, chlorine for water purification, medicines and household cleaners; and petroleum products such as gasoline, home heating oil, and propane. Many of these materials are regulated as hazardous materials by the U.S. Department of Transportation (USDOT).

What is a Hazardous Material?

A ***hazardous material*** is a substance or material that is capable of posing an unreasonable risk to health, safety, and property when transported in commerce.

Hazardous materials include hazardous wastes, and designated hazardous substances and marine pollutants. Some of the hazard classes are explosives, flammable and toxic gases, flammable liquids, flammable solids, oxidizers, poisons, infectious substances, radioactive materials, and corrosive materials.

The vast majority of hazardous materials are transported safely on our highways. However, the possibility of serious consequences resulting from accidents involving hazardous materials is a major concern. Over 500,000 daily shipments (more than 1 billion tons per year) of hazardous materials are transported by commercial motor vehicle in the United States. This includes transportation by private motor carrier, i.e., transportation in furtherance of any business activity that is other than transportation for hire.

What is HM-200?

Concern about the safe handling and transportation of hazardous materials on our highways, and the need for a uniform system of regulation, prompted an amendment to the Hazardous Materials Transportation Act of 1990. The amendment required that the Federal hazardous materials regulations apply to transportation in intrastate commerce by highway in the same manner they have applied for many years to transportation by railroad, aircraft, vessels and transportation by highway in interstate commerce. Following a rulemaking proceeding in which special provisions were adopted for materials of trade, small cargo tanks, and certain operations of farmers, the Research and Special Programs Administration (RSPA) published a final rule--HM-200--on January 8, 1997, extending application of the regulations to all hazardous materials in ***intra**state* transportation by motor vehicle. Since 1980, the regulations have applied to hazardous substances and hazardous wastes transported by intrastate motor vehicle.

Effective October 1, 1998, the Federal ***Hazardous Materials Regulations*** (HMR; 49 CFR Parts 171-180] apply to transportation by motor vehicle in ***intra**state* commerce.

Are there requirements for packaging and marking MOTs?

Yes — except for tanks containing diluted mixtures of a Class 9 material, the packaging must be either the manufacturer's original packaging or a package of equal or greater strength and integrity. The packaging must be marked with a common name (such as "gas" or "spray paint") or a proper shipping name from the HMR (such as Isopropyl alcohol).

In addition, the following requirements apply to MOTs:

- packagings must be leak tight for liquids and gases and sift proof for solids;
- packages must be securely closed, secured against movement and protected against damage;
- outer packagings are not required for receptacles (such as cans or bottles) that are secured against movement in cages, bins, boxes or compartments;
- gasoline must be in DOT or OSHA approved metal or plastic cans;
- cylinders and pressure vessels must conform to the HMR except that outer packagings are not required -- These cylinders must be marked with the proper shipping name and identification number and have a hazard class label;
- if the package contains a reportable quantity of a hazardous substance, it must be marked "RQ"; and
- a tank containing a diluted mixture (not more than 2% concentration) of a Class 9 material must be marked on two opposing sides with the identification number for the material on orange panels or a white square on point configuration.

Where can I learn more?

Visit RSPA's Hazmat Safety Homepage on the Internet to view the HMR, copies of the latest rulemakings, exemptions, clarifications of the regulations, hazmat publications and training schedules.

http://hazmat.dot.gov

Download or print related brochures for Agricultural Operations and Intrastate Transportation.

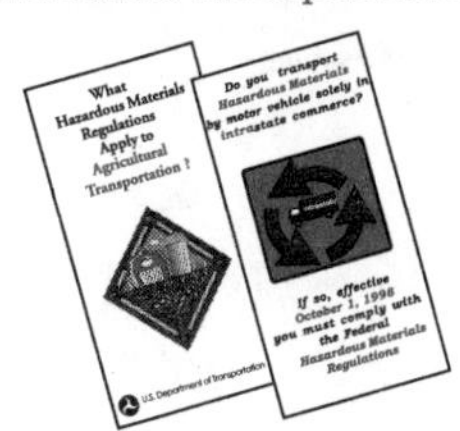

US Department of Transportation
Research and Special Programs Administration
400 Seventh St., SW, DHM-50
Washington, DC 20590
E-Mail: Training@rspa.dot.gov

What Hazardous Materials Regulations Apply to Materials of Trade?

The Hazardous Materials Regulations (HMR) set forth requirements that you must follow if you ship or transport a hazardous material in the course of your business. The HMR tell you:

- how to classify and package a hazardous material;
- how the package must be marked and labeled;
- how to complete a shipping paper;
- how to provide emergency response information that must accompany a hazardous material shipment;
- whether the vehicle in which a hazardous material shipment is being transported must be placarded and the specific placards that must be used; and
- about training requirements for persons who transport hazardous materials or prepare hazardous materials for shipment.

The HMR are published in Title 49, Code of Federal Regulations (49 CFR) Parts 171-180.

Certain hazardous materials transported in small quantities as part of a business are subject to less regulation because of their lesser hazards.

What are Materials of Trade?

Materials of Trade (MOTs) are hazardous materials that are carried on a motor vehicle for at least one of the following purposes:

- to protect the health and safety of the motor vehicle operator or passengers (*examples include: insect repellant, self-contained breathing apparatus, and fire extinguishers*);
- to support the operation or maintenance of a motor vehicle or auxiliary equipment *(examples include: engine starting fluid, spare battery, and gasoline)*; or
- when carried by a private motor carrier to directly support a principal business that is not transportation *(examples include: lawn care, pest control, plumbing, welding, painting, door-to-door sales)*.

What Regulations apply to Materials of Trade?

The rules that apply to MOTs are found in 49 CFR 173.6 and include:

- general knowledge of MOTs regulations,
- quantity limitations,
- packaging requirements, and
- marking and labeling requirements.

MOTs do not require:

- shipping papers,
- emergency response information,
- placarding, or
- formal training or recordkeeping.

Must I be aware that I am transporting MOTs?

Yes — if you operate a motor vehicle containing MOTs you must know the materials are hazardous, and you must be aware of the requirements for MOTs. However, no formal training, recordkeeping or recurrent training is required.

What Hazardous Materials qualify as MOTs?

Materials of trade are limited to the hazardous materials in the following classes and divisions:

- flammable or combustible liquids (Class 3), *such as paint, paint thinner, or gasoline;*
- corrosive materials (Class 8), *such as muriatic acid, battery fluid, or drain cleaners;*
- miscellaneous hazard materials (Class 9), *such as asbestos or self inflating life boats;*
- flammable gases (Division 2.1), *such as acetylene or propane;*
- non-flammable compressed gases (Division 2.2), *such as oxygen or nitrogen;*
- flammable solids (Division 4.1), *such as charcoal;*
- spontaneously combustible materials (Division 4.3), *such as test kits;*
- oxidizers (Division 5.1), *such as bleaching compounds;*
- organic peroxides (Division 5.2), *such as benzoyl peroxide;*
- poisons (Division 6.1), *such as certain pesticides;* or
- Consumer commodities (ORM-D), *such as hair spray or spray paint.*

Are there any quantity limits for hazardous materials being transported as MOTs?

Yes — except for tanks containing diluted mixtures of a Class 9 material, you may not transport more than 440 pounds (200 kg) of MOTs on any one vehicle, and there are size limits for individual packages:

- if the hazardous material is a high hazard (Packing Group I) material, the maximum amount of material in one package is 1 pound (.5 kg) or 1 pint (.5 L);.
- if the hazardous material is a medium or lower hazard (Packing Group II or III) material (other than Division 4.3 or Consumer commodities) the maximum amount of material in one package is 66 pounds (30 kg) or 8 gallons (30 L);
- if the hazardous material is in Division 4.3 (only Packing Group II or III materials are allowed) the maximum amount of material in each package is 1 ounce (30 ml);
- there are no individual package limits for Consumer commodity (ORM-D) materials; and
- each cylinder containing a gas (Division 2.1 or 2.2) may not weigh more than 220 pounds (100 kg).

A diluted mixture of a Class 9 material (not exceeding 2% concentration) may be transported in a tank having a capacity of up to 400 gallons.

Offices of Hazardous Materials Enforcement

Central Region
Office of Hazardous Materials Enforcement
2300 East Devon Avenue, Suite 478
Des Plaines, Illinois 60018-4696
(847) 294-8580
Fax: (847) 294-8590
Areas Covered:
Illinois	Indiana	Iowa	Kentucky	Michigan
Minnesota	Missouri	Nebraska	North Dakota
Ohio	South Dakota	Wisconsin

Southern Region
Office of Hazardous Materials Enforcement
1701 Columbia Avenue, Suite 520
College Park, Georgia 30337
(404) 305-6120
Fax: (404) 305-6125
Areas Covered:
| Alabama | Florida | Georgia | Mississippi |
| North Carolina | Puerto Rico | South Carolina |
| Tennessee |

Western Region
Office of Hazardous Materials Enforcement
3401 Centrelake Drive, Suite 550B
Ontario, California 91761
(909) 937-3279
Fax: (909) 390-5142
Areas Covered:
| Alaska | Arizona | California | Hawaii | Idaho | Montana |
| Nevada | Oregon | Utah | Washington | Wyoming |

Eastern Region
Office of Hazardous Materials Enforcement
820 Bear Tavern Road, Suite 306
West Trenton, New Jersey 08628
(609) 989-2256
Fax: (609) 989-2277
Areas Covered:
Connecticut	Delaware	Maine	Maryland
Massachusetts	New Hampshire	New Jersey
New York	Pennsylvania	Rhode Island	Vermont
Virginia	Washington DC	West Virginia

Southwest Region
Office of Hazardous Materials Enforcement
2320 LaBranch Street, Suite 2100
Houston, Texas 77004
(713) 718-3950
Fax: (713) 718-3952
Areas Covered:
| Arkansas | Colorado | Kansas | Louisiana |
| New Mexico | Oklahoma | Texas |

Special Investigations

Office of Hazardous Materials Enforcement
DHM-40
400 7th St., S.W.
Washington, DC 20590
(202) 366-4700
Fax: (202) 366-2784

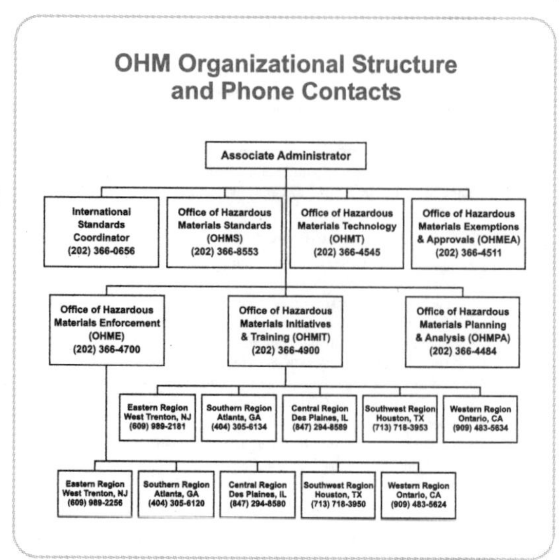

Offices of Hazardous Materials Initiatives and Training

Central Region
Office of Hazardous Materials Initiatives and Training
2300 East Devon Avenue, Suite 478
Des Plaines, Illinois 60018-4696
(847) 294-8589
Fax: (847) 294-8590
Areas Covered:
Illinois	Indiana	Iowa	Kentucky	Michigan
Minnesota	Missouri	Nebraska	North Dakota
Ohio	South Dakota	Wisconsin

Southwest Region
Office of Hazardous Materials Initiatives and Training
2320 LaBranch Street, Suite 2100
Houston, Texas 77004
(713) 718-3953
Fax: (713) 718-3952
Areas Covered:
| Arkansas | Colorado | Kansas | Louisiana |
| New Mexico | Oklahoma | Texas |

Eastern Region
Office of Hazardous Materials Initiatives and Training
820 Bear Tavern Road, Suite 306
West Trenton, New Jersey 08628
(609) 989-2181
Fax: (609) 989-2277
Areas Covered:
Connecticut	Delaware	Maine	Maryland
Massachusetts	New Hampshire	New Jersey
New York	Pennsylvania	Rhode Island	Vermont
Virginia	Washington DC	West Virginia

Western Region
Office of Hazardous Materials Initiatives and Training
3401 Centrelake Drive, Suite 550B
Ontario, California 91761
(909) 937-3279
Fax: (909) 390-5142
Areas Covered:
| Alaska | Arizona | California | Hawaii | Idaho | Montana |
| Nevada | Oregon | Utah | Washington | Wyoming |

Southern Region
Office of Hazardous Materials Initiatives and Training
1701 Columbia Avenue, Suite 520
College Park, Georgia 30337
(404) 305-6134
Fax: (404) 305-6125
Areas Covered:
| Alabama | Florida | Georgia | Mississippi |
| North Carolina | Puerto Rico | South Carolina |
| Tennessee |

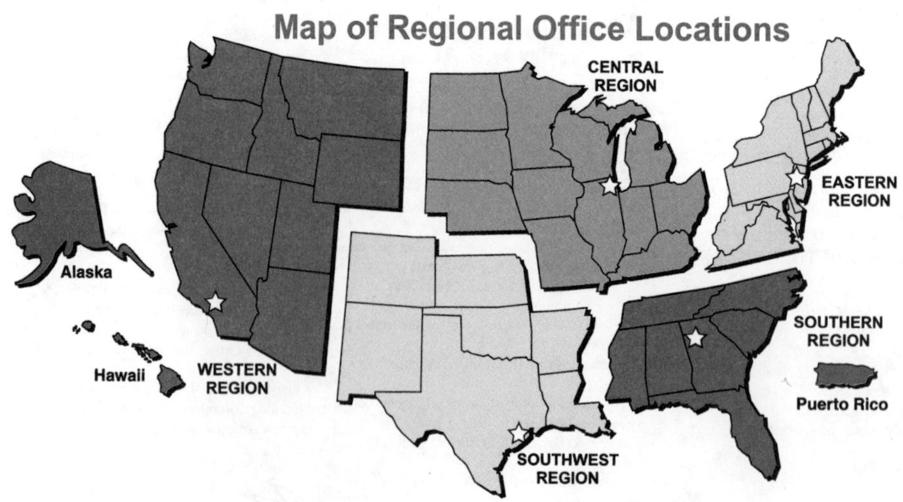

Index

A

B

IX Subject Index

C

IX Subject Index

D

E

F

G

H

I

J

K

L

M

N

O

P

R

S

T

U

V

GCIU